" *Do not be shaped by this world; instead be changed within by a new way of thinking.* "

—ROMANS 12:2

The editors of *The Maximized Living Bible,* along with our great friends at the Global Pastors Network, are pleased to dedicate this devotional Bible to the late Dr. Adrian Rogers, whose passion for the inerrant Word of God—and its relevance for maximized living—is an ongoing source of inspiration for millions around the world.

Known for his evangelistic zeal and uncompromising commitment to the Word of God, Adrian Rogers was one of the greatest preachers, respected Bible teachers, and Christian leaders of our time. For over fifty years, he consistently presented the Good News of Jesus Christ with strong conviction, compassion, and integrity.

He was a devoted family man—husband to his childhood sweetheart Joyce, father to four children, grandfather to nine, and great-grandfather to one. Of all his accomplishments, Dr. Rogers often said his greatest joy centered in his relationship to Jesus Christ, his wife and family, and the church he pastored.

On the day of his death, his final pastorate at Bellevue Baptist Church in Memphis stood more than 29,000 members strong, housed on a scenic landscape of more than 400 acres.

The broadcast arm of his ministry, *Love Worth Finding,* took his preaching and teaching to nearly 12,000 television stations and 2,100 radio stations in more than 150 countries.

The Lord used Dr. Rogers, when he served as President of the Southern Baptist Convention and beyond, to unify the Southern Baptist Convention around unequivocal allegiance to the inerrant Word of God. Throughout his dynamic leadership, and with the team he built around him, liberal theology was removed from seminaries and the preaching of "sound doctrine" was consistently heard throughout the Convention again.

Dr. Rogers once said, "I would rather stand alone in the light of truth than in the crowd filled with error." On the back cover of his official biography, written by Joyce, are these words, "I'm willing to compromise about many things, but not the Word of God. So far as getting together is concerned, we don't have to get together. The Southern Baptist Convention, as it is, does not have to survive. I don't have to be the pastor of Bellevue Baptist Church. I don't have to be loved; I don't even have to live. But I will not compromise the Word of God."

We are honored to be able to dedicate the Book he loved so well to the memory of a servant of God who fought the good fight and finished his race with excellence on every track, Dr. Adrian Rogers.

> Dr. Ben Lerner
> Dr. James O. Davis
> Dr. Greg Loman
> Dr. Rob Schiffman
> Dr. Skip Moen

Online

116 TRAINING COURSES, CHURCH PLANTING RESOURCES, AND WORLD-CLASS LEADERSHIP COLLECTIONS IN AN INTERNET LEARNING ENVIRONMENT.

One of the greatest crises in pastoral ministry today is equipping enough pastors fast enough to keep up with the rapid, exponential growth of Christianity. Both new and seasoned pastors desperately need around-the-clock teaching and training made available to them anywhere, anytime, in their language and on their education level.

When the leaders of NASA were planning to launch the first rocket to the moon, they were not so much concerned about where the moon was at the time of the launch as where the moon would be in order for them to hit their target.

The Holy Spirit has sovereignly brought together a world-class Global Pastors Network Board, not only to ask where our society is today, but to acquire an understanding of where our societal landscape will be in the years to come.

GPN has become the third most trafficked site for pastors on the Internet.

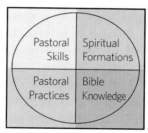

| Pastoral Skills | Spiritual Formations |
| Pastoral Practices | Bible Knowledge |

DIVISION OF STUDIES

Global Pastors Network Ministry Board

On-Air

THE GLOBAL TRAINING HOUR IS AVAILABLE IN 217 NATIONS BY SATELLITE.

There are more than 10,000 seminaries, Bible colleges, and training institutes in the world. These institutions are able, however, only to produce 5 to 7 percent of the ministers needed now.

GPN is an ever-developing, ever-expanding technological presence that thrives on simplicity and user-friendliness. GPN is offering in 217 nations the finest vision-casting and training to pastors who may not have easy access to the Internet. Due to the size of this global vision, synergistic thinking from many different viewpoints has produced the scope, substance, and strategy required to complete the Great Commission in our lifetime.

Satellite broadcasting has become a powerful means of communication in our day. The GPN Training Hour is seen around the world. Pastors and their ministry teams are able to view and learn from some of God's finest ministers in the world today.

GPN Board Member Larry Stockstill and GPN President James O. Davis

On-Ground

WORLD-CLASS PASTORS CONFERENCES AND CHURCH PLANTING CONGRESSES.

More than eighty denominations and parachurch organizations and more than two hundred different ministries throughout the world are coming together in strategic events for the fulfillment of the Great Commission. In the last few years, more than 20,000 leaders have attended GPN events from more than seventy nations. World-class leaders from Mel Gibson to remote church planters have been ministered to at GPN-sponsored events.

GPN is leading a Billion Soul Tour in North America in four strategic cities each year, plus international Regional Church Planting Congresses. Each Church Planting Congress is designed to canvass every nation on earth to involve all in the billion-soul harvest. Thousands of pastors have received scholarships in order to bring the finest training to them.

On-Time

A GLOBAL NETWORKING STRATEGY FOR EXPONENTIAL CHURCH GROWTH.

The Global Pastors Network is in the leadership position in order:

- To Provide Relationship-building opportunities for the fulfillment of the Great Commission.
- To Promote Resources for kingdom-minded leaders and make them available everywhere.
- To Publish Research for successful evangelism and church planting models and methods worldwide.
- To Prepare Recommendations for global partners on a bimonthly basis.
- To Produce Reports measuring the progress of the Billion Soul Initiative in real time.

"The goal of one billion new followers of Christ sets a good minimum number from which to start. People who seek the will of God are overrun by those who do the will of God."
Reinhard Bonnke, Evangelist, Christ for All Nations, Orlando, FL

"God is aligning his forces around the world for the greatest evangelism thrust in church history."
Steve Douglass, President, Campus Crusade for Christ, Orlando, FL

"GPN is allowing leaders to rub their minds together and break down barriers. I am thrilled to join this great movement!"
Sunday Adelaja, Pastor, Embassy of God, Kiev, Ukraine

"Evangelism, discipleship, and church-planting are worldwide efforts. God is going to get it all done with the people who are willing to do the work."
Billy Joe Daugherty, Pastor, Victory Christian Center, Tulsa, OK

"God is doing great works around the world, and a lot of Christians do not know what he is doing. GPN has become the communication portal for church leaders to know what is happening on a global basis toward the fulfillment of the Great Commission."
John Maxwell, Chairman, Global Pastors Network

GLOBAL PASTORS NETWORK IS BUILDING THE PREMIER COMMUNITY OF SUCCESSFUL PASTORS ONLINE, ON-AIR, ON-GROUND, ON-TIME.

why the Bible is true

BY DR. ADRIAN ROGERS

The Power of the Word of God

There is a great battle today over the Word of God. Some people think we ought not to get excited about it. But John Calvin wrote a long time ago, "A dog barks when his master is attacked. I would be a coward if I saw that God's truth is attacked and yet would remain silent without giving any sound."

I want to tell you of the power of the Word of God, and why the Bible is so important. First Peter 1:17–25 contains a very good illustration with solid proof that the Good News, the Word of God, the Bible, is the truth.

You were conceived by the Word of God.

First Peter 1:23 tells us: "You have been born again, and this new life did not come from something that dies, but from something that cannot die. You were born again through God's living message that continues forever." When you were conceived and born from your mother, your birth was a result of your physical father. When you were born again, your new life was the result of your heavenly Father. It was God's living message that acted as your father. "You were born again through God's living message [that's the Bible] that continues forever." You cannot get a new birth without the Word of God, the Good News, any more than you can get corn by planting marbles.

Again, you can read in James 1:18: "God decided to give us life through the word of truth [that means the Bible] so we might be the most important of all the things he made." Isn't that why the Bible is so important? And this life-giving truth cannot be bought; it won't fade or wear out; and it will never change or break down. It is incorruptible.

You are cleansed by the Word of God.

Look at 1 Peter 1:22: "Now that your obedience to the truth has purified your souls. . . ." It's the Word of God that gives you life. It's the Word of God that gives you purity and makes you clean.

How can you stay clean? In the Old Testament, in the outer courts of the tabernacle or the Temple, there was a big basin of water. It was called a laver. Before the priests went into the inner tabernacle to minister, they washed in that laver. The laver represents the Word of God. And the priests washed before they could work and before they could serve. The washing made them clean. The way that I stay clean and the way that you stay clean is by washing daily in the Word of God. Read it, listen to it, study it. We're purified by the Word. God's Word is like living water that washes and cleanses and purifies us.

You are completed by the Word of God.

Now look at 1 Peter 2:1–2: "So then, rid yourselves of all evil, all lying, hypocrisy, jealousy, and evil speech. As newborn babies want milk, you should want the pure and simple teaching. By it you can mature in your salvation. . . ."

One night I met a man—a grown, mature man—and he said, "I've just given my life to Christ. I have just been baptized." He said, "There is so much that I don't understand. It's all new to me." I thought, *I'm almost envious of you—all of the wonderful, sweet things you're going to learn if you'll just keep your heart open to the truth.*

How do you grow up in Jesus? How do you come to maturity? By feeding on the Word of God!

Many folks are so spiritually weak and malnourished, they look like they are anorexic. I say to them, "Well, what's wrong with you?"

"I don't know, Pastor. I just don't have any power in my prayer. I don't have any joy in my life. I don't have any zip in my testimony. I just don't have any of whatever it takes to live the Christian life."

Well, what could be wrong with this person?

Suppose you came to me and rather than talking about your spiritual life, you talked about your physical life. Suppose I said, "You look mighty weak."

You might say, "Yeah, I can hardly get up out of this chair. I'm just tired all the time. My hands tremble. I have palpitations. I have headaches. I just feel so weak, my knees are about to buckle."

I would ask, "My! What are you eating?"

"Well, I'm not eating anything."

"What?"

"No, I just don't eat. Well, I take a snack every Sunday at 11:00, but that's all. Other than that, I just don't eat."

I would further ask, "You're not feeding yourself? You're not getting regular meals?"

Now, I don't even have to be a physician to tell you what's wrong. And, friend, there are some of you who are not strong spiritually, and I don't have to tell you what's wrong with you—you are not feeding on the Word of God!

The Bible is to you spiritually what food is to you physically. A lot of folks go to church on Sunday and get a thimble full of milk, and they spill half of that on the way out of church! That's not enough food to grow up strong and healthy.

The Purity of the Word of God

Notice verse 22 declares: "Now that your obedience to the truth has purified your souls. . . ." Please, get a pen or marker and underline that phrase, "the truth." Verse 23 continues: "You have been born again, and this new life did not come from something that dies, but from something that cannot die."

How did the Word of God come to us? The Word of God came to us *by the Holy Spirit.* Men wrote it down, but the Holy Spirit moved, motivated, and compelled what they said.

First Peter 1:10 talks about our salvation: "The prophets searched carefully and tried to learn about salvation. They prophesied about the grace that was coming to you." This verse is saying that prophets wrote something down and then said to themselves, *I wonder what that means.* They in-

quired, they asked, they studied and looked for the answers. They prophesied about the coming Messiah—*our Messiah.* They wrote about our salvation. They were writing about the new birth, restoration, and all of this. But they did not even understand fully and completely what they were writing.

And verse 11 says, "The Spirit of Christ was in the prophets, telling in advance about the sufferings of Christ and about the glory that would follow those sufferings. The prophets tried to learn about what the Spirit was showing them. . . ." They were saying, "What does the Holy Spirit mean? Why did the Holy Spirit tell me to write that? What time is this going to take place? When is Messiah going to come? When will all of this be?" They did not even have a complete understanding of what they were writing. Why? Because the Bible says it was the Spirit in them that was testifying.

The Bible is the writing of the Holy Spirit. It used humans as instruments. Many times they understood exactly what they were writing. Sometimes they did not. Therefore, it is not called the word of man; it is the Word of God. And the author of the Bible is the Holy Spirit. This is important to know.

Look at verse 11 again: "The Spirit of Christ was in the prophets. . . ." That's talking about the Holy Spirit of God. We talk about the Word of God; we speak of its *inerrancy.* What does that mean? That it cannot err. It is God's Word. And a God of truth cannot speak error.

Dr. Lewis Sperry Chafer, a great theologian who is now in heaven, wrote this about the Bible: "It is not such a book as man would write if he could because it condemns him, or could write if he would because it surpasses him." This is exactly right.

The Word of God has authority.

Look again at verse 23: "You have been born again, and this new life did not come from something that dies, but from something that cannot die. You were born again through God's living message that continues forever."

A big question in any order or demand is this: Says who? It is not the word of man. It is the Word of God—God's living message that continues forever. It is absolutely, totally trustworthy and dependable. God's favorite terminology for this Book is "The Word of God." That's what it is called. And, therefore, because it is the Word of God, there can be no stutter, no stammer, no apology, and no retreat.

In 2 Timothy 3:16, Paul says: "All Scripture is inspired by God and is useful for teaching, for showing people what is wrong in their lives, for correcting faults, and for teaching how to live right."

Dr. Billy Graham gave this testimony. He said when he was studying in his earlier years, he had questions and problems about the Word of God. There were many things hard to understand about the Bible. He found himself wavering, and he felt that he had doubts about the Word of God. So, he went off to the mountains to pray. He wanted to get it settled in his heart.

He said to himself, *I know that the Bible has to be the Word of God. I've seen its transforming power in many lives.* He laid it on a stump and backed off, and said, "God, I accept it as your Word. What I understand and what I do not understand I accept as your Word. I take it by faith, and I will trust you to make it clear to me what it means." And he began to have power, incredible power, on his ministry.

Dr. Billy Graham, through the years and before multiplied millions, has pointed that index finger of his out and said, "The Bible says, the Bible says. . . . " That's where the power is.

The Word of God has vitality.

Look at verse 23: " . . . and this new life did not come from something that dies, but from something that cannot die. You were born again through God's living message that continues forever." This is not like any other book. This Book is alive.

Hebrews 4:12 says, "God's word is alive and working and is sharper than a double-edged sword. It cuts all the way into us, where the soul and the spirit are joined, to the center of our joints and bones. And it judges the thoughts and feelings in our hearts." It is quick and energizes, powerful. It pulsates with power. Not only do you read the Bible; the Bible reads you.

When I was a younger preacher, I had a fear that I would run out of material to preach. Really. I thought someday I would say: *Well, I've preached all there is in the Bible to preach, and I've just run out.* But, now I'm afraid I won't live long enough to even step inside the door of God's Word.

New light is constantly breaking forth from the Word of God. The fact that it has proved itself beyond measure for centuries is positive proof of the infinite treasures of the wisdom of God that are found in it. The Word of God has truth, authority, and vitality.

The Word of God will last for eternity.

Look again at verse 23: " . . . and this new life did not come from something that dies, but from something that cannot die. You were born again through God's living message that continues forever."

The Bible cannot fade or decay. It is timeless truth. And the gnawing tooth of time and the foul breath of decay cannot erode its blessings. Thank God, the Bible has withstood all of the assaults and insults of the centuries: the cults who twist it, the liberals who water it down, the humanists who ignore it, the atheists who deny it, and those who try to distort it.

Friend, it is the Word of God. It is not to be tinkered with. It is not to be added to or taken from. Psalm 119:89 says, "LORD, your word is everlasting; it continues forever in heaven." Forever!

In my office, I have a big Bible near the door where I walk out to the pulpit. That Bible stays open to Psalm 119. I look at a verse from Psalm 119 each day before I step out to preach because it's all about the Word of God. I want to give you one verse that put a fire in my bones. I want you to look at verse 111 and see if you don't love this great, great verse from the Word of God: "I will follow your rules forever, because they make me happy." That's right—they make me happy!

The Bible, my friend, is timeless, ultimate, indestructible, and infallible; it is *eternal*. That is the eternity of the Word of God.

The Proclamation of the Word of God

Go back to 1 Peter 1 and read verse 25: "'but the word of the Lord will live forever.' And this is the word that was preached to you."

As believers, we proclaim it faithfully, no matter what happens. *Proclaim* means to announce, declare, broadcast, make known, or say in public. Romans 1:16 says, "I am not ashamed of the Good News, because it is the power God uses to save everyone who believes. . . ."

I want to say to you younger people who are members of the great believing body of Christ, for God's sake, for your sake, for Jesus' sake, for the church's sake, don't forsake the Word of God. Stay with it! Be faithful to God's Word. I don't care what the secular scholars say. I don't care what the politicians say. I don't care what your peers and neighbors say. I don't care what cults and gangs proclaim. You stick with the Word.

There are two reasons I preach the Bible. Number one: I'd run out of cleansing power if I had to draw from my own well. But, thank God, I've got a bottomless reservoir to draw from. And I'm not smart enough to preach anything else.

Number two: I'm too smart to preach anything else because I know the power of the Word of God. I've preached it long enough now, folks, it's not a theory to me. I know the power of the Word of God. I've been standing by it, preaching it, loving it, and watching it change both my life and other lives in time and for eternity.

You need to know and understand it fully. It deals with every area of life. Yes, read the newspapers and listen to the television news. Yes, study human nature. Yes, understand current events and search the Internet. But see everything through the lens of the Word of God.

Search the Word of God fully. And take the Bible's wisdom freely. "But the word of the Lord will live forever." No other thought or notion or theory or book will.

Do you know what the word "gospel" means? It means "good news." What do you do with good news? Folks, you use it faithfully, fully, and freely. Stand up for Jesus and his Word. As God gives you breath, live by it.

do you know?

Do you know for sure that you are going to be with God in heaven? What would you say if God were to ask you, "Why should I let you into my heaven?"

You don't know? Then the following pages contain the best news you could ever hear!

The few minutes it will take you to read these pages may be the most important time you will ever spend! Did you know that the Bible tells how you can know for sure that you have eternal life and will go to be with God in heaven?

Here's how:

The Bible says there are five things you need to know about eternal life.

"I write this letter to you . . . so you will know you have eternal life" (1 John 5:13). Here's how:

1. Heaven

Eternal life is a gift!

The Bible says, "God gives us the free gift of life forever in Christ Jesus our Lord" (Romans 6:23).

And because heaven is a gift, like any other genuine gift . . . it is not earned or deserved.

No amount of personal effort, good works, or religious deeds can earn a place in heaven for you.

"I mean that you have been saved by grace through believing. You did not save yourselves; it was a gift from God" (Ephesians 2:8–9).

Why is it that people cannot earn their way to heaven? Because . . .

2. Human Beings

Human beings are sinners!

"Everyone has sinned and fallen short of God's glorious standard" (Romans 3:23).

Sin is transgressing God's law and includes such things as lying, lusting, cheating, deceiving, thinking evil thoughts, and behaving immorally.

And because of this, people cannot save themselves.

If you wanted to save yourself by good deeds, do you know how good you would have to be?

"So you must be perfect, just as your Father in heaven is perfect" (Matthew 5:48).

With such a high standard, no one can save himself or herself.

However, in spite of our sin . . .

3. God

God is merciful; therefore, he doesn't want to punish us.

This is because "God is love" (1 John 4:8). And he says, "I love you people with a love that will last forever" (Jeremiah 31:3).

But the same Bible that tells us God loves us also tells us that God is just and so must punish sin.

The Bible says . . .

"He does not forget to punish guilty people" (Exodus 34:7).

"The person who sins is the one who will die" (Ezekiel 18:4).

We have a problem, but God solved this problem for us in the Person of . . .

4. Jesus Christ

Who is he?

The Bible tells us clearly that Jesus is the infinite God-Man.

"In the beginning there was the Word [Jesus] . . . and the Word [Jesus] was God. The Word [Jesus] became a human and lived among us" (John 1:1, 14).

Jesus Christ came to earth and lived a sinless life, but while on earth, what did he do?

He died on the cross to pay the penalty for our sins and rose from the grave to purchase a place for us in heaven.

"We all have wandered away like sheep; each of us has gone his own way. But the LORD has put on him [Jesus] the punishment for all the evil we have done" (Isaiah 53:6).

Jesus Christ bore our sin in his body on the cross and now offers you eternal life (heaven) as a gift.

This gift is received by . . .

5. Faith, the key that opens the door to heaven

Many people mistake two things for saving faith:

1. Saving faith is not mere head knowledge, like believing certain historical facts. The Bible says that the devil believes there is one God, so believing that there is one God is not saving faith.

2. Saving faith is not mere temporal faith; that is, trusting God during temporary crises, such as financial, family, or physical needs. Yes, it is good to trust Christ during such challenges, but this is not saving faith!

Saving faith is trusting in Jesus Christ alone for eternal life. It means resting upon Christ alone and what he has done rather than in what you have done to get into heaven.

"Believe in the Lord Jesus and you will be saved" (Acts 16:31).

You have just read the greatest story ever told about the greatest offer ever made by the greatest Person who ever lived—Jesus Christ.

The question that God is asking you now is . . .

Would you like to receive the gift of eternal life?

Because this is such an important matter, let's clarify just what it involves.

It means that you need to:

•Transfer your trust from what you have been doing to what Christ has done for you on the cross.

•Accept Christ as Savior by opening your heart and inviting him to enter your life.

He says: "I stand at the door and knock. If you hear my voice and open the door, I will come in" (Revelation 3:20).

•Receive Jesus Christ as Lord by giving him the "driver's seat" of your life, not the "back seat."

•Repent and be willing to turn from anything that is not pleasing to him. He will reveal his will to you as you grow in your relationship with him.

Now, if this is what you really want . . .

You can go to God in prayer right where you are. You can receive his gift of eternal life through Jesus Christ right now.

"We believe with our hearts, and so we are made right with God. And we declare with our mouths that we believe, and so we are saved. 'Anyone who calls on the Lord will be saved'" (Romans 10:10, 13).

If you want to receive the gift of eternal life through Jesus Christ, then call on him and ask him for this gift right now.

Here's a suggested prayer:

"Lord Jesus, thank you for your gift of eternal life. I know I'm a sinner and do not deserve eternal life. But you loved me, so you died and rose from the grave to purchase a place in heaven for me. I now trust in you alone for eternal life, and I repent of my sin. Please take control as Lord of my life. Thank you. I pray in your name, amen."

If this prayer is the sincere desire of your heart, look at what Jesus promises to those who believe in him:

"I tell you the truth, whoever believes has eternal life" (John 6:47).

Welcome to the family of God!

If you have truly repented (forsaken and turned away) from your sins, placed your trust in Jesus Christ's sacrificial death, and received the gift of eternal life, you are now a child of God—forever!

"But to all who did accept him and believe in him he gave the right to become children of God" (John 1:12).

Today is your spiritual birthday! *It is a day you will always want to remember!*

The Bible speaks of those who receive eternal life in these words:

"They did not become his children in any human way—by any human parents or human desire. They were born of God" (John 1:13).

When you were physically born, the day of your birth was attested by a birth certificate. And so, today, to help you recall what God has done in your life on this important day, we invite you to sign and keep the following "spiritual birth certificate."

Spiritual Birth Certificate

"Anyone who calls on the Lord will be saved." (ROMANS 10:13)

Knowing that I have sinned, and I need the Lord Jesus Christ as my Savior, I now turn from my sins and trust him for my eternal life. I ask Jesus Christ to forgive me and to deliver me from sin's power and to give me eternal life. I now give Jesus Christ control of my life. From this time forward, as he gives me strength, I will seek to trust him and obey him in all areas of my life.

Date: _____

Signature: _____

What's next?

Just as a newborn baby grows physically, in a similar way you can grow spiritually by taking the following steps:

• Read the Bible.

Starting with the Gospel of John, read a chapter each day.

"As newborn babies want milk, you should want the pure and simple teaching" (1 Peter 2:2).

• Pray.

Spend time each day talking with God.

"Do not worry about anything, but pray and ask God for everything you need, always giving thanks" (Philippians 4:6).

• Worship.

Regularly attend a church that honors Jesus Christ and teaches you the Bible.

"I was happy when they said to me, 'Let's go to the Temple of the LORD'" (Psalm 122:1).

"God is spirit, and those who worship him must worship in spirit and truth" (John 4:24).

• Fellowship.

Spend time with Christians who will help you grow in faith.

"We announce to you what we have seen and heard, because we want you also to have fellowship with us. Our fellowship is with God the Father and with his Son, Jesus Christ" (1 John 1:3).

• Witness.

Tell others what Jesus Christ means to you!

"But when the Holy Spirit comes to you, you will receive power. You will be my witnesses" (Acts 1:8).

how to share Christ with a friend[1]

Witness in the power of the Holy Spirit:

Never try to share the Good News in your own power. We must realize it is God who draws people to himself (John 1:12–13). That's his part. Our part is to determine where he is working and intentionally join him in it.

How to determine where God is working:

- Sow a thought like, "Have you ever experienced something and wondered if maybe God had something to do with it?"
- See if your friend responds positively. If not, just change the subject. If so, God may be working!
- Share one of your own God-stories, such as something you have seen God do in your life. End your story with a positive statement about your assurance of eternal life. For example, "The greatest thing of all is that I have come to a place in my life where I now know for certain that I have eternal life. When I die, I will go to heaven." Is there still a positive response? God IS working!

To determine the spiritual condition of your friend, you might begin with one of these approaches:

- May I ask you a question? Have you come to the place in your spiritual life where you know for certain that you have eternal life? That is to say, if you were to die today, do you know for certain that you would go to heaven? Or is that something you would say you are still working on?
- May I share with you how I came to know I have eternal life and how you can know it, too? (Yes?) May I ask you another question first? Suppose you were to die today and find yourself standing before God and he were to ask you, "Why should I let you into my heaven?" What would you say to him?

Clarify the answer to determine where this person is placing his or her trust. Is this person trusting in Jesus Christ or in himself or herself?

How to share the Good News:

Share the five points of the Good News using scripture and illustrations as appropriate.

Grace

Heaven is a gift (Romans 6:23). It is not earned or deserved.

People

We all have a problem called sin (Romans 3:23). We cannot solve it ourselves (Romans 3:24).

God

God is love and doesn't want to hurt us (1 John 4:8b), but he is also just and so must punish our sin (Exodus 34:7b).

Christ

Christ is both God and human being (John 1:1, 14). He died on the cross and rose from the dead to pay the penalty for our sins and purchase a place in heaven for us (Isaiah 53:6).

Faith

Faith is not just head knowledge (James 2:19), nor is it just temporal faith. True saving faith is trusting in Jesus Christ alone for our eternal life (Acts 16:31).

---

[1]

How to lead in commitment:

Ask, "Does this make sense to you?" (Yes?) "Would you like to receive this gift of eternal life?"

Clarify everything so that your friend understands that a true commitment to Christ involves:

1. Transferring trust to Jesus Christ alone for eternal life (John 6:47).
2. Receiving the resurrected and living Christ as Savior (John 3:16).
3. Receiving Christ as Lord and Master of one's life (John 13:16–17).
4. Repenting from sin and choosing right living with the help of the Holy Spirit (2 Timothy 2:20–21).

Lead your friend in prayer as he or she places his or her trust in Jesus Christ alone for eternal life.

How to assist with spiritual growth:

- The Bible: Read a portion of the Bible every day. A good place to begin is with the Gospel of John, often called the "Gospel of Belief" (John 20:30–31).
- Prayer: Talk to God often (John 16:24).
- Worship: Join a Bible teaching church were you can learn to honor God with other believers (Psalm 34:1).
- Fellowship: Meet regularly with other believers for mutual support and encouragement (Hebrews 10:24).
- Witness: Experience the privilege and joy of telling others about Jesus (John 1:40–41).

The Maximized Living Bible

LEARNING TO LIVE THE ABUNDANT LIFE
ONE STEP AT A TIME!

Dr. Ben Lerner, Senior Editor

Dr. Greg Loman, Dr. Rob Schiffman, and

Skip Moen, Ph.D., General Editors

IN PARTNERSHIP WITH

JAMES O. DAVIS

AND THE GLOBAL PASTORS NETWORK

NCV
NEW CENTURY VERSION
www.myfaithandlife.com

NELSON BIBLES
A Division of Thomas Nelson Publishers
Since 1798
www.thomasnelson.com

contents

BOOKS OF THE OLD AND NEW TESTAMENTS

THE OLD TESTAMENT

THE NEW TESTAMENT

contributors

NAME	ORGANIZATION
Sunday Adelaja, Senior Pastor	Embassy of God Church, Kiev, Ukraine
Matthew Barnett, Senior Pastor	Angelus Temple/Los Angeles Dream Center
Tommy Barnett, Senior Pastor	Phoenix First Assembly and Los Angeles Dream Center
Robert Barriger, Senior Pastor	Camino de Vida, Lima, Peru
Reinhard Bonnke, Evangelist	Christ for All Nations
Chantelle Casey, Lay Leader	Granger Community Church, Granger, Indiana
S. Truett Cathy, CEO & Founder	Chick-fil-A, Inc.
Dr. Gary D. Chapman, Director	Marriage and Family Life Consultants, Inc.
Dr. Mark Chironna	Mark Chironna Ministries
Edwin Louis Cole, Father of the Christian Men's Movement	Ed Cole Library
Paul Louis Cole, President	Christian Men's Network
Dr. Wayne Cordeiro, Senior Pastor & Founder	New Hope Christian Fellowship, Oahu, Hawaii
Dr. Billy Joe Daugherty, Senior Pastor	Victory Christian Center, Tulsa, Oklahoma
Dr. James O. Davis, Co-founder/President/CEO	Global Pastors Network
Howard Dayton, Co-founder	Crown Financial Ministries
Lynne Dugan, Founder & President	Ministry Wives Network International
Rev. Gary Edmonds	Breakthrough Partners
Jimmy Evans, Founder & CEO	Marriage Today
Dale Evrist, Senior Pastor	New Song Christian Fellowship, Brentwood, Tennessee
Dr. Ronnie W. Floyd, Senior Pastor	First Baptist Church of Springdale, Arkansas; The Church at Pinnacle Hills, Rogers, Arkansas
Leon Fontaine, Senior Pastor	Springs Church, Winnipeg, Alberta, Canada
Dr. Claudio Freidzon, Senior Pastor	King of Kings Church, Buenos Aires, Argentina
Dr. Jim Garlow, Senior Pastor	Skyline Wesleyan Church, La Mesa, California
Rick Goad	Rick Goad Ministries
Diana Hagee, Chief of Staff	John Hagee Ministries
John Hagee, Founder and Senior Pastor	Cornerstone Church and President, Global Evangelism Television
Dr. Jack Hayford, Chancellor	The King's College & Seminary
Rev. Dr. Kong Hee, Senior Pastor	City Harvest Church, Singapore
Stephen L. Hill, Senior Pastor	Heartland World Ministries Church, Las Colinas, Texas
Larry Huch, Senior Pastor	DFW New Beginnings, Dallas, Texas

Becky Hunter, President .... Global Pastors' Wives Network
Dr. Joel C. Hunter, Senior Pastor .... Northland, A Church Distributed, Longwood, Florida
Dr. D. James Kennedy, Senior Pastor........... Coral Ridge Presbyterian Church, Fort Lauderdale, Florida
Dr. Ben Lerner .... Maximized Living Health Center, Celebration, Florida
Dr. Sheri Lerner .... Celebration Family Chiropractic
Dr. Greg Loman .... Maximized Living Health Center, Naples, Florida
H. B. London, Jr. .... Pastor to Pastor, Focus on the Family
Peter Lowe, CEO .... Get Motivated Seminars, Inc.
Dr. John Ed Mathison, Senior Minister .... Frazer Memorial United Methodist Church, Montgomery, Alabama
Bill McCartney .... The Road to Jerusalem
Dr. Joseph Mercola, Founder.................. Mercola.com
Dr. James Merritt, Senior Pastor............... Cross Pointe—The Church at Gwinnett Center, Duluth, Georgia
Skip Moen, Ph.D............................ Founder of At God's Table, Executive Director of BlueSky Ministries, Dean of the Department of Biblical Leadership at Master's International Divinity School
Dr. Tom Mullins, Senior Pastor .... Christ Fellowship Church, Palm Beach Gardens, Florida
Rick Nash .... Get Motivated Seminars, Inc.
Drs. Les & Leslie Parrott .... Seattle Pacific University
Dr. Phil Pringle, Senior Pastor .... Christian City Church, Oxford Falls, New South Wales, Australia
Bob Roberts, Jr.,
    Founder and Senior Pastor.................. NorthWood Church, Keller, Texas
James Robison, President & Founder .... LIFE Outreach International
Dr. Adrian Rogers........................... Love Worth Finding
Bob Russell, Retired Senior Minister........... Southeast Christian Church, Louisville, Kentucky
Dr. Rob Schiffman .... Get The Big Idea, Southbend, Indiana
Steve Sjogren, Senior Leader .... Coastland Tampa, Tampa, Florida
Dr. Gary Smalley, Author/Speaker .... Founder of Smalley Relationship Center
Virginia Smith, Executive Pastor .... The City Church, Kirkland, Washington
Wendell Smith, Senior Pastor .... The City Church, Kirkland, Washington
Larry Stockstill, Senior Pastor .... Bethany World Prayer Center, Baton Rouge, Louisiana
Joseph M. Stowell, Teaching Pastor............ Harvest Bible Chapel/RBC Ministries
Doug Stringer, Founder/President............. Somebody Cares America/International
Dr. Elmer L. Towns, Dean..................... School of Religion, Liberty University, Lynchburg, Virginia
Bishop Kenneth C. Ulmer,
    Senior Pastor/Teacher...................... Faithful Central Bible Church, Inglewood, California
Dr. Paul L. Walker, Executive Bishop .... Church of God International, Cleveland, Tennessee
Darlene Zschech, Worship Pastor .... Hillsong Church, Baulkham Hills, New South Wales, Australia

the maximized life

On the first day of January, millions of people make resolutions hoping to change their lives in some way. Unfortunately, by January 4 (possibly the highest chocolate consumption day of the year), most of these resolutions have disappeared. Change is difficult. The next year, the holidays show up again and the same pattern is repeated. In the dictionary, the term "resolution" actually means "fixed purpose." That definition makes the reality of resolutions either humorous or sad. We clearly need to change what we call these oaths, or we need to amend the term "resolution." Maybe we should call it something like this year's "passing fancy" or "temporary whim."

Sometime shortly after the fourth day of January, life goes on; but our dreams, goals, and plans don't survive the rest of the journey. For many of us, it's not so much what happens in January as it is what's taken place during a lifetime. Our search for significance, for meaning, and for buried treasure has met with so much struggle and failure that we've either given up altogether or we've ended up on the wrong track. At the beginning of the journey, we were off just a few degrees, but by the time we arrived at the destination, we were miles from our intended location. We may have left New York on the way to Florida but ended up in New Mexico.

Getting off track and ending up at the wrong destination is a tragic consequence. Our desire to fulfill our God-given potential—to live life to the max—and to reach our destination (nation of destiny, land of dreams) is authentic and important. The dreams, goals, and plans God gives us are meant to pull us toward our future and bring us closer to him. Those desires that motivate our resolutions are often placed there by God. If we go after these deeper desires, we can gain a closer walk with him.

It's not uncommon for people to admire their own survival skills. When trial, tribulation, hardship, failure, and setbacks have come into their lives, they've endured. But there is a big difference between enduring and actually living a maximized life. If ideals are sacrificed, purposes denied, important plans changed, and dreams relinquished, are we left with anything but existing? We keep breathing, but if we are no longer moving toward our real destiny, something important has been forgotten.

For most of us, it's past time for resolutions. Resolutions come from a temporary motivation for change. They're emotional, and emotions change with the day and season. It's not time for a resolution. It's time for a revolution—and, for that, we need inspiration, not motivation. This can only occur when we no longer rely on the latest motivational materials and fad programs. We need the transforming, inspiring power of God that turns simple emotional change into commitment. To live maximized lives we need to be more than survivors!

The Bible gives us plenty of inspiration not to give up. There are many accounts of men and women who failed dramatically *before* and *as* they were working to get on track with God. This should give us encouragement. Some of the Bible's greatest examples of leaders made big mistakes. This fact tells us that we cannot succeed with resolution and self-motivation alone. We need the awe-inspiring, life-transforming power of the Word of God.

You might think you have messed up your past life, but it's highly unlikely you will have made as many mistakes as our patriarchs did. David had a man killed to cover up his adultery. Saul (Paul) dedicated his early life to the persecution and death of the Christians. Along with many others, they discovered that God loves giving second chances. Paul says in Romans 7:18, "I want to do the things that are good, but I do not do them." Paul knew that in his own strength he was finished. But he tells us that he gained victory over his "body of death" through Jesus Christ. Paul discovered transformation, the real revolution of God. He realized his potential—he was a great deal more than a survivor.

The Bible guides us to a joyful, healthy, peaceful life in the presence of God. With God's help, we can face trial, tribulation, and severe hardship with hope and our heads held high. But too often our lives don't reflect this joyful existence. Even though we are believers, religion can turn our relationship with Christ into nothing more than a ritual.

We end up with obligations to attend church, to tithe without cheerfulness, to read the Bible without personal inspiration, to enter marriages that are relationships of fear and doubt, to accept addictions, poor health, depression, and anxiety. From the outside, Christians who don't live maximized lives start to look just like the rest of the world, or worse. Although we're called by God to be light, we can slip into worldly darkness.

The maximized life is not simply material prosperity. Jesus calls us to take up our cross daily and to move toward the peace of spiritual aspiration and away from the war for material accumulation. If you are a follower of the Man from Galilee, you should make a difference—and people who know you should see a difference. Christians are beacons of light in a world of darkness. That means they stand out, not because they accumulate more of what the world counts as treasure, but because they seek to distribute the gifts from a God who owns the world and everything in it. If your Christian life isn't radically different from that of the best nonbeliever you know, then you're not maximized for God.

Conversion and repentance actually mean to turn 180 degrees and start heading down a brand-new path, completely different from the old one. Where there was once spiritual exhaustion and despair, there is now joy and direction. Where there was hopelessness and worthlessness, there is now power and self-worth. But transformation only begins with redirection. Transformation is conversion to a journey that will take you the rest of your life to complete. It is not a journey of drudgery but rather a journey of adventure and joy, a chance to explore yourself, and an opportunity to become confident that God is at your side.

Are the ideals, the dreams, and the future you set out to experience still intact? Or have the challenge to find your path and the frustrations of the deferred discovery of your destiny caused you to lead a less than authentic life? Have you forgotten where you were headed?

Remember that you have a destiny that can only come through purposefully and prayerfully searching for your redeemer Messiah—a Messiah who redeems you not only from sin but also from every aspect of a sin-filled world; a Messiah who came to set you free. You can realize your maximized life as long as you believe that what's inside of you is more powerful than any circumstance outside of you!

The turbulence, speed bumps, and steep hills that the world means for bad, God uses for good to strengthen, shape, and mold you for the future. At times, it may seem like it's taking too long to reach your land of dreams. But, as Dr. James Davis, president of the Global Pastors Network, puts it, "Live life by the compass and not the clock. You'd rather be going the right way slowly, than the wrong way fast!"

We want you to inherit the life you were born to live. Welcome to *The Maximized Living Bible*. It is our heart's desire that Jesus, the Christ, will transform everyone. We want that transformation to affect your fulfillment, future, finances, fitness, family, and faith. We want you to be MAXIMIZED: "To have life and have it to the max!"

Using the Word of God, we want to show you how to maximize your life in these six vital areas:

1. Faith (personal and corporate)
2. Family (marriage and children)
3. Fitness (health and wellness)
4. Finances (stewardship and security)
5. Future (purpose and mission)
6. Fulfillment (stress and time management)

The Maximized Living Bible will take you through each of these areas. In addition to devotionals from us, your editors (Dr. Ben Lerner, Dr. Greg Loman, Dr. Rob Schiffman, and Dr. Skip Moen), you'll find exciting content from some of the best Christian thinkers in the world, of both yesterday and today, on these subjects. Join us on a daily journey in maximized living throughout the next year. Within only five to six weeks (40 days), you'll begin to form new habits, develop new skills, and experience real change. There are major articles to read on the six "F's" and then devotionals to read linked to these topics.

You have enough here to give you an inspirational and illuminating message every day of the year. In the process, you'll discover that maximized living is about more than just your spiritual growth. It's about how you achieve your goals; how you eat and exercise; how you live at home; how you rear your children; what you do for work and school; what you do with your money; what the world looks like from God's point of view; and what to do when life tests you.

Throughout our lives, we're told we're not worthy, that we don't look good enough, that we're not funny or popular, that we aren't famous or rich or even spiritual enough, or that we're not doing what we should. Rather than feeling loved, we experience regret, guilt, the pain of poor self-images, and inauthentic lives that can only lead to unhappiness, anxiety, and a constant burning emptiness.

That's why Paul said, "Do not be shaped by this world; instead be changed within by a new way of thinking" (Romans 12:2). Above all else, realize that God loves you just as you are, no matter what you do, what you weigh, what you look like, or what you possess right now. You've likely done the best you could with what you've had to work with. God calls us to improve and to do our best—not on our own, but through him and with him—to become more like his Son. And that's the ultimate goal of maximized living—to be like Jesus.

Maximized blessings from
Dr. Ben, Dr. Greg, Dr. Rob, and Dr. Skip

index

TO ARTICLES AND RELATED DEVOTIONALS
for Maximized Living

To be MAXIMIZED in every part of your life—your faith, family, finances, fitness, fulfillment, and future—see what the Word of God has to say about them. You'll find fifty-two introductory articles on these key areas with several related devotionals positioned near the scripture locations listed with each. Again, remember that we want you to be MAXIMIZED: "To have life and have it to the max!"

acknowledgments

We acknowledge and greatly appreciate the privilege to use materials from these sources in *The Maximized Living Bible*:

Adapted by permission. *The Body by God*. Dr. Ben Lerner, copyright © 2003, Thomas Nelson, Inc., Nashville, Tennessee. All rights reserved.

Adapted by permission. *Bouncing Back from Pregnancy*. Sheri Lerner, copyright © 2005, Thomas Nelson, Inc., Nashville, Tennessee. All rights reserved.

Adapted by permission. B&H Publishing Group, Nashville, TN. Excerpt taken from the book *Covenant Marriage*, by Gary Chapman. © 2003. All rights reserved.

Adapted by permission. *Free at Last*. Larry Huch, copyright © 2004, Whitaker House Publishing, New Kensington, PA. All rights reserved.

Adapted by permission. *One-Minute Wellness*. Ben Lerner, copyright © 2005, Thomas Nelson, Inc., Nashville, Tennessee. All rights reserved.

God intended for everyone to be able to read and understand his Word. The Old Testament is written in Hebrew, the language of the people of Israel. Through the use of vivid stories based on real events and beautiful poetry, it appeals to the minds and hearts of the educated and the uneducated. The New Testament was first written in the simple Greek of everyday life, not in the Latin of Roman courts or the classical Greek of the academies. Even Jesus, the Master Teacher, taught spiritual principles by comparing them to such familiar terms as pearls, seeds, rocks, trees, and sheep. Likewise, the New Century Version translates the Scriptures in familiar, everyday words of our times.

The New Century Version is a translation of God's Word from the original Hebrew and Greek languages. A previous edition of the complete New Century Version, the International Children's Bible, was published in 1986.

A Trustworthy Translation

Two basic premises guided the translation process of the New Century Version. The first concern was that the translation be faithful to the manuscripts in the original languages. A team composed of the World Bible Translation Center and fifty additional, highly qualified and experienced Bible scholars and translators was assembled. The team included people with translation experience on such accepted versions as the New International Version, the New American Standard Bible, and the New King James Version. The most recent scholarship and the best available Hebrew and Greek texts were used, principally the third edition of the United Bible Societies' Greek text and the latest edition of the *Biblia Hebraica,* along with the Septuagint.

A Clear Translation

The second concern was to make the language clear enough for anyone to read the Bible and understand it. In maintaining clear language, several guidelines were followed. Vocabulary choice has been based upon *The Living Word Vocabulary* by Dr. Edgar Dale and Dr. Joseph O'Rourke (Worldbook-Childcraft International, 1981), which is the standard used by the editors of *The World Book Encyclopedia* to determine appropriate vocabulary. For difficult words that have no simpler synonyms, footnotes, references, and dictionary definitions are provided. Footnotes appear at the bottom of the page and are indicated in the text by an [n] (for "note").

The New Century Version aids understanding by putting concepts into natural terms. Modern measurements and geographical locations have been used as much as possible. For instance, terms such as "shekels," "cubits," "omer," and "hin" have been converted to modern equivalents of weights and measures. Where geographical references are identical, the modern name has been used, such as the "Mediterranean Sea" instead of "Great Sea" or "Western Sea." Also, to minimize confusion, the most familiar name for a place is used consistently instead of using variant names for the same place. "Lake Galilee" is used throughout the text rather than its variant forms, "Sea of Kinnereth," "Lake Gennesaret," and "Sea of Tiberias."

Ancient customs are often unfamiliar to modern readers. Customs such as shaving a man's beard to shame him or walking between the halves of a dead animal to seal an agreement are meaningless to most people today. So these are clarified either in the text or in a footnote.

Since *meanings* of words change with time, care has been taken to avoid potential misunderstandings. Frequently in the Old Testament God tells his people to "devote" something to him, as when he tells the Israelites to devote Jericho and everything in it to him. While we might understand this to mean he is telling them to keep it safe and holy, the exact opposite is true. He is telling them to destroy it totally as an offering to him. The New Century Version communicates the idea clearly by translating "devoted" in these situations as "destroyed as an offering to the LORD."

Rhetorical questions in many instances have been stated according to their implied answer. The psalmist's question "What god is so great as our God?" has been stated more directly as "No god is as great as our God."

Figures of speech have been translated according to their meanings. For instance, the expression "the Virgin Daughter of Zion," which is frequently used in the Old Testament, is simply translated "the people of Jerusalem."

Idiomatic expressions of the biblical languages are translated to communicate the same meaning to today's reader that would have been understood by the original audience. For example, the Hebrew idiom "he rested with his fathers" is translated by its meaning—"he died."

Obscure terms have been clarified. In the Old Testament God frequently condemns the people for their "high places" and "Asherah poles." The New Century Version translates these according to their meanings, which would have been understood by the Hebrews. "High places" is translated "places where gods were worshiped," and "Asherah poles" is translated "Asherah idols."

Gender language has been rendered in keeping with the principles of meaning-based translation. In the interest of providing the best rendering of the original Hebrew and Greek texts in contemporary English, appropriate gender terms are used whenever it is possible to do so without hindering clarity or accuracy. Masculine terms are used when the meaning of the original has to do with males, including references to deity and to male cultural situations such as the military and the priesthood. Feminine terms are used when the meaning of the original has to do with females. When the meaning of the original has to do with both males and females, nongendered terms are used. (In such cases, the masculine resumptive pronoun has sometimes been preferred to changing person or number.)

The divine name YHWH, *the tetragrammaton,* has been indicated in the New Century Version by putting "LORD," and sometimes "GOD," in capital letters, following the tradition of other English versions. This is to distinguish it from *Adonai,* another Hebrew word that is translated "Lord."

Proper English style has been maintained while clarifying concepts and communication. The beauty of the Hebrew parallelism in poetry and the wordplays have been retained, and the images of the ancient languages have been captured in equivalent English images wherever possible.

Study Aids

Other features to enhance understanding of the text include subject headings throughout the text to identify speakers and topics, book subheadings to give a synopsis of each book's theme, and footnotes offering additional information on selected verses.

Our Prayer

It is with great humility and prayerfulness that this Bible is presented. We acknowledge the infallibility of God's Word, as well as our own human frailty. We pray that God has worked through us as his vessels so that we all might better learn his truth for ourselves and that it might richly grow in our lives. It is to his glory that this Bible is given.

THE PUBLISHER

the **old testament**

THE BEGINNING OF THE WORLD

1 In the beginning God created the sky and the earth. ²The earth was empty and had no form. Darkness covered the ocean, and God's Spirit was moving over the water.

³Then God said, "Let there be light," and there was light. ⁴God saw that the light was good, so he divided the light from the darkness. ⁵God named the light "day" and the darkness "night." Evening passed, and morning came. This was the first day.

⁶Then God said, "Let there be something to divide the water in two." ⁷So God made the air and placed some of the water above the air and some below it. ⁸God named the air "sky." Evening passed, and morning came. This was the second day.

⁹Then God said, "Let the water under the sky be gathered together so the dry land will appear." And it happened. ¹⁰God named the dry land "earth" and the water that was gathered together "seas." God saw that this was good.

¹¹Then God said, "Let the earth produce plants—some to make grain for seeds and others to make fruits with seeds in them. Every seed will produce more of its own kind of plant." And it happened. ¹²The earth produced plants with grain for seeds and trees that made fruits with seeds in them. Each seed grew its own kind of plant. God saw that all this was good. ¹³Evening passed, and morning came. This was the third day.

¹⁴Then God said, "Let there be lights in the sky to separate day from night. These lights will be used for signs, seasons, days, and years. ¹⁵They will be in the sky to give light to the earth." And it happened.

¹⁶So God made the two large lights. He made the brighter light to rule the day and made the smaller light to rule the night. He also made the stars. ¹⁷God put all these in the sky to shine on the earth, ¹⁸to rule over the day and over the night, and to separate the light from the darkness. God saw that all these things were good. ¹⁹Evening passed, and morning came. This was the fourth day.

²⁰Then God said, "Let the water be filled with living things, and let birds fly in the air above the earth."

²¹So God created the large sea animals and every living thing that moves in the sea. The sea is filled with these living things, with each one producing more of its own kind. He also made every bird that flies, and each bird produced more of its own kind. God saw that this was good. ²²God blessed them and said, "Have many young ones so that you may grow in number. Fill the water of the seas, and let the birds grow in number on the earth." ²³Evening passed, and morning came. This was the fifth day.

²⁴Then God said, "Let the earth be filled with animals, each producing more of its own kind. Let there be tame animals and small crawling animals and wild animals, and let each produce more of its kind." And it happened.

²⁵So God made the wild animals, the tame animals, and all the small crawling animals to produce more of their own kind. God saw that this was good.

²⁶Then God said, "Let us make human beings in our image and likeness. And let them rule over the fish in the sea and the birds in the sky, over the tame animals, over all the earth, and over all the small crawling animals on the earth."

²⁷So God created human beings in his image. In the image of God he created them. He created them male and female. ²⁸God blessed them and said, "Have many children and grow in number. Fill the earth and be its master. Rule over the fish in the sea and over the birds in the sky and over every living thing that moves on the earth."

²⁹God said, "Look, I have given you all the plants that have grain for seeds and all the trees whose fruits have seeds in them. They will be food for you. ³⁰I have given all the green plants as food for every wild animal,

every bird of the air, and every small crawling animal." And it happened. ³¹God looked at everything he had made, and it was very good. Evening passed, and morning came. This was the sixth day.

THE SEVENTH DAY—REST

2 So the sky, the earth, and all that filled them were finished. ²By the seventh day God finished the work he had been doing, so he rested from all his work. ³God blessed the seventh day and made it a holy day, because on that day he rested from all the work he had done in creating the world.

THE FIRST PEOPLE

⁴This is the story of the creation of the sky and the earth. When the LORD God first made the earth and the sky, ⁵there were still no plants on the earth. Nothing was growing in the fields because the LORD God had not yet made it rain on the land. And there was no person to care for the ground, ⁶but a mist would rise up from the earth and water all the ground.

⁷Then the LORD God took dust from the ground and formed a man from it. He breathed the breath of life into the man's nose, and the man became a living person.

WHEN YOUR WAY ISN'T GOD'S WAY

FITNESS

smart food

GENESIS 1:11

When God developed the body, he specifically created certain foods for its use. These are the foods that grow and exist in nature. God has built into natural foods everything that is necessary in just the right amounts and in the perfect balance needed for proper digestion, distribution of nutrients, and elimination of waste.

The digestive system is an intricate network of food-processing organs whose purpose is to break down and utilize the food you eat. Each component of the digestive system is so divinely complex that no human could create it. Every part is a universe to itself.

All the organs of this system have unique cells, glands, fluids, and functions that are divinely formulated to play a specific role in the amazing manner in which the body processes food. When you take in food in its natural state, the digestive system easily breaks it down, dispenses the nutrients to body cells, and quickly eliminates leftover toxins and by-products.

Natural food is packed with living vitamins, minerals, water, fiber, and the enzymes needed to digest the food itself. These various elements, and all the other elements natural food contains, are designed by God. And food designed by God is smart food for us to eat.

reflect: Consider the types of foods you eat and try to eat more natural foods if needed.
Go to **Genesis 1:31**.

8Then the LORD God planted a garden in the east, in a place called Eden, and put the man he had formed into it. 9The LORD God caused every beautiful tree and every tree that was good for food to grow out of the ground. In the middle of the garden, God put the tree that gives life and also the tree that gives the knowledge of good and evil.

10A river flowed through Eden and watered the garden. From there the river branched out to become four rivers. 11The first river, named Pishon, flows around the whole land of Havilah, where there is gold. 12The gold of that land is excellent. Bdellium and onyx[n] are also found there. 13The second river, named Gihon, flows around the whole land of Cush. 14The third river, named Tigris, flows out of Assyria toward the east. The fourth river is the Euphrates.

15The LORD God put the man in the garden of Eden to care for it and work it. 16The LORD God commanded him, "You may eat the fruit from any tree in the garden, 17but you must

---

2:12 bdellium and onyx Bdellium is an expensive, sweet-smelling resin like myrrh, and onyx is a gem.

WHEN YOUR WAY ISN'T GOD'S WAY

no help, just no interference

FITNESS

GENESIS 1:31

If we got rid of the ozone, the rainforests, the oceans, and the endangered species, humankind would die. However, if we get rid of human beings, the ozone, rainforests, and endangered species would flourish. So what do we need to save these things from? Ourselves, of course. God did not need our help to create these things, and he doesn't need our help to restore these things. He just needs us to stop destroying them.

Because we do not understand all of the processes, protocols, and purposes for creation, any time we drastically remove or alter something we create chaos. Life is a process of an infinite number of chemical combinations and reactions at precise moments with varying speeds. For example, altering or changing body chemistry by living out of alignment with God and constantly placing various drugs and chemicals into the system will have negative and potentially hazardous (if not lethal) effects on the body.

By interfering with God's design, we contribute to decay, depression, and disease that he never intended for us to experience. He created health, and our interference causes disease. When it comes to our lives, we must align with God in order to experience health. He needs no help, just no interference.

reflect: Learn to take better care of yourself and to show respect for creation.
Go to **Genesis 2:7.**

not eat the fruit from the tree which gives the knowledge of good and evil. If you ever eat fruit from that tree, you will die!"

THE FIRST WOMAN

18Then the LORD God said, "It is not good for the man to be alone. I will make a helper who is right for him."

19From the ground God formed every wild animal and every bird in the sky, and he brought them to the man so the man could name them. Whatever the man called each living thing, that became its name. 20The man gave names to all the tame animals, to the birds in the sky, and to all the wild animals. But Adam[n] did not find a helper that was right for him. 21So the LORD God caused the man to sleep very deeply, and while he was asleep, God removed one of the man's ribs. Then God closed up the man's skin at the place where he took the rib. 22The LORD God used the rib from the man to make a woman, and then he brought the woman to the man.

2:20 Adam This is the name of the first man. It also means "humans," including men and women.

WHEN YOUR WAY ISN'T GOD'S WAY

FITNESS

the breath of life

GENESIS 2:7

Breath is life! The body's most important nutrient is oxygen. While you can survive weeks without food and days without water, you can go only a few minutes without oxygen. Our bodies survive by drawing in oxygen through the lungs. Once the lungs have the oxygen, the heart and blood vessels pump it out to the rest of the organs.

During aerobic activity, the body needs more oxygen than during inactivity, and it needs it faster than usual, causing the body to adapt by increasing the efficiency of the lungs, heart, and blood vessels to draw, deliver, absorb, and store oxygen. In essence, our bodies become highly efficient "oxygen-utilizing machines." Aerobic exercise is also called "cardiovascular" exercise because it conditions two of the most important muscles: the heart and the lungs.

If you regularly perform aerobic or cardiovascular activities, every function needed for you to move for longer periods of time improves. By regularly moving vigorously for fifteen to twenty minutes, all the organs, vessels and glands of the cardiovascular system adapt in a healthy way. They get stronger, more flexible, and better at using the God-given gift of a "breath."

reflect: Exercise your cardiovascular system for increased efficiency in breathing.
Go to **Joshua 1:7.**

23And the man said,

"Now, this is someone whose bones came
from my bones,
whose body came from my body.
I will call her 'woman,'
because she was taken out of man."

24So a man will leave his father and
mother and be united with his wife, and the
two will become one body. 25The man and his wife were naked, but
they were not ashamed.

THE BEGINNING OF SIN

3 Now the snake was the most clever of
all the wild animals the LORD God had
made. One day the snake said to the woman,
"Did God really say that you must not eat
fruit from any tree in the garden?"

2The woman answered the snake, "We
may eat fruit from the trees in the garden.
3But God told us, 'You must not eat fruit from
the tree that is in the middle of the garden.
You must not even touch it, or you will die.'"

GUILT AND GRACE

God's perfect plan
for marriage

FAMILY

By Jimmy Evans

GENESIS 2:18

G od has a perfect plan for marriage. Polls show that most people say having a
happy, stable marriage for a lifetime is very important, yet few people believe it is
possible. People have not lost the dream of having a happy marriage, but they have lost
the hope of making it a reality. For a fact, it *is* possible to have that happy marriage you
dream about.

No matter your past experience, God can forgive you and make it possible for you to
have a happy marriage. Even if you have failed at marriage before, God has not given
up on you. His perfect plan for marriage works for everyone. This plan is outlined in
the Book of Ephesians. Husbands must love their wives as Christ loves the church, and
wives are to submit to their husbands as to the Lord.

Most people do not like that Bible passage. But this plan is the only one that works. It
may be threatening Scripture to us, but it is God's only plan for marriage. The husband
must lay his life down and love his wife, or he will not succeed in marriage. The wife
must honor and submit to her husband, or the marriage will fail.

All of us struggle with these concepts. Men struggle with loving sacrificially, and
women struggle with being submissive. Why does the plan work? The plan works
because the roles described in Ephesians disable our sin nature and keep our sin from
destroying our marriage.

reflect: Do you need to change how you are relating to your spouse?
Go to **1 Corinthians 11:7–9.**

4But the snake said to the woman, "You will not die. 5God knows that if you eat the fruit from that tree, you will learn about good and evil and you will be like God!"

6The woman saw that the tree was beautiful, that its fruit was good to eat, and that it would make her wise. So she took some of its fruit and ate it. She also gave some of the fruit to her husband who was with her, and he ate it.

7Then, it was as if their eyes were opened. They realized they were naked, so they sewed fig leaves together and made something to cover themselves.

8Then they heard the LORD God walking in the garden during the cool part of the day, and the man and his wife hid from the LORD God among the trees in the garden. 9But the LORD God called to the man and said, "Where are you?"

10The man answered, "I heard you walking in the garden, and I was afraid because I was naked, so I hid."

11God asked, "Who told you that you were naked? Did you eat fruit from the tree from which I commanded you not to eat?"

12The man said, "You gave this woman to me and she gave me fruit from the tree, so I ate it."

13Then the LORD God said to the woman, "How could you have done such a thing?"

She answered, "The snake tricked me, so I ate the fruit."

14The LORD God said to the snake,
"Because you did this,
    a curse will be put on you.
You will be cursed as no other animal,
    tame or wild, will ever be.
You will crawl on your stomach,
    and you will eat dust all the days of your
        life.
15 I will make you and the woman
    enemies to each other.
Your descendants and her descendants
    will be enemies.
One of her descendants will crush your
        head,
    and you will bite his heel."
16Then God said to the woman,
"I will cause you to have much trouble
    when you are pregnant,
and when you give birth to children,
    you will have great pain.

You will greatly desire your husband,
    but he will rule over you."

17Then God said to the man, "You listened to what your wife said, and you ate fruit from the tree from which I commanded you not to eat.
"So I will put a curse on the ground,
    and you will have to work very hard for
        your food.
In pain you will eat its food
    all the days of your life.
18 The ground will produce thorns and
        weeds for you,
    and you will eat the plants of the field.
19 You will sweat and work hard for your
        food.
Later you will return to the ground,
    because you were taken from it.
You are dust,
    and when you die, you will return to the
        dust."
20The man named his wife Eve,[n] because she was the mother of all the living.

21The LORD God made clothes from animal skins for the man and his wife and dressed them. 22Then the LORD God said, "Humans have become like one of us; they know good and evil. We must keep them from eating some of the fruit from the tree of life, or they will live forever." 23So the LORD God forced Adam out of the garden of Eden to work the ground from which he was taken. 24After God forced humans out of the garden, he placed angels and a sword of fire that flashed around in every direction on its eastern border. This kept people from getting to the tree of life.

THE FIRST FAMILY

4 Adam had sexual relations with his wife Eve, and she became pregnant and gave birth to Cain.[n] Eve said, "With the LORD's help, I have given birth to a man." 2After that, Eve gave birth to Cain's brother Abel. Abel took care of flocks, and Cain became a farmer.

3Later, Cain brought some food from the ground as a gift to God. 4Abel brought the best parts from some of the firstborn of

---

3:20 Eve This name sounds like the Hebrew word meaning "alive." **4:1 Cain** This name sounds like the Hebrew word for "I have given birth."

his flock. The Lord accepted Abel and his gift, 5but he did not accept Cain and his gift. So Cain became very angry and felt rejected.

6The Lord asked Cain, "Why are you angry? Why do you look so unhappy? 7If you do things well, I will accept you, but if you do not do them well, sin is ready to attack you. Sin wants you, but you must rule over it."

8Cain said to his brother Abel, "Let's go out into the field." While they were out in the field, Cain attacked his brother Abel and killed him.

9Later, the Lord said to Cain, "Where is your brother Abel?"

Cain answered, "I don't know. Is it my job to take care of my brother?"

10Then the Lord said, "What have you done? Your brother's blood is crying out to me from the ground. 11And now you will be cursed in your work with the ground, the same ground where your brother's blood fell and where your hands killed him. 12You will

WHEN YOUR WAY ISN'T GOD'S WAY

mastering your emotions

FITNESS

GENESIS 4:7

This verse is located in the context of the story of Cain and Abel. As the story suggests, God knows that emotional situations can become the seedbed for sinful acts. He saw Cain's depression and knew that Cain faced two monumental choices. Cain could agree with God's assessment of the situation and take steps to repair the relationship. Or Cain could defend himself, refuse God's assistance, and let his emotional state carry him into action.

God closed the conversation with this remark, "Sin wants you, but you must rule over it." Sin wants control. Sin needs control. The word for desire used here occurs only three times in the Old Testament. In both of the other occurrences, it is about sexual desire. Is there any stronger form of desire to take over someone than sexual desire? Is there any stronger emotion than the emotion of wanting to possess the object of our lust?

God makes it very clear. Sin wants to own us. Sin wants a controlling, intimate involvement with us. And it will use the emotional gateway to get what it wants. But God says that Cain could be sin's master. It was up to him. Cain could reverse the emotional roller coaster he was on and prevent the downhill slide into sin. Alas, Cain chose poorly and suffered the consequences of his actions, but we can learn from his mistake and choose wisely.

reflect: Thank God for the grace to overcome sin and its destructive power.
Go to **Leviticus 3:17**.

work the ground, but it will not grow good crops for you anymore, and you will wander around on the earth."

¹³Then Cain said to the LORD, "This punishment is more than I can stand! ¹⁴Today you have forced me to stop working the ground, and now I must hide from you. I must wander around on the earth, and anyone who meets me can kill me."

¹⁵The LORD said to Cain, "No! If anyone kills you, I will punish that person seven times more." Then the LORD put a mark on Cain warning anyone who met him not to kill him.

CAIN'S FAMILY

¹⁶So Cain went away from the LORD and lived in the land of Nod,ⁿ east of Eden. ¹⁷He had sexual relations with his wife, and she became pregnant and gave birth to Enoch. At that time Cain was building a city, which he named after his son Enoch. ¹⁸Enoch had a son named Irad, Irad had a son named Mehujael, Mehujael had a son named Methushael, and Methushael had a son named Lamech.

¹⁹Lamech married two women, Adah and Zillah. ²⁰Adah gave birth to Jabal, who became the first person to live in tents and raise cattle. ²¹Jabal's brother was Jubal, the first person to play the harp and flute. ²²Zillah gave birth to Tubal-Cain, who made tools out of bronze and iron. The sister of Tubal-Cain was Naamah.

²³Lamech said to his wives:

"Adah and Zillah, hear my voice!
    You wives of Lamech, listen to what I
    say.
I killed a man for wounding me,
    a young man for hitting me.
²⁴ If Cain's killer is punished seven times,
    then Lamech's killer will be punished
    seventy-seven times."

ADAM AND EVE HAVE A NEW SON

²⁵Adam had sexual relations with his wife Eve again, and she gave birth to a son. She named him Sethⁿ and said, "God has given me another child. He will take the place of Abel, who was killed by Cain." ²⁶Seth also had a son, and they named him Enosh. At that time people began to pray to the LORD.

ADAM'S FAMILY HISTORY

5 This is the family history of Adam. When God created human beings, he made them in his own likeness. ²He created them male and female, and on that day he blessed them and named them human beings.

³When Adam was 130 years old, he became the father of another son in his likeness and image, and Adam named him Seth. ⁴After Seth was born, Adam lived 800 years and had other sons and daughters. ⁵So Adam lived a total of 930 years, and then he died.

⁶When Seth was 105 years old, he had a son named Enosh. ⁷After Enosh was born, Seth lived 807 years and had other sons and daughters. ⁸So Seth lived a total of 912 years, and then he died.

⁹When Enosh was 90 years old, he had a son named Kenan. ¹⁰After Kenan was born, Enosh lived 815 years and had other sons and daughters. ¹¹So Enosh lived a total of 905 years, and then he died.

¹²When Kenan was 70 years old, he had a son named Mahalalel. ¹³After Mahalalel was born, Kenan lived 840 years and had other sons and daughters. ¹⁴So Kenan lived a total of 910 years, and then he died.

¹⁵When Mahalalel was 65 years old, he had a son named Jared. ¹⁶After Jared was born, Mahalalel lived 830 years and had other sons and daughters. ¹⁷So Mahalalel lived a total of 895 years, and then he died.

¹⁸When Jared was 162 years old, he had a son named Enoch. ¹⁹After Enoch was born, Jared lived 800 years and had other sons and daughters. ²⁰So Jared lived a total of 962 years, and then he died.

²¹When Enoch was 65 years old, he had a son named Methuselah. ²²After Methuselah was born, Enoch walked with God 300 years more and had other sons and daughters. ²³So Enoch lived a total of 365 years. ²⁴Enoch walked with God; one day Enoch could not be found, because God took him.

²⁵When Methuselah was 187 years old, he had a son named Lamech. ²⁶After Lamech was born, Methuselah lived 782 years and had other sons and daughters. ²⁷So Methu-

---

4:16 Nod This name sounds like the Hebrew word for "wander." **4:25 Seth** This name sounds like the Hebrew word for "to give."

selah lived a total of 969 years, and then he died.

[28]When Lamech was 182, he had a son. [29]Lamech named his son Noah[n] and said, "He will comfort us in our work, which comes from the ground the LORD has cursed." [30]After Noah was born, Lamech lived 595 years and had other sons and daughters. [31]So Lamech lived a total of 777 years, and then he died.

[32]After Noah was 500 years old, he became the father of Shem, Ham, and Japheth.

THE HUMAN RACE BECOMES EVIL

6 The number of people on earth began to grow, and daughters were born to them. [2]When the sons of God saw that these girls were beautiful, they married any of them they chose. [3]The LORD said, "My Spirit will not remain in human beings forever, because they are flesh. They will live only 120 years."

[4]The Nephilim were on the earth in those days and also later. That was when the sons of God had sexual relations with the daughters of human beings. These women gave birth to children, who became famous and were the mighty warriors of long ago.

[5]The LORD saw that the human beings on the earth were very wicked and that everything they thought about was evil. [6]He was sorry he had made human beings on the earth, and his heart was filled with pain. [7]So the LORD said, "I will destroy all human beings that I made on the earth. And I will destroy every animal and everything that crawls on the earth and the birds of the air, because I am sorry I have made them." [8]But Noah pleased the LORD.

NOAH AND THE GREAT FLOOD

[9]This is the family history of Noah. Noah was a good man, the most innocent man of his time, and he walked with God. [10]He had three sons: Shem, Ham, and Japheth.

[11]People on earth did what God said was evil, and violence was everywhere. [12]When God saw that everyone on the earth did only evil, [13]he said to Noah, "Because people have made the earth full of violence, I will destroy all of them from the earth. [14]Build a boat of cypress wood for yourself. Make rooms in it and cover it inside and outside with tar. [15]This is how big I want you to build the boat: four hundred fifty feet long, seventy-five

feet wide, and forty-five feet high. [16]Make an opening around the top of the boat that is eighteen inches high from the edge of the roof down. Put a door in the side of the boat. Make an upper, middle, and lower deck in it. [17]I will bring a flood of water on the earth to destroy all living things that live under the sky, including everything that has the breath of life. Everything on the earth will die. [18]But I will make an agreement with you—you, your sons, your wife, and your sons' wives will all go into the boat. [19]Also, you must bring into the boat two of every living thing, male and female. Keep them alive with you. [20]Two of every kind of bird, animal, and crawling thing will come to you to be kept alive. [21]Also gather some of every kind of food and store it on the boat as food for you and the animals."

[22]Noah did everything that God commanded him.

THE FLOOD BEGINS

7 Then the LORD said to Noah, "I have seen that you are the best person among the people of this time, so you and your family can go into the boat. [2]Take with you seven pairs, each male with its female, of every kind of clean animal, and take one pair, each male with its female, of every kind of unclean animal. [3]Take seven pairs of all the birds of the sky, each male with its female. This will allow all these animals to continue living on the earth after the flood. [4]Seven days from now I will send rain on the earth. It will rain forty days and forty nights, and I will wipe off from the earth every living thing that I have made."

[5]Noah did everything the LORD commanded him.

[6]Noah was six hundred years old when the flood came. [7]He and his wife and his sons and their wives went into the boat to escape the waters of the flood. [8]The clean animals, the unclean animals, the birds, and everything that crawls on the ground [9]came to Noah. They went into the boat in groups of two, male and female, just as God had commanded Noah. [10]Seven days later the flood started.

[11]When Noah was six hundred years old,

the flood started. On the seventeenth day of the second month of that year the underground springs split open, and the clouds in the sky poured out rain. [12]The rain fell on the earth for forty days and forty nights.

[13]On that same day Noah and his wife, his sons Shem, Ham, and Japheth, and their wives went into the boat. [14]They had every kind of wild and tame animal, every kind of animal that crawls on the earth, and every kind of bird. [15]Every creature that had the breath of life came to Noah in the boat in groups of two. [16]One male and one female of every living thing came, just as God had commanded Noah. Then the LORD closed the door behind them.

[17]Water flooded the earth for forty days, and as it rose it lifted the boat off the ground. [18]The water continued to rise, and the boat floated on it above the earth. [19]The water rose so much that even the highest mountains under the sky were covered by it. [20]It continued to rise until it was more than twenty feet above the mountains.

[21]All living things that moved on the earth died. This included all the birds, tame animals, wild animals, and creatures that swarm on the earth, as well as all human beings. [22]So everything on dry land that had the breath of life in it died. [23]God destroyed from the earth every living thing that was on the land—every man, animal, crawling thing, and bird of the sky. All that was left was Noah and what was with him in the boat. [24]And the waters continued to cover the earth for one hundred fifty days.

THE FLOOD ENDS

8 But God remembered Noah and all the wild and tame animals with him in the boat. He made a wind blow over the earth, and the water went down. [2]The underground springs stopped flowing, and the clouds in the sky stopped pouring down rain. [3-4]The water that covered the earth began to go down. After one hundred fifty days it had gone down so much that the boat touched land again. It came to rest on one of the mountains of Ararat[n] on the seventeenth day of the seventh month. [5]The water continued to go down so that by the first day of the tenth month the tops of the mountains could be seen.

[6]Forty days later Noah opened the window he had made in the boat, and [7]he sent out a raven. It flew here and there until the water had dried up from the earth. [8]Then Noah sent out a dove to find out if the water had dried up from the ground. [9]The dove could not find a place to land because water still covered the earth, so it came back to the boat. Noah reached out his hand and took the bird and brought it back into the boat.

[10]After seven days Noah again sent out the dove from the boat, [11]and that evening it came back to him with a fresh olive leaf in its mouth. Then Noah knew that the ground was almost dry. [12]Seven days later he sent the dove out again, but this time it did not come back.

[13]When Noah was six hundred and one years old, in the first day of the first month of that year, the water was dried up from the land. Noah removed the covering of the boat and saw that the land was dry. [14]By the twenty-seventh day of the second month the land was completely dry.

[15]Then God said to Noah, [16]"You and your wife, your sons, and their wives should go out of the boat. [17]Bring every animal out of the boat with you—the birds, animals, and everything that crawls on the earth. Let them have many young ones so that they might grow in number."

[18]So Noah went out with his sons, his wife, and his sons' wives. [19]Every animal, everything that crawls on the earth, and every bird went out of the boat by families.

[20]Then Noah built an altar to the LORD. He took some of all the clean birds and animals, and he burned them on the altar as offerings to God. [21]The LORD was pleased with these sacrifices and said to himself, "I will never again curse the ground because of human beings. Their thoughts are evil even when they are young, but I will never again destroy every living thing on the earth as I did this time.

[22] "As long as the earth continues,
    planting and harvest,
    cold and hot,
    summer and winter,

8:3–4 Ararat The ancient land of Urartu, an area in Eastern Turkey.

day and night will not stop."

THE NEW BEGINNING

9 Then God blessed Noah and his sons and said to them, "Have many children; grow in number and fill the earth. ²Every animal on earth, every bird in the sky, every animal that crawls on the ground, and every fish in the sea will respect and fear you. I have given them to you.

³"Everything that moves, everything that is alive, is yours for food. Earlier I gave you the green plants, but now I give you everything for food. ⁴But you must not eat meat that still has blood in it, because blood gives life. ⁵I will demand blood for life. I will demand the life of any animal that kills a person, and I will demand the life of anyone who takes another person's life.

⁶ "Whoever kills a human being
    will be killed by a human being,
    because God made humans
    in his own image.

⁷"As for you, Noah, I want you and your

SOWING AND REAPING

expecting
the increase

FINANCES

By Larry Stockstill

GENESIS 8:22

When you look to God as your source, you cannot help but anticipate something. It is as if you are eagerly leaning forward and expecting to see something on the horizon. Expectation in God is really faith in him. Expectation comes from vision. Let the Holy Spirit give you vision. When you have a vision, you become a channel of blessing for God. For example, later we read that Joseph's vision was for a massive harvest and the best use of it for Egypt and many other countries (Genesis 41).

After God gives you a vision, expect him to give you the seed you need to plant for a harvest to fulfill it. He will give you all you need and make it grow (2 Corinthians 9:10). Once you receive the vision from God, prepare a storehouse to receive it. Then plant according to the size of your vision. Be constantly on the lookout for seed to sow, and then be faithful to plant it. If you do all of these things, your harvest will come (Genesis 8:22).

Hold on to your expectations of seeing blessings in your life. If you need love, sow love into the life of someone else. Show mercy to others, and you will receive mercy. Give forgiveness, and you will be granted forgiveness. Everyone can live in the Father's abundance and without any lack. Be faithful with your tithe, and give offerings, and you will be able to help others. Wait for God, and expect him to pour out a blessing so large you cannot contain it!

reflect: What type of harvest are you expecting to reap?
Go to **1 Corinthians 10:13.**

family to have many children, to grow in number on the earth, and to become many."

⁸Then God said to Noah and his sons, ⁹"Now I am making my agreement with you and your people who will live after you, ¹⁰and with every living thing that is with you—the birds, the tame and the wild animals, and with everything that came out of the boat with you—with every living thing on earth. ¹¹I make this agreement with you: I will never again destroy all living things by a flood. A flood will never again destroy the earth."

¹²And God said, "This is the sign of the agreement between me and you and every living creature that is with you. ¹³I am putting my rainbow in the clouds as the sign of the agreement between me and the earth. ¹⁴When I bring clouds over the earth and a rainbow appears in them, ¹⁵I will remember my agreement between me and you and every living thing. Floods will never again destroy all life on the earth. ¹⁶When the rainbow appears in the clouds, I will see it and I will remember the agreement that continues forever between me and every living thing on the earth."

¹⁷So God said to Noah, "The rainbow is a sign of the agreement that I made with all living things on earth."

NOAH AND HIS SONS

¹⁸The sons of Noah who came out of the boat with him were Shem, Ham, and Japheth. (Ham was the father of Canaan.) ¹⁹These three men were Noah's sons, and all the people on earth came from these three sons.

²⁰Noah became a farmer and planted a vineyard. ²¹When he drank wine made from his grapes, he became drunk and lay naked in his tent. ²²Ham, the father of Canaan, looked at his naked father and told his brothers outside. ²³Then Shem and Japheth got a coat and, carrying it on both their shoulders, they walked backwards into the tent and covered their father. They turned their faces away so that they did not see their father's nakedness.

²⁴Noah was sleeping because of the wine. When he woke up and learned what his youngest son, Ham, had done to him, ²⁵he said,

"May there be a curse on Canaan!
  May he be the lowest slave to his
    brothers."
²⁶Noah also said,
"May the LORD, the God of Shem, be
    praised!
  May Canaan be Shem's slave.
²⁷ May God give more land to Japheth.
  May Japheth live in Shem's tents,
  and may Canaan be their slave."

²⁸After the flood Noah lived 350 years. ²⁹He lived a total of 950 years, and then he died.

NATIONS GROW AND SPREAD

10 This is the family history of Shem, Ham, and Japheth, the sons of Noah. After the flood these three men had sons.

JAPHETH'S SONS

²The sons of Japheth were Gomer, Magog, Madai, Javan, Tubal, Meshech, and Tiras. ³The sons of Gomer were Ashkenaz, Riphath, and Togarmah. ⁴The sons of Javan were Elishah, Tarshish, Kittim,ⁿ and Rodanim. ⁵Those who lived in the lands around the Mediterranean Sea came from these sons of Japheth. All the families grew and became different nations, each nation with its own land and its own language.

HAM'S SONS

⁶The sons of Ham were Cush, Mizraim,ⁿ Put, and Canaan. ⁷The sons of Cush were Seba, Havilah, Sabtah, Raamah, and Sabteca.

The sons of Raamah were Sheba and Dedan.

⁸Cush also had a descendant named Nimrod, who became a very powerful man on earth. ⁹He was a great hunter before the LORD, which is why people say someone is "like Nimrod, a great hunter before the LORD." ¹⁰At first Nimrod's kingdom covered Babylon, Erech, Akkad, and Calneh in the land of Babylonia. ¹¹From there he went to Assyria, where he built the cities of Nineveh, Rehoboth Ir, and Calah. ¹²He also built Resen, the great city between Nineveh and Calah.

10:4 Kittim His descendants were the people of Cyprus. **10:6 Mizraim** This is another name for Egypt.

¹³Mizraim was the father of the Ludites, Anamites, Lehabites, Naphtuhites, ¹⁴Pathrusites, Casluhites, and the people of Crete. (The Philistines came from the Casluhites.)

¹⁵Canaan was the father of Sidon, his first son, and of Heth. ¹⁶He was also the father of the Jebusites, Amorites, Girgashites, ¹⁷Hivites, Arkites, Sinites, ¹⁸Arvadites, Zemarites, and Hamathites. The families of the Canaanites scattered. ¹⁹Their land reached from Sidon to Gerar as far as Gaza, and then to Sodom, Gomorrah, Admah, and Zeboiim, as far as Lasha.

²⁰All these people were the sons of Ham, and all these families had their own languages, their own lands, and their own nations.

SHEM'S SONS

²¹Shem, Japheth's older brother, also had sons. One of his descendants was the father of all the sons of Eber.

²²The sons of Shem were Elam, Asshur, Arphaxad, Lud, and Aram.

²³The sons of Aram were Uz, Hul, Gether, and Meshech.

²⁴Arphaxad was the father of Shelah, who was the father of Eber. ²⁵Eber was the father of two sons—one named Peleg,ⁿ because the earth was divided during his life, and the other was named Joktan.

²⁶Joktan was the father of Almodad, Sheleph, Hazarmaveth, Jerah, ²⁷Hadoram, Uzal, Diklah, ²⁸Obal, Abimael, Sheba, ²⁹Ophir, Havilah, and Jobab. All these people were the sons of Joktan. ³⁰They lived in the area between Mesha and Sephar in the hill country in the East.

³¹These are the people from the family of Shem, arranged by families, languages, countries, and nations.

³²This is the list of the families from the sons of Noah, arranged according to their nations. From these families came all the nations who spread across the earth after the flood.

THE LANGUAGES CONFUSED

11 At this time the whole world spoke one language, and everyone used the same words. ²As people moved from the east, they found a plain in the land of Babylonia and settled there.

³They said to each other, "Let's make bricks and bake them to make them hard." So they used bricks instead of stones, and tar instead of mortar. ⁴Then they said to each other, "Let's build a city and a tower for ourselves, whose top will reach high into the sky. We will become famous. Then we will not be scattered over all the earth."

⁵The LORD came down to see the city and the tower that the people had built. ⁶The LORD said, "Now, these people are united, all speaking the same language. This is only the beginning of what they will do. They will be able to do anything they want. ⁷Come, let us go down and confuse their language so they will not be able to understand each other."

⁸So the LORD scattered them from there over all the earth, and they stopped building the city. ⁹The place is called Babelⁿ since that is where the LORD confused the language of the whole world. So the LORD caused them to spread out from there over the whole world.

THE STORY OF SHEM'S FAMILY

¹⁰This is the family history of Shem. Two years after the flood, when Shem was 100 years old, his son Arphaxad was born. ¹¹After that, Shem lived 500 years and had other sons and daughters.

¹²When Arphaxad was 35 years old, his son Shelah was born. ¹³After that, Arphaxad lived 403 years and had other sons and daughters.

¹⁴When Shelah was 30 years old, his son Eber was born. ¹⁵After that, Shelah lived 403 years and had other sons and daughters.

¹⁶When Eber was 34 years old, his son Peleg was born. ¹⁷After that, Eber lived 430 years and had other sons and daughters.

¹⁸When Peleg was 30 years old, his son Reu was born. ¹⁹After that, Peleg lived 209 years and had other sons and daughters.

²⁰When Reu was 32 years old, his son Serug was born. ²¹After that, Reu lived 207 years and had other sons and daughters.

²²When Serug was 30 years old, his son Nahor was born. ²³After that, Serug lived 200 years and had other sons and daughters.

²⁴When Nahor was 29 years old, his son

10:25 **Peleg** This name sounds like the Hebrew word for "divided." 11:9 **Babel** This name sounds like the Hebrew word for "confused."

Terah was born. 25After that, Nahor lived 119 years and had other sons and daughters.

26After Terah was 70 years old, his sons Abram, Nahor, and Haran were born.

THE STORY OF TERAH'S FAMILY

27This is the family history of Terah. Terah was the father of Abram, Nahor, and Haran. Haran was the father of Lot. 28While his father, Terah, was still alive, Haran died in Ur in Babylonia, where he was born. 29Abram and Nahor both married. Abram's wife was named Sarai, and Nahor's wife was named Milcah. She was the daughter of Haran, who was the father of both Milcah and Iscah. 30Sarai was not able to have children.

31Terah took his son Abram, his grandson Lot (Haran's son), and his daughter-in-law Sarai (Abram's wife) and moved out of Ur of Babylonia. They had planned to go to the land of Canaan, but when they reached the city of Haran, they settled there.

32Terah lived to be 205 years old, and then he died in Haran.

GOD CALLS ABRAM

12 The LORD said to Abram, "Leave your country, your relatives, and your father's family, and go to the land I will show you.

2 I will make you a great nation,
  and I will bless you.
I will make you famous,
  and you will be a blessing to others.
3 I will bless those who bless you,
  and I will place a curse on those who
    harm you.
And all the people on earth
  will be blessed through you."

4So Abram left Haran as the LORD had told him, and Lot went with him. At this time Abram was 75 years old. 5He took his wife Sarai, his nephew Lot, and everything they owned, as well as all the servants they had gotten in Haran. They set out from Haran, planning to go to the land of Canaan, and in time they arrived there.

6Abram traveled through that land as far as the great tree of Moreh at Shechem. The Canaanites were living in the land at that time. 7The LORD appeared to Abram and said, "I will give this land to your descendants." So Abram built an altar there to the LORD, who had appeared to him. 8Then he traveled from Shechem to the mountain east of Bethel and set up his tent there. Bethel was to the west, and Ai was to the east. There Abram built another altar to the LORD and worshiped him. 9After this, he traveled on toward southern Canaan.

ABRAM GOES TO EGYPT

10At this time there was not much food in the land, so Abram went down to Egypt to live because there was so little food. 11Just before they arrived in Egypt, he said to his wife Sarai, "I know you are a very beautiful woman. 12When the Egyptians see you, they will say, 'This woman is his wife.' Then they will kill me but let you live. 13Tell them you are my sister so that things will go well with me and I may be allowed to live because of you."

14When Abram came to Egypt, the Egyptians saw that Sarai was very beautiful. 15The Egyptian officers saw her and told the king of Egypt how beautiful she was. They took her to the king's palace, and 16the king was kind to Abram because he thought Abram was her brother. He gave Abram sheep, cattle, male and female donkeys, male and female servants, and camels.

17But the LORD sent terrible diseases on the king and all the people in his house because of Abram's wife Sarai. 18So the king sent for Abram and said, "What have you done to me? Why didn't you tell me Sarai was your wife? 19Why did you say, 'She is my sister' so that I made her my wife? Now, here is your wife. Take her and leave!" 20Then the king commanded his men to make Abram leave Egypt; so Abram and his wife left with everything they owned.

ABRAM AND LOT SEPARATE

13 So Abram, his wife, and Lot left Egypt, taking everything they owned, and traveled to southern Canaan. 2Abram was very rich in cattle, silver, and gold.

3He left southern Canaan and went back to Bethel where he had camped before, between Bethel and Ai, 4and where he had built an altar. So he worshiped the LORD there.

5During this time Lot was traveling with Abram, and Lot also had flocks, herds, and tents. 6Abram and Lot had so many animals that the land could not support both of them together, 7so Abram's herdsmen and Lot's herdsmen began to argue. The Canaanites and the Perizzites were living in the land at this time.

⁸Abram said to Lot, "There should be no arguing between you and me, or between your herdsmen and mine, because we are brothers. ⁹We should separate. The whole land is there in front of you. If you go to the left, I will go to the right. If you go to the right, I will go to the left."

¹⁰Lot looked all around and saw the whole

THE FAVOR OF GOD

God's riches

FINANCES

By Mark Chironna

GENESIS 13:2, 5

While Lot had a lot of livestock, his riches were not as abundant as his Uncle Abraham's. Abraham had a good relationship with God and had faith that God would provide all he required. Abraham trusted and worshiped God, and God gave him the power to become rich.

Lot's wealth grew; however, since his was a competitive increase, what he had was far less than what Abraham created in his life. Abraham's wealth grew because the power of God enhanced Abraham's skills (Deuteronomy 8:18).

Lot was not walking with faith, but with a competitive spirit, and his wealth was restricted to his natural abilities. The stress of maintaining the wealth he did have helped bring about Lot's separation from Abraham.

Those who compete for wealth in their own abilities never attain the supernatural abundance and peace of those who create wealth by faith in God's power.

Here are some things to consider about faith in God and all his blessings:

• Faith progresses by the power of choice to trust God.

• Faith is a fact; in order to come to God, you have to believe that he is God and that he rewards those who look to him.

• Faith is active; it is an act of the will to set your hopes and thoughts on God and his purposes.

The difference between Abraham's awesome legacy and personal wealth and Lot's troubles was accepting and acting in faith upon God's instructions. This faith allowed God to give Abraham the power to become rich.

reflect: Are you focused on your wealth instead of on God?
Go to **Genesis 18:14.**

Jordan Valley and that there was much water there. It was like the LORD's garden, like the land of Egypt in the direction of Zoar. (This was before the LORD destroyed Sodom and Gomorrah.) ¹¹So Lot chose to move east and live in the Jordan Valley. In this way Abram and Lot separated. ¹²Abram lived in the land of Canaan, but Lot lived among the cities in the Jordan Valley, very near to Sodom. ¹³Now the people of Sodom were very evil and were always sinning against the LORD.

¹⁴After Lot left, the LORD said to Abram, "Look all around you—to the north and south and east and west. ¹⁵All this land that you see I will give to you and your descendants forever. ¹⁶I will make your descendants as many as the dust of the earth. If anyone could count the dust on the earth, he could count your people. ¹⁷Get up! Walk through all this land because I am now giving it to you."

¹⁸So Abram moved his tents and went to live near the great trees of Mamre at the city of Hebron. There he built an altar to the LORD.

LOT IS CAPTURED

14 Now Amraphel was king of Babylonia, Arioch was king of Ellasar, Kedor-

---

FUTURE

THE PRODUCT OF PRESENT OBEDIENCE

taking territory
for God

GENESIS 13:17

There is a procedure that a person goes through in order to purchase a piece of property today. After picking out the property, the person looks at what it is and what is on it. Then he will verify where the boundaries are on the property, whether it is done by a survey or accepting what the seller tells him. After coming to an agreement on the price, the paperwork begins to clear the property of any previous liens on it to make sure the buyer is receiving a clean piece of land. The day comes for a closing of all the procedures, and the property is handed over to the buyer with paperwork in hand.

In Bible days, the procedure was a little different, with not as much documented legally. However, the buyer and seller would come to an agreement before going before the city elders. When the elders had approved the transaction, the buyer was actually given a sample of the soil as a promise note. The buyer then would walk the length and breadth of the property to take possession of it.

You can do that in the spiritual realm at your own home and at your workplace. Take possession in the spirit and claim that area as what God has given you. Give the powers of darkness "notice" that the area is off limits to them and a change of ownership has taken place. Commission ministering spirits to guard the region in order to keep the Enemy off of it. You will see God work for you.

reflect: Trust God to expand your territory of influence.
Go to **Genesis 39:2-5.**

laomer was king of Elam, and Tidal was king of Goiim. ²All these kings went to war against several other kings: Bera king of Sodom, Birsha king of Gomorrah, Shinab king of Admah, Shemeber king of Zeboiim, and the king of Bela. (Bela is also called Zoar.)

³These kings who were attacked united their armies in the Valley of Siddim (now the Dead Sea). ⁴They had served Kedorlaomer for twelve years, but in the thirteenth year, they all turned against him. ⁵Then in the fourteenth year, Kedorlaomer and the kings with him came and defeated the Rephaites in Ashteroth Karnaim, the Zuzites in Ham, and the Emites in Shaveh Kiriathaim. ⁶They also defeated the Horites in the mountains of Edom to El Paran (near the desert). ⁷Then they turned back and went to En Mishpat (that is, Kadesh). They defeated all the Amalekites, as well as the Amorites who lived in Hazazon Tamar.

⁸At that time the kings of Sodom, Gomorrah, Admah, Zeboiim, and Bela went out to fight in the Valley of Siddim. (Bela is called Zoar.) ⁹They fought against Kedorlaomer king of Elam, Tidal king of Goiim, Amraphel king of Babylonia, and Arioch king of Ellasar—four kings fighting against five. ¹⁰There were many tar pits in the Valley of Siddim. When the kings of Sodom and Gomorrah and their armies ran away, some of the soldiers fell into the tar pits, but the others ran away to the mountains.

¹¹Now Kedorlaomer and his armies took everything the people of Sodom and Gomorrah owned, including their food. ¹²They took Lot, Abram's nephew who was living in Sodom, and everything he owned. Then they left. ¹³One of the men who was not captured went to Abram, the Hebrew, and told him what had happened. At that time Abram was camped near the great trees of Mamre the Amorite. Mamre was a brother of Eshcol and Aner, and they had all made an agreement to help Abram.

ABRAM RESCUES LOT

¹⁴When Abram learned that Lot had been captured, he called out his 318 trained men who had been born in his camp. He led the men and chased the enemy all the way to the town of Dan. ¹⁵That night he divided his men into groups, and they made a surprise attack against the enemy. They chased them all the way to Hobah, north of Damascus. ¹⁶Then Abram brought back everything the enemy had stolen, the women and the other people, and Lot, and everything Lot owned.

¹⁷After defeating Kedorlaomer and the kings who were with him, Abram went home. As he was returning, the king of Sodom came out to meet him in the Valley of Shaveh (now called King's Valley).

¹⁸Melchizedek king of Salem brought out bread and wine. He was a priest for God Most High ¹⁹and blessed Abram, saying,

"Abram, may you be blessed by God Most
   High,
   the God who made heaven and earth.
²⁰ And we praise God Most High,
   who has helped you to defeat your
   enemies."

Then Abram gave Melchizedek a tenth of everything he had brought back from the battle.

²¹The king of Sodom said to Abram, "You may keep all these things for yourself. Just give me my people who were captured."

²²But Abram said to the king of Sodom, "I make a promise to the LORD, the God Most High, who made heaven and earth. ²³I promise that I will not keep anything that is yours. I will not keep even a thread or a sandal strap so that you cannot say, 'I made Abram rich.' ²⁴I will keep nothing but the food my young men have eaten. But give Aner, Eshcol, and Mamre their share of what we won, because they went with me into battle."

GOD'S AGREEMENT WITH ABRAM

15 After these things happened, the LORD spoke his word to Abram in a vision: "Abram, don't be afraid. I will defend you, and I will give you a great reward."

²But Abram said, "Lord GOD, what can you give me? I have no son, so my slave Eliezer from Damascus will get everything I own after I die." ³Abram said, "Look, you have given me no son, so a slave born in my house will inherit everything I have."

⁴Then the LORD spoke his word to Abram: "He will not be the one to inherit what you have. You will have a son of your own who will inherit what you have."

⁵Then God led Abram outside and said, "Look at the sky. There are so many stars you

cannot count them. Your descendants also will be too many to count."

6Abram believed the LORD. And the LORD accepted Abram's faith, and that faith made him right with God.

7God said to Abram, "I am the LORD who led you out of Ur of Babylonia so that I could give you this land to own."

8But Abram said, "Lord GOD, how can I be sure that I will own this land?"

9The LORD said to Abram, "Bring me a three-year-old cow, a three-year-old goat, a three-year-old male sheep, a dove, and a young pigeon."

10Abram brought them all to God. Then Abram killed the animals and cut each of them into two pieces, laying each half opposite the other half. But he did not cut the birds in half. 11Later, large birds flew down to eat the animals, but Abram chased them away.

12As the sun was going down, Abram fell into a deep sleep. While he was asleep, a very terrible darkness came. 13Then the LORD said to Abram, "You can be sure that your descendants will be strangers and travel in a land they don't own. The people there will make them slaves and be cruel to them for four hundred years. 14But I will punish the nation where they are slaves. Then your descendants will leave that land, taking great wealth with them. 15And you, Abram, will die in peace and will be buried at an old age. 16After your great-great-grandchildren are born, your people will come to this land again. It will take that long, because I am not yet going to punish the Amorites for their evil behavior."

17After the sun went down, it was very dark. Suddenly a smoking firepot and a blazing torch passed between the halves of the dead animals.n 18So on that day the LORD made an agreement with Abram and said, "I will give to your descendants the land between the river of Egypt and the great river Euphrates. 19This is the land of the Kenites, Kenizzites, Kadmonites, 20Hittites, Perizzites, Rephaites, 21Amorites, Canaanites, Girgashites, and Jebusites."

ISHMAEL IS BORN

16 Sarai, Abram's wife, had no children, but she had a slave girl from Egypt named Hagar. 2Sarai said to Abram, "Look, the LORD has not allowed me to have children, so have sexual relations with my slave girl. If she has a child, maybe I can have my own family through her."

Abram did what Sarai said. 3It was after he had lived ten years in Canaan that Sarai gave Hagar to her husband Abram. (Hagar was her slave girl from Egypt.)

4Abram had sexual relations with Hagar, and she became pregnant. When Hagar learned she was pregnant, she began to treat her mistress Sarai badly. 5Then Sarai said to Abram, "This is your fault. I gave my slave girl to you, and when she became pregnant, she began to treat me badly. Let the LORD decide who is right—you or me."

6But Abram said to Sarai, "You are Hagar's mistress. Do anything you want to her." Then Sarai was hard on Hagar, and Hagar ran away.

7The angel of the LORD found Hagar beside a spring of water in the desert, by the road to Shur. 8The angel said, "Hagar, Sarai's slave girl, where have you come from? Where are you going?"

Hagar answered, "I am running away from my mistress Sarai."

9The angel of the LORD said to her, "Go home to your mistress and obey her." 10The angel also said, "I will give you so many descendants they cannot be counted."

11The angel added,

"You are now pregnant,
  and you will have a son.
You will name him Ishmael,n
  because the LORD has heard your cries.
12 Ishmael will be like a wild donkey.
He will be against everyone,
  and everyone will be against him.
He will attack all his brothers."

13The slave girl gave a name to the LORD who spoke to her: "You are 'God who sees me,'" because she said to herself, "Have I really seen God who sees me?" 14So the well there, between Kadesh and Bered, was called Beer Lahai Roi.n

15Hagar gave birth to a son for Abram, and

15:17 passed . . . animals This showed that God sealed the agreement between himself and Abram. 16:11 Ishmael The Hebrew words for "Ishmael" and "has heard" sound similar. 16:14 Beer Lahai Roi This means "the well of the Living One who sees me."

The **Favor** of God

By Diana Hagee

GENESIS 16:1-13

Many of us have heard the story of Hagar numerous times. Hagar was Sarai's hand-maiden who bore Abram a son named Ishmael. However, few of us have thought about her relationship with the God of Abram.

Hagar was an unbeliever living in the household of believers. How unwanted she must have felt when rejected and cast off by Sarai. Then God did something very unusual for this disheartened woman. He gave Hagar the opportunity to hear his voice—Hagar actually heard the voice of God!

Imagine it for a moment—heartbroken and alone, Hagar hears her name called by the God of Abram and Sarai! Jehovah Jireh—the God who "sees," met her needs. His watchful eye was upon her just as it is upon us.

• After her amazing encounter with Hashem, the Name above all names, she made a choice and returned to her idols. Going back was "safe" and comfortable. Hagar heard the voice of God and tasted of his favor only to walk back to the familiarity of her old life.
• Once we have experienced the favor of God we must never "go back." It's spiritually illogical to go back to the old way of life—back to the pleasures of this world—back to the idols we once worshiped. Walking the way of repentance and redemption is the path our God would have us take, and "going back" is never an option.
• The God of Abraham, Isaac, and Jacob is the God of provision. He is an action God, and we are his children. We have a great and incomparable birthright, and once we accept our inheritance as a child of the living God we can begin walking in the benefits of our relationship with him. Our lives will change dramatically for the good, and we will never be the same again. The Promise

Keeper of all promise keepers gives his children great assurances in his Word concerning his favor.

When you read his promises given in his Word and believe them to be true, then you can learn to walk in the inheritance he has already provided for you. Remember this truth always—you are a child of the King—and the promises of his Word are for you. Believe fully in God's favor—learn to trust in it—have the faith to ask for it—and finally, learn to act on it, and you will live in his favor forevermore!

• Genesis 39:21. Favor garners supernatural increase and promotion.
• Exodus 3:21. Favor restores everything the enemy has stolen.
• Exodus 11:3. Favor gives us honor in the midst of our adversaries.
• Deuteronomy 33:23. Favor increases our assets.
• 1 Samuel 16:22. Favor provides recognition in the midst of many.
• 2 Chronicles 20:15-30. Favor secures great victory in the midst of daunting odds.
• Esther 2:18. Favor denotes prominence and preferential treatment.
• Esther 5:8. Favor grants petitions, even by ungodly authorities.
• Esther 8:5, 8. Favor changes policies, rules, regulations, and laws on our behalf.
• Psalm 5:11-12. Favor provides a protective shield over our life.
• Psalm 37:5. Favor lasts for a lifetime, and it gives us confidence.
• Psalm 44:3. Favor is territory gained for our belief in God's intervention.
• Psalm 106:4-5. Favor provides salvation, prosperity, and joy.

TO LEARN MORE ON WHAT THE BIBLE HAS TO SAY ABOUT **FINANCES,** READ THE SCRIPTURES AND DEVOTIONALS AT **GENESIS 13:2, 5, GENESIS 18:14, GENESIS 28:15, EXODUS 22:29,** AND **LEVITICUS 27:30.**

Abram named him Ishmael. [16]Abram was eighty-six years old when Hagar gave birth to Ishmael.

PROOF OF THE AGREEMENT

17 When Abram was ninety-nine years old, the LORD appeared to him and said, "I am God Almighty. Obey me and do what is right. [2]I will make an agreement between us, and I will make you the ancestor of many people."

[3]Then Abram bowed facedown on the ground. God said to him, [4]"I am making my agreement with you: I will make you the father of many nations. [5]I am changing your name from Abram[n] to Abraham[n] because I am making you a father of many nations. [6]I will give you many descendants. New nations will be born from you, and kings will come from you. [7]And I will make an agreement between me and you and all your descendants from now on: I will be your God and the God of all your descendants. [8]You live in the land of Canaan now as a stranger, but I will give you and your descendants all this land forever. And I will be the God of your descendants."

[9]Then God said to Abraham, "You and your descendants must keep this agreement from now on. [10]This is my agreement with you and all your descendants, which you must obey: Every male among you must be circumcised. [11]Cut away your foreskin to show that you are prepared to follow the agreement between me and you. [12]From now on when a baby boy is eight days old, you will circumcise him. This includes any boy born among your people or any who is your slave, who is not one of your descendants. [13]Circumcise every baby boy whether he is born in your family or bought as a slave. Your bodies will be marked to show that you are part of my agreement that lasts forever. [14]Any male who is not circumcised will be cut off from his people, because he has broken my agreement."

ISAAC—THE PROMISED SON

[15]God said to Abraham, "I will change the name of Sarai,[n] your wife, to Sarah.[n] [16]I will bless her and give her a son, and you will be the father. She will be the mother of many nations. Kings of nations will come from her."

[17]Abraham bowed facedown on the ground and laughed. He said to himself, "Can a man have a child when he is a hundred years old? Can Sarah give birth to a child when she is ninety?" [18]Then Abraham said to God, "Please let Ishmael be the son you promised."

[19]God said, "No, Sarah your wife will have a son, and you will name him Isaac.[n] I will make my agreement with him to be an agreement that continues forever with all his descendants.

[20]"As for Ishmael, I have heard you. I will bless him and give him many descendants. And I will cause their numbers to grow greatly. He will be the father of twelve great leaders, and I will make him into a great nation. [21]But I will make my agreement with Isaac, the son whom Sarah will have at this same time next year." [22]After God finished talking with Abraham, God rose and left him.

[23]Then Abraham gathered Ishmael, all the males born in his camp, and the slaves he had bought. So that day Abraham circumcised every man and boy in his camp as God had told him to do. [24]Abraham was ninety-nine years old when he was circumcised. [25]And Ishmael, his son, was thirteen years old when he was circumcised. [26]Abraham and his son were circumcised on the same day. [27]Also on that day all the men in Abraham's camp were circumcised, including all those born in his camp and all the slaves he had bought from other nations.

THE THREE VISITORS

18 Later, the LORD again appeared to Abraham near the great trees of Mamre. Abraham was sitting at the entrance of his tent during the hottest part of the day. [2]He looked up and saw three men standing near him. When Abraham saw them, he ran from his tent to meet them. He bowed facedown on the ground before them [3]and said, "Sir, if you think well of me, please stay awhile with me, your servant. [4]I will bring some water so

---

17:5 Abram This name means "honored father." **17:5 Abraham** The end of the Hebrew word for "Abraham" sounds like the beginning of the Hebrew word for "many." **17:15 Sarai** An Aramaic name meaning "princess." **17:15 Sarah** A Hebrew name meaning "princess." **17:19 Isaac** The Hebrew words for "he laughed" (v. 17) and "Isaac" sound the same.

all of you can wash your feet. You may rest under the tree, ⁵and I will get some bread for you so you can regain your strength. Then you may continue your journey."

The three men said, "That is fine. Do as you said."

⁶Abraham hurried to the tent where Sarah was and said to her, "Hurry, prepare twenty quarts of fine flour, and make it into loaves of bread." ⁷Then Abraham ran to his herd and took one of his best calves. He gave it to a servant, who hurried to kill it and to

prepare it for food. ⁸Abraham gave the three men the calf that had been cooked and milk curds and milk. While they ate, he stood under the tree near them.

⁹The men asked Abraham, "Where is your wife Sarah?"

"There, in the tent," said Abraham.

¹⁰Then the LORD said, "I will certainly return to you about this time a year from now. At that time your wife Sarah will have a son."

Sarah was listening at the entrance of the

THE FAVOR OF GOD

believe in the incredible

FINANCES

GENESIS 18:14

What dreams are you willing to chase after? God poses a question to Abraham. Actually, it's more than a question. It is a shift in focus, from the helplessness of man to the sufficiency of God. Here, the Hebrew word for "hard" is pala. In some cases, this word is translated "wonderful" or "demanding."

Try substituting these two possible translations and you will start to understand the majesty of God's statement. Abraham and Sarah were consumed with the problems of human conception, but God reminded them that he was responsible for all of creation. Their concerns were much too small to thwart God's purposes.

Faith is an act. If you'll act on the incredible, God will do the impossible. He'll help you fulfill dreams that completely oppose physical law. God left all of these stories in the Bible about human beings who just didn't get it because he knows that we are just as doubtful. We fret over our problems as if they were insurmountable impossibilities.

We agonize and worry and cry and blame and sink into depression—all because we have not understood who God is. We are just like Abraham and Sarah. Pregnant at ninety? No way! How quickly we forget that God simply spoke and the world came into being. He can handle our problems with no trouble. Is anything too demanding, too wonderful, or too difficult? Of course not! This is GOD speaking.

reflect: Trust your financial concerns to the God who is more than enough.
Go to **Genesis 28:15**.

tent which was behind him. ¹¹Abraham and Sarah were very old. Since Sarah was past the age when women normally have children, ¹²she laughed to herself, "My husband and I are too old to have a baby."

¹³Then the LORD said to Abraham, "Why did Sarah laugh? Why did she say, 'I am too old to have a baby'? ¹⁴Is anything too hard for the LORD? No! I will return to you at the right time a year from now, and Sarah will have a son."

¹⁵Sarah was afraid, so she lied and said, "I didn't laugh."

But the LORD said, "No. You did laugh."

¹⁶Then the men got up to leave and started out toward Sodom. Abraham walked along with them a short time to send them on their way.

ABRAHAM'S BARGAIN WITH GOD

¹⁷The LORD said, "Should I tell Abraham what I am going to do now? ¹⁸Abraham's children will certainly become a great and powerful nation, and all nations on earth will be blessed through him. ¹⁹I have chosen him so he would command his children and his descendants to live the way the LORD wants them to, to live right and be fair. Then I, the LORD, will give Abraham what I promised him."

²⁰Then the LORD said, "I have heard many complaints against the people of Sodom and Gomorrah. They are very evil. ²¹I will go down and see if they are as bad as I have heard. If not, I will know."

²²So the men turned and went toward Sodom, but Abraham stood there before the LORD. ²³Then Abraham approached him and asked, "Do you plan to destroy the good people along with the evil ones? ²⁴What if there are fifty good people in that city? Will you still destroy it? Surely you will save the city for the fifty good people living there. ²⁵Surely you will not destroy the good people along with the evil ones; then they would be treated the same. You are the judge of all the earth. Won't you do what is right?"

²⁶The LORD said, "If I find fifty good people in the city of Sodom, I will save the whole city because of them."

²⁷Then Abraham said, "Though I am only dust and ashes, I have been brave to speak to the Lord. ²⁸What if there are only forty-five good people in the city? Will you destroy the whole city for the lack of five good people?"

The LORD said, "If I find forty-five there, I will not destroy the city."

²⁹Again Abraham said to him, "If you find only forty good people there, will you destroy the city?"

The LORD said, "If I find forty, I will not destroy it."

³⁰Then Abraham said, "Lord, please don't be angry with me, but let me ask you this. If you find only thirty good people in the city, will you destroy it?"

He said, "If I find thirty good people there, I will not destroy the city."

³¹Then Abraham said, "I have been brave to speak to the Lord. But what if there are twenty good people in the city?"

He answered, "If I find twenty there, I will not destroy the city."

³²Then Abraham said, "Lord, please don't be angry with me, but let me bother you this one last time. What if you find ten there?"

He said, "If I find ten there, I will not destroy it."

³³When the LORD finished speaking to Abraham, he left, and Abraham returned home.

LOT LEAVES SODOM

19 The two angels came to Sodom in the evening as Lot was sitting near the city gate. When he saw them, he got up and went to them and bowed facedown on the ground. ²Lot said, "Sirs, please come to my house and spend the night. There you can wash your feet, and then tomorrow you may continue your journey."

The angels answered, "No, we will spend the night in the city's public square."

³But Lot begged them to come, so they agreed and went to his house. Then Lot prepared a meal for them. He baked bread without yeast, and they ate it.

⁴Before bedtime, men both young and old and from every part of Sodom surrounded Lot's house. ⁵They called to Lot, "Where are the two men who came to you tonight? Bring them out to us so we can have sexual relations with them."

⁶Lot went outside to them, closing the door behind him. ⁷He said, "No, my brothers! Do not do this evil thing. ⁸Look! I have two

daughters who have never slept with a man. I will give them to you, and you may do anything you want with them. But please don't do anything to these men. They have come to my house, and I must protect them."

⁹The men around the house answered, "Move out of the way!" Then they said to each other, "This man Lot came to our city as a stranger, and now he wants to tell us what to do!" They said to Lot, "We will do worse things to you than to them." They started pushing him back and were ready to break down the door.

¹⁰But the two men staying with Lot opened the door, pulled him back inside the house, and then closed the door. ¹¹They struck those outside the door with blindness, so the men, both young and old, could not find the door.

¹²The two men said to Lot, "Do you have any other relatives in this city? Do you have any sons-in-law, sons, daughters, or any other relatives? If you do, tell them to leave now, ¹³because we are about to destroy this city. The LORD has heard of all the evil that is here, so he has sent us to destroy it."

¹⁴So Lot went out and said to his future sons-in-law who were pledged to marry his daughters, "Hurry and leave this city! The LORD is about to destroy it!" But they thought Lot was joking.

¹⁵At dawn the next morning, the angels begged Lot to hurry. They said, "Go! Take your wife and your two daughters with you so you will not be destroyed when the city is punished."

¹⁶But Lot delayed. So the two men took the hands of Lot, his wife, and his two daughters and led them safely out of the city. So the LORD was merciful to Lot and his family. ¹⁷After they brought them out of the city, one of the men said, "Run for your lives! Don't look back or stop anywhere in the valley. Run to the mountains, or you will be destroyed."

¹⁸But Lot said to one of them, "Sir, please don't force me to go so far! ¹⁹You have been merciful and kind to me and have saved my life. But I can't run to the mountains. The disaster will catch me, and I will die. ²⁰Look, that little town over there is not too far away. Let me run there. It's really just a little town, and I'll be safe there."

²¹The angel said to Lot, "Very well, I will allow you to do this also. I will not destroy that town. ²²But run there fast, because I cannot destroy Sodom until you are safely in that town." (That town is named Zoar,ⁿ because it is little.)

SODOM AND GOMORRAH ARE DESTROYED

²³The sun had already come up when Lot entered Zoar. ²⁴The LORD sent a rain of burning sulfur down from the sky on Sodom and Gomorrah ²⁵and destroyed those cities. He also destroyed the whole Jordan Valley, everyone living in the cities, and even all the plants.

²⁶At that point Lot's wife looked back. When she did, she became a pillar of salt.

²⁷Early the next morning, Abraham got up and went to the place where he had stood before the LORD. ²⁸He looked down toward Sodom and Gomorrah and all the Jordan Valley and saw smoke rising from the land, like smoke from a furnace.

²⁹God destroyed the cities in the valley, but he remembered what Abraham had asked. So God saved Lot's life, but he destroyed the city where Lot had lived.

LOT AND HIS DAUGHTERS

³⁰Lot was afraid to continue living in Zoar, so he and his two daughters went to live in the mountains in a cave. ³¹One day the older daughter said to the younger, "Our father is old. Everywhere on the earth women and men marry, but there are no men around here for us to marry. ³²Let's get our father drunk and have sexual relations with him. We can use him to have children and continue our family."

³³That night the two girls got their father drunk, and the older daughter went and had sexual relations with him. But Lot did not know when she lay down or when she got up.

³⁴The next day the older daughter said to the younger, "Last night I had sexual relations with my father. Let's get him drunk again tonight so you can go and have sexual relations with him, too. In this way we can use our father to have children to continue our family." ³⁵So that night they got their father drunk again, and the younger daughter

---

19:22 Zoar This name sounds like the Hebrew word for "little."

went and had sexual relations with him. Again, Lot did not know when she lay down or when she got up.

36So both of Lot's daughters became pregnant by their father. 37The older daughter gave birth to a son and named him Moab. He is the ancestor of all the Moabite people who are still living today. 38The younger daughter also gave birth to a son and named him Ben-Ammi. He is the father of all the Ammonite people who are still living today.

ABRAHAM TRICKS ABIMELECH

20 Abraham left Hebron and traveled to southern Canaan where he stayed awhile between Kadesh and Shur. When he moved to Gerar, 2he told people that his wife Sarah was his sister. Abimelech king of Gerar heard this, so he sent some servants to take her. 3But one night God spoke to Abimelech in a dream and said, "You will die. The woman you took is married."

4But Abimelech had not gone near Sarah, so he said, "Lord, would you destroy an innocent nation? 5Abraham himself told me, 'This woman is my sister,' and she also said, 'He is my brother.' I am innocent. I did not know I was doing anything wrong."

6Then God said to Abimelech in the dream, "Yes, I know you did not realize what you were doing. So I did not allow you to sin against me and touch her. 7Give Abraham his wife back. He is a prophet. He will pray for you, and you will not die. But if you do not give Sarah back, you and all your family will surely die."

8So early the next morning, Abimelech called all his officers and told them everything that had happened in the dream. They were very afraid. 9Then Abimelech called Abraham to him and said, "What have you done to us? What wrong did I do against you? Why did you bring this trouble to my kingdom? You should not have done these things to me. 10What were you thinking that caused you to do this?"

11Then Abraham answered, "I thought no one in this place respected God and that someone would kill me to get Sarah. 12And it is true that she is my sister. She is the daughter of my father, but she is not the daughter of my mother. 13When God told me to leave my father's house and wander in many different places, I told Sarah, 'You must do a special favor for me. Everywhere we go tell people I am your brother.'"

14Then Abimelech gave Abraham some sheep, cattle, and male and female slaves. He also gave Sarah, Abraham's wife, back to him 15and said, "Look around you at my land. You may live anywhere you want."

16Abimelech said to Sarah, "I gave your brother Abraham twenty-five pounds of silver to make up for any wrong that people may think about you. I want everyone to know that you are innocent."

17Then Abraham prayed to God, and God healed Abimelech, his wife, and his servant girls so they could have children. 18The LORD had kept all the women in Abimelech's house from having children as a punishment on Abimelech for taking Abraham's wife Sarah.

A BABY FOR SARAH

21 The LORD cared for Sarah as he had said and did for her what he had promised. 2Sarah became pregnant and gave birth to a son for Abraham in his old age. Everything happened at the time God had said it would. 3Abraham named his son Isaac, the son Sarah gave birth to. 4He circumcised Isaac when he was eight days old as God had commanded.

5Abraham was one hundred years old when his son Isaac was born. 6And Sarah said, "God has made me laugh.[n] Everyone who hears about this will laugh with me. 7No one thought that I would be able to have Abraham's child, but even though Abraham is old I have given him a son."

HAGAR AND ISHMAEL LEAVE

8Isaac grew, and when he became old enough to eat food, Abraham gave a great feast. 9But Sarah saw Ishmael making fun of Isaac. (Ishmael was the son of Abraham by Hagar, Sarah's Egyptian slave.) 10So Sarah said to Abraham, "Throw out this slave woman and her son. Her son should not inherit anything; my son Isaac should receive it all."

11This troubled Abraham very much because Ishmael was also his son. 12But God said to Abraham, "Don't be troubled about the boy and the slave woman. Do whatever

---

21:6 laugh The Hebrew words for "he laughed" and "Isaac" sound the same.

Sarah tells you. The descendants I promised you will be from Isaac. [13]I will also make the descendants of Ishmael into a great nation because he is your son, too."

[14]Early the next morning Abraham took some food and a leather bag full of water. He gave them to Hagar and sent her away. Carrying these things and her son, Hagar went and wandered in the desert of Beersheba.

[15]Later, when all the water was gone from the bag, Hagar put her son under a bush. [16]Then she went away a short distance and sat down. She thought, "My son will die, and I cannot watch this happen." She sat there and began to cry.

[17]God heard the boy crying, and God's angel called to Hagar from heaven. He said, "What is wrong, Hagar? Don't be afraid! God has heard the boy crying there. [18]Help him up and take him by the hand. I will make his descendants into a great nation."

[19]Then God showed Hagar a well of water. So she went to the well and filled her bag with water and gave the boy a drink.

[20]God was with the boy as he grew up. Ishmael lived in the desert and became an archer. [21]He lived in the Desert of Paran, and his mother found a wife for him in Egypt.

ABRAHAM'S BARGAIN WITH ABIMELECH

[22]Then Abimelech came with Phicol, the commander of his army, and said to Abraham, "God is with you in everything you do. [23]So make a promise to me here before God that you will be fair with me and my children and my descendants. Be kind to me and to this land where you have lived as a stranger—as kind as I have been to you."

[24]And Abraham said, "I promise." [25]Then Abraham complained to Abimelech about Abimelech's servants who had seized a well of water.

[26]But Abimelech said, "I don't know who did this. You never told me about this before today."

[27]Then Abraham gave Abimelech some sheep and cattle, and they made an agreement. [28]Abraham also put seven female lambs in front of Abimelech.

[29]Abimelech asked Abraham, "Why did you put these seven female lambs by themselves?"

[30]Abraham answered, "Accept these lambs from me to prove that you believe I dug this well."

[31]So that place was called Beersheba[n] because they made a promise to each other there.

[32]After Abraham and Abimelech made the agreement at Beersheba, Abimelech and Phicol, the commander of his army, went back to the land of the Philistines.

[33]Abraham planted a tamarisk tree at Beersheba and prayed to the LORD, the God who lives forever. [34]And Abraham lived as a stranger in the land of the Philistines for a long time.

GOD TESTS ABRAHAM

22After these things God tested Abraham's faith. God said to him, "Abraham!"

And he answered, "Here I am."

[2]Then God said, "Take your only son, Isaac, the son you love, and go to the land of Moriah. Kill him there and offer him as a whole burnt offering on one of the mountains I will tell you about."

[3]Abraham got up early in the morning and saddled his donkey. He took Isaac and two servants with him. After he cut the wood for the sacrifice, they went to the place God had told them to go. [4]On the third day Abraham looked up and saw the place in the distance. [5]He said to his servants, "Stay here with the donkey. My son and I will go over there and worship, and then we will come back to you."

[6]Abraham took the wood for the sacrifice and gave it to his son to carry, but he himself took the knife and the fire. So he and his son went on together.

[7]Isaac said to his father Abraham, "Father!"

Abraham answered, "Yes, my son."

Isaac said, "We have the fire and the wood, but where is the lamb we will burn as a sacrifice?"

[8]Abraham answered, "God will give us the lamb for the sacrifice, my son."

So Abraham and his son went on together [9]and came to the place God had told him about. Abraham built an altar there. He laid

---

21:31 Beersheba This name means "well of the promise" or "well of seven."

the wood on it and then tied up his son Isaac and laid him on the wood on the altar. ¹⁰Then Abraham took his knife and was about to kill his son.

¹¹But the angel of the LORD called to him from heaven and said, "Abraham! Abraham!"

Abraham answered, "Yes."

¹²The angel said, "Don't kill your son or hurt him in any way. Now I can see that you trust God and that you have not kept your son, your only son, from me."

¹³Then Abraham looked up and saw a male sheep caught in a bush by its horns. So Abraham went and took the sheep and killed it. He offered it as a whole burnt offering to God, and his son was saved. ¹⁴So Abraham named that place The LORD Provides. Even today people say, "On the mountain of the LORD it will be provided."

¹⁵The angel of the LORD called to Abraham from heaven a second time ¹⁶and said, "The LORD says, 'Because you did not keep back your son, your only son, from me, I make you this promise by my own name: ¹⁷I will surely bless you and give you many descendants. They will be as many as the stars in the sky and the sand on the seashore, and they will capture the cities of their enemies. ¹⁸Through your descendants all the nations on the earth will be blessed, because you obeyed me.'"

¹⁹Then Abraham returned to his servants. They all traveled back to Beersheba, and Abraham stayed there.

²⁰After these things happened, someone told Abraham: "Your brother Nahor and his wife Milcah have children now. ²¹The first son is Uz, and the second is Buz. The third son is Kemuel (the father of Aram). ²²Then there are Kesed, Hazo, Pildash, Jidlaph, and Bethuel." ²³Bethuel became the father of Rebekah. Milcah was the mother of these eight sons, and Nahor, Abraham's brother, was the father. ²⁴Also Nahor had four other sons by his slave woman Reumah. Their names were Tebah, Gaham, Tahash, and Maacah.

SARAH DIES

23 Sarah lived to be one hundred twenty-seven years old. ²She died in Kiriath Arba (that is, Hebron) in the land of Canaan. Abraham was very sad and cried because of her. ³After a while he got up from the side of his wife's body and went to talk to the Hittites. He said, ⁴"I am only a stranger and a foreigner here. Sell me some of your land so that I can bury my dead wife."

⁵The Hittites answered Abraham, ⁶"Sir, you are a great leader among us. You may have the best place we have to bury your dead. You may have any of our burying places that you want, and none of us will stop you from burying your dead wife."

⁷Abraham rose and bowed to the people of the land, the Hittites. ⁸He said to them, "If you truly want to help me bury my dead wife here, speak to Ephron, the son of Zohar for me. ⁹Ask him to sell me the cave of Machpelah at the edge of his field. I will pay him the full price. You can be the witnesses that I am buying it as a burial place."

¹⁰Ephron was sitting among the Hittites at the city gate. He answered Abraham, ¹¹"No, sir. I will give you the land and the cave that is in it, with these people as witnesses. Bury your dead wife."

¹²Then Abraham bowed down before the Hittites. ¹³He said to Ephron before all the people, "Please let me pay you the full price for the field. Accept my money, and I will bury my dead there."

¹⁴Ephron answered Abraham, ¹⁵"Sir, the land is worth ten pounds of silver, but I won't argue with you over the price. Take the land, and bury your dead wife."

¹⁶Abraham agreed and paid Ephron in front of the Hittite witnesses. He weighed out the full price, ten pounds of silver, and they counted the weight as the traders normally did.

¹⁷⁻¹⁸So Ephron's field in Machpelah, east of Mamre, was sold. Abraham became the owner of the field, the cave in it, and all the trees that were in the field. The sale was made at the city gate, with the Hittites as witnesses. ¹⁹After this, Abraham buried his wife Sarah in the cave in the field of Machpelah, near Mamre. (Mamre was later called Hebron in the land of Canaan.) ²⁰So Abraham bought the field and the cave in it from the Hittites to use as a burying place.

A WIFE FOR ISAAC

24 Abraham was now very old, and the LORD had blessed him in every way. ²Abraham said to his oldest servant, who was in charge of everything he owned, "Put your hand under my leg." ³Make a promise to me before the LORD, the God of heaven and earth. Don't get a wife for my son from the Canaanite girls who live around here. ⁴Instead, go back to my country, to the land of my relatives, and get a wife for my son Isaac."

⁵The servant said to him, "What if this woman does not want to return with me to this land? Then, should I take your son with me back to your homeland?"

⁶Abraham said to him, "No! Don't take my son back there. ⁷The LORD, the God of heaven, brought me from the home of my father and the land of my relatives. And he promised me, 'I will give this land to your descendants.' The LORD will send his angel before you to help you get a wife for my son there. ⁸If the girl won't come back with you, you will be free from this promise. But you must not take my son back there." ⁹So the servant put his hand under his master's leg and made a promise to Abraham about this.

¹⁰The servant took ten of Abraham's camels and left, carrying with him many different kinds of beautiful gifts. He went to Northwest Mesopotamia to Nahor's city. ¹¹In the evening, when the women come out to get water, he made the camels kneel down at the well outside the city.

¹²The servant said, "LORD, God of my master Abraham, allow me to find a wife for his son today. Please show this kindness to my master Abraham. ¹³Here I am, standing by the spring, and the girls from the city are coming out to get water. ¹⁴I will say to one of them, 'Please put your jar down so I can drink.' Then let her say, 'Drink, and I will also give water to your camels.' If that happens, I will know she is the right one for your servant Isaac and that you have shown kindness to my master."

¹⁵Before the servant had finished praying, Rebekah, the daughter of Bethuel, came out of the city. (Bethuel was the son of Milcah and Nahor, Abraham's brother.) Rebekah was carrying her water jar on her shoulder. ¹⁶She was very pretty, a virgin; she had never had sexual relations with a man. She went down to the spring and filled her jar, then came back up. ¹⁷The servant ran to her and said, "Please give me a little water from your jar."

¹⁸Rebekah said, "Drink, sir." She quickly lowered the jar from her shoulder and gave him a drink. ¹⁹After he finished drinking, Rebekah said, "I will also pour some water for your camels." ²⁰So she quickly poured all the water from her jar into the drinking trough for the camels. Then she kept running to the well until she had given all the camels enough to drink.

²¹The servant quietly watched her. He wanted to be sure the LORD had made his trip successful. ²²After the camels had finished drinking, he gave Rebekah a gold ring weighing one-fifth of an ounce and two gold arm bracelets weighing about four ounces each. ²³He asked, "Who is your father? Is there a place in his house for me and my men to spend the night?"

²⁴Rebekah answered, "My father is Bethuel, the son of Milcah and Nahor." ²⁵Then she said, "And, yes, we have straw for your camels and a place for you to spend the night."

²⁶The servant bowed and worshiped the LORD ²⁷and said, "Blessed is the LORD, the God of my master Abraham. The LORD has been kind and truthful to him and has led me to my master's relatives."

²⁸Then Rebekah ran and told her mother's family about all these things. ²⁹She had a brother named Laban, who ran out to Abraham's servant, who was still at the spring. ³⁰Laban had heard what she had said and had seen the ring and the bracelets on his sister's arms. So he ran out to the well, and there was the man standing by the camels at the spring. ³¹Laban said, "Sir, you are welcome to come in; you don't have to stand outside. I have prepared the house for you and also a place for your camels."

³²So Abraham's servant went into the house. After Laban unloaded the camels and gave them straw and food, he gave water to Abraham's servant so he and the men with him could wash their feet. ³³Then Laban gave the servant food, but the servant said, "I will not eat until I have told you why I came."

So Laban said, "Then tell us."

³⁴He said, "I am Abraham's servant. ³⁵The LORD has greatly blessed my master in everything, and he has become a rich man. The

---

24:2 Put...leg This showed that a person would keep the promise.

LORD has given him many flocks of sheep, herds of cattle, silver and gold, male and female servants, camels, and horses. ³⁶Sarah, my master's wife, gave birth to a son when she was old, and my master has given everything he owns to that son. ³⁷My master had me make a promise to him and said, 'Don't get a wife for my son from the Canaanite girls who live around here. ³⁸Instead, you must go to my father's people and to my family. There you must get a wife for my son.' ³⁹I said to my master, 'What if the woman will not

---

FINANCES

GOD'S MANAGEMENT PLAN

you are worth your weight in wealth

GENESIS 24:35

By Mark Chironna

Abraham was a rich man. He was wealthy with livestock, silver, and gold. He managed well all that the Lord had given him. His herds were healthy and expansive, and he found good pastures where there was abundant food and water. His servants were trained to be diligent shepherds and to protect and control his flocks wisely.

However, his excellent administration skills were not the reason Abraham prospered. The best grazing lands alone were not the reason Abraham's herds increased. Environment has nothing to do with creating wealth: Abraham became wealthy in the least opportune environment.

Abraham walked with God and lived in harmony with FAITH. "Because the Scripture says, 'Abraham believed God, and God accepted Abraham's faith, and that faith made him right with God'" (Romans 4:3).

God caused Abraham to become wealthy. Abraham's ownership of money and property was the result of doing things God's way, as described in Deuteronomy 8:18: "but remember the Lord your God! It is he who gives you the power to become rich, keeping the agreement he promised to your ancestors, as it is today."

God not only blessed Abraham with a herd of fine animals and sacks of gold; he also gave him the power, the potential, and the capacity to become rich. Abraham's part in this creative act was to remain in fellowship and obedience to God, to take delivery of the power and provisions, and then to act in faith. He had to believe and to trust that God actually intended for him to be wealthy.

---

reflect: What are the results of obeying God in the area of finances?
Go to **Deuteronomy 28.**

come back with me?' ⁴⁰But he said, 'I serve the LORD, who will send his angel with you and will help you. You will get a wife for my son from my family and my father's people. ⁴¹Then you will be free from the promise. But if they will not give you a wife for my son, you will be free from this promise.'

⁴²"Today I came to this spring. I said, 'LORD, God of my master Abraham, please make my trip successful. ⁴³I am standing by this spring. I will wait for a young woman to come out to get water, and I will say, "Please give me water from your jar to drink." ⁴⁴Then let her say, "Drink this water, and I will also get water for your camels." By this I will know the LORD has chosen her for my master's son.'

⁴⁵"Before I finished my silent prayer, Rebekah came out of the city with her water jar on her shoulder. She went down to the spring and got water. I said to her, 'Please give me a drink.' ⁴⁶She quickly lowered the jar from her shoulder and said, 'Drink this. I will also get water for your camels.' So I drank, and she gave water to my camels too. ⁴⁷When I asked her, 'Who is your father?' she answered, 'My father is Bethuel son of Milcah and Nahor.' Then I put the ring in her nose and the bracelets on her arms, ⁴⁸and I bowed my head and thanked the LORD. I praised the LORD, the God of my master Abraham, because he led me on the right road to get the granddaughter of my master's brother for his son. ⁴⁹Now, tell me, will you be kind and truthful to my master? And if not, tell me so. Then I will know what I should do."

⁵⁰Laban and Bethuel answered, "This is clearly from the LORD, and we cannot change what must happen. ⁵¹Rebekah is yours. Take her and go. Let her marry your master's son as the LORD has commanded."

⁵²When Abraham's servant heard these words, he bowed facedown on the ground before the LORD. ⁵³Then he gave Rebekah gold and silver jewelry and clothes. He also gave expensive gifts to her brother and mother. ⁵⁴The servant and the men with him ate and drank and spent the night there. When they got up the next morning, the servant said, "Now let me go back to my master."

⁵⁵Rebekah's mother and her brother said, "Let Rebekah stay with us at least ten days. After that she may go."

⁵⁶But the servant said to them, "Do not make me wait, because the LORD has made my trip successful. Now let me go back to my master."

⁵⁷Rebekah's brother and mother said, "We will call Rebekah and ask her what she wants to do." ⁵⁸They called her and asked her, "Do you want to go with this man now?"

She said, "Yes, I do."

⁵⁹So they allowed Rebekah and her nurse to go with Abraham's servant and his men. ⁶⁰They blessed Rebekah and said,

"Our sister, may you be the mother of
   thousands of people,
   and may your descendants capture the
   cities of their enemies."

⁶¹Then Rebekah and her servant girls got on the camels and followed the servant and his men. So the servant took Rebekah and left.

⁶²At this time Isaac had left Beer Lahai Roi and was living in southern Canaan. ⁶³One evening when he went out to the field to think, he looked up and saw camels coming. ⁶⁴Rebekah also looked and saw Isaac. Then she jumped down from the camel ⁶⁵and asked the servant, "Who is that man walking in the field to meet us?"

The servant answered, "That is my master." So Rebekah covered her face with her veil.

⁶⁶The servant told Isaac everything that had happened. ⁶⁷Then Isaac brought Rebekah into the tent of Sarah, his mother, and she became his wife. Isaac loved her very much, and so he was comforted after his mother's death.

ABRAHAM'S FAMILY

25 Abraham married again, and his new wife was Keturah. ²She gave birth to Zimran, Jokshan, Medan, Midian, Ishbak, and Shuah. ³Jokshan was the father of Sheba and Dedan. Dedan's descendants were the people of Assyria, Letush, and Leum. ⁴The sons of Midian were Ephah, Epher, Hanoch, Abida, and Eldaah. All these were descendants of Keturah. ⁵Abraham left everything he owned to Isaac. ⁶But before Abraham died, he did give gifts to the sons of his other wives, then sent them to the East to be away from Isaac.

⁷Abraham lived to be one hundred

seventy-five years old. [8]He breathed his last breath and died at an old age, after a long and satisfying life. [9]His sons Isaac and Ishmael buried him in the cave of Machpelah in the field of Ephron east of Mamre. (Ephron was the son of Zohar the Hittite.) [10]So Abraham was buried with his wife Sarah in the same field that he had bought from the Hittites. [11]After Abraham died, God blessed his son Isaac. Isaac was now living at Beer Lahai Roi.

[12]This is the family history of Ishmael, Abraham's son. (Hagar, Sarah's Egyptian servant, was Ishmael's mother.) [13]These are the names of Ishmael's sons in the order they were born: Nebaioth, the first son, then Kedar, Adbeel, Mibsam, [14]Mishma, Dumah, Massa, [15]Hadad, Tema, Jetur, Naphish, and Kedemah. [16]These were Ishmael's sons, and these are the names of the tribal leaders listed according to their settlements and camps. [17]Ishmael lived one hundred thirty-seven years and then breathed his last breath and died. [18]His descendants lived from Havilah to Shur, which is east of Egypt stretching toward Assyria. They often attacked the descendants of his brothers.

ISAAC'S FAMILY

[19]This is the family history of Isaac. Abraham had a son named Isaac. [20]When Isaac was forty years old, he married Rebekah, who came from Northwest Mesopotamia. She was Bethuel's daughter and the sister of Laban the Aramean. [21]Isaac's wife could not have children, so Isaac prayed to the LORD for her. The LORD heard Isaac's prayer, and Rebekah became pregnant.

[22]While she was pregnant, the babies struggled inside her. She asked, "Why is this happening to me?" Then she went to get an answer from the LORD.

[23]The LORD said to her,

"Two nations are in your body,
    and two groups of people will be taken
        from you.
One group will be stronger than the other,
    and the older will serve the younger."

[24]When the time came, Rebekah gave birth to twins. [25]The first baby was born red. Since his skin was like a hairy robe, he was named Esau.[n] [26]When the second baby was born, he was holding on to Esau's heel, so that baby was named Jacob.[n] Isaac was sixty years old when they were born.

[27]When the boys grew up, Esau became a skilled hunter. He loved to be out in the fields. But Jacob was a quiet man and stayed among the tents. [28]Isaac loved Esau because he hunted the wild animals that Isaac enjoyed eating. But Rebekah loved Jacob.

[29]One day Jacob was boiling a pot of vegetable soup. Esau came in from hunting in the fields, weak from hunger. [30]So Esau said to Jacob, "Let me eat some of that red soup, because I am weak with hunger." (That is why people call him Edom.[n])

[31]But Jacob said, "You must sell me your rights as the firstborn son."[n]

[32]Esau said, "I am almost dead from hunger. If I die, all of my father's wealth will not help me."

[33]But Jacob said, "First, promise me that you will give it to me." So Esau made a promise to Jacob and sold his part of their father's wealth to Jacob. [34]Then Jacob gave Esau bread and vegetable soup, and he ate and drank, and then left. So Esau showed how little he cared about his rights as the firstborn son.

ISAAC LIES TO ABIMELECH

26 Now there was a time of hunger in the land, besides the time of hunger that happened during Abraham's life. So Isaac went to the town of Gerar to see Abimelech king of the Philistines. [2]The LORD appeared to Isaac and said, "Don't go down to Egypt, but live in the land where I tell you to live. [3]Stay in this land, and I will be with you and bless you. I will give you and your descendants all these lands, and I will keep the oath I made to Abraham your father. [4]I will give you many descendants, as hard to count as the stars in the sky, and I will give them all these lands. Through your descendants all the nations on the earth will be blessed. [5]I will do this because your father Abraham

---

25:25 Esau This name may mean "hairy." **25:26 Jacob** This name sounds like the Hebrew word for "heel." "Grabbing someone's heel" is a Hebrew saying for tricking someone. **25:30 Edom** This name sounds like the Hebrew word for "red." **25:31 rights ... son** Usually the firstborn son had a high rank in the family. The firstborn son usually became the new head of the family.

obeyed me. He did what I said and obeyed my commands, my teachings, and my rules."

[6]So Isaac stayed in Gerar. [7]His wife Rebekah was very beautiful, and the men of that place asked Isaac about her. Isaac said, "She is my sister," because he was afraid to tell them she was his wife. He thought they might kill him so they could have her.

[8]Isaac lived there a long time. One day as Abimelech king of the Philistines looked out his window, he saw Isaac holding his wife Rebekah tenderly. [9]Abimelech called for Isaac and said, "This woman is your wife. Why did you say she was your sister?"

Isaac said to him, "I was afraid you would kill me so you could have her."

[10]Abimelech said, "What have you done to us? One of our men might have had sexual relations with your wife. Then we would have been guilty of a great sin."

[11]So Abimelech warned everyone, "Anyone who touches this man or his wife will be put to death."

ISAAC BECOMES RICH

[12]Isaac planted seed in that land, and that year he gathered a great harvest. The LORD blessed him very much, [13]and he became rich. He gathered more wealth until he became a very rich man. [14]He had so many slaves and flocks and herds that the Philistines envied him. [15]So they stopped up all the wells the servants of Isaac's father Abraham had dug. (They had dug them when Abraham was alive.) The Philistines filled those wells with dirt. [16]And Abimelech said to Isaac, "Leave our country because you have become much more powerful than we are."

[17]So Isaac left that place and camped in the Valley of Gerar and lived there. [18]Long before this time Abraham had dug many wells, but after he died, the Philistines filled them with dirt. So Isaac dug those wells again and gave them the same names his father had given them. [19]Isaac's servants dug a well in the valley, from which a spring of water flowed. [20]But the herdsmen of Gerar argued with them and said, "This water is ours." So Isaac named that well Argue because they argued with him. [21]Then his servants dug another well. When the people also argued about it, Isaac named that well Fight. [22]He moved from there and dug another well. No one

argued about this one, so he named it Room Enough. Isaac said, "Now the LORD has made room for us, and we will be successful in this land."

[23]From there Isaac went to Beersheba. [24]The LORD appeared to him that night and said, "I am the God of your father Abraham. Don't be afraid, because I am with you. I will bless you and give you many descendants because of my servant Abraham." [25]So Isaac built an altar and worshiped the LORD there. He also made a camp there, and his servants dug a well.

[26]Abimelech came from Gerar to see Isaac. He brought with him Ahuzzath, who advised him, and Phicol, the commander of his army. [27]Isaac asked them, "Why have you come to see me? You were my enemy and forced me to leave your country."

[28]They answered, "Now we know that the LORD is with you. Let us swear an oath to each other. Let us make an agreement with you [29]that since we did not hurt you, you will not hurt us. We were good to you and sent you away in peace. Now the LORD has blessed you."

[30]So Isaac prepared food for them, and they all ate and drank. [31]Early the next morning the men swore an oath to each other. Then Isaac sent them away, and they left in peace.

[32]That day Isaac's servants came and told him about the well they had dug, saying, "We found water in that well." [33]So Isaac named it Shibah[n] and that city is called Beersheba even now.

[34]When Esau was forty years old, he married two Hittite women—Judith daughter of Beeri and Basemath daughter of Elon. [35]These women brought much sorrow to Isaac and Rebekah.

JACOB TRICKS ISAAC

27 When Isaac was old, his eyesight was poor, so he could not see clearly. One day he called his older son Esau to him and said, "Son."

Esau answered, "Here I am."

[2]Isaac said, "I am old and don't know when I might die. [3]So take your bow and

---

26:33 Shibah This name sounds like the Hebrew words for "seven" and "promise."

arrows and go hunting in the field for an animal for me to eat. ⁴When you prepare the tasty food that I love, bring it to me, and I will eat. Then I will bless you before I die." ⁵So Esau went out in the field to hunt.

Rebekah was listening as Isaac said this to his son Esau. ⁶She said to her son Jacob, "Listen, I heard your father saying to your brother Esau, ⁷'Kill an animal and prepare some tasty food for me to eat. Then I will bless you in the presence of the LORD before I die.' ⁸So obey me, my son, and do what I tell you. ⁹Go out to our goats and bring me two of the best young ones. I will prepare them just the way your father likes them. ¹⁰Then you will take the food to your father, and he will bless you before he dies."

¹¹But Jacob said to his mother Rebekah, "My brother Esau is a hairy man, and I am smooth! ¹²If my father touches me, he will know I am not Esau. Then he will not bless me but will place a curse on me because I tried to trick him."

¹³So Rebekah said to him, "If your father puts a curse on you, I will accept the blame. Just do what I said. Go get the goats for me."

¹⁴So Jacob went out and got two goats and brought them to his mother, and she cooked them in the special way Isaac enjoyed. ¹⁵She took the best clothes of her older son Esau that were in the house and put them on the younger son Jacob. ¹⁶She also took the skins of the goats and put them on Jacob's hands and neck. ¹⁷Then she gave Jacob the tasty food and the bread she had made.

¹⁸Jacob went in to his father and said, "Father."

And his father said, "Yes, my son. Who are you?"

¹⁹Jacob said to him, "I am Esau, your first son. I have done what you told me. Now sit up and eat some meat of the animal I hunted for you. Then bless me."

²⁰But Isaac asked his son, "How did you find and kill the animal so quickly?"

Jacob answered, "Because the LORD your God helped me to find it."

²¹Then Isaac said to Jacob, "Come near so I can touch you, my son. Then I will know if you are really my son Esau."

²²So Jacob came near to Isaac his father. Isaac touched him and said, "Your voice sounds like Jacob's voice, but your hands are hairy like the hands of Esau." ²³Isaac did not know it was Jacob, because his hands were hairy like Esau's hands, so Isaac blessed him. ²⁴Isaac asked, "Are you really my son Esau?"

Jacob answered, "Yes, I am."

²⁵Then Isaac said, "Bring me the food, and I will eat it and bless you." So Jacob gave him the food, and he ate. Jacob gave him wine, and he drank. ²⁶Then Isaac said to him, "My son, come near and kiss me." ²⁷So Jacob went to his father and kissed him. When Isaac smelled Esau's clothes, he blessed him and said,

"The smell of my son
     is like the smell of the field
     that the LORD has blessed.
²⁸ May God give you plenty of rain
     and good soil
   so that you will have plenty of grain and
     new wine.
²⁹ May nations serve you
     and peoples bow down to you.
May you be master over your brothers,
     and may your mother's sons bow down
     to you.
May everyone who curses you be cursed,
     and may everyone who blesses you be
     blessed."

³⁰Isaac finished blessing Jacob. Then, just as Jacob left his father Isaac, Esau came in from hunting. ³¹He also prepared some tasty food and brought it to his father. He said, "Father, rise and eat the food that your son killed for you and then bless me."

³²Isaac asked, "Who are you?"

He answered, "I am your son—your first-born son—Esau."

³³Then Isaac trembled greatly and said, "Then who was it that hunted the animals and brought me food before you came? I ate it, and I blessed him, and it is too late now to take back my blessing."

³⁴When Esau heard the words of his father, he let out a loud and bitter cry. He said to his father, "Bless me—me, too, my father!"

³⁵But Isaac said, "Your brother came and tricked me. He has taken your blessing."

³⁶Esau said, "Jacob[n] is the right name for him. He has tricked me these two times. He

---

27:36 Jacob This name sounds like the Hebrew word for "heel." "Grabbing someone's heel" is a Hebrew saying for tricking someone.

took away my share of everything you own, and now he has taken away my blessing." Then Esau asked, "Haven't you saved a blessing for me?"

37Isaac answered, "I gave Jacob the power to be master over you, and all his brothers will be his servants. And I kept him strong with grain and new wine. There is nothing left to give you, my son."

38But Esau continued, "Do you have only one blessing, Father? Bless me, too, Father!" Then Esau began to cry out loud.

39Isaac said to him,

"You will live far away from the best land,
   far from the rain.
40 You will live by using your sword,
   and you will be a slave to your brother.
But when you struggle,
   you will break free from him."

41After that Esau hated Jacob because of the blessing from Isaac. He thought to himself, "My father will soon die, and I will be sad for him. Then I will kill Jacob."

42Rebekah heard about Esau's plan to kill Jacob. So she sent for Jacob and said to him, "Listen, your brother Esau is comforting himself by planning to kill you. 43So, my son, do what I say. My brother Laban is living in Haran. Go to him at once! 44Stay with him for a while, until your brother is not so angry. 45In time, your brother will not be angry, and he will forget what you did to him. Then I will send a servant to bring you back. I don't want to lose both of my sons on the same day."

46Then Rebekah said to Isaac, "I am tired of Hittite women. If Jacob marries one of these Hittite women here in this land, I want to die."

JACOB SEARCHES FOR A WIFE

28 Isaac called Jacob and blessed him and commanded him, "You must not marry a Canaanite woman. 2Go to the house of Bethuel, your mother's father, in Northwest Mesopotamia. Laban, your mother's brother, lives there. Marry one of his daughters. 3May God Almighty bless you and give you many children, and may you become a group of many peoples. 4May he give you and your descendants the blessing of Abraham so that you may own the land where you are now living as a stranger, the land God gave to Abraham." 5So Isaac sent Jacob to Northwest Mesopotamia, to Laban the brother of Rebekah. Bethuel the Aramean was the father of Laban and Rebekah, and Rebekah was the mother of Jacob and Esau.

6Esau learned that Isaac had blessed Jacob and sent him to Northwest Mesopotamia to find a wife there. He also learned that Isaac had commanded Jacob not to marry a Canaanite woman 7and that Jacob had obeyed his father and mother and had gone to Northwest Mesopotamia. 8So Esau saw that his father Isaac did not want his sons to marry Canaanite women. 9Now Esau already had wives, but he went to Ishmael son of Abraham, and he married Mahalath, Ishmael's daughter. Mahalath was the sister of Nebaioth.

JACOB'S DREAM AT BETHEL

10Jacob left Beersheba and set out for Haran. 11When he came to a place, he spent the night there because the sun had set. He found a stone and laid his head on it to go to sleep. 12Jacob dreamed that there was a ladder resting on the earth and reaching up into heaven, and he saw angels of God going up and coming down the ladder. 13Then Jacob saw the LORD standing above the ladder, and he said, "I am the LORD, the God of Abraham your grandfather, and the God of Isaac. I will give you and your descendants the land on which you are now sleeping. 14Your descendants will be as many as the dust of the earth. They will spread west and east, north and south, and all the families of the earth will be blessed through you and your descendants. 15I am with you and will protect you everywhere you go and will bring you back to this land. I will not leave you until I have done what I have promised you."

16Then Jacob woke from his sleep and said, "Surely the LORD is in this place, but I did not know it." 17He was afraid and said, "This place frightens me! It is surely the house of God and the gate of heaven."

18Jacob rose early in the morning and took the stone he had slept on and set it up on its end. Then he poured olive oil on the top of it. 19At first, the name of that city was Luz, but Jacob named it Bethel.[n]

28:19 Bethel This name means "house of God."

²⁰Then Jacob made a promise. He said, "I want God to be with me and to protect me on this journey. I want him to give me food to eat and clothes to wear ²¹so I will be able to return in peace to my father's house. If the LORD does these things, he will be my God. ²²This stone which I have set up on its end will be the house of God. And I will give God one-tenth of all he gives me."

JACOB ARRIVES IN NORTHWEST MESOPOTAMIA

29 Then Jacob continued his journey and came to the land of the people of the East. ²He looked and saw a well in the field and three flocks of sheep lying nearby, because they drank water from this well. A large stone covered the mouth of the well. ³When all the flocks would gather there, the shepherds would roll the stone away from the well and water the sheep. Then they would put the stone back in its place.

⁴Jacob said to the shepherds there, "My brothers, where are you from?"

They answered, "We are from Haran."

⁵Then Jacob asked, "Do you know Laban, grandson of Nahor?"

They answered, "We know him."

⁶Then Jacob asked, "How is he?"

THE FAVOR OF GOD

FINANCES

what's reliable?

GENESIS 28:15

God spoke to Jacob at the site of Bethel. God reassured Jacob that he had more than temporary use of Jacob. There was permanence in God's plans. God was not going to stop dealing with Jacob until everything God had said he would do had been done. What we discover as we read the story of Jacob is this: God's promise was good for as long as Jacob lived.

God has made the same promise to his children: "I will never leave you; I will never abandon you." The most important fact of this promise is that it is *unconditional*. God does not say, "I'll stick around as long as you obey me." He doesn't put any conditions on his faithfulness toward us. He is with us for the duration, no matter what.

How many times have we let the truth of these words slip from our minds? We start worrying about the "what ifs" of life. We take on the burden of all of our cares. We think we have to do it ourselves. Our panic over security, shelter, food, and money drives us to forget just how incredibly faithful God really is. That panic is just a symptom of our unfaithfulness. We act as if God is lying to us. If God says that he will not leave us, who are we to argue with him? Live according to God's promises. He never tells a lie. You can count on him.

reflect: Do you need to reflect upon the goodness of God?
Go to **Exodus 22:29**.

They answered, "He is well. Look, his daughter Rachel is coming now with his sheep."

7 Jacob said, "But look, it is still the middle of the day. It is not time for the sheep to be gathered for the night, so give them water and let them go back into the pasture."

8 But they said, "We cannot do that until all the flocks are gathered. Then we will roll away the stone from the mouth of the well and water the sheep."

9 While Jacob was talking with the shepherds, Rachel came with her father's sheep, because it was her job to care for the sheep. 10 When Jacob saw Laban's daughter Rachel and Laban's sheep, he went to the well and rolled the stone from its mouth and watered Laban's sheep. Now Laban was the brother of Rebekah, Jacob's mother. 11 Then Jacob kissed Rachel and cried. 12 He told her that he was from her father's family and that he was the son of Rebekah. So Rachel ran home and told her father.

13 When Laban heard the news about his sister's son Jacob, he ran to meet him. Laban hugged him and kissed him and brought him to his house, where Jacob told Laban everything that had happened.

14 Then Laban said, "You are my own flesh and blood."

JACOB IS TRICKED

Jacob stayed there a month. 15 Then Laban said to Jacob, "You are my relative, but it is not right for you to work for me without pay. What would you like me to pay you?"

16 Now Laban had two daughters. The older was Leah, and the younger was Rachel. 17 Leah had weak eyes, but Rachel was very beautiful. 18 Jacob loved Rachel, so he said to Laban, "Let me marry your younger daughter Rachel. If you will, I will work seven years for you."

19 Laban said, "It would be better for her to marry you than someone else, so stay here with me." 20 So Jacob worked for Laban seven years so he could marry Rachel. But they seemed like just a few days to him because he loved Rachel very much.

21 After seven years Jacob said to Laban, "Give me Rachel so that I may marry her. The time I promised to work for you is over."

22 So Laban gave a feast for all the people there. 23 That evening he brought his daughter Leah to Jacob, and they had sexual relations. 24 (Laban gave his slave girl Zilpah to his daughter to be her servant.) 25 In the morning when Jacob saw that he had had sexual relations with Leah, he said to Laban, "What have you done to me? I worked hard for you so that I could marry Rachel! Why did you trick me?"

26 Laban said, "In our country we do not allow the younger daughter to marry before the older daughter. 27 But complete the full week of the marriage ceremony with Leah, and I will give you Rachel to marry also. But you must serve me another seven years."

28 So Jacob did this, and when he had completed the week with Leah, Laban gave him his daughter Rachel as a wife. 29 (Laban gave his slave girl Bilhah to his daughter Rachel to be her servant.) 30 So Jacob had sexual relations with Rachel also, and Jacob loved Rachel more than Leah. Jacob worked for Laban for another seven years.

JACOB'S FAMILY GROWS

31 When the LORD saw that Jacob loved Rachel more than Leah, he made it possible for Leah to have children, but not Rachel. 32 Leah became pregnant and gave birth to a son. She named him Reuben,[n] because she said, "The LORD has seen my troubles. Surely now my husband will love me."

33 Leah became pregnant again and gave birth to another son. She named him Simeon[n] and said, "The LORD has heard that I am not loved, so he has given me this son."

34 Leah became pregnant again and gave birth to another son. She named him Levi[n] and said, "Now, surely my husband will be close to me, because I have given him three sons."

35 Then Leah gave birth to another son. She named him Judah,[n] because she said, "Now I will praise the LORD." Then Leah stopped having children.

30 When Rachel saw that she was not having children for Jacob, she envied her sister Leah. She said to Jacob, "Give me

---

29:32 Reuben This name sounds like the Hebrew word for "he has seen my troubles." **29:33 Simeon** This name sounds like the Hebrew word for "has heard." **29:34 Levi** This name sounds like the Hebrew word for "be close to." **29:35 Judah** This name sounds like the Hebrew word for "praise."

children, or I'll die!" [2]Jacob became angry with her and said, "Can I do what only God can do? He is the one who has kept you from having children."

[3]Then Rachel said, "Here is my slave girl Bilhah. Have sexual relations with her so she can give birth to a child for me. Then I can have my own family through her."

[4]So Rachel gave Bilhah, her slave girl, to Jacob as a wife, and he had sexual relations with her. [5]She became pregnant and gave Jacob a son. [6]Rachel said, "God has judged me innocent. He has listened to my prayer and has given me a son," so she named him Dan.[n]

[7]Bilhah became pregnant again and gave Jacob a second son. [8]Rachel said, "I have struggled hard with my sister, and I have won." So she named that son Naphtali.[n]

[9]Leah saw that she had stopped having children, so she gave her slave girl Zilpah to Jacob as a wife. [10]When Zilpah had a son, [11]Leah said, "I am lucky," so she named him Gad.[n] [12]Zilpah gave birth to another son, [13]and Leah said, "I am very happy! Now women will call me happy," so she named him Asher.[n]

[14]During the wheat harvest Reuben went into the field and found some mandrake[n] plants and brought them to his mother Leah. But Rachel said to Leah, "Please give me some of your son's mandrakes."

[15]Leah answered, "You have already taken away my husband, and now you are trying to take away my son's mandrakes."

But Rachel answered, "If you will give me your son's mandrakes, you may sleep with Jacob tonight."

[16]When Jacob came in from the field that night, Leah went out to meet him. She said, "You will have sexual relations with me tonight because I have paid for you with my son's mandrakes." So Jacob slept with her that night.

[17]Then God answered Leah's prayer, and she became pregnant again. She gave birth to a fifth son [18]and said, "God has given me what I paid for, because I gave my slave girl to my husband." So Leah named her son Issachar.[n]

[19]Leah became pregnant again and gave birth to a sixth son. [20]She said, "God has given me a fine gift. Now surely Jacob will honor me, because I have given him six sons," so she named him Zebulun.[n] [21]Later Leah gave birth to a daughter and named her Dinah.

[22]Then God remembered Rachel and answered her prayer, making it possible for her to have children. [23]When she became pregnant and gave birth to a son, she said, "God has taken away my shame," [24]and she named him Joseph.[n] Rachel said, "I wish the LORD would give me another son."

JACOB TRICKS LABAN

[25]After the birth of Joseph, Jacob said to Laban, "Now let me go to my own home and country. [26]Give me my wives and my children and let me go. I have earned them by working for you, and you know that I have served you well."

[27]Laban said to him, "If I have pleased you, please stay. I know the LORD has blessed me because of you. [28]Tell me what I should pay you, and I will give it to you."

[29]Jacob answered, "You know that I have worked hard for you, and your flocks have grown while I cared for them. [30]When I came, you had little, but now you have much. Every time I did something for you, the LORD blessed you. But when will I be able to do something for my own family?"

[31]Laban asked, "Then what should I give you?"

Jacob answered, "I don't want you to give me anything. Just do this one thing, and I will come back and take care of your flocks. [32]Today let me go through all your flocks. I will take every speckled or spotted sheep, every black lamb, and every spotted or speckled goat. That will be my pay. [33]In the future you can easily see if I am honest. When you come to look at my flocks, if I have any goat that isn't speckled or spotted or any lamb that isn't black, you will know I stole it."

[34]Laban answered, "Agreed! We will do what you ask." [35]But that day Laban took away all the male goats that had streaks or

---

30:6 Dan This name means "he has judged." **30:8 Naphtali** This name sounds like the Hebrew word for "my struggle." **30:11 Gad** This name may mean "lucky." **30:13 Asher** This name may mean "happy." **30:14 mandrake** A plant which was believed to cause a woman to become pregnant. **30:18 Issachar** This name sounds like the Hebrew word for "paid for." **30:20 Zebulun** This name sounds like the Hebrew word for "honor." **30:24 Joseph** This name sounds like the Hebrew word for "he adds."

spots, all the speckled and spotted female goats (all those that had white on them), and all the black sheep. He told his sons to watch over them. 36Then he took these animals to a place that was three days' journey away from Jacob. Jacob took care of all the flocks that were left.

37So Jacob cut green branches from poplar, almond, and plane trees and peeled off some of the bark so that the branches had white stripes on them. 38He put the branches in front of the flocks at the watering places. When the animals came to drink, they also mated there, 39so the flocks mated in front of the branches. Then the young that were born were streaked, speckled, or spotted. 40Jacob separated the young animals from the others, and he made them face the streaked and dark animals in Laban's flock. Jacob kept his animals separate from Laban's. 41When the stronger animals in the flock were mating, Jacob put the branches before their eyes so they would mate near the branches. 42But when the weaker animals mated, Jacob did not put the branches there. So the animals born from the weaker animals were Laban's, and those born from the stronger animals were Jacob's. 43In this way Jacob became very rich. He had large flocks, many male and female servants, camels, and donkeys.

JACOB RUNS AWAY

31 One day Jacob heard Laban's sons talking. They said, "Jacob has taken everything our father owned, and in this way he has become rich." 2Then Jacob noticed that Laban was not as friendly as he had been before. 3The LORD said to Jacob, "Go back to the land where your ancestors lived, and I will be with you."

4So Jacob told Rachel and Leah to meet him in the field where he kept his flocks. 5He said to them, "I have seen that your father is not as friendly with me as he used to be, but the God of my father has been with me. 6You both know that I have worked as hard as I could for your father, 7but he cheated me and changed my pay ten times. But God has not allowed your father to harm me. 8When Laban said, 'You can have all the speckled animals as your pay,' all the animals gave birth to speckled young ones. But when he said, 'You can have all the streaked animals as your pay,'

all the flocks gave birth to streaked babies. 9So God has taken the animals away from your father and has given them to me.

10"I had a dream during the season when the flocks were mating. I saw that the only male goats who were mating were streaked, speckled, or spotted. 11The angel of God spoke to me in that dream and said, 'Jacob!' I answered, 'Yes!' 12The angel said, 'Look! Only the streaked, speckled, or spotted male goats are mating. I have seen all the wrong things Laban has been doing to you. 13I am the God who appeared to you at Bethel, where you poured olive oil on the stone you set up on end and where you made a promise to me. Now I want you to leave here and go back to the land where you were born.'"

14Rachel and Leah answered Jacob, "Our father has nothing to give us when he dies. 15He has treated us like strangers. He sold us to you, and then he spent all of the money you paid for us. 16God took all this wealth from our father, and now it belongs to us and our children. So do whatever God has told you to do."

17So Jacob put his children and his wives on camels, 18and they began their journey back to Isaac, his father, in the land of Canaan. All the flocks of animals that Jacob owned walked ahead of them. He carried everything with him that he had gotten while he lived in Northwest Mesopotamia.

19While Laban was gone to cut the wool from his sheep, Rachel stole the idols that belonged to him. 20And Jacob tricked Laban the Aramean by not telling him he was leaving. 21Jacob and his family left quickly, crossed the Euphrates River, and traveled toward the mountains of Gilead.

22Three days later Laban learned that Jacob had run away, 23so he gathered his relatives and began to chase him. After seven days Laban found him in the mountains of Gilead. 24That night God came to Laban the Aramean in a dream and said, "Be careful! Do not say anything to Jacob, good or bad."

THE SEARCH FOR THE STOLEN IDOLS

25So Laban caught up with Jacob. Now Jacob had made his camp in the mountains, so Laban and his relatives set up their camp in the mountains of Gilead. 26Laban said to Jacob, "What have you done? You cheated me and took my daughters as if you had captured them in a war. 27Why did you run away secretly and trick me? Why didn't you tell me? Then I could have sent you away with joy and singing and with the music of tambourines and harps. 28You did not even let me kiss my grandchildren and my daughters good-bye. You were very foolish to do this! 29I have the power to harm you, but last night the God of your father spoke to me and warned me not to say anything to you, good or bad. 30I know you want to go back to your home, but why did you steal my idols?"

31Jacob answered Laban, "I left without telling you, because I was afraid you would take your daughters away from me. 32If you find anyone here who has taken your idols, that person will be killed! Your relatives will be my witnesses. You may look for anything that belongs to you and take anything that is yours." (Now Jacob did not know that Rachel had stolen Laban's idols.)

33So Laban looked in Jacob's tent, in Leah's tent, and in the tent where the two slave women stayed, but he did not find his idols. When he left Leah's tent, he went into Rachel's tent. 34Rachel had hidden the idols inside her camel's saddle and was sitting on them. Although Laban looked through the whole tent, he did not find them.

35Rachel said to her father, "Father, don't be angry with me. I am not able to stand up before you because I am having my monthly period." So Laban looked through the camp, but he did not find his idols.

36Then Jacob became very angry and said, "What wrong have I done? What law have I broken to cause you to chase me? 37You have looked through everything I own, but you have found nothing that belongs to you. If you have found anything, show it to everyone. Put it in front of your relatives and my relatives, and let them decide which one of us is right. 38I have worked for you now for twenty years. During all that time none of the lambs and kids died during birth, and I have not eaten any of the male sheep from your flocks. 39Any time an animal was killed by wild beasts, I did not bring it to you, but made up for the loss myself. You made me pay for any animal that was stolen during the day or night. 40In the daytime the sun took away my strength, and at night I was cold and could

not sleep. 41I worked like a slave for you for twenty years—the first fourteen to get your two daughters and the last six to earn your flocks. During that time you changed my pay ten times. 42But the God of my father, the God of Abraham and the God of Isaac, was with me. Otherwise, you would have sent me away with nothing. But he saw the trouble I had and the hard work I did, and last night he corrected you."

JACOB AND LABAN'S AGREEMENT

43Laban said to Jacob, "These girls are my daughters. Their children belong to me, and these flocks are mine. Everything you see here belongs to me, but I can do nothing to keep my daughters and their children. 44Let us make an agreement, and let us set up a pile of stones to remind us of it."

45So Jacob took a large rock and set it up on its end. 46He told his relatives to gather rocks, so they took the rocks and piled them up; then they ate beside the pile. 47Laban named that place in his language A Pile to Remind Us, and Jacob gave the place the same name in Hebrew.

48Laban said to Jacob, "This pile of rocks will remind us of the agreement between us." That is why the place was called A Pile to Remind Us. 49It was also called Mizpah,[n] because Laban said, "Let the LORD watch over us while we are separated from each other. 50Remember that God is our witness even if no one else is around us. He will know if you harm my daughters or marry other women. 51Here is the pile of rocks that I have put between us and here is the rock I set up on end. 52This pile of rocks and this rock set on end will remind us of our agreement. I will never go past this pile to hurt you, and you must never come to my side of them to hurt me. 53Let the God of Abraham, who is the God of Nahor and the God of their ancestors, punish either of us if we break this agreement."

So Jacob made a promise in the name of the God whom his father Isaac worshiped. 54Then Jacob killed an animal and offered it as a sacrifice on the mountain, and he invited his relatives to share in the meal. After they finished eating, they spent the night on the

---

31:49 Mizpah This name sounds like the Hebrew word for "watch."

mountain. [55]Early the next morning Laban kissed his grandchildren and his daughters and blessed them, and then he left to return home.

JACOB MEETS ESAU

32 When Jacob also went his way, the angels of God met him. [2]When he saw them, he said, "This is the camp of God!" So he named that place Mahanaim.[n]

[3]Jacob's brother Esau was living in the area called Seir in the country of Edom. Jacob sent messengers to Esau, [4]telling them,

"Give this message to my master Esau: 'This is what Jacob, your servant, says: I have lived with Laban and have remained there until now. [5]I have cattle, donkeys, flocks, and male and female servants. I send this message to you and ask you to accept us.'"

[6]The messengers returned to Jacob and said, "We went to your brother Esau. He is coming to meet you and has four hundred men with him."

32:2 Mahanaim This name means "two camps."

THE EXTRAORDINARY IN THE MUNDANE

bribing God?

FAITH

GENESIS 32:20

In ancient times, there were no erasers. To change an agreement meant to "cover over" the old one. The "covering" was a way of altering the character of the original. It was like "whiting it out." God established a sacrificial system that "covered over" the sins of the people. The sacrifice did not erase the sins. It simply painted them over with the blood of the sacrifice.

In this scripture, Jacob literally means, "I will *cover over* his face." He means that his gifts will alter the face of the one set against him. He will cover over the anger of Esau and alter Esau's face so that it will become the face of acceptance rather than rejection. This is also part of the forgiveness of sins through a "covering" sacrifice. God's wrath is turned away. His face is changed toward his people. Instead of a face of anger, he shows a face of love.

But God is not waiting for us to bring gifts to him before he will forgive. The actual idea in what he has done for us in Christ is "expiate." That means "to pay the penalty." And the reason this is so important is because Christ paid the penalty for us; sin is *removed,* not just covered over, by expiation. God is not mad at us, waiting for us to be good enough to be forgiven. He is holding out his hands, waiting for us to see that we have been forgiven by the sacrifice of his Son. We come to God with *thankfulness,* not with bribes.

reflect: Remember to thank God today for the gift of forgiveness through Christ.
Go to **Exodus 24:8.**

Brave Joy

FAITH

By Robert Barriger

GENESIS 32:22–32

Webster's Dictionary defines "peace" as "the absence of war." However, the definition of peace in the Bible is the presence of God. Peace is not withdrawing from a conflict. Giving in to a point of view or situation contrary to God narrows your life. When others build your world, they always make it too small. Peace is victory in the presence of God. No matter how hard the problem is, his grace and peace will guide you through.

Faith helps you move forward in the presence of fear. There are many times when circumstances conflict with the purpose and will of God. At times, what you see as an impossible struggle can paralyze you with fear, but God promises to sustain you from beginning to end. Simply knowing that he supplies his power and strength enables you to move ahead from fear to faith. Courageous faith is not the absence of fear. It is the result of applying God's faith principles in the face of danger. Our struggles strengthen us.

For example, Isaac's son, Jacob, lived like he was defeated, running from his brother, his marriage problems, and his past. He was in danger of remaining weak. When he was alone and scared one night on the banks of the Jabbok River (Genesis 32:22–32), God did not send an angel to comfort him in his defeated attitude. God had

a better destiny and sent an angel to fight with him all night long. He learned to be strong in the Lord's grace and wrestle with the things of God until he could ask face-to-face for a blessing. God has a better destiny for your life; let his peace be with you so he can strengthen you with joy.

On the battlefield a healthy fear warns a soldier of very real dangers. An experienced soldier uses fear to keep his senses vigilant and alert to every detail and noise about him. A trained soldier moves ahead regardless of his feelings and trusts in his training and fellow soldiers at his side.

As Christians, we also use fear wisely to alert us to possible dangers. A well-trained Christian prays with all senses on alert and trusts in God's Word and his Son. An experienced Christian joins other Christians to stand on God's promises until he gives the victory over danger and over fear.

Joy unspeakable is yours when you conquer a situation that looks impossible. Hold onto the promises of God in a difficult battle, even when you don't feel victorious, and joy will be one of your rewards. God's presence with you triumphs over this life's battles. He plans for you to find peace and joy through victory, and he promises to see you through to the end. Trust in God, who is powerful and ready to move you through your fear into victory.

TO LEARN MORE ON WHAT THE BIBLE HAS TO SAY ABOUT **FAITH,** READ THE SCRIPTURES AND DEVOTIONALS AT **JOHN 4:10, JOHN 13:34–35, JOHN 14:16–17, JOHN 15:7, MATTHEW 7:13–14,** AND **ROMANS 6:23.**

7Then Jacob was very afraid and worried. He divided the people who were with him and all the flocks, herds, and camels into two camps. 8Jacob thought, "Esau might come and destroy one camp, but the other camp can run away and be saved."

9Then Jacob said, "God of my father Abraham! God of my father Isaac! LORD, you told me to return to my country and my family. You said that you would treat me well. 10I am not worthy of the kindness and continual goodness you have shown me. The first time I traveled across the Jordan River, I had only my walking stick, but now I own enough to have two camps. 11Please save me from my brother Esau. I am afraid he will come and kill all of us, even the mothers with the children. 12You said to me, 'I will treat you well and will make your children as many as the sand

---

ALWAYS ON HIS MIND

your heavenly name

FULFILLMENT

GENESIS 32:28

The phrase "What's in a name?" is a common way these days for saying that names are not really important. But in God's world, names definitely matter. In fact, they are so important that God sometimes changes a person's name to mark a change in that person.

In ancient Middle Eastern cultures, a person's name said something important about the character of that person. The Book of Genesis is full of names that carry very specific meanings. From Adam to Noah, names told the story of the man. Throughout the Bible, some men's names reflected changes in their character. In the Old Testament, Abram became Abraham and Jacob became Israel. In the New Testament, Simon became Peter and Saul became Paul.

Today, we choose names because of relatives or friends or even a favorite song or month. Names no longer associate us with who we are. They have become badges at a business conference or a school meeting. But that is not how God looks at a name. God sees *who* we are, not *what* we happen to call ourselves.

We need to recognize that when God enters our lives, we become someone new. We get a new name, based on our new family tradition. When God recreates us, we get a name that marks our status as a new person. "Christian" is a name that tells everyone exactly who we have become through the new birth, and it's a name that shows our true godly character.

reflect: Remind yourself of the value of your new name in Christ Jesus.
Go to **Exodus 14:2**.

of the seashore. There will be too many to count.'"

13Jacob stayed there for the night and prepared a gift for Esau from what he had with him: 14two hundred female goats and twenty male goats, two hundred female sheep and twenty male sheep, 15thirty female camels and their young, forty cows and ten bulls, twenty female donkeys, and ten male donkeys. 16Jacob gave each separate flock of animals to one of his servants and said to them, "Go ahead of me and keep some space between each herd." 17Jacob gave them their orders. To the servant with the first group of animals he said, "My brother Esau will come to you and ask, 'Whose servant are you? Where are you going and whose animals are these?' 18Then you will answer, 'They belong to your servant Jacob. He sent them as a gift to you, my master Esau, and he also is coming behind us.'"

19Jacob ordered the second servant, the third servant, and all the other servants to do the same thing. He said, "Say the same thing to Esau when you meet him. 20Say, 'Your servant Jacob is coming behind us.'" Jacob thought, "If I send these gifts ahead of me, maybe Esau will forgive me. Then when I see him, perhaps he will accept me." 21So Jacob sent the gifts to Esau, but he himself stayed that night in the camp.

JACOB WRESTLES WITH GOD

22During the night Jacob rose and crossed the Jabbok River at the crossing, taking with him his two wives, his two slave girls, and his eleven sons. 23He sent his family and everything he had across the river. 24So Jacob was alone, and a man came and wrestled with him until the sun came up. 25When the man saw he could not defeat Jacob, he struck Jacob's hip and put it out of joint. 26Then he said to Jacob, "Let me go. The sun is coming up."

But Jacob said, "I will let you go if you will bless me."

27The man said to him, "What is your name?"

And he answered, "Jacob."

28Then the man said, "Your name will no longer be Jacob. Your name will now be Israel,[n] because you have wrestled with God and with people, and you have won."

29Then Jacob asked him, "Please tell me your name."

But the man said, "Why do you ask my name?" Then he blessed Jacob there.

30So Jacob named that place Peniel,[n] saying, "I have seen God face to face, but my life was saved." 31Then the sun rose as he was leaving that place, and Jacob was limping because of his leg. 32So even today the people of Israel do not eat the muscle that is on the hip joint of animals, because Jacob was touched there.

JACOB SHOWS HIS BRAVERY

33 Jacob looked up and saw Esau coming, and with him were four hundred men. So Jacob divided his children among Leah, Rachel, and the two slave girls. 2Jacob put the slave girls with their children first, then Leah and her children behind them, and Rachel and Joseph last. 3Jacob himself went out in front of them and bowed down flat on the ground seven times as he was walking toward his brother.

4But Esau ran to meet Jacob and put his arms around him and hugged him. Then Esau kissed him, and they both cried. 5When Esau looked up and saw the women and children, he asked, "Who are these people with you?"

Jacob answered, "These are the children God has given me. God has been good to me, your servant."

6Then the two slave girls and their children came up to Esau and bowed down flat on the earth before him. 7Leah and her children also came up to Esau and also bowed down flat on the earth. Last of all, Joseph and Rachel came up to Esau, and they, too, bowed down flat before him.

8Esau said, "I saw many herds as I was coming here. Why did you bring them?"

Jacob answered, "They were to please you, my master."

9But Esau said, "I already have enough, my brother. Keep what you have."

10Jacob said, "No! Please! If I have pleased you, then accept the gift I give you. I am very happy to see your face again. It is like seeing the face of God, because you have accepted

---

32:28 Israel This name means "he wrestles with God."
32:30 Peniel This name means "the face of God."

me. [11]So I beg you to accept the gift I give you. God has been very good to me, and I have more than I need." And because Jacob begged, Esau accepted the gift.

[12]Then Esau said, "Let us be going. I will travel with you."

[13]But Jacob said to him, "My master, you know that the children are weak. And I must be careful with my flocks and their young ones. If I force them to go too far in one day, all the animals will die. [14]So, my master, you go on ahead of me, your servant. I will follow you slowly and let the animals and the children set the speed at which we travel. I will meet you, my master, in Edom."

[15]So Esau said, "Then let me leave some of my people with you."

"No, thank you," said Jacob. "I only want to please you, my master." [16]So that day Esau started back to Edom. [17]But Jacob went to Succoth, where he built a house for himself and shelters for his animals. That is why the place was named Succoth.[n]

[18]Jacob left Northwest Mesopotamia and arrived safely at the city of Shechem in the land of Canaan. There he camped east of the city. [19]He bought a part of the field where he had camped from the sons of Hamor father of Shechem for one hundred pieces of silver. [20]He built an altar there and named it after God, the God of Israel.

DINAH IS ATTACKED

34 At this time Dinah, the daughter of Leah and Jacob, went out to visit the women of the land. [2]When Shechem son of Hamor the Hivite, the ruler of the land, saw her, he took her and forced her to have sexual relations with him. [3]Shechem fell in love with Dinah, and he spoke kindly to her. [4]He told his father, Hamor, "Please get this girl for me so I can marry her."

[5]Jacob learned how Shechem had disgraced his daughter, but since his sons were out in the field with the cattle, Jacob said nothing until they came home. [6]While he waited, Hamor father of Shechem went to talk with Jacob.

[7]When Jacob's sons heard what had happened, they came in from the field. They were very angry that Shechem had done such a wicked thing to Israel. It was wrong for him to have sexual relations with Jacob's daughter; a thing like this should not be done.

[8]But Hamor talked to Dinah's brothers and said, "My son Shechem is deeply in love with Dinah. Please let him marry her. [9]Marry our people. Give us your women to our men as wives and take our women for your men as wives. [10]You can live in the same land with us. You will be free to own land and to trade here."

[11]Shechem also talked to Jacob and to Dinah's brothers and said, "Please accept my offer. I will give anything you ask. [12]Ask as much as you want for the payment for the bride, and I will give it to you. Just let me marry Dinah."

[13]Jacob's sons answered Shechem and his father with lies, because Shechem had disgraced their sister Dinah. [14]The brothers said to them, "We cannot allow you to marry our sister, because you are not circumcised. That would be a disgrace to us. [15]But we will allow you to marry her if you do this one thing: Every man in your town must be circumcised like us. [16]Then your men can marry our women, and our men can marry your women, and we will live in your land and become one people. [17]If you refuse to be circumcised, we will take Dinah and leave."

[18]What they asked seemed fair to Hamor and Shechem. [19]So Shechem quickly went to be circumcised because he loved Jacob's daughter.

Now Shechem was the most respected man in his family. [20]So Hamor and Shechem went to the gate of their city and spoke to the men of their city, saying, [21]"These people want to be friends with us. So let them live in our land and trade here. There is enough land for all of us. Let us marry their women, and we can let them marry our women. [22]But we must agree to one thing: All our men must be circumcised as they are. Then they will agree to live in our land, and we will be one people. [23]If we do this, their cattle and their animals will belong to us. Let us do what they say, and they will stay in our land." [24]All the people who had come to the city gate heard this. They agreed with Hamor and Shechem, and every man was circumcised.

[25]Three days later the men who were

33:17 Succoth This name means "shelters."

circumcised were still in pain. Two of Jacob's sons, Simeon and Levi (Dinah's brothers), took their swords and made a surprise attack on the city, killing all the men there. 26They killed Hamor and his son Shechem and then took Dinah out of Shechem's house and left. 27Jacob's sons came upon the dead bodies and stole everything that was in the city, to pay them back for what Shechem had done to their sister. 28So the brothers took the flocks, herds, and donkeys, and everything in the city and in the fields. 29They took every valuable thing the people owned, even their wives and children and everything in the houses.

30Then Jacob said to Simeon and Levi, "You have caused me a lot of trouble. Now the Canaanites and the Perizzites who live in the land will hate me. Since there are only a few of us, if they join together to attack us, my people and I will be destroyed."

31But the brothers said, "We will not allow our sister to be treated like a prostitute."

JACOB IN BETHEL

35 God said to Jacob, "Go to the city of Bethel and live there. Make an altar to the God who appeared to you there when you were running away from your brother Esau."

2So Jacob said to his family and to all who were with him, "Put away the foreign gods you have, and make yourselves clean, and change your clothes. 3We will leave here and go to Bethel. There I will build an altar to God, who has helped me during my time of trouble. He has been with me everywhere I have gone." 4So they gave Jacob all the foreign gods they had, and the earrings they were wearing, and he hid them under the great tree near the town of Shechem. 5Then Jacob and his sons left there. But God caused the people in the nearby cities to be afraid, so they did not follow them. 6And Jacob and all the people who were with him went to Luz, which is now called Bethel, in the land of Canaan. 7There Jacob built an altar and named the place Bethel, after God, because God had appeared to him there when he was running from his brother.

8Deborah, Rebekah's nurse, died and was buried under the oak tree at Bethel, so they named that place Oak of Crying.

JACOB'S NEW NAME

9When Jacob came back from Northwest Mesopotamia, God appeared to him again and blessed him. 10God said to him, "Your name is Jacob, but you will not be called Jacob any longer. Your new name will be Israel." So he called him Israel. 11God said to him, "I am God Almighty. Have many children and grow in number as a nation. You will be the ancestor of many nations and kings. 12The same land I gave to Abraham and Isaac I will give to you and your descendants." 13Then God left him. 14Jacob set up a stone on edge in that place where God had talked to him, and he poured a drink offering and olive oil on it to make it special for God. 15And Jacob named the place Bethel.

RACHEL DIES GIVING BIRTH

16Jacob and his group left Bethel. Before they came to Ephrath, Rachel began giving birth to her baby, 17but she was having much trouble. When Rachel's nurse saw this, she said, "Don't be afraid, Rachel. You are giving birth to another son." 18Rachel gave birth to the son, but she herself died. As she lay dying, she named the boy Son of My Suffering, but Jacob called him Benjamin.[n]

19Rachel was buried on the road to Ephrath, a district of Bethlehem, 20and Jacob set up a rock on her grave to honor her. That rock is still there. 21Then Israel[n] continued his journey and camped just south of Migdal Eder.

22While Israel was there, Reuben had sexual relations with Israel's slave woman Bilhah, and Israel heard about it.

THE FAMILY OF ISRAEL

Jacob had twelve sons. 23He had six sons by his wife Leah: Reuben, his first son, then Simeon, Levi, Judah, Issachar, and Zebulun.

24He had two sons by his wife Rachel: Joseph and Benjamin.

25He had two sons by Rachel's slave girl Bilhah: Dan and Naphtali.

26And he had two sons by Leah's slave girl Zilpah: Gad and Asher.

These are Jacob's sons who were born in Northwest Mesopotamia.

27Jacob went to his father Isaac at Mamre

35:18 **Benjamin** This name means "right-hand son" or "favorite son." **35:21 Israel** Also called Jacob.

near Hebron, where Abraham and Isaac had lived. ²⁸Isaac lived one hundred eighty years. ²⁹So Isaac breathed his last breath and died when he was very old, and his sons Esau and Jacob buried him.

ESAU'S FAMILY

36 This is the family history of Esau (also called Edom). ²Esau married women from the land of Canaan: Adah daughter of Elon the Hittite; and Oholibamah daughter of Anah, the son of Zibeon the Hivite; ³and Basemath, Ishmael's daughter, the sister of Nebaioth.

⁴Adah gave birth to Eliphaz for Esau. Basemath gave him Reuel, ⁵and Oholibamah gave him Jeush, Jalam, and Korah. These were Esau's sons who were born in the land of Canaan.

⁶Esau took his wives, his sons, his daughters, and all the people who lived with him, his herds and other animals, and all the belongings he had gotten in Canaan, and he went to a land away from his brother Jacob. ⁷Esau and Jacob's belongings were becoming too many for them to live in the same land. The land where they had lived could not support both of them, because they had too many herds. ⁸So Esau lived in the mountains of Edom. (Esau is also named Edom.)

⁹This is the family history of Esau. He is the ancestor of the Edomites, who live in the mountains of Edom.

¹⁰Esau's sons were Eliphaz, son of Adah and Esau, and Reuel, son of Basemath and Esau.

¹¹Eliphaz had five sons: Teman, Omar, Zepho, Gatam, and Kenaz. ¹²Eliphaz also had a slave woman named Timna, and Timna and Eliphaz gave birth to Amalek. These were Esau's grandsons by his wife Adah.

¹³Reuel had four sons: Nahath, Zerah, Shammah, and Mizzah. These were Esau's grandsons by his wife Basemath.

¹⁴Esau's third wife was Oholibamah the daughter of Anah. (Anah was the son of Zibeon.) Esau and Oholibamah gave birth to Jeush, Jalam, and Korah.

¹⁵These were the leaders that came from Esau: Esau's first son was Eliphaz. From him came these leaders: Teman, Omar, Zepho, Kenaz, ¹⁶Korah, Gatam, and Amalek. These were the leaders that came from Eliphaz in

the land of Edom. They were the grandsons of Adah.

¹⁷Esau's son Reuel was the father of these leaders: Nahath, Zerah, Shammah, and Mizzah. These were the leaders that came from Reuel in the land of Edom. They were the grandsons of Esau's wife Basemath.

¹⁸Esau's wife Oholibamah gave birth to these leaders: Jeush, Jalam, and Korah. These are the leaders that came from Esau's wife Oholibamah the daughter of Anah. ¹⁹These were the sons of Esau (also called Edom), and these were their leaders.

²⁰These were the sons of Seir the Horite, who were living in the land: Lotan, Shobal, Zibeon, Anah, ²¹Dishon, Ezer, and Dishan. These sons of Seir were the leaders of the Horites in Edom.

²²The sons of Lotan were Hori and Homam. (Timna was Lotan's sister.)

²³The sons of Shobal were Alvan, Manahath, Ebal, Shepho, and Onam.

²⁴The sons of Zibeon were Aiah and Anah. Anah is the man who found the hot springs in the desert while he was caring for his father's donkeys.

²⁵The children of Anah were Dishon and Oholibamah daughter of Anah.

²⁶The sons of Dishon were Hemdan, Eshban, Ithran, and Keran.

²⁷The sons of Ezer were Bilhan, Zaavan, and Akan.

²⁸The sons of Dishan were Uz and Aran.

²⁹These were the names of the Horite leaders: Lotan, Shobal, Zibeon, Anah, ³⁰Dishon, Ezer, and Dishan.

These men were the leaders of the Horite families who lived in the land of Edom.

³¹These are the kings who ruled in the land of Edom before the Israelites ever had a king:

³²Bela son of Beor was the king of Edom. He came from the city of Dinhabah.

³³When Bela died, Jobab son of Zerah became king. Jobab was from Bozrah.

³⁴When Jobab died, Husham became king. He was from the land of the Temanites.

³⁵When Husham died, Hadad son of Bedad, who had defeated Midian in the country of Moab, became king. Hadad was from the city of Avith.

³⁶When Hadad died, Samlah became king. He was from Masrekah.

37When Samlah died, Shaul became king. He was from Rehoboth on the Euphrates River.

38When Shaul died, Baal-Hanan son of Acbor became king.

39When Baal-Hanan son of Acbor died, Hadad became king. He was from the city of Pau. His wife's name was Mehetabel daughter of Matred, who was the daughter of Me-Zahab.

40These Edomite leaders, listed by their families and regions, came from Esau. Their names were Timna, Alvah, Jetheth, 41Oholibamah, Elah, Pinon, 42Kenaz, Teman, Mibzar, 43Magdiel, and Iram. They were the leaders of Edom. (Esau was the father of the Edomites.) The area where each of these families lived was named after that family.

JOSEPH THE DREAMER

37 Jacob lived in the land of Canaan, where his father had lived. 2This is the family history of Jacob:

Joseph was a young man, seventeen years old. He and his brothers, the sons of Bilhah and Zilpah, his father's wives, cared for the flocks. Joseph gave his father bad reports about his brothers. 3Since Joseph was born when his father Israel[n] was old, Israel loved him more than his other sons. He made Joseph a special robe with long sleeves. 4When Joseph's brothers saw that their father loved him more than he loved them, they hated their brother and could not speak to him politely.

5One time Joseph had a dream, and when he told his brothers about it, they hated him even more. 6Joseph said, "Listen to the dream I had. 7We were in the field tying bundles of wheat together. My bundle stood up, and your bundles of wheat gathered around it and bowed down to it."

8His brothers said, "Do you really think you will be king over us? Do you truly think you will rule over us?" His brothers hated him even more because of his dreams and what he had said.

9Then Joseph had another dream, and he told his brothers about it also. He said, "Listen, I had another dream. I saw the sun, moon, and eleven stars bowing down to me."

10Joseph also told his father about this dream, but his father scolded him, saying, "What kind of dream is this? Do you really believe that your mother, your brothers, and I will bow down to you?" 11Joseph's brothers were jealous of him, but his father thought about what all these things could mean.

12One day Joseph's brothers went to Shechem to graze their father's flocks. 13Israel said to Joseph, "Go to Shechem where your brothers are grazing the flocks."

Joseph answered, "I will go."

14His father said, "Go and see if your brothers and the flocks are all right. Then come back and tell me." So Joseph's father sent him from the Valley of Hebron.

When Joseph came to Shechem, 15a man found him wandering in the field and asked him, "What are you looking for?"

16Joseph answered, "I am looking for my brothers. Can you tell me where they are grazing the flocks?"

17The man said, "They have already gone. I heard them say they were going to Dothan." So Joseph went to look for his brothers and found them in Dothan.

JOSEPH SOLD INTO SLAVERY

18Joseph's brothers saw him coming from far away. Before he reached them, they made a plan to kill him. 19They said to each other, "Here comes that dreamer. 20Let's kill him and throw his body into one of the wells. We can tell our father that a wild animal killed him. Then we will see what will become of his dreams."

21But Reuben heard their plan and saved Joseph, saying, "Let's not kill him. 22Don't spill any blood. Throw him into this well here in the desert, but don't hurt him!" Reuben planned to save Joseph later and send him back to his father. 23So when Joseph came to his brothers, they pulled off his robe with long sleeves 24and threw him into the well. It was empty, and there was no water in it.

25While Joseph was in the well, the brothers sat down to eat. When they looked up, they saw a group of Ishmaelites traveling from Gilead to Egypt. Their camels were carrying spices, balm, and myrrh.

26Then Judah said to his brothers, "What will we gain if we kill our brother and hide his death? 27Let's sell him to these Ishmael-

---

37:3 **Israel** Also called Jacob.

ites. Then we will not be guilty of killing our own brother. After all, he is our brother, our own flesh and blood." And the other brothers agreed. 28So when the Midianite traders came by, the brothers took Joseph out of the well and sold him to the Ishmaelites for eight ounces of silver. And the Ishmaelites took him to Egypt.

29When Reuben came back to the well and Joseph was not there, he tore his clothes to show he was upset. 30Then he went back to his brothers and said, "The boy is not there! What shall I do?" 31The brothers killed a goat and dipped Joseph's robe in its blood. 32Then they brought the long-sleeved robe to their father and said, "We found this robe. Look it over carefully and see if it is your son's robe."

33Jacob looked it over and said, "It is my son's robe! Some savage animal has eaten him. My son Joseph has been torn to pieces!" 34Then Jacob tore his clothes and put on rough cloth to show that he was upset, and he continued to be sad about his son for a long time. 35All of his sons and daughters tried to comfort him, but he could not be comforted. He said, "I will be sad about my son until the day I die." So Jacob cried for his son Joseph.

36Meanwhile the Midianites who had bought Joseph had taken him to Egypt. There they sold him to Potiphar, an officer to the king of Egypt and captain of the palace guard.

JUDAH AND TAMAR

38 About that time, Judah left his brothers and went to stay with a man named Hirah in the town of Adullam. 2There Judah met a Canaanite girl, the daughter of a man named Shua, and married her. Judah had sexual relations with her, 3and she became pregnant and gave birth to a son, whom Judah named Er. 4Later she gave birth to another son and named him Onan. 5Still later she had another son and named him Shelah. She was at Kezib when this third son was born.

6Judah chose a girl named Tamar to be the wife of his first son Er. 7But Er, Judah's oldest son, did what the LORD said was evil, so the LORD killed him. 8Then Judah said to Er's brother Onan, "Go and have sexual relations with your dead brother's wife.[n]

It is your duty to provide children for your brother in this way."

9But Onan knew that the children would not belong to him, so when he was supposed to have sexual relations with Tamar he did not complete the sex act. This made it impossible for Tamar to become pregnant and for Er to have descendants. 10The LORD was displeased by this wicked thing Onan had done, so the LORD killed Onan also. 11Then Judah said to his daughter-in-law Tamar, "Go back to live in your father's house, and don't marry until my young son Shelah grows up." Judah was afraid that Shelah also would die like his brothers. So Tamar returned to her father's home.

12After a long time Judah's wife, the daughter of Shua, died. After Judah had gotten over his sorrow, he went to Timnah to his men who were cutting the wool from his sheep. His friend Hirah from Adullam went with him. 13Tamar learned that Judah, her father-in-law, was going to Timnah to cut the wool from his sheep. 14So she took off the clothes that showed she was a widow and covered her face with a veil to hide who she was. Then she sat down by the gate of Enaim on the road to Timnah. She did this because Judah's younger son Shelah had grown up, but Judah had not made plans for her to marry him.

15When Judah saw her, he thought she was a prostitute, because she had covered her face with a veil. 16So Judah went to her and said, "Let me have sexual relations with you." He did not know that she was Tamar, his daughter-in-law.

She asked, "What will you give me if I let you have sexual relations with me?"

17Judah answered, "I will send you a young goat from my flock."

She answered, "First give me something to keep as a deposit until you send the goat."

18Judah asked, "What do you want me to give you as a deposit?"

Tamar answered, "Give me your seal and its cord,[n] and give me your walking stick." So

---

38:8 Go . . . wife It was a custom in Israel that if a man died without children, one of his brothers would marry the widow. If a child was born, it would be considered the dead man's child. **38:18 seal . . . cord** A seal was used like a rubber stamp, and people ran a string through it to tie around the neck. They wrote a contract, folded it, put wax or clay on the contract, and pressed the seal onto it as a signature.

Judah gave these things to her. Then Judah and Tamar had sexual relations, and Tamar became pregnant. ¹⁹When Tamar went home, she took off the veil that covered her face and put on the clothes that showed she was a widow.

²⁰Judah sent his friend Hirah with the young goat to find the woman and get back his seal and the walking stick he had given her, but Hirah could not find her. ²¹He asked some of the people at the town of Enaim, "Where is the prostitute who was here by the road?"

They answered, "There has never been a prostitute here."

²²So he went back to Judah and said, "I could not find the woman, and the people who lived there said, 'There has never been a prostitute here.'"

²³Judah said, "Let her keep the things. I don't want people to laugh at us. I sent her the goat as I promised, but you could not find her."

²⁴About three months later someone told Judah, "Tamar, your daughter-in-law, is guilty of acting like a prostitute, and now she is pregnant."

Then Judah said, "Bring her out and let her be burned to death."

²⁵When the people went to bring Tamar out, she sent a message to her father-in-law that said, "The man who owns these things has made me pregnant. Look at this seal and its cord and this walking stick, and tell me whose they are."

²⁶Judah recognized them and said, "She is more in the right than I. She did this because I did not give her to my son Shelah as I promised." And Judah did not have sexual relations with her again.

²⁷When the time came for Tamar to give birth, there were twins in her body. ²⁸While she was giving birth, one baby put his hand out. The nurse tied a red string on his hand and said, "This baby came out first." ²⁹But he pulled his hand back in, so the other baby was born first. The nurse said, "So you are able to break out first," and they named him Perez.ⁿ ³⁰After this, the baby with the red string on his hand was born, and they named him Zerah.

JOSEPH IS SOLD TO POTIPHAR

39 Now Joseph had been taken down to Egypt. An Egyptian named Potiphar was an officer to the king of Egypt and the captain of the palace guard. He bought Joseph from the Ishmaelites who had brought him down there. ²The LORD was with Joseph, and he became a successful man. He lived in the house of his master, Potiphar the Egyptian.

³Potiphar saw that the LORD was with Joseph and that the LORD made Joseph successful in everything he did. ⁴So Potiphar was very happy with Joseph and allowed him to be his personal servant. He put Joseph in charge of the house, trusting him with everything he owned. ⁵When Joseph was put in charge of the house and everything Potiphar owned, the LORD blessed the people in Potiphar's house because of Joseph. And the LORD blessed everything that belonged to Potiphar, both in the house and in the field. ⁶So Potiphar left Joseph in charge of everything he owned and was not concerned about anything except the food he ate.

JOSEPH IS PUT INTO PRISON

Now Joseph was well built and handsome. ⁷After some time the wife of Joseph's master began to desire Joseph, and one day she said to him, "Have sexual relations with me."

⁸But Joseph refused and said to her, "My master trusts me with everything in his house. He has put me in charge of everything he owns. ⁹There is no one in his house greater than I. He has not kept anything from me except you, because you are his wife. How can I do such an evil thing? It is a sin against God."

¹⁰The woman talked to Joseph every day, but he refused to have sexual relations with her or even spend time with her.

¹¹One day Joseph went into the house to do his work as usual and was the only man in the house at that time. ¹²His master's wife grabbed his coat and said to him, "Come and have sexual relations with me." But Joseph left his coat in her hand and ran out of the house.

¹³When she saw that Joseph had left his

38:29 Perez This name means "breaking out."

THE PRODUCT OF PRESENT OBEDIENCE

thinking like
a winner

FUTURE

By Jim Garlow

GENESIS 39:2-5

Do you want a great future? It's God's will for every Christian to be a winner. He has given us everything we need to fulfill his purpose for our lives, but we have to do our part. Here are some practical things you must do to achieve God's best for your life:

• Have the vision to see what you can become.

• Make decisions that yield good results.

• Be ready to change when necessary.

• Keep accurate daily records; it's a way of saying you value life.

• Have the discipline needed to give you the dreams of your heart. Lack of discipline is a "dream-destroyer."

• In order to break from a destructive "rut," be willing to accept the routine needed to establish new and healthy habits.

• Appreciate compliments from others, but choose to live your life by principles rather than by what others think of you.

• Although you must avoid unhealthy fears, you must embrace healthy fears that restrain you from doing those things that will ultimately be harmful.

• Depend on the endurance God will provide to outlast any problem.

• Have convictions you will die for, even though you may choose to live by some of your preferences.

• Let your mind rule over your body.

• Allow the Holy Spirit to rule over your mind, which rules over your body.

• Focus on wholesome thoughts that take you to healthy results.

• Pray. Your spirit was created for communion with God and for thinking higher thoughts.

• Accept the fact that you must always "keep on keeping on."

reflect: Are you willing to do what is necessary to become a winner?
Go to **1 Samuel 2:6–10.**

coat in her hands and had run outside, ¹⁴she called to the servants in her house and said, "Look! This Hebrew slave was brought here to shame us. He came in and tried to have sexual relations with me, but I screamed. ¹⁵My scream scared him and he ran away, but he left his coat with me." ¹⁶She kept his coat until her husband came home, ¹⁷and she told him the same story. She said, "This Hebrew slave you brought here came in to shame me! ¹⁸When he came near me, I screamed. He ran away, but he left his coat."

¹⁹When Joseph's master heard what his wife said Joseph had done, he became very angry. ²⁰So Potiphar arrested Joseph and put him into the prison where the king's prisoners were put. And Joseph stayed there in the prison.

²¹But the LORD was with Joseph and showed him kindness and caused the prison warden to like Joseph. ²²The prison warden chose Joseph to take care of all the prisoners, and he was responsible for whatever was done in the prison. ²³The warden paid no attention to anything that was in Joseph's care because the LORD was with Joseph and made him successful in everything he did.

JOSEPH INTERPRETS TWO DREAMS

40 After these things happened, two of the king's officers displeased the king—the man who served wine to the king and the king's baker. ²The king became angry with his officer who served him wine and his baker, ³so he put them in the prison of the captain of the guard, the same prison where Joseph was kept. ⁴The captain of the guard put the two prisoners in Joseph's care, and they stayed in prison for some time.

⁵One night both the king's officer who served him wine and the baker had a dream. Each had his own dream with its own meaning. ⁶When Joseph came to them the next morning, he saw they were worried. ⁷He asked the king's officers who were with him, "Why do you look so unhappy today?"

⁸The two men answered, "We both had dreams last night, but no one can explain their meaning to us."

Joseph said to them, "God is the only One who can explain the meaning of dreams. Tell me your dreams."

⁹So the man who served wine to the king told Joseph his dream. He said, "I dreamed I saw a vine, and ¹⁰on the vine were three branches. I watched the branches bud and blossom, and then the grapes ripened. ¹¹I was holding the king's cup, so I took the grapes and squeezed the juice into the cup. Then I gave it to the king."

¹²Then Joseph said, "I will explain the dream to you. The three branches stand for three days. ¹³Before the end of three days the king will free you, and he will allow you to return to your work. You will serve the king his wine just as you did before. ¹⁴But when you are free, remember me. Be kind to me, and tell the king about me so I can get out of this prison. ¹⁵I was taken by force from the land of the Hebrews, and I have done nothing here to deserve being put in prison."

¹⁶The baker saw that Joseph's explanation of the dream was good, so he said to him, "I also had a dream. I dreamed there were three bread baskets on my head. ¹⁷In the top basket were all kinds of baked food for the king, but the birds were eating this food out of the basket on my head."

¹⁸Joseph answered, "I will tell you what the dream means. The three baskets stand for three days. ¹⁹Before the end of three days, the king will cut off your head! He will hang your body on a pole, and the birds will eat your flesh."

²⁰Three days later, on his birthday, the king gave a feast for all his officers. In front of his officers, he released from prison the chief officer who served his wine and the chief baker. ²¹The king gave his chief officer who served wine his old position, and once again he put the king's cup of wine into the king's hand. ²²But the king hanged the baker on a pole. Everything happened just as Joseph had said it would, ²³but the officer who served wine did not remember Joseph. He forgot all about him.

THE KING'S DREAMS

41 Two years later the king dreamed he was standing on the bank of the Nile River. ²He saw seven fat and beautiful cows come up out of the river, and they stood there, eating the grass. ³Then seven more cows came up out of the river, but they were thin and ugly. They stood beside the seven beautiful cows on the bank of the Nile. ⁴The seven thin and ugly cows ate the seven beautiful fat cows. Then the king woke up. ⁵The king slept again and dreamed a second time. In his dream he saw seven full and good heads of grain growing on one stalk. ⁶After that, seven more heads of grain sprang up, but they were thin and burned by the hot east wind. ⁷The thin heads of grain ate the seven full and good heads. Then the king woke up again, and he realized it was only a dream. ⁸The next morning the king was troubled about these dreams, so he sent for all the magicians and wise men of Egypt. The king told them his dreams, but no one could explain their meaning to him.

⁹Then the chief officer who served wine to the king said to him, "Now I remember something I promised to do, but I forgot about it. ¹⁰There was a time when you were angry with the baker and me, and you put us in prison in the house of the captain of the guard. ¹¹In prison we each had a dream on the same night, and each dream had a different meaning. ¹²A young Hebrew man, a servant of the captain of the guard, was in the prison with us. When we told him our dreams, he explained their meanings to us. He told each man the meaning of his dream, and ¹³things happened exactly as he said they would: I was given back my old position, and the baker was hanged."

¹⁴So the king called for Joseph. The guards quickly brought him out of the prison, and he shaved, put on clean clothes, and went before the king.

¹⁵The king said to Joseph, "I have had a dream, but no one can explain its meaning to me. I have heard that you can explain a dream when someone tells it to you."

¹⁶Joseph answered the king, "I am not able to explain the meaning of dreams, but God will do this for the king."

¹⁷Then the king said to Joseph, "In my dream I was standing on the bank of the Nile River. ¹⁸I saw seven fat and beautiful cows that came up out of the river and ate the grass. ¹⁹Then I saw seven more cows come out of the river that were thin and lean and ugly—the worst looking cows I have seen in all the land of Egypt. ²⁰And these thin and ugly cows ate the first seven fat cows, ²¹but after they had eaten the seven cows, no one could tell they had eaten them. They looked just as thin and ugly as they did in the beginning. Then I woke up.

²²"I had another dream. I saw seven full and good heads of grain growing on one stalk. ²³Then seven more heads of grain sprang up after them, but these heads were thin and ugly and were burned by the hot east wind. ²⁴Then the thin heads ate the seven good heads. I told this dream to the magicians, but no one could explain its meaning to me."

JOSEPH TELLS THE DREAMS' MEANING

²⁵Then Joseph said to the king, "Both of these dreams mean the same thing. God is telling you what he is about to do. ²⁶The seven good cows stand for seven years, and the seven good heads of grain stand for seven years. Both dreams mean the same thing. ²⁷The seven thin and ugly cows stand for seven years, and the seven thin heads of grain burned by the hot east wind stand for seven years of hunger. ²⁸This will happen as I told you. God is showing the king what he is about to do. ²⁹You will have seven years of good crops and plenty to eat in all the land of Egypt. ³⁰But after those seven years, there will come seven years of hunger, and all the food that grew in the land of Egypt will be forgotten. The time of hunger will eat up the land. ³¹People will forget what it was like to have plenty of food, because the hunger that follows will be so great. ³²You had two dreams which mean the same thing. This shows that God has firmly decided that this will happen, and he will make it happen soon.

³³"So let the king choose a man who is very wise and understanding and set him over the land of Egypt. ³⁴And let the king also appoint officers over the land, who should take one-fifth of all the food that is grown during the seven good years. ³⁵They should gather all the food that is produced during the good years that are coming, and under the king's authority they should store the grain in the cities and guard it. ³⁶That food should be saved to use during the seven years of hunger that will come on the land of Egypt. Then the people in Egypt will not die during the seven years of hunger."

JOSEPH IS MADE RULER OVER EGYPT

³⁷This seemed like a very good idea to the king, and all his officers agreed. ³⁸And the

king asked them, "Can we find a better man than Joseph to take this job? God's spirit is truly in him!"

³⁹So the king said to Joseph, "God has shown you all this. There is no one as wise and understanding as you are, so ⁴⁰I will put you in charge of my palace. All the people will obey your orders, and only I will be greater than you."

⁴¹Then the king said to Joseph, "Look! I have put you in charge of all the land of Egypt." ⁴²Then the king took off from his own finger his ring with the royal seal on it, and he put it on Joseph's finger. He gave Joseph fine linen clothes to wear, and he put a gold chain around Joseph's neck. ⁴³The king had Joseph ride in the second royal chariot, and people walked ahead of his chariot calling, "Bow down!" By doing these things, the king put Joseph in charge of all of Egypt.

⁴⁴The king said to him, "I am the king, and I say that no one in all the land of Egypt may lift a hand or a foot without your permission." ⁴⁵The king gave Joseph the name Zaphenath-Paneah. He also gave Joseph a wife named Asenath, who was the daughter of Potiphera, priest of On. So Joseph traveled through all the land of Egypt.

⁴⁶Joseph was thirty years old when he began serving the king of Egypt. And he left the king's court and traveled through all the land of Egypt. ⁴⁷During the seven good years, the crops in the land grew well. ⁴⁸And Joseph gathered all the food produced in Egypt during those seven years of good crops and stored the food in the cities. In every city he stored grain that had been grown in the fields around that city. ⁴⁹Joseph stored much grain, as much as the sand of the seashore—so much that he could not measure it.

⁵⁰Joseph's wife was Asenath daughter of Potiphera, the priest of On. Before the years of hunger came, Joseph and Asenath had two sons. ⁵¹Joseph named the first son Manasseh[n] and said, "God has made me forget all the troubles I have had and all my father's family." ⁵²Joseph named the second son Ephraim[n] and said, "God has given me children in the land of my troubles."

⁵³The seven years of good crops came to an end in the land of Egypt. ⁵⁴Then the seven years of hunger began, just as Joseph had said. In all the lands people had nothing to eat, but in Egypt there was food. ⁵⁵The time of hunger became terrible in all of Egypt, and the people cried to the king for food. He said to all the Egyptians, "Go to Joseph and do whatever he tells you."

⁵⁶The hunger was everywhere in that part of the world. And Joseph opened the storehouses and sold grain to the people of Egypt, because the time of hunger became terrible in Egypt. ⁵⁷And all the people in that part of the world came to Joseph in Egypt to buy grain because the hunger was terrible everywhere in that part of the world.

THE DREAMS COME TRUE

42 Jacob learned that there was grain in Egypt, so he said to his sons, "Why are you just sitting here looking at one another? ²I have heard that there is grain in Egypt. Go down there and buy grain for us to eat, so that we will live and not die."

³So ten of Joseph's brothers went down to buy grain from Egypt. ⁴But Jacob did not send Benjamin, Joseph's brother, with them, because he was afraid that something terrible might happen to him. ⁵Along with many other people, the sons of Israel[n] went to Egypt to buy grain, because the people in the land of Canaan were also hungry.

⁶Now Joseph was governor over Egypt. He was the one who sold the grain to people who came to buy it. So Joseph's brothers came to him and bowed facedown on the ground before him. ⁷When Joseph saw his brothers, he knew who they were, but he acted as if he didn't know them. He asked unkindly, "Where do you come from?"

They answered, "We have come from the land of Canaan to buy food."

⁸Joseph knew they were his brothers, but they did not know who he was. ⁹And Joseph remembered his dreams about his brothers bowing to him. He said to them, "You are spies! You came to learn where the nation is weak!"

¹⁰But his brothers said to him, "No, my master. We come as your servants just to buy food. ¹¹We are all sons of the same father. We are honest men, not spies."

41:51 **Manasseh** This name sounds like the Hebrew word for "made me forget." 41:52 **Ephraim** This name sounds like the Hebrew word for "given me children." 42:5 **Israel** Also called Jacob.

¹²Then Joseph said to them, "No! You have come to learn where this nation is weak!"

¹³And they said, "We are ten of twelve brothers, sons of the same father, and we live in the land of Canaan. Our youngest brother is there with our father right now, and our other brother is gone."

¹⁴But Joseph said to them, "I can see I was right! You are spies! ¹⁵But I will give you a way to prove you are telling the truth. As surely as the king lives, you will not leave this place until your youngest brother comes here. ¹⁶One of you must go and get your brother. The rest of you will stay here in prison. We will see if you are telling the truth. If not, as surely as the king lives, you are spies." ¹⁷Then Joseph put them all in prison for three days.

¹⁸On the third day Joseph said to them, "I am a God-fearing man. Do this and I will let you live: ¹⁹If you are honest men, let one of your brothers stay here in prison while the rest of you go and carry grain back to feed your hungry families. ²⁰Then bring your youngest brother back here to me. If you do this, I will know you are telling the truth, and you will not die."

The brothers agreed to this. ²¹They said to each other, "We are being punished for what we did to our brother. We saw his trouble, and he begged us to save him, but we refused to listen. That is why we are in this trouble now."

²²Then Reuben said to them, "I told you not to harm the boy, but you refused to listen to me. So now we are being punished for what we did to him."

²³When Joseph talked to his brothers, he used an interpreter, so they did not know that Joseph understood what they were saying. ²⁴Then Joseph left them and cried. After a short time he went back and spoke to them. He took Simeon and tied him up while the other brothers watched. ²⁵Joseph told his servants to fill his brothers' bags with grain and to put the money the brothers had paid for the grain back in their bags. The servants were also to give them what they would need for their trip back home. And the servants did this.

²⁶So the brothers put the grain on their donkeys and left. ²⁷When they stopped for the night, one of the brothers opened his sack to get food for his donkey. Then he saw his money in the top of the sack. ²⁸He said to the other brothers, "The money I paid for the grain has been put back. Here it is in my sack!"

The brothers were very frightened. They said to each other, "What has God done to us?"

THE BROTHERS RETURN TO JACOB

²⁹The brothers went to their father Jacob in the land of Canaan and told him everything that had happened. ³⁰They said, "The master of that land spoke unkindly to us. He accused us of spying on his country, ³¹but we told him that we were honest men, not spies. ³²We told him that we were ten of twelve brothers—sons of one father. We said that one of our brothers was gone and that our youngest brother was with our father in Canaan.

³³"Then the master of the land said to us, 'Here is a way I can know you are honest men: Leave one of your brothers with me, and take grain to feed your hungry families, and go. ³⁴And bring your youngest brother to me so I will know you are not spies but honest men. Then I will give you back your brother whom you leave with me, and you can move about freely in our land.'"

³⁵As the brothers emptied their sacks, each of them found his money in his sack. When they and their father saw it, they were afraid.

³⁶Their father Jacob said to them, "You are robbing me of all my children. Joseph is gone, Simeon is gone, and now you want to take Benjamin away, too. Everything is against me."

³⁷Then Reuben said to his father, "You may put my two sons to death if I don't bring Benjamin back to you. Trust him to my care, and I will bring him back to you."

³⁸But Jacob said, "I will not allow Benjamin to go with you. His brother is dead, and he is the only son left from my wife Rachel. I am afraid something terrible might happen to him during the trip to Egypt. Then I would be sad until the day I die."

THE BROTHERS GO BACK TO EGYPT

43 Still no food grew in the land of Canaan. ²When Jacob's family had eaten all the grain they had brought from Egypt, Jacob said to them, "Go to Egypt again and buy a little more grain for us to eat."

³But Judah said to Jacob, "The governor of that country strongly warned us, 'If you don't bring your brother back with you, you will not be allowed to see me.' ⁴If you will send Benjamin with us, we will go down and buy food for you. ⁵But if you refuse to send Benjamin, we will not go. The governor of that country warned us that we would not see him if we didn't bring Benjamin with us."

⁶Israel[n] said, "Why did you tell the man you had another brother? You have caused me a lot of trouble."

⁷The brothers answered, "He questioned us carefully about ourselves and our family. He asked us, 'Is your father still alive? Do you have another brother?' We just answered his questions. How could we know he would ask us to bring our other brother to him?"

⁸Then Judah said to his father Jacob, "Send Benjamin with me, and we will go at once so that we, you, and our children may live and not die. ⁹I will guarantee you that he will be safe, and I will be personally responsible for him. If I don't bring him back to you, you can blame me all my life. ¹⁰If we had not wasted all this time, we could have already made two trips."

¹¹Then their father Jacob said to them, "If it has to be that way, then do this: Take some of the best foods in our land in your packs. Give them to the man as a gift: some balm, some honey, spices, myrrh, pistachio nuts, and almonds. ¹²Take twice as much money with you this time, and take back the money that was returned to you in your sacks last time. Maybe it was a mistake. ¹³And take Benjamin with you. Now leave and go to the man. ¹⁴I pray that God Almighty will cause the governor to be merciful to you and that he will allow Simeon and Benjamin to come back with you. If I am robbed of my children, then I am robbed of them!"

¹⁵So the brothers took the gifts. They also took twice as much money as they had taken the first time, and they took Benjamin. They hurried down to Egypt and stood before Joseph.

¹⁶When Joseph saw Benjamin with them, he said to the servant in charge of his house, "Bring those men into my house. Kill an animal and prepare a meal. Those men will eat with me today at noon." ¹⁷The servant did as Joseph told him and brought the men to Joseph's house.

¹⁸The brothers were afraid when they were brought to Joseph's house and thought, "We were brought here because of the money that was put in our sacks on the first trip. He wants to attack us, make us slaves, and take our donkeys." ¹⁹So the brothers went to the servant in charge of Joseph's house and spoke to him at the door of the house. ²⁰They said, "Master, we came here once before to buy food. ²¹While we were going home, we stopped for the night and when we opened our sacks each of us found all his money in his sack. We brought that money with us to give it back to you. ²²And we have brought more money to pay for the food we want to buy this time. We don't know who put that money in our sacks."

²³But the servant answered, "It's all right. Don't be afraid. Your God, the God of your father, must have put the money in your sacks. I got the money you paid me for the grain last time." Then the servant brought Simeon out to them.

²⁴The servant led the men into Joseph's house and gave them water, and they washed their feet. Then he gave their donkeys food to eat. ²⁵The men prepared their gift to give to Joseph when he arrived at noon, because they had heard they were going to eat with him there.

²⁶When Joseph came home, the brothers gave him the gift they had brought into the house and bowed down to the ground in front of him. ²⁷Joseph asked them how they were doing. He said, "How is your aged father you told me about? Is he still alive?"

²⁸The brothers answered, "Your servant, our father, is well. He is still alive." And they bowed low before Joseph to show him respect.

²⁹When Joseph saw his brother Benjamin, who had the same mother as he, Joseph asked, "Is this your youngest brother you told me about?" Then he said to Benjamin, "God be good to you, my son!" ³⁰Then Joseph hurried off because he had to hold back the tears when he saw his brother Benjamin. So Joseph went into his room and cried there. ³¹Then he

---

43:6 Israel Also called Jacob.

washed his face and came out. He controlled himself and said, "Serve the meal."

³²So they served Joseph at one table, his brothers at another table, and the Egyptians who ate with him at another table. This was because Egyptians did not like Hebrews and never ate with them. ³³Joseph's brothers were seated in front of him in order of their ages, from oldest to youngest. They looked at each other because they were so amazed. ³⁴Food from Joseph's table was taken to them, but Benjamin was given five times more food than the others. Joseph's brothers ate and drank freely with him.

JOSEPH SETS A TRAP

44 Then Joseph gave a command to the servant in charge of his house. He said, "Fill the men's sacks with as much grain as they can carry, and put each man's money into his sack with the grain. ²Put my silver cup in the sack of the youngest brother, along with his money for the grain." The servant did what Joseph told him.

³At dawn the brothers were sent away with their donkeys. ⁴They were not far from the city when Joseph said to the servant in charge of his house, "Go after the men. When you catch up with them, say, 'Why have you paid back evil for good? ⁵The cup you have stolen is the one my master uses for drinking and for explaining dreams. You have done a very wicked thing!'"

⁶So the servant caught up with the brothers and said to them what Joseph had told him to say.

⁷But the brothers said to the servant, "Why do you say these things? We would not do anything like that! ⁸We brought back to you from the land of Canaan the money we found in our sacks. So surely we would not steal silver or gold from your master's house. ⁹If you find that silver cup in the sack of one of us, then let him die, and we will be your slaves."

¹⁰The servant said, "We will do as you say, but only the man who has taken the cup will become my slave. The rest of you may go free."

¹¹Then every brother quickly lowered his sack to the ground and opened it. ¹²The servant searched the sacks, going from the oldest brother to the youngest, and found the cup in Benjamin's sack. ¹³The brothers tore their clothes to show they were afraid. Then they put their sacks back on the donkeys and returned to the city.

¹⁴When Judah and his brothers went back to Joseph's house, Joseph was still there, so the brothers bowed facedown on the ground before him. ¹⁵Joseph said to them, "What have you done? Didn't you know that a man like me can learn things by signs and dreams?"

¹⁶Judah said, "Master, what can we say? And how can we show we are not guilty? God has uncovered our guilt, so all of us will be your slaves, not just Benjamin."

¹⁷But Joseph said, "I will not make you all slaves! Only the man who stole the cup will be my slave. The rest of you may go back safely to your father."

¹⁸Then Judah went to Joseph and said, "Master, please let me speak plainly to you, and please don't be angry with me. I know that you are as powerful as the king of Egypt himself. ¹⁹When we were here before, you asked us, 'Do you have a father or a brother?' ²⁰And we answered you, 'We have an old father. And we have a younger brother, who was born when our father was old. This youngest son's brother is dead, so he is the only one of his mother's children left alive, and our father loves him very much.' ²¹Then you said to us, 'Bring that brother to me. I want to see him.' ²²And we said to you, 'That young boy cannot leave his father, because if he leaves him, his father would die.' ²³But you said to us, 'If you don't bring your youngest brother, you will not be allowed to see me again.' ²⁴So we went back to our father and told him what you had said.

²⁵"Later, our father said, 'Go again and buy us a little more food.' ²⁶We said to our father, 'We cannot go without our youngest brother. Without our youngest brother, we will not be allowed to see the governor.' ²⁷Then my father said to us, 'You know that my wife Rachel gave me two sons. ²⁸When one son left me, I thought, "Surely he has been torn apart by a wild animal," and I haven't seen him since. ²⁹Now you want to take this son away from me also. But something terrible might happen to him, and I would be miserable until the day I die.' ³⁰Now what will happen if we go home to our father without

our youngest brother? He is so important in our father's life that [31]when our father sees the young boy is not with us, he will die. And it will be our fault. We will cause the great sorrow that kills our father.

[32]"I gave my father a guarantee that the young boy would be safe. I said to my father, 'If I don't bring him back to you, you can blame me all my life.' [33]So now, please allow me to stay here and be your slave, and let the young boy go back home with his brothers. [34]I cannot go back to my father if the boy is not with me. I couldn't stand to see my father that sad."

JOSEPH REVEALS WHO HE IS

45 Joseph could not control himself in front of his servants any longer, so he cried out, "Have everyone leave me." When only the brothers were left with Joseph, he told them who he was. [2]Joseph cried so loudly that the Egyptians heard him, and the people in the king's palace heard about it. [3]He said to his brothers, "I am Joseph. Is my father still alive?" But the brothers could not answer him, because they were very afraid of him.

[4]So Joseph said to them, "Come close to me." When the brothers came close to him, he said to them, "I am your brother Joseph, whom you sold as a slave to go to Egypt. [5]Now don't be worried or angry with yourselves because you sold me here. God sent me here ahead of you to save people's lives. [6]No food has grown on the land for two years now, and there will be five more years without planting or harvest. [7]So God sent me here ahead of you to make sure you have some descendants left on earth and to keep you alive in an amazing way. [8]So it was not you who sent me here, but God. God has made me the highest officer of the king of Egypt. I am in charge of his palace, and I am the master of all the land of Egypt.

[9]"So leave quickly and go to my father. Tell him, 'Your son Joseph says: God has made me master over all Egypt. Come down to me quickly. [10]Live in the land of Goshen where you will be near me. Your children, your grandchildren, your flocks and herds, and all that you have will also be near me. [11]I will care for you during the next five years of hunger so that you and your family and all that you have will not starve.'

[12]"Now you can see for yourselves, and so can my brother Benjamin, that the one speaking to you is really Joseph. [13]So tell my father about how powerful I have become in Egypt. Tell him about everything you have seen. Now hurry and bring him back to me." [14]Then Joseph hugged his brother Benjamin and cried, and Benjamin cried also. [15]And Joseph kissed all his brothers and cried as he hugged them. After this, his brothers talked with him.

[16]When the king of Egypt and his officers learned that Joseph's brothers had come, they were very happy. [17]So the king said to Joseph, "Tell your brothers to load their animals and go back to the land of Canaan [18]and bring their father and their families back here to me. I will give them the best land in Egypt, and they will eat the best food we have here. [19]Tell them to take some wagons from Egypt for their children and their wives and to bring their father back also. [20]Tell them not to worry about bringing any of their things with them, because we will give them the best of what we have in Egypt."

[21]So the sons of Israel did this. Joseph gave them wagons as the king had ordered and food for their trip. [22]He gave each brother a change of clothes, but he gave Benjamin five changes of clothes and about seven and one-half pounds of silver. [23]Joseph also sent his father ten donkeys loaded with the best things from Egypt and ten female donkeys loaded with grain, bread, and other food for his father on his trip back. [24]Then Joseph told his brothers to go. As they were leaving, he said to them, "Don't quarrel on the way home."

[25]So the brothers left Egypt and went to their father Jacob in the land of Canaan. [26]They told him, "Joseph is still alive and is the ruler over all the land of Egypt." Their father was shocked and did not believe them. [27]But when the brothers told him everything Joseph had said, and when Jacob saw the wagons Joseph had sent to carry him back to Egypt, he felt better. [28]Israel[n] said, "Now I believe you. My son Joseph is still alive, and I will go and see him before I die."

45:28 Israel Also called Jacob.

JACOB GOES TO EGYPT

46 So Israel[n] took all he had and started his trip. He went to Beersheba, where he offered sacrifices to the God of his father Isaac. ²During the night God spoke to Israel in a vision and said, "Jacob, Jacob."

And Jacob answered, "Here I am."

³Then God said, "I am God, the God of your father. Don't be afraid to go to Egypt, because I will make your descendants a great nation there. ⁴I will go to Egypt with you, and I will bring you out of Egypt again. Joseph's own hands will close your eyes when you die."

⁵Then Jacob left Beersheba. The sons of Israel loaded their father, their children, and their wives in the wagons the king of Egypt had sent. ⁶They also took their farm animals and everything they had gotten in Canaan. So Jacob went to Egypt with all his descendants— ⁷his sons and grandsons, his daughters and granddaughters. He took all his family to Egypt with him.

JACOB'S FAMILY

⁸Now these are the names of the children of Israel who went into Egypt (Jacob and his descendants).

Reuben was Jacob's first son. ⁹Reuben's sons were Hanoch, Pallu, Hezron, and Carmi.

¹⁰Simeon's sons were Jemuel, Jamin, Ohad, Jakin, Zohar, and Shaul (Simeon's son by a Canaanite woman).

¹¹Levi's sons were Gershon, Kohath, and Merari.

¹²Judah's sons were Er, Onan, Shelah, Perez, and Zerah (but Er and Onan had died in the land of Canaan). Perez's sons were Hezron and Hamul.

¹³Issachar's sons were Tola, Puah, Jashub, and Shimron.

¹⁴Zebulun's sons were Sered, Elon, and Jahleel.

¹⁵These are the sons of Leah and Jacob born in Northwest Mesopotamia, in addition to his daughter Dinah. There were thirty-three persons in this part of Jacob's family.

¹⁶Gad's sons were Zephon, Haggi, Shuni, Ezbon, Eri, Arodi, and Areli.

¹⁷Asher's sons were Imnah, Ishvah, Ishvi, and Beriah, and their sister was Serah. Beriah's sons were Heber and Malkiel.

¹⁸These are Jacob's sons by Zilpah, the slave girl whom Laban gave to his daughter Leah. There were sixteen persons in this part of Jacob's family.

¹⁹The sons of Jacob's wife Rachel were Joseph and Benjamin. ²⁰In Egypt, Joseph became the father of Manasseh and Ephraim by his wife Asenath, the daughter of Potiphera, priest of On.

²¹Benjamin's sons were Bela, Beker, Ashbel, Gera, Naaman, Ehi, Rosh, Muppim, Huppim, and Ard.

²²These are the sons of Jacob by his wife Rachel. There were fourteen persons in this part of Jacob's family.

²³Dan's son was Hushim.

²⁴Naphtali's sons were Jahziel, Guni, Jezer, and Shillem.

²⁵These are Jacob's sons by Bilhah, the slave girl whom Laban gave to his daughter Rachel. There were seven persons in this part of Jacob's family.

²⁶So the total number of Jacob's direct descendants who went to Egypt was sixty-six, not counting the wives of Jacob's sons. ²⁷Joseph had two sons born in Egypt, so the total number in the family of Jacob in Egypt was seventy.

JACOB ARRIVES IN EGYPT

²⁸Jacob sent Judah ahead of him to see Joseph in Goshen. When Jacob and his people came into the land of Goshen, ²⁹Joseph prepared his chariot and went to meet his father Israel in Goshen. As soon as Joseph saw his father, he hugged him, and cried there for a long time.

³⁰Then Israel said to Joseph, "Now I am ready to die, because I have seen your face and I know you are still alive."

³¹Joseph said to his brothers and his father's family, "I will go and tell the king you are here. I will say, 'My brothers and my father's family have left the land of Canaan and have come here to me. ³²They are shepherds and take care of farm animals, and they have brought their flocks and their herds and everything they own with them.' ³³When the king calls you, he will ask, 'What work do you do?' ³⁴This is what you should tell him: 'We, your servants, have taken care of farm

---

46:1 Israel Also called Jacob.

animals all our lives. Our ancestors did the same thing.' Then the king will allow you to settle in the land of Goshen, away from the Egyptians, because they don't like to be near shepherds."

JACOB SETTLES IN GOSHEN

47 Joseph went in to the king and said, "My father and my brothers have arrived from Canaan with their flocks and herds and everything they own. They are now in the land of Goshen." ²Joseph chose five of his brothers to introduce to the king.

³The king said to the brothers, "What work do you do?"

And they said to him, "We, your servants, are shepherds, just as our ancestors were." ⁴They said to the king, "We have come to live in this land, because there is no grass in the land of Canaan for our animals to eat, and the hunger is terrible there. So please allow us to live in the land of Goshen."

⁵Then the king said to Joseph, "Your father and your brothers have come to you, ⁶and you may choose any place in Egypt for them to live. Give your father and your brothers the best land; let them live in the land of Goshen. And if any of them are skilled shepherds, put them in charge of my sheep and cattle."

⁷Then Joseph brought in his father Jacob and introduced him to the king, and Jacob blessed the king.

⁸Then the king said to Jacob, "How old are you?"

⁹Jacob said to him, "My life has been spent wandering from place to place. It has been short and filled with trouble—only one hundred thirty years. My ancestors lived much longer than I." ¹⁰Then Jacob blessed the king and left.

¹¹Joseph obeyed the king and gave his father and brothers the best land in Egypt, near the city of Rameses. ¹²And Joseph gave his father, his brothers, and everyone who lived with them the food they needed.

JOSEPH BUYS LAND FOR THE KING

¹³The hunger became worse, and since there was no food anywhere in the land, Egypt and Canaan became very poor. ¹⁴Joseph collected all the money that was to be found in Egypt and Canaan. People paid for the grain they were buying, and he brought that money to the king's palace. ¹⁵After some time, when the people in Egypt and Canaan had no money left, they went to Joseph and said, "Please give us food. Our money is gone, and if we don't eat, we will die here in front of you."

¹⁶Joseph answered, "Since you have no money, give me your farm animals, and I will give you food in return." ¹⁷So people brought their farm animals to Joseph, and he gave them food in exchange for their horses, sheep, goats, cattle, and donkeys. And he kept them alive by trading food for their farm animals that year.

¹⁸The next year the people came to Joseph and said, "You know we have no money left, and all our animals belong to you. We have nothing left except our bodies and our land. ¹⁹Surely both we and our land will die here in front of you. Buy us and our land in exchange for food, and we will be slaves to the king, together with our land. Give us seed to plant so that we will live and not die, and the land will not become a desert."

²⁰So Joseph bought all the land in Egypt for the king. Every Egyptian sold Joseph his field, because the hunger was very great. So the land became the king's, ²¹and Joseph made the people slaves from one end of Egypt to the other. ²²The only land he did not buy was the land the priests owned. They did not need to sell their land because the king paid them for their work. So they had money to buy food.

²³Joseph said to the people, "Now I have bought you and your land for the king, so I will give you seed and you can plant your fields. ²⁴At harvest time you must give one-fifth to the king. You may keep four-fifths for yourselves to use as seed for the field and as food for yourselves, your families, and your children."

²⁵The people said, "You have saved our lives. If you like, we will become slaves of the king."

²⁶So Joseph made a law in Egypt, which continues today: One-fifth of everything from the land belongs to the king. The only land the king did not get was the priests' land.

"DON'T BURY ME IN EGYPT"

²⁷The Israelites continued to live in the land of Goshen in Egypt. There they got pos-

sessions and had many children and grew in number.

[28]Jacob[n] lived in Egypt seventeen years, so he lived to be one hundred forty-seven years old. [29]When Israel knew he soon would die, he called his son Joseph to him and said to him, "If you love me, put your hand under my leg.[n] Promise me you will not bury me in Egypt. [30]When I die, carry me out of Egypt, and bury me where my ancestors are buried."

Joseph answered, "I will do as you say."

[31]Then Jacob said, "Promise me." And Joseph promised him that he would do this. Then Israel worshiped as he leaned on the top of his walking stick.

BLESSINGS FOR MANASSEH AND EPHRAIM

48 Some time later Joseph learned that his father was very sick, so he took his two sons Manasseh and Ephraim and went to his father. [2]When Joseph arrived, someone told Jacob,[n] "Your son Joseph has come to see you." Jacob was weak, so he used all his strength and sat up on his bed.

[3]Then Jacob said to Joseph, "God Almighty appeared to me at Luz in the land of Canaan and blessed me there. [4]He said to me, 'I will give you many children. I will make you the father of many peoples, and I will give your descendants this land forever.' [5]Your two sons, who were born here in Egypt before I came, will be counted as my own sons. Ephraim and Manasseh will be my sons just as Reuben and Simeon are my sons. [6]But if you have other children, they will be your own, and their land will be part of the land given to Ephraim and Manasseh. [7]When I came from Northwest Mesopotamia, Rachel died in the land of Canaan, as we were traveling toward Ephrath. This made me very sad, and I buried her there beside the road to Ephrath." (Today Ephrath is Bethlehem.)

[8]Then Israel saw Joseph's sons and said, "Who are these boys?"

[9]Joseph said to his father, "They are my sons that God has given me here in Egypt."

Israel said, "Bring your sons to me so I may bless them."

[10]At this time Israel's eyesight was bad because he was old. So Joseph brought the boys close to him, and Israel kissed the boys and put his arms around them. [11]He said to Joseph, "I thought I would never see you alive again, and now God has let me see you and also your children." [12]Then Joseph moved his sons off Israel's lap and bowed facedown to the ground. [13]He put Ephraim on his right side and Manasseh on his left. (So Ephraim was near Israel's left hand, and Manasseh was near Israel's right hand.) Joseph brought the boys close to Israel. [14]But Israel crossed his arms and put his right hand on the head of Ephraim, who was younger. He put his left hand on the head of Manasseh, the firstborn son. [15]And Israel blessed Joseph and said,

"My ancestors Abraham and Isaac served
    our God,
  and like a shepherd God has led me all
    my life.
[16] He was the Angel who saved me from all
    my troubles.
  Now I pray that he will bless these boys.
May my name be known through these
    boys,
  and may the names of my ancestors
    Abraham and Isaac be known
    through them.
May they have many descendants
  on the earth."

[17]When Joseph saw that his father put his right hand on Ephraim's head, he didn't like it. So he took hold of his father's hand, wanting to move it from Ephraim's head to Manasseh's head. [18]Joseph said to his father, "You are doing it wrong, Father. Manasseh is the firstborn son. Put your right hand on his head."

[19]But his father refused and said, "I know, my son, I know. Manasseh will be great and have many descendants. But his younger brother will be greater, and his descendants will be enough to make a nation."

[20]So Israel blessed them that day and said,

"When a blessing is given in Israel, they
    will say:

  'May God make you like Ephraim and
    Manasseh.'"

In this way he made Ephraim greater than Manasseh.

[21]Then Israel said to Joseph, "Look at me;

47:28; 48:2 **Jacob** Also called Israel.   47:29 **put . . . leg** This showed that a person would keep a promise.

I am about to die. But God will be with you and will take you back to the land of your fathers. 22I have given you something that I did not give your brothers—the land of Shechem that I took from the Amorite people with my sword and my bow."

JACOB BLESSES HIS SONS

49 Then Jacob called his sons to him. He said, "Come here to me, and I will tell you what will happen to you in the future.
2 "Come together and listen, sons of Jacob.
    Listen to Israel, your father."

3 "Reuben, my first son, you are my
        strength.
    Your birth showed I could be a father.
    You have the highest position among my
        sons,
    and you are the most powerful.
4 But you are uncontrolled like water,
    so you will no longer lead your
        brothers.
This is because you got into your father's
        bed
    and shamed me by having sexual
        relations with my slave girl.

5 "Simeon and Levi are brothers
    who used their swords to do violence.
6 I will not join their secret talks,
    and I will not meet with them to plan
        evil.
They killed men because they were angry,
    and they crippled oxen just for fun.
7 May their anger be cursed, because it is
        too violent.
    May their violence be cursed, because it
        is too cruel.
I will divide them up among the tribes of
        Jacob
    and scatter them through all the tribes
        of Israel.

8 "Judah, your brothers will praise you.
    You will grab your enemies by the neck,
    and your brothers will bow down to
        you.
9 Judah is like a young lion.
    You have returned from killing, my son.
    Like a lion, he stretches out and lies down
        to rest,
    and no one is brave enough to wake
        him.
10 Kings will come from Judah's family;

someone from Judah will always be on
        the throne.
Judah will rule until Shiloh comes,
    and the nations will obey him.
11 He ties his donkey to a grapevine,
    his young donkey to the best branch.
He can afford to use wine to wash his
        clothes
    and the best wine to wash his robes.
12 His eyes are dark like the color of wine,
    and his teeth are as white as the color
        of milk.

13 "Zebulun will live near the sea.
    His shore will be a safe place for ships,
    and his land will reach as far as Sidon.

14 "Issachar is like a strong donkey
    who lies down while carrying his load.
15 When he sees his resting place is good
    and how pleasant his land is,
he will put his back to the load
    and become a slave.

16 "Dan will rule his own people
    like the other tribes in Israel.
17 Dan will be like a snake by the side of the
        road,
    a dangerous snake lying near the path.
    That snake bites a horse's leg,
    and the rider is thrown off backward.

18 "LORD, I wait for your salvation.

19 "Robbers will attack Gad,
    but he will defeat them and drive them
        away.

20 "Asher's land will grow much good food;
    he will grow food fit for a king.

21 "Naphtali is like a female deer that runs
        free,
    that has beautiful fawns.

22 "Joseph is like a grapevine that produces
        much fruit,
    a healthy vine watered by a spring,
    whose branches grow over the wall.
23 Archers attack him violently
    and shoot at him angrily,
24 but he aims his bow well.
    His arms are made strong.
He gets his power from the Mighty God
        of Jacob
    and his strength from the Shepherd, the
        Rock of Israel.

25 Your father's God helps you.
God Almighty blesses you.
He blesses you with rain from above,
with water from springs below,
with many babies born to your wives,
and many young ones born to your
animals.
26 The blessings of your father are greater
than the blessings of the oldest
mountains,
greater than the good things of the
long-lasting hills.
May these blessings rest on the head of
Joseph,
on the forehead of the one who was
separated from his brothers.

27 "Benjamin is like a hungry wolf.
In the morning he eats what he has
caught,
and in the evening he divides what he
has taken."

28 These are the twelve tribes of Israel, and this is what their father said to them. He gave each son the blessing that was right for him. 29 Then Israel gave them a command and said, "I am about to die. Bury me with my ancestors in the cave in the field of Ephron the Hittite. 30 That cave is in the field of Machpelah east of Mamre in the land of Canaan. Abraham bought the field and cave from Ephron the Hittite for a burying place. 31 Abraham and Sarah his wife are buried there. Isaac and Rebekah his wife are buried there, and I buried my wife Leah there. 32 The field and the cave in it were bought from the Hittite people." 33 After Jacob finished talking to his sons, he lay down. He put his feet back on the bed, took his last breath, and died.

JACOB'S BURIAL

50 When Jacob died, Joseph hugged his father and cried over him and kissed him. 2 He commanded the doctors who served him to prepare his father's body, so the doctors prepared Jacob's body to be buried. 3 It took the doctors forty days to prepare his body (the usual time it took). And the Egyptians had a time of sorrow for Jacob that lasted seventy days.

4 When this time of sorrow had ended, Joseph spoke to the king's officers and said, "If you think well of me, please tell this to the king: 5 'When my father was near death, I made a promise to him that I would bury him in a cave in the land of Canaan, in a burial place that he cut out for himself. So please let me go and bury my father, and then I will return.'"

6 The king answered, "Keep your promise. Go and bury your father."

7 So Joseph went to bury his father. All the king's officers, the elders of his court, and all the elders of Egypt went with Joseph. 8 Everyone who lived with Joseph and his brothers went with him, as well as everyone who lived with his father. They left only their children, their flocks, and their herds in the land of Goshen. 9 They went with Joseph in chariots and on horses. It was a very large group.

10 When they came to the threshing floor of Atad, near the Jordan River, they cried loudly and bitterly for his father. Joseph's time of sorrow continued for seven days. 11 The people that lived in Canaan saw the sadness at the threshing floor of Atad and said, "Those Egyptians are showing great sorrow!" So now that place is named Sorrow of the Egyptians.

12 So Jacob's sons did as their father commanded. 13 They carried his body to the land of Canaan and buried it in the cave in the field of Machpelah near Mamre. Abraham had bought this cave and field from Ephron the Hittite to use as a burial place. 14 After Joseph buried his father, he returned to Egypt, along with his brothers and everyone who had gone with him to bury his father.

THE BROTHERS FEAR JOSEPH

15 After Jacob died, Joseph's brothers said, "What if Joseph is still angry with us? We did many wrong things to him. What if he plans to pay us back?" 16 So they sent a message to Joseph that said, "Your father gave this command before he died. 17 He said to us, 'You have done wrong and have sinned and done evil to Joseph. Tell Joseph to forgive you, his brothers.' So now, Joseph, we beg you to forgive our wrong. We are the servants of the God of your father." When Joseph received the message, he cried.

18 And his brothers went to him and bowed low before him and said, "We are your slaves."

19 Then Joseph said to them, "Don't be afraid. Can I do what only God can do? 20 You meant to hurt me, but God turned your evil

into good to save the lives of many people, which is being done. 21So don't be afraid. I will take care of you and your children." So Joseph comforted his brothers and spoke kind words to them.

22Joseph continued to live in Egypt with all his father's family. He died when he was one hundred ten years old. 23During Joseph's life Ephraim had children and grandchildren, and Joseph's son Manasseh had a son named Makir. Joseph accepted Makir's children as his own.

THE DEATH OF JOSEPH

24Joseph said to his brothers, "I am about to die, but God will take care of you. He will lead you out of this land to the land he promised to Abraham, Isaac, and Jacob." 25Then Joseph had the sons of Israel make a promise. He said, "Promise me that you will carry my bones with you out of Egypt."

26Joseph died when he was one hundred ten years old. Doctors prepared his body for burial, and then they put him in a coffin in Egypt.

exodus

ESCAPE FROM EGYPT

JACOB'S FAMILY GROWS STRONG

1 When Jacob[n] went to Egypt, he took his sons, and each son took his own family with him. These are the names of the sons of Israel: [2]Reuben, Simeon, Levi, Judah, [3]Issachar, Zebulun, Benjamin, [4]Dan, Naphtali, Gad, and Asher. [5]There was a total of seventy people who were descendants of Jacob. Jacob's son Joseph was already in Egypt.

[6]Some time later, Joseph and his brothers died, along with all the people who had lived at that same time. [7]But the people of Israel had many children, and their number grew greatly. They became very strong, and the country of Egypt was filled with them.

TROUBLE FOR THE PEOPLE OF ISRAEL

[8]Then a new king began to rule Egypt, who did not know who Joseph was. [9]This king said to his people, "Look! The people of Israel are too many and too strong for us to handle! [10]If we don't make plans against them, the number of their people will grow even more. Then if there is a war, they might join our enemies and fight us and escape from the country!"

[11]So the Egyptians made life hard for the Israelites. They put slave masters over them, who forced the Israelites to build the cities Pithom and Rameses as supply centers for the king. [12]But the harder the Egyptians forced the Israelites to work, the more the Israelites grew in number and spread out. So the Egyptians became very afraid of them [13]and demanded even more of them. [14]They made their lives bitter. They forced the Israelites to work hard to make bricks and mortar and to do all kinds of work in the fields. The Egyptians were not merciful to them in all their painful work.

[15]Two Hebrew nurses, named Shiphrah and Puah, helped the Israelite women give birth to their babies. The king of Egypt said to the nurses, [16]"When you are helping the Hebrew women give birth to their babies, watch! If the baby is a girl, let her live, but if it is a boy, kill him!" [17]But the nurses feared God, so they did not do as the king told them; they let all the boy babies live. [18]Then the king of Egypt sent for the nurses and said, "Why did you do this? Why did you let the boys live?"

[19]The nurses said to him, "The Hebrew women are much stronger than the Egyptian women. They give birth to their babies before we can get there." [20]God was good to the nurses. And the Hebrew people continued to grow in number, so they became even stronger. [21]Because the nurses feared God, he gave them families of their own.

[22]So the king commanded all his people, "Every time a boy is born to the Hebrews, you must throw him into the Nile River, but let all the girl babies live."

BABY MOSES

2 Now a man from the family of Levi married a woman who was also from the family of Levi. [2]She became pregnant and gave birth to a son. When she saw how wonderful the baby was, she hid him for three months. [3]But after three months she was not able to hide the baby any longer, so she got a basket made of reeds and covered it with tar so that it would float. She put the baby in the basket. Then she put the basket among the tall stalks of grass at the edge of the Nile River. [4]The baby's sister stood a short distance away to see what would happen to him.

[5]Then the daughter of the king of Egypt came to the river to take a bath, and her servant girls were walking beside the river. When she saw the basket in the tall grass, she sent her slave girl to get it. [6]The king's daughter opened the basket and saw the baby boy. He was crying, so she felt sorry for him and said, "This is one of the Hebrew babies."

[7]Then the baby's sister asked the king's daughter, "Would you like me to go and find a Hebrew woman to nurse the baby for you?"

1:1 **Jacob** Also called Israel.

8The king's daughter said, "Go!" So the girl went and got the baby's own mother.

9The king's daughter said to the woman, "Take this baby and nurse him for me, and I will pay you." So the woman took her baby and nursed him. 10When the child grew older, the woman took him to the king's daughter, and she adopted the baby as her own son. The king's daughter named him Moses,[n] because she had pulled him out of the water.

MOSES TRIES TO HELP

11Moses grew and became a man. One day he visited his people and saw that they were forced to work very hard. He saw an Egyptian beating a Hebrew man, one of Moses' own people. 12Moses looked all around and saw that no one was watching, so he killed the Egyptian and hid his body in the sand.

13The next day Moses returned and saw two Hebrew men fighting each other. He said to the one that was in the wrong, "Why are you hitting one of your own people?"

14The man answered, "Who made you our ruler and judge? Are you going to kill me as you killed the Egyptian?"

Moses was afraid and thought, "Now everyone knows what I did."

15When the king heard what Moses had done, he tried to kill him. But Moses ran away from the king and went to live in the land of Midian. There he sat down near a well.

MOSES IN MIDIAN

16There was a priest in Midian who had seven daughters. His daughters went to that well to get water to fill the water troughs for their father's flock. 17Some shepherds came and chased the girls away, but Moses defended the girls and watered their flock.

18When they went back to their father Reuel,[n] he asked them, "Why have you come home early today?"

19The girls answered, "The shepherds chased us away, but an Egyptian defended us. He got water for us and watered our flock."

20He asked his daughters, "Where is this man? Why did you leave him? Invite him to eat with us."

21Moses agreed to stay with Jethro, and he gave his daughter Zipporah to Moses to be his wife. 22Zipporah gave birth to a son. Moses named him Gershom,[n] because Moses was a stranger in a land that was not his own.

23After a long time, the king of Egypt died. The people of Israel groaned, because they were forced to work very hard. When they cried for help, God heard them. 24God heard their cries, and he remembered the agreement he had made with Abraham, Isaac, and Jacob. 25He saw the troubles of the people of Israel, and he was concerned about them.

THE BURNING BUSH

3One day Moses was taking care of Jethro's flock. (Jethro was the priest of Midian and also Moses' father-in-law.) When Moses led the flock to the west side of the desert, he came to Sinai, the mountain of God. 2There the angel of the LORD appeared to him in flames of fire coming out of a bush. Moses saw that the bush was on fire, but it was not burning up. 3So he said, "I will go closer to this strange thing. How can a bush continue burning without burning up?"

4When the LORD saw Moses was coming to look at the bush, God called to him from the bush, "Moses, Moses!"

And Moses said, "Here I am."

5Then God said, "Do not come any closer. Take off your sandals, because you are standing on holy ground. 6I am the God of your ancestors—the God of Abraham, the God of Isaac, and the God of Jacob." Moses covered his face because he was afraid to look at God.

7The LORD said, "I have seen the troubles my people have suffered in Egypt, and I have heard their cries when the Egyptian slave masters hurt them. I am concerned about their pain, 8and I have come down to save them from the Egyptians. I will bring them out of that land and lead them to a good land with lots of room—a fertile land. It is the land of the Canaanites, Hittites, Amorites, Perizzites, Hivites, and Jebusites. 9I have heard the cries of the people of Israel, and I have seen the way the Egyptians have made life hard for them. 10So now I am sending you to

2:10 Moses The name "Moses" sounds like the Hebrew word for "to pull out." **2:18 Reuel** He was also called Jethro. **2:22 Gershom** This name sounds like the Hebrew word meaning "a stranger there."

the king of Egypt. Go! Bring my people, the Israelites, out of Egypt!"

[11]But Moses said to God, "I am not a great man! How can I go to the king and lead the Israelites out of Egypt?"

[12]God said, "I will be with you. This will be the proof that I am sending you: After you lead the people out of Egypt, all of you will worship me on this mountain."

[13]Moses said to God, "When I go to the Israelites, I will say to them, 'The God of your ancestors sent me to you.' What if the people say, 'What is his name?' What should I tell them?"

[14]Then God said to Moses, "I AM WHO I AM.[n] When you go to the people of Israel, tell them, 'I AM sent me to you.'"

[15]God also said to Moses, "This is what you should tell the people: 'The LORD is the God of your ancestors—the God of Abraham, the God of Isaac, and the God of Jacob. He sent me to you.' This will always be my name, by which people from now on will know me.

[16]"Go and gather the elders and tell them this: 'The LORD, the God of your ancestors Abraham, Isaac, and Jacob, has appeared to me. He said, I care about you, and I have seen what has happened to you in Egypt. [17]I promised I would take you out of your troubles in Egypt. I will lead you to the land of the Canaanites, Hittites, Amorites, Perizzites, Hivites, and Jebusites—a fertile land.'

[18]"The elders will listen to you. And then you and the elders of Israel will go to the king of Egypt and tell him, 'The LORD, the God of the Hebrews, appeared to us. Let us travel three days into the desert to offer sacrifices to the LORD our God.'

[19]"But I know that the king of Egypt will not let you go. Only a great power will force him to let you go, [20]so I will use my great power against Egypt. I will strike Egypt with all the miracles that will happen in that land. After I do that, he will let you go. [21]I will cause the Egyptians to think well of the Israelites. So when you leave, they will give gifts to your people. [22]Each woman should ask her Egyptian neighbor and any Egyptian woman living in her house for gifts—silver, gold, and clothing. You should put those gifts on your children when you leave Egypt. In this way you will take with you the riches of the Egyptians."

PROOF FOR MOSES

4 Then Moses answered, "What if the people of Israel do not believe me or listen to me? What if they say, 'The LORD did not appear to you'?"

[2]The LORD said to him, "What is that in your hand?"

Moses answered, "It is my walking stick."

[3]The LORD said, "Throw it on the ground."

So Moses threw it on the ground, and it became a snake. Moses ran from the snake, [4]but the LORD said to him, "Reach out and grab the snake by its tail." When Moses reached out and took hold of the snake, it again became a stick in his hand. [5]The LORD said, "This is so that the Israelites will believe that the LORD appeared to you. I am the God of their ancestors, the God of Abraham, the God of Isaac, and the God of Jacob."

[6]Then the LORD said to Moses, "Put your hand inside your coat." So Moses put his hand inside his coat. When he took it out, it was white with a skin disease.

[7]Then he said, "Now put your hand inside your coat again." So Moses put his hand inside his coat again. When he took it out, his hand was healthy again, like the rest of his skin.

[8]Then the LORD said, "If the people do not believe you or pay attention to the first miracle, they may believe you when you show them this second miracle. [9]After these two miracles, if they still do not believe or listen to you, take some water from the Nile River and pour it on the dry ground. The water will become blood when it touches the ground."

[10]But Moses said to the LORD, "Please, Lord, I have never been a skilled speaker. Even now, after talking to you, I cannot speak well. I speak slowly and can't find the best words."

[11]Then the LORD said to him, "Who made a person's mouth? And who makes someone deaf or not able to speak? Or who gives a person sight or blindness? It is I, the LORD. [12]Now go! I will help you speak, and I will teach you what to say."

3:14 I . . . I AM The Hebrew words are like the name "Yahweh." This Hebrew name for God, usually called "LORD," shows that God always lives and is always with his people.

13But Moses said, "Please, Lord, send someone else."

14The Lord became angry with Moses and said, "Your brother Aaron, from the family of Levi, is a skilled speaker. He is already coming to meet you, and he will be happy when he sees you. 15You will speak to Aaron and tell him what to say. I will help both of you to speak and will teach you what to do. 16Aaron will speak to the people for you. You will tell him what God says, and he will speak for you. 17Take your walking stick with you, and use it to do the miracles."

MOSES RETURNS TO EGYPT

18Moses went back to Jethro, his father-in-law, and said to him, "Let me go back to my people in Egypt. I want to see if they are still alive."

Jethro said to Moses, "Go! I wish you well."

19While Moses was still in Midian, the Lord said to him, "Go back to Egypt, because the men who wanted to kill you are dead now."

20So Moses took his wife and his sons, put them on a donkey, and started back to Egypt. He took with him the walking stick of God.

21The Lord said to Moses, "When you get back to Egypt, do all the miracles I have given you the power to do. Show them to the king of Egypt. But I will make the king very stubborn, and he will not let the people go. 22Then say to the king, 'This is what the Lord says: Israel is my firstborn son. 23I told you to let my son go so he may worship me. But you refused to let Israel go, so I will kill your firstborn son.'"

24As Moses was on his way to Egypt, he stopped at a resting place for the night. The Lord met him there and tried to kill him. 25But Zipporah took a flint knife and circumcised her son. Taking the skin, she touched Moses' feet with it and said to him, "You are a bridegroom of blood to me." 26She said, "You are a bridegroom of blood," because she had to circumcise her son. So the Lord let Moses alone.

27Meanwhile the Lord said to Aaron, "Go out into the desert to meet Moses." When Aaron went, he met Moses at Sinai, the mountain of God, and kissed him. 28Moses told Aaron everything the Lord had said to him when he sent him to Egypt. He also told him about the miracles which the Lord had commanded him to do.

29Moses and Aaron gathered all the elders of the Israelites, 30and Aaron told them everything that the Lord had told Moses. Then Moses did the miracles for all the people to see, 31and the Israelites believed. When they heard that the Lord was concerned about them and had seen their troubles, they bowed down and worshiped him.

MOSES AND AARON BEFORE THE KING

5After Moses and Aaron talked to the people, they went to the king of Egypt and said, "This is what the Lord, the God of Israel, says: 'Let my people go so they may hold a feast for me in the desert.'"

2But the king of Egypt said, "Who is the Lord? Why should I obey him and let Israel go? I do not know the Lord, and I will not let Israel go."

3Then Aaron and Moses said, "The God of the Hebrews has met with us. Now let us travel three days into the desert to offer sacrifices to the Lord our God. If we don't do this, he may kill us with a disease or in war."

4But the king said to them, "Moses and Aaron, why are you taking the people away from their work? Go back to your jobs! 5There are very many Hebrews, and now you want them to quit working!"

6That same day the king gave a command to the slave masters and foremen. 7He said, "Don't give the people straw to make bricks as you used to do. Let them gather their own straw. 8But they must still make the same number of bricks as they did before. Do not accept fewer. They have become lazy, and that is why they are asking me, 'Let us go to offer sacrifices to our God.' 9Make these people work harder and keep them busy; then they will not have time to listen to the lies of Moses."

10So the slave masters and foremen went to the Israelites and said, "This is what the king says: I will no longer give you straw. 11Go and get your own straw wherever you can find it. But you must make as many bricks as you made before." 12So the people went everywhere in Egypt looking for dry stalks to use for straw. 13The slave masters kept forcing the people to work harder. They said,

"You must make just as many bricks as you did when you were given straw." [14]The king's slave masters had made the Israelite foremen responsible for the work the people did. The Egyptian slave masters beat these men and asked them, "Why aren't you making as many bricks as you made in the past?"

[15]Then the Israelite foremen went to the king and complained, "Why are you treating us, your servants, this way? [16]You give us no straw, but we are commanded to make bricks. Our slave masters beat us, but it is your own people's fault."

[17]The king answered, "You are lazy! You don't want to work! That is why you ask to leave here and make sacrifices to the LORD. [18]Now, go back to work! We will not give you any straw, but you must make just as many bricks as you did before."

[19]The Israelite foremen knew they were in trouble, because the king had told them, "You must make just as many bricks each day as you did before." [20]As they were leaving the meeting with the king, they met Moses and Aaron, who were waiting for them. [21]So they said to Moses and Aaron, "May the LORD punish you. You caused the king and his officers to hate us. You have given them an excuse to kill us."

MOSES COMPLAINS TO GOD

[22]Then Moses returned to the LORD and said, "Lord, why have you brought this trouble on your people? Is this why you sent me here? [23]I went to the king and said what you told me to say, but ever since that time he has made the people suffer. And you have done nothing to save them."

6 Then the LORD said to Moses, "Now you will see what I will do to the king of Egypt. I will use my great power against him, and he will let my people go. Because of my power, he will force them out of his country."

[2]Then God said to Moses, "I am the LORD. [3]I appeared to Abraham, Isaac, and Jacob by the name God Almighty, but they did not know me by my name, the LORD. [4]I also made my agreement with them to give them the land of Canaan. They lived in that land, but it was not their own. [5]Now I have heard the cries of the Israelites, whom the Egyptians are treating as slaves, and I remember my agreement. [6]So tell the people of Israel that I say to them, 'I am the LORD. I will save you from the hard work the Egyptians force you to do. I will make you free, so you will not be slaves to the Egyptians. I will free you by my great power, and I will punish the Egyptians terribly. [7]I will make you my own people, and I will be your God. You will know that I am the LORD your God, the One who saves you from the hard work the Egyptians force you to do. [8]I will lead you to the land that I promised to Abraham, Isaac, and Jacob, and I will give you that land to own. I am the LORD.'"

[9]So Moses told this to the Israelites, but they would not listen to him. They were discouraged, and their slavery was hard.

[10]Then the LORD said to Moses, [11]"Go tell the king of Egypt that he must let the Israelites leave his land."

[12]But Moses answered, "The Israelites will not listen to me, so surely the king will not listen to me either. I am not a good speaker."

[13]But the LORD spoke to Moses and Aaron and gave them orders about the Israelites and the king of Egypt. He commanded them to lead the Israelites out of Egypt.

FAMILIES OF ISRAEL

[14]These are the leaders of the families of Israel:

Israel's first son, Reuben, had four sons: Hanoch, Pallu, Hezron, and Carmi. These are the family groups of Reuben.

[15]Simeon's sons were Jemuel, Jamin, Ohad, Jakin, Zohar, and Shaul, the son of a Canaanite woman. These are the family groups of Simeon.

[16]Levi lived one hundred thirty-seven years. These are the names of his sons according to their family history: Gershon, Kohath, and Merari.

[17]Gershon had two sons, Libni and Shimei, with their families.

[18]Kohath lived one hundred thirty-three years. The sons of Kohath were Amram, Izhar, Hebron, and Uzziel.

[19]The sons of Merari were Mahli and Mushi.

These are the family groups of Levi, according to their family history.

[20]Amram married his father's sister Jochebed, who gave birth to Aaron and

Moses. Amram lived one hundred thirty-seven years.

²¹Izhar's sons were Korah, Nepheg, and Zicri.

²²Uzziel's sons were Mishael, Elzaphan, and Sithri.

²³Aaron married Elisheba, the daughter of Amminadab and the sister of Nahshon. Elisheba gave birth to Nadab, Abihu, Eleazar, and Ithamar.

²⁴The sons of Korah were Assir, Elkanah, and Abiasaph. These are the family groups of the Korahites.

²⁵Eleazar son of Aaron married a daughter of Putiel, and she gave birth to Phinehas.

These are the leaders of the family groups of the Levites.

²⁶This was the Aaron and Moses to whom the LORD said, "Lead the people of Israel out of Egypt by their divisions." ²⁷Aaron and Moses are the ones who talked to the king of Egypt and told him to let the Israelites leave Egypt.

GOD REPEATS HIS CALL TO MOSES

²⁸The LORD spoke to Moses in the land of Egypt ²⁹and said, "I am the LORD. Tell the king of Egypt everything I tell you."

³⁰But Moses answered, "I am not a good speaker. The king will not listen to me."

7 The LORD said to Moses, "I have made you like God to the king of Egypt, and your brother Aaron will be like a prophet for you. ²Tell Aaron your brother everything that I command you, and let him tell the king of Egypt to let the Israelites leave his country. ³But I will make the king stubborn. I will do many miracles in Egypt, ⁴but he will still refuse to listen. So then I will punish Egypt terribly, and I will lead my divisions, my people the Israelites, out of that land. ⁵I will punish Egypt with my power, and I will bring the Israelites out of that land. Then they will know I am the LORD."

⁶Moses and Aaron did just as the LORD had commanded them. ⁷Moses was eighty years old and Aaron was eighty-three when they spoke to the king.

AARON'S WALKING STICK BECOMES A SNAKE

⁸The LORD said to Moses and Aaron, ⁹"Moses, when the king asks you to do a miracle, tell Aaron to throw his walking stick

down in front of the king, and it will become a snake."

¹⁰So Moses and Aaron went to the king as the LORD had commanded. Aaron threw his walking stick down in front of the king and his officers, and it became a snake.

¹¹So the king called in his wise men and his magicians, and with their tricks the Egyptian magicians were able to do the same thing. ¹²They threw their walking sticks on the ground, and their sticks became snakes. But Aaron's stick swallowed theirs. ¹³Still the king was stubborn and refused to listen to Moses and Aaron, just as the LORD had said.

THE WATER BECOMES BLOOD

¹⁴Then the LORD said to Moses, "The king is being stubborn and refuses to let the people go. ¹⁵In the morning the king will go out to the Nile River. Go meet him by the edge of the river, and take with you the walking stick that became a snake. ¹⁶Tell him: The LORD, the God of the Hebrews, sent me to you. He said, 'Let my people go worship me in the desert.' Until now you have not listened. ¹⁷This is what the LORD says: 'This is how you will know that I am the LORD. I will strike the water of the Nile River with this stick in my hand, and the water will change into blood. ¹⁸Then the fish in the Nile will die, and the river will begin to stink. The Egyptians will not be able to drink the water from the Nile.'"

¹⁹The LORD said to Moses, "Tell Aaron: 'Take the walking stick in your hand and stretch your hand over the rivers, canals, ponds, and pools in Egypt.' The water will become blood everywhere in Egypt, both in wooden buckets and in stone jars."

²⁰So Moses and Aaron did just as the LORD had commanded. In front of the king and his officers, Aaron raised his walking stick and struck the water in the Nile River. So all the water in the Nile changed into blood. ²¹The fish in the Nile died, and the river began to stink, so the Egyptians could not drink water from it. Blood was everywhere in the land of Egypt.

²²Using their tricks, the magicians of Egypt did the same thing. So the king was stubborn and refused to listen to Moses and Aaron, just as the LORD had said. ²³The king turned and went into his palace and ignored

what Moses and Aaron had done. ²⁴The Egyptians could not drink the water from the Nile, so all of them dug along the bank of the river, looking for water to drink.

THE FROGS

²⁵Seven days passed after the LORD changed the Nile River.

8 Then the LORD told Moses, "Go to the king of Egypt and tell him, 'This is what the LORD says: Let my people go to worship me. ²If you refuse, I will punish Egypt with frogs. ³The Nile River will be filled with frogs. They will come up into your palace, into your bedroom, on your bed, into the houses of your officers, and onto your people. They will come into your ovens and into your baking pans. ⁴The frogs will jump all over you, your people, and your officers.'"

⁵Then the LORD said to Moses, "Tell Aaron to hold his walking stick in his hand over the rivers, canals, and ponds. Make frogs come up out of the water onto the land of Egypt."

⁶So Aaron held his hand over all the waters of Egypt, and the frogs came up out of the water and covered the land of Egypt. ⁷The magicians used their tricks to do the same thing, so even more frogs came up onto the land of Egypt.

⁸The king called for Moses and Aaron and said, "Pray to the LORD to take the frogs away from me and my people. I will let your people go to offer sacrifices to the LORD."

⁹Moses said to the king, "Please set the time when I should pray for you, your people, and your officers. Then the frogs will leave you and your houses and will remain only in the Nile."

¹⁰The king answered, "Tomorrow."

Moses said, "What you want will happen. By this you will know that there is no one like the LORD our God. ¹¹The frogs will leave you, your houses, your officers, and your people. They will remain only in the Nile."

¹²After Moses and Aaron left the king, Moses asked the LORD about the frogs he had sent to the king. ¹³And the LORD did as Moses asked. The frogs died in the houses, in the yards, and in the fields. ¹⁴The Egyptians put them in piles, and the whole country began to stink. ¹⁵But when the king saw that they were free of the frogs, he became stubborn

again. He did not listen to Moses and Aaron, just as the LORD had said.

THE GNATS

¹⁶Then the LORD said to Moses, "Tell Aaron to raise his walking stick and strike the dust on the ground. Then everywhere in Egypt the dust will change into gnats." ¹⁷They did this, and when Aaron raised the walking stick that was in his hand and struck the dust on the ground, everywhere in Egypt the dust changed into gnats. The gnats got on the people and animals. ¹⁸Using their tricks, the magicians tried to do the same thing, but they could not make the dust change into gnats. The gnats remained on the people and animals. ¹⁹So the magicians told the king that the power of God had done this. But the king was stubborn and refused to listen to them, just as the LORD had said.

THE FLIES

²⁰The LORD told Moses, "Get up early in the morning, and meet the king of Egypt as he goes out to the river. Tell him, 'This is what the LORD says: Let my people go so they can worship me. ²¹If you don't let them go, I will send swarms of flies into your houses. The flies will be on you, your officers, and your people. The houses of Egypt will be full of flies, and they will be all over the ground, too. ²²But I will not treat the Israelites the same as the Egyptian people. There will not be any flies in the land of Goshen, where my people live. By this you will know that I, the LORD, am in this land. ²³I will treat my people differently from your people. This miracle will happen tomorrow.'"

²⁴So the LORD did as he had said, and great swarms of flies came into the king's palace and his officers' houses. All over Egypt flies were ruining the land. ²⁵The king called for Moses and Aaron and told them, "Offer sacrifices to your God here in this country."

²⁶But Moses said, "It wouldn't be right to do that, because the Egyptians hate the sacrifices we offer to the LORD our God. If they see us offering sacrifices they hate, they will throw stones at us and kill us. ²⁷Let us make a three-day journey into the desert. We must offer sacrifices to the LORD our God there, as the LORD told us to do."

²⁸The king said, "I will let you go so that you may offer sacrifices to the LORD your

God in the desert, but you must not go very far away. Now go and pray for me."

²⁹Moses said, "I will leave and pray to the LORD, and he will take the flies away from you, your officers, and your people tomorrow. But do not try to trick us again. Do not stop the people from going to offer sacrifices to the LORD."

³⁰So Moses left the king and prayed to the LORD, ³¹and the LORD did as he asked. He removed the flies from the king, his officers, and his people so that not one fly was left. ³²But the king became stubborn again and did not let the people go.

THE DISEASE ON THE FARM ANIMALS

9 Then the LORD told Moses, "Go to the king of Egypt and tell him, 'This is what the LORD, the God of the Hebrews, says: Let my people go to worship me. ²If you refuse to let them go and continue to hold them, ³the LORD will punish you. He will send a terrible disease on your farm animals that are in the fields. He will cause your horses, donkeys, camels, cattle, goats, and sheep to become sick. ⁴But the LORD will treat Israel's animals differently from the animals of Egypt. None of the animals that belong to the Israelites will die. ⁵The LORD has set tomorrow as the time he will do this in the land.'" ⁶The next day the LORD did as he promised. All the farm animals in Egypt died, but none of the animals belonging to Israelites died. ⁷The king sent people to see what had happened to the animals of Israel, and they found that not one of them had died. But the king was still stubborn and did not let the people go.

THE BOILS

⁸The LORD said to Moses and Aaron, "Fill your hands with ashes from a furnace. Moses, throw the ashes into the air in front of the king of Egypt. ⁹The ashes will spread like dust through all the land of Egypt. They will cause boils to break out and become sores on the skin of people and animals everywhere in the land."

¹⁰So Moses and Aaron took ashes from a furnace and went and stood before the king. Moses threw ashes into the air, which caused boils to break out and become sores on people and animals. ¹¹The magicians could not stand before Moses, because all the Egyptians had boils, even the magicians. ¹²But the

LORD made the king stubborn, so he refused to listen to Moses and Aaron, just as the LORD had said.

THE HAIL

¹³Then the LORD said to Moses, "Get up early in the morning and go to the king of Egypt. Tell him, 'This is what the LORD, the God of the Hebrews, says: Let my people go to worship me. ¹⁴If you don't, this time I will punish you, your officers, and your people, with all my power. Then you will know there is no one in the whole land like me. ¹⁵By now I could have used my power and caused a terrible disease that would have destroyed you and your people from the earth. ¹⁶But I have let you live for this reason: to show you my power so that my name will be talked about in all the earth. ¹⁷You are still against my people and do not want to let them go. ¹⁸So at this time tomorrow, I will send a terrible hailstorm, the worst in Egypt since it became a nation. ¹⁹Now send for your animals and whatever you have in the fields, and bring them into a safe place. The hail will fall on every person or animal that is still in the fields. If they have not been brought in, they will die.'" ²⁰Some of the king's officers respected the word of the LORD and hurried to bring their slaves and animals inside. ²¹But others ignored the LORD's message and left their slaves and animals in the fields.

²²The LORD told Moses, "Raise your hand toward the sky. Then the hail will start falling in all the land of Egypt. It will fall on people, animals, and on everything that grows in the fields of Egypt." ²³When Moses raised his walking stick toward the sky, the LORD sent thunder and hail, and lightning flashed down to the earth. So he caused hail to fall upon the land of Egypt. ²⁴There was hail, and lightning flashed as it hailed—the worst hailstorm in Egypt since it had become a nation. ²⁵The hail destroyed all the people and animals that were in the fields in all the land of Egypt. It also destroyed everything that grew in the fields and broke all the trees in the fields. ²⁶The only place it did not hail was in the land of Goshen, where the Israelites lived.

²⁷The king sent for Moses and Aaron and told them, "This time I have sinned. The LORD is in the right, and I and my people are in the wrong. ²⁸Pray to the LORD. We have

had enough of God's thunder and hail. I will let you go; you do not have to stay here any longer."

29Moses told the king, "When I leave the city, I will raise my hands to the LORD in prayer, and the thunder and hail will stop. Then you will know that the earth belongs to the LORD. 30But I know that you and your officers do not yet fear the LORD God."

31The flax was in bloom, and the barley had ripened, so these crops were destroyed. 32But both wheat crops ripen later, so they were not destroyed.

33Moses left the king and went outside the city. He raised his hands to the LORD, and the thunder and hail stopped. The rain also stopped falling to the ground. 34When the king saw that the rain, hail, and thunder had stopped, he sinned again, and he and his officers became stubborn. 35So the king became stubborn and refused to let the Israelites go, just as the LORD had said through Moses.

THE LOCUSTS

10 The LORD said to Moses, "Go to the king of Egypt. I have made him and his officers stubborn so I could show them my powerful miracles. 2I also did this so you could tell your children and your grandchildren how I was hard on the Egyptians. Tell them about the miracles I did among them so that all of you will know that I am the LORD."

3So Moses and Aaron went to the king and told him, "This is what the LORD, the God of the Hebrews, says: 'How long will you refuse to be sorry for what you have done? Let my people go to worship me. 4If you refuse to let my people go, tomorrow I will bring locusts into your country. 5They will cover the land so that no one will be able to see the ground. They will eat anything that was left from the hailstorm and the leaves from every tree growing in the field. 6They will fill your palaces and all your officers' houses, as well as the houses of all the Egyptians. There will be more locusts than your fathers or ancestors have ever seen—more than there have been since people began living in Egypt.'" Then Moses turned and walked away from the king.

7The king's officers asked him, "How long will this man make trouble for us? Let the Israelites go to worship the LORD their God. Don't you know that Egypt is ruined?"

8So Moses and Aaron were brought back to the king. He said to them, "Go and worship the LORD your God. But tell me, just who is going?"

9Moses answered, "We will go with our young and old people, our sons and daughters, and our flocks and herds, because we are going to have a feast to honor the LORD."

10The king said to them, "The LORD will really have to be with you if ever I let you and all of your children leave Egypt. See, you are planning something evil! 11No! Only the men may go and worship the LORD, which is what you have been asking for." Then the king forced Moses and Aaron out of his palace.

12The LORD told Moses, "Raise your hand over the land of Egypt, and the locusts will come. They will spread all over the land of Egypt and will eat all the plants the hail did not destroy."

13So Moses raised his walking stick over the land of Egypt, and the LORD caused a strong wind to blow from the east. It blew across the land all that day and night, and when morning came, the east wind had brought the locusts. 14Swarms of locusts covered all the land of Egypt and settled everywhere. There were more locusts than ever before or after, 15and they covered the whole land so that it was black. They ate everything that was left after the hail—every plant in the field and all the fruit on the trees. Nothing green was left on any tree or plant anywhere in Egypt.

16The king quickly called for Moses and Aaron. He said, "I have sinned against the LORD your God and against you. 17Now forgive my sin this time. Pray to the LORD your God, and ask him to stop this punishment that kills."

18Moses left the king and prayed to the LORD. 19So the LORD changed the wind. He made a very strong wind blow from the west, and it blew the locusts away into the Red Sea. Not one locust was left anywhere in Egypt. 20But the LORD caused the king to be stubborn again, and he did not let the Israelites go.

THE DARKNESS

21Then the LORD told Moses, "Raise your hand toward the sky, and darkness will cover the land of Egypt. It will be so dark you will be able to feel it." ²²Moses raised his hand toward the sky, and total darkness was everywhere in Egypt for three days. ²³No one could see anyone else, and no one could go anywhere for three days. But the Israelites had light where they lived.

²⁴Again the king of Egypt called for Moses. He said, "All of you may go and worship the LORD. You may take your women and children with you, but you must leave your flocks and herds here."

²⁵Moses said, "You must let us have animals to use as sacrifices and burnt offerings, because we have to offer them to the LORD our God. ²⁶So we must take our animals with us; not a hoof will be left behind. We have to use some of the animals to worship the LORD our God. We won't know exactly what we will need to worship the LORD until we get there."

²⁷But the LORD made the king stubborn again, so he refused to let them go. ²⁸Then he told Moses, "Get out of here, and don't come again! The next time you see me, you will die."

²⁹Then Moses told the king, "I'll do what you say. I will not come to see you again."

THE DEATH OF THE FIRSTBORN

11 Now the LORD had told Moses, "I have one more way to punish the king and the people of Egypt. After this, the king will send all of you away from Egypt. When he does, he will force you to leave completely. ²Tell the men and women of Israel to ask their neighbors for things made of silver and gold." ³The LORD had caused the Egyptians to respect the Israelites, and both the king's officers and the Egyptian people considered Moses to be a great man.

⁴So Moses said to the king, "This is what the LORD says: 'About midnight tonight I will go through all Egypt. ⁵Every firstborn son in the land of Egypt will die—from the firstborn son of the king, who sits on his throne, to the firstborn of the slave girl grinding grain. Also the firstborn farm animals will die. ⁶There will be loud outcries everywhere in Egypt, worse than any time before or after this. ⁷But not even a dog will bark at the Israelites or their animals.' Then you will know that the LORD treats Israel differently from Egypt.

⁸All your officers will come to me. They will bow facedown to the ground before me and say, 'Leave and take all your people with you.' After that, I will leave." Then Moses very angrily left the king.

⁹The LORD had told Moses, "The king will not listen to you and Aaron so that I may do many miracles in the land of Egypt." ¹⁰Moses and Aaron did all these great miracles in front of the king. But the LORD made him stubborn, and the king would not let the Israelites leave his country.

THE FIRST PASSOVER

12 The LORD spoke to Moses and Aaron in the land of Egypt: ²"This month will be the beginning of months, the first month of the year for you. ³Tell the whole community of Israel that on the tenth day of this month each man must get one lamb for the people in his house. ⁴If there are not enough people in his house to eat a whole lamb, he must share it with his closest neighbor, considering the number of people. There must be enough lamb for everyone to eat. ⁵The lamb must be a one-year-old male that has nothing wrong with it. This animal can be either a young sheep or a young goat. ⁶Take care of the animals until the fourteenth day of the month. On that day all the people of the community of Israel will kill them in the evening before dark. ⁷The people must take some of the blood and put it on the sides and tops of the doorframes of the houses where they eat the lambs. ⁸On this night they must roast the lamb over a fire. They must eat it with bitter herbs and bread made without yeast. ⁹Do not eat the lamb raw or boiled in water. Roast the whole lamb over a fire—with its head, legs, and inner organs. ¹⁰You must not leave any of it until morning, but if any of it is left over until morning, you must burn it with fire.

¹¹"This is the way you must eat it: You must be fully dressed as if you were going on a trip. You must have your sandals on and your walking stick in your hand. You must eat it in a hurry; this is the LORD's Passover.

¹²"That night I will go through the land of Egypt and kill all the firstborn animals and people in the land of Egypt. I will also punish all the gods of Egypt. I am the LORD. ¹³But the blood will be a sign on the houses where you

are. When I see the blood, I will pass over you. Nothing terrible will hurt you when I punish the land of Egypt.

¹⁴"You are always to remember this day and celebrate it with a feast to the LORD. Your descendants are to honor the LORD with this feast from now on. ¹⁵For this feast you must eat bread made without yeast for seven days. On the first day, you are to remove all the yeast from your houses. No one should eat any yeast for the full seven days of the feast, or that person will be cut off from Israel. ¹⁶You are to have holy meetings on the first and last days of the feast. You must not do any work on these days; the only work you may do is to prepare your meals. ¹⁷You must celebrate the Feast of Unleavened Bread, because on this very day I brought your divisions of people out of Egypt. So all of your descendants must celebrate this day. This is a law that will last from now on. ¹⁸In the first month of the year you are to eat bread made without yeast, from the evening of the fourteenth day until the evening of the twenty-first day. ¹⁹For seven days there must not be any yeast in your houses. Anybody who eats yeast during this time, either an Israelite or non-Israelite, must be cut off from the community of Israel. ²⁰During this feast you must not eat anything made with yeast. You must eat only bread made without yeast wherever you live."

²¹Then Moses called all the elders of Israel together and told them, "Get the animals for your families and kill the lamb for the Passover. ²²Take a branch of the hyssop plant, dip it into the bowl filled with blood, and then wipe the blood on the sides and tops of the doorframes. No one may leave that house until morning. ²³When the LORD goes through Egypt to kill the Egyptians, he will see the blood on the sides and tops of the doorframes, and he will pass over that house. He will not let the one who brings death come into your houses and kill you.

²⁴"You must keep this command as a law for you and your descendants from now on. ²⁵Do this when you go to the land the LORD has promised to give you. ²⁶When your children ask you, 'Why are we doing these things?' ²⁷you will say, 'This is the Passover sacrifice to honor the LORD. When we were in Egypt, the LORD passed over the houses of Israel, and when he killed the Egyptians, he saved our homes.'" Then the people bowed down and worshiped the LORD. ²⁸They did just as the LORD commanded Moses and Aaron.

²⁹At midnight the LORD killed all the firstborn sons in the land of Egypt—from the firstborn of the king who sat on the throne to the firstborn of the prisoner in jail. Also, all the firstborn farm animals died. ³⁰The king, his officers, and all the Egyptians got up during the night because someone had died in every house. So there was a loud outcry everywhere in Egypt.

ISRAEL LEAVES EGYPT

³¹During the night the king called for Moses and Aaron and said, "Get up and leave my people. You and your people may do as you have asked; go and worship the LORD. ³²Take all of your flocks and herds as you have asked, and go. And also bless me." ³³The Egyptians also asked the Israelites to hurry and leave, saying, "If you don't leave, we will all die!"

³⁴So the people took their dough before the yeast was added. They wrapped the bowls for making dough in clothing and carried them on their shoulders. ³⁵The Israelites did what Moses told them to do and asked their Egyptian neighbors for things made of silver and gold and for clothing. ³⁶The LORD caused the Egyptians to think well of them, and the Egyptians gave the people everything they asked for. So the Israelites took rich gifts from them.

³⁷The Israelites traveled from Rameses to Succoth. There were about six hundred thousand men walking, not including the women and children. ³⁸Many other people who were not Israelites went with them, as well as a large number of sheep, goats, and cattle. ³⁹The Israelites used the dough they had brought out of Egypt to bake loaves of bread without yeast. The dough had no yeast in it, because they had been rushed out of Egypt and had no time to get food ready for their trip.

⁴⁰The people of Israel had lived in Egypt for four hundred thirty years; ⁴¹on the very day the four hundred thirty years ended, the LORD's divisions of people left Egypt. ⁴²That night the LORD kept watch to bring them out of Egypt, and so on this same night the

Israelites are to keep watch to honor the LORD from now on.

43The LORD told Moses and Aaron, "Here are the rules for Passover: No foreigner is to eat the Passover. 44If someone buys a slave and circumcises him, the slave may eat the Passover. 45But neither a person who lives for a short time in your country nor a hired worker may eat it.

46"The meal must be eaten inside a house; take none of the meat outside the house. Don't break any of the bones. 47The whole community of Israel must take part in this feast. 48A foreigner who lives with you may share in the LORD's Passover if all the males in his house become circumcised. Then, since he will be like a citizen of Israel, he may share in the meal. But a man who is not circumcised may not eat the Passover meal. 49The same rules apply to an Israelite born in the country or to a foreigner living there."

50So all the Israelites did just as the LORD had commanded Moses and Aaron. 51On that same day the LORD led the Israelites out of Egypt by their divisions.

THE LAW OF THE FIRSTBORN

13 Then the LORD said to Moses, 2"Give every firstborn male to me. Every firstborn male among the Israelites belongs to me, whether human or animal."

3Moses said to the people, "Remember this day, the day you left Egypt. You were slaves in that land, but the LORD with his great power brought you out of it. You must not eat bread made with yeast. 4Today, in the month of Abib, you are leaving Egypt. 5The LORD will lead you to the land of the Canaanites, Hittites, Amorites, Hivites, and Jebusites. This is the land he promised your ancestors he would give you, a fertile land. There you must celebrate this feast during the first month of every year. 6For seven days you must eat bread made without yeast, and on the seventh day there will be a feast to honor the LORD. 7So for seven days you must not eat any bread made with yeast. There must be no bread made with yeast anywhere in your land. 8On that day you should tell your son: 'We are having this feast because of what the LORD did for me when I came out of Egypt.' 9This feast will help you remember, like a mark on your hand or a reminder

on your forehead. This feast will remind you to speak the LORD's teachings, because the LORD used his great power to bring you out of Egypt. 10So celebrate this feast every year at the right time.

11"And when the LORD takes you into the land of the Canaanites, the land he promised to give you and your ancestors, 12you must give him every firstborn male. Also every firstborn male animal must be given to the LORD. 13Buy back every firstborn donkey by offering a lamb. But if you don't want to buy the donkey back, then break its neck. You must buy back from the LORD every firstborn of your sons.

14"From now on when your son asks you, 'What does this mean?' you will answer, 'With his great power, the LORD brought us out from Egypt, the land where we were slaves. 15The king of Egypt was stubborn and refused to let us leave. But the LORD killed every firstborn male in Egypt, both human and animal. That is why I sacrifice every firstborn male animal to the LORD, and that is why I buy back each of my firstborn sons from the LORD.' 16This feast is like a mark on your hand and a reminder on your forehead to help you remember that the LORD brought us out of Egypt with his great power."

THE WAY OUT OF EGYPT

17When the king sent the people out of Egypt, God did not lead them on the road through the Philistine country, though that was the shortest way. God said, "If they have to fight, they might change their minds and go back to Egypt." 18So God led them through the desert toward the Red Sea. The Israelites were dressed for fighting when they left the land of Egypt.

19Moses carried the bones of Joseph with him, because before Joseph died, he had made the Israelites promise to do this. He had said, "When God saves you, remember to carry my bones with you out of Egypt."

20The Israelites left Succoth and camped at Etham, on the edge of the desert. 21The LORD showed them the way; during the day he went ahead of them in a pillar of cloud, and during the night he was in a pillar of fire to give them light. In this way they could travel during the day or night. 22The pillar of cloud was always with them during the day, and the pillar of fire was always with them at night.

14 Then the LORD said to Moses, 2"Tell the Israelites to turn back to Pi Hahiroth and to camp between Migdol and the Red Sea. Camp across from Baal Zephon, on the shore of the sea. 3The king will think, 'The Israelites are lost, trapped by the desert.' 4I will make the king stubborn again so he will chase after them, but I will defeat the king and his army. This will bring honor to me, and the Egyptians will know that I am the LORD." The Israelites did just as they were told.

THE KING CHASES THE ISRAELITES

5When the king of Egypt was told that the Israelites had left, he and his officers changed

ALWAYS ON HIS MIND

dead ends

FULFILLMENT

EXODUS 14:2

God would not necessarily make a very good general in today's army. He doesn't act according to any of the usual military strategies. In fact, in this instance, he leads his people right into a dead end.

Bayin, the Hebrew word for "between," indicates that God directed the Israelites to make camp with their backs to the sea and their flanks to the wilderness. They might as well as have walked into a trap. There was no way out for them. And that is exactly what God wanted them to see.

It wasn't military prowess or advance planning or clever escapes that would save them. It was God. But in order for the message to get through loud and clear, the Israelites had to be led to a dead end. The king of Egypt thought it was a colossal mistake. God had something else in mind.

Has God led you to a dead end? When you looked around and saw "no exit," did you cry out like the faithless Israelites, "Oh, God, why did you bring me here? I was so much better off in my old imprisoned lifestyle. Even though I was a slave, I didn't have to deal with this dreadful anxiety. I knew what to expect."

It is *always* a mistake to underestimate the salvation of the Lord. God doesn't make mistakes. If you are standing with your back to the wall and the enemy is coming, don't you think that God realizes your predicament? How will you ever be able to see the strength of the Lord if you are always planning the next move? God likes dead ends. That's when he does some of his best work.

reflect: Stand strong in the power of the Lord and await his deliverance.
Go to **Exodus 14:13-14.**

their minds about them. They said, "What have we done? We have let the Israelites leave. We have lost our slaves!" [6]So the king prepared his war chariot and took his army with him. [7]He took six hundred of his best chariots, together with all the other chariots of Egypt, each with an officer in it. [8]The LORD made the king of Egypt stubborn, so he chased the Israelites, who were leaving victoriously. [9]The Egyptians—with all the king's horses, chariot drivers, and army—chased the Israelites. They caught up with them while they were camped by the Red Sea, near Pi Hahiroth and Baal Zephon.

[10]When the Israelites saw the king and his army coming after them, they were very frightened and cried to the LORD for help. [11]They said to Moses, "What have you done

ALWAYS ON HIS MIND

FULFILLMENT

no panic

EXODUS 14:13-14

By Dale Evrist

Have you ever experienced an intensely frightening situation? Remember how the feeling of panic numbed you or clouded your thinking? Panic releases overwhelming amounts of the chemical adrenaline into your system and, if uncontrolled, causes you to scurry about with no clear sense of direction or design for dealing with the situation. However, keeping the proper perspective kills panic.

Extreme situations demand extreme relationships with God and other people. Deepen your commitment to God in dynamic devotion and abiding intimacy by spending time in prayer and worship and studying his Word. Godly companionship also helps you maintain your security and strength and keeps your perspective true.

Take the time now to develop deep associations with the people God has placed in your life. Build strong fellowships with other Christians who will take responsibility for each other and help each other relate rightly to any situation. Surround yourself with like-minded believers and a pastor who truly loves his flock and stands up to defend it when necessary. Your spiritual leaders are accountable to assume covering authority over you.

Ignore any suggestion that you are a helpless victim. Stand in faith on and in God's delivering power, keep in mind his promise never to leave you, and you will defeat panic. In the midst of intimidating circumstances, you will be able to fight off fear as if it were a burglar. How dare any demonic powers lay a hand on God's beloved or anything that belongs to them!

reflect: Whom do you entrust with your safety and security?
Go to **Exodus 15:2.**

to us? Why did you bring us out of Egypt to die in the desert? There were plenty of graves for us in Egypt. ¹²We told you in Egypt, 'Let us alone; we will stay and serve the Egyptians.' Now we will die in the desert."

¹³But Moses answered, "Don't be afraid! Stand still and you will see the LORD save you today. You will never see these Egyptians again after today. ¹⁴You only need to remain calm; the LORD will fight for you."

¹⁵Then the LORD said to Moses, "Why are you crying out to me? Command the Israelites to start moving. ¹⁶Raise your walking stick and hold it over the sea so that the sea will split and the people can cross it on dry land. ¹⁷I will make the Egyptians stubborn so they will chase the Israelites, but I will be honored when I defeat the king and all of his chariot drivers and chariots. ¹⁸When I defeat the king, his chariot drivers, and chariots, the Egyptians will know that I am the LORD."

¹⁹Now the angel of God that usually traveled in front of Israel's army moved behind them. Also, the pillar of cloud moved from in front of the people and stood behind them. ²⁰So the cloud came between the Egyptians and the Israelites. This made it dark for the Egyptians but gave light to the Israelites. So the cloud kept the two armies apart all night.

²¹Then Moses held his hand over the sea. All that night the LORD drove back the sea with a strong east wind, making the sea become dry ground. The water was split, ²²and the Israelites went through the sea on dry land, with a wall of water on their right and on their left.

²³Then all the king's horses, chariots, and chariot drivers followed them into the sea. ²⁴When morning came, the LORD looked down from the pillar of cloud and fire at the Egyptian army and made them panic. ²⁵He kept the wheels of the chariots from turning, making it hard to drive the chariots. The Egyptians shouted, "Let's get away from the Israelites! The LORD is fighting for them and against Egypt."

²⁶Then the LORD told Moses, "Hold your hand over the sea so that the water will come back over the Egyptians, their chariots, and chariot drivers." ²⁷So Moses raised his hand over the sea, and at dawn the sea returned to its place. The Egyptians tried to run from it, but the LORD swept them away into the sea. ²⁸The water returned, covering the chariots, chariot drivers, and all the king's army that had followed the Israelites into the sea. Not one of them survived.

²⁹But the Israelites crossed the sea on dry land, with a wall of water on their right and on their left. ³⁰So that day the LORD saved the Israelites from the Egyptians, and the Israelites saw the Egyptians lying dead on the seashore. ³¹When the Israelites saw the great power the LORD had used against the Egyptians, they feared the LORD, and they trusted him and his servant Moses.

THE SONG OF MOSES

15 Then Moses and the Israelites sang this song to the LORD:

"I will sing to the LORD,
  because he is worthy of great honor.
He has thrown the horse and its rider
  into the sea.
² The LORD gives me strength and makes
    me sing;
  he has saved me.
He is my God,
  and I will praise him.
He is the God of my ancestors,
  and I will honor him.
³ The LORD is a warrior;
  the LORD is his name.
⁴ The chariots and soldiers of the king of
    Egypt
  he has thrown into the sea.
The king's best officers
  are drowned in the Red Sea.
⁵ The deep waters covered them,
  and they sank to the bottom like a
    rock.
⁶ Your right hand, LORD,
  is amazingly strong.
LORD, your right hand
  broke the enemy to pieces.
⁷ In your great victory
  you destroyed those who were against
    you.
Your anger destroyed them,
  like fire burning straw.
⁸ Just a blast of your breath,
  and the waters piled up.
The moving water stood like a wall;
  the deep waters became solid in the
    middle of the sea.

9 "The enemy bragged,
  'I'll chase them and catch them.
I'll take all their riches;
  I'll take all I want.
I'll pull out my sword,
  and my hand will destroy them.'
10 But you blew on them with your
    breath
  and covered them with the sea.

They sank like lead
  in the raging water.
11 "Are there any gods like you, LORD?
  There are no gods like you.
You are wonderfully holy,
  amazingly powerful,
  a worker of miracles.
12 You reached out with your right hand,

ALWAYS ON HIS MIND

praise the shackles
off your feet

FULFILLMENT

EXODUS 15:2

During the travel from Egypt to the Promised Land, the children of Israel complained and moaned. They wanted to go back to Egypt because they were afraid and didn't see their means of salvation. When Moses and the children of Israel were standing at the Red Sea, with the king of Egypt and his army bearing down on them, Moses encouraged the people to not be afraid. He told them to stand firm in order to see the deliverance of the Lord.

Moses was confident that God would deliver them. After they had crossed the Red Sea, Moses' sister, Miriam, sang a song of praise. She sang of the Lord's great works and what he had done on their behalf. What would have happened if the children of Israel had praised God before he had done the great wonders?

In the Book of Acts, the Scriptures talk about the time when Paul and Silas were in prison and locked in chains. Paul and Silas did not look at their circumstances, but rather began to sing and praise the Lord. God allowed the earth to quake and the ground to shake so that their chains fell off and they were freed.

It doesn't matter what the circumstances in your life are, if you will only praise the Lord and give him thanks, you will see him do great wonders for you. God is not a respecter of persons. God loves your praises, and Psalm 22:3 says that the praises of his people are his throne. He is a fair and just God, and he will work mightily on your behalf, if only you will trust in him and praise him for what he is doing in your life.

reflect: Praise the Lord when you are faced with trials.
Go to **Psalm 9:9**.

and the earth swallowed our enemies.
13 You keep your loving promise
and lead the people you have saved.
With your strength you will guide them
to your holy place.

14 "The other nations will hear this and
tremble with fear;
terror will take hold of the Philistines.
15 The leaders of the tribes of Edom will be
very frightened;
the powerful men of Moab will shake
with fear;
the people of Canaan will lose all their
courage.
16 Terror and horror will fall on them.
When they see your strength,
they will be as still as a rock.
They will be still until your people pass
by, LORD.
They will be still until the people you
have taken as your own pass by.
17 You will lead your people and place them
on your very own mountain,
the place that you, LORD, made for
yourself to live,
the temple, Lord, that your hands have
made.
18 The LORD will be king forever!"

19 The horses, chariot drivers, and chariots of the king of Egypt went into the sea, and the LORD covered them with water from the sea. But the Israelites walked through the sea on dry land. 20 Then Aaron's sister Miriam, a prophetess, took a tambourine in her hand. All the women followed her, playing tambourines and dancing. 21 Miriam told them:

"Sing to the LORD,
because he is worthy of great honor;
he has thrown the horse and its rider
into the sea."

BITTER WATER BECOMES GOOD

22 Moses led the Israelites away from the Red Sea into the Desert of Shur. They traveled for three days in the desert but found no water. 23 Then they came to Marah, where there was water, but they could not drink it because it was too bitter. (That is why the place was named Marah.[n]) 24 The people grumbled to Moses and asked, "What will we drink?"

25 So Moses cried out to the LORD, and the LORD showed him a tree. When Moses threw

the tree into the water, the water became good to drink.

There the LORD gave the people a rule and a law to live by, and there he tested their loyalty to him. 26 He said, "You must obey the LORD your God and do what he says is right. If you obey all his commands and keep his rules, I will not bring on you any of the sicknesses I brought on the Egyptians. I am the LORD who heals you."

27 Then the people traveled to Elim, where there were twelve springs of water and seventy palm trees. So the people camped there near the water.

THE PEOPLE DEMAND FOOD

16 The whole Israelite community left Elim and came to the Desert of Sin, which was between Elim and Sinai; they arrived there on the fifteenth day of the second month after they had left Egypt. 2 Then the whole Israelite community grumbled to Moses and Aaron in the desert. 3 They said to them, "It would have been better if the LORD had killed us in the land of Egypt. There we had meat to eat and all the food we wanted. But you have brought us into this desert to starve us to death."

4 Then the LORD said to Moses, "I will cause food to fall like rain from the sky for all of you. Every day the people must go out and gather what they need for that day. I want to see if the people will do what I teach them. 5 On the sixth day of each week, they are to gather twice as much as they gather on other days. Then they are to prepare it."

6 So Moses and Aaron said to all the Israelites: "This evening you will know that the LORD is the one who brought you out of Egypt. 7 Tomorrow morning you will see the glory of the LORD, because he has heard you grumble against him. We are nothing, so you are not grumbling against us, but against the LORD." 8 And Moses said, "Each evening the LORD will give you meat to eat, and every morning he will give you all the bread you want, because he has heard you grumble against him. You are not grumbling against Aaron and me, because we are nothing; you are grumbling against the LORD."

9 Then Moses said to Aaron, "Speak to

15:23 Marah This name means "bitter."

the whole community of the Israelites, and say to them, 'Meet together in the presence of the LORD, because he has heard your grumblings.'"

10 While Aaron was speaking to the whole community of the Israelites, they looked toward the desert. There the glory of the LORD appeared in a cloud.

11 The LORD said to Moses, 12 "I have heard the grumblings of the people of Israel. So tell them, 'At twilight you will eat meat, and every morning you will eat all the bread you want. Then you will know I am the LORD your God.'"

13 That evening quail came and covered the camp, and in the morning dew lay around the camp. 14 When the dew was gone, thin flakes like frost were on the desert ground. 15 When the Israelites saw it, they asked each other, "What is it?" because they did not know what it was.

So Moses told them, "This is the bread the LORD has given you to eat. 16 The LORD has commanded, 'Each one of you must gather what he needs, about two quarts for every person in your family.'"

17 So the people of Israel did this; some people gathered much, and some gathered little. 18 Then they measured it. The person who gathered more did not have too much, nor did the person who gathered less have too little. Each person gathered just as much as he needed.

19 Moses said to them, "Don't keep any of it to eat the next day." 20 But some of the people did not listen to Moses and kept part of it to eat the next morning. It became full of worms and began to stink, so Moses was angry with those people.

21 Every morning each person gathered as much food as he needed, but when the sun became hot, it melted away.

22 On the sixth day the people gathered twice as much food—four quarts for every person. When all the leaders of the community came and told this to Moses, 23 he said to them, "This is what the LORD commanded, because tomorrow is the Sabbath, the LORD's holy day of rest. Bake what you want to bake, and boil what you want to boil today. Save the rest of the food until tomorrow morning."

24 So the people saved it until the next morning, as Moses had commanded, and none of it began to stink or have worms in it. 25 Moses told the people, "Eat the food you gathered yesterday. Today is a Sabbath, the LORD's day of rest; you will not find any out in the field today. 26 You should gather the food for six days, but the seventh day is a Sabbath day. On that day there will not be any food on the ground."

27 On the seventh day some of the people went out to gather food, but they couldn't find any. 28 Then the LORD said to Moses, "How long will you people refuse to obey my commands and teachings? 29 Look, the LORD has made the Sabbath a day of rest for you. So on the sixth day he will give you enough food for two days, but on the seventh day each of you must stay where you are. Do not go anywhere." 30 So the people rested on the seventh day.

31 The people of Israel called the food manna. It was like small white seeds and tasted like wafers made with honey.

32 Then Moses said, "The LORD said, 'Save two quarts of this food for your descendants. Then they can see the food I gave you to eat in the desert when I brought you out of Egypt.'"

33 Moses told Aaron, "Take a jar and fill it with two quarts of manna. Then place it before the LORD, and save it for your descendants." 34 So Aaron did what the LORD had commanded Moses. He put the jar of manna in front of the Agreement to keep it safe. 35 The Israelites ate manna for forty years, until they came to the land where they settled—the edge of the land of Canaan. 36 The measure they used for the manna was two quarts, or one-tenth of an ephah.[n]

WATER FROM A ROCK

17 The whole Israelite community left the Desert of Sin and traveled from place to place, as the LORD commanded. They camped at Rephidim, but there was no water there for the people to drink. 2 So they quarreled with Moses and said, "Give us water to drink."

Moses said to them, "Why do you quarrel with me? Why are you testing the LORD?"

3 But the people were very thirsty for

16:36 **ephah** An ephah was a measure that equaled twenty quarts.

water, so they grumbled against Moses. They said, "Why did you bring us out of Egypt? Was it to kill us, our children, and our farm animals with thirst?"

⁴So Moses cried to the LORD, "What can I do with these people? They are almost ready to stone me to death."

⁵The LORD said to Moses, "Go ahead of the people, and take some of the elders of Israel with you. Carry with you the walking stick that you used to strike the Nile River. Now go! ⁶I will stand in front of you on a rock at Mount Sinai. Hit that rock with the stick, and water will come out of it so that the people can drink." Moses did these things as the elders of Israel watched. ⁷He named that place Massah,ⁿ because the Israelites tested the LORD when they asked, "Is the LORD with us or not?" He also named it Meribah,ⁿ because they quarreled.

THE AMALEKITES FIGHT ISRAEL

⁸At Rephidim the Amalekites came and fought the Israelites. ⁹So Moses said to Joshua, "Choose some men and go and fight the Amalekites. Tomorrow I will stand on the top of the hill, holding the walking stick of God in my hands."

¹⁰Joshua obeyed Moses and went to fight the Amalekites, while Moses, Aaron, and Hur went to the top of the hill. ¹¹As long as Moses held his hands up, the Israelites would win the fight, but when Moses put his hands down, the Amalekites would win. ¹²Later, when Moses' arms became tired, the men put a large rock under him, and he sat on it. Then Aaron and Hur held up Moses' hands— Aaron on one side and Hur on the other. They kept his hands steady until the sun went down. ¹³So Joshua defeated the Amalekites in this battle.

¹⁴Then the LORD said to Moses, "Write about this battle in a book so people will remember. And be sure to tell Joshua, because I will completely destroy the Amalekites from the earth."

¹⁵Then Moses built an altar and named it The LORD Is My Banner. ¹⁶Moses said, "I lifted my hands toward the LORD's throne. The LORD will fight against the Amalekites forever."

JETHRO VISITS MOSES

18 Jethro, Moses' father-in-law, was the priest of Midian. He heard about everything that God had done for Moses and his people, the Israelites, and how the LORD had led the Israelites out of Egypt. ²Now Moses had sent his wife Zipporah to Jethro, his father-in-law, ³along with his two sons. The first son was named Gershom,ⁿ because when he was born, Moses said, "I am a stranger in a foreign country." ⁴The other son was named Eliezer,ⁿ because when he was born, Moses said, "The God of my father is my help. He saved me from the king of Egypt."

⁵So Jethro, Moses' father-in-law, took Moses' wife and his two sons and went to Moses. He was camped in the desert near the mountain of God. ⁶Jethro had sent a message ahead to Moses that said, "I, Jethro, your father-in-law, am coming to you with your wife and her two sons."

⁷So Moses went out to meet his father-in-law and bowed down and kissed him. After the two men asked about each other's health, they went into Moses' tent. ⁸Moses told his father-in-law everything the LORD had done to the king and the Egyptians to help Israel. He told about all the problems they had faced along the way and how the LORD had saved them.

⁹Jethro was very happy to hear all the good things the LORD had done for Israel when he had saved them from the Egyptians. ¹⁰He said, "Praise the LORD. He has saved you from the Egyptians and their king, and he has saved the people from the power of the Egyptians. ¹¹Now I know the LORD is greater than all gods, because he did this to those who looked down on Israel." ¹²Then Jethro, Moses' father-in-law, gave a whole burnt offering and other sacrifices to God. Aaron and all the elders of Israel came to Moses' father-in-law to eat the holy meal together before God.

¹³The next day Moses solved disagreements among the people, and the people

---

17:7 Massah This name is the Hebrew word for "testing." **17:7 Meribah** This name is the Hebrew word for "quarrel." **18:3 Gershom** This name sounds like the Hebrew word for "a stranger there." **18:4 Eliezer** This name sounds like the Hebrew words "My God is my help."

God's Management Plan

By Leon Fontaine

EXODUS 18:13–27

In today's world, people are very clever at managing phenomenal responsibilities, such as businesses, corporations, governments, and armies. God wants us to become just as smart and creative when handling the incredible resources he provides.

The first manager or administrator on earth was Adam. When God planted a garden within the boundaries of Eden, he left the rest of the planet for Adam to subdue and fill. God delegated management of the garden to Adam and instructed him to spread it around the earth. Adam knew without a doubt what his orders were: cultivate, protect, exercise dominion, and multiply what God had given him.

God gave Adam authority and power before he created Eve; she was not around when Adam received his assignment as manager. God made man first to be the foundation of the home. The devil wanted to destroy God's perfect plan, so in the form of a snake he deceived Eve, and she ate from the tree that God had specifically told them not to. Though Adam had the authority and power to dominate everything on earth, he let that snake wiggle in and lie to his wife.

Adam lost his garden and his spiritual relationship with God because of irresponsible management. But because of the redemptive work of Jesus, men can reinstate loving authority to family households by managing relationships properly, applying God's Word, and seeking whatever help is needed. Women can help men to lead righteously by blessing, supporting, loving, and encouraging them. Together, men and women can become excellent managers again.

On another note, clever spiritual managers learn how to be smart in handling their community and social issues, as well as their families and businesses. God is calling Christian doctors and nurses to rise up and influence the healthcare system, corporate administrators to influence finance, and neighbors to use their influence in communities. No matter what part you play in your home, business, or community, reach out and positively influence everyone around you!

God expects you to manage everything he has given you with excellence. A great attitude and careful study of Scripture to learn the simple Bible principles will empower you to manage the blessings God has given you. Prayer is the beginning, but you cannot pray promotion into existence. God moves you on to the next level after you prove to be responsible where you are. Pray for wisdom to grow and change as you learn God's Word!

Your tithe is an important part of management. Give to God what belongs to God, and manage the rest with excellence and you will have increase. Use wisdom in making decisions that affect your life, your marriage, your children, your job, your home, and your nation. If you are faithful with the little things, then there is no limit to God's blessing in your life.

TO LEARN MORE ON WHAT THE BIBLE HAS TO SAY ABOUT **FINANCES,** READ THE SCRIPTURES AND DEVOTIONALS AT **GENESIS 24:35, DEUTERONOMY 28, DEUTERONOMY 31:6, RUTH 2:12,** AND **1 CHRONICLES 4:10.**

stood around him from morning until night. ¹⁴When Moses' father-in-law saw all that Moses was doing for the people, he asked, "What is all this you are doing for the people? Why are you the only one to solve disagreements? All the people are standing around you from morning until night!"

¹⁵Then Moses said to his father-in-law, "It is because the people come to me for God's help in solving their disagreements. ¹⁶When people have a disagreement, they come to me, and I decide who is right. I tell them God's laws and teachings."

¹⁷Moses' father-in-law said to him, "You are not doing this right. ¹⁸You and the people who come to you will get too tired. This is too much work for you; you can't do it by yourself. ¹⁹Now listen to me, and I will give you some advice. I want God to be with you. You must speak to God for the people and tell him about their disagreements. ²⁰Warn them about the laws and teachings, and teach them the right way to live and what they should do. ²¹But choose some capable men from among the people—men who respect God, who can be trusted, and who will not change their decisions for money. Make these men officers over the people, to rule over groups of thousands, hundreds, fifties, and tens. ²²Let these officers solve the disagreements among the people all the time. They can bring the hard cases to you, but they can decide the simple cases themselves. That will make it easier for you, because they will share the work with you. ²³If you do this as God commands you, then you will be able to do your job, and all the people will go home with their disagreements solved."

²⁴So Moses listened to his father-in-law and did everything he said. ²⁵He chose capable men from all the Israelites and made them leaders over the people; they were officers over groups of thousands, hundreds, fifties, and tens. ²⁶These officers solved disagreements among the people all the time. They brought the hard cases to Moses, but they decided the simple cases themselves.

²⁷So Moses sent his father-in-law on his way, and Jethro went back to his own home.

ISRAEL CAMPS AT SINAI

19 Exactly three months after the Israelites had left Egypt, they reached the Desert of Sinai. ²When they left Rephidim, they came to the Desert of Sinai and camped in the desert in front of the mountain. ³Then Moses went up on the mountain to God. The Lord called to him from the mountain and said, "Say this to the family of Jacob, and tell the people of Israel: ⁴'Every one of you has seen what I did to the people of Egypt. You saw how I carried you out of Egypt, as if on eagle's wings. And I brought you here to me. ⁵So now if you obey me and keep my agreement, you will be my own possession, chosen from all nations. Even though the whole earth is mine, ⁶you will be my kingdom of priests and a holy nation.' You must tell the Israelites these words."

⁷So Moses went down and called the elders of the people together. He told them all the words the Lord had commanded him to say. ⁸All the people answered together, "We will do everything he has said." Then Moses took their answer back to the Lord.

⁹And the Lord said to Moses, "I will come to you in a thick cloud and speak to you. The people will hear me speaking with you and will always trust you." Then Moses told the Lord what the people had said.

¹⁰The Lord said to Moses, "Go to the people and have them spend today and tomorrow preparing themselves. They must wash their clothes ¹¹and be ready by the day after tomorrow. On that day I, the Lord, will come down on Mount Sinai, and all the people will see me. ¹²But you must set a limit around the mountain that the people are not to cross. Tell them not to go up on the mountain and not to touch the foot of it. Anyone who touches the mountain must be put to death ¹³with stones or shot with arrows. No one is allowed to touch him. Whether it is a person or an animal, he will not live. But the trumpet will make a long blast, and only then may the people go up on the mountain."

¹⁴After Moses went down from the mountain to the people, he made them prepare themselves for service to God, and they washed their clothes. ¹⁵Then Moses said to the people, "Be ready in three days. Do not have sexual relations during this time."

¹⁶On the morning of the third day, there was thunder and lightning with a thick cloud on the mountain. There was a very loud blast from a trumpet, and all the people in the

camp trembled. ¹⁷Then Moses led the people out of the camp to meet God, and they stood at the foot of the mountain. ¹⁸Mount Sinai was covered with smoke, because the LORD came down on it in fire. The smoke rose from the mountain like smoke from a furnace, and the whole mountain shook wildly. ¹⁹The sound from the trumpet became louder. Then Moses spoke, and the voice of God answered him.

²⁰When the LORD came down on top of Mount Sinai, he called Moses to come up to the top of the mountain, and Moses went up. ²¹The LORD said to Moses, "Go down and warn the people that they must not force their way through to see me. If they do, many of them will die. ²²Even the priests, who may come near me, must first prepare themselves. If they don't, I, the LORD, will punish them."

²³Moses told the LORD, "The people cannot come up on Mount Sinai, because you yourself told us, 'Set a limit around the mountain, and set it apart as holy.'"

²⁴The LORD said to him, "Go down and bring Aaron up with you, but don't allow the priests or the people to force their way through. They must not come up to the LORD, or I will punish them."

²⁵So Moses went down to the people and told them these things.

THE TEN COMMANDMENTS

20 Then God spoke all these words:

²"I am the LORD your God, who brought you out of the land of Egypt where you were slaves.

³"You must not have any other gods except me.

⁴"You must not make for yourselves an idol that looks like anything in the sky above or on the earth below or in the water below the land. ⁵You must not worship or serve any idol, because I, the LORD your God, am a jealous God. If you hate me, I will punish your children, and even your grandchildren and great-grandchildren. ⁶But I show kindness to thousands who love me and obey my commands.

⁷"You must not use the name of the LORD your God thoughtlessly; the LORD will punish anyone who misuses his name.

⁸"Remember to keep the Sabbath holy. ⁹Work and get everything done during six days each week, ¹⁰but the seventh day is a day of rest to honor the LORD your God. On that day no one may do any work: not you, your son or daughter, your male or female slaves, your animals, or the foreigners living in your cities. ¹¹The reason is that in six days the LORD made everything—the sky, the earth, the sea, and everything in them. On the seventh day he rested. So the LORD blessed the Sabbath day and made it holy.

¹²"Honor your father and your mother so that you will live a long time in the land that the LORD your God is going to give you.

¹³"You must not murder anyone.

¹⁴"You must not be guilty of adultery.

¹⁵"You must not steal.

¹⁶"You must not tell lies about your neighbor.

¹⁷"You must not want to take your neighbor's house. You must not want his wife or his male or female slaves, or his ox or his donkey, or anything that belongs to your neighbor."

¹⁸When the people heard the thunder and the trumpet, and when they saw the lightning and the smoke rising from the mountain, they shook with fear and stood far away from the mountain. ¹⁹Then they said to Moses, "Speak to us yourself, and we will listen. But don't let God speak to us, or we will die."

²⁰Then Moses said to the people, "Don't be afraid, because God has come to test you. He wants you to respect him so you will not sin."

²¹The people stood far away from the mountain while Moses went near the dark cloud where God was. ²²Then the LORD told Moses to say these things to the Israelites: "You yourselves have seen that I talked with you from heaven. ²³You must not use gold or silver to make idols for yourselves; do not worship these gods in addition to me.

²⁴"Make an altar of dirt for me, and sacrifice on it your whole burnt offerings and fellowship offerings, your sheep and your cattle. Worship me in every place that I choose, and I will come and bless you. ²⁵If you use stones to make an altar for me, don't use stones that you have shaped with tools. When you use any tools on them, you make them unsuitable for use in worship. ²⁶And you must not go up to my altar on steps, or people will be able to see under your clothes."

LAWS FOR LIVING

21 Then God said to Moses, "These are the laws for living that you will give to the Israelites:

²"If you buy a Hebrew slave, he will serve you for six years. In the seventh year you are to set him free, and he will have to pay nothing. ³If he is not married when he becomes your slave, he must leave without a wife. But if he is married when he becomes your slave, he may take his wife with him. ⁴If the slave's master gives him a wife, and she gives birth to sons or daughters, the woman and her children will belong to the master. When the slave is set free, only he may leave.

⁵"But if the slave says, 'I love my master, my wife and my children, and I don't want to go free,' ⁶then the slave's master must take him to God. The master is to take him to a door or doorframe and punch a hole through the slave's ear using a sharp tool. Then the slave will serve that master all his life.

⁷"If a man sells his daughter as a slave, the rules for setting her free are different from the rules for setting the male slaves free. ⁸If the master wanted to marry her but then decided he was not pleased with her, he must let one of her close relatives buy her back. He has no right to sell her to foreigners, because he has treated her unfairly. ⁹If the man who bought her promises to let the woman marry his son, he must treat her as a daughter. ¹⁰If the man who bought her marries another woman, he must not keep his first wife from having food or clothing or sexual relations. ¹¹If he does not give her these three things, she may go free, and she owes him no money.

LAWS ABOUT INJURIES

¹²"Anyone who hits a person and kills him must be put to death. ¹³But if a person kills someone accidentally, God allowed that to happen, so the person must go to a place I will choose. ¹⁴But if someone plans and murders another person on purpose, put him to death, even if he has run to my altar for safety.

¹⁵"Anyone who hits his father or his mother must be put to death.

¹⁶"Anyone who kidnaps someone and either sells him as a slave or still has him when he is caught must be put to death.

¹⁷"Anyone who says cruel things to his father or mother must be put to death.

¹⁸"If two men argue, and one hits the other with a rock or with his fist, the one who is hurt but not killed might have to stay in bed. ¹⁹Later if he is able to get up and walk around outside with his walking stick, the one who hit him is not to be punished. But he must pay the injured man for the loss of his time, and he must support the injured man until he is completely healed.

²⁰"If a man beats his male or female slave with a stick, and the slave dies on the spot, the owner must be punished. ²¹But if the slave gets well after a day or two, the owner will not be punished since the slave belongs to him.

²²"Suppose two men are fighting and hit a pregnant woman, causing the baby to come out. If there is no further injury, the man who caused the accident must pay money—whatever amount the woman's husband says and the court allows. ²³But if there is further injury, then the punishment that must be paid is life for life, ²⁴eye for eye, tooth for tooth, hand for hand, foot for foot, ²⁵burn for burn, wound for wound, and bruise for bruise.

²⁶"If a man hits his male or female slave in the eye, and the eye is blinded, the man is to free the slave to pay for the eye. ²⁷If a master knocks out a tooth of his male or female slave, the man is to free the slave to pay for the tooth.

²⁸"If a man's bull kills a man or woman, you must kill that bull by throwing stones at it, and you should not eat the bull. But the owner of the bull is not guilty. ²⁹However, suppose the bull has hurt people in the past and the owner, though warned, did not keep it in a pen. Then if it kills a man or woman, the bull must be stoned to death, and the owner must also be put to death. ³⁰But if the family of the dead person accepts money, the one who owned the bull may buy back his life, but he must pay whatever is demanded. ³¹Use this same law if the bull kills a person's son or daughter. ³²If the bull kills a male or female slave, the owner must pay the master the price for a new slave, or twelve ounces of silver, and the bull must also be stoned to death.

³³"If a man takes the cover off a pit, or digs a pit and does not cover it, and another

man's ox or donkey comes and falls into it, [34]the owner of the pit must pay the owner of the animal for the loss. The dead animal will belong to the one who pays.

[35]"If a man's bull kills another man's bull, they must sell the bull that is alive. Both men will get half of the money and half of the bull that was killed. [36]But if a person's bull has hurt other animals in the past and the owner did not keep it in a pen, that owner must pay bull for bull, and the dead animal is his.

PROPERTY LAWS

22 "If a man steals a bull or a sheep and kills or sells it, he must pay back five bulls for the one bull he stole and four sheep for the one sheep he stole.

[2-4]"The robber who is caught must pay back what he stole. If he owns nothing, he must be sold as a slave to pay for what he stole. If the stolen animal is found alive with the robber, he must give the owner two animals for every animal he stole, whether it was a bull, donkey, or sheep.

"If a thief is killed while breaking into a house at night, the one who killed him is not guilty of murder. But if this happens during the day, he is guilty of murder.

[5]"If a man lets his farm animal graze in his field or vineyard, and it wanders into another man's field or vineyard, the owner of the animal must pay back the loss from the best of his crop.

[6]"Suppose a man starts a fire that spreads through the thornbushes to his neighbor's field. If the fire burns his neighbor's growing grain or grain that has been stacked, or if it burns his whole field, the person who started the fire must pay for what was burned.

[7]"Suppose a man gives his neighbor money or other things to keep for him and those things are stolen from the neighbor's house. If the thief is caught, he must pay back twice as much as he stole. [8]But if the thief is never found, the owner of the house must make a promise before God that he has not stolen his neighbor's things.

[9]"Suppose two men disagree about who owns something—whether ox, donkey, sheep, clothing, or something else that is lost. If each says, 'This is mine,' each man must bring his case to God. God's judges will decide who is guilty, and that person must pay the other man twice as much as the object is worth.

[10]"Suppose a man asks his neighbor to keep his donkey, ox, sheep, or some other animal for him, and that animal dies, gets hurt, or is taken away, without anyone seeing what happened. [11]That neighbor must promise before the Lord that he did not harm or kill the other man's animal, and the owner of the animal must accept his promise made before God. The neighbor does not have to pay the owner for the animal. [12]But if the animal was stolen from the neighbor, he must pay the owner for it. [13]If wild animals killed it, the neighbor must bring the body as proof, and he will not have to pay for the animal that was killed.

[14]"If a man borrows an animal from his neighbor, and it gets hurt or dies while the owner is not there, the one who borrowed it must pay the owner for the animal. [15]But if the owner is with the animal, the one who borrowed it does not have to pay. If the animal was rented, the rental price covers the loss.

LAWS AND RELATIONSHIPS

[16]"Suppose a man finds a woman who is not pledged to be married and has never had sexual relations with a man. If he tricks her into having sexual relations with him, he must give her family the payment to marry her, and she will become his wife. [17]But if her father refuses to allow his daughter to marry him, the man must still give the usual payment for a bride who has never had sexual relations.

[18]"Put to death any woman who does evil magic.

[19]"Put to death anyone who has sexual relations with an animal.

[20]"Destroy completely any person who makes a sacrifice to any god except the Lord.

[21]"Do not cheat or hurt a foreigner, because you were foreigners in the land of Egypt.

[22]"Do not cheat a widow or an orphan. [23]If you do, and they cry out to me for help, I certainly will hear their cry. [24]And I will be very angry and kill you in war. Then your wives will become widows, and your children will become orphans.

²⁵"If you lend money to one of my people who is poor, do not treat him as a money-lender would. Charge him nothing for using your money. ²⁶If your neighbor gives you his coat as a promise for the money he owes you, you must give it back to him by sunset, ²⁷because it is the only cover to keep his body warm. He has nothing else to sleep in. If he cries out to me for help, I will listen, because I am merciful.

²⁸"You must not speak against God or curse a leader of your people.

²⁹"Do not hold back your offering from the first of your harvest and the first wine that you make. Also, you must give me your firstborn sons. ³⁰You must do the same with your bulls and your sheep. Let the firstborn males stay with their mothers for seven days, and on the eighth day you must give them to me.

³¹"You are to be my holy people. You must not eat the meat of any animal that has been killed by wild animals. Instead, give it to the dogs.

THE FAVOR OF GOD

the principle
of tithing

FINANCES

EXODUS 22:29

Christians understand the principle of tithing. God graciously gives us 100 percent of what he owns and only requires that we give 10 percent back to him. But God is also very practical about this requirement. He knows that the pressures of this world may cause us to think that we will take care of this responsibility a little later, when things are more under control.

As a result, God instructs his people to bring the tithe without delay. We are to make it the first thing on the list, not the last. Don't wait to tithe. God knows that when we think we'll take care of it tomorrow, tomorrow has a way of demanding more than we have. Today is the day to honor the Lord with the first of our harvest.

Get into the habit of tithing as soon as you have the time, money, or talent. Tithing is not just about money. It's about whatever God gives you as gain. You might discover that you have more time than you used to. Give 10 percent back to God. You may be blessed with additional abilities or position or power. Give 10 percent to his agenda.

Do it now, before the pressures of the world snatch it from you. If you get into the habit of making the first decision the tithing decision, soon you will find it a more joyful experience. You'll be looking forward to that increase so that you will have another opportunity to provide God with your thankfulness.

reflect: Practice giving God the firstfruits of your increase, including your time and talent.

Go to **Leviticus 27:30**.

LAWS ABOUT FAIRNESS

23 "You must not tell lies. If you are a witness in court, don't help a wicked person by telling lies.

2"You must not do wrong just because everyone else is doing it. If you are a witness in court, you must not ruin a fair trial. You must not tell lies just because everyone else is. 3If a poor person is in court, you must not take his side just because he is poor.

4"If you see your enemy's ox or donkey wandering away, you must return it to him. 5If you see that your enemy's donkey has fallen because its load is too heavy, do not leave it there. You must help your enemy get the donkey back on its feet.

6"You must not be unfair to a poor person when he is in court. 7You must not lie when you accuse someone in court. Never allow an innocent or honest person to be put to death as punishment, because I will not treat guilty people as if they were innocent.

8"You must not accept money from a person who wants you to lie in court, because such money will not let you see what is right. Such money makes good people tell lies.

9"You must not mistreat a foreigner. You know how it feels to be a foreigner, because you were foreigners in Egypt.

LAWS FOR THE SABBATH

10"For six years you are to plant and harvest crops on your land. 11Then during the seventh year, do not plow or plant your land. If any food grows there, allow the poor people to have it, and let the wild animals eat what is left. You should do the same with your vineyards and your orchards of olive trees.

12"You should work six days a week, but on the seventh day you must rest. This lets your ox and your donkey rest, and it also lets the slave born in your house and the foreigner be refreshed.

13"Be sure to do all that I have said to you. You must not even say the names of other gods; those names must not come out of your mouth.

THREE YEARLY FEASTS

14"Three times each year you must hold a feast to honor me. 15You must celebrate the Feast of Unleavened Bread in the way I commanded you. For seven days you must eat bread that is made without yeast at the set time during the month of Abib, the month when you came out of Egypt. No one is to come to worship me without bringing an offering.

16"You must celebrate the Feast of Weeks. Offer to God the first things you harvest from the crops you planted in your fields.

"You must celebrate the Feast of Shelters in the fall, when you gather all the crops from your fields.

17"So three times during every year all your males must come to worship the LORD God.

18"You must not offer animal blood along with anything that has yeast in it.

"You must not save any of the fat from the sacrifice for the next day.

19"You must bring the best of the first-fruits of your land to the Holy Tent[n] of the LORD your God.

"You must not cook a young goat in its mother's milk.

GOD WILL HELP ISRAEL

20"I am sending an angel ahead of you, who will protect you as you travel. He will lead you to the place I have prepared. 21Pay attention to the angel and obey him. Do not turn against him; he will not forgive such turning against him because my power is in him. 22If you listen carefully to all he says and do everything that I tell you, I will be an enemy to your enemies. I will fight all who fight against you. 23My angel will go ahead of you and take you into the land of the Amorites, Hittites, Perizzites, Canaanites, Hivites, and Jebusites, and I will destroy them.

24"You must not bow down to their gods or worship them. You must not live the way those people live. You must destroy their idols, breaking into pieces the stone pillars they use in worship. 25If you worship the LORD your God, I will bless your bread and your water. I will take away sickness from you. 26None of your women will have her baby die before it is born, and all women will have children. I will allow you to live long lives.

27"I will make your enemies afraid of me. I will confuse any people you fight against,

---

23:19 Holy Tent Literally, "house of the LORD your God." See Exodus 25:9.

and I will make all your enemies run away from you. ²⁸I will send terror ahead of you that will force the Hivites, Canaanites, and Hittites out of your way. ²⁹But I will not force all those people out in only one year. If I did, the land would become a desert and the wild animals would become too many for you. ³⁰Instead, I will force those people out slowly, until there are enough of you to take over the land.

³¹"I will give you the land from the Red Sea to the Mediterranean Sea, and from the desert to the Euphrates River. I will give you power over the people who now live in the land, and you will force them out ahead of you. ³²You must not make an agreement with those people or with their gods. ³³You must not let them live in your land, or they will make you sin against me. If you worship their gods, you will be caught in a trap."

GOD AND ISRAEL MAKE THEIR AGREEMENT

24 The LORD told Moses, "You, Aaron, Nadab, Abihu, and seventy of the elders of Israel must come up to me and worship me from a distance. ²Then Moses alone must come near me; the others must not come near. The rest of the people must not come up the mountain with Moses."

³Moses told the people all the LORD's words and laws for living. Then all of the people answered out loud together, "We will do all the things the LORD has said." ⁴So Moses wrote down all the words of the LORD. And he got up early the next morning and built an altar near the bottom of the mountain. He set up twelve stones, one stone for each of the twelve tribes of Israel. ⁵Then Moses sent young Israelite men to offer whole burnt offerings and to sacrifice young bulls as fellowship offerings to the LORD. ⁶Moses put half of the blood of these animals in bowls, and he sprinkled the other half of the blood on the altar. ⁷Then he took the Book of the Agreement and read it so the people could hear him. And they said, "We will do everything that the LORD has said; we will obey."

⁸Then Moses took the blood from the bowls and sprinkled it on the people, saying, "This is the blood that begins the Agreement, the Agreement which the LORD has made with you about all these words."

⁹Moses, Aaron, Nadab, Abihu, and seventy of the elders of Israel went up the mountain ¹⁰and saw the God of Israel. Under his feet was a surface that looked as if it were paved with blue sapphire stones, and it was as clear as the sky! ¹¹These leaders of the Israelites saw God, but God did not destroy them. Then they ate and drank together.

GOD PROMISES MOSES THE STONE TABLETS

¹²The LORD said to Moses, "Come up the mountain to me. Wait there, and I will give you two stone tablets. On these are the teachings and the commands I have written to instruct the people."

¹³So Moses and his helper Joshua set out, and Moses went up to Sinai, the mountain of God. ¹⁴Moses said to the elders, "Wait here for us until we come back to you. Aaron and Hur are with you, and anyone who has a disagreement with others can take it to them."

MOSES MEETS WITH GOD

¹⁵When Moses went up on the mountain, the cloud covered it. ¹⁶The glory of the LORD came down on Mount Sinai, and the cloud covered it for six days. On the seventh day the LORD called to Moses from inside the cloud. ¹⁷To the Israelites the glory of the LORD looked like a fire burning on top of the mountain. ¹⁸Then Moses went into the cloud and went higher up the mountain. He was on the mountain for forty days and forty nights.

GIFTS FOR THE LORD

25 The LORD said to Moses, ²"Tell the Israelites to bring me gifts. Receive for me the gifts each person wants to give. ³These are the gifts that you should receive from them: gold, silver, bronze; ⁴blue, purple, and red thread; fine linen, goat hair, ⁵sheepskins that are dyed red; fine leather; acacia wood; ⁶olive oil to burn in the lamps; spices for sweet-smelling incense, and the special olive oil poured on a person's head to make him a priest; ⁷onyx stones, and other jewels to be put on the holy vest and the chest covering.

⁸"The people must build a holy place for me so that I can live among them. ⁹Build this Holy Tent and everything in it by the plan I will show you.

THE ARK OF THE AGREEMENT

¹⁰"Use acacia wood and build an Ark forty-five inches long, twenty-seven inches

wide, and twenty-seven inches high. ¹¹Cover the Ark inside and out with pure gold, and put a gold strip all around it. ¹²Make four gold rings for the Ark and attach them to its four feet, two rings on each side. ¹³Then make poles from acacia wood and cover them with gold. ¹⁴Put the poles through the rings on the sides of the Ark, and use these poles to carry it. ¹⁵These poles must always stay in the rings of the Ark. Do not take them out. ¹⁶Then put in the Ark the Agreement which I will make with you.

¹⁷"Then make a lid of pure gold for the Ark; this is the mercy seat. Make it forty-five inches long and twenty-seven inches wide. ¹⁸Then hammer gold to make two creatures with wings, and put one on each end of the lid. ¹⁹Attach one creature on one end of the lid and the other creature on the other end. Make them to be one piece with the lid at

---

THE EXTRAORDINARY IN THE MUNDANE

FAITH

God's mark on you

EXODUS 24:8

In our world, we do everything we can to prevent scars. We hire the best plastic surgeons, we look for the finest techniques, and we demand perfectly seamless incisions. We want an unblemished appearance after the cuts have been made. But some scars are much too important to conceal.

The Hebrew word *karat*, translated "made," is really a word that means "to cut." God cut an agreement with his people. When an agreement was made, both parties cut a line across the arm. They wanted a reminder of the agreement to be permanently etched into the body. There were two reasons for this action. The first was a personal sign of the promise to someone else. Every time a person looked at his arm, he saw the mark of promise. When God instructed the men of Israel to be circumcised, he wanted them to have a permanent reminder of the promise.

But there is another reason. If an enemy saw the mark of an agreement on a person's arm, that enemy would know that someone else stood behind the person. If the enemy harmed that person, he would also have to deal with the other party in the agreement. The cut of the agreement was a sign of protection.

Have you let God inscribe his agreement on your heart? Are you a living sacrifice, marked by the blood of the Lamb? Do you live with the confidence that the God of all creation is behind you? What is there to fear? Who would dare harm someone protected by his cut?

reflect: Consider all the many benefits of being in agreement with almighty God.
Go to **Deuteronomy 23:5.**

the ends. 20The creatures' wings should be spread upward, covering the lid, and the creatures are to face each other across the lid. 21Put this lid on top of the Ark, and put in the Ark the Agreement which I will make with you. 22I will meet with you there, above the lid between the two winged creatures on the Ark of the Agreement. There I will give you all my commands for the Israelites.

THE TABLE

23"Make a table out of acacia wood, thirty-six inches long, eighteen inches wide, and twenty-seven inches high. 24Cover it with pure gold, and put a gold strip around it. 25Make a frame three inches high that stands up all around the edge, and put a gold strip around it. 26Then make four gold rings. Attach them to the four corners of the table where the four legs are. 27Put the rings close to the frame around the top of the table, because they will hold the poles for carrying it. 28Make the poles out of acacia wood, cover them with gold, and carry the table with these poles. 29Make the plates and bowls for the table, as well as the jars and cups, out of pure gold. They will be used for pouring out the drink offerings. 30On this table put the bread that shows you are in my presence so that it is always there in front of me.

THE LAMPSTAND

31"Hammer pure gold to make a lampstand. Its base, stand, flower-like cups, buds, and petals must all be joined together in one piece. 32The lampstand must have six branches going out from its sides—three on one side and three on the other. 33Each branch must have three cups shaped like almond flowers on it. Each cup must have a bud and a petal. Each of the six branches going out from the lampstand must be the same. 34And there must be four more cups made like almond flowers on the lampstand itself. These cups must also have buds and petals. 35Put a bud under each pair of branches that goes out from the lampstand. Each of the six branches going out from the lampstand must be the same. 36The branches, buds, and lampstand must be made of one piece, hammered out of pure gold.

37"Then make seven small oil lamps and put them on the lampstand so that they give light to the area in front of it. 38The wick trimmers and trays must be made of pure gold. 39Use seventy-five pounds of pure gold to make the lampstand and everything with it. 40Be very careful to make them by the plan I showed you on the mountain.

THE HOLY TENT

26 "Make for the Holy Tent ten curtains of fine linen and blue, purple, and red thread. Have a skilled craftsman sew designs of creatures with wings on the pieces of cloth. 2Make each curtain the same size—forty-two feet long and six feet wide. 3Sew five curtains together for one set, and sew the other curtains together for the second set. 4Make loops of blue cloth on the edge of the end curtain of one set, and do the same for the end curtain of the other set. 5Make fifty loops on the end curtain of the first set and fifty loops on the end curtain of the second set. These loops must be opposite each other. 6And make fifty gold hooks to join the two sets of curtains so that the Holy Tent is one piece.

7"Then make another tent that will cover the Holy Tent, using eleven curtains made from goat hair. 8All these curtains must be the same size—forty-five feet long and six feet wide. 9Sew five of the curtains together into one set. Then sew the other six curtains together into the second set. Fold the sixth curtain double over the front of the Tent. 10Make fifty loops down the edge of the end curtain of one set, and do the same for the end curtain of the other set. 11Then make fifty bronze hooks and put them in the loops to join the tent together so that the covering is one piece. 12Let the extra half piece of cloth hang over the back of the Holy Tent. 13There will be eighteen inches hanging over the sides of the Holy Tent, to protect it. 14Make a covering for the Holy Tent from sheepskins colored red, and over that make a covering from fine leather.

15"Use acacia wood to make upright frames for the Holy Tent. 16Each frame must be fifteen feet long and twenty-seven inches wide, 17with two pegs side by side. Every frame must be made the same way. 18Make twenty frames for the south side of the Holy Tent. 19Each frame must have two silver bases to go under it, a peg fitting into each base. You must make forty silver bases for the frames. ²⁰Make twenty more frames for the north side of the Holy Tent ²¹and forty silver bases for them—two bases for each frame. ²²You must make six frames for the rear or west end of the Holy Tent ²³and two frames for each corner at the rear. ²⁴The two frames are to be doubled at the bottom and joined at the top with a metal ring. Both corner frames must be made this way. ²⁵So there will be a total of eight frames at the rear of the Tent, and there will be sixteen silver bases—two bases under each frame.

²⁶"Make crossbars of acacia wood to connect the upright frames of the Holy Tent. Make five crossbars to hold the frames together on one side ²⁷and five to hold the frames together on the other side. Also make five crossbars to hold the frames together on the west end, at the rear. ²⁸The middle crossbar is to be set halfway up the frames, and it is to run along the entire length of each side and rear. ²⁹Make gold rings on the sides of the frames to hold the crossbars, and cover the frames and the crossbars with gold. ³⁰Set up the Holy Tent by the plan shown to you on the mountain.

³¹"Make a curtain of fine linen and blue, purple, and red thread, and have a skilled craftsman sew designs of creatures with wings on it. ³²Hang the curtain by gold hooks on four posts of acacia wood that are covered with gold, and set them in four silver bases. ³³Hang the curtain from the hooks in the roof, and put the Ark of the Agreement containing the two stone tablets behind it. This curtain will separate the Holy Place from the Most Holy Place. ³⁴Put the lid on the Ark of the Agreement in the Most Holy Place.

³⁵"Outside the curtain, put the table on the north side of the Holy Tent. Put the lampstand on the south side of the Holy Tent across from the table.

THE ENTRANCE OF THE HOLY TENT

³⁶"Then, for the entrance of the Tent, make a curtain with fine linen and blue, purple, and red thread. Someone who can sew well is to sew designs on it. ³⁷Make five posts of acacia wood covered with gold. Make gold hooks for them on which to hang the curtain, and make five bronze bases for them.

THE ALTAR FOR BURNT OFFERINGS

27 "Make an altar of acacia wood, four and one-half feet high. It should be square—seven and one-half feet long and seven and one-half feet wide. ²Make each of the four corners of the altar stick out like a horn, in such a way that the corners with their horns are all one piece. Then cover the whole altar with bronze.

³"Use bronze to make all the tools and dishes that will be used on the altar: the pots to remove the ashes, the shovels, the bowls for sprinkling blood, the meat forks, and the pans for carrying the burning wood.

⁴"Make a large bronze screen to hold the burning wood, and put a bronze ring at each of the four corners of it. ⁵Put the screen inside the altar, under its rim, halfway up from the bottom.

⁶"Make poles of acacia wood for the altar, and cover them with bronze. ⁷Put the poles through the rings on both sides of the altar to carry it. ⁸Make the altar out of boards and leave the inside hollow. Make it as you were shown on the mountain.

THE COURTYARD OF THE HOLY TENT

⁹"Make a wall of curtains to form a courtyard around the Holy Tent. The south side should have a wall of fine linen curtains one hundred fifty feet long. ¹⁰Hang the curtains with silver hooks and bands on twenty bronze posts with twenty bronze bases. ¹¹The north side must also be one hundred fifty feet long. Hang its curtains on silver hooks and bands on twenty bronze posts with twenty bronze bases.

¹²"The west end of the courtyard must have a wall of curtains seventy-five feet long, with ten posts and ten bases on that wall. ¹³The east end of the courtyard must also be seventy-five feet long. ¹⁴On one side of the entry, there is to be a wall of curtains twenty-two and one-half feet long, held up by three posts on three bases. ¹⁵On the other side of the entry, there is also to be a wall of curtains twenty-two and one-half feet long, held up by three posts on three bases.

¹⁶"The entry to the courtyard is to be a curtain thirty feet wide, made of fine linen with blue, purple, and red thread. Someone who can sew well is to sew designs on it. It is to be held up by four posts on four bases. ¹⁷All the

posts around the courtyard must have silver bands and hooks and bronze bases. ¹⁸The courtyard must be one hundred fifty feet long and seventy-five feet wide, with a wall of curtains around it seven and one-half feet high, made of fine linen. The bases in which the posts are set must be bronze. ¹⁹All the things used in the Holy Tent and all the tent pegs for the Holy Tent and the wall around the courtyard must be made of bronze.

OIL FOR THE LAMP

²⁰"Command the people of Israel to bring you pure olive oil, made from pressed olives, to keep the lamps on the lampstand burning. ²¹Aaron and his sons must keep the lamps burning before the LORD from evening till morning. This will be in the Meeting Tent, outside the curtain which is in front of the Ark. The Israelites and their descendants must obey this rule from now on.

CLOTHES FOR THE PRIESTS

28 "Tell your brother Aaron to come to you, along with his sons Nadab, Abihu, Eleazar, and Ithamar. Separate them from the other Israelites to serve me as priests. ²Make holy clothes for your brother Aaron to give him honor and beauty. ³Tell all the skilled craftsmen to whom I have given wisdom to make special clothes for Aaron—clothes to show that he belongs to me so that he may serve me as a priest. ⁴These are the clothes they must make: a chest covering, a holy vest, an outer robe, a woven inner robe, a turban, and a cloth belt. The craftsmen must make these holy clothes for your brother Aaron and his sons. Then they may serve me as priests. ⁵The craftsmen must use gold and blue, purple and red thread, and fine linen.

THE HOLY VEST

⁶"Use gold and blue, purple and red thread, and fine linen to make the holy vest; skilled craftsmen are to make it. ⁷At each top corner of this holy vest there will be a pair of shoulder straps tied together over each shoulder.

⁸"The craftsmen will very carefully weave a belt on the holy vest that is made with the same materials—gold and blue, purple and red thread, and fine linen.

⁹"Take two onyx stones and write the names of the twelve sons of Israel on them, ¹⁰six on one stone and six on the other. Write the names in order, from the oldest son to the youngest. ¹¹Carve the names of the sons of Israel on these stones in the same way a person carves words and designs on a seal. Put gold around the stones to hold them on the holy vest. ¹²Then put the two stones on the two straps of the holy vest as reminders of the twelve sons of Israel. Aaron is to wear their names on his shoulders in the presence of the LORD as reminders of the sons of Israel. ¹³Make two gold pieces to hold the stones ¹⁴and two chains of pure gold, twisted together like a rope. Attach the chains to the two gold pieces that hold the stones.

THE CHEST COVERING

¹⁵"Make a chest covering to help in making decisions. The craftsmen should make it as they made the holy vest, using gold and blue, purple and red thread, and fine linen. ¹⁶The chest covering must be square—nine inches long and nine inches wide—and folded double to make a pocket. ¹⁷Put four rows of beautiful gems on the chest covering: The first row must have a ruby, topaz, and yellow quartz; ¹⁸the second must have turquoise, a sapphire, and an emerald; ¹⁹the third must have a jacinth, an agate, and an amethyst; ²⁰the fourth must have a chrysolite, an onyx, and a jasper. Put gold around these jewels to attach them to the chest covering. ²¹There must be twelve jewels on the chest covering—one jewel for each of the names of the sons of Israel. Carve the name of one of the twelve tribes on each of the stones as you would carve a seal.

²²"Make chains of pure gold, twisted together like rope, for the chest covering. ²³Make two gold rings and put them on the two upper corners of the chest covering. ²⁴Attach the two gold chains to the two rings at the upper corners of the chest covering. ²⁵Attach the other ends of the two chains to the two gold pieces on the shoulder straps in the front of the holy vest.

²⁶"Make two gold rings and put them at the two lower corners of the chest covering, on the inside edge next to the holy vest. ²⁷Make two more gold rings and attach them to the bottom of the shoulder straps in the front of the holy vest. Put them close to the seam above the woven belt of the holy vest.

28Join the rings of the chest covering to the rings of the holy vest with blue ribbon, connecting it to the woven belt so the chest covering will not swing out from the holy vest.

29"When Aaron enters the Holy Place, he will wear the names of the sons of Israel over his heart, on the chest covering that helps in making decisions. This will be a continual reminder before the LORD. 30And put the Urim and Thummim inside the chest covering so that they will be on Aaron's heart when he goes before the LORD. They will help in making decisions for the Israelites. So Aaron will always carry them with him when he is before the LORD.

31"Make the outer robe to be worn under the holy vest, using only blue cloth. 32Make a hole in the center for Aaron's head, with a woven collar around the hole so it will not tear. 33Make balls like pomegranates of blue, purple, and red thread, and hang them around the bottom of the outer robe with gold bells between them. 34All around the bottom of the outer robe there should be a gold bell and a pomegranate ball, a gold bell and a pomegranate ball. 35Aaron must wear this robe when he serves as priest. The ringing of the bells will be heard when he enters and leaves the Holy Place before the LORD so that Aaron will not die.

36"Make a strip of pure gold and carve these words on it as you would carve a seal: 'Holy to the LORD.' 37Use blue ribbon to tie it to the turban; put it on the front of the turban. 38Aaron must wear this on his forehead. In this way, he will be blamed if anything is wrong with the gifts of the Israelites. Aaron must always wear this on his head so the LORD will accept the gifts of the people.

39"Make the woven inner robe of fine linen, and make the turban of fine linen also. Make the cloth belt with designs sewn on it. 40Also make woven inner robes, cloth belts, and headbands for Aaron's sons, to give them honor and beauty. 41Put these clothes on your brother Aaron and his sons, and pour olive oil on their heads to appoint them as priests. Make them belong to me so they may serve me as priests.

42"Make for them linen underclothes to cover them from the waist to the upper parts of the legs. 43Aaron and his sons must wear these underclothes when they enter the Meeting Tent and anytime they come near the altar to serve as priests in the Holy Place. If they do not wear these clothes, they will be guilty of wrong, and they will die. This will be a law that will last from now on for Aaron and all his descendants.

APPOINTING THE PRIESTS

29 "This is what you must do to appoint Aaron and his sons to serve me as priests. Take one young bull and two male sheep that have nothing wrong with them. 2Use fine wheat flour without yeast to make bread, cakes mixed with olive oil, and wafers brushed with olive oil. 3Put these in one basket, and bring them along with the bull and two male sheep. 4Bring Aaron and his sons to the entrance of the Meeting Tent and wash them with water. 5Take the clothes and dress Aaron in the inner robe and the outer robe of the holy vest. Then put on him the holy vest and the chest covering, and tie the holy vest on him with its skillfully woven belt. 6Put the turban on his head, and put the holy crown on the turban. 7Take the special olive oil and pour it on his head to make him a priest.

8"Then bring his sons and put the inner robes on them. 9Put the headbands on their heads, and tie cloth belts around their waists. Aaron and his descendants will be priests in Israel, according to a rule that will continue from now on. This is how you will appoint Aaron and his sons as priests.

10"Bring the bull to the front of the Meeting Tent, and Aaron and his sons must put their hands on the bull's head. 11Then kill the bull before the LORD at the entrance to the Meeting Tent. 12Use your finger to put some of the bull's blood on the corners of the altar, and then pour the blood that is left at the bottom of the altar. 13Take all the fat that covers the inner organs, as well as the best part of the liver, both kidneys, and the fat around them, and burn them on the altar. 14Take the bull's meat, skin, and intestines, and burn them outside the camp. This is an offering to take away sin.

15"Take one of the male sheep, and have Aaron and his sons put their hands on its head. 16Kill it, and take its blood and sprinkle it on all four sides of the altar. 17Then cut it into pieces and wash its inner organs and its legs, putting them with its head and its other pieces. [18]Burn the whole sheep on the altar; it is a burnt offering made by fire to the LORD. Its smell is pleasing to the LORD.

[19]"Take the other male sheep, and have Aaron and his sons put their hands on its head. [20]Kill it and take some of its blood. Put the blood on the bottom of the right ears of Aaron and his sons and on the thumbs of their right hands and on the big toes of their right feet. Then sprinkle the rest of the blood against all four sides of the altar. [21]Take some of the blood from the altar, and mix it with the special oil used in appointing priests. Sprinkle this on Aaron and his clothes and on his sons and their clothes. This will show that Aaron and his sons and their clothes are given to my service.

[22]"Then take the fat from the male sheep, the fat tail, and the fat that covers the inner organs. In addition, take the best part of the liver, both kidneys, and the fat around them, and the right thigh. (This is the male sheep to be used in appointing priests.)

[23]"Then take the basket of bread that you made without yeast, which you put before the LORD. From it take a loaf of bread, a cake made with olive oil, and a wafer. [24]Put all of these in the hands of Aaron and his sons, and tell them to present them as an offering to the LORD. [25]Then take them from their hands and burn them on the altar with the whole burnt offering. This is an offering made by fire to the LORD; its smell is pleasing to the LORD. [26]Then take the breast of the male sheep used to appoint Aaron as priest, and present it before the LORD as an offering. This part of the animal will be your share. [27]Set aside the breast and the thigh of the sheep that were used to appoint Aaron and his sons as priests. These parts belong to them. [28]They are to be the regular share which the Israelites will always give to Aaron and his sons. It is the gift the Israelites must give to the LORD from their fellowship offerings.

[29]"The holy clothes made for Aaron will belong to his descendants so that they can wear these clothes when they are appointed as priests. [30]Aaron's son, who will become high priest after Aaron, will come to the Meeting Tent to serve in the Holy Place. He is to wear these clothes for seven days.

[31]"Take the male sheep used to appoint priests and boil its meat in a place that is holy. [32]Then at the entrance of the Meeting Tent, Aaron and his sons must eat the meat of the sheep and the bread that is in the basket. [33]They should eat these offerings that were used to remove their sins and to make them holy when they were made priests. But no one else is to eat them, because they are holy things. [34]If any of the meat from that sheep or any of the bread is left the next morning, it must be burned. It must not be eaten, because it is holy.

[35]"Do all these things that I commanded you to do to Aaron and his sons, and spend seven days appointing them. [36]Each day you are to offer a bull to remove the sins of Aaron and his sons so they will be given for service to the LORD. Make the altar ready for service to the LORD, and pour oil on it to make it holy. [37]Spend seven days making the altar ready for service to God and making it holy. Then the altar will become very holy, and anything that touches it must be holy.

THE DAILY SACRIFICES

[38]"Every day from now on, offer on the altar two lambs that are one year old. [39]Offer one lamb in the morning and the other in the evening before dark. [40]In the morning, when you offer the first lamb, offer also two quarts of fine flour mixed with one quart of oil from pressed olives. Pour out a quart of wine as a drink offering. [41]Offer the second lamb in the evening with the same grain offering and drink offering as you did in the morning. This is an offering made by fire to the LORD, and its smell is pleasing to him.

[42]"You must burn these things as an offering to the LORD every day, from now on, at the entrance of the Meeting Tent before the LORD. When you make the offering, I, the LORD, will meet you there and speak to you. [43]I will meet with the people of Israel there, and that place will be holy because of my glory.

[44]"So I will make the Meeting Tent and the altar holy; I will also make Aaron and his sons holy so they may serve me as priests. [45]I will live with the people of Israel and be their God. [46]And they will know that I am the LORD their God who led them out of Egypt so that I could live with them. I am the LORD their God.

THE ALTAR FOR BURNING INCENSE

30 "Make an altar out of acacia wood for burning incense. [2]Make it square—eighteen inches long and eighteen inches wide—and make it thirty-six inches high. The corners that stick out like horns must be one piece with the altar. [3]Cover its top, its sides, and its corners with pure gold, and put a gold strip all around the altar. [4]Make two gold rings beneath the gold strip on opposite sides of the altar, and slide poles through them to carry the altar. [5]Make the poles from acacia wood and cover them with gold. [6]Put the altar of incense in front of the curtain that is near the Ark of the Agreement, in front of the lid that covers that Ark. There I will meet with you.

[7]"Aaron must burn sweet-smelling incense on the altar every morning when he comes to take care of the oil lamps. [8]He must burn incense again in the evening when he lights the lamps, so incense will burn before the LORD every day from now on. [9]Do not use this altar for offering any other incense, or burnt offering, or any kind of grain offering, or drink offering. [10]Once a year Aaron must make the altar ready for service to God by putting blood on its corners—the blood of the animal offered to remove sins. He is to do this once a year from now on. This altar belongs completely to the LORD's service."

THE TAX FOR THE MEETING TENT

[11]The LORD said to Moses, [12]"When you count the people of Israel, every person must buy back his life from the LORD so that no terrible things will happen to the people when you number them. [13]Every person who is counted must pay one-fifth of an ounce of silver. (This is set by using one-half of the Holy Place measure, which weighs two-fifths of an ounce.) This amount is a gift to the LORD. [14]Every person who is counted and is twenty years old or older must give this amount to the LORD. [15]A rich person must not give more than one-fifth of an ounce, and a poor person must not give less. You are paying this to the LORD to buy back your lives. [16]Gather from the people of Israel this money paid to buy back their lives, and spend it on things for the service in the Meeting Tent. This payment will remind the LORD that the Israelites' lives have been bought back."

THE BRONZE BOWL

[17]The LORD said to Moses, [18]"Make a bronze bowl, on a bronze stand, for washing. Put the bowl and stand between the Meeting Tent and the altar, and put water in the bowl. [19]Aaron and his sons must wash their hands and feet with the water from this bowl. [20]Each time they enter the Meeting Tent they must wash with water so they will not die. Whenever they approach the altar to serve as priests and offer a sacrifice to the LORD by fire, [21]they must wash their hands and their feet so they will not die. This is a rule which Aaron and his descendants are to keep from now on."

OIL FOR APPOINTING

[22]Then the LORD said to Moses, [23]"Take the finest spices: twelve pounds of liquid myrrh, half that amount (that is, six pounds) of sweet-smelling cinnamon, six pounds of sweet-smelling cane, [24]and twelve pounds of cassia. Weigh all these by the Holy Place measure. Also take four quarts of olive oil, [25]and mix all these things like a perfume to make a holy olive oil. This special oil must be put on people and things to make them ready for service to God. [26]Put this oil on the Meeting Tent and the Ark of the Agreement, [27]on the table and all its dishes, on the lampstand and all its tools, and on the incense altar. [28]Also, put the oil on the altar for burnt offerings and on all its tools, as well as on the bowl and the stand under the bowl. [29]You will prepare all these things for service to God, and they will be very holy. Anything that touches these things must be holy.

[30]"Put the oil on Aaron and his sons to give them for service to me, that they may serve me as priests. [31]Tell the Israelites, 'This is to be my holy olive oil from now on. It is to be put on people and things to make them ready for service to God. [32]Do not pour it on the bodies of ordinary people, and do not make perfume the same way you make this oil. It is holy, and you must treat it as holy. [33]If anyone makes perfume like it or puts it on someone who is not a priest, that person must be cut off from his people.'"

INCENSE

[34]Then the LORD said to Moses, "Take these sweet-smelling spices: resin, onycha, galbanum, and pure frankincense. Be sure

that you have equal amounts of each. ³⁵Make incense as a person who makes perfume would do. Add salt to it to keep it pure and holy. ³⁶Beat some of the incense into a fine powder, and put it in front of the Ark of the Agreement in the Meeting Tent, where I will meet with you. You must use this incense powder only for its very special purpose. ³⁷Do not make incense for yourselves the same way you make this incense. Treat it as holy to the LORD. ³⁸Whoever makes incense like this to use as perfume must be cut off from his people."

BEZALEL AND OHOLIAB HELP

31 Then the LORD said to Moses, ²"See, I have chosen Bezalel son of Uri from the tribe of Judah. (Uri was the son of Hur.) ³I have filled Bezalel with the Spirit of God and have given him the skill, ability, and knowledge to do all kinds of work. ⁴He is able to design pieces to be made from gold, silver, and bronze, ⁵to cut jewels and put them in metal, to carve wood, and to do all kinds of work. ⁶I have also chosen Oholiab son of Ahisamach from the tribe of Dan to work with Bezalel. I have given skills to all the craftsmen, and they will be able to make all these things I have commanded you: ⁷the Meeting Tent, the Ark of the Agreement, the lid that covers the Ark, and everything in the Tent. ⁸This includes the table and everything on it, the pure gold lampstand and everything with it, the altar of incense, ⁹the altar for burnt offerings and everything used with it, and the bowl and the stand under it. ¹⁰They will make the woven clothes and the holy clothes for Aaron and the clothes for his sons to wear when they serve as priests. ¹¹They will also make the special olive oil used in appointing people and things to the service of the LORD, and the sweet-smelling incense for the Holy Place.

"These workers will make all these things just as I have commanded you."

THE DAY OF REST

¹²Then the LORD said to Moses, ¹³"Tell the Israelites, 'You must keep the rules about my Sabbaths, because they will be a sign between you and me from now on. In this way you will know that I, the LORD, make you holy.

¹⁴"'Make the Sabbath a holy day. If anyone treats the Sabbath like any other day, that person must be put to death; anyone who works on the Sabbath day must be cut off from his people. ¹⁵There are six days for working, but the seventh day is a day of rest, a day holy for the LORD. Anyone who works during the Sabbath day must be put to death. ¹⁶The Israelites must remember the Sabbath day as an agreement between them and me that will continue from now on. ¹⁷The Sabbath day will be a sign between me and the Israelites forever, because in six days I, the LORD, made the sky and the earth. On the seventh day I did not work; I rested.'"

¹⁸When the LORD finished speaking to Moses on Mount Sinai, he gave him the two stone tablets with the Agreement written on them, written by the finger of God.

THE PEOPLE MAKE A GOLD CALF

32 The people saw that a long time had passed and Moses had not come down from the mountain. So they gathered around Aaron and said, "Moses led us out of Egypt, but we don't know what has happened to him. Make us gods who will lead us."

²Aaron said to the people, "Take off the gold earrings that your wives, sons, and daughters are wearing, and bring them to me." ³So all the people took their gold earrings and brought them to Aaron. ⁴He took the gold from the people and formed it with a tool and made a statue of a calf. Then the people said, "Israel, these are your gods who brought you out of the land of Egypt!"

⁵When Aaron saw all this, he built an altar before the calf and announced, "Tomorrow there will be a special feast to honor the LORD." ⁶The people got up early the next morning and offered whole burnt offerings and fellowship offerings. They sat down to eat and drink, and then they got up and sinned sexually.

⁷Then the LORD said to Moses, "Go down from this mountain, because your people, the people you brought out of the land of Egypt, have ruined themselves. ⁸They have quickly turned away from the things I commanded them to do. They have made for themselves a calf covered with gold, and they have worshiped it and offered sacrifices to it. They have said, 'Israel, these are your gods who brought you out of Egypt.'"

⁹The LORD said to Moses, "I have seen

these people, and I know that they are very stubborn. ¹⁰So now do not stop me. I am so angry with them that I am going to destroy them. Then I will make you and your descendants a great nation."

¹¹But Moses begged the LORD his God and said, "LORD, don't let your anger destroy your people, whom you brought out of Egypt with your great power and strength. ¹²Don't let the people of Egypt say, 'The LORD brought the Israelites out of Egypt for an evil purpose. He planned to kill them in the mountains and destroy them from the earth.' So stop being angry, and don't destroy your people. ¹³Remember the men who served you—Abraham, Isaac, and Israel. You promised with an oath to them and said, 'I will make your descendants as many as the stars in the sky. I will give your descendants all this land that I have promised them, and it will be theirs forever.'" ¹⁴So the LORD changed his mind and did not destroy the people as he had said he might.

¹⁵Then Moses went down the mountain, and in his hands he had the two stone tablets with the Agreement on them. The commands were written on both sides of each stone, front and back. ¹⁶God himself had made the tablets, and God himself had written the commands on the tablets.

¹⁷When Joshua heard the sound of the people shouting, he said to Moses, "It sounds like war down in the camp."

¹⁸Moses answered:

"It is not a shout of victory;
    it is not a cry of defeat.
    It is the sound of singing that I hear."

¹⁹When Moses came close to the camp, he saw the gold calf and the dancing, and he became very angry. He threw down the stone tablets that he was carrying and broke them at the bottom of the mountain. ²⁰Then he took the calf that the people had made and melted it in the fire. He ground it into powder. Then he threw the powder into the water and forced the Israelites to drink it.

²¹Moses said to Aaron, "What did these people do to you? Why did you cause them to do such a terrible sin?"

²²Aaron answered, "Don't be angry, master. You know that these people are always ready to do wrong. ²³The people said to me, 'Moses led us out of Egypt, but we don't know what has happened to him. Make us gods who will lead us.' ²⁴So I told the people, 'Take off your gold jewelry.' When they gave me the gold, I threw it into the fire and out came this calf!"

²⁵Moses saw that the people were acting wildly. Aaron had let them get out of control and become fools in front of their enemies. ²⁶So Moses stood at the entrance to the camp and said, "Let anyone who wants to follow the LORD come to me." And all the people from the family of Levi gathered around Moses.

²⁷Then Moses said to them, "The LORD, the God of Israel, says this: 'Every man must put on his sword and go through the camp from one end to the other. Each man must kill his brother, his friend, and his neighbor.'" ²⁸The people from the family of Levi obeyed Moses, and that day about three thousand of the Israelites died. ²⁹Then Moses said, "Today you have been given for service to the LORD. You were willing to kill your own sons and brothers, and God has blessed you for this."

³⁰The next day Moses told the people, "You have done a terrible sin. But now I will go up to the LORD. Maybe I can do something so your sins will be removed." ³¹So Moses went back to the LORD and said, "How terribly these people have sinned! They have made for themselves gods from gold. ³²Now, please forgive them of this sin. If you will not, then erase my name from the book in which you have written the names of your people."

³³But the LORD told Moses, "I will erase from my book the names of the people who sin against me. ³⁴So now, go. Lead the people where I have told you, and my angel will lead you. When the time comes to punish, I will punish them for their sin."

³⁵So the LORD caused terrible things to happen to the people because of what they did with the calf Aaron had made.

33

Then the LORD said to Moses, "You and the people you brought out of Egypt must leave this place. Go to the land that I promised with an oath to give to Abraham, Isaac, and Jacob when I said, 'I will give that land to your descendants.' ²I will send an angel to lead you, and I will force these people out of the land: the Canaanites, Amorites, Hittites, Perizzites, Hivites, and Jebusites.

³Go up to a fertile land. But I will not go with you, because I might destroy you on the way, since you are such a stubborn people."

⁴When the people heard this bad news, they became very sad, and none of them put on jewelry. ⁵This was because the LORD had said to Moses, "Tell the Israelites, 'You are a stubborn people. If I were to go with you even for a moment, I would destroy you. So take off all your jewelry, and I will decide what to do with you.'" ⁶So the people of Israel took off their jewelry at Mount Sinai.

THE MEETING TENT

⁷Moses used to take a tent and set it up a long way outside the camp; he called it the "Meeting Tent." Anyone who wanted to ask the LORD about something would go to the Meeting Tent outside the camp. ⁸Whenever Moses went out to the Tent, all the people would rise and stand at the entrances of their tents, watching him until he entered the Meeting Tent. ⁹When Moses went into the Tent, the pillar of cloud would always come down and stay at the entrance of the Tent while the LORD spoke with Moses. ¹⁰Whenever the people saw the pillar of cloud at the entrance of the Tent, they stood and worshiped, each person at the entrance of his own tent.

¹¹The LORD spoke to Moses face to face as a man speaks with his friend. Then Moses would return to the camp, but Moses' young helper, Joshua son of Nun, did not leave the Tent.

¹²Moses said to the LORD, "You have told me to lead these people, but you did not say whom you would send with me. You have said to me, 'I know you very well, and I am pleased with you.' ¹³If I have truly pleased you, show me your plans so that I may know you and continue to please you. Remember that this nation is your people."

¹⁴The LORD answered, "I myself will go with you, and I will give you victory."

¹⁵Then Moses said to him, "If you yourself don't go with us, then don't send us away from this place. ¹⁶If you don't go with us, no one will know that you are pleased with me and with your people. These people and I will be no different from any other people on earth."

¹⁷Then the LORD said to Moses, "I will do what you ask, because I know you very well, and I am pleased with you."

MOSES SEES GOD'S GLORY

¹⁸Then Moses said, "Now, please show me your glory."

¹⁹The LORD answered, "I will cause all my goodness to pass in front of you, and I will announce my name, the LORD, so you can hear it. I will show kindness to anyone to whom I want to show kindness, and I will show mercy to anyone to whom I want to show mercy. ²⁰But you cannot see my face, because no one can see me and live.

²¹"There is a place near me where you may stand on a rock. ²²When my glory passes that place, I will put you in a large crack in the rock and cover you with my hand until I have passed by. ²³Then I will take away my hand, and you will see my back. But my face must not be seen."

MOSES GETS NEW STONE TABLETS

34 The LORD said to Moses, "Cut two more stone tablets like the first two, and I will write the same words on them that were on the first two stones which you broke. ²Be ready tomorrow morning, and then come up on Mount Sinai. Stand before me there on the top of the mountain. ³No one may come with you or even be seen any place on the mountain. Not even the flocks or herds may eat grass near that mountain."

⁴So Moses cut two stone tablets like the first ones. Then early the next morning he went up Mount Sinai, just as the LORD had commanded him, carrying the two stone tablets with him. ⁵Then the LORD came down in the cloud and stood there with Moses, and the LORD called out his name: the LORD.

⁶The LORD passed in front of Moses and said, "I am the LORD. The LORD is a God who shows mercy, who is kind, who doesn't become angry quickly, who has great love and faithfulness ⁷and is kind to thousands of people. The LORD forgives people for evil, for sin, and for turning against him, but he does not forget to punish guilty people. He will punish not only the guilty people, but also their children, their grandchildren, their great-grandchildren, and their great-great-grandchildren."

⁸Then Moses quickly bowed to the ground and worshiped. ⁹He said, "Lord, if

you are pleased with me, please go with us. I know that these are stubborn people, but forgive our evil and our sin. Take us as your own people."

¹⁰Then the LORD said, "I am making this agreement with you. I will do miracles in front of all your people—things that have never before been done for any other nation on earth—and the people with you will see my work. I, the LORD, will do wonderful things for you. ¹¹Obey the things I command you today, and I will force out the Amorites, Canaanites, Hittites, Perizzites, Hivites, and Jebusites ahead of you. ¹²Be careful that you don't make an agreement with the people who live in the land where you are going, because it will bring you trouble. ¹³Destroy their altars, break their stone pillars, and cut down their Asherah idols. ¹⁴Don't worship any other god, because I, the LORD, the Jealous One, am a jealous God.

¹⁵"Be careful that you don't make an

FAMILY

GUILT AND GRACE

the parents of your past

EXODUS 34:6–7

By Jimmy Evans

Parents are a tremendous force in our lives, regardless of whether positive or negative. God put parents in our lives to help us, nurture us, and be his influence. However, in the process of growing up, negative things sometimes happen to us. How do we deal with these issues correctly?

The Hebrew word for "evil" is *avon*, which means a sin created in you because of the same sin being in your parents' lives. Just like a tree that is blown by the wind becomes bent in the direction it is blown, so is a child bent in the direction he sees in the behavior of his parents. Everything we say and do affects our children and our grandchildren for four generations.

We repeat the behavior, even if we recognize it as wrong, because it is what we constantly witnessed. We need to understand how to deal with and break the negative effects. All of us have baggage that we need to get free from. It is never too late to break the tradition and model righteousness for our children.

Recognize the problem, but don't go through life blaming your parents. Forgive your parents. Remember that they had baggage from their parents, too. You can't get free from your bondage until you forgive your parents. Focus on the good things they did. When a righteous person breaks a negative pattern and does what is right, God extends righteousness to a thousand generations.

reflect: Have you dealt properly with the things your parents did wrong?
Go to **FAMILY:** "Boys Will Be . . . " at **Proverbs 22:6.**

agreement with the people who live in that land. When they worship their gods, they will invite you to join them. Then you will eat their sacrifices. 16If you choose some of their daughters as wives for your sons and those daughters worship gods, they will lead your sons to do the same thing.

17"Do not make gods of melted metal.

18"Celebrate the Feast of Unleavened Bread. For seven days you must eat bread made without yeast as I commanded you. Do this during the month I have chosen, the month of Abib, because in that month you came out of Egypt.

19"The firstborn of every mother belongs to me, including every firstborn male animal that is born in your flocks and herds. 20You may buy back a donkey by paying for it with a lamb, but if you don't want to buy back a donkey, you must break its neck. You must buy back all your firstborn sons.

"No one is to come before me without a gift.

21"You must work for six days, but on the seventh day you must rest—even during the planting season and the harvest season.

22"Celebrate the Feast of Weeks when you gather the first grain of the wheat harvest. And celebrate the Feast of Shelters in the fall.

23"Three times each year all your males must come before the Lord GOD, the God of Israel. 24I will force out nations ahead of you and expand the borders of your land. You will go before the LORD your God three times each year, and at that time no one will try to take your land from you.

25"Do not offer the blood of a sacrifice to me with anything containing yeast, and do not leave any of the sacrifice of the Feast of Passover until the next morning.

26"Bring the best first crops that you harvest from your ground to the Tent of the LORD your God.

"You must not cook a young goat in its mother's milk."

27Then the LORD said to Moses, "Write down these words, because with these words I have made an agreement with you and Israel."

28Moses stayed there with the LORD forty days and forty nights, and during that time he did not eat food or drink water. And Moses wrote the words of the Agreement—the Ten Commandments—on the stone tablets.

THE FACE OF MOSES SHINES

29Then Moses came down from Mount Sinai, carrying the two stone tablets of the Agreement in his hands. But he did not know that his face was shining because he had talked with the LORD. 30When Aaron and all the people of Israel saw that Moses' face was shining, they were afraid to go near him. 31But Moses called to them, so Aaron and all the leaders of the people returned to Moses, and he talked with them. 32After that, all the people of Israel came near him, and he gave them all the commands that the LORD had given him on Mount Sinai.

33When Moses finished speaking to the people, he put a covering over his face. 34Anytime Moses went before the LORD to speak with him, Moses took off the covering until he came out. Then Moses would come out and tell the Israelites what the LORD had commanded. 35They would see that Moses' face was shining. So he would cover his face again until the next time he went in to speak with the LORD.

RULES ABOUT THE SABBATH

35 Moses gathered all the Israelite community together and said to them, "These are the things the LORD has commanded you to do. 2You are to work for six days, but the seventh day will be a holy day, a Sabbath of rest to honor the LORD. Anyone who works on that day must be put to death. 3On the Sabbath day you must not light a fire in any of your houses."

4Moses said to all the Israelites, "This is what the LORD has commanded: 5From what you have, take an offering for the LORD. Let everyone who is willing bring this offering to the LORD: gold, silver, bronze, 6blue, purple and red thread, and fine linen, goat hair 7and male sheepskins that are colored red. They may also bring fine leather, acacia wood, 8olive oil for the lamps, spices for the special olive oil used for appointing priests and for the sweet-smelling incense, 9onyx stones, and other jewels to be put on the holy vest and chest covering of the priests.

10"Let all the skilled workers come and make everything the LORD commanded: 11the Holy Tent, its outer tent and its covering, the hooks, frames, crossbars, posts, and bases; [12]the Ark of the Agreement, its poles, lid, and the curtain in front of it; [13]the table, and its poles, all the things that go with the table, and the bread that shows we are in God's presence; [14]the lampstand for the light and all the things that go with it, the lamps, and olive oil for the light; [15]the altar of incense and its poles, the special oil and the sweet-smelling incense, the curtain for the entrance of the Meeting Tent; [16]the altar of burnt offering and its bronze screen, its poles and all its tools, the bronze bowl and its base; [17]the curtains around the courtyard, their posts and bases, and the curtain at the entry to the courtyard; [18]the pegs of the Holy Tent and of the courtyard and their ropes; [19]the special clothes that the priest will wear in the Holy Place. These are the holy clothes for Aaron the priest and his sons to wear when they serve as priests."

[20]Then all the people of Israel went away from Moses. [21]Everyone who wanted to give came and brought a gift to the LORD for making the Meeting Tent, all the things in the Tent, and the special clothes. [22]All the men and women who wanted to give brought gold jewelry of all kinds—pins, earrings, rings, and bracelets. They all presented their gold to the LORD. [23]Everyone who had blue, purple, and red thread, and fine linen, and anyone who had goat hair or male sheepskins colored red or fine leather brought them to the LORD. [24]Everyone who could give silver or bronze brought that as a gift to the LORD, and everyone who had acacia wood to be used in the work brought it. [25]Every skilled woman used her hands to make the blue, purple, and red thread, and fine linen, and they brought what they had made. [26]All the women who were skilled and wanted to help made thread of the goat hair. [27]The leaders brought onyx stones and other jewels to put on the holy vest and chest covering for the priest. [28]They also brought spices and olive oil for the sweet-smelling incense, the special oil, and the oil to burn in the lamps. [29]All the men and women of Israel who wanted to help brought gifts to the LORD for all the work the LORD had commanded Moses and the people to do.

[30]Then Moses said to the Israelites, "Look, the LORD has chosen Bezalel son of Uri the son of Hur, from the tribe of Judah.

[31]The LORD has filled Bezalel with the Spirit of God and has given him the skill, ability, and knowledge to do all kinds of work. [32]He is able to design pieces to be made of gold, silver, and bronze, [33]to cut stones and jewels and put them in metal, to carve wood, and to do all kinds of work. [34]Also, the LORD has given Bezalel and Oholiab, the son of Ahisamach from the tribe of Dan, the ability to teach others. [35]The LORD has given them the skill to do all kinds of work. They are able to cut designs in metal and stone. They can plan and sew designs in the fine linen with the blue, purple, and red thread. And they are also able to weave things. **36** [1]So Bezalel, Oholiab, and every skilled person will do the work the LORD has commanded, because he gave them the wisdom and understanding to do all the skilled work needed to build the Holy Tent."

[2]Then Moses called Bezalel, Oholiab, and all the other skilled people to whom the LORD had given skills, and they came because they wanted to help with the work. [3]They received from Moses everything the people of Israel had brought as gifts to build the Holy Tent. The people continued to bring gifts each morning because they wanted to. [4]So all the skilled workers left the work they were doing on the Holy Tent, [5]and they said to Moses, "The people are bringing more than we need to do the work the LORD commanded."

[6]Then Moses sent this command throughout the camp: "No man or woman should make anything else as a gift for the Holy Tent." So the people were kept from giving more, [7]because what they had was already more than enough to do all the work.

THE HOLY TENT

[8]Then the skilled workers made the Holy Tent. They made the ten curtains of blue, purple, and red cloth, and they sewed designs of creatures with wings on the curtains. [9]Each curtain was the same size—forty-two feet long and six feet wide. [10]Five of the curtains were fastened together to make one set, and the other five were fastened together to make another set. [11]Then they made loops of blue cloth along the edge of the end curtain on the first set of five, and they did the same thing with the other set of five. [12]There were fifty loops on one curtain and fifty loops on

the other curtain, with the loops opposite each other. ¹³They made fifty gold hooks to join the two curtains together so that the Holy Tent was joined together as one piece.

¹⁴Then the workers made another tent of eleven curtains made of goat hair, to put over the Holy Tent. ¹⁵All eleven curtains were the same size—forty-five feet long and six feet wide. ¹⁶The workers sewed five curtains together into one set and six together into another set. ¹⁷They made fifty loops along the edge of the outside curtain of one set and fifty loops along the edge of the outside curtain of the other set. ¹⁸Then they made fifty bronze rings to join the two sets of cloth together and make the tent one piece. ¹⁹They made two more coverings for the outer tent—one made of male sheepskins colored red and the other made of fine leather.

²⁰Then they made upright frames of acacia wood for the Holy Tent. ²¹Each frame was fifteen feet tall and twenty-seven inches wide, ²²and there were two pegs side by side on each one. Every frame of the Holy Tent was made this same way. ²³They made twenty frames for the south side of the Tent, ²⁴and they made forty silver bases that went under the twenty frames. There were two bases for every frame—one for each peg of each frame. ²⁵They also made twenty frames for the north side of the Holy Tent ²⁶and forty silver bases—two to go under each frame. ²⁷They made six frames for the rear or west end of the Holy Tent ²⁸and two frames for the corners at the rear of the Holy Tent. ²⁹These two frames were doubled at the bottom and joined at the top with a metal ring. They did this for each of these corners. ³⁰So there were eight frames and sixteen silver bases—two bases under each frame.

³¹Then they made crossbars of acacia wood to connect the upright frames of the Holy Tent. Five crossbars held the frames together on one side of the Tent, ³²and five held the frames together on the other side. Also, five crossbars held the frames together on the west end, at the rear of the Tent. ³³They made the middle crossbar run along the entire length of each side and rear of the Tent. It was set halfway up the frames. ³⁴They made gold rings on the sides of the frames to hold the crossbars, and they covered the frames and the crossbars with gold.

³⁵Then they made the curtain of blue, purple, and red thread, and fine linen. A skilled craftsman sewed designs of creatures with wings on it. ³⁶They made four posts of acacia wood for it and covered them with gold. Then they made gold hooks for the posts, as well as four silver bases in which to set the posts. ³⁷For the entrance to the Tent, they made a curtain of blue, purple, and red thread, and fine linen. A person who sewed well sewed designs on it. ³⁸Then they made five posts and hooks for it. They covered the tops of the posts and their bands with gold, and they made five bronze bases for the posts.

THE ARK OF THE AGREEMENT

37 Bezalel made the Ark of acacia wood; it was forty-five inches long, twenty-seven inches wide, and twenty-seven inches high. ²He covered it, both inside and out, with pure gold, and he put a gold strip around it. ³He made four gold rings for it and attached them to its four feet, with two rings on each side. ⁴Then he made poles of acacia wood and covered them with gold. ⁵He put the poles through the rings on each side of the Ark to carry it. ⁶Then he made a lid of pure gold that was forty-five inches long and twenty-seven inches wide. ⁷Then Bezalel hammered gold to make two creatures with wings and attached them to each end of the lid. ⁸He made one creature on one end of the lid and the other creature on the other end. He attached them to the lid so that it would be one piece. ⁹The creatures' wings were spread upward, covering the lid, and the creatures faced each other across the lid.

THE TABLE

¹⁰Then he made the table of acacia wood; it was thirty-six inches long, eighteen inches wide, and twenty-seven inches high. ¹¹He covered it with pure gold and put a gold strip around it. ¹²He made a frame three inches high that stood up all around the edge, and he put a gold strip around it. ¹³Then he made four gold rings for the table and attached them to the four corners of the table where the four legs were. ¹⁴The rings were put close to the frame around the top of the table, because they held the poles for carrying it. ¹⁵The poles for carrying the table were made of acacia wood and were covered with gold.

16He made of pure gold all the things that were used on the table: the plates, bowls, cups, and jars used for pouring the drink offerings.

THE LAMPSTAND

17Then he made the lampstand of pure gold, hammering out its base and stand. Its flower-like cups, buds, and petals were joined together in one piece with the base and stand. 18Six branches went out from the sides of the lampstand—three on one side and three on the other. 19Each branch had three cups shaped like almond flowers, and each cup had a bud and a petal. Each of the six branches going out from the lampstand was the same. 20There were four more cups shaped like almond flowers on the lampstand itself, each with its buds and petals. 21Three pairs of branches went out from the lampstand. A bud was under the place where each pair was attached to the lampstand. Each of the six branches going out from the lampstand was the same. 22The buds, branches, and lampstand were all one piece of pure, hammered gold. 23He made seven pure gold lamps for this lampstand, and he made pure gold wick trimmers and trays. 24He used about seventy-five pounds of pure gold to make the lampstand and all the things that go with it.

THE ALTAR FOR BURNING INCENSE

25Then he made the altar of incense out of acacia wood. It was square—eighteen inches long and eighteen inches wide—and it was thirty-six inches high. Each corner that stuck out like a horn was joined into one piece with the altar. 26He covered the top and all the sides and the corners with pure gold, and he put gold trim around the altar. 27He made two gold rings and put them below the trim on opposite sides of the altar; these rings held the poles for carrying it. 28He made the poles of acacia wood and covered them with gold.

29Then he made the holy olive oil for appointing the priests and the pure, sweet-smelling incense. He made them like a person who mixes perfumes.

THE ALTAR FOR BURNT OFFERINGS

38 Then he built the altar for burnt offerings out of acacia wood. The altar was square—seven and one-half feet long and seven and one-half feet wide—and it was four and one-half feet high. 2He made each corner stick out like a horn so that the horns and the altar were joined together in one piece. Then he covered the altar with bronze. 3He made all the tools of bronze to use on the altar: the pots, shovels, bowls for sprinkling blood, meat forks, and pans for carrying the fire. 4He made a large bronze screen to hold the burning wood for the altar and put it inside the altar, under its rim, halfway up from the bottom. 5He made bronze rings to hold the poles for carrying the altar, and he put them at the four corners of the screen. 6Then he made poles of acacia wood and covered them with bronze. 7He put the poles through the rings on both sides of the altar, to carry it. He made the altar of boards and left the inside hollow.

THE BRONZE BOWL

8He made the bronze bowl for washing, and he built it on a bronze stand. He used the bronze from mirrors that belonged to the women who served at the entrance to the Meeting Tent.

THE COURTYARD OF THE HOLY TENT

9Then he made a wall of curtains to form a courtyard around the Holy Tent. On the south side the curtains were one hundred fifty feet long and were made of fine linen. 10The curtains hung on silver hooks and bands, placed on twenty bronze posts with twenty bronze bases. 11On the north side the wall of curtains was also one hundred fifty feet long, and it hung on silver hooks and bands on twenty posts with twenty bronze bases.

12On the west side of the courtyard, the wall of curtains was seventy-five feet long. It was held up by silver hooks and bands on ten posts with ten bases. 13The east side was also seventy-five feet long. 14On one side of the entry there was a wall of curtains twenty-two and one-half feet long, held up by three posts and three bases. 15On the other side of the entry there was also a wall of curtains twenty-two and one-half feet long, held up by three posts and three bases. 16All the curtains around the courtyard were made of fine linen. 17The bases for the posts were made of bronze. The hooks and the bands on the posts were made of silver, and the tops of the posts were covered with silver also. All the posts in the courtyard had silver bands.

¹⁸The curtain for the entry of the courtyard was made of blue, purple, and red thread, and fine linen, sewn by a person who could sew well. The curtain was thirty feet long and seven and one-half feet high, the same height as the curtains around the courtyard. ¹⁹It was held up by four posts and four bronze bases. The hooks and bands on the posts were made of silver, and the tops on the posts were covered with silver. ²⁰All the tent pegs for the Holy Tent and for the curtains around the courtyard were made of bronze.

²¹This is a list of the materials used to make the Holy Tent, where the Agreement was kept. Moses ordered the Levites to make this list, and Ithamar son of Aaron was in charge of keeping it. ²²Bezalel son of Uri, the son of Hur of the tribe of Judah, made everything the LORD commanded Moses. ²³Oholiab son of Ahisamach of the tribe of Dan helped him. He could cut designs into metal and stone; he was a designer and also skilled at sewing the blue, purple, and red thread, and fine linen.

²⁴The total amount of gold used to build the Holy Tent was presented to the LORD. It weighed over 2,000 pounds, as set by the Holy Place measure.

²⁵The silver was given by the members of the community who were counted. It weighed 7,550 pounds, as set by the Holy Place measure. ²⁶All the men twenty years old or older were counted. There were 603,550 men, and each man had to pay one-fifth of an ounce of silver, as set by the Holy Place measure. ²⁷Of this silver, 7,500 pounds were used to make the one hundred bases for the Holy Tent and for the curtain—75 pounds of silver in each base. ²⁸They used 50 pounds of silver to make the hooks for the posts and to cover the tops of the posts and to make the bands on them.

²⁹The bronze which was presented to the LORD weighed about 5,000 pounds. ³⁰They used the bronze to make the bases at the entrance of the Meeting Tent, to make the altar and the bronze screen, and to make all the tools for the altar. ³¹This bronze was also used to make bases for the wall of curtains around the courtyard and bases for curtains

at the entry to the courtyard, as well as to make the tent pegs for the Holy Tent and the curtains that surrounded the courtyard.

CLOTHES FOR THE PRIESTS

39 They used blue, purple, and red thread to make woven clothes for the priests to wear when they served in the Holy Place. They made the holy clothes for Aaron as the LORD had commanded Moses.

²They made the holy vest of gold, and blue, purple, and red thread, and fine linen. ³They hammered the gold into sheets and then cut it into long, thin strips. They worked the gold into the blue, purple, and red thread, and fine linen. This was done by skilled craftsmen. ⁴They made the shoulder straps for the holy vest, which were attached to the top corners of the vest and tied together over each shoulder. ⁵The skillfully woven belt was made in the same way; it was joined to the holy vest as one piece. It was made of gold, and blue, purple, and red thread, and fine linen, the way the LORD commanded Moses.

⁶They put gold around the onyx stones and then wrote the names of the sons of Israel on these gems, as a person carves words and designs on a seal. ⁷Then they attached the gems on the shoulder straps of the holy vest, as reminders of the twelve sons of Israel. This was done just as the LORD had commanded Moses.

⁸The skilled craftsmen made the chest covering like the holy vest; it was made of gold, and blue, purple, and red thread, and fine linen. ⁹The chest covering was square—nine inches long and nine inches wide—and it was folded double to make a pocket. ¹⁰Then they put four rows of beautiful jewels on it: In the first row there was a ruby, a topaz, and a yellow quartz; ¹¹in the second there was a turquoise, a sapphire, and an emerald; ¹²in the third there was a jacinth, an agate, and an amethyst; ¹³in the fourth there was a chrysolite, an onyx, and a jasper. Gold was put around these jewels to attach them to the chest covering, ¹⁴and the names of the sons of Israel were carved on these twelve jewels as a person carves a seal. Each jewel had the name of one of the twelve tribes of Israel.

¹⁵They made chains of pure gold, twisted together like a rope, for the chest covering. ¹⁶The workers made two gold pieces and

two gold rings. They put the two gold rings on the two upper corners of the chest covering. ¹⁷Then they put two gold chains in the two rings at the ends of the chest covering, ¹⁸and they fastened the other two ends of the chains to the two gold pieces. They attached these gold pieces to the two shoulder straps in the front of the holy vest. ¹⁹They made two gold rings and put them at the lower corners of the chest covering on the inside edge next to the holy vest. ²⁰They made two more gold rings on the bottom of the shoulder straps in front of the holy vest, near the seam, just above the woven belt of the holy vest. ²¹They used a blue ribbon and tied the rings of the chest covering to the rings of the holy vest, connecting it to the woven belt. In this way the chest covering would not swing out from the holy vest. They did all these things the way the LORD commanded.

²²Then they made the outer robe to be worn under the holy vest. It was woven only of blue cloth. ²³They made a hole in the center of the outer robe, with a woven collar sewn around it so it would not tear. ²⁴Then they made balls like pomegranates of blue, purple, and red thread, and fine linen and hung them around the bottom of the outer robe. ²⁵They also made bells of pure gold and hung these around the bottom of the outer robe between the balls. ²⁶So around the bottom of the outer robe there was a bell and a pomegranate ball, a bell and a pomegranate ball. The priest wore this outer robe when he served as priest, just as the LORD had commanded Moses.

²⁷They wove inner robes of fine linen for Aaron and his sons, ²⁸and they made turbans, headbands, and underclothes of fine linen. ²⁹Then they made the cloth belt of fine linen, and blue, purple, and red thread, and designs were sewn onto it, just as the LORD had commanded Moses.

³⁰They made a strip of pure gold, which is the holy crown, and carved these words in the gold, as one might carve on a seal: "Holy to the LORD." ³¹Then they tied this flat piece to the turban with a blue ribbon, as the LORD had commanded Moses.

³²So all the work on the Meeting Tent was finished. The Israelites did everything just as the LORD had commanded Moses. ³³Then they brought the Holy Tent to Moses: the Tent and all its furniture, hooks, frames, crossbars, posts, and bases; ³⁴the covering made of male sheepskins colored red, the covering made of fine leather, and the curtain that covered the entrance to the Most Holy Place; ³⁵the Ark of the Agreement, its poles and lid; ³⁶the table, all its containers, and the bread that showed they were in God's presence; ³⁷the pure gold lampstand with its lamps in a row, all its tools, and the olive oil for the light; ³⁸the gold altar, the special olive oil used for appointing priests, the sweet-smelling incense, and the curtain that covered the entrance to the Tent; ³⁹the bronze altar and its screen, its poles and all its tools, the bowl and its stand; ⁴⁰the curtains for the courtyard with their posts and bases, the curtain that covered the entry to the courtyard, the cords, pegs, and all the things in the Meeting Tent. ⁴¹They brought the clothes for the priests to wear when they served in the Holy Tent—the holy clothes for Aaron the priest and the clothes for his sons, which they wore when they served as priests.

⁴²The Israelites had done all this work just as the LORD had commanded Moses. ⁴³Moses looked closely at all the work and saw they had done it just as the LORD had commanded. So Moses blessed them.

SETTING UP THE HOLY TENT

40 Then the LORD said to Moses: ²"On the first day of the first month, set up the Holy Tent, which is the Meeting Tent. ³Put the Ark of the Agreement in it and hang the curtain in front of the Ark. ⁴Bring in the table and arrange everything on the table that should be there. Then bring in the lampstand and set up its lamps. ⁵Put the gold altar for burning incense in front of the Ark of the Agreement, and put the curtain at the entrance to the Holy Tent.

⁶"Put the altar of burnt offerings in front of the entrance of the Holy Tent, the Meeting Tent. ⁷Put the bowl between the Meeting Tent and the altar, and put water in it. ⁸Set up the courtyard around the Holy Tent, and put the curtain at the entry to the courtyard.

⁹"Use the special olive oil and pour it on the Holy Tent and everything in it, in order to give the Tent and all that is in it for service to the LORD. They will be holy. ¹⁰Pour the special oil on the altar for burnt offerings

and on all its tools. Give the altar for service to God, and it will be very holy. ¹¹Then pour the special olive oil on the bowl and the base under it so that they will be given for service to God.

¹²"Bring Aaron and his sons to the entrance of the Meeting Tent, and wash them with water. ¹³Then put the holy clothes on Aaron. Pour the special oil on him, and give him for service to God so that he may serve me as a priest. ¹⁴Bring Aaron's sons and put the inner robes on them. ¹⁵Pour the special oil on them in the same way that you appointed their father as priest so that they may also serve me as priests. Pouring oil on them will make them a family of priests, they and their descendants from now on." ¹⁶Moses did everything that the LORD commanded him.

¹⁷So the Holy Tent was set up on the first day of the first month during the second year after they left Egypt. ¹⁸When Moses set up the Holy Tent, he put the bases in place, and he put the frames on the bases. Next he put the crossbars through the rings of the frames and set up the posts. ¹⁹After that, Moses spread the cloth over the Holy Tent and put the covering over it, just as the LORD commanded.

²⁰Moses put the stone tablets that had the Agreement written on them into the Ark. He put the poles through the rings of the Ark and put the lid on it. ²¹Next he brought the Ark into the Tent and hung the curtain to cover the Ark, just as the LORD commanded him.

²²Moses put the table in the Meeting Tent on the north side of the Holy Tent in front of the curtain. ²³Then he put the bread on the table before the LORD, just as the LORD commanded him. ²⁴Moses put the lampstand in the Meeting Tent on the south side of the Holy Tent across from the table. ²⁵Then he put the lamps on the lampstand before the LORD, just as the LORD commanded him.

²⁶Moses put the gold altar for burning incense in the Meeting Tent in front of the curtain. ²⁷Then he burned sweet-smelling incense on it, just as the LORD commanded him. ²⁸Then he hung the curtain at the entrance to the Holy Tent.

²⁹He put the altar for burnt offerings at the entrance to the Holy Tent, the Meeting Tent, and offered a whole burnt offering and grain offerings on it, just as the LORD commanded him. ³⁰Moses put the bowl between the Meeting Tent and the altar for burnt offerings, and he put water in it for washing. ³¹Moses, Aaron, and Aaron's sons used this water to wash their hands and feet. ³²They washed themselves every time they entered the Meeting Tent and every time they went near the altar for burnt offerings, just as the LORD commanded Moses.

³³Then Moses set up the courtyard around the Holy Tent and the altar, and he put up the curtain at the entry to the courtyard. So Moses finished the work.

THE CLOUD OVER THE HOLY TENT

³⁴Then the cloud covered the Meeting Tent, and the glory of the LORD filled the Holy Tent. ³⁵Moses could not enter the Meeting Tent, because the cloud had settled on it, and the glory of the LORD filled the Holy Tent.

³⁶When the cloud rose from the Holy Tent, the Israelites would begin to travel, ³⁷but as long as the cloud stayed on the Holy Tent, they did not travel. They stayed in that place until the cloud rose. ³⁸So the cloud of the LORD was over the Holy Tent during the day, and there was a fire in the cloud at night. So all the Israelites could see the cloud while they traveled.

leviticus

THE BURNT OFFERING

1 The LORD called to Moses and spoke to him from the Meeting Tent, saying, ²"Tell the people of Israel: 'When you bring an offering to the LORD, bring as your offering an animal from the herd or flock.

³"'If the offering is a whole burnt offering from the herd, it must be a male that has nothing wrong with it. The person must take the animal to the entrance of the Meeting Tent so that the LORD will accept the offering. ⁴He must put his hand on the animal's head, and the LORD will accept it to remove the person's sin so he will belong to God. ⁵He must kill the young bull before the LORD, and Aaron's sons, the priests, must bring its blood and sprinkle it on all sides of the altar at the entrance to the Meeting Tent. ⁶After that he will skin the animal and cut it into pieces. ⁷The priests, when they have put wood and fire on the altar, ⁸are to lay the head, the fat, and other pieces on the wood that is on the fire of the altar. ⁹The animal's inner organs and legs must be washed with water. Then the priest must burn all the animal's parts on the altar. It is a whole burnt offering, an offering made by fire, and its smell is pleasing to the LORD.

¹⁰"'If the burnt offering is a sheep or a goat from the flock, it must be a male that has nothing wrong with it. ¹¹The person must kill the animal on the north side of the altar before the LORD, and Aaron's sons, the priests, must sprinkle its blood on all sides of the altar. ¹²The person must cut the animal into pieces, and the priest must lay them, with the head and fat, on the wood that is on the fire of the altar. ¹³The person must wash the animal's inner organs and legs with water, and then the priest must burn all its parts on the altar. It is a whole burnt offering, an offering made by fire, and its smell is pleasing to the LORD.

¹⁴"'If the whole burnt offering for the LORD is a bird, it must be a dove or a young pigeon. ¹⁵The priest will bring it to the altar and pull off its head, which he will burn on the altar; the bird's blood must be drained out on the side of the altar. ¹⁶The priest must remove the bird's crop[n] and its contents and throw them on the east side of the altar, where the ashes are. ¹⁷Then he must tear the bird open by its wings without dividing it into two parts. He must burn the bird on the altar, on the wood which is on the fire. It is a whole burnt offering, an offering made by fire, and its smell is pleasing to the LORD.

THE GRAIN OFFERING

2 "'When anyone offers a grain offering to the LORD, it must be made from fine flour. The person must pour oil on it, put incense on it, ²and then take it to Aaron's sons, the priests. The priest must take a handful of the fine flour and oil and all the incense, and burn it on the altar as a memorial portion. It is an offering made by fire, and its smell is pleasing to the LORD. ³The rest of the grain offering will belong to Aaron and the priests; it is a most holy part of the offerings made by fire to the LORD.

⁴"'If you bring a grain offering that was baked in the oven, it must be made from fine flour. It may be loaves made without yeast and mixed with oil, or it may be wafers made without yeast that have oil poured over them. ⁵If your grain offering is cooked on a griddle, it must be made, without yeast, of fine flour mixed with oil. ⁶Crumble it and pour oil over it; it is a grain offering. ⁷If your grain offering is cooked in a pan, it must be made from fine flour and oil. ⁸Bring the grain offering made of these things to the LORD. Give it to the priest, and he will take it to the altar. ⁹He will take out the memorial portion from the grain offering and burn it on the altar, as an offering made by fire. Its smell is pleasing to the LORD. ¹⁰The rest of the grain offering belongs

---

1:16 crop A small bag inside a bird's throat. When a bird eats, its food goes into this part first. There, the food is made soft before it goes into the stomach.

to Aaron and the priests. It is a most holy part of the offerings made to the LORD by fire.

11 "'Every grain offering you bring to the LORD must be made without yeast, because you must not burn any yeast or honey in an offering made by fire to the LORD. 12You may bring yeast and honey to the LORD as an offering from the first harvest, but they must not be burned on the altar as a pleasing smell. 13You must also put salt on all your grain offerings. Salt stands for your agreement with God that will last forever; do not leave it out of your grain offering. You must add salt to all your offerings.

14 "'If you bring a grain offering from the first harvest to the LORD, bring crushed heads of new grain roasted in the fire. 15Put oil and incense on it; it is a grain offering. 16The priest will burn the memorial portion of the crushed grain and oil, with the incense on it. It is an offering by fire to the LORD.

THE FELLOWSHIP OFFERING

3 "If a person's fellowship offering to the LORD is from the herd, it may be a male or female, but it must have nothing wrong with it. 2The person must put his hand on the animal's head and kill it at the entrance to the Meeting Tent. Then Aaron's sons, the priests, must sprinkle the blood on all sides of the altar. 3From the fellowship offering he must make a sacrifice by fire to the LORD. He must offer the fat of the animal's inner organs (both the fat that is in them and that covers them), 4both kidneys with the fat that is on them near the lower back muscle, and the best part of the liver, which he will remove with the kidneys. 5Then the priests will burn these parts on the altar, on the whole burnt offering that is on the wood of the fire. It is an offering made by fire, and its smell is pleasing to the LORD.

6 "If a person's fellowship offering to the LORD is a lamb or a goat, it may be a male or female, but it must have nothing wrong with it. 7If he offers a lamb, he must bring it before the LORD 8and put his hand on its head. Then he must kill the animal in front of the Meeting Tent, and the priests must sprinkle its blood on all sides of the altar. 9From the fellowship offering the person must make a sacrifice by fire to the LORD. He must bring the fat, the whole fat tail cut off close to the backbone, the fat of the inner organs (both the fat that is in them and that covers them), 10both kidneys with the fat that is on them, near the lower back muscle, and the best part of the liver, which he will remove with the kidneys. 11Then the priest will burn these parts on the altar as food; it will be an offering made by fire to the LORD.

12 "If a person's offering is a goat, he must offer it before the LORD 13and put his hand on its head. Then he must kill it in front of the Meeting Tent, and the priests must sprinkle its blood on all sides of the altar. 14From this offering the person must make a sacrifice by fire to the LORD. He must offer all the fat of the goat's inner organs (both the fat that is in them and that covers them), 15both kidneys with the fat that is on them near the lower back muscle, and the best part of the liver, which he will remove with the kidneys. 16The priest will burn these parts on the altar as food. It is an offering made by fire, and its smell is pleasing to the LORD. All the fat belongs to the LORD.

17 "'This law will continue for people from now on, wherever you live: You must not eat any fat or blood.'"

THE SIN OFFERING

4 The LORD said to Moses, 2"Tell the people of Israel this: 'When a person sins by accident and does some things the LORD has commanded not to be done, that person must do these things:

3 "If the appointed priest sins so that he brings guilt on the people, then he must offer a young bull to the LORD, one that has nothing wrong with it, as a sin offering for the sin he has done. 4He will bring the bull to the entrance of the Meeting Tent in front of the LORD, put his hand on its head, and kill it before the LORD. 5Then the appointed priest must bring some of the bull's blood into the Meeting Tent. 6The priest is to dip his finger into the blood and sprinkle it seven times before the LORD in front of the curtain of the Most Holy Place. 7The priest must also put some of the blood on the corners of the altar of incense that stands before the LORD in the Meeting Tent. The rest of the blood he must pour out at the bottom of the altar of burnt offering, which is at the entrance of the Meeting Tent. 8He must remove all the

fat from the bull of the sin offering—the fat on and around the inner organs, 9both kidneys with the fat that is on them near the lower back muscle, and the best part of the liver which he will remove with the kidneys. 10(He must do this in the same way the fat is removed from the bull of the fellowship offering.) Then the priest must burn the animal parts on the altar of burnt offering. 11But the priest must carry off the skin of the bull and all its meat, along with the rest of the bull—its head, legs, intestines, and other inner organs. 12He must take it outside the camp to the special clean place where the ashes are poured out. He must burn it on a wood fire on the pile of ashes.

13"If the whole nation of Israel sins accidentally without knowing it and does something the LORD has commanded not to be done, they are guilty. 14When they learn about the sin they have done, they must offer a young bull as a sin offering and bring it before the Meeting Tent. 15The elders of the group of people must put their hands on the bull's head before the LORD, and it must be killed before the LORD. 16Then the appointed priest must bring some of the bull's blood into the Meeting Tent. 17Dipping his

---

FITNESS

WHEN YOUR WAY ISN'T GOD'S WAY

your estimated
transit time

LEVITICUS 3:17

Excessive obesity and the extremely high rates of malnutrition and disease among Americans are related less to "how much" food we eat than to "how processed" those foods are. It is the highly processed fast foods, prepared with an abundance of chemicals, additives, and preservatives not even allowed in other parts of the world—things that make up such a high percentage of the calories consumed by Americans—that cause us such problems.

Outside of America, meals are more often prepared fresh, from scratch, and with natural food, instead of convenience foods out of a box. Convenient, processed foods contain sugar-based and other types of additives that make food impossible to digest or to break down adequately. These foods, which aren't really food at all, stay in your system. The longer anything stays in your system, the more problems it will cause.

There is a digestive trait known as the ETT, which stands for the Estimated Transit Time. The longer it takes for food to get in and out of the system, the less healthy the diet is. Food should be eaten, broken down into its basic nutrients, utilized by the body, and quickly eliminated. The edible products created by God are high in fiber and water, the two elements necessary for a speedy and successful ETT. Processed, high fat foods that contain additives make for slow ETT.

reflect: Consider changing your diet to include more foods high in fiber and water.
Go to **Deuteronomy 10:14.**

finger in the blood, he must sprinkle it seven times before the Lord in front of the curtain. 18Then he must put some of the blood on the corners of the altar that is before the Lord in the Meeting Tent. The priest must pour out the rest of the blood at the bottom of the altar of burnt offering, which is at the entrance to the Meeting Tent. 19He must remove all the fat from the animal and burn it on the altar; 20he will do the same thing with this bull that he did with the first bull of the sin offering. In this way the priest removes the sins of the people so they will belong to the Lord and be forgiven. 21Then the priest must carry the bull outside the camp and burn it, just as he did with the first bull. This is the sin offering for the whole community.

22"If a ruler sins by accident and does something the Lord his God has commanded must not be done, he is guilty. 23When he learns about his sin, he must bring a male goat that has nothing wrong with it as his offering. 24The ruler must put his hand on the goat's head and kill it in the place where they kill the whole burnt offering before the Lord; it is a sin offering. 25The priest must take some of the blood of the sin offering on his finger and put it on the corners of the altar of burnt offering. He must pour out the rest of the blood at the bottom of the altar of burnt offering. 26He must burn all the goat's fat on the altar in the same way he burns the fat of the fellowship offerings. In this way the priest removes the ruler's sin so he belongs to the Lord, and the Lord will forgive him.

27"If any person in the community sins by accident and does something which the Lord has commanded must not be done, he is guilty. 28When the person learns about his sin, he must bring a female goat that has nothing wrong with it as an offering for his sin. 29He must put his hand on the animal's head and kill it at the place of the whole burnt offering. 30Then the priest must take some of the goat's blood on his finger and put it on the corners of the altar of burnt offering. He must pour out the rest of the goat's blood at the bottom of the altar. 31Then the priest must remove all the goat's fat in the same way the fat is removed from the fellowship offerings. He must burn it on the altar as a smell pleasing to the Lord. In this way the priest will remove that person's sin so he

will belong to the Lord, and the Lord will forgive him.

32"If this person brings a lamb as his offering for sin, he must bring a female that has nothing wrong with it. 33He must put his hand on the animal's head and kill it as a sin offering in the place where the whole burnt offering is killed. 34The priest must take some of the blood from the sin offering on his finger and put it on the corners of the altar of burnt offering. He must pour out the rest of the lamb's blood at the bottom of the altar. 35Then the priest must remove all the lamb's fat in the same way that the lamb's fat is removed from the fellowship offerings. He must burn the pieces on the altar on top of the offerings made by fire for the Lord. In this way the priest will remove that person's sins so he will belong to the Lord, and the Lord will forgive him.

SPECIAL TYPES OF ACCIDENTAL SINS

5 "If a person is ordered to tell in court what he has seen or what he knows and he does not tell the court, he is guilty of sin.

2"Or someone might touch something unclean, such as the dead body of an unclean wild animal or an unclean farm animal or an unclean crawling animal. Even if he does not know that he touched it, he will still be unclean and guilty of sin.

3"Someone might touch human uncleanness—anything that makes someone unclean—and not know it. But when he learns about it, he will be guilty.

4"Or someone might make a promise before the Lord without thinking. It might be a promise to do something bad or something good; it might be about anything. Even if he forgets about it, when he remembers, he will be guilty.

5"When anyone is guilty of any of these things, he must tell how he sinned. 6He must bring an offering to the Lord as a penalty for sin; it must be a female lamb or goat from the flock. The priest will perform the acts to remove that person's sin so he will belong to the Lord.

7"But if the person cannot afford a lamb, he must bring two doves or two young pigeons to the Lord as the penalty for his sin. One bird must be for a sin offering, and the other must be for a whole burnt offering. 8He must bring them to the priest, who will first offer the one for the sin offering. He will pull the bird's head from its neck, but he will not pull it completely off. 9He must sprinkle the blood from the sin offering on the side of the altar, and then he must pour the rest of the blood at the bottom of the altar; it is a sin offering. 10Then the priest must offer the second bird as a whole burnt offering, as the law says. In this way the priest will remove the person's sin so he will belong to the LORD, and the LORD will forgive him.

11"'If the person cannot afford two doves or two pigeons, he must bring about two quarts of fine flour as an offering for sin. He must not put oil or incense on the flour, because it is a sin offering. 12He must bring the flour to the priest. The priest will take a handful of the flour as a memorial offering and burn it on the altar on top of the offerings made by fire to the LORD; it is a sin offering. 13In this way the priest will remove the person's sins so he will belong to the LORD, and the LORD will forgive him. What is left of the sin offering belongs to the priest, like the grain offering.'"

THE PENALTY OFFERING

14The LORD said to Moses, 15"If a person accidentally sins and does something against the holy things of the LORD, he must bring from the flock a male sheep that has nothing wrong with it. This will be his penalty offering to the LORD. Its value in silver must be correct as set by the Holy Place measure. It is a penalty offering. 16That person must pay for the sin he did against the holy thing, adding one-fifth to its value. Then he must give it all to the priest. In this way the priest will remove the person's sin so he will belong to the LORD, by using the male sheep as the penalty offering. And the LORD will forgive the person.

17"If a person sins and does something the LORD has commanded not to be done, even if he does not know it, he is still guilty. He is responsible for his sin. 18He must bring the priest a male sheep from the flock, one that has nothing wrong with it and that is worth the correct amount. It will be a penalty offering. Though the person sinned without knowing it, with this offering the priest will remove the sin so the person will belong to

the LORD, and the LORD will forgive him. 19The person is guilty of doing wrong, so he must give the penalty offering to the LORD."

6 The LORD said to Moses, 2"A person might sin against the LORD by doing one of these sins: He might lie about what happened to something he was taking care of for someone else, or he might lie about a promise he made. He might steal something or cheat someone. 3He might find something that had been lost and then lie about it. He might make a promise before the LORD about something and not mean it, or he might do some other sin. 4If he does any of these things, he is guilty of sin. He must bring back whatever he stole or whatever he took by cheating. He must bring back the thing he took care of for someone else. He must bring back what he found and lied about 5or what he made a false promise about. He must pay the full price plus an extra one-fifth of the value of what he took. He must give the money to the true owner on the day he brings his penalty offering. 6He must bring his penalty to the priest—a male sheep from the flock, one that does not have anything wrong with it and that is worth the correct amount. It will be a penalty offering to the LORD. 7Then the priest will perform the acts to remove that person's sin so he will belong to the LORD, and the LORD will forgive him for the sins that made him guilty."

THE WHOLE BURNT OFFERING

8The LORD said to Moses, 9"Give this command to Aaron and the priests: 'These are the teachings about the whole burnt offering: The burnt offering must stay on the altar all night until morning, and the altar's fire must be kept burning. 10The priest must put on his linen robe and linen underclothes next to his body. Then he will remove the ashes from the burnt offering on the altar and put them beside the altar. 11Then he must take off those clothes and put on others and carry the ashes outside the camp to a special clean place. 12But the fire must be kept burning on the altar; it must not be allowed to go out. The priest must put more firewood on the altar every morning, place the whole burnt offering on the fire, and burn the fat of the fellowship offerings. 13The fire must be kept burning on the altar all the time; it must not go out.

THE GRAIN OFFERING

14 " 'These are the teachings about the grain offering: The priests must bring it to the LORD in front of the altar. 15 The priest must take a handful of fine flour, with the oil and all of the incense on it, and burn the grain offering on the altar as a memorial offering to the LORD. Its smell is pleasing to him. 16 Aaron and the priests may eat what is left, but it must be eaten without yeast in a holy place. They must eat it in the courtyard of the Meeting Tent. 17 It must not be cooked with yeast. I have given it as their share of the offerings made to me by fire; it is most holy, like the sin offering and the penalty offering. 18 Any male descendant of Aaron may eat it as his share of the offerings made to the LORD by fire, and this will continue from now on. Whatever touches these offerings shall become holy.' "

19 The LORD said to Moses, 20 "This is the offering Aaron and the priests must bring to the LORD on the day they appoint Aaron as high priest: They must bring two quarts of fine flour for a continual grain offering, half of it in the morning and half in the evening. 21 The fine flour must be mixed with oil and cooked on a griddle. Bring it when it is well mixed. Present the grain offering that is broken into pieces, and it will be a smell that is pleasing to the LORD. 22 One of the priests appointed to take Aaron's place as high priest must make the grain offering. It is a rule forever that the grain offering must be completely burned to the LORD. 23 Every grain offering made by a priest must be completely burned; it must not be eaten."

THE SIN OFFERING

24 The LORD said to Moses, 25 "Tell Aaron and the priests: 'These are the teachings about the sin offering: The sin offering must be killed in front of the LORD in the same place the whole burnt offering is killed; it is most holy. 26 The priest who offers the sin offering must eat it in a holy place, in the courtyard of the Meeting Tent. 27 Whatever touches the meat of the sin offering must be holy, and if the blood is sprinkled on any clothes, you must wash them in a holy place. 28 The clay pot the meat is cooked in must be broken, or if a bronze pot is used, it must be scrubbed and rinsed with water. 29 Any male

in a priest's family may eat the offering; it is most holy. 30 But if the blood of the sin offering is taken into the Meeting Tent and used to remove sin in the Holy Place, that sin offering must be burned with fire. It must not be eaten.

THE PENALTY OFFERING

7 " 'These are the teachings about the penalty offering, which is most holy: 2 The penalty offering must be killed where the whole burnt offering is killed. Then the priest must sprinkle its blood on all sides of the altar. 3 He must offer all the fat from the penalty offering—the fat tail, the fat that covers the inner organs, 4 both kidneys with the fat that is on them near the lower back muscle, and the best part of the liver, which is to be removed with the kidneys. 5 The priest must burn all these things on the altar as an offering made by fire to the LORD. It is a penalty offering. 6 Any male in a priest's family may eat it. It is most holy, so it must be eaten in a holy place.

7 " 'The penalty offering is like the sin offering in that the teachings are the same for both. The priest who offers the sacrifice to remove sins will get the meat for food. 8 The priest who offers the burnt offering may also have the skin from it. 9 Every grain offering that is baked in an oven, cooked on a griddle, or baked in a dish belongs to the priest who offers it. 10 Every grain offering, either dry or mixed with oil, belongs to the priests, and all priests will share alike.

THE FELLOWSHIP OFFERING

11 " 'These are the teachings about the fellowship offering a person may offer to the LORD: 12 If he brings the fellowship offering to show his thanks, he should also bring loaves of bread made without yeast that are mixed with oil, wafers made without yeast that have oil poured over them, and loaves of fine flour that are mixed with oil. 13 He must also offer loaves of bread made with yeast along with his fellowship offering, which he gives to show thanks. 14 One of each kind of offering will be for the LORD; it will be given to the priest who sprinkles the blood of the fellowship offering. 15 When the fellowship offering is given to thank the LORD, the meat from it must be eaten the same day it is offered; none of it must be left until morning.

16"'If a person brings a fellowship offering just to give a gift to God or because of a special promise to him, the sacrifice should be eaten the same day he offers it. If there is any left, it may be eaten the next day. 17If any meat from this sacrifice is left on the third day, it must be burned up. 18Any meat of the fellowship offering eaten on the third day will not be accepted, nor will the sacrifice count for the person who offered it. It will become unclean, and anyone who eats the meat will be guilty of sin.

19"'People must not eat meat that touches anything unclean; they must burn this meat with fire. Anyone who is clean may eat other meat. 20But if anyone is unclean and eats the meat from the fellowship offering that belongs to the LORD, he must be cut off from his people.

21"'If anyone touches something unclean—uncleanness that comes from people, from an animal, or from some hated thing—touching it will make him unclean. If he then eats meat from the fellowship offering that belongs to the LORD, he must be cut off from his people.'"

22The LORD said to Moses, 23"Tell the people of Israel: 'You must not eat any of the fat from cattle, sheep, or goats. 24If an animal is found dead or torn by wild animals, you may use its fat for other things, but you must not eat it. 25If someone eats fat from an animal offering made by fire to the LORD, he must be cut off from his people. 26No matter where you live, you must not eat blood from any bird or animal. 27Anyone who eats blood must be cut off from his people.'"

THE PRIESTS' SHARE

28The LORD said to Moses, 29"Tell the people of Israel: 'If someone brings a fellowship offering to the LORD, he must give part of it as his sacrifice to the LORD. 30He must carry that part of the gift in his own hands as an offering made by fire to the LORD. He must bring the fat and the breast of the animal to the priest, to be presented to the LORD as the priests' share. 31Then the priest must burn the fat on the altar, but the breast of the animal will belong to Aaron and the priests. 32You must also give the right thigh from the fellowship offering to the priest as a gift; 33it will belong to the priest who offers the blood

and fat of the fellowship offering. 34I have taken the breast and the thigh from the fellowship offerings of the Israelites, and I have given these parts to Aaron and the priests as their share for all time from the Israelites.'"

35This is the portion that belongs to Aaron and his sons from the offerings made by fire to the LORD. They were given this share on the day they were presented to the LORD as priests. 36On the day the LORD appointed the priests, he commanded Israel to give this share to them, and it is to be given to the priests as their share from now on.

37These are the teachings about the whole burnt offering, the grain offering, the sin offering, the penalty offering, the offering for the appointment of priests, and the fellowship offering. 38The LORD gave these teachings to Moses on Mount Sinai on the day he commanded the Israelites to bring their offerings to the LORD in the Sinai Desert.

AARON AND HIS SONS APPOINTED

8 The LORD said to Moses, 2"Bring Aaron and his sons and their clothes, the special olive oil used in appointing people and things to the service of the LORD, the bull of the sin offering and the two male sheep, and the basket of bread made without yeast. 3Then gather the people together at the entrance to the Meeting Tent." 4Moses did as the LORD commanded him, and the people met together at the entrance to the Meeting Tent.

5Then Moses spoke to the people and said, "This is what the LORD has commanded to be done." 6Bringing Aaron and his sons forward, Moses washed them with water. 7He put the inner robe on Aaron and tied the cloth belt around him. Then Moses put the outer robe on him and placed the holy vest on him. He tied the skillfully woven belt around him so that the holy vest was tied to Aaron. 8Then Moses put the chest covering on him and put the Urim and the Thummim in the chest covering. 9He also put the turban on Aaron's head. He put the strip of gold, the holy crown, on the front of the turban, as the LORD commanded him to do.

10Then Moses put the special oil on the Holy Tent and everything in it, making them holy for the LORD. 11He sprinkled some oil on the altar seven times, sprinkling the altar and all its tools and the large bowl and its base. In this way he made them holy for the LORD. 12He poured some of the special oil on Aaron's head to make Aaron holy for the LORD. 13Then Moses brought Aaron's sons forward. He put the inner robes on them, tied cloth belts around them, and put headbands on them, as the LORD had commanded him.

14Then Moses brought the bull for the sin offering, and Aaron and his sons put their hands on its head. 15Moses killed the bull, took the blood, and with his finger put some of it on all the corners of the altar, to make it pure. Then he poured out the rest of the blood at the bottom of the altar. In this way he made it holy and ready for service to God. 16Moses took all the fat from the inner organs of the bull, the best part of the liver, and both kidneys with the fat that is on them, and he burned them on the altar. 17But he took the bull's skin, its meat, and its intestines and burned them in a fire outside the camp, as the LORD had commanded him.

18Next Moses brought the male sheep of the burnt offering, and Aaron and his sons put their hands on its head. 19Then Moses killed it and sprinkled the blood on all sides of the altar. 20He cut the male sheep into pieces and burned the head, the pieces, and the fat. 21He washed the inner organs and legs with water and burned the whole sheep on the altar as a burnt offering made by fire to the LORD; its smell was pleasing to the LORD. Moses did these things as the LORD had commanded him.

22Then Moses brought the other male sheep, the one used in appointing Aaron and his sons as priests, and Aaron and his sons put their hands on its head. 23Then Moses killed the sheep and put some of its blood on the bottom of Aaron's right ear, some on the thumb of Aaron's right hand, and some on the big toe of his right foot. 24Then Moses brought Aaron's sons close to the altar. He put some of the blood on the bottom of their right ears, some on the thumbs of their right hands, and some on the big toes of their right feet. Then he sprinkled blood on all sides of the altar. 25He took the fat, the fat tail, all the fat on the inner organs, the best part of the liver, both kidneys with their fat, and the right thigh. 26From the basket of bread made without yeast that is put before the LORD each day, Moses took a loaf of bread, a loaf made with

oil, and a wafer. He put these pieces of bread on the fat and right thigh of the male sheep. 27All these things he put in the hands of Aaron and his sons and presented them as an offering before the LORD. 28Then Moses took them from their hands and burned them on the altar on top of the burnt offering. So this was the offering for appointing Aaron and his sons as priests. It was an offering made by fire to the LORD, and its smell was pleasing to him. 29Moses also took the breast and presented it as an offering before the LORD. It was Moses' share of the male sheep used in appointing the priests, as the LORD had commanded him.

30Moses took some of the special oil and some of the blood which was on the altar, and he sprinkled them on Aaron and Aaron's clothes and on Aaron's sons and their clothes. In this way Moses made Aaron, his clothes, his sons, and their clothes holy for the LORD.

31Then Moses said to Aaron and his sons, "I gave you a command, saying, 'Aaron and his sons will eat these things.' So take the meat and basket of bread from the offering for appointing priests. Boil the meat at the door of the Meeting Tent, and eat it there with the bread. 32If any of the meat or bread is left, burn it. 33The time of appointing will last seven days; you must not go outside the entrance of the Meeting Tent until that time is up. Stay there until the time of your appointing is finished. 34The LORD commanded the things that were done today to remove your sins so you will belong to him. 35You must stay at the entrance of the Meeting Tent day and night for seven days. If you don't obey the LORD's commands, you will die. The LORD has given me these commands."

36So Aaron and his sons did everything the LORD had commanded through Moses.

AARON AND HIS SONS OFFER SACRIFICES

9 On the eighth day after the time of appointing, Moses called for Aaron and his sons and for the elders of Israel. 2He said to Aaron, "Take a bull calf and a male sheep that have nothing wrong with them, and offer them to the LORD. The calf will be a sin offering, and the male sheep will be a whole burnt offering. 3Tell the people of Israel, 'Take a male goat for a sin offering and a calf and a lamb for a whole burnt offering;

each must be one year old, and it must have nothing wrong with it. ⁴Also take a bull and a male sheep for fellowship offerings, along with a grain offering mixed with oil. Offer all these things to the LORD, because the LORD will appear to you today.'"

⁵So all the people came to the front of the Meeting Tent, bringing the things Moses had commanded them to bring, and they stood before the LORD. ⁶Moses said, "You have done what the LORD commanded, so you will see the LORD's glory."

⁷Then Moses told Aaron, "Go to the altar and offer sin offerings and whole burnt offerings. Do this to remove your sins and the people's sins so you will belong to God. Offer the sacrifices for the people and perform the acts to remove their sins for them so they will belong to the LORD, as the LORD has commanded."

⁸So Aaron went to the altar and killed the bull calf as a sin offering for himself. ⁹Then his sons brought the blood to him, and he dipped his finger in the blood and put it on the corners of the altar. He poured out the rest of the blood at the bottom of the altar. ¹⁰Aaron took the fat, the kidneys, and the best part of the liver from the sin offering and burned them on the altar, in the way the LORD had commanded Moses. ¹¹The meat and skin he burned outside the camp.

¹²Then Aaron killed the animal for the whole burnt offering. His sons brought the blood to him, and he sprinkled it on all sides of the altar. ¹³As they gave him the pieces and head of the burnt offering, Aaron burned them on the altar. ¹⁴He also washed the inner organs and the legs of the burnt offering and burned them on top of the burnt offering on the altar.

¹⁵Then Aaron brought the offering that was for the people. He took the goat of the people's sin offering and killed it and offered it for the sin offering, just as he had done the first sin offering.

¹⁶Then Aaron brought the whole burnt offering and offered it in the way that the LORD had commanded. ¹⁷He also brought the grain offering to the altar. He took a handful of the grain and burned it on the altar, in addition to the morning's burnt offering.

¹⁸Aaron also killed the bull and the male sheep as the fellowship offerings for the people. His sons brought him the blood, and he sprinkled it on all sides of the altar. ¹⁹Aaron's sons also brought to Aaron the fat of the bull and the male sheep—the fat tail, the fat covering the inner organs, the kidneys, and the best part of the liver. ²⁰Aaron's sons put them on the breasts of the bull and the sheep. Then Aaron burned these fat parts on the altar. ²¹He presented the breasts and the right thigh before the LORD as the priests' share of the offering, as Moses had commanded.

²²Then Aaron lifted his hands toward the people and blessed them. When he had finished offering the sin offering, the burnt offering, and the fellowship offering, he stepped down from the altar.

²³Moses and Aaron went into the Meeting Tent. Then they came out and blessed the people, and the LORD's glory came to all the people. ²⁴Fire came out from the LORD and burned up the burnt offering and fat on the altar. When the people saw this, they shouted with joy and bowed facedown on the ground.

GOD DESTROYS NADAB AND ABIHU

10 Aaron's sons Nadab and Abihu took their pans for burning incense, put fire in them, and added incense; but they did not use the special fire Moses had commanded them to use in the presence of the LORD. ²So fire came down from the LORD and destroyed Nadab and Abihu, and they died in front of the LORD. ³Then Moses said to Aaron, "This is what the LORD was speaking about when he said,

'I must be respected as holy
    by those who come near me;
before all the people
    I must be given honor.'"

So Aaron did not say anything about the death of his sons.

⁴Aaron's uncle Uzziel had two sons named Mishael and Elzaphan. Moses said to them, "Come here and pick up your cousins' bodies. Carry them outside the camp away from the front of the Holy Place." ⁵So Mishael and Elzaphan obeyed Moses and carried the bodies of Nadab and Abihu, still clothed in the special priest's inner robes, outside the camp.

⁶Then Moses said to Aaron and his other sons, Eleazar and Ithamar, "Don't show sad-

ness by tearing your clothes or leaving your hair uncombed. If you do, you will die, and the LORD will be angry with all the people. All the people of Israel, your relatives, may cry loudly about the LORD burning Nadab and Abihu, 7but you must not even leave the Meeting Tent. If you go out of the entrance, you will die, because the LORD has appointed you to his service." So Aaron, Eleazar, and Ithamar obeyed Moses.

8Then the LORD said to Aaron, 9"You and your sons must not drink wine or beer when you go into the Meeting Tent. If you do, you will die. This law will continue from now on. 10You must keep what is holy separate from what is not holy; you must keep what is clean separate from what is unclean. 11You must teach the people all the laws that the LORD gave to them through Moses."

12Moses said to Aaron and his remaining sons, Eleazar and Ithamar, "Eat the part of the grain offering that is left from the sacrifices offered by fire to the LORD, but do not add yeast to it. Eat it near the altar because it is most holy. 13You must eat it in a holy place, because this part of the offerings made by fire to the LORD belongs to you and your sons. I have been commanded to tell you this.

14"Also, you and your sons and daughters may eat the breast and thigh of the fellowship offering that was presented to the LORD. You must eat them in a clean place; they are your share of the fellowship offerings given by the Israelites. 15The people must bring the fat from their animals that was part of the offering made by fire, and they must present it to the LORD along with the thigh and the breast of the fellowship offering. They will be the regular share of the offerings for you and your children, as the LORD has commanded."

16Moses looked for the goat of the sin offering, but it had already been burned up. So he became very angry with Eleazar and Ithamar, Aaron's remaining sons. He said, 17"Why didn't you eat that goat in a holy place? It is most holy, and the LORD gave it to you to take away the guilt of the people, to remove their sins so they will belong to the LORD. 18You didn't bring the goat's blood inside the Holy Place. You were supposed to eat the goat in a holy place, as I commanded!"

19But Aaron said to Moses, "Today they brought their sin offering and burnt offering before the LORD, but these terrible things have still happened to me! Do you think the LORD would be any happier if I ate the sin offering today?" 20When Moses heard this, he was satisfied.

RULES ABOUT WHAT MAY BE EATEN

11 The LORD said to Moses and Aaron, 2"Tell the Israelites this: 'These are the land animals you may eat: 3You may eat any animal that has split hoofs completely divided and that chews the cud.

4"'Some animals only chew the cud or only have split hoofs, and you must not eat them. The camel chews the cud but does not have a split hoof; it is unclean for you. 5The rock badger chews the cud but does not have a split hoof; it is unclean for you. 6The rabbit chews the cud but does not have a split hoof; it is unclean for you. 7Now the pig has a split hoof that is completely divided, but it does not chew the cud; it is unclean for you. 8You must not eat the meat from these animals or even touch their dead bodies; they are unclean for you.

9"'Of the animals that live in the sea or in a river, if the animal has fins and scales, you may eat it. 10But whatever lives in the sea or in a river and does not have fins and scales—including the things that fill the water and all other things that live in it—you should hate. 11You must not eat any meat from them or even touch their dead bodies, because you should hate them. 12You must hate any animal in the water that does not have fins and scales.

13"'Also, these are the birds you are to hate. They are hateful and should not be eaten. You must not eat eagles, vultures, black vultures, 14kites, any kind of falcon, 15any kind of raven, 16horned owls, screech owls, sea gulls, any kind of hawk, 17little owls, cormorants, great owls, 18white owls, desert owls, ospreys, 19storks, any kind of heron, hoopoes, or bats.

20"'Don't eat insects that have wings and walk on all four feet; they also are to be hated.

21"'But you may eat certain insects that have wings and walk on four feet. You may eat those that have legs with joints above their feet so they can jump. 22These are the insects you may eat: all kinds of locusts, winged locusts, crickets, and grasshoppers. 23But all other insects that have wings and walk on four feet you are to hate. 24Those insects will make you unclean, and anyone who touches the dead body of one of these insects will become unclean until evening. 25Anyone who picks up one of these dead insects must wash his clothes and be unclean until evening.

26"Some animals have split hoofs, but the hoofs are not completely divided; others do not chew the cud. They are unclean for you, and anyone who touches the dead body of one of these animals will become unclean. 27Of all the animals that walk on four feet, the animals that walk on their paws are unclean for you. Anyone who touches the dead body of one of these animals will become unclean until evening. 28Anyone who picks up their dead bodies must wash his clothes and be unclean until evening; these animals are unclean for you.

29"These crawling animals are unclean for you: moles, rats, all kinds of great lizards, 30geckos, crocodiles, lizards, sand reptiles, and chameleons. 31These crawling animals are unclean for you; anyone who touches their dead bodies will be unclean until evening.

32"If an unclean animal dies and falls on something, that item will also become unclean. This includes anything made from wood, cloth, leather, or rough cloth, regardless of its use. Whatever the animal falls on must be washed with water and be unclean until evening; then it will become clean again. 33If the dead, unclean animal falls into a clay bowl, anything in the bowl will become unclean, and you must break the bowl. 34If water from the unclean clay bowl gets on any food, that food will become unclean. 35If any dead, unclean animal falls on something, it becomes unclean. If it is a clay oven or a clay baking pan, it must be broken into pieces. These things will be unclean; they are unclean for you.

36"A spring or well that collects water will stay clean, but anyone who touches the dead body of any unclean animal will become unclean. 37If a dead, unclean animal falls on a seed to be planted, that seed is still clean. 38But if you put water on some seeds and a dead, unclean animal falls on them, they are unclean for you.

39"Also, if an animal which you use for food dies, anyone who touches its body will be unclean until evening. 40Anyone who eats meat from this animal's dead body must wash his clothes and be unclean until evening. Anyone who picks up the animal's dead body must wash his clothes and be unclean until evening.

41"Every animal that crawls on the ground is to be hated; it must not be eaten. 42You must not eat any of the animals that crawl on the ground, including those that crawl on their stomachs, that walk on all four feet, or on many feet. They are to be hated. 43Do not make yourself unclean by these animals; you must not become unclean by them. 44I am the LORD your God. Keep yourselves holy for me because I am holy. Don't make yourselves unclean with any of these crawling animals. 45I am the LORD who brought you out of Egypt to be your God; you must be holy because I am holy.

46"These are the teachings about all of the cattle, birds, and other animals on earth, as well as the animals in the sea and those that crawl on the ground. 47These teachings help people know the difference between unclean animals and clean animals; they help people know which animals may be eaten and which ones must not be eaten.'"

RULES FOR NEW MOTHERS

12 The LORD said to Moses, 2"Tell the people of Israel this: 'If a woman gives birth to a son, she will become unclean for seven days, as she is unclean during her monthly period. 3On the eighth day the boy must be circumcised. 4Then it will be thirty-three days before she becomes clean from her loss of blood. She must not touch anything that is holy or enter the Holy Tent until her time of cleansing is finished. 5But if she gives birth to a daughter, the mother will be unclean for two weeks, as she is unclean during her monthly period. It will be sixty-six days before she becomes clean from her loss of blood.

6"After she has a son or daughter and her days of cleansing are over, the new mother must bring certain sacrifices to the Meeting Tent. She must give the priest at the entrance a year-old lamb for a burnt offering and a dove or young pigeon for a sin offering. [7]He will offer them before the LORD to make her clean so she will belong to the LORD again; then she will be clean from her loss of blood. These are the teachings for a woman who gives birth to a boy or girl.

[8] 'If she cannot afford a lamb, she is to bring two doves or two young pigeons, one for a burnt offering and one for a sin offering. In this way the priest will make her clean so she will belong to the LORD again, and she will be clean.'"

RULES ABOUT SKIN DISEASES

13 The LORD said to Moses and Aaron, [2]"Someone might have on his skin a swelling or a rash or a bright spot. If the sore looks like a harmful skin disease, the person must be brought to Aaron the priest or to one of Aaron's sons, the priests. [3]The priest must look at the sore on the person's skin. If the hair in the sore has become white, and the sore seems deeper than the person's skin, it is a harmful skin disease. When he has finished looking at the person, the priest must announce that the person is unclean.

[4]"If there is a white spot on a person's skin, but the spot does not seem deeper than the skin, and if the hair from the spot has not turned white, the priest must separate that person from other people for seven days. [5]On the seventh day the priest must look at the person again. If he sees that the sore has not changed and it has not spread on the skin, the priest must keep the person separated for seven more days. [6]On the seventh day the priest must look at the person again. If the sore has faded and has not spread on the skin, the priest must announce that the person is clean. The sore is only a rash. The person must wash his clothes, and he will become clean again.

[7]"But if the rash spreads again after the priest has announced him clean, the person must come again to the priest. [8]The priest must look at him, and if the rash has spread on the skin, the priest must announce that the person is unclean; it is a harmful skin disease.

[9]"If a person has a harmful skin disease, he must be brought to the priest, [10]and the priest must look at him. If there is a white swelling in the skin, and the hair has become white, and the skin looks raw in the swelling, [11]it is a harmful skin disease. It is one he has had for a long time. The priest must announce that the person is unclean. He will not need to separate that person from other people, because everyone already knows that the person is unclean.

[12]"If the skin disease spreads all over a person's body, covering his skin from his head to his feet, as far as the priest can see, the priest must look at the person's whole body. [13]If the priest sees that the disease covers the whole body and has turned all of the person's skin white, he must announce that the person is clean.

[14]"But when the person has an open sore, he is unclean. [15]When the priest sees the open sore, he must announce that the person is unclean. The open sore is not clean; it is a harmful skin disease. [16]If the open sore becomes white again, the person must come to the priest. [17]The priest must look at him, and if the sores have become white, the priest must announce that the person with the sores is clean. Then he will be clean.

[18]"Someone may have a boil on his skin that is healed. [19]If in the place where the boil was, there is a white swelling or a bright red spot, this place on the skin must be shown to the priest. [20]And the priest must look at it. If the spot seems deeper than the skin and the hair on it has become white, the priest must announce that the person is unclean. The spot is a harmful skin disease that has broken out from inside the boil. [21]But if the priest looks at the spot and there are no white hairs in it and the spot is not deeper than the skin and it has faded, the priest must separate the person from other people for seven days. [22]If the spot spreads on the skin, the priest must announce that the person is unclean; it is a disease that will spread. [23]But if the bright spot does not spread or change, it is only the scar from the old boil. Then the priest must announce that the person is clean.

[24]"When a person gets a burn on his skin, if the open sore becomes white or red, [25]the priest must look at it. If the white spot seems deeper than the skin and the hair at that spot has become white, it is a harmful skin disease. The disease has broken out in the burn, and the priest must announce that the person

is unclean. It is a harmful skin disease. 26But if the priest looks at the spot and there is no white hair in the bright spot, and the spot is no deeper than the skin and has faded, the priest must separate the person from other people for seven days. 27On the seventh day the priest must look at him again. If the spot has spread on the skin, the priest must announce that the person is unclean. It is a harmful skin disease. 28But if the bright spot has not spread on the skin but has faded, it is the swelling from the burn. The priest must announce that the person is clean, because the spot is only a scar from the burn.

29"When a man or a woman gets a sore on the scalp or on the chin, 30a priest must look at the sore. If it seems deeper than the skin and the hair around it is thin and yellow, the priest must announce that the person is unclean. It is an itch, a harmful skin disease of the head or chin. 31But if the priest looks at it and it does not seem deeper than the skin and there is no black hair in it, the priest must separate the person from other people for seven days. 32On the seventh day the priest must look at the sore. If it has not spread, and there are no yellow hairs growing in it, and the sore does not seem deeper than the skin, 33the person must shave himself, but he must not shave the sore place. The priest must separate that person from other people for seven more days. 34On the seventh day the priest must look at the sore. If it has not spread on the skin and it does not seem deeper than the skin, the priest must announce that the person is clean. So the person must wash his clothes and become clean. 35But if the sore spreads on the skin after the person has become clean, 36the priest must look at him again. If the sore has spread on the skin, the priest doesn't need to look for the yellowish hair; the person is unclean. 37But if the priest thinks the sore has stopped spreading, and black hair is growing in it, the sore has healed. The person is clean, and the priest must announce that he is clean.

38"When a man or a woman has white spots on the skin, 39a priest must look at them. If the spots on the skin are dull white, the disease is only a harmless rash. That person is clean.

40"When anyone loses hair from his head and is bald, he is clean. 41If he loses hair from the front of his head and has a bald forehead, he is clean. 42But if there is a red-white sore on his bald head or forehead, it is a skin disease breaking out in those places. 43A priest must look at that person. If the swelling of the sore on his bald head or forehead is red-white, like a skin disease that spreads, 44that person has a skin disease. He is unclean. The priest must announce that the person is unclean because of the sore on his head.

45"If a person has a skin disease that spreads, he must warn other people by shouting, 'Unclean, unclean!' His clothes must be torn at the seams, he must let his hair stay uncombed, and he must cover his mouth. 46That person will be unclean the whole time he has the disease; he is unclean. He must live alone outside the camp.

RULES ABOUT MILDEW

47"Clothing might have mildew on it. It might be clothing made of linen or wool 48(either woven or knitted), or of leather, or something made from leather. 49If the mildew in the clothing, leather, or woven or knitted material is green or red, it is a spreading mildew. It must be shown to the priest. 50The priest must look at the mildew, and he must put that piece of clothing in a separate place for seven days. 51On the seventh day he must look at the mildew again. If the mildew has spread on the cloth (either woven or knitted) or the leather, no matter what the leather was used for, it is a mildew that destroys; it is unclean. 52The priest must burn the clothing. It does not matter if it is woven or knitted, wool or linen, or made of leather, because the mildew is spreading. It must be burned.

53"If the priest sees that the mildew has not spread in the cloth (either knitted or woven) or leather, 54he must order the people to wash that piece of leather or cloth. Then he must separate the clothing for seven more days. 55After the piece with the mildew has been washed, the priest must look at it again. If the mildew still looks the same, the piece is unclean, even if the mildew has not spread. You must burn it in fire; it does not matter if the mildew is on one side or the other.

56"But when the priest looks at that piece of leather or cloth, the mildew might have faded after the piece has been washed. Then the priest must tear the mildew out of the piece of leather or cloth (either woven or knitted). ⁵⁷But if the mildew comes back to that piece of leather or cloth (either woven or knitted), the mildew is spreading. And whatever has the mildew must be burned with fire. ⁵⁸When the cloth (either woven or knitted) or the leather is washed and the mildew is gone, it must be washed again; then it will be clean.

⁵⁹"These are the teachings about mildew on pieces of cloth (either woven or knitted) or leather, to decide if they are clean or unclean."

RULES FOR CLEANSING FROM SKIN DISEASES

14 The LORD said to Moses, ²"These are the teachings for the time at which people who had a harmful skin disease are made clean.

"The person shall be brought to the priest, ³and the priest must go outside the camp and look at the one who had the skin disease. If the skin disease is healed, ⁴the priest will command that two living, clean birds, a piece of cedar wood, a piece of red string, and a hyssop plant be brought for cleansing the person with the skin disease.

⁵"The priest must order one bird to be killed in a clay bowl containing fresh water. ⁶Then he will take the living bird, the piece of cedar wood, the red string, and the hyssop; all these he will dip into the blood of the bird that was killed over the fresh water. ⁷The priest will sprinkle the blood seven times on the person being cleansed from the skin disease. He must announce that the person is clean and then go to an open field and let the living bird go free.

⁸"The person to be cleansed must wash his clothes, shave off all his hair, and bathe in water. Then he will be clean and may go into the camp, though he must stay outside his tent for the first seven days. ⁹On the seventh day he must shave off all his hair—the hair from his head, his beard, his eyebrows, and the rest of his hair. He must wash his clothes and bathe his body in water, and he will be clean.

¹⁰"On the eighth day the person who had the skin disease must take two male lambs that have nothing wrong with them and a year-old female lamb that has nothing wrong with it. He must also take six quarts of fine flour mixed with oil for a grain offering and two-thirds of a pint of olive oil. ¹¹The priest who is to announce that the person is clean must bring him and his sacrifices before the LORD at the entrance of the Meeting Tent. ¹²The priest will take one of the male lambs and offer it with the olive oil as a penalty offering; he will present them before the LORD as an offering. ¹³Then he will kill the male lamb in the holy place, where the sin offering and the whole burnt offering are killed. The penalty offering is like the sin offering—it belongs to the priest and it is most holy.

¹⁴"The priest will take some of the blood of the penalty offering and put it on the bottom of the right ear of the person to be made clean. He will also put some of it on the thumb of the person's right hand and on the big toe of the person's right foot. ¹⁵Then the priest will take some of the oil and pour it into his own left hand. ¹⁶He will dip a finger of his right hand into the oil that is in his left hand, and with his finger he will sprinkle some of the oil seven times before the LORD. ¹⁷The priest will put some oil from his hand on the bottom of the right ear of the person to be made clean, some on the thumb of the person's right hand, and some on the big toe of the person's right foot. The oil will go on these places on top of the blood for the penalty offering. ¹⁸He will put the rest of the oil that is in his left hand on the head of the person to be made clean. In this way the priest will make that person clean so he can belong to the LORD again.

¹⁹"Next the priest will offer the sin offering to make that person clean so he can belong to the LORD again. After this the priest will kill the animal for the whole burnt offering, ²⁰and he will offer the burnt offering and grain offering on the altar. In this way he will make that person clean so he can belong to the LORD again.

²¹"But if the person is poor and unable to afford these offerings, he must take one male lamb for a penalty offering. It will be presented to the LORD to make him clean so he can belong to the LORD again. The person must also take two quarts of fine flour mixed with oil for a grain offering. He must also take two-thirds of a pint of olive oil ²²and two doves or two young pigeons, which he can afford. One bird is for a sin offering and

the other for a whole burnt offering. ²³On the eighth day the person will bring them for his cleansing to the priest at the entrance of the Meeting Tent, before the Lord. ²⁴The priest will take the lamb for the penalty offering and the oil, and he will present them as an offering before the Lord. ²⁵Then he will kill the lamb of the penalty offering, take some of its blood, and put it on the bottom of the right ear of the person to be made clean. The priest will put some of this blood on the thumb of the person's right hand and some on the big toe of the person's right foot. ²⁶He will also pour some of the oil into his own left hand. ²⁷Then with a finger of his right hand, he will sprinkle some of the oil from his left hand seven times before the Lord. ²⁸The priest will take some of the oil from his hand and put it on the bottom of the right ear of the person to be made clean. He will also put some of it on the thumb of the person's right hand and some on the big toe of the person's right foot. The oil will go on these places on top of the blood from the penalty offering. ²⁹The priest must put the rest of the oil that is in his hand on the head of the person to be made clean, to make him clean so he can belong to the Lord again. ³⁰Then the priest will offer one of the doves or young pigeons, which the person can afford. ³¹He must offer one of the birds for a sin offering and the other for a whole burnt offering, along with the grain offering. In this way the priest will make the person clean so he can belong to the Lord again; he will become clean.

³²"These are the teachings for making a person clean after he has had a skin disease, if he cannot afford the regular sacrifices for becoming clean."

RULES FOR CLEANING MILDEW

³³The Lord also said to Moses and Aaron, ³⁴"I am giving the land of Canaan to your people. When they enter that land, if I cause mildew to grow in someone's house in that land, ³⁵the owner of that house must come and tell the priest. He should say, 'I have seen something like mildew in my house.' ³⁶Then the priest must order the people to empty the house before he goes in to look at the mildew. This is so he will not have to say that everything in the house is unclean. After this, the priest will go in to look at it. ³⁷He will look at

the mildew, and if the mildew on the walls of the house is green or red and goes into the wall's surface, ³⁸he must go out and close up the house for seven days. ³⁹On the seventh day the priest must come back and check the house. If the mildew has spread on the walls of the house, ⁴⁰the priest must order the people to tear out the stones with the mildew on them. They should throw them away, at a certain unclean place outside the city. ⁴¹Then the priest must have all the inside of the house scraped. The people must throw away the plaster they scraped off the walls, at a certain unclean place outside the city. ⁴²Then the owner must put new stones in the walls, and he must cover the walls with new clay plaster.

⁴³"Suppose a person has taken away the old stones and plaster and put in new stones and plaster. If mildew again appears in his house, ⁴⁴the priest must come back and check the house again. If the mildew has spread in the house, it is a mildew that destroys things; the house is unclean. ⁴⁵Then the owner must tear down the house, remove all its stones, plaster, and wood, and take them to the unclean place outside the city. ⁴⁶Anyone who goes into that house while it is closed up will be unclean until evening. ⁴⁷Anyone who eats in that house or lies down there must wash his clothes.

⁴⁸"Suppose after new stones and plaster have been put in a house, the priest checks it again and the mildew has not spread. Then the priest will announce that the house is clean, because the mildew is gone.

⁴⁹"Then, to make the house clean, the priest must take two birds, a piece of cedar wood, a piece of red string, and a hyssop plant. ⁵⁰He will kill one bird in a clay bowl containing fresh water. ⁵¹Then he will take the bird that is still alive, the cedar wood, the hyssop, and the red string, and he will dip them into the blood of the bird that was killed over the fresh water. The priest will sprinkle the blood on the house seven times. ⁵²He will use the bird's blood, the fresh water, the live bird, the cedar wood, the hyssop, and the red string to make the house clean. ⁵³He will then go to an open field outside the city and let the living bird go free. This is how the priest makes the house clean and ready for service to the Lord."

54These are the teachings about any kind of skin disease, 55mildew on pieces of cloth or in a house, 56swellings, rashes, or bright spots on the skin; 57they help people decide when things are unclean and when they are clean. These are the teachings about all these kinds of diseases.

RULES ABOUT A PERSON'S BODY

15 The LORD also said to Moses and Aaron, 2"Say to the people of Israel: 'When a fluid comes from a person's body, the fluid is unclean. 3It doesn't matter if the fluid flows freely or if it is blocked from flowing; the fluid will make him unclean. This is the way the fluid makes him unclean:

4"'If the person who discharges the body fluid lies on a bed, that bed becomes unclean, and everything he sits on becomes unclean. 5Anyone who touches his bed must wash his clothes and bathe in water, and the person will be unclean until evening. 6Whoever sits on something that the person who discharges the fluid sat on must wash his clothes and bathe in water; he will be unclean until evening. 7Anyone who touches the person who discharges the body fluid must wash his clothes and bathe in water; he will be unclean until evening.

8"'If the person who discharges the body fluid spits on someone who is clean, that person must wash his clothes and bathe in water; he will be unclean until evening. 9Everything on which the person who is unclean sits when riding will become unclean. 10Anyone who touches something that was under him will be unclean until evening. And anyone who carries these things must wash his clothes and bathe in water; he will be unclean until evening.

11"'If the person who discharges a body fluid has not washed his hands in water and touches another person, that person must wash his clothes and bathe in water; he will be unclean until evening.

12"'If a person who discharges a body fluid touches a clay bowl, that bowl must be broken. If he touches a wooden bowl, that bowl must be washed in water.

13"'When a person who discharges a body fluid is made clean, he must count seven days for himself for his cleansing. He must wash his clothes and bathe his body in fresh water,

and he will be clean. 14On the eighth day he must take two doves or two young pigeons before the LORD at the entrance of the Meeting Tent. He will give the two birds to the priest. 15The priest will offer the birds, one for a sin offering and the other for a burnt offering. And the priest will make that person clean so he can belong to the LORD again.

16"'If semen[n] goes out from a man, he must bathe in water; he will be unclean until evening. 17If the fluid gets on any clothing or leather, it must be washed with water; it will be unclean until evening.

18"'If a man has sexual relations with a woman and semen comes out, both people must bathe in water; they will be unclean until evening.

RULES ABOUT A WOMAN'S BODY

19"'When a woman has her monthly period, she is unclean for seven days; anyone who touches her will be unclean until evening. 20Anything she lies on during this time will be unclean, and everything she sits on during this time will be unclean. 21Anyone who touches her bed must wash his clothes and bathe in water; that person will be unclean until evening. 22Anyone who touches something she has sat on must wash his clothes and bathe in water; that person will be unclean until evening. 23It does not matter if the person touched the woman's bed or something she sat on; he will be unclean until evening.

24"'If a man has sexual relations with a woman and her monthly period touches him, he will be unclean for seven days; every bed he lies on will be unclean.

25"'If a woman has a loss of blood for many days and it is not during her regular monthly period, or if she continues to have a loss of blood after her regular period, she will be unclean, as she is during her monthly period. She will be unclean for as long as she continues to bleed. 26Any bed she lies on during all the time of her bleeding will be like her bed during her regular monthly period. Everything she sits on will be unclean, as during her regular monthly period.

27"'Whoever touches those things will be

15:16 semen A man's body fluid by which he can make a woman pregnant.

123

unclean and must wash his clothes and bathe in water; he will be unclean until evening. 28When the woman becomes clean from her bleeding, she must wait seven days, and after this she will be clean. 29Then on the eighth day she must take two doves or two young pigeons and bring them to the priest at the entrance of the Meeting Tent. 30The priest must offer one bird for a sin offering and the other for a whole burnt offering. In this way the priest will make her clean so she can belong to the LORD again.

31"'So you must warn the people of Israel to stay separated from things that make them unclean. If you don't warn the people, they might make my Holy Tent unclean, and then they would have to die!'"

32These are the teachings for the person who discharges a body fluid and for the man who becomes unclean from semen[n] coming out of his body. 33These are the teachings for the woman who becomes unclean from her monthly period, for a man or woman who has a discharge, and for a man who becomes unclean by having sexual relations with a woman who is unclean.

THE DAY OF CLEANSING

16 Now two of Aaron's sons had died while offering incense to the LORD, and after that time the LORD spoke to Moses. 2The LORD said to him, "Tell your brother Aaron that there are times when he cannot go behind the curtain into the Most Holy Place where the Ark is. If he goes in when I appear in a cloud over the lid on the Ark, he will die.

3"This is how Aaron may enter the Most Holy Place: Before he enters, he must offer a bull for a sin offering and a male sheep for a whole burnt offering. 4He must put on the holy linen inner robe, with the linen underclothes next to his body. His belt will be the cloth belt, and he will wear the linen turban. These are holy clothes, so he must bathe his body in water before he puts them on.

5"Aaron must take from the people of Israel two male goats for a sin offering and one male sheep for a burnt offering. 6Then he will offer the bull for the sin offering for himself to remove sins from him and his family so they will belong to the LORD.

7"Next Aaron will take the two goats and bring them before the LORD at the entrance to the Meeting Tent. 8He will throw lots for the two goats—one will be for the LORD and the other for the goat that removes sin. 9Then Aaron will take the goat that was chosen for the LORD by throwing the lot, and he will offer it as a sin offering. 10The other goat, which was chosen by lot to remove the sin, must be brought alive before the LORD. The priest will use it to perform the acts that remove Israel's sin so they will belong to the LORD. Then this goat will be sent out into the desert as a goat that removes sin.

11"Then Aaron will offer the bull as a sin offering for himself, to remove the sins from him and his family so they will belong to the LORD; he will kill the bull for the sin offering for himself. 12Then he must take a pan full of burning coals from the altar before the LORD and two handfuls of sweet incense that has been ground into powder. He must bring it into the room behind the curtain. 13He must put the incense on the fire before the LORD so that the cloud of incense will cover the lid on the Ark. Then when Aaron comes in, he will not die. 14Also, he must take some of the blood from the bull and sprinkle it with his finger on the front of the lid; with his finger he will sprinkle the blood seven times in front of the lid.

15"Then Aaron must kill the goat of the sin offering for the people and bring its blood into the room behind the curtain. He must do with the goat's blood as he did with the bull's blood, sprinkling it on the lid and in front of the lid. 16Because the people of Israel have been unclean, Aaron will perform the acts to make the Most Holy Place ready for service to the LORD. Then it will be clean from the sins and crimes of the Israelites. He must also do this for the Meeting Tent, because it stays in the middle of unclean people. 17When Aaron makes the Most Holy Place ready for service to the LORD, no one is allowed in the Meeting Tent until he comes out. So Aaron will perform the acts to remove sins from himself, his family, and all the people of Israel, so they will belong to the LORD. 18Afterward he will go out to the altar that is before the LORD and will make it ready for service to the LORD.

15:32 semen A man's body fluid by which he can make a woman pregnant.

Aaron will take some of the bull's blood and some of the goat's blood and put it on the corners of the altar on all sides. ¹⁹Then, with his finger, he will sprinkle some of the blood on the altar seven times to make the altar holy for the LORD and clean from all the sins of the Israelites.

²⁰"When Aaron has finished making the Most Holy Place, the Meeting Tent, and the altar ready for service to the LORD, he will offer the living goat. ²¹He will put both his hands on the head of the living goat, and he will confess over it all the sins and crimes of Israel. In this way Aaron will put the people's sins on the goat's head. Then he will send the goat away into the desert, and a man who has been appointed will lead the goat away. ²²So the goat will carry on itself all the people's sins to a lonely place in the desert. The man who leads the goat will let it loose there.

²³"Then Aaron will enter the Meeting Tent and take off the linen clothes he had put on before he went into the Most Holy Place; he must leave these clothes there. ²⁴He will bathe his body in water in a holy place and put on his regular clothes. Then he will come

---

DO YOU KNOW HIM?

crooked behavior
equals crooked results

FULFILLMENT

LEVITICUS 16:20–22

There is one significant difference between the contemporary understanding of iniquity and the Old Testament usage. In the Old Testament, this word encompassed both the sinful action and the punishment of that action, whereas today we separate these two events. Within the umbrella of this word, the actions that are designated as bent or crooked entail processes that result in distressing penalties. Acting in ways that distort God's intentions automatically causes distorted consequences.

Our godless behaviors are living examples of this coupling process in our own lives. When we let sin run our lives, the inevitable results are distress, distortion, and disaster. There are no exceptions. Crooked behavior equals crooked results. Christ bore these inevitable consequences for us as foreshadowed in these verses by the goat released in the desert. Our twisted actions that should have inflicted automatic penalties on us produced penalties that he bore for us instead.

This is the very essence of forgiveness: that God would take upon himself the consequences that we not only deserved but also actually initiated. God undid the eternal law of cause and effect for us, but only because the effect fell on Christ. In spite of our guilt, we do not get punished.

reflect: Praise God for sending Jesus to die for your sins in your place on the cross.
Go to **Jeremiah 3:22.**

out and offer the whole burnt offering for himself and for the people, to remove sins from himself and the people so they will belong to the LORD. 25Then he will burn the fat of the sin offering on the altar.

26"The person who led the goat, the goat to remove sins, into the desert must wash his clothes and bathe his body in water. After that, he may come back into the camp. 27"The bull and the goat for the sin offerings, whose blood was brought into the Most Holy Place to make it ready for service to the LORD, must be taken outside the camp; the animals' skins, bodies, and intestines will be burned in the fire. 28Then the one who burns them must wash his clothes and bathe his body in water. After that, he may come back into the camp.

29"This law will always continue for you: On the tenth day of the seventh month, you must deny yourself and you must not do any work. The travelers or foreigners living with you must not work either. 30It is on this day that the priests will make you clean so you will belong to the LORD again. All your sins will be removed. 31This is a very important day of rest for you, and you must deny yourselves. This law will continue forever.

32"The priest appointed to take his father's place, on whom the oil was poured, will perform the acts for making things ready for service to the LORD. He must put on the holy linen clothes 33and make the Most Holy Place, the Meeting Tent, and the altar ready for service to the LORD. He must also remove the sins of the priests and all the people of Israel so they will belong to the LORD. 34That law for removing the sins of the Israelites so they will belong to the LORD will continue forever. You will do these things once a year."

So they did the things the LORD had commanded Moses.

OFFERING SACRIFICES

17 The LORD said to Moses, 2"Speak to Aaron, his sons, and all the people of Israel. Tell them: 'This is what the LORD has commanded. 3If an Israelite kills an ox, a lamb, or a goat either inside the camp or outside it, 4when he should have brought the animal to the entrance of the Meeting Tent as a gift to the LORD in front of the LORD's Holy Tent, he is guilty of killing. He has killed, and he must be cut off from the people. 5This rule is so people will bring their sacrifices, which they have been sacrificing in the open fields, to the LORD. They must bring those animals to the LORD at the entrance of the Meeting Tent; they must bring them to the priest and offer them as fellowship offerings. 6Then the priest will sprinkle the blood from those animals on the LORD's altar near the entrance of the Meeting Tent. And he will burn the fat from those animals on the altar, as a smell pleasing to the LORD. 7They must not offer any more sacrifices to their goat idols, which they have chased like prostitutes. These rules will continue for people from now on.'

8"Tell the people this: 'If any citizen of Israel or foreigner living with you offers a burnt offering or sacrifice, 9that person must take his sacrifice to the entrance of the Meeting Tent to offer it to the LORD. If he does not do this, he must be cut off from the people.

10"'I will be against any citizen of Israel or foreigner living with you who eats blood. I will cut off that person from the people. 11This is because the life of the body is in the blood, and I have given you rules for pouring that blood on the altar to remove your sins so you will belong to the LORD. It is the blood that removes the sins, because it is life. 12So I tell the people of Israel this: "None of you may eat blood, and no foreigner living among you may eat blood."

13"'If any citizen of Israel or foreigner living among you catches a wild animal or bird that can be eaten, that person must pour the blood on the ground and cover it with dirt. 14If blood is still in the meat, the animal's life is still in it. So I give this command to the people of Israel: "Don't eat meat that still has blood in it, because the animal's life is in its blood. Anyone who eats blood must be cut off."

15"'If a person, either a citizen or a foreigner, eats an animal that died by itself or was killed by another animal, he must wash his clothes and bathe in water. He will be unclean until evening; then he will be clean. 16If he does not wash his clothes and bathe his body, he will be guilty of sin.'"

RULES ABOUT SEXUAL RELATIONS

18 The LORD said to Moses, ²"Tell the people of Israel: 'I am the LORD your God. ³In the past you lived in Egypt, but you must not do what was done in that country. And you must not do as they do in the land of Canaan, where I am bringing you. Do not follow their customs. ⁴You must obey my rules and follow them. I am the LORD your God. ⁵Obey my laws and rules; a person who obeys them will live because of them. I am the LORD.

⁶"You must never have sexual relations with your close relatives. I am the LORD.

⁷"You must not shame your father by having sexual relations with your mother. She is your mother; do not have sexual relations with her. ⁸You must not have sexual relations with your father's wife; that would shame your father.

⁹"You must not have sexual relations with your sister, either the daughter of your father or your mother. It doesn't matter if she was born in your house or somewhere else.

¹⁰"You must not have sexual relations with your son's daughter or your daughter's daughter; that would bring shame on you.

¹¹"If your father and his wife have a daughter, she is your sister. You must not have sexual relations with her.

¹²"You must not have sexual relations with your father's sister; she is your father's close relative. ¹³You must not have sexual relations with your mother's sister; she is your mother's close relative. ¹⁴You must not have sexual relations with the wife of your father's brother, because this would shame him. She is your aunt.

¹⁵"You must not have sexual relations with your daughter-in-law; she is your son's wife. Do not have sexual relations with her.

¹⁶"You must not have sexual relations with your brother's wife. That would shame your brother.

¹⁷"You must not have sexual relations with both a woman and her daughter. And do not have sexual relations with this woman's granddaughter, either the daughter of her son or her daughter; they are her close relatives. It is evil to do this.

¹⁸"While your wife is still living, you must not take her sister as another wife. Do not have sexual relations with her.

¹⁹"You must not go near a woman to have sexual relations with her during her monthly period, when she is unclean.

²⁰"You must not have sexual relations with your neighbor's wife and make yourself unclean with her.

²¹"You must not give any of your children to be sacrificed to Molech, because this would show that you do not respect your God. I am the LORD.

²²"You must not have sexual relations with a man as you would a woman. That is a hateful sin.

²³"You must not have sexual relations with an animal and make yourself unclean with it. Also a woman must not have sexual relations with an animal; it is not natural.

²⁴"Don't make yourself unclean by any of these wrong things. I am forcing nations out of their countries because they did these sins, and I am giving their land to you. ²⁵The land has become unclean, and I punished it for its sins, so the land is throwing out those people who live there.

²⁶"You must obey my laws and rules, and you must not do any of these hateful sins. These rules are for the citizens of Israel and for the people who live with you. ²⁷The people who lived in the land before you did all these hateful things and made the land unclean. ²⁸If you do these things, you will also make the land unclean, and it will throw you out as it threw out the nations before you. ²⁹Anyone who does these hateful sins must be cut off from the people. ³⁰Keep my command not to do these hateful sins that were done by the people who lived in the land before you. Don't make yourself unclean by doing them. I am the LORD your God.'"

OTHER LAWS

19 The LORD said to Moses, ²"Tell all the people of Israel: 'I am the LORD your God. You must be holy because I am holy.

³"You must respect your mother and father, and you must keep my Sabbaths. I am the LORD your God.

⁴"Do not worship idols or make statues of gods for yourselves. I am the LORD your God.

⁵"When you sacrifice a fellowship offering to the LORD, offer it in such a way that will be accepted. ⁶You may eat it the same

day you offer it or on the next day. But if any is left on the third day, you must burn it up. 7If any of it is eaten on the third day, it is unclean, and it will not be accepted. 8Anyone who eats it then will be guilty of sin, because he did not respect the holy things that belong to the LORD. He must be cut off from the people.

9"When you harvest your crops on your land, do not harvest all the way to the corners of your fields. If grain falls onto the ground, don't gather it up. 10Don't pick all the grapes in your vineyards, and don't pick up the grapes that fall to the ground. You must leave those things for poor people and for people traveling through your country. I am the LORD your God.

11"You must not steal. You must not cheat people, and you must not lie to each other. 12You must not make a false promise by my name, or you will show that you don't respect your God. I am the LORD.

13"You must not cheat your neighbor or rob him. You must not keep a hired worker's salary all night until morning. 14You must not curse a deaf person or put something in front of a blind person to make him fall. But you must respect your God. I am the LORD.

15"Be fair in your judging. You must not show special favor to poor people or great people, but be fair when you judge your neighbor. 16You must not spread false stories against other people, and you must not do anything that would put your neighbor's life in danger. I am the LORD.

17"You must not hate your fellow citizen in your heart. If your neighbor does something wrong, tell him about it, or you will be partly to blame. 18Forget about the wrong things people do to you, and do not try to get even. Love your neighbor as you love yourself. I am the LORD.

19"Obey my laws. You must not mate two different kinds of cattle or sow your field with two different kinds of seed. You must not wear clothing made from two different kinds of material mixed together.

20"If a man has sexual relations with a slave girl of another man, but this slave girl has not been bought or given her freedom, there must be punishment. But they are not to be put to death, because the woman was not free. 21The man must bring a male sheep as his penalty offering to the LORD at the entrance to the Meeting Tent. 22The priest will offer the sheep as a penalty offering before the LORD for the man's sin, to remove the sins of the man so he will belong to the LORD. Then he will be forgiven for his sin.

23"In the future, when you enter your country, you will plant many kinds of trees for food. After planting a tree, wait three years before using its fruit. 24In the fourth year the fruit from the tree will be the LORD's, a holy offering of praise to him. 25Then in the fifth year, you may eat the fruit from the tree. The tree will then produce more fruit for you. I am the LORD your God.

26"You must not eat anything with the blood in it.

"You must not try to tell the future by signs or black magic.

27"You must not cut the hair on the sides of your heads or cut the edges of your beard. 28You must not cut your body to show sadness for someone who died or put tattoo marks on yourselves. I am the LORD.

29"Do not dishonor your daughter by making her become a prostitute. If you do this, the country will be filled with all kinds of sin.

30"Obey the laws about Sabbaths, and respect my Most Holy Place. I am the LORD.

31"Do not go to mediums or fortune-tellers for advice, or you will become unclean. I am the LORD your God.

32"Show respect to old people; stand up in their presence. Show respect also to your God. I am the LORD.

33"Do not mistreat foreigners living in your country, 34but treat them just as you treat your own citizens. Love foreigners as you love yourselves, because you were foreigners one time in Egypt. I am the LORD your God.

35"Do not cheat when you measure the length or weight or amount of something. 36Your weights and balances should weigh correctly, with your weighing baskets the right size and your jars holding the right amount of liquid. I am the LORD your God. I brought you out of the land of Egypt.

37"Remember all my laws and rules, and obey them. I am the LORD.'"

A Family Changed

FAMILY

By Gary Smalley

LEVITICUS 19:18

When Cherryl was growing up, a simple plaque hung in the family room. The plaque belonged to Cherryl's grandfather and had become a kind of unspoken "family motto." It carried only two hand-painted words: STAND UP. Just two words—yet these two words had written volumes of hurt into three generations of Cherryl's family.

The words were originally part of a longer sentence, a motto that went something like this: "Don't take anything off anyone. Stand up and fight." This slogan may have been a helpful frontier slogan, but it did nothing but damage personal relationships in Cherryl's family.

Cherryl's father had been infected with the "never give an inch" attitude of his father. "I'm sorry" or "You're right" were not in the vocabulary of someone who based his life on the words "Stand up and fight." Also absent were words that were not useful in a fight. Words like "I love you," "Will you forgive me?" and "You're important to me."

While following his family rule of "never give an inch" pushed Cherryl's father ahead in business, it pushed him into a corner with his wife and children. Under this rule he may have believed that other people would take advantage of him or would withhold something he needed—the fear of being cheated. He was also teaching this fear to his wife and children.

Cherryl's mother and father fought constantly, each an expert on the other's faults and the other's fear buttons. Therefore, the two usually ended up in a full-blown Fear Dance. When all

of Cherryl's four brothers and sisters grew old enough to dislike "taking orders" from their father, they joined the battle, too. Soon there were seven people under the same roof following the family rule of "Stand up and fight" and participating in the same deadly dance. None were able to recognize how they were responsible for their own actions, but, instead, continually pointed the finger at one another.

One summer, Cherryl went away to Young Life camp and trusted Christ as her Lord and Savior. The first thing she noticed when she came back home was the two-word plaque "Stand Up." She thought about how Jesus had laid down his life and how tired she was of following this family rule. Little by little, Cherryl began to break some "family rules." Right in the middle of a fight, Cherryl would say, "I'm sorry. You're right. Would you forgive me?" and end the argument. She even began saying, "Love you, Mom. Love you, Dad," and then giving them a hug as she left for school.

During the next two years, Cherryl's father learned how to receive love from Cherryl. Cherryl's younger sister was so taken with Cherryl's changed life that she also trusted Christ. Soon Cherryl's older brother followed, and the plaque on the wall was beginning to shake. Last Christmas, as a baby Christian, her father took down the plaque. The dance of fear had stopped.

What a testimony to God's power to break even the deepest core fears! And what a help to Cherryl's family to have new dance steps to follow!

TO LEARN MORE ON WHAT THE BIBLE HAS TO SAY ABOUT **FAMILY,** READ THE SCRIPTURES AND DEVOTIONALS AT **PSALM 78:1–4, PROVERBS 1:7, JOSHUA 3:1–17, 1 CORINTHIANS 15:34, PROVERBS 12:14,** AND **PROVERBS 13:1.**

WARNINGS ABOUT VARIOUS SINS

20 The LORD said to Moses, ²"You must also tell the people of Israel these things: 'If a person in your country gives one of his children to Molech, that person must be killed. It doesn't matter if he is a citizen or a foreigner living in Israel; you must throw stones at him and kill him. ³I will be against him and cut him off from his people, because he gave his children to Molech. He showed that he did not respect my holy name, and he made my Holy Place unclean. ⁴The people of the community might ignore that person and not kill the one who gave his children to Molech. ⁵But I will be against him and his family, and I will cut him off from his people. I will do this to anyone who follows him in being unfaithful to me by worshiping Molech.

⁶"'I will be against anyone who goes to mediums and fortune-tellers for advice, because that person is being unfaithful to me. So I will cut him off from his people.

⁷"'Be my holy people. Be holy because I am the LORD your God. ⁸Remember and obey my laws. I am the LORD, and I have made you holy.

⁹"'Anyone who curses his father or mother must be put to death. He has cursed his father or mother, so he has brought his own death on himself.

PUNISHMENTS FOR SEXUAL SINS

¹⁰"'If a man has sexual relations with his neighbor's wife, both the man and the woman are guilty of adultery and must be put to death. ¹¹If a man has sexual relations with his father's wife, he has shamed his father, and both the man and his father's wife must be put to death. They have brought it on themselves.

¹²"'If a man has sexual relations with his daughter-in-law, both of them must be put to death. What they have done is not natural. They have brought their own deaths on themselves.

¹³"'If a man has sexual relations with another man as a man does with a woman, these two men have done a hateful sin. They must be put to death. They have brought it on themselves.

¹⁴"'If a man has sexual relations with both a woman and her mother, this is evil. The people must burn that man and the two women in fire so that your people will not be evil.

¹⁵"'If a man has sexual relations with an animal, he must be put to death. You must also kill the animal. ¹⁶If a woman approaches an animal and has sexual relations with it, you must kill the woman and the animal. They must be put to death. They have brought it on themselves.

¹⁷"'It is shameful for a brother to marry his sister, the daughter of either his father or his mother, and to have sexual relations with her. In front of everyone they must both be cut off from their people. The man has shamed his sister, and he is guilty of sin.

¹⁸"'If a man has sexual relations with a woman during her monthly period, both the woman and the man must be cut off from their people. They sinned because they showed the source of her blood.

¹⁹"'Do not have sexual relations with your mother's sister or your father's sister, because that would shame a close relative. Both of you are guilty of this sin.

²⁰"'If a man has sexual relations with his uncle's wife, he has shamed his uncle. That man and his uncle's wife will die without children; they are guilty of sin.

²¹"'It is unclean for a man to marry his brother's wife. That man has shamed his brother, and they will have no children.

²²"'Remember all my laws and rules, and obey them. I am leading you to your own land, and if you obey my laws and rules, that land will not throw you out. ²³I am forcing out ahead of you the people who live there. Because they did all these sins, I have hated them. Do not live the way those people lived.

²⁴"'I have told you that you will get their land, which I will give to you as your very own; it is a fertile land. I am the LORD your God, and I have set you apart from other people and made you my own. ²⁵So you must treat clean animals and birds differently from unclean animals and birds. Do not make yourselves unclean by any of these unclean birds or animals or things that crawl on the ground, which I have made unclean for you. ²⁶So you must be holy to me because I, the LORD, am holy, and I have set you apart from other people to be my own.

27"'A man or woman who is a medium or a fortune-teller must be put to death. You must stone them to death; they have brought it on themselves.'"

HOW PRIESTS MUST BEHAVE

21 The LORD said to Moses, "Tell these things to Aaron's sons, the priests: 'A priest must not make himself unclean by touching a dead person. 2But if the dead person was one of his close relatives, he may touch him. The priest may make himself unclean if the dead person is his mother or father, son or daughter, brother or 3unmarried sister who is close to him because she has no husband. The priest may make himself unclean for her if she dies. 4But a priest must not make himself unclean if the dead person was only related to him by marriage.

5"'Priests must not shave their heads, or shave off the edges of their beards, or cut their bodies. 6They must be holy to their God and show respect for God's name, because they present the offerings made by fire to the LORD, which is the food of their God. So they must be holy.

7"'A priest must not marry an unclean prostitute or a divorced woman, because he is holy to his God. 8Treat him as holy, because he offers up the food of your God. Think of him as holy; I am the LORD who makes you holy, and I am holy.

9"'If a priest's daughter makes herself unclean by becoming a prostitute, she shames her father. She must be burned with fire.

10"'The high priest, who was chosen from among his brothers, had the special olive oil poured on his head. He was also appointed to wear the priestly clothes. So he must not show his sadness by letting his hair go uncombed or tearing his clothes. 11He must not go into a house where there is a dead body. He must not make himself unclean, even if it is for his own father or mother. 12The high priest must not go out of the Holy Place, because if he does and becomes unclean, he will make God's Holy Place unclean. The special oil used in appointing priests was poured on his head to separate him from the rest of the people. I am the LORD.

13"'The high priest must marry a woman who is a virgin. 14He must not marry a widow, a divorced woman, or a prostitute. He must marry a virgin from his own people 15so the people will respect his children as his own. I am the LORD. I have set the high priest apart for his special job.'"

16The LORD said to Moses, 17"Tell Aaron: 'If any of your descendants have something wrong with them, they must never come near to offer the special food of their God. 18Anyone who has something wrong with him must not come near: blind men, crippled men, men with damaged faces, deformed men, 19men with a crippled foot or hand, 20hunchbacks, dwarfs, men who have something wrong with their eyes, men who have an itching disease or a skin disease, or men who have damaged sex glands.

21"'If one of Aaron's descendants has something wrong with him, he cannot come near to make the offerings made by fire to the LORD. He has something wrong with him; he cannot offer the food of his God. 22He may eat the most holy food and also the holy food. 23But he may not go through the curtain into the Most Holy Place, and he may not go near the altar, because he has something wrong with him. He must not make my Holy Place unfit. I am the LORD who makes these places holy.'"

24So Moses told these things to Aaron, Aaron's sons, and all the people of Israel.

22 The LORD said to Moses, 2"Tell Aaron and his sons: 'The people of Israel will give offerings to me. These offerings are holy, and they are mine, so you must respect them to show that you respect my holy name. I am the LORD.' 3Say to them: 'If any one of your descendants from now on is unclean and comes near the offerings that the Israelites made holy for me, that person must be cut off from appearing before me. I am the LORD.

4"'If one of Aaron's descendants has a harmful skin disease, or if he discharges a body fluid, he cannot eat the holy offerings until he becomes clean. He could also become unclean from touching a dead body, from his own semen,[n] 5from touching any unclean crawling animal, or from touching an unclean person (no matter what made the person unclean). 6Anyone who touches those things will become unclean until evening.

22:4 **semen** A man's body fluid by which he can make a woman pregnant.

That person must not eat the holy offerings unless he washes with water. ⁷He will be clean only after the sun goes down. Then he may eat the holy offerings; the offerings are his food.

⁸"If a priest finds an animal that died by itself or that was killed by some other animal, he must not eat it. If he does, he will become unclean. I am the LORD.

⁹"If the priests keep all the rules I have given, they will not become guilty; if they are careful, they will not die. I am the LORD who has made them holy. ¹⁰Only people in a priest's family may eat the holy offering. A visitor staying with the priest or a hired worker must not eat it. ¹¹But if the priest buys a slave with his own money, that slave may eat the holy offerings; slaves who were born in his house may also eat his food. ¹²If a priest's daughter marries a person who is not a priest, she must not eat any of the holy offerings. ¹³But if the priest's daughter becomes widowed or divorced, with no children to support her, and if she goes back to her father's house where she lived as a child, she may eat some of her father's food. But only people from a priest's family may eat this food.

¹⁴"If someone eats some of the holy offering by mistake, that person must pay back the priest for that holy food, adding another one-fifth of the price of that food.

¹⁵"When the Israelites give their holy offerings to the LORD, the priest must not treat these holy things as though they were not holy. ¹⁶The priests must not allow those who are not priests to eat the holy offerings. If they do, they cause the ones who eat the holy offerings to become guilty, and they will have to pay for it. I am the LORD, who makes them holy.'"

¹⁷The LORD said to Moses, ¹⁸"Tell Aaron and his sons and all the people of Israel: 'A citizen of Israel or a foreigner living in Israel might want to bring a whole burnt offering, either for some special promise he has made or for a special gift he wants to give to the LORD. ¹⁹If he does, he must bring a male animal that has nothing wrong with it—a bull, a sheep, or a goat—so it might be accepted for him. ²⁰He must not bring an animal that has something wrong with it, or it will not be accepted for him.

²¹"If someone brings a fellowship offering to the LORD, either as payment for a special promise the person has made or as a special gift the person wants to give the LORD, it might be from the herd or from the flock. But it must be healthy, with nothing wrong with it, so that it will be accepted. ²²You must not offer to the LORD any animal that is blind, that has broken bones or is crippled, that has running sores or any sort of skin disease. You must not offer any animals like these on the altar as an offering by fire to the LORD.

²³"If an ox or lamb is smaller than normal or is not perfectly formed, you may give it as a special gift to the LORD; it will be accepted. But it will not be accepted as payment for a special promise you have made.

²⁴"If an animal has bruised, crushed, torn, or cut sex glands, you must not offer it to the LORD. You must not do this in your own land, ²⁵and you must not take such animals from foreigners as sacrifices to the LORD. Because the animals have been hurt in some way and have something wrong with them, they will not be accepted for you.'"

²⁶The LORD said to Moses, ²⁷"When an ox, a sheep, or a goat is born, it must stay seven days with its mother. But from the eighth day on, this animal will be accepted as a sacrifice by fire to the LORD. ²⁸But you must not kill the animal and its mother on the same day, either an ox or a sheep.

²⁹"If you want to offer some special offering of thanks to the LORD, you must do it in a way that pleases him. ³⁰You must eat the whole animal that same day and not leave any of the meat for the next morning. I am the LORD.

³¹"Remember my commands and obey them; I am the LORD. ³²Show respect for my holy name. You Israelites must remember that I am holy; I am the LORD, who has made you holy. ³³I brought you out of Egypt to be your God. I am the LORD."

SPECIAL HOLIDAYS

23 The LORD said to Moses, ²"Tell the people of Israel: 'You will announce the LORD's appointed feasts as holy meetings. These are my special feasts.

THE SABBATH

³"'There are six days for you to work, but the seventh day will be a special day of rest.

It is a day for a holy meeting; you must not do any work. It is a Sabbath to the LORD in all your homes.

THE PASSOVER AND UNLEAVENED BREAD

4 " 'These are the LORD's appointed feasts, the holy meetings, which you will announce at the times set for them. 5The LORD's Passover is on the fourteenth day of the first month, beginning at twilight. 6The Feast of Unleavened Bread begins on the fifteenth day of the same month. You will eat bread made without yeast for seven days. 7On the first day of this feast you will have a holy meeting, and you must not do any work. 8For seven days you will bring an offering made by fire to the LORD. There will be a holy meeting on the seventh day, and on that day you must not do any regular work.' "

THE FIRST OF THE HARVEST

9The LORD said to Moses, 10"Tell the people of Israel: 'You will enter the land I will give you and gather its harvest. At that time you must bring the first bundle of grain from your harvest to the priest. 11The priest will present the bundle before the LORD, and it will be accepted for you; he will present the bundle on the day after the Sabbath.

12 " 'On the day when you present the bundle of grain, offer a male lamb, one year old, that has nothing wrong with it, as a burnt offering to the LORD. 13You must also offer a grain offering—four quarts of fine flour mixed with olive oil as an offering made by fire to the LORD; its smell will be pleasing to him. You must also offer a quart of wine as a drink offering. 14Until the day you bring your offering to your God, do not eat any new grain, roasted grain, or bread made from new grain. This law will always continue for people from now on, wherever you live.

THE FEAST OF WEEKS

15 " 'Count seven full weeks from the morning after the Sabbath. (This is the Sabbath that you bring the bundle of grain to present as an offering.) 16On the fiftieth day, the first day after the seventh week, you will bring a new grain offering to the LORD. 17On that day bring two loaves of bread from your homes to be presented as an offering. Use yeast and four quarts of flour to make those loaves of bread; they will be your gift to the LORD from the first wheat of your harvest.

18 " 'Offer with the bread one young bull, two male sheep, and seven male lambs that are one year old and have nothing wrong with them. Offer them with their grain offerings and drink offerings, as a burnt offering to the LORD. They will be an offering made by fire, and the smell will be pleasing to the LORD. 19You must also offer one male goat for a sin offering and two male, one-year-old lambs as a fellowship offering.

20 " 'The priest will present the two lambs as an offering before the LORD, along with the bread from the first wheat of the harvest. They are holy to the LORD, and they will belong to the priest. 21On that same day you will call a holy meeting; you must not do any work that day. This law will continue for you from now on, wherever you live.

22 " 'When you harvest your crops on your land, do not harvest all the way to the corners of your field. If grain falls onto the ground, don't gather it up. Leave it for poor people and foreigners in your country. I am the LORD your God.' "

THE FEAST OF TRUMPETS

23Again the LORD said to Moses, 24"Tell the people of Israel: 'On the first day of the seventh month you must have a special day of rest, a holy meeting, when you blow the trumpet for a special time of remembering. 25Do not do any work, and bring an offering made by fire to the LORD.' "

THE DAY OF CLEANSING

26The LORD said to Moses, 27"The Day of Cleansing will be on the tenth day of the seventh month. There will be a holy meeting, and you will deny yourselves and bring an offering made by fire to the LORD. 28Do not do any work on that day, because it is the Day of Cleansing. On that day the priests will go before the LORD and perform the acts to make you clean from sin so you will belong to the LORD.

29"Anyone who refuses to give up food on this day must be cut off from the people. 30If anyone works on this day, I will destroy that person from among the people. 31You must not do any work at all; this law will continue for people from now on wherever you live. 32It will be a special day of rest for you, and you must deny yourselves. You will start this special day of rest on the evening after the ninth day of the month, and it will continue from that evening until the next evening."

THE FEAST OF SHELTERS

33Again the LORD said to Moses, 34"Tell the people of Israel: 'On the fifteenth day of the seventh month is the Feast of Shelters. This feast to the LORD will continue for seven days. 35There will be a holy meeting on the first day; do not do any work. 36You will bring an offering made by fire to the LORD each day for seven days. On the eighth day you will have another holy meeting, and you will bring an offering made by fire to the LORD. This will be a holy meeting; do not do any work.

37("'These are the LORD's special feasts, when there will be holy meetings and when you bring offerings made by fire to the LORD. You will bring whole burnt offerings, grain offerings, sacrifices, and drink offerings— each at the right time. 38These offerings are in addition to those for the LORD's Sabbath days, in addition to offerings you give as payment for special promises, and in addition to special offerings you want to give to the LORD.)

39"'So on the fifteenth day of the seventh month, after you have gathered in the crops of the land, celebrate the LORD's festival for seven days. You must rest on the first day and the eighth day. 40On the first day you will take good fruit from the fruit trees, as well as branches from palm trees, poplars, and other leafy trees. You will celebrate before the LORD your God for seven days. 41Celebrate this festival to the LORD for seven days each year. This law will continue from now on; you will celebrate it in the seventh month. 42Live in shelters for seven days. All the people born in Israel must live in shelters 43so that all your descendants will know I made Israel live in shelters during the time I brought them out of Egypt. I am the LORD your God.'"

44So Moses told the people of Israel about all of the LORD's appointed feast days.

THE LAMPSTAND AND THE HOLY BREAD

24 The LORD said to Moses, 2"Command the people of Israel to bring you pure oil from crushed olives. That oil is for the lamps so that these lamps may never go out.

3Aaron will keep the lamps burning in the Meeting Tent from evening until morning before the LORD; this is in front of the curtain of the Ark of the Agreement. This law will continue from now on. 4Aaron must always keep the lamps burning on the lampstands of pure gold before the LORD.

5"Take fine flour and bake twelve loaves of bread with it, using four quarts of flour for each loaf. 6Put them in two rows on the golden table before the LORD, six loaves in each row. 7Put pure incense on each row as the memorial portion to take the place of the bread. It is an offering made by fire to the LORD. 8Every Sabbath day Aaron will put the bread in order before the LORD, as an agreement with the people of Israel that will continue forever. 9That bread will belong to Aaron and his sons. They will eat it in a holy place, because it is a most holy part of the offerings made by fire to the LORD. That bread is their share forever."

THE MAN WHO CURSED GOD

10Now there was a son of an Israelite woman and an Egyptian father who was walking among the Israelites. A fight broke out in the camp between him and an Israelite. 11The son of the Israelite woman began cursing and speaking against the LORD, so the people took him to Moses. (The mother's name was Shelomith, the daughter of Dibri from the family of Dan.) 12The people held him as a prisoner while they waited for the LORD's command to be made clear to them.

13Then the LORD said to Moses, 14"Take the one who spoke against me outside the camp. Then all the people who heard him must put their hands on his head, and all the people must throw stones at him and kill him. 15Tell the people of Israel this: 'If anyone curses his God, he is guilty of sin. 16Anyone who speaks against the LORD must be put to death; all the people must kill him by throwing stones at him. Foreigners must be punished just like the people born in Israel; if they speak against the LORD, they must be put to death.

17"'Whoever kills another person must be put to death. 18Whoever kills an animal that belongs to another person must give that person another animal to take its place. 19And whoever causes an injury to a neighbor must receive the same kind of injury in return: [20]Broken bone for broken bone, eye for eye, tooth for tooth. Anyone who injures another person must be injured in the same way in return. [21]Whoever kills another person's animal must give that person another animal to take its place. But whoever kills another person must be put to death.

[22]"'The law will be the same for the foreigner as for those from your own country. I am the LORD your God.'"

[23]Then Moses spoke to the people of Israel, and they took the person who had cursed outside the camp and killed him by throwing stones at him. So the people of Israel did as the LORD had commanded Moses.

THE TIME OF REST FOR THE LAND

25 The LORD said to Moses at Mount Sinai, [2]"Tell the people of Israel this: 'When you enter the land I will give you, let it have a special time of rest, to honor the LORD. [3]You may plant seed in your field for six years, and you may trim your vineyards for six years and bring in their fruits. [4]But during the seventh year, you must let the land rest. This will be a special time to honor the LORD. You must not plant seed in your field or trim your vineyards. [5]You must not cut the crops that grow by themselves after harvest, or gather the grapes from your vines that are not trimmed. The land will have a year of rest.

[6]"'You may eat whatever the land produces during that year of rest. It will be food for your men and women servants, for your hired workers, and for the foreigners living in your country. [7]It will also be food for your cattle and the wild animals of your land. Whatever the land produces may be eaten.

THE YEAR OF JUBILEE

[8]"'Count off seven groups of seven years, or forty-nine years. During that time there will be seven years of rest for the land. [9]On the Day of Cleansing, you must blow the horn of a male sheep; this will be on the tenth day of the seventh month. You must blow the horn through the whole country. [10]Make the fiftieth year a special year, and announce freedom for all the people living in your country. This time will be called Jubilee.[n] You will each go back to your own property, each to your own family and family group.

[11]The fiftieth year will be a special time for you to celebrate. Don't plant seeds, or harvest the crops that grow by themselves, or gather grapes from the vines that are not trimmed. [12]That year is Jubilee; it will be a holy time for you. You may eat only the crops that come from the field. [13]In the year of Jubilee you each must go back to your own property.

[14]"'If you sell your land to your neighbor, or if you buy land from your neighbor, don't cheat each other. [15]If you want to buy your neighbor's land, count the number of years since the last Jubilee, and use that number to decide the right price. If your neighbor sells the land to you, count the number of years left for harvesting crops, and use that number to decide the right price. [16]If there are many years, the price will be high. But if there are only a few years, lower the price, because your neighbor is really selling only a few crops to you. [17]You must not cheat each other, but you must respect your God. I am the LORD your God.

[18]"'Remember my laws and rules, and obey them so that you will live safely in the land. [19]The land will give good crops to you, and you will eat as much as you want and live safely in the land.

[20]"'But you might ask, "If we don't plant seeds or gather crops, what will we eat the seventh year?" [21]I will send you such a great blessing during the sixth year that the land will produce enough crops for three years. [22]When you plant in the eighth year, you will still be eating from the old crop; you will eat the old crop until the harvest of the ninth year.

PROPERTY LAWS

[23]"'The land really belongs to me, so you can't sell it for all time. You are only foreigners and travelers living for a while on my land. [24]People might sell their land, but it must always be possible for the family to get its land back. [25]If a person in your country becomes very poor and sells some land, then close relatives must come and buy it back. [26]If there is not a close relative to buy the land back, but if the person makes enough money to be able to buy it back, [27]the years must be

---

25:10 Jubilee This word comes from the Hebrew word for a horn of a male sheep.

counted since the land was sold. That number must be used to decide how much the first owner should pay back the one who bought it. Then the land will belong to the first owner again. ²⁸But if there is not enough money to buy it back, the one who bought it will keep it until the year of Jubilee. During that celebration, the land will go back to the first owner's family.

²⁹"'If someone sells a home in a walled city, for a full year after it is sold, the person has the right to buy it back. ³⁰But if the owner does not buy back the house before a full year is over, it will belong to the one who bought it and to his future sons. The house will not go back to the first owner at Jubilee. ³¹But houses in small towns without walls are like open country; they can be bought back, and they must be returned to their first owner at Jubilee.

³²"'The Levites may always buy back their houses in the cities that belong to them. ³³If someone buys a house from a Levite, that house in the Levites' city will again belong to the Levites in the Jubilee. This is because houses in Levite cities belong to the people of Levi; the Israelites gave these cities to them. ³⁴Also the fields and pastures around the Levites' cities cannot be sold, because those fields belong to the Levites forever.

RULES FOR SLAVE OWNERS

³⁵"'If anyone from your country becomes too poor to support himself, help him to live among you as you would a stranger or foreigner. ³⁶Do not charge him any interest on money you loan to him, but respect your God; let the poor live among you. ³⁷Don't lend him money for interest, and don't try to make a profit from the food he buys. ³⁸I am the LORD your God, who brought you out of the land of Egypt to give the land of Canaan to you and to become your God.

³⁹"'If anyone from your country becomes very poor and sells himself as a slave to you, you must not make him work like a slave. ⁴⁰He will be like a hired worker and a visitor with you until the year of Jubilee. ⁴¹Then he may leave you, take his children, and go back to his family and the land of his ancestors. ⁴²This is because the Israelites are my servants, and I brought them out of slavery in Egypt. They must not become slaves again.

⁴³You must not rule this person cruelly, but you must respect your God.

⁴⁴"'Your men and women slaves must come from other nations around you; from them you may buy slaves. ⁴⁵Also you may buy as slaves children from the families of foreigners living in your land. These child slaves will belong to you, ⁴⁶and you may even pass them on to your children after you die; you can make them slaves forever. But you must not rule cruelly over your own people, the Israelites.

⁴⁷"'Suppose a foreigner or visitor among you becomes rich. If someone in your country becomes so poor that he has to sell himself as a slave to the foreigner living among you or to a member of the foreigner's family, ⁴⁸the poor person has the right to be bought back and become free. One of his relatives may buy him back: ⁴⁹His uncle, his uncle's son, or any one of his close relatives may buy him back. Or, if he gets enough money, he may pay the money to free himself.

⁵⁰"'He and the one who bought him must count the time from when he sold himself up to the next year of Jubilee. Use that number to decide the price, because the person really only hired himself out for a certain number of years. ⁵¹If there are still many years before the year of Jubilee, the person must pay back a large part of the price. ⁵²If there are only a few years left until Jubilee, the person must pay a small part of the first price. ⁵³But he will live like a hired person with the foreigner every year; don't let the foreigner rule cruelly over him.

⁵⁴"'Even if no one buys him back, at the year of Jubilee, he and his children will become free. ⁵⁵This is because the people of Israel are servants to me. They are my servants, whom I brought out of Egypt. I am the LORD your God.

REWARDS FOR OBEYING GOD

26 "'Don't make idols for yourselves or set up statues or memorials. Don't put stone statues in your land to bow down to, because I am the LORD your God.

²"'Remember my Sabbaths, and respect my Holy Place. I am the LORD.

³"'If you remember my laws and commands and obey them, ⁴I will give you rains at the right season; the land will produce crops,

and the trees of the field will produce their fruit. [5]Your threshing will continue until the grape harvest, and your grape harvest will continue until it is time to plant. Then you will have plenty to eat and live safely in your land. [6]I will give peace to your country; you will lie down in peace, and no one will make you afraid. I will keep harmful animals out of your country, and armies will not pass through it.

[7]"You will chase your enemies and defeat them, killing them with your sword. [8]Five of you will chase a hundred men; a hundred of you will chase ten thousand men. You will defeat your enemies and kill them with your sword.

[9]"Then I will show kindness to you and let you have many children; I will keep my agreement with you. [10]You will have enough crops to last for more than a year. When you harvest the new crops, you will have to throw out the old ones to make room for them. [11]Also I will place my Holy Tent among you, and I will not turn away from you. [12]I will walk with you and be your God, and you will be my people. [13]I am the LORD your God, who brought you out of Egypt, where you were slaves. I broke the heavy weights that were on your shoulders and let you walk proudly again.

PUNISHMENT FOR NOT OBEYING GOD

[14]"But if you do not obey me and keep all my commands, [15]and if you turn away from my rules and hate my laws, refusing to obey all my commands, you have broken our agreement. [16]As a result, I will do this to you: I will cause terrible things to happen to you. I will cause you to have disease and fever that will destroy your eyes and slowly kill you. You will not have success when you plant your seed, and your enemy will eat your crops. [17]I will be against you, and your enemies will defeat you. These people who hate you will rule over you, and you will run away even when no one is chasing you.

[18]"If after all this you still do not obey me, I will punish you seven times more for your sins. [19]I will break your great pride, and I will make the sky like iron and the earth like bronze.[n] [20]You will work hard, but it will not help. Your land will not grow any crops, and your trees will not give their fruit.

[21]"If you still turn against me and refuse to obey me, I will beat you seven times harder. The more you sin, the more you will be punished. [22]I will send wild animals to attack you, and they will take your children away from you and destroy your cattle. They will make you so few in number the roads will be empty.

[23]"If you don't learn your lesson after all these things, and if you still turn against me, [24]I will also turn against you. I will punish you seven more times for your sins. [25]You broke my agreement, and I will punish you. I will bring armies against you, and if you go into your cities for safety, I will cause diseases to spread among you so that your enemy will defeat you. [26]There will be very little bread to eat; ten women will be able to cook all your bread in one oven. They will measure each piece of bread, and you will eat, but you will still be hungry.

[27]"If you still refuse to listen to me and still turn against me, [28]I will show my great anger; I will punish you seven more times for your sins. [29]You will eat the bodies of your sons and daughters. [30]I will destroy your places where gods are worshiped and cut down your incense altars. I will pile your dead bodies on the lifeless forms of your idols. I will hate you. [31]I will destroy your cities and make your holy places empty, and I will not smell the pleasing smell of your offerings. [32]I will make the land empty so that your enemies who come to live in it will be shocked at it. [33]I will scatter you among the nations, and I will pull out my sword and destroy you. Your land will become empty, your cities a waste. [34]When you are taken to your enemy's country, your land will finally get its rest. It will enjoy its time of rest all the time it lies empty. [35]During the time the land is empty, it will have the rest you should have given it while you lived in it.

[36]"Those of you who are left alive will lose their courage in the land of their enemies. They will be frightened by the sound of a leaf being blown by the wind. They will run as if someone were chasing them with a sword, and they will fall even when no one

---

26:19 sky . . . bronze This means the sky will give no rain and the earth will produce no crops.

The Laws of Increase

By Larry Stockstill

LEVITICUS 26:1-13

Everybody wants more! Babies demand more milk, mothers crave more time, fathers strive to make more money, and churches try to attract more members. It seems an inescapable part of life to want more. This desire for more, however, is not necessarily bad; in fact, God wants to give us more in every area of life.

The problem is that we don't know how to receive that increase. We are ignorant of the laws that God has put in place to bless and increase us. There are spiritual laws that govern our ability to increase, so we need to learn them in order to live the abundant, overflowing life that is ours as children of God.

If we take the word **SOWER** and use it as an acronym, we can discover five basic laws of increase:

S – Sacrifice. If we want God to bless us, we are going to have to be willing to sacrifice. Sacrifice is the opposite of greed, and God can never bless greediness. Instead, a sower is someone who will plant a seed in the lives of others. A seed is God's potential miracle. But you first have to relinquish control and allow the seed to die. That's sacrifice. One way to do that is by being faithful to tithe 10 percent of your income.

O – Offering. Tithing is good, but it is only the beginning. The next level is to give offerings above and beyond the tithe! In the Greek, the word "offering" actually means "presenting" or "making a present." In other words, it is a gift freely given. Think of the offering as worship to God, an investment into the kingdom and into the lives of others.

W – Waiting. In the spiritual realm, waiting is an integral part of the process of seeing God's increase come into your life. It assumes patience, which to some of us is a dirty word. Through waiting, God has the opportunity to test your obedience (Deuteronomy 8:2), your faithfulness (Luke 16:10), and your patience (Hebrews 6:12).

E – Expecting. If you don't learn how to expect your increase, you'll be stymied. That, unfortunately, is what happens to many people. They lose their expectancy of ever seeing an increase in their lives. Keep your eyes on the Lord and look for the breakthrough as though it could happen any moment.

R – Receiving. This is a critical step. God knows how to bless, but so many don't know how to receive. The key is to remain humble and childlike in your relationship with the Lord. You've got to say, "Lord, I don't care what I have on this earth. I'm just a pilgrim passing through. Whatever you give me on the journey, I'll be a good steward of it."

Never give up on the vision of increase God has given you. Once you grasp it in your heart, make provision for it in your life. Commit today to being a sower in the kingdom of God and maintain the sower's heart!

TO LEARN MORE ON WHAT THE BIBLE HAS TO SAY ABOUT **FINANCES,** READ THE SCRIPTURES AND DEVOTIONALS AT **PROVERBS 7:4, PROVERBS 30:5, ECCLESIASTES 7:12, ECCLESIASTES 11:4-6, ISAIAH 33:6,** AND **DANIEL 4:30-37.**

is chasing them. ³⁷They will fall over each other, as if someone were chasing them with a sword, even though no one is chasing them. You will not be strong enough to stand up against your enemies. ³⁸You will die among other nations and disappear in your enemies' countries. ³⁹So those who are left alive will rot away in their enemies' countries because of their sins. They will also rot away because of their ancestors' sins.

THERE IS ALWAYS HOPE

⁴⁰"But maybe the people will confess their sins and the sins of their ancestors; maybe they will admit they turned against me and sinned against me, ⁴¹which made me turn against them and send them into the land of their enemies. If these disobedient people are sorry for what they did and accept punishment for their sin, ⁴²I will remember my agreement with Jacob, my agreement with Isaac, and my agreement with Abraham, and I will remember the land. ⁴³The land will be left empty by its people, and it will enjoy its time of rest as it lies bare without them. Then those who are left alive will accept the punishment for their sins. They will learn that they were punished because they hated my laws and refused to obey my rules. ⁴⁴But even though this is true, I will not turn away from them when they are in the land of their enemies. I will not hate them so much that I completely destroy them and break my agreement with them, because I am the LORD their God. ⁴⁵For their good I will remember the agreement with their ancestors, whom I brought out of the land of Egypt so I could become their God; the other nations saw these things. I am the LORD.'"

⁴⁶These are the laws, rules, and teachings the LORD made between himself and the Israelites through Moses at Mount Sinai.

PROMISES ARE IMPORTANT

27 The LORD said to Moses, ²"Speak to the people of Israel and tell them: 'If someone makes a special promise to give a person as a servant to the LORD by paying a price that is the same value as that person, ³the price for a man twenty to sixty years old is about one and one-fourth pounds of silver. (You must use the measure as set by the Holy Place.) ⁴The price for a woman twenty to sixty years old is about twelve ounces of silver. ⁵The price for a man five to twenty years old is about eight ounces of silver; for a woman it is about four ounces of silver. ⁶The price for a baby boy one month to five years old is about two ounces of silver; for a baby girl the price is about one and one-half ounces of silver. ⁷The price for a man sixty years old or older is about six ounces of silver; for a woman it is about four ounces of silver.

⁸"If anyone is too poor to pay the price, bring him to the priest, and the priest will set the price. The priest will decide how much money the person making the vow can afford to pay.

GIFTS TO THE LORD

⁹"Some animals may be used as sacrifices to the LORD. If someone promises to bring one of these to the LORD, it will become holy. ¹⁰That person must not try to put another animal in its place or exchange it, a good animal for a bad one, or a bad animal for a good one. If this happens, both animals will become holy.

¹¹"Unclean animals cannot be offered as sacrifices to the LORD, and if someone brings one of them to the LORD, that animal must be brought to the priest. ¹²The priest will decide a price for the animal, according to whether it is good or bad; as the priest decides, that is the price for the animal. ¹³If the person wants to buy back the animal, an additional one-fifth must be added to the price.

VALUE OF A HOUSE

¹⁴"If a person gives a house as holy to the LORD, the priest must decide its value, according to whether the house is good or bad; as the priest decides, that is the price for the house. ¹⁵But if the person who gives the house wants to buy it back, an additional one-fifth must be added to the price. Then the house will belong to that person again.

VALUE OF LAND

¹⁶"If a person gives some family property to the LORD, the value of the fields will depend on how much seed is needed to plant them. It will cost about one and one-fourth pounds of silver for each six bushels of barley seed needed. ¹⁷If the person gives a field at the year of Jubilee, its value will stay at what the priest has decided. ¹⁸But if the person

gives the field after the Jubilee, the priest must decide the exact price by counting the number of years to the next year of Jubilee. Then he will subtract that number from its value. ¹⁹If the person who gave the field wants to buy it back, one-fifth must be added

THE FAVOR OF GOD

the power
of tithing

FINANCES

LEVITICUS 27:30

By Kong Hee

The principle of tithing is important because it is the most basic Bible test of your faithfulness as a servant of God. It also qualifies or disqualifies you from God's wealth and abundance.

Tithing predates the Mosaic Law because Abraham tithed faithfully long before the Law was established on Mount Sinai. When he met Melchizedek, he gave him "a tenth of everything" (Genesis 14:19–20). Abraham's faithful stewardship resulted in his becoming the richest man of his generation.

Jacob tithed. When he came to Bethel, he made a vow to the Lord, "I will give God one-tenth of all he gives me" (Genesis 28:22). Jacob's faithful stewardship resulted in his becoming the richest man of his generation.

Abraham and Jacob started tithing long before Moses gave the law about tithing. Tithing has to do with your heart and love for God. You tithe not because you have to, but because you want to.

In Malachi 3:10–12, Malachi the prophet told about five great blessings that you can experience if you tithe regularly:

• Your church will be a blessing to disciple you and evangelize the world.

• You will hear from the Lord clearly, and his presence and power will be readily available to you at all times.

• God will protect your finances from being "eaten away" by Satan and the financial system of the world.

• Your hard work will prosper.

• The wise investments you make will bring back a good return.

reflect: Are you ready to tithe regularly and give faithfully?
Go to **FINANCES:** "God's Management Plan" at **Exodus 18:13–27.**

to that price, and the field will belong to the first owner again.

20"If the person does not buy back the field, or if it is sold to someone else, the first person cannot ever buy it back. **21**When the land is released at the year of Jubilee, it will become holy to the LORD, like land specially given to him. It will become the property of the priests.

22"If someone gives to the LORD a field he has bought, which is not a part of his family land, **23**the priest must count the years to the next Jubilee. He must decide the price for the land, and the price must be paid on that day. Then that land will be holy to the LORD. **24**At the year of Jubilee, the land will go back to its first owner, to the family who sold the land.

25"You must use the measure as set by the Holy Place in paying these prices; it weighs two-fifths of an ounce.

VALUE OF ANIMALS

26"If an animal is the first one born to its parent, it already belongs to the LORD, so people may not give it again. If it is a cow or a sheep, it is the LORD's. **27**If the animal is unclean, the person must buy it back for the price set by the priest, and the person must add one-fifth to that price. If it is not bought back, the priest must sell it for the price he had decided.

28"There is a special kind of gift that people set apart to give to the LORD; it may be a person, animal, or field from the family property. That gift cannot be bought back or sold. Every special kind of gift is most holy to the LORD.

29"If anyone is given for the purpose of being destroyed, he cannot be bought back; he must be put to death.

30"One-tenth of all crops belongs to the LORD, including the crops from fields and the fruit from trees. That one-tenth is holy to the LORD. **31**If a person wants to get back that tenth, one-fifth must be added to its price.

32"The priest will take every tenth animal from a person's herd or flock, and it will be holy to the LORD. **33**The owner should not pick out the good animals from the bad or exchange one animal for another. If that happens, both animals will become holy; they cannot be bought back.'"

34These are the commands the LORD gave to Moses at Mount Sinai for the people of Israel.

numbers

WANDERING IN THE DESERT

THE PEOPLE OF ISRAEL ARE COUNTED

1 The LORD spoke to Moses in the Meeting Tent in the Desert of Sinai. This was on the first day of the second month in the second year after the Israelites left Egypt. He said to Moses: 2"You and Aaron must count all the people of Israel by families and family groups, listing the name of each man. 3You and Aaron must count every man twenty years old or older who will serve in the army of Israel, and list them by their divisions. 4One man from each tribe, the leader of his family, will help you. 5These are the names of the men who will help you:

from the tribe of Reuben—Elizur son of Shedeur;

6 from the tribe of Simeon—Shelumiel son of Zurishaddai;

7 from the tribe of Judah—Nahshon son of Amminadab;

8 from the tribe of Issachar—Nethanel son of Zuar;

9 from the tribe of Zebulun—Eliab son of Helon;

10 from the tribe of Ephraim son of Joseph—Elishama son of Ammihud;

from the tribe of Manasseh son of Joseph—Gamaliel son of Pedahzur;

11 from the tribe of Benjamin—Abidan son of Gideoni;

12 from the tribe of Dan—Ahiezer son of Ammishaddai;

13 from the tribe of Asher—Pagiel son of Ocran;

14 from the tribe of Gad—Eliasaph son of Deuel;

15 from the tribe of Naphtali—Ahira son of Enan."

16These were the men chosen from the people to be leaders of their tribes, the heads of Israel's family groups.

17Moses and Aaron took these men who had been picked 18and called all the people of Israel together on the first day of the second month. Then the people were listed by their families and family groups, and all the men who were twenty years old or older were listed by name. 19Moses did exactly what the LORD had commanded and listed the people while they were in the Desert of Sinai.

20The tribe of Reuben, the first son born to Israel, was counted; all the men twenty years old or older who were able to serve in the army were listed by name with their families and family groups. 21The tribe of Reuben totaled 46,500 men.

22The tribe of Simeon was counted; all the men twenty years old or older who were able to serve in the army were listed by name with their families and family groups. 23The tribe of Simeon totaled 59,300 men.

24The tribe of Gad was counted; all the men twenty years old or older who were able to serve in the army were listed by name with their families and family groups. 25The tribe of Gad totaled 45,650 men.

26The tribe of Judah was counted; all the men twenty years old or older who were able to serve in the army were listed by name with their families and family groups. 27The tribe of Judah totaled 74,600 men.

28The tribe of Issachar was counted; all the men twenty years old or older who were able to serve in the army were listed by name with their families and family groups. 29The tribe of Issachar totaled 54,400 men.

30The tribe of Zebulun was counted; all the men twenty years old or older who were able to serve in the army were listed by name with their families and family groups. 31The tribe of Zebulun totaled 57,400 men.

32The tribe of Ephraim, a son of Joseph, was counted; all the men twenty years old or older who were able to serve in the army were listed by name with their families and family groups. 33The tribe of Ephraim totaled 40,500 men.

34The tribe of Manasseh, also a son of Joseph, was counted; all the men twenty years old or older who were able to serve in the army were listed by name with their families and family groups. ³⁵The tribe of Manasseh totaled 32,200 men.

³⁶The tribe of Benjamin was counted; all the men twenty years old or older who were able to serve in the army were listed by name with their families and family groups. ³⁷The tribe of Benjamin totaled 35,400 men.

³⁸The tribe of Dan was counted; all the men twenty years old or older who were able to serve in the army were listed by name with their families and family groups. ³⁹The tribe of Dan totaled 62,700 men.

⁴⁰The tribe of Asher was counted; all the men twenty years old or older who were able to serve in the army were listed by name with their families and family groups. ⁴¹The tribe of Asher totaled 41,500 men.

⁴²The tribe of Naphtali was counted; all the men twenty years old or older who were able to serve in the army were listed by name with their families and family groups. ⁴³The tribe of Naphtali totaled 53,400 men.

⁴⁴Moses, Aaron, and the twelve leaders of Israel, one from each of the families, counted these men. ⁴⁵Every man of Israel twenty years old or older who was able to serve in the army was counted and listed with his family. ⁴⁶The total number of men was 603,550.

⁴⁷The families from the tribe of Levi were not listed with the others, because ⁴⁸the LORD had told Moses: ⁴⁹"Do not count the tribe of Levi or include them with the other Israelites. ⁵⁰Instead put the Levites in charge of the Holy Tent of the Agreement and everything that is with it. They must carry the Holy Tent and everything in it, and they must take care of it and make their camp around it. ⁵¹Any time the Holy Tent is moved, the Levites must take it down, and any time it is set up, the Levites must do it. Anyone else who goes near the Holy Tent will be put to death. ⁵²The Israelites will make their camps in separate divisions, each family near its flag. ⁵³But the Levites must make their camp around the Holy Tent of the Agreement so that I will not be angry with the Israelites. The Levites will take care of the Holy Tent of the Agreement."

⁵⁴So the Israelites did everything just as the LORD commanded Moses.

THE CAMP ARRANGEMENT

2 The LORD said to Moses and Aaron: ²"The Israelites should make their camps around the Meeting Tent, but they should not camp too close to it. They should camp under their family flag and banners."

³The camp of Judah will be on the east side, where the sun rises, and they will camp by divisions there under their flag. The leader of the people of Judah is Nahshon son of Amminadab. ⁴There are 74,600 men in his division.

⁵Next to them the tribe of Issachar will camp. The leader of the people of Issachar is Nethanel son of Zuar. ⁶There are 54,400 men in his division.

⁷Next is the tribe of Zebulun. The leader of the people of Zebulun is Eliab son of Helon. ⁸There are 57,400 men in his division.

⁹There are a total of 186,400 men in the camps of Judah and its neighbors, in all their divisions. They will be the first to march out of camp.

¹⁰The divisions of the camp of Reuben will be on the south side, where they will camp under their flag. The leader of the people of Reuben is Elizur son of Shedeur. ¹¹There are 46,500 men in his division.

¹²Next to them the tribe of Simeon will camp. The leader of the people of Simeon is Shelumiel son of Zurishaddai. ¹³There are 59,300 men in his division.

¹⁴Next is the tribe of Gad. The leader of the people of Gad is Eliasaph son of Deuel. ¹⁵There are 45,650 men in his division.

¹⁶There are a total of 151,450 men in the camps of Reuben and its neighbors, in all their divisions. They will be the second group to march out of camp.

¹⁷When the Levites march out with the Meeting Tent, they will be in the middle of the other camps. The tribes will march out in the same order as they camp, each in its place under its flag.

¹⁸The divisions of the camp of Ephraim will be on the west side, where they will camp under their flag. The leader of the people of Ephraim is Elishama son of Ammihud. ¹⁹There are 40,500 men in his division.

²⁰Next to them the tribe of Manasseh will camp. The leader of the people of Manasseh is Gamaliel son of Pedahzur. ²¹There are 32,200 men in his division.

²²Next is the tribe of Benjamin. The leader of the people of Benjamin is Abidan son of Gideoni. ²³There are 35,400 men in his division.

²⁴There are a total of 108,100 men in the camps of Ephraim and its neighbors, in all their divisions. They will be the third group to march out of camp.

²⁵The divisions of the camp of Dan will be on the north side, where they will camp under their flag. The leader of the people of Dan is Ahiezer son of Ammishaddai. ²⁶There are 62,700 men in his division.

²⁷Next to them the tribe of Asher will camp. The leader of the people of Asher is Pagiel son of Ocran. ²⁸There are 41,500 men in his division.

²⁹Next is the tribe of Naphtali. The leader of the people of Naphtali is Ahira son of Enan. ³⁰There are 53,400 men in his division.

³¹There are 157,600 men in the camps of Dan and its neighbors. They will be the last to march out of camp, and they will travel under their own flag.

³²These are the Israelites who were counted by families. The total number of Israelites in the camps, counted by divisions, is 603,550. ³³Moses obeyed the LORD and did not count the Levites among the other people of Israel.

³⁴So the Israelites obeyed everything the LORD commanded Moses. They camped under their flags and marched out by families and family groups.

AARON'S FAMILY, THE PRIESTS

3 This is the family history of Aaron and Moses at the time the LORD talked to Moses on Mount Sinai.

²Aaron had four sons: Nadab, the oldest, Abihu, Eleazar, and Ithamar. ³These were the names of Aaron's sons, who were appointed to serve as priests. ⁴But Nadab and Abihu died in the presence of the LORD when they offered the wrong kind of fire before the LORD in the Desert of Sinai. They had no sons. So Eleazar and Ithamar served as priests during the lifetime of their father Aaron.

⁵The LORD said to Moses, ⁶"Bring the tribe of Levi and present them to Aaron the priest to help him. ⁷They will help him and all the Israelites at the Meeting Tent, doing the work in the Holy Tent. ⁸The Levites must take care of everything in the Meeting Tent and serve the people of Israel by doing the work in the Holy Tent. ⁹Give the Levites to Aaron and his sons; of all the Israelites, the Levites are given completely to him. ¹⁰Appoint Aaron and his sons to serve as priests, but anyone else who comes near the holy things must be put to death."

¹¹The LORD also said to Moses, ¹²"I am choosing the Levites from all the Israelites to take the place of all the firstborn children of Israel. The Levites will be mine, ¹³because the firstborn are mine. When you were in Egypt, I killed all the firstborn children of the Egyptians and took all the firstborn of Israel to be mine, both animals and children. They are mine. I am the LORD."

¹⁴The LORD again said to Moses in the Desert of Sinai, ¹⁵"Count the Levites by families and family groups. Count every male one month old or older." ¹⁶So Moses obeyed the LORD and counted them all.

¹⁷Levi had three sons, whose names were Gershon, Kohath, and Merari.

¹⁸The Gershonite family groups were Libni and Shimei.

¹⁹The Kohathite family groups were Amram, Izhar, Hebron, and Uzziel.

²⁰The Merarite family groups were Mahli and Mushi.

These were the family groups of the Levites.

²¹The family groups of Libni and Shimei belonged to Gershon; they were the Gershonite family groups. ²²The number that was counted was 7,500 males one month old or older. ²³The Gershonite family groups camped on the west side, behind the Holy Tent. ²⁴The leader of the families of Gershon was Eliasaph son of Lael. ²⁵In the Meeting Tent the Gershonites were in charge of the Holy Tent, its covering, the curtain at the entrance to the Meeting Tent, ²⁶the curtains in the courtyard, the curtain at the entry to the courtyard around the Holy Tent and the altar, the ropes, and all the work connected with these items.

²⁷The family groups of Amram, Izhar, Hebron, and Uzziel belonged to Kohath; they were the Kohathite family groups. ²⁸They had 8,600 males one month old or older, and they were responsible for taking care of the Holy Place. ²⁹The Kohathite family groups

camped south of the Holy Tent. ³⁰The leader of the Kohathite families was Elizaphan son of Uzziel. ³¹They were responsible for the Ark, the table, the lampstand, the altars, the tools of the Holy Place which they were to use, the curtain, and all the work connected with these items. ³²The main leader of the Levites was Eleazar son of Aaron, the priest, who was in charge of all those responsible for the Holy Place.

³³The family groups of Mahli and Mushi belonged to Merari; they were the Merarite family groups. ³⁴The number that was counted was 6,200 males one month old or older. ³⁵The leader of the Merari families was Zuriel son of Abihail, and they were to camp north of the Holy Tent. ³⁶The Merarites were responsible for the frames of the Holy Tent, the braces, the posts, the bases, and all the work connected with these items. ³⁷They were also responsible for the posts in the courtyard around the Holy Tent and their bases, tent pegs, and ropes.

³⁸Moses, Aaron, and his sons camped east of the Holy Tent, toward the sunrise, in front of the Meeting Tent. They were responsible for the Holy Place for the Israelites. Anyone else who came near the Holy Place was to be put to death.

³⁹Moses and Aaron counted the Levite men by their families, as the LORD commanded, and there were 22,000 males one month old or older.

LEVITES TAKE THE PLACE OF THE FIRSTBORN SONS

⁴⁰The LORD said to Moses, "Count all the firstborn sons in Israel one month old or older, and list their names. ⁴¹Take the Levites for me instead of the firstborn sons of Israel; take the animals of the Levites instead of the firstborn animals from the rest of Israel. I am the LORD."

⁴²So Moses did what the LORD commanded and counted all the firstborn sons of the Israelites. ⁴³When he listed all the firstborn sons one month old or older, there were 22,273 names.

⁴⁴The LORD also said to Moses, ⁴⁵"Take the Levites instead of all the firstborn sons of the Israelites, and take the animals of the Levites instead of the animals of the other people. The Levites are mine. I am the LORD.

⁴⁶Since there are 273 more firstborn sons than Levites, ⁴⁷collect two ounces of silver for each of the 273 sons. Use the measure as set by the Holy Place, which is two-fifths of an ounce. ⁴⁸Give the silver to Aaron and his sons as the payment for the 273 Israelites."

⁴⁹So Moses collected the money for the people the Levites could not replace. ⁵⁰From the firstborn of the Israelites, he collected thirty-five pounds of silver, using the measure set by the Holy Place. ⁵¹Moses obeyed the command of the LORD and gave the silver to Aaron and his sons.

THE JOBS OF THE KOHATH FAMILY

4 The LORD said to Moses and Aaron, ²"Count the Kohathites among the Levites by family groups and families. ³Count the men from thirty to fifty years old, all who come to serve in the Meeting Tent.

⁴"The Kohathites are responsible for the most holy things in the Meeting Tent. ⁵When the Israelites are ready to move, Aaron and his sons must go into the Holy Tent, take down the curtain, and cover the Ark of the Agreement with it. ⁶Over this they must put a covering made from fine leather, then spread the solid blue cloth over that, and put the poles in place.

⁷"Then they must spread a blue cloth over the table for the bread that shows a person is in God's presence. They must put the plates, pans, bowls, and the jars for drink offerings on the table; they must leave the bread that is always there on the table. ⁸Then they must put a red cloth over all of these things, cover everything with fine leather, and put the poles in place.

⁹"With a blue cloth they must cover the lampstand, its lamps, its wick trimmers, its trays, and all the jars for the oil used in the lamps. ¹⁰Then they must wrap everything in fine leather and put all these things on a frame for carrying them.

¹¹"They must spread a blue cloth over the gold altar, cover it with fine leather, and put the poles in place.

¹²"They must gather all the things used for serving in the Holy Place and wrap them in a blue cloth. Then they must cover that with fine leather and put these things on a frame for carrying them.

13"They must clean the ashes off the bronze altar and spread a purple cloth over it. 14They must gather all the things used for serving at the altar—the pans for carrying the fire, the meat forks, the shovels, and the bowls—and put them on the bronze altar. Then they must spread a covering of fine leather over it and put the poles in place.

15"When the Israelites are ready to move, and when Aaron and his sons have covered the holy furniture and all the holy things, the Kohathites may go in and carry them away. In this way they won't touch the holy things and die. It is the Kohathites' job to carry the things that are in the Meeting Tent.

16"Eleazar son of Aaron, the priest, will be responsible for the Holy Tent and for everything in it, for all the holy things it has: the oil for the lamp, the sweet-smelling incense, the continual grain offering, and the oil used to appoint priests and things to the LORD's service."

17The LORD said to Moses and Aaron, 18"Don't let the Kohathites be cut off from the Levites. 19Do this for the Kohathites so that they may go near the Most Holy Place and not die: Aaron and his sons must go in and show each Kohathite what to do and what to carry. 20The Kohathites must not enter and look at the holy things, even for a second, or they will die."

THE JOBS OF THE GERSHON FAMILY

21The LORD said to Moses, 22"Count the Gershonites by families and family groups. 23Count the men from thirty to fifty years old, all who have a job to do in the Meeting Tent.

24"This is what the Gershonite family groups must do and what they must carry. 25They must carry the curtains of the Holy Tent, the Meeting Tent, its covering, and its outer covering made from fine leather. They must also carry the curtains for the entrance to the Meeting Tent, 26the curtains of the courtyard that go around the Holy Tent and the altar, the curtain for the entry to the courtyard, the ropes, and all the things used with the curtains. They must do everything connected with these things. 27Aaron and his sons are in charge of what the Gershonites do or carry; you tell them what they are responsible for carrying. 28This is the work of the Gershonite family group at the Meeting Tent. Ithamar son of Aaron, the priest, will direct their work.

THE JOBS OF THE MERARI FAMILY

29"Count the Merarite families and family groups. 30Count the men from thirty to fifty years old, all who work at the Meeting Tent. 31It is their job to carry the following as they serve in the Meeting Tent: the frames of the Holy Tent, the crossbars, the posts, and bases, 32in addition to the posts that go around the courtyard, their bases, tent pegs, ropes, and everything that is used with the poles around the courtyard. Tell each man exactly what to carry. 33This is the work the Merarite family group will do for the Meeting Tent. Ithamar son of Aaron, the priest, will direct their work."

THE LEVITE FAMILIES

34Moses, Aaron, and the leaders of Israel counted the Kohathites by families and family groups, 35the men from thirty to fifty years old who were to work at the Meeting Tent. 36There were 2,750 men in the family groups. 37This was the total of the Kohath family groups who worked at the Meeting Tent, whom Moses and Aaron counted as the LORD had commanded Moses.

38Also, the Gershonites were counted by families and family groups, 39the men from thirty to fifty years old who were given work at the Meeting Tent. 40The families and family groups had 2,630 men. 41This was the total of the Gershon family groups who worked at the Meeting Tent, whom Moses and Aaron counted as the LORD had commanded.

42Also, the men in the families and family groups of the Merari family were counted, 43the men from thirty to fifty years old who were to work at the Meeting Tent. 44The family groups had 3,200 men. 45This was the total of the Merari family groups, whom Moses and Aaron counted as the LORD had commanded Moses.

46So Moses, Aaron, and the leaders of Israel counted all the Levites by families and family groups. 47They counted the men from thirty to fifty who were given work at the Meeting Tent and who carried the Tent. 48The total number of these men was 8,580. 49Each man was counted as the LORD had commanded Moses; each man was given his work and told what to carry as the LORD had commanded Moses.

RULES ABOUT CLEANLINESS

5 The LORD said to Moses, 2"Command the Israelites to send away from camp anyone with a harmful skin disease. Send away anyone who gives off body fluid or who has become unclean by touching a dead body. 3Send both men and women outside the camp so that they won't spread the disease there, where I am living among you." 4So Israel obeyed the LORD's command and sent those people outside the camp. They did just as the LORD had told Moses.

PAYING FOR DOING WRONG

5The LORD said to Moses, 6"Tell the Israelites: 'When a man or woman does something wrong to another person, that is really sinning against the LORD. That person is guilty 7and must admit the wrong that has been done. The person must fully pay for the wrong that has been done, adding one-fifth to it, and giving it to the person who was wronged. 8But if that person is dead and does not have any close relatives to receive the payment, the one who did wrong owes the LORD and must pay the priest. In addition, the priest must sacrifice a male sheep to remove the wrong so that the person will belong to the LORD. 9When an Israelite brings a holy gift, it should be given to the priest. 10No one has to give these holy gifts, but if someone does give them, they belong to the priest.'"

SUSPICIOUS HUSBANDS

11Then the LORD said to Moses, 12"Tell the Israelites: 'A man's wife might be unfaithful to him 13and have sexual relations with another man. Her sin might be kept hidden from her husband so that he does not know about the wrong she did. Perhaps no one saw it, and she wasn't caught. 14But if her husband has feelings of jealousy and suspects she has sinned—whether she has or not— 15he should take her to the priest. The husband must also take an offering for her of two quarts of barley flour. He must not pour oil or incense on it, because this is a grain offering for jealousy, an offering of remembrance. It is to find out if she is guilty.

16"The priest will bring in the woman and make her stand before the LORD. 17He will take some holy water in a clay jar, and he will put some dirt from the floor of the Holy Tent into the water. 18The priest will make the woman stand before the LORD, and he will loosen her hair. He will hand her the offering of remembrance, the grain offering for jealousy; he will hold the bitter water that brings a curse. 19The priest will make her take an oath and ask her, "Has another man had sexual relations with you? Have you been unfaithful to your husband? If you haven't, this bitter water that brings a curse won't hurt you. 20But if you have been unfaithful to your husband and have had sexual relations with a man besides him"— 21the priest will then put on her the curse that the oath will bring—"the LORD will make the people curse and reject you. He will make your stomach get big, and he will make your body unable to give birth to another baby. 22This water that brings a curse will go inside you and make your body unable to give birth to another baby."

"'The woman must say, "I agree."

23"'The priest should write these curses on a scroll, wash the words off into the bitter water, 24and make the woman drink the bitter water that brings a curse. If she is guilty, the water will make her sick. 25Then the priest will take the grain offering for jealousy from her. He will present it before the LORD and bring it to the altar. 26He will take a handful of the grain, which is a memorial offering, and burn it on the altar. After that he will make the woman drink the water 27to see if she is not pure and if she has sinned against her husband. When it goes into her, if her stomach gets big and she is not able to have another baby, her people will reject her. 28But if the woman has not sinned, she is pure. She is not guilty, and she will be able to have babies.

29"'So this is the teaching about jealousy. This is what to do when a woman does wrong and is unfaithful while she is married to her husband. 30It also should be done if the man gets jealous because he suspects his wife. The priest will have her stand before the LORD, and he will do all these things, just as the teaching commands. 31In this way the husband can be proven correct, and the woman will suffer if she has done wrong.'"

RULES FOR THE NAZIRITES

6 The Lord said to Moses, ²"Tell the Israelites: 'If men or women want to promise to belong to the Lord in a special way, they will be called Nazirites. ³During this time, they must not drink wine or beer, or vinegar made from wine or beer. They must not even drink grape juice or eat grapes or rai-sins. ⁴While they are Nazirites, they must not eat anything that comes from the grapevine, even the seeds or the skin.

⁵"'During the time they have promised to belong to the Lord, they must not cut their hair. They must be holy until this special time is over. They must let their hair grow long. ⁶During their special time of belonging to the

---

FAMILY

BOYS WILL BE . . .

God watches
over you

NUMBERS 6:22-27

The Book of Numbers is God's accounting ledger. The name in English comes from the fact that this document *numbers* the tribes of Israel. It is a mix of historical records and laws. In this general ledger is one of the most often used blessings of Scripture. If you read the context, you will find that God himself tells Moses to use this blessing for the people of Israel. God gives Moses the exact words that he wants Aaron to use because God wants his children to know who is watching over them.

This is not a blessing for God's one-time interaction with you. It is a blessing to have God constantly watch over you, every moment of every day. Even more interesting is the fact that this blessing is practically a command. God tells Aaron, "Use precisely these words. Don't give a sort of general paraphrase of what I mean. Tell the people that this is *exactly* what I will do."

Think about it. God says, "May the Lord bless you and keep you." God commands himself to look after us in everything we do. If you thought you just had a guardian angel, you're wrong. You've got someone a lot more important than an angel looking over you.

It might help to think of the other meanings of *shamar*. Picture a fortress wall protecting you. Think of a guard tower fully manned. Then remember that this word is also used in another famous passage: "Is it my job to take care of my brother?" We have guard duty, too. God watches over you so that you can fulfill your guard duty to those he puts under you.

---

reflect: Thank God today that he blesses and keeps you at all times.
Go to **FAMILY:** "The Extra Mile Marriage" at **Amos 3:3.**

LORD, Nazirites must not go near a dead body. ⁷Even if their own father, mother, brother, or sister dies, they must not touch them, or they will become unclean. They must still keep their promise to belong to God in a special way. ⁸While they are Nazirites, they belong to the LORD in a special way.

⁹"If they are next to someone who dies suddenly, their hair, which was part of their promise, has been made unclean. So they must shave their head seven days later to be clean. ¹⁰Then on the eighth day, they must bring two doves or two young pigeons to the priest at the entrance to the Meeting Tent. ¹¹The priest will offer one as a sin offering and the other as a burnt offering. This removes sin so they will belong to the LORD. (They had sinned because they were near a dead body.) That same day they will again promise to let their hair grow ¹²and give themselves to the LORD for another special time. They must bring a male lamb a year old as a penalty offering. The days of the special time before don't count, because they became unclean during their first special time.

¹³"This is the teaching for the Nazirites. When the promised time is over, they must go to the entrance of the Meeting Tent ¹⁴and give their offerings to the LORD. They must offer a year-old male lamb that has nothing wrong with it, as a burnt offering, a year-old female lamb that has nothing wrong with it, as a sin offering, and a male sheep that has nothing wrong with it, for a fellowship offering. ¹⁵They must also bring the grain offerings and drink offerings that go with them. And they must bring a basket of bread made without yeast, loaves made with fine flour mixed with oil, and wafers made without yeast spread with oil.

¹⁶"The priest will give these offerings to the LORD and make the sin offering and the burnt offering. ¹⁷Then he will kill the male sheep as a fellowship offering to the LORD; along with it, he will present the basket of bread made without yeast, the grain offering, and the drink offering.

¹⁸"The Nazirites must go to the entrance of the Meeting Tent and shave off their hair that they grew for their promise. The hair will be put in the fire that is under the sacrifice of the fellowship offering.

¹⁹"After the Nazirites cut off their hair, the priest will give them a boiled shoulder from the male sheep. From the basket he will also give a loaf and a wafer, both made without yeast. ²⁰Then the priest will present them to the LORD. They are holy and belong to the priest. Also, he is to present the breast and the thigh from the male sheep. After that, the Nazirites may drink wine.

²¹"This is the teaching for the Nazirites who make a promise. Everyone who makes the Nazirite promise must give all of these gifts to the LORD. If they promised to do more, they must keep their promise, according to the teaching of the Nazirites.'"

THE PRIESTS' BLESSINGS

²²The LORD said to Moses, ²³"Tell Aaron and his sons, 'This is how you should bless the Israelites. Say to them:
²⁴ "May the LORD bless you and keep you.
²⁵ May the LORD show you his kindness
  and have mercy on you.
²⁶ May the LORD watch over you
  and give you peace." '
²⁷"So Aaron and his sons will bless the Israelites with my name, and I will bless them."

THE HOLY TENT

7 When Moses finished setting up the Holy Tent, he gave it for service to the LORD by pouring olive oil on the Tent and on everything used in it. He also poured oil on the altar and all its tools to prepare them for service to the LORD. ²Then the leaders of Israel made offerings. These were the heads of the families, the leaders of each tribe who counted the people. ³They brought to the LORD six covered carts and twelve oxen—each leader giving an ox, and every two leaders giving a cart. They brought these to the Holy Tent.

⁴The LORD said to Moses, ⁵"Accept these gifts from the leaders and use them in the work of the Meeting Tent. Give them to the Levites as they need them."

⁶So Moses accepted the carts and the oxen and gave them to the Levites. ⁷He gave two carts and four oxen to the Gershonites, which they needed for their work. ⁸Then Moses gave four carts and eight oxen to the Merarites, which they needed for their work. Ithamar son of Aaron, the priest, directed the work of all of them. ⁹Moses did not give any oxen or carts to the Kohathites, because

their job was to carry the holy things on their shoulders.

¹⁰When the oil was poured on the altar, the leaders brought their offerings to it to give it to the LORD's service; they presented them in front of the altar. ¹¹The LORD told Moses, "Each day one leader must bring his gift to make the altar ready for service to me."

¹²⁻⁸³Each of the twelve leaders brought these gifts. Each leader brought one silver plate that weighed about three and one-fourth pounds, and one silver bowl that weighed about one and three-fourths pounds. These weights were set by the Holy Place measure. The bowl and the plate were filled with fine flour mixed with oil for a grain offering. Each leader also brought a large gold dish that weighed about four ounces and was filled with incense.

In addition, each of the leaders brought one young bull, one male sheep, and one male lamb a year old for a burnt offering; one male goat for a sin offering; and two oxen, five male sheep, five male goats, and five male lambs a year old for a fellowship offering.

On the first day Nahshon son of Amminadab brought his gifts. He was the leader of the tribe of Judah.

On the second day Nethanel son of Zuar brought his gifts. He was the leader of the tribe of Issachar.

On the third day Eliab son of Helon brought his gifts. He was the leader of the tribe of Zebulun.

On the fourth day Elizur son of Shedeur brought his gifts. He was the leader of the tribe of Reuben.

On the fifth day Shelumiel son of Zurishaddai brought his gifts. He was the leader of the tribe of Simeon.

On the sixth day Eliasaph son of Deuel brought his gifts. He was the leader of the tribe of Gad.

On the seventh day Elishama son of Ammihud brought his gifts. He was the leader of the tribe of Ephraim.

On the eighth day Gamaliel son of Pedahzur brought his gifts. He was the leader of the tribe of Manasseh.

On the ninth day Abidan son of Gideoni brought his gifts. He was the leader of the tribe of Benjamin.

On the tenth day Ahiezer son of Ammishaddai brought his gifts. He was the leader of the tribe of Dan.

On the eleventh day Pagiel son of Ocran brought his gifts. He was the leader of the tribe of Asher.

On the twelfth day Ahira son of Enan brought his gifts. He was the leader of the tribe of Naphtali.

⁸⁴So these were the gifts from the Israelite leaders when oil was poured on the altar and it was given for service to the LORD: twelve silver plates, twelve silver bowls, and twelve gold dishes. ⁸⁵Each silver plate weighed about three and one-fourth pounds, and each bowl weighed about one and three-fourths pounds. All the silver plates and silver bowls together weighed about sixty pounds according to a weight set by the Holy Place measure. ⁸⁶The twelve gold dishes filled with incense weighed four ounces each, according to the weight set by the Holy Place measure. Together the gold dishes weighed about three pounds. ⁸⁷The total number of animals for the burnt offering was twelve bulls, twelve male sheep, and twelve male lambs a year old. There was also a grain offering, and there were twelve male goats for a sin offering. ⁸⁸The total number of animals for the fellowship offering was twenty-four bulls, sixty male sheep, sixty male goats, and sixty male lambs a year old. All these offerings were for giving the altar to the service of the LORD after the oil had been poured on it.

⁸⁹When Moses went into the Meeting Tent to speak with the LORD, he heard the LORD speaking to him. The voice was coming from between the two gold creatures with wings that were above the lid of the Ark of the Agreement. In this way the LORD spoke with him.

THE LAMPSTAND

8 The LORD said to Moses, ²"Speak to Aaron and tell him, 'Put the seven lamps where they can light the area in front of the lampstand.'"

³Aaron did this, putting the lamps so they lighted the area in front of the lampstand; he obeyed the command the LORD gave Moses. ⁴The lampstand was made from hammered gold, from its base to the flowers. It was made exactly the way the LORD had showed Moses.

THE LEVITES ARE GIVEN TO GOD

⁵The LORD said to Moses, ⁶"Take the Levites away from the other Israelites and make them clean. ⁷This is what you should do to make them clean: Sprinkle the cleansing water on them, and have them shave their bodies and wash their clothes so they will be clean. ⁸They must take a young bull and the grain offering of flour mixed with oil that goes with it. Then take a second young bull for a sin offering. ⁹Bring the Levites to the front of the Meeting Tent, and gather all the Israelites around. ¹⁰When you bring the Levites before the LORD, the Israelites should put their hands on them.ⁿ ¹¹Aaron will present the Levites before the LORD as an offering presented from the Israelites. Then the Levites will be ready to do the work of the LORD.

¹²"The Levites will put their hands on the bulls' heads—one bull will be a sin offering to the LORD, and the other will be a burnt offering, to remove the sins of the Levites so they will belong to the LORD. ¹³Make the Levites stand in front of Aaron and his sons and present the Levites as an offering to the LORD. ¹⁴In this way you must set apart the Levites from the other Israelites; the Levites will be mine.

¹⁵"Make the Levites pure, and present them as an offering so that they may come to work at the Meeting Tent. ¹⁶They will be given completely to me from the Israelites; I have taken them for myself instead of the firstborn of every Israelite woman. ¹⁷All the firstborn in Israel—people or animals—are mine. When I killed all the firstborn in Egypt, I set the firstborn in Israel aside for myself. ¹⁸But I have taken the Levites instead of all the firstborn in Israel. ¹⁹From all the Israelites I have given the Levites to Aaron and his sons so that they may serve the Israelites at the Meeting Tent. They will help remove the Israelites' sins so they will belong to the LORD and so that no disaster will strike the Israelites when they approach the Holy Place."

²⁰So Moses, Aaron, and all the Israelites obeyed and did with the Levites what the LORD commanded Moses. ²¹The Levites made themselves clean and washed their clothes. Then Aaron presented them as an offering to the LORD. He also removed their sins so they would be pure. ²²After that, the Levites came to the Meeting Tent to work, and Aaron and his sons told them what to do. They did with the Levites what the LORD commanded Moses.

²³The LORD said to Moses, ²⁴"This command is for the Levites. Everyone twenty-five years old or older must come to the Meeting Tent, because they all have jobs to do there. ²⁵At the age of fifty, they must retire from their jobs and not work again. ²⁶They may help their fellow Levites with their work at the Meeting Tent, but they must not do the work themselves. This is the way you are to give the Levites their jobs."

THE PASSOVER IS CELEBRATED

9 The LORD spoke to Moses in the Desert of Sinai in the first month of the second year after the Israelites left Egypt. He said, ²"Tell the Israelites to celebrate the Passover at the appointed time. ³That appointed time is the fourteenth day of this month at twilight; they must obey all the rules about it."

⁴So Moses told the Israelites to celebrate the Passover, ⁵and they did; it was in the Desert of Sinai at twilight on the fourteenth day of the first month. The Israelites did everything just as the LORD commanded Moses.

⁶But some of the people could not celebrate the Passover on that day because they were unclean from touching a dead body. So they went to Moses and Aaron that day and ⁷said to Moses, "We are unclean because of touching a dead body. But why should we be kept from offering gifts to the LORD at this appointed time? Why can't we join the other Israelites?"

⁸Moses said to them, "Wait, and I will find out what the LORD says about you."

⁹Then the LORD said to Moses, ¹⁰"Tell the Israelites this: 'If you or your descendants become unclean because of a dead body, or if you are away on a trip during the Passover, you must still celebrate the LORD's Passover. ¹¹But celebrate it at twilight on the fourteenth day of the second month. Eat the lamb with bitter herbs and bread made without yeast. ¹²Don't leave any of it until the next morning or break any of its bones. When you celebrate the Passover, follow all the rules.

8:10 put . . . them This showed that the people had a part in giving the Levites their special work.

[13]Anyone who is clean and is not away on a trip but does not eat the Passover must be cut off from the people. That person did not give an offering to the LORD at the appointed time and must be punished for the sin.

[14]"'Foreigners among you may celebrate the LORD's Passover, but they must follow all the rules. You must have the same rules for foreigners as you have for yourselves.'"

THE CLOUD ABOVE THE TENT

[15]On the day the Holy Tent, the Tent of the Agreement, was set up, a cloud covered it. From dusk until dawn the cloud above the Tent looked like fire. [16]The cloud stayed above the Tent, and at night it looked like fire. [17]When the cloud moved from its place over the Tent, the Israelites moved, and wherever the cloud stopped, the Israelites camped. [18]So the Israelites moved at the LORD's command, and they camped at his command. While the cloud stayed over the Tent, they remained camped. [19]Sometimes the cloud stayed over the Tent for a long time, but the Israelites obeyed the LORD and did not move. [20]Sometimes the cloud was over it only a few days. At the LORD's command the people camped, and at his command they moved. [21]Sometimes the cloud stayed only from dusk until dawn; when the cloud lifted the next morning, the people moved. When the cloud lifted, day or night, the people moved. [22]The cloud might stay over the Tent for two days, a month, or a year. As long as it stayed, the people camped, but when it lifted, they moved. [23]At the LORD's command the people camped, and at his command they moved. They obeyed the LORD's order that he commanded through Moses.

THE SILVER TRUMPETS

10 The LORD said to Moses, [2]"Make two trumpets of hammered silver, and use them to call the people together and to march out of camp. [3]When both trumpets are blown, the people should gather before you at the entrance to the Meeting Tent. [4]If you blow only one trumpet, the leaders, the heads of the family groups of Israel, should meet before you. [5]When you loudly blow the trumpets, the tribes camping on the east should move. [6]When you loudly blow them again, the tribes camping on the south should move; the loud sound will tell them to move.

[7]When you want to gather the people, blow the trumpets, but don't blow them as loudly.

[8]"Aaron's sons, the priests, should blow the trumpets. This is a law for you and your descendants from now on. [9]When you are fighting an enemy who attacks you in your own land, blow the trumpets loudly. The LORD your God will take notice of you and will save you from your enemies. [10]Also blow your trumpets at happy times and during your feasts and at New Moon festivals. Blow them over your burnt offerings and fellowship offerings, because they will help you remember your God. I am the LORD your God."

THE ISRAELITES MOVE CAMP

[11]The cloud lifted from the Tent of the Agreement on the twentieth day of the second month of the second year. [12]So the Israelites moved from the Desert of Sinai and continued until the cloud stopped in the Desert of Paran. [13]This was their first time to move, and they did it as the LORD had commanded Moses.

[14]The divisions from the camp of Judah moved first under their flag. Nahshon son of Amminadab was the commander. [15]Nethanel son of Zuar was over the division of the tribe of Issachar. [16]Eliab son of Helon was over the division of the tribe of Zebulun. [17]Then the Holy Tent was taken down, and the Gershonites and Merarites, who carried it, moved next.

[18]Then came the divisions from the camp of Reuben under their flag, and Elizur son of Shedeur was the commander. [19]Shelumiel son of Zurishaddai was over the division of the tribe of Simeon. [20]Eliasaph son of Deuel was over the division of the tribe of Gad. [21]Then came the Kohathites, who carried the holy things; the Holy Tent was to be set up before they arrived.

[22]Next came the divisions from the camp of Ephraim under their flag, and Elishama son of Ammihud was the commander. [23]Gamaliel son of Pedahzur was over the division of the tribe of Manasseh, [24]and Abidan son of Gideoni was over the division of the tribe of Benjamin.

[25]The last ones were the rear guard for all the tribes. These were the divisions from the camp of Dan under their flag, and Ahiezer

son of Ammishaddai was the commander. 26Pagiel son of Ocran was over the division of the tribe of Asher; 27Ahira son of Enan was over the division of the tribe of Naphtali. 28This was the order the Israelite divisions marched in when they moved.

29Hobab was the son of Reuel the Midianite,[n] who was Moses' father-in-law. Moses said to Hobab, "We are moving to the land the LORD promised to give us. Come with us and we will be good to you, because the LORD has promised good things to Israel."

30But Hobab answered, "No, I will not go. I will go back to my own land where I was born."

31But Moses said, "Please don't leave us. You know where we can camp in the desert, and you can be our guide. 32Come with us. We will share with you all the good things the LORD gives us." 33So they left the mountain of the LORD and traveled for three days. The Ark of the LORD's Agreement went in front of the people for those three days, as they looked for a place to camp. 34The LORD's cloud was over them during the day when they left their camp.

35When the Ark left the camp, Moses said,

"Rise up, LORD!
Scatter your enemies:
make those who hate you run from
you."

36And when the Ark was set down, Moses said,

"Return, LORD,
to the thousands of people of Israel."

FIRE FROM THE LORD

11 Now the people complained to the LORD about their troubles, and when he heard them, he became angry. Then fire from the LORD burned among the people at the edge of the camp. 2The people cried out to Moses, and when he prayed to the LORD, the fire stopped burning. 3So that place was called Taberah,[n] because the LORD's fire had burned among them.

SEVENTY ELDERS HELP MOSES

4Some troublemakers among them wanted better food, and soon all the Israelites began complaining. They said, "We want meat! 5We remember the fish we ate for free in Egypt. We also had cucumbers, melons, leeks, onions, and garlic. 6But now we have lost our appetite; we never see anything but this manna!"

7The manna was like small white seeds. 8The people would go to gather it, and then grind it in handmills, or crush it between stones. After they cooked it in a pot or made cakes with it, it tasted like bread baked with olive oil. 9When the dew fell on the camp each night, so did the manna.

10Moses heard every family crying as they stood in the entrances of their tents. Then the LORD became very angry, and Moses got upset. 11He asked the LORD, "Why have you brought me, your servant, this trouble? What have I done wrong that you made me responsible for all these people? 12I am not the father of all these people, and I didn't give birth to them. So why do you make me carry them to the land you promised to our ancestors? Must I carry them in my arms as a nurse carries a baby? 13Where can I get meat for all these people? They keep crying to me, 'We want meat!' 14I can't take care of all these people alone. It is too much for me. 15If you are going to continue doing this to me, then kill me now. If you care about me, put me to death, and then I won't have any more troubles."

16The LORD said to Moses, "Bring me seventy of Israel's elders, men that you know are leaders among the people. Bring them to the Meeting Tent, and have them stand there with you. 17I will come down and speak with you there. I will take some of the Spirit that is in you, and I will give it to them. They will help you care for the people so that you will not have to care for them alone.

18"Tell the people this: 'Make yourselves holy for tomorrow, and you will eat meat. You cried to the LORD, "We want meat! We were better off in Egypt!" So now the LORD will give you meat to eat. 19You will eat it not for just one, two, five, ten, or even twenty days, 20but you will eat that meat for a whole month. You will eat it until it comes out your nose, and you will grow to hate it. This is because you have rejected the LORD, who is with you. You have cried to him, saying, "Why did we ever leave Egypt?" '"

10:29 Reuel the Midianite Also called Jethro.
11:3 Taberah This name means "burning."

21Moses said, "LORD, here are six hundred thousand people standing around me, and you say, 'I will give them enough meat to eat for a month!' 22If we killed all the flocks and herds, that would not be enough. If we caught all the fish in the sea, that would not be enough."

23But the LORD said to Moses, "Do you think I'm weak? Now you will see if I can do what I say."

24So Moses went out to the people and told them what the LORD had said. He gathered seventy of the elders together and had them stand around the Tent. 25Then the LORD came down in the cloud and spoke to Moses. The LORD took some of the Spirit Moses had, and he gave it to the seventy leaders. With the Spirit in them, they prophesied, but just that one time.

26Two men named Eldad and Medad were also listed as leaders, but they did not go to the Tent. They stayed in the camp, but the Spirit was also given to them, and they prophesied in the camp. 27A young man ran to Moses and said, "Eldad and Medad are prophesying in the camp."

28Joshua son of Nun said, "Moses, my master, stop them!" (Ever since he was a young boy, Joshua had been Moses' assistant.)

29But Moses answered, "Are you jealous for me? I wish all the LORD's people could prophesy. I wish the LORD would give his Spirit to all of them!" 30Then Moses and the leaders of Israel went back to the camp.

THE LORD SENDS QUAIL

31The LORD sent a strong wind from the sea, and it blew quail into the area all around the camp. The quail were about three feet deep on the ground, and there were quail a day's walk in any direction. 32The people went out and gathered quail all that day, that night, and the next day. Everyone gathered at least sixty bushels, and they spread them around the camp. 33But the LORD became very angry, and he gave the people a terrible sickness that came while the meat was still in their mouths. 34So the people named that place Kibroth Hattaavah,n because there they buried those who wanted other food.

35From Kibroth Hattaavah the people went to stay at Hazeroth.

MIRIAM AND AARON SPEAK AGAINST MOSES

12 Miriam and Aaron began to talk against Moses because of his Cushite wife (he had married a Cushite). 2They said, "Is Moses the only one the LORD speaks through? Doesn't he also speak through us?" And the LORD heard this.

3(Now Moses was very humble. He was the least proud person on earth.)

4So the LORD suddenly spoke to Moses, Aaron, and Miriam and said, "All three of you come to the Meeting Tent." So they went. 5The LORD came down in a pillar of cloud and stood at the entrance to the Tent. He called to Aaron and Miriam, and they both came near. 6He said, "Listen to my words:

When prophets are among you,
   I, the LORD, will show myself to them in
      visions;
   I will speak to them in dreams.
7 But this is not true with my servant
      Moses.
   I trust him to lead all my people.
8 I speak face to face with him—
   clearly, not with hidden meanings.
   He has even seen the form of the LORD.
You should be afraid
   to speak against my servant Moses."

9The LORD was very angry with them, and he left.

10When the cloud lifted from the Tent and Aaron turned toward Miriam, she was as white as snow; she had a skin disease. 11Aaron said to Moses, "Please, my master, forgive us for our foolish sin. 12Don't let her be like a baby who is born dead. (Sometimes a baby is born with half of its flesh eaten away.)"

13So Moses cried out to the LORD, "God, please heal her!"

14The LORD answered Moses, "If her father had spit in her face, she would have been shamed for seven days, so put her outside the camp for seven days. After that, she may come back." 15So Miriam was put outside of the camp for seven days, and the people did not move on until she came back.

16After that, the people left Hazeroth and camped in the Desert of Paran.

11:34 Kibroth Hattaavah This name in Hebrew means "graves of wanting."

THE SPIES EXPLORE CANAAN

13 The LORD said to Moses, ²"Send men to explore the land of Canaan, which I will give to the Israelites. Send one leader from each tribe."

³So Moses obeyed the LORD's command and sent the Israelite leaders out from the Desert of Paran. ⁴These are their names: from the tribe of Reuben, Shammua son of Zaccur; ⁵from the tribe of Simeon, Shaphat son of Hori; ⁶from the tribe of Judah, Caleb son of Jephunneh; ⁷from the tribe of Issachar, Igal son of Joseph; ⁸from the tribe of Ephraim, Hoshea son of Nun; ⁹from the tribe of Benjamin, Palti son of Raphu; ¹⁰from the tribe of Zebulun, Gaddiel son of Sodi; ¹¹from the tribe of Manasseh (a tribe of Joseph), Gaddi son of Susi; ¹²from the tribe of Dan, Ammiel son of Gemalli; ¹³from the tribe of Asher, Sethur son of Michael; ¹⁴from the tribe of Naphtali, Nahbi son of Vophsi; ¹⁵from the tribe of Gad, Geuel son of Maki.

¹⁶These are the names of the men Moses sent to explore the land. (Moses gave Hoshea son of Nun the new name Joshua.)

¹⁷Moses sent them to explore Canaan and said, "Go through southern Canaan and then into the mountains. ¹⁸See what the land looks like. Are the people who live there strong or weak? Are there a few or many? ¹⁹What kind of land do they live in? Is it good or bad? What about the towns they live in—are they open like camps, or do they have walls? ²⁰What about the soil? Is it fertile or poor? Are there trees there? Try to bring back some of the fruit from that land." (It was the season for the first grapes.)

²¹So they went up and explored the land, from the Desert of Zin all the way to Rehob by Lebo Hamath. ²²They went through the southern area to Hebron, where Ahiman, Sheshai, and Talmai, the descendants of Anak lived. (The city of Hebron had been built seven years before Zoan in Egypt.) ²³In the Valley of Eshcol, they cut off a branch of a grapevine that had one bunch of grapes on it and carried that branch on a pole between two of them. They also got some pomegranates and figs. ²⁴That place was called the Valley of Eshcol,ⁿ because the Israelites cut off the bunch of grapes there. ²⁵After forty days of exploring the land, the men returned to the camp.

²⁶They came back to Moses and Aaron and all the Israelites at Kadesh, in the Desert of Paran. The men reported to them and showed everybody the fruit from the land. ²⁷They told Moses, "We went to the land where you sent us, and it is a fertile land! Here is some of its fruit. ²⁸But the people who live there are strong. Their cities are walled and very large. We even saw some Anakites there. ²⁹The Amalekites live in the southern area; the Hittites, Jebusites, and Amorites live in the mountains; and the Canaanites live near the sea and along the Jordan River."

³⁰Then Caleb told the people near Moses to be quiet, and he said, "We should certainly go up and take the land for ourselves. We can certainly do it."

³¹But the men who had gone with him said, "We can't attack those people; they are stronger than we are." ³²And those men gave the Israelites a bad report about the land they explored, saying, "The land that we explored is too large to conquer. All the people we saw are very tall. ³³We saw the Nephilim people there. (The Anakites come from the Nephilim people.) We felt like grasshoppers, and we looked like grasshoppers to them."

THE PEOPLE COMPLAIN AGAIN

14 That night all the people in the camp began crying loudly. ²All the Israelites complained against Moses and Aaron, and all the people said to them, "We wish we had died in Egypt or in this desert. ³Why is the LORD bringing us to this land to be killed with swords? Our wives and children will be taken away. We would be better off going back to Egypt." ⁴They said to each other, "Let's choose a leader and go back to Egypt."

⁵Then Moses and Aaron bowed facedown in front of all the Israelites gathered there. ⁶Joshua son of Nun and Caleb son of Jephunneh, who had explored the land, tore their clothes. ⁷They said to all of the Israelites, "The land we explored is very good. ⁸If the LORD is pleased with us, he will lead us into that land and give us that fertile land. ⁹Don't turn against the LORD! Don't be afraid of the people in that land! We will chew them up. They have no protection, but the LORD is with us. So don't be afraid of them."

13:24 Eshcol This name in Hebrew means "bunch."

¹⁰Then all the people talked about killing them with stones. But the glory of the LORD appeared at the Meeting Tent to all the Israelites. ¹¹The LORD said to Moses, "How long will these people ignore me? How long will they not believe me in spite of the miracles I have done among them? ¹²I will give them a terrible sickness and get rid of them. But I will make you into a great nation that will be stronger than they are."

¹³Then Moses said to the LORD, "The Egyptians will hear about it! You brought these people from there by your great power, ¹⁴and the Egyptians will tell this to those who live in this land. They have already heard about you, LORD. They know that you are with your people and that you were seen face to face. They know that your cloud stays over your people and that you lead your people with that cloud during the day and with fire at night. ¹⁵If you put these people to death all at once, the nations who have heard about your power will say, ¹⁶'The LORD was not able to bring them into the land he promised them. So he killed them in the desert.'

¹⁷"So show your strength now, Lord. Do what you said: ¹⁸'The LORD doesn't become angry quickly, but he has great love. He forgives sin and law breaking. But the LORD never forgets to punish guilty people. When parents sin, he will also punish their children, their grandchildren, their great-grandchildren, and their great-great-grandchildren.' ¹⁹By your great love, forgive these people's sin, just as you have forgiven them from the time they left Egypt until now."

²⁰The LORD answered, "I have forgiven them as you asked. ²¹But, as surely as I live and as surely as my glory fills the whole earth, I make this promise: ²²All these people saw my glory and the miracles I did in Egypt and in the desert, but they disobeyed me and tested me ten times. ²³So not one of them will see the land I promised to their ancestors. No one who rejected me will see that land. ²⁴But my servant Caleb thinks differently and follows me completely. So I will bring him into the land he has already seen, and his children will own that land. ²⁵Since the Amalekites and the Canaanites are living in the valleys, leave tomorrow and follow the desert road toward the Red Sea."

THE LORD PUNISHES THE PEOPLE

²⁶The LORD said to Moses and Aaron, ²⁷"How long will these evil people complain about me? I have heard the grumbling and complaining of these Israelites. ²⁸So tell them, 'This is what the LORD says. I heard what you said, and as surely as I live, I will do those very things to you: ²⁹You will die in this desert. Every one of you who is twenty years old or older and who was counted with the people—all of you who complained against me—will die. ³⁰Not one of you will enter the land where I promised you would live; only Caleb son of Jephunneh and Joshua son of Nun will go in. ³¹You said that your children would be taken away, but I will bring them into the land to enjoy what you refused. ³²As for you, you will die in this desert. ³³Your children will be shepherds here for forty years. Because you were not loyal, they will suffer until you lie dead in the desert. ³⁴For forty years you will suffer for your sins—a year for each of the forty days you explored the land. You will know me as your enemy.' ³⁵I, the LORD, have spoken, and I will certainly do these things to all these evil people who have come together against me. So they will all die here in this desert."

³⁶The men Moses had sent to explore the land had returned and spread complaints among all the people. They had given a bad report about the land. ³⁷The men who gave a very bad report died; the LORD killed them with a terrible sickness. ³⁸Only two of the men who explored the land did not die—Joshua son of Nun and Caleb son of Jephunneh.

³⁹When Moses told these things to all the Israelites, they were very sad. ⁴⁰Early the next morning they started to go toward the top of the mountains, saying, "We have sinned. We will go where the LORD told us."

⁴¹But Moses said, "Why are you disobeying the LORD's command? You will not win! ⁴²Don't go, because the LORD is not with you and you will be beaten by your enemies. ⁴³You will run into the Amalekites and Canaanites, who will kill you with swords. You have turned away from the LORD, so the LORD will not be with you."

⁴⁴But they were proud. They went toward the top of the mountains, but Moses and the Ark of the Agreement with the LORD

did not leave the camp. 45The Amalekites and the Canaanites who lived in those mountains came down and attacked the Israelites and beat them back all the way to Hormah.

RULES ABOUT SACRIFICES

15 The LORD said to Moses, 2"Speak to the Israelites and say to them, 'When you enter the land that I am giving you as a home, 3give the LORD offerings made by fire. These may be from your herds or flocks, as a smell pleasing to the LORD. These may be burnt offerings or sacrifices for special promises, or as gifts to him, or as festival offerings. 4The one who brings the offering shall also give the LORD a grain offering. It should be two quarts of fine flour mixed with one quart of olive oil. 5Each time you offer a lamb as a burnt offering or sacrifice, also prepare a quart of wine as a drink offering.

6"'If you are giving a male sheep, also prepare a grain offering of four quarts of fine flour mixed with one and one-fourth quarts of olive oil. 7Also prepare one and one-fourth quarts of wine as a drink offering. Its smell will be pleasing to the LORD.

8"'If you prepare a young bull as a burnt offering or sacrifice, whether it is for a special promise or a fellowship offering to the LORD, 9bring a grain offering with the bull. It should be six quarts of fine flour mixed with two quarts of olive oil. 10Also bring two quarts of wine as a drink offering. This offering is made by fire, and its smell will be pleasing to the LORD. 11Prepare each bull or male sheep, lamb or young goat this way. 12Do this for every one of the animals you bring.

13"'All citizens must do these things in this way, and the smell of their offerings by fire will be pleasing to the LORD. 14From now on if foreigners who live among you want to make offerings by fire so the smell will be pleasing to the LORD, they must offer them the same way you do. 15The law is the same for you and for foreigners, and it will be from now on; you and the foreigners are alike before the LORD. 16The teachings and rules are the same for you and for the foreigners among you.'"

17The LORD said to Moses, 18"Tell the Israelites: 'You are going to another land, where I am taking you. 19When you eat the food there, offer part of it to the LORD. 20Of-fer a loaf of bread from the first of your grain, which will be your offering from the threshing floor. 21From now on offer to the LORD the first part of your grain.

22"'Now what if you forget to obey any of these commands the LORD gave Moses? 23These are the LORD's commands given to you through Moses, which began the day the LORD gave them to you and will continue from now on. 24If the people forget to obey one of these commands, all the people must offer a young bull as a burnt offering, a smell pleasing to the LORD. By law you must also give the grain offering and the drink offering with it, and you must bring a male goat as a sin offering.

25"'The priest will remove that sin for all the Israelites so they will belong to the LORD. They are forgiven, because they didn't know they were sinning. For the wrong they did they brought offerings to the LORD, an offering by fire and a sin offering. 26So all of the people of Israel and the foreigners living among them will be forgiven. No one meant to do wrong.

27"'If just one person sins without meaning to, a year-old female goat must be brought for a sin offering. 28The priest will remove the sin of the person who sinned accidentally. He will remove it before the LORD, and the person will be forgiven. 29The same teaching is for everyone who sins accidentally—for those born Israelites and for foreigners living among you.

30"'But anyone who sins on purpose is against the LORD and must be cut off from the people, whether it is someone born among you or a foreigner. 31That person has turned against the LORD's word and has not obeyed his commands. Such a person must surely be cut off from the others. He is guilty.'"

A MAN WORKED ON THE SABBATH

32When the Israelites were still in the desert, they found a man gathering wood on the Sabbath day. 33Those who found him gathering wood brought him to Moses and Aaron and all the people. 34They held the man under guard, because they did not know what to do with him. 35Then the LORD said to Moses, "The man must surely die. All the people must kill him by throwing stones at him outside the camp." 36So all the people took him outside the camp and stoned him to death, as the LORD commanded Moses.

THE TASSELS

37The LORD said to Moses, 38"Speak to the Israelites and tell them this: 'Tie several pieces of thread together and attach them to the corners of your clothes. Put a blue thread in each one of these tassels. Wear them from now on. 39You will have these tassels to look at to remind you of all the LORD's commands. Then you will obey them and not be disloyal by following what your bodies and eyes want. 40Then you will remember to obey all my commands, and you will be God's holy people. 41I am the LORD your God, who brought you out of Egypt to be your God. I am the LORD your God.'"

KORAH, DATHAN, ABIRAM, AND ON

16 Korah, Dathan, Abiram, and On turned against Moses. (Korah was the son of Izhar, the son of Kohath, the son of Levi; Dathan and Abiram were brothers, the sons of Eliab; and On was the son of Peleth; Dathan, Abiram, and On were from the tribe of Reuben.) 2These men gathered two hundred fifty other Israelite men, well-known leaders chosen by the community, and challenged Moses. 3They came as a group to speak to Moses and Aaron and said, "You have gone too far. All the people are holy, every one of them, and the LORD is among them. So why do you put yourselves above all the people of the LORD?"

4When Moses heard this, he bowed facedown. 5Then he said to Korah and all his followers: "Tomorrow morning the LORD will show who belongs to him. He will bring the one who is holy near to him; he will bring to himself the person he chooses. 6So Korah, you and all your followers do this: Get some pans for burning incense. 7Tomorrow put fire and incense in them and take them before the LORD. He will choose the man who is holy. You Levites have gone too far."

8Moses also said to Korah, "Listen, you Levites. 9The God of Israel has separated you from the rest of the Israelites. He brought you near to himself to do the work in the LORD's Holy Tent and to stand before all the Israelites and serve them. Isn't that enough? 10He has brought you and all your fellow Levites near to himself, yet now you want to be

priests. 11You and your followers have joined together against the LORD. Your complaint is not against Aaron."

12Then Moses called Dathan and Abiram, the sons of Eliab, but they said, "We will not come! 13You have brought us out of a fertile land to this desert to kill us, and now you want to order us around. 14You haven't brought us into a fertile land; you haven't given us any land with fields and vineyards. Will you put out the eyes of these men? No! We will not come!"

15Then Moses became very angry and said to the LORD, "Don't accept their gifts. I have not taken anything from them, not even a donkey, and I have not done wrong to any of them."

16Then Moses said to Korah, "You and all your followers must stand before the LORD tomorrow. And Aaron will stand there with you and them. 17Each of you must take your pan and put incense in it; present these two hundred fifty pans before the LORD. You and Aaron must also present your pans." 18So each man got his pan and put burning incense in it and stood with Moses and Aaron at the entrance to the Meeting Tent. 19Korah gathered all his followers who were against Moses and Aaron, and they stood at the entrance to the Meeting Tent. Then the glory of the LORD appeared to everyone.

20The LORD said to Moses and Aaron, 21"Move away from these men so I can destroy them quickly."

22But Moses and Aaron bowed facedown and cried out, "God, you are the God over the spirits of all people. Please don't be angry with this whole group. Only one man has really sinned."

23Then the LORD said to Moses, 24"Tell everyone to move away from the tents of Korah, Dathan, and Abiram."

25Moses stood and went to Dathan and Abiram; the elders of Israel followed him. 26Moses warned the people, "Move away from the tents of these evil men! Don't touch anything of theirs, or you will be destroyed because of their sins." 27So they moved away from the tents of Korah, Dathan, and Abiram. Dathan and Abiram were standing outside their tents with their wives, children, and little babies.

28Then Moses said, "Now you will know

that the LORD has sent me to do all these things; it was not my idea. ²⁹If these men die a normal death—the way men usually die—then the LORD did not really send me. ³⁰But if the LORD does something new, you will know they have insulted the LORD. The ground will open and swallow them. They will be buried alive and will go to the place of the dead, and everything that belongs to them will go with them."

³¹When Moses finished saying these things, the ground under the men split open. ³²The earth opened and swallowed them and all their families. All Korah's men and everything they owned went down. ³³They were buried alive, going to the place of the dead, and everything they owned went with them. Then the earth covered them. They died and were gone from the community. ³⁴The people of Israel around them heard their screams and ran away, saying, "The earth will swallow us, too!"

³⁵Then a fire came down from the LORD and destroyed the two hundred fifty men who had presented the incense.

³⁶The LORD said to Moses, ³⁷"Tell Eleazar son of Aaron, the priest, to take all the incense pans out of the fire. Have him scatter the coals a long distance away. But the incense pans are still holy. ³⁸Take the pans of these men who sinned and lost their lives, and hammer them into flat sheets that will be used to cover the altar. They are holy, because they were presented to the LORD, and they will be a sign to the Israelites."

³⁹So Eleazar the priest gathered all the bronze pans that had been brought by the men who were burned up. He had the pans hammered into flat sheets to put on the altar, ⁴⁰as the LORD had commanded him through Moses. These sheets were to remind the Israelites that only descendants of Aaron should burn incense before the LORD. Anyone else would die like Korah and his followers.

AARON SAVES THE PEOPLE

⁴¹The next day all the Israelites complained against Moses and Aaron and said, "You have killed the LORD's people."

⁴²When the people gathered to complain against Moses and Aaron, they turned toward the Meeting Tent, and the cloud covered it. The glory of the LORD appeared.

⁴³Then Moses and Aaron went in front of the Meeting Tent.

⁴⁴The LORD said to Moses, ⁴⁵"Move away from these people so I can destroy them quickly." So Moses and Aaron bowed facedown.

⁴⁶Then Moses said to Aaron, "Get your pan, and put fire from the altar and incense in it. Hurry to the people and remove their sin. The LORD is angry with them; the sickness has already started." ⁴⁷So Aaron did as Moses said. He ran to the middle of the people, where the sickness had already started among them. So Aaron offered the incense to remove their sin. ⁴⁸He stood between the dead and the living, and the sickness stopped there. ⁴⁹But 14,700 people died from that sickness, in addition to those who died because of Korah. ⁵⁰Then Aaron went back to Moses at the entrance to the Meeting Tent. The terrible sickness had been stopped.

AARON'S WALKING STICK BUDS

17 The LORD said to Moses, ²"Speak to the people of Israel and get twelve walking sticks from them—one from the leader of each tribe. Write the name of each man on his stick, and ³on the stick from Levi, write Aaron's name. There must be one stick for the head of each tribe. ⁴Put them in the Meeting Tent in front of the Ark of the Agreement, where I meet with you. ⁵I will choose one man whose walking stick will begin to grow leaves; in this way I will stop the Israelites from always complaining against you."

⁶So Moses spoke to the Israelites. Each of the twelve leaders gave him a walking stick—one from each tribe—and Aaron's walking stick was among them. ⁷Moses put them before the LORD in the Tent of the Agreement.

⁸The next day, when Moses entered the Tent, he saw that Aaron's stick (which stood for the family of Levi) had grown leaves. It had even budded, blossomed, and produced almonds. ⁹So Moses brought out to the Israelites all the walking sticks from the LORD's presence. They all looked, and each man took back his stick.

¹⁰Then the LORD said to Moses, "Put Aaron's walking stick back in front of the Ark of the Agreement. It will remind these people who are always turning against me to stop their complaining against me so they won't

die." ¹¹So Moses obeyed what the LORD commanded him.

¹²The people of Israel said to Moses, "We are going to die! We are destroyed. We are all destroyed! ¹³Anyone who even comes near the Holy Tent of the LORD will die. Will we all die?"

THE WORK OF THE PRIESTS AND LEVITES

18 The LORD said to Aaron, "You, your sons, and your family are now responsible for any wrongs done against the Holy Place; you and your sons are responsible for any wrongs done against the priests. ²Bring with you your fellow Levites from your tribe, and they will help you and your sons serve in the Tent of the Agreement. ³They are under your control, to do all the work that needs to be done in the Tent. But they must not go near the things in the Holy Place or near the altar. If they do, both you and they will die. ⁴They will join you in taking care of the Meeting Tent. They must do the work at the Tent, and no one else may come near you.

⁵"You must take care of the Holy Place and the altar so that I won't become angry with the Israelites again. ⁶I myself chose your fellow Levites from among the Israelites as a gift given for you to the LORD, to work at the Meeting Tent. ⁷But only you and your sons may serve as priests. Only you may serve at the altar or go behind the curtain. I am giving you this gift of serving as a priest, and anyone else who comes near the Holy Place will be put to death."

⁸Then the LORD said to Aaron, "I myself make you responsible for the offerings given to me. All the holy offerings that the Israelites give to me, I give to you and your sons as your share, your continual portion. ⁹Your share of the holy offerings is that part which is not burned. When the people bring me gifts as most holy offerings, whether they are grain or sin or penalty offerings, they will be set apart for you and your sons. ¹⁰You must eat the offering in a most holy place. Any male may eat it, but you must respect it as holy.

¹¹"I also give you the offerings the Israelites present to me. I give these to you and your sons and daughters as your continual share. Anyone in your family who is clean may eat it.

¹²"And I give you all the best olive oil and all the best new wine and grain. This is what the Israelites give to me, the LORD, from the first crops they harvest. ¹³When they bring to the LORD all the first things they harvest, they will be yours. Anyone in your family who is clean may eat these things.

¹⁴"Everything in Israel that is given to the LORD is yours. ¹⁵The first one born to any family, whether people or animals, will be offered to the LORD. And that will be yours. But you must make a payment for every firstborn child and every firstborn animal that is unclean. ¹⁶When they are one month old, you must make a payment for them of two ounces of silver, as set by the Holy Place measure.

¹⁷"But you must not make a payment for the firstborn ox or sheep or goat. Those animals are holy. Sprinkle their blood on the altar and burn their fat as an offering made by fire. The smell is pleasing to the LORD. ¹⁸But the meat will be yours, just as the breast that is presented and the right thigh will be yours. ¹⁹Anything the Israelites present as holy gifts I, the LORD, give to you, your sons and daughters as your continual portion. This is a lasting agreement of salt[n] before the LORD for you and your children forever."

²⁰The LORD also said to Aaron, "You will not inherit any of the land, and you will not own any land among the other people. I will be yours. Out of all the Israelites, only you will inherit me.

²¹"When the people of Israel give me a tenth of what they make, I will give that tenth to the Levites. This is their payment for the work they do serving at the Meeting Tent. ²²But the other Israelites must never go near the Meeting Tent, or they will die for their sin. ²³Only the Levites should work in the Meeting Tent and be responsible for any sins against it. This is a rule from now on. The Levites will not inherit any land among the other Israelites, ²⁴but when the Israelites give a tenth of everything they make to me, I will give that tenth to the Levites as a reward. That is why I said about the Levites: 'They will not inherit any land among the Israelites.'"

18:19 agreement of salt The meaning is not clear, but Leviticus 2:13 says, "Salt stands for your agreement with God that will last forever."

²⁵The Lord said to Moses, ²⁶"Speak to the Levites and tell them: 'You will receive a tenth of everything the Israelites make, which I will give to you. But you must give a tenth of that back to the Lord. ²⁷I will accept your offering just as much as I accept the offerings from others, who give new grain or new wine. ²⁸In this way you will present an offering to the Lord as the other Israelites do. When you receive a tenth from the Israelites, you will give a tenth of that to Aaron, the priest, as the Lord's share. ²⁹Choose the best and holiest part from what you are given as the portion you must give to the Lord.'

³⁰"Say to the Levites: 'When you present the best, it will be accepted as much as the grain and wine from the other people. ³¹You and your families may eat all that is left anywhere, because it is your pay for your work in the Meeting Tent. ³²And if you always give the best part to the Lord, you will never be guilty. If you do not sin against the holy offerings of the Israelites, you will not die.'"

THE OFFERING FOR CLEANSING

19 The Lord said to Moses and Aaron, ²"These are the teachings that the Lord commanded. Tell the Israelites to get a young red cow that does not have anything wrong with it and that has never been worked. ³Give the cow to Eleazar the priest; he will take it outside the camp and kill it. ⁴Then Eleazar the priest must put some of its blood on his finger and sprinkle it seven times toward the front of the Meeting Tent. ⁵The whole cow must be burned while he watches; the skin, the meat, the blood, and the intestines must all be burned. ⁶Then the priest must take a cedar stick, a hyssop branch, and a red string and throw them onto the burning cow. ⁷After the priest has washed himself and his clothes with water, he may come back into the camp, but he will be unclean until evening. ⁸The man who burns the cow must wash himself and his clothes in water; he will be unclean until evening.

⁹"Then someone who is clean will collect the ashes from the cow and put them in a clean place outside the camp. The Israelites will keep these ashes to use in the cleansing water, in a special ceremony to cleanse away sin. ¹⁰The man who collected the cow's ashes must wash his clothes and be unclean until evening. This is a lasting rule for the Israelites and for the foreigners among them.

¹¹"Those who touch a dead person's body will be unclean for seven days. ¹²They must wash themselves with the cleansing water on the third day and on the seventh day; then they will be clean. But if they do not wash themselves on the third day and the seventh day, they cannot be clean. ¹³If those who touch a dead person's body stay unclean and go to the Lord's Holy Tent, it becomes unclean; they must be cut off from Israel. If the cleansing water is not sprinkled on them, they are unclean and will stay unclean.

¹⁴"This is the teaching about someone who dies in a tent: Anyone in the tent or anyone who enters it will be unclean for seven days. ¹⁵And every open jar or pot without a cover becomes unclean. ¹⁶If anyone is outside and touches someone who was killed by a sword or who died a natural death, or if anyone touches a human bone or a grave, that person will be unclean for seven days.

¹⁷"So you must use the ashes from the burnt offering to make that person clean again. Pour fresh water over the ashes into a jar. ¹⁸A clean person must take a hyssop branch and dip it into the water, and then he must sprinkle it over the tent and all its objects. He must also sprinkle the people who were there, as well as anyone who touched a bone, or the body of someone who was killed, or a dead person, or a grave. ¹⁹The person who is clean must sprinkle this water on the unclean people on the third day and on the seventh day. On the seventh day they will become clean. They must wash their clothes and take a bath, and they will be clean that evening. ²⁰If any who are unclean do not become clean, they must be cut off from the community. Since they were not sprinkled with the cleansing water, they stay unclean, and they could make the Lord's Holy Tent unclean. ²¹This is a lasting rule. Those who sprinkle the cleansing water must also wash their clothes, and anyone who touches the water will be unclean until evening. ²²Anything an unclean person touches becomes unclean, and whoever touches it will be unclean until evening."

MOSES DISOBEYS GOD

20 In the first month all the people of Israel arrived at the Desert of Zin, and they stayed at Kadesh. There Miriam died and was buried. ²There was no water for the people, so they came together against Moses and Aaron. ³They argued with Moses and said, "We should have died in front of the LORD as our brothers did. ⁴Why did you bring the LORD's people into this desert? Are we and our animals to die here? ⁵Why did you bring us from Egypt to this terrible place? It has no grain, figs, grapevines, or pomegranates, and there's no water to drink!"

⁶So Moses and Aaron left the people and went to the entrance of the Meeting Tent. There they bowed facedown, and the glory of the LORD appeared to them. ⁷The LORD said to Moses, ⁸"Take your walking stick, and you and your brother Aaron should gather the people. Speak to that rock in front of them so that its water will flow from it. When you bring the water out from that rock, give it to the people and their animals."

⁹So Moses took the stick from in front of the LORD, as he had said. ¹⁰Moses and Aaron gathered the people in front of the rock, and Moses said, "Now listen to me, you who turn against God! Do you want us to bring water out of this rock?" ¹¹Then Moses lifted his hand and hit the rock twice with his stick. Water began pouring out, and the people and their animals drank it.

¹²But the LORD said to Moses and Aaron, "Because you did not believe me, and because you did not honor me as holy before the people, you will not lead them into the land I will give them."

¹³These are the waters of Meribah,ⁿ where the Israelites argued with the LORD and where he showed them he was holy.

EDOM WILL NOT LET ISRAEL PASS

¹⁴From Kadesh, Moses sent messengers to the king of Edom. He said, "Your brothers, the Israelites, say to you: You know about all the troubles we have had, ¹⁵how our ancestors went down into Egypt and we lived there for many years. The people of Egypt were cruel to us and our ancestors, ¹⁶but when we cried out to the LORD, he heard us and sent us an angel to bring us out of Egypt.

"Now we are here at Kadesh, a town on the edge of your land. ¹⁷Please let us pass through your country. We will not touch any fields of grain or vineyards, and will not drink water from the wells. We will travel only along the king's road, not turning right or left until we have passed through your country."

¹⁸But the king of Edom answered: "You may not pass through here. If you try, I will come and meet you with swords."

¹⁹The Israelites answered: "We will go along the main road, and if we or our animals drink any of your water, we will pay for it. We only want to walk through. That's all."

²⁰But he answered: "You may not pass through here."

Then the Edomites went out to meet the Israelites with a large and powerful army. ²¹The Edomites refused to let them pass through their country, so the Israelites turned back.

AARON DIES

²²All the Israelites moved from Kadesh to Mount Hor, ²³near the border of Edom. There the LORD said to Moses and Aaron, ²⁴"Aaron will die. He will not enter the land that I'm giving to the Israelites, because you both acted against my command at the waters of Meribah. ²⁵Take Aaron and his son Eleazar up on Mount Hor, ²⁶and take off Aaron's special clothes and put them on his son Eleazar. Aaron will die there; he will join his ancestors."

²⁷Moses obeyed the LORD's command. They climbed up Mount Hor, and all the people saw them go. ²⁸Moses took off Aaron's clothes and put them on Aaron's son Eleazar. Then Aaron died there on top of the mountain. Moses and Eleazar came back down the mountain, ²⁹and when all the people learned that Aaron was dead, everyone in Israel cried for him for thirty days.

WAR WITH THE CANAANITES

21 The Canaanite king of Arad lived in the southern area. When he heard that the Israelites were coming on the road to Atharim, he attacked them and captured some of them. ²Then the Israelites made this promise to the LORD: "If you will help us defeat these people, we will completely destroy their

20:13 **Meribah** This name in Hebrew means "argument."

cities." [3]The LORD listened to the Israelites, and he let them defeat the Canaanites. The Israelites completely destroyed the Canaanites and their cities, so the place was named Hormah.[n]

THE BRONZE SNAKE

[4]The Israelites left Mount Hor and went on the road toward the Red Sea, in order to go around the country of Edom. But the people became impatient on the way [5]and grumbled at God and Moses. They said, "Why did you bring us out of Egypt to die in this desert? There is no bread and no water, and we hate this terrible food!"

[6]So the LORD sent them poisonous snakes; they bit the people, and many of the Israelites died. [7]The people came to Moses and said, "We sinned when we grumbled at you and the LORD. Pray that the LORD will take away these snakes." So Moses prayed for the people.

[8]The LORD said to Moses, "Make a bronze snake, and put it on a pole. When anyone who is bitten looks at it, that person will live." [9]So Moses made a bronze snake and put it on a pole. Then when a snake bit anyone, that person looked at the bronze snake and lived.

THE JOURNEY TO MOAB

[10]The Israelites went and camped at Oboth. [11]They went from Oboth to Iye Abarim, in the desert east of Moab. [12]From there they went and camped in the Zered Valley. [13]From there they went and camped across the Arnon, in the desert just inside the Amorite country. The Arnon is the border between the Moabites and the Amorites. [14]That is why the Book of the Wars of the LORD says:

"... and Waheb in Suphah, and the
    ravines,
  the Arnon, [15]and the slopes of the
    ravines
that lead to the settlement of Ar.
  These places are at the border of Moab."

[16]The Israelites went from there to Beer; a well is there where the LORD said to Moses, "Gather the people and I will give them water."

[17]Then the Israelites sang this song:
"Pour out water, well!
  Sing about it.
[18] Princes dug this well.

Important men made it.
  With their scepters and poles, they
    dug it."
The people went from the desert to Mattanah. [19]From Mattanah they went to Nahaliel and on to Bamoth. [20]From Bamoth they went to the valley of Moab where the top of Mount Pisgah looks over the desert.

ISRAEL KILLS SIHON AND OG

[21]The Israelites sent messengers to Sihon, king of the Amorites, saying, [22]"Let us pass through your country. We will not go through any fields of grain or vineyards, or drink water from the wells. We will travel only along the king's road until we have passed through your country."

[23]But King Sihon would not let the Israelites pass through his country. He gathered his whole army together, and they marched out to meet Israel in the desert. At Jahaz they fought the Israelites. [24]Israel killed the king and captured his land from the Arnon River to the Jabbok River. They took the land as far as the Ammonite border, which was strongly defended. [25]Israel captured all the Amorite cities and lived in them, taking Heshbon and all the towns around it. [26]Heshbon was the city where Sihon, the Amorite king, lived. In the past he had fought with the king of Moab and had taken all the land as far as the Arnon.

[27]That is why the poets say:
"Come to Heshbon
  and rebuild it;
  rebuild Sihon's city.
[28] A fire began in Heshbon;
  flames came from Sihon's city.
It destroyed Ar in Moab,
  and it burned the Arnon highlands.
[29] How terrible for you, Moab!
  The people of Chemosh are ruined.
His sons ran away
  and his daughters were captured
  by Sihon, king of the Amorites.
[30] But we defeated those Amorites.
  We ruined their towns from Heshbon
    to Dibon,
  and we destroyed them as far as
    Nophah, near Medeba."

21:3 Hormah This name in Hebrew means "completely destroyed."

³¹So Israel lived in the land of the Amorites. ³²After Moses sent spies to the town of Jazer, they captured the towns around it, forcing out the Amorites who lived there. ³³Then the Israelites went up the road toward Bashan. Og king of Bashan and his whole army marched out to meet the Israelites, and they fought at Edrei.

³⁴The LORD said to Moses, "Don't be afraid of him. I will hand him, his whole army, and his land over to you. Do to him what you did to Sihon, the Amorite king who lived in Heshbon." ³⁵So the Israelites killed Og and his sons and all his army; no one was left alive. And they took his land.

BALAK SENDS FOR BALAAM

22 Then the people of Israel went to the plains of Moab, and they camped near the Jordan River across from Jericho.

²Balak son of Zippor saw everything the Israelites had done to the Amorites. ³And Moab was scared of so many Israelites; truly, Moab was terrified by them. ⁴The Moabites said to the elders of Midian, "These people will take everything around us like an ox eating grass."

Balak son of Zippor was the king of Moab at this time. ⁵He sent messengers to Balaam son of Beor at Pethor, near the Euphrates River in his native land. Balak said, "A nation has come out of Egypt that covers the land. They have camped next to me, ⁶and they are too powerful for me. So come and put a curse on them. Maybe then I can defeat them and make them leave the area. I know that if you bless someone, the blessings happen, and if you put a curse on someone, it happens."

⁷The elders of Moab and Midian went with payment in their hands. When they found Balaam, they told him what Balak had said. ⁸Balaam said to them, "Stay here for the night, and I will tell you what the LORD tells me." So the Moabite leaders stayed with him.

⁹God came to Balaam and asked, "Who are these men with you?"

¹⁰Balaam said to God, "The king of Moab, Balak son of Zippor, sent them to me with this message: ¹¹'A nation has come out of Egypt that covers the land. So come and put a curse on them, and maybe I can fight them and force them out of my land.'"

¹²But God said to Balaam, "Do not go with them. Don't put a curse on those people, because I have blessed them."

¹³The next morning Balaam awoke and said to Balak's leaders, "Go back to your own country; the LORD has refused to let me go with you."

¹⁴So the Moabite leaders went back to Balak and said, "Balaam refused to come with us."

¹⁵So Balak sent other leaders—this time there were more of them, and they were more important. ¹⁶They went to Balaam and said, "Balak son of Zippor says this: Please don't let anything stop you from coming to me. ¹⁷I will pay you very well, and I will do what you say. Come and put a curse on these people for me."

¹⁸But Balaam answered Balak's servants, "King Balak could give me his palace full of silver and gold, but I cannot disobey the LORD my God in anything, great or small. ¹⁹You stay here tonight as the other men did, and I will find out what more the LORD tells me."

²⁰That night God came to Balaam and said, "These men have come to ask you to go with them. Go, but only do what I tell you."

BALAAM'S DONKEY SPEAKS

²¹Balaam got up the next morning and put a saddle on his donkey. Then he went with the Moabite leaders. ²²But God became angry because Balaam went, so the angel of the LORD stood in the road to stop Balaam. Balaam was riding his donkey, and he had two servants with him. ²³When the donkey saw the angel of the LORD standing in the road with a sword in his hand, the donkey left the road and went into the field. Balaam hit the donkey to force her back on the road.

²⁴Later, the angel of the LORD stood on a narrow path between two vineyards, with walls on both sides. ²⁵Again the donkey saw the angel of the LORD, and she walked close to one wall, crushing Balaam's foot against it. So he hit her again.

²⁶The angel of the LORD went ahead again and stood at a narrow place, too narrow to turn left or right. ²⁷When the donkey saw the angel of the LORD, she lay down under

Balaam. This made him so angry that he hit her with his stick. ²⁸Then the LORD made the donkey talk, and she said to Balaam, "What have I done to make you hit me three times?"

²⁹Balaam answered the donkey, "You have made me look foolish! I wish I had a sword in my hand! I would kill you right now!"

³⁰But the donkey said to Balaam, "I am your very own donkey, which you have ridden for years. Have I ever done this to you before?"

"No," Balaam said.

³¹Then the LORD let Balaam see the angel of the LORD, who was standing in the road with his sword drawn. Then Balaam bowed facedown on the ground.

³²The angel of the LORD asked Balaam, "Why have you hit your donkey three times? I have stood here to stop you, because what you are doing is wrong. ³³The donkey saw me and turned away from me three times. If she had not turned away, I would have killed you by now, but I would have let her live."

³⁴Then Balaam said to the angel of the LORD, "I have sinned; I did not know you were standing in the road to stop me. If I am wrong, I will go back."

³⁵The angel of the LORD said to Balaam, "Go with these men, but say only what I tell you." So Balaam went with Balak's leaders.

³⁶When Balak heard that Balaam was coming, he went out to meet him at Ar in Moab, which was beside the Arnon, at the edge of his country. ³⁷Balak said to Balaam, "I had asked you before to come quickly. Why didn't you come to me? I am able to reward you well."

³⁸But Balaam answered, "I have come to you now, but I can't say just anything. I can only say what God tells me to say."

³⁹Then Balaam went with Balak to Kiriath Huzoth. ⁴⁰Balak offered cattle and sheep as a sacrifice and gave some meat to Balaam and the leaders with him.

⁴¹The next morning Balak took Balaam to Bamoth Baal; from there he could see the edge of the Israelite camp.

BALAAM'S FIRST MESSAGE

23 Balaam said to Balak, "Build me seven altars here, and prepare seven bulls and seven male sheep for me." ²Balak did what Balaam asked, and they offered a bull and a male sheep on each of the altars.

³Then Balaam said to Balak, "Stay here beside your burnt offering and I will go. If the LORD comes to me, I will tell you whatever he shows me." Then Balaam went to a higher place.

⁴God came to Balaam there, and Balaam said to him, "I have prepared seven altars, and I have offered a bull and a male sheep on each altar."

⁵The LORD told Balaam what he should say. Then the LORD said, "Go back to Balak and give him this message."

⁶So Balaam went back to Balak. Balak and all the leaders of Moab were still standing beside his burnt offering ⁷when Balaam gave them this message:

"Balak brought me here from Aram;
   the king of Moab brought me from the
     eastern mountains.
Balak said, 'Come, put a curse on the
   people of Jacob for me.
Come, call down evil on the people of
   Israel.'
⁸ But God has not cursed them,
   so I cannot curse them.
The LORD has not called down evil on
   them,
   so I cannot call down evil on them.
⁹ I see them from the top of the mountains;
   I see them from the hills.
I see a people who live alone,
   who think they are different from other
     nations.
¹⁰ No one can number the many people of
   Jacob,
   and no one can count a fourth of Israel.
Let me die like good men,
   and let me end up like them!"

¹¹Balak said to Balaam, "What have you done to me? I brought you here to curse my enemies, but you have only blessed them!"

¹²But Balaam answered, "I must say what the LORD tells me to say."

BALAAM'S SECOND MESSAGE

¹³Then Balak said to him, "Come with me to another place, where you can also see the people. But you can only see part of them, not all of them. Curse them for me from there." ¹⁴So Balak took Balaam to the field of Zophim, on top of Mount Pisgah. There Balak

built seven altars and offered a bull and a male sheep on each altar.

¹⁵So Balaam said to Balak, "Stay here by your burnt offering, and I will meet with God over there."

¹⁶So the LORD came to Balaam and told him what to say. Then he said, "Go back to Balak and say such and such."

¹⁷So Balaam went to Balak, where he and the leaders of Moab were standing beside his burnt offering. Balak asked him, "What did the LORD say?"

¹⁸Then Balaam gave this message:
"Stand up, Balak, and listen.
  Hear me, son of Zippor.
¹⁹ God is not a human being, and he will not
    lie.
  He is not a human, and he does not
    change his mind.
What he says he will do, he does.
  What he promises, he makes come true.
²⁰ He told me to bless them,
  so I cannot change the blessing.
²¹ He has found no wrong in the people of
    Jacob;
  he saw no fault in Israel.
The LORD their God is with them,
  and they praise their King.
²² God brought them out of Egypt;
  they are as strong as a wild ox.
²³ No tricks will work on the people of
    Jacob,
  and no magic will work against Israel.
People now say about them,
  'Look what God has done for Israel!'
²⁴ The people rise up like a lioness;
  they get up like a lion.
Lions don't rest until they have eaten,
  until they have drunk their enemies'
    blood."

²⁵Then Balak said to Balaam, "You haven't cursed these people, so at least don't bless them!"

²⁶Balaam answered Balak, "I told you before that I can only do what the LORD tells me."

BALAAM'S THIRD MESSAGE

²⁷Then Balak said to Balaam, "Come, I will take you to another place. Maybe God will be pleased to let you curse them from there." ²⁸So Balak took Balaam to the top of Peor, the mountain that looks over the desert.

²⁹Balaam told Balak, "Build me seven altars here and prepare for me seven bulls and seven male sheep." ³⁰Balak did what Balaam asked, and he offered a bull and a male sheep on each altar.

24 Balaam saw that the LORD wanted to bless Israel, so he did not try to use any magic but looked toward the desert. ²When Balaam saw the Israelites camped in their tribes, the Spirit of God took control of him, ³and he gave this message:

"This is the message of Balaam son of
    Beor,
  the message of a man who sees clearly;
⁴ this is the message of a man who hears
    the words of God.
I see a vision from the Almighty,
  and my eyes are open as I fall before
    him.
⁵ Your tents are beautiful, people of Jacob!
  So are your homes, Israel!
⁶ Your tents spread out like valleys,
  like gardens beside a river.
They are like spices planted by the LORD,
  like cedar trees growing by the water.
⁷ Israel's water buckets will always be full,
  and their crops will have plenty of
    water.
Their king will be greater than Agag;
  their kingdom will be very great.
⁸ God brought them out of Egypt;
  they are as strong as a wild ox.
They will defeat their enemies
  and break their enemies' bones;
  they will shoot them with arrows.
⁹ Like a lion, they lie waiting to attack;
  like a lioness, no one would be brave
    enough to wake them.
Anyone who blesses you will be blessed,
  and anyone who curses you will be
    cursed."

¹⁰Then Balak was angry with Balaam, and he pounded his fist. He said to Balaam, "I called you here to curse my enemies, but you have continued to bless them three times. ¹¹Now go home! I said I would pay you well, but the LORD has made you lose your reward."

¹²Balaam said to Balak, "When you sent messengers to me, I told them, ¹³'Balak could give me his palace filled with silver and gold, but I still cannot go against the LORD's commands. I could not do anything, good or bad,

on my own, but I must say what the LORD says.' ¹⁴Now I am going back to my own people, but I will tell you what these people will do to your people in the future."

BALAAM'S FINAL MESSAGE

¹⁵Then Balaam gave this message:

"This is the message of Balaam son of Beor,

the message of a man who sees clearly;
¹⁶ this is the message of a man who hears the words of God.

I know well the Most High God.
I see a vision from the Almighty,
and my eyes are open as I fall before him.
¹⁷ I see someone who will come someday,
someone who will come, but not soon.

A star will come from Jacob;
a ruler will rise from Israel.
He will crush the heads of the Moabites
and smash the skulls of the sons of Sheth.
¹⁸ Edom will be conquered;
his enemy Edom will be conquered,
but Israel will grow wealthy.
¹⁹ A ruler will come from the descendants of Jacob
and will destroy those left in the city."

²⁰Then Balaam saw Amalek and gave this message:

"Amalek was the most important nation,
but Amalek will be destroyed at last."

²¹Then Balaam saw the Kenites and gave this message:

"Your home is safe,
like a nest on a cliff.
²² But you Kenites will be burned up;
Assyria will keep you captive."

²³Then Balaam gave this message:

"No one can live when God does this.
²⁴ Ships will sail from the shores of Cyprus
and defeat Assyria and Eber,
but they will also be destroyed."

²⁵Then Balaam got up and returned home, and Balak also went on his way.

ISRAEL WORSHIPS BAAL AT PEOR

25 While the people of Israel were still camped at Acacia, the men began sinning sexually with Moabite women. ²The women invited them to their sacrifices to their gods, and the Israelites ate food there and worshiped these gods. ³So the Israelites began to worship Baal of Peor, and the LORD was very angry with them.

⁴The LORD said to Moses, "Get all the leaders of the people and kill them in open daylight in the presence of the LORD. Then the LORD will not be angry with the people of Israel."

⁵So Moses said to Israel's judges, "Each of you must put to death your people who have become worshipers of Baal of Peor."

⁶Moses and the Israelites were gathered at the entrance to the Meeting Tent, crying there. Then an Israelite man brought a Midianite woman to his brothers in plain sight of Moses and all the people. ⁷Phinehas son of Eleazar, the son of Aaron, the priest, saw this, so he left the meeting and got his spear. ⁸He followed the Israelite into his tent and drove his spear through both the Israelite man and the Midianite woman. Then the terrible sickness among the Israelites stopped. ⁹This sickness had killed twenty-four thousand people.

¹⁰The LORD said to Moses, ¹¹"Phinehas son of Eleazar, the son of Aaron, the priest, has saved the Israelites from my anger. He hates sin as much as I do. Since he tried to save my honor among them, I will not kill them. ¹²So tell Phinehas that I am making my peace agreement with him. ¹³He and his descendants will always be priests, because he had great concern for the honor of his God. He removed the sins of the Israelites so they would belong to God."

¹⁴The Israelite man who was killed with the Midianite woman was named Zimri son of Salu. He was the leader of a family in the tribe of Simeon. ¹⁵And the name of the Midianite woman who was put to death was Cozbi daughter of Zur, who was the chief of a Midianite family.

¹⁶The LORD said to Moses, ¹⁷"The Midianites are your enemies, and you should kill them. ¹⁸They have already made you their enemies, because they tricked you at Peor and because of their sister Cozbi, the daughter of a Midianite leader. She was the woman who was killed when the sickness came because the people sinned at Peor."

THE PEOPLE ARE COUNTED

26 After the great sickness, the LORD said to Moses and Eleazar son of Aaron, the priest, ²"Count all the people of Israel by families. Count all the men who are twenty years old or older who will serve in the army of Israel." ³Moses and Eleazar the priest spoke to the people on the plains of Moab near the Jordan River, across from Jericho. They said, ⁴"Count the men twenty years old or older, as the LORD commanded Moses."

Here are the Israelites who came out of Egypt:

⁵The tribe of Reuben, the first son born to Israel, was counted. From Hanoch came the Hanochite family group; from Pallu came the Palluite family group; ⁶from Hezron came the Hezronite family group; from Carmi came the Carmite family group. ⁷These were the family groups of Reuben, and the total number of men was 43,730.

⁸The son of Pallu was Eliab, ⁹and Eliab's sons were Nemuel, Dathan, and Abiram. Dathan and Abiram were the leaders who turned against Moses and Aaron and followed Korah when he turned against the LORD. ¹⁰The earth opened up and swallowed them and Korah; they died at the same time the fire burned up the 250 men. This was a warning, ¹¹but the children of Korah did not die.

¹²These were the family groups in the tribe of Simeon: From Nemuel came the Nemuelite family group; from Jamin came the Jaminite family group; from Jakin came the Jakinite family group; ¹³from Zerah came the Zerahite family group; from Shaul came the Shaulite family group. ¹⁴These were the family groups of Simeon, and the total number of men was 22,200.

¹⁵These were the family groups in the tribe of Gad: From Zephon came the Zephonite family group; from Haggi came the Haggite family group; from Shuni came the Shunite family group; ¹⁶from Ozni came the Oznite family group; from Eri came the Erite family group; ¹⁷from Arodi came the Arodite family group; from Areli came the Arelite family group. ¹⁸These were the family groups of Gad, and the total number of men was 40,500.

¹⁹Two of Judah's sons, Er and Onan, died in Canaan.

²⁰These were the family groups in the tribe of Judah: From Shelah came the Shelanite family group; from Perez came the Perezite family group; from Zerah came the Zerahite family group. ²¹These were the family groups from Perez: From Hezron came the Hezronite family group; from Hamul came the Hamulite family group. ²²These were the family groups of Judah, and the total number of men was 76,500.

²³These were the family groups in the tribe of Issachar: From Tola came the Tolaite family group; from Puah came the Puite family group; ²⁴from Jashub came the Jashubite family group; from Shimron came the Shimronite family group. ²⁵These were the family groups of Issachar, and the total number of men was 64,300.

²⁶These were the family groups in the tribe of Zebulun: From Sered came the Seredite family group; from Elon came the Elonite family group; from Jahleel came the Jahleelite family group. ²⁷These were the family groups of Zebulun, and the total number of men was 60,500.

²⁸These were the family groups of Joseph through Manasseh and Ephraim.

²⁹These were the family groups of Manasseh: From Makir came the Makirite family group (Makir was the father of Gilead); from Gilead came the Gileadite family group. ³⁰These were the family groups that came from Gilead: From Iezer came the Iezerite family group; from Helek came the Helekite family group; ³¹from Asriel came the Asrielite family group; from Shechem came the Shechemite family group; ³²from Shemida came the Shemidaite family group; from Hepher came the Hepherite family group. ³³(Zelophehad son of Hepher had no sons; he had only daughters, and their names were Mahlah, Noah, Hoglah, Milcah, and Tirzah.) ³⁴These were the family groups of Manasseh, and the total number of men was 52,700.

³⁵These were the family groups in the tribe of Ephraim: From Shuthelah came the Shuthelahite family group; from Beker came the Bekerite family group; from Tahan came the Tahanite family group. ³⁶This was the family group from Shuthelah: From Eran came the Eranite family group. ³⁷These were the family groups of Ephraim, and the total

number of men was 32,500. These are the family groups that came from Joseph.

³⁸These were the family groups in the tribe of Benjamin: From Bela came the Belaite family group; from Ashbel came the Ashbelite family group; from Ahiram came the Ahiramite family group; ³⁹from Shupham came the Shuphamite family group; from Hupham came the Huphamite family group. ⁴⁰These were the family groups from Bela through Ard and Naaman: From Ard came the Ardite family group; from Naaman came the Naamite family group. ⁴¹These were the family groups of Benjamin, and the total number of men was 45,600.

⁴²This was the family group in the tribe of Dan: From Shuham came the Shuhamite family group. That was the family of Dan, ⁴³and the total number of men in the Shuhamite family group of Dan was 64,400.

⁴⁴These were the family groups in the tribe of Asher: From Imnah came the Imnite

---

THE EXTRA MILE MARRIAGE

community and history

FAMILY

NUMBERS 26:58

Did you ever wonder why there are so many lists of families in the Bible? Most of these genealogies seem like nothing more than endless repetitions of fathers and sons. Why would they be included in the Holy Scriptures? There are many historical reasons for these statements of heritage, but perhaps there is another reason that has something to teach us.

Each of these genealogies reminds us that we stand in a long line of people who have been involved with God. We are not individuals standing alone in the universe. We represent God's unwavering interaction with our community. In fact, our identity is really wrapped up in the community that he calls his own.

The paradigm of the modern world emphasizes the individual. But God's world is a world of community. God directed his activity through a community when he involved the nation of Israel. Today, he continues that involvement through the community he calls the church, the body of believers around the world.

We are one family, all children of the Father. Our individual identities are caught up in the great family of God. I am not all that I am apart from this family of believers. I participate as a part of the body, not a separate independent part, but a part intimately connected to every other part, functioning together for God's purposes. Family is God's history with us made manifest in other people.

reflect: Consider what it means to be part of the worldwide family of God today.
Go to **Ruth 1:16.**

family group; from Ishvi came the Ishvite family group; from Beriah came the Beriite family group. 45These were the family groups that came from Beriah: From Heber came the Heberite family group; from Malkiel came the Malkielite family group. 46(Asher also had a daughter named Serah.) 47These were the family groups of Asher, and the total number of men was 53,400.

48These were the family groups in the tribe of Naphtali: From Jahzeel came the Jahzeelite family group; from Guni came the Gunite family group; 49from Jezer came the Jezerite family group; from Shillem came the Shillemite family group. 50These were the family groups of Naphtali, and the total number of men was 45,400.

51So the total number of the men of Israel was 601,730.

52The LORD said to Moses, 53"Divide the land among these people by the number of names. 54A large tribe will get more land, and a small tribe will get less land; the amount of land each tribe gets will depend on the number of its people. 55Divide the land by drawing lots, and the land each tribe gets will be named for that tribe. 56Divide the land between large and small groups by drawing lots."

57The tribe of Levi was also counted. These were the family groups of Levi: From Gershon came the Gershonite family group; from Kohath came the Kohathite family group; from Merari came the Merarite family group. 58These also were Levite family groups: the Libnite family group, the Hebronite family group, the Mahlite family group, the Mushite family group, and the Korahite family group. (Kohath was the ancestor of Amram, 59whose wife was named Jochebed. She was from the tribe of Levi and she was born in Egypt. She and Amram had two sons, Aaron and Moses, and their sister Miriam. 60Aaron was the father of Nadab, Abihu, Eleazar, and Ithamar. 61But Nadab and Abihu died because they made an offering before the LORD with the wrong kind of fire.)

62The total number of male Levites one month old or older was 23,000. But these men were not counted with the other Israelites, because they were not given any of the land among the other Israelites.

63Moses and Eleazar the priest counted all these people. They counted the Israelites on the plains of Moab across the Jordan River from Jericho. 64Moses and Aaron the priest had counted the Israelites in the Desert of Sinai, but no one Moses counted on the plains of Moab was in the first counting. 65The LORD had told the Israelites they would all die in the desert, and the only two left were Caleb son of Jephunneh and Joshua son of Nun.

ZELOPHEHAD'S DAUGHTERS

27 Then the daughters of Zelophehad came near. Zelophehad was the son of Hepher, the son of Gilead, the son of Makir, the son of Manasseh. Zelophehad's daughters belonged to the family groups of Manasseh son of Joseph. The daughters' names were Mahlah, Noah, Hoglah, Milcah, and Tirzah. 2They went to the entrance of the Meeting Tent and stood before Moses, Eleazar the priest, the leaders, and all the people. They said, 3"Our father died in the desert. He was not one of Korah's followers who came together against the LORD, but he died because of his own sin, and he had no sons. 4Our father's name will die out because he had no sons. Give us property among our father's relatives."

5So Moses brought their case to the LORD, 6and the LORD said to him, 7"The daughters of Zelophehad are right; they should certainly get what their father owned. Give them property among their father's relatives.

8"Tell the Israelites, 'If a man dies and has no son, then everything he owned should go to his daughter. 9If he has no daughter, then everything he owned should go to his brothers. 10If he has no brothers, then everything he owned should go to his father's brothers. 11And if his father had no brothers, then everything he owned should go to the nearest relative in his family group. This should be a rule among the people of Israel, as the LORD has given this command to Moses.'"

JOSHUA IS THE NEW LEADER

12Then the LORD said to Moses, "Climb this mountain in the Abarim Mountains, and look at the land I have given to the Israelites. 13After you have seen it, you will die and join your ancestors as your brother Aaron did, 14because you both acted against my command in the Desert of Zin. You did not honor me as holy before the people at the waters of Meribah." (This was at Meribah in Kadesh in the Desert of Zin.)

15Moses said to the LORD, 16"The LORD is the God of the spirits of all people. May he choose a leader for these people, 17who will go in and out before them. He must lead them out like sheep and bring them in; the LORD's people must not be like sheep without a shepherd."

18So the LORD said to Moses, "Take Joshua son of Nun, because my Spirit is in him. Put your hand on him, 19and have him stand before Eleazar the priest and all the people. Then give him his orders as they watch. 20Let him share your honor so that all the Israelites will obey him. 21He must stand before Eleazar the priest, and Eleazar will get advice from the LORD by using the Urim. At his command all the Israelites will go out, and at his command they will all come in."

22Moses did what the LORD told him. He took Joshua and had him stand before Eleazar the priest and all the people, 23and he put his hands on him and gave him orders, just as the LORD had told him.

DAILY OFFERINGS

28 The LORD said to Moses, 2"Give this command to the Israelites. Tell them: 'Bring me food offerings made by fire, for a smell that is pleasing to me, and be sure to bring them at the right time.' 3Say to them, 'These are the offerings you must bring to the LORD: two male lambs, a year old, as a burnt offering each day. They must have nothing wrong with them. 4Offer one lamb in the morning and the other lamb at twilight. 5Also bring a grain offering of two quarts of fine flour, mixed with one quart of oil from pressed olives. 6This is the daily burnt offering which began at Mount Sinai; its smell is pleasing to the LORD. 7Offer one quart of wine with each lamb as a drink offering; pour it out to the LORD at the Holy Place. 8Offer the second lamb at twilight. As in the morning, also give a grain offering and a drink offering. This offering is made by fire, and its smell is pleasing to the LORD.

SABBATH OFFERINGS

9"'On the Sabbath day you must give two male lambs, a year old, that have nothing wrong with them. Also give a drink offering and a grain offering; the grain offering must be four quarts of fine flour mixed with olive oil. 10This is the burnt offering for every Sabbath, in addition to the daily burnt offering and drink offering.

MONTHLY OFFERINGS

11"'On the first day of each month bring a burnt offering to the LORD. This will be two young bulls, one male sheep, and seven male lambs a year old, and they must have nothing wrong with them. 12Give a grain offering with each bull of six quarts of fine flour mixed with olive oil. Also give a grain offering with the male sheep. It must be four quarts of fine flour mixed with olive oil. 13And give a grain offering with each lamb of two quarts of fine flour mixed with olive oil. This is a burnt offering, and its smell is pleasing to the LORD. 14The drink offering with each bull will be two quarts of wine, with the male sheep it will be one and one-third quarts, and with each lamb it will be one quart of wine. This is the burnt offering that must be offered each month of the year. 15Besides the daily burnt offerings and drink offerings, bring a sin offering of one goat to the LORD.

THE PASSOVER

16"'The LORD's Passover will be on the fourteenth day of the first month. 17The Feast of Unleavened Bread begins on the fifteenth day of that month. For seven days, you may eat only bread made without yeast. 18Have a holy meeting on the first day of the festival, and don't work that day. 19Bring to the LORD an offering made by fire, a burnt offering of two young bulls, one male sheep, and seven male lambs a year old. They must have nothing wrong with them. 20With each bull give a grain offering of six quarts of fine flour mixed with olive oil. With the male sheep it must be four quarts of fine flour mixed with oil. 21With each of the seven lambs, it must be two quarts of fine flour mixed with oil. 22Bring one goat as a sin offering, to remove your sins so you will belong to God. 23Bring these offerings in addition to the burnt offerings you give every morning. 24So bring food for the offering made by fire each day for seven days, for a smell that is pleasing to the LORD. Do it in addition to the daily burnt offering and its drink offering. 25On the seventh day have a holy meeting, and don't work that day.

THE FEAST OF WEEKS

26"'On the day of firstfruits when you bring new grain to the LORD during the Feast of Weeks, have a holy meeting. Don't work that day. 27Bring this burnt offering to the LORD: two young bulls, one male sheep, and seven male lambs a year old. This smell is pleasing to the LORD. 28Also, with each bull give a grain offering of six quarts of fine flour mixed with oil. With the male sheep, it must be four quarts of flour, 29and with each of the seven lambs offer two quarts of flour. 30Offer one male goat to remove your sins so you will belong to God. 31Bring these offerings and their drink offerings in addition to the daily burnt offering and its grain offering. The animals must have nothing wrong with them.

THE FEAST OF TRUMPETS

29 "'Have a holy meeting on the first day of the seventh month, and don't work on that day. That is the day you blow the trumpets. 2Bring these burnt offerings as a smell pleasing to the LORD: one young bull, one male sheep, and seven male lambs a year old. They must have nothing wrong with them. 3With the bull give a grain offering of six quarts of fine flour mixed with oil. With the male sheep offer four quarts, 4and with each of the seven lambs offer two quarts. 5Offer one male goat for a sin offering to remove your sins so you will belong to God. 6These offerings are in addition to the monthly and daily burnt offerings. Their grain offerings and drink offerings must be done as you have been told. These offerings are made by fire to the LORD, and their smell is pleasing to him.

THE DAY OF CLEANSING

7"'Have a holy meeting on the tenth day of the seventh month. On that day do not eat and do not work. 8Bring these burnt offerings as a smell pleasing to the LORD: one young bull, one male sheep, and seven male lambs a year old. They must have nothing wrong with them. 9With the bull give a grain offering of six quarts of fine flour mixed with oil. With the male sheep it must be four quarts, 10and with each of the seven lambs it must be two quarts. 11Offer one male goat as a sin offering. This will be in addition to the sin offering which removes your sins, the daily burnt offering with its grain offering, and the drink offerings.

THE FEAST OF SHELTERS

12"'Have a holy meeting on the fifteenth day of the seventh month, and do not work on that day. Celebrate a festival to the LORD for seven days. 13Bring these burnt offerings, made by fire, as a smell pleasing to the LORD: thirteen young bulls, two male sheep, and fourteen male lambs a year old. They must have nothing wrong with them. 14With each of the thirteen bulls offer a grain offering of six quarts of fine flour mixed with oil. With each of the two male sheep it must be four quarts, 15and with each of the fourteen lambs it must be two quarts. 16Offer one male goat as a sin offering in addition to the daily burnt offering with its grain and drink offerings.

17"'On the second day of this festival give an offering of twelve bulls, two male sheep, and fourteen male lambs a year old. They must have nothing wrong with them. 18Bring the grain and drink offerings for the bulls, sheep, and lambs, according to the number required. 19Offer one male goat as a sin offering, in addition to the daily burnt offering with its grain and drink offerings.

20"'On the third day offer eleven bulls, two male sheep, and fourteen male lambs a year old. They must have nothing wrong with them. 21Bring the grain and drink offerings for the bulls, sheep, and lambs, according to the number required. 22Offer one male goat as a sin offering, in addition to the daily burnt offering with its grain and drink offerings.

23"'On the fourth day offer ten bulls, two male sheep, and fourteen male lambs a year old. They must have nothing wrong with them. 24Bring the grain and drink offerings for the bulls, sheep, and lambs, according to the number required. 25Offer one male goat as a sin offering, in addition to the daily burnt offering with its grain and drink offerings.

26"'On the fifth day offer nine bulls, two male sheep, and fourteen male lambs a year old. They must have nothing wrong with them. 27Bring the grain and drink offerings for the bulls, sheep, and lambs, according to the number required. 28Offer one male goat as a sin offering, in addition to the daily burnt offering with its grain and drink offerings.

29"'On the sixth day offer eight bulls, two male sheep, and fourteen male lambs a year old. They must have nothing wrong with them. 30Bring the grain and drink offerings for the bulls, sheep, and lambs, according to the number required. 31Offer one male goat as a sin offering, in addition to the daily burnt offering with its grain and drink offerings.

32"'On the seventh day offer seven bulls, two male sheep, and fourteen male lambs a year old. They must have nothing wrong with them. 33Bring the grain and drink offerings for the bulls, sheep, and lambs, according to the number required. 34Offer one male goat as a sin offering, in addition to the daily burnt offering with its grain and drink offerings.

35"'On the eighth day have a closing meeting, and do not work on that day. 36Bring an offering made by fire, a burnt offering, as a smell pleasing to the LORD. Offer one bull, one male sheep, and seven male lambs a year old. They must have nothing wrong with them. 37Bring the grain and drink offerings for the bull, the male sheep, and the lambs, according to the number required. 38Offer one male goat as a sin offering, in addition to the daily burnt offering with its grain and drink offerings.

39"'At your festivals you should bring these to the LORD: your burnt offerings, grain offerings, drink offerings and fellowship offerings. These are in addition to other promised offerings and special gifts you want to give to the LORD.'"

40Moses told the Israelites everything the LORD had commanded him.

RULES ABOUT SPECIAL PROMISES

30 Moses spoke with the leaders of the Israelite tribes. He told them these commands from the LORD.

2"If a man makes a promise to the LORD or says he will do something special, he must keep his promise. He must do what he said. 3If a young woman still living at home makes a promise to the LORD or pledges to do something special, 4and if her father hears about the promise or pledge and says nothing, she must do what she promised. She must keep her pledge. 5But if her father hears about the promise or pledge and does not allow it, then the promise or pledge does not have to be kept. Her father would not allow it,

so the LORD will free her from her promise.

6"If a woman makes a pledge or a careless promise and then gets married, 7and if her husband hears about it and says nothing, she must keep her promise or the pledge she made. 8But if her husband hears about it and does not allow it, he cancels her pledge or the careless promise she made. The LORD will free her from keeping it.

9"If a widow or divorced woman makes a promise, she must do whatever she promised.

10"If a woman makes a promise or pledge while she is married, 11and if her husband hears about it but says nothing and does not stop her, she must keep her promise or pledge. 12But if her husband hears about it and cancels it, she does not have to do what she said. Her husband has canceled it, so the LORD will free her from it. 13A woman's husband may make her keep or cancel any promise or pledge she has made. 14If he says nothing to her about it for several days, she must keep her promises. If he hears about them and says nothing, she must keep her promises. 15But if he cancels them long after he heard about them, he is responsible if she breaks her promise."

16These are commands that the LORD gave to Moses for husbands and wives, and for fathers with daughters living at home.

ISRAEL ATTACKS THE MIDIANITES

31 The LORD spoke to Moses and said, 2"Pay back the Midianites for what they did to the Israelites; after that you will die."

3So Moses said to the people, "Get some men ready for war. The LORD will use them to pay back the Midianites. 4Send to war a thousand men from each of the tribes of Israel." 5So twelve thousand men got ready for war, a thousand men from each tribe. 6Moses sent those men to war; Phinehas son of Eleazar the priest was with them. He took with him the holy things and the trumpets for giving the alarm. 7They fought the Midianites as the LORD had commanded Moses, and they killed every Midianite man. 8Among those they killed were Evi, Rekem, Zur, Hur, and Reba, who were the five kings of Midian. They also killed Balaam son of Beor with a sword.

⁹The Israelites captured the Midianite women and children, and they took all their flocks, herds, and goods. ¹⁰They burned all the Midianite towns where they had settled and all their camps, ¹¹but they took all the people and animals and goods. ¹²Then they brought the captives, the animals, and the goods back to Moses and Eleazar the priest and all the Israelites. Their camp was on the plains of Moab near the Jordan River, across from Jericho.

¹³Moses, Eleazar the priest, and all the leaders of the people went outside the camp to meet them. ¹⁴Moses was angry with the army officers, the commanders over a thousand men, and those over a hundred men, who returned from war.

¹⁵He asked them, "Why did you let the women live? ¹⁶They were the ones who followed Balaam's advice and turned the Israelites from the LORD at Peor. Then a terrible sickness struck the LORD's people. ¹⁷Kill all the Midianite boys, and kill all the Midianite women who have had sexual relations. ¹⁸But save for yourselves the girls who have not had sexual relations with a man.

¹⁹"All you men who killed anyone or touched a dead body must stay outside the camp for seven days. On the third and seventh days you and your captives must make yourselves clean. ²⁰You must clean all your clothes and anything made of leather, goat hair, or wood."

²¹Then Eleazar the priest said to the soldiers who had gone to war, "These are the teachings that the LORD gave to Moses: ²²Put any gold, silver, bronze, iron, tin, or lead— ²³anything that will not burn—into the fire, and then it will be clean. But also purify those things with the cleansing water. Then they will be clean. If something cannot stand the fire, wash it with the water. ²⁴On the seventh day wash your clothes, and you will be clean. After that you may come into the camp."

DIVIDING THE GOODS

²⁵The LORD said to Moses, ²⁶"You, Eleazar the priest, and the leaders of the family groups should take a count of the goods, the men, and the animals that were taken. ²⁷Then divide those possessions between the soldiers who went to war and the rest of the people. ²⁸From the soldiers who went to war, take a tax for the LORD of one item out of every five hundred. This includes people, cattle, donkeys, or sheep. ²⁹Take it from the soldiers' half, and give it to Eleazar the priest as the LORD's share. ³⁰And from the people's half, take one item out of every fifty. This includes people, cattle, donkeys, sheep, or other animals. Give that to the Levites, who take care of the LORD's Holy Tent." ³¹So Moses and Eleazar did as the LORD commanded Moses.

³²There remained from what the soldiers had taken 675,000 sheep, ³³72,000 cattle, ³⁴61,000 donkeys, ³⁵and 32,000 women who had not had sexual relations with a man. ³⁶The soldiers who went to war got 337,500 sheep, ³⁷and they gave 675 of them to the LORD. ³⁸They got 36,000 cattle, and they gave 72 of them to the LORD. ³⁹They got 30,500 donkeys, and they gave 61 of them to the LORD. ⁴⁰They got 16,000 people, and they gave 32 of them to the LORD. ⁴¹Moses gave the LORD's share to Eleazar the priest, as the LORD had commanded him.

⁴²Moses separated the people's half from the soldiers' half. ⁴³The people got 337,500 sheep, ⁴⁴36,000 cattle, ⁴⁵30,500 donkeys, ⁴⁶and 16,000 people. ⁴⁷From the people's half Moses took one item out of every fifty for the LORD. This included the animals and the people. Then he gave them to the Levites, who took care of the LORD's Holy Tent. This was what the LORD had commanded Moses.

⁴⁸Then the officers of the army, the commanders of a thousand men and commanders of a hundred men, came to Moses. ⁴⁹They told Moses, "We, your servants, have counted our soldiers under our command, and not one of them is missing. ⁵⁰So we have brought the LORD a gift of the gold things that each of us found: arm bands, bracelets, signet rings, earrings, and necklaces. These are to remove our sins so we will belong to the LORD."

⁵¹So Moses and Eleazar the priest took the gold from them, which had been made into all kinds of objects. ⁵²The commanders of a thousand men and the commanders of a hundred men gave the LORD the gold, and all of it together weighed about 420 pounds; ⁵³each soldier had taken something for himself. ⁵⁴Moses and Eleazar the priest took the gold from the commanders of a thousand

men and the commanders of a hundred men. Then they put it in the Meeting Tent as a memorial before the LORD for the people of Israel.

THE TRIBES EAST OF THE JORDAN

32 The people of Reuben and Gad had large flocks and herds. When they saw that the lands of Jazer and Gilead were good for the animals, ²they came to Moses, Eleazar the priest, and the leaders of the people. ³⁻⁴They said, "We, your servants, have flocks and herds. The LORD has captured for the Israelites a land that is good for animals—the land around Ataroth, Dibon, Jazer, Nimrah, Heshbon, Elealeh, Sebam, Nebo, and Beon. ⁵If it pleases you, we would like this land to be given to us. Don't make us cross the Jordan River."

⁶Moses told the people of Gad and Reuben, "Shall your brothers go to war while you stay behind? ⁷You will discourage the Israelites from going over to the land the LORD has given them. ⁸Your ancestors did the same thing. I sent them from Kadesh Barnea to look at the land. ⁹They went as far as the Valley of Eshcol, and when they saw the land, they discouraged the Israelites from going into the land the LORD had given them. ¹⁰The LORD became very angry that day and made this promise: ¹¹'None of the people who came from Egypt and who are twenty years old or older will see the land that I promised to Abraham, Isaac, and Jacob. These people have not followed me completely. ¹²Only Caleb son of Jephunneh the Kenizzite and Joshua son of Nun followed the LORD completely.'

¹³"The LORD was angry with Israel, so he made them wander in the desert for forty years. Finally all the people who had sinned against the LORD died, ¹⁴and now you are acting just like your ancestors! You sinful people are making the LORD even more angry with Israel. ¹⁵If you quit following him, it will add to their stay in the desert, and you will destroy all these people."

¹⁶Then the Reubenites and Gadites came up to Moses and said, "We will build pens for our animals and cities for our children here. ¹⁷Then our children will be in strong, walled cities, safe from the people who live in this land. Then we will prepare for war. We will help the other Israelites get their land, ¹⁸and we will not return home until every Israelite has received his land. ¹⁹We won't take any of the land west of the Jordan River; our part of the land is east of the Jordan."

²⁰So Moses told them, "You must do these things. You must go before the LORD into battle ²¹and cross the Jordan River armed, until the LORD forces out the enemy. ²²After the LORD helps us take the land, you may return home. You will have done your duty to the LORD and Israel, and you may have this land as your own.

²³"But if you don't do these things, you will be sinning against the LORD; know for sure that you will be punished for your sin. ²⁴Build cities for your children and pens for your animals, but then you must do what you promised."

²⁵The Gadites and Reubenites said to Moses, "We are your servants, and we will do what you, our master, command. ²⁶Our children, wives, and all our cattle will stay in the cities of Gilead, ²⁷but we, your servants, will prepare for battle. We will go over and fight for the LORD, as you, our master, have said."

²⁸So Moses gave orders about them to Eleazar the priest, to Joshua son of Nun, and to the leaders of the tribes of Israel. ²⁹Moses said to them, "If the Gadites and Reubenites prepare for battle and cross the Jordan River with you, to go before the LORD and help you take the land, give them the land of Gilead for their own. ³⁰But if they do not go over armed, they will not receive it; their land will be in Canaan with you."

³¹The Gadites and Reubenites answered, "We are your servants, and we will do as the LORD said. ³²We will cross over into Canaan and go before the LORD ready for battle. But our land will be east of the Jordan River."

³³So Moses gave that land to the tribes of Gad, Reuben, and East Manasseh. (Manasseh was Joseph's son.) That land had been the kingdom of Sihon, king of the Amorites, and the kingdom of Og, king of Bashan, as well as all the cities and the land around them.

³⁴The Gadites rebuilt the cities of Dibon, Ataroth, Aroer, ³⁵Atroth Shophan, Jazer, Jogbehah, ³⁶Beth Nimrah, and Beth Haran. These were strong, walled cities. And they built sheep pens.

³⁷The Reubenites rebuilt Heshbon, Elealeh, Kiriathaim, ³⁸Nebo, Baal Meon, and

Sibmah. They renamed Nebo and Baal Meon when they rebuilt them.

³⁹The descendants of Makir son of Manasseh went and captured Gilead and forced out the Amorites who were there. ⁴⁰So Moses gave Gilead to the family of Makir son of Manasseh, and they settled there. ⁴¹Jair son of Manasseh went out and captured the small towns there, and he called them the Towns of Jair. ⁴²Nobah went and captured Kenath and the small towns around it; then he named it Nobah after himself.

ISRAEL'S JOURNEY FROM EGYPT

33 These are the places the Israelites went as Moses and Aaron led them out of Egypt in divisions. ²At the LORD's command Moses recorded the places they went, and these are the places they went.

³On the fifteenth day of the first month, the day after the Passover, the Israelites left Rameses and marched out boldly in front of all the Egyptians. ⁴The Egyptians were burying their firstborn sons, whom the LORD had killed; the LORD showed that the gods of Egypt were false.

⁵The Israelites left Rameses and camped at Succoth.

⁶They left Succoth and camped at Etham, at the edge of the desert.

⁷They left Etham and went back to Pi Hahiroth, to the east of Baal Zephon, and camped near Migdol.

⁸They left Pi Hahiroth and walked through the sea into the desert. After going three days through the Desert of Etham, they camped at Marah.

⁹They left Marah and went to Elim; there were twelve springs of water and seventy palm trees where they camped.

¹⁰They left Elim and camped near the Red Sea.

¹¹They left the Red Sea and camped in the Desert of Sin.

¹²They left the Desert of Sin and camped at Dophkah.

¹³They left Dophkah and camped at Alush.

¹⁴They left Alush and camped at Rephidim, where the people had no water to drink.

¹⁵They left Rephidim and camped in the Desert of Sinai.

¹⁶They left the Desert of Sinai and camped at Kibroth Hattaavah.

¹⁷They left Kibroth Hattaavah and camped at Hazeroth.

¹⁸They left Hazeroth and camped at Rithmah.

¹⁹They left Rithmah and camped at Rimmon Perez.

²⁰They left Rimmon Perez and camped at Libnah.

²¹They left Libnah and camped at Rissah.

²²They left Rissah and camped at Kehelathah.

²³They left Kehelathah and camped at Mount Shepher.

²⁴They left Mount Shepher and camped at Haradah.

²⁵They left Haradah and camped at Makheloth.

²⁶They left Makheloth and camped at Tahath.

²⁷They left Tahath and camped at Terah.

²⁸They left Terah and camped at Mithcah.

²⁹They left Mithcah and camped at Hashmonah.

³⁰They left Hashmonah and camped at Moseroth.

³¹They left Moseroth and camped at Bene Jaakan.

³²They left Bene Jaakan and camped at Hor Haggidgad.

³³They left Hor Haggidgad and camped at Jotbathah.

³⁴They left Jotbathah and camped at Abronah.

³⁵They left Abronah and camped at Ezion Geber.

³⁶They left Ezion Geber and camped at Kadesh in the Desert of Zin.

³⁷They left Kadesh and camped at Mount Hor, on the border of Edom. ³⁸Aaron the priest obeyed the LORD and went up Mount Hor. There he died on the first day of the fifth month in the fortieth year after the Israelites left Egypt. ³⁹Aaron was 123 years old when he died on Mount Hor.

⁴⁰The Canaanite king of Arad, who lived in the southern area of Canaan, heard that the Israelites were coming.

⁴¹The people left Mount Hor and camped at Zalmonah.

⁴²They left Zalmonah and camped at Punon.

⁴³They left Punon and camped at Oboth.

⁴⁴They left Oboth and camped at Iye Abarim, on the border of Moab.

⁴⁵They left Iye Abarim and camped at Dibon Gad.

⁴⁶They left Dibon Gad and camped at Almon Diblathaim.

⁴⁷They left Almon Diblathaim and camped in the mountains of Abarim, near Nebo.

⁴⁸They left the mountains of Abarim and camped on the plains of Moab near the Jordan River across from Jericho. ⁴⁹They camped along the Jordan on the plains of Moab, and their camp went from Beth Jeshimoth to Abel Acacia.

⁵⁰On the plains of Moab by the Jordan River across from Jericho, the LORD spoke to Moses. He said, ⁵¹"Speak to the Israelites and tell them, 'When you cross the Jordan River and go into Canaan, ⁵²force out all the people who live there. Destroy all of their carved statues and metal idols. Wreck all of their places of worship. ⁵³Take over the land and settle there, because I have given this land to you to own. ⁵⁴Throw lots to divide up the land by family groups, giving larger portions to larger family groups and smaller portions to smaller family groups. The land will be given as the lots decide; each tribe will get its own land.'

⁵⁵"'But if you don't force those people out of the land, they will bring you trouble. They will be like sharp hooks in your eyes and thorns in your sides. They will bring trouble to the land where you live. ⁵⁶Then I will punish you as I had planned to punish them.'"

THE BORDERS OF CANAAN

34 The LORD said to Moses, ²"Give this command to the people of Israel: 'You will soon enter Canaan and it will be yours. These shall be the borders: ³On the south you will get part of the Desert of Zin near the border of Edom. On the east side your southern border will start at the south end of the Dead Sea, ⁴cross south of Scorpion Pass, and go through the Desert of Zin and south of Kadesh Barnea. Then it will go to Hazar Addar and over to Azmon. ⁵From Azmon it will go to the brook of Egypt, and it will end at the Mediterranean Sea.

⁶"'Your western border will be the Mediterranean Sea.

⁷"'Your northern border will begin at the Mediterranean Sea and go to Mount Hor. ⁸From Mount Hor it will go to Lebo Hamath, and on to Zedad. ⁹Then the border will go to Ziphron, and it will end at Hazar Enan. This will be your northern border.

¹⁰"'Your eastern border will begin at Hazar Enan and go to Shepham. ¹¹From Shepham the border will go east of Ain to Riblah and along the hills east of Lake Galilee. ¹²Then the border will go down along the Jordan River and end at the Dead Sea.

"'These are the borders around your country.'"

¹³So Moses gave this command to the Israelites: "This is the land you will receive. Throw lots to divide it among the nine and one-half tribes, because the LORD commanded that it should be theirs. ¹⁴The tribes of Reuben, Gad, and East Manasseh have already received their land. ¹⁵These two and one-half tribes received land east of the Jordan River, across from Jericho."

¹⁶Then the LORD said to Moses, ¹⁷"These are the men who will divide the land: Eleazar the priest and Joshua son of Nun. ¹⁸Also take one leader from each tribe to help divide the land. ¹⁹These are the names of the leaders: from the tribe of Judah, Caleb son of Jephunneh; ²⁰from the tribe of Simeon, Shemuel son of Ammihud; ²¹from the tribe of Benjamin, Elidad son of Kislon; ²²from the tribe of Dan, Bukki son of Jogli; ²³from the tribe of Manasseh son of Joseph, Hanniel son of Ephod; ²⁴from the tribe of Ephraim son of Joseph, Kemuel son of Shiphtan; ²⁵from the tribe of Zebulun, Elizaphan son of Parnach; ²⁶from the tribe of Issachar, Paltiel son of Azzan; ²⁷from the tribe of Asher, Ahihud son of Shelomi; ²⁸from the tribe of Naphtali, Pedahel son of Ammihud."

²⁹The LORD commanded these men to divide the land of Canaan among the Israelites.

THE LEVITES' TOWNS

35 The LORD spoke to Moses on the plains of Moab across from Jericho by the Jordan River. He said, ²"Command the Israelites to give the Levites cities to live in from the land they receive. Also give the Levites the pastureland around these cities. ³Then the Levites will have cities where they may live and pastureland for their cattle, flocks, and other animals. ⁴The pastureland you give the Levites will extend fifteen hundred feet from the city wall. ⁵Also measure three thousand feet in each direction outside the city wall—three thousand feet east of the city, three thousand feet south of the city, three thousand feet west of the city, and three thousand feet north of the city, with the city in the center. This will be pastureland for the Levites' cities.

CITIES OF SAFETY

⁶"Six of the cities you give the Levites will be cities of safety. A person who accidentally kills someone may run to one of those cities for safety. You must also give forty-two other cities to the Levites; ⁷give the Levites a total of forty-eight cities and their pastures. ⁸The larger tribes of Israel must give more cities, and the smaller tribes must give fewer cities. Each tribe must give some of its cities to the Levites, but the number of cities they give will depend on the size of their land."

⁹Then the LORD said to Moses, ¹⁰"Tell the Israelites these things: 'When you cross the Jordan River and go into Canaan, ¹¹you must choose cities to be cities of safety, so that a person who accidentally kills someone may run to them for safety. ¹²There the person will be safe from the dead person's relative who has the duty of punishing the killer. He will not die before he receives a fair trial in court. ¹³The six cities you give will be cities of safety. ¹⁴Give three cities east of the Jordan River and three cities in Canaan as cities of safety. ¹⁵These six cities will be places of safety for citizens of Israel, as well as for foreigners and other people living with you. Any of these people who accidentally kills someone may run to one of these cities.

¹⁶"Anyone who uses an iron weapon to kill someone is a murderer. He must be put to death. ¹⁷Anyone who takes a rock and kills a person with it is a murderer. He must be put to death. ¹⁸Anyone who picks up a piece of wood and kills someone with it is a murderer. He must be put to death. ¹⁹A relative of the dead person must put the murderer to death;

when they meet, the relative must kill the murderer. ²⁰A person might shove someone or throw something at someone and cause death. ²¹Or a person might hit someone with his hand and cause death. If it were done from hate, the person is a murderer and must be put to death. A relative of the dead person must kill the murderer when they meet.

²²"But a person might suddenly shove someone, and not from hatred. Or a person might accidentally throw something and hit someone. ²³Or a person might drop a rock on someone he couldn't see and kill that person. There was no plan to hurt anyone and no hatred for the one who was killed. ²⁴If that happens, the community must judge between the relative of the dead person and the killer, according to these rules. ²⁵They must protect the killer from the dead person's relative, sending the killer back to the original city of safety, to stay there until the high priest dies (the high priest had the holy oil poured on him).

²⁶"Such a person must never go outside the limits of the city of safety. ²⁷If a relative of the dead person finds the killer outside the city, the relative may kill that person and not be guilty of murder. ²⁸The killer must stay in the city of safety until the high priest dies. After the high priest dies, the killer may go home.

²⁹"These laws are for you from now on, wherever you live.

³⁰"If anyone kills a person, the murderer may be put to death only if there are witnesses. No one may be put to death with only one witness.

³¹"Don't take money to spare the life of a murderer who should be put to death. A murderer must be put to death.

³²"If someone has run to a city of safety, don't take money to let the person go back home before the high priest dies.

³³"Don't let murder spoil your land. The only way to remove the sin of killing an innocent person is for the murderer to be put to death. ³⁴I am the LORD, and I live among the Israelites. I live in that land with you, so do not spoil it with murder.'"

LAND FOR ZELOPHEHAD'S DAUGHTERS

36 The leaders of Gilead's family group went to talk to Moses and the leaders of the families of Israel. (Gilead was the son of Makir, the son of Manasseh, the son of Joseph.) ²They said, "The LORD commanded you, our master, to give the land to the Israelites by throwing lots, and the LORD commanded you to give the land of Zelophehad, our brother, to his daughters. ³But if his daughters marry men from other tribes of Israel, then that land will leave our family, and the people of the other tribes will get that land. So we will lose some of our land. ⁴When the time of Jubilee comes for the Israelites, their land will go to the tribes of the people they marry; their land will be taken away from us, the land we received from our fathers."

⁵Then Moses gave the Israelites this command from the LORD: "These men from the tribe of Joseph are right. ⁶This is the LORD's command to Zelophehad's daughters: You may marry anyone you wish, as long as the person is from your own tribe. ⁷In this way

the Israelites' land will not pass from tribe to tribe, and each Israelite will keep the land in the tribe that belonged to his ancestors. ⁸A woman who inherits her father's land may marry, but she must marry someone from her own tribe. In this way every Israelite will keep the land that belonged to his ancestors. ⁹The land must not pass from tribe to tribe, and each Israelite tribe will keep the land it received from its ancestors."

¹⁰Zelophehad's daughters obeyed the LORD's command to Moses. ¹¹So Zelophehad's daughters—Mahlah, Tirzah, Hoglah, Milcah, and Noah—married their cousins, their father's relatives. ¹²Their husbands were from the tribe of Manasseh son of Joseph, so their land stayed in their father's family group and tribe.

¹³These were the laws and commands that the LORD gave to the Israelites through Moses on the plains of Moab by the Jordan River, across from Jericho.

deuteronomy

MOSES' LAST MESSAGE TO ISRAEL

MOSES TALKS TO THE ISRAELITES

1 This is the message Moses gave to all the people of Israel in the desert east of the Jordan River. They were in the desert area near Suph, between Paran and the towns of Tophel, Laban, Hazeroth, and Dizahab.

²(The trip from Mount Sinai to Kadesh Barnea on the Mount Seir road takes eleven days.) ³Forty years after the Israelites had left Egypt, on the first day of the eleventh month, Moses told the people of Israel everything the LORD had commanded him to tell them. ⁴This was after the LORD had defeated Sihon and Og. Sihon was king of the Amorite people and lived in Heshbon. Og was king of Bashan and lived in Ashteroth and Edrei.

⁵Now the Israelites were east of the Jordan River in the land of Moab, and there Moses began to explain what God had commanded. He said:

⁶The LORD our God spoke to us at Mount Sinai and said, "You have stayed long enough at this mountain. ⁷Get ready, and go to the mountain country of the Amorites, and to all the places around there—the Jordan Valley, the mountains, the western hills, the southern area, the seacoast, the land of Canaan, and Lebanon. Go as far as the great river, the Euphrates. ⁸See, I have given you this land, so go in and take it for yourselves. The LORD promised it to your ancestors—Abraham, Isaac, and Jacob and their descendants."

MOSES APPOINTS LEADERS

⁹At that time I said, "I am not able to take care of you by myself. ¹⁰The LORD your God has made you grow in number so that there are as many of you as there are stars in the sky. ¹¹I pray that the LORD, the God of your ancestors, will give you a thousand times more people and do all the wonderful things he promised. ¹²But I cannot take care of your problems, your troubles, and your arguments by myself. ¹³So choose some men from each tribe—wise men who have understanding and experience—and I will make them leaders over you."

¹⁴And you said, "That's a good thing to do."

¹⁵So I took the wise and experienced leaders of your tribes, and I made them your leaders. I appointed commanders over a thousand people, over a hundred people, over fifty people, and over ten people and made them officers over your tribes. ¹⁶Then I told your leaders, "Listen to the arguments between your people. Judge fairly between two Israelites or between an Israelite and a foreigner. ¹⁷When you judge, be fair to everyone; don't act as if one person is more important than another, and don't be afraid of anyone, because your decision comes from God. Bring the hard cases to me, and I will judge them." ¹⁸At that time I told you everything you must do.

SPIES ENTER THE LAND

¹⁹Then, as the LORD our God commanded us, we left Mount Sinai and went toward the mountain country of the Amorite people. We went through that large and terrible desert you saw, and then we came to Kadesh Barnea. ²⁰I said to you, "You have now come to the mountain country of the Amorites, to the land the LORD our God will give us. ²¹Look, here it is! Go up and take it. The LORD, the God of your ancestors, told you to do this, so don't be afraid and don't worry."

²²Then all of you came to me and said, "Let's send men before us to spy out the land. They can come back and tell us about the way we should go and the cities we will find."

²³I thought that was a good idea, so I chose twelve of your men, one for each tribe. ²⁴They left and went up to the mountains, and when they came to the Valley of Eshcol they explored it. ²⁵They took some of the fruit from that land and brought it down to us, saying, "It is a good land that the LORD our God is giving us."

ISRAEL REFUSES TO ENTER

²⁶But you refused to go. You would not obey the command of the LORD your God,

27but grumbled in your tents, saying, "The LORD hates us. He brought us out of Egypt just to give us to the Amorites, who will destroy us. 28Where can we go now? The spies we sent have made us afraid, because they said, 'The people there are stronger and taller than we are. The cities are big, with walls up to the sky. And we saw the Anakites there!'"

29Then I said to you, "Don't be frightened; don't be afraid of those people. 30The LORD your God will go ahead of you and fight for you as he did in Egypt; you saw him do it. 31And in the desert you saw how the LORD your God carried you, like one carries a child. And he has brought you safely all the way to this place."

32But you still did not trust the LORD your God, even though 33he had always gone

THE ROAD TO SUCCESS

crossing over to your promised land

FUTURE

DEUTERONOMY 1:8

God led the people forth from Egypt with awesome signs and miracles, yet their faith failed them at the first real test put to them.

It was important that they remember not to be like their forefathers, rebellious and stubborn, with their hearts not right and spirits that did not trust God.

The children of Israel saw the awesome miracles of God and what he did for them. They crossed the Red Sea on dry ground; God gave them a cloud by day and a pillar of fire by night; he gave them water from a rock and fed them manna and quail for sustenance. God met all their needs; even the clothes on their backs and the shoes on their feet were all in good condition during this time. God showed them he would take care of them; but when it came time to trust him in taking care of them in battle, they doubted him. They forgot his works; they were armed for battle but they limited God through their fear.

God gave so much in spite of all the Israelites' murmuring and complaining, but due to their doubt, God could not do what he wanted for them. Today God has given us marvelous blessings, especially when it comes to forgiveness of sins and the gift of salvation, yet when it comes to daily battles, doubt and unbelief creep in and the cares of the world often keep us from being victorious. To survive in today's society, we need to trust him in all things. Unbelief and doubt will limit God. Don't make your own way or make decisions without God. Arm yourself for battle and have faith that God will be your defense.

reflect: Trust God to provide all your needs today.

Go to **FUTURE:** "Mentoring World Changers for Christ" at **Mark 4:13–20.**

before you to find places for you to camp. In a fire at night and in a cloud during the day, he showed you which way to go.

³⁴When the Lord heard what you said, he was angry and made an oath, saying, ³⁵"I promised a good land to your ancestors, but none of you evil people will see it. ³⁶Only Caleb son of Jephunneh will see it. I will give him and his descendants the land he walked on, because he followed the Lord completely."

³⁷Because of you, the Lord was also angry with me and said, "You won't enter the land either, ³⁸but your assistant, Joshua son of Nun, will enter it. Encourage him, because he will lead Israel to take the land for their own.

³⁹"Your little children that you said would be captured, who do not know right from wrong at this time, will go into the land. I will give the land to them, and they will take it for their own. ⁴⁰But you must turn around and follow the desert road toward the Red Sea."

⁴¹Then you said to me, "We have sinned against the Lord, but now we will go up and fight, as the Lord our God commanded us." Then all of you put on weapons, thinking it would be easy to go into the mountains.

⁴²But the Lord said to me, "Tell the people, 'You must not go up there and fight. I will not be with you, and your enemies will defeat you.'"

⁴³So I told you, but you would not listen. You would not obey the Lord's command. You were proud, so you went on up into the mountains, ⁴⁴and the Amorites who lived in those mountains came out and fought you. They chased you like bees and defeated you from Edom to Hormah. ⁴⁵So you came back and cried before the Lord, but the Lord did not listen to you; he refused to pay attention to you. ⁴⁶So you stayed in Kadesh a long time.

ISRAEL WANDERS IN THE DESERT

2 Then we turned around, and we traveled on the desert road toward the Red Sea, as the Lord had told me to do. We traveled through the mountains of Edom for many days.

²Then the Lord said to me, ³"You have traveled through these mountains long enough. Turn north ⁴and give the people this command: 'You will soon go through the land that belongs to your relatives, the descendants of Esau who live in Edom. They will be afraid of you, but be very careful. ⁵Do not go to war against them. I will not give you any of their land—not even a foot of it, because I have given the mountains of Edom to Esau as his own. ⁶You must pay them in silver for any food you eat or water you drink.'"

⁷The Lord your God has blessed everything you have done; he has protected you while you traveled through this great desert. The Lord your God has been with you for the past forty years, and you have had everything you needed.

⁸So we passed by our relatives, the descendants of Esau who lived in Edom. We turned off the Jordan Valley road that comes from the towns of Elath and Ezion Geber and traveled along the desert road to Moab.

THE LAND OF AR

⁹Then the Lord said to me, "Don't bother the people of Moab. Don't go to war against them, because I will not give you any of their land as your own; I have given Ar to the descendants of Lot as their own." ¹⁰(The Emites, who lived in Ar before, were strong people, and there were many of them. They were very tall, like the Anakites. ¹¹The Emites were thought to be Rephaites, like the Anakites, but the Moabite people called them Emites. ¹²The Horites also lived in Edom before, but the descendants of Esau forced them out and destroyed them, taking their place as Israel did in the land the Lord gave them as their own.)

¹³And the Lord said to me, "Now get up and cross the Zered Valley." So we crossed the valley. ¹⁴It had been thirty-eight years from the time we left Kadesh Barnea until we crossed the Zered Valley. By then, all the fighting men from that time had died, as the Lord had promised would happen. ¹⁵The Lord continued to work against them to remove them from the camp until they were all dead.

¹⁶When the last of those fighting men had died, ¹⁷the Lord said to me, ¹⁸"Today you will pass by Ar, on the border of Moab. ¹⁹When you come near the people of Ammon, don't bother them or go to war against them, because I will not give you any of their land as

your own. I have given it to the descendants of Lot for their own."

20(That land was also thought to be a land of the Rephaites, because those people used to live there, but the Ammonites called them Zamzummites. 21They were strong people, and there were many of them; they were very tall, like the Anakites. The LORD destroyed the Zamzummites, and the Ammonites forced them out of the land and took their place. 22The LORD did the same thing for the descendants of Esau, who lived in Edom, when he destroyed the Horites. The Edomites forced them out of the land and took their place, and they live there to this day. 23The Cretan people came from Crete and destroyed the Avvites, who lived in towns all the way to Gaza; the Cretans destroyed them and took their place.)

FIGHTING THE AMORITES

24The LORD said, "Get up and cross the Arnon Ravine. See, I am giving you the power to defeat Sihon the Amorite, king of Heshbon, and I am giving you his land. So fight against him and begin taking his land. 25Today I will begin to make all the people in the world afraid of you. When they hear reports about you, they will shake with fear, and they will be terrified of you."

26I sent messengers from the desert of Kedemoth to Sihon king of Heshbon. They offered him peace, saying, 27"If you let us pass through your country, we will stay on the road and not turn right or left. 28We will pay you in silver for any food we eat or water we drink. We only want to walk through your country. 29The descendants of Esau in Edom let us go through their land, and so did the Moabites in Ar. We want to cross the Jordan River into the land the LORD our God has given us." 30But Sihon king of Heshbon would not let us pass, because the LORD your God had made him stubborn. The LORD wanted you to defeat Sihon, and now this has happened.

31The LORD said to me, "See, I have begun to give Sihon and his country to you. Begin taking the land as your own."

32Then Sihon and all his army came out and fought us at Jahaz, 33but the LORD our God gave Sihon to us. We defeated him, his sons, and all his army. 34We captured all his cities at that time and completely destroyed them, as well as the men, women, and children. We left no one alive. 35But we kept the cattle and valuable things from the cities for ourselves. 36We defeated Aroer on the edge of the Arnon Ravine, and we defeated the town in the ravine, and even as far as Gilead. No town was too strong for us; the LORD our God gave us all of them. 37But you did not go near the land of the Ammonites, on the shores of the Jabbok River, or the towns in the mountains, as the LORD our God had commanded.

THE BATTLE AT BASHAN

3 When we turned and went up the road toward Bashan, Og king of Bashan and all his army came out to fight us at Edrei. 2The LORD said to me, "Don't be afraid of Og, because I will hand him, his whole army, and his land over to you. Do to him what you did to Sihon king of the Amorites, who ruled in Heshbon."

3So the LORD our God gave us Og king of Bashan and all his army; we defeated them and left no one alive. 4Then we captured all of Og's cities, all sixty of them, and took the whole area of Argob, Og's kingdom in Bashan. 5All these were strong cities, with high walls and gates with bars. And there were also many small towns with no walls. 6We completely destroyed them, just like the cities of Sihon king of Heshbon. We killed all the men, women, and children, 7but we kept all the cattle and valuable things from the cities for ourselves.

8So at that time we took the land east of the Jordan River, from the Arnon Ravine to Mount Hermon, from these two Amorite kings. 9(Hermon is called Sirion by the Sidonian people, but the Amorites call it Senir.) 10We captured all the cities on the high plain and all of Gilead, and we took all of Bashan as far as Salecah and Edrei, towns in Og's kingdom of Bashan. 11(Only Og king of Bashan was left of the few Rephaites. His bed was made of iron, and it was more than thirteen feet long and six feet wide! It is still in the Ammonite city of Rabbah.)

THE LAND IS DIVIDED

12At that time we took this land to be our own. I gave the people of Reuben and Gad the land from Aroer by the Arnon Ravine, as well as half of the mountain country of

Gilead and the cities in it. [13]To the people of East Manasseh I gave the rest of Gilead and all of Bashan, the kingdom of Og. (The area of Argob in Bashan was called the land of the Rephaites. [14]Jair, a descendant of Manasseh, took the whole area of Argob, all the way to the border of the Geshurites and Maacathites. So that land was named for Jair, and even today Bashan is called the Towns of Jair.) [15]I gave Gilead to Makir. [16]I gave the Reubenites and the Gadites the land that begins at Gilead and goes from the Arnon Ravine (the middle of the Arnon is the border) to the Jabbok River, which is the Ammonite border. [17]The border on the west was the Jordan River in the Jordan Valley, and it goes from Lake Galilee to the Dead Sea west of Mount Pisgah.

[18]At that time I gave you this command: "The LORD your God has given you this land as your own. Now your fighting men must take their weapons, and you must lead the other Israelites across the river. [19]Your wives, your young children, and your cattle may stay here. I know you have many cattle, and they may stay here in the cities I have given you, [20]until the LORD also gives your Israelite relatives a place to rest. They will receive the land the LORD your God has given them on the other side of the Jordan River. After that, you may each return to the land I have given you."

[21]Then I gave this command to Joshua: "You have seen for yourself all that the LORD your God has done to these two kings. The LORD will do the same thing to all the kingdoms where you are going. [22]Don't be afraid of them, because the LORD your God will fight for you."

MOSES CANNOT ENTER THE LAND

[23]Then I begged the LORD: [24]"Lord GOD, you have begun to show me, your servant, how great you are. You have great strength, and no other god in heaven or on earth can do the powerful things you do. There is no other god like you. [25]Please let me cross the Jordan River so that I may see the good land by the Jordan. I want to see the beautiful mountains and Lebanon."

[26]But the LORD was angry with me because of you, and he would not listen to me. The LORD said to me, "That's enough. Don't talk to me anymore about it. [27]Climb to the top of Mount Pisgah and look west, north, south, and east. You can look at the land, but you will not cross the Jordan River. [28]Appoint Joshua and help him be brave and strong. He will lead the people across the river and give them the land that they are to inherit, but you can only look at it." [29]So we stayed in the valley opposite Beth Peor.

MOSES TELLS ISRAEL TO OBEY

4 Now, Israel, listen to the laws and commands I will teach you. Obey them so that you will live and so that you will go over and take the land the LORD, the God of your ancestors, is giving to you. [2]Don't add to these commands, and don't leave anything out, but obey the commands of the LORD your God that I give you.

[3]You have seen for yourselves what the LORD did at Baal Peor, how the LORD your God destroyed everyone among you who followed Baal in Peor. [4]But all of you who continued following the LORD your God are still alive today.

[5]Look, I have taught you the laws and rules the LORD my God commanded me. Now you can obey the laws in the land you are entering, in the land you will take. [6]Obey these laws carefully, in order to show the other nations that you have wisdom and understanding. When they hear about these laws, they will say, "This great nation of Israel is wise and understanding." [7]No other nation is as great as we are. Their gods do not come near them, but the LORD our God comes near when we pray to him. [8]And no other nation has such good teachings and commands as those I am giving to you today.

[9]But be careful! Watch out and don't forget the things you have seen. Don't forget them as long as you live, but teach them to your children and grandchildren. [10]Remember the day you stood before the LORD your God at Mount Sinai. He said to me, "Bring the people together so I can tell them what I have to say. Then they will respect me as long as they live in the land, and they will teach these things to their children." [11]When you came and stood at the bottom of the mountain, it blazed with fire that reached to the sky, and black clouds made it very dark. [12]The LORD spoke to you from the fire. You heard the sound of words, but you did not see him;

there was only a voice. ¹³The LORD told you about his Agreement, the Ten Commandments. He told you to obey them, and he wrote them on two stone tablets. ¹⁴Then the LORD commanded me to teach you the laws and rules that you must obey in the land you will take when you cross the Jordan River.

LAWS ABOUT IDOLS

¹⁵Since the LORD spoke to you from the fire at Mount Sinai, but you did not see him, watch yourselves carefully! ¹⁶Don't sin by making idols of any kind, and don't make statues—of men or women, ¹⁷of animals on earth or birds that fly in the air, ¹⁸of anything that crawls on the ground, or of fish in the water below. ¹⁹When you look up at the sky, you see the sun, moon, and stars, and everything in the sky. But don't bow down and worship them, because the LORD your God has made these things for all people everywhere. ²⁰But the LORD brought you out of Egypt, which tested you like a furnace for melting iron, and he made you his very own people, as you are now.

²¹The LORD was angry with me because of you, and he swore that I would not cross the Jordan River to go into the good land the LORD your God is giving you as your own. ²²I will die here in this land and not cross the Jordan, but you will soon go across and take that good land. ²³Be careful. Don't forget the Agreement of the LORD your God that he made with you, and don't make any idols for yourselves, as the LORD your God has commanded you not to do. ²⁴The LORD your God is a jealous God, like a fire that burns things up.

²⁵Even after you have lived in the land a long time and have had children and grandchildren, don't do evil things. Don't make any kind of idol, and don't do what the LORD your God says is evil, because that will make him angry. ²⁶If you do, I ask heaven and earth to speak against you this day that you will quickly be removed from this land that you are crossing the Jordan River to take. You will not live there long after that, but you will be completely destroyed. ²⁷The LORD will scatter you among the other nations. Only a few of you will be left alive, and those few will be in other nations where the LORD will send you. ²⁸There you will worship gods made by people, gods made of wood and stone, that cannot see, hear, eat, or smell. ²⁹But even there you can look for the LORD your God, and you will find him if you look for him with your whole being. ³⁰It will be hard when all these things happen to you. But after that you will come back to the LORD your God and obey him, ³¹because the LORD your God is a merciful God. He will not leave you or destroy you. He will not forget the Agreement with your ancestors, which he swore to them.

THE LORD IS GREAT

³²Nothing like this has ever happened before! Look at the past, long before you were even born. Go all the way back to when God made humans on the earth, and look from one end of heaven to the other. Nothing like this has ever been heard of! ³³No other people have ever heard God speak from a fire and have still lived. But you have. ³⁴No other god has ever taken for himself one nation out of another. But the LORD your God did this for you in Egypt, right before your own eyes. He did it with tests, signs, miracles, war, and great sights, by his great power and strength.

³⁵He showed you things so you would know that the LORD is God, and there is no other God besides him. ³⁶He spoke to you from heaven to teach you. He showed you his great fire on earth, and you heard him speak from the fire. ³⁷Because the LORD loved your ancestors, he chose you, their descendants, and he brought you out of Egypt himself by his great strength. ³⁸He forced nations out of their land ahead of you, nations that were bigger and stronger than you were. The LORD did this so he could bring you into their land and give it to you as your own, and this land is yours today.

³⁹Know and believe today that the LORD is God. He is God in heaven above and on the earth below. There is no other god! ⁴⁰Obey his laws and commands that I am giving you today so that things will go well for you and your children. Then you will live a long time in the land that the LORD your God is giving to you forever.

CITIES OF SAFETY

⁴¹Moses chose three cities east of the Jordan River, ⁴²where a person who accidentally killed someone could go. If the person was not killed because of hatred, the murderer's

life could be saved by running to one of these cities. ⁴³These were the cities: Bezer in the desert high plain was for the Reubenites; Ramoth in Gilead was for the Gadites; and Golan in Bashan was for the Manassites.

THE LAWS MOSES GAVE

⁴⁴These are the teachings Moses gave to the people of Israel. ⁴⁵They are the rules, commands, and laws he gave them when they came out of Egypt. ⁴⁶They were in the valley near Beth Peor, east of the Jordan River, in the land of Sihon. Sihon king of the Amorites ruled in Heshbon and was defeated by Moses and the Israelites as they came out of Egypt. ⁴⁷The Israelites took his land and the land of Og king of Bashan, the two Amorite kings east of the Jordan River. ⁴⁸This land went from Aroer, on the edge of the Arnon Ravine, to Mount Hermon. ⁴⁹It included all the Jordan Valley east of the Jordan River, and it went as far as the Dead Sea below Mount Pisgah.

THE TEN COMMANDMENTS

5 Moses called all the people of Israel together and said: Listen, Israel, to the commands and laws I am giving you today. Learn them and obey them carefully. ²The LORD our God made an Agreement with us at Mount Sinai. ³He did not make this Agreement with our ancestors, but he made it with us, with all of us who are alive here today. ⁴The LORD spoke to you face to face from the fire on the mountain. ⁵(At that time I stood between you and the LORD in order to tell you what the LORD said; you were afraid of the fire, so you would not go up on the mountain.) The LORD said:

⁶"I am the LORD your God; I brought you out of the land of Egypt where you were slaves.

⁷"You must not have any other gods except me.

⁸"You must not make for yourselves any idols or anything to worship that looks like something in the sky above or on the earth below or in the water below the land. ⁹You must not worship or serve any idol, because I, the LORD your God, am a jealous God. If people sin against me and hate me, I will punish their children, even their grandchildren and great-grandchildren. ¹⁰But I will be very kind for a thousand lifetimes to those who love me and obey my commands.

¹¹"You must not use the name of the LORD your God thoughtlessly, because the LORD will punish anyone who uses his name in this way.

¹²"Keep the Sabbath as a holy day, as the LORD your God has commanded you. ¹³You may work and get everything done during six days each week, ¹⁴but the seventh day is a day of rest to honor the LORD your God. On that day no one may do any work: not you, your son or daughter, your male or female slaves, your ox, your donkey, or any of your animals, or the foreigners living in your cities. That way your servants may rest as you do. ¹⁵Remember that you were slaves in Egypt and that the LORD your God brought you out of there by his great power and strength. So the LORD your God has commanded you to rest on the Sabbath day.

¹⁶"Honor your father and your mother as the LORD your God has commanded you. Then you will live a long time, and things will go well for you in the land that the LORD your God is going to give you.

¹⁷"You must not murder anyone.

¹⁸"You must not be guilty of adultery.

¹⁹"You must not steal.

²⁰"You must not tell lies about your neighbor.

²¹"You must not want to take your neighbor's wife. You must not want to take your neighbor's house or land, his male or female slaves, his ox or his donkey, or anything that belongs to your neighbor."

²²The LORD spoke these commands to all of you on the mountain in a loud voice out of the fire, the cloud, and the deep darkness; he did not say anything else. Then he wrote them on two stone tablets, and he gave them to me.

²³When you heard the voice from the darkness, as the mountain was blazing with fire, all the leaders of your tribes and your elders came to me. ²⁴And you said, "The LORD our God has shown us his glory and majesty, and we have heard his voice from the fire. Today we have seen that a person can live even if God speaks to him. ²⁵But now, we will die! This great fire will burn us up, and we will die if we hear the LORD our God speak anymore. ²⁶No human being has ever heard the living God speaking from a fire and still lived, but we have. ²⁷Moses, you go near and

listen to everything the LORD our God says. Then you tell us what the LORD our God tells you, and we will listen and obey."

²⁸The LORD heard what you said to me, and he said to me, "I have heard what the people said to you. Everything they said was good. ²⁹I wish their hearts would always respect me and that they would always obey my commands so that things would go well for them and their children forever!

³⁰"Go and tell the people to return to their tents, ³¹but you stay here with me so that I may give you all the commands, rules, and laws that you must teach the people to obey in the land I am giving them as their own."

³²So be careful to do what the LORD your God has commanded you, and follow the commands exactly. ³³Live the way the LORD your God has commanded you so that you may live and have what is good and have a long life in the land you will take.

THE COMMAND TO LOVE GOD

6 These are the commands, rules, and laws that the LORD your God told me to teach you to obey in the land you are crossing the Jordan River to take. ²You, your children, and your grandchildren must respect the LORD your God as long as you live. Obey all his rules and commands I give you so that you will live a long time. ³Listen, Israel, and carefully obey these laws. Then all will go well for you, and you will become a great nation in a fertile land, just as the LORD, the God of your ancestors, has promised you.

⁴Listen, people of Israel! The LORD our God is the only LORD. ⁵Love the LORD your God with all your heart, all your soul, and all your strength. ⁶Always remember these commands I give you today. ⁷Teach them to your children, and talk about them when you sit at home and walk along the road, when you lie down and when you get up. ⁸Write them down and tie them to your hands as a sign. Tie them on your forehead to remind you, ⁹and write them on your doors and gates.

¹⁰The LORD your God will bring you into the land he promised to your ancestors, to Abraham, Isaac, and Jacob, and he will give it to you. The land has large, growing cities you did not build, ¹¹houses full of good things you did not buy, wells you did not dig, and vineyards and olive trees you did not plant. You will eat as much as you want. ¹²But be careful! Do not forget the LORD, who brought you out of the land of Egypt where you were slaves.

¹³Respect the LORD your God. You must worship him and make your promises only in his name. ¹⁴Do not worship other gods as the people around you do, ¹⁵because the LORD your God is a jealous God. He is present with you, and if you worship other gods, he will become angry with you and destroy you from the earth. ¹⁶Do not test the LORD your God as you did at Massah. ¹⁷Be sure to obey the commands of the LORD your God and the rules and laws he has given you. ¹⁸Do what the LORD says is good and right so that things will go well for you. Then you may go in and take the good land the LORD promised to your ancestors. ¹⁹He will force all your enemies out as you go in, as the LORD has said.

²⁰In the future when your children ask you, "What is the meaning of the laws, commands, and rules the LORD our God gave us?" ²¹tell them, "We were slaves to the king of Egypt, but the LORD brought us out of Egypt by his great power. ²²The LORD showed us great and terrible signs and miracles, which he did to Egypt, the king, and his whole family. ²³The LORD brought us out of Egypt to lead us here and to give us the land he promised our ancestors. ²⁴The LORD ordered us to obey all these commands and to respect the LORD our God so that we will always do well and stay alive, as we are today. ²⁵The right thing for us to do is this: Obey all these rules in the presence of the LORD our God, as he has commanded."

YOU ARE GOD'S PEOPLE

7 The LORD your God will bring you into the land that you are entering and that you will have as your own. As you go in, he will force out these nations: the Hittites, Girgashites, Amorites, Canaanites, Perizzites, Hivites, and Jebusites—seven nations that are stronger than you. ²The LORD your God will hand these nations over to you, and when you defeat them, you must destroy them completely. Do not make a peace treaty with them or show them any mercy. ³Do not marry any of them, or let your daughters marry their sons, or let your sons marry their daughters. ⁴If you do, those people will turn your children away from me, to begin serving

other gods. Then the LORD will be very angry with you, and he will quickly destroy you. ⁵This is what you must do to those people: Tear down their altars, smash their holy stone pillars, cut down their Asherah idols, and burn their idols in the fire. ⁶You are holy people who belong to the LORD your God. He has chosen you from all the people on earth to be his very own.

⁷The LORD did not care for you and choose you because there were many of you—you are the smallest nation of all. ⁸But the LORD chose you because he loved you, and he kept his promise to your ancestors. So he brought you out of Egypt by his great power and freed you from the land of slavery, from the power of the king of Egypt. ⁹So know that the LORD your God is God, the faithful God. He will keep his agreement of love for a thousand lifetimes for people who

FAMILY

BOYS WILL BE . . .

be vigilant
parents

DEUTERONOMY 6:6–9

By Bob Russell

Three children were watching television with their grandparents when they came upon a children's program that was in progress. It immediately caught the grandparents' attention because it was a skillful promotion for evolution.

The announcer said, "Billions of years ago, the first apelike creatures learned that if they stood up on their back legs in the face of danger, they looked bigger and more intimidating. Soon they stood up all the time and began to cooperate with each other." The program had animated characters that looked very real. After a half hour of indoctrination, the announcer said, "These creatures are our ancestors." Evolution was presented as a fact. The grandparents were understandably alarmed.

Children today are getting a steady diet of politically correct doctrine from cartoons, music, classrooms, and movies. One magazine predicted that most citizens of this century will have no knowledge of, interest in, or need for God. Some say that school children in the near future will be taught "Christian mythology," much like children fifty years ago were taught about Greek and Roman gods.

Parents need to realize that an hour in Sunday school each week and a brief Bible story before bedtime are not enough to counter this constant barrage of propaganda. Parents must be continually vigilant in screening their children's television viewing, monitoring their entertainment, and selecting their schools and teachers. That is what Moses meant when he said to teach God's commands to our children.

reflect: How can you exercise more vigilance when it comes to the mass media?
Go to **Deuteronomy 7:8–15.**

love him and obey his commands. ¹⁰But he will pay back those people who hate him. He will destroy them, and he will not be slow to pay back those who hate him. ¹¹So be careful to obey the commands, rules, and laws I give you today.

¹²If you pay attention to these laws and obey them carefully, the LORD your God will keep his agreement and show his love to you, as he promised your ancestors. ¹³He will love and bless you. He will make the number of your people grow; he will bless you with children. He will bless your fields with good crops and will give you grain, new wine, and oil. He will bless your herds with calves and your flocks with lambs in the land he promised your ancestors he would give you. ¹⁴You will be blessed more than any other people.

BOYS WILL BE . . .

growing your family
on purpose

FAMILY

By Jimmy Evans

DEUTERONOMY 7:8–15

Vision is so important in marriage. It's amazing that we have vision about everything else in life, but not for our marriage. Hardly anybody knows what they are trying to accomplish in their marriage. Most of us are just plodding along, hoping that it will all work out.

The challenge is to grow your marriage "on purpose." You need a defined vision to know what you are trying to accomplish in your marriage. Vision without action is merely a dream. Action without vision just passes the time. Vision with action can change the world. Vision is everything. Today's vision becomes tomorrow's reality.

The greatest threat to marriages today is having two visions. When God put you and your spouse together, two became one, and one vision is what you need. Division and strife work against what God wants to do in your family. Having vision is critical for what you want and where you want to go.

Part of the problem in our society is that we are present-oriented; it's hard for us to think about future generations. In Bible times, people thought about future generations. Vision helps you do that.

Who are you as a family? What are some important things you want to instill in your children? What are the core values and beliefs in your family? What will your family look like if it turns out well? Discover your family vision. Develop a vision statement to help define to your children what your family is about.

reflect: Are you communicating your core beliefs to your family?
Go to **Deuteronomy 12:12.**

Every husband and wife will have children, and all your cattle will have calves. ¹⁵The LORD will take away all disease from you; you will not have the terrible diseases that were in Egypt, but he will give them to all the people who hate you. ¹⁶You must destroy all the people the LORD your God hands over to you. Do not feel sorry for them, and do not worship their gods, or they will trap you.

¹⁷You might say to yourselves, "Because these nations are stronger than we are, we can't force them out." ¹⁸But don't be afraid of them. Remember what the LORD your God did to all of Egypt and its king. ¹⁹You saw for yourselves the troubles, signs, and miracles he did, how the LORD's great power and strength brought you out of Egypt. The LORD your God will do the same thing to all the nations you now fear. ²⁰The LORD your God will also send terror among them so that even those who are alive and hiding from you will die. ²¹Don't be afraid of them, because the LORD your God is with you; he is a great God and people are afraid of him. ²²When the LORD your God forces those nations out of the land, he will do it little by little ahead of you. You won't be able to destroy them all at once; otherwise, the wild animals will grow too many in number. ²³But the LORD your God will hand those nations over to you, confusing them until they are destroyed. ²⁴The LORD will help you defeat their kings, and the world will forget who they were. No one will be able to stop you; you will destroy them all. ²⁵Burn up their idols in the fire. Do not wish for the silver and gold they have, and don't take it for yourselves, or you will be trapped by it. The LORD your God hates it. ²⁶Do not bring one of those hateful things into your house, or you will be completely destroyed along with it. Hate and reject those things; they must be completely destroyed.

REMEMBER THE LORD

8 Carefully obey every command I give you today. Then you will live and grow in number, and you will enter and take the land the LORD promised your ancestors. ²Remember how the LORD your God has led you in the desert for these forty years, taking away your pride and testing you, because he wanted to know what was in your heart. He wanted to know if you would obey his commands. ³He took away your pride when he let you get hungry, and then he fed you with manna, which neither you nor your ancestors had ever seen. This was to teach you that a person does not live on bread alone, but by everything the LORD says. ⁴During these forty years, your clothes did not wear out, and your feet did not swell. ⁵Know in your heart that the LORD your God corrects you as a parent corrects a child.

⁶Obey the commands of the LORD your God, living as he has commanded you and respecting him. ⁷The LORD your God is bringing you into a good land, a land with rivers and pools of water, with springs that flow in the valleys and hills, ⁸a land that has wheat and barley, vines, fig trees, pomegranates, olive oil, and honey. ⁹It is a land where you will have plenty of food, where you will have everything you need, where the rocks are iron, and where you can dig copper out of the hills.

¹⁰When you have all you want to eat, then praise the LORD your God for giving you a good land. ¹¹Be careful not to forget the LORD your God so that you fail to obey his commands, laws, and rules that I am giving to you today. ¹²When you eat all you want and build nice houses and live in them, ¹³when your herds and flocks grow large and your silver and gold increase, when you have more of everything, ¹⁴then your heart will become proud. You will forget the LORD your God, who brought you out of the land of Egypt, where you were slaves. ¹⁵He led you through the large and terrible desert that was dry and had no water, and that had poisonous snakes and stinging insects. He gave you water from a solid rock ¹⁶and manna to eat in the desert. Manna was something your ancestors had never seen. He did this to take away your pride and to test you, so things would go well for you in the end. ¹⁷You might say to yourself, "I am rich because of my own power and strength," ¹⁸but remember the LORD your God! It is he who gives you the power to become rich, keeping the agreement he promised to your ancestors, as it is today.

¹⁹If you ever forget the LORD your God and follow other gods and worship them and bow down to them, I warn you today that you will be destroyed. ²⁰Just as the LORD destroyed the other nations for you, you can be

The **Longevity** Factor

FITNESS

By Dr. Ben Lerner

DEUTERONOMY 8:11–19

I n developed countries, on the average, women live five to seven years longer than men. Is this the fate of men, or can something be done about it?

As any doctor or person in the health and wellness field will tell you, more than 75 percent of all visits, purchases, Web site hits, or memberships are from women. *This additional focus on health is the logical key reason women outdistance the men.*

How can men close the gap?

The Importance of Exercise

A recent study in England found that 70-year-old men had the hearts of 70-year-olds but their female peers had the hearts of 20-year-olds. Men lose one-third of the contractile muscle cells in the walls of their hearts between the ages of 20 and 70, while women lose hardly any. There is a strong link between the number of these cells and the function of the heart.

But there's hope! The study also discovered that the hearts of veteran male athletes were equal to those of inactive 20-year-old males.

Remember, exercise doesn't have to be boring, can be done in some cases in less than three minutes, doesn't require a gym membership or fancy equipment, and should never hurt. You owe it to God, your family, yourself, and everyone who is depending on you!

Keeping First Things First

In an effort to get ahead and fend for their families, men will often become classic workaholics.

Jesus talks about how a man works and works to fill his barn, never making time for what is important. God's verdict is this: "Foolish man! Tonight your life will be taken from you. So who will get those things you have prepared for yourself?" (Luke 12:20)

Think about it: a man works long and hard at his business to get ahead. Although he rarely spends enough time with his wife or children, he convinces himself that he is doing it all for them and he will give them more time "as soon as things settle down."

Throughout the years his waistline starts getting bigger and his neck and back hurt after about three or four hours at the computer. His wife starts bugging him about it, but he thinks, *Who has time to exercise or go to a doctor now? I'll start as soon as things settle down.* One night working late on his laptop at home, his wife notices that it's 3:00 in the morning and he is still not in bed. She goes down to get him and sees him slumped over his computer—dead of a massive heart attack.

At his funeral, everyone talked about what an "innovator" he was, a "leader in industry," and a "great husband and father." But, according to the parable, he was a "foolish man!" No one wants to end up with this verdict on his life—and you don't have to. There's no time like right now to start taking care of your body and to make time for what's really important.

TO LEARN MORE ON WHAT THE BIBLE HAS TO SAY ABOUT **FITNESS**, READ THE SCRIPTURES AND DEVOTIONALS AT **MATTHEW 6:33, LUKE 6:12, LUKE 19:1-6, JOHN 5:6, ACTS 2:24,** AND **ACTS 10:14–15.**

destroyed if you do not obey the LORD your God.

THE LORD WILL BE WITH ISRAEL

9 Listen, Israel. You will soon cross the Jordan River to go in and force out nations that are bigger and stronger than you. They have large cities with walls up to the sky. ²The people there are Anakites, who are strong and tall. You know about them, and you have heard it said: "No one can stop the Anakites." ³But today remember that the LORD your God goes in before you to destroy them like a fire that burns things up. He will defeat them ahead of you, and you will force them out and destroy them quickly, just as the LORD has said.

⁴After the LORD your God has forced those nations out ahead of you, don't say to yourself, "The LORD brought me here to take this land because I am so good." No! It is because these nations are evil that the LORD will force them out ahead of you. ⁵You are going in to take the land, not because you are good and honest, but because these nations are evil. That is why the LORD your God will force them out ahead of you, to keep his promise to your ancestors, to Abraham, Isaac, and Jacob. ⁶The LORD your God is giving you this good land to take as your own. But know this: It is not because you are good; you are a stubborn people.

REMEMBER THE LORD'S ANGER

⁷Remember this and do not forget it: You made the LORD your God angry in the desert. You would not obey the LORD from the day you left Egypt until you arrived here. ⁸At Mount Sinai you made the LORD angry—angry enough to destroy you. ⁹When I went up on the mountain to receive the stone tablets, the tablets with the Agreement the LORD had made with you, I stayed on the mountain for forty days and forty nights; I did not eat bread or drink water. ¹⁰The LORD gave me two stone tablets, which God had written on with his own finger. On them were all the commands that the LORD gave to you on the mountain out of the fire, on the day you were gathered there.

¹¹When the forty days and forty nights were over, the LORD gave me the two stone tablets, the tablets with the Agreement on them. ¹²Then the LORD told me, "Get up and go down quickly from here, because the people you brought out from Egypt are ruining themselves. They have quickly turned away from what I commanded and have made an idol for themselves."

¹³The LORD said to me, "I have watched these people, and they are very stubborn! ¹⁴Get away so that I may destroy them and make the whole world forget who they are. Then I will make another nation from you that will be bigger and stronger than they are."

¹⁵So I turned and came down the mountain that was burning with fire, and the two stone tablets with the Agreement were in my hands. ¹⁶When I looked, I saw you had sinned against the LORD your God and had made an idol in the shape of a calf. You had quickly turned away from what the LORD had told you to do. ¹⁷So I took the two stone tablets and threw them down, breaking them into pieces right in front of you.

¹⁸Then I again bowed facedown on the ground before the LORD for forty days and forty nights; I did not eat bread or drink water. You had sinned by doing what the LORD said was evil, and you made him angry. ¹⁹I was afraid of the LORD's anger and rage, because he was angry enough with you to destroy you, but the LORD listened to me again. ²⁰And the LORD was angry enough with Aaron to destroy him, but then I prayed for Aaron, too. ²¹I took that sinful calf idol you had made and burned it in the fire. I crushed it into a powder like dust and threw the dust into a stream that flowed down the mountain.

²²You also made the LORD angry at Taberah, Massah, and Kibroth Hattaavah.

²³Then the LORD sent you away from Kadesh Barnea and said, "Go up and take the land I have given you." But you rejected the command of the LORD your God. You did not trust him or obey him. ²⁴You have refused to obey the LORD as long as I have known you.

²⁵The LORD had said he would destroy you, so I threw myself down in front of him for those forty days and forty nights. ²⁶I prayed to the LORD and said, "Lord GOD, do not destroy your people, your own people, whom you freed and brought out of Egypt by your great power and strength. ²⁷Remember your servants Abraham, Isaac, and Jacob. Don't look at how stubborn these people are,

and don't look at their sin and evil. ²⁸Otherwise, Egypt will say, 'It was because the LORD was not able to take his people into the land he promised them, and it was because he hated them that he took them into the desert to kill them.' ²⁹But they are your people, LORD, your own people, whom you brought out of Egypt with your great power and strength."

NEW STONE TABLETS

10 At that time the LORD said to me, "Cut two stone tablets like the first ones and come up to me on the mountain. Also make a wooden Ark. ²I will write on the tablets the same words that were on the first tablets, which you broke, and you will put the new tablets in the Ark."

³So I made the Ark out of acacia wood, and I cut out two stone tablets like the first ones. Then I went up on the mountain with the two tablets in my hands. ⁴The LORD wrote the same things on these tablets he had written before —the Ten Commandments that he had told you on the mountain from the fire, on the day you were gathered there. And the LORD gave them to me. ⁵Then I turned and came down the mountain; I put the tablets in the Ark I had made, as the LORD had commanded, and they are still there.

⁶(The people of Israel went from the wells of the Jaakanites to Moserah. Aaron died there and was buried; his son Eleazar became priest in his place. ⁷From Moserah they went to Gudgodah, and from Gudgodah they went to Jotbathah, a place with streams of water. ⁸At that time the LORD chose the tribe of Levi to carry the Ark of the Agreement with the LORD. They were to serve the LORD and to bless the people in

---

WHEN YOUR WAY ISN'T GOD'S WAY

spiritual way
to worship

FITNESS

DEUTERONOMY 10:14

G od is not only the Producer; he is also the Executive Director. His power, which created and resides in all things, created you and resides within you. His power is constantly on the job controlling, sustaining, healing, creating, and recreating every part and system of your body.

Your body is a miraculous gift that God has handed over to you for the relatively brief duration of your lifetime. Showing respect for this physical gift is the "spiritual way for you to worship" (Romans 12:1). Your body is not your own! Your body is not only by God, it is for God, and it is God's.

Everything and everyone on earth was placed here for a reason. God chooses specific people to perform specific tasks for him. Therefore, you want to be the most resonant vessel for God you can be because, while you are spirit, your body is the vehicle that carries out those tasks.

reflect: Think of a specific way to glorify God with your body today.
Go to **FITNESS:** "Anger Management" at **Psalm 118:24.**

his name, which they still do today. ⁹That is why the Levites did not receive any land of their own; instead, they received the LORD himself as their gift, as the LORD your God told them.)

¹⁰I stayed on the mountain forty days and forty nights just like the first time, and the LORD listened to me this time also. He did not want to destroy you. ¹¹The LORD said to me, "Go and lead the people so that they will go in and take the land I promised their ancestors."

WHAT THE LORD WANTS YOU TO DO

¹²Now, Israel, this is what the LORD your God wants you to do: Respect the LORD your God, and do what he has told you to do. Love him. Serve the LORD your God with your whole being, ¹³and obey the LORD's commands and laws that I am giving you today for your own good.

¹⁴The LORD owns the world and everything in it—the heavens, even the highest heavens, are his. ¹⁵But the LORD cared for and loved your ancestors, and he chose you, their descendants, over all the other nations, just as it is today. ¹⁶Give yourselves completely to serving him, and do not be stubborn any longer. ¹⁷The LORD your God is God of all gods and Lord of all lords. He is the great God, who is strong and wonderful. He does not take sides, and he will not be talked into doing evil. ¹⁸He helps orphans and widows, and he loves foreigners and gives them food and clothes. ¹⁹You also must love foreigners, because you were foreigners in Egypt. ²⁰Respect the LORD your God and serve him. Be loyal to him and make your promises in his name. ²¹He is the one you should praise; he is your God, who has done great and wonderful things for you, which you have seen with your own eyes. ²²There were only seventy of your ancestors when they went down to Egypt, and now the LORD your God has made you as many as the stars in the sky.

GREAT THINGS ISRAEL SAW

11 Love the LORD your God and always obey his orders, rules, laws, and commands. ²Remember today it was not your children who saw and felt the correction of the LORD your God. They did not see his majesty, his power, his strength, ³or his signs and the things he did in Egypt to the king and his whole country. ⁴They did not see what he did to the Egyptian army, its horses and chariots, when he drowned them in the Red Sea as they were chasing you. The LORD ruined them forever. ⁵They did not see what he did for you in the desert until you arrived here. ⁶They did not see what he did to Dathan and Abiram, the sons of Eliab the Reubenite, when the ground opened up and swallowed them, their families, their tents, and everyone who stood with them in Israel. ⁷It was you who saw all these great things the LORD has done.

⁸So obey all the commands I am giving you today so that you will be strong and can go in and take the land you are going to take as your own. ⁹Then you will live a long time in the land that the LORD promised to give to your ancestors and their descendants, a fertile land. ¹⁰The land you are going to take is not like Egypt, where you were. There you had to plant your seed and water it, like a vegetable garden, by using your feet. ¹¹But the land that you will soon cross the Jordan River to take is a land of hills and valleys, a land that drinks rain from heaven. ¹²It is a land the LORD your God cares for. His eyes are on it continually, and he watches it from the beginning of the year to the end.

¹³If you carefully obey the commands I am giving you today and love the LORD your God and serve him with your whole being, ¹⁴then he will send rain on your land at the right time, in the fall and spring, and you will be able to gather your grain, new wine, and oil. ¹⁵He will put grass in the fields for your cattle, and you will have plenty to eat.

¹⁶Be careful, or you will be fooled and will turn away to serve and worship other gods. ¹⁷If you do, the LORD will become angry with you and will shut the heavens so it will not rain. Then the land will not grow crops, and you will soon die in the good land the LORD is giving you. ¹⁸Remember my words with your whole being. Write them down and tie them to your hands as a sign; tie them on your foreheads to remind you. ¹⁹Teach them well to your children, talking about them when you sit at home and walk along the road, when you lie down and when you get up. ²⁰Write them on your doors and gates ²¹so that both you and your children will live a long time in the land the LORD promised

your ancestors, as long as the skies are above the earth.

²²If you are careful to obey every command I am giving you to follow, and love the LORD your God, and do what he has told you to do, and are loyal to him, ²³then the LORD will force all those nations out of the land ahead of you, and you will take the land from nations that are bigger and stronger than you. ²⁴Everywhere you step will be yours. Your land will go from the desert to Lebanon and from the Euphrates River to the Mediterranean Sea. ²⁵No one will be able to stop you. The LORD your God will do what he promised and will make the people afraid everywhere you go.

²⁶See, today I am letting you choose a blessing or a curse. ²⁷You will be blessed if you obey the commands of the LORD your God that I am giving you today. ²⁸But you will be cursed if you disobey the commands of the LORD your God. So do not disobey the commands I am giving you today, and do not worship other gods you do not know. ²⁹When the LORD your God brings you into the land you will take as your own, you are to announce the blessings from Mount Gerizim and the curses from Mount Ebal. ³⁰(These mountains are on the other side of the Jordan River, to the west, toward the sunset. They are near the great trees of Moreh in the land of the Canaanites who live in the Jordan Valley opposite Gilgal.) ³¹You will soon cross the Jordan River to enter and take the land the LORD your God is giving you. When you take it over and live there, ³²be careful to obey all the commands and laws I am giving you today.

COVENANT MARRIAGE

quantity and quality time

FAMILY

DEUTERONOMY 11:18-25

Do you think your kids would rather have a bigger allowance than more time with you? Think again. According to a new study published by The Australia Institute, if given the choice between more money from their parents and more time spent with their parents, most kids prefer the time rather than the money.

There's an old saying related to exercise: "Showing up is half the battle." This is because if you can just get to the gym, you'll usually have a great workout. The tough part is convincing yourself to get there.

It's said, "God doesn't need your ability as much as he needs your availability." One of the most important things you can do for your family is just show up. That's a good summary of what God expects from us in all the areas of living. Jesus made it abundantly clear that encouraging children to come to him was critically important. Availability is a sign of the kingdom of God.

reflect: Make it a priority to be available to those who need your presence.
Go to **Psalm 19:7-11.**

THE PLACE FOR WORSHIP

12 These are the commands and laws you must carefully obey in the land the LORD, the God of your ancestors, is giv- ing you. Obey them as long as you live in the land. ²When you inherit the lands of these nations, you must completely destroy all the places where they serve their gods, on high

FUTURE

GOD'S PURPOSE FOR YOUR LIFE

positive generational transference

DEUTERONOMY 11:19

By Jimmy Evans

An extraordinary truth found in this Scripture is the fact that writing down a vision and reading it regularly energizes our lives and our children's future. Vision is a motivating and powerful force.

Without a vision for our lives, marriages, families, finances, and ministries, we don't know where we are going. Every day is filled with "going through the motions." When we have no vision, our lives naturally degrade. Living this way for a long time creates a meaningless life that fails to transfer anything positive to our children.

It is critical that we have a plan and know what we are trying to accomplish. Here are some important questions to ask yourself so you can have a positive generational effect upon your family:

• What is God's call for your life?

• What do you want your children to remember about you after you're gone?

• What do you want said about you at your funeral?

• What is the purpose of your marriage?

• If you died today, what would be your greatest regret?

• What do you want your children to become, and what are you doing to help them accomplish it?

When you sit down and consider these questions, lift your eyes above the fray of everyday life to see the big picture. Seeing the picture, keeping that picture before you, and making sure it's the picture God wants for you are major factors in deciding your future and that of your children and grandchildren.

reflect: Are you willing to change your actions to follow the will of God?
Go to **1 Chronicles 16:34–36.**

mountains and hills and under every green tree. ³Tear down their altars, smash their holy stone pillars, and burn their Asherah idols in the fire. Cut down their idols and destroy their names from those places.

⁴Don't worship the LORD your God that way, ⁵but look for the place the LORD your God will choose—a place among your tribes where he is to be worshiped. Go there, ⁶and bring to that place your burnt offerings and sacrifices; bring a tenth of what you gain and your special gifts; bring what you have promised and the special gifts you want to give the LORD, and bring the first animals born to your herds and flocks.

⁷There you will be together with the LORD your God. There you and your families will eat, and you will enjoy all the good things for which you have worked, because the LORD your God has blessed you.

⁸Do not worship the way we have been doing today, each person doing what he

---

BOYS WILL BE . . .

practicing
priorities

FAMILY

DEUTERONOMY 12:12

God is a God of families. It is no accident that his creation of community includes every member of the household, even those who are not part of the immediate bloodline. God knows that the families that worship together create a strong hedge protecting them from disintegration by the world's pressures. Here in the Law, God says that rejoicing is a family affair. Everyone is involved in the process of enjoying his favor and celebrating who he is.

This is more than going to church or delivering the children to the Sunday school. This is practicing the presence of God in the activities of daily life together at home. In our busy world, we have a tendency to let the priorities of work, school, and activities squeeze out the celebration of God in our families. But celebrating God is an eternal, kingdom-building exercise that has significant consequences for you and your children. Paint some yellow lines around a special time of the day when God takes the center stage for your whole family. It's not meant to be only a once-a-week exercise.

Do you make time for each member of your family to celebrate God and rejoice over his goodness? Do you share experiences and replay them from a biblical perspective? Do you go over family decisions, disputes, and life's challenges and discuss them in the context of God's will for your lives? If God commands us to do this, he must know just how important it is. Bring all the children. Let's praise God together.

---

reflect: Practice the presence of God by worshiping the Lord together as a family.
Go to **Numbers 6:22–27.**

thinks is right. ⁹You have not yet come to a resting place, to the land the LORD your God will give you as your own. ¹⁰But soon you will cross the Jordan River to live in the land the LORD your God is giving you as your own, where he will give you rest from all your enemies and you will live in safety. ¹¹Then the LORD your God will choose a place where he is to be worshiped. To that place you must bring everything I tell you: your burnt offerings and sacrifices, your offerings of a tenth of what you gain, your special gifts, and all your best things you promised to the LORD. ¹²There rejoice before the LORD your God. Everyone should rejoice: you, your sons and daughters, your male and female servants, and the Levites from your towns who have no land of their own. ¹³Be careful that you don't sacrifice your burnt offerings just anywhere you please. ¹⁴Offer them only in the place the LORD will choose. He will choose a place in one of your tribes, and there you must do everything I am commanding you.

¹⁵But you may kill your animals in any of your towns and eat as much of the meat as you want, as if it were a deer or a gazelle; this is the blessing the LORD your God is giving you. Anyone, clean or unclean, may eat this meat, ¹⁶but do not eat the blood. Pour it out on the ground like water. ¹⁷Do not eat in your own towns what belongs to the LORD: one-tenth of your grain, new wine, or oil; the first animals born to your herds or flocks; whatever you have promised to give; the special gifts you want to give to the LORD, or any other gifts. ¹⁸Eat these things when you are together with the LORD your God, in the place the LORD your God chooses to be worshiped. Everyone must do this: you, your sons and daughters, your male and female servants, and the Levites from your towns. Rejoice in the LORD your God's presence about the things you have worked for. ¹⁹Be careful not to forget the Levites as long as you live in the land.

²⁰When the LORD your God enlarges your country as he has promised, and you want some meat so you say, "I want some meat," you may eat as much meat as you want. ²¹If the LORD your God chooses a place where he is to be worshiped that is too far away from you, you may kill animals from your herds and flocks, which the LORD has given to you.

I have commanded that you may do this. You may eat as much of them as you want in your own towns, ²²as you would eat gazelle or deer meat. Both clean and unclean people may eat this meat, ²³but be sure you don't eat the blood, because the life is in the blood. Don't eat the life with the meat. ²⁴Don't eat the blood, but pour it out on the ground like water. ²⁵If you don't eat it, things will go well for you and your children, because you will be doing what the LORD says is right.

²⁶Take your holy things and the things you have promised to give, and go to the place the LORD will choose. ²⁷Present your burnt offerings on the altar of the LORD your God, both the meat and the blood. The blood of your sacrifices should be poured beside the altar of the LORD your God, but you may eat the meat. ²⁸Be careful to obey all the rules I am giving you so that things will always go well for you and your children, and you will be doing what the LORD your God says is good and right.

²⁹You will enter the land and take it away from the nations that the LORD your God will destroy ahead of you. When you force them out and live in their land, ³⁰they will be destroyed for you, but be careful not to be trapped by asking about their gods. Don't say, "How do these nations worship? I will do the same." ³¹Don't worship the LORD your God that way, because the LORD hates the evil ways they worship their gods. They even burn their sons and daughters as sacrifices to their gods!

³²Be sure to do everything I have commanded you. Do not add anything to it, and do not take anything away from it.

FALSE PROPHETS

13 Prophets or those who tell the future with dreams might come to you and say they will show you a miracle or a sign. ²The miracle or sign might even happen, and then they might say, "Let's serve other gods" (gods you have not known) "and let's worship them." ³But you must not listen to those prophets or dreamers. The LORD your God is testing you, to find out if you love him with your whole being. ⁴Serve only the LORD your God. Respect him, keep his commands, and obey him. Serve him and be loyal to him. ⁵The prophets or dreamers must be killed, because they said you should turn against the Lord your God, who brought you out of Egypt and saved you from the land where you were slaves. They tried to turn you from doing what the Lord your God commanded you to do. You must get rid of the evil among you.

⁶Someone might try to lead you to serve other gods—it might be your brother, your son or daughter, the wife you love, or a close friend. The person might say, "Let's go and worship other gods." (These are gods that neither you nor your ancestors have known, ⁷gods of the people who live around you, either nearby or far away, from one end of the land to the other.) ⁸Do not give in to such people. Do not listen or feel sorry for them, and do not let them go free or protect them. ⁹You must put them to death. You must be the first one to start to kill them, and then everyone else must join in. ¹⁰You must throw stones at them until they die, because they tried to turn you away from the Lord your God, who brought you out of the land of Egypt, where you were slaves. ¹¹Then everyone in Israel will hear about this and be afraid, and no one among you will ever do such an evil thing again.

CITIES TO DESTROY

¹²The Lord your God is giving you cities in which to live, and you might hear something about one of them. Someone might say ¹³that evil people have moved in among you. And they might lead the people of that city away from God, saying, "Let's go and worship other gods." (These are gods you have not known.) ¹⁴Then you must ask about it, looking into the matter and checking carefully whether it is true. If it is proved that a hateful thing has happened among you, ¹⁵you must kill with a sword everyone who lives in that city. Destroy the city completely and kill everyone in it, as well as the animals, with a sword. ¹⁶Gather up everything those people owned, and put it in the middle of the city square. Then completely burn the city and everything they owned as a burnt offering to the Lord your God. That city should never be rebuilt; let it be ruined forever. ¹⁷Don't keep for yourselves any of the things found in that city, so the Lord will not be angry anymore. He will give you mercy and feel sorry for you,

and he will make your nation grow larger, as he promised to your ancestors. ¹⁸You will have obeyed the Lord your God by keeping all his commands that I am giving to you today, and you will be doing what the Lord says is right.

GOD'S SPECIAL PEOPLE

14 You are the children of the Lord your God. When someone dies, do not cut yourselves or shave your heads to show your sadness. ²You are holy people, who belong to the Lord your God. He has chosen you from all the people on earth to be his very own.

³Do not eat anything the Lord hates. ⁴These are the animals you may eat: oxen, sheep, goats, ⁵deer, gazelle, roe deer, wild goats, ibex, antelope, and mountain sheep. ⁶You may eat any animal that has a split hoof and chews the cud, ⁷but you may not eat camels, rabbits, or rock badgers. These animals chew the cud, but they do not have split hoofs, so they are unclean for you. ⁸Pigs are also unclean for you; they have split hoofs, but they do not chew the cud. Do not eat their meat or touch their dead bodies.

⁹There are many things that live in the water. You may eat anything that has fins and scales, ¹⁰but do not eat anything that does not have fins and scales. It is unclean for you.

¹¹You may eat any clean bird. ¹²But do not eat these birds: eagles, vultures, black vultures, ¹³red kites, falcons, any kind of kite, ¹⁴any kind of raven, ¹⁵horned owls, screech owls, sea gulls, any kind of hawk, ¹⁶little owls, great owls, white owls, ¹⁷desert owls, ospreys, cormorants, ¹⁸storks, any kind of heron, the hoopoes, or bats.

¹⁹All insects with wings are unclean for you; do not eat them. ²⁰Other things with wings are clean, and you may eat them.

²¹Do not eat anything you find that is already dead. You may give it to a foreigner living in your town, and he may eat it, or you may sell it to a foreigner. But you are holy people, who belong to the Lord your God.

Do not cook a baby goat in its mother's milk.

GIVING ONE-TENTH

²²Be sure to save one-tenth of all your crops each year. ²³Take it to the place the Lord your God will choose where he is to be worshiped. There, where you will be

together with the LORD, eat the tenth of your grain, new wine, and oil, and eat the animals born first to your herds and flocks. Do this so that you will learn to respect the LORD your God always. 24But if the place the LORD will choose to be worshiped is too far away and he has blessed you so much you cannot carry a tenth, 25exchange your one-tenth for silver. Then take the silver with you to the place the LORD your God shall choose. 26Use the silver to buy anything you wish—cattle, sheep, wine, beer, or anything you wish. Then you and your family will eat and celebrate there before the LORD your God. 27Do not forget the Levites in your town, because they have no land of their own among you.

28At the end of every third year, everyone should bring one-tenth of that year's crop and store it in your towns. 29This is for the Levites so they may eat and be full. (They have no land of their own among you.) It is also for strangers, orphans, and widows who live in your towns so that all of them may eat and be full. Then the LORD your God will bless you and all the work you do.

THE SPECIAL SEVENTH YEAR

15 At the end of every seven years, you must tell those who owe you anything that they do not have to pay you back. 2This is how you must do it: Everyone who has loaned money must cancel the loan and not make a neighbor or relative pay it back. This is the LORD's time for canceling what people owe. 3You may make a foreigner pay what is owed to you, but you must not collect what another Israelite owes you. 4But there should be no poor people among you, because the LORD your God will richly bless you in the land he is giving you as your own. 5He will bless you if you obey the LORD your God completely, but you must be careful to obey all the commands I am giving you today. 6The LORD your God will bless you as he promised, and you will lend to other nations, but you will not need to borrow from them. You will rule over many nations, but none will rule over you.

7If there are poor among you, in one of the towns of the land the LORD your God is giving you, do not be selfish or greedy toward them. 8But give freely to them, and freely lend them whatever they need. 9Beware of evil thoughts. Don't think, "The seventh year is near, the year to cancel what people owe." You might be mean to the needy and not give them anything. Then they will complain to the LORD about you, and he will find you guilty of sin. 10Give freely to the poor person, and do not wish that you didn't have to give. The LORD your God will bless your work and everything you touch. 11There will always be poor people in the land, so I command you to give freely to your neighbors and to the poor and needy in your land.

LETTING SLAVES GO FREE

12If one of your own people sells himself to you as a slave, whether it is a Hebrew man or woman, that person will serve you for six years. But in the seventh year you must let the slave go free. 13When you let slaves go, don't send them away without anything. 14Give them some of your flock, your grain, and your wine, giving to them as the LORD has given to you. 15Remember that you were slaves in Egypt, and the LORD your God saved you. That is why I am commanding this to you today.

16But if your slave says to you, "I don't want to leave you," because he loves you and your family and has a good life with you, 17stick an awl[n] through his ear into the door; he will be your slave for life. Also do this to a female slave.

18Do not think of it as a hard thing when you let your slaves go free. After all, they served you six years and did twice the work of a hired person. The LORD your God will bless you in everything you do.

RULES ABOUT FIRSTBORN ANIMALS

19Save all the first male animals born to your herds and flocks. They are for the LORD your God. Do not work the first calf born to your oxen, and do not cut off the wool from the first lamb born to your sheep. 20Each year you and your family are to eat these animals in the presence of the LORD your God, in the place he will choose to be worshiped. 21If an animal is crippled or blind or has something else wrong, do not sacrifice it to the LORD your God. 22But you may eat that animal in your own town. Both

---

15:17 awl A tool like a big needle with a handle at one end.

Handling Money
God's Way

FINANCES

By Howard Dayton

DEUTERONOMY 15:6

If we are bound up by consumer debt, mortgage payments, and trying to gain recognition from our neighbors, we will have little time or money left over for what is really important—fulfilling God's plan for our lives and financially supporting the work of the church. If we carefully and prayerfully consider the vanity of working year after year and decade after decade to earn enough money to make costly payments on expensive cars, homes, and gadgets, we will be compelled to immediately begin to take steps to become financially free to serve Christ. When we break free of the bondage to monthly payments and compulsion to have the latest and biggest that money can buy, we break free to do what God has called us to do rather than continuing on in slavery to what the world is calling us to do.

When our own priorities don't match God's priorities, money competes with Jesus for lordship of our lives. After accepting Christ, Christians must decide whom they are going to serve. The Bible teaches that no one can serve two masters. We can't serve God and money. Sadly, millions of Christians serve money to the point that there is almost no distinction between how Christians and non-Christians handle their money. Christians have adopted our culture's perspective, so we continue to increase our consumer debt, while the rate of our savings declines. Because of this, giving to God's work has declined almost every year.

Having learned biblical principles on giving from an eternal viewpoint, one family made choices to downsize. They purchased a secondhand diesel automobile and used it as the wife's transportation for seventeen years. They built a home and lived in it for twenty-nine years. They paid off their consumer debt and then focused on paying off the home. They began to give aggressively and save aggressively and began working toward becoming financially free.

The husband's car was a homely yellow station wagon. The children called it the Cheetah! When the husband came home from work one day, the neighborhood kids playing basketball all stopped and laughed at his Cheetah. Our culture says it's not enough to have a car that provides transportation; it has to look good, too.

Even though the car appeared ridiculous to the outside world, the husband had wonderful experiences driving it because he used his driving time to worship the Lord. Whether you're driving an old yellow station wagon or a Ferrari, the deepest joy in life can be experienced in the Lord's presence.

The challenge is to gain the same perspective for your lifestyle with an eternal view and work toward becoming free to serve Christ. Every time a debt is paid, that is time you don't have to earn money. You don't have to service that debt. Every time you save and invest, those assets are earning money to free you to serve the Lord in whatever he has called you to do.

TO LEARN MORE ON WHAT THE BIBLE HAS TO SAY ABOUT **FINANCES,** READ THE SCRIPTURES AND DEVOTIONALS AT **HAGGAI 2:8, MALACHI 3:3, 1 TIMOTHY 3:1-4, MALACHI 3:8-12, MATTHEW 5:5,** AND **SONG OF SONGS 8:6-7.**

clean and unclean people may eat it, as they would eat a gazelle or a deer. ²³But don't eat its blood; pour it out on the ground like water.

THE PASSOVER

16 Celebrate the Passover of the LORD your God during the month of Abib, because it was during Abib that he brought you out of Egypt at night. ²As the sacrifice for the Passover to the LORD your God, offer an animal from your flock or herd at the place the LORD will choose to be worshiped. ³Do not eat it with bread made with yeast. But for seven days eat bread made without yeast, the bread of suffering, because you left Egypt in a hurry. So all your life you will remember the time you left Egypt. ⁴There must be no yeast anywhere in your land for seven days. Offer the sacrifice on the evening of the first day, and eat all the meat before morning; do not leave it overnight.

⁵Do not offer the Passover sacrifice in just any town the LORD your God gives you, ⁶but offer it in the place he will choose to be worshiped. Offer it in the evening as the sun goes down, which is when you left Egypt. ⁷Roast the meat and eat it at the place the LORD your God will choose. The next morning go back to your tents. ⁸Eat bread made without yeast for six days. On the seventh day have a special meeting for the LORD your God, and do not work that day.

THE FEAST OF WEEKS

⁹Count seven weeks from the time you begin to harvest the grain, ¹⁰and then celebrate the Feast of Weeks for the LORD your God. Bring an offering as a special gift to him, giving to him just as he has blessed you. ¹¹Rejoice before the LORD your God at the place he will choose to be worshiped. Everybody should rejoice: you, your sons and daughters, your male and female servants, the Levites in your town, the strangers, orphans, and widows living among you. ¹²Remember that you were slaves in Egypt, and carefully obey all these laws.

THE FEAST OF SHELTERS

¹³Celebrate the Feast of Shelters for seven days, after you have gathered your harvest from the threshing floor and winepress. ¹⁴Everybody should rejoice at your Feast: you, your sons and daughters, your male and female servants, the Levites, strangers, orphans, and widows who live in your towns. ¹⁵Celebrate the Feast to the LORD your God for seven days at the place he will choose, because the LORD your God will bless all your harvest and all the work you do, and you will be completely happy.

¹⁶All your men must come before the LORD three times a year to the place he will choose. They must come at these times: the Feast of Unleavened Bread, the Feast of Weeks, and the Feast of Shelters. No man should come before the LORD without a gift. ¹⁷Each of you must bring a gift that will show how much the LORD your God has blessed you.

JUDGES FOR THE PEOPLE

¹⁸Appoint judges and officers for your tribes in every town the LORD your God is giving you; they must judge the people fairly. ¹⁹Do not judge unfairly or take sides. Do not let people pay you to make wrong decisions, because that kind of payment makes wise people seem blind, and it changes the words of good people. ²⁰Always do what is right so that you will live and always have the land the LORD your God is giving you.

GOD HATES IDOLS

²¹Do not set up a wooden Asherah idol next to the altar you build for the LORD your God, ²²and do not set up holy stone pillars. The LORD your God hates them.

17 If an ox or sheep has something wrong with it, do not offer it as a sacrifice to the LORD your God. He would hate that.

²A man or woman in one of the towns the LORD gave you might be found doing something evil and breaking the Agreement. ³That person may have served other gods and bowed down to them or to the sun or moon or stars of the sky, which I have commanded should not be done. ⁴If someone has told you about it, you must look into the matter carefully. If it is true that such a hateful thing has happened in Israel, ⁵take the man or woman who has done the evil thing to the city gates and throw stones at that person until he dies. ⁶There must be two or three witnesses that it is true before the person is put to death; if there is only one witness, the person should not be put to death. ⁷The witnesses must be the first to throw stones at the person, and

then everyone else will follow. You must get rid of the evil among you.

COURTS OF LAW

[8]Some cases that come before you, such as murder, quarreling, or attack, may be too difficult to judge. Take these cases to the place the LORD your God will choose. [9]Go to the priests who are Levites and to the judge who is on duty at that time. Ask them about the case, and they will decide. [10]You must follow the decision they give you at the place the LORD your God will choose. Be careful to do everything they tell you. [11]Follow the teachings they give you, and do whatever they decide, exactly as they tell you. [12]The person who does not show respect for the judge or priest who is there serving the LORD your God must be put to death. You must get rid of that evil from Israel. [13]Then everyone will hear about this and will be afraid, and they will not show disrespect anymore.

CHOOSING A KING

[14]When you enter the land the LORD your God is giving you, taking it as your own and living in it, you will say, "Let's appoint a king over us like the nations all around us." [15]Be sure to appoint over you the king the LORD your God chooses. He must be one of your own people. Do not appoint as your king a foreigner who is not a fellow Israelite. [16]The king must not have too many horses for himself, and he must not send people to Egypt to get more horses, because the LORD has told you, "Don't return that way again." [17]The king must not have many wives, or his heart will be led away from God. He must not have too much silver and gold.

[18]When he becomes king, he should write a copy of the teachings on a scroll for himself, a copy taken from the priests and Levites. [19]He should keep it with him all the time and read from it every day of his life. Then he will learn to respect the LORD his God, and he will obey all the teachings and commands. [20]He should not think he is better than his fellow Israelites, and he must not stop obeying the law in any way so that he and his descendants may rule the kingdom for a long time.

SHARES FOR PRIESTS AND LEVITES

18 The priests are from the tribe of Levi, and that tribe will not receive a share of the land with the Israelites. They will eat the offerings made to the LORD by fire, which is their share. [2]They will not inherit any of the land like their brothers, but they will inherit the LORD himself, as he has promised them.

[3]When you offer a bull or sheep as a sacrifice, you must share with the priests, giving them the shoulder, the cheeks, and the inner organs. [4]Give them the first of your grain, new wine, and oil, as well as the first wool you cut from your sheep. [5]The LORD your God has chosen the priests and their descendants out of all your tribes to stand and serve the LORD always.

[6]If a Levite moves from one of your towns anywhere in Israel where he lives and comes to the place the LORD will choose, because he wants to serve the LORD there, [7]he may serve the LORD his God. He will be like his fellow Levites who serve there before the LORD. [8]They all will have an equal share of the food. That is separate from what he has received from the sale of family possessions.

DO NOT FOLLOW OTHER NATIONS

[9]When you enter the land the LORD your God is giving you, don't learn to do the hateful things the other nations do. [10]Don't let anyone among you offer a son or daughter as a sacrifice in the fire. Don't let anyone use magic or witchcraft, or try to explain the meaning of signs. [11]Don't let anyone try to control others with magic, and don't let them be mediums or try to talk with the spirits of dead people. [12]The LORD hates anyone who does these things. Because the other nations do these things, the LORD your God will force them out of the land ahead of you. [13]But you must be innocent in the presence of the LORD your God.

THE LORD'S SPECIAL PROPHET

[14]The nations you will force out listen to people who use magic and witchcraft, but the LORD your God will not let you do those things. [15]The LORD your God will give you a prophet like me, who is one of your own people. Listen to him. [16]This is what you asked the LORD your God to do when you were gathered at Mount Sinai. You said, "Don't

make us listen to the voice of the LORD our God again, and don't make us look at this terrible fire anymore, or we will die."

17So the LORD said to me, "What they have said is good. 18So I will give them a prophet like you, who is one of their own people. I will tell him what to say, and he will tell them everything I command. 19This prophet will speak for me; anyone who does not listen when he speaks will answer to me. 20But if a prophet says something I did not tell him to say as though he were speaking for me, or if a prophet speaks in the name of other gods, that prophet must be killed."

21You might be thinking, "How can we know if a message is not from the LORD?" 22If what a prophet says in the name of the LORD does not happen, it is not the LORD's message. That prophet was speaking his own ideas. Don't be afraid of him.

CITIES OF SAFETY

19 When the LORD your God gives you land that belongs to the other nations, nations that he will destroy, you will force them out and live in their cities and houses. 2Then choose three cities in the middle of the land the LORD your God is giving you as your own. 3Build roads to these cities, and divide the land the LORD is giving you into three parts so that someone who kills another person may run to these cities.

4This is the rule for someone who kills another person and runs to one of these cities in order to save his life. But the person must have killed a neighbor without meaning to, not out of hatred. 5For example, suppose someone goes into the forest with a neighbor to cut wood and swings an ax to cut down a tree. If the ax head flies off the handle, hitting and killing the neighbor, the one who killed him may run to one of these cities to save his life. 6Otherwise, the dead person's relative who has the duty of punishing a murderer might be angry and chase him. If the city is far away, the relative might catch and kill the person, even though he should not be killed because there was no intent to kill his neighbor. 7This is why I command you to choose these three cities.

8-9Carefully obey all these laws I'm giving you today. Love the LORD your God, and always do what he wants you to do. Then the LORD your God will enlarge your land as he promised your ancestors, giving you the whole land he promised to them. After that, choose three more cities of safety 10so that innocent people will not be killed in your land, the land that the LORD your God is giving you as your own. By doing this you will not be guilty of allowing the death of innocent people.

11But if a person hates his neighbor and, after hiding and waiting, attacks and kills him and then runs to one of these cities for safety, 12the elders of his own city should send for the murderer. They should bring the person back from the city of safety and hand him over to the relative who has the duty of punishing the murderer. 13Show no mercy. You must remove from Israel the guilt of murdering innocent people so that things will go well for you.

14Do not move the stone that marks the border of your neighbor's land, which people long ago set in place. It marks what you inherit in the land the LORD your God is giving you as your own.

RULES ABOUT WITNESSES

15One witness is not enough to accuse a person of a crime or sin. A case must be proved by two or three witnesses.

16If a witness lies and accuses a person of a crime, 17the two people who are arguing must stand in the presence of the LORD before the priests and judges who are on duty. 18The judges must check the matter carefully. The witness who is a liar, lying about a fellow Israelite, 19must be punished. He must be punished in the same way the other person would have been punished. You must get rid of the evil among you. 20The rest of the people will hear about this and be afraid, and no one among you will ever do such an evil thing again. 21Show no mercy. A life must be paid for a life, an eye for an eye, a tooth for a tooth, a hand for a hand, a foot for a foot.

LAWS FOR WAR

20 When you go to war against your enemies and you see horses and chariots and an army that is bigger than yours, don't be afraid of them. The LORD your God, who brought you out of Egypt, will be with you. 2The priest must come and speak to the army before you go into battle. 3He will say, "Listen, Israel! Today you are going into battle against your enemies. Don't lose your courage or be afraid. Don't panic or be frightened, 4because the LORD your God goes with you, to fight for you against your enemies and to save you."

5The officers should say to the army, "Has anyone built a new house but not given it to God? He may go home, because he might die in battle and someone else would get to give his house to God. 6Has anyone planted a vineyard and not begun to enjoy it? He may go home, because he might die in battle and someone else would enjoy his vineyard. 7Is any man engaged to a woman and not yet married to her? He may go home, because he might die in battle and someone else would marry her." 8Then the officers should also say, "Is anyone here afraid? Has anyone lost his courage? He may go home so that he will not cause others to lose their courage, too." 9When the officers finish speaking to the army, they should appoint commanders to lead it.

10When you march up to attack a city, first make them an offer of peace. 11If they accept your offer and open their gates to you, all the people of that city will become your slaves and work for you. 12But if they do not make peace with you and fight you in battle, you should surround that city. 13The LORD your God will give it to you. Then kill all the men with your swords, 14and you may take everything else in the city for yourselves. Take the women, children, and animals, and you may use these things the LORD your God gives you from your enemies. 15Do this to all the cities that are far away, that do not belong to the nations nearby.

16But leave nothing alive in the cities of the land the LORD your God is giving you. 17Completely destroy these people: the Hittites, Amorites, Canaanites, Perizzites, Hivites, and Jebusites, as the LORD your God has commanded. 18Otherwise, they will teach you what they do for their gods, and if you do these hateful things, you will sin against the LORD your God.

19If you surround and attack a city for a long time, trying to capture it, do not destroy its trees with an ax. You can eat the fruit from the trees, but do not cut them down. These trees are not the enemy, so don't make war against them. 20But you may cut down trees that you know are not fruit trees and use them to build devices to attack the city walls, until the city is captured.

A PERSON FOUND MURDERED

21 Suppose someone is found murdered, lying in a field in the land the LORD your God is giving you as your own, and no one knows who killed the person. 2Your elders and judges should go to where the body was found, and they should measure how far it is to the nearby cities. 3The elders of the city nearest the body must take a young cow that has never worked or worn a yoke, 4and they must lead her down to a valley that has never been plowed or planted, with a stream flowing through it. There they must break the young cow's neck. 5The priests, the sons of Levi, should come forward, because they have been chosen by the LORD your God to serve him and to give blessings in the LORD's name. They are the ones who decide cases of quarreling and attacks. 6Then all the elders of the city nearest the murdered person should wash their hands over the young cow whose neck was broken in the valley. 7They should declare: "We did not kill this person, and we did not see it happen. 8LORD, remove this sin from your people Israel, whom you have saved. Don't blame your people, the Israelites, for the murder of this innocent person." And so the murder will be paid for. 9Then you will have removed from yourselves the guilt of murdering an innocent person, because you will be doing what the LORD says is right.

CAPTIVE WOMEN AS WIVES

10When you go to war against your enemies, the LORD will help you defeat them so that you will take them captive. 11If you see a beautiful woman among the captives and are attracted to her, you may take her as your wife. 12Bring her into your home, where she must shave her head and cut her nails 13and change the clothes she was wearing when you captured her. After she has lived in your house and cried for her parents for a month, you may marry her. You will be her husband, and she will be your wife. 14But if you are not pleased with her, you must let her go anywhere she wants. You must not sell her for money or make her a slave, because you have taken away her honor.

THE OLDEST SON

[15]A man might have two wives, one he loves and one he doesn't. Both wives might have sons by him. If the older son belongs to the wife he does not love, [16]when that man wills his property to his sons he must not give the son of the wife he loves what belongs to the older son, the son of the wife he does not love. [17]He must agree to give the older son two shares of everything he owns, even though the older son is from the wife he does not love. That son was the first to prove his father could have children, so he has the rights that belong to the older son.

SONS WHO REFUSE TO OBEY

[18]If someone has a son who is stubborn, who turns against his father and mother and doesn't obey them or listen when they correct him, [19]his parents must take him to the elders at the city gate. [20]They will say to the elders, "Our son is stubborn and turns against us. He will not obey us. He eats too much, and he is always drunk." [21]Then all the men in his town must throw stones at him until he dies. Get rid of the evil among you, because then all the people of Israel will hear about this and be afraid.

OTHER LAWS

[22]If someone is guilty of a sin worthy of death, he must be put to death and his body displayed on a tree. [23]But don't leave his body hanging on the tree overnight; be sure to bury him that same day, because anyone whose body is displayed on a tree is cursed by God. You must not ruin the land the LORD your God is giving you as your own.

22 If you see your fellow Israelite's ox or sheep wandering away, don't ignore it. Take it back to its owner. [2]If the owner does not live close to you, or if you do not know who the owner is, take the animal home with you. Keep it until the owner comes looking for it; then give it back. [3]Do the same thing if you find a donkey or coat or anything someone lost. Don't just ignore it.

[4]If you see your fellow Israelite's donkey or ox fallen on the road, don't ignore it. Help the owner get it up.

[5]A woman must not wear men's clothes, and a man must not wear women's clothes. The LORD your God hates anyone who does that.

[6]If you find a bird's nest by the road, either in a tree or on the ground, and the mother bird is sitting on the young birds or eggs, do not take the mother bird with the young birds. [7]You may take the young birds, but you must let the mother bird go free. Then things will go well for you, and you will live a long time.

[8]When you build a new house, build a low wall around the edge of the roof [n] so you will not be guilty if someone falls off the roof.

[9]Don't plant two different kinds of seeds in your vineyard. Otherwise, both crops will be ruined.

[10]Don't plow with an ox and a donkey tied together.

[11]Don't wear clothes made of wool and linen woven together.

[12]Tie several pieces of thread together; then put these tassels on the four corners of your coat.

MARRIAGE LAWS

[13]If a man marries a girl and has sexual relations with her but then decides he does not like her, [14]he might talk badly about her and give her a bad name. He might say, "I married this woman, but when I had sexual relations with her, I did not find that she was a virgin." [15]Then the girl's parents must bring proof that she was a virgin to the elders at the city gate. [16]The girl's father will say to the elders, "I gave my daughter to this man to be his wife, but now he does not want her. [17]This man has told lies about my daughter. He has said, 'I did not find your daughter to be a virgin,' but here is the proof that my daughter was a virgin." Then her parents are to show the sheet to the elders of the city, [18]and the elders must take the man and punish him. [19]They must make him pay about two and one-half pounds of silver to the girl's father, because the man has given an Israelite virgin a bad name. The girl will continue to be the man's wife, and he may not divorce her as long as he lives.

22:8 roof In Bible times houses were built with flat roofs. The roof was used for drying things such as flax and fruit. And it was used as an extra room, as a place for worship, and as a cool place to sleep in the summer.

²⁰But if the things the husband said about his wife are true, and there is no proof that she was a virgin, ²¹the girl must be brought to the door of her father's house. Then the men of the town must put her to death by throwing stones at her. She has done a disgraceful thing in Israel by having sexual relations before she was married. You must get rid of the evil among you.

²²If a man is found having sexual relations with another man's wife, both the woman and the man who had sexual relations with her must die. Get rid of this evil from Israel.

²³If a man meets a virgin in a city and has sexual relations with her, but she is engaged to another man, ²⁴you must take both of them to the city gate and put them to death by throwing stones at them. Kill the girl, because she was in a city and did not scream for help. And kill the man for having sexual relations with another man's wife. You must get rid of the evil among you.

²⁵But if a man meets an engaged girl out in the country and forces her to have sexual relations with him, only the man who had sexual relations with her must be put to death. ²⁶Don't do anything to the girl, because she has not done a sin worthy of death. This is like the person who attacks and murders a neighbor; ²⁷the man found the engaged girl in the country and she screamed, but no one was there to save her.

²⁸If a man meets a virgin who is not engaged to be married and forces her to have sexual relations with him and people find out about it, ²⁹the man must pay the girl's father about one and one-fourth pounds of silver. He must also marry the girl, because he has dishonored her, and he may never divorce her for as long as he lives.

³⁰A man must not marry his father's wife; he must not dishonor his father in this way.

THE LORD'S PEOPLE

23 No man who has had part of his sex organ cut off may come into the meeting to worship the LORD.

²No one born to parents who were forbidden by law to marry may come into the meeting to worship the LORD. The descendants for ten generations may not come in either.

³No Ammonite or Moabite may come into the meeting to worship the LORD, and none of their descendants for ten generations may come in. ⁴This is because the Ammonites and Moabites did not give you bread and water when you came out of Egypt. And they hired Balaam son of Beor, from Pethor in Northwest Mesopotamia, to put a curse on you. ⁵But the LORD your God would not listen to Balaam. He turned the curse into a blessing for you, because the LORD your God loves you. ⁶Don't wish for their peace or success as long as you live.

⁷Don't hate Edomites; they are your close relatives. Don't hate Egyptians, because you were foreigners in their country. ⁸The great-grandchildren of these two peoples may come into the meeting to worship the LORD.

KEEPING THE CAMP CLEAN

⁹When you are camped in time of war, keep away from unclean things. ¹⁰If a man becomes unclean during the night, he must go outside the camp and not come back. ¹¹But when evening comes, he must wash himself, and at sunset he may come back into the camp.

¹²Choose a place outside the camp where people may go to relieve themselves. ¹³Carry a tent peg with you, and when you relieve yourself, dig a hole and cover up your dung. ¹⁴The LORD your God moves around through your camp to protect you and to defeat your enemies for you, so the camp must be holy. He must not see anything unclean among you so that he will not leave you.

OTHER LAWS

¹⁵If an escaped slave comes to you, do not hand over the slave to his master. ¹⁶Let the slave live with you anywhere he likes, in any town he chooses. Do not mistreat him.

¹⁷No Israelite man or woman must ever become a temple prostitute. ¹⁸Do not bring a male or female prostitute's pay to the Temple of the LORD your God to pay what you have promised to the LORD, because the LORD your God hates prostitution.

¹⁹If you loan your fellow Israelites money or food or anything else, don't make them pay back more than you loaned them. ²⁰You may charge foreigners, but not fellow Israelites. Then the LORD your God will bless everything you do in the land you are entering to take as your own.

²¹If you make a promise to give something

to the LORD your God, do not be slow to pay it, because the LORD your God demands it from you. Do not be guilty of sin. ²²But if you do not make the promise, you will not be guilty. ²³You must do whatever you say you will do, because you chose to make the promise to the LORD your God.

²⁴If you go into your neighbor's vineyard, you may eat as many grapes as you wish, but do not put any grapes into your basket. ²⁵If you go into your neighbor's grainfield, you may pick grain with your hands, but you must not cut down your neighbor's grain with your sickle.

24 A man might marry a woman but later decide she doesn't please him because he has found something bad about her. He writes out divorce papers for her, gives them to her, and sends her away from his house. ²After she leaves his house, she

---

FAITH

THE EXTRAORDINARY IN THE MUNDANE

temptations and blessings

DEUTERONOMY 23:5

To receive a blessing is to receive something favorable from someone greater. The paradigm of this action is a blessing from God to man. Throughout the Old Testament the central idea of God's blessing is that bountiful life depends solely upon the goodness and faithfulness of God. God is the only source of blessing because God gives life itself. No man, no ritual, no religion, no other power is capable of giving and sustaining life. Amazingly, God is not stingy with his desire to offer this blessing. He does not have to be talked into giving it. He is more than willing to provide blessing to all who trust him.

It's been said, "Were it not for the numbing effects of our addictions, we would probably all have committed suicide." However, the temporary anesthetic of addictions can stop us from facing our powerlessness and seeking help. The result of the addiction, from God's perspective, is simply getting us to the place where we are used up and ready in our weakness to turn to his strength.

Addictions have no power to give life, only to take it away. They are lies of the highest magnitude, disguising death as something worth having. God offers us a complete turnaround, taking what was a curse to us and turning it into the doorway to his grace. Maybe that's why James says that we should count it a blessing when we fall into temptation. Each temptation is a reminder that God took our personal hell and made heavenly joy from it.

reflect: Thank God today for reversing the curse on your life and blessing you with his love instead.

Go to **Deuteronomy 25:1.**

goes and marries another man, ³but her second husband does not like her either. So he writes out divorce papers for her, gives them to her, and sends her away from his house. Or the second husband might die. ⁴In either case, her first husband who divorced her must not marry her again, because she has become unclean. The LORD would hate this. Don't bring this sin into the land the LORD your God is giving you as your own.

⁵A man who has just married must not be sent to war or be given any other duty. He should be free to stay home for a year to make his new wife happy.

⁶If someone owes you something, do not take his two stones for grinding grain—not even the upper one—in place of what he owes, because this is how the person makes a living.

⁷If someone kidnaps a fellow Israelite, either to make him a slave or sell him, the kidnapper must be killed. You must get rid of the evil among you.

⁸Be careful when someone has a skin disease. Do exactly what the priests, the Levites, teach you, being careful to do what I have commanded them. ⁹Remember what the LORD your God did to Miriam on your way out of Egypt.

¹⁰When you make a loan to your neighbors, don't go into their homes to get something in place of it. ¹¹Stay outside and let them go in and get what they promised you. ¹²If a poor person gives you a coat to show he will pay the loan back, don't keep it overnight. ¹³Give the coat back at sunset, because your neighbor needs that coat to sleep in, and he will be grateful to you. And the LORD your God will see that you have done a good thing.

¹⁴Don't cheat hired servants who are poor and needy, whether they are fellow Israelites or foreigners living in one of your towns. ¹⁵Pay them each day before sunset, because they are poor and need the money. Otherwise, they may complain to the LORD about you, and you will be guilty of sin.

¹⁶Parents must not be put to death if their children do wrong, and children must not be put to death if their parents do wrong. Each person must die for his own sin.

¹⁷Do not be unfair to a foreigner or an orphan. Don't take a widow's coat to make sure she pays you back. ¹⁸Remember that you were slaves in Egypt, and the LORD your God saved you from there. That is why I am commanding you to do this.

¹⁹When you are gathering your harvest in the field and leave behind a bundle of grain, don't go back and get it. Leave it there for foreigners, orphans, and widows so that the LORD your God can bless everything you do. ²⁰When you beat your olive trees to knock the olives off, don't beat the trees a second time. Leave what is left for foreigners, orphans, and widows. ²¹When you harvest the grapes in your vineyard, don't pick the vines a second time. Leave what is left for foreigners, orphans, and widows. ²²Remember that you were slaves in Egypt; that is why I am commanding you to do this.

25 If two people have an argument and go to court, the judges will decide the case. They will declare one person right and the other guilty. ²If the guilty person has to be punished with a beating, the judge will make that person lie down and be beaten in front of him. The number of lashes should match the crime. ³But don't hit a person more than forty times, because more than that would disgrace him before others.

⁴When an ox is working in the grain, do not cover its mouth to keep it from eating.

⁵If two brothers are living together, and one of them dies without having a son, his widow must not marry someone outside her husband's family. Her husband's brother must marry her, which is his duty to her as a brother-in-law. ⁶The first son she has counts as the son of the dead brother so that his name will not be forgotten in Israel.

⁷But if a man does not want to marry his brother's widow, she should go to the elders at the town gate. She should say, "My brother-in-law will not carry on his brother's name in Israel. He refuses to do his duty for me."

⁸Then the elders of the town must call for the man and talk to him. But if he is stubborn and says, "I don't want to marry her," ⁹the woman must go up to him in front of the elders. She must take off one of his sandals and spit in his face and say, "This is for the man who won't continue his brother's family!" ¹⁰Then that man's family shall be known in Israel as the Family of the Unsandaled.

¹¹If two men are fighting and one man's wife comes to save her husband from his attacker, grabbing the attacker by his sex organs, ¹²you must cut off her hand. Show her no mercy.

¹³Don't carry two sets of weights with you, one heavy and one light. ¹⁴Don't have two different sets of measures in your house, one large and one small. ¹⁵You must have true and honest weights and measures so that you will live a long time in the land the LORD your God is giving you. ¹⁶The LORD your God hates anyone who is dishonest and uses dishonest measures.

¹⁷Remember what the Amalekites did to you when you came out of Egypt. ¹⁸When you were tired and worn out, they met you on the road and attacked all those lagging behind. They were not afraid of God. ¹⁹When the LORD your God gives you rest from all the enemies around you in the land he is giving you as your own, you shall destroy any memory of the Amalekites on the earth. Do not forget!

FAITH

THE EXTRAORDINARY IN THE MUNDANE

God's courtroom
declaration

DEUTERONOMY 25:1

Righteousness is not a quality, but rather a relation. If you go to court, you are declared right, or righteous; that is, the court grants you the status of "not guilty." Righteousness is a description of your personal relationship to the norm. You are either guilty (not righteous) or not guilty (righteous). You are either justified or you are condemned.

Too often we are confused about this point. We think that righteousness is some sort of quality of life that we have to earn. We start to believe that our righteousness is really like being virtuous. We imagine that God measures us by how virtuous we are—that is, how good we are—as though he is looking for some inward moral quality in our lives.

To understand the word properly, we have to imagine that we are in God's court. Jesus pleads our case. We are guilty, that's for sure, because we have broken the moral law. But God declares us not guilty because Jesus volunteers to take our place. There is no double jeopardy, even in God's court. If Jesus takes my guilt and my punishment, then I am given the status of no longer guilty. That means I am now seen as righteous. This verse says it all. We go to court, and the court says that we are justified. We have been given a new lease on life because we have been declared "not guilty."

---

reflect: Meditate on the goodness of God, and celebrate his gift of righteousness.
Go to **1 Samuel 16:7.**

THE FIRST HARVEST

26 When you go into the land the LORD your God is giving you as your own, to take it over and live in it, ²you must take some of the first harvest of crops that grow from the land the LORD your God is giving you. Put the food in a basket and go to the place where the LORD your God will choose to be worshiped. ³Say to the priest on duty at that time, "Today I declare before the LORD your God that I have come into the land the LORD promised our ancestors that he would give us." ⁴The priest will take your basket and set it down in front of the altar of the LORD your God. ⁵Then you shall announce before the LORD your God: "My father was a wandering Aramean. He went down to Egypt with only a few people, but they became a great, powerful, and large nation there. ⁶But the Egyptians were cruel to us, making us suffer and work very hard. ⁷So we prayed to the LORD, the God of our ancestors, and he heard us. When he saw our trouble, hard work, and suffering, ⁸the LORD brought us out of Egypt with his great power and strength, using great terrors, signs, and miracles. ⁹Then he brought us to this place and gave us this fertile land. ¹⁰Now I bring part of the first harvest from this land that you, LORD, have given me." Place the basket before the LORD your God and bow down before him. ¹¹Then you and the Levites and foreigners among you should rejoice, because the LORD your God has given good things to you and your family.

¹²Bring a tenth of all your harvest the third year (the year to give a tenth of your harvest). Give it to the Levites, foreigners, orphans, and widows so that they may eat in your towns and be full. ¹³Then say to the LORD your God, "I have taken out of my house the part of my harvest that belongs to God, and I have given it to the Levites, foreigners, orphans, and widows. I have done everything you commanded me; I have not broken your commands, and I have not forgotten any of them. ¹⁴I have not eaten any of the holy part while I was in sorrow. I have not removed any of it while I was unclean, and I have not offered it for dead people. I have obeyed you, the LORD my God, and have done everything you commanded me. ¹⁵So look down from heaven, your holy home. Bless your people Israel and bless the land you have given us, which you promised to our ancestors—a fertile land."

OBEY THE LORD'S COMMANDS

¹⁶Today the LORD your God commands you to obey all these rules and laws; be careful to obey them with your whole being. ¹⁷Today you have said that the LORD is your God, and you have promised to do what he wants you to do—to keep his rules, commands, and laws. You have said you will obey him. ¹⁸And today the LORD has said that you are his very own people, as he has promised you. But you must obey his commands. ¹⁹He will make you greater than all the other nations he made. He will give you praise, fame, and honor, and you will be a holy people to the LORD your God, as he has said.

THE LAW WRITTEN ON STONES

27 Then Moses, along with the elders of Israel, commanded the people, saying, "Keep all the commands I have given you today. ²Soon you will cross the Jordan River to go into the land the LORD your God is giving you. On that day set up some large stones and cover them with plaster. ³When you cross over, write all the words of these teachings on them. Then you may enter the land the LORD your God is giving you, a fertile land, just as the LORD, the God of your ancestors, promised. ⁴After you have crossed the Jordan River, set up these stones on Mount Ebal, as I command you today, and cover them with plaster. ⁵Build an altar of stones there to the LORD your God, but don't use any iron tool to cut the stones; ⁶build the altar of the LORD your God with stones from the field. Offer burnt offerings on it to the LORD your God, ⁷and offer fellowship offerings there, and eat them and rejoice before the LORD your God. ⁸Then write clearly all the words of these teachings on the stones."

CURSES OF THE LAW

⁹Then Moses and the Levites who were priests spoke to all Israel and said, "Be quiet, Israel. Listen! Today you have become the people of the LORD your God. ¹⁰Obey the LORD your God, and keep his commands and laws that I give you today."

¹¹That day Moses also gave the people this command:

¹²When you cross the Jordan River, these

tribes must stand on Mount Gerizim to bless the people: Simeon, Levi, Judah, Issachar, Joseph and Benjamin. [13]And these tribes must stand on Mount Ebal to announce the curses: Reuben, Gad, Asher, Zebulun, Dan, and Naphtali.

[14]The Levites will say to all the people of Israel in a loud voice:

[15]"Anyone will be cursed who makes an idol or statue and secretly sets it up, because the LORD hates the idols people make."

Then all the people will say, "Amen!"

[16]"Anyone will be cursed who dishonors his father or mother."

Then all the people will say, "Amen!"

[17]"Anyone will be cursed who moves the stone that marks a neighbor's border."

Then all the people will say, "Amen!"

[18]"Anyone will be cursed who sends a blind person down the wrong road."

Then all the people will say, "Amen!"

[19]"Anyone will be cursed who is unfair to foreigners, orphans, or widows."

Then all the people will say, "Amen!"

[20]"A man will be cursed who has sexual relations with his father's wife, because it is a dishonor to his father."

Then all the people will say, "Amen!"

[21]"Anyone will be cursed who has sexual relations with an animal."

Then all the people will say, "Amen!"

[22]"A man will be cursed who has sexual relations with his sister, whether she is his father's daughter or his mother's daughter."

Then all the people will say, "Amen!"

[23]"A man will be cursed who has sexual relations with his mother-in-law."

Then all the people will say, "Amen!"

[24]"Anyone will be cursed who kills a neighbor secretly."

Then all the people will say, "Amen!"

[25]"Anyone will be cursed who takes money to murder an innocent person."

Then all the people will say, "Amen!"

[26]"Anyone will be cursed who does not agree with the words of these teachings and does not obey them."

Then all the people will say, "Amen!"

BLESSINGS FOR OBEYING

28 You must completely obey the LORD your God, and you must carefully follow all his commands I am giving you to-day. Then the LORD your God will make you greater than any other nation on earth. [2]Obey the LORD your God so that all these blessings will come and stay with you:

[3]You will be blessed in the city and blessed in the country.

[4]Your children will be blessed, as well as your crops; your herds will be blessed with calves and your flocks with lambs.

[5]Your basket and your kitchen will be blessed.

[6]You will be blessed when you come in and when you go out.

[7]The LORD will help you defeat the enemies that come to fight you. They will attack you from one direction, but they will run from you in seven directions.

[8]The LORD your God will bless you with full barns, and he will bless everything you do. He will bless the land he is giving you.

[9]The LORD will make you his holy people, as he promised. But you must obey his commands and do what he wants you to do. [10]Then everyone on earth will see that you are the LORD's people, and they will be afraid of you. [11]The LORD will make you rich: You will have many children, your animals will have many young, and your land will give good crops. It is the land that the LORD promised your ancestors he would give to you.

[12]The LORD will open up his heavenly storehouse so that the skies send rain on your land at the right time, and he will bless every-thing you do. You will lend to other nations, but you will not need to borrow from them. [13]The LORD will make you like the head and not like the tail; you will be on top and not on bottom. But you must obey the commands of the LORD your God that I am giving you today, being careful to keep them. [14]Do not disobey anything I command you today. Do exactly as I command, and do not follow other gods or serve them.

CURSES FOR DISOBEYING

[15]But if you do not obey the LORD your God and carefully follow all his commands and laws I am giving you today, all these curses will come upon you and stay:

[16]You will be cursed in the city and cursed in the country.

[17]Your basket and your kitchen will be cursed.

[18]Your children will be cursed, as well as your crops; the calves of your herds and the lambs of your flocks will be cursed.

[19]You will be cursed when you go in and when you go out.

[20]The LORD will send you curses, confusion, and punishment in everything you do. You will be destroyed and suddenly ruined because you did wrong when you left him. [21]The LORD will give you terrible diseases and destroy you from the land you are going to take. [22]The LORD will punish you with disease, fever, swelling, heat, lack of rain, plant diseases, and mildew until you die. [23]The sky above will be like bronze, and the ground below will be like iron.[n] [24]The LORD will turn the rain into dust and sand, which will fall from the skies until you are destroyed.

[25]The LORD will help your enemies defeat you. You will attack them from one direction, but you will run from them in seven directions. And you will become a thing of horror among all the kingdoms on earth. [26]Your dead bodies will be food for all the birds and wild animals, and there will be

---

28:23 sky . . . iron This means the sky will give no rain and the earth will produce no crops.

GOD'S MANAGEMENT PLAN

blessings and curses

FINANCES

DEUTERONOMY 28

Look over the list of blessings that God promises to provide. There's hardly a category that isn't covered. There's a blessing for national favor, geographical location, family prosperity, financial gain, economic abundance, daily provision, property assets, travel, protection, reputation, legacy, leadership, and respect.

Everything that matters in life is covered by God's promises. Notice here that the only requirement necessary to enjoy all of them is obedience. God doesn't require management training, career counseling, higher education, or business networking. He simply requires obedience to his precepts.

Now, notice what follows. For the next several verses, God describes the consequences of disobedience. There are some pretty terrible things in the list of curses. But if you reflect on the state of the world, you'll see that most of these punishments are evident today, and all because people choose not to obey God.

Financial success is one of the promises of God. But if money or any of the material possessions money provides becomes the focal point of our attention instead of obedience to the principles of God, then we won't experience the promises of God as he designed.

reflect: Decide to obey God's principles, and you'll inherit his promises.
Go to **Deuteronomy 31:6.**

no one to scare them away. ²⁷The LORD will punish you with boils like those the Egyptians had. You will have bad growths, sores, and itches that can't be cured. ²⁸The LORD will give you madness, blindness, and a confused mind. ²⁹You will have to feel around in the daylight like a blind person. You will fail in everything you do. People will hurt you and steal from you every day, and no one will save you.

³⁰You will be engaged to a woman, but another man will force her to have sexual relations with him. You will build a house, but you will not live in it. You will plant a vineyard, but you will not get its grapes. ³¹Your ox will be killed before your eyes, but you will not eat any of it. Your donkey will be taken away from you, and it will not be brought back. Your sheep will be given to your enemies, and no one will save you. ³²Your sons and daughters will be given to another nation, and you will grow tired looking for them every day, but there will be nothing you can do. ³³People you don't know will eat the crops your land and hard work have produced. You will be mistreated and abused all your life. ³⁴The things you see will cause you to go mad. ³⁵The LORD will give you sore boils on your knees and legs that cannot be cured, and they will go from the soles of your feet to the tops of your heads.

³⁶The LORD will send you and your king away to a nation neither you nor your ancestors know, where you will serve other gods made of wood and stone. ³⁷You will become a hated thing to the nations where the LORD sends you; they will laugh at you and make fun of you.

³⁸You will plant much seed in your field, but your harvest will be small, because locusts will eat the crop. ³⁹You will plant vineyards and work hard in them, but you will not pick the grapes or drink the wine, because the worms will eat them. ⁴⁰You will have olive trees in all your land, but you will not get any olive oil, because the olives will drop off the trees. ⁴¹You will have sons and daughters, but you will not be able to keep them, because they will be taken captive. ⁴²Locusts will destroy all your trees and crops.

⁴³The foreigners who live among you will get stronger and stronger, and you will get weaker and weaker. ⁴⁴Foreigners will lend money to you, but you will not be able to lend to them. They will be like the head, and you will be like the tail.

⁴⁵All these curses will come upon you. They will chase you and catch you and destroy you, because you did not obey the LORD your God and keep the commands and laws he gave you. ⁴⁶The curses will be signs and miracles to you and your descendants forever. ⁴⁷You had plenty of everything, but you did not serve the LORD your God with joy and a pure heart, ⁴⁸so you will serve the enemies the LORD sends against you. You will be hungry, thirsty, naked, and poor, and the LORD will put a load on you until he has destroyed you.

THE CURSE OF AN ENEMY NATION

⁴⁹The LORD will bring a nation against you from far away, from the end of the world, and it will swoop down like an eagle. You won't understand their language, ⁵⁰and they will look mean. They will not respect old people or feel sorry for the young. ⁵¹They will eat the calves from your herds and the harvest of your field, and you will be destroyed. They will not leave you any grain, new wine or oil, or any calves from your herds or lambs from your flocks. You will be ruined. ⁵²That nation will surround and attack all your cities. You trust in your high, strong walls, but they will fall down. That nation will surround all your cities everywhere in the land the LORD your God is giving you.

⁵³Your enemy will surround you. Those people will make you starve so that you will eat your own babies, the bodies of the sons and daughters the LORD your God gave you. ⁵⁴Even the most gentle and kind man among you will become cruel to his brother, his wife whom he loves, and his children who are still alive. ⁵⁵He will not even give them any of the flesh of his children he is eating, because it will be all he has left. Your enemy will surround you and make you starve in all your cities. ⁵⁶The most gentle and kind woman among you, so gentle and kind she would hardly even walk on the ground, will be cruel to her husband whom she loves and to her son and daughter. ⁵⁷She will give birth to a baby, but she will plan to eat the baby and what comes after the birth itself. She will eat them secretly while the enemy surrounds

the city. Those people will make you starve in all your cities.

58Be careful to obey everything in these teachings that are written in this book. You must respect the glorious and wonderful name of the LORD your God, 59or the LORD will give terrible diseases to you and your descendants. You will have long and serious diseases, and long and miserable sicknesses. 60He will give you all the diseases of Egypt that you dread, and the diseases will stay with you. 61The LORD will also give you every disease and sickness not written in this Book of the Teachings, until you are destroyed. 62You people may have outnumbered the stars, but only a few of you will be left, because you did not obey the LORD your God. 63Just as the LORD was once happy with you and gave you good things and made you grow in number, so then the LORD will be happy to ruin and destroy you, and you will be removed from the land you are entering to take as your own.

64Then the LORD will scatter you among the nations—from one end of the earth to the other. There you will serve other gods of wood and stone, gods that neither you nor your ancestors have known. 65You will have no rest among those nations and no place that is yours. The LORD will make your mind worried, your sight weak, and your soul sad. 66You will live with danger and be afraid night and day. You will not be sure that you will live. 67In the morning you will say, "I wish it were evening," and in the evening you will say, "I wish it were morning." Terror will be in your heart, and the things you have seen will scare you. 68The LORD will send you back to Egypt in ships, even though I, Moses, said you would never go back to Egypt. And there you will try to sell yourselves as slaves to your enemies, but no one will buy you.

THE AGREEMENT IN MOAB

29 The LORD commanded Moses to make an agreement with the Israelites in Moab in addition to the agreement he had made with them at Mount Sinai. These are the words of that agreement.

2Moses called all the Israelites together and said to them:

You have seen everything the LORD did before your own eyes to the king of Egypt and to the king's leaders and to the whole country. 3With your own eyes you saw the great troubles, signs, and miracles. 4But to this day the LORD has not given you a mind that understands; you don't really understand what you see with your eyes or hear with your ears. 5I led you through the desert for forty years, and during that time neither your clothes nor sandals wore out. 6You ate no bread and drank no wine or beer. This was so you would understand that I am the LORD your God.

7When you came to this place, Sihon king of Heshbon and Og king of Bashan came out to fight us, but we defeated them. 8We captured their land and gave it to the tribes of Reuben, Gad, and East Manasseh to be their own.

9You must carefully obey everything in this agreement so that you will succeed in everything you do. 10Today you are all standing here before the LORD your God—your leaders and important men, your elders, officers, and all the other men of Israel, 11your wives and children and the foreigners who live among you, who chop your wood and carry your water. 12You are all here to enter into an agreement and a promise with the LORD your God, an agreement the LORD your God is making with you today. 13This will make you today his own people. He will be your God, as he told you and as he promised your ancestors Abraham, Isaac, and Jacob. 14But I am not just making this agreement and its promises with you 15who are standing here before the LORD your God today, but also with those who are not here today.

16You know how we lived in Egypt and how we passed through the countries when we came here. 17You saw their hateful idols made of wood, stone, silver, and gold. 18Make sure no man, woman, family group, or tribe among you leaves the LORD our God to go and serve the gods of those nations. They would be to you like a plant that grows bitter, poisonous fruit.

19These are the kind of people who hear these curses but bless themselves, thinking, "We will be safe even though we continue doing what that we want to do." Those people may destroy all of your land, both wet and dry. 20The LORD will not forgive them. His anger will be like a burning fire against those people, and all the curses written in this book will come on them. The LORD will destroy any memory of them on the earth. ²¹He will separate them from all the tribes of Israel for punishment. All the curses of the Agreement that are written in this Book of the Teachings will happen to them.

²²Your children who will come after you, as well as foreigners from faraway lands, will see the disasters that come to this land and the diseases the LORD will send on it. They will say, ²³"The land is nothing but burning cinders and salt. Nothing is planted, nothing grows, and nothing blooms. It is like Sodom and Gomorrah, and Admah and Zeboiim, which the LORD destroyed because he was very angry." ²⁴All the other nations will ask, "Why has the LORD done this to the land? Why is he so angry?"

²⁵And the answer will be, "It is because the people broke the Agreement of the LORD, the God of their ancestors, which he made with them when he brought them out of Egypt. ²⁶They went and served other gods and bowed down to gods they did not even know. The LORD did not allow that, ²⁷so he became very angry at the land and brought all the curses on it that are written in this book. ²⁸Since the LORD became angry and furious with them, he took them out of their land and put them in another land where they are today."

²⁹There are some things the LORD our God has kept secret, but there are some things he has let us know. These things belong to us and our children forever so that we will do everything in these teachings.

THE ISRAELITES WILL RETURN

30 When all these blessings and curses I have described happen to you, and the LORD your God has sent you away to other nations, think about these things. ²Then you and your children will return to the LORD your God, and you will obey him with your whole being in everything I am commanding you today. ³Then the LORD your God will give you back your freedom. He will feel sorry for you, and he will bring you back again from the nations where he scattered you. ⁴He may send you to the ends of the earth, but he will gather you and bring you back from there, ⁵back to the land that belonged to your ancestors. It will be yours. He will give you success, and there will be more of you than there were of your ancestors. ⁶The LORD your God will prepare you and your descendants to love him with your whole being so that you will live. ⁷The LORD your God will put all these curses on your enemies, who hate you and are cruel to you. ⁸And you will again obey the LORD, keeping all his commands that I give you today. ⁹The LORD your God will make you successful in everything you do. You will have many children, your cattle will have many calves, and your fields will produce good crops, because the LORD will again be happy with you, just as he was with your ancestors. ¹⁰But you must obey the LORD your God by keeping all his commands and rules that are written in this Book of the Teachings. You must return to the LORD your God with your whole being.

CHOOSE LIFE OR DEATH

¹¹This command I give you today is not too hard for you; it is not beyond what you can do. ¹²It is not up in heaven. You do not have to ask, "Who will go up to heaven and get it for us so we can obey it and keep it?" ¹³It is not on the other side of the sea. You do not have to ask, "Who will go across the sea and get it? Who will tell it to us so we can keep it?" ¹⁴No, the word is very near you. It is in your mouth and in your heart so you may obey it.

¹⁵Look, today I offer you life and success, death and destruction. ¹⁶I command you today to love the LORD your God, to do what he wants you to do, and to keep his commands, his rules, and his laws. Then you will live and grow in number, and the LORD your God will bless you in the land you are entering to take as your own.

¹⁷But if you turn away from the LORD and do not obey him, if you are led to bow and serve other gods, ¹⁸I tell you today that you will surely be destroyed. And you will not live long in the land you are crossing the Jordan River to enter and take as your own.

¹⁹Today I ask heaven and earth to be witnesses. I am offering you life or death, blessings or curses. Now, choose life! Then you and your children may live. ²⁰To choose life is to love the LORD your God, obey him, and stay close to him. He is your life, and he will let you live many years in the land, the land

he promised to give your ancestors Abraham, Isaac, and Jacob.

JOSHUA TAKES MOSES' PLACE

31 Then Moses went and spoke these words to all the Israelites: ²"I am now one hundred twenty years old, and I cannot lead you anymore. The LORD told me I would not cross the Jordan River; ³the LORD your God will lead you across himself. He will destroy those nations for you, and you will take over their land. Joshua will also lead you across, as the LORD has said. ⁴The LORD will do to those nations what he did to Sihon and Og, the kings of the Amorites, when he destroyed them and their land. ⁵The LORD will give those nations to you; do to them everything I told you. ⁶Be strong and brave. Don't be afraid of them and don't be frightened, because the LORD your God will go with you. He will not leave you or forget you."

⁷Then Moses called Joshua and said to him in front of the people, "Be strong and brave, because you will lead these people into the land the LORD promised to give their ancestors, and help them take it as their own. ⁸The LORD himself will go before you. He will be with you; he will not leave you or forget you. Don't be afraid and don't worry."

GOD'S MANAGEMENT PLAN

success and failure

FINANCES

DEUTERONOMY 31:6

The Hebrew word for "fail" can mean to let go, to let drop, or to sink down. It also may mean weakening. In other places, it means to slack or dishearten, to faint in the day of adversity. It is interesting that some of the derivatives of this word are used to refer to the ghosts of the dead or to death itself.

All of these different nuances of the word hold important meanings for our spiritual growth. God promises not to let us down, or abandon us, or leave us alone. He is not slack or absent in the day of adversity. And he is ready to stand by us until death.

God has set life up as a course in learning. Every day and every experience is an opportunity to learn. It is not to be considered failure if we learn from our mistakes. Many times we may have felt that the ghosts of our past are so overwhelming that we might never become what we envision.

And many of us may have cowered under the weight of our old life. But the failures of the past are no longer to be feared, only learned from. After all is said and done, success does not depend on our frailties, but rather on the abilities of God through us.

reflect: Lean on the ability of God to bring you success in your endeavors.
Go to **Ruth 2:12.**

MOSES WRITES THE TEACHINGS

9So Moses wrote down these teachings and gave them to the priests and all the elders of Israel. (The priests are the sons of Levi, who carry the Ark of the Agreement with the LORD.) 10-11Then Moses commanded them: "Read these teachings for all Israel to hear at the end of every seven years, which is the year to cancel what people owe. Do it during the Feast of Shelters, when all the Israelites will come to appear before the LORD your God and stand at the place he will choose. 12Gather all the people: the men, women, children, and foreigners living in your towns so that they can listen and learn to respect the LORD your God and carefully obey everything in this law. 13Since their children do not know this law, they must hear it. They must learn to respect the LORD your God for as long as they live in the land you are crossing the Jordan River to take for your own."

THE LORD CALLS MOSES AND JOSHUA

14The LORD said to Moses, "Soon you will die. Get Joshua and come to the Meeting Tent so that I may command him." So Moses and Joshua went to the Meeting Tent.

15The LORD appeared at the Meeting Tent in a cloud; the cloud stood over the entrance of the Tent. 16And the LORD said to Moses, "You will soon die. Then these people will not be loyal to me but will worship the foreign gods of the land they are entering. They will leave me, breaking the Agreement I made with them. 17Then I will become very angry at them, and I will leave them. I will turn away from them, and they will be destroyed. Many terrible things will happen to them. Then they will say, 'It is because God is not with us that these terrible things are happening.' 18I will surely turn away from them then, because they have done wrong and have turned to other gods.

19"Now write down this song and teach it to the Israelites. Then have them sing it, because it will be my witness against them. 20When I bring them into the land I promised to their ancestors, a fertile land, they will eat as much as they want and get fat. Then they will turn to other gods and serve them. They will reject me and break my Agreement. 21Then when many troubles and terrible things happen to them, this song will testify against them, because the song will not be forgotten by their descendants. I know what they plan to do, even before I take them into the land I promised them." 22So Moses wrote down the song that day, and he taught it to the Israelites.

23Then the LORD gave this command to Joshua son of Nun: "Be strong and brave, because you will lead the people of Israel to the land I promised them, and I will be with you."

24After Moses finished writing all the words of the teachings in a book, 25he gave a command to the Levites, who carried the Ark of the Agreement with the LORD. 26He said, "Take this Book of the Teachings and put it beside the Ark of the Agreement with the LORD your God. It must stay there as a witness against you. 27I know how stubborn and disobedient you are. You have disobeyed the LORD while I am alive and with you, and you will disobey even more after I die! 28Gather all the elders of your tribes and all your officers to me so that I may say these things for them to hear, and so that I may ask heaven and earth to testify against them. 29I know that after I die you will become completely evil. You will turn away from the commands I have given you. Terrible things will happen to you in the future when you do what the LORD says is evil, and you will make him angry with the idols you have made."

MOSES' SONG

30And Moses spoke this whole song for all the people of Israel to hear:

32 Hear, heavens, and I will speak.
Listen, earth, to what I say.
2 My teaching will drop like rain;
   my words will fall like dew.
They will be like showers on the grass;
   they will pour down like rain on young
      plants.
3 I will announce the name of the LORD.
   Praise God because he is great!
4 He is like a rock; what he does is perfect,
   and he is always fair.
He is a faithful God who does no wrong,
   who is right and fair.

5 They have done evil against him.
   To their shame they are no longer his
      children;
   they are an evil and lying people.

⁶ This is not the way to repay the LORD,
   you foolish and unwise people.
He is your Father and Maker,
   who made you and formed you.

⁷ Remember the old days.
   Think of the years already passed.
Ask your father and he will tell you;
   ask your elders and they will inform
   you.

⁸ God Most High gave the nations their
   lands,
   dividing up the human race.
He set up borders for the people
   and even numbered the Israelites.

⁹ The LORD took his people as his share,
   the people of Jacob as his very own.

¹⁰ He found them in a desert,
   a windy, empty land.
He surrounded them and brought them
   up,
   guarding them as those he loved very
   much.

¹¹ He was like an eagle building its nest
   that flutters over its young.
It spreads its wings to catch them
   and carries them on its feathers.

¹² The LORD alone led them,
   and there was no foreign god helping
   him.

¹³ The LORD brought them to the heights of
   the land
   and fed them the fruit of the fields.
He gave them honey from the rocks,
   bringing oil from the solid rock.

¹⁴ There were milk curds from the cows and
   milk from the flock;
   there were fat sheep and goats.
There were sheep and goats from Bashan
   and the best of the wheat.
You drank the juice of grapes.

¹⁵ Israel grew fat and kicked;
   they were fat and full and firm.
They left the God who made them
   and rejected the Rock who saved them.

¹⁶ They made God jealous with foreign gods
   and angry with hateful idols.

¹⁷ They made sacrifices to demons, not God,
   to gods they had never known,
   new gods from nearby,
   gods your ancestors did not fear.

¹⁸ You left God who is the Rock, your Father,

and you forgot the God who gave you
   birth.

¹⁹ The LORD saw this and rejected them;
   his sons and daughters had made him
   angry.

²⁰ He said, "I will turn away from them
   and see what will happen to them.
They are evil people,
   unfaithful children.

²¹ They used things that are not gods to
   make me jealous
   and worthless idols to make me angry.
So I will use those who are not a nation to
   make them jealous;
   I will use a nation that does not
   understand to make them angry.

²² My anger has started a fire
   that burns down to the place of the
   dead.
It will burn up the ground and its crops,
   and it will set fire to the base of the
   mountains.

²³ "I will pile troubles upon them
   and shoot my arrows at them.

²⁴ They will be starved and sick,
   destroyed by terrible diseases.
I will send them vicious animals
   and gliding, poisonous snakes.

²⁵ In the streets the sword will kill;
   in their homes there will be terror.
Young men and women will die,
   and so will babies and gray-haired
   men.

²⁶ I will scatter them as I said,
   and no one will remember them.

²⁷ But I didn't want their enemy to brag;
   their enemy might misunderstand
and say, 'We have won!
   The LORD has done none of this.'"

²⁸ Israel has no sense;
   they do not understand.

²⁹ I wish they were wise and understood
   this;
   I wish they could see what will happen
   to them.

³⁰ One person cannot chase a thousand
   people,
   and two people cannot fight ten
   thousand
unless their Rock has sold them,
   unless the LORD has given them up.

31 The rock of these people is not like our
  Rock;
    our enemies agree to that.
32 Their vine comes from Sodom,
    and their fields are like Gomorrah.
  Their grapes are full of poison;
    their bunches of grapes are bitter.
33 Their wine is like snake poison,
    like the deadly poison of cobras.

34 "I have been saving this,
    and I have it locked in my storehouses.
35 I will punish those who do wrong; I will
  repay them.
    Soon their foot will slip,
  because their day of trouble is near,
    and their punishment will come
      quickly."

36 The LORD will defend his people
    and have mercy on his servants.
  He will see that their strength is gone,
    that nobody is left, slaves or free.
37 Then he will say, "Where are their gods?
    Where is the rock they trusted?
38 Who ate the fat from their sacrifices,
    and who drank the wine of their drink
      offerings?
  Let those gods come to help you!
    Let them protect you!

39 "Now you will see that I am the one God!
    There is no god but me.
  I send life and death;
    I can hurt, and I can heal.
  No one can escape from me.
40 I raise my hand toward heaven and make
    this promise:
    As surely as I live forever,
41 I will sharpen my flashing sword,
    and I will take it in my hand to judge.
  I will punish my enemies
    and pay back those who hate me.
42 My arrows will be covered with their
    blood;
    my sword will eat their flesh.
  The blood will flow from those who are
    killed and the captives.
  The heads of the enemy leaders will be
    cut off."

43 Be happy, nations, with his people,
    because he will repay you for the blood
      of his servants.
  He will punish his enemies,

and he will remove the sin of his land
    and people.

44 Moses came with Joshua son of Nun,
and they spoke all the words of this song for
the people to hear. 45 When Moses finished
speaking these words to all Israel, 46 he said to
them: "Pay careful attention to all the words
I have said to you today, and command your
children to obey carefully everything in these
teachings. 47 These should not be unimportant words for you, but rather they mean life
for you! By these words you will live a long
time in the land you are crossing the Jordan
River to take as your own."

MOSES GOES UP TO MOUNT NEBO

48 The LORD spoke to Moses again that
same day and said, 49 "Go up the Abarim
Mountains, to Mount Nebo in the country of
Moab, across from Jericho. Look at the land
of Canaan that I am giving to the Israelites
as their own. 50 On that mountain that you
climb, you will die and join your ancestors,
just as your brother Aaron died on Mount
Hor and joined his ancestors. 51 You both
sinned against me at the waters of Meribah
Kadesh in the Desert of Zin, and you did not
honor me as holy there among the Israelites.
52 So now you will only look at the land from
far away. You will not enter the land I am giving the people of Israel."

MOSES BLESSES THE PEOPLE

33 Moses, the man of God, gave this
blessing to the Israelites before he
died. 2 He said:
  "The LORD came from Mount Sinai
    and rose like the sun from Edom;
    he showed his greatness from Mount
      Paran.
  He came with thousands of angels
    from the southern mountains.
3 The LORD surely loves his people
    and takes care of all those who belong
      to him.
  They bow down at his feet,
    and they are taught by him.
4 Moses gave us the teachings
    that belong to the people of Jacob.
5 The LORD became king of Israel
    when the leaders of the people
      gathered,
    when the tribes of Israel came together.

6 "Let the people of Reuben live and not
die,
but let the people be few."

7Moses said this about the people of
Judah:
"LORD, listen to Judah's prayer;
bring them back to their people.
They defend themselves with their
hands.
Help them fight their enemies!"

8Moses said this about the people of
Levi:
"LORD, your Thummim and Urim belong
to Levi, whom you love.
LORD, you tested him at Massah
and argued with him at the waters of
Meribah.
9 He said about his father and mother,
'I don't care about them.'
He did not treat his brothers as favorites
or give special favors to his children,
but he protected your word
and guarded your agreement.
10 He teaches your laws to the people of
Jacob
and your teachings to the people of
Israel.
He burns incense before you
and makes whole burnt offerings on
your altar.
11 LORD, make them strong;
be pleased with the work they do.
Defeat those who attack them,
and don't let their enemies rise up
again."

12Moses said this about the people of
Benjamin:
"The LORD's loved ones will lie down in
safety,
because he protects them all day long.
The ones he loves rest with him."

13Moses said this about the people of
Joseph:
"May the LORD bless their land with
wonderful dew from heaven,
with water from the springs below,
14 with the best fruits that the sun brings,
and with the best fruits that the moon
brings.
15 Let the old mountains give the finest
crops,

and let the everlasting hills give the best
fruits.
16 Let the full earth give the best fruits,
and let the LORD who lived in the
burning bush be pleased.
May these blessings rest on the head of
Joseph,
on the forehead of the one who was
blessed among his brothers.
17 Joseph has the majesty of a firstborn bull;
he is as strong as a wild ox.
He will stab other nations,
even those nations far away.
These are the ten thousands of Ephraim,
and these are the thousands of
Manasseh."

18Moses said this about the people of
Zebulun:
"Be happy when you go out, Zebulun,
and be happy in your tents, Issachar.
19 They will call the people to the mountain,
and there they will offer the right
sacrifices.
They will do well from all that is in the
sea,
and they will do well from the treasures
hidden in the sand on the shore."

20Moses said this about the people of
Gad:
"Praise God who gives Gad more land!
Gad lives there like a lion,
who tears off arms and heads.
21 They chose the best land for themselves.
They received a large share, like that
given to an officer.
When the leaders of the people gathered,
the people of Gad did what the LORD
said was right,
and they judged Israel fairly."

22Moses said this about the people of
Dan:
"Dan is like a lion's cub,
who jumps out of Bashan."

23Moses said this about the people of
Naphtali:
"Naphtali enjoys special kindnesses,
and they are full of the LORD's blessings.
Take as your own the west and south."

24Moses said this about the people of
Asher:

"Asher is the most blessed of the sons;
　　let him be his brothers' favorite.
　　Let him bathe his feet in olive oil.
25 Your gates will have locks of iron and
　　　bronze,
　　and you will be strong as long as you
　　　live.

26 "There is no one like the God of Israel,
　　who rides through the skies to help you,
　　who rides on the clouds in his majesty.
27 The everlasting God is your place of
　　　safety,
　　and his arms will hold you up forever.
　He will force your enemy out ahead of
　　　you,
　　saying, 'Destroy the enemy!'
28 The people of Israel will lie down in
　　　safety.
　　Jacob's spring is theirs alone.
　Theirs is a land full of grain and new
　　　wine,
　　where the skies drop their dew.
29 Israel, you are blessed!
　　No one else is like you,
　　because you are a people saved by the
　　　LORD.
　He is your shield and helper,
　　your glorious sword.
　Your enemies will be afraid of you,
　　and you will walk all over their holy
　　　places."

MOSES DIES

34 Then Moses climbed Mount Nebo from the plains of Moab to the top of Mount Pisgah, across from Jericho. From there the LORD showed him all the land from Gilead to Dan, 2all of Naphtali and the lands of Ephraim and Manasseh, all the land of Judah as far as the Mediterranean Sea, 3as well as the southern desert and the whole Valley of Jericho up to Zoar. (Jericho is called the city of palm trees.) 4Then the LORD said to Moses, "This is the land I promised to Abraham, Isaac, and Jacob when I said to them, 'I will give this land to your descendants.' I have let you look at it, Moses, but you will not cross over there."

5Then Moses, the servant of the LORD, died there in Moab, as the LORD had said. 6He buried Moses in Moab in the valley opposite Beth Peor, but even today no one knows where his grave is. 7Moses was one hundred twenty years old when he died. His eyes were not weak, and he was still strong. 8The Israelites cried for Moses for thirty days, staying in the plains of Moab until the time of sadness was over.

9Joshua son of Nun was then filled with wisdom, because Moses had put his hands on him. So the Israelites listened to Joshua, and they did what the LORD had commanded Moses.

10There has never been another prophet in Israel like Moses. The LORD knew Moses face to face 11and sent him to do signs and miracles in Egypt—to the king, to all his officers, and to the whole land of Egypt. 12Moses had great power, and he did great and wonderful things for all the Israelites to see.

joshua

GOD'S COMMAND TO JOSHUA

1 After Moses, the servant of the LORD, died, the LORD spoke to Joshua son of Nun, Moses' assistant. ²The LORD said, "My servant Moses is dead. Now you and all these people go across the Jordan River into the land I am giving to the Israelites. ³I promised Moses I would give you this land, so I will give you every place you go in the land. ⁴All the land from the desert in the south to Lebanon in the north will be yours. All the land from the great river, the Euphrates, in the east, to the Mediterranean Sea in the west will be yours, too, including the land of the Hittites. ⁵No

---

WHEN YOUR WAY ISN'T GOD'S WAY

exercise
by God

FITNESS

JOSHUA 1:7

In the beginning, God created man and woman to move. He gave them joints that bend, hands that grab, arms that swing, legs that run, feet that kick, and muscles that stretch . . . and he saw that this was good.

Before the use of technology, our survival required movement. Building shelter, traveling, growing food, and hunting for dinner, all required physical action. Today you can do just about everything without moving more than your hand or finger. You can buy a house, make travel arrangements, and order lunch and never have to leave your desk . . . and God saw that this was bad.

In this passage, Joshua was about to lead Israel into the promised land—an intensely physical task that required walking, climbing, and fighting—so he *had to be strong* not only spiritually, but emotionally and physically as well. And so do you.

Exercise should be safe, natural, and fun! A child's play produces hours of aerobic and resistance training along with a fun activity so that he or she does not even realize he or she is getting a workout. Ask yourself what you can do to get exercise every day, the way you were created to, and enjoy yourself at the same time. That is your exercise by God.

---

reflect: Start an exercise program that is both enjoyable and energizing.
Go to **Genesis 4:7.**

God's Purpose for Your Life

FUTURE

By Dr. D. James Kennedy

JOSHUA 1:1–9

I have a question for you—a very, very important question—and that is this: What are you living for? What is the purpose of your life?

Socrates said that an unexamined life is not worth living, but I'm afraid the situation is more serious than that. An unexamined life might bring us into disastrous conflict with God, who calls us to examine ourselves. What is your purpose for living?

The famed preacher, Dr. Louis Evans of the great Hollywood Presbyterian Church, some years ago was invited to a frat house at UCLA to speak. A large number of young men had gathered there to hear him, for he was a fascinating speaker. They were sitting on couches, occupying every chair, even sitting on the floor or just leaning against the wall. He asked them, "Gentlemen, what is your purpose for living?"

One of the young men raised his hand and said, "Well, I'm studying business. I plan to go on and get an MBA, and I want to have a successful business one day."

He said, "That's very commendable. However, that is how you are going to *make* your living. What are you living *for*?"

"Oh."

Another man raised his hand and said, "Well, you see, pastor, I'm looking for the girl of my dreams. When I find her I'm going to get married, and we're going to have six kids, because I love kids and I'm going to live for my family."

He said, "That's wonderful. Those are the people you are going to be living *with*, but what are you living *for*?"

Another said, "I want a big beautiful home in the suburbs with a swimming pool and all of the modern conveniences."

He said, "That's nice, but that's *where* you are going to be living. But what are you living *for*?"

You see, purpose is very important. There are eight different Greek words in the New Testament that are translated "purpose." In its various forms, "purpose" is used sixty-two times in the Bible. God acts by purpose. He is fulfilling his purposes. The angels of God act according to his purpose. And because we are rational creatures, everything we do we do on purpose. Unfortunately, most of us don't examine our purposes very carefully.

By contrast, listen carefully to the words of America's Founding Fathers, recorded in 1643 at the New England Confederation: "Whereas we all came into these parts of America with one and the same end and aim, namely, to advance the Kingdom of our Lord Jesus Christ." You won't hear that in any public school today, but that is why they came.

Like those frat students, the Founding Fathers dreamt of and succeeded in making a living, rearing families and building homes—but those were not their reasons for living. They were living to advance the Kingdom of our Lord Jesus Christ.

Dear friend, what is *your* purpose for life? May your purpose be the same as our Founding Fathers and of Christ himself—to seek and save those who are lost and, thus, to advance the Kingdom of God.

TO LEARN MORE ON WHAT THE BIBLE HAS TO SAY ABOUT **FUTURE,** READ THE SCRIPTURES AND DEVOTIONALS AT **EZEKIEL 36:25–27, DEUTERONOMY 11:19, 1 CHRONICLES 16:34–36, LAMENTATIONS 5:7, MATTHEW 19:26,** AND **MATTHEW 22:21.**

one will be able to defeat you all your life. Just as I was with Moses, so I will be with you. I will not leave you or forget you.

6"Joshua, be strong and brave! You must lead these people so they can take the land that I promised their fathers I would give them. 7Be strong and brave. Be sure to obey all the teachings my servant Moses gave you. If you follow them exactly, you will be successful in everything you do. 8Always remember what is written in the Book of the Teachings. Study it day and night to be sure to obey everything that is written there. If you do this, you will be wise and successful in everything. 9Remember that I commanded you to be strong and brave. Don't be afraid, because the LORD your God will be with you everywhere you go."

JOSHUA'S ORDERS TO THE PEOPLE

10Then Joshua gave orders to the officers of the people: 11"Go through the camp and tell the people, 'Get your supplies ready. Three days from now you will cross the Jordan River and take the land the LORD your God is giving you.'"

12Then Joshua said to the people of Reuben, Gad, and East Manasseh, 13"Remember what Moses, the servant of the LORD, told you. He said the LORD your God would give you rest and would give you this land. 14Now the LORD has given you this land east of the Jordan River. Your wives, children, and animals may stay here, but your fighting men must dress for war and cross the Jordan River ahead of your brothers to help them. 15The LORD has given you a place to rest and will do the same for your brothers. But you must help them until they take the land the LORD their God is giving them. Then you may return to your own land east of the Jordan River, the land that Moses, the servant of the LORD, gave you."

16Then the people answered Joshua, "Anything you command us to do, we will do. Any place you send us, we will go. 17Just as we fully obeyed Moses, we will obey you. We ask only that the LORD your God be with you just as he was with Moses. 18Whoever refuses to obey your commands or turns against you will be put to death. Just be strong and brave!"

SPIES SENT TO JERICHO

2 Joshua son of Nun secretly sent out two spies from Acacia and said to them, "Go and look at the land, particularly at the city of Jericho."

So the men went to Jericho and stayed at the house of a prostitute named Rahab.

2Someone told the king of Jericho, "Some men from Israel have come here tonight to spy out the land."

3So the king of Jericho sent this message to Rahab: "Bring out the men who came to you and entered your house. They have come to spy out our whole land."

4But the woman had hidden the two men. She said, "They did come here, but I didn't know where they came from. 5In the evening, when it was time to close the city gate, they left. I don't know where they went, but if you go quickly, maybe you can catch them." 6(The woman had taken the men up to the roof [n] and had hidden them there under stalks of flax that she had spread out.) 7So the king's men went out looking for the spies on the road that leads to the crossings of the Jordan River. The city gate was closed just after the king's men left the city.

8Before the spies went to sleep for the night, Rahab went up to the roof. 9She said to them, "I know the LORD has given this land to your people. You frighten us very much. Everyone living in this land is terribly afraid of you 10because we have heard how the LORD dried up the Red Sea when you came out of Egypt. We have heard how you destroyed Sihon and Og, two Amorite kings who lived east of the Jordan. 11When we heard this, we were very frightened. Now our men are afraid to fight you because the LORD your God rules the heavens above and the earth below! 12So now, promise me before the LORD that you will show kindness to my family just as I showed kindness to you. Give me some proof that you will do this. 13Allow my father, mother, brothers, sisters, and all of their families to live. Save us from death."

14The men agreed and said, "It will be our lives for your lives if you don't tell anyone

---

2:6 roof In Bible times houses were built with flat roofs. The roof was used for drying things such as flax and fruit. And it was used as an extra room, as a place for worship, and as a cool place to sleep in the summer.

The **Extraordinary** in the **Mundane**

By Wayne Cordeiro

JOSHUA 2:1–21

I was catching a plane in Honolulu to Hilo. A lady, obviously flustered, pushed her way to the front of the line with a box full of bank records.

"I need to get on this plane!" she said gasping.

"Well, you could stand in line, Ma'am, and get your ticket," replied the ticketing agent. "The plane will leave in fifteen minutes."

"That's the problem," she said. "I have to take my rental car back. I have to be in Hilo for a meeting. These are the records our bank officers are waiting for. If I don't make this meeting, I will get fired!"

The ticketing agent wasn't moved. "I'm sorry, Ma'am, you're not going to make this plane. You can catch the next one. It's in two hours."

At this point, I could no longer stand by and observe. "Give me that," I said as I grabbed the box of records from her. "What are you doing?" she replied, taken completely off guard.

"Go take your car back. Go right now! I'll get your ticket, and I'll wait for you at the gate. Go!"

Both dumbfounded and appreciative, she ran and turned in her car. By the time she returned, I had her ticket and was waiting at the gate.

"You saved my life! How can I thank you?"

"No problem," I said. "I'm glad to help."

"At least, tell me your name," she said. I told her my name: Wayne Cordeiro.

"O God!" she exclaimed.

"No," I replied, "just Wayne Cordeiro."

"No, you don't understand," she said. "For the past two months, people from your church have been trying to get me to come with them, but I have been refusing. And now this has happened! I have to go to your church now!"

That was a simple thing that seemed quite unspiritual. I was just helping somebody. She came to church the next Sunday, and she dragged her husband with her. Both of them received Christ that day! What was extraordinary was hidden in a very simple act.

Remember Rahab, the prostitute? The people of Israel sent spies into Jericho because God said, "You're going to take this city." When the officials of the city heard that the Israelite spies were there, they wanted to capture and kill them. Rahab sneaked them out of the city another way. Now, that may seem simple and not very spiritual, but God hid the extraordinary in the simple.

Because of that simple act, God saved Israel, Israel defeated Jericho and, later on, Rahab married into the lineage of the Israelites! One of her great-great-grandchildren was King David. She was grafted into the very lineage that Jesus Christ was born into. And it all began with something seemingly very small.

You might not see immediate results as I did, but it doesn't do any harm to be kind. And you never know what extraordinary thing God might hide inside your simple act of obedience.

TO LEARN MORE ON WHAT THE BIBLE HAS TO SAY ABOUT **FAITH,** READ THE SCRIPTURES AND DEVOTIONALS AT **GENESIS 32:20, EXODUS 24:8, DEUTERONOMY 23:5, DEUTERONOMY 25:1, 1 SAMUEL 16:7,** AND **1 SAMUEL 21:8-9.**

what we are doing. When the LORD gives us the land, we will be kind and true to you."

15The house Rahab lived in was built on the city wall, so she used a rope to let the men down through a window. 16She said to them, "Go into the hills so the king's men will not find you. Hide there for three days. After the king's men return, you may go on your way."

17The men said to her, "You must do as we say. If not, we cannot be responsible for keeping this oath you have made us swear. 18When we return to this land, you must tie this red rope in the window through which you let us down. Bring your father, mother, brothers, and all your family into your house. 19If anyone leaves your house and is killed, it is his own fault. We cannot be responsible for him. If anyone in your house is hurt, we will be responsible. 20But if you tell anyone about this, we will be free from the oath you made us swear."

21Rahab answered, "I agree to this." So she sent them away, and they left. Then she tied the red rope in the window.

22The men left and went into the hills where they stayed for three days. The king's men looked for them all along the road, but after three days, they returned to the city without finding them. 23Then the two men started back. They left the hills and crossed the river and came to Joshua son of Nun and told him everything that had happened to them. 24They said, "The LORD surely has given us all of the land. All the people in that land are terribly afraid of us."

CROSSING THE JORDAN

3 Early the next morning Joshua and all the Israelites left Acacia. They traveled to the Jordan River and camped there before crossing it. 2After three days the officers went through the camp 3and gave orders to the people: "When you see the priests and Levites carrying the Ark of the Agreement with the LORD your God, leave where you are and follow it. 4That way you will know which way to go since you have never been here before. But do not follow too closely. Stay about a thousand yards behind the Ark."

5Then Joshua told the people, "Make yourselves holy, because tomorrow the LORD will do amazing things among you."

6Joshua said to the priests, "Take the Ark of the Agreement and go ahead of the people." So the priests lifted the Ark and carried it ahead of the people.

7Then the LORD said to Joshua, "Today I will begin to make you great in the opinion of all the Israelites so the people will know I am with you just as I was with Moses. 8Tell the priests who carry the Ark of the Agreement to go to the edge of the Jordan River and stand in the water."

9Then Joshua said to the Israelites, "Come here and listen to the words of the LORD your God. 10Here is proof that the living God is with you and that he will force out the Canaanites, Hittites, Hivites, Perizzites, Girgashites, Amorites, and Jebusites. 11The Ark of the Agreement with the Lord of the whole world will go ahead of you into the Jordan River. 12Now choose twelve men from among you, one from each of the twelve tribes of Israel. 13The priests will carry the Ark of the LORD, the Master of the whole world, into the Jordan ahead of you. When they step into the water, it will stop. The river will stop flowing and will stand up in a heap."

14So the people left the place where they had camped, and they followed the priests who carried the Ark of the Agreement across the Jordan River. 15During harvest the Jordan overflows its banks. When the priests carrying the Ark came to the edge of the river and stepped into the water, 16the water upstream stopped flowing. It stood up in a heap a great distance away at Adam, a town near Zarethan. The water flowing down to the Sea of Arabah (the Dead Sea) was completely cut off. So the people crossed the river near Jericho. 17The priests carried the Ark of the Agreement with the LORD to the middle of the river and stood there on dry ground. They waited there while all the people of Israel walked across the Jordan River on dry land.

ROCKS TO REMIND THE PEOPLE

4 After all the people had finished crossing the Jordan, the LORD said to Joshua, 2"Choose twelve men from among the people, one from each tribe. 3Tell them to get twelve rocks from the middle of the river, from where the priests stood. Carry the rocks and put them down where you stay tonight."

4So Joshua chose one man from each

tribe. Then he called the twelve men together ⁵and said to them, "Go out into the river where the Ark of the LORD your God is. Each of you bring back one rock, one for each tribe of Israel, and carry it on your shoulder. ⁶They will be a sign among you. In the future your children will ask you, 'What do these rocks mean?' ⁷Tell them the water stopped flowing in the Jordan when the Ark of the Agreement with the LORD crossed the river. These rocks will always remind the Israelites of this."

⁸So the Israelites obeyed Joshua and carried twelve rocks from the middle of the Jordan River, one rock for each of the twelve tribes of Israel, just as the LORD had commanded Joshua. They carried the rocks with them and put them down where they made their camp. ⁹Joshua also put twelve rocks in the middle of the Jordan River where the priests had stood while carrying the Ark of the Agreement. These rocks are still there today.

A FAMILY CHANGED

grace and truth

FAMILY

JOSHUA 3:1–17

By Jimmy Evans

God commanded Moses to build two pieces of furniture that when put together would be a physical representation of God to Israel. The first piece was the Ark. The Ark was a trunklike receptacle that Moses was instructed to fill with the Ten Commandments, his brother Aaron's rod that budded, and a pot of manna. Therefore, when completed, the Ark and its contents were a powerful representation of the unchangeable standards of God's perfection.

Another piece of furniture was built to cover the Ark and its priceless contents. Unlike the plain, rectangular Ark below, the piece of furniture built to cover the Ark was magnificent. It was called the "mercy seat." Once a year, an unblemished lamb was sacrificed, and its blood was poured on the mercy seat for the forgiveness of sins for the tribes of Israel.

The Ark and the mercy seat together were called the "Ark of the Agreement." God was communicating to Israel through the Ark about his nature and the way he related to man. The point was this: God is both grace and truth.

The Ark of the Agreement symbolized the coming sacrifice of Christ. Jesus is full of grace and truth, so we are drawn to him, and his influence is redemptive and powerful. The family full of grace and truth will also be a place where family members are drawn. The function of a balanced family will be redemptive and powerful. It will be a place of lasting joy and loving progress.

reflect: What does the Ark of the Agreement communicate to you about God?
Go to **1 Corinthians 15:34.**

¹⁰The priests carrying the Ark continued standing in the middle of the river until everything was done that the LORD had commanded Joshua to tell the people, just as Moses had told Joshua. The people hurried across the river. ¹¹After they finished crossing the river, the priests carried the Ark of the LORD to the other side as the people watched. ¹²The men from the tribes of Reuben, Gad, and East Manasseh obeyed what Moses had told them. They were dressed for war, and they crossed the river ahead of the other people. ¹³About forty thousand soldiers prepared for war passed before the LORD as they marched across the river, going toward the plains of Jericho.

¹⁴That day the LORD made Joshua great in the opinion of all the Israelites. They respected Joshua all his life, just as they had respected Moses.

¹⁵Then the LORD said to Joshua, ¹⁶"Command the priests to bring the Ark of the Agreement out of the river."

¹⁷So Joshua commanded the priests, "Come up out of the Jordan."

¹⁸Then the priests carried the Ark of the Agreement with the LORD out of the river. As soon as their feet touched dry land, the water began flowing again. The river again overflowed its banks, just as it had before they crossed.

¹⁹The people crossed the Jordan on the tenth day of the first month and camped at Gilgal, east of Jericho. ²⁰They carried with them the twelve rocks taken from the Jordan, and Joshua set them up at Gilgal. ²¹Then he spoke to the Israelites: "In the future your children will ask you, 'What do these rocks mean?' ²²Tell them, 'Israel crossed the Jordan River on dry land. ²³The LORD your God caused the water to stop flowing until you finished crossing it, just as the LORD did to the Red Sea. He stopped the water until we crossed it. ²⁴The LORD did this so all people would know he has great power and so you would always respect the LORD your God.'"

5 All the kings of the Amorites west of the Jordan and the Canaanite kings living by the Mediterranean Sea heard that the LORD dried up the Jordan River until the Israelites had crossed it. After that they were scared and too afraid to face the Israelites.

THE ISRAELITES ARE CIRCUMCISED

²At that time the LORD said to Joshua, "Make knives from flint stones and circumcise the Israelites." ³So Joshua made knives from flint stones and circumcised the Israelites at Gibeath Haaraloth.

⁴This is why Joshua circumcised the men: After the Israelites left Egypt, all the men old enough to serve in the army died in the desert on the way out of Egypt. ⁵The men who had come out of Egypt had been circumcised, but none of those who were born in the desert on the trip from Egypt had been circumcised. ⁶The Israelites had moved about in the desert for forty years. During that time all the fighting men who had left Egypt had died because they had not obeyed the LORD. So the LORD swore they would not see the land he had promised their ancestors to give them, a fertile land. ⁷Their sons took their places. But none of the sons born on the trip from Egypt had been circumcised, so Joshua circumcised them. ⁸After all the Israelites had been circumcised, they stayed in camp until they were healed.

⁹Then the LORD said to Joshua, "As slaves in Egypt you were ashamed, but today I have removed that shame." So Joshua named that place Gilgal, which it is still named today.

¹⁰The people of Israel were camped at Gilgal on the plains of Jericho. It was there, on the evening of the fourteenth day of the month, they celebrated the Passover Feast. ¹¹The day after the Passover, the people ate food grown on that land: bread made without yeast and roasted grain. ¹²The day they ate this food, the manna stopped coming. The Israelites no longer got the manna from heaven. They ate the food grown in the land of Canaan that year.

¹³Joshua was near Jericho when he looked up and saw a man standing in front of him with a sword in his hand. Joshua went to him and asked, "Are you a friend or an enemy?"

¹⁴The man answered, "I am neither. I have come as the commander of the LORD's army."

Then Joshua bowed facedown on the ground and asked, "Does my master have a command for me, his servant?"

¹⁵The commander of the LORD's army answered, "Take off your sandals, because

the place where you are standing is holy." So Joshua did.

THE FALL OF JERICHO

6 The people of Jericho were afraid because the Israelites were near. They closed the city gates and guarded them. No one went into the city, and no one came out.

²Then the LORD said to Joshua, "Look, I have given you Jericho, its king, and all its fighting men. ³March around the city with your army once a day for six days. ⁴Have seven priests carry trumpets made from horns of male sheep and have them march in front of the Ark. On the seventh day march around the city seven times and have the priests blow the trumpets as they march. ⁵They will make one long blast on the trumpets. When you hear that sound, have all the people give a loud shout. Then the walls of the city will fall so the people can go straight into the city."

⁶So Joshua son of Nun called the priests together and said to them, "Carry the Ark of the Agreement. Tell seven priests to carry trumpets and march in front of it." ⁷Then Joshua ordered the people, "Now go! March around the city. The soldiers with weapons should march in front of the Ark of the Agreement with the LORD."

⁸When Joshua finished speaking to the people, the seven priests began marching before the LORD. They carried the seven trumpets and blew them as they marched. The priests carrying the Ark of the Agreement with the LORD followed them. ⁹Soldiers with weapons marched in front of the priests, and armed men walked behind the Ark. The priests were blowing their trumpets. ¹⁰But Joshua had told the people not to give a war cry. He said, "Don't shout. Don't say a word until the day I tell you. Then shout." ¹¹So Joshua had the Ark of the LORD carried around the city one time. Then they went back to camp for the night.

¹²Early the next morning Joshua got up, and the priests carried the Ark of the LORD again. ¹³The seven priests carried the seven trumpets and marched in front of the Ark of the LORD, blowing their trumpets. Soldiers with weapons marched in front of them, and other soldiers walked behind the Ark of the LORD. All this time the priests were blowing their trumpets. ¹⁴So on the second day they marched around the city one time and then went back to camp. They did this every day for six days.

¹⁵On the seventh day they got up at dawn and marched around the city, just as they had on the days before. But on that day they marched around the city seven times. ¹⁶The seventh time around the priests blew their trumpets. Then Joshua gave the command: "Now, shout! The LORD has given you this city! ¹⁷The city and everything in it are to be destroyed as an offering to the LORD. Only Rahab the prostitute and everyone in her house should remain alive. They must not be killed, because Rahab hid the two spies we sent out. ¹⁸Don't take any of the things that are to be destroyed as an offering to the LORD. If you take them and bring them into our camp, you yourselves will be destroyed, and you will bring trouble to all of Israel. ¹⁹All the silver and gold and things made from bronze and iron belong to the LORD and must be saved for him."

²⁰When the priests blew the trumpets, the people shouted. At the sound of the trumpets and the people's shout, the walls fell, and everyone ran straight into the city. So the Israelites defeated that city. ²¹They completely destroyed with the sword every living thing in the city—men and women, young and old, cattle, sheep, and donkeys.

²²Joshua said to the two men who had spied out the land, "Go into the prostitute's house. Bring her out and bring out those who are with her, because of the promise you made to her." ²³So the two men went into the house and brought out Rahab, her father, mother, brothers, and all those with her. They put all of her family in a safe place outside the camp of Israel.

²⁴Then Israel burned the whole city and everything in it, but they did not burn the things made from silver, gold, bronze, and iron. These were saved for the LORD. ²⁵Joshua saved Rahab the prostitute, her family, and all who were with her, because Rahab had helped the men he had sent to spy out Jericho. Rahab still lives among the Israelites today.

²⁶Then Joshua made this oath:

"Anyone who tries to rebuild this city of
    Jericho

will be cursed by the LORD.
The one who lays the foundation of this
city
will lose his oldest son,
and the one who sets up the gates
will lose his youngest son."

²⁷So the LORD was with Joshua, and Joshua became famous through all the land.

THE SIN OF ACHAN

7 But the Israelites did not obey the LORD. There was a man from the tribe of Judah named Achan. (He was the son of Carmi and grandson of Zabdi, who was the son of Zerah.) Because Achan kept some of the things that were to be given to the LORD, the LORD became very angry at the Israelites.

²Joshua sent some men from Jericho to Ai, which was near Beth Aven, east of Bethel. He told them, "Go to Ai and spy out the area." So the men went to spy on Ai.

³Later they came back to Joshua and said, "There are only a few people in Ai, so we will not need all our people to defeat them. Send only two or three thousand men to fight. There is no need to send all of our people." ⁴So about three thousand men went up to Ai, but the people of Ai beat them badly. ⁵The people of Ai killed about thirty-six Israelites and then chased the rest from the city gate all the way down to the canyon, killing them as they went down the hill. When the Israelites saw this, they lost their courage.

⁶Then Joshua tore his clothes in sorrow. He bowed facedown on the ground before the Ark of the LORD and stayed there until evening. The leaders of Israel did the same thing. They also threw dirt on their heads to show their sorrow. ⁷Then Joshua said, "Lord GOD, you brought our people across the Jordan River. Why did you bring us this far and then let the Amorites destroy us? We would have been happy to stay on the other side of the Jordan. ⁸Lord, there is nothing I can say now. Israel has been beaten by the enemy. ⁹The Canaanites and all the other people in this country will hear about this and will surround and kill us all! Then what will you do for your own great name?"

¹⁰The LORD said to Joshua, "Stand up! Why are you down on your face? ¹¹The Israelites have sinned; they have broken the agreement I commanded them to obey.

They took some of the things I commanded them to destroy. They have stolen and lied and have taken those things for themselves. ¹²That is why the Israelites cannot face their enemies. They turn away from the fight and run, because I have commanded that they be destroyed. I will not help you anymore unless you destroy everything as I commanded you.

¹³"Now go! Make the people holy. Tell them, 'Set yourselves apart to the LORD for tomorrow. The LORD, the God of Israel, says some of you are keeping things he commanded you to destroy. You will never defeat your enemies until you throw away those things.

¹⁴"'Tomorrow morning you must be present with your tribes. The LORD will choose one tribe to stand alone before him. Then the LORD will choose one family group from that tribe to stand before him. Then the LORD will choose one family from that family group to stand before him, person by person. ¹⁵The one who is keeping what should have been destroyed will himself be destroyed by fire. Everything he owns will be destroyed with him. He has broken the agreement with the LORD and has done a disgraceful thing among the people of Israel!'"

¹⁶Early the next morning Joshua led all of Israel to present themselves in their tribes, and the LORD chose the tribe of Judah. ¹⁷So the family groups of Judah presented themselves, and the LORD then chose the family group of Zerah. When all the families of Zerah presented themselves, the family of Zabdi was chosen. ¹⁸And Joshua told all the men in that family to present themselves. The LORD chose Achan son of Carmi. (Carmi was the son of Zabdi, who was the son of Zerah.)

¹⁹Then Joshua said to Achan, "My son, tell the truth. Confess to the LORD, the God of Israel. Tell me what you did, and don't try to hide anything from me."

²⁰Achan answered, "It is true! I have sinned against the LORD, the God of Israel. This is what I did: ²¹Among the things I saw was a beautiful coat from Babylonia and about five pounds of silver and more than one and one-fourth pounds of gold. I wanted these things very much for myself, so I took them. You will find them buried in

the ground under my tent, with the silver underneath."

²²So Joshua sent men who ran to the tent and found the things hidden there, with the silver. ²³The men brought them out of the tent, took them to Joshua and all the Israelites, and spread them out on the ground before the LORD. ²⁴Then Joshua and all the people led Achan son of Zerah to the Valley of Trouble. They also took the silver, the coat, the gold, Achan's sons, daughters, cattle, donkeys, sheep, tent, and everything he owned. ²⁵Joshua said, "I don't know why you caused so much trouble for us, but now the LORD will bring trouble to you." Then all the people threw stones at Achan and his family until they died. Then the people burned them. ²⁶They piled rocks over Achan's body, and they are still there today. That is why it is called the Valley of Trouble. After this the LORD was no longer angry.

AI IS DESTROYED

8 Then the LORD said to Joshua, "Don't be afraid or give up. Lead all your fighting men to Ai. I will help you defeat the king of Ai, his people, his city, and his land. ²You will do to Ai and its king what you did to Jericho and its king. Only this time you may take all the wealth and keep it for yourselves. Now tell some of your soldiers to set up an ambush behind the city."

³So Joshua led his whole army toward Ai. Then he chose thirty thousand of his best fighting men and sent them out at night. ⁴Joshua gave them these orders: "Listen carefully. You must set up an ambush behind the city. Don't go far from it, but continue to watch and be ready. ⁵I and the men who are with me will march toward the city, and the men in the city will come out to fight us, just as they did before. Then we will turn and run away from them. ⁶They will chase us away from the city, thinking we are running away from them as we did before. When we run away, ⁷come out from your ambush and take the city. The LORD your God will give you the power to win. ⁸After you take the city, burn it. See to it! You have your orders."

⁹Then Joshua sent them to wait in ambush between Bethel and Ai, to the west of Ai. But Joshua stayed the night with his people.

¹⁰Early the next morning Joshua gathered his men together. He and the older leaders of Israel led them up to Ai. ¹¹All of the soldiers who were with Joshua marched up to Ai and stopped in front of the city and made camp north of it. There was a valley between them and the city. ¹²Then Joshua chose about five thousand men and set them in ambush in the area west of the city between Bethel and Ai. ¹³So the people took their positions; the main camp was north of the city, and the other men were hiding to the west. That night Joshua went down into the valley.

¹⁴Now when the king of Ai saw the army of Israel, he and his people got up early the next morning and hurried out to fight them. They went out to a place east of the city, but the king did not know soldiers were waiting in ambush behind the city. ¹⁵Joshua and all the men of Israel let the army of Ai push them back. Then they ran toward the desert. ¹⁶The men in Ai were called to chase Joshua and his men, so they left the city and went after them. ¹⁷All the men of Ai and Bethel chased the army of Israel. The city was left open; not a man stayed to protect it.

¹⁸Then the LORD said to Joshua, "Hold your spear toward Ai, because I will give you that city." So Joshua held his spear toward the city of Ai. ¹⁹When the Israelites who were in ambush saw this, they quickly came out of their hiding place and hurried toward the city. They entered the city, took control of it, and quickly set it on fire.

²⁰When the men of Ai looked back, they saw smoke rising from their city. At the same time the Israelites stopped running and turned against the men of Ai, who could not escape in any direction. ²¹When Joshua and all his men saw that the army had taken control of the city and saw the smoke rising from it, they stopped running and turned to fight the men of Ai. ²²The men who were in ambush also came out of the city to help with the fight. So the men of Ai were caught between the armies of Israel. None of the enemy escaped. The Israelites fought until not one of the men of Ai was left alive, except ²³the king of Ai, and they brought him to Joshua.

A REVIEW OF THE FIGHTING

²⁴During the fighting the army of Israel chased the men of Ai into the fields and des-

ert and killed all of them. Then they went back to Ai and killed everyone there. 25All the people of Ai died that day, twelve thousand men and women. 26Joshua had held his spear toward Ai, as a sign to destroy the city, and did not draw it back until all the people of Ai were destroyed. 27The people of Israel kept for themselves the animals and the other things the people of Ai had owned, as the LORD had commanded Joshua to do.

28Then Joshua burned the city of Ai and made it a pile of ruins. And it is still like that today. 29Joshua hanged the king of Ai on a tree and left him there until evening. At sunset Joshua told his men to take the king's body down from the tree and to throw it down at the city gate. Then they covered it with a pile of rocks, which is still there today.

30Joshua built an altar for the LORD, the God of Israel, on Mount Ebal, as 31Moses, the LORD's servant, had commanded. Joshua built the altar as it was explained in the Book of the Teachings of Moses. It was made from uncut stones; no tool was ever used on them. On that altar the Israelites offered burnt offerings to the LORD and fellowship offerings. 32There Joshua wrote the teachings of Moses on stones for all the people of Israel to see. 33The elders, officers, judges, and all the Israelites were there; Israelites and non-Israelites were all standing around the Ark of the Agreement with the LORD in front of the priests, the Levites who had carried the Ark. Half of the people stood in front of Mount Ebal, and half stood in front of Mount Gerizim. This was the way the LORD's servant Moses had earlier commanded the people to be blessed.

34Then Joshua read all the words of the teachings, the blessings and the curses, exactly as they were written in the Book of the Teachings. 35All the Israelites were gathered together—men, women, and children—along with the non-Israelites who lived among them. Joshua read every command that Moses had given.

THE GIBEONITE TRICKERY

9 All the kings west of the Jordan River heard about these things: the kings of the Hittites, Amorites, Canaanites, Perizzites, Hivites, and Jebusites. They lived in the mountains and on the western hills and along the whole Mediterranean Sea coast. 2So all these kings gathered to fight Joshua and the Israelites.

3When the people of Gibeon heard how Joshua had defeated Jericho and Ai, 4they decided to trick the Israelites. They gathered old sacks and old leather wine bags that were cracked and mended, and they put them on the backs of their donkeys. 5They put old sandals on their feet and wore old clothes, and they took some dry, moldy bread. 6Then they went to Joshua in the camp near Gilgal.

The men said to Joshua and the Israelites, "We have traveled from a faraway country. Make a peace agreement with us."

7The Israelites said to these Hivites, "Maybe you live near us. How can we make a peace agreement with you?"

8The Hivites said to Joshua, "We are your servants."

But Joshua asked, "Who are you? Where do you come from?"

9The men answered, "We are your servants who have come from a far country, because we heard of the fame of the LORD your God. We heard about what he has done and everything he did in Egypt. 10We heard that he defeated the two kings of the Amorites from the east side of the Jordan River—Sihon king of Heshbon and Og king of Bashan who ruled in Ashtaroth. 11So our elders and our people said to us, 'Take food for your journey and go and meet the Israelites. Tell them, "We are your servants. Make a peace agreement with us." '

12"Look at our bread. On the day we left home to come to you it was warm and fresh, but now it is dry and moldy. 13Look at our leather wine bags. They were new and filled with wine, but now they are cracked and old. Our clothes and sandals are worn out from the long journey."

14The men of Israel tasted the bread, but they did not ask the LORD what to do. 15So Joshua agreed to make peace with the Gibeonites and to let them live. And the leaders of the Israelites swore an oath to keep the agreement.

16Three days after they had made the agreement, the Israelites learned that the Gibeonites lived nearby. 17So the Israelites went to where they lived and on the third day came to their cities: Gibeon, Kephirah,

Beeroth, and Kiriath Jearim. ¹⁸But the Israelites did not attack those cities, because they had made a promise to them before the LORD, the God of Israel.

All the Israelites grumbled against the leaders. ¹⁹But the leaders answered, "We have given our promise before the LORD, the God of Israel, so we cannot attack them now. ²⁰This is what we must do. We must let them live. Otherwise, God's anger will be against us for breaking the oath we swore to them. ²¹So let them live, but they will cut wood and carry water for our people." So the leaders kept their promise to them.

²²Joshua called for the Gibeonites and asked, "Why did you lie to us? Your land was near our camp, but you told us you were from a far country. ²³Now, you will be placed under a curse to be our slaves. You will have to cut wood and carry water for the house of my God."

²⁴The Gibeonites answered Joshua, "We lied to you because we were afraid you would kill us. We heard that the LORD your God commanded his servant Moses to give you all of this land and to kill all the people who lived in it. That is why we did this. ²⁵Now you can decide what to do with us, whatever you think is right."

²⁶So Joshua saved their lives by not allowing the Israelites to kill them, ²⁷but he made the Gibeonites slaves. They cut wood and carried water for the Israelites, and they did it for the altar of the LORD—wherever he chose it to be. They are still doing this today.

THE SUN STANDS STILL

10 At this time Adoni-Zedek king of Jerusalem heard that Joshua had defeated Ai and completely destroyed it, as he had also done to Jericho and its king. The king also learned that the Gibeonites had made a peace agreement with Israel and that they lived nearby. ²Adoni-Zedek and his people were very afraid because of this. Gibeon was not a little town like Ai; it was a large city, as big as a city that had a king, and all its men were good fighters. ³So Adoni-Zedek king of Jerusalem sent a message to Hoham king of Hebron, Piram king of Jarmuth, Japhia king of Lachish, and Debir king of Eglon. He begged them, ⁴"Come with me and help me attack Gibeon, which has

made a peace agreement with Joshua and the Israelites."

⁵Then these five Amorite kings—the kings of Jerusalem, Hebron, Jarmuth, Lachish, and Eglon—gathered their armies, went to Gibeon, surrounded it, and attacked it.

⁶The Gibeonites sent this message to Joshua in his camp at Gilgal: "Don't let us, your servants, be destroyed. Come quickly and help us! Save us! All the Amorite kings from the mountains have joined their armies and are fighting against us."

⁷So Joshua marched out of Gilgal with his whole army, including his best fighting men. ⁸The LORD said to Joshua, "Don't be afraid of those armies, because I will hand them over to you. None of them will be able to stand against you."

⁹Joshua and his army marched all night from Gilgal for a surprise attack. ¹⁰The LORD confused those armies when Israel attacked, so Israel defeated them in a great victory at Gibeon. They chased them along the road going up to Beth Horon and killed men all the way to Azekah and Makkedah. ¹¹As they chased the enemy down the Beth Horon Pass to Azekah, the LORD threw large hailstones on them from the sky and killed them. More people were killed by the hailstones than by the Israelites' swords.

¹²On the day that the LORD gave up the Amorites to the Israelites, Joshua stood before all the people of Israel and said to the LORD:

"Sun, stand still over Gibeon.
    Moon, stand still over the Valley of
        Aijalon."

¹³ So the sun stood still,
    and the moon stopped
        until the people defeated their enemies.
These words are written in the Book of Jashar.

The sun stopped in the middle of the sky and waited to go down for a full day. ¹⁴That has never happened at any time before that day or since. That was the day the LORD listened to a human being. Truly the LORD was fighting for Israel!

¹⁵After this, Joshua and his army went back to the camp at Gilgal.

¹⁶During the fight the five kings ran away and hid in a cave near Makkedah, ¹⁷but someone found them hiding in the cave at Makke-

dah and told Joshua. ¹⁸So he said, "Cover the opening of the cave with large rocks. Put some men there to guard it, ¹⁹but don't stay there yourselves. Continue chasing the enemy and attacking them from behind. Don't let them get to their cities, because the LORD your God will hand them over to you."

²⁰So Joshua and the Israelites killed the enemy, but a few were able to get back to their strong, walled cities. ²¹After the fighting, Joshua's men came back safely to him at Makkedah. No one was brave enough to say a word against the Israelites.

²²Joshua said, "Move the rocks that are covering the opening of the cave and bring those five kings out to me." ²³So Joshua's men brought the five kings out of the cave— the kings of Jerusalem, Hebron, Jarmuth, Lachish, and Eglon. ²⁴When they brought the five kings out to Joshua, he called for all his men. He said to the commanders of his army, "Come here! Put your feet on the necks of these kings." So they came close and put their feet on their necks.

²⁵Joshua said to his men, "Be strong and brave! Don't be afraid, because I will show you what the LORD will do to the enemies you will fight in the future." ²⁶Then Joshua killed the five kings and hung their bodies on five trees, where he left them until evening.

²⁷At sunset Joshua told his men to take the bodies down from the trees. Then they threw them into the same cave where they had been hiding and covered the opening of the cave with large rocks, which are still there today.

²⁸That day Joshua defeated Makkedah. He killed the king and completely destroyed all the people in that city as an offering to the LORD; no one was left alive. He did the same thing to the king of Makkedah that he had done to the king of Jericho.

DEFEATING SOUTHERN CITIES

²⁹Joshua and all the Israelites traveled from Makkedah to Libnah and attacked it. ³⁰The LORD handed over the city and its king. They killed every person in the city; no one was left alive. And they did the same thing to that king that they had done to the king of Jericho.

³¹Then Joshua and all the Israelites left Libnah and went to Lachish, which they surrounded and attacked. ³²The LORD handed over Lachish on the second day. The Israelites killed everyone in that city just as they had done to Libnah. ³³During this same time Horam king of Gezer came to help Lachish, but Joshua also defeated him and his army; no one was left alive.

³⁴Then Joshua and all the Israelites went from Lachish to Eglon. They surrounded Eglon, attacked it, and ³⁵captured it the same day. They killed all its people and completely destroyed everything in it as an offering to the LORD, just as they had done to Lachish.

³⁶Then Joshua and the Israelites went from Eglon to Hebron and attacked it, ³⁷capturing it and all the little towns near it. The Israelites killed everyone in Hebron; no one was left alive there. Just as they had done to Eglon, they completely destroyed the city and all its people as an offering to the LORD.

³⁸Then Joshua and the Israelites went back to Debir and attacked it. ³⁹They captured that city, its king, and all the little towns near it, completely destroying everyone in Debir as an offering to the LORD; no one was left alive there. Israel did to Debir and its king just as they had done to Libnah and its king, just as they had done to Hebron.

⁴⁰So Joshua defeated all the kings of the cities of these areas: the mountains, southern Canaan, the western hills, and the slopes. The LORD, the God of Israel, had told Joshua to completely destroy all the people as an offering to the LORD, so he left no one alive in those places. ⁴¹Joshua captured all the cities from Kadesh Barnea to Gaza, and from Goshen to Gibeon. ⁴²He captured all these cities and their kings on one trip, because the LORD, the God of Israel, was fighting for Israel.

⁴³Then Joshua and all the Israelites returned to their camp at Gilgal.

DEFEATING NORTHERN KINGS

11 When Jabin king of Hazor heard about all that had happened, he sent messages to Jobab king of Madon, to the king of Shimron, and to the king of Acshaph. ²He sent messages to the kings in the northern mountains and also to the kings in the Jordan Valley south of Lake Galilee and in the western hills. He sent a message to the king of Naphoth Dor in the west ³and to the kings of the Canaanites in the east and in the west.

He sent messages to the Amorites, Hittites, Perizzites, and Jebusites in the mountains. Jabin also sent one to the Hivites, who lived below Mount Hermon in the area of Mizpah. 4So the armies of all these kings came together with their horses and chariots. There were as many soldiers as grains of sand on the seashore.

5All of these kings met together at the waters of Merom, joined their armies together into one camp, and made plans to fight against the Israelites.

6Then the LORD said to Joshua, "Don't be afraid of them, because at this time tomorrow I will give them to you. You will cripple their horses and burn all their chariots."

7So Joshua and his whole army surprised the enemy by attacking them at the waters of Merom. 8The LORD handed them over to Israel. They chased them to Greater Sidon, Misrephoth Maim, and the Valley of Mizpah in the east. Israel fought until none of the enemy was left alive. 9Joshua did what the LORD said to do; he crippled their horses and burned their chariots.

10Then Joshua went back and captured the city of Hazor and killed its king. (Hazor had been the leader of all the kingdoms that fought against Israel.) 11Israel killed everyone in Hazor, completely destroying them; no one was left alive. Then they burned Hazor itself.

12Joshua captured all of these cities, killed all of their kings, and completely destroyed everything in these cities. He did this just as Moses, the servant of the LORD, had commanded. 13But the Israelites did not burn any cities that were built on their mounds, except Hazor; only that city was burned by Joshua. 14The people of Israel kept for themselves everything they found in the cities, including all the animals. But they killed all the people there; they left no one alive. 15Long ago the LORD had commanded his servant Moses to do this, and then Moses had commanded Joshua to do it. Joshua did everything the LORD had commanded Moses.

16So Joshua defeated all the people in the land. He had control of the mountains and the area of southern Canaan, all the areas of Goshen, the western hills, and the Jordan Valley. He controlled the mountains of Israel and all the hills near them. 17Joshua con-trolled all the land from Mount Halak near Edom to Baal Gad in the Valley of Lebanon, below Mount Hermon. Joshua also captured all the kings in the land and killed them. 18He fought against them for many years. 19The people of only one city in all the land had made a peace agreement with Israel—the Hivites living in Gibeon. All the other cities were defeated in war. 20The LORD made those people stubborn so they would fight against Israel and he could completely destroy them without mercy. This is what the LORD had commanded Moses to do.

21Now Joshua fought the Anakites who lived in the mountains of Hebron, Debir, Anab, Judah, and Israel, and he completely destroyed them and their towns. 22There were no Anakites left living in the land of the Israelites and only a few were left in Gaza, Gath, and Ashdod. 23Joshua took control of all the land of Israel as the LORD had told Moses to do long ago. He gave the land to Israel, because he had promised it to them. Then Joshua divided the land among the tribes of Israel, and there was peace in the land.

KINGS DEFEATED BY ISRAEL

12 The Israelites took control of the land east of the Jordan River from the Arnon Ravine to Mount Hermon and all the land along the eastern side of the Jordan Valley. These lands belonged to the kings whom the Israelites defeated.

2Sihon king of the Amorites lived in the city of Heshbon and ruled the land from Aroer at the Arnon Ravine to the Jabbok River. His land started in the middle of the ravine, which was their border with the Ammonites. Sihon ruled over half the land of Gilead 3and over the eastern side of the Jordan Valley from Lake Galilee to the Dead Sea. And he ruled from Beth Jeshimoth south to the slopes of Pisgah.

4Og king of Bashan was one of the last of the Rephaites. He ruled the land in Ashtaroth and Edrei. 5He ruled over Mount Hermon, Salecah, and all the area of Bashan up to where the people of Geshur and Maacah lived. Og also ruled half the land of Gilead up to the border of Sihon king of Heshbon.

6The LORD's servant Moses and the Israelites defeated all these kings, and Moses gave that land to the tribes of Reuben and Gad and to East Manasseh as their own.

7Joshua and the Israelites also defeated kings in the land west of the Jordan River. He gave the people the land and divided it among the twelve tribes to be their own. It was between Baal Gad in the Valley of Lebanon and Mount Halak near Edom. 8This included the mountains, the western hills, the Jordan Valley, the slopes, the desert, and southern Canaan. This was the land where the Hittites, Amorites, Canaanites, Perizzites, Hivites, and Jebusites had lived. The Israelites defeated the king of each of the following cities: 9Jericho, Ai (near Bethel), 10Jerusalem, Hebron, 11Jarmuth, Lachish, 12Eglon, Gezer, 13Debir, Geder, 14Hormah, Arad, 15Libnah, Adullam, 16Makkedah, Bethel, 17Tappuah, Hepher, 18Aphek, Lasharon, 19Madon, Hazor, 20Shimron Meron, Acshaph, 21Taanach, Megiddo, 22Kedesh, Jokneam in Carmel, 23Dor (in Naphoth Dor), Goyim in Gilgal, and 24Tirzah.

The total number of kings was thirty-one.

LAND STILL TO BE TAKEN

13 When Joshua was very old, the LORD said to him, "Joshua, you have grown old, but there is still much land for you to take. 2This is what is left: the regions of Geshur and of the Philistines; 3the area from the Shihor River at the border of Egypt to Ekron in the north, which belongs to the Canaanites; the five Philistine leaders at Gaza, Ashdod, Ashkelon, Gath, and Ekron; the Avites, 4who live south of the Canaanite land; 5the Gebalites, and the area of Lebanon east of Baal Gad below Mount Hermon to Lebo Hamath.

6"The Sidonians are living in the hill country from Lebanon to Misrephoth Maim, but I will force all of them out ahead of the Israelites. Be sure to remember this land when you divide the land among the Israelites, as I told you.

7"Now divide the land among the nine tribes and West Manasseh."

DIVIDING THE LAND

8East Manasseh and the tribes of Reuben and Gad had received their land. The LORD's servant Moses had given them the land east of the Jordan River. 9Their land started at Aroer at the Arnon Ravine and continued to the town in the middle of the ravine, and it included the whole plain from Medeba to Dibon. 10All the towns ruled by Sihon king of the Amorites, who ruled in the city of Heshbon, were in that land. The land continued to the area where the Ammonites lived. 11Gilead was also there, as well as the area where the people of Geshur and Maacah lived, and all of Mount Hermon and Bashan as far as Salecah. 12All the kingdom of Og king of Bashan was in the land. Og was one of the last of the Rephaites, and in the past he ruled in Ashtaroth and Edrei. Moses had defeated them and had taken their land. 13Because the Israelites did not force out the people of Geshur and Maacah, they still live among the Israelites today.

14The tribe of Levi was the only one that did not get any land. Instead, they were given all the burned sacrifices made to the LORD, the God of Israel, as he had promised them.

15Moses had given each family group from the tribe of Reuben some land: 16Theirs was the land from Aroer near the Arnon Ravine to the town of Medeba, including the whole plain and the town in the middle of the ravine; 17Heshbon and all the towns on the plain: Dibon, Bamoth Baal, and Beth Baal Meon, 18Jahaz, Kedemoth, Mephaath, 19Kiriathaim, Sibmah, Zereth Shahar on the hill in the valley, 20Beth Peor, the hills of Pisgah, and Beth Jeshimoth. 21So that land included all the towns on the plain and all the area that Sihon king of the Amorites had ruled from the town of Heshbon. Moses had defeated him along with the leaders of the Midianites, including Evi, Rekem, Zur, Hur, and Reba. All these leaders fought together with Sihon and lived in that country. 22The Israelites killed many people during the fighting, including Balaam of Beor, who tried to use magic to tell the future. 23The land given to Reuben stopped at the shore of the Jordan River. So the land given to the family groups of Reuben included all these towns and their villages that were listed.

24This is the land Moses gave to the tribe of Gad, to all its family groups: 25the land of Jazer and all the towns of Gilead; half the land of the Ammonites that went as far as Aroer near Rabbah; 26the area from Heshbon to Ramath Mizpah and Betonim; the area from Mahanaim to the land of Debir;

27in the valley, Beth Haram, Beth Nimrah, Succoth, and Zaphon, the other land Sihon king of Heshbon had ruled east of the Jordan River and continuing to the end of Lake Galilee. 28All this land went to the family groups of Gad, including all these towns and their villages.

29This is the land Moses had given to East Manasseh. Half of all the family groups in the tribe of Manasseh were given this land: 30The land started at Mahanaim and included all of Bashan and the land ruled by Og king of Bashan; all the towns of Jair in Bashan, sixty cities in all; 31half of Gilead, Ashtaroth, and Edrei, the cities where Og king of Bashan had ruled. All this went to the family of Makir son of Manasseh, and half of all his sons were given this land.

32Moses had given this land to these tribes on the plains of Moab across the Jordan River east of Jericho. 33But Moses had given no land to the tribe of Levi because the LORD, the God of Israel, promised that he himself would be the gift for the Levites.

14 Eleazar the priest, Joshua son of Nun, and the leaders of all the tribes of Israel decided what land to give to the people in the land of Canaan. 2The LORD had commanded Moses long ago how he wanted the people to choose their land. The people of the nine-and-a-half tribes threw lots to decide which land they would receive. 3Moses had already given the two-and-a-half tribes their land east of the Jordan River. But the tribe of Levi was not given any land like the others. 4The sons of Joseph had divided into two tribes—Manasseh and Ephraim. The tribe of Levi was not given any land. It was given only some towns in which to live and pastures for its animals. 5The LORD had told Moses how to give the land to the tribes of Israel, and the Israelites divided the land.

CALEB'S LAND

6One day some men from the tribe of Judah went to Joshua at Gilgal. Among them was Caleb son of Jephunneh the Kenizzite. He said to Joshua, "You remember what the LORD said at Kadesh Barnea when he was speaking to the prophet Moses about you and me. 7Moses, the LORD's servant, sent me to look at the land where we were going. I was forty years old then. When I came back, I told Moses what I thought about the land. 8The other men who went with me frightened the people, but I fully believed the LORD would allow us to take the land. 9So that day Moses promised me, 'The land where you went will become your land, and your children will own it forever. I will give you that land because you fully believed in the LORD, my God.'

10"Now then, the LORD has kept his promise. He has kept me alive for forty-five years from the time he said this to Moses during the time we all wandered in the desert. Now here I am, eighty-five years old. 11I am still as strong today as I was the day Moses sent me out, and I am just as ready to fight now as I was then. 12So give me the mountain country the LORD promised me that day long ago. Back then you heard that the Anakite people lived there and the cities were large and well protected. But now with the LORD helping me, I will force them out, just as the LORD said."

13Joshua blessed Caleb son of Jephunneh and gave him the city of Hebron as his own. 14Hebron still belongs to the family of Caleb son of Jephunneh the Kenizzite because he had faith and obeyed the LORD, the God of Israel. 15(In the past it was called Kiriath Arba, named for Arba, the greatest man among the Anakites.)

After this there was peace in the land.

LAND FOR JUDAH

15 The land that was given to the tribe of Judah was divided among all the family groups. It went all the way to the Desert of Zin in the far south, at the border of Edom.

2The southern border of Judah's land started at the south end of the Dead Sea 3and went south of Scorpion Pass to Zin. From there it passed to the south of Kadesh Barnea and continued past Hezron to Addar. From Addar it turned and went to Karka. 4It continued to Azmon, the brook of Egypt, and then to the Mediterranean Sea. This was the southern border.

5The eastern border was the shore of the Dead Sea, as far as the mouth of the Jordan River.

The northern border started at the bay of the sea at the mouth of the Jordan River. 6Then it went to Beth Hoglah and continued north of Beth Arabah to the stone of Bohan son of Reuben. 7Then the northern border went through the Valley of Achor to Debir where it turned toward the north and went to Gilgal. Gilgal is across from the road that goes through Adummim Pass, on the south side of the ravine. The border continued to the waters of En Shemesh and stopped at En Rogel. 8Then it went through the Valley of Ben Hinnom, next to the southern side of the Jebusite city (which is called Jerusalem). There the border went to the top of the hill on the west side of Hinnom Valley, at the northern end of the Valley of Giants. 9From there it went to the spring of the waters of Nephtoah and then it went to the cities near Mount Ephron. There it turned and went toward Baalah, which is called Kiriath Jearim. 10At Baalah the border turned west and went toward Mount Seir. It continued along the north side of Mount Jearim (also called Kesalon) and came to Beth Shemesh. From there it went past Timnah 11to the hill north of Ekron. Then it turned toward Shikkeron and went past Mount Baalah and continued on to Jabneel, ending at the sea. 12The Mediterranean Sea was the western border. Inside these borders lived the family groups of Judah.

13The LORD had commanded Joshua to give Caleb son of Jephunneh part of the land in Judah, so he gave Caleb the town of Kiriath Arba, also called Hebron. (Arba was the father of Anak.) 14Caleb forced out the three Anakite families living in Hebron: Sheshai, Ahiman, and Talmai, the descendants of Anak. 15Then he left there and went to fight against the people living in Debir. (In the past Debir had been called Kiriath Sepher.) 16Caleb said, "I will give Acsah, my daughter, as a wife to the man who attacks and captures the city of Kiriath Sepher." 17Othniel son of Kenaz, Caleb's brother, captured the city, so Caleb gave his daughter Acsah to Othniel to be his wife. 18When Acsah came to Othniel, she told him to ask her father for a field. So Acsah went to her father. When she got down from her donkey, Caleb asked her, "What do you want?"

19Acsah answered, "Do me a special favor. Since you have given me land in southern Canaan, also give me springs of water." So Caleb gave her the upper and lower springs.

20The tribe of Judah got the land God had promised them. Each family group got part of the land.

21The tribe of Judah got all these towns in the southern part of Canaan near the border of Edom: Kabzeel, Eder, Jagur, 22Kinah, Dimonah, Adadah, 23Kedesh, Hazor, Ithnan, 24Ziph, Telem, Bealoth, 25Hazor Hadattah, Kerioth Hezron (also called Hazor), 26Amam, Shema, Moladah, 27Hazar Gaddah, Heshmon, Beth Pelet, 28Hazar Shual, Beersheba, Biziothiah, 29Baalah, Iim, Ezem, 30Eltolad, Kesil, Hormah, 31Ziklag, Madmannah, Sansannah, 32Lebaoth, Shilhim, Ain, and Rimmon. There were twenty-nine towns and their villages.

33The tribe of Judah got these towns in the western hills: Eshtaol, Zorah, Ashnah, 34Zanoah, En Gannim, Tappuah, Enam, 35Jarmuth, Adullam, Socoh, Azekah, 36Shaaraim, Adithaim, and Gederah (also called Gederothaim). There were fourteen towns and their villages.

37Judah was also given these towns in the western hills: Zenan, Hadashah, Migdal Gad, 38Dilean, Mizpah, Joktheel, 39Lachish, Bozkath, Eglon, 40Cabbon, Lahmas, Kitlish, 41Gederoth, Beth Dagon, Naamah, and Makkedah. There were sixteen towns and their villages.

42Judah was also given these towns in the western hills: Libnah, Ether, Ashan, 43Iphtah, Ashnah, Nezib, 44Keilah, Aczib, and Mareshah. There were nine towns and their villages.

45The tribe of Judah was also given these towns: Ekron and all the small towns and villages near it; 46the area west of Ekron and all the villages and small towns near Ashdod; 47Ashdod and the small towns and villages around it; the villages and small towns around Gaza as far as the brook of Egypt and along the coast of the Mediterranean Sea.

48The tribe of Judah was also given these towns in the mountains: Shamir, Jattir, Socoh, 49Dannah, Kiriath Sannah (also called Debir), 50Anab, Eshtemoh, Anim, 51Goshen, Holon, and Giloh. There were eleven towns and their villages.

52They were also given these towns in the mountains: Arab, Dumah, Eshan, 53Janim, Beth Tappuah, Aphekah, 54Humtah, Kiriath Arba (also called Hebron), and Zior. There were nine towns and their villages.

⁵⁵Judah was also given these towns in the mountains: Maon, Carmel, Ziph, Juttah, ⁵⁶Jezreel, Jokdeam, Zanoah, ⁵⁷Kain, Gibeah, and Timnah. There were ten towns and their villages.

⁵⁸They were also given these towns in the mountains: Halhul, Beth Zur, Gedor, ⁵⁹Maarath, Beth Anoth, and Eltekon. There were six towns and their villages.

⁶⁰The people of Judah were also given the two towns of Rabbah and Kiriath Baal (also called Kiriath Jearim) and their villages.

⁶¹Judah was given these towns in the desert: Beth Arabah, Middin, Secacah, ⁶²Nibshan, the City of Salt, and En Gedi. There were six towns and all their villages.

⁶³The army of Judah was not able to force out the Jebusites living in Jerusalem, so the Jebusites still live among the people of Judah to this day.

LAND FOR EPHRAIM AND MANASSEH

16 This is the land the tribe of Joseph received. It started at the Jordan River near Jericho and continued to the waters of Jericho, just east of the city. The border went up from Jericho to the mountains of Bethel. ²Then it continued from Bethel (also called Luz) to the Arkite border at Ataroth. ³From there it went west to the border of the Japhletites and continued to the area of the Lower Beth Horon. Then it went to Gezer and ended at the sea.

⁴So Manasseh and Ephraim, sons of Joseph, received their land.

⁵This is the land that was given to the family groups of Ephraim: Their border started at Ataroth Addar in the east, went to Upper Beth Horon, ⁶and then to the sea. From Micmethath it turned eastward toward Taanath Shiloh and continued eastward to Janoah. ⁷Then it went down from Janoah to Ataroth and to Naarah. It continued until it touched Jericho and stopped at the Jordan River. ⁸The border went from Tappuah west to Kanah Ravine and ended at the sea. This is all the land that was given to each family group in the tribe of the Ephraimites. ⁹Many of the towns were actually within Manasseh's borders, but the people of Ephraim got those towns and their villages. ¹⁰The Ephraimites could not force the Canaanites to leave Gezer, so the Canaanites still live among the Ephraimites today, but they became slaves of the Ephraimites.

17 Then land was given to the tribe of Manasseh, Joseph's first son. Manasseh's first son was Makir, the father of Gilead. Makir was a great soldier, so the lands of Gilead and Bashan were given to his family. ²Land was also given to the other family groups of Manasseh—Abiezer, Helek, Asriel, Shechem, Hepher, and Shemida. These were all the other sons of Manasseh son of Joseph.

³Zelophehad was the son of Hepher, who was the son of Gilead, who was the son of Makir, who was the son of Manasseh. Zelophehad had no sons, but he had five daughters, named Mahlah, Noah, Hoglah, Milcah, and Tirzah. ⁴They went to Eleazar the priest and to Joshua son of Nun and all the leaders. They said, "The LORD told Moses to give us land like the men received." So Eleazar obeyed the LORD and gave the daughters some land, just like the brothers of their father. ⁵So the tribe of Manasseh had ten sections of land west of the Jordan River and two more sections, Gilead and Bashan, on the east side of the Jordan River. ⁶The daughters of Manasseh received land just as the sons did. Gilead was given to the rest of the families of Manasseh.

⁷The lands of Manasseh were in the area between Asher and Micmethath, near Shechem. The border went south to the En Tappuah area, ⁸which belonged to Manasseh, except for the town of Tappuah. It was along the border of Manasseh's land and belonged to the sons of Ephraim. ⁹The border of Manasseh continued south to Kanah Ravine. The cities in this area of Manasseh belonged to Ephraim. Manasseh's border was on the north side of the ravine and went to the sea. ¹⁰The land to the south belonged to Ephraim, and the land to the north belonged to Manasseh. The Mediterranean Sea was the western border. The border touched Asher's land on the north and Issachar's land on the east.

¹¹In the areas of Issachar and Asher, the people of Manasseh owned these towns: Beth Shan and its small towns; Ibleam and its small towns; the people who lived in Dor and its small towns; the people in Naphoth Dor and its small towns; the people who lived in

Taanach and its small towns; the people in Megiddo and its small towns. ¹²Manasseh was not able to defeat those cities, so the Canaanites continued to live there. ¹³When the Israelites grew strong, they forced the Canaanites to work for them, although they did not force them to leave the land.

¹⁴The people from the tribes of Joseph said to Joshua, "You gave us only one area of land, but we are many people. Why did you give us only one part of all the land the LORD gave his people?"

¹⁵And Joshua answered them, "If you have too many people, go up to the forest and make a place for yourselves to live there in the land of the Perizzites and the Rephaites. The mountain country of Ephraim is too small for you."

¹⁶The people of Joseph said, "It is true. The mountain country of Ephraim is not enough for us, but the land where the Canaanites live is dangerous. They are skilled fighters. They have powerful weapons in Beth Shan and all the small towns in that area, and they are also in the Valley of Jezreel."

¹⁷Then Joshua said to the people of Joseph—to Ephraim and Manasseh, "There are many of you, and you have great power. You should be given more than one share of land. ¹⁸You also will have the mountain country. It is a forest, but you can cut down the trees and make it a good place to live. You will own all of it because you will force the Canaanites to leave the land even though they have powerful weapons and are strong."

THE REST OF THE LAND DIVIDED

18 All of the Israelites gathered together at Shiloh where they set up the Meeting Tent. The land was now under their control. ²But there were still seven tribes of Israel that had not yet received their land.

³So Joshua said to the Israelites: "Why do you wait so long to take your land? The LORD, the God of your ancestors, has given this land to you. ⁴Choose three men from each tribe, and I will send them out to study the land. They will describe in writing the land their tribe wants as its share, and then they will come back to me. ⁵They will divide the land into seven parts. The people of Judah will keep their land in the south, and the people of Joseph will keep their land in the north.

⁶You should describe the seven parts of land in writing and bring what you have written to me. Then I will throw lots in the presence of the LORD our God. ⁷But the Levites do not get any part of these lands, because they are priests, and their work is to serve the LORD. Gad, Reuben, and East Manasseh have received the land promised to them, which is east of the Jordan River. Moses, the servant of the LORD, gave it to them."

⁸So the men who were chosen to map the land started out. Joshua told them, "Go and study the land and describe it in writing. Then come back to me, and I will throw lots in the presence of the LORD here in Shiloh." ⁹So the men left and went into the land. They described in a scroll each town in the seven parts of the land. Then they came back to Joshua, who was still at the camp at Shiloh. ¹⁰There Joshua threw lots in the presence of the LORD to choose the lands that should be given to each tribe.

LAND FOR BENJAMIN

¹¹The first part of the land was given to the tribe of Benjamin. Each family group received some land between the land of Judah and the land of Joseph. This is the land chosen for Benjamin: ¹²The northern border started at the Jordan River and went along the northern edge of Jericho, and then it went west into the mountains. That boundary continued until it was just east of Beth Aven. ¹³From there it went south to Luz (also called Bethel) and then down to Ataroth Addar, which is on the hill south of Lower Beth Horon.

¹⁴At the hill to the south of Beth Horon, the border turned and went south near the western side of the hill. It went to Kiriath Baal (also called Kiriath Jearim), a town where people of Judah lived. This was the western border.

¹⁵The southern border started near Kiriath Jearim and went west to the waters of Nephtoah. ¹⁶Then it went down to the bottom of the hill, which was near the Valley of Ben Hinnom, on the north side of the Valley of Rephaim. The border continued down the Hinnom Valley just south of the Jebusite city to En Rogel. ¹⁷There it turned north and went to En Shemesh. It continued to Geliloth near the Adummim Pass. Then

it went down to the great Stone of Bohan son of Reuben. ¹⁸The border continued to the northern part of Beth Arabah and went down into the Jordan Valley. ¹⁹From there it went to the northern part of Beth Hoglah and ended at the north shore of the Dead Sea, where the Jordan River flows into the sea. This was the southern border.

²⁰The Jordan River was the border on the eastern side. So this was the land given to the family groups of Benjamin with the borders on all sides.

²¹The family groups of Benjamin received these cities: Jericho, Beth Hoglah, Emek Keziz, ²²Beth Arabah, Zemaraim, Bethel, ²³Avvim, Parah, Ophrah, ²⁴Kephar Ammoni, Ophni, and Geba. There were twelve towns and all their villages.

²⁵The tribe of Benjamin also received Gibeon, Ramah, Beeroth, ²⁶Mizpah, Kephirah, Mozah, ²⁷Rekem, Irpeel, Taralah, ²⁸Zelah, Haeleph, the Jebusite city (Jerusalem), Gibeah, and Kiriath. There were fourteen towns and their villages. All these areas are the lands the family groups of Benjamin were given.

LAND FOR SIMEON

19 The second part of the land was given to the tribe of Simeon. Each family group received some of the land inside the area of Judah. ²They received Beersheba (also called Sheba), Moladah, ³Hazar Shual, Balah, Ezem, ⁴Eltolad, Bethul, Hormah, ⁵Ziklag, Beth Marcaboth, Hazar Susah, ⁶Beth Lebaoth, and Sharuhen. There were thirteen towns and their villages.

⁷They received the towns of Ain, Rimmon, Ether, and Ashan, four towns and their villages. ⁸They also received all the very small areas with people living in them as far as Baalath Beer (this is the same as Ramah in southern Canaan). So these were the lands given to the family groups in the tribe of Simeon. ⁹The land of the Simeonites was taken from part of the land of Judah. Since Judah had much more land than they needed, the Simeonites received part of their land.

LAND FOR ZEBULUN

¹⁰The third part of the land was given to the tribe of Zebulun. Each family group of Zebulun received some of the land. The border of Zebulun went as far as Sarid. ¹¹Then

it went west to Maralah and came near Dabbesheth and then near Jokneam. ¹²Then it turned to the east. It went from Sarid to the area of Kisloth Tabor and on to Daberath and to Japhia. ¹³It continued eastward to Gath Hepher and Eth Kazin, ending at Rimmon. There the border turned and went toward Neah. ¹⁴At Neah it turned again and went to the north to Hannathon and continued to the Valley of Iphtah El. ¹⁵Inside this border were the cities of Kattath, Nahalal, Shimron, Idalah, and Bethlehem. There were twelve towns and their villages.

¹⁶So these are the towns and the villages that were given to the family groups of Zebulun.

LAND FOR ISSACHAR

¹⁷The fourth part of the land was given to the tribe of Issachar. Each family group of Issachar received some of the land. ¹⁸Their land included Jezreel, Kesulloth, Shunem, ¹⁹Hapharaim, Shion, Anaharath, ²⁰Rabbith, Kishion, Ebez, ²¹Remeth, En Gannim, En Haddah, and Beth Pazzez.

²²The border of their land touched the area called Tabor, Shahazumah, and Beth Shemesh and stopped at the Jordan River. There were sixteen towns and their villages.

²³These cities and towns were part of the land that was given to the family groups of Issachar.

LAND FOR ASHER

²⁴The fifth part of the land was given to the tribe of Asher. Each family group of Asher received some of the land. ²⁵Their land included Helkath, Hali, Beten, Acshaph, ²⁶Allammelech, Amad, and Mishal.

The western border touched Mount Carmel and Shihor Libnath. ²⁷Then it turned east and went to Beth Dagon, touching Zebulun and the Valley of Iphtah El. Then it went north of Beth Emek and Neiel and passed north to Cabul. ²⁸From there it went to Abdon, Rehob, Hammon, and Kanah and continued to Greater Sidon. ²⁹Then the border went back south toward Ramah and continued to the strong, walled city of Tyre. There it turned and went toward Hosah, ending at the sea. This was in the area of Aczib, ³⁰Ummah, Aphek, and Rehob. There were twenty-two towns and their villages.

³¹These cities and their villages were

part of the land that was given to the family groups of Asher.

LAND FOR NAPHTALI

³²The sixth part of the land was given to the tribe of Naphtali. Each family group of Naphtali received some of the land. ³³The border of their land started at the large tree in Zaanannim, which is near Heleph. Then it went through Adami Nekeb and Jabneel, as far as Lakkum, and ended at the Jordan River. ³⁴Then it went to the west through Aznoth Tabor and stopped at Hukkok. It went to the area of Zebulun on the south, Asher on the west, and Judah, at the Jordan River, on the east. ³⁵The strong, walled cities inside these borders were called Ziddim, Zer, Hammath, Rakkath, Kinnereth, ³⁶Adamah, Ramah, Hazor, ³⁷Kedesh, Edrei, En Hazor, ³⁸Iron, Migdal El, Horem, Beth Anath, and Beth Shemesh. There were nineteen towns and all their villages.

³⁹The towns and the villages around them were in the land that was given to the family groups of Naphtali.

LAND FOR DAN

⁴⁰The seventh part of the land was given to the tribe of Dan. Each family group of Dan received some of the land. ⁴¹Their land included Zorah, Eshtaol, Ir Shemesh, ⁴²Shaalabbin, Aijalon, Ithlah, ⁴³Elon, Timnah, Ekron, ⁴⁴Eltekeh, Gibbethon, Baalath, ⁴⁵Jehud, Bene Berak, Gath Rimmon, ⁴⁶Me Jarkon, Rakkon, and the area near Joppa.

⁴⁷(But the Danites had trouble taking their land. They went and fought against Leshem, defeated it, and killed the people who lived there. So the Danites moved into the town of Leshem and changed its name to Dan, because he was the father of their tribe.) ⁴⁸All of these towns and villages were given to the family groups of Dan.

LAND FOR JOSHUA

⁴⁹After the leaders finished dividing the land and giving it to the different tribes, the Israelites gave Joshua son of Nun his land also. ⁵⁰They gave Joshua the town he asked for, Timnath Serah in the mountains of Ephraim, just as the LORD commanded. He built up the town and lived there.

⁵¹So these lands were given to the different tribes of Israel. Eleazar the priest, Joshua

son of Nun, and the leaders of each tribe divided up the land by lots at Shiloh. They met in the presence of the LORD at the entrance to the Meeting Tent. Now they were finished dividing the land.

CITIES OF SAFETY

20 Then the LORD said to Joshua: ²"Tell the Israelites to choose the special cities of safety, as I had Moses command you to do. ³If a person kills someone accidentally and without meaning to kill him, that person may go to a city of safety to hide. There the killer will be safe from the relative who has the duty of punishing a murderer.

⁴"When the killer runs to one of those cities, he must stop at the entrance gate, stand there, and tell the leaders of the people what happened. Then that person will be allowed to enter the city and will be given a place to live among them. ⁵But if the one who is chasing him follows him to that city, the leaders of the city must not hand over the killer. It was an accident. He did not hate him beforehand or kill him on purpose. ⁶The killer must stay in the city until a court comes to a decision and until the high priest dies. Then he may go back home to the town from which he ran away."

⁷So the Israelites chose these cities to be cities of safety: Kedesh in Galilee in the mountains of Naphtali; Shechem in the mountains of Ephraim; Kiriath Arba (also called Hebron) in the mountains of Judah; ⁸Bezer on the east side of the Jordan River near Jericho in the desert in the land of Reuben; Ramoth in Gilead in the land of Gad; and Golan in Bashan in the land of Manasseh. ⁹Any Israelite or anyone living among them who killed someone accidentally was to be allowed to run to one of these cities of safety. There he would not be killed, before he was judged, by the relative who had the duty of punishing a murderer.

TOWNS FOR THE LEVITES

21 The heads of the Levite families went to talk to Eleazar the priest, to Joshua son of Nun, and to the heads of the families of all the tribes of Israel. ²At Shiloh in the land of Canaan, the heads of the Levite families said to them, "The LORD commanded Moses that you give us towns where we may live and pastures for our animals." ³So the Israelites obeyed this command of the LORD and gave the Levite people these towns and pastures for their own land: ⁴The Kohath family groups were part of the tribe of Levi. Some of the Levites in the Kohath family groups were from the family of Aaron the priest. To these Levites were given thirteen towns in the areas of Judah, Simeon, and Benjamin. ⁵The other family groups of Kohath were given ten towns in the areas of Ephraim, Dan, and West Manasseh.

⁶The people from the Gershon family groups were given thirteen towns in the land of Issachar, Asher, Naphtali, and the East Manasseh in Bashan.

⁷The family groups of Merari were given twelve towns in the areas of Reuben, Gad, and Zebulun.

⁸So the Israelites gave the Levites these towns and the pastures around them, just as the LORD had commanded Moses.

⁹These are the names of the towns that came from the lands of Judah and Simeon. ¹⁰The first choice of towns was given to the Kohath family groups of the Levites. ¹¹They gave them Kiriath Arba, also called Hebron, and all its pastures in the mountains of Judah. (Arba was the father of Anak.) ¹²But the fields and the villages around Kiriath Arba had been given to Caleb son of Jephunneh.

¹³So they gave the city of Hebron to the descendants of Aaron (Hebron was a city of safety). They also gave them the towns of Libnah, ¹⁴Jattir, Eshtemoa, ¹⁵Holon, Debir, ¹⁶Ain, Juttah, and Beth Shemesh, and all the pastures around them. Nine towns were given from these two tribes.

¹⁷They also gave the people of Aaron these cities that belonged to the tribe of Benjamin: Gibeon, Geba, ¹⁸Anathoth, and Almon. They gave them these four towns and the pastures around them.

¹⁹So these thirteen towns with their pastures were given to the priests, who were from the family of Aaron.

²⁰The other Kohathite family groups of the Levites were given these towns from the tribe of Ephraim: ²¹Shechem in the mountains of Ephraim (which was a city of safety), Gezer, ²²Kibzaim, and Beth Horon. There were four towns and their pastures.

²³The tribe of Dan gave them Eltekeh, Gibbethon, ²⁴Aijalon, and Gath Rimmon. There were four towns and their pastures.

²⁵West Manasseh gave them Taanach and Gath Rimmon and the pastures around these two towns.

²⁶So these ten towns and the pastures around them were given to the rest of the Kohathite family groups.

²⁷The Gershonite family groups of the Levite tribe were given these towns: East Manasseh gave them Golan in Bashan, which was a city of safety, and Be Eshtarah, and the pastures around these two towns.

²⁸The tribe of Issachar gave them Kishion, Daberath, ²⁹Jarmuth, and En Gannim, and the pastures around these four towns.

³⁰The tribe of Asher gave them Mishal, Abdon, ³¹Helkath, and Rehob, and the pastures around these four towns.

³²The tribe of Naphtali gave them Kedesh in Galilee (a city of safety), Hammoth Dor, and Kartan, and the pastures around these three towns.

³³So the Gershonite family groups received thirteen towns and the pastures around them.

³⁴The Merarite family groups (the rest of the Levites) were given these towns: The tribe of Zebulun gave them Jokneam, Kartah, ³⁵Dimnah, and Nahalal, and the pastures around these four towns.

³⁶The tribe of Reuben gave them Bezer, Jahaz, ³⁷Kedemoth, and Mephaath, along with the pastures around these four towns.

³⁸The tribe of Gad gave them Ramoth in Gilead (a city of safety), Mahanaim, ³⁹Heshbon, and Jazer, and the pastures around these four towns.

⁴⁰So the total number of towns given to the Merarite family groups was twelve.

⁴¹A total of forty-eight towns with their pastures in the land of Israel were given to the Levites. ⁴²Each town had pastures around it.

⁴³So the LORD gave the people all the land he had promised their ancestors. The people took the land and lived there. ⁴⁴The LORD gave them peace on all sides, as he had promised their ancestors. None of their enemies defeated them; the LORD handed all their enemies over to them. ⁴⁵He kept every promise he had made to the Israelites; each one came true.

THREE TRIBES GO HOME

22 Then Joshua called a meeting of all the people from the tribes of Reuben, Gad, and East Manasseh. ²He said to them, "You have done everything Moses, the LORD's servant, told you to do. You have also obeyed all my commands. ³For a long time you have supported the other Israelites. You have been careful to obey the commands the LORD your God gave you. ⁴The LORD your God promised to give the Israelites peace, and he has kept his promise. Now you may go back to your homes, to the land that Moses, the LORD's servant, gave you, on the east side of the Jordan River. ⁵But be careful to obey the teachings and laws Moses, the LORD's servant, gave you: to love the LORD your God and obey his commands, to continue to follow him and serve him the very best you can."

⁶Then Joshua said good-bye to them, and they left and went away to their homes. ⁷Moses had given the land of Bashan to East Manasseh. Joshua gave land on the west side of the Jordan River to West Manasseh. And he sent them to their homes and he blessed them. ⁸He said, "Go back to your homes and your riches. You have many animals, silver, gold, bronze, and iron, and many beautiful clothes. Also, you have taken many things from your enemies that you should divide among yourselves."

⁹So the people from the tribes of Reuben, Gad, and East Manasseh left the other Israelites at Shiloh in Canaan and went back to Gilead. It was their own land, given to them by Moses as the LORD had commanded.

¹⁰The people of Reuben, Gad, and East Manasseh went to Geliloth, near the Jordan River in the land of Canaan. There they built a beautiful altar. ¹¹The other Israelites still

---

GOD'S ULTIMATE SACRIFICE

just do it!

FAITH

JOSHUA 22:5

If God tells you to do something, do it. Don't hesitate. Don't debate. Don't launch an internal process of questioning why or how or when. Just do it!

Here's a key point: something we often fail to acknowledge is the consistency of God's character. He *always* does what is right. So there is never any need to second-guess his motives or his directions. Following his orders will always result in just the right thing.

That's why Joshua instructed his listeners to "be careful to obey the teachings and laws." That's why he said to "follow [God] and serve him the very best you can." Unquestioning, instantaneous, joyful obedience is what ushers in the blessing.

This is something we need to heed today. We are God's chosen people—but the Father is our commander-in-chief. There is no room for questioning or debating. There is only room for obedience. Follow Joshua's admonition, and just do it!

reflect: Consider the areas of your life where you could follow Jesus more closely.
Go to **John 3:31–36.**

at Shiloh heard about the altar these three tribes built at the border of Canaan at Geliloth, near the Jordan River on Israel's side. ¹²All the Israelites became very angry at these three tribes, so they met together and decided to fight them.

¹³The Israelites sent Phinehas son of Eleazar the priest to Gilead to talk to the people of Reuben, Gad, and East Manasseh. ¹⁴They also sent one leader from each of the ten tribes at Shiloh. Each of them was a leader of his family group of Israelites.

¹⁵These leaders went to Gilead to talk to the people of Reuben, Gad, and East Manasseh. They said: ¹⁶"All the Israelites ask you: 'Why did you turn against the God of Israel by building an altar for yourselves? You know that this is against God's law. ¹⁷Remember what happened at Peor? We still suffer today because of that sin, for which God made many Israelites very sick. ¹⁸And now are you turning against the LORD and refusing to follow him?

" 'If you don't stop what you're doing today, the LORD will be angry with everyone in Israel tomorrow. ¹⁹If your land is unclean, come over into our land where the LORD's Tent is. Share it with us. But don't turn against the LORD and us by building another altar for the LORD our God. ²⁰Remember how Achan son of Zerah refused to obey the command about what must be completely destroyed. That one man broke God's law, but all the Israelites were punished. Achan died because of his sin, but others also died.' "

²¹The people from Reuben, Gad, and East Manasseh answered, ²²"The LORD is God of gods! The LORD is God of gods! God knows, and we want you to know also. If we have done something wrong, you may kill us. ²³If we broke God's law, we ask the LORD himself to punish us. We did not build this altar to offer burnt offerings or grain and fellowship offerings.

²⁴"We did not build it for that reason. We feared that someday your people would not accept us as part of your nation. Then they might say, 'You cannot worship the LORD, the God of Israel. ²⁵The LORD made the Jordan River a border between us and you people of Reuben and Gad. You cannot worship the LORD.' So we feared that your children might make our children stop worshiping the LORD.

²⁶"That is why we decided to build this altar. But it is not for burnt offerings and sacrifices. ²⁷This altar is proof to you and us and to all our children who will come after us that we worship the LORD with our whole burnt offerings, grain, and fellowship offerings. This was so your children would not say to our children, 'You are not the LORD's.'

²⁸"In the future if your children say that, our children can say, 'See the altar made by our ancestors. It is exactly like the LORD's altar, but we do not use it for sacrifices. It shows that we are part of Israel.'

²⁹"Truly, we don't want to be against the LORD or to stop following him by building an altar for burnt offerings, grain offerings, or sacrifices. We know the only true altar to the LORD our God is in front of the Holy Tent."

³⁰When Phinehas the priest and the ten leaders heard the people of Reuben, Gad, and East Manasseh, they were pleased. ³¹So Phinehas, son of Eleazar the priest, said, "Now we know the LORD is with us and that you didn't turn against him. Now the Israelites will not be punished by the LORD."

³²Then Phinehas and the leaders left the people of Reuben and Gad in Gilead and went back to Canaan where they told the Israelites what had happened. ³³They were pleased and thanked God. So they decided not to fight the people of Reuben and Gad and destroy those lands.

³⁴And the people of Reuben and Gad named the altar Proof That We Believe the LORD Is God.

THE LAST WORDS OF JOSHUA

23 The LORD gave Israel peace from their enemies around them. Many years passed, and Joshua grew very old. ²He called a meeting of all the elders, heads of families, judges, and officers of Israel. He said, "I am now very old. ³You have seen what the LORD has done to our enemies to help us. The LORD your God fought for you. ⁴Remember that your people have been given their land between the Jordan River and the Mediterranean Sea in the west, the land I promised to give you. ⁵The LORD your God will force out the people living there. The LORD will push them out ahead of you. And you

19 "The kings came, and they fought.
At that time the kings of Canaan fought
at Taanach, by the waters of Megiddo.
But they took away no silver or
possessions of Israel.
20 The stars fought from heaven;
from their paths, they fought Sisera.
21 The Kishon River swept Sisera's men
away,
that old river, the Kishon River.
March on, my soul, with strength!
22 Then the horses' hoofs beat the ground.
Galloping, galloping go Sisera's mighty
horses.
23 'May the town of Meroz be cursed,' said
the angel of the LORD.
'Bitterly curse its people,
because they did not come to help the
LORD.
They did not fight the strong enemy.'

24 "May Jael, the wife of Heber the Kenite,
be blessed above all women who live in
tents.
25 Sisera asked for water,
but Jael gave him milk.
In a bowl fit for a ruler,
she brought him cream.
26 Jael reached out and took the tent peg.
Her right hand reached for the
workman's hammer.
She hit Sisera! She smashed his head!
She crushed and pierced the side of his
head!
27 At Jael's feet he sank.
He fell, and he lay there.
At her feet he sank. He fell.
Where Sisera sank, there he fell, dead!

28 "Sisera's mother looked out through the
window.
She looked through the curtains and
cried out,
'Why is Sisera's chariot so late in coming?
Why are sounds of his chariots' horses
delayed?'
29 The wisest of her servant ladies answer
her,
and Sisera's mother says to herself,
30 'Surely they are robbing the people they
defeated!
Surely they are dividing those things
among themselves!
Each soldier is given a girl or two.

Maybe Sisera is taking pieces of dyed
cloth.
Maybe they are even taking
pieces of dyed, embroidered cloth for
the necks of the victors!'
31 "Let all your enemies die this way, LORD!
But let all the people who love you
be as strong as the rising sun!"
Then there was peace in the land for forty
years.

THE MIDIANITES ATTACK ISRAEL

6 Again the Israelites did what the LORD said was wrong. So for seven years the LORD handed them over to Midian. 2Because the Midianites were very powerful and were cruel to Israel, the Israelites made hiding places in the mountains, in caves, and in safe places. 3Whenever the Israelites planted crops, the Midianites, Amalekites, and other peoples from the east would come and attack them. 4They camped in the land and destroyed the crops that the Israelites had planted as far away as Gaza. They left nothing for Israel to eat, and no sheep, cattle, or donkeys. 5The Midianites came with their tents and their animals like swarms of locusts to ruin the land. There were so many people and camels they could not be counted. 6Israel became very poor because of the Midianites, so they cried out to the LORD.

7When the Israelites cried out to the LORD against the Midianites, 8the LORD sent a prophet to them. He said, "This is what the LORD, the God of Israel, says: I brought you out of Egypt, the land of slavery. 9I saved you from the Egyptians and from all those who were against you. I forced the Canaanites out of their land and gave it to you. 10Then I said to you, 'I am the LORD your God. Live in the land of the Amorites, but do not worship their gods.' But you did not obey me."

THE ANGEL OF THE LORD VISITS GIDEON

11The angel of the LORD came and sat down under the oak tree at Ophrah that belonged to Joash, one of the Abiezrite people. Gideon, Joash's son, was separating some wheat from the chaff in a winepress to keep the wheat from the Midianites. 12The angel of the LORD appeared to Gideon and said, "The LORD is with you, mighty warrior!" 13Then Gideon said, "Sir, if the LORD is with us, why are we having so much trouble? Where are the miracles our ancestors told us he did when the LORD brought them out of Egypt? But now he has left us and has handed us over to the Midianites."

¹⁴The LORD turned to Gideon and said, "Go with your strength and save Israel from the Midianites. I am the one who is sending you."

¹⁵But Gideon answered, "Lord, how can I save Israel? My family group is the weakest in Manasseh, and I am the least important member of my family."

¹⁶The LORD answered him, "I will be with you. It will seem as if the Midianites you are fighting are only one man."

¹⁷Then Gideon said to the LORD, "If you are pleased with me, give me proof that it is really you talking with me. ¹⁸Please wait here until I come back to you. Let me bring my offering and set it in front of you."

And the LORD said, "I will wait until you return."

¹⁹So Gideon went in and cooked a young goat, and with twenty quarts of flour, made bread without yeast. Then he put the meat into a basket and the broth into a pot. He brought them out and gave them to the angel under the oak tree.

²⁰The angel of God said to Gideon, "Put the meat and the bread without yeast on that rock over there. Then pour the broth on them." And Gideon did as he was told. ²¹The angel of the LORD touched the meat and the bread with the end of the stick that was in his hand. Then fire jumped up from the rock and completely burned up the meat and the bread! And the angel of the LORD disappeared! ²²Then Gideon understood he had been talking to the angel of the LORD. So Gideon cried out, "Lord GOD! I have seen the angel of the LORD face to face!"

²³But the LORD said to Gideon, "Calm down! Don't be afraid! You will not die!"

²⁴So Gideon built an altar there to worship the LORD and named it The LORD Is Peace. It still stands at Ophrah, where the Abiezrites live.

GIDEON TEARS DOWN THE ALTAR OF BAAL

²⁵That same night the LORD said to Gideon, "Take the bull that belongs to your father and a second bull seven years old. Pull down your father's altar to Baal, and cut down the Asherah idol beside it. ²⁶Then build an altar to the LORD your God with its stones in the right order on this high ground. Kill and burn a second bull on this altar, using the wood from the Asherah idol."

²⁷So Gideon got ten of his servants and did what the LORD had told him to do. But Gideon was afraid that his family and the men of the city might see him, so he did it at night, not in the daytime.

²⁸When the men of the city got up the next morning, they saw that the altar for Baal had been destroyed and that the Asherah idol beside it had been cut down! They also saw the altar Gideon had built and the second bull that had been sacrificed on it. ²⁹The men of the city asked each other, "Who did this?"

After they asked many questions, someone told them, "Gideon son of Joash did this."

³⁰So they said to Joash, "Bring your son out. He has pulled down the altar of Baal and cut down the Asherah idol beside it. He must die!"

³¹But Joash said to the angry crowd around him, "Are you going to take Baal's side? Are you going to defend him? Anyone who takes Baal's side will be killed by morning! If Baal is a god, let him fight for himself. It's his altar that has been pulled down." ³²So on that day Gideon got the name Jerub-Baal, which means "let Baal fight against him," because Gideon pulled down Baal's altar.

GIDEON DEFEATS MIDIAN

³³All the Midianites, the Amalekites, and other peoples from the east joined together and came across the Jordan River and camped in the Valley of Jezreel. ³⁴But the Spirit of the LORD entered Gideon, and he blew a trumpet to call the Abiezrites to follow him. ³⁵He sent messengers to all of Manasseh, calling them to follow him. He also sent messengers to the people of Asher, Zebulun, and Naphtali. So they also went up to meet Gideon and his men.

³⁶Then Gideon said to God, "You said you would help me save Israel. ³⁷I will put some wool on the threshing floor. If there is dew only on the wool but all of the ground is dry, then I will know that you will use me to save

will own the land, as he has promised you.

⁶"Be strong. You must be careful to obey everything commanded in the Book of the Teachings of Moses. Do not stray from it either from the left or the right. ⁷Don't become friends with the people living among us who are not Israelites. Don't say the names of their gods or make anyone swear by them. Don't serve or worship them. ⁸You must continue to follow the LORD your God, as you have done in the past.

⁹"The LORD has forced many great and powerful nations to leave ahead of you. No nation has been able to defeat you. ¹⁰With his help, one Israelite could defeat a thousand, because the LORD your God fights for you, as he promised to do. ¹¹So you must be careful to love the LORD your God.

¹²"If you turn away from the way of the LORD and become friends with these people who are not part of Israel and marry them, ¹³the LORD your God will not help you defeat your enemies. They will be like traps for you, like whips on your back and thorns in your eyes, and none of you will be left in this good land the LORD your God has given you.

¹⁴"It's almost time for me to die. You know and fully believe that the LORD has done great things for you. You know that he has not failed to keep any of his promises. ¹⁵Every good promise that the LORD your God made has come true, and in the same way, his other promises will come true. He promised that evil will come to you and that he will destroy you from this good land that he gave you. ¹⁶This will happen if you don't keep your

---

MENTORING WORLD CHANGERS FOR CHRIST

doing God's will

FUTURE

JOSHUA 23:6

If you can get your pride and your ego out of the way, God will use you to do remarkable things. Your heart will overflow with love when you realize you *are* loved. The true "you" will be revealed to you—and *through* you. Once you get out of the way and stop fighting the will of God for your life, your true potential will be realized.

You can do this! You can do it every day of your life. Be used by God. Believe that through him all things are possible. Be strong and courageous and your life will bless others, you will be blessed in all things, and most of all . . . his *will* can be done and you *will* glorify the Lord.

This does not advocate a lack of preparation and responsible living. This promotes giving it your best effort while recognizing the difference between what God wants and what you want. You will see a lot in life, but none of it will matter if you lose sight of what's important. Start by asking yourself, "Do my actions, reactions, relationships, and life praise the Lord?"

reflect: Live in such a way that your life praises God in all things.
Go to **Proverbs 3:5–6.**

agreement with the LORD your God. If you go and serve other gods and worship them, the LORD will become very angry with you. Then none of you will be left in this good land he has given you."

24 Joshua gathered all the tribes of Israel together at Shechem. He called the elders, heads of families, judges, and officers of Israel to stand before God.

²Then Joshua said to all the people, "Here's what the LORD, the God of Israel, says to you: 'A long time ago your ancestors lived on the other side of the Euphrates River. Terah, the father of Abraham and Nahor, worshiped other gods. ³But I, the LORD, took your ancestor Abraham from the other side of the river and led him through the land of Canaan. And I gave him many children, including his son Isaac. ⁴I gave Isaac two sons named Jacob and Esau. I gave the land around the mountains of Edom to Esau, but Jacob and his sons went down to Egypt. ⁵Then I sent Moses and Aaron to Egypt, where I brought many disasters on the Egyptians. Afterwards I brought you out. ⁶When I brought your ancestors out of Egypt, they came to the Red Sea, and the Egyptians chased them with chariots and men on horses. ⁷So the people called out to the LORD. And I brought darkness between you and the Egyptians and made the sea to cover them. You yourselves saw what I did to the army of Egypt. After that, you lived in the desert for a long time.

⁸"'Then I brought you to the land of the Amorites, east of the Jordan River. They fought against you, but I handed them over to you. I destroyed them before you, and you took control of that land. ⁹But the king of Moab, Balak son of Zippor, prepared to fight against the Israelites. The king sent for Balaam son of Beor to curse you, ¹⁰but I refused to listen to Balaam. So he asked for good things to happen to you! I saved you and brought you out of his power.

¹¹"'Then you crossed the Jordan River and came to Jericho, where the people of Jericho fought against you. Also, the Amorites, Perizzites, Canaanites, Hittites, Girgashites, Hivites, and Jebusites fought against you. But I handed them over to you. ¹²I sent terror ahead of you to force out two Amorite kings. You took the land without using swords and bows. ¹³I gave you that land where you

did not have to work. I gave you cities that you did not have to build. And now you live in that land and in those cities, and you eat from vineyards and olive trees that you did not plant.'"

¹⁴Then Joshua said to the people, "Now respect the LORD and serve him fully and sincerely. Throw away the gods that your ancestors worshiped on the other side of the Euphrates River and in Egypt. Serve the LORD. ¹⁵But if you don't want to serve the LORD, you must choose for yourselves today whom you will serve. You may serve the gods that your ancestors worshiped when they lived on the other side of the Euphrates River, or you may serve the gods of the Amorites who lived in this land. As for me and my family, we will serve the LORD."

¹⁶Then the people answered, "We will never stop following the LORD to serve other gods! ¹⁷It was the LORD our God who brought our ancestors out of Egypt. We were slaves in that land, but the LORD did great things for us there. He brought us out and protected us while we traveled through other lands. ¹⁸Then he forced out all the people living in these lands, even the Amorites. So we will serve the LORD, because he is our God."

¹⁹Then Joshua said, "You are not able to serve the LORD, because he is a holy God and a jealous God. If you turn against him and sin, he will not forgive you. ²⁰If you leave the LORD and serve other gods, he will send you great trouble. The LORD may have been good to you, but if you turn against him, he will destroy you."

²¹But the people said to Joshua, "No! We will serve the LORD."

²²Then Joshua said, "You are your own witnesses that you have chosen to serve the LORD."

The people said, "Yes, we are."

²³Then Joshua said, "Now throw away the gods that you have. Love the LORD, the God of Israel, with all your heart."

²⁴Then the people said to Joshua, "We will serve the LORD our God, and we will obey him."

²⁵On that day at Shechem Joshua made an agreement for the people. He made rules and laws for them to follow. ²⁶Joshua wrote these things in the Book of the Teachings of God. Then he took a large stone and set it

up under the oak tree near the LORD's Holy Tent.

27Joshua said to all the people, "See this stone! It will remind you of what we did today. It was here the LORD spoke to us today. It will remind you of what happened so you will not turn against your God."

JOSHUA DIES

28Then Joshua sent the people back to their land.

29After that, Joshua son of Nun died at the age of one hundred ten. 30They buried him in his own land at Timnath Serah, in the mountains of Ephraim, north of Mount Gaash.

31The Israelites served the LORD during the lifetime of Joshua and during the lifetimes of the elders who lived after Joshua who had seen what the LORD had done for Israel.

JOSEPH COMES HOME

32When the Israelites left Egypt, they carried the bones of Joseph with them. They buried them at Shechem, in the land Jacob had bought for a hundred pieces of silver from the sons of Hamor (Hamor was the father of Shechem). This land now belonged to Joseph's children.

33And Eleazar son of Aaron died and was buried at Gibeah in the mountains of Ephraim, which had been given to Eleazar's son Phinehas.

judges

GREAT LEADERS RESCUE ISRAEL

JUDAH FIGHTS THE CANAANITES

1 After Joshua died, the Israelites asked the LORD, "Who will be first to go and fight for us against the Canaanites?"

2 The LORD said to them, "The tribe of Judah will go. I have handed the land over to them."

3 The men of Judah said to the men of Simeon, their relatives, "Come and help us fight the Canaanites for our land. If you do, we will go and help you fight for your land." So the men of Simeon went with them.

4 When Judah attacked, the LORD handed over the Canaanites and the Perizzites to them, and they defeated ten thousand men at the city of Bezek. 5 There they found Adoni-Bezek, the ruler of the city, and fought him. The men of Judah defeated the Canaanites and the Perizzites, 6 but Adoni-Bezek ran away. The men of Judah chased him, and when they caught him, they cut off his thumbs and big toes.

7 Adoni-Bezek said, "Seventy kings whose thumbs and big toes had been cut off used to eat scraps that fell from my table. Now God has paid me back for what I did to them." The men of Judah took Adoni-Bezek to Jerusalem, and he died there.

8 Then the men of Judah fought against Jerusalem and captured it. They attacked with their swords and burned the city.

9 Later, they went down to fight the Canaanites who lived in the mountains, in the dry country to the south, and in the western hills. 10 The men of Judah went to fight against the Canaanites in the city of Hebron (which used to be called Kiriath Arba). And they defeated Sheshai, Ahiman, and Talmai.

CALEB AND HIS DAUGHTER

11 Then they left there and went to fight against the people living in Debir. (In the past Debir had been called Kiriath Sepher.) 12 Before attacking the city, Caleb said, "I will give Acsah, my daughter, as a wife to the man who attacks and captures the city of Kiriath Sepher." 13 Othniel son of Kenaz, Caleb's younger brother, captured the city, so Caleb gave his daughter Acsah to Othniel to be his wife. 14 When Acsah came to Othniel, she told him to ask her father for a field. When she got down from her donkey, Caleb asked her, "What do you want?"

15 Acsah answered him, "Do me a special favor. Since you have given me land in southern Canaan, also give me springs of water." So Caleb gave her the upper and lower springs.

FIGHTS WITH THE CANAANITES

16 The Kenite people, who were from the family of Moses' father-in-law, left Jericho, the city of palm trees. They went with the men of Judah to the Desert of Judah to live with them there in southern Judah near the city of Arad.

17 The men of Judah and the men of Simeon, their relatives, defeated the Canaanites who lived in Zephath. They completely destroyed the city, so they called it Hormah.ⁿ 18 The men of Judah captured Gaza, Ashkelon, Ekron, and the lands around them.

19 The LORD was with the men of Judah. They took the land in the mountains, but they could not force out the people living on the plain, because they had iron chariots. 20 As Moses had promised, Hebron was given to Caleb, and Caleb forced out the three sons of Anak. 21 But the people of Benjamin could not make the Jebusite people leave Jerusalem. Since that time the Jebusites have lived with the Benjaminites in Jerusalem.

22 The men of Joseph went to fight against the city of Bethel, and the LORD was with them. 23 They sent some spies to Bethel (which used to be called Luz). 24 The spies saw a man coming out of the city and said to him, "Show us a way into the city, and we will be kind to you." 25 So the man showed them the way into the city. The men of Joseph attacked with swords the people in Bethel, but

---

1:17 Hormah Hormah sounds like the Hebrew word meaning "to destroy completely."

they let the man and his family go free. ²⁶He went to the land where the Hittites lived and built a city. He named it Luz, which it is called even today.

²⁷There were Canaanites living in the cities of Beth Shan, Taanach, Dor, Ibleam, Megiddo, and the small towns around them. The people of Manasseh did not force those people out of their towns, because the Canaanites were determined to stay there. ²⁸Later, the Israelites grew strong and forced the Canaanites to work as slaves, but they did not make all the Canaanites leave their land. ²⁹The people of Ephraim did not force out all of the Canaanites living in Gezer. So the Canaanites continued to live in Gezer with the people of Ephraim. ³⁰The people of Zebulun did not force out the Canaanites living in the cities of Kitron and Nahalol. They stayed and lived with the people of Zebulun, but Zebulun made them work as slaves.

³¹The people of Asher did not force the Canaanites from the cities of Acco, Sidon, Ahlab, Aczib, Helbah, Aphek, and Rehob. ³²Since the people of Asher did not force them out, the Canaanites continued to live with them. ³³The people of Naphtali did not force out the people of the cities of Beth Shemesh and Beth Anath. So they continued to live with the Canaanites in those cities, and the Canaanites worked as slaves. ³⁴The Amorites forced the Danites back into the mountains and would not let them come down to live in the plain. ³⁵The Amorites were determined to stay in Mount Heres, Aijalon, and Shaalbim. But when the Israelites grew stronger, they made the Amorites work as slaves. ³⁶The land of the Amorites was from Scorpion Pass to Sela and beyond.

THE ANGEL OF THE LORD AT BOKIM

2 The angel of the LORD went up from Gilgal to Bokim and said, "I brought you up from Egypt and led you to the land I promised to give your ancestors. I said, 'I will never break my agreement with you. ²But you must not make an agreement with the people who live in this land. You must destroy their altars.' But you did not obey me. How could you do this? ³Now I tell you, 'I will not force out the people in this land. They will be your

enemies, and their gods will be a trap for you.'"

⁴After the angel gave Israel this message from the LORD, they cried loudly. ⁵So they named the place Bokim.ⁿ There they offered sacrifices to the LORD.

JOSHUA DIES

⁶Then Joshua sent the people back to their land. ⁷The people served the LORD during the lifetime of Joshua and during the lifetimes of the elders who lived after Joshua and who had seen what great things the LORD had done for Israel. ⁸Joshua son of Nun, the servant of the LORD, died at the age of one hundred ten. ⁹They buried him in his own land at Timnath Serah in the mountains of Ephraim, north of Mount Gaash.

THE PEOPLE DISOBEY

¹⁰After those people had died, their children grew up and did not know the LORD or what he had done for Israel. ¹¹So they did what the LORD said was wrong, and they worshiped the Baal idols. ¹²They quit following the LORD, the God of their ancestors who had brought them out of Egypt. They began to worship the gods of the people who lived around them, and that made the LORD angry. ¹³The Israelites quit following the LORD and worshiped Baal and Ashtoreth. ¹⁴The LORD was angry with the people of Israel, so he handed them over to robbers who took their possessions. He let their enemies who lived around them defeat them; they could not protect themselves. ¹⁵When the Israelites went out to fight, they always lost, because the LORD was not with them. The LORD had sworn to them this would happen. So the Israelites suffered very much.

GOD CHOOSES JUDGES

¹⁶Then the LORD chose leaders called judges,ⁿ who saved the Israelites from the robbers. ¹⁷But the Israelites did not listen to their judges. They were not faithful to God but worshiped other gods instead. Their ancestors had obeyed the LORD's commands, but they quickly turned away and did not obey. ¹⁸When their enemies hurt them, the

---

2:5 Bokim This name means "crying." **2:16 judges** They were not judges in courts of law, but leaders of the people in times of emergency.

Israelites cried for help. So the LORD felt sorry for them and sent judges to save them from their enemies. The LORD was with those judges all their lives. 19But when the judges died, the Israelites again sinned and worshiped other gods. They became worse than their ancestors. The Israelites were very stubborn and refused to change their evil ways.

20So the LORD became angry with the Israelites. He said, "These people have broken the agreement I made with their ancestors. They have not listened to me. 21I will no longer defeat the nations who were left when Joshua died. 22I will use them to test Israel, to see if Israel will keep the LORD's commands as their ancestors did." 23In the past the LORD had permitted those nations to stay in the land. He did not quickly force them out or help Joshua's army defeat them.

3 These are the nations the LORD did not force to leave. He wanted to test the Israelites who had not fought in the wars of Canaan. 2(The only reason the LORD left those nations in the land was to teach the descendants of the Israelites who had not fought in those wars how to fight.) 3These are the nations: the five rulers of the Philistines, all the Canaanites, the people of Sidon, and the Hivites who lived in the Lebanon mountains from Mount Baal Hermon to Lebo Hamath. 4Those nations were in the land to test the Israelites—to see if they would obey the commands the LORD had given to their ancestors by Moses.

5The people of Israel lived with the Canaanites, Hittites, Amorites, Perizzites, Hivites, and Jebusites. 6The Israelites began to marry the daughters of those people, and they allowed their daughters to marry the sons of those people. Israel also served their gods.

OTHNIEL, THE FIRST JUDGE

7The Israelites did what the LORD said was wrong. They forgot about the LORD their God and served the idols of Baal and Asherah. 8So the LORD was angry with Israel and allowed Cushan-Rishathaim king of Northwest Mesopotamia to rule over the Israelites for eight years. 9When Israel cried to the LORD, the LORD sent someone to save them. Othniel son of Kenaz, Caleb's younger brother, saved the Israelites. 10The Spirit of the LORD entered Othniel, and he became Israel's judge. When he went to war, the LORD handed over to him Cushan-Rishathaim king of Northwest Mesopotamia. 11So the land was at peace for forty years. Then Othniel son of Kenaz died.

EHUD, THE JUDGE

12Again the people of Israel did what the LORD said was wrong. So the LORD gave Eglon king of Moab power to defeat Israel because of the evil Israel did. 13Eglon got the Ammonites and the Amalekites to join him. Then he attacked Israel and took Jericho, the city of palm trees. 14So the people of Israel were ruled by Eglon king of Moab for eighteen years.

15When the people cried to the LORD, he sent someone to save them. He was Ehud, son of Gera from the people of Benjamin, who was left-handed. Israel sent Ehud to give Eglon king of Moab the payment he demanded. 16Ehud made himself a sword with two edges, about eighteen inches long, and he tied it to his right hip under his clothes. 17Ehud gave Eglon king of Moab the payment he demanded. Now Eglon was a very fat man. 18After he had given Eglon the payment, Ehud sent away the people who had carried it. 19When he passed the statues near Gilgal, he turned around and said to Eglon, "I have a secret message for you, King Eglon."

The king said, "Be quiet!" Then he sent all of his servants out of the room. 20Ehud went to King Eglon, as he was sitting alone in the room above his summer palace.

Ehud said, "I have a message from God for you." As the king stood up from his chair, 21Ehud reached with his left hand and took out the sword that was tied to his right hip. Then he stabbed the sword deep into the king's belly! 22Even the handle sank in, and the blade came out his back. The king's fat covered the whole sword, so Ehud left the sword in Eglon. 23Then he went out of the room and closed and locked the doors behind him.

24When the servants returned just after Ehud left, they found the doors to the room locked. So they thought the king was relieving himself. 25They waited for a long time. Finally they became worried because he still had not opened the doors. So they got the key and unlocked them and saw their king lying dead on the floor!

26While the servants were waiting, Ehud had escaped. He passed by the statues and went to Seirah. 27When he reached the mountains of Ephraim he blew the trumpet. The people of Israel heard it and went down from the hills with Ehud leading them.

28He said to them, "Follow me! The LORD has helped you to defeat your enemies, the Moabites." So Israel followed Ehud and captured the crossings of the Jordan River. They did not allow the Moabites to cross the Jordan River. 29Israel killed about ten thousand strong and able men from Moab; not one escaped. 30So that day Moab was forced to be under the rule of Israel, and there was peace in the land for eighty years.

SHAMGAR, THE JUDGE

31After Ehud, Shamgar son of Anath saved Israel. Shamgar killed six hundred Philistines with a sharp stick used to guide oxen.

DEBORAH, THE WOMAN JUDGE

4 After Ehud died, the Israelites again did what the LORD said was wrong. 2So he let Jabin, a king of Canaan who ruled in the city of Hazor, defeat Israel. Sisera, who lived in Harosheth Haggoyim, was the commander of Jabin's army. 3Because he had nine hundred iron chariots and was very cruel to the people of Israel for twenty years, they cried to the LORD for help.

4A prophetess named Deborah, the wife of Lappidoth, was judge of Israel at that time. 5Deborah would sit under the Palm Tree of Deborah, which was between the cities of Ramah and Bethel, in the mountains of Ephraim. And the people of Israel would come to her to settle their arguments.

6Deborah sent a message to Barak son of Abinoam. Barak lived in the city of Kedesh, which is in the area of Naphtali. Deborah said to Barak, "The LORD, the God of Israel, commands you: 'Go and gather ten thousand men of Naphtali and Zebulun and lead them to Mount Tabor. 7I will make Sisera, the commander of Jabin's army, and his chariots, and his army meet you at the Kishon River. I will hand Sisera over to you.'"

8Then Barak said to Deborah, "I will go if you will go with me, but if you won't go with me, I won't go."

9"Of course I will go with you," Deborah answered, "but you will not get credit for the victory. The LORD will let a woman defeat Sisera." So Deborah went with Barak to Kedesh. 10At Kedesh, Barak called the people of Zebulun and Naphtali together. From them, he gathered ten thousand men to follow him, and Deborah went with him also.

11Now Heber the Kenite had left the other Kenites, the descendants of Hobab, Moses' brother-in-law. Heber had put up his tent by the great tree in Zaanannim, near Kedesh.

12When Sisera was told that Barak son of Abinoam had gone to Mount Tabor, 13Sisera gathered his nine hundred iron chariots and all the men with him, from Harosheth Haggoyim to the Kishon River.

14Then Deborah said to Barak, "Get up! Today is the day the LORD will hand over Sisera. The LORD has already cleared the way for you." So Barak led ten thousand men down Mount Tabor. 15As Barak approached, the LORD confused Sisera and his army and chariots. The LORD defeated them with the sword, but Sisera left his chariot and ran away on foot. 16Barak and his men chased Sisera's chariots and army to Harosheth Haggoyim. With their swords they killed all of Sisera's men; not one of them was left alive.

17But Sisera himself ran away to the tent where Jael lived. She was the wife of Heber, one of the Kenite family groups. Heber's family was at peace with Jabin king of Hazor. 18Jael went out to meet Sisera and said to him, "Come into my tent, master! Come in. Don't be afraid." So Sisera went into Jael's tent, and she covered him with a rug.

19Sisera said to Jael, "I am thirsty. Please give me some water to drink." So she opened a leather bag of milk and gave him a drink. Then she covered him up.

20He said to her, "Go stand at the entrance to the tent. If anyone comes and asks you, 'Is anyone here?' say, 'No.'"

21But Jael, the wife of Heber, took a tent peg and a hammer and quietly went to Sisera. Since he was very tired, he was in a deep sleep. She hammered the tent peg through the side of Sisera's head and into the ground. And so Sisera died.

22At that very moment Barak came by

Jael's tent, chasing Sisera. Jael went out to meet him and said, "Come. I will show you the man you are looking for." So Barak entered her tent, and there Sisera lay dead, with the tent peg in his head.

23On that day God defeated Jabin king of Canaan in the sight of Israel.

24Israel became stronger and stronger against Jabin king of Canaan until finally they destroyed him.

THE SONG OF DEBORAH

5 On that day Deborah and Barak son of Abinoam sang this song:

2 "The leaders led Israel.
  The people volunteered to go to battle.
  Praise the LORD!

3 Listen, kings.
  Pay attention, rulers!
I myself will sing to the LORD.
  I will make music to the LORD, the God of Israel.

4 "LORD, when you came from Edom,
  when you marched from the land of Edom,
the earth shook,
  the skies rained,
and the clouds dropped water.

5 The mountains shook before the LORD,
  the God of Mount Sinai,
before the LORD, the God of Israel!

6 "In the days of Shamgar son of Anath,
  in the days of Jael, the main roads were empty.
  Travelers went on the back roads.

7 There were no warriors in Israel
  until I, Deborah, arose,
  until I arose to be a mother to Israel.

8 At that time they chose to follow new gods.
  Because of this, enemies fought us at our city gates.
No one could find a shield or a spear
  among the forty thousand people of Israel.

9 My heart is with the commanders of Israel.
  They volunteered freely from among the people.
  Praise the LORD!

10 "You who ride on white donkeys
  and sit on saddle blankets,
and you who walk along the road,
  listen!

11 Listen to the sound of the singers
  at the watering holes.
There they tell about the victories of the LORD,
  the victories of the LORD's warriors in Israel.
Then the LORD's people went down to the city gates.

12 "Wake up, wake up, Deborah!
  Wake up, wake up, sing a song!
Get up, Barak!
  Go capture your enemies, son of Abinoam!

13 "Then those who were left came down to the important leaders.
  The LORD's people came down to me with strong men.

14 They came from Ephraim in the mountains of Amalek.
  Benjamin was among the people who followed you.
From the family group of Makir, the commanders came down.
  And from Zebulun came those who lead.

15 The princes of Issachar were with Deborah.
  The people of Issachar were loyal to Barak
  and followed him into the valley.
The Reubenites thought hard
  about what they would do.

16 Why did you stay by the sheepfold?
  Was it to hear the music played for your sheep?
The Reubenites thought hard
  about what they would do.

17 The people of Gilead stayed east of the Jordan River.
  People of Dan, why did you stay by the ships?
The people of Asher stayed at the seashore,
  at their safe harbors.

18 But the people of Zebulun risked their lives,
  as did the people of Naphtali on the battlefield.

Israel, as you said." ³⁸And that is just what happened. When Gideon got up early the next morning and squeezed the wool, he got a full bowl of water from it.

³⁹Then Gideon said to God, "Don't be angry with me if I ask just one more thing. Please let me make one more test. Let only the wool be dry while the ground around it gets wet with dew." ⁴⁰That night God did that very thing. Just the wool was dry, but the ground around it was wet with dew.

7 Early in the morning Jerub-Baal (also called Gideon) and all his men set up their camp at the spring of Harod. The Midianites were camped north of them in the valley at the bottom of the hill called Moreh. ²Then the LORD said to Gideon, "You have too many men to defeat the Midianites. I don't want the Israelites to brag that they saved themselves. ³So now, announce to the people, 'Anyone who is afraid may leave Mount Gilead and go back home.'" So twenty-two thousand men returned home, but ten thousand remained.

⁴Then the LORD said to Gideon, "There are still too many men. Take the men down to the water, and I will test them for you there. If I say, 'This man will go with you, he will go. But if I say, 'That one will not go with you,' he will not go."

⁵So Gideon led the men down to the water. There the LORD said to him, "Separate them into those who drink water by lapping it up like a dog and those who bend down to drink." ⁶There were three hundred men who used their hands to bring water to their mouths, lapping it as a dog does. All the rest got down on their knees to drink.

⁷Then the LORD said to Gideon, "Using the three hundred men who lapped the water, I will save you and hand Midian over to you. Let all the others go home." ⁸So Gideon sent the rest of Israel to their homes. But he kept three hundred men and took the jars and the trumpets of those who left.

Now the camp of Midian was in the valley below Gideon. ⁹That night the LORD said to Gideon, "Get up. Go down and attack the camp of the Midianites, because I will give them to you. ¹⁰But if you are afraid to go down, take your servant Purah with you. ¹¹When you come to the camp of Midian, you will hear what they are saying. Then you will not be afraid to attack the camp."

GIDEON IS ENCOURAGED

So Gideon and his servant Purah went down to the edge of the enemy camp. ¹²The Midianites, the Amalekites, and all the peoples from the east were camped in that valley. There were so many of them they seemed like locusts. Their camels could not be counted because they were as many as the grains of sand on the seashore!

¹³When Gideon came to the enemy camp, he heard a man telling his friend about a dream. He was saying, "I dreamed that a loaf of barley bread rolled into the camp of Midian. It hit the tent so hard that the tent turned over and fell flat!"

¹⁴The man's friend said, "Your dream is about the sword of Gideon son of Joash, a man of Israel. God will hand Midian and the whole army over to him!"

¹⁵When Gideon heard about the dream and what it meant, he worshiped God. Then Gideon went back to the camp of Israel and called out to them, "Get up! The LORD has handed the army of Midian over to you!" ¹⁶Gideon divided the three hundred men into three groups. He gave each man a trumpet and an empty jar with a burning torch inside.

¹⁷Gideon told the men, "Watch me and do what I do. When I get to the edge of the camp, do what I do. ¹⁸Surround the enemy camp. When I and everyone with me blow our trumpets, you blow your trumpets, too. Then shout, 'For the LORD and for Gideon!'"

MIDIAN IS DEFEATED

¹⁹So Gideon and the one hundred men with him came to the edge of the enemy camp just after they had changed guards. It was during the middle watch of the night. Then Gideon and his men blew their trumpets and smashed their jars. ²⁰All three groups of Gideon's men blew their trumpets and smashed their jars. They held the torches in their left hands and the trumpets in their right hands. Then they shouted, "A sword for the LORD and for Gideon!" ²¹Each of Gideon's men stayed in his place around the camp, but the Midianites began shouting and running to escape.

²²When Gideon's three hundred men blew their trumpets, the LORD made all the Midianites fight each other with their

swords! The enemy army ran away to the city of Beth Shittah toward Zererah. They ran as far as the border of Abel Meholah, near the city of Tabbath. ²³Then men of Israel from Naphtali, Asher, and all of Manasseh were called out to chase the Midianites. ²⁴Gideon sent messengers through all the mountains of Ephraim, saying, "Come down and attack the Midianites. Take control of the Jordan River as far as Beth Barah before the Midianites can get to it."

So they called out all the men of Ephraim, who took control of the Jordan River as far as Beth Barah. ²⁵The men of Ephraim captured two princes of Midian named Oreb and Zeeb. They killed Oreb at the rock of Oreb and Zeeb at the winepress of Zeeb, and they continued chasing the Midianites. They brought the heads of Oreb and Zeeb to Gideon, who was east of the Jordan River.

8 The men of Ephraim asked Gideon, "Why did you treat us this way? Why didn't you call us when you went to fight against Midian?" They argued angrily with Gideon.

²But he answered them, "I have not done as well as you! The small part you did was better than all that my people of Abiezer did. ³God let you capture Oreb and Zeeb, the princes of Midian. How can I compare what I did with what you did?" When the men of Ephraim heard Gideon's answer, they were not as angry anymore.

GIDEON CAPTURES TWO KINGS

⁴When Gideon and his three hundred men came to the Jordan River, they were tired, but they chased the enemy across to the other side. ⁵Gideon said to the men of Succoth, "Please give my soldiers some bread because they are very tired. I am chasing Zebah and Zalmunna, the kings of Midian."

⁶But the leaders of Succoth said, "Why should we give your soldiers bread? You haven't caught Zebah and Zalmunna yet."

⁷Then Gideon said, "The LORD will surrender Zebah and Zalmunna to me. After that, I will whip your skin with thorns and briers from the desert."

⁸Gideon left Succoth and went to the city of Peniel and asked them for food. But the people of Peniel gave him the same answer as the people of Succoth. ⁹So Gideon said to the men of Peniel, "After I win the victory, I will return and pull down this tower."

¹⁰Zebah and Zalmunna and their army were in the city of Karkor. About fifteen thousand men were left of the armies of the peoples of the east. Already one hundred twenty thousand soldiers had been killed. ¹¹Gideon went up the road of those who live in tents east of Nobah and Jogbehah, and he attacked the enemy army when they did not expect it. ¹²Zebah and Zalmunna, the kings of Midian, ran away, but Gideon chased and captured them and frightened away their army.

¹³Then Gideon son of Joash returned from the battle by the Pass of Heres. ¹⁴Gideon captured a young man from Succoth and asked him some questions. So the young man wrote down for Gideon the names of seventy-seven officers and elders of Succoth.

GIDEON PUNISHES SUCCOTH

¹⁵When Gideon came to Succoth, he said to the people of that city, "Here are Zebah and Zalmunna. You made fun of me by saying, 'Why should we give bread to your tired men? You have not caught Zebah and Zalmunna yet.'" ¹⁶So Gideon took the elders of the city and punished them with thorns and briers from the desert. ¹⁷He also pulled down the tower of Peniel and killed the people in that city.

¹⁸Gideon asked Zebah and Zalmunna, "What were the men like that you killed on Mount Tabor?"

They answered, "They were like you. Each one of them looked like a prince."

¹⁹Gideon said, "Those were my brothers, my mother's sons. As surely as the LORD lives, I would not kill you if you had spared them." ²⁰Then Gideon said to Jether, his oldest son, "Kill them." But Jether was only a boy and was afraid, so he did not take out his sword.

²¹Then Zebah and Zalmunna said to Gideon, "Come on. Kill us yourself. As the saying goes, 'It takes a man to do a man's job.'" So Gideon got up and killed Zebah and Zalmunna and took the decorations off their camels' necks.

GIDEON MAKES AN IDOL

²²The people of Israel said to Gideon, "You saved us from the Midianites. Now, we want you and your son and your grandson to rule over us."

[23]But Gideon told them, "The LORD will be your ruler. I will not rule over you, nor will my son rule over you." [24]He said, "I want you to do this one thing for me. I want each of you to give me a gold earring from the things you took in the fighting." (The Ishmaelites[n] wore gold earrings.)

[25]They said, "We will gladly give you what you want." So they spread out a coat, and everyone threw down an earring from what he had taken. [26]The gold earrings weighed about forty-three pounds. This did not count the decorations, necklaces, and purple robes worn by the kings of Midian, nor the chains from the camels' necks. [27]Gideon used the gold to make a holy vest, which he put in his hometown of Ophrah. But all the Israelites were unfaithful to God and worshiped it, so it became a trap for Gideon and his family.

THE DEATH OF GIDEON

[28]So Midian was under the rule of Israel; they did not cause trouble anymore. And the land had peace for forty years, as long as Gideon was alive.

[29]Gideon[n] son of Joash went to his home to live. [30]He had seventy sons of his own, because he had many wives. [31]He had a slave woman who lived in Shechem, and he had a son by her, whom he named Abimelech. [32]So Gideon son of Joash died at a good old age. He was buried in the tomb of Joash, his father, in Ophrah, where the Abiezrites live.

[33]As soon as Gideon died, the people of Israel were again unfaithful to God and followed the Baals. They made Baal-Berith their god. [34]The Israelites did not remember the LORD their God, who had saved them from all their enemies living all around them. [35]And they were not kind to the family of Jerub-Baal, also called Gideon, for all the good he had done for Israel.

ABIMELECH BECOMES KING

9 Abimelech son of Gideon went to his uncles in the city of Shechem. He said to his uncles and all of his mother's family group, [2]"Ask the leaders of Shechem, 'Is it better for the seventy sons of Gideon to rule over you or for one man to rule?' Remember, I am your relative."

[3]Abimelech's uncles spoke to all the leaders of Shechem about this. And they decided to follow Abimelech, because they said, "He is our relative." [4]So the leaders of Shechem gave Abimelech about one and three-quarter pounds of silver from the temple of the god Baal-Berith. Abimelech used the silver to hire some worthless, reckless men, who followed him wherever he went. [5]He went to Ophrah, the hometown of his father, and murdered his seventy brothers, the sons of Gideon. He killed them all on one stone. But Gideon's youngest son, Jotham, hid from Abimelech and escaped. [6]Then all of the leaders of Shechem and Beth Millo gathered beside the great tree standing in Shechem. There they made Abimelech their king.

JOTHAM'S STORY

[7]When Jotham heard this, he went and stood on the top of Mount Gerizim. He shouted to the people: "Listen to me, you leaders of Shechem, so that God will listen to you! [8]One day the trees decided to appoint a king to rule over them. They said to the olive tree, 'You be king over us!'

[9]"But the olive tree said, 'Men and gods are honored by my oil. Should I stop making it and go and sway over the other trees?'

[10]"Then the trees said to the fig tree, 'Come and be king over us!'

[11]"But the fig tree answered, 'Should I stop making my sweet and good fruit and go and sway over the other trees?'

[12]"Then the trees said to the vine, 'Come and be king over us!'

[13]"But the vine answered, 'My new wine makes men and gods happy. Should I stop making it and go and sway over the trees?'

[14]"Then all the trees said to the thornbush, 'Come and be king over us.'

[15]"But the thornbush said to the trees, 'If you really want to appoint me king over you, come and find shelter in my shade! But if not, let fire come out of the thornbush and burn up the cedars of Lebanon!'

[16]"Now, were you completely honest and sincere when you made Abimelech king? Have you been fair to Gideon[n] and his family? Have you treated Gideon as you should? [17]Remember, my father fought for you and risked his life to save you from the power of

---

8:24 Ishmaelites Another name for the Midianites. See Genesis 37:25–28. **8:29; 9:16 Gideon** Also called Jerub-Baal.

the Midianites. [18]But now you have turned against my father's family and have killed his seventy sons on one stone. You have made Abimelech, the son of my father's slave girl, king over the leaders of Shechem just because he is your relative! [19]So then, if you have been honest and sincere to Gideon and his family today, be happy with Abimelech as your king. And may he be happy with you! [20]But if not, may fire come out of Abimelech and completely burn you leaders of Shechem and Beth Millo! Also may fire come out of the leaders of Shechem and Beth Millo and burn up Abimelech!"

[21]Then Jotham ran away and escaped to the city of Beer. He lived there because he was afraid of his brother Abimelech.

ABIMELECH FIGHTS AGAINST SHECHEM

[22]Abimelech ruled Israel for three years. [23]Then God sent an evil spirit to make trouble between Abimelech and the leaders of Shechem so that the leaders of Shechem turned against him. [24]Abimelech had killed Gideon's[n] seventy sons, his own brothers, and the leaders of Shechem had helped him. So God sent the evil spirit to punish them. [25]The leaders of Shechem were against Abimelech then. They put men on the hilltops in ambush who robbed everyone going by. And Abimelech was told.

[26]A man named Gaal son of Ebed and his brothers moved into Shechem, and the leaders of Shechem trusted him. [27]They went out to the vineyards to pick grapes, and they squeezed the grapes. Then they had a feast in the temple of their god, where they ate and drank and cursed Abimelech. [28]Gaal son of Ebed said, "We are the men of Shechem. Who is Abimelech that we should serve him? Isn't he one of Gideon's sons, and isn't Zebul his officer? We should serve the men of Hamor, Shechem's father. Why should we serve Abimelech? [29]If you made me commander of these people, I would get rid of Abimelech. I would say to him, 'Get your army ready and come out to battle.'"

[30]Now when Zebul, the ruler of Shechem, heard what Gaal son of Ebed said, he was very angry. [31]He sent secret messengers to Abimelech, saying, "Gaal son of Ebed and Gaal's brothers have come to Shechem, and they are turning the city against you!

[32]You and your men should get up during the night and hide in the fields outside the city. [33]As soon as the sun comes up in the morning, attack the city. When Gaal and his men come out to fight you, do what you can to them."

[34]So Abimelech and all his soldiers got up during the night and hid near Shechem in four groups. [35]Gaal son of Ebed went out and was standing at the entrance to the city gate. As he was standing there, Abimelech and his soldiers came out of their hiding places.

[36]When Gaal saw the soldiers, he said to Zebul, "Look! There are people coming down from the mountains!"

But Zebul said, "You are seeing the shadows of the mountains. The shadows just look like people."

[37]But again Gaal said, "Look, there are people coming down from the center of the land, and there is a group coming from the fortune-tellers' tree!"

[38]Zebul said to Gaal, "Where is your bragging now? You said, 'Who is Abimelech that we should serve him?' You made fun of these men. Now go out and fight them."

[39]So Gaal led the men of Shechem out to fight Abimelech. [40]Abimelech and his men chased them, and many of Gaal's men were killed before they could get back to the city gate. [41]While Abimelech stayed at Arumah, Zebul forced Gaal and his brothers to leave Shechem.

[42]The next day the people of Shechem went out to the fields. When Abimelech was told about it, [43]he separated his men into three groups and hid them in the fields. When he saw the people coming out of the city, he jumped up and attacked them. [44]Abimelech and his group ran to the entrance gate to the city. The other two groups ran out to the people in the fields and struck them down. [45]Abimelech and his men fought the city of Shechem all day until they captured it and killed its people. Then he tore it down and threw salt[n] over the ruins.

THE TOWER OF SHECHEM BURNS

[46]When the leaders who were in the Tower of Shechem heard what had happened

---

9:24 Gideon Also called Jerub-Baal. **9:45 salt** The salt would keep crops from growing there.

to Shechem, they gathered in the safest room of the temple of El Berith. ⁴⁷Abimelech heard that all the leaders of the Tower of Shechem had gathered there. ⁴⁸So he and all his men went up Mount Zalmon, near Shechem. Abimelech took an ax and cut some branches and put them on his shoulders. He said to all those with him, "Hurry! Do what I have done!" ⁴⁹So all those men cut branches and followed Abimelech and piled them against the safest room of the temple. Then they set them on fire and burned the people inside. So all the people who were at the Tower of Shechem also died—about a thousand men and women.

ABIMELECH'S DEATH

⁵⁰Then Abimelech went to the city of Thebez. He surrounded the city, attacked it, and captured it. ⁵¹But inside the city was a strong tower, so all the men, women, and leaders of that city ran to the tower. When they got inside, they locked the door behind them. Then they climbed up to the roof of the tower. ⁵²Abimelech came to the tower to attack it. He approached the door of the tower to set it on fire, ⁵³but as he came near, a woman dropped a grinding stone on his head, crushing his skull.

⁵⁴He quickly called to the officer who carried his armor and said, "Take out your sword and kill me. I don't want people to say, 'A woman killed Abimelech.'" So the officer stabbed Abimelech, and he died. ⁵⁵When the people of Israel saw Abimelech was dead, they all returned home.

⁵⁶In that way God punished Abimelech for all the evil he had done to his father by killing his seventy brothers. ⁵⁷God also punished the men of Shechem for the evil they had done. So the curse spoken by Jotham, the youngest son of Gideon,ⁿ came true.

TOLA, THE JUDGE

10 After Abimelech died, another judge came to save Israel. He was Tola son of Puah, the son of Dodo. Tola was from the people of Issachar and lived in the city of Shamir in the mountains of Ephraim. ²Tola was a judge for Israel for twenty-three years. Then he died and was buried in Shamir.

JAIR, THE JUDGE

³After Tola died, Jair from the region of Gilead became judge. He was a judge for Israel for twenty-two years. ⁴Jair had thirty sons, who rode thirty donkeys. These thirty sons controlled thirty towns in Gilead, which are called the Towns of Jair to this day. ⁵Jair died and was buried in the city of Kamon.

THE AMMONITES TROUBLE ISRAEL

⁶Again the Israelites did what the LORD said was wrong. They worshiped Baal and Ashtoreth, the gods of Aram, Sidon, Moab, and Ammon, and the gods of the Philistines. The Israelites left the LORD and stopped serving him. ⁷So the LORD was angry with them and handed them over to the Philistines and the Ammonites. ⁸In the same year those people destroyed the Israelites who lived east of the Jordan River in the region of Gilead, where the Amorites lived. So the Israelites suffered for eighteen years. ⁹The Ammonites then crossed the Jordan River to fight the people of Judah, Benjamin, and Ephraim, causing much trouble to the people of Israel. ¹⁰So the Israelites cried out to the LORD, "We have sinned against you. We left our God and worshiped the Baal idols."

¹¹The LORD answered the Israelites, "When the Egyptians, Amorites, Ammonites, Philistines, ¹²Sidonians, Amalekites, and Maonites were cruel to you, you cried out to me, and I saved you. ¹³But now you have left me again and have worshiped other gods. So I refuse to save you again. ¹⁴You have chosen those gods. So go call to them for help. Let them save you when you are in trouble."

¹⁵But the people of Israel said to the LORD, "We have sinned. Do to us whatever you want, but please save us today!" ¹⁶Then the Israelites threw away the foreign gods among them, and they worshiped the LORD again. So he felt sorry for them when he saw their suffering.

¹⁷The Ammonites gathered for war and camped in Gilead. The Israelites gathered and camped at Mizpah. ¹⁸The leaders of the people of Gilead said, "Who will lead us to attack the Ammonites? He will become the head of all those who live in Gilead."

9:57 Gideon Also called Jerub-Baal.

JEPHTHAH IS CHOSEN AS LEADER

11 Jephthah was a strong soldier from Gilead. His father was named Gilead, and his mother was a prostitute. ²Gilead's wife had several sons. When they grew up, they forced Jephthah to leave his home, saying to him, "You will not get any of our father's property, because you are the son of another woman." ³So Jephthah ran away from his brothers and lived in the land of Tob. There some worthless men began to follow him.

⁴After a time the Ammonites fought against Israel. ⁵When the Ammonites made war against Israel, the elders of Gilead went to Jephthah to bring him back from Tob. ⁶They said to him, "Come and lead our army so we can fight the Ammonites."

⁷But Jephthah said to them, "Didn't you hate me? You forced me to leave my father's house. Why are you coming to me now that you are in trouble?"

⁸The elders of Gilead said to Jephthah, "It is because of those troubles that we come to you now. Please come with us and fight against the Ammonites. You will be the ruler over everyone who lives in Gilead."

⁹Then Jephthah answered, "If you take me back to Gilead to fight the Ammonites and the LORD helps me win, I will be your ruler."

¹⁰The elders of Gilead said to him, "The LORD is listening to everything we are saying. We promise to do all that you tell us to do." ¹¹So Jephthah went with the elders of Gilead, and the people made him their leader and commander of their army. Jephthah repeated all of his words in front of the LORD at Mizpah.

JEPHTHAH SENDS MESSENGERS TO THE AMMONITE KING

¹²Jephthah sent messengers to the king of the Ammonites, asking, "What have you got against Israel? Why have you come to attack our land?"

¹³The king of the Ammonites answered the messengers of Jephthah, "We are fighting Israel because you took our land when you came up from Egypt. You took our land from the Arnon River to the Jabbok River to the Jordan River. Now give our land back to us peacefully."

¹⁴Jephthah sent the messengers to the Ammonite king again. ¹⁵They said:

"This is what Jephthah says: Israel did not take the land of the people of Moab or Ammon. ¹⁶When the Israelites came out of Egypt, they went into the desert to the Red Sea and then to Kadesh. ¹⁷Israel sent messengers to the king of Edom, saying, 'Let the people of Israel go across your land.' But the king of Edom refused. We sent the same message to the king of Moab, but he also refused. So the Israelites stayed at Kadesh.

¹⁸"Then the Israelites went into the desert around the borders of the lands of Edom and Moab. Israel went east of the land of Moab and camped on the other side of the Arnon River, the border of Moab. They did not cross it to go into the land of Moab.

¹⁹"Then Israel sent messengers to Sihon king of the Amorites, king of the city of Heshbon, asking, 'Let the people of Israel pass through your land to go to our land.' ²⁰But Sihon did not trust the Israelites to cross his land. So he gathered all of his people and camped at Jahaz and fought with Israel.

²¹"But the LORD, the God of Israel, handed Sihon and his army over to Israel. All the land of the Amorites became the property of Israel. ²²So Israel took all the land of the Amorites from the Arnon River to the Jabbok River, from the desert to the Jordan River.

²³"It was the LORD, the God of Israel, who forced out the Amorites ahead of the people of Israel. So do you think you can make them leave? ²⁴Take the land that your god Chemosh has given you. We will live in the land the LORD our God has given us!

²⁵"Are you any better than Balak son of Zippor, king of Moab? Did he ever quarrel or fight with the people of Israel? ²⁶For three hundred years the Israelites have lived in Heshbon and Aroer and the towns around them and in all the cities along the Arnon River. Why have you not taken these cities back in all that time? ²⁷I have not sinned against you, but you are sinning against me by making war on me. May the LORD, the Judge, decide whether the Israelites or the Ammonites are right."

²⁸But the king of the Ammonites ignored this message from Jephthah.

JEPHTHAH'S PROMISE

²⁹Then the Spirit of the LORD entered Jephthah. Jephthah passed through Gilead and Manasseh and the city of Mizpah in Gilead to the land of the Ammonites. ³⁰Jephthah made a promise to the LORD, saying, "If you will hand over the Ammonites to me, ³¹I will give you as a burnt offering the first thing that comes out of my house to meet me when I return from the victory. It will be the LORD's."

³²Then Jephthah went over to fight the Ammonites, and the LORD handed them over to him. ³³In a great defeat Jephthah struck them down from the city of Aroer to the area of Minnith, and twenty cities as far as the city of Abel Keramim. So the Ammonites were defeated by the Israelites.

³⁴When Jephthah returned to his home in Mizpah, his daughter was the first one to come out to meet him, playing a tambourine and dancing. She was his only child; he had no other sons or daughters. ³⁵When Jephthah saw his daughter, he tore his clothes to show his sorrow. He said, "My daughter! You have made me so sad because I made a promise to the LORD, and I cannot break it!"

³⁶Then his daughter said, "Father, you made a promise to the LORD. So do to me just what you promised, because the LORD helped you defeat your enemies, the Ammonites." ³⁷She also said, "But let me do one thing. Let me be alone for two months to go to the mountains. Since I will never marry, let me and my friends go and cry together."

³⁸Jephthah said, "Go." So he sent her away for two months. She and her friends stayed in the mountains and cried for her because she would never marry. ³⁹After two months she returned to her father, and Jephthah did to her what he had promised. Jephthah's daughter never had a husband.

From this came a custom in Israel that ⁴⁰every year the young women of Israel would go out for four days to remember the daughter of Jephthah from Gilead.

JEPHTHAH AND EPHRAIM

12 The men of Ephraim called all their soldiers together and crossed the river to the town of Zaphon. They said to Jephthah, "Why didn't you call us to help you fight the Ammonites? We will burn your house down with you in it."

²Jephthah answered them, "My people and I fought a great battle against the Ammonites. I called you, but you didn't come to help me. ³When I saw that you would not help me, I risked my own life and went against the Ammonites. The LORD handed them over to me. So why have you come to fight against me today?"

⁴Then Jephthah called the men of Gilead together and fought the men of Ephraim. The men of Gilead struck them down because the Ephraimites had said, "You men of Gilead are nothing but deserters from Ephraim—living between Ephraim and Manasseh." ⁵The men of Gilead captured the crossings of the Jordan River that led to the country of Ephraim. A person from Ephraim trying to escape would say, "Let me cross the river." Then the men of Gilead would ask him, "Are you from Ephraim?" If he replied no, ⁶they would say to him, "Say the word 'Shibboleth.'" The men of Ephraim could not say that word correctly. So if the person from Ephraim said, "Sibboleth," the men of Gilead would kill him at the crossing. So forty-two thousand people from Ephraim were killed at that time.

⁷Jephthah was a judge for Israel for six years. Then Jephthah, the man from Gilead, died and was buried in a town in Gilead.

IBZAN, THE JUDGE

⁸After Jephthah died, Ibzan from Bethlehem was a judge for Israel. ⁹He had thirty sons and thirty daughters. He let his daughters marry men who were not in his family group, and he brought thirty women who were not in his tribe to be wives for his sons. Ibzan judged Israel for seven years. ¹⁰Then he died and was buried in Bethlehem.

ELON, THE JUDGE

¹¹After Ibzan died, Elon from the tribe of Zebulun was a judge for Israel. He judged Israel for ten years. ¹²Then Elon, the man of Zebulun, died and was buried in the city of Aijalon in the land of Zebulun.

ABDON, THE JUDGE

¹³After Elon died, Abdon son of Hillel from the city of Pirathon was a judge for Israel. ¹⁴He had forty sons and thirty grandsons, who rode on seventy donkeys. He judged

Israel for eight years. ¹⁵Then Abdon son of Hillel died and was buried in Pirathon in the land of Ephraim, in the mountains where the Amalekites lived.

THE BIRTH OF SAMSON

13 Again the people of Israel did what the LORD said was wrong. So he handed them over to the Philistines for forty years.

²There was a man named Manoah from the tribe of Dan, who lived in the city of Zorah. He had a wife, but she could not have children. ³The angel of the LORD appeared to Manoah's wife and said, "You have not been able to have children, but you will become pregnant and give birth to a son. ⁴Be careful not to drink wine or beer or eat anything that is unclean, ⁵because you will become pregnant and have a son. You must never cut his hair, because he will be a Nazirite, given to God from birth. He will begin to save Israel from the power of the Philistines."

⁶Then Manoah's wife went to him and told him what had happened. She said, "A man from God came to me. He looked like an angel from God; his appearance was frightening. I didn't ask him where he was from, and he didn't tell me his name. ⁷But he said to me, 'You will become pregnant and will have a son. Don't drink wine or beer or eat anything that is unclean, because the boy will be a Nazirite to God from his birth until the day of his death.'"

⁸Then Manoah prayed to the LORD: "Lord, I beg you to let the man of God come to us again. Let him teach us what we should do for the boy who will be born to us."

⁹God heard Manoah's prayer, and the angel of God came to Manoah's wife again while she was sitting in the field. But her husband Manoah was not with her. ¹⁰So she ran to tell him, "He is here! The man who appeared to me the other day is here!"

¹¹Manoah got up and followed his wife. When he came to the man, he said, "Are you the man who spoke to my wife?"

The man said, "I am."

¹²So Manoah asked, "When what you say happens, what kind of life should the boy live? What should he do?"

¹³The angel of the LORD said, "Your wife must be careful to do everything I told her to do. ¹⁴She must not eat anything that grows on a grapevine, or drink any wine or beer, or eat anything that is unclean. She must do everything I have commanded her."

¹⁵Manoah said to the angel of the LORD, "We would like you to stay awhile so we can cook a young goat for you."

¹⁶The angel of the LORD answered, "Even if I stay awhile, I would not eat your food. But if you want to prepare something, offer a burnt offering to the LORD." (Manoah did not understand that the man was really the angel of the LORD.)

¹⁷Then Manoah asked the angel of the LORD, "What is your name? Then we will honor you when what you have said really happens."

¹⁸The angel of the LORD said, "Why do you ask my name? It is too amazing for you to understand." ¹⁹So Manoah sacrificed a young goat on a rock and offered some grain as a gift to the LORD. Then an amazing thing happened as Manoah and his wife watched. ²⁰The flames went up to the sky from the altar. As the fire burned, the angel of the LORD went up to heaven in the flame. When Manoah and his wife saw that, they bowed facedown on the ground. ²¹The angel of the LORD did not appear to them again. Then Manoah understood that the man was really the angel of the LORD. ²²Manoah said, "We have seen God, so we will surely die."

²³But his wife said to him, "If the LORD wanted to kill us, he would not have accepted our burnt offering or grain offering. He would not have shown us all these things or told us all this."

²⁴So the woman gave birth to a boy and named him Samson. He grew, and the LORD blessed him. ²⁵The Spirit of the LORD began to work in Samson while he was in the city of Mahaneh Dan, between the cities of Zorah and Eshtaol.

SAMSON'S FIRST MARRIAGE

14 Samson went down to the city of Timnah where he saw a Philistine woman. ²When he returned home, he said to his father and mother, "I saw a Philistine woman in Timnah. I want you to get her for me so I can marry her."

³His father and mother answered, "Surely there is a woman from Israel you can marry. Do you have to marry a woman from

the Philistines, who are not circumcised?"

But Samson said, "Get that woman for me! She is the one I want!" [4](Samson's parents did not know that the LORD wanted this to happen because he was looking for a way to challenge the Philistines, who were ruling over Israel at this time.) [5]Samson went down with his father and mother to Timnah, as far as the vineyard near there. Suddenly, a young lion came roaring toward Samson! [6]The Spirit of the LORD entered Samson with great power, and he tore the lion apart with his bare hands. For him it was as easy as tearing apart a young goat. But Samson did not tell his father or mother what he had done. [7]Then he went down to the city and talked to the Philistine woman, and he liked her.

[8]Several days later Samson went back to marry her. On his way he went over to look at the body of the dead lion and found a swarm of bees and honey in it. [9]Samson got some of the honey with his hands and walked along eating it. When he came to his parents, he gave some to them. They ate it, too, but Samson did not tell them he had taken the honey from the body of the dead lion.

[10]Samson's father went down to see the Philistine woman. And Samson gave a feast, as was the custom for the bridegroom. [11]When the people saw him, they sent thirty friends to be with him.

SAMSON'S RIDDLE

[12]Samson said to them, "Let me tell you a riddle. Try to find the answer during the seven days of the feast. If you can, I will give you thirty linen shirts and thirty changes of clothes. [13]But if you can't, you must give me thirty linen shirts and thirty changes of clothes."

So they said, "Tell us your riddle so we can hear it."

[14]Samson said,

"Out of the eater comes something to eat.
  Out of the strong comes something
      sweet."

After three days, they had not found the answer.

[15]On the fourth[n] day they said to Samson's wife, "Did you invite us here to make us poor? Trick your husband into telling us the answer to the riddle. If you don't, we will burn you and everyone in your father's house."

[16]So Samson's wife went to him, crying, and said, "You hate me! You don't really love me! You told my people a riddle, but you won't tell me the answer."

Samson said, "I haven't even told my father or mother. Why should I tell you?"

[17]Samson's wife cried for the rest of the seven days of the feast. So he finally gave her the answer on the seventh day, because she kept bothering him. Then she told her people the answer to the riddle.

[18]Before sunset on the seventh day of the feast, the Philistine men had the answer. They came to Samson and said,

"What is sweeter than honey?
  What is stronger than a lion?"

Then Samson said to them,

"If you had not plowed with my young
      cow,
  you would not have solved my riddle!"

[19]Then the Spirit of the LORD entered Samson and gave him great power. Samson went down to the city of Ashkelon and killed thirty of its men and took all that they had and gave the clothes to the men who had answered his riddle. Then he went to his father's house very angry. [20]And Samson's wife was given to his best man.

SAMSON TROUBLES THE PHILISTINES

15 At the time of the wheat harvest, Samson went to visit his wife, taking a young goat with him. He said, "I'm going to my wife's room," but her father would not let him go in.

[2]He said to Samson, "I thought you really hated your wife, so I gave her to your best man. Her younger sister is more beautiful. Take her instead."

[3]But Samson said to them, "This time no one will blame me for hurting you Philistines!" [4]So Samson went out and caught three hundred foxes. He took two foxes at a time, tied their tails together, and then tied a torch to the tails of each pair of foxes. [5]After he lit the torches, he let the foxes loose in the grainfields of the Philistines so that he burned up their standing grain, the piles of grain, their vineyards, and their olive trees.

14:15 fourth The Hebrew word is "seventh." Some old translations say "fourth," which fits the order of events better.

6 The Philistines asked, "Who did this?"

Someone told them, "Samson, the son-in-law of the man from Timnah, did because his father-in-law gave his wife to his best man."

So the Philistines burned Samson's wife and her father to death. 7 Then Samson said to the Philistines, "Since you did this, I won't stop until I pay you back!" 8 Samson attacked the Philistines and killed many of them. Then he went down and stayed in a cave in the rock of Etam.

9 The Philistines went up and camped in the land of Judah, near a place named Lehi. 10 The men of Judah asked them, "Why have you come here to fight us?"

They answered, "We have come to make Samson our prisoner, to pay him back for what he did to our people."

11 Then three thousand men of Judah went to the cave in the rock of Etam and said to Samson, "What have you done to us? Don't you know that the Philistines rule over us?"

Samson answered, "I only paid them back for what they did to me."

12 Then they said to him, "We have come to tie you up and to hand you over to the Philistines."

Samson said to them, "Promise me you will not hurt me yourselves."

13 The men from Judah said, "We agree. We will just tie you up and give you to the Philistines. We will not kill you." So they tied Samson with two new ropes and led him up from the cave in the rock. 14 When Samson came to the place named Lehi, the Philistines came to meet him, shouting for joy. Then the Spirit of the LORD entered Samson and gave him great power. The ropes on him weakened like burned strings and fell off his hands! 15 Samson found the jawbone of a dead donkey, took it, and killed a thousand men with it!

16 Then Samson said,

"With a donkey's jawbone
    I made donkeys out of them.
With a donkey's jawbone
    I killed a thousand men!"

17 When he finished speaking, he threw away the jawbone. So that place was named Ramath Lehi.[n]

18 Samson was very thirsty, so he cried out to the LORD, "You gave me, your servant, this great victory. Do I have to die of thirst now?

Do I have to be captured by people who are not circumcised?" 19 Then God opened up a hole in the ground at Lehi, and water came out. When Samson drank, he felt better; he felt strong again. So he named that spring Caller's Spring, which is still in Lehi.

20 Samson judged Israel for twenty years in the days of the Philistines.

SAMSON GOES TO THE CITY OF GAZA

16 One day Samson went to Gaza and saw a prostitute there. He went in to spend the night with her. 2 When the people of Gaza heard, "Samson has come here!" they surrounded the place and waited for him near the city gate all night. They whispered to each other, "When dawn comes, we will kill Samson!"

3 But Samson only stayed with the prostitute until midnight. Then he got up and took hold of the doors and the two posts of the city gate and tore them loose, along with the bar. He put them on his shoulders and carried them to the top of the hill that faces the city of Hebron.

SAMSON AND DELILAH

4 After this, Samson fell in love with a woman named Delilah, who lived in the Valley of Sorek. 5 The Philistine rulers went to Delilah and said, "Find out what makes Samson so strong. Trick him into telling you how we can overpower him and capture him and tie him up. If you do this, each one of us will give you twenty-eight pounds of silver."

6 So Delilah said to Samson, "Tell me why you are so strong. How can someone tie you up and capture you?"

7 Samson answered, "Someone would have to tie me up with seven new bowstrings that have not been dried. Then I would be as weak as any other man."

8 The Philistine rulers brought Delilah seven new bowstrings that had not been dried, and she tied Samson with them. 9 Some men were hiding in another room. Delilah said to him, "Samson, the Philistines are here!" But Samson broke the bowstrings like pieces of burned string. So the Philistines did not find out the secret of Samson's strength.

10 Then Delilah said to Samson, "You made

15:17 Ramath Lehi This name means "Jawbone Hill."

a fool of me. You lied to me. Now tell me how someone can tie you up."

¹¹Samson said, "They would have to tie me with new ropes that have not been used before. Then I would become as weak as any other man."

¹²So Delilah took new ropes and tied Samson. Some men were hiding in another room. She called out to him, "Samson, the Philistines are here!" But he broke the ropes as easily as if they were threads.

¹³Then Delilah said to Samson, "Again you have made a fool of me. You lied to me. Tell me how someone can tie you up."

He said, "Using the loom,ⁿ weave the seven braids of my hair into the cloth, and tighten it with a pin. Then I will be as weak as any other man."

While Samson slept, Delilah wove the seven braids of his hair into the cloth. ¹⁴Then she fastened it with a pin.

Again she said to him, "Samson, the Philistines are here!" Samson woke up and pulled out the pin and the loom with the cloth.

¹⁵Then Delilah said to him, "How can you

16:13 loom A machine for making cloth from thread.

ANGER MANAGEMENT

for healthy muscles,
you must resist

FITNESS

JUDGES 16:3

Due to the Law of Adaptation, muscles that are continuously under "resistance" become stronger, leaner, and better developed. Muscles adapt to whatever force you apply to them. Or don't. If you consistently put a strain on a certain muscle group, it will adapt by getting more powerful and developing better tone. If you do not consistently put strain on your muscles, they will become weaker and flabbier. While Samson was endowed with supernatural strength, there is no doubt that he used his muscles—a lot.

To be healthy, lean muscle mass must increase and fat must decrease. You can't just get smaller. Getting smaller without getting fitter may just mean a smaller coffin. While aerobic exercise will cause some resistance to the set of muscles being used, it is not enough. Resistance needs to be applied throughout the entire body so that you will remove fat and increase leanness in all or most of the muscles.

Resistance exercise occurs when you apply sustained or repetitive strain to muscle. The most effective way to create resistance against the muscles, and thus produce predictable results, is a properly applied weight-lifting program. However, God designed us to walk, run, climb, play, plant, and build. Perform such daily activities for stronger muscles.

---

reflect: Exercise regularly by doing daily household activities with zest.
Go to **Job 10:10–11.**

say, 'I love you,' when you don't even trust me? This is the third time you have made a fool of me. You haven't told me the secret of your great strength." [16]She kept bothering Samson about his secret day after day until he felt he was going to die!

[17]So he told her everything. He said, "I have never had my hair cut, because I have been set apart to God as a Nazirite since I was born. If someone shaved my head, I would lose my strength and be as weak as any other man."

[18]When Delilah saw that he had told her everything sincerely, she sent a message to the Philistine rulers. She said, "Come back one more time, because he has told me everything." So the Philistine rulers came back to Delilah and brought the silver with them. [19]Delilah got Samson to sleep, lying in her lap. Then she called in a man to shave off the seven braids of Samson's hair. In this way she began to make him weak, and his strength left him.

[20]Then she said, "Samson, the Philistines are here!"

He woke up and thought, "I'll leave as I did before and shake myself free." But he did not know that the LORD had left him.

[21]Then the Philistines captured Samson and tore out his eyes. They took him down to Gaza, where they put bronze chains on him and made him grind grain in the prison. [22]But his hair began to grow again.

SAMSON DIES

[23]The Philistine rulers gathered to celebrate and to offer a great sacrifice to their god Dagon. They said, "Our god has handed Samson our enemy over to us." [24]When the people saw him, they praised their god, saying,

"This man destroyed our country.
    He killed many of us!
But our god handed over
    our enemy to us."

[25]While the people were enjoying the celebration, they said, "Bring Samson out to perform for us." So they brought Samson from the prison, and he performed for them. They made him stand between the pillars. [26]Samson said to the servant holding his hand, "Let me feel the pillars that hold up the temple so I can lean against them." [27]Now

the temple was full of men and women. All the Philistine rulers were there, and about three thousand men and women were on the roof [n] watching Samson perform. [28]Then Samson prayed to the LORD, "Lord GOD, remember me. God, please give me strength one more time so I can pay these Philistines back for putting out my two eyes!" [29]Then Samson turned to the two center pillars that supported the whole temple. He braced himself between the two pillars, with his right hand on one and his left hand on the other. [30]Samson said, "Let me die with these Philistines!" Then he pushed as hard as he could, causing the temple to fall on the rulers and all the people in it. So Samson killed more of the Philistines when he died than when he was alive.

[31]Samson's brothers and his whole family went down to get his body. They brought him back and buried him in the tomb of Manoah, his father, between the cities of Zorah and Eshtaol. Samson was a judge for the people of Israel for twenty years.

MICAH'S IDOLS

17 There was a man named Micah who lived in the mountains of Ephraim. [2]He said to his mother, "I heard you speak a curse about the twenty-eight pounds of silver that were taken from you. I have the silver with me; I took it."

His mother said, "The LORD bless you, my son!"

[3]Micah gave the twenty-eight pounds of silver to his mother. Then she said, "I will give this silver to the LORD. I will have my son make an idol and a statue. So I will give the silver back to you."

[4]When he gave the silver back to his mother, she took about five pounds and gave it to a silversmith. With it he made an idol and a statue, which stood in Micah's house. [5]Micah had a special holy place, and he made a holy vest and some household idols. Then Micah chose one of his sons to be his priest. [6]At that time Israel did not have a king, so everyone did what seemed right.

[7]There was a young man who was a

16:27 roof In Bible times houses were built with flat roofs. The roof was used for drying things such as flax and fruit. And it was used as an extra room, as a place for worship, and as a cool place to sleep in the summer.

Levite[n] from the city of Bethlehem in Judah who was from the people of Judah. [8]He left Bethlehem to look for another place to live, and on his way he came to Micah's house in the mountains of Ephraim. [9]Micah asked him, "Where are you from?"

He answered, "I'm a Levite from Bethlehem in Judah. I'm looking for a place to live."

[10]Micah said to him, "Live with me and be my father and my priest. I will give you four ounces of silver each year and clothes and food." So the Levite went in. [11]He agreed to live with Micah and became like one of Micah's own sons. [12]Micah made him a priest, and he lived in Micah's house. [13]Then Micah said, "Now I know the LORD will be good to me, because I have a Levite as my priest."

DAN'S FAMILY CAPTURES LAISH

18 At that time Israel did not have a king. And at that time the tribe of Dan was still looking for a land where they could live, a land of their own. The Danites had not yet been given their own land among the tribes of Israel. [2]So, from their family groups, they chose five soldiers from the cities of Zorah and Eshtaol to spy out and explore the land. They were told, "Go, explore the land."

They came to the mountains of Ephraim, to Micah's house, where they spent the night. [3]When they came near Micah's house, they recognized the voice of the young Levite.[n] So they stopped there and asked him, "Who brought you here? What are you doing here? Why are you here?"

[4]He told them what Micah had done for him, saying, "He hired me. I am his priest."

[5]They said to him, "Please ask God if our journey will be successful."

[6]The priest said to them, "Go in peace. The LORD is pleased with your journey."

[7]So the five men left. When they came to the city of Laish, they saw that the people there lived in safety, like the people of Sidon. They thought they were safe and had plenty of everything. They lived a long way from the Sidonians and had no dealings with anyone else.

[8]When the five men returned to Zorah and Eshtaol, their relatives asked them, "What did you find?"

[9]They answered, "We have seen the land, and it is very good. We should attack them. Aren't you going to do something? Don't wait! Let's go and take that land! [10]When you go, you will see there is plenty of land—plenty of everything! The people are not expecting an attack. Surely God has handed that land over to us!"

[11]So six hundred Danites left Zorah and Eshtaol ready for war. [12]On their way they set up camp near the city of Kiriath Jearim in Judah. That is why the place west of Kiriath Jearim is named Mahaneh Dan[n] to this day. [13]From there they traveled on to the mountains of Ephraim. Then they came to Micah's house.

[14]The five men who had explored the land around Laish said to their relatives, "Do you know in one of these houses there are a holy vest, household gods, an idol, and a statue? You know what to do." [15]So they stopped at the Levite's house, which was also Micah's house, and greeted the Levite. [16]The six hundred Danites stood at the entrance gate, wearing their weapons of war. [17]The five spies went into the house and took the idol, the holy vest, the household idols, and the statue. The priest and the six hundred men armed for war stood by the entrance gate.

[18]When the spies went into Micah's house and took the image, the holy vest, the household idols, and the statue, the priest asked them, "What are you doing?"

[19]They answered, "Be quiet! Don't say a word. Come with us and be our father and priest. Is it better for you to be a priest for one man's house or for a tribe and family group in Israel?" [20]This made the priest happy. So he took the holy vest, the household idols, and the idol and went with the Danites. [21]They left Micah's house, putting their little children, their animals, and everything they owned in front of them.

[22]When they had gone a little way from Micah's house, the men who lived near Micah were called out and caught up with them. [23]The men with Micah shouted at the Danites, who turned around and said to

---

17:7; 18:3 Levite The Levites were the only ones God had appointed as priests. **18:12 Mahaneh Dan** This name means "the camp of Dan."

Micah, "What's the matter with you? Why have you been called out to fight?"

²⁴Micah answered, "You took my gods that I made and my priest. What do I have left? How can you ask me, 'What's the matter?'"

²⁵The Danites answered, "You should not argue with us. Some of our angry men might attack you, killing you and your family." ²⁶Then the Danites went on their way. Micah knew they were too strong for him, so he turned and went back home.

²⁷Then the Danites took what Micah had made and his priest and went on to Laish. They attacked those peaceful people and killed them with their swords and then burned the city. ²⁸There was no one to save the people of Laish. They lived too far from Sidon, and they had no dealings with anyone else. Laish was in a valley near Beth Rehob.

The people of Dan rebuilt the city and lived there. ²⁹They changed the name of Laish to Dan, naming it for their ancestor Dan, one of the sons of Israel.

³⁰The people of Dan set up the idols in the city of Dan. Jonathan son of Gershom, Moses' son, and his sons served as priests for the tribe of Dan until the land was captured. ³¹The people of Dan set up the idols Micah had made as long as the Holy Tent of God was in Shiloh.

A LEVITE AND HIS SERVANT

19 At that time Israel did not have a king. There was a Levite who lived in the faraway mountains of Ephraim. He had taken a slave woman from the city of Bethlehem in the land of Judah to live with him, ²but she was unfaithful to him. She left him and went back to her father's house in Bethlehem in Judah and stayed there for four months. ³Then her husband went to ask her to come back to him, taking with him his servant and two donkeys. When the Levite came to her father's house, she invited him to come in, and her father was happy to see him. ⁴The father-in-law, the young woman's father, asked him to stay. So he stayed for three days and ate, drank, and slept there.

⁵On the fourth day they got up early in the morning. The Levite was getting ready to leave, but the woman's father said to his son-in-law, "Refresh yourself by eating some-thing. Then go." ⁶So the two men sat down to eat and drink together. After that, the father said to him, "Please stay tonight. Relax and enjoy yourself." ⁷When the man got up to go, his father-in-law asked him to stay. So he stayed again that night. ⁸On the fifth day the man got up early in the morning to leave. The woman's father said, "Refresh yourself. Wait until this afternoon." So the two men ate together.

⁹When the Levite, his slave woman, and his servant got up to leave, the father-in-law, the young woman's father, said, "It's almost night. The day is almost gone. Spend the night here and enjoy yourself. Tomorrow morning you can get up early and go home." ¹⁰But the Levite did not want to stay another night. So he took his two saddled donkeys and his slave woman and traveled toward the city of Jebus (also called Jerusalem).

¹¹As the day was almost over, they came near Jebus. So the servant said to his master, "Let's stop at this city of the Jebusites, and spend the night here."

¹²But his master said, "No. We won't go inside a foreign city. Those people are not Israelites. We will go on to the city of Gibeah." ¹³He said, "Come on. Let's try to make it to Gibeah or Ramah so we can spend the night in one of those cities." ¹⁴So they went on. The sun went down as they came near Gibeah, which belongs to the tribe of Benjamin. ¹⁵They stopped there to spend the night. They came to the public square of the city and sat down, but no one invited them home to spend the night.

¹⁶Finally, in the evening an old man came in from his work in the fields. His home was in the mountains of Ephraim, but now he was living in Gibeah. (The people of Gibeah were from the tribe of Benjamin.) ¹⁷He saw the traveler in the public square and asked, "Where are you going? Where did you come from?"

¹⁸The Levite answered, "We are traveling from Bethlehem in Judah to my home in the mountains of Ephraim. I have been to Bethlehem in Judah, but now I am going to the Holy Tent of the LORD. No one has invited me to stay in his house. ¹⁹We already have straw and food for our donkeys and bread and wine for me, the young woman, and my servant. We don't need anything."

20The old man said, "You are welcome to stay at my house. Let me give you anything you need, but don't spend the night in the public square." 21So the old man took the Levite into his house, and he fed their donkeys. They washed their feet and had something to eat and drink.

22While they were enjoying themselves, some wicked men of the city surrounded the house and beat on the door. They shouted to the old man who owned the house, "Bring out the man who came to your house. We want to have sexual relations with him."

23The owner of the house went outside and said to them, "No, my friends. Don't be so evil. This man is a guest in my house. Don't do this terrible thing! 24Look, here are my daughter, who has never had sexual relations before, and the man's slave woman. I will bring them out to you now. Do anything you want with them, but don't do such a terrible thing to this man."

25But the men would not listen to him. So the Levite took his slave woman and sent her outside to them. They forced her to have sexual relations with them, and they abused her all night long. Then, at dawn, they let her go. 26She came back to the house where her master was staying and fell down at the door and lay there until daylight.

27In the morning when the Levite got up, he opened the door of the house and went outside to go on his way. But his slave woman was lying at the doorway of the house, with her hands on the doorsill. 28The Levite said to her, "Get up; let's go." But she did not answer. So he put her on his donkey and went home.

29When the Levite got home, he took a knife and cut his slave woman into twelve parts, limb by limb. Then he sent a part to each area of Israel. 30Everyone who saw this said, "Nothing like this has ever happened before, not since the people of Israel came out of Egypt. Think about it. Tell us what to do."

THE WAR BETWEEN ISRAEL AND BENJAMIN

20 So all the Israelites from Dan to Beersheba,[n] including the land of Gilead, joined together before the Lord in the city of Mizpah. 2The leaders of all the tribes of Israel took their places in the meeting of the people of God. There were 400,000 soldiers with swords. 3(The people of Benjamin heard that the Israelites had gone up to Mizpah.) Then the Israelites said to the Levite, "Tell us how this evil thing happened."

4So the husband of the murdered woman answered, "My slave woman and I came to Gibeah in Benjamin to spend the night. 5During the night the men of Gibeah came after me. They surrounded the house and wanted to kill me. They forced my slave woman to have sexual relations and she died. 6I took her and cut her into parts and sent one part to each area of Israel because the people of Benjamin did this wicked and terrible thing in Israel. 7Now, all you Israelites, speak up. What is your decision?"

8Then all the people stood up at the same time, saying, "None of us will go home. Not one of us will go back to his house! 9Now this is what we will do to Gibeah. We will throw lots. 10That way we will choose ten men from every hundred men from all the tribes of Israel, and we will choose a hundred men from every thousand, and a thousand men from every ten thousand. These will find supplies for the army. Then the army will go to the city of Gibeah of Benjamin to repay them for the terrible thing they have done in Israel." 11So all the men of Israel were united and gathered against the city.

12The tribes of Israel sent men throughout the tribe of Benjamin demanding, "What is this evil thing some of your men have done? 13Hand over the wicked men in Gibeah so that we can put them to death. We must remove this evil from Israel."

But the Benjaminites would not listen to their fellow Israelites. 14The Benjaminites left their own cities and met at Gibeah to fight the Israelites. 15In only one day the Benjaminites got 26,000 soldiers together who were trained with swords. They also had 700 chosen men from Gibeah. 16Seven hundred of these trained soldiers were left-handed, each of whom could sling a stone at a hair and not miss!

17The Israelites, except for the Benjaminites, gathered 400,000 soldiers with swords.

20:1 Dan...Beersheba Dan was the city farthest north in Israel. Beersheba was the city farthest south. So this means all the people of Israel.

18The Israelites went up to the city of Bethel and asked God, "Which tribe shall be first to attack the Benjaminites?"

The LORD answered, "Judah shall go first."

19The next morning the Israelites got up and made a camp near Gibeah. 20The men of Israel went out to fight the Benjaminites and took their battle position at Gibeah. 21Then the Benjaminites came out of Gibeah and killed 22,000 Israelites during the battle that day. 22-23The Israelites went before the LORD and cried until evening. They asked the LORD, "Shall we go to fight our relatives, the Benjaminites, again?"

The LORD answered, "Go up and fight them." The men of Israel encouraged each other. So they took the same battle positions they had taken the first day.

24The Israelites came to fight the Benjaminites the second day. 25The Benjaminites came out of Gibeah to attack the Israelites. This time, the Benjaminites killed 18,000 Israelites, all of whom carried swords.

26Then the Israelites went up to Bethel. There they sat down and cried to the LORD and fasted all day until evening. They also brought burnt offerings and fellowship offerings to the LORD. 27The Israelites asked the LORD a question. (In those days the Ark of the Agreement with God was there at Bethel. 28A priest named Phinehas son of Eleazar, the son of Aaron, served before the Ark of the Agreement.) They asked, "Shall we go to fight our relatives, the Benjaminites, again, or shall we stop fighting?"

The LORD answered, "Go, because tomorrow I will hand them over to you."

29Then the Israelites set up ambushes all around Gibeah. 30They went to fight against the Benjaminites at Gibeah on the third day, getting into position for battle as they had done before. 31When the Benjaminites came out to fight them, the Israelites backed up and led the Benjaminites away from the city. The Benjaminites began to kill some of the Israelites as they had done before. About thirty Israelites were killed—some in the fields and some on the roads leading to Bethel and to Gibeah.

32The Benjaminites said, "We are winning as before!"

But the Israelites said, "Let's run. Let's trick them into going farther away from their city and onto the roads."

33All the Israelites moved from their places and got into battle positions at a place named Baal Tamar. Then the Israelites ran out from their hiding places west of Gibeah. 34Ten thousand of the best trained soldiers from all of Israel attacked Gibeah. The battle was very hard. The Benjaminites did not know disaster was about to come to them. 35The LORD used the Israelites to defeat the Benjaminites. On that day the Israelites killed 25,100 Benjaminites, all armed with swords. 36Then the Benjaminites saw that they were defeated.

The Israelites had moved back because they were depending on the surprise attack they had set up near Gibeah. 37The men in hiding rushed into Gibeah, spread out, and killed everyone in the city with their swords. 38Now the Israelites had set up a signal with the men in hiding. The men in the surprise attack were to send up a cloud of smoke from the city. 39Then the army of Israel turned around in the battle.

The Benjaminites had killed about thirty Israelites. They were saying, "We are winning, as in the first battle!" 40But then a cloud of smoke began to rise from the city. The Benjaminites turned around and saw that the whole city was going up in smoke. 41Then the Israelites turned and began to fight. The Benjaminites were terrified because they knew that disaster was coming to them. 42So the Benjaminites ran away from the Israelites toward the desert, but they could not escape the battle. And the Israelites who came out of the cities killed them. 43They surrounded the Benjaminites and chased them and caught them in the area east of Gibeah. 44So 18,000 brave Benjaminite fighters were killed. 45The Benjaminites ran toward the desert to the rock of Rimmon, but the Israelites killed 5,000 Benjaminites along the roads. They chased them as far as Gidom and killed 2,000 more Benjaminites there.

46On that day 25,000 Benjaminites were killed, all of whom had fought bravely with swords. 47But 600 Benjaminites ran to the rock of Rimmon in the desert, where they stayed for four months. 48Then the Israelites went back to the land of Benjamin and killed the people in every city and also the animals and everything they could find. And they burned every city they found.

WIVES FOR THE MEN OF BENJAMIN

21 At Mizpah the men of Israel had sworn, "Not one of us will let his daughter marry a man from the tribe of Benjamin."

²The people went to the city of Bethel and sat before God until evening, crying loudly. ³They said, "LORD, God of Israel, why has this terrible thing happened to us so that one tribe of Israel is missing today?"

⁴Early the next day the people built an altar and put burnt offerings and fellowship offerings to God on it.

⁵Then the Israelites asked, "Did any tribe of Israel not come here to meet with us in the presence of the LORD?" They asked this question because they had sworn that anyone who did not meet with them at Mizpah would be killed.

⁶The Israelites felt sorry for their relatives, the Benjaminites. They said, "Today one tribe has been cut off from Israel. ⁷We swore before the LORD that we would not allow our daughters to marry a Benjaminite. How can we make sure that the remaining men of Benjamin will have wives?" ⁸Then they asked, "Which one of the tribes of Israel did not come here to Mizpah?" They found that no one from the city of Jabesh Gilead had come. ⁹The people of Israel counted everyone, but there was no one from Jabesh Gilead.

¹⁰So the whole group of Israelites sent twelve thousand soldiers to Jabesh Gilead to kill the people with their swords, even the women and children.

¹¹"This is what you must do: Kill every man in Jabesh Gilead and every married woman." ¹²The soldiers found four hundred young unmarried women in Jabesh Gilead, so they brought them to the camp at Shiloh in Canaan.

¹³Then the whole group of Israelites sent a message to the men of Benjamin, who were at the rock of Rimmon, offering to make peace with them. ¹⁴So the men of Benjamin came back at that time. The Israelites gave them the women from Jabesh Gilead who had not been killed, but there were not enough women.

¹⁵The people of Israel felt sorry for the Benjaminites because the LORD had separated the tribes of Israel. ¹⁶The elders of the Israelites said, "The women of Benjamin have been killed. Where can we get wives for the men of Benjamin who are still alive? ¹⁷These men must have children to continue their families so a tribe in Israel will not die out. ¹⁸But we cannot allow our daughters to marry them, because we swore, 'Anyone who gives a wife to a man of Benjamin is cursed.' ¹⁹We have an idea! There is a yearly festival of the LORD at Shiloh, which is north of the city of Bethel, east of the road that goes from Bethel to Shechem, and south of the city of Lebonah."

²⁰So the elders told the men of Benjamin, "Go and hide in the vineyards. ²¹Watch for the young women from Shiloh to come out to join the dancing. Then run out from the vineyards and take one of the young Shiloh women and return to the land of Benjamin. ²²If their fathers or brothers come to us and complain, we will say: 'Be kind to the men of Benjamin. We did not get wives for Benjamin during the war, and you did not give the women to the men from Benjamin. So you are not guilty.'"

²³So that is what the Benjaminites did. While the young women were dancing, each man caught one of them, took her away, and married her. Then they went back to the land God had given them and rebuilt their cities and lived there.

²⁴Then the Israelites went home to their own tribes and family groups, to their own land that God had given them.

²⁵In those days Israel did not have a king. All the people did whatever seemed right in their own eyes.

ruth

THE STORY OF A GIRL FROM MOAB

1 Long ago when the judges[n] ruled Israel, there was a shortage of food in the land. [2]So a man named Elimelech left the town of Bethlehem in Judah to live in the country of Moab with his wife and his two sons. His wife was named Naomi, and his two sons were named Mahlon and Kilion. They were Ephrathahites from Bethlehem in Judah. When they came to Moab, they settled there.

1:1 judges They were not judges in courts of law, but leaders of the people in times of emergency.

THE EXTRA MILE MARRIAGE

FAMILY

rights or devotion?

RUTH 1:16

Would you volunteer to give up your rights of citizenship in order to be a comfort to an old woman who had no support and an uncertain future? Would you be ready to leave your hometown and your country, your family and friends just because you were worried about what might happen to someone else? Would you give up the life you know to be a support to someone who had nothing to offer?

Ruth knew the meaning of *agape* love long before the word found its way into the New Testament. Ruth not only refused to leave Naomi; she deliberately gave up her rights to become what Naomi needed most: family.

The Hebrew sentence is powerfully emphatic: Your people are *my people*. Your God is *my God*. It is a voluntary transfer of identity. I am no longer my own person. From now on, I belong to your tribe, and I serve your God. The Old Testament hardly contains a more powerful statement of commitment.

Ruth is described as "clinging" to Naomi. When we decide to give up our own rights and our native citizenship in order to identify with the tribe of Jesus, it is because we love him so much we cannot let him go. We say to him, "Your people are my people." If Jesus' people are now our people, what does that say about how we should treat them? Our devotion to his people ought to be like our devotion to him.

---

reflect: Treat the people of God as you treat God personally.
Go to **2 Samuel 12:7-15**.

³Then Naomi's husband, Elimelech, died, and she was left with her two sons. ⁴These sons married women from Moab. One was named Orpah, and the other was named Ruth. Naomi and her sons had lived in Moab about ten years ⁵when Mahlon and Kilion also died. So Naomi was left alone without her husband or her two sons.

⁶While Naomi was in Moab, she heard that the LORD had come to help his people and had given them food again. So she and her daughters-in-law got ready to leave Moab and return home. ⁷Naomi and her daughters-in-law left the place where they had lived and started back to the land of Judah. ⁸But Naomi said to her two daughters-in-law, "Go back home, each of you to your own mother's house. May the LORD be as kind to you as you have been to me and my sons who are now dead. ⁹May the LORD give you another happy home and a new husband."

When Naomi kissed the women good-bye, they began to cry out loud. ¹⁰They said to her, "No, we want to go with you to your people."

¹¹But Naomi said, "My daughters, return to your own homes. Why do you want to go with me? I cannot give birth to more sons to give you new husbands; ¹²go back, my daughters, to your own homes. I am too old to have another husband. Even if I told myself, 'I still have hope' and had another husband tonight, and even if I had more sons, ¹³should you wait until they were grown into men? Should you live for so many years without husbands? Don't do that, my daughters. My life is much too sad for you to share, because the LORD has been against me!"

¹⁴The women cried together out loud again. Then Orpah kissed her mother-in-law Naomi good-bye, but Ruth held on to her tightly.

¹⁵Naomi said to Ruth, "Look, your sister-in-law is going back to her own people and her own gods. Go back with her."

RUTH STAYS WITH NAOMI

¹⁶But Ruth said, "Don't beg me to leave you or to stop following you. Where you go, I will go. Where you live, I will live. Your people will be my people, and your God will be my God. ¹⁷And where you die, I will die, and there I will be buried. I ask the LORD to pun-

ish me terribly if I do not keep this promise: Not even death will separate us."

¹⁸When Naomi saw that Ruth had firmly made up her mind to go with her, she stopped arguing with her. ¹⁹So Naomi and Ruth went on until they came to the town of Bethlehem. When they entered Bethlehem, all the people became very excited. The women of the town said, "Is this really Naomi?"

²⁰Naomi answered the people, "Don't call me Naomi.ⁿ Call me Mara,ⁿ because the Almighty has made my life very sad. ²¹When I left, I had all I wanted, but now, the LORD has brought me home with nothing. Why should you call me Naomi when the LORD has spoken against me and the Almighty has given me so much trouble?"

²²So Naomi and her daughter-in-law Ruth, the Moabite, returned from Moab and arrived at Bethlehem at the beginning of the barley harvest.

RUTH MEETS BOAZ

2 Now Naomi had a rich relative named Boaz, from Elimelech's family.

²One day Ruth, the Moabite, said to Naomi, "I am going to the fields. Maybe someone will be kind enough to let me gather the grain he leaves behind."

Naomi said, "Go, my daughter."

³So Ruth went to the fields and gathered the grain that the workers cutting the grain had left behind. It just so happened that the field belonged to Boaz, from Elimelech's family.

⁴Soon Boaz came from Bethlehem and greeted his workers, "The LORD be with you!"

And the workers answered, "May the LORD bless you!"

⁵Then Boaz asked his servant in charge of the workers, "Whose girl is that?"

⁶The servant answered, "She is the young Moabite woman who came back with Naomi from the country of Moab. ⁷She said, 'Please let me follow the workers cutting grain and gather what they leave behind.' She came and has remained here, from morning until just now. She has stopped only a few moments to rest in the shelter."

1:20 Naomi This name means "happy" or "pleasant."
1:20 Mara This name means "bitter" or "sad."

⁸Then Boaz said to Ruth, "Listen, my daughter. Don't go to gather grain for yourself in another field. Don't even leave this field at all, but continue following closely behind my women workers. ⁹Watch to see into which fields they go to cut grain and follow them. I have warned the young men not to bother you. When you are thirsty, you may go and drink from the water jugs that the young men have filled."

¹⁰Then Ruth bowed low with her face to the ground and said to him, "I am not an Israelite. Why have you been so kind to notice me?"

¹¹Boaz answered her, "I know about all the help you have given your mother-in-law

GOD'S MANAGEMENT PLAN

working
for God

FINANCES

RUTH 2:12

From the world's perspective, Ruth was a transient. She had no job. That's why she was gleaning the fields. She was living under the law of God for the protection of widows and strangers. Ruth was today's homeless woman, caring for her widowed mother-in-law. Neither woman had the favor or protection of a man. And that meant real hardship.

Boaz had heard the story. He knew that Ruth hadn't had to come with her mother-in-law to that strange land. He knew that Ruth had embraced a new God and was seeking to serve him. But Boaz did not offer her wages.

Instead, he offered her something of far more value: acceptance. He told Ruth that the one who was going to reward her was God himself. Boaz saw immediately that the service Ruth was performing meant she was in the employ of God, and God never misses a paycheck.

Boaz's comment to Ruth establishes a critical principle. No matter where the money comes from, we work for God. He is the real boss. He may use someone else to do the distribution, but the vault is his, and he hands out the wages.

This principle works no matter what kind of job we are doing. Self-sacrificing service for others never goes unnoticed by the Father of those seeking refuge. The story of Ruth turns our attention toward real service and her service puts the spotlight on the real employer. The company name on your paycheck isn't really paying your wages. In God's world, you work for him.

reflect: Is your work worthy of your wages?
Go to **1 Chronicles 4:10.**

after your husband died. You left your father and mother and your own country to come to a nation where you did not know anyone. ¹²May the LORD reward you for all you have done. May your wages be paid in full by the LORD, the God of Israel, under whose wings you have come for shelter."

¹³Then Ruth said, "I hope I can continue to please you, sir. You have said kind and encouraging words to me, your servant, though I am not one of your servants."

¹⁴At mealtime Boaz told Ruth, "Come here. Eat some of our bread and dip it in our sauce."

So Ruth sat down beside the workers. Boaz handed her some roasted grain, and she ate until she was full; she even had some food left over. ¹⁵When Ruth rose and went back to work, Boaz commanded his workers, "Let her gather even around the piles of cut grain. Don't tell her to go away. ¹⁶In fact, drop some full heads of grain for her from what you have in your hands, and let her gather them. Don't tell her to stop."

¹⁷So Ruth gathered grain in the field until evening. Then she separated the grain from the chaff, and there was about one-half bushel of barley. ¹⁸Ruth carried the grain into town, and her mother-in-law saw how much she had gathered. Ruth also took out the food that was left over from lunch and gave it to Naomi.

¹⁹Naomi asked her, "Where did you gather all this grain today? Where did you work? Blessed be whoever noticed you!"

Ruth told her mother-in-law whose field she had worked in. She said, "The man I worked with today is named Boaz."

²⁰Naomi told her daughter-in-law, "The LORD bless him! He continues to be kind to us—both the living and the dead!" Then Naomi told Ruth, "Boaz is one of our close relatives,ⁿ one who should take care of us."

²¹Then Ruth, the Moabite, said, "Boaz also told me, 'Keep close to my workers until they have finished my whole harvest.'"

²²But Naomi said to her daughter-in-law Ruth, "It is better for you to continue working with his women workers. If you work in another field, someone might hurt you." ²³So Ruth continued working closely with the workers of Boaz, gathering grain until the barley harvest and the wheat harvest were finished. And she continued to live with Naomi, her mother-in-law.

NAOMI'S PLAN

3 Then Naomi, Ruth's mother-in-law, said to her, "My daughter, I must find a suitable home for you, one that will be good for you. ²Now Boaz, whose young women you worked with, is our close relative.ⁿ Tonight he will be working at the threshing floor. ³Wash yourself, put on perfume, change your clothes, and go down to the threshing floor. But don't let him know you're there until he has finished his dinner. ⁴Watch him so you will know where he lies down to sleep. When he lies down, go and lift the cover off his feetⁿ and lie down. He will tell you what you should do."

⁵Then Ruth answered, "I will do everything you say."

⁶So Ruth went down to the threshing floor and did all her mother-in-law told her to do. ⁷After his evening meal, Boaz felt good and went to sleep lying beside the pile of grain. Ruth went to him quietly and lifted the cover from his feet and lay down.

⁸About midnight Boaz was startled and rolled over. There was a woman lying near his feet! ⁹Boaz asked, "Who are you?"

She said, "I am Ruth, your servant girl. Spread your cover over me, because you are a relative who is supposed to take care of me."ⁿ

¹⁰Then Boaz said, "The LORD bless you, my daughter. This act of kindness is greater than the kindness you showed to Naomi in the beginning. You didn't look for a young man to marry, either rich or poor. ¹¹Now, my daughter, don't be afraid. I will do everything you ask, because all the people in our town know you are a good woman. ¹²It is true that I am a relative who is to take care of you, but you have a closer relative than I. ¹³Stay here tonight, and in the morning we will see if he will take care of you. If he decides to take care of you, that is fine. But if he refuses, I

2:20; 3:2 close relatives In Bible times the closest relative could marry a widow without children so she could have children. He would care for this family, but they and their property would not belong to him. They would belong to the dead husband. **3:4 lift . . . feet** This showed Ruth was asking him to be her husband. **3:9 Spread . . . me** By this, Ruth was asking Boaz to marry her.

will take care of you myself, as surely as the LORD lives. So stay here until morning."

¹⁴So Ruth stayed near his feet until morning but got up while it was still too dark to recognize anyone. Boaz thought, "People in town must not know that the woman came here to the threshing floor." ¹⁵So Boaz said to Ruth, "Bring me your shawl and hold it open."

So Ruth held her shawl open, and Boaz poured six portions of barley into it. Boaz then put it on her head and went back to the city.

¹⁶When Ruth went back to her mother-in-law, Naomi asked, "How did you do, my daughter?"

Ruth told Naomi everything that Boaz did for her. ¹⁷She said, "Boaz gave me these six portions of barley, saying, 'You must not go home without a gift for your mother-in-law.'"

¹⁸Naomi answered, "Ruth, my daughter, wait here until you see what happens. Boaz will not rest until he has finished doing what he should do today."

BOAZ MARRIES RUTH

4 Boaz went to the city gate and sat there until the close relative he had mentioned passed by. Boaz called to him, "Come here, friend, and sit down." So the man came over and sat down. ²Boaz gathered ten of the elders of the city and told them, "Sit down here!" So they sat down.

³Then Boaz said to the close relative, "Naomi, who has come back from the country of Moab, wants to sell the piece of land that belonged to our relative Elimelech. ⁴So I decided to tell you about it: If you want to buy back the land, then buy it in front of the people who are sitting here and in front of the elders of my people. But if you don't want to buy it, tell me, because you are the only one who can buy it, and I am next after you."

The close relative answered, "I will buy back the land."

⁵Then Boaz explained, "When you buy the land from Naomi, you must also marry Ruth, the Moabite, the dead man's wife. That way, the land will stay in the dead man's name."

⁶The close relative answered, "I can't buy back the land. If I did, I might harm what I can pass on to my own sons. I cannot buy the land back, so buy it yourself."

⁷Long ago in Israel when people traded or bought back something, one person took off his sandal and gave it to the other person. This was the proof of ownership in Israel.

⁸So the close relative said to Boaz, "Buy the land yourself," and he took off his sandal.

⁹Then Boaz said to the elders and to all the people, "You are witnesses today. I am buying from Naomi everything that belonged to Elimelech and Kilion and Mahlon. ¹⁰I am also taking Ruth, the Moabite who was the wife of Mahlon, as my wife. I am doing this so her dead husband's property will stay in his name and his name will not be separated from his family and his hometown. You are witnesses today."

¹¹So all the people and elders who were at the city gate said, "We are witnesses. May the LORD make this woman, who is coming into your home, like Rachel and Leah, who had many children and built up the people of Israel. May you become powerful in the district of Ephrathah and famous in Bethlehem. ¹²As Tamar gave birth to Judah's son Perez,ⁿ may the LORD give you many children through Ruth. May your family be great like his."

¹³So Boaz took Ruth home as his wife and had sexual relations with her. The LORD let her become pregnant, and she gave birth to a son. ¹⁴The women told Naomi, "Praise the LORD who gave you this grandson. May he become famous in Israel. ¹⁵He will give you new life and will take care of you in your old age because of your daughter-in-law who loves you. She is better for you than seven sons, because she has given birth to your grandson."

¹⁶Naomi took the boy, held him in her arms, and cared for him. ¹⁷The neighbors gave the boy his name, saying, "This boy was born for Naomi." They named him Obed. Obed was the father of Jesse, and Jesse was the father of David.

¹⁸This is the family history of Perez, the father of Hezron. ¹⁹Hezron was the father

---

4:12 Perez One of Boaz's ancestors.

of Ram, who was the father of Amminadab. [20]Amminadab was the father of Nahshon, who was the father of Salmon. [21]Salmon was the father of Boaz, who was the father of Obed. [22]Obed was the father of Jesse, and Jesse was the father of David.

1 samuel

SAMUEL AND KING SAUL

of Ram, who was the father of Amminadab.
Amminadab was the father of Nahshon,
who was the father of Salmon. Salmon

SAMUEL'S BIRTH

1 There was a man named Elkanah son of Jeroham from Ramathaim in the mountains of Ephraim. Elkanah was from the family of Zuph. (Jeroham was Elihu's son. Elihu was Tohu's son, and Tohu was the son of Zuph from the family group of Ephraim.) ²Elkanah had two wives named Hannah and Peninnah. Peninnah had children, but Hannah had none.

³Every year Elkanah left his town of Ramah and went up to Shiloh to worship the LORD All-Powerful and to offer sacrifices to him. Shiloh was where Hophni and Phinehas, the sons of Eli, served as priests of the LORD. ⁴When Elkanah offered sacrifices, he always gave a share of the meat to his wife Peninnah and to her sons and daughters. ⁵But Elkanah always gave a special share of the meat to Hannah, because he loved Hannah and because the LORD had kept her from having children. ⁶Peninnah would tease Hannah and upset her, because the LORD had made her unable to have children. ⁷This happened every year when they went up to the house of the LORD at Shiloh. Peninnah would upset Hannah until Hannah would cry and not eat anything. ⁸Her husband Elkanah would say to her, "Hannah, why are you crying and why won't you eat? Why are you sad? Don't I mean more to you than ten sons?"

⁹Once, after they had eaten their meal in Shiloh, Hannah got up. Now Eli the priest was sitting on a chair near the entrance to the LORD's house. ¹⁰Hannah was so sad that she cried and prayed to the LORD. ¹¹She made a promise, saying, "LORD All-Powerful, see how sad I am. Remember me and don't forget me. If you will give me a son, I will give him back to you all his life, and no one will ever cut his hair with a razor." [n]

¹²While Hannah kept praying, Eli watched her mouth. ¹³She was praying in her heart so her lips moved, but her voice was not heard. Eli thought she was drunk ¹⁴and said to her, "Stop getting drunk! Throw away your wine!"

¹⁵Hannah answered, "No, sir, I have not drunk any wine or beer. I am a deeply troubled woman, and I was telling the LORD about all my problems. ¹⁶Don't think I am an evil woman. I have been praying because I have many troubles and am very sad."

¹⁷Eli answered, "Go! I wish you well. May the God of Israel give you what you asked of him."

¹⁸Hannah said, "May I always please you." When she left and ate something, she was not sad anymore.

¹⁹Early the next morning Elkanah's family got up and worshiped the LORD. Then they went back home to Ramah. Elkanah had sexual relations with his wife Hannah, and the LORD remembered her. ²⁰So Hannah became pregnant, and in time she gave birth to a son. She named him Samuel,[n] saying, "His name is Samuel because I asked the LORD for him."

HANNAH GIVES SAMUEL TO GOD

²¹Every year Elkanah went with his whole family to Shiloh to offer sacrifices and to keep the promise he had made to God. ²²But one time Hannah did not go with him. She told him, "When the boy is old enough to eat solid food, I will take him to Shiloh. Then I will give him to the LORD, and he will always live there."

²³Elkanah, Hannah's husband, said to her, "Do what you think is best. You may stay home until the boy is old enough to eat. May the LORD do what you have said." So Hannah stayed at home to nurse her son until he was old enough to eat.

1:11 cut . . . razor People who made special promises not to cut their hair or to drink wine or beer were called Nazirites. These people gave a specific time in their lives, or sometimes their entire lives, to the Lord. See Numbers 6:1–5. **1:20 Samuel** This name sounds like the Hebrew word for "God heard."

²⁴When Samuel was old enough to eat, Hannah took him to the house of the LORD at Shiloh, along with a three-year-old bull, one-half bushel of flour, and a leather bag filled with wine. ²⁵After they had killed the bull for the sacrifice, Hannah brought Samuel to Eli. ²⁶She said to Eli, "As surely as you live, sir, I am the same woman who stood near you praying to the LORD. ²⁷I prayed for this child, and the LORD answered my prayer and gave him to me. ²⁸Now I give him back to the LORD. He will belong to the LORD all his life." And he worshiped the LORD there.

HANNAH GIVES THANKS

2 Hannah prayed:
"The LORD has filled my heart with
joy;
I feel very strong in the LORD.
I can laugh at my enemies;
I am glad because you have helped me!

² "There is no one holy like the LORD.
There is no God but you;
there is no Rock like our God.

³ "Don't continue bragging,
don't speak proud words.

THE PRODUCT OF PRESENT OBEDIENCE

live a
prioritized life

FUTURE

By Dr. Ronnie Floyd

1 SAMUEL 2:6–10

If you will exalt God in your heart above anything and everyone in your life—even your family—he will exalt you. But, God will only help you reach your maximum potential in life if you honor him above all else. Is your relationship with God more important to you than anyone and anything else? For this to be the case, there are two battles that must be won in your heart, first and continually.

The first is that what's important to you is what's important to God. Too often these priorities are both different and conflicting. Think about your own battles as you consider Paul's description of the battle between the flesh and the Spirit in Galatians 5:16–26.

The second is that you are going after what lasts forever rather than what lasts for a while. Is most of what you are chasing eternal or temporary? The result is that we lack the time, energy, or resources to chase the eternal.

You cannot win this battle on your own. Let God be your companion and your guide as you evaluate what you value most. Ask God to help you prioritize your life so that he is given the honor of being your first priority. This battle is not for today only; God will need to be your companion in this struggle each day.

reflect: Is God the first priority in every area of your life?
Go to **2 Chronicles 20.**

The LORD is a God who knows everything,
  and he judges what people do.

4 "The bows of warriors break,
  but weak people become strong.
5 Those who once had plenty of food now
    must work for food,
  but people who were hungry are
    hungry no more.
The woman who could not have children
    now has seven,
  but the woman who had many children
    now is sad.

6 "The LORD sends death,
  and he brings to life.
He sends people to the grave,
  and he raises them to life again.
7 The LORD makes some people poor,
  and others he makes rich.
He makes some people humble,
  and others he makes great.
8 The LORD raises the poor up from the dust,
  and he lifts the needy from the ashes.
He lets the poor sit with princes
  and receive a throne of honor.

"The foundations of the earth belong to
    the LORD,
  and the LORD set the world upon them.
9 He protects those who are loyal to him,
  but evil people will be silenced in
    darkness.
  Power is not the key to success.
10 The LORD destroys his enemies;
  he will thunder in heaven against them.
The LORD will judge all the earth.
  He will give power to his king
  and make his appointed king strong."

ELI'S EVIL SONS

11 Then Elkanah went home to Ramah, but the boy continued to serve the LORD under Eli the priest.

12 Now Eli's sons were evil men; they did not care about the LORD. 13 This is what the priests would normally do to the people: Every time someone brought a sacrifice, the meat would be cooked in a pot. The priest's servant would then come carrying a fork that had three prongs. 14 He would plunge the fork into the pot or the kettle. Whatever the fork brought out of the pot belonged to the priest. But this is how they treated all the Israelites who came to Shiloh to offer sacrifices. 15 Even before the fat was burned, the priest's servant would come to the person offering sacrifices and say, "Give the priest some meat to roast. He won't accept boiled meat from you, only raw meat."

16 If the one who offered the sacrifice said, "Let the fat be burned up first as usual, and then take anything you want," the priest's servant would answer, "No, give me the meat now. If you don't, I'll take it by force."

17 The LORD saw that the sin of the servants was very great because they did not show respect for the offerings made to the LORD.

SAMUEL GROWS UP

18 But Samuel obeyed the LORD. As a boy he wore a linen holy vest. 19 Every year Samuel's mother made a little coat for him and took it to him when she went with her husband to Shiloh for the sacrifice. 20 When Eli blessed Elkanah and his wife, he would say, "May the LORD repay you with children through Hannah to take the place of the boy Hannah prayed for and gave back to the LORD." Then Elkanah and Hannah would go home. 21 The LORD was kind to Hannah, so she became the mother of three sons and two daughters. And the boy Samuel grew up serving the LORD.

22 Now Eli was very old. He heard about everything his sons were doing to all the Israelites and how his sons had sexual relations with the women who served at the entrance to the Meeting Tent. 23 Eli said to his sons, "Why do you do these evil things that the people tell me about? 24 No, my sons. The LORD's people are spreading a bad report about you. 25 If you sin against someone, God can help you. But if you sin against the LORD himself, no one can help you!" But Eli's sons would not listen to him, because the LORD had decided to put them to death.

26 The boy Samuel grew physically. He pleased the LORD and the people.

27 A man of God came to Eli and said, "This is what the LORD says: 'I clearly showed myself to the family of your ancestor Aaron when they were slaves to the king of Egypt. 28 I chose them from all the tribes of Israel to be my priests. I wanted them to go up to my altar, to burn incense, and to wear the holy vest. I also let the family of your ancestor

have part of all the offerings sacrificed by the Israelites. ²⁹So why don't you respect the sacrifices and gifts? You honor your sons more than me. You grow fat on the best parts of the meat the Israelites bring to me.'

³⁰"So the LORD, the God of Israel, says: 'I promised that your family and your ancestor's family would serve me always.' But now the LORD says: 'This must stop! I will honor those who honor me, but I will dishonor those who ignore me. ³¹The time is coming when I will destroy the descendants of both you and your ancestors. No man will grow old in your family. ³²You will see trouble in my house. No matter what good things happen to Israel, there will never be an old man in your family. ³³I will not totally cut off your family from my altar. But your eyes will cry and your heart be sad, because all your descendants will die.

³⁴"'I will give you a sign. Both your sons, Hophni and Phinehas, will die on the same day. ³⁵I will choose a loyal priest for myself who will listen to me and do what I want. I will make his family continue, and he will always serve before my appointed king. ³⁶Then everyone left in your family will come and bow down before him. They will beg for a little money or a little food and say, "Please give me a job as priest so I can have food to eat."'"

GOD CALLS SAMUEL

3 The boy Samuel served the LORD under Eli. In those days the LORD did not speak directly to people very often; there were very few visions.

²Eli's eyes were so weak he was almost blind. One night he was lying in bed. ³Samuel was also in bed in the LORD's house, where the Ark of the Agreement was. God's lamp was still burning.

⁴Then the LORD called Samuel, and Samuel answered, "I am here!" ⁵He ran to Eli and said, "I am here. You called me."

But Eli said, "I didn't call you. Go back to bed." So Samuel went back to bed.

⁶The LORD called again, "Samuel!"

Samuel again went to Eli and said, "I am here. You called me."

Again Eli said, "I didn't call you. Go back to bed."

⁷Samuel did not yet know the LORD, and the LORD had not spoken directly to him yet.

⁸The LORD called Samuel for the third time. Samuel got up and went to Eli and said, "I am here. You called me."

Then Eli realized the LORD was calling the boy. ⁹So he told Samuel, "Go to bed. If he calls you again, say, 'Speak, LORD. I am your servant and I am listening.'" So Samuel went and lay down in bed.

¹⁰The LORD came and stood there and called as he had before, "Samuel, Samuel!"

Samuel said, "Speak, LORD. I am your servant and I am listening."

¹¹The LORD said to Samuel, "Watch, I am going to do something in Israel that will shock those who hear about it. ¹²At that time I will do to Eli and his family everything I promised, from beginning to end. ¹³I told Eli I would punish his family always, because he knew his sons were evil. They acted without honor, but he did not stop them. ¹⁴So I swore to Eli's family, 'Your guilt will never be removed by sacrifice or offering.'"

¹⁵Samuel lay down until morning. Then he opened the doors of the house of the LORD. He was afraid to tell Eli about the vision, ¹⁶but Eli called to him, "Samuel, my son!"

Samuel answered, "I am here."

¹⁷Eli asked, "What did the LORD say to you? Don't hide it from me. May God punish you terribly if you hide from me anything he said to you." ¹⁸So Samuel told Eli everything and did not hide anything from him. Then Eli said, "He is the LORD. Let him do what he thinks is best."

¹⁹The LORD was with Samuel as he grew up; he did not let any of Samuel's messages fail to come true. ²⁰Then all Israel, from Dan to Beersheba,[n] knew Samuel was a true prophet of the LORD. ²¹And the LORD continued to show himself at Shiloh, and he showed himself to Samuel through his word.

4 So, news about Samuel spread through all of Israel.

THE PHILISTINES CAPTURE THE ARK OF THE AGREEMENT

At that time the Israelites went out to fight the Philistines. The Israelites camped

---

3:20 Dan to Beersheba Dan was the city farthest north in Israel, and Beersheba was the city farthest south. So this means all the people of Israel.

at Ebenezer and the Philistines at Aphek. ²The Philistines went to meet the Israelites in battle. And as the battle spread, they defeated the Israelites, killing about four thousand soldiers on the battlefield. ³When some Israelite soldiers went back to their camp, the elders of Israel asked, "Why did the LORD let the Philistines defeat us? Let's bring the Ark of the Agreement with the LORD here from Shiloh and take it with us into battle. Then God will save us from our enemies."

⁴So the people sent men to Shiloh. They brought back the Ark of the Agreement with the LORD All-Powerful, who sits between the gold creatures with wings. Eli's two sons, Hophni and Phinehas, were there with the Ark.

⁵When the Ark of the Agreement with the LORD came into the camp, all the Israelites gave a great shout of joy that made the ground shake. ⁶When the Philistines heard Israel's shout, they asked, "What's all this shouting in the Hebrew camp?"

Then the Philistines found out that the Ark of the LORD had come into the Hebrew camp. ⁷They were afraid and said, "A god has come into the Hebrew camp! We're in trouble! This has never happened before! ⁸How terrible it will be for us! Who can save us from these powerful gods? They are the ones who struck the Egyptians with all kinds of disasters in the desert. ⁹Be brave, Philistines! Fight like men! In the past they were our slaves. So fight like men, or we will become their slaves."

¹⁰So the Philistines fought hard and defeated the Israelites, and every Israelite soldier ran away to his own home. It was a great defeat for Israel, because thirty thousand Israelite soldiers were killed. ¹¹The Ark of God was taken by the Philistines, and Eli's two sons, Hophni and Phinehas, died.

¹²That same day a man from the tribe of Benjamin ran from the battle. He tore his clothes and put dust on his head to show his great sadness. ¹³When he arrived in Shiloh, Eli was by the side of the road. He was sitting there in a chair, watching, because he was worried about the Ark of God. When the Benjaminite entered Shiloh, he told the bad news. Then all the people in town cried loudly. ¹⁴Eli heard the crying and asked, "What's all this noise?"

The Benjaminite ran to Eli and told him what had happened. ¹⁵Eli was now ninety-eight years old, and he was blind. ¹⁶The Benjaminite told him, "I have come from the battle. I ran all the way here today."

Eli asked, "What happened, my son?"

¹⁷The Benjaminite answered, "Israel ran away from the Philistines, and the Israelite army has lost many soldiers. Your two sons are both dead, and the Philistines have taken the Ark of God."

¹⁸When he mentioned the Ark of God, Eli fell backward off his chair. He fell beside the gate, broke his neck, and died, because he was old and fat. He had led Israel for forty years.

THE GLORY IS GONE

¹⁹Eli's daughter-in-law, the wife of Phinehas, was pregnant and was about to give birth. When she heard the news that the Ark of God had been taken and that Eli, her father-in-law, and Phinehas, her husband, were both dead, she began to give birth to her child. The child was born, but the mother had much trouble in giving birth. ²⁰As she was dying, the women who helped her said, "Don't worry! You've given birth to a son!" But she did not answer or pay attention. ²¹She named the baby Ichabod,[n] saying, "Israel's glory is gone." She said this because the Ark of God had been taken and her father-in-law and husband were dead. ²²She said, "Israel's glory is gone, because the Ark of God has been taken away."

TROUBLE FOR THE PHILISTINES

5 After the Philistines had captured the Ark of God, they took it from Ebenezer to Ashdod. ²They carried it into Dagon's temple and put it next to Dagon. ³When the people of Ashdod rose early the next morning, they found that Dagon had fallen on his face on the ground before the Ark of the LORD. So they put Dagon back in his place. ⁴The next morning when they rose, they again found Dagon fallen on the ground before the Ark of the LORD. His head and hands had broken off and were lying in the doorway. Only his body was still in one piece. ⁵So, even today, Dagon's priests and others who enter his temple at Ashdod refuse to step on the doorsill.

4:21 Ichabod This name means "no glory."

⁶The LORD was hard on the people of Ashdod and their neighbors. He caused them to suffer and gave them growths on their skin. ⁷When the people of Ashdod saw what was happening, they said, "The Ark of the God of Israel can't stay with us. God is punishing us and Dagon our god." ⁸The people of Ashdod called all five Philistine kings together and asked them, "What should we do with the Ark of the God of Israel?"

The rulers answered, "Move the Ark of the God of Israel to Gath." So the Philistines moved it to Gath.

⁹But after they moved it to Gath, there was a great panic. The LORD was hard on that city also, and he gave both old and young people in Gath growths on their skin. ¹⁰Then the Philistines sent the Ark of God to Ekron.

But when it came into Ekron, the people of Ekron yelled, "Why are you bringing the Ark of the God of Israel to our city? Do you want to kill us and our people?" ¹¹So they called all the kings of the Philistines together and said, "Send the Ark of the God of Israel back to its place before it kills us and our people!" All the people in the city were struck with terror because God was so hard on them there. ¹²The people who did not die were troubled with growths on their skin. So the people of Ekron cried loudly to heaven.

THE ARK OF GOD IS SENT HOME

6 The Philistines kept the Ark of God in their land seven months. ²Then they called for their priests and magicians and said, "What should we do with the Ark of the LORD? Tell us how to send it back home!"

³The priests and magicians answered, "If you send back the Ark of the God of Israel, don't send it back empty. You must give a penalty offering. If you are then healed, you will know that it was because of the Ark that you had such trouble."

⁴The Philistines asked, "What kind of penalty offering should we send to Israel's God?"

They answered, "Make five gold models of the growths on your skin and five gold models of rats. The number of models must match the number of Philistine kings, because the same sickness has come on you and your kings. ⁵Make models of the growths and the rats that are ruining the country, and give honor to Israel's God. Then maybe he will stop being so hard on you, your gods, and your land. ⁶Don't be stubborn like the king of Egypt and the Egyptians. After God punished them terribly, they let the Israelites leave Egypt.

⁷"You must build a new cart and get two cows that have just had calves. These must be cows that have never had yokes on their necks. Hitch the cows to the cart, and take the calves home, away from their mothers. ⁸Put the Ark of the LORD on the cart and the gold models for the penalty offering in a box beside the Ark. Then send the cart straight on its way. ⁹Watch the cart. If it goes toward Beth Shemesh in Israel's own land, the LORD has given us this great sickness. But if it doesn't, we will know that Israel's God has not punished us. Our sickness just happened by chance."

¹⁰The Philistines did what the priests and magicians said. They took two cows that had just had calves and hitched them to the cart, but they kept their calves at home. ¹¹They put the Ark of the LORD and the box with the gold rats and models of growths on the cart. ¹²Then the cows went straight toward Beth Shemesh. They stayed on the road, mooing all the way, and did not turn right or left. The Philistine kings followed the cows as far as the border of Beth Shemesh.

¹³Now the people of Beth Shemesh were harvesting their wheat in the valley. When they looked up and saw the Ark of the LORD, they were very happy. ¹⁴The cart came to the field belonging to Joshua of Beth Shemesh and stopped near a large rock. The people of Beth Shemesh chopped up the wood of the cart. Then they sacrificed the cows as burnt offerings to the LORD. ¹⁵The Levites took down the Ark of the LORD and the box that had the gold models, and they put both on the large rock. That day the people of Beth Shemesh offered whole burnt offerings and made sacrifices to the LORD. ¹⁶After the five Philistine kings saw this, they went back to Ekron the same day.

¹⁷The Philistines had sent these gold models of the growths as penalty offerings to the LORD. They sent one model for each Philistine town: Ashdod, Gaza, Ashkelon, Gath, and Ekron. ¹⁸And the Philistines also sent gold models of rats. The number of rats

matched the number of towns belonging to the Philistine kings, including both strong, walled cities and country villages. The large rock on which they put the Ark of the LORD is still there in the field of Joshua of Beth Shemesh.

¹⁹But some of the men of Beth Shemesh looked into the Ark of the LORD. So God killed seventy of them. The people of Beth Shemesh cried because the LORD had struck them down. ²⁰They said, "Who can stand before the LORD, this holy God? Whom will he strike next?"

²¹Then they sent messengers to the people of Kiriath Jearim, saying, "The Philistines have brought back the Ark of the LORD. Come down and take it to your city."

7 The men of Kiriath Jearim came and took the Ark of the LORD to Abinadab's house on a hill. There they made Abinadab's son Eleazar holy for the LORD so he could guard the Ark of the LORD.

THE LORD SAVES THE ISRAELITES

²The Ark stayed at Kiriath Jearim a long time—twenty years in all. And the people of Israel began to follow the LORD again. ³Samuel spoke to the whole group of Israel, saying, "If you're turning back to the LORD with all your hearts, you must remove your foreign gods and your idols of Ashtoreth. You must give yourselves fully to the LORD and serve only him. Then he will save you from the Philistines."

⁴So the Israelites put away their idols of Baal and Ashtoreth, and they served only the LORD.

⁵Samuel said, "All Israel must meet at Mizpah, and I will pray to the LORD for you." ⁶So the Israelites met together at Mizpah. They drew water from the ground and poured it out before the LORD and fasted that day. They confessed, "We have sinned against the LORD." And Samuel served as judge of Israel at Mizpah.

⁷The Philistines heard the Israelites were meeting at Mizpah, so the Philistine kings came up to attack them. When the Israelites heard they were coming, they were afraid. ⁸They said to Samuel, "Don't stop praying to the LORD our God for us! Ask him to save us from the Philistines!" ⁹Then Samuel took a baby lamb and offered it to the LORD as a whole burnt offering. He called to the LORD for Israel's sake, and the LORD answered him.

¹⁰While Samuel was burning the offering, the Philistines came near to attack Israel. But the LORD thundered against them with loud thunder. They were so frightened they became confused. So the Israelites defeated the Philistines in battle. ¹¹The men of Israel ran out of Mizpah and chased the Philistines almost to Beth Car, killing the Philistines along the way.

PEACE COMES TO ISRAEL

¹²After this happened Samuel took a stone and set it up between Mizpah and Shen. He named the stone Ebenezer,ⁿ saying, "The LORD has helped us to this point." ¹³So the Philistines were defeated and did not enter the Israelites' land again.

The LORD was against the Philistines all Samuel's life. ¹⁴Earlier the Philistines had taken towns from the Israelites, but the Israelites won them back, from Ekron to Gath. They also took back from the Philistines the lands near these towns. There was peace also between Israel and the Amorites.

¹⁵Samuel continued as judge of Israel all his life. ¹⁶Every year he went from Bethel to Gilgal to Mizpah and judged the Israelites in all these towns. ¹⁷But Samuel always went back to Ramah, where his home was. There he judged Israel and built an altar to the LORD.

ISRAEL ASKS FOR A KING

8 When Samuel was old, he made his sons judges for Israel. ²His first son was named Joel, and his second son was named Abijah. Joel and Abijah were judges in Beersheba. ³But Samuel's sons did not live as he did. They tried to get money dishonestly, and they accepted money secretly to make wrong judgments.

⁴So all the elders came together and met Samuel at Ramah. ⁵They said to him, "You're old, and your sons don't live as you do. Give us a king to rule over us like all the other nations."

⁶When the elders said that, Samuel was not pleased. He prayed to the LORD, ⁷and the

---

7:12 Ebenezer This name means "stone of help."

LORD told Samuel, "Listen to whatever the people say to you. They have not rejected you. They have rejected me from being their king. 8They are doing as they have always done. When I took them out of Egypt, they left me and served other gods. They are doing the same to you. 9Now listen to the people, but warn them what the king who rules over them will do."

10So Samuel told those who had asked him for a king what the LORD had said. 11Samuel said, "If you have a king ruling over you, this is what he will do: He will take your sons and make them serve with his chariots and his horses, and they will run in front of the king's chariot. 12The king will make some of your sons commanders over thousands or over fifties. He will make some of your other sons plow his ground and reap his harvest. He will take others to make weapons of war and equipment for his chariots. 13He will take your daughters to make perfume and cook and bake for him. 14He will take your best fields, vineyards, and olive groves and give them to his servants. 15He will take one-tenth of your grain and grapes and give it to his officers and servants. 16He will take your male and female servants, your best cattle, and your donkeys and use them all for his own work. 17He will take one-tenth of your flocks, and you yourselves will become his slaves. 18When that time comes, you will cry out because of the king you chose. But the LORD will not answer you then."

19But the people would not listen to Samuel. They said, "No! We want a king to rule over us. 20Then we will be the same as all the other nations. Our king will judge for us and go with us and fight our battles."

21After Samuel heard all that the people said, he repeated their words to the LORD. 22The LORD answered, "You must listen to them. Give them a king."

Then Samuel told the people of Israel, "Go back to your towns."

SAUL LOOKS FOR HIS FATHER'S DONKEYS

9 Kish, son of Abiel from the tribe of Benjamin, was an important man. (Abiel was the son of Zeror, who was the son of Becorath, who was the son of Aphiah of Benjamin.) 2Kish had a son named Saul, who was a fine young man. There was no Israelite

better than he. Saul stood a head taller than any other man in Israel.

3Now the donkeys of Saul's father, Kish, were lost. So Kish said to Saul, his son, "Take one of the servants, and go and look for the donkeys." 4Saul went through the mountains of Ephraim and the land of Shalisha, but he and the servant could not find the donkeys. They went into the land of Shaalim, but the donkeys were not there. They went through the land of Benjamin, but they still did not find them. 5When they arrived in the area of Zuph, Saul said to his servant, "Let's go back or my father will stop thinking about the donkeys and will start worrying about us."

6But the servant answered, "A man of God is in this town. People respect him because everything he says comes true. Let's go into the town now. Maybe he can tell us something about the journey we have taken."

7Saul said to his servant, "If we go into the town, what can we give him? The food in our bags is gone. We have no gift to give him. Do we have anything?"

8Again the servant answered Saul. "Look, I have one-tenth of an ounce of silver. Give it to the man of God. Then he will tell us about our journey." 9(In the past, if someone in Israel wanted to ask something from God, he would say, "Let's go to the seer." We call the person a prophet today, but in the past he was called a seer.)

10Saul said to his servant, "That's a good idea. Come, let's go." So they went toward the town where the man of God was.

11As Saul and the servant were going up the hill to the town, they met some young women coming out to get water. Saul and the servant asked them, "Is the seer here?"

12The young women answered, "Yes, he's here. He's ahead of you. Hurry now. He has just come to our town today, because the people will offer a sacrifice at the place of worship. 13As soon as you enter the town, you will find him before he goes up to the place of worship to eat. The people will not begin eating until the seer comes, because he must bless the sacrifice. After that, the guests will eat. Go now, and you should find him."

SAUL MEETS SAMUEL

14Saul and the servant went up to the town. Just as they entered it, they saw Samuel coming toward them on his way up to the place of worship.

15The day before Saul came, the LORD had told Samuel: 16"About this time tomorrow I will send you a man from the land of Benjamin. Appoint him to lead my people Israel. He will save my people from the Philistines. I have seen the suffering of my people, and I have listened to their cry."

17When Samuel first saw Saul, the LORD said to Samuel, "This is the man I told you about. He will organize my people."

18Saul approached Samuel at the gate and said, "Please tell me where the seer's house is."

19Samuel answered, "I am the seer. Go with me to the place of worship. Today you and your servant are to eat with me. Tomorrow morning I will answer all your questions and send you home. 20Don't worry about the donkeys you lost three days ago, because they have been found. Soon all the wealth of Israel will belong to you and your family."

21Saul answered, "But I am from the tribe of Benjamin, the smallest tribe in Israel. And my family group is the smallest in the tribe of Benjamin. Why are you saying such things?"

22Then Samuel took Saul and his servant into a large room and gave them a choice place at the table. About thirty guests were there. 23Samuel said to the cook, "Bring the meat I gave you, the portion I told you to set aside."

24So the cook took the thigh and put it on the table in front of Saul. Samuel said, "This is the meat saved for you. Eat it, because it was set aside for you for this special time. As I said, 'I had invited the people.'" So Saul ate with Samuel that day.

25After they finished eating, they came down from the place of worship and went to the town. Then Samuel talked with Saul on the roof[n] of his house. 26At dawn they got up, and Samuel called to Saul on the roof. He said, "Get up, and I will send you on your way." So Saul got up and went out of the house with Samuel. 27As Saul, his servant, and Samuel were getting near the edge of the city, Samuel said to Saul, "Tell the servant to go on ahead of us, but you stay, because I have a message from God for you."

SAMUEL APPOINTS SAUL

10 Samuel took a jar of olive oil and poured it on Saul's head. He kissed Saul and said, "The LORD has appointed you to lead his people. 2After you leave me today, you will meet two men near Rachel's tomb on the border of Benjamin at Zelzah. They will say to you, 'The donkeys you were looking for have been found. But now your father has stopped thinking about his donkeys and is worrying about you. He is asking, "What will I do about my son?"'

3"Then you will go on until you reach the big tree at Tabor. Three men on their way to worship God at Bethel will meet you there. One man will be carrying three goats. Another will be carrying three loaves of bread. And the third will have a leather bag full of wine. 4They will greet you and offer you two loaves of bread, which you must accept. 5Then you will go to Gibeah of God, where a Philistine camp is. When you approach this town, a group of prophets will come down from the place of worship. They will be playing harps, tambourines, flutes, and lyres, and they will be prophesying. 6Then the Spirit of the LORD will rush upon you with power. You will prophesy with these prophets, and you will be changed into a different man. 7After these signs happen, do whatever you find to do, because God will help you.

8"Go ahead of me to Gilgal. I will come down to you to offer whole burnt offerings and fellowship offerings. But you must wait seven days. Then I will come and tell you what to do."

SAUL MADE KING

9When Saul turned to leave Samuel, God changed Saul's heart. All these signs came true that day. 10When Saul and his servant arrived at Gibeah, Saul met a group of prophets. The Spirit of God rushed upon him, and he prophesied with the prophets. 11When people who had known Saul before saw him prophesying with the prophets, they asked each other, "What has happened to Kish's son? Is even Saul one of the prophets?"

9:25 roof In Bible times houses were built with flat roofs. The roof was used for drying things such as flax and fruit. And it was used as an extra room, as a place for worship, and as a cool place to sleep in the summer. See Deuteronomy 22:8.

¹²A man who lived there said, "Who is the father of these prophets?" So this became a famous saying: "Is even Saul one of the prophets?" ¹³When Saul finished prophesying, he entered the place of worship.

¹⁴Saul's uncle asked him and his servant, "Where have you been?"

Saul said, "We were looking for the donkeys. When we couldn't find them, we went to talk to Samuel."

¹⁵Saul's uncle asked, "Please tell me. What did Samuel say to you?"

¹⁶Saul answered, "He told us the donkeys had already been found." But Saul did not tell his uncle what Samuel had said about his becoming king.

¹⁷Samuel called all the people of Israel to meet with the LORD at Mizpah. ¹⁸He said, "This is what the LORD, the God of Israel, says: 'I led Israel out of Egypt. I saved you from Egypt's control and from other kingdoms that were troubling you.' ¹⁹But now you have rejected your God. He saves you from all your troubles and problems, but you said, 'No! We want a king to rule over us.' Now come, stand before the LORD in your tribes and family groups."

²⁰When Samuel gathered all the tribes of Israel, the tribe of Benjamin was picked. ²¹Samuel had them pass by in family groups, and Matri's family was picked. Then he had each man of Matri's family pass by, and Saul son of Kish was picked. But when they looked for Saul, they could not find him. ²²They asked the LORD, "Has Saul come here yet?"

The LORD said, "Yes. He's hiding behind the baggage."

²³So they ran and brought him out. When Saul stood among the people, he was a head taller than anyone else. ²⁴Then Samuel said to the people, "See the man the LORD has chosen. There is no one like him among all the people."

Then the people shouted, "Long live the king!"

²⁵Samuel explained the rights and duties of the king and then wrote them in a book and put it before the LORD. Then he told the people to go to their homes.

²⁶Saul also went to his home in Gibeah. God touched the hearts of certain brave men who went along with him. ²⁷But some troublemakers said, "How can this man save

us?" They disapproved of Saul and refused to bring gifts to him. But Saul kept quiet.

NAHASH TROUBLES JABESH GILEAD

11 About a month later Nahash the Ammonite and his army surrounded the city of Jabesh in Gilead. All the people of Jabesh said to Nahash, "Make a treaty with us, and we will serve you."

²But he answered, "I will make a treaty with you only if I'm allowed to poke out the right eye of each of you. Then all Israel will be ashamed!"

³The elders of Jabesh said to Nahash, "Give us seven days to send messengers through all Israel. If no one comes to help us, we will give ourselves up to you."

⁴When the messengers came to Gibeah where Saul lived and told the people the news, they cried loudly. ⁵Saul was coming home from plowing the fields with his oxen when he heard the people crying. He asked, "What's wrong with the people that they are crying?" Then they told Saul what the messengers from Jabesh had said. ⁶When Saul heard their words, God's Spirit rushed upon him with power, and he became very angry. ⁷So he took a pair of oxen and cut them into pieces. Then he gave the pieces of the oxen to messengers and ordered them to carry them through all the land of Israel.

The messengers said, "This is what will happen to the oxen of anyone who does not follow Saul and Samuel." So the people became very afraid of the LORD. They all came together as if they were one person. ⁸Saul gathered the people together at Bezek. There were three hundred thousand men from Israel and thirty thousand men from Judah.

⁹They said to the messengers who had come, "Tell the people at Jabesh Gilead this: 'Before the day warms up tomorrow, you will be saved.'" So the messengers went and reported this to the people at Jabesh, and they were very happy. ¹⁰The people said to Nahash the Ammonite, "Tomorrow we will come out to meet you. Then you can do anything you want to us."

¹¹The next morning Saul divided his soldiers into three groups. At dawn they entered the Ammonite camp and defeated them before the heat of the day. The Ammonites who

escaped were scattered; no two of them were still together.

¹²Then the people said to Samuel, "Who didn't want Saul as king? Bring them here and we will kill them!"

¹³But Saul said, "No! No one will be put to death today. Today the LORD has saved Israel!"

¹⁴Then Samuel said to the people, "Come, let's go to Gilgal. There we will again promise to obey the king." ¹⁵So all the people went to Gilgal, and there, before the LORD, the people made Saul king. They offered fellowship offerings to the LORD, and Saul and all the Israelites had a great celebration.

SAMUEL'S FAREWELL SPEECH

12 Samuel said to all Israel, "I have done everything you wanted me to do and have put a king over you. ²Now you have a king to lead you. I am old and gray, and my sons are here with you. I have been your leader since I was young. ³Here I am. If I have done anything wrong, you must testify against me before the LORD and his appointed king. Did I steal anyone's ox or donkey? Did I hurt or cheat anyone? Did I ever secretly accept money to pretend not to see something wrong? If I did any of these things, I will make it right."

⁴The Israelites answered, "You have not cheated us, or hurt us, or taken anything unfairly from anyone."

⁵Samuel said to them, "The LORD is a witness to what you have said. His appointed king is also a witness today that you did not find anything wrong in me."

"He is our witness," they said.

⁶Then Samuel said to the people, "It is the LORD who chose Moses and Aaron and brought your ancestors out of Egypt. ⁷Now, stand there, and I will remind you of all the good things the LORD did for you and your ancestors.

⁸"After Jacob entered Egypt, his descendants cried to the LORD for help. So the LORD sent Moses and Aaron, who took your ancestors out of Egypt and brought them to live in this place.

⁹"But they forgot the LORD their God. So he handed them over as slaves to Sisera, the commander of the army of Hazor, and as slaves to the Philistines and the king of Moab. They all fought against your ancestors. ¹⁰Then your ancestors cried to the LORD and said, 'We have sinned. We have left the LORD and served the Baals and the Ashtoreths. But now save us from our enemies, and we will serve you.' ¹¹So the LORD sent Gideon,ⁿ Barak, Jephthah, and Samuel. He saved you from your enemies around you, and you lived in safety. ¹²But when you saw Nahash king of the Ammonites coming against you, you said, 'No! We want a king to rule over us!'—even though the LORD your God was your king. ¹³Now here is the king you chose, the one you asked for. The LORD has put him over you. ¹⁴You must honor the LORD and serve him. You must obey his word and not turn against his commands. Both you and the king ruling over you must follow the LORD your God. If you do, it will be well with you. ¹⁵But if you don't obey the LORD, and if you turn against his commands, he will be against you. He will do to you what he did to your ancestors.

¹⁶"Now stand still and see the great thing the LORD will do before your eyes. ¹⁷It is now the time of the wheat harvest.ⁿ I will pray for the LORD to send thunder and rain. Then you will know what an evil thing you did against the LORD when you asked for a king."

¹⁸Then Samuel prayed to the LORD, and that same day the LORD sent thunder and rain. So the people were very afraid of the LORD and Samuel. ¹⁹They said to Samuel, "Pray to the LORD your God for us, your servants! Don't let us die! We've added to all our sins the evil of asking for a king."

²⁰Samuel answered, "Don't be afraid. It's true that you did wrong, but don't turn away from the LORD. Serve the LORD with all your heart. ²¹Idols are of no use, so don't worship them. They can't help you or save you. They are useless! ²²For his own sake, the LORD won't leave his people. Instead, he was pleased to make you his own people. ²³I will surely not stop praying for you, because that would be sinning against the LORD. I will teach you what is good and right. ²⁴You must honor the LORD and truly serve him with all your heart. Remember the wonderful things

---

12:11 Gideon Also called Jerub-Baal. **12:17 time . . . harvest** This was a dry time in the summer when no rains fell.

he did for you! ²⁵But if you are stubborn and do evil, he will sweep you and your king away."

13
Saul was thirty years old when he became king, and he was king over Israel forty-two years.ⁿ ²Saul chose three thousand men from Israel. Two thousand men stayed with him at Micmash in the mountains of Bethel, and one thousand men stayed with Jonathan at Gibeah in Benjamin. Saul sent the other men in the army back home.

³Jonathan attacked the Philistine camp in Geba, and the other Philistines heard about it. Saul said, "Let the Hebrews hear what happened." So he told the men to blow trumpets through all the land of Israel. ⁴All the Israelites heard the news. The men said, "Saul has defeated the Philistine camp. Now the Philistines will really hate us!" Then the Israelites were called to join Saul at Gilgal.

⁵The Philistines gathered to fight Israel with three thousandⁿ chariots and six thousand men to ride in them. Their soldiers were as many as the grains of sand on the seashore. The Philistines went and camped at Micmash, which is east of Beth Aven. ⁶When the Israelites saw that they were in trouble, they went to hide in caves and bushes, among the rocks, and in pits and wells. ⁷Some Hebrews even went across the Jordan River to the land of Gad and Gilead.

But Saul stayed at Gilgal, and all the men in his army were shaking with fear. ⁸Saul waited seven days, because Samuel had said he would meet him then. But Samuel did not come to Gilgal, and the soldiers began to leave.

⁹So Saul said, "Bring me the whole burnt offering and the fellowship offerings." Then Saul offered the whole burnt offering. ¹⁰Just as he finished, Samuel arrived, and Saul went to greet him.

¹¹Samuel asked, "What have you done?"

Saul answered, "I saw the soldiers leaving me, and you were not here when you said you would be. The Philistines were gathering at Micmash. ¹²Then I thought, 'The Philistines will come against me at Gilgal, and I haven't asked for the LORD's approval.' So I forced myself to offer the whole burnt offering."

¹³Samuel said, "You acted foolishly! You haven't obeyed the command of the LORD your God. If you had obeyed him, the LORD would have made your kingdom continue in Israel always, ¹⁴but now your kingdom will not continue. The LORD has looked for the kind of man he wants. He has appointed him to rule his people, because you haven't obeyed his command."

¹⁵Then Samuel left Gilgal and went to Gibeah in Benjamin. Saul counted the men who were still with him, and there were about six hundred.

HARD TIMES FOR ISRAEL

¹⁶Saul and his son Jonathan and the soldiers with him stayed in Gibeah in the land of Benjamin. The Philistines made their camp at Micmash. ¹⁷Three groups went out from the Philistine camp to make raids. One group went on the Ophrah road in the land of Shual. ¹⁸The second group went on the Beth Horon road. The third group went on the border road that overlooks the Valley of Zeboim toward the desert.

¹⁹The whole land of Israel had no blacksmith because the Philistines had said, "The Hebrews might make swords and spears." ²⁰So all the Israelites had to go down to the Philistines to have their plows, hoes, axes, and sickles sharpened. ²¹The Philistine blacksmiths charged about one-fourth of an ounce of silver for sharpening plows and hoes. And they charged one-eighth of an ounce of silver for sharpening picks, axes, and the sticks used to guide oxen.

²²So when the battle came, the soldiers with Saul and Jonathan had no swords or spears. Only Saul and his son Jonathan had them.

ISRAEL DEFEATS THE PHILISTINES

²³A group from the Philistine army had gone out to the pass at Micmash.

14
One day Jonathan, Saul's son, said to the officer who carried his armor, "Come, let's go over to the Philistine camp on the other side." But Jonathan did not tell his father.

²Saul was sitting under a pomegranate tree at the threshing floor near Gibeah. He had about six hundred men with him. ³One

---

13:1 **Saul . . . years** This is how the verse is worded in some early Greek copies. The Hebrew is not clear here.
13:5 **three thousand** Some Greek copies say three thousand. The Hebrew copies say thirty thousand.

man was Ahijah who was wearing the holy vest. (Ahijah was a son of Ichabod's brother Ahitub. Ichabod was the son of Phinehas, the son of Eli, the LORD's priest in Shiloh.) No one knew Jonathan had left.

⁴There was a steep slope on each side of the pass that Jonathan planned to go through to reach the Philistine camp. The cliff on one side was named Bozez, and the cliff on the other side was named Seneh. ⁵One cliff faced north toward Micmash. The other faced south toward Geba.

⁶Jonathan said to his officer who carried his armor, "Come. Let's go to the camp of those men who are not circumcised. Maybe the LORD will help us. The LORD can give us victory if we have many people, or just a few."

⁷The officer who carried Jonathan's armor said to him, "Do whatever you think is best. Go ahead. I'm with you."

⁸Jonathan said, "Then come. We will cross over to the Philistines and let them see us. ⁹If they say to us, 'Stay there until we come to you,' we will stay where we are. We won't go up to them. ¹⁰But if they say, 'Come up to us,' we will climb up, and the LORD will let us defeat them. This will be the sign for us."

¹¹When both Jonathan and his officer let the Philistines see them, the Philistines said, "Look! The Hebrews are crawling out of the holes they were hiding in!" ¹²The Philistines in the camp shouted to Jonathan and his officer, "Come up to us. We'll teach you a lesson!"

Jonathan said to his officer, "Climb up behind me, because the LORD has given the Philistines to Israel!" ¹³So Jonathan climbed up, using his hands and feet, and his officer climbed just behind him. Jonathan struck down the Philistines as he went, and his officer killed them as he followed behind him. ¹⁴In that first fight Jonathan and his officer killed about twenty Philistines over a half acre of ground.

¹⁵All the Philistine soldiers panicked—those in the camp and those in the raiding party. The ground itself shook! God had caused the panic.

¹⁶Saul's guards were at Gibeah in the land of Benjamin when they saw the Philistine soldiers running in every direction. ¹⁷Saul said to his army, "Check to see who has left our camp." When they checked, they learned that Jonathan and his officer were gone.

¹⁸So Saul said to Ahijah the priest, "Bring the Ark of God." (At that time it was with the Israelites.) ¹⁹While Saul was talking to the priest, the confusion in the Philistine camp was growing. Then Saul said to Ahijah, "Put your hand down!"

²⁰Then Saul gathered his army and entered the battle. They found the Philistines confused, striking each other with their swords! ²¹Earlier, there were Hebrews who had served the Philistines and had stayed in their camp, but now they joined the Israelites with Saul and Jonathan. ²²When all the Israelites hidden in the mountains of Ephraim heard that the Philistine soldiers were running away, they also joined the battle and chased the Philistines. ²³So the LORD saved the Israelites that day, and the battle moved on past Beth Aven.

SAUL MAKES ANOTHER MISTAKE

²⁴The men of Israel were miserable that day because Saul had made an oath for all of them. He had said, "No one should eat food before evening and before I finish defeating my enemies. If he does, he will be cursed!" So no Israelite soldier ate food.

²⁵Now the army went into the woods, where there was some honey on the ground. ²⁶They came upon some honey, but no one took any because they were afraid of the oath. ²⁷Jonathan had not heard the oath Saul had put on the army, so he dipped the end of his stick into the honey and lifted some out and ate it. Then he felt better. ²⁸Then one of the soldiers told Jonathan, "Your father made an oath for all the soldiers. He said any man who eats today will be cursed! That's why they are so weak."

²⁹Jonathan said, "My father has made trouble for the land! See how much better I feel after just tasting a little of this honey! ³⁰It would have been much better for the men to eat the food they took from their enemies today. We could have killed many more Philistines!"

³¹That day the Israelites defeated the Philistines from Micmash to Aijalon. After that, they were very tired. ³²They had taken sheep, cattle, and calves from the Philistines. Now they were so hungry they killed the animals

on the ground and ate them, without draining the blood from them! 33Someone said to Saul, "Look! The men are sinning against the LORD. They're eating meat without draining the blood from it!"

Saul said, "You have sinned! Roll a large stone over here now!" 34Then he said, "Go to the men and tell them that each person must bring his ox and sheep to me and kill it here and eat it. Don't sin against the LORD by eating meat without draining the blood from it."

That night everyone brought his animals and killed them there. 35Then Saul built an altar to the LORD. It was the first altar he had built to the LORD.

36Saul said, "Let's go after the Philistines tonight and rob them. We won't let any of them live!"

The men answered, "Do whatever you think is best."

But the priest said, "Let's ask God."

37So Saul asked God, "Should I chase the Philistines? Will you let us defeat them?" But God did not answer Saul at that time. 38Then Saul said to all the leaders of his army, "Come here. Let's find out what sin has been done today. 39As surely as the LORD lives who has saved Israel, even if my son Jonathan did the sin, he must die." But no one in the army spoke.

40Then Saul said to all the Israelites, "You stand on this side. I and my son Jonathan will stand on the other side."

The men answered, "Do whatever you think is best."

41Then Saul prayed to the LORD, the God of Israel, "Give me the right answer."

And Saul and Jonathan were picked; the other men went free. 42Saul said, "Now let us discover if it is I or Jonathan my son who is guilty." And Jonathan was picked.

43Saul said to Jonathan, "Tell me what you have done."

So Jonathan told Saul, "I only tasted a little honey from the end of my stick. And must I die now?"

44Saul said, "Jonathan, if you don't die, may God punish me terribly."

45But the soldiers said to Saul, "Must Jonathan die? Never! He is responsible for saving Israel today! As surely as the LORD lives, not even a hair of his head will fall to the ground! Today Jonathan fought against the Philistines with God's help!" So the army saved Jonathan, and he did not die.

46Then Saul stopped chasing the Philistines, and they went back to their own land.

SAUL FIGHTS ISRAEL'S ENEMIES

47When Saul became king over Israel, he fought against Israel's enemies all around. He fought Moab, the Ammonites, Edom, the king of Zobah, and the Philistines. Everywhere Saul went he defeated Israel's enemies. 48He fought bravely and defeated the Amalekites. He saved the Israelites from their enemies who had robbed them.

49Saul's sons were Jonathan, Ishvi, and Malki-Shua. His older daughter was named Merab, and his younger daughter was named Michal. 50Saul's wife was Ahinoam daughter of Ahimaaz. The commander of his army was Abner son of Ner, Saul's uncle. 51Saul's father Kish and Abner's father Ner were sons of Abiel.

52All Saul's life he fought hard against the Philistines. When he saw strong or brave men, he took them into his army.

SAUL REJECTED AS KING

15 Samuel said to Saul, "The LORD sent me to appoint you king over Israel. Now listen to his message. 2This is what the LORD All-Powerful says: 'When the Israelites came out of Egypt, the Amalekites tried to stop them from going to Canaan. So I will punish them. 3Now go, attack the Amalekites and destroy everything they own as an offering to the LORD. Don't let anything live. Put to death men and women, children and small babies, cattle and sheep, camels and donkeys.'"

4So Saul called the army together at Telaim. There were two hundred thousand foot soldiers and ten thousand men from Judah. 5Then Saul went to the city of Amalek and set up an ambush in the ravine. 6He said to the Kenites, "Go away. Leave the Amalekites so that I won't destroy you with them, because you showed kindness to the Israelites when they came out of Egypt." So the Kenites moved away from the Amalekites.

7Then Saul defeated the Amalekites. He fought them all the way from Havilah to Shur, at the border of Egypt. 8He took King Agag of the Amalekites alive, but he killed all of Agag's army with the sword. ⁹Saul and the army let Agag live, along with the best sheep, fat cattle, and lambs. They let every good animal live, because they did not want to destroy them. But when they found an animal that was weak or useless, they killed it.

¹⁰Then the Lord spoke his word to Samuel: ¹¹"I am sorry I made Saul king, because he has stopped following me and has not obeyed my commands." Samuel was upset, and he cried out to the Lord all night long.

¹²Early the next morning Samuel got up and went to meet Saul. But the people told Samuel, "Saul has gone to Carmel, where he has put up a monument in his own honor. Now he has gone down to Gilgal."

¹³When Samuel came to Saul, Saul said, "May the Lord bless you! I have obeyed the Lord's commands."

¹⁴But Samuel said, "Then why do I hear cattle mooing and sheep bleating?"

¹⁵Saul answered, "The soldiers took them from the Amalekites. They saved the best sheep and cattle to offer as sacrifices to the Lord your God, but we destroyed all the other animals."

¹⁶Samuel said to Saul, "Stop! Let me tell you what the Lord said to me last night."

Saul answered, "Tell me."

¹⁷Samuel said, "Once you didn't think much of yourself, but now you have become the leader of the tribes of Israel. The Lord appointed you to be king over Israel. ¹⁸And he sent you on a mission. He said, 'Go and destroy those evil people, the Amalekites. Make war on them until all of them are dead.' ¹⁹Why didn't you obey the Lord? Why did you take the best things? Why did you do what the Lord said was wrong?"

²⁰Saul said, "But I did obey the Lord. I did what the Lord told me to do. I destroyed all the Amalekites, and I brought back Agag their king. ²¹The soldiers took the best sheep and cattle to sacrifice to the Lord your God at Gilgal."

²²But Samuel answered,

"What pleases the Lord more:
  burnt offerings and sacrifices
  or obedience to his voice?
It is better to obey than to sacrifice.
  It is better to listen to God than to offer
    the fat of sheep.

²³ Disobedience is as bad as the sin of
    sorcery.
  Pride is as bad as the sin of worshiping
    idols.
You have rejected the Lord's command.
  Now he rejects you as king."

²⁴Then Saul said to Samuel, "I have sinned. I didn't obey the Lord's commands and your words. I was afraid of the people, and I did what they said. ²⁵Now, I beg you, forgive my sin. Come back with me so I may worship the Lord."

²⁶But Samuel said to Saul, "I won't go back with you. You rejected the Lord's command, and now he rejects you as king of Israel."

²⁷As Samuel turned to leave, Saul caught his robe, and it tore. ²⁸Samuel said to him, "The Lord has torn the kingdom of Israel from you today and has given it to one of your neighbors who is better than you. ²⁹The Lord is the Eternal One of Israel. He does not lie or change his mind. He is not a human being, so he does not change his mind."

³⁰Saul answered, "I have sinned. But please honor me in front of the elders of my people and in front of the Israelites. Come back with me so that I can worship the Lord your God." ³¹So Samuel went back with Saul, and Saul worshiped the Lord.

³²Then Samuel said, "Bring me King Agag of the Amalekites."

Agag came to Samuel in chains, but Agag thought, "Surely the threat of death has passed."

³³Samuel said to him, "Your sword made other mothers lose their children. Now your mother will have no children." And Samuel cut Agag to pieces before the Lord at Gilgal.

³⁴Then Samuel left and went to Ramah, but Saul went up to his home in Gibeah. ³⁵And Samuel never saw Saul again the rest of his life, but he was sad for Saul. And the Lord was very sorry he had made Saul king of Israel.

SAMUEL GOES TO BETHLEHEM

16 The Lord said to Samuel, "How long will you continue to feel sorry for Saul? I have rejected him as king of Israel. Fill your container with olive oil and go. I am sending you to Jesse who lives in Bethlehem, because I have chosen one of his sons to be king."

Authority Over Darkness Begins at Home

FAMILY

By Jimmy Evans

1 SAMUEL 15:22–23

The focus of the Christian life is to submit to the authority and will of God daily. In this way, we live in the blessing of God's peace and presence. The Bible teaches us that authority is from God and is for our good (Romans 13:1–3). Submission to authority is considered a virtue, and rebellion is serious sin (1 Samuel 15:22–23). Therefore, parental authority is a necessary, righteous influence that promotes God's will and prevents our sin nature from destroying the potential of each family member and the family as a whole.

The Bible commands children to obey and honor their parents. This is the first of the Ten Commandments God gave Moses that carried a profound promise (Exodus 20:12). God is trying to communicate something to us concerning the values of his kingdom, as well as the importance of authority and submission. Therefore, parents who do not exercise righteous authority by requiring their children to obey and honor them aren't only creating problems for themselves and society; they are also cursing their children with a life of problems, separated from the blessings and promises of God.

In order for us to begin to stop the wholesale destruction of the marriages and families in America and to build solid foundations for family life, we must totally reject the rebellious message of the world around us and begin to pray for God's righteous authority in our homes. When proper parental authority is present, it creates the framework for lasting, loving relationships.

Rather than standing up to the forces that are wreaking havoc in our homes and neighborhoods, many are casually observing as Satan destroys an entire generation. We are often irresponsible in our duty to resist and "subdue" the forces of darkness.

God has given us authority. It isn't just a blessing; it is a responsibility. Speaking to his church, Jesus says, "I will give you the keys of the kingdom of heaven; the things you don't allow on earth will be the things that God does not allow, and the things you allow on earth will be the things that God allows" (Matthew 16:19).

You can bind the evil in your home. You can kick the devil out the front door, or you can let him in; it's totally in *your* power, not his. You have the authority to rule your home righteously. Furthermore, the church has the power to take authority over evil forces in our cities.

Mayors and city commissioners don't have the greatest authority in our cities; the church does. Paul says in Ephesians 6:12 that we are not fighting against people. He says that our real battle is against "the spiritual powers of evil in the heavenly world."

Only the church can do something about evil powers in the heavenlies. As God's church, we have the authority to come against those powers, subdue them, and take dominion over them in Jesus' name. The only question is, will we do something, or will we stand back and say nothing?

TO LEARN MORE ON WHAT THE BIBLE HAS TO SAY ABOUT **FAMILY,** READ THE SCRIPTURES AND DEVOTIONALS AT **PROVERBS 31:10–31, PROVERBS 14:26, PROVERBS 15:4, PROVERBS 18:21, PROVERBS 20:11,** AND **PROVERBS 23:24.**

²But Samuel said, "If I go, Saul will hear the news and will try to kill me."

The LORD said, "Take a young calf with you. Say, 'I have come to offer a sacrifice to the LORD.' ³Invite Jesse to the sacrifice. Then I will tell you what to do. You must appoint the one I show you."

⁴Samuel did what the LORD told him to do. When he arrived at Bethlehem, the elders of Bethlehem shook with fear. They met him and asked, "Are you coming in peace?"

⁵Samuel answered, "Yes, I come in peace. I have come to make a sacrifice to the LORD. Set yourselves apart to the LORD and come to the sacrifice with me." Then he set Jesse and his sons apart to the LORD, and he invited them to come to the sacrifice.

⁶When they arrived, Samuel saw Eliab, and he thought, "Surely the LORD has

---

THE EXTRAORDINARY IN THE MUNDANE

FAITH

no secrets

1 SAMUEL 16:7

Notice that God tells Samuel that people do not see what they think they see. They look at the outward appearance and make judgments on that basis. Even when people gather personal information and insight about you, they still do not know everything there is to know about who you really are. But God is different. He puts no stock in outward appearance. He looks for the real self, the inner being of who we really are.

Implicit in this idea is the fact that God alone knows us thoroughly. Nothing is hidden from him. Most of us would rather not have everyone know all about us. There are thoughts and deeds that each of us would rather keep secret. But God knows them all.

Amazingly, in spite of this complete knowledge of who we are, he stands ready to accept us exactly as we are. God is well aware of our faults, mistakes, and sins. But he still opens his arms to us and says, "Come to me." This invitation overcomes the greatest of all fears: "If you knew all about me, you wouldn't love me." God says just the opposite: "I know all about you, and I love you just the same."

In a way, the fact that God does know all about us is vital to our redemption. What good would it really do us if God could only forgive what we wished to reveal? We would still be left with the fear that knowing all about us would turn him away. Thank God he knows everything. There is nothing left for us to hide. We can put away the secrets that hold us back. God knows them all, and he still loves us.

reflect: Give thanks to God for knowing all about you, yet loving you just the same.
Go to **1 Samuel 21:8-9.**

appointed this person standing here before him."

⁷But the LORD said to Samuel, "Don't look at how handsome Eliab is or how tall he is, because I have not chosen him. God does not see the same way people see. People look at the outside of a person, but the LORD looks at the heart."

⁸Then Jesse called Abinadab and told him to pass by Samuel. But Samuel said, "The LORD has not chosen this man either. ⁹Then Jesse had Shammah pass by. But Samuel said, "No, the LORD has not chosen this one." ¹⁰Jesse had seven of his sons pass by Samuel. But Samuel said to him, "The LORD has not chosen any of these."

¹¹Then he asked Jesse, "Are these all the sons you have?"

Jesse answered, "I still have the youngest son. He is out taking care of the sheep."

Samuel said, "Send for him. We will not sit down to eat until he arrives."

¹²So Jesse sent and had his youngest son brought in. He was a fine boy, tanned, and handsome.

The LORD said to Samuel, "Go, appoint him, because he is the one."

¹³So Samuel took the container of olive oil and poured it on Jesse's youngest son to appoint him in front of his brothers. From that day on, the LORD's Spirit worked in David. Samuel then went back to Ramah.

DAVID SERVES SAUL

¹⁴But the LORD's Spirit had left Saul, and an evil spirit from the LORD troubled him.

¹⁵Saul's servants said to him, "See, an evil spirit from God is troubling you. ¹⁶Give us the command to look for someone who can play the harp. When the evil spirit from God troubles you, he will play, and you will feel better."

¹⁷So Saul said to his servants, "Find someone who can play well and bring him to me." ¹⁸One of the servants said, "I have seen a son of Jesse of Bethlehem play the harp. He is brave and courageous. He is a good speaker and handsome, and the LORD is with him."

¹⁹Then Saul sent messengers to Jesse, saying, "Send me your son David, who is with the sheep." ²⁰So Jesse loaded a donkey with bread, a leather bag full of wine, and a young goat, and he sent them with his son David to Saul.

²¹When David came to Saul, he began to serve him. Saul liked David and made him the officer who carried his armor. ²²Saul sent a message to Jesse, saying, "Let David stay and serve me because I like him."

²³When the evil spirit from God troubled Saul, David would take his harp and play. Then the evil spirit would leave him, and Saul would feel better.

DAVID AND GOLIATH

17 The Philistines gathered their armies for war. They met at Socoh in Judah and camped at Ephes Dammim between Socoh and Azekah. ²Saul and the Israelites gathered in the Valley of Elah and camped there and took their positions to fight the Philistines. ³The Philistines controlled one hill while the Israelites controlled another. The valley was between them.

⁴The Philistines had a champion fighter from Gath named Goliath. He was about nine feet, four inches tall. He came out of the Philistine camp ⁵with a bronze helmet on his head and a coat of bronze armor that weighed about one hundred twenty-five pounds. ⁶He wore bronze protectors on his legs, and he had a bronze spear on his back. ⁷The wooden part of his larger spear was like a weaver's rod, and its blade weighed about fifteen pounds. The officer who carried his shield walked in front of him.

⁸Goliath stood and shouted to the Israelite soldiers, "Why have you taken positions for battle? I am a Philistine, and you are Saul's servants! Choose a man and send him to fight me. ⁹If he can fight and kill me, we will be your servants. But if I can kill him, you will be our servants." ¹⁰Then he said, "Today I stand and dare the army of Israel! Send one of your men to fight me!" ¹¹When Saul and the Israelites heard the Philistine's words, they were very scared.

¹²Now David was the son of Jesse, an Ephrathite from Bethlehem in Judah. Jesse had eight sons. In Saul's time Jesse was an old man. ¹³His three oldest sons followed Saul to the war. The first son was Eliab, the second was Abinadab, and the third was Shammah. ¹⁴David was the youngest. Jesse's three oldest sons followed Saul, ¹⁵but David went back

and forth from Saul to Bethlehem, where he took care of his father's sheep.

¹⁶For forty days the Philistine came out every morning and evening and stood before the Israelite army.

¹⁷Jesse said to his son David, "Take this half bushel of cooked grain and ten loaves of bread to your brothers in the camp. ¹⁸Also take ten pieces of cheese to the commander and to your brothers. See how your brothers are and bring back some proof to show me that they are all right. ¹⁹Your brothers are with Saul and the army in the Valley of Elah, fighting against the Philistines."

²⁰Early in the morning David left the sheep with another shepherd. He took the food and left as Jesse had told him. When David arrived at the camp, the army was going out to their battle positions, shouting their war cry. ²¹The Israelites and Philistines were lining up their men to face each other in battle.

²²David left the food with the man who kept the supplies and ran to the battle line to talk to his brothers. ²³While he was talking with them, Goliath, the Philistine champion from Gath, came out. He shouted things against Israel as usual, and David heard him. ²⁴When the Israelites saw Goliath, they were very much afraid and ran away.

²⁵They said, "Look at this man! He keeps coming out to challenge Israel. The king will give much money to whoever kills him. He will also let whoever kills him marry his daughter. And his father's family will not have to pay taxes in Israel."

²⁶David asked the men who stood near him, "What will be done to reward the man who kills this Philistine and takes away the shame from Israel? Who does this uncircumcised Philistine think he is? Does he think he can speak against the armies of the living God?"

²⁷The Israelites told David what would be done for the man who would kill Goliath.

²⁸When David's oldest brother Eliab heard David talking with the soldiers, he was angry with David. He asked David, "Why did you come here? Who's taking care of those few sheep of yours in the desert? I know you are proud and wicked at heart. You came down here just to watch the battle."

²⁹David asked, "Now what have I done wrong? Can't I even talk?" ³⁰When he turned to other people and asked the same questions, they gave him the same answer as before. ³¹Yet what David said was told to Saul, and he sent for David.

³²David said to Saul, "Don't let anyone be discouraged. I, your servant, will go and fight this Philistine!"

³³Saul answered, "You can't go out against this Philistine and fight him. You're only a boy. Goliath has been a warrior since he was a young man."

³⁴But David said to Saul, "I, your servant, have been keeping my father's sheep. When a lion or bear came and took a sheep from the flock, ³⁵I would chase it. I would attack it and save the sheep from its mouth. When it attacked me, I caught it by its fur and hit it and killed it. ³⁶I, your servant, have killed both a lion and a bear! This uncircumcised Philistine will be like them, because he has spoken against the armies of the living God. ³⁷The LORD who saved me from a lion and a bear will save me from this Philistine."

Saul said to David, "Go, and may the LORD be with you." ³⁸Saul put his own clothes on David. He put a bronze helmet on his head and dressed him in armor. ³⁹David put on Saul's sword and tried to walk around, but he was not used to all the armor Saul had put on him.

He said to Saul, "I can't go in this, because I'm not used to it." Then David took it all off. ⁴⁰He took his stick in his hand and chose five smooth stones from a stream. He put them in his shepherd's bag and grabbed his sling. Then he went to meet the Philistine.

⁴¹At the same time, the Philistine was coming closer to David. The man who held his shield walked in front of him. ⁴²When Goliath looked at David and saw that he was only a boy, tanned and handsome, he looked down on David with disgust. ⁴³He said, "Do you think I am a dog, that you come at me with a stick?" He used his gods' names to curse David. ⁴⁴He said to David, "Come here. I'll feed your body to the birds of the air and the wild animals!"

⁴⁵But David said to him, "You come to me using a sword and two spears. But I come to you in the name of the LORD All-Powerful, the God of the armies of Israel! You have spoken against him. ⁴⁶Today the LORD will

hand you over to me, and I'll kill you and cut off your head. Today I'll feed the bodies of the Philistine soldiers to the birds of the air and the wild animals. Then all the world will know there is a God in Israel! ⁴⁷Everyone gathered here will know the LORD does not need swords or spears to save people. The battle belongs to him, and he will hand you over to us."

⁴⁸As Goliath came near to attack him, David ran quickly to meet him. ⁴⁹He took a stone from his bag, put it into his sling, and slung it. The stone hit the Philistine and went deep into his forehead, and Goliath fell face-down on the ground.

⁵⁰So David defeated the Philistine with only a sling and a stone. He hit him and killed him. He did not even have a sword in his hand. ⁵¹Then David ran and stood beside him. He took Goliath's sword out of its holder and killed him by cutting off his head.

When the Philistines saw that their champion was dead, they turned and ran. ⁵²The men of Israel and Judah shouted and chased the Philistines all the way to the entrance of the city of Gath and to the gates of Ekron.

The Philistines' bodies lay on the Shaaraim road as far as Gath and Ekron. ⁵³The Israelites returned after chasing the Philistines and robbed their camp. ⁵⁴David took Goliath's head to Jerusalem and put Goliath's weapons in his own tent.

⁵⁵When Saul saw David go out to meet Goliath, Saul asked Abner, commander of the army, "Abner, who is that young man's father?"

Abner answered, "As surely as you live, my king, I don't know."

⁵⁶The king said, "Find out whose son he is."

⁵⁷When David came back from killing Goliath, Abner brought him to Saul. David was still holding Goliath's head.

⁵⁸Saul asked him, "Young man, who is your father?"

David answered, "I am the son of your servant Jesse of Bethlehem."

SAUL FEARS DAVID

18 When David finished talking with Saul, Jonathan felt very close to David. He loved David as much as he loved himself. ²Saul kept David with him from that day on and did not let him go home to his father's house. ³Jonathan made an agreement with David, because he loved David as much as himself. ⁴He took off his coat and gave it to David, along with his armor, including his sword, bow, and belt.

⁵Saul sent David to fight in different battles, and David was very successful. Then Saul put David over the soldiers, which pleased Saul's officers and all the other people.

⁶After David had killed the Philistine, he and the men returned home. Women came out from all the towns of Israel to meet King Saul. They sang songs of joy, danced, and played tambourines and stringed instruments. ⁷As they played, they sang,

"Saul has killed thousands of his
    enemies,
  but David has killed tens of thousands."

⁸The women's song upset Saul, and he became very angry. He thought, "The women say David has killed tens of thousands, but they say I have killed only thousands. The only thing left for him to have is the kingdom!" ⁹So Saul watched David closely from then on, because he was jealous.

¹⁰The next day an evil spirit from God rushed upon Saul, and he prophesied in his house. David was playing the harp as he usually did, but Saul had a spear in his hand. ¹¹He threw the spear, thinking, "I'll pin David to the wall." But David escaped from him twice.

¹²The LORD was with David but had left Saul. So Saul was afraid of David. ¹³He sent David away and made him commander of a thousand soldiers. So David led them in battle. ¹⁴He had great success in everything he did because the LORD was with him. ¹⁵When Saul saw that David was very successful, he feared David even more. ¹⁶But all the people of Israel and Judah loved David because he led them well in battle.

SAUL'S DAUGHTER MARRIES DAVID

¹⁷Saul said to David, "Here is my older daughter Merab. I will let you marry her. All I ask is that you remain brave and fight the LORD's battles." Saul thought, "I won't have to kill David. The Philistines will do that."

¹⁸But David answered Saul, saying, "Who am I? My family is not important enough for me to become the king's son-in-law." ¹⁹So,

when the time came for Saul's daughter Merab to marry David, Saul gave her instead to Adriel of Meholah.

20Now Saul's other daughter, Michal, loved David. When they told Saul, he was pleased. 21He thought, "I will let her marry David. Then she will be a trap for him, and the Philistines will defeat him." So Saul said to David a second time, "You may become my son-in-law."

22And Saul ordered his servants to talk with David in private and say, "Look, the king likes you. His servants love you. You should be his son-in-law."

23Saul's servants said these words to David, but David answered, "Do you think it is easy to become the king's son-in-law? I am poor and unimportant."

24When Saul's servants told him what David had said, 25Saul said, "Tell David, 'The king doesn't want money for the bride. All he wants is a hundred Philistine foreskins to get even with his enemies.'" Saul planned to let the Philistines kill David.

26When Saul's servants told this to David, he was pleased to become the king's son-in-law. 27So he and his men went out and killed two hundred Philistines. David brought all their foreskins to Saul so he could be the king's son-in-law. Then Saul gave him his daughter Michal for his wife. 28Saul saw that the LORD was with David and that his daughter Michal loved David. 29So he grew even more afraid of David, and he was David's enemy all his life.

30The Philistine commanders continued to go out to fight the Israelites, but every time, David was more skillful than Saul's officers. So he became famous.

SAUL TRIES TO KILL DAVID

19 Saul told his son Jonathan and all his servants to kill David, but Jonathan liked David very much. 2So he warned David, "My father Saul is looking for a chance to kill you. Watch out in the morning. Hide in a secret place. 3I will go out and stand with my father in the field where you are hiding, and I'll talk to him about you. Then I'll let you know what I find out."

4When Jonathan talked to Saul his father, he said good things about David. Jonathan said, "The king should do no wrong to your servant David since he has done nothing wrong to you. What he has done has helped you greatly. 5David risked his life when he killed Goliath the Philistine, and the LORD won a great victory for all Israel. You saw it and were happy. Why would you do wrong against David? He's innocent. There's no reason to kill him!"

6Saul listened to Jonathan and then made this promise: "As surely as the LORD lives, David won't be put to death."

7So Jonathan called to David and told him everything that had been said. He brought David to Saul, and David was with Saul as before.

8When war broke out again, David went out to fight the Philistines. He defeated them, and they ran away from him.

9But once again an evil spirit from the LORD rushed upon Saul as he was sitting in his house with his spear in his hand. David was playing the harp. 10Saul tried to pin David to the wall with his spear, but David jumped out of the way. So Saul's spear went into the wall, and David ran away that night.

11Saul sent messengers to David's house to watch it and to kill him in the morning. But Michal, David's wife, warned him, saying, "Tonight you must run for your life. If you don't, you will be dead in the morning." 12So she let David down out of a window, and he ran away and escaped. 13Then Michal took an idol, laid it on the bed, covered it with clothes, and put goats' hair at its head.

14Saul sent messengers to take David prisoner, but Michal said, "He is sick."

15Saul sent them back to see David, saying, "Bring him to me on his bed so I can kill him."

16When the messengers entered David's house, they found just an idol on the bed with goats' hair on its head.

17Saul said to Michal, "Why did you trick me this way? You let my enemy go so he could run away!"

Michal answered Saul, "David told me if I did not help him escape, he would kill me."

18After David had escaped from Saul, he went to Samuel at Ramah and told him everything Saul had done to him. Then David and Samuel went to Naioth and stayed there. 19Saul heard that David was in Naioth at Ramah. 20So he sent messengers to capture him. But they met a group of prophets prophesying, with Samuel standing there leading them. So the Spirit of God entered Saul's men, and they also prophesied.

²¹When Saul heard the news, he sent more messengers, but they also prophesied. Then he sent messengers a third time, but they also prophesied. ²²Finally, Saul himself went to Ramah, to the well at Secu. He asked, "Where are Samuel and David?"

The people answered, "In Naioth at Ramah."

²³When Saul went to Naioth at Ramah, the Spirit of God also rushed upon him. And he walked on, prophesying until he came to Naioth at Ramah. ²⁴He took off his robes and prophesied in front of Samuel. He lay that way all day and all night. That is why people ask, "Is even Saul one of the prophets?"

JONATHAN HELPS DAVID

20 Then David ran away from Naioth in Ramah. He went to Jonathan and asked, "What have I done? What is my crime? How did I sin against your father? Why is he trying to kill me?"

²Jonathan answered, "No! You won't die! See, my father doesn't do anything great or small without first telling me. Why would he keep this from me? It's not true!"

³But David took an oath, saying, "Your father knows very well that you like me. He says to himself, 'Jonathan must not know about it, or he will tell David.' As surely as the LORD lives and as you live, I am only a step away from death!"

⁴Jonathan said to David, "I'll do anything you want me to do."

⁵So David said, "Look, tomorrow is the New Moon festival. I am supposed to eat with the king, but let me hide in the field until the third evening. ⁶If your father notices I am gone, tell him, 'David begged me to let him go to his hometown of Bethlehem. Every year at this time his family group offers a sacrifice.' ⁷If your father says, 'Fine,' I am safe. But if he becomes angry, you will know that he wants to hurt me. ⁸Jonathan, be loyal to me, your servant. You have made an agreement with me before the LORD. If I am guilty, you may kill me yourself! Why hand me over to your father?"

⁹Jonathan answered, "No, never! If I learn that my father plans to hurt you, I will warn you!"

¹⁰David asked, "Who will let me know if your father answers you unkindly?"

¹¹Then Jonathan said, "Come, let's go out into the field." So the two of them went out into the field.

¹²Jonathan said to David, "I promise this before the LORD, the God of Israel: At this same time the day after tomorrow, I will find out how my father feels. If he feels good toward you, I will send word to you and let you know. ¹³But if my father plans to hurt you, I will let you know and send you away safely. May the LORD punish me terribly if I don't do this. And may the LORD be with you as he has been with my father. ¹⁴But show me the kindness of the LORD as long as I live so that I may not die. ¹⁵You must never stop showing your kindness to my family, even when the LORD has destroyed all your enemies from the earth."

¹⁶So Jonathan made an agreement with David. He said, "May the LORD hold David's enemies responsible." ¹⁷And Jonathan asked David to repeat his promise of love for him, because he loved David as much as he loved himself.

¹⁸Jonathan said to David, "Tomorrow is the New Moon festival. Your seat will be empty, so my father will miss you. ¹⁹On the third day go to the place where you hid when this trouble began. Wait by the rock Ezel. ²⁰On the third day I will shoot three arrows to the side of the rock as if I am shooting at a target. ²¹Then I will send a boy to find the arrows. If I say to him, 'The arrows are near you; bring them here,' you may come out of hiding. You are safe. As the LORD lives, there is no danger. ²²But if I say to the boy, 'Look, the arrows are beyond you,' you must go, because the LORD is sending you away. ²³Remember what we talked about. The LORD is a witness between you and me forever."

²⁴So David hid in the field. When the New Moon festival came, the king sat down to eat. ²⁵He sat where he always sat, near the wall. Jonathan sat across from him, and Abner sat next to Saul, but David's place was empty. ²⁶That day Saul said nothing. He thought, "Maybe something has happened to David so that he is unclean." ²⁷But the next day was the second day of the month, and David's

place was still empty. So Saul said to Jonathan, "Why hasn't the son of Jesse come to the feast yesterday or today?"

28Jonathan answered, "David begged me to let him go to Bethlehem. 29He said, 'Let me go, because our family has a sacrifice in the town, and my brother has ordered me to be there. Now if I am your friend, please let me go to see my brothers.' That is why he has not come to the king's table."

30Then Saul became very angry with Jonathan. He said, "You son of a wicked, worthless woman! I know you are on the side of David son of Jesse! You bring shame on yourself and on your mother who gave birth to you. 31As long as Jesse's son lives, you will never be king or have a kingdom. Now send for David and bring him to me. He must die!"

32Jonathan asked his father, "Why should David be killed? What wrong has he done?" 33Then Saul threw his spear at Jonathan, trying to kill him. So Jonathan knew that his father really wanted to kill David. 34Jonathan was very angry and left the table. That second day of the month he refused to eat. He was ashamed of his father and upset over David.

35The next morning Jonathan went out to the field to meet David as they had agreed. He had a young boy with him. 36Jonathan said to the boy, "Run and find the arrows I shoot." When he ran, Jonathan shot an arrow beyond him. 37The boy ran to the place where Jonathan's arrow fell, but Jonathan called, "The arrow is beyond you!" 38Then he shouted, "Hurry! Go quickly! Don't stop!" The boy picked up the arrow and brought it back to his master. 39(The boy knew nothing about what this meant; only Jonathan and David knew.) 40Then Jonathan gave his weapons to the boy and told him, "Go back to town."

41When the boy left, David came out from the south side of the rock. He bowed facedown on the ground before Jonathan three times. Then David and Jonathan kissed each other and cried together, but David cried the most.

42Jonathan said to David, "Go in peace. We have promised by the Lord that we will be friends. We said, 'The Lord will be a witness between you and me, and between our descendants always.'" Then David left, and Jonathan went back to town.

DAVID GOES TO SEE AHIMELECH

21 David went to Nob to see Ahimelech the priest. Ahimelech shook with fear when he saw David, and he asked, "Why are you alone? Why is no one with you?"

2David answered him, "The king gave me a special order. He told me, 'No one must know what I am sending you to do or what I told you to do.' I told my men where to meet me. 3Now, what food do you have with you? Give me five loaves of bread or anything you find."

4The priest said to David, "I don't have any plain bread here, but I do have some holy bread.⊓ You may eat it if your men have kept themselves from women."

5David answered, "No women have been near us for days. My men always keep themselves holy, even when we do ordinary work. And this is especially true when the work is holy."

6So the priest gave David the holy bread from the presence of God because there was no other. Each day the holy bread was replaced with hot bread.

7One of Saul's servants happened to be there that day. He had been held there before the Lord. He was Doeg the Edomite, the chief of Saul's shepherds.

8David asked Ahimelech, "Do you have a spear or sword here? The king's business was very important, so I left without my sword or any other weapon."

9The priest answered, "The sword of Goliath the Philistine, the one you killed in the Valley of Elah, is here. It is wrapped in a cloth behind the holy vest. If you want it, you may take it. There's no other sword here but that one."

David said, "There is no other sword like it. Give it to me."

DAVID GOES TO GATH

10That day David ran away from Saul and went to Achish king of Gath. 11But the servants of Achish said to him, "This is David,

---

21:4 holy bread This was the bread that showed the people were in the presence of God. Normally only the priests ate this bread.

the king of the Israelites. He's the man they dance and sing about, saying:

'Saul has killed thousands of his
  enemies,
but David has killed tens of
  thousands.'"

¹²David paid attention to these words and was very much afraid of Achish king of Gath. ¹³So he pretended to be crazy in front of Achish and his servants. While he was with them, he acted like a madman and clawed on the doors of the gate and let spit run down his beard.

¹⁴Achish said to his servants, "Look at the man! He's crazy! Why do you bring him to me? ¹⁵I have enough madmen. I don't need you to bring him here to act like this in front of me! Don't let him in my house!"

DAVID AT ADULLAM AND MIZPAH

22 David left Gath and escaped to the cave of Adullam. When his brothers and other relatives heard that he was there,

---

THE EXTRAORDINARY IN THE MUNDANE

Goliath's sword

FAITH

By Matthew Barnett

1 SAMUEL 21:8-9

You've probably heard the story of David and Goliath a thousand times. But what you may not know is that in his "early fugitive days," David found himself on the run and in need of a weapon. The next thing you know here came a priest dragging Goliath's sword behind him. And he said to David, "Here's Goliath's sword . . . ."

Now, here's the great part. David took Goliath's sword—the same sword that was intended to kill him—and used the sword of Goliath as an aid rather than a liability.

You need to understand what I'm saying here: David didn't succeed in spite of Goliath's sword. He used Goliath's sword to succeed!

Like it or not, Goliath's sword is coming at every one of us. It may be in the form of sickness, persecution, an inner struggle, or a broken heart. It may be the loss of a job, or your past coming back to haunt you. Whatever the form, Goliath's sword may serve as your weapon of personal destruction.

Now you can do one of two things: You can let that weapon destroy you, or you can take that sword and use it! Say to yourself, "This sword, this tragedy, this heartache, this sorrow, has come my way, but it will not destroy me. I'm going to use it to be something I could have never been. I'll use it to win victories that I could not win any other way." Use the sword that was a means of destruction for liberation instead. And thank God for Goliath's sword!

---

reflect: What are the "swords" you can use to win your victory?
Go to **FAITH:** "Early, First, or Nothing" at **Acts 13:22.**

they went to see him. ²Everyone who was in trouble, or who owed money, or who was unsatisfied gathered around David, and he became their leader. About four hundred men were with him.

³From there David went to Mizpah in Moab and spoke to the king of Moab. He said, "Please let my father and mother come and stay with you until I learn what God is going to do for me." ⁴So he left them with the king of Moab, and they stayed with him as long as David was hiding in the stronghold.

⁵But the prophet Gad said to David, "Don't stay in the stronghold. Go to the land of Judah." So David left and went to the forest of Hereth.

SAUL DESTROYS AHIMELECH'S FAMILY

⁶Saul heard that David and his men had been seen. Saul was sitting under the tamarisk tree on the hill at Gibeah, and all his officers were standing around him. He had a spear in his hand. ⁷Saul said to them, "Listen, men of Benjamin! Do you think the son of Jesse will give all of you fields and vineyards? Will David make you commanders over thousands of men or hundreds of men? ⁸You have all made plans against me! No one tells me when my son makes an agreement with the son of Jesse! No one cares about me! No one tells me when my son has encouraged my servant to ambush me this very day!"

⁹Doeg the Edomite, who was standing there with Saul's officers, said, "I saw the son of Jesse. He came to see Ahimelech son of Ahitub at Nob. ¹⁰Ahimelech prayed to the LORD for David and gave him food and gave him the sword of Goliath the Philistine."

¹¹Then the king sent for the priest Ahimelech son of Ahitub and for all of Ahimelech's relatives who were priests at Nob. And they all came to the king. ¹²Saul said to Ahimelech, "Listen now, son of Ahitub."

Ahimelech answered, "Yes, master."

¹³Saul said, "Why are you and Jesse's son against me? You gave him bread and a sword! You prayed to God for him. David has turned against me and is waiting to attack me even now!"

¹⁴Ahimelech answered, "You have no other servant who is as loyal as David, your own son-in-law and captain of your bodyguards. Everyone in your house respects

him. ¹⁵That was not the first time I prayed to God for David. Don't blame me or any of my relatives. I, your servant, know nothing about what is going on."

¹⁶But the king said, "Ahimelech, you and all your relatives must die!" ¹⁷Then he told the guards at his side, "Go and kill the priests of the LORD, because they are on David's side. They knew he was running away, but they didn't tell me."

But the king's officers refused to kill the priests of the LORD.

¹⁸Then the king ordered Doeg, "Go and kill the priests." So Doeg the Edomite went and killed the priests. That day he killed eighty-five men who wore the linen holy vest. ¹⁹He also killed the people of Nob, the city of the priests. With the sword he killed men, women, children, babies, cattle, donkeys, and sheep.

²⁰But Abiathar, a son of Ahimelech, who was the son of Ahitub, escaped. He ran away and joined David. ²¹He told David that Saul had killed the LORD's priests. ²²Then David told him, "Doeg the Edomite was there at Nob that day. I knew he would surely tell Saul. So I am responsible for the death of all your father's family. ²³Stay with me. Don't be afraid. The man who wants to kill you also wants to kill me. You will be safe with me."

DAVID SAVES THE PEOPLE OF KEILAH

23 Someone told David, "Look, the Philistines are fighting against Keilah and stealing grain from the threshing floors."

²David asked the LORD, "Should I go and fight these Philistines?"

The LORD answered him, "Go. Attack them, and save Keilah."

³But David's men said to him, "We're afraid here in Judah. We will be more afraid if we go to Keilah where the Philistine army is."

⁴David again asked the LORD, and the LORD answered, "Go down to Keilah. I will help you defeat the Philistines." ⁵So David and his men went to Keilah and fought the Philistines and took their cattle. David killed many Philistines and saved the people of Keilah. ⁶(Now Abiathar son of Ahimelech had brought the holy vest with him when he came to David at Keilah.)

SAUL CHASES DAVID

[7]Someone told Saul that David was now at Keilah. Saul said, "God has handed David over to me! He has trapped himself, because he has entered a town with gates and bars." [8]Saul called all his army together for battle, and they prepared to go down to Keilah to attack David and his men.

[9]David learned Saul was making evil plans against him. So he said to Abiathar the priest, "Bring the holy vest." [10]David prayed, "LORD, God of Israel, I have heard that Saul plans to come to Keilah to destroy the town because of me. [11]Will the leaders of Keilah hand me over to Saul? Will Saul come down to Keilah, as I heard? LORD, God of Israel, tell me, your servant!"

The LORD answered, "Saul will come down."

[12]Again David asked, "Will the leaders of Keilah hand me and my men over to Saul?"

The LORD answered, "They will."

[13]So David and his six hundred men left Keilah and kept moving from place to place. When Saul found out that David had escaped from Keilah, he did not go there.

[14]David stayed in the desert hideouts and in the hills of the Desert of Ziph. Every day Saul looked for David, but the LORD did not surrender David to him.

[15]While David was at Horesh in the Desert of Ziph, he learned that Saul was coming to kill him. [16]But Saul's son Jonathan went to David at Horesh and strengthened his faith in God. [17]Jonathan told him, "Don't be afraid, because my father won't touch you. You will be king of Israel, and I will be second to you. Even my father Saul knows this." [18]The two of them made an agreement before the LORD. Then Jonathan went home, but David stayed at Horesh.

[19]The people from Ziph went to Saul at Gibeah and told him, "David is hiding in our land. He's at the hideouts of Horesh, on the hill of Hakilah, south of Jeshimon. [20]Now, our king, come down anytime you want. It's our duty to hand David over to you."

[21]Saul answered, "The LORD bless you for helping me. [22]Go and learn more about him. Find out where he is staying and who has seen him there. I have heard that he is clever. [23]Find all the hiding places he uses, and come back and tell me everything. Then I'll go with you. If David is in the area, I will track him down among all the families in Judah."

[24]So they went back to Ziph ahead of Saul. Now David and his men were in the Desert of Maon[n] in the desert area south of Jeshimon. [25]Saul and his men went to look for David, but David heard about it and went down to a rock and stayed in the Desert of Maon. When Saul heard that, he followed David into the Desert of Maon.

[26]Saul was going along one side of the mountain, and David and his men were on the other side. They were hurrying to get away from Saul, because Saul and his men were closing in on them. [27]But a messenger came to Saul, saying, "Come quickly! The Philistines are attacking our land!" [28]So Saul stopped chasing David and went to challenge the Philistines. That is why people call this place Rock of Parting. [29]David also left the Desert of Maon and stayed in the hideouts of En Gedi.

DAVID SHAMES SAUL

24 After Saul returned from chasing the Philistines, he was told, "David is in the Desert of En Gedi." [2]So he took three thousand chosen men from all Israel and began looking for David and his men near the Rocks of the Wild Goats.

[3]Saul came to the sheep pens beside the road. A cave was there, and he went in to relieve himself. Now David and his men were hiding far back in the cave. [4]The men said to David, "Today is the day the LORD spoke of when he said, 'I will give your enemy over to you. Do anything you want with him.'"

Then David crept up to Saul and quietly cut off a corner of Saul's robe. [5]Later David felt guilty because he had cut off a corner of Saul's robe. [6]He said to his men, "May the LORD keep me from doing such a thing to my master! Saul is the LORD's appointed king. I should not do anything against him, because he is the LORD's appointed king!" [7]David used these words to stop his men; he did not let them attack Saul. Then Saul left the cave and went his way.

[8]When David came out of the cave, he shouted to Saul, "My master and king!" Saul

---

23:24 **Maon** Some early Greek copies say "Maon." The Hebrew copies say "Paran."

looked back, and David bowed facedown on the ground. 9He said to Saul, "Why do you listen when people say, 'David wants to harm you'? 10You have seen something with your own eyes today. The LORD put you in my power in the cave. They said I should kill you, but I was merciful. I said, 'I won't harm my master, because he is the LORD's appointed king.' 11My father, look at this piece of your robe in my hand! I cut off the corner of your robe, but I didn't kill you. Now understand and know I am not planning any evil against you. I did nothing wrong to you, but you are hunting me to kill me. 12May the LORD judge between us, and may he punish you for the wrong you have done to me! But I am not against you. 13There is an old saying: 'Evil things come from evil people.' But I am not against you. 14Whom is the king of Israel coming out against? Whom are you chasing? It's as if you are chasing a dead dog or a flea. 15May the LORD be our judge and decide between you and me. May he support me and show that I am right. May he save me from you!"

16When David finished saying these words, Saul asked, "Is that your voice, David my son?" And he cried loudly. 17He said, "You are a better man than I am. You have been good to me, but I have done wrong to you. 18You told me what good things you did. The LORD handed me over to you, but you did not kill me. 19People don't normally let an enemy get away like this, do they? May the LORD reward you because you were good to me today. 20I know you will surely be king, and you will rule the kingdom of Israel. 21Now swear to me by the LORD that you will not kill my descendants and that you won't wipe out my name from my father's family."

22So David made the promise to Saul. Then Saul went back home, and David and his men went up to their hideout.

NABAL INSULTS DAVID

25 Now Samuel died, and all the Israelites met and had a time of sadness for him. Then they buried him at his home in Ramah.

David moved to the Desert of Maon.[n] 2A man in Maon who had land at Carmel was very rich. He had three thousand sheep and a thousand goats. He was cutting the wool off his sheep at Carmel. 3His name was Nabal, and he was a descendant of Caleb. His wife was named Abigail. She was wise and beautiful, but Nabal was cruel and mean.

4While David was in the desert, he heard that Nabal was cutting the wool from his sheep. 5So he sent ten young men and told them, "Go to Nabal at Carmel, and greet him for me. 6Say to Nabal, 'May you and your family and all who belong to you have good health! 7I have heard that you are cutting the wool from your sheep. When your shepherds were with us, we did not harm them. All the time your shepherds were at Carmel, we stole nothing from them. 8Ask your servants, and they will tell you. We come at a happy time, so be kind to my young men. Please give anything you can find for them and for your son David.'"

9When David's men arrived, they gave the message to Nabal, but Nabal insulted them. 10He answered them, "Who is David? Who is this son of Jesse? Many slaves are running away from their masters today! 11I have bread and water, and I have meat that I killed for my servants who cut the wool. But I won't give it to men I don't know."

12David's men went back and told him all Nabal had said. 13Then David said to them, "Put on your swords!" So they put on their swords, and David put on his also. About four hundred men went with David, but two hundred men stayed with the supplies.

14One of Nabal's servants said to Abigail, Nabal's wife, "David sent messengers from the desert to greet our master, but Nabal insulted them. 15These men were very good to us. They did not harm us. They stole nothing from us during all the time we were out in the field with them. 16Night and day they protected us. They were like a wall around us while we were with them caring for the sheep. 17Now think about it, and decide what you can do. Terrible trouble is coming to our master and all his family. Nabal is such a wicked man that no one can even talk to him."

18Abigail hurried. She took two hundred loaves of bread, two leather bags full of wine, five cooked sheep, a bushel of cooked grain,

---

25:1 Maon Some early Greek copies say "Maon." The Hebrew copies say "Paran."

a hundred cakes of raisins, and two hundred cakes of pressed figs and put all these on donkeys. ¹⁹Then she told her servants, "Go on. I'll follow you." But she did not tell her husband.

²⁰Abigail rode her donkey and came down toward the mountain hideout. There she met David and his men coming down toward her.

²¹David had just said, "It's been useless! I watched over Nabal's property in the desert. I made sure none of his sheep was missing. I did good to him, but he has paid me back with evil. ²²May God punish my enemies even more. I will not leave one of Nabal's men alive until morning."

²³When Abigail saw David, she quickly got off her donkey and bowed facedown on the ground before him. ²⁴She fell at David's feet and said, "My master, let the blame be on me! Please let me talk to you. Listen to what I say. ²⁵My master, don't pay attention to this worthless man Nabal. He is like his name. His name means 'fool,' and he is truly a fool. But I, your servant, didn't see the men you sent. ²⁶The LORD has kept you from killing and punishing anyone. As surely as the LORD lives and as surely as you live, may your enemies become like Nabal! ²⁷I have brought a gift to you for the men who follow you. ²⁸Please forgive my wrong. The LORD will certainly let your family have many kings, because you fight his battles. As long as you live, may you do nothing bad. ²⁹Someone might chase you to kill you, but the LORD your God will keep you alive. He will throw away your enemies' lives as he would throw a stone from a sling. ³⁰The LORD will keep all his promises of good things for you. He will make you leader over Israel. ³¹Then you won't feel guilty or troubled because you killed innocent people and punished them. Please remember me when the LORD brings you success."

³²David answered Abigail, "Praise the LORD, the God of Israel, who sent you to meet me. ³³May you be blessed for your wisdom. You have kept me from killing or punishing people today. ³⁴As surely as the LORD, the God of Israel, lives, he has kept me from hurting you. If you hadn't come quickly to meet me, not one of Nabal's men would have lived until morning."

³⁵Then David accepted Abigail's gifts. He told her, "Go home in peace. I have heard your words, and I will do what you have asked."

NABAL'S DEATH

³⁶When Abigail went back to Nabal, he was in the house, eating like a king. He was very drunk and in a good mood. So she told him nothing until the next morning. ³⁷In the morning when he was not drunk, his wife told him everything. His heart stopped, and he became like stone. ³⁸About ten days later the LORD struck Nabal and he died.

³⁹When David heard that Nabal was dead, he said, "Praise the LORD! Nabal insulted me, but the LORD has supported me! He has kept me from doing wrong. The LORD has punished Nabal for his wrong."

Then David sent a message to Abigail, asking her to be his wife. ⁴⁰His servants went to Carmel and said to Abigail, "David sent us to take you so you can become his wife."

⁴¹Abigail bowed facedown on the ground and said, "I am your servant. I'm ready to serve you and to wash the feet of my master's servants." ⁴²Abigail quickly got on a donkey and went with David's messengers, with her five maids following her. And she became David's wife.

⁴³David also had married Ahinoam of Jezreel. So they were both David's wives. ⁴⁴Saul's daughter Michal was also David's wife, but Saul had given her to Paltiel son of Laish, who was from Gallim.

DAVID SHAMES SAUL AGAIN

26 The people of Ziph went to Saul at Gibeah and said to him, "David is hiding on the hill of Hakilah opposite Jeshimon."

²So Saul went down to the Desert of Ziph with three thousand chosen men of Israel to look for David there. ³Saul made his camp beside the road on the hill of Hakilah opposite Jeshimon, but David stayed in the desert. When he heard Saul had followed him, ⁴he sent out spies and learned for certain that Saul had come to Hakilah.

⁵Then David went to the place where Saul had camped. He saw where Saul and Abner son of Ner, the commander of Saul's army, were sleeping. Saul was sleeping in the middle of the camp with all the army around him.

⁶David asked Ahimelech the Hittite and Abishai son of Zeruiah, Joab's brother, "Who will go down into Saul's camp with me?"

Abishai answered, "I'll go with you."

⁷So that night David and Abishai went into Saul's camp. Saul was asleep in the middle of the camp with his spear stuck in the ground near his head. Abner and the army were sleeping around Saul. ⁸Abishai said to David, "Today God has handed your enemy over to you. Let me pin Saul to the ground with my spear. I'll only have to do it once. I won't need to hit him twice."

⁹But David said to Abishai, "Don't kill Saul! No one can harm the Lord's appointed king and still be innocent! ¹⁰As surely as the Lord lives, the Lord himself will punish Saul. Maybe Saul will die naturally, or maybe he will go into battle and be killed. ¹¹But may the Lord keep me from harming his appointed king! Take the spear and water jug that are near Saul's head. Then let's go."

¹²So David took the spear and water jug that were near Saul's head, and they left. No one saw them or knew about it or woke up, because the Lord had put them sound asleep.

¹³David crossed over to the other side of the hill and stood on top of the mountain far from Saul's camp. They were a long way away from each other. ¹⁴David shouted to the army and to Abner son of Ner, "Won't you answer me, Abner?"

Abner answered, "Who is calling for the king? Who are you?"

¹⁵David said, "You're the greatest man in Israel. Isn't that true? Why didn't you guard your master the king? Someone came into your camp to kill your master the king! ¹⁶You have not done well. As surely as the Lord lives, you and your men should die. You haven't guarded your master, the Lord's appointed king. Look! Where are the king's spear and water jug that were near his head?"

¹⁷Saul knew David's voice. He said, "Is that your voice, David my son?"

David answered, "Yes, it is, my master and king." ¹⁸David also said, "Why are you chasing me, my master? What wrong have I done? What evil am I guilty of? ¹⁹My master and king, listen to me. If the Lord made you angry with me, let him accept an offer-

ing. But if people did it, may the Lord curse them! They have made me leave the land the Lord gave me. They have told me, 'Go and serve other gods.' ²⁰Now don't let me die far away from the Lord's presence. The king of Israel has come out looking for a flea! You're just hunting a bird in the mountains!"

²¹Then Saul said, "I have sinned. Come back, David my son. Today you respected my life, so I will not try to hurt you. I have been very stupid and foolish."

²²David answered, "Here is your spear. Let one of your young men come here and get it. ²³The Lord rewards us for the things we do right and for our loyalty to him. The Lord handed you over to me today, but I wouldn't harm the Lord's appointed king. ²⁴As I respected your life today, may the Lord also respect my life and save me from all trouble."

²⁵Then Saul said to David, "You are blessed, my son David. You will do great things and succeed."

So David went on his way, and Saul went back home.

DAVID LIVES WITH THE PHILISTINES

27 But David thought to himself, "Saul will catch me someday. The best thing I can do is escape to the land of the Philistines. Then he will give up looking for me in Israel, and I can get away from him."

²So David and his six hundred men left Israel and went to Achish son of Maoch, king of Gath. ³David, his men, and their families made their home in Gath with Achish. David had his two wives with him—Ahinoam of Jezreel and Abigail of Carmel, the widow of Nabal. ⁴When Saul heard that David had run away to Gath, he stopped looking for him.

⁵Then David said to Achish, "If you are pleased with me, give me a place in one of the country towns where I can live. I don't need to live in the royal city with you."

⁶That day Achish gave David the town of Ziklag, and Ziklag has belonged to the kings of Judah ever since. ⁷David lived in the Philistine land a year and four months.

⁸David and his men raided the people of Geshur, Girzi, and Amalek. (These people had lived for a long time in the land that reached to Shur and Egypt.) ⁹When David fought them, he killed all the men and women and

took their sheep, cattle, donkeys, camels, and clothes. Then he returned to Achish.

¹⁰Achish would ask David, "Where did you go raiding today?" And David would tell him that he had gone to the southern part of Judah, or Jerahmeel, or to the land of the Kenites. ¹¹David never brought a man or woman alive to Gath. He thought, "If we bring people alive, they may tell Achish, 'This is what David really did.'" David did this all the time he lived in the Philistine land. ¹²So Achish trusted David and said to himself, "David's own people, the Israelites, now hate him very much. He will serve me forever."

SAUL AND THE MEDIUM OF ENDOR

28 Later, the Philistines gathered their armies to fight against Israel. Achish said to David, "You understand that you and your men must join my army."

²David answered, "You will see for yourself what I, your servant, can do!"

Achish said, "Fine, I'll make you my permanent bodyguard."

³Now Samuel was dead, and all the Israelites had shown their sadness for him. They had buried Samuel in his hometown of Ramah.

And Saul had forced out the mediums and fortune-tellers from the land.

⁴The Philistines came together and made camp at Shunem. Saul gathered all the Israelites and made camp at Gilboa. ⁵When he saw the Philistine army, he was afraid, and his heart pounded with fear. ⁶He prayed to the Lord, but the Lord did not answer him through dreams, Urim, or prophets. ⁷Then Saul said to his servants, "Find me a woman who is a medium so I may go and ask her what will happen."

His servants answered, "There is a medium in Endor."

⁸Then Saul put on other clothes to disguise himself, and at night he and two of his men went to see the woman. Saul said to her, "Talk to a spirit for me. Bring up the person I name."

⁹But the woman said to him, "Surely you know what Saul has done. He has forced the mediums and fortune-tellers from the land. You are trying to trap me and get me killed."

¹⁰Saul made a promise to the woman in the name of the Lord. He said, "As surely as the Lord lives, you won't be punished for this."

¹¹The woman asked, "Whom do you want me to bring up?"

He answered, "Bring up Samuel."

¹²When the woman saw Samuel, she screamed. She said, "Why have you tricked me? You are Saul!"

¹³The king said to the woman, "Don't be afraid! What do you see?"

The woman said, "I see a spirit coming up out of the ground."

¹⁴Saul asked, "What does he look like?"

The woman answered, "An old man wearing a coat is coming up."

Then Saul knew it was Samuel, and he bowed facedown on the ground.

¹⁵Samuel asked Saul, "Why have you disturbed me by bringing me up?"

Saul said, "I am greatly troubled. The Philistines are fighting against me, and God has left me. He won't answer me anymore, either by prophets or in dreams. That's why I called for you. Tell me what to do."

¹⁶Samuel said, "The Lord has left you and has become your enemy. So why do you call on me? ¹⁷He has done what he said he would do—the things he said through me. He has torn the kingdom out of your hands and given it to one of your neighbors, David. ¹⁸You did not obey the Lord; you did not show the Amalekites how angry he was with them. That's why he has done this to you today. ¹⁹The Lord will hand over both Israel and you to the Philistines. Tomorrow you and your sons will be with me. The Lord will hand over the army of Israel to the Philistines."

²⁰Saul quickly fell flat on the ground and was afraid of what Samuel had said. He was also very weak because he had eaten nothing all that day and night.

²¹Then the woman came to Saul and saw that he was really frightened. She said, "Look, I, your servant, have obeyed you. I have risked my life and done what you told me to do. ²²Now please listen to me. Let me give you some food so you may eat and have enough strength to go on your way."

²³But Saul refused, saying, "I won't eat."

His servants joined the woman in asking him to eat, and he listened to them. So he got up from the ground and sat on the bed.

²⁴At the house the woman had a fat calf, which she quickly killed. She took some flour and mixed dough with her hands. Then she baked some bread without yeast. ²⁵She put the food before them, and they ate. That same night they got up and left.

DAVID GOES BACK TO ZIKLAG

29 The Philistines gathered all their soldiers at Aphek. Israel camped by the spring at Jezreel. ²The Philistine kings were marching with their groups of a hundred and a thousand men. David and his men were marching behind Achish. ³The Philistine commanders asked, "What are these Hebrews doing here?"

Achish told them, "This is David. He served Saul king of Israel, but he has been with me for over a year now. I have found nothing wrong in David since the time he left Saul."

⁴But the Philistine commanders were angry with Achish and said, "Send David back to the city you gave him. He cannot go with us into battle. If he does, we'll have an enemy in our own camp. He could please his king by killing our own men. ⁵David is the one the Israelites dance and sing about, saying:

'Saul has killed thousands of his
       enemies,
    but David has killed tens of thousands.'"

⁶So Achish called David and said to him, "As surely as the LORD lives, you are loyal. I would be pleased to have you serve in my army. Since the day you came to me, I have found no wrong in you. But the other kings don't trust you. ⁷Go back in peace. Don't do anything to displease the Philistine kings."

⁸David asked, "What wrong have I done? What evil have you found in me from the day I came to you until now? Why can't I go fight your enemies, my lord and king?"

⁹Achish answered, "I know you are as good as an angel from God. But the Philistine commanders have said, 'David must not go with us into battle.' ¹⁰Early in the morning you and your master's servants should leave. Get up as soon as it is light and go."

¹¹So David and his men got up early in the morning and went back to the country of the Philistines. And the Philistines went up to Jezreel.

DAVID'S WAR WITH THE AMALEKITES

30 On the third day, when David and his men arrived at Ziklag, he found that the Amalekites had raided southern Judah and Ziklag, attacking Ziklag and burning it. ²They captured the women and everyone, young and old, but they had not killed anyone. They had only taken them away.

³When David and his men came to Ziklag, they found the town had been burned and their wives, sons, and daughters had been taken as prisoners. ⁴Then David and his army cried loudly until they were too weak to cry anymore. ⁵David's two wives had also been taken—Ahinoam of Jezreel and Abigail the widow of Nabal from Carmel. ⁶The men in the army were threatening to kill David with stones, which greatly upset David. Each man was sad and angry because his sons and daughters had been captured, but David found strength in the LORD his God. ⁷David said to Abiathar the priest, "Bring me the holy vest."

⁸Then David asked the LORD, "Should I chase the people who took our families? Will I catch them?"

The LORD answered, "Chase them. You will catch them, and you will succeed in saving your families."

⁹David and the six hundred men with him came to the Besor Ravine, where some of the men stayed. ¹⁰David and four hundred men kept up the chase. The other two hundred men stayed behind because they were too tired to cross the ravine.

¹¹They found an Egyptian in a field and brought him to David. They gave the Egyptian some water to drink and some food to eat. ¹²And they gave him a piece of a fig cake and two clusters of raisins. Then he felt better, because he had not eaten any food or drunk any water for three days and nights.

¹³David asked him, "Who is your master? Where do you come from?"

He answered, "I'm an Egyptian, the slave of an Amalekite. Three days ago my master left me, because I was sick. ¹⁴We had raided the southern area of the Kerethites, the land of Judah, and the southern area of Caleb. We burned Ziklag, as well."

¹⁵David asked him, "Can you lead me to the people who took our families?"

He answered, "Yes, if you promise me

before God that you won't kill me or give me back to my master. Then I will take you to them."

¹⁶So the Egyptian led David to the Amalekites. They were lying around on the ground, eating and drinking and celebrating with the things they had taken from the land of the Philistines and from Judah. ¹⁷David fought them from sunset until the evening of the next day. None of them escaped, except four hundred young men who rode off on their camels. ¹⁸David got his two wives back and everything the Amalekites had taken. ¹⁹Nothing was missing. David brought back everyone, young and old, sons and daughters. He recovered the valuable things and everything the Amalekites had taken. ²⁰David took all the sheep and cattle, and his men made these animals go in front, saying, "They are David's prize."

²¹Then David came to the two hundred men who had been too tired to follow him, who had stayed at the Besor Ravine. They came out to meet David and the people with him. When he came near, David greeted the men at the ravine.

²²But the evil men and troublemakers among those who followed David said, "Since these two hundred men didn't go with us, we shouldn't give them any of the things we recovered. Just let each man take his wife and children and go."

²³David answered, "No, my brothers. Don't do that after what the LORD has given us. He has protected us and given us the enemy who attacked us. ²⁴Who will listen to what you say? The share will be the same for the one who stayed with the supplies as for the one who went into battle. All will share alike." ²⁵David made this an order and rule for Israel, which continues even today.

²⁶When David arrived in Ziklag, he sent some of the things he had taken from the Amalekites to his friends, the leaders of Judah. He said, "Here is a present for you from the things we took from the LORD's enemies."

²⁷David also sent some things to the leaders in Bethel, Ramoth in the southern part of Judah, Jattir, ²⁸Aroer, Siphmoth, Eshtemoa,

²⁹Racal, the cities of the Jerahmeelites and the Kenites, ³⁰Hormah, Bor Ashan, Athach, ³¹Hebron, and to the people in all the other places where he and his men had been.

THE DEATH OF SAUL

31 The Philistines fought against Israel, and the Israelites ran away from them. Many Israelites were killed on Mount Gilboa. ²The Philistines fought hard against Saul and his sons, killing his sons Jonathan, Abinadab, and Malki-Shua. ³The fighting was heavy around Saul. The archers shot him, and he was badly wounded. ⁴He said to the officer who carried his armor, "Pull out your sword and kill me. Then those uncircumcised men won't make fun of me and kill me." But Saul's officer refused, because he was afraid. So Saul took his own sword and threw himself on it. ⁵When the officer saw that Saul was dead, he threw himself on his own sword, and he died with Saul. ⁶So Saul, his three sons, and the officer who carried his armor died together that day.

⁷When the Israelites who lived across the Jezreel Valley and those who lived across the Jordan River saw how the Israelite army had run away, and that Saul and his sons were dead, they left their cities and ran away. Then the Philistines came and lived there.

⁸The next day when the Philistines came to take all the valuable things from the dead soldiers, they found Saul and his three sons dead on Mount Gilboa. ⁹They cut off Saul's head and took off his armor. Then they sent messengers through all the land of the Philistines to tell the news in the temple of their idols and to their people. ¹⁰They put Saul's armor in the temple of the Ashtoreths and hung his body on the wall of Beth Shan.

¹¹When the people living in Jabesh Gilead heard what the Philistines had done to Saul, ¹²the brave men of Jabesh marched all night and came to Beth Shan. They removed the bodies of Saul and his sons from the wall of Beth Shan and brought them to Jabesh. There they burned the bodies. ¹³They took their bones and buried them under the tamarisk tree in Jabesh. Then the people of Jabesh fasted for seven days.

2 samuel

DAVID, THE GREATEST KING

DAVID LEARNS ABOUT SAUL'S DEATH

1 Now Saul was dead. After David had defeated the Amalekites, he returned to Ziklag and stayed there two days. ²On the third day a young man from Saul's camp came to Ziklag. To show his sadness, his clothes were torn and he had dirt on his head. He came and bowed facedown on the ground before David.

³David asked him, "Where did you come from?"

The man answered, "I escaped from the Israelite camp."

⁴David asked him, "What happened? Please tell me!"

The man answered, "The people have run away from the battle, and many of them have fallen and are dead. Saul and his son Jonathan are dead also."

⁵David asked him, "How do you know Saul and his son Jonathan are dead?"

⁶The young man answered, "I happened to be on Mount Gilboa. There I saw Saul leaning on his spear. The Philistine chariots and the men riding in them were coming closer to Saul. ⁷When he looked back and saw me, he called to me. I answered him, 'Here I am!'

⁸"Then Saul asked me, 'Who are you?'

"I told him, 'I am an Amalekite.'

⁹"Then Saul said to me, 'Please come here and kill me. I am badly hurt and am almost dead already.'

¹⁰"So I went over and killed him. He had been hurt so badly I knew he couldn't live. Then I took the crown from his head and the bracelet from his arm, and I have brought them here to you, my master."

¹¹Then David tore his clothes to show his sorrow, and all the men with him did also. ¹²They were very sad and cried and fasted until evening. They cried for Saul and his son Jonathan and for all the people of the LORD and for all the Israelites who had died in the battle.

DAVID ORDERS THE AMALEKITE KILLED

¹³David asked the young man who brought the report, "Where are you from?"

The young man answered, "I am the son of a foreigner, an Amalekite."

¹⁴David asked him, "Why were you not afraid to kill the LORD's appointed king?"

¹⁵Then David called one of his men and told him, "Go! Kill the Amalekite!" So the Israelite killed him. ¹⁶David had said to the Amalekite, "You are responsible for your own death. You confessed by saying, 'I have killed the LORD's appointed king.'"

DAVID'S SONG ABOUT SAUL AND JONATHAN

¹⁷David sang a funeral song about Saul and his son Jonathan, ¹⁸and he ordered that the people of Judah be taught this song. It is called "The Bow," and it is written in the Book of Jashar:

¹⁹ "Israel, your leaders have been killed on
　　the hills.
　　How the mighty have fallen in battle!
²⁰ Don't tell it in Gath.
　　Don't announce it in the streets of
　　Ashkelon.
　If you do, the Philistine women will be
　　happy.
　The daughters of the Philistines will
　　rejoice.

²¹ "May there be no dew or rain on the
　　mountains of Gilboa,
　　and may their fields produce no grain,
　because there the mighty warrior's shield
　　was dishonored.
　Saul's shield will no longer be rubbed
　　with oil.
²² Jonathan's bow did not fail
　　to kill many soldiers.
　Saul's sword did not fail
　　to wound many strong men.

²³ "We loved Saul and Jonathan
　　and enjoyed them while they lived.
　　They are together even in death.

They were faster than eagles.
They were stronger than lions.

24 "You daughters of Israel, cry for Saul.
Saul clothed you with red dresses
and put gold decorations on them.

25 "How the mighty have fallen in battle!
Jonathan is dead on Gilboa's hills.
26 I cry for you, my brother Jonathan.
I enjoyed your friendship so much.
Your love to me was wonderful,
better than the love of women.

27 "How the mighty have fallen!
The weapons of war are gone."

DAVID IS MADE KING OF JUDAH

2 Later, David prayed to the LORD, saying, "Should I go up to any of the cities of Judah?"

The LORD said to David, "Go."

David asked, "Where should I go?"

The LORD answered, "To Hebron."

2So David went up to Hebron with his two wives: Ahinoam from Jezreel and Abigail, the widow of Nabal from Carmel. 3David also brought his men and their families, and they all made their homes in the cities of Hebron. 4Then the men of Judah came to Hebron and appointed David king over Judah.

They told David that the men of Jabesh Gilead had buried Saul. 5So David sent messengers to the men of Jabesh Gilead and said to them, "The LORD bless you. You have shown loyalty to your master Saul by burying him. 6May the LORD now be loyal and true to you. I will also treat you well because you have done this. 7Now be strong and brave. Saul your master is dead, and the people of Judah have appointed me their king."

WAR BETWEEN JUDAH AND ISRAEL

8Abner son of Ner was the commander of Saul's army. Abner took Saul's son Ish-Bosheth to Mahanaim 9and made him king of Gilead, Ashuri, Jezreel, Ephraim, Benjamin, and all Israel. 10Saul's son Ish-Bosheth was forty years old when he became king over Israel, and he ruled two years. But the people of Judah followed David. 11David was king in Hebron for seven years and six months.

12Abner son of Ner and the servants of Ish-Bosheth son of Saul left Mahanaim and went to Gibeon. 13Joab son of Zeruiah and

David's men also went there and met Abner and Ish-Bosheth's men at the pool of Gibeon. Abner's group sat on one side of the pool; Joab's group sat on the other. 14Abner said to Joab, "Let the young men have a contest here."

Joab said, "Yes, let them have a contest."

15Then the men got up and were counted—twelve from the people of Benjamin for Ish-Bosheth son of Saul, and twelve from David's men. 16Each man grabbed the one opposite him by the head and stabbed him in the side with a knife. So the men fell down together. For that reason, that place in Gibeon is called the Field of Knives. 17That day there was a terrible battle, and David's men defeated Abner and the Israelites.

ABNER KILLS ASAHEL

18Zeruiah's three sons, Joab, Abishai, and Asahel, were there. Now Asahel was a fast runner, as fast as a deer in the field. 19Asahel chased Abner, going straight toward him. 20Abner looked back and asked, "Is that you, Asahel?"

Asahel said, "Yes, it is."

21Then Abner said to Asahel, "Turn to your right or left and catch one of the young men and take his armor." But Asahel refused to stop chasing him.

22Abner again said to Asahel, "Stop chasing me! If you don't stop, I'll have to kill you! Then I won't be able to face your brother Joab again!"

23But Asahel refused to stop chasing Abner. So using the back end of his spear, Abner stabbed Asahel in the stomach, and the spear came out of his back. Asahel died right there, and everyone stopped when they came to the place where Asahel's body lay.

24But Joab and Abishai continued chasing Abner. As the sun was going down, they arrived at the hill of Ammah, near Giah on the way to the desert near Gibeon. 25The men of Benjamin came to Abner, and all stood together at the top of the hill.

26Abner shouted to Joab, "Must the sword kill forever? Surely you must know this will only end in sadness! Tell the people to stop chasing their own brothers!"

27Then Joab said, "As surely as God lives, if you had not said anything, the people would have chased their brothers until morning."

28Then Joab blew a trumpet, and his people stopped chasing the Israelites. They did not fight them anymore.

29Abner and his men marched all night through the Jordan Valley. They crossed the Jordan River, and after marching all day, arrived at Mahanaim.

30After he had stopped chasing Abner, Joab came back and gathered the people together. Asahel and nineteen of David's men were missing. 31But David's men had killed three hundred sixty Benjaminites who had followed Abner. 32David's men took Asahel and buried him in the tomb of his father at Bethlehem. Then Joab and his men marched all night. The sun came up as they reached Hebron.

3 There was a long war between the people who supported Saul's family and those who supported David's family. The supporters of David's family became stronger and stronger, but the supporters of Saul's family became weaker and weaker.

DAVID'S SONS

2Sons were born to David at Hebron. The first was Amnon, whose mother was Ahinoam from Jezreel. 3The second son was Kileab, whose mother was Abigail, the widow of Nabal from Carmel. The third son was Absalom, whose mother was Maacah daughter of Talmai, the king of Geshur. 4The fourth son was Adonijah, whose mother was Haggith. The fifth son was Shephatiah, whose mother was Abital. 5The sixth son was Ithream, whose mother was Eglah, David's wife. These sons were born to David at Hebron.

ABNER JOINS DAVID

6During the war between the supporters of Saul's family and the supporters of David's family, Abner made himself a main leader among the supporters of Saul.

7Saul once had a slave woman named Rizpah, who was the daughter of Aiah. Ish-Bosheth said to Abner, "Why did you have sexual relations with my father's slave woman?"

8Abner was very angry because of what Ish-Bosheth said, and he replied, "I have been loyal to Saul and his family and friends! I didn't hand you over to David. I am not a traitor working for Judah! But now you are say-ing I did something wrong with this woman! 9May God help me if I don't join David! I will make sure that what the LORD promised does happen! 10I will take the kingdom from the family of Saul and make David king of Israel and Judah, from Dan to Beersheba!"[n]

11Ish-Bosheth couldn't say anything to Abner, because he was afraid of him.

12Then Abner sent messengers to ask David, "Who is going to rule the land? Make an agreement with me, and I will help you unite all Israel."

13David answered, "Good! I will make an agreement with you, but I ask you one thing. I will not meet with you unless you bring Saul's daughter Michal to me." 14Then David sent messengers to Saul's son Ish-Bosheth, saying, "Give me my wife Michal. She was promised to me, and I killed a hundred Philistines to get her."

15So Ish-Bosheth sent men to take Michal from her husband Paltiel son of Laish. 16Michal's husband went with her, crying as he followed her to Bahurim. But Abner said to Paltiel, "Go back home." So he went home.

17Abner sent this message to the elders of Israel: "You have been wanting to make David your king. 18Now do it! The LORD said of David, 'Through my servant David, I will save my people Israel from the Philistines and all their enemies.'"

19Abner also said these things to the people of Benjamin. He then went to Hebron to tell David what the Benjaminites and Israel wanted to do. 20Abner came with twenty men to David at Hebron. There David prepared a feast for them. 21Abner said to David, "My master and king, I will go and bring all the Israelites to you. Then they will make an agreement with you so you will rule over all Israel as you wanted." So David let Abner go, and he left in peace.

ABNER'S DEATH

22Just then Joab and David's men came from a battle, bringing many valuable things they had taken from the enemy. David had let Abner leave in peace, so he was not with David at Hebron. 23When Joab and all his

---

3:10 Dan to Beersheba Dan was the city farthest north in Israel, and Beersheba was the city farthest south. So this means all the people of Israel.

army arrived at Hebron, the army said to Joab, "Abner son of Ner came to King David, and David let him leave in peace."

24Joab came to the king and said, "What have you done? Abner came to you. Why did you let him go? Now he's gone. 25You know Abner son of Ner! He came to trick you! He came to learn about everything you are doing!"

26After Joab left David, he sent messengers after Abner, and they brought him back from the well of Sirah. But David did not know this. 27When Abner arrived at Hebron, Joab took him aside into the gateway. He acted as though he wanted to talk with Abner in private, but Joab stabbed him in the stomach, and Abner died. Abner had killed Joab's brother Asahel, so Joab killed Abner to pay him back.

28Later when David heard the news, he said, "My kingdom and I are innocent forever of the death of Abner son of Ner. The LORD knows this. 29Joab and his family are responsible for this. May his family always have someone with sores or with a skin disease. May they always have someone who must lean on a crutch. May some of his family be killed in war. May they always have someone without food to eat."

30(Joab and his brother Abishai killed Abner, because he had killed their brother Asahel in the battle at Gibeon.)

31Then David said to Joab and to all the people with Joab, "Tear your clothes and put on rough cloth to show how sad you are. Cry for Abner." King David himself followed the body of Abner. 32They buried Abner in Hebron, and David and all the people cried at Abner's grave.

33King David sang this funeral song for Abner.

"Did Abner die like a fool?
34   His hands were not tied.
    His feet were not in chains.
He fell at the hands of evil men."

Then all the people cried again for Abner. 35They came to encourage David to eat while it was still day. But he made a promise, saying, "May God punish me terribly if I eat bread or anything else before the sun sets!"

36All the people saw what happened, and they agreed with what the king was doing, just as they agreed with everything he did.

37That day all the people of Judah and Israel understood that David did not order the killing of Abner son of Ner.

38David said to his officers, "You know that a great man died today in Israel. 39Even though I am the appointed king, I feel empty. These sons of Zeruiah are too much for me. May the LORD give them the punishment they should have."

ISH-BOSHETH'S DEATH

4 When Ish-Bosheth son of Saul heard that Abner had died at Hebron, he was shocked and all Israel became frightened. 2Two men who were captains in Saul's army came to Ish-Bosheth. One was named Baanah, and the other was named Recab. They were the sons of Rimmon of Beeroth, who was a Benjaminite. (The town Beeroth belonged to the tribe of Benjamin. 3The people of Beeroth ran away to Gittaim, and they still live there as foreigners today.)

4(Saul's son Jonathan had a son named Mephibosheth, who was crippled in both feet. He was five years old when the news came from Jezreel that Saul and Jonathan were dead. Mephibosheth's nurse had picked him up and run away. But as she hurried to leave, she dropped him, and now he was lame.)

5Recab and Baanah, sons of Rimmon from Beeroth, went to Ish-Bosheth's house in the afternoon while he was taking a nap. 6-7They went into the middle of the house as if to get some wheat. Ish-Bosheth was lying on his bed in his bedroom. Then Recab and Baanah stabbed him in the stomach, killed him, cut off his head, and took it with them. They escaped and traveled all night through the Jordan Valley. 8When they arrived at Hebron, they gave his head to David and said to the king, "Here is the head of Ish-Bosheth son of Saul, your enemy. He tried to kill you! Today the LORD has paid back Saul and his family for what they did to you!"

9David answered Recab and his brother Baanah, the sons of Rimmon of Beeroth, "As surely as the LORD lives, he has saved me from all trouble! 10Once a man thought he was bringing me good news. When he told me, 'Saul is dead!' I seized him and killed him at Ziklag. That was the reward I gave him for his news! 11So even more I must put you evil men to death because you have killed an innocent man on his own bed in his own house!"

12So David commanded his men to kill Recab and Baanah. They cut off the hands and feet of Recab and Baanah and hung them over the pool of Hebron. Then they took Ish-Bosheth's head and buried it in Abner's tomb at Hebron.

DAVID IS MADE KING OF ISRAEL

5 Then all the tribes of Israel came to David at Hebron and said to him, "Look, we are your own family. 2Even when Saul was king, you were the one who led Israel in battle. The LORD said to you, 'You will be a shepherd for my people Israel. You will be their leader.'"

3So all the elders of Israel came to King David at Hebron, and he made an agreement with them in Hebron in the presence of the LORD. Then they poured oil on David to make him king over Israel.

4David was thirty years old when he became king, and he ruled forty years. 5He was king over Judah in Hebron for seven years and six months, and he was king over all Israel and Judah in Jerusalem for thirty-three years.

6When the king and his men went to Jerusalem to attack the Jebusites who lived there, the Jebusites said to David, "You can't get inside our city. Even the blind and the crippled can stop you." They thought David could not enter their city. 7But David did take the city of Jerusalem with its strong walls, and it became the City of David.

8That day David said to his men, "To defeat the Jebusites you must go through the water tunnel. Then you can reach those 'crippled' and 'blind' enemies. This is why people say, 'The blind and the crippled may not enter the palace.'"

9So David lived in the strong, walled city and called it the City of David. David built more buildings around it, beginning where the land was filled in. He also built more buildings inside the city. 10He became stronger and stronger, because the LORD God All-Powerful was with him.

11Hiram king of the city of Tyre sent messengers to David, along with cedar logs, carpenters, and stonecutters. They built a palace for David. 12Then David knew that the LORD really had made him king of Israel and that the LORD had made his kingdom great because the LORD loved his people Israel.

13After he came from Hebron, David took for himself more slave women and wives in Jerusalem. More sons and daughters were born to David. 14These are the names of the sons born to David in Jerusalem: Shammua, Shobab, Nathan, Solomon, 15Ibhar, Elishua, Nepheg, Japhia, 16Elishama, Eliada, and Eliphelet.

DAVID DEFEATS THE PHILISTINES

17When the Philistines heard that David had been made king over Israel, all the Philistines went to look for him. But when David heard the news, he went down to the stronghold. 18The Philistines came and camped in the Valley of Rephaim. 19David asked the LORD, "Should I attack the Philistines? Will you hand them over to me?"

The LORD said to David, "Go! I will certainly hand them over to you."

20So David went to Baal Perazim and defeated the Philistines there. David said, "Like a flood of water, the LORD has broken through my enemies in front of me." So David named the place Baal Perazim.[n] 21The Philistines left their idols behind at Baal Perazim, so David and his men carried them away.

22Once again the Philistines came and camped at the Valley of Rephaim. 23When David prayed to the LORD, he answered, "Don't attack the Philistines from the front. Instead, go around and attack them in front of the balsam trees. 24When you hear the sound of marching in the tops of the balsam trees, act quickly. I, the LORD, will have gone ahead of you to defeat the Philistine army." 25So David did what the LORD commanded. He defeated the Philistines and chased them all the way from Gibeon to Gezer.

THE ARK IS BROUGHT TO JERUSALEM

6 David again gathered all the chosen men of Israel—thirty thousand of them. 2Then he and all his people went to Baalah in Judah[n] to bring back the Ark of God. The Ark is called by the Name, the name of the LORD All-Powerful, whose throne is between the gold creatures with wings. 3They put the

---

5:20 Baal Perazim This name means "the Lord breaks through." **6:2 Baalah in Judah** Another name for Kiriath Jearim.

Ark of God on a new cart and brought it out of Abinadab's house on the hill. Uzzah and Ahio, sons of Abinadab, led the new cart ⁴which had the Ark of God on it. Ahio was walking in front of it. ⁵David and all the Israelites were celebrating in the presence of the LORD. They were playing wooden instruments: lyres, harps, tambourines, rattles, and cymbals.

⁶When David's men came to the threshing floor of Nacon, the oxen stumbled. So Uzzah reached out to steady the Ark of God. ⁷The LORD was angry with Uzzah and killed him because of what he did. So Uzzah died there beside the Ark of God. ⁸David was angry because the LORD had killed Uzzah. Now that place is called the Punishment of Uzzah.

⁹David was afraid of the LORD that day, and he said, "How can the Ark of the LORD come to me now?" ¹⁰So David would not move the Ark of the LORD to be with him in Jerusalem. Instead, he took it to the house of Obed-Edom, a man from Gath. ¹¹The Ark of the LORD stayed in Obed-Edom's house for three months, and the LORD blessed Obed-Edom and all his family.

¹²The people told David, "The LORD has blessed the family of Obed-Edom and all that belongs to him, because the Ark of God is there." So David went and brought it up from Obed-Edom's house to Jerusalem with joy. ¹³When the men carrying the Ark of the LORD had walked six steps, David sacrificed a bull and a fat calf. ¹⁴Then David danced with all his might before the LORD. He had on a holy linen vest. ¹⁵David and all the Israelites shouted with joy and blew the trumpets as they brought the Ark of the LORD to the city.

¹⁶As the Ark of the LORD came into the city, Saul's daughter Michal looked out the window. When she saw David jumping and dancing in the presence of the LORD, she hated him.

¹⁷David put up a tent for the Ark of the LORD, and then the Israelites put it in its place inside the tent. David offered whole burnt offerings and fellowship offerings before the LORD. ¹⁸When David finished offering the whole burnt offerings and the fellowship offerings, he blessed the people in the name of the LORD All-Powerful. ¹⁹David gave a loaf of bread, a cake of dates, and a cake of raisins to every Israelite, both men and women. Then all the people went home.

²⁰David went back to bless the people in his home, but Saul's daughter Michal came out to meet him. She said, "With what honor the king of Israel acted today! You took off your clothes in front of the servant girls of your officers like one who takes off his clothes without shame!"

²¹Then David said to Michal, "I did it in the presence of the LORD. The LORD chose me, not your father or anyone from Saul's family. The LORD appointed me to be over Israel. So I will celebrate in the presence of the LORD. ²²Maybe I will lose even more honor, and maybe I will be brought down in my own opinion, but the girls you talk about will honor me!"

²³And Saul's daughter Michal had no children to the day she died.

DAVID WANTS TO BUILD A TEMPLE

7 King David was living in his palace, and the LORD had given him peace from all his enemies around him. ²Then David said to Nathan the prophet, "Look, I am living in a palace made of cedar wood, but the Ark of God is in a tent!"

³Nathan said to the king, "Go and do what you really want to do, because the LORD is with you."

⁴But that night the LORD spoke his word to Nathan, ⁵"Go and tell my servant David, 'This is what the LORD says: Will you build a house for me to live in? ⁶From the time I brought the Israelites out of Egypt until now I have not lived in a house. I have been moving around all this time with a tent as my home. ⁷As I have moved with the Israelites, I have never said to the tribes, whom I commanded to take care of my people Israel, "Why haven't you built me a house of cedar?" '

⁸"You must tell my servant David, 'This is what the LORD All-Powerful says: I took you from the pasture and from tending the sheep and made you leader of my people Israel. ⁹I have been with you everywhere you have gone and have defeated your enemies for you. I will make you as famous as any of the great people on the earth. ¹⁰Also I will choose a place for my people Israel, and I will plant them so they can live in their own homes. They will not be bothered anymore.

Wicked people will no longer bother them as they have in the past ¹¹when I chose judges for my people Israel. But I will give you peace from all your enemies. I also tell you that I will make your descendants kings of Israel after you.

¹²" 'When you die and join your ancestors, I will make one of your sons the next king, and I will set up his kingdom. ¹³He will build a house for me, and I will let his kingdom rule always. ¹⁴I will be his father, and he will be my son. When he sins, I will use other people to punish him. They will be my whips. ¹⁵I took away my love from Saul, whom I removed before you, but I will never stop loving your son. ¹⁶But your family and your kingdom will continue always before me. Your throne will last forever.' "

¹⁷Nathan told David everything God had said in this vision.

DAVID PRAYS TO GOD

¹⁸Then King David went in and sat in front of the LORD. David said, "Lord GOD, who am I? What is my family? Why did you bring me to this point? ¹⁹But even this is not enough for you, Lord GOD. You have also made promises about my future family. This is extraordinary, Lord GOD.

²⁰"What more can I say to you, Lord GOD, since you know me, your servant, so well! ²¹You have done this great thing because you said you would and because you wanted to, and you have let me know about it. ²²This is why you are great, Lord GOD! There is no one like you. There is no God except you. We have heard all this ourselves! ²³There is no nation like your people Israel. They are the only people on earth that God chose to be his own. You made your name well known. You did great and wonderful miracles for them. You went ahead of them and forced other nations and their gods out of the land. You freed your people from slavery in Egypt. ²⁴You made the people of Israel your very own people forever, and, LORD, you are their God.

²⁵"Now, LORD God, keep the promise forever that you made about my family and me, your servant. Do what you have said. ²⁶Then you will be honored always, and people will say, 'The LORD All-Powerful is God over Israel!' And the family of your servant David will continue before you.

²⁷"LORD All-Powerful, the God of Israel, you have said to me, 'I will make your family great.' So I, your servant, am brave enough to pray to you. ²⁸Lord GOD, you are God, and your words are true. And you have promised these good things to me, your servant. ²⁹Please, bless my family. Let it continue before you always. Lord GOD, you have said so. With your blessing let my family always be blessed."

DAVID WINS MANY WARS

8 Later, David defeated the Philistines, conquered them, and took the city of Metheg Ammah.

²He also defeated the people of Moab. He made them lie on the ground, and then he used a rope to measure them. Those who were measured within two rope lengths were killed, but those who were within the next rope length were allowed to live. So the people of Moab became servants of David and gave him the payment he demanded.

³David also defeated Hadadezer son of Rehob, king of Zobah, as he went to take control again at the Euphrates River. ⁴David captured one thousand chariots, seven thousand men who rode in chariots, and twenty thousand foot soldiers. He crippled all but a hundred of the chariot horses.

⁵Arameans from Damascus came to help Hadadezer king of Zobah, but David killed twenty-two thousand of them. ⁶Then David put groups of soldiers in Damascus in Aram. The Arameans became David's servants and gave him the payment he demanded. The LORD gave David victory everywhere he went.

⁷David took the shields of gold that had belonged to Hadadezer's officers and brought them to Jerusalem. ⁸David also took many things made of bronze from Tebah and Berothai, which had been cities under Hadadezer's control.

⁹Toi king of Hamath heard that David had defeated all the army of Hadadezer. ¹⁰So Toi sent his son Joram to greet and congratulate King David for defeating Hadadezer. (Hadadezer had been at war with Toi.) Joram brought items made of silver, gold, and bronze. ¹¹King David gave them to the LORD, along with the silver and gold he had taken from the other nations he had defeated. ¹²These nations were Edom, Moab, Ammon,

Philistia, and Amalek. David also gave the LORD what he had taken from Hadadezer son of Rehob, king of Zobah.

¹³David was famous after he returned from defeating eighteen thousand Arameans in the Valley of Salt. ¹⁴He put groups of soldiers all over Edom, and all the Edomites became his servants. The LORD gave David victory everywhere he went.

¹⁵David was king over all Israel, and he did what was fair and right for all his people. ¹⁶Joab son of Zeruiah was commander over the army. Jehoshaphat son of Ahilud was the recorder. ¹⁷Zadok son of Ahitub and Abiathar son of Ahimelech were priests. Seraiah was the royal secretary. ¹⁸Benaiah son of Jehoiada was over the Kerethites and Pelethites.ⁿ And David's sons were priests.

DAVID HELPS SAUL'S FAMILY

9 David asked, "Is anyone still left in Saul's family? I want to show kindness to that person for Jonathan's sake!"

²Now there was a servant named Ziba from Saul's family. So David's servants called Ziba to him. King David said to him, "Are you Ziba?"

He answered, "Yes, I am your servant."

³The king asked, "Is anyone left in Saul's family? I want to show God's kindness to that person."

Ziba answered the king, "Jonathan has a son still living who is crippled in both feet."

⁴The king asked Ziba, "Where is this son?"

Ziba answered, "He is at the house of Makir son of Ammiel in Lo Debar."

⁵Then King David had servants bring Jonathan's son from the house of Makir son of Ammiel in Lo Debar. ⁶Mephibosheth, Jonathan's son, came before David and bowed facedown on the floor.

David said, "Mephibosheth!"

Mephibosheth said, "I am your servant."

⁷David said to him, "Don't be afraid. I will be kind to you for your father Jonathan's sake. I will give you back all the land of your grandfather Saul, and you will always eat at my table."

⁸Mephibosheth bowed to David again and said, "You are being very kind to me, your servant! And I am no better than a dead dog!"

⁹Then King David called Saul's servant Ziba. David said to him, "I have given your master's grandson everything that belonged to Saul and his family. ¹⁰You, your sons, and your servants will farm the land and harvest the crops. Then your family will have food to eat. But Mephibosheth, your master's grandson, will always eat at my table."

(Now Ziba had fifteen sons and twenty servants.) ¹¹Ziba said to King David, "I, your servant, will do everything my master, the king, commands me."

So Mephibosheth ate at David's table as if he were one of the king's sons. ¹²Mephibosheth had a young son named Mica. Everyone in Ziba's family became Mephibosheth's servants. ¹³Mephibosheth lived in Jerusalem, because he always ate at the king's table. And he was crippled in both feet.

WAR WITH THE AMMONITES AND ARAMEANS

10 When Nahash king of the Ammonites died, his son Hanun became king after him. ²David said, "Nahash was loyal to me, so I will be loyal to his son Hanun." So David sent his messengers to comfort Hanun about his father's death.

David's officers went to the land of the Ammonites. ³But the Ammonite leaders said to Hanun, their master, "Do you think David wants to honor your father by sending men to comfort you? No! David sent them to study the city and spy it out and capture it!" ⁴So Hanun arrested David's officers. To shame them he shaved off half their beards and cut off their clothes at the hips. Then he sent them away.

⁵When the people told David, he sent messengers to meet his officers because they were very ashamed. King David said, "Stay in Jericho until your beards have grown back. Then come home."

⁶The Ammonites knew that they had insulted David. So they hired twenty thousand Aramean foot soldiers from Beth Rehob and Zobah. They also hired the king of Maacah with a thousand men and twelve thousand men from Tob.

8:18 Kerethites and Pelethites These were probably special units of the army that were responsible for the king's safety, a kind of palace guard.

7When David heard about this, he sent Joab with the whole army. 8The Ammonites came out and prepared for battle at the city gate. The Arameans from Zobah and Rehob and the men from Tob and Maacah were out in the field by themselves.

9Joab saw that there were enemies both in front of him and behind him. So he chose some of the best soldiers of Israel and sent them out to fight the Arameans. 10Joab put the rest of the army under the command of Abishai, his brother. Then he sent them out to fight the Ammonites. 11Joab said to Abishai, "If the Arameans are too strong for me, you must help me. Or, if the Ammonites are too strong for you, I will help you. 12Be strong. We must fight bravely for our people and the cities of our God. The LORD will do what he thinks is right."

13Then Joab and the army with him went to attack the Arameans, and the Arameans ran away. 14When the Ammonites saw that the Arameans were running away, they also ran away from Abishai and went back to their city. So Joab returned from the battle with the Ammonites and came to Jerusalem.

15When the Arameans saw that Israel had defeated them, they came together into one big army. 16Hadadezer sent messengers to bring the Arameans from east of the Euphrates River, and they went to Helam. Their leader was Shobach, the commander of Hadadezer's army.

17When David heard about this, he gathered all the Israelites together. They crossed over the Jordan River and went to Helam. There the Arameans prepared for battle and attacked him. 18But the Arameans ran away from the Israelites. David killed seven hundred Aramean chariot drivers and forty thousand Aramean horsemen. He also killed Shobach, the commander of the Aramean army.

19When the kings who served Hadadezer saw that the Israelites had defeated them, they made peace with the Israelites and served them. And the Arameans were afraid to help the Ammonites again.

DAVID SINS WITH BATHSHEBA

11 In the spring, when the kings normally went out to war, David sent out Joab, his servants, and all the Israelites. They de-stroyed the Ammonites and attacked the city of Rabbah. But David stayed in Jerusalem. 2One evening David got up from his bed and walked around on the roof ^{n} of his palace. While he was on the roof, he saw a woman bathing. She was very beautiful. 3So David sent his servants to find out who she was. A servant answered, "That woman is Bathsheba daughter of Eliam. She is the wife of Uriah the Hittite." 4So David sent messengers to bring Bathsheba to him. When she came to him, he had sexual relations with her. (Now Bathsheba had purified herself from her monthly period.) Then she went back to her house. 5But Bathsheba became pregnant and sent word to David, saying, "I am pregnant."

6So David sent a message to Joab: "Send Uriah the Hittite to me." And Joab sent Uriah to David. 7When Uriah came to him, David asked him how Joab was, how the soldiers were, and how the war was going. 8Then David said to Uriah, "Go home and rest."

So Uriah left the palace, and the king sent a gift to him. 9But Uriah did not go home. Instead, he slept outside the door of the palace as all the king's officers did.

10The officers told David, "Uriah did not go home."

Then David said to Uriah, "You came from a long trip. Why didn't you go home?"

11Uriah said to him, "The Ark and the soldiers of Israel and Judah are staying in tents. My master Joab and his officers are camping out in the fields. It isn't right for me to go home to eat and drink and have sexual relations with my wife!"

12David said to Uriah, "Stay here today. Tomorrow I'll send you back to the battle." So Uriah stayed in Jerusalem that day and the next. 13Then David called Uriah to come to see him, so Uriah ate and drank with David. David made Uriah drunk, but he still did not go home. That evening Uriah again slept with the king's officers.

14The next morning David wrote a letter to Joab and sent it by Uriah. 15In the letter David wrote, "Put Uriah on the front lines

---

11:2 roof In Bible times houses were built with flat roofs. The roof was used for drying things such as flax and fruit. And it was used as an extra room, as a place for worship, and as a cool place to sleep in the summer.

where the fighting is worst and leave him there alone. Let him be killed in battle."

¹⁶Joab watched the city and saw where its strongest defenders were and put Uriah there. ¹⁷When the men of the city came out to fight against Joab, some of David's men were killed. And Uriah the Hittite was one of them.

¹⁸Then Joab sent David a complete account of the war. ¹⁹Joab told the messenger, "Tell King David what happened in the war. ²⁰After you finish, the king may be angry and ask, 'Why did you go so near the city to fight? Didn't you know they would shoot arrows from the city wall? ²¹Do you remember who killed Abimelech son of Jerub-Besheth?[n] It was a woman on the city wall. She threw a large stone for grinding grain on Abimelech and killed him there in Thebez. Why did you go so near the wall?' If King David asks that, tell him, 'Your servant Uriah the Hittite also died.'"

²²The messenger left and went to David and told him everything Joab had told him to say. ²³The messenger told David, "The men of Ammon were winning. They came out and attacked us in the field, but we fought them back to the city gate. ²⁴The archers on the city wall shot at your servants, and some of your men were killed. Your servant Uriah the Hittite also died."

²⁵David said to the messenger, "Say this to Joab: 'Don't be upset about this. The sword kills everyone the same. Make a stronger attack against the city and capture it.' Encourage Joab with these words."

²⁶When Bathsheba heard that her husband was dead, she cried for him. ²⁷After she finished her time of sadness, David sent servants to bring her to his house. She became David's wife and gave birth to his son, but the LORD did not like what David had done.

DAVID'S SON DIES

12 The LORD sent Nathan to David. When he came to David, he said, "There were two men in a city. One was rich, but the other was poor. ²The rich man had many sheep and cattle. ³But the poor man had nothing except one little female lamb he had bought. The poor man fed the lamb, and it grew up with him and his children. It shared his food and

drank from his cup and slept in his arms. The lamb was like a daughter to him.

⁴"Then a traveler stopped to visit the rich man. The rich man wanted to feed the traveler, but he didn't want to take one of his own sheep or cattle. Instead, he took the lamb from the poor man and cooked it for his visitor."

⁵David became very angry at the rich man. He said to Nathan, "As surely as the LORD lives, the man who did this should die! ⁶He must pay for the lamb four times for doing such a thing. He had no mercy!"

⁷Then Nathan said to David, "You are the man! This is what the LORD, the God of Israel, says: 'I appointed you king of Israel and saved you from Saul. ⁸I gave you his kingdom and his wives. And I made you king of Israel and Judah. And if that had not been enough, I would have given you even more. ⁹So why did you ignore the LORD's command? Why did you do what he says is wrong? You killed Uriah the Hittite with the sword of the Ammonites and took his wife to be your wife! ¹⁰Now there will always be people in your family who will die by a sword, because you did not respect me; you took the wife of Uriah the Hittite for yourself!'

¹¹"This is what the LORD says: 'I am bringing trouble to you from your own family. While you watch, I will take your wives from you and give them to someone who is very close to you. He will have sexual relations with your wives, and everyone will know it. ¹²You had sexual relations with Bathsheba in secret, but I will do this so all the people of Israel can see it.'"

¹³Then David said to Nathan, "I have sinned against the LORD."

Nathan answered, "The LORD has taken away your sin. You will not die. ¹⁴But what you did caused the LORD's enemies to lose all respect for him. For this reason the son who was born to you will die."

¹⁵Then Nathan went home. And the LORD caused the son of David and Bathsheba, Uriah's widow, to be very sick. ¹⁶David prayed to God for the baby. David fasted and went into his house and stayed there, lying on the ground all night. ¹⁷The elders of David's family came to him and tried to pull him up from

---

11:21 Jerub-Besheth Another name for Gideon.

the ground, but he refused to get up or to eat food with them.

¹⁸On the seventh day the baby died. David's servants were afraid to tell him that the baby was dead. They said, "Look, we tried to talk to David while the baby was alive, but he refused to listen to us. If we tell him the baby is dead, he may do something awful."

¹⁹When David saw his servants whispering, he knew that the baby was dead. So he asked them, "Is the baby dead?"

They answered, "Yes, he is dead."

²⁰Then David got up from the floor, washed himself, put lotions on, and changed his clothes. Then he went into the LORD's house to worship. After that, he went home and asked for something to eat. His servants gave him some food, and he ate.

²¹David's servants said to him, "Why are you doing this? When the baby was still alive, you fasted and you cried. Now that the baby is dead, you get up and eat food."

THE EXTRA MILE MARRIAGE

FAMILY

consequences

2 SAMUEL 12:7–15

David's sin with Bathsheba had grave consequences. In spite of David's repentance, the child he had by her died. There is a great and powerful lesson here. God's forgiveness does not mean that the consequences of our sins are erased. God's forgiveness removes our guilt, but it does not remove the consequences.

We want to think that if we are forgiven we go back to zero. All debts are repaid. All obligations removed. But that is not the way God made the world. Actions produce consequences. That is the law of the moral order. God and I may settle the debts for eternity, but I will still have to face the facts here.

This principle is so important in the development of children that God reminds us about it over and over in Proverbs. Children cannot learn to function in this world without understanding that actions have consequences. Every time we intervene in the automatic and natural relationship between actions and consequences, we interfere with God's order for living.

Whenever parents make a concerted effort to remove the consequences from a child's behavior, they are teaching that child to live with a deceptive and dangerous myth. Eventually life will catch up with this bad education and enforce self-correction. But there is no need for the delay. Parents have been given the right rules from the beginning. Consequences matter.

---

reflect: Consider the potential consequences of your actions in order to avoid foolish behavior.

Go to **1 Chronicles 29:11–12.**

[22]David said, "While the baby was still alive, I fasted, and I cried. I thought, 'Who knows? Maybe the LORD will feel sorry for me and let the baby live.' [23]But now that the baby is dead, why should I fast? I can't bring him back to life. Someday I will go to him, but he cannot come back to me."

[24]Then David comforted Bathsheba his wife. He slept with her and had sexual relations with her. She became pregnant again and had another son, whom David named Solomon. The LORD loved Solomon. [25]The LORD sent word through Nathan the prophet to name the baby Jedidiah,[n] because the LORD loved the child.

DAVID CAPTURES RABBAH

[26]Joab fought against Rabbah, a royal city of the Ammonites, and he was about to capture it. [27]Joab sent messengers to David and said, "I have fought against Rabbah and have captured its water supply. [28]Now bring the other soldiers together and attack this city. Capture it before I capture it myself and it is called by my name!"

[29]So David gathered all the army and went to Rabbah and fought against it and captured it. [30]David took the crown off their king's head and had it placed on his own head. That gold crown weighed about seventy-five pounds, and it had valuable gems in it. And David took many valuable things from the city. [31]He also brought out the people of the city and forced them to work with saws, iron picks, and axes. He also made them build with bricks. David did this to all the Ammonite cities. Then David and all his army returned to Jerusalem.

AMNON AND TAMAR

13 David had a son named Absalom and a son named Amnon. Absalom had a beautiful sister named Tamar, and Amnon loved her. [2]Tamar was a virgin. Amnon made himself sick just thinking about her, because he could not find any chance to be alone with her.

[3]Amnon had a friend named Jonadab son of Shimeah, David's brother. Jonadab was a very clever man. [4]He asked Amnon, "Son of the king, why do you look so sad day after day? Tell me what's wrong!"

Amnon told him, "I love Tamar, the sister of my half-brother Absalom."

[5]Jonadab said to Amnon, "Go to bed and act as if you are sick. Then your father will come to see you. Tell him, 'Please let my sister Tamar come in and give me food to eat. Let her make the food in front of me so I can watch and eat it from her hand.'"

[6]So Amnon went to bed and acted sick. When King David came in to see him, Amnon said to him, "Please let my sister Tamar come in. Let her make two of her special cakes for me while I watch. Then I will eat them from her hands."

[7]David sent for Tamar in the palace, saying, "Go to your brother Amnon's house and make some food for him." [8]So Tamar went to her brother Amnon's house, and he was in bed. Tamar took some dough and pressed it together with her hands. She made some special cakes while Amnon watched. Then she baked them. [9]Next she took the pan and served him, but he refused to eat.

He said to his servants, "All of you, leave me alone!" So they all left him alone. [10]Amnon said to Tamar, "Bring the food into the bedroom so I may eat from your hand."

Tamar took the cakes she had made and brought them to her brother Amnon in the bedroom. [11]She went to him so he could eat from her hands, but Amnon grabbed her. He said, "Sister, come and have sexual relations with me."

[12]Tamar said to him, "No, brother! Don't force me! This should never be done in Israel! Don't do this shameful thing! [13]I could never get rid of my shame! And you will be like the shameful fools in Israel! Please talk with the king, and he will let you marry me."

[14]But Amnon refused to listen to her. He was stronger than she was, so he forced her to have sexual relations with him. [15]After that, Amnon hated Tamar. He hated her more than he had loved her before. Amnon said to her, "Get up and leave!"

[16]Tamar said to him, "No! Sending me away would be worse than what you've already done!"

But he refused to listen to her. [17]He called his young servant back in and said, "Get this woman out of here and away from me! Lock the door after her." [18]So his servant led her

---

12:25 Jedidiah This name means "loved by the LORD."

out of the room and bolted the door after her.

Tamar was wearing a special robe with long sleeves, because the king's virgin daughters wore this kind of robe. 19To show how upset she was, Tamar put ashes on her head and tore her special robe and put her hand on her head. Then she went away, crying loudly.

20Absalom, Tamar's brother, said to her, "Has Amnon, your brother, forced you to have sexual relations with him? For now, sister, be quiet. He is your half-brother. Don't let this upset you so much!" So Tamar lived in her brother Absalom's house and was sad and lonely.

21When King David heard the news, he was very angry. 22Absalom did not say a word, good or bad, to Amnon. But he hated Amnon for disgracing his sister Tamar.

ABSALOM'S REVENGE

23Two years later Absalom had some men come to Baal Hazor, near Ephraim, to cut the wool from his sheep. Absalom invited all the king's sons to come also. 24Absalom went to the king and said, "I have men coming to cut the wool. Please come with your officers and join me."

25King David said to Absalom, "No, my son. We won't all go, because it would be too much trouble for you." Although Absalom begged David, he would not go, but he did give his blessing.

26Absalom said, "If you don't want to come, then please let my brother Amnon come with us."

King David asked, "Why should he go with you?"

27Absalom kept begging David until he let Amnon and all the king's sons go with Absalom.

28Then Absalom instructed his servants, "Watch Amnon. When he is drunk, I will tell you, 'Kill Amnon.' Right then, kill him! Don't be afraid, because I have commanded you! Be strong and brave!" 29So Absalom's young men killed Amnon as Absalom commanded, but all of David's other sons got on their mules and escaped.

30While the king's sons were on their way, the news came to David, "Absalom has killed all of the king's sons! Not one of them is left

alive!" 31King David tore his clothes and lay on the ground to show his sadness. All his servants standing nearby tore their clothes also.

32Jonadab son of Shimeah, David's brother, said to David, "Don't think all the young men, your sons, are killed. No, only Amnon is dead! Absalom has planned this ever since Amnon forced his sister Tamar to have sexual relations with him. 33My master and king, don't think that all of the king's sons are dead. Only Amnon is dead!"

34In the meantime Absalom had run away.

A guard standing on the city wall saw many people coming from the other side of the hill. 35So Jonadab said to King David, "Look, I was right! The king's sons are coming!"

36As soon as Jonadab had said this, the king's sons arrived, crying loudly. David and all his servants began crying also. 37David cried for his son every day.

But Absalom ran away to Talmai[n] son of Ammihud, the king of Geshur. 38After Absalom ran away to Geshur, he stayed there for three years. 39When King David got over Amnon's death, he missed Absalom greatly.

JOAB SENDS A WISE WOMAN TO DAVID

14 Joab son of Zeruiah knew that King David missed Absalom very much. 2So Joab sent messengers to Tekoa to bring a wise woman from there. He said to her, "Pretend to be very sad. Put on funeral clothes and don't put lotion on yourself. Act like a woman who has been crying many days for someone who died. 3Then go to the king and say these words." Then Joab told her what to say.

4So the woman from Tekoa spoke to the king. She bowed facedown on the ground to show respect and said, "My king, help me!"

5King David asked her, "What is the matter?"

The woman said, "I am a widow; my husband is dead. 6I had two sons. They were out in the field fighting, and no one was there to stop them. So one son killed the other son. 7Now all the family group is against me. They said to me, 'Bring the son who killed his brother so we may kill him for killing his

---

13:37 Talmai He was Absalom's grandfather.

brother. That way we will also get rid of the one who would receive what belonged to his father.' My son is like the last spark of a fire. He is all I have left. If they kill him, my husband's name and property will be gone from the earth."

⁸Then the king said to the woman, "Go home. I will take care of this for you."

⁹The woman of Tekoa said to him, "Let the blame be on me and my father's family. My master and king, you and your throne are innocent."

¹⁰King David said, "Bring me anyone who says anything bad to you. Then he won't bother you again."

¹¹The woman said, "Please promise in the name of the LORD your God. Then my relative who has the duty of punishing a murderer won't add to the destruction by killing my son."

David said, "As surely as the LORD lives, no one will hurt your son. Not one hair from his head will fall to the ground."

¹²The woman said, "Let me say something to you, my master and king."

The king said, "Speak."

¹³Then the woman said, "Why have you decided this way against the people of God? When you judge this way, you show that you are guilty for not bringing back your son who was forced to leave home. ¹⁴We will all die someday. We're like water spilled on the ground; no one can gather it back. But God doesn't take away life. Instead, he plans ways that those who have been sent away will not have to stay away from him! ¹⁵My master and king, I came to say this to you because the people have made me afraid! I thought, 'Let me talk to the king. Maybe he will do what I ask. ¹⁶Maybe he will listen. Perhaps he will save me from those who want to keep both me and my son from getting what God gave us.'

¹⁷"Now I say, 'May the words of my master the king give me rest. Like an angel of God, you know what is good and what is bad. May the LORD your God be with you!' "

¹⁸Then King David said, "Do not hide the truth. Answer me one question."

The woman said, "My master the king, please ask your question."

¹⁹The king said, "Did Joab tell you to say all these things?"

The woman answered, "As you live, my master the king, no one could avoid that question. You are right. Your servant Joab did tell me to say these things. ²⁰Joab did it so you would see things differently. My master, you are wise like an angel of God who knows everything that happens on earth."

ABSALOM RETURNS TO JERUSALEM

²¹The king said to Joab, "Look, I will do what I promised. Bring back the young man Absalom."

²²Joab bowed facedown on the ground and blessed the king. Then he said, "Today I know you are pleased with me, because you have done what I asked."

²³Then Joab got up and went to Geshur and brought Absalom back to Jerusalem. ²⁴But King David said, "Absalom must go to his own house. He may not come to see me." So Absalom went to his own house and did not go to see the king.

²⁵Absalom was greatly praised for his handsome appearance. No man in Israel was as handsome as he. No blemish was on him from his head to his foot. ²⁶At the end of every year, Absalom would cut his hair, because it became too heavy. When he weighed it, it would weigh about five pounds by the royal measure.

²⁷Absalom had three sons and one daughter. His daughter's name was also Tamar, and she was a beautiful woman.

²⁸Absalom lived in Jerusalem for two full years without seeing King David. ²⁹Then Absalom sent for Joab so he could send him to the king, but Joab would not come. Absalom sent a message a second time, but Joab still refused to come. ³⁰Then Absalom said to his servants, "Look, Joab's field is next to mine, and he has barley growing there. Go burn it." So Absalom's servants set fire to Joab's field.

³¹Then Joab went to Absalom's house and said to him, "Why did your servants burn my field?"

³²Absalom said to Joab, "I sent a message to you, asking you to come here. I wanted to send you to the king to ask him why he brought me home from Geshur. It would have been better for me to stay there! Now let me see the king. If I have sinned, he can put me to death!"

³³So Joab went to the king and told him

Absalom's words. Then the king called for Absalom. Absalom came and bowed face-down on the ground before the king, and the king kissed him.

ABSALOM PLANS TO TAKE DAVID'S KINGDOM

15 After this, Absalom got a chariot and horses for himself and fifty men to run before him. [2]Absalom would get up early and stand near the city gate.[n] Anyone who had a problem for the king to settle would come here. When someone came, Absalom would call out and say, "What city are you from?"

The person would answer, "I'm from one of the tribes of Israel."

[3]Then Absalom would say, "Look, your claims are right, but the king has no one to listen to you." [4]Absalom would also say, "I wish someone would make me judge in this land! Then people with problems could come to me, and I could help them get justice."

[5]People would come near Absalom to bow to him. When they did, Absalom would reach out his hand and take hold of them and kiss them. [6]Absalom did that to all the Israelites who came to King David for decisions. In this way, Absalom stole the hearts of all Israel.

[7]After four years Absalom said to King David, "Please let me go to Hebron. I want to carry out my promise that I made to the LORD [8]while I was living in Geshur in Aram. I said, 'If the LORD takes me back to Jerusalem, I will worship him in Hebron.'"

[9]The king said, "Go in peace."

So Absalom went to Hebron. [10]But he sent secret messengers through all the tribes of Israel. They told the people, "When you hear the trumpets, say this: 'Absalom is the king at Hebron!'"

[11]Absalom had invited two hundred men to go with him. So they went from Jerusalem with him, but they didn't know what he was planning. [12]While Absalom was offering sacrifices, he sent for Ahithophel, one of the people who advised David, to come from his hometown of Giloh. So Absalom's plans were working very well. More and more people began to support him.

[13]A messenger came to David, saying, "The Israelites are giving their loyalty to Absalom."

[14]Then David said to all his officers who were with him in Jerusalem, "We must leave quickly! If we don't, we won't be able to get away from Absalom. We must hurry before he catches us and destroys us and kills the people of Jerusalem."

[15]The king's officers said to him, "We will do anything you say."

[16]The king set out with everyone in his house, but he left ten slave women to take care of the palace. [17]The king left with all his people following him, and they stopped at a house far away. [18]All the king's servants passed by him—the Kerethites and Pelethites,[n] all those from Gath, and the six hundred men who had followed him.

[19]The king said to Ittai, a man from Gath, "Why are you also going with us? Turn back and stay with King Absalom because you are a foreigner. This is not your homeland. [20]You joined me only a short time ago. Should I make you wander with us when I don't even know where I'm going? Turn back and take your brothers with you. May kindness and loyalty be shown to you."

[21]But Ittai said to the king, "As surely as the LORD lives and as you live, I will stay with you, whether it means life or death."

[22]David said to Ittai, "Go, march on." So Ittai from Gath and all his people with their children marched on. [23]All the people cried loudly as everyone passed by. King David crossed the Kidron Valley, and then all the people went on to the desert. [24]Zadok and all the Levites with him carried the Ark of the Agreement with God. They set it down, and Abiathar offered sacrifices until all the people had left the city.

[25]The king said to Zadok, "Take the Ark of God back into the city. If the LORD is pleased with me, he will bring me back and will let me see both it and Jerusalem again. [26]But if the LORD says he is not pleased with me, I am ready. He can do what he wants with me."

[27]The king also said to Zadok the priest, "Aren't you a seer? Go back to the city in peace and take your son Ahimaaz and Abiathar's son Jonathan with you. [28]I will wait

---

15:2 city gate People came here to conduct business. Public meetings and court cases were also held here. **15:18 Kerethites and Pelethites** These were probably special units of the army that were responsible for the king's safety, a kind of palace guard.

near the crossings into the desert until I hear from you." ²⁹So Zadok and Abiathar took the Ark of God back to Jerusalem and stayed there.

³⁰David went up the Mount of Olives, crying as he went. He covered his head and went barefoot. All the people with David covered their heads also and cried as they went. ³¹Someone told David, "Ahithophel is one of the people with Absalom who made secret plans against you."

So David prayed, "Lord, please make Ahithophel's advice foolish."

³²When David reached the top of the mountain where people used to worship God, Hushai the Arkite came to meet him. Hushai's coat was torn, and there was dirt on his head to show how sad he was. ³³David said to Hushai, "If you go with me, you will be just one more person for me to take care of. ³⁴But if you return to the city, you can make Ahithophel's advice useless. Tell Absalom, 'I am your servant, my king. In the past I served your father, but now I will serve you.' ³⁵The priests Zadok and Abiathar will be with you. Tell them everything you hear in the royal palace. ³⁶Zadok's son Ahimaaz and Abiathar's son Jonathan are with them. Send them to tell me everything you hear." ³⁷So David's friend Hushai entered Jerusalem just as Absalom arrived.

ZIBA MEETS DAVID

16 When David had passed a short way over the top of the Mount of Olives, Ziba, Mephibosheth's servant, met him. Ziba had a row of donkeys loaded with two hundred loaves of bread, one hundred cakes of raisins, one hundred cakes of figs, and leather bags full of wine. ²The king asked Ziba, "What are these things for?"

Ziba answered, "The donkeys are for your family to ride. The bread and cakes of figs are for the servants to eat. And the wine is for anyone to drink who might become weak in the desert."

³The king asked, "Where is Mephibosheth?"

Ziba answered him, "Mephibosheth is staying in Jerusalem because he thinks, 'Today the Israelites will give my father's kingdom back to me!'"

⁴Then the king said to Ziba, "All right. Everything that belonged to Mephibosheth, I now give to you!"

Ziba said, "I bow to you. I hope I will always be able to please you."

SHIMEI CURSES DAVID

⁵As King David came to Bahurim, a man came out and cursed him. He was from Saul's family group, and his name was Shimei son of Gera. ⁶He threw stones at David and his officers, but the people and soldiers gathered all around David. ⁷Shimei cursed David, saying, "Get out, get out, you murderer, you troublemaker. ⁸The Lord is punishing you for the people in Saul's family you killed! You took Saul's place as king, but now the Lord has given the kingdom to your son Absalom! Now you are ruined because you are a murderer!"

⁹Abishai son of Zeruiah said to the king, "Why should this dead dog curse you, the king? Let me go over and cut off his head!"

¹⁰But the king answered, "This does not concern you, sons of Zeruiah! If he is cursing me because the Lord told him to, who can question him?"

¹¹David also said to Abishai and all his officers, "My own son is trying to kill me! This man is a Benjaminite and has more right to kill me! Leave him alone, and let him curse me because the Lord told him to do this. ¹²Maybe the Lord will see my misery and repay me with something good for Shimei's curses today!"

¹³So David and his men went on down the road, but Shimei followed on the nearby hillside. He kept cursing David and throwing stones and dirt at him. ¹⁴When the king and all his people arrived at the Jordan, they were very tired, so they rested there.

¹⁵Meanwhile, Absalom, Ahithophel, and all the Israelites arrived at Jerusalem. ¹⁶David's friend Hushai the Arkite came to Absalom and said to him, "Long live the king! Long live the king!"

¹⁷Absalom asked, "Why are you not loyal to your friend David? Why didn't you leave Jerusalem with your friend?"

¹⁸Hushai said, "I belong to the one chosen by the Lord and by these people and everyone in Israel. I will stay with you. ¹⁹In the past I served your father. So whom should I

serve now? David's son! I will serve you as I served him."

AHITHOPHEL'S ADVICE

20Absalom said to Ahithophel, "Tell us what we should do."

21Ahithophel said, "Your father left behind some of his slave women to take care of the palace. Have sexual relations with them. Then all Israel will hear that your father is your enemy, and all your people will be encouraged to give you more support." 22So they put up a tent for Absalom on the roofⁿ of the palace where everyone in Israel could see it. And Absalom had sexual relations with his father's slave women.

23At that time people thought Ahithophel's advice was as reliable as God's own word. Both David and Absalom thought it was that reliable.

17 Ahithophel said to Absalom, "Let me choose twelve thousand men and chase David tonight. 2I'll catch him while he is tired and weak, and I'll frighten him so all his people will run away. But I'll kill only King David. 3Then I'll bring everyone back to you. If the man you are looking for is dead, everyone else will return safely." 4This plan seemed good to Absalom and to all the leaders of Israel.

5But Absalom said, "Now call Hushai the Arkite, so I can hear what he says." 6When Hushai came to Absalom, Absalom said to him, "This is the plan Ahithophel gave. Should we follow it? If not, tell us."

7Hushai said to Absalom, "Ahithophel's advice is not good this time." 8Hushai added, "You know your father and his men are strong. They are as angry as a bear that is robbed of its cubs. Your father is a skilled fighter. He won't stay all night with the army. 9He is probably already hiding in a cave or some other place. If the first attack fails, people will hear the news and think, 'Absalom's followers are losing!' 10Then even the men who are as brave as lions will be frightened, because all the Israelites know your father is a fighter. They know his men are brave!

11"This is what I suggest: Gather all the Israelites from Dan to Beersheba.ⁿ There will be as many people as grains of sand by the sea. Then you yourself must go into the battle. 12We will go to David wherever he is

hiding. We will fall on him as dew falls on the ground. We will kill him and all of his men so that no one will be left alive. 13If David escapes into a city, all the Israelites will bring ropes to that city and pull it into the valley. Not a stone will be left!"

14Absalom and all the Israelites said, "The advice of Hushai the Arkite is better than that of Ahithophel." (The LORD had planned to destroy the good advice of Ahithophel so the LORD could bring disaster on Absalom.)

15Hushai told Zadok and Abiathar, the priests, what Ahithophel had suggested to Absalom and the elders of Israel. He also reported to them what he himself had suggested. Hushai said, 16"Quickly! Send a message to David. Tell him not to stay tonight at the crossings into the desert but to cross over the Jordan River at once. If he crosses the river, he and all his people won't be destroyed."

17Jonathan and Ahimaaz were waiting at En Rogel. They did not want to be seen going into the city, so a servant girl would go out to them and give them messages. Then Jonathan and Ahimaaz would go and tell King David.

18But a boy saw Jonathan and Ahimaaz and told Absalom. So Jonathan and Ahimaaz left quickly and went to a man's house in Bahurim. He had a well in his courtyard, and they climbed down into it. 19The man's wife spread a sheet over the opening of the well and covered it with grain. No one could tell that anyone was hiding there.

20Absalom's servants came to the woman at the house and asked, "Where are Ahimaaz and Jonathan?"

She said to them, "They have already crossed the brook."

Absalom's servants then went to look for Jonathan and Ahimaaz, but they could not find them. So they went back to Jerusalem.

21After Absalom's servants left, Jonathan and Ahimaaz climbed out of the well and went to tell King David. They said, "Hurry,

---

16:22 roof In Bible times houses were built with flat roofs. The roof was used for drying things such as flax and fruit. And it was used as an extra room, as a place for worship, and as a cool place to sleep in the summer.
17:11 Dan to Beersheba Dan was the city farthest north in Israel, and Beersheba was the city farthest south. So this means all the people of Israel.

cross over the river! Ahithophel has said these things against you!" ²²So David and all his people crossed the Jordan River. By dawn, everyone had crossed the Jordan.

²³When Ahithophel saw that the Israelites did not accept his advice, he saddled his donkey and went to his hometown. He left orders for his family and property, and then he hanged himself. He died and was buried in his father's tomb.

WAR BETWEEN DAVID AND ABSALOM

²⁴David arrived at Mahanaim. And Absalom and all his Israelites crossed over the Jordan River. ²⁵Absalom had made Amasa captain of the army instead of Joab. Amasa was the son of a man named Jether the Ishmaelite. Amasa's mother was Abigail daughter of Nahash and sister of Zeruiah, Joab's mother. ²⁶Absalom and the Israelites camped in the land of Gilead.

²⁷Shobi, Makir, and Barzillai were at Mahanaim when David arrived. Shobi son of Nahash was from the Ammonite town of Rabbah. Makir son of Ammiel was from Lo Debar, and Barzillai was from Rogelim in Gilead. ²⁸They brought beds, bowls, clay pots, wheat, barley, flour, roasted grain, beans, small peas, ²⁹honey, milk curds, sheep, and cheese made from cows' milk for David and his people. They said, "The people are hungry and tired and thirsty in the desert."

18 David counted his men and placed over them commanders of thousands and commanders of hundreds. ²He sent the troops out in three groups. Joab commanded one-third of the men. Joab's brother Abishai son of Zeruiah commanded another third. And Ittai from Gath commanded the last third. King David said to them, "I will also go with you."

³But the men said, "You must not go with us! If we run away in the battle, Absalom's men won't care. Even if half of us are killed, Absalom's men won't care. But you're worth ten thousand of us! You can help us most by staying in the city."

⁴The king said to his people, "I will do what you think is best." So the king stood at the side of the gate as the army went out in groups of a hundred and a thousand.

⁵The king commanded Joab, Abishai, and Ittai, "Be gentle with young Absalom for my sake." Everyone heard the king's orders to the commanders about Absalom.

⁶David's army went out into the field against Absalom's Israelites, and they fought in the forest of Ephraim. ⁷There David's army defeated the Israelites. Many died that day—twenty thousand men. ⁸The battle spread through all the country, but that day more men died in the forest than in the fighting.

ABSALOM DIES

⁹Then Absalom happened to meet David's troops. As Absalom was riding his mule, it went under the thick branches of a large oak tree. Absalom's head got caught in the tree, and his mule ran out from under him. So Absalom was left hanging above the ground.

¹⁰When one of the men saw it happen, he told Joab, "I saw Absalom hanging in an oak tree!"

¹¹Joab said to him, "You saw him? Why didn't you kill him and let him fall to the ground? I would have given you a belt and four ounces of silver!"

¹²The man answered, "I wouldn't touch the king's son even if you gave me twenty-five pounds of silver. We heard the king command you, Abishai, and Ittai, 'Be careful not to hurt young Absalom.' ¹³If I had killed him, the king would have found out, and you would not have protected me!"

¹⁴Joab said, "I won't waste time here with you!" Absalom was still alive in the oak tree, so Joab took three spears and stabbed him in the heart. ¹⁵Ten young men who carried Joab's armor also gathered around Absalom and struck him and killed him.

¹⁶Then Joab blew the trumpet, so the troops stopped chasing the Israelites. ¹⁷Then Joab's men took Absalom's body and threw it into a large pit in the forest and filled the pit with many stones. All the Israelites ran away to their homes.

¹⁸When Absalom was alive, he had set up a pillar for himself in the King's Valley. He said, "I have no son to keep my name alive." So he named the pillar after himself, and it is called Absalom's Monument even today.

¹⁹Ahimaaz son of Zadok said to Joab, "Let me run and take the news to King David. I'll tell him the LORD has saved him from his enemies."

²⁰Joab answered Ahimaaz, "No, you are

not the one to take the news today. You may do it another time, but do not take it today, because the king's son is dead."

²¹Then Joab said to a man from Cush, "Go, tell the king what you have seen." The Cushite bowed to Joab and ran to tell David.

²²But Ahimaaz son of Zadok begged Joab again, "No matter what happens, please let me go along with the Cushite!"

Joab said, "Son, why do you want to carry the news? You won't get any reward."

²³Ahimaaz answered, "No matter what happens, I will run."

So Joab said to Ahimaaz, "Run!" Then Ahimaaz ran by way of the Jordan Valley and passed the Cushite.

²⁴David was sitting between the inner and outer gates of the city. The watchman went up to the roof of the gate by the walls, and as he looked up, he saw a man running alone. ²⁵He shouted the news to the king.

The king said, "If he is alone, he is bringing good news!"

The man came nearer and nearer to the city. ²⁶Then the watchman saw another man running, and he called to the gatekeeper, "Look! Another man is running alone!"

The king said, "He is also bringing good news!"

²⁷The watchman said, "I think the first man runs like Ahimaaz son of Zadok."

The king said, "Ahimaaz is a good man. He must be bringing good news!"

²⁸Then Ahimaaz called a greeting to the king. He bowed facedown on the ground before the king and said, "Praise the LORD your God! The LORD has defeated those who were against you, my king."

²⁹The king asked, "Is young Absalom all right?"

Ahimaaz answered, "When Joab sent me, I saw some great excitement, but I don't know what it was."

³⁰The king said, "Step over here and wait." So Ahimaaz stepped aside and stood there.

³¹Then the Cushite arrived. He said, "Master and king, hear the good news! Today the LORD has punished those who were against you!"

³²The king asked the Cushite, "Is young Absalom all right?"

The Cushite answered, "May your enemies and all who come to hurt you be like that young man!"

³³Then the king was very upset, and he went to the room over the city gate and cried. As he went, he cried out, "My son Absalom, my son Absalom! I wish I had died and not you. Absalom, my son, my son!"

JOAB SCOLDS DAVID

19 People told Joab, "Look, the king is sad and crying because of Absalom." ²David's army had won the battle that day. But it became a very sad day for all the people, because they heard that the king was very sad for his son. ³The people came into the city quietly that day. They were like an army that had been defeated in battle and had run away. ⁴The king covered his face and cried loudly, "My son Absalom! Absalom, my son, my son!"

⁵Joab went into the king's house and said, "Today you have shamed all your men. They saved your life and the lives of your sons, daughters, wives, and slave women. ⁶You have shamed them because you love those who hate you, and you hate those who love you. Today you have made it clear that your commanders and men mean nothing to you. What if Absalom had lived and all of us were dead? I can see you would be pleased. ⁷Now go out and encourage your servants. I swear by the LORD that if you don't go out, no man will be left with you by tonight! That will be worse than all the troubles you have had from your youth until today."

⁸So the king went to the city gate.ⁿ When the news spread that the king was at the gate, everyone came to see him.

DAVID GOES BACK TO JERUSALEM

All the Israelites who had followed Absalom had run away to their homes. ⁹People in all the tribes of Israel began to argue, saying, "The king saved us from the Philistines and our other enemies, but he left the country because of Absalom. ¹⁰We appointed Absalom to rule us, but now he has died in battle. We should make David the king again."

¹¹King David sent a message to Zadok and Abiathar, the priests, that said, "Speak to the elders of Judah. Say, 'Even in my house

---

19:8 city gate People came here to conduct business. Public meetings and court cases were also held here.

I have heard what all the Israelites are saying. So why are you the last tribe to bring the king back to his palace? 12You are my brothers, my own family. Why are you the last tribe to bring back the king?' 13And say to Amasa, 'You are part of my own family. May God punish me terribly if I don't make you commander of the army in Joab's place!'"

14David touched the hearts of all the people of Judah at once. They sent a message to the king that said, "Return with all your men." 15Then the king returned as far as the Jordan River. The men of Judah came to Gilgal to meet him and to bring him across the Jordan.

16Shimei son of Gera, a Benjaminite who lived in Bahurim, hurried down with the men of Judah to meet King David. 17With Shimei came a thousand Benjaminites. Ziba, the servant from Saul's family, also came, bringing his fifteen sons and twenty servants with him. They all hurried to the Jordan River to meet the king. 18The people went across the Jordan to help bring the king's family back to Judah and to do whatever the king wanted. As the king was crossing the river, Shimei son of Gera came to him and bowed facedown on the ground in front of the king. 19He said to the king, "My master, don't hold me guilty. Don't remember the wrong I did when you left Jerusalem! Don't hold it against me. 20I know I have sinned. That is why I am the first person from Joseph's family to come down and meet you today, my master and king!"

21But Abishai son of Zeruiah said, "Shimei should die because he cursed you, the LORD's appointed king!"

22David said, "This does not concern you, sons of Zeruiah! Today you're against me! No one will be put to death in Israel today. Today I know I am king over Israel!" 23Then the king promised Shimei, "You won't die."

24Mephibosheth, Saul's grandson, also went down to meet King David. Mephibosheth had not cared for his feet, cut his beard, or washed his clothes from the time the king had left Jerusalem until he returned safely. 25When Mephibosheth came from Jerusalem to meet the king, the king asked him, "Mephibosheth, why didn't you go with me?"

26He answered, "My master, my servant Ziba tricked me! I said to Ziba, 'I am crippled, so saddle a donkey. Then I will ride it so I can go with the king.' 27But he lied about me to you. You, my master and king, are like an angel from God. Do what you think is good. 28You could have killed all my grandfather's family. Instead, you put me with those people who eat at your own table. So I don't have a right to ask anything more from the king!"

29The king said to him, "Don't say anything more. I have decided that you and Ziba will divide the land."

30Mephibosheth said to the king, "Let Ziba take all the land now that my master the king has arrived safely home."

31Barzillai of Gilead came down from Rogelim to cross the Jordan River with the king. 32Barzillai was a very old man, eighty years old. He had taken care of the king when David was staying at Mahanaim, because Barzillai was a very rich man. 33David said to Barzillai, "Cross the river with me. Come with me to Jerusalem, and I will take care of you."

34But Barzillai answered the king, "Do you know how old I am? Do you think I can go with you to Jerusalem? 35I am eighty years old! I am too old to taste what I eat or drink. I am too old to hear the voices of men and women singers. Why should you be bothered with me? 36I am not worthy of a reward from you, but I will cross the Jordan River with you. 37Then let me go back so I may die in my own city near the grave of my father and mother. But here is Kimham, your servant. Let him go with you, my master and king. Do with him whatever you want."

38The king answered, "Kimham will go with me. I will do for him anything you wish, and I will do anything for you that you wish." 39The king kissed Barzillai and blessed him. Then Barzillai returned home, and the king and all the people crossed the Jordan.

40When the king crossed over to Gilgal, Kimham went with him. All the troops of Judah and half the troops of Israel led David across the river.

41Soon all the Israelites came to the king and said to him, "Why did our relatives, the people of Judah, steal you away? Why did they bring you and your family across the Jordan River with your men?"

42All the people of Judah answered the Israelites, "We did this because the king is our close relative. Why are you angry about it? We have not eaten food at the king's expense or taken anything for ourselves!"

⁴³The Israelites answered the people of Judah, "We have ten tribes in the kingdom, so we have more right to David than you do! But you ignored us! We were the first ones to talk about bringing our king back!"

But the people of Judah spoke even more unkindly than the people of Israel.

SHEBA LEADS ISRAEL AWAY FROM DAVID

20 It happened that a troublemaker named Sheba son of Bicri from the tribe of Benjamin was there. He blew the trumpet and said:

"We have no share in David!
    We have no part in the son of Jesse!
People of Israel, let's go home!"

²So all the Israelites left David and followed Sheba son of Bicri. But the people of Judah stayed with their king all the way from the Jordan River to Jerusalem.

³David came back to his palace in Jerusalem. He had left ten of his slave women there to take care of the palace. Now he put them in a locked house. He gave them food, but he did not have sexual relations with them. So they lived like widows until they died.

⁴The king said to Amasa, "Tell the men of Judah to meet with me in three days, and you must also be here." ⁵So Amasa went to call the men of Judah together, but he took more time than the king had said.

⁶David said to Abishai, "Sheba son of Bicri is more dangerous to us than Absalom was. Take my men and chase him before he finds walled cities and escapes from us." ⁷So Joab's men, the Kerethites and the Pelethites,ⁿ and all the soldiers went with Abishai. They went out from Jerusalem to chase Sheba son of Bicri.

⁸When Joab and the army came to the great rock at Gibeon, Amasa came out to meet them. Joab was wearing his uniform, and at his waist he wore a belt that held his sword in its case. As Joab stepped forward, his sword fell out of its case. ⁹Joab asked Amasa, "Brother, is everything all right with you?" Then with his right hand he took Amasa by the beard to kiss him. ¹⁰Amasa was not watching the sword in Joab's hand. So Joab pushed the sword into Amasa's stom-

ach, causing Amasa's insides to spill onto the ground. Joab did not have to stab Amasa again; he was already dead. Then Joab and his brother Abishai continued to chase Sheba son of Bicri.

¹¹One of Joab's young men stood by Amasa's body and said, "Everyone who is for Joab and David should follow Joab!" ¹²Amasa lay in the middle of the road, covered with his own blood. When the young man saw that everyone was stopping to look at the body, he dragged it from the road, laid it in a field, and put a cloth over it. ¹³After Amasa's body was taken off the road, all the men followed Joab to chase Sheba son of Bicri.

¹⁴Sheba went through all the tribes of Israel to Abel Beth Maacah. All the Berites also came together and followed him. ¹⁵So Joab and his men came to Abel Beth Maacah and surrounded it. They piled dirt up against the city wall, and they began hacking at the walls to bring them down.

¹⁶But a wise woman shouted out from the city, "Listen! Listen! Tell Joab to come here. I want to talk to him!"

¹⁷So Joab came near her. She asked him, "Are you Joab?"

He answered, "Yes, I am."

Then she said, "Listen to what I say."

Joab said, "I'm listening."

¹⁸Then the woman said, "In the past people would say, 'Ask for advice at Abel,' and the problem would be solved. ¹⁹I am one of the peaceful, loyal people of Israel. You are trying to destroy an important city of Israel. Why must you destroy what belongs to the LORD?"

²⁰Joab answered, "I would prefer not to destroy or ruin anything! ²¹That is not what I want. But there is a man here from the mountains of Ephraim, who is named Sheba son of Bicri. He has turned against King David. If you bring him to me, I will leave the city alone."

The woman said to Joab, "His head will be thrown over the wall to you."

²²Then the woman spoke very wisely to all the people of the city. They cut off the head of Sheba son of Bicri and threw it over

---

20:7 Kerethites and Pelethites These were probably special units of the army that were responsible for the king's safety, a kind of palace guard.

the wall to Joab. So he blew the trumpet, and the army left the city. Every man returned home, and Joab went back to the king in Jerusalem.

23Joab was commander of all the army of Israel. Benaiah son of Jehoiada led the Kerethites and Pelethites. 24Adoniram was in charge of the men who were forced to do hard work. Jehoshaphat son of Ahilud was the recorder. 25Sheba was the royal secretary. Zadok and Abiathar were the priests, 26and Ira the Jairite was David's priest.

THE GIBEONITES PUNISH SAUL'S FAMILY

21 During the time David was king, there was a shortage of food that lasted for three years. So David prayed to the LORD.

The LORD answered, "Saul and his family of murderers are the reason for this shortage, because he killed the Gibeonites." 2(Now the Gibeonites were not Israelites; they were a group of Amorites who were left alive. The Israelites had promised not to hurt the Gibeonites, but Saul had tried to kill them, because he was eager to help the people of Israel and Judah.)

King David called the Gibeonites together and spoke to them. 3He asked, "What can I do for you? How can I make up for the harm done so you can bless the LORD's people?"

4The Gibeonites said to David, "We cannot demand silver or gold from Saul or his family. And we don't have the right to kill anyone in Israel."

Then David asked, "What do you want me to do for you?"

5The Gibeonites said, "Saul made plans against us and tried to destroy all our people who are left in the land of Israel. 6So bring seven of his sons to us. Then we will kill them and hang them on stakes in the presence of the LORD at Gibeah, the hometown of Saul, the LORD's chosen king."

The king said, "I will give them to you." 7But the king protected Mephibosheth, the son of Jonathan, the son of Saul, because of the promise he had made to Jonathan in the LORD's name. 8The king did take Armoni and Mephibosheth,[n] sons of Rizpah and Saul. (Rizpah was the daughter of Aiah.) And the king took the five sons of Saul's daughter Merab. (Adriel son of Barzillai the Meholathite was the father of Merab's five sons.)

9David gave these seven sons to the Gibeonites. Then the Gibeonites killed them and hung them on stakes on a hill in the presence of the LORD. All seven sons died together. They were put to death during the first days of the harvest season at the beginning of barley harvest.

10Aiah's daughter Rizpah took the rough cloth that was worn to show sadness and put it on a rock for herself. She stayed there from the beginning of the harvest until the rain fell on her sons' bodies. During the day she did not let the birds of the sky touch her sons' bodies, and during the night she did not let the wild animals touch them.

11People told David what Aiah's daughter Rizpah, Saul's slave woman, was doing. 12Then David took the bones of Saul and Jonathan from the men of Jabesh Gilead. (The Philistines had hung the bodies of Saul and Jonathan in the public square of Beth Shan after they had killed Saul at Gilboa. Later the men of Jabesh Gilead had secretly taken them from there.) 13David brought the bones of Saul and his son Jonathan from Gilead. Then the people gathered the bodies of Saul's seven sons who were hanged on stakes. 14The people buried the bones of Saul and his son Jonathan at Zela in Benjamin in the tomb of Saul's father Kish. The people did everything the king commanded.

Then God answered the prayers for the land.

WARS WITH THE PHILISTINES

15Again there was war between the Philistines and Israel. David and his men went out to fight the Philistines, but David became tired. 16Ishbi-Benob, one of the sons of Rapha, had a bronze spearhead weighing about seven and one-half pounds and a new sword. He planned to kill David, 17but Abishai son of Zeruiah killed the Philistine and saved David's life.

Then David's men made a promise to him, saying, "Never again will you go out with us to battle. If you were killed, Israel would lose its greatest leader."

18Later, at Gob, there was another battle with the Philistines. Sibbecai the Hushathite

---

21:8 Mephibosheth This is not Jonathan's son but another man with the same name.

killed Saph, another one of the sons of Rapha.

19Later, there was another battle at Gob with the Philistines. Elhanan son of Jaare-Oregim from Bethlehem killed Goliath[n] from Gath. His spear was as large as a weaver's rod.

20At Gath another battle took place. A huge man was there; he had six fingers on each hand and six toes on each foot—twenty-four fingers and toes in all. This man also was one of the sons of Rapha. 21When he challenged Israel, Jonathan son of Shimeah, David's brother, killed him.

22These four sons of Rapha from Gath were killed by David and his men.

DAVID'S SONG OF PRAISE

22 David sang this song to the LORD when the LORD saved him from Saul and all his other enemies. 2He said:

"The LORD is my rock, my fortress, my Savior.
3 My God is my rock.
  I can run to him for safety.
He is my shield and my saving strength,
  my defender and my place of safety.
The LORD saves me from those who
  want to harm me.
4 I will call to the LORD, who is worthy of
  praise,
  and I will be saved from my enemies.

5 "The waves of death came around me;
  the deadly rivers overwhelmed me.
6 The ropes of death wrapped around me.
  The traps of death were before me.
7 In my trouble I called to the LORD;
  I cried out to my God.
From his temple he heard my voice;
  my call for help reached his ears.

8 "The earth trembled and shook.
  The foundations of heaven began to
  shake.
  They trembled because the LORD was
  angry.
9 Smoke came out of his nose,
  and burning fire came out of his mouth.
  Burning coals went before him.
10 He tore open the sky and came down
  with dark clouds under his feet.
11 He rode a creature with wings and flew.
  He raced on the wings of the wind.

12 He made darkness his shelter,
  surrounded by fog and clouds.
13 Out of the brightness of his presence
  came flashes of lightning.
14 The LORD thundered from heaven;
  the Most High raised his voice.
15 He shot his arrows and scattered his
  enemies.
  His bolts of lightning confused them
  with fear.
16 The LORD spoke strongly.
  The wind blew from his nose.
Then the valleys of the sea appeared,
  and the foundations of the earth were
  seen.

17 "The LORD reached down from above and
  took me;
  he pulled me from the deep water.
18 He saved me from my powerful enemies,
  from those who hated me, because they
  were too strong for me.
19 They attacked me at my time of trouble,
  but the LORD supported me.
20 He took me to a safe place.
  Because he delights in me, he saved me.

21 "The LORD spared me because I did what
  was right.
  Because I have not done evil, he has
  rewarded me.
22 I have followed the ways of the LORD;
  I have not done evil by turning from my
  God.
23 I remember all his laws
  and have not broken his rules.
24 I am innocent before him;
  I have kept myself from doing evil.
25 The LORD rewarded me because I did
  what was right,
  because I did what the LORD said was
  right.

26 "LORD, you are loyal to those who are
  loyal,
  and you are good to those who are good.
27 You are pure to those who are pure,
  but you are against those who are evil.
28 You save the humble,
  but you bring down those who are
  proud.

21:19 Goliath In 1 Chronicles 20:5 he is called Lahmi, brother of Goliath.

29 LORD, you give light to my lamp.
    The LORD brightens the darkness
        around me.
30 With your help I can attack an army.
    With God's help I can jump over a wall.

31 "The ways of God are without fault;
    the LORD's words are pure.
    He is a shield to those who trust him.
32 Who is God? Only the LORD.
    Who is the Rock? Only our God.
33 God is my protection.
    He makes my way free from fault.
34 He makes me like a deer that does not
        stumble;
    he helps me stand on the steep
        mountains.
35 He trains my hands for battle

so my arms can bend a bronze bow.
36 You protect me with your saving shield.
    You have stooped to make me great.
37 You give me a better way to live,
    so I live as you want me to.
38 I chased my enemies and destroyed them.
    I did not quit till they were destroyed.
39 I destroyed and crushed them
    so they couldn't rise up again.
    They fell beneath my feet.
40 You gave me strength in battle.
    You made my enemies bow before me.
41 You made my enemies turn back,
    and I destroyed those who hated me.
42 They called for help,
    but no one came to save them.
    They called to the LORD,

UNWAVERING FAITH

celebrate God's gift
of life

FAITH

By Chantelle Casey

2 SAMUEL 22:4

By being thankful for all the things we *get* to do rather than complaining about all the things we *have* to do, we take back the power that stress once had over us. When we anchor our perspective in being thankful for the activities that are part of God's gift of life to us, joy and peace rule in our lives instead of stress. Jesus' words instruct us: "Don't let your hearts be troubled or afraid."

My own perspective on life dramatically reduced my stress level after I met four-year-old Kary, who had been diagnosed with terminal cancer. As I watched this little ambassador of Christ brighten the lives of the people around him with his solid belief that God had a special plan for his life, he became my hero. Seeing little Kary's faith at work before he went home to be with Jesus increased my own faith.

Now, instead of worrying about all I *have* to do, I am happy about all I *get* to do as I pray for God's help. Why be downtrodden when there is so much to be happy about? Why worry when we can pray? Why complain when God has given us the gift of another day to live?

reflect: Are you willing to give thanks no matter the circumstances?
Go to **2 Thessalonians 2:13–15.**

but he did not answer them.
43 I beat my enemies into pieces,
like dust on the ground.
I poured them out and walked on them
like mud in the streets.

44 "You saved me when my people attacked
me.
You kept me as the leader of nations.
People I never knew serve me.
45 Foreigners obey me.
As soon as they hear me, they obey me.
46 They all become afraid
and tremble in their hiding places.

47 "The LORD lives!
May my Rock be praised!
Praise God, the Rock, who saves me!
48 God gives me victory over my enemies
and brings people under my rule.
49 He frees me from my enemies.

"You set me over those who hate me.
You saved me from violent people.
50 So I will praise you, LORD, among the
nations.
I will sing praises to your name.
51 The LORD gives great victories to his king.
He is loyal to his appointed king,
to David and his descendants forever."

DAVID'S LAST WORDS

23 These are the last words of David.
This is the message of David son of
Jesse.
The man made great by the Most High
God speaks.
He is the appointed king of the God of
Jacob;
he is the sweet singer of Israel:

2 "The LORD's Spirit spoke through me,
and his word was on my tongue.
3 The God of Israel spoke;
the Rock of Israel said to me:
'Whoever rules fairly over people,
who rules with respect for God,
4 is like the morning light at dawn,
like a morning without clouds.
He is like sunshine after a rain
that makes the grass sprout from the
ground.'

5 "This is how God has cared for my family.
God made a lasting agreement with me,
right and sure in every way.

He will accomplish my salvation
and satisfy all my desires.
6 "But all evil people will be thrown away
like thorns
that cannot be held in a hand.
7 No one can touch them
except with a tool of iron or wood.
They will be thrown in the fire and
burned where they lie."

DAVID'S ARMY

8 These are the names of David's warriors:
Josheb-Basshebeth, the Tahkemonite,
was head of the Three.[n] He killed eight hundred men at one time.

9 Next was Eleazar son of Dodai the
Ahohite. Eleazar was one of the three soldiers who were with David when they challenged the Philistines. The Philistines were
gathered for battle, and the Israelites drew
back. 10 But Eleazar stayed where he was and
fought the Philistines until he was so tired
his hand stuck to his sword. The LORD gave
a great victory for the Israelites that day. The
troops came back after Eleazar had won the
battle, but only to take weapons and armor
from the enemy.

11 Next there was Shammah son of Agee
the Hararite. The Philistines came together
to fight in a vegetable field. Israel's troops ran
away from the Philistines, 12 but Shammah
stood in the middle of the field and fought
for it and killed the Philistines. And the LORD
gave a great victory.

13 Once, three of the Thirty, David's chief
soldiers, came down to him at the cave of
Adullam during harvest. The Philistine army
had camped in the Valley of Rephaim. 14 At
that time David was in the stronghold, and
some of the Philistines were in Bethlehem.

15 David had a strong desire for some water. He said, "Oh, I wish someone would get
me water from the well near the city gate of
Bethlehem!" 16 So the three warriors broke
through the Philistine army and took water
from the well near the city gate of Bethlehem.
Then they brought it to David, but he refused
to drink it. He poured it out before the LORD,
17 saying, "May the LORD keep me from drink-

23:8 Three These were David's most powerful soldiers.
See 1 Chronicles 11:11.

ing this water! It would be like drinking the blood of the men who risked their lives!" So David refused to drink it. These were the brave things that the three warriors did.

[18]Abishai, brother of Joab son of Zeruiah, was captain of the Three. Abishai fought three hundred soldiers with his spear and killed them. He became as famous as the Three [19]and was more honored than the Three. He became their commander even though he was not one of them.

[20]Benaiah son of Jehoiada was a brave fighter from Kabzeel who did mighty things. He killed two of the best warriors from Moab. He also went down into a pit and killed a lion on a snowy day. [21]Benaiah killed a large Egyptian who had a spear in his hand. Benaiah had a club, but he grabbed the spear from the Egyptian's hand and killed him with his own spear. [22]These were the things Benaiah son of Jehoiada did. He was as famous as the Three. [23]He received more honor than the Thirty, but he did not become a member of the Three. David made him leader of his bodyguards.

THE THIRTY CHIEF SOLDIERS

[24]The following men were among the Thirty:

Asahel brother of Joab;
Elhanan son of Dodo from Bethlehem;
[25] Shammah the Harodite;
Elika the Harodite;
[26] Helez the Paltite;
Ira son of Ikkesh from Tekoa;
[27] Abiezer the Anathothite;
Mebunnai the Hushathite;
[28] Zalmon the Ahohite;
Maharai the Netophathite;
[29] Heled son of Baanah the Netophathite;
Ithai son of Ribai from Gibeah in Benjamin;
[30] Benaiah the Pirathonite;
Hiddai from the ravines of Gaash;
[31] Abi-Albon the Arbathite;
Azmaveth the Barhumite;
[32] Eliahba the Shaalbonite;
the sons of Jashen;
Jonathan [33]son of Shammah the Hararite;
Ahiam son of Sharar the Hararite;
[34] Eliphelet son of Ahasbai the Maacathite;

Eliam son of Ahithophel the Gilonite;
[35] Hezro the Carmelite;
Paarai the Arbite;
[36] Igal son of Nathan of Zobah;
the son of Hagri;
[37] Zelek the Ammonite;
Naharai the Beerothite, who carried the armor of Joab son of Zeruiah;
[38] Ira the Ithrite;
Gareb the Ithrite,
[39] and Uriah the Hittite.
There were thirty-seven in all.

DAVID COUNTS HIS ARMY

24 The LORD was angry with Israel again, and he caused David to turn against the Israelites. He said, "Go, count the people of Israel and Judah."

[2]So King David said to Joab, the commander of the army, "Go through all the tribes of Israel, from Dan to Beersheba,[n] and count the people. Then I will know how many there are."

[3]But Joab said to the king, "May the LORD your God give you a hundred times more people, and may my master the king live to see this happen. Why do you want to do this?"

[4]But the king commanded Joab and the commanders of the army, so they left the king to count the Israelites.

[5]After crossing the Jordan River, they camped near Aroer on the south side of the city in the ravine. They went through Gad and on to Jazer. [6]Then they went to Gilead and the land of Tahtim Hodshi and to Dan Jaan and around to Sidon. [7]They went to the strong, walled city of Tyre and to all the cities of the Hivites and Canaanites. Finally, they went to southern Judah, to Beersheba. [8]After nine months and twenty days, they had gone through all the land. Then they came back to Jerusalem.

[9]Joab gave the list of the people to the king. There were eight hundred thousand men in Israel who could use the sword and five hundred thousand men in Judah.

[10]David felt ashamed after he had counted the people. He said to the LORD, "I have

---

24:2 Dan to Beersheba Dan was the city farthest north in Israel, and Beersheba was the city farthest south. So this means all the people of Israel.

sinned greatly by what I have done. LORD, I beg you to forgive me, your servant, because I have been very foolish."

[11]When David got up in the morning, the LORD spoke his word to Gad, who was a prophet and David's seer. [12]The LORD told Gad, "Go and tell David, 'This is what the LORD says: I offer you three choices. Choose one of them and I will do it to you.'"

[13]So Gad went to David and said to him, "Should three years of hunger come to you and your land? Or should your enemies chase you for three months? Or should there be three days of disease in your land? Think about it. Then decide which of these things I should tell the LORD who sent me."

[14]David said to Gad, "I am in great trouble. Let the LORD punish us, because the LORD is very merciful. Don't let my punishment come from human beings!"

[15]So the LORD sent a terrible disease on Israel. It began in the morning and continued until the chosen time to stop. From Dan to Beersheba seventy thousand people died. [16]When the angel raised his arm toward Jerusalem to destroy it, the LORD felt very sorry about the terrible things that had happened. He said to the angel who was destroying the people, "That is enough! Put down your arm!" The angel of the LORD was then by the threshing floor of Araunah the Jebusite.

[17]When David saw the angel that killed the people, he said to the LORD, "I am the one who sinned and did wrong. These people only followed me like sheep. They did nothing wrong. Please punish me and my family."

[18]That day Gad came to David and said, "Go and build an altar to the LORD on the threshing floor of Araunah the Jebusite." [19]So David did what Gad told him to do, just as the LORD commanded.

[20]Araunah looked and saw the king and his servants coming to him. So he went out and bowed facedown on the ground before the king. [21]He said, "Why has my master the king come to me?"

David answered, "To buy the threshing floor from you so I can build an altar to the LORD. Then the terrible disease will stop."

[22]Araunah said to David, "My master and king, you may take anything you want for a sacrifice. Here are some oxen for the whole burnt offering and the threshing boards and the yokes for the wood. [23]My king, I give everything to you." Araunah also said to the king, "May the LORD your God be pleased with you."

[24]But the king answered Araunah, "No, I will pay you for the land. I won't offer to the LORD my God burnt offerings that cost me nothing."

So David bought the threshing floor and the oxen for one and one-fourth pounds of silver. [25]He built an altar to the LORD there and offered whole burnt offerings and fellowship offerings. Then the LORD answered his prayer for the country, and the disease in Israel stopped.

ADONIJAH TRIES TO BECOME KING

1 At this time King David was very old, and although his servants covered him with blankets, he could not keep warm. ²They said to him, "We will look for a young woman to care for you. She will lie close to you and keep you warm." ³After searching everywhere in Israel for a beautiful young woman, they found a girl named Abishag from Shunam and brought her to the king. ⁴The girl was very beautiful, and she cared for the king and served him. But the king did not have sexual relations with her.

⁵Adonijah was the son of King David and Haggith, and he was very proud. "I will be the king," he said. So he got chariots and horses for himself and fifty men for his personal bodyguard. ⁶Now David had never interfered with Adonijah by questioning what he did. Born next after Absalom, Adonijah was a very handsome man.

⁷Adonijah spoke with Joab son of Zeruiah and Abiathar the priest, and they agreed to help him. ⁸But Zadok the priest, Benaiah son of Jehoiada, Nathan the prophet, Shimei, Rei, and King David's special guard did not join Adonijah.

⁹Then Adonijah killed some sheep, cows, and fat calves for sacrifices at the Stone of Zoheleth near the spring of Rogel. He invited all his brothers, the other sons of King David, to come, as well as all the men of Judah. ¹⁰But Adonijah did not invite Nathan the prophet, Benaiah, his father's special guard, or his brother Solomon.

¹¹When Nathan heard about this, he went to Bathsheba, Solomon's mother. "Have you heard that Adonijah, Haggith's son, has made himself king?" Nathan asked. "Our real king, David, does not know it. ¹²I strongly advise you to save yourself and your sons. ¹³Go to King David and tell him, 'My master and king, you promised that my son Solomon would be king and would rule on your throne after you. Why then has Adonijah become king?' ¹⁴While you are still talking to the king, I will come in and tell him that what you have said about Adonijah is true."

¹⁵So Bathsheba went in to see the aged king in his bedroom, where Abishag, the girl from Shunam, was caring for him. ¹⁶Bathsheba bowed and knelt before the king. He asked, "What do you want?"

¹⁷She answered, "My master, you made a promise to me in the name of the LORD your God. You said, 'Your son Solomon will become king after me, and he will rule on my throne.' ¹⁸But now, unknown to you, Adonijah has become king. ¹⁹He has killed many cows, fat calves, and sheep for sacrifices. And he has invited all your sons, as well as Abiathar the priest and Joab the commander of the army, but he did not invite Solomon, who serves you. ²⁰My master and king, all the Israelites are watching you, waiting for you to decide who will be king after you. ²¹As soon as you die, Solomon and I will be treated as criminals."

²²While Bathsheba was still talking with the king, Nathan the prophet arrived. ²³The servants told the king, "Nathan the prophet is here." So Nathan went to the king and bowed facedown on the ground before him.

²⁴Nathan said, "My master and king, have you said that Adonijah will be the king after you and that he will rule on your throne? ²⁵Today he has sacrificed many cows, fat calves, and sheep, and he has invited all your other sons, the commanders of the army, and Abiathar the priest. Right now they are eating and drinking with him. They are saying, 'Long live King Adonijah!' ²⁶But he did not invite me, your own servant, or Zadok the priest, or Benaiah son of Jehoiada, or your son Solomon. ²⁷Did you do this? Since we are your servants, why didn't you tell us who should be king after you?"

DAVID MAKES SOLOMON KING

²⁸Then the king said, "Tell Bathsheba to come in!" So she came in and stood before the king.

²⁹Then the king made this promise, "The LORD has saved me from all trouble. As surely as he lives, ³⁰I will do today what I have promised you in the name of the LORD, the God of Israel. I promised that your son Solomon would be king after me and rule on my throne in my place."

³¹Then Bathsheba bowed facedown on the ground and knelt before the king and said, "Long live my master King David!"

³²Then King David said, "Tell Zadok the priest, Nathan the prophet, and Benaiah son of Jehoiada to come in." When they came before the king, ³³he said to them, "Take my servants with you and put my son Solomon on my own mule. Take him down to the spring called Gihon. ³⁴There Zadok the priest and Nathan the prophet should pour olive oil on him and make him king over Israel. Blow the trumpet and shout, 'Long live King Solomon!' ³⁵Then come back up here with him. He will sit on my throne and rule in my place, because he is the one I have chosen to be the ruler over Israel and Judah."

³⁶Benaiah son of Jehoiada answered the king, "Amen! This is what the LORD, the God of my master, has declared! ³⁷The LORD has always helped you, our king. May he also help Solomon and make King Solomon's throne an even greater throne than yours."

³⁸So Zadok the priest, Nathan the prophet, and Benaiah son of Jehoiada left with the Kerethites and Pelethites.ⁿ They put Solomon on King David's mule and took him to the spring called Gihon. ³⁹Zadok the priest took the container of olive oil from the Holy Tent and poured the oil on Solomon's head to show he was the king. Then they blew the trumpet, and all the people shouted, "Long live King Solomon!" ⁴⁰All the people followed Solomon into the city. Playing flutes and shouting for joy, they made so much noise the ground shook.

⁴¹At this time Adonijah and all the guests with him were finishing their meal. When he heard the sound from the trumpet, Joab asked, "What does all that noise from the city mean?"

⁴²While Joab was speaking, Jonathan son of Abiathar the priest arrived. Adonijah said, "Come in! You are an important man, so you must be bringing good news."

⁴³But Jonathan answered, "No! Our master King David has made Solomon the new king. ⁴⁴King David sent Zadok the priest, Nathan the prophet, Benaiah son of Jehoiada, and all the king's bodyguards with him, and they have put Solomon on the king's own mule. ⁴⁵Then Zadok the priest and Nathan the prophet poured olive oil on Solomon at Gihon to make him king. After that they went into the city, shouting with joy. Now the whole city is excited, and that is the noise you hear. ⁴⁶Solomon has now become the king. ⁴⁷All the king's officers have come to tell King David that he has done a good thing. They are saying, 'May your God make Solomon even more famous than you and an even greater king than you.'" Jonathan continued, "And King David bowed down on his bed to worship God, ⁴⁸saying, 'Bless the LORD, the God of Israel. Today he has made one of my sons the king and allowed me to see it.'"

⁴⁹Then all of Adonijah's guests were afraid, and they left quickly and scattered. ⁵⁰Adonijah was also afraid of Solomon, so he went and took hold of the corners of the altar.ⁿ ⁵¹Then someone told Solomon, "Adonijah is afraid of you, so he is at the altar, holding on to its corners. He says, 'Tell King Solomon to promise me today that he will not kill me.'"

⁵²So Solomon answered, "Adonijah must show that he is a man of honor. If he does that, I promise he will not lose even a single hair from his head. But if he does anything wrong, he will die." ⁵³Then King Solomon sent some men to get Adonijah. When he was brought from the altar, he came before King Solomon and bowed down. Solomon told him, "Go home."

THE DEATH OF DAVID

2 Since it was almost time for David to die, he gave his son Solomon his last commands. ²David said, "My time to die is near. Be a good and strong leader. ³Obey the LORD your God. Follow him by obeying his demands, his commands, his laws, and his rules

---

1:38 Kerethites and Pelethites These were probably special units of the army that were responsible for the king's safety, a kind of palace guard. **1:50 corners of the altar** If a person was innocent of a crime, he could run into the Holy Place where the altar was. If he held on to the corners of the altar, which looked like horns, he would be safe.

that are written in the teachings of Moses. If you do these things, you will be successful in all you do and wherever you go. 4And if you obey the LORD, he will keep the promise he made to me. He said: 'If your descendants live as I tell them and have complete faith in me, a man from your family will always be king over the people of Israel.'

5"Also, you remember what Joab son of Zeruiah did to me. He killed the two commanders of Israel's armies: Abner son of Ner and Amasa son of Jether. He did this as if he and they were at war, although it was a time of peace. He put their blood on the belt around his waist and on his sandals on his feet. 6Punish him in the way you think is wisest, but do not let him die peacefully of old age.

7"Be kind to the children of Barzillai of Gilead, and allow them to eat at your table. They welcomed me when I ran away from your brother Absalom.

8"And remember, Shimei son of Gera, the Benjaminite, is here with you. He cursed me the day I went to Mahanaim. But when he came down to meet me at the Jordan River, I promised him before the Lord, 'Shimei, I will not kill you.' 9But you should not leave him unpunished. You are a wise man, and you will know what to do to him, but you must be sure he is killed."

10Then David died and was buried with his ancestors in Jerusalem. 11He had ruled over Israel forty years—seven years in Hebron and thirty-three years in Jerusalem.

SOLOMON TAKES CONTROL AS KING

12Solomon became king after David, his father, and he was in firm control of his kingdom.

13At this time Adonijah son of Haggith went to Bathsheba, Solomon's mother. "Do you come in peace?" Bathsheba asked.

"Yes. This is a peaceful visit," Adonijah answered. 14"I have something to say to you."

"You may speak," she said.

15"You remember that at one time the kingdom was mine," Adonijah said. "All the people of Israel recognized me as their king, but things have changed. Now my brother is the king, because the LORD chose him. 16Now I have one thing to ask you; please do not refuse me."

Bathsheba answered, "What do you want?"

17"I know King Solomon will do anything you ask him," Adonijah continued. "Please ask him to give me Abishag the Shunammite to be my wife."

18"Very well," she answered. "I will speak to the king for you."

19So Bathsheba went to King Solomon to speak to him for Adonijah. When Solomon saw her, he stood up to meet her, then bowed down, and sat on the throne. He told some servants to bring another throne for his mother. Then she sat down at his right side.

20Bathsheba said, "I have one small thing to ask you. Please do not refuse me."

"Ask, mother," the king answered. "I will not refuse you."

21So she said, "Allow Abishag the Shunammite to marry your brother Adonijah."

22King Solomon answered his mother, "Why do you ask me to give him Abishag? Why don't you also ask for him to become the king since he is my older brother? Abiathar the priest and Joab son of Zeruiah would support him!"

23Then King Solomon swore by the name of the LORD, saying, "May God punish me terribly if this doesn't cost Adonijah his life! 24By the LORD who has given me the throne that belonged to my father David and who has kept his promise and given the kingdom to me and my people, Adonijah will die today!" 25Then King Solomon gave orders to Benaiah son of Jehoiada, and he went and killed Adonijah.

26King Solomon said to Abiathar the priest, "I should kill you too, but I will allow you to go back to your fields in Anathoth. I will not kill you at this time, because you helped carry the Ark of the Lord GOD while marching with my father David. And I know you shared in all the hard times with him." 27Then Solomon removed Abiathar from being the LORD's priest. This happened as the LORD had said it would, when he was speaking in Shiloh about the priest Eli and his descendants.

28When Joab heard about what had happened, he was afraid. He had supported Adonijah but not Absalom. So Joab ran to the Tent of the LORD and took hold of the corners of the altar.ⁿ ²⁹Someone told King Solomon that Joab had run to the Tent of the LORD and was beside the altar. Then Solomon ordered Benaiah to go and kill him.

³⁰Benaiah went into the Tent of the LORD and said to Joab, "The king says, 'Come out!'"

But Joab answered, "No, I will die here."

So Benaiah went back to the king and told him what Joab had said. ³¹Then the king ordered Benaiah, "Do as he says! Kill him there and bury him. Then my family and I will be free of the guilt of Joab, who has killed innocent people. ³²Without my father knowing it, he killed two men who were much better than he was—Abner son of Ner, the commander of Israel's army, and Amasa son of Jether, the commander of Judah's army. So the LORD will pay him back for those deaths. ³³Joab and his family will be forever guilty for their deaths, but there will be peace from the LORD for David, his descendants, his family, and his throne forever."

³⁴So Benaiah son of Jehoiada killed Joab, and he was buried near his home in the desert. ³⁵The king then made Benaiah son of Jehoiada commander of the army in Joab's place. He also made Zadok the new high priest in Abiathar's place.

³⁶Next the king sent for Shimei. Solomon said to him, "Build a house for yourself in Jerusalem and live there. Don't leave the city. ³⁷The very day you leave and cross the Kidron Valley, someone will kill you, and it will be your own fault."

³⁸So Shimei answered the king, "I agree with what you say. I will do what you say, my master and king." So Shimei lived in Jerusalem for a long time.

³⁹But three years later two of Shimei's slaves ran away to Achish king of Gath, who was the son of Maacah. Shimei heard that his slaves were in Gath, ⁴⁰so he put his saddle on his donkey and went to Achish at Gath to find them. Then he brought them back from Gath.

⁴¹Someone told Solomon that Shimei had gone from Jerusalem to Gath and had returned. ⁴²So Solomon sent for Shimei and said, "I made you promise in the name of the LORD not to leave Jerusalem. I warned you if you went out anywhere you would die, and you agreed to what I said. ⁴³Why did you

break your promise to the LORD and disobey my command?" ⁴⁴The king also said, "You know the many wrong things you did to my father David, so now the LORD will punish you for those wrongs. ⁴⁵But the LORD will bless me and make the rule of David safe before the LORD forever."

⁴⁶Then the king ordered Benaiah to kill Shimei, and he did. Now Solomon was in full control of his kingdom.

SOLOMON ASKS FOR WISDOM

3 Solomon made an agreement with the king of Egypt by marrying his daughter and bringing her to Jerusalem. At this time Solomon was still building his palace and the Temple of the LORD, as well as a wall around Jerusalem. ²The Temple for the worship of the LORD had not yet been finished, so people were still sacrificing at altars in many places of worship. ³Solomon showed he loved the LORD by following the commands his father David had given him, except many other places of worship were still used to offer sacrifices and to burn incense.

⁴King Solomon went to Gibeon to offer a sacrifice, because it was the most important place of worship. He offered a thousand burnt offerings on that altar. ⁵While he was at Gibeon, the LORD appeared to him in a dream during the night. God said, "Ask for whatever you want me to give you."

⁶Solomon answered, "You were very kind to your servant, my father David. He obeyed you, and he was honest and lived right. You showed great kindness to him when you allowed his son to be king after him. ⁷LORD my God, now you have made me, your servant, king in my father's place. But I am like a little child; I don't know how to do what must be done. ⁸I, your servant, am here among your chosen people, and there are too many of them to count. ⁹I ask that you give me a heart that understands, so I can rule the people in the right way and will know the difference between right and wrong. Otherwise, it is impossible to rule this great people of yours."

¹⁰The Lord was pleased that Solomon had

2:28 corners of the altar If a person were innocent of a crime, he could run into the Holy Place where the altar was. If he held on to the corners of the altar, which looked like horns, he would be safe.

asked this. ¹¹So God said to him, "You did not ask for a long life, or riches for yourself, or the death of your enemies. Since you asked for wisdom to make the right decisions, ¹²I will do what you asked. I will give you wisdom and understanding that is greater than anyone has had in the past or will have in the future. ¹³I will also give you what you did not ask for: riches and honor. During your life no other king will be as great as you. ¹⁴If you follow me and obey my laws and commands, as your father David did, I will also give you a long life."

¹⁵After Solomon woke up from the dream, he went to Jerusalem. He stood before the Ark of the Agreement with the LORD, where he made burnt offerings and fellowship offerings. After that, he gave a feast for all his leaders and officers.

SOLOMON MAKES A WISE DECISION

¹⁶One day two women who were prostitutes came to Solomon. As they stood before him, ¹⁷one of the women said, "My master, this woman and I live in the same house. I gave birth to a baby while she was there with me. ¹⁸Three days later this woman also gave birth to a baby. No one else was in the house with us; it was just the two of us. ¹⁹One night this woman rolled over on her baby, and he died. ²⁰So she took my son from my bed during the night while I was asleep, and she carried him to her bed. Then she put the dead baby in my bed. ²¹The next morning when I got up to feed my baby, I saw that he was dead! When I looked at him more closely, I realized he was not my son."

²²"No!" the other woman cried. "The living baby is my son, and the dead baby is yours!"

But the first woman said, "No! The dead baby is yours, and the living one is mine!" So the two women argued before the king.

²³Then King Solomon said, "One of you says, 'My son is alive and your son is dead.' Then the other one says, 'No! Your son is dead and my son is alive.'"

²⁴The king sent his servants to get a sword. When they brought it to him, ²⁵he said, "Cut the living baby into two pieces, and give each woman half."

²⁶The real mother of the living child was full of love for her son. So she said to the king,

"Please, my master, don't kill him! Give the baby to her!"

But the other woman said, "Neither of us will have him. Cut him into two pieces!"

²⁷Then King Solomon said, "Don't kill him. Give the baby to the first woman, because she is the real mother."

²⁸When the people of Israel heard about King Solomon's decision, they respected him very much. They saw he had wisdom from God to make the right decisions.

SOLOMON'S OFFICERS

4 King Solomon ruled over all Israel. ²These are the names of his leading officers:

Azariah son of Zadok was the priest;

³Elihoreph and Ahijah, sons of Shisha, recorded what happened in the courts;

Jehoshaphat son of Ahilud recorded the history of the people;

⁴Benaiah son of Jehoiada was commander of the army;

Zadok and Abiathar were priests;

⁵Azariah son of Nathan was in charge of the district governors;

Zabud son of Nathan was a priest and adviser to the king;

⁶Ahishar was responsible for everything in the palace;

Adoniram son of Abda was in charge of the labor force.

⁷Solomon placed twelve governors over the districts of Israel, who gathered food from their districts for the king and his family. Each governor was responsible for bringing food to the king one month of each year. ⁸These are the names of the twelve governors:

Ben-Hur was governor of the mountain country of Ephraim.

⁹Ben-Deker was governor of Makaz, Shaalbim, Beth Shemesh, and Elon Bethhanan.

¹⁰Ben-Hesed was governor of Arubboth, Socoh, and all the land of Hepher.

¹¹Ben-Abinadab was governor of Naphoth Dor. (He was married to Taphath, Solomon's daughter.)

¹²Baana son of Ahilud was governor of Taanach, Megiddo, and all of Beth Shan next to Zarethan. This was below Jezreel from

Beth Shan to Abel Meholah across from Jokmeam.

13Ben-Geber was governor of Ramoth in Gilead. (He was governor of all the towns of Jair in Gilead. Jair was the son of Manasseh. Ben-Geber was also over the district of Argob in Bashan, which had sixty large, walled cities with bronze bars on their gates.)

14Ahinadab son of Iddo was governor of Mahanaim.

15Ahimaaz was governor of Naphtali. (He was married to Basemath, Solomon's daughter.)

16Baana son of Hushai was governor of Asher and Aloth.

17Jehoshaphat son of Paruah was governor of Issachar.

18Shimei son of Ela was governor of Benjamin.

19Geber son of Uri was governor of Gilead. Gilead had been the country of Sihon king of the Amorites and Og king of Bashan. But Geber was the only governor over this district.

SOLOMON'S KINGDOM

20There were as many people in Judah and Israel as grains of sand on the seashore. The people ate, drank, and were happy. 21Solomon ruled over all the kingdoms from the Euphrates River to the land of the Philistines, as far as the border of Egypt. These countries brought Solomon the payments he demanded, and they were under his control all his life.

22Solomon needed much food each day to feed himself and all the people who ate at his table: one hundred ninety-five bushels of fine flour, three hundred ninety bushels of grain, 23ten cows that were fed on good grain, twenty cows that were raised in the fields, one hundred sheep, three kinds of deer, and fattened birds.

24Solomon controlled all the countries west of the Euphrates River—the land from Tiphsah to Gaza. And he had peace on all sides of his kingdom. 25During Solomon's life Judah and Israel, from Dan to Beersheba,[n] also lived in peace; all of his people were able to sit under their own fig trees and grapevines.

26Solomon had four thousand stalls for his chariot horses and twelve thousand horses. 27Each month one of the district governors gave King Solomon all the food he needed—enough for every person who ate at the king's table. The governors made sure he had everything he needed. 28They also brought enough barley and straw for Solomon's chariot and work horses; each person brought this grain to the right place.

SOLOMON'S WISDOM

29God gave Solomon great wisdom so he could understand many things. His wisdom was as hard to measure as the grains of sand on the seashore. 30His wisdom was greater than any wisdom of the East, or any wisdom in Egypt. 31He was wiser than anyone on earth. He was even wiser than Ethan the Ezrahite, as well as Heman, Calcol, and Darda—the three sons of Mahol. King Solomon became famous in all the surrounding countries. 32During his life he spoke three thousand wise sayings and also wrote one thousand five songs. 33He taught about many kinds of plants—everything from the great cedar trees of Lebanon to the weeds that grow out of the walls. He also taught about animals, birds, crawling things, and fish. 34People from all nations came to listen to King Solomon's wisdom. The kings of all nations sent them to him, because they had heard of Solomon's wisdom.

PREPARING TO BUILD THE TEMPLE

5 Hiram, the king of Tyre, had always been David's friend. When Hiram heard that Solomon had been made king in David's place, he sent his messengers to Solomon. 2Solomon sent this message back to King Hiram: 3"You remember my father David had to fight many wars with the countries around him, so he was never able to build a temple for worshiping the LORD his God. David was waiting until the LORD allowed him to defeat all his enemies. 4But now the LORD my God has given me peace on all sides of my country. I have no enemies now, and no danger threatens my people.

5"The LORD promised my father David, 'I will make your son king after you, and he will build a temple for worshiping me.' Now, I plan to build that temple for worshiping

---

4:25 Dan to Beersheba Dan was the city farthest north in Israel, and Beersheba was the city farthest south. So this means all the people of Israel.

the LORD my God. ⁶So send your men to cut down cedar trees for me from Lebanon. My servants will work with yours, and I will pay them whatever wages you decide. We don't have anyone who can cut down trees as well as the people of Sidon."

⁷When Hiram heard what Solomon asked, he was very happy. He said, "Praise the LORD today! He has given David a wise son to rule over this great nation!" ⁸Then Hiram sent back this message to Solomon: "I received the message you sent, and I will give you all the cedar and pine trees you want. ⁹My servants will bring them down from Lebanon to the sea. There I will tie them together and float them along the shore to the place you choose. Then I will separate the logs there, and you can take them away. In return it is my wish that you give food to all those who live with me." ¹⁰So Hiram gave Solomon as much cedar and pine as he wanted. ¹¹And Solomon gave Hiram about one hundred twenty-five thousand bushels of wheat each year to feed the people who lived with him. Solomon also gave him about one hundred fifteen thousand gallons of pure olive oil every year.

¹²The LORD gave Solomon wisdom as he had promised. And there was peace between Hiram and Solomon; these two kings made a treaty between themselves.

¹³King Solomon forced thirty thousand men of Israel to help in this work. ¹⁴He sent a group of ten thousand men each month to Lebanon. Each group worked in Lebanon one month, then went home for two months. A man named Adoniram was in charge. ¹⁵Solomon forced eighty thousand men to work in the hill country, cutting stone, and he had seventy thousand men to carry the stones. ¹⁶There were also thirty-three hundred men who directed the workers. ¹⁷King Solomon commanded them to cut large blocks of fine stone to be used for the foundation of the Temple. ¹⁸Solomon's and Hiram's builders and the men from Byblos carved the stones and prepared the stones and the logs for building the Temple.

SOLOMON BUILDS THE TEMPLE

6 Solomon began to build the Temple four hundred eighty years after the people of Israel had left Egypt. This was during the fourth year of King Solomon's rule over Is-

rael. It was the second month, the month of Ziv.

²The Temple was ninety feet long, thirty feet wide, and forty-five feet high. ³The porch in front of the main room of the Temple was fifteen feet deep and thirty feet wide. This room ran along the front of the Temple itself. Its width was equal to that of the Temple. ⁴The Temple also had windows that opened and closed. ⁵Solomon also built some side rooms against the walls of the main room and the inner room of the Temple. He built rooms all around. ⁶The rooms on the bottom floor were seven and one-half feet wide. Those on the middle floor were nine feet wide, and the rooms above them were ten and one-half feet wide. The Temple wall that formed the side of each room was thinner than the wall in the room below. These rooms were pushed against the Temple wall, but they did not have their main beams built into this wall.

⁷The stones were prepared at the same place where they were cut from the ground. Since these stones were the only ones used to build the Temple, there was no noise of hammers, axes, or any other iron tools at the Temple.

⁸The entrance to the lower rooms beside the Temple was on the south side. From there, stairs went up to the second-floor rooms. And from there, stairs went on to the third-floor rooms. ⁹Solomon put a roof made from beams and cedar boards on the Temple. So he finished building the Temple ¹⁰as well as the bottom floor that was beside the Temple. This bottom floor was seven and one-half feet high and was attached to the Temple by cedar beams.

¹¹The LORD said to Solomon: ¹²"If you obey all my laws and commands, I will do for you what I promised your father David. ¹³I will live among the Israelites in this Temple, and I will never leave my people Israel."

¹⁴So Solomon finished building the Temple. ¹⁵The inside walls were covered from floor to ceiling with cedar boards. The floor was made from pine boards. ¹⁶A room thirty feet long was built in the back part of the Temple. This room, called the Most Holy Place, was separated from the rest of the Temple by cedar boards which reached from floor to ceiling. ¹⁷The main room, the one in

front of the Most Holy Place, was sixty feet long. ¹⁸Everything inside the Temple was covered with cedar, which was carved with pictures of flowers and plants. A person could not see the stones of the wall, only the cedar.

¹⁹Solomon prepared the inner room at the back of the Temple to keep the Ark of the Agreement with the LORD. ²⁰This inner room was thirty feet long, thirty feet wide, and thirty feet high. He covered this room with pure gold, and he also covered the altar of cedar. ²¹He covered the inside of the Temple with pure gold, placing gold chains across the front of the inner room, which was also covered with gold. ²²So all the inside of the Temple, as well as the altar of the Most Holy Place, was covered with gold.

²³Solomon made two creatures from olive wood and placed them in the Most Holy Place. Each creature was fifteen feet tall ²⁴and had two wings. Each wing was seven and one-half feet long, so it was fifteen feet from the end of one wing to the end of the other. ²⁵The creatures were the same size and shape; ²⁶each was fifteen feet tall. ²⁷These creatures were put beside each other in the Most Holy Place with their wings spread out. One creature's wing touched one wall, and the other creature's wing touched the other wall with their wings touching each other in the middle of the room. ²⁸These two creatures were covered with gold.

²⁹All the walls around the Temple were carved with pictures of creatures with wings, as well as palm trees and flowers. This was true for both the main room and the inner room. ³⁰The floors of both rooms were covered with gold.

³¹Doors made from olive wood were placed at the entrance to the Most Holy Place. These doors had five-sided frames. ³²Creatures with wings, as well as palm trees and flowers, were also carved on the two olive wood doors that were covered with gold. The creatures and the palm trees on the doors were covered with gold as well. ³³At the entrance to the main room there was a square door frame made of olive wood. ³⁴Two doors were made from pine. Each door had two parts so the doors folded. ³⁵The doors were covered with pictures of creatures with wings, as well as palm trees and flowers.

All of the carvings were covered with gold, which was evenly spread over them.

³⁶The inner courtyard was enclosed by walls, which were made of three rows of cut stones and one row of cedar boards.

³⁷Work began on the Temple in Ziv, the second month, during the fourth year Solomon was king over Israel. ³⁸The Temple was finished during the eleventh year he was king, in the eighth month, the month of Bul. It was built exactly as it was planned. Solomon had spent seven years building it.

SOLOMON'S PALACE

7 King Solomon also built a palace for himself; it took him thirteen years to finish it. ²Built of cedars from the Forest of Lebanon, it was one hundred fifty feet long, seventy-five feet wide, and forty-five feet high. It had four rows of cedar columns which supported the cedar beams. ³There were forty-five beams on the roof, with fifteen beams in each row, and the ceiling was covered with cedar above the beams. ⁴Windows were placed in three rows facing each other. ⁵All the doors were square, and the three doors at each end faced each other.

⁶Solomon also built the porch that had pillars. This porch was seventy-five feet long and forty-five feet wide. Along the front of the porch was a roof supported by pillars.

⁷Solomon also built a throne room where he judged people, called the Hall of Justice. This room was covered with cedar from the floor to the ceiling. ⁸The palace where Solomon lived was built like the Hall of Justice, and it was behind this hall. Solomon also built the same kind of palace for his wife, who was the daughter of the king of Egypt.

⁹All these buildings were made with blocks of fine stone. First they were carefully cut. Then they were trimmed with a saw in the front and back. These fine stones went from the foundations of the buildings to the top of the walls. Even the courtyard was made with blocks of stone. ¹⁰The foundations were made with large blocks of fine stone, some as long as fifteen feet. Others were twelve feet long. ¹¹On top of these foundation stones were other blocks of fine stone and cedar beams. ¹²The palace courtyard, the courtyard inside the Temple, and the porch of the Temple were surrounded by walls. All

of these walls had three rows of stone blocks and one row of cedar beams.

THE TEMPLE IS COMPLETED INSIDE

¹³King Solomon sent to Tyre and had Huram brought to him. ¹⁴Huram's mother was a widow from the tribe of Naphtali. His father was from Tyre and had been skilled in making things from bronze. Huram was also very skilled and experienced in bronze work. So he came to King Solomon and did all the bronze work.

¹⁵He made two bronze pillars, each one twenty-seven feet tall and eighteen feet around. ¹⁶He also made two bronze capitals that were seven and one-half feet tall, and he put them on top of the pillars. ¹⁷Then he made a net of seven chains for each capital, which covered the capitals on top of the two pillars. ¹⁸He made two rows of bronze pomegranates to go on the nets. These covered the capitals at the top of the pillars. ¹⁹The capitals on top of the pillars in the porch were shaped like lilies, and they were six feet tall. ²⁰The capitals were on top of both pillars, above the bowl-shaped section and next to the nets. At that place there were two hundred pomegranates in rows all around the capitals. ²¹Huram put these two bronze pillars at the porch of the Temple. He named the south pillar He Establishes and the north pillar In Him Is Strength. ²²The capitals on top of the pillars were shaped like lilies. So the work on the pillars was finished.

²³Then Huram made from bronze a large round bowl, which was called the Sea. It was forty-five feet around, fifteen feet across, and seven and one-half feet deep. ²⁴Around the outer edge of the bowl was a rim. Under this rim were two rows of bronze plants which surrounded the bowl. There were ten plants every eighteen inches, and these plants were made in one piece with the bowl. ²⁵The bowl rested on the backs of twelve bronze bulls that faced outward from the center of the bowl. Three bulls faced north, three faced west, three faced south, and three faced east. ²⁶The sides of the bowl were four inches thick, and it held about eleven thousand gallons. The rim of the bowl was like the rim of a cup or like a lily blossom.

²⁷Then Huram made ten bronze stands, each one six feet long, six feet wide, and four and one-half feet high. ²⁸The stands were made from square sides, which were put on frames. ²⁹On the sides were bronze lions, bulls, and creatures with wings. On the frames above and below the lions and bulls were designs of flowers hammered into the bronze. ³⁰Each stand had four bronze wheels with bronze axles. At the corners there were bronze supports for a large bowl, and the supports had designs of flowers. ³¹There was a frame on top of the bowls, eighteen inches high above the bowls. The opening of the bowl was round, twenty-seven inches deep. Designs were carved into the bronze on the frame, which was square, not round. ³²The four wheels, placed under the frame, were twenty-seven inches high. The axles between the wheels were made as one piece with the stand. ³³The wheels were like a chariot's wheels. Everything on the wheels— the axles, rims, spokes, and hubs—were made of bronze.

³⁴The four supports were on the four corners of each stand. They were made as one piece with the stand. ³⁵A strip of bronze around the top of each stand was nine inches deep. It was also made as one piece with the stand. ³⁶The sides of the stand and the frames were covered with carvings of creatures with wings, as well as lions, palm trees, and flowers. ³⁷This is the way Huram made the ten stands. The bronze for each stand was melted and poured into a mold, so all the stands were the same size and shape.

³⁸Huram also made ten bronze bowls, one bowl for each of the ten stands. Each bowl was six feet across and could hold about two hundred thirty gallons. ³⁹Huram put five stands on the south side of the Temple and five on the north side. He put the large bowl in the southeast corner of the Temple. ⁴⁰Huram also made bowls, shovels, and small bowls.

So Huram finished all his work for King Solomon on the Temple of the Lord:
⁴¹two pillars;
   two large bowls for the capitals on top of the pillars;
   two nets to cover the two large bowls for the capitals on top of the pillars;
⁴²four hundred pomegranates for the two nets (there were two rows of pomegranates for each net covering the

bowls for the capitals on top of the pillars);

43 ten stands with a bowl on each stand;

44 the large bowl with twelve bulls under it;

45 the pots, shovels, small bowls, and all the utensils for the Temple of the LORD.

Huram made everything King Solomon wanted from polished bronze. 46The king had these things poured into clay molds that were made in the plain of the Jordan River between Succoth and Zarethan. 47Solomon never weighed the bronze used to make these things, because there was too much to weigh. So the total weight of all the bronze was never known.

48Solomon also made all the items for the Temple of the LORD:

the golden altar;

the golden table which held the bread that shows God's people are in his presence;

49 the lampstands of pure gold (five on the right side and five on the left side in front of the Most Holy Place);

the flowers, lamps, and tongs of gold;

50 the pure gold bowls, wick trimmers, small bowls, pans, and dishes used to carry coals;

the gold hinges for the doors of the Most Holy Place and the main room of the Temple.

51Finally the work King Solomon did for the Temple of the LORD was finished. Solomon brought in everything his father David had set apart for the Temple—silver, gold, and other articles. He put everything in the treasuries of the Temple of the LORD.

THE ARK IS BROUGHT INTO THE TEMPLE

8 King Solomon called for the elders of Israel, the heads of the tribes, and the leaders of the families to come to him in Jerusalem. He wanted them to bring the Ark of the Agreement with the LORD from the older part of the city. 2So all the Israelites came together with King Solomon during the festival in the month of Ethanim, the seventh month.

3When all the elders of Israel arrived, the priests lifted up the Ark. 4They carried the Ark of the LORD, the Meeting Tent, and the holy utensils; the priests and the Levites brought them up. 5King Solomon and all the Israelites gathered before the Ark and sacrificed so many sheep and cattle no one could count them all. 6Then the priests put the Ark of the Agreement with the LORD in its place inside the Most Holy Place in the Temple, under the wings of the golden creatures. 7The wings of these creatures were spread out over the place for the Ark, covering it and its carrying poles. 8The carrying poles were so long that anyone standing in the Holy Place in front of the Most Holy Place could see the ends of the poles, but no one could see them from outside the Holy Place. The poles are still there today. 9The only things inside the Ark were two stone tablets[n] that Moses had put in the Ark at Mount Sinai. That was where the LORD made his agreement with the Israelites after they came out of Egypt.

10When the priests left the Holy Place, a cloud filled the Temple of the LORD. 11The priests could not continue their work, because the Temple was filled with the glory of the LORD.

SOLOMON SPEAKS TO THE PEOPLE

12Then Solomon said, "The LORD said he would live in a dark cloud. 13LORD, I have truly built a wonderful Temple for you—a place for you to live forever."

14While all the Israelites were standing there, King Solomon turned to them and blessed them.

15Then he said, "Praise the LORD, the God of Israel. He has done what he promised to my father David. The LORD said, 16'Since the time I brought my people Israel out of Egypt, I have not chosen a city in any tribe of Israel where a temple will be built for me. But I have chosen David to lead my people Israel.'

17"My father David wanted to build a temple for the LORD, the God of Israel. 18But the LORD said to my father David, 'It was good that you wanted to build a temple for me. 19But you are not the one to build it. Your son, who comes from your own body, is the one who will build my temple.'

20"Now the LORD has kept his promise.

8:9 stone tablets They were the two tablets on which God wrote the Ten Commandments.

I am the king now in place of David my father. Now I rule Israel as the LORD promised, and I have built the Temple for the LORD, the God of Israel. 21I have made a place there for the Ark, in which is the Agreement the LORD made with our ancestors when he brought them out of Egypt."

SOLOMON'S PRAYER

22Then Solomon stood facing the LORD's altar, and all the Israelites were standing behind him. He spread out his hands toward the sky 23and said:

"LORD, God of Israel, there is no god like you in heaven above or on earth below. You keep your agreement of love with your servants who truly follow you. 24You have kept the promise you made to your servant David, my father. You spoke it with your own mouth and finished it with your hands today. 25Now LORD, God of Israel, keep the promise you made to your servant David, my father. You said, 'If your sons are careful to obey me as you have obeyed me, there will always be someone from your family ruling Israel.' 26Now, God of Israel, please continue to keep that promise you made to your servant David, my father.

27"But, God, can you really live here on the earth? The sky and the highest place in heaven cannot contain you. Surely this house which I have built cannot contain you. 28But please listen to my prayer and my request, because I am your servant. LORD my God, hear this prayer your servant prays to you today. 29Night and day please watch over this Temple where you have said, 'I will be worshiped there.' Hear the prayer I pray facing this Temple. 30Hear my prayers and the prayers of your people Israel when we pray facing this place. Hear from your home in heaven, and when you hear, forgive us.

31"If someone wrongs another person, he will be brought to the altar in this Temple. If he swears an oath that he is not guilty, 32then hear in heaven. Judge the case, punish the guilty, but declare that the innocent person is not guilty.

33"When your people, the Israelites, sin against you, their enemies will defeat them. But if they come back to you and praise you and pray to you in this Temple, 34then hear them in heaven. Forgive the sins of your people Israel, and bring them back to the land you gave to their ancestors.

35"When they sin against you, you will stop the rain from falling on their land. Then they will pray, facing this place and praising you; they will stop sinning when you make them suffer. 36When this happens, please hear their prayer in heaven, and forgive the sins of your servants, the Israelites. Teach them to do what is right. Then please send rain to this land you have given particularly to them.

37"At times the land will become so dry that no food will grow, or a great sickness will spread among the people. Sometimes all the crops will be destroyed by locusts or grasshoppers. Your people will be attacked in their cities by their enemy or will become sick. 38When any of these things happen, the people will become truly sorry. If your people spread their hands in prayer toward this Temple, 39then hear their prayers from your home in heaven. Forgive and treat each person as he should be treated because you know what is in a person's heart. Only you know what is in everyone's heart. 40Then your people will respect you as long as they live in this land you gave to our ancestors.

41-42"People who are not Israelites, foreigners from other lands, will hear about your greatness and power. They will come from far away to pray at this Temple. 43Then hear from your home in heaven, and do whatever they ask you. Then people everywhere will know you and respect you, just as your people in Israel do. Then everyone will know I built this Temple as a place to worship you.

44"When your people go out to fight their enemies along some road on which you send them, your people will pray to you, facing the city which you have chosen and the Temple I have built for you. 45Then hear in heaven their prayers, and do what is right.

46"Everyone sins, so your people will also sin against you. You will become angry with them and hand them over to their enemies. Their enemies will capture them and take them away to their countries far or near. 47Your people will be sorry for their sins when they are held as prisoners in another country. They will be sorry and pray to you in the land where they are held as prisoners, saying, 'We have sinned. We have done

349

wrong and acted wickedly.' ⁴⁸They will truly turn back to you in the land of their enemies. They will pray to you, facing this land you gave their ancestors, this city you have chosen, and the Temple I have built for you. ⁴⁹Then hear their prayers from your home in heaven, and do what is right. ⁵⁰Forgive your people of all their sins and for turning against you. Make those who have captured them show them mercy. ⁵¹Remember, they are your special people. You brought them out of Egypt, as if you were pulling them out of a blazing furnace.

⁵²"Give your attention to my prayers and the prayers of your people Israel. Listen to them anytime they ask you for help. ⁵³You chose them from all the nations on earth to be your very own people. This is what you promised through Moses your servant when you brought our ancestors out of Egypt, Lord GOD."

⁵⁴Solomon prayed this prayer to the LORD, kneeling in front of the altar with his arms raised toward heaven. When he finished praying, he got up. ⁵⁵Then, in a loud voice, he stood and blessed all the people of Israel, saying: ⁵⁶"Praise the LORD! He promised he would give rest to his people Israel, and he has given us rest. The LORD has kept all the good promises he gave through his servant Moses. ⁵⁷May the LORD our God be with us as he was with our ancestors. May he never leave us, ⁵⁸and may he turn us to himself so we will follow him. Let us obey all the laws and commands he gave our ancestors. ⁵⁹May the LORD our God remember this prayer day and night and do what is right for his servant and his people Israel day by day. ⁶⁰Then all the people of the world will know the LORD is the only true God. ⁶¹You must fully obey the LORD our God and follow all his laws and commands. Continue to obey in the future as you do now."

SACRIFICES ARE OFFERED

⁶²Then King Solomon and all Israel with him offered sacrifices to the LORD. ⁶³Solomon killed twenty-two thousand cattle and one hundred twenty thousand sheep as fellowship offerings. So the king and all the people gave the Temple to the LORD.

⁶⁴On that day King Solomon made holy the middle part of the courtyard which is in front of the Temple of the LORD. There he offered whole burnt offerings, grain offerings, and the fat of the fellowship offerings. He offered them in the courtyard, because the bronze altar before the LORD was too small to hold all the burnt offerings, the grain offerings, and the fat of the fellowship offerings.

⁶⁵Solomon and all the Israelites celebrated the other festival that came at that time. People came from as far away as Lebo Hamath and the brook of Egypt. A great many people celebrated before the LORD for seven days, then seven more days, for a total of fourteen days. ⁶⁶On the following day Solomon sent the people home. They blessed the king as they went, happy because of all the good things the LORD had done for his servant David and his people Israel.

THE LORD APPEARS TO SOLOMON AGAIN

9 Solomon finished building the Temple of the LORD and his royal palace and everything he wanted to build. ²Then the LORD appeared to him again just as he had done before, in Gibeon. ³The LORD said to him: "I have heard your prayer and what you have asked me to do. You built this Temple, and I have made it a holy place. I will be worshiped there forever and will watch over it and protect it always.

⁴"But you must serve me as your father David did; he was fair and sincere. You must obey all I have commanded and keep my laws and rules. ⁵If you do, I will make your kingdom strong. This is the promise I made to your father David—that someone from his family would always rule Israel.

⁶"But you and your children must follow me and obey the laws and commands I have given you. You must not serve or worship other gods. ⁷If you do, I will force Israel to leave the land I have given them, and I will leave this Temple that I have made holy. All the nations will make fun of Israel and speak evil about them. ⁸If the Temple is destroyed, everyone who passes by will be shocked. They will make fun of you and ask, 'Why did the LORD do this terrible thing to this land and this Temple?' ⁹People will answer, 'This happened because they left the LORD their

God. This was the God who brought their ancestors out of Egypt, but they decided to follow other gods. They worshiped and served those gods, so the LORD brought all this disaster on them.'"

SOLOMON'S OTHER ACHIEVEMENTS

[10] By the end of twenty years, King Solomon had built two buildings—the Temple of the LORD and the royal palace. [11] At that time King Solomon gave twenty towns in Galilee

---

ALWAYS ON HIS MIND

who's talking?

FULFILLMENT

1 KINGS 9:1–5

The human mind kicks out millions of "self-talk" words every day. Our job is to figure out which of these words are from God and which are not. Here's a tip: if it is uplifting, encouraging, inspiring, and comforting, it's from God. If it is negative, destructive, fearful, and depressing, it's not!

To overcome negative self-talk, make time for the "Spiritual Triathlon" every day:

1. Bible Time
2. Prayer Time
3. Quiet Time

BIBLE TIME:
While the words of your head can come from anywhere, the words in the Bible come from God. By reading his words every day, you condition yourself to hear from him.

PRAYER TIME:
Prayer is a proven way to make a change in your body, your heart, and your relationships. Talk to God. He loves to hear from you, and he'll never turn a deaf ear to your petition.

QUIET TIME:
In the noisy world we live in today, we will never hear what God is trying to tell us if we do not commit to finding some quiet time to listen to his voice and to obey his directives.

By spending five to ten minutes a day in each area of the Spiritual Triathlon (fifteen to thirty minutes total), every part of your life will get in better shape. This will allow you to give the appropriate response to the voices in your head that are not God's.

---

reflect: Spend some time with God today, and reap the rewards of faithfulness.
Go to **2 Chronicles 16:9.**

to Hiram king of Tyre, because Hiram had helped with the buildings. Hiram had given Solomon all the cedar, pine, and gold he wanted. ¹²So Hiram traveled from Tyre to see the towns Solomon had given him, but when he saw them, he was not pleased. ¹³He asked, "What good are these towns you have given me, my brother?" So he named them the Land of Cabul,ⁿ and they are still called that today. ¹⁴Hiram had sent Solomon about nine thousand pounds of gold.

¹⁵This is the account of the forced labor Solomon used to build the Temple and the palace. He had them fill in the land and build the wall around Jerusalem. He also had them rebuild the cities of Hazor, Megiddo, and Gezer. ¹⁶(In the past the king of Egypt had attacked and captured Gezer. After burning it, he killed the Canaanites who lived there. Then he gave it as a wedding present to his daughter, who married Solomon. ¹⁷So Solomon rebuilt it.) He also built the cities of Lower Beth Horon ¹⁸and Baalath, as well as Tadmor, which is in the desert. ¹⁹King Solomon also built cities for storing grain and supplies and cities for his chariots and horses. He built whatever he wanted in Jerusalem, Lebanon, and everywhere he ruled.

²⁰There were other people in the land who were not Israelites—Amorites, Hittites, Perizzites, Hivites, and Jebusites. ²¹They were descendants of people that the Israelites had not destroyed. Solomon forced them to work for him as slaves, as is still true today. ²²But Solomon did not make slaves of the Israelites. They were his soldiers, government leaders, officers, captains, chariot commanders, and drivers.

²³These were his most important officers over the work. There were five hundred fifty supervisors over the people who did the work on Solomon's projects.

²⁴The daughter of the king of Egypt moved from the old part of Jerusalem to the palace that Solomon had built for her. Then Solomon filled in the surrounding land.

²⁵Three times each year Solomon offered whole burnt offerings and fellowship offerings on the altar he had built for the LORD. He also burned incense before the LORD. So he finished the work on the Temple.

²⁶King Solomon also built ships at Ezion Geber, a town near Elath on the shore of the Red Sea, in the land of Edom. ²⁷Hiram had skilled sailors, so he sent them to serve in these ships with Solomon's men. ²⁸The ships sailed to Ophir and brought back about thirty-two thousand pounds of gold to King Solomon.

THE QUEEN OF SHEBA VISITS SOLOMON

10 When the queen of Sheba heard about Solomon, she came to test him with hard questions. ²She traveled to Jerusalem with a large group of servants and camels carrying spices, jewels, and much gold. When she came to Solomon, she talked with him about all she had in mind, ³and Solomon answered all her questions. Nothing was too hard for him to explain to her. ⁴The queen of Sheba learned that Solomon was very wise. She saw the palace he had built, ⁵the food on his table, his many officers, the palace servants, and their good clothes. She saw the servants who served him at feasts and the whole burnt offerings he made in the Temple of the LORD. All these things amazed her.

⁶So she said to King Solomon, "What I heard in my own country about your achievements and wisdom is true. ⁷I could not believe it then, but now I have come and seen it with my own eyes. I was not told even half of it! Your wisdom and wealth are much greater than I had heard. ⁸Your men and officers are very lucky, because in always serving you, they are able to hear your wisdom. ⁹Praise the LORD your God, who was pleased to make you king of Israel. The LORD has constant love for Israel, so he made you king to keep justice and to rule fairly."

¹⁰Then she gave the king about nine thousand pounds of gold and many spices and jewels. No one since that time has brought more spices than the queen of Sheba gave to King Solomon.

¹¹(Hiram's ships brought gold from Ophir, as well as much juniper wood and jewels. ¹²Solomon used the juniper wood to build supports for the Temple of the LORD and the palace, and to make harps and lyres for the musicians. Such fine juniper wood has not been brought in or been seen since that time.)

9:13 **Cabul** This name sounds like the Hebrew word for "worthless."

¹³King Solomon gave the queen of Sheba everything she wanted and asked for, in addition to what he had already given her of his wealth. Then she and her servants returned to her own country.

SOLOMON'S WEALTH

¹⁴Every year King Solomon received about fifty thousand pounds of gold. ¹⁵Besides that, he also received gold from the traders and merchants, as well as from the kings of Arabia and governors of the land.

¹⁶King Solomon made two hundred large shields of hammered gold, each of which contained about seven and one-half pounds of gold. ¹⁷He also made three hundred smaller shields of hammered gold, each of which contained about four pounds of gold. The king put them in the Palace of the Forest of Lebanon.

¹⁸The king built a large throne of ivory and covered it with fine gold. ¹⁹The throne had six steps on it, and its back was round at the top. There were armrests on both sides of the chair, and each armrest had a lion beside it. ²⁰Twelve lions stood on the six steps, one lion at each end of each step. Nothing like this had ever been made for any other kingdom. ²¹All of Solomon's drinking cups, as well as the dishes in the Palace of the Forest of Lebanon, were made of pure gold. Nothing was made from silver, because silver was not valuable in Solomon's time.

²²King Solomon also had many trading ships at sea, along with Hiram's ships. Every three years the ships returned, bringing back gold, silver, ivory, apes, and baboons.

²³So Solomon had more riches and wisdom than all the other kings on earth. ²⁴People everywhere wanted to see King Solomon and listen to the wisdom God had given him. ²⁵Every year those who came brought gifts of silver and gold, clothes, weapons, spices, horses, and mules.

²⁶Solomon had fourteen hundred chariots and twelve thousand horses. He kept some in special cities for the chariots, and others he kept with him in Jerusalem. ²⁷In Jerusalem Solomon made silver as common as stones and cedar trees as common as the fig trees on the western hills. ²⁸He imported horses from Egypt and Kue. His traders bought them in Kue. ²⁹A chariot from Egypt cost about fif-teen pounds of silver, and a horse cost nearly four pounds of silver. Solomon's traders also sold horses and chariots to all the kings of the Hittites and the Arameans.

SOLOMON'S MANY WIVES

11 King Solomon loved many women who were not from Israel. He loved the daughter of the king of Egypt, as well as women of the Moabites, Ammonites, Edomites, Sidonians, and Hittites. ²The LORD had told the Israelites, "You must not marry people of other nations. If you do, they will cause you to follow their gods." But Solomon fell in love with these women. ³He had seven hundred wives who were from royal families and three hundred slave women who gave birth to his children. His wives caused him to turn away from God. ⁴As Solomon grew old, his wives caused him to follow other gods. He did not follow the LORD completely as his father David had done. ⁵Solomon worshiped Ashtoreth, the goddess of the people of Sidon, and Molech, the hated god of the Ammonites. ⁶So Solomon did what the LORD said was wrong and did not follow the LORD completely as his father David had done.

⁷On a hill east of Jerusalem, Solomon built two places for worship. One was a place to worship Chemosh, the hated god of the Moabites, and the other was a place to worship Molech, the hated god of the Ammonites. ⁸Solomon did the same thing for all his foreign wives so they could burn incense and offer sacrifices to their gods.

⁹The LORD had appeared to Solomon twice, but the king turned away from following the LORD, the God of Israel. The LORD was angry with Solomon, ¹⁰because he had commanded Solomon not to follow other gods. But Solomon did not obey the LORD's command. ¹¹So the LORD said to Solomon, "Because you have chosen to break your agreement with me and have not obeyed my commands, I will tear your kingdom away from you and give it to one of your officers. ¹²But I will not take it away while you are alive because of my love for your father David. I will tear it away from your son when he becomes king. ¹³I will not tear away all the kingdom from him, but I will leave him one tribe to rule. I will do this because of David,

my servant, and because of Jerusalem, the city I have chosen."

SOLOMON'S ENEMIES

¹⁴The LORD caused Hadad the Edomite, a member of the family of the king of Edom, to become Solomon's enemy. ¹⁵Earlier, David had defeated Edom. When Joab, the commander of David's army, went into Edom to bury the dead, he killed all the males. ¹⁶Joab and all the Israelites stayed in Edom for six months and killed every male in Edom. ¹⁷At that time Hadad was only a young boy, so he ran away to Egypt with some of his father's officers. ¹⁸They left Midian and went to Paran, where they were joined by other men. Then they all went to Egypt to see the king, who gave Hadad a house, some food, and some land.

¹⁹The king liked Hadad so much he gave Hadad a wife—the sister of Tahpenes, the king's wife. ²⁰They had a son named Genubath. Queen Tahpenes brought him up in the royal palace with the king's own children.

²¹While he was in Egypt, Hadad heard that David had died and that Joab, the commander of the army, was dead also. So Hadad said to the king, "Let me go; I will return to my own country."

²²"Why do you want to go back to your own country?" the king asked. "What haven't I given you here?"

"Nothing," Hadad answered, "but please, let me go."

²³God also caused another man to be Solomon's enemy—Rezon son of Eliada. Rezon had run away from his master, Hadadezer king of Zobah. ²⁴After David defeated the army of Zobah, Rezon gathered some men and became the leader of a small army. They went to Damascus and settled there, and Rezon became king of Damascus. ²⁵Rezon ruled Aram, and he hated Israel. So he was an enemy of Israel all the time Solomon was alive. Both Rezon and Hadad made trouble for Israel.

²⁶Jeroboam son of Nebat was one of Solomon's officers. He was an Ephraimite from the town of Zeredah, and he was the son of a widow named Zeruah. Jeroboam turned against the king.

²⁷This is the story of how Jeroboam turned against the king. Solomon was filling in the land and repairing the wall of Jerusalem, the city of David, his father. ²⁸Jeroboam was a capable man, and Solomon saw that this young man was a good worker. So Solomon put him over all the workers from the tribes of Ephraim and Manasseh.

²⁹One day as Jeroboam was leaving Jerusalem, Ahijah, the prophet from Shiloh, who was wearing a new coat, met him on the road. The two men were alone out in the country. ³⁰Ahijah took his new coat and tore it into twelve pieces. ³¹Then he said to Jeroboam, "Take ten pieces of this coat for yourself. The LORD, the God of Israel, says: 'I will tear the kingdom away from Solomon and give you ten tribes. ³²But I will allow him to control one tribe. I will do this for the sake of my servant David and for Jerusalem, the city I have chosen from all the tribes of Israel. ³³I will do this because Solomon has stopped following me and has worshiped the Sidonian god Ashtoreth, the Moabite god Chemosh, and the Ammonite god Molech. Solomon has not obeyed me by doing what I said is right and obeying my laws and commands, as his father David did.

³⁴"'But I will not take all the kingdom away from Solomon. I will let him rule all his life because of my servant David, whom I chose, who obeyed all my commands and laws. ³⁵But I will take the kingdom away from his son, and I will allow you to rule over the ten tribes. ³⁶I will allow Solomon's son to continue to rule over one tribe so that there will always be a descendant of David, my servant, in Jerusalem, the city where I chose to be worshiped. ³⁷But I will make you rule over everything you want. You will rule over all of Israel, ³⁸and I will always be with you if you do what I say is right. You must obey all my commands. If you obey my laws and commands as David did, I will be with you. I will make your family a lasting family of kings, as I did for David, and give Israel to you. ³⁹I will punish David's children because of this, but I will not punish them forever.'"

SOLOMON'S DEATH

⁴⁰Solomon tried to kill Jeroboam, but he ran away to Egypt, to Shishak king of Egypt, where he stayed until Solomon died.

⁴¹Everything else King Solomon did, and the wisdom he showed, is written in the book

of the history of Solomon. ⁴²Solomon ruled in Jerusalem over all Israel for forty years. ⁴³Then he died and was buried in Jerusalem, the city of David, his father. And his son Rehoboam became king in his place.

ISRAEL TURNS AGAINST REHOBOAM

12 Rehoboam went to Shechem, where all the Israelites had gone to make him king. ²Jeroboam son of Nebat was still in Egypt, where he had gone to escape from Solomon. When Jeroboam heard about Rehoboam being made king, he was living in Egypt. ³After the people sent for him, he and the people went to Rehoboam and said to him, ⁴"Your father forced us to work very hard. Now, make it easier for us, and don't make us work as hard as he did. Then we will serve you."

⁵Rehoboam answered, "Go away for three days, and then come back to me." So the people left.

⁶King Rehoboam asked the elders who had advised Solomon during his lifetime, "How do you think I should answer these people?"

⁷They said, "You should be like a servant to them today. If you serve them and give them a kind answer, they will serve you always."

⁸But Rehoboam rejected this advice. Instead, he asked the young men who had grown up with him and who served as his advisers. ⁹Rehoboam asked them, "What is your advice? How should we answer these people who said, 'Don't make us work as hard as your father did'?"

¹⁰The young men who had grown up with him answered, "Those people said to you, 'Your father forced us to work very hard. Now make our work easier.' You should tell them, 'My little finger is bigger than my father's legs. ¹¹He forced you to work hard, but I will make you work even harder. My father beat you with whips, but I will beat you with whips that have sharp points.'"

¹²Rehoboam had told the people, "Come back to me in three days." So after three days Jeroboam and all the people returned to Rehoboam. ¹³King Rehoboam spoke cruel words to them, because he had rejected the advice the elders had given him. ¹⁴He followed the advice of the young men and said to the people, "My father forced you to work hard, but I will make you work even harder. My father beat you with whips, but I will beat you with whips that have sharp points." ¹⁵So the king did not listen to the people. The LORD caused this to happen to keep the promise he had made to Jeroboam son of Nebat through Ahijah, a prophet from Shiloh.

¹⁶When all the Israelites saw that the new king refused to listen to them, they said to the king,

"We have no share in David!
    We have no part in the son of Jesse!
People of Israel, let's go to our own
      homes!
    Let David's son rule his own people!"

So the Israelites went home. ¹⁷But Rehoboam still ruled over the Israelites who lived in the towns of Judah.

¹⁸Adoniram was in charge of the forced labor. When Rehoboam sent him to the people of Israel, they threw stones at him until he died. But King Rehoboam ran to his chariot and escaped to Jerusalem. ¹⁹Since then, Israel has been against the family of David.

²⁰When all the Israelites heard that Jeroboam had returned, they called him to a meeting and made him king over all Israel. Only the tribe of Judah continued to follow the family of David.

²¹When Rehoboam arrived in Jerusalem, he gathered one hundred eighty thousand of the best soldiers from the tribes of Judah and Benjamin. As son of Solomon, Rehoboam wanted to fight the people of Israel to take back his kingdom.

²²But God spoke his word to Shemaiah, a man of God, saying, ²³"Speak to Solomon's son Rehoboam, the king of Judah, and to all the people of Judah and Benjamin and the rest of the people. Say to them, ²⁴'The LORD says you must not go to war against your brothers, the Israelites. Every one of you should go home, because I made all these things happen.'" So they obeyed the LORD's command and went home as the LORD had commanded.

²⁵Then Jeroboam made Shechem in the mountains of Ephraim a very strong city, and he lived there. He also went to the city of Peniel and made it stronger.

JEROBOAM BUILDS GOLDEN CALVES

²⁶Jeroboam said to himself, "The kingdom will probably go back to David's family. ²⁷If the people continue going to the Temple of the LORD in Jerusalem to offer sacrifices, they will want to be ruled again by Rehoboam. Then they will kill me and follow Rehoboam king of Judah."

²⁸King Jeroboam asked for advice. Then he made two golden calves. "It is too long a journey for you to go to Jerusalem to worship," he said to the people. "Israel, here are your gods who brought you out of Egypt." ²⁹Jeroboam put one golden calf in the city of Bethel and the other in the city of Dan. ³⁰This became a very great sin, because the people traveled as far as Dan to worship the calf there.

³¹Jeroboam built temples on the places of worship. He also chose priests from all the people, not just from the tribe of Levi. ³²And he started a new festival on the fifteenth day of the eighth month, just like the festival in Judah. During that time the king offered sacrifices on the altar, along with sacrifices to the calves in Bethel he had made. He also chose priests in Bethel to serve at the places of worship he had made. ³³So Jeroboam chose his own time for a festival for the Israelites—the fifteenth day of the eighth month. During that time he offered sacrifices on the altar he had built in Bethel. He set up a festival for the Israelites and offered sacrifices on the altar.

THE MAN OF GOD SPEAKS AGAINST BETHEL

13 The LORD commanded a man of God from Judah to go to Bethel. When he arrived, Jeroboam was standing by the altar to offer a sacrifice. ²The LORD had commanded the man of God to speak against the altar. The man said, "Altar, altar, the LORD says to you: 'David's family will have a son named Josiah. The priests for the places of worship now make their sacrifices on you, but Josiah will sacrifice those priests on you. Human bones will be burned on you.'" ³That same day the man of God gave proof that these things would happen. "This is the LORD's sign that this will happen," he said. "This altar will break apart, and the ashes on it will fall to the ground."

⁴When King Jeroboam heard what the man of God said about the altar in Bethel, the king raised his hand from the altar and pointed at the man. "Take him!" he said. But when the king said this, his arm was paralyzed, and he could not move it. ⁵The altar also broke into pieces, and its ashes fell to the ground. This was the sign the LORD had told the man of God to give.

⁶Then the king said to the man of God, "Please pray to the LORD your God for me, and ask him to heal my arm."

So the man of God prayed to the LORD, and the king's arm was healed, becoming as it was before.

⁷Then the king said to the man of God, "Please come home and eat with me, and I will give you a gift."

⁸But the man of God answered the king, "Even if you gave me half of your kingdom, I would not go with you. I will not eat or drink anything in this place. ⁹The LORD commanded me not to eat or drink anything nor to return on the same road by which I came." ¹⁰So he took a different road and did not return on the same road by which he had come to Bethel.

¹¹Now an old prophet was living in Bethel. His sons came and told him what the man of God had done there that day. They also told their father what he had said to King Jeroboam. ¹²The father asked, "Which road did he use when he left?" So his sons showed him the road the man of God from Judah had taken. ¹³Then the prophet told his sons to put a saddle on his donkey. So they saddled the donkey, and he left.

¹⁴He went after the man of God and found him sitting under an oak tree. The prophet asked, "Are you the man of God who came from Judah?"

The man answered, "Yes, I am."

¹⁵The prophet said, "Please come home and eat with me."

¹⁶"I can't go home with you," the man of God answered. "I can't eat or drink with you in this place. ¹⁷The LORD said to me, 'Don't eat or drink anything there or return on the same road by which you came.'"

¹⁸Then the old prophet said, "But I also am a prophet like you." Then he told a lie. He said, "An angel from the LORD came to me and told me to bring you to my home. He said you should eat and drink with me." ¹⁹So the

man of God went to the old prophet's house, and he ate and drank with him there.

20While they were sitting at the table, the LORD spoke his word to the old prophet. 21The old prophet cried out to the man of God from Judah, "The LORD said you did not obey him! He said you did not do what the LORD your God commanded you. 22The LORD commanded you not to eat or drink anything in this place, but you came back and ate and drank. So your body will not be buried in your family grave."

23After the man of God finished eating and drinking, the prophet put a saddle on his donkey for him, and the man left. 24As he was traveling home, a lion attacked and killed him. His body lay on the road, with the donkey and the lion standing nearby. 25Some men who were traveling on that road saw the body and the lion standing nearby. So they went to the city where the old prophet lived and told what they had seen.

26The old prophet who had brought back the man of God heard what had happened. "It is the man of God who did not obey the LORD's command," he said. "So the LORD sent a lion to kill him, just as he said he would."

27Then the prophet said to his sons, "Put a saddle on my donkey," which they did. 28The old prophet went out and found the body lying on the road, with the donkey and the lion still standing nearby. The lion had not eaten the body or hurt the donkey. 29The prophet put the body on his donkey and carried it back to the city to have a time of sadness for him and to bury him. 30The prophet buried the body in his own family grave, and they were sad for the man of God and said, "Oh, my brother."

31After the prophet buried the body, he said to his sons, "When I die, bury me in this same grave. Put my bones next to his. 32Through him the LORD spoke against the altar at Bethel and against the places of worship in the towns of Samaria. What the LORD spoke through him will certainly come true."

33After this incident King Jeroboam did not stop doing evil. He continued to choose priests for the places of worship from among all the people. Anyone who wanted to be a priest for the places of worship was allowed to be one. 34In this way the family of Jeroboam sinned, and this sin caused its ruin and destruction from the earth.

JEROBOAM'S SON DIES

14 At that time Jeroboam's son Abijah became very sick. 2So Jeroboam said to his wife, "Go to Shiloh to see the prophet Ahijah. He is the one who said I would become king of Israel. But dress yourself so people won't know you are my wife. 3Take the prophet ten loaves of bread, some cakes, and a jar of honey. Then ask him what will happen to our son, and he will tell you." 4So the king's wife did as he said and went to Ahijah's home in Shiloh.

Now Ahijah was very old and blind. 5The LORD said to him, "Jeroboam's son is sick, and Jeroboam's wife is coming to ask you about him. When she arrives, she will pretend to be someone else." Then the LORD told Ahijah what to say.

6When Ahijah heard her walking to the door, he said, "Come in, wife of Jeroboam. Why are you pretending to be someone else? I have bad news for you. 7Go back and tell Jeroboam that this is what the LORD, the God of Israel, says: 'Jeroboam, I chose you from among all the people and made you the leader of my people Israel. 8I tore the kingdom away from David's family, and I gave it to you. But you are not like my servant David, who always obeyed my commands and followed me with all his heart. He did only what I said was right. 9But you have done more evil than anyone who ruled before you. You have quit following me and have made other gods and idols of metal. This has made me very angry, 10so I will soon bring disaster to your family. I will kill all the men in your family, both slaves and free men. I will destroy your family as completely as fire burns up manure. 11Anyone from your family who dies in the city will be eaten by dogs, and those who die in the fields will be eaten by the birds. The LORD has spoken.'"

12Then Ahijah said to Jeroboam's wife, "Go home now. As soon as you enter your city, your son will die, 13and all Israel will be sad for him and bury him. He is the only one of Jeroboam's family who will be buried, because he is the only one in the king's family who pleased the LORD, the God of Israel.

14"The LORD will put a new king over

Israel, who will destroy Jeroboam's family, and this will happen soon. [15]Then the LORD will punish Israel, which will be like reeds swaying in the water. The LORD will pull up Israel from this good land, the land he gave their ancestors. He will scatter Israel beyond the Euphrates River, because he is angry with the people. They made the LORD angry when they set up idols to worship Asherah. [16]Jeroboam sinned, and then he made the people of Israel sin. So the LORD will let the people of Israel be defeated."

[17]Then Jeroboam's wife left and returned to Tirzah. As soon as she entered her home, the boy died. [18]After they buried him, all Israel had a time of sadness for him, just as the LORD had said through his servant, the prophet Ahijah.

[19]Everything else Jeroboam did is written in the book of the history of the kings of Israel. He fought wars and continued to rule the people, [20]serving as king for twenty-two years. Then he died, and his son Nadab became king in his place.

THE DEATH OF REHOBOAM

[21]Solomon's son Rehoboam was forty-one years old when he became king of Judah. His mother was Naamah from Ammon. Rehoboam ruled in Jerusalem for seventeen years. (The LORD had chosen that city from all the land of Israel as the place where he would be worshiped.)

[22]The people of Judah did what the LORD said was wrong. Their sins made the LORD very angry, even more angry than he had been at their ancestors. [23]The people built stone pillars and places to worship gods and Asherah idols on every high hill and under every green tree. [24]There were even male prostitutes in the land. They acted like the people who had lived in the land before the Israelites. They had done many evil things, and God had taken the land away from them.

[25]During the fifth year Rehoboam was king, Shishak king of Egypt attacked Jerusalem. [26]He took the treasures from the Temple of the LORD and the king's palace. He took everything, even the gold shields Solomon had made. [27]So King Rehoboam made bronze shields to put in their place and gave them to the commanders of the guards for the palace gates. [28]Whenever the king went to the

Temple of the LORD, the guards carried the shields. Later, they would put them back in the guardroom.

[29]Everything else King Rehoboam did is written in the book of the history of the kings of Judah. [30]There was war between Rehoboam and Jeroboam the whole time. [31]Rehoboam, son of Naamah from Ammon, died and was buried with his ancestors in Jerusalem, and his son Abijam[n] became king in his place.

ABIJAM KING OF JUDAH

15 Abijam became king of Judah during the eighteenth year Jeroboam son of Nebat was king of Israel. [2]Abijam ruled in Jerusalem for three years. His mother was Maacah daughter of Abishalom. [3]He did all the same sins his father before him had done. Abijam was not faithful to the LORD his God as David, his great-grandfather, had been. [4]Because the LORD loved David, the LORD gave him a kingdom in Jerusalem and allowed him to have a son to be king after him. The LORD also kept Jerusalem safe. [5]David always did what the LORD said was right and obeyed his commands all his life, except the one time when David sinned against Uriah the Hittite.

[6]There was war between Abijam and Jeroboam during Abijam's lifetime. [7]Everything else Abijam did is written in the book of the history of the kings of Judah. During the time Abijam ruled, there was war between Abijam and Jeroboam. [8]Abijam died and was buried in Jerusalem, and his son Asa became king in his place.

ASA KING OF JUDAH

[9]During the twentieth year Jeroboam was king of Israel, Asa became king of Judah. [10]His grandmother's name was Maacah, the daughter of Abishalom. Asa ruled in Jerusalem for forty-one years.

[11]Asa did what the LORD said was right, as his ancestor David had done. [12]He forced the male prostitutes at the worship places to leave the country. He also took away the idols that his ancestors had made. [13]His grandmother Maacah had made a terrible Asherah idol, so Asa removed her from be-

---

14:31 **Abijam** A negative name for Abijah. See 2 Chronicles 13.

ing queen mother. He cut down that idol and burned it in the Kidron Valley. ¹⁴The places of worship to gods were not removed. Even so, Asa was faithful to the LORD all his life. ¹⁵Asa brought into the Temple of the LORD the gifts he and his father had given: gold, silver, and utensils.

¹⁶There was war between Asa and Baasha king of Israel all the time they were kings. ¹⁷Baasha attacked Judah, and he made the town of Ramah strong so he could keep people from leaving or entering Judah, Asa's country.

¹⁸Asa took the rest of the silver and gold from the treasuries of the Temple of the LORD and his own palace and gave it to his officers. Then he sent them to Ben-Hadad son of Tabrimmon, who was the son of Hezion. Ben-Hadad was the king of Aram and ruled in the city of Damascus. Asa said, ¹⁹"Let there be a treaty between you and me as there was between my father and your father. I am sending you a gift of silver and gold. Break your treaty with Baasha king of Israel so he will leave my land."

²⁰Ben-Hadad agreed with King Asa, so he sent the commanders of his armies to attack the towns of Israel. They defeated the towns of Ijon, Dan, and Abel Beth Maacah, as well as all Galilee and the area of Naphtali. ²¹When Baasha heard about these attacks, he stopped building up Ramah and returned to Tirzah. ²²Then King Asa gave an order to all the people of Judah; everyone had to help. They carried away all the stones and wood Baasha had been using in Ramah, and they used them to build up Geba and Mizpah in the land of Benjamin.

²³Everything else Asa did—his victories and the cities he built—is written in the book of the history of the kings of Judah. When he became old, he got a disease in his feet. ²⁴After Asa died, he was buried with his ancestors in Jerusalem, the city of David, his ancestor. Then Jehoshaphat, Asa's son, became king in his place.

NADAB KING OF ISRAEL

²⁵Nadab son of Jeroboam became king of Israel during the second year Asa was king of Judah. Nadab was king of Israel for two years, ²⁶and he did what the LORD said was wrong. Jeroboam had led the people of Israel to sin, and Nadab sinned in the same way as his father Jeroboam.

²⁷Baasha son of Ahijah, from the tribe of Issachar, made plans to kill Nadab. Nadab and all Israel were attacking the Philistine town of Gibbethon, so Baasha killed Nadab there. ²⁸This happened during Asa's third year as king of Judah, and Baasha became the next king of Israel.

BAASHA KING OF ISRAEL

²⁹As soon as Baasha became king, he killed all of Jeroboam's family, leaving no one in Jeroboam's family alive. He destroyed them all as the LORD had said would happen through his servant Ahijah from Shiloh. ³⁰King Jeroboam had sinned very much and had led the people of Israel to sin, so he made the LORD, the God of Israel, very angry.

³¹Everything else Nadab did is written in the book of the history of the kings of Israel. ³²There was war between Asa king of Judah and Baasha king of Israel all the time they ruled.

³³Baasha son of Ahijah became king of Israel during Asa's third year as king of Judah. Baasha ruled in Tirzah for twenty-four years, ³⁴and he did what the LORD said was wrong. Jeroboam had led the people of Israel to sin, and Baasha sinned in the same way as Jeroboam.

16 Jehu son of Hanani spoke the word of the LORD against King Baasha. ²The LORD said, "You were nothing, but I took you and made you a leader over my people Israel. But you have followed the ways of Jeroboam and have led my people Israel to sin. Their sins have made me angry, ³so, Baasha, I will soon destroy you and your family. I will do to you what I did to the family of Jeroboam son of Nebat. ⁴Anyone from your family who dies in the city will be eaten by dogs, and anyone from your family who dies in the fields will be eaten by birds."

⁵Everything else Baasha did and all his victories are written down in the book of the history of the kings of Israel. ⁶So Baasha died and was buried in Tirzah, and his son Elah became king in his place.

⁷The LORD spoke his word against Baasha and his family through the prophet Jehu son of Hanani. Baasha had done many things the LORD said were wrong, which made the

LORD very angry. He did the same evil deeds that Jeroboam's family had done before him. The LORD also spoke against Baasha because he killed all of Jeroboam's family.

ELAH KING OF ISRAEL

8Elah son of Baasha became king of Israel during Asa's twenty-sixth year as king of Judah, and Elah ruled in Tirzah for two years.

9Zimri, one of Elah's officers, commanded half of Elah's chariots. Zimri made plans against Elah while the king was in Tirzah, getting drunk at Arza's home. (Arza was in charge of the palace at Tirzah.) 10Zimri went into Arza's house and killed Elah during Asa's twenty-seventh year as king of Judah. Then Zimri became king of Israel in Elah's place.

ZIMRI KING OF ISRAEL

11As soon as Zimri became king, he killed all of Baasha's family, not allowing any of Baasha's family or friends to live. 12So Zimri destroyed all of Baasha's family just as the LORD had said it would happen through the prophet Jehu. 13Baasha and his son Elah sinned and led the people of Israel to sin, and they made the LORD, the God of Israel, angry because of their worthless idols.

14Everything else Elah did is written in the book of the history of the kings of Israel.

15So during Asa's twenty-seventh year as king of Judah, Zimri became king of Israel and ruled in Tirzah seven days.

The army of Israel was camped near Gibbethon, a Philistine town. 16The men in the camp heard that Zimri had made secret plans against King Elah and had killed him. So that day in the camp they made Omri, the commander of the army, king over Israel. 17So Omri and all the Israelite army left Gibbethon and attacked Tirzah. 18When Zimri saw that the city had been captured, he went into the palace and set it on fire, burning the palace and himself with it. 19So Zimri died because he had sinned by doing what the LORD said was wrong. Jeroboam had led the people of Israel to sin, and Zimri sinned in the same way as Jeroboam.

20Everything else Zimri did and the story of how he turned against King Elah are written down in the book of the history of the kings of Israel.

OMRI KING OF ISRAEL

21The people of Israel were divided into two groups. Half of the people wanted Tibni son of Ginath to be king, while the other half wanted Omri. 22Omri's followers were stronger than the followers of Tibni son of Ginath, so Tibni died, and Omri became king.

23Omri became king of Israel during the thirty-first year Asa was king of Judah. Omri ruled Israel for twelve years, six of those years in the city of Tirzah. 24He bought the hill of Samaria from Shemer for about one hundred fifty pounds of silver. Omri built a city on that hill and called it Samaria after the name of its earlier owner, Shemer.

25But Omri did what the LORD said was wrong; he did more evil than all the kings who came before him. 26Jeroboam son of Nebat had led the people of Israel to sin, and Omri sinned in the same way as Jeroboam. The Israelites made the LORD, the God of Israel, very angry because they worshiped worthless idols.

27Everything else Omri did and all his successes are written in the book of the history of the kings of Israel. 28So Omri died and was buried in Samaria, and his son Ahab became king in his place.

AHAB KING OF ISRAEL

29Ahab son of Omri became king of Israel during Asa's thirty-eighth year as king of Judah, and Ahab ruled Israel in the city of Samaria for twenty-two years. 30More than any king before him, Ahab son of Omri did many things the LORD said were wrong. 31He sinned in the same ways as Jeroboam son of Nebat, but he did even worse things. He married Jezebel daughter of Ethbaal, the king of Sidon. Then Ahab began to serve Baal and worship him. 32He built a temple in Samaria for worshiping Baal and put an altar there for Baal. 33Ahab also made an idol for worshiping Asherah. He did more things to make the LORD, the God of Israel, angry than all the other kings before him.

34During the time of Ahab, Hiel from Bethel rebuilt the city of Jericho. It cost Hiel the life of Abiram, his oldest son, to begin work on the city, and it cost the life of Segub, his youngest son, to build the city gates. This happened just as the LORD, speaking through Joshua son of Nun, said it would happen.[n]

ELIJAH STOPS THE RAIN

17 Now Elijah the Tishbite was a prophet from the settlers in Gilead. "I serve the LORD, the God of Israel," Elijah said to Ahab. "As surely as the LORD lives, no rain or dew will fall during the next few years unless I command it."

2 Then the LORD spoke his word to Elijah: 3 "Leave this place and go east and hide near Kerith Ravine east of the Jordan River. 4 You may drink from the stream, and I have commanded ravens to bring you food there." 5 So Elijah did what the LORD said; he went to Kerith Ravine, east of the Jordan, and lived there. 6 The birds brought Elijah bread and meat every morning and evening, and he drank water from the stream.

7 After a while the stream dried up because there was no rain. 8 Then the LORD spoke his word to Elijah, 9 "Go to Zarephath in Sidon and live there. I have commanded a widow there to take care of you."

10 So Elijah went to Zarephath. When he reached the town gate, he saw a widow gathering wood for a fire. Elijah asked her, "Would you bring me a little water in a cup so I may have a drink?" 11 As she was going to get his water, Elijah said, "Please bring me a piece of bread, too."

12 The woman answered, "As surely as the LORD your God lives, I have no bread. I have only a handful of flour in a jar and only a little olive oil in a jug. I came here to gather some wood so I could go home and cook our last meal. My son and I will eat it and then die from hunger."

13 "Don't worry," Elijah said to her. "Go home and cook your food as you have said. But first make a small loaf of bread from the flour you have, and bring it to me. Then cook something for yourself and your son. 14 The LORD, the God of Israel, says, 'That jar of flour will never be empty, and the jug will always have oil in it, until the day the LORD sends rain to the land.'"

15 So the woman went home and did what Elijah told her to do. And the woman and her son and Elijah had enough food every day. 16 The jar of flour and the jug of oil were never empty, just as the LORD, through Elijah, had promised.

ELIJAH BRINGS A BOY BACK TO LIFE

17 Some time later the son of the woman who owned the house became sick. He grew worse and worse and finally stopped breathing. 18 The woman said to Elijah, "Man of God, what have you done to me? Did you come here to remind me of my sin and to kill my son?"

19 Elijah said to her, "Give me your son." Elijah took the boy from her, carried him upstairs, and laid him on the bed in the room where he was staying. 20 Then he prayed to the LORD: "LORD my God, this widow is letting me stay in her house. Why have you done this terrible thing to her and caused her son to die?" 21 Then Elijah lay on top of the boy three times. He prayed to the LORD, "LORD my God, let this boy live again!"

22 The LORD answered Elijah's prayer; the boy began breathing again and was alive. 23 Elijah carried the boy downstairs and gave him to his mother and said, "See! Your son is alive!"

24 "Now I know you really are a man from God," the woman said to Elijah. "I know that the LORD truly speaks through you!"

ELIJAH KILLS THE PROPHETS OF BAAL

18 During the third year without rain, the LORD spoke his word to Elijah: "Go and meet King Ahab, and I will soon send rain." 2 So Elijah went to meet Ahab.

By this time there was no food in Samaria. 3 King Ahab sent for Obadiah, who was in charge of the king's palace. (Obadiah was a true follower of the LORD. 4 When Jezebel was killing all the LORD's prophets, Obadiah hid a hundred of them in two caves, fifty in one cave and fifty in another. He also brought them food and water.) 5 Ahab said to Obadiah, "Let's check every spring and valley in the land. Maybe we can find enough grass to keep our horses and mules alive and not have to kill our animals." 6 So each one chose a part of the country to search; Ahab went in one direction and Obadiah in another.

16:34 the LORD . . . happen When Joshua destroyed Jericho, he said whoever rebuilt the city would lose his oldest and youngest sons. See Joshua 6:26.

7While Obadiah was on his way, Elijah met him. Obadiah recognized Elijah, so he bowed down to the ground and said, "Elijah? Is it really you, master?"

8"Yes," Elijah answered. "Go tell your master that I am here."

9Then Obadiah said, "What wrong have I done for you to hand me over to Ahab like this? He will put me to death. 10As surely as the LORD your God lives, the king has sent people to every country to search for you. If the ruler said you were not there, Ahab forced the ruler to swear you could not be found in his country. 11Now you want me to go to my master and tell him, 'Elijah is here'? 12The Spirit of the LORD may carry you to some other place after I leave. If I go tell King Ahab you are here, and he comes and doesn't find you, he will kill me! I have followed the LORD since I was a boy. 13Haven't you been told what I did? When Jezebel was killing the LORD's prophets, I hid a hundred of them, fifty in one cave and fifty in another. I brought them food and water. 14Now you want me to go and tell my master you are here? He will kill me!"

15Elijah answered, "As surely as the LORD All-Powerful lives, whom I serve, I will be seen by Ahab today."

16So Obadiah went to Ahab and told him where Elijah was. Then Ahab went to meet Elijah.

17When he saw Elijah, he asked, "Is it you—the biggest troublemaker in Israel?"

18Elijah answered, "I have not made trouble in Israel. You and your father's family have made all this trouble by not obeying the LORD's commands. You have gone after the Baals. 19Now tell all Israel to meet me at Mount Carmel. Also bring the four hundred fifty prophets of Baal and the four hundred prophets of Asherah, who eat at Jezebel's table."

20So Ahab called all the Israelites and those prophets to Mount Carmel. 21Elijah approached the people and said, "How long will you not decide between two choices? If the LORD is the true God, follow him, but if Baal is the true God, follow him!" But the people said nothing.

22Elijah said, "I am the only prophet of the LORD here, but there are four hundred fifty prophets of Baal. 23Bring two bulls. Let the prophets of Baal choose one bull and kill it and cut it into pieces. Then let them put the meat on the wood, but they are not to set fire to it. I will prepare the other bull, putting the meat on the wood but not setting fire to it. 24You prophets of Baal, pray to your god, and I will pray to the LORD. The god who answers by setting fire to his wood is the true God."

All the people agreed that this was a good idea.

25Then Elijah said to the prophets of Baal, "There are many of you, so you go first. Choose a bull and prepare it. Pray to your god, but don't start the fire."

26So they took the bull that was given to them and prepared it. They prayed to Baal from morning until noon, shouting "Baal, answer us!" But there was no sound, and no one answered. They danced around the altar they had built.

27At noon Elijah began to make fun of them. "Pray louder!" he said. "If Baal really is a god, maybe he is thinking, or busy, or traveling! Maybe he is sleeping so you will have to wake him!" 28The prophets prayed louder, cutting themselves with swords and spears until their blood flowed, which was the way they worshiped. 29The afternoon passed, and the prophets continued to act like this until it was time for the evening sacrifice. But no voice was heard; Baal did not answer, and no one paid attention.

30Then Elijah said to all the people, "Now come to me." So they gathered around him, and Elijah rebuilt the altar of the LORD, which had been torn down. 31He took twelve stones, one stone for each of the twelve tribes, the number of Jacob's sons. (The LORD changed Jacob's name to Israel.) 32Elijah used these stones to rebuild the altar in honor of the LORD. Then he dug a ditch around the altar that was big enough to hold about thirteen quarts of seed. 33Elijah put the wood on the altar, cut the bull into pieces, and laid the pieces on the wood. 34Then he said, "Fill four jars with water, and pour it on the meat and on the wood." Then Elijah said, "Do it again," and they did it again. Then he said, "Do it a third time," and they did it the third time. 35So the water ran off the altar and filled the ditch.

36At the time for the evening sacrifice, the prophet Elijah went near the altar.

"LORD, you are the God of Abraham, Isaac, and Israel," he prayed. "Prove that you are the God of Israel and that I am your servant. Show these people that you commanded me to do all these things. ³⁷LORD, answer my prayer so these people will know that you, LORD, are God and that you will change their minds."

³⁸Then fire from the LORD came down and burned the sacrifice, the wood, the stones, and the ground around the altar. It also dried up the water in the ditch. ³⁹When all the people saw this, they fell down to the ground, crying, "The LORD is God! The LORD is God!"

⁴⁰Then Elijah said, "Capture the prophets of Baal! Don't let any of them run away!" The people captured all the prophets. Then Elijah led them down to the Kishon Valley, where he killed them.

INSPIRE YOUR TEAM TO REALIZE THE DREAM

eat my dust

FUTURE

By Claudio Freidzon

1 KINGS 18:41-46

God called the prophet Elijah in a time of apostasy and duplicity to raise up a standard of righteousness and boldly confront King Ahab and his lies. As Elijah and the king raced toward Jezreel, Elijah did not trail behind Ahab, following his path and eating his dust. Through the power of God, he outpaced Ahab and his chariot and blazed his own trail (1 Kings 18:41-46).

While the cloud of dust stirred up by Ahab's chariot represents the influence of the kingdom of darkness that soils everything in its path, the swiftness of Elijah shows that it is possible by the power of God to go in a new direction—one unsoiled by the world.

Today the spirit of Ahab is broadcast through mass media. Our age is perverse, wicked, and tolerant of evil. Yet, in the midst of all this, the Lord is raising up a generation that walks in his Word and his power and Spirit. He is calling you to rise up and to run ahead of the failing precepts of this world. You may feel like an "ordinary" person—but God is calling ordinary people just like you to an "extra" prayer life, an "extra" level of obedience and commitment, and an "extra" anointing. And, as a result, you can be "extra"ordinary in every area of life.

This holy generation burns with God's fire to confront the "Ahabs" of this day. This generation shows a different way and leads men to repent and turn back to the one true God. Never forget that the favor of God is upon you. Stir up a great dust cloud for God and watch the Enemy eat *your* dust!

reflect: Have you made the decision to overcome what oppresses you?
Go to **Jeremiah 29:14.**

THE RAIN COMES AGAIN

⁴¹Then Elijah said to Ahab, "Now, go, eat, and drink, because a heavy rain is coming." ⁴²So King Ahab went to eat and drink. At the same time Elijah climbed to the top of Mount Carmel, where he bent down to the ground with his head between his knees.

⁴³Then Elijah said to his servant, "Go and look toward the sea."

The servant went and looked. "I see nothing," he said.

Elijah told him to go and look again. This happened seven times. ⁴⁴The seventh time, the servant said, "I see a small cloud, the size of a human fist, coming from the sea."

Elijah told the servant, "Go to Ahab and tell him to get his chariot ready and go home now. Otherwise, the rain will stop him."

⁴⁵After a short time the sky was covered with dark clouds. The wind began to blow, and soon a heavy rain began to fall. Ahab got in his chariot and started back to Jezreel. ⁴⁶The LORD gave his power to Elijah, who tightened his clothes around him and ran ahead of King Ahab all the way to Jezreel.

ELIJAH RUNS AWAY

19 King Ahab told Jezebel every thing Elijah had done and how Elijah had killed all the prophets with a sword. ²So Jezebel sent a messenger to Elijah, saying, "May the gods punish me terribly if by this time tomorrow I don't kill you just as you killed those prophets."

³When Elijah heard this, he was afraid and ran for his life, taking his servant with him. When they came to Beersheba in Judah, Elijah left his servant there. ⁴Then Elijah walked for a whole day into the desert. He sat down under a bush and asked to die. "I have had enough, LORD," he prayed. "Let me die. I am no better than my ancestors." ⁵Then he lay down under the tree and slept.

Suddenly an angel came to him and touched him. "Get up and eat," the angel said. ⁶Elijah saw near his head a loaf baked over coals and a jar of water, so he ate and drank. Then he went back to sleep.

⁷Later the LORD's angel came to him a second time. The angel touched him and said, "Get up and eat. If you don't, the journey will be too hard for you." ⁸So Elijah got up and ate and drank. The food made him strong enough to walk for forty days and nights to Mount Sinai, the mountain of God. ⁹There Elijah went into a cave and stayed all night.

Then the LORD spoke his word to him: "Elijah! Why are you here?"

¹⁰He answered, "LORD God All-Powerful, I have always served you as well as I could. But the people of Israel have broken their agreement with you, destroyed your altars, and killed your prophets with swords. I am the only prophet left, and now they are trying to kill me, too."

¹¹The LORD said to Elijah, "Go, stand in front of me on the mountain, and I will pass by you." Then a very strong wind blew until it caused the mountains to fall apart and large rocks to break in front of the LORD. But the LORD was not in the wind. After the wind, there was an earthquake, but the LORD was not in the earthquake. ¹²After the earthquake, there was a fire, but the LORD was not in the fire. After the fire, there was a quiet, gentle sound. ¹³When Elijah heard it, he covered his face with his coat and went out and stood at the entrance to the cave.

Then a voice said to him, "Elijah! Why are you here?"

¹⁴He answered, "LORD God All-Powerful, I have always served you as well as I could. But the people of Israel have broken their agreement with you, destroyed your altars, and killed your prophets with swords. I am the only prophet left, and now they are trying to kill me, too."

¹⁵The LORD said to him, "Go back on the road that leads to the desert around Damascus. Enter that city, and pour olive oil on Hazael to make him king over Aram. ¹⁶Then pour oil on Jehu son of Nimshi to make him king over Israel. Next, pour oil on Elisha son of Shaphat from Abel Meholah to make him a prophet in your place. ¹⁷Jehu will kill anyone who escapes from Hazael's sword, and Elisha will kill anyone who escapes from Jehu's sword. ¹⁸I have seven thousand people left in Israel who have never bowed down before Baal and whose mouths have never kissed his idol."

ELISHA BECOMES A PROPHET

¹⁹So Elijah left that place and found Elisha son of Shaphat plowing a field with a team of

The **Product** of **Present Obedience**

By Edwin Louis Cole

1 KINGS 19:1–18

Elijah acted obediently on what God said, and his future became secure. *The basic art of communication is the ability to hear.* God waited to speak until Elijah was ready to hear. As Elijah sat commiserating under a juniper tree, it wasn't until he stopped feeling sorry for himself, was rested in his mind and spirit, that God spoke to him.

It would do no good for God to try to talk to Elijah while Elijah was still speaking because he wouldn't be able to hear. God spoke to Elijah in a "quiet, gentle sound." In quietness, Elijah again possessed his soul, heard from God, and became ready to receive the new revelation that would change and multiply his ministry.

The beauty of the relationship between God and Elijah was not just in Elijah's willingness to be identified with God, but also in God's willingness to be identified with Elijah—both on the mount and under the juniper tree. God would simply not let go of his prophet.

Under God's direction, Elijah left the mount and found Elisha, tutored and schooled him in the ways of faith, and eventually left the mantle of ministry with him. The spiritual tides in Israel changed and Elijah's adversaries, Ahab and Jezebel, died the dishonorable deaths due them. Elijah, a man who once desired to die under a juniper tree, ended his life without tasting death on this earth.

When God's purposes for Elijah were accomplished, *Elijah exchanged his juniper tree for a chariot of fire* that ushered him into heaven.

The turning point for Elijah was that in the midst of his aloneness, facing his most trying temptations, Elijah was able to hear God's voice. Once he heard, he obeyed. *God's power is released in our lives to the degree of our obedience, and no more.*

Obedience is not based on emotion, but on faith. Faith is always the key element in obedience. When Elijah obeyed God's Word, his emotions changed. The principle is: *Emotions follow actions.* Righteousness means "right standing" before God. There is no emotional quality to righteousness. It is a state of being. However, when the righteousness of Christ is imparted, the result is peace and joy, both of which have powerful emotional qualities.

Like righteousness, obedience and faith have no emotional qualities, but they have the ability to change a person's emotions. In other words, *to change your emotions, change your actions.* Obedience is an act of faith. Faith is belief in action. Belief is not faith until it is acted upon. Faith is like wind—*it cannot be seen, only its results.* Obedience is God's method of protection for our lives.

Living within his will, Word, and way is a life of obedient faith. God will take what is meant for harm and make it work for our ultimate good. God will take our most difficult times and make them work for our ultimate good when they are committed and submitted to him. Our obedience secures our future.

TO LEARN MORE ON WHAT THE BIBLE HAS TO SAY ABOUT **FUTURE,** READ THE SCRIPTURES AND DEVOTIONALS AT **GENESIS 13:17, GENESIS 39:2-5, 1 SAMUEL 2:6-10, 2 CHRONICLES 20,** AND **ESTHER 4:14.**

oxen. He owned twelve teams of oxen and was plowing with the twelfth team. Elijah came up to Elisha, took off his coat, and put it on Elisha. ²⁰Then Elisha left his oxen and ran to follow Elijah. "Let me kiss my father and my mother good-bye," Elisha said. "Then I will go with you."

Elijah answered, "Go back. It does not matter to me."

²¹So Elisha went back and took his pair of oxen and killed them. He used their wooden yoke for a fire. Then he cooked the meat and gave it to the people. After they ate it, Elisha left and followed Elijah and became his helper.

BEN-HADAD AND AHAB GO TO WAR

20 Ben-Hadad king of Aram gathered together all his army. There were thirty-two kings with their horses and chariots who went with him and surrounded Samaria and attacked it. ²The king sent messengers into the city to Ahab king of Israel.

This was his message: "Ben-Hadad says, ³'Your silver and gold belong to me, as well as the best of your wives and children.'"

⁴Ahab king of Israel answered, "My master and king, I agree to what you say. I and everything I have belong to you."

⁵Then the messengers came to Ahab again. They said, "Ben-Hadad says, 'I told you before that you must give me your silver and gold, your wives and your children. ⁶About this time tomorrow I will send my men, who will search everywhere in your palace and in the homes of your officers. Whatever they want they will take and carry off.'"

⁷Then Ahab called a meeting of all the elders of his country. He said, "Ben-Hadad is looking for trouble. First he said I had to give him my wives, my children, my silver, and my gold, and I have not refused him."

⁸The elders and all the people said, "Don't listen to him or agree to this."

⁹So Ahab said to Ben-Hadad's messengers, "Tell my master the king: 'I will do what you said at first, but I cannot allow this second command.'" And King Ben-Hadad's men carried the message back to him.

¹⁰Then Ben-Hadad sent another message to Ahab: "May the gods punish me terribly if I don't completely destroy Samaria. There won't be enough left for each of my men to get a handful of dust!"

¹¹Ahab answered, "Tell Ben-Hadad, 'The man who puts on his armor should not brag. It's the man who lives to take it off who has the right to brag.'"

¹²Ben-Hadad was drinking in his tent with the other rulers when the message came from Ahab. Ben-Hadad commanded his men to prepare to attack the city, and they moved into place for battle.

¹³At the same time a prophet came to Ahab king of Israel. The prophet said, "Ahab, the LORD says to you, 'Do you see that big army? I will hand it over to you today so you will know I am the LORD.'"

¹⁴Ahab asked, "Who will you use to defeat them?"

The prophet answered, "The LORD says, 'The young officers of the district governors will defeat them.'"

Then the king asked, "Who will command the main army?"

The prophet answered, "You will."

¹⁵So Ahab gathered the young officers of the district governors, two hundred thirty-two of them. Then he called together the army of Israel, about seven thousand people in all.

¹⁶They marched out at noon, while Ben-Hadad and the thirty-two rulers helping him were getting drunk in their tents. ¹⁷The young officers of the district governors attacked first. Ben-Hadad sent out scouts who told him that soldiers were coming from Samaria. ¹⁸Ben-Hadad said, "They may be coming to fight, or they may be coming to ask for peace. In either case capture them alive."

¹⁹The young officers of the district governors led the attack, followed by the army of Israel. ²⁰Each officer of Israel killed the man who came against him. The men from Aram ran away as Israel chased them, but Ben-Hadad king of Aram escaped on a horse with some of his horsemen. ²¹Ahab king of Israel led the army and destroyed the Arameans' horses and chariots. King Ahab thoroughly defeated the Aramean army.

²²Then the prophet went to Ahab king of Israel and said, "The king of Aram will attack you again next spring. So go home now and strengthen your army and see what you need to do."

²³Meanwhile the officers of Ben-Hadad king of Aram said to him, "The gods of Israel are mountain gods. Since we fought in a mountain area, Israel won. Let's fight them on the flat land, and then we will win. ²⁴This is what you should do. Don't allow the thirty-two rulers to command the armies, but put other commanders in their places. ²⁵Gather an army like the one that was destroyed and as many horses and chariots as before. We will fight the Israelites on flat land, and then we will win." Ben-Hadad agreed with their advice and did what they said.

²⁶The next spring Ben-Hadad gathered the army of Aram and went up to Aphek to fight against Israel.

²⁷The Israelites also had prepared for war. They marched out to meet the Arameans and camped opposite them. The Israelites looked like two small flocks of goats, but the Arameans covered the area.

²⁸A man of God came to the king of Israel with this message: "The LORD says, 'The people of Aram say that I, the LORD, am a god of the mountains, not a god of the valleys. So I will allow you to defeat this huge army, and then you will know I am the LORD.'"

²⁹The armies were camped across from each other for seven days. On the seventh day the battle began. The Israelites killed one hundred thousand Aramean soldiers in one day. ³⁰The rest of them ran away to the city of Aphek, where a city wall fell on twenty-seven thousand of them. Ben-Hadad also ran away to the city and hid in a room.

³¹His officers said to him, "We have heard that the kings of Israel are trustworthy. Let's dress in rough cloth to show our sadness, and wear ropes on our heads. Then we will go to the king of Israel, and perhaps he will let you live."

³²So they dressed in rough cloth and wore ropes on their heads and went to the king of Israel. They said, "Your servant Ben-Hadad says, 'Please let me live.'"

Ahab answered, "Is he still alive? He is my brother."

³³Ben-Hadad's men had wanted a sign from Ahab. So when Ahab called Ben-Hadad his brother, they quickly said, "Yes! Ben-Hadad is your brother."

Ahab said, "Bring him to me." When Ben-Hadad came, Ahab asked him to join him in the chariot.

³⁴Ben-Hadad said to him, "Ahab, I will give you back the cities my father took from your father. And you may put shops in Damascus, as my father did in Samaria."

Ahab said, "If you agree to this, I will allow you to go free." So the two kings made a peace agreement. Then Ahab let Ben-Hadad go free.

A PROPHET SPEAKS AGAINST AHAB

³⁵One prophet from one of the groups of prophets told another, "Hit me!" He said this because the LORD had commanded it, but the other man refused. ³⁶The prophet said, "You did not obey the LORD's command, so a lion will kill you as soon as you leave me." When the man left, a lion found him and killed him.

³⁷The prophet went to another man and said, "Hit me, please!" So the man hit him and hurt him. ³⁸The prophet wrapped his face in a cloth so no one could tell who he was. Then he went and waited by the road for the king. ³⁹As Ahab king of Israel passed by, the prophet called out to him. "I went to fight in the battle," the prophet said. "One of our men brought an enemy soldier to me. Our man said, 'Guard this man. If he runs away, you will have to give your life in his place. Or, you will have to pay a fine of seventy-five pounds of silver.' ⁴⁰But I was busy doing other things, so the man ran away."

The king of Israel answered, "You have already said what the punishment is. You must do what the man said."

⁴¹Then the prophet quickly took the cloth from his face. When the king of Israel saw him, he knew he was one of the prophets. ⁴²The prophet said to the king, "This is what the LORD says: 'You freed the man I said should die, so your life will be taken instead of his. The lives of your people will also be taken instead of the lives of his people.'"

⁴³Then King Ahab went back to his palace in Samaria, angry and upset.

AHAB TAKES NABOTH'S VINEYARD

21 After these things had happened, this is what followed. A man named Naboth owned a vineyard in Jezreel, near the palace of Ahab king of Israel. ²One day Ahab said to Naboth, "Give me your vineyard. It is near my palace, and I want to make it into a vegetable garden. I will give you a better vineyard in its place, or, if you prefer, I will pay you what it is worth."

³Naboth answered, "May the Lord keep me from ever giving my land to you. It belongs to my family."

⁴Ahab went home angry and upset, because he did not like what Naboth from Jezreel had said. (Naboth had said, "I will not give you my family's land.") Ahab lay down on his bed, turned his face to the wall, and refused to eat.

⁵His wife, Jezebel, came in and asked him, "Why are you so upset that you refuse to eat?"

⁶Ahab answered, "I talked to Naboth, the man from Jezreel. I said, 'Sell me your vineyard, or, if you prefer, I will give you another vineyard for it.' But Naboth refused."

⁷Jezebel answered, "Is this how you rule as king over Israel? Get up, eat something, and cheer up. I will get Naboth's vineyard for you."

⁸So Jezebel wrote some letters, signed Ahab's name to them, and used his own seal to seal them. Then she sent them to the elders and important men who lived in Naboth's town. ⁹The letter she wrote said: "Declare a day during which the people are to fast. Call the people together, and give Naboth a place of honor among them. ¹⁰Seat two troublemakers across from him, and have them say they heard Naboth speak against God and the king. Then take Naboth out of the city and kill him with stones."

¹¹The elders and important men of Jezreel obeyed Jezebel's command, just as she wrote in the letters. ¹²They declared a special day on which the people were to fast. And they put Naboth in a place of honor before the people. ¹³Two troublemakers sat across from Naboth and said in front of everybody that they had heard him speak against God and the king. So the people carried Naboth out of the city and killed him with stones. ¹⁴Then the leaders sent a message to Jezebel, saying, "Naboth has been killed."

¹⁵When Jezebel heard that Naboth had been killed, she told Ahab, "Naboth of Jezreel is dead. Now you may go and take for yourself the vineyard he would not sell to you." ¹⁶When Ahab heard that Naboth of Jezreel

was dead, he got up and went to the vineyard to take it for his own.

¹⁷At this time the Lord spoke his word to the prophet Elijah the Tishbite. The Lord said, ¹⁸"Go to Ahab king of Israel in Samaria. He is at Naboth's vineyard, where he has gone to take it as his own. ¹⁹Tell Ahab that I, the Lord, say to him, 'You have murdered Naboth and taken his land. So I tell you this: In the same place the dogs licked up Naboth's blood, they will also lick up your blood!'"

²⁰When Ahab saw Elijah, he said, "So you have found me, my enemy!"

Elijah answered, "Yes, I have found you. You have always chosen to do what the Lord says is wrong. ²¹So the Lord says to you, 'I will soon destroy you. I will kill you and every male in your family, both slave and free. ²²Your family will be like the family of King Jeroboam son of Nebat and like the family of King Baasha son of Ahijah. I will destroy you, because you have made me angry and have led the people of Israel to sin.'

²³"And the Lord also says, 'Dogs will eat the body of Jezebel in the city of Jezreel.'

²⁴"Anyone in your family who dies in the city will be eaten by dogs, and anyone who dies in the fields will be eaten by birds."

²⁵There was no one like Ahab who had chosen so often to do what the Lord said was wrong, because his wife Jezebel influenced him to do evil. ²⁶Ahab sinned terribly by worshiping idols, just as the Amorite people did. And the Lord had taken away their land and given it to the people of Israel.

²⁷After Elijah finished speaking, Ahab tore his clothes. He put on rough cloth, fasted, and even slept in the rough cloth to show how sad and upset he was.

²⁸The Lord spoke his word to Elijah the Tishbite: ²⁹"I see that Ahab is now sorry for what he has done. So I will not cause the trouble to come to him during his life, but I will wait until his son is king. Then I will bring this trouble to Ahab's family."

THE DEATH OF AHAB

22 For three years there was peace between Israel and Aram. ²During the third year Jehoshaphat king of Judah went to visit Ahab king of Israel.

³At that time Ahab asked his officers, "Do you remember that the king of Aram took

Ramoth in Gilead from us? Why have we done nothing to get it back?" ⁴So Ahab asked King Jehoshaphat, "Will you go with me to fight at Ramoth in Gilead?"

"I will go with you," Jehoshaphat answered. "My soldiers are yours, and my horses are yours." ⁵Jehoshaphat also said to Ahab, "But first we should ask if this is the LORD's will."

⁶Ahab called about four hundred prophets together and asked them, "Should I go to war against Ramoth in Gilead or not?"

They answered, "Go, because the Lord will hand them over to you."

⁷But Jehoshaphat asked, "Isn't there a prophet of the LORD here? Let's ask him what we should do."

⁸Then King Ahab said to Jehoshaphat, "There is one other prophet. We could ask the LORD through him, but I hate him. He never prophesies anything good about me, but something bad. He is Micaiah son of Imlah."

Jehoshaphat said, "King Ahab, you shouldn't say that!"

⁹So Ahab king of Israel told one of his officers to bring Micaiah to him at once.

¹⁰Ahab king of Israel and Jehoshaphat king of Judah had on their royal robes and were sitting on their thrones at the threshing floor, near the entrance to the gate of Samaria. All the prophets were standing before them, speaking their messages. ¹¹Zedekiah son of Kenaanah had made some iron horns. He said to Ahab, "This is what the LORD says, 'You will use these horns to fight the Arameans until they are destroyed.'"

¹²All the other prophets said the same thing. "Attack Ramoth in Gilead and win, because the LORD will hand the Arameans over to you."

¹³The messenger who had gone to get Micaiah said to him, "All the other prophets are saying King Ahab will succeed. You should agree with them and give the king a good answer."

¹⁴But Micaiah answered, "As surely as the LORD lives, I can tell him only what the LORD tells me."

¹⁵When Micaiah came to Ahab, the king asked him, "Micaiah, should we attack Ramoth in Gilead or not?"

Micaiah answered, "Attack and win!

The LORD will hand them over to you."

¹⁶But Ahab said to Micaiah, "How many times do I have to tell you to speak only the truth to me in the name of the LORD?"

¹⁷So Micaiah answered, "I saw the army of Israel scattered over the hills like sheep without a shepherd. The LORD said, 'They have no leaders. They should go home and not fight.'"

¹⁸Then Ahab king of Israel said to Jehoshaphat, "I told you! He never prophesies anything good about me, but only bad."

¹⁹But Micaiah said, "Hear the message from the LORD: I saw the LORD sitting on his throne with his heavenly army standing near him on his right and on his left. ²⁰The LORD said, 'Who will trick Ahab into attacking Ramoth in Gilead where he will be killed?'

"Some said one thing; some said another. ²¹Then one spirit came and stood before the LORD and said, 'I will trick him.'

²²"The LORD asked, 'How will you do it?'

"The spirit answered, 'I will go to Ahab's prophets and make them tell lies.'

"So the LORD said, 'You will succeed in tricking him. Go and do it.'"

²³Micaiah said, "Ahab, the LORD has made your prophets lie to you, and the LORD has decided that disaster should come to you."

²⁴Then Zedekiah son of Kenaanah went up to Micaiah and slapped him in the face. Zedekiah said, "Has the LORD's spirit left me to speak through you?"

²⁵Micaiah answered, "You will find out on the day you go to hide in an inside room."

²⁶Then Ahab king of Israel ordered, "Take Micaiah and send him to Amon, the governor of the city, and to Joash, the king's son. ²⁷Tell them I said to put this man in prison and give him only bread and water until I return safely from the battle."

²⁸Micaiah said, "Ahab, if you come back safely from battle, the LORD has not spoken through me. Remember my words, all you people!"

²⁹So Ahab king of Israel and Jehoshaphat king of Judah went to Ramoth in Gilead. ³⁰King Ahab said to Jehoshaphat, "I will go into battle, but I will wear other clothes so no one will recognize me. But you wear your royal clothes." So Ahab wore other clothes and went into battle.

³¹The king of Aram had ordered his thirty-two chariot commanders, "Don't fight with anyone—important or unimportant—except the king of Israel." ³²When these commanders saw Jehoshaphat, they thought he was certainly the king of Israel, so they turned to attack him. But Jehoshaphat began shouting. ³³When they saw he was not King Ahab, they stopped chasing him.

³⁴By chance, a soldier shot an arrow, but he hit Ahab king of Israel between the pieces of his armor. King Ahab said to his chariot driver, "Turn around and get me out of the battle, because I am hurt!" ³⁵The battle continued all day. King Ahab was held up in his chariot and faced the Arameans. His blood flowed down to the bottom of the chariot. That evening he died. ³⁶Near sunset a cry went out through the army of Israel: "Each man go back to his own city and land."

³⁷In that way King Ahab died. His body was carried to Samaria and buried there. ³⁸The men cleaned Ahab's chariot at a pool in Samaria where prostitutes bathed, and the dogs licked his blood from the chariot. These things happened as the LORD had said they would.

³⁹Everything else Ahab did is written in the book of the history of the kings of Israel. It tells about the palace Ahab built and decorated with ivory and the cities he built. ⁴⁰So Ahab died, and his son Ahaziah became king in his place.

JEHOSHAPHAT KING OF JUDAH

⁴¹Jehoshaphat son of Asa became king of Judah during Ahab's fourth year as king of Israel. ⁴²Jehoshaphat was thirty-five years old when he became king, and he ruled in Jerusalem for twenty-five years. His mother's name was Azubah daughter of Shilhi. ⁴³Jehoshaphat was good, like his father Asa, and he did what the LORD said was right. But Jehoshaphat did not destroy the places where gods were worshiped, so the people continued offering sacrifices and burning incense there. ⁴⁴Jehoshaphat was at peace with the king of Israel. ⁴⁵Jehoshaphat fought many wars, and these wars and his successes are written in the book of the history of the kings of Judah. ⁴⁶There were male prostitutes still in the places of worship from the days of his father, Asa. So Jehoshaphat forced them to leave.

⁴⁷During this time the land of Edom had no king; it was ruled by a governor.

⁴⁸King Jehoshaphat built trading ships to sail to Ophir for gold. But the ships were wrecked at Ezion Geber, so they never set sail. ⁴⁹Ahaziah son of Ahab went to help Jehoshaphat, offering to give Jehoshaphat some men to sail with his men, but Jehoshaphat refused.

⁵⁰Jehoshaphat died and was buried with his ancestors in Jerusalem, the city of David, his ancestor. Then his son Jehoram became king in his place.

AHAZIAH KING OF ISRAEL

⁵¹Ahaziah son of Ahab became king of Israel in Samaria during Jehoshaphat's seventeenth year as king over Judah. Ahaziah ruled Israel for two years, ⁵²and he did what the LORD said was wrong. He did the same evil his father Ahab, his mother Jezebel, and Jeroboam son of Nebat had done. All these rulers led the people of Israel into more sin. ⁵³Ahaziah worshiped and served the god Baal, and this made the LORD, the God of Israel, very angry. In these ways Ahaziah did what his father had done.

ELIJAH AND KING AHAZIAH

1 After Ahab died, Moab broke away from Israel's rule. ²Ahaziah fell down through the wooden bars in his upstairs room in Samaria and was badly hurt. He sent messengers and told them, "Go, ask Baal-Zebub, god of Ekron, if I will recover from my injuries."

³But the LORD's angel said to Elijah the Tishbite, "Go up and meet the messengers sent by the king of Samaria. Ask them, 'Why are you going to ask questions of Baal-Zebub, god of Ekron? Is it because you think there is no God in Israel?' ⁴This is what the LORD says: 'You will never get up from the bed you are lying on; you will die.'" Then Elijah left.

⁵When the messengers returned to Ahaziah, he asked them, "Why have you returned?"

⁶They said, "A man came to meet us. He said, 'Go back to the king who sent you and tell him what the LORD says: "Why do you send messengers to ask questions of Baal-Zebub, god of Ekron? Is it because you think there is no God in Israel? You will never get up from the bed you are lying on; you will die."'"

⁷Ahaziah asked them, "What did the man look like who met you and told you this?"

⁸They answered, "He was a hairy man and wore a leather belt around his waist."

Ahaziah said, "It was Elijah the Tishbite."

⁹Then he sent a captain with his fifty men to Elijah. The captain went to Elijah, who was sitting on top of the hill, and said to him, "Man of God, the king says, 'Come down!'"

¹⁰Elijah answered the captain, "If I am a man of God, let fire come down from heaven and burn up you and your fifty men." Then fire came down from heaven and burned up the captain and his fifty men.

¹¹Ahaziah sent another captain and fifty men to Elijah. The captain said to him, "Man of God, this is what the king says: 'Come down quickly!'"

¹²Elijah answered, "If I am a man of God, let fire come down from heaven and burn up you and your fifty men!" Then fire came down from heaven and burned up the captain and his fifty men.

¹³Ahaziah then sent a third captain with his fifty men. The third captain came and fell down on his knees before Elijah and begged, "Man of God, please respect my life and the lives of your fifty servants. ¹⁴See, fire came down from heaven and burned up the first two captains of fifty with all their men. But now, respect my life."

¹⁵The LORD's angel said to Elijah, "Go down with him and don't be afraid of him." So Elijah got up and went down with him to see the king.

¹⁶Elijah told Ahaziah, "This is what the LORD says: 'You have sent messengers to ask questions of Baal-Zebub, god of Ekron. Is it because you think there is no God in Israel to ask? Because of this, you will never get up from your bed; you will die.'" ¹⁷So Ahaziah died, just as the LORD, through Elijah, had said he would.

Joram became king in Ahaziah's place during the second year Jehoram son of Jehoshaphat was king of Judah. Joram ruled because Ahaziah had no son to take his place. ¹⁸The other things Ahaziah did are written in the book of the history of the kings of Israel.

ELIJAH IS TAKEN TO HEAVEN

2 It was almost time for the LORD to take Elijah by a whirlwind up into heaven. While Elijah and Elisha were leaving Gilgal, ²Elijah said to Elisha, "Please stay here. The LORD has told me to go to Bethel."

But Elisha said, "As the LORD lives, and as you live, I won't leave you." So they went down to Bethel. ³The groups of prophets at Bethel came out to Elisha and said to him, "Do you know the LORD will take your master away from you today?"

Elisha said, "Yes, I know, but don't talk about it."

⁴Elijah said to him, "Stay here, Elisha, because the LORD has sent me to Jericho."

But Elisha said, "As the LORD lives, and as you live, I won't leave you."

So they went to Jericho. ⁵The groups of prophets at Jericho came to Elisha and said, "Do you know that the LORD will take your master away from you today?"

Elisha answered, "Yes, I know, but don't talk about it."

⁶Elijah said to Elisha, "Stay here. The LORD has sent me to the Jordan River."

Elisha answered, "As the LORD lives, and as you live, I won't leave you."

So the two of them went on. ⁷Fifty men of the groups of prophets came and stood far from where Elijah and Elisha were by the Jordan. ⁸Elijah took off his coat, rolled it up, and hit the water. The water divided to the right and to the left, and Elijah and Elisha crossed over on dry ground.

⁹After they had crossed over, Elijah said to Elisha, "What can I do for you before I am taken from you?"

Elisha said, "Leave me a double share of your spirit."ⁿ

¹⁰Elijah said, "You have asked a hard thing. But if you see me when I am taken from you, it will be yours. If you don't, it won't happen."

¹¹As they were walking and talking, a chariot and horses of fire appeared and separated Elijah from Elisha. Then Elijah went up to heaven in a whirlwind. ¹²Elisha saw it and shouted, "My father! My father! The chariots of Israel and their horsemen!" And Elisha did not see him anymore. Then Elisha grabbed his own clothes and tore them to show how sad he was.

¹³He picked up Elijah's coat that had fallen from him. Then he returned and stood on the bank of the Jordan. ¹⁴Elisha hit the water with Elijah's coat and said, "Where is the LORD, the God of Elijah?" When he hit the water, it divided to the right and to the left, and Elisha crossed over.

¹⁵The groups of prophets at Jericho were watching and said, "Elisha now has the spirit Elijah had." And they came to meet him, bowing down to the ground before him. ¹⁶They said to him, "There are fifty strong men with us. Please let them go and look for your master. Maybe the Spirit of the LORD has taken

Elijah up and set him down on some mountain or in some valley."

But Elisha answered, "No, don't send them."

¹⁷When the groups of prophets had begged Elisha until he couldn't refuse them anymore, he said, "Send them." So they sent fifty men who looked for three days, but they could not find him. ¹⁸Then they came back to Elisha at Jericho where he was staying. He said to them, "I told you not to go, didn't I?"

ELISHA MAKES THE WATER PURE

¹⁹The people of the city said to Elisha, "Look, master, this city is a nice place to live as you can see. But the water is so bad the land cannot grow crops."

²⁰Elisha said, "Bring me a new bowl and put salt in it." So they brought it to him.

²¹Then he went out to the spring and threw the salt in it. He said, "This is what the LORD says: 'I have healed this water. From now on it won't cause death, and it won't keep the land from growing crops.'" ²²So the water has been healed to this day just as Elisha had said.

BOYS MAKE FUN OF ELISHA

²³From there Elisha went up to Bethel. On the way some boys came out of the city and made fun of him. They said to him, "Go up too, you baldhead! Go up too, you baldhead!" ²⁴Elisha turned around, looked at them, and put a curse on them in the name of the LORD. Then two mother bears came out of the woods and tore forty-two of the boys to pieces. ²⁵Elisha went to Mount Carmel and from there he returned to Samaria.

WAR BETWEEN ISRAEL AND MOAB

3 Joram son of Ahab became king over Israel at Samaria in Jehoshaphat's eighteenth year as king of Judah. And Joram ruled twelve years. ²He did what the LORD said was wrong, but he was not like his father and mother; he removed the stone pillars his father had made for Baal. ³But he continued to sin like Jeroboam son of Nebat who had

---

2:9 Leave . . . spirit By law, the first son in a family would inherit a double share of his father's possessions. Elisha is asking to inherit a share of his master's power as his follower. He is not asking for twice as much power as Elijah had.

led Israel to sin. Joram did not stop doing these same sins.

⁴Mesha king of Moab raised sheep. He paid the king of Israel one hundred thousand lambs and the wool of one hundred thousand sheep. ⁵But when Ahab died, the king of Moab turned against the king of Israel. ⁶So King Joram went out from Samaria and gathered Israel's army. ⁷He also sent messengers to Jehoshaphat king of Judah. "The king of Moab has turned against me," he said. "Will you go with me to fight Moab?"

Jehoshaphat replied, "I will go with you. My soldiers and my horses are yours."

⁸Jehoshaphat asked, "Which way should we attack?"

Joram answered, "Through the Desert of Edom."

⁹So the king of Israel went with the king of Judah and the king of Edom. After they had marched seven days, there was no more water for the army or for their animals that were with them. ¹⁰The king of Israel said, "This is terrible! The LORD has called us three kings together to hand us over to the Moabites!"

¹¹But Jehoshaphat asked, "Is there a prophet of the LORD here? We can ask the LORD through him."

An officer of the king of Israel answered, "Elisha son of Shaphat is here. He was Elijah's servant."

¹²Jehoshaphat said, "He speaks the LORD's truth." So the king of Israel and Jehoshaphat and the king of Edom went down to see Elisha.

¹³Elisha said to the king of Israel, "I have nothing to do with you. Go to the prophets of your father and to the prophets of your mother!"

The king of Israel said to Elisha, "No, the LORD has called us three kings together to hand us over to the Moabites."

¹⁴Elisha said, "As surely as the LORD All-Powerful lives, whom I serve, I tell you the truth. I wouldn't even look at you or notice you if Jehoshaphat king of Judah were not here. I respect him. ¹⁵Now bring me someone who plays the harp."

While the harp was being played, the LORD gave Elisha power. ¹⁶Then Elisha said, "The LORD says to dig holes in the valley. ¹⁷The LORD says you won't see wind or rain, but the valley will be filled with water. Then you, your cattle, and your other animals can drink. ¹⁸This is easy for the LORD to do; he will also hand Moab over to you. ¹⁹You will destroy every strong, walled city and every important town. You will cut down every good tree and stop up all springs. You will ruin every good field with rocks."

²⁰The next morning, about the time the sacrifice was offered, water came from the direction of Edom and filled the valley.

²¹All the Moabites heard that the kings had come up to fight against them. So they gathered everyone old enough to put on armor and waited at the border. ²²But when the Moabites got up early in the morning, the sun was shining on the water. They saw the water across from them, and it looked as red as blood. ²³Then they said, "This is blood! The kings must have fought and killed each other! Come, Moabites, let's take the valuables from the dead bodies!"

²⁴When the Moabites came to the camp of Israel, the Israelites came out and fought them until they ran away. Then the Israelites went on into the land, killing the Moabites. ²⁵They tore down the cities and threw rocks all over every good field. They stopped up all the springs and cut down all the good trees. Kir Hareseth was the only city with its stones still in place, but the men with slingshots surrounded it and conquered it, too.

²⁶When the king of Moab saw that the battle was too much for him, he took seven hundred men with swords to try to break through to the king of Edom. But they could not break through. ²⁷Then the king of Moab took his oldest son, who would have been king after him, and offered him as a burnt offering on the wall. So there was great anger against the Israelites, who left and went back to their own land.

A WIDOW ASKS ELISHA FOR HELP

4 The wife of a man from the groups of prophets said to Elisha, "Your servant, my husband, is dead. You know he honored the LORD. But now the man he owes money to is coming to take my two boys as his slaves!"

²Elisha answered, "How can I help you? Tell me, what do you have in your house?"

The woman said, "I don't have anything there except a pot of oil."

³Then Elisha said, "Go and get empty jars from all your neighbors. Don't ask for just a few. ⁴Then go into your house and shut the door behind you and your sons. Pour oil into all the jars, and set the full ones aside."

⁵So she left Elisha and shut the door behind her and her sons. As they brought the jars to her, she poured out the oil. ⁶When the jars were all full, she said to her son, "Bring me another jar."

But he said, "There are no more jars." Then the oil stopped flowing.

⁷She went and told Elisha. And the prophet said to her, "Go, sell the oil and pay what you owe. You and your sons can live on what is left."

THE SHUNAMMITE WOMAN

⁸One day Elisha went to Shunem, where an important woman lived. She begged Elisha to stay and eat. So every time Elisha passed by, he stopped there to eat. ⁹The woman said to her husband, "I know that this is a holy man of God who passes by our house all the time. ¹⁰Let's make a small room on the roof [n] and put a bed in the room for him. We can put a table, a chair, and a lampstand there. Then when he comes by, he can stay there."

¹¹One day Elisha came to the woman's house. After he went to his room and rested, ¹²he said to his servant Gehazi, "Call the Shunammite woman."

When the servant had called her, she stood in front of him. ¹³Elisha had told his servant, "Now say to her, 'You have gone to all this trouble for us. What can I do for you? Do you want me to speak to the king or the commander of the army for you?'"

She answered, "I live among my own people."

¹⁴Elisha said to Gehazi, "But what can we do for her?"

He answered, "She has no son, and her husband is old."

¹⁵Then Elisha said to Gehazi, "Call her." When he called her, she stood in the doorway. ¹⁶Then Elisha said, "About this time next year, you will hold a son in your arms."

The woman said, "No, master, man of God, don't lie to me, your servant!"

¹⁷But the woman became pregnant and gave birth to a son at that time the next year, just as Elisha had told her.

¹⁸The boy grew up and one day went out to his father, who was with the grain harvesters. ¹⁹The boy said to his father, "My head! My head!"

The father said to his servant, "Take him to his mother!" ²⁰The servant took him to his mother, and he lay on his mother's lap until noon. Then he died. ²¹So she took him up and laid him on Elisha's bed. Then she shut the door and left.

²²She called to her husband, "Send me one of the servants and one of the donkeys. Then I can go quickly to the man of God and return."

²³The husband said, "Why do you want to go to him today? It isn't the New Moon or the Sabbath day."

She said, "It will be all right."

²⁴Then she saddled the donkey and said to her servant, "Lead on. Don't slow down for me unless I tell you." ²⁵So she went to Elisha, the man of God, at Mount Carmel.

When he saw her coming from far away, he said to his servant Gehazi, "Look, there's the Shunammite woman! ²⁶Run to meet her and ask, 'Are you all right? Is your husband all right? Is the boy all right?'"

She answered, "Everything is all right."

²⁷Then she came to Elisha at the hill and grabbed his feet. Gehazi came near to pull her away, but Elisha said to him, "Leave her alone. She's very upset, and the LORD has not told me about it. He has hidden it from me."

²⁸She said, "Master, did I ask you for a son? Didn't I tell you not to lie to me?"

²⁹Then Elisha said to Gehazi, "Get ready. Take my walking stick in your hand and go quickly. If you meet anyone, don't say hello. If anyone greets you, don't respond. Lay my walking stick on the boy's face."

³⁰The boy's mother said, "As surely as the LORD lives and as you live, I won't leave you!" So Elisha got up and followed her.

³¹Gehazi went on ahead and laid the walking stick on the boy's face, but the boy did not talk or move. Then Gehazi went back to meet Elisha. "The boy has not awakened," he said. ³²When Elisha came into the house, the

---

4:10 roof In Bible times houses were built with flat roofs. The roof was used for drying things such as flax and fruit. And it was used as an extra room, as a place for worship, and as a cool place to sleep in the summer.

boy was lying dead on his bed. ³³Elisha entered the room and shut the door, so only he and the boy were in the room. Then he prayed to the LORD. ³⁴He went to the bed and lay on the boy, putting his mouth on the boy's mouth, his eyes on the boy's eyes, and his hands on the boy's hands. He stretched himself out on top of the boy. Soon the boy's skin became warm. ³⁵Elisha turned away and walked around the room. Then he went back and put himself on the boy again. The boy sneezed seven times and opened his eyes.

³⁶Elisha called Gehazi and said, "Call the Shunammite!" So he did. When she came, Elisha said, "Pick up your son." ³⁷She came in and fell at Elisha's feet, bowing facedown to the floor. Then she picked up her son and went out.

ELISHA AND THE STEW

³⁸When Elisha returned to Gilgal, there was a shortage of food in the land. While the groups of prophets were sitting in front of him, he said to his servant, "Put the large pot on the fire, and boil some stew for these men."

³⁹One of them went out into the field to gather plants. Finding a wild vine, he picked fruit from the vine and filled his robe with it. Then he came and cut up the fruit into the pot. But they didn't know what kind of fruit it was. ⁴⁰They poured out the stew for the others to eat. When they began to eat it, they shouted, "Man of God, there's death in the pot!" And they could not eat it.

⁴¹Elisha told them to bring some flour. He threw it into the pot and said, "Pour it out for the people to eat." Then there was nothing harmful in the pot.

ELISHA FEEDS THE PEOPLE

⁴²A man from Baal Shalishah came to Elisha, bringing him twenty loaves of barley bread from the first harvest. He also brought fresh grain in his sack. Elisha said, "Give it to the people to eat."

⁴³Elisha's servant asked, "How can I feed a hundred people with so little?"

"Give the bread to the people to eat," Elisha said. "This is what the LORD says: 'They will eat and will have food left over.'" ⁴⁴After he gave it to them, the people ate and had food left over, as the LORD had said.

NAAMAN IS HEALED

5 Naaman was commander of the army of the king of Aram. He was honored by his master, and he had much respect because the LORD used him to give victory to Aram. He was a mighty and brave man, but he had a skin disease.

²The Arameans had gone out to raid the Israelites and had taken a little girl as a captive. This little girl served Naaman's wife. ³She said to her mistress, "I wish my master would meet the prophet who lives in Samaria. He would cure him of his disease."

⁴Naaman went to the king and told him what the girl from Israel had said. ⁵The king of Aram said, "Go ahead, and I will send a letter to the king of Israel." So Naaman left and took with him about seven hundred fifty pounds of silver, as well as one hundred fifty pounds of gold and ten changes of clothes. ⁶He brought the letter to the king of Israel, which read, "I am sending my servant Naaman to you so you can heal him of his skin disease."

⁷When the king of Israel read the letter, he tore his clothes to show how upset he was. He said, "I'm not God! I can't kill and make alive again! Why does this man send someone with a skin disease for me to heal? You can see that the king of Aram is trying to start trouble with me."

⁸When Elisha, the man of God, heard that the king of Israel had torn his clothes, he sent the king this message: "Why have you torn your clothes? Let Naaman come to me. Then he will know there is a prophet in Israel." ⁹So Naaman went with his horses and chariots to Elisha's house and stood outside the door.

¹⁰Elisha sent Naaman a messenger who said, "Go and wash in the Jordan River seven times. Then your skin will be healed, and you will be clean."

¹¹Naaman became angry and left. He said, "I thought Elisha would surely come out and stand before me and call on the name of the LORD his God. I thought he would wave his hand over the place and heal the disease. ¹²The Abana and the Pharpar, the rivers of Damascus, are better than all the waters of Israel. Why can't I wash in them and become clean?" So Naaman went away very angry.

¹³Naaman's servants came near and said to him, "My father, if the prophet had told

you to do some great thing, wouldn't you have done it? Doesn't it make more sense just to do it? After all, he only told you, 'Wash, and you will be clean.'" ¹⁴So Naaman went down and dipped in the Jordan seven times, just as Elisha had said. Then his skin became new again, like the skin of a child. And he was clean.

¹⁵Naaman and all his group returned to Elisha. He stood before Elisha and said, "Look, I now know there is no God in all the earth except in Israel. Now please accept a gift from me."

¹⁶But Elisha said, "As surely as the LORD lives whom I serve, I won't accept anything." Naaman urged him to take the gift, but he refused.

¹⁷Then Naaman said, "If you won't take the gift, then please give me some soil—as much as two of my mules can carry. From now on I'll not offer any burnt offering or sacrifice to any other gods but the LORD. ¹⁸But let the LORD pardon me for this: When my master goes into the temple of Rimmon[n] to worship, he leans on my arm. Then I must bow in that temple. May the LORD pardon me when I do that."

¹⁹Elisha said to him, "Go in peace."

Naaman left Elisha and went a short way. ²⁰Gehazi, the servant of Elisha the man of God, thought, "My master has not accepted what Naaman the Aramean brought. As surely as the LORD lives, I'll run after him and get something from him." ²¹So Gehazi went after Naaman.

When Naaman saw someone running after him, he got off the chariot to meet Gehazi. He asked, "Is everything all right?"

²²Gehazi said, "Everything is all right. My master has sent me. He said, 'Two young men from the groups of prophets in the mountains of Ephraim just came to me. Please give them seventy-five pounds of silver and two changes of clothes.'"

²³Naaman said, "Please take one hundred fifty pounds," and he urged Gehazi to take it. He tied one hundred fifty pounds of silver in two bags with two changes of clothes. Then he gave them to two of his servants to carry for Gehazi. ²⁴When they came to the hill, Gehazi took these things from Naaman's servants and put them in the house. Then he let Naaman's servants go, and they left.

²⁵When he came in and stood before his master, Elisha said to him, "Where have you been, Gehazi?"

"I didn't go anywhere," he answered.

²⁶But Elisha said to him, "My spirit was with you. I knew when the man turned from his chariot to meet you. This isn't a time to take money, clothes, olives, grapes, sheep, oxen, male servants, or female servants. ²⁷So Naaman's skin disease will come on you and your children forever." When Gehazi left Elisha, he had the disease and was as white as snow.

AN AXHEAD FLOATS

6 The groups of prophets said to Elisha, "The place where we meet with you is too small for us. ²Let's go to the Jordan River. There everyone can get a log, and let's build a place there to live."

Elisha said, "Go."

³One of them said, "Please go with us."

Elisha answered, "I will go," ⁴so he went with them. When they arrived at the Jordan, they cut down some trees. ⁵As one man was cutting down a tree, the head of his ax fell into the water. He yelled, "Oh, my master! I borrowed that ax!"

⁶Elisha asked, "Where did it fall?" The man showed him the place. Then Elisha cut down a stick and threw it into the water, and it made the iron head float. ⁷Elisha said, "Pick up the axhead." Then the man reached out and took it.

ELISHA AND THE BLINDED ARAMEANS

⁸The king of Aram was at war with Israel. He had a council meeting with his officers and said, "I will set up my camp in this place."

⁹Elisha, the man of God, sent a message to the king of Israel, saying, "Be careful! Don't pass that place, because the Arameans are going down there!"

¹⁰The king of Israel checked the place about which Elisha had warned him. Elisha warned him several times, so the king protected himself there.

¹¹The king of Aram was angry about this. He called his officers together and de-

---

5:18 temple of Rimmon The place where the Aramean people worshiped the god Rimmon.

manded, "Tell me who of us is working for the king of Israel."

12One of the officers said, "None, my master and king. It's Elisha, the prophet from Israel. He can tell you what you speak in your bedroom."

13The king said, "Go and find him so I can send men and catch him."

The servants came back and reported, "He is in Dothan."

14Then the king sent horses, chariots, and many troops to Dothan. They arrived at night and surrounded the city.

15Elisha's servant got up early, and when he went out, he saw an army with horses and chariots all around the city. The servant said to Elisha, "Oh, my master, what can we do?"

16Elisha said, "Don't be afraid. The army that fights for us is larger than the one against us."

17Then Elisha prayed, "LORD, open my servant's eyes, and let him see."

The LORD opened the eyes of the young man, and he saw that the mountain was full of horses and chariots of fire all around Elisha.

18As the enemy came down toward Elisha, he prayed to the LORD, "Make these people blind." So he made the Aramean army blind, as Elisha had asked.

19Elisha said to them, "This is not the right road or the right city. Follow me and I'll take you to the man you are looking for." Then Elisha led them to Samaria.

20After they entered Samaria, Elisha said, "LORD, open these men's eyes so they can see." So the LORD opened their eyes, and the Aramean army saw that they were inside the city of Samaria!

21When the king of Israel saw the Aramean army, he said to Elisha, "My father, should I kill them? Should I kill them?"

22Elisha answered, "Don't kill them. You wouldn't kill people whom you captured with your sword and bow. Give them food and water, and let them eat and drink and then go home to their master." 23So he prepared a great feast for the Aramean army. After they ate and drank, the king sent them away, and they went home to their master. The soldiers of Aram did not come anymore into the land of Israel.

A SHORTAGE OF FOOD

24Later, Ben-Hadad king of Aram gathered his whole army and surrounded and attacked Samaria. 25There was a shortage of food in Samaria. It was so bad that a donkey's head sold for about two pounds of silver, and half of a pint of dove's dung sold for about two ounces of silver.

26As the king of Israel was passing by on the wall, a woman yelled out to him, "Help me, my master and king!"

27The king said, "If the LORD doesn't help you, how can I? Can I get help from the threshing floor or from the winepress?" 28Then the king said to her, "What is your trouble?"

She answered, "This woman said to me, 'Give up your son so we can eat him today. Then we will eat my son tomorrow.' 29So we boiled my son and ate him. Then the next day I said to her, 'Give up your son so we can eat him.' But she had hidden him."

30When the king heard the woman's words, he tore his clothes in grief. As he walked along the wall, the people looked and saw he had on rough cloth under his clothes to show his sadness. 31He said, "May God punish me terribly if the head of Elisha son of Shaphat isn't cut off from his body today!"

32The king sent a messenger to Elisha, who was sitting in his house with the elders. But before the messenger arrived, Elisha said to them, "See, this murderer is sending men to cut off my head. When the messenger arrives, shut the door and hold it; don't let him in. The sound of his master's feet is behind him."

33Elisha was still talking with the leaders when the messenger arrived. The king said, "This trouble has come from the LORD. Why should I wait for the LORD any longer?"

7 Elisha said, "Listen to the LORD's word. This is what the LORD says: 'About this time tomorrow seven quarts of fine flour will be sold for two-fifths of an ounce of silver, and thirteen quarts of barley will be sold for two-fifths of an ounce of silver. This will happen at the gate of Samaria.'"

2Then the officer who was close to the king answered Elisha, "Even if the LORD opened windows in the sky, that couldn't happen."

Elisha said, "You will see it with your eyes, but you will not eat any of it."

³There were four men with a skin disease at the entrance to the city gate. They said to each other, "Why do we sit here until we die? ⁴There is no food in the city. So if we go into the city, we will die there. If we stay here, we will die. So let's go to the Aramean camp. If they let us live, we will live. If they kill us, we die."

⁵So they got up at twilight and went to the Aramean camp, but when they arrived, no one was there. ⁶The Lord had caused the Aramean army to hear the sound of chariots, horses, and a large army. They had said to each other, "The king of Israel has hired the Hittite and Egyptian kings to attack us!" ⁷So they got up and ran away in the twilight, leaving their tents, horses, and donkeys. They left the camp standing and ran for their lives.

⁸When the men with the skin disease came to the edge of the camp, they went into one of the tents and ate and drank. They carried silver, gold, and clothes out of the camp and hid them. Then they came back and entered another tent. They carried things from this tent and hid them, also. ⁹Then they said to each other, "We're doing wrong. Today we have good news, but we are silent. If we wait until the sun comes up, we'll be discovered. Let's go right now and tell the people in the king's palace."

¹⁰So they went and called to the gatekeepers of the city. They said, "We went to the Aramean camp, but no one is there; we didn't hear anyone. The horses and donkeys were still tied up, and the tents were still standing." ¹¹Then the gatekeepers shouted out and told the people in the palace.

¹²The king got up in the night and said to his officers, "I'll tell you what the Arameans are doing to us. They know we are starving. They have gone out of the camp to hide in the field. They're saying, 'When the Israelites come out of the city, we'll capture them alive. Then we'll enter the city.'" ¹³One of his officers answered, "Let some men take five of the horses that are still left in the city. These men are like all the Israelites who are left; they are also about to die. Let's send them to see what has happened."

¹⁴So the men took two chariots with horses. The king sent them after the Aramean army, saying, "Go and see what has happened." ¹⁵The men followed the Aramean army as far as the Jordan River. The road was full of clothes and equipment that the Arameans had thrown away as they had hurriedly left. So the messengers returned and told the king. ¹⁶Then the people went out and took valuables from the Aramean camp. So seven quarts of fine flour were sold for two-fifths of an ounce of silver, and thirteen quarts of barley were sold for two-fifths of an ounce of silver, just as the Lord had said.

¹⁷The king chose the officer who was close to him to guard the gate, but the people trampled the officer to death. This happened just as Elisha had told the king when the king came to his house. ¹⁸He had said, "Thirteen quarts of barley and seven quarts of fine flour will each sell for two-fifths of an ounce of silver about this time tomorrow at the gate of Samaria."

¹⁹But the officer had answered, "Even if the Lord opened windows in the sky, that couldn't happen." And Elisha had told him, "You will see it with your eyes, but you won't eat any of it." ²⁰It happened to the officer just that way. The people trampled him in the gateway, and he died.

THE SHUNAMMITE REGAINS HER LAND

8 Elisha spoke to the woman whose son he had brought back to life. He said, "Get up and go with your family. Stay any place you can, because the Lord has called for a time without food that will last seven years." ²So the woman got up and did as the man of God had said. She left with her family, and they stayed in the land of the Philistines for seven years. ³After seven years she returned from the land of the Philistines and went to beg the king for her house and land. ⁴The king was talking with Gehazi, the servant of the man of God. The king had said, "Please tell me all the great things Elisha has done." ⁵Gehazi was telling the king how Elisha had brought a dead boy back to life. Just then the woman whose son Elisha had brought back to life came and begged the king for her house and land.

Gehazi said, "My master and king, this is the woman, and this is the son Elisha brought back to life."

⁶The king asked the woman, and she told

him about it. Then the king chose an officer to help her. "Give the woman everything that is hers," the king said. "Give her all the money made from her land from the day she left until now."

BEN-HADAD IS KILLED

[7]Then Elisha went to Damascus, where Ben-Hadad king of Aram was sick. Someone told him, "The man of God has arrived."

[8]The king said to Hazael, "Take a gift in your hand and go meet him. Ask the LORD through him if I will recover from my sickness."

[9]So Hazael went to meet Elisha, taking with him a gift of forty camels loaded with every good thing in Damascus. He came and stood before Elisha and said, "Your son Ben-Hadad king of Aram sent me to you. He asks if he will recover from his sickness."

[10]Elisha said to Hazael, "Go and tell Ben-Hadad, 'You will surely recover,' but the LORD has told me he will really die." [11]Hazael stared at Elisha until he felt ashamed. Then Elisha cried.

[12]Hazael asked, "Why are you crying, master?"

Elisha answered, "Because I know what evil you will do to the Israelites. You will burn their strong, walled cities with fire and kill their young men with swords. You will throw their babies to the ground and split open their pregnant women."

[13]Hazael said, "Am I a dog? How could I do such things?"

Elisha answered, "The LORD has shown me that you will be king over Aram."

[14]Then Hazael left Elisha and came to his master. Ben-Hadad said to him, "What did Elisha say to you?"

Hazael answered, "He told me that you will surely recover." [15]But the next day Hazael took a blanket and dipped it in water. Then he put it over Ben-Hadad's face, and he died. So Hazael became king in Ben-Hadad's place.

JEHORAM KING OF JUDAH

[16]While Jehoshaphat was king in Judah, Jehoram son of Jehoshaphat became king of Judah. This was during the fifth year Joram son of Ahab was king of Israel. [17]Jehoram was thirty-two years old when he began to rule, and he ruled eight years in Jerusalem. [18]He followed the ways of the kings of Israel, just as the family of Ahab had done, because he married Ahab's daughter. Jehoram did what the LORD said was wrong. [19]But the LORD would not destroy Judah because of his servant David. The LORD had promised that one of David's descendants would always rule.

[20]In Jehoram's time Edom broke away from Judah's rule and chose their own king. [21]So Jehoram and all his chariots went to Zair. The Edomites surrounded him and his chariot commanders. Jehoram got up and attacked the Edomites at night, but his army ran away to their tents. [22]From then until now the country of Edom has fought against the rule of Judah. At the same time Libnah also broke away from Judah's rule.

[23]The other acts of Jehoram and all the things he did are written in the book of the history of the kings of Judah. [24]Jehoram died and was buried with his ancestors in Jerusalem, and Jehoram's son Ahaziah ruled in his place.

[25]Ahaziah son of Jehoram became king of Judah during the twelfth year Joram son of Ahab was king of Israel. [26]Ahaziah was twenty-two years old when he became king, and he ruled one year in Jerusalem. His mother's name was Athaliah, a granddaughter of Omri king of Israel. [27]Ahaziah followed the ways of Ahab's family. He did what the LORD said was wrong, as Ahab's family had done, because he was a son-in-law to Ahab.

[28]Ahaziah went with Joram son of Ahab to Ramoth in Gilead, where they fought against Hazael king of Aram. The Arameans wounded Joram. [29]So King Joram returned to Jezreel to heal from the wound he had received from the Arameans at Ramoth when he fought Hazael king of Aram. Ahaziah son of Jehoram king of Judah went down to visit Joram son of Ahab at Jezreel, because he had been wounded.

JEHU IS CHOSEN KING

9 At the same time, Elisha the prophet called a man from the groups of prophets. Elisha said, "Get ready, and take this small bottle of olive oil in your hand. Go to Ramoth in Gilead. [2]When you arrive, find Jehu son of Jehoshaphat, the son of Nimshi. Go in and make Jehu get up from among his brothers, and take him to an inner room. [3]Then take the bottle and pour the oil on Jehu's head and say, 'This is what the LORD says: I have appointed you king over Israel.' Then open the door and run away. Don't wait!"

⁴So the young man, the prophet, went to Ramoth in Gilead. ⁵When he arrived, he saw the officers of the army sitting together. He said, "Commander, I have a message for you."

Jehu asked, "For which one of us?"

The young man said, "For you, commander."

⁶Jehu got up and went into the house. Then the young prophet poured the olive oil on Jehu's head and said to him, "This is what the LORD, the God of Israel says: 'I have appointed you king over the LORD's people Israel. ⁷You must destroy the family of Ahab your master. I will punish Jezebel for the deaths of my servants the prophets and for all the LORD's servants who were murdered. ⁸All of Ahab's family must die. I will not let any male child in Ahab's family live in Israel, whether slave or free. ⁹I will make Ahab's family like the family of Jeroboam son of Nebat and like the family of Baasha son of Ahijah. ¹⁰The dogs will eat Jezebel at Jezreel, and no one will bury her.' "

Then the young prophet opened the door and ran away.

¹¹When Jehu went back to his master's officers, one of them said to Jehu, "Is everything all right? Why did this crazy man come to you?"

Jehu answered, "You know the man and how he talks."

¹²They answered, "That's not true. Tell us."

Jehu said, "He said to me, 'This is what the LORD says: I have appointed you to be king over Israel.' "

¹³Then the officers hurried, and each man took off his own coat and put it on the stairs for Jehu. They blew the trumpet and shouted, "Jehu is king!"

JORAM AND AHAZIAH ARE KILLED

¹⁴So Jehu son of Jehoshaphat, the son of Nimshi, made plans against Joram. Now Joram and all Israel had been defending Ramoth in Gilead from Hazael king of Aram. ¹⁵But King Joram had to return to Jezreel to heal from the injuries the Arameans had

given him when he fought against Hazael king of Aram.

Jehu said, "If you agree with this, don't let anyone leave the city. They might tell the news in Jezreel." ¹⁶Then he got into his chariot and set out for Jezreel, where Joram was resting. Ahaziah king of Judah had gone down to see him.

¹⁷The lookout was standing on the watchtower in Jezreel when he saw Jehu's troops coming. He said, "I see some soldiers!"

Joram said, "Take a horseman and send him to meet them. Tell him to ask, 'Is all in order?' "

¹⁸The horseman rode out to meet Jehu, and he said, "This is what the king says: 'Is all in order?' "

Jehu said, "Why bother yourself with order? Come along behind me."

The lookout reported, "The messenger reached them, but he is not coming back."

¹⁹Then Joram sent out a second horseman. This rider came to Jehu's group and said, "This is what the king says: 'Is all in order?' "

Jehu answered, "Why bother yourself with order? Come along behind me."

²⁰The lookout reported, "The second man reached them, but he is not coming back. The man in the chariot is driving like Jehu son of Nimshi. He drives as if he were crazy!"

²¹Joram said, "Get my chariot ready." Then the servant got Joram's chariot ready. Joram king of Israel and Ahaziah king of Judah went out, each in his own chariot, to meet Jehu at the property of Naboth the Jezreelite.

²²When Joram saw Jehu, he said, "Is all in order, Jehu?"

Jehu answered, "There will never be any order as long as your mother Jezebel worships idols and uses witchcraft."

²³Joram turned the horses to run away and yelled to Ahaziah, "It's a trick, Ahaziah!"

²⁴Then Jehu drew his bow and shot Joram between his shoulders. The arrow went through Joram's heart, and he fell down in his chariot.

²⁵Jehu ordered Bidkar, his chariot officer, "Pick up Joram's body, and throw it into the field of Naboth the Jezreelite. Remember when you and I rode together with Joram's father Ahab. The LORD made this prophecy

against him: 26'Yesterday I saw the blood of Naboth and his sons, says the LORD, so I will punish Ahab in his field, says the LORD.' Take Joram's body and throw it into the field, as the LORD has said."

27When Ahaziah king of Judah saw this, he ran away toward Beth Haggan. Jehu chased him, saying, "Shoot Ahaziah, too!" Ahaziah was wounded in his chariot on the way up to Gur near Ibleam. He got as far as Megiddo but died there. 28Ahaziah's servants carried his body in a chariot to Jerusalem and buried him with his ancestors in his tomb in Jerusalem. 29(Ahaziah had become king over Judah in the eleventh year Joram son of Ahab was king.)

DEATH OF JEZEBEL

30When Jehu came to Jezreel, Jezebel heard about it. She put on her eye makeup and fixed her hair. Then she looked out the window. 31When Jehu entered the city gate, Jezebel said, "Have you come in peace, you Zimri,[n] you who killed your master?"

32Jehu looked up at the window and said, "Who is on my side? Who?" Two or three servants looked out the window at Jehu. 33He said to them, "Throw her down." So they threw Jezebel down, and the horses ran over her. Some of her blood splashed on the wall and on the horses.

34Jehu went into the house and ate and drank. Then he said, "Now see about this cursed woman. Bury her, because she is a king's daughter."

35The men went to bury Jezebel, but they could not find her. They found only her skull, feet, and the palms of her hands. 36When they came back and told Jehu, he said, "The LORD said this through his servant Elijah the Tishbite: 'The dogs will eat Jezebel at Jezreel. 37Her body will be like manure on the field in the land at Jezreel. No one will be able to say that this is Jezebel.'"

FAMILIES OF AHAB AND AHAZIAH KILLED

10 Ahab had seventy sons in Samaria. Jehu wrote letters and sent them to Samaria to the officers and elders of Jezreel and to the guardians of the sons of Ahab. Jehu said, 2"You have your master's sons with you, and you have chariots, horses, a city with strong walls, and weapons. When you get this letter, 3choose the best and most worthy per-

son among your master's sons, and make him king. Then fight for your master's family."

4But the officers and leaders of Jezreel were frightened. They said, "Two kings could not stand up to Jehu, so how can we?"

5The palace manager, the city governor, the leaders, and the guardians sent a message to Jehu. "We are your servants," they said. "We will do everything you tell us to do. We won't make any man king, so do whatever you think is best."

6Then Jehu wrote a second letter, saying, "If you are on my side and will obey me, cut off the heads of your master's sons and come to me at Jezreel tomorrow about this time."

Now the seventy sons of the king's family were with the leading men of the city who were their guardians. 7When the leaders received the letter, they took the king's sons and killed all seventy of them. They put their heads in baskets and sent them to Jehu at Jezreel. 8The messenger came to Jehu and told him, "They have brought the heads of the king's sons."

Then Jehu said, "Lay the heads in two piles at the city gate until morning."

9In the morning, Jehu went out and stood before the people and said to them, "You are innocent. Look, I made plans against my master and killed him. But who killed all these? 10You should know that everything the LORD said about Ahab's family will come true. The LORD has spoken through his servant Elijah, and the LORD has done what he said." 11So Jehu killed everyone of Ahab's family in Jezreel who was still alive. He also killed all Ahab's leading men, close friends, and priests. No one who had helped Ahab was left alive.

12Then Jehu left and went to Samaria by way of the road to Beth Eked of the Shepherds. 13There Jehu met some relatives of Ahaziah king of Judah. Jehu asked, "Who are you?"

They answered, "We are relatives of Ahaziah. We have come down to get revenge for the families of the king and the king's mother."

14Then Jehu said, "Take them alive!" So they captured Ahaziah's relatives alive and

---

9:31 Zimri He was the man who killed Elah and the family of Baasha. Read 1 Kings 16:8–12.

killed them at the well near Beth Eked—forty-two of them. Jehu did not leave anyone alive.

¹⁵After Jehu left there, he met Jehonadab son of Recab, who was also on his way to meet Jehu. Jehu greeted him and said, "Are you as good a friend to me as I am to you?"

Jehonadab answered, "Yes, I am."

Jehu said, "If you are, then give me your hand." So Jehonadab gave him his hand, and Jehu pulled him into the chariot. ¹⁶"Come with me," Jehu said. "You can see how strong my feelings are for the LORD." So Jehu had Jehonadab ride in his chariot.

¹⁷When Jehu came to Samaria, he killed all of Ahab's family in Samaria. He destroyed all those who were left, just as the LORD had told Elijah it would happen.

BAAL WORSHIPERS KILLED

¹⁸Then Jehu gathered all the people together and said to them, "Ahab served Baal a little, but Jehu will serve Baal much. ¹⁹Now call for me all Baal's prophets and priests and all the people who worship Baal. Don't let anyone miss this meeting, because I have a great sacrifice for Baal. Anyone who is not there will not live." But Jehu was tricking them so he could destroy the worshipers of Baal. ²⁰He said, "Prepare a holy meeting for Baal." So they announced the meeting. ²¹Then Jehu sent word through all Israel, and all the worshipers of Baal came; not one stayed home. They came into the temple of Baal, and the temple was filled from one side to the other.

²²Jehu said to the man who kept the robes, "Bring out robes for all the worshipers of Baal." After he brought out robes for them, ²³Jehu and Jehonadab son of Recab went into the temple of Baal. Jehu said to the worshipers of Baal, "Look around, and make sure there are no servants of the LORD with you. Be sure there are only worshipers of Baal." ²⁴Then the worshipers of Baal went in to offer sacrifices and burnt offerings.

Jehu had eighty men waiting outside. He had told them, "Don't let anyone escape. If you do, you must pay with your own life."

²⁵As soon as Jehu finished offering the burnt offering, he ordered the guards and the captains, "Go in and kill the worshipers of Baal. Don't let anyone come out." So the guards and captains killed the worshipers of Baal with the sword and threw their bodies out. Then they went to the inner rooms of the temple ²⁶and brought out the pillars of the temple of Baal and burned them. ²⁷They tore down the stone pillar of Baal, as well as the temple of Baal. And they made it into a sewage pit, as it is today.

²⁸So Jehu destroyed Baal worship in Israel, ²⁹but he did not stop doing the sins Jeroboam son of Nebat had done. Jeroboam had led Israel to sin by worshiping the golden calves in Bethel and Dan.

³⁰The LORD said to Jehu, "You have done well in obeying what I said was right. You have done to the family of Ahab as I wanted. Because of this, your descendants as far as your great-great-grandchildren will be kings of Israel." ³¹But Jehu was not careful to follow the teachings of the LORD, the God of Israel, with all his heart. He did not stop doing the same sins Jeroboam had done, by which he had led Israel to sin.

³²At that time the LORD began to make Israel smaller. Hazael defeated the Israelites in all the land of Israel, ³³taking all the land of the Jordan known as the land of Gilead. (It was the region of Gad, Reuben, and Manasseh.) He took land from Aroer by the Arnon Ravine through Gilead to Bashan.

³⁴The other things Jehu did—everything he did and all his victories—are recorded in the book of the history of the kings of Israel. ³⁵Jehu died and was buried in Samaria, and his son Jehoahaz became king in his place. ³⁶Jehu was king over Israel in Samaria for twenty-eight years.

ATHALIAH AND JOASH

11 When Ahaziah's mother, Athaliah, saw that her son was dead, she killed all the royal family. ²But Jehosheba, King Jehoram's daughter and Ahaziah's sister, took Joash, Ahaziah's son. She stole him from among the other sons of the king who were about to be murdered. She put Joash and his nurse in a bedroom to hide him from Athaliah, so he was not killed. ³He hid with her in the Temple of the LORD for six years. During that time Athaliah ruled the land.

⁴In the seventh year Jehoiada sent for the commanders of groups of a hundred

men, as well as the Carites.[n] He brought them together in the Temple of the LORD and made an agreement with them. There, in the Temple of the LORD, he made them promise loyalty, and then he showed them the king's son. [5]He commanded them, "This is what you must do. A third of you who go on duty on the Sabbath will guard the king's palace. [6]A third of you will be at the Sur Gate, and another third will be at the gate behind the guard. This way you will guard the Temple. [7]The two groups who go off duty on the Sabbath must protect the Temple of the LORD for the king. [8]All of you must stand around the king, with weapons in hand. Kill anyone who comes near. Stay close to the king when he goes out and when he comes in."

[9]The commanders over a hundred men obeyed everything Jehoiada the priest had commanded. Each one took his men who came on duty on the Sabbath and those who went off duty on the Sabbath, and they came to Jehoiada the priest. [10]He gave the commanders the spears and shields that had belonged to King David and that were kept in the Temple of the LORD.

JOASH BECOMES KING

[11]Then each guard took his place with his weapons in his hand. There were guards from the south side of the Temple to the north side. They stood by the altar and the Temple and around the king. [12]Jehoiada brought out the king's son and put the crown on him and gave him a copy of the agreement. They appointed him king and poured olive oil on him. Then they clapped their hands and said, "Long live the king!"

[13]When Athaliah heard the noise of the guards and the people, she went to them at the Temple of the LORD. [14]She looked, and there was the king, standing by the pillar, as the custom was. The officers and trumpeters were standing beside him, and all the people of the land were very happy and were blowing trumpets. Then Athaliah tore her clothes and screamed, "Traitors! Traitors!"

[15]Jehoiada the priest gave orders to the commanders of a hundred men, who led the army. He said, "Surround her with soldiers and kill with a sword anyone who follows her." He commanded this because he had said, "Don't put Athaliah to death in the Temple of the LORD." [16]So they caught her when she came to the horses' entrance near the palace. There she was put to death.

[17]Then Jehoiada made an agreement between the LORD and the king and the people that they would be the LORD's special people. He also made an agreement between the king and the people. [18]All the people of the land went to the temple of Baal and tore it down, smashing the altars and idols. They also killed Mattan, the priest of Baal, in front of the altars.

Then Jehoiada the priest placed guards at the Temple of the LORD. [19]He took with him the commanders of a hundred men and the Carites, the royal bodyguards, as well as the guards and all the people of the land. Together they took the king out of the Temple of the LORD and went into the palace through the gate of the guards. Then the king sat on the royal throne. [20]So all the people of the land were very happy, and Jerusalem had peace, because Athaliah had been put to death with the sword at the palace.

[21]Joash was seven years old when he became king.

12 Joash became king of Judah in Jehu's seventh year as king of Israel, and he ruled for forty years in Jerusalem. His mother's name was Zibiah, and she was from Beersheba. [2]Joash did what the LORD said was right as long as Jehoiada the priest taught him. [3]But the places where gods were worshiped were not removed; the people still made sacrifices and burned incense there.

JOASH REPAIRS THE TEMPLE

[4]Joash said to the priests, "Take all the money brought as offerings to the Temple of the LORD. This includes the money each person owes in taxes and the money each person promises or brings freely to the LORD. [5]Each priest will take the money from the people he serves. Then the priests must repair any damage they find in the Temple."

[6]But by the twenty-third year Joash was king, the priests still had not repaired the Temple. [7]So King Joash called for Jehoiada the priest and the other priests and said to

---

11:4 Carites This was probably a special unit of the army that was responsible for the king's safety, a kind of palace guard similar to the Kerethites and the Pelethites.

them, "Why aren't you repairing the damage of the Temple? Don't take any more money from the people you serve, but hand over the money for the repair of the Temple." ⁸The priests agreed not to take any more money from the people and not to repair the Temple themselves.

⁹Jehoiada the priest took a box and made a hole in the top of it. Then he put it by the altar, on the right side as the people came into the Temple of the LORD. The priests guarding the doorway put all the money brought to the Temple of the LORD into the box.

¹⁰Each time the priests saw that the box was full of money, the king's royal secretary and the high priest came. They counted the money that had been brought to the Temple of the LORD, and they put it into bags. ¹¹Next they weighed the money and gave it to the people in charge of the work on the Temple. With it they paid the carpenters and the builders who worked on the Temple of the LORD, ¹²as well as the bricklayers and stonecutters. They also used the money to buy timber and cut stone to repair the damage of the Temple of the LORD. It paid for everything.

¹³The money brought into the Temple of the LORD was not used to make silver cups, wick trimmers, bowls, trumpets, or gold or silver vessels. ¹⁴They paid the money to the workers, who used it to repair the Temple of the LORD. ¹⁵They did not demand to know how the money was spent, because the workers were honest. ¹⁶The money from the penalty offerings and sin offerings was not brought into the Temple of the LORD, because it belonged to the priests.

JOASH SAVES JERUSALEM

¹⁷About this time Hazael king of Aram attacked Gath and captured it. Then he went to attack Jerusalem. ¹⁸Joash king of Judah took all the holy things given by his ancestors, the kings of Judah—Jehoshaphat, Jehoram, and Ahaziah. He also took his own holy things as well as the gold that was found in the treasuries of the Temple of the LORD and the gold from the palace. Joash sent all this treasure to Hazael king of Aram, who turned away from Jerusalem.

¹⁹Everything else Joash did is written in the book of the history of the kings of Judah.

²⁰His officers made plans against him and killed him at Beth Millo on the road down to Silla. ²¹The officers who killed him were Jozabad son of Shimeath and Jehozabad son of Shomer. Joash was buried with his ancestors in Jerusalem, and Amaziah, his son, became king in his place.

JEHOAHAZ KING OF ISRAEL

13 Jehoahaz son of Jehu became king over Israel in Samaria during the twenty-third year Joash son of Ahaziah was king of Judah. Jehoahaz ruled seventeen years, ²and he did what the LORD said was wrong. Jehoahaz did the same sins Jeroboam son of Nebat had done. Jeroboam had led Israel to sin, and Jehoahaz did not stop doing these same sins. ³So the LORD was angry with Israel and handed them over to Hazael king of Aram and his son Ben-Hadad for a long time.

⁴Then Jehoahaz begged the LORD, and the LORD listened to him. The LORD had seen the troubles of Israel; he saw how terribly the king of Aram was treating them. ⁵He gave Israel a man to save them, and they escaped from the Arameans. The Israelites then lived in their own homes as they had before, ⁶but they still did not stop doing the same sins that the family of Jeroboam had done. He had led Israel to sin, and they continued doing those sins. The Asherah idol also was left standing in Samaria.

⁷Nothing was left of Jehoahaz's army except fifty horsemen, ten chariots, and ten thousand foot soldiers. The king of Aram had destroyed them and made them like chaff.

⁸Everything else Jehoahaz did and all his victories are written in the book of the history of the kings of Israel. ⁹Jehoahaz died and was buried in Samaria, and his son Jehoash became king in his place.

JEHOASH KING OF ISRAEL

¹⁰Jehoash son of Jehoahaz became king of Israel in Samaria during Joash's thirty-seventh year as king of Judah. Jehoash ruled sixteen years, ¹¹and he did what the LORD said was wrong. He did not stop doing the same sins Jeroboam son of Nebat had done. Jeroboam had led Israel to sin, and Jehoash continued to do the same thing. ¹²Everything else he did and all his victories, including his war against Amaziah king of Judah, are written in the book of the history of the kings of

Israel. [13]Jehoash died, and Jeroboam took his place on the throne. Jehoash was buried in Samaria with the kings of Israel.

THE DEATH OF ELISHA

[14]At this time Elisha became sick. Before he died, Jehoash king of Israel went to Elisha and cried for him. Jehoash said, "My father, my father! The chariots of Israel and their horsemen!"

[15]Elisha said to Jehoash, "Take a bow and arrows." So he took a bow and arrows. [16]Then Elisha said to him, "Put your hand on the bow." So Jehoash put his hand on the bow. Then Elisha put his hands on the king's hands. [17]Elisha said, "Open the east window." So Jehoash opened the window. Then Elisha said, "Shoot," and Jehoash shot. Elisha said, "The LORD's arrow of victory over Aram! You will defeat the Arameans at Aphek until you destroy them."

[18]Elisha said, "Take the arrows." So Jehoash took them. Then Elisha said to him, "Strike the ground." So Jehoash struck the ground three times and stopped. [19]The man of God was angry with him. "You should have struck five or six times!" Elisha said. "Then you would have struck Aram until you had completely destroyed it. But now you will defeat it only three times."

[20]Then Elisha died and was buried.

At that time groups of Moabites would rob the land in the springtime. [21]Once as some Israelites were burying a man, suddenly they saw a group of Moabites coming. The Israelites threw the dead man into Elisha's grave. When the man touched Elisha's bones, the man came back to life and stood on his feet.

WAR WITH ARAM

[22]During all the days Jehoahaz was king, Hazael king of Aram troubled Israel. [23]But the LORD was kind to the Israelites; he had mercy on them and helped them because of his agreement with Abraham, Isaac, and Jacob. To this day he has never wanted to destroy them or reject them.

[24]When Hazael king of Aram died, his son Ben-Hadad became king in his place. [25]During a war Hazael had taken some cities from Jehoahaz, Jehoash's father. Now Jehoash took back those cities from Hazael's son Ben-Hadad. He defeated Ben-Hadad three times and took back the cities of Israel.

AMAZIAH KING OF JUDAH

14 Amaziah son of Joash became king of Judah during the second year Jehoash son of Jehoahaz was king of Israel. [2]Amaziah was twenty-five years old when he became king, and he ruled twenty-nine years in Jerusalem. His mother was named Jehoaddin, and she was from Jerusalem. [3]Amaziah did what the LORD said was right. He did everything his father Joash had done, but he did not do as his ancestor David had done. [4]The places where gods were worshiped were not removed, so the people still sacrificed and burned incense there.

[5]As soon as Amaziah took control of the kingdom, he executed the officers who had murdered his father the king. [6]But he did not put to death the children of the murderers because of the rule written in the Book of the Teachings of Moses. The LORD had commanded: "Parents must not be put to death when their children do wrong, and children must not be put to death when their parents do wrong. Each must die for his own sins."[n]

[7]In battle Amaziah killed ten thousand Edomites in the Valley of Salt. He also took the city of Sela. He called it Joktheel, as it is still called today.

[8]Amaziah sent messengers to Jehoash son of Jehoahaz, the son of Jehu, king of Israel. They said, "Come, let's meet face to face."

[9]Then Jehoash king of Israel answered Amaziah king of Judah, "A thornbush in Lebanon sent a message to a cedar tree in Lebanon. It said, 'Let your daughter marry my son.' But then a wild animal from Lebanon came by, walking on and crushing the thornbush. [10]You have defeated Edom, but you have become proud. Stay at home and brag. Don't ask for trouble, or you and Judah will be defeated."

[11]But Amaziah would not listen, so Jehoash king of Israel went to attack. He and Amaziah king of Judah faced each other in battle at Beth Shemesh in Judah. [12]Israel defeated Judah, and every man of Judah ran away to his home. [13]At Beth Shemesh Jehoash king of Israel captured Amaziah king of Judah. (Amaziah was the son of Joash, who was the son of Ahaziah.) Jehoash went

---

14:6 "Parents . . . sins." See Deuteronomy 24:16.

up to Jerusalem and broke down the wall of Jerusalem from the Gate of Ephraim to the Corner Gate, which was about six hundred feet. [14]He took all the gold and silver and all the utensils in the Temple of the LORD, and he took the treasuries of the palace and some hostages. Then he returned to Samaria.

[15]The other acts of Jehoash and his victories, including his war against Amaziah king of Judah, are written in the book of history of the kings of Israel. [16]Jehoash died and was buried in Samaria with the kings of Israel, and his son Jeroboam became king in his place.

[17]Amaziah son of Joash, the king of Judah, lived fifteen years after the death of Jehoash son of Jehoahaz, the king of Israel. [18]The other things Amaziah did are written in the book of the history of the kings of Judah. [19]The people in Jerusalem made plans against him. So he ran away to the town of Lachish, but they sent men after him to Lachish and killed him. [20]They brought his body back on horses, and he was buried with his ancestors in Jerusalem, in the city of David.

[21]Then all the people of Judah made Uzziah[n] king in place of his father Amaziah. Uzziah was sixteen years old. [22]He rebuilt the town of Elath and made it part of Judah again after Amaziah died.

JEROBOAM KING OF ISRAEL

[23]Jeroboam son of Jehoash became king of Israel in Samaria during the fifteenth year Amaziah was king of Judah. (Amaziah was the son of Joash.) Jeroboam ruled forty-one years, [24]and he did what the LORD said was wrong. Jeroboam son of Nebat had led Israel to sin, and Jeroboam son of Jehoash did not stop doing the same sins. [25]Jeroboam won back Israel's border from Lebo Hamath to the Dead Sea. This happened as the LORD, the God of Israel, had said through his servant Jonah son of Amittai, the prophet from Gath Hepher. [26]The LORD had seen how the Israelites, both slave and free, were suffering terribly. No one was left who could help Israel. [27]The LORD had not said he would completely destroy Israel from the world, so he saved the Israelites through Jeroboam son of Jehoash.

[28]Everything else Jeroboam did is written down—all his victories and how he won back from Judah the towns of Damascus and Hamath for Israel. All this is written in the book of the history of the kings of Israel. [29]Jeroboam died and was buried with his ancestors, the kings of Israel. Jeroboam's son Zechariah became king in his place.

UZZIAH KING OF JUDAH

15 Uzziah son of Amaziah became king of Judah during Jeroboam's twenty-seventh year as king of Israel. [2]Uzziah was sixteen years old when he became king, and he ruled fifty-two years in Jerusalem. His mother was named Jecoliah, and she was from Jerusalem. [3]He did what the LORD said was right, just as his father Amaziah had done. [4]But the places where gods were worshiped were not removed, so the people still made sacrifices and burned incense there.

[5]The LORD struck Uzziah with a skin disease, which he had until the day he died. So he had to live in a separate house. Jotham, the king's son, was in charge of the palace, and he governed the people of the land.

[6]All the other things Uzziah did are written in the book of the history of the kings of Judah. [7]Uzziah died and was buried near his ancestors in Jerusalem, and his son Jotham became king in his place.

ZECHARIAH KING OF ISRAEL

[8]Zechariah son of Jeroboam was king over Israel in Samaria. He ruled for six months during Uzziah's[n] thirty-eighth year as king of Judah. [9]Zechariah did what the LORD said was wrong, just as his ancestors had done. Jeroboam son of Nebat had led the people of Israel to sin, and Zechariah did not stop doing the same sins.

[10]Shallum son of Jabesh made plans against Zechariah and killed him in front of the people. Then Shallum became king in his place. [11]The other acts of Zechariah are written in the book of the history of the kings of Israel. [12]The LORD had told Jehu: "Your sons down to your great-great-grandchildren will be kings of Israel," and the LORD's word came true.

14:21; 15:8 Uzziah Also called Azariah.

SHALLUM KING OF ISRAEL

13Shallum son of Jabesh became king during Uzziah's thirty-ninth year as king of Judah. Shallum ruled for a month in Samaria. 14Then Menahem son of Gadi came up from Tirzah to Samaria and attacked Shallum son of Jabesh in Samaria. He killed him and became king in Shallum's place.

15The other acts of Shallum and his secret plans are written in the book of the history of the kings of Israel.

MENAHEM KING OF ISRAEL

16Menahem started out from Tirzah and attacked Tiphsah, destroying the city and the area nearby. This was because the people had refused to open the city gate for him. He defeated them and ripped open all their pregnant women.

17Menahem son of Gadi became king over Israel during Uzziah's thirty-ninth year as king of Judah. Menahem ruled ten years in Samaria, 18and he did what the LORD said was wrong. Jeroboam son of Nebat had led Israel to sin, and all the time Menahem was king, he did not stop doing the same sins.

19Pul king of Assyria came to attack the land. Menahem gave him about seventy-four thousand pounds of silver so Pul would support him and make his hold on the kingdom stronger. 20Menahem taxed Israel to pay about one and one-fourth pounds of silver to each soldier of the king of Assyria. So the king left and did not stay in the land.

21Everything else Menahem did is written in the book of the history of the kings of Israel. 22Then Menahem died, and his son Pekahiah became king in his place.

PEKAHIAH KING OF ISRAEL

23Pekahiah son of Menahem became king over Israel in Samaria during Uzziah's[n] fiftieth year as king of Judah. Pekahiah ruled two years, 24and he did what the LORD said was wrong. Jeroboam son of Nebat had led Israel to sin, and Pekahiah did not stop doing the same sins.

25Pekah son of Remaliah was one of Pekahiah's captains, and he made plans against Pekahiah. He took fifty men of Gilead with him and killed Pekahiah, as well as Argob and Arieh, in the palace at Samaria. Then Pekah became king in Pekahiah's place.

26Everything else Pekahiah did is written in the book of the history of the kings of Israel.

PEKAH KING OF ISRAEL

27Pekah son of Remaliah became king over Israel in Samaria during Uzziah's[n] fifty-second year as king of Judah. Pekah ruled twenty years, 28and he did what the LORD said was wrong. Jeroboam son of Nebat had led Israel to sin, and Pekah did not stop doing the same sins.

29Tiglath-Pileser[n] was king of Assyria. He attacked while Pekah was king of Israel, capturing the cities of Ijon, Abel Beth Maacah, Janoah, Kedesh, and Hazor. He also captured Gilead and Galilee and all the land of Naphtali and carried the people away to Assyria. 30Then Hoshea son of Elah made plans against Pekah son of Remaliah and attacked and killed him. Then Hoshea became king in Pekah's place during the twentieth year Jotham son of Uzziah was king.

31Everything else Pekah did is written in the book of the history of the kings of Israel.

JOTHAM KING OF JUDAH

32Jotham son of Uzziah became king of Judah during the second year Pekah son of Remaliah was king of Israel. 33Jotham was twenty-five years old when he became king, and he ruled sixteen years in Jerusalem. His mother's name was Jerusha daughter of Zadok. 34Jotham did what the LORD said was right, just as his father Uzziah had done. 35But the places where gods were worshiped were not removed, and the people still made sacrifices and burned incense there. Jotham rebuilt the Upper Gate of the Temple of the LORD.

36The other things Jotham did while he was king are written in the book of the history of the kings of Judah. 37At that time the LORD began to send Rezin king of Aram and Pekah son of Remaliah against Judah. 38Jotham died and was buried with his ancestors in Jerusalem, the city of David, his ancestor. Then Jotham's son Ahaz became king in his place.

15:23, 27 Uzziah Also called Azariah. **15:29 Tiglath-Pileser** Also called Pul.

AHAZ KING OF JUDAH

16 Ahaz was the son of Jotham king of Judah. Ahaz became king of Judah in the seventeenth year Pekah son of Remaliah was king of Israel. ²Ahaz was twenty years old when he became king, and he ruled sixteen years in Jerusalem. Unlike his ancestor David, he did not do what the LORD his God said was right. ³Ahaz did the same things the kings of Israel had done. He even made his son pass through fire. He did the same hateful sins as the nations had done whom the LORD had forced out of the land ahead of the Israelites. ⁴Ahaz offered sacrifices and burned incense at the places where gods were worshiped, on the hills, and under every green tree.

⁵Rezin king of Aram and Pekah son of Remaliah, the king of Israel, came up to attack Jerusalem. They surrounded Ahaz but could not defeat him. ⁶At that time Rezin king of Aram took back the city of Elath for Aram, and he forced out all the people of Judah. Then Edomites moved into Elath, and they still live there today.

⁷Ahaz sent messengers to Tiglath-Pileser king of Assyria, saying, "I am your servant and your friend. Come and save me from the king of Aram and the king of Israel, who are attacking me." ⁸Ahaz took the silver and gold that was in the Temple of the LORD and in the treasuries of the palace, and he sent these as a gift to the king of Assyria. ⁹So the king of Assyria listened to Ahaz. He attacked Damascus and captured it and sent all its people away to Kir. And he killed Rezin.

¹⁰Then King Ahaz went to Damascus to meet Tiglath-Pileser king of Assyria. Ahaz saw an altar at Damascus, and he sent plans and a pattern of this altar to Uriah the priest. ¹¹So Uriah the priest built an altar, just like the plans King Ahaz had sent him from Damascus. Uriah finished the altar before King Ahaz came back from Damascus. ¹²When the king arrived from Damascus, he saw the altar and went near and offered sacrifices on it. ¹³He burned his burnt offerings and grain offerings and poured out his drink offering. He also sprinkled the blood of his fellowship offerings on the altar.

¹⁴Ahaz moved the bronze altar that was before the LORD at the front of the Temple. It was between Ahaz's altar and the Temple of the LORD, but he put it on the north side of his altar. ¹⁵King Ahaz commanded Uriah the priest, "On the large altar burn the morning burnt offering, the evening grain offering, the king's burnt offering and grain offering, and the whole burnt offering, the grain offering, and the drink offering for all the people of the land. Sprinkle on the altar all the blood of the burnt offering and of the sacrifice. But I will use the bronze altar to ask questions of God." ¹⁶So Uriah the priest did everything as King Ahaz commanded him.

¹⁷Then King Ahaz took off the side panels from the bases and removed the washing bowls from the top of the bases. He also took the large bowl, which was called the Sea, off the bronze bulls that held it up, and he put it on a stone base. ¹⁸Ahaz took away the platform for the royal throne, which had been built at the Temple of the LORD. He also took away the outside entrance for the king. He did these things because of the king of Assyria.

¹⁹The other things Ahaz did as king are written in the book of the history of the kings of Judah. ²⁰Ahaz died and was buried with his ancestors in Jerusalem, and Ahaz's son Hezekiah became king in his place.

HOSHEA, LAST KING OF ISRAEL

17 Hoshea son of Elah became king over Israel during Ahaz's twelfth year as king of Judah. Hoshea ruled in Samaria nine years. ²He did what the LORD said was wrong, but he was not as bad as the kings of Israel who had ruled before him.

³Shalmaneser king of Assyria came to attack Hoshea. Hoshea had been Shalmaneser's servant and had made the payments to Shalmaneser that he had demanded. ⁴But the king of Assyria found out that Hoshea had made plans against him by sending messengers to So, the king of Egypt. Hoshea had also stopped giving Shalmaneser the payments, which he had paid every year in the past. For that, the king put Hoshea in prison. ⁵Then the king of Assyria came and attacked all the land of Israel. He surrounded Samaria and attacked it for three years. ⁶He defeated Samaria in the ninth year Hoshea was king, and he took the Israelites away to Assyria. He settled them in Halah, in Gozan on the Habor River, and in the cities of the Medes.

ISRAELITES PUNISHED FOR SIN

⁷All these things happened because the Israelites had sinned against the LORD their God. He had brought them out of Egypt and had rescued them from the power of the king of Egypt, but the Israelites had honored other gods. ⁸They lived like the nations the LORD had forced out of the land ahead of them. They lived as their evil kings had shown them, ⁹secretly sinning against the LORD their God. They built places to worship gods in all their cities, from the watchtower to the strong, walled city. ¹⁰They put up stone pillars to gods and Asherah idols on every high hill and under every green tree. ¹¹The Israelites burned incense everywhere gods were worshiped, just as the nations who lived there before them had done, whom the LORD had forced out of the land. The Israelites did wicked things that made the LORD angry. ¹²They served idols when the LORD had said, "You must not do this." ¹³The LORD used every prophet and seer to warn Israel and Judah. He said, "Stop your evil ways and obey my commands and laws. Follow all the teachings that I commanded your ancestors, the teachings that I gave you through my servants the prophets."

¹⁴But the people would not listen. They were stubborn, just as their ancestors had been who did not believe in the LORD their God. ¹⁵They rejected the LORD's laws and the agreement he had made with their ancestors. And they refused to listen to his warnings. They worshiped useless idols and became useless themselves. They did what the nations around them did, which the LORD had warned them not to do.

¹⁶The people rejected all the commands of the LORD their God. They molded statues of two calves, and they made an Asherah idol. They worshiped all the stars of the sky and served Baal. ¹⁷They made their sons and daughters pass through fire and tried to find out the future by magic and witchcraft. They always chose to do what the LORD said was wrong, which made him angry. ¹⁸Because he was very angry with the people of Israel, he removed them from his presence. Only the tribe of Judah was left.

JUDAH IS ALSO GUILTY

¹⁹But even Judah did not obey the commands of the LORD their God. They did what the Israelites had done, ²⁰so the LORD rejected all the people of Israel. He punished them and let others destroy them; he threw them out of his presence. ²¹When the LORD separated them from the family of David, the Israelites made Jeroboam son of Nebat their king. Jeroboam led the Israelites away from the LORD and led them to sin greatly. ²²So they continued to do all the sins Jeroboam did. They did not stop doing these sins ²³until the LORD removed the Israelites from his presence, just as he had said through all his servants the prophets. So the Israelites were taken out of their land to Assyria, and they have been there to this day.

THE BEGINNING OF THE SAMARITAN PEOPLE

²⁴The king of Assyria brought people from Babylon, Cuthah, Avva, Hamath, and Sepharvaim and put them in the cities of Samaria to replace the Israelites. These people took over Samaria and lived in the cities. ²⁵At first they did not worship the LORD, so he sent lions among them which killed some of them. ²⁶The king of Assyria was told, "You sent foreigners into the cities of Samaria who do not know the law of the god of the land. This is why he has sent lions among them. The lions are killing them because they don't know what the god wants."

²⁷Then the king of Assyria commanded, "Send back one of the priests you took away. Let him live there and teach the people what the god wants." ²⁸So one of the priests who had been carried away from Samaria returned to live in Bethel. And he taught the people how to honor the LORD.

²⁹But each nation made gods of its own and put them in the cities where they lived and in the temples where gods were worshiped. These temples had been built by the Samaritans. ³⁰The people from Babylon made Succoth Benoth their god. The people from Cuthah worshiped Nergal. The people of Hamath worshiped Ashima. ³¹The Avites worshiped Nibhaz and Tartak. The Sepharvites burned their children in the fire, sacrificing them to Adrammelech and Anammelech, the gods of Sepharvaim. ³²They also honored the LORD, but they chose priests for the places where gods were worshiped. The priests were chosen from

among themselves, and they made sacrifices for the people. ³³The people honored the LORD but also served their own gods, just as the nations did from which they had been brought. ³⁴Even today they do as they did in the past. They do not worship the LORD nor obey his rules and commands. They do not obey the teachings or the commands of the LORD, which he gave to the children of Jacob, whom he had named Israel. ³⁵The LORD had made an agreement with them and had commanded them, "Do not honor other gods. Do not bow down to them or worship them or offer sacrifices to them. ³⁶Worship the LORD who brought you up out of the land of Egypt with great power and strength. Bow down to him and offer sacrifices to him. ³⁷Always obey the rules, orders, teachings, and commands he wrote for you. Do not honor other gods. ³⁸Do not forget the agreement I made with you, and do not honor other gods. ³⁹Instead worship the LORD your God, who will save you from all your enemies."

⁴⁰But the Israelites did not listen. They kept on doing the same things they had done before. ⁴¹So these nations honored the LORD but also worshiped their idols, and their children and grandchildren still do as their ancestors did.

HEZEKIAH KING OF JUDAH

18 Hezekiah son of Ahaz king of Judah became king during the third year Hoshea son of Elah was king of Israel. ²Hezekiah was twenty-five years old when he became king, and he ruled twenty-nine years in Jerusalem. His mother's name was Abijah daughter of Zechariah. ³Hezekiah did what the LORD said was right, just as his ancestor David had done. ⁴He removed the places where gods were worshiped. He smashed the stone pillars and cut down the Asherah idols. Also the Israelites had been burning incense to Nehushtan, the bronze snake Moses had made. But Hezekiah broke it into pieces.

⁵Hezekiah trusted in the LORD, the God of Israel. There was no one like him among all the kings of Judah, either before him or after him. ⁶Hezekiah was loyal to the LORD and did not stop following him; he obeyed the commands the LORD had given Moses. ⁷And the LORD was with Hezekiah, so he had success in everything he did. He turned

against the king of Assyria and stopped serving him. ⁸Hezekiah defeated the Philistines all the way to Gaza and its borders, including the watchtowers and the strong, walled cities.

THE ASSYRIANS CAPTURE SAMARIA

⁹Shalmaneser king of Assyria surrounded Samaria and attacked it in the fourth year Hezekiah was king. This was the seventh year Hoshea son of Elah was king of Israel. ¹⁰After three years the Assyrians captured Samaria. This was in the sixth year Hezekiah was king, which was Hoshea's ninth year as king of Israel. ¹¹The king of Assyria took the Israelites away to Assyria and settled them in Halah, in Gozan on the Habor River, and in the cities of the Medes. ¹²This happened because they did not obey the LORD their God. They broke his agreement and did not obey all that Moses, the LORD's servant, had commanded. They would not listen to the commands or do them.

ASSYRIA ATTACKS JUDAH

¹³During Hezekiah's fourteenth year as king, Sennacherib king of Assyria attacked all the strong, walled cities of Judah and captured them. ¹⁴Then Hezekiah king of Judah sent a message to the king of Assyria at Lachish. He said, "I have done wrong. Leave me alone, and I will pay anything you ask." So the king of Assyria made Hezekiah pay about twenty-two thousand pounds of silver and two thousand pounds of gold. ¹⁵Hezekiah gave him all the silver that was in the Temple of the LORD and in the palace treasuries. ¹⁶Hezekiah stripped all the gold that covered the doors and doorposts of the Temple of the LORD. Hezekiah had put gold on these doors himself, but he gave it all to the king of Assyria.

¹⁷The king of Assyria sent out his supreme commander, his chief officer, and his field commander. They went with a large army from Lachish to King Hezekiah in Jerusalem. When they came near the waterway from the upper pool on the road where people do their laundry, they stopped. ¹⁸They called for the king, so the king sent Eliakim, Shebna, and Joah out to meet them. Eliakim son of Hilkiah was the palace manager, Shebna was the royal secretary, and Joah son of Asaph was the recorder.

[19]The field commander said to them, "Tell Hezekiah this:

"'The great king, the king of Assyria, says: What can you trust in now? [20]You say you have battle plans and power for war, but your words mean nothing. Whom are you trusting for help so that you turn against me? [21]Look, you are depending on Egypt to help you, but Egypt is like a splintered walking stick. If you lean on it for help, it will stab your hand and hurt you. The king of Egypt will hurt all those who depend on him. [22]You might say, "We are depending on the LORD our God," but Hezekiah destroyed the LORD's altars and the places of worship. Hezekiah told Judah and Jerusalem, "You must worship only at this one altar in Jerusalem."

[23]"'Now make an agreement with my master, the king of Assyria: I will give you two thousand horses if you can find enough men to ride them. [24]You cannot defeat one of my master's least important officers, so why do you depend on Egypt to give you chariots and horsemen? [25]I have not come to attack and destroy this place without an order from the LORD. The LORD himself told me to come to this country and destroy it.'"

[26]Then Eliakim son of Hilkiah, Shebna, and Joah said to the field commander, "Please speak to us in the Aramaic language. We understand it. Don't speak to us in Hebrew, because the people on the city wall can hear you."

[27]"No," the commander said, "my master did not send me to tell these things only to you and your king. He sent me to speak also to those people sitting on the wall who will have to eat their own dung and drink their own urine like you."

[28]Then the commander stood and shouted loudly in the Hebrew language, "Listen to what the great king, the king of Assyria, says! [29]The king says you should not let Hezekiah fool you, because he can't save you from my power. [30]Don't let Hezekiah talk you into trusting the LORD by saying, 'The LORD will surely save us. This city won't be handed over to the king of Assyria.'

[31]"Don't listen to Hezekiah. The king of Assyria says, 'Make peace with me, and come out of the city to me. Then everyone will be free to eat the fruit from his own grapevine and fig tree and to drink water from his own well. [32]After that I will come and take you to a land like your own—a land with grain and new wine, bread and vineyards, olives, and honey. Choose to live and not to die!'

"Don't listen to Hezekiah. He is fooling you when he says, 'The LORD will save us.' [33]Has a god of any other nation saved his people from the power of the king of Assyria? [34]Where are the gods of Hamath and Arpad? Where are the gods of Sepharvaim, Hena, and Ivvah? They did not save Samaria from my power. [35]Not one of all the gods of these countries has saved his people from me. Neither can the LORD save Jerusalem from my power."

[36]The people were silent. They didn't answer the commander at all, because King Hezekiah had ordered, "Don't answer him."

[37]Then Eliakim, Shebna, and Joah tore their clothes to show how upset they were. (Eliakim son of Hilkiah was the palace manager, Shebna was the royal secretary, and Joah son of Asaph was the recorder.) The three men went to Hezekiah and told him what the field commander had said.

JERUSALEM WILL BE SAVED

19 When King Hezekiah heard the message, he tore his clothes and put on rough cloth to show how sad he was. Then he went into the Temple of the LORD. [2]Hezekiah sent Eliakim, the palace manager, and Shebna, the royal secretary, and the older priests to Isaiah. They were all wearing rough cloth when they came to Isaiah the prophet, the son of Amoz. [3]They told Isaiah, "This is what Hezekiah says: Today is a day of sorrow and punishment and disgrace, as when a child should be born, but the mother is not strong enough to give birth to it. [4]The king of Assyria sent his field commander to make fun of the living God. Maybe the LORD your God will hear what the commander said and will punish him for it. So pray for the few of us who are left alive."

[5]When Hezekiah's officers came to Isaiah, [6]he said to them, "Tell your master this: The LORD says, 'Don't be afraid of what you have heard. Don't be frightened by the words the servants of the king of Assyria have spoken against me. [7]Listen! I am going to put a spirit in the king of Assyria. He will hear a report that will make him return to his own

country, and I will cause him to die by the sword there.'"

8The field commander heard that the king of Assyria had left Lachish. When he went back, he found the king fighting against the city of Libnah.

9The king received a report that Tirhakah, the Cushite king of Egypt, was coming to attack him. When the king of Assyria heard this, he sent messengers to Hezekiah, saying, 10"Tell Hezekiah king of Judah: Don't be fooled by the god you trust. Don't believe him when he says Jerusalem will not be handed over to the king of Assyria. 11You have heard what the kings of Assyria have done. They have completely defeated every country, so do not think you will be saved. 12Did the gods of those people save them? My ancestors destroyed them, defeating the cities of Gozan, Haran, and Rezeph, and the people of Eden living in Tel Assar. 13Where are the kings of Hamath and Arpad? Where are the kings of Sepharvaim, Hena, and Ivvah?"

HEZEKIAH PRAYS TO THE LORD

14When Hezekiah received the letter from the messengers and read it, he went up to the Temple of the LORD. He spread the letter out before the LORD 15and prayed to the LORD: "LORD, God of Israel, whose throne is between the gold creatures with wings, only you are God of all the kingdoms of the earth. You made the heavens and the earth. 16Hear, LORD, and listen. Open your eyes, LORD, and see. Listen to the words Sennacherib has said to insult the living God. 17It is true, LORD, that the kings of Assyria have destroyed these countries and their lands. 18They have thrown the gods of these nations into the fire, but they were only wood and rock statues that people made. So the kings have destroyed them. 19Now, LORD our God, save us from the king's power so that all the kingdoms of the earth will know that you, LORD, are the only God."

GOD ANSWERS HEZEKIAH

20Then Isaiah son of Amoz sent a message to Hezekiah that said, "This is what the LORD, the God of Israel, says: I have heard your prayer to me about Sennacherib king of Assyria. 21This is what the LORD has said against Sennacherib:

'The people of Jerusalem

hate you and make fun of you.
The people of Jerusalem
    laugh at you as you run away.
22 You have insulted me and spoken against me;
    you have raised your voice against me.
You have a proud look on your face,
    which is against me, the Holy One of Israel.
23 You have sent your messengers to insult the Lord.
    You have said, "With my many chariots
I have gone to the tops of the mountains,
    to the highest mountains of Lebanon.
I have cut down its tallest cedars
    and its best pine trees.
I have gone to its farthest places
    and to its best forests.
24 I have dug wells in foreign countries
    and drunk water there.
By the soles of my feet,
    I have dried up all the rivers of Egypt."

25 "'King of Assyria, surely you have heard.
    Long ago I, the LORD, planned these things.
Long ago I designed them,
    and now I have made them happen.
I allowed you to turn those strong, walled cities
    into piles of rocks.
26 The people in those cities were weak;
    they were frightened and put to shame.
They were like grass in the field,
    like tender, young grass,
like grass on the housetop
    that is burned by the wind before it can grow.

27 "'I know when you rest,
    when you come and go,
    and how you rage against me.
28 Because you rage against me,
    and because I have heard your proud words,
I will put my hook in your nose
    and my bit in your mouth.
Then I will force you to leave my country
    the same way you came.'

29"Then the LORD said, 'Hezekiah, I will give you this sign:
    This year you will eat the grain that grows wild,

and the second year you will eat what grows wild from that.

But in the third year, plant grain and harvest it.

Plant vineyards and eat their fruit.

³⁰ Some of the people in the family of Judah will escape.

Like plants that take root, they will grow strong and have many children.

³¹ A few people will come out of Jerusalem alive;

a few from Mount Zion will live.

The strong love of the LORD All-Powerful will make this happen.'

³²"So this is what the LORD says about the king of Assyria:

'He will not enter this city or even shoot an arrow here.

He will not fight against it with shields or build a ramp to attack the city walls.

³³ He will return to his country the same way he came,

and he will not enter this city,' says the LORD.

³⁴ 'I will defend and save this city for my sake and for the sake of David, my servant.'"

³⁵That night the angel of the LORD went out and killed one hundred eighty-five thousand men in the Assyrian camp. When the people got up early the next morning, they saw all the dead bodies. ³⁶So Sennacherib king of Assyria left and went back to Nineveh and stayed there.

³⁷One day as Sennacherib was worshiping in the temple of his god Nisroch, his sons Adrammelech and Sharezer killed him with a sword. Then they escaped to the land of Ararat. So Sennacherib's son Esarhaddon became king of Assyria.

HEZEKIAH'S ILLNESS

20 At that time Hezekiah became so sick he almost died. The prophet Isaiah son of Amoz went to see him and told him, "This is what the LORD says: Make arrangements because you are not going to live, but die."

²Hezekiah turned toward the wall and prayed to the LORD, ³"LORD, please remember that I have always obeyed you. I have given myself completely to you and have done what you said was right." Then Hezekiah cried loudly.

⁴Before Isaiah had left the middle courtyard, the LORD spoke his word to Isaiah: ⁵"Go back and tell Hezekiah, the leader of my people: 'This is what the LORD, the God of your ancestor David, says: I have heard your prayer and seen your tears, so I will heal you. Three days from now you will go up to the Temple of the LORD. ⁶I will add fifteen years to your life. I will save you and this city from the king of Assyria; I will protect the city for my sake and for the sake of my servant David.'"

⁷Then Isaiah said, "Make a paste from figs." So they made it and put it on Hezekiah's boil, and he got well.

⁸Hezekiah had asked Isaiah, "What will be the sign that the LORD will heal me and that I will go up to the Temple of the LORD on the third day?"

⁹Isaiah said, "The LORD will do what he says. This is the sign from the LORD to show you: Do you want the shadow to go forward ten steps or back ten steps?"

¹⁰Hezekiah answered, "It's easy for the shadow to go forward ten steps. Instead, let it go back ten steps."

¹¹Then Isaiah the prophet called to the LORD, and the LORD brought the shadow ten steps back up the stairway of Ahaz that it had gone down.

MESSENGERS FROM BABYLON

¹²At that time Merodach-Baladan son of Baladan was king of Babylon. He sent letters and a gift to Hezekiah, because he had heard that Hezekiah was sick. ¹³Hezekiah listened to the messengers, so he showed them what was in his storehouses: the silver, gold, spices, expensive perfumes, his swords and shields, and all his wealth. He showed them everything in his palace and his kingdom.

¹⁴Then Isaiah the prophet went to King Hezekiah and asked him, "What did these men say? Where did they come from?"

Hezekiah said, "They came from a faraway country—from Babylon."

¹⁵So Isaiah asked him, "What did they see in your palace?"

Hezekiah said, "They saw everything in my palace. I showed them all my wealth."

¹⁶Then Isaiah said to Hezekiah, "Listen to the words of the LORD: ¹⁷'In the future everything in your palace and everything your ancestors have stored up until this day will be taken away to Babylon. Nothing will be left,' says the LORD. ¹⁸'Some of your own children, those who will be born to you, will be taken away. And they will become servants in the palace of the king of Babylon.'"

¹⁹Hezekiah told Isaiah, "These words from the LORD are good." He said this because he thought, "There will be peace and security in my lifetime."

²⁰Everything else Hezekiah did—all his victories, his work on the pool, his work on the tunnel to bring water into the city—is written in the book of the history of the kings of Judah. ²¹Then Hezekiah died, and his son Manasseh became king in his place.

MANASSEH KING OF JUDAH

21 Manasseh was twelve years old when he became king, and he was king fifty-five years in Jerusalem. His mother's name was Hephzibah. ²He did what the LORD said was wrong. He did the hateful things the other nations had done—the nations that the LORD had forced out of the land ahead of the Israelites. ³Manasseh's father, Hezekiah, had destroyed the places where gods were worshiped, but Manasseh rebuilt them. He built altars for Baal, and he made an Asherah idol as Ahab king of Israel had done. Manasseh also worshiped all the stars of the sky and served them. ⁴The LORD had said about the Temple, "I will be worshiped in Jerusalem," but Manasseh built altars in the Temple of the LORD. ⁵He built altars to worship the stars in the two courtyards of the Temple of the LORD. ⁶He made his own son pass through fire. He practiced magic and told the future by explaining signs and dreams, and he got advice from mediums and fortune-tellers. He did many things the LORD said were wrong, which made the LORD angry.

⁷Manasseh carved an Asherah idol and put it in the Temple. The LORD had said to David and his son Solomon about the Temple, "I will be worshiped forever in this Temple and in Jerusalem, which I have chosen from all the tribes of Israel. ⁸I will never again make the Israelites wander out of the land I gave their ancestors. But they must

obey everything I have commanded them and all the teachings my servant Moses gave them." ⁹But the people did not listen. Manasseh led them to do more evil than the nations the LORD had destroyed ahead of the Israelites.

¹⁰The LORD said through his servants the prophets, ¹¹"Manasseh king of Judah has done these hateful things. He has done more evil than the Amorites before him. He also has led Judah to sin with his idols. ¹²So this is what the LORD, the God of Israel, says: 'I will bring so much trouble on Jerusalem and Judah that anyone who hears about it will be shocked. ¹³I will stretch the measuring line of Samaria over Jerusalem, and the plumb line used against Ahab's family will be used on Jerusalem. I will wipe out Jerusalem as a person wipes a dish and turns it upside down. ¹⁴I will throw away the rest of my people who are left. I will give them to their enemies, and they will be robbed by all their enemies, ¹⁵because my people did what I said was wrong. They have made me angry from the day their ancestors left Egypt until now.'"

¹⁶Manasseh also killed many innocent people, filling Jerusalem from one end to the other with their blood. This was besides the sin he led Judah to do; he led Judah to do what the LORD said was wrong.

¹⁷The other things Manasseh did as king, even the sin he did, are written in the book of the history of the kings of Judah. ¹⁸Manasseh died and was buried in the garden of his own palace, the garden of Uzza. Then Manasseh's son Amon became king in his place.

AMON KING OF JUDAH

¹⁹Amon was twenty-two years old when he became king, and he was king for two years in Jerusalem. His mother's name was Meshullemeth daughter of Haruz, who was from Jotbah. ²⁰Amon did what the LORD said was wrong, as his father Manasseh had done. ²¹He lived in the same way his father had lived: he worshiped the idols his father had worshiped, and he bowed down before them. ²²Amon rejected the LORD, the God of his ancestors, and did not follow the ways of the LORD.

²³Amon's officers made plans against him and killed him in his palace. ²⁴Then the people of the land killed all those who had made

plans to kill King Amon, and they made his son Josiah king in his place.

25Everything else Amon did is written in the book of the history of the kings of Judah. 26He was buried in his grave in the garden of Uzza, and his son Josiah became king in his place.

JOSIAH KING OF JUDAH

22 Josiah was eight years old when he became king, and he ruled thirty-one years in Jerusalem. His mother's name was Jedidah daughter of Adaiah, who was from Bozkath. 2Josiah did what the LORD said was right. He lived as his ancestor David had lived, and he did not stop doing what was right.

3In Josiah's eighteenth year as king, he sent Shaphan to the Temple of the LORD. Shaphan son of Azaliah, the son of Meshullam, was the royal secretary. Josiah said, 4"Go up to Hilkiah the high priest, and have him empty out the money the gatekeepers have gathered from the people. This is the money they have brought into the Temple of the LORD. 5Have him give the money to the supervisors of the work on the Temple of the LORD. They must pay the workers who repair the Temple of the LORD— 6the carpenters, builders, and bricklayers. Also use the money to buy timber and cut stone to repair the Temple. 7They do not need to report how they use the money given to them, because they are working honestly."

THE BOOK OF THE TEACHINGS IS FOUND

8Hilkiah the high priest said to Shaphan the royal secretary, "I've found the Book of the Teachings in the Temple of the LORD." He gave it to Shaphan, who read it.

9Then Shaphan the royal secretary went to the king and reported to Josiah, "Your officers have paid out the money that was in the Temple of the LORD. They have given it to the workers and supervisors at the Temple." 10Then Shaphan the royal secretary told the king, "Hilkiah the priest has given me a book." And Shaphan read from the book to the king.

11When the king heard the words of the Book of the Teachings, he tore his clothes to show how upset he was. 12He gave orders to Hilkiah the priest, Ahikam son of Shaphan, Acbor son of Micaiah, Shaphan the royal sec-

retary, and Asaiah the king's servant. These were the orders: 13"Go and ask the LORD about the words in the book that was found. Ask for me, for all the people, and for all Judah. The LORD's anger is burning against us, because our ancestors did not obey the words of this book; they did not do all the things written for us to do."

14So Hilkiah the priest, Ahikam, Acbor, Shaphan, and Asaiah went to talk to Huldah the prophetess. She was the wife of Shallum son of Tikvah, the son of Harhas, who took care of the king's clothes. Huldah lived in Jerusalem, in the new area of the city.

15She said to them, "This is what the LORD, the God of Israel, says: Tell the man who sent you to me, 16'This is what the LORD says: I will bring trouble to this place and to the people living here, as it is written in the book which the king of Judah has read. 17The people of Judah have left me and have burned incense to other gods. They have made me angry by all that they have done. My anger burns against this place like a fire, and it will not be put out.' 18Tell the king of Judah, who sent you to ask the LORD, 'This is what the LORD, the God of Israel, says about the words you heard: 19When you heard my words against this place and its people, you became sorry for what you had done and humbled yourself before me. I said they would be cursed and would be destroyed. You tore your clothes to show how upset you were, and you cried in my presence. This is why I have heard you, says the LORD. 20So I will let you die, and you will be buried in peace. You won't see all the trouble I will bring to this place.'"

So they took her message back to the king.

THE PEOPLE HEAR THE AGREEMENT

23 Then the king gathered all the elders of Judah and Jerusalem together. 2He went up to the Temple of the LORD, and all the people from Judah and Jerusalem went with him. The priests, prophets, and all the people—from the least important to the most important—went with him. He read to them all the words of the Book of the Agreement that was found in the Temple of the LORD. 3The king stood by the pillar and made an agreement in the presence of the LORD to follow the LORD and obey his commands, rules,

and laws with his whole being, and to obey the words of the agreement written in this book. Then all the people promised to obey the agreement.

JOSIAH DESTROYS THE PLACES FOR IDOL WORSHIP

⁴The king commanded Hilkiah the high priest and the priests of the next rank and the gatekeepers to bring out of the Temple of the LORD everything made for Baal, Asherah, and all the stars of the sky. Then Josiah burned them outside Jerusalem in the open country of the Kidron Valley and carried their ashes to Bethel. ⁵The kings of Judah had chosen priests for these gods. These priests burned incense in the places where gods were worshiped in the cities of Judah and the towns around Jerusalem. They burned incense to Baal, the sun, the moon, the planets, and all the stars of the sky. But Josiah took those priests away. ⁶He removed the Asherah idol from the Temple of the LORD and took it outside Jerusalem to the Kidron Valley, where he burned it and beat it into dust. Then he threw the dust on the graves of the common people. ⁷He also tore down the houses of the male prostitutes who were in the Temple of the LORD, where the women did weaving for Asherah.

⁸King Josiah brought all the false priests from the cities of Judah. He ruined the places where gods were worshiped, where the priests had burned incense, from Geba to Beersheba. He destroyed the places of worship at the entrance to the Gate of Joshua, the ruler of the city, on the left side of the city gate. ⁹The priests at the places where gods were worshiped were not allowed to serve at the LORD's altar in Jerusalem. But they could eat bread made without yeast with their brothers.

¹⁰Josiah ruined Topheth, in the Valley of Ben Hinnom, so no one could sacrifice his son or daughter to Molech. ¹¹Judah's kings had placed horses at the front door of the Temple of the LORD in the courtyard near the room of Nathan-Melech, an officer. These horses were for the worship of the sun. So Josiah removed them and burned the chariots that were for sun worship also.

¹²The kings of Judah had built altars on the roof*ⁿ* of the upstairs room of Ahaz. Jo-

siah broke down these altars and the altars Manasseh had made in the two courtyards of the Temple of the LORD. Josiah smashed them to pieces and threw their dust into the Kidron Valley. ¹³King Josiah ruined the places where gods were worshiped east of Jerusalem, south of the Mount of Olives.*ⁿ* Solomon king of Israel had built these places. One was for Ashtoreth, the hated goddess of the Sidonians. One was for Chemosh, the hated god of Moab. And one was for Molech, the hated god of the Ammonites. ¹⁴Josiah smashed to pieces the stone pillars they worshiped, and he cut down the Asherah idols. Then he covered the places with human bones.

¹⁵Josiah also broke down the altar at Bethel—the place of worship made by Jeroboam son of Nebat, who had led Israel to sin. Josiah burned that place, broke the stones of the altar into pieces, then beat them into dust. He also burned the Asherah idol. ¹⁶When he turned around, he saw the graves on the mountain. He had the bones taken from the graves, and he burned them on the altar to ruin it. This happened as the LORD had said it would through the man of God.

¹⁷Josiah asked, "What is that monument I see?"

The people of the city answered, "It's the grave of the man of God who came from Judah. This prophet announced the things you have done against the altar of Bethel."

¹⁸Josiah said, "Leave the grave alone. No one may move this man's bones." So they left his bones and the bones of the prophet who had come from Samaria.

¹⁹The kings of Israel had built temples for worshiping gods in the cities of Samaria, which had caused the LORD to be angry. Josiah removed all those temples and did the same things as he had done at Bethel. ²⁰He killed all the priests of those places of worship; he killed them on the altars and burned human bones on the altars. Then he went back to Jerusalem.

23:12 roof In Bible times houses were built with flat roofs. The roof was used for drying things such as flax and fruit. And it was used as an extra room, as a place for worship, and as a cool place to sleep in the summer. **23:13 Mount of Olives** Literally, "The Mountain of Ruin."

JOSIAH CELEBRATES THE PASSOVER

²¹The king commanded all the people, "Celebrate the Passover to the LORD your God as it is written in this Book of the Agreement." ²²The Passover had not been celebrated like this since the judges led Israel. Nor had one like it happened while there were kings of Israel and kings of Judah. ²³This Passover was celebrated to the LORD in Jerusalem in the eighteenth year of King Josiah's rule.

²⁴Josiah destroyed the mediums, fortune-tellers, house gods, and idols. He also destroyed all the hated gods seen in the land of Judah and Jerusalem. This was to obey the words of the teachings written in the book Hilkiah the priest had found in the Temple of the LORD.

²⁵There was no king like Josiah before or after him. He obeyed the LORD with all his heart, soul, and strength, following all the Teachings of Moses.

²⁶Even so, the LORD did not stop his strong and terrible anger. His anger burned against Judah because of all Manasseh had done to make him angry. ²⁷The LORD said, "I will send Judah out of my sight, as I have sent Israel away. I will reject Jerusalem, which I chose. And I will take away the Temple about which I said, 'I will be worshiped there.'"

²⁸Everything else Josiah did is written in the book of the history of the kings of Judah. ²⁹While Josiah was king, Neco king of Egypt went to help the king of Assyria at the Euphrates River. King Josiah marched out to fight against Neco, but at Megiddo, Neco faced him and killed him. ³⁰Josiah's servants carried his body in a chariot from Megiddo to Jerusalem and buried him in his own grave. Then the people of Judah chose Josiah's son Jehoahaz and poured olive oil on him to make him king in his father's place.

JEHOAHAZ KING OF JUDAH

³¹Jehoahaz was twenty-three years old when he became king, and he was king in Jerusalem for three months. His mother's name was Hamutal, who was the daughter of Jeremiah from Libnah. ³²Jehoahaz did what the LORD said was wrong, just as his ancestors had done.

³³King Neco took Jehoahaz prisoner at Riblah in the land of Hamath so that Jehoahaz could not rule in Jerusalem. Neco made the people of Judah pay about seventy-five hundred pounds of silver and about seventy-five pounds of gold.

³⁴King Neco made Josiah's son Eliakim the king in place of Josiah his father. Then Neco changed Eliakim's name to Jehoiakim. But Neco took Jehoahaz to Egypt, where he died. ³⁵Jehoiakim gave King Neco the silver and gold he demanded. Jehoiakim taxed the land and took silver and gold from the people of the land to give to King Neco. Each person had to pay his share.

JEHOIAKIM KING OF JUDAH

³⁶Jehoiakim was twenty-five years old when he became king, and he was king in Jerusalem for eleven years. His mother's name was Zebidah daughter of Pedaiah, who was from Rumah. ³⁷Jehoiakim did what the LORD said was wrong, just as his ancestors had done.

24 While Jehoiakim was king, Nebuchadnezzar king of Babylon attacked the land of Judah. So Jehoiakim became Nebuchadnezzar's servant for three years. Then he turned against Nebuchadnezzar and broke away from his rule. ²The LORD sent raiding parties from Babylon, Aram, Moab, and Ammon against Jehoiakim to destroy Judah. This happened as the LORD had said it would through his servants the prophets.

³The LORD commanded this to happen to the people of Judah, to remove them from his presence, because of all the sins of Manasseh. ⁴He had killed many innocent people and had filled Jerusalem with their blood. And the LORD would not forgive these sins.

⁵The other things that happened while Jehoiakim was king and all he did are written in the book of the history of the kings of Judah. ⁶Jehoiakim died, and his son Jehoiachin became king in his place.

⁷The king of Egypt did not leave his land again, because the king of Babylon had captured all that belonged to the king of Egypt, from the brook of Egypt to the Euphrates River.

JEHOIACHIN KING OF JUDAH

⁸Jehoiachin was eighteen years old when he became king, and he was king three months in Jerusalem. His mother's name was Nehushta daughter of Elnathan from Jerusalem. ⁹Jehoiachin did what the LORD

said was wrong, just as his father had done.

¹⁰At that time the officers of Nebuchadnezzar king of Babylon came up to Jerusalem. When they reached the city, they attacked it. ¹¹Nebuchadnezzar himself came to the city while his officers were attacking it. ¹²Jehoiachin king of Judah surrendered to the king of Babylon, along with Jehoiachin's mother, servants, nobles, and officers. So Nebuchadnezzar made Jehoiachin a prisoner in the eighth year he was king of Babylon. ¹³Nebuchadnezzar took all the treasures from the Temple of the LORD and from the palace. He cut up all the gold objects Solomon king of Israel had made for the Temple of the LORD. This happened as the LORD had said it would. ¹⁴Nebuchadnezzar took away all the people of Jerusalem, including all the leaders, all the wealthy people, and all the craftsmen and metal workers. There were ten thousand prisoners in all. Only the poorest people in the land were left. ¹⁵Nebuchadnezzar carried away Jehoiachin to Babylon, as well as the king's mother and his wives, the officers, and the leading men of the land. They were taken captive from Jerusalem to Babylon. ¹⁶The king of Babylon also took all seven thousand soldiers, who were strong and able to fight in war, and about a thousand craftsmen and metal workers. Nebuchadnezzar took them as prisoners to Babylon. ¹⁷Then he made Mattaniah, Jehoiachin's uncle, king in Jehoiachin's place. He also changed Mattaniah's name to Zedekiah.

ZEDEKIAH KING OF JUDAH

¹⁸Zedekiah was twenty-one years old when he became king, and he was king in Jerusalem for eleven years. His mother's name was Hamutal daughter of Jeremiah[n] from Libnah. ¹⁹Zedekiah did what the LORD said was wrong, just as Jehoiakim had done. ²⁰All this happened in Jerusalem and Judah because the LORD was angry with them. Finally, he threw them out of his presence.

THE FALL OF JERUSALEM

Zedekiah turned against the king of Babylon.

25 Nebuchadnezzar king of Babylon marched against Jerusalem with his whole army during Zedekiah's ninth year as king, on the tenth day of the tenth month. He made a camp around the city and piled

dirt against the city walls to attack it. ²The city was under attack until Zedekiah's eleventh year as king. ³By the ninth day of the fourth month, the hunger was terrible in the city. There was no food for the people to eat. ⁴Then the city was broken into, and the whole army ran away at night through the gate between the two walls by the king's garden. While the Babylonians were still surrounding the city, Zedekiah and his men ran away toward the Jordan Valley. ⁵But the Babylonian army chased King Zedekiah and caught up with him in the plains of Jericho. All of his army was scattered from him, ⁶so they captured Zedekiah and took him to the king of Babylon at Riblah. There he passed sentence on Zedekiah. ⁷They killed Zedekiah's sons as he watched. Then they put out his eyes and put bronze chains on him and took him to Babylon.

⁸Nebuzaradan was the commander of the king's special guards. This officer of the king of Babylon came to Jerusalem on the seventh day of the fifth month, in Nebuchadnezzar's nineteenth year as king of Babylon. ⁹Nebuzaradan set fire to the Temple of the LORD and the palace and all the houses of Jerusalem. Every important building was burned.

¹⁰The whole Babylonian army, led by the commander of the king's special guards, broke down the walls around Jerusalem. ¹¹Nebuzaradan, the commander of the guards, captured the people left in Jerusalem, those who had surrendered to the king of Babylon, and the rest of the people. ¹²But the commander left behind some of the poorest people of the land to take care of the vineyards and fields.

¹³The Babylonians broke up the bronze pillars, the bronze stands, and the large bronze bowl, which was called the Sea, in the Temple of the LORD. Then they carried the bronze to Babylon. ¹⁴They also took the pots, shovels, wick trimmers, dishes, and all the bronze objects used to serve in the Temple. ¹⁵The commander of the king's special guards took away the pans for carrying hot coals, the bowls, and everything made of pure gold or silver. ¹⁶There were two pillars and the large bronze bowl and the movable

---

24:18 Jeremiah This is not the prophet Jeremiah, but a different man with the same name.

stands which Solomon had made for the Temple of the LORD. There was so much bronze that it could not be weighed. ¹⁷Each pillar was about twenty-seven feet high. The bronze capital on top of the pillar was about four and one-half feet high. It was decorated with a net design and bronze pomegranates all around it. The other pillar also had a net design and was like the first pillar.

JUDAH IS TAKEN PRISONER

¹⁸The commander of the guards took some prisoners—Seraiah the chief priest, Zephaniah the priest next in rank, and the three doorkeepers. ¹⁹Of the people who were still in the city, he took the officer in charge of the fighting men, as well as five people who advised the king. He took the royal secretary who selected people for the army and sixty other men who were in the city. ²⁰Nebuzaradan, the commander, took all these people and brought them to the king of Babylon at Riblah. ²¹There at Riblah, in the land of Hamath, the king had them killed. So the people of Judah were led away from their country as captives.

GEDALIAH BECOMES GOVERNOR

²²Nebuchadnezzar king of Babylon left some people in the land of Judah. He appointed Gedaliah son of Ahikam, the son of Shaphan, as governor. ²³The army captains and their men heard that the king of Babylon had made Gedaliah

governor, so they came to Gedaliah at Mizpah. They were Ishmael son of Nethaniah, Johanan son of Kareah, Seraiah son of Tanhumeth the Netophathite, Jaazaniah son of the Maacathite, and their men. ²⁴Then Gedaliah promised these army captains and their men, "Don't be afraid of the Babylonian officers. Live in the land and serve the king of Babylon, and everything will go well for you."

²⁵In the seventh month Ishmael son of Nethaniah, son of Elishama from the king's family, came with ten men and killed Gedaliah. They also killed the men of Judah and Babylon who were with Gedaliah at Mizpah. ²⁶Then all the people, from the least important to the most important, along with the army leaders, ran away to Egypt, because they were afraid of the Babylonians.

JEHOIACHIN IS SET FREE

²⁷Jehoiachin king of Judah was held in Babylon for thirty-seven years. In the thirty-seventh year Evil-Merodach became king of Babylon, and he let Jehoiachin out of prison on the twenty-seventh day of the twelfth month. ²⁸Evil-Merodach spoke kindly to Jehoiachin and gave him a seat of honor above the seats of the other kings who were with him in Babylon. ²⁹So Jehoiachin put away his prison clothes. For the rest of his life, he ate at the king's table. ³⁰Every day, for as long as Jehoiachin lived, the king gave him an allowance.

1 chronicles

ISRAEL'S HISTORY FROM ADAM TO DAVID

FROM ADAM TO ABRAHAM

1 Adam was the father of Seth. Seth was the father of Enosh. Enosh was the father of Kenan. [2]Kenan was the father of Mahalalel. Mahalalel was the father of Jared. Jared was the father of Enoch. [3]Enoch was the father of Methuselah. Methuselah was the father of Lamech, and Lamech was the father of Noah.

[4]The sons of Noah were Shem, Ham, and Japheth.

[5]Japheth's sons were Gomer, Magog, Madai, Javan, Tubal, Meshech, and Tiras.

[6]Gomer's sons were Ashkenaz, Riphath, and Togarmah.

[7]Javan's sons were Elishah, Tarshish, Kittim,[n] and Rodanim.

[8]Ham's sons were Cush, Mizraim,[n] Put, and Canaan.

[9]Cush's sons were Seba, Havilah, Sabta, Raamah, and Sabteca.

Raamah's sons were Sheba and Dedan.

[10]Cush was the father of Nimrod, who grew up to become a mighty warrior on the earth.

[11]Mizraim was the father of the Ludites, Anamites, Lehabites, and Naphtuhites, [12]Pathrusites, Casluhites, and Caphtorites. (The Philistines came from the Casluhites.)

[13]Canaan's first child was Sidon. He was also the father of the Hittites, [14]Jebusites, Amorites, Girgashites, [15]Hivites, Arkites, Sinites, [16]Arvadites, Zemarites, and Hamathites.

[17]Shem's sons were Elam, Asshur, Arphaxad, Lud, and Aram.

Aram's sons were Uz, Hul, Gether, and Meshech.

[18]Arphaxad was the father of Shelah, who was the father of Eber.

[19]Eber had two sons. One son was named Peleg,[n] because the people on the earth were divided into different languages during his life. Peleg's brother was named Joktan.

[20]Joktan was the father of Almodad, Sheleph, Hazarmaveth, Jerah, [21]Hadoram, Uzal, Diklah, [22]Obal, Abimael, Sheba, [23]Ophir, Havilah, and Jobab. All these were Joktan's sons. [24]The family line included Shem, Arphaxad, Shelah, [25]Eber, Peleg, Reu, [26]Serug, Nahor, Terah, [27]and Abram, who was called Abraham.

ABRAHAM'S FAMILY

[28]Abraham's sons were Isaac and Ishmael.

[29]These were the sons of Isaac and Ishmael. Ishmael's first son was Nebaioth. His other sons were Kedar, Adbeel, Mibsam, [30]Mishma, Dumah, Massa, Hadad, Tema, [31]Jetur, Naphish, and Kedemah. These were Ishmael's sons. [32]Keturah, Abraham's slave woman, gave birth to Zimran, Jokshan, Medan, Midian, Ishbak, and Shuah.

Jokshan's sons were Sheba and Dedan.

[33]Midian's sons were Ephah, Epher, Hanoch, Abida, and Eldaah. All these were descendants of Keturah.

[34]Abraham was the father of Isaac, and Isaac's sons were Esau and Israel.

[35]Esau's sons were Eliphaz, Reuel, Jeush, Jalam, and Korah.

[36]Eliphaz's sons were Teman, Omar, Zepho, Gatam, Kenaz, Timna, and Amalek.

[37]Reuel's sons were Nahath, Zerah, Shammah, and Mizzah.

THE EDOMITES FROM SEIR

[38]Seir's sons were Lotan, Shobal, Zibeon, Anah, Dishon, Ezer, and Dishan.

[39]Lotan's sons were Hori and Homam, and his sister was Timna.

[40]Shobal's sons were Alvan, Manahath, Ebal, Shepho, and Onam.

Zibeon's sons were Aiah and Anah.

[41]Anah's son was Dishon.

Dishon's sons were Hemdan, Eshban, Ithran, and Keran.

1:7 Kittim His descendants were the people of Cyprus. **1:8 Mizraim** This is another name for Egypt. **1:19 Peleg** This name sounds like the Hebrew word for "divided."

⁴²Ezer's sons were Bilhan, Zaavan, and Akan.

Dishan's sons were Uz and Aran.

THE KINGS OF EDOM

⁴³These kings ruled in Edom before there were kings in Israel. Bela son of Beor was king of Edom, and his city was named Dinhabah. ⁴⁴When Bela died, Jobab son of Zerah became king. He was from Bozrah. ⁴⁵When Jobab died, Husham became king. He was from the land of the Temanites. ⁴⁶When Husham died, Hadad son of Bedad became king, and his city was named Avith. Hadad defeated Midian in the country of Moab. ⁴⁷When Hadad died, Samlah became king. He was from Masrekah. ⁴⁸When Samlah died, Shaul became king. He was from Rehoboth by the river. ⁴⁹When Shaul died, Baal-Hanan son of Acbor became king. ⁵⁰When Baal-Hanan died, Hadad became king, and his city was named Pau. Hadad's wife was named Mehetabel, and she was the daughter of Matred, who was the daughter of Me-Zahab. ⁵¹Then Hadad died.

The leaders of the family groups of Edom were Timna, Alvah, Jetheth, ⁵²Oholibamah, Elah, Pinon, ⁵³Kenaz, Teman, Mibzar, ⁵⁴Magdiel, and Iram. These were the leaders of Edom.

ISRAEL'S FAMILY

2 The sons of Israel[n] were Reuben, Simeon, Levi, Judah, Issachar, Zebulun, ²Dan, Joseph, Benjamin, Naphtali, Gad, and Asher.

JUDAH'S FAMILY

³Judah's sons were Er, Onan, and Shelah. A Canaanite woman, the daughter of Shua, was their mother. Judah's first son, Er, did what the LORD said was wicked, so the LORD put him to death. ⁴Judah's daughter-in-law Tamar gave birth to Perez and Zerah. Judah was the father, so Judah had five sons.

⁵Perez's sons were Hezron and Hamul. ⁶Zerah had five sons: Zimri, Ethan, Heman, Calcol, and Darda. ⁷Carmi's son was Achan, who caused trouble for Israel because he took things that had been given to the LORD to be destroyed. ⁸Ethan's son was Azariah.

⁹Hezron's sons were Jerahmeel, Ram, and Caleb. ¹⁰Ram was Amminadab's father, and Amminadab was Nahshon's father. Nahshon was the leader of the people of Judah. ¹¹Nahshon was the father of Salmon, who was the father of Boaz. ¹²Boaz was the father of Obed, and Obed was the father of Jesse.

¹³Jesse's first son was Eliab. His second son was Abinadab, his third was Shimea, ¹⁴his fourth was Nethanel, his fifth was Raddai, ¹⁵his sixth was Ozem, and his seventh son was David. ¹⁶Their sisters were Zeruiah and Abigail. Zeruiah's three sons were Abishai, Joab, and Asahel. ¹⁷Abigail was the mother of Amasa, and his father was Jether, an Ishmaelite.

CALEB'S FAMILY

¹⁸Caleb son of Hezron had children by his wife Azubah and by Jerioth. Caleb and Azubah's sons were Jesher, Shobab, and Ardon. ¹⁹When Azubah died, Caleb married Ephrath. They had a son named Hur, ²⁰who was the father of Uri, who was the father of Bezalel.

²¹Later, when Hezron was sixty years old, he married the daughter of Makir, Gilead's father. Hezron had sexual relations with Makir's daughter, and she had a son named Segub. ²²Segub was the father of Jair. Jair controlled twenty-three cities in the country of Gilead. ²³(But Geshur and Aram captured the Towns of Jair, as well as Kenath and the small towns around it—sixty towns in all.) All these were descendants of Makir, the father of Gilead.

²⁴After Hezron died in Caleb Ephrathah, his wife Abijah had his son, named Ashhur. Ashhur became the father of Tekoa.

JERAHMEEL'S FAMILY

²⁵Hezron's first son was Jerahmeel. Jerahmeel's sons were Ram, Bunah, Oren, Ozem, and Ahijah. Ram was Jerahmeel's first son. ²⁶Jerahmeel had another wife, named Atarah. She was the mother of Onam.

²⁷Jerahmeel's first son, Ram, had sons. They were Maaz, Jamin, and Eker. ²⁸Onam's sons were Shammai and Jada.

2:1 **Israel** Another name for Jacob.

401

Shammai's sons were Nadab and Abishur.

²⁹Abishur's wife was named Abihail, and their sons were Ahban and Molid.

³⁰Nadab's sons were Seled and Appaim. Seled died without having children.

³¹Appaim's son was Ishi, who became the father of Sheshan.

Sheshan was the father of Ahlai.

³²Jada was Shammai's brother, and Jada's sons were Jether and Jonathan. Jether died without having children.

³³Jonathan's sons were Peleth and Zaza.

These were Jerahmeel's descendants.

³⁴Sheshan did not have any sons, only daughters. He had a servant from Egypt named Jarha. ³⁵Sheshan let his daughter marry his servant Jarha, and she had a son named Attai.

³⁶Attai was the father of Nathan. Nathan was the father of Zabad. ³⁷Zabad was the father of Ephlal. Ephlal was the father of Obed. ³⁸Obed was the father of Jehu. Jehu was the father of Azariah. ³⁹Azariah was the father of Helez. Helez was the father of Eleasah. ⁴⁰Eleasah was the father of Sismai. Sismai was the father of Shallum. ⁴¹Shallum was the father of Jekamiah, and Jekamiah was the father of Elishama.

CALEB'S FAMILY

⁴²Caleb was Jerahmeel's brother. Caleb's first son was Mesha. Mesha was the father of Ziph, and his son Mareshah was the father of Hebron.

⁴³Hebron's sons were Korah, Tappuah, Rekem, and Shema. ⁴⁴Shema was the father of Raham, who was the father of Jorkeam. Rekem was the father of Shammai. ⁴⁵Shammai was the father of Maon, and Maon was the father of Beth Zur.

⁴⁶Caleb's slave woman was named Ephah, and she was the mother of Haran, Moza, and Gazez. Haran was the father of Gazez.

⁴⁷Jahdai's sons were Regem, Jotham, Geshan, Pelet, Ephah, and Shaaph.

⁴⁸Caleb had another slave woman named Maacah. She was the mother of Sheber, Tirhanah, ⁴⁹Shaaph, and Sheva. Shaaph was the father of Madmannah. Sheva was the father of Macbenah and Gibea. Caleb's daughter was Acsah.

⁵⁰⁻⁵¹These were Caleb's descendants:

Caleb's son Hur was the first son of his mother Ephrathah. Hur's sons were Shobal, Salma, and Hareph. Shobal was the father of Kiriath Jearim. Salma was the father of Bethlehem. And Hareph was the father of Beth Gader.

⁵²Shobal was the father of Kiriath Jearim. Shobal's descendants were Haroeh, half the Manahathites, ⁵³and the family groups of Kiriath Jearim: the Ithrites, Puthites, Shumathites, and Mishraites. The Zorathites and the Eshtaolites came from the Mishraite people.

⁵⁴Salma's descendants were Bethlehem, the Netophathites, Atroth Beth Joab, half the Manahathites, and the Zorites. ⁵⁵His descendants included the families who lived at Jabez, who wrote and copied important papers. They were called the Tirathites, Shimeathites, and Sucathites and were from the Kenite family group who came from Hammath. He was the father of the people living in Recab.

DAVID'S FAMILY

3 These are David's sons who were born in Hebron. The first was Amnon, whose mother was Ahinoam from Jezreel. The second son was Daniel, whose mother was Abigail from Carmel. ²The third son was Absalom, whose mother was Maacah daughter of Talmai, the king of Geshur. The fourth son was Adonijah, whose mother was Haggith. ³The fifth son was Shephatiah, whose mother was Abital. The sixth son was Ithream, whose mother was Eglah. ⁴These six sons of David were born to him in Hebron, where David ruled for seven and one-half years.

David ruled in Jerusalem thirty-three years. ⁵These were his children who were born in Jerusalem: Shammua, Shobab, Nathan, and Solomon—the four children of David and Bathsheba, Ammiel's daughter. ⁶⁻⁸David's other nine children were Ibhar, Elishua, Eliphelet, Nogah, Nepheg, Japhia, Elishama, Eliada, and Eliphelet. ⁹These were all of David's sons, except for those born to his slave women. David also had a daughter named Tamar.

THE KINGS OF JUDAH

¹⁰Solomon's son was Rehoboam. Rehoboam's son was Abijah. Abijah's son was Asa. Asa's son was Jehoshaphat. ¹¹Jehoshaphat's

son was Jehoram. Jehoram's son was Ahaziah. Ahaziah's son was Joash. 12Joash's son was Amaziah. Amaziah's son was Azariah. Azariah's son was Jotham. 13Jotham's son was Ahaz. Ahaz's son was Hezekiah. Hezekiah's son was Manasseh. 14Manasseh's son was Amon, and Amon's son was Josiah.

15These were Josiah's sons: His first son was Johanan, his second was Jehoiakim, his third was Zedekiah, and his fourth was Shallum.

16Jehoiakim was followed by Jehoiachin, and he was followed by Zedekiah.

DAVID'S DESCENDANTS AFTER THE BABYLONIAN CAPTIVITY

17Jehoiachin was taken as a prisoner. His sons were Shealtiel, 18Malkiram, Pedaiah, Shenazzar, Jekamiah, Hoshama, and Nedabiah.

19Pedaiah's sons were Zerubbabel and Shimei.

Zerubbabel's sons were Meshullam and Hananiah, and their sister was Shelomith. 20Zerubbabel also had five other sons: Hashubah, Ohel, Berekiah, Hasadiah, and Jushab-Hesed.

21Hananiah's descendants were Pelatiah and Jeshaiah, and the sons of Rephaiah, Arnan, Obadiah, and Shecaniah.

22Shecaniah's son was Shemaiah. Shemaiah's sons were Hattush, Igal, Bariah, Neariah, and Shaphat. There were six in all.

23Neariah had three sons: Elioenai, Hizkiah, and Azrikam.

24Elioenai had seven sons: Hodaviah, Eliashib, Pelaiah, Akkub, Johanan, Delaiah, and Anani.

OTHER FAMILY GROUPS OF JUDAH

4 Judah's descendants were Perez, Hezron, Carmi, Hur, and Shobal.

2Reaiah was Shobal's son. Reaiah was the father of Jahath, and Jahath was the father of Ahumai and Lahad. They were the family groups of the Zorathite people.

3-4Hur was the oldest son of Caleb and his wife Ephrathah. Hur was the leader of Bethlehem. His three sons were Etam, Penuel, and Ezer. Etam's sons were Jezreel, Ishma, and Idbash. They had a sister named Hazzelelponi. Penuel was the father of Gedor, and Ezer was the father of Hushah.

5Tekoa's father was Ashhur. Ashhur had two wives named Helah and Naarah.

6The sons of Ashhur and Naarah were Ahuzzam, Hepher, Temeni, and Haahashtari. These were the descendants of Naarah.

7Helah's sons were Zereth, Zohar, Ethnan, 8and Koz. Koz was the father of Anub, Hazzobebah, and the Aharhel family group. Aharhel was the son of Harum.

9There was a man named Jabez, who was respected more than his brothers. His mother named him Jabez[n] because she said, "I was in much pain when I gave birth to him." 10Jabez prayed to the God of Israel, "Please do good things for me and give me more land. Stay with me, and don't let anyone hurt me. Then I won't have any pain." And God did what Jabez had asked.

11Kelub, Shuhah's brother, was the father of Mehir. Mehir was the father of Eshton. 12Eshton was the father of Beth Rapha, Paseah, and Tehinnah. Tehinnah was the father of the people from the town of Nahash. These people were from Recah.

13The sons of Kenaz were Othniel and Seraiah.

Othniel's sons were Hathath and Meonothai. 14Meonothai was the father of Ophrah.

Seraiah was the father of Joab. Joab was the ancestor of the people from Craftsmen's Valley, named that because the people living there were craftsmen.

15Caleb was Jephunneh's son. Caleb's sons were Iru, Elah, and Naam. Elah's son was Kenaz.

16Jehallelel's sons were Ziph, Ziphah, Tiria, and Asarel.

17-18Ezrah's sons were Jether, Mered, Epher, and Jalon. Mered married Bithiah, the daughter of the king of Egypt. The children of Mered and Bithiah were Miriam, Shammai, and Ishbah. Ishbah was the father of Eshtemoa. Mered also had a wife from Judah, who gave birth to Jered, Heber, and Jekuthiel. Jered became the father of Gedor. Heber became the father of Soco. And Jekuthiel became the father of Zanoah.

19Hodiah's wife was Naham's sister. The sons of Hodiah's wife were Eshtemoa and the father of Keilah. Keilah was from the

---

4:9 **Jabez** This name in Hebrew sounds like the word for "pain."

Garmite people, and Eshtemoa was from the Maacathite people.

²⁰Shimon's sons were Amnon, Rinnah, Ben-Hanan, and Tilon.

Ishi's sons were Zoheth and Ben-Zoheth.

²¹⁻²²Shelah was Judah's son. Shelah's sons were Er, Laadah, Jokim, the men from Cozeba, Joash, and Saraph. Er was the father of Lecah. Laadah was the father of Mareshah and the family groups of linen workers at Beth Ashbea. Joash and Saraph ruled in Moab and Jashubi Lehem. The writings about this family are very old. ²³These sons of Shelah were potters. They lived in Netaim and Gederah and worked for the king.

SIMEON'S CHILDREN

²⁴Simeon's sons were Nemuel, Jamin, Jarib, Zerah, and Shaul. ²⁵Shaul's son was Shallum. Shallum's son was Mibsam. Mibsam's son was Mishma.

²⁶Mishma's son was Hammuel. Hammuel's son was Zaccur. Zaccur's son was Shimei. ²⁷Shimei had sixteen sons and six daughters, but his brothers did not have many children, so there were not as many people in their family group as there were in Judah.

²⁸Shimei's children lived in Beersheba, Moladah, Hazar Shual, ²⁹Bilhah, Ezem, Tolad, ³⁰Bethuel, Hormah, Ziklag, ³¹Beth Marcaboth, Hazar Susim, Beth Biri, and Shaaraim.

FINANCES

GOD'S MANAGEMENT PLAN

explosive
growth

1 CHRONICLES 4:10

The Hebrew word for "enlarge" is a word about multiplying physical assets. We find it first in God's command to his creation: "be fruitful and multiply." It is also translated "increase, gather much, heap up, give more, be many." But in one special use it is the name for a kind of locust.

Jabez asked God to explode his growth. He said, "God, make my assets multiply like locusts. Let them overrun their accounts. Let them burst their borders. Make them grow so much that they can't be contained. Let them go wild." That's quite a request. But Jabez knew that the basis of his request was his willingness to acknowledge both parts of the word "bless": the gift and the act of bowing down.

Jabez said, "God, I acknowledge that all favor comes from you. You are the only source of my prosperity. And I know that my prosperity means that I submit to you. I bow my knee in worship. Make your blessing big. Give me all you've got for me." There are obligations in blessings. Jabez did not waver in asking because he knew God. Do you know God well enough to boldly ask him to make your assets explode with growth?

reflect: Ask God to bless specially your life beyond its present boundaries.
Go to **FINANCES:** "The Ultimate Investment" at **Matthew 19:21.**

They lived in these cities until David became king. ³²The five villages near these cities were Etam, Ain, Rimmon, Token, and Ashan. ³³There were also other villages as far away as Baalath. This is where they lived. And they wrote the history of their family.

³⁴⁻³⁸The men in this list were leaders of their family groups: Meshobab, Jamlech, Joshah son of Amaziah, Joel, Jehu son of Joshibiah (Joshibiah was the son of Seraiah, who was the son of Asiel), Elioenai, Jaakobah, Jeshohaiah, Asaiah, Adiel, Jesimiel, Benaiah, and Ziza. (Ziza was the son of Shiphi, who was the son of Allon. Allon was the son of Jedaiah, who was the son of Shimri. And Shimri was the son of Shemaiah.)

These families grew very large. ³⁹They went outside the city of Gedor to the east side of the valley to look for pasture for their flocks. ⁴⁰They found good pastures with plenty of grass, and the land was open country and peaceful and quiet. Ham's descendants had lived there in the past.

⁴¹These men who were listed came to Gedor while Hezekiah was king of Judah. They fought against the Hamites, destroying their tents, and also against the Meunites who lived there, and completely destroyed them. So there are no Meunites there even today. Then these men began to live there, because there was pasture for their flocks. ⁴²Ishi's sons, Pelatiah, Neariah, Rephaiah, and Uzziel, led five hundred of the Simeonites and attacked the people living in the mountains of Edom. ⁴³They killed the few Amalekites who were still alive. From that time until now these Simeonites have lived in Edom.

REUBEN'S CHILDREN

5 Reuben was Israel's first son. Reuben should have received the special privileges of the oldest son, but he had sexual relations with his father's slave woman. So those special privileges were given to Joseph's sons. (Joseph was a son of Israel.) In the family history Reuben's name is not listed as the first son. ²Judah became stronger than his brothers, and a leader came from his family. But Joseph's family received the privileges that belonged to the oldest son. ³Reuben was Israel's first son. Reuben's sons were Hanoch, Pallu, Hezron, and Carmi.

⁴These were the children of Joel: Shemaiah was Joel's son. Gog was Shemaiah's son. Shimei was Gog's son. ⁵Micah was Shimei's son. Reaiah was Micah's son. Baal was Reaiah's son. ⁶Beerah was Baal's son. Beerah was a leader of the tribe of Reuben. Tiglath-Pileser king of Assyria captured him and took him away.

⁷Joel's brothers and all his family groups are listed just as they are written in their family histories: Jeiel was the first, then Zechariah, ⁸and Bela. (Bela was the son of Azaz. Azaz was the son of Shema, and Shema was the son of Joel.) They lived in the area of Aroer all the way to Nebo and Baal Meon. ⁹Bela's people lived to the east—as far as the edge of the desert, which is beside the Euphrates River—because they had too many cattle for the land of Gilead.

¹⁰When Saul was king, Bela's people fought a war against the Hagrite people and defeated them. Then Bela's people lived in the tents that had belonged to the Hagrites in all the area east of Gilead.

GAD'S CHILDREN

¹¹The people from the tribe of Gad lived near the Reubenites. The Gadites lived in the area of Bashan all the way to Salecah. ¹²Joel was the main leader, Shapham was second, and then Janai and Shaphat were leaders in Bashan.

¹³The seven relatives in their families were Michael, Meshullam, Sheba, Jorai, Jacan, Zia, and Eber. ¹⁴They were the descendants of Abihail. Abihail was Huri's son. Huri was Jaroah's son. Jaroah was Gilead's son. Gilead was Michael's son. Michael was Jeshishai's son. Jeshishai was Jahdo's son, and Jahdo was the son of Buz. ¹⁵Ahi was Abdiel's son, and Abdiel was Guni's son. Ahi was the leader of their family.

¹⁶The Gadites lived in Gilead, Bashan and the small towns around it, and on all the pasturelands in the Plain of Sharon all the way to the borders.

¹⁷All these names were written in the family history of Gad during the time Jotham was king of Judah and Jeroboam was king of Israel.

SOLDIERS SKILLED IN WAR

¹⁸There were forty-four thousand seven hundred sixty soldiers from the tribes of Reuben and Gad and East Manasseh who

carried shields and swords and bows. They were skilled in war. ¹⁹They started a war against the Hagrites and the people of Jetur, Naphish, and Nodab. ²⁰The men from the tribes of Manasseh, Reuben, and Gad prayed to God during the war, asking him to help them. So he helped them because they trusted him. He handed over to them the Hagrites and all those who were with them. ²¹They took the animals that belonged to the Hagrites: fifty thousand camels, two hundred fifty thousand sheep, and two thousand donkeys. They also captured one hundred thousand people. ²²Many Hagrites were killed because God helped the people of Reuben, Gad, and Manasseh. Then they lived there until Babylon captured them and took them away.

EAST MANASSEH

²³There were many people in East Manasseh, and they lived in the area of Bashan all the way to Baal Hermon, Senir, and Mount Hermon.

²⁴These were the family leaders: Epher, Ishi, Eliel, Azriel, Jeremiah, Hodaviah, and Jahdiel. They were all strong, brave, and famous men, and leaders in their families. ²⁵But they sinned against the God that their ancestors had worshiped. They began worshiping the gods of the people in that land, and those were the people God was destroying. ²⁶So the God of Israel made Pul king of Assyria want to go to war. (Pul was also called Tiglath-Pileser.) He captured the people of Reuben, Gad, and East Manasseh, and he took them away to Halah, Habor, Hara, and near the Gozan River. They have lived there from that time until this day.

LEVI'S CHILDREN

6 Levi's sons were Gershon, Kohath, and Merari.

²Kohath's sons were Amram, Izhar, Hebron, and Uzziel.

³Amram's children were Aaron, Moses, and Miriam.

Aaron's sons were Nadab, Abihu, Eleazar, and Ithamar. ⁴Eleazar was the father of Phinehas. Phinehas was the father of Abishua. ⁵Abishua was the father of Bukki. Bukki was the father of Uzzi. ⁶Uzzi was the father of Zerahiah. Zerahiah was the father of Meraioth. ⁷Meraioth was the father of

Amariah. Amariah was the father of Ahitub. ⁸Ahitub was the father of Zadok. Zadok was the father of Ahimaaz. ⁹Ahimaaz was the father of Azariah. Azariah was the father of Johanan. ¹⁰Johanan was the father of Azariah. (Azariah was a priest in the Temple Solomon built in Jerusalem.) ¹¹Azariah was the father of Amariah. Amariah was the father of Ahitub. ¹²Ahitub was the father of Zadok. Zadok was the father of Shallum. ¹³Shallum was the father of Hilkiah. Hilkiah was the father of Azariah. ¹⁴Azariah was the father of Seraiah, and Seraiah was the father of Jehozadak.

¹⁵Jehozadak was forced to leave his home when the LORD sent Judah and Jerusalem into captivity under the control of Nebuchadnezzar.

¹⁶Levi's sons were Gershon, Kohath, and Merari.

¹⁷The names of Gershon's sons were Libni and Shimei.

¹⁸Kohath's sons were Amram, Izhar, Hebron, and Uzziel.

¹⁹Merari's sons were Mahli and Mushi.

This is a list of the family groups of Levi, listed by the name of the father of each group.

²⁰Gershon's son was Libni. Libni's son was Jehath. Jehath's son was Zimmah. ²¹Zimmah's son was Joah. Joah's son was Iddo. Iddo's son was Zerah. And Zerah's son was Jeatherai.

²²Kohath's son was Amminadab. Amminadab's son was Korah. Korah's son was Assir. ²³Assir's son was Elkanah. Elkanah's son was Ebiasaph. Ebiasaph's son was Assir. ²⁴Assir's son was Tahath. Tahath's son was Uriel. Uriel's son was Uzziah, and Uzziah's son was Shaul.

²⁵Elkanah's sons were Amasai and Ahimoth. ²⁶Ahimoth's son was Elkanah. Elkanah's son was Zophai. Zophai's son was Nahath. ²⁷Nahath's son was Eliab. Eliab's son was Jeroham. Jeroham's son was Elkanah, and Elkanah's son was Samuel.

²⁸Samuel's sons were Joel, the first son, and Abijah, the second son.

²⁹Merari's son was Mahli. Mahli's son was Libni. Libni's son was Shimei. Shimei's son was Uzzah. ³⁰Uzzah's son was Shimea. Shimea's son was Haggiah, and Haggiah's son was Asaiah.

THE TEMPLE MUSICIANS

³¹David chose some people to be in charge of the music in the house of the LORD. They began their work after the Ark of the Agreement was put there. ³²They served by making music at the Holy Tent (also called the Meeting Tent), and they served until Solomon built the Temple of the LORD in Jerusalem. They followed the rules for their work.

³³These are the musicians and their sons: From Kohath's family there was Heman the singer. Heman was Joel's son. Joel was Samuel's son. ³⁴Samuel was Elkanah's son. Elkanah was Jeroham's son. Jeroham was Eliel's son. Eliel was Toah's son. ³⁵Toah was Zuph's son. Zuph was Elkanah's son. Elkanah was Mahath's son. Mahath was Amasai's son. ³⁶Amasai was Elkanah's son. Elkanah was Joel's son. Joel was Azariah's son. Azariah was Zephaniah's son. ³⁷Zephaniah was Tahath's son. Tahath was Assir's son. Assir was Ebiasaph's son. Ebiasaph was Korah's son. ³⁸Korah was Izhar's son. Izhar was Kohath's son. Kohath was Levi's son. Levi was Israel's son.

³⁹There was Heman's helper Asaph, whose group stood by Heman's right side. Asaph was Berekiah's son. Berekiah was Shimea's son. ⁴⁰Shimea was Michael's son. Michael was Baaseiah's son. Baaseiah was Malkijah's son. ⁴¹Malkijah was Ethni's son. Ethni was Zerah's son. Zerah was Adaiah's son. ⁴²Adaiah was Ethan's son. Ethan was Zimmah's son. Zimmah was Shimei's son. ⁴³Shimei was Jahath's son. Jahath was Gershon's son, and Gershon was Levi's son.

⁴⁴Merari's family were the helpers of Heman and Asaph, and they stood by Heman's left side. In this group was Ethan son of Kishi. Kishi was Abdi's son. Abdi was Malluch's son. ⁴⁵Malluch was Hashabiah's son. Hashabiah was Amaziah's son. Amaziah was Hilkiah's son. ⁴⁶Hilkiah was Amzi's son. Amzi was Bani's son. Bani was Shemer's son. ⁴⁷Shemer was Mahli's son. Mahli was Mushi's son. Mushi was Merari's son, and Merari was Levi's son.

⁴⁸The other Levites served by doing their own special work in the Holy Tent, the house of God. ⁴⁹Aaron and his descendants offered the sacrifices on the altar of burnt offering and burned the incense on the altar of incense. They offered the sacrifices that removed the Israelites' sins so they could belong to God. They did all the work in the Most Holy Place and followed all the laws that Moses, God's servant, had commanded.

⁵⁰These were Aaron's sons: Eleazar was Aaron's son. Phinehas was Eleazar's son. Abishua was Phinehas' son. ⁵¹Bukki was Abishua's son. Uzzi was Bukki's son. Zerahiah was Uzzi's son. ⁵²Meraioth was Zerahiah's son. Amariah was Meraioth's son. Ahitub was Amariah's son. ⁵³Zadok was Ahitub's son, and Ahimaaz was Zadok's son.

LAND FOR THE LEVITES

⁵⁴These are the places where Aaron's descendants lived. His descendants from the Kohath family group received the first share of the land.

⁵⁵They were given the city of Hebron in Judah and the pastures around it, ⁵⁶but the fields farther from the city and the villages near Hebron were given to Caleb son of Jephunneh. ⁵⁷So the descendants of Aaron were given Hebron, one of the cities of safety. They also received the towns and pastures of Libnah, Jattir, Eshtemoa, ⁵⁸Hilen, Debir, ⁵⁹Ashan, Juttah, and Beth Shemesh. ⁶⁰They also received these towns and pastures from the tribe of Benjamin: Gibeon, Geba, Alemeth, and Anathoth.

The Kohath family groups received a total of thirteen towns.

⁶¹The rest of the Kohath family group was given ten towns from the family groups of West Manasseh. The towns were chosen by throwing lots.

⁶²The Gershon family group received thirteen towns from the tribes of Issachar, Asher, Naphtali, and the part of Manasseh living in Bashan.

⁶³The Merari family group received twelve towns from the tribes of Reuben, Gad, and Zebulun. Those towns were chosen by throwing lots.

⁶⁴So the Israelites gave these towns and their pastures to the Levites. ⁶⁵The towns from the tribes of Judah, Simeon, and Benjamin, which were named, were chosen by throwing lots.

⁶⁶Some of the Kohath family groups received towns and pastures from the tribe of Ephraim. ⁶⁷They received Shechem, one of

the cities of safety,[n] with its pastures in the mountains of Ephraim. They also received the towns and pastures of Gezer, 68Jokmeam, Beth Horon, 69Aijalon, and Gath Rimmon.

70The rest of the people in the Kohath family group received the towns of Aner and Bileam and their pastures from West Manasseh.

71From East Manasseh, the Gershon family received the towns and pastures of Golan in Bashan and Ashtaroth.

72-73From the tribe of Issachar, the Gershon family received the towns and pastures of Kedesh, Daberath, Ramoth, and Anem.

74-75From the tribe of Asher, the Gershon family received the towns and pastures of Mashal, Abdon, Hukok, and Rehob.

76From the tribe of Naphtali, the Gershon family received the towns and pastures of Kedesh in Galilee, Hammon, and Kiriathaim.

77The rest of the Levites, the people from the Merari family, received from the tribe of Zebulun the towns and pastures of Jokneam, Kartah, Rimmono, and Tabor.

78-79From the tribe of Reuben, the Merari family received the towns and pastures of Bezer in the desert, Jahzah, Kedemoth, and Mephaath. (The tribe of Reuben lived east of the Jordan River, across from Jericho.)

80-81From the tribe of Gad, the Merari family received the towns and pastures of Ramoth in Gilead, Mahanaim, Heshbon, and Jazer.

ISSACHAR'S CHILDREN

7 Issachar had four sons: Tola, Puah, Jashub, and Shimron.

2Tola's sons were Uzzi, Rephaiah, Jeriel, Jahmai, Ibsam, and Samuel, and they were leaders of their families. In the family history of Tola's descendants, twenty-two thousand six hundred men were listed as fighting men during the time David was king.

3Uzzi's son was Izrahiah.

Izrahiah's sons were Michael, Obadiah, Joel, and Isshiah. All five of them were leaders. 4Their family history shows they had thirty-six thousand men ready to serve in the army, because they had many wives and children.

5The records of the family groups of Issa-char show there were eighty-seven thousand fighting men.

BENJAMIN'S CHILDREN

6Benjamin had three sons: Bela, Beker, and Jediael.

7Bela had five sons: Ezbon, Uzzi, Uzziel, Jerimoth, and Iri, and they were leaders of their families. Their family history shows they had twenty-two thousand thirty-four fighting men.

8Beker's sons were Zemirah, Joash, Eliezer, Elioenai, Omri, Jeremoth, Abijah, Anathoth, and Alemeth. They all were Beker's sons. 9Their family history listed the family leaders and twenty thousand two hundred fighting men.

10Jediael's son was Bilhan.

Bilhan's sons were Jeush, Benjamin, Ehud, Kenaanah, Zethan, Tarshish, and Ahishahar. 11All these sons of Jediael were leaders of their families. They had seventeen thousand two hundred fighting men ready to serve in the army.

12The Shuppites and Huppites were descendants of Ir, and the Hushites were descendants of Aher.

NAPHTALI'S CHILDREN

13Naphtali's sons were Jahziel, Guni, Jezer, and Shillem. They were Bilhah's grandsons.

MANASSEH'S CHILDREN

14These are Manasseh's descendants. Manasseh had an Aramean slave woman, who was the mother of Asriel and Makir. Makir was Gilead's father. 15Makir took a wife from the Huppites and Shuppites. His sister was named Maacah. His second son was named Zelophehad, and he had only daughters. 16Makir's wife Maacah had a son whom she named Peresh. Peresh's brother was named Sheresh. Sheresh's sons were Ulam and Rakem.

17Ulam's son was Bedan.

These were the sons of Gilead, who was the son of Makir. Makir was Manasseh's son. 18Makir's sister Hammoleketh gave birth to Ishhod, Abiezer, and Mahlah.

6:67 cities of safety A person who had accidentally killed someone could go to one of the six cities of safety to receive protection and a fair trial.

[19]The sons of Shemida were Ahian, Shechem, Likhi, and Aniam.

EPHRAIM'S CHILDREN

[20]These are the names of Ephraim's descendants. Ephraim's son was Shuthelah. Shuthelah's son was Bered. Bered's son was Tahath. Tahath's son was Eleadah. Eleadah's son was Tahath. [21]Tahath's son was Zabad. Zabad's son was Shuthelah.

Ezer and Elead went to Gath to steal cows and sheep and were killed by some men who grew up in that city. [22]Their father Ephraim cried for them many days, and his family came to comfort him. [23]Then he had sexual relations with his wife again. She became pregnant and gave birth to a son whom Ephraim named Beriah[n] because of the trouble that had happened to his family. [24]Ephraim's daughter was Sheerah. She built Lower Beth Horon, Upper Beth Horon, and Uzzen Sheerah.

[25]Rephah was Ephraim's son. Resheph was Rephah's son. Telah was Resheph's son. Tahan was Telah's son. [26]Ladan was Tahan's son. Ammihud was Ladan's son. Elishama was Ammihud's son. [27]Nun was Elishama's son, and Joshua was the son of Nun.

[28]Ephraim's descendants lived in these lands and towns: Bethel and the villages near it, Naaran on the east, Gezer and the villages near it on the west, and Shechem and the villages near it. These villages went all the way to Ayyah and its villages. [29]Along the borders of Manasseh's land were the towns of Beth Shan, Taanach, Megiddo, and Dor, and the villages near them. The descendants of Joseph son of Israel lived in these towns.

ASHER'S CHILDREN

[30]Asher's sons were Imnah, Ishvah, Ishvi, and Beriah. Their sister was Serah.

[31]Beriah's sons were Heber and Malkiel. Malkiel was Birzaith's father.

[32]Heber was the father of Japhlet, Shomer, Hotham, and their sister Shua.

[33]Japhlet's sons were Pasach, Bimhal, and Ashvath. They were Japhlet's children.

[34]Japhlet's brother was Shomer. Shomer's sons were Rohgah, Hubbah, and Aram.

[35]Shomer's brother was Hotham. Hotham's sons were Zophah, Imna, Shelesh, and Amal.

[36]Zophah's sons were Suah, Harnepher, Shual, Beri, Imrah, [37]Bezer, Hod, Shamma, Shilshah, Ithran, and Beera.

[38]Jether's sons were Jephunneh, Pispah, and Ara.

[39]Ulla's sons were Arah, Hanniel, and Rizia.

[40]All these men were descendants of Asher and leaders of their families. They were powerful warriors and outstanding leaders. Their family history lists that they had twenty-six thousand soldiers ready to serve in the army.

THE FAMILY HISTORY OF KING SAUL

8 Benjamin was the father of Bela, his first son. Ashbel was his second son, Aharah was his third, [2]Nohah was his fourth, and Rapha was his fifth son.

[3]Bela's sons were Addar, Gera, Abihud, [4]Abishua, Naaman, Ahoah, [5]Gera, Shephuphan, and Huram.

[6]These were the descendants of Ehud and leaders of their families in Geba. They were forced to move to Manahath. [7]Ehud's descendants were Naaman, Ahijah, and Gera. Gera forced them to leave. He was the father of Uzza and Ahihud.

[8-11]Shaharaim and his wife Hushim had sons named Abitub and Elpaal. In Moab, Shaharaim divorced his wives Hushim and Baara. Shaharaim and his wife Hodesh had these sons: Jobab, Zibia, Mesha, Malcam, Jeuz, Sakia, and Mirmah. They were leaders of their families.

[12-13]Elpaal's sons were Eber, Misham, Shemed, Beriah, and Shema. Shemed built the towns of Ono and Lod and the villages around them. Beriah and Shema were leaders of the families living in Aijalon, and they forced out the people who lived in Gath.

[14]Beriah's sons were Ahio, Shashak, Jeremoth, [15]Zebadiah, Arad, Eder, [16]Michael, Ishpah, and Joha.

[17]Elpaal's sons were Zebadiah, Meshullam, Hizki, Heber, [18]Ishmerai, Izliah, and Jobab.

[19]Shimei's sons were Jakim, Zicri, Zabdi, [20]Elienai, Zillethai, Eliel, [21]Adaiah, Beraiah, and Shimrath.

[22]Shashak's sons were Ishpan, Eber, Eliel,

7:23 Beriah This name sounds like the Hebrew word for "trouble."

23Abdon, Zicri, Hanan, 24Hananiah, Elam, Anthothijah, 25Iphdeiah, and Penuel.

26Jeroham's sons were Shamsherai, Shehariah, Athaliah, 27Jaareshiah, Elijah, and Zicri.

28The family histories show that all these men were leaders of their families and lived in Jerusalem.

29Jeiel lived in the town of Gibeon, where he was the leader. His wife was named Maacah. 30Jeiel's first son was Abdon. His other sons were Zur, Kish, Baal, Ner, Nadab, 31Gedor, Ahio, Zeker, 32and Mikloth. Mikloth was the father of Shimeah. These sons also lived near their relatives in Jerusalem.

33Ner was the father of Kish. Kish was the father of Saul, and Saul was the father of Jonathan, Malki-Shua, Abinadab, and Esh-Baal.

34Jonathan's son was Merib-Baal, who was the father of Micah.

35Micah's sons were Pithon, Melech, Tarea, and Ahaz. 36Ahaz was the father of Jehoaddah. Jehoaddah was the father of Alemeth, Azmaveth, and Zimri. Zimri was the father of Moza. 37Moza was the father of Binea. Raphah was Binea's son. Eleasah was Raphah's son, and Azel was Eleasah's son.

38Azel had six sons: Azrikam, Bokeru, Ishmael, Sheariah, Obadiah, and Hanan. All these were Azel's sons.

39Azel's brother was Eshek. Eshek's first son was Ulam, his second was Jeush, and Eliphelet was his third. 40Ulam's sons were mighty warriors and good archers. They had many sons and grandsons—one hundred fifty of them in all.

All these men were Benjamin's descendants.

9 The names of all the people of Israel were listed in their family histories, and those family histories were put in the book of the kings of Israel.

THE PEOPLE IN JERUSALEM

The people of Judah were captured and forced to go to Babylon, because they were not faithful to God. 2The first people to come back and live in their own lands and towns were some Israelites, priests, Levites, and Temple servants.

3People from the tribes of Judah, Benjamin, Ephraim, and Manasseh lived in Jerusalem. This is a list of those people.

4There was Uthai son of Ammihud. (Ammihud was Omri's son. Omri was Imri's son. Imri was Bani's son. Bani was a descendant of Perez, and Perez was Judah's son.)

5Of the Shilonite people there were Asaiah and his sons. Asaiah was the oldest son in his family.

6Of the Zerahite people there were Jeuel and other relatives of Zerah. There were six hundred ninety of them in all.

7From the tribe of Benjamin there was Sallu son of Meshullam. (Meshullam was Hodaviah's son, and Hodaviah was Hassenuah's son.) 8There was also Ibneiah son of Jeroham and Elah son of Uzzi. (Uzzi was Micri's son.) And there was Meshullam son of Shephatiah. (Shephatiah was Reuel's son, and Reuel was Ibnijah's son.) 9The family history of Benjamin lists nine hundred fifty-six people living in Jerusalem, and all these were leaders of their families.

10Of the priests there were Jedaiah, Jehoiarib, Jakin, and 11Azariah son of Hilkiah. (Hilkiah was Meshullam's son. Meshullam was Zadok's son. Zadok was Meraioth's son. Meraioth was Ahitub's son. Ahitub was the officer responsible for the Temple of God.) 12Also there was Adaiah son of Jeroham. (Jeroham was Pashhur's son, and Pashhur was Malkijah's son.) And there was Maasai son of Adiel. (Adiel was Jahzerah's son. Jahzerah was Meshullam's son. Meshullam was Meshillemith's son, and Meshillemith was Immer's son.) 13There were one thousand seven hundred sixty priests. They were leaders of their families, and they were responsible for serving in the Temple of God.

14Of the Levites there was Shemaiah son of Hasshub. (Hasshub was Azrikam's son, and Azrikam was Hashabiah's son. Hashabiah was from the family of Merari.) 15There were also Bakbakkar, Heresh, Galal, and Mattaniah son of Mica. (Mica was Zicri's son, and Zicri was Asaph's son.) 16There was also Obadiah son of Shemaiah. (Shemaiah was Galal's son, and Galal was Jeduthun's son.) And there was Berekiah son of Asa. (Asa was the son of Elkanah, who lived in the villages of the Netophathites.)

17Of the gatekeepers there were Shallum, Akkub, Talmon, Ahiman, and their relatives. Shallum was their leader. 18These gatekeepers from the tribe of Levi still stand next to the King's Gate on the east side of the city. ¹⁹Shallum was Kore's son. Kore was Ebiasaph's son, and Ebiasaph was Korah's son. Shallum and his relatives from the family of Korah were gatekeepers and were responsible for guarding the gates of the Temple. Their ancestors had also been responsible for guarding the entrance to the Temple of the LORD. ²⁰In the past Phinehas, Eleazar's son, was in charge of the gatekeepers, and the LORD was with Phinehas. ²¹Zechariah son of Meshelemiah was the gatekeeper at the entrance to the Temple.

²²In all, two hundred twelve men were chosen to guard the gates, and their names were written in their family histories in their villages. David and Samuel the seer chose these men because they were dependable. ²³The gatekeepers and their descendants had to guard the gates of the Temple of the LORD. (The Temple took the place of the Holy Tent.) ²⁴There were gatekeepers on all four sides of the Temple: east, west, north, and south. ²⁵The gatekeepers' relatives who lived in the villages had to come and help them at times. Each time they came they helped the gatekeepers for seven days. ²⁶Because they were dependable, four gatekeepers were made the leaders of all the gatekeepers. They were Levites, and they were responsible for the rooms and treasures in the Temple of God. ²⁷They stayed up all night guarding the Temple of God, and they opened it every morning.

²⁸Some of the gatekeepers were responsible for the utensils used in the Temple services. They counted these utensils when people took them out and when they brought them back. ²⁹Other gatekeepers were chosen to take care of the furniture and utensils in the Holy Place. They also took care of the flour, wine, oil, incense, and spices, ³⁰but some of the priests took care of mixing the spices. ³¹There was a Levite named Mattithiah who was dependable and had the job of baking the bread used for the offerings. He was the first son of Shallum, who was from the family of Korah. ³²Some of the gatekeepers from the Kohath family had the job of preparing the special bread that was put on the table every Sabbath day.

³³Some of the Levites were musicians in the Temple. The leaders of these families stayed in the rooms of the Temple. Since they were on duty day and night, they did not do other work in the Temple.

³⁴These are the leaders of the Levite families. Their names were listed in their family histories, and they lived in Jerusalem.

THE FAMILY HISTORY OF KING SAUL

³⁵Jeiel lived in the town of Gibeon, where he was the leader. His wife was named Maacah. ³⁶Jeiel's first son was Abdon. His other sons were Zur, Kish, Baal, Ner, Nadab, ³⁷Gedor, Ahio, Zechariah, and Mikloth. ³⁸Mikloth was Shimeam's father. Jeiel's family lived near their relatives in Jerusalem.

³⁹Ner was Kish's father. Kish was Saul's father. Saul was the father of Jonathan, Malki-Shua, Abinadab, and Esh-Baal.

⁴⁰Jonathan's son was Merib-Baal, who was the father of Micah.

⁴¹Micah's sons were Pithon, Melech, Tahrea, and Ahaz. ⁴²Ahaz was Jadah's father. Jadah was the father of Alemeth, Azmaveth, and Zimri. Zimri was Moza's father. ⁴³Moza was Binea's father. Rephaiah was Binea's son. Eleasah was Rephaiah's son, and Azel was Eleasah's son.

⁴⁴Azel had six sons: Azrikam, Bokeru, Ishmael, Sheariah, Obadiah, and Hanan. They were Azel's sons.

THE DEATH OF KING SAUL

10 The Philistines fought against Israel, and the Israelites ran away from them. Many Israelites were killed on Mount Gilboa. ²The Philistines fought hard against Saul and his sons, killing his sons Jonathan, Abinadab, and Malki-Shua. ³The fighting was heavy around Saul, and the archers shot him with their arrows and wounded him.

⁴Then Saul said to the officer who carried his armor, "Pull out your sword and stab me. If you don't, these Philistines who are not circumcised will come and hurt me." But Saul's officer refused, because he was afraid. So Saul took his own sword and threw himself on it. ⁵When the officer saw that Saul was dead, he threw himself on his own sword and died. ⁶So Saul and three of his sons died; all his family died together.

⁷When the Israelites living in the valley saw that their army had run away and that Saul and his sons were dead, they left their

towns and ran away. Then the Philistines came and settled in them.

8The next day when the Philistines came to strip the dead soldiers, they found Saul and his sons dead on Mount Gilboa. 9The Philistines stripped Saul's body and took his head and his armor. Then they sent messengers through all their country to tell the news to their idols and to their people. 10The Philistines put Saul's armor in the temple of their idols and hung his head in the temple of Dagon.

11All the people in Jabesh Gilead heard what the Philistines had done to Saul. 12So the brave men of Jabesh went and got the bodies of Saul and his sons and brought them to Jabesh. They buried their bones under the large tree in Jabesh. Then the people of Jabesh fasted for seven days.

13Saul died because he was not faithful to the LORD and did not obey the LORD. He even went to a medium and asked her for advice 14instead of asking the LORD. This is why the LORD put Saul to death and gave the kingdom to Jesse's son David.

DAVID BECOMES KING

11 Then the people of Israel came to David at the town of Hebron and said, "Look, we are your own family. 2Even when Saul was king, you were the one who led Israel in battle. The LORD your God said to you, 'You will be the shepherd for my people Israel. You will be their leader.'"

3So all the elders of Israel came to King David at Hebron. He made an agreement with them in Hebron in the presence of the LORD. Then they poured oil on David to make him king over Israel. The LORD had promised through Samuel that this would happen.

DAVID CAPTURES JERUSALEM

4David and all the Israelites went to the city of Jerusalem. At that time Jerusalem was called Jebus, and the people living there were named Jebusites. 5They said to David, "You can't get inside our city." But David did take the city of Jerusalem with its strong walls, and it became the City of David.

6David had said, "The person who leads the attack against the Jebusites will become the commander over all my army." Joab son of Zeruiah led the attack, so he became the commander of the army.

7Then David made his home in the strong, walled city, which is why it was named the City of David. 8David rebuilt the city, beginning where the land was filled in and going to the wall that was around the city. Joab repaired the other parts of the city. 9David became stronger and stronger, and the LORD All-Powerful was with him.

DAVID'S MIGHTY WARRIORS

10This is a list of the leaders over David's warriors who helped make David's kingdom strong. All the people of Israel also supported David's kingdom. These heroes and all the people of Israel made David king, just as the LORD had promised.

11This is a list of David's warriors:

Jashobeam was from the Hacmonite people. He was the head of the Three,n David's most powerful soldiers. He used his spear to fight three hundred men at one time, and he killed them all.

12Next was Eleazar, one of the Three. Eleazar was Dodai's son from the Ahohite people. 13Eleazar was with David at Pas Dammim when the Philistines came there to fight. There was a field of barley at that place. The Israelites ran away from the Philistines, 14but they stopped in the middle of that field and fought for it and killed the Philistines. The LORD gave them a great victory.

15Once, three of the Thirty, David's chief soldiers, came down to him at the rock by the cave near Adullam. At the same time the Philistine army had camped in the Valley of Rephaim.

16At that time David was in a stronghold, and some of the Philistines were in Bethlehem. 17David had a strong desire for some water. He said, "Oh, I wish someone would get me water from the well near the city gate of Bethlehem!" 18So the Three broke through the Philistine army and took water from the well near the city gate in Bethlehem. Then they brought it to David, but he refused to drink it. He poured it out before the LORD, 19saying, "May God keep me from drinking this water! It would be like drinking the blood of the men who risked their lives to bring it to me!" So David refused to drink it.

11:11 Three Or maybe "Thirty." These were David's most powerful soldiers. See 2 Samuel 23:8.

These were the brave things that the three warriors did.

20Abishai brother of Joab was the captain of the Three. Abishai fought three hundred soldiers with his spear and killed them. He became as famous as the Three 21and was more honored than the Three. He became their commander even though he was not one of them.

22Benaiah son of Jehoiada was a brave fighter from Kabzeel who did mighty things. He killed two of the best warriors from Moab. He also went down into a pit and killed a lion on a snowy day. 23Benaiah killed an Egyptian who was about seven and one-half feet tall and had a spear as large as a weaver's rod. Benaiah had a club, but he grabbed the spear from the Egyptian's hand and killed him with his own spear. 24These were the things Benaiah son of Jehoiada did. He was as famous as the Three. 25He received more honor than the Thirty, but he did not become a member of the Three. David made him leader of his bodyguards.

THE THIRTY CHIEF SOLDIERS

26These were also mighty warriors:
Asahel brother of Joab;
Elhanan son of Dodo from Bethlehem;
27 Shammoth the Harorite;
Helez the Pelonite;
28 Ira son of Ikkesh from Tekoa;
Abiezer the Anathothite;
29 Sibbecai the Hushathite;
Ilai the Ahohite;
30 Maharai the Netophathite;
Heled son of Baanah the Netophathite;
31 Ithai son of Ribai from Gibeah in Benjamin;
Benaiah the Pirathonite;
32 Hurai from the ravines of Gaash;
Abiel the Arbathite;
33 Azmaveth the Baharumite;
Eliahba the Shaalbonite;
34 the sons of Hashem the Gizonite;
Jonathan son of Shagee the Hararite;
35 Ahiam son of Sacar the Hararite;
Eliphal son of Ur;
36 Hepher the Mekerathite;
Ahijah the Pelonite;
37 Hezro the Carmelite;
Naarai son of Ezbai;
38 Joel brother of Nathan;

Mibhar son of Hagri;
39 Zelek the Ammonite;
Naharai the Berothite, the officer who carried the armor for Joab son of Zeruiah;
40 Ira the Ithrite;
Gareb the Ithrite;
41 Uriah the Hittite;
Zabad son of Ahlai;
42 Adina son of Shiza the Reubenite, who was the leader of the Reubenites, and his thirty soldiers;
43 Hanan son of Maacah;
Joshaphat the Mithnite;
44 Uzzia the Ashterathite;
Shama and Jeiel sons of Hotham the Aroerite;
45 Jediael son of Shimri;
Joha, Jediael's brother, the Tizite;
46 Eliel the Mahavite;
Jeribai and Joshaviah, Elnaam's sons;
Ithmah the Moabite;
47 Eliel, Obed, and Jaasiel the Mezobaites.

WARRIORS JOIN DAVID

12 These were the men who came to David at Ziklag when David was hiding from Saul son of Kish. They were among the warriors who helped David in battle. 2They came with bows for weapons and could use either their right or left hands to shoot arrows or to sling rocks. They were Saul's relatives from the tribe of Benjamin. 3Ahiezer was their leader, and there was Joash. (Ahiezer and Joash were sons of Shemaah, who was from the town of Gibeah.) There were also Jeziel and Pelet, the sons of Azmaveth. There were Beracah and Jehu from the town of Anathoth. 4And there was Ishmaiah from the town of Gibeon; he was one of the Thirty. In fact, he was the leader of the Thirty. There were Jeremiah, Jahaziel, Johanan, and Jozabad from Gederah. 5There were Eluzai, Jerimoth, Bealiah, and Shemariah. There was Shephatiah from Haruph. 6There were Elkanah, Isshiah, Azarel, Joezer, and Jashobeam from the family group of Korah. 7And there were Joelah and Zebadiah, the sons of Jeroham, from the town of Gedor.

8Part of the people of Gad joined David at his stronghold in the desert. They were brave warriors trained for war and skilled with shields and spears. They were as fierce as lions and as fast as gazelles over the hills.

⁹Ezer was the leader of Gad's army, and Obadiah was second in command. Eliab was third, ¹⁰Mishmannah was fourth, Jeremiah was fifth, ¹¹Attai was sixth, Eliel was seventh, ¹²Johanan was eighth, Elzabad was ninth, ¹³Jeremiah was tenth, and Macbannai was eleventh in command.

¹⁴They were the commanders of the army from Gad. The least of these leaders was in charge of a hundred soldiers, and the greatest was in charge of a thousand. ¹⁵They crossed the Jordan River and chased away the people living in the valleys, to the east and to the west. This happened in the first month of the year when the Jordan floods the valley.

¹⁶Other people from the tribes of Benjamin and Judah also came to David at his stronghold. ¹⁷David went out to meet them and said to them, "If you have come peacefully to help me, I welcome you. Join me. But if you have come to turn me over to my enemies, even though I have done nothing wrong, the God of our ancestors will see this and punish you."

¹⁸Then the Spirit entered Amasai, the leader of the Thirty, and he said:

"We belong to you, David.
    We are with you, son of Jesse.
  Success, success to you.
    Success to those who help you,
    because your God helps you."

So David welcomed these men and made them leaders of his army.

¹⁹Some of the men from Manasseh also joined David when he went with the Philistines to fight Saul. But David and his men did not really help the Philistines. After talking about it, the Philistine leaders decided to send David away. They said, "If David goes back to his master Saul, we will be killed." ²⁰These are the men from Manasseh who joined David when he went to Ziklag: Adnah, Jozabad, Jediael, Michael, Jozabad, Elihu, and Zillethai. Each of them was a leader of a thousand men from Manasseh. ²¹All these men of Manasseh were brave soldiers, and they helped David fight against groups of men who went around the country robbing people. These soldiers became commanders in David's army. ²²Every day more men joined David, and his army became large, like the army of God.

OTHERS JOIN DAVID AT HEBRON

²³These are the numbers of the soldiers ready for battle who joined David at Hebron. They came to help turn the kingdom of Saul over to David, just as the LORD had said.

²⁴There were sixty-eight hundred men with their weapons from Judah. They carried shields and spears.

²⁵There were seventy-one hundred men from Simeon. They were warriors ready for war.

²⁶There were forty-six hundred men from Levi. ²⁷Jehoiada, a leader from Aaron's family, was in that group. There were thirty-seven hundred with him. ²⁸Zadok was also in that group. He was a strong young warrior, and with him came twenty-two leaders from his family.

²⁹There were three thousand men from Benjamin, who were Saul's relatives. Most of them had remained loyal to Saul's family until then.

³⁰There were twenty thousand eight hundred men from Ephraim. They were brave warriors and were famous men in their own family groups.

³¹There were eighteen thousand men from West Manasseh. Each one was especially chosen to make David king.

³²There were two hundred leaders from Issachar. They knew what Israel should do, and they knew the right time to do it. Their relatives were with them and under their command.

³³There were fifty thousand men from Zebulun. They were trained soldiers and knew how to use every kind of weapon of war. They followed David completely.

³⁴There were one thousand officers from Naphtali. They had thirty-seven thousand soldiers with them who carried shields and spears.

³⁵There were twenty-eight thousand six hundred men from Dan, who were ready for war.

³⁶There were forty thousand trained soldiers from Asher, who were ready for war.

³⁷There were one hundred twenty thousand soldiers from the east side of the Jordan River from the people of Reuben, Gad, and East Manasseh. They had every kind of weapon.

³⁸All these fighting men were ready to go

to war. They came to Hebron fully agreed to make David king of all Israel. All the other Israelites also agreed to make David king. ³⁹They spent three days there with David, eating and drinking, because their relatives had prepared food for them. ⁴⁰Also, their neighbors came from as far away as Issachar, Zebulun, and Naphtali, bringing food on donkeys, camels, mules, and oxen. They brought much flour, fig cakes, raisins, wine, oil, cows, and sheep, because the people of Israel were very happy.

BRINGING BACK THE ARK

13 David talked with all the officers of his army, the commanders of a hundred men and the commanders of a thousand men. ²Then David called the people of Israel together and said, "If you think it is a good idea, and if it is what the LORD our God wants, let's send a message. Let's tell our fellow Israelites in all the areas of Israel and the priests and Levites living with them in their towns and pastures to come and join us. ³Let's bring the Ark of our God back to us. We did not use it to ask God for help while Saul was king." ⁴All the people agreed with David, because they all thought it was the right thing to do.

⁵So David gathered all the Israelites, from the Shihor River in Egypt to Lebo Hamath, to bring the Ark of God back from the town of Kiriath Jearim. ⁶David and all the Israelites with him went to Baalah of Judah, which is Kiriath Jearim, to get the Ark of God the LORD. God's throne is between the golden, winged creatures on the Ark, and the Ark is called by his name.

⁷The people carried the Ark of God from Abinadab's house on a new cart, and Uzzah and Ahio guided it. ⁸David and all the Israelites were celebrating in the presence of God. With all their strength they were singing and playing lyres, harps, tambourines, cymbals, and trumpets.

⁹When David's men came to the threshing floor of Kidon, the oxen stumbled, and Uzzah reached out his hand to steady the Ark. ¹⁰The LORD was angry with Uzzah and killed him, because he had touched the Ark. So Uzzah died there in the presence of God.

¹¹David was angry because the LORD had punished Uzzah in his anger. Now that place is called The Punishment of Uzzah.

¹²David was afraid of God that day and asked, "How can I bring the Ark of God home to me?" ¹³So David did not take the Ark with him to Jerusalem. Instead, he took it to the house of Obed-Edom who was from Gath. ¹⁴The Ark of God stayed with Obed-Edom's family in his house for three months, and the LORD blessed Obed-Edom's family and everything he owned.

DAVID'S KINGDOM GROWS

14 Hiram king of the city of Tyre sent messengers to David. He also sent cedar logs, bricklayers, and carpenters to build a palace for David. ²Then David knew that the LORD really had made him king of Israel and that he had made his kingdom great. The LORD did this because he loved his people Israel.

³David married more women in Jerusalem and had more sons and daughters. ⁴These are the names of David's children born in Jerusalem: Shammua, Shobab, Nathan, Solomon, ⁵Ibhar, Elishua, Elpelet, ⁶Nogah, Nepheg, Japhia, ⁷Elishama, Beeliada, and Eliphelet.

DAVID DEFEATS THE PHILISTINES

⁸When the Philistines heard that David had been made king of all Israel, they went to look for him. But David heard about it and went out to fight them. ⁹The Philistines had attacked and robbed the people in the Valley of Rephaim. ¹⁰David asked God, "Should I go and attack the Philistines? Will you hand them over to me?"

The LORD answered him, "Go, I will hand them over to you."

¹¹So David and his men went up to the town of Baal Perazim and defeated the Philistines. David said, "Like a flood of water, God has broken through my enemies by using me." So that place was named Baal Perazim.ⁿ ¹²The Philistines had left their idols there, so David ordered his men to burn them.

¹³Soon the Philistines attacked the people in the valley again. ¹⁴David prayed to God again, and God answered him, saying, "Don't attack the Philistines from the front. Instead, go around them and attack them in front of the balsam trees. ¹⁵When you hear the sound

---

14:11 Baal Perazim This name means "the Lord breaks through."

of marching in the tops of the balsam trees, then attack. I, God, will have gone out before you to defeat the Philistine army." [16]David did as God commanded, and he and his men defeated the Philistine army all the way from Gibeon to Gezer.

[17]So David became famous in all the countries, and the LORD made all nations afraid of him.

THE ARK IS BROUGHT TO JERUSALEM

15 David built houses for himself in Jerusalem. Then he prepared a place for the Ark of God, and he set up a tent for it. [2]David said, "Only the Levites may carry the Ark of God. The LORD chose them to carry the Ark of the LORD and to serve him forever."

[3]David called all the people of Israel to come to Jerusalem. He wanted to bring the Ark of the LORD to the place he had made for it. [4]David called together the descendants of Aaron and the Levites. [5]There were one hundred twenty people from Kohath's family group, with Uriel as their leader. [6]There were two hundred twenty people from Merari's family group, with Asaiah as their leader. [7]There were one hundred thirty people from Gershon's family group, with Joel as their leader. [8]There were two hundred people from Elizaphan's family group, with Shemaiah as their leader. [9]There were eighty people from Hebron's family group, with Eliel as their leader. [10]And there were one hundred twelve people from Uzziel's family group, with Amminadab as their leader.

[11]Then David asked the priests Zadok and Abiathar and these Levites to come to him: Uriel, Asaiah, Joel, Shemaiah, Eliel, and Amminadab. [12]David said to them, "You are the leaders of the families of Levi. You and the other Levites must give yourselves for service to the LORD. Bring up the Ark of the LORD, the God of Israel, to the place I have made for it. [13]The last time we did not ask the LORD how to carry it. You Levites didn't carry it, so the LORD our God punished us."

[14]Then the priests and Levites prepared themselves for service to the LORD so they could carry the Ark of the LORD, the God of Israel. [15]The Levites used special poles to carry the Ark of God on their shoulders, as Moses had commanded, just as the LORD had said they should.

[16]David told the leaders of the Levites to appoint their brothers as singers to play their lyres, harps, and cymbals and to sing happy songs.

[17]So the Levites appointed Heman and his relatives Asaph and Ethan. Heman was Joel's son. Asaph was Berekiah's son. And Ethan, from the Merari family group, was Kushaiah's son. [18]There was also a second group of Levites: Zechariah, Jaaziel, Shemiramoth, Jehiel, Unni, Eliab, Benaiah, Maaseiah, Mattithiah, Eliphelehu, Mikneiah, Obed-Edom, and Jeiel. They were the Levite guards.

[19]The singers Heman, Asaph, and Ethan played bronze cymbals. [20]Zechariah, Jaaziel, Shemiramoth, Jehiel, Unni, Eliab, Maaseiah, and Benaiah played the lyres. [21]Mattithiah, Eliphelehu, Mikneiah, Obed-Edom, Jeiel, and Azaziah played the harps. [22]The Levite leader Kenaniah was in charge of the singing, because he was very good at it.

[23]Berekiah and Elkanah were two of the guards for the Ark of the Agreement. [24]The priests Shebaniah, Joshaphat, Nethanel, Amasai, Zechariah, Benaiah, and Eliezer had the job of blowing trumpets in front of the Ark of God. Obed-Edom and Jehiah were also guards for the Ark.

[25]David, the leaders of Israel, and the commanders of a thousand soldiers went to get the Ark of the Agreement with the LORD. They all went to bring the Ark from Obed-Edom's house with great joy. [26]Because God helped the Levites who carried the Ark of the Agreement with the LORD, they sacrificed seven bulls and seven male sheep. [27]All the Levites who carried the Ark, and Kenaniah, the man in charge of the singing, and all the singers wore robes of fine linen. David also wore a robe of fine linen and a holy vest of fine linen. [28]So all the people of Israel brought up the Ark of the Agreement with the LORD. They shouted, blew horns and trumpets, and played cymbals, lyres, and harps.

[29]As the Ark of the Agreement with the LORD entered Jerusalem, Saul's daughter Michal watched from a window. When she saw King David dancing and celebrating, she hated him.

16 They brought the Ark of God and put it inside the tent that David had set up for it. Then they offered burnt offerings and fellowship offerings to God. [2]When David had finished giving the burnt offerings and fellowship offerings, he blessed the people in the name of the LORD. ³He gave a loaf of bread, some dates, and raisins to every Israelite man and woman.

⁴Then David appointed some of the Levites to serve before the Ark of the LORD. They had the job of leading the worship and giving thanks and praising the LORD, the God of Israel. ⁵Asaph, who played the cymbals, was the leader. Zechariah was second to him. The other Levites were Jaaziel, Shemiramoth, Jehiel, Mattithiah, Eliab, Benaiah, Obed-Edom, and Jeiel. They played the lyres and harps. ⁶Benaiah and Jahaziel were priests who blew the trumpets regularly before the Ark of the Agreement with God. ⁷That day David first gave Asaph and his relatives the job of singing praises to the LORD.

DAVID'S SONG OF THANKS

⁸ Give thanks to the LORD and pray to him.
　　Tell the nations what he has done.
⁹ Sing to him; sing praises to him.
　　Tell about all his miracles.
¹⁰ Be glad that you are his;
　　let those who seek the LORD be happy.
¹¹ Depend on the LORD and his strength;
　　always go to him for help.
¹² Remember the miracles he has done,
　　his wonders, and his decisions.
¹³ You are the descendants of his servant, Israel;
　　you are the children of Jacob, his chosen people.

¹⁴ He is the LORD our God.
　　His laws are for all the world.
¹⁵ He will keep his agreement forever;
　　he will keep his promises always.
¹⁶ He will keep the agreement he made with Abraham
　　and the promise he made to Isaac.
¹⁷ He made it a law for the people of Jacob;
　　he made it an agreement with Israel to last forever.
¹⁸ He said, "I will give the land of Canaan to you,
　　to belong to you."

¹⁹ Then God's people were few in number,
　　and they were strangers in the land.
²⁰ They went from one nation to another,
　　from one kingdom to another.

²¹ But he did not let anyone hurt them;
　　he warned kings not to harm them.
²² He said, "Don't touch my chosen people,
　　and don't harm my prophets."

²³ Sing to the LORD, all the earth.
　　Every day tell how he saves us.
²⁴ Tell the nations about his glory;
　　tell all peoples the miracles he does.
²⁵ The LORD is great; he should be praised.
　　He should be respected more than all the gods.
²⁶ All the gods of the nations are only idols,
　　but the LORD made the skies.
²⁷ He has glory and majesty;
　　he has power and joy in his Temple.

²⁸ Praise the LORD, all nations on earth.
　　Praise the LORD's glory and power;
²⁹ 　　praise the glory of the LORD's name.
　　Bring an offering and come to him.
　　Worship the LORD because he is holy.
³⁰ Tremble before him, everyone on earth.
　　The earth is set, and it cannot be moved.
³¹ Let the skies rejoice and the earth be glad.
　　Let people everywhere say, "The LORD is king!"
³² Let the sea and everything in it shout;
　　let the fields and everything in them rejoice.
³³ Then the trees of the forest will sing
　　for joy before the LORD.
　　They will sing because he is coming to judge the world.

³⁴ Thank the LORD because he is good.
　　His love continues forever.
³⁵ Say to him, "Save us, God our Savior,
　　and bring us back and save us from other nations.
　　Then we will thank you
　　and will gladly praise you."
³⁶ Praise the LORD, the God of Israel.
　　He always was and always will be.

All the people said "Amen" and praised the LORD.

³⁷Then David left Asaph and the other Levites there in front of the Ark of the Agreement with the LORD. They were to serve there every day. ³⁸David also left Obed-Edom and sixty-eight other Levites to serve with them. Hosah and Obed-Edom son of Jeduthun were guards.

FUTURE

the **meaning**
of **"saved"**

1 CHRONICLES 16:34-36

"**A** re you saved?" Unless you understand what that word saved means, this question doesn't make much sense, does it? Saved from what? The Greek verb *sozo* is used fifty-four times in the Gospels. About half of those times it means to be rescued from some impending danger to physical life. We could all answer the question if it was, Did someone rescue you from death? That is a "yes" or "no" question. If you were drowning and someone pulled you out of the water, you would know right away you had been saved. But the other half of the fifty-four times is not so clear. How can anyone be *saved* from sins?

Once we see that the first meaning of the word *sozo* is to be rescued, we understand that *sozo* means to protect, to keep alive, and to deliver. The Bible tells us that we need to be rescued from more than physical perils. If we are going to stay alive, we need to be rescued from the consequences of sin. Those consequences are spiritual death, punishment, and eternal misery. Salvation is a lot more than an admission ticket to heaven. If Jesus is going to save his people from their sins, he has to rescue them from their spiritual death, from the punishment they deserve, and from the misery that is bound to follow.

Salvation is about so much more than getting into heaven. It is all about staying alive spiritually. If you thought you were *saved* just in order to get a heavenly gate pass, you missed the point. Jesus rescues people who are in deep, deep trouble. They are not just drowning. They are already dead. Unless he shows up with life, they will remain dead. Salvation is what is necessary because they need to live again.

Twenty centuries ago a man was born whom God sent to rescue us from death. Jesus did not come to sell tickets to heaven. He came to give us artificial respiration. He came because we had been in a life-and-death struggle—and we had lost. It is his work, not ours, that produces life. And for two thousand years he has been doing just that—rescuing people who were dead. If you have been rescued, you can weep for joy today. The lifeguard has arrived.

reflect: Thank God for rescuing your soul from spiritual death, punishment, and eternal misery.
Go to **Lamentations 5:7.**

³⁹David left Zadok the priest and the other priests who served with him in front of the Tent of the LORD at the place of worship in Gibeon. ⁴⁰Every morning and evening they offered burnt offerings on the altar of burnt offerings, following the rules written in the Teachings of the LORD, which he had given Israel. ⁴¹With them were Heman and Jeduthun and other Levites. They were chosen by name to sing praises to the LORD because his love continues forever. ⁴²Heman and Jeduthun also had the job of playing the trumpets and cymbals and other musical instruments when songs were sung to God. Jeduthun's sons guarded the gates.

⁴³Then all the people left. Each person went home, and David also went home to bless the people in his home.

GOD'S PROMISE TO DAVID

17 When David moved into his palace, he said to Nathan the prophet, "Look, I am living in a palace made of cedar, but the Ark of the Agreement with the LORD sits in a tent."

²Nathan said to David, "Do what you want to do, because God is with you."

³But that night God spoke his word to Nathan, saying, ⁴"Go and tell David my servant, 'This is what the LORD says: You are not the person to build a house for me to live in. ⁵From the time I brought Israel out of Egypt until now I have not lived in a house. I have moved from one tent site to another and from one place to another. ⁶As I have moved with the Israelites to different places, I have never said to the leaders, whom I commanded to take care of my people, "Why haven't you built me a house of cedar?" '

⁷"Now, tell my servant David: 'This is what the LORD All-Powerful says: I took you from the pasture and from tending the sheep and made you king of my people Israel. ⁸I have been with you everywhere you have gone. I have defeated your enemies for you. I will make you as famous as any of the great people on the earth. ⁹I will choose a place for my people Israel, and I will plant them so they can live in their own homes. They will not be bothered anymore. Wicked people will no longer hurt them as they have in the past ¹⁰when I chose judges for my people Israel. I will defeat all your enemies.

" 'I tell you that the LORD will make your descendants kings of Israel after you. ¹¹When you die and join your ancestors, I will make one of your sons the new king, and I will set up his kingdom. ¹²He will build a house for me, and I will let his kingdom rule always. ¹³I will be his father, and he will be my son. I took away my love from Saul, who ruled before you, but I will never stop loving your son. ¹⁴I will put him in charge of my house and kingdom forever. His family will rule forever.' "

¹⁵Nathan told David everything God had said in this vision.

DAVID PRAYS TO GOD

¹⁶Then King David went in and sat in front of the LORD. David said, "LORD God, who am I? What is my family? Why did you bring me to this point? ¹⁷But that was not enough for you, God. You have also made promises about my future family. LORD God, you have treated me like a very important person.

¹⁸"What more can I say to you for honoring me, your servant? You know me so well. ¹⁹LORD, you have done this wonderful thing for my sake and because you wanted to. You have made known all these great things.

²⁰"There is no one like you, LORD. There is no God except you. We have heard all this ourselves! ²¹There is no nation like your people Israel. They are the only people on earth that God chose to be his own. You made your name well known by the great and wonderful things you did for them. You went ahead of them and forced other nations out of the land. You freed your people from slavery in Egypt. ²²You made the people of Israel your very own people forever, and, LORD, you are their God.

²³"LORD, keep the promise forever that you made about my family and me, your servant. Do what you have said. ²⁴Then you will be honored always, and people will say, 'The LORD All-Powerful, the God over Israel, is Israel's God!' And the family of your servant David will continue before you.

²⁵"My God, you have told me that you would make my family great. So I, your servant, am brave enough to pray to you. ²⁶LORD, you are God, and you have promised these good things to me, your servant. ²⁷You have chosen to bless my family. Let it continue

before you always. LORD, you have blessed my family, so it will always be blessed."

DAVID DEFEATS NATIONS

18 Later, David defeated the Philistines, conquered them, and took the city of Gath and the small towns around it.

2He also defeated the people of Moab. So the people of Moab became servants of David and gave him the payment he demanded.

3David also defeated Hadadezer king of Zobah all the way to the town of Hamath as he tried to spread his kingdom to the Euphrates River. 4David captured one thousand of his chariots, seven thousand men who rode in chariots, and twenty thousand foot soldiers. He crippled all but a hundred of the chariot horses.

5Arameans from Damascus came to help Hadadezer king of Zobah, but David killed twenty-two thousand of them. 6Then David put groups of soldiers in Damascus in Aram. The Arameans became David's servants and gave him the payments he demanded. So the LORD gave David victory everywhere he went.

7David took the shields of gold that had belonged to Hadadezer's officers and brought them to Jerusalem. 8David also took many things made of bronze from Tebah and Cun, which had been cities under Hadadezer's control. Later, Solomon used this bronze to make things for the Temple: the large bronze bowl, which was called the Sea, the pillars, and other bronze utensils.

9Toi king of Hamath heard that David had defeated all the army of Hadadezer king of Zobah. 10So Toi sent his son Hadoram to greet and congratulate King David for defeating Hadadezer. (Hadadezer had been at war with Toi.) Hadoram brought items made of gold, silver, and bronze. 11King David gave them to the LORD, along with the silver and gold he had taken from these nations: Edom, Moab, the Ammonites, the Philistines, and Amalek.

12Abishai son of Zeruiah killed eighteen thousand Edomites in the Valley of Salt. 13David put groups of soldiers in Edom, and all the Edomites became his servants. The LORD gave David victory everywhere he went.

DAVID'S IMPORTANT OFFICERS

14David was king over all of Israel, and he did what was fair and right for all his people. 15Joab son of Zeruiah was commander over the army. Jehoshaphat son of Ahilud was the recorder. 16Zadok son of Ahitub and Abiathar son of Ahimelech were priests. Shavsha was the royal secretary. 17Benaiah son of Jehoiada was over the Kerethites and Pelethites.[n] And David's sons were important officers who served at his side.

WAR WITH THE AMMONITES AND ARAMEANS

19 When Nahash king of the Ammonites died, his son became king after him. 2David said, "Nahash was loyal to me, so I will be loyal to his son Hanun." So David sent messengers to comfort Hanun about his father's death.

David's officers went to the land of the Ammonites to comfort Hanun. 3But the Ammonite leaders said to Hanun, "Do you think David wants to honor your father by sending men to comfort you? No! David sent them to study the land and capture it and spy it out." 4So Hanun arrested David's officers. To shame them he shaved their beards and cut off their clothes at the hips. Then he sent them away.

5When the people told David what had happened to his officers, he sent messengers to meet them, because they were very ashamed. King David said, "Stay in Jericho until your beards have grown back. Then come home."

6The Ammonites knew that they had insulted David. So Hanun and the Ammonites sent about seventy-four thousand pounds of silver to hire chariots and chariot drivers from Northwest Mesopotamia, Aram Maacah, and Zobah. 7The Ammonites hired thirty-two thousand chariots and the king of Maacah and his army. So they came and set up camp near the town of Medeba. The Ammonites themselves came out of their towns and got ready for battle.

8When David heard about this, he sent Joab with the whole army. 9The Ammonites came out and prepared for battle at the city

---

18:17 Kerethites and Pelethites These were probably special units of the army that were responsible for the king's safety, a kind of palace guard.

gate. The kings who had come to help were out in the field by themselves.

¹⁰Joab saw that there were enemies both in front of him and behind him. So he chose some of the best soldiers of Israel and sent them out to fight the Arameans. ¹¹Joab put the rest of the army under the command of Abishai, his brother. Then they went out to fight the Ammonites. ¹²Joab said to Abishai, "If the Arameans are too strong for me, you must help me. Or, if the Ammonites are too strong for you, I will help you. ¹³Be strong. We must fight bravely for our people and the cities of our God. The LORD will do what he thinks is right."

¹⁴Then Joab and the army with him went to attack the Arameans, and the Arameans ran away. ¹⁵When the Ammonites saw that the Arameans were running away, they also ran away from Joab's brother Abishai and went back to their city. So Joab went back to Jerusalem.

¹⁶When the Arameans saw that Israel had defeated them, they sent messengers to bring other Arameans from east of the Euphrates River. Their leader was Shophach, the commander of Hadadezer's army.

¹⁷When David heard about this, he gathered all the Israelites, and they crossed over the Jordan River. He prepared them for battle, facing the Arameans. The Arameans fought with him, ¹⁸but they ran away from the Israelites. David killed seven thousand Aramean chariot drivers and forty thousand Aramean foot soldiers. He also killed Shophach, the commander of the Aramean army.

¹⁹When those who served Hadadezer saw that the Israelites had defeated them, they made peace with David and served him. So the Arameans refused to help the Ammonites again.

JOAB DESTROYS THE AMMONITES

20 In the spring, the time of year when kings normally went out to battle, Joab led out the army of Israel. But David stayed in Jerusalem. The army of Israel destroyed the land of Ammon and went to the city of Rabbah and attacked it. ²David took the crown off the head of their king,[n] and had it placed on his own head. That gold crown weighed about seventy-five pounds, and it had valuable gems in it. And David

took many valuable things from the city. ³He also brought out the people of the city and forced them to work with saws, iron picks, and axes. David did this to all the Ammonite cities. Then David and all his army returned to Jerusalem.

PHILISTINE GIANTS ARE KILLED

⁴Later, at Gezer, war broke out with the Philistines. Sibbecai the Hushathite killed Sippai, who was one of the descendants of the Rephaites. So those Philistines were defeated.

⁵Later, there was another battle with the Philistines. Elhanan son of Jair killed Lahmi, the brother of Goliath, who was from the town of Gath. His spear was as large as a weaver's rod.

⁶At Gath another battle took place. A huge man was there; he had six fingers on each hand and six toes on each foot—twenty-four fingers and toes in all. This man also was one of the sons of Rapha. ⁷When he spoke against Israel, Jonathan son of Shimea, David's brother, killed him.

⁸These descendants of Rapha from Gath were killed by David and his men.

DAVID COUNTS THE ISRAELITES

21 Satan was against Israel, and he caused David to count the people of Israel. ²So David said to Joab and the commanders of the troops, "Go and count all the Israelites from Beersheba to Dan.[n] Then tell me so I will know how many there are."

³But Joab said, "May the LORD give the nation a hundred times more people. My master the king, all the Israelites are your servants. Why do you want to do this, my master? You will make Israel guilty of sin."

⁴But the king commanded Joab, so Joab left and went through all Israel. Then he returned to Jerusalem. ⁵Joab gave the list of the people to David. There were one million one hundred thousand men in all of Israel who could use the sword, and there were four hundred seventy thousand men in Judah who could use the sword. ⁶But Joab did not count the tribes of Levi and Benjamin, because he

---

20:2 their king Or, "Milcom," the god of the Ammonite people. **21:2 Beersheba to Dan** Beersheba was the city farthest south in Israel. Dan was the city farthest north. So this means all the people of Israel.

didn't like King David's order. 7David had done something God had said was wrong, so God punished Israel.

8Then David said to God, "I have sinned greatly by what I have done! Now, I beg you to forgive me, your servant, because I have been very foolish."

9The LORD said to Gad, who was David's seer, 10"Go and tell David, 'This is what the LORD says: I offer you three choices. Choose one of them and I will do it.'"

11So Gad went to David and said to him, "This is what the LORD says: 'Choose for yourself 12three years of hunger. Or choose three months of running from your enemies as they chase you with their swords. Or choose three days of punishment from the LORD, in which a terrible disease will spread through the country. The angel of the LORD will go through Israel destroying the people.' Now, David, decide which of these things I should tell the LORD who sent me."

13David said to Gad, "I am in great trouble. Let the LORD punish me, because the LORD is very merciful. Don't let my punishment come from human beings."

14So the LORD sent a terrible disease on Israel, and seventy thousand people died. 15God sent an angel to destroy Jerusalem, but when the angel started to destroy it, the LORD saw it and felt very sorry about the terrible things that had happened. So he said to the angel who was destroying, "That is enough! Put down your arm!" The angel of the LORD was then standing at the threshing floor of Araunah the Jebusite.

16David looked up and saw the angel of the LORD in the sky, holding his sword drawn and pointed at Jerusalem. Then David and the elders bowed facedown on the ground. They were wearing rough cloth to show their grief. 17David said to God, "I am the one who sinned and did wrong. I gave the order for the people to be counted. These people only followed me like sheep. They did nothing wrong. LORD my God, please punish me and my family, but stop the terrible disease that is killing your people."

18Then the angel of the LORD told Gad to tell David that he should build an altar to the LORD on the threshing floor of Araunah the Jebusite. 19So David did what Gad told him to do, in the name of the LORD.

20Araunah was separating the wheat from the straw. When he turned around, he saw the angel. Araunah's four sons who were with him hid. 21David came to Araunah, and when Araunah saw him, he left the threshing floor and bowed facedown on the ground before David.

22David said to him, "Sell me your threshing floor so I can build an altar to the LORD here. Then the terrible disease will stop. Sell it to me for the full price."

23Araunah said to David, "Take this threshing floor. My master the king, do anything you want. Look, I will also give you oxen for the whole burnt offerings, the threshing boards for the wood, and wheat for the grain offering. I give everything to you."

24But King David answered Araunah, "No, I will pay the full price for the land. I won't take anything that is yours and give it to the LORD. I won't offer a burnt offering that costs me nothing."

25So David paid Araunah about fifteen pounds of gold for the place. 26David built an altar to the LORD there and offered whole burnt offerings and fellowship offerings. David prayed to the LORD, and he answered him by sending down fire from heaven on the altar of burnt offering. 27Then the LORD commanded the angel to put his sword back into its holder.

28When David saw that the LORD had answered him on the threshing floor of Araunah, he offered sacrifices there. 29The Holy Tent that Moses made while the Israelites were in the desert and the altar of burnt offerings were in Gibeon at the place of worship. 30But David could not go to the Holy Tent to speak with God, because he was afraid of the angel of the LORD and his sword.

22 David said, "The Temple of the LORD God and the altar for Israel's burnt offerings will be built here."

DAVID MAKES PLANS FOR THE TEMPLE

2So David ordered all foreigners living in Israel to gather together. From that group David chose stonecutters to cut stones to be used in building the Temple of God. 3David supplied a large amount of iron to be used for making nails and hinges for the gate doors. He also supplied more bronze than could be weighed, 4and he supplied more cedar logs than could be counted. Much of the cedar had been brought to David by the people from Sidon and Tyre.

5David said, "We should build a great Temple for the LORD, which will be famous everywhere for its greatness and beauty. But my son Solomon is young. He hasn't yet learned what he needs to know, so I will prepare for the building of it." So David got many of the materials ready before he died.

6Then David called for his son Solomon and told him to build the Temple for the LORD, the God of Israel. 7David said to him, "My son, I wanted to build a temple for worshiping the LORD my God. 8But the LORD spoke his word to me, 'David, you have killed many people. You have fought many wars. You cannot build a temple for worship to me, because you have killed many people. 9But, you will have a son, a man of peace and rest. I will give him rest from all his enemies around him. His name will be Solomon,n and I will give Israel peace and quiet while he is king. 10Solomon will build a temple for worship to me. He will be my son, and I will be his father. I will make his kingdom strong; someone from his family will rule Israel forever.' "

11David said, "Now, my son, may the LORD be with you. May you build a temple for the LORD your God, as he said you would. 12He will make you the king of Israel. May the LORD give you wisdom and understanding so you will be able to obey the teachings of the LORD your God. 13Be careful to obey the rules and laws the LORD gave Moses for Israel. If you obey them, you will have success. Be strong and brave. Don't be afraid or discouraged.

14"Solomon, I have worked hard getting many of the materials for building the Temple of the LORD. I have supplied about seven and one-half million pounds of gold, about seventy-five million pounds of silver, so much bronze and iron it cannot be weighed, and wood and stone. You may add to them. 15You have many workmen—stonecutters, bricklayers, carpenters, and people skilled in every kind of work. 16They are skilled in working with gold, silver, bronze, and iron. You have more craftsmen than can be counted. Now begin the work, and may the LORD be with you."

17Then David ordered all the leaders of Israel to help his son Solomon. 18David said to them, "The LORD your God is with you. He has given you rest from our enemies. He has handed over to me the people living around us. The LORD and his people are in control of this land. 19Now give yourselves completely to obeying the LORD your God. Build the holy place of the LORD God; build the Temple for worship to the LORD. Then bring the Ark of the Agreement with the LORD and the holy items that belong to God into the Temple."

THE LEVITES

23 After David had lived long and was old, he made his son Solomon the new king of Israel. 2David gathered all the leaders of Israel, along with the priests and Levites. 3He counted the Levites who were thirty years old and older. In all, there were thirty-eight thousand Levites. 4David said, "Of these, twenty-four thousand Levites will direct the work of the Temple of the LORD, six thousand Levites will be officers and judges, 5four thousand Levites will be gatekeepers, and four thousand Levites will praise the LORD with musical instruments I made for giving praise."

6David separated the Levites into three groups that were led by Levi's three sons: Gershon, Kohath, and Merari.

THE PEOPLE OF GERSHON

7From the people of Gershon, there were Ladan and Shimei.

8Ladan had three sons. His first son was Jehiel, and his other sons were Zetham and Joel.

9Shimei's sons were Shelomoth, Haziel, and Haran. These three sons were leaders of Ladan's families. 10Shimei had four sons: Jahath, Ziza, Jeush, and Beriah. 11Jahath was the first son, and Ziza was the second son. But Jeush and Beriah did not have many children, so they were counted as if they were one family.

THE PEOPLE OF KOHATH

12Kohath had four sons: Amram, Izhar, Hebron, and Uzziel.

13Amram's sons were Aaron and Moses. Aaron and his descendants were chosen to

---

22:9 **Solomon** This name sounds like the Hebrew word for "peace."

be special forever. They were chosen to prepare the holy things for the LORD's service, to offer sacrifices before the LORD, and to serve him as priests. They were to give blessings in his name forever.

14Moses was the man of God, and his sons were counted as part of the tribe of Levi. 15Moses' sons were Gershom and Eliezer. 16Gershom's first son was Shubael. 17Eliezer's first son was Rehabiah. Eliezer had no other sons, but Rehabiah had many sons.

18Izhar's first son was Shelomith.

19Hebron's first son was Jeriah, his second was Amariah, his third was Jahaziel, and his fourth was Jekameam.

20Uzziel's first son was Micah and his second was Isshiah.

THE PEOPLE OF MERARI

21Merari's sons were Mahli and Mushi. Mahli's sons were Eleazar and Kish. 22Eleazar died without sons; he had only daughters. Eleazar's daughters married their cousins, the sons of Kish. 23Mushi's three sons were Mahli, Eder, and Jerimoth.

THE LEVITES' WORK

24These were Levi's descendants listed by their families. They were the leaders of families. Each person who was twenty years old or older was listed. They served in the LORD's Temple.

25David had said, "The LORD, the God of Israel, has given rest to his people. He has come to live in Jerusalem forever. 26So the Levites don't need to carry the Holy Tent or any of the things used in its services anymore." 27David's last instructions were to count the Levites who were twenty years old and older.

28The Levites had the job of helping Aaron's descendants in the service of the Temple of the LORD. They cared for the Temple courtyard and side rooms, and they made all the holy things pure. Their job was to serve in the Temple of God. 29They were responsible for putting the holy bread on the table, for the flour in the grain offerings, for the bread made without yeast, for the baking and mixing, and for the measuring. 30The Levites also stood every morning and gave thanks and praise to the LORD. They also did this every evening. 31The Levites offered all the burnt offerings to the LORD on the special days of rest, at the New Moon festivals, and at all appointed feasts. They served before the LORD every day. They were to follow the rules for how many Levites should serve each time. 32So the Levites took care of the Meeting Tent and the Holy Place. And they helped their relatives, Aaron's descendants, with the services at the Temple of the LORD.

THE GROUPS OF THE PRIESTS

24 These were the groups of Aaron's sons: Aaron's sons were Nadab, Abihu, Eleazar, and Ithamar. 2But Nadab and Abihu died before their father did, and they had no sons. So Eleazar and Ithamar served as the priests. 3David, with the help of Zadok, a descendant of Eleazar, and Ahimelech, a descendant of Ithamar, separated their family groups into two different groups. Each group had certain duties. 4There were more leaders from Eleazar's family than from Ithamar's—sixteen leaders from Eleazar's family and eight leaders from Ithamar's family. 5Men were chosen from Eleazar's and Ithamar's families by throwing lots. Some men from each family were chosen to be in charge of the Holy Place, and some were chosen to serve as priests.

6Shemaiah son of Nethanel, from the tribe of Levi, was the secretary. He recorded the names of those descendants in front of King David, the officers, Zadok the priest, Ahimelech son of Abiathar, and the leaders of the families of the priests and Levites. The work was divided by lots among the families of Eleazar and Ithamar. The following men with their groups were chosen.

7The first one chosen was Jehoiarib. The second was Jedaiah. 8The third was Harim. The fourth was Seorim. 9The fifth was Malkijah. The sixth was Mijamin. 10The seventh was Hakkoz. The eighth was Abijah. 11The ninth was Jeshua. The tenth was Shecaniah. 12The eleventh was Eliashib. The twelfth was Jakim. 13The thirteenth was Huppah. The fourteenth was Jeshebeab. 14The fifteenth was Bilgah. The sixteenth was Immer. 15The seventeenth was Hezir. The eighteenth was Happizzez. 16The nineteenth was Pethahiah. The twentieth was Jehezkel. 17The twenty-first was Jakin. The twenty-second was Gamul. 18The twenty-third was Delaiah. The twenty-fourth was Maaziah.

[19]These were the groups chosen to serve in the Temple of the LORD. They obeyed the rules given them by Aaron, just as the LORD, the God of Israel, had commanded him.

THE OTHER LEVITES

[20]These are the names of the rest of Levi's descendants:

Shubael was a descendant of Amram, and Jehdeiah was a descendant of Shubael.

[21]Isshiah was the first son of Rehabiah.

[22]From the Izhar family group, there was Shelomoth, and Jahath was a descendant of Shelomoth.

[23]Hebron's first son was Jeriah, Amariah was his second, Jahaziel was his third, and Jekameam was his fourth.

[24]Uzziel's son was Micah. Micah's son was Shamir. [25]Micah's brother was Isshiah, and Isshiah's son was Zechariah.

[26]Merari's descendants were Mahli and Mushi. Merari's son was Jaaziah. [27]Jaaziah son of Merari had sons named Shoham, Zaccur, and Ibri. [28]Mahli's son was Eleazar, but Eleazar did not have any sons.

[29]Kish's son was Jerahmeel.

[30]Mushi's sons were Mahli, Eder, and Jerimoth.

These are the Levites, listed by their families. [31]They were chosen for special jobs by throwing lots in front of King David, Zadok, Ahimelech, the leaders of the families of the priests, and the Levites. They did this just as their relatives, the priests, Aaron's descendants, had done. The families of the oldest brother and the youngest brother were treated the same.

THE MUSIC GROUPS

25 David and the commanders of the army chose some of the sons of Asaph, Heman, and Jeduthun to preach and play harps, lyres, and cymbals. Here is a list of the men who served in this way:

[2]Asaph's sons who served were Zaccur, Joseph, Nethaniah, and Asarelah. King David chose Asaph to preach, and Asaph directed his sons.

[3]Jeduthun's sons who served were Gedaliah, Zeri, Jeshaiah, Shimei, Hashabiah, and Mattithiah. There were six of them, and Jeduthun directed them. He preached and used a harp to give thanks and praise to the LORD.

[4]Heman's sons who served were Bukkiah, Mattaniah, Uzziel, Shubael, Jerimoth, Hananiah, Hanani, Eliathah, Giddalti, Romamti-Ezer, Joshbekashah, Mallothi, Hothir, and Mahazioth. [5]All these were sons of Heman, David's seer. God promised to make Heman strong, so Heman had many sons. God gave him fourteen sons and three daughters. [6]Heman directed all his sons in making music for the Temple of the LORD with cymbals, lyres, and harps; that was their way of serving in the Temple of God. King David was in charge of Asaph, Jeduthun, and Heman. [7]These men and their relatives were trained and skilled in making music for the LORD. There were two hundred eighty-eight of them. [8]Everyone threw lots to choose the time his family was to serve at the Temple. The young and the old, the teacher and the student, had to throw lots.

[9]First, the lot fell to Joseph, from the family of Asaph.

Second, twelve men were chosen from Gedaliah, his sons and relatives.

[10]Third, twelve men were chosen from Zaccur, his sons and relatives.

[11]Fourth, twelve men were chosen from Izri, his sons and relatives.

[12]Fifth, twelve men were chosen from Nethaniah, his sons and relatives.

[13]Sixth, twelve men were chosen from Bukkiah, his sons and relatives.

[14]Seventh, twelve men were chosen from Jesarelah, his sons and relatives.

[15]Eighth, twelve men were chosen from Jeshaiah, his sons and relatives.

[16]Ninth, twelve men were chosen from Mattaniah, his sons and relatives.

[17]Tenth, twelve men were chosen from Shimei, his sons and relatives.

[18]Eleventh, twelve men were chosen from Azarel, his sons and relatives.

[19]Twelfth, twelve men were chosen from Hashabiah, his sons and relatives.

[20]Thirteenth, twelve men were chosen from Shubael, his sons and relatives.

[21]Fourteenth, twelve men were chosen from Mattithiah, his sons and relatives.

[22]Fifteenth, twelve men were chosen from Jerimoth, his sons and relatives.

[23]Sixteenth, twelve men were chosen from Hananiah, his sons and relatives.

²⁴Seventeenth, twelve men were chosen from Joshbekashah, his sons and relatives.

²⁵Eighteenth, twelve men were chosen from Hanani, his sons and relatives.

²⁶Nineteenth, twelve men were chosen from Mallothi, his sons and relatives.

²⁷Twentieth, twelve men were chosen from Eliathah, his sons and relatives.

²⁸Twenty-first, twelve men were chosen from Hothir, his sons and relatives.

²⁹Twenty-second, twelve men were chosen from Giddalti, his sons and relatives.

³⁰Twenty-third, twelve men were chosen from Mahazioth, his sons and relatives.

³¹Twenty-fourth, twelve men were chosen from Romamti-Ezer, his sons and relatives.

THE GATEKEEPERS

26 These are the groups of the gatekeepers. From the family of Korah, there was Meshelemiah son of Kore, who was from Asaph's family. ²Meshelemiah had sons. Zechariah was his first son, Jediael was second, Zebadiah was third, Jathniel was fourth, ³Elam was fifth, Jehohanan was sixth, and Eliehoenai was seventh.

⁴Obed-Edom had sons. Shemaiah was his first son, Jehozabad was second, Joah was third, Sacar was fourth, Nethanel was fifth, ⁵Ammiel was sixth, Issachar was seventh, and Peullethai was eighth. God blessed Obed-Edom with children.

⁶Obed-Edom's son Shemaiah also had sons. They were leaders in their father's family because they were capable men. ⁷Shemaiah's sons were Othni, Rephael, Obed, Elzabad, Elihu, and Semakiah. Elihu, and Semakiah were skilled workers. ⁸All these were Obed-Edom's descendants. They and their sons and relatives were capable men and strong workers. Obed-Edom had sixty-two descendants in all.

⁹Meshelemiah had sons and relatives who were skilled workers. In all, there were eighteen.

¹⁰From the Merari family, Hosah had sons. Shimri was chosen to be in charge. Although he was not the oldest son, his father chose him to be in charge. ¹¹Hilkiah was his second son, Tabaliah was third, and Zechariah was fourth. In all, Hosah had thirteen sons and relatives.

¹²These were the leaders of the groups of gatekeepers, and they served in the Temple of the LORD. Their relatives also worked in the Temple. ¹³By throwing lots, each family chose a gate to guard. Young and old threw lots.

¹⁴Meshelemiah was chosen by lot to guard the East Gate. Then lots were thrown for Meshelemiah's son Zechariah. He was a wise counselor and was chosen for the North Gate. ¹⁵Obed-Edom was chosen for the South Gate, and Obed-Edom's sons were chosen to guard the storehouse. ¹⁶Shuppim and Hosah were chosen for the West Gate and the Shalleketh Gate on the upper road.

Guards stood side by side with guards. ¹⁷Six Levites stood guard every day at the East Gate; four Levites stood guard every day at the North Gate; four Levites stood guard every day at the South Gate; and two Levites at a time guarded the storehouse. ¹⁸There were two guards at the western court and four guards on the road to the court.

¹⁹These were the groups of the gatekeepers from the families of Korah and Merari.

OTHER LEADERS

²⁰Other Levites were responsible for guarding the treasuries of the Temple of God and for the places where the holy items were kept.

²¹Ladan was Gershon's son and the ancestor of several family groups. Jehiel was a leader of one of the family groups. ²²His sons were Zetham and Joel his brother, and they were responsible for the treasuries of the Temple of the LORD.

²³Other leaders were chosen from the family groups of Amram, Izhar, Hebron, and Uzziel. ²⁴Shubael, the descendant of Gershom, who was Moses' son, was the leader responsible for the treasuries. ²⁵These were Shubael's relatives from Eliezer: Eliezer's son Rehabiah, Rehabiah's son Jeshaiah, Jeshaiah's son Joram, Joram's son Zicri, and Zicri's son Shelomith. ²⁶Shelomith and his relatives were responsible for everything that had been collected for the Temple by King David, by the heads of families, by the commanders of a thousand men and of a hundred men, and by other army commanders. ²⁷They also gave some of the things they had taken in wars to be used in repairing the Temple of the LORD. ²⁸Shelomith and his relatives took

care of all the holy items. Some had been given by Samuel the seer, Saul son of Kish, Abner son of Ner, and Joab son of Zeruiah.

29Kenaniah was from the Izhar family. He and his sons worked outside the Temple as officers and judges in different places in Israel.

30Hashabiah was from the Hebron family. He and his relatives were responsible for the LORD's work and the king's business in Israel west of the Jordan River. There were seventeen hundred skilled men in Hashabiah's group. 31The history of the Hebron family shows that Jeriah was their leader. In David's fortieth year as king, the records were searched, and some capable men of the Hebron family were found living at Jazer in Gilead. 32Jeriah had twenty-seven hundred relatives who were skilled men and leaders of families. King David gave them the responsibility of directing the tribes of Reuben, Gad, and East Manasseh in God's work and the king's business.

ARMY DIVISIONS

27 This is the list of the Israelites who served the king in the army. Each division was on duty one month each year. There were leaders of families, commanders of a hundred men, commanders of a thousand men, and other officers. Each division had twenty-four thousand men.

2Jashobeam son of Zabdiel was in charge of the first division for the first month. There were twenty-four thousand men in his division. 3Jashobeam, one of the descendants of Perez, was leader of all the army officers for the first month.

4Dodai, from the Ahohites, was in charge of the division for the second month. Mikloth was a leader in the division. There were twenty-four thousand men in Dodai's division.

5The third commander, for the third month, was Benaiah son of Jehoiada the priest. There were twenty-four thousand men in his division. 6He was the Benaiah who was one of the Thirty[n] soldiers. Benaiah was a brave warrior who led those men. Benaiah's son Ammizabad was in charge of Benaiah's division.

7The fourth commander, for the fourth month, was Asahel, the brother of Joab. Later,

Asahel's son Zebadiah took his place as commander. There were twenty-four thousand men in his division.

8The fifth commander, for the fifth month, was Shamhuth, from Izrah's family. There were twenty-four thousand men in his division.

9The sixth commander, for the sixth month, was Ira son of Ikkesh from the town of Tekoa. There were twenty-four thousand men in his division.

10The seventh commander, for the seventh month, was Helez. He was from the Pelonites and a descendant of Ephraim. There were twenty-four thousand men in his division.

11The eighth commander, for the eighth month, was Sibbecai. He was from Hushah and was from Zerah's family. There were twenty-four thousand men in his division.

12The ninth commander, for the ninth month, was Abiezer. He was from Anathoth in Benjamin. There were twenty-four thousand men in his division.

13The tenth commander, for the tenth month, was Maharai. He was from Netophah and was from Zerah's family. There were twenty-four thousand men in his division.

14The eleventh commander, for the eleventh month, was Benaiah. He was from Pirathon in Ephraim. There were twenty-four thousand men in his division.

15The twelfth commander, for the twelfth month, was Heldai. He was from Netophah and was from Othniel's family. There were twenty-four thousand men in his division.

LEADERS OF THE TRIBES

16These were the leaders of the tribes of Israel. Eliezer son of Zicri was over the tribe of Reuben. Shephatiah son of Maacah was over the tribe of Simeon. 17Hashabiah son of Kemuel was over the tribe of Levi. Zadok was over the people of Aaron. 18Elihu, one of David's brothers, was over the tribe of Judah. Omri son of Michael was over the tribe of Issachar. 19Ishmaiah son of Obadiah was over the tribe of Zebulun. Jerimoth son of Azriel was over the tribe of Naphtali. 20Hoshea son of Azaziah was over the tribe of Ephraim.

27:6 Thirty These were David's most powerful soldiers. See 2 Samuel 23:24.

Joel son of Pedaiah was over West Manasseh. 21Iddo son of Zechariah was over East Manasseh. Jaasiel son of Abner was over the tribe of Benjamin. 22Azarel son of Jeroham was over the tribe of Dan.

These were the leaders of the tribes of Israel.

23The LORD had promised to make the Israelites as many as the stars in the sky. So David only counted the men who were twenty years old and older. 24Joab son of Zeruiah began to count the people, but he did not finish. God became angry with Israel for counting the people, so the number of the people was not put in the history book about King David's rule.

THE KING'S DIRECTORS

25Azmaveth son of Adiel was in charge of the royal storehouses.

Jonathan son of Uzziah was in charge of the storehouses in the country, towns, villages, and towers.

26Ezri son of Kelub was in charge of the field workers who farmed the land.

27Shimei, from the town of Ramah, was in charge of the vineyards.

Zabdi, from Shapham, was in charge of storing the wine that came from the vineyards.

28Baal-Hanan, from Geder, was in charge of the olive trees and sycamore trees in the western hills.

Joash was in charge of storing the olive oil.

29Shitrai, from Sharon, was in charge of the herds that fed in the Plain of Sharon.

Shaphat son of Adlai was in charge of the herds in the valleys.

30Obil, an Ishmaelite, was in charge of camels.

Jehdeiah, from Meronoth, was in charge of the donkeys.

31Jaziz, from the Hagrites, was in charge of the flocks.

All these men were the officers who took care of King David's property.

32Jonathan was David's uncle, and he advised David. Jonathan was a wise man and a teacher of the law. Jehiel son of Hacmoni took care of the king's sons. 33Ahithophel advised the king. Hushai, from the Arkite people, was the king's friend. 34Jehoiada

and Abiathar later took Ahithophel's place in advising the king. Jehoiada was Benaiah's son. Joab was the commander of the king's army.

DAVID'S PLANS FOR THE TEMPLE

28 David commanded all the leaders of Israel to come to Jerusalem. There were the leaders of the tribes, commanders of the divisions serving the king, commanders of a thousand men and of a hundred men, leaders who took care of the property and animals that belonged to the king and his sons, men over the palace, the powerful men, and all the brave warriors.

2King David stood up and said, "Listen to me, my relatives and my people. I wanted to build a place to keep the Ark of the Agreement with the LORD. I wanted it to be God's footstool. So I made plans to build a temple. 3But God said to me, 'You must not build a temple for worshiping me, because you are a soldier and have killed many people.'

4"But the LORD, the God of Israel, chose me from my whole family to be king of Israel forever. He chose the tribe of Judah to lead, and from the people of Judah, he chose my father's family. From that family God was pleased to make me king of Israel. 5The LORD has given me many sons, and from those sons he has chosen Solomon to be the new king of Israel. Israel is the LORD's kingdom. 6The LORD said to me, 'Your son Solomon will build my Temple and its courtyards. I have chosen Solomon to be my son, and I will be his father. 7He is obeying my laws and commands now. If he continues to obey them, I will make his kingdom strong forever.'"

8David said, "Now, in front of all Israel, the assembly of the LORD, and in the hearing of God, I tell you these things: Be careful to obey all the commands of the LORD your God. Then you will keep this good land and pass it on to your descendants forever.

9"And you, my son Solomon, accept the God of your father. Serve him completely and willingly, because the LORD knows what is in everyone's mind. He understands everything you think. If you go to him for help, you will get an answer. But if you turn away from him, he will leave you forever. 10Solomon, you must understand this. The LORD has chosen you to build the Temple as his holy place. Be strong and finish the job."

¹¹Then David gave his son Solomon the plans for building the Temple and the courtyard around the Temple. They included its buildings, its storerooms, its upper rooms, its inside rooms, and the place where the people's sins were removed. ¹²David gave him plans for everything he had in mind: the courtyards around the Lord's Temple and all the rooms around it, the Temple treasuries, and the treasuries of the holy items used in the Temple. ¹³David gave Solomon directions for the groups of the priests and Levites. David told him about all the work of serving in the Temple of the Lord and about the items to be used in the Temple service ¹⁴that were made of gold or silver. David told Solomon how much gold or silver should be used to make each thing. ¹⁵David told him how much gold to use for each gold lampstand and its lamps and how much silver to use for each silver lampstand and its lamps. The different lampstands were to be used where needed. ¹⁶David told how much gold should be used for each table that held the holy bread and how much silver should be used for the silver tables. ¹⁷He told how much pure gold should be used to make the forks, bowls, and pitchers and how much gold should be used to make each gold dish. He told how much silver should be used to make each silver dish ¹⁸and how much pure gold should be used for the altar of incense. He also gave Solomon the plans for the chariot of the golden creatures that spread their wings over the Ark of the Agreement with the Lord.

¹⁹David said, "All these plans were written with the Lord guiding me. He helped me understand everything in the plans."

²⁰David also said to his son Solomon, "Be strong and brave, and do the work. Don't be afraid or discouraged, because the Lord God, my God, is with you. He will not fail you or leave you until all the work for the Temple of the Lord is finished. ²¹The groups of the priests and Levites are ready for all the work on the Temple of God. Every skilled worker is ready to help you with all the work. The leaders and all the people will obey every command you give."

GIFTS FOR BUILDING THE TEMPLE

29 King David said to all the Israelites who were gathered, "God chose my son Solomon, who is young and hasn't yet learned what he needs to know, but the work is important. This palace is not for people; it is for the Lord God. ²I have done my best to prepare for building the Temple of God. I have given gold for the things made of gold and silver for the things made of silver. I have given bronze for the things made of bronze and iron for the things made of iron. I have given wood for the things made of wood and onyx for the settings. I have given turquoise gems of many different colors, valuable stones, and white marble. I have given much of all these things. ³I have already given this for the Temple, but now I am also giving my own treasures of gold and silver, because I really want the Temple of my God to be built. ⁴I have given about two hundred twenty thousand pounds of pure gold from Ophir and about five hundred twenty thousand pounds of pure silver. They will be used to cover the walls of the buildings ⁵and for all the gold and silver work. Skilled men may use the gold and silver to make things for the Temple. Now, who is ready to give himself to the service of the Lord today?"

⁶The family leaders and the leaders of the tribes of Israel, the commanders of a thousand men and of a hundred men, and the leaders responsible for the king's work gave their valuable things. ⁷They donated about three hundred eighty thousand pounds of gold, about seven hundred fifty thousand pounds of silver, about one million three hundred fifty thousand pounds of bronze, and about seven million five hundred thousand pounds of iron to the Temple of God. ⁸People who had valuable gems gave them to the treasury of the Temple of the Lord, and Jehiel, from the Gershon family, took care of the valuable gems. ⁹The leaders gave willingly and completely to the Lord. The people rejoiced to see their leaders give so gladly, and King David was also very happy.

DAVID'S PRAYER

¹⁰David praised the Lord in front of all the people who were gathered. He said:

"We praise you, Lord,
    God of our father Israel.

We praise you forever and ever.
¹¹ LORD, you are great and powerful.
You have glory, victory, and honor.
Everything in heaven and on earth
belongs to you.
The kingdom belongs to you, LORD;
you are the ruler over everything.
¹² Riches and honor come from you.
You rule everything.
You have the power and strength
to make anyone great and strong.
¹³ Now, our God, we thank you
and praise your glorious name.

¹⁴ "These things did not really come from
me and my people.
Everything comes from you;
we have given you back what you gave
us.
¹⁵ We are like foreigners and strangers,
as our ancestors were.
Our time on earth is like a shadow.
There is no hope.
¹⁶ LORD our God, we have gathered all this
to build your Temple for worship to
you.
But everything has come from you;

THE EXTRA MILE MARRIAGE

FAMILY

giving God
the deed

1 CHRONICLES 29:11–12

Living life for God gives you both freedom and power. When talking about your business, say: "It's God's office, business, practice," and so on. If you're talking about your customers, say: "They are God's customers, clients, patients," and so on.

When you turn your life and everything in it over to God, you grant him the opportunity and authority to bless it and, in his way and his time, take care of it. So, when things are not going as quickly or smoothly as you would like, turn it all over to God. Better yet, turn it over to God from the beginning.

When you take ownership over things, you take control away from God and do not allow his perfect will and plan to unfold in your life. You stop the blessings. So call your spouse "God's spouse," call your money "God's money," call your children "God's children," call your work "God's work," call your body "God's body," and call your life "God's life." When you turn everything over to him, the right things will happen in God's timing and according to his plan rather than yours.

When everything becomes God's, you ultimately have your best chance to defeat any enemy and accomplish any task. As you work with him instead of against him, his desires become your desires and life becomes much sweeter in the process.

reflect: Give your life to God today, and watch with amazement what becomes of it.
Go to **Job 12:12.**

everything belongs to you. [17] I know, my God, that you test people's hearts.

You are happy when people do what is right.

I was happy to give all these things,
and I gave with an honest heart.

Your people gathered here are happy to give to you,
and I rejoice to see their giving.

[18] LORD, you are the God of our ancestors, the God of Abraham, Isaac, and Jacob.

Make your people want to serve you always,
and make them want to obey you.

[19] Give my son Solomon a desire to serve you.

Help him always obey your commands, laws, and rules.

Help him build the Temple
for which I have prepared."

[20] Then David said to all the people who were gathered, "Praise the LORD your God." So they all praised the LORD, the God of their ancestors, and they bowed to the ground to give honor to the LORD and the king.

SOLOMON BECOMES KING

[21] The next day the people sacrificed to the LORD. They offered burnt offerings to him of a thousand bulls, a thousand male sheep, and a thousand male lambs. They also brought drink offerings. Many sacrifices were made for all the people of Israel. [22] That day the people ate and drank with much joy, and the LORD was with them.

And they made David's son Solomon king for the second time. They poured olive oil on Solomon to appoint him king in the presence of the LORD. And they poured oil on Zadok to appoint him as priest. [23] Then Solomon sat on the LORD's throne as king and took his father David's place. Solomon was very successful, and all the people of Israel obeyed him. [24] All the leaders and soldiers and King David's sons accepted Solomon as king and promised to obey him. [25] The LORD made Solomon great before all the Israelites and gave Solomon much honor. No king of Israel before Solomon had such honor.

DAVID'S DEATH

[26] David son of Jesse was king over all Israel. [27] He had ruled over Israel forty years—seven years in Hebron and thirty-three years in Jerusalem. [28] David died when he was old. He had lived a good, long life and had received many riches and honors. His son Solomon became king after him.

[29] Everything David did as king, from beginning to end, is recorded in the records of Samuel the seer, the records of Nathan the prophet, and the records of Gad the seer. [30] Those writings tell what David did as king of Israel. They tell about his power and what happened to him and to Israel and to all the kingdoms around them.

2 chronicles

ISRAEL'S HISTORY FROM SOLOMON TO THE CAPTIVITY

SOLOMON ASKS FOR WISDOM

1 Solomon, David's son, became a powerful king, because the LORD his God was with him and made him very great.

2Solomon spoke to all the people of Israel—the commanders of a hundred men and of a thousand men, the judges, every leader in all Israel, and the leaders of the families. 3Then Solomon and all the people with him went to the place of worship at the town of Gibeon. God's Meeting Tent, which Moses the LORD's servant had made in the desert, was there. 4David had brought the Ark of God from Kiriath Jearim to Jerusalem, where he had made a place for it and had set up a tent for it. 5The bronze altar that Bezalel son of Uri, who was the son of Hur, had made was in Gibeon in front of the Holy Tent. So Solomon and the people worshiped there. 6Solomon went up to the bronze altar in the presence of the LORD at the Meeting Tent and offered a thousand burnt offerings on it.

7That night God appeared to Solomon and said to him, "Ask for whatever you want me to give you."

8Solomon answered, "You have been very kind to my father David, and you have made me king in his place. 9Now, LORD God, may your promise to my father David come true. You have made me king of a people who are as many as the dust of the earth. 10Now give me wisdom and knowledge so I can lead these people in the right way, because no one can rule them without your help."

11God said to Solomon, "You have not asked for wealth or riches or honor, or for the death of your enemies, or for a long life. But since you have asked for wisdom and knowledge to lead my people, over whom I have made you king, 12I will give you wisdom and knowledge. I will also give you more wealth, riches, and honor than any king who has lived before you or any who will live after you."

13Then Solomon left the place of worship, the Meeting Tent, at Gibeon and went back to Jerusalem. There King Solomon ruled over Israel.

SOLOMON'S WEALTH

14Solomon had fourteen hundred chariots and twelve thousand horses. He kept some in special cities for the chariots, and others he kept with him in Jerusalem. 15In Jerusalem Solomon made silver and gold as plentiful as stones and cedar trees as plentiful as the fig trees on the western hills. 16He imported horses from Egypt and Kue; his traders bought them in Kue. 17They imported chariots from Egypt for about fifteen pounds of silver apiece, and horses cost nearly four pounds of silver apiece. Then they sold the horses and chariots to all the kings of the Hittites and the Arameans.

SOLOMON PREPARES FOR THE TEMPLE

2 Solomon decided to build a temple as a place to worship the LORD and also a palace for himself. 2He chose seventy thousand men to carry loads, eighty thousand men to cut stone in the hill country, and thirty-six hundred men to direct the workers.

3Solomon sent this message to Hiram king of the city of Tyre: "Help me as you helped my father David by sending him cedar logs so he could build himself a palace to live in. 4I will build a temple for worshiping the LORD my God, and I will give this temple to him. There we will burn sweet-smelling spices in his presence. We will continually set out the holy bread in God's presence. And we will burn sacrifices every morning and evening, on Sabbath days and New Moons, and on the other feast days commanded by the LORD our God. This is a rule for Israel to obey forever.

5"The temple I build will be great, because our God is greater than all gods. 6But no one can really build a house for our God. Not even the highest of heavens can hold him. How then can I build a temple for him except as a place to burn sacrifices to him?

7"Now send me a man skilled in working with gold, silver, bronze, and iron, and with purple, red, and blue thread. He must also know how to make engravings. He will work with my skilled craftsmen in Judah and Jerusalem, whom my father David chose.

8"Also send me cedar, pine, and juniper logs from Lebanon. I know your servants are experienced at cutting down the trees in Lebanon, and my servants will help them. 9Send me a lot of wood, because the temple I am going to build will be large and wonderful. 10I will give your servants who cut the wood one hundred twenty-five thousand bushels of wheat, one hundred twenty-five thousand bushels of barley, one hundred fifteen thousand gallons of wine, and one hundred fifteen thousand gallons of oil."

11Then Hiram king of Tyre answered Solomon with this letter: "Solomon, because the LORD loves his people, he chose you to be their king." 12Hiram also said: "Praise the LORD, the God of Israel, who made heaven and earth! He has given King David a wise son, one with wisdom and understanding, who will build a temple for the LORD and a palace for himself.

13"I will send you a skilled and wise man named Huram-Abi. 14His mother was from the people of Dan, and his father was from Tyre. Huram-Abi is skilled in working with gold, silver, bronze, iron, stone, and wood, and with purple, blue, and red thread, and expensive linen. He is skilled in making engravings and can make any design you show him. He will help your craftsmen and the craftsmen of your father David.

15"Now send my servants the wheat, barley, oil, and wine you promised. 16We will cut as much wood from Lebanon as you need and will bring it on rafts by sea to Joppa. Then you may carry it to Jerusalem."

17Solomon counted all the foreigners living in Israel. (This was after the time his father David had counted the people.) There were one hundred fifty-three thousand six hundred foreigners in the country. 18Solomon chose seventy thousand of them to carry loads, eighty thousand of them to cut stone in the mountains, and thirty-six hundred of them to direct the workers and to keep the people working.

SOLOMON BUILDS THE TEMPLE

3 Then Solomon began to build the Temple of the LORD in Jerusalem on Mount Moriah. This was where the LORD had appeared to David, Solomon's father. Solomon built the Temple on the place David had prepared on the threshing floor of Araunah the Jebusite. 2Solomon began building in the second month of the fourth year he ruled Israel.

3Solomon used these measurements for building the Temple of God. It was ninety feet long and thirty feet wide, using the old measurement. 4The porch in front of the main room of the Temple was thirty feet long and thirty feet high.

He covered the inside of the porch with pure gold. 5He put panels of pine on the walls of the main room and covered them with pure gold. Then he put designs of palm trees and chains in the gold. 6He decorated the Temple with gems and gold from Parvaim.[n] 7He put gold on the Temple's ceiling beams, doorposts, walls, and doors, and he carved creatures with wings on the walls.

8Then he made the Most Holy Place. It was thirty feet long and thirty feet wide, as wide as the Temple. He covered its walls with about forty-six thousand pounds of pure gold. 9The gold nails weighed over a pound. He also covered the upper rooms with gold.

10He made two creatures with wings for the Most Holy Place and covered them with gold. 11The wings of the gold creatures were thirty feet across. One wing of one creature was seven and one-half feet long and touched the Temple wall. The creature's other wing was also seven and one-half feet long, and it touched a wing of the second creature. 12One wing of the second creature touched the other side of the room and was also seven and one-half feet long. The second creature's other wing touched the first creature's wing, and it was also seven and one-half feet long. 13Together, the creatures' wings were thirty feet across. The creatures stood on their feet, facing the main room.

14He made the curtain of blue, purple, and red thread, and expensive linen, and he put designs of creatures with wings in it.

15He made two pillars to stand in front of

3:6 Parvaim There was much gold there. It may have been in the country of Ophir.

the Temple. They were about fifty-two feet tall, and the capital of each pillar was over seven feet tall. [16]He made a net of chains and put them on the tops of the pillars. He made a hundred pomegranates and put them on the chains. [17]Then he put the pillars up in front of the Temple. One pillar stood on the south side, the other on the north. He named the south pillar He Establishes and the north pillar In Him Is Strength.

THINGS FOR THE TEMPLE

4 He made a bronze altar thirty feet long, thirty feet wide, and fifteen feet tall. [2]Then he made from bronze a large round bowl, which was called the Sea. It was forty-five feet around, fifteen feet across, and seven and one-half feet deep. [3]There were carvings of bulls under the rim of the bowl—ten bulls every eighteen inches. They were in two rows and were made in one piece with the bowl.

[4]The bowl rested on the backs of twelve bronze bulls that faced outward from the center of the bowl. Three bulls faced north, three faced west, three faced south, and three faced east. [5]The sides of the bowl were four inches thick, and it held about seventeen thousand five hundred gallons. The rim of the bowl was like the rim of a cup or like a lily blossom.

[6]He made ten smaller bowls and put five on the south side and five on the north. They were for washing the animals for the burnt offerings, but the large bowl was for the priests to wash in.

[7]He made ten lampstands of gold, following the plans. He put them in the Temple, five on the south side and five on the north.

[8]He made ten tables and put them in the Temple, five on the south side and five on the north. And he used gold to make a hundred other bowls.

[9]He also made the priests' courtyard and the large courtyard. He made the doors that opened to the courtyard and covered them with bronze. [10]Then he put the large bowl in the southeast corner of the Temple.

[11]Huram also made bowls, shovels, and small bowls. So he finished his work for King Solomon on the Temple of God:

[12] two pillars;

two large bowls for the capitals on top of the pillars;

two nets to cover the two large bowls for the capitals on top of the pillars;

[13] four hundred pomegranates for the two nets (there were two rows of pomegranates for each net covering the bowls for the capitals on top of the pillars);

[14] the stands with a bowl on each stand;

[15] the large bowl with twelve bulls under it;

[16] the pots, shovels, forks, and all the things to go with them.

All the things that Huram-Abi made for King Solomon for the Temple of the LORD were made of polished bronze. [17]The king had these things poured into clay molds that were made in the plain of the Jordan River between Succoth and Zarethan. [18]Solomon had so many things made that the total weight of all the bronze was never known.

[19]Solomon also made all the things for God's Temple: the golden altar; tables which held the bread that shows God's people are in his presence; [20]the lampstands and their lamps of pure gold, to burn in front of the Most Holy Place as planned; [21]the flowers, lamps, and tongs of pure gold; [22]the pure gold wick trimmers, small bowls, pans, and dishes used to carry coals, the gold doors for the Temple, and the inside doors of the Most Holy Place and of the main room.

5 Finally all the work Solomon did for the Temple of the LORD was finished. He brought in everything his father David had set apart for the Temple—all the silver and gold and other articles. And he put everything in the treasuries of God's Temple.

THE ARK IS BROUGHT INTO THE TEMPLE

[2]Solomon called for the elders of Israel, the heads of the tribes, and the leaders of the families to come to him in Jerusalem. He wanted them to bring the Ark of the Agreement with the LORD from the older part of the city. [3]So all the Israelites came together with the king during the festival in the seventh month.

[4]When all the elders of Israel arrived, the Levites lifted up the Ark. [5]They carried the Ark of the Agreement, the Meeting Tent, and the holy utensils in it; the priests and the Levites brought them up. [6]King Solomon and all the Israelites gathered before the Ark of

the Agreement and sacrificed so many sheep and bulls no one could count them.

[7]Then the priests put the Ark of the Agreement with the LORD in its place inside the Most Holy Place in the Temple, under the wings of the golden creatures. [8]The wings of these creatures were spread out over the place for the Ark, covering it and its carrying poles. [9]The carrying poles were so long that anyone standing in the Holy Place in front of the Most Holy Place could see the ends of the poles. But no one could see them from outside the Holy Place. The poles are still there today. [10]The only things inside the Ark were two stone tablets[n] that Moses had put in the Ark at Mount Sinai. That was where the LORD made his agreement with the Israelites after they came out of Egypt.

[11]Then all the priests left the Holy Place. (All the priests from each group had made themselves ready to serve the LORD.) [12]All the Levite musicians—Asaph, Heman, Jeduthun, and all their sons and relatives—stood on the east side of the altar. They were dressed in white linen and played cymbals, harps, and lyres. With them were one hundred twenty priests who blew trumpets. [13]Those who blew the trumpets and those who sang together sounded like one person as they praised and thanked the LORD. They sang as others played their trumpets, cymbals, and other instruments. They praised the LORD with this song:

"He is good;

his love continues forever."

Then the Temple of the LORD was filled with a cloud. [14]The priests could not continue their work because of the cloud, because the LORD's glory filled the Temple of God.

SOLOMON SPEAKS TO THE PEOPLE

6 Then Solomon said, "The LORD said he would live in the dark cloud. [2]LORD, I have built a wonderful Temple for you—a place for you to live forever."

[3]While all the Israelites were standing there, King Solomon turned to them and blessed them. [4]Then he said, "Praise the LORD, the God of Israel. He has done what he promised to my father David. The LORD said, [5]'Since the time I brought my people out of Egypt, I have not chosen a city in any tribe of Israel where a temple will be built for me. I did not choose a man to lead my people Israel. [6]But now I have chosen Jerusalem as the place I am to be worshiped, and I have chosen David to lead my people Israel.'

[7]"My father David wanted to build a temple for the LORD, the God of Israel. [8]But the LORD said to my father David, 'It was good that you wanted to build a temple for me. [9]But you are not the one to build it. Your son, who comes from your own body, is the one who will build my temple.'

[10]"Now the LORD has kept his promise. I am the king now in place of David my father. Now I rule Israel as the LORD promised, and I have built the Temple for the LORD, the God of Israel. [11]There I have put the Ark, in which is the Agreement the LORD made with the Israelites."

SOLOMON'S PRAYER

[12]Then Solomon stood facing the LORD's altar, and all the Israelites were standing behind him. He spread out his hands. [13]He had made a bronze platform seven and one-half feet long, seven and one-half feet wide, and seven and one-half feet high, and he had placed it in the middle of the outer courtyard. Solomon stood on the platform. Then he kneeled in front of all the people of Israel gathered there, and he spread out his hands toward the sky. [14]He said, "LORD, God of Israel, there is no god like you in heaven or on earth. You keep your agreement of love with your servants who truly follow you. [15]You have kept the promise you made to your servant David, my father. You spoke it with your own mouth and finished it with your hands today.

[16]"Now, LORD, God of Israel, keep the promise you made to your servant David, my father. You said, 'If your sons are careful to obey my teachings as you have obeyed, there will always be someone from your family ruling Israel.' [17]Now, LORD, God of Israel, please continue to keep that promise you made to your servant.

[18]"But, God, can you really live here on the earth with people? The sky and the highest place in heaven cannot contain you. Surely this house which I have built cannot contain

---

5:10 stone tablets They were the two stone tablets on which God wrote the Ten Commandments.

you. ¹⁹But please listen to my prayer and my request, because I am your servant. LORD my God, hear this prayer your servant prays to you. ²⁰Day and night please watch over this Temple where you have said you would be worshiped. Hear the prayer I pray facing this Temple. ²¹Hear my prayers and the prayers of your people Israel when we pray facing this place. Hear from your home in heaven, and when you hear, forgive us.

²²"If someone wrongs another person, he will be brought to the altar in this Temple. If he swears an oath that he is not guilty, ²³then hear in heaven. Judge the case, punish the guilty, but declare that the innocent person is not guilty.

²⁴"When your people, the Israelites, sin against you, their enemies will defeat them. But if they come back to you and praise you and pray to you in this Temple, ²⁵then listen from heaven. Forgive the sin of your people Israel, and bring them back to the land you gave to them and their ancestors.

²⁶"When they sin against you, you will stop the rain from falling on their land. Then they will pray, facing this place and praising you; they will stop sinning when you make them suffer. ²⁷When this happens, hear their prayer in heaven, and forgive the sins of your servants, the Israelites. Teach them to do what is right. Then please send rain to this land you have given particularly to them.

²⁸"At times the land will get so dry that no food will grow, or a great sickness will spread among the people. Sometimes the crops will be destroyed by locusts or grasshoppers. Your people will be attacked in their cities by their enemies, or will become sick. ²⁹When any of these things happens, the people will become truly sorry. If your people spread their hands in prayer toward this Temple, ³⁰then hear their prayers from your home in heaven. Forgive and treat each person as he should be treated because you know what is in a person's heart. Only you know what is in people's hearts. ³¹Then the people will respect and obey you as long as they live in this land you gave our ancestors.

³²"People who are not Israelites, foreigners from other lands, will hear about your greatness and power. They will come from far away to pray at this Temple. ³³Then hear from your home in heaven, and do whatever they ask you. Then people everywhere will know you and respect you, just as your people Israel do. Then everyone will know that I built this Temple as a place to worship you.

³⁴"When your people go out to fight their enemies along some road on which you send them, your people will pray to you, facing this city which you have chosen and the Temple I have built for you. ³⁵Then hear in heaven their prayers, and do what is right.

³⁶"Everyone sins, so your people will also sin against you. You will become angry with them and will hand them over to their enemies. Their enemies will capture them and take them away to a country far or near. ³⁷Your people will be sorry for their sins when they are held as prisoners in another country. They will be sorry and pray to you in the land where they are held as prisoners, saying, 'We have sinned. We have done wrong and acted wickedly.' ³⁸They will truly turn back to you in the land where they are captives. They will pray, facing this land you gave their ancestors, this city you have chosen, and the Temple I have built for you. ³⁹Then hear their prayers from your home in heaven and do what is right. Forgive your people who have sinned against you.

⁴⁰"Now, my God, look at us. Listen to the prayers we pray in this place.
⁴¹ Now, rise, LORD God, and come to your
    resting place.
  Come with the Ark of the Agreement
    that shows your strength.
Let your priests receive your salvation,
  LORD God,
  and may your holy people be happy
    because of your goodness.
⁴² LORD God, do not reject your appointed
  one.
  Remember your love for your servant
  David."

THE TEMPLE IS GIVEN TO THE LORD

7 When Solomon finished praying, fire came down from the sky and burned up the burnt offering and the sacrifices. The LORD's glory filled the Temple. ²The priests could not enter the Temple of the LORD, because the LORD's glory filled it. ³When all the people of Israel saw the fire come down from heaven and the LORD's glory on the Temple, they bowed down on the pavement with their faces to the ground. They worshiped and thanked the LORD, saying,

"He is good;
      his love continues forever."

⁴Then King Solomon and all the people offered sacrifices to the LORD. ⁵King Solomon offered a sacrifice of twenty-two thousand cattle and one hundred twenty thousand sheep. So the king and all the people gave the Temple to God. ⁶The priests stood ready to do their work. The Levites also stood with the instruments of the LORD's music that King David had made for praising the LORD. The priests and Levites were saying, "His love continues forever." The priests, who stood across from the Levites, blew their trumpets, and all the Israelites were standing.

⁷Solomon made holy the middle part of the courtyard, which is in front of the Temple of the LORD. There he offered whole burnt offerings and the fat of the fellowship offerings. He offered them in the courtyard, because the bronze altar he had made could not hold the burnt offerings, grain offerings, and fat.

⁸Solomon and all the Israelites celebrated the festival for seven days. There were many people, and they came from as far away as Lebo Hamath and the brook of Egypt. ⁹For seven days they celebrated giving the altar for the worship of God. Then they celebrated the festival for seven days. On the eighth day they had a meeting. ¹⁰On the twenty-third day of the seventh month Solomon sent the people home, full of joy. They were happy because the LORD had been so good to David, Solomon, and his people Israel.

THE LORD APPEARS TO SOLOMON

¹¹Solomon finished the Temple of the LORD and his royal palace. He had success in doing everything he planned in the Temple of the LORD and his own palace. ¹²Then the LORD appeared to Solomon at night and said to him, "I have heard your prayer and have chosen this place for myself to be a Temple for sacrifices.

¹³"I may stop the sky from sending rain. I may command the locusts to destroy the land. I may send sicknesses to my people. ¹⁴Then if my people, who are called by my name, will humble themselves, if they will pray and seek me and stop their evil ways, I will hear them

from heaven. I will forgive their sin, and I will heal their land. ¹⁵Now I will see them, and I will listen to the prayers prayed in this place. ¹⁶I have chosen this Temple and made it holy. So I will be worshiped there forever. Yes, I will always watch over it and love it.

¹⁷"But you must serve me as your father David did. You must obey all I have commanded and keep my laws and rules. ¹⁸If you do, I will make your kingdom strong. This is the agreement I made with your father David, saying, 'Someone from your family will always rule in Israel.'

¹⁹"But you must follow me and obey the laws and commands I have given you. You must not serve or worship other gods. ²⁰If you do, I will take the Israelites out of my land, the land I have given them, and I will leave this Temple that I have made holy. All the nations will make fun of it and speak evil about it. ²¹This Temple is honored now, but then, everyone who passes by will be shocked. They will ask, 'Why did the LORD do this terrible thing to this land and this Temple?' ²²People will answer, 'This happened because they left the LORD, the God of their ancestors, the God who brought them out of Egypt. They decided to follow other gods and worshiped and served them, so he brought all this disaster on them.'"

SOLOMON'S OTHER ACHIEVEMENTS

8 By the end of twenty years, Solomon had built the Temple of the LORD and the royal palace. ²Solomon rebuilt the towns that Hiram had given him, and Solomon sent Israelites to live in them. ³Then he went to Hamath Zobah and captured it. ⁴Solomon also built the town of Tadmor in the desert, and he built all the towns in Hamath as towns for storing grain and supplies. ⁵He rebuilt the towns of Upper Beth Horon and Lower Beth Horon, protecting them with strong walls, gates, and bars in the gates. ⁶He also rebuilt the town of Baalath. And he built all the other towns for storage and all the cities for his chariots and horses. He built all he wanted in Jerusalem, Lebanon, and everywhere he ruled.

⁷There were other people in the land who were not Israelites—the Hittites, Amorites, Perizzites, Hivites, and Jebusites. ⁸They were descendants of the people that the Israelites

had not destroyed. Solomon forced them to be slave workers, as is still true today. ⁹But Solomon did not make slaves of the Israelites. They were his soldiers, chief captains, commanders of his chariots, and his chariot drivers. ¹⁰These were his most important officers. There were two hundred fifty of them to direct the people.

¹¹Solomon brought the daughter of the king of Egypt from the older part of Jerusalem to the palace he had built for her. Solomon said, "My wife must not live in King David's palace, because the places where the Ark of the Agreement has been are holy."

¹²Then Solomon offered burnt offerings to the LORD on the altar he had built for the LORD in front of the Temple porch. ¹³He offered sacrifices every day as Moses had commanded. They were offered on the Sabbath days, New Moons, and the three yearly feasts—the Feast of Unleavened Bread, the Feast of Weeks, and the Feast of Shelters. ¹⁴Solomon followed his father David's instructions and chose the groups of priests for their service and the Levites to lead the praise and to help the priests do their daily work. And he chose the gatekeepers by their groups to serve at each gate, as David, the man of God, had commanded. ¹⁵They obeyed all of Solomon's commands to the priests and Levites, as well as his commands about the treasuries.

¹⁶All Solomon's work was done as he had said from the day the foundation of the Temple of the LORD was begun, until it was finished. So the Temple was finished.

¹⁷Then Solomon went to the towns of Ezion Geber and Elath near the Red Sea in the land of Edom. ¹⁸Hiram sent ships to Solomon that were commanded by his own men, who were skilled sailors. Hiram's men went with Solomon's men to Ophir and brought back about thirty-four thousand pounds of gold to King Solomon.

THE QUEEN OF SHEBA VISITS

9 When the queen of Sheba heard about Solomon's fame, she came to Jerusalem to test him with hard questions. She had a large group of servants with her and camels carrying spices, jewels, and much gold. When she came to Solomon, she talked with him about all she had in mind, ²and Solomon answered all her questions. Nothing was too hard for him to explain to her. ³The queen of Sheba saw that Solomon was very wise. She saw the palace he had built, ⁴the food on his table, his many officers, the palace servants and their good clothes, the servants who served Solomon his wine and their good clothes. She saw the whole burnt offerings he made in the Temple of the LORD. All these things amazed her.

⁵So she said to King Solomon, "What I heard in my own country about your achievements and wisdom is true. ⁶I did not believe it then, but now I have come and seen it with my own eyes. I was not told even half of your great wisdom! You are much greater than I had heard. ⁷Your people and officials are very lucky, because in always serving you, they are able to hear your wisdom. ⁸Praise the LORD your God who was pleased to make you king. He has put you on his throne to rule for the LORD your God, because your God loves the people of Israel and supports them forever. He has made you king over them to keep justice and to rule fairly."

⁹Then she gave the king about nine thousand pounds of gold and many spices and jewels. No one had ever given such spices as the queen of Sheba gave to King Solomon.

¹⁰Hiram's men and Solomon's men brought gold from Ophir, juniper wood, and jewels. ¹¹King Solomon used the juniper wood to build steps for the Temple of the LORD and the palace and to make lyres and harps for the musicians. No one in Judah had ever seen such beautiful things as these.

¹²King Solomon gave the queen of Sheba everything she wanted and asked for, even more than she had brought to him. Then she and her servants returned to her own country.

SOLOMON'S WEALTH

¹³Every year King Solomon received about fifty thousand pounds of gold. ¹⁴Besides that, he also received gold from traders and merchants. All the kings of Arabia and the governors of the land also brought gold and silver.

¹⁵King Solomon made two hundred large shields of hammered gold, each of which contained about seven and one-half pounds of hammered gold. ¹⁶He also made three hundred smaller shields of hammered gold,

each of which contained about four pounds of gold. The king put them in the Palace of the Forest of Lebanon.

17The king built a large throne of ivory and covered it with pure gold. 18The throne had six steps on it and a gold footstool. There were armrests on both sides of the chair, and each armrest had a lion beside it. 19Twelve lions stood on the six steps, one lion at each end of each step. Nothing like this had ever been made for any other kingdom. 20All of Solomon's drinking cups, as well as the dishes in the Palace of the Forest of Lebanon, were made of pure gold. In Solomon's time people did not think silver was valuable.

21King Solomon had many ships that he sent out to trade, with Hiram's men as the crews. Every three years the ships returned, bringing back gold, silver, ivory, apes, and baboons.

22King Solomon had more riches and wisdom than all the other kings on earth. 23All the kings of the earth wanted to see Solomon and listen to the wisdom God had given him. 24Year after year everyone who came brought gifts of silver and gold, clothes, weapons, spices, horses, and mules.

25Solomon had four thousand stalls for horses and chariots, and he had twelve thousand horses. He kept some in special cities for the chariots, and others he kept with him in Jerusalem. 26Solomon ruled over all the kingdoms from the Euphrates River to the land of the Philistines, as far as the border of Egypt. 27In Jerusalem the king made silver as common as stones and cedar trees as plentiful as the fig trees on the western hills. 28Solomon imported horses from Egypt and all other countries.

SOLOMON'S DEATH

29Everything else Solomon did, from the beginning to the end, is written in the records of Nathan the prophet, and in the prophecy of Ahijah the Shilonite, and in the visions of Iddo the seer, who wrote about Jeroboam, Nebat's son. 30Solomon ruled in Jerusalem over all Israel for forty years. 31Then Solomon died and was buried in Jerusalem, the city of David, his father. And Solomon's son Rehoboam became king in his place.

ISRAEL TURNS AGAINST REHOBOAM

10 Rehoboam went to Shechem, where all the Israelites had gone to make him king. 2Jeroboam son of Nebat was in Egypt, where he had gone to escape from King Solomon. When Jeroboam heard about Rehoboam being made king, he returned from Egypt. 3After the people sent for him, he and the people went to Rehoboam and said to him, 4"Your father forced us to work very hard. Now, make it easier for us, and don't make us work as he did. Then we will serve you."

5Rehoboam answered, "Come back to me in three days." So the people left.

6King Rehoboam asked the elders who had advised Solomon during his lifetime, "How do you think I should answer these people?"

7They answered, "Be kind to these people. If you please them and give them a kind answer, they will serve you always."

8But Rehoboam rejected this advice. Instead, he asked the young men who had grown up with him and who served as his advisers. 9Rehoboam asked them, "What is your advice? How should we answer these people who said, 'Don't make us work as hard as your father did'?"

10The young men who had grown up with him answered, "The people said to you, 'Your father forced us to work very hard. Now make our work easier.' You should tell them, 'My little finger is bigger than my father's legs. 11He forced you to work hard, but I will make you work even harder. My father beat you with whips, but I will beat you with whips that have sharp points.'"

12Rehoboam had told the people, "Come back to me in three days." So after three days Jeroboam and all the people returned to Rehoboam. 13King Rehoboam spoke cruel words to them, because he had rejected the advice of the elders. 14He followed the advice of the young men and said, "My father forced you to work hard, but I will make you work even harder. My father beat you with whips, but I will beat you with whips that have sharp points." 15So the king did not listen to the people. God caused this to happen so that the LORD could keep the promise he had made to Jeroboam son of Nebat through Ahijah, a prophet from Shiloh.

16When all the Israelites saw that the king refused to listen to them, they said to the king,

"We have no share in David!
   We have no part in the son of Jesse!
People of Israel, let's go to our own
      homes!
   Let David's son rule his own people."

So all the Israelites went home. 17But Rehoboam still ruled over the Israelites who lived in the towns of Judah.

18Adoniram was in charge of the forced labor. When Rehoboam sent him to the people, they threw stones at him until he died. But King Rehoboam ran to his chariot and escaped to Jerusalem. 19Since then, Israel has been against the family of David.

11 When Rehoboam arrived in Jerusalem, he gathered one hundred eighty thousand of the best soldiers from Judah and Benjamin. He wanted to fight Israel to take back his kingdom. 2But the LORD spoke his word to Shemaiah, a man of God, saying, 3"Speak to Solomon's son Rehoboam, the king of Judah, and to all the Israelites living in Judah and Benjamin. Say to them, 4'The LORD says you must not go to war against your brothers. Every one of you should go home, because I made all these things happen.'" So they obeyed the LORD's command and turned back and did not attack Jeroboam.

REHOBOAM MAKES JUDAH STRONG

5Rehoboam lived in Jerusalem and built strong cities in Judah to defend it. 6He built up the cities of Bethlehem, Etam, Tekoa, 7Beth Zur, Soco, Adullam, 8Gath, Mareshah, Ziph, 9Adoraim, Lachish, Azekah, 10Zorah, Aijalon, and Hebron. These were strong, walled cities in Judah and Benjamin. 11When Rehoboam made those cities strong, he put commanders and supplies of food, oil, and wine in them. 12Also, Rehoboam put shields and spears in all the cities and made them very strong. Rehoboam kept the people of Judah and Benjamin under his control.

13The priests and the Levites from all over Israel joined Rehoboam. 14The Levites even left their pasturelands and property and came to Judah and Jerusalem, because Jeroboam and his sons refused to let them serve as priests to the LORD. 15Jeroboam chose his own priests for the places of worship and for the goat and calf idols he had made. 16There were people from all the tribes of Israel who wanted to obey the LORD, the God of Israel. So they went to Jerusalem with the Levites to sacrifice to the LORD, the God of their ancestors. 17These people made the kingdom of Judah strong, and they supported Solomon's son Rehoboam for three years. During this time they lived the way David and Solomon had lived.

REHOBOAM'S FAMILY

18Rehoboam married Mahalath, the daughter of Jerimoth and Abihail. Jerimoth was David's son, and Abihail was the daughter of Eliab, Jesse's son. 19Mahalath gave Rehoboam these sons: Jeush, Shemariah, and Zaham. 20Then Rehoboam married Absalom's daughter Maacah, and she gave Rehoboam these children: Abijah, Attai, Ziza, and Shelomith. 21Rehoboam loved Maacah more than his other wives and slave women. Rehoboam had eighteen wives and sixty slave women and was the father of twenty-eight sons and sixty daughters.

22Rehoboam chose Abijah son of Maacah to be the leader of his own brothers, because he planned to make Abijah king. 23Rehoboam acted wisely. He spread his sons through all the areas of Judah and Benjamin, sending them to every strong, walled city. He gave plenty of supplies to his sons, and he also found wives for them.

SHISHAK ATTACKS JERUSALEM

12 After Rehoboam's kingdom was set up and he became strong, he and the people of Judah stopped obeying the teachings of the LORD. 2During the fifth year Rehoboam was king, Shishak king of Egypt attacked Jerusalem, because Rehoboam and the people were unfaithful to the LORD. 3Shishak had twelve hundred chariots and sixty thousand horsemen. He brought troops of Libyans, Sukkites, and Cushites from Egypt with him, so many they couldn't be counted. 4Shishak captured the strong, walled cities of Judah and came as far as Jerusalem.

5Then Shemaiah the prophet came to Rehoboam and the leaders of Judah who had gathered in Jerusalem because they were afraid of Shishak. Shemaiah said to them, "This is what the LORD says: 'You have left me, so now I will leave you to face Shishak alone.'"

6Then the leaders of Judah and King Rehoboam were sorry for what they had done. They said, "The LORD does what is right."

7When the LORD saw they were sorry for what they had done, the LORD spoke his word to Shemaiah, saying, "The king and the leaders are sorry. So I will not destroy them but will save them soon. I will not use Shishak to punish Jerusalem in my anger. 8But the people of Jerusalem will become Shishak's servants so they may learn that serving me is different than serving the kings of other nations."

9Shishak king of Egypt attacked Jerusalem and took the treasures from the Temple of the LORD and the king's palace. He took everything, even the gold shields Solomon had made. 10So King Rehoboam made bronze shields to take their place and gave them to the commanders of the guards for the palace gates. 11Whenever the king went to the Temple of the LORD, the guards went with him, carrying the shields. Later, they would put them back in the guardroom.

12When Rehoboam was sorry for what he had done, the LORD held his anger back and did not fully destroy Rehoboam. There was some good in Judah.

13King Rehoboam made himself a strong king in Jerusalem. He was forty-one years old when he became king, and he was king in Jerusalem for seventeen years. Jerusalem is the city that the LORD chose from all the tribes of Israel in which he was to be worshiped. Rehoboam's mother was Naamah from the country of Ammon. 14Rehoboam did evil because he did not want to obey the LORD.

15The things Rehoboam did as king, from the beginning to the end, are written in the records of Shemaiah the prophet and Iddo the seer, in the family histories. There were wars between Rehoboam and Jeroboam all the time they ruled. 16Rehoboam died and was buried in Jerusalem, and his son Abijah became king in his place.

ABIJAH KING OF JUDAH

13 Abijah became the king of Judah during the eighteenth year Jeroboam was king of Israel. 2Abijah ruled in Jerusalem for three years. His mother was Maacah daughter of Uriel from the town of Gibeah.

And there was war between Abijah and Jeroboam. 3Abijah led an army of four hundred thousand capable soldiers into battle, and Jeroboam prepared to fight him with eight hundred thousand capable soldiers.

4Abijah stood on Mount Zemaraim in the mountains of Ephraim and said, "Jeroboam and all Israel, listen to me! 5You should know that the LORD, the God of Israel, gave David and his sons the right to rule Israel forever by an agreement of salt. 6But Jeroboam son of Nebat, one of the officers of Solomon, David's son, turned against his master. 7Then worthless, evil men joined Jeroboam against Rehoboam, Solomon's son. He was young and didn't know what to do, so he could not stop them.

8"Now you people are making plans against the LORD's kingdom, which belongs to David's sons. There are many of you, and you have the gold calves Jeroboam made for you as gods. 9You have thrown out the Levites and the LORD's priests, Aaron's sons. You have chosen your own priests as people in other countries do. Anyone who comes with a young bull and seven male sheep can become a priest of idols that are not gods.

10"But as for us, the LORD is our God; we have not left him. The priests who serve the LORD are Aaron's sons, and the Levites help them. 11They offer burnt offerings and sweet-smelling incense to the LORD every morning and evening. They put the bread on the special table in the Temple. And they light the lamps on the gold lampstand every evening. We obey the command of the LORD our God, but you have left him. 12God himself is with us as our ruler. His priests blow the trumpet to call us to war against you. Men of Israel, don't fight against the LORD, the God of your ancestors, because you won't succeed."

13But Jeroboam had sent some troops to sneak behind Judah's army. So while Jeroboam was in front of Judah's army, Jeroboam's soldiers were behind them. 14When the soldiers of Judah turned around, they saw Jeroboam's army attacking both in front and back. So they cried out to the LORD, and the priests blew the trumpets. 15Then the men of Judah gave a battle cry. When they shouted, God caused Jeroboam and the army of Israel to run away from Abijah and the army of Judah. ¹⁶When the army of Israel ran away from the men of Judah, God handed them over to Judah. ¹⁷Abijah's army struck Israel so that five hundred thousand of Israel's best men were killed. ¹⁸So at that time the people of Israel were defeated. And the people of Judah won, because they depended on the LORD, the God of their ancestors.

¹⁹Abijah's army chased Jeroboam's army and captured from him the towns of Bethel, Jeshanah, and Ephron, and the small villages near them. ²⁰Jeroboam never became strong again while Abijah was alive. The LORD struck Jeroboam, and he died.

²¹But Abijah became strong. He married fourteen women and was the father of twenty-two sons and sixteen daughters. ²²Everything else Abijah did—what he said and what he did—is recorded in the writings of the prophet Iddo.

14 Abijah died and was buried in Jerusalem. His son Asa became king in his place, and there was peace in the country for ten years during Asa's time.

ASA KING OF JUDAH

²Asa did what the LORD his God said was good and right. ³He removed the foreign altars and the places where gods were worshiped. He smashed the stone pillars that honored other gods, and he tore down the Asherah idols. ⁴Asa commanded the people of Judah to follow the LORD, the God of their ancestors, and to obey his teachings and commandments. ⁵He also removed the places where gods were worshiped and the incense altars from every town in Judah. So the kingdom had peace while Asa was king. ⁶Asa built strong, walled cities in Judah during the time of peace. He had no war in these years, because the LORD gave him peace.

⁷Asa said to the people of Judah, "Let's build up these towns and put walls around them. Let's make towers, gates, and bars in the gates. This country is ours, because we have obeyed the LORD our God. We have followed him, and he has given us peace all around." So they built and had success.

⁸Asa had an army of three hundred thousand men from Judah and two hundred eighty thousand men from Benjamin. The men from Judah carried large shields

and spears. The men from Benjamin carried small shields and bows and arrows. All of them were brave fighting men.

⁹Then Zerah from Cush came out to fight them with an enormous army and three hundred chariots. They came as far as the town of Mareshah. ¹⁰So Asa went out to fight Zerah and prepared for battle in the Valley of Zephathah at Mareshah.

¹¹Asa called out to the LORD his God, saying, "LORD, only you can help weak people against the strong. Help us, LORD our God, because we depend on you. We fight against this enormous army in your name. LORD, you are our God. Don't let anyone win against you."

¹²So the LORD defeated the Cushites when Asa's army from Judah attacked them, and the Cushites ran away. ¹³Asa's army chased them as far as the town of Gerar. So many Cushites were killed that the army could not fight again; they were crushed by the LORD and his army. Asa and his army carried many valuable things away from the enemy. ¹⁴They destroyed all the towns near Gerar, because the people living in these towns were afraid of the LORD. Since these towns had many valuable things, Asa's army took them away. ¹⁵Asa's army also attacked the camps where the shepherds lived and took many sheep and camels. Then they returned to Jerusalem.

ASA'S CHANGES

15 The Spirit of God entered Azariah son of Oded. ²Azariah went to meet Asa and said, "Listen to me, Asa and all you people of Judah and Benjamin. The LORD is with you when you are with him. If you obey him, you will find him, but if you leave him, he will leave you. ³For a long time Israel was without the true God and without a priest to teach them and without the teachings. ⁴But when they were in trouble, they turned to the LORD, the God of Israel. They looked for him and found him. ⁵In those days no one could travel safely. There was much trouble in all the nations. ⁶One nation would destroy another nation, and one city would destroy another city, because God troubled them with all kinds of distress. ⁷But you should be strong. Don't give up, because you will get a reward for your good work."

⁸Asa felt brave when he heard these

words and the message from Azariah son of Oded the prophet. So he removed the hateful idols from all of Judah and Benjamin and from the towns he had captured in the hills of Ephraim. He repaired the LORD's altar that was in front of the porch of the Temple of the LORD.

⁹Then Asa gathered all the people from Judah and Benjamin and from the tribes of Ephraim, Manasseh, and Simeon who were living in Judah. Many people came to Asa even from Israel, because they saw that the LORD, Asa's God, was with him.

¹⁰Asa and these people gathered in Jerusalem in the third month of the fifteenth year of Asa's rule. ¹¹At that time they sacrificed to the LORD seven hundred bulls and seven thousand sheep and goats from the valuable things Asa's army had taken from their enemies. ¹²Then they made an agreement to obey the LORD, the God of their ancestors, with their whole being. ¹³Anyone who refused to obey the LORD, the God of Israel, was to be killed. It did not matter if that person was important or unimportant, a man or woman. ¹⁴Then Asa and the people made a promise before the LORD, shouting with a loud voice and blowing trumpets and sheep's horns. ¹⁵All the people of Judah were happy about the promise, because they had promised with all their heart. They looked for God and found him. So the LORD gave them peace in all the country.

¹⁶King Asa also removed Maacah, his grandmother, from being queen mother, because she had made a terrible Asherah idol. Asa cut down that idol, smashed it into pieces, and burned it in the Kidron Valley. ¹⁷But the places of worship to gods were not removed from Judah. Even so, Asa was faithful all his life. ¹⁸Asa brought into the Temple of God the gifts he and his father had given: silver, gold, and utensils. ¹⁹There was no more war until the thirty-fifth year of Asa's rule.

ASA'S LAST YEARS

16 In the thirty-sixth year of Asa's rule, Baasha king of Israel attacked Judah. He made the town of Ramah strong so he could keep people from leaving or entering Judah, Asa's country.

²Asa took silver and gold from the treasuries of the Temple of the LORD and out of his own palace. Then he sent it with messengers to Ben-Hadad king of Aram, who lived in Damascus. Asa said, ³"Let there be a treaty between you and me as there was between my father and your father. I am sending you silver and gold. Break your treaty with Baasha king of Israel so he will leave my land."

⁴Ben-Hadad agreed with King Asa and sent the commanders of his armies to attack the towns of Israel. They defeated the towns of Ijon, Dan, and Abel Beth Maacah, and all the towns in Naphtali where treasures were stored. ⁵When Baasha heard about this, he stopped building up Ramah and left his work. ⁶Then King Asa brought all the people of Judah to Ramah, and they carried away the rocks and wood that Baasha had used. And they used them to build up Geba and Mizpah.

⁷At that time Hanani the seer came to Asa king of Judah and said to him, "You depended on the king of Aram to help you and not on the LORD your God. So the king of Aram's army escaped from you. ⁸The Cushites and Libyans had a large and powerful army and many chariots and horsemen. But you depended on the LORD to help you, so he handed them over to you. ⁹The LORD searches all the earth for people who have given themselves completely to him. He wants to make them strong. Asa, you did a foolish thing, so from now on you will have wars."

¹⁰Asa was angry with Hanani the seer because of what he had said; he was so angry that he put Hanani in prison. And Asa was cruel to some of the people at the same time.

¹¹Everything Asa did as king, from the beginning to the end, is written in the book of the kings of Judah and Israel. ¹²In the thirty-ninth year of his rule, Asa got a disease in his feet. Though his disease was very bad, he did not ask for help from the LORD, but only from the doctors. ¹³Then Asa died in the forty-first year of his rule. ¹⁴The people buried Asa in the tomb he had made for himself in Jerusalem. They laid him on a bed filled with spices and different kinds of mixed perfumes, and they made a large fire to honor him.

JEHOSHAPHAT KING OF JUDAH

17 Jehoshaphat, Asa's son, became king of Judah in his place. Jehoshaphat made Judah strong so they could fight against Israel. ²He put troops in all the strong, walled cities of Judah, in the land of Judah, and in the towns of Ephraim that his father Asa had captured.

³The LORD was with Jehoshaphat, because he lived as his ancestor David had lived when he first became king. Jehoshaphat did not ask for help from the Baal idols, ⁴but from the God of his father. He obeyed God's commands and did not live as the people of Israel lived. ⁵The LORD made Jehoshaphat a strong king over Judah. All the people of Judah brought gifts to Jehoshaphat, so he had much wealth and honor. ⁶He wanted very much to obey the LORD. He also removed the places for worshiping gods and the Asherah idols from Judah.

⁷During the third year of his rule, Jehoshaphat sent his officers to teach in the towns of Judah. These officers were Ben-Hail, Obadiah, Zechariah, Nethanel, and Micaiah. ⁸Jehoshaphat sent with them these Levites: Shemaiah, Nethaniah, Zebadiah, Asahel, Shemiramoth, Jehonathan, Adonijah, Tobijah, and Tob-Adonijah. He also sent the priests Elishama and Jehoram. ⁹These leaders, Levites, and priests taught the people in Judah. They took the Book of the Teachings of the LORD and went through all the towns of Judah and taught the people.

ALWAYS ON HIS MIND

FULFILLMENT

the great hunter

2 CHRONICLES 16:9

This verse contains two amazing thoughts:

First, God searches the earth to find us. He is constantly looking for those whose hearts are in right relationship to him. This is one of the most important differences between the Judeo-Christian God and every other religion. God is the Great Hunter searching for us. Every other religion is about people searching for God. What a difference it makes to have God looking for us!

Second, God powerfully supports those whose hearts are perfect toward him. God does not leave those he finds in desperate straits. And if God is supporting you, who is going to overcome you? No one! This is the God who created it all. He says that he is looking for you in order to give you his strong support. Failure is impossible. God cannot lose!

God is searching the earth for people who are in the midst of catastrophe. God tells us that he will offer his strong support. And nothing can overcome him. Insurmountable obstacles are opportunities for his declaration of power. So trust him to deliver you, too!

reflect: Rejoice in the fact that God is searching for ways to help and bless you.
Go to **FULFILLMENT:** "Fear of the Future" at **Matthew 6:25–34.**

[10]The nations near Judah were afraid of the LORD, so they did not start a war against Jehoshaphat. [11]Some of the Philistines brought gifts and silver to Jehoshaphat as he demanded. Some Arabs brought him flocks: seventy-seven hundred sheep and seventy-seven hundred goats.

[12]Jehoshaphat grew more and more powerful. He built strong, walled cities and towns for storing supplies in Judah. [13]He kept many supplies in the towns of Judah, and he kept trained soldiers in Jerusalem. [14]These soldiers were listed by families. From the families of Judah, these were the commanders of groups of a thousand men: Adnah was the commander of three hundred thousand soldiers; [15]Jehohanan was the commander of two hundred eighty thousand soldiers; [16]Amasiah was the commander of two hundred thousand soldiers. Amasiah son of Zicri had volunteered to serve the LORD.

[17]These were the commanders from the families of Benjamin: Eliada, a brave soldier, had two hundred thousand soldiers who used bows and shields. [18]And Jehozabad had one hundred eighty thousand men armed for war.

[19]All these soldiers served King Jehoshaphat. The king also put other men in the strong, walled cities through all of Judah.

MICAIAH WARNS KING AHAB

18 Jehoshaphat had much wealth and honor, and he made an agreement with King Ahab through marriage.[n] [2]A few years later Jehoshaphat went to visit Ahab in Samaria. Ahab sacrificed many sheep and cattle as a great feast to honor Jehoshaphat and the people with him. He encouraged Jehoshaphat to attack Ramoth in Gilead. [3]Ahab king of Israel asked Jehoshaphat king of Judah, "Will you go with me to attack Ramoth in Gilead?"

Jehoshaphat answered, "I will go with you, and my soldiers are yours. We will join you in the battle." [4]Jehoshaphat also said to Ahab, "But first we should ask if this is the LORD's will."

[5]So King Ahab called four hundred prophets together and asked them, "Should we go to war against Ramoth in Gilead or not?"

They answered, "Go, because God will hand them over to you."

[6]But Jehoshaphat asked, "Isn't there a prophet of the LORD here? Let's ask him what we should do."

[7]Then King Ahab said to Jehoshaphat, "There is one other prophet. We could ask the LORD through him, but I hate him. He never prophesies anything good about me, but always something bad. He is Micaiah son of Imlah."

Jehoshaphat said, "King Ahab, you shouldn't say that!"

[8]So Ahab king of Israel told one of his officers to bring Micaiah to him at once.

[9]Ahab king of Israel and Jehoshaphat king of Judah had on their royal robes and were sitting on their thrones at the threshing floor, near the entrance to the gate of Samaria. All the prophets were standing before them speaking their messages. [10]Zedekiah son of Kenaanah had made some iron horns. He said to Ahab, "This is what the LORD says: 'You will use these horns to fight the Arameans until they are destroyed.'"

[11]All the other prophets said the same thing, "Attack Ramoth in Gilead and win, because the LORD will hand the Arameans over to you."

[12]The messenger who had gone to get Micaiah said to him, "All the other prophets are saying King Ahab will win. You should agree with them and give the king a good answer."

[13]But Micaiah answered, "As surely as the LORD lives, I can tell him only what my God says."

[14]When Micaiah came to Ahab, the king asked him, "Micaiah, should we attack Ramoth in Gilead or not?"

Micaiah answered, "Attack and win! They will be handed over to you."

[15]But Ahab said to Micaiah, "How many times do I have to tell you to speak only the truth to me in the name of the LORD?"

[16]So Micaiah answered, "I saw the army of Israel scattered over the hills like sheep without a shepherd. The LORD said, 'They have no leaders. They should go home and not fight.'"

[17]Then Ahab king of Israel said to

18:1 agreement . . . through marriage Jehoshaphat's son Jehoram married Athaliah, Ahab's daughter. See 2 Chronicles 21:6.

Jehoshaphat, "I told you! He never prophesies anything good about me, but only bad."

¹⁸But Micaiah said, "Hear the message from the LORD: I saw the LORD sitting on his throne with his heavenly army standing on his right and on his left. ¹⁹The LORD said, 'Who will trick King Ahab of Israel into attacking Ramoth in Gilead where he will be killed?'

"Some said one thing; some said another. ²⁰Then one spirit came and stood before the LORD and said, 'I will trick him.'

"The LORD asked, 'How will you do it?'

²¹"The spirit answered, 'I will go to Ahab's prophets and make them tell lies.'

"So the LORD said, 'You will succeed in tricking him. Go and do it.'"

²²Micaiah said, "Ahab, the LORD has made your prophets lie to you, and the LORD has decided that disaster should come to you."

²³Then Zedekiah son of Kenaanah went up to Micaiah and slapped him in the face. Zedekiah said, "Has the LORD's Spirit left me to speak through you?"

²⁴Micaiah answered, "You will find out on the day you go to hide in an inside room."

²⁵Then Ahab king of Israel ordered, "Take Micaiah and send him to Amon, the governor of the city, and to Joash, the king's son. ²⁶Tell them I said to put this man in prison and give him only bread and water until I return safely from the battle."

²⁷Micaiah said, "Ahab, if you come back safely from the battle, the LORD has not spoken through me. Remember my words, all you people!"

AHAB IS KILLED

²⁸So Ahab king of Israel and Jehoshaphat king of Judah went to Ramoth in Gilead. ²⁹King Ahab said to Jehoshaphat, "I will go into battle, but I will wear other clothes so no one will recognize me. But you wear your royal clothes." So Ahab wore other clothes, and they went into battle.

³⁰The king of Aram ordered his chariot commanders, "Don't fight with anyone—important or unimportant—except the king of Israel." ³¹When these commanders saw Jehoshaphat, they thought he was the king of Israel, so they turned to attack him. But Jehoshaphat began shouting, and the LORD helped him. God made the chariot command-

ers turn away from Jehoshaphat. ³²When they saw he was not King Ahab, they stopped chasing him.

³³By chance, a soldier shot an arrow which hit Ahab king of Israel between the pieces of his armor. King Ahab said to his chariot driver, "Turn around and get me out of the battle, because I am hurt!" ³⁴The battle continued all day. King Ahab held himself up in his chariot and faced the Arameans until evening. Then he died at sunset.

19 Jehoshaphat king of Judah came back safely to his palace in Jerusalem. ²Jehu son of Hanani, a seer, went out to meet him and said to the king, "Why did you help evil people? Why do you love those who hate the LORD? That is the reason the LORD is angry with you. ³But there is some good in you. You took the Asherah idols out of this country, and you have tried to obey God."

JEHOSHAPHAT CHOOSES JUDGES

⁴Jehoshaphat lived in Jerusalem. He went out again to be with the people, from Beersheba to the mountains of Ephraim, and he turned them back to the LORD, the God of their ancestors. ⁵Jehoshaphat appointed judges in all the land, in each of the strong, walled cities of Judah. ⁶Jehoshaphat said to them, "Watch what you do, because you are not judging for people but for the LORD. He will be with you when you make a decision. ⁷Now let each of you fear the LORD. Watch what you do, because the LORD our God wants people to be fair. He wants all people to be treated the same, and he doesn't want decisions influenced by money."

⁸And in Jerusalem Jehoshaphat appointed some of the Levites, priests, and leaders of Israelite families to be judges. They were to decide cases about the law of the LORD and settle problems between the people who lived in Jerusalem. ⁹Jehoshaphat commanded them, "You must always serve the LORD completely, and you must fear him. ¹⁰Your people living in the cities will bring you cases about killing, about the teachings, commands, rules, or some other law. In all these cases you must warn the people not to sin against the LORD. If you don't, he will be angry with you and your people. But if you warn them, you won't be guilty.

¹¹"Amariah, the leading priest, will be

over you in all cases about the Lord. Zebadiah son of Ishmael, a leader in the tribe of Judah, will be over you in all cases about the king. Also, the Levites will serve as officers for you. Have courage. May the Lord be with those who do what is right."

JEHOSHAPHAT FACES WAR

20 Later the Moabites, Ammonites, and some Meunites came to start a war with Jehoshaphat. ²Messengers came and told Jehoshaphat, "A large army is coming against you from Edom, from the other side of the Dead Sea. They are already in Hazazon Tamar!" (Hazazon Tamar is also called En Gedi.) ³Jehoshaphat was afraid, so he decided to ask the Lord what to do. He announced that everyone in Judah should fast during this special time of prayer to God.

⁴The people of Judah came together to ask the Lord for help; they came from every town in Judah.

⁵The people of Judah and Jerusalem met in front of the new courtyard in the Temple of the Lord. Then Jehoshaphat stood up, ⁶and he said, "Lord, God of our ancestors, you are the God in heaven. You rule over all the kingdoms of the nations. You have power and strength, so no one can stand against you. ⁷Our God, you forced out the people who lived in this land as your people Israel moved in. And you gave this land forever to the descendants of your friend Abraham. ⁸They lived in this land and built a Temple for you. They said, ⁹'If trouble comes upon us, or war, punishment, sickness, or hunger, we will stand before you and before this Temple where you have chosen to be worshiped. We

---

THE PRODUCT OF PRESENT OBEDIENCE

in all things

FUTURE

By Rick Goad

2 CHRONICLES 20

There may be a moment for you, as there was for me, when everything in your life changes in a flash, or so it seems. You may have a day of such grief that you do not think you will be able to bear it, or you may hear those words you never thought you would ever hear because those things only happen to other people.

In my moment of great trouble, God spoke to me and said, "What seems to be a season of great trouble over your life is really the season of my great love over you." You see, God takes what is broken into a million pieces, and what looks as though can never be mended again, and he builds a monument of his great love. If we allow him to, he will build a monument of love, peace, and trust, and show us that he as Father can take even the worst of the troubled times and turn our sorrow into dancing.

"In All Things" was a song I wrote many years before my battle really began. God knew even then that he would write a song for me to keep me strong in my faith . . . for the battle is the Lord's.

reflect: Can you honestly say that you trust the Lord in all things?
Go to **Esther 4:14.**

will cry out to you when we are in trouble. Then you will hear and save us.'

10"But now here are men from Ammon, Moab, and Edom. You wouldn't let the Israelites enter their lands when the Israelites came from Egypt. So the Israelites turned away and did not destroy them. 11But see how they repay us for not destroying them! They have come to force us out of your land, which you gave us as our own. 12Our God, punish those people. We have no power against this large army that is attacking us. We don't know what to do, so we look to you for help."

13All the men of Judah stood before the LORD with their babies, wives, and children. 14Then the Spirit of the LORD entered Jahaziel. (Jahaziel was Zechariah's son. Zechariah was Benaiah's son. Benaiah was Jeiel's son, and Jeiel was Mattaniah's son.) Jahaziel, a Levite and a descendant of Asaph, stood up in the meeting. 15He said, "Listen to me, King Jehoshaphat and all you people living in Judah and Jerusalem. The LORD says this to you: 'Don't be afraid or discouraged because of this large army. The battle is not your battle, it is God's. 16Tomorrow go down there and fight those people. They will come up through the Pass of Ziz. You will find them at the end of the ravine that leads to the Desert of Jeruel. 17You won't need to fight in this battle. Just stand strong in your places, and you will see the LORD save you. Judah and Jerusalem, don't be afraid or discouraged, because the LORD is with you. So go out against those people tomorrow.'"

18Jehoshaphat bowed facedown on the ground. All the people of Judah and Jerusalem bowed down before the LORD and worshiped him. 19Then some Levites from the Kohathite and Korahite people stood up and praised the LORD, the God of Israel, with very loud voices.

20Jehoshaphat's army went out into the Desert of Tekoa early in the morning. As they were starting out, Jehoshaphat stood and said, "Listen to me, people of Judah and Jerusalem. Have faith in the LORD your God, and you will stand strong. Have faith in his prophets, and you will succeed." 21Jehoshaphat listened to the people's advice. Then he chose men to be singers to the LORD, to praise him because he is holy and wonderful. As they marched in front of the army, they said,

"Thank the LORD,
    because his love continues forever."

22As they began to sing and praise God, the LORD set ambushes for the people of Ammon, Moab, and Edom who had come to attack Judah. And they were defeated. 23The Ammonites and Moabites attacked the Edomites, destroying them completely. After they had killed the Edomites, they killed each other.

24When the men from Judah came to a place where they could see the desert, they looked at the enemy's large army. But they only saw dead bodies lying on the ground; no one had escaped. 25When Jehoshaphat and his army came to take their valuables, they found many supplies, much clothing, and other valuable things. There was more than they could carry away; there was so much it took three days to gather it all. 26On the fourth day Jehoshaphat and his army met in the Valley of Beracah and praised the LORD. That is why that place has been called the Valley of Beracah[n] to this day.

27Then Jehoshaphat led all the men from Judah and Jerusalem back to Jerusalem. The LORD had made them happy because their enemies were defeated. 28They entered Jerusalem with harps, lyres, and trumpets and went to the Temple of the LORD.

29When all the kingdoms of the lands around them heard how the LORD had fought Israel's enemies, they feared God. 30So Jehoshaphat's kingdom was not at war. His God gave him peace from all the countries around him.

JEHOSHAPHAT'S RULE ENDS

31Jehoshaphat ruled over the country of Judah. He was thirty-five years old when he became king, and he ruled in Jerusalem for twenty-five years. His mother's name was Azubah daughter of Shilhi. 32Jehoshaphat was good like his father Asa, and he did what the LORD said was right. 33But the places where gods were worshiped were not removed, and the people did not really want to follow the God of their ancestors.

34The other things Jehoshaphat did as king, from the beginning to the end, are writ-

---

20:26 Beracah This name means "blessing" or "praise."

ten in the records of Jehu son of Hanani, which are in the book of the kings of Israel.

³⁵Later, Jehoshaphat king of Judah made a treaty with Ahaziah king of Israel, which was a wrong thing to do. ³⁶Jehoshaphat agreed with Ahaziah to build trading ships, which they built in the town of Ezion Geber. ³⁷Then Eliezer son of Dodavahu from the town of Mareshah spoke against Jehoshaphat. He said, "Jehoshaphat, because you joined with Ahaziah, the LORD will destroy what you have made." The ships were wrecked so they could not sail out to trade.

21 Jehoshaphat died and was buried with his ancestors in Jerusalem, the city of David. Then his son Jehoram became king in his place. ²Jehoram's brothers were Azariah, Jehiel, Zechariah, Azariahu, Michael, and Shephatiah. They were the sons of Jehoshaphat king of Judah. ³Jehoshaphat gave his sons many gifts of silver, gold, and valuable things, and he gave them strong, walled cities in Judah. But Jehoshaphat gave the kingdom to Jehoram, because he was the first son.

JEHORAM KING OF JUDAH

⁴When Jehoram took control of his father's kingdom, he killed all his brothers with a sword and also killed some of the leaders of Judah. ⁵He was thirty-two years old when he began to rule, and he ruled eight years in Jerusalem. ⁶He followed in the ways of the kings of Israel, just as the family of Ahab had done, because he married Ahab's daughter. Jehoram did what the LORD said was wrong. ⁷But the LORD would not destroy David's family because of the agreement he had made with David. He had promised that one of David's descendants would always rule.

⁸In Jehoram's time, Edom broke away from Judah's rule and chose their own king. ⁹So Jehoram went to Edom with all his commanders and chariots. The Edomites surrounded him and his chariot commanders, but Jehoram got up and attacked the Edomites at night. ¹⁰From then until now the country of Edom has fought against the rule of Judah. At the same time the people of Libnah also broke away from Jehoram because Jehoram left the LORD, the God of his ancestors.

¹¹Jehoram also built places to worship gods on the hills in Judah. He led the people of Jerusalem to sin, and he led the people of Judah away from the LORD. ¹²Then Jehoram received this letter from Elijah the prophet:

This is what the LORD, the God of your ancestor David, says, "Jehoram, you have not lived as your father Jehoshaphat lived and as Asa king of Judah lived. ¹³But you have lived as the kings of Israel lived, leading the people of Judah and Jerusalem to sin against God, as Ahab and his family did. You have killed your brothers, and they were better than you. ¹⁴So now the LORD is about to punish your people, your children, wives, and everything you own. ¹⁵You will have a terrible disease in your intestines that will become worse every day. Finally it will cause your intestines to come out."

¹⁶The LORD caused the Philistines and the Arabs who lived near the Cushites to be angry with Jehoram. ¹⁷So the Philistines and Arabs attacked Judah and carried away all the wealth of Jehoram's palace, as well as his sons and wives. Only Jehoram's youngest son, Ahaziah, was left.

¹⁸After these things happened, the LORD gave Jehoram a disease in his intestines that could not be cured. ¹⁹After he was sick for two years, Jehoram's intestines came out because of the disease, and he died in terrible pain. The people did not make a fire to honor Jehoram as they had done for his ancestors.

²⁰Jehoram was thirty-two years old when he became king, and he ruled eight years in Jerusalem. No one was sad when he died. He was buried in Jerusalem, but not in the graves for the kings.

AHAZIAH KING OF JUDAH

22 The people of Jerusalem chose Ahaziah, Jehoram's youngest son, to be king in his place. The robbers who had come with the Arabs to attack Jehoram's camp had killed all of Jehoram's older sons. So Ahaziah began to rule Judah. ²Ahaziah was twenty-two years old when he became king, and he ruled one year in Jerusalem. His mother's name was Athaliah, a granddaughter of Omri. ³Ahaziah followed the ways of Ahab's family, because his mother encouraged him to do wrong. ⁴Ahaziah did what the LORD said was wrong, as Ahab's family had done. They gave advice to Ahaziah after his father died, and their bad advice led to his death. ⁵Following their advice, Ahaziah went with Joram son of Ahab to Ramoth in Gilead, where they fought against Hazael king of Aram. The Arameans wounded Joram. ⁶So Joram returned to Jezreel to heal from the wounds he received at Ramoth when he fought Hazael king of Aram.

Ahaziah son of Jehoram and king of Judah went down to visit Joram son of Ahab at Jezreel because he had been wounded.

⁷God caused Ahaziah's death when he went to visit Joram. Ahaziah arrived and went out with Joram to meet Jehu son of Nimshi, whom the LORD had appointed to destroy Ahab's family. ⁸While Jehu was punishing Ahab's family, he found the leaders of Judah and the sons of Ahaziah's relatives who served Ahaziah, and Jehu killed them all. ⁹Then Jehu looked for Ahaziah. Jehu's men caught him hiding in Samaria, so they brought him to Jehu. Then they killed and buried him. They said, "Ahaziah is a descendant of Jehoshaphat, and Jehoshaphat obeyed the LORD with all his heart." No one in Ahaziah's family had the power to take control of the kingdom of Judah.

ATHALIAH AND JOASH

¹⁰When Ahaziah's mother, Athaliah, saw that her son was dead, she killed all the royal family in Judah. ¹¹But Jehosheba, King Jehoram's daughter, took Joash, Ahaziah's son. She stole him from among the other sons of the king who were going to be murdered and put him and his nurse in a bedroom. So Jehosheba, who was King Jehoram's daughter and Ahaziah's sister and the wife of Jehoiada the priest, hid Joash so Athaliah could not kill him. ¹²He hid with them in the Temple of God for six years. During that time Athaliah ruled the land.

23 In the seventh year Jehoiada decided to do something. He made an agreement with the commanders of the groups of a hundred men: Azariah son of Jeroham, Ishmael son of Jehohanan, Azariah son of Obed, Maaseiah son of Adaiah, and Elishaphat son of Zicri. ²They went around in Judah and gathered the Levites from all the towns, and they gathered the leaders of the families of Judah. Then they went to Jerusalem. ³All the people together made an agreement with the king in the Temple of God.

Jehoiada said to them, "The king's son will rule, as the LORD promised about David's descendants. ⁴Now this is what you must do: You priests and Levites go on duty on the Sabbath. A third of you will guard the doors. ⁵A third of you will be at the king's palace, and a third of you will be at the Foundation Gate. All the other people will stay in the courtyards of the Temple of the LORD. ⁶Don't let anyone come into the Temple of the LORD except the priests and Levites who serve. They may come because they have been made ready to serve the LORD, but all the others must do the job the LORD has given them. ⁷The Levites must stay near the king, each man with his weapon in his hand. If anyone tries to enter the Temple, kill him. Stay close to the king when he goes in and when he goes out."

JOASH BECOMES KING

⁸The Levites and all the people of Judah obeyed everything Jehoiada the priest had commanded. He did not excuse anyone from the groups of the priests. So each commander took his men who came on duty on the Sabbath with those who went off duty on the Sabbath. ⁹Jehoiada gave the commanders of a hundred men the spears and the large and small shields that had belonged to King David and that were kept in the Temple of God. ¹⁰Then Jehoiada told the soldiers where to stand with weapon in hand. There were guards from the south side of the Temple to the north side. They stood by the altar and the Temple and around the king.

¹¹Jehoiada and his sons brought out the king's son and put the crown on him and gave him a copy of the agreement. Then they appointed him king and poured olive oil on him and shouted, "Long live the king!"

¹²When Athaliah heard the noise of the people running and praising the king, she went to them at the Temple of the LORD. ¹³She looked, and there was the king standing by his pillar at the entrance. The officers and the trumpeters were standing beside him, and all the people of the land were happy and blowing trumpets. The singers were playing musical instruments and leading

praises. Then Athaliah tore her clothes and screamed, "Traitors! Traitors!"

¹⁴Jehoiada the priest sent out the commanders of a hundred men, who led the army. He said, "Surround her with soldiers and take her out of the Temple area. Kill with a sword anyone who follows her." He had said, "Don't put Athaliah to death in the Temple of the Lord." ¹⁵So they caught her when she came to the entrance of the Horse Gate near the palace. There they put her to death.

¹⁶Then Jehoiada made an agreement with the people and the king that they would be the Lord's special people. ¹⁷All the people went to the temple of Baal and tore it down, smashing the altars and idols. They killed Mattan, the priest of Baal, in front of the altars.

¹⁸Then Jehoiada chose the priests, who were Levites, to be responsible for the Temple of the Lord. David had given them duties in the Temple of the Lord. They were to offer the burnt offerings to the Lord as the Teachings of Moses commanded, and they were to offer them with much joy and singing as David had commanded. ¹⁹Jehoiada put guards at the gates of the Temple of the Lord so that anyone who was unclean in any way could not enter.

²⁰Jehoiada took with him the commanders of a hundred men, the important men, the rulers of the people, and all the people of the land to take the king out of the Temple of the Lord. They went through the Upper Gate into the palace, and then they seated the king on the throne. ²¹So all the people of the land were very happy, and Jerusalem had peace, because Athaliah had been put to death with the sword.

JOASH REPAIRS THE TEMPLE

24 Joash was seven years old when he became king, and he ruled forty years in Jerusalem. His mother's name was Zibiah, and she was from Beersheba. ²Joash did what the Lord said was right as long as Jehoiada the priest was alive. ³Jehoiada chose two wives for Joash, and Joash had sons and daughters.

⁴Later, Joash decided to repair the Temple of the Lord. ⁵He called the priests and the Levites together and said to them, "Go to the towns of Judah and gather the money all the Israelites have to pay every year. Use it to repair the Temple of your God. Do this now." But the Levites did not hurry.

⁶So King Joash called for Jehoiada the leading priest and said to him, "Why haven't you made the Levites bring in from Judah and Jerusalem the tax money that Moses, the Lord's servant, and the people of Israel used for the Holy Tent?"

⁷In the past the sons of wicked Athaliah had broken into the Temple of God and used its holy things for worshiping the Baal idols.

⁸King Joash commanded that a box for contributions be made. They put it outside, at the gate of the Temple of the Lord. ⁹Then the Levites made an announcement in Judah and Jerusalem, telling people to bring to the Lord the tax money Moses, the servant of God, had made the Israelites give while they were in the desert. ¹⁰All the officers and people were happy to bring their money, and they put it in the box until the box was full. ¹¹When the Levites would take the box to the king's officers, they would see that it was full of money. Then the king's royal secretary and the leading priest's officer would come and take out the money and return the box to its place. They did this often and gathered much money. ¹²King Joash and Jehoiada gave the money to the people who worked on the Temple of the Lord. And they hired stoneworkers and carpenters to repair the Temple of the Lord. They also hired people to work with iron and bronze to repair the Temple.

¹³The people worked hard, and the work to repair the Temple went well. They rebuilt the Temple of God to be as it was before, but even stronger. ¹⁴When the workers finished, they brought the money that was left to King Joash and Jehoiada. They used that money to make utensils for the Temple of the Lord, utensils for the service in the Temple and for the burnt offerings, and bowls and other utensils from gold and silver. Burnt offerings were given every day in the Temple of the Lord while Jehoiada was alive.

¹⁵Jehoiada grew old and lived many years. Then he died when he was one hundred thirty years old. ¹⁶Jehoiada was buried in Jerusalem with the kings, because he had done much good in Judah for God and his Temple.

JOASH DOES EVIL

17After Jehoiada died, the officers of Judah came and bowed down to King Joash, and he listened to them. 18The king and these leaders stopped worshiping in the Temple of the LORD, the God of their ancestors. Instead, they began to worship the Asherah idols and other idols. Because they did wrong, God was angry with the people of Judah and Jerusalem. 19Even though the LORD sent prophets to the people to turn them back to him and even though the prophets warned them, they refused to listen.

20Then the Spirit of God entered Zechariah son of Jehoiada the priest. Zechariah stood before the people and said, "This is what God says: 'Why do you disobey the LORD's commands? You will not be successful. Because you have left the LORD, he has also left you.'"

21But the king and his officers made plans against Zechariah. At the king's command they threw stones at him in the courtyard of the Temple of the LORD until he died. 22King Joash did not remember Jehoiada's kindness to him, so Joash killed Zechariah, Jehoiada's son. Before Zechariah died, he said, "May the LORD see what you are doing and punish you."

23At the end of the year, the Aramean army came against Joash. They attacked Judah and Jerusalem, killed all the leaders of the people, and sent all the valuable things to their king in Damascus. 24The Aramean army came with only a small group of men, but the LORD handed over to them a very large army from Judah, because the people of Judah had left the LORD, the God of their ancestors. So Joash was punished. 25When the Arameans left, Joash was badly wounded. His own officers made plans against him because he had killed Zechariah son of Jehoiada the priest. So they killed Joash in his own bed. He died and was buried in Jerusalem but not in the graves of the kings.

26The officers who made plans against Joash were Jozabad and Jehozabad. Jozabad was the son of Shimeath, a woman from Ammon. And Jehozabad was the son of Shimrith, a woman from Moab. 27The story of Joash's sons, the great prophecies against him, and how he repaired the Temple of God are written in the book of the kings. Joash's son Amaziah became king in his place.

AMAZIAH KING OF JUDAH

25Amaziah was twenty-five years old when he became king, and he ruled for twenty-nine years in Jerusalem. His mother's name was Jehoaddin, and she was from Jerusalem. 2Amaziah did what the LORD said was right, but he did not really want to obey him. 3As soon as Amaziah took strong control of the kingdom, he executed the officers who had murdered his father the king. 4But Amaziah did not put to death their children. He obeyed what was written in the Book of Moses, where the LORD commanded, "Parents must not be put to death when their children do wrong, and children must not be put to death when their parents do wrong. Each must die for his own sins."[n]

5Amaziah gathered the people of Judah together. He grouped all the people of Judah and Benjamin by families, and he put commanders over groups of a thousand and over groups of a hundred. He counted the men who were twenty years old and older. In all there were three hundred thousand soldiers ready to fight and skilled with spears and shields. 6Amaziah also hired one hundred thousand soldiers from Israel for about seventy-five hundred pounds of silver. 7But a man of God came to Amaziah and said, "My king, don't let the army of Israel go with you. The LORD is not with Israel or the people from the tribe of Ephraim. 8You can make yourself strong for war, but God will defeat you. He has the power to help you or to defeat you."

9Amaziah said to the man of God, "But what about the seventy-five hundred pounds of silver I paid to the Israelite army?"

The man of God answered, "The LORD can give you much more than that."

10So Amaziah sent the Israelite army back home to Ephraim. They were very angry with the people of Judah and went home angry.

11Then Amaziah became very brave and led his army to the Valley of Salt in the country of Edom. There Amaziah's army killed ten thousand Edomites. 12The army of Judah also captured ten thousand and took them to

---

25:4 **"Parents...sins."** See Deuteronomy 24:16.

the top of a cliff and threw them off so that they split open.

¹³At the same time the Israelite troops that Amaziah had not let fight in the war were robbing towns in Judah. From Samaria to Beth Horon they killed three thousand people and took many valuable things.

¹⁴When Amaziah came home after defeating the Edomites, he brought back the idols they worshiped and started to worship them himself. He bowed down to them and offered sacrifices to them. ¹⁵The LORD was very angry with Amaziah, so he sent a prophet to him who said, "Why have you asked their gods for help? They could not even save their own people from you!"

¹⁶As the prophet spoke, Amaziah said to him, "We never gave you the job of advising the king. Stop, or you will be killed."

The prophet stopped speaking except to say, "I know that God has decided to destroy you because you have done this. You did not listen to my advice."

¹⁷Amaziah king of Judah talked with those who advised him. Then he sent a message to Jehoash son of Jehoahaz, who was the son of Jehu king of Israel. Amaziah said to Jehoash, "Come, let's meet face to face."

¹⁸Then Jehoash king of Israel answered Amaziah king of Judah, "A thornbush in Lebanon sent a message to a cedar tree in Lebanon. It said, 'Let your daughter marry my son.' But then a wild animal from Lebanon came by, walking on and crushing the thornbush. ¹⁹You say to yourself that you have defeated Edom, but you have become proud, and you brag. But you stay at home! Don't ask for trouble, or you and Judah will be defeated."

²⁰But Amaziah would not listen. God caused this to happen so that Jehoash would defeat Judah, because Judah asked for help from the gods of Edom. ²¹So Jehoash king of Israel went to attack. He and Amaziah king of Judah faced each other in battle at Beth Shemesh in Judah. ²²Israel defeated Judah, and every man of Judah ran away to his home. ²³At Beth Shemesh Jehoash king of Israel captured Amaziah king of Judah. (Amaziah was the son of Joash, who was the son of Ahaziah.) Then Jehoash brought him to Jerusalem. Jehoash broke down the wall of Jerusalem, from the Gate of Ephraim to the Corner Gate, about six hundred feet. ²⁴He took all the gold and silver and all the utensils from the Temple of God that Obed-Edom had taken care of. He also took the treasures from the palace and some hostages. Then he returned to Samaria.

²⁵Amaziah son of Joash, the king of Judah, lived fifteen years after the death of Jehoash son of Jehoahaz, the king of Israel. ²⁶The other things Amaziah did as king, from the beginning to the end, are written in the book of the kings of Judah and Israel. ²⁷When Amaziah stopped obeying the LORD, the people in Jerusalem made plans against him. So he ran away to the town of Lachish, but they sent men after him to Lachish and killed him. ²⁸They brought his body back on horses, and he was buried with his ancestors in Jerusalem, the city of David.

UZZIAH KING OF JUDAH

26 Then all the people of Judah made Uzziah[n] king in place of his father Amaziah. Uzziah was sixteen years old. ²He rebuilt the town of Elath and made it part of Judah again after Amaziah died.

³Uzziah was sixteen years old when he became king, and he ruled fifty-two years in Jerusalem. His mother's name was Jecoliah, and she was from Jerusalem. ⁴He did what the LORD said was right, just as his father Amaziah had done. ⁵Uzziah obeyed God while Zechariah was alive, because he taught Uzziah how to respect and obey God. And as long as Uzziah obeyed the LORD, God gave him success.

⁶Uzziah fought a war against the Philistines. He tore down the walls around their towns of Gath, Jabneh, and Ashdod and built new towns near Ashdod and in other places among the Philistines. ⁷God helped Uzziah fight the Philistines, the Arabs living in Gur Baal, and the Meunites. ⁸Also, the Ammonites made the payments Uzziah demanded. He was very powerful, so his name became famous all the way to the border of Egypt.

⁹Uzziah built towers in Jerusalem at the Corner Gate, the Valley Gate, and where the wall turned, and he made them strong. ¹⁰He also built towers in the desert and dug many wells, because he had many cattle on the

---

26:1 **Uzziah** Also called Azariah.

western hills and in the plains. He had people who worked his fields and vineyards in the hills and in the fertile lands, because he loved the land.

11Uzziah had an army of trained soldiers. They were counted and put in groups by Jeiel the royal secretary and Maaseiah the officer. Hananiah, one of the king's commanders, was their leader. 12There were twenty-six hundred leaders over the soldiers. 13They were in charge of an army of three hundred seven thousand five hundred men who fought with great power to help the king against the enemy. 14Uzziah gave his army shields, spears, helmets, armor, bows, and stones for their slings. 15In Jerusalem Uzziah made cleverly designed devices. These devices on the towers and corners of the city walls were used to shoot arrows and large rocks. So Uzziah became famous in faraway places, because he had much help until he became powerful.

16But when Uzziah became powerful, his pride led to his ruin. He was unfaithful to the LORD his God; he went into the Temple of the LORD to burn incense on the altar for incense. 17Azariah and eighty other brave priests who served the LORD followed Uzziah into the Temple. 18They told him he was wrong and said to him, "You don't have the right to burn incense to the LORD. Only the priests, Aaron's descendants, should burn the incense, because they have been made holy. Leave this holy place. You have been unfaithful, and the LORD God will not honor you for this."

19Uzziah was standing beside the altar for incense in the Temple of the LORD, and in his hand was a pan for burning incense. He was very angry with the priests. As he was standing in front of the priests, a skin disease broke out on his forehead. 20Azariah, the leading priest, and all the other priests looked at him and saw the skin disease on his forehead. So they hurried him out of the Temple. Uzziah also rushed out, because the LORD was punishing him. 21So King Uzziah had the skin disease until the day he died. He had to live in a separate house and could not enter the Temple of the LORD. His son Jotham was in charge of the palace, and he governed the people of the land.

22The other things Uzziah did as king, from beginning to end, were written down by the prophet Isaiah son of Amoz. 23Uzziah died and was buried near his ancestors in a graveyard that belonged to the kings. This was because people said, "He had a skin disease." And his son Jotham became king in his place.

JOTHAM KING OF JUDAH

27 Jotham was twenty-five years old when he became king, and he ruled sixteen years in Jerusalem. His mother's name was Jerusha daughter of Zadok. 2Jotham did what the LORD said was right, just as his father Uzziah had done. But Jotham did not enter the Temple of the LORD to burn incense as his father had. But the people continued doing wrong. 3Jotham rebuilt the Upper Gate of the Temple of the LORD, and he added greatly to the wall at Ophel. 4He also built towns in the hill country of Judah, as well as walled cities and towers in the forests.

5Jotham also fought the king of the Ammonites and defeated them. So each year for three years they gave Jotham about seventy-five hundred pounds of silver, about sixty-two thousand bushels of wheat, and about sixty-two thousand bushels of barley. 6Jotham became powerful, because he always obeyed the LORD his God.

7The other things Jotham did while he was king and all his wars are written in the book of the kings of Israel and Judah. 8Jotham was twenty-five years old when he became king, and he ruled sixteen years in Jerusalem. 9Jotham died and was buried in Jerusalem, the city of David. Then Jotham's son Ahaz became king in his place.

AHAZ KING OF JUDAH

28 Ahaz was twenty years old when he became king, and he ruled sixteen years in Jerusalem. Unlike his ancestor David, he did not do what the LORD said was right. 2Ahaz did the same things the kings of Israel had done. He made metal idols to worship Baal. 3He burned incense in the Valley of Ben Hinnom and made his children pass through the fire. He did the same hateful sins as the nations had done whom the LORD had forced out of the land ahead of the Israelites. 4Ahaz offered sacrifices and burned incense at the places where gods were worshiped, and on the hills, and under every green tree.

⁵So the LORD his God handed over Ahaz to the king of Aram. The Arameans defeated Ahaz and took many people of Judah as prisoners to Damascus.

He also handed over Ahaz to Pekah king of Israel, and Pekah's army killed many soldiers of Ahaz. ⁶The army of Pekah son of Remaliah killed one hundred twenty thousand brave soldiers from Judah in one day. Pekah defeated them because they had left the LORD, the God of their ancestors. ⁷Zicri, a warrior from Ephraim, killed King Ahaz's son Maaseiah. He also killed Azrikam, the officer in charge of the palace, and Elkanah, who was second in command to the king. ⁸The Israelite army captured two hundred thousand of their own relatives. They took women, sons and daughters, and many valuable things from Judah and carried them back to Samaria. ⁹But a prophet of the LORD named Oded was there. He met the Israelite army when it returned to Samaria and said to them, "The LORD, the God of your ancestors, handed Judah over to you, because he was angry with those people. But God has seen the cruel way you killed them. ¹⁰Now you plan to make the people of Judah and Jerusalem your slaves, but you also have sinned against the LORD your God. ¹¹Now listen to me. Send back your brothers and sisters whom you captured, because the LORD is very angry with you."

¹²Then some of the leaders in Ephraim—Azariah son of Jehohanan, Berekiah son of Meshillemoth, Jehizkiah son of Shallum, and Amasa son of Hadlai—met the Israelite soldiers coming home from war. ¹³They warned the soldiers, "Don't bring the prisoners from Judah here. If you do, we will be guilty of sin against the LORD, and that will make our sin and guilt even worse. Our guilt is already so great that he is angry with Israel."

¹⁴So the soldiers left the prisoners and valuable things in front of the officers and people there. ¹⁵The leaders who were named took the prisoners and gave those who were naked the clothes that the Israelite army had taken. They gave the prisoners clothes, sandals, food, drink, and medicine. They put the weak prisoners on donkeys and took them back to their families in Jericho, the city of palm trees. Then they returned home to Samaria.

¹⁶⁻¹⁷At that time the Edomites came again and attacked Judah and carried away prisoners. So King Ahaz sent to the king of Assyria for help. ¹⁸The Philistines also robbed the towns in the western hills and in southern Judah. They captured the towns of Beth Shemesh, Aijalon, Gederoth, Soco, Timnah, and Gimzo, and the villages around them. Then the Philistines lived in those towns. ¹⁹The LORD brought trouble on Judah because Ahaz their king led the people of Judah to sin, and he was unfaithful to the LORD. ²⁰Tiglath-Pileser king of Assyria came to Ahaz, but he gave Ahaz trouble instead of help. ²¹Ahaz took some valuable things from the Temple of the LORD, from the palace, and from the princes, and he gave them to the king of Assyria, but it did not help.

²²During Ahaz's troubles he was even more unfaithful to the LORD. ²³He offered sacrifices to the gods of the people of Damascus, who had defeated him. He thought, "The gods of the kings of Aram helped them. If I offer sacrifices to them, they will help me also." But this brought ruin to Ahaz and all Israel.

²⁴Ahaz gathered the things from the Temple of God and broke them into pieces. Then he closed the doors of the Temple of the LORD. He made altars and put them on every street corner in Jerusalem. ²⁵In every town in Judah, Ahaz made places for burning sacrifices to worship other gods. So he made the LORD, the God of his ancestors, very angry.

²⁶The other things Ahaz did as king, from beginning to end, are written in the book of the kings of Judah and Israel. ²⁷Ahaz died and was buried in the city of Jerusalem, but not in the graves of the kings of Israel. Ahaz's son Hezekiah became king in his place.

HEZEKIAH PURIFIES THE TEMPLE

29 Hezekiah was twenty-five years old when he became king, and he ruled twenty-nine years in Jerusalem. His mother's name was Abijah daughter of Zechariah. ²Hezekiah did what the LORD said was right, just as his ancestor David had done.

³Hezekiah opened the doors of the Temple of the LORD and repaired them in the first

month of the first year he was king. ⁴Hezekiah brought in the priests and Levites and gathered them in the courtyard on the east side of the Temple. ⁵Hezekiah said, "Listen to me, Levites. Make yourselves ready for the LORD's service, and make holy the Temple of the LORD, the God of your ancestors. Remove from the Temple everything that makes it impure. ⁶Our ancestors were unfaithful to God and did what the LORD said was wrong. They left the LORD and stopped worshiping at the Temple where he lives. They rejected him. ⁷They shut the doors of the porch of the Temple, and they let the fire go out in the lamps. They stopped burning incense and offering burnt offerings in the holy place to the God of Israel. ⁸So the LORD became very angry with the people of Judah and Jerusalem, and he punished them. Other people are frightened and shocked by what he did to them. So they insult the people of Judah. You know these things are true. ⁹That is why our ancestors were killed in battle and our sons, daughters, and wives were taken captive. ¹⁰Now I, Hezekiah, have decided to make an agreement with the LORD, the God of Israel, so he will not be angry with us anymore. ¹¹My sons, don't waste any more time. The LORD chose you to stand before him, to serve him, to be his servants, and to burn incense to him."

¹²These are the Levites who started to work. From the Kohathite family there were Mahath son of Amasai and Joel son of Azariah. From the Merarite family there were Kish son of Abdi and Azariah son of Jehallelel. From the Gershonite family there were Joah son of Zimmah and Eden son of Joah. ¹³From Elizaphan's family there were Shimri and Jeiel. From Asaph's family there were Zechariah and Mattaniah. ¹⁴From Heman's family there were Jehiel and Shimei. From Jeduthun's family there were Shemaiah and Uzziel.

¹⁵These Levites gathered their brothers together and made themselves holy for service in the Temple. Then they went into the Temple of the LORD to purify it. They obeyed the king's command that had come from the LORD. ¹⁶When the priests went into the Temple of the LORD to purify it, they took out all the unclean things they found in the Temple of the LORD and put them in the Temple courtyard. Then the Levites took these things out to the Kidron Valley. ¹⁷Beginning on the first day of the first month, they made the Temple holy for the LORD's service. On the eighth day of the month, they came to the porch of the Temple, and for eight more days they made the Temple of the LORD holy. So they finished on the sixteenth day of the first month.

¹⁸Then they went to King Hezekiah and said, "We have purified the entire Temple of the LORD, the altar for burnt offerings and its utensils, and the table for the holy bread and all its utensils. ¹⁹When Ahaz was king, he was unfaithful to God and removed some things from the Temple. But we have put them back and made them holy for the LORD. They are now in front of the LORD's altar."

²⁰Early the next morning King Hezekiah gathered the leaders of the city and went up to the Temple of the LORD. ²¹They brought seven bulls, seven male sheep, seven lambs, and seven male goats. These animals were an offering to remove the sin of the people and the kingdom of Judah and to make the Temple ready for service to God. King Hezekiah commanded the priests, the descendants of Aaron, to offer these animals on the LORD's altar. ²²So the priests killed the bulls and sprinkled their blood on the altar. They killed the sheep and sprinkled their blood on the altar. Then they killed the lambs and sprinkled their blood on the altar. ²³Then the priests brought the male goats for the sin offering before the king and the people there. After the king and the people put their hands on the goats, ²⁴the priests killed them. With the goats' blood they made an offering on the altar to remove the sins of the Israelites so they would belong to God. The king had said that the burnt offering and sin offering should be made for all Israel.

²⁵King Hezekiah put the Levites in the Temple of the LORD with cymbals, harps, and lyres, as David, Gad, and Nathan had commanded. (Gad was the king's seer, and Nathan was a prophet.) This command came from the LORD through his prophets. ²⁶So the Levites stood ready with David's instruments of music, and the priests stood ready with their trumpets.

²⁷Then Hezekiah gave the order to sacrifice the burnt offering on the altar. When

the burnt offering began, the singing to the LORD also began. The trumpets were blown, and the musical instruments of David king of Israel were played. 28All the people worshiped, the singers sang, and the trumpeters blew their trumpets until the burnt offering was finished.

29When the sacrifices were completed, King Hezekiah and everyone with him bowed down and worshiped. 30King Hezekiah and his officers ordered the Levites to praise the LORD, using the words David and Asaph the seer had used. So they praised God with joy and bowed down and worshiped.

31Then Hezekiah said, "Now that you people of Judah have given yourselves to the LORD, come near to the Temple of the LORD. Bring sacrifices and offerings, to show thanks to him." So the people brought sacrifices and thank offerings, and anyone who was willing also brought burnt offerings. 32For burnt offerings they brought a total of seventy bulls, one hundred male sheep, and two hundred lambs; all these animals were sacrificed as burnt offerings to the LORD. 33The holy offerings totaled six hundred bulls and three thousand sheep and goats. 34There were not enough priests to skin all the animals for the burnt offerings. So their relatives the Levites helped them until the work was finished and other priests could be made holy. The Levites had been more careful to make themselves holy for the LORD's service than the priests. 35There were many burnt offerings along with the fat of fellowship offerings and drink offerings. So the service in the Temple of the LORD began again. 36And Hezekiah and the people were very happy that God had made it happen so quickly for his people.

THE PASSOVER CELEBRATION

30 King Hezekiah sent messages to all the people of Israel and Judah, and he wrote letters to the people of Ephraim and Manasseh. Hezekiah invited all these people to come to the Temple of the LORD in Jerusalem to celebrate the Passover for the LORD, the God of Israel. 2King Hezekiah, his officers, and all the people in Jerusalem agreed to celebrate the Passover in the second month. 3They could not celebrate it at the normal time, because not enough priests had made themselves ready to serve the

LORD, and the people had not yet gathered in Jerusalem. 4This plan satisfied King Hezekiah and all the people. 5So they made an announcement everywhere in Israel, from Beersheba to Dan,[n] telling the people to come to Jerusalem to celebrate the Passover for the LORD, the God of Israel. For a long time most of the people had not celebrated the Passover as the law commanded. 6At the king's command, the messengers took letters from him and his officers all through Israel and Judah. This is what the letters said:

People of Israel, return to the LORD, the God of Abraham, Isaac, and Israel. Then God will return to you who are still alive, who have escaped from the kings of Assyria. 7Don't be like your ancestors or your relatives. They turned against the LORD, the God of their ancestors, so he caused other people to be disgusted with them. You know this is true. 8Don't be stubborn as your ancestors were, but obey the LORD willingly. Come to the Temple, which he has made holy forever. Serve the LORD your God so he will not be angry with you. 9Come back to the LORD. Then the people who captured your relatives and children will be kind to them and will let them return to this land. The LORD your God is kind and merciful. He will not turn away from you if you return to him.

10The messengers went to every town in Ephraim and Manasseh, and all the way to Zebulun, but the people laughed at them and made fun of them. 11But some men from Asher, Manasseh, and Zebulun were sorry for what they had done and went to Jerusalem. 12And God united all the people of Judah in obeying King Hezekiah and his officers, because their command had come from the LORD.

13In the second month a large crowd came together in Jerusalem to celebrate the Feast of Unleavened Bread. 14The people removed the altars and incense altars to gods in Jerusalem and threw them into the Kidron Valley.

15They killed the Passover lamb on the

30:5 Beersheba to Dan Dan was the city farthest north in Israel, and Beersheba was the city farthest south. So this means all the people of Israel.

fourteenth day of the second month. The priests and the Levites were ashamed, so they made themselves holy and brought burnt offerings into the Temple of the LORD. ¹⁶They took their regular places in the Temple as the Teachings of Moses, the man of God, commanded. The Levites gave the blood of the sacrifices to the priests, who sprinkled it on the altar. ¹⁷Since many people in the crowd had not made themselves holy, the Levites killed the Passover lambs for everyone who was not clean. The Levites made each lamb holy for the LORD. ¹⁸⁻¹⁹Although many people from Ephraim, Manasseh, Issachar, and Zebulun had not purified themselves for the feast, they ate the Passover even though it was against the law. So Hezekiah prayed for them, saying, "LORD, you are good. You are the LORD, the God of our ancestors. Please forgive all those who try to obey you even if they did not make themselves clean as the rules of the Temple command." ²⁰The LORD listened to Hezekiah's prayer, and he healed the people. ²¹The Israelites in Jerusalem celebrated the Feast of Unleavened Bread for seven days with great joy to the LORD. The Levites and priests praised the LORD every day with loud music. ²²Hezekiah encouraged all the Levites who showed they understood well how to do their service for the LORD. The people ate the feast for seven days, offered fellowship offerings, and praised the LORD, the God of their ancestors.

²³Then all the people agreed to stay seven more days, so they celebrated with joy for seven more days. ²⁴Hezekiah king of Judah gave one thousand bulls and seven thousand sheep to the people. The officers gave one thousand bulls and ten thousand sheep to the people. Many priests made themselves holy. ²⁵All the people of Judah, the priests, the Levites, those who came from Israel, the foreigners from Israel, and the foreigners living in Judah were very happy. ²⁶There was much joy in Jerusalem, because there had not been a celebration like this since the time of Solomon son of David and king of Israel. ²⁷The priests and Levites stood up and blessed the people, and God heard them because their prayer reached heaven, his holy home.

THE COLLECTION FOR THE PRIESTS

31 When the Passover celebration was finished, all the Israelites in Jerusalem went out to the towns of Judah. There they smashed the stone pillars used to worship gods. They cut down the Asherah idols and destroyed the altars and places for worshiping gods in all of Judah, Benjamin, Ephraim, and Manasseh. After they had destroyed all of them, the Israelites returned to their own towns and homes.

²King Hezekiah appointed groups of priests and Levites for their special duties. They were to offer burnt offerings and fellowship offerings, to worship, and to give thanks and praise at the gates of the LORD's house. ³Hezekiah gave some of his own animals for the burnt offerings, which were given every morning and evening, on Sabbath days, during New Moons, and at other feasts commanded in the LORD's Teachings.

⁴Hezekiah commanded the people living in Jerusalem to give the priests and Levites the portion that belonged to them. Then the priests and Levites could give all their time to the LORD's Teachings. ⁵As soon as the king's command went out to the Israelites, they gave freely of the first portion of their grain, new wine, oil, honey, and everything they grew in their fields. They brought a large amount, one-tenth of everything. ⁶The people of Israel and Judah who lived in Judah also brought one-tenth of their cattle and sheep and one-tenth of the holy things that were given to the LORD their God, and they put all of them in piles. ⁷The people began the piles in the third month and finished in the seventh month. ⁸When Hezekiah and his officers came and saw the piles, they praised the LORD and his people, the people of Israel. ⁹Hezekiah asked the priests and Levites about the piles. ¹⁰Azariah, the leading priest from Zadok's family, answered Hezekiah, "Since the people began to bring their offerings to the Temple of the LORD, we have had plenty to eat and plenty left over, because the LORD has blessed his people. So we have all this left over."

¹¹Then Hezekiah commanded the priests to prepare the storerooms in the Temple of the LORD. So this was done. ¹²Then the priests brought in the offerings and the things given to the LORD and one-tenth of everything the

people had given. Conaniah the Levite was in charge of these things, and his brother Shimei was second to him. [13]Conaniah and his brother Shimei were over these supervisors: Jehiel, Azaziah, Nahath, Asahel, Jerimoth, Jozabad, Eliel, Ismakiah, Mahath, and Benaiah. King Hezekiah and Azariah the officer in charge of the Temple of God had chosen them.

[14]Kore son of Imnah the Levite was in charge of the special gifts the people wanted to give to God. He was responsible for giving out the contributions made to the LORD and the holy gifts. Kore was the guard at the East Gate. [15]Eden, Miniamin, Jeshua, Shemaiah, Amariah, and Shecaniah helped Kore in the towns where the priests lived. They gave from what was collected to the other groups of priests, both young and old.

[16]From what was collected, these men also gave to the males three years old and older who had their names in the Levite family histories. They were to enter the Temple of the LORD for their daily service, each group having its own responsibilities. [17]The priests were given their part of the collection, by families, as listed in the family histories. The Levites twenty years old and older were given their part of the collection, based on their responsibilities and their groups. [18]The Levites' babies, wives, sons, and daughters also got part of the collection. This was done for all the Levites who were listed in the family histories, because they always kept themselves ready to serve the LORD.

[19]Some of Aaron's descendants, the priests, lived on the farmlands near the towns or in the towns. Men were chosen by name to give part of the collection to these priests. All the males and those named in the family histories of the Levites received part of the collection.

[20]This is what King Hezekiah did in Judah. He did what was good and right and obedient before the LORD his God. [21]Hezekiah tried to obey God in his service of the Temple of God, and he tried to obey God's teachings and commands. He gave himself fully to his work for God. So he had success.

ASSYRIA ATTACKS JUDAH

32 After Hezekiah did all these things to serve the LORD, Sennacherib king of Assyria came and attacked Judah. He and his army surrounded and attacked the strong, walled cities, hoping to take them for himself. [2]Hezekiah knew that Sennacherib had come to Jerusalem to attack it. [3]So Hezekiah and his officers and army commanders decided to cut off the water from the springs outside the city. So the officers and commanders helped Hezekiah. [4]Many people came and cut off all the springs and the stream that flowed through the land. They said, "The king of Assyria will not find much water when he comes here." [5]Then Hezekiah made Jerusalem stronger. He rebuilt all the broken parts of the wall and put towers on it. He also built another wall outside the first one and strengthened the area that was filled in on the east side of the old part of Jerusalem. He also made many weapons and shields.

[6]Hezekiah put army commanders over the people and met with them at the open place near the city gate. Hezekiah encouraged them, saying, [7]"Be strong and brave. Don't be afraid or worried because of the king of Assyria or his large army. There is a greater power with us than with him. [8]He only has men, but we have the LORD our God to help us and to fight our battles." The people were encouraged by the words of Hezekiah king of Judah.

[9]After this King Sennacherib of Assyria and all his army surrounded and attacked Lachish. Then he sent his officers to Jerusalem with this message for King Hezekiah of Judah and all the people of Judah in Jerusalem:

[10]Sennacherib king of Assyria says this: "You have nothing to trust in to help you. It is no use for you to stay in Jerusalem under attack. [11]Hezekiah says to you, 'The LORD our God will save us from the king of Assyria,' but he is fooling you. If you stay in Jerusalem, you will die from hunger and thirst. [12]Hezekiah himself removed your LORD's places of worship and altars. He told you people of Judah and Jerusalem that you must worship and burn incense on only one altar.

[13]"You know what my ancestors and I have done to all the people in other nations. The gods of those nations could not save their people from my power. [14]My ancestors destroyed those nations; none

of their gods could save them from me. So your god cannot save you from my power. [15]Do not let Hezekiah fool you or trick you, and do not believe him. No god of any nation or kingdom has been able to save his people from me or my ancestors. Your god is even less able to save you from me."

[16]Sennacherib's officers said worse things against the LORD God and his servant Hezekiah. [17]King Sennacherib also wrote letters insulting the LORD, the God of Israel. They spoke against him, saying, "The gods of the other nations could not save their people from me. In the same way Hezekiah's god won't be able to save his people from me." [18]Then the king's officers shouted in Hebrew, calling out to the people of Jerusalem who were on the city wall. The officers wanted to scare the people away so they could capture Jerusalem. [19]They spoke about the God of Jerusalem as though he were like the gods the people of the world worshiped, which are made by human hands.

[20]King Hezekiah and the prophet Isaiah son of Amoz prayed to heaven about this. [21]Then the LORD sent an angel who killed all the soldiers, leaders, and officers in the camp of the king of Assyria. So the king went back to his own country in disgrace. When he went into the temple of his god, some of his own sons killed him with a sword.

[22]So the LORD saved Hezekiah and the people in Jerusalem from Sennacherib king of Assyria and from all other people. He took care of them on every side. [23]Many people brought gifts for the LORD to Jerusalem, and they also brought valuable gifts to King Hezekiah of Judah. From then on all the nations respected Hezekiah.

HEZEKIAH DIES

[24]At that time Hezekiah became so sick he almost died. When he prayed to the LORD, the LORD spoke to him and gave him a sign.[n] [25]But Hezekiah did not thank God for his kindness, because he was so proud. So the LORD was angry with him and the people of Judah and Jerusalem. [26]But later Hezekiah and the people of Jerusalem were sorry and stopped being proud, so the LORD did not punish them while Hezekiah was alive.

[27]Hezekiah had many riches and much honor. He made treasuries for his silver,

gold, gems, spices, shields, and other valuable things. [28]He built storage buildings for grain, new wine, and oil and stalls for all the cattle and pens for the sheep. [29]He also built many towns. He had many flocks and herds, because God had given Hezekiah much wealth.

[30]It was Hezekiah who cut off the upper pool of the Gihon spring and made those waters flow straight down to the west side of the older part of Jerusalem. And Hezekiah was successful in everything he did. [31]But one time the leaders of Babylon sent messengers to Hezekiah, asking him about a strange sign that had happened in the land. When they came, God left Hezekiah alone to test him so he could know everything that was in Hezekiah's heart.[n]

[32]Hezekiah's love for God and the other things he did as king are written in the vision of the prophet Isaiah son of Amoz. This is in the book of the kings of Judah and Israel. [33]Hezekiah died and was buried on a hill, where the graves of David's ancestors are. All the people of Judah and Jerusalem honored Hezekiah when he died, and his son Manasseh became king in his place.

MANASSEH KING OF JUDAH

33 Manasseh was twelve years old when he became king, and he was king for fifty-five years in Jerusalem. [2]He did what the LORD said was wrong. He did the hateful things the nations had done—the nations that the LORD had forced out of the land ahead of the Israelites. [3]Manasseh's father, Hezekiah, had torn down the places where gods were worshiped, but Manasseh rebuilt them. He also built altars for the Baal gods, and he made Asherah idols and worshiped all the stars of the sky and served them. [4]The LORD had said about the Temple, "I will be worshiped in Jerusalem forever," but Manasseh built altars in the Temple of the LORD. [5]He built altars to worship the stars in the two courtyards of the Temple of the LORD. [6]He made his children pass through fire in the Valley of Ben Hinnom. He practiced magic and witchcraft and told the future by explaining

---

32:24 sign See Isaiah 38:1–8. It tells the story about the sign and how the Lord gave Hezekiah fifteen more years to live. **32:31 God . . . heart** See 2 Kings 20:12–19.

signs and dreams. He got advice from mediums and fortune-tellers. He did many things the LORD said were wrong, which made the LORD angry.

7Manasseh carved an idol and put it in the Temple of God. God had said to David and his son Solomon about the Temple, "I will be worshiped forever in this Temple and in Jerusalem, which I have chosen from all the tribes of Israel. 8I will never again make the Israelites leave the land I gave to their ancestors. But they must obey everything I have commanded them in all the teachings, rules, and commands I gave them through Moses." 9But Manasseh led the people of Judah and Jerusalem to do wrong. They did more evil than the nations the LORD had destroyed ahead of the Israelites.

10The LORD spoke to Manasseh and his people, but they did not listen. 11So the LORD brought the king of Assyria's army commanders to attack Judah. They captured Manasseh, put hooks in him, placed bronze chains on his hands, and took him to Babylon. 12As Manasseh suffered, he begged the LORD his God for help and humbled himself before the God of his ancestors. 13When Manasseh prayed, the LORD heard him and had pity on him. So the LORD let him return to Jerusalem and to his kingdom. Then Manasseh knew that the LORD is the true God.

14After that happened, Manasseh rebuilt the outer wall of Jerusalem and made it higher. It was in the valley on the west side of the Gihon spring and went to the entrance of the Fish Gate and around the hill of Ophel. Then he put commanders in all the strong, walled cities in Judah.

15Manasseh removed the idols of other nations, including the idol in the Temple of the LORD. He removed all the altars he had built on the Temple hill and in Jerusalem and threw them out of the city. 16Then he set up the LORD's altar and sacrificed on it fellowship offerings and offerings to show thanks to God. Manasseh commanded all the people of Judah to serve the LORD, the God of Israel. 17The people continued to offer sacrifices at the places of worship, but their sacrifices were only to the LORD their God. 18The other things Manasseh did as king, his prayer to his God, and what the seers said to him in the name of the LORD, the God of Israel—all

are recorded in the book of the history of the kings of Israel. 19Manasseh's prayer and God's pity for him, his sins, his unfaithfulness, the places he built for worshiping gods and the Asherah idols before he humbled himself—all are written in the book of the seers. 20Manasseh died and was buried in his palace. Then Manasseh's son Amon became king in his place.

AMON KING OF JUDAH

21Amon was twenty-two years old when he became king, and he was king for two years in Jerusalem. 22He did what the LORD said was wrong, as his father Manasseh had done. Amon worshiped and offered sacrifices to all the carved idols Manasseh had made. 23Amon did not humble himself before the LORD as his father Manasseh had done. Instead, Amon sinned even more.

24King Amon's officers made plans against him and killed him in his palace. 25Then the people of the land killed all those who had made plans to kill King Amon, and they made his son Josiah king in his place.

JOSIAH KING OF JUDAH

34 Josiah was eight years old when he became king, and he ruled thirty-one years in Jerusalem. 2He did what the LORD said was right. He lived as his ancestor David had lived, and he did not stop doing what was right.

3In his eighth year as king while he was still young, Josiah began to obey the God of his ancestor David. In his twelfth year as king, Josiah began to remove from Judah and Jerusalem the gods, the places for worshiping gods, the Asherah idols, and the wooden and metal idols. 4The people tore down the altars for the Baal gods as Josiah directed. Then Josiah cut down the incense altars that were above them. He broke up the Asherah idols and the wooden and metal idols and beat them into powder. Then he sprinkled the powder on the graves of the people who had offered sacrifices to these gods. 5He burned the bones of their priests on their own altars. So Josiah removed idol worship from Judah and Jerusalem, 6and from the towns in the areas of Manasseh, Ephraim, and Simeon all the way to Naphtali, and in the ruins near these towns. 7Josiah broke down the altars and Asherah idols and beat the idols into powder. He cut down all the incense altars in all of Israel. Then he went back to Jerusalem.

⁸In Josiah's eighteenth year as king, he made Judah and the Temple pure again. He sent Shaphan son of Azaliah, Maaseiah the city leader, and Joah son of Joahaz the recorder to repair the Temple of the LORD, the God of Josiah. ⁹These men went to Hilkiah the high priest and gave him the money the Levite gatekeepers had gathered from the people of Manasseh, Ephraim, and all the Israelites who were left alive, and also from all the people of Judah, Benjamin, and Jerusalem. This is the money they had brought into the Temple of God. ¹⁰Then the Levites gave it to the supervisors of the work on the Temple of the LORD, and they paid the workers who rebuilt and repaired the Temple. ¹¹They gave money to carpenters and builders to buy cut stone and wood. The wood was used to rebuild the buildings and to make beams for them, because the kings of Judah had let the buildings fall into ruin. ¹²The men did their work well. Their supervisors were Jahath and Obadiah, who were Levites from the family of Merari, and Zechariah and Meshullam, who were from the family of Kohath. These Levites were all skilled musicians. ¹³They were also in charge of the workers who carried loads and all the other workers. Some Levites worked as secretaries, officers, and gatekeepers.

THE BOOK OF THE TEACHINGS IS FOUND

¹⁴The Levites brought out the money that was in the Temple of the LORD. As they were doing this, Hilkiah the priest found the Book of the LORD's Teachings that had been given through Moses. ¹⁵Hilkiah said to Shaphan the royal secretary, "I've found the Book of the Teachings in the Temple of the LORD!" Then he gave it to Shaphan.

¹⁶Shaphan took the book to the king and reported to Josiah, "Your officers are doing everything you told them to do. ¹⁷They have paid out the money that was in the Temple of the LORD and have given it to the supervisors and the workers." ¹⁸Then Shaphan the royal secretary told the king, "Hilkiah the priest has given me a book." And Shaphan read from the book to the king.

¹⁹When the king heard the words of the Teachings, he tore his clothes to show how upset he was. ²⁰He gave orders to Hilkiah, Ahikam son of Shaphan, Acbor son of Micaiah, Shaphan the royal secretary, and Asaiah, the king's servant. These were the orders: ²¹"Go and ask the LORD about the words in the book that was found. Ask for me and for the people who are left alive in Israel and Judah. The LORD is very angry with us, because our ancestors did not obey the LORD's word; they did not do everything this book says to do."

²²So Hilkiah and those the king sent with him went to talk to Huldah the prophetess. She was the wife of Shallum son of Tikvah, the son of Harhas, who took care of the king's clothes. Huldah lived in Jerusalem, in the new area of the city.

²³She said to them, "This is what the LORD, the God of Israel, says: Tell the man who sent you to me, ²⁴'This is what the LORD says: I will bring trouble to this place and to the people living here. I will bring all the curses that are written in the book that was read to the king of Judah. ²⁵The people of Judah have left me and have burned incense to other gods. They have made me angry by all the evil things they have made. So I will punish them in my anger, which will not be put out.' ²⁶Tell the king of Judah, who sent you to ask the LORD, 'This is what the LORD, the God of Israel, says about the words you heard: ²⁷When you heard my words against this place and its people, you became sorry for what you had done and you humbled yourself before me. You tore your clothes to show how upset you were, and you cried in my presence. This is why I have heard you, says the LORD. ²⁸So I will let you die and be buried in peace. You won't see all the trouble I will bring to this place and the people living here.'"

So they took her message back to the king.

²⁹Then the king gathered all the elders of Judah and Jerusalem together. ³⁰He went up to the Temple of the LORD, and all the people from Judah and from Jerusalem went with him. The priests, the Levites, and all the people—from the most important to the least important—went with him. He read to them all the words in the Book of the Agreement that was found in the Temple of the LORD.

³¹The king stood by his pillar and made an agreement in the presence of the LORD to follow the LORD and obey his commands, rules, and laws with his whole being and to obey the words of the agreement written in this book. ³²Then Josiah made all the people in Jerusalem and Benjamin promise to accept the agreement. So the people of Jerusalem obeyed the agreement of God, the God of their ancestors.

³³And Josiah threw out the hateful idols from all the land that belonged to the Israelites. He led everyone in Israel to serve the LORD their God. While Josiah lived, the people obeyed the LORD, the God of their ancestors.

JOSIAH CELEBRATES THE PASSOVER

35 King Josiah celebrated the Passover to the LORD in Jerusalem. The Passover lamb was killed on the fourteenth day of the first month. ²Josiah chose the priests to do their duties, and he encouraged them as they served in the Temple of the LORD. ³The Levites taught the Israelites and were made holy for service to the LORD. Josiah said to them, "Put the Holy Ark in the Temple that David's son Solomon, the king of Israel, built. Do not carry it from place to place on your shoulders anymore. Now serve the LORD your God and his people Israel. ⁴Prepare yourselves by your family groups for service, and do the jobs that King David and his son Solomon gave you to do.

⁵"Stand in the holy place with a group of the Levites for each family group of the people. ⁶Kill the Passover lambs, and make yourselves holy to the LORD. Prepare the lambs for your relatives, the people of Israel, as the LORD through Moses commanded us to do."

⁷Josiah gave the Israelites thirty thousand sheep and goats to kill for the Passover sacrifices, and he gave them three thousand cattle. They were all his own animals.

⁸Josiah's officers also gave willingly to the people, the priests, and the Levites. Hilkiah, Zechariah, and Jehiel, the officers in charge of the Temple, gave the priests twenty-six hundred lambs and goats and three hundred cattle for Passover sacrifices. ⁹Conaniah, his brothers Shemaiah and Nethanel, and Hashabiah, Jeiel, and Jozabad gave the Levites five thousand sheep and goats and five hundred cattle for Passover sacrifices. These men were leaders of the Levites.

¹⁰When everything was ready for the Passover service, the priests and Levites went to their places, as the king had commanded. ¹¹The Passover lambs were killed. Then the Levites skinned the animals and gave the blood to the priests, who sprinkled it on the altar. ¹²Then they gave the animals for the burnt offerings to the different family groups so the burnt offerings could be offered to the LORD as was written in the book of Moses. They also did this with the cattle. ¹³The Levites roasted the Passover sacrifices over the fire as they were commanded, and they boiled the holy offerings in pots, kettles, and pans. Then they quickly gave the meat to the people. ¹⁴After this was finished, the Levites prepared meat for themselves and for the priests, the descendants of Aaron. The priests worked until night, offering the burnt offerings and burning the fat of the sacrifices.

¹⁵The Levite singers from Asaph's family stood in the places chosen for them by King David, Asaph, Heman, and Jeduthun, the king's seer. The gatekeepers at each gate did not have to leave their places, because their fellow Levites had prepared everything for them for the Passover.

¹⁶So everything was done that day for the worship of the LORD, as King Josiah commanded. The Passover was celebrated, and the burnt offerings were offered on the LORD's altar. ¹⁷The Israelites who were there celebrated the Passover and the Feast of Unleavened Bread for seven days. ¹⁸The Passover had not been celebrated like this in Israel since the prophet Samuel was alive. None of the kings of Israel had ever celebrated a Passover like it was celebrated by King Josiah, the priests, the Levites, the people of Judah and Israel who were there, and the people of Jerusalem. ¹⁹This Passover was celebrated in the eighteenth year Josiah was king.

THE DEATH OF JOSIAH

²⁰After Josiah did all this for the Temple, Neco king of Egypt led an army to attack Carchemish, a town on the Euphrates River. And Josiah marched out to fight against Neco. ²¹But Neco sent messengers to Josiah,

saying, "King Josiah, there should not be war between us. I did not come to fight you, but my enemies. God told me to hurry, and he is on my side. So don't fight God, or he will destroy you."

22But Josiah did not go away. He wore different clothes so no one would know who he was. Refusing to listen to what Neco said at God's command, Josiah went to fight on the plain of Megiddo. 23In the battle King Josiah was shot by archers. He told his servants, "Take me away because I am badly wounded." 24So they took him out of his chariot and put him in another chariot and carried him to Jerusalem. There he died and was buried in the graves where his ancestors were buried. All the people of Judah and Jerusalem were very sad because he was dead.

25Jeremiah wrote some sad songs about Josiah. Even to this day all the men and women singers remember and honor Josiah with these songs. It became a custom in Israel to sing these songs that are written in the collection of sad songs.

26-27The other things Josiah did as king, from beginning to end, are written in the book of the kings of Israel and Judah. It tells how he loved what was written in the LORD's teachings.

JEHOAHAZ KING OF JUDAH

36 The people of Judah chose Josiah's son Jehoahaz and made him king in Jerusalem in his father's place.

2Jehoahaz was twenty-three years old when he became king, and he was king in Jerusalem for three months. 3Then King Neco of Egypt removed Jehoahaz from being king in Jerusalem. Neco made the people of Judah pay about seventy-five hundred pounds of silver and about seventy-five pounds of gold. 4The king of Egypt made Jehoahaz's brother Eliakim the king of Judah and Jerusalem and changed his name to Jehoiakim. But Neco took his brother Jehoahaz to Egypt.

JEHOIAKIM KING OF JUDAH

5Jehoiakim was twenty-five years old when he became king, and he was king in Jerusalem for eleven years. He did what the LORD his God said was wrong. 6King Nebuchadnezzar of Babylon attacked Judah, captured Jehoiakim, put bronze chains on him, and took him to Babylon. 7Nebuchadnezzar removed some of the things from the Temple of the LORD, took them to Babylon, and put them in his own palace.

8The other things Jehoiakim did as king, the hateful things he did, and everything he was guilty of doing, are written in the book of the kings of Israel and Judah. And Jehoiakim's son Jehoiachin became king in his place.

JEHOIACHIN KING OF JUDAH

9Jehoiachin was eighteen years old when he became king of Judah, and he was king in Jerusalem for three months and ten days. He did what the LORD said was wrong. 10In the spring King Nebuchadnezzar sent for Jehoiachin and brought him and some valuable treasures from the Temple of the LORD to Babylon. Then Nebuchadnezzar made Jehoiachin's uncle Zedekiah the king of Judah and Jerusalem.

ZEDEKIAH KING OF JUDAH

11Zedekiah was twenty-one years old when he became king of Judah, and he was king in Jerusalem for eleven years. 12Zedekiah did what the LORD his God said was wrong. The prophet Jeremiah spoke messages from the LORD, but Zedekiah did not obey. 13Zedekiah turned against King Nebuchadnezzar, who had forced him to swear in God's name to be loyal to him. But Zedekiah became stubborn and refused to obey the LORD, the God of Israel. 14Also, all the leaders of the priests and the people of Judah became more wicked, following the evil example of the other nations. The LORD had made the Temple in Jerusalem holy, but the leaders made it unholy.

THE FALL OF JERUSALEM

15The LORD, the God of their ancestors, sent prophets again and again to warn his people, because he had pity on them and on his Temple. 16But they made fun of God's prophets and hated God's messages. They refused to listen to the prophets until, finally, the LORD became so angry with his people that he could not be stopped. 17So God brought the king of Babylon to attack them. The king killed the young men even when they were in the Temple. He had no mercy on the young men or women, the old men or those who were sick. God handed all of them over to Nebuchadnezzar. [18]Nebuchadnezzar carried away to Babylon all the things from the Temple of God, both large and small, and all the treasures from the Temple of the LORD and from the king and his officers. [19]Nebuchadnezzar and his army set fire to God's Temple and broke down Jerusalem's wall and burned all the palaces. They took or destroyed every valuable thing in Jerusalem. [20]Nebuchadnezzar took captive to Babylon the people who were left alive, and he forced them to be slaves for him and his descendants. They remained there as slaves until the Persian kingdom defeated Babylon. [21]And so what the LORD had told Israel through the prophet Jeremiah happened: The country was an empty wasteland for seventy years to make up for the years of Sabbath rest[n] that the people had not kept.

[22]In the first year Cyrus was king of Persia, the LORD had Cyrus send an announcement to his whole kingdom. This happened so the LORD's message spoken by Jeremiah would come true. He wrote:

[23]This is what Cyrus king of Persia says:

The LORD, the God of heaven, has given me all the kingdoms of the earth, and he has appointed me to build a Temple for him at Jerusalem in Judah. Now may the LORD your God be with all of you who are his people. You are free to go to Jerusalem.

36:21 Sabbath rest The law said that every seventh year the land was not to be farmed. See Leviticus 25:1–7.

ezra

THE RETURN FROM CAPTIVITY

CYRUS HELPS THE CAPTIVES RETURN

1 In the first year Cyrus was king of Persia, the LORD caused Cyrus to send an announcement to his whole kingdom and to put it in writing. This happened so the LORD's message spoken by Jeremiah would come true. He wrote:

²This is what Cyrus king of Persia says:

The LORD, the God of heaven, has given all the kingdoms of the earth to me, and he has appointed me to build a Temple for him at Jerusalem in Judah. ³May God be with all of you who are his people. You are free to go to Jerusalem in Judah and build the Temple of the LORD, the God of Israel, who is in Jerusalem. ⁴Those who stay behind, wherever they live, should support those who want to go. Give them silver and gold, supplies and cattle, and special gifts for the Temple of God in Jerusalem.

⁵Then the family leaders of Judah and Benjamin and the priests and Levites got ready to go to Jerusalem—everyone God had caused to want to go to Jerusalem to build the Temple of the LORD. ⁶All their neighbors helped them, giving them things made of silver and gold, along with supplies, cattle, valuable gifts, and special gifts for the Temple. ⁷Also, King Cyrus brought out the bowls and pans that belonged in the Temple of the LORD, which Nebuchadnezzar had taken from Jerusalem and put in the temple of his own god. ⁸Cyrus king of Persia had Mithredath the treasurer bring them and count them out for Sheshbazzar, the prince of Judah.

⁹He listed thirty gold dishes, one thousand silver dishes, twenty-nine pans, ¹⁰thirty gold bowls, four hundred ten matching silver bowls, and one thousand other pieces. ¹¹There was a total of fifty-four hundred pieces of gold and silver. Sheshbazzar brought all these things along when the captives went from Babylon to Jerusalem.

THE CAPTIVES WHO RETURNED

2 These are the people of the area who returned from captivity, whom Nebuchadnezzar king of Babylon had taken away to Babylon. They returned to Jerusalem and Judah, each going back to his own town. ²These people returned with Zerubbabel, Jeshua, Nehemiah, Seraiah, Reelaiah, Mordecai, Bilshan, Mispar, Bigvai, Rehum, and Baanah.

These are the people from Israel: ³the descendants of Parosh—2,172; ⁴the descendants of Shephatiah—372; ⁵the descendants of Arah—775; ⁶the descendants of Pahath-Moab (through the family of Jeshua and Joab)—2,812; ⁷the descendants of Elam—1,254; ⁸the descendants of Zattu—945; ⁹the descendants of Zaccai—760; ¹⁰the descendants of Bani—642; ¹¹the descendants of Bebai—623; ¹²the descendants of Azgad—1,222; ¹³the descendants of Adonikam—666; ¹⁴the descendants of Bigvai—2,056; ¹⁵the descendants of Adin—454; ¹⁶the descendants of Ater (through the family of Hezekiah)—98; ¹⁷the descendants of Bezai—323; ¹⁸the descendants of Jorah—112; ¹⁹the descendants of Hashum—223; ²⁰the descendants of Gibbar—95.

²¹These are the people from the towns: of Bethlehem—123; ²²of Netophah—56; ²³of Anathoth—128; ²⁴of Azmaveth—42; ²⁵of Kiriath Jearim, Kephirah, and Beeroth—743; ²⁶of Ramah and Geba—621; ²⁷of Micmash—122; ²⁸of Bethel and Ai—223; ²⁹of Nebo—52; ³⁰of Magbish—156; ³¹of the other town of Elam—1,254; ³²of Harim—320; ³³of Lod, Hadid and Ono—725; ³⁴of Jericho—345; ³⁵of Senaah—3,630.

³⁶These are the priests: the descendants of Jedaiah (through the family of Jeshua)—973; ³⁷the descendants of Immer—1,052; ³⁸the descendants of Pashhur—1,247; ³⁹the descendants of Harim—1,017.

⁴⁰These are the Levites: the descendants of Jeshua and Kadmiel (through the family of Hodaviah)—74.

⁴¹These are the singers: the descendants of Asaph—128.

⁴²These are the gatekeepers of the Temple: the descendants of Shallum, Ater, Talmon, Akkub, Hatita, and Shobai—139.

⁴³These are the Temple servants: the descendants of Ziha, Hasupha, Tabbaoth, ⁴⁴Keros, Siaha, Padon, ⁴⁵Lebanah, Hagabah, Akkub, ⁴⁶Hagab, Shalmai, Hanan, ⁴⁷Giddel, Gahar, Reaiah, ⁴⁸Rezin, Nekoda, Gazzam, ⁴⁹Uzza, Paseah, Besai, ⁵⁰Asnah, Meunim, Nephussim, ⁵¹Bakbuk, Hakupha, Harhur, ⁵²Bazluth, Mehida, Harsha, ⁵³Barkos, Sisera, Temah, ⁵⁴Neziah, and Hatipha.

⁵⁵These are the descendants of the servants of Solomon: the descendants of Sotai, Hassophereth, Peruda, ⁵⁶Jaala, Darkon, Giddel, ⁵⁷Shephatiah, Hattil, Pokereth-Hazzebaim, and Ami.

⁵⁸The Temple servants and the descendants of the servants of Solomon numbered 392.

⁵⁹Some people came to Jerusalem from the towns of Tel Melah, Tel Harsha, Kerub, Addon, and Immer, but they could not prove that their ancestors came from Israel. ⁶⁰They were the descendants of Delaiah, Tobiah, and Nekoda—652.

⁶¹Also these priests: the descendants of Hobaiah, Hakkoz, and Barzillai, who had married a daughter of Barzillai from Gilead and was called by her family name.

⁶²These people searched for their family records but could not find them. So they could not be priests, because they were thought to be unclean. ⁶³The governor ordered them not to eat any of the food offered to God until a priest had settled this matter by using the Urim and Thummim.

⁶⁴The total number of those who returned was 42,360. ⁶⁵This is not counting their 7,337 male and female servants and the 200 male and female singers they had with them. ⁶⁶They had 736 horses, 245 mules, ⁶⁷435 camels, and 6,720 donkeys.

⁶⁸When they arrived at the Temple of the LORD in Jerusalem, some of the leaders of families gave offerings to rebuild the Temple of God on the same site as before. ⁶⁹They gave as much as they could to the treasury to rebuild the Temple—about 1,100 pounds of gold, about 6,000 pounds of silver, and 100 pieces of clothing for the priests.

⁷⁰All the Israelites settled in their hometowns. The priests, Levites, singers, gatekeepers, and Temple servants, along with some of the other people, settled in their own towns as well.

REBUILDING THE ALTAR

3 In the seventh month, after the Israelites were settled in their hometowns, they met together in Jerusalem. ²Then Jeshua son of Jozadak and his fellow priests joined Zerubbabel son of Shealtiel and began to build the altar of the God of Israel where they could offer burnt offerings, just as it is written in the Teachings of Moses, the man of God. ³Even though they were afraid of the people living around them, they built the altar where it had been before. And they offered burnt offerings on it to the LORD morning and evening. ⁴Then, to obey what was written, they celebrated the Feast of Shelters. They offered the right number of sacrifices for each day of the festival. ⁵After the Feast of Shelters, they had regular sacrifices every day, as well as sacrifices for the New Moon and all the festivals commanded by the LORD. Also there were special offerings brought as gifts to the LORD. ⁶On the first day of the seventh month they began to bring burnt offerings to the LORD, but the foundation of the LORD's Temple had not yet been laid.

REBUILDING THE TEMPLE

⁷Then they gave money to the bricklayers and carpenters. They also gave food, wine, and oil to the cities of Sidon and Tyre so they would float cedar logs from Lebanon to the seacoast town of Joppa. Cyrus king of Persia had given permission for this.

⁸In the second month of the second year after their arrival at the Temple of God in Jerusalem, Zerubbabel son of Shealtiel, Jeshua son of Jozadak, their fellow priests and Levites, and all who had returned from captivity to Jerusalem began to work. They chose Levites twenty years old and older to be in charge of the building of the Temple of the LORD. ⁹These men were in charge of the work of building the Temple of God: Jeshua and his sons and brothers; Kadmiel and his sons who were the descendants of Hodaviah; and the sons of Henadad and their sons and brothers. They were all Levites.

¹⁰The builders finished laying the foundation of the Temple of the LORD. Then the priests, dressed in their robes, stood with their trumpets, and the Levites, the sons of Asaph, stood with their cymbals. They all took their places and praised the LORD just as David king of Israel had said to do. ¹¹With praise and thanksgiving, they sang to the LORD:

"He is good;

his love for Israel continues forever."
And then all the people shouted loudly, "Praise the LORD! The foundation of his Temple has been laid." ¹²But many of the older priests, Levites, and family leaders who had seen the first Temple cried when they saw the foundation of this Temple. Most of the other people were shouting with joy. ¹³The people made so much noise it could be heard far away, and no one could tell the difference between the joyful shouting and the sad crying.

ENEMIES OF THE REBUILDING

4 When the enemies of the people of Judah and Benjamin heard that the returned captives were building a Temple for the LORD, the God of Israel, ²they came to Zerubbabel and the leaders of the families. The enemies said, "Let us help you build, because we are like you and want to worship your God. We have been offering sacrifices to him since the time of Esarhaddon king of Assyria, who brought us here."

³But Zerubbabel, Jeshua, and the leaders of Israel answered, "You will not help us build a Temple to our God. We will build it ourselves for the LORD, the God of Israel, as King Cyrus, the king of Persia, commanded us to do."

⁴Then the people around them tried to discourage the people of Judah by making them afraid to build. ⁵Their enemies hired others to delay the building plans during the time Cyrus was king of Persia. And it continued to the time Darius was king of Persia.

MORE PROBLEMS FOR THE BUILDERS

⁶When Xerxes first became king, those enemies wrote a letter against the people of Judah and Jerusalem.

⁷When Artaxerxes became king of Persia, Bishlam, Mithredath, Tabeel, and those with them wrote a letter to Artaxerxes. It was written in the Aramaic language and translated.

⁸Rehum the governor and Shimshai the governor's secretary wrote a letter against Jerusalem to Artaxerxes the king. It said:

⁹This letter is from Rehum the governor, Shimshai the secretary, and their fellow workers—the judges and important officers over the men who came from Tripolis, Persia, Erech, and Babylon, the Elamite people of Susa, ¹⁰and those whom the great and honorable Ashurbanipal forced out of their countries and settled in the city of Samaria and in other places of the Trans-Euphrates.

¹¹(This is a copy of the letter they sent to Artaxerxes.)

To King Artaxerxes.
From your servants who live in Trans-Euphrates.

¹²King Artaxerxes, you should know that the Jewish people who came to us from you have gone to Jerusalem to rebuild that evil city that refuses to obey. They are fixing the walls and repairing the foundations of the buildings.

¹³Now, King Artaxerxes, you should know that if Jerusalem is built and its walls are fixed, Jerusalem will not pay taxes of any kind. Then the amount of money your government collects will be less. ¹⁴Since we must be loyal to the government, we don't want to see the king dishonored. So we are writing to let the king know. ¹⁵We suggest you search the records of the kings who ruled before you. You will find out that the city of Jerusalem refuses to obey and makes trouble for kings and areas controlled by Persia. Since long ago it has been a place where disobedience has started. That is why it was destroyed. ¹⁶We want you to know, King Artaxerxes, that if this city is rebuilt and its walls fixed, you will be left with nothing in Trans-Euphrates.

¹⁷King Artaxerxes sent this answer:

To Rehum the governor and Shimshai the secretary, to all their fellow workers living in Samaria, and to those in other places in Trans-Euphrates.

Greetings.

[18]The letter you sent to us has been translated and read to me. [19]I ordered the records to be searched, and it was done. We found that Jerusalem has a history of disobedience to kings and has been a place of problems and trouble. [20]Jerusalem has had powerful kings who have ruled over the whole area of Trans-Euphrates, and taxes of all kinds have been paid to them. [21]Now, give an order for those men to stop work. The city of Jerusalem will not be rebuilt until I say so. [22]Make sure you do this, because if they continue, it will hurt the government.

[23]A copy of the letter that King Artaxerxes sent was read to Rehum and Shimshai the secretary and the others. Then they quickly went to the Jewish people in Jerusalem and forced them to stop building.

[24]So the work on the Temple of God in Jerusalem stopped until the second year Darius was king of Persia.

TATTENAI'S LETTER TO DARIUS

5 The prophets Haggai and Zechariah, a descendant of Iddo, prophesied to the Jewish people in Judah and Jerusalem in the name of the God of Israel, who was over them. [2]Then Zerubbabel son of Shealtiel and Jeshua son of Jozadak started working again to rebuild the Temple of God in Jerusalem. And the prophets of God were there, helping them.

[3]At that time Tattenai, the governor of Trans-Euphrates, and Shethar-Bozenai, and their fellow workers went to the Jewish people and asked, "Who gave you permission to rebuild this Temple and fix these walls?" [4]They also asked, "What are the names of the men working on this building?" [5]But their God was watching over the elders of the Jewish people. The builders were not stopped until a report could go to King Darius and his written answer could be received.

[6]This is a copy of the letter that was sent to King Darius by Tattenai, the governor of Trans-Euphrates, Shethar-Bozenai, and the other important officers of Trans-Euphrates. [7]This is what was said in the report they sent to him:

To King Darius.

Greetings. May you have peace.

[8]King Darius, you should know that we went to the district of Judah where the Temple of the great God is. The people are building that Temple with large stones, and they are putting timbers in the walls. They are working very hard and are building very fast.

[9]We asked their elders, "Who gave you permission to rebuild this Temple and these walls?" [10]We also asked for their names, and we wrote down the names of their leaders so you would know who they are.

[11]This is the answer they gave to us: "We are the servants of the God of heaven and earth. We are rebuilding the Temple that a great king of Israel built and finished many years ago. [12]But our ancestors made the God of heaven angry, so he handed them over to Nebuchadnezzar king of Babylon, who destroyed this Temple and took the people to Babylon as captives.

[13]"Later, in the first year Cyrus was king of Babylon, he gave a special order for this Temple to be rebuilt. [14]Cyrus brought out from the temple in Babylon the gold and silver bowls and pans that came from the Temple of God. Nebuchadnezzar had taken them from the Temple in Jerusalem and had put them in the temple in Babylon.

"Then King Cyrus gave them to Sheshbazzar, his appointed governor. [15]Cyrus said to him, 'Take these gold and silver bowls and pans, and put them back in the Temple in Jerusalem and rebuild the Temple of God where it was.' [16]So Sheshbazzar came and laid the foundations of the Temple of God in Jerusalem. From that day until now the work has been going on, but it is not yet finished."

[17]Now, if the king wishes, let a search be made in the royal records of Babylon. See if King Cyrus gave an order to rebuild this Temple in Jerusalem. Then let the king write us and tell us what he has decided.

THE ORDER OF DARIUS

6 So King Darius gave an order to search the records kept in the treasury in Babylon. [2]A scroll was found in Ecbatana, the capital city of Media. This is what was written on it:

Note:

[3]King Cyrus gave an order about the Temple of God in Jerusalem in the first year he was king. This was the order:

"Let the Temple be rebuilt as a place to present sacrifices. Let its foundations be laid; it should be ninety feet high and ninety feet wide. [4]It must have three layers of large stones and then one layer of timbers. The costs should be paid from the king's treasury. [5]The gold and silver utensils from the Temple of God should be put back in their places. Nebuchadnezzar took them from the Temple in Jerusalem and brought them to Babylon, but they are to be put back in the Temple of God in Jerusalem."

[6]Now then, Tattenai, governor of Trans-Euphrates, Shethar-Bozenai, and all the officers of that area, stay away from there. [7]Do not bother the work on that Temple of God. Let the governor of the Jewish people and the Jewish elders rebuild this Temple where it was before.

[8]Also, I order you to do this for those elders of the Jewish people who are building this Temple: The cost of the building is to be fully paid from the royal treasury, from taxes collected from Trans-Euphrates. Do this so the work will not stop. [9]Give those people anything they need—young bulls, male sheep, or lambs for burnt offerings to the God of heaven, or wheat, salt, wine, or olive oil. Give the priests in Jerusalem anything they ask for every day without fail. [10]Then they may offer sacrifices pleasing to the God of heaven, and they may pray for the life of the king and his sons.

[11]Also, I give this order: If anyone changes this order, a wood beam is to be pulled from his house and driven through his body. Because of his crime, make his house a pile of ruins. [12]God has chosen Jerusalem as the place he is to be worshiped. May he punish any king or person who tries to change this order and destroy this Temple.

I, Darius, have given this order. Let it be obeyed quickly and carefully.

COMPLETION OF THE TEMPLE

[13]So, Tattenai, the governor of Trans-Euphrates, Shethar-Bozenai, and their fellow workers carried out King Darius' order quickly and carefully. [14]The Jewish elders continued to build and were successful because of the preaching of Haggai the prophet and Zechariah, a descendant of Iddo. They finished building the Temple as the God of Israel had commanded and as kings Cyrus, Darius, and Artaxerxes of Persia had ordered. [15]The Temple was finished on the third day of the month of Adar in the sixth year Darius was king.

[16]Then the people of Israel celebrated and gave the Temple to God to honor him. Everybody was happy: the priests, the Levites, and the rest of the Jewish people who had returned from captivity. [17]They gave the Temple to God by offering a hundred bulls, two hundred male sheep, and four hundred lambs as sacrifices. And as an offering to forgive the sins of all Israel, they offered twelve male goats, one goat for each tribe in Israel. [18]Then they put the priests and the Levites into their separate groups. Each group had a certain time to serve God in the Temple at Jerusalem as it is written in the Book of Moses.

THE PASSOVER IS CELEBRATED

[19]The Jewish people who returned from captivity celebrated the Passover on the fourteenth day of the first month. [20]The priests and Levites had made themselves clean. Then the Levites killed the Passover lambs for all the people who had returned from captivity, for their relatives the priests, and for themselves. [21]So all the people of Israel who returned from captivity ate the Passover lamb. So did the people who had given up the unclean ways of their non-Jewish neighbors in order to worship the Lord, the God of Israel. [22]For seven days they celebrated the Feast of Unleavened Bread in a very joyful way. The Lord had made them happy by changing the mind of the king of Assyria so that he helped them in the work on the Temple of the God of Israel.

EZRA COMES TO JERUSALEM

7 After these things[n] during the rule of Artaxerxes king of Persia, Ezra came up from Babylon. Ezra was the son of Seraiah, the son of Azariah, the son of Hilkiah, ²the son of Shallum, the son of Zadok, the son of Ahitub, ³the son of Amariah, the son of Azariah, the son of Meraioth, ⁴the son of Zerahiah, the son of Uzzi, the son of Bukki, ⁵the son of Abishua, the son of Phinehas, the son of Eleazar, the son of Aaron the high priest. ⁶This Ezra came to Jerusalem from Babylon. He was a teacher and knew well the Teachings of Moses that had been given by the LORD, the God of Israel. Ezra received everything he asked for from the king, because the LORD his God was helping him. ⁷In the seventh year of King Artaxerxes more Israelites came to Jerusalem. Among them were priests, Levites, singers, gatekeepers, and Temple servants.

⁸Ezra arrived in Jerusalem in the fifth month of Artaxerxes' seventh year as king. ⁹Ezra had left Babylon on the first day of the first month, and he arrived in Jerusalem on the first day of the fifth month, because God was helping him. ¹⁰Ezra had worked hard to know and obey the Teachings of the LORD and to teach his rules and commands to the Israelites.

ARTAXERXES' LETTER TO EZRA

¹¹King Artaxerxes had given a letter to Ezra, a priest and teacher who taught about the commands and laws the LORD gave Israel. This is a copy of the letter:

¹²From Artaxerxes, king of kings, to Ezra the priest, a teacher of the Law of the God of heaven.

Greetings.

¹³Now I give this order: Any Israelite in my kingdom who wishes may go with you to Jerusalem, including priests and Levites. ¹⁴Ezra, you are sent by the king and the seven people who advise him to ask how Judah and Jerusalem are obeying the Law of your God, which you are carrying with you. ¹⁵Also take with you the silver and gold that the king and those who advise him have given freely to the God of Israel, whose Temple is in Jerusalem. ¹⁶Also take the silver and gold you receive from the area of Babylon. Take the offerings the Israelites and their priests have given as gifts for the Temple of your God in Jerusalem. ¹⁷With this money buy bulls, male sheep, and lambs, and the grain offerings and drink offerings that go with those sacrifices. Then sacrifice them on the altar in the Temple of your God in Jerusalem.

¹⁸You and your fellow Jews may spend the silver and gold left over as you want and as God wishes. ¹⁹Take to the God of Jerusalem all the utensils for worship in the Temple of your God, ²⁰which we have given you. Use the royal treasury to pay for anything else you need for the Temple of your God.

²¹Now I, King Artaxerxes, give this order to all the men in charge of the treasury of Trans-Euphrates: Give Ezra, a priest and a teacher of the Law of the God of heaven, whatever he asks for. ²²Give him up to seventy-five hundred pounds of silver, six hundred bushels of wheat, six hundred gallons of wine, and six hundred gallons of olive oil. And give him as much salt as he wants. ²³Carefully give him whatever the God of heaven wants for the Temple of the God of heaven. We do not want God to be angry with the king and his sons. ²⁴Remember, you must not make these people pay taxes of any kind: priests, Levites, singers, gatekeepers, Temple servants, and other workers in this Temple of God.

²⁵And you, Ezra, use the wisdom you have from your God to choose judges and lawmakers to rule the Jewish people of Trans-Euphrates. They know the laws of your God, and you may teach anyone who does not know them. ²⁶Whoever does not obey the law of your God or of the king must be punished. He will be killed, or sent away, or have his property taken away, or be put in jail.

²⁷Praise the LORD, the God of our ancestors. He caused the king to want to honor the Temple of the LORD in Jerusalem. ²⁸The LORD has shown me, Ezra, his love in the presence

---

7:1 After these things There is a time period of about sixty years between chapters six and seven.

of the king, those who advise the king, and the royal officers. Because the LORD my God was helping me, I had courage, and I gathered the leaders of Israel to return with me.

LEADERS WHO RETURNED WITH EZRA

8 These are the leaders of the family groups and those who were listed with them who came back with me from Babylon during the rule of King Artaxerxes.

²From the descendants of Phinehas: Gershom.

From the descendants of Ithamar: Daniel.

From the descendants of David: Hattush ³of the descendants of Shecaniah.

From the descendants of Parosh: Zechariah, with one hundred fifty men.

⁴From the descendants of Pahath-Moab: Eliehoenai son of Zerahiah, with two hundred men.

⁵From the descendants of Zattu: Shecaniah son of Jahaziel, with three hundred men.

⁶From the descendants of Adin: Ebed son of Jonathan, with fifty men.

⁷From the descendants of Elam: Jeshaiah son of Athaliah, with seventy men.

⁸From the descendants of Shephatiah: Zebadiah son of Michael, with eighty men.

⁹From the descendants of Joab: Obadiah son of Jehiel, with two hundred eighteen men.

¹⁰From the descendants of Bani: Shelomith son of Josiphiah, with one hundred sixty men.

¹¹From the descendants of Bebai: Zechariah son of Bebai, with twenty-eight men.

¹²From the descendants of Azgad: Johanan son of Hakkatan, with one hundred ten men.

¹³From the descendants of Adonikam, these were the last ones: Eliphelet, Jeuel, and Shemaiah, with sixty men.

¹⁴From the descendants of Bigvai: Uthai and Zaccur, with seventy men.

THE RETURN TO JERUSALEM

¹⁵I called all those people together at the canal that flows toward Ahava, where we camped for three days. I checked all the people and the priests, but I did not find any Levites. ¹⁶So I called these leaders: Eliezer, Ariel, Shemaiah, Elnathan, Jarib, Elnathan, Nathan, Zechariah, and Meshullam. And I called Joiarib and Elnathan, who were teachers. ¹⁷I sent these men to Iddo, the leader at Casiphia, and told them what to say to Iddo and his relatives, who are the Temple servants in Casiphia. I sent them to bring servants to us for the Temple of our God. ¹⁸Our God was helping us, so Iddo's relatives gave us Sherebiah, a wise man from the descendants of Mahli son of Levi, who was the son of Israel. And they brought Sherebiah's sons and brothers, for a total of eighteen men. ¹⁹And they brought to us Hashabiah and Jeshaiah from the descendants of Merari, and his brothers and nephews. In all there were twenty men. ²⁰They also brought two hundred twenty of the Temple servants, a group David and the officers had set up to help the Levites. All of those men were listed by name.

²¹There by the Ahava Canal, I announced we would all fast and deny ourselves before our God. We would ask God for a safe trip for ourselves, our children, and all our possessions. ²²I was ashamed to ask the king for soldiers and horsemen to protect us from enemies on the road. We had said to the king, "Our God helps everyone who obeys him, but he is very angry with all who reject him." ²³So we fasted and prayed to our God about our trip, and he answered our prayers.

²⁴Then I chose twelve of the priests who were leaders, Sherebiah, Hashabiah, and ten of their relatives. ²⁵I weighed the offering of silver and gold and the utensils given for the Temple of our God, and I gave them to the twelve priests I had chosen. The king, the people who advised him, his officers, and all the Israelites there with us had given these things for the Temple. ²⁶I weighed out and gave them about fifty thousand pounds of silver, about seventy-five hundred pounds of silver objects, and about seventy-five hundred pounds of gold. ²⁷I gave them twenty gold bowls that weighed about nineteen pounds and two fine pieces of polished bronze that were as valuable as gold.

²⁸Then I said to the priests, "You and these utensils belong to the LORD for his service. The silver and gold are gifts to the LORD, the God of your ancestors. ²⁹Guard these things carefully. In Jerusalem, weigh them in front of the leading priests, Levites, and the leaders

of the family groups of Israel in the rooms of the Temple of the LORD." ³⁰So the priests and Levites accepted the silver, the gold, and the utensils that had been weighed to take them to the Temple of our God in Jerusalem.

³¹On the twelfth day of the first month we left the Ahava Canal and started toward Jerusalem. Our God helped us and protected us from enemies and robbers along the way. ³²Finally we arrived in Jerusalem where we rested three days.

³³On the fourth day we weighed out the silver, the gold, and the utensils in the Temple of our God. We handed them to the priest Meremoth son of Uriah. Eleazar son of Phinehas was with him, as were the Levites Jozabad son of Jeshua and Noadiah son of Binnui. ³⁴We checked everything by number and by weight, and the total weight was written down.

³⁵Then the captives who returned made burnt offerings to the God of Israel. They sacrificed twelve bulls for all Israel, ninety-six male sheep, and seventy-seven lambs. For a sin offering there were twelve male goats. All this was a burnt offering to the LORD. ³⁶They took King Artaxerxes' orders to the royal officers and to the governors of Trans-Euphrates. Then these men gave help to the people and the Temple of God.

EZRA'S PRAYER

9 After these things had been done, the leaders came to me and said, "Ezra, the Israelites, including the priests and Levites, have not kept themselves separate from the people around us. Those neighbors do evil things, as the Canaanites, Hittites, Perizzites, Jebusites, Ammonites, Moabites, Egyptians, and Amorites did. ²The Israelite men and their sons have married these women. They have mixed the people who belong to God with the people around them. The leaders and officers of Israel have led the rest of the Israelites to do this unfaithful thing."

³When I heard this, I angrily tore my robe and coat, pulled hair from my head and beard, and sat down in shock. ⁴Everyone who trembled in fear at the word of the God of Israel gathered around me because of the unfaithfulness of the captives who had returned. I sat there in shock until the evening sacrifice.

⁵At the evening sacrifice I got up from where I had shown my shame. My robe and coat were torn, and I fell on my knees with my hands spread out to the LORD my God. ⁶I prayed,

"My God, I am too ashamed and embarrassed to lift up my face to you, my God, because our sins are so many. They are higher than our heads. Our guilt even reaches up to the sky. ⁷From the days of our ancestors until now, our guilt has been great. Because of our sins, we, our kings, and our priests have been punished by the sword and captivity. Foreign kings have taken away our things and shamed us, even as it is today.

⁸"But now, for a short time, the LORD our God has been kind to us. He has let some of us come back from captivity and has let us live in safety in his holy place. And so our God gives us hope and a little relief from our slavery. ⁹Even though we are slaves, our God has not left us. He caused the kings of Persia to be kind to us and has given us new life. We can rebuild the Temple and repair its ruins. And he has given us a wall to protect us in Judah and Jerusalem.

¹⁰"But now, our God, what can we say after you have done all this? We have disobeyed your commands ¹¹that you gave through your servants the prophets. You said, 'The land you are entering to own is ruined; the people living there have spoiled it by the evil they do. Their evil filled the land with uncleanness from one end to the other. ¹²So do not let your daughters marry their sons, and do not let their daughters marry your sons. Do not wish for their peace or success. Then you will be strong and eat the good things of the land. Then you can leave this land to your descendants forever.'

¹³"What has happened to us is our own fault. We have done evil things, and our guilt is great. But you, our God, have punished us less than we deserve; you have left a few of us alive. ¹⁴We should not again break your commands by allowing marriages with these wicked people. If we did, you would get angry enough to destroy us, and none of us would be left alive. ¹⁵LORD, God of Israel, by your goodness a few of us are left alive today. We admit that we are guilty and none of us should be allowed to stand before you."

THE PEOPLE CONFESS SIN

10 As Ezra was praying and confessing and crying and throwing himself down in front of the Temple, a large group of Israelite men, women, and children gathered around him who were also crying loudly. ²Then Shecaniah son of Jehiel the Elamite said to Ezra, "We have been unfaithful to our God by marrying women from the peoples around us. But even so, there is still hope for Israel. ³Now let us make an agreement before our God. We will send away all these women and their children as you and those who respect the commands of our God advise. Let it be done to obey God's Teachings. ⁴Get up, Ezra. You are in charge, and we will support you. Have courage and do it."

⁵So Ezra got up and made the priests, Levites, and all the people of Israel promise to do what was suggested; and they promised. ⁶Then Ezra left the Temple and went to the room of Jehohanan son of Eliashib. While Ezra was there, he did not eat or drink, because he was still sad about the unfaithfulness of the captives who had returned.

⁷They sent an order in Judah and Jerusalem for all the captives who had returned to meet together in Jerusalem. ⁸Whoever did not come to Jerusalem within three days would lose his property and would no longer be a member of the community of the returned captives. That was the decision of the officers and elders.

⁹So within three days all the men of Judah and Benjamin gathered in Jerusalem. It was the twentieth day of the ninth month. All the men were sitting in the open place in front of the Temple and were upset because of the meeting and because it was raining. ¹⁰Ezra the priest stood up and said to them, "You have been unfaithful and have married non-Jewish women. You have made Israel more guilty. ¹¹Now, confess it to the LORD, the God of your ancestors. Do his will and separate yourselves from the people living around you and from your non-Jewish wives."

¹²Then the whole group answered Ezra with a loud voice, "Ezra, you're right! We must do what you say. ¹³But there are many people here, and it's the rainy season. We can't stand outside, and this problem can't be solved in a day or two, because we have sinned badly. ¹⁴Let our officers make a decision for the whole group. Then let everyone in our towns who has married a non-Jewish woman meet with the elders and judges of each town at a planned time, until the hot anger of our God turns away from us." ¹⁵Only Jonathan son of Asahel, Jahzeiah son of Tikvah, Meshullam, and Shabbethai the Levite were against the plan.

¹⁶So the returned captives did what was suggested. Ezra the priest chose men who were leaders of the family groups and named one from each family division. On the first day of the tenth month they sat down to study each case. ¹⁷By the first day of the first month, they had finished with all the men who had married non-Jewish women.

THOSE GUILTY OF MARRYING NON-JEWISH WOMEN

¹⁸These are the descendants of the priests who had married foreign women:

From the descendants of Jeshua son of Jozadak and Jeshua's brothers: Maaseiah, Eliezer, Jarib, and Gedaliah. ¹⁹(They all promised to divorce their wives, and each one brought a male sheep from the flock as a penalty offering.)

²⁰From the descendants of Immer: Hanani and Zebadiah.

²¹From the descendants of Harim: Maaseiah, Elijah, Shemaiah, Jehiel, and Uzziah.

²²From the descendants of Pashhur: Elioenai, Maaseiah, Ishmael, Nethanel, Jozabad, and Elasah.

²³Among the Levites: Jozabad, Shimei, Kelaiah (also called Kelita), Pethahiah, Judah, and Eliezer.

²⁴Among the singers: Eliashib.

Among the gatekeepers: Shallum, Telem, and Uri.

²⁵And among the other Israelites, these married non-Jewish women:

From the descendants of Parosh: Ramiah, Izziah, Malkijah, Mijamin, Eleazar, Malkijah, and Benaiah.

²⁶From the descendants of Elam: Mattaniah, Zechariah, Jehiel, Abdi, Jeremoth, and Elijah.

²⁷From the descendants of Zattu: Elioenai, Eliashib, Mattaniah, Jeremoth, Zabad, and Aziza.

²⁸From the descendants of Bebai: Jehohanan, Hananiah, Zabbai, and Athlai.

²⁹From the descendants of Bani: Meshullam, Malluch, Adaiah, Jashub, Sheal, and Jeremoth.

³⁰From the descendants of Pahath-Moab: Adna, Kelal, Benaiah, Maaseiah, Mattaniah, Bezalel, Binnui, and Manasseh.

³¹From the descendants of Harim: Eliezer, Ishijah, Malkijah, Shemaiah, Shimeon, ³²Benjamin, Malluch, and Shemariah.

³³From the descendants of Hashum: Mattenai, Mattattah, Zabad, Eliphelet, Jeremai, Manasseh, and Shimei.

³⁴From the descendants of Bani: Maadai, Amram, Uel, ³⁵Benaiah, Bedeiah, Keluhi, ³⁶Vaniah, Meremoth, Eliashib, ³⁷Mattaniah, Mattenai, and Jaasu.

³⁸From the descendants of Binnui: Shimei, ³⁹Shelemiah, Nathan, Adaiah, ⁴⁰Macnadebai, Shashai, Sharai, ⁴¹Azarel, Shelemiah, Shemariah, ⁴²Shallum, Amariah, and Joseph.

⁴³From the descendants of Nebo: Jeiel, Mattithiah, Zabad, Zebina, Jaddai, Joel, and Benaiah.

⁴⁴All these men had married non-Jewish women, and some of them had children by these wives.

nehemiah

REBUILDING THE WALLS OF JERUSALEM

NEHEMIAH'S PRAYER

1 These are the words of Nehemiah son of Hacaliah.

In the month of Kislev in the twentieth year,[n] I, Nehemiah, was in the capital city of Susa. [2]One of my brothers named Hanani came with some other men from Judah. I asked them about Jerusalem and the Jewish people who lived through the captivity.

[3]They answered me, "Those who are left from the captivity are back in Judah, but they are in much trouble and are full of shame. The wall around Jerusalem is broken down, and its gates have been burned."

[4]When I heard these things, I sat down and cried for several days. I was sad and fasted. I prayed to the God of heaven, [5]"LORD, God of heaven, you are the great God who is to be respected. You are loyal, and you keep your agreement with those who love you and obey your commands. [6]Look and listen carefully. Hear the prayer that I, your servant, am praying to you day and night for your servants, the Israelites. I confess the sins we Israelites have done against you. My father's family and I have sinned against you. [7]We have been wicked toward you and have not obeyed the commands, rules, and laws you gave your servant Moses.

[8]"Remember what you taught your servant Moses, saying, 'If you are unfaithful, I will scatter you among the nations. [9]But if you return to me and obey my commands, I will gather your people from the far ends of the earth. And I will bring them from captivity to where I have chosen to be worshiped.'

[10]"They are your servants and your people, whom you have saved with your great strength and power. [11]Lord, listen carefully to the prayer of your servant and the prayers of your servants who love to honor you. Give me, your servant, success today; allow this king to show kindness to me."

I was the one who served wine to the king.

NEHEMIAH IS SENT TO JERUSALEM

2 It was the month of Nisan in the twentieth year Artaxerxes was king. He wanted some wine, so I took some and gave it to the king. I had not been sad in his presence before. [2]So the king said, "Why does your face look sad even though you are not sick? Your heart must be sad."

Then I was very afraid. [3]I said to the king, "May the king live forever! My face is sad because the city where my ancestors are buried lies in ruins, and its gates have been destroyed by fire."

[4]Then the king said to me, "What do you want?"

First I prayed to the God of heaven. [5]Then I answered the king, "If you are willing and if I have pleased you, send me to the city in Judah where my ancestors are buried so I can rebuild it."

[6]The queen was sitting next to the king. He asked me, "How long will your trip take, and when will you get back?" It pleased the king to send me, so I set a time.

[7]I also said to him, "If you are willing, give me letters for the governors of Trans-Euphrates. Tell them to let me pass safely through their lands on my way to Judah. [8]And may I have a letter for Asaph, the keeper of the king's forest, telling him to give me timber? I will need it to make boards for the gates of the palace, which is by the Temple, and for the city wall, and for the house in which I will live." So the king gave me the letters, because God was showing kindness to me. [9]Then I went to the governors of Trans-Euphrates and gave them the king's letters. The king had also sent army officers and soldiers on horses with me.

[10]When Sanballat the Horonite and Tobiah the Ammonite officer heard about this, they were upset that someone had come to help the Israelites.

1:1 twentieth year This is probably referring to the twentieth year King Artaxerxes I ruled Persia.

NEHEMIAH INSPECTS JERUSALEM

[11]I went to Jerusalem and stayed there three days. [12]Then at night I started out with a few men. I had not told anyone what God had caused me to do for Jerusalem. There were no animals with me except the one I was riding.

[13]I went out at night through the Valley Gate. I rode toward the Dragon Well and the Trash Gate, inspecting the walls of Jerusalem that had been broken down and the gates that had been destroyed by fire. [14]Then I rode on toward the Fountain Gate and the King's Pool, but there was not enough room for the animal I was riding to pass through. [15]So I went up the valley at night, inspecting the wall. Finally, I turned and went back in through the Valley Gate. [16]The guards did not know where I had gone or what I was doing. I had not yet said anything to the Jewish people, the priests, the important men, the officers, or any of the others who would do the work.

[17]Then I said to them, "You can see the trouble we have here. Jerusalem is a pile of ruins, and its gates have been burned. Come, let's rebuild the wall of Jerusalem so we won't be full of shame any longer." [18]I also told them how God had been kind to me and what the king had said to me.

Then they answered, "Let's start rebuilding." So they began to work hard.

[19]But when Sanballat the Horonite, Tobiah the Ammonite officer, and Geshem the Arab heard about it, they made fun of us and laughed at us. They said, "What are you doing? Are you turning against the king?"

[20]But I answered them, "The God of heaven will give us success. We, his servants, will start rebuilding, but you have no share, claim, or memorial in Jerusalem."

BUILDERS OF THE WALL

3 Eliashib the high priest and his fellow priests went to work and rebuilt the Sheep Gate. They gave it to the Lord's service and set its doors in place. They worked as far as the Tower of the Hundred and gave it to the Lord's service. Then they went on to the Tower of Hananel. [2]Next to them, the people of Jericho built part of the wall, and Zaccur son of Imri built next to them.

[3]The sons of Hassenaah rebuilt the Fish Gate, laying its boards and setting its doors, bolts, and bars in place. [4]Meremoth son of Uriah, the son of Hakkoz, made repairs next to them. Meshullam son of Berekiah, the son of Meshezabel, made repairs next to Meremoth. And Zadok son of Baana made repairs next to Meshullam. [5]The people from Tekoa made repairs next to them, but the leading men of Tekoa would not work under their supervisors.

[6]Joiada son of Paseah and Meshullam son of Besodeiah repaired the Old Gate. They laid its boards and set its doors, bolts, and bars in place. [7]Next to them, Melatiah from Gibeon, other men from Gibeon and Mizpah, and Jadon from Meronoth made repairs. These places were ruled by the governor of Trans-Euphrates. [8]Next to them, Uzziel son of Harhaiah, a goldsmith, made repairs. And next to him, Hananiah, a perfume maker, made repairs. These men rebuilt Jerusalem as far as the Broad Wall. [9]The next part of the wall was repaired by Rephaiah son of Hur, the ruler of half of the district of Jerusalem. [10]Next to him, Jedaiah son of Harumaph made repairs opposite his own house. And next to him, Hattush son of Hashabneiah made repairs. [11]Malkijah son of Harim and Hasshub son of Pahath-Moab repaired another part of the wall and the Tower of the Ovens. [12]Next to them Shallum son of Hallohesh, the ruler of half of the district of Jerusalem, and his daughters made repairs.

[13]Hanun and the people of Zanoah repaired the Valley Gate, rebuilding it and setting its doors, bolts, and bars in place. They also repaired the five hundred yards of the wall to the Trash Gate.

[14]Malkijah son of Recab, the ruler of the district of Beth Hakkerem, repaired the Trash Gate. He rebuilt that gate and set its doors, bolts, and bars in place.

[15]Shallun son of Col-Hozeh, the ruler of the district of Mizpah, repaired the Fountain Gate. He rebuilt it, put a roof over it, and set its doors, bolts, and bars in place. He also repaired the wall of the Pool of Siloam next to the King's Garden all the way to the steps that went down from the older part of the city. [16]Next to Shallun was Nehemiah[n] son of

---

3:16 Nehemiah This is a different Nehemiah than the one who wrote this book.

Azbuk, the ruler of half of the district of Beth Zur. He made repairs opposite the tombs of David and as far as the man-made pool and the House of the Heroes.

17Next to him, the Levites made repairs, working under Rehum son of Bani. Next to him, Hashabiah, the ruler of half of the district of Keilah, for his district. 18Next to him, Binnui son of Henadad and his relatives made repairs. Binnui was the ruler of the other half of the district of Keilah. 19Next to them, Ezer son of Jeshua, the ruler of Mizpah, repaired another part of the wall. He worked across from the way up to the armory, as far as the bend. 20Next to him, Baruch son of Zabbai worked hard on the wall that went from the bend to the entrance to the house of Eliashib, the high priest. 21Next to him, Meremoth son of Uriah, the son of Hakkoz, repaired the wall that went from the entrance to Eliashib's house to the far end of it.

22Next to him worked the priests from the surrounding area. 23Next to them, Benjamin and Hasshub made repairs in front of their own house. Next to them, Azariah son of Maaseiah, the son of Ananiah, made repairs beside his own house. 24Next to him, Binnui son of Henadad repaired the wall that went from Azariah's house to the bend and on to the corner. 25Palal son of Uzai worked across from the bend and by the tower on the upper palace, which is near the courtyard of the king's guard. Next to Palal, Pedaiah son of Parosh made repairs. 26The Temple servants who lived on the hill of Ophel made repairs as far as a point opposite the Water Gate. They worked toward the east and the tower that extends from the palace. 27Next to them, the people of Tekoa repaired the wall from the great tower that extends from the palace to the wall of Ophel.

28The priests made repairs above the Horse Gate, each working in front of his own house. 29Next to them, Zadok son of Immer made repairs across from his own house. Next to him, Shemaiah son of Shecaniah, the guard of the East Gate, made repairs. 30Next to him, Hananiah son of Shelemiah, and Hanun, the sixth son of Zalaph, made repairs on another part of the wall. Next to them, Meshullam son of Berekiah made repairs across from where he lived. 31Next to him, Malkijah, one of the goldsmiths, made

repairs. He worked as far as the house of the Temple servants and the traders, which is across from the Inspection Gate, and as far as the room above the corner of the wall. 32The goldsmiths and the traders made repairs between the room above the corner of the wall and the Sheep Gate.

THOSE AGAINST THE REBUILDING

4 When Sanballat heard we were rebuilding the wall, he was very angry, even furious. He made fun of the Jewish people. 2He said to his friends and those with power in Samaria, "What are these weak Jews doing? Will they rebuild the wall? Will they offer sacrifices? Can they finish it in one day? Can they bring stones back to life from piles of trash and ashes?"

3Tobiah the Ammonite, who was next to Sanballat, said, "If a fox climbed up on the stone wall they are building, it would break it down."

4I prayed, "Hear us, our God. We are hated. Turn the insults of Sanballat and Tobiah back on their own heads. Let them be captured and stolen like valuables. 5Do not hide their guilt or take away their sins so that you can't see them, because they have insulted the builders."

6So we rebuilt the wall to half its height, because the people were willing to work.

7But Sanballat, Tobiah, the Arabs, the Ammonites, and the people from Ashdod were very angry when they heard that the repairs to Jerusalem's walls were continuing and that the holes in the wall were being closed. 8So they all made plans to come to Jerusalem and fight and stir up trouble. 9But we prayed to our God and appointed guards to watch for them day and night.

10The people of Judah said, "The workers are getting tired. There is so much trash we cannot rebuild the wall."

11And our enemies said, "The Jews won't know or see anything until we come among them and kill them and stop the work."

12Then the Jewish people who lived near our enemies came and told us ten times, "Everywhere you turn, the enemy will attack us." 13So I put people behind the lowest places along the wall—the open places—and I put families together with their swords, spears, and bows. 14Then I looked around and stood up and said to the important men, the leaders, and the rest of the people: "Don't be afraid of them. Remember the Lord, who is great and powerful. Fight for your brothers, your sons and daughters, your wives, and your homes."

15Then our enemies heard that we knew about their plans and that God had ruined their plans. So we all went back to the wall, each to his own work.

16From that day on, half my people worked on the wall. The other half was ready with spears, shields, bows, and armor. The officers stood in back of the people of Judah 17who were building the wall. Those who carried materials did their work with one hand and carried a weapon with the other. 18Each builder wore his sword at his side as he worked. The man who blew the trumpet to warn the people stayed next to me.

19Then I said to the important people, the leaders, and everyone else, "This is a very big job. We are spreading out along the wall so that we are far apart. 20Wherever you hear the sound of the trumpet, assemble there. Our God will fight for us."

21So we continued to work with half the men holding spears from sunrise till the stars came out. 22At that time I also said to the people, "Let every man and his helper stay inside Jerusalem at night. They can be our guards at night and workmen during the day." 23Neither I, my brothers, my workers, nor the guards with me ever took off our clothes. Each person carried his weapon even when he went for water.

NEHEMIAH HELPS POOR PEOPLE

5 The men and their wives complained loudly against their fellow Jews. 2Some of them were saying, "We have many sons and daughters in our families. To eat and stay alive, we need grain."

3Others were saying, "We are borrowing money against our fields, vineyards, and homes to get grain because there is not much food."

4And still others were saying, "We are borrowing money to pay the king's tax on our fields and vineyards. 5We are just like our fellow Jews, and our sons are like their sons. But we have to sell our sons and daughters as slaves. Some of our daughters have already been sold. But there is nothing we can do, because our fields and vineyards already belong to other people."

6When I heard their complaints about these things, I was very angry. 7After I thought about it, I accused the important people and the leaders, "You are charging your own brothers too much interest." So I called a large meeting to deal with them. 8I said to them, "As much as possible, we have bought freedom for our fellow Jews who had been sold to foreigners. Now you are selling your fellow Jews to us!" The leaders were quiet and had nothing to say.

9Then I said, "What you are doing is not right. Don't you fear God? Don't let our foreign enemies shame us. 10I, my brothers, and my men are also lending money and grain to the people. But stop charging them so much for this. 11Give back their fields, vineyards, olive trees, and houses right now. Also give back the extra amount you charged—the hundredth part of the money, grain, new wine, and oil."

12They said, "We will give it back and not demand anything more from them. We will do as you say."

Then I called for the priests, and I made the important people and leaders take an oath to do what they had said. 13Also I shook out the folds of my robe and said, "In this way may God shake out everyone who does not keep his promise. May God shake him out of his house and out of the things that are his. Let that person be shaken out and emptied!"

Then the whole group said, "Amen," and they praised the LORD. So the people did what they had promised.

14I was appointed governor in the land of Judah in the twentieth year of King Artaxerxes' rule. I was governor of Judah for twelve years, until his thirty-second year. During that time neither my brothers nor I ate the food that was allowed for a governor. 15But the governors before me had placed a heavy load on the people. They took about one pound of silver from each person, along with food and wine. The governors' helpers before me also controlled the people, but I did not do that, because I feared God. 16I worked on the wall, as did all my men who were gathered there. We did not buy any fields.

17Also, I fed one hundred fifty Jewish

people and officers at my table, as well as those who came from the nations around us. 18This is what was prepared every day: one ox, six good sheep, and birds. And every ten days there were all kinds of wine. But I never demanded the food that was due a governor, because the people were already working very hard.

19Remember to be kind to me, my God, for all the good I have done for these people.

MORE PROBLEMS FOR NEHEMIAH

6 Then Sanballat, Tobiah, Geshem the Arab, and our other enemies heard that I had rebuilt the wall and that there was not one gap in it. But I had not yet set the doors in the gates. 2So Sanballat and Geshem sent me this message: "Come, Nehemiah, let's meet together in Kephirim on the plain of Ono."

But they were planning to harm me. 3So I sent messengers to them with this answer: "I am doing a great work, and I can't come down. I don't want the work to stop while I leave to meet you." 4Sanballat and Geshem sent the same message to me four times, and each time I sent back the same answer.

5The fifth time Sanballat sent his helper to me with the message, and in his hand was an unsealed letter. 6This is what was written:

A report is going around to all the nations, and Geshem says it is true, that you and the Jewish people are planning to turn against the king and that you are rebuilding the wall. They say you are going to be their king 7and that you have appointed prophets to announce in Jerusalem: "There is a king of Judah!" The king will hear about this. So come, let's discuss this together.

8So I sent him back this answer: "Nothing you are saying is really happening. You are just making it up in your own mind."

9Our enemies were trying to scare us, thinking, "They will get too weak to work. Then the wall will not be finished."

But I prayed, "God, make me strong."

10One day I went to the house of Shemaiah son of Delaiah, the son of Mehetabel. Shemaiah had to stay at home. He said, "Nehemiah, let's meet in the Temple of God. Let's go inside the Temple and close the doors, because men are coming at night to kill you."

11But I said, "Should a man like me run away? Should I run for my life into the Temple? I will not go." 12I knew that God had not sent him but that Tobiah and Sanballat had paid him to prophesy against me. 13They paid him to frighten me so I would do this and sin. Then they could give me a bad name to shame me.

14I prayed, "My God, remember Tobiah and Sanballat and what they have done. Also remember the prophetess Noadiah and the other prophets who have been trying to frighten me."

THE WALL IS FINISHED

15The wall of Jerusalem was completed on the twenty-fifth day of the month of Elul. It took fifty-two days to rebuild. 16When all our enemies heard about it and all the nations around us saw it, they were shamed. They then understood that the work had been done with the help of our God.

17Also in those days the important people of Judah sent many letters to Tobiah, and he answered them. 18Many Jewish people had promised to be faithful to Tobiah, because he was the son-in-law of Shecaniah son of Arah. And Tobiah's son Jehohanan had married the daughter of Meshullam son of Berekiah. 19These important people kept telling me about the good things Tobiah was doing, and then they would tell Tobiah what I said about him. So Tobiah sent letters to frighten me.

7 After the wall had been rebuilt and I had set the doors in place, the gatekeepers, singers, and Levites were chosen. 2I put my brother Hanani, along with Hananiah, the commander of the palace, in charge of Jerusalem. Hananiah was honest and feared God more than most people. 3I said to them, "The gates of Jerusalem should not be opened until the sun is hot. While the gatekeepers are still on duty, have them shut and bolt the doors. Appoint people who live in Jerusalem as guards, and put some at guard posts and some near their own houses."

THE CAPTIVES WHO RETURNED

4The city was large and roomy, but there were few people in it, and the houses had not yet been rebuilt. 5Then my God caused me to gather the important people, the leaders, and the common people so I could register them by families. I found the family history of those who had returned first. This is what I found written there:

6These are the people of the area who returned from captivity, whom Nebuchadnezzar king of Babylon had taken away. They returned to Jerusalem and Judah, each going back to his own town. 7These people returned with Zerubbabel, Jeshua, Nehemiah, Azariah, Raamiah, Nahamani, Mordecai, Bilshan, Mispereth, Bigvai, Nehum, and Baanah.

These are the people from Israel: 8the descendants of Parosh—2,172; 9the descendants of Shephatiah—372; 10the descendants of Arah—652; 11the descendants of Pahath-Moab (through the family of Jeshua and Joab)—2,818; 12the descendants of Elam—1,254; 13the descendants of Zattu—845; 14the descendants of Zaccai—760; 15the descendants of Binnui—648; 16the descendants of Bebai—628; 17the descendants of Azgad—2,322; 18the descendants of Adonikam—667; 19the descendants of Bigvai—2,067; 20the descendants of Adin—655; 21the descendants of Ater (through Hezekiah)—98; 22the descendants of Hashum—328; 23the descendants of Bezai—324; 24the descendants of Hariph—112; 25the descendants of Gibeon—95.

26These are the people from the towns of Bethlehem and Netophah—188; 27of Anathoth—128; 28of Beth Azmaveth—42; 29of Kiriath Jearim, Kephirah, and Beeroth—743; 30of Ramah and Geba—621; 31of Micmash—122; 32of Bethel and Ai—123; 33of the other Nebo—52; 34of the other Elam—1,254; 35of Harim—320; 36of Jericho—345; 37of Lod, Hadid, and Ono—721; 38of Senaah—3,930.

39These are the priests: the descendants of Jedaiah (through the family of Jeshua)—973; 40the descendants of Immer—1,052; 41the descendants of Pashhur—1,247; 42the descendants of Harim—1,017.

43These are the Levites: the descendants of Jeshua (through Kadmiel through the family of Hodaviah)—74.

44These are the singers: the descendants of Asaph—148.

45These are the gatekeepers: the descendants of Shallum, Ater, Talmon, Akkub, Hatita, and Shobai—138.

46These are the Temple servants: the descendants of Ziha, Hasupha, Tabbaoth, 47Keros, Sia, Padon, 48Lebana, Hagaba, Shalmai, 49Hanan, Giddel, Gahar, 50Reaiah, Rezin, Nekoda, 51Gazzam, Uzza, Paseah, 52Besai, Meunim, Nephussim, 53Bakbuk, Hakupha, Harhur, 54Bazluth, Mehida, Harsha, 55Barkos, Sisera, Temah, 56Neziah, and Hatipha.

57These are the descendants of the servants of Solomon: the descendants of Sotai, Sophereth, Perida, 58Jaala, Darkon, Giddel, 59Shephatiah, Hattil, Pokereth-Hazzebaim, and Amon.

60The Temple servants and the descendants of the servants of Solomon totaled 392 people.

61Some people came to Jerusalem from the towns of Tel Melah, Tel Harsha, Kerub, Addon, and Immer, but they could not prove that their ancestors came from Israel. Here are their names and their number: 62the descendants of Delaiah, Tobiah, and Nekoda—642.

63And these priests could not prove that their ancestors came from Israel: the descendants of Hobaiah, Hakkoz, and Barzillai. (He had married a daughter of Barzillai from Gilead and was called by her family name.)

64These people searched for their family records, but they could not find them. So they could not be priests, because they were thought to be unclean. 65The governor ordered them not to eat any of the holy food until a priest settled this matter by using the Urim and Thummim.

66The total number of those who returned was 42,360. 67This is not counting their 7,337 male and female servants and the 245 male and female singers with them. 68They had 736 horses, 245 mules, 69435 camels, and 6,720 donkeys.

70Some of the family leaders gave to the work. The governor gave to the treasury about 19 pounds of gold, 50 bowls, and 530 pieces of clothing for the priests. 71Some of the family leaders gave about 375 pounds of gold and about 2,660 pounds of silver to the treasury for the work. 72The total of what the other people gave was about 375 pounds of gold, about 2,250 pounds of silver, and 67 pieces of clothing for the priests. 73So these people all settled in their own towns: the priests, the Levites, the gatekeepers, the singers, the Temple servants, and all the other people of Israel.

EZRA READS THE TEACHINGS

By the seventh month the Israelites were settled in their own towns.

8 All the people of Israel gathered together in the square by the Water Gate. They asked Ezra the teacher to bring out the Book of the Teachings of Moses, which the LORD had given to Israel.

²So on the first day of the seventh month, Ezra the priest brought out the Teachings for the crowd. Men, women, and all who could listen and understand had gathered. ³At the square by the Water Gate Ezra read the Teachings out loud from early morning until noon to the men, women, and everyone who could listen and understand. All the people listened carefully to the Book of the Teachings.

⁴Ezra the teacher stood on a high wooden platform that had been built just for this time. On his right were Mattithiah, Shema, Anaiah, Uriah, Hilkiah, and Maaseiah. And on his left were Pedaiah, Mishael, Malkijah, Hashum, Hashbaddanah, Zechariah, and Meshullam.

⁵Ezra opened the book in full view of everyone, because he was above them. As he opened it, all the people stood up. ⁶Ezra praised the LORD, the great God, and all the people held up their hands and said, "Amen! Amen!" Then they bowed down and worshiped the LORD with their faces to the ground.

⁷These Levites explained the Teachings to the people as they stood there: Jeshua, Bani, Sherebiah, Jamin, Akkub, Shabbethai, Hodiah, Maaseiah, Kelita, Azariah, Jozabad, Hanan, and Pelaiah. ⁸They read from the Book of the Teachings of God and explained what it meant so the people understood what was being read.

⁹Then Nehemiah the governor, Ezra the priest and teacher, and the Levites who were teaching said to all the people, "This is a holy day to the LORD your God. Don't be sad or cry." All the people had been crying as they listened to the words of the Teachings.

¹⁰Nehemiah said, "Go and enjoy good food and sweet drinks. Send some to people who have none, because today is a holy day to the Lord. Don't be sad, because the joy of the LORD will make you strong."

¹¹The Levites helped calm the people, saying, "Be quiet, because this is a holy day. Don't be sad."

¹²Then all the people went away to eat and drink, to send some of their food to others, and to celebrate with great joy. They finally understood what they had been taught.

¹³On the second day of the month, the leaders of all the families, the priests, and the Levites met with Ezra the teacher. They gathered to study the words of the Teachings. ¹⁴This is what they found written in the Teachings: The LORD commanded through Moses that the people of Israel were to live in shelters during the feast of the seventh month. ¹⁵The people were supposed to preach this message and spread it through all their towns and in Jerusalem: "Go out into the mountains, and bring back branches from olive and wild olive trees, myrtle trees, palms, and shade trees. Make shelters with them, as it is written."

¹⁶So the people went out and got tree branches. They built shelters on their roofs,ⁿ in their courtyards, in the courtyards of the Temple, in the square by the Water Gate, and in the square next to the Gate of Ephraim. ¹⁷The whole group that had come back from captivity built shelters and lived in them. The Israelites had not done this since the time of Joshua son of Nun. And they were very happy.

¹⁸Ezra read to them every day from the Book of the Teachings, from the first day to the last. The people of Israel celebrated the feast for seven days, and then on the eighth day the people gathered as the law said.

ISRAEL CONFESSES SINS

9 On the twenty-fourth day of that same month, the people of Israel gathered. They fasted, and they wore rough cloth and put dust on their heads to show their sadness. ²Those people whose ancestors were from Israel had separated themselves from all foreigners. They stood and confessed their sins and their ancestors' sins. ³For a fourth of

---

8:16 roofs In Bible times houses were built with flat roofs. The roof was used for drying things such as flax and fruit. And it was used as an extra room, as a place for worship, and as a cool place to sleep in the summer.

the day they stood where they were and read from the Book of the Teachings of the LORD their God. For another fourth of the day they confessed their sins and worshiped the LORD their God. 4These Levites were standing on the stairs: Jeshua, Bani, Kadmiel, Shebaniah, Bunni, Sherebiah, Bani, and Kenani. They called out to the LORD their God with loud voices. 5Then these Levites spoke: Jeshua, Kadmiel, Bani, Hashabneiah, Sherebiah, Hodiah, Shebaniah, and Pethahiah. They said, "Stand up and praise the LORD your God, who lives forever and ever."

THE PEOPLE'S PRAYER

"Blessed be your wonderful name.
It is more wonderful than all blessing
and praise.
6 You are the only LORD.
You made the heavens, even the highest
heavens,
with all the stars.
You made the earth and everything on it,
the seas and everything in them;
you give life to everything.
The heavenly army worships you.

7 "You are the LORD,
the God who chose Abram
and brought him out of Ur in Babylonia
and named him Abraham.
8 You found him faithful to you,
so you made an agreement with him
to give his descendants the land of the
Canaanites,
Hittites, Amorites,
Perizzites, Jebusites, and Girgashites.
You have kept your promise,
because you do what is right.

9 "You saw our ancestors suffering in Egypt
and heard them cry out at the Red Sea.
10 You did signs and miracles against the
king of Egypt,
and against all his officers and all his
people,
because you knew how proud they
were.
You became as famous as you are today.
11 You divided the sea in front of our
ancestors;
they walked through on dry ground.
But you threw the people chasing them
into the deep water,

like a stone thrown into mighty waters.
12 You led our ancestors with a pillar of
cloud by day
and with a pillar of fire at night.
It lit the way
they were supposed to go.
13 You came down to Mount Sinai
and spoke from heaven to our ancestors.
You gave them fair rules and true
teachings,
good orders and commands.
14 You told them about your holy Sabbath
and gave them commands, orders, and
teachings
through your servant Moses.
15 When they were hungry, you gave them
bread from heaven.
When they were thirsty, you brought
them water from the rock.
You told them to enter and take over
the land you had promised to give them.

16 "But our ancestors were proud and
stubborn
and did not obey your commands.
17 They refused to listen;
they forgot the miracles you did for
them.
So they became stubborn and turned
against you,
choosing a leader to take them back to
slavery.
But you are a forgiving God.
You are kind and full of mercy.
You do not become angry quickly, and you
have great love.
So you did not leave them.
18 Our ancestors even made an idol of a calf
for themselves.
They said, 'This is your god, Israel,
who brought you up out of Egypt.'
They spoke against you.

19 "You have great mercy,
so you did not leave them in the desert.
The pillar of cloud guided them by day,
and the pillar of fire led them at night,
lighting the way they were to go.
20 You gave your good Spirit to teach them.
You gave them manna to eat
and water when they were thirsty.
21 You took care of them for forty years in
the desert;
they needed nothing.

Their clothes did not wear out,
and their feet did not swell.

22 "You gave them kingdoms and nations;
you gave them more land.
They took over the country of Sihon king
of Heshbon
and the country of Og king of Bashan.
23 You made their children as many as the
stars in the sky,
and you brought them into the land
that you told their ancestors to enter
and take over.
24 So their children went into the land and
took over.
The Canaanites lived there, but you
defeated them for our ancestors.
You handed over to them the Canaanites,
their kings, and the people of the
land.
Our ancestors could do what they
wanted with them.
25 They captured strong, walled cities and
fertile land.
They took over houses full of good
things,
wells that were already dug,
vineyards, olive trees, and many fruit
trees.
They ate until they were full and grew fat;
they enjoyed your great goodness.

26 "But they were disobedient and turned
against you
and ignored your teachings.
Your prophets warned them to come back
to you,
but they killed those prophets
and spoke against you.
27 So you handed them over to their
enemies,
and their enemies treated them badly.
But in this time of trouble our ancestors
cried out to you,
and you heard from heaven.
You had great mercy
and gave them saviors who saved them
from the power of their enemies.
28 But as soon as they had rest,
they again did what was evil.
So you left them to their enemies
who ruled over them.
When they cried out to you again,
you heard from heaven.

Because of your mercy, you saved them
again and again.
29 You warned them to return to your
teachings,
but they were proud and did not obey
your commands.
If someone obeys your laws, he will live,
but they sinned against your laws.
They were stubborn, unwilling, and
disobedient.
30 You were patient with them for many
years
and warned them by your Spirit
through the prophets,
but they did not pay attention.
So you handed them over to other
countries.
31 But because your mercy is great, you did
not kill them all or leave them.
You are a kind and merciful God.

32 "And so, our God, you are the great and
mighty and wonderful God.
You keep your agreement of love.
Do not let all our trouble seem
unimportant to you.
This trouble has come to us, to our kings
and our leaders,
to our priests and prophets,
to our ancestors and all your people
from the days of the kings of Assyria until
today.
33 You have been fair in everything that has
happened to us;
you have been loyal, but we have been
wicked.
34 Our kings, leaders, priests, and ancestors
did not obey your teachings;
they did not pay attention to the
commands and warnings you gave
them.
35 Even when our ancestors were living in
their kingdom,
enjoying all the good things you had
given them,
enjoying the land that was fertile and
full of room,
they did not stop their evil ways.

36 "Look, we are slaves today
in the land you gave our ancestors.
They were to enjoy its fruit and its good
things,
but look, we are slaves here.

37 The land's great harvest belongs to the
    kings you have put over us
  because of our sins.
Those kings rule over us and our cattle as
    they please,
  so we are in much trouble.

THE PEOPLE'S AGREEMENT

38"Because of all this, we are making an agreement in writing, and our leaders, Levites, and priests are putting their seals on it."

10 These are the men who sealed the agreement:

Nehemiah the governor, son of Hacaliah. Zedekiah, 2Seraiah, Azariah, Jeremiah, 3Pashhur, Amariah, Malkijah, 4Hattush, Shebaniah, Malluch, 5Harim, Meremoth, Obadiah, 6Daniel, Ginnethon, Baruch, 7Meshullam, Abijah, Mijamin, 8Maaziah, Bilgai, and Shemaiah. These are the priests.

9These are the Levites who sealed it: Jeshua son of Azaniah, Binnui of the sons of Henadad, Kadmiel, 10and their fellow Levites: Shebaniah, Hodiah, Kelita, Pelaiah, Hanan, 11Mica, Rehob, Hashabiah, 12Zaccur, Sherebiah, Shebaniah, 13Hodiah, Bani, and Beninu.

14These are the leaders of the people who sealed the agreement: Parosh, Pahath-Moab, Elam, Zattu, Bani, 15Bunni, Azgad, Bebai, 16Adonijah, Bigvai, Adin, 17Ater, Hezekiah, Azzur, 18Hodiah, Hashum, Bezai, 19Hariph, Anathoth, Nebai, 20Magpiash, Meshullam, Hezir, 21Meshezabel, Zadok, Jaddua, 22Pelatiah, Hanan, Anaiah, 23Hoshea, Hananiah, Hasshub, 24Hallohesh, Pilha, Shobek, 25Rehum, Hashabnah, Maaseiah, 26Ahiah, Hanan, Anan, 27Malluch, Harim, and Baanah.

28The rest of the people took an oath. They were the priests, Levites, gatekeepers, singers, Temple servants, all those who separated themselves from foreigners to keep the Teachings of God, and also their wives and their sons and daughters who could understand. 29They joined their fellow Israelites and their leading men in taking an oath, which was tied to a curse in case they broke the oath. They promised to follow the Teachings of God, which they had been given through Moses the servant of God, and to obey all the commands, rules, and laws of the LORD our God.

30They said:

We promise not to let our daughters marry foreigners nor to let our sons marry their daughters. 31Foreigners may bring goods or grain to sell on the Sabbath, but we will not buy on the Sabbath or any holy day. Every seventh year we will not plant, and that year we will forget all that people owe us.

32We will be responsible for the commands to pay for the service of the Temple of our God. We will give an eighth of an ounce of silver each year. 33It is for the bread that is set out on the table; the regular grain offerings and burnt offerings; the offerings on the Sabbaths, New Moon festivals, and special feasts; the holy offerings; the offerings to remove the sins of the Israelites so they will belong to God; and for the work of the Temple of our God.

34We, the priests, the Levites, and the people, have thrown lots to decide at what time of year each family must bring wood to the Temple. The wood is for burning on the altar of the LORD our God, and we will do this as it is written in the Teachings.

35We also will bring the firstfruits from our crops and the firstfruits of every tree to the Temple each year.

36We will bring to the Temple our firstborn sons and cattle and the firstborn of our herds and flocks, as it is written in the Teachings. We will bring them to the priests who are serving in the Temple.

37We will bring to the priests at the storerooms of the Temple the first of our ground meal, our offerings, the fruit from all our trees, and our new wine and oil. And we will bring a tenth of our crops to the Levites, who will collect these things in all the towns where we work. 38A priest of Aaron's family must be with the Levites when they receive the tenth of the people's crops. The Levites must bring a tenth of all they receive to the Temple of our God to put in the storerooms of the treasury. 39The people of Israel and the Levites are to bring to the storerooms the gifts of grain, new wine, and oil. That is where the utensils for the Temple are kept and where the priests who are serving, the gatekeepers, and singers stay.

We will not ignore the Temple of our God.

NEW PEOPLE MOVE INTO JERUSALEM

11 The leaders of Israel lived in Jerusalem. But the rest of the people threw lots to choose one person out of every ten to come and live in Jerusalem, the holy city. The other nine could stay in their own cities. 2The people blessed those who volunteered to live in Jerusalem.

3These are the area leaders who lived in Jerusalem. (Some people lived on their own land in the cities of Judah. These included Israelites, priests, Levites, Temple servants, and descendants of Solomon's servants. 4Others from the families of Judah and Benjamin lived in Jerusalem.)

These are the descendants of Judah who moved into Jerusalem. There was Athaiah son of Uzziah. (Uzziah was the son of Zechariah, the son of Amariah. Amariah was the son of Shephatiah, the son of Mahalalel. Mahalalel was a descendant of Perez.) 5There was also Maaseiah son of Baruch. (Baruch was the son of Col-Hozeh, the son of Hazaiah. Hazaiah was the son of Adaiah, the son of Joiarib. Joiarib was the son of Zechariah, a descendant of Shelah.) 6All the descendants of Perez who lived in Jerusalem totaled 468 men. They were soldiers.

7These are descendants of Benjamin who moved into Jerusalem. There was Sallu son of Meshullam. (Meshullam was the son of Joed, the son of Pedaiah. Pedaiah was the son of Kolaiah, the son of Maaseiah. Maaseiah was the son of Ithiel, the son of Jeshaiah.) 8Following him were Gabbai and Sallai, for a total of 928 men. 9Joel son of Zicri was appointed over them, and Judah son of Hassenuah was second in charge of the new area of the city.

10These are the priests who moved into Jerusalem. There was Jedaiah son of Joiarib, Jakin, 11and Seraiah son of Hilkiah, the supervisor in the Temple. (Hilkiah was the son of Meshullam, the son of Zadok. Zadok was the son of Meraioth, the son of Ahitub.) 12And there were others with them who did the work for the Temple. All together there were 822 men. Also there was Adaiah son of Jeroham. (Jeroham was the son of Pelaliah, the son of Amzi. Amzi was the son of Zechariah, the son of Pashhur. Pashhur was the son of Malkijah.) 13And there were family heads with him. All together there were 242 men. Also there was Amashsai son of Azarel. (Azarel was the son of Ahzai, the son of Meshillemoth. Meshillemoth was the son of Immer.) 14And there were brave men with Amashsai. All together there were 128 men. Zabdiel son of Haggedolim was appointed over them.

15These are the Levites who moved into Jerusalem. There was Shemaiah son of Hasshub. (Hasshub was the son of Azrikam, the son of Hashabiah. Hashabiah was the son of Bunni.) 16And there were Shabbethai and Jozabad, two of the leaders of the Levites who were in charge of the work outside the Temple. 17There was Mattaniah son of Mica. (Mica was the son of Zabdi, the son of Asaph.) Mattaniah was the director who led the people in thanksgiving and prayer. There was Bakbukiah, who was second in charge over his fellow Levites. And there was Abda son of Shammua. (Shammua was the son of Galal, the son of Jeduthun.) 18All together 284 Levites lived in the holy city of Jerusalem.

19The gatekeepers who moved into Jerusalem were Akkub, Talmon, and others with them. There was a total of 172 men who guarded the city gates.

20The other Israelites, priests, and Levites lived on their own land in all the cities of Judah.

21The Temple servants lived on the hill of Ophel, and Ziha and Gishpa were in charge of them.

22Uzzi son of Bani was appointed over the Levites in Jerusalem. (Bani was the son of Hashabiah, the son of Mattaniah. Mattaniah was the son of Mica.) Uzzi was one of Asaph's descendants, who were the singers responsible for the service of the Temple. 23The singers were under the king's orders, which regulated them day by day.

24Pethahiah son of Meshezabel was the king's spokesman. (Meshezabel was a descendant of Zerah, the son of Judah.)

25Some of the people of Judah lived in villages with their surrounding fields. They lived in Kiriath Arba and its surroundings, in Dibon and its surroundings, in Jekabzeel and its surroundings, 26in Jeshua, Moladah, Beth Pelet, 27Hazar Shual, Beersheba and its surroundings, 28in Ziklag and Meconah and its surroundings, ²⁹in En Rimmon, Zorah, Jarmuth, ³⁰Zanoah, Adullam and their villages, in Lachish and the fields around it, and in Azekah and its surroundings. So they settled from Beersheba all the way to the Valley of Hinnom.

³¹The descendants of the Benjaminites from Geba lived in Micmash, Aija, Bethel and its surroundings, ³²in Anathoth, Nob, Ananiah, ³³Hazor, Ramah, Gittaim, ³⁴Hadid, Zeboim, Neballat, ³⁵Lod, Ono, and in the Valley of the Craftsmen.

³⁶Some groups of the Levites from Judah settled in the land of Benjamin.

PRIESTS AND LEVITES

12 These are the priests and Levites who returned with Zerubbabel son of Shealtiel and with Jeshua. There were Seraiah, Jeremiah, Ezra, ²Amariah, Malluch, Hattush, ³Shecaniah, Rehum, Meremoth, ⁴Iddo, Ginnethon, Abijah, ⁵Mijamin, Moadiah, Bilgah, ⁶Shemaiah, Joiarib, Jedaiah, ⁷Sallu, Amok, Hilkiah, and Jedaiah. They were the leaders of the priests and their relatives in the days of Jeshua.

⁸The Levites were Jeshua, Binnui, Kadmiel, Sherebiah, Judah, and Mattaniah. Mattaniah and his relatives were in charge of the songs of thanksgiving. ⁹Bakbukiah and Unni, their relatives, stood across from them in the services.

¹⁰Jeshua was the father of Joiakim. Joiakim was the father of Eliashib. Eliashib was the father of Joiada. ¹¹Joiada was the father of Jonathan, and Jonathan was the father of Jaddua.

¹²In the days of Joiakim, these priests were the leaders of the families of priests: Meraiah, from Seraiah's family; Hananiah, from Jeremiah's family; ¹³Meshullam, from Ezra's family; Jehohanan, from Amariah's family; ¹⁴Jonathan, from Malluch's family; Joseph, from Shecaniah's family; ¹⁵Adna, from Harim's family; Helkai, from Meremoth's family; ¹⁶Zechariah, from Iddo's family; Meshullam, from Ginnethon's family; ¹⁷Zicri, from Abijah's family; Piltai, from Miniamin's and Moadiah's families; ¹⁸Shammua, from Bilgah's family; Jehonathan, from Shemaiah's family; ¹⁹Mattenai, from Joiarib's family; Uzzi, from Jedaiah's family; ²⁰Kallai, from Sallu's family; Eber, from Amok's family; ²¹Hashabiah, from Hilkiah's family; and Nethanel, from Jedaiah's family.

²²The leaders of the families of the Levites and the priests were written down in the days of Eliashib, Joiada, Johanan, and Jaddua, while Darius the Persian was king. ²³The family leaders among the Levites were written down in the history book, but only up to the time of Johanan son of Eliashib. ²⁴The leaders of the Levites were Hashabiah, Sherebiah, Jeshua son of Kadmiel, and their relatives. Their relatives stood across from them and gave praise and thanksgiving to God. One group answered the other group, as David, the man of God, had commanded.

²⁵These were the gatekeepers who guarded the storerooms next to the gates: Mattaniah, Bakbukiah, Obadiah, Meshullam, Talmon, and Akkub. ²⁶They served in the days of Joiakim son of Jeshua, the son of Jozadak. They also served in the days of Nehemiah the governor and Ezra the priest and teacher.

THE WALL OF JERUSALEM

²⁷When the wall of Jerusalem was offered as a gift to God, they asked the Levites to come from wherever they lived to Jerusalem to celebrate with joy the gift of the wall. They were to celebrate with songs of thanksgiving and with the music of cymbals, harps, and lyres. ²⁸They also brought together singers from all around Jerusalem, from the Netophathite villages, ²⁹from Beth Gilgal, and from the areas of Geba and Azmaveth. The singers had built villages for themselves around Jerusalem. ³⁰The priests and Levites made themselves pure, and they also made the people, the gates, and the wall of Jerusalem pure.

³¹I had the leaders of Judah go up on top of the wall, and I appointed two large choruses to give thanks. One chorus went to the right on top of the wall, toward the Trash Gate. ³²Behind them went Hoshaiah and half the leaders of Judah. ³³Azariah, Ezra, Meshullam, ³⁴Judah, Benjamin, Shemaiah, and Jeremiah also went. ³⁵Some priests with trumpets also went, along with Zechariah son of Jonathan. (Jonathan was the son of Shemaiah, the son of Mattaniah. Mattaniah was the son of Micaiah, the son of Zaccur. Zaccur was the son of Asaph.) ³⁶Zechariah's

relatives also went. They were Shemaiah, Azarel, Milalai, Gilalai, Maai, Nethanel, Judah, and Hanani. These men played the musical instruments of David, the man of God, and Ezra the teacher walked in front of them. [37]They went from the Fountain Gate straight up the steps to the highest part of the wall by the older part of the city. They went on above the house of David to the Water Gate on the east.

[38]The second chorus went to the left, while I followed them on top of the wall with half the people. We went from the Tower of the Ovens to the Broad Wall, [39]over the Gate of Ephraim to the Old Gate and the Fish Gate, to the Tower of Hananel and the Tower of the Hundred. We went as far as the Sheep Gate and stopped at the Gate of the Guard.

[40]The two choruses took their places at the Temple. Half of the leaders and I did also. [41]These priests were there with their trumpets: Eliakim, Maaseiah, Miniamin, Micaiah, Elioenai, Zechariah, and Hananiah. [42]These people were also there: Maaseiah, Shemaiah, Eleazar, Uzzi, Jehohanan, Malkijah, Elam, and Ezer. The choruses sang, led by Jezrahiah. [43]The people offered many sacrifices that day and were happy because God had given them great joy. The women and children were happy. The sound of happiness in Jerusalem could be heard far away.

[44]At that time the leaders appointed men to be in charge of the storerooms. These rooms were for the gifts, the firstfruits, and the ten percent that the people brought. The Teachings said they should bring a share for the priests and Levites from the fields around the towns. The people of Judah were happy to do this for the priests and Levites who served. [45]They performed the service of their God in making things pure. The singers and gatekeepers also did their jobs, as David had commanded his son Solomon. [46]Earlier, in the time of David and Asaph, there was a leader of the singers and of the songs of praise and thanksgiving to God. [47]So it was in the days of Zerubbabel and Nehemiah. All the people of Israel gave something to the singers and gatekeepers, and they also set aside part for the Levites. Then the Levites set aside part for the descendants of Aaron.

FOREIGN PEOPLE ARE SENT AWAY

13 On that day they read the Book of Moses to the people, and they found that it said no Ammonite or Moabite should ever be allowed in the meeting to worship. [2]The Ammonites and Moabites had not welcomed the Israelites with food and water. Instead, they had hired Balaam to put a curse on Israel. (But our God turned the curse into a blessing.) [3]When the people heard this teaching, they separated all foreigners from Israel.

NEHEMIAH RETURNS TO JERUSALEM

[4]Before that happened, Eliashib the priest, who was in charge of the Temple storerooms, was friendly with Tobiah. [5]Eliashib let Tobiah use one of the large storerooms. Earlier it had been used for grain offerings, incense, the utensils, and the tenth offerings of grain, new wine, and olive oil that belonged to the Levites, singers, and gatekeepers. It had also been used for gifts for the priests.

[6]I was not in Jerusalem when this happened. I had gone back to Artaxerxes king of Babylon in the thirty-second year he was king. Finally I asked the king to let me leave. [7]When I returned to Jerusalem, I found out the evil Eliashib had done by letting Tobiah have a room in the Temple courtyard. [8]I was very upset at this, so I threw all of Tobiah's goods out of the room. [9]I ordered the rooms to be purified, and I brought back the utensils for God's Temple, the grain offerings, and the incense.

[10]Then I found out the people were not giving the Levites their shares. So the Levites and singers who served had gone back to their own farms. [11]I argued with the officers, saying, "Why haven't you taken care of the Temple?" Then I gathered the Levites and singers and put them back at their places.

[12]All the people of Judah then brought to the storerooms a tenth of their crops, new wine, and olive oil. [13]I put these men in charge of the storerooms: Shelemiah the priest, Zadok the teacher, and Pedaiah a Levite. I made Hanan son of Zaccur, the son of Mattaniah, their helper. Everyone knew they were honest. They gave out the portions that went to their relatives.

[14]Remember me, my God, for this. Do

not ignore my love for the Temple and its service.

15In those days I saw people in Judah working in the winepresses on the Sabbath day. They were bringing in grain and loading it on donkeys. And they were bringing loads of wine, grapes, and figs into Jerusalem on the Sabbath day. So I warned them about selling food on that day. 16People from the city of Tyre who were living in Jerusalem brought in fish and other things and sold them there on the Sabbath day to the people of Judah. 17I argued with the important men of Judah and said to them, "What is this evil thing you are doing? You are ruining the Sabbath day. 18This is just what your ancestors did. So our God did terrible things to us and this city. Now you are making him even more angry at Israel by ruining the Sabbath day."

19So I ordered that the doors be shut at sunset before the Sabbath and not be opened until the Sabbath was over. I put my servants at the gates so no load could come in on the Sabbath. 20Once or twice traders and sellers of all kinds of goods spent the night outside Jerusalem. 21So I warned them, "Why are you spending the night by the wall? If you do it again, I will force you away." After that, they did not come back on the Sabbath. 22Then I ordered the Levites to purify themselves and to guard the city gates to make sure the Sabbath remained holy.

Remember me, my God, for this. Have mercy on me because of your great love.

23In those days I saw men of Judah who had married women from Ashdod, Ammon, and Moab. 24Half their children were speaking the language of Ashdod or some other place, and they couldn't speak the language of Judah. 25I argued with those people, put curses on them, hit some of them, and pulled out their hair. I forced them to make a promise to God, saying, "Do not let your daughters marry the sons of foreigners, and do not take the daughters of foreigners as wives for your sons or yourselves. 26Foreign women made King Solomon of Israel sin. There was never a king like him in any of the nations. God loved Solomon and made him king over all Israel, but foreign women made him sin. 27And now you are not obedient when you do this evil thing. You are unfaithful to our God when you marry foreign wives."

28Joiada was the son of Eliashib the high priest. One of Joiada's sons married a daughter of Sanballat the Horonite, so I sent him away from me.

29Remember them, my God, because they made the priesthood unclean and the agreement of the priests and Levites unclean.

30So I purified them of everything that was foreign. I appointed duties for the priests and Levites, giving each man his own job. 31I also made sure wood was brought for the altar at regular times and that the firstfruits were brought.

Remember me, my God; be kind to me.

esther

ESTHER SAVES HER PEOPLE

QUEEN VASHTI DISOBEYS THE KING

1 This is what happened during the time of King Xerxes, the king who ruled the one hundred twenty-seven states from India to Cush. ²In those days King Xerxes ruled from his capital city of Susa. ³In the third year of his rule, he gave a banquet for all his important men and royal officers. The army leaders from the countries of Persia and Media and the important men from all Xerxes' empire were there.

⁴The banquet lasted one hundred eighty days. All during that time King Xerxes was showing off the great wealth of his kingdom and his own great riches and glory. ⁵When the one hundred eighty days were over, the king gave another banquet. It was held in the courtyard of the palace garden for seven days, and it was for everybody in the palace at Susa, from the greatest to the least. ⁶The courtyard had fine white curtains and purple drapes that were tied to silver rings on marble pillars by white and purple cords. And there were gold and silver couches on a floor set with tiles of white marble, shells, and gems. ⁷Wine was served in gold cups of various kinds. And there was plenty of the king's wine, because he was very generous. ⁸The king commanded that the guests be permitted to drink as much as they wished. He told the wine servers to serve each man what he wanted.

⁹Queen Vashti also gave a banquet for the women in the royal palace of King Xerxes.

¹⁰On the seventh day of the banquet, King Xerxes was very happy, because he had been drinking much wine. He gave a command to the seven eunuchs who served him—Mehuman, Biztha, Harbona, Bigtha, Abagtha, Zethar, and Carcas. ¹¹He commanded them to bring him Queen Vashti, wearing her royal crown. She was to come to show her beauty to the people and important men, because she was very beautiful. ¹²The eunuchs told Queen Vashti about the king's command, but she refused to come. Then the king became very angry; his anger was like a burning fire.

¹³It was a custom for the king to ask advice from experts about law and order. So King Xerxes spoke with the wise men who would know the right thing to do. ¹⁴The wise men the king usually talked to were Carshena, Shethar, Admatha, Tarshish, Meres, Marsena, and Memucan, seven of the important men of Persia and Media. These seven had special privileges to see the king and had the highest rank in the kingdom. ¹⁵The king asked them, "What does the law say must be done to Queen Vashti? She has not obeyed the command of King Xerxes, which the eunuchs took to her."

¹⁶Then Memucan said to the king and the other important men, "Queen Vashti has not done wrong to the king alone. She has also done wrong to all the important men and all the people in all the empire of King Xerxes. ¹⁷All the wives of the important men of Persia and Media will hear about the queen's actions. Then they will no longer honor their husbands. They will say, 'King Xerxes commanded Queen Vashti to be brought to him, but she refused to come.' ¹⁸Today the wives of the important men of Persia and Media have heard about the queen's actions. So they will speak in the same way to their husbands, and there will be no end to disrespect and anger.

¹⁹"So, our king, if it pleases you, give a royal order, and let it be written in the laws of Persia and Media, which cannot be changed. The law should say Vashti is never again to enter the presence of King Xerxes. Also let the king give her place as queen to someone who is better than she is. ²⁰And let the king's order be announced everywhere in his enormous kingdom. Then all the women will respect their husbands, from the greatest to the least."

²¹The king and his important men were happy with this advice, so King Xerxes did as Memucan suggested. ²²He sent letters to all the states of the kingdom in the writing of

each state and in the language of each group of people. These letters announced that each man was to be the ruler of his own family.

ESTHER IS MADE QUEEN

2 Later, when King Xerxes was not so angry, he remembered Vashti and what she had done and his order about her. ²Then the king's personal servants suggested, "Let a search be made for beautiful young girls for the king. ³Let the king choose supervisors in every state of his kingdom to bring every beautiful young girl to the palace at Susa. They should be taken to the women's quarters and put under the care of Hegai, the king's eunuch in charge of the women. And let beauty treatments be given to them. ⁴Then let the girl who most pleases the king become queen in place of Vashti." The king liked this idea, so he did as they said.

⁵Now there was a Jewish man in the palace of Susa whose name was Mordecai son of Jair. Jair was the son of Shimei, the son of Kish. Mordecai was from the tribe of Benjamin, ⁶which had been taken captive from Jerusalem by Nebuchadnezzar king of Babylon. They were part of the group taken into captivity with Jehoiachin king of Judah. ⁷Mordecai had a cousin named Hadassah, who had no father or mother, so Mordecai took care of her. Hadassah was also called Esther, and she had a very pretty figure and face. Mordecai had adopted her as his own daughter when her father and mother died.

⁸When the king's command and order had been heard, many girls had been brought to the palace in Susa and put under the care of Hegai. Esther was also taken to the king's palace and put under the care of Hegai, who was in charge of the women. ⁹Esther pleased Hegai, and he liked her. So Hegai quickly began giving Esther her beauty treatments and special food. He gave her seven servant girls chosen from the king's palace. Then he moved her and her seven servant girls to the best part of the women's quarters.

¹⁰Esther did not tell anyone about her family or who her people were, because Mordecai had told her not to. ¹¹Every day Mordecai walked back and forth near the courtyard where the king's women lived to find out how Esther was and what was happening to her.

¹²Before a girl could take her turn with King Xerxes, she had to complete twelve months of beauty treatments that were ordered for the women. For six months she was treated with oil and myrrh and for six months with perfumes and cosmetics. ¹³Then she was ready to go to the king. Anything she asked for was given to her to take with her from the women's quarters to the king's palace. ¹⁴In the evening she would go to the king's palace, and in the morning she would return to another part of the women's quarters. There she would be placed under the care of Shaashgaz, the king's eunuch in charge of the slave women. The girl would not go back to the king again unless he was pleased with her and asked for her by name.

¹⁵The time came for Esther daughter of Abihail, Mordecai's uncle, who had been adopted by Mordecai, to go to the king. She asked for only what Hegai suggested she should take. (Hegai was the king's eunuch who was in charge of the women.) Everyone who saw Esther liked her. ¹⁶So Esther was taken to King Xerxes in the royal palace in the tenth month, the month of Tebeth, during Xerxes' seventh year as king.

¹⁷And the king was pleased with Esther more than with any of the other virgins. He liked her more than any of the others, so he put a royal crown on her head and made her queen in place of Vashti. ¹⁸Then the king gave a great banquet for Esther and invited all his important men and royal officers. He announced a holiday for all the empire and had the government give away gifts.

MORDECAI DISCOVERS AN EVIL PLAN

¹⁹Now Mordecai was sitting at the king's gate when the girls were gathered the second time. ²⁰Esther still had not told anyone about her family or who her people were, just as Mordecai had commanded her. She obeyed Mordecai just as she had done when she was under his care.

²¹Now Bigthana and Teresh were two of the king's eunuchs who guarded the doorway. While Mordecai was sitting at the king's gate, they became angry and began to make plans to kill King Xerxes. ²²But Mordecai found out about their plans and told Queen Esther. Then Esther told the king how Mordecai had discovered the evil plan. ²³When

the report was investigated, it was found to be true, and the two officers who had planned to kill the king were hanged. All this was written down in the daily court record in the king's presence.

HAMAN PLANS TO DESTROY THE JEWISH PEOPLE

3 After these things happened, King Xerxes honored Haman son of Hammedatha the Agagite. He gave him a new rank that was higher than all the important men. ²All the royal officers at the king's gate would bow down and kneel before Haman, as the king had ordered. But Mordecai would not bow down or show him honor.

³Then the royal officers at the king's gate asked Mordecai, "Why don't you obey the king's command?" ⁴And they said this to him every day. When he did not listen to them, they told Haman about it. They wanted to see if Haman would accept Mordecai's behavior because Mordecai had told them he was Jewish.

⁵When Haman saw that Mordecai would not bow down to him or honor him, he became very angry. ⁶He thought of himself as too important to try to kill only Mordecai. He had been told who the people of Mordecai were, so he looked for a way to destroy all of Mordecai's people, the Jews, in all of Xerxes' kingdom.

⁷It was in the first month of the twelfth year of King Xerxes' rule—the month of Nisan. Pur (that is, the lot) was thrown before Haman to choose a day and a month. So the twelfth month, the month of Adar, was chosen.

⁸Then Haman said to King Xerxes, "There is a certain group of people scattered among the other people in all the states of your kingdom. Their customs are different from those of all the other people, and they do not obey the king's laws. It is not right for you to allow them to continue living in your kingdom. ⁹If it pleases the king, let an order be given to destroy those people. Then I will pay seven hundred fifty thousand pounds of silver to those who do the king's business, and they will put it into the royal treasury."

¹⁰So the king took his signet ring off and gave it to Haman son of Hammedatha, the Agagite, the enemy of the Jewish people. ¹¹Then the king said to Haman, "The money and the people are yours. Do with them as you please."

¹²On the thirteenth day of the first month, the royal secretaries were called, and they wrote out all of Haman's orders. They wrote to the king's governors and to the captains of the soldiers in each state and to the important men of each group of people. The orders were written in the writing of each state and in the language of each people. They were written in the name of King Xerxes and sealed with his signet ring. ¹³Letters were sent by messengers to all the king's empire ordering them to destroy, kill, and completely wipe out all the Jewish people. That meant young and old, women and little children, too. It was to happen on a single day—the thirteenth day of the twelfth month, which was Adar. And they could take everything the Jewish people owned. ¹⁴A copy of the order was given out as a law in every state so all the people would be ready for that day.

¹⁵The messengers set out, hurried by the king's command, as soon as the order was given in the palace at Susa. The king and Haman sat down to drink, but the city of Susa was in confusion.

MORDECAI ASKS ESTHER TO HELP

4 When Mordecai heard about all that had been done, he tore his clothes, put on rough cloth and ashes, and went out into the city crying loudly and painfully. ²But Mordecai went only as far as the king's gate, because no one was allowed to enter that gate dressed in rough cloth. ³As the king's order reached every area, there was great sadness and loud crying among the Jewish people. They fasted and cried out loud, and many of them lay down on rough cloth and ashes to show how sad they were.

⁴When Esther's servant girls and eunuchs came to her and told her about Mordecai, she was very upset and afraid. She sent clothes for Mordecai to put on instead of the rough cloth, but he would not wear them. ⁵Then Esther called for Hathach, one of the king's eunuchs chosen by the king to serve her. Esther ordered him to find out what was bothering Mordecai and why.

⁶So Hathach went to Mordecai, who was in the city square in front of the king's gate. ⁷Mordecai told Hathach everything that had

happened to him, and he told Hathach about the amount of money Haman had promised to pay into the king's treasury for the killing of the Jewish people. ⁸Mordecai also gave him a copy of the order to kill the Jewish people, which had been given in Susa. He wanted Hathach to show it to Esther and to tell her about it. And Mordecai told him to order Esther to go into the king's presence to beg for mercy and to plead with him for her people.

⁹Hathach went back and reported to Esther everything Mordecai had said. ¹⁰Then Esther told Hathach to tell Mordecai, ¹¹"All

the royal officers and people of the royal states know that no man or woman may go to the king in the inner courtyard without being called. There is only one law about this: Anyone who enters must be put to death unless the king holds out his gold scepter. Then that person may live. And I have not been called to go to the king for thirty days."

¹²Esther's message was given to Mordecai. ¹³Then Mordecai sent back word to Esther: "Just because you live in the king's palace, don't think that out of all the Jewish people you alone will escape. ¹⁴If you keep quiet at this time, someone else will help and save

---

THE PRODUCT OF PRESENT OBEDIENCE

for such a time
as this

FUTURE

By Claudio Freidzon

ESTHER 4:14

God has something special planned for you, something great that only you can do. He has been preparing you all along for this thing. The opportunity you have been waiting for, the change, the blessing you have been desperate for, is now upon you.

The Lord says, "Come into my presence and enjoy my friendship. I will not reject you. I love you." He is reaching out to you. Come to him with joy and expectation, seek his company, and he will do the rest. He places your enemies under your feet and takes you where you need to go. Do not rely on your strategies or religious methods but on the powerful presence of God to accomplish God's will.

God chose you; he has trained you because you are a willing and surrendered believer. You look for his face and study his ways and believe in his promises. He provides the breakthrough. God gives you the ability, the wisdom, and the strength. His Word guides and encourages you. His Son's authority opens doors, and his Holy Spirit blesses it all.

Don't listen to discouragement; it is from the devil. The Enemy will try to distract or confront you. All that you need is already planned and in place to heal, restore, and lift you. God's holy fire and his never-ending love lead you and finish what he plans for you. The Lord is waiting for you to ask, so he can bless everything that is important to you.

reflect: How might you trust God in a fresh way today?

Go to **FUTURE:** "The Road to Success" at **1 Corinthians 15:58.**

the Jewish people, but you and your father's family will all die. And who knows, you may have been chosen queen for just such a time as this."

15Then Esther sent this answer to Mordecai: 16"Go and get all the Jewish people in Susa together. For my sake, fast; do not eat or drink for three days, night and day. I and my servant girls will also fast. Then I will go to the king, even though it is against the law, and if I die, I die."

17So Mordecai went away and did everything Esther had told him to do.

ESTHER SPEAKS TO THE KING

5 On the third day Esther put on her royal robes and stood in the inner courtyard of the king's palace, facing the king's hall. The king was sitting on his royal throne in the hall, facing the doorway. 2When the king saw Queen Esther standing in the courtyard, he was pleased. He held out to her the gold scepter that was in his hand, so Esther went forward and touched the end of it.

3The king asked, "What is it, Queen Esther? What do you want to ask me? I will give you as much as half of my kingdom."

4Esther answered, "My king, if it pleases you, come today with Haman to a banquet that I have prepared for you."

5Then the king said, "Bring Haman quickly so we may do what Esther asks."

So the king and Haman went to the banquet Esther had prepared for them. 6As they were drinking wine, the king said to Esther, "Now, what are you asking for? I will give it to you. What is it you want? I will give you as much as half of my kingdom."

7Esther answered, "This is what I want and what I ask for. 8My king, if you are pleased with me and if it pleases you, give me what I ask for and do what I want. Come with Haman tomorrow to the banquet I will prepare for you. Then I will answer your question about what I want."

HAMAN'S PLANS AGAINST MORDECAI

9Haman left the king's palace that day happy and content. But when he saw Mordecai at the king's gate and saw that Mordecai did not stand up or tremble with fear before him, Haman became very angry with Mordecai. 10But he controlled his anger and went home.

Then Haman called together his friends and his wife, Zeresh. 11He told them how wealthy he was and how many sons he had. He also told them all the ways the king had honored him and how the king had placed him higher than his important men and his royal officers. 12He also said, "I'm the only person Queen Esther invited to come with the king to the banquet she gave. And tomorrow also the queen has asked me to be her guest with the king. 13But all this does not really make me happy when I see that Jew Mordecai sitting at the king's gate."

14Then Haman's wife, Zeresh, and all his friends said, "Have a seventy-five foot platform built, and in the morning ask the king to have Mordecai hanged on it. Then go to the banquet with the king and be happy." Haman liked this suggestion, so he ordered the platform to be built.

MORDECAI IS HONORED

6 That same night the king could not sleep. So he gave an order for the daily court record to be brought in and read to him. 2It was found recorded that Mordecai had warned the king about Bigthana and Teresh, two of the king's officers who guarded the doorway and who had planned to kill the king.

3The king asked, "What honor and reward have been given to Mordecai for this?"

The king's personal servants answered, "Nothing has been done for Mordecai."

4The king said, "Who is in the courtyard?" Now Haman had just entered the outer court of the king's palace. He had come to ask the king about hanging Mordecai on the platform he had prepared.

5The king's personal servants said, "Haman is standing in the courtyard."

The king said, "Bring him in."

6So Haman came in. And the king asked him, "What should be done for a man whom the king wants very much to honor?"

And Haman thought to himself, "Whom would the king want to honor more than me?" 7So he answered the king, "This is what you could do for the man you want very much to honor. 8Have the servants bring a royal robe that the king himself has worn. And also bring a horse with a royal crown on its head, a horse that the king himself has ridden. 9Let the robe and the horse be given to one of the king's most important men. Let the servants put the robe on the man the king wants to honor, and let them lead him on the horse through the city streets. As they are leading him, let them announce: 'This is what is done for the man whom the king wants to honor!'"

[10]The king commanded Haman, "Go quickly. Take the robe and the horse just as you have said, and do all this for Mordecai the Jew who sits at the king's gate. Do not leave out anything you have suggested."

[11]So Haman took the robe and the horse, and he put the robe on Mordecai. Then he led him on horseback through the city streets, announcing before Mordecai: "This is what is done for the man whom the king wants to honor!"

[12]Then Mordecai returned to the king's gate, but Haman hurried home with his head covered, because he was embarrassed and ashamed. [13]He told his wife, Zeresh, and all his friends everything that had happened to him.

Haman's wife and the men who gave him advice said, "You are starting to lose power to Mordecai. Since he is a Jew, you cannot win against him. You will surely be ruined." [14]While they were still talking, the king's eunuchs came to Haman's house and made him hurry to the banquet Esther had prepared.

HAMAN IS HANGED

7 So the king and Haman went in to eat with Queen Esther. [2]As they were drinking wine on the second day, the king asked Esther again, "What are you asking for? I will give it to you. What is it you want? I will give you as much as half of my kingdom."

[3]Then Queen Esther answered, "My king, if you are pleased with me, and if it pleases you, let me live. This is what I ask. And let my people live, too. This is what I want. [4]My people and I have been sold to be destroyed, to be killed and completely wiped out. If we had been sold as male and female slaves, I would have kept quiet, because that would not be enough of a problem to bother the king."

[5]Then King Xerxes asked Queen Esther, "Who is he, and where is he? Who has done such a thing?"

[6]Esther said, "Our enemy and foe is this wicked Haman!"

Then Haman was filled with terror before the king and queen. [7]The king was very angry, so he got up, left his wine, and went out into the palace garden. But Haman stayed inside to beg Queen Esther to save his life. He could see that the king had already decided to kill him.

[8]When the king returned from the palace garden to the banquet hall, he saw Haman falling on the couch where Esther was lying. The king said, "Will he even attack the queen while I am in the house?"

As soon as the king said that, servants came in and covered Haman's face. [9]Harbona, one of the eunuchs there serving the king, said, "Look, a seventy-five foot platform stands near Haman's house. This is the one Haman had prepared for Mordecai, who gave the warning that saved the king."

The king said, "Hang Haman on it!" [10]So they hanged Haman on the platform he had prepared for Mordecai. Then the king was not so angry anymore.

THE KING HELPS THE JEWISH PEOPLE

8 That same day King Xerxes gave Queen Esther everything Haman, the enemy of the Jewish people, had left when he died. And Mordecai came in to see the king, because Esther had told the king how he was related to her. [2]Then the king took off his signet ring that he had taken back from Haman, and he gave it to Mordecai. Esther put Mordecai in charge of everything Haman left when he died.

[3]Once again Esther spoke to the king. She fell at the king's feet and cried and begged him to stop the evil plan that Haman the Agagite had planned against the Jews. [4]The king held out the gold scepter to Esther. So Esther got up and stood in front of him.

[5]She said, "My king, if you are pleased with me, and if it pleases you to do this, if you think it is the right thing to do, and if you are happy with me, let an order be written to cancel the letters Haman wrote. Haman the Agagite sent messages to destroy all the Jewish people in all of your kingdom. [6]I could not stand to see that terrible thing happen to my people. I could not stand to see my family killed."

7King Xerxes answered Queen Esther and Mordecai the Jew, "Because Haman was against the Jewish people, I have given his things to Esther, and my soldiers have hanged him. 8Now, in the king's name, write another order to the Jewish people as it seems best to you. Then seal the order with the king's signet ring, because no letter written in the king's name and sealed with his signet ring can be canceled."

9At that time the king's secretaries were called. This was the twenty-third day of the third month, which is Sivan. The secretaries wrote out all of Mordecai's orders to the Jews, to the governors, to the captains of the soldiers in each state, and to the important men of the one hundred twenty-seven states that reached from India to Cush. They wrote in the writing of each state and in the language of each people. They also wrote to the Jewish people in their own writing and language. 10Mordecai wrote orders in the name of King Xerxes and sealed the letters with the king's signet ring. Then he sent the king's orders by messengers on fast horses, horses that were raised just for the king.

11These were the king's orders: The Jewish people in every city have the right to gather together to protect themselves. They may destroy, kill, and completely wipe out the army of any state or people who attack them. And they are to do the same to the women and children of that army. They may also take by force the property of their enemies. 12The one day set for the Jewish people to do this in all the empire of King Xerxes was the thirteenth day of the twelfth month, the month of Adar. 13A copy of the king's order was to be sent out as a law in every state. It was to be made known to the people of every nation living in the kingdom so the Jewish people would be ready on that set day to strike back at their enemies.

14The messengers hurried out, riding on the royal horses, because the king commanded those messengers to hurry. And the order was also given in the palace at Susa.

15Mordecai left the king's presence wearing royal clothes of blue and white and a large gold crown. He also had a purple robe made of the best linen. And the people of Susa shouted for joy. 16It was a time of happiness, joy, gladness, and honor for the Jewish people. 17As the king's order went to every state and city, there was joy and gladness among the Jewish people. In every state and city to which the king's order went, they were having feasts and celebrating. And many people through all the empire became Jews, because they were afraid of the Jewish people.

VICTORY FOR THE JEWISH PEOPLE

9 The order the king had commanded was to be done on the thirteenth day of the twelfth month, the month of Adar. That was the day the enemies of the Jewish people had hoped to defeat them, but that was changed. So the Jewish people themselves defeated those who hated them. 2The Jews met in their cities in all the empire of King Xerxes in order to attack those who wanted to harm them. No one was strong enough to fight against them, because all the other people living in the empire were afraid of them. 3All the important men of the states, the governors, captains of the soldiers, and the king's officers helped the Jewish people, because they were afraid of Mordecai. 4Mordecai was very important in the king's palace. He was famous in all the empire, because he was becoming a leader of more and more people.

5And, with their swords, the Jewish people defeated all their enemies, killing and destroying them. And they did what they wanted with those people who hated them. 6In the palace at Susa, they killed and destroyed five hundred men. 7They also killed: Parshandatha, Dalphon, Aspatha, 8Poratha, Adalia, Aridatha, 9Parmashta, Arisai, Aridai, and Vaizatha, 10the ten sons of Haman, son of Hammedatha, the enemy of the Jewish people. But the Jewish people did not take their belongings.

11On that day the number killed in the palace at Susa was reported to the king. 12The king said to Queen Esther, "The Jewish people have killed and destroyed five hundred people in the palace at Susa, and they have also killed Haman's ten sons. What have they done in the rest of the king's empire! Now what else are you asking? I will do it! What else do you want? It will be done!"

13Esther answered, "If it pleases the king, give the Jewish people who are in Susa permission to do again tomorrow what the king ordered for today. And let the bodies of Haman's ten sons be hanged on the platform."

[14]So the king ordered that it be done. A law was given in Susa, and the bodies of the ten sons of Haman were hanged. [15]The Jewish people in Susa came together on the fourteenth day of the month of Adar. They killed three hundred people in Susa, but they did not take their belongings.

[16]At that same time, all the Jewish people in the king's empire also met to protect themselves and get rid of their enemies. They killed seventy-five thousand of those who hated them, but they did not take their belongings. [17]This happened on the thirteenth day of the month of Adar. On the fourteenth day they rested and made it a day of joyful feasting.

THE FEAST OF PURIM

[18]But the Jewish people in Susa met on the thirteenth and fourteenth days of the month of Adar. Then they rested on the fifteenth day and made it a day of joyful feasting.

[19]This is why the Jewish people who live in the country and small villages celebrate on the fourteenth day of the month of Adar. It is a day of joyful feasting and a day for exchanging gifts.

[20]Mordecai wrote down everything that had happened. Then he sent letters to all the Jewish people in all the empire of King Xerxes, far and near. [21]He told them to celebrate every year on the fourteenth and fifteenth days of the month of Adar, [22]because that was when the Jewish people got rid of their enemies. They were also to celebrate it as the month their sadness was turned to joy and their crying for the dead was turned into celebration. He told them to celebrate those days as days of joyful feasting and as a time for giving food to each other and presents to the poor.

[23]So the Jewish people agreed to do what Mordecai had written to them, and they agreed to hold the celebration every year. [24]Haman son of Hammedatha, the Agagite, was the enemy of all the Jewish people. He had made an evil plan against the Jewish people to destroy them, and he had thrown the Pur (that is, the lot) to choose a day to ruin and destroy them. [25]But when the king learned of the evil plan, he sent out written

orders that the evil plans Haman had made against the Jewish people would be used against him. And those orders said that Haman and his sons should be hanged on the platform. [26]So these days were called Purim, which comes from the word "Pur" (the lot). Because of everything written in this letter and what they had seen and what happened to them, [27]the Jewish people set up this custom. They and their descendants and all those who join them are always to celebrate these two days every year. They should do it in the right way and at the time Mordecai had ordered them in the letter. [28]These two days should be remembered and celebrated from now on in every family, in every state, and in every city. These days of Purim should always be celebrated by the Jewish people, and their descendants should always remember to celebrate them, too.

[29]So Queen Esther daughter of Abihail, along with Mordecai the Jew, wrote this second letter about Purim. Using the power they had, they wrote to prove the first letter was true. [30]And Mordecai sent letters to all the Jewish people in the one hundred twenty-seven states of the kingdom of Xerxes, writing them a message of peace and truth. [31]He wrote to set up these days of Purim at the chosen times. Mordecai the Jew and Queen Esther had sent out the order for the Jewish people, just as they had set up things for themselves and their descendants: On these two days the people should fast and cry loudly. [32]Esther's letter set up the rules for Purim, and they were written down in the records.

THE GREATNESS OF MORDECAI

10 King Xerxes demanded taxes everywhere, even from the cities on the seacoast. [2]And all the great things Xerxes did by his power and strength are written in the record books of the kings of Media and Persia. Also written in those record books are all the things done by Mordecai, whom the king made great. [3]Mordecai the Jew was second in importance to King Xerxes, and he was the most important man among the Jewish people. His fellow Jews respected him very much, because he worked for the good of his people and spoke up for the safety of all the Jewish people.

job

A GOOD MAN SUFFERS

JOB, THE GOOD MAN

1 A man named Job lived in the land of Uz. He was an honest and innocent man; he honored God and stayed away from evil. ²Job had seven sons and three daughters. ³He owned seven thousand sheep, three thousand camels, five hundred teams of oxen, and five hundred female donkeys. He also had a large number of servants. He was the greatest man among all the people of the East.

⁴Job's sons took turns holding feasts in their homes and invited their sisters to eat and drink with them. ⁵After a feast was over, Job would send and have them made clean. Early in the morning Job would offer a burnt offering for each of them, because he thought, "My children may have sinned and cursed God in their hearts." Job did this every time.

SATAN APPEARS BEFORE THE LORD

⁶One day the angels came to show themselves before the LORD, and Satan[n] was with them. ⁷The LORD said to Satan, "Where have you come from?"

Satan answered the LORD, "I have been wandering around the earth, going back and forth in it."

⁸Then the LORD said to Satan, "Have you noticed my servant Job? No one else on earth is like him. He is an honest and innocent man, honoring God and staying away from evil."

⁹But Satan answered the LORD, "Job honors God for a good reason. ¹⁰You have put a wall around him, his family, and everything he owns. You have blessed the things he has done. His flocks and herds are so large they almost cover the land. ¹¹But reach out your hand and destroy everything he has, and he will curse you to your face."

¹²The LORD said to Satan, "All right, then. Everything Job has is in your power, but you must not touch Job himself." Then Satan left the LORD's presence.

¹³One day Job's sons and daughters were eating and drinking wine together at the oldest brother's house. ¹⁴A messenger came to Job and said, "The oxen were plowing and the donkeys were eating grass nearby, ¹⁵when the Sabeans attacked and carried them away. They killed the servants with swords, and I am the only one who escaped to tell you!"

¹⁶The messenger was still speaking when another messenger arrived and said, "Lightning from God fell from the sky. It burned up the sheep and the servants, and I am the only one who escaped to tell you!"

¹⁷The second messenger was still speaking when another messenger arrived and said, "The Babylonians sent three groups of attackers that swept down and stole your camels and killed the servants. I am the only one who escaped to tell you!"

¹⁸The third messenger was still speaking when another messenger arrived and said, "Your sons and daughters were eating and drinking wine together at the oldest brother's house. ¹⁹Suddenly a great wind came from the desert, hitting all four corners of the house at once. The house fell in on the young people, and they are all dead. I am the only one who escaped to tell you!"

²⁰When Job heard this, he got up and tore his robe and shaved his head to show how sad he was. Then he bowed down to the ground to worship God. ²¹He said:

"I was naked when I was born,
    and I will be naked when I die.
The LORD gave these things to me,
    and he has taken them away.
    Praise the name of the LORD."

²²In all this Job did not sin or blame God.

SATAN APPEARS BEFORE THE LORD AGAIN

2 On another day the angels came to show themselves before the LORD, and Satan was with them again. ²The LORD said to Satan, "Where have you come from?"

Satan answered the LORD, "I have been wandering around the earth, going back and forth in it."

1:6 Satan Or "the accuser."

³Then the LORD said to Satan, "Have you noticed my servant Job? No one else on earth is like him. He is an honest and innocent man, honoring God and staying away from evil. You caused me to ruin him for no good reason, but he continues to be without blame."

⁴"One skin for another!" Satan answered. "A man will give all he has to save his own life. ⁵But reach out your hand and destroy his flesh and bones, and he will curse you to your face."

⁶The LORD said to Satan, "All right, then. Job is in your power, but you may not take his life."

⁷So Satan left the LORD's presence. He put painful sores on Job's body, from the top of his head to the soles of his feet. ⁸Job took a piece of broken pottery to scrape himself, and he sat in ashes in misery.

⁹Job's wife said to him, "Why are you trying to stay innocent? Curse God and die!"

¹⁰Job answered, "You are talking like a foolish woman. Should we take only good things from God and not trouble?" In spite of all this Job did not sin in what he said.

JOB'S THREE FRIENDS COME TO HELP

¹¹Now Job had three friends: Eliphaz the Temanite, Bildad the Shuhite, and Zophar the Naamathite. When these friends heard about Job's troubles, they agreed to meet and visit him. They wanted to show their concern and to comfort him. ¹²They saw Job from far away, but he looked so different they almost didn't recognize him. They began to cry loudly and tore their robes and put dirt on their heads to show how sad they were. ¹³Then they sat on the ground with Job seven days and seven nights. No one said a word to him because they saw how much he was suffering.

JOB CURSES HIS BIRTH

3 After seven days Job cried out and cursed the day he had been born, ²saying:

³ "Let the day I was born be destroyed,
    and the night it was said, 'A boy is born!'
⁴ Let that day turn to darkness.
    Don't let God care about it.
    Don't let light shine on it.
⁵ Let darkness and gloom have that day.
    Let a cloud hide it.
    Let thick darkness cover its light.

⁶ Let thick darkness capture that night.
    Don't count it among the days of the
        year
    or put it in any of the months.
⁷ Let that night be empty,
    with no shout of joy to be heard.
⁸ Let those who curse days curse that day.
    Let them prepare to wake up the sea
        monster Leviathan.
⁹ Let that day's morning stars never appear;
    let it wait for daylight that never comes.
    Don't let it see the first light of dawn,
¹⁰ because it allowed me to be born
    and did not hide trouble from my eyes.

¹¹ "Why didn't I die as soon as I was born?
    Why didn't I die when I came out of the
        womb?
¹² Why did my mother's knees receive me,
    and my mother's breasts feed me?
¹³ If they had not been there,
    I would be lying dead in peace;
    I would be asleep and at rest
¹⁴ with kings and wise men of the earth
    who built places for themselves that are
        now ruined.
¹⁵ I would be asleep with rulers
    who filled their houses with gold and
        silver.
¹⁶ Why was I not buried like a child born
        dead,
    like a baby who never saw the light of
        day?
¹⁷ In the grave the wicked stop making
        trouble,
    and the weary workers are at rest.
¹⁸ In the grave there is rest for the captives
    who no longer hear the shout of the
        slave driver.
¹⁹ People great and small are in the grave,
    and the slave is freed from his master.

²⁰ "Why is light given to those in misery?
    Why is life given to those who are so
        unhappy?
²¹ They want to die, but death does not come.
    They search for death more than for
        hidden treasure.
²² They are very happy
    when they get to the grave.
²³ They cannot see where they are going.
    God has hidden the road ahead.
²⁴ I make sad sounds as I eat;
    my groans pour out like water.

25 Everything I feared and dreaded
   has happened to me.
26 I have no peace or quietness.
   I have no rest, only trouble."

ELIPHAZ SPEAKS

4 Then Eliphaz the Temanite answered:
   2 "If someone tried to speak with you,
      would you be upset?
   I cannot keep from speaking.
3 Think about the many people you have
      taught
   and the weak hands you have made
      strong.
4 Your words have comforted those who
      fell,
   and you have strengthened those who
      could not stand.
5 But now trouble comes to you, and you
      are discouraged;
   trouble hits you, and you are terrified.
6 You should have confidence because you
      respect God;
   you should have hope because you are
      innocent.

7 "Remember that the innocent will not
      die;
   honest people will never be destroyed.
8 I have noticed that people who plow evil
   and plant trouble, harvest it.
9 God's breath destroys them,
   and a blast of his anger kills them.
10 Lions may roar and growl,
   but when the teeth of a strong lion are
      broken,
11 that lion dies of hunger.
   The cubs of the mother lion are
      scattered.

12 "A word was brought to me in secret,
   and my ears heard a whisper of it.
13 It was during a nightmare
   when people are in deep sleep.
14 I was trembling with fear;
   all my bones were shaking.
15 A spirit glided past my face,
   and the hair on my body stood on end.
16 The spirit stopped,
   but I could not see what it was.
   A shape stood before my eyes,
   and I heard a quiet voice.
17 It said, 'Can a human be more right than
      God?

Can a person be pure before his maker?
18 God does not trust his angels;
   he blames them for mistakes.
19 So he puts even more blame on people
      who live in clay houses,[n]
   whose foundations are made of dust,
   who can be crushed like a moth.
20 Between dawn and sunset many people
      are broken to pieces;
   without being noticed, they die and are
      gone forever.
21 The ropes of their tents are pulled up,
   and they die without wisdom.'

5 "Call if you want to, Job, but no one will
      answer you.
   You can't turn to any of the holy ones.
2 Anger kills the fool,
   and jealousy slays the stupid.
3 I have seen a fool succeed,
   but I cursed his home immediately.
4 His children are far from safety
   and are crushed in court with no
      defense.
5 The hungry eat his harvest,
   even taking what grew among the
      thorns,
   and thirsty people want his wealth.
6 Hard times do not come up from the
      ground,
   and trouble does not grow from the
      earth.
7 People produce trouble
   as surely as sparks fly upward.

8 "But if I were you, I would call on God
   and bring my problem before him.
9 God does wonders that cannot be
      understood;
   he does so many miracles they cannot
      be counted.
10 He gives rain to the earth
   and sends water on the fields.
11 He makes the humble person important
   and lifts the sad to places of safety.
12 He ruins the plans of those who trick
      others
   so they have no success.
13 He catches the wise in their own clever
      traps

4:19 clay houses This is probably talking about people's
bodies.

and sweeps away the plans of those
who try to trick others.
¹⁴ Darkness covers them up in the daytime;
even at noon they feel around in the
dark.
¹⁵ God saves the needy from their lies
and from the harm done by powerful
people.
¹⁶ So the poor have hope,
while those who are unfair are silenced.

¹⁷ "The one whom God corrects is happy,
so do not hate being corrected by the
Almighty.
¹⁸ God hurts, but he also bandages up;
he injures, but his hands also heal.
¹⁹ He will save you from six troubles;
even seven troubles will not harm you.
²⁰ God will buy you back from death in times
of hunger,
and in battle he will save you from the
sword.
²¹ You will be protected from the tongue
that strikes like a whip,
and you will not be afraid when
destruction comes.
²² You will laugh at destruction and
hunger,
and you will not fear the wild animals,
²³ because you will have an agreement with
the stones in the field,
and the wild animals will be at peace
with you.
²⁴ You will know that your tent is safe,
because you will check the things you
own and find nothing missing.
²⁵ You will know that you will have many
children,
and your descendants will be like the
grass on the earth.
²⁶ You will come to the grave with all your
strength,
like bundles of grain gathered at the
right time.

²⁷ "We have checked this, and it is true,
so hear it and decide what it means to
you."

JOB ANSWERS ELIPHAZ

6 Then Job answered:
² "I wish my suffering could be
weighed
and my misery put on scales.

³ My sadness would be heavier than the
sand of the seas.
No wonder my words seem careless.
⁴ The arrows of the Almighty are in me;
my spirit drinks in their poison;
God's terrors are gathered against me.
⁵ A wild donkey does not bray when it has
grass to eat,
and an ox is quiet when it has feed.
⁶ Tasteless food is not eaten without salt,
and there is no flavor in the white of an
egg.
⁷ I refuse to touch it;
such food makes me sick.

⁸ "How I wish that I might have what I ask
for
and that God would give me what I
hope for.
⁹ How I wish God would crush me
and reach out his hand to destroy me.
¹⁰ Then I would have this comfort
and be glad even in this unending pain,
because I would know I did not reject
the words of the Holy One.

¹¹ "I do not have the strength to wait.
There is nothing to hope for,
so why should I be patient?
¹² I do not have the strength of stone;
my flesh is not bronze.
¹³ I have no power to help myself,
because success has been taken away
from me.

¹⁴ "They say, 'A person's friends should be
kind to him when he is in trouble,
even if he stops fearing the Almighty.'
¹⁵ But my brothers cannot be counted on.
They are like streams that do not always
flow,
streams that sometimes run over.
¹⁶ They are made dark by melting ice
and rise with melting snow.
¹⁷ But they stop flowing in the dry season;
they disappear when it is hot.
¹⁸ Travelers turn away from their paths
and go into the desert and die.
¹⁹ The groups of travelers from Tema look
for water,
and the traders of Sheba look
hopefully.
²⁰ They are upset because they had been
sure;

when they arrive, they are
    disappointed.
21 You also have been no help.
    You see something terrible, and you are
        afraid.
22 I have never said, 'Give me a gift.
    Use your wealth to pay my debt.
23 Save me from the enemy's power.
    Buy me back from the clutches of cruel
        people.'

24 "Teach me, and I will be quiet.
    Show me where I have been wrong.
25 Honest words are painful,
    but your arguments prove nothing.
26 Do you mean to correct what I say?
    Will you treat the words of a troubled
        man as if they were only wind?
27 You would even gamble for orphans
    and would trade away your friend.

28 "But now please look at me.
    I would not lie to your face.
29 Change your mind; do not be unfair;
    think again, because my innocence is
        being questioned.
30 What I am saying is not wicked;
    I can tell the difference between right
        and wrong.

7 "People have a hard task on earth,
    and their days are like those of a
        laborer.
2 They are like a slave wishing for the
    evening shadows,
    like a laborer waiting to be paid.
3 But I am given months that are empty,
    and nights of misery have been given
        to me.
4 When I lie down, I think, 'How long until
    I get up?'
    The night is long, and I toss until dawn.
5 My body is covered with worms and scabs,
    and my skin is broken and full of sores.

6 "My days go by faster than a weaver's tool,
    and they come to an end without hope.
7 Remember, God, that my life is only a
    breath.
    My eyes will never see happy times
        again.
8 Those who see me now will see me no
    more;
    you will look for me, but I will be gone.
9 As a cloud disappears and is gone,

people go to the grave and never return.
10 They will never come back to their houses
    again,
    and their places will not know them
        anymore.

11 "So I will not stay quiet;
    I will speak out in the suffering of my
        spirit.
    I will complain because I am so
        unhappy.
12 I am not the sea or the sea monster.
    So why have you set a guard over me?
13 Sometimes I think my bed will comfort me
    or that my couch will stop my
        complaint.
14 Then you frighten me with dreams
    and terrify me with visions.
15 My throat prefers to be choked;
    my bones welcome death.
16 I hate my life; I don't want to live forever.
    Leave me alone, because my days have
        no meaning.

17 "Why do you make people so important
    and give them so much attention?
18 You examine them every morning
    and test them every moment.
19 Will you never look away from me
    or leave me alone even long enough to
        swallow?
20 If I have sinned, what have I done to you,
    you watcher of humans?
    Why have you made me your target?
    Have I become a heavy load for you?
21 Why don't you pardon my wrongs
    and forgive my sins?
    I will soon lie down in the dust of death.
    Then you will search for me, but I will
        be no more."

BILDAD SPEAKS TO JOB

8 Then Bildad the Shuhite answered:
2 "How long will you say such things?
    Your words are no more than wind.
3 God does not twist justice;
    the Almighty does not make wrong
        what is right.
4 Your children sinned against God,
    and he punished them for their sins.
5 But you should ask God for help
    and pray to the Almighty for mercy.
6 If you are good and honest,
    he will stand up for you

and bring you back where you belong.

7 Where you began will seem unimportant,
because your future will be so
successful.

8 "Ask old people;
find out what their ancestors learned,

9 because we were only born yesterday and
know nothing.
Our days on earth are only a shadow.

10 Those people will teach you and tell you
and speak about what they know.

11 Papyrus plants cannot grow where there
is no swamp,
and reeds cannot grow tall without
water.

12 While they are still growing and not yet
cut,
they will dry up quicker than grass.

13 That is what will happen to those who
forget God;
the hope of the wicked will be gone.

14 What they hope in is easily broken;
what they trust is like a spider's web.

15 They lean on the spider's web, but it
breaks.
They grab it, but it does not hold up.

16 They are like well-watered plants in the
sunshine
that spread their roots all through the
garden.

17 They wrap their roots around a pile of
rocks
and look for a place among the stones.

18 But if a plant is torn from its place,
then that place rejects it and says, 'I
never saw you.'

19 Now joy has gone away;
other plants grow up from the same
dirt.

20 "Surely God does not reject the innocent
or give strength to those who do evil.

21 God will yet fill your mouth with laughter
and your lips with shouts of joy.

22 Your enemies will be covered with shame,
and the tents of the wicked will be
gone."

JOB ANSWERS BILDAD

9 Then Job answered:

2 "Yes, I know that this is true,
but how can anyone be right in the
presence of God?

3 Someone might want to argue with God,
but no one could answer God,
not one time out of a thousand.

4 God's wisdom is deep, and his power is
great;
no one can fight him without getting
hurt.

5 God moves mountains without anyone
knowing it
and turns them over when he is angry.

6 He shakes the earth out of its place
and makes its foundations tremble.

7 He commands the sun not to shine
and shuts off the light of the stars.

8 He alone stretches out the skies
and walks on the waves of the sea.

9 It is God who made the Bear, Orion, and
the Pleiades[n]
and the groups of stars in the southern
sky.

10 He does wonders that cannot be
understood;
he does so many miracles they cannot
be counted.

11 When he passes me, I cannot see him;
when he goes by me, I do not recognize
him.

12 If he snatches something away, no one can
stop him
or say to him, 'What are you doing?'

13 God will not hold back his anger.
Even the helpers of the monster Rahab
lie at his feet in fear.

14 So how can I argue with God,
or even find words to argue with him?

15 Even if I were right, I could not answer
him;
I could only beg God, my Judge, for
mercy.

16 If I called to him and he answered,
I still don't believe he would listen to
me.

17 He would crush me with a storm
and multiply my wounds for no reason.

18 He would not let me catch my breath
but would overwhelm me with misery.

19 When it comes to strength, God is
stronger than I;
when it comes to justice, no one can
accuse him.

9:9 Bear . . . Pleiades Names of well-known groups
of stars.

20 Even if I were right, my own mouth
  would say I was wrong;
 if I were innocent, my mouth would say
  I was guilty.

21 "I am innocent,
 but I don't care about myself.
 I hate my own life.
22 It is all the same. That is why I say,
 'God destroys both the innocent and the
  guilty.'
23 If the whip brings sudden death,
 God will laugh at the suffering of the
  innocent.
24 When the land falls into the hands of evil
  people,
 he covers the judges' faces so they can't
  see it.
 If it is not God who does this, then who
  is it?

25 "My days go by faster than a runner;
 they fly away without my seeing any
  joy.
26 They glide past like paper boats.
 They attack like eagles swooping down
  to feed.
27 Even though I say, 'I will forget my
  complaint;
 I will change the look on my face and
  smile,'
28 I still dread all my suffering.
 I know you will hold me guilty.
29 I have already been found guilty,
 so why should I struggle for no reason?
30 I might wash myself with soap
 and scrub my hands with strong soap,
31 but you would push me into a dirty pit,
 and even my clothes would hate me.

32 "God is not human like me, so I cannot
  answer him.
 We cannot meet each other in court.
33 I wish there were someone to make peace
  between us,
 someone to decide our case.
34 Maybe he could remove God's
  punishment
 so his terror would no longer frighten
  me.
35 Then I could speak without being afraid,
 but I am not able to do that.

10 "I hate my life,
  so I will complain without holding
   back;
 I will speak because I am so unhappy.
2 I will say to God: Do not hold me guilty,
 but tell me what you have against me.
3 Does it make you happy to trouble me?
 Don't you care about me, the work of
  your hands?
 Are you happy with the plans of evil
  people?
4 Do you have human eyes
 that see as we see?
5 Are your days like the days of humans,
 and your years like our years?
6 You look for the evil I have done
 and search for my sin.
7 You know I am not guilty,
 but no one can save me from your
  power.

8 "Your hands shaped and made me.
 Do you now turn around and destroy
  me?
9 Remember that you molded me like a
  piece of clay.
 Will you now turn me back into dust?
10 You formed me inside my mother
 like cheese formed from milk.
11 You dressed me with skin and flesh;
 you sewed me together with bones and
  muscles.
12 You gave me life and showed me kindness,
 and in your care you watched over my
  life.

13 "But in your heart you hid other plans.
 I know this was in your mind.
14 If I sinned, you would watch me
 and would not let my sin go
  unpunished.
15 How terrible it will be for me if I am
  guilty!
 Even if I am right, I cannot lift my head.
 I am full of shame
 and experience only pain.
16 If I hold up my head, you hunt me like a
  lion
 and again show your terrible power
  against me.
17 You bring new witnesses against me
 and increase your anger against me.
 Your armies come against me.

When Your Way
Isn't God's Way

FITNESS

By Dr. Ben Lerner

JOB 10:8-9

When I graduated from high school, I wanted to be one thing and one thing only: an orthopedic surgeon. As a student athlete who played only collision sports, I had developed numerous health problems, and I practically lived in orthopedists' offices throughout my childhood. As a result, I one day wanted to be a doctor who helped young athletes like myself.

I wrestled in college and desired one day to make the Olympic wrestling team. Unfortunately, by my sophomore year, at the age of nineteen, the problems I had in high school had worsened. I couldn't move my right arm, and I had a bleeding ulcer from the anti-inflammatory medications my orthopedist had given me. Despite endless physical therapy, drugs, and orthopedic care, I became an eighty-year-old in the body of a teenager. Eventually, the orthopedist told me to quit sports altogether, and I had arthritis and would need invasive surgery. I couldn't understand it. I ate healthy, worked out every day, and was under the best of medical care; yet I felt like I could die at any minute.

At that time, one thing became crystal clear— I was not following God's directions for healing. I didn't have to read it somewhere or hear it from an expert; I simply realized I couldn't possibly be in alignment with God's will. I didn't feel stricken or victimized; something inside told me I was simply doing it wrong. I have nothing against orthopedists, physical therapists, or trainers; it just wasn't working for me, and, in truth, it was beginning to hurt.

Right before I was scheduled for surgery, I noticed that two teammates had completely recovered from the same or similar problems that I had and were back in practice. Both of them had stopped going to the team doctor like I was and, instead, had gone to a chiropractor. Immediately, I knew chiropractic was the right way to go. Not just because of their testimony, but because when I asked my coaches, my doctors, and my parents about seeing a chiropractor, they all told me in a variety of overly cynical ways that there was no way I should ever see a chiropractor.

Within a few months, five years of shoulder and back problems were completely gone. Within a year, I no longer had ulcers or any of my ongoing immune system issues. I became a wrestling All-American and I am in better shape at thirty-nine than I was at nineteen. When going with the flow of society's current beliefs isn't working out for you, a good question to ask is whether what you're doing is humankind's way or God's way. God's people shouldn't be afraid to swim upstream against the current of common beliefs. When a million people believe in the wrong idea, it's still the wrong idea. God's way is always the right way.

TO LEARN MORE ON WHAT THE BIBLE HAS TO SAY ABOUT **FITNESS,** READ THE SCRIPTURES AND DEVOTIONALS AT **GENESIS 1:11, GENESIS 1:31, GENESIS 2:7, JOSHUA 1:7, GENESIS 4:7, LEVITICUS 3:17,** AND **DEUTERONOMY 10:14.**

18 "So why did you allow me to be born?
  I wish I had died before anyone saw
  me.
19 I wish I had never lived,
  but had been carried straight from birth
  to the grave.
20 The few days of my life are almost over.
  Leave me alone so I can have a moment
  of joy.
21 Soon I will leave; I will not return
  from the land of darkness and gloom,
22 the land of darkest night,
  from the land of gloom and confusion,
  where even the light is darkness."

ZOPHAR SPEAKS TO JOB

11 Then Zophar the Naamathite answered:
  2 "Should these words go
      unanswered?
  Is this talker in the right?
3 Your lies do not make people quiet;
  people should correct you when you
  make fun of God.
4 You say, 'My teachings are right,
  and I am clean in God's sight.'
5 I wish God would speak
  and open his lips against you
6 and tell you the secrets of wisdom,
  because wisdom has two sides.

ANGER MANAGEMENT

FITNESS

your lifeline

JOB 10:10–11

In the past, if your head jutted out and you developed a humped back and your hips rolled under, you were just getting older or simply had bad posture. Today medical science has uncovered a whole new meaning to losing or overly accentuating your curves.

A shocking study in the *Journal of the American Geriatrics Society* revealed that mortality could be predicted by hyperkyphosis (increased curve or "hump" in the middle back). An elite group of medical scientists found that as the curve in the middle back, the kyphosis, became greater than normal, death came sooner.

Another groundbreaking study published in the medical journal *Spine* revealed that progressive kyphosis of the cervical spine (a loss or reversing of the neck's normal curve) resulted in destruction of nerve fibers and resulting pathology (disease) due to chronic compression of the spinal cord.

God created us to live upright against gravity. As your posture worsens, muscles weaken, and the spine moves out of its optimum position, life quickly slips away. Your spine is your lifeline. Therefore, regular exercise doesn't just keep you pain-free and healthy; it helps keep you alive.

reflect: Exercise regularly to help maintain proper posture and overall health.
Go to **Job 11:18.**

Know this: God has even forgotten some of your sin.

7 "Can you understand the secrets of God? Can you search the limits of the Almighty?

8 His limits are higher than the heavens; you cannot reach them! They are deeper than the grave; you cannot understand them!

9 His limits are longer than the earth and wider than the sea.

ANGER MANAGEMENT

a good night's
sleep

FITNESS

By Dr. Joseph Mercola

JOB 11:18

Did you know that a good night's sleep is just one of the many ways that God wants to bless his children? So if you are having sleep problems or simply want to improve the quality of your sleep, try as many of the following techniques as possible:

1. **Exercise and lose weight**. Being overweight can increase the risk of sleep apnea.

2. **Avoid before-bed snacks.** Snacks will raise blood sugar and inhibit sleep.

3. **Take a hot bath or shower before bed.** When body temperature is raised in the late evening, it will fall at bedtime, facilitating sleep.

4. **Respect your bedtime.** You should go to bed and wake up at the same times each day, even on the weekends. This will help your body get into a sleep rhythm and will make it easier to fall asleep and get up in the morning.

5. **Move the television.** If you are used to watching television in bed, you may find it harder to relax and to think of the bed as a place to sleep.

6. **Adjust the temperature.** Keep the temperature in the bedroom no higher than 70 degrees F. Many people keep their homes and particularly the upstairs bedrooms too hot.

7. **Sleep in complete darkness (or as close as possible).** When light hits the eyes, it disrupts the circadian rhythm of the pineal gland and production of melatonin and serotonin.

8. **Avoid using loud alarm clocks.** It is very stressful on the body to be awakened suddenly. If you are regularly getting enough sleep, alarms should be unnecessary.

reflect: Thank God for the gift of sweet sleep, and do your part to facilitate it.
Go to **Psalm 6:2.**

10 "If God comes along and puts you in
prison
or calls you into court, no one can stop
him.
11 God knows who is evil,
and when he sees evil, he takes note of
it.
12 A fool cannot become wise
any more than a wild donkey can be
born tame.

13 "You must give your whole heart to him
and hold out your hands to him for
help.
14 Put away the sin that is in your hand;
let no evil remain in your tent.
15 Then you can lift up your face without
shame,
and you can stand strong without fear.
16 You will forget your trouble
and remember it only as water gone by.
17 Your life will be as bright as the noonday
sun,
and darkness will seem like morning.
18 You will feel safe because there is hope;
you will look around and rest in safety.
19 You will lie down, and no one will scare
you.
Many people will want favors from you.
20 But the wicked will not be able to see,
so they will not escape.
Their only hope will be to die."

JOB ANSWERS ZOPHAR

12 Then Job answered:
2 "You really think you are the only
wise people
and that when you die, wisdom will die
with you!
3 But my mind is as good as yours;
you are not better than I am.
Everyone knows all these things.
4 My friends all laugh at me
when I call on God and expect him to
answer me;
they laugh at me even though I am right
and innocent!
5 Those who are comfortable don't care
that others have trouble;
they think it right that those people
should have troubles.
6 The tents of robbers are not bothered,
and those who make God angry are safe.
They have their god in their pocket.

7 "But ask the animals, and they will teach
you,
or ask the birds of the air, and they will
tell you.
8 Speak to the earth, and it will teach you,
or let the fish of the sea tell you.
9 Every one of these knows
that the hand of the LORD has done this.
10 The life of every creature
and the breath of all people are in God's
hand.
11 The ear tests words
as the tongue tastes food.
12 Older people are wise,
and long life brings understanding.

13 "But only God has wisdom and power,
good advice and understanding.
14 What he tears down cannot be rebuilt;
anyone he puts in prison cannot be let
out.
15 If God holds back the waters, there is no
rain;
if he lets the waters go, they flood the
land.
16 He is strong and victorious;
both the one who fools others and the
one who is fooled belong to him.
17 God leads the wise away as captives
and turns judges into fools.
18 He takes off chains that kings put on
and puts a garment on their bodies.
19 He leads priests away naked
and destroys the powerful.
20 He makes trusted people be silent
and takes away the wisdom of elders.
21 He brings disgrace on important people
and takes away the weapons of the
strong.
22 He uncovers the deep things of darkness
and brings dark shadows into the light.
23 He makes nations great and then destroys
them;
he makes nations large and then
scatters them.
24 He takes understanding away from the
leaders of the earth
and makes them wander through a
pathless desert.
25 They feel around in darkness with no
light;
he makes them stumble like drunks.

13 "Now my eyes have seen all this;
  my ears have heard and
    understood it.

2 What you know, I also know.
  You are not better than I am.

3 But I want to speak to the Almighty
  and to argue my case with God.

4 But you smear me with lies.
  You are worthless doctors, all of you!

5 I wish you would just stop talking;
  then you would really be wise!

6 Listen to my argument,
  and hear the pleading of my lips.

7 You should not speak evil in the name of
    God;
  you cannot speak God's truth by telling
    lies.

8 You should not unfairly choose his side
    against mine;
  you should not argue the case for God.

9 You will not do well if he examines
    you;

THE EXTRA MILE MARRIAGE

the wisdom of having marriage mentors

FAMILY

By Drs. Les and Leslie Parrott

JOB 12:12

Chaim Potok's novel, *The Chosen,* tells the story of a young boy born to a Hasidic rabbi. As the child matures, the father begins to realize that his son is especially clever and gifted, if not already a little arrogant and impatient. The father fears that his son's analytic brilliance and arrogance will rob him of the capacity to love others.

Knowing that the boy was likely to become the rabbi of his people, the father makes a mysterious and difficult decision. He chooses not to speak to the boy. He raises his son in a house without the comfort of a speaking relationship.

As the story closes, Potok reveals that the father has chosen this unconventional path of parenthood with the boy because he wants to create in him the capacity for understanding and compassion. He wants him to minister from a heart that knows pain—a heart that can identify with and feel the heartache of others.

The father in Potok's novel intuitively understands how keen analytic abilities not softened by emotional tenderness lead to manipulation rather than ministry, how they lead to control rather than compassion. You may not agree with this father's methods, but it is difficult to dispute his insight.

This powerful novel has reminded us as a couple to consider the "wisdom found among the aged." God's wisdom often comes from those who have traveled the path before us. For this reason, we do not take marriage mentors for granted. How about you?

reflect: Whom would you identify as marriage mentors in your life?
Go to **Psalm 37:24.**

you cannot fool God as you might fool
humans.
10 God would surely scold you
if you unfairly took one person's side.
11 His bright glory would scare you,
and you would be very much afraid of
him.
12 Your wise sayings are worth no more than
ashes,
and your arguments are as weak as
clay.

13 "Be quiet and let me speak.
Let things happen to me as they will.
14 Why should I put myself in danger
and take my life in my own hands?
15 Even if God kills me, I have hope in him;
I will still defend my ways to his face.
16 This is my salvation.
The wicked cannot come before him.
17 Listen carefully to my words;
let your ears hear what I say.
18 See, I have prepared my case,
and I know I will be proved right.

FUTURE

WHO ARE YOU?

the goodness
of God

JOB 13:15

Trust God. Believe him in all your times of blessing. Believe him in times of troubles. Believe him and trust in him. When you put your trust in God, you show him your reverence. You acknowledge him to be supreme, operating all according to the counsel of his will, and working all together for the good of those who love him.

When you trust him, you know that he will give you the strength and courage to overcome all sorts of trials. Praise God that nothing is allowed to separate us from his love. In the Old Testament, Job is the name that stands out as an example of endurance in suffering. Even when his friends turned their backs on him, he still endured. The type of suffering that Job went through made him realize that God is good, and if you will trust him in all types of afflictions, he will sustain you.

At the end of Job's trials, he was able to say of God that he knew the faithfulness of God firsthand. Job was faithful till the end, and he trusted God; and because of that, God blessed him more in the latter part of his life than in the former. So remember that no matter what you go through, God is there; he will sustain you and keep you if you don't faint. Trials are beneficial for our growth, and we may glory in them, as such, realizing that they produce endurance, and endurance will produce character, and with that we will receive hope. So remember to not grieve about your trials and sufferings but to rejoice in all things because God is good.

reflect: Consider the goodness of God in your own life today.
Go to **FUTURE:** "Building Momentum Through Teamwork" at **Acts 6:1-7.**

19 No one can accuse me of doing wrong.
  If someone can, I will be quiet and die.

20 "God, please just give me these two things,
  and then I will not hide from you:
21 Take your punishment away from me,
  and stop frightening me with your
    terrors.
22 Then call me, and I will answer,
  or let me speak, and you answer.
23 How many evil things and sins have I
    done?
  Show me my wrong and my sin.
24 Don't hide your face from me;
  don't think of me as your enemy.
25 Don't punish a leaf that is blown by the
    wind;
  don't chase after straw.
26 You write down cruel things against me
  and make me suffer for my boyhood
    sins.
27 You put my feet in chains
  and keep close watch wherever I go.
  You even mark the soles of my feet.

28 "Everyone wears out like something
    rotten,
  like clothing eaten by moths.

14

"All of us born to women
  live only a few days and have lots
    of trouble.
2 We grow up like flowers and then dry up
    and die.
  We are like a passing shadow that does
    not last.
3 Lord, do you need to watch me like this?
  Must you bring me before you to be
    judged?
4 No one can bring something clean from
    something dirty.
5 Our time is limited.
  You have given us only so many months
    to live
  and have set limits we cannot go
    beyond.
6 So look away from us and leave us alone
  until we put in our time like a laborer.

7 "If a tree is cut down,
  there is hope that it will grow again
  and will send out new branches.
8 Even if its roots grow old in the ground,
  and its stump dies in the dirt,

9 at the smell of water it will bud
  and put out new shoots like a plant.
10 But we die, and our bodies are laid in the
    ground;
  we take our last breath and are gone.
11 Water disappears from a lake,
  and a river loses its water and dries up.
12 In the same way, we lie down and do not
    rise again;
  we will not get up or be awakened
  until the heavens disappear.

13 "I wish you would hide me in the grave;
  hide me until your anger is gone.
  I wish you would set a time
  and then remember me!
14 Will the dead live again?
  All my days are a struggle;
  I will wait until my change comes.
15 You will call, and I will answer you;
  you will desire the creature your hands
    have made.
16 Then you will count my steps,
  but you will not keep track of my sin.
17 My wrongs will be closed up in a bag,
  and you will cover up my sin.

18 "A mountain washes away and crumbles;
  and a rock can be moved from its place.
19 Water washes over stones and wears them
    down,
  and rushing waters wash away the dirt.
  In the same way, you destroy hope.
20 You defeat people forever, and they are
    gone;
  you change their appearance and send
    them away.
21 Their children are honored, but they do
    not know it;
  their children are disgraced, but they do
    not see it.
22 They only feel the pain of their body
  and feel sorry for themselves."

ELIPHAZ ANSWERS JOB

15

Then Eliphaz the Temanite answered:
2 "A wise person would not answer
    with empty words
  or fill his stomach with the hot east
    wind.
3 He would not argue with useless words
  or make speeches that have no value.
4 But you even destroy respect for God
  and limit the worship of him.

5 Your sin teaches your mouth what to say;
   you use words to trick others.
6 It is your own mouth, not mine, that
      shows you are wicked;
   your own lips testify against you.

7 "You are not the first man ever born;
   you are not older than the hills.
8 You did not listen in on God's secret
      council.
   But you limit wisdom to yourself.
9 You don't know any more than we know.
   You don't understand any more than we
      understand.
10 Old people with gray hair are on our side;
   they are even older than your father.
11 Is the comfort God gives you not enough
      for you,
   even when words are spoken gently to
      you?
12 Has your heart carried you away from God?
   Why do your eyes flash with anger?
13 Why do you speak out your anger against
      God?
   Why do these words pour out of your
      mouth?

14 "How can anyone be pure?
   How can someone born to a woman be
      good?
15 God places no trust in his holy ones,
   and even the heavens are not pure in
      his eyes.
16 How much less pure is one who is terrible
      and rotten
   and drinks up evil as if it were water!

17 "Listen to me, and I will tell you about it;
   I will tell you what I have seen.
18 These are things wise men have told;
   their ancestors told them, and they have
      hidden nothing.
19 (The land was given to their fathers only,
   and no foreigner lived among them.)
20 The wicked suffer pain all their lives;
   the cruel suffer during all the years
      saved up for them.
21 Terrible sounds fill their ears,
   and when things seem to be going well,
      robbers attack them.
22 Evil people give up trying to escape from
      the darkness;
   it has been decided that they will die by
      the sword.

23 They wander around and will become
      food for vultures.
   They know darkness will soon come.
24 Worry and suffering terrify them;
   they overwhelm them, like a king ready
      to attack,
25 because they shake their fists at God
   and try to get their own way against the
      Almighty.
26 They stubbornly charge at God
   with thick, strong shields.

27 "Although the faces of the wicked are
      thick with fat,
   and their bellies are fat with flesh,
28 they will live in towns that are ruined,
   in houses where no one lives,
   which are crumbling into ruins.
29 The wicked will no longer get rich,
   and the riches they have will not last;
   the things they own will no longer
      spread over the land.
30 They will not escape the darkness.
   A flame will dry up their branches;
   God's breath will carry the wicked
      away.
31 The wicked should not fool themselves by
      trusting what is useless.
   If they do, they will get nothing in
      return.
32 Their branches will dry up before they
      finish growing
   and will never turn green.
33 They will be like a vine whose grapes are
      pulled off before they are ripe,
   like an olive tree that loses its blossoms.
34 People without God can produce
      nothing.
   Fire will destroy the tents of those who
      take money to do evil,
35 who plan trouble and give birth to evil,
   whose hearts plan ways to trick others."

JOB ANSWERS ELIPHAZ

16 Then Job answered:
2 "I have heard many things like these.
   You are all painful comforters!
3 Will your long-winded speeches never
      end?
   What makes you keep on arguing?
4 I also could speak as you do
   if you were in my place.
   I could make great speeches against you
      and shake my head at you.

5 But, instead, I would encourage you,
  and my words would bring you relief.

6 "Even if I speak, my pain is not less,
  and if I don't speak, it still does not go
  away.
7 God, you have surely taken away my
  strength
  and destroyed my whole family.
8 You have made me thin and weak,
  and this shows I have done wrong.
9 God attacks me and tears me with anger;
  he grinds his teeth at me;
  my enemy stares at me with his angry
  eyes.
10 People open their mouths to make fun of
  me
  and hit my cheeks to insult me.
  They join together against me.
11 God has turned me over to evil people
  and has handed me over to the wicked.
12 Everything was fine with me,
  but God broke me into pieces;
  he held me by the neck and crushed me.
  He has made me his target;
13 his archers surround me.
  He stabs my kidneys without mercy;
  he spills my blood on the ground.
14 Again and again God attacks me;
  he runs at me like a soldier.

15 "I have sewed rough cloth over my skin to
  show my sadness
  and have buried my face in the dust.
16 My face is red from crying;
  I have dark circles around my eyes.
17 Yet my hands have never done anything
  cruel,
  and my prayer is pure.

18 "Earth, please do not cover up my blood.
  Don't let my cry ever stop being heard!
19 Even now I have one who speaks for me
  in heaven;
  the one who is on my side is high above.
20 The one who speaks for me is my friend.
  My eyes pour out tears to God.
21 He begs God on behalf of a human
  as a person begs for his friend.

22 "Only a few years will pass
  before I go on the journey of no return.
17 My spirit is broken;
  the days of my life are almost gone.
  The grave is waiting for me.

2 Those who laugh at me surround me;
  I watch them insult me.

3 "God, make me a promise.
  No one will make a pledge for me.
4 You have closed their minds to
  understanding.
  Do not let them win over me.
5 People might speak against their friends
  for money,
  but if they do, the eyes of their children
  go blind.

6 "God has made my name a curse word;
  people spit in my face.
7 My sight has grown weak because of my
  sadness,
  and my body is as thin as a shadow.
8 Honest people are upset about this;
  innocent people are upset with those
  who do wrong.
9 But those who do right will continue to do
  right,
  and those whose hands are not dirty
  with sin will grow stronger.

10 "But, all of you, come and try again!
  I do not find a wise person among you.
11 My days are gone, and my plans have been
  destroyed,
  along with the desires of my heart.
12 These men think night is day;
  when it is dark, they say, 'Light is near.'
13 If the only home I hope for is the grave,
  if I spread out my bed in darkness,
14 if I say to the grave, 'You are my father,'
  and to the worm, 'You are my mother'
  or 'You are my sister,'
15 where, then, is my hope?
  Who can see any hope for me?
16 Will hope go down to the gates of death?
  Will we go down together into the
  dust?"

BILDAD ANSWERS JOB

18 Then Bildad the Shuhite answered:
2 "When will you stop these speeches?
  Be sensible, and then we can talk.
3 You think of us as cattle,
  as if we are stupid.
4 You tear yourself to pieces in your anger.
  Should the earth be vacant just for you?
  Should the rocks move from their
  places?

5 "The lamp of the wicked will be put out,
and the flame in their lamps will stop
burning.

6 The light in their tents will grow dark,
and the lamps by their sides will go out.

7 Their strong steps will grow weak;
they will fall into their own evil traps.

8 Their feet will be caught in a net
when they walk into its web.

9 A trap will catch them by the heel
and hold them tight.

10 A trap for them is hidden on the ground,
right in their path.

11 Terrible things startle them from every
side
and chase them at every step.

12 Hunger takes away their strength,
and disaster is at their side.

13 Disease eats away parts of their skin;
death gnaws at their arms and legs.

14 They are torn from the safety of their
tents
and dragged off to Death, the King of
Terrors.

15 Their tents are set on fire,
and sulfur is scattered over their homes.

16 Their roots dry up below ground,
and their branches die above ground.

17 People on earth will not remember them;
their names will be forgotten in the
land.

18 They will be driven from light into
darkness
and chased out of the world.

19 They have no children or descendants
among their people,
and no one will be left alive where they
once lived.

20 People of the west will be shocked at what
has happened to them,
and people of the east will be very
frightened.

21 Surely this is what will happen to the
wicked;
such is the place of one who does not
know God."

JOB ANSWERS BILDAD

19 Then Job answered:

2 "How long will you hurt me
and crush me with your words?

3 You have insulted me ten times now
and attacked me without shame.

4 Even if I have sinned,
it is my worry alone.

5 If you want to make yourselves look
better than I,
you can blame me for my suffering.

6 Then know that God has wronged me
and pulled his net around me.

7 "I shout, 'I have been wronged!'
But I get no answer.
I scream for help
but I get no justice.

8 God has blocked my way so I cannot pass;
he has covered my paths with
darkness.

9 He has taken away my honor
and removed the crown from my head.

10 He beats me down on every side until I
am gone;
he destroys my hope like a fallen tree.

11 His anger burns against me,
and he treats me like an enemy.

12 His armies gather;
they prepare to attack me.
They camp around my tent.

13 "God has made my brothers my enemies,
and my friends have become strangers.

14 My relatives have gone away,
and my friends have forgotten me.

15 My guests and my female servants treat
me like a stranger;
they look at me as if I were a foreigner.

16 I call for my servant, but he does not
answer,
even when I beg him with my own
mouth.

17 My wife can't stand my breath,
and my own family dislikes me.

18 Even the little boys hate me
and talk about me when I leave.

19 All my close friends hate me;
even those I love have turned against
me.

20 I am nothing but skin and bones;
I have escaped by the skin of my teeth.

21 Pity me, my friends, pity me,
because the hand of God has hit me.

22 Why do you chase me as God does?
Haven't you hurt me enough?

23 "How I wish my words were written
down,
written on a scroll.

24 I wish they were carved with an iron pen into lead,
or carved into stone forever.
25 I know that my Defender lives,
and in the end he will stand upon the earth.
26 Even after my skin has been destroyed,
in my flesh I will see God.
27 I will see him myself;
I will see him with my very own eyes.
How my heart wants that to happen!

28 "If you say, 'We will continue to trouble Job,
because the problem lies with him,'
29 you should be afraid of the sword yourselves.
God's anger will bring punishment by the sword.
Then you will know there is judgment."

ZOPHAR ANSWERS

20 Then Zophar the Naamathite answered:
2 "My troubled thoughts cause me to answer,
because I am very upset.
3 You correct me and I am insulted,
but I understand how to answer you.

4 "You know how it has been for a long time,
ever since people were first put on the earth.
5 The happiness of evil people is brief,
and the joy of the wicked lasts only a moment.
6 Their pride may be as high as the heavens,
and their heads may touch the clouds,
7 but they will be gone forever, like their own dung.
People who knew them will say, 'Where are they?'
8 They will fly away like a dream
and not be found again;
they will be chased away like a vision in the night.
9 Those who saw them will not see them again;
the places where they lived will see them no more.
10 Their children will have to pay back the poor,

and they will have to give up their wealth.
11 They had the strength of their youth in their bones,
but it will lie with them in the dust of death.

12 "Evil may taste sweet in their mouths,
and they may hide it under their tongues.
13 They cannot stand to let go of it;
they keep it in their mouths.
14 But their food will turn sour in their stomachs,
like the poison of a snake inside them.
15 They have swallowed riches, but they will spit them out;
God will make them vomit their riches up.
16 They will suck the poison of snakes,
and the snake's fangs will kill them.
17 They will not admire the sparkling streams
or the rivers flowing with honey and cream.
18 They must give back what they worked for without eating it;
they will not enjoy the money they made from their trading,
19 because they troubled the poor and left them with nothing.
They have taken houses they did not build.

20 "Evil people never lack an appetite,
and nothing escapes their selfishness.
21 But nothing will be left for them to eat;
their riches will not continue.
22 When they still have plenty, trouble will catch up to them,
and great misery will come down on them.
23 When the wicked fill their stomachs,
God will send his burning anger against them,
and blows of punishment will fall on them like rain.
24 The wicked may run away from an iron weapon,
but a bronze arrow will stab them.
25 They will pull the arrows out of their backs
and pull the points out of their livers.
Terrors will come over them;

26   total darkness waits for their
         treasure.
     A fire not fanned by people will destroy
         them
         and burn up what is left of their tents.
27 The heavens will show their guilt,
         and the earth will rise up against them.
28 A flood will carry their houses away,
         swept away on the day of God's anger.
29 This is what God plans for evil people;
         this is what he has decided they will
         receive."

JOB ANSWERS ZOPHAR

21 Then Job answered:
     2 "Listen carefully to my words,
         and let this be the way you comfort me.
3 Be patient while I speak.
     After I have finished, you may continue
         to make fun of me.

4 "My complaint is not just against people;
     I have reason to be impatient.
5 Look at me and be shocked;
     put your hand over your mouth in
         shock.
6 When I think about this, I am terribly
     afraid
     and my body shakes.
7 Why do evil people live a long time?
     They grow old and become more
         powerful.
8 They see their children around them;
     they watch them grow up.
9 Their homes are safe and without fear;
     God does not punish them.
10 Their bulls never fail to mate;
     their cows have healthy calves.
11 They send out their children like a flock;
     their little ones dance about.
12 They sing to the music of tambourines
         and harps,
     and the sound of the flute makes them
         happy.
13 Evil people enjoy successful lives
     and then go peacefully to the grave.
14 They say to God, 'Leave us alone!
     We don't want to know your ways.
15 Who is the Almighty that we should serve
         him?
     What would we gain by praying to
         him?'
16 The success of the wicked is not their
     own doing.

Their way of thinking is different from
         mine.
17 Yet how often are the lamps of evil people
         turned off?
     How often does trouble come to them?
     How often do they suffer God's angry
         punishment?
18 How often are they like straw in the wind
     or like chaff that is blown away by a
         storm?
19 It is said, 'God saves up a person's
     punishment for his children.'
     But God should punish the wicked
         themselves so they will know it.
20 Their eyes should see their own
         destruction,
     and they should suffer the anger of the
         Almighty.
21 They do not care about the families they
         leave behind
     when their lives have come to an end.

22 "No one can teach knowledge to God;
     he is the one who judges even the most
         important people.
23 One person dies while he still has all his
         strength,
     feeling completely safe and
         comfortable.
24 His body was well fed,
     and his bones were strong and healthy.
25 But another person dies with an unhappy
         heart,
     never enjoying any happiness.
26 They are buried next to each other,
     and worms cover them both.

27 "I know very well your thoughts
     and your plans to wrong me.
28 You ask about me, 'Where is this great
         man's house?
     Where are the tents where the wicked
         live?'
29 Have you never asked those who travel?
     Have you never listened to their stories?
30 On the day of God's anger and
         punishment,
     it is the wicked who are spared.
31 Who will accuse them to their faces?
     Who will pay them back for the evil
         they have done?
32 They are carried to their graves,
     and someone keeps watch over their
         tombs.

33 The dirt in the valley seems sweet to them.
  Everybody follows after them,
  and many people go before them.

34 "So how can you comfort me with this
  nonsense?
  Your answers are only lies!"

ELIPHAZ ANSWERS

22 Then Eliphaz the Temanite answered:
2 "Can anyone be of real use to God?
  Can even a wise person do him good?
3 Does it help the Almighty for you to be
  good?
  Does he gain anything if you are
  innocent?

4 Does God punish you for respecting him?
  Does he bring you into court for this?
5 No! It is because your evil is without
  limits
  and your sins have no end.
6 You took your brothers' things for a debt
  they didn't owe;
  you took clothes from people and left
  them naked.
7 You did not give water to tired people,
  and you kept food from the hungry.
8 You were a powerful man who owned
  land;
  you were honored and lived in the land.
9 But you sent widows away empty-handed,

FEAR OF THE FUTURE

looking up

FULFILLMENT

JOB 22:26

Faces don't lie. We might hear lying words, but we rarely see lying eyes. If you look carefully, most people reveal all you need to know just in the face. It's a natural reaction. You get caught. You are confronted. What do you do? You look down or away. Every mother knows this secret. "Now, look me in the face and tell me the truth."

For years we had to look away from God. Confronted with our sins, we were not able to raise our faces to him because the truth stood between us. Job captures a wonderful moment when God's presence becomes our delight and we lift up our faces to his countenance.

When the Hebrew root *nasa* ("look up") is used in this figurative way, it carries an important nuance. It is a sign of good conscience and acceptance. This feeling has two sides. We discover that our burdens, those lies that kept us separated from God, are removed. We are free to look up because the weight is gone.

Once we look up, we discover that God accepts us. The burden that kept us staring at the ground never let us see the face of our Redeemer. We only saw the dirt of our sins and the dust of our grave. We didn't know that the Son was shining.

reflect: Look up toward heaven and see the Son shining brightly on you today.
Go to **Psalm 4:4–5.**

and you mistreated orphans.

10 That is why traps are all around you
and sudden danger frightens you.

11 That is why it is so dark you cannot see
and a flood of water covers you.

12 "God is in the highest part of heaven.
See how high the highest stars are!

13 But you ask, 'What does God know?
Can he judge us through the dark
clouds?

14 Thick clouds cover him so he cannot see
us
as he walks around high up in the sky.'

15 Are you going to stay on the old path
where evil people walk?

16 They were carried away before their time
was up,
and their foundations were washed
away by a flood.

17 They said to God, 'Leave us alone!
The Almighty can do nothing to us.'

18 But it was God who filled their houses
with good things.
Their way of thinking is different from
mine.

19 "Good people can watch and be glad;
the innocent can laugh at them and say,

20 'Surely our enemies are destroyed,
and fire burns up their wealth.'

21 "Obey God and be at peace with him;
this is the way to happiness.

22 Accept teaching from his mouth,
and keep his words in your heart.

23 If you return to the Almighty, you will be
blessed again.
So remove evil from your house.

24 Throw your gold nuggets into the dust
and your fine gold among the rocks in
the ravines.

25 Then the Almighty will be your gold
and the best silver for you.

26 You will find pleasure in the Almighty,
and you will look up to him.

27 You will pray to him, and he will hear you,
and you will keep your promises to him.

28 Anything you decide will be done,
and light will shine on your ways.

29 When people are made humble and you
say, 'Have courage,'
then the humble will be saved.

30 Even a guilty person will escape

and be saved because your hands are
clean."

JOB ANSWERS

23 Then Job answered:

2 "My complaint is still bitter today.
I groan because God's heavy hand is on
me.

3 I wish I knew where to find God
so I could go to where he lives.

4 I would present my case before him
and fill my mouth with arguments.

5 I would learn how he would answer me
and would think about what he would
say.

6 Would he not argue strongly against
me?
No, he would really listen to me.

7 Then an honest person could present his
case to God,
and I would be saved forever by my
judge.

8 "If I go to the east, God is not there;
if I go to the west, I do not see him.

9 When he is at work in the north, I catch
no sight of him;
when he turns to the south, I cannot
see him.

10 But God knows the way that I take,
and when he has tested me, I will come
out like gold.

11 My feet have closely followed his steps;
I have stayed in his way;
I did not turn aside.

12 I have never left the commands he has
spoken;
I have treasured his words more than
my own.

13 "But he is the only God.
Who can come against him?
He does anything he wants.

14 He will do to me what he said he would
do,
and he has many plans like this.

15 That is why I am frightened of him;
when I think of this, I am afraid of
him.

16 God has made me afraid;
the Almighty terrifies me.

17 But I am not hidden by the darkness,
by the thick darkness that covers my
face.

24

"I wish the Almighty would set a time for judging.
Those who know God do not see such a day.

2 Wicked people take other people's land;
they steal flocks and take them to new pastures.

3 They chase away the orphan's donkey
and take the widow's ox when she has no money.

4 They push needy people off the path;
all the poor of the land hide from them.

5 The poor become like wild donkeys in the desert
who go about their job of finding food.
The desert gives them food for their children.

6 They gather hay and straw in the fields
and pick up leftover grapes from the vineyard of the wicked.

7 They spend the night naked, because they have no clothes,
nothing to cover themselves in the cold.

8 They are soaked from mountain rains
and stay near the large rocks because they have no shelter.

9 The fatherless child is grabbed from its mother's breast;
they take a poor mother's baby to pay for what she owes.

10 So the poor go around naked without any clothes;
they carry bundles of grain but still go hungry;

11 they crush olives to get oil
and grapes to get wine, but they still go thirsty.

12 Dying people groan in the city,
and the injured cry out for help,
but God accuses no one of doing wrong.

13 "Those who fight against the light
do not know God's ways
or stay in his paths.

14 When the day is over, the murderers get up
to kill the poor and needy.
At night they go about like thieves.

15 Those who are guilty of adultery watch for the night,
thinking, 'No one will see us,'
and they keep their faces covered.

16 In the dark, evil people break into houses.
In the daytime they shut themselves up in their own houses,
because they want nothing to do with the light.

17 Darkness is like morning to all these evil people
who make friends with the terrors of darkness.

18 "They are like foam floating on the water.
Their part of the land is cursed;
no one uses the road that goes by their vineyards.

19 As heat and dryness quickly melt the snow,
so the grave quickly takes away the sinners.

20 Their mothers forget them,
and worms will eat their bodies.
They will not be remembered,
so wickedness is broken in pieces like a stick.

21 These evil people abuse women who cannot have children
and show no kindness to widows.

22 But God drags away the strong by his power.
Even though they seem strong, they do not know how long they will live.

23 God may let these evil people feel safe,
but he is watching their ways.

24 For a little while they are important, and then they die;
they are laid low and buried like everyone else;
they are cut off like the heads of grain.

25 If this is not true, who can prove I am wrong?
Who can show that my words are worth nothing?"

BILDAD ANSWERS

25

Then Bildad the Shuhite answered:

2 "God rules and he must be honored;
he set up order in his high heaven.

3 No one can count God's armies.
His light shines on all people.

4 So no one can be good in the presence of God,
and no one born to a woman can be pure.

5 Even the moon is not bright
and the stars are not pure in his eyes.

6 People are much less! They are like
  insects.
  They are only worms!"

JOB ANSWERS BILDAD

26 Then Job answered:
  2 "You are no help to the helpless!
  You have not aided the weak!
3 Your advice lacks wisdom!
  You have shown little understanding!
4 Who has helped you say these words?
  And where did you get these ideas?

5 "The spirits of the dead tremble,
  those who are beneath and in the
  waters.
6 Death is naked before God;
  destruction is uncovered before him.
7 God stretches the northern sky out over
  empty space
  and hangs the earth on nothing.
8 He wraps up the waters in his thick
  clouds,
  but the clouds do not break under their
  weight.
9 He covers the face of the moon,
  spreading his clouds over it.
10 He draws the horizon like a circle on the
  water
  at the place where light and darkness
  meet.
11 Heaven's foundations shake
  when he thunders at them.
12 With his power he quiets the sea;
  by his wisdom he destroys Rahab, the
  sea monster.
13 He breathes, and the sky clears.
  His hand stabs the fleeing snake.
14 And these are only a small part of God's
  works.
  We only hear a small whisper of him.
  Who could understand God's
  thundering power?"

27 And Job continued speaking:
  2 "As surely as God lives, who has
  taken away my rights,
  the Almighty, who has made me
  unhappy,
3 as long as I am alive
  and God's breath of life is in my nose,
4 my lips will not speak evil,
  and my tongue will not tell a lie.
5 I will never agree you are right;

until I die, I will never stop saying I am
  innocent.
6 I will insist that I am right; I will not back
  down.
  My conscience will never bother me.

7 "Let my enemies be like evil people,
  my foes like those who are wrong.
8 What hope do the wicked have when they
  die,
  when God takes their life away?
9 God will not listen to their cries
  when trouble comes to them.
10 They will not find joy in the Almighty,
  even though they call out to God all the
  time.

11 "I will teach you about the power of God
  and will not hide the ways of the
  Almighty.
12 You have all seen this yourselves.
  So why are we having all this talk that
  means nothing?

13 "Here is what God has planned for evil
  people,
  and what the Almighty will give to cruel
  people:
14 They may have many children, but the
  sword will kill them.
  Their children who are left will never
  have enough to eat.
15 Then they will die of disease and be
  buried,
  and the widows will not even cry for
  them.
16 The wicked may heap up silver like piles
  of dirt
  and have so many clothes they are like
  piles of clay.
17 But good people will wear what evil
  people have gathered,
  and the innocent will divide up their
  silver.
18 The houses the wicked build are like a
  spider's web,
  like a hut that a guard builds.
19 The wicked are rich when they go to bed,
  but they are rich for the last time;
  when they open their eyes, everything
  is gone.
20 Fears come over them like a flood,
  and a storm snatches them away in the
  night.

²¹ The east wind will carry them away, and
then they are gone,
    because it sweeps them out of their
    place.
²² The wind will hit them without mercy
    as they try to run away from its power.
²³ It will be as if the wind is clapping its
    hands;
    it will whistle at them as they run from
    their place.

28
"There are mines where people dig
    silver
    and places where gold is made pure.
² Iron is taken from the ground,
    and copper is melted out of rocks.
³ Miners bring lights
    and search deep into the mines
    for ore in thick darkness.
⁴ Miners dig a tunnel far from where
    people live,
    where no one has ever walked;
    they work far from people, swinging
    and swaying from ropes.
⁵ Food grows on top of the earth,
    but below ground things are changed as
    if by fire.
⁶ Sapphires are found in rocks,
    and gold dust is also found there.
⁷ No hawk knows that path;
    the falcon has not seen it.
⁸ Proud animals have not walked there,
    and no lions cross over it.
⁹ Miners hit the rocks of flint
    and dig away at the bottom of the
    mountains.
¹⁰ They cut tunnels through the rock
    and see all the treasures there.
¹¹ They search for places where rivers begin
    and bring things hidden out into the
    light.

¹² "But where can wisdom be found,
    and where does understanding live?
¹³ People do not understand the value of
    wisdom;
    it cannot be found among those who
    are alive.
¹⁴ The deep ocean says, 'It's not in me;'
    the sea says, 'It's not in me.'
¹⁵ Wisdom cannot be bought with gold,
    and its cost cannot be weighed in silver.
¹⁶ Wisdom cannot be bought with fine gold

or with valuable onyx or sapphire gems.
¹⁷ Gold and crystal are not as valuable as
    wisdom,
    and you cannot buy it with jewels of
    gold.
¹⁸ Coral and jasper are not worth talking
    about,
    and the price of wisdom is much
    greater than rubies.
¹⁹ The topaz from Cush cannot compare to
    wisdom;
    it cannot be bought with the purest
    gold.

²⁰ "So where does wisdom come from,
    and where does understanding live?
²¹ It is hidden from the eyes of every living
    thing,
    even from the birds of the air.
²² The places of destruction and death say,
    'We have heard reports about it.'
²³ Only God understands the way to
    wisdom,
    and he alone knows where it lives,
²⁴ because he looks to the farthest parts of
    the earth
    and sees everything under the sky.
²⁵ When God gave power to the wind
    and measured the water,
²⁶ when he made rules for the rain
    and set a path for a thunderstorm to
    follow,
²⁷ then he looked at wisdom and decided its
    worth;
    he set wisdom up and tested it.
²⁸ Then he said to humans,
    'The fear of the Lord is wisdom;
    to stay away from evil is
    understanding.'"

JOB CONTINUES

29
Job continued to speak:
² "How I wish for the months that
    have passed
    and the days when God watched over
    me.
³ God's lamp shined on my head,
    and I walked through darkness by his
    light.
⁴ I wish for the days when I was strong,
    when God's close friendship blessed my
    house.
⁵ The Almighty was still with me,
    and my children were all around me.

6 It was as if my path were covered with
    cream
    and the rocks poured out olive oil for
    me.
7 I would go to the city gate
    and sit in the public square.
8 When the young men saw me, they would
    step aside,
    and the old men would stand up in
    respect.
9 The leading men stopped speaking
    and covered their mouths with their
    hands.
10 The voices of the important men were
    quiet,
    as if their tongues stuck to the roof of
    their mouths.
11 Anyone who heard me spoke well of me,
    and those who saw me praised me,
12 because I saved the poor who called out
    and the orphan who had no one to help.
13 The dying person blessed me,
    and I made the widow's heart sing.
14 I put on right living as if it were clothing;
    I wore fairness like a robe and a turban.
15 I was eyes for the blind
    and feet for the lame.
16 I was like a father to needy people,
    and I took the side of strangers who
    were in trouble.
17 I broke the fangs of evil people
    and snatched the captives from their
    teeth.
18 "I thought, 'I will live for as many days as
    there are grains of sand,
    and I will die in my own house.
19 My roots will reach down to the water.
    The dew will lie on the branches all
    night.
20 New honors will come to me continually,
    and I will always have great strength.'
21 "People listened to me carefully
    and waited quietly for my advice.
22 After I finished speaking, they spoke no
    more.
    My words fell very gently on their ears.
23 They waited for me as they would for
    rain
    and drank in my words like spring rain.
24 I smiled at them when they doubted,
    and my approval was important to
    them.

25 I chose the way for them and was their
    leader.
    I lived like a king among his army,
    like a person who comforts sad people.

30 "But now those who are younger
        than I
    make fun of me.
    I would not have even let their fathers
    sit with my sheep dogs.
2 What use did I have for their strength
    since they had lost their strength to
    work?
3 They were thin from hunger
    and wandered the dry and ruined land
    at night.
4 They gathered desert plants among the
    brush
    and ate the root of the broom tree.
5 They were forced to live away from
    people;
    people shouted at them as if they were
    thieves.
6 They lived in dried-up streambeds,
    in caves, and among the rocks.
7 They howled like animals among the
    bushes
    and huddled together in the brush.
8 They are worthless people without
    names
    and were forced to leave the land.

9 "Now they make fun of me with songs;
    my name is a joke among them.
10 They hate me and stay far away from me,
    but they do not mind spitting in my
    face.
11 God has taken away my strength and
    made me suffer,
    so they attack me with all their anger.
12 On my right side they rise up like a mob.
    They lay traps for my feet
    and prepare to attack me.
13 They break up my road
    and work to destroy me,
    and no one helps me.
14 They come at me as if through a hole in
    the wall,
    and they roll in among the ruins.
15 Great fears overwhelm me.
    They blow my honor away as if by a
    great wind,
    and my safety disappears like a cloud.

16 "Now my life is almost over;
  my days are full of suffering.
17 At night my bones ache;
  gnawing pains never stop.
18 In his great power God grabs hold of my
    clothing
  and chokes me with the collar of my
    coat.
19 He throws me into the mud,
  and I become like dirt and ashes.

20 "I cry out to you, God, but you do not
    answer;
  I stand up, but you just look at me.
21 You have turned on me without mercy;
  with your powerful hand you attacked
    me.
22 You snatched me up and threw me into
    the wind
  and tossed me about in the storm.
23 I know you will bring me down to death,
  to the place where all living people
    must go.

24 "Surely no one would hurt those who are
    ruined
  when they cry for help in their time of
    trouble.
25 I cried for those who were in trouble;
  I have been very sad for poor people.
26 But when I hoped for good, only evil came
    to me;
  when I looked for light, darkness came.
27 I never stop being upset;
  days of suffering are ahead of me.
28 I have turned black, but not by the sun.
  I stand up in public and cry for help.
29 I have become a brother to wild dogs
  and a friend to ostriches.
30 My skin has become black and peels off,
  as my body burns with fever.
31 My harp is tuned to sing a sad song,
  and my flute is tuned to moaning.

31

"But I made an agreement with my
    eyes
  not to look with desire at a girl.
2 What has God above promised for people?
  What has the Almighty planned from
    on high?
3 It is ruin for evil people
  and disaster for those who do wrong.
4 God sees my ways
  and counts every step I take.

5 "If I have been dishonest
  or lied to others,
6 then let God weigh me on honest scales.
  Then he will know I have done nothing
    wrong.
7 If I have turned away from doing what is
    right,
  or my heart has been led by my eyes to
    do wrong,
  or my hands have been made unclean,
8 then let other people eat what I have
    planted,
  and let my crops be plowed up.

9 "If I have desired another woman
  or have waited at my neighbor's door
    for his wife,
10 then let my wife grind another man's
    grain,
  and let other men have sexual relations
    with her.
11 That would be shameful,
  a sin to be punished.
12 It is like a fire that burns and destroys;
  all I have done would be plowed up.

13 "If I have been unfair to my male and
    female slaves
  when they had a complaint against me,
14 how could I tell God what I did?
  What will I answer when he asks me to
    explain what I've done?
15 God made me in my mother's womb, and
    he also made them;
  the same God formed both of us in our
    mothers' wombs.

16 "I have never refused the appeals of the
    poor
  or let widows give up hope while
    looking for help.
17 I have not kept my food to myself
  but have given it to the orphans.
18 Since I was young, I have been like a
    father to the orphans.
  From my birth I guided the widows.
19 I have not let anyone die for lack of
    clothes
  or let a needy person go without a coat.
20 That person's heart blessed me,
  because I warmed him with the wool of
    my sheep.
21 I have never hurt an orphan
  even when I knew I could win in court.

22 If I have, then let my arm fall off my
   shoulder
      and be broken at the joint.
23 I fear destruction from God,
      and I fear his majesty, so I could not do
      such things.

24 "I have not put my trust in gold
      or said to pure gold, 'You are my
      security.'
25 I have not celebrated my great wealth
      or the riches my hands had gained.
26 I have not thought about worshiping the
   sun in its brightness
      nor admired the moon moving in glory
27 so that my heart was pulled away from
   God.
      My hand has never offered the sun and
      moon a kiss of worship.
28 If I had, these also would have been sins
   to be punished,
      because I would have been unfaithful
      to God.

29 "I have not been happy when my enemies
   fell
      or laughed when they had trouble.
30 I have not let my mouth sin
      by cursing my enemies' life.
31 The servants of my house have always
   said,
      'All have eaten what they want of Job's
      food.'
32 No stranger ever had to spend the night in
   the street,
      because I always let travelers stay in my
      home.
33 I have not hidden my sin as others do,
      secretly keeping my guilt to myself.
34 I was not so afraid of the crowd
   that I kept quiet and stayed inside
      because I feared being hated by other
      families.

35 ("How I wish a court would hear my
   case!
      Here I sign my name to show I have
      told the truth.
   Now let the Almighty answer me;
      let the one who accuses me write it
      down.
36 I would wear the writing on my shoulder;
      I would put it on like a crown.
37 I would explain to God every step I took,

and I would come near to him like a
   prince.)

38 "If my land cries out against me
      and its plowed rows are not wet with
      tears,
39 if I have taken the land's harvest without
   paying
      or have broken the spirit of those who
      worked the land,
40 then let thorns come up instead of wheat,
      and let weeds come up instead of
      barley."
   The words of Job are finished.

ELIHU SPEAKS

32 These three men stopped trying to answer Job, because he was so sure he was right. 2But Elihu son of Barakel the Buzite, from the family of Ram, became very angry with Job, because Job claimed he was right instead of God. 3Elihu was also angry with Job's three friends who had no answer to show that Job was wrong, yet continued to blame him. 4Elihu had waited before speaking to Job, because the three friends were older than he was. 5But when Elihu saw that the three men had nothing more to say, he became very angry.

6So Elihu son of Barakel the Buzite said this:
   "I am young,
      and you are old.
   That is why I was afraid
      to tell you what I know.
7 I thought, 'Older people should speak,
      and those who have lived many years
      should teach wisdom.'
8 But it is the spirit in a person,
      the breath of the Almighty, that gives
      understanding.
9 It is not just older people who are wise;
      they are not the only ones who
      understand what is right.
10 So I say, listen to me.
      I too will tell you what I know.
11 I waited while you three spoke,
      and listened to your explanations.
   While you looked for words to use,
12   I paid close attention to you.
   But not one of you has proved Job wrong;
      none of you has answered his
      arguments.
13 Don't say, 'We have found wisdom;

only God will show Job to be wrong,
not people.'

14 Job has not spoken his words against me,
so I will not use your arguments to
answer Job.

15 "These three friends are defeated and
have no more to say;
words have failed them.

16 Now they are standing there with no
answers for Job.
Now that they are quiet, must I wait to
speak?

17 No, I too will speak
and tell what I know.

18 I am full of words,
and the spirit in me causes me to speak.

19 I am like wine that has been bottled up;
I am ready to burst like a new leather
wine bag.

20 I must speak so I will feel relief;
I must open my mouth and answer.

21 I will be fair to everyone
and not flatter anyone.

22 I don't know how to flatter,
and if I did, my Maker would quickly
take me away.

33

"Now, Job, listen to my words.
Pay attention to everything I say.

2 I open my mouth
and am ready to speak.

3 My words come from an honest heart,
and I am sincere in saying what I
know.

4 The Spirit of God created me,
and the breath of the Almighty gave me
life.

5 Answer me if you can;
get yourself ready and stand before me.

6 I am just like you before God;
I too am made out of clay.

7 Don't be afraid of me;
I will not be hard on you.

8 "But I heard what you have said;
I heard every word.

9 You said, 'I am pure and without sin;
I am innocent and free from guilt.

10 But God has found fault with me;
he considers me his enemy.

11 He locks my feet in chains
and closely watches everywhere I go.'

12 "But I tell you, you are not right in saying
this,
because God is greater than we are.

13 Why do you accuse God
of not answering anyone?

14 God does speak—sometimes one way and
sometimes another—
even though people may not
understand it.

15 He speaks in a dream or a vision of the
night
when people are in a deep sleep,
lying on their beds.

16 He speaks in their ears
and frightens them with warnings

17 to turn them away from doing wrong
and to keep them from being proud.

18 God does this to save people from death,
to keep them from dying.

19 People may be corrected while in bed in
great pain;
they may have continual pain in their
very bones.

20 They may be in such pain that they even
hate food,
even the very best meal.

21 Their body becomes so thin there is
almost nothing left of it,
and their bones that were hidden now
stick out.

22 They are near death,
and their life is almost over.

23 "But there may be an angel to speak for
him,
one out of a thousand, who will tell him
what to do.

24 The angel will beg for mercy and say:
'Save him from death.
I have found a way to pay for his life.'

25 Then his body is made new like a child's.
It will return to the way it was when he
was young.

26 That person will pray to God, and God
will listen to him.
He will see God's face and will shout
with happiness.
And God will set things right for him
again.

27 Then he will say to others,
'I sinned and twisted what was right,
but I did not receive the punishment I
should have received.

28 God bought my life back from death,
   and I will continue to enjoy life.'

29 "God does all these things to a person
   two or even three times
30 so he won't die as punishment for his sins
   and so he may still enjoy life.

31 "Job, pay attention and listen to me;
   be quiet, and I will speak.
32 If you have anything to say, answer me;
   speak up, because I want to prove you
   right.
33 But if you have nothing to say, then listen
   to me;
   be quiet, and I will teach you wisdom."

34

Then Elihu said:
2 "Hear my words, you wise men;
   listen to me, you who know a lot.
3 The ear tests words
   as the tongue tastes food.
4 Let's decide for ourselves what is right,
   and let's learn together what is good.

5 "Job says, 'I am not guilty,
   and God has refused me a fair trial.
6 Instead of getting a fair trial,
   I am called a liar.
I have been seriously hurt,
   even though I have not sinned.'
7 There is no other man like Job;
   he takes insults as if he were drinking
   water.
8 He keeps company with those who do evil
   and spends time with wicked men,
9 because he says, 'It is no use
   to try to please God.'

10 "So listen to me, you who can understand.
   God can never do wrong!
   It is impossible for the Almighty to do
   evil.
11 God pays people back for what they have
   done
   and gives them what their actions
   deserve.
12 Truly God will never do wrong;
   the Almighty will never twist what is
   right.
13 No one chose God to rule over the earth
   or put him in charge of the whole
   world.
14 If God should decide
   to take away life and breath,

15 then everyone would die together
   and turn back into dust.

16 "If you can understand, hear this;
   listen to what I have to say.
17 Can anyone govern who hates what is
   right?
   How can you blame God who is both
   fair and powerful?
18 God is the one who says to kings, 'You are
   worthless,'
   or to important people, 'You are evil.'
19 He is not nicer to princes than other
   people,
   nor kinder to rich people than poor
   people,
   because he made them all with his own
   hands.
20 They can die in a moment, in the middle
   of the night.
   They are struck down, and then they
   pass away;
   powerful people die without help.

21 "God watches where people go;
   he sees every step they take.
22 There is no dark place or deep shadow
   where those who do evil can hide from
   him.
23 He does not set a time
   for people to come before him for
   judging.
24 Without asking questions, God breaks
   powerful people into pieces
   and puts others in their place.
25 Because God knows what people do,
   he defeats them in the night, and they
   are crushed.
26 He punishes them for the evil they do
   so that everyone else can watch,
27 because they stopped following God
   and did not care about any of his ways.
28 The cry of the poor comes to God;
   he hears the cry of the needy.
29 But if God keeps quiet, who can blame
   him?
   If he hides his face, who can see him?
   God still rules over both nations and
   persons alike.
30   He keeps the wicked from ruling
   and from trapping others.

31 "But suppose someone says to God,
   'I am guilty, but I will not sin anymore.

32 Teach me what I cannot see.
  If I have done wrong, I will not do it
    again.'
33 So, Job, should God reward you as you
    want
  when you refuse to change?
  You must decide, not I,
    so tell me what you know.

34 "Those who understand speak,
  and the wise who hear me say,
35 'Job speaks without knowing what is
    true;
  his words show he does not
    understand.'
36 I wish Job would be tested completely,
  because he answered like an evil man!
37 Job now adds to his sin by turning against
    God.
  He claps his hands in protest,
  speaking more and more against God."

35

Then Elihu said:
2 "Do you think this is fair?
  You say, 'God will show that I am right,'
3 but you also ask, 'What's the use?
  I don't gain anything by not sinning.'

4 "I will answer you
  and your friends who are with you.
5 Look up at the sky
  and see the clouds so high above you.
6 If you sin, it does nothing to God;
  even if your sins are many, they do
    nothing to him.
7 If you are good, you give nothing to God;
  he receives nothing from your hand.
8 Your evil ways only hurt others like
    yourself,
  and the good you do only helps other
    human beings.

9 "People cry out when they are in trouble;
  they beg for relief from powerful
    people.
10 But no one asks, 'Where is God, my
    Maker,
  who gives us songs in the night,
11 who makes us smarter than the animals of
    the earth
  and wiser than the birds of the air?'
12 God does not answer evil people when
    they cry out,
  because the wicked are proud.

13 God does not listen to their useless
    begging;
  the Almighty pays no attention to them.
14 He will listen to you even less
  when you say that you do not see him,
  that your case is before him,
  that you must wait for him,
15 that his anger never punishes,
  and that he doesn't notice evil.
16 So Job is only speaking nonsense,
  saying many words without knowing
    what is true."

ELIHU'S SPEECH CONTINUES

36

Elihu continued:
2 "Listen to me a little longer, and
    I will show you
  that there is more to be said for God.
3 What I know comes from far away.
  I will show that my Maker is right.
4 You can be sure that my words are not
    false;
  one who really knows is with you.

5 "God is powerful, but he does not hate
    people;
  he is powerful and sure of what he
    wants to do.
6 He will not keep evil people alive,
  but he gives the poor their rights.
7 He always watches over those who do
    right;
  he sets them on thrones with kings
  and they are honored forever.
8 If people are bound in chains,
  or if trouble, like ropes, ties them up,
9 God tells them what they have done,
  that they have sinned in their pride.
10 God makes them listen to his warning
  and commands them to change from
    doing evil.
11 If they obey and serve him,
  the rest of their lives will be successful,
  and the rest of their years will be happy.
12 But if they do not listen,
  they will die by the sword,
  and they will die without knowing why.

13 "Those who have wicked hearts hold on
    to anger.
  Even when God punishes them, they do
    not cry for help.
14 They die while they are still young,
  and their lives end in disgrace.

15 But God saves those who suffer through
their suffering;
he gets them to listen through their
pain.

16 "God is gently calling you from the jaws of
trouble
to an open place of freedom
where he has set your table full of the
best food.

17 But now you are being punished like the
wicked;
you are getting justice.

18 Be careful! Don't be led away from God by
riches;
don't let much money turn you away.

19 Neither your wealth nor all your great
strength
will keep you out of trouble.

20 Don't wish for the night
when people are taken from their
homes.

21 Be careful not to turn to evil,
which you seem to want more than
suffering.

22 "God is great and powerful;
no other teacher is like him.

23 No one has planned his ways for him;
no one can say to God, 'You have done
wrong.'

24 Remember to praise his work,
about which people have sung.

25 Everybody has seen it;
people look at it from far off.

26 God is so great, greater than we can
understand!
No one knows how old he is.

27 "He evaporates the drops of water from
the earth
and turns them into rain.

28 The rain then pours down from the
clouds,
and showers fall on people.

29 No one understands how God spreads out
the clouds
or how he sends thunder from where
he lives.

30 Watch how God scatters his lightning
around him,
lighting up the deepest parts of the sea.

31 This is the way God governs the nations;
this is how he gives us enough food.

32 God fills his hands with lightning
and commands it to strike its target.

33 His thunder announces the coming storm,
and even the cattle know it is near.

37

"At the sound of his thunder, my
heart pounds
as if it will jump out of my chest.

2 Listen! Listen to the thunder of God's
voice
and to the rumbling that comes from
his mouth.

3 He turns his lightning loose under the
whole sky
and sends it to the farthest parts of the
earth.

4 After that you can hear the roar
when he thunders with a great sound.
He does not hold back the flashing
when his voice is heard.

5 God's voice thunders in wonderful ways;
he does great things we cannot
understand.

6 He says to the snow, 'Fall on the earth,'
and to the shower, 'Be a heavy rain.'

7 With it, he stops everyone from working
so everyone knows it is the work of
God.

8 The animals take cover from the rain
and stay in their dens.

9 The storm comes from where it was
stored;
the cold comes with the strong winds.

10 The breath of God makes ice,
and the wide waters become frozen.

11 He fills the clouds with water
and scatters his lightning through them.

12 At his command they swirl around
over the whole earth,
doing whatever he commands.

13 He uses the clouds to punish people
or to water his earth and show his love.

14 "Job, listen to this:
Stop and notice God's miracles.

15 Do you know how God controls the
clouds
and makes his lightning flash?

16 Do you know how the clouds hang in the
sky?
Do you know the miracles of God, who
knows everything?

17 You suffer in your clothes

when the land is silenced by the hot, south wind.

¹⁸ You cannot stretch out the sky like God
and make it look as hard as polished bronze.

¹⁹ Tell us what we should say to him;
we cannot get our arguments ready
because we do not have enough understanding.

²⁰ Should God be told that I want to speak?
Would a person ask to be swallowed up?

²¹ No one can look at the sun
when it is bright in the sky
after the wind has blown all the clouds away.

²² God comes out of the north in golden light,
in overwhelming greatness.

²³ The Almighty is too high for us to reach.
He has great strength;
he is always right and never punishes unfairly.

²⁴ That is why people honor him;
he does not respect those who say they are wise."

THE LORD QUESTIONS JOB

38 Then the LORD answered Job from the storm. He said:

² "Who is this that makes my purpose unclear
by saying things that are not true?

³ Be strong like a man!
I will ask you questions,
and you must answer me.

⁴ Where were you when I made the earth's foundation?
Tell me, if you understand.

⁵ Who marked off how big it should be?
Surely you know!
Who stretched a ruler across it?

⁶ What were the earth's foundations set on,
or who put its cornerstone in place

⁷ while the morning stars sang together
and all the angels shouted with joy?

⁸ "Who shut the doors to keep the sea in
when it broke through and was born,

⁹ when I made the clouds like a coat for the sea
and wrapped it in dark clouds,

¹⁰ when I put limits on the sea
and put its doors and bars in place,

¹¹ when I said to the sea, 'You may come this far, but no farther;
this is where your proud waves must stop'?

¹² "Have you ever ordered the morning to begin,
or shown the dawn where its place was

¹³ in order to take hold of the earth by its edges
and shake evil people out of it?

¹⁴ At dawn the earth changes like clay being pressed by a seal;
the hills and valleys stand out like folds in a coat.

¹⁵ Light is not given to evil people;
their arm is raised to do harm, but it is broken.

¹⁶ "Have you ever gone to where the sea begins
or walked in the valleys under the sea?

¹⁷ Have the gates of death been opened to you?
Have you seen the gates of the deep darkness?

¹⁸ Do you understand how wide the earth is?
Tell me, if you know all these things.

¹⁹ "What is the path to light's home,
and where does darkness live?

²⁰ Can you take them to their places?
Do you know the way to their homes?

²¹ Surely you know, if you were already born when all this happened!
Have you lived that many years?

²² "Have you ever gone into the storehouse of the snow
or seen the storehouses for hail,

²³ which I save for times of trouble,
for days of war and battle?

²⁴ Where is the place from which light comes?
Where is the place from which the east winds blow over the earth?

²⁵ Who cuts a waterway for the heavy rains
and sets a path for the thunderstorm?

²⁶ Who waters the land where no one lives,
the desert that has no one in it?

²⁷ Who sends rain to satisfy the empty land
so the grass begins to grow?

²⁸ Does the rain have a father?
Who is father to the drops of dew?

²⁹ Who is the mother of the ice?

Who gives birth to the frost from the
sky

30 when the water becomes hard as stone,
and even the surface of the ocean is
frozen?

31 "Can you tie up the stars of the Pleiades
or loosen the ropes of the stars in
Orion?

32 Can you bring out the stars on time
or lead out the stars of the Bear with its
cubs?

33 Do you know the laws of the sky
and understand their rule over the
earth?

34 "Can you shout an order to the clouds
and cover yourself with a flood of
water?

35 Can you send lightning bolts on their
way?
Do they come to you and say, 'Here we
are'?

36 Who put wisdom inside the mind
or understanding in the heart?

37 Who has the wisdom to count the clouds?
Who can pour water from the jars of
the sky

38 when the dust becomes hard
and the clumps of dirt stick together?

39 "Do you hunt food for the female lion
to satisfy the hunger of the young lions

40 while they lie in their dens
or hide in the bushes waiting to attack?

41 Who gives food to the birds
when their young cry out to God
and wander about without food?

39 "Do you know when the mountain
goats give birth?
Do you watch when the deer gives birth
to her fawn?

2 Do you count the months until they give
birth
and know the right time for them to
give birth?

3 They lie down, their young are born,
and then the pain of giving birth is over.

4 Their young ones grow big and strong in
the wild country.
Then they leave their homes and do not
return.

5 "Who let the wild donkey go free?

Who untied its ropes?

6 I am the one who gave the donkey the
desert as its home;
I gave it the desert lands as a place to
live.

7 The wild donkey laughs at the confusion
in the city,
and it does not hear the drivers shout.

8 It roams the hills looking for pasture,
looking for anything green to eat.

9 "Will the wild ox agree to serve you
and stay by your feeding box at night?

10 Can you hold it to the plowed row with a
harness
so it will plow the valleys for you?

11 Will you depend on the wild ox for its
great strength
and leave your heavy work for it to do?

12 Can you trust the ox to bring in your grain
and gather it to your threshing floor?

13 "The wings of the ostrich flap happily,
but they are not like the feathers of the
stork.

14 The ostrich lays its eggs on the ground
and lets them warm in the sand.

15 It does not stop to think that a foot might
step on them and crush them;
it does not care that some animal might
walk on them.

16 The ostrich is cruel to its young, as if they
were not even its own.
It does not care that its work is for
nothing,

17 because God did not give the ostrich
wisdom;
God did not give it a share of good
sense.

18 But when the ostrich gets up to run, it is
so fast
that it laughs at the horse and its rider.

19 "Job, are you the one who gives the horse
its strength
or puts a flowing mane on its neck?

20 Do you make the horse jump like a locust?
It scares people with its proud snorting.

21 It paws wildly, enjoying its strength,
and charges into battle.

22 It laughs at fear and is afraid of nothing;
it does not run away from the sword.

23 The bag of arrows rattles against the
horse's side,

along with the flashing spears and swords.
24 With great excitement, the horse races over the ground;
and it cannot stand still when it hears the trumpet.
25 When the trumpet blows, the horse snorts, 'Aha!'
It smells the battle from far away;
it hears the shouts of commanders and the battle cry.

26 "Is it through your wisdom that the hawk flies
and spreads its wings toward the south?
27 Are you the one that commands the eagle to fly
and build its nest so high?
28 It lives on a high cliff and stays there at night;
the rocky peak is its protected place.
29 From there it looks for its food;
its eyes can see it from far away.
30 Its young eat blood,
and where there is something dead, the eagle is there."

40 The LORD said to Job:
2 "Will the person who argues with the Almighty correct him?
Let the person who accuses God answer him."

3 Then Job answered the LORD:
4 "I am not worthy; I cannot answer you anything,
so I will put my hand over my mouth.
5 I spoke one time, but I will not answer again;
I even spoke two times, but I will say nothing more."

6 Then the LORD spoke to Job from the storm:
7 "Be strong, like a man!
I will ask you questions,
and you must answer me.
8 Would you say that I am unfair?
Would you blame me to make yourself look right?
9 Are you as strong as God?
Can your voice thunder like his?
10 If so, then decorate yourself with glory and beauty;

dress in honor and greatness as if they were clothing.
11 Let your great anger punish;
look at the proud and bring them down.
12 Look at the proud and make them humble.
Crush the wicked wherever they are.
13 Bury them all in the dirt together;
cover their faces in the grave.
14 If you can do that, then I myself will praise you,
because you are strong enough to save yourself.

15 "Look at Behemoth,[n]
which I made just as I made you.
It eats grass like an ox.
16 Look at the strength it has in its body;
the muscles of its stomach are powerful.
17 Its tail is like a cedar tree;
the muscles of its thighs are woven together.
18 Its bones are like tubes of bronze;
its legs are like bars of iron.
19 It is one of the first of God's works,
but its Maker can destroy it.
20 The hills, where the wild animals play, provide food for it.
21 It lies under the lotus plants,
hidden by the tall grass in the swamp.
22 The lotus plants hide it in their shadow;
the poplar trees by the streams surround it.
23 If the river floods, it will not be afraid;
it is safe even if the Jordan River rushes to its mouth.
24 Can anyone blind its eyes and capture it?
Can anyone put hooks in its nose?

41 "Can you catch Leviathan[n] on a fishhook
or tie its tongue down with a rope?
2 Can you put a cord through its nose
or a hook in its jaw?
3 Will it keep begging you for mercy
and speak to you with gentle words?
4 Will it make an agreement with you
and let you take it as your slave for life?
5 Can you make a pet of Leviathan as you would a bird

40:15 Behemoth A large land animal, exact identity unknown. **41:1 Leviathan** A sea creature, exact identity unknown.

531

or put it on a leash for your girls?

6 Will traders try to bargain with you for it?
  Will they divide it up among the
    merchants?

7 Can you stick darts all over its skin
  or fill its head with fishing spears?

8 If you put one hand on it,
  you will never forget the battle,
  and you will never do it again!

9 There is no hope of defeating it;
  just seeing it overwhelms people.

10 No one is brave enough to make it angry,
  so who would be able to stand up
    against me?

11 No one has ever given me anything that I
    must pay back,
  because everything under the sky
    belongs to me.

12 "I will speak about Leviathan's arms and
    legs,
  its great strength and well-formed body.

13 No one can tear off its outer hide
  or poke through its double armor.

14 No one can force open its great jaws;
  they are filled with frightening teeth.

15 It has rows of shields on its back
  that are tightly sealed together.

16 Each shield is so close to the next one
  that no air can go between them.

17 They are joined strongly to one another;
  they hold on to each other and cannot
    be separated.

18 When it snorts, flashes of light are thrown
    out,
  and its eyes look like the light at dawn.

19 Flames blaze from its mouth;
  sparks of fire shoot out.

20 Smoke pours out of its nose,
  as if coming from a large pot over a hot
    fire.

21 Its breath sets coals on fire,
  and flames come out of its mouth.

22 There is great strength in its neck.
  People are afraid and run away.

23 The folds of its skin are tightly joined;
  they are set and cannot be moved.

24 Its chest is as hard as a rock,
  even as hard as a grinding stone.

25 The powerful fear its terrible looks
  and draw back in fear as it moves.

26 The sword that hits it does not hurt it,
  nor the arrows, darts, and spears.

27 It treats iron as if it were straw
  and bronze metal as if it were rotten
    wood.

28 It does not run away from arrows;
  stones from slings are like chaff to it.

29 Clubs feel like pieces of straw to it,
  and it laughs when they shake a spear
    at it.

30 The underside of its body is like broken
    pieces of pottery.
  It leaves a trail in the mud like a
    threshing board.

31 It makes the deep sea bubble like a boiling
    pot;
  it stirs up the sea like a pot of oil.

32 When it swims, it leaves a shining path in
    the water
  that makes the sea look as if it had
    white hair.

33 Nothing else on earth is equal to it;
  it is a creature without fear.

34 It looks down on all those who are too
    proud;
  it is king over all proud creatures."

JOB ANSWERS THE LORD

42 Then Job answered the LORD:
2 "I know that you can do all things
  and that no plan of yours can be ruined.

3 You asked, 'Who is this that made my
    purpose unclear by saying things that
    are not true?'
  Surely I spoke of things I did not
    understand;
  I talked of things too wonderful for me
    to know.

4 You said, 'Listen now, and I will speak.
  I will ask you questions,
  and you must answer me.'

5 My ears had heard of you before,
  but now my eyes have seen you.

6 So now I hate myself;
  I will change my heart and life.
  I will sit in the dust and ashes."

END OF THE STORY

7 After the LORD had said these things to
Job, he said to Eliphaz the Temanite, "I am
angry with you and your two friends, because you have not said what is right about
me, as my servant Job did. 8 Now take seven
bulls and seven male sheep, and go to my servant Job, and offer a burnt offering for yourselves. My servant Job will pray for you, and

I will listen to his prayer. Then I will not punish you for being foolish. You have not said what is right about me, as my servant Job did." ⁹So Eliphaz the Temanite, Bildad the Shuhite, and Zophar the Naamathite did as the Lord said, and the Lord listened to Job's prayer.

¹⁰After Job had prayed for his friends, the Lord gave him success again. The Lord gave Job twice as much as he had owned before. ¹¹Job's brothers and sisters came to his house, along with everyone who had known him before, and they all ate with him there. They comforted him and made him feel better about the trouble the Lord had brought on him, and each one gave Job a piece of silver and a gold ring.

¹²The Lord blessed the last part of Job's life even more than the first part. Job had fourteen thousand sheep, six thousand camels, a thousand teams of oxen, and a thousand female donkeys. ¹³Job also had seven sons and three daughters. ¹⁴He named the first daughter Jemimah, the second daughter Keziah, and the third daughter Keren-Happuch. ¹⁵There were no other women in all the land as beautiful as Job's daughters. And their father Job gave them land to own along with their brothers.

¹⁶After this, Job lived one hundred forty years. He lived to see his children, grandchildren, great-grandchildren, and great-great-grandchildren. ¹⁷Then Job died; he was old and had lived many years.

THE ULTIMATE INVESTMENT

the only
safe place

FINANCES

JOB 42:2

The imagery in this verse is all about forts. Fortified cites were a significant part of the ancient world. They provided safety and refuge. Job used this metaphor to describe the plans of God. This verse tells us to think of God's purposes as a great fortress. It is so well constructed that nothing can prevail against it. No attack will ever break its gates or overrun its walls. God's purposes will stand against anything.

Job discovered the mighty hand of God was the only safe place. All he had was stripped away. Yet he refused to turn away from his faith in the Lord. Most of us would have crumbled just like those towering walls of false security. Broke, sick, and wretched, we would have complained. Sometimes it takes disaster to show us how insane it is to trust our lives to anything but God's purposes.

Do you want to live in a fortress that will never be overrun? Do you want security that will never fail? Give up your own fortifications. They are never secure. Put your life entirely in his hands, no matter how you feel about your circumstances. It is a deliberate choice to say, "Yes, Lord, I know that you are the only one I can really trust."

reflect: What lessons can you learn from the life of Job?
Go to **Ecclesiastes 9:7–9.**

psalms

THE SONGBOOK OF ISRAEL

Book 1

TWO WAYS TO LIVE

1 Happy are those who don't listen to the
  wicked,
   who don't go where sinners go,
   who don't do what evil people do.
2 They love the LORD's teachings,
   and they think about those teachings
     day and night.
3 They are strong, like a tree planted by a
     river.
   The tree produces fruit in season,
   and its leaves don't die.
 Everything they do will succeed.

4 But wicked people are not like that.
   They are like chaff that the wind blows
     away.
5 So the wicked will not escape God's
     punishment.
   Sinners will not worship with God's
     people.
6 This is because the LORD takes care of his
     people,
   but the wicked will be destroyed.

THE LORD'S CHOSEN KING

2 Why are the nations so angry?
   Why are the people making useless
     plans?
2 The kings of the earth prepare to fight,
   and their leaders make plans together
 against the LORD
   and his appointed one.
3 They say, "Let's break the chains that hold
     us back
   and throw off the ropes that tie us
     down."

4 But the one who sits in heaven laughs;
   the Lord makes fun of them.
5 Then the LORD warns them
   and frightens them with his anger.
6 He says, "I have appointed my own king
   to rule in Jerusalem on my holy
     mountain, Zion."

7 Now I will tell you what the LORD has
     declared:
 He said to me, "You are my son.
   Today I have become your father.
8 If you ask me, I will give you the nations;
   all the people on earth will be yours.
9 You will rule over them with an iron rod.
   You will break them into pieces like
     pottery."

10 So, kings, be wise;
   rulers, learn this lesson.
11 Obey the LORD with great fear.
   Be happy, but tremble.
12 Show that you are loyal to his son,
   or you will be destroyed by his anger,
 because he can quickly become angry.
   But happy are those who trust him for
     protection.

A MORNING PRAYER

David sang this when he ran away from his son
Absalom.

3 LORD, I have many enemies!
   Many people have turned against me.
2 Many are saying about me,
   "God won't rescue him."   *Selah*

3 But, LORD, you are my shield,
   my wonderful God who gives me
     courage.
4 I will pray to the LORD,
   and he will answer me from his holy
     mountain.   *Selah*

5 I can lie down and go to sleep,
   and I will wake up again,
   because the LORD gives me strength.
6 Thousands of troops may surround me,
   but I am not afraid.

7 LORD, rise up!
   My God, come save me!
 You have struck my enemies on the cheek;
   you have broken the teeth of the
     wicked.
8 The LORD can save his people.
   LORD, bless your people.   *Selah*

AN EVENING PRAYER
For the director of music. With stringed instruments. A psalm of David.

4 Answer me when I pray to you,
my God who does what is right.
Make things easier for me when I am in trouble.
Have mercy on me and hear my prayer.

² People, how long will you turn my honor into shame?
How long will you love what is false
and look for new lies?   *Selah*

³ You know that the LORD has chosen for himself those who are loyal to him.
The LORD listens when I pray to him.

⁴ When you are angry, do not sin.
Think about these things quietly
as you go to bed.   *Selah*

⁵ Do what is right as a sacrifice to the LORD
and trust the LORD.

⁶ Many people ask,
"Who will give us anything good?"
LORD, be kind to us.

⁷ But you have made me very happy,
happier than they are,
even with all their grain and new wine.

FEAR OF THE FUTURE

the evening
psalm

FULFILLMENT

By Darlene Zschech

PSALM 4:4–5

We have affectionately come to know this psalm as "the evening psalm," for David's words are quoted again in Ephesians 4:26–27. "When you are angry, do not sin, and be sure to stop being angry before the end of the day. Do not give the devil a way to defeat you."

David had realized that when he was outraged, or his emotions were about to overtake him, wisdom shouted, "Wait! Take a moment, pause, think, and be still." This is an example of a yielded vessel. This is self-control.

Psalm 4:5 sums up this decision-making process quite bluntly: "Do what is right as a sacrifice to the LORD." When you decide to walk in the way of righteousness, this may require you to close your mouth and say nothing when you feel you have much to say. Think of those words: "Trust in the LORD."

Never lose sight of the Lord as you read this psalm. He is your righteousness. As you approach his throne, always be mindful that he is far greater than life itself. He fills you; you inherit substance and peace in all seasons, and you can rest in him. Every evening, commit all your concerns to the faithful, loving hand of the Lord.

reflect: Do you need to make some changes when it comes to anger control?
Go to **Psalm 7:11–17.**

8 I go to bed and sleep in peace,
because, LORD, only you keep me safe.

A MORNING PRAYER FOR PROTECTION
For the director of music. For flutes. A psalm
of David.

5 LORD, listen to my words.
Understand my sadness.
2 Listen to my cry for help, my King and my
God,
because I pray to you.
3 LORD, every morning you hear my voice.
Every morning, I tell you what I need,
and I wait for your answer.

4 You are not a God who is pleased with the
wicked;
you do not live with those who do evil.
5 Those people who make fun of you cannot
stand before you.

You hate all those who do evil.
6 You destroy liars;
the LORD hates those who kill and trick
others.

7 Because of your great love,
I can come into your Temple.
Because I fear and respect you,
I can worship in your holy Temple.
8 LORD, since I have many enemies,
show me the right thing to do.
Show me clearly how you want me to
live.

9 My enemies' mouths do not tell the truth;
in their hearts they want to destroy
others.
Their throats are like open graves;
they use their tongues for telling lies.
10 God, declare them guilty!
Let them fall into their own traps.

ANGER MANAGEMENT

-◠◡◠-

FITNESS

healing power

PSALM 6:2

If you get to the scene of an accident and you find two victims, one who is dead
and one who is barely surviving, which one has a chance of making it? Obviously,
only the one who is surviving. Whether or not you pump oxygen into the dead person,
he is still dead. Only the person who still has life in his body has a chance to recover.

That is because oxygen and other elements don't heal the body. The body can only heal
from within, yet what heals it is not the body itself but rather God's power *inside* of the
body. Without his power, our bodies are virtually nothing more than dust and water.

For example, vitamins are not a cure for what ails us. Yet our bodily defense system's
organs of immunity do require vitamins and many other nutrients to keep us well—or
get us well after we've been sick. Consequently, when we take vitamins, the vitamins
don't heal us; they just provide the nourishment necessary so that God's power within
us can heal our bodies.

reflect: Thank God that his healing power flows through your body daily.
Go to **Isaiah 12:2.**

Send them away because their sins are
many;
they have turned against you.

11 But let everyone who trusts you be happy;
let them sing glad songs forever.
Protect those who love you
and who are happy because of you.
12 LORD, you bless those who do what is
right;
you protect them like a soldier's shield.

A PRAYER FOR MERCY IN TROUBLED TIMES

For the director of music. With stringed
instruments. Upon the sheminith. A psalm of
David.

6 LORD, don't correct me when you are
angry;
don't punish me when you are very
angry.
2 LORD, have mercy on me because I am
weak.
Heal me, LORD, because my bones ache.
3 I am very upset.
LORD, how long will it be?

4 LORD, return and save me;
save me because of your kindness.
5 Dead people don't remember you;
those in the grave don't praise you.

6 I am tired of crying to you.
Every night my bed is wet with tears;
my bed is soaked from my crying.
7 My eyes are weak from so much crying;
they are weak from crying about my
enemies.

8 Get away from me, all you who do evil,
because the LORD has heard my crying.
9 The LORD has heard my cry for help;
the LORD will answer my prayer.
10 All my enemies will be ashamed and
troubled.
They will turn and suddenly leave in
shame.

A PRAYER FOR FAIRNESS

A shiggaion of David which he sang to the LORD
about Cush, from the tribe of Benjamin.

7 LORD my God, I trust in you for
protection.
Save me and rescue me

from those who are chasing me.
2 Otherwise, like a lion they will tear me
apart.
They will rip me to pieces, and no one
can save me.

3 LORD my God, what have I done?
Have my hands done something
wrong?
4 Have I done wrong to my friend
or stolen without reason from my
enemy?
5 If I have, let my enemy chase me and
capture me.
Let him trample me into the dust
and bury me in the ground.   *Selah*

6 LORD, rise up in your anger;
stand up against my enemies' anger.
Get up and demand fairness.
7 Gather the nations around you
and rule them from above.
8 LORD, judge the people.
LORD, defend me because I am right,
because I have done no wrong, God
Most High.
9 God, you do what is right.
You know our thoughts and feelings.
Stop those wicked actions done by evil
people,
and help those who do what is right.

10 God protects me like a shield;
he saves those whose hearts are
right.
11 God judges by what is right,
and God is always ready to punish the
wicked.
12 If they do not change their lives,
God will sharpen his sword;
he will string his bow and take aim.
13 He has prepared his deadly weapons;
he has made his flaming arrows.

14 There are people who think up evil
and plan trouble and tell lies.
15 They dig a hole to trap others,
but they will fall into it themselves.
16 They will get themselves into trouble;
the violence they cause will hurt only
themselves.

17 I praise the LORD because he does what is
right.
I sing praises to the LORD Most High.

THE LORD'S GREATNESS

For the director of music. On the gittith. A psalm of David.

8 LORD our Lord,
   your name is the most wonderful
      name in all the earth!
   It brings you praise in heaven above.
² You have taught children and babies
      to sing praises to you
   because of your enemies.
And so you silence your enemies
   and destroy those who try to get even.

³ I look at your heavens,
      which you made with your fingers.
I see the moon and stars,
      which you created.
⁴ But why are people even important to
      you?
   Why do you take care of human
      beings?
⁵ You made them a little lower than the
      angels
   and crowned them with glory and
      honor.

FULFILLMENT

FEAR OF THE FUTURE

how's your
heart?

PSALM 7:11–17   By Darlene Zschech

In these verses, notice how much God hates sin; he searches minds and hearts and makes a vow to protect the upright. Being upright is about valuing and pursuing spiritual and moral integrity; it does not mean being sinless. God promises, "Whoever loves me, I will save. I will protect those who know me" (Psalm 91:14). Those who have devised wicked schemes need to know that God is sharpening his sword to protect his loved ones. When a sword is sharpened, it is to cut deeper, and when a bow is bent, it is to kill. Get the picture?

When you are unfairly treated, don't fight for your rights. Think of what is happening in the unseen world. God is overseeing your trial, and he destroys evil workers. In the final verses, the deviser falls into his own trap. If you are feeling overwhelmed by a sense of injustice, picture God with a sharp sword, his heart crazy for you, and dirt on the face of the evildoer!

Before evil is carried out, it is devised in the heart of a person. The Lord wants us to stop the thought processes that would lead us to devise wicked schemes! How's your heart doing? Ask God to reveal the weak areas of your heart. Ask him to continue to change your intent. In verse 17, David brings all his thoughts, limitations, and humanity to a crescendo of praise, thankful for the righteousness of God. Rest in the strength of your King today!

---

reflect: What areas of your heart do you need to ask God for his help with?
Go to **Psalm 23:5.**

⁶ You put them in charge of everything you made.
  You put all things under their control:
⁷ all the sheep, the cattle,
    and the wild animals,
⁸ the birds in the sky,
    the fish in the sea,
    and everything that lives under water.
⁹ LORD our Lord,
    your name is the most wonderful name
    in all the earth!

THANKSGIVING FOR VICTORY
For the director of music. To the tune of "The Death of the Son." A psalm of David.

9 I will praise you, LORD, with all my heart.

  I will tell all the miracles you have done.
² I will be happy because of you;
    God Most High, I will sing praises to your name.

³ My enemies turn back;
    they are overwhelmed and die because of you.
⁴ You have heard my complaint;
    you sat on your throne and judged by what was right.
⁵ You spoke strongly against the foreign nations and destroyed the wicked;
    you wiped out their names forever and ever.
⁶ The enemy is gone forever.

ALWAYS ON HIS MIND

got my back

FULFILLMENT

PSALM 9:9

In the oldest song in recorded history, Moses proclaims something quite spectacular. This song of praise and triumph contains the sternest of warnings—something that we seem to have forgotten. Moses stands on the edge of the Red Sea. The waters are filled with dead Egyptian soldiers. God has rescued the Israelites in a spectacular way. And Moses draws the correct conclusion: the enemies of God's children are the enemies of God.

Notice that Moses does not say, "You destroyed those who were against *us*." He sees that if someone stands against God's elect, that person opposes God himself. And he had better watch out. God judges harshly those who oppose him.

There is comfort in this thought. Those who oppose you oppose God. And God will not remain complacent about their opposition. God protects his own. He may not protect us the way that we expect (the Israelites didn't really expect the sea to open). But God is faithful to preserve and protect his own. The next time you face opposition, remind yourself: "God's got my back!"

---

reflect: Remember that if God is for you, no one can stand against you.
Go to **1 Kings 9:1–5.**

You destroyed their cities;
no one even remembers them.

7 But the LORD rules forever.
He sits on his throne to judge,
8 and he will judge the world in fairness;
he will decide what is fair for the
nations.
9 The LORD defends those who suffer;
he defends them in times of trouble.
10 Those who know the LORD trust him,
because he will not leave those who
come to him.

11 Sing praises to the LORD who is king on
Mount Zion.
Tell the nations what he has done.
12 He remembers who the murderers are;
he will not forget the cries of those who
suffer.
13 LORD, have mercy on me.
See how my enemies hurt me.
Do not let me go through the gates of
death.
14 Then, at the gates of Jerusalem, I will
praise you;
I will rejoice because you saved me.

15 The nations have fallen into the pit they
dug.
Their feet are caught in the nets they
laid.
16 The LORD has made himself known by his
fair decisions;
the wicked get trapped by what they do.
Higgaion. Selah

17 Wicked people will go to the grave,
and so will all those who forget God.
18 But those who have troubles will not be
forgotten.
The hopes of the poor will never die.

19 LORD, rise up and judge the nations.
Don't let people think they are strong.
20 Teach them to fear you, LORD.
The nations must learn that they are
only human.   *Selah*

A COMPLAINT ABOUT EVIL PEOPLE

10 LORD, why are you so far away?
Why do you hide when there is
trouble?
2 Proudly the wicked chase down those
who suffer.
Let them be caught in their own traps.

3 They brag about the things they want.
They bless the greedy but hate the
LORD.
4 The wicked people are too proud.
They do not look for God;
there is no room for God in their
thoughts.
5 They always succeed.
They are far from keeping your laws;
they make fun of their enemies.
6 They say to themselves, "Nothing bad will
ever happen to me;
I will never be ruined."
7 Their mouths are full of curses, lies, and
threats;
they use their tongues for sin and evil.
8 They hide near the villages.
They look for innocent people to kill;
they watch in secret for the helpless.
9 They wait in hiding like a lion.
They wait to catch poor people;
they catch the poor in nets.
10 The poor are thrown down and crushed;
they are defeated because the others are
stronger.
11 The wicked think, "God has forgotten us.
He doesn't see what is happening."

12 LORD, rise up and punish the wicked.
Don't forget those who need help.
13 Why do wicked people hate God?
They say to themselves, "God won't
punish us."
14 LORD, surely you see these cruel and evil
things;
look at them and do something.
People in trouble look to you for help.
You are the one who helps the orphans.
15 Break the power of wicked people.
Punish them for the evil they have
done.

16 The LORD is King forever and ever.
Destroy from your land those nations
that do not worship you.
17 LORD, you have heard what the poor
people want.
Do what they ask, and listen to them.
18 Protect the orphans and put an end to
suffering
so they will no longer be afraid of evil
people.

TRUST IN THE LORD
For the director of music. Of David.

11 I trust in the LORD for protection.
So why do you say to me,
"Fly like a bird to your mountain.
2 Like hunters, the wicked string their
bows;
they set their arrows on the bowstrings.
They shoot from dark places
at those who are honest.
3 When the foundations for good collapse,
what can good people do?"

4 The LORD is in his holy temple;
the LORD sits on his throne in heaven.
He sees what people do;
he keeps his eye on them.
5 The LORD tests those who do right,
but he hates the wicked and those who
love to hurt others.
6 He will send hot coals and burning sulfur
on the wicked.
A whirlwind is what they will get.
7 The LORD does what is right, and he loves
justice,
so honest people will see his face.

A PRAYER AGAINST LIARS
For the director of music. Upon the sheminith.
A psalm of David.

12 Save me, LORD, because the good
people are all gone;
no true believers are left on earth.
2 Everyone lies to his neighbors;
they say one thing and mean another.

3 The LORD will stop those flattering lips
and cut off those bragging tongues.
4 They say, "Our tongues will help us win.
We can say what we wish; no one is our
master."

5 But the LORD says,
"I will now rise up,
because the poor are being hurt.
Because of the moans of the helpless,
I will give them the help they want."
6 The LORD's words are pure,
like silver purified by fire,
like silver purified seven times over.

7 LORD, you will keep us safe;
you will always protect us from such
people.

8 But the wicked are all around us;
everyone loves what is wrong.

A PRAYER FOR GOD TO BE NEAR
For the director of music. A psalm of David.

13 How long will you forget me, LORD?
Forever?
How long will you hide from me?
2 How long must I worry
and feel sad in my heart all day?
How long will my enemy win over me?

3 LORD, look at me.
Answer me, my God;
tell me, or I will die.
4 Otherwise my enemy will say, "I have
won!"
Those against me will rejoice that I've
been defeated.

5 I trust in your love.
My heart is happy because you saved
me.
6 I sing to the LORD
because he has taken care of me.

THE UNBELIEVING FOOL
For the director of music. Of David.

14 Fools say to themselves,
"There is no God."
Fools are evil and do terrible things;
there is no one who does anything good.

2 The LORD looked down from heaven on
all people
to see if anyone understood,
if anyone was looking to God for help.
3 But all have turned away.
Together, everyone has become evil.
There is no one who does anything good,
not even one.

4 Don't the wicked understand?
They destroy my people as if they were
eating bread.
They do not ask the LORD for help.
5 But the wicked are filled with terror,
because God is with those who do what
is right.
6 The wicked upset the plans of the poor,
but the LORD will protect them.

7 I pray that victory will come to Israel
from Mount Zion!
May the LORD bring them back.

Then the people of Jacob will rejoice,
and the people of Israel will be glad.

WHAT THE LORD DEMANDS
A psalm of David.

15 LORD, who may enter your Holy Tent?
Who may live on your holy
mountain?

2 Only those who are innocent
and who do what is right.
Such people speak the truth from their
hearts
3 and do not tell lies about others.
They do no wrong to their neighbors
and do not gossip.
4 They do not respect hateful people
but honor those who honor the
LORD.
They keep their promises to their
neighbors,
even when it hurts.
5 They do not charge interest on money
they lend
and do not take money to hurt innocent
people.

Whoever does all these things will never
be destroyed.

THE LORD TAKES CARE OF HIS PEOPLE
A miktam of David.

16 Protect me, God,
because I trust in you.
2 I said to the LORD, "You are my Lord.
Every good thing I have comes from
you."
3 As for the godly people in the world,
they are the wonderful ones I
enjoy.
4 But those who turn to idols
will have much pain.
I will not offer blood to those idols
or even speak their names.

5 No, the LORD is all I need.
He takes care of me.
6 My share in life has been pleasant;
my part has been beautiful.

7 I praise the LORD because he advises me.
Even at night, I feel his leading.
8 I keep the LORD before me always.
Because he is close by my side,
I will not be hurt.

9 So I rejoice and am glad.
Even my body has hope,
10 because you will not leave me in the
grave.
You will not let your holy one rot.
11 You will teach me how to live a holy life.
Being with you will fill me with joy;
at your right hand I will find pleasure
forever.

A PRAYER FOR PROTECTION
A prayer of David.

17 LORD, hear me begging for fairness;
listen to my cry for help.
Pay attention to my prayer,
because I speak the truth.
2 You will judge that I am right;
your eyes can see what is true.
3 You have examined my heart;
you have tested me all night.
You questioned me without finding
anything wrong;
I have not sinned with my mouth.
4 I have obeyed your commands,
so I have not done what evil people do.
5 I have done what you told me;
I have not failed.

6 I call to you, God,
and you answer me.
Listen to me now,
and hear what I say.
7 Your love is wonderful.
By your power you save those who trust
you
from their enemies.
8 Protect me as you would protect your
own eye.
Hide me under the shadow of your
wings.
9 Keep me from the wicked who attack me,
from my enemies who surround me.
10 They are selfish
and brag about themselves.
11 They have chased me until they have
surrounded me.
They plan to throw me to the ground.
12 They are like lions ready to kill;
like lions, they sit in hiding.

13 LORD, rise up, face the enemy, and throw
them down.
Save me from the wicked with your
sword.

¹⁴ LORD, save me by your power
   from those whose reward is in this life.
   They have plenty of food.
      They have many sons
      and leave much money to their
         children.

¹⁵ Because I have lived right, I will see your
      face.
   When I wake up, I will see your likeness
      and be satisfied.

A SONG OF VICTORY

For the director of music. By the LORD's servant,
David. David sang this song to the LORD when the
LORD had saved him from Saul and all his other
enemies.

18 I love you, LORD. You are my strength.
   ² The LORD is my rock, my protection,
         my Savior.
   My God is my rock.
   I can run to him for safety.

THE ROAD TO SUCCESS

following
the way

FUTURE

PSALM 16:11

Too many times we think of God's way as something obscure or difficult to find. We all have the tendency to question whether or not we are really following God's will. But the Bible doesn't portray God's path as a hard-to-follow trail in the brush.

In fact, the words used to describe the path of God ("how to live a holy life") are words that picture elevated roadways, clear and straight highways, and easy-to-see trails. God did not leave us in this world to wander around hoping we could find the right path. He did all he could to make it as clear as possible.

The psalmist emphasizes this point when he says that God himself will make the path known to us. We don't have to rely on intuition, trial and error, or bad road maps. God wants us to walk on the right path, and he will take us each step of the way. The only requirement that we have is to follow where he goes.

That isn't as easy as it sounds. We often start to think, *You can't really be going that way, can you, God? And you especially can't be going that slowly!* Yet God does know where he's going. We can count on him. Clear directions are his specialty. But we have to be willing to listen, follow, and be patient.

Some great questions to ask in the all-important areas of our lives include: "Am I going my way or God's way?" "Is this a good idea or a God idea?" "Am I going at my speed or at God's speed?"

reflect: Pray about the path and the pace that your life is following.
Go to **Psalm 23:1.**

He is my shield and my saving strength,
my defender.
3 I will call to the LORD, who is worthy of
praise,
and I will be saved from my enemies.

4 The ropes of death came around me;
the deadly rivers overwhelmed me.
5 The ropes of death wrapped around me.
The traps of death were before me.
6 In my trouble I called to the LORD.
I cried out to my God for help.
From his temple he heard my voice;
my call for help reached his ears.

7 The earth trembled and shook.
The foundations of the mountains
began to shake.
They trembled because the LORD was
angry.

8 Smoke came out of his nose,
and burning fire came out of his
mouth.
Burning coals went before him.
9 He tore open the sky and came down
with dark clouds under his feet.
10 He rode a creature with wings and flew.
He raced on the wings of the wind.
11 He made darkness his covering, his
shelter around him,
surrounded by fog and clouds.
12 Out of the brightness of his presence
came clouds
with hail and lightning.
13 The LORD thundered from heaven;
the Most High raised his voice,
and there was hail and lightning.
14 He shot his arrows and scattered his
enemies.

EARLY, FIRST, OR NOTHING

FAITH

examining
and testing

PSALM 17:3

The words "examined" and "tested" combine two different ideas. The first is the idea of being inspected to be found good or worthy. The second is to be refined in order to be purified. David says to God, "You have examined my heart; you have tested me all night." It is an example of what we need to do sometimes.

We need to ask God to look right through our pretensions and excuses, and all our equivocations and denials. We need his help to face our faults and secrets so that we can walk pure and blameless at all times.

Most of us don't like to let go of our secrets. Rather, we allow our pride, our arrogance, and our fear of repercussion to get in the way of our honesty with God and the people in our life. We recognize some level of vulnerability to certain sins. But what we really need is for God to examine our hearts fully. We need a periodic spiritual check-up for our own good and for the sake of others we love.

reflect: Ask God to show you areas of your life that need his changing grace.
Go to **Psalm 28:6–7.**

His many bolts of lightning confused them with fear.

15 LORD, you spoke strongly.
The wind blew from your nose.
Then the valleys of the sea appeared,
and the foundations of the earth were seen.

16 The LORD reached down from above and took me;
he pulled me from the deep water.
17 He saved me from my powerful enemies,
from those who hated me, because they were too strong for me.
18 They attacked me at my time of trouble,
but the LORD supported me.
19 He took me to a safe place.
Because he delights in me, he saved me.

20 The LORD spared me because I did what was right.
Because I have not done evil, he has rewarded me.
21 I have followed the ways of the LORD;
I have not done evil by turning away from my God.
22 I remember all his laws
and have not broken his rules.
23 I am innocent before him;
I have kept myself from doing evil.
24 The LORD rewarded me because I did what was right,
because I did what the LORD said was right.

25 LORD, you are loyal to those who are loyal,
and you are good to those who are good.
26 You are pure to those who are pure,
but you are against those who are bad.
27 You save the humble,
but you bring down those who are proud.
28 LORD, you give light to my lamp.
My God brightens the darkness around me.
29 With your help I can attack an army.
With God's help I can jump over a wall.

30 The ways of God are without fault.
The LORD's words are pure.
He is a shield to those who trust him.
31 Who is God? Only the LORD.
Who is the Rock? Only our God.
32 God is my protection.
He makes my way free from fault.

33 He makes me like a deer that does not stumble;
he helps me stand on the steep mountains.
34 He trains my hands for battle
so my arms can bend a bronze bow.
35 You protect me with your saving shield.
You support me with your right hand.
You have stooped to make me great.
36 You give me a better way to live,
so I live as you want me to.
37 I chased my enemies and caught them.
I did not quit until they were destroyed.
38 I crushed them so they couldn't rise up again.
They fell beneath my feet.
39 You gave me strength in battle.
You made my enemies bow before me.
40 You made my enemies turn back,
and I destroyed those who hated me.
41 They called for help,
but no one came to save them.
They called to the LORD,
but he did not answer them.
42 I beat my enemies into pieces, like dust in the wind.
I poured them out like mud in the streets.

43 You saved me when the people attacked me.
You made me the leader of nations.
People I never knew serve me.
44 As soon as they hear me, they obey me.
Foreigners obey me.
45 They all become afraid
and tremble in their hiding places.

46 The LORD lives!
May my Rock be praised.
Praise the God who saves me!
47 God gives me victory over my enemies
and brings people under my rule.
48 He saves me from my enemies.

You set me over those who hate me.
You saved me from violent people.
49 So I will praise you, LORD, among the nations.
I will sing praises to your name.
50 The LORD gives great victories to his king.
He is loyal to his appointed king,
to David and his descendants forever.

GOD'S WORKS AND WORD

For the director of music. A psalm of David.

19 The heavens declare the glory of God,
and the skies announce what his
hands have made.
2 Day after day they tell the story;
night after night they tell it again.
3 They have no speech or words;
they have no voice to be heard.

4 But their message goes out through all
the world;
their words go everywhere on
earth.
The sky is like a home for the sun.
5 The sun comes out like a bridegroom
from his bedroom.
It rejoices like an athlete eager to run
a race.
6 The sun rises at one end of the sky

FAMILY

COVENANT MARRIAGE

a correct priority structure

PSALM 19:7-11

By Jimmy Evans

Successful families are always families with a correct priority structure purposefully entrenched in their lives. It doesn't happen by accident. It happens because they make the choice to arrange their decisions, practices, and lifestyles to honor God first and then family. There are three priorities that are essential, universal, and unchanging: God, family, and church. Our devotion to God is a personal issue. It has to do with personal prayer, obedience to God's word, and giving God the first and best of our lives every day in every arena of life.

Our devotion to our family starts with our marriage. Our spouses intuitively know that they should have priority above everything other than God. Our children will also reflect whether they feel they have a position of priority. Even though all children have their problems, children who feel unloved and rejected by their parents have much greater problems and cause much more heartache. Except for God and our spouses, nothing should be valued greater than our children.

For people who have made a commitment to God and family, it is essential to have a support network of like-minded people. The church is not only an institution ordained by God to spread the Good News, but it is also a relational base of accountability, spiritual support, and encouragement for the saints. As we establish daily disciplines in our lives, we must also establish regular weekly times for church. If you haven't already done so, make a commitment now to God, your family, and your church.

reflect: Are your family priorities in their proper places?
Go to **Mark 3:25.**

and follows its path to the other end.
Nothing hides from its heat.

7 The teachings of the LORD are perfect;
they give new strength.
The rules of the LORD can be trusted;
they make plain people wise.
8 The orders of the LORD are right;
they make people happy.
The commands of the LORD are pure;
they light up the way.
9 Respect for the LORD is good;
it will last forever.
The judgments of the LORD are true;
they are completely right.
10 They are worth more than gold,
even the purest gold.
They are sweeter than honey,
even the finest honey.
11 By them your servant is warned.
Keeping them brings great reward.

12 People cannot see their own mistakes.
Forgive me for my secret sins.
13 Keep me from the sins of pride;
don't let them rule me.
Then I can be pure
and innocent of the greatest of sins.

14 I hope my words and thoughts please you.
LORD, you are my Rock, the one who
saves me.

A PRAYER FOR THE KING
For the director of music. A psalm of David.

20 May the LORD answer you in times
of trouble.
May the God of Jacob protect you.
2 May he send you help from his Temple
and support you from Mount Zion.
3 May he remember all your offerings
and accept all your sacrifices.   *Selah*
4 May he give you what you want
and make all your plans succeed,
5 and we will shout for joy when you
succeed,
and we will raise a flag in the name of
our God.
May the LORD give you all that you ask for.

6 Now I know the LORD helps his appointed
king.
He answers him from his holy heaven
and saves him with his strong right
hand.

7 Some trust in chariots, others in horses,
but we trust the LORD our God.
8 They are overwhelmed and defeated,
but we march forward and win.
9 LORD, save the king!
Answer us when we call for help.

THANKSGIVING FOR THE KING
For the director of music. A psalm of David.

21 LORD, the king rejoices because of
your strength;
he is so happy when you save him!
2 You gave the king what he wanted
and did not refuse what he asked for.
Selah
3 You put good things before him
and placed a gold crown on his head.
4 He asked you for life,
and you gave it to him,
so his years go on and on.
5 He has great glory because you gave him
victories;
you gave him honor and praise.
6 You always gave him blessings;
you made him glad because you were
with him.
7 The king truly trusts the LORD.
Because God Most High always loves
him,
he will not be overwhelmed.
8 Your hand is against all your enemies;
those who hate you will feel your
power.
9 When you appear,
you will burn them as in a furnace.
In your anger you will swallow them up,
and fire will burn them up.
10 You will destroy their families from the
earth;
their children will not live.
11 They made evil plans against you,
but their traps won't work.
12 You will make them turn their backs
when you aim your arrows at them.
13 Be supreme, LORD, in your power.
We sing and praise your greatness.

THE PRAYER OF A SUFFERING MAN
For the director of music. To the tune of "The Doe
of Dawn." A psalm of David.

22 My God, my God, why have you
abandoned me?
You seem far from saving me,

far away from my groans.
2 My God, I call to you during the day,
but you do not answer.
I call at night;
I am not silent.

3 You sit as the Holy One.
The praises of Israel are your throne.
4 Our ancestors trusted you;
they trusted, and you saved them.
5 They called to you for help
and were rescued.
They trusted you
and were not disappointed.

6 But I am like a worm instead of a man.
People make fun of me and hate me.
7 Those who look at me laugh.
They stick out their tongues and shake
their heads.
8 They say, "Turn to the LORD for help.
Maybe he will save you.
If he likes you,
maybe he will rescue you."

9 You had my mother give birth to me.
You made me trust you
while I was just a baby.
10 I have leaned on you since the day I was
born;
you have been my God since my mother
gave me birth.
11 So don't be far away from me.
Now trouble is near,
and there is no one to help.
12 People have surrounded me like angry
bulls.
Like the strong bulls of Bashan, they are
on every side.
13 Like hungry, roaring lions
they open their mouths at me.
14 My strength is gone,
like water poured out onto the ground,
and my bones are out of joint.
My heart is like wax;
it has melted inside me.
15 My strength has dried up like a clay pot,
and my tongue sticks to the top of my
mouth.
You laid me in the dust of death.
16 Evil people have surrounded me;
like dogs they have trapped me.
They have bitten my arms and legs.
17 I can count all my bones;

people look and stare at me.
18 They divided my clothes among them,
and they threw lots for my clothing.

19 But, LORD, don't be far away.
You are my strength; hurry to help me.
20 Save me from the sword;
save my life from the dogs.
21 Rescue me from the lion's mouth;
save me from the horns of the bulls.

22 Then I will tell my brothers and sisters
about you;
I will praise you in the public meeting.
23 Praise the LORD, all you who respect him.
All you descendants of Jacob, honor
him;
fear him, all you Israelites.
24 He does not ignore those in trouble.
He doesn't hide from them
but listens when they call out to him.
25 LORD, I praise you in the great meeting of
your people;
these worshipers will see me do what I
promised.
26 Poor people will eat until they are full;
those who look to the LORD will praise
him.
May your hearts live forever!
27 People everywhere will remember
and will turn to the LORD.
All the families of the nations
will worship him
28 because the LORD is King,
and he rules the nations.

29 All the powerful people on earth will eat
and worship.
Everyone will bow down to him,
all who will one day die.
30 The people in the future will serve him;
they will always be told about the Lord.
31 They will tell that he does what is right.
People who are not yet born
will hear what God has done.

THE LORD THE SHEPHERD
A psalm of David.

23 The LORD is my shepherd;
I have everything I need.
2 He lets me rest in green pastures.
He leads me to calm water.
3 He gives me new strength.
He leads me on paths that are right

for the good of his name.
4 Even if I walk through a very dark valley,
   I will not be afraid,
because you are with me.
   Your rod and your shepherd's staff
      comfort me.

5 You prepare a meal for me
   in front of my enemies.
You pour oil of blessing on my head;[n]
   you fill my cup to overflowing.
6 Surely your goodness and love will be
      with me
   all my life,
and I will live in the house of the LORD
   forever.

A WELCOME FOR GOD INTO THE TEMPLE
A psalm of David.

24 The earth belongs to the LORD, and
      everything in it—
   the world and all its people.
2 He built it on the waters
   and set it on the rivers.

3 Who may go up on the mountain of the
      LORD?
   Who may stand in his holy Temple?
4 Only those with clean hands and pure
      hearts,

23:5 pour oil . . . head This can mean that God gave him
great wealth and blessed him.

THE ROAD TO SUCCESS

the Good Shepherd

FUTURE

By Darlene Zschech

PSALM 23:1

Psalm 23 is not only one of the most popular of all the psalms, it is also one of great comfort, full of kindness and strength, as the psalmist sings this poetic, powerful song of safety and security. This passage reminds us that just as the shepherd leads his flock to fields of safety and well-being, so does our Good Shepherd guide us in ways that lead to security and prosperity.

Notice that the Lord's heavenly hand of protection and authority is an instrument of support; it does not cause fear, but gives great confidence and incredible comfort—just as the shepherd uses his rod to count, guide, rescue, and protect his precious sheep.

Customary treatment of the honored guest at the table would be to anoint his head with oil, but it gets better. To be considered a friend of God is much more than accepting an invitation that lasts for a day. It is to live with him—for our journey on earth and our journey home—for the courts of the Lord are, indeed, our true home.

We will dwell in the house of the Lord forever. We will dwell as children of God, in the home of our God, forever! Psalm 23 is a chapter we *must* put to memory and allow to feed our soul with life, promise, comfort, and security.

reflect: How does it feel to know that the Lord is on your side?
Go to **Psalm 32:8.**

who have not worshiped idols,
who have not made promises in the
name of a false god.
⁵ They will receive a blessing from the
LORD;
the God who saves them will declare
them right.
⁶ They try to follow God;

they look to the God of Jacob for help.
Selah

⁷ Open up, you gates.
Open wide, you aged doors
and the glorious King will come in.
⁸ Who is this glorious King?
The LORD, strong and mighty.
The LORD, the powerful warrior.

FEAR OF THE FUTURE

FULFILLMENT

is your cup half full
or half empty?

PSALM 23:5

By Dr. Sheri Lerner

There are the *haves* and the *have-nots* in life. The *haves* are those who have so much positive energy and happiness that they seem to bubble over and touch the lives of others in a life-giving way. The *have-nots* appear always to be drained from negativity, stress, and unhappiness. Because they have nothing left to give to others, they instead feed upon the positive energy from those around them.

What's the difference between these two groups of people? The *haves* choose to control their responses and react in a nonstressful manner, allowing them to perceive life as positive—their cups are *half full*. The *have-nots* allow stress to take control, creating negative responses—seeing their cups as *half empty*.

Even if you look at only a portion of what God has given you, you will find that your life is not just half full—it is *overflowing* with blessings.

When you stop focusing on the one small area of distress in your life and take time to look at the big picture, you will find things aren't as bad as you had originally thought. You can focus on the damaged bumper of your car after a fender bender, or you can focus on the fact that no one was harmed. Focusing on one causes you negative stress; focusing on the other will cause you peace and relief.

When you start to become more aware and critical of your responses, you will give yourself an opportunity to choose peace and positive thoughts over stress and negative thoughts.

reflect: How about taking a moment to count the many blessings in your life?
Go to **Psalm 30:5.**

⁹ Open up, you gates.
  Open wide, you aged doors
  and the glorious King will come in.
¹⁰ Who is this glorious King?
  The LORD All-Powerful—
  he is the glorious King.   *Selah*

A PRAYER FOR GOD TO GUIDE
Of David.

25 LORD, I give myself to you;
  ² my God, I trust you.
  Do not let me be disgraced;
    do not let my enemies laugh at me.
³ No one who trusts you will be disgraced,
    but those who sin without excuse will
      be disgraced.

⁴ LORD, tell me your ways.
    Show me how to live.
⁵ Guide me in your truth,
    and teach me, my God, my Savior.
    I trust you all day long.
⁶ LORD, remember your mercy and love
    that you have shown since long ago.
⁷ Do not remember the sins
    and wrong things I did when I was
      young.
  But remember to love me always
    because you are good, LORD.

⁸ The LORD is good and right;
    he points sinners to the right way.
⁹ He shows those who are humble how to
      do right,
    and he teaches them his ways.
¹⁰ All the LORD's ways are loving and true
    for those who follow the demands of his
      agreement.
¹¹ For the sake of your name, LORD,
    forgive my many sins.
¹² Are there those who respect the LORD?
    He will point them to the best way.
¹³ They will enjoy a good life,
    and their children will inherit the land.
¹⁴ The LORD tells his secrets to those who
      respect him;
    he tells them about his agreement.
¹⁵ My eyes are always looking to the LORD
      for help.
    He will keep me from any traps.
¹⁶ Turn to me and have mercy on me,
    because I am lonely and hurting.
¹⁷ My troubles have grown larger;

free me from my problems.
¹⁸ Look at my suffering and troubles,
    and take away all my sins.
¹⁹ Look at how many enemies I have!
    See how much they hate me!
²⁰ Protect me and save me.
    I trust you, so do not let me be
      disgraced.
²¹ My hope is in you,
    so may goodness and honesty guard
      me.
²² God, save Israel from all their troubles!

THE PRAYER OF AN INNOCENT BELIEVER
Of David.

26 LORD, defend me because I have
    lived an innocent life.
  I have trusted the LORD and never
    doubted.
² LORD, try me and test me;
    look closely into my heart and mind.
³ I see your love,
    and I live by your truth.
⁴ I do not spend time with liars,
    nor do I make friends with those who
      hide their sin.
⁵ I hate the company of evil people,
    and I won't sit with the wicked.
⁶ I wash my hands to show I am innocent,
    and I come to your altar, LORD.
⁷ I raise my voice in praise
    and tell of all the miracles you have
      done.
⁸ LORD, I love the Temple where you live,
    where your glory is.
⁹ Do not kill me with those sinners
    or take my life with those murderers.
¹⁰ Evil is in their hands,
    and they do wrong for money.
¹¹ But I have lived an innocent life,
    so save me and have mercy on me.
¹² I stand in a safe place.
    LORD, I praise you in the great meeting.

A SONG OF TRUST IN GOD
Of David.

27 The LORD is my light and the one
    who saves me.
  So why should I fear anyone?
  The LORD protects my life.
  So why should I be afraid?
² Evil people may try to destroy my body.

My enemies and those who hate me
attack me,
but they are overwhelmed and defeated.
3 If an army surrounds me,
I will not be afraid.
If war breaks out,
I will trust the LORD.

4 I ask only one thing from the LORD.
This is what I want:
Let me live in the LORD's house
all my life.
Let me see the LORD's beauty
and look with my own eyes at his
Temple.
5 During danger he will keep me safe in his
shelter.

He will hide me in his Holy Tent,
or he will keep me safe on a high
mountain.
6 My head is higher than my enemies
around me.
I will offer joyful sacrifices in his Holy
Tent.
I will sing and praise the LORD.

7 LORD, hear me when I call;
have mercy and answer me.
8 My heart said of you, "Go, worship him."
So I come to worship you, LORD.
9 Do not turn away from me.
Do not turn your servant away in anger;
you have helped me.
Do not push me away or leave me alone,

FAITH

EARLY, FIRST, OR NOTHING

light dependence

PSALM 27:1

Everything living depends on light. It's a physical fact. In this universe, light is the fundamental ingredient of existence. This Hebrew word *or* is linked directly to life and happiness. Light is also used to describe a happy face, a good day, a successful life, and the Light of the world. This word has physical and spiritual connections.

Ancient religions often worshiped the sources of light: the sun, the moon, and the stars. Some of that idolatry is still with us today. Arrangements of stars and planets do not control destiny. God does. This is the reason the creation story in Genesis is so completely different from all of the other ancient cosmologies. God creates light. Light is not the source; it is the product. God is the source.

Just as everything in the physical universe depends on light (and on the source of light), so everything in the spiritual universe depends on the source of light. When David says, "The LORD is my light," he is saying that everything he is depends on this one source. His physical and spiritual being depends on God alone. David is saying much more than "God is my guide" or "God shows my way." David is saying that without the Lord, he ceases to exist.

---

reflect: Thank the Lord for being the light that guides and sustains you.
Go to **Psalm 41:4.**

God, my Savior.
10 If my father and mother leave me,
   the LORD will take me in.
11 LORD, teach me your ways,
   and guide me to do what is right
   because I have enemies.
12 Do not hand me over to my enemies,
   because they tell lies about me
   and say they will hurt me.

13 I truly believe
   I will live to see the LORD's goodness.
14 Wait for the LORD's help.
   Be strong and brave,
   and wait for the LORD's help.

A PRAYER IN TROUBLED TIMES
Of David.

28 LORD, my Rock, I call out to you for
   help.
   Do not be deaf to me.
   If you are silent,
   I will be like those in the grave.
2 Hear the sound of my prayer,
   when I cry out to you for help.
   I raise my hands
   toward your Most Holy Place.
3 Don't drag me away with the wicked,
   with those who do evil.
   They say "Peace" to their neighbors,
   but evil is in their hearts.
4 Pay them back for what they have done,
   for their evil deeds.
   Pay them back for what they have done;
   give them their reward.
5 They don't understand what the LORD has
   done
   or what he has made.
   So he will knock them down
   and not lift them up.

6 Praise the LORD,
   because he heard my prayer for help.
7 The LORD is my strength and shield.
   I trust him, and he helps me.
   I am very happy,
   and I praise him with my song.
8 The LORD is powerful;
   he gives victory to his chosen one.
9 Save your people
   and bless those who are your own.
   Be their shepherd and carry them
   forever.

GOD IN THE THUNDERSTORM
A psalm of David.

29 Praise the LORD, you angels;
   praise the LORD's glory and power.
2 Praise the LORD for the glory of his name;
   worship the LORD because he is holy.

3 The LORD's voice is heard over the sea.
   The glorious God thunders;
   the LORD thunders over the ocean.
4 The LORD's voice is powerful;
   the LORD's voice is majestic.
5 The LORD's voice breaks the trees;
   the LORD breaks the cedars of Lebanon.
6 He makes the land of Lebanon dance like
   a calf
   and Mount Hermon jump like a baby
   bull.
7 The LORD's voice makes the lightning
   flash.
8 The LORD's voice shakes the desert;
   the LORD shakes the Desert of Kadesh.
9 The LORD's voice shakes the oaks
   and strips the leaves off the trees.
   In his Temple everyone says, "Glory to
   God!"

10 The LORD controls the flood.
   The LORD will be King forever.
11 The LORD gives strength to his people;
   the LORD blesses his people with peace.

THANKSGIVING FOR ESCAPING DEATH
A psalm of David. A song for giving the Temple to
the LORD.

30 I will praise you, LORD,
   because you rescued me.
   You did not let my enemies laugh at me.
2 LORD, my God, I prayed to you,
   and you healed me.
3 You lifted me out of the grave;
   you spared me from going down to the
   place of the dead.

4 Sing praises to the LORD, you who belong
   to him;
   praise his holy name.
5 His anger lasts only a moment,
   but his kindness lasts for a lifetime.
   Crying may last for a night,
   but joy comes in the morning.

6 When I felt safe, I said,
   "I will never fear."

FAITH

praising God

PSALM 28:6-7

By Wendell Smith

David's majestic poetry, his songs of praise to God, weren't telling God anything new. God knows who he is, how great he is, and he knows what he can do. He knows he is the maker of the earth and has proven nothing is too difficult for him.

Praise is for us. It gives us pause in his presence and reminds us of who God is and what he has done and can do. Like David, when we meditate and contemplate God, the Lord is magnified to us, and his very presence brings us ever closer to who God intends for us to become. Exalting him does something for us. We remember that we serve a mighty God.

The names of God reveal that he is:

- El Olam (Everlasting God)
- El Elyon (the Most High God)
- Adonai (Master)
- El Shaddai (Almighty God, the strength giver)
- Jehovah/Yahweh (the self-existent one: I AM)
- Jehovah-Elohim (the Lord God)
- Jehovah-jireh (the Lord will provide)
- Jehovah-rapha (the Lord who heals)
- Jehovah-nissi (the Lord our banner)
- Jehovah-shalom (the Lord our peace)
- Jehovah-ra-ah (the Lord my shepherd)
- Jehovah-tsidkenu (the Lord our righteousness)
- Jehovah-shammah (the Lord is present)
- Jehovah Sabaoth (the Lord of hosts)

He is the Lord our salvation. Jesus said, "I am the resurrection, the way, the truth, the life, the light of the world, the bread of life, the good shepherd, the door of the sheep, the true vine." And "Before Abraham was even born, I AM." Praise is for us!

reflect: What one name for God is your very favorite?
Go to **Psalm 27:1.**

7 LORD, in your kindness you made my
  mountain safe.
    But when you turned away, I was
    frightened.

8 I called to you, LORD,
    and asked you to have mercy on me.
9 I said, "What good will it do if I die
    or if I go down to the grave?
  Dust cannot praise you;
    it cannot speak about your truth.
10 LORD, hear me and have mercy on me.
    LORD, help me."

11 You changed my sorrow into dancing.
    You took away my clothes of sadness,
    and clothed me in happiness.
12 I will sing to you and not be silent.
    LORD, my God, I will praise you
    forever.

A PRAYER OF FAITH IN TROUBLED TIMES
For the director of music. A psalm of David.

31 LORD, I trust in you;
    let me never be disgraced.
  Save me because you do what is right.
2 Listen to me
    and save me quickly.

FEAR OF THE FUTURE

joy in the morning

FULFILLMENT

By Darlene Zschech

PSALM 30:5

Psalm 30 was probably written because of the events of 1 Chronicles 21:1—22:6. This is when David tried to take a census of the Israelites. The account in Chronicles refers to David's sin of trusting in a large army, instead of in God. It then refers to God's favor in delivering David. It also boasts about the mercy of God, since David was rescued again! David was offered a shortcut to bring his offering before the Lord, but he bravely and passionately replied, "I won't offer a burnt offering that costs me nothing" (1 Chronicles 21:24).

The message in Psalm 30 closely follows what David expressed in other psalms: that life's storms will most certainly be followed by God's peace and joy. David says that in his prosperity he had forgotten where his strength and security came from. Isn't it amazing how quickly we forget the hand of God on our lives? Isn't it true that the heart is deceitful above all things? To trust in wealth or riches is certainly not what the Scripture teaches, nor are we to trust in the vain thoughts of man.

If you face a challenge, don't become overconfident in your ability to find the answer. Be wise, ask God for direction, and learn to praise. Don't allow disappointment or self-righteous thinking to rob you of all God has in store for your life. This song was for the dedication of the Temple. Make it your song, for the dedication of yourself to the Lord.

reflect: Do you need to return to the Lord overdue thanks and praise?
Go to **Psalm 46:1.**

Be my rock of protection,
a strong city to save me.
3 You are my rock and my protection.
For the good of your name, lead me and
guide me.
4 Set me free from the trap they set for me,
because you are my protection.
5 I give you my life.
Save me, LORD, God of truth.

6 I hate those who worship false gods.
I trust only in the LORD.
7 I will be glad and rejoice in your love,
because you saw my suffering;
you knew my troubles.
8 You have not handed me over to my
enemies
but have set me in a safe place.

9 LORD, have mercy, because I am in
misery.
My eyes are weak from so much crying,
and my whole being is tired from grief.
10 My life is ending in sadness,
and my years are spent in crying.
My troubles are using up my strength,
and my bones are getting weaker.
11 Because of all my troubles, my enemies
hate me,
and even my neighbors look down on
me.
When my friends see me,
they are afraid and run.
12 I am like a piece of a broken pot.
I am forgotten as if I were dead.
13 I have heard many insults.
Terror is all around me.
They make plans against me
and want to kill me.

14 LORD, I trust you.
I have said, "You are my God."
15 My life is in your hands.
Save me from my enemies
and from those who are chasing me.
16 Show your kindness to me, your servant.
Save me because of your love.
17 LORD, I called to you,
so do not let me be disgraced.
Let the wicked be disgraced
and lie silent in the grave.
18 With pride and hatred
they speak against those who do right.
So silence their lying lips.

19 How great is your goodness
that you have stored up for those who
fear you,
that you have given to those who trust
you.
You do this for all to see.
20 You protect them by your presence
from what people plan against
them.
You shelter them from evil words.
21 Praise the LORD.
His love to me was wonderful
when my city was attacked.
22 In my distress, I said,
"God cannot see me!"
But you heard my prayer
when I cried out to you for help.
23 Love the LORD, all you who belong to
him.
The LORD protects those who truly
believe,
but he punishes the proud as much as
they have sinned.
24 All you who put your hope in the LORD
be strong and brave.

IT IS BETTER TO CONFESS SIN
A maskil of David.

32 Happy is the person
whose sins are forgiven,
whose wrongs are pardoned.
2 Happy is the person
whom the LORD does not consider
guilty
and in whom there is nothing false.

3 When I kept things to myself,
I felt weak deep inside me.
I moaned all day long.
4 Day and night you punished me.
My strength was gone as in the summer
heat.   *Selah*
5 Then I confessed my sins to you
and didn't hide my guilt.
I said, "I will confess my sins to the
LORD,"
and you forgave my guilt.   *Selah*

6 For this reason, all who obey you
should pray to you while they still can.
When troubles rise like a flood,
they will not reach them.
7 You are my hiding place.
You protect me from my troubles

and fill me with songs of salvation.

Selah

8 The LORD says, "I will make you wise and show you where to go. I will guide you and watch over you. 9 So don't be like a horse or donkey,

that doesn't understand. They must be led with bits and reins, or they will not come near you."

10 Wicked people have many troubles, but the LORD's love surrounds those who trust him.

THE ROAD TO SUCCESS

the principles of God's school

FUTURE

PSALM 32:8

God is always teaching and always watching. While the principles of academic schools include reading, writing, and arithmetic, the Bible teaches the meaning of life. The principles taught by God are life itself. God is looking for people of principle who:

- Do not have a price at which they can be bought.

- Do what is right whether or not it is expedient.

- Are honest in every transaction whether big or small.

- Make decisions that account for the well-being of others.

- See past what is temporal to that which is eternal.

- Never pay their expenses at the expense of others.

- Desire to be successful in their mission.

- Do not fear rejection, failure, or popular opinion.

- Are willing to do what has never been done before.

- Are inspired to be obedient to their calling.

- Are faithful and hopeful in all circumstances.

- Are uncompromising in their leadership.

- Are committed to seeing their goals accomplished.

reflect: Commit yourself to living according to the principles of God.
Go to **Psalm 58:1-3.**

11 Good people, rejoice and be happy in the
   LORD.
   Sing all you whose hearts are right.

PRAISE GOD WHO CREATES AND SAVES

33 Sing to the LORD, you who do what is
   right;
   honest people should praise him.
2 Praise the LORD on the harp;
   make music for him on a ten-stringed
   lyre.
3 Sing a new song to him;
   play well and joyfully.

4 God's word is true,
   and everything he does is right.
5 He loves what is right and fair;
   the LORD's love fills the earth.

6 The sky was made at the LORD's
   command.
   By the breath from his mouth, he made
   all the stars.
7 He gathered the water of the sea into a
   heap.
   He made the great ocean stay in its
   place.
8 All the earth should worship the LORD;
   the whole world should fear him.
9 He spoke, and it happened.
   He commanded, and it appeared.
10 The LORD upsets the plans of nations;
   he ruins all their plans.
11 But the LORD's plans will stand forever;
   his ideas will last from now on.
12 Happy is the nation whose God is the
   LORD,
   the people he chose for his very
   own.
13 The LORD looks down from heaven
   and sees every person.
14 From his throne he watches
   all who live on earth.
15 He made their hearts
   and understands everything they do.
16 No king is saved by his great army.
   No warrior escapes by his great
   strength.
17 Horses can't bring victory;
   they can't save by their strength.
18 But the LORD looks after those who fear
   him,
   those who put their hope in his love.
19 He saves them from death

and spares their lives in times of
   hunger.
20 So our hope is in the LORD.
   He is our help, our shield to protect us.
21 We rejoice in him,
   because we trust his holy name.
22 LORD, show your love to us
   as we put our hope in you.

PRAISE GOD WHO JUDGES AND SAVES

David's song from the time he acted crazy so
Abimelech would send him away, and David
did leave.

34 I will praise the LORD at all times;
   his praise is always on my lips.
2 My whole being praises the LORD.
   The poor will hear and be glad.
3 Glorify the LORD with me,
   and let us praise his name together.

4 I asked the LORD for help, and he
   answered me.
   He saved me from all that I feared.
5 Those who go to him for help are happy,
   and they are never disgraced.
6 This poor man called, and the LORD heard
   him
   and saved him from all his troubles.
7 The angel of the LORD camps around
   those who fear God,
   and he saves them.

8 Examine and see how good the LORD is.
   Happy is the person who trusts him.
9 You who belong to the LORD, fear him!
   Those who fear him will have
   everything they need.
10 Even lions may get weak and hungry,
   but those who look to the LORD will
   have every good thing.
11 Children, come and listen to me.
   I will teach you to worship the LORD.
12 You must do these things
   to enjoy life and have many happy days.
13 You must not say evil things,
   and you must not tell lies.
14 Stop doing evil and do good.
   Look for peace and work for it.

15 The LORD sees the good people
   and listens to their prayers.
16 But the LORD is against those who do
   evil;
   he makes the world forget them.

17 The LORD hears good people when they
cry out to him,
and he saves them from all their
troubles.
18 The LORD is close to the brokenhearted,
and he saves those whose spirits have
been crushed.

19 People who do what is right may have
many problems,
but the LORD will solve them all.
20 He will protect their very bones;
not one of them will be broken.
21 Evil will kill the wicked;
those who hate good people will be
judged guilty.
22 But the LORD saves his servants' lives;
no one who trusts him will be judged
guilty.

A PRAYER FOR HELP
Of David.

35

LORD, battle with those who battle
with me.
Fight against those who fight against
me.
2 Pick up the shield and armor.
Rise up and help me.
3 Lift up your spears, both large and small,
against those who chase me.
Tell me, "I will save you."

4 Make those who want to kill me
be ashamed and disgraced.
Make those who plan to harm me
turn back and run away.
5 Make them like chaff blown by the wind
as the angel of the LORD forces them
away.
6 Let their road be dark and slippery
as the angel of the LORD chases them.
7 For no reason they spread out their net to
trap me;
for no reason they dug a pit for me.
8 So let ruin strike them suddenly.
Let them be caught in their own nets;
let them fall into the pit and *die*.
9 Then I *will rejoice in the LORD*;
I *will* be happy when he saves me.
10 Even my bones will say,
"LORD, who is like you?
You save the weak from the strong,
the weak and poor from robbers."

11 Men without mercy stand up to testify.
They ask me things I do not know.
12 They repay me with evil for the good I
have done,
and they make me very sad.
13 Yet when they were sick, I put on clothes
of sadness
and showed my sorrow by fasting.
But my prayers were not answered.
14 I acted as if they were my friends or
brothers.
I bowed in sadness as if I were crying for
my mother.
15 But when I was in trouble, they gathered
and laughed;
they gathered to attack before I knew it.
They insulted me without stopping.
16 They made fun of me and were cruel to
me
and ground their teeth at me in anger.

17 Lord, how long will you watch this
happen?
Save my life from their attacks;
save me from these people who are like
lions.
18 I will praise you in the great meeting.
I will praise you among crowds of
people.
19 Do not let my enemies laugh at me;
they hate me for no reason.
Do not let them make fun of me;
they have no cause to hate me.
20 Their words are not friendly
but are lies about peace-loving people.
21 They speak against me
and say, "Aha! We saw what you did!"

22 LORD, you have been watching. Do not
keep quiet.
Lord, do not leave me alone.
23 Wake up! Come and defend me!
My God and Lord, fight for me!
24 LORD my God, defend me with your
justice.
Don't let them laugh at me.
25 Don't let them think, "Aha! We got what
we wanted!"
Don't let them say, "We destroyed him."
26 Let them be ashamed and embarrassed,
because they were happy when I hurt.
Cover them with shame and disgrace,
because they thought they were better
than I was.

27 May my friends sing and shout for joy.
   May they always say, "Praise the
      greatness of the LORD,
   who loves to see his servants do
      well."
28 I will tell of your goodness
   and will praise you every day.

WICKED PEOPLE AND A GOOD GOD
For the director of music. Of David, the servant
of the LORD.

36 Sin speaks to the wicked in their
      hearts.
   They have no fear of God.
2 They think too much of themselves
   so they don't see their sin and hate it.
3 Their words are wicked lies;
   they are no longer wise or good.
4 At night they make evil plans;
   what they do leads to nothing good.
   They don't refuse things that are evil.

5 LORD, your love reaches to the heavens,
   your loyalty to the skies.
6 Your goodness is as high as the
      mountains.
   Your justice is as deep as the great
      ocean.
   LORD, you protect both people and
      animals.
7 God, your love is so precious!
   You protect people in the shadow of
      your wings.
8 They eat the rich food in your house,
   and you let them drink from your river
      of pleasure.
9 You are the giver of life.
   Your light lets us enjoy life.

10 Continue to love those who know you
   and to do good to those who are good.
11 Don't let proud people attack me
   and the wicked force me away.
12 Those who do evil have been defeated.
   They are overwhelmed;
   they cannot do evil any longer.

GOD WILL REWARD FAIRLY
Of David.

37 Don't be upset because of evil people.
      Don't be jealous of those who do
         wrong,
2 because like the grass, they will soon dry
      up.

Like green plants, they will soon die
      away.
3 Trust the LORD and do good.
   Live in the land and feed on truth.
4 Enjoy serving the LORD,
   and he will give you what you want.
5 Depend on the LORD;
   trust him, and he will take care of you.
6 Then your goodness will shine like the
      sun,
   and your fairness like the noonday sun.

7 Wait and trust the LORD.
   Don't be upset when others get rich
   or when someone else's plans succeed.
8 Don't get angry.
   Don't be upset; it only leads to trouble.
9 Evil people will be sent away,
   but those who trust the LORD will
      inherit the land.
10 In a little while the wicked will be no
      more.
   You may look for them, but they will be
      gone.
11 People who are not proud will inherit the
      land
   and will enjoy complete peace.

12 The wicked make evil plans against good
      people.
   They grind their teeth at them in anger.
13 But the Lord laughs at the wicked,
   because he sees that their day is
      coming.
14 The wicked draw their swords
   and bend their bows
   to kill the poor and helpless,
   to kill those who are honest.
15 But their swords will stab their own
      hearts,
   and their bows will break.

16 It is better to have little and be right
   than to have much and be wrong.
17 The power of the wicked will be broken,
   but the LORD supports those who do
      right.
18 The LORD watches over the lives of the
      innocent,
   and their reward will last forever.
19 They will not be ashamed when trouble
      comes.
   They will be full in times of hunger.
20 But the wicked will die.

The LORD's enemies will be like the
  flowers of the fields;
they will disappear like smoke.
21 The wicked borrow and don't pay back,
  but those who do right give freely to
    others.
22 Those whom the LORD blesses will inherit
    the land,
  but those he curses will be sent away.

23 When people's steps follow the LORD,
  God is pleased with their ways.
24 If they stumble, they will not fall,
  because the LORD holds their hand.

25 I was young, and now I am old,
  but I have never seen good people left
    helpless

or their children begging for food.
26 Good people always lend freely to others,
  and their children are a blessing.

27 Stop doing evil and do good,
  so you will live forever.
28 The LORD loves justice
  and will not leave those who worship
    him.
He will always protect them,
  but the children of the wicked will die.
29 Good people will inherit the land
  and will live in it forever.

30 Good people speak with wisdom,
  and they say what is fair.
31 The teachings of their God are in their
    heart,

THE EXTRA MILE MARRIAGE

holding hands

FAMILY

PSALM 37:24

The Bible teaches that our support must come from God, not from other people, for it is by God's power that we will dwell in a place of safety and righteousness despite those times when we fall. One of the characteristics of children is that they typically like to hold the hands of their parents. It is a bond of safety and protection for them, and an assurance of love for parents.

Lovers hold hands for the same reasons, along with the aspect of personal intimacy and vulnerability. Did you know that God loves to hold hands with us? After all, he is our perfect Father and our greatest admirer. His handholding is the deepest expression of care and concern for us.

Does your family hold hands naturally? It is a sure sign of bonding and protection. God wants us to have the same attitude with him. We need to offer our hand to him. If we do, we can walk through life just like our own children, safe and secure in the comfort of that strong hand holding ours. He will guide us in the right way if we just hold on to his grip.

reflect: Reach out to God today, and grasp his outstretched hand of love and support.
Go to **FAMILY:** "A Family Changed" at **Leviticus 19:18.**

so they do not fail to keep them.
32 The wicked watch for good people
so that they may kill them.
33 But the Lord will not take away his
protection
or let good people be judged guilty.

34 Wait for the Lord's help
and follow him.
He will honor you and give you the land,
and you will see the wicked sent away.

35 I saw a wicked and cruel man
who looked strong like a healthy tree in
good soil.
36 But he died and was gone;
I looked for him, but he couldn't be
found.

37 Think of the innocent person,
and watch the honest one.
The man who has peace
will have children to live after him.
38 But sinners will be destroyed;
in the end the wicked will die.

39 The Lord saves good people;
he is their strength in times of trouble.
40 The Lord helps them and saves them;
he saves them from the wicked,
because they trust in him for protection.

A PRAYER IN TIME OF SICKNESS
A psalm of David to remember.

38 Lord, don't correct me when you are
angry.
Don't punish me when you are furious.
2 Your arrows have wounded me,
and your hand has come down on me.
3 My body is sick from your punishment.
Even my bones are not healthy because
of my sin.
4 My guilt has overwhelmed me;
like a load it weighs me down.

5 My sores stink and become infected
because I was foolish.
6 I am bent over and bowed down;
I am sad all day long.
7 I am burning with fever,
and my whole body is sore.
8 I am weak and faint.
I moan from the pain I feel.

9 Lord, you know everything I want;
my cries are not hidden from you.

10 My heart pounds, and my strength is
gone.
I am losing my sight.
11 Because of my wounds, my friends and
neighbors avoid me,
and my relatives stay far away.
12 Some people set traps to kill me.
Those who want to hurt me plan
trouble;
all day long they think up lies.

13 I am like the deaf; I cannot hear.
Like the mute, I cannot speak.
14 I am like those who do not hear,
who have no answer to give.
15 I trust you, Lord.
You will answer, my Lord and God.
16 I said, "Don't let them laugh at me
or brag when I am defeated."

17 I am about to die,
and I cannot forget my pain.
18 I confess my guilt;
I am troubled by my sin.
19 My enemies are strong and healthy,
and many hate me for no reason.
20 They repay me with evil for the good I
did.
They lie about me because I try to do
good.

21 Lord, don't leave me;
my God, don't go away.
22 Quickly come and help me,
my Lord and Savior.

LIFE IS SHORT
For the director of music. For Jeduthun. A psalm
of David.

39 I said, "I will be careful how I act
and will not sin by what I say.
I will be careful what I say
around wicked people."
2 So I kept very quiet.
I didn't even say anything good,
but I became even more upset.
3 I became very angry inside,
and as I thought about it, my anger
burned.
So I spoke:
4 "Lord, tell me when the end will come
and how long I will live.
Let me know how long I have.
5 You have given me only a short life;
my lifetime is like nothing to you.

Everyone's life is only a breath.　　*Selah*

6 People are like shadows moving about.
All their work is for nothing;
they collect things but don't know who
will get them.

7 "So, Lord, what hope do I have?
You are my hope.
8 Save me from all my sins.
Don't let wicked fools make fun of me.
9 I am quiet; I do not open my mouth,
because you are the one who has done
this.
10 Quit punishing me;
your beating is about to kill me.
11 You correct and punish people for their
sins;
like a moth, you destroy what they love.
Everyone's life is only a breath.　　*Selah*

12 "Lord, hear my prayer,
and listen to my cry.
Do not ignore my tears.
I am like a visitor with you.
Like my ancestors, I'm only here a short
time.
13 Leave me alone so I can be happy
before I leave and am no more."

PRAISE AND PRAYER FOR HELP

For the director of music. A psalm of David.

40 I waited patiently for the Lord.
He turned to me and heard my cry.
2 He lifted me out of the pit of destruction,
out of the sticky mud.
He stood me on a rock
and made my feet steady.
3 He put a new song in my mouth,
a song of praise to our God.
Many people will see this and worship
him.
Then they will trust the Lord.

4 Happy is the person
who trusts the Lord,
who doesn't turn to those who are proud
or to those who worship false gods.
5 Lord my God, you have done many
miracles.
Your plans for us are many.
If I tried to tell them all,
there would be too many to count.

6 You do not want sacrifices and offerings.
But you have made a hole in my ear

to show that my body and life are
yours.
You do not ask for burnt offerings
and sacrifices to take away sins.
7 Then I said, "Look, I have come.
It is written about me in the book.
8 My God, I want to do what you want.
Your teachings are in my heart."

9 I will tell about your goodness in the great
meeting of your people.
Lord, you know my lips are not silent.
10 I do not hide your goodness in my heart;
I speak about your loyalty and salvation.
I do not hide your love and truth
from the people in the great meeting.

11 Lord, do not hold back your mercy from
me;
let your love and truth always protect
me.
12 Troubles have surrounded me;
there are too many to count.
My sins have caught me
so that I cannot see a way to escape.
I have more sins than hairs on my head,
and I have lost my courage.
13 Please, Lord, save me.
Hurry, Lord, to help me.
14 People are trying to kill me.
Shame them and disgrace them.
People want to hurt me.
Let them run away in disgrace.
15 People are making fun of me.
Let them be shamed into silence.
16 But let those who follow you
be happy and glad.
They love you for saving them.
May they always say, "Praise the Lord!"

17 Lord, because I am poor and helpless,
please remember me.
You are my helper and savior.
My God, do not wait.

A PRAYER IN TIME OF SICKNESS

For the director of music. A psalm of David.

41 Happy are those who think about the
poor.
When trouble comes, the Lord will
save them.
2 The Lord will protect them and spare
their life
and will bless them in the land.

He will not let their enemies take them.
³ The LORD will give them strength when
they are sick,
and he will make them well again.

⁴ I said, "LORD, have mercy on me.
Heal me, because I have sinned against
you."
⁵ My enemies are saying evil things about
me.
They say, "When will he die and be
forgotten?"

⁶ Some people come to see me,
but they lie.
They just come to get bad news.
Then they go and gossip.
⁷ All my enemies whisper about me
and think the worst about me.
⁸ They say, "He has a terrible disease.
He will never get out of bed again."
⁹ My best and truest friend, who ate at my
table,
has even turned against me.

FAITH

EARLY, FIRST, OR NOTHING

rules or
relationship?

PSALM 41:4

We are a culture of list makers. Do you know anyone who doesn't have a "to do" list somewhere? We have lists for nearly everything, from grocery shopping to career building. Our thought patterns are conditioned by a reductionist view of the universe—a view that breaks everything down into smaller parts so that we can get a handle on each piece of the bigger picture. This isn't the only way to look at things, but it is certainly our dominant way, even when it comes to thinking about sin.

For most of us, sin is a long list of things we aren't supposed to do. The Ten Commandments are a primary example. Don't do this. Don't do that. Jesus met a man once who was a real list freak. He wanted to know what he needed to have on his list in order to get into heaven. Jesus replied, "Obey the commands." This man instantly responded, "Oh, yes. I know that list. I already do everything on that list." His statement revealed that he had no real understanding of the commandments. They were not a list of rules. They were reflections of God's character.

It is easy to tie our Christian values to lists of rules. It's much more convenient simply to have a checklist for being good. Then we don't have to deal with inner attitudes, deep-seated personality issues, or hidden agendas. But God would rather have a relationship with someone who was a murderer, an adulterer, a liar, and a thief than with someone who kept the list but didn't know the list maker. Simply look at the life of David, who was all these things, but God called him a man after his own heart.

reflect: Enjoy your relationship with God, and you'll end up keeping the rules, also.
Go to **Psalm 50:12.**

51 God killed all the firstborn sons in Egypt,
the oldest son of each family of Ham.[n]
52 But God led his people out like sheep
and he guided them like a flock through
the desert.
53 He led them to safety so they had nothing
to fear,
but their enemies drowned in the sea.
54 So God brought them to his holy land,
to the mountain country he took with
his own power.
55 He forced out the other nations,
and he had his people inherit the land.
He let the tribes of Israel settle there in
tents.

56 But they tested God
and turned against God Most High;
they did not keep his rules.
57 They turned away and were disloyal just
like their ancestors.
They were like a crooked bow that does
not shoot straight.
58 They made God angry by building places
to worship gods;
they made him jealous with their idols.
59 When God heard them, he became very
angry
and rejected the people of Israel
completely.
60 He left his dwelling at Shiloh,
the Tent where he lived among the
people.
61 He let the Ark, his power, be captured;
he let the Ark, his glory, be taken by
enemies.
62 He let his people be killed;
he was very angry with his children.
63 The young men died by fire,
and the young women had no one to
marry.
64 Their priests fell by the sword,
but their widows were not allowed to
cry.
65 Then the Lord got up as if he had been
asleep;
he awoke like a man who had been
drunk with wine.
66 He struck down his enemies
and disgraced them forever.
67 But God rejected the family of Joseph;
he did not choose the tribe of Ephraim.
68 Instead, he chose the tribe of Judah

and Mount Zion, which he loves.
69 And he built his Temple high like the
mountains.
Like the earth, he built it to last forever.
70 He chose David to be his servant
and took him from the sheep pens.
71 He brought him from tending the sheep
so he could lead the flock, the people of
Jacob,
his own people, the people of Israel.
72 And David led them with an innocent
heart
and guided them with skillful hands.

THE NATION CRIES FOR JERUSALEM
A psalm of Asaph.

79
God, nations have come against your
chosen people.
They have ruined your holy Temple.
They have turned Jerusalem into ruins.
2 They have given the bodies of your
servants as food to the wild birds.
They have given the bodies of those who
worship you to the wild animals.
3 They have spilled blood like water all
around Jerusalem.
No one was left to bury the dead.
4 We are a joke to the other nations;
they laugh and make fun of us.

5 LORD, how long will this last?
Will you be angry forever?
How long will your jealousy burn like
a fire?
6 Be angry with the nations that do not
know you
and with the kingdoms that do not
honor you.
7 They have gobbled up the people of Jacob
and destroyed their land.
8 Don't punish us for our past sins.
Show your mercy to us soon,
because we are helpless!
9 God our Savior, help us
so people will praise you.
Save us and forgive our sins
so people will honor you.
10 Why should the nations say,
"Where is their God?"
Tell the other nations in our presence

78:51 Ham The people in Egypt were descendants of
Ham, one of Noah's sons. See Genesis 10:6.

that you punish those who kill your
  servants.
[11] Hear the moans of the prisoners.
  Use your great power
  to save those sentenced to die.

[12] Repay those around us seven times over
  for their insults to you, Lord.
[13] We are your people, the sheep of your
  flock.
  We will thank you always;
  forever and ever we will praise you.

A PRAYER TO BRING ISRAEL BACK

For the director of music. To the tune of "Lilies of
the Agreement." A psalm of Asaph.

80 Shepherd of Israel, listen to us.
  You lead the people of Joseph like a
  flock.
  You sit on your throne between the gold
  creatures with wings.
  Show your greatness [2]to the people of
  Ephraim, Benjamin, and Manasseh.
  Use your strength,
  and come to save us.

[3] God, take us back.
  Show us your kindness so we can be
  saved.

[4] Lord God All-Powerful,
  how long will you be angry
  at the prayers of your people?
[5] You have fed your people with tears;
  you have made them drink many tears.
[6] You made those around us fight over us,
  and our enemies make fun of us.

[7] God All-Powerful, take us back.
  Show us your kindness so we can be
  saved.

[8] You brought us out of Egypt as if we were
  a vine.
  You forced out other nations and
  planted us in the land.
[9] You cleared the ground for us.
  Like a vine, we took root and filled the
  land.
[10] We covered the mountains with our
  shade.
  We had limbs like the mighty cedar
  tree.
[11] Our branches reached the Mediterranean
  Sea,

and our shoots went to the Euphrates
  River.
[12] So why did you pull down our walls?
  Now everyone who passes by steals
  from us.
[13] Like wild pigs they walk over us;
  like wild animals they feed on us.

[14] God All-Powerful, come back.
  Look down from heaven and see.
  Take care of us, your vine.
[15] You planted this shoot with your own
  hands
  and strengthened this child.
[16] Now it is cut down and burned with fire;
  you destroyed us by your angry looks.
[17] With your hand,
  strengthen the one you have chosen for
  yourself.
[18] Then we will not turn away from you.
  Give us life again, and we will call to
  you for help.

[19] Lord God All-Powerful, take us back.
  Show us your kindness so we can be
  saved.

A SONG FOR A HOLIDAY

For the director of music. By the gittith. A psalm
of Asaph.

81 Sing for joy to God, our strength;
  shout out loud to the God of Jacob.
[2] Begin the music. Play the tambourines.
  Play pleasant music on the harps and
  lyres.
[3] Blow the trumpet at the time of the New
  Moon,
  when the moon is full, when our feast
  begins.
[4] This is the law for Israel;
  it is the command of the God of Jacob.
[5] He gave this rule to the people of Joseph
  when they went out of the land of
  Egypt.

I heard a language I did not know,
  saying:
[6] "I took the load off their shoulders;
  I let them put down their baskets.
[7] When you were in trouble, you called, and
  I saved you.
  I answered you with thunder.
  I tested you at the waters of Meribah.
  Selah

¹⁰ Lord, have mercy on me.
  Give me strength so I can pay them
    back.
¹¹ Because my enemies do not defeat me,
  I know you are pleased with me.
¹² Because I am innocent, you support me
  and will let me be with you forever.

¹³ Praise the Lord, the God of Israel.
  He has always been,
  and he will always be.
    Amen and amen.

Book 2

WISHING TO BE NEAR GOD

For the director of music. A maskil of the sons
of Korah.

42 As a deer thirsts for streams of water,
    so I thirst for you, God.
² I thirst for the living God.
  When can I go to meet with him?
³ Day and night, my tears have been my
    food.
  People are always saying,
    "Where is your God?"
⁴ When I remember these things,
  I speak with a broken heart.
  I used to walk with the crowd
    and lead them to God's Temple
    with songs of praise.

⁵ Why am I so sad?
  Why am I so upset?
  I should put my hope in God
    and keep praising him,
    my Savior and ⁶my God.

I am very sad.
  So I remember you where the Jordan
    River begins,
  near the peaks of Hermon and Mount
    Mizar.
⁷ Troubles have come again and again,
    sounding like waterfalls.
  Your waves are crashing all around me.
⁸ The Lord shows his true love every day.
  At night I have a song,
    and I pray to my living God.
⁹ I say to God, my Rock,
  "Why have you forgotten me?
  Why am I sad
    and troubled by my enemies?"
¹⁰ My enemies' insults make me feel

as if my bones were broken.
  They are always saying,
    "Where is your God?"

¹¹ Why am I so sad?
  Why am I so upset?
  I should put my hope in God
    and keep praising him,
    my Savior and my God.

A PRAYER FOR PROTECTION

43 God, defend me.
    Argue my case against those who
      don't follow you.
  Save me from liars and those who do
    evil.
² God, you are my strength.
  Why have you rejected me?
  Why am I sad
    and troubled by my enemies?
³ Send me your light and truth
    to guide me.
  Let them lead me to your holy mountain,
    to where you live.
⁴ Then I will go to the altar of God,
    to God who is my joy and happiness.
  I will praise you with a harp,
    God, my God.

⁵ Why am I so sad?
  Why am I so upset?
  I should put my hope in God
    and keep praising him,
    my Savior and my God.

A PRAYER FOR HELP

For the director of music. A maskil of the sons of
Korah.

44 God, we have heard about you.
    Our ancestors told us
  what you did in their days,
    in days long ago.
² With your power you forced the nations
    out of the land
  and placed our ancestors here.
  You destroyed those other nations,
    but you made our ancestors grow
      strong.
³ It wasn't their swords that took the land.
  It wasn't their power that gave them
    victory.
  But it was your great power and strength.
  You were with them because you loved
    them.

4 My God, you are my King.
Your commands led Jacob's people to
victory.
5 With your help we pushed back our
enemies.
In your name we trampled those who
came against us.
6 I don't trust my bow to help me,
and my sword can't save me.
7 You saved us from our foes,
and you made our enemies ashamed.
8 We will praise God every day;
we will praise your name forever. *Selah*

9 But you have rejected us and shamed us.
You don't march with our armies
anymore.
10 You let our enemies push us back,
and those who hate us have taken our
wealth.
11 You gave us away like sheep to be eaten
and have scattered us among the
nations.
12 You sold your people for nothing
and made no profit on the sale.
13 You made us a joke to our neighbors;
those around us laugh and make fun of
us.
14 You made us a joke to the other nations;
people shake their heads.
15 I am always in disgrace,
and I am covered with shame.
16 My enemy is getting even
with insults and curses.

17 All these things have happened to us,
but we have not forgotten you
or failed to keep our agreement with
you.
18 Our hearts haven't turned away from you,
and we haven't stopped following you.
19 But you crushed us in this place where
wild dogs live,
and you covered us with deep darkness.
20 If we had forgotten our God
or lifted our hands in prayer to foreign
gods,
21 God would have known,
because he knows what is in our hearts.
22 But for you we are in danger of death all
the time.
People think we are worth no more
than sheep to be killed.

23 Wake up, Lord! Why are you sleeping?
Get up! Don't reject us forever.
24 Why do you hide from us?
Have you forgotten our pain and
troubles?
25 We have been pushed down into the dirt;
we are flat on the ground.
26 Get up and help us.
Because of your love, save us.

A SONG FOR THE KING'S WEDDING
For the director of music. To the tune of "Lilies."
A maskil. A love song of the sons of Korah.

45 Beautiful words fill my mind.
I am speaking of royal things.
My tongue is like the pen of a skilled
writer.

2 You are more handsome than anyone,
and you are an excellent speaker,
so God has blessed you forever.
3 Put on your sword, powerful warrior.
Show your glory and majesty.
4 In your majesty win the victory
for what is true and right.
Your power will do amazing things.
5 Your sharp arrows will enter
the hearts of the king's enemies.
Nations will be defeated before you.
6 God, your throne will last forever and
ever.
You will rule your kingdom with
fairness.
7 You love right and hate evil,
so God has chosen you from among
your friends;
he has set you apart with much joy.
8 Your clothes smell like myrrh, aloes, and
cassia.
From palaces of ivory
music comes to make you happy.
9 Kings' daughters are among your honored
women.
Your bride stands at your right side
wearing gold from Ophir.
10 Listen to me, daughter; look and pay
attention.
Forget your people and your father's
family.
11 The king loves your beauty.
Because he is your master, you should
obey him.

¹² People from the city of Tyre have brought
a gift.
Wealthy people will want to meet you.

¹³ The princess is very beautiful.
Her gown is woven with gold.
¹⁴ In her beautiful clothes she is brought to
the king.
Her bridesmaids follow behind her,
and they are also brought to him.
¹⁵ They come with happiness and joy;
they enter the king's palace.

¹⁶ You will have sons to replace your fathers.
You will make them rulers through all
the land.

¹⁷ I will make your name famous from now
on,
so people will praise you forever and
ever.

GOD PROTECTS HIS PEOPLE

For the director of music. By alamoth. A psalm of
the sons of Korah.

46 God is our protection and our
strength.
He always helps in times of trouble.
² So we will not be afraid even if the earth
shakes,
or the mountains fall into the sea,
³ even if the oceans roar and foam,

FEAR OF THE FUTURE

God's protection

FULFILLMENT

By Darlene Zschech   PSALM 46:1

The first two words in this psalm instill great confidence: God is . . . our
protection, our strength, our help. Do you believe beyond a shadow of a doubt
that God is all he says he is? God alone IS our All in All and a very present help. Though
many trials will come, we will stand, knowing our God IS near. Even when heaven and
earth pass away, *even then*, God *IS!*

Later, the psalmist declares: Come and see what God did to overthrow our enemies.
He was faithful again to his Word and his character. He crushed even the greatest
enemies until they could not wreak havoc ever again.

One word from God is all it takes to still the storm. That's why you need to have the
Word of God *in you.*

Another uplifting verse is Psalm 46:10: "Be still and know that I am God." The great I
AM says he will be exalted among the heathen and exalted on the earth. Why do we
hesitate to trust in God? Truly to trust, you've got to let go of trying to work everything
out yourself. Learn to let go and trust God. Be confident in his ability to hold your life in
his hands, for you are his greatest pleasure.

---

reflect: What do you need to let go of so God can handle it for you?
Go to **Psalm 51:10.**

or the mountains shake at the raging
    sea.   *Selah*

4 There is a river that brings joy to the city
    of God,
    the holy place where God Most High
      lives.
5 God is in that city, and so it will not be
    shaken.
    God will help her at dawn.
6 Nations tremble and kingdoms shake.
    God shouts and the earth crumbles.

7 The LORD All-Powerful is with us;
    the God of Jacob is our defender.
          Selah

8 Come and see what the LORD has done,
    the amazing things he has done on the
      earth.
9 He stops wars everywhere on the earth.
    He breaks all bows and spears
    and burns up the chariots with fire.
10 God says, "Be still and know that I am
    God.
    I will be praised in all the nations;
    I will be praised throughout the earth."

11 The LORD All-Powerful is with us;
    the God of Jacob is our defender.
          Selah

GOD, THE KING OF THE WORLD
For the director of music. A psalm of the sons
of Korah.

47 Clap your hands, all you people.
    Shout to God with joy.
2 The LORD Most High is wonderful.
    He is the great King over all the
      earth!
3 He defeated nations for us
    and put them under our control.
4 He chose the land we would inherit.
    We are the children of Jacob, whom he
      loved.   *Selah*

5 God has risen with a shout of joy;
    the LORD has risen as the trumpets
      sounded.
6 Sing praises to God. Sing praises.
    Sing praises to our King. Sing praises.
7 God is King of all the earth,
    so sing a song of praise to him.
8 God is King over the nations.
    God sits on his holy throne.

9 The leaders of the nations meet
    with the people of the God of
      Abraham,
    because the leaders of the earth belong to
      God.
    He is supreme.

JERUSALEM, THE CITY OF GOD
A psalm of the sons of Korah.

48 The LORD is great; he should be
    praised
    in the city of our God, on his holy
      mountain.
2 It is high and beautiful
    and brings joy to the whole world.
    Mount Zion is like the high mountains of
      the north;
    it is the city of the Great King.
3 God is within its palaces;
    he is known as its defender.
4 Kings joined together
    and came to attack the city.
5 But when they saw it, they were
    amazed.
    They ran away in fear.
6 Fear took hold of them;
    they hurt like a woman having a baby.
7 You destroyed the large trading ships
    with an east wind.

8 First we heard
    and now we have seen
    that God will always keep his city safe.
    It is the city of the LORD All-Powerful,
    the city of our God.   *Selah*

9 God, we come into your Temple
    to think about your love.
10 God, your name is known everywhere;
    all over the earth people praise you.
    Your right hand is full of goodness.
11 Mount Zion is happy
    and all the towns of Judah rejoice,
    because your decisions are fair.

12 Walk around Jerusalem
    and count its towers.
13 Notice how strong they are.
    Look at the palaces.
    Then you can tell your children about
      them.
14 This God is our God forever and ever.
    He will guide us from now on.

TRUSTING MONEY IS FOOLISH

For the director of music. A psalm of the sons of Korah.

49 Listen to this, all you nations;
listen, all you who live on earth.
2 Listen, both great and small,
rich and poor together.
3 What I say is wise,
and my heart speaks with
understanding.
4 I will pay attention to a wise saying;
I will explain my riddle on the harp.

5 Why should I be afraid of bad days?
Why should I fear when evil people
surround me?
6 They trust in their money
and brag about their riches.
7 No one can buy back the life of another.
No one can pay God for his own life,
8 because the price of a life is high.
No payment is ever enough.
9 Do people live forever?
Don't they all face death?

10 See, even wise people die.
Fools and stupid people also die
and leave their wealth to others.
11 Their graves will always be their homes.
They will live there from now on,
even though they named places after
themselves.
12 Even rich people do not live forever;
like the animals, people die.

13 This is what will happen to those who
trust in themselves
and to their followers who believe
them. *Selah*
14 Like sheep, they must die,
and death will be their shepherd.
Honest people will rule over them in the
morning,
and their bodies will rot in a grave far
from home.
15 But God will save my life
and will take me from the grave. *Selah*

16 Don't be afraid of rich people
because their houses are more
beautiful.
17 They don't take anything to the grave;
their wealth won't go down with
them.

18 Even though they were praised when they
were alive—
and people may praise you when you
succeed—
19 they will go to where their ancestors are.
They will never see light again.
20 Rich people with no understanding
are just like animals that die.

GOD WANTS TRUE WORSHIP

A psalm of Asaph.

50 The God of gods, the LORD, speaks.
He calls the earth from the rising to
the setting sun.
2 God shines from Jerusalem,
whose beauty is perfect.
3 Our God comes, and he will not be silent.
A fire burns in front of him,
and a powerful storm surrounds him.
4 He calls to the sky above and to the earth
that he might judge his people.
5 He says, "Gather around, you who
worship me,
who have made an agreement with me,
using a sacrifice."
6 God is the judge,
and even the skies say he is right.
Selah

7 God says, "My people, listen to me;
Israel, I will testify against you.
I am God, your God.
8 I do not scold you for your sacrifices.
You always bring me your burnt
offerings.
9 But I do not need bulls from your stalls
or goats from your pens,
10 because every animal of the forest is
already mine.
The cattle on a thousand hills are mine.
11 I know every bird on the mountains,
and every living thing in the fields is
mine.
12 If I were hungry, I would not tell you,
because the earth and everything in it
are mine.
13 I don't eat the meat of bulls
or drink the blood of goats.
14 Give an offering to show thanks to God.
Give God Most High what you have
promised.
15 Call to me in times of trouble.
I will save you, and you will honor me."

16 But God says to the wicked,
  "Why do you talk about my laws?
    Why do you mention my agreement?
17 You hate my teachings
    and turn your back on what I say.
18 When you see a thief, you join him.
    You take part in adultery.
19 You don't stop your mouth from speaking
      evil,
    and your tongue makes up lies.
20 You speak against your brother
    and lie about your mother's son.
21 I have kept quiet while you did these
      things,
    so you thought I was just like you.
  But I will scold you
    and accuse you to your face.

22 "Think about this, you who forget God.
    Otherwise, I will tear you apart,
    and no one will save you.
23 Those people honor me
    who bring me offerings to show thanks.
  And I, God, will save those who do that."

A PRAYER FOR FORGIVENESS
For the director of music. A psalm of David when
the prophet Nathan came to David after David's
sin with Bathsheba.

51 God, be merciful to me
    because you are loving.
  Because you are always ready to be
      merciful,
    wipe out all my wrongs.
2 Wash away all my guilt
    and make me clean again.

3 I know about my wrongs,
    and I can't forget my sin.
4 You are the only one I have sinned
      against;
  I have done what you say is wrong.
  You are right when you speak
    and fair when you judge.
5 I was brought into this world in sin.
    In sin my mother gave birth to me.

6 You want me to be completely truthful,
    so teach me wisdom.

EARLY, FIRST, OR NOTHING

FAITH

true worship

PSALM 50:12

By Darlene Zschech

The first half of this psalm talks of the true meaning of sacrifice—that God
  doesn't *need* our worship; he *wants* our worship because he wants *us!* It's not
out of obligation, but out of love and commitment to him. In verse 12, God is saying to
us that he has need of nothing, for the world is his, and everything in it, *but* we are to
sacrifice offerings of gratitude to him, fulfill our vows to him, and honor him.

The second half of the psalm addresses the plight of those who refuse to obey his will.
Too many people live a life where their seen and unseen lives do not remotely look like
each other, and defeat will always be the fruit of a life like that. But God is saying here,
"Do not blame me. You cast my wisdom, the Word of God, behind you, as if it held no
worth."

reflect: Is there compromise in your character that needs to be corrected?
Go to **FAITH:** "Have Faith in God" at **Mark 11:22-24.**

7 Take away my sin, and I will be clean.
Wash me, and I will be whiter than
snow.
8 Make me hear sounds of joy and gladness;
let the bones you crushed be happy
again.
9 Turn your face from my sins
and wipe out all my guilt.
10 Create in me a pure heart, God,
and make my spirit right again.
11 Do not send me away from you
or take your Holy Spirit away from me.
12 Give me back the joy of your salvation.

Keep me strong by giving me a willing
spirit.
13 Then I will teach your ways to those who
do wrong,
and sinners will turn back to you.
14 God, save me from the guilt of murder,
God of my salvation,
and I will sing about your goodness.
15 Lord, let me speak
so I may praise you.
16 You are not pleased by sacrifices, or I
would give them.
You don't want burnt offerings.

FEAR OF THE FUTURE

confession
of sin

FULFILLMENT

By Darlene Zschech

PSALM 51:10

Psalm 51 is the fourth of seven penitential psalms (psalms of regret or sorrow). This is a very passionate psalm, one where David acknowledges his sin with Bathsheba and takes full responsibility for his actions. His heart cries out to the tender mercy and loving kindness of God, and he offers a broken spirit as a sacrifice for his sin.

All of us have sinned and fallen short of the glory of God, and, hopefully, every one of us knows what it is like to humble ourselves before God, confess our sins and ask him to wash us clean again. Critical to the life of a follower of Christ is this act of obedience. All other acts of obedience seem to pale in comparison to confessing our need of the power of the cross in our lives.

A God-honoring life is one of dependence, not independence. Dependence on God is how we were designed to function. Confess any known sin to God daily (1 John 1:7–9). The sacrifice that is desired by God is that of a clean heart—one that is broken, humbled by his presence, and willing to obey his will.

Whether or not you repent, you *cannot* hide sin from God or simply dismiss it as insignificant. Sin left in the dark will eventually bring rot to your life, to your bones, to your heart, or to those you love. Deal with it, my friends. The Lord will wash you clean. Beautiful is the sweet fragrance of forgiveness!

reflect: What act of sin do you need to confess to the Lord?
Go to **FULFILLMENT:** "For Your Own Good" at **Mark 2:27.**

17 The sacrifice God wants is a broken spirit.
God, you will not reject a heart that is
broken and sorry for sin.

18 Do whatever good you wish for
Jerusalem.
Rebuild the walls of Jerusalem.
19 Then you will be pleased with right
sacrifices and whole burnt offerings,
and bulls will be offered on your altar.

GOD WILL PUNISH THE PROUD

For the director of music. A maskil of David.
When Doeg the Edomite came to Saul and said to
him, "David is in Ahimelech's house."

52

Mighty warrior, why do you brag
about the evil you do?
God's love will continue forever.
2 You think up evil plans.
Your tongue is like a sharp razor,
making up lies.
3 You love wrong more than right
and lies more than truth.   *Selah*
4 You love words that bite
and tongues that lie.

5 But God will ruin you forever.
He will grab you and throw you out of
your tent;
he will tear you away from the land of
the living.   *Selah*
6 Those who do right will see this and fear
God.
They will laugh at you and say,
7 "Look what happened to the man
who did not depend on God
but depended on his money.
He grew strong by his evil plans."

8 But I am like an olive tree
growing in God's Temple.
I trust God's love
forever and ever.
9 God, I will thank you forever for what you
have done.
With those who worship you, I will
trust you because you are good.

THE UNBELIEVING FOOL

For the director of music. By mahalath. A maskil
of David.

53

Fools say to themselves,
"There is no God."
Fools are evil and do terrible things;
none of them does anything good.

2 God looked down from heaven on all
people
to see if anyone was wise,
if anyone was looking to God for help.
3 But all have turned away.
Together, everyone has become evil;
none of them does anything good.
Not a single person.

4 Don't the wicked understand?
They destroy my people as if they were
eating bread.
They do not ask God for help.
5 The wicked are filled with terror
where there had been nothing to fear.
God will scatter the bones of your
enemies.
You will defeat them,
because God has rejected them.

6 I pray that victory will come to Israel
from Mount Zion!
May God bring them back.
Then the people of Jacob will rejoice,
and the people of Israel will be glad.

A PRAYER FOR HELP

For the director of music. With stringed
instruments. A maskil of David when the Ziphites
went to Saul and said, "We think David is hiding
among our people."

54

God, save me because of who you
are.
By your strength show that I am
innocent.
2 Hear my prayer, God;
listen to what I say.
3 Strangers turn against me,
and cruel people want to kill me.
They do not care about God.   *Selah*

4 See, God will help me;
the Lord will support me.
5 Let my enemies be punished with their
own evil.
Destroy them because you are loyal to
me.

6 I will offer a sacrifice as a special gift to
you.
I will thank you, LORD, because you are
good.
7 You have saved me from all my troubles,
and I have seen my enemies defeated.

A PRAYER ABOUT A FALSE FRIEND

For the director of music. With stringed instruments. A maskil of David.

55 God, listen to my prayer
and do not ignore my cry for
help.
2 Pay attention to me and answer me.
I am troubled and upset
3 by what the enemy says
and how the wicked look at me.
They bring troubles down on me,
and in anger they attack me.

4 I am frightened inside;
the terror of death has attacked me.
5 I am scared and shaking,
and terror grips me.
6 I said, "I wish I had wings like a dove.
Then I would fly away and rest.
7 I would wander far away
and stay in the desert.   *Selah*
8 I would hurry to my place of escape,
far away from the wind and storm."

9 Lord, destroy and confuse their words,
because I see violence and fighting in
the city.
10 Day and night they are all around its
walls,
and evil and trouble are everywhere
inside.
11 Destruction is everywhere in the city;
trouble and lying never leave its
streets.

12 It was not an enemy insulting me.
I could stand that.
It was not someone who hated me.
I could hide from him.
13 But it is you, a person like me,
my companion and good friend.
14 We had a good friendship
and walked together to God's Temple.

15 Let death take away my enemies.
Let them die while they are still
young
because evil lives with them.
16 But I will call to God for help,
and the LORD will save me.
17 Morning, noon, and night I am troubled
and upset,
but he will listen to me.
18 Many are against me,

but he keeps me safe in battle.
19 God who lives forever
will hear me and punish them.   *Selah*
But they will not change;
they do not fear God.

20 The one who was my friend attacks his
friends
and breaks his promises.
21 His words are slippery like butter,
but war is in his heart.
His words are smoother than oil,
but they cut like knives.

22 Give your worries to the LORD,
and he will take care of you.
He will never let good people
down.
23 But, God, you will bring down
the wicked to the grave.
Murderers and liars will live
only half a lifetime.
But I will trust in you.

TRUSTING GOD FOR HELP

For the director of music. To the tune of "The Dove in the Distant Oak." A miktam of David when the Philistines captured him in Gath.

56 God, be merciful to me because
people are chasing me;
the battle has pressed me all day long.
2 My enemies have chased me all day;
there are many proud people fighting
me.
3 When I am afraid,
I will trust you.
4 I praise God for his word.
I trust God, so I am not afraid.
What can human beings do to me?

5 All day long they twist my words;
all their evil plans are against me.
6 They wait. They hide.
They watch my steps,
hoping to kill me.
7 God, do not let them escape;
punish the foreign nations in your
anger.
8 You have recorded my troubles.
You have kept a list of my tears.
Aren't they in your records?

9 On the day I call for help, my enemies will
be defeated.
I know that God is on my side.

¹⁰ I praise God for his word to me;
    I praise the LORD for his word.
¹¹ I trust in God. I will not be afraid.
    What can people do to me?

¹² God, I must keep my promises to you.
    I will give you my offerings to thank
    you,
¹³ because you have saved me from death.
    You have kept me from being defeated.
    So I will walk with God
    in light among the living.

A PRAYER IN TROUBLED TIMES
For the director of music. To the tune of "Do Not
Destroy." A miktam of David when he escaped
from Saul in the cave.

57 Be merciful to me, God; be merciful
    to me
because I come to you for
    protection.
Let me hide under the shadow of your
    wings
until the trouble has passed.

FULFILLMENT

FOR YOUR OWN GOOD
trusting God
for help

PSALM 56:11

By Darlene Zschech

What a psalm! For David to have fled from Saul straight to Gath, the hometown of Goliath, shows how down David was feeling and how he had no confidence in who he was in the eyes of the people. His followers at this stage were very few; the four hundred mentioned in 1 Samuel were yet to be gathered.

The beginning indicates that David is encountering tremendous pressure. Interestingly, he is not yet crushed; when he is afraid, he puts his trust in God. How great a statement of faith this was! He really had nowhere to hide.

We know how to handle pressure in small or intermittent doses, but pressure with no end is what causes many to break down. As David states, he is misrepresented, which is often the kind of pressure you can do nothing about, so you need to know how to rise above it!

When David states, "I trust in God," we find him sharing how the enemy continues to hunt, intimidate, and weaken him. But now, compared to God, David observes that the enemy is frail flesh and can ultimately do nothing to defeat him.

We come to the crescendo at the end of the psalm with the thanksgiving offering. It is being offered to celebrate answered prayer and the promise made in adversity. Thank offerings can be literal sacrifices (Leviticus 7:12) or songs of gratitude (Psalm 26:7). Here is a great example of how to live: thankful and faithful.

---

reflect: What areas of life do you need to trust God for help with today?
Go to **Psalm 61:1–4.**

2 I cry out to God Most High,
to the God who does everything for me.
3 He sends help from heaven and saves me.
He punishes those who chase me.

Selah

God sends me his love and truth.

4 Enemies, like lions, are all around me;
I must lie down among them.
Their teeth are like spears and arrows,
their tongues as sharp as swords.

5 God is supreme over the skies;
his majesty covers the earth.

6 They set a trap for me.
I am very worried.
They dug a pit in my path,
but they fell into it themselves.   *Selah*

7 My heart is steady, God; my heart is
steady.
I will sing and praise you.
8 Wake up, my soul.
Wake up, harp and lyre!
I will wake up the dawn.
9 Lord, I will praise you among the nations;
I will sing songs of praise about you to
all the nations.
10 Your great love reaches to the skies,
your truth to the clouds.
11 God, you are supreme above the skies.
Let your glory be over all the earth.

UNFAIR JUDGES

For the director of music. To the tune of "Do Not
Destroy." A miktam of David.

58 Do you rulers really say what is
right?
Do you judge people fairly?
2 No, in your heart you plan evil;
you think up violent crimes in the
land.
3 From birth, evil people turn away from
God;
they wander off and tell lies as soon as
they are born.
4 They are like poisonous snakes,
like deaf cobras that stop up their ears
5 so they cannot hear the music of the snake
charmer
no matter how well he plays.
6 God, break the teeth in their mouths!
Tear out the fangs of those lions, LORD!

7 Let them disappear like water that flows
away.
Let them be cut short like a broken
arrow.
8 Let them be like snails that melt as they
move.
Let them be like a child born dead who
never saw the sun.
9 His anger will blow them away alive
faster than burning thorns can heat a
pot.
10 Good people will be glad when they see
him get even.
They will wash their feet in the blood of
the wicked.
11 Then people will say,
"There really are rewards for doing
what is right.
There really is a God who judges the
world."

A PRAYER FOR PROTECTION

For the director of music. To the tune of "Do Not
Destroy." A miktam of David when Saul sent men
to watch David's house to kill him.

59 God, save me from my enemies.
Protect me from those who come
against me.
2 Save me from those who do evil
and from murderers.

3 Look, they are waiting to ambush me.
Cruel people attack me,
but I have not sinned or done wrong,
LORD.
4 I have done nothing wrong, but they are
ready to attack me.
Wake up to help me, and look.
5 You are the LORD God All-Powerful, the
God of Israel.
Arise and punish those people.
Do not give those traitors any mercy.

Selah

6 They come back at night.
Like dogs they growl and roam around
the city.
7 Notice what comes from their mouths.
Insults come from their lips,
because they say, "Who's listening?"
8 But, LORD, you laugh at them;
you make fun of all of them.

⁹ God, my strength, I am looking to you,
   because God is my defender.
¹⁰ My God loves me, and he goes in front of
   me.
   He will help me defeat my enemies.
¹¹ Lord, our protector, do not kill them, or
   my people will forget.
   With your power scatter them and
   defeat them.
¹² They sin by what they say;
   they sin with their words.
   They curse and tell lies,
   so let their pride trap them.

¹³ Destroy them in your anger;
   destroy them completely!
   Then they will know
   that God rules over Israel
   and to the ends of the earth.   *Selah*
¹⁴ They come back at night.
   Like dogs they growl
   and roam around the city.
¹⁵ They wander about looking for food,
   and they howl if they do not find
   enough.
¹⁶ But I will sing about your strength.

THE ROAD TO SUCCESS

FUTURE

a cry against injustice

PSALM 58:1-3   By Darlene Zschech

This is another of the great psalms—a cry against injustice. The psalmist does not allow us to get complacent when it comes to bringing justice. An unjust judge, or anyone for that matter, can bring wrongful complaints against you, but God, the supreme judge, will always judge rightly.

Here David points out something very interesting: in their hearts, they were forming wicked schemes, and their hands were working out the calculated ruthlessness in their hearts. Hearts and hands have always been critical in the lives of the righteous. Before you feel puffed up, you've got to remember where you came from and that the sin nature is in all of us, which is why we needed a Savior in the first place!

David says that if he cannot convince the enemies to bring truth to light, or right the wrong, he at least wants to deprive them of their ability for evil. To that end, David continues to speak right over every wrong that the enemy tries to throw his way.

The great news is that the righteous will never be forsaken and given over to their enemies, as all men will be forced by the final judgment to see that there is a God, the righteous ruler over the universe. Time will remove doubts, solve difficulties, and reveal secrets; meanwhile, faith's foreseeing eye discerns the truth even now and rejoices in the midst of any trial.

reflect: Do you ever cry out against the injustices you witness around you?
Go to **Deuteronomy 1:8.**

In the morning I will sing about your
love.
You are my defender,
my place of safety in times of trouble.
¹⁷ God, my strength, I will sing praises to you.
God, my defender, you are the God who
loves me.

A PRAYER AFTER A DEFEAT

For the director of music. To the tune of "Lily of
the Agreement." A miktam of David. For teaching.
When David fought the Arameans of Northwest
Mesopotamia and Zobah, and when Joab
returned and defeated twelve thousand Edomites
at the Valley of Salt.

60 God, you have rejected us and
scattered us.
You have been angry, but please come
back to us.
² You made the earth shake and crack.
Heal its breaks because it is shaking.
³ You have given your people trouble.
You made us unable to walk straight,
like people drunk with wine.
⁴ You have raised a banner to gather those
who fear you.
Now they can stand up against the
enemy. *Selah*

⁵ Answer us and save us by your power
so the people you love will be rescued.

⁶ God has said from his Temple,
"When I win, I will divide Shechem
and measure off the Valley of Succoth.
⁷ Gilead and Manasseh are mine.
Ephraim is like my helmet.
Judah holds my royal scepter.

ANGER MANAGEMENT

easier exercise

FITNESS

PSALM 59:9

Here are a few tips on making exercise easier:

1. **The Power of Ten Minutes:** Experts have found that exercising twice for ten minutes has almost the same positive effects on overall health as working out for twenty minutes straight.

2. **No Pain, No Pain:** It turns out that moderate, regular exercise is better for your health than rigorous, painful exercise.

3. **The Three-Minute Solution:** You can get a body part in shape by working it out for only three minutes every five to seven days. Try working out during the television commercials. Since you can do this at virtually any time, there are no excuses for not exercising on a regular basis.

God created you to move, so get moving!

reflect: Start with simple exercises that you can do anytime and anywhere.
Go to **Philemon 17–21.**

8 Moab is like my washbowl.
   I throw my sandals at Edom.
   I shout at Philistia."

9 Who will bring me to the strong, walled
      city?
   Who will lead me to Edom?
10 God, surely you have rejected us;
   you do not go out with our armies.
11 Help us fight the enemy.
   Human help is useless,

12 but we can win with God's help.
   He will defeat our enemies.

A PRAYER FOR PROTECTION
For the director of music. With stringed
instruments. Of David.

61 God, hear my cry;
   listen to my prayer.
2 I call to you from the ends of the earth
   when I am afraid.
   Carry me away to a high mountain.

FOR YOUR OWN GOOD

FULFILLMENT

God has heard me

PSALM 61:1-4

By Darlene Zschech

In these verses of Scripture, David is crying out to God—it is not the prayer of a casual worshiper, but the cry of a man who has learned to trust in the Lord. Perhaps the psalm was written during David's enforced exile from the Tabernacle, the visible home of God.

In these times, to be absent from the place of divine worship was like having your breath taken away, an absolute disconnection to anything that truly mattered. So David may have felt like he was banished to the ends of the earth. Beautifully, the Maker of heaven and earth still reached down to find him.

Many people reach for temporary emotional fixes, rather than reaching out to God or looking at some of the real issues. But our lovely friend, the Holy Spirit, has the amazing ability to lead us to a high mountain, that great towering providential Rock that towers over *any* situation going on in our lives.

Psalm 61:4 finishes with a needful pause as we contemplate the faithfulness of God. David is now in the land of "God Has Heard Me." His language has changed to confidence, for God is with this banished king and will lead him back to where he needs to be. He is again captivated by the future and everything that God had promised to him for that season and to all generations. Through Jesus Christ, we are part of that spiritual lineage today.

reflect: Whom do you turn to when your heart is overwhelmed?
Go to **Psalm 100.**

3 You have been my protection,
  like a strong tower against my enemies.

4 Let me live in your Holy Tent forever.
  Let me find safety in the shelter of your
    wings. *Selah*

5 God, you have heard my promises.
  You have given me what belongs to
    those who fear you.

6 Give the king a long life;
  let him live many years.

7 Let him rule in the presence of God
    forever.
  Protect him with your love and truth.

8 Then I will praise your name forever,
  and every day I will keep my promises.

TRUST ONLY IN GOD

For the director of music. For Jeduthun. A psalm
of David.

62 I find rest in God;
    only he can save me.

2 He is my rock and my salvation.
  He is my defender;
  I will not be defeated.

3 How long will you attack someone?
  Will all of you kill that person?
  Who is like a leaning wall, like a fence
    ready to fall?

4 They are planning to make that person
    fall.
  They enjoy telling lies.
  With their mouths they bless,
    but in their hearts they curse. *Selah*

5 I find rest in God;
  only he gives me hope.

6 He is my rock and my salvation.
  He is my defender;
  I will not be defeated.

7 My honor and salvation come from God.
  He is my mighty rock and my
    protection.

8 People, trust God all the time.
  Tell him all your problems,
  because God is our protection. *Selah*

9 The least of people are only a breath,
  and even the greatest are just a lie.
  On the scales, they weigh nothing;
    together they are only a breath.

10 Do not trust in force.

Stealing is of no use.
  Even if you gain more riches,
    don't put your trust in them.

11 God has said this,
  and I have heard it over and over:
  God is strong.

12 The Lord is loving.
  You reward people for what they have
    done.

WISHING TO BE NEAR GOD

A psalm of David when he was in the desert of
Judah.

63 God, you are my God.
    I search for you.
  I thirst for you
    like someone in a dry, empty land
    where there is no water.

2 I have seen you in the Temple
  and have seen your strength and glory.

3 Because your love is better than life,
  I will praise you.

4 I will praise you as long as I live.
  I will lift up my hands in prayer to your
    name.

5 I will be content as if I had eaten the best
    foods.
  My lips will sing, and my mouth will
    praise you.

6 I remember you while I'm lying in bed;
  I think about you through the night.

7 You are my help.
  Because of your protection, I sing.

8 I stay close to you;
  you support me with your right hand.

9 Some people are trying to kill me,
  but they will go down to the grave.

10 They will be killed with swords
  and eaten by wild dogs.

11 But the king will rejoice in his God.
  All who make promises in his name will
    praise him,
  but the mouths of liars will be shut.

A PRAYER AGAINST ENEMIES

For the director of music. A psalm of David.

64 God, listen to my complaint.
    I am afraid of my enemies;
  protect my life from them.

2 Hide me from those who plan wicked
    things,

from that gang who does evil.

3 They sharpen their tongues like swords
and shoot bitter words like arrows.
4 From their hiding places they shoot at
innocent people;
they shoot suddenly and are not afraid.
5 They encourage each other to do wrong.
They talk about setting traps,
thinking no one will see them.
6 They plan wicked things and say,
"We have a perfect plan."
The mind of human beings is hard to
understand.

7 But God will shoot them with arrows;
they will suddenly be struck down.
8 Their own words will be used against
them.
All who see them will shake their
heads.
9 Then everyone will fear God.
They will tell what God has done,
and they will learn from what he has
done.
10 Good people will be happy in the LORD
and will find protection in him.
Let everyone who is honest praise the
LORD.

A HYMN OF THANKSGIVING
For the director of music. A psalm of David.
A song.

65 God, you will be praised in
Jerusalem.
We will keep our promises to you.
2 You hear our prayers.
All people will come to you.
3 Our guilt overwhelms us,
but you forgive our sins.
4 Happy are the people you choose
and invite to stay in your court.
We are filled with good things in your
house,
your holy Temple.

5 You answer us in amazing ways,
God our Savior.
People everywhere on the earth
and beyond the sea trust you.
6 You made the mountains by your strength;
you are dressed in power.
7 You stopped the roaring seas,
the roaring waves,
and the uproar of the nations.

8 Even those people at the ends of the earth
fear your miracles.
You are praised from where the sun
rises to where it sets.
9 You take care of the land and water it;
you make it very fertile.
The rivers of God are full of water.
Grain grows because you make it grow.
10 You send rain to the plowed fields;
you fill the rows with water.
You soften the ground with rain,
and then you bless it with crops.
11 You give the year a good harvest,
and you load the wagons with many
crops.
12 The desert is covered with grass
and the hills with happiness.
13 The pastures are full of flocks,
and the valleys are covered with grain.
Everything shouts and sings for joy.

PRAISE GOD FOR WHAT HE HAS DONE
For the director of music. A song. A psalm.

66 Everything on earth, shout with joy
to God!
2 Sing about his glory!
Make his praise glorious!
3 Say to God, "Your works are amazing!
Because your power is great,
your enemies fall before you.
4 All the earth worships you
and sings praises to you.
They sing praises to your name." *Selah*

5 Come and see what God has done,
the amazing things he has done for
people.
6 He turned the sea into dry land.
The people crossed the river on foot.
So let us rejoice because of what he did.
7 He rules forever with his power.
He keeps his eye on the nations,
so people should not turn against him.
Selah

8 You people, praise our God;
loudly sing his praise.
9 He protects our lives
and does not let us be defeated.
10 God, you have tested us;
you have purified us like silver.
11 You let us be trapped
and put a heavy load on us.

12 You let our enemies walk on our heads.
We went through fire and flood,
but you brought us to a place with good
things.

13 I will come to your Temple with burnt
offerings.
I will give you what I promised,
14 things I promised when I was in
trouble.
15 I will bring you offerings of fat animals,
and I will offer sheep, bulls, and goats.
Selah

16 All of you who fear God, come and
listen,
and I will tell you what he has done for
me.
17 I cried out to him with my mouth
and praised him with my tongue.
18 If I had known of any sin in my heart,
the Lord would not have listened
to me.
19 But God has listened;
he has heard my prayer.
20 Praise God,
who did not ignore my prayer
or hold back his love from me.

EVERYONE SHOULD PRAISE GOD

For the director of music. With stringed
instruments. A psalm. A song.

67 God, have mercy on us and bless us
and show us your kindness
Selah

2 so the world will learn your ways,
and all nations will learn that you can
save.
3 God, the people should praise you;
all people should praise you.
4 The nations should be glad and sing
because you judge people fairly.
You guide all the nations on earth.
Selah
5 God, the people should praise you;
all people should praise you.
6 The land has given its crops.
God, our God, blesses us.
7 God blesses us
so people all over the earth will fear
him.

PRAISE GOD WHO SAVED THE NATION

For the director of music. A psalm of David.
A song.

68 Let God rise up and scatter his
enemies;
let those who hate him run away from
him.
2 Blow them away as smoke
is driven away by the wind.
As wax melts before a fire,
let the wicked be destroyed before God.
3 But those who do right should be glad
and should rejoice before God;
they should be happy and glad.

4 Sing to God; sing praises to his name.
Prepare the way for him
who rides through the desert,
whose name is the LORD.
Rejoice before him.
5 God is in his holy Temple.
He is a father to orphans,
and he defends the widows.
6 God gives the lonely a home.
He leads prisoners out with joy,
but those who turn against God will live
in a dry land.

7 God, you led your people out
when you marched through the desert.
Selah

8 The ground shook
and the sky poured down rain
before God, the God of Mount Sinai,
before God, the God of Israel.
9 God, you sent much rain;
you refreshed your tired land.
10 Your people settled there.
God, in your goodness
you took care of the poor.

11 The Lord gave the command,
and a great army told the news:
12 "Kings and their armies run away.
In camp they divide the wealth taken
in war.
13 Those who stayed by the campfires
will share the riches taken in battle."
14 The Almighty scattered kings
like snow on Mount Zalmon.

15 The mountains of Bashan are high;
the mountains of Bashan have many
peaks.

16 Why do you mountains with many peaks
 look with envy
 on the mountain that God chose for his
 home?
 The LORD will live there forever.
17 God comes with millions of chariots;
 the Lord comes from Mount Sinai to his
 holy place.
18 When you went up to the heights,
 you led a parade of captives.
 You received gifts from the people,
 even from those who turned against you.
 And the LORD God will live there.

19 Praise the Lord, God our Savior,
 who helps us every day.   *Selah*
20 Our God is a God who saves us;
 the LORD God saves us from death.

21 God will crush his enemies' heads,
 the hairy skulls of those who continue
 to sin.
22 The Lord said, "I will bring the enemy
 back from Bashan;
 I will bring them back from the depths
 of the sea.
23 Then you can stick your feet in their
 blood,
 and your dogs can lick their share."

24 God, people have seen your victory
 march;
 God my King marched into the holy
 place.
25 The singers are in front and the
 instruments are behind.
 In the middle are the girls with the
 tambourines.
26 Praise God in the meeting place;
 praise the LORD in the gathering of
 Israel.
27 There is the smallest tribe, Benjamin,
 leading them.
 And there are the leaders of Judah with
 their group.
 There also are the leaders of Zebulun
 and of Naphtali.

28 God, order up your power;
 show the mighty power you have used
 for us before.
29 Kings will bring their wealth to you,
 to your Temple in Jerusalem.
30 Punish Egypt, the beast in the tall grass
 along the river.

Punish the leaders of nations, those
 bulls among the cows.
 Defeated, they will bring you their silver.
 Scatter those nations that love war.
31 Messengers will come from Egypt;
 the people of Cush will pray to God.

32 Kingdoms of the earth, sing to God;
 sing praises to the Lord.   *Selah*
33 Sing to the one who rides through the
 skies, which are from long ago.
 He speaks with a thundering voice.
34 Announce that God is powerful.
 He rules over Israel,
 and his power is in the skies.
35 God, you are wonderful in your Temple.
 The God of Israel gives his people
 strength and power.

Praise God!

A CRY FOR HELP

For the director of music. To the tune of "Lilies."
A psalm of David.

69

God, save me,
 because the water has risen to my
 neck.
2 I'm sinking down into the mud,
 and there is nothing to stand on.
I am in deep water,
 and the flood covers me.
3 I am tired from calling for help;
 my throat is sore.
My eyes are tired from waiting
 for God to help me.
4 There are more people who hate me for
 no reason than hairs on my head;
 powerful enemies want to destroy me
 for no reason.
They make me pay back
 what I did not steal.

5 God, you know what I have done wrong;
 I cannot hide my guilt from you.
6 Lord GOD All-Powerful,
 do not let those who hope in you be
 ashamed because of me.
God of Israel,
 do not let your worshipers be disgraced
 because of me.
7 For you, I carry this shame,
 and my face is covered with disgrace.
8 I am like a stranger to my closest relatives
 and a foreigner to my mother's children.

⁹ My strong love for your Temple
    completely controls me.
  When people insult you, it hurts me.
¹⁰ When I cry and fast,
    they make fun of me.
¹¹ When I wear clothes of sadness,
    they joke about me.
¹² They make fun of me in public places,
    and the drunkards make up songs
    about me.

¹³ But I pray to you, LORD, for favor.
  God, because of your great love,
    answer me.
  You are truly able to save.

¹⁴ Pull me from the mud,
    and do not let me sink.
  Save me from those who hate me
    and from the deep water.
¹⁵ Do not let the flood drown me
    or the deep water swallow me
    or the grave close its mouth over me.
¹⁶ LORD, answer me because your love is so
    good.
  Because of your great kindness, turn
    to me.
¹⁷ Do not hide from me, your servant.
  I am in trouble. Hurry to help me!
¹⁸ Come near and save me;
  rescue me from my enemies.

THE ULTIMATE INVESTMENT

are you listening?

FINANCES

PSALM 69:33

This Hebrew verb for "listens to" is used over a thousand times in the Old Testament. It can be translated "to hear, listen to, pay attention, obey, examine, and understand," depending on the context. In its basic use, it has the same meaning as the English translation—to comprehend a sound or message. When it is used in connection with God's commandments, it usually carries the stronger sense of "listen to, obey, respond to, or answer."

There is an important connection between God's proclamations to us and our perception and response to his words. Jeremiah tells us that refusing to listen to God carries the consequence of finding God silent when we try to seek him later. True hearing entails understanding that is exhibited in action.

This Old Testament context was foremost in Jesus' mind when he said those peculiar words, "Let those with ears use them and listen!" In this verse, the psalmist declares that the Lord is not like men who hear the sound of affliction and desperation but do not respond. The Lord hears and acts. He pays attention to our cries for help and demonstrates his care by rescuing us. He is not put off by the fact that we are prisoners to ourselves.

reflect: Are you listening to the voice of God for direction in your life?
Go to **Psalm 106:3.**

¹⁹ You see my shame and disgrace.
    You know all my enemies and what
        they have said.
²⁰ Insults have broken my heart
    and left me weak.
I looked for sympathy, but there was
        none;
    I found no one to comfort me.
²¹ They put poison in my food
    and gave me vinegar to drink.

²² Let their own feasts cause their ruin;
    let their feasts trap them and pay them
        back.
²³ Let their eyes be closed so they cannot see
    and their backs be forever weak from
        troubles.
²⁴ Pour your anger out on them;
    let your anger catch up with them.
²⁵ May their place be empty;
    leave no one to live in their tents.
²⁶ They chase after those you have hurt,
    and they talk about the pain of those
        you have wounded.
²⁷ Charge them with crime after crime,
    and do not let them have anything good.
²⁸ Wipe their names from the book of life,
    and do not list them with those who do
        what is right.

²⁹ I am sad and hurting.
    God, save me and protect me.

³⁰ I will praise God in a song
    and will honor him by giving thanks.
³¹ That will please the LORD more than
        offering him cattle,
    more than sacrificing a bull with horns
        and hoofs.
³² Poor people will see this and be glad.
    Be encouraged, you who worship God.
³³ The LORD listens to those in need
    and does not look down on captives.

³⁴ Heaven and earth should praise him,
    the seas and everything in them.
³⁵ God will save Jerusalem
    and rebuild the cities of Judah.
Then people will live there and own the
        land.
³⁶   The descendants of his servants will
        inherit that land,
    and those who love him will live there.

A CRY FOR GOD TO HELP QUICKLY

For the director of music. A psalm of David.
To help people remember.

70 God, come quickly and save me.
    LORD, hurry to help me.
² Let those who are trying to kill me
    be ashamed and disgraced.
Let those who want to hurt me
    run away in disgrace.
³ Let those who make fun of me
    stop because of their shame.
⁴ But let all those who worship you
    rejoice and be glad.
Let those who love your salvation
    always say, "Praise the greatness of
        God."
⁵ I am poor and helpless;
    God, hurry to me.
You help me and save me.
    LORD, do not wait.

AN OLD PERSON'S PRAYER

71 In you, LORD, is my protection.
    Never let me be ashamed.
² Because you do what is right, save and
        rescue me;
    listen to me and save me.
³ Be my place of safety
    where I can always come.
Give the command to save me,
    because you are my rock and my strong,
        walled city.
⁴ My God, save me from the power of the
        wicked
    and from the hold of evil and cruel
        people.
⁵ LORD, you are my hope.
    LORD, I have trusted you since I was
        young.
⁶ I have depended on you since I was born;
    you helped me even on the day of my
        birth.
    I will always praise you.

⁷ I am an example to many people,
    because you are my strong protection.
⁸ I am always praising you;
    all day long I honor you.
⁹ Do not reject me when I am old;
    do not leave me when my strength is
        gone.
¹⁰ My enemies make plans against me,
    and they meet together to kill me.

11 They say, "God has left him.
Go after him and take him,
because no one will save him."

12 God, don't be far off.
My God, hurry to help me.
13 Let those who accuse me
be ashamed and destroyed.
Let those who are trying to hurt me
be covered with shame and disgrace.
14 But I will always have hope
and will praise you more and more.
15 I will tell how you do what is right.
I will tell about your salvation all day
long,
even though it is more than I can tell.
16 I will come and tell about your powerful
works, Lord God.
I will remind people that only you do
what is right.
17 God, you have taught me since I was
young.
To this day I tell about the miracles you
do.
18 Even though I am old and gray,
do not leave me, God.
I will tell the children about your power;
I will tell those who live after me about
your might.
19 God, your justice reaches to the skies.
You have done great things;
God, there is no one like you.
20 You have given me many troubles and bad
times,
but you will give me life again.
When I am almost dead,
you will keep me alive.
21 You will make me greater than ever,
and you will comfort me again.

22 I will praise you with the harp.
I trust you, my God.
I will sing to you with the lyre,
Holy One of Israel.
23 I will shout for joy when I sing praises to
you.
You have saved me.
24 I will tell about your justice all day
long.
And those who want to hurt me
will be ashamed and disgraced.

A PRAYER FOR THE KING

Of Solomon.

72 God, give the king your good
judgment
and the king's son your goodness.
2 Help him judge your people fairly
and decide what is right for the poor.
3 Let there be peace on the mountains
and goodness on the hills for the
people.
4 Help him be fair to the poor
and save the needy
and punish those who hurt them.

5 May they respect you as long as the sun
shines
and as long as the moon glows.
6 Let him be like rain on the grass,
like showers that water the earth.
7 Let goodness be plentiful while he lives.
Let peace continue as long as there is a
moon.

8 Let his kingdom go from sea to sea,
and from the Euphrates River to the
ends of the earth.
9 Let the people of the desert bow down to
him,
and make his enemies lick the dust.
10 Let the kings of Tarshish and the faraway
lands
bring him gifts.
Let the kings of Sheba and Seba
bring their presents to him.
11 Let all kings bow down to him
and all nations serve him.

12 He will help the poor when they cry out
and will save the needy when no one
else will help.
13 He will be kind to the weak and poor,
and he will save their lives.
14 He will save them from cruel people who
try to hurt them,
because their lives are precious to
him.

15 Long live the king!
Let him receive gold from Sheba.
Let people always pray for him
and bless him all day long.
16 Let the fields grow plenty of grain
and the hills be covered with crops.
Let the land be as fertile as Lebanon,

and let the cities grow like the grass in
a field.
17 Let the king be famous forever;
let him be remembered as long as the
sun shines.
Let the nations be blessed because of him,
and may they all bless him.

18 Praise the LORD God, the God of Israel,
who alone does such miracles.
19 Praise his glorious name forever.
Let his glory fill the whole world.
Amen and amen.

20 This ends the prayers of David son of
Jesse.

Book 3

SHOULD THE WICKED BE RICH?
A psalm of Asaph.

73 God is truly good to Israel,
to those who have pure hearts.
2 But I had almost stopped believing;
I had almost lost my faith
3 because I was jealous of proud people.
I saw wicked people doing well.

4 They are not suffering;
they are healthy and strong.
5 They don't have troubles like the rest of
us;
they don't have problems like other
people.
6 They wear pride like a necklace
and put on violence as their clothing.
7 They are looking for profits
and do not control their selfish desires.
8 They make fun of others and speak evil;
proudly they speak of hurting others.
9 They brag to the sky.
They say that they own the earth.
10 So their people turn to them
and give them whatever they want.
11 They say, "How can God know?
What does God Most High know?"
12 These people are wicked,
always at ease, and getting richer.
13 So why have I kept my heart pure?
Why have I kept my hands from doing
wrong?
14 I have suffered all day long;
I have been punished every morning.

15 God, if I had decided to talk like this,

I would have let your people down.
16 I tried to understand all this,
but it was too hard for me to see
17 until I went to the Temple of God.
Then I understood what will happen to
them.
18 You have put them in danger;
you cause them to be destroyed.
19 They are destroyed in a moment;
they are swept away by terrors.
20 It will be like waking from a dream.
Lord, when you rise up, they will
disappear.

21 When my heart was sad
and I was angry,
22 I was senseless and stupid.
I acted like an animal toward you.
23 But I am always with you;
you have held my hand.
24 You guide me with your advice,
and later you will receive me in honor.
25 I have no one in heaven but you;
I want nothing on earth besides you.
26 My body and my mind may become weak,
but God is my strength.
He is mine forever.

27 Those who are far from God will die;
you destroy those who are unfaithful.
28 But I am close to God, and that is good.
The Lord GOD is my protection.
I will tell all that you have done.

A NATION IN TROUBLE PRAYS
A maskil of Asaph.

74 God, why have you rejected us for so
long?
Why are you angry with us, the sheep of
your pasture?
2 Remember the people you bought long
ago.
You saved us, and we are your very own.
After all, you live on Mount Zion.
3 Make your way through these old ruins;
the enemy wrecked everything in the
Temple.

4 Those who were against you shouted in
your meeting place
and raised their flags there.
5 They came with axes raised
as if to cut down a forest of trees.
6 They smashed the carved panels

with their axes and hatchets.
7 They burned your Temple to the ground;
they have made the place where you
live unclean.
8 They thought, "We will completely crush
them!"
They burned every place where God
was worshiped in the land.
9 We do not see any signs.
There are no more prophets,
and no one knows how long this will
last.
10 God, how much longer will the enemy
make fun of you?
Will they insult you forever?
11 Why do you hold back your power?
Bring your power out in the open and
destroy them!

12 God, you have been our king for a long
time.
You bring salvation to the earth.
13 You split open the sea by your power
and broke the heads of the sea monster.
14 You smashed the heads of the monster
Leviathan
and gave it to the desert creatures as
food.
15 You opened up the springs and streams
and made the flowing rivers run dry.
16 Both the day and the night are yours;
you made the sun and the moon.
17 You set all the limits on the earth;
you created summer and winter.

18 LORD, remember how the enemy insulted
you.
Remember how those foolish people
made fun of you.
19 Do not give us, your doves, to those wild
animals.
Never forget your poor people.
20 Remember the agreement you made with
us,
because violence fills every dark corner
of this land.
21 Do not let your suffering people be
disgraced.
Let the poor and helpless praise you.

22 God, arise and defend yourself.
Remember the insults that come from
those foolish people all day long.
23 Don't forget what your enemies said;

don't forget their roar as they rise
against you always.

GOD THE JUDGE
For the director of music. To the tune of "Do Not
Destroy." A psalm of Asaph. A song.

75 God, we thank you;
we thank you because you are near.
We tell about the miracles you do.

2 You say, "I set the time for trial,
and I will judge fairly.
3 The earth with all its people may shake,
but I am the one who holds it steady.
Selah
4 I say to those who are proud, 'Don't brag,'
and to the wicked, 'Don't show your
power.
5 Don't try to use your power against
heaven.
Don't be stubborn.'"

6 No one from the east or the west
or the desert can judge you.
7 God is the judge;
he judges one person as guilty and
another as innocent.
8 The LORD holds a cup of anger in his
hand;
it is full of wine mixed with spices.
He pours it out even to the last drop,
and the wicked drink it all.

9 I will tell about this forever;
I will sing praise to the God of Jacob.
10 He will take all power away from the
wicked,
but the power of good people will grow.

THE GOD WHO ALWAYS WINS
For the director of music. With stringed
instruments. A psalm of Asaph. A song.

76 People in Judah know God;
his fame is great in Israel.
2 His Tent is in Jerusalem;
his home is on Mount Zion.
3 There God broke the flaming arrows,
the shields, the swords, and the
weapons of war. *Selah*
4 God, how wonderful you are!
You are more splendid than the hills full
of animals.
5 The brave soldiers were stripped
as they lay asleep in death.

Not one warrior
   had the strength to stop it.
6 God of Jacob, when you spoke strongly,
   horses and riders fell dead.
7 You are feared;
   no one can stand against you when you
   are angry.
8 From heaven you gave the decision,
   and the earth was afraid and silent.
9 God, you stood up to judge
   and to save the needy people of the
   earth.   *Selah*
10 People praise you for your anger against
   evil.
   Those who live through your anger are
   stopped from doing more evil.

11 Make and keep your promises to the LORD
   your God.
   From all around, gifts should come to
   the God we worship.
12 God breaks the spirits of great leaders;
   the kings on earth fear him.

REMEMBERING GOD'S HELP
For the director of music. For Jeduthun. A psalm
of Asaph.

77
I cry out to God;
   I call to God, and he will hear me.
2 I look for the Lord on the day of trouble.
   All night long I reach out my hands,
   but I cannot be comforted.
3 When I remember God, I become upset;
   when I think, I become afraid.   *Selah*

4 You keep my eyes from closing.
   I am too upset to say anything.
5 I keep thinking about the old days,
   the years of long ago.
6 At night I remember my songs.
   I think and I ask myself:
7 "Will the Lord reject us forever?
   Will he never be kind to us again?
8 Is his love gone forever?
   Has he stopped speaking for all time?
9 Has God forgotten mercy?
   Is he too angry to pity us?"   *Selah*
10 Then I say, "This is what makes me sad:
   For years the power of God Most High
   was with us."

11 I remember what the LORD did;
   I remember the miracles you did long
   ago.

12 I think about all the things you did
   and consider your deeds.
13 God, your ways are holy.
   No god is as great as our God.
14 You are the God who does miracles;
   you have shown people your power.
15 By your power you have saved your
   people,
   the descendants of Jacob and Joseph.
        Selah

16 God, the waters saw you;
   they saw you and became afraid;
   the deep waters shook with fear.
17 The clouds poured down their rain.
   The sky thundered.
   Your lightning flashed back and forth
   like arrows.
18 Your thunder sounded in the whirlwind.
   Lightning lit up the world.
   The earth trembled and shook.
19 You made a way through the sea
   and paths through the deep waters,
   but your footprints were not seen.
20 You led your people like a flock
   by using Moses and Aaron.

GOD SAVED ISRAEL FROM EGYPT
A maskil of Asaph.

78
My people, listen to my teaching;
   listen to what I say.
2 I will speak using stories;
   I will tell secret things from long ago.
3 We have heard them and known them
   by what our ancestors have told us.
4 We will not keep them from our children;
   we will tell those who come later
   about the praises of the LORD.
   We will tell about his power
   and the miracles he has done.

5 The LORD made an agreement with Jacob
   and gave the teachings to Israel,
   which he commanded our ancestors
   to teach to their children.
6 Then their children would know them,
   even their children not yet born.
   And they would tell their children.
7 So they would all trust God
   and would not forget what he had done
   but would obey his commands.
8 They would not be like their ancestors
   who were stubborn and disobedient.

Their hearts were not loyal to God,
and they were not true to him.

⁹ The men of Ephraim had bows for
weapons,
but they ran away on the day of
battle.
¹⁰ They didn't keep their agreement with
God
and refused to live by his teachings.
¹¹ They forgot what he had done

and the miracles he had shown them.
¹² He did miracles while their ancestors
watched,
in the fields of Zoan in Egypt.
¹³ He divided the Red Sea and led them
through.
He made the water stand up like a wall.
¹⁴ He led them with a cloud by day
and by the light of a fire by night.
¹⁵ He split the rocks in the desert

A FAMILY CHANGED

passing the baton
of faith

FAMILY

By Bob Russell

PSALM 78:1-4

I t has been said that Christianity is just one generation from extinction. Because of this, it is the primary responsibility of godly parents to pass along the baton of faith to their children. That's more important than teaching children good manners, providing a sound education, or preparing them to be self-reliant.

Teaching children the Bible is not an option; it is a commandment. When we stand before God, he will hold us accountable. Since the Bible is rarely taught in the public arena, it is crucial that we be intentional in teaching our children about God and the way he has worked in history. With all the tools available today, we are without excuse.

There are excellent Bible storybooks in Christian bookstores and church libraries. Entertaining videos can inspire children with God's truth and teach moral values. Old-fashioned Bible drills and modern games can occupy kids and inform at the same time. Christian music can teach kids catchy Scripture choruses. Wise parents also review memory verses with their children and place Scripture in prominent places in their homes.

Today, television programming, movies, music, literature, and education are largely anti-Christ. Godly parents need to counter Satan's deceptive ways by being proactive and demonstrating that "when sin grew worse, God's grace increased" (Romans 5:20). In doing so, we potentially affect the lives of millions and leave an eternal legacy to the glory of God.

reflect: How are you training the next generation to live a godly lifestyle?
Go to **Proverbs 1:7.**

and gave them more than enough water,
  as if from the deep ocean.
16 He brought streams out of the rock
  and caused water to flow down like
    rivers.

17 But the people continued to sin against
    him;
  in the desert they turned against God
    Most High.
18 They decided to test God
  by asking for the food they wanted.
19 Then they spoke against God,
  saying, "Can God prepare food in the
    desert?
20 When he hit the rock, water poured out
  and rivers flowed down.
  But can he give us bread also?
  Will he provide his people with meat?"
21 When the LORD heard them, he was very
    angry.
  His anger was like fire to the people of
    Jacob;
  his anger grew against the people of
    Israel.
22 They had not believed God
  and had not trusted him to save them.
23 But he gave a command to the clouds
    above
  and opened the doors of heaven.
24 He rained manna down on them to eat;
  he gave them grain from heaven.
25 So they ate the bread of angels.
  He sent them all the food they could
    eat.
26 He sent the east wind from heaven
  and led the south wind by his power.
27 He rained meat on them like dust.
  The birds were as many as the sand of
    the sea.
28 He made the birds fall inside the camp,
  all around the tents.
29 So the people ate and became very full.
  God had given them what they
    wanted.
30 While they were still eating,
  and while the food was still in their
    mouths,
31 God became angry with them.
  He killed some of the healthiest of
    them;
  he struck down the best young men of
    Israel.

32 But they kept on sinning;
  they did not believe even with the
    miracles.
33 So he ended their days without meaning
  and their years in terror.
34 Anytime he killed them, they would look
    to him for help;
  they would come back to God and
    follow him.
35 They would remember that God was their
    Rock,
  that God Most High had saved them.
36 But their words were false,
  and their tongues lied to him.
37 Their hearts were not really loyal to God;
  they did not keep his agreement.
38 Still God was merciful.
  He forgave their sins
  and did not destroy them.
Many times he held back his anger
  and did not stir up all his anger.
39 He remembered that they were only
    human,
  like a wind that blows and does not
    come back.

40 They turned against God so often in the
    desert
  and grieved him there.
41 Again and again they tested God
  and brought pain to the Holy One of
    Israel.
42 They did not remember his power
  or the time he saved them from the
    enemy.
43 They forgot the signs he did in Egypt
  and his wonders in the fields of Zoan.
44 He turned their rivers to blood
  so no one could drink the water.
45 He sent flies that bit the people.
  He sent frogs that destroyed them.
46 He gave their crops to grasshoppers
  and what they worked for to locusts.
47 He destroyed their vines with hail
  and their sycamore trees with sleet.
48 He killed their animals with hail
  and their cattle with lightning.
49 He showed them his hot anger.
  He sent his strong anger against them,
  his destroying angels.
50 He found a way to show his anger.
  He did not keep them from dying
  but let them die by a terrible disease.

8 My people, listen. I am warning you.
   Israel, please listen to me!
9 You must not have foreign gods;
   you must not worship any false god.
10 I, the LORD, am your God,
   who brought you out of Egypt.
   Open your mouth and I will feed you.

11 "But my people did not listen to me;
   Israel did not want me.
12 So I let them go their stubborn way
   and follow their own advice.
13 I wish my people would listen to me;
   I wish Israel would live my way.
14 Then I would quickly defeat their
   enemies
   and turn my hand against their foes.
15 Those who hate the LORD would bow
   before him.
   Their punishment would continue
   forever.
16 But I would give you the finest wheat
   and fill you with honey from the rocks."

A CRY FOR JUSTICE
A psalm of Asaph.

82
God is in charge of the great meeting;
   he judges among the "gods."
2 He says, "How long will you defend evil
   people?
   How long will you show greater
   kindness to the wicked?   *Selah*
3 Defend the weak and the orphans;
   defend the rights of the poor and
   suffering.
4 Save the weak and helpless;
   free them from the power of the wicked.

5 "You know nothing. You don't understand.
   You walk in the dark,
   while the world is falling apart.
6 I said, 'You are "gods."
   You are all sons of God Most High.'
7 But you will die like any other person;
   you will fall like all the leaders."

8 God, come and judge the earth,
   because you own all the nations.

A PRAYER AGAINST THE ENEMIES
A song. A psalm of Asaph.

83
God, do not keep quiet;
   God, do not be silent or still.
2 Your enemies are making noises;

those who hate you are getting ready to
   attack.
3 They are making secret plans against your
   people;
   they plot against those you love.
4 They say, "Come, let's destroy them as a
   nation.
   Then no one will ever remember the
   name 'Israel.'"
5 They are united in their plan.
   These have made an agreement against
   you:
6 the families of Edom and the Ishmaelites,
   Moab and the Hagrites,
7 the people of Byblos, Ammon, Amalek,
   Philistia, and Tyre.
8 Even Assyria has joined them
   to help Ammon and Moab, the
   descendants of Lot.   *Selah*

9 God, do to them what you did to Midian,
   what you did to Sisera and Jabin at the
   Kishon River.
10 They died at Endor,
   and their bodies rotted on the ground.
11 Do to their important leaders what you
   did to Oreb and Zeeb.
   Do to their princes what you did to
   Zebah and Zalmunna.
12 They said, "Let's take for ourselves
   the pasturelands that belong to God."
13 My God, make them like tumbleweed,
   like chaff blown away by the wind.
14 Be like a fire that burns a forest
   or like flames that blaze through the
   hills.
15 Chase them with your storm,
   and frighten them with your wind.
16 Cover them with shame.
   Then people will look for you, LORD.
17 Make them afraid and ashamed forever.
   Disgrace them and destroy them.
18 Then they will know that you are the
   LORD,
   that only you are God Most High over
   all the earth.

WISHING TO BE IN THE TEMPLE
For the director of music. On the gittith. A psalm
of the sons of Korah.

84
LORD All-Powerful,
   how lovely is your Temple!
2 I want more than anything

to be in the courtyards of the LORD's
Temple.
My whole being wants
to be with the living God.
3 The sparrows have found a home,
and the swallows have nests.
They raise their young near your altars,
LORD All-Powerful, my King and my
God.
4 Happy are the people who live at your
Temple;
they are always praising you.　　*Selah*

5 Happy are those whose strength comes
from you,
who want to travel to Jerusalem.
6 As they pass through the Valley of Baca,
they make it like a spring.
The autumn rains fill it with pools of
water.
7 The people get stronger as they go,
and everyone meets with God in
Jerusalem.

8 LORD God All-Powerful, hear my prayer;
God of Jacob, listen to me.　　*Selah*
9 God, look at our shield;
be kind to your appointed king.

10 One day in the courtyards of your Temple
is better
than a thousand days anywhere else.
I would rather be a doorkeeper in the
Temple of my God
than live in the homes of the wicked.
11 The LORD God is like a sun and shield;
the LORD gives us kindness and honor.
He does not hold back anything good
from those whose lives are innocent.
12 LORD All-Powerful,
happy are the people who trust you!

A PRAYER FOR THE NATION

For the director of music. A psalm of the sons
of Korah.

85 LORD, you have been kind to your
land;
you brought back the people of Jacob.
2 You forgave the guilt of the people
and covered all their sins.　　*Selah*
3 You stopped all your anger;
you turned back from your strong anger.

4 God our Savior, bring us back again.
Stop being angry with us.

5 Will you be angry with us forever?
Will you stay angry from now on?
6 Won't you give us life again?
Your people would rejoice in you.
7 LORD, show us your love,
and save us.

8 I will listen to God the LORD.
He has ordered peace for those who
worship him.
Don't let them go back to foolishness.
9 God will soon save those who respect
him,
and his glory will be seen in our land.
10 Love and truth belong to God's people;
goodness and peace will be theirs.
11 On earth people will be loyal to God,
and God's goodness will shine down
from heaven.
12 The LORD will give his goodness,
and the land will give its crops.
13 Goodness will go before God
and prepare the way for him.

A CRY FOR HELP

A prayer of David.

86 LORD, listen to me and answer me.
I am poor and helpless.
2 Protect me, because I worship you.
My God, save me, your servant who
trusts in you.
3 Lord, have mercy on me,
because I have called to you all day.
4 Give happiness to me, your servant,
because I give my life to you, Lord.
5 Lord, you are kind and forgiving
and have great love for those who call
to you.
6 LORD, hear my prayer,
and listen when I ask for mercy.
7 I call to you in times of trouble,
because you will answer me.

8 Lord, there is no god like you
and no works like yours.
9 Lord, all the nations you have made
will come and worship you.
They will honor you.
10 You are great and you do miracles.
Only you are God.
11 LORD, teach me what you want me
to do,
and I will live by your truth.
Teach me to respect you completely.

¹² Lord, my God, I will praise you with all
　　my heart,
　　and I will honor your name forever.
¹³ You have great love for me.
　　You have saved me from death.

¹⁴ God, proud people are attacking me;
　　a gang of cruel people is trying to kill
　　me.
　　They do not respect you.
¹⁵ But, Lord, you are a God who shows
　　mercy and is kind.
　　You don't become angry quickly.
　　You have great love and faithfulness.
¹⁶ Turn to me and have mercy.
　　Give me, your servant, strength.
　　Save me, the son of your female servant.
¹⁷ Show me a sign of your goodness.
　　When my enemies look, they will be
　　ashamed.
　　You, Lord, have helped me and
　　comforted me.

GOD LOVES JERUSALEM
A song. A psalm of the sons of Korah.

87 The Lord built Jerusalem on the
　　holy mountain.
² 　He loves its gates more than any other
　　place in Israel.
³ City of God,
　　wonderful things are said about you.
　　　　　　　　　　Selah
⁴ God says, "I will put Egypt and Babylonia
　　on the list of nations that know me.
　　People from Philistia, Tyre, and Cush
　　will be born there."

⁵ They will say about Jerusalem,
　　"This one and that one were born there.
　　God Most High will strengthen her."
⁶ The Lord will keep a list of the nations.
　　He will note, "This person was born
　　there."　　　　　　　*Selah*

⁷ They will dance and sing,
　　"All good things come from Jerusalem."

A SAD COMPLAINT
A song. A psalm of the sons of Korah. For the
director of music. By the mahalath leannoth.
A maskil of Heman the Ezrahite.

88 Lord, you are the God who saves me.
　　I cry out to you day and night.
² Receive my prayer,
　　and listen to my cry.

³ My life is full of troubles,
　　and I am nearly dead.
⁴ They think I am on the way to my grave.
　　I am like a man with no strength.
⁵ I have been left as dead,
　　like a body lying in a grave
　　whom you don't remember anymore,
　　cut off from your care.
⁶ You have brought me close to death;
　　I am almost in the dark place of the
　　dead.
⁷ You have been very angry with me;
　　all your waves crush me.　　*Selah*
⁸ You have taken my friends away from me
　　and have made them hate me.
　　I am trapped and cannot escape.
⁹ 　My eyes are weak from crying.
　　Lord, I have prayed to you every day;
　　I have lifted my hands in prayer to you.

¹⁰ Do you show your miracles for the dead?
　　Do their spirits rise up and praise you?
　　　　　　　　　　Selah

¹¹ Will your love be told in the grave?
　　Will your loyalty be told in the place of
　　death?
¹² Will your miracles be known in the dark
　　grave?
　　Will your goodness be known in the
　　land of forgetfulness?

¹³ But, Lord, I have called out to you for
　　help;
　　every morning I pray to you.
¹⁴ Lord, why do you reject me?
　　Why do you hide from me?
¹⁵ I have been weak and dying since I was
　　young.
　　I suffer from your terrors, and I am
　　helpless.
¹⁶ You have been angry with me,
　　and your terrors have destroyed me.
¹⁷ They surround me daily like a flood;
　　they are all around me.
¹⁸ You have taken away my loved ones and
　　friends.
　　Darkness is my only friend.

A SONG ABOUT GOD'S LOYALTY
A maskil of Ethan the Ezrahite.

89 I will always sing about the Lord's
　　love;
　　I will tell of his loyalty from now on.

2 I will say, "Your love continues forever;
　　your loyalty goes on and on like the
　　sky."
3 You said, "I made an agreement with the
　　man of my choice;
　　I made a promise to my servant David.
4 I told him, 'I will make your family
　　continue forever.
　　Your kingdom will go on and on.'"

Selah

5 LORD, the heavens praise you for your
　　miracles
　　and for your loyalty in the meeting of
　　your holy ones.
6 Who in heaven is equal to the LORD?
　　None of the angels is like the LORD.
7 When the holy ones meet, it is God they
　　fear.
　　He is more frightening than all who
　　surround him.
8 LORD God All-Powerful, who is like you?
　　LORD, you are powerful and completely
　　trustworthy.
9 You rule the mighty sea
　　and calm the stormy waves.
10 You crushed the sea monster Rahab;
　　by your power you scattered your
　　enemies.
11 The skies and the earth belong to you.
　　You made the world and everything in
　　it.
12 You created the north and the south.
　　Mount Tabor and Mount Hermon sing
　　for joy at your name.
13 Your arm has great power.
　　Your hand is strong; your right hand is
　　lifted up.
14 Your kingdom is built on what is right and
　　fair.
　　Love and truth are in all you do.

15 Happy are the people who know how to
　　praise you.
　　LORD, let them live in the light of your
　　presence.
16 In your name they rejoice
　　and continually praise your goodness.
17 You are their glorious strength,
　　and in your kindness you honor our
　　king.
18 Our king, our shield, belongs to the LORD,
　　to the Holy One of Israel.

19 Once, in a vision, you spoke
　　to those who worship you.
　　You said, "I have given strength to a
　　warrior;
　　I have raised up a young man from my
　　people.
20 I have found my servant David;
　　I appointed him by pouring holy oil on
　　him.
21 I will steady him with my hand
　　and strengthen him with my arm.
22 No enemy will make him give forced
　　payments,
　　and wicked people will not defeat him.
23 I will crush his enemies in front of him;
　　I will defeat those who hate him.
24 My loyalty and love will be with him.
　　Through me he will be strong.
25 I will give him power over the sea
　　and control over the rivers.
26 He will say to me, 'You are my father,
　　my God, the Rock, my Savior.'
27 I will make him my firstborn son,
　　the greatest king on earth.
28 My love will watch over him forever,
　　and my agreement with him will never
　　end.
29 I will make his family continue,
　　and his kingdom will last as long as the
　　skies.

30 "If his descendants reject my teachings
　　and do not follow my laws,
31 if they ignore my demands
　　and disobey my commands,
32 then I will punish their sins with a rod
　　and their wrongs with a whip.
33 But I will not hold back my love from
　　David,
　　nor will I stop being loyal.
34 I will not break my agreement
　　nor change what I have said.
35 I have promised by my holiness,
　　I will not lie to David.
36 His family will go on forever.
　　His kingdom will last before me like the
　　sun.
37 It will continue forever, like the moon,
　　like a dependable witness in the sky."

Selah

38 But now you have refused and rejected
　　your appointed king.
　　You have been angry with him.

39 You have abandoned the agreement with
   your servant
   and thrown his crown to the ground.
40 You have torn down all his city walls;
   you have turned his strong cities into
   ruins.
41 Everyone who passes by steals from him.
   His neighbors insult him.
42 You have given strength to his enemies
   and have made them all happy.
43 You have made his sword useless;
   you did not help him stand in battle.
44 You have kept him from winning
   and have thrown his throne to the
   ground.
45 You have cut his life short
   and covered him with shame.   *Selah*

46 LORD, how long will this go on?
   Will you ignore us forever?
   How long will your anger burn like a
   fire?
47 Remember how short my life is.
   Why did you create us? For nothing?
48 What person alive will not die?
   Who can escape the grave?   *Selah*

49 Lord, where is your love from times past,
   which in your loyalty you promised to
   David?
50 Lord, remember how they insulted your
   servant;
   remember how I have suffered the
   insults of the nations.
51 LORD, remember how your enemies
   insulted you
   and how they insulted your appointed
   king wherever he went.

52 Praise the LORD forever!
   Amen and amen.

Book 4

GOD IS ETERNAL, AND WE ARE NOT
A prayer of Moses, the man of God.

90 Lord, you have been our home
       since the beginning.
2 Before the mountains were born
   and before you created the earth and
   the world,
you are God.
   You have always been, and you will
   always be.

3 You turn people back into dust.
   You say, "Go back into dust, human
   beings."
4 To you, a thousand years
   is like the passing of a day,
   or like a few hours in the night.
5 While people sleep, you take their lives.
   They are like grass that grows up in the
   morning.
6 In the morning they are fresh and new,
   but by evening they dry up and die.
7 We are destroyed by your anger;
   we are terrified by your hot anger.
8 You have put the evil we have done right
   in front of you;
   you clearly see our secret sins.
9 All our days pass while you are angry.
   Our years end with a moan.
10 Our lifetime is seventy years
   or, if we are strong, eighty years.
   But the years are full of hard work and
   pain.
   They pass quickly, and then we are
   gone.
11 Who knows the full power of your anger?
   Your anger is as great as our fear of you
   should be.
12 Teach us how short our lives really are
   so that we may be wise.
13 LORD, how long before you return
   and show kindness to your servants?
14 Fill us with your love every morning.
   Then we will sing and rejoice all our
   lives.
15 We have seen years of trouble.
   Now give us as much joy as you gave us
   sorrow.
16 Show your servants the wonderful things
   you do;
   show your greatness to their children.
17 Lord our God, treat us well.
   Give us success in what we do;
   yes, give us success in what we do.

SAFE IN THE LORD

91 Those who go to God Most High for
       safety
   will be protected by the Almighty.
2 I will say to the LORD, "You are my place
   of safety and protection.
   You are my God and I trust you."

3 God will save you from hidden traps
and from deadly diseases.
4 He will cover you with his feathers,
and under his wings you can hide.
His truth will be your shield and
protection.
5 You will not fear any danger by night
or an arrow during the day.
6 You will not be afraid of diseases that
come in the dark
or sickness that strikes at noon.
7 At your side one thousand people may die,
or even ten thousand right beside you,
but you will not be hurt.
8 You will only watch
and see the wicked punished.

9 The LORD is your protection;
you have made God Most High your
place of safety.
10 Nothing bad will happen to you;
no disaster will come to your home.
11 He has put his angels in charge of you
to watch over you wherever you go.
12 They will catch you in their hands
so that you will not hit your foot on a
rock.
13 You will walk on lions and cobras;
you will step on strong lions and
snakes.

14 The LORD says, "Whoever loves me, I will
save.
I will protect those who know me.
15 They will call to me, and I will answer
them.
I will be with them in trouble;
I will rescue them and honor them.
16 I will give them a long, full life,
and they will see how I can save."

THANKSGIVING FOR GOD'S GOODNESS
A psalm. A song for the Sabbath day.

92 It is good to praise you, LORD,
to sing praises to God Most High.
2 It is good to tell of your love in the
morning
and of your loyalty at night.
3 It is good to praise you with the ten-
stringed lyre
and with the soft-sounding harp.

4 LORD, you have made me happy by what
you have done;

I will sing for joy about what your
hands have done.
5 LORD, you have done such great things!
How deep are your thoughts!
6 Stupid people don't know these things,
and fools don't understand.
7 Wicked people grow like the grass.
Evil people seem to do well,
but they will be destroyed forever.
8 But, LORD, you will be honored forever.

9 LORD, surely your enemies,
surely your enemies will be destroyed,
and all who do evil will be scattered.
10 But you have made me as strong as an ox.
You have poured fine oils on me.
11 When I looked, I saw my enemies;
I heard the cries of those who are
against me.

12 But good people will grow like palm trees;
they will be tall like the cedars of
Lebanon.
13 Like trees planted in the Temple of the
LORD,
they will grow strong in the courtyards
of our God.
14 When they are old, they will still produce
fruit;
they will be healthy and fresh.
15 They will say that the LORD is good.
He is my Rock, and there is no wrong
in him.

THE MAJESTY OF THE LORD

93 The LORD is king. He is clothed in
majesty.
The LORD is clothed in majesty
and armed with strength.
The world is set,
and it cannot be moved.
2 LORD, your kingdom was set up long ago;
you are everlasting.

3 LORD, the seas raise,
the seas raise their voice.
The seas raise up their pounding waves.
4 The sound of the water is loud;
the ocean waves are powerful,
but the LORD above is much greater.

5 LORD, your laws will stand forever.
Your Temple will be holy forevermore.

GOD WILL PAY BACK HIS ENEMIES

94 The LORD is a God who punishes.
God, show your greatness and
punish!

2 Rise up, Judge of the earth,
and give the proud what they deserve.

3 How long will the wicked be happy?
How long, LORD?

4 They are full of proud words;
those who do evil brag about what they
have done.

5 LORD, they crush your people
and make your children suffer.

6 They kill widows and foreigners
and murder orphans.

7 They say, "The LORD doesn't see;
the God of Jacob doesn't notice."

8 You stupid ones among the people, pay
attention.
You fools, when will you understand?

9 Can't the creator of ears hear?
Can't the maker of eyes see?

10 Won't the one who corrects nations
punish you?
Doesn't the teacher of people know
everything?

MENTORING WORLD CHANGERS FOR CHRIST

correcting nature—
not behavior

FUTURE

PSALM 94:12

Proper punishment is an essential part of the process of learning to make the right decisions and aligning with the Creator. Without correction and uncomfortable consequences, we would all maintain a tendency to continue down the pathway of personal and social destruction. Children need to understand the Bible tells us to honor and obey our mother and father. When they don't listen, they fall short of what God has demanded for their lives.

When the child does what is correct, his or her life becomes much easier and more pleasant. God intended families to be the practice field of discipline. Your family is the place where you first learn about correction. It's the place where you first practice obedience. It's the place where you first experience the joy of submission. Within the context of the family, we experience what it means to delight under authority. It changes the heart of a child. It changes his nature.

Rather than correcting behavior, we need to be correcting nature. When the inner nature changes, the outer behavior changes. This kind of correction brings contentment and peace. We know that the purpose of discipline is not punishment, but purpose. It's a reminder to stay on track with God's best interests for our nature, which ultimately changes our behavior.

---

reflect: Learn to follow God by submitting to his plans and purposes for your life.
Go to **Psalm 133:1-3.**

11 The LORD knows what people think.
  He knows their thoughts are just a puff
  of wind.

12 LORD, those you correct are happy;
  you teach them from your law.
13 You give them rest from times of trouble
  until a pit is dug for the wicked.
14 The LORD won't leave his people
  nor give up his children.
15 Judgment will again be fair,
  and all who are honest will follow it.

16 Who will help me fight against the
  wicked?
  Who will stand with me against those
  who do evil?
17 If the LORD had not helped me,
  I would have died in a minute.
18 I said, "I am about to fall,"
  but, LORD, your love kept me safe.
19 I was very worried,
  but you comforted me and made me
  happy.

20 Crooked leaders cannot be your friends.
  They use the law to cause suffering.
21 They join forces against people who do
  right
  and sentence to death the innocent.
22 But the LORD is my defender;
  my God is the rock of my protection.
23 God will pay them back for their sins
  and will destroy them for their evil.
  The LORD our God will destroy them.

A CALL TO PRAISE AND OBEDIENCE

95 Come, let's sing for joy to the LORD.
  Let's shout praises to the Rock who
  saves us.
2 Let's come to him with thanksgiving.
  Let's sing songs to him,
3 because the LORD is the great God,
  the great King over all gods.
4 The deepest places on earth are his,
  and the highest mountains belong to
  him.
5 The sea is his because he made it,
  and he created the land with his own
  hands.

6 Come, let's worship him and bow down.
  Let's kneel before the LORD who made
  us,
7 because he is our God

and we are the people he takes care of,
  the sheep that he tends.

Today listen to what he says:
8 "Do not be stubborn, as your ancestors
  were at Meribah,
  as they were that day at Massah in the
  desert.
9 There your ancestors tested me
  and tried me even though they saw
  what I did.
10 I was angry with those people for forty
  years.
  I said, 'They are not loyal to me
  and have not understood my ways.'
11 I was angry and made a promise,
  'They will never enter my rest.'"

PRAISE FOR THE LORD'S GLORY

96 Sing to the LORD a new song;
  sing to the LORD, all the earth.
2 Sing to the LORD and praise his name;
  every day tell how he saves us.
3 Tell the nations of his glory;
  tell all peoples the miracles he does,

4 because the LORD is great; he should be
  praised at all times.
  He should be honored more than all the
  gods,
5 because all the gods of the nations are
  only idols,
  but the LORD made the heavens.
6 The LORD has glory and majesty;
  he has power and beauty in his Temple.

7 Praise the LORD, all nations on earth;
  praise the LORD's glory and power.
8 Praise the glory of the LORD's name.
  Bring an offering and come into his
  Temple courtyards.
9 Worship the LORD because he is holy.
  Tremble before him, everyone on earth.
10 Tell the nations, "The LORD is king."
  The earth is set, and it cannot be
  moved.
  He will judge the people fairly.
11 Let the skies rejoice and the earth be glad;
  let the sea and everything in it shout.
12 Let the fields and everything in them
  rejoice.
  Then all the trees of the forest will sing
  for joy
13 before the LORD, because he is coming.
  He is coming to judge the world;

he will judge the world with fairness
and the peoples with truth.

A HYMN ABOUT THE LORD'S POWER

97 The LORD is king. Let the earth
rejoice;
faraway lands should be glad.
2 Thick, dark clouds surround him.
His kingdom is built on what is right
and fair.
3 A fire goes before him
and burns up his enemies all around.
4 His lightning lights up the world;
when the people see it, they tremble.
5 The mountains melt like wax before the
LORD,
before the Lord of all the earth.
6 The heavens tell about his goodness,
and all the people see his glory.

7 Those who worship idols should be
ashamed;
they brag about their gods.
All the gods should worship the LORD.
8 When Jerusalem hears this, she is glad,
and the towns of Judah rejoice.
They are happy because of your
judgments, LORD.
9 You are the LORD Most High over all the
earth;
you are supreme over all gods.

10 People who love the LORD hate evil.
The LORD watches over those who
follow him
and frees them from the power of the
wicked.
11 Light shines on those who do right;
joy belongs to those who are honest.
12 Rejoice in the LORD, you who do right.
Praise his holy name.

THE LORD OF POWER AND JUSTICE

A psalm.

98 Sing to the LORD a new song,
because he has done miracles.
By his right hand and holy arm
he has won the victory.
2 The LORD has made known his power to
save;
he has shown the other nations his
victory for his people.
3 He has remembered his love
and his loyalty to the people of Israel.

All the ends of the earth have seen
God's power to save.

4 Shout with joy to the LORD, all the earth;
burst into songs and make music.
5 Make music to the LORD with harps,
with harps and the sound of singing.
6 Blow the trumpets and the sheep's horns;
shout for joy to the LORD the King.

7 Let the sea and everything in it shout;
let the world and everyone in it sing.
8 Let the rivers clap their hands;
let the mountains sing together for joy.
9 Let them sing before the LORD,
because he is coming to judge the
world.
He will judge the world fairly;
he will judge the peoples with fairness.

THE LORD, THE FAIR AND HOLY KING

99 The LORD is king.
Let the peoples shake with fear.
He sits between the gold creatures with
wings.
Let the earth shake.
2 The LORD in Jerusalem is great;
he is supreme over all the peoples.
3 Let them praise your name;
it is great, holy and to be feared.

4 The King is powerful and loves justice.
LORD, you made things fair;
you have done what is fair and right
for the people of Jacob.
5 Praise the LORD our God,
and worship at the Temple, his
footstool.
He is holy.

6 Moses and Aaron were among his priests,
and Samuel was among his worshipers.
They called to the LORD,
and he answered them.
7 He spoke to them from the pillar of cloud.
They kept the rules and laws he gave
them.

8 LORD our God, you answered them.
You showed them that you are a
forgiving God,
but you punished them for their
wrongs.
9 Praise the LORD our God,
and worship at his holy mountain,
because the LORD our God is holy.

A CALL TO PRAISE THE LORD
A psalm of thanks.

100 Shout to the LORD, all the earth.
² Serve the LORD with joy;
come before him with singing.
³ Know that the LORD is God.
He made us, and we belong to him;
we are his people, the sheep he tends.

⁴ Come into his city with songs of
thanksgiving
and into his courtyards with songs of
praise.

Thank him and praise his name.
⁵ The LORD is good. His love is forever,
and his loyalty goes on and on.

A PROMISE TO RULE WELL
A psalm of David.

101 I will sing of your love and fairness;
LORD, I will sing praises to you.
² I will be careful to live an innocent life.
When will you come to me?

I will live an innocent life in my house.
³ I will not look at anything wicked.

FULFILLMENT

FOR YOUR OWN GOOD

powerful
prayer time

PSALM 100

There are many ways to pray, but it is good to be given examples at times. These are a few ways that can help you with your prayer life and personal time with the Lord:

1. Come before the Lord with a humble heart, and be sincere in what you say. Give the Lord praise, and take time to thank him for what he has done for you. Ask the Lord to forgive you for what you have done wrong in thought, word, and deed. Lay your heart out before him so he can show you what is needed in your life. As you do this, it opens the channel of communication, and the Lord loves to hear and answer your prayers.

2. Bring to the Lord the petitions you have and be specific with them. Do not generalize your requests because vague requests are more like wishes than prayers. God knows you, and he knows your heart; so be open and honest with him in all your prayers. God loves to be reminded of his Word, so use it as a tool to communicate with him.

3. Give the Lord thanks for handling the challenges in your life. Be mindful of such matters, but continually thank him for taking care of them. Be a thanks giver. Whenever doubt or unbelief comes into your mind about your prayers, begin to praise the Lord. You will see your prayers being answered when you least expect it. He is a good God and a faithful one. It is the Lord's delight to bless us.

reflect: Pray for the will of God to be done in your life today.
Go to **Jonah 4:2.**

I hate those who turn against you;
  they will not be found near me.
4 Let those who want to do wrong stay
    away from me;
  I will have nothing to do with evil.
5 If anyone secretly says things against his
    neighbor,
  I will stop him.
I will not allow people
  to be proud and look down on others.

6 I will look for trustworthy people
  so I can live with them in the land.
Only those who live innocent lives
  will be my servants.
7 No one who is dishonest will live in my
    house;
  no liars will stay around me.
8 Every morning I will destroy the wicked
    in the land.
  I will rid the LORD's city of people who
    do evil.

A CRY FOR HELP

A prayer of a person who is suffering when he is
discouraged and tells the LORD his complaints.

102

LORD, listen to my prayer;
  let my cry for help come to you.
2 Do not hide from me
  in my time of trouble.
Pay attention to me.
  When I cry for help, answer me quickly.

3 My life is passing away like smoke,
  and my bones are burned up with fire.
4 My heart is like grass
  that has been cut and dried.
  I forget to eat.
5 Because of my grief,
  my skin hangs on my bones.
6 I am like a desert owl,
  like an owl living among the ruins.
7 I lie awake.
  I am like a lonely bird on a housetop.
8 All day long enemies insult me;
  those who make fun of me use my name
    as a curse.
9 I eat ashes for food,
  and my tears fall into my drinks.
10 Because of your great anger,
  you have picked me up and thrown me
    away.
11 My days are like a passing shadow;
  I am like dried grass.

12 But, LORD, you rule forever,
  and your fame goes on and on.
13 You will come and have mercy on
    Jerusalem,
  because the time has now come to be
    kind to her;
  the right time has come.
14 Your servants love even her stones;
  they even care about her dust.
15 Nations will fear the name of the LORD,
  and all the kings on earth will honor you.
16 The LORD will rebuild Jerusalem;
  there his glory will be seen.
17 He will answer the prayers of the needy;
  he will not reject their prayers.

18 Write these things for the future
  so that people who are not yet born will
    praise the LORD.
19 The LORD looked down from his holy
    place above;
  from heaven he looked down at the
    earth.
20 He heard the moans of the prisoners,
  and he freed those sentenced to die.
21 The name of the LORD will be heard in
    Jerusalem;
  his praise will be heard there.
22 People will come together,
  and kingdoms will serve the LORD.

23 God has made me tired of living;
  he has cut short my life.
24 So I said, "My God, do not take me in the
    middle of my life.
  Your years go on and on.
25 In the beginning you made the earth,
  and your hands made the skies.
26 They will be destroyed, but you will
    remain.
  They will all wear out like clothes.
  And, like clothes, you will change them
    and throw them away.
27 But you never change,
  and your life will never end.
28 Our children will live in your presence,
  and their children will remain with
    you."

PRAISE TO THE LORD OF LOVE
Of David.

103

All that I am, praise the LORD;
  everything in me, praise his holy
    name.

2 My whole being, praise the LORD
and do not forget all his kindnesses.
3 He forgives all my sins
and heals all my diseases.
4 He saves my life from the grave
and loads me with love and mercy.
5 He satisfies me with good things
and makes me young again, like the
eagle.

6 The LORD does what is right and fair
for all who are wronged by others.
7 He showed his ways to Moses
and his deeds to the people of Israel.
8 The LORD shows mercy and is kind.
He does not become angry quickly, and
he has great love.

9 He will not always accuse us,
and he will not be angry forever.
10 He has not punished us as our sins should
be punished;
he has not repaid us for the evil we have
done.
11 As high as the sky is above the earth,
so great is his love for those who
respect him.
12 He has taken our sins away from us
as far as the east is from west.
13 The LORD has mercy on those who
respect him,
as a father has mercy on his children.
14 He knows how we were made;
he remembers that we are dust.

FAITH

HAVE FAITH IN GOD

attending
the banquet

PSALM 103:8

The story of the Old Testament is a divine love story. It is a story of God's unfailing pursuit of his wayward and disobedient children. Throughout the Bible, we are given a picture of a God who passionately loves what he has created and actively engages in reconciling and renewing this broken love relationship.

Here the psalmist tells us that God is compassionate and gracious toward us. Even though we have spurned his love over and over, even though we have mocked his sovereignty by acting as though we control our own destiny, he does not give up on us. Not only does he restrain anger about our rebelliousness, he actually offers abundantly more than we could ever deserve.

Paul states the same principle when he suggests that even when we were enemies of God, he was acting in ways that would heal the breach between us. Here we see that it is not just love that God demonstrates. It is more. It is love that expresses itself in benevolence toward us. God has prepared a banquet feast of gifts for us. He has given an invitation. All we need to do is wholeheartedly accept his invitation and attend the banquet of love.

reflect: Think about how much God loves and cherishes you today.
Go to **Jeremiah 12:3.**

15 Human life is like grass;
    we grow like a flower in the field.
16 After the wind blows, the flower is gone,
    and there is no sign of where it was.
17 But the Lord's love for those who respect
    him
    continues forever and ever,
    and his goodness continues to their
      grandchildren
18 and to those who keep his agreement
    and who remember to obey his orders.

19 The Lord has set his throne in heaven,
    and his kingdom rules over everything.
20 You who are his angels, praise the Lord.
    You are the mighty warriors who do
      what he says
    and who obey his voice.
21 You, his armies, praise the Lord;
    you are his servants who do what he
      wants.
22 Everything the Lord has made
    should praise him in all the places he
      rules.
My whole being, praise the Lord.

PRAISE TO GOD WHO MADE THE WORLD

104 My whole being, praise the Lord.
    Lord my God, you are very
      great.
You are clothed with glory and majesty;
2   you wear light like a robe.
You stretch out the skies like a tent.
3   You build your room above the clouds.
You make the clouds your chariot,
    and you ride on the wings of the wind.
4 You make the winds your messengers,
    and flames of fire are your servants.
5 You built the earth on its foundations
    so it can never be moved.
6 You covered the earth with oceans;
    the water was above the mountains.
7 But at your command, the water rushed
    away.
    When you thundered your orders, it
      hurried away.
8 The mountains rose; the valleys sank.
    The water went to the places you made
      for it.
9 You set borders for the seas that they
    cannot cross,
    so water will never cover the earth
      again.

10 You make springs pour into the ravines;
    they flow between the mountains.
11 They water all the wild animals;
    the wild donkeys come there to drink.
12 Wild birds make nests by the water;
    they sing among the tree branches.
13 You water the mountains from above.
    The earth is full of the things you made.
14 You make the grass for cattle
    and vegetables for the people.
    You make food grow from the earth.
15 You give us wine that makes happy hearts
    and olive oil that makes our faces shine.
    You give us bread that gives us strength.
16 The Lord's trees have plenty of water;
    they are the cedars of Lebanon, which
      he planted.
17 The birds make their nests there;
    the stork's home is in the fir trees.
18 The high mountains belong to the wild
    goats.
    The rocks are hiding places for the
      badgers.
19 You made the moon to mark the seasons,
    and the sun always knows when to set.
20 You make it dark, and it becomes night.
    Then all the wild animals creep around.
21 The lions roar as they attack.
    They look to God for food.
22 When the sun rises, they leave
    and go back to their dens to lie down.
23 Then people go to work
    and work until evening.

24 Lord, you have made many things;
    with your wisdom you made them all.
    The earth is full of your riches.
25 Look at the sea, so big and wide,
    with creatures large and small that
      cannot be counted.
26 Ships travel over the ocean,
    and there is the sea monster Leviathan,
    which you made to play there.

27 All these things depend on you
    to give them their food at the right time.
28 When you give it to them,
    they gather it up.
    When you open your hand,
    they are filled with good food.
29 When you turn away from them,
    they become frightened.
    When you take away their breath,

who had done great things in
Egypt,
22 who had done miracles in Egypt[n]
and amazing things by the Red Sea.
23 So God said he would destroy them.
But Moses, his chosen one, stood before
him
and stopped God's anger from
destroying them.

24 Then they refused to go into the beautiful
land of Canaan;
they did not believe what God
promised.
25 They grumbled in their tents
and did not obey the LORD.

26 So he swore to them
that they would die in the desert.
27 He said their children would be killed by
other nations
and that they would be scattered among
other countries.

28 They joined in worshiping Baal at Peor
and ate meat that had been sacrificed to
lifeless statues.
29 They made the LORD angry by what they
did,

106:22 Egypt Literally, "the land of Ham." The people
in Egypt were descendants of Ham, one of Noah's sons.
See Genesis 10:6.

THE ULTIMATE INVESTMENT

FINANCES

are you blessed?

PSALM 106:3

This beatitude is not about receiving a reward. It has nothing to do with what I am
going to get. It is about a state of bliss (happiness). It describes an inner character,
not an outward reward.

The primary characteristic of living according to the plan and purposes of God is inner
harmony and bliss. It is not the expectation of reward.

The reward is the change in our own hearts, brought about by the gracious intervention
of God. Blessings have much less to do with what we are going to get than with what
we discover within ourselves. Just as God looks on the inner motivation when he
searches for repentance, he begins renewal from within our own character.

If you serve in order to receive, you have probably missed the point. Serving changes
our character. It is not about collecting rewards, rather about an attitude toward
life. The men and women who make God the priority are blessed, not because God
showers them with possessions, comfort, or ease, but because their lives take on a
new perspective, a view from the realm of eternity. They live in calm reliance under the
authority of God.

reflect: Look at life through the lens of eternity for its message and meaning.
Go to **Psalm 144:13–15.**

15 Human life is like grass;
   we grow like a flower in the field.
16 After the wind blows, the flower is gone,
   and there is no sign of where it was.
17 But the LORD's love for those who respect
      him
   continues forever and ever,
   and his goodness continues to their
      grandchildren
18 and to those who keep his agreement
   and who remember to obey his orders.

19 The LORD has set his throne in heaven,
   and his kingdom rules over everything.
20 You who are his angels, praise the LORD.
   You are the mighty warriors who do
      what he says
   and who obey his voice.
21 You, his armies, praise the LORD;
   you are his servants who do what he
      wants.
22 Everything the LORD has made
   should praise him in all the places he
      rules.
   My whole being, praise the LORD.

PRAISE TO GOD WHO MADE THE WORLD

104 My whole being, praise the LORD.
   LORD my God, you are very
      great.
   You are clothed with glory and majesty;
2   you wear light like a robe.
   You stretch out the skies like a tent.
3   You build your room above the clouds.
   You make the clouds your chariot,
      and you ride on the wings of the wind.
4 You make the winds your messengers,
   and flames of fire are your servants.

5 You built the earth on its foundations
   so it can never be moved.
6 You covered the earth with oceans;
   the water was above the mountains.
7 But at your command, the water rushed
      away.
   When you thundered your orders, it
      hurried away.
8 The mountains rose; the valleys sank.
   The water went to the places you made
      for it.
9 You set borders for the seas that they
      cannot cross,
   so water will never cover the earth
      again.

10 You make springs pour into the ravines;
   they flow between the mountains.
11 They water all the wild animals;
   the wild donkeys come there to drink.
12 Wild birds make nests by the water;
   they sing among the tree branches.
13 You water the mountains from above.
   The earth is full of the things you made.
14 You make the grass for cattle
   and vegetables for the people.
   You make food grow from the earth.
15 You give us wine that makes happy hearts
   and olive oil that makes our faces shine.
   You give us bread that gives us strength.
16 The LORD's trees have plenty of water;
   they are the cedars of Lebanon, which
      he planted.
17 The birds make their nests there;
   the stork's home is in the fir trees.
18 The high mountains belong to the wild
      goats.
   The rocks are hiding places for the
      badgers.

19 You made the moon to mark the seasons,
   and the sun always knows when to set.
20 You make it dark, and it becomes night.
   Then all the wild animals creep around.
21 The lions roar as they attack.
   They look to God for food.
22 When the sun rises, they leave
   and go back to their dens to lie down.
23 Then people go to work
   and work until evening.

24 LORD, you have made many things;
   with your wisdom you made them all.
   The earth is full of your riches.
25 Look at the sea, so big and wide,
   with creatures large and small that
      cannot be counted.
26 Ships travel over the ocean,
   and there is the sea monster Leviathan,
   which you made to play there.

27 All these things depend on you
   to give them their food at the right time.
28 When you give it to them,
   they gather it up.
   When you open your hand,
   they are filled with good food.
29 When you turn away from them,
   they become frightened.
   When you take away their breath,

they die and turn to dust.
30 When you breathe on them,
they are created,
and you make the land new again.

31 May the glory of the LORD be forever.
May the LORD enjoy what he has made.
32 He just looks at the earth, and it shakes.
He touches the mountains, and they
smoke.

33 I will sing to the LORD all my life;
I will sing praises to my God as long as
I live.
34 May my thoughts please him;
I am happy in the LORD.
35 Let sinners be destroyed from the earth,
and let the wicked live no longer.

My whole being, praise the LORD.
Praise the LORD.

GOD'S LOVE FOR ISRAEL

105 Give thanks to the LORD and pray
to him.
Tell the nations what he has done.
2 Sing to him; sing praises to him.
Tell about all his miracles.
3 Be glad that you are his;
let those who seek the LORD be happy.
4 Depend on the LORD and his strength;
always go to him for help.
5 Remember the miracles he has done;
remember his wonders and his
decisions.
6 You are descendants of his servant
Abraham,
the children of Jacob, his chosen
people.
7 He is the LORD our God.
His laws are for all the world.

8 He will keep his agreement forever;
he will keep his promises always.
9 He will keep the agreement he made with
Abraham
and the promise he made to Isaac.
10 He made it a law for the people of Jacob;
he made it an agreement with Israel to
last forever.
11 The LORD said, "I will give you the land of
Canaan,
and it will belong to you."

12 Then God's people were few in number.
They were strangers in the land.

13 They went from one nation to another,
from one kingdom to another.
14 But the LORD did not let anyone hurt
them;
he warned kings not to harm them.
15 He said, "Don't touch my chosen people,
and don't harm my prophets."

16 God ordered a time of hunger in the land,
and he destroyed all the food.
17 Then he sent a man ahead of them—
Joseph, who was sold as a slave.
18 They put chains around his feet
and an iron ring around his neck.
19 Then the time he had spoken of came,
and the LORD's words proved that
Joseph was right.
20 The king of Egypt sent for Joseph and
freed him;
the ruler of the people set him free.
21 He made him the master of his house;
Joseph was in charge of his riches.
22 He could order the princes as he wished.
He taught the older men to be wise.
23 Then his father Israel came to Egypt;
Jacob[n] lived in Egypt.[n]
24 The LORD made his people grow in
number,
and he made them stronger than their
enemies.
25 He caused the Egyptians to hate his
people
and to make plans against his servants.
26 Then he sent his servant Moses,
and Aaron, whom he had chosen.
27 They did many signs among the Egyptians
and worked wonders in Egypt.
28 The LORD sent darkness and made the
land dark,
but the Egyptians turned against what
he said.
29 So he changed their water into blood
and made their fish die.
30 Then their country was filled with frogs,
even in the bedrooms of their rulers.
31 The LORD spoke and flies came,
and gnats were everywhere in the
country.
32 He made hail fall like rain

105:23 **Jacob** Also called Israel. **105:23 Egypt** Liter-
ally, "the land of Ham." Also in verse 27. The people in
Egypt were descendants of Ham, one of Noah's sons. See
Genesis 10:6.

and sent lightning through their land.
³³ He struck down their grapevines and fig trees,
and he destroyed every tree in the country.
³⁴ He spoke and grasshoppers came;
the locusts were too many to count.
³⁵ They ate all the plants in the land
and everything the earth produced.
³⁶ The LORD also killed all the firstborn sons in the land,
the oldest son of each family.

³⁷ Then he brought his people out,
and they carried with them silver and gold.
Not one of his people stumbled.
³⁸ The Egyptians were glad when they left,
because the Egyptians were afraid of them.
³⁹ The LORD covered them with a cloud
and lit up the night with fire.
⁴⁰ When they asked, he brought them quail
and filled them with bread from heaven.
⁴¹ God split the rock, and water flowed out;
it ran like a river through the desert.
⁴² He remembered his holy promise
to his servant Abraham.

⁴³ So God brought his people out with joy,
his chosen ones with singing.
⁴⁴ He gave them lands of other nations,
so they received what others had worked for.
⁴⁵ This was so they would keep his orders
and obey his teachings.

Praise the LORD!

ISRAEL'S FAILURE TO TRUST GOD

106
Praise the LORD!

Thank the LORD because he is good.
His love continues forever.
² No one can tell all the mighty things the LORD has done;
no one can speak all his praise.
³ Happy are those who do right,
who do what is fair at all times.

⁴ LORD, remember me when you are kind to your people;
help me when you save them.
⁵ Let me see the good things you do for your chosen people.

Let me be happy along with your happy nation;
let me join your own people in praising you.

⁶ We have sinned just as our ancestors did.
We have done wrong; we have done evil.
⁷ Our ancestors in Egypt
did not learn from your miracles.
They did not remember all your kindnesses,
so they turned against you at the Red Sea.
⁸ But the LORD saved them for his own sake,
to show his great power.
⁹ He commanded the Red Sea, and it dried up.
He led them through the deep sea as if it were a desert.
¹⁰ He saved them from those who hated them.
He saved them from their enemies,
¹¹ and the water covered their foes.
Not one of them escaped.
¹² Then the people believed what the LORD said,
and they sang praises to him.

¹³ But they quickly forgot what he had done;
they did not wait for his advice.
¹⁴ They became greedy for food in the desert,
and they tested God there.
¹⁵ So he gave them what they wanted,
but he also sent a terrible disease among them.

¹⁶ The people in the camp were jealous of Moses
and of Aaron, the holy priest of the LORD.
¹⁷ Then the ground opened up and swallowed Dathan
and closed over Abiram's group.
¹⁸ A fire burned among their followers,
and flames burned up the wicked.

¹⁹ The people made a gold calf at Mount Sinai
and worshiped a metal statue.
²⁰ They exchanged their glorious God
for a statue of a bull that eats grass.
²¹ They forgot the God who saved them,

who had done great things in
Egypt,
22 who had done miracles in Egypt[n]
and amazing things by the Red Sea.
23 So God said he would destroy them.
But Moses, his chosen one, stood before
him
and stopped God's anger from
destroying them.

24 Then they refused to go into the beautiful
land of Canaan;
they did not believe what God
promised.
25 They grumbled in their tents
and did not obey the LORD.

26 So he swore to them
that they would die in the desert.
27 He said their children would be killed by
other nations
and that they would be scattered among
other countries.

28 They joined in worshiping Baal at Peor
and ate meat that had been sacrificed to
lifeless statues.
29 They made the LORD angry by what they
did,

106:22 Egypt Literally, "the land of Ham." The people
in Egypt were descendants of Ham, one of Noah's sons.
See Genesis 10:6.

THE ULTIMATE INVESTMENT

FINANCES

are you blessed?

PSALM 106:3

This beatitude is not about receiving a reward. It has nothing to do with what I am going to get. It is about a state of bliss (happiness). It describes an inner character, not an outward reward.

The primary characteristic of living according to the plan and purposes of God is inner harmony and bliss. It is not the expectation of reward.

The reward is the change in our own hearts, brought about by the gracious intervention of God. Blessings have much less to do with what we are going to get than with what we discover within ourselves. Just as God looks on the inner motivation when he searches for repentance, he begins renewal from within our own character.

If you serve in order to receive, you have probably missed the point. Serving changes our character. It is not about collecting rewards, rather about an attitude toward life. The men and women who make God the priority are blessed, not because God showers them with possessions, comfort, or ease, but because their lives take on a new perspective, a view from the realm of eternity. They live in calm reliance under the authority of God.

reflect: Look at life through the lens of eternity for its message and meaning.
Go to **Psalm 144:13-15.**

so many people became sick with a terrible disease.

30 But Phinehas prayed to the LORD, and the disease stopped.

31 Phinehas did what was right, and it will be remembered from now on.

32 The people also made the LORD angry at Meribah, and Moses was in trouble because of them.

33 The people turned against the Spirit of God, so Moses spoke without stopping to think.

34 The people did not destroy the other nations as the LORD had told them to do.

35 Instead, they mixed with the other nations and learned their customs.

36 They worshiped other nations' idols and were trapped by them.

37 They even killed their sons and daughters as sacrifices to demons.

38 They killed innocent people, their own sons and daughters, as sacrifices to the idols of Canaan. So the land was made unholy by their blood.

39 The people became unholy by their sins; they were unfaithful to God in what they did.

40 So the LORD became angry with his people and hated his own children.

41 He handed them over to other nations and let their enemies rule over them.

42 Their enemies were cruel to them and kept them under their power.

43 The LORD saved his people many times, but they continued to turn against him. So they became even more wicked.

44 But God saw their misery when he heard their cry.

45 He remembered his agreement with them, and he felt sorry for them because of his great love.

46 He caused them to be pitied by those who held them captive.

47 LORD our God, save us and bring us back from other nations. Then we will thank you and will gladly praise you.

48 Praise the LORD, the God of Israel. He always was and always will be. Let all the people say, "Amen!"

Praise the LORD!

Book 5

GOD SAVES FROM MANY DANGERS

107 Thank the LORD because he is good. His love continues forever.

2 That is what those whom the LORD has saved should say. He has saved them from the enemy

3 and has gathered them from other lands, from east and west, north and south.

4 Some people had wandered in the desert lands. They found no city in which to live.

5 They were hungry and thirsty, and they were discouraged.

6 In their misery they cried out to the LORD, and he saved them from their troubles.

7 He led them on a straight road to a city where they could live.

8 Let them give thanks to the LORD for his love and for the miracles he does for people.

9 He satisfies the thirsty and fills up the hungry.

10 Some sat in gloom and darkness; they were prisoners suffering in chains.

11 They had turned against the words of God and had refused the advice of God Most High.

12 So he broke their pride by hard work. They stumbled, and no one helped.

13 In their misery they cried out to the LORD, and he saved them from their troubles.

14 He brought them out of their gloom and darkness and broke their chains.

15 Let them give thanks to the LORD for his love and for the miracles he does for people.

16 He breaks down bronze gates and cuts apart iron bars.

17 Some fools turned against God
and suffered for the evil they did.
18 They refused to eat anything,
so they almost died.
19 In their misery they cried out to the LORD,
and he saved them from their troubles.
20 God gave the command and healed them,
so they were saved from dying.
21 Let them give thanks to the LORD for his
love
and for the miracles he does for people.
22 Let them offer sacrifices to thank him.
With joy they should tell what he has
done.

23 Others went out to sea in ships
and did business on the great oceans.
24 They saw what the LORD could do,
the miracles he did in the deep oceans.
25 He spoke, and a storm came up,
which blew up high waves.
26 The ships were tossed as high as the sky
and fell low to the depths.
The storm was so bad that they lost
their courage.
27 They stumbled and fell like people who
were drunk.
They did not know what to do.
28 In their misery they cried out to the LORD,
and he saved them from their troubles.
29 He stilled the storm
and calmed the waves.
30 They were happy that it was quiet,
and God guided them to the port they
wanted.
31 Let them give thanks to the LORD for his
love
and for the miracles he does for people.
32 Let them praise his greatness in the
meeting of the people;
let them praise him in the meeting of
the elders.

33 He changed rivers into a desert
and springs of water into dry ground.
34 He made fertile land salty,
because the people there did evil.
35 He changed the desert into pools of water
and dry ground into springs of water.
36 He had the hungry settle there
so they could build a city in which to
live.
37 They planted seeds in the fields and
vineyards,

and they had a good harvest.
38 God blessed them, and they grew in
number.
Their cattle did not become fewer.

39 Because of disaster, troubles, and sadness,
their families grew smaller and weaker.
40 He showed he was displeased with their
leaders
and made them wander in a pathless
desert.
41 But he lifted the poor out of their
suffering
and made their families grow like flocks
of sheep.
42 Good people see this and are happy,
but the wicked say nothing.

43 Whoever is wise will remember these
things
and will think about the love of the
LORD.

A PRAYER FOR VICTORY
A song. A psalm of David.

108
God, my heart is steady.
I will sing and praise you with all
my being.
2 Wake up, harp and lyre!
I will wake up the dawn.
3 LORD, I will praise you among the nations;
I will sing songs of praise about you to
all the nations.
4 Your great love reaches to the skies,
your truth to the heavens.
5 God, you are supreme above the skies.
Let your glory be over all the earth.

6 Answer us and save us by your power
so the people you love will be rescued.
7 God has said from his Temple,
"When I win, I will divide Shechem
and measure off the Valley of Succoth.
8 Gilead and Manasseh are mine.
Ephraim is like my helmet.
Judah holds my royal scepter.
9 Moab is like my washbowl.
I throw my sandals at Edom.
I shout at Philistia."

10 Who will bring me to the strong, walled
city?
Who will lead me to Edom?
11 God, surely you have rejected us;
you do not go out with our armies.

¹² Help us fight the enemy.
    Human help is useless,
¹³ but we can win with God's help.
    He will defeat our enemies.

A PRAYER AGAINST AN ENEMY
For the director of music. A psalm of David.

109 God, I praise you.
        Do not be silent.
² Wicked people and liars have spoken
    against me;
    they have told lies about me.
³ They have said hateful things about me
    and attack me for no reason.
⁴ They attacked me, even though I loved
    them
    and prayed for them.
⁵ I was good to them, but they repay me
    with evil.
    I loved them, but they hate me in
    return.

⁶ They say about me, "Have an evil person
    work against him,
    and let an accuser stand against him.
⁷ When he is judged, let him be found
    guilty,
    and let even his prayers show his
    guilt.
⁸ Let his life be cut short,
    and let another man replace him as
    leader.
⁹ Let his children become orphans
    and his wife a widow.
¹⁰ Make his children wander around,
    begging for food.
    Let them be forced out of the ruins in
    which they live.
¹¹ Let the people to whom he owes money
    take everything he owns,
    and let strangers steal everything he has
    worked for.
¹² Let no one show him love
    or have mercy on his orphaned
    children.
¹³ Let all his descendants die
    and be forgotten by those who live after
    him.
¹⁴ LORD, remember how wicked his
    ancestors were,
    and don't let the sins of his mother be
    wiped out.
¹⁵ LORD, always remember their sins.

Then make people forget about them
    completely.

¹⁶ "He did not remember to be loving.
    He hurt the poor, the needy, and those
    who were sad
    until they were nearly dead.
¹⁷ He loved to put curses on others,
    so let those same curses fall on him.
    He did not like to bless others,
    so do not let good things happen to him.
¹⁸ He cursed others as often as he wore
    clothes.
    Cursing others filled his body and his
    life,
    like drinking water and using olive oil.
¹⁹ So let curses cover him like clothes
    and wrap around him like a belt."
²⁰ May the LORD do these things to those
    who accuse me,
    to those who speak evil against me.

²¹ But you, Lord GOD,
    be kind to me so others will know you
    are good.
    Because your love is good, save me.
²² I am poor and helpless
    and very sad.
²³ I am dying like an evening shadow;
    I am shaken off like a locust.
²⁴ My knees are weak from fasting,
    and I have grown thin.
²⁵ My enemies insult me;
    they look at me and shake their heads.

²⁶ LORD my God, help me;
    because you are loving, save me.
²⁷ Then they will know that your power has
    done this;
    they will know that you have done it,
    LORD.
²⁸ They may curse me, but you bless me.
    They may attack me, but they will be
    disgraced.
    Then I, your servant, will be glad.
²⁹ Let those who accuse me be disgraced
    and covered with shame like a coat.

³⁰ I will thank the LORD very much;
    I will praise him in front of many
    people.
³¹ He defends the helpless
    and saves them from those who accuse
    them.

THE LORD APPOINTS A KING
A psalm of David.

110 The LORD said to my Lord,
"Sit by me at my right side
until I put your enemies under your
control."
2 The LORD will enlarge your kingdom
beyond Jerusalem,
and you will rule over your enemies.
3 Your people will join you on your day of
battle.
You have been dressed in holiness from
birth;
you have the freshness of a child.

4 The LORD has made a promise
and will not change his mind.
He said, "You are a priest forever,
a priest like Melchizedek."

5 The Lord is beside you to help you.
When he becomes angry, he will crush
kings.
6 He will judge those nations, filling them
with dead bodies;
he will defeat rulers all over the world.
7 The king will drink from the brook on the
way.
Then he will be strengthened.

PRAISE THE LORD'S GOODNESS
111 Praise the LORD!

I will thank the LORD with all my
heart
in the meeting of his good people.
2 The LORD does great things;
those who enjoy them seek them.
3 What he does is glorious and splendid,
and his goodness continues forever.
4 His miracles are unforgettable.
The LORD is kind and merciful.
5 He gives food to those who fear him.
He remembers his agreement forever.
6 He has shown his people his power
when he gave them the lands of other
nations.

7 Everything he does is good and fair;
all his orders can be trusted.
8 They will continue forever.
They were made true and right.
9 He sets his people free.
He made his agreement everlasting.
He is holy and wonderful.

10 Wisdom begins with respect for the LORD;
those who obey his orders have good
understanding.
He should be praised forever.

HONEST PEOPLE ARE BLESSED
112 Praise the LORD!

Happy are those who respect the
LORD,
who want what he commands.
2 Their descendants will be powerful in the
land;
the children of honest people will be
blessed.
3 Their houses will be full of wealth and
riches,
and their goodness will continue
forever.
4 A light shines in the dark for honest
people,
for those who are merciful and kind and
good.
5 It is good to be merciful and generous.
Those who are fair in their business
6 will never be defeated.
Good people will always be
remembered.
7 They won't be afraid of bad news;
their hearts are steady because they
trust the LORD.
8 They are confident and will not be
afraid;
they will look down on their enemies.
9 They give freely to the poor.
The things they do are right and will
continue forever.
They will be given great honor.

10 The wicked will see this and become
angry;
they will grind their teeth in anger and
then disappear.
The wishes of the wicked will come to
nothing.

PRAISE FOR THE LORD'S KINDNESS
113 Praise the LORD!

Praise him, you servants of the
LORD;
praise the name of the LORD.
2 The LORD's name should be praised
now and forever.
3 The LORD's name should be praised

from where the sun rises to where it
  sets.
4 The LORD is supreme over all the nations;
  his glory reaches to the skies.

5 No one is like the LORD our God,
  who rules from heaven,
6 who bends down to look
  at the skies and the earth.
7 The LORD lifts the poor from the dirt
  and takes the helpless from the ashes.
8 He seats them with princes,
  the princes of his people.
9 He gives children to the woman who has
  none
  and makes her a happy mother.

Praise the LORD!

GOD BROUGHT ISRAEL FROM EGYPT

114 When the Israelites went out of
  Egypt,
  the people of Jacob left that foreign
  country.
2 Then Judah became God's holy place;
  Israel became the land he ruled.

3 The Red Sea looked and ran away;
  the Jordan River turned back.
4 The mountains danced like sheep
  and the hills like little lambs.
5 Sea, why did you run away?
  Jordan, why did you turn back?
6 Mountains, why did you dance like sheep?
  Hills, why did you dance like little
  lambs?

7 Earth, shake with fear before the Lord,
  before the God of Jacob.
8 He turned a rock into a pool of water,
  a hard rock into a spring of water.

THE ONE TRUE GOD

115 It does not belong to us, LORD.
  The glory belongs to you
  because of your love and loyalty.

2 Why do the nations ask,
  "Where is their God?"
3 Our God is in heaven.
  He does what he pleases.
4 Their idols are made of silver and gold,
  the work of human hands.
5 They have mouths, but they cannot speak.
  They have eyes, but they cannot see.
6 They have ears, but they cannot hear.

They have noses, but they cannot smell.
7 They have hands, but they cannot feel.
  They have feet, but they cannot walk.
  No sounds come from their throats.
8 People who make idols will be like them,
  and so will those who trust them.

9 Family of Israel, trust the LORD;
  he is your helper and your protection.
10 Family of Aaron, trust the LORD;
  he is your helper and your protection.
11 You who respect the LORD should trust
  him;
  he is your helper and your protection.

12 The LORD remembers us and will bless us.
  He will bless the family of Israel;
  he will bless the family of Aaron.
13 The LORD will bless those who respect
  him,
  from the smallest to the greatest.

14 May the LORD give you success,
  and may he give you and your children
  success.
15 May you be blessed by the LORD,
  who made heaven and earth.

16 Heaven belongs to the LORD,
  but he gave the earth to people.
17 Dead people do not praise the LORD;
  those in the grave are silent.
18 But we will praise the LORD
  now and forever.

Praise the LORD!

THANKSGIVING FOR ESCAPING DEATH

116 I love the LORD,
  because he listens to my prayers
  for help.
2 He paid attention to me,
  so I will call to him for help as long as
  I live.
3 The ropes of death bound me,
  and the fear of the grave took hold of
  me.
  I was troubled and sad.
4 Then I called out the name of the LORD.
  I said, "Please, LORD, save me!"

5 The LORD is kind and does what is right;
  our God is merciful.
6 The LORD watches over the foolish;
  when I was helpless, he saved me.
7 I said to myself, "Relax,

because the LORD takes care of you."

8 LORD, you saved me from death.
You stopped my eyes from crying;
    you kept me from being defeated.
9 So I will walk with the LORD
    in the land of the living.
10 I believed, so I said,
    "I am completely ruined."
11 In my distress I said,
    "All people are liars."

12 What can I give the LORD
    for all the good things he has given to
        me?
13 I will lift up the cup of salvation,
    and I will pray to the LORD.
14 I will give the LORD what I promised
    in front of all his people.

15 The death of one that belongs to the
        LORD
    is precious in his sight.
16 LORD, I am your servant;
    I am your servant and the son of your
        female servant.
    You have freed me from my chains.
17 I will give you an offering to show thanks
        to you,
    and I will pray to the LORD.
18 I will give the LORD what I promised
    in front of all his people,
19 in the Temple courtyards
    in Jerusalem.

Praise the LORD!

A HYMN OF PRAISE

117 All you nations, praise the LORD.
    All you people, praise him
2 because the LORD loves us very much,
    and his truth is everlasting.

Praise the LORD!

THANKSGIVING FOR VICTORY

118 Thank the LORD because he is good.
    His love continues forever.
2 Let the people of Israel say,
    "His love continues forever."
3 Let the family of Aaron say,
    "His love continues forever."
4 Let those who respect the LORD say,
    "His love continues forever."

5 I was in trouble, so I called to the LORD.
    The LORD answered me and set me free.

6 I will not be afraid, because the LORD is
        with me.
    People can't do anything to me.
7 The LORD is with me to help me,
    so I will see my enemies defeated.
8 It is better to trust the LORD
    than to trust people.
9 It is better to trust the LORD
    than to trust princes.

10 All the nations surrounded me,
    but I defeated them in the name of the
        LORD.
11 They surrounded me on every side,
    but with the LORD's power I defeated
        them.
12 They surrounded me like a swarm of
        bees,
    but they died as quickly as thorns burn.
    By the LORD's power, I defeated them.
13 They chased me until I was almost
        defeated,
    but the LORD helped me.
14 The LORD gives me strength and a song.
    He has saved me.

15 Shouts of joy and victory
    come from the tents of those who do
        right:
    "The LORD has done powerful things."
16 The power of the LORD has won the
        victory;
    with his power the LORD has done
        mighty things.

17 I will not die, but live,
    and I will tell what the LORD has done.
18 The LORD has taught me a hard lesson,
    but he did not let me die.

19 Open for me the Temple gates.
    Then I will come in and thank the
        LORD.
20 This is the LORD's gate;
    only those who are good may enter
        through it.
21 LORD, I thank you for answering me.
    You have saved me.

22 The stone that the builders rejected
    became the cornerstone.
23 The LORD did this,
    and it is wonderful to us.
24 This is the day that the LORD has made.
    Let us rejoice and be glad today!

Anger
Management

By Dr. Ben Lerner

PSALM 118:24

Science has finally caught up with the Bible. The *Journal of Circulation* reported in May 2004 that even if you're healthy and routinely test in the "normal" blood pressure range, if you've got an anger management problem, you put yourself at high risk of not only emotional explosion but also valve explosion.

It isn't clear precisely how or why anger raises the risk of heart disease, but many studies have reported a link between the two. Even the Associated Press has sounded the cry, reporting that, "Hotheaded men who explode with anger seem to be at greater risk of having a stroke or dying."

One theory posits that the secretion of stress hormones (epinephrine, norepinephrine, and dopamine) when someone is angry can damage the layer of thin, flattened cells that line the arteries and can accelerate the development of atherosclerosis, the condition which is ultimately responsible for most heart attacks. Excess amounts of stress hormones can also disrupt the electrical rhythm of the heart and may lead to blockages in veins and arteries.

The bottom line: *What you eat* may not be as important as *what's eating you!* Of course, students of God's Word probably know this already. Proverbs 17:22 says that "a happy heart is like good medicine, but a broken spirit drains your strength."

In other words, you cannot separate your wellness from your emotions. Every feeling you have

affects some part of your body. Skin, heart rate, digestion, joints, muscle energy levels, the hair on your head, and endless cells and systems you don't even know about change with every emotion. That's why an angry, stressed-out individual will be very likely to experience illness despite following other important rules of wellness.

That is not God's grand scheme for your life . . . that is why I've come to believe that Peace Management is more important than nutrition or fitness. Again, God's Word provides the answer: "Do not worry about anything, but pray and ask God for everything you need, always giving thanks. And God's peace, which is so great we cannot understand it, will keep your hearts and minds in Christ Jesus" (Philippians 4:6–7).

Notice where peace has the greatest effect: the heart and mind. Whereas stress and anger can cause you to deteriorate physically and mentally, the peace of God can protect you physically and mentally!

So the next time you find yourself in a stressful situation and you feel your blood pressure beginning to rise, don't become like the guy in the express aisle blowing his top when he spots someone with thirteen items. Don't follow the example of the gal yelling and cursing the cars in front of her. Instead, do yourself a big favor and remember the advice of your Great Physician: Pray! Then God will not only help you through the situation, but he also will protect your heart and mind against deadly stress and anger.

TO LEARN MORE ON WHAT THE BIBLE HAS TO SAY ABOUT **FITNESS,** READ THE SCRIPTURES AND DEVOTIONALS AT **JUDGES 16:3, JOB 10:10–11, JOB 11:18, PSALM 6:2, ISAIAH 12:2, PSALM 59:9,** AND **PHILEMON 17–21.**

25 Please, LORD, save us;
  please, LORD, give us success.
26 God bless the one who comes in the name
    of the LORD.
  We bless all of you from the Temple of
    the LORD.
27 The LORD is God,
    and he has shown kindness to us.
  With branches in your hands, join the
    feast.
  Come to the corners of the altar.

28 You are my God, and I will thank you;
    you are my God, and I will praise your
    greatness.

29 Thank the LORD because he is good.
    His love continues forever.

THE WORD OF GOD

119 Happy are those who live pure
    lives,
  who follow the LORD's teachings.
2 Happy are those who keep his rules,
    who try to obey him with their whole
    heart.
3 They don't do what is wrong;
    they follow his ways.
4 LORD, you gave your orders
    to be obeyed completely.
5 I wish I were more loyal
    in obeying your demands.
6 Then I would not be ashamed
    when I study your commands.
7 When I learned that your laws are fair,
    I praised you with an honest heart.
8 I will obey your demands,
    so please don't ever leave me.

9 How can a young person live a pure life?
    By obeying your word.
10 With all my heart I try to obey you.
    Don't let me break your commands.
11 I have taken your words to heart
    so I would not sin against you.
12 LORD, you should be praised.
    Teach me your demands.
13 My lips will tell about
    all the laws you have spoken.
14 I enjoy living by your rules
    as people enjoy great riches.
15 I think about your orders
    and study your ways.
16 I enjoy obeying your demands,
    and I will not forget your word.

17 Do good to me, your servant, so I can live,
    so I can obey your word.
18 Open my eyes to see
    the miracles in your teachings.
19 I am a stranger on earth.
    Do not hide your commands from me.
20 I wear myself out with desire
    for your laws all the time.
21 You scold proud people;
    those who ignore your commands are
    cursed.
22 Don't let me be insulted and hated
    because I keep your rules.
23 Even if princes speak against me,
    I, your servant, will think about your
    demands.
24 Your rules give me pleasure;
    they give me good advice.

25 I am about to die.
    Give me life, as you have promised.
26 I told you about my life, and you
    answered me.
  Teach me your demands.
27 Help me understand your orders.
    Then I will think about your miracles.
28 I am sad and tired.
  Make me strong again as you have
    promised.
29 Don't let me be dishonest;
    have mercy on me by helping me obey
    your teachings.
30 I have chosen the way of truth;
    I have obeyed your laws.
31 I hold on to your rules.
    LORD, do not let me be disgraced.
32 I will quickly obey your commands,
    because you have made me happy.

33 LORD, teach me your demands,
    and I will keep them until the end.
34 Help me understand, so I can keep your
    teachings,
  obeying them with all my heart.
35 Lead me in the path of your commands,
    because that makes me happy.
36 Make me want to keep your rules
    instead of wishing for riches.
37 Keep me from looking at worthless
    things.
  Let me live by your word.
38 Keep your promise to me, your servant,
    so you will be respected.
39 Take away the shame I fear,

because your laws are good.
40 How I want to follow your orders.
  Give me life because of your goodness.

41 LORD, show me your love,
  and save me as you have promised.
42 I have an answer for people who insult
    me,
  because I trust what you say.
43 Never keep me from speaking your truth,
  because I depend on your fair laws.
44 I will obey your teachings
  forever and ever.
45 So I will live in freedom,
  because I want to follow your orders.
46 I will discuss your rules with kings
  and will not be ashamed.
47 I enjoy obeying your commands,
  which I love.
48 I praise your commands, which I love,
  and I think about your demands.

49 Remember your promise to me, your
    servant;
  it gives me hope.
50 When I suffer, this comforts me:
  Your promise gives me life.
51 Proud people always make fun of me,
  but I do not reject your teachings.
52 I remember your laws from long ago,
  and they comfort me, LORD.
53 I become angry with wicked people
  who do not keep your teachings.
54 I sing about your demands
  wherever I live.
55 LORD, I remember you at night,
  and I will obey your teachings.
56 This is what I do:
  I follow your orders.

57 LORD, you are my share in life;
  I have promised to obey your words.
58 I prayed to you with all my heart.
  Have mercy on me as you have
    promised.
59 I thought about my life,
  and I decided to follow your rules.
60 I hurried and did not wait
  to obey your commands.
61 Wicked people have tied me up,
  but I have not forgotten your teachings.
62 In the middle of the night, I get up to
    thank you
  because your laws are right.

63 I am a friend to everyone who fears you,
  to anyone who obeys your orders.
64 LORD, your love fills the earth.
  Teach me your demands.

65 You have done good things for your
    servant,
  as you have promised, LORD.
66 Teach me wisdom and knowledge
  because I trust your commands.
67 Before I suffered, I did wrong,
  but now I obey your word.
68 You are good, and you do what is good.
  Teach me your demands.
69 Proud people have made up lies about me,
  but I will follow your orders with all my
    heart.
70 Those people have no feelings,
  but I love your teachings.
71 It was good for me to suffer
  so I would learn your demands.
72 Your teachings are worth more to me
  than thousands of pieces of gold and
    silver.

73 You made me and formed me with your
    hands.
  Give me understanding so I can learn
    your commands.
74 Let those who respect you rejoice when
    they see me,
  because I put my hope in your word.
75 LORD, I know that your laws are right
  and that it was right for you to punish
    me.
76 Comfort me with your love,
  as you promised me, your servant.
77 Have mercy on me so that I may live.
  I love your teachings.
78 Make proud people ashamed because
    they lied about me.
  But I will think about your orders.
79 Let those who respect you return to me,
  those who know your rules.
80 Let me obey your demands perfectly
  so I will not be ashamed.

81 I am weak from waiting for you to save me,
  but I hope in your word.
82 My eyes are tired from looking for your
    promise.
  When will you comfort me?
83 Even though I am like a wine bag going
    up in smoke,

I do not forget your demands.

84 How long will I live?
   When will you judge those who are
      hurting me?

85 Proud people have dug pits to trap me.
   They have nothing to do with your
      teachings.

86 All of your commands can be trusted.
   Liars are hurting me. Help me!

87 They have almost put me in the grave,
   but I have not rejected your orders.

88 Give me life by your love
   so I can obey your rules.

89 LORD, your word is everlasting;
   it continues forever in heaven.

90 Your loyalty will go on and on;
   you made the earth, and it still stands.

91 All things continue to this day because of
      your laws,
   because all things serve you.

92 If I had not loved your teachings,
   I would have died from my sufferings.

93 I will never forget your orders,
   because you have given me life by them.

94 I am yours. Save me.
   I want to obey your orders.

95 Wicked people are waiting to destroy
      me,
   but I will think about your rules.

96 Everything I see has its limits,
   but your commands have none.

97 How I love your teachings!
   I think about them all day long.

98 Your commands make me wiser than my
      enemies,
   because they are mine forever.

99 I am wiser than all my teachers,
   because I think about your rules.

100 I have more understanding than the
      elders,
   because I follow your orders.

101 I have avoided every evil way
   so I could obey your word.

102 I haven't walked away from your laws,
   because you yourself are my teacher.

103 Your promises are sweet to me,
   sweeter than honey in my mouth!

104 Your orders give me understanding,
   so I hate lying ways.

105 Your word is like a lamp for my feet
   and a light for my path.

106 I will do what I have promised
   and obey your fair laws.

107 I have suffered for a long time.
   LORD, give me life by your word.

108 LORD, accept my willing praise
   and teach me your laws.

109 My life is always in danger,
   but I haven't forgotten your teachings.

110 Wicked people have set a trap for me,
   but I haven't strayed from your orders.

111 I will follow your rules forever,
   because they make me happy.

112 I will try to do what you demand
   forever, until the end.

113 I hate disloyal people,
   but I love your teachings.

114 You are my hiding place and my shield;
   I hope in your word.

115 Get away from me, you who do evil,
   so I can keep my God's commands.

116 Support me as you promised so I can live.
   Don't let me be embarrassed because of
      my hopes.

117 Help me, and I will be saved.
   I will always respect your demands.

118 You reject those who ignore your
      demands,
   because their lies mislead them.

119 You throw away the wicked of the world
      like trash.
   So I will love your rules.

120 I shake in fear of you;
   I respect your laws.

121 I have done what is fair and right.
   Don't leave me to those who wrong me.

122 Promise that you will help me, your
      servant.
   Don't let proud people wrong me.

123 My eyes are tired from looking for your
      salvation
   and for your good promise.

124 Show your love to me, your servant,
   and teach me your demands.

125 I am your servant. Give me wisdom
   so I can understand your rules.

126 LORD, it is time for you to do something,
   because people have disobeyed your
      teachings.

127 I love your commands
   more than the purest gold.

128 I respect all your orders,
   so I hate lying ways.

129 Your rules are wonderful.
That is why I keep them.
130 Learning your words gives wisdom
and understanding for the foolish.
131 I am nearly out of breath.
I really want to learn your commands.
132 Look at me and have mercy on me
as you do for those who love you.
133 Guide my steps as you promised;
don't let any sin control me.
134 Save me from harmful people
so I can obey your orders.
135 Show your kindness to me, your servant.
Teach me your demands.
136 Tears stream from my eyes,
because people do not obey your
teachings.

137 LORD, you do what is right,
and your laws are fair.
138 The rules you commanded are right
and completely trustworthy.
139 I am so upset I am worn out,
because my enemies have forgotten
your words.
140 Your promises are proven,
so I, your servant, love them.
141 I am unimportant and hated,
but I have not forgotten your orders.
142 Your goodness continues forever,
and your teachings are true.
143 I have had troubles and misery,
but I love your commands.
144 Your rules are always good.
Help me understand so I can live.

145 LORD, I call to you with all my heart.
Answer me, and I will keep your
demands.
146 I call to you.
Save me so I can obey your rules.
147 I wake up early in the morning and cry
out.
I hope in your word.
148 I stay awake all night
so I can think about your promises.
149 Listen to me because of your love;
LORD, give me life by your laws.
150 Those who love evil are near,
but they are far from your teachings.
151 But, LORD, you are also near,
and all your commands are true.
152 Long ago I learned from your rules
that you made them to continue forever.

153 See my suffering and rescue me,
because I have not forgotten your
teachings.
154 Argue my case and save me.
Let me live by your promises.
155 Wicked people are far from being saved,
because they do not want your
demands.
156 LORD, you are very kind;
give me life by your laws.
157 Many enemies are after me,
but I have not rejected your rules.
158 I see those traitors, and I hate them,
because they do not obey what you
say.
159 See how I love your orders.
LORD, give me life by your love.
160 Your words are true from the start,
and all your laws will be fair forever.

161 Leaders attack me for no reason,
but I fear your law in my heart.
162 I am as happy over your promises
as if I had found a great treasure.
163 I hate and despise lies,
but I love your teachings.
164 Seven times a day I praise you
for your fair laws.
165 Those who love your teachings will find
true peace,
and nothing will defeat them.
166 I am waiting for you to save me, LORD.
I will obey your commands.
167 I obey your rules,
and I love them very much.
168 I obey your orders and rules,
because you know everything I do.

169 Hear my cry to you, LORD.
Let your word help me understand.
170 Listen to my prayer;
save me as you promised.
171 Let me speak your praise,
because you have taught me your
demands.
172 Let me sing about your promises,
because all your commands are fair.
173 Give me your helping hand,
because I have chosen your commands.
174 I want you to save me, LORD.
I love your teachings.
175 Let me live so I can praise you,
and let your laws help me.
176 I have wandered like a lost sheep.

Look for your servant, because I have
    not forgotten your commands.

A PRAYER OF SOMEONE FAR FROM HOME
A psalm for going up to worship.

120 When I was in trouble, I called to
    the LORD,
    and he answered me.
2 LORD, save me from liars
    and from those who plan evil.

3 You who plan evil, what will God do to
    you?
    How will he punish you?
4 He will punish you with the sharp arrows
    of a warrior
    and with burning coals of wood.

5 How terrible it is for me to live in the land
    of Meshech,
    to live among the people of Kedar.
6 I have lived too long
    with people who hate peace.
7 When I talk peace,
    they want war.

THE LORD GUARDS HIS PEOPLE
A song for going up to worship.

121 I look up to the hills,
    but where does my help come
        from?
2 My help comes from the LORD,
    who made heaven and earth.

3 He will not let you be defeated.
    He who guards you never sleeps.
4 He who guards Israel
    never rests or sleeps.
5 The LORD guards you.
    The LORD is the shade that protects you
        from the sun.
6 The sun cannot hurt you during the day,
    and the moon cannot hurt you at night.
7 The LORD will protect you from all
        dangers;
    he will guard your life.
8 The LORD will guard you as you come
        and go,
    both now and forever.

HAPPY PEOPLE IN JERUSALEM
A song for going up to worship. Of David.

122 I was happy when they said to me,
    "Let's go to the Temple of the
        LORD."

2 Jerusalem, we are standing
    at your gates.
3 Jerusalem is built as a city
    with the buildings close together.
4 The tribes go up there,
    the tribes who belong to the LORD.
    It is the rule in Israel
    to praise the LORD at Jerusalem.
5 There the descendants of David
    set their thrones to judge the people.

6 Pray for peace in Jerusalem:
    "May those who love her be safe.
7 May there be peace within her walls
    and safety within her strong towers."
8 To help my relatives and friends,
    I say, "Let Jerusalem have peace."
9 For the sake of the Temple of the LORD
        our God,
    I wish good for her.

A PRAYER FOR MERCY
A song for going up to worship.

123 LORD, I look upward to you,
    you who live in heaven.
2 Slaves depend on their masters,
    and a female servant depends on her
        mistress.
    In the same way, we depend on the LORD
        our God;
    we wait for him to show us mercy.

3 Have mercy on us, LORD. Have mercy on
    us,
    because we have been insulted.
4 We have suffered many insults from lazy
        people
    and much cruelty from the proud.

THE LORD SAVES HIS PEOPLE
A song for going up to worship. Of David.

124 What if the LORD had not been on
        our side?
    (Let Israel repeat this.)
2 What if the LORD had not been on our
        side
    when we were attacked?
3 When they were angry with us,
    they would have swallowed us alive.
4 They would have been like a flood
        drowning us;
    they would have poured over us like a
        river.

5   They would have swept us away like a
    mighty stream.

6 Praise the LORD,
    who did not let them chew us up.
7 We escaped like a bird
    from the hunter's trap.
  The trap broke,
    and we escaped.
8 Our help comes from the LORD,
    who made heaven and earth.

GOD PROTECTS THOSE WHO TRUST HIM
A song for going up to worship.

125 Those who trust the LORD are like
      Mount Zion,
  which sits unmoved forever.
2 As the mountains surround Jerusalem,
    the LORD surrounds his people
    now and forever.

3 The wicked will not rule
    over those who do right.
  If they did, the people who do right
    might use their power to do evil.

4 LORD, be good to those who are good,
    whose hearts are honest.
5 But, LORD, when you remove those who
    do evil,
  also remove those who stop following
    you.

Let there be peace in Israel.

LORD, BRING YOUR PEOPLE BACK
A song for going up to worship.

126 When the LORD brought the
      prisoners back to Jerusalem,
  it seemed as if we were dreaming.
2 Then we were filled with laughter,
    and we sang happy songs.
  Then the other nations said,
    "The LORD has done great things for
    them."
3 The LORD has done great things for us,
    and we are very glad.

4 LORD, return our prisoners again,
    as you bring streams to the desert.
5 Those who cry as they plant crops
    will sing at harvest time.
6 Those who cry
    as they carry out the seeds
  will return singing
    and carrying bundles of grain.

ALL GOOD THINGS COME FROM GOD
A song for going up to worship. Of Solomon.

127 If the LORD doesn't build the
      house,
  the builders are working for nothing.
  If the LORD doesn't guard the city,
    the guards are watching for nothing.
2 It is no use for you to get up early
    and stay up late,
  working for a living.
    The LORD gives sleep to those he loves.
3 Children are a gift from the LORD;
    babies are a reward.
4 Children who are born to a young man
    are like arrows in the hand of a warrior.
5 Happy is the man
    who has his bag full of arrows.
  They will not be defeated
    when they fight their enemies at the
    city gate.

THE HAPPY HOME
A song for going up to worship.

128 Happy are those who respect the
      LORD and obey him.
2 You will enjoy what you work for,
    and you will be blessed with good
    things.
3 Your wife will give you many children,
    like a vine that produces much fruit.
  Your children will bring you much good,
    like olive branches that produce many
    olives.
4 This is how the man who respects the
    LORD
  will be blessed.
5 May the LORD bless you from Mount
    Zion;
  may you enjoy the good things of
    Jerusalem all your life.
6 May you see your grandchildren.

Let there be peace in Israel.

A PRAYER AGAINST THE ENEMIES
A song for going up to worship.

129 They have treated me badly all my
      life.
  (Let Israel repeat this.)
2 They have treated me badly all my life,
    but they have not defeated me.
3 Like farmers plowing, they plowed over
    my back,

making long wounds.
⁴ But the LORD does what is right;
he has set me free from those wicked
people.

⁵ Let those who hate Jerusalem
be turned back in shame.
⁶ Let them be like the grass on the roof
that dries up before it has grown.
⁷ There is not enough of it to fill a hand
or to make into a bundle to fill one's
arms.
⁸ Let those who pass by them not say,
"May the LORD bless you.
We bless you by the power of the
LORD."

A PRAYER FOR MERCY
A song for going up to worship.

130 LORD, I am in great trouble,
so I call out to you.
² Lord, hear my voice;
listen to my prayer for help.
³ LORD, if you punished people for all their
sins,
no one would be left, Lord.
⁴ But you forgive us,
so you are respected.

⁵ I wait for the LORD to help me,
and I trust his word.
⁶ I wait for the Lord to help me
more than night watchmen wait for the
dawn,
more than night watchmen wait for the
dawn.

⁷ People of Israel, put your hope in the
LORD
because he is loving
and able to save.
⁸ He will save Israel
from all their sins.

CHILDLIKE TRUST IN THE LORD
A song for going up to worship. Of David.

131 LORD, my heart is not proud;
I don't look down on others.
I don't do great things,
and I can't do miracles.
² But I am calm and quiet,
like a baby with its mother.

I am at peace, like a baby with its
mother.

³ People of Israel, put your hope in the LORD
now and forever.

IN PRAISE OF THE TEMPLE
A song for going up to worship.

132 LORD, remember David
and all his suffering.
² He made an oath to the LORD,
a promise to the Mighty God of Jacob.
³ He said, "I will not go home to my house,
or lie down on my bed,
⁴ or close my eyes,
or let myself sleep
⁵ until I find a place for the LORD.
I want to provide a home for the Mighty
God of Jacob."

⁶ We heard about the Ark in Bethlehem.
We found it at Kiriath Jearim.
⁷ Let's go to the LORD's house.
Let's worship at his footstool.
⁸ Rise, LORD, and come to your resting
place;
come with the Ark that shows your
strength.
⁹ May your priests do what is right.
May your people sing for joy.

¹⁰ For the sake of your servant David,
do not reject your appointed king.
¹¹ The LORD made a promise to David,
a sure promise that he will not take
back.
He promised, "I will make one of your
descendants
rule as king after you.
¹² If your sons keep my agreement
and the rules that I teach them,
then their sons after them will rule
on your throne forever and ever."

¹³ The LORD has chosen Jerusalem;
he wants it for his home.
¹⁴ He says, "This is my resting place
forever.
Here is where I want to stay.
¹⁵ I will bless her with plenty;
I will fill her poor with food.
¹⁶ I will cover her priests with salvation,
and those who worship me will really
sing for joy.

10 He killed the firstborn sons of the
  Egyptians.
    His love continues forever.
11 He brought the people of Israel out of
  Egypt.
    His love continues forever.
12 He did it with his great power and
  strength.
    His love continues forever.
13 He parted the water of the Red Sea.
    His love continues forever.
14 He brought the Israelites through the
  middle of it.
    His love continues forever.
15 But the king of Egypt and his army
  drowned in the Red Sea.
    His love continues forever.

16 He led his people through the desert.
    His love continues forever.
17 He defeated great kings.
    His love continues forever.
18 He killed powerful kings.
    His love continues forever.
19 He defeated Sihon king of the Amorites.
    His love continues forever.
20 He defeated Og king of Bashan.
    His love continues forever.
21 He gave their land as a gift.
    His love continues forever.
22 It was a gift to his servants, the Israelites.
    His love continues forever.

23 He remembered us when we were in
  trouble.
    His love continues forever.
24 He freed us from our enemies.
    His love continues forever.
25 He gives food to every living creature.
    His love continues forever.

26 Give thanks to the God of heaven.
    His love continues forever.

ISRAELITES IN CAPTIVITY

137 By the rivers in Babylon we sat and
  cried
    when we remembered Jerusalem.
2 On the poplar trees nearby
  we hung our harps.
3 Those who captured us asked us to sing;
  our enemies wanted happy songs.
  They said, "Sing us a song about
  Jerusalem!"

4 But we cannot sing songs about the LORD
  while we are in this foreign country!
5 Jerusalem, if I forget you,
  let my right hand lose its skill.
6 Let my tongue stick to the roof of my
  mouth
  if I do not remember you,
  if I do not think about Jerusalem
  as my greatest joy.

7 LORD, remember what the Edomites did
  on the day Jerusalem fell.
  They said, "Tear it down!
  Tear it down to its foundations!"

8 People of Babylon, you will be destroyed.
  The people who pay you back for what
  you did to us will be happy.
9 They will grab your babies
  and throw them against the rocks.

A HYMN OF THANKSGIVING
A psalm of David.

138 LORD, I will thank you with all my
  heart;
  I will sing to you before the gods.
2 I will bow down facing your holy Temple,
  and I will thank you for your love and
  loyalty.
  You have made your name and your word
  greater than anything.
3 On the day I called to you, you answered
  me.
  You made me strong and brave.

4 LORD, let all the kings of the earth praise
  you
  when they hear the words you speak.
5 They will sing about what the LORD has
  done,
  because the LORD's glory is great.

6 Though the LORD is supreme,
  he takes care of those who are humble,
  but he stays away from the proud.
7 LORD, even when I have trouble all
  around me,
  you will keep me alive.
  When my enemies are angry,
  you will reach down and save me by
  your power.
8 LORD, you do everything for me.
  LORD, your love continues forever.
  Do not leave us, whom you made.

GOD KNOWS EVERYTHING
For the director of music. A psalm of David.

139

LORD, you have examined me
and know all about me.
2 You know when I sit down and when I get
up.
You know my thoughts before I think
them.
3 You know where I go and where I lie
down.
You know everything I do.
4 LORD, even before I say a word,
you already know it.
5 You are all around me—in front and in
back—
and have put your hand on me.
6 Your knowledge is amazing to me;
it is more than I can understand.

7 Where can I go to get away from your
Spirit?
Where can I run from you?
8 If I go up to the heavens, you are there.
If I lie down in the grave, you are there.
9 If I rise with the sun in the east
and settle in the west beyond the sea,
10 even there you would guide me.
With your right hand you would hold
me.
11 I could say, "The darkness will hide me.
Let the light around me turn into
night."
12 But even the darkness is not dark to you.
The night is as light as the day;
darkness and light are the same to you.

13 You made my whole being;
you formed me in my mother's body.
14 I praise you because you made me in an
amazing and wonderful way.
What you have done is wonderful.
I know this very well.
15 You saw my bones being formed
as I took shape in my mother's body.
When I was put together there,
16 you saw my body as it was formed.

THE LIFE YOU WERE BORN TO LIVE

〰〰

FITNESS

you're wonderful

PSALM 139:14

Inside your body designed by God is a wonderful, beautiful symphony of thousands of functions and chemical reactions we know about, and endless ones only God knows about. All these functions and reactions happen at precisely the right time, at the right place, and for all the right reasons. Each moment of each day, the body is repairing tissue, creating new cells, and balancing billions of tiny little operating systems.

Because we have no idea what is actually happening, all we can do is respect the body God has given us, admire its vast potential, appreciate its brilliance, and place no interference on its natural path of development. When appreciated and well taken care of, the body knows precisely what to do to keep or get itself well, without side effects.

reflect: Trust God to help you learn how to take proper care of your body.
Go to **Proverbs 3:1–2.**

¹⁷ "I will make a king come from the family of David.
I will provide my appointed one descendants to rule after him.
¹⁸ I will cover his enemies with shame,
but his crown will shine."

THE LOVE OF GOD'S PEOPLE
A song for going up to worship. Of David.

133 It is good and pleasant
when God's people live together in peace!
² It is like perfumed oil poured on the priest's head

MENTORING WORLD CHANGERS FOR CHRIST

successful
team building

FUTURE

PSALM 133:1–3

It is essential in the working environment to have teamwork. If your office is centered on Christian principles, then you need a group that shares the same spirit. God designed his kingdom so that we can work together with kindred spirits as team members. It is exciting when you find someone who shares the same vision as you. Working together as a team creates an atmosphere where unity prevails. Often, God will bring a Christian believer to work alongside you who will help you in the work that God has set before you.

God is looking for people who will work together in unity. He releases a powerful dimension of his presence when hearts and minds are united. The Scriptures say that when two or more Christians discuss matters concerning him, he is pleased to listen and respond to their discussion. When you are in agreement, that is when God chooses to respond to your unity by making his presence known. He will hear your petitions and answer them.

If you are carrying concerns about your family or coworkers, surround yourself with believers who have the same vision or goals as you do. This will unite you as a team and help to dispel any attacks from outside influences that could cause turmoil in your business or in your family. Don't attempt to bear the burden on your own.

You may pray about them by yourself, but you will miss the blessing of being united with others. Being united as a team and praying together as a unit multiplies your ability to enjoy the presence of God. No person is an island in the kingdom of God. He wants you to depend on him and to work with fellow believers to achieve your goals and to overcome your challenges.

---

reflect: Work with others as a team so that together everyone achieves more.
Go to **Joshua 23:6.**

and running down his beard.
It ran down Aaron's beard
and on to the collar of his robes.
³ It is like the dew of Mount Hermon
falling on the hills of Jerusalem.
There the LORD gives his blessing
of life forever.

TEMPLE GUARDS, PRAISE THE LORD

A song for going up to worship.

134 Praise the LORD, all you servants of
the LORD,
you who serve at night in the Temple of
the LORD.
² Raise your hands in the Temple
and praise the LORD.

³ May the LORD bless you from Mount
Zion,
he who made heaven and earth.

THE LORD SAVES, IDOLS DO NOT

135 Praise the LORD!

Praise the name of the LORD;
praise him, you servants of the LORD,
² you who stand in the LORD's Temple
and in the Temple courtyards.
³ Praise the LORD, because he is good;
sing praises to him, because it is
pleasant.

⁴ The LORD has chosen the people of Jacob
for himself;
he has chosen the people of Israel for
his very own.
⁵ I know that the LORD is great.
Our Lord is greater than all the gods.
⁶ The LORD does what he pleases,
in heaven and on earth,
in the seas and the deep oceans.
⁷ He brings the clouds from the ends of the
earth.
He sends the lightning with the rain.
He brings out the wind from his
storehouses.
⁸ He destroyed the firstborn sons in Egypt
the firstborn of both people and
animals.
⁹ He did many signs and miracles in Egypt
against the king and his servants.
¹⁰ He defeated many nations

and killed powerful kings:
¹¹ Sihon king of the Amorites,
Og king of Bashan,
and all the kings of Canaan.
¹² Then he gave their land as a gift,
a gift to his people, the Israelites.

¹³ LORD, your name is everlasting;
LORD, you will be remembered forever.
¹⁴ The LORD defends his people
and has mercy on his servants.

¹⁵ The idols of other nations are made of
silver and gold,
the work of human hands.
¹⁶ They have mouths, but they cannot
speak.
They have eyes, but they cannot see.
¹⁷ They have ears, but they cannot hear.
They have no breath in their mouths.
¹⁸ People who make idols will be like them,
and so will those who trust them.

¹⁹ Family of Israel, praise the LORD.
Family of Aaron, praise the LORD.
²⁰ Family of Levi, praise the LORD.
You who respect the LORD should
praise him.
²¹ You people of Jerusalem, praise the LORD
on Mount Zion.
Praise the LORD!

GOD'S LOVE CONTINUES FOREVER

136 Give thanks to the LORD because
he is good.
His love continues forever.
² Give thanks to the God of gods.
His love continues forever.
³ Give thanks to the Lord of lords.
His love continues forever.

⁴ Only he can do great miracles.
His love continues forever.
⁵ With his wisdom he made the skies.
His love continues forever.
⁶ He spread out the earth on the seas.
His love continues forever.
⁷ He made the sun and the moon.
His love continues forever.
⁸ He made the sun to rule the day.
His love continues forever.
⁹ He made the moon and stars to rule the
night.
His love continues forever.

10 He killed the firstborn sons of the
   Egyptians.
   His love continues forever.
11 He brought the people of Israel out of
   Egypt.
   His love continues forever.
12 He did it with his great power and
   strength.
   His love continues forever.
13 He parted the water of the Red Sea.
   His love continues forever.
14 He brought the Israelites through the
   middle of it.
   His love continues forever.
15 But the king of Egypt and his army
   drowned in the Red Sea.
   His love continues forever.

16 He led his people through the desert.
   His love continues forever.
17 He defeated great kings.
   His love continues forever.
18 He killed powerful kings.
   His love continues forever.
19 He defeated Sihon king of the Amorites.
   His love continues forever.
20 He defeated Og king of Bashan.
   His love continues forever.
21 He gave their land as a gift.
   His love continues forever.
22 It was a gift to his servants, the Israelites.
   His love continues forever.

23 He remembered us when we were in
   trouble.
   His love continues forever.
24 He freed us from our enemies.
   His love continues forever.
25 He gives food to every living creature.
   His love continues forever.

26 Give thanks to the God of heaven.
   His love continues forever.

ISRAELITES IN CAPTIVITY

137 By the rivers in Babylon we sat and
   cried
   when we remembered Jerusalem.
2 On the poplar trees nearby
   we hung our harps.
3 Those who captured us asked us to sing;
   our enemies wanted happy songs.
   They said, "Sing us a song about
   Jerusalem!"

4 But we cannot sing songs about the LORD
   while we are in this foreign country!
5 Jerusalem, if I forget you,
   let my right hand lose its skill.
6 Let my tongue stick to the roof of my
   mouth
   if I do not remember you,
   if I do not think about Jerusalem
   as my greatest joy.

7 LORD, remember what the Edomites did
   on the day Jerusalem fell.
   They said, "Tear it down!
   Tear it down to its foundations!"

8 People of Babylon, you will be destroyed.
   The people who pay you back for what
   you did to us will be happy.
9 They will grab your babies
   and throw them against the rocks.

A HYMN OF THANKSGIVING
A psalm of David.

138 LORD, I will thank you with all my
   heart;
   I will sing to you before the gods.
2 I will bow down facing your holy Temple,
   and I will thank you for your love and
   loyalty.
   You have made your name and your word
   greater than anything.
3 On the day I called to you, you answered
   me.
   You made me strong and brave.

4 LORD, let all the kings of the earth praise
   you
   when they hear the words you speak.
5 They will sing about what the LORD has
   done,
   because the LORD's glory is great.

6 Though the LORD is supreme,
   he takes care of those who are humble,
   but he stays away from the proud.
7 LORD, even when I have trouble all
   around me,
   you will keep me alive.
   When my enemies are angry,
   you will reach down and save me by
   your power.
8 LORD, you do everything for me.
   LORD, your love continues forever.
   Do not leave us, whom you made.

GOD KNOWS EVERYTHING
For the director of music. A psalm of David.

139
¹ LORD, you have examined me
and know all about me.
² You know when I sit down and when I get
up.
You know my thoughts before I think
them.
³ You know where I go and where I lie
down.
You know everything I do.
⁴ LORD, even before I say a word,
you already know it.
⁵ You are all around me—in front and in
back—
and have put your hand on me.
⁶ Your knowledge is amazing to me;
it is more than I can understand.

⁷ Where can I go to get away from your
Spirit?
Where can I run from you?
⁸ If I go up to the heavens, you are there.

If I lie down in the grave, you are there.
⁹ If I rise with the sun in the east
and settle in the west beyond the sea,
¹⁰ even there you would guide me.
With your right hand you would hold
me.

¹¹ I could say, "The darkness will hide me.
Let the light around me turn into
night."
¹² But even the darkness is not dark to you.
The night is as light as the day;
darkness and light are the same to you.

¹³ You made my whole being;
you formed me in my mother's body.
¹⁴ I praise you because you made me in an
amazing and wonderful way.
What you have done is wonderful.
I know this very well.
¹⁵ You saw my bones being formed
as I took shape in my mother's body.
When I was put together there,
¹⁶ you saw my body as it was formed.

THE LIFE YOU WERE BORN TO LIVE

FITNESS

you're wonderful

PSALM 139:14

I nside your body designed by God is a wonderful, beautiful symphony of thousands of functions and chemical reactions we know about, and endless ones only God knows about. All these functions and reactions happen at precisely the right time, at the right place, and for all the right reasons. Each moment of each day, the body is repairing tissue, creating new cells, and balancing billions of tiny little operating systems.

Because we have no idea what is actually happening, all we can do is respect the body God has given us, admire its vast potential, appreciate its brilliance, and place no interference on its natural path of development. When appreciated and well taken care of, the body knows precisely what to do to keep or get itself well, without side effects.

reflect: Trust God to help you learn how to take proper care of your body.
Go to **Proverbs 3:1–2.**

All the days planned for me
were written in your book
before I was one day old.
17 God, your thoughts are precious to me.
They are so many!
18 If I could count them,
they would be more than all the grains
of sand.
When I wake up,
I am still with you.

19 God, I wish you would kill the wicked!
Get away from me, you murderers!
20 They say evil things about you.
Your enemies use your name
thoughtlessly.
21 LORD, I hate those who hate you;
I hate those who rise up against you.
22 I feel only hate for them;
they are my enemies.

23 God, examine me and know my heart;
test me and know my anxious
thoughts.
24 See if there is any bad thing in me.
Lead me on the road to everlasting
life.

A PRAYER FOR PROTECTION
For the director of music. A psalm of David.

140 LORD, rescue me from evil people;
protect me from cruel people
2 who make evil plans,
who always start fights.
3 They make their tongues sharp as a
snake's;
their words are like snake poison. *Selah*

4 LORD, guard me from the power of wicked
people;
protect me from cruel people
who plan to trip me up.
5 The proud hid a trap for me.
They spread out a net beside the road;
they set traps for me. *Selah*

6 I said to the LORD, "You are my God."
LORD, listen to my prayer for help.
7 LORD God, my mighty savior,
you protect me in battle.
8 LORD, do not give the wicked what they
want.
Don't let their plans succeed,
or they will become proud. *Selah*

9 Those around me have planned trouble.
Now let it come to them.
10 Let burning coals fall on them.
Throw them into the fire
or into pits from which they cannot
escape.
11 Don't let liars settle in the land.
Let evil quickly hunt down cruel
people.

12 I know the LORD will get justice for the
poor
and will defend the needy in court.
13 Good people will praise his name;
honest people will live in his presence.

A PRAYER NOT TO SIN
A psalm of David.

141 LORD, I call to you. Come quickly.
Listen to me when I call to you.
2 Let my prayer be like incense placed
before you,
and my praise like the evening
sacrifice.

3 LORD, help me control my tongue;
help me be careful about what I say.
4 Take away my desire to do evil
or to join others in doing wrong.
Don't let me eat tasty food
with those who do evil.

5 If a good person punished me, that would
be kind.
If he corrected me, that would be like
perfumed oil on my head.
I shouldn't refuse it.
But I pray against those who do evil.
6 Let their leaders be thrown down the
cliffs.
Then people will know that I have
spoken correctly:
7 "The ground is plowed and broken up.
In the same way, our bones have been
scattered at the grave."

8 GOD, I look to you for help.
I trust in you, LORD. Don't let me die.
9 Protect me from the traps they set for me
and from the net that evil people have
spread.
10 Let the wicked fall into their own nets,
but let me pass by safely.

627

A PRAYER FOR SAFETY

A maskil of David when he was in the cave.
A prayer.

142
I cry out to the LORD;
  I pray to the LORD for mercy.
2 I pour out my problems to him;
  I tell him my troubles.
3 When I am afraid,
  you, LORD, know the way out.
In the path where I walk,
  a trap is hidden for me.
4 Look around me and see.
  No one cares about me.
I have no place of safety;
  no one cares if I live.
5 LORD, I cry out to you.
  I say, "You are my protection.
  You are all I want in this life."
6 Listen to my cry,
  because I am helpless.
Save me from those who are chasing me,
  because they are too strong for me.
7 Free me from my prison,
  and then I will praise your name.
Then good people will surround me,
  because you have taken care of me.

A PRAYER NOT TO BE KILLED

A psalm of David.

143
LORD, hear my prayer;
  listen to my cry for mercy.
Answer me
  because you are loyal and good.
2 Don't judge me, your servant,
  because no one alive is right before you.
3 My enemies are chasing me;
  they crushed me to the ground.
They made me live in darkness
  like those long dead.
4 I am afraid;
  my courage is gone.
5 I remember what happened long ago;
  I consider everything you have done.
  I think about all you have made.
6 I lift my hands to you in prayer.
  As a dry land needs rain, I thirst for you.
                                    Selah
7 LORD, answer me quickly,
  because I am getting weak.
Don't turn away from me,
  or I will be like those who are dead.

8 Tell me in the morning about your love,
  because I trust you.
Show me what I should do,
  because my prayers go up to you.
9 LORD, save me from my enemies;
  I hide in you.
10 Teach me to do what you want,
  because you are my God.
Let your good Spirit
  lead me on level ground.

11 LORD, let me live
  so people will praise you.
In your goodness
  save me from my troubles.
12 In your love defeat my enemies.
  Destroy all those who trouble me,
  because I am your servant.

A PRAYER FOR VICTORY

Of David.

144
Praise the LORD, my Rock,
  who trains me for war,
  who trains me for battle.
2 He protects me like a strong, walled city,
  and he loves me.
He is my defender and my Savior,
  my shield and my protection.
He helps me keep my people under
  control.

3 LORD, why are people important to you?
  Why do you even think about human
  beings?
4 People are like a breath;
  their lives are like passing shadows.

5 LORD, tear open the sky and come down.
  Touch the mountains so they will
  smoke.
6 Send the lightning and scatter my enemies.
  Shoot your arrows and force them away.
7 Reach down from above.
  Save me and rescue me out of this sea of
  enemies,
  from these foreigners.
8 They are liars;
  they are dishonest.

9 God, I will sing a new song to you;
  I will play to you on the ten-stringed
  harp.
10 You give victory to kings.
  You save your servant David from cruel
  swords.

11 Save me, rescue me from these foreigners.
　They are liars; they are dishonest.

12 Let our sons in their youth
　grow like plants.
　Let our daughters be
　like the decorated stones in the Temple.

13 Let our barns be filled
　with crops of all kinds.
　Let our sheep in the fields have
　thousands and tens of thousands of
　lambs.

14 　Let our cattle be strong.

Let no one break in.
　Let there be no war,
　no screams in our streets.

15 Happy are those who are like this;
　happy are the people whose God is the
　Lord.

PRAISE TO GOD THE KING
A psalm of praise. Of David.

145 I praise your greatness, my God
　the King;
　I will praise you forever and ever.

THE ULTIMATE INVESTMENT

the freedom
principle

FINANCES

PSALM 144:13–15

David knew poverty and wealth. He knew failure and victory. He knew scorn and acclaim. But one thing David wants us all to know is this: God is the only sure foundation for all that we have.

We often think that financial security will make our lives easier and better. We seek power and position to ensure our goals. But life's lessons are brutal realizations that the only sure foundation is the one given and sustained by God. Make yourself a list of the top five things you pursue. Then ask yourself the question: Is there any set of circumstances or any person in the world who can take these away from me?

If you find that you can imagine a scenario where the prizes you value most can be snatched away, then you need to ask yourself why you are spending so much effort to achieve them. God wants you to prize those things that cannot be taken from you. What we discover is that the things that cannot be taken away almost always were never ours. They were gifts given to us by our Father.

David knew that wealth, fame, and power are God's gifts, not our achievements. God provides them according to his purposes. There is incredible freedom in this divine principle. I need only be a good steward of what God grants me. I am not the producer; I am the caretaker. Life is much easier when I get the right perspective.

reflect: Do you need to change your perspective of life?
Go to **Mark 10:21.**

2 I will praise you every day;
  I will praise you forever and ever.
3 The LORD is great and worthy of our
    praise;
  no one can understand how great he is.

4 Parents will tell their children what you
    have done.
  They will retell your mighty acts,
5 wonderful majesty, and glory.
  And I will think about your miracles.
6 They will tell about the amazing things
    you do,
  and I will tell how great you are.
7 They will remember your great goodness
  and will sing about your fairness.

8 The LORD is kind and shows mercy.
  He does not become angry quickly but
    is full of love.
9 The LORD is good to everyone;
  he is merciful to all he has made.
10 LORD, everything you have made will
    praise you;
  those who belong to you will bless you.
11 They will tell about the glory of your
    kingdom
  and will speak about your power.
12 Then everyone will know the mighty
    things you do
  and the glory and majesty of your
    kingdom.
13 Your kingdom will go on and on,
  and you will rule forever.

  The LORD will keep all his promises;
  he is loyal to all he has made.
14 The LORD helps those who have been
    defeated
  and takes care of those who are in
    trouble.
15 All living things look to you for food,
  and you give it to them at the right time.
16 You open your hand,
  and you satisfy all living things.
17 Everything the LORD does is right.
  He is loyal to all he has made.
18 The LORD is close to everyone who prays
    to him,
  to all who truly pray to him.
19 He gives those who respect him what they
    want.
  He listens when they cry, and he saves
    them.

20 The LORD protects everyone who loves
    him,
  but he will destroy the wicked.
21 I will praise the LORD.
  Let everyone praise his holy name
    forever.

PRAISE GOD WHO HELPS THE WEAK

146 Praise the LORD!
    My whole being, praise the LORD.
2 I will praise the LORD all my life;
  I will sing praises to my God as long as
    I live.

3 Do not put your trust in princes
  or other people, who cannot save you.
4 When people die, they are buried.
  Then all of their plans come to an end.
5 Happy are those who are helped by the
    God of Jacob.
  Their hope is in the LORD their God.
6 He made heaven and earth,
  the sea and everything in it.
  He remains loyal forever.
7 He does what is fair for those who have
    been wronged.
  He gives food to the hungry.
  The LORD sets the prisoners free.
8 The LORD gives sight to the blind.
  The LORD lifts up people who are in
    trouble.
  The LORD loves those who do right.
9 The LORD protects the foreigners.
  He defends the orphans and widows,
  but he blocks the way of the wicked.

10 The LORD will be King forever.
  Jerusalem, your God is everlasting.

  Praise the LORD!

PRAISE GOD WHO HELPS HIS PEOPLE

147 Praise the LORD!
    It is good to sing praises to our
      God;
  it is good and pleasant to praise him.
2 The LORD rebuilds Jerusalem;
  he brings back the captured Israelites.
3 He heals the brokenhearted
  and bandages their wounds.

4 He counts the stars
  and names each one.
5 Our Lord is great and very powerful.

There is no limit to what he knows.
6 The LORD defends the humble,
but he throws the wicked to the ground.

7 Sing praises to the LORD;
praise our God with harps.
8 He fills the sky with clouds
and sends rain to the earth
and makes grass grow on the hills.
9 He gives food to cattle
and to the little birds that call.

10 He is not impressed with the strength of a
horse
or with human might.
11 The LORD is pleased with those who
respect him,
with those who trust his love.

12 Jerusalem, praise the LORD;
Jerusalem, praise your God.
13 He makes your city gates strong
and blesses your children inside.
14 He brings peace to your country
and fills you with the finest grain.

15 He gives a command to the earth,
and it quickly obeys him.
16 He spreads the snow like wool
and scatters the frost like ashes.
17 He throws down hail like rocks.
No one can stand the cold he sends.
18 Then he gives a command, and it melts.
He sends the breezes, and the waters
flow.

19 He gave his word to Jacob,
his laws and demands to Israel.
20 He didn't do this for any other nation.
They don't know his laws.

Praise the LORD!

THE WORLD SHOULD PRAISE THE LORD

148 Praise the LORD!
Praise the LORD from the skies.
Praise him high above the earth.
2 Praise him, all you angels.
Praise him, all you armies of heaven.
3 Praise him, sun and moon.
Praise him, all you shining stars.
4 Praise him, highest heavens
and you waters above the sky.
5 Let them praise the LORD,
because they were created by his
command.

6 He put them in place forever and ever;
he made a law that will never change.

7 Praise the LORD from the earth,
you large sea animals and all the
oceans,
8 lightning and hail, snow and mist,
and stormy winds that obey him,
9 mountains and all hills,
fruit trees and all cedars,
10 wild animals and all cattle,
crawling animals and birds,
11 kings of the earth and all nations,
princes and all rulers of the earth,
12 young men and women,
old people and children.

13 Praise the LORD,
because he alone is great.
He is more wonderful than heaven and
earth.
14 God has given his people a king.
He should be praised by all who belong
to him;
he should be praised by the Israelites,
the people closest to his heart.

Praise the LORD!

PRAISE THE GOD OF ISRAEL

149 Praise the LORD!
Sing a new song to the LORD;
sing his praise in the meeting of his
people.

2 Let the Israelites be happy because of
God, their Maker.
Let the people of Jerusalem rejoice
because of their King.
3 They should praise him with dancing.
They should sing praises to him with
tambourines and harps.
4 The LORD is pleased with his people;
he saves the humble.
5 Let those who worship him rejoice in his
glory.
Let them sing for joy even in bed!

6 Let them shout his praise
with their two-edged swords in their
hands.
7 They will punish the nations
and defeat the people.
8 They will put those kings in chains
and those important men in iron bands.

⁹ They will punish them as God has
written.
God is honored by all who worship him.

Praise the LORD!

PRAISE THE LORD WITH MUSIC

150 Praise the LORD!
Praise God in his Temple;
praise him in his mighty heaven.
² Praise him for his strength;
praise him for his greatness.

³ Praise him with trumpet blasts;
praise him with harps and lyres.
⁴ Praise him with tambourines and
dancing;
praise him with stringed instruments
and flutes.
⁵ Praise him with loud cymbals;
praise him with crashing cymbals.
⁶ Let everything that breathes praise the
LORD.

Praise the LORD!

FOR YOUR OWN GOOD

FULFILLMENT

a zeal for God

PSALM 150:6

After the Wesley brothers had graduated from Oxford University, they sailed to America with the goal of evangelizing the rugged colonists and the savage Indians. However, after a short time, they became very distraught with their effort and felt they were getting nowhere, so they sailed back to England.

While crossing the Atlantic Ocean, they had time to observe a group of passengers who were with them on the voyage. They were very impressed with the spiritual depth these people had. They both realized that they did not have what those people had. When they reached their homeland, they took time to search for these men and talk with them about what they had observed upon the voyage. The men shared what they had and in May of 1738, John and Charles Wesley each had life-changing experiences.

They discovered the forgiveness of the true, living God and, for the first time in their lives, received real joy. The zeal that they had when they first left England had not come from a true relationship with the Father. After their life-changing experiences, their ministries displayed a higher level of spiritual power. That spiritual power did not come from their own zeal, but from God. It was then that they could worship God with the passion that King David and other psalmists displayed in the Book of Psalms. You need to have that desire and zeal in your life. Praise him from the depths of your heart. Recognize that he is the eternal, immortal, and invincible God. He is the only true God, so serve him with your whole being.

reflect: Worship God with your entire being: spirit, soul, and body.
Go to **Proverbs 2:1-5.**

proverbs

THE IMPORTANCE OF PROVERBS

1 These are the wise words of Solomon son of David, king of Israel.

2 They teach wisdom and self-control;
  they will help you understand wise
    words.

3 They will teach you how to be wise and
    self-controlled
  and will teach you to do what is honest
    and fair and right.

4 They make the uneducated wise
  and give knowledge and sense to the
    young.

5 Wise people can also listen and learn;
  even they can find good advice in these
    words.

6 Then anyone can understand wise words
    and stories,
  the words of the wise and their riddles.

7 Knowledge begins with respect for the
    LORD,
  but fools hate wisdom and discipline.

WARNINGS AGAINST EVIL

8 My child, listen to your father's teaching
  and do not forget your mother's advice.

9 Their teaching will be like flowers in your
    hair
  or a necklace around your neck.

10 My child, if sinners try to lead you into
    sin,
  do not follow them.

11 They will say, "Come with us.
  Let's ambush and kill someone;
  let's attack some innocent people just
    for fun.

12 Let's swallow them alive, as death does;
  let's swallow them whole, as the grave
    does.

13 We will take all kinds of valuable things
  and fill our houses with stolen goods.

14 Come join us,
  and we will share with you stolen
    goods."

15 My child, do not go along with them;

do not do what they do.

16 They are eager to do evil
  and are quick to kill.

17 It is useless to spread out a net
  right where the birds can see it.

18 But sinners will fall into their own traps;
  they will only catch themselves!

19 All greedy people end up this way;
  greed kills selfish people.

WISDOM SPEAKS

20 Wisdom is like a woman shouting in the
    street;
  she raises her voice in the city squares.

21 She cries out in the noisy street
  and shouts at the city gates:

22 "You fools, how long will you be foolish?
  How long will you make fun of wisdom
    and hate knowledge?

23 If only you had listened when I corrected
    you,
  I would have told you what's in my
    heart;
  I would have told you what I am
    thinking.

24 I called, but you refused to listen;
  I held out my hand, but you paid no
    attention.

25 You did not follow my advice
  and did not listen when I corrected you.

26 So I will laugh when you are in trouble.
  I will make fun when disaster strikes
    you,

27 when disaster comes over you like a
    storm,
  when trouble strikes you like a
    whirlwind,
  when pain and trouble overwhelm you.

28 "Then you will call to me,
  but I will not answer.
  You will look for me,
  but you will not find me.

29 It is because you rejected knowledge
  and did not choose to respect the LORD.

30 You did not accept my advice,
  and you rejected my correction.

³¹ So you will get what you deserve;
   you will get what you planned for
      others.
³² Fools will die because they refuse to
      listen;
   they will be destroyed because they do
      not care.
³³ But those who listen to me will live in
      safety

and be at peace, without fear of
   injury."

REWARDS OF WISDOM

2 My child, listen to what I say
   and remember what I command you.
² Listen carefully to wisdom;
   set your mind on understanding.
³ Cry out for wisdom,

A FAMILY CHANGED

FAMILY

wise up

PROVERBS 1:7   By Drs. Les and Leslie Parrott

Losing one's mind is a common danger in love. The emotional force of love can override the capacity to think clearly and drive one to become "crazy." What's more, when one's romantic passions are appreciated and returned by another, wisdom is all but put on ice.

Once the spark of attraction catches flame, love quickly turns into a raging, out-of-control fire. Engulfed by its heat, the couple, madly in love, becomes oblivious to sound judgment. Even after the heat dies down and a couple settles into a healthy marriage, there is no guarantee of sound judgment returning.

For this reason, God calls every couple to wise up. The Hebrew root word translated as "wise" or "wisdom" occurs more than three hundred times in the Old Testament, and many of those are in Proverbs. In the Greek New Testament, "wisdom" is found more than sixty times. The word implies having special knowledge and sound judgment, like a carpenter who knows his trade well and makes good decisions.

A wise couple knows marriage well and works together on important decisions such as financial management and child rearing. According to the *American Heritage Dictionary*, "wisdom" is "a common sense understanding of what is true, right, and lasting." Did you catch that? It is built on common sense.

Unfortunately, it appears that Horace Greeley was right when he said, "Common sense is very uncommon." Every year around Christmas, some churches display a sign with an insightful message: "Wise men still seek him." So do wise couples.

reflect: How can you exercise some common sense in your marriage?
Go to **Joshua 3:1–17.**

and beg for understanding.
⁴ Search for it like silver,
    and hunt for it like hidden treasure.
⁵ Then you will understand respect for the
    LORD,
    and you will find that you know God.
⁶ Only the LORD gives wisdom;
    he gives knowledge and understanding.
⁷ He stores up wisdom for those who are
    honest.

Like a shield he protects the innocent.
⁸ He makes sure that justice is done,
    and he protects those who are loyal to
    him.

⁹ Then you will understand what is honest
    and fair
    and what is the good and right thing to
    do.
¹⁰ Wisdom will come into your mind,
    and knowledge will be pleasing to you.

FOR YOUR OWN GOOD

don't be afraid

FULFILLMENT

PROVERBS 2:1–5

There is a sense in which fear (respect) is the basis of all our interaction with God. We see this when the people reacted to one of Jesus' miracles of healing. They were afraid. They wanted Jesus to leave them alone. In spite of their recognition that God was acting in startling ways right in front of them, they could not cope with the situation.

This gives us a clue to understanding what fear has to do with our reactions to God. Just for a moment, think about this: God made everything. Everything actually stays in existence from one second to the next because God sustains everything. God has a purpose for everything. And God will judge everything by his standard. Now imagine that this one finite and fragile being called *man* stands before the God of everything.

This is not like meeting a friend or even a stranger. This is meeting the Being who is all-powerful, all-knowing, and all-present. He is the Being who could, if he chose to, end our existence and that of everything else with a single act. Is it any wonder that anyone who comes into contact with such a Being falls to the ground trembling?

The truly amazing fact of Scripture is that this God, whom we rightly fear, actually wants us to love him. More amazing still is that he loves us. He is not out to get us. He really wants to care for us. Who could be better at that than God? The God we are prone to fear tells us, "Don't be afraid."

reflect: Consider the amazing fact that God loves you and cares for you as one of his very own.
Go to **Ecclesiastes 2:24–26**.

¹¹ Good sense will protect you;
    understanding will guard you.
¹² It will keep you from the wicked,
    from those whose words are bad,
¹³ who don't do what is right
    but what is evil.
¹⁴ They enjoy doing wrong
    and are happy to do what is crooked
    and evil.
¹⁵ What they do is wrong,
    and their ways are dishonest.

¹⁶ It will save you from the unfaithful
    wife

who tries to lead you into adultery with
    pleasing words.
¹⁷ She leaves the husband she married when
    she was young.
    She ignores the promise she made
    before God.
¹⁸ Her house is on the way to death;
    those who took that path are now all
    dead.
¹⁹ No one who goes to her comes back
    or walks the path of life again.

²⁰ But wisdom will help you be good
    and do what is right.

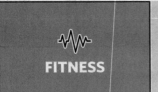

THE LIFE YOU WERE BORN TO LIVE

FITNESS

no hurt exercise

PROVERBS 3:1–2

If the mere thought of exercise makes your joints sore and your stomach queasy, there is good news. You do not have to hurt yourself with exercise to be doing some good. Moderate, nonpainful, regular exercise actually extends your life more than anything else. In fact, one interesting statistic shows that professional and Olympic athletes have an average life expectancy much lower than the average population. The reason is obvious: top athletes simply overdo it.

However, the bottom line for us is that if we do not exercise, we are likely to die early. That is one of life's unfortunate tendencies. On the other hand, regular exercise will give us energy and quality throughout our lives. God created us to move, so we owe it to him and our loved ones to get moving.

Studies have shown that as little as ten minutes of exercise is beneficial and that if you do ten minutes in the morning and ten minutes in the evening it is almost as beneficial as twenty minutes straight through. Stress, even if it's from exercising, is still stress. That's why it's important to find exercise you enjoy. If you are moving at a moderate to brisk pace or intensity level, make sure to drink water while you exercise. This will prevent, and even help reverse, pain and fatigue.

reflect: Select a type of exercise that you enjoy, and it'll help you endure the pain.
Go to **Proverbs 12:25**.

²¹ Those who are honest will live in the
    land,
    and those who are innocent will remain
    in it.
²² But the wicked will be removed from the
    land,
    and the unfaithful will be thrown out
    of it.

ADVICE TO CHILDREN

3 My child, do not forget my teaching,
    but keep my commands in mind.
² Then you will live a long time,
    and your life will be successful.

³ Don't ever forget kindness and
    truth.
    Wear them like a necklace.
    Write them on your heart as if on a
    tablet.
⁴ Then you will be respected
    and will please both God and
    people.
⁵ Trust the Lord with all your heart,
    and don't depend on your own
    understanding.
⁶ Remember the Lord in all you do,
    and he will give you success.

MENTORING WORLD CHANGERS FOR CHRIST

the straight path

FUTURE

PROVERBS 3:5-6

Some translations of verse 6 read "he shall direct your path," but that isn't quite the right sense. God doesn't push you out on your way without making the road ahead straight, level, and clear. It is both the work of God for people and also the work of people for God.

God grants us the ability to recognize his law and to walk in it. The person who is judged to have straight paths from God's viewpoint is said to have that quality of heart that enables him or her to be obedient to God's will. This promise claims that our dependence on (trust in) God will allow him to straighten our lives.

We do not need to struggle with the mechanics of how this will be done. We are asked only to trust him and not ourselves, and he will do the rest. It is a blessing for us to know that God is willing and able to repair what we have damaged if we will only surrender ourselves to him in all our endeavors.

After years of struggling, it is a wonderful promise of grace to realize that our lives can be characterized by blamelessness and discernment. God does work miracles. Verse 6 makes it clear. All of the crooked paths, all of the bends and curves, all of the messes we have made, he will straighten. The result will be a life of blameless freedom.

reflect: Trust God to make the crooked paths of your life straight, level, and clear.
Go to **Proverbs 16:18–19.**

Guilt and Grace

FAMILY

By Drs. Les and Leslie Parrott

PROVERBS 3:13-18

At a conference on laughter in the ballroom of the Disneyland Hotel, Dr. Steve Allen, Jr., the son of the famous comedian, handed out three scarves and then went through about a dozen steps to teach this room full of psychologists the art of juggling. The first step was to hold one of the scarves out at arm's length—then drop it.

Everyone thought he was joking. Nobody dropped their scarf. "C'mon now, drop it!" Dr. Allen commanded. One by one, people reluctantly released their scarves and they fluttered to the carpeted floor. "There now, doesn't that feel better?" asked Dr. Allen. "You have gotten your mistake over with. This is the first step in learning to juggle. We call it the guilt-free drop." Isn't that a wonderful and wise principle? Do you need a guilt-free drop? Does your partner? We apply the guilt-free drop to our marriage almost daily.

Marriage offers a lot of opportunities for partners to feel guilty. In a survey assessing "who makes you feel most guilty," the majority of respondents confessed they were the key perpetrators of their own guilt. But next on the list was "my spouse." Research has also revealed that much of the guilt we experience is undeserved. It is false guilt, where we suffer self-punishment needlessly. Our internal tape recorder says, "You should always have the house clean. You should never come home late. You should never make a mistake."

It's time we wise up in our marriages. Look at Proverbs 3:13–18 and imagine the word "mar-riage" inserted and substituted: "Happy is the [marriage which] finds wisdom, the one [which] gets understanding. Wisdom is worth more than silver; it brings more profit [to your marriage] than gold. Wisdom is more precious [to your marriage] than rubies; nothing you could want is equal to it. With her right hand wisdom offers you a long [marriage], and with her left hand she gives [your marriage] riches and honor. Wisdom will make your [marriage] pleasant and will bring you peace. As a tree produces fruit, wisdom gives life to those who use it, and everyone who uses it will be happy" (Proverbs 3:13–18).

Amazing thought, isn't it, that a simple thing such as wisdom could combat guilt and frustration in our marriages. The Hebrew root word translated as "wise" or "wisdom" occurs more than three hundred times in the Old Testament. And in the Greek New Testament, "wisdom" is found more than sixty times. It is a word that implies having special knowledge and sound judgment.

A wise couple is one who knows marriage well and works together to offer plenty of guilt-free drops. On the other hand, ignoring or nurturing constant feelings of guilt is anything but wise. That's why it is important for soul mates to offer grace to each other. We need to help each other see reality as it is. A little wisdom will go a long way in making our marriages pleasant and peaceful for the long haul.

TO LEARN MORE ON WHAT THE BIBLE HAS TO SAY ABOUT **FAMILY,** READ THE SCRIPTURES AND DEVOTIONALS AT **GENESIS 2:18, 1 CORINTHIANS 11:7–9, SONG OF SONGS 5:1, MALACHI 2:15,** AND **EXODUS 34:6–7.**

⁷ Don't depend on your own wisdom.
　Respect the LORD and refuse to do
　wrong.
⁸ Then your body will be healthy,
　and your bones will be strong.

⁹ Honor the LORD with your wealth
　and the firstfruits from all your crops.
¹⁰ Then your barns will be full,
　and your wine barrels will overflow
　with new wine.

¹¹ My child, do not reject the LORD's
　discipline,
　and don't get angry when he corrects
　you.
¹² The LORD corrects those he loves,

just as parents correct the child they
　delight in.

¹³ Happy is the person who finds
　wisdom,
　the one who gets understanding.
¹⁴ Wisdom is worth more than silver;
　it brings more profit than gold.
¹⁵ Wisdom is more precious than rubies;
　nothing you could want is equal to it.
¹⁶ With her right hand wisdom offers you a
　long life,
　and with her left hand she gives you
　riches and honor.
¹⁷ Wisdom will make your life pleasant
　and will bring you peace.

HAVE FAITH IN GOD

no bending

FAITH

PROVERBS 3:21

Did you know that gravity bends light? When you watch the sun setting over a flat horizon, the image that you see just before the sun vanishes is really not where you think it is. The gravity of the earth bends the light you see. The sun has actually already dipped below the horizon, but the light is curved by the mass of the earth, so you still see it.

Sometimes we take the same "bending" approach with God's instruction. We keep his word on our horizon where we think we are still being exposed to his wisdom. But the closer we come to letting his instruction slip out of sight, the more bending our moral gravity affects his straight message.

The Hebrew word here is *luz*. It means "to bend or deviate." It is used to describe a crooked or perverse person, someone who opposes the straight paths of the Lord. Of course, bends in the line of sight mean that we are no longer able to see what's really there. Gravity might bend light in the physical world, but in the spiritual world, bending God's instructions will definitely leave us in the dark. If you find yourself on the edge of a moral horizon, better check the line of sight. God's directions for living don't bend.

reflect: Work to keep the Word of God in your line of sight at all times.
Go to **Isaiah 44:21.**

18 As a tree produces fruit, wisdom gives life
to those who use it,
and everyone who uses it will be happy.

19 The LORD made the earth, using his
wisdom.
He set the sky in place, using his
understanding.
20 With his knowledge, he made springs
flow into rivers
and the clouds drop rain on the earth.

21 My child, hold on to wisdom and good
sense.
Don't let them out of your sight.
22 They will give you life
and beauty like a necklace around your
neck.
23 Then you will go your way in safety,
and you will not get hurt.
24 When you lie down, you won't be afraid;
when you lie down, you will sleep in
peace.
25 You won't be afraid of sudden trouble;
you won't fear the ruin that comes to
the wicked,
26 because the LORD will keep you safe.
He will keep you from being trapped.

27 Whenever you are able,
do good to people who need help.
28 If you have what your neighbor asks
for,
don't say, "Come back later.
I will give it to you tomorrow."
29 Don't make plans to hurt your neighbor
who lives nearby and trusts you.
30 Don't accuse a person for no good reason;
don't accuse someone who has not
harmed you.

31 Don't be jealous of those who use
violence,
and don't choose to be like them.
32 The LORD hates those who do wrong,
but he is a friend to those who are
honest.
33 The LORD will curse the evil person's
house,
but he will bless the home of those who
do right.
34 The LORD laughs at those who laugh at
him,
but he gives grace to those who are not
proud.

35 Wise people will receive honor,
but fools will be disgraced.

WISDOM IS IMPORTANT

4 My children, listen to your father's
teaching;
pay attention so you will understand.
2 What I am telling you is good,
so do not forget what I teach you.
3 When I was a young boy in my father's
house
and like an only child to my mother,
4 my father taught me and said,
"Hold on to my words with all your
heart.
Keep my commands and you will live.
5 Get wisdom and understanding.
Don't forget or ignore my words.
6 Hold on to wisdom, and it will take care of
you.
Love it, and it will keep you safe.
7 Wisdom is the most important thing; so
get wisdom.
If it costs everything you have, get
understanding.
8 Treasure wisdom, and it will make you
great;
hold on to it, and it will bring you
honor.
9 It will be like flowers in your hair
and like a beautiful crown on your
head."

10 My child, listen and accept what I say.
Then you will have a long life.
11 I am guiding you in the way of wisdom,
and I am leading you on the right
path.
12 Nothing will hold you back;
you will not be overwhelmed.
13 Always remember what you have been
taught,
and don't let go of it.
Keep all that you have learned;
it is the most important thing in life.
14 Don't follow the ways of the wicked;
don't do what evil people do.
15 Avoid their ways, and don't follow them.
Stay away from them and keep on
going,
16 because they cannot sleep until they do
evil.
They cannot rest until they harm
someone.

Turning Revelations
into Revolutions

By Dr. Ben Lerner

PROVERBS 4:20–22

Do you have a "Disease Mentality"? Often people think that this is living with a mind-set that creates illness. However, it's exactly the opposite. Here's what it means: to think (and act) like you would if you just found out you had a deadly disease and you were going to do everything possible to heal from it.

When proactive people get sick, they:

- Change their diet
- Stop doing abusive things like smoking, drinking, and overworking
- Start praying full time
- Attempt to start controlling stress levels
- Read, watch, and listen to all they can on healing
- Do healthy forms of exercise
- Are very careful with how they use time
- Become very open to non-medical approaches to health

When a patient comes to us with a life threatening illness, we do all we can to create maximized living so that he or she can have the best shot at defeating the disease. Additionally, we have an entire cancer regime of care, nutrients, and dietary advice. However, wouldn't it have been smart to have lived that way all along? Everything a proactive person does to get well from being sick represents the regimen we all should be focusing on every day so as not to get sick in the first place!

But how do we start living this way instead of merely *knowing* that we should? How do we keep from falling back into our old habits? The answer is profoundly simple: to truly become different your *heart* has to become different.

A change in heart makes you different at the very core of your being. You truly look at life and other people in a more accepting, loving, patient, and compassionate way. With a real change of heart, your perception of everything improves and so do others' perception of you.

In order to bring about real change, it is going to take some time. However, more time does not mean more wisdom, maturity, and victory. If it did, then older people would be the happiest and least stressed. Usually, it is just the opposite.

Growing more healthy, wise, and mature takes more than just growing old. Real growth requires learning through reading, practicing stress and time management techniques, and constantly examining your life and your reaction to stressors in it. Getting healthier takes a constant commitment to better eating, exercise, and making sure your spine and nervous system are in proper shape and free from interference.

I remember when I first read the Bible, I was only mildly impressed. Then as I grew, I would read the same books and passages over again, and this time I'd find them life changing. The Bible didn't change—I grew in faith. I experienced a personal revolution!

In time, with the right effort and discipline, you continue to grow all of your life. That is called acquiring wisdom—and it will revolutionize your health, your thoughts, and your life.

TO LEARN MORE ON WHAT THE BIBLE HAS TO SAY ABOUT **FITNESS**, READ THE SCRIPTURES AND DEVOTIONALS AT **ISAIAH 27:5**, **ISAIAH 46:3–4, ISAIAH 53:5, ISAIAH 59:16–17, DANIEL 1:8–16, AMOS 6:1–6,** AND **MATTHEW 6:21.**

¹⁷ They feast on wickedness and cruelty
as if they were eating bread and
drinking wine.

¹⁸ The way of the good person is like the
light of dawn,
growing brighter and brighter until full
daylight.
¹⁹ But the wicked walk around in the dark;
they can't even see what makes them
stumble.

²⁰ My child, pay attention to my words;
listen closely to what I say.
²¹ Don't ever forget my words;
keep them always in mind.
²² They are the key to life for those who find
them;
they bring health to the whole body.
²³ Be careful what you think,
because your thoughts run your life.
²⁴ Don't use your mouth to tell lies;
don't ever say things that are not true.
²⁵ Keep your eyes focused on what is right,
and look straight ahead to what is
good.
²⁶ Be careful what you do,
and always do what is right.
²⁷ Don't turn off the road of goodness;
keep away from evil paths.

WARNING ABOUT ADULTERY

5 My son, pay attention to my wisdom;
listen to my words of understanding.
² Be careful to use good sense,
and watch what you say.
³ The words of another man's wife may
seem sweet as honey;
they may be as smooth as olive oil.
⁴ But in the end she will bring you sorrow,
causing you pain like a two-edged
sword.
⁵ She is on the way to death;
her steps are headed straight to the
grave.
⁶ She gives little thought to life.
She doesn't even know that her ways
are wrong.
⁷ Now, my sons, listen to me,
and don't ignore what I say.
⁸ Stay away from such a woman.
Don't even go near the door of her
house,
⁹ or you will give your riches to others,

and the best years of your life will be
given to someone cruel.
¹⁰ Strangers will enjoy your wealth,
and what you worked so hard for will
go to someone else.
¹¹ You will groan at the end of your life
when your health is gone.
¹² Then you will say, "I hated being told
what to do!
I would not listen to correction!
¹³ I would not listen to my teachers
or pay attention to my instructors.
¹⁴ I came close to being completely ruined
in front of a whole group of people."

¹⁵ Be faithful to your own wife,
just as you drink water from your own
well.
¹⁶ Don't pour your water in the streets;
don't give your love to just any woman.
¹⁷ These things are yours alone
and shouldn't be shared with strangers.
¹⁸ Be happy with the wife you married when
you were young.
She gives you joy, as your fountain gives
you water.
¹⁹ She is as lovely and graceful as a deer.
Let her love always make you happy;
let her love always hold you captive.
²⁰ My son, don't be held captive by a woman
who takes part in adultery.
Don't fondle a woman who is not your
wife.

²¹ The LORD sees everything you do,
and he watches where you go.
²² An evil man will be caught in his wicked
ways;
the ropes of his sins will tie him up.
²³ He will die because he does not control
himself,
and he will be held captive by his
foolishness.

DANGERS OF BEING FOOLISH

6 My child, be careful about giving a
guarantee for somebody else's loan,
about promising to pay what someone
else owes.
² You might get trapped by what you say;
you might be caught by your own
words.
³ My child, if you have done this and are
under your neighbor's control,

here is how to get free.
Don't be proud. Go to your neighbor
and beg to be free from your promise.
4 Don't go to sleep
or even rest your eyes,
5 but free yourself like a deer running from
a hunter,
like a bird flying away from a trapper.

6 Go watch the ants, you lazy person.
Watch what they do and be wise.
7 Ants have no commander,
no leader or ruler,
8 but they store up food in the summer
and gather their supplies at harvest.
9 How long will you lie there, you lazy
person?
When will you get up from sleeping?
10 You sleep a little; you take a nap.
You fold your hands and lie down to
rest.
11 So you will be as poor as if you had been
robbed;
you will have as little as if you had been
held up.

12 Some people are wicked and no good.
They go around telling lies,
13 winking with their eyes, tapping with
their feet,
and making signs with their fingers.
14 They make evil plans in their hearts
and are always starting arguments.
15 So trouble will strike them in an instant;
suddenly they will be so hurt no one
can help them.

16 There are six things the LORD hates.
There are seven things he cannot stand:
17 a proud look,
a lying tongue,
hands that kill innocent people,
18 a mind that thinks up evil plans,
feet that are quick to do evil,
19 a witness who lies,
and someone who starts arguments
among families.

WARNING ABOUT ADULTERY
20 My son, keep your father's commands,
and don't forget your mother's teaching.
21 Keep their words in mind forever
as though you had them tied around
your neck.
22 They will guide you when you walk.

They will guard you when you sleep.
They will speak to you when you are
awake.
23 These commands are like a lamp;
this teaching is like a light.
And the correction that comes from them
will help you have life.
24 They will keep you from sinful women
and from the pleasing words of another
man's unfaithful wife.
25 Don't desire her because she is beautiful.
Don't let her capture you by the way
she looks at you.
26 A prostitute will treat you like a loaf of
bread,
and a woman who takes part in adultery
may cost you your life.
27 You cannot carry hot coals against your
chest
without burning your clothes,
28 and you cannot walk on hot coals
without burning your feet.
29 The same is true if you have sexual
relations with another man's wife.
Anyone who does so will be punished.

30 People don't hate a thief
when he steals because he is hungry.
31 But if he is caught, he must pay back
seven times what he stole,
and it may cost him everything he owns.
32 A man who takes part in adultery has no
sense;
he will destroy himself.
33 He will be beaten up and disgraced,
and his shame will never go away.
34 Jealousy makes a husband very angry,
and he will have no pity when he gets
revenge.
35 He will accept no payment for the wrong;
he will take no amount of money.

THE WOMAN OF ADULTERY
7 My son, remember what I say, and
treasure my commands.
2 Obey my commands, and you will live.
Guard my teachings as you would your
own eyes.
3 Remind yourself of them;
write them on your heart as if on a
tablet.
4 Treat wisdom as a sister,
and make understanding your closest
friend.

⁵ Wisdom and understanding will keep you
away from adultery,
away from the unfaithful wife and her
pleasing words.

⁶ Once while I was at the window of my
house
I looked out through the shutters
⁷ and saw some foolish, young men.
I noticed one of them had no wisdom.

⁸ He was walking down the street near the
corner
on the road leading to her house.
⁹ It was the twilight of the evening;
the darkness of the night was just
beginning.
¹⁰ Then the woman approached him,
dressed like a prostitute
and planning to trick him.

THE LAWS OF INCREASE

financial advice
from God

FINANCES

PROVERBS 7:4

Let's face it: life is much easier when there is money in our pockets. Yet, if you had to choose between money and wisdom, which would you choose? Many would say money. However, nothing is more valuable than wisdom, and nothing is more expensive than ignorance.

Money has a way of coming in, but it also has a way of going out quickly. Money talks, but for many people it only says, "Good-bye." When you use your money wisely, it will provide for all the needs you have. Financial advisors will show you that even on the most modest of salaries, you can retire with wealth if you use wisdom. However, a lack of wisdom leads people to make wrong choices that can cause sickness, poverty, or confusion. There are times when it can even lead to death.

Through his Word and the power of his Holy Spirit, God offers insight and wisdom on all matters of financial transactions. If you're struggling with finances, business, or any other important area of your fiscal world, you need knowledge and can turn to the Bible. Yet God will also work through the testimony of others. Therefore, don't just pray for money; pray for someone who can show you how to make it and keep it. Don't ask for gold only; ask for the leaders and mentors who can help you mine it from the ground.

Proverbs 7:4 says that wisdom is your sister and understanding, or insight, is your intimate friend. The Bible and the people you have around you are signs that God is crying out to you in order to show you how to make and keep the money he gives you.

reflect: Ask God to send you wise counselors in the area of finances.
Go to **Proverbs 30:5**.

¹¹ She was loud and stubborn
    and never stayed at home.
¹² She was always out in the streets or in the
        city squares,
    waiting around on the corners of the
        streets.
¹³ She grabbed him and kissed him.
    Without shame she said to him,
¹⁴ "I made my fellowship offering and took
        some of the meat home.
    Today I have kept my special promises.
¹⁵ So I have come out to meet you;
    I have been looking for you and have
        found you.
¹⁶ I have covered my bed
    with colored sheets from Egypt.
¹⁷ I have made my bed smell sweet
    with myrrh, aloes, and cinnamon.
¹⁸ Come, let's make love until morning.
    Let's enjoy each other's love.
¹⁹ My husband is not home;
    he has gone on a long trip.
²⁰ He took a lot of money with him
    and won't be home for weeks."
²¹ By her clever words she made him give in;
    by her pleasing words she led him into
        doing wrong.
²² All at once he followed her,
    like an ox led to the butcher,
    like a deer caught in a trap
²³ and shot through the liver with an
        arrow.
    Like a bird caught in a trap,
    he didn't know what he did would kill
        him.

²⁴ Now, my sons, listen to me;
    pay attention to what I say.
²⁵ Don't let yourself be tricked by such a
        woman;
    don't go where she leads you.
²⁶ She has ruined many good men,
    and many have died because of her.
²⁷ Her house is on the road to death,
    the road that leads down to the grave.

LISTEN TO WISDOM

8 Wisdom calls to you like someone
        shouting;
    understanding raises her voice.
² On the hilltops along the road
    and at the crossroads, she stands
        calling.
³ Beside the city gates,

at the entrances into the city, she calls
    out:
⁴ "Listen, everyone, I'm calling out to you;
    I am shouting to all people.
⁵ You who are uneducated, seek wisdom.
    You who are foolish, get understanding.
⁶ Listen, because I have important things to
        say,
    and what I tell you is right.
⁷ What I say is true,
    I refuse to speak evil.
⁸ Everything I say is honest;
    nothing I say is crooked or false.
⁹ People with good sense know what I say
        is true;
    and those with knowledge know my
        words are right.
¹⁰ Choose my teachings instead of silver,
    and knowledge rather than the finest
        gold.
¹¹ Wisdom is more precious than rubies.
    Nothing you could want is equal to it.

¹² "I am wisdom, and I have good judgment.
    I also have knowledge and good sense.
¹³ If you respect the LORD, you will also hate
        evil.
    I hate pride and bragging,
    evil ways and lies.
¹⁴ I have good sense and advice,
    and I have understanding and power.
¹⁵ I help kings to govern
    and rulers to make fair laws.
¹⁶ Princes use me to lead,
    and so do all important people who
        judge fairly.
¹⁷ I love those who love me,
    and those who seek me find me.
¹⁸ Riches and honor are mine to give.
    So are wealth and lasting success.
¹⁹ What I give is better than the finest gold,
    better than the purest silver.
²⁰ I do what is right
    and follow the path of justice.
²¹ I give wealth to those who love me,
    filling their houses with treasures.

²² "I, wisdom, was with the LORD when he
        began his work,
    long before he made anything else.
²³ I was created in the very beginning,
    even before the world began.
²⁴ I was born before there were oceans,
    or springs overflowing with water,

25 before the hills were there,
  before the mountains were put in place.
26 God had not made the earth or fields,
  not even the first dust of the earth.
27 I was there when God put the skies in
    place,
  when he stretched the horizon over the
    oceans,
28 when he made the clouds above
  and put the deep underground springs
    in place.
29 I was there when he ordered the sea
  not to go beyond the borders he had set.
  I was there when he laid the earth's
    foundation.
30   I was like a child by his side.
  I was delighted every day,
    enjoying his presence all the time,
31 enjoying the whole world,
  and delighted with all its people.

32 "Now, my children, listen to me,
  because those who follow my ways are
    happy.
33 Listen to my teaching, and you will be
    wise;
  do not ignore it.
34 Happy are those who listen to me,
  watching at my door every day,
  waiting at my open doorway.
35 Those who find me find life,
  and the LORD will be pleased with
    them.
36 Those who do not find me hurt
    themselves.
  Those who hate me love death."

BEING WISE OR FOOLISH

9 Wisdom has built her house;
  she has made its seven columns.
2 She has prepared her food and wine;
  she has set her table.
3 She has sent out her servant girls,
  and she calls out from the highest place
    in the city.
4 She says to those who are uneducated,
  "Come in here, you foolish people!
5 Come and eat my food
  and drink the wine I have prepared.
6 Stop your foolish ways, and you will live;
  take the road of understanding.

7 "If you correct someone who makes fun of
    wisdom, you will be insulted.

If you correct an evil person, you will
    get hurt.
8 Do not correct those who make fun of
    wisdom, or they will hate you.
  But correct the wise, and they will love
    you.
9 Teach the wise, and they will become
    even wiser;
  teach good people, and they will learn
    even more.

10 "Wisdom begins with respect for the
    LORD,
  and understanding begins with
    knowing the Holy One.
11 If you live wisely, you will live a long
    time;
  wisdom will add years to your life.
12 The wise person is rewarded by wisdom,
  but whoever makes fun of wisdom will
    suffer for it."

13 Foolishness is like a loud woman;
  she does not have wisdom or
    knowledge.
14 She sits at the door of her house
  at the highest place in the city.
15 She calls out to those who are passing by,
  who are going along, minding their own
    business.
16 She says to those who are uneducated,
  "Come in here, you foolish people!
17 Stolen water is sweeter,
  and food eaten in secret tastes better."
18 But these people don't know that
  everyone who goes there dies,
  that her guests end up deep in the
    grave.

THE WISE WORDS OF SOLOMON

10 These are the wise words of Solomon:
  Wise children make their father
    happy,
  but foolish children make their mother
    sad.

2 Riches gotten by doing wrong have no
    value,
  but right living will save you from
    death.

3 The LORD does not let good people go
    hungry,
  but he keeps evil people from getting
    what they want.

⁴ A lazy person will end up poor,
  but a hard worker will become rich.

⁵ Those who gather crops on time are wise,
  but those who sleep through the
    harvest are a disgrace.

⁶ Good people will have rich blessings,
  but the wicked will be overwhelmed by
    violence.

⁷ Good people will be remembered as a
    blessing,
  but evil people will soon be forgotten.

⁸ The wise do what they are told,
  but a talkative fool will be ruined.

⁹ The honest person will live in safety,
  but the dishonest will be caught.

¹⁰ A wink may get you into trouble,
  and foolish talk will lead to your ruin.

¹¹ The words of a good person give life, like
    a fountain of water,
  but the words of the wicked contain
    nothing but violence.

¹² Hatred stirs up trouble,
  but love forgives all wrongs.

¹³ Wise people speak with understanding,
  but people without wisdom should be
    punished.

¹⁴ The wise don't tell everything they know,
  but the foolish talk too much and are
    ruined.

¹⁵ Having lots of money protects the rich,
  but having no money destroys the poor.

¹⁶ Good people are rewarded with life,
  but evil people are paid with
    punishment.

¹⁷ Whoever accepts correction is on the way
    to life,
  but whoever ignores correction will
    lead others away from life.

¹⁸ Whoever hides hate is a liar.
  Whoever tells lies is a fool.

¹⁹ If you talk a lot, you are sure to sin;
  if you are wise, you will keep quiet.

²⁰ The words of a good person are like pure
    silver,
but an evil person's thoughts are worth
    very little.

²¹ Good people's words will help many
    others,
  but fools will die because they don't
    have wisdom.

²² The LORD's blessing brings wealth,
  and no sorrow comes with it.

²³ A foolish person enjoys doing wrong,
  but a person with understanding enjoys
    doing what is wise.

²⁴ Evil people will get what they fear most,
  but good people will get what they want
    most.

²⁵ A storm will blow the evil person away,
  but a good person will always be safe.

²⁶ A lazy person affects the one he works for
  like vinegar on the teeth or smoke in
    the eyes.

²⁷ Whoever respects the LORD will have a
    long life,
  but the life of an evil person will be cut
    short.

²⁸ A good person can look forward to
    happiness,
  but an evil person can expect nothing.

²⁹ The LORD will protect good people
  but will ruin those who do evil.

³⁰ Good people will always be safe,
  but evil people will not remain in the
    land.

³¹ A good person says wise things,
  but a liar's tongue will be stopped.

³² Good people know the right thing to say,
  but evil people only tell lies.

11 The LORD hates dishonest scales,
  but he is pleased with honest
    weights.

² Pride leads only to shame;
  it is wise to be humble.

³ Good people will be guided by honesty;
  dishonesty will destroy those who are
    not trustworthy.

⁴ Riches will not help when it's time to
    die,

but right living will save you from
death.

⁵ The goodness of the innocent makes life
easier,
but the wicked will be destroyed by
their wickedness.

⁶ Doing right brings freedom to honest
people,
but those who are not trustworthy will
be caught by their own desires.

⁷ When the wicked die, hope dies with
them;
their hope in riches will come to
nothing.

⁸ The good person is saved from trouble;
it comes to the wicked instead.

⁹ With words an evil person can destroy a
neighbor,
but a good person will escape by being
resourceful.

FINANCES

ATTAINING FINANCIAL FREEDOM

from an eternal
perspective

PROVERBS 11:28   By Howard Dayton

Life on earth is very short, but eternity is very long. What we do with our time
counts forever. This came home to one man when he learned that one of his closest
friends, in his mid-forties, had died in a plane crash. A distinctive in the friend's life had
been that he had an eternal perspective. Over the doorway to his workout room was a
quote: *"Take care of your body as if you will live forever. Take care of your soul as if you will
die tomorrow."*

For a perspective of eternity, imagine a cable that runs in two directions. One direction
represents millions of light years as eternity-past. The other direction represents
millions of light years as eternity-future. Place a mark in the middle of that cable
to represent our brief time on earth. The challenge is, we often live as if that mark
is all there is, forgetting eternity-future. Only those who know Christ and have his
perspective can live a life that counts for eternity.

Thinking about this had an impact on one family's members as they learned God's
financial principles, which are tied to a perspective of eternity. They decided, by God's
grace, to live a modest lifestyle, to eradicate all their debt and work toward putting
themselves in a position of financial freedom so they could follow Christ in whatever
he wanted them to do. This was God's design to put them into a position to begin a
successful ministry without the necessity of a salary.

reflect: How can you develop more of an eternal perspective of life?
Go to **Ephesians 6:5-8.**

10 When good people succeed, the city is
  happy.
  When evil people die, there are shouts
  of joy.

11 Good people bless and build up their city,
  but the wicked can destroy it with their
  words.

12 People without good sense find fault with
  their neighbors,
  but those with understanding keep
  quiet.

13 Gossips can't keep secrets,
  but a trustworthy person can.

14 Without leadership a nation falls,
  but lots of good advice will save it.

15 Whoever guarantees to pay somebody
  else's loan will suffer.
  It is safer to avoid such promises.

16 A kind woman gets respect,
  but cruel men get only wealth.

17 Kind people do themselves a favor,
  but cruel people bring trouble on
  themselves.

18 An evil person really earns nothing,
  but a good person will surely be
  rewarded.

19 Those who are truly good will live,
  but those who chase after evil will die.

20 The LORD hates those with evil hearts
  but is pleased with those who are
  innocent.

21 Evil people will certainly be punished,
  but those who do right will be set free.

22 A beautiful woman without good sense
  is like a gold ring in a pig's snout.

23 Those who do right only wish for good,
  but the wicked can expect to be
  defeated by God's anger.

24 Some people give much but get back even
  more.
  Others don't give what they should and
  end up poor.

25 Whoever gives to others will get richer;
  those who help others will themselves
  be helped.

26 People curse those who keep all the grain,
  but they bless the one who is willing to
  sell it.

27 Whoever looks for good will find
  kindness,
  but whoever looks for evil will find
  trouble.

28 Those who trust in riches will be ruined,
  but a good person will be healthy like a
  green leaf.

29 Whoever brings trouble to his family
  will be left with nothing but the wind.
  A fool will be a servant to the wise.

30 A good person gives life to others;
  the wise person teaches others how to
  live.

31 Good people will be rewarded on earth,
  and the wicked and the sinners will be
  punished.

12 Anyone who loves learning accepts
  correction,
  but a person who hates being corrected
  is stupid.

2 The LORD is pleased with a good person,
  but he will punish anyone who plans
  evil.

3 Doing evil brings no safety at all,
  but a good person has safety and
  security.

4 A good wife is like a crown for her
  husband,
  but a disgraceful wife is like a disease in
  his bones.

5 The plans that good people make are fair,
  but the advice of the wicked will trick
  you.

6 The wicked talk about killing people,
  but the words of good people will save
  them.

7 Wicked people die and they are no more,
  but a good person's family continues.

8 The wisdom of the wise wins praise,
  but there is no respect for the stupid.

9 A person who is not important but has a
  servant is better off

than someone who acts important but has no food.

¹⁰ Good people take care of their animals,
   but even the kindest acts of the wicked are cruel.

¹¹ Those who work their land will have plenty of food,
   but the one who chases empty dreams is not wise.

¹² The wicked want what other evil people have stolen,
   but good people want to give what they have to others.

¹³ Evil people are trapped by their evil talk,
   but good people stay out of trouble.

¹⁴ People will be rewarded for what they say,
   and they will also be rewarded for what they do.

¹⁵ Fools think they are doing right,
   but the wise listen to advice.

¹⁶ Fools quickly show that they are upset,
   but the wise ignore insults.

¹⁷ An honest witness tells the truth,
   but a dishonest witness tells lies.

¹⁸ Careless words stab like a sword,
   but wise words bring healing.

¹⁹ Truth will continue forever,
   but lies are only for a moment.

FAMILY

A FAMILY CHANGED

the "hold your tongue" rule

PROVERBS 12:14

When God speaks, things happen. God's speech brought the world into existence. We are the products of his words. And God always speaks the truth. That's why God tells us that the words from our mouths are very important in life. You were made in his image and likeness, and that image should reflect its Creator.

Life and death are in the power of your tongue, the Bible says. It's possible to harm and even kill another person with words. Therefore, learn the "hold your tongue" rule. If the kids tell you they wrecked the car or a customer loudly expresses his or her discontentment, try holding your tongue whenever the words about to come out of your mouth could potentially ruin a relationship.

When we speak without considering the image of God in ourselves and in the ones we address, we can crush their spirits. Yet, God's words are uplifting and as sweet as honey. Likewise, our speech can reflect the grace of God to our children. We have the awesome opportunity to speak life into our surroundings. Whatever you want for your family, business, and relationships, speak into existence!

reflect: Proclaim life to yourself and all those around you on a daily basis.
Go to **Proverbs 13:1.**

²⁰ Those who plan evil are full of lies,
  but those who plan peace are happy.

²¹ No harm comes to a good person,
  but an evil person's life is full of trouble.

²² The LORD hates those who tell lies
  but is pleased with those who keep
  their promises.

²³ Wise people keep what they know to
  themselves,

but fools can't keep from showing how
  foolish they are.

²⁴ Hard workers will become leaders,
  but those who are lazy will be
  slaves.

²⁵ Worry is a heavy load,
  but a kind word cheers you up.

²⁶ Good people take advice from their
  friends,

THE LIFE YOU WERE BORN TO LIVE

fitness, family, and fun

FITNESS

By Leon Fontaine

PROVERBS 12:25

Life with God is incredible—being part of a life-giving church, exploring and learning the Word of God, and loving him is awesome, but it doesn't just end there . . . there's something vital missing!

It's very important that the areas of your life be prioritized. Faith always comes first, but then, secondly, you've got to stay healthy to live long and enjoy life! Are you looking after your physical health with the same intensity as your spiritual health? God wants you to be healthy and whole—in spirit, mind, *and* body.

You've got to change what's become normal to you and take care of yourself. Improper diet and poor fitness routines have to change. And when you're fit and in shape, you will then be able to have an exciting and long life, enjoying and taking care of yourself and your family!

Learn to appreciate and delight in the life that God has given you! Ask yourself: When is the last time I had a good laugh? God designed laughter, and Jesus came to bring exceeding joy. He was irresistible, and people couldn't help but follow him! Be full of joy, and have fun wherever you go! Having fun and laughing often multiplies peace and strengthens not only yourself, but also everyone around you.

Be healthy. Lighten up! God created our senses of humor, so go ahead and smile—grin, laugh, giggle, chuckle, burst out laughing. Have fun, be creative, and do something!

reflect: How can you make sure to have fun more often?
Go to **Proverbs 17:22.**

but an evil person is easily led to do wrong.

27 The lazy catch no food to cook,
but a hard worker will have great wealth.

28 Doing what is right is the way to life,
but there is another way that leads to death.

13 Wise children take their parents' advice,
but whoever makes fun of wisdom won't listen to correction.

2 People will be rewarded for what they say,

but those who can't be trusted want only violence.

3 Those who are careful about what they say protect their lives,
but whoever speaks without thinking will be ruined.

4 The lazy will not get what they want,
but those who work hard will.

5 Good people hate what is false,
but the wicked do shameful and disgraceful things.

6 Doing what is right protects the honest person,
but doing evil ruins the sinner.

A FAMILY CHANGED

FAMILY

choosing friends

PROVERBS 13:1

Do you want to make a powerful difference in the lives of your children? Then pray for their friends. They influence your child's development in all sorts of ways. Pray for the spirit of wisdom to help your children choose the friends who are honoring to the Lord and will help them walk obediently. Ask the Holy Spirit for discernment in influencing and guiding your children.

Encourage them to stay away from foolish people who will lead them in paths of destruction. Pray that they will listen to God's voice when it is time to make choices. When you do this, you will be following the good advice of Solomon. And God will smile.

Today's peer pressure is so great that parents may feel as if they have no real power against it. But God says otherwise. The sovereign God we serve is Lord of all relationships, including the friends of your children. Prayer is the real source of protection for your child. A parent's job is not done until the child's world is securely placed in the Father's hands. Take up the challenge. Bring every influence to God's throne in prayer.

reflect: Pray that your children will make good decisions and choose their friends wisely.

Go to **FAMILY:** "Authority Over Darkness Begins at Home" at **1 Samuel 15:22–23.**

7 Some people pretend to be rich but really
　　have nothing.
　　Others pretend to be poor but really are
　　wealthy.

8 The rich may have to pay a ransom for
　　their lives,
　　but the poor will face no such danger.

9 Good people can look forward to a bright
　　future,
　　but the future of the wicked is like a
　　flame going out.

10 Pride only leads to arguments,
　　but those who take advice are wise.

11 Money that comes easily disappears
　　quickly,
　　but money that is gathered little by little
　　will grow.

12 It is sad not to get what you hoped for.
　　But wishes that come true are like
　　eating fruit from the tree of life.

13 Those who reject what they are taught
　　will pay for it,
　　but those who obey what they are told
　　will be rewarded.

14 The teaching of a wise person gives life.
　　It is like a fountain that can save people
　　from death.

15 People with good understanding will be
　　well liked,
　　but the lives of those who are not
　　trustworthy are hard.

16 Every wise person acts with good sense,
　　but fools show how foolish they are.

17 A wicked messenger brings nothing but
　　trouble,
　　but a trustworthy one makes everything
　　right.

18 A person who refuses correction will end
　　up poor and disgraced,
　　but the one who accepts correction will
　　be honored.

19 It is so good when wishes come true,
　　but fools hate to stop doing evil.

20 Spend time with the wise and you will
　　become wise,
　　but the friends of fools will suffer.

21 Trouble always comes to sinners,
　　but good people enjoy success.

22 Good people leave their wealth to their
　　grandchildren,
　　but a sinner's wealth is stored up for
　　good people.

23 A poor person's field might produce
　　plenty of food,
　　but others often steal it away.

24 If you do not punish your children, you
　　don't love them,
　　but if you love your children, you will
　　correct them.

25 Good people have enough to eat,
　　but the wicked will go hungry.

14 A wise woman strengthens her family,
　　but a foolish woman destroys hers
　　by what she does.

2 People who live good lives respect the
　　LORD,
　　but those who live evil lives don't.

3 Fools will be punished for their proud
　　words,
　　but the words of the wise will protect
　　them.

4 When there are no oxen, no food is in the
　　barn.
　　But with a strong ox, much grain can be
　　grown.

5 A truthful witness does not lie,
　　but a false witness tells nothing but lies.

6 Those who make fun of wisdom look for it
　　and do not find it,
　　but knowledge comes easily to those
　　with understanding.

7 Stay away from fools,
　　because they can't teach you anything.

8 A wise person will understand what to do,
　　but a foolish person is dishonest.

9 Fools don't care if they sin,
　　but honest people work at being right.

10 No one else can know your sadness,
　　and strangers cannot share your joy.

11 The wicked person's house will be
　　destroyed,

but a good person's tent will still be
standing.

¹² Some people think they are doing
right,
but in the end it leads to death.

¹³ Someone who is laughing may be sad
inside,
and joy may end in sadness.

¹⁴ Evil people will be paid back for their evil
ways,

and good people will be rewarded for
their good ones.

¹⁵ Fools will believe anything,
but the wise think about what they do.

¹⁶ Wise people are careful and stay out of
trouble,
but fools are careless and quick to
act.

¹⁷ Someone with a quick temper does
foolish things,

AUTHORITY OVER DARKNESS BEGINS AT HOME

FAMILY

life as cake

PROVERBS 14:26

The movie character Forrest Gump famously said, **"Life is like a box of chocolates.
You never know what you are going to get."** Yet, this statement is misleading, and
believing it is destroying humanity. As long as we continue thinking that life is a flip of a
coin, we will likely have no better than an even chance of having a successful family life.

We need to change the metaphor. We must begin to look at our life like baking a
cake. Imagine what would happen if we just guessed at the ingredients and the
measurements when we baked a cake. Failure would be certain. But if we use a recipe,
we can always bake something tasty.

Family success is exactly like baking a cake. There are certain ingredients that must
be present. It is also very important to make sure there is a proper amount of each
ingredient. To make a family rise to the occasion of life we must have proper balance in
these areas:

• Spending time with your spouse without the children.

• Spending quality time with your children individually.

• Discovering the plans and purposes God has created for each member's life.

• Developing each family member's God-given passion in life and ministry.

reflect: Acknowledge God as the one who brings all the ingredients of life together.
Go to **Proverbs 15:4.**

but someone with understanding
remains calm.

18 Fools are rewarded with nothing but more
foolishness,
but the wise are rewarded with
knowledge.

19 Evil people will bow down to those who
are good;
the wicked will bow down at the door
of those who do right.

20 The poor are rejected, even by their
neighbors,
but the rich have many friends.

21 It is a sin to hate your neighbor,
but being kind to the needy brings
happiness.

22 Those who make evil plans will be
ruined,
but those who plan to do good will be
loved and trusted.

23 Those who work hard make a profit,
but those who only talk will be poor.

24 Wise people are rewarded with
wealth,
but fools only get more foolishness.

25 A truthful witness saves lives,
but a false witness is a traitor.

26 Those who respect the LORD will have
security,
and their children will be protected.

27 Respect for the LORD gives life.
It is like a fountain that can save people
from death.

28 A king is honored when he has many
people to rule,
but a prince is ruined if he has none.

29 Patient people have great understanding,
but people with quick tempers show
their foolishness.

30 Peace of mind means a healthy body,
but jealousy will rot your bones.

31 Whoever mistreats the poor insults their
Maker,
but whoever is kind to the needy
honors God.

32 The wicked are ruined by their own
evil,
but those who do right are protected
even in death.

33 Wisdom lives in those with
understanding,
and even fools recognize it.

34 Doing what is right makes a nation great,
but sin will bring disgrace to any
people.

35 A king is pleased with a wise servant,
but he will become angry with one who
causes him shame.

15 A gentle answer will calm a person's
anger,
but an unkind answer will cause more
anger.

2 Wise people use knowledge when they
speak,
but fools pour out foolishness.

3 The LORD's eyes see everything;
he watches both evil and good people.

4 As a tree gives fruit, healing words give
life,
but dishonest words crush the spirit.

5 Fools reject their parents' correction,
but anyone who accepts correction is
wise.

6 Much wealth is in the houses of good
people,
but evil people get nothing but trouble.

7 Wise people use their words to spread
knowledge,
but there is no knowledge in the
thoughts of fools.

8 The LORD hates the sacrifice that the
wicked offer,
but he likes the prayers of honest
people.

9 The LORD hates what evil people do,
but he loves those who do what is right.

10 The person who quits doing what is right
will be punished,
and the one who hates to be corrected
will die.

¹¹ The Lᴏʀᴅ knows what is happening in the
   world of the dead,
   so he surely knows the thoughts of the
   living.

¹² Those who make fun of wisdom don't like
   to be corrected;
   they will not ask the wise for advice.

¹³ Happiness makes a person smile,
   but sadness can break a person's spirit.

¹⁴ People with understanding want more
   knowledge,
   but fools just want more foolishness.

¹⁵ Every day is hard for those who suffer,
   but a happy heart is like a continual
   feast.

¹⁶ It is better to be poor and respect the
   Lᴏʀᴅ
   than to be wealthy and have much
   trouble.

¹⁷ It is better to eat vegetables with those
   who love you
   than to eat meat with those who hate
   you.

¹⁸ People with quick tempers cause trouble,
   but those who control their tempers
   stop a quarrel.

¹⁹ A lazy person's life is like a patch of
   thorns,
   but an honest person's life is like a
   smooth highway.

FAMILY

AUTHORITY OVER DARKNESS BEGINS AT HOME

positive
communication

PROVERBS 15:4   By Jimmy Evans

Words are very powerful. Because of this, the Bible is full of directives concerning
the manner in which we communicate. In Matthew 12:36–37, Jesus warns,
"People will be responsible for every careless thing they have said. The words you have
said will be used to judge you." This scripture surprises many people because they
think that words can be used casually without consequence.

Another very significant scripture related to the power of communication is Proverbs
18:21. It says, "What you say can mean life or death. Those who speak with care will
be rewarded." All of us have experienced pain by the words someone has spoken to
us. In fact, some of the deepest wounds we've had came from the careless, insensitive
speech of the people close to us.

Many people live in families where words are used to hurt and destroy. Sarcasm,
criticism, verbal abuse, shame, and anger all manifest themselves as negative forces
that kill relationships. As easily as words can kill, they can also bring life. The choice is
ours, moment by moment.

reflect: How can you change your speech to better reflect your values?
Go to **Proverbs 18:21.**

20 Wise children make their father happy,
   but foolish children disrespect their
   mother.

21 A person without wisdom enjoys being
   foolish,
   but someone with understanding does
   what is right.

22 Plans fail without good advice,
   but they succeed with the advice of
   many others.

23 People enjoy giving good advice.
   Saying the right word at the right time
   is so pleasing.

24 Wise people's lives get better and better.
   They avoid whatever would cause their
   death.

25 The LORD will tear down the proud
   person's house,
   but he will protect the widow's
   property.

26 The LORD hates evil thoughts
   but is pleased with kind words.

27 Greedy people bring trouble to their
   families,
   but the person who can't be paid to do
   wrong will live.

28 Good people think before they answer,
   but the wicked simply pour out evil.

29 The LORD does not listen to the wicked,
   but he hears the prayers of those who
   do right.

30 Good news makes you feel better.
   Your happiness will show in your eyes.

31 If you listen to correction to improve your
   life,
   you will live among the wise.

32 Those who refuse correction hate
   themselves,
   but those who accept correction gain
   understanding.

33 Respect for the LORD will teach you
   wisdom.
   If you want to be honored, you must be
   humble.

16 People may make plans in their minds,
   but only the LORD can make them
   come true.

2 You may believe you are doing right,
   but the LORD will judge your reasons.

3 Depend on the LORD in whatever you do,
   and your plans will succeed.

4 The LORD makes everything go as he
   pleases.
   He has even prepared a day of disaster
   for evil people.

5 The LORD hates those who are proud.
   They will surely be punished.

6 Love and truth bring forgiveness of sin.
   By respecting the LORD you will avoid
   evil.

7 When people live so that they please the
   LORD,
   even their enemies will make peace
   with them.

8 It is better to be poor and right
   than to be wealthy and dishonest.

9 People may make plans in their minds,
   but the LORD decides what they will do.

10 The words of a king are like a message
   from God,
   so his decisions should be fair.

11 The LORD wants honest balances and
   scales;
   all the weights are his work.

12 Kings hate those who do wrong,
   because governments only continue if
   they are fair.

13 Kings like honest people;
   they value someone who speaks the
   truth.

14 An angry king can put someone to death,
   so a wise person will try to make him
   happy.

15 A smiling king can give people life;
   his kindness is like a spring shower.

16 It is better to get wisdom than gold,
   and to choose understanding rather
   than silver!

¹⁷ Good people stay away from evil.
   By watching what they do, they protect
   their lives.

¹⁸ Pride leads to destruction;
   a proud attitude brings ruin.

¹⁹ It is better to be humble and be with those
   who suffer
   than to share stolen property with the
   proud.

²⁰ Whoever listens to what is taught will
   succeed,

and whoever trusts the LORD will be
   happy.

²¹ The wise are known for their
   understanding.
   Their pleasant words make them better
   teachers.

²² Understanding is like a fountain which
   gives life to those who use it,
   but foolishness brings punishment to
   fools.

²³ Wise people's minds tell them what to say,

MENTORING WORLD CHANGERS FOR CHRIST

FUTURE

from good
to great

PROVERBS 16:18–19   By Bill McCartney

Jim Collins wrote a best-seller called *From Good to Great* on how to make a
company great. He researched 1,435 Fortune 500 companies. His criteria for
greatness: you had to outdistance the competition and triple your productivity for
fifteen consecutive years. He listed eleven companies that had done that.

Then he asked an obvious question: What did these companies have in common? He
found that their leaders had two unmistakable qualities. One of those qualities was
humility. The leaders made sure everyone shared in the success, but when anything
went bad, they looked at themselves first, instead of pointing fingers.

The origin of the word "humility" means "harnessed power." Originally, a humility was
the implement put on horses in chariot races to get them to run together. If someone is
genuinely humble, he is a person you can follow. On the other hand, if humility is all he
has, you won't follow him for very long.

The other quality of these leaders was resolve. It didn't matter what had happened in
the past; they could get up and bring fresh fire to their work. Past failures did not keep
them down. The first mark of leadership is one who can lead and motivate himself. If a
leader has focus, you can follow him. A leader can help you do what you can't do alone.
Great leadership is all about a balance between humility and resolve. "Good to great" is
found in people who have this balance in their lives.

---

reflect: Who in your life exemplifies good leadership characteristics?
Go to **2 Thessalonians 3:5.**

and that helps them be better teachers.

24 Pleasant words are like a honeycomb, making people happy and healthy.

25 Some people think they are doing right, but in the end it leads to death.

26 The workers' hunger helps them, because their desire to eat makes them work.

27 Useless people make evil plans, and their words are like a burning fire.

28 A useless person causes trouble, and a gossip ruins friendships.

29 Cruel people trick their neighbors and lead them to do wrong.

30 Someone who winks is planning evil, and the one who grins is planning something wrong.

31 Gray hair is like a crown of honor; it is earned by living a good life.

32 Patience is better than strength. Controlling your temper is better than capturing a city.

33 People throw lots to make a decision, but the answer comes from the LORD.

17 It is better to eat a dry crust of bread in peace than to have a feast where there is quarreling.

2 A wise servant will rule over the master's disgraceful child and will even inherit a share of what the master leaves his children.

3 A hot furnace tests silver and gold, but the LORD tests hearts.

4 Evil people listen to evil words. Liars pay attention to cruel words.

5 Whoever mistreats the poor insults their Maker; whoever enjoys someone's trouble will be punished.

6 Old people are proud of their grandchildren, and children are proud of their parents.

7 Fools should not be proud, and rulers should not be liars.

8 Some people think they can pay others to do anything they ask. They think it will work every time.

9 Whoever forgives someone's sin makes a friend, but gossiping about the sin breaks up friendships.

10 A wise person will learn more from a warning than a fool will learn from a hundred lashings.

11 Disobedient people look only for trouble, so a cruel messenger will be sent against them.

12 It is better to meet a bear robbed of her cubs than to meet a fool doing foolish things.

13 Whoever gives evil in return for good will always have trouble at home.

14 Starting a quarrel is like a leak in a dam, so stop it before a fight breaks out.

15 The LORD hates both of these things: freeing the guilty and punishing the innocent.

16 It won't do a fool any good to try to buy wisdom, because he doesn't have the ability to be wise.

17 A friend loves you all the time, and a brother helps in time of trouble.

18 It is not wise to promise to pay what your neighbor owes.

19 Whoever loves to argue loves to sin. Whoever brags a lot is asking for trouble.

20 A person with an evil heart will find no success, and the person whose words are evil will get into trouble.

21 It is sad to have a foolish child; there is no joy in being the parent of a fool.

²² A happy heart is like good medicine,
    but a broken spirit drains your strength.

²³ When the wicked accept money to do
    wrong
    there can be no justice.

²⁴ The person with understanding is always
    looking for wisdom,
    but the mind of a fool wanders
    everywhere.

²⁵ Foolish children make their father sad
    and cause their mother great sorrow.

²⁶ It is not good to punish the innocent
    or to beat leaders for being honest.

²⁷ The wise say very little,
    and those with understanding stay
    calm.

²⁸ Even fools seem to be wise if they keep
    quiet;

THE LIFE YOU WERE BORN TO LIVE

FITNESS

healthy laughter

PROVERBS 17:22

By Bob Russell

Aren't you glad God gave us a sense of humor? Aren't you thankful that he gave us the capacity to laugh? Humor can bring comic relief, grab attention, assist unity, and bring comfort to troubled hearts. "A happy heart is like good medicine" (Proverbs 17:22).

In Psalm 126, the Israelites had experienced a great victory. They were returning from a long captivity to reoccupy Jerusalem. They celebrated their restored community and liberty with exultant laughter and songs of joy. Other nations saw the celebration and knew it was all made possible by the God of the Israelites.

As Christians, we have much to celebrate. Any time a loving couple marries, a baby is born, a financial goal is reached, a new believer is baptized, or a respected couple celebrates many years of marriage, there should be healthy laughter in the church. This genuine, healthy laughter among Christians is a positive witness to unbelievers. Laughter attracts attention and draws others like a magnet, just as other nations noticed the laughter of the returning Israelites. This kind of laughter glorifies God.

Solomon said, "There is a time to cry and a time to laugh" (Ecclesiastes 3:4). Even though the church may have plenty to cry about, Christians should not miss any opportunity to celebrate with healthy laughter. Look for, and take advantage of, opportunities to celebrate joyous occasions and give the glory to God.

reflect: When was the last time you enjoyed some hearty laughter?
Go to **Proverbs 22:6.**

if they don't speak, they appear to understand.

18 Unfriendly people are selfish and hate all good sense.

² Fools do not want to understand anything. They only want to tell others what they think.

³ Do something evil, and people won't like you.
Do something shameful, and they will make fun of you.

⁴ Spoken words can be like deep water, but wisdom is like a flowing stream.

⁵ It is not good to honor the wicked or to be unfair to the innocent.

AUTHORITY OVER DARKNESS BEGINS AT HOME

communication
in marriage

FAMILY

By Jimmy Evans   PROVERBS 18:21

Communication is one of the most critical issues that determines the success of a marriage. You cannot have an intimate marriage without open, honest communication. Communication is the means by which to share information and reach agreement about important issues, activities, and priorities. It is how we avoid and resolve conflicts.

Words are powerful. We must be careful with our words and use them for good. We fall in love because we are careful and respectful, and we fall out of love because we are careless and insensitive. We must use our words as bricks to build instead of as stones to destroy, as scalpels to heal instead of as swords to kill, and as food to nourish instead of as poison to punish.

One understanding we must have is the difference between women and men. Women have a deep *need* for communication; it is not just a *want*. This need is as great as a man's need for sex. A man opens up emotionally through sex, but if a man wants his wife to be sexually responsive, he must meet her emotional needs by communicating.

Another understanding we must have is that men are emotionally modest, while women are emotionally immodest. Women are in touch with their emotions, but men are not. Women are modest sexually, but men are modest in communication. A man needs a private and honoring atmosphere in which his wife will respect him and not repeat what he shares. Then he opens up, and genuine communication takes place.

---

reflect: How can you improve communication in your marriage?
Go to **Proverbs 20:11.**

6 The words of fools start quarrels.
    They make people want to beat them.

7 The words of fools will ruin them;
    their own words will trap them.

8 The words of a gossip are like tasty bits of
        food.
    People like to gobble them up.

9 A person who doesn't work hard
    is just like someone who destroys
        things.

10 The LORD is like a strong tower;
    those who do right can run to him for
        safety.

11 Rich people trust their wealth to protect
        them.
    They think it is like the high walls of a
        city.

12 Proud people will be ruined,
    but the humble will be honored.

13 Anyone who answers without listening
    is foolish and confused.

14 The will to live can get you through
        sickness,
    but no one can live with a broken
        spirit.

15 The mind of a person with understanding
        gets knowledge;
    the wise person listens to learn more.

16 Taking gifts to important people
    will help get you in to see them.

17 The person who tells one side of a story
        seems right,
    until someone else comes and asks
        questions.

18 Throwing lots can settle arguments
    and keep the two sides from fighting.

19 A brother who has been insulted is harder
        to win back than a walled city,
    and arguments separate people like the
        barred gates of a palace.

20 People will be rewarded for what they
        say;
    they will be rewarded by how they
        speak.

21 What you say can mean life or death.

Those who speak with care will be
    rewarded.

22 When a man finds a wife, he finds
        something good.
    It shows that the LORD is pleased with
        him.

23 The poor beg for mercy,
    but the rich give rude answers.

24 Some friends may ruin you,
    but a real friend will be more loyal than
        a brother.

19 It is better to be poor and honest
        than to be foolish and tell lies.

2 Enthusiasm without knowledge is not
        good.
    If you act too quickly, you might make a
        mistake.

3 People's own foolishness ruins their lives,
    but in their minds they blame the LORD.

4 Wealthy people are always finding more
        friends,
    but the poor lose all theirs.

5 A witness who lies will not go free;
    liars will never escape.

6 Many people want to please a leader,
    and everyone is friends with those who
        give gifts.

7 Poor people's relatives avoid them;
    even their friends stay far away.
    They run after them, begging,
    but they are gone.

8 Those who get wisdom do themselves a
        favor,
    and those who love learning will
        succeed.

9 A witness who lies will not go free,
    liars will die.

10 A fool should not live in luxury.
    A slave should not rule over princes.

11 The wise are patient;
    they will be honored if they ignore
        insults.

12 An angry king is like a roaring lion,
    but his kindness is like the dew on the
        grass.

¹³ A foolish child brings disaster to a father,
   and a quarreling wife is like dripping
   water.

¹⁴ Houses and wealth are inherited from
   parents,
   but a wise wife is a gift from the LORD.

¹⁵ Lazy people sleep a lot,
   and idle people will go hungry.

¹⁶ Those who obey the commands protect
   themselves,
   but those who are careless will die.

¹⁷ Being kind to the poor is like lending to
   the LORD;
   he will reward you for what you have
   done.

¹⁸ Correct your children while there is still
   hope;
   do not let them destroy themselves.

¹⁹ People with quick tempers will have to
   pay for it.
   If you help them out once, you will have
   to do it again.

²⁰ Listen to advice and accept correction,
   and in the end you will be wise.

²¹ People can make all kinds of plans,
   but only the LORD's plan will happen.

²² People want others to be loyal,
   so it is better to be poor than to be a liar.

²³ Those who respect the LORD will live
   and be satisfied, unbothered by trouble.

²⁴ Though the lazy person puts his hand in
   the dish,
   he won't lift the food to his mouth.

²⁵ Whip those who make fun of wisdom, and
   perhaps foolish people will gain some
   wisdom.
   Correct those with understanding, and
   they will gain knowledge.

²⁶ A child who robs his father and sends
   away his mother
   brings shame and disgrace on himself.

²⁷ Don't stop listening to correction, my
   child,
   or you will forget what you have already
   learned.

²⁸ An evil witness makes fun of fairness,
   and wicked people love what is evil.

²⁹ People who make fun of wisdom will be
   punished,
   and the backs of foolish people will be
   beaten.

20 Wine and beer make people loud
   and uncontrolled;
   it is not wise to get drunk on them.

² An angry king is like a roaring lion.
   Making him angry may cost you your
   life.

³ Foolish people are always fighting,
   but avoiding quarrels will bring you
   honor.

⁴ Lazy farmers don't plow when they
   should;
   they expect a harvest, but there is none.

⁵ People's thoughts can be like a deep well,
   but someone with understanding can
   find the wisdom there.

⁶ Many people claim to be loyal,
   but it is hard to find a trustworthy
   person.

⁷ The good people who live honest lives
   will be a blessing to their children.

⁸ When a king sits on his throne to judge,
   he knows evil when he sees it.

⁹ No one can say, "I am innocent;
   I have never done anything wrong."

¹⁰ The LORD hates both these things:
   dishonest weights and dishonest
   measures.

¹¹ Even children are known by their
   behavior;
   their actions show if they are innocent
   and good.

¹² The LORD has made both these things:
   ears to hear and eyes to see.

¹³ If you love to sleep, you will be poor.
   If you stay awake, you will have plenty
   of food.

¹⁴ Buyers say, "This is bad. It's no good."
   Then they go away and brag about what
   they bought.

15 There is gold and plenty of rubies,
  but only a few people speak with
    knowledge.

16 Take the coat of someone who promises
    to pay a stranger's debts,
  and keep it until he pays what the
    stranger owes.

17 Stolen food may taste sweet at first,

but later it will feel like a mouth full of
    gravel.

18 Get advice if you want your plans to
    work.
  If you go to war, get the advice of
    others.

19 Gossips can't keep secrets,
  so avoid people who talk too much.

FAMILY

AUTHORITY OVER DARKNESS BEGINS AT HOME

praying in advance

PROVERBS 20:11

How can anyone send kids into the world today? With all of the dangers, you'd want armed guards, or at least chaperones, to accompany them everywhere. Unfortunately, we can't do this. Even if we did, it still wouldn't be enough. Fortunately, there's a more powerful force to protect your kids above and beyond police or your presence. It is praying in advance.

Parents understand that praying for children is one of the most important responsibilities God has given them. Every godly parent wants a child to have a lasting relationship with God. But too often we forget that the chain of spiritual intervention begins long before a child is born. Godly children are the product of godly parents, and godly parents are the product of godly individuals. When your children marry, you want them to find the godly mates they need to continue the chain.

So it's never too soon to begin praying for your children's spouses. Jesus must be the first important decision your child will make. The next decision is whom they shall marry. Not only will their choice of spouse affect their own lives, but the lives of their families, as well. Choosing the wrong mate can cause pain and misery for all those involved.

So pray and ask God to bring the right person into your child's life. God will make the way for your child to meet the best possible marriage partner. If you want your child to be strong in the Lord and partnered with the right spouse, start that prayer today. Your faithfulness will help your children in the years to come.

reflect: Pray for your children and their selection of a godly spouse one day.
Go to **Proverbs 23:24.**

20 Those who curse their father or mother
    will be like a light going out in darkness.

21 Wealth inherited quickly in the beginning
    will do you no good in the end.

22 Don't say, "I'll pay you back for the wrong
    you did."
    Wait for the LORD, and he will make
    things right.

23 The LORD hates dishonest weights,
    and dishonest scales do not please him.

24 The LORD decides what a person will do;
    no one understands what his life is all
    about.

25 It's dangerous to promise something to
    God too quickly.
    After you've thought about it, it may be
    too late.

26 A wise king sorts out the evil people,
    and he punishes them as they deserve.

27 The LORD looks deep inside people
    and searches through their thoughts.

28 Loyalty and truth keep a king in power;
    he continues to rule if he is loyal.

29 The young glory in their strength,
    and the old are honored for their gray
    hair.

30 Hard punishment will get rid of evil,
    and whippings can change an evil heart.

21 The LORD can control a king's mind as
    he controls a river;
    he can direct it as he pleases.

2 You may believe you are doing right,
    but the LORD judges your reasons.

3 Doing what is right and fair
    is more important to the LORD than
    sacrifices.

4 Proud looks, proud thoughts,
    and evil actions are sin.

5 The plans of hard-working people earn a
    profit,
    but those who act too quickly become
    poor.

6 Wealth that comes from telling lies
    vanishes like a mist and leads to death.

7 The violence of the wicked will destroy
    them,
    because they refuse to do what is right.

8 Guilty people live dishonest lives,
    but honest people do right.

9 It is better to live in a corner on the roof[n]
    than inside the house with a quarreling
    wife.

10 Evil people only want to harm others.
    Their neighbors get no mercy from
    them.

11 If you punish those who make fun of
    wisdom, a foolish person may gain
    some wisdom.
    But if you teach the wise, they will get
    knowledge.

12 God, who is always right, watches the
    house of the wicked
    and brings ruin on every evil person.

13 Whoever ignores the poor when they cry
    for help
    will also cry for help and not be
    answered.

14 A secret gift will calm an angry person;
    a present given in secrecy will quiet
    great anger.

15 When justice is done, good people are
    happy,
    but evil people are ruined.

16 Whoever does not use good sense
    will end up among the dead.

17 Whoever loves pleasure will become
    poor;
    whoever loves wine and perfume will
    never be rich.

18 Wicked people will suffer instead of good
    people,
    and those who cannot be trusted will
    suffer instead of those who do right.

19 It is better to live alone in the desert
    than with a quarreling and complaining
    wife.

21:9 roof In Bible times houses were built with flat
roofs. The roof was used for drying things such as flax
and fruit. And it was used as an extra room, as a place for
worship, and as a cool place to sleep in the summer.

20 Wise people's houses are full of the best
foods and olive oil,
but fools waste everything they have.

21 Whoever tries to live right and be loyal
finds life, success, and honor.

22 A wise person can defeat a city full of
warriors
and tear down the defenses they trust
in.

23 Those who are careful about what they
say
keep themselves out of trouble.

24 People who act with stubborn pride
are called "proud," "bragger," and
"mocker."

25 Lazy people's desire for sleep will kill
them,
because they refuse to work.

26 All day long they wish for more,
but good people give without holding
back.

27 The LORD hates sacrifices brought by evil
people,
particularly when they offer them for
the wrong reasons.

28 A lying witness will be forgotten,
but a truthful witness will speak on.

29 Wicked people are stubborn,
but good people think carefully about
what they do.

30 There is no wisdom, understanding, or
advice
that can succeed against the LORD.

31 You can get the horses ready for battle,
but it is the LORD who gives the
victory.

22 Being respected is more important
than having great riches.
To be well thought of is better than
silver or gold.

2 The rich and the poor are alike
in that the LORD made them all.

3 The wise see danger ahead and avoid it,
but fools keep going and get into
trouble.

4 Respecting the LORD and not being proud
will bring you wealth, honor, and life.

5 Evil people's lives are like paths covered
with thorns and traps.
People who guard themselves don't
have such problems.

6 Train children to live the right way,
and when they are old, they will not
stray from it.

7 The rich rule over the poor,
and borrowers are servants to lenders.

8 Those who plan evil will receive trouble.
Their cruel anger will come to an end.

9 Generous people will be blessed,
because they share their food with the
poor.

10 Get rid of the one who makes fun of
wisdom.
Then fighting, quarrels, and insults will
stop.

11 Whoever loves pure thoughts and kind
words
will have even the king as a friend.

12 The LORD guards knowledge,
but he destroys false words.

13 The lazy person says, "There's a lion
outside!
I might get killed out in the street!"

14 The words of an unfaithful wife are like a
deep trap.
Those who make the LORD angry will
get caught by them.

15 Every child is full of foolishness,
but punishment can get rid of it.

16 Whoever gets rich by mistreating the
poor,
and gives presents to the wealthy, will
become poor.

OTHER WISE SAYINGS

17 Listen carefully to what wise people say;
pay attention to what I am teaching
you.

18 It will be good to keep these things in
mind
so that you are ready to repeat them.

19 I am teaching them to you now

Boys Will Be . . .

By Becky Hunter

PROVERBS 22:6

As her sons jumped on the couch, turned up the television volume as loud as it would go, ransacked the refrigerator, and tossed their popcorn in the air to see "who could juggle the most," my friend just smiled and said, "Boys will be boys."

That phrase—"boys will be boys." I had heard it before, but it bounced around in my head for days after that experience. Nothing about that scene looked quite right to me, but, as my friend graciously had pointed out, I didn't have any children—yet. "You'll see," she said.

A few years later, Joel and I had our first son, Joshua. As he neared his second birthday, our second son, Isaac, made his appearance. By the time our third son, Joel, arrived, some three years after that, I thought about that old saying, "Boys will be boys,"—and I realized it was a lie.

The truth is, boys will be *men*. Confirmation of that truth came to me in a roundabout way. One morning, as I was feeding our youngest son and watching the older two playing together, an interview with Lillian Carter came on television. "Ms. Lillian" was the mother of four. Her oldest, Jimmy, and youngest, Billy, were often in the news because Jimmy Carter was president of the United States and Billy Carter, well, suffice it to say, was not the president. His outrageous behavior, though, warranted the attention of the press.

When the interviewer asked Ms. Lillian, "To what do you attribute the difference between your son Jimmy, our president, and your son Billy?" I leaned forward to hear her response. Rocking back in her chair and crossing her arms, she spoke only after she had thoroughly pondered the question, "You know, I was just plumb worn out by the time I got to Billy."

Her answer profoundly impacted my parenting, giving me the confirmation I needed to remember that boys will be *men*. Proverbs 22:6 says it best: "Train children to live the right way, and when they are old, they will not stray from it." In other words, train them to be godly boys so that they will one day be godly men!

No, it isn't *easy*—or at least it isn't for most parents. For Joel and me, we needed a future-oriented point of view in order to deal effectively with the present behaviors and attitudes that might have limited our sons' relationship with God or with others. We needed continually to remind ourselves that each boy would one day be someone's husband, someone's father, someone's employee, someone's boss, and quite possibly someone's only look at what it means to be a Christian. We needed to stay on task and be the parents God intended, picturing each boy as the godly man we hoped he would become.

Having a vision for your child's future is powerful motivation to be faithful and consistent in child rearing. In fact, a vision is more than motivating—it is essential.

TO LEARN MORE ON WHAT THE BIBLE HAS TO SAY ABOUT **FAMILY,** READ THE SCRIPTURES AND DEVOTIONALS AT **DEUTERONOMY 6:6–9, DEUTERONOMY 7:8–15, DEUTERONOMY 12:12,** AND **NUMBERS 6:22–27.**

so that you will put your trust in the
LORD.

²⁰ I have written thirty sayings for you,
which give knowledge and good
advice.

²¹ I am teaching you true and reliable
words
so that you can give true answers to
anyone who asks.

²² Do not abuse poor people because they
are poor,

and do not take away the rights of the
needy in court.

²³ The LORD will defend them in court
and will take the life of those who take
away their rights.

²⁴ Don't make friends with quick-tempered
people
or spend time with those who have bad
tempers.

²⁵ If you do, you will be like them.
Then you will be in real danger.

THE LIFE YOU WERE BORN TO LIVE

FITNESS

a conscious person

PROVERBS 22:6

Our basic, natural human tendencies interfere with God. Some of the greatest examples of our self-destructive nature can be found in children. Most children under the age of five would perish within fifteen minutes if left alone. One reason for this is that no matter how dangerous or disgusting it is, kids have this bizarre desire to put everything inside their mouth. If you have small children or have seen them operate, then you know that anything within reach is considered fair game for an oral deposit.

As with kids, wanting to do good and healthful things is extremely unnatural for us. Good nutritional choices, exercising regularly, or improving any area of your lifestyle that deals with health, appearance, and longevity are things that you know are necessary. However, the natural tendency is not to do them or to quit even thinking about them altogether. It's as if we all move through our lives asleep or unconscious.

It is incredibly important that we discipline ourselves to set aside time on a weekly basis for objectively evaluating our results in life. This will allow us to consciously think through what we do with our time and what we put into our bodies. We want to consciously choose not to eat rubbish, to schedule exercise, and to meet our family's needs. We do not want to go through life unconsciously popping junk food, wasting time, and neglecting people in our lives who need us. The key is to wake up early and go for it!

---

reflect: Plan to awaken early enough each day to exercise and pray.
Go to **Ecclesiastes 3:1.**

26 Don't promise to pay what someone else
owes,
and don't guarantee anyone's loan.
27 If you cannot pay the loan,
your own bed may be taken right out
from under you.
28 Don't move an old stone that marks a
border,
because those stones were set up by
your ancestors.

29 Do you see people skilled in their work?
They will work for kings, not for
ordinary people.

23 If you sit down to eat with a ruler,
notice the food that is in front of
you.
2 Control yourself
if you have a big appetite.
3 Don't be greedy for his fine foods,
because that food might be a trick.

4 Don't wear yourself out trying to get rich;
be wise enough to control yourself.
5 Wealth can vanish in the wink of an eye.
It can seem to grow wings
and fly away like an eagle.

6 Don't eat the food of selfish people;
don't be greedy for their fine foods.
7 Selfish people are always worrying
about how much the food costs.
They tell you, "Eat and drink,"
but they don't really mean it.
8 You will throw up the little you have
eaten,
and you will have wasted your kind
words.

9 Don't speak to fools;
they will only ignore your wise words.

10 Don't move an old stone that marks a
border,
and don't take fields that belong to
orphans.
11 God, their defender, is strong;
he will take their side against you.

12 Remember what you are taught,
and listen carefully to words of
knowledge.

13 Don't fail to punish children.
If you spank them, they won't die.

14 If you spank them,
you will save them from death.

15 My child, if you are wise,
then I will be happy.
16 I will be so pleased
if you speak what is right.

17 Don't envy sinners,
but always respect the LORD.
18 Then you will have hope for the future,
and your wishes will come true.

19 Listen, my child, and be wise.
Keep your mind on what is right.
20 Don't drink too much wine
or eat too much food.
21 Those who drink and eat too much
become poor.
They sleep too much and end up
wearing rags.

22 Listen to your father, who gave you life,
and do not forget your mother when
she is old.
23 Learn the truth and never reject it.
Get wisdom, self-control, and
understanding.
24 The father of a good child is very happy;
parents who have wise children are
glad because of them.
25 Make your father and mother happy;
give your mother a reason to be glad.

26 My son, pay attention to me,
and watch closely what I do.
27 A prostitute is as dangerous as a deep pit,
and an unfaithful wife is like a narrow
well.
28 They ambush you like robbers
and cause many men to be unfaithful to
their wives.

29 Who has trouble? Who has pain?
Who fights? Who complains?
Who has unnecessary bruises?
Who has bloodshot eyes?
30 It is people who drink too much wine,
who try out all different kinds of strong
drinks.
31 Don't stare at the wine when it is red,
when it sparkles in the cup,
when it goes down smoothly.
32 Later it bites like a snake
with poison in its fangs.
33 Your eyes will see strange sights,

and your mind will be confused.
³⁴ You will feel dizzy as if you're in a storm
on the ocean,
as if you're on top of a ship's sails.
³⁵ You will think, "They hit me, but I'm not
hurt.
They beat me up, but I don't remember
it.
I wish I could wake up.
Then I would get another drink."

24 Don't envy evil people
or try to be friends with them.
² Their minds are always planning violence,
and they always talk about making
trouble.

³ It takes wisdom to have a good family,
and it takes understanding to make it
strong.
⁴ It takes knowledge to fill a home
with rare and beautiful treasures.
⁵ Wise people have great power,
and those with knowledge have great
strength.
⁶ So you need advice when you go to war.
If you have lots of good advice, you will
win.

FAMILY

AUTHORITY OVER DARKNESS BEGINS AT HOME

life as an open book

PROVERBS 23:24

Do you want to rejoice over your child? Solomon suggests that the secret to happiness over your children is not found in what they do but in who *you* are. If you live a life of obedience to the Lord so that your children see the hand of God on your life, God will honor you with children who will reflect your obedience. Training your children in the way of God is first and foremost about disciplining yourself to be his follower. Paraphrasing a thought by St. Francis of Assisi, teach your kids about God whenever possible, and when necessary, use words.

There are many stories in the Bible about parents who failed to live according to God's righteousness. The result was usually disaster for their children. God is gracious, and a child may still find the right path without a godly example. But the lives of parents teach more to children than any other lessons. If you want children of righteousness, be righteous yourself.

God's plan for happy families is quite simple. God does not ask us to change the lives of others. He knows that the only life we really control is our own. The life we live is the book our children will read. Nothing is more effective as a training tool for children than the behavior of parents. As we commit ourselves to following the direction of God in our own lives, we will be able to rejoice over our children.

reflect: Live godly before your children today, and sow the seeds of contentment.
Go to **FAMILY:** "Understanding Authority" at **Romans 1:28-32.**

they are like sparrows or swallows that fly around and never land.

3 Whips are for horses, and harnesses are for donkeys,
  so paddles are good for fools.

4 Don't answer fools when they speak foolishly,
  or you will be just like them.

5 Answer fools when they speak foolishly,
  or they will think they are really wise.

6 Sending a message by a foolish person
  is like cutting off your feet or drinking poison.

7 A wise saying spoken by a fool
  is as useless as the legs of a crippled person.

8 Giving honor to a foolish person
  is like tying a stone in a slingshot.

9 A wise saying spoken by a fool
  is like a thorn stuck in the hand of a drunk.

10 Hiring a foolish person or anyone just passing by
  is like an archer shooting at just anything.

11 A fool who repeats his foolishness
  is like a dog that goes back to what it has thrown up.

12 There is more hope for a foolish person
  than for those who think they are wise.

13 The lazy person says, "There's a lion in the road!
  There's a lion in the streets!"

14 Like a door turning back and forth on its hinges,
  the lazy person turns over and over in bed.

15 Lazy people may put their hands in the dish,
  but they are too tired to lift the food to their mouths.

16 The lazy person thinks he is wiser
  than seven people who give sensible answers.

17 Interfering in someone else's quarrel as you pass by
  is like grabbing a dog by the ears.

18 Like a madman shooting
  deadly, burning arrows

19 is the one who tricks a neighbor
  and then says, "I was just joking."

20 Without wood, a fire will go out,
  and without gossip, quarreling will stop.

21 Just as charcoal and wood keep a fire going,
  a quarrelsome person keeps an argument going.

22 The words of a gossip are like tasty bits of food;
  people like to gobble them up.

23 Kind words from a wicked mind
  are like a shiny coating on a clay pot.

24 Those who hate you may try to fool you with their words,
  but in their minds they are planning evil.

25 People's words may be kind, but don't believe them,
  because their minds are full of evil thoughts.

26 Lies can hide hate,
  but the evil will be plain to everyone.

27 Whoever digs a pit for others will fall into it.
  Whoever tries to roll a boulder down on others will be crushed by it.

28 Liars hate the people they hurt,
  and false praise can ruin others.

27

Don't brag about tomorrow;
  you don't know what may happen then.

2 Don't praise yourself. Let someone else do it.
  Let the praise come from a stranger and not from your own mouth.

3 Stone is heavy, and sand is weighty,
  but a complaining fool is worse than either.

4 Anger is cruel and destroys like a flood,
  but no one can put up with jealousy!

⁵ It is better to correct someone openly
than to have love and not show it.

⁶ The slap of a friend can be trusted to help
you,
but the kisses of an enemy are nothing
but lies.

⁷ When you are full, not even honey tastes
good,
but when you are hungry, even
something bitter tastes sweet.

⁸ A person who leaves his home
is like a bird that leaves its nest.

⁹ The sweet smell of perfume and oils is
pleasant,
and so is good advice from a friend.

¹⁰ Don't forget your friend or your parent's
friend.
Don't always go to your family for help
when trouble comes.

FAMILY

UNDERSTANDING AUTHORITY

extraordinary
harmony

PROVERBS 27:17   By Larry Stockstill

People who have extraordinary relationships have problems just like everybody
else, but they have learned how to face their problems head-on to resolve them
in a godly manner. Everyone's natural tendency when facing a problem is to become
defensive and to blame others. You want the other person to change, not you. God
intends for your relationships, however, to refine both of you.

When iron sharpens iron, the contact and friction between two surfaces causes
sparks to fly. When you are in relationships, sparks fly when other people rub against
the grain, like a file sharpening a blade, to smooth out your rough edges. This is not
necessarily bad; just do not give in to hatred or pride.

God sends people into your life to develop your character. God is going to bring people
into your life to challenge you in areas where you have flaws. If you are impatient, he
might send people to try your patience. If you are overly regimented, he may surround
you with very disorganized and impulsive people. Whatever your blemish, he wants to
polish your character and hone your cutting edge.

It is easier to stop resenting conflict and cooperate when you learn to recognize God's
hand at work. He has given you the people around you to sharpen and refine you. He
does not mean for you to live in constant conflict; he wants all your conflicts to find
solutions at the cross. Facing and settling conflicts in an open and caring manner allows
God to strengthen and restore your relationships.

---

reflect: How do you deal with people who upset you?
Go to **Ecclesiastes 4:12.**

A neighbor close by is better than a
family far away.

11 Be wise, my child, and make me happy.
Then I can respond to any insult.

12 The wise see danger ahead and avoid it,
but fools keep going and get into
trouble.

13 Take the coat of someone who promises
to pay a stranger's loan,
and keep it until he pays what the
stranger owes.

14 If you loudly greet your neighbor early in
the morning,
he will think of it as a curse.

15 A quarreling wife is as bothersome
as a continual dripping on a rainy day.
16 Stopping her is like stopping the wind
or trying to grab oil in your hand.

17 As iron sharpens iron,
so people can improve each other.

18 Whoever tends a fig tree gets to eat its
fruit,
and whoever takes care of his master
will receive honor.

19 As water reflects your face,
so your mind shows what kind of
person you are.

20 People will never stop dying and being
destroyed,
and they will never stop wanting more
than they have.

21 A hot furnace tests silver and gold,
and people are tested by the praise they
receive.

22 Even if you ground up a foolish person
like grain in a bowl,
you couldn't remove the foolishness.

23 Be sure you know how your sheep are
doing,
and pay attention to the condition of
your cattle.
24 Riches will not go on forever,
nor do governments go on forever.
25 Bring in the hay, and let the new grass
appear.
Gather the grass from the hills.
26 Make clothes from the lambs' wool,

and sell some goats to buy a field.
27 There will be plenty of goat's milk
to feed you and your family
and to make your servant girls healthy.

28 Evil people run even though no one
is chasing them,
but good people are as brave as a lion.

2 When a country is lawless, it has one ruler
after another;
but when it is led by a leader with
understanding and knowledge, it
continues strong.

3 Rulers who mistreat the poor
are like a hard rain that destroys the
crops.

4 Those who disobey what they have been
taught praise the wicked,
but those who obey what they have
been taught are against them.

5 Evil people do not understand justice,
but those who follow the LORD
understand it completely.

6 It is better to be poor and innocent
than to be rich and wicked.

7 Children who obey what they have been
taught are wise,
but friends of troublemakers disgrace
their parents.

8 Some people get rich by overcharging
others,
but their wealth will be given to those
who are kind to the poor.

9 If you refuse to obey what you have been
taught,
your prayers will not be heard.

10 Those who lead good people to do wrong
will be ruined by their own evil,
but the innocent will be rewarded with
good things.

11 Rich people may think they are wise,
but the poor with understanding will
prove them wrong.

12 When good people triumph, there is great
happiness,
but when the wicked get control,
everybody hides.

13 If you hide your sins, you will not succeed.
If you confess and reject them, you will receive mercy.

14 Those who are always respectful will be happy,
but those who are stubborn will get into trouble.

15 A wicked ruler is as dangerous to poor people
as a roaring lion or a charging bear.

16 A ruler without wisdom will be cruel,
but the one who refuses to take dishonest money will rule a long time.

17 Don't help those who are guilty of murder;
let them run until they die.

18 Innocent people will be kept safe,
but those who are dishonest will suddenly be ruined.

19 Those who work their land will have plenty of food,
but the ones who chase empty dreams instead will end up poor.

20 A truthful person will have many blessings,
but those eager to get rich will be punished.

21 It is not good for a judge to take sides,
but some will sin for only a piece of bread.

22 Selfish people are in a hurry to get rich
and do not realize they soon will be poor.

23 Those who correct others will later be liked
more than those who give false praise.

24 Whoever robs father or mother
and says, "It's not wrong,"
is just like someone who destroys things.

25 A greedy person causes trouble,
but the one who trusts the LORD will succeed.

26 Those who trust in themselves are foolish,
but those who live wisely will be kept safe.

27 Whoever gives to the poor will have everything he needs,
but the one who ignores the poor will receive many curses.

28 When the wicked get control, everybody hides,
but when they die, good people do well.

29 Whoever is stubborn after being corrected many times
will suddenly be hurt beyond cure.

2 When good people do well, everyone is happy,
but when evil people rule, everyone groans.

3 Those who love wisdom make their parents happy,
but friends of prostitutes waste their money.

4 If a king is fair, he makes his country strong,
but if he takes gifts dishonestly, he tears his country down.

5 Those who give false praise to their neighbors
are setting a trap for them.

6 Evil people are trapped by their own sin,
but good people can sing and be happy.

7 Good people care about justice for the poor,
but the wicked are not concerned.

8 People who make fun of wisdom cause trouble in a city,
but wise people calm anger down.

9 When a wise person takes a foolish person to court,
the fool only shouts or laughs, and there is no peace.

10 Murderers hate an honest person
and try to kill those who do right.

11 Foolish people lose their tempers,
but wise people control theirs.

12 If a ruler pays attention to lies,
all his officers will become wicked.

13 The poor person and the cruel person are
alike
in that the LORD gave eyes to both of
them.

14 If a king judges poor people fairly,
his government will continue forever.

15 Correction and punishment make
children wise,
but those left alone will disgrace their
mother.

16 When there are many wicked people,
there is much sin,
but those who do right will see them
destroyed.

17 Correct your children, and you will be
proud;
they will give you satisfaction.

18 Where there is no word from God, people
are uncontrolled,
but those who obey what they have
been taught are happy.

19 Words alone cannot correct a servant,
because even if they understand, they
won't respond.

20 Do you see people who speak too quickly?
There is more hope for a foolish person
than for them.

21 If you spoil your servants when they are
young,
they will bring you grief later on.

22 An angry person causes trouble;
a person with a quick temper sins a
lot.

23 Pride will ruin people,
but those who are humble will be
honored.

24 Partners of thieves are their own worst
enemies.
If they have to testify in court, they are
afraid to say anything.

25 Being afraid of people can get you into
trouble,
but if you trust the LORD, you will be
safe.

26 Many people want to speak to a ruler,
but justice comes only from the LORD.

27 Good people hate those who are
dishonest,
and the wicked hate those who are
honest.

WISE WORDS FROM AGUR

30 These are the words of Agur son of
Jakeh.
This is his message to Ithiel and Ucal:

2 "I am the most stupid person there is,
and I have no understanding.

3 I have not learned to be wise,
and I don't know much about God, the
Holy One.

4 Who has gone up to heaven and come
back down?
Who can hold the wind in his hand?
Who can gather up the waters in his coat?
Who has set in place the ends of the
earth?
What is his name or his son's name?
Tell me, if you know!

5 "Every word of God is true.
He guards those who come to him for
safety.

6 Do not add to his words,
or he will correct you and prove you are
a liar.

7 "I ask two things from you, LORD.
Don't refuse me before I die.

8 Keep me from lying and being dishonest.
And don't make me either rich or
poor;
just give me enough food for each day.

9 If I have too much, I might reject you
and say, 'I don't know the LORD.'
If I am poor, I might steal
and disgrace the name of my God.

10 "Do not say bad things about servants to
their masters,
or they will curse you, and you will
suffer for it.

11 "Some people curse their fathers
and do not bless their mothers.

12 Some people think they are pure,
but they are not really free from
evil.

13 Some people have such a proud look!
They look down on others.

14 Some people have teeth like swords;
their jaws seem full of knives.

They want to remove the poor from the
earth
and the needy from the land.

15 "Greed has two daughters
named 'Give' and 'Give.'
There are three things that are never
satisfied,
really four that never say, 'I've had
enough!':

16 the cemetery, the childless mother,
the land that never gets enough rain,
and fire that never says, 'I've had
enough!'

17 "If you make fun of your father
and refuse to obey your mother,
the birds of the valley will peck out your
eyes,
and the vultures will eat them.

THE LAWS OF INCREASE

FINANCES

God's shield

PROVERBS 30:5

The Hebrew word for "guard" comes from a root that means "to defend." In its various forms, it can mean enclosure, garden, covering, and shield. The root word is exclusively used in reference to God's protection, never to the protection of men or things. It isn't surprising that in many translations God would then be described as a shield (from the same root word).

There are actually several words for different kinds of shields, but they are all translated by the same English word in the Bible. The particular type of shield described by the Hebrew word used here did not cover the whole body. It was the kind of shield used by light infantry to defend against arrows and blows. In Proverbs 2:7, God is called a shield for those who walk with moral integrity ("the innocent").

So often we act as though we must defend ourselves against the onslaughts of the world. Troubles come our way, and we immediately begin plans of defense. Lawyers, police, doctors, counselors, soldiers, bankers, and a host of other men or women are called to our aid. Even when the troubles are only verbal, we seek the right words to justify ourselves. But God says something different. If we walk in his light, he will be our defense. He will act on our behalf, shielding us from the attacks that try to overwhelm us.

If the God who knows all things says that we do not need to be afraid because he is personally going to shield us, what reason can we possibly have for self-protection? Instead of jumping to defend ourselves, we need to rest in the peace that God is the defender of those who trust in him.

---

reflect: Thank God for guarding you and personally securing your safety.
Go to **Ecclesiastes 7:12.**

18 "There are three things that are too hard
for me,
really four I don't understand:
19 the way an eagle flies in the sky,
the way a snake slides over a rock,
the way a ship sails on the sea,
and the way a man and a woman fall in
love.

20 "This is the way of a woman who takes
part in adultery:
She acts as if she had eaten and washed
her face;
she says, 'I haven't done anything
wrong.'

21 "There are three things that make the
earth tremble,
really four it cannot stand:
22 a servant who becomes a king,
a foolish person who has plenty to eat,
23 a hated woman who gets married,
and a maid who replaces her mistress.

24 "There are four things on earth that are
small,
but they are very wise:
25 Ants are not very strong,
but they store up food in the summer.
26 Rock badgers are not very powerful,
but they can live among the rocks.
27 Locusts have no king,
but they all go forward in formation.
28 Lizards can be caught in the hand,
but they are found even in kings'
palaces.

29 "There are three things that strut proudly,
really four that walk as if they were
important:
30 a lion, the proudest animal,
which is strong and runs from nothing,
31 a rooster, a male goat,
and a king when his army is around him.

32 "If you have been foolish and proud,
or if you have planned evil, shut your
mouth.
33 Just as stirring milk makes butter,
and twisting noses makes them bleed,
so stirring up anger causes trouble."

WISE WORDS OF KING LEMUEL

31 These are the words of King Lemuel,
the message his mother taught him:
2 "My son, I gave birth to you.

You are the son I prayed for.
3 Don't waste your strength on women
or your time on those who ruin kings.

4 "Kings should not drink wine, Lemuel,
and rulers should not desire beer.
5 If they drink, they might forget the law
and keep the needy from getting their
rights.
6 Give beer to people who are dying
and wine to those who are sad.
7 Let them drink and forget their need
and remember their misery no more.

8 "Speak up for those who cannot speak for
themselves;
defend the rights of all those who have
nothing.
9 Speak up and judge fairly,
and defend the rights of the poor and
needy."

THE GOOD WIFE

10 It is hard to find a good wife,
because she is worth more than
rubies.
11 Her husband trusts her completely.
With her, he has everything he needs.
12 She does him good and not harm
for as long as she lives.
13 She looks for wool and flax
and likes to work with her hands.
14 She is like a trader's ship,
bringing food from far away.
15 She gets up while it is still dark
and prepares food for her family
and feeds her servant girls.
16 She inspects a field and buys it.
With money she earned, she plants a
vineyard.
17 She does her work with energy,
and her arms are strong.
18 She knows that what she makes is
good.
Her lamp burns late into the night.
19 She makes thread with her hands
and weaves her own cloth.
20 She welcomes the poor
and helps the needy.
21 She does not worry about her family
when it snows,
because they all have fine clothes to
keep them warm.
22 She makes coverings for herself;

her clothes are made of linen and other expensive material.
²³ Her husband is known at the city meetings,
where he makes decisions as one of the leaders of the land.
²⁴ She makes linen clothes and sells them and provides belts to the merchants.
²⁵ She is strong and is respected by the people.
She looks forward to the future with joy.
²⁶ She speaks wise words and teaches others to be kind.

FAMILY

AUTHORITY OVER DARKNESS BEGINS AT HOME

mother coordinates
the family

PROVERBS 31:10–31   By Elmer Towns

Some church leaders preach against the "working mother." They give women a guilt trip for not staying home. Many of these women would love to stay home but are forced to work by necessity. These women may become hurt and angry if their church has a condemning attitude. They need not feel this way.

In Proverbs 31, the ideal woman purchased a field, implying she was into real estate investment. Furthermore, Lydia was a seller of goods, and Priscilla worked with her husband as owner and manager of a tent-making business. Scripture makes no condemnation of these endeavors.

A mother, whether she works outside the home or not, plays three major roles in coordinating the family. One of the basic contributions of the mother is her role as a friend to her husband and children. She listens to everyone, encourages everyone, and becomes the *emotional glue* of the home.

Second, mothers teach children foundational life lessons regarding social interaction, character, and responsibility. Most lessons learned in life are learned before the child goes to school. Mothers are the *moral glue* of the home.

Third, mothers are usually responsible for meeting the basic needs of each family member. They are most often the parent who is involved in food preparation and making sure each child gets three nutritious meals a day. Since mothers are the managers of the home, they are the *administrative glue* of the home. Whether they work outside the home or not, it is important for mothers to fulfill these roles and to feel validated in them.

reflect: Do you validate the role of women in your life?
Go to **Proverbs 14:26.**

27 She watches over her family
and never wastes her time.
28 Her children speak well of her.
Her husband also praises her,
29 saying, "There are many fine women,
but you are better than all of
them."

30 Charm can fool you, and beauty can trick
you,
but a woman who respects the LORD
should be praised.
31 Give her the reward she has earned;
she should be praised in public for what
she has done.

ecclesiastes

A WISE MAN BELIEVES IN GOD

1 These are the words of the Teacher, a son of David, king in Jerusalem.

2 The Teacher says,
> "Useless! Useless!
> Completely useless!
> Everything is useless."

3 What do people really gain
> from all the hard work they do here on
> earth?

THINGS NEVER CHANGE

4 People live, and people die,
> but the earth continues forever.
5 The sun rises, the sun sets,
> and then it hurries back to where it
> rises again.
6 The wind blows to the south;
> it blows to the north.
> It blows from one direction and then
> another.
> Then it turns around and repeats the
> same pattern, going nowhere.
7 All the rivers flow to the sea,
> but the sea never becomes full.
8 Everything is boring,
> so boring that you don't even want to
> talk about it.
> Words come again and again to our ears,
> but we never hear enough,
> nor can we ever really see all we want
> to see.
9 All things continue the way they have
> been since the beginning.
> What has happened will happen again;
> there is nothing new here on earth.
10 Someone might say,
> "Look, this is new,"
> but really it has always been here.
> It was here before we were.
11 People don't remember what happened
> long ago,
> and in the future people will not
> remember what happens now.
> Even later, other people will not
> remember what was done before
> them.

DOES WISDOM BRING HAPPINESS?

12 I, the Teacher, was king over Israel in Jerusalem. 13 I decided to use my wisdom to learn about everything that happens on earth. I learned that God has given us terrible things to face. 14 I looked at everything done on earth and saw that it is all useless, like chasing the wind.

15 If something is crooked,
> you can't make it straight.
> If something is missing,
> you can't say it is there.

16 I said to myself, "I have become very wise and am now wiser than anyone who ruled Jerusalem before me. I know what wisdom and knowledge really are." 17 So I decided to find out about wisdom and knowledge and also about foolish thinking, but this turned out to be like chasing the wind.

18 With much wisdom comes much
> disappointment;
> the person who gains more knowledge
> also gains more sorrow.

DOES "HAVING FUN" BRING HAPPINESS?

2 I said to myself, "I will try having fun. I will enjoy myself." But I found that this is also useless. 2 It is foolish to laugh all the time, and having fun doesn't accomplish anything. 3 I decided to cheer myself up with wine while my mind was still thinking wisely. I wanted to find a way to enjoy myself and see what was good for people to do during their few days of life.

DOES HARD WORK BRING HAPPINESS?

4 Then I did great things: I built houses and planted vineyards for myself. 5 I made gardens and parks, and I planted all kinds of fruit trees in them. 6 I made pools of water for myself and used them to water my growing trees. 7 I bought male and female slaves, and slaves were also born in my house. I had large herds and flocks, more than anyone in Jerusalem had ever had before. 8 I also gathered silver and gold for myself, treasures from kings and other areas. I had male and female

singers and all the women a man could ever want. ⁹I became very famous, even greater than anyone who had lived in Jerusalem before me. My wisdom helped me in all this.

¹⁰ Anything I saw and wanted, I got for
> myself;
> I did not miss any pleasure I desired.
> I was pleased with everything I did,
> and this pleasure was the reward for all
> my hard work.

¹¹ But then I looked at what I had done,
> and I thought about all the hard
> work.
> Suddenly I realized it was useless, like
> chasing the wind.

> There is nothing to gain from anything
> we do here on earth.

MAYBE WISDOM IS THE ANSWER

¹² Then I began to think again about being
> wise,
> and also about being foolish and doing
> crazy things.
> But after all, what more can anyone do?
> He can't do more than what the other
> king has already done.

¹³ I saw that being wise is certainly better
> than being foolish,
> just as light is better than darkness.

¹⁴ Wise people see where they are going,
> but fools walk around in the dark.

FOR YOUR OWN GOOD

point of view

FULFILLMENT

ECCLESIASTES 2:24–26

Sometimes we just can't understand the reward systems of this world. Good people seem to get the worst of the deal while bad people seem to prosper. The world doesn't seem to honor justice, even when we know that God is ultimately in charge. And too often it looks as if the only real purpose in life is to "eat, drink, and enjoy."

When Solomon wrote this verse, he reflected on all these disparities. He concluded that even when it all looks out of proportion, an intelligent person sees that even the most basic pleasures of life are still gifts from God. When life's turmoil begins to cast doubts on our worth, Solomon suggests we change our point of view.

The wisest man who ever lived saw how easily we might slip into despair. He saw how tempting it could be to fall into apathy. But he knew that careful examination shows God's handiwork in even the simplest of things. There is no escaping the fact that life itself is God's gift. That should lead us to see that if the simplest of life's activities are tied to God's goodness, our lofty and noble endeavors certainly have his hand upon them, also.

reflect: Enjoy the life that God has blessed you with and praise him for it.
Go to **FULFILLMENT:** "Do You Know Him?" at **Luke 9:28–29.**

Yet I saw that
> both wise and foolish people end the
> same way.

15 I thought to myself,
> "What happens to a fool will happen to
> me, too,
> so what is the reward for being wise?"
> I said to myself,
> "Being wise is also useless."
16 The wise person and the fool
> will both die,
> and no one will remember either one for
> long.
> In the future, both will be forgotten.

IS THERE REAL HAPPINESS IN LIFE?

17So I hated life. It made me sad to think that everything here on earth is useless, like chasing the wind. 18I hated all the things I had worked for here on earth, because I must leave them to someone who will live after me. 19Someone else will control everything for which I worked so hard here on earth, and I don't know if he will be wise or foolish. This is also useless. 20So I became sad about all the hard work I had done here on earth. 21People can work hard using all their wisdom, knowledge, and skill, but they will die, and other people will get the things for which they worked. They did not do the work, but they will get everything. This is also unfair and useless. 22What do people get for all their work and struggling here on earth? 23All of their lives their work is full of pain and sorrow, and even at night their minds don't rest. This is also useless.

24The best that people can do is eat, drink, and enjoy their work. I saw that even this comes from God, 25because no one can eat or enjoy life without him. 26If people please God, God will give them wisdom, knowledge, and joy. But sinners will get only the work of gathering and storing wealth that they will have to give to the ones who please God. So all their work is useless, like chasing the wind.

THERE IS A TIME FOR EVERYTHING

3 There is a time for everything,
> and everything on earth has its special
> season.
2 There is a time to be born
> and a time to die.

There is a time to plant
> and a time to pull up plants.
3 There is a time to kill
> and a time to heal.
There is a time to destroy
> and a time to build.
4 There is a time to cry
> and a time to laugh.
There is a time to be sad
> and a time to dance.
5 There is a time to throw away stones
> and a time to gather them.
There is a time to hug
> and a time not to hug.
6 There is a time to look for something
> and a time to stop looking for it.
There is a time to keep things
> and a time to throw things away.
7 There is a time to tear apart
> and a time to sew together.
There is a time to be silent
> and a time to speak.
8 There is a time to love
> and a time to hate.
There is a time for war
> and a time for peace.

GOD CONTROLS HIS WORLD

9Do people really gain anything from their work? 10I saw the hard work God has given people to do. 11God has given them a desire to know the future. He does everything just right and on time, but people can never completely understand what he is doing. 12So I realize that the best thing for them is to be happy and enjoy themselves as long as they live. 13God wants all people to eat and drink and be happy in their work, which are gifts from God. 14I know that everything God does will continue forever. People cannot add anything to what God has done, and they cannot take anything away from it. God does it this way to make people respect him.
15 What happens now has happened in the
> past,
> and what will happen in the future has
> happened before.
> God makes the same things happen
> again and again.

UNFAIRNESS ON EARTH

16 I also saw this here on earth:
> Where there should have been justice,
> there was evil;

where there should have been right,
there was wrong.
¹⁷ I said to myself,
God has planned a time for every thing
and every action,
so he will judge both good people and
bad.
¹⁸I decided that God leaves it the way it
is to test people and to show them they are
just like animals. ¹⁹The same thing happens
to animals and to people; they both have the
same breath, so they both die. People are no
better off than the animals, because everything is useless. ²⁰Both end up the same way;
both came from dust and both will go back to
dust. ²¹Who can be sure that the human spirit
goes up to God and that the spirit of an animal goes down into the ground? ²²So I saw
that the best thing people can do is to enjoy
their work, because that is all they have. No
one can help another person see what will
happen in the future.

IS IT BETTER TO BE DEAD?

4 Again I saw all the people who were mistreated here on earth.
I saw their tears
and that they had no one to comfort
them.
Cruel people had all the power,
and there was no one to comfort those
they hurt.
² I decided that the dead
are better off than the living.
³ But those who have never been born
are better off still;
they have not seen the evil
that is done here on earth.

THE LIFE YOU WERE BORN TO LIVE

there's a *why* for everything

FITNESS

ECCLESIASTES 3:1

There's a saying, "If you know the why, you can endure almost any how." This
is because why you do certain things is often more important than how you do
them. When dieting and exercising, if the "why" is to lose weight, you'll never endure
the "how."

On the other hand, if the "why" is to become healthier, live longer, be there for your
family, serve God at a greater capacity, and educate yourself on being a good custodian
of your body, you'll be adequately prepared to withstand virtually any "how."

Dieting or exercising because you want to lose weight is like mopping up a wet floor
rather than covering up the hole in the roof. It's a very temporary, useless solution.
However, eating well and engaging in regular physical activity as a conscientious,
caring, godly person is a long-term solution because it's a great reason for doing the
right thing.

reflect: Examine why you do the things you do on a daily basis, and make changes if
necessary.
Go to **FITNESS:** "Turning Revelations into Revolutions" at **Proverbs 4:20-22.**

WHY WORK SO HARD?

⁴I realized the reason people work hard and try to succeed: They are jealous of each other. This, too, is useless, like chasing the wind.

⁵ Some say it is foolish to fold your hands
 and do nothing,
 because you will starve to death.
⁶ Maybe so, but I say it is better to be
 content
 with what little you have.

Otherwise, you will always be struggling
 for more,
 and that is like chasing the wind.

⁷ Again I saw something here on earth that
 was useless:
⁸ I saw a man who had no family,
 no son or brother.
He always worked hard
 but was never satisfied with what he had.
He never asked himself, "For whom am I
 working so hard?"

UNDERSTANDING AUTHORITY

FAMILY

bonded together

ECCLESIASTES 4:12

What binds you to your spouse and your children? Is it the marriage contract? Is it the social expectation? Is it the desire to be a parent? Is it mutual advantage and cooperation? The truth is that none of these things will guarantee protection against the pressures on the family. Divorce rates are the same inside and outside the church. Just trying to do everything right isn't enough.

That's why Solomon gives us the metaphor of the three-strand cord. It is a picture of the blended unity and strength of relationships that weave God into every part of the bond. All of the reasons for marriage and family continuity are good ones, but unless God saturates the relationship, a vital part of the cord will be missing. You're really married to God more than to each other.

The verse actually says that a cord of three strands is not easily torn apart. Isn't that precisely the way we talk about family pressures today? So many times we feel torn apart. Something wants to break that bond and it stretches and pulls and picks at the family in an effort to tear the cord. God offers a permanent solution: surrender to him.

Weave invincibility into your marriage by making God the solid strand in everything you do. When your commitment is to not only a vulnerable person, but also to God, how you react to the challenges of married life changes. With God as your partner, the odds are in your favor.

reflect: Commit your marriage to God by inviting him to partner with you and your spouse.

Go to **Jeremiah 3:19.**

Why don't I let myself enjoy life?"
This also is very sad and useless.

FRIENDS AND FAMILY GIVE STRENGTH

9 Two people are better than one,
   because they get more done by working
   together.
10 If one falls down,
   the other can help him up.
But it is bad for the person who is alone
   and falls,
   because no one is there to help.
11 If two lie down together, they will be
   warm,
   but a person alone will not be warm.
12 An enemy might defeat one person,
   but two people together can defend
   themselves;
a rope that is woven of three strings is
   hard to break.

FAME AND POWER ARE USELESS

13 A poor but wise boy is better than a foolish but old king who doesn't listen to advice.
14 A boy became king. He had been born poor
in the kingdom and had even gone to prison
before becoming king. 15 I watched all the
people who live on earth follow him and
make him their king. 16 Many followed him at
first, but later, they did not like him, either.
So fame and power are useless, like chasing
the wind.

BE CAREFUL ABOUT MAKING PROMISES

5 Be careful when you go to worship at the
Temple. It is better to listen than to offer
foolish sacrifices without even knowing you
are doing wrong.
 2 Think before you speak,
   and be careful about what you say to
   God.
God is in heaven,
   and you are on the earth,
   so say only a few words to God.
3 The saying is true: Bad dreams come from
   too much worrying,
   and too many words come from foolish
   people.
4 If you make a promise to God, don't be
slow to keep it. God is not happy with fools,
so give God what you promised. 5 It is better not to promise anything than to promise something and not do it. 6 Don't let your
words cause you to sin, and don't say to the

priest at the Temple, "I didn't mean what I
promised." If you do, God will become angry
with your words and will destroy everything
you have worked for. 7 Many useless promises
are like so many dreams; they mean nothing.
You should respect God.

OFFICERS CHEAT EACH OTHER

8 In some places you will see poor people
mistreated. Don't be surprised when they are
not treated fairly or given their rights. One
officer is cheated by a higher officer who in
turn is cheated by even higher officers. 9 The
wealth of the country is divided up among
them all. Even the king makes sure he gets
his share of the profits.

WEALTH CANNOT BUY HAPPINESS

10 Whoever loves money
   will never have enough money;
Whoever loves wealth
   will not be satisfied with it.
   This is also useless.
11 The more wealth people have,
   the more friends they have to help
   spend it.
So what do people really gain?
   They gain nothing except to look at
   their riches.
12 Those who work hard sleep in peace;
   it is not important if they eat little or
   much.
But rich people worry about their wealth
   and cannot sleep.
13 I have seen real misery here on earth:
   Money saved is a curse to its owners.
14   They lose it all in a bad deal
and have nothing to give to their children.
15 People come into this world with nothing,
   and when they die they leave with
   nothing.
In spite of all their hard work,
   they leave just as they came.
16 This, too, is real misery:
   They leave just as they came.
   So what do they gain from chasing the
   wind?
17 All they get are days full of sadness and
   sorrow,
   and they end up sick, defeated, and
   angry.

ENJOY YOUR LIFE'S WORK

¹⁸I have seen what is best for people here on earth. They should eat and drink and enjoy their work, because the life God has given them on earth is short. ¹⁹God gives some people the ability to enjoy the wealth and property he gives them, as well as the ability to accept their state in life and enjoy their work. ²⁰They do not worry about how short life is, because God keeps them busy with what they love to do.

6 I have seen something else wrong here on earth that causes serious problems for people. ²God gives great wealth, riches, and honor to some people; they have everything they want. But God does not let them enjoy such things; a stranger enjoys them instead. This is useless and very wrong. ³A man might have a hundred children and live a long time, but what good is it if he can't enjoy the good God gives him or have a proper burial? I say a baby born dead is better off than he is. ⁴A baby born dead is useless. It returns to darkness without even a name. ⁵That baby never saw the sun and never knew anything, but it finds more rest than that man. ⁶Even if he lives two thousand years, he doesn't enjoy the good God gives him. Everyone is going to the same place.

⁷ People work just to feed themselves,
　but they never seem to get enough to
　　eat.
⁸ In this way a wise person
　is no better off than a fool.
Then, too, it does a poor person little good
　to know how to get along in life.
⁹ It is better to see what you have
　than to want more.
Wanting more is useless—
　like chasing the wind.

WHO CAN UNDERSTAND GOD'S PLAN?

¹⁰ Whatever happens was planned long
　　ago.
Everyone knows what people are like.
No one can argue with God,
　who is stronger than anyone.
¹¹ The more you say,
　the more useless it is.
What good does it do?
¹²People have only a few useless days of life on the earth; their short life passes like a shadow. Who knows what is best for them while they live? Who can tell them what the future will bring?

SOME BENEFITS OF SERIOUS THINKING

7 It is better to have respect than good
　　perfume.
The day of death is better than the day of
　　birth.
² It is better to go to a funeral
　than to a party.
We all must die,
　and everyone living should think about
　　this.
³ Sorrow is better than laughter,
　and sadness has a good influence on
　　you.
⁴ A wise person thinks about death,
　but a fool thinks only about having a
　　good time.
⁵ It is better to be criticized by a wise
　　person
　than to be praised by a fool.
⁶ The laughter of fools
　is like the crackling of thorns in a
　　cooking fire.
Both are useless.

⁷ Even wise people are fools
　if they let money change their thinking.

⁸ It is better to finish something
　than to start it.
It is better to be patient
　than to be proud.
⁹ Don't become angry quickly,
　because getting angry is foolish.

¹⁰ Don't ask, "Why was life better in the
　'good old days'?"
It is not wise to ask such questions.

¹¹ Wisdom is better when it comes with
　　money.
They both help those who are alive.
¹² Wisdom is like money:
　they both help.
But wisdom is better,
　because it can save whoever has it.

¹³ Look at what God has done:
　No one can straighten what he has bent.
¹⁴ When life is good, enjoy it.
　But when life is hard, remember:
God gives good times and hard times,
　and no one knows what tomorrow will
　　bring.

IT IS IMPOSSIBLE TO BE TRULY GOOD

15 In my useless life I have seen both of
these:

I have seen good people die in spite of
their goodness

and evil people live a long time in spite
of their evil.

16 Don't be too right,
and don't be too wise.
Why destroy yourself?

17 Don't be too wicked,
and don't be foolish.
Why die before your time?

18 It is good to grab the one and not let go of
the other;
those who honor God will hold them
both.

19 Wisdom makes a person stronger
than ten leaders in a city.

20 Surely there is not a good person on earth
who always does good and never sins.

21 Don't listen to everything people say,
or you might hear your servant
insulting you.

THE LAWS OF INCREASE

money as a gift

FINANCES

ECCLESIASTES 7:12

One of the purposes of money is defense. God does not want his people to
suffer under the oppression of debt or waste away from the lack of resources.
God is the great provider. He demonstrated his care every day for forty years while
the Israelites crossed the wilderness. Money is one of the ways God provides a defense
against the evil of this world. But it's easy to slip from the defensive posture to the
belief that money is intended to make us self-sufficient. Solomon warns us about this
mistake.

Solomon, the richest man who ever lived, recognized the legitimate purpose of money.
But he also saw that the only real treasure is something that cannot be purchased:
wisdom. In the Bible, the word for "wisdom" does not mean the astute application
of information. Wisdom is the biblical term for behavior that pleases God. Wisdom
is godly thinking in action. Solomon knew that money is no security at all if it is not
backed by a life devoted to God. Money is God's gift, not anyone's reward.

If I live my life with the accumulation of money as my highest priority, I will soon
discover that the gift giver requires more of me than a large bank account. I will wake
up one day only to realize that in spite of my wealth, I am desperately poor in the
things that matter most. For what will a man trade for his soul? Money has its uses, but
it is not the ultimate goal at all.

reflect: Do you maintain a proper perspective of money?
Go to **Ecclesiastes 11:4-6.**

22 You know that many times
    you have insulted others.

23 I used wisdom to test all these things.
    I wanted to be wise,
        but it was too hard for me.
24 I cannot understand why things are as
        they are.
    It is too hard for anyone to understand.
25 I studied and tried very hard to find
        wisdom,
    to find some meaning for everything.
    I learned that it is foolish to be evil,
        and it is crazy to act like a fool.

26 I found that some women are worse than
        death
    and are as dangerous as traps.
    Their love is like a net,
        and their arms hold men like chains.
    A man who pleases God will be saved
        from them,
    but a sinner will be caught by them.

27 The Teacher says, "This is what I learned:
    I added all these things together
        to find some meaning for everything.
28 While I was searching,
    I did not find one man among the
        thousands I found.
    Nor did I find a woman among all these.
29 One thing I have learned:
    God made people good,
        but they have found all kinds of ways to
        be bad."

OBEY THE KING

8 No one is like the wise person
    who can understand what things
        mean.
Wisdom brings happiness;
    it makes sad faces happy.
    2 Obey the king's command, because you
made a promise to God. 3 Don't be too quick
to leave the king. Don't support something
that is wrong, because the king does whatever he pleases. 4 What the king says is law;
no one tells him what to do.
5 Whoever obeys the king's command will
        be safe.
    A wise person does the right thing at
        the right time.
6 There is a right time and a right way for
        everything,
    yet people often have many troubles.

7 They do not know what the future holds,
    and no one can tell them what will
        happen.
8 No one can control the wind
    or stop his own death.
    No soldier is released in times of war,
        and evil does not set free those who do
        evil.

JUSTICE, REWARDS, AND PUNISHMENT

9 I saw all of this as I considered all that is
done here on earth. Sometimes people harm
those they control. 10 I saw the funerals of evil
people who used to go in and out of the holy
place. They were honored in the same towns
where they had done evil. This is useless,
too.

11 When evil people are not punished right
away, it makes others want to do evil, too.
12 Though a sinner might do a hundred evil
things and might live a long time, I know it
will be better for those who honor God. 13 I
also know it will not go well for evil people, because they do not honor God. Like
a shadow, they will not last. 14 Sometimes
something useless happens on earth. Bad
things happen to good people, and good
things happen to bad people. I say that this
is also useless. 15 So I decided it was more important to enjoy life. The best that people can
do here on earth is to eat, drink, and enjoy
life, because these joys will help them do the
hard work God gives them here on earth.

WE CANNOT UNDERSTAND ALL GOD DOES

16 I tried to understand all that happens
on earth. I saw how busy people are, working
day and night and hardly ever sleeping. 17 I
also saw all that God has done. Nobody can
understand what God does here on earth. No
matter how hard people try to understand
it, they cannot. Even if wise people say they
understand, they cannot; no one can really
understand it.

IS DEATH FAIR?

9 I thought about all this and tried to un-
    derstand it. I saw that God controls good
people and wise people and what they do,
but no one knows if they will experience love
or hate.
2 Good and bad people end up the same—
    those who are right and those who are
        wrong,

those who are good and those who are
evil,
those who are clean and those who are
unclean,
those who sacrifice and those who do
not.
The same things happen to a good person
as happen to a sinner,
to a person who makes promises to God
and to one who does not.

³This is something wrong that happens here on earth: What happens to one happens to all. So people's minds are full of evil and foolish thoughts while they live. After that, they join the dead. ⁴But anyone still alive has hope; even a live dog is better off than a dead lion!

⁵ The living know they will die,
but the dead know nothing.
Dead people have no more reward,
and people forget them.
⁶ After people are dead,
they can no longer love or hate or envy.

They will never again share
in what happens here on earth.

ENJOY LIFE WHILE YOU CAN

⁷ So go eat your food and enjoy it;
drink your wine and be happy,
because that is what God wants you to do.
⁸ Put on nice clothes
and make yourself look good.
⁹Enjoy life with the wife you love. Enjoy all the useless days of this useless life God has given you here on earth, because it is all you have. So enjoy the work you do here on earth. ¹⁰Whatever work you do, do your best, because you are going to the grave, where there is no working, no planning, no knowledge, and no wisdom.

TIME AND CHANCE

¹¹ I also saw something else here on earth:
The fastest runner does not always win
the race,
the strongest soldier does not always
win the battle,

THE ULTIMATE INVESTMENT

be ambitious
but content

FINANCES

ECCLESIASTES 9:7–9

David understood something we all need to learn. Be ambitious but content. We tend to focus on the circumference of life. We look at the things, the people, and the worries of life. God is focused on the center. People, appearances, and problems are on the exterior. God does not look at the exterior; he scrutinizes only the interior.

Dissatisfied people are the ones yelling in traffic, getting aggravated in lines at the grocery store, and giving clerks, waitresses, and their families a hard time. What you are on the inside is usually what people are seeing on the *outside*. Getting satisfied and healthy does not come from doing or getting *more*. It comes from allowing God to change you from the inside out.

reflect: Meditate on the fact that the Lord is your caretaker and all your needs are
covered.
Go to **Psalm 69:33.**

the wisest does not always have food,
the smartest does not always become
wealthy,
and the talented one does not always
receive praise.
Time and chance happen to everyone.
12 No one knows what will happen next.
Like a fish caught in a net,
or a bird caught in a trap,
people are trapped by evil
when it suddenly falls on them.

WISDOM DOES NOT ALWAYS WIN

13I also saw something wise here on earth that impressed me. 14There was a small town with only a few people in it. A great king fought against it and put his armies all around it. 15Now there was a poor but wise man in the town who used his wisdom to save his town. But later on, everyone forgot about him. 16I still think wisdom is better than strength. But those people forgot about the poor man's wisdom and stopped listening to what he said.
17 The quiet words of a wise person are
better
than the shouts of a foolish ruler.
18 Wisdom is better than weapons of war,
but one sinner can destroy much good.

10 Dead flies can make even perfume
stink.
In the same way, a little foolishness can
spoil wisdom.
2 The heart of the wise leads to right,
but the heart of a fool leads to wrong.
3 Even in the way fools walk along the road,
they show they are not wise;
they show everyone how stupid they
are.
4 Don't leave your job
just because your boss is angry with
you.
Remaining calm solves great problems.

5 There is something else wrong that
happens here on earth.
It is the kind of mistake rulers make:
6 Fools are given important positions
while gifted people are given lower
ones;
7 I have seen servants ride horses
while princes walk like servants on foot.
8 Anyone who digs a pit might fall into it;

anyone who knocks down a wall might
be bitten by a snake;
9 anyone who moves boulders might be
hurt by them;
and anyone who cuts logs might be
harmed by them.
10 A dull ax means
harder work.
Being wise will make it easier.
11 If a snake bites the tamer before it is
tamed,
what good is the tamer?

12 The words of the wise bring them praise,
but the words of a fool will destroy
them.
13 A fool begins by saying foolish things
and ends by saying crazy and wicked
things.
14 A fool talks too much.
No one knows the future,
and no one can tell what will happen
after death.
15 Work wears fools out;
they don't even know how to get
home.

THE VALUE OF WORK

16 How terrible it is for a country whose
king is a child
and whose leaders eat all morning.
17 How lucky a country is whose king comes
from a good family,
whose leaders eat only at mealtime
and for strength, not to get drunk.

18 If someone is lazy, the roof will begin to
fall.
If he doesn't fix it, the house will leak.

19 A party makes you feel good,
wine makes you feel happy,
and money buys anything.

20 Don't make fun of the king,
and don't make fun of rich people, even
in your bedroom.
A little bird might carry your words;
a bird might fly and tell what you said.

BOLDLY FACE THE FUTURE

11 Invest what you have,
because after a while you will get a
return.
2 Invest what you have in several different
businesses,

because you don't know what disasters might happen.

³ If clouds are full of rain,
  they will shower on the earth.
A tree can fall to the north or south,
  but it will stay where it falls.
⁴ Those who wait for perfect weather
  will never plant seeds;
those who look at every cloud
  will never harvest crops.

⁵ You don't know where the wind will blow,
  and you don't know how a baby grows
    inside the mother.
In the same way, you don't know what
    God is doing,
  or how he created everything.
⁶ Plant early in the morning,
  and work until evening,
because you don't know if this or that will
    succeed.
  They might both do well.

THE LAWS OF INCREASE

the sacrificial sower

FINANCES

By Larry Stockstill

ECCLESIASTES 11:4–6

A sower in the kingdom of God is a person of sacrifice, someone who will plant a seed in the lives of others. A little seed of corn by itself will not satisfy anybody's appetite. However, if you plant that seed, it produces thousands of kernels. You can eat your fill and still have plenty to bless others.

A seed is God's potential miracle, but before it can produce anything, it has to die. As long as you hold it in your hand, it cannot multiply. A sower plants sacrificially with no strings attached, no demands made, and all control of the seed surrendered.

You are not planting your seeds when you do not tithe. The tithe belongs to God, so when you keep it for yourself, you are stealing from God. He cannot give you more seeds if you eat the seeds you have. If you do not plant, nothing can grow.

The size of your harvest is up to you. Sacrificial giving has nothing to do with the amount you give. God knows your financial situation, and he will bless any seed that you cheerfully sow, whether it is small or large. The more you sow, the bigger will be your harvest. It is all relative, but he wants you to give cheerfully.

Sow your seed! Plant it cheerfully in the morning, in the evening, whenever and wherever the Holy Spirit leads. You might not know which seed will prosper, but God does; and he will bless you according to his wonderful riches and not according to the economy or your paycheck!

reflect: What is in your hand today that you could sow into the life of another?
Go to **Isaiah 33:6.**

SERVE GOD WHILE YOU ARE YOUNG

7 Sunshine is sweet;
  it is good to see the light of day.
8 People ought to enjoy every day of their
      lives,
  no matter how long they live.
  But they should also remember this:
  You will be dead a long time.
  Everything that happens then is useless.
9 Young people, enjoy yourselves while you
      are young;
  be happy while you are young.
  Do whatever your heart desires,
  whatever you want to do.
  But remember that God will judge you
  for everything you do.
10 Don't worry,
    and forget the troubles of your body,
    because youth and childhood are
      useless.

THE PROBLEMS OF OLD AGE

12 Remember your Creator
      while you are young,
  before the days of trouble come
  and the years when you say,
  "I find no pleasure in them."
2 When you get old,
    the light from the sun, moon, and stars
      will grow dark;
    the rain clouds will never seem to go
      away.
3 At that time your arms will shake
    and your legs will become weak.
  Your teeth will fall out so you cannot
      chew,
    and your eyes will not see clearly.
4 Your ears will be deaf to the noise in the
      streets,
    and you will barely hear the millstone
      grinding grain.
  You'll wake up when a bird starts singing,
    but you will barely hear singing.
5 You will fear high places
    and will be afraid to go for a walk.

Your hair will become white like the
    flowers on an almond tree.
  You will limp along like a grasshopper
    when you walk.
  Your appetite will be gone.
  Then you will go to your everlasting
    home,
  and people will go to your funeral.
6 Soon your life will snap like a silver chain
    or break like a golden bowl.
  You will be like a broken pitcher at a
    spring,
  or a broken wheel at a well.
7 You will turn back into the dust of the
    earth again,
  but your spirit will return to God who
    gave it.

8 Everything is useless!
  The Teacher says that everything is
    useless.

CONCLUSION: HONOR GOD

9The Teacher was very wise and taught
the people what he knew. He very carefully
thought about, studied, and set in order many
wise teachings. 10The Teacher looked for just
the right words to write what is dependable
and true.

11Words from wise people are like sharp
sticks used to guide animals. They are like
nails that have been driven in firmly. Altogether they are wise teachings that come
from one Shepherd. 12So be careful, my son,
about other teachings. People are always
writing books, and too much study will make
you tired.
13 Now, everything has been heard,
    so I give my final advice:
  Honor God and obey his commands,
    because this is all people must do.
14 God will judge everything,
    even what is done in secret,
  the good and the evil.

song of songs

A LOVE SONG

1 Solomon's Song of Songs.

THE WOMAN SPEAKS TO THE MAN SHE LOVES

2 Kiss me with the kisses of your mouth,
   because your love is better than wine.
3 The smell of your perfume is pleasant,
   and your name is pleasant like
      expensive perfume.
   That's why the young women love you.
4 Take me with you; let's run together.
   The king takes me into his rooms.

FRIENDS SPEAK TO THE MAN

   We will rejoice and be happy with you;
   we praise your love more than wine.
   With good reason, the young women
      love you.

THE WOMAN SPEAKS

5 I'm dark but lovely,
   women of Jerusalem,
   dark like the tents of Kedar,
   like the curtains of Solomon.
6 Don't look at how dark I am,
   at how dark the sun has made me.
   My brothers were angry with me
   and made me tend the vineyards,
   so I haven't tended my own vineyard!
7 Tell me, you whom I love,
   where do you feed your sheep?
   Where do you let them rest at noon?
   Why should I look for you near your
      friend's sheep,
   like a woman who wears a veil?[n]

THE MAN SPEAKS TO THE WOMAN

8 You are the most beautiful of women.
   Surely you know to follow the sheep
   and feed your young goats
      near the shepherds' tents.
9 My darling, you are like a mare
   among the king's stallions.
10 Your cheeks are beautiful with ornaments,
   and your neck with jewels.
11 We will make for you gold earrings
   with silver hooks.

THE WOMAN SPEAKS

12 The smell of my perfume spreads out
   to the king on his couch.
13 My lover is like a bag of myrrh
   that lies all night between my breasts.
14 My lover is like a bunch of flowers
   from the vineyards at En Gedi.

THE MAN SPEAKS

15 My darling, you are beautiful!
   Oh, you are beautiful,
   and your eyes are like doves.

THE WOMAN ANSWERS THE MAN

16 You are so handsome, my lover,
   and so pleasant!
   Our bed is the grass.
17 Cedar trees form our roof;
   our ceiling is made of juniper wood.

THE WOMAN SPEAKS AGAIN

2 I am a rose in the Plain of Sharon,
   a lily in the valleys.

THE MAN SPEAKS AGAIN

2 Among the young women, my darling
   is like a lily among thorns!

THE WOMAN ANSWERS

3 Among the young men, my lover
   is like an apple tree in the woods!
   I enjoy sitting in his shadow;
      his fruit is sweet to my taste.
4 He brought me to the banquet room,
   and his banner over me is love.
5 Strengthen me with raisins,
   and refresh me with apples,
   because I am weak with love.
6 My lover's left hand is under my head,
   and his right arm holds me tight.

THE WOMAN SPEAKS TO THE FRIENDS

7 Women of Jerusalem, promise me
   by the gazelles and the deer
not to awaken
   or excite my feelings of love
   until it is ready.

1:7 veil This was the way a prostitute usually dressed.

THE WOMAN SPEAKS AGAIN

8 I hear my lover's voice.
Here he comes jumping across the
mountains,
skipping over the hills.
9 My lover is like a gazelle or a young deer.
Look, he stands behind our wall
peeking through the windows,
looking through the blinds.
10 My lover spoke and said to me,
"Get up, my darling;
let's go away, my beautiful one.
11 Look, the winter is past;
the rains are over and gone.
12 Blossoms appear through all the land.
The time has come to sing;
the cooing of doves is heard in our land.
13 There are young figs on the fig trees,
and the blossoms on the vines smell
sweet.
Get up, my darling;
let's go away, my beautiful one."

THE MAN SPEAKS

14 My beloved is like a dove hiding in the
cracks of the rock,
in the secret places of the cliff.
Show me your face,
and let me hear your voice.
Your voice is sweet,
and your face is lovely.
15 Catch the foxes for us—
the little foxes that ruin the vineyards
while they are in blossom.

THE WOMAN SPEAKS

16 My lover is mine, and I am his.
He feeds among the lilies
17 until the day dawns
and the shadows disappear.
Turn, my lover.
Be like a gazelle or a young deer
on the mountain valleys.

THE WOMAN DREAMS

3 At night on my bed,
I looked for the one I love;
I looked for him, but I could not find
him.
2 I got up and went around the city,
in the streets and squares,
looking for the one I love.
I looked for him, but I could not find
him.

3 The watchmen found me as they patrolled
the city,
so I asked, "Have you seen the one I
love?"
4 As soon as I had left them,
I found the one I love.
I held him and would not let him go
until I brought him to my mother's
house,
to the room where I was born.

THE WOMAN SPEAKS TO THE FRIENDS

5 Women of Jerusalem, promise me
by the gazelles and the deer
not to awaken
or excite my feelings of love
until it is ready.
6 Who is this coming out of the desert
like a cloud of smoke?
Who is this that smells like myrrh,
incense,
and other spices?
7 Look, it's Solomon's couch[n]
with sixty soldiers around it,
the finest soldiers of Israel.
8 These soldiers all carry swords
and have been trained in war.
Every man wears a sword at his side
and is ready for the dangers of the
night.
9 King Solomon had a couch made for
himself
of wood from Lebanon.
10 He made its posts of silver
and its braces of gold.
The seat was covered with purple cloth
that the women of Jerusalem wove with
love.
11 Women of Jerusalem, go out and see King
Solomon.
He is wearing the crown his mother put
on his head
on his wedding day,
when his heart was happy!

THE MAN SPEAKS TO THE WOMAN

4 How beautiful you are, my darling!
Oh, you are beautiful!
Your eyes behind your veil are like doves.
Your hair is like a flock of goats
streaming down Mount Gilead.

3:7 couch Something like a bed carried by slaves on
which the king lay or sat while traveling.

2 Your teeth are white like newly sheared
sheep
  just coming from their bath.
Each one has a twin,
  and none of them is missing.
3 Your lips are like red silk thread,
  and your mouth is lovely.
Your cheeks behind your veil
  are like slices of a pomegranate.
4 Your neck is like David's tower,
  built with rows of stones.
A thousand shields hang on its walls;
  each shield belongs to a strong soldier.
5 Your breasts are like two fawns,
  like twins of a gazelle,
    feeding among the lilies.
6 Until the day dawns
  and the shadows disappear,
I will go to that mountain of myrrh
  and to that hill of incense.
7 My darling, everything about you is
  beautiful,
    and there is nothing at all wrong with
    you.
8 Come with me from Lebanon, my bride.
  Come with me from Lebanon,
from the top of Mount Amana,
  from the tops of Mount Senir and
    Mount Hermon.
Come from the lions' dens
  and from the leopards' hills.
9 My sister, my bride,
  you have thrilled my heart;
you have thrilled my heart
  with a glance of your eyes,
  with one sparkle from your necklace.
10 Your love is so sweet, my sister, my bride.
  Your love is better than wine,
  and your perfume smells better than
    any spice.
11 My bride, your lips drip honey;
  honey and milk are under your tongue.
Your clothes smell like the cedars of
  Lebanon.
12 My sister, my bride, you are like a garden
  locked up,
  like a walled-in spring, a closed-up
    fountain.
13 Your limbs are like an orchard
  of pomegranates with all the best fruit,
filled with flowers and nard,
14 nard and saffron, calamus, and cinnamon,
  with trees of incense, myrrh, and aloes—

all the best spices.
15 You are like a garden fountain—
  a well of fresh water
  flowing down from the mountains of
    Lebanon.

THE WOMAN SPEAKS
16 Awake, north wind.
  Come, south wind.
Blow on my garden,
  and let its sweet smells flow out.
Let my lover enter the garden
  and eat its best fruits.

THE MAN SPEAKS
5 I have entered my garden, my sister, my
  bride.
  I have gathered my myrrh with my
    spice.
  I have eaten my honeycomb and my
    honey.
  I have drunk my wine and my milk.

THE FRIENDS SPEAK
Eat, friends, and drink;
  yes, drink deeply, lovers.

THE WOMAN DREAMS
2 I sleep, but my heart is awake.
  I hear my lover knocking.
"Open to me, my sister, my darling,
  my dove, my perfect one.
My head is wet with dew,
  and my hair with the dampness of the
    night."
3 I have taken off my garment
  and don't want to put it on again.
I have washed my feet
  and don't want to get them dirty again.
4 My lover put his hand through the
  opening,
  and I felt excited inside.
5 I got up to open the door for my lover.
  Myrrh was dripping from my hands
and flowing from my fingers,
  onto the handles of the lock.
6 I opened the door for my lover,
  but my lover had left and was gone.
  When he spoke, he took my breath
    away.
I looked for him, but I could not find him;
  I called for him, but he did not answer.
7 The watchmen found me
  as they patrolled the city.
They hit me and hurt me;

the guards on the wall took away my
veil.
⁸ Promise me, women of Jerusalem,
if you find my lover,
tell him I am weak with love.

THE FRIENDS ANSWER THE WOMAN
⁹ How is your lover better than other
lovers,

most beautiful of women?
How is your lover better than other
lovers?
Why do you want us to promise this?

THE WOMAN ANSWERS THE FRIENDS
¹⁰ My lover is healthy and tan,
the best of ten thousand men.
¹¹ His head is like the finest gold;

FAMILY

GUILT AND GRACE

extraordinary
intimacy

SONG OF SONGS 5:1

By Larry Stockstill

God intentionally created Adam and Eve to complement each other perfectly in
every way. This included their physical bodies. Genesis 2:24 tells us the union
God desires is so complete that the two individuals become one body. When intimate
physical contact takes place, a supernatural, spiritual connection occurs. Inside the
framework of marriage, this union is pure, holy, and powerful; however, physical
intimacy outside of marriage is not innocent, and it brings shame. Anytime Satan can
entice a person to enter into improper activities, shame is always the result.

Today's sexually charged society falsely views the act of sex without marriage as
acceptable, normal, and desired. Sex is a primary selling force in the media and in
business. Premarital sex, homosexuality, and extramarital affairs are presented as
preferable, and purity is openly mocked. We are constantly bombarded with an erroneous
message of sex as something with no bounds, no standards, and no restraints.

Do not be deceived. Despite what popular culture says, it is possible to maintain your
purity and innocence. You are not just a victim of uncontrollable passion. You do not
have to go from one relationship to another, giving away your heart and your body over
and over again. There is a better way.

From the very beginning, God designed man and woman for physical intimacy in
marriage. Trust the guidelines in God's Word and quit filling your mind with distorted
garbage. You can resolve to be innocent and pure. Ask the Lord to help you fulfill his
design.

reflect: Are you suffering because of a compromised lifestyle?
Go to **Malachi 2:15.**

his hair is wavy and black like a raven.
12 His eyes are like doves
  by springs of water.
They seem to be bathed in cream
  and are set like jewels.
13 His cheeks are like beds of spices;
  they smell like mounds of perfume.
His lips are like lilies
  flowing with myrrh.
14 His hands are like gold hinges,
  filled with jewels.
His body is like shiny ivory
  covered with sapphires.
15 His legs are like large marble posts,
  standing on bases of fine gold.
He is like a cedar of Lebanon,
  like the finest of the trees.
16 His mouth is sweet to kiss,
  and I desire him very much.
Yes, daughters of Jerusalem,
  this is my lover
  and my friend.

THE FRIENDS SPEAK TO THE WOMAN

6 Where has your lover gone,
  most beautiful of women?
Which way did your lover turn?
  We will look for him with you.

THE WOMAN ANSWERS THE FRIENDS

2 My lover has gone down to his garden,
  to the beds of spices,
to feed in the gardens
  and to gather lilies.
3 I belong to my lover,
  and my lover belongs to me.
He feeds among the lilies.

THE MAN SPEAKS TO THE WOMAN

4 My darling, you are as beautiful as the city
  of Tirzah,
  as lovely as the city of Jerusalem,
  like an army flying flags.
5 Turn your eyes from me,
  because they excite me too much.
Your hair is like a flock of goats
  streaming down Mount Gilead.
6 Your teeth are white like sheep
  just coming from their bath;
each one has a twin,
  and none of them is missing.
7 Your cheeks behind your veil
  are like slices of a pomegranate.

8 There may be sixty queens and eighty
  slave women
  and so many girls you cannot count
  them,
9 but there is only one like my dove, my
  perfect one.
She is her mother's only daughter,
  the brightest of the one who gave her
  birth.
The young women saw her and called her
  happy;
  the queens and the slave women also
  praised her.

THE YOUNG WOMEN PRAISE THE WOMAN

10 Who is that young woman
  that shines out like the dawn?
She is as pretty as the moon,
  as bright as the sun,
  as wonderful as an army flying flags.

THE MAN SPEAKS

11 I went down into the orchard of nut trees
  to see the blossoms of the valley,
to look for buds on the vines,
  to see if the pomegranate trees had
  bloomed.
12 Before I realized it, my desire for you
  made me feel
  like a prince in a chariot.

THE FRIENDS CALL TO THE WOMAN

13 Come back, come back, woman of
  Shulam.
Come back, come back,
  so we may look at you!

THE WOMAN ANSWERS THE FRIENDS

Why do you want to look at the woman of
  Shulam
  as you would at the dance of two
  armies?

THE MAN SPEAKS TO THE WOMAN

7 Your feet are beautiful in sandals,
  you daughter of a prince.
Your round thighs are like jewels
  shaped by an artist.
2 Your navel is like a round drinking cup
  always filled with wine.
Your stomach is like a pile of wheat
  surrounded with lilies.
3 Your breasts are like two fawns,
  like twins of a gazelle.
4 Your neck is like an ivory tower.

Your eyes are like the pools in Heshbon
near the gate of Bath Rabbim.
Your nose is like the mountain of Lebanon
that looks down on Damascus.
5 Your head is like Mount Carmel,
and your hair is like purple cloth;
the king is captured in its folds.
6 You are beautiful and pleasant;
my love, you are full of delights.
7 You are tall like a palm tree,

and your breasts are like its bunches of
fruit.
8 I said, "I will climb up the palm tree
and take hold of its fruit."
Let your breasts be like bunches of grapes,
the smell of your breath like apples,
9 and your mouth like the best wine.

THE WOMAN SPEAKS TO THE MAN
Let this wine go down sweetly for my
lover;

FAMILY

LOVE IS MORE THAN GIVING

the law
of possession

SONG OF SONGS 7:10

By Jimmy Evans

God designed marriage partners to become one: emotionally, mentally, spiritually, and physically. For oneness to occur, complete surrender must take place. Things that were individually owned and administrated before marriage must now become co-owned and co-administrated. The only way two things can become one is for there to be a total melding of both parts into one.

Anything we will not surrender to our spouse to co-own and co-administrate will seriously hinder or even destroy our relationship. The marriage relationship parallels our relationship with Jesus, as stated in Ephesians 5. Anything we will not give up for Jesus is an idol and will prevent an intimate relationship with him. For intimacy to occur, there must be total surrender.

There are some common violations of the law of possession. One is dominance: a disproportionate control of the marriage and those elements common to the relationship. Another common violation is independence. The reason America leads the world in the number of broken families is that we worship our independence and have developed a selfish spirit.

Everything we do affects our spouse. Therefore, he/she has a need and a right to speak about our lives and to share decisions. Possession communicates value. If you will not give up ownership in a certain area of your life, you are telling your spouse that he/she does not have as much value as the issue at hand.

reflect: How is your relationship with your spouse today?
Go to **1 Corinthians 7:4.**

may it flow gently past the lips and
teeth.
¹⁰ I belong to my lover,
and he desires only me.
¹¹ Come, my lover,
let's go out into the country
and spend the night in the fields.
¹² Let's go early to the vineyards
and see if the buds are on the vines.
Let's see if the blossoms have already
opened
and if the pomegranates have bloomed.
There I will give you my love.
¹³ The mandrake flowers give their sweet
smell,
and all the best fruits are at our gates.
I have saved them for you, my lover,
the old delights and the new.

8 I wish you were like my brother
who fed at my mother's breasts.
If I found you outside,
I would kiss you,
and no one would look down on me.
² I would lead you and bring you
to my mother's house;
she is the one who taught me.
I would give you a drink of spiced wine
from my pomegranates.

THE WOMAN SPEAKS TO THE FRIENDS
³ My lover's left hand is under my head,
and his right arm holds me tight.
⁴ Women of Jerusalem,
promise not to awaken
or excite my feelings of love
until it is ready.

THE FRIENDS SPEAK
⁵ Who is this coming out of the desert,
leaning on her lover?

THE MAN SPEAKS TO THE WOMAN
I woke you under the apple tree
where you were born;
there your mother gave birth to you.
⁶ Put me like a seal on your heart,
like a seal on your arm.
Love is as strong as death;

jealousy is as strong as the grave.
Love bursts into flames
and burns like a hot fire.
⁷ Even much water cannot put out the
flame of love;
floods cannot drown love.
If a man offered everything in his house
for love,
people would totally reject it.

THE WOMAN'S BROTHERS SPEAK
⁸ We have a little sister,
and her breasts are not yet grown.
What should we do for our sister
on the day she becomes engaged?
⁹ If she is a wall,
we will put silver towers on her.
If she is a door,
we will protect her with cedar boards.

THE WOMAN SPEAKS
¹⁰ I am a wall,
and my breasts are like towers.
So I was to him,
as one who brings happiness.
¹¹ Solomon had a vineyard at Baal Hamon.
He rented the vineyards for others to
tend,
and everyone who rented had to pay
twenty-five pounds of silver for the
fruit.
¹² But my own vineyard is mine to give.
Solomon, the twenty-five pounds of
silver are for you,
and five pounds are for those who tend
the fruit.

THE MAN SPEAKS TO THE WOMAN
¹³ You who live in the gardens,
my friends are listening for your
voice;
let me hear it.

THE WOMAN SPEAKS TO THE MAN
¹⁴ Hurry, my lover,
be like a gazelle
or a young deer
on the mountains where spices grow.

FINANCES

the secrets of successful financial management in marriage

SONG OF SONGS 8:6-7

By Jimmy Evans

Even though being married gives us better financial potential, money problems are the primary reason people list as the reason for divorce. When there are financial problems or disagreements, they create incredible stress and resentment. If not settled quickly and correctly, financial problems can destroy intimacy and trust.

In learning to manage money in marriage, we must look at five common dangers to avoid. The first danger is disrespect of your spouse's financial perspective and input. Most married couples view money differently. Money "symbolizes" different things to us. Unless we realize this and respect it, we end up judging and resenting each other.

The second danger is dominance of money and financial decisions. Dominance is disproportionate control. It always creates damage because God designed men and women as equals and marriage as an intimate partnership.

The third danger is disagreement about financial decisions, priorities, and values. Unity in financial decisions is critical for financial success, as well as intimacy and trust. As soon as division sets in, financial problems are inevitable, and they take a toll on the relationship.

The fourth danger is debt. Even though the Bible doesn't say that borrowing is a sin, it does talk about it in cautionary terms. We must be careful about debt and how we borrow.

The fifth danger is disregarding the lordship of Jesus in your finances and his power to work in your marriage and money.

reflect: What can you do to improve financial management in your marriage?
Go to **FINANCES:** "Understanding Freedom" at **Romans 12:2.**

isaiah

GOD'S MESSAGE IN TROUBLED TIMES

1 This is the vision Isaiah son of Amoz saw about what would happen to Judah and Jerusalem. Isaiah saw these things while Uzziah, Jotham, Ahaz, and Hezekiah were kings of Judah.

GOD'S CASE AGAINST HIS CHILDREN

2 Heaven and earth, listen,
  because the LORD is speaking:
"I raised my children and helped them
    grow up,
  but they have turned against me.
3 An ox knows its master,
    and a donkey knows where its owner
    feeds it,
  but the people of Israel do not know me;
    my people do not understand."

4 How terrible! Israel is a nation of sin,
  a people loaded down with guilt,
a group of children doing evil,
  children who are full of evil.
They have left the LORD;
  they hate God, the Holy One of Israel,
  and have turned away from him as if he
    were a stranger.

5 Why should you continue to be punished?
  Why do you continue to turn against
    him?
Your whole head is hurt,
  and your whole heart is sick.
6 There is no healthy spot
  from the bottom of your foot to the top
    of your head;
  you are covered with wounds, hurts,
    and open sores
that are not cleaned and covered,
  and no medicine takes away the pain.

7 Your land is ruined;
  your cities have been burned with fire.
While you watch,
  your enemies are stealing everything
    from your land;
  it is ruined like a country destroyed by
    enemies.
8 Jerusalem is left alone

like an empty shelter in a vineyard,
  like a hut left in a field of melons,
  like a city surrounded by enemies.
9 The LORD All-Powerful
  allowed a few of our people to live.
Otherwise we would have been
    completely destroyed
  like the cities of Sodom and Gomorrah.

10 Jerusalem, your rulers are like those of
    Sodom,
  and your people are like those of
    Gomorrah.
Hear the word of the LORD;
  listen to the teaching of our God!
11 The LORD says,
  "I do not want all these sacrifices.
I have had enough of your burnt sacrifices
  of male sheep and fat from fine animals.
I am not pleased
  by the blood of bulls, lambs, and goats.
12 You come to meet with me,
  but who asked you to do
  all this running in and out of my
    Temple's rooms?
13 Don't continue bringing me worthless
    sacrifices!
  I hate the incense you burn.
I can't stand your New Moons, Sabbaths,
    and other feast days;
  I can't stand the evil you do in your holy
    meetings.
14 I hate your New Moon feasts
  and your other yearly feasts.
They have become a heavy weight on me,
  and I am tired of carrying it.
15 When you raise your arms to me in prayer,
  I will refuse to look at you.
Even if you say many prayers,
  I will not listen to you,
because your hands are full of blood.
16 Wash yourselves and make yourselves
    clean.
  Stop doing the evil things I see you do.
Stop doing wrong.
17   Learn to do good.

Seek justice.
  Punish those who hurt others.
Help the orphans.
  Stand up for the rights of widows."

18 The LORD says,
  "Come, let us talk about these things.
Though your sins are like scarlet,
  they can be as white as snow.
Though your sins are deep red,
  they can be white like wool.
19 If you become willing and obey me,
  you will eat good crops from the land.
20 But if you refuse to obey and if you turn
    against me,
  you will be destroyed by your enemies'
    swords."
The LORD himself said these things.

JERUSALEM IS NOT LOYAL TO GOD

21 The city of Jerusalem once followed the
    LORD,
  but she is no longer loyal to him.
She used to be filled with fairness;
  people there lived the way God wanted.
But now, murderers live there.
22 Jerusalem, you have become like the scum
    left when silver is purified;
  you are like wine mixed with water.
23 Your rulers are rebels
  and friends of thieves.
They all accept money for doing
    wrong,
  and they are paid to cheat people.
They don't seek justice for the orphans
  or listen to the widows' needs.
24 So the Lord GOD All-Powerful,
  the Mighty One of Israel, says:
"You, my enemies, will not cause me any
    more trouble.
  I will pay you back for what you did.
25 I will turn against you
  and clean away all your wrongs as if
    with soap;
  I will take all the worthless things out
    of you.
26 I will bring back judges as you had long
    ago;
  your counselors will be like those you
    had in the beginning.
Then you will be called the City That Is
    Right with God,
  the Loyal City."

27 By doing what is fair,
  Jerusalem will be free again.
By doing what is right,
  her people who come back to the LORD
    will have freedom.
28 But sinners and those who turn against
    him will be destroyed;
  those who have left the LORD will die.

29 "You will be ashamed,
  because you have worshiped gods
    under the oak trees.
You will be disgraced,
  because you have worshiped idols in
    your gardens.
30 You will be like an oak whose leaves are
    dying
  or like a garden without water.
31 Powerful people will be like small, dry
    pieces of wood,
  and their works will be like sparks.
They will burn together,
  and no one will be able to put out that
    fire."

THE MESSAGE ABOUT JERUSALEM

2 Isaiah son of Amoz saw this message
  about Judah and Jerusalem:
2   In the last days
  the mountain on which the LORD's
    Temple stands
  will become the most important of all
    mountains.
It will be raised above the hills,
  and people from all nations will come
    streaming to it.
3 Many nations will come and say,
  "Come, let us go up to the mountain of
    the LORD,
  to the Temple of the God of Jacob.
Then God will teach us his ways,
  and we will obey his teachings."
His teachings will go out from
    Jerusalem;
  the message of the LORD will go out
    from Jerusalem.
4 He will settle arguments among the
    nations
  and will make decisions for many
    nations.
Then they will make their swords into
    plows
  and their spears into hooks for
    trimming trees.

Nations will no longer fight other nations,
  nor will they train for war anymore.

⁵ Come, family of Jacob,
  and let us follow the way of the LORD.

A TERRIBLE DAY IS COMING

⁶ LORD, you have left your people,
    the family of Jacob,
  because they have become filled with
      wrong ideas from people in the
      East.
    They try to tell the future like the
      Philistines,
    and they have completely accepted
      those foreign ideas.
⁷ Their land has been filled with silver and
    gold;
  there are a great many treasures there.
  Their land has been filled with horses;
    there are many chariots there.
⁸ Their land is full of idols.
    The people worship these idols they
      made with their own hands
    and shaped with their own fingers.
⁹ People will not be proud any longer
    but will bow low with shame.
  God, do not forgive them.

¹⁰ Go into the caves of the cliffs;
    dig holes and hide in the ground
  from the anger of the LORD
    and from his great power!
¹¹ Proud people will be made humble,
    and they will bow low with shame.
  At that time only the LORD will still be
    praised.

¹² The LORD All-Powerful has a certain day
    planned
    when he will punish the proud and
      those who brag,
  and they will no longer be important.
¹³ He will bring down the tall cedar trees
      from Lebanon
  and the great oak trees of Bashan,
¹⁴ all the tall mountains
    and the high hills,
¹⁵ every tall tower
    and every high, strong wall,
¹⁶ all the trading ships
    and the beautiful ships.
¹⁷ At that time proud people will be made
    humble,
    and they will bow low with shame.

At that time only the LORD will be praised,
¹⁸   but all the idols will be gone.

¹⁹ People will run to caves in the rocky cliffs
    and will dig holes and hide in the
      ground
  from the anger of the LORD
    and his great power,
    when he stands to shake the earth.
²⁰ At that time people will throw away
    their gold and silver idols,
  which they made for themselves to
      worship;
    they will throw them away to the bats
      and moles.
²¹ Then the people will hide in caves
    and cracks in the rocks
  from the anger of the LORD
    and his great power,
    when he stands to shake the earth.

²² You should stop trusting in people to save
    you,
  because people are only human;
  they aren't able to help you.

GOD WILL PUNISH JUDAH AND JERUSALEM

3 Understand this:
  The Lord GOD All-Powerful
  will take away everything Judah and
      Jerusalem need—
    all the food and water,
² the heroes and great soldiers,
    the judges and prophets,
  people who do magic and elders,
³ the military leaders and government
      leaders,
    the counselors, the skilled craftsmen,
    and those who try to tell the future.
⁴ The LORD says, "I will cause young boys
    to be your leaders,
  and foolish children will rule over you.
⁵ People will be against each other;
    everyone will be against his neighbor.
  Young people will not respect older
      people,
  and common people will not respect
      important people."
⁶ At that time a man will grab one of his
    brothers
  from his own family and say,
  "You have a coat, so you will be our leader.
  These ruins will be under your control."
⁷ But that brother will stand up and say,

"I cannot help you,
because I do not have food or clothes in
my house.
You will not make me your leader."
8 This will happen because Jerusalem has
stumbled,
and Judah has fallen.
The things they say and do are against the
LORD;
they turn against him.
9 The look on their faces shows they are
guilty;
like the people of Sodom, they are
proud of their sin.
They don't care who sees it.
How terrible it will be for them,
because they have brought much
trouble on themselves.

10 Tell those who do what is right that things
will go well for them,
because they will receive a reward for
what they do.
11 But how terrible it will be for the
wicked!
They will be punished for all the wrong
they have done.
12 Children treat my people cruelly,
and women rule over them.
My people, your guides lead you in the
wrong way
and turn you away from what is right.

13 The LORD takes his place in court
and stands to judge the people.
14 The LORD presents his case
against the elders and other leaders of
his people:
"You have burned the vineyard.
Your houses are full of what you took
from the poor.
15 What gives you the right to crush my
people
and grind the faces of the poor into the
dirt?"
The Lord GOD All-Powerful says this.

A WARNING TO WOMEN OF JERUSALEM
16 The LORD says,
"The women of Jerusalem are proud.
They walk around with their heads held
high,
and they flirt with their eyes.
They take quick, short steps,

making noise with their ankle
bracelets."
17 So the Lord will put sores on the heads of
those women in Jerusalem,
and he will make them lose their hair.
18 At that time the Lord will take away
everything that makes them proud: their
beautiful ankle bracelets, their headbands,
their necklaces shaped like the moon, 19their
earrings, bracelets, and veils, 20their scarves,
ankle chains, the cloth belts worn around
their waists, their bottles of perfume, and
charms, 21their signet rings, nose rings,
22their fine robes, capes, shawls, and purses,
23their mirrors, linen dresses, turbans, and
long shawls.
24 Instead of wearing sweet-smelling
perfume, they will stink.
Instead of fine cloth belts, they will
wear the ropes of captives.
Instead of having their hair fixed in fancy
ways, they will be bald.
Instead of fine clothes, they will wear
clothes of sadness.
Instead of being beautiful, they will
wear the brand of a captive.
25 At that time your men will be killed with
swords,
and your heroes will die in war.
26 There will be crying and sadness near the
city gates.
Jerusalem will be like a woman who
has lost everything and sits on the
ground.

4 At that time seven women will grab one
man
and say, "We will eat our own bread
and make our own clothes,
but please marry us!
Please, take away our shame."

THE BRANCH OF THE LORD
2At that time the LORD's branch will be
very beautiful and great. The people still living in Israel will be proud of what the land
grows. 3Those who are still living in Jerusalem will be called holy; their names are
recorded among the living in Jerusalem.
4The Lord will wash away the filth from
the women of Jerusalem. He will wash the
bloodstains out of Jerusalem and clean the
city with the spirit of fairness and the spirit

of fire. 5Then the LORD will cover Mount Zion and the people who meet there with a cloud of smoke during the day and with a bright, flaming fire at night. There will be a covering over every person. 6This covering will protect the people from the heat of the sun and will provide a safe place to hide from the storm and rain.

ISRAEL, THE LORD'S VINEYARD

5 Now I will sing for my friend a song
about his vineyard.
My friend had a vineyard
on a hill with very rich soil.
2 He dug and cleared the field of stones
and planted the best grapevines there.
He built a tower in the middle of it
and cut out a winepress as well.
He hoped good grapes would grow there,
but only bad ones grew.

3 My friend says, "You people living in
Jerusalem,
and you people of Judah,
judge between me and my vineyard.
4 What more could I have done for my
vineyard
than I have already done?
Although I expected good grapes to grow,
why were there only bad ones?
5 Now I will tell you
what I will do to my vineyard:
I will remove the hedge,
and it will be burned.
I will break down the stone wall,
and it will be walked on.
6 I will ruin my field.
It will not be trimmed or hoed,
and weeds and thorns will grow there.
I will command the clouds
not to rain on it."

7 The vineyard belonging to the LORD
All-Powerful
is the nation of Israel;
the garden that he loves
is the people of Judah.
He looked for justice, but there was only
killing.
He hoped for right living, but there
were only cries of pain.

8 How terrible it will be for you who add
more houses to your houses
and more fields to your fields

until there is no room left for other
people.
Then you are left alone in the land.

9The LORD All-Powerful said this to me:
"The fine houses will be destroyed;
the large and beautiful houses will be
left empty.
10 At that time a ten-acre vineyard will make
only six gallons of wine,
and ten bushels of seed will grow only
half a bushel of grain."

11 How terrible it will be for people who rise
early in the morning
to look for strong drink,
who stay awake late at night,
becoming drunk with wine.
12 At their parties they have lyres, harps,
tambourines, flutes, and wine.
They don't see what the LORD has done
or notice the work of his hands.
13 So my people will be captured and taken
away,
because they don't really know me.
All the great people will die of hunger,
and the common people will die of
thirst.
14 So the place of the dead wants more and
more people,
and it opens wide its mouth.
Jerusalem's important people and
common people will go down into it,
with their happy and noisy ones.
15 So the common people and the great
people will be brought down;
those who are proud will be humbled.
16 The LORD All-Powerful will receive glory
by judging fairly;
the holy God will show himself holy by
doing what is right.
17 Then the sheep will go anywhere they
want,
and lambs will feed on the land that
rich people once owned.
18 How terrible it will be for those
people!
They pull their guilt and sins behind
them
as people pull wagons with ropes.
19 They say, "Let God hurry;
let him do his work soon
so we may see it.

Let the plan of the Holy One of Israel
happen soon
so that we will know what it is."

20 How terrible it will be for people who call
good things bad
and bad things good,
who think darkness is light
and light is darkness,
who think sour is sweet
and sweet is sour.

21 How terrible it will be for people who
think they are wise
and believe they are clever.

22 How terrible it will be for people who are
famous for drinking wine
and are champions at mixing drinks.

23 They take money to set the guilty free
and don't allow good people to be
judged fairly.

24 They will be destroyed
just as fire burns straw or dry grass.
They will be destroyed
like a plant whose roots rot
and whose flower dies and blows away
like dust.
They have refused to obey the teachings
of the LORD All-Powerful
and have hated the message from the
Holy God of Israel.

25 So the LORD has become very angry with
his people,
and he has raised his hand to punish
them.
Even the mountains are frightened.
Dead bodies lie in the streets like
garbage.

But the LORD is still angry;
his hand is still raised to strike down
the people.

26 He raises a banner for the nations far
away.
He whistles to call those people from
the ends of the earth.
Look! The enemy comes quickly!

27 Not one of them becomes tired or falls
down.
Not one of them gets sleepy and falls
asleep.
Their weapons are close at hand,
and their sandal straps are not broken.

28 Their arrows are sharp,
and all of their bows are ready to shoot.
The horses' hoofs are hard as rocks,
and their chariot wheels move like a
whirlwind.

29 Their shout is like the roar of a lion;
it is loud like a young lion.
They growl as they grab their captives.
There is no one to stop them from
taking their captives away.

30 On that day they will roar
like the waves of the sea.
And when people look at the land,
they will see only darkness and pain;
all light will become dark in this thick
cloud.

ISAIAH BECOMES A PROPHET

6 In the year that King Uzziah died, I saw
the Lord sitting on a very high throne.
His long robe filled the Temple. 2Heavenly
creatures of fire stood above him. Each creature had six wings: It used two wings to cover
its face, two wings to cover its feet, and two
wings for flying. 3Each creature was calling
to the others:

"Holy, holy, holy is the LORD All-Powerful.
His glory fills the whole earth."

4Their calling caused the frame around the
door to shake, as the Temple filled with
smoke.

5I said, "Oh, no! I will be destroyed. I am
not pure, and I live among people who are
not pure, but I have seen the King, the LORD
All-Powerful."

6One of the heavenly creatures used a pair
of tongs to take a hot coal from the altar. Then
he flew to me with the hot coal in his hand.
7The creature touched my mouth with the
hot coal and said, "Look, your guilt is taken
away, because this hot coal has touched your
lips. Your sin is taken away."

8Then I heard the Lord's voice, saying,
"Whom can I send? Who will go for us?"

So I said, "Here I am. Send me!"

9Then the Lord said, "Go and tell this to
the people:

'You will listen and listen, but you will not
understand.
You will look and look, but you will not
learn.'

10 Make the minds of these people dumb.
Shut their ears. Cover their eyes.

Otherwise, they might really understand
what they see with their eyes
and hear with their ears.
They might really understand in their
minds
and come back to me and be healed."

[11]Then I asked, "Lord, how long should I
do this?"

He answered,

"Until the cities are destroyed
and the people are gone,
until there are no people left in the
houses,
until the land is destroyed and left
empty.
[12] The LORD will send the people far
away,
and the land will be left empty.
[13] One-tenth of the people will be left in the
land,
but it will be destroyed again.
These people will be like an oak tree
whose stump is left when the tree is
chopped down.
The people who remain will be like a
stump that will sprout again."

TROUBLE WITH ARAM

7 Now Ahaz was the son of Jotham, who
was the son of Uzziah. When Ahaz was
king of Judah, Rezin king of Aram and Pekah
son of Remaliah, the king of Israel, went up
to Jerusalem to fight against it. But they were
not able to defeat the city.

[2]Ahaz king of Judah received a message
saying, "The armies of Aram and Israel[n] have
joined together."

When Ahaz heard this, he and the people
were frightened. They shook with fear like
trees of the forest blown by the wind.

[3]Then the LORD told Isaiah, "You and
your son Shear-Jashub[n] should go and meet
Ahaz at the place where the water flows into
the upper pool, on the road where people
do their laundry. [4]Tell Ahaz, 'Be careful. Be
calm and don't worry. Don't let those two
men, Rezin and Pekah son of Remaliah, scare
you. Don't be afraid of their anger or Aram's
anger, because they are like two barely burning sticks that are ready to go out. [5]They
have made plans against you, saying, [6]"Let's
fight against Judah and tear it apart. We will
divide the land for ourselves and make the

son of Tabeel the new king of Judah." [7]But I,
the Lord GOD, say,

"'Their plan will not succeed;
it will not happen,
[8] because Aram is led by the city of
Damascus,
and Damascus is led by its weak king,
Rezin.
Within sixty-five years Israel will no
longer be a nation.
[9] Israel is led by the city of Samaria,
and Samaria is led by its weak king, the
son of Remaliah.
If your faith is not strong,
you will not have strength enough to
last.'"

IMMANUEL—GOD IS WITH US

[10]Then the LORD spoke to Ahaz again, saying, [11]"Ask for a sign from the LORD your God
to prove to yourself that these things are true.
It may be a sign from as deep as the place of
the dead or as high as the heavens."

[12]But Ahaz said, "I will not ask for a sign
or test the LORD."

[13]Then Isaiah said, "Ahaz, descendant of
David, listen carefully! Isn't it bad enough
that you wear out the patience of people? Do
you also have to wear out the patience of my
God? [14]The Lord himself will give you a sign:
The virgin[n] will be pregnant. She will have a
son, and she will name him Immanuel.[n] [15]He
will be eating milk curds and honey when
he learns to reject what is evil and to choose
what is good. [16]You are afraid of the kings of
Israel and Aram now. But before the child
learns to choose good and reject evil, the
lands of Israel and Aram will be empty. [17]The
LORD will bring troubled times to you, your
people, and to the people of your father's
family. They will be worse than anything that
has happened since Israel separated from Judah. The LORD will bring the king of Assyria
to fight against you.

[18]"At that time the LORD will whistle
for the Egyptians, and they will come like

7:2 Israel Literally, "Ephraim." Isaiah often uses "Ephraim"
to mean all of Israel. **7:3 Shear-Jashub** This name means
"a part of the people will come back." **7:14 virgin** The
Hebrew word means "a young woman." Often this meant
a girl who was not married and had not yet had sexual
relations with anyone. **7:14 Immanuel** This name
means "God is with us."

flies from Egypt's faraway streams. He will call for the Assyrians, and they will come like bees. ¹⁹These enemies will camp in the deep ravines and in the cliffs, by the thorn-bushes and watering holes. ²⁰The Lord will hire Assyria and use it like a razor to punish Judah. It will be as if the Lord is shaving the hair from Judah's head and legs and removing Judah's beard.

²¹"At that time a person will be able to keep only one young cow and two sheep alive. ²²There will be only enough milk for that person to eat milk curds. All who remain in the land will go back to eating just milk curds and honey. ²³In this land there are now vineyards that have a thousand grapevines, which are worth about twenty-five pounds of silver. But these fields will become full of weeds and thorns. ²⁴The land will become wild and useful only as a hunting ground. ²⁵People once worked and grew food on these hills, but at that time people will not go there, because the land will be filled with weeds and thorns. Only sheep and cattle will go to those places."

ASSYRIA WILL COME SOON

8 The LORD told me, "Take a large scroll and write on it with an ordinary pen: 'Maher-Shalal-Hash-Baz.' ²I will gather some men to be reliable witnesses: Uriah the priest and Zechariah son of Jeberekiah."

³Then I went to the prophetess, and she became pregnant and had a son. The LORD told me, "Name the boy Maher-Shalal-Hash-Baz,ⁿ ⁴because the king of Assyria will take away all the wealth and possessions of Damascus and Samaria before the boy learns to say 'my father' or 'my mother.'"

⁵Again the LORD spoke to me, saying,

⁶ "These people refuse to accept
   the slow-moving waters of the pool of
      Shiloah
 and are terrified of Rezin
   and Pekah son of Remaliah.
⁷ So I, the Lord, will bring
   the king of Assyria and all his power
      against them,
   like a powerful flood of water from the
      Euphrates River.
The Assyrians will be like water rising
      over the banks of the river,
   flowing over the land.

⁸ That water will flow into Judah and pass
      through it,
   rising to Judah's throat.
Immanuel, this army will spread its wings
      like a bird
   until it covers your whole country."

⁹ Be broken, all you nations,
   and be smashed to pieces.
Listen, all you faraway countries.
   Prepare for battle and be smashed to
      pieces!
   Prepare for battle and be smashed to
      pieces!
¹⁰ Make your plans for the fight,
   but they will be defeated.
Give orders to your armies,
   but they will be useless,
because God is with us.

WARNINGS TO ISAIAH

¹¹The LORD spoke to me with his great power and warned me not to follow the lead of the rest of the people. He said,

¹² "People are saying that others make plans
      against them,
   but you should not believe them.
Don't be afraid of what they fear;
   do not dread those things.
¹³ But remember that the LORD All-Powerful
      is holy.
He is the one you should fear;
   he is the one you should dread.
¹⁴ Then he will be a place of safety for you.
   But for the two families of Israel,
he will be like a stone that causes people
      to stumble,
   like a rock that makes them fall.
He will be like a trap for the people of
      Jerusalem,
   and he will catch them in his trap.
¹⁵ Many people will fall over this rock.
   They will fall and be broken;
   they will be trapped and caught."

¹⁶ Make an agreement.
   Seal up the teaching while my followers
      are watching.
¹⁷ I will wait for the LORD to help us,
   the LORD who is ashamed of the family
      of Israel.
I will wait for him.

8:3 Maher-Shalal-Hash-Baz This name means "there will soon be looting and stealing."

18I am here, and with me are the children the LORD has given me. We are signs and proofs for the people of Israel from the LORD All-Powerful, who lives on Mount Zion.

19Some people say, "Ask the mediums and fortune-tellers, who whisper and mutter, what to do." But I tell you that people should ask their God for help. Why should people who are still alive ask something from the dead? 20You should follow the teachings and the agreement with the LORD. The mediums and fortune-tellers do not speak the word of the LORD, so their words are worth nothing.

21People will wander through the land troubled and hungry. When they become hungry, they will become angry and will look up and curse their king and their God. 22They will look around them at their land and see only trouble, darkness, and awful gloom. And they will be forced into the darkness.

A NEW DAY IS COMING

9 But suddenly there will be no more gloom for the land that suffered. In the past God made the lands of Zebulun and Naphtali hang their heads in shame, but in the future those lands will be made great. They will stretch from the road along the Mediterranean Sea to the land beyond the Jordan River and north to Galilee, the land of people who are not Israelites.

2 Before those people lived in darkness,
  but now they have seen a great light.
They lived in a dark land,
  but a light has shined on them.
3 God, you have caused the nation to grow
  and made the people happy.
And they have shown their happiness to you,
  like the joy during harvest time,
like the joy of people
  taking what they have won in war.
4 Like the time you defeated Midian,
  you have taken away their heavy load
and the heavy pole from their backs
  and the rod the enemy used to punish them.
5 Every boot that marched in battle
  and every uniform stained with blood
  has been thrown into the fire.
6 A child has been born to us;
  God has given a son to us.
He will be responsible for leading the people.
His name will be Wonderful Counselor,
  Powerful God,
Father Who Lives Forever, Prince of Peace.
7 Power and peace will be in his kingdom
  and will continue to grow forever.
He will rule as king on David's throne
  and over David's kingdom.
He will make it strong
  by ruling with justice and goodness
  from now on and forever.
The LORD All-Powerful will do this
  because of his strong love for his people.

GOD WILL PUNISH ISRAEL

8 The Lord sent a message against the people of Jacob;
  it says that God will judge Israel.
9 Then everyone in Israel, even the leaders in Samaria,
  will know that God has sent it.
Those people are proud and brag by saying,
10 "These bricks have fallen,
  but we will build again with cut stones.
These small trees have been chopped down,
  but we will put great cedars there."
11 But the LORD has brought the enemies of Rezin against them;
  he has stirred up their enemies against them.
12 The Arameans came from the east
  and the Philistines from the west,
and they ate up Israel with their armies.
But the LORD was still angry;
  his hand was still raised to punish the people.
13 But the people did not return to the one who had struck them;
  they did not follow the LORD All-Powerful.
14 So the LORD cut off Israel's head and tail,
  taking away both the branch and stalk in one day.
15 The elders and important men were the head,
  and the prophets who speak lies were the tail.

711

16 Those who led the people led them in the
  wrong direction,
  and those who followed them were
    destroyed.
17 So the Lord is not happy with the young
    people,
  nor will he show mercy to the orphans
    and widows.
All the people are separated from God and
    are very evil;
  they all speak lies.

But the Lord is still angry;
  his hand is still raised to strike down
    the people.

18 Evil is like a small fire.
  First, it burns weeds and thorns.
Next, it burns the larger bushes in the
    forest,
  and they all go up in a column of smoke.
19 The Lord All-Powerful is angry,
  so the land will be burned.
The people are like fuel for the fire;
  no one will try to save his brother or
    sister.
20 People will grab something on the right,
  but they will still be hungry.
They will eat something on the left,
  but they will not be filled.
Then they will each turn and eat their
    own children.
21 The people of Manasseh will fight against
  the people of Ephraim,
  and Ephraim will fight against
    Manasseh.
  Then both of them will turn against
    Judah.

But the Lord is still angry;
  his hand is still raised to strike down
    the people.

10 How terrible it will be for those who
    make unfair laws,
  and those who write laws that make life
    hard for people.
2 They are not fair to the poor,
  and they rob my people of their rights.
They allow people to steal from widows
  and to take from orphans what really
    belongs to them.
3 How will you explain the things you have
    done?

What will you do when your
  destruction comes from far away?
Where will you run for help?
  Where will you hide your riches then?
4 You will have to bow down among the
    captives
  or fall down among the dead bodies.
But the Lord is still angry;
  his hand is still raised to strike down
    the people.

GOD WILL PUNISH ASSYRIA

5 God says, "How terrible it will be for the
    king of Assyria.
  I use him like a rod to show my anger;
  in anger I use Assyria like a club.
6 I send it to fight against a nation that is
    separated from God.
  I am angry with those people,
  so I command Assyria to fight against
    them,
to take their wealth from them,
  to trample them down like dirt in the
    streets.
7 But Assyria's king doesn't understand that
    I am using him;
  he doesn't know he is a tool for me.
He only wants to destroy other people
  and to defeat many nations.
8 The king of Assyria says to himself,
  'All of my commanders are like kings.
9 The city Calno is like the city Carchemish.
  The city Hamath is like the city Arpad.
  The city Samaria is like the city
    Damascus.
10 I defeated those kingdoms that worship
    idols,
  and those idols were more than the
    idols of Jerusalem and Samaria.
11 As I defeated Samaria and her idols,
  I will also defeat Jerusalem and her
    idols.' "

12 When the Lord finishes doing what
he planned to Mount Zion and Jerusalem,
he will punish Assyria. The king of Assyria is
very proud, and his pride has made him do
these evil things, so God will punish him.
13 The king of Assyria says this:

"By my own power I have done these
    things;
  by my wisdom I have defeated many
    nations.
I have taken their wealth,

and, like a mighty one, I have taken
their people.

14 I have taken the riches of all these people,
like a person reaching into a bird's nest.
I have taken these nations,
like a person taking eggs.
Not one raised a hand
or opened its mouth to stop me."

15 An ax is not better than the person who
swings it.
A saw is not better than the one who
uses it.
A stick cannot control the person who
picks it up.
A club cannot pick up the person!

16 So the Lord GOD All-Powerful
will send a terrible disease upon
Assyria's soldiers.
The strength of Assyria will be burned up
like a fire burning until everything is
gone.

17 God, the Light of Israel, will be like a fire;
the Holy One will be like a flame.
He will be like a fire
that suddenly burns the weeds and
thorns.

18 The fire burns away the great trees and
rich farmlands,
destroying everything.
It will be like a sick person who wastes
away.

19 The trees left standing will be so few
that even a child could count them.

20 At that time some people will be left alive
in Israel
from the family of Jacob.
They will not continue to depend
on the person who defeated them.
They will learn truly to depend on the
LORD,
the Holy One of Israel.

21 Those who are left alive in Jacob's family
will again follow the powerful God.

22 Israel, your people are many,
like the grains of sand by the sea.
But only a few of them will be left alive
to return to the LORD.
God has announced that he will destroy
the land
completely and fairly.

23 The Lord GOD All-Powerful will certainly
destroy this land,
as he has announced.

24 This is what the Lord GOD All-Powerful
says:

"My people living in Jerusalem,
don't be afraid of the Assyrians,
who beat you with a rod
and raise a stick against you, as Egypt
did.

25 After a short time my anger against you
will stop,
and then I will turn my anger to
destroying them."

26 Then the LORD All-Powerful will beat the
Assyrians with a whip
as he defeated Midian at the rock of
Oreb.
He will raise his stick over the waters
as he did in Egypt.

27 Then the troubles that Assyria puts on
you
will be removed,
and the load they make you carry
will be taken away.

ASSYRIA INVADES ISRAEL

28 The army of Assyria will enter near
Aiath.
Its soldiers will walk through Migron.
They will store their food in Micmash.

29 The army will go over the pass.
The soldiers will sleep at Geba.
The people of Ramah will be afraid,
and the people at Gibeah of Saul will
run away.

30 Cry out, Bath Gallim!
Laishah, listen!
Poor Anathoth!

31 The people of Madmenah are running
away;
the people of Gebim are hiding.

32 This day the army will stop at Nob.
They will shake their fist at Mount
Zion,
at the hill of Jerusalem.

33 Watch! The Lord GOD All-Powerful
with his great power will chop them
down like a great tree.
Those who are great will be cut down;
those who are important will fall to the
ground.

34 He will cut them down
as a forest is cut down with an ax.
And the great trees of Lebanon

will fall by the power of the Mighty One.

THE KING OF PEACE IS COMING

11 A new branch will grow
from a stump of a tree;
so a new king will come
from the family of Jesse.[n]

2 The Spirit of the LORD will rest upon that king.
The Spirit will give him wisdom and understanding, guidance and power.
The Spirit will teach him to know and respect the LORD.
3 This king will be glad to obey the LORD.
He will not judge by the way things look or decide by what he hears.
4 But he will judge the poor honestly;
he will be fair in his decisions for the poor people of the land.
At his command evil people will be punished,
and by his words the wicked will be put to death.
5 Goodness and fairness will give him strength,
like a belt around his waist.

6 Then wolves will live in peace with lambs,
and leopards will lie down to rest with goats.
Calves, lions, and young bulls will eat together,
and a little child will lead them.
7 Cows and bears will eat together in peace.
Their young will lie down to rest together.
Lions will eat hay as oxen do.
8 A baby will be able to play near a cobra's hole,
and a child will be able to put his hand into the nest of a poisonous snake.
9 They will not hurt or destroy each other on all my holy mountain,
because the earth will be full of the knowledge of the LORD,
as the sea is full of water.

10 At that time the new king from the family of Jesse will stand as a banner for all peoples. The nations will come together around him, and the place where he lives will be filled with glory. 11 At that time the Lord will again reach out and take his people who are left alive in Assyria, North Egypt, South Egypt, Cush, Elam, Babylonia, Hamath, and all the islands of the sea.

12 God will raise a banner as a sign for all nations,
and he will gather the people of Israel who were forced from their country.
He will gather the scattered people of Judah
from all parts of the earth.
13 At that time Israel will not be jealous anymore,
and Judah will have no more enemies.
Israel will not be jealous of Judah,
and Judah will not hate Israel.
14 But Israel and Judah will attack the Philistines on the west.
Together they will take the riches from the people of the east.
They will conquer Edom and Moab,
and the people of Ammon will be under their control.
15 The LORD will dry up
the Red Sea of Egypt.
He will wave his arm over the Euphrates River
and dry it up with a scorching wind.
He will divide it into seven small rivers
so that people can walk across them with their sandals on.
16 So God's people who are left alive will have a way to leave Assyria,
just like the time the Israelites came out of Egypt.

A SONG OF PRAISE TO GOD

12 At that time you will say:
"I praise you, LORD!
You were angry with me,
but you are not angry with me now!
You have comforted me.
2 God is the one who saves me;
I will trust him and not be afraid.
The LORD, the LORD gives me strength and makes me sing.
He has saved me."
3 You will receive your salvation with joy
as you would draw water from a well.
4 At that time you will say,
"Praise the LORD and worship him.
Tell everyone what he has done
and how great he is.

11:1 Jesse King David's father.

⁵ Sing praise to the LORD, because he has
    done great things.
  Let all the world know what he has
    done.
⁶ Shout and sing for joy, you people of
    Jerusalem,
  because the Holy One of Israel does
    great things before your eyes."

GOD'S MESSAGE TO BABYLON

13 God showed Isaiah son of Amoz this
message about Babylon:

² Raise a flag on the bare mountain.
  Call out to the men.
  Raise your hand to signal them
    to enter through the gates for important
    people.
³ I myself have commanded those people
  whom I have separated as mine.
  I have called those warriors to carry out
    my anger.
  They rejoice and are glad to do my will.

⁴ Listen to the loud noise in the mountains,
  the sound of many people.
  Listen to the noise among the kingdoms,
    the sound of nations gathering
    together.
  The LORD All-Powerful is calling
    his army together for battle.
⁵ This army is coming from a faraway land,
  from the edge of the horizon.
  In anger the LORD is using this army like
    a weapon
    to destroy the whole country.

⁶ Cry, because the LORD's day of judging is
    near;
  the Almighty is sending destruction.
⁷ People will be weak with fear,
  and their courage will melt away.
⁸ Everyone will be afraid.
  Pain and hurt will grab them;
  they will hurt like a woman giving birth
    to a baby.

ANGER MANAGEMENT

planned intervals

FITNESS

ISAIAH 12:2

G od is the only source of restoration. It is God who brings renewal and restoration
to life. God returns both physical and spiritual wellness.

Little by little, the journey of life dissipates our vitality. Often we don't notice how tired
we really are until we stop doing things. That's when we recognize that we need a
return to wellness. Yet restoration requires planned intervals.

If you feel like you're in a marathon, you might consider your need for regular
restoration along the way. Without it, damage is inevitable. God is able to return your
whole person to vitality if you take what he offers. He's right there, holding out the cup.
Don't pass by without taking it. Planned restoration is the only way to finish the race
alive and well.

reflect: Rejoice in the fact that God is in the personal restoration business.
Go to **Psalm 59:9.**

They will look at each other in fear,
  with their faces red like fire.

GOD'S JUDGMENT AGAINST BABYLON

⁹ Look, the LORD's day of judging is
    coming—
  a terrible day, a day of God's anger.
He will destroy the land
  and the sinners who live in it.
¹⁰ The stars will not show their light;
  the skies will be dark.
The sun will grow dark as it rises,
  and the moon will not give its light.

¹¹ The LORD says, "I will punish the world
    for its evil
  and wicked people for their sins.
I will cause proud people to lose their
    pride,
  and I will destroy the pride of those
    who are cruel to others.
¹² People will be harder to find than pure
    gold;
  there will be fewer people than there is
    fine gold in Ophir.
¹³ I will make the sky shake,
  and the earth will be moved from its
    place
by the anger of the LORD All-Powerful
  at the time of his burning anger.

¹⁴ "Then the people from Babylon will run
    away like hunted deer
  or like sheep who have no shepherd.
Everyone will turn back to his own
    people;
  each will run back to his own land.
¹⁵ Everyone who is captured will be killed;
  everyone who is caught will be killed
    with a sword.
¹⁶ Their little children will be beaten to
    death in front of them.
  Their houses will be robbed
    and their wives raped.

¹⁷ "Look, I will cause the armies of Media to
    attack Babylon.
  They do not care about silver
    or delight in gold.
¹⁸ Their soldiers will shoot the young men
    with arrows;
  they will show no mercy on children,
    nor will they feel sorry for little ones.
¹⁹ Babylon is the most beautiful of all
    kingdoms,

and the Babylonians are very proud of
    it.
But God will destroy it
  like Sodom and Gomorrah.
²⁰ No one will ever live there
  or settle there again.
No Arab will put a tent there;
  no shepherd will bring sheep there.
²¹ Only desert animals will live there,
  and their houses will be full of wild
    dogs.
Owls will live there,
  and wild goats will leap about in the
    houses.
²² Wolves will howl within the strong walls,
  and wild dogs will bark in the beautiful
    buildings.
The end of Babylon is near;
  its time is almost over."

ISRAEL WILL RETURN HOME

14 The LORD will show mercy to the people of Jacob, and he will again choose
the people of Israel. He will settle them in
their own land. Then non-Israelite people
will join the Israelites and will become a part
of the family of Jacob. ²Nations will take the
Israelites back to their land. Then those men
and women from the other nations will become slaves to Israel in the LORD's land. In
the past the Israelites were their slaves, but
now the Israelites will defeat those nations
and rule over them.

THE KING OF BABYLON WILL FALL

³The LORD will take away the Israelites'
hard work and will comfort them. They will
no longer have to work hard as slaves. ⁴On
that day Israel will sing this song about the
king of Babylon:
  The cruel king who ruled us is finished;
    his angry rule is finished!
⁵ The LORD has broken the scepter of evil
    rulers
  and taken away their power.
⁶ The king of Babylon struck people in
    anger
  again and again.
He ruled nations in anger
  and continued to hurt them.
⁷ But now, the whole world rests and is
    quiet.
  Now the people begin to sing.
⁸ Even the pine trees are happy,

and the cedar trees of Lebanon rejoice.
They say, "The king has fallen,
so no one will ever cut us down again."

9 The place of the dead is excited
to meet you when you come.
It wakes the spirits of the dead,
the leaders of the world.
It makes kings of all nations
stand up from their thrones to greet
you.
10 All these leaders will make fun of you
and will say,
"Now you are weak, as we are.
Now you are just like us."
11 Your pride has been sent down to the
place of the dead.
The music from your harps goes with it.
Flies are spread out like your bed beneath
you,
and worms cover your body like a
blanket.
12 King of Babylon, morning star, you have
fallen from heaven,
even though you were as bright as the
rising sun!
In the past all the nations on earth bowed
down before you,
but now you have been cut down.
13 You told yourself,
"I will go up to heaven.
I will put my throne
above God's stars.
I will sit on the mountain of the gods,
on the slopes of the sacred mountain.
14 I will go up above the tops of the clouds.
I will be like God Most High."
15 But you were brought down to the grave,
to the deep places where the dead are.

16 Those who see you stare at you.
They think about what has happened
to you
and say, "Is this the same man who caused
great fear on earth,
who shook the kingdoms,
17 who turned the world into a desert,
who destroyed its cities,
who captured people in war
and would not let them go home?"

18 Every king of the earth has been buried
with honor,
each in his own grave.

19 But you are thrown out of your grave,
like an unwanted branch.
You are covered by bodies
that died in battle,
by bodies to be buried in a rocky pit.
You are like a dead body other soldiers
walk on.
20 You will not be buried with those
bodies,
because you ruined your own country
and killed your own people.
The children of evil people
will never be mentioned again.

21 Prepare to kill his children,
because their father is guilty.
They will never again take control of the
earth;
they will never again fill the world with
their cities.

22 The LORD All-Powerful says this:
"I will fight against those people;
I will destroy Babylon and its people,
its children and their descendants," says
the LORD.
23 "I will make Babylon fit only for owls
and for swamps.
I will sweep Babylon as with a broom of
destruction,"
says the LORD All-Powerful.

GOD WILL PUNISH ASSYRIA

24 The LORD All-Powerful has made this
promise:
"These things will happen exactly as I
planned them;
they will happen exactly as I set them
up.
25 I will destroy the king of Assyria in my
country;
I will trample him on my mountains.
He placed a heavy load on my people,
but that weight will be removed.

26 "This is what I plan to do for all the earth.
And this is the hand that I have raised
over all nations."

27 When the LORD All-Powerful makes a
plan,
no one can stop it.
When the LORD raises his hand to punish
people,
no one can stop it.

GOD'S MESSAGE TO PHILISTIA

28This message was given in the year that King Ahaz died:

29 Country of Philistia, don't be happy
 that the king who struck you is now
 dead.
He is like a snake that will give birth to
 another dangerous snake.
 The new king will be like a quick,
 dangerous snake to bite you.
30 Even the poorest of my people will be able
 to eat safely,
 and people in need will be able to lie
 down in safety.
But I will kill your family with hunger,
 and all your people who are left will die.

31 People near the city gates, cry out!
 Philistines, be frightened,
because a cloud of dust comes from the
 north.
 It is an army, full of men ready to fight.
32 What shall we tell the messengers from
 Philistia?
Say that the LORD has made Jerusalem
 strong
 and that his poor people will go there
 for safety.

GOD'S MESSAGE TO MOAB

15 This is a message about Moab:
 In one night armies took the wealth
 from Ar in Moab,
 and it was destroyed.
In one night armies took the wealth from
 Kir in Moab,
 and it was destroyed.
2 The people of Dibon go to the places of
 worship to cry.
 The people of Moab cry for the cities of
 Nebo and Medeba.
Every head and beard has been shaved to
 show how sad Moab is.
3 In the streets they wear rough cloth to
 show their sadness.
 On the roofs[n] and in the public squares,
they are crying loudly.
4 People in the cities Heshbon and Elealeh
 cry out loud.
 You can hear their voices far away in
 the city Jahaz.
Even the soldiers are frightened;
 they are shaking with fear.

5 My heart cries with sorrow for Moab.
 Its people run away to Zoar for safety;
 they run to Eglath Shelishiyah.
People are going up the mountain road to
 Luhith,
 crying as they go.
People are going on the road to Horonaim,
 crying over their destruction.
6 But the water of Nimrim has dried up.
 The grass has dried up,
and all the plants are dead;
 nothing green is left.
7 So the people gather up what they have
 saved
 and carry it across the Ravine of the
 Poplars.
8 Crying is heard everywhere in Moab.
 Their crying is heard as far away as the
 city Eglaim;
 it is heard as far away as Beer Elim.
9 The water of the city Dibon is full of
 blood,
 and I, the LORD, will bring even more
 troubles to Dibon.
A few people living in Moab have escaped
 the enemy,
 but I will send lions to kill them.

16 Send the king of the land
 the payment he demands.
Send a lamb from Sela through the
 desert
 to the mountain of Jerusalem.
2 The women of Moab
 try to cross the river Arnon
like little birds
 that have fallen from their nest.

3 They say: "Help us.
 Tell us what to do.
Protect us from our enemies
 as shade protects us from the noon sun.
Hide us, because we are running for
 safety!
 Don't give us to our enemies.
4 Let those of us who were forced out of
 Moab live in your land.
 Hide us from our enemies."

15:3 roofs In Bible times houses were built with flat roofs. The roof was used for drying things such as flax and fruit. And it was used as an extra room, as a place for worship, and as a cool place to sleep in the summer.

The robbing of Moab will stop.
The enemy will be defeated;
those who hurt others will disappear
from the land.
5 Then a new loyal king will come;
this faithful king will be from the family
of David.
He will judge fairly
and do what is right.

6 We have heard that the people of Moab
are proud
and very conceited.
They are very proud and angry,
but their bragging means nothing.
7 So the people of Moab will cry;
they will all be sad.
They will moan and groan
for the raisin cakes they had in Kir
Hareseth.
8 But the fields of Heshbon and the vines of
Sibmah cannot grow grapes;
foreign rulers have destroyed the
grapevines.
The grapevines once spread as far as the
city of Jazer and into the desert;
they had spread as far as the sea.
9 I cry with the people of Jazer
for the grapevines of Sibmah.
I will cry with the people of Heshbon and
Elealeh.
There will be no shouts of joy,
because there will be no harvest or ripe
fruit.
10 There will be no joy and happiness in the
orchards
and no songs or shouts of joy in the
vineyards.
No one makes wine in the winepresses,
because I have put an end to shouts of
joy.
11 My heart cries for Moab like a harp
playing a funeral song;
I am very sad for Kir Hareseth.
12 The people of Moab will go to their places
of worship
and will try to pray.
But when they go to their temple to pray,
they will not be able.

13 Earlier the LORD said these things about
Moab. 14 Now the LORD says, "In three years
all those people and what they take pride in
will be hated. (This is three years as a hired

helper would count time.) There will be a
few people left, but they will be weak."

GOD'S MESSAGE TO ARAM

17 This is a message about Damascus:
"The city of Damascus will be
destroyed;
only ruins will remain.
2 People will leave the cities of Aroer.
Flocks will wander freely in those
empty towns,
and there will be no one to bother them.
3 The strong, walled cities of Israel will be
destroyed.
The government in Damascus will end.
Those left alive of Aram will be
like the glory of Israel," says the LORD
All-Powerful.

4 "At that time Israel's wealth will all be
gone.
Israel will be like someone who has lost
much weight from sickness.
5 That time will be like the grain harvest in
the Valley of Rephaim.
The workers cut the wheat.
Then they cut the heads of grain from
the plants
and collect the grain.
6 That time will also be like the olive
harvest,
when a few olives are left.
Two or three olives are left in the top
branches.
Four or five olives are left on full
branches," says the LORD, the God of
Israel.

7 At that time people will look to God, their
Maker;
their eyes will see the Holy One of
Israel.
8 They will not trust the altars they have
made,
nor will they trust what their hands
have made,
not even the Asherah idols and altars.
9 In that day all their strong cities will
be empty. They will be like the cities the
Hivites and the Amorites left when the Israelites came to take the land. Everything will
be ruined.
10 You have forgotten the God who saves
you;

you have not remembered that God is
your place of safety.
You plant the finest grapevines
and grapevines from faraway places.
11 You plant your grapevines one day and try
to make them grow,
and the next day you make them
blossom.
But at harvest time everything will be
dead;
a sickness will kill all the plants.

12 Listen to the many people!
Their crying is like the noise from the
sea.
Listen to the nations!
Their crying is like the crashing of great
waves.
13 The people roar like the waves,
but when God speaks harshly to them,
they will run away.
They will be like chaff on the hills being
blown by the wind,
or like tumbleweeds blown away by a
storm.
14 At night the people will be very
frightened.
Before morning, no one will be left.
So our enemies will come to our land,
but they will become nothing.

GOD'S MESSAGE TO CUSH

18 How terrible it will be for the land
beyond the rivers of Cush.
It is filled with the sound of wings.
2 That land sends messengers across the
sea;
they go on the water in boats made of
reeds.

Go, quick messengers,
to a people who are tall and
smooth-skinned,
who are feared everywhere.
They are a powerful nation that defeats
other nations.
Their land is divided by rivers.

3 All you people of the world, look!
Everyone who lives in the world, look!
You will see a banner raised on a
mountain.
You will hear a trumpet sound.
4 The LORD said to me,
"I will quietly watch from where I live,

like heat in the sunshine,
like the dew in the heat of harvest
time."
5 The time will come, after the flowers have
bloomed and before the harvest,
when new grapes will be budding and
growing.
The enemy will cut the plants with
knives;
he will cut down the vines and take
them away.
6 They will be left for the birds of the
mountains
and for the wild animals.
Birds will feed on them all summer,
and wild animals will eat them that
winter."

7 At that time a gift will be brought to the
LORD All-Powerful
from the people who are tall and
smooth-skinned,
who are feared everywhere.
They are a powerful nation that defeats
other nations.
Their land is divided by rivers.
These gifts will be brought to the place of
the LORD All-Powerful,
to Mount Zion.

GOD'S MESSAGE TO EGYPT

19 This is a message about Egypt:
Look, the LORD is coming on a fast
cloud
to enter Egypt.
The idols of Egypt will tremble before
him,
and Egypt's courage will melt away.

2 The LORD says, "I will cause the Egyptians
to fight against themselves.
People will fight with their relatives;
neighbors will fight neighbors;
cities will fight cities;
kingdoms will fight kingdoms.
3 The Egyptians will be afraid,
and I will ruin their plans.
They will ask advice from their idols and
spirits of the dead,
from their mediums and
fortune-tellers."
4 The Lord GOD All-Powerful says,
"I will hand Egypt over to a hard
master,

and a powerful king will rule over
them."

5 The sea will become dry,
and the water will disappear from the
Nile River.
6 The canals will stink;
the streams of Egypt will decrease and
dry up.
All the water plants will rot;
7   all the plants along the banks of the
Nile will die.
Even the planted fields by the Nile
will dry up, blow away, and disappear.
8 The fishermen, all those who catch fish
from the Nile,
will groan and cry;
those who fish in the Nile will be sad.
9 All the people who make cloth from flax
will be sad,
and those who weave linen will lose
hope.
10 Those who weave cloth will be broken.
All those who work for money will be
sad.

11 The officers of the city of Zoan are fools;
the wise men who advise the king of
Egypt give wrong advice.
How can you say to him, 'I am wise'?
How can you say, 'I am from the old
family of the kings'?
12 Egypt, where are your wise men?
Let them show you
what the LORD All-Powerful has planned
for Egypt.
13 The officers of Zoan have been fooled;
the leaders of Memphis have believed
false things.
So the leaders of Egypt
lead that nation the wrong way.
14 The LORD has made the leaders confused.
They have led Egypt to wander in the
wrong ways,
like drunk people stumbling in their
own vomit.
15 There is nothing Egypt can do;
no one there can help.

16In that day the Egyptians will be like
women. They will be afraid of the LORD All-
Powerful, because he will raise his hand to
strike them down. 17The land of Judah will
bring fear to Egypt. Anyone there who hears
the name Judah will be afraid, because the
LORD All-Powerful has planned terrible
things for them. 18At that time five cities in
Egypt will speak Hebrew, the language of
Canaan, and they will promise to be loyal to
the LORD All-Powerful. One of these cities
will be named the City of Destruction. 19At
that time there will be an altar for the LORD
in the middle of Egypt and a monument to the
LORD at the border of Egypt. 20This will be a
sign and a witness to the LORD All-Powerful
in the land of Egypt. When the people cry to
the LORD for help, he will send someone to
save and defend them. He will rescue them
from those who hurt them.

21So the LORD will show himself to the
Egyptians, and then they will know he is the
LORD. They will worship God and offer many
sacrifices. They will make promises to the
LORD and will keep them. 22The LORD will
punish the Egyptians, but then he will heal
them. They will come back to the LORD, and
he will listen to their prayers and heal them.

23At that time there will be a highway
from Egypt to Assyria, and the Assyrians
will go to Egypt, and the Egyptians will go
to Assyria. The Egyptians and Assyrians will
worship God together. 24At that time Israel,
Assyria, and Egypt will join together, which
will be a blessing for the earth. 25The LORD
All-Powerful will bless them, saying, "Egypt,
you are my people. Assyria, I made you. Israel, I own you. You are all blessed!"

ASSYRIA WILL DEFEAT EGYPT AND CUSH

20 Sargon king of Assyria sent a military commander to Ashdod to attack
that city. So the commander attacked and
captured it. 2Then the LORD spoke through
Isaiah son of Amoz, saying, "Take the rough
cloth off your body, and take your sandals
off your feet." So Isaiah obeyed and walked
around naked and barefoot.

3Then the LORD said, "Isaiah my servant has walked around naked and barefoot
for three years as a sign against Egypt and
Cush. 4The king of Assyria will carry away
prisoners from Egypt and Cush. Old people
and young people will be led away naked
and barefoot, with their buttocks bare. So
the Egyptians will be shamed. 5People who
looked to Cush for help will be afraid, and
those who were amazed by Egypt's glory
will be shamed. 6People who live near the

sea will say, 'Look at those countries. We trusted them to help us. We ran to them so they would save us from the king of Assyria. So how will we be able to escape?'"

GOD'S MESSAGE TO BABYLON

21 This is a message about the Desert by the Sea:[n]
Disaster is coming from the desert
like wind blowing in the south.
It is coming from a terrible country.
2 I have seen a terrible vision.
I see traitors turning against you
and people taking your wealth.

Elam, attack the people!
Media, surround the city and attack it!
I will bring an end to the pain the city
causes.

3 I saw those terrible things, and now I am
in pain;
my pains are like the pains of giving
birth.
What I hear makes me very afraid;
what I see causes me to shake with fear.
4 I am worried,
and I am shaking with fear.
My pleasant evening
has become a night of fear.

5 They set the table;
they spread the rugs;
they eat and drink.
Leaders, stand up.
Prepare the shields for battle!

6 The Lord said to me,
"Go, place a lookout for the city
and have him report what he sees.
7 If he sees chariots and teams of horses,
donkeys, or camels,
he should pay very close attention."

8 Then the lookout called out,
"My master, each day I stand in the
watchtower watching;
every night I have been on guard.
9 Look, I see a man coming in a chariot
with a team of horses."
The man gives back the answer,
"Babylon has fallen. It has fallen!
All the statues of her gods
lie broken on the ground."
10 My people are crushed like grain on the
threshing floor.

My people, I tell you what I have heard
from the LORD All-Powerful,
from the God of Israel.

GOD'S MESSAGE TO EDOM

11 This is a message about Dumah:[n]
Someone calls to me from Edom,
"Watchman, how much of the night is
left?
Watchman, how much longer will it be
night?"
12 The watchman answers,
"Morning is coming, but then night will
come again.
If you have something to ask,
then come back and ask."

GOD'S MESSAGE TO ARABIA

13 This is a message about Arabia:
A group of traders from Dedan
spent the night near some trees in
Arabia.
14 They gave water to thirsty travelers;
the people of Tema gave food
to those who were escaping.
15 They were running from swords,
from swords ready to kill,
from bows ready to shoot,
from a hard battle.
16 This is what the Lord said to me: "In
one year all the glory of the country of Kedar will be gone. (This is a year as a hired helper counts time.) 17 At that time only a few of the archers, the soldiers of Kedar, will be left alive." The LORD, the God of Israel, has spoken.

GOD'S MESSAGE TO JERUSALEM

22 This is a message about the Valley of Vision:[n]
What is wrong with you people?
Why are you on your roofs?[n]
2 This city was a very busy city,
full of noise and wild parties.
Now your people have been killed,
but not with swords,
nor did they die in battle.

21:1 **Desert by the Sea** Probably Babylon. 21:11 **Dumah** Another name for Edom. 22:1 **Valley of Vision** This probably means a valley near Jerusalem. 22:1 **roofs** In Bible times houses were built with flat roofs. The roof was used for drying things such as flax and fruit. And it was used as an extra room, as a place for worship, and as a cool place to sleep in the summer.

³ All your leaders ran away together,
> but they have been captured without
> using a bow.
> All you who were captured
> tried to run away before the enemy
> came.
⁴ So I say, "Don't look at me.
> Let me cry loudly.
> Don't hurry to comfort me
> about the destruction of Jerusalem."
⁵ The Lord GOD All-Powerful has chosen a
> special day
> of riots and confusion.
> People will trample each other in the
> Valley of Vision.
> The city walls will be knocked down,
> and the people will cry out to the
> mountain.
⁶ The soldiers from Elam will gather their
> arrows
> and their chariots and men on horses.
> Kir will prepare their shields.
⁷ Your nicest valleys will be filled with
> chariots.
> Horsemen will be ordered to guard the
> gates of the city.
⁸ The walls protecting Judah will fall.

> At that time the people of Jerusalem
> depended on
> the weapons kept at the Palace of the
> Forest.
⁹ You saw that the walls of Jerusalem
> had many cracks that needed repairing.
> You stored up water in the lower pool.
¹⁰ You counted the houses of Jerusalem,
> and you tore down houses to repair the
> walls with their stones.
¹¹ You made a pool between the two walls
> to save water from the old pool,
> but you did not trust the God who made
> these things;
> you did not respect the One who
> planned them long ago.
¹² The Lord GOD All-Powerful told the
> people
> to cry and be sad,
> to shave their heads and wear rough
> cloth.
¹³ But look, the people are happy
> and are having wild parties.
> They kill the cattle and the sheep;
> they eat the food and drink the wine.

> They say, "Let us eat and drink,
> because tomorrow we will die."
¹⁴ The LORD All-Powerful said to me: "You
people will die before this guilt is forgiven."
The Lord GOD All-Powerful said this.

GOD'S MESSAGE TO SHEBNA

¹⁵ This is what the Lord GOD All-Powerful
says:

> "Go to this servant Shebna,
> the manager of the palace.
¹⁶ Say to him, 'What are you doing here?
> Who said you could cut out a tomb for
> yourself here?
> Why are you preparing your tomb in a
> high place?
> Why are you carving out a tomb from
> the rock?
¹⁷ Look, mighty one! The LORD will throw
> you away.
> He will take firm hold of you
¹⁸ and roll you tightly into a ball
> and throw you into another country.
> There you will die,
> and there your fine chariots will
> remain.
> You are a disgrace to your master's
> house.
¹⁹ I will force you out of your important job,
> and you will be thrown down from your
> important place.'

²⁰ "At that time I will call for my servant
Eliakim son of Hilkiah. ²¹ I will take your robe
and put it on him and give him your belt. I
will hand over to him the important job you
have, and he will be like a father to the people
of Jerusalem and the family of Judah. ²² I will
put the key to the house of David around his
neck. If he opens a door, no one will be able
to close it; if he closes a door, no one will be
able to open it. ²³ He will be like an honored
chair in his father's house. I will make him
strong like a peg that is hammered into a
strong board. ²⁴ All the honored and important things of his family will depend on him;
all the adults and little children will depend
on him. They will be like bowls and jars
hanging on him.

²⁵ "At that time," says the LORD All-
Powerful, "the peg hammered into the strong
board will weaken. It will break and fall, and
everything hanging on it will be destroyed."
The LORD says this.

GOD'S MESSAGE TO LEBANON

23 This is a message about Tyre:
You trading ships, cry!
The houses and harbor of Tyre are
destroyed.
This news came to the ships
from the land of Cyprus.
2 Be silent, you who live on the island of
Tyre;
you merchants of Sidon, be silent.
Sailors have made you rich.
3 They traveled the sea to bring grain from
Egypt;
the sailors of Tyre brought grain from
the Nile Valley
and sold it to other nations.

4 Sidon, be ashamed.
Strong city of the sea, be ashamed,
because the sea says:
"I have not felt the pain of giving birth;
I have not reared young men or
women."
5 Egypt will hear the news about Tyre,
and it will make Egypt hurt with
sorrow.

6 You ships should return to Tarshish.
You people living near the sea should
be sad.
7 Look at your once happy city!
Look at your old, old city!
People from that city have traveled
far away to live.
8 Who planned Tyre's destruction?
Tyre made others rich.
Its merchants were treated like princes,
and its traders were greatly respected.
9 It was the LORD All-Powerful who
planned this.
He decided to make these proud people
unimportant;
he decided to disgrace those who were
greatly respected.
10 Go through your land, people of Tarshish,
like the Nile goes through Egypt.
There is no harbor for you now!
11 The LORD has stretched his hand over the
sea
and made its kingdoms tremble.
He commands that Canaan's
strong, walled cities be destroyed.
12 He said, "Sidon, you will not rejoice any
longer,

because you are destroyed.
Even if you cross the sea to Cyprus,
you will not find a place to rest."
13 Look at the land of the Babylonians;
it is not a country now.
Assyria has made it a place for wild
animals.
Assyria built towers to attack it;
the soldiers took all the treasures from its
cities,
and they turned it into ruins.
14 So be sad, you trading ships,
because your strong city is destroyed.

15 At that time people will forget about
Tyre for seventy years, which is the length of
a king's life. After seventy years, Tyre will be
like the prostitute in this song:
16 "Oh woman, you are forgotten.
Take your harp and walk through the
city.
Play your harp well. Sing your song often.
Then people will remember you."

17 After seventy years the LORD will deal
with Tyre, and it will again have trade. It
will be like a prostitute for all the nations
of the earth. 18 The profits will be saved for
the LORD. Tyre will not keep the money she
earns but will give them to the people who
serve the LORD, so they will have plenty of
food and nice clothes.

THE LORD WILL PUNISH THE WORLD

24 Look! The LORD will destroy the
earth and leave it empty;
he will ruin the surface of the land and
scatter its people.
2 At that time the same thing will happen to
everyone:
to common people and priests,
to slaves and masters,
to women slaves and their women
masters,
to buyers and sellers,
to those who borrow and those who
lend,
to bankers and those who owe the bank.
3 The earth will be completely empty.
The wealth will all be taken,
because the LORD has commanded it.
4 The earth will dry up and die;
the world will grow weak and die;
the great leaders in this land will
become weak.

5 The people of the earth have ruined it,
  because they do not follow God's
    teachings
  or obey God's laws
  or keep their agreement with God that
    was to last forever.
6 So a curse will destroy the earth.
  The people of the world are guilty,
  so they will be burned up;
  only a few will be left.
7 The new wine will be bad, and the
    grapevines will die.
  People who were happy will be sad.
8 The happy music of the tambourines will
    end.
  The happy sounds of wild parties will
    stop.
  The joyful music from the harps will
    end.
9 People will no longer sing while they
    drink their wine.
  The beer will taste bitter to those who
    drink it.
10 The ruined city will be empty,
  and people will hide behind closed
    doors.
11 People in the streets will ask for wine,
  but joy will have turned to sadness;
  all the happiness will have left.
12 The city will be left in ruins,
  and its gates will be smashed to pieces.
13 This is what will happen all over the earth
  and to all the nations.
  The earth will be like an olive tree after
    the harvest
  or like the few grapes left on a vine after
    harvest.
14 The people shout for joy.
  From the west they praise the greatness
    of the LORD.
15 People in the east, praise the LORD.
  People in the islands of the sea,
  praise the name of the LORD, the God
    of Israel.
16 We hear songs from every part of the
    earth
  praising God, the Righteous One.

But I said, "I am dying! I am dying!
  How terrible it will be for me!
Traitors turn against people;
  with their dishonesty, they turn against
    people."

17 There are terrors, holes, and traps
  for the people of the earth.
18 Anyone who tries to escape from the
    sound of terror
  will fall into a hole.
  Anyone who climbs out of the hole
  will be caught in a trap.
  The clouds in the sky will pour out rain,
  and the foundations of the earth will
    shake.
19 The earth will be broken up;
  the earth will split open;
  the earth will shake violently.
20 The earth will stumble around like
    someone who is drunk;
  it will shake like a hut in a storm.
  Its sin is like a heavy weight on its back;
  it will fall and never rise again.
21 At that time the LORD will punish
  the powers in the sky above
  and the rulers on earth below.
22 They will be gathered together
  like prisoners thrown into a dungeon;
  they will be shut up in prison.
  After much time they will be punished.
23 The moon will be embarrassed,
  and the sun will be ashamed,
because the LORD All-Powerful will rule
    as king
  on Mount Zion in Jerusalem.
  Jerusalem's leaders will see his
    greatness.

A SONG OF PRAISE TO GOD

25 LORD, you are my God.
  I honor you and praise you,
because you have done amazing things.
  You have always done what you said
    you would do;
  you have done what you planned long
    ago.
2 You have made the city a pile of rocks
  and have destroyed her walls.
  The city our enemies built with strong
    walls is gone;
  it will never be built again.
3 People from powerful nations will honor
    you;
  cruel people from strong cities will fear
    you.
4 You protect the poor;
  you protect the helpless when they are
    in danger.

You are like a shelter from storms,
    like shade that protects them from the
       heat.
The cruel people attack
    like a rainstorm beating against the
       wall,
5 like the heat in the desert.
But you, God, stop their violent attack.
    As a cloud cools a hot day,
    you silence the songs of those who have
       no mercy.

GOD'S BANQUET FOR HIS SERVANTS

6 The LORD All-Powerful will prepare a
    feast
    on this mountain for all people.
It will be a feast with all the best food and
    wine,
    the finest meat and wine.
7 On this mountain God will destroy
    the veil that covers all nations,
the veil that stretches over all peoples;
8 he will destroy death forever.
The Lord GOD will wipe away every tear
    from every face.
    He will take away the shame of his
      people from the earth.
The LORD has spoken.

9 At that time people will say,
    "Our God is doing this!
We have waited for him, and he has come
    to save us.
    This is the LORD. We waited for him,
so we will rejoice and be happy when he
    saves us."

10 The LORD will protect Jerusalem,
    but he will crush our enemy Moab
like straw that is trampled down in the
    manure.
11 They will spread their arms in it
    like a person who is swimming.
But God will bring down their pride,
    and all the clever things they have made
      will mean nothing.
12 Moab's high walls protect them,
    but God will destroy these walls.
He will throw them down to the ground,
    even to the dust.

A SONG OF PRAISE TO GOD

26 At that time people will sing this song
in Judah:
We have a strong city.

God protects us with its strong walls
    and defenses.
2 Open the gates,
    and the good people will enter,
    those who follow God.
3 You, LORD, give true peace
    to those who depend on you,
    because they trust you.
4 So, trust the LORD always,
    because he is our Rock forever.
5 He will destroy the proud city,
    and he will punish the people living
      there.
He will bring that high city down to the
    ground
    and throw it down into the dust.
6 Then those who were hurt by the city will
    walk on its ruins;
    those who were made poor by the city
      will trample it under their feet.
7 The path of life is level for those who are
    right with God;
    LORD, you make the way of life smooth
      for those people.
8 But, LORD, we are waiting
    for your way of justice.
Our souls want to remember
    you and your name.
9 My soul wants to be with you at night,
    and my spirit wants to be with you at
      the dawn of every day.
When your way of justice comes to the
    land,
    people of the world will learn the right
      way of living.
10 Evil people will not learn to do good
    even if you show them kindness.
They will continue doing evil, even if they
    live in a good world;
    they never see the LORD's greatness.
11 LORD, you are ready to punish those
    people,
    but they do not see that.
Show them your strong love for your
    people.
    Then those who are evil will be
      ashamed.
Burn them in the fire
    you have prepared for your enemies.
12 LORD, all our success is because of what
    you have done,
    so give us peace.

13 LORD, our God, other masters besides you
　　have ruled us,
　　but we honor only you.
14 Those masters are now dead;
　　their ghosts will not rise from death.
　　You punished and destroyed them
　　and erased any memory of them.
15 LORD, you multiplied the number of your
　　people;
　　you multiplied them and brought honor
　　to yourself.

You made the borders of the land wide.
16 LORD, people remember you when they
　　are in trouble;
　　they say quiet prayers to you when you
　　punish them.
17 LORD, when we are with you,
　　we are like a woman giving birth to a
　　baby;
　　she cries and has pain from the birth.
18 In the same way, we had pain.
　　We gave birth, but only to wind.

PEACE BY GOD

turn off the news

FULFILLMENT

ISAIAH 26:3

I t is very easy in today's society to hear the news of what has happened all the
way on the other side of the country. No matter where we live, even if it is on the
other side of the world, the news is broadcast to us. The access to the news is almost
immediate, and the news is often brought directly to us via satellites. It enables us
actually to see the incident right after a calamity has occurred.

Not only can we hear about the news right away, but we have so many choices that we
can go back and forth between news networks and saturate ourselves with all sorts of
stories. A few years ago that was not a possibility. People in the past might have had to
wait days before the news reached them.

It is wonderful to have all this technology, but at times it becomes overwhelming. A
person has many media outlets, and it is easy to get so engrossed in the news that all
one thinks about is doom and gloom. It is okay to hear the news, but do not dwell on
its negative message.

It is no wonder that we often feel discouraged by the things we see and hear. Praise
God that he has made a way for us not to become distraught with the chaos of what
life brings. We are not to be consumed by what we see or hear, but rather to meditate
on what God's Word says by focusing on the good, which takes putting down the
newspaper and turning off the news.

reflect: Focus more on the Good News than on the bad news.
Go to **FULFILLMENT:** "Beating the Burnout Blues" at **2 Corinthians 11:21–33.**

We don't bring salvation to the land
  or make new people for the world.
¹⁹ Your people have died, but they will live
    again;
  their bodies will rise from death.
You who lie in the ground,
  wake up and be happy!
The dew covering you is like the dew of a
    new day;
  the ground will give birth to the dead.

JUDGMENT: REWARD OR PUNISHMENT
²⁰ My people, go into your rooms
  and shut your doors behind you.
Hide in your rooms for a short time
  until God's anger is finished.
²¹ The LORD will leave his place

to punish the people of the world for
    their sins.
The earth will show the blood of the
  people who have been killed;
  it will not cover the dead any longer.
27 At that time the LORD will punish
      Leviathan, the gliding snake.
He will punish Leviathan, the coiled
    snake,
with his great and hard and powerful
    sword.
He will kill the monster in the sea.

² At that time
  people will sing about the pleasant
    vineyard.
³ "I, the LORD, will care for that vineyard;

TURNING REVELATIONS INTO REVOLUTIONS

FITNESS

fitness and spiritual safety

ISAIAH 27:5

The Hebrew word often translated "strength" is a word that means "a place of refuge." It suggests a place of safety that we can get to in a hurry. God expects each of us to make a decision about our safety zone. He tells us that we must choose if we are going to rely on our own efforts in this world or if we are going to rely entirely on him.

There is no intermediate ground. We can't have a little bit of the world's safety and a little bit of God's, just in case. This is a matter of ultimate concern. We either live in a world that is safe because we trust the Creator, or we live in a world of our own making. God tells us that living in a world of our own making will always mean living with fear and risk.

When we choose to find our place of safety with God, we have his strength behind us. That is a comfortable and secure environment, but it isn't a lazy one. God expects us to take care of his creation, and that includes the body that he made for us. While we are secure in his strength, we are obligated to serve him. Our well being, in body, mind, and spirit, is work God expects us to do. We are called to be caretakers of who we are.

reflect: Spend time caring for yourself today, spiritually, mentally, and physically.
Go to **Isaiah 46:3–4.**

I will water it at the right time.
No one will hurt it,
because I will guard it day and night.
4 I am not angry.
If anyone builds a wall of thornbushes in war,
I will march to it and burn it.
5 But if anyone comes to me for safety
and wants to make peace with me,
he should come and make peace with me."
6 In the days to come, the people of Jacob
will be like a plant with good roots;
Israel will grow like a plant beginning to bloom.
Then the world will be filled with their children.

THE LORD WILL SEND ISRAEL AWAY

7 The Lord has not hurt his people as he hurt their enemies;
his people have not been killed like those who tried to kill them.
8 He will settle his argument with Israel by sending it far away.
Like a hot desert wind, he will drive it away.
9 This is how Israel's guilt will be forgiven;
this is how its sins will be taken away:
Israel will crush the rocks of the altar to dust,
and no statues or altars will be left standing for the Asherah idols.
10 At that time the strong, walled city will be empty
like a desert.
Calves will eat grass there.
They will lie down there
and eat leaves from the branches.
11 The limbs will become dry and break off,
so women will use them for firewood.
The people refuse to understand,
so God will not comfort them;
their Maker will not be kind to them.
12 At that time the Lord will begin gathering his people one by one from the Euphrates River to the brook of Egypt. He will separate them from others as grain is separated from chaff. 13 Many of my people are now lost in Assyria. Some have run away to Egypt. But at that time a great trumpet will be blown, and all those people will come and worship the Lord on that holy mountain in Jerusalem.

WARNINGS TO ISRAEL

28 How terrible it will be for Samaria,
the pride of Israel's drunken people!
That beautiful crown of flowers is just a dying plant
set on a hill above a rich valley where drunkards live.
2 Look, the Lord has someone who is strong and powerful.
Like a storm of hail and strong wind,
like a sudden flood of water pouring over the country,
he will throw Samaria down to the ground.
3 That city, the pride of Israel's drunken people,
will be trampled underfoot.
4 That beautiful crown of flowers is just a dying plant
set on a hill above a rich valley.
That city will be like the first fig of summer.
Anyone who sees it
quickly picks it and eats it.

5 At that time the Lord All-Powerful
will be like a beautiful crown,
like a wonderful crown of flowers
for his people who are left alive.
6 Then he will give wisdom to the judges
who must decide cases
and strength to those who battle at the city gate.
7 But now those leaders are drunk with wine;
they stumble from drinking too much beer.
The priests and prophets are drunk with beer
and are filled with wine.
They stumble from too much beer.
The prophets are drunk when they see their visions;
the judges stumble when they make their decisions.
8 Every table is covered with vomit,
so there is not a clean place anywhere.

9 The Lord is trying to teach the people a lesson;
he is trying to make them understand his teachings.

But the people are like babies too old for
  breast milk,
    like those who no longer nurse at their
    mother's breast.
10 So they make fun of the LORD's prophet
  and say:
    "A command here, a command there.
    A rule here, a rule there.
    A little lesson here, a little lesson there."
11 So the LORD will use strange words and
    foreign languages
  to speak to these people.
12 God said to them,
  "Here is a place of rest;
    let the tired people come and rest.
  This is the place of peace."
    But the people would not listen.
13 So the words of the LORD will be,
  "A command here, a command there.
    A rule here, a rule there.
    A little lesson here, a little lesson there."
  They will fall back and be defeated;
    they will be trapped and captured.

14 So listen to the LORD's message, you who
    brag,
  you leaders in Jerusalem.
15 You say, "We have made an agreement
    with death;
  we have a contract with death.
  When terrible punishment passes by,
    it won't hurt us.
  Our lies will keep us safe,
    and our tricks will hide us."
16 Because of these things, this is what the
Lord GOD says:
  "I will put a stone in the ground in
    Jerusalem,
    a tested stone.
  Everything will be built on this important
    and precious rock.
    Anyone who trusts in it will never be
    disappointed.
17 I will use justice as a measuring line
    and goodness as the standard.
  The lies you hide behind will be destroyed
    as if by hail.
  They will be washed away as if in a
    flood.
18 Your agreement with death will be erased;
  your contract with death will not help
    you.
  When terrible punishment comes,

you will be crushed by it.
19 Whenever punishment comes, it will take
    you away.
  It will come morning after morning;
    it will defeat you by day and by night.
  Those who understand this punishment
    will be terrified."
20 You will be like the person who tried to
    sleep
  on a bed that was too short
  and with a blanket that was too narrow
    to wrap around himself.
21 The LORD will fight as he did at Mount
    Perazim.
  He will be angry as he was in the Valley
    of Gibeon.
  He will do his work, his strange work.
  He will finish his job, his strange job.
22 Now, you must not make fun of these
    things,
  or the ropes around you will become
    tighter.
  The Lord GOD All-Powerful has told me
    how the whole earth will be destroyed.

THE LORD PUNISHES FAIRLY

23 Listen closely to what I tell you;
    listen carefully to what I say.
24 A farmer does not plow his field all the
    time;
  he does not go on working the soil.
25 He makes the ground flat and smooth.
    Then he plants the dill and scatters the
    cumin.
  He plants the wheat in rows,
    the barley in its special place,
    and other wheat as a border around the
    field.
26 His God teaches him
    and shows him the right way.
27 A farmer doesn't use heavy boards to
    crush dill;
  he doesn't use a wagon wheel to crush
    cumin.
  He uses a small stick to break open the
    dill,
    and with a stick he opens the cumin.
28 The grain is ground to make bread.
  People do not ruin it by crushing it
    forever.
  The farmer separates the wheat from the
    chaff with his cart,
    but he does not let his horses grind it.

²⁹ This lesson also comes from the LORD
All-Powerful,
who gives wonderful advice, who is
very wise.

WARNINGS TO JERUSALEM

29 How terrible it will be for you,
Jerusalem,
the city where David camped.
Your festivals have continued
year after year.
² I will attack Jerusalem,
and that city will be filled with sadness
and crying.
It will be like an altar to me.
³ I will put armies all around you,
Jerusalem;
I will surround you with towers
and with devices to attack you.
⁴ You will be pulled down and will speak
from the ground;
I will hear your voice rising from the
ground.
It will sound like the voice of a ghost;
your words will come like a whisper
from the dirt.
⁵ Your many enemies will become like fine
dust;
the many cruel people will be like chaff
that is blown away.
Everything will happen very quickly.
⁶ The LORD All-Powerful will come
with thunder, earthquakes, and great
noises,
with storms, strong winds, and a fire
that destroys.
⁷ Then all the nations that fight against
Jerusalem
will be like a dream;
all the nations that attack her
will be like a vision in the night.
⁸ They will be like a hungry man who
dreams he is eating,
but when he awakens, he is still hungry.
They will be like a thirsty man who
dreams he is drinking,
but when he awakens, he is still weak
and thirsty.
It will be the same way with all the
nations
who fight against Mount Zion.
⁹ Be surprised and amazed.

Blind yourselves so that you cannot see.
Become drunk, but not from wine.
Trip and fall, but not from beer.
¹⁰ The LORD has made you go into a deep
sleep.
He has closed your eyes. (The prophets
are your eyes.)
He has covered your heads. (The seers
are your heads.)
¹¹ This vision is like the words of a book
that is closed and sealed. You may give the
book to someone who can read and tell that
person to read it. But he will say, "I can't read
the book, because it is sealed." ¹²Or you may
give the book to someone who cannot read
and tell him to read it. But he will say, "I don't
know how to read."
¹³The Lord says:

"These people worship me with their
mouths,
and honor me with their lips,
but their hearts are far from me.
Their worship is based on
nothing but human rules.
¹⁴ So I will continue to amaze these people
by doing more and more miracles.
Their wise men will lose their wisdom;
their wise men will not be able to
understand."

WARNINGS ABOUT OTHER NATIONS

¹⁵ How terrible it will be for those who try
to hide things from the LORD
and who do their work in darkness.
They think no one will see them or
know what they do.
¹⁶ You are confused.
You think the clay is equal to the
potter.
You think that an object can tell the one
who made it,
"You didn't make me."
This is like a pot telling its maker,
"You don't know anything."

A BETTER TIME IS COMING

¹⁷ In a very short time, Lebanon will become
rich farmland,
and the rich farmland will seem like a
forest.
¹⁸ At that time the deaf will hear the words
in a book.
Instead of having darkness and gloom,
the blind will see.

19 The LORD will make the poor people
happy;
they will rejoice in the Holy One of
Israel.
20 Then the people without mercy will come
to an end;
those who do not respect God will
disappear.
Those who enjoy doing evil will be
gone:
21 those who lie about others in court,
those who trap people in court,
those who lie and take justice from
innocent people in court.
22 This is what the LORD who set Abraham
free says to the family of Jacob:
"Now the people of Jacob will not be
ashamed
or disgraced any longer.
23 When they see all their children,
the children I made with my hands,
they will say my name is holy.
They will agree that the Holy One of
Jacob is holy,
and they will respect the God of
Israel.
24 People who do wrong will now
understand.
Those who complain will accept being
taught."

WARNINGS TO THE STUBBORN NATION

30 The LORD said,
"How terrible it will be for these
stubborn children.
They make plans, but they don't ask me to
help them.
They make agreements with other
nations, without asking my Spirit.
They are adding more and more sins to
themselves.
2 They go down to Egypt for help
without asking me about it first.
They hope they will be saved by the king
of Egypt;
they want Egypt to protect them.
3 But hiding in Egypt will bring you only
shame;
Egypt's protection will only disappoint
you.
4 Your officers have gone to Zoan,
and your messengers have gone to
Hanes,

5 but they will be put to shame,
because Egypt is useless to them.
It will give no help and will be of no use;
it will cause them only shame and
embarrassment."

GOD'S MESSAGE TO JUDAH

6 This is a message about the animals in
southern Judah:
Southern Judah is a dangerous place
full of lions and lionesses,
poisonous snakes and darting snakes.
The messengers travel through there with
their wealth on the backs of donkeys
and their treasure on the backs of
camels.
They carry them to a nation that cannot
help them,
7 to Egypt whose help is useless.
So I call that country Rahab the
Do-Nothing.

8 Now write this on a sign for the people,
write this on a scroll,
so that for the days to come
this will be a witness forever.
9 These people are like children who lie
and refuse to obey;
they refuse to listen to the LORD's
teachings.
10 They tell the seers,
"Don't see any more visions!"
They say to the prophets,
"Don't tell us the truth!
Say things that will make us feel good;
see only good things for us.
11 Stop blocking our path.
Get out of our way.
Stop telling us
about God, the Holy One of Israel."
12 So this is what the Holy One of Israel
says:
"You people have refused to accept this
message
and have depended on cruelty and lies
to help you.
13 You are guilty of these things.
So you will be like a high wall with
cracks in it
that falls suddenly and breaks into small
pieces.
14 You will be like a clay jar that breaks,
smashed into many pieces.
Those pieces will be too small

INSPIRE YOUR TEAM TO REALIZE THE DREAM

a journey
with God

FUTURE

By Diana Hagee   ISAIAH 30:21

S omeone described a relationship with God as being similar to a ride on a tandem bicycle. This person was in the front seat directing the course, and God was in the back helping to peddle the bicycle.

From time to time, I have imagined this journey. I tried my very best to find my own way, while depending on God to peddle from behind, and hoping he would support all the choices I was making along life's path. I can clearly remember the day I finally exchanged places with him and let him take the lead. Life has been so much better for me since I let that exchange take place.

God knows all the bicycling secrets—he knows how to take sharp turns around corners that suddenly creep up on our journey. He dodges big boulders on life's highway and even masters "slippery when wet" conditions. Somehow, these hindrances do not seem to bother him at all. He knows how to pedal through the scary passages, just slowly enough so I won't fall off.

I finally learned to believe he loved me enough to stay with me, no matter how difficult the course. I've also learned to stay quiet and listen as I sit behind him and pedal through life. He has taken me to many places—beautiful places, strange places, lonely places, scary places—even to divine places, but never to a place he has not gone before.

I so take pleasure in the journey now that I let him lead. I worry less. I have confidence in him, and I am secure about my future, for fear does not control my direction anymore. I can feel the cool breeze on my face, and I am actually enjoying the view.

Remember, God is too wise to make a mistake and too loving to be unkind. He knew the paths you would travel long before you began your journey. He knows everything about you: he knows your limitations and your potentials. And, most of all, he believes in you!

reflect: Will you let him lead you in the paths he has chosen for you?
Go to **1 Kings 18:41–46.**

to take coals from the fire
or to get water from a well."

¹⁵This is what the Lord GOD, the Holy One of Israel, says:

"If you come back to me and trust me, you
will be saved.
If you will be calm and trust me, you
will be strong."
But you don't want to do that.
¹⁶ You say, "No, we need horses to run away
on."
So you will run away on horses.
You say, "We will ride away on fast
horses."
So those who chase you will be fast.
¹⁷ One enemy will make threats,
and a thousand of your men will run
away.
Five enemies will make threats,
and all of you will run from them.
You will be left alone like a flagpole on a
hilltop,
like a banner on a hill.
¹⁸ The LORD wants to show his mercy to
you.
He wants to rise and comfort you.
The LORD is a fair God,
and everyone who waits for his help
will be happy.

THE LORD WILL HELP HIS PEOPLE

¹⁹You people who live on Mount Zion in Jerusalem will not cry anymore. The LORD will hear your crying, and he will comfort you. When he hears you, he will help you. ²⁰The Lord has given you sorrow and hurt like the bread and water you ate every day. He is your teacher; he will not continue to hide from you, but you will see your teacher with your own eyes. ²¹If you go the wrong way—to the right or to the left—you will hear a voice behind you saying, "This is the right way. You should go this way." ²²You have statues covered with silver and gold, but you will ruin them for further use. You will throw them away like filthy rags and say, "Go away!"

²³At that time the LORD will send rain for the seeds you plant in the ground, and the ground will grow food for you. The harvest will be rich and great, and you will have plenty of food in the fields for your animals. ²⁴Your oxen and donkeys that work the soil will have all the food they need. You will

have to use shovels and pitchforks to spread all their food. ²⁵Every mountain and hill will have streams filled with water. These things will happen after many people are killed and the towers are pulled down. ²⁶At that time the light from the moon will be bright like the sun, and the light from the sun will be seven times brighter than now, like the light of seven days. These things will happen when the LORD bandages his broken people and heals the hurts he gave them.

²⁷ Look! The LORD comes from far away.
His anger is like a fire with thick clouds
of smoke.
His mouth is filled with anger,
and his tongue is like a burning fire.
²⁸ His breath is like a rushing river,
which rises to the throat.
He will judge the nations as if he is
sifting them through the strainer of
destruction.
He will place in their mouths a bit that
will lead them the wrong way.
²⁹ You will sing happy songs
as on the nights you begin a festival.
You will be happy like people listening to
flutes
as they come to the mountain of the
LORD,
to the Rock of Israel.
³⁰ The LORD will cause all people to hear his
great voice
and to see his powerful arm come down
with anger,
like a great fire that burns everything,
like a great storm with much rain and
hail.
³¹ Assyria will be afraid when it hears the
voice of the LORD,
because he will strike Assyria with a
rod.
³² When the LORD punishes Assyria with a
rod,
he will beat them to the music of
tambourines and harps;
he will fight against them with his
mighty weapons.
³³ Topheth[n] has been made ready for a long
time;

30:33 Topheth Gehenna; the Valley of Hinnom. Here people burned the bodies of criminals and animals, along with garbage.

it is ready for the king.
It was made deep and wide
  with much wood and fire.
And the LORD's breath will come
  like a stream of burning sulfur and set
  it on fire.

WARNINGS ABOUT RELYING ON EGYPT

31 How terrible it will be for those
  people who go down to Egypt for
  help.
They think horses will save them.
They think their many chariots
  and strong horsemen will save them.
But they don't trust God, the Holy One of
  Israel,
  or ask the LORD for help.
2 But he is wise and can bring them
  disaster.
He does not change his warnings.
He will rise up and fight against the evil
  people
  and against those who try to help evil
  people.
3 The Egyptians are only people and are not
  God.
Their horses are only animals and are
  not spirit.
The LORD will stretch out his arm,
  and the one who helps will stumble,
  and the people who wanted help will
  fall.
All of them will be destroyed together.
4 The LORD says this to me:
"When a lion or a lion's cub kills an
  animal to eat,
  it stands over the dead animal and
  roars.
A band of shepherds
  may be assembled against it,
but the lion will not be afraid of their
  yelling
  or upset by their noise.
So the LORD All-Powerful will come down
  to fight on Mount Zion and on its hill.
5 The LORD All-Powerful will defend
  Jerusalem
  like birds flying over their nests.
He will defend and save it;
  he will 'pass over' and save Jerusalem."
6 You children of Israel, come back to the
God you fought against. 7 The time is coming when each of you will stop worshiping

idols of gold and silver, which you sinned by
making.
8 "Assyria will be defeated by a sword, but
  not the sword of a person;
  Assyria will be destroyed, but not by a
  person's sword.
Assyria will run away from the sword of
  God,
  but its young men will be caught and
  made slaves.
9 They will panic, and their protection will
  be destroyed.
Their commanders will be terrified
  when they see God's battle flag,"
says the LORD,
  whose fire is in Jerusalem
  and whose furnace is in Jerusalem.

A GOOD KINGDOM IS COMING

32 A king will rule in a way that brings
  justice,
  and leaders will make fair decisions.
2 Then each ruler will be like a shelter from
  the wind,
  like a safe place in a storm,
like streams of water in a dry land,
  like a cool shadow from a large rock in
  a hot land.

3 People will look to the king for help,
  and they will truly listen to what he
  says.
4 People who are now worried will be able
  to understand.
Those who cannot speak clearly now
  will then be able to speak clearly and
  quickly.
5 Fools will not be called great,
  and people will not respect the
  wicked.
6 A fool says foolish things,
  and in his mind he plans evil.
A fool does things that are wicked,
  and he says wrong things about the
  LORD.
A fool does not feed the hungry
  or let thirsty people drink water.
7 The wicked person uses evil like a tool.
  He plans ways to take everything from
  the poor.
He destroys the poor with lies,
  even when the poor person is in the
  right.
8 But a good leader plans to do good,

735

and those good things make him a good
leader.

HARD TIMES ARE COMING

9 You women who are calm now,
stand up and listen to me.
You women who feel safe now,
hear what I say.
10 You women feel safe now,
but after one year you will be afraid.
There will be no grape harvest
and no summer fruit to gather.
11 Women, you are calm now, but you should
shake with fear.
Women, you feel safe now, but you
should tremble.
Take off your nice clothes
and put rough cloth around your waist
to show your sadness.
12 Beat your breasts in grief, because the
fields that were pleasant are now
empty.
Cry, because the vines that once had
fruit now have no more grapes.
13 Cry for the land of my people,
in which only thorns and weeds now
grow.
Cry for the city that once was happy
and for all the houses that once were
filled with joy.
14 The palace will be empty;
people will leave the noisy city.
Strong cities and towers will be empty.
Wild donkeys will love to live there, and
sheep will go there to eat.

THINGS WILL GET BETTER

15 This will continue until God pours his
Spirit from above upon us.
Then the desert will be like a fertile
field
and the fertile field like a forest.
16 Justice will be found even in the desert,
and fairness will be found in the fertile
fields.
17 That fairness will bring peace,
and it will bring calm and safety
forever.
18 My people will live in peaceful places
and in safe homes
and in calm places of rest.
19 Hail will destroy the forest,
and the city will be completely
destroyed.

20 But you will be happy as you plant seeds
near every stream
and as you let your cattle and donkeys
wander freely.

**WARNINGS TO ASSYRIA AND PROMISES TO
GOD'S PEOPLE**

33 How terrible it will be for you who
destroy others
but have not been destroyed yet.
How terrible it will be for you, traitor,
whom no one has turned against yet.
When you stop destroying,
others will destroy you.
When you stop turning against others,
they will turn against you.

2 Lord, be kind to us.
We have waited for your help.
Give us strength every morning.
Save us when we are in trouble.
3 Your powerful voice makes people run
away in fear;
your greatness causes the nations to run
away.
4 Like locusts, your enemies will take away
the things you stole in war.
Like locusts rushing about, they will
take your wealth.
5 The Lord is very great, and he lives in a
high place.
He fills Jerusalem with fairness and
justice.
6 He will be your safety.
He is full of salvation, wisdom, and
knowledge.
Respect for the Lord is the greatest
treasure.

7 See, brave people are crying out in the
streets;
those who tried to bring peace are
weeping loudly.
8 There is no one on the roads,
no one walking in the paths.
People have broken the agreements they
made.
They refuse to believe the proof from
witnesses.
No one respects other people.
9 The land is sick and dying;
Lebanon is ashamed and dying.
The Plain of Sharon is dry like the
desert,

and the trees of Bashan and Carmel are
  dying.

10 The LORD says, "Now, I will stand up
    and show my greatness.
  Now, I will become important to the
    people.
11 You people do useless things
    that are like hay and straw.
  A destructive wind will burn you like fire.
12 People will be burned until their bones
    become like lime;
  they will burn quickly like dry
    thornbushes."

13 You people in faraway lands, hear what I
    have done.

You people who are near me, learn
  about my power.
14 The sinners in Jerusalem are afraid;
    those who are separated from God
      shake with fear.
  They say, "Can any of us live through this
    fire that destroys?
  Who can live near this fire that burns
    on and on?"
15 A person who does what is right
    and speaks what is right,
  who refuses to take money unfairly,
    who refuses to take money to hurt
      others,
  who does not listen to plans of murder,
    who refuses to think about evil—

THE LAWS OF INCREASE

real treasure

FINANCES

ISAIAH 33:6

For most of us, financial success means fat bank accounts. In biblical times, this
usually meant agricultural abundance. The storehouse was the bank and when it
was full, life seemed secure. But Isaiah reminds us that full warehouses and fat bank
accounts do not provide any real security at all. Those things are always subject to
catastrophe, theft, or economic collapse. Real treasure is found only in one place:
reverence for God.

It's really a matter of trust. If we think of the world as a risky and unpredictable place,
we will try to reduce that risk and eliminate our fears by controlling our environment.
We will be tempted to think that we can come up with the perfect plan to insure our
future. It's all foolishness, isn't it?

Nothing can guarantee a secure future except the will of God. So Isaiah points out
that the only really secure world is a world where I serve as a steward under God's
authority. Unless God is running my life and my business, I will always have something
to fear. So are you worrying about your future? Or are you confident in your obedience
to God, relaxing under his protection?

reflect: What areas of your life do you need to entrust to God?
Go to **Daniel 4:30-37.**

16 this is the kind of person who will be safe.
He will be protected as he would be in a high, walled city.
He will always have bread,
and he will not run out of water.
17 Your eyes will see the king in his beauty.
You will see the land that stretches far away.
18 You will think about the terror of the past:
"Where is that officer?
Where is the one who collected the taxes?
Where is the officer in charge of our defense towers?"
19 No longer will you see those proud people from other countries,
whose strange language you couldn't understand.

GOD WILL PROTECT JERUSALEM

20 Look at Jerusalem, the city of our festivals.
Look at Jerusalem, that beautiful place of rest.
It is like a tent that will never be moved;
the pegs that hold her in place will never be pulled up,
and her ropes will never be broken.
21 There the LORD will be our Mighty One.
That land is a place with streams and wide rivers,
but there will be no enemy boats on those rivers;
no powerful ship will sail on them.
22 This is because the LORD is our judge.
The LORD makes our laws.
The LORD is our king.
He will save us.
23 You sailors from other lands, hear:
The ropes on your boats hang loose.
The mast is not held firm.
The sails are not spread open.
Then your great wealth will be divided.
There will be so much wealth that even the crippled people will carry off a share.
24 No one living in Jerusalem will say, "I am sick."
The people who live there will have their sins forgiven.

GOD WILL PUNISH HIS ENEMIES

34 All you nations, come near and listen.
Pay attention, you peoples!
The earth and all the people in it should listen,
the world and everything in it.
2 The LORD is angry with all the nations;
he is angry with their armies.
He will destroy them and kill them all.
3 Their bodies will be thrown outside.
The stink will rise from the bodies,
and the blood will flow down the mountains.
4 The sun, moon, and stars will dissolve,
and the sky will be rolled up like a scroll.
The stars will fall
like dead leaves from a vine
or dried-up figs from a fig tree.
5 The LORD's sword in the sky is covered with blood.
It will cut through Edom
and destroy those people as an offering to the LORD.
6 The LORD's sword will be covered with blood;
it will be covered with fat,
with the blood from lambs and goats,
with the fat from the kidneys of sheep.
This is because the LORD decided there will be a sacrifice in Bozrah
and much killing in Edom.
7 The oxen will be killed,
and the cattle and the strong bulls.
The land will be filled with their blood,
and the dirt will be covered with their fat.

8 The LORD has chosen a time for punishment.
He has chosen a year when people must pay for the wrongs they did to Jerusalem.
9 Edom's rivers will be like hot tar.
Its dirt will be like burning sulfur.
Its land will be like burning tar.
10 The fires will burn night and day;
the smoke will rise from Edom forever.
Year after year that land will be empty;
no one will ever travel through that land again.
11 Birds and small animals will own that land,
and owls and ravens will live there.
God will make it an empty wasteland;
it will have nothing left in it.

¹² The important people will have no one
 left to rule them;
 the leaders will all be gone.
¹³ Thorns will take over the strong towers,
 and wild bushes will grow in the walled
 cities.
It will be a home for wild dogs
 and a place for owls to live.
¹⁴ Desert animals will live with the hyenas,
 and wild goats will call to their friends.
Night animals will live there
 and find a place of rest.
¹⁵ Owls will nest there and lay eggs.
 When they hatch open, the owls will
 gather their young under their wings.
Hawks will gather
 with their own kind.
¹⁶ Look at the LORD's scroll and read what
is written there:
None of these will be missing;
 none will be without its mate.
God has given the command,
 so his Spirit will gather them together.
¹⁷ God has divided the land among them,
 and he has given them each their
 portion.
So they will own that land forever
 and will live there year after year.

GOD WILL COMFORT HIS PEOPLE

35 The desert and dry land will become
 happy;
 the desert will be glad and will produce
 flowers.
Like a flower, ²it will have many blooms.
 It will show its happiness, as if it were
 shouting with joy.
It will be beautiful like the forest of
 Lebanon,
 as beautiful as the hill of Carmel and
 the Plain of Sharon.
Everyone will see the glory of the LORD
 and the splendor of our God.
³ Make the weak hands strong
 and the weak knees steady.
⁴ Say to people who are frightened,
 "Be strong. Don't be afraid.
Look, your God will come,
 and he will punish your enemies.
He will make them pay for the wrongs
 they did,
 but he will save you."
⁵ Then the blind people will see again,

and the deaf will hear.
⁶ Crippled people will jump like deer,
 and those who can't talk now will shout
 with joy.
Water will flow in the desert,
 and streams will flow in the dry land.
⁷ The burning desert will have pools of
 water,
 and the dry ground will have springs.
Where wild dogs once lived,
 grass and water plants will grow.
⁸ A road will be there;
 this highway will be called "The Road
 to Being Holy."
Evil people will not be allowed to walk on
 that road;
 only good people will walk on it.
No fools will go on it.
⁹ No lions will be there,
 nor will dangerous animals be on that
 road.
They will not be found there.
That road will be for the people God
 saves;
¹⁰ the people the LORD has freed will
 return there.
They will enter Jerusalem with joy,
 and their happiness will last forever.
Their gladness and joy will fill them
 completely,
 and sorrow and sadness will go far
 away.

THE ASSYRIANS INVADE JUDAH

36 During Hezekiah's fourteenth year as
 king, Sennacherib king of Assyria attacked all the strong, walled cities of Judah
and captured them. ²The king of Assyria sent
out his field commander with a large army
from Lachish to King Hezekiah in Jerusalem. When the commander came near the
waterway from the upper pool on the road
where people do their laundry, he stopped.
³Eliakim, Shebna, and Joah went out to meet
him. Eliakim son of Hilkiah was the palace
manager, Shebna was the royal secretary, and
Joah son of Asaph was the recorder.

⁴The field commander said to them, "Tell
Hezekiah this:

"'The great king, the king of Assyria, says:
What can you trust in now? ⁵You say you
have battle plans and power for war, but your
words mean nothing. Whom are you trusting

for help so that you turn against me? ⁶Look, you are depending on Egypt to help you, but Egypt is like a splintered walking stick. If you lean on it for help, it will stab your hand and hurt you. The king of Egypt will hurt all those who depend on him. ⁷You might say, "We are depending on the LORD our God," but Hezekiah destroyed the LORD's altars and the places of worship. Hezekiah told Judah and Jerusalem, "You must worship only at this one altar."

⁸"Now make an agreement with my master, the king of Assyria: I will give you two thousand horses if you can find enough men to ride them. ⁹You cannot defeat one of my master's least important officers, so why do you depend on Egypt to give you chariots and horsemen? ¹⁰I have not come to attack and destroy this country without an order from the LORD. The LORD himself told me to come to this country and destroy it.'"

¹¹Then Eliakim, Shebna, and Joah said to the field commander, "Please speak to us in the Aramaic language. We understand it. Don't speak to us in Hebrew, because the people on the city wall can hear you."

¹²But the commander said, "My master did not send me to tell these things only to you and your king. He sent me to speak also to those people sitting on the wall who will have to eat their own dung and drink their own urine like you."

¹³Then the commander stood and shouted loudly in the Hebrew language, "Listen to what the great king, the king of Assyria says, ¹⁴The king says you should not let Hezekiah fool you, because he can't save you. ¹⁵Don't let Hezekiah talk you into trusting the LORD by saying, 'The LORD will surely save us. This city won't be handed over to the king of Assyria.'

¹⁶"Don't listen to Hezekiah. The king of Assyria says, 'Make peace with me, and come out of the city to me. Then everyone will be free to eat the fruit from his own grapevine and fig tree and to drink water from his own well. ¹⁷After that I will come and take you to a land like your own—a land with grain and new wine, bread and vineyards.'

¹⁸"Don't let Hezekiah fool you, saying, 'The LORD will save us.' Has a god of any other nation saved his people from the power of the king of Assyria? ¹⁹Where are the gods

of Hamath and Arpad? Where are the gods of Sepharvaim? They did not save Samaria from my power. ²⁰Not one of all the gods of these countries has saved his people from me. Neither can the LORD save Jerusalem from my power."

²¹The people were silent. They didn't answer the commander at all, because King Hezekiah had ordered, "Don't answer him."

²²Then Eliakim, Shebna, and Joah tore their clothes to show how upset they were. (Eliakim son of Hilkiah was the palace manager, Shebna was the royal secretary, and Joah son of Asaph was the recorder.) The three men went to Hezekiah and told him what the field commander had said.

HEZEKIAH ASKS GOD TO HELP

37 When King Hezekiah heard the message, he tore his clothes and put on rough cloth to show how sad he was. Then he went into the Temple of the LORD. ²Hezekiah sent Eliakim, the palace manager, and Shebna, the royal secretary, and the older priests to Isaiah. They were all wearing rough cloth when they came to Isaiah the prophet, the son of Amoz. ³They told Isaiah, "This is what Hezekiah says: Today is a day of sorrow and punishment and disgrace, as when a child should be born, but the mother is not strong enough to give birth to it. ⁴The king of Assyria sent his field commander to make fun of the living God. Maybe the LORD your God will hear what the commander said and will punish him for it. So pray for the few of us who are left alive."

⁵When Hezekiah's officers came to Isaiah, ⁶he said to them, "Tell your master this: The LORD says, 'Don't be afraid of what you have heard. Don't be frightened by the words the servants of the king of Assyria have spoken against me. ⁷Listen! I am going to put a spirit in the king of Assyria. He will hear a report that will make him return to his own country, and I will cause him to die by the sword there.'"

⁸The field commander heard that the king of Assyria had left Lachish. When he went back, he found the king fighting against the city of Libnah.

⁹The king received a report that Tirhakah, the Cushite king of Egypt, was coming to attack him. When the king of Assyria heard

this, he sent messengers to Hezekiah, saying, [10]"Tell Hezekiah king of Judah: Don't be fooled by the god you trust. Don't believe him when he says Jerusalem will not be handed over to the king of Assyria. [11]You have heard what the kings of Assyria have done. They have completely defeated every country, so do not think you will be saved. [12]Did the gods of those people save them? My ancestors destroyed them, defeating the cities of Gozan, Haran, and Rezeph, and the people of Eden living in Tel Assar. [13]Where are the kings of Hamath and Arpad? Where are the kings of Sepharvaim, Hena, and Ivvah?"

HEZEKIAH PRAYS TO THE LORD

[14]When Hezekiah received the letter from the messengers and read it, he went up to the Temple of the LORD. He spread the letter out before the LORD [15]and prayed to the LORD: [16]"LORD All-Powerful, you are the God of Israel, whose throne is between the gold creatures with wings, only you are God of all the kingdoms of the earth. You made the heavens and the earth. [17]Hear, LORD, and listen. Open your eyes, LORD, and see. Listen to all the words Sennacherib has said to insult the living God.

[18]"It is true, LORD, that the kings of Assyria have destroyed all these countries and their lands. [19]They have thrown the gods of these nations into the fire, but they were only wood and rock statues that people made. So the kings have destroyed them. [20]Now, LORD our God, save us from the king's power so that all the kingdoms of the earth will know that you, LORD, are the only God."

THE LORD ANSWERS HEZEKIAH

[21]Then Isaiah son of Amoz sent a message to Hezekiah that said, "This is what the LORD, the God of Israel, says: 'You prayed to me about Sennacherib king of Assyria. [22]So this is what the LORD has said against Sennacherib:

The people of Jerusalem
    hate you and make fun of you;
the people of Jerusalem
    laugh at you as you run away.
[23]You have insulted me and spoken against me;
    you have raised your voice against me.
You have a proud look on your face,

which is against me, the Holy One of Israel!
[24]You have sent your messengers to insult the Lord.
You have said, "With my many chariots
I have gone to the tops of the mountains,
    to the highest mountains of Lebanon.
I have cut down its tallest cedars
    and its best pine trees.
I have gone to its greatest heights
    and its best forests.
[25]I have dug wells in foreign countries
    and drunk water there.
By the soles of my feet,
    I have dried up all the rivers of Egypt."

[26]"'King of Assyria, surely you have heard.
    Long ago I, the LORD, planned these things.
Long ago I designed them,
    and now I have made them happen.
I allowed you to turn those strong, walled cities
    into piles of rocks.
[27]The people in those cities were weak;
    they were frightened and put to shame.
They were like grass in the field,
    like tender, young grass,
like grass on the housetop
    that is burned by the wind before it can grow.

[28]"'I know when you rest,
    when you come and go,
    and how you rage against me.
[29]Because you rage against me,
    and because I have heard your proud words,
I will put my hook in your nose
    and my bit in your mouth.
Then I will force you to leave my country
    the same way you came.'

[30]"Then the LORD said, 'Hezekiah, I will give you this sign:
This year you will eat the grain that grows wild,
    and the second year you will eat what grows wild from that.
But in the third year, plant grain and harvest it.
    Plant vineyards and eat their fruit.
[31]Some of the people in the family of Judah will escape.
Like plants that take root,

they will grow strong and have many
children.
32 A few people will come out of Jerusalem
alive;
a few from Mount Zion will live.
The strong love of the LORD All-Powerful
will make this happen.'

33"So this is what the LORD says about the
king of Assyria:
'He will not enter this city
or even shoot an arrow here.
He will not fight against it with shields
or build a ramp to attack the city walls.
34 He will return to his country the same
way he came,
and he will not enter this city,'
says the LORD.
35 'I will defend and save this city
for my sake and for David, my servant.'"

36Then the angel of the LORD went out
and killed one hundred eighty-five thousand
men in the Assyrian camp. When the people
got up early the next morning, they saw all
the dead bodies. 37So Sennacherib king of
Assyria left and went back to Nineveh and
stayed there.

38One day as Sennacherib was worshiping in the temple of his god Nisroch, his sons
Adrammelech and Sharezer killed him with
a sword. Then they escaped to the land of
Ararat. So Sennacherib's son Esarhaddon became king of Assyria.

HEZEKIAH'S ILLNESS

38 At that time Hezekiah became very
sick; he was almost dead. The prophet
Isaiah son of Amoz went to see him and told
him, "This is what the LORD says: Make arrangements, because you are not going to
live, but die."

2Hezekiah turned toward the wall and
prayed to the LORD, 3"LORD, please remember that I have always obeyed you. I have
given myself completely to you and have
done what you said was right." Then Hezekiah cried loudly.

4Then the LORD spoke his word to Isaiah:
5"Go to Hezekiah and tell him: 'This is what
the LORD, the God of your ancestor David,
says: I have heard your prayer and seen your
tears. So I will add fifteen years to your life.
6I will save you and this city from the king of
Assyria; I will defend this city.

7"'The LORD will do what he says. This
is the sign from the LORD to show you: 8The
sun has made a shadow go down the stairway
of Ahaz, but I will make it go back ten steps.'"
So the shadow made by the sun went back up
the ten steps it had gone down.

9After Hezekiah king of Judah got well,
he wrote this song:
10 I said, "I am in the middle of my life.
Do I have to go through the gates of
death?
Will I have the rest of my life taken
away from me?"
11 I said, "I will not see the LORD
in the land of the living again.
I will not again see the people
who live on the earth.
12 Like a shepherd's tent,
my home has been pulled down and
taken from me.
I am finished
like the cloth a weaver rolls up and cuts
from the loom."n
In one day you brought me to this end.
13 All night I cried loudly.
Like a lion, he crushed all my bones.
In one day you brought me to this end.
14 I cried like a bird
and moaned like a dove.
My eyes became tired as I looked to the
heavens.
Lord, I have troubles. Please help me."

15 What can I say?
The Lord told me what would happen
and then made it happen.
I have had these troubles in my soul,
so now I will be humble all my life.
16 Lord, because of you, people live.
Because of you, my spirit also lives;
you made me well and let me live.
17 It was for my own good
that I had such troubles.
Because you love me very much,
you did not let me die
but threw my sins
far away.
18 People in the place of the dead cannot
praise you;
those who have died cannot sing praises
to you;

38:12 **loom** A machine for making cloth from thread.

those who die don't trust you
to help them.
19 The people who are alive are the ones
who praise you.
They praise you as I praise you today.
A father should tell his children
that you provide help.
20 The LORD saved me,
so we will play songs on stringed
instruments
in the Temple of the LORD
all the days of our lives.

21 Then Isaiah said, "Make a paste from figs and put it on Hezekiah's boil. Then he will get well." 22 Hezekiah then asked Isaiah, "What will be the sign? What will show that I will go up to the Temple of the LORD?"

MESSENGERS FROM BABYLON

39 At that time Merodach-Baladan son of Baladan was king of Babylon. He sent letters and a gift to Hezekiah, because he had heard that Hezekiah had been sick and was now well. 2 Hezekiah was pleased and showed the messengers what was in his storehouses: the silver, gold, spices, expensive perfumes, his swords and shields, and all his wealth. He showed them everything in his palace and in his kingdom.

3 Then Isaiah the prophet went to King Hezekiah and asked him, "What did these men say? Where did they come from?"

Hezekiah said, "They came from a faraway country—from Babylon."

4 So Isaiah asked him, "What did they see in your palace?"

Hezekiah said, "They saw everything in my palace. I showed them all my wealth."

5 Then Isaiah said to Hezekiah: "Listen to the words of the LORD All-Powerful: 6 'In the future everything in your palace and everything your ancestors have stored up until this day will be taken away to Babylon. Nothing will be left,' says the LORD. 7 Some of your own children, those who will be born to you, will be taken away, and they will become servants in the palace of the king of Babylon."

8 Hezekiah told Isaiah, "These words from the LORD are good." He said this because he thought, "There will be peace and security in my lifetime."

ISRAEL'S PUNISHMENT WILL END

40 Your God says,
"Comfort, comfort my people.
2 Speak kindly to the people of Jerusalem
and tell them
that their time of service is finished,
that they have paid for their sins,
that the LORD has punished Jerusalem
twice for every sin they did."

3 This is the voice of one who calls out:
"Prepare in the desert
the way for the LORD.
Make a straight road in the dry lands
for our God.
4 Every valley should be raised up,
and every mountain and hill should be
made flat.
The rough ground should be made level,
and the rugged ground should be made
smooth.
5 Then the glory of the LORD will be shown,
and all people together will see it.
The LORD himself said these things."

6 A voice says, "Cry out!"
Then I said, "What shall I cry out?"

"Say all people are like the grass,
and all their glory is like the flowers of
the field.
7 The grass dies and the flowers fall
when the breath of the LORD blows on
them.
Surely the people are like grass.
8 The grass dies and the flowers fall,
but the word of our God will live
forever."

9 Jerusalem, you have good news to tell.
Go up on a high mountain.
Jerusalem, you have good news to tell.
Shout out loud the good news.
Shout it out and don't be afraid.
Say to the towns of Judah,
"Here is your God."
10 Look, the Lord GOD is coming with power
to rule all the people.
Look, he will bring reward for his people;
he will have their payment with him.
11 He takes care of his people like a
shepherd.
He gathers them like lambs in his arms
and carries them close to him.
He gently leads the mothers of the lambs.

GOD IS SUPREME

¹² Who has measured the oceans in the palm
of his hand?
Who has used his hand to measure the
sky?
Who has used a bowl to measure all the
dust of the earth
and scales to weigh the mountains and
hills?

¹³ Who has known the mind of the LORD
or been able to give him advice?
¹⁴ Whom did he ask for help?
Who taught him the right way?
Who taught him knowledge
and showed him the way to
understanding?

¹⁵ The nations are like one small drop in a
bucket;

FUTURE

INSPIRE YOUR TEAM TO REALIZE THE DREAM

healthy
dependency

ISAIAH 40:11   By Jimmy Evans

All through the Bible, humanity is compared to sheep. Since the Scriptures are
divinely inspired, we need to understand what God means when he compares
us to sheep. Sheep are cuddly-looking animals, but they are beset with weaknesses
and limitations. They are absolutely vulnerable in regard to being able to protect
themselves. They have no sharp hooves or sharp teeth, and they are not aggressive.
They also have no navigational ability.

Unlike homing pigeons, whales, or other migratory animals that have the ability to
wander hundreds or even thousands of miles and find their way back, sheep can't
travel any significant distance without help. They also cannot provide for themselves.
They're not hunters; therefore, they lack the predatory skills needed to gather food
independently.

When God looks at us and says, "You're my sheep," what does he mean? In essence,
he is saying, "I created you without the ability to get where you're going. You need me.
I created you without the ability to provide for yourself. You need me." Jesus refers
to himself as the Good Shepherd, and he declares his willingness to lay down his life
for us.

The life of a person who has understood and accepted his or her weakness and has
turned to Christ for guidance, protection, and provision is a life of incredible blessing
and fullness. Probably the best description of the life dependent upon God was written
by David in Psalm 23:1: "The Lord is my shepherd; I have everything I need."

reflect: Have you entrusted total care for your life to the Good Shepherd?
Go to **Isaiah 42:10–16.**

they are no more than the dust on his
measuring scales.
To him the islands are no more than
fine dust on his scales.
16 All the trees in Lebanon are not enough
for the altar fires,
and all the animals in Lebanon are not
enough for burnt offerings.
17 Compared to the LORD all the nations are
worth nothing;
to him they are less than nothing.

18 Can you compare God to anything?
Can you compare him to an image of
anything?
19 An idol is formed by a craftsman,
and a goldsmith covers it with gold
and makes silver chains for it.
20 A poor person cannot buy those expensive
statues,
so he finds a tree that will not rot.
Then he finds a skilled craftsman
to make it into an idol that will not fall
over.

21 Surely you know. Surely you have heard.
Surely from the beginning someone
told you.
Surely you understand how the earth
was created.
22 God sits on his throne above the circle of
the earth,
and compared to him, people are like
grasshoppers.
He stretches out the skies like a piece of
cloth
and spreads them out like a tent to sit
under.
23 He makes rulers unimportant
and the judges of this world worth
nothing.
24 They are like plants that are placed in the
ground,
like seeds that are planted.
As soon as they begin to grow strong,
he blows on them and they die,
and the wind blows them away like
chaff.

25 God, the Holy One, says, "Can you
compare me to anyone?
Is anyone equal to me?"
26 Look up to the skies.
Who created all these stars?

He leads out the army of heaven one by
one
and calls all the stars by name.
Because he is strong and powerful,
not one of them is missing.

27 People of Jacob, why do you complain?
People of Israel, why do you say,
"The LORD does not see what happens to
me;
he does not care if I am treated fairly"?
28 Surely you know.
Surely you have heard.
The LORD is the God who lives forever,
who created all the world.
He does not become tired or need to rest.
No one can understand how great his
wisdom is.
29 He gives strength to those who are tired
and more power to those who are
weak.
30 Even children become tired and need to
rest,
and young people trip and fall.
31 But the people who trust the LORD will
become strong again.
They will rise up as an eagle in the sky;
they will run and not need rest;
they will walk and not become tired.

THE LORD WILL HELP ISRAEL

41 The LORD says, "Faraway countries,
listen to me.
Let the nations become strong.
Come to me and speak;
we will meet together to decide who is
right.

2 "Who caused the one to come from the
east?
Who gives him victories everywhere he
goes?
The one who brought him gives nations
over to him
and defeats kings.
He uses his sword, and kings become like
dust.
He uses his bow, and they are blown
away like chaff.
3 He chases them and is never hurt,
going places he has never been before.
4 Who caused this to happen?
Who has controlled history since the
beginning?

I, the LORD, am the one. I was here at the beginning,
and I will be here when all things are finished."

⁵ All you faraway places, look and be afraid;
all you places far away on the earth, shake with fear.
Come close and listen to me.
⁶ The workers help each other
and say to each other, "Be strong!"
⁷ The craftsman encourages the goldsmith,
and the workman who smooths the metal with a hammer encourages the one who shapes the metal.
He says, "This metal work is good."
He nails the statue to a base so it can't fall over.

ONLY THE LORD CAN SAVE US
⁸ The LORD says, "People of Israel, you are my servants.
People of Jacob, I chose you.
You are from the family of my friend Abraham.

FULFILLMENT

DO YOU KNOW HIM?

looking over
your shoulder

ISAIAH 41:10

Hebrew is a language that often uses parallel expressions to emphasize a point. This is God's version of a double take. God starts us off with a command about giving up fear. "Don't be afraid," he says. "You live in a world that is under my care. Decide to trust me." Then he gives us a *behavioral parallel*. "Don't shift your gaze from one thing to another, worrying about what might happen to you," he says. It's the Hebrew way of describing "looking over your shoulder." God says, "Trust me. I've got your back."

We all want someone to watch over us. We can't always see what's coming. But God can. He reminds us that one of the behavioral consequences of trusting him is to give up our anxiety and the actions that come from anxiety. If you really live in a world where God cares for you, do you need to be anxious about what might happen next? If you live in a world where God loves you and always does what is best for you, do you really need to worry about your life?

Red flag theology needs to become part of our daily walk. Whenever we discover we are behaving on the basis of a worrisome world, we need to see a big red flag. The world of worry is the world that says, "God doesn't care about me." That's a lie! And who wants to live life based on a lie?

reflect: Rest in the knowledge that God is watching out for you always.
Go to **Isaiah 43:1.**

9 I took you from places far away on the
   earth
   and called you from a faraway country.
   I said, 'You are my servants.'
   I have chosen you and have not turned
      against you.
10 So don't worry, because I am with you.
   Don't be afraid, because I am your God.
   I will make you strong and will help you;
   I will support you with my right hand
      that saves you.

11 "All those people who are angry with you
      will be ashamed and disgraced.
   Those who are against you
      will disappear and be lost.
12 You will look for your enemies,
      but you will not find them.
   Those who fought against you
      will vanish completely.
13 I am the LORD your God,
      who holds your right hand,
   and I tell you, 'Don't be afraid.
   I will help you.'
14 You few people of Israel who are left,
      do not be afraid even though you are
         weak as a worm.
   I myself will help you," says the LORD.
      "The one who saves you is the Holy One
         of Israel.
15 Look, I have made you like a new
      threshing board
   with many sharp teeth.
   So you will walk on mountains and crush
      them;
   you will make the hills like chaff.
16 You will throw them into the air, and the
      wind will carry them away;
   a windstorm will scatter them.
   Then you will be happy in the LORD;
   you will be proud of the Holy One of
      Israel.

17 "The poor and needy people look for
      water,
   but they can't find any.
   Their tongues are dry with thirst.
   But I, the LORD, will answer their prayers;
   I, the God of Israel, will not leave them
      to die.
18 I will make rivers flow on the dry hills
   and springs flow through the valleys.
   I will change the desert into a lake of
      water

and the dry land into fountains of water.
19 I will make trees grow in the desert—
   cedars, acacia, myrtle, and olive trees.
   I will put pine, fir, and cypress trees
      growing together in the desert.
20 People will see these things and
      understand;
   they will think carefully about these
      things and learn
   that the LORD's power did this,
      that the Holy One of Israel made these
         things."

THE LORD CHALLENGES FALSE GODS
21 The LORD says, "Present your case."
      The King of Jacob says, "Tell me your
         arguments.
22 Bring in your idols to tell us
      what is going to happen.
   Have them tell us what happened in the
      beginning.
   Then we will think about these things,
      and we will know how they will turn out.
   Or tell us what will happen in the future.
23   Tell us what is coming next
      so we will believe that you are gods.
   Do something, whether it is good or bad,
      and make us afraid.
24 You gods are less than nothing;
      you can't do anything.
   Those who worship you should be
      hated.

25 "I have brought someone to come out of
      the north[n]
   I have called by name a man from the
      east, and he knows me.
   He walks on kings as if they were mud,
      just as a potter walks on the clay.
26 Who told us about this before it
      happened?
   Who told us ahead of time so we could
      say, 'He was right'?
   None of you told us anything;
      none of you told us before it happened;
      no one heard you tell about it.
27 I, the LORD, was the first one to tell
      Jerusalem that the people were
         coming home.
   I sent a messenger to Jerusalem with
      the good news.

41:25 someone . . . north This probably means Cyrus,
a king of Persia.

747

28 I look at the idols, but there is not one that
   can answer.
   None of them can give advice;
   none of them can answer my questions.
29 Look, all these idols are false.
   They cannot do anything;
   they are worth nothing.

THE LORD'S SPECIAL SERVANT

42 "Here is my servant, the one I
   support.
   He is the one I chose, and I am pleased
      with him.
   I have put my Spirit upon him,
      and he will bring justice to all nations.
2 He will not cry out or yell
      or speak loudly in the streets.
3 He will not break a crushed blade of grass
      or put out even a weak flame.
   He will truly bring justice;
4   he will not lose hope or give up
   until he brings justice to the world.
      And people far away will trust his
         teachings."

5 God, the LORD, said these things.
   He created the skies and stretched them
      out.
   He spread out the earth and everything
      on it.
   He gives life to all people on earth,
      to everyone who walks on the earth.
6 The LORD says, "I, the LORD, called you to
      do right,
      and I will hold your hand
   and protect you.
   You will be the sign of my agreement
      with the people,
      a light to shine for all people.
7 You will help the blind to see.
   You will free those who are in prison,
      and you will lead those who live in
         darkness out of their prison.

8 "I am the LORD. That is my name.
   I will not give my glory to another;
   I will not let idols take the praise that
      should be mine.
9 The things I said would happen have
      happened,
      and now I tell you about new things.
   Before those things happen,
      I tell you about them."

A SONG OF PRAISE TO THE LORD

10 Sing a new song to the LORD;
   sing his praise everywhere on the earth.
   Praise him, you people who sail on the
      seas and you animals who live in
         them.
   Praise him, you people living in faraway
      places.
11 The deserts and their cities should praise
      him.
   The settlements of Kedar should praise
      him.
   The people living in Sela should sing for
      joy;
      they should shout from the
         mountaintops.
12 They should give glory to the LORD.
   People in faraway lands should praise
      him.
13 The LORD will march out like a strong
      soldier;
      he will be excited like a man ready to
         fight a war.
   He will shout out the battle cry
      and defeat his enemies.

14 The LORD says, "For a long time I have
      said nothing;
      I have been quiet and held myself
         back.
   But now I will cry out
      and strain like a woman giving birth to
         a child.
15 I will destroy the hills and mountains
      and dry up all their plants.
   I will make the rivers become dry land
      and dry up the pools of water.
16 Then I will lead the blind along a way
      they never knew;
      I will guide them along paths they have
         not known.
   I will make the darkness become light for
      them,
      and the rough ground smooth.
   These are the things I will do;
      I will not leave my people.
17 But those who trust in idols,
      who say to their statues,
   'You are our gods'
      will be rejected in disgrace.

ISRAEL REFUSED TO LISTEN TO THE LORD

18 "You who are deaf, hear me.
   You who are blind, look and see.

¹⁹ No one is more blind than my servant
  Israel
    or more deaf than the messenger I send.
  No one is more blind than the person I
  own
    or more blind than the servant of the
    LORD.
²⁰ Israel, you have seen much, but you have
    not obeyed.

You hear, but you refuse to listen."
²¹ The LORD made his teachings wonderful,
    because he is good.
²² These people have been defeated and
    robbed.
  They are trapped in pits
    or locked up in prison.
  Like robbers, enemies have taken them
    away,

INSPIRE YOUR TEAM TO REALIZE THE DREAM

a new day

FUTURE

By Claudio Freidzon

ISAIAH 42:10-16

Has it been a bitter night of great frustrations because the harvests you expected never came, the strategies you planned never succeeded, or the changes you expected in your life, family, or finances never took place? Then you can understand the pressures and doubts Simon Peter and his crew faced when their empty nets held no answers (Luke 5:5).

Now, when you have nothing left, Jesus appears at the dawn of the new day and directs you to overflowing nets. Jesus is not just talking about financial prosperity, but also an abundance of open doors, favor, forgiveness, power, and authority. He declares a new grace, a new time, and a new harvest.

Your strategies or the system's methods cannot create success; only a visitation by God can. Coincidence does not have anything to do with it. Your new day has nothing to do with your own talents or worthiness. It is Jesus! His power is what fills you and gives you ability.

The Lord is announcing a new day to all those who worship him and recognize his voice. Run to Jesus, give him credit, and rejoice loudly! Your lonely night of sorrow and scarcity is ending. Tell your circumstances and the devil, "I have left all my sins at the cross of Jesus. I have left the past behind, and I am not staying in the bitter night. I will not delay in the shadows because Jesus has announced my new day, and I declare abundance of anointing, joy, open doors, favor, and all that I need."

reflect: What influences do you want to leave in the past?
Go to **Isaiah 57:15.**

and there is no one to save them.
Enemies carried them off,
    and no one said, "Bring them back."

23 Will any of you listen to this?
    Will you listen carefully in the future?
24 Who let the people of Jacob be carried off?
    Who let robbers take Israel away?
The LORD allowed this to happen,
    because we sinned against him.
We did not live the way he wanted us to
        live
    and did not obey his teaching.
25 So he became very angry with us
    and brought terrible wars against us.

It was as if the people of Israel had fire all
        around them,
    but they didn't know what was
        happening.
It was as if they were burning,
    but they didn't pay any attention.

GOD IS ALWAYS WITH HIS PEOPLE

43 Now this is what the LORD says.
    He created you, people of Jacob;
    he formed you, people of Israel.
He says, "Don't be afraid, because I have
        saved you.
    I have called you by name, and you are
        mine.

FULFILLMENT

DO YOU KNOW HIM?

the name
he knows

ISAIAH 43:1

God actually requests that we call on his name, not only in times when our lives are uncontrollable, but also as an ordinary practice of acknowledging our **powerlessness.** He's not just looking for desperation prayers when we're surrounded in a crisis. We are to rely on him totally, never taking him for granted regarding any details of our lives.

God specifically acknowledges that he has named each of us as his own, that our lives are in his hands, and that he is our absolute Lord. This promise of God's sovereignty over us is not generalized, but quite specific; so specific, in fact, that he names each one of us individually. Two important truths reside in this promise. The first is that we are not insignificant or obscure. God himself has called us by name.

The second is that God's calling for us is tailored precisely to who we are. He knows us each by the name he has called us. No wonder the Bible can say that God knows us better than we know ourselves. If God knows that much about us, and he still says that he wants to make us whole, to forgive us, to pick us up and help us, how can we refuse such an offer! God knows us by name. That means he has a claim on us. Since we belong to him, we don't have to be afraid, for he takes care of his own.

reflect: Give God thanks for naming you and claiming you as his very own.
Go to Isaiah 52:7.

2 When you pass through the waters, I will
be with you.
When you cross rivers, you will not
drown.
When you walk through fire, you will not
be burned,
nor will the flames hurt you.
3 This is because I, the LORD, am your God,
the Holy One of Israel, your Savior.
I gave Egypt to pay for you,
and I gave Cush and Seba to make you
mine.
4 Because you are precious to me,
because I give you honor and love you,
I will give other people in your place;
I will give other nations to save your
life.
5 Don't be afraid, because I am with you.
I will bring your children from the east
and gather you from the west.
6 I will tell the north: Give my people to me.
I will tell the south: Don't keep my
people in prison.
Bring my sons from far away
and my daughters from faraway places.
7 Bring to me all the people who are mine,
whom I made for my glory,
whom I formed and made."

JUDAH IS GOD'S WITNESS

8 Bring out the people who have eyes but
don't see
and those who have ears but don't hear.
9 All the nations gather together,
and all the people come together.
Which of their gods said this would
happen?
Which of their gods can tell what
happened in the beginning?
Let them bring their witnesses to prove
they were right.
Then others will say, "It is true."
10 The LORD says, "You are my witnesses
and the servant I chose.
I chose you so you would know and
believe me,
so you would understand that I am the
true God.
There was no God before me,
and there will be no God after me.
11 I myself am the LORD;
I am the only Savior.
12 I myself have spoken to you, saved you,

and told you these things.
It was not some foreign god among you.
You are my witnesses, and I am God,"
says the LORD.
13 "I have always been God.
No one can save people from my power;
when I do something, no one can
change it."

14 This is what the LORD, who saves you,
the Holy One of Israel, says:
"I will send armies to Babylon for you,
and I will knock down all its locked
gates.
The Babylonians will shout their cries of
sorrow.
15 I am the LORD, your Holy One,
the Creator of Israel, your King."

GOD WILL SAVE HIS PEOPLE AGAIN

16 This is what the LORD says.
He is the one who made a road through
the sea
and a path through rough waters.
17 He is the one who defeated the chariots
and horses
and the mighty armies.
They fell together and will never rise
again.
They were destroyed as a flame is put
out.
18 The LORD says, "Forget what happened
before,
and do not think about the past.
19 Look at the new thing I am going to do.
It is already happening. Don't you see
it?
I will make a road in the desert
and rivers in the dry land.
20 Even the wild animals will be thankful to
me—
the wild dogs and owls.
They will honor me when I put water in
the desert
and rivers in the dry land
to give water to my people, the ones I
chose.
21 The people I made
will sing songs to praise me.

22 "People of Jacob, you have not called to
me;
people of Israel, you have become tired
of me.

23 You have not brought me your sacrifices
of sheep
nor honored me with your sacrifices.
I did not weigh you down with sacrifices
to offer
or make you tired with incense to burn.
24 So you did not buy incense for me;
you did not freely bring me fat from
your sacrifices.
Instead you have weighed me down with
your many sins;
you have made me tired of your many
wrongs.

25 "I, I am the One who erases all your sins,
for my sake;
I will not remember your sins.
26 But you should remind me.
Let's meet and decide what is right.
Tell what you have done and show you
are right.
27 Your first father sinned,
and your leaders have turned against
me.
28 So I will make your holy rulers unholy.
I will bring destruction on the people
of Jacob,
and I will let Israel be insulted."

THE LORD IS THE ONLY GOD

44 The LORD says, "People of Jacob, you
are my servants. Listen to me!
People of Israel, I chose you."
2 This is what the LORD says, who made
you,
who formed you in your mother's body,
who will help you:
"People of Jacob, my servants, don't be
afraid.
Israel, I chose you.
3 I will pour out water for the thirsty land
and make streams flow on dry land.
I will pour out my Spirit into your
children
and my blessing on your descendants.
4 Your children will grow like a tree in the
grass,
like poplar trees growing beside
streams of water.
5 One person will say, 'I belong to the LORD,'
and another will use the name Jacob.
Another will sign his name 'I am the
LORD's,'
and another will use the name Israel."

6 The LORD, the king of Israel,
is the LORD All-Powerful, who saves
Israel.
This is what he says: "I am the beginning
and the end.
I am the only God.
7 Who is a god like me?
That god should come and prove it.
Let him tell and explain all that has
happened since I set up my ancient
people.
He should also tell what will happen in
the future.
8 Don't be afraid! Don't worry!
I have always told you what will
happen.
You are my witnesses.
There is no other God but me.
I know of no other Rock; I am the only
One."

IDOLS ARE USELESS

9 Some people make idols, but they are
worth nothing.
People treasure them, but they are
useless.
Those people are witnesses for the
statues, but those people cannot
see.
They know nothing, so they will be
ashamed.
10 Who made these gods?
Who made these useless idols?
11 The workmen who made them will be
ashamed,
because they are only human.
If they all would come together,
they would all be ashamed and afraid.

12 One workman uses tools to heat iron,
and he works over hot coals.
With his hammer he beats the metal and
makes a statue,
using his powerful arms.
But when he becomes hungry, he loses his
power.
If he does not drink water, he becomes
tired.

13 Another workman uses a line and a
compass
to draw on the wood.
Then he uses his chisels to cut a statue
and his calipers to measure the statue.

In this way, the workman makes the wood
 look exactly like a person,
and this statue of a person sits in the
 house.

¹⁴ He cuts down cedars
 or cypress or oak trees.
Those trees grew by their own power in
 the forest.
Or he plants a pine tree, and the rain
 makes it grow.

¹⁵ Then he burns the tree.
He uses some of the wood for a fire to
 keep himself warm.
He also starts a fire to bake his bread.
But he uses part of the wood to make a
 god, and then he worships it!
He makes the idol and bows down to it!

¹⁶ The man burns half of the wood in the
 fire.
He uses the fire to cook his meat,
 and he eats the meat until he is full.
He also burns the wood to keep himself
 warm. He says,
 "Good! Now I am warm. I can see
 because of the fire's light."

¹⁷ But he makes a statue from the wood that
 is left and calls it his god.
He bows down to it and worships it.
He prays to it and says,
 "You are my god. Save me!"

¹⁸ Those people don't know what they are
 doing. They don't understand!
It is as if their eyes are covered so they
 can't see.

HAVE FAITH IN GOD

God and slavery

FAITH

ISAIAH 44:21

Slave! That's the primary meaning of this verse. But slavery in the Hebrew culture was not like our modern version of slavery. In the Hebrew culture, a person could only be held as a slave for six years. The seventh year, the Year of Jubilee, was a year of freedom. Slaves had rights and could attain position and power.

However (and it's a *big* "however"), we should not think that the relationship between master and slave was reduced to nothing more than employer and employee. Notice the context of God's proclamation in this verse. Why are we, the chosen ones, his servants? Because he made us. We owe a great deal more to him than six years service for the payment of a debt. We owe our very existence to him. He has an absolute claim over us. God is no tyrant, but he is the absolute ruler.

This concept of slavery is an important one. It is not about forced surrender. It is about voluntary submission. Jesus came to earth to model the role of a servant, and we are to follow his godly example. The good news is that Jesus no longer calls us mere slaves, but his "friends."

reflect: Think about how awesome it is to be considered a personal friend of God!
Go to **Mark 15:34.**

Their minds don't understand.

19 They have not thought about these things;
they don't understand.
They have never thought to themselves,
"I burned half of the wood in the fire
and used the hot coals to bake my
bread.
I cooked and ate my meat.
And I used the wood that was left to make
this hateful thing.
I am worshiping a block of wood!"

20 He doesn't know what he is doing;
his confused mind leads him the wrong
way.
He cannot save himself
or say, "This statue I am holding is a
false god."

THE LORD IS THE TRUE GOD

21 "People of Jacob, remember these things!
People of Israel, remember you are my
servants.
I made you, and you are my servants.
So Israel, I will not forget you.

22 I have swept away your sins like a big
cloud;
I have removed your sins like a cloud
that disappears into the air.
Come back to me because I saved you."

23 Skies, sing for joy because the LORD did
great things!
Earth, shout for joy, even in your
deepest parts!
Sing, you mountains, with thanks to God.
Sing, too, you trees in the forest!
The LORD saved the people of Jacob!
He showed his glory when he saved
Israel.

24 This is what the LORD says, who saved
you,
who formed you in your mother's
body:
"I, the LORD, made everything,
stretching out the skies by myself
and spreading out the earth all alone.

25 I show that the signs of the lying prophets
are false;
I make fools of those who do magic.
I confuse even the wise;
they think they know much, but I make
them look foolish.

26 I make the messages of my servants come
true;

I make the advice of my messengers
come true.
I say to Jerusalem,
'People will live in you again!'
I say to the towns of Judah,
'You will be built again!'
I say to Jerusalem's ruins,
'I will repair you.'

27 I tell the deep waters, 'Become dry!
I will make your streams become dry!'

28 I say of Cyrus,[n] 'He is my shepherd
and will do all that I want him to do.
He will say to Jerusalem, "You will be
built again!"
He will tell the Temple, "Your
foundations will be rebuilt."'"

GOD CHOOSES CYRUS TO FREE ISRAEL

45 This is what the LORD says to Cyrus,
his appointed king:
"I hold your right hand
and will help you defeat nations
and take away other kings' power.
I will open doors for you
so city gates will not stop you.

2 I will go before you
and make the mountains flat.
I will break down the bronze gates of the
cities
and cut through their iron bars.

3 I will give you the wealth that is stored
away
and the hidden riches
so you will know I am the LORD,
the God of Israel, who calls you by
name.

4 I do these things for my servants, the
people of Jacob,
and for my chosen people, the Israelites.
Cyrus, I call you by name,
and I give you a title of honor even
though you don't know me.

5 I am the LORD. There is no other God;
I am the only God.
I will make you strong,
even though you don't know me,

6 so that everyone will know
there is no other God.
From the east to the west they will know
I alone am the LORD.

44:28 Cyrus A king of Persia who ruled from about
550–530 B.C.

7 I made the light and the darkness.
  I bring peace, and I cause troubles.
  I, the LORD, do all these things.

8 "Sky above, make victory fall like
    rain;
  clouds, pour down victory.
  Let the earth receive it,
    and let salvation grow,

and let victory grow with it.
  I, the LORD, have created it.

9 "How terrible it will be for those who
    argue with the God who made them.
  They are like a piece of broken pottery
    among many pieces.
  The clay does not ask the potter,
  'What are you doing?'

PEACE BY GOD

take back your peace

By Dr. Sheri Lerner

FULFILLMENT

ISAIAH 45:7

There's a popular story about two artists who were asked to paint their conceptions of peace. One painted a tranquil lake at sunrise with mist hovering over the placid water. The other painted a raging torrent of a stream plunging over a waterfall with the storm clouds blackening the sky and the rain pelting down. On the branch of a tree hanging way out over the treacherous water was a bird's nest. In it sat a small bird, hunkered down against the wind and rain, with her eyes shut . . . sleeping. That painting truly illustrated peace: calmness and trust in the middle of the storms of life.

When you focus on stress and give it power over you through your improper reactions, you are not in control. Stress is. That is the opposite of what God intended. God gave you the power to be peaceful; you have surrendered it by turning around and giving it to others or situations. There's only one thing to do: take it back.

Here's how:

• Understand it.

• Accept it.

• Teach it to others.

When life is just too much, your gift of peace by God is right there within you, waiting for you to use it. It's helpful to think of it as a savings account that God opened in your name, just sitting there, waiting for you to make withdrawals as you need them. You take what you need at the moment, but there's plenty more where that came from.

reflect: Do you need to unwrap the gift of peace that is yours today?
Go to **Isaiah 26:3**.

The thing that is made doesn't say to its
maker,
'You have no hands.'
10 How terrible it will be for the child who
says to his father,
'Why are you giving me life?'
How terrible it will be for the child who
says to his mother,
'Why are you giving birth to me?'"

11 This is what the LORD,
the Holy One of Israel, and its Maker,
says:
"You ask me about what will happen.
You question me about my children.
You give me orders about what I have
made.
12 I made the earth
and all the people living on it.
With my own hands I stretched out the
skies,
and I commanded all the armies in the
sky.
13 I will bring Cyrus to do good things,
and I will make his work easy.
He will rebuild my city
and set my people free
without any payment or reward.
The LORD All-Powerful says this."

14 The LORD says,
"The goods made in Egypt and Cush
and the tall people of Seba
will come to you
and will become yours.
The Sabeans will walk behind you,
coming along in chains.
They will bow down before you
and pray to you, saying,
'God is with you,
and there is no other God.'"

15 God and Savior of Israel,
you are a God that people cannot see.
16 All the people who make idols will be put
to great shame;
they will go off together in disgrace.
17 But Israel will be saved by the LORD,
and that salvation will continue forever.
Never again will Israel be put to shame.

18 The LORD created the heavens.
He is the God who formed the earth
and made it.
He did not want it to be empty,

but he wanted life on the earth.
This is what the LORD says:
"I am the LORD. There is no other God.
19 I did not speak in secret
or hide my words in some dark place.
I did not tell the family of Jacob
to look for me in empty places.
I am the LORD, and I speak the truth;
I say what is right.

20 "You people who have escaped from other
nations,
gather together and come before me;
come near together.
People who carry idols of wood don't
know what they are doing.
They pray to a god who cannot save
them.
21 Tell these people to come to me.
Let them talk about these things
together.
Who told you long ago that this would
happen?
Who told about it long ago?
I, the LORD, said these things.
There is no other God besides me.
I am the only good God. I am the Savior.
There is no other God.

22 "All people everywhere,
follow me and be saved.
I am God. There is no other God.
23 I will make a promise by my own power,
and my promise is true;
what I say will not be changed.
I promise that everyone will bow before
me
and will promise to follow me.
24 People will say about me, 'Goodness and
power
come only from the LORD.'"
Everyone who has been angry with him
will come to him and be ashamed.
25 But with the LORD's help, the people of
Israel
will be found to be good,
and they will praise him.

FALSE GODS ARE USELESS

46 Bel and Nebo bow down.
Their idols are carried by animals.
The statues are only heavy loads that must
be carried;
they only make people tired.

2 These gods will all bow down.
  They cannot save themselves
  but will all be carried away like
    prisoners.

3 "Family of Jacob, listen to me!
  All you people from Israel who are still
    alive, listen!
  I have carried you since you were born;

TURNING REVELATIONS INTO REVOLUTIONS

use it or lose it

FITNESS

ISAIAH 46:3-4

God created you to survive this rough world you inhabit. God structured your body with the capacity to develop survival strength through what is called the Law of Adaptation. This law states that, over time, your body will *adapt* to the stress imposed on it by the environment it inhabits or the challenges it regularly encounters. For instance, desert cultures that are regularly exposed to the sun have adapted the dark skin pigmentation needed to more safely absorb the abundance of ultraviolet rays.

Similarly, in other parts of the world, the immune systems of the indigenous people have naturally adapted to deal with the local germs, their respiratory systems have adapted to the local altitude, and other parts of their bodies have adapted to the climate, the workload, and even the food of the region.

Part of the Law of Adaptation states as your body adapts to certain stresses, it further *un*adapts to opposing stresses. For instance, people used to warm climates are not prepared for cold weather, while people in colder climates often cannot stand extreme heat. Likewise, people at lower altitudes have a great deal of trouble at high altitudes.

Due to the *un*adaptation that is part and parcel of the Law of Adaptation, as people enter any totally new environment or different way of life, their bodies will often not be able to handle the nutrition, the bacteria, the time zone, or anything else they are not used to dealing with on a regular basis.

For better or worse, your body will adapt to whatever forces you impose, or don't impose, upon it. In the case of exercise, if you participate in a regular fitness program, the forces you apply will cause you to adapt and get stronger, leaner, and healthier. If you rarely move, however, the lack of forces will cause you to adapt and get weaker, fatter, and sicker. For that reason, part of the Law of Adaptation is: "Use it or you lose it."

reflect: Do some type of exercise today that strengthens your ability to adapt.
Go to **Isaiah 53:5.**

I have taken care of you from your
birth.
4 Even when you are old, I will be the same.
Even when your hair has turned gray, I
will take care of you.
I made you and will take care of you.
I will carry you and save you.

5 "Can you compare me to anyone?
No one is equal to me or like me.
6 Some people are rich with gold
and weigh their silver on the scales.
They hire a goldsmith, and he makes it
into a god.
Then they bow down and worship it.
7 They put it on their shoulders and carry
it.
They set it in its place, and there it
stands;
it cannot move from its place.
People may yell at it, but it cannot answer.
It cannot save them from their troubles.

8 "Remember this, and do not forget it!
Think about these things, you who turn
against God.
9 Remember what happened long ago.
Remember that I am God, and there is
no other God.
I am God, and there is no one like me.
10 From the beginning I told you what
would happen in the end.
A long time ago I told you things that
have not yet happened.
When I plan something, it happens.
What I want to do, I will do.
11 I am calling a man from the east to carry
out my plan;
he will come like a hawk from a country
far away.
I will make what I have said come true;
I will do what I have planned.
12 Listen to me, you stubborn people,
who are far from what is right.
13 I will soon do the things that are right.
I will bring salvation soon.
I will save Jerusalem
and bring glory to Israel."

GOD WILL DESTROY BABYLON

47 The LORD says, "City of Babylon, go
down and sit in the dirt.
People of Babylon, sit on the ground.
You are no longer the ruler.

You will no longer be called
tender or beautiful.
2 You must use large stones to grind grain
into flour.
Remove your veil and your nice skirts.
Uncover your legs and cross the rivers.
3 People will see your nakedness;
they will see your shame.
I will punish you;
I will punish every one of you."

4 Our Savior is named the LORD
All-Powerful;
he is the Holy One of Israel.

5 "Babylon, sit in darkness and say nothing.
You will no longer be called the queen
of kingdoms.
6 I was angry with my people,
so I rejected those who belonged
to me.
I gave them to you,
but you showed them no mercy.
You even made the old people
work very hard.
7 You said, 'I will live forever
as the queen.'
But you did not think about these things
or consider what would happen.

8 "Now, listen, you lover of pleasure.
You think you are safe.
You tell yourself,
'I am the only important person.
I will never be a widow
or lose my children.'
9 Two things will happen to you suddenly,
in a single day.
You will lose your children and your
husband.
These things will truly happen to you,
in spite of all your magic,
in spite of your powerful tricks.
10 You do evil things, but you feel safe
and say, 'No one sees what I do.'
Your wisdom and knowledge
have fooled you.
You say to yourself,
'I am God, and no one is equal to me.'
11 But troubles will come to you,
and you will not know how to stop
them.
Disaster will fall on you,
and you will not be able to keep it away.

You will be destroyed quickly;
you will not even see it coming.

12 "Keep on using your tricks
and doing all your magic
that you have used since you were
young.
Maybe they will help you;
maybe you will be able to scare
someone.
13 You are tired of the advice you have
received.
So let those who study the sky—
those who tell the future by looking at the
stars and the new moons—
let them save you from what is about to
happen to you.
14 But they are like straw;
fire will quickly burn them up.
They cannot save themselves
from the power of the fire.
They are not like coals that give warmth
nor like a fire that you may sit beside.
15 You have worked with these people,
and they have been with you since you
were young,
but they will not be able to help you.
Everyone will go his own way,
and there will be no one left to save
you."

GOD CONTROLS THE FUTURE

48 The LORD says, "Family of Jacob,
listen to me.
You are called Israel,
and you come from the family of Judah.
You swear by the LORD's name
and praise the God of Israel,
but you are not honest or sincere.
2 You call yourselves people of the holy city,
and you depend on the God of Israel,
who is named the LORD All-Powerful.
3 Long ago I told you what would happen.
I said these things and made them
known;
suddenly I acted, and these things
happened.
4 I knew you were stubborn;
your neck was like an iron muscle,
and your head was like bronze.
5 So a long time ago I told you about these
things;
I told you about them before they
happened

so you couldn't say, 'My idols did this,
and my wooden and metal statues made
these things happen.'

6 "You heard and saw everything that
happened,
so you should tell this news to others.
Now I will tell you about new things,
hidden things that you don't know yet.
7 These things are happening now, not long
ago;
you have not heard about them before
today.
So you cannot say, 'We already knew
about that.'
8 But you have not heard me; you have not
understood.
Even long ago you did not listen to me.
I knew you would surely turn against me;
you have fought against me since you
were born.
9 But for my own sake I will be patient.
People will praise me for not becoming
angry
and destroying you.
10 I have made you pure, but not by fire, as
silver is made pure.
I have purified you by giving you
troubles.
11 I do this for myself, for my own sake.
I will not let people speak evil against
me,
and I will not let some god take my
glory.

ISRAEL WILL BE FREE

12 "People of Jacob, listen to me.
People of Israel, I have called you to be
my people.
I am God;
I am the beginning and the end.
13 I made the earth with my own hands.
With my right hand I spread out the
skies.
When I call them,
they come together before me."

14 All of you, come together and listen.
None of the gods said these things
would happen.
The LORD has chosen someone
to attack the Babylonians;
he will carry out his wishes against
Babylon.

15 "I have spoken; I have called him.[n]
   I have brought him, and I will make
      him successful.
16 Come to me and listen to this.
   From the beginning I have spoken
      openly.
   From the time it began, I was there."

   Now, the Lord GOD
      has sent me with his Spirit.

17 This is what the LORD, who saves you,
      the Holy One of Israel, says:
   "I am the LORD your God,
      who teaches you to do what is good,
      who leads you in the way you should go.
18 If you had obeyed me,
      you would have had peace like a full-
         flowing river.
   Good things would have flowed to you
      like the waves of the sea.
19 You would have had many children,
      as many as the grains of sand.
   They would never have died out
      nor been destroyed."

20 My people, leave Babylon!
   Run from the Babylonians!
   Tell this news with shouts of joy to the
      people;
   spread it everywhere on earth.
   Say, "The LORD has saved his servants, the
      people of Jacob."
21 They did not become thirsty when he led
      them through the deserts.
   He made water flow from a rock for
      them.
   He split the rock,
      and water flowed out.

22 "There is no peace for evil people," says
      the LORD.

GOD CALLS HIS SPECIAL SERVANT

49 All of you people in faraway places,
      listen to me.
   Listen, all you nations far away.
   Before I was born, the LORD called me to
      serve him.
   The LORD named me while I was still in
      my mother's womb.
2 He made my tongue like a sharp sword.
   He hid me in the shadow of his hand.
   He made me like a sharp arrow.
   He hid me in the holder for his arrows.

3 He told me, "Israel, you are my servant.
   I will show my glory through you."
4 But I said, "I have worked hard for
      nothing;
   I have used all my power, but I did
      nothing useful.
   But the LORD will decide what my work
      is worth;
   God will decide my reward."

5 The LORD made me in the body of my
      mother
   to be his servant,
   to lead the people of Jacob back to him
      so that Israel might be gathered to him.
   The LORD will honor me,
      and I will get my strength from my
         God.
6 Now he told me,
   "You are an important servant to me
      to bring back the tribes of Jacob,
      to bring back the people of Israel who
         are left alive.
   But, more importantly, I will make you a
      light for all nations
      to show people all over the world the
         way to be saved."

7 The LORD who saves you
      is the Holy One of Israel.
   He speaks to the one who is hated by the
      people,
      to the servant of rulers.
   This is what he says: "Kings will see you
      and stand to honor you;
   great leaders will bow down before you,
   because the LORD can be trusted.
   He is the Holy One of Israel, who has
      chosen you."

THE DAY OF SALVATION

8 This is what the LORD says:
   "At the right time I will hear your prayers.
      On the day of salvation I will help you.
   I will protect you,
      and you will be the sign of my
         agreement with the people.
   You will bring back the people to the land
      and give the land that is now ruined
         back to its owners.
9 You will tell the prisoners, 'Come out of
      your prison.'

48:15 **him** This probably refers to Cyrus king of Persia.

You will tell those in darkness, 'Come
   into the light.'
The people will eat beside the roads,
   and they will find food even on bare
   hills.
10 They will not be hungry or thirsty.
   Neither the hot sun nor the desert wind
   will hurt them.
The God who comforts them will lead
   them
   and guide them by springs of water.
11 I will make my mountains into roads,
   and the roads will be raised up.
12 Look, people are coming to me from far
   away,
   from the north and from the west,
   from Aswan in southern Egypt."

13 Heavens and earth, be happy.
   Mountains, shout with joy,
because the LORD comforts his people
   and will have pity on those who
   suffer.

JERUSALEM AND HER CHILDREN

14 But Jerusalem said, "The LORD has left
   me;
   the Lord has forgotten me."

15 The LORD answers, "Can a woman forget
   the baby she nurses?
   Can she feel no kindness for the child to
   which she gave birth?
Even if she could forget her children,
   I will not forget you.
16 See, I have written your name on my
   hand.
   Jerusalem, I always think about your
   walls.
17 Your children will soon return to you,
   and the people who defeated you and
   destroyed you will leave.
18 Look up and look around you.
   All your children are gathering to
   return to you."
The LORD says, "As surely as I live,
   your children will be like jewels
   that a bride wears proudly.

19 "You were destroyed and defeated,
   and your land was made useless.
But now you will have more people than
   the land can hold,
   and those people who destroyed you
   will be far away.

20 Children were born to you while you were
   sad,
   but they will say to you,
   'This place is too small for us.
   Give us a bigger place to live.'
21 Then you will say to yourself,
   'Who gave me all these children?
I was sad and lonely,
   defeated and separated from my people.
So who reared these children?
I was left all alone.
   Where did all these children come
   from?'"

22 This is what the Lord GOD says:
"See, I will lift my hand to signal the
   nations;
   I will raise my banner for all the people
   to see.
Then they will bring your sons back to
   you in their arms,
   and they will carry your daughters on
   their shoulders.
23 Kings will teach your children,
   and daughters of kings will take care of
   them.
They will bow down before you
   and kiss the dirt at your feet.
Then you will know I am the LORD.
   Anyone who trusts in me will not be
   disappointed."

24 Can the wealth a soldier wins in war be
   taken away from him?
   Can a prisoner be freed from a powerful
   soldier?
25 This is what the LORD says:
"The prisoners will be taken from the
   strong soldiers.
   What the soldiers have taken will be
   saved.
I will fight your enemies,
   and I will save your children.
26 I will force those who trouble you to eat
   their own flesh.
   Their own blood will be the wine that
   makes them drunk.
Then everyone will know
   I, the LORD, am the One who saves you;
   I am the Powerful One of Jacob who
   saves you."

ISRAEL WAS PUNISHED FOR ITS SIN

50 This is what the LORD says:
"People of Israel, you say I divorced
your mother.
Then where is the paper that proves it?
Or do you think I sold you
to pay a debt?
Because of the evil things you did, I sold
you.
Because of the times she turned against
me, your mother was sent away.
2 I came home and found no one there;
I called, but no one answered.
Do you think I am not able to save you?
Do I not have the power to save you?
Look, I need only to shout and the sea
becomes dry.
I change rivers into a desert,
and their fish rot because there is no
water;
they die of thirst.
3 I can make the skies dark;
I can make them black like clothes of
sadness."

GOD'S SERVANT OBEYS

4 The Lord GOD gave me the ability to teach
so that I know what to say to make the
weak strong.
Every morning he wakes me.
He teaches me to listen like a student.
5 The Lord GOD helps me learn,
and I have not turned against him
nor stopped following him.
6 I offered my back to those who beat me.
I offered my cheeks to those who pulled
my beard.
I won't hide my face from them
when they make fun of me and spit at
me.
7 The Lord GOD helps me,
so I will not be ashamed.
I will be determined,
and I know I will not be disgraced.
8 He shows that I am innocent, and he is
close to me.
So who can accuse me?
If there is someone, let us go to court
together.
If someone wants to prove I have done
wrong,
he should come and tell me.
9 Look! It is the Lord GOD who helps me.

So who can prove me guilty?
Look! All those who try will become
useless like old clothes;
moths will eat them.

10 Who among you fears the LORD
and obeys his servant?
That person may walk in the dark
and have no light.
Then let him trust in the LORD
and yet depend on his God.
11 But instead, some of you want to light
your own fires
and make your own light.
So, go, walk in the light of your fires,
and trust your own light to guide you.
But this is what you will receive from me:
You will lie down in a place of pain.

JERUSALEM WILL BE SAVED

51 The LORD says, "Listen to me,
those of you who try to live right
and follow the LORD.
Look at the rock from which you were
cut;
look at the stone quarry from which you
were dug.
2 Look at Abraham, your ancestor,
and Sarah, who gave birth to your
ancestors.
Abraham had no children when I called
him,
but I blessed him and gave him many
descendants.
3 So the LORD will comfort Jerusalem;
he will show mercy to those who live in
her ruins.
He will change her deserts into a garden
like Eden;
he will make her empty lands like the
garden of the LORD.
People there will be very happy;
they will give thanks and sing songs.

4 "My people, listen to me;
my nation, pay attention to me.
I will give the people my teachings,
and my decisions will be like a light to
all people.
5 I will soon show that I do what is right.
I will soon save you.
I will use my power and judge all
nations.
All the faraway places are waiting for me;

762

they wait for my power to help them.
⁶ Look up to the heavens.
  Look around you at the earth below.
The skies will disappear like clouds of
    smoke.
  The earth will become useless like old
    clothes,
  and its people will die like flies.
But my salvation will continue forever,
  and my goodness will never end.

⁷ "You people who know what is right
    should listen to me;
  you people who follow my teachings
    should hear what I say.
Don't be afraid of the evil things people
    say,
  and don't be upset by their insults.
⁸ Moths will eat those people as if they
    were clothes,
  and worms will eat them as if they were
    wool.
But my goodness will continue forever,
  and my salvation will continue from
    now on."

⁹ Wake up, wake up, and use your strength,
    powerful LORD.
Wake up as you did in the old times,
  as you did a long time ago.
With your own power, you cut Rahab into
    pieces
  and killed that sea monster.
¹⁰ You dried up the sea
  and the waters of the deep ocean.
You made the deepest parts of the sea into
    a road
  for your people to cross over and be
    saved.
¹¹ The people the LORD has freed will return
    and enter Jerusalem with joy.
  Their happiness will last forever.
They will have joy and gladness,
  and all sadness and sorrow will be gone
    far away.
¹² The LORD says, "I am the one who
    comforts you.
  So why should you be afraid of people,
    who die?
  Why should you fear people who die
    like the grass?
¹³ Have you forgotten the LORD who made
    you,

who stretched out the skies
  and made the earth?
Why are you always afraid
  of those angry people who trouble you
  and who want to destroy?
But where are those angry people now?
¹⁴ People in prison will soon be set free;
  they will not die in prison,
  and they will have enough food.
¹⁵ I am the LORD your God,
  who stirs the sea and makes the waves
    roar.
  My name is the LORD All-Powerful.
¹⁶ I will give you the words I want you to
    say.
  I will cover you with my hands and
    protect you.
I made the heavens and the earth,
  and I say to Jerusalem, 'You are my
    people.'"

GOD PUNISHED ISRAEL

¹⁷ Awake! Awake!
  Get up, Jerusalem.
The LORD was very angry with you;
  your punishment was like wine in a
    cup.
The LORD made you drink that wine;
  you drank the whole cup until you
    stumbled.
¹⁸ Jerusalem had many people,
  but there was not one to lead her.
Of all the people who grew up there,
  no one was there to guide her.
¹⁹ Troubles came to you two by two,
  but no one will feel sorry for you.
There was ruin and disaster, great hunger
    and fighting.
  No one can comfort you.
²⁰ Your people have become weak.
  They fall down and lie on every street
    corner,
  like animals caught in a net.
They have felt the full anger of the
    LORD
  and have heard God's angry shout.

²¹ So listen to me, poor Jerusalem,
  you who are drunk but not from
    wine.
²² Your God will defend his people.
  This is what the LORD your God says:
"The punishment I gave you is like a cup
    of wine.

You drank it and could not walk
straight.
But I am taking that cup of my anger away
from you,
and you will never be punished by my
anger again.
²³ I will now give that cup of punishment to
those who gave you pain,
who told you,
'Bow down so we can walk over you.'
They made your back like dirt for them to
walk on;
you were like a street for them to travel
on."

JERUSALEM WILL BE SAVED

52 Wake up, wake up, Jerusalem!
Become strong!
Be beautiful again,
holy city of Jerusalem.
The people who do not worship God and
who are not pure
will not enter you again.
² Jerusalem, you once were a prisoner.
Now shake off the dust and stand up.
Jerusalem, you once were a prisoner.
Now free yourself from the chains
around your neck.
³ This is what the LORD says:

FULFILLMENT

DO YOU KNOW HIM?

complete spiritual makeover

ISAIAH 52:7

By Diana Hagee

Imagine yourself walking to the cross of your Redeemer. The spirit of the living God has drawn you to this place of repentance. Everyone who has accepted Christ as Savior has been there. No faults are showing, no pain is exposed, and no rejection is revealed. Everything is in place as you answer Jesus' call.

This should be a safe and noble journey. However, something unexpected happens on your way to the cross of Jesus Christ. Masks and facades begin to fall away until the real you is exposed. On your way, Satan reminds you of your past, your mistakes, and your failures, and he tries to steer you away from your eternal destiny.

Then something remarkable happens. Jesus comes off the cross where his redemptive blood was shed for your transgressions. He takes his pure robe of righteousness and drapes it over your life, hiding all your ugliness. At that instant, you become beautiful! Not because of what you have or have not done but because of what was done *for* you.

Now you stand accepted, loved, and made whole. You begin to see yourself as Christ sees you. He sees you made in his image. He sees your full potential. He sees your God-given destiny. You have just had a complete spiritual makeover. Now you should see yourself as Jesus sees you...beautiful!

reflect: How does receiving a complete spiritual makeover change you?
Go to **Leviticus 16:20–22.**

"You were not sold for a price,
so you will be saved without cost."
⁴ This is what the Lord GOD says:
"First my people went down to Egypt to
live.
Later Assyria made them slaves.

⁵ "Now see what has happened," says the
LORD.
"Another nation has taken away my
people for nothing.
This nation who rules them makes fun of
me," says the LORD.
"All day long they speak against me.
⁶ This has happened so my people will
know who I am,
and so, on that future day, they will
know
that I am the one speaking to them.
It will really be me."

⁷ How beautiful is the person
who comes over the mountains to bring
good news,
who announces peace
and brings good news,
who announces salvation
and says to Jerusalem,
"Your God is King."
⁸ Listen! Your guards are shouting.
They are all shouting for joy!
They all will see with their own eyes
when the LORD returns to Jerusalem.
⁹ Jerusalem, your buildings are destroyed
now,
but shout and rejoice together,
because the LORD has comforted his
people.
He has saved Jerusalem.
¹⁰ The LORD will show his holy power
to all the nations.
Then everyone on earth
will see the salvation of our God.

¹¹ You people, leave, leave; get out of
Babylon!
Touch nothing that is unclean.
You men who carry the LORD's things
used in worship,
leave there and make yourselves pure.
¹² You will not be forced to leave Babylon
quickly;
you will not be forced to run away,
because the LORD will go before you,

and the God of Israel will guard you
from behind.

THE LORD'S SUFFERING SERVANT

¹³ The LORD says, "See, my servant will act
wisely.
People will greatly honor and respect
him.
¹⁴ Many people were shocked when they
saw him.
His appearance was so damaged he did
not look like a man;
his form was so changed they could
barely tell he was human.
¹⁵ But now he will surprise many nations.
Kings will be amazed and shut their
mouths.
They will see things they had not been
told about him,
and they will understand things they
had not heard."

53 Who would have believed what we
heard?
Who saw the LORD's power in this?
² He grew up like a small plant before the
LORD,
like a root growing in a dry land.
He had no special beauty or form to make
us notice him;
there was nothing in his appearance to
make us desire him.
³ He was hated and rejected by people.
He had much pain and suffering.
People would not even look at him.
He was hated, and we didn't even
notice him.

⁴ But he took our suffering on him
and felt our pain for us.
We saw his suffering
and thought God was punishing him.
⁵ But he was wounded for the wrong we
did;
he was crushed for the evil we did.
The punishment, which made us well,
was given to him,
and we are healed because of his
wounds.
⁶ We all have wandered away like sheep;
each of us has gone his own way.
But the LORD has put on him the
punishment
for all the evil we have done.

7 He was beaten down and punished,
  but he didn't say a word.
He was like a lamb being led to be killed.
  He was quiet, as a sheep is quiet while
    its wool is being cut;
  he never opened his mouth.
8 Men took him away roughly and unfairly.

He died without children to continue
  his family.
He was put to death;
  he was punished for the sins of my
    people.
9 He was buried with wicked men,
  and he died with the rich.

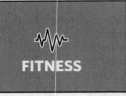

FITNESS

TURNING REVELATIONS INTO REVOLUTIONS

Jesus won back our health

ISAIAH 53:5

By Larry Huch

Come boldly and confidently to God for healing. Your healing is so important to him that he made a promise to you in the blood of his Son more than two thousand years ago. Jesus paid the price for your perfect health, and God is still delivering your healing. He is not finished yet.

God takes great pleasure in blessing you and does not send sickness into your life. It is the devil who comes to kill, steal, and destroy. All sickness, no matter where it first started—birth, inheritance, injury—is sent from the devil. There was no sickness or injury in the Garden of Eden.

When Adam sinned, the curse of sin entered. The wage of sin is death, and the spirit of infirmity is one symptom. However, everyone who is born again is freed from that curse. If there is sickness, disease, or injury, Satan is trespassing on legally paid-for property.

Jesus spoke directly to spirits of sickness and commanded them to leave people alone many times during his ministry (see Mark 9:17–27 and Luke 13:10–12). He told us we could do the same, and even greater, works (John 14:12). You have the authority to say, "By the blood of Jesus Christ, I am healed."

Jesus shed his blood at the whipping post. Every time the devil put the whip to Jesus' back, blood was shed to overcome disease until every illness brought on humanity was conquered. We no longer live under the curse of sickness and disease. The precious blood of Jesus has set us free! (From *Free at Last*)

reflect: What type of healing do you need so that you can serve others?
Go to **Isaiah 59:16–17.**

He had done nothing wrong,
and he had never lied.

10 But it was the LORD who decided
to crush him and make him suffer.
The LORD made his life a penalty
offering,
but he will still see his descendants and
live a long life.
He will complete the things the LORD
wants him to do.

11 "After his soul suffers many things,
he will see life and be satisfied.
My good servant will make many people
right with God;
he will carry away their sins.

12 For this reason I will make him a great
man among people,
and he will share in all things with
those who are strong.
He willingly gave his life
and was treated like a criminal.
But he carried away the sins of many
people
and asked forgiveness for those who
sinned."

PEOPLE WILL RETURN TO JERUSALEM

54 The LORD says, "Sing, Jerusalem.
You are like a woman who never
gave birth to children.
Start singing and shout for joy.
You never felt the pain of giving birth,
but you will have more children
than the woman who has a husband.

2 Make your tent bigger;
stretch it out and make it wider.
Do not hold back.
Make the ropes longer
and its stakes stronger,

3 because you will spread out to the right
and to the left.
Your children will take over other
nations,
and they will again live in cities that
once were destroyed.

4 "Don't be afraid, because you will not be
ashamed.
Don't be embarrassed, because you will
not be disgraced.
You will forget the shame you felt earlier;
you will not remember the shame you
felt when you lost your husband.

5 The God who made you is like your
husband.
His name is the LORD All-Powerful.
The Holy One of Israel is the one who
saves you.
He is called the God of all the earth.

6 You were like a woman whose husband
left her,
and you were very sad.
You were like a wife who married young
and then her husband left her.
But the LORD called you to be his,"
says your God.

7 God says, "I left you for a short time,
but with great kindness I will bring you
back again.

8 I became very angry
and hid from you for a time,
but I will show you mercy with kindness
forever,"
says the LORD who saves you.

9 The LORD says, "This day is like the time
of Noah to me.
I promised then that I would never
flood the world again.
In the same way, I promise I will not be
angry with you
or punish you again.

10 The mountains may disappear,
and the hills may come to an end,
but my love will never disappear;
my promise of peace will not come to
an end,"
says the LORD who shows mercy to you.

11 "You poor city. Storms have hurt you,
and you have not been comforted.
But I will rebuild you with turquoise
stones,
and I will build your foundations with
sapphires.

12 I will use rubies to build your walls
and shining jewels for the gates
and precious jewels for all your outer
walls.

13 All your children will be taught by the
LORD,
and they will have much peace.

14 I will build you using fairness.
You will be safe from those who would
hurt you,
so you will have nothing to fear.
Nothing will come to make you afraid.

15 I will not send anyone to attack you,
and you will defeat those who do attack
you.

16 "See, I made the blacksmith.
He fans the fire to make it hotter,
and he makes the kind of tool he wants.
In the same way I have made the
destroyer to destroy.

17 So no weapon that is used against you
will defeat you.
You will show that those who speak
against you are wrong.
These are the good things my servants
receive.
Their victory comes from me," says the
LORD.

GOD GIVES WHAT IS GOOD

55 The LORD says, "All you who are
thirsty,
come and drink.
Those of you who do not have money,
come, buy and eat!
Come buy wine and milk
without money and without cost.

2 Why spend your money on something
that is not real food?
Why work for something that doesn't
really satisfy you?
Listen closely to me, and you will eat what
is good;
your soul will enjoy the rich food that
satisfies.

3 Come to me and listen;
listen to me so you may live.
I will make an agreement with you that
will last forever.
I will give you the blessings I promised
to David.

4 I made David a witness of my power for
all nations,
a ruler and commander of many
nations.

5 You will call for nations that you don't yet
know.
And these nations that do not know you
will run to you
because of the LORD your God,
because of the Holy One of Israel who
honors you."

6 So you should look for the LORD before it
is too late;

you should call to him while he is near.

7 The wicked should stop doing wrong,
and they should stop their evil
thoughts.
They should return to the LORD so he may
have mercy on them.
They should come to our God, because
he will freely forgive them.

8 The LORD says, "My thoughts are not like
your thoughts.
Your ways are not like my ways.

9 Just as the heavens are higher than the
earth,
so are my ways higher than your ways
and my thoughts higher than your
thoughts.

10 Rain and snow fall from the sky
and don't return without watering the
ground.
They cause the plants to sprout and grow,
making seeds for the farmer
and bread for the people.

11 The same thing is true of the words I
speak.
They will not return to me empty.
They make the things happen that I want
to happen,
and they succeed in doing what I send
them to do.

12 "So you will go out with joy
and be led out in peace.
The mountains and hills will burst into
song before you,
and all the trees in the fields will clap
their hands.

13 Large cypress trees will grow where
thornbushes were.
Myrtle trees will grow where weeds
were.
These things will be a reminder of the
LORD's promise,
and this reminder will never be
destroyed."

ALL NATIONS WILL OBEY THE LORD

56 This is what the LORD says:
"Give justice to all people,
and do what is right,
because my salvation will come to you
soon.
Soon everyone will know that I do what
is right.

² The person who obeys the law about the Sabbath
will be blessed,
and the person who does no evil
will be blessed."

³ Foreigners who have joined the LORD
should not say,
"The LORD will not accept me with his
people."
The eunuch should not say,

"Because I cannot have children, the
LORD will not accept me."
⁴ This is what the LORD says:
"The eunuchs should obey the law about
the Sabbath
and do what I want
and keep my agreement.
⁵ If they do, I will make their names
remembered
within my Temple and its walls.
It will be better for them than children.

SERVANT EVANGELISM

God and prayer

FAITH

ISAIAH 56:7

Is your church really a "house of prayer"? This is not a trivial question. God himself gave us the picture of his Temple. Is prayer the central focus of your house of worship? Does it matter more than the sermon or the music or the offering? If everything else were pushed aside except prayer, would you still find that vital connection?

When Jesus uttered these words, he was driving out those who were desecrating his Father's house. The Temple of Jerusalem no longer stands. It has been replaced with another temple—the permanent dwelling place of the Most High. But the purpose of this new "house" is still the same. It is still a house of prayer.

The difference is that now it is found *inside* you. As it reads in 1 Corinthians 3:16, "Don't you know that you are God's temple and that God's Spirit lives in you?" If that's true, then prayer should dominate our lives. If we are God's dwelling place, then the one thing that we cannot do without should be prayer.

A deep relationship depends on full, emotional, expressive, open communication. If we are in a relationship with God, then prayer is the principal means of communication. How deep is your connection with God? Is he your best friend? Is he the one you can't wait to talk to? Feel free to share all your thoughts, hurts, joys, struggles, and tears with him.

reflect: Commune with God today, and share whatever it is you are experiencing.
Go to **Isaiah 61:8.**

I will give them a name that will last
forever,
that will never be forgotten.

6 Foreigners will join the LORD
to worship him and love him,
to serve him,
to obey the law about the Sabbath,
and to keep my agreement.

7 I will bring these people to my holy
mountain
and give them joy in my house of prayer.
The offerings and sacrifices
they place on my altar will please me,
because my Temple will be called
a house for prayer for people from all
nations."

8 The Lord GOD says—
he who gathers the Israelites that were
forced to leave their country:
"I will bring together other people
to join those who are already gathered."

ISRAEL'S LEADERS ARE EVIL

9 All you animals of the field,
all you animals of the forest, come to
eat.

10 The leaders who are to guard the people
are blind;
they don't know what they are doing.
All of them are like quiet dogs
that don't know how to bark.
They lie down and dream
and love to sleep.

11 They are like hungry dogs
that are never satisfied.
They are like shepherds
who don't know what they are doing.
They all have gone their own way;
all they want to do is satisfy themselves.

12 They say, "Come, let's drink some wine;
let's drink all the beer we want.
And tomorrow we will do this again,
or, maybe we will have an even better
time."

ISRAEL DOES NOT FOLLOW GOD

57 Those who are right with God may
die,
but no one pays attention.
Good people are taken away,
but no one understands.
Those who do right are being taken away
from evil

2 and are given peace.

Those who live as God wants
find rest in death.

3 "Come here, you magicians!
Come here, you children of prostitutes
and those who take part in adultery!

4 Of whom are you making fun?
Whom are you insulting?
At whom do you stick out your
tongue?
You turn against God,
and you are liars.

5 You have sexual relations under every
green tree
to worship your gods.
You kill children in the ravines
and sacrifice them in the rocky places.

6 You take the smooth rocks from the
ravines
as your portion.
You pour drink offerings on them to
worship them,
and you give grain offerings to them.
Do you think this makes me want to
show you mercy?

7 You make your bed on every hill and
mountain,
and there you offer sacrifices.

8 You have hidden your idols
behind your doors and doorposts.
You have left me, and you have uncovered
yourself.
You have pulled back the covers and
climbed into bed.
You have made an agreement with those
whose beds you love,
and you have looked at their
nakedness.

9 You use your oils and perfumes
to look nice for Molech.
You have sent your messengers to faraway
lands;
you even tried to send them to the place
of the dead.

10 You were tired from doing these things,
but you never gave up.
You found new strength,
so you did not quit.

11 "Whom were you so afraid of
that you lied to me?
You have not remembered me
or even thought about me.
I have been quiet for a long time.

Is that why you are not afraid of me?
¹² I will tell about your 'goodness' and what
you do,
and those things will do you no good.
¹³ When you cry out for help,
let the gods you have gathered help
you.
The wind will blow them all away;
just a puff of wind will take them away.
But the person who depends on me will
receive the land
and own my holy mountain."

THE LORD WILL SAVE HIS PEOPLE
¹⁴ Someone will say, "Build a road! Build a
road! Prepare the way!
Make the way clear for my people."
¹⁵ And this is the reason: God lives forever
and is holy.
He is high and lifted up.
He says, "I live in a high and holy place,
but I also live with people who are sad
and humble.
I give new life to those who are humble
and to those whose hearts are broken.

INSPIRE YOUR TEAM TO REALIZE THE DREAM

living in fellowship
with God

FUTURE

By Claudio Freidzon

ISAIAH 57:15

Moses knew better than to attempt to lead the Israelites without God accompanying him (Exodus 33:14-15). He asked for God to go with them and God answered. Today's Christians often face similar situations where the very real presence of God is needed. In fact, we need God constantly in all our affairs. No matter how many books we read to learn how to do something, it is the presence of God that makes a difference. God wants and expects us to seek his company on a daily basis.

Do you want him to show himself to you? Have you been searching for and desiring a very real personal relationship with God? In this passage, God tells us he requires a humble heart before he can live with us. A humble heart is not rebellious, but obeys God's instructions and submits to his guidance. It is a heart that learns from Jesus and accepts the influence of Christ into every area of life. If you have a humble heart, you will look upon others as superior to yourself and you will respect the presence of God with others.

Close companionship with God heals and delivers you absolutely. His fellowship strengthens your faith and keeps you in the will of God. God gives you the strength to face stressful situations and not to be fearful so that you will not need to surrender to circumstances. The presence of God will be with you through everything. His mercies will go with you. Simply be like Moses, and ask.

reflect: Do you remember to ask God for help in making decisions?
Go to **Isaiah 30:21.**

16 I will not accuse forever,
  nor will I always be angry,
because then human life would grow
    weak.
  Human beings, whom I created, would
    die.
17 I was angry because they were dishonest
    in order to make money.
  I punished them and turned away from
    them in anger,
  but they continued to do evil.
18 I have seen what they have done, but I
    will heal them.
  I will guide them and comfort them and
    those who felt sad for them.
  They will all praise me.
19 I will give peace, real peace, to those far
    and near,
  and I will heal them," says the LORD.
20 But evil people are like the angry sea,
    which cannot rest,
  whose waves toss up waste and mud.
21 "There is no peace for evil people," says
    my God.

HOW TO HONOR GOD

58 The LORD says, "Shout out loud.
    Don't hold back.
  Shout out loud like a trumpet.
Tell my people what they have done
    against their God;
  tell the family of Jacob about their sins.
2 They still come every day looking for me
    and want to learn my ways.
  They act just like a nation that does what
    is right,
    that obeys the commands of its God.
  They ask me to judge them fairly.
  They want God to be near them.
3 They say, 'To honor you we had special
    days when we fasted,
  but you didn't see.
  We humbled ourselves to honor you,
    but you didn't notice.'"

But the LORD says, "You do what pleases
    yourselves on these special days,
  and you are unfair to your workers.
4 On these special days when you fast, you
    argue and fight
  and hit each other with your fists.
  You cannot do these things as you do now
  and believe your prayers are heard in
    heaven.

5 This kind of special day is not what I
    want.
  This is not the way I want people to be
    sorry for what they have done.
I don't want people just to bow their
    heads like a plant
  and wear rough cloth and lie in ashes to
    show their sadness.
This is what you do on your special days
    when you fast,
  but do you think this is what the LORD
    wants?

6 "I will tell you the kind of fast I want:
Free the people you have put in prison
    unfairly
  and undo their chains.
Free those to whom you are unfair
  and stop their hard labor.
7 Share your food with the hungry
  and bring poor, homeless people into
    your own homes.
When you see someone who has no
    clothes, give him yours,
  and don't refuse to help your own
    relatives.
8 Then your light will shine like the dawn,
  and your wounds will quickly heal.
Your God will walk before you,
  and the glory of the LORD will protect
    you from behind.
9 Then you will call out, and the LORD will
    answer.
  You will cry out, and he will say, 'Here
    I am.'

"If you stop making trouble for others,
  if you stop using cruel words and
    pointing your finger at others,
10 if you feed those who are hungry
  and take care of the needs of those who
    are troubled,
then your light will shine in the darkness,
  and you will be bright like sunshine at
    noon.
11 The LORD will always lead you.
  He will satisfy your needs in dry lands
  and give strength to your bones.
You will be like a garden that has much
    water,
  like a spring that never runs dry.
12 Your people will rebuild the old cities that
    are now in ruins;
  you will rebuild their foundations.

You will be known for repairing the
broken places
and for rebuilding the roads and houses.

13 "You must obey God's law about the
Sabbath
and not do what pleases yourselves on
that holy day.
You should call the Sabbath a joyful day
and honor it as the LORD's holy day.
You should honor it by not doing
whatever you please
nor saying whatever you please on that
day.
14 Then you will find joy in the LORD,
and I will carry you to the high places
above the earth.
I will let you eat the crops of the land
your ancestor Jacob had."
The LORD has said these things.

THE EVIL THAT PEOPLE DO

59 Surely the LORD's power is enough to
save you.
He can hear you when you ask him for
help.
2 It is your evil that has separated
you from your God.
Your sins cause him to turn away from
you,
so he does not hear you.
3 With your hands you have killed others,
and with your fingers you have done
wrong.
With your lips you have lied,
and with your tongue you say evil
things.
4 People take each other to court unfairly,
and no one tells the truth in arguing his
case.
They accuse each other falsely and tell
lies.
They cause trouble and create more
evil.
5 They hatch evil like eggs from poisonous
snakes.
If you eat one of those eggs, you will
die,
and if you break one open, a poisonous
snake comes out.
People tell lies as they would spin a
spider's web.
6 The webs they make cannot be used for
clothes;

you can't cover yourself with those
webs.
The things they do are evil,
and they use their hands to hurt others.
7 They eagerly run to do evil,
and they are always ready to kill
innocent people.
They think evil thoughts.
Everywhere they go they cause ruin
and destruction.
8 They don't know how to live in peace,
and there is no fairness in their lives.
They are dishonest.
Anyone who lives as they live will never
have peace.

ISRAEL'S SIN BRINGS TROUBLE

9 Fairness has gone far away;
goodness is nowhere to be found.
We wait for the light, but there is only
darkness now.
We hope for a bright light, but all we
have is darkness.
10 We are like the blind feeling our way
along a wall.
We feel our way as if we had no eyes.
In the brightness of day we trip as if it
were night.
We are like dead men among the strong.
11 All of us growl like the bears.
We call out sadly like the doves.
We look for justice, but there isn't any.
We want to be saved, but salvation is far
away.
12 We have done many wrong things against
our God;
our sins show we are wrong.
We know we have turned against God;
we know the evil things we have done:
13 sinning and rejecting the LORD,
turning away from our God,
planning to hurt others and to disobey
God,
planning and speaking lies.
14 So we have driven away justice,
and we have kept away from what is
right.
Truth is not spoken in the streets;
what is honest is not allowed to enter
the city.
15 Truth cannot be found anywhere,
and people who refuse to do evil are
attacked.

The LORD looked and could not find any justice,
and he was displeased.
16 He could not find anyone to help the people,
and he was surprised that there was no one to help.
So he used his own power to save the people;
his own goodness gave him strength.
17 He covered himself with goodness like armor.
He put the helmet of salvation on his head.
He put on his clothes for punishing
and wrapped himself in the coat of his strong love.

18 The LORD will pay back his enemies for what they have done.
He will show his anger to those who were against him;
he will punish the people in faraway places as they deserve.
19 Then people from the west will fear the LORD,
and people from the east will fear his glory.
The LORD will come quickly like a fast-flowing river,
driven by the breath of the LORD.

20 "Then a Savior will come to Jerusalem
and to the people of Jacob who have turned from sin,"
says the LORD.

TURNING REVELATIONS INTO REVOLUTIONS

FITNESS

integrated health

ISAIAH 59:16–17

You've heard it before, "I can't believe he died prematurely. I thought he took such good care of himself." Why does premature death usually happen? Often, it's a hole or several holes in the "health armor."

Maybe people worked out hard, but did not take in the right nutrients. Or vice versa, maybe they did manage to eat well, but exercised inconsistently. Perhaps they were physically fit, but did not have their spiritual lives in order and, therefore, suffered from overpowering levels of stress. Spinal health, mental health, toxicity, medications, poor relationships, and the like, if not under control, can all lead to holes in the armor of one's health.

True prosperity is success in all areas of your life, and not just one or two. To be a healthy, happy person, you have to consider ALL of you—and all of the things that will make you that way. To be the person God created you to be, and to live long enough and well enough to accomplish all of the wonderful tasks you were born to achieve, you must realize that you are a body, a mind, and a spirit. You must care for them all.

reflect: Remember to take good care of your entire being: spirit, soul, and body.
Go to **Daniel 1:8–16.**

²¹The LORD says, "This is my agreement with these people: My Spirit and my words that I give you will never leave you or your children or your grandchildren, now and forever."

JERUSALEM WILL BE GREAT

60 "Jerusalem, get up and shine, because your light has come, and the glory of the LORD shines on you.
² Darkness now covers the earth;
deep darkness covers her people.
But the LORD shines on you,
and people see his glory around you.
³ Nations will come to your light;
kings will come to the brightness of
your sunrise.

⁴ "Look around you.
People are gathering and coming to you.
Your sons are coming from far away,
and your daughters are coming with
them.
⁵ When you see them, you will shine with
happiness;
you will be excited and full of joy,
because the wealth of the nations across
the seas will be given to you;
the riches of the nations will come to
you.
⁶ Herds of camels will cover your land,
young camels from Midian and Ephah.
People will come from Sheba
bringing gold and incense,
and they will sing praises to the LORD.
⁷ All the sheep from Kedar will be given to
you;
the sheep from Nebaioth will be
brought to you.
They will be pleasing sacrifices on my
altar,
and I will make my beautiful Temple
more beautiful.

⁸ "The people are returning to you like
clouds,
like doves flying to their nests.
⁹ People in faraway lands are waiting for
me.
The great trading ships will come
first,
bringing your children from faraway
lands,
and with them silver and gold.

This will honor the LORD your God,
the Holy One of Israel,
who does wonderful things for you.

¹⁰ "Jerusalem, foreigners will rebuild your
walls,
and their kings will serve you.
When I was angry, I hurt you,
but now I want to be kind to you and
comfort you.
¹¹ Your gates will always be open;
they will not be closed day or night
so the nations can bring their wealth to
you,
and their kings will be led to you.
¹² The nation or kingdom that doesn't serve
you will be destroyed;
it will be completely ruined.

¹³ "The great trees of Lebanon will be given
to you:
its pine, fir, and cypress trees together.
You will use them to make my Temple
beautiful,
and I will give much honor to this place
where I rest my feet.
¹⁴ The people who have hurt you will bow
down to you;
those who hated you will bow down at
your feet.
They will call you The City of the LORD,
Jerusalem, city of the Holy One of
Israel.

¹⁵ "You have been hated and left empty
with no one passing through.
But I will make you great from now on;
you will be a place of happiness forever
and ever.
¹⁶ You will be given what you need from the
nations,
like a child drinking milk from its
mother.
Then you will know that it is I, the LORD,
who saves you.
You will know that the Powerful One of
Jacob protects you.
¹⁷ I will bring you gold in place of bronze,
silver in place of iron,
bronze in place of wood,
iron in place of rocks.
I will change your punishment into
peace,
and you will be ruled by what is right.

18 There will be no more violence in your
country;
it will not be ruined or destroyed.
You will name your walls Salvation
and your gates Praise.
19 The sun will no longer be your light
during the day
nor will the brightness from the moon
be your light,
because the LORD will be your light
forever,
and your God will be your glory.
20 Your sun will never set again,
and your moon will never be dark,
because the LORD will be your light
forever,
and your time of sadness will end.
21 All of your people will do what is right.
They will receive the earth forever.
They are the plant I have planted,
the work of my own hands
to show my greatness.
22 The smallest family will grow to a
thousand.
The least important of you will become
a powerful nation.
I am the LORD,
and when it is time, I will make these
things happen quickly."

THE LORD'S MESSAGE OF FREEDOM

61 The Lord GOD has put his Spirit in
me,
because the LORD has appointed me
to tell the good news to the poor.
He has sent me to comfort those whose
hearts are broken,
to tell the captives they are free,
and to tell the prisoners they are
released.
2 He has sent me to announce the time
when the LORD will show his
kindness
and the time when our God will punish
evil people.
He has sent me to comfort all those who
are sad
3 and to help the sorrowing people of
Jerusalem.
I will give them a crown to replace their
ashes,
and the oil of gladness to replace their
sorrow,

and clothes of praise to replace their
spirit of sadness.
Then they will be called Trees of
Goodness,
trees planted by the LORD to show his
greatness.

4 They will rebuild the old ruins
and restore the places destroyed long
ago.
They will repair the ruined cities
that were destroyed for so long.
5 My people, foreigners will come to tend
your sheep.
People from other countries will tend
your fields and vineyards.
6 You will be called priests of the LORD;
you will be named the servants of our
God.
You will have riches from all the nations
on earth,
and you will take pride in them.
7 Instead of being ashamed, my people will
receive twice as much wealth.
Instead of being disgraced, they will be
happy because of what they receive.
They will receive a double share of the
land,
so their happiness will continue
forever.
8 "I, the LORD, love justice.
I hate stealing and everything that is
wrong.
I will be fair and give my people what
they should have,
and I will make an agreement with
them that will continue forever.
9 Everyone in all nations will know the
children of my people,
and their children will be known among
the nations.
Anyone who sees them will know
that they are people the LORD has
blessed."

10 The LORD makes me very happy;
all that I am rejoices in my God.
He has covered me with clothes of
salvation
and wrapped me with a coat of
goodness,
like a bridegroom dressed for his
wedding,

like a bride dressed in jewels.
¹¹ The earth causes plants to grow,
    and a garden causes the seeds planted
        in it to grow.
In the same way the Lord GOD will make
    goodness and praise
    come from all the nations.

NEW JERUSALEM

62 Because I love Jerusalem, I will
        continue to speak for her;
for Jerusalem's sake I will not stop
    speaking
until her goodness shines like a bright
    light,

until her salvation burns bright like a
    flame.
² Jerusalem, the nations will see your
        goodness,
    and all kings will see your glory.
Then you will have a new name,
    which the LORD himself will give you.
³ You will be like a beautiful crown in the
        LORD's hand,
    like a king's crown in your God's hand.
⁴ You will never again be called the People
        that God Left,
    nor your land the Land that God
        Destroyed.
You will be called the People God Loves,

---

chief of the tribe

FAITH

ISAIAH 61:8

In our Western world, we think of the law as a system of rules that stands above any individual. That's why we say, "No man is above the law." But the people of Israel had a different view of the law. All of their law was contained within the leader of the tribe. They were a people governed by a person, not by a book of rules. The chief of the tribe ruled everything about them. Justice was whatever he decided.

For Israel, God was the personal representation of all the government. He was the source and the administration of law. God controlled life, administered life, and made the decisions regarding life. God's government was nothing more than his decision making. And Christ assumed the role of the Chief of the tribe—the tribe of God's elected and the people under his leadership.

If you belong to his tribe, God's personal decisions become your government. He invites you to be a member of his tribe, to relax, surrender, and confidently live your life under his decisions. When you choose to accept his invitation, he promises to guide you in every aspect of your life. His government covers everything about you. That's why you could summarize the whole idea in a single word: "trust." "In God we trust." Not political leaders and presidents, but the real ruler of the tribe.

reflect: Allow God to rule and reign over every aspect of your life today.
Go to **Jeremiah 17:9.**

and your land will be called the Bride
    of God,
because the LORD loves you.
    And your land will belong to him as a
        bride belongs to her husband.
5 As a young man marries a woman,
    so your children will marry your land.
As a man rejoices over his new wife,
    so your God will rejoice over you.

6 Jerusalem, I have put guards on the walls
    to watch.
    They must not be silent day or night.
You people who remind the LORD of your
    needs in prayer
    should never be quiet.
7 You should not stop praying to him until
    he builds up Jerusalem
and makes it a city all people will praise.

8 The LORD has made a promise,
    and by his power he will keep his
        promise.
He said, "I will never again give your grain
    as food to your enemies.
I will not let your enemies drink the new
    wine
    that you have worked to make.
9 Those who gather food will eat it,
    and they will praise the LORD.
Those who gather the grapes will drink
    the wine
    in the courts of my Temple."

10 Go through, go through the gates!
    Make the way ready for the people.
Build up, build up the road!
    Move all the stones off the road.
    Raise the banner as a sign for the people.

11 The LORD is speaking
    to all the faraway lands:
"Tell the people of Jerusalem,
    'Look, your Savior is coming.
He is bringing your reward to you;
    he is bringing his payment with him.'"
12 His people will be called the Holy
    People,
    the Saved People of the LORD,
and Jerusalem will be called the City God
    Wants,
    the City God Has Not Rejected.

THE LORD JUDGES HIS PEOPLE

63 Who is this coming from Edom,
    from the city of Bozrah, dressed in
    red?
Who is this dressed in fine clothes
    and marching forward with his great
        power?

He says, "I, the LORD, speak what is right.
    I have the power to save you."

2 Someone asks, "Why are your clothes
    bright red
    as if you had walked on the grapes to
        make wine?"

3 The LORD answers, "I have walked in the
    winepress alone,
    and no one among the nations helped
        me.
I was angry and walked on the nations
    and crushed them because of my anger.
Blood splashed on my clothes,
    and I stained all my clothing.
4 I chose a time to punish people,
    and the time has come for me to save.
5 I looked around, but I saw no one to help
    me.
    I was surprised that no one supported
        me.
So I used my own power to save my
    people;
    my own anger supported me.
6 While I was angry, I walked on the
    nations.
    In my anger I punished them
    and poured their blood on the ground."

THE LORD'S KINDNESS TO HIS PEOPLE

7 I will tell about the LORD's kindness
    and praise him for everything he has
        done.
I will praise the LORD for the many good
    things he has given us
    and for his goodness to the people of
        Israel.
He has shown great mercy to us
    and has been very kind to us.
8 He said, "These are my people;
    my children will not lie to me."
So he saved them.
9 When they suffered, he suffered also.
    He sent his own angel to save them.
Because of his love and kindness, he saved
    them.

Since long ago he has picked them up
and carried them.
¹⁰ But they turned against him
and made his Holy Spirit very sad.
So he became their enemy,
and he fought against them.

¹¹ But then his people remembered what
happened long ago,
in the days of Moses and the Israelites
with him.
Where is the LORD who brought the
people through the sea,
with the leaders of his people?
Where is the one
who put his Holy Spirit among them,
¹² who led Moses by the right hand
with his wonderful power,
who divided the water before them
to make his name famous forever,
¹³ who led the people through the deep
waters?
Like a horse walking through a desert,
the people did not stumble.
¹⁴ Like cattle that go down to the valley,
the Spirit of the LORD gave the people a
place to rest.
LORD, that is the way you led your
people,
and by this you won for yourself
wonderful fame.

A PRAYER FOR HELP

¹⁵ LORD, look down from the heavens and
see;
look at us from your wonderful and
holy home in heaven.
Where is your strong love and power?
Why are you keeping your love and
mercy from us?
¹⁶ You are our father.
Abraham doesn't know we are his
children,
and Israel doesn't recognize us.
LORD, you are our father.
You are called "the one who has always
saved us."
¹⁷ LORD, why are you making us wander
from your ways?
Why do you make us stubborn so that
we don't honor you?
For our sake come back to us,
your servants, who belong to you.
¹⁸ Your people had your Temple for a while,

but now our enemies have walked on
your holy place and crushed it.
¹⁹ We have become like people you never
ruled over,
like those who have never worn your
name.

64 Tear open the skies and come down
to earth
so that the mountains will tremble
before you.
² Like a fire that burns twigs,
like a fire that makes water boil,
let your enemies know who you are.
Then all nations will shake with fear
when they see you.
³ You have done amazing things we did not
expect.
You came down, and the mountains
trembled before you.
⁴ From long ago no one has ever heard of a
God like you.
No one has ever seen a God besides you,
who helps the people who trust you.
⁵ You help those who enjoy doing good,
who remember how you want them to
live.
But you were angry because we sinned.
For a long time we disobeyed,
so how can we be saved?
⁶ All of us are dirty with sin.
All the right things we have done are
like filthy pieces of cloth.
All of us are like dead leaves,
and our sins, like the wind, have carried
us away.
⁷ No one worships you
or even asks you to help us.
That is because you have turned away
from us
and have let our sins destroy us.
⁸ But LORD, you are our father.
We are like clay, and you are the potter;
your hands made us all.
⁹ LORD, don't continue to be angry with us;
don't remember our sins forever.
Please, look at us,
because we are your people.
¹⁰ Your holy cities are empty like the desert.
Jerusalem is like a desert;
it is destroyed.
¹¹ Our ancestors worshiped you
in our holy and wonderful Temple,

but now it has been burned with fire,
and all our precious things have been
destroyed.
¹² When you see these things, will you hold
yourself back from helping us, LORD?
Will you be silent and punish us beyond
what we can stand?

ALL PEOPLE WILL LEARN ABOUT GOD

65 The LORD says, "I made myself
known to people who were not
looking for me.
I was found by those who were not
asking me for help.
I said, 'Here I am. Here I am,'
to a nation that was not praying to me.
² All day long I stood ready to accept
people who turned against me,
but the way they continue to live is not
good;
they do anything they want to do.
³ Right in front of me
they continue to do things that make
me angry.
They offer sacrifices to their gods in
their gardens,
and they burn incense on altars of brick.
⁴ They sit among the graves
and spend their nights waiting to get
messages from the dead.
They eat the meat of pigs,
and their pots are full of soup made
from meat that is wrong to eat.
⁵ But they tell others, 'Stay away, and don't
come near me.
I am too holy for you.'
These people are like smoke in my nose.
Like a fire that burns all the time, they
continue to make me angry.

⁶ "Look, it is written here before me.
I will not be quiet; instead, I will repay
you in full.
I will punish you for what you have
done.
⁷ I will punish you for your sins and your
ancestors' sins,"
says the LORD.
"They burned incense to gods on the
mountains
and shamed me on those hills.
So I will punish them as they should be
punished
for what they did."

⁸ This is what the LORD says:
"When there is juice left in the grapes,
people do not destroy them,
because they know there is good left in
them.
So I will do the same thing to my
servants—
I will not completely destroy them.
⁹ I will leave some of the children of Jacob,
and some of the people of Judah will
receive my mountain.
I will choose the people who will live
there;
my servants will live there.
¹⁰ Then the Plain of Sharon will be a field
for flocks,
and the Valley of Achor will be a place
for herds to rest.
They will be for the people who want to
follow me.

¹¹ "But as for you who left the LORD,
who forgot about my holy mountain,
who worship the god Luck,
who hold religious feasts for the god
Fate,
¹² I decide your fate, and I will punish you
with my sword.
You will all be killed,
because I called you, but you refused to
answer.
I spoke to you, but you wouldn't listen.
You did the things I said were evil
and chose to do things that displease
me."

¹³ So this is what the Lord GOD says:
"My servants will eat,
but you evil people will be hungry.
My servants will drink,
but you evil people will be thirsty.
My servants will be happy,
but you evil people will be shamed.
¹⁴ My servants will shout for joy
because of the goodness of their hearts,
but you evil people will cry,
because you will be sad.
You will cry loudly, because your spirits
will be broken.
¹⁵ Your names will be like curses to my
servants,
and the Lord GOD will put you to death.
But he will call his servants by another
name.

16 People in the land who ask for blessings
will ask for them from the faithful God.
And people in the land who make a
promise
will promise in the name of the faithful
God,
because the troubles of the past will be
forgotten.
I will make those troubles go away.

A NEW TIME IS COMING

17 "Look, I will make new heavens and a
new earth,
and people will not remember the past
or think about those things.
18 My people will be happy forever
because of the things I will make.
I will make a Jerusalem that is full of
joy,
and I will make her people a delight.
19 Then I will rejoice over Jerusalem
and be delighted with my people.
There will never again be heard in that
city
the sounds of crying and sadness.
20 There will never be a baby from that city
who lives only a few days.
And there will never be an older person
who doesn't have a long life.
A person who lives a hundred years will
be called young,
and a person who dies before he is
a hundred will be thought of as a
sinner.
21 In that city those who build houses will
live there.
Those who plant vineyards will get to
eat their grapes.
22 No more will one person build a house
and someone else live there.
One person will not plant a garden and
someone else eat its fruit.
My people will live a long time,
as trees live long.
My chosen people will live there
and enjoy the things they make.
23 They will never again work for nothing.
They will never again give birth to
children who die young.
All my people will be blessed by the LORD;
they and their children will be blessed.
24 I will provide for their needs before they
ask,

and I will help them while they are still
asking for help.
25 Wolves and lambs will eat together in
peace.
Lions will eat hay like oxen,
and a snake on the ground will not hurt
anyone.
They will not hurt or destroy each other
on all my holy mountain,"
says the LORD.

THE LORD WILL JUDGE ALL NATIONS

66 This is what the LORD says:
"Heaven is my throne,
and the earth is my footstool.
So do you think you can build a house for
me?
Do I need a place to rest?
2 My hand made all things.
All things are here because I made
them,"
says the LORD.

"These are the people I am pleased with:
those who are not proud or stubborn
and who fear my word.
3 But those people who kill bulls as a
sacrifice to me
are like those who kill people.
Those who kill sheep as a sacrifice
are like those who break the necks of
dogs.
Those who give me grain offerings
are like those who offer me the blood
of pigs.[n]
Those who burn incense
are like those who worship idols.
These people choose their own ways, not
mine,
and they love the terrible things they
do.
4 So I will choose their punishments,
and I will punish them with what they
fear most.
This is because I called to them, but they
did not listen.
I spoke to them, but they did not hear
me.
They did things I said were evil;
they chose to do things I did not like."

66:3 dogs . . . pigs God did not want his people to offer
dogs and pigs as sacrifices because they were unclean
animals.

5 You people who obey the words of the
LORD,
    listen to what he says:
"Your brothers hated you
    and turned against you because you
    followed me.
Your brothers said, 'Let the LORD be
    honored
    so we may see you rejoice,'
    but they will be punished.
6 Listen to the loud noise coming from the
    city;
    hear the noise from the Temple.
It is the LORD punishing his enemies,
    giving them the punishment they
    should have.

7 "A woman does not give birth before she
    feels the pain;
    she does not give birth to a son before
    the pain starts.
8 No one has ever heard of that happening;
    no one has ever seen that happen.
In the same way no one ever saw a
    country begin in one day;
    no one has ever heard of a new nation
    beginning in one moment.
But Jerusalem will give birth to her
    children
    just as soon as she feels the birth pains.
9 In the same way I will not cause pain
    without allowing something new to be
    born," says the LORD.
"If I cause you the pain,
    I will not stop you from giving birth to
    your new nation," says your God.
10 "Jerusalem, rejoice.
    All you people who love Jerusalem, be
    happy.
Those of you who felt sad for Jerusalem
    should now feel happy with her.
11 You will take comfort from her and be
    satisfied,
    as a child is nursed by its mother.
You will receive her good things
    and enjoy her wealth."
12 This is what the LORD says:
"I will give her peace that will flow to her
    like a river.
The wealth of the nations will come to
    her like a river overflowing its banks.
Like babies you will be nursed and held in
    my arms

and bounced on my knees.
13 I will comfort you
    as a mother comforts her child.
    You will be comforted in Jerusalem."

14 When you see these things, you will be
    happy,
    and you will grow like the grass.
The LORD's servants will see his power,
    but his enemies will see his anger.
15 Look, the LORD is coming with fire
    and his armies with clouds of dust.
He will punish those people with his
    anger;
    he will punish them with flames of
    fire.
16 The LORD will judge the people with
    fire,
    and he will destroy many people with
    his sword;
    he will kill many people.

17 "These people make themselves holy
and pure to go to worship their gods in their
gardens. Following each other into their special gardens, they eat the meat of pigs and
rats and other hateful things. But they will all
be destroyed together," says the LORD.

18 "I know they have evil thoughts and do
evil things, so I am coming to punish them.
I will gather all nations and all people, and
they will come together and see my glory.

19 "I will put a mark on some of the people, and I will send some of these saved people to the nations: to Tarshish, Libya, Lud
(the land of archers), Tubal, Greece, and all
the faraway lands. These people have never
heard about what I have done nor seen my
glory. So the saved people will tell the nations about my glory. 20 And they will bring
all your fellow Israelites from all nations to
my holy mountain in Jerusalem. Your fellow Israelites will come on horses, donkeys,
and camels and in chariots and wagons.
They will be like the grain offerings that
the people bring in clean containers to the
Temple," says the LORD. 21 "And I will choose
even some of these people to be priests and
Levites," says the LORD.

22 "I will make new heavens and the new
earth, which will last forever," says the LORD.
"In the same way, your names and your children will always be with me. 23 All people will
come to worship me every Sabbath and every

New Moon," says the LORD. 24"They will go out and see the dead bodies of the people who sinned against me. The worms that eat them will never die, and the fires that burn them will never stop, and everyone will hate to see those bodies."

jeremiah

A WARNING ABOUT CAPTIVITY

1 These are the words of Jeremiah son of Hilkiah. He belonged to the family of priests who lived in the town of Anathoth in the land of Benjamin. ²The LORD spoke his word to Jeremiah during the thirteenth year that Josiah son of Amon was king of Judah. ³The LORD also spoke to Jeremiah while Jehoiakim son of Josiah was king of Judah and during the eleven years that Zedekiah son of Josiah was king of Judah. In the fifth month of his last year, the people of Jerusalem were taken away as captives.

THE LORD CALLS JEREMIAH

⁴The LORD spoke his word to me, saying:
⁵ "Before I made you in your mother's
womb, I chose you.
Before you were born, I set you apart
for a special work.
I appointed you as a prophet to the
nations."

⁶Then I said, "But Lord GOD, I don't know how to speak. I am only a boy."

⁷But the LORD said to me, "Don't say, 'I am only a boy.' You must go everywhere I send you, and you must say everything I tell you to say. ⁸Don't be afraid of anyone, because I am with you to protect you," says the LORD.

⁹Then the LORD reached out his hand and touched my mouth. He said to me, "See, I am putting my words in your mouth. ¹⁰Today I have put you in charge of nations and kingdoms. You will pull up and tear down, destroy and overthrow, build up and plant."

JEREMIAH SEES TWO VISIONS

¹¹The LORD spoke his word to me, saying: "Jeremiah, what do you see?"

I answered, "I see a stick of almond wood."

¹²The LORD said to me, "You have seen correctly, because I am watching to make sure my words come true."

¹³The LORD spoke his word to me again: "What do you see?"

I answered, "I see a pot of boiling water, tipping over from the north."

¹⁴The LORD said to me, "Disaster will come from the north and strike all the people who live in this country. ¹⁵In a short time I will call all of the people in the northern kingdoms," said the LORD.

"Those kings will come and set up their
thrones
near the entrance of the gates of
Jerusalem.
They will attack all the city walls around
Jerusalem
and all the cities in Judah.
¹⁶ And I will announce my judgments
against my people
because of their evil in turning away
from me.
They offered sacrifices to other gods
and worshiped idols they had made
with their own hands.

¹⁷"Jeremiah, get ready. Stand up and tell them everything I command you to say. Don't be afraid of the people, or I will give you good reason to be afraid of them. ¹⁸Today I am going to make you a strong city, an iron pillar, a bronze wall. You will be able to stand against everyone in the land: Judah's kings, officers, priests, and the people of the land. ¹⁹They will fight against you, but they will not defeat you, because I am with you to protect you!" says the LORD.

ISRAEL TURNS FROM GOD

2 The LORD spoke his word to me, saying: ²"Go and speak to the people of Jerusalem, saying: This is what the LORD says:

'I remember how faithful you were to me
when you were a young nation.
You loved me like a young bride.
You followed me through the desert,
a land that had never been planted.
³ The people of Israel were holy to the
LORD,
like the firstfruits from his harvest.
Those who tried to hurt Israel were
judged guilty.
Disasters struck them,'" says the LORD.

⁴ Hear the word of the LORD, family of
Jacob,
  all you family groups of Israel.
⁵This is what the LORD says:
"I was fair to your ancestors,
  so why did they turn away from me?
Your ancestors worshiped useless idols
  and became useless themselves.
⁶ Your ancestors didn't say,
  'Where is the LORD who brought us out
    of Egypt?
He led us through the desert,
  through a dry and rocky land,
through a dark and dangerous land.
He led us where no one travels or
  lives.'
⁷ I brought you into a fertile land
  so you could eat its fruit and produce.
But you came and made my land unclean;
  you made it a hateful place.
⁸ The priests didn't ask,
  'Where is the LORD?'
The people who know the teachings
  didn't know me.
The leaders turned against me.
The prophets prophesied in the name of
  Baal
  and worshiped useless idols.

⁹ "So now I will again tell what I have
  against you," says the LORD.
  "And I will tell what I have against your
    grandchildren.
¹⁰ Go across the sea to the island of Cyprus
  and see.
  Send someone to the land of Kedar to
    look closely.
  See if there has ever been anything like
    this.
¹¹ Has a nation ever exchanged its gods?
  (Of course, its gods are not really gods
    at all.)
But my people have exchanged their
  glorious God
  for idols worth nothing.
¹² Skies, be shocked at the things that have
  happened
  and shake with great fear!" says the
    LORD.
¹³ "My people have done two evils:
They have turned away from me,
  the spring of living water.
And they have dug their own wells,

which are broken wells that cannot
  hold water.
¹⁴ Have the people of Israel become slaves?
  Have they become like someone who
    was born a slave?
  Why were they taken captive?
¹⁵ Enemies have roared like lions at Israel;
  they have growled at Israel.
They have destroyed the land of Israel.
  The cities of Israel lie in ruins,
  and all the people have left.
¹⁶ The men from the cities of Memphis and
  Tahpanhes
  have disgraced you by shaving the top
    of your head.
¹⁷ Haven't you brought this on yourselves
  by turning away from the LORD your
    God
  when he was leading you in the right
    way?
¹⁸ It did not help to go to Egypt
  and drink from the Shihor River.
  It did not help to go to Assyria
  and drink from the Euphrates River.
¹⁹ Your evil will bring punishment to you,
  and the wrong you have done will teach
    you a lesson.
Think about it and understand
  that it is a terrible evil to turn away from
    the LORD your God.
  It is wrong not to fear me,"
  says the Lord GOD All-Powerful.

²⁰ "Long ago you refused to obey me as an ox
    breaks its yoke.
  You broke the ropes I used to hold you
  and said, 'I will not serve you!'
In fact, on every high hill
  and under every green tree
  you lay down as a prostitute.
²¹ But I planted you as a special vine,
  as a very good seed.
How then did you turn
  into a wild vine that grows bad fruit?
²² Although you wash yourself with cleanser
  and use much soap,
  I can still see the stain of your guilt,"
  says the Lord GOD.
²³ "How can you say to me, 'I am not guilty.
  I have not worshiped the Baal idols'?
Look at the things you did in the valley.
  Think about what you have done.
You are like a she-camel in mating season

that runs from place to place.
²⁴ You are like a wild donkey that lives in the
desert
and sniffs the wind at mating time.
At that time who can hold her back?
Any male who chases her will easily catch
her;
at mating time, it is easy to find her.
²⁵ Don't run until your feet are bare
or until your throat is dry.
But you say, 'It's no use!
I love those other gods,
and I must chase them!'

²⁶ "A thief is ashamed when someone
catches him stealing.
In the same way, the family of Israel is
ashamed—
they, their kings, their officers,
their priests, and their prophets.
²⁷ They say to things of wood, 'You are my
father,'
and to idols of stone, 'You gave birth to
me.'
Those people won't look at me;
they have turned their backs to me.
But when they get into trouble, they
say,
'Come and save us!'
²⁸ Where are the idols you made for
yourselves?
Let them come and save you
when you are in trouble!
People of Judah, you have as many idols
as you have towns!

²⁹ "Why do you complain to me?
All of you have turned against me," says
the LORD.
³⁰ "I punished your people, but it did not
help.
They didn't come back when they were
punished.
With your swords you killed your
prophets
like a hungry lion.
³¹"People of Judah, pay attention to the
word of the LORD:
Have I been like a desert to the people of
Israel
or like a dark and dangerous land?
Why do my people say, 'We are free to
wander.
We won't come to you anymore'?

³² A young woman does not forget her
jewelry,
and a bride does not forget the
decorations for her dress.
But my people have forgotten me
for more days than can be counted.
³³ You really know how to chase after love.
Even the worst women can learn evil
ways from you.
³⁴ Even on your clothes you have the blood
of poor and innocent people,
but they weren't thieves you caught
breaking in.
You do all these things,
³⁵ but you say, 'I am innocent.
God is not angry with me.'
But I will judge you guilty of lying,
because you say, 'I have not sinned.'
³⁶ It is so easy for you to change your
mind.
Even Egypt will let you down,
as Assyria let you down.
³⁷ You will eventually leave that place
with your hands on your head, like
captives.
You trusted those countries,
but you will not be helped by them,
because the LORD has rejected them.

JUDAH IS UNFAITHFUL

3 "If a man divorces his wife
and she leaves him and marries
another man,
should her first husband come back to her
again?
If he went back to her, wouldn't the
land become completely unclean?
But you have acted like a prostitute with
many lovers,
and now you want to come back to me?"
says the LORD.
² "Look up to the bare hilltops, Judah.
Is there any place where you have not
been a prostitute?
You have sat by the road waiting for
lovers,
like an Arab in the desert.
You made the land unclean,
because you did evil and were like a
prostitute.
³ So the rain has not come,
and there have not been any spring
rains.

But your face still looks like the face of a
   prostitute.
You refuse even to be ashamed of what
   you did.
⁴ Now you are calling to me,
   'My father, you have been my friend
     since I was young.
⁵ Will you always be angry at me?
   Will your anger last forever?'
Judah, you said this,
   but you did as much evil as you could!"

JUDAH AND ISRAEL ARE LIKE SISTERS

⁶When King Josiah was ruling Judah, the LORD said to me, "Did you see what unfaithful Israel did? She was like a prostitute with her idols on every hill and under every green tree. ⁷I said to myself, 'Israel will come back to me after she does this evil,' but she didn't come back. And Israel's wicked sister Judah saw what she did. ⁸Judah saw that I divorced unfaithful Israel because of her adultery, but that didn't make Israel's wicked sister Judah afraid. She also went out and acted like

UNDERSTANDING AUTHORITY

family forgiveness

FAMILY

JEREMIAH 3:19

Possibly the best description of our Heavenly Father's willingness to forgive is that he offers "a gift that we don't deserve." Jesus' parable of the prodigal son only reflects something that God the Father spoke to his prophet Jeremiah centuries before. God has always been the patient Father, waiting for the return of his disobedient children. In this passage in Jeremiah, God proclaims that he will gladly treat us all as his special children if we will only come back to him.

When families are broken, every person experiences the pain. Too often that pain leads to more separation. In our world, it is rare to see reconciliation and forgiveness. But God desires us to demonstrate a different kind of spirit. He wants us to reflect his heart. That means we must stand ready to welcome back any member of the family who returns in repentance. We are to give them a gift they don't deserve. Not one of us can claim we did not need personal repentance.

God's call to us only demonstrates how far we were from his holiness. When we look into the eyes of someone who has hurt us or who has abandoned us, we should see ourselves standing in front of God in need of his welcome blessing. The family that reflects the heart of God when someone returns will discover great joy in spite of the pain. Families that forgive are families that know what it means to be forgiven by the Father.

reflect: Practice the fine art of forgiveness toward those who don't deserve it today.
Go to **Jeremiah 31:33.**

a prostitute! ⁹And she didn't care that she was acting like a prostitute. So she made her country unclean and was guilty of adultery, because she worshiped idols made of stone and wood. ¹⁰Israel's wicked sister didn't even come back to me with her whole heart, but only pretended," says the Lord.

¹¹The Lord said to me, "Unfaithful Israel had a better excuse than wicked Judah. ¹²Go and speak this message toward the north:

'Come back, unfaithful people of Israel,'
    says the Lord.
'I will stop being angry at you,
because I am full of mercy,' says the
    Lord.
'I will not be angry with you forever.
¹³ All you have to do is admit your sin—

that you turned against the Lord your
    God
and worshiped gods under every green
    tree
and didn't obey me,'" says the Lord.

¹⁴"Come back to me, you unfaithful children," says the Lord, "because I am your master. I will take one person from every city and two from every family group, and I will bring you to Jerusalem. ¹⁵Then I will give you new rulers who will be faithful to me, who will lead you with knowledge and understanding. ¹⁶In those days there will be many of you in the land," says the Lord. "At that time people will no longer say, 'I remember the Ark of the Agreement.' They won't think about it anymore or remember it or miss it or

---

DO YOU KNOW HIM?

FULFILLMENT

restoration

JEREMIAH 3:22

The Hebrew word *rapa* appears more than sixty times in the Old Testament. In almost every case, it means restoring or making healthy. It is most often used of human subjects but can sometimes be used for the restoration of an object (for example, restoring salt water to fresh in 2 Kings 2:22).

Here God promises that our lives can be repaired and restored. He will do it, if we only surrender ourselves to him. We are not asked to repair ourselves, only to return to him. God does not ask for success, only for obedience. We do not need to come to him after we have fixed everything. He asks only one thing of us and that is that we return. The rest is up to him.

What a relief to find that God is ready and willing to take over the life that we could not take care of and that he doesn't expect us to make it right before we come to him for help. The water has already passed under the bridge, and the damage is already done. But God says, "Return to me, and I'll repair the damage." All we need to do is come back, willing to let him go to work on us.

reflect: Allow God to restore the broken parts of your heart and life.
Go to **Jeremiah 31:3.**

make another one. ¹⁷At that time people will call Jerusalem The Throne of the LORD, and all nations will come together in Jerusalem to show respect to the LORD. They will not follow their stubborn, evil hearts anymore. ¹⁸In those days the family of Judah will join the family of Israel. They will come together from a land in the north to the land I gave their ancestors.

¹⁹"I, the LORD, said,
'How happy I would be to treat you as my
    own children
  and give you a pleasant land,
  a land more beautiful than that of any
    other nation.'
I thought you would call me 'My Father'
  and not turn away from me.
²⁰ But like a woman who is unfaithful to her
    husband,
  family of Israel, you have been
    unfaithful to me," says the LORD.

²¹ You can hear crying on the bare hilltops.
  It is the people of Israel crying and
    praying for mercy.
  They have become very evil
    and have forgotten the LORD their
      God.
²² "Come back to me, you unfaithful
    children,
  and I will forgive you for being
    unfaithful."

  "Yes, we will come to you,
    because you are the LORD our God.
²³ It was foolish to worship idols on the
    hills
  and on the mountains.
  Surely the salvation of Israel
    comes from the LORD our God.
²⁴ Since our youth, shameful gods have
    eaten up in sacrifice
  everything our ancestors worked for—
    their flocks and herds,
    their sons and daughters.
²⁵ Let us lie down in our shame,
  and let our disgrace cover us like a
    blanket.
  We have sinned against the LORD our
    God,
  both we and our ancestors.
  From our youth until now,
    we have not obeyed the LORD our God."

⁴ "If you will return, Israel,
  then return to me," says the LORD.
"If you will throw away your idols that I
    hate,
  then don't wander away from me.
² If you say when you make a promise,
    'As surely as the LORD lives,'
  and you can say it in a truthful, honest,
    and right way,
  then the nations will be blessed by him,
    and they will praise him for what he has
      done."

³This is what the LORD says to the people of Judah and to Jerusalem:
  "Plow your unplowed fields,
    and don't plant seeds among thorns.
⁴ Give yourselves to the service of the
    LORD,
  and decide to obey him,
  people of Judah and people of
    Jerusalem.
If you don't, my anger will spread among
    you like a fire,
  and no one will be able to put it out,
  because of the evil you have done.

TROUBLE FROM THE NORTH

⁵ "Announce this message in Judah and say
    it in Jerusalem:
  'Blow the trumpet throughout the
    country!'
Shout out loud and say,
  'Come together!
  Let's all escape to the strong, walled
    cities!'
⁶ Raise the signal flag toward Jerusalem!
  Run for your lives, and don't wait,
  because I am bringing disaster from the
    north
  There will be terrible destruction."

⁷ A lion has come out of his den;
  a destroyer of nations has begun to
    march.
He has left his home
  to destroy your land.
Your towns will be destroyed
  with no one left to live in them.
⁸ So put on rough cloth,
  show how sad you are, and cry
    loudly.
The terrible anger of the LORD
  has not turned away from us.

9 "When this happens," says the LORD,
"the king and officers will lose their
courage.
The priests will be terribly afraid,
and the prophets will be shocked!"

10 Then I said, "Lord GOD, you have tricked
the people of Judah and Jerusalem. You said,
'You will have peace,' but now the sword is
pointing at our throats!"

11 At that time this message will be given
to Judah and Jerusalem: "A hot wind blows
from the bare hilltops of the desert toward
the LORD's people. It is not a gentle wind to
separate grain from chaff. 12 I feel a stronger
wind than that. Now even I will announce
judgments against the people of Judah."

13 Look! The enemy rises up like a cloud,
and his chariots come like a tornado.
His horses are faster than eagles.
How terrible it will be for us! We are
ruined!

14 People of Jerusalem, clean the evil from
your hearts so that you can be saved.
Don't continue making evil plans.

15 A voice from Dan makes an
announcement
and brings bad news from the
mountains of Ephraim.

16 "Report this to the nations.
Spread this news in Jerusalem:
'Invaders are coming from a faraway
country,
shouting words of war against the cities
of Judah.

17 The enemy has surrounded Jerusalem as
men guard a field,
because Judah turned against me,'" says
the LORD.

18 "The way you have lived and acted
has brought this trouble to you.
This is your punishment.
How terrible it is!
The pain stabs your heart!"

JEREMIAH'S CRY

19 Oh, how I hurt! How I hurt!
I am bent over in pain.
Oh, the torture in my heart!
My heart is pounding inside me.
I cannot keep quiet,
because I have heard the sound of the
trumpet.
I have heard the shouts of war.

20 Disaster follows disaster;
the whole country has been destroyed.
My tents are destroyed in only a moment.
My curtains are torn down quickly.

21 How long must I look at the war flag?
How long must I listen to the war
trumpet?

22 The LORD says, "My people are foolish.
They do not know me.
They are stupid children;
they don't understand.
They are skillful at doing evil,
but they don't know how to do good."

DISASTER IS COMING

23 I looked at the earth,
and it was empty and had no shape.
I looked at the sky,
and its light was gone.

24 I looked at the mountains,
and they were shaking.
All the hills were trembling.

25 I looked, and there were no people.
Every bird in the sky had flown away.

26 I looked, and the good, rich land had
become a desert.
All its towns had been destroyed
by the LORD and his great anger.

27 This is what the LORD says:
"All the land will be ruined,
but I will not completely destroy it.

28 So the people in the land will cry loudly,
and the sky will grow dark,
because I have spoken and will not
change my mind.
I have made a decision, and I will not
change it."

29 At the sound of the horsemen and the
archers,
all the people in the towns run away.
They hide in the thick bushes
and climb up into the rocks.
All of the cities of Judah are empty;
no one lives in them.

30 Judah, you destroyed nation, what are you
doing?
Why do you put on your finest dress
and decorate yourself with gold
jewelry?
Why do you put color around your eyes?
You make yourself beautiful, but it is all
useless.

Your lovers hate you;
they want to kill you.

31 I hear a cry like a woman having a baby,
distress like a woman having her first
child.
It is the sound of Jerusalem gasping for
breath.
She lifts her hands in prayer and says,
"Oh! I am about to faint
before my murderers!"

NO ONE IS RIGHT

5 The LORD says, "Walk up and down the
streets of Jerusalem.
Look around and discover these things.
Search the public squares of the city.
If you can find one person who does
honest things,
who searches for the truth,
I will forgive this city.
2 Although the people say, 'As surely as the
LORD lives!'
they don't really mean it."

3 LORD, don't you look for truth in people?
You struck the people of Judah,
but they didn't feel any pain.
You crushed them,
but they refused to learn what is right.
They became more stubborn than a rock;
they refused to turn back to God.
4 But I thought,
"These are only the poor, foolish
people.
They have not learned the way of the
LORD
and what their God wants them to do.
5 So I will go to the leaders of Judah
and talk to them.
Surely they understand the way of the
LORD
and know what God wants them to do."
But even the leaders had all joined
together to break away from the
LORD;
they had broken their ties with him.
6 So a lion from the forest will attack
them.
A wolf from the desert will kill them.
A leopard is waiting for them near their
towns.
It will tear to pieces anyone who comes
out of the city,

because the people of Judah have sinned
greatly.
They have wandered away from the
LORD many times.

7 The LORD said, "Tell me why I should
forgive you.
Your children have left me
and have made promises to idols that
are not gods at all.
I gave your children everything they
needed,
but they still were like an unfaithful
wife to me.
They spent much time in houses of
prostitutes.
8 They are like well-fed horses filled with
sexual desire;
each one wants another man's wife.
9 Shouldn't I punish the people of Judah for
doing these things?" says the LORD.
"Shouldn't I give a nation such as this
the punishment it deserves?

10 "Go along and cut down Judah's
vineyards,
but do not completely destroy them.
Cut off all her people as if they were
branches,
because they do not belong to the LORD.
11 The families of Israel and Judah
have been completely unfaithful to me,"
says the LORD.

12 Those people have lied about the LORD
and said, "He will not do anything to us!
Nothing bad will happen to us!
We will never see war or hunger!
13 The prophets are like an empty wind;
the word of God is not in them.
Let the bad things they say happen to
them."
14 So this is what the LORD God All-
Powerful says:
"The people said I would not punish
them.
So, the words I give you will be like fire,
and these people will be like wood that
it burns up.

15 Listen, family of Israel," says the LORD,
"I will soon bring a nation from far
away to attack you.
It is an old nation that has lasted a long
time.

The people there speak a language you
do not know;
you cannot understand what they say.
16 Their arrows bring death.
All their people are strong warriors.
17 They will eat your crops and your food.
They will eat your sons and daughters.
They will eat your flocks and herds.
They will eat your grapes and figs.
They will destroy with their swords
the strong, walled cities you trust.

18"Yet even then," says the LORD, "I will
not destroy you completely. 19When the people of Judah ask, 'Why has the LORD our God
done all these terrible things to us?' then give
them this answer: 'You have left the LORD
and served foreign idols in your own land. So
now you will serve foreigners in a land that
does not belong to you.'

20 "Announce this message to the family of
Jacob,
and tell it to the nation of Judah:
21 Hear this message, you foolish people
who have no sense.
They have eyes, but they don't really
see.
They have ears, but they don't really
listen.
22 Surely you are afraid of me," says the
LORD.
"You should shake with fear in my
presence.
I am the one who made the beaches to be
a border for the sea,
a border the water can never go past.
The waves may pound the beach, but they
can't win over it.
They may roar, but they cannot go
beyond it.
23 But the people of Judah are stubborn and
have turned against me.
They have turned aside and gone away
from me.
24 They do not say to themselves,
'We should fear the LORD our God,
who gives us autumn and spring rains in
their seasons,
who makes sure we have the harvest at
the right time.'
25 But your evil has kept away both rain and
harvest.
Your sins have kept you from enjoying
good things.

26 There are wicked men among my people.
Like those who make nets for catching
birds,
they set their traps to catch people.
27 Like cages full of birds,
their houses are full of lies.
They have become rich and powerful.
28 They have grown big and fat.
There is no end to the evil things they do.
They won't plead the case of the
orphan
or help the poor be judged fairly.
29 Shouldn't I punish the people of Judah for
doing these things?" says the LORD.
"Shouldn't I give a nation such as this
the punishment it deserves?

30 "A terrible and shocking thing
has happened in the land of Judah:
31 The prophets speak lies,
and the priests take power into their
own hands,
and my people love it this way.
But what will you do when the end
comes?

JERUSALEM IS SURROUNDED

6 "Run for your lives, people of Benjamin!
Run away from Jerusalem!
Blow the war trumpet in the town of
Tekoa!
Raise the warning flag over the town of
Beth Hakkerem!
Disaster is coming from the north;
terrible destruction is coming to you.
2 Jerusalem, I will destroy you,
you who are fragile and gentle.
3 Shepherds with their flocks will come
against Jerusalem.
They will set up their tents all around
her,
each shepherd taking care of his own
section."
4 They say, "Get ready to fight against
Jerusalem!
Get up! We will attack at noon!
But it is already getting late;
the evening shadows are growing long.
5 So get up! We will attack at night.
We will destroy the strong towers of
Jerusalem!"
6This is what the LORD All-Powerful
says:
"Cut down the trees around Jerusalem,

and build an attack ramp to the top of
    its walls.
This city must be punished.
    Inside it is nothing but slavery.
7 Jerusalem pours out her evil
    as a well pours out its water.
The sounds of violence and destruction
    are heard within her.
I can see the sickness and hurts of
    Jerusalem.
8 Listen to this warning, Jerusalem,
    or I will turn my back on you
and make your land an empty desert
    where no one can live."
9 This is what the LORD All-Powerful
says:
"Gather the few people of Israel who are
    left alive,
    as you would gather the last grapes on a
        grapevine.
Check each vine again,
    like someone who gathers grapes."

10 To whom can I speak? Whom can I warn?
    Who will listen to me?
The people of Israel have closed ears,
    so they cannot hear my warnings.
They don't like the word of the LORD;
    they don't want to listen to it!
11 But I am full of the anger of the LORD,
    and I am tired of holding it in.

"Pour out my anger on the children who
    play in the street
and on the young men gathered
    together.
A husband and his wife will both be
    caught in his anger,
    as will the very old.
12 Their houses will be turned over to
    others,
    along with their fields and wives,
because I will raise my hand
    and punish the people of Judah," says
        the LORD.
13 "Everyone, from the least important to the
    greatest,
    is greedy for money.
Even the prophets and priests
    all tell lies.
14 They tried to heal my people's serious
    injuries
as if they were small wounds.
They said, 'It's all right, it's all right.'

But really, it is not all right.
15 They should be ashamed of the terrible
    way they act,
    but they are not ashamed at all.
They don't even know how to blush
    about their sins.
So they will fall, along with everyone else.
    They will be thrown to the ground
    when I punish them," says the LORD.
16 This is what the LORD says:
"Stand where the roads cross and look.
    Ask where the old way is,
where the good way is, and walk on it.
    If you do, you will find rest for
        yourselves.
But they have said, 'We will not walk on
    the good way.'
17 I set watchmen over you
    and told you, 'Listen for the sound of
        the war trumpet!'
But they said, 'We will not listen.'
18 So listen, all you nations,
    and pay attention, you witnesses.
Watch what I will do to the people of
    Judah.
19 Hear this, people of the earth:
    I am going to bring disaster to the
        people of Judah
    because of the evil they plan.
They have not listened to my messages
    and have rejected my teachings.
20 Why do you bring me offerings of incense
    from the land of Sheba?
Why do you bring me sweet-smelling
    cane from a faraway land?
Your burnt offerings will not be accepted;
    your sacrifices do not please me."
21 So this is what the LORD says:
"I will put problems in front of Judah.
    Fathers and sons will stumble over
        them together.
    Neighbors and friends will die."
22 This is what the LORD says:
"Look, an army is coming
    from the land of the north;
a great nation is coming
    from the far sides of the earth.
23 The soldiers carry bows and spears.
    They are cruel and show no mercy.
They sound like the roaring ocean
    when they ride their horses.
That army is coming lined up for battle,
    ready to attack you, Jerusalem."

24 We have heard the news about that army
and are helpless from fear.
We are gripped by our pain,
like a woman having a baby.
25 Don't go out into the fields
or walk down the roads,
because the enemy has swords.
There is terror on every side.
26 My people, put on rough cloth
and roll in the ashes to show how sad
you are.
Cry loudly for those who are dead,
as if your only son were dead,
because the destroyer
will soon come against us.

27 "Jeremiah, I have made you like a worker
who tests metal,
and my people are like the ore.
You must observe their ways
and test them.
28 All my people have turned against me and
are stubborn.
They go around telling lies about
others.
They are like bronze and iron
that became covered with rust.
They all act dishonestly.
29 The fire is fanned to make it hotter,
but the lead does not melt.
The pure metal does not come out;
the evil is not removed from my
people.
30 My people will be called rejected silver,
because the LORD has rejected them."

JEREMIAH'S TEMPLE MESSAGE

7 This is the word that the LORD spoke to
Jeremiah: 2"Stand at the gate of the Temple and preach this message there:

"'Hear the word of the LORD, all you people of the nation of Judah! All you who come through these gates to worship the LORD, listen to this message! 3This is what the LORD All-Powerful, the God of Israel, says: Change your lives and do what is right! Then I will let you live in this place. 4Don't trust the lies of people who say, "This is the Temple of the LORD. This is the Temple of the LORD. This is the Temple of the LORD!" 5You must change your lives and do what is right. Be fair to each other. 6You must not be hard on strangers, orphans, and widows. Don't kill innocent

people in this place! Don't follow other gods, or they will ruin your lives. 7If you do these things, I will let you live in this land that I gave to your ancestors to keep forever.

8"'But look, you are trusting lies, which is useless. 9Will you steal and murder and be guilty of adultery? Will you falsely accuse other people? Will you burn incense to the god Baal and follow other gods you have not known? 10If you do that, do you think you can come before me and stand in this place where I have chosen to be worshiped? Do you think you can say, "We are safe!" when you do all these hateful things? 11This place where I have chosen to be worshiped is nothing more to you than a hideout for robbers. I have been watching you, says the LORD.

12"'You people of Judah, go now to the town of Shiloh, where I first made a place to be worshiped. See what I did to it because of the evil things the people of Israel had done. 13You people of Judah have done all these evil things too, says the LORD. I spoke to you again and again, but you did not listen to me. I called you, but you did not answer. 14So I will destroy the place where I have chosen to be worshiped in Jerusalem. You trust in that place, which I gave to you and your ancestors, but I will destroy it just as I destroyed Shiloh. 15I will push you away from me just as I pushed away your relatives, the people of Israel!'

16"As for you, Jeremiah, don't pray for these people. Don't cry out for them or ask anything for them or beg me to help them, because I will not listen to you. 17Don't you see what they are doing in the towns of Judah and in the streets of Jerusalem? 18The children gather wood, and the fathers use the wood to make a fire. The women make the dough for cakes of bread, and they offer them to the Queen Goddess. They pour out drink offerings to other gods to make me angry. 19But I am not the one the people of Judah are really hurting, says the LORD. They are only hurting themselves and bringing shame upon themselves.

20"'So this is what the Lord GOD says: I will pour out my anger on this place, on people and animals, on the trees in the field and the crops in the ground. My anger will be like a hot fire that no one can put out.

OBEDIENCE IS MORE THAN SACRIFICE

21"This is what the LORD All-Powerful, the God of Israel, says: Offer burnt offerings along with your other sacrifices, and eat the meat yourselves! 22When I brought your ancestors out of Egypt, I did not speak to them and give them commands only about burnt offerings and sacrifices. 23I also gave them this command: Obey me, and I will be your God and you will be my people. Do all that I command so that good things will happen to you. 24But your ancestors did not listen or pay attention to me. They were stubborn and did whatever their evil hearts wanted. They went backward, not forward. 25Since the day your ancestors left Egypt, I have sent my servants, the prophets again and again to you. 26But your ancestors did not listen or pay attention to me. They were very stubborn and did more evil than their ancestors.'

27"Jeremiah, you will tell all these things to the people of Judah, but they will not listen to you. You will call to them, but they will not answer you. 28So say to them, 'This is the nation that has not obeyed the LORD its God. The people do nothing when I correct them. They do not tell the truth; it has disappeared from their lips.

VALLEY OF KILLING

THE Lord says, cut off your hair and throw it away. Go up on the bare hilltop and cry out, because the LORD has rejected these people. He has turned his back on them, and in his anger he will punish them. 30The people of Judah have done what I said was evil, says the LORD. They have set up their hateful idols in the place where I have chosen to be worshiped and have made it unclean. 31The people of Judah have built places of worship at Topheth in the Valley of Ben Hinnom. There they burned their own sons and daughters as sacrifices, something I never commanded. It never even entered my mind. 32So, I warn you. The days are coming, says the LORD, when people will not call this place Topheth or the Valley of Ben Hinnom anymore. They will call it the Valley of Killing. They will bury the dead in Topheth until there is no room to bury anyone else. 33Then the bodies of the dead will become food for the birds of the sky and for the wild animals. There will be no one left alive to chase them away. 34I

will end the happy sounds of the bride and bridegroom. There will be no happy sounds in the cities of Judah or in the streets of Jerusalem, because the land will become an empty desert!

8 "'The LORD says: At that time they will remove from their tombs the bones of Judah's kings and officers, priests and prophets, and the people of Jerusalem. 2The bones will be spread on the ground under the sun, moon, and stars that the people loved and served and went after and searched for and worshiped. No one will gather up the bones and bury them. So they will be like dung thrown on the ground. 3I will force the people of Judah to leave their homes and their land. Those of this evil family who are not dead will wish they were, says the LORD All-Powerful.'

SIN AND PUNISHMENT

4"Say to the people of Judah: 'This is what the LORD says:

When people fall down, don't they get up
    again?
  And when someone goes the wrong
    way, doesn't he turn back?
5 Why, then, have the people of Jerusalem
    gone the wrong way
  and not turned back?
They believe their own lies
  and refuse to turn around and come
    back.
6 I have listened to them very carefully,
  but they do not say what is right.
They do not feel sorry about their wicked
    ways,
  saying, "What have I done?"
Each person goes his own way,
  like a horse charging into a battle.
7 Even the birds in the sky
  know the right times to do things.
The storks, doves, swifts, and thrushes
  know when it is time to migrate.
But my people don't know
  what the LORD wants them to do.

8 "'You keep saying, "We are wise,
  because we have the teachings of the
    LORD."
But actually, those who explain the
    Scriptures
  have written lies with their pens.

9 These wise teachers refused to listen to
 the word of the LORD,
 so they are not really wise at all.
They will be ashamed.
 They will be shocked and trapped.
10 So I will give their wives to other men
 and their fields to new owners.
Everyone, from the least important to the
 greatest,
 is greedy for money.
Even the prophets and priests
 all tell lies.
11 They tried to heal my people's serious
 injuries
 as if they were small wounds.
They said, "It's all right, it's all right."
 But really, it is not all right.
12 They should be ashamed of the terrible
 way they act,
 but they are not ashamed at all.
 They don't even know how to blush
 about their sins.
So they will fall, along with everyone else.
 They will be thrown to the ground
 when I punish them, says the LORD.
13 "'I will take away their crops, says the
 LORD.
 There will be no grapes on the vine
and no figs on the fig tree.
 Even the leaves will dry up and die.
I will take away what I gave them.'"

14 "Why are we just sitting here?
 Let's get together!
We have sinned against the LORD,
 so he has given us poisoned water to
 drink.
Come, let's run to the strong, walled
 cities.
 The LORD our God has decided that we
 must die,
 so let's die there.
15 We hoped to have peace,
 but nothing good has come.
We hoped for a time when he would heal
 us,
 but only terror has come.
16 From the land of Dan,
 the snorting of the enemy's horses is
 heard.
 The ground shakes from the neighing of
 their large horses.
They have come and destroyed

the land and everything in it,
 the city and all who live there."

17 "Look! I am sending poisonous snakes to
 attack you.
 These snakes cannot be charmed,
 and they will bite you," says the LORD.

JEREMIAH'S SADNESS

18 God, you are my comfort when I am very
 sad
 and when I am afraid.
19 Listen to the sound of my people.
 They cry from a faraway land:
 "Isn't the LORD still in Jerusalem?
 Isn't Jerusalem's king still there?"

But God says, "Why did the people make
 me angry by worshiping idols,
 useless foreign idols?"

20 And the people say, "Harvest time is
 over;
 summer has ended,
 and we have not been saved."

21 Because my people are crushed, I am
 crushed.
 I cry loudly and am afraid for them.
22 Isn't there balm in the land of Gilead?
 Isn't there a doctor there?
So why aren't the hurts of my people
 healed?

9 I wish my head were like a spring of
 water
 and my eyes like a fountain of tears!
Then I could cry day and night
 for my people who have been killed.
2 I wish I had a place in the desert—
 a house where travelers spend the
 night—
so I could leave my people.
 I could go away from them,
because they are all unfaithful to God;
 they are all turning against him.

JUDAH'S FAILURES

3 "They use their tongues like a bow,
 shooting lies from their mouths like
 arrows.
Lies, not truth,
 have grown strong in the land.
They go from one evil thing to another.
 They do not know who I am," says the
 LORD.
4 "Watch out for your friends,

and don't trust your own relatives,
because every relative is a cheater,
and every friend tells lies about you.
5 Everyone lies to his friend,
and no one speaks the truth.
The people of Judah have taught their
tongues to lie.
They have become tired from sinning.
6 Jeremiah, you live in the middle of lies.
With their lies the people refuse to
know me," says the LORD.
7 So this is what the LORD All-Powerful
says:
"I will test the people of Judah as a person
tests metal in a fire.
I have no other choice
because my people has sinned.
8 Their tongues are like sharp arrows.
Their mouths speak lies.
Everyone speaks nicely his neighbor,
but he is secretly planning to attack
him.
9 Shouldn't I punish the people for doing
this?" says the LORD.
"Shouldn't I give a nation like this the
punishment it deserves?"

10 I, Jeremiah, will cry loudly for the
mountains
and sing a funeral song the empty
fields.
They are empty, and no one goes
through.
The mooing of cattle is not heard.
The birds have flown away,
and the animals are gone.

11 "I, the LORD, will make the
Jerusalem a heap of ruins,
a home for wild dogs.
I will destroy the cities of Judah
so no one can live there."

12 What person is wise enough to understand these things? Is there anyone who
has been taught by the LORD who can explain
them? Why was the land ruined? Why has it
been made like an empty desert where no
one goes?

13 The LORD answered, "It is because Judah quit following my teaching that I gave
them. They have not obeyed me or done
what I told them to do. 14 Instead, they were
stubborn and followed the Baals as their ancestors taught them to do." This is why

the LORD All-Powerful, the God of Israel,
says: "I will soon make the people of Judah
eat bitter food and drink poisoned water. 16 I
will scatter them through other nations that
they and their ancestors never knew about.
I will chase the people of Judah with the
sword until they are all killed."

17 This is what the LORD All-Powerful
says:
"Now, think about these things!
Call for the women who cry at funerals
to come.
Send for those women who are good at
that job.
18 Let them come quickly
and cry loudly for us.
Then our eyes will fill with tears,
and streams of water will flow from our
eyelids.
19 The sound of loud crying is heard from
Jerusalem:
'We are truly ruined!
We are truly ashamed!
We must leave our land,
because our houses are in ruins.'"

20 Now, women of Judah, listen to the word
of the LORD;
open your ears to hear the words of his
mouth.
Teach your daughters how to cry loudly.
Teach one another a funeral song.
21 Death has climbed in through our
windows
and has entered our strong cities.
Death has taken away our children who
play in the streets
and the young men who meet in the city
squares.
22 Say, "This is what the LORD says:
'The dead bodies of people will lie
in the open field like dung.
They will lie like grain a farmer has cut,
but there will be no one to gather
them.'"
23 This is what the LORD says:
"The wise must not brag about their
wisdom.
The strong must not brag about their
strength.
The rich must not brag about their
money.
24 But if people want to brag, let them brag

that they understand and know me.
Let them brag that I am the LORD,
   and that I am kind and fair,
   and that I do things that are right on
      earth.
This kind of bragging pleases me," says
   the LORD.

²⁵The LORD says, "The time is coming when I will punish all those who are circumcised only in the flesh: ²⁶the people of Egypt, Judah, Edom, Ammon, Moab, and the desert people who cut their hair short. The men in all those countries are not circumcised. And the whole family of Israel does not give itself to serving me."

THE LORD AND THE IDOLS

10 Family of Israel, listen to what the LORD says to you. ²This is what he says:
"Don't live like the people from other
      nations,
   and don't be afraid of special signs in
      the sky,
   even though the other nations are afraid
      of them.
³ The customs of other people are worth
      nothing.
   Their idols are just wood cut from the
      forest,
   shaped by a worker with his chisel.
⁴ They decorate their idols with silver and
      gold.
   With hammers and nails they fasten
      them down
   so they won't fall over.
⁵ Their idols are like scarecrows in melon
      fields;
   they cannot talk.
Since they cannot walk,
   they must be carried.
Do not be afraid of those idols,
   because they can't hurt you,
   and they can't help you either."

⁶ LORD, there is no one like you.
   You are great,
   and your name is great and powerful.
⁷ Everyone should respect you, King of the
      nations;
   you deserve respect.
Of all the wise people among the nations
   and in all the kingdoms,
   none of them is as wise as you.

⁸Those wise people are stupid and
   foolish.
Their teachings come from worthless
   wooden idols.
⁹ Hammered silver is brought from
   Tarshish
   and gold from Uphaz,
so the idols are made by craftsmen and
   goldsmiths.
They put blue and purple clothes on the
   idols.
All these things are made by skilled
   workers.
¹⁰ But the LORD is the only true God.
   He is the only living God, the King
      forever.
The earth shakes when he is angry,
   and the nations cannot stand up to his
      anger.

¹¹"Tell them this message: 'These gods did not make heaven and earth; they will be destroyed and disappear from heaven and earth.'"

¹² God made the earth by his power.
   He used his wisdom to build the world
   and his understanding to stretch out the
      skies.
¹³ When he thunders, the waters in the skies
      roar.
   He makes clouds rise in the sky all over
      the earth.
   He sends lightning with the rain
   and brings out the wind from his
      storehouses.
¹⁴ People are so stupid and know so little.
   Goldsmiths are ashamed by their
      idols,
   because these idols are only false gods.
   They have no breath in them.
¹⁵ They are worth nothing; people make fun
      of them.
   When they are judged, they will be
      destroyed.
¹⁶ But God, who is Jacob's Portion, is not like
      those idols.
   He made everything,
   and Israel is his special people.
   The LORD All-Powerful is his name.

DESTRUCTION IS COMING
¹⁷ Gather up everything you own and prepare to

you people who are trapped by your
enemies.

[18] This is what the LORD says:

"At this time I will throw out the people
who live in this land.
I will bring trouble to them
so that they may be captured."

[19] How terrible it will be for me because of
my injury.
My wound cannot be healed.
Yet I told myself,
"This is my sickness; I must suffer
through it."

[20] My tent is ruined,
and all its ropes are broken.
My children have gone away and left me.
No one is left to put up my tent again
or to set up a shelter for me.

[21] The shepherds are stupid
and don't ask the LORD for advice.
So they do not have success,
and all their flocks are scattered and
lost.

[22] Listen! The news is coming.
A loud noise comes from the north
to make the towns of Judah an empty
desert
and a home for wild dogs!

JEREMIAH'S PRAYER

[23] LORD, I know that our lives don't really
belong to us.
We can't control our own lives.

[24] LORD, correct me, but be fair.
Don't punish me in your anger,
or you will destroy me.

[25] Pour out your anger on other nations
that do not know you
and do not pray to you.
Those nations have destroyed the people
of Jacob.
They have eaten them up completely
and destroyed their homeland.

THE AGREEMENT IS BROKEN

11 These are the words that the LORD
spoke to Jeremiah: [2]"Listen to the words
of this agreement and tell them to the people of Judah and those living in Jerusalem.
[3]Tell them this is what the LORD, the God of
Israel, says: 'Cursed is the person who does
not obey the words of this agreement [4]that
I made with your ancestors when I brought

them out of Egypt. Egypt was like a furnace
for melting iron!' I told them, 'Obey me and
do everything I command you. Then you will
be my people, and I will be your God. [5]Then
I will keep the promise I made to your ancestors to give them a fertile land.' And you are
living in that country today."

I answered, "Amen, LORD."

[6]The LORD said to me, "Announce this
message in the towns of Judah and in the
streets of Jerusalem: 'Listen to the words of
this agreement and obey them. [7]I warned
your ancestors to obey me when I brought
them out of Egypt. I have warned them again
and again to this very day: 'Obey me!' [8]But
your ancestors did not listen to me. They
were stubborn and did what their own evil
hearts wanted. So I made all the curses of
this agreement come upon them. I commanded them to obey the agreement, but
they did not.'"

[9]Then the LORD said to me, "I know the
people of Judah and those living in Jerusalem have made secret plans. [10]They have
gone back to the same sins their ancestors
did. Their ancestors refused to listen to my
message and followed and worshiped other
gods instead. The families of Israel and Judah have broken the agreement I made with
their ancestors. [11]So this is what the LORD
says: 'I will soon bring a disaster on the
people of Judah which they will not be able
to escape. They will cry to me for help, but
I will not listen to them. [12]The people living
in the towns of Judah and the city of Jerusalem will pray to their idols to whom they
burn incense. But those idols will not be able
to help when disaster comes. [13]Look, people
of Judah, you have as many idols as there are
towns in Judah. You have built as many altars
to burn incense to that shameful god Baal as
there are streets in Jerusalem.'

[14]"As for you, Jeremiah, don't pray for
these people or cry out for them or ask anything for them. I will not listen when they
call to me in the time of their trouble.

[15] "What is my beloved Judah doing in my
Temple
when she makes many evil plans?
Do you think animal sacrifices will stop
your punishment?
When you do your evil, then you are
happy."

16 The LORD called you "a leafy olive tree,
   with beautiful fruit and shape."
   But with the roar of a strong storm
   he will set that tree on fire,
   and its branches will be burned up.

17 The LORD All-Powerful, who planted you, has announced that disaster will come to you. This is because the families of Israel and Judah have done evil and have made him angry by burning incense to Baal.

EVIL PLANS AGAINST JEREMIAH

18 The LORD showed me that people were making plans against me. Because he showed me what they were doing, I knew they were against me. 19 Before this, I was like a gentle lamb waiting to be butchered. I did not know they had made plans against me, saying:

   "Let us destroy the tree and its fruit.
   Let's kill him so people will forget him."
20 But, LORD All-Powerful, you are a fair
      judge.
   You know how to test peoples' hearts
      and minds.
   I have told you what I have against them.
   So let me see you give them the
      punishment they deserve.

21 So the LORD speaks about the people from Anathoth who plan to kill Jeremiah and say, "Don't prophesy in the name of the LORD, or we will kill you!" 22 So this is what the LORD All-Powerful says: "I will soon punish the men from Anathoth. Their young men will die in war. Their sons and daughters will die from hunger. 23 No one from the city of Anathoth will be left alive, because I will cause a disaster to happen to them that year."

JEREMIAH'S FIRST COMPLAINT

12 LORD, when I bring my case to you,
      you are always right.
   But I want to ask you about the justice
      you give.
   Why are evil people successful?
   Why do dishonest people have such
      easy lives?
2 You have put the evil people here
   like plants with strong roots.
   They grow and produce fruit.
   With their mouths they speak well of you,
   but their hearts are really far away from
      you.
3 But you know my heart, LORD.

You see me and test my thoughts about
   you.
Drag the evil people away like sheep to be
   butchered.
Set them aside for the day of killing.
4 How much longer will the land stay dried
   up
   and the grass in every field be dead?
The animals and birds in the land have
   died,
   because the people are evil.
Yes, they are even saying,
   "God does not see what happens to us."

THE LORD'S ANSWER TO JEREMIAH

5 "If you get tired while racing against
      people,
   how can you race against horses?
   If you stumble in a country that is safe,
      what will you do in the thick
         thornbushes along the Jordan River?
6 Even your own brothers and members of
      your own family
   are making plans against you.
   They are crying out against you.
Don't trust them,
   even when they say nice things to you!

7 "I have left Israel;
   I have left my people.
I have given the people I love
   over to their enemies.
8 My people have become to me
   like a lion in the forest.
They roar at me,
   so I hate them.
9 My people have become to me
   like a speckled bird attacked on all sides
      by hawks.
Go, gather the wild animals.
   Bring them to get something to eat.
10 Many shepherds have ruined my
      vineyards
   and trampled the plants in my field.
They have turned my beautiful field
   into an empty desert.
11 They have turned my field into a desert
   that is wilted and dead.
The whole country is an empty desert,
   because no one who lives there cares.
12 Many soldiers have marched over those
      barren hills.
   The LORD is using the armies to punish
      that land

from one end to the other.
No one is safe.
13 The people have planted wheat,
but they have harvested only thorns.
They have worked hard until they were
very tired,
but they have nothing for all their work.
They are ashamed of their poor harvest,
because the LORD's terrible anger has
caused this."

14This is what the LORD said to me: "Here is what I will do to all my wicked neighbors who take the land I gave my people Israel. I will pull them up and throw them out of their land. And I will pull up the people of Judah from among them. 15But after I pull them up, I will feel sorry for them again. I will bring each person back to his own property and to his own land. 16I want them to learn their lessons well. In the past they taught my people to swear by Baal's name. But if they will now learn to swear by my name, saying, 'As surely as the LORD lives...' I will allow them to rebuild among my people. 17But if a nation will not listen to my message, I will pull it up completely and destroy it," says the LORD.

JEREMIAH'S LINEN BELT

13 This is what the LORD said to me: "Go and buy a linen belt and put it around your waist. Don't let the belt get wet."

2So I bought a linen belt, just as the LORD told me, and put it around my waist. 3Then

---

HAVE FAITH IN GOD

what **God** knows

FAITH

JEREMIAH 12:3

The root word for "know" occurs in the Bible nearly a thousand times. It signifies the many contexts of gaining information through the senses. It is used to describe God's understanding of people, as well as our understanding of God. It describes the context of being acquainted with other persons, of distinguishing between good and evil, of moral insight and judgment, and of the prophetic revelation of God's will directly to people. It is also used euphemistically to describe sexual intercourse.

The Bible uses this word to proclaim God's complete knowledge of creation. Nothing can be hidden from his understanding. God's perception and recognition extend to every act and circumstance. For all believers, this has the powerful consequence that none of our secrets are unknown to God. No matter how much we try to cover up our sinful attitudes and actions, God knows all about us.

This truth may be terrifying if we perceive God as the proverbial taskmaster. But we need not fear if we have come to see that God's full recognition of who we are is not about punishment but affirmation. God loves us in spite of our sinful addictions. He knows everything about what we have done, and he still forgives, cares, and blesses us.

reflect: Consider the goodness of God toward you and your family today.
Go to **Jeremiah 23:24**.

the LORD spoke his word to me a second time: ⁴"Take the belt you bought and are wearing, and go to Perath. Hide the belt there in a crack in the rocks." ⁵So I went to Perath and hid the belt there, just as the LORD told me.

⁶Many days later the LORD said to me, "Now go to Perath and get the belt I told you to hide there." ⁷So I went to Perath and dug up the belt and took it from where I had hidden it. But now it was ruined; it was good for nothing.

⁸Then the LORD spoke his word to me. ⁹This is what the LORD said: "In the same way I will ruin the pride of the people of Judah and the great pride of Jerusalem. ¹⁰These evil people refuse to listen to my warnings. They stubbornly do only what they want to do, and they follow other gods to serve and worship them. So they will become like this linen belt—good for nothing. ¹¹As a belt is wrapped tightly around a person's waist, I wrapped the families of Israel and Judah around me," says the LORD. "I did that so they would be my people and bring fame, praise, and honor to me. But my people would not listen.

WARNINGS ABOUT LEATHER WINE BAGS

¹²"Say to them: 'This is what the LORD, the God of Israel, says: All leather bags for holding wine should be filled with wine.' People will say to you: 'Of course, we know all wine bags should be filled with wine.' ¹³Then you will say to them, 'This is what the LORD says: I will make everyone in this land like a drunken person—the kings who sit on David's throne, the priests and the prophets, and all the people who live in Jerusalem. ¹⁴I will make them smash against one another, fathers and sons alike, says the LORD. I will not feel sorry or have pity on them or show mercy that would stop me from destroying them.'"

THREAT OF SLAVERY

¹⁵ Listen and pay attention.
　　Don't be too proud,
　　　because the LORD has spoken to you.
¹⁶ Give glory to the LORD your God
　　before he brings darkness
　and before you slip and fall
　　on the dark hills.
　You hope for light,
　　but he will turn it into thick darkness;
　he will change it into deep gloom.

¹⁷ If you don't listen to him,
　　I will cry secretly
　　　because of your pride.
　I will cry painfully,
　　and my eyes will overflow with tears,
　　　because the LORD's people will be
　　　　captured.

¹⁸ Tell this to the king and the queen
　　　mother:
　　"Come down from your thrones,
　because your beautiful crowns
　　have fallen from your heads."
¹⁹ The cities of southern Judah are locked
　　　up,
　　and no one can open them.
　All Judah will be taken as captives to a
　　　foreign land;
　　they will be carried away completely.

²⁰ Jerusalem, look up and see
　　the people coming from the north.
　Where is the flock God gave you to care
　　　for,
　　the flock you bragged about?
²¹ What will you say when they appoint as
　　　your heads
　　those you had thought were your
　　　friends?
　Won't you have much pain and trouble,
　　like a woman giving birth to a baby?
²² You might ask yourself,
　　"Why has this happened to me?"
　It happened because of your many sins.
　　Because of your sins, your skirt was
　　　torn off
　　and your body has been treated badly.
²³ Can a person from Cush change the color
　　　of his skin?
　　Can a leopard change his spots?
　In the same way, Jerusalem, you cannot
　　　change and do good,
　　because you are accustomed to doing
　　　evil.

²⁴ "I will scatter you like chaff that is blown
　　　away by the desert wind.
²⁵ This is what will happen to you;
　　this is your part in my plans," says the
　　　LORD.
　"Because you forgot me
　　and trusted in false gods,
²⁶ I will pull your skirts up over your face
　　so everyone will see your shame.

27 I have seen the terrible things you have
    done:
  your acts of adultery and your snorting,
  your prostitution,
your hateful acts
  on the hills and in the fields.
How terrible it will be for you, Jerusalem.
  How long will you continue being
    unclean?"

A TIME WITHOUT RAIN

14 These are the words that the LORD
    spoke to Jeremiah about the time when
there was no rain:

2 "The nation of Judah cries as if someone
    has died,
  and her cities are very sad.
They are distressed over the land.
  A cry goes up to God from Jerusalem.
3 The important men send their servants to
    get water.
  They go to the wells,
  but they find no water.
So they return with empty jars.
  They are ashamed and embarrassed
  and cover their heads in shame.
4 The ground is dry and cracked open,
  because no rain falls on the land.
The farmers are upset and sad,
  so they cover their heads in shame.
5 Even the mother deer in the field
  leaves her newborn fawn to die,
  because there is no grass.
6 Wild donkeys stand on the bare hills
  and sniff the wind like wild dogs.
But their eyes go blind,
  because there is no food."

7 We know that we suffer because of our
    sins.
  LORD, do something to help us for the
    good of your name.
We have left you many times;
  we have sinned against you.
8 God, the Hope of Israel,
  you have saved Israel in times of
    trouble.
Why are you like a stranger in the land,
  or like a traveler who only stays one
    night?
9 Why are you like someone who has been
    attacked by surprise,
  like a warrior who is not able to save
    anyone?

But you are among us, LORD,
  and we are called by your name
  so don't leave us without help!
10 This is what the LORD says about the
people of Judah:
  "They really love to wander from me;
  they don't stop themselves from leaving
    me.
So now the LORD will not accept them.
  He will now remember the evil they do
  and will punish them for their sins."

11 Then the LORD said, "Don't pray for
good things to happen to the people of Judah. 12 Even if they fast, I will not listen to
their prayers. Even if they offer burnt offerings and grain offerings to me, I will not
accept them. Instead, I will destroy the people of Judah with war, hunger, and terrible
diseases."

13 But I said, "Oh, Lord GOD, the prophets
keep telling the people, 'You will not suffer
from an enemy's sword or from hunger. I, the
LORD, will give you peace in this land.'"

14 Then the LORD said to me, "Those
prophets are prophesying lies in my name. I
did not send them or appoint them or speak
to them. They have been prophesying false
visions, idolatries, worthless magic, and
their own wishful thinking. 15 So this is what
I say about the prophets who are prophesying in my name. I did not send them. They
say, 'No enemy will attack this country with
swords. There will never be hunger in this
land.' So those prophets will die from hunger
and from an enemy's sword. 16 And the people
to whom the prophets speak will be thrown
into the streets of Jerusalem. There they will
die from hunger and from an enemy's sword.
And no one will be there to bury them, or
their wives, or their sons, or their daughters.
I will punish them.

17 "Jeremiah, speak this message to the
people of Judah:
  'Let my eyes be filled with tears
  night and day, without stopping.
My people have received a terrible
    blow;
  they have been hurt badly.
18 If I go into the country,
  I see people killed by swords.
If I go into the city,
  I see much sickness, because the people
  have no food.

803

Both the priests and the prophets
   have been taken to a foreign land.'"

19 LORD, have you completely rejected the
   nation of Judah?
  Do you hate Jerusalem?
Why have you hurt us so badly
   that we cannot be made well again?
We hoped for peace,
  but nothing good has come.
We looked for a time of healing,
  but only terror came.
20 LORD, we admit that we are wicked
   and that our ancestors did evil things.
  We have sinned against you.
21 For your sake, do not hate us.
  Do not take away the honor from your
   glorious throne.
Remember your agreement with us,
  and do not break it.
22 Do foreign idols have the power to bring
   rain?
  Does the sky itself have the power to
   send down showers?
No, it is you, LORD our God.
  You are our only hope,
   because you are the one who made all
   these things.

15 Then the LORD said to me: "I would
not feel sorry for the people of Judah
even if Moses and Samuel prayed for them.
Send them away from me! Tell them to go!
2When they ask you, 'Where will we go?' tell
them: 'This is what the LORD says:

  Those who are meant to die
   will die.
  Those who are meant to die in war
   will die in war.
  Those who are meant to die from hunger
   will die from hunger.
  Those who are meant to be taken captive
   will be taken captive.'

3"I will send four kinds of destroyers
against them," says the LORD. "I will send
war to kill, dogs to drag the bodies away,
and the birds of the air and wild animals to
eat and destroy the bodies. 4I will make the
people of Judah hated by everyone on earth
because of what Manasseh did in Jerusalem.
(Manasseh son of Hezekiah was king of the
nation of Judah.)

5 "Who will feel sorry for you, Jerusalem?
  Who will be sad and cry for you?

Who will go out of his way to ask how
  you are?
6 Jerusalem, you have left me," says the
  LORD.
  "You keep going farther and farther
   away,
so I have taken hold of you and destroyed
  you.
  I was tired of holding back my anger.
7 I have separated the people of Judah with
  my pitchfork
  and scattered them at the city gates of
   the land.
My people haven't changed their ways.
  So I have destroyed them
  and taken away their children.
8 There are more widows than grains of
  sand in the sea.
I brought a destroyer at noontime
  against the mothers of the young men
   of Judah.
I suddenly brought pain and fear
  on the people of Judah.
9 When the enemy attacked, a woman with
  seven sons felt faint because they
   would all die.
  She became weak and unable to
   breathe.
Her bright day became dark from sadness.
  She felt shame and disgrace.
And everyone else left alive in Judah
  I will hand over to the enemies, too!"
   says the LORD.

JEREMIAH'S SECOND COMPLAINT

10 Mother, I am sorry that you gave birth to
  me
  since I must accuse and criticize the
   whole land.
I have not loaned or borrowed anything,
  but everyone curses me.
11 The LORD said,
  "I have saved you for a good reason.
I have made your enemies beg you
  in times of disaster and trouble.
12 No one can smash a piece of iron or
  bronze
  that comes from the north.
13 Your wealth and treasures
  I will give to others free of charge,
because the people of Judah have sinned
  throughout the country.
14 I will make you slaves to your enemies

in a land you have never known.
My anger is like a hot fire,
and it will burn against you."

15 LORD, you understand.
Remember me and take care of me.
Punish for me those who are hurting
me.
Don't destroy me while you remain
patient with them.
Think about the shame I suffer for you.
16 Your words came to me, and I listened
carefully to them.
Your words made me very happy,
because I am called by your name,
LORD God All-Powerful.
17 I never sat with the crowd
as they laughed and had fun.
I sat by myself, because you were there,
and you filled me with anger at the evil
around me.
18 I don't understand why my pain has no
end.
I don't understand why my injury is not
cured or healed.
Will you be like a brook that goes dry?
Will you be like a spring that stops
flowing?
19 So this is what the LORD says:
"If you change your heart and return to
me, I will take you back.
Then you may serve me.
And if you speak things that have worth,
not useless words,
then you may speak for me.
Let the people of Judah turn to you,
but you must not change and be like
them.
20 I will make you as strong as a wall to this
people,
as strong as a wall of bronze.
They will fight against you,
but they will not defeat you,
because I am with you.
I will rescue you and save you," says the
LORD.
21 "I will save you from these wicked people
and rescue you from these cruel
people."

THE DAY OF DISASTER

16 Then the LORD spoke his word to me:
2"You must not get married or have
sons or daughters in this place."

3The LORD says this about the sons and
daughters born in this land and their mothers and fathers: 4"They will die of terrible
diseases, and no one will cry for them or bury
them. Their bodies will lie on the ground like
dung. They will die in war, or they will starve
to death. Their bodies will be food for the
birds of the sky and for the wild animals."

5So this is what the LORD says: "Jeremiah,
do not go into a house where there is a funeral
meal. Do not go there to cry for the dead or to
show your sorrow for them, because I have
taken back my blessing, my love, and my pity
from these people," says the LORD. 6"Important people and common people will die in
the land of Judah. No one will bury them or
cry for them or cut himself or shave his head
to show sorrow for them. 7No one will bring
food to comfort those who are crying for the
dead. No one will offer a drink to comfort
someone whose mother or father has died.

8"Do not go into a house where the people are having a feast to sit down to eat and
drink, 9because this is what the LORD All-
Powerful, the God of Israel, says: I will soon
stop the sounds of joy and gladness and the
happy sounds of brides and bridegrooms
in this place. This will happen during your
lifetime.

10"When you tell the people of Judah
these things, they will ask you, 'Why has the
LORD said these terrible things to us? What
have we done wrong? What sin have we done
against the LORD our God?'

11"Then say to them: 'This is because your
ancestors quit following me,' says the LORD.
'And they followed other gods and served
and worshiped them. Your ancestors left
me and quit obeying my teaching. 12But you
have done even more evil than your ancestors. You are very stubborn and do only what
you want to do; you have not obeyed me. 13So
I will throw you out of this country and send
you into a land that you and your ancestors
never knew. There you can serve other gods
day and night, because I will not help you or
show you any favors.'

14"People say, 'As surely as the LORD
lives, who brought the people of Israel out
of Egypt...' But the time is coming," says the
LORD, "when people will not say this anymore. 15They will say instead, 'As surely as
the LORD lives, who brought the Israelites

from the northern land and from all the countries where he had sent them…' And I will bring them back to the land I gave to their ancestors.

16"I will soon send for many fishermen to come to this land," says the LORD. "And they will catch the people of Judah. After that, I will send for many hunters to come to this land. And they will hunt the people of Judah on every mountain and hill and in the cracks of the rocks. 17I see everything they do. They cannot hide from me the things they do; their sin is not hidden from my eyes. 18I will pay back the people of Judah twice for every one of their sins, because they have made my land unclean. They have filled my country with their hateful idols."

19 LORD, you are my strength and my
    protection,
  my safe place in times of trouble.
The nations will come to you from all over
    the world
  and say, "Our ancestors had only false
    gods,
  useless idols that didn't help them.
20 Can people make gods for themselves?
  They will not really be gods!"
21 The LORD says, "So I will teach those who
    make idols.
This time I will teach them
  about my power and my strength.
Then they will know
  that my name is the LORD.

JUDAH'S GUILTY HEART

17 "The sin of the people of Judah is
    written with an iron tool.
Their sins were cut with a hard point
    into the stone that is their hearts.
Their sins were cut into the corners of
    their altars.
2 Even their children remember
  their altars to idols and their Asherah
    idols
beside the green trees
  and on the high hills.
3 My mountain in the open country
  and your wealth and treasures
I will give away to other people.
  I will give away the places of worship in
    your country,
because you sinned by worshiping
  there.

4 You will lose the land I gave you,
  and it is your own fault.
I will let your enemies take you as their
    slaves
  to a land you have never known.
This is because you have made my anger
    burn like a hot fire,
  and it will burn forever."

TRUSTING IN HUMANS OR GOD

5This is what the LORD says:
"A curse is placed on those who trust
    other people,
  who depend on humans for strength,
  who have stopped trusting the LORD.
6 They are like a bush in a desert
  that grows in a land where no one lives,
  a hot and dry land with bad soil.
They don't know about the good things
  God can give.

7 "But the person who trusts in the LORD
  will be blessed.
The LORD will show him that he can be
  trusted.
8 He will be strong, like a tree planted near
    water
  that sends its roots by a stream.
It is not afraid when the days are hot;
  its leaves are always green.
It does not worry in a year when no rain
    comes;
  it always produces fruit.

9 "More than anything else, a person's mind
    is evil
  and cannot be healed.
Who can understand it?
10 But I, the LORD, look into a person's heart
  and test the mind.
So I can decide what each one deserves;
  I can give each one the right payment
    for what he does."

11 Like a bird hatching an egg it did not lay,
  so are the people who get rich by
    cheating.
When their lives are half finished, they
    will lose their riches.
At the end of their lives, it will be clear
    they were fools.

12 From the beginning, our Temple has been
    honored
  as a glorious throne for God.

¹³ LORD, hope of Israel,
those who leave you will be shamed.
People who quit following the LORD will
be like a name written in the dust,
because they have left the LORD, the
spring of living water.

JEREMIAH'S THIRD COMPLAINT

¹⁴ LORD, heal me, and I will truly be healed.
Save me, and I will truly be saved.
You are the one I praise.
¹⁵ The people of Judah keep asking me,

"Where is the word from the LORD?
Let's see that message come true!"

¹⁶ LORD, I didn't run away from being the
shepherd you wanted.
I didn't want the terrible day to
come.
You know everything I have said;
you see all that is happening.
¹⁷ Don't be a terror to me.
I run to you for safety in times of
trouble.

SERVANT EVANGELISM

believe in God

FAITH

By Elmer Towns

JEREMIAH 17:9

People give many different reasons for not coming to Christ. One of the reasons is
demonstrated in this story:

A man came to Dwight L. Moody, the great evangelist of the 1800s, and said, "I cannot
believe." Moody said, "Who?" The man again said to Moody, "I said I cannot believe."

"Who?" Moody asked again. "Who can you not believe . . . God?" "Oh, yes, I believe
God, but I cannot believe myself," answered the man.

Surprised, Mr. Moody answered, "Well, you do not want to believe yourself. Your 'heart is
deceitful above all things, and desperately wicked' (Jeremiah 17:9). Put no confidence in
the flesh. Don't believe yourself; call yourself a liar, and let God be true. Believe in God."

God provided the way to salvation through sending his only begotten Son, Jesus Christ,
to die on the cross for our sins and in our place, but it is our responsibility to believe.
As we draw near to God, our capacity to believe increases. We find that God is faithful
and true.

When we see God in his holiness and perfection, we see our own sinfulness even more.
This should move us toward salvation, not away from it. The man who spoke to Dwight
Moody had come to an important realization: his own feelings and thoughts could not
be trusted. He needed to put all his trust in God.

reflect: Do you need to change your focus from yourself to faith in God?
Go to **Daniel 3:16-30.**

18 Make those who are hurting me be
   ashamed,
   but don't bring shame to me.
Let them be terrified,
   but keep me from terror.
Bring the day of disaster on my enemies.
   Destroy them, and destroy them again.

KEEPING THE SABBATH HOLY

19This is what the LORD said to me: "Go
and stand at the People's Gate of Jerusalem,
where the kings of Judah go in and out. And
then go to all the other gates of Jerusalem.
20Say to them there: 'Hear the word of the
LORD, kings of Judah, all you people of Judah, and all who live in Jerusalem, who come
through these gates into the city. 21This is
what the LORD says: Be careful not to carry
a load on the Sabbath day or bring it through
the gates of Jerusalem. 22Don't take a load
out of your houses on the Sabbath or do any
work on that day. But keep the Sabbath as a
holy day, as I commanded your ancestors.
23But your ancestors did not listen or pay attention to me. They were very stubborn and
did not listen. I punished them, but it didn't
do any good. 24But you must be careful to
obey me, says the LORD. You must not bring
a load through the gates of Jerusalem on the
Sabbath, but you must keep the Sabbath as a
holy day and not do any work on that day.

25"'If you obey this command, kings who
sit on David's throne will come through the
gates of Jerusalem with their officers. They
will come riding in chariots and on horses,
along with the people of Judah and Jerusalem. And the city of Jerusalem will have people living in it forever. 26People will come to
Jerusalem from the villages around it, from
the towns of Judah, from the land of Benjamin, from the western hills, from the mountains, and from southern Judah. They will all
bring to the Temple of the LORD burnt offerings, sacrifices, grain offerings, incense, and
offerings to show thanks to God. 27But you
must obey me and keep the Sabbath day as
a holy day. You must not carry any loads into
Jerusalem on the Sabbath. If you don't obey
me, I will start a fire at the gates of Jerusalem, and it will burn until it burns even the
strong towers. And it will not be put out.'"

THE POTTER AND THE CLAY

18 This is the word the LORD spoke to
Jeremiah: 2"Go down to the potter's
house, and I will give you my message there."
3So I went down to the potter's house and
saw him working at the potter's wheel. 4He
was using his hands to make a pot from clay,
but something went wrong with it. So he
used that clay to make another pot the way
he wanted it to be.

5Then the LORD spoke his word to me:
6"Family of Israel, can't I do the same thing
with you?" says the LORD. "You are in my
hands like the clay in the potter's hands.
7There may come a time when I will speak
about a nation or a kingdom that I will pull
up by its roots or that I will pull down to destroy it. 8But if the people of that nation stop
doing the evil they have done, I will change
my mind and not carry out my plans to bring
disaster to them. 9There may come another
time when I will speak about a nation that I
will build up and plant. 10But if I see it doing evil by not obeying me, I will change my
mind and not carry out my plans to do good
for them.

11"So, say this to the people of Judah and
those who live in Jerusalem: 'This is what
the LORD says: I am preparing disaster for
you and making plans against you. So stop
doing evil. Change your ways and do what is
right.' 12But the people of Judah will answer,
'It won't do any good to try! We will continue
to do what we want. Each of us will do what
his stubborn, evil heart wants!'"

13So this is what the LORD says:
"Ask the people in other nations this
      question:
   'Have you ever heard anything like
      this?'
   The people of Israel have done a
      horrible thing.
14 The snow on the mountains of Lebanon
      never melts from the rocks.
   Its cool, flowing streams
      do not dry up.
15 But my people have forgotten me.
      They burn incense to worthless idols
   and have stumbled in what they do
      and in the old ways of their
         ancestors.
   They walk along back roads
      and on poor highways.

16 So Judah's country will become an empty desert.

People will not stop making fun of it.
They will shake their heads as they pass by;
they will be shocked at how the country was destroyed.

17 Like a strong east wind,
I will scatter them before their enemies.
At that awful time they will not see me coming to help them;
they will see me leaving."

JEREMIAH'S FOURTH COMPLAINT

18 Then the people said, "Come, let's make plans against Jeremiah. Surely the teaching of the law by the priest will not be lost. We will still have the advice from the wise teachers and the words of the prophets. So let's ruin him by telling lies about him. We won't pay attention to anything he says."

19 LORD, listen to me.

Listen to what my accusers are saying!

20 Good should not be paid back with evil,
but they have dug a pit in order to kill me.

Remember that I stood before you
and asked you to do good things for these people
and to turn your anger away from them.

21 So now, let their children starve,
and let their enemies kill them with swords.

Let their wives lose their children and husbands.

Let the men from Judah be put to death
and the young men be killed with swords in battle.

22 Let them cry out in their houses
when you bring an enemy against them suddenly.

Let all this happen, because my enemies have dug
a pit to capture me and have hidden traps for my feet.

23 LORD, you know
about all their plans to kill me.

Don't forgive their crimes
or erase their sins from your mind.

Make them fall from their places;
punish them while you are angry.

JUDAH IS LIKE A BROKEN JAR

19 This is what the LORD said to me: "Go and buy a clay jar from a potter. 2 Take some of the elders of the people and the priests, and go out to the Valley of Ben Hinnom, near the front of the Potsherd Gate. There speak the words I tell you. 3 Say, 'Kings of Judah and people of Jerusalem, listen to this message from the LORD. This is what the LORD All-Powerful, the God of Israel, says: I will soon bring a disaster on this place that will amaze and frighten everyone who hears about it. 4 The people of Judah have quit following me. They have made this a place for foreign gods. They have burned sacrifices to other gods that neither they, nor their ancestors, nor the kings of Judah had ever known before. They filled this place with the blood of innocent people. 5 They have built places on hilltops to worship Baal, where they burn their children in the fire to Baal. That is something I did not command or speak about; it never even entered my mind. 6 Now people call this place the Valley of Ben Hinnom or Topheth, but the days are coming, says the LORD, when people will call it the Valley of Killing.

7 "'At this place I will ruin the plans of the people of Judah and Jerusalem. The enemy will chase them, and I will have them killed with swords. I will make their dead bodies food for the birds and wild animals. 8 I will completely destroy this city. People will make fun of it and shake their heads when they pass by. They will be shocked when they see how the city was destroyed. 9 An enemy army will surround the city and will not let anyone go out to get food. I will make the people so hungry that they will eat the bodies of their own sons and daughters, and then they will begin to eat each other.'

10 "While the people with you are watching, break that jar. 11 Then say this: 'The LORD All-Powerful says: I will break this nation and this city just as someone breaks a clay jar that cannot be put back together again. The dead people will be buried here in Topheth, because there is no other place for them. 12 This is what I will do to these people and to this place, says the LORD. I will make this city like Topheth. 13 The houses in Jerusalem and the king's palaces will become as unclean as this place, Topheth, because the

people worshiped gods on the roofs[n] of their houses. They worshiped the stars and burned incense to honor them and gave drink offerings to gods.'"

14When Jeremiah left Topheth where the LORD had sent him to prophesy, he went to the LORD's Temple, stood in the courtyard, and said to all the people: 15"This is what the LORD All-Powerful, the God of Israel, says: 'I will soon bring disaster to Jerusalem and the villages around it, as I said I would. This will happen because the people are very stubborn and do not listen at all to what I say.'"

PASHHUR WILL BE CAPTURED

20 Pashhur son of Immer was a priest and the highest officer in the Temple of the LORD. When he heard Jeremiah prophesying in the Temple courtyard, 2he had Jeremiah the prophet beaten. And he locked Jeremiah's hands and feet between large blocks of wood at the Upper Gate of Benjamin of the LORD's Temple. 3The next day when Pashhur took Jeremiah out of the blocks of wood, Jeremiah said to him, "The LORD's name for you is not Pashhur. Now his name for you is Terror on Every Side. 4This is what the LORD says: 'I will soon make you a terror to yourself and to all your friends. You will watch enemies killing your friends with swords. And I will give all the people of Judah to the king of Babylon, who will take them away as captives to Babylon and then will kill them with swords. 5I will give all the wealth of this city to its enemies—its goods, its valuables, and the treasures of the kings of Judah. The enemies will carry all those valuables off to Babylon. 6And Pashhur, you and everyone in your house will be taken captive. You will be forced to go to Babylon, where you will die and be buried, you and your friends to whom you have prophesied lies.'"

JEREMIAH'S FIFTH COMPLAINT

7 LORD, you tricked me, and I was fooled.
   You are stronger than I am, so you won.
I have become a joke;
   everyone makes fun of me all day long.
8 Every time I speak, I shout.
   I am always shouting about violence
      and destruction.
I tell the people about the message I
      received from the LORD,
   but this only brings me insults.

The people make fun of me all day long.
9 Sometimes I say to myself,
   "I will forget about the LORD.
   I will not speak anymore in his name."
But then his message becomes like a
      burning fire inside me,
   deep within my bones.
I get tired of trying to hold it inside of me,
   and finally, I cannot hold it in.
10 I hear many people whispering about me:
   "Terror on every side!
   Tell on him! Let's tell the rulers about
      him."
My friends are all just waiting for me to
      make some mistake.
   They are saying,
"Maybe we can trick him
   so we can defeat him
   and pay him back."

11 But the LORD is with me like a strong
      warrior,
   so those who are chasing me will trip
      and fall;
   they will not defeat me.
They will be ashamed because they have
      failed,
   and their shame will never be forgotten.

12 LORD All-Powerful, you test good people;
   you look deeply into the heart and mind
      of a person.
I have told you my arguments against
      these people,
   so let me see you give them the
      punishment they deserve.

13 Sing to the LORD!
   Praise the LORD!
He saves the life of the poor
   from the power of the wicked.

JEREMIAH'S SIXTH COMPLAINT

14 Let there be a curse on the day I was born;
   let there be no blessing on the day when
      my mother gave birth to me.
15 Let there be a curse on the man
   who brought my father the news:
"You have a son!"
   This made my father very glad.

19:13 roofs In Bible times houses were built with flat roofs. The roof was used for drying things such as flax and fruit. And it was used as an extra room, as a place for worship, and as a cool place to sleep in the summer.

[16] Let that man be like the towns
   the LORD destroyed without pity.
Let him hear loud crying in the morning
   and battle cries at noon,
[17] because he did not kill me before I was
      born.
Then my mother would have been my
      grave;
   she would have stayed pregnant forever.
[18] Why did I have to come out of my
      mother's body?
All I have known is trouble and sorrow,
   and my life will end in shame.

GOD REJECTS KING ZEDEKIAH'S REQUEST

21 This is the word that the LORD spoke to Jeremiah. It came when Zedekiah king of Judah sent Pashhur son of Malkijah and the priest Zephaniah son of Maaseiah to Jeremiah. [2]They said, "Ask the LORD for us what will happen, because Nebuchadnezzar king of Babylon is attacking us. Maybe the LORD will do miracles for us as he did in the past so Nebuchadnezzar will stop attacking us and leave."

[3]But Jeremiah answered them, "Tell King Zedekiah this: [4]'Here is what the LORD, the God of Israel, says: You have weapons of war in your hands to defend yourselves against the king of Babylon and the Babylonians, who are all around the city wall. But I will make those weapons useless. Soon I will bring them into the center of this city. [5]In my anger, my very great anger, I myself will fight against you with my great power and strength. [6]I will kill everything living in Jerusalem—both people and animals. They will die from terrible diseases. [7]Then, says the LORD, I'll hand over Zedekiah king of Judah, his officers, and the people in Jerusalem who do not die from the terrible diseases or battle or hunger, to Nebuchadnezzar king of Babylon. I will let those win who want to kill the people of Judah, so the people of Judah and Jerusalem will be killed in war. Nebuchadnezzar will not show any mercy or pity or feel sorry for them!'

[8]"Also tell this to the people of Jerusalem: 'This is what the LORD says: I will let you choose to live or die. [9]Anyone who stays in Jerusalem will die in war or from hunger or from a terrible disease. But anyone who goes out of Jerusalem and surrenders to the Babylonians who are attacking you will live. Anyone who leaves the city will save his life as if it were a prize won in war. [10]I have decided to make trouble for this city and not to help it, says the LORD. I will give it to the king of Babylon, and he will burn it with fire.'

[11]"Say to Judah's royal family: 'Hear the word of the LORD. [12]Family of David, this is what the LORD says:

You must judge people fairly every
      morning.
Save the person who has been robbed
   from the power of his attacker.
If you don't, I will become very angry.
   My anger will be like a fire that no one
      can put out,
because you have done evil things.

[13] "'Jerusalem, I am against you,
   you who live on top of the mountain
      over this valley, says the LORD.
You say, "No one can attack us
   or come into our strong city."
[14] But I will give you the punishment you
      deserve, says the LORD.
I will start a fire in your forests
   that will burn up everything around
      you!'"

JUDGMENT AGAINST EVIL KINGS

22 This is what the LORD says: "Go down to the palace of the king of Judah and prophesy this message there: [2]'Hear the word of the LORD, king of Judah, who rules from David's throne. You and your officers, and your people who come through these gates, listen! [3]This is what the LORD says: Do what is fair and right. Save the one who has been robbed from the power of his attacker. Don't mistreat or hurt the foreigners, orphans, or widows. Don't kill innocent people here. [4]If you carefully obey these commands, kings who sit on David's throne will come through the gates of this palace with their officers and people, riding in chariots and on horses. [5]But if you don't obey these commands, says the LORD, I swear by my own name that this king's palace will become a ruin.'

[6]This is what the LORD says about the palace where the king of Judah lives:

"You are tall like the forests of Gilead,
   like the mountaintops of Lebanon.
But I will truly make you into a desert,
   into towns where no one lives.

7 I will send men to destroy the palace,
  each with his weapons.
They will cut up your strong, beautiful
    cedar beams
  and throw them into the fire.

8"People from many nations will pass by this city and ask each other, 'Why has the LORD done such a terrible thing to Jerusalem, this great city?' 9And the answer will be: 'Because the people of Judah quit following the agreement with the LORD their God. They worshiped and served other gods.'"

JUDGMENT AGAINST JEHOAHAZ

10 Don't cry for the dead king or be sad
    about him.
  But cry painfully for the king who is
    being taken away,
because he will never return
  or see his homeland again.

11This is what the LORD says about Jehoahaz son of Josiah who became king of Judah after his father died and who has left this place: "He will never return. 12He will die where he has been taken captive, and he will not see this land again."

JUDGMENT AGAINST JEHOIAKIM

13 "How terrible it will be for one who
    builds his palace by doing evil,
  who cheats people so he can build its
    upper rooms.
He makes his own people work for
    nothing
  and does not pay them.
14 He says, 'I will build a great palace for
    myself
  with large upper rooms.'
So he builds it with large windows
  and uses cedar wood for the walls,
    which he paints red.

15 "Does having a lot of cedar in your house
    make you a great king?
  Your father was satisfied to have food and
    drink.
He did what was right and fair,
  so everything went well for him.
16 He helped those who were poor and
    needy,
  so everything went well for him.
That is what it means to know God,"
  says the LORD.
17 "But you only look for and think about

what you can get dishonestly.
You are even willing to kill innocent
    people to get it.
  You feel free to hurt people and to steal
    from them."

18So this is what the LORD says to Jehoiakim son of Josiah king of Judah:

"The people of Judah will not cry when
    Jehoiakim dies,
  saying: 'Oh, my brother,' or 'Oh, my
    sister.'
They will not cry for him, saying:
  'Oh, master,' or 'Oh, my king.'
19 They will bury him like a donkey,
    dragging his body away
  and throwing it outside the gates of
    Jerusalem.

20 "Judah, go up to Lebanon and cry out.
  Let your voice be heard in Bashan.
Cry out from Abarim,
  because all your friends are destroyed!
21 Judah, when you were successful, I
    warned you,
  but you said, 'I won't listen.'
You have acted like this since you were
    young;
  you have not obeyed me.
22 Like a storm, my punishment will blow all
    your shepherds away
  and send your friends into captivity.
Then you will really be ashamed and
    disgraced
  because of all the wicked things you
    did.
23 King, you live in your palace,
  cozy in your rooms of cedar.
But when your punishment comes, how
    you will groan
  like a woman giving birth to a baby!

JUDGMENT UPON JEHOIACHIN

24"As surely as I live," says the LORD, "Jehoiachin son of Jehoiakim king of Judah, even if you were a signet ring on my right hand, I would still pull you off. 25I will hand you over to Nebuchadnezzar king of Babylon and to the Babylonians—those people you fear because they want to kill you. 26I will throw you and your mother into another country. Neither of you was born there, but both of you will die there. 27They will want to come back, but they will never be able to return."

28 Jehoiachin is like a broken pot someone
threw away;
  he is like something no one wants.
Why will Jehoiachin and his children be
    thrown out
  and sent into a foreign land?
29 Land, land, land of Judah,
  hear the word of the LORD!
30 This is what the LORD says:
"Write this down in the record about
    Jehoiachin:
  He is a man without children,
  a man who will not be successful in his
    lifetime.
And none of his descendants will be
    successful;
  none will sit on the throne of David
  or rule in Judah."

THE EVIL LEADERS OF JUDAH

23 "How terrible it will be for the leaders of Judah, who are scattering and
destroying my people," says the LORD.
²They are responsible for the people, so
the LORD, the God of Israel, says to them:
"You have scattered my people and forced
them away and not taken care of them. So I
will punish you for the evil things you have
done," says the LORD. ³"I sent my people to
other countries, but I will gather those who
are left alive and bring them back to their
own country. Then they will have many children and grow in number. ⁴I will place new
leaders over my people, who will take care
of them. And my people will not be afraid
or terrified again, and none of them will be
lost," says the LORD.

THE GOOD BRANCH WILL COME

5 "The days are coming," says the LORD,
  "when I will raise up a good branch in
    David's family.
He will be a king who will rule in a wise
    way;
  he will do what is fair and right in the
    land.
6 In his time Judah will be saved,
  and Israel will live in safety.
This will be his name:
  The LORD Does What Is Right.
7"So the days are coming," says the LORD,
"when people will not say again: 'As surely
as the LORD lives, who brought Israel out
of Egypt…' ⁸But people will say something

new: 'As surely as the LORD lives, who brought
the descendants of Israel from the land of
the north and from all the countries where
he had sent them away…' Then the people
of Israel will live in their own land."

FALSE PROPHETS WILL BE PUNISHED

⁹A message to the prophets:
My heart is broken.
  All my bones shake.
I'm like someone who is drunk,
  like someone who has been overcome
    with wine.
This is because of the LORD
  and his holy words.
10 The land of Judah is full of people who
    are guilty of adultery.
  Because of this, the LORD cursed the
    land.
  It has become a very sad place,
  and the pastures have dried up.
The people are evil
  and use their power in the wrong way.

11 "Both the prophets and the priests live as
    if there were no God.
  I have found them doing evil things
    even in my own Temple," says the
    LORD.
12 "So they will be in danger.
  They will be forced into darkness
  where they will be defeated.
I will bring disaster on them
  in the year I punish them," says the
    LORD.

13 "I saw the prophets of Samaria
  do something wrong.
Those prophets prophesied by Baal
  and led my people Israel away.
14 And I have seen the prophets of
    Jerusalem
  do terrible things.
They are guilty of adultery
  and live by lies.
They encourage evil people to keep on
    doing evil,
  so the people don't stop sinning.
All of those people are like the city of
    Sodom.
  The people of Jerusalem are like the
    city of Gomorrah to me!"
15So this is what the LORD All-Powerful
says about the prophets:

"I will make those prophets eat bitter
food
and drink poisoned water,
because the prophets of Jerusalem spread
wickedness
through the whole country."
¹⁶This is what the LORD All-Powerful
says:
"Don't pay attention to what those
prophets are saying to you.
They are trying to fool you.
They talk about visions their own minds
made up,
not about visions from me.
¹⁷ They say to those who hate me:
'The LORD says: You will have peace.'

They say to all those who are stubborn
and do as they please:
'Nothing bad will happen to you.'
¹⁸ But none of these prophets has stood in
the meeting of angels
to see or hear the message of the LORD.
None of them has paid close attention
to his message.
¹⁹ Look, the punishment from the LORD
will come like a storm.
His anger will be like a hurricane.
It will come swirling down on the heads
of those wicked people.
²⁰ The LORD's anger will not stop
until he finishes what he plans to do.
When that day is over,

FAITH

HAVE FAITH IN GOD

how close
is he?

JEREMIA 23:24

Faith is the process of putting into action what we trust about God's character. Faith makes real what the heart believes to be true. Faith certainly isn't blind. You can't commit yourself wholeheartedly to something you don't believe is the truth. Ultimately, faith comes down to trust. The better I know someone, the more confidence I will have that he or she really is who I think that person to be. Unfortunately, we know human beings well enough to know that sometimes the more we know, the less we are able to trust.

But have you ever thought about it from God's perspective?

This verse tells us that God knows *everything* about us, right down to the smallest detail. God is never in doubt about who we are or what we can do. Yet, here's the amazing conclusion: God knows things about us that no one else knows, and he *still* trusts us to follow him. He still loves us. He still invites us to join his family. He still seeks after us. What an incredible God he is! Who could imagine such trust among mere mortals? God knows *everything*, and he still wants to be with us. That should give us reason for a great sigh of relief—and a great song of thanksgiving.

reflect: Praise God for knowing all about you and loving you just the same.
Go to **Proverbs 3:21**.

you will understand this clearly.
²¹ I did not send those prophets,
    but they ran to tell their message.
I did not speak to them,
    but they prophesied anyway.
²² But if they had stood in the meeting of
    angels,
    they would have told my message to my
    people.
They would have turned the people from
    their evil ways
    and from doing evil.

²³ "I am a God who is near," says the LORD.
    "I am also a God who is far away.
²⁴ No one can hide
    where I cannot see him," says the LORD.
    "I fill all of heaven and earth," says the
    LORD.

²⁵"I have heard the prophets who prophesy lies in my name. They say, 'I have had a dream! I have had a dream!' ²⁶How long will this continue in the minds of these lying prophets? They prophesy from their own wishful thinking. ²⁷They are trying to make the people of Judah forget me by telling each other these dreams. In the same way, their ancestors forgot me and worshiped Baal. ²⁸Is straw the same thing as wheat?" says the LORD. "If a prophet wants to tell about his dreams, let him! But let the person who hears my message speak it truthfully! ²⁹Isn't my message like a fire?" says the LORD. "Isn't it like a hammer that smashes a rock?

³⁰"So I am against the false prophets," says the LORD. "They keep stealing words from each other and say they are from me. ³¹I am against the false prophets," says the LORD. "They use their own words and pretend it is a message from me. ³²I am against the prophets who prophesy false dreams," says the LORD. "They mislead my people with their lies and false teachings! I did not send them or command them to do anything for me. They can't help the people of Judah at all," says the LORD.

THE SAD MESSAGE FROM THE LORD

³³"Suppose the people of Judah, a prophet, or a priest asks you: 'Jeremiah, what is the message from the LORD?' You will answer them and say, 'You are a heavy load to the LORD, and I will throw you down, says the LORD.' ³⁴A prophet or a priest or one of

the people might say, 'This is a message from the LORD.' That person has lied, so I will punish him and his whole family. ³⁵This is what you will say to each other: 'What did the LORD answer?' or 'What did the LORD say?' ³⁶But you will never again say, 'The message of the LORD,' because the only message you speak is your own words. You have changed the words of our God, the living God, the LORD All-Powerful. ³⁷This is how you should speak to the prophets: 'What answer did the LORD give you?' or 'What did the LORD say?' ³⁸But don't say, 'The message from the LORD.' If you use these words, this is what the LORD says: Because you called it a 'message from the LORD,' though I told you not to use those words, ³⁹I will pick you up and throw you away from me, along with Jerusalem, which I gave to your ancestors and to you. ⁴⁰And I will make a disgrace of you forever; your shame will never be forgotten."

THE GOOD AND BAD FIGS

24 Nebuchadnezzar king of Babylon captured Jehoiachin son of Jehoiakim and king of Judah, his officers, and all the craftsmen and metalworkers of Judah. He took them away from Jerusalem and brought them to Babylon. It was then that the LORD showed me two baskets of figs arranged in front of the Temple of the LORD. ²One of the baskets had very good figs in it, like figs that ripen early in the season. But the other basket had figs too rotten to eat.

³The LORD said to me, "What do you see, Jeremiah?"

I answered, "I see figs. The good figs are very good, but the rotten figs are too rotten to eat."

⁴Then the LORD spoke his word to me: ⁵"This is what the LORD, the God of Israel, says: 'I sent the people of Judah out of their country to live in the country of Babylon. I think of those people as good, like these good figs. ⁶I will look after them and bring them back to the land of Judah. I will not tear them down, but I will build them up. I will not pull them up, but I will plant them so they can grow. ⁷I will make them want to know me, that I am the LORD. They will be my people, and I will be their God, because they will return to me with their whole hearts.

⁸"But the bad figs are too rotten to eat.'

So this is what the LORD says: 'Zedekiah king of Judah, his officers, and all the people from Jerusalem who are left alive, even those who live in Egypt, will be like those rotten figs. ⁹I will make those people hated as an evil people by all the kingdoms of the earth. People will make fun of them and tell jokes about them and point fingers at them and curse them everywhere I scatter them. ¹⁰I will send war, hunger, and disease against them. I will attack them until they have all been killed. Then they will no longer be in the land I gave to them and their ancestors.'"

A SUMMARY OF JEREMIAH'S PREACHING

25 This is the message that came to Jeremiah concerning all the people of Judah. It came in the fourth year that Jehoiakim son of Josiah was king of Judah and the first year Nebuchadnezzar was king of Babylon. ²This is the message Jeremiah the prophet spoke to all the people of Judah and Jerusalem:

³The LORD has spoken his word to me again and again for these past twenty-three years. I have been a prophet since the thirteenth year of Josiah son of Amon king of Judah. I have spoken messages from the LORD to you from that time until today, but you have not listened.

⁴The LORD has sent all his servants the prophets to you over and over again, but you have not listened or paid any attention to them. ⁵Those prophets have said, "Stop your evil ways. Stop doing what is wrong so you can stay in the land that the LORD gave to you and your ancestors to live in forever. ⁶Don't follow other gods to serve them or to worship them. Don't make me, the LORD, angry by worshiping idols that are the work of your own hands, or I will punish you."

⁷"But you people of Judah did not listen to me," says the LORD. "You made me angry by worshiping idols that were the work of your own hands, so I punished you."

⁸So this is what the LORD All-Powerful says: "Since you have not listened to my messages, ⁹I will send for all the peoples of the north," says the LORD, "along with my servant Nebuchadnezzar king of Babylon. I will bring them all against Judah, those who live there, and all the nations around you, too. I will completely destroy all those countries and leave them in ruins forever. People will be shocked when they see how badly I have destroyed those countries. ¹⁰I will bring an end to the sounds of joy and happiness, the sounds of brides and bridegrooms, and the sound of people grinding meal. And I will take away the light of the lamp. ¹¹That whole area will be an empty desert, and these nations will be slaves of the king of Babylon for seventy years.

¹²"But when the seventy years have passed, I will punish the king of Babylon and his entire nation for their evil," says the LORD. "I will make that land a desert forever. ¹³I will make happen all the terrible things I said about Babylonia—everything Jeremiah prophesied about all those foreign nations, the warnings written in this book. ¹⁴Even the Babylonians will have to serve many nations and many great kings. I will give them the punishment they deserve for all their own hands have done."

JUDGMENT ON THE NATIONS

¹⁵The LORD, the God of Israel, said this to me: "My anger is like the wine in a cup. Take it from my hand and make all the nations, to whom I am sending you, drink all of my anger from this cup. ¹⁶They will drink my anger and stumble about and act like madmen because of the war I am going to send among them."

¹⁷So I took the cup from the LORD's hand and went to those nations and made them drink from it. ¹⁸I served this wine to the people of Jerusalem and the towns of Judah, and the kings and officers of Judah, so they would become a ruin. Then people would be shocked and would insult them and speak evil of them. And so it has been to this day. ¹⁹I also made these people drink of the LORD's anger: the king of Egypt, his servants, his officers, all his people, ²⁰and all the foreigners there; all the kings of the land of Uz; all the kings of the Philistines (the kings of the cities of Ashkelon, Gaza, Ekron, and the people left at Ashdod); ²¹the people of Edom, Moab, and Ammon; ²²all the kings of Tyre and Sidon; all the kings of the coastal countries to the west; ²³the people of Dedan and Tema and Buz; all who cut their hair short; ²⁴all the kings of Arabia; and the kings of the people who live in the desert; ²⁵all the

kings of Zimri, Elam, and Media; 26and all the kings of the north, near and far, one after the other. I made all the kingdoms on earth drink from the cup of the LORD's anger, but the king of Babylon will drink from this cup after all the others.

27"Then say to them, 'This is what the LORD All-Powerful, the God of Israel, says: Drink this cup of my anger. Get drunk from it and vomit. Fall down and don't get up because of the war I am sending among you!'

28"If they refuse to take the cup from your hand and drink, say to them, 'The LORD All-Powerful says this: You must drink from this cup. 29Look! I am already bringing disaster on Jerusalem, the city that is called by my name. Do you think you will not be punished? You will be punished! I am sending war on all the people of the earth, says the LORD All-Powerful.'

30"You, Jeremiah, will prophesy against them with all these words. Say to them:

'The LORD will roar from heaven
    and will shout from his Holy Temple.
He will roar loudly against his land.
He will shout like people who walk on
        grapes to make wine;
    he will shout against all who live on the
        earth.
31 The noise will spread all over the earth,
    because the LORD will accuse all the
        nations.
He will judge and tell what is wrong with
        all people,
    and he will kill the evil people with a
        sword,'" says the LORD.

32This is what the LORD All-Powerful says:

"Disasters will soon spread
    from nation to nation.
They will come like a powerful storm
    from the faraway places on earth."

33At that time those killed by the LORD will reach from one end of the earth to the other. No one will cry for them or gather up their bodies and bury them. They will be left lying on the ground like dung.

34 Cry, you leaders! Cry out loud!
    Roll around in the dust, leaders of the
        people!
It is now time for you to be killed.
    You will fall and be scattered,
        like pieces of a broken jar.

35 There will be no place for the leaders to
        hide;
    they will not escape.
36 I hear the sound of the leaders shouting.
    I hear the leaders of the people crying
        loudly,
    because the LORD is destroying their
        land.
37 Those peaceful pastures will be like an
        empty desert,
    because the LORD is very angry.
38 Like a lion, he has left his den.
    Their land has been destroyed
because of the terrible war he brought,
    because of his fierce anger.

JEREMIAH'S LESSON AT THE TEMPLE

26 This message came from the LORD soon after Jehoiakim son of Josiah became king of Judah. 2This is what the LORD said: "Jeremiah, stand in the courtyard of the Temple of the LORD. Give this message to all the people of the towns of Judah who are coming to worship at the Temple of the LORD. Tell them everything I tell you to say; don't leave out a word. 3Maybe they will listen and stop their evil ways. If they will, I will change my mind about bringing on them the disaster that I am planning because of the evil they have done. 4Say to them: 'This is what the LORD says: You must obey me and follow my teachings that I gave you. 5You must listen to what my servants the prophets say to you. I have sent them to you again and again, but you did not listen. 6If you don't obey me, I will destroy my Temple in Jerusalem as I destroyed my Holy Tent at Shiloh. When I do, people all over the world will curse Jerusalem.'"

7The priests, the prophets, and all the people heard Jeremiah speaking these words in the Temple of the LORD. 8When Jeremiah finished speaking everything the LORD had commanded him to say, the priests, prophets, and all the people grabbed Jeremiah. They said, "You must die! 9How dare you prophesy in the name of the LORD that this Temple will be destroyed like the one at Shiloh! How dare you say that Jerusalem will become a desert without anyone to live in it!" And all the people crowded around Jeremiah in the Temple of the LORD.

10Now when the officers of Judah heard

about what was happening, they came out of the king's palace and went up to the Temple of the LORD and took their places at the entrance of the New Gate. ¹¹Then the priests and prophets said to the officers and all the other people, "Jeremiah should be killed. He prophesied against Jerusalem, and you heard him yourselves."

¹²Then Jeremiah spoke these words to all the officers of Judah and all the other people: "The LORD sent me to say everything you have heard about this Temple and this city. ¹³Now change your lives and start doing good and obey the LORD your God. Then he will change his mind and not bring on you the disaster he has told you about. ¹⁴As for me, I am in your power. Do to me what you think is good and right. ¹⁵But be sure of one thing. If you kill me, you will be guilty of killing an innocent person. You will make this city and everyone who lives in it guilty, too! The LORD truly sent me to you to give you this message."

¹⁶Then the officers and all the people said to the priests and the prophets, "Jeremiah must not be killed. What he told us comes from the LORD our God."

¹⁷Then some of the elders of Judah stood up and said to all the people, ¹⁸"Micah, from the city of Moresheth, was a prophet during the time Hezekiah was king of Judah. Micah said to all the people of Judah, 'This is what the LORD All-Powerful says:

Jerusalem will be plowed like a field.
  It will become a pile of rocks,
  and the hill where the Temple stands
    will be covered with bushes.'

¹⁹"Hezekiah king of Judah and the people of Judah did not kill Micah. You know that Hezekiah feared the LORD and tried to please the LORD. So the LORD changed his mind and did not bring on Judah the disaster he had promised. If we hurt Jeremiah, we will bring a terrible disaster on ourselves!"

²⁰(Now there was another man who prophesied in the name of the LORD. His name was Uriah son of Shemaiah from the city of Kiriath Jearim. He preached the same things against Jerusalem and the land of Judah that Jeremiah did. ²¹When King Jehoiakim, all his army officers, and all the leaders of Judah heard Uriah preach, King Jehoiakim wanted to kill Uriah. But Uriah heard about it and was afraid. So he escaped to Egypt. ²²Then King Jehoiakim sent Elnathan son of Acbor and some other men to Egypt, ²³and they brought Uriah back from Egypt. Then they took him to King Jehoiakim, who had Uriah killed with a sword. His body was thrown into the burial place where poor people are buried.)

²⁴Ahikam son of Shaphan supported Jeremiah. So Ahikam did not hand Jeremiah over to be killed by the people.

NEBUCHADNEZZAR IS MADE RULER

27 The LORD spoke his word to Jeremiah soon after Zedekiah son of Josiah was made king of Judah. ²This is what the LORD said to me: "Make a yoke out of straps and poles, and put it on the back of your neck. ³Then send messages to the kings of Edom, Moab, Ammon, Tyre, and Sidon by their messengers who have come to Jerusalem to see Zedekiah king of Judah. ⁴Tell them to give this message to their masters: 'The LORD All-Powerful, the God of Israel, says: "Tell your masters: ⁵I made the earth, its people, and all its animals with my great power and strength. I can give the earth to anyone I want. ⁶Now I have given all these lands to Nebuchadnezzar king of Babylon, my servant. I will make even the wild animals obey him. ⁷All nations will serve Nebuchadnezzar and his son and grandson. Then the time will come for Babylon to be defeated, and many nations and great kings will make Babylon their servant.

⁸"'"But if some nations or kingdoms refuse to serve Nebuchadnezzar king of Babylon and refuse to be under his control, I will punish them with war, hunger, and terrible diseases, says the LORD. I will use Nebuchadnezzar to destroy them. ⁹So don't listen to your false prophets, those who use magic to tell the future, those who explain dreams, the mediums, or magicians. They all tell you, 'You will not be slaves to the king of Babylon.' ¹⁰They are telling you lies that will cause you to be taken far from your homeland. I will force you to leave your homes, and you will die in another land. ¹¹But the nations who put themselves under the control of the king of Babylon and serve him I will let stay in their own country, says the LORD. The people from those nations will live in their own land and farm it."'"

12I gave the same message to Zedekiah king of Judah. I said, "Put yourself under the control of the king of Babylon and serve him, and you will live. 13Why should you and your people die from war, hunger, or disease, as the LORD said would happen to those who do not serve the king of Babylon? 14But the false prophets are saying, 'You will never be slaves to the king of Babylon.' Don't listen to them because they are prophesying lies to you! 15'I did not send them,' says the LORD. 'They are prophesying lies and saying the message is from me. So I will send you away, Judah. And you and those prophets who prophesy to you will die.'"

16Then I, Jeremiah, said to the priests and all the people, "This is what the LORD says: Those false prophets are saying, 'The Babylonians will soon return what they took from the Temple of the LORD.' Don't listen to them! They are prophesying lies to you. 17Don't listen to those prophets. But serve the king of Babylon, and you will live. There is no reason for you to cause Jerusalem to become a ruin. 18If they are prophets and have the message from the LORD, let them pray to the LORD All-Powerful. Let them ask that the items which are still in the Temple of the LORD and in the king's palace and in Jerusalem not be taken away to Babylon.

19"This is what the LORD All-Powerful says about those items left in Jerusalem: the pillars, the large bronze bowl, which is called the Sea, the stands that can be moved, and other things. 20Nebuchadnezzar king of Babylon did not take these away when he took as captives Jehoiachin son of Jehoiakim king of Judah and all the other important people from Judah and Jerusalem to Babylon. 21This is what the LORD All-Powerful, the God of Israel, says about the items left in the Temple of the LORD and in the king's palace and in Jerusalem: 22'All of them will also be taken to Babylon. And they will stay there until the day I go to get them,' says the LORD. 'Then I will bring them back and return them to this place.'"

THE FALSE PROPHET HANANIAH

28 It was in that same year, in the fifth month of Zedekiah's fourth year as king of Judah, soon after he began to rule. The prophet Hananiah son of Azzur, from the town of Gibeon, spoke to me in the Temple of the LORD in front of the priests and all the people. He said: 2"The LORD All-Powerful, the God of Israel, says: 'I have broken the yoke the king of Babylon has put on Judah. 3Before two years are over, I will bring back everything that Nebuchadnezzar king of Babylon took to Babylon from the LORD's Temple. 4I will also bring back Jehoiachin son of Jehoiakim king of Judah and all the other captives from Judah who went to Babylon,' says the LORD. 'So I will break the yoke the king of Babylon put on Judah.'"

5Then the prophet Jeremiah spoke to the prophet Hananiah in front of the priests and all the people who were standing in the Temple of the LORD. 6He said, "Amen! Let the LORD really do that! May the LORD make the message you prophesy come true. May he bring back here everything from the LORD's Temple and all the people who were taken as captives to Babylon.

7"But listen to what I am going to say to you and all the people. 8There were prophets long before we became prophets, Hananiah. They prophesied that war, hunger, and terrible diseases would come to many countries and great kingdoms. 9But if a prophet prophesies that we will have peace and that message comes true, he can be recognized as one truly sent by the LORD."

10Then the prophet Hananiah took the yoke off Jeremiah's neck and broke it. 11Hananiah said in front of all the people, "This is what the LORD says: 'In the same way I will break the yoke of Nebuchadnezzar king of Babylon. He put that yoke on all the nations of the world, but I will break it before two years are over.'" After Hananiah had said that, Jeremiah left the Temple.

12The LORD spoke his word to Jeremiah after the prophet Hananiah had broken the yoke off of the prophet Jeremiah's neck. 13The LORD said, "Go and tell Hananiah, 'This is what the LORD says: You have broken a wooden yoke, but I will make a yoke of iron in its place! 14The LORD All-Powerful, the God of Israel, says: I will put a yoke of iron on the necks of all these nations to make them serve Nebuchadnezzar king of Babylon, and they will be slaves to him. I will even give Nebuchadnezzar control over the wild animals.'"

¹⁵Then the prophet Jeremiah said to the prophet Hananiah, "Listen, Hananiah! The LORD did not send you, and you have made the people of Judah trust in lies. ¹⁶So this is what the LORD says: 'Soon I will remove you from the earth. You will die this year, because you taught the people to turn against the LORD.'"

¹⁷Hananiah died in the seventh month of that same year.

A LETTER TO THE CAPTIVES IN BABYLON

29 This is the letter that Jeremiah the prophet sent from Jerusalem to the elders who were among the captives, the priests, and the prophets. He sent it to all the other people Nebuchadnezzar had taken as captives from Jerusalem to Babylon. ²(This letter was sent after all these people were taken away: Jehoiachin the king and the queen mother; the officers and leaders of Judah and Jerusalem; and the craftsmen and metalworkers from Jerusalem.) ³Zedekiah king of Judah sent Elasah son of Shaphan and Gemariah son of Hilkiah to Babylon to Nebuchadnezzar king of Babylon. So Jeremiah gave them this letter to carry to Babylon:

⁴This is what the LORD All-Powerful, the God of Israel, says to all those people I sent away from Jerusalem as captives to Babylon: ⁵"Build houses and settle in the land. Plant gardens and eat the food they grow. ⁶Get married and have sons and daughters. Find wives for your sons, and let your daughters be married so they also may have sons and daughters. Have many children in Babylon; don't become fewer in number. ⁷Also do good things for the city where I sent you as captives. Pray to the LORD for the city where you are living, because if good things happen in the city, good things will happen to you also." ⁸The LORD All-Powerful, the God of Israel, says: "Don't let the prophets among you and the people who do magic fool you. Don't listen to their dreams. ⁹They are prophesying lies to you, saying that their message is from me. But I did not send them," says the LORD.

¹⁰This is what the LORD says: "Babylon will be powerful for seventy years. After that time I will come to you, and I will keep my promise to bring you back to Je-

rusalem. ¹¹I say this because I know what I am planning for you," says the LORD. "I have good plans for you, not plans to hurt you. I will give you hope and a good future. ¹²Then you will call my name. You will come to me and pray to me, and I will listen to you. ¹³You will search for me. And when you search for me with all your heart, you will find me! ¹⁴I will let you find me," says the LORD. "And I will bring you back from your captivity. I forced you to leave this place, but I will gather you from all the nations, from the places I have sent you as captives," says the LORD. "And I will bring you back to this place."

¹⁵You might say, "The LORD has given us prophets here in Babylon."

¹⁶But the LORD says this about the king who is sitting on David's throne now and all the other people still in Jerusalem, your relatives who did not go as captives to Babylon with you. ¹⁷The LORD All-Powerful says: "I will soon send war, hunger, and terrible diseases against those still in Jerusalem. I will make them like bad figs that are too rotten to eat. ¹⁸I will chase them with war, hunger, and terrible diseases. I will make them hated by all the kingdoms of the earth. People will curse them and be shocked and will use them as a shameful example wherever I make them go. ¹⁹This is because they have not listened to my message," says the LORD. "I sent my message to them again and again through my servants, the prophets, but they did not listen," says the LORD.

²⁰You captives, whom I forced to leave Jerusalem and go to Babylon, listen to the message from the LORD. ²¹The LORD All-Powerful, the God of Israel, says this about Ahab son of Kolaiah and Zedekiah son of Maaseiah: "These two men have been prophesying lies to you, saying that their message is from me. But soon I will hand over those two prophets to Nebuchadnezzar king of Babylon, and he will kill them in front of you. ²²Because of them, all the captives from Judah in Babylon will use this curse: 'May the LORD treat you like Zedekiah and Ahab, whom the king of Babylon burned in the fire.' ²³They have done evil things among the people of Israel. They are guilty of adultery with their

The Life You Were Born **to Live**

FITNESS

By Dr. Ben Lerner

JEREMIAH 29:11

According to common beliefs in genetics, God has a plan to give you hope and a future only if you've chosen your grandparents carefully. The popular belief is that if you have bad genetics, you are cursed. The fact is, however, that even science now agrees with the discovery that, despite your genes, there is hope and a future for you.

In a study called *Balancing Life-style and Genomics Research for Disease Prevention*, Dr. W. C. Willet reveals that only 5 percent of all cancer and heart disease comes from hereditary factors. The rest comes from lifestyle . . . how we think, live, and eat. When it comes to cellular success, it's nurture and not nature that makes the biggest difference.

The vast majority of diseases we face aren't due to our poor DNA. Single gene disorders affect less than 2 percent of the population. That means that 95 percent to 98 percent of us are born with the ability to live with outrageous health and incredible happiness. Mostly, we're born with hope and a future.

These new discoveries show us that there is an ongoing creative power in our life and we are not "fated" at birth to feel a certain way, act a certain way, behave a certain way, and die a certain way at a certain time. The diseases, sicknesses, aches, and pains we face today are not as a result of dysfunctional grandparents, but because we've lived and thought in such a way that created disharmony in our bodies.

It's your environment and not your genes that make the difference. If your lifestyle lines up with God's plan for your body and you provide a healthy environment for your cells, they will thrive. Get off of the plan and the cells will falter. By the grace of God, if you've been causing your cells to suffer in a less than advantageous environment and they have become sick, you can improve that environment so that they can become well again. It's a plan with hope and a future.

TO LEARN MORE ON WHAT THE BIBLE HAS TO SAY ABOUT **FITNESS,** READ THE SCRIPTURES AND DEVOTIONALS AT **MARK 14:3–9, PSALM 139:14, PROVERBS 3:1–2, PROVERBS 12:25, PROVERBS 17:22, PROVERBS 22:6,** AND **ECCLESIASTES 3:1.**

neighbors' wives. They have also spoken lies and said those lies were a message from me. I did not tell them to do that. I know what they have done; I am a witness to it," says the LORD.

²⁴Also give a message to Shemaiah from the Nehelamite family. ²⁵The LORD All-Powerful, the God of Israel, says: "Shemaiah, you sent letters in your name to all the people in Jerusalem, to the priest Zephaniah son of Maaseiah, and to all the priests. ²⁶You said to Zephaniah, 'The LORD has made you priest

in place of Jehoiada. You are to be in charge of the Temple of the LORD. You should arrest any madman who acts like a prophet. Lock his hands and feet between wooden blocks, and put iron rings around his neck. ²⁷Now Jeremiah from Anathoth is acting like a prophet. So why haven't you arrested him? ²⁸Jeremiah has sent this message to us in Babylon: You will be there for a long time, so build houses and settle down. Plant gardens and eat what they grow.' "

²⁹Zephaniah the priest read the letter

INSPIRE YOUR TEAM TO REALIZE THE DREAM

FUTURE

how about a comeback?

JEREMIAH 29:14

I'm a sucker for a Cinderella story. I've got the original *Rocky* movie poster hanging in front of my treadmill at home. I love it because of the motivational saying, "His whole life was a million-to-one shot." Did you ever feel like that? Like all of the odds have been or still are against you. As a kid, maybe it was the family you came from, the place you lived, or the grades you got. Or as an adult, maybe you've lost money, faced rejection, experienced divorce, become overweight, gotten depressed, or suffered alienation.

Rocky said, "If when that bell rings at the end of the fifteenth round and I'm still standing, for the first time in my life, I'll be a somebody." He didn't know if he could do it, but he was willing to go for it. Once there, he called on all his past pain, all his unmet desires, and all his hopelessness and, rather than letting those emotions block him as they had in the past, he used them to discover newfound hope, access deep resources, and go the distance.

Rocky's life wasn't a "million-to-one shot" because of his circumstances or abilities; it was because only one in a million people will ever believe enough in God's plan to go for it and reach their potential. As the old saying goes, "It's not the size of the dog in the fight, but the size of the fight in the dog." Don't you think it's about time for your comeback?

reflect: What step can you take today toward your comeback?
Go to **FUTURE:** "God's Purpose for Your Life" at **Joshua 1:1-9.**

to Jeremiah the prophet. ³⁰Then the LORD spoke his word to Jeremiah: ³¹"Send this message to all the captives in Babylon: 'This is what the LORD says about Shemaiah the Nehelamite: Shemaiah has prophesied to you, but I did not send him. He has made you believe a lie. ³²So the LORD says, I will soon punish Shemaiah the Nehelamite and his family. He will not see the good things I will do for my people, says the LORD. None of his family will be left alive among the people, because he has taught the people to turn against me.'"

PROMISES OF HOPE

30 These are the words that the LORD spoke to Jeremiah. ²The LORD, the God of Israel, said: "Jeremiah, write in a book all the words I have spoken to you. ³The days will come when I will bring Israel and Judah back from captivity," says the LORD. "I will return them to the land I gave their ancestors, and they will own it!" says the LORD.

⁴The LORD spoke this message about the people of Israel and Judah: ⁵This is what the LORD said:

"We hear people crying from fear.
    They are afraid; there is no peace.
⁶ Ask this question, and consider it:
    A man cannot have a baby.
So why do I see every strong man
    holding his stomach in pain like a
    woman having a baby?
    Why is everyone's face turning white
    like a dead man's face?
⁷ This will be a terrible day!
    There will never be another time like
    this.
This is a time of great trouble for the
    people of Jacob,
    but they will be saved from it."

⁸ The LORD All-Powerful says, "At that
    time
    I will break the yoke from their necks
and tear off the ropes that hold them.
    Foreign people will never again make
    my people slaves.
⁹ They will serve the LORD their God
    and David their king,
    whom I will send to them.

¹⁰ "So people of Jacob, my servants, don't be
    afraid.

Israel, don't be frightened," says the
    LORD.
"I will soon save you from that faraway
    place where you are captives.
    I will save your family from that land.
The people of Jacob will be safe and have
    peace again;
    there will be no enemy to frighten
    them.
¹¹ I am with you and will save you,"
    says the LORD.
"I will completely destroy all those
    nations
    where I scattered you,
    but I will not completely destroy you.
I will punish you fairly,
    but I will still punish you."
¹²This is what the LORD said:
"You people have a wound that cannot be
    cured;
    your injury will not heal.
¹³ There is no one to argue your case
    and no cure for your sores.
    So you will not be healed.
¹⁴ All those nations who were your friends
    have forgotten you.
    They don't care about you.
I have hurt you as an enemy would.
    I punished you very hard,
because your guilt was so great
    and your sins were so many.
¹⁵ Why are you crying out about your injury?
    There is no cure for your pain.
I did these things to you because of your
    great guilt,
    because of your many sins.
¹⁶ But all those nations that destroyed you
    will now be destroyed.
    All your enemies will become captives
    in other lands.
Those who stole from you will have their
    own things stolen.
    Those who took things from you in war
    will have their own things taken.
¹⁷ I will bring back your health
    and heal your injuries," says the LORD,
"because other people forced you away.
    They said about you, 'No one cares
    about Jerusalem!'"
¹⁸This is what the LORD said:
"I will soon make the tents of Jacob's
    people as they used to be,
    and I will have pity on Israel's houses.

The city will be rebuilt on its hill of ruins,
and the king's palace will stand in its
proper place.
19 People in those places will sing songs of
praise.
There will be the sound of laughter.
I will give them many children
so their number will not be small.
I will bring honor to them
so no one will look down on them.
20 Their descendants will be as they were in
the old days.
I will set them up as a strong people
before me,
and I will punish the nations who have
hurt them.
21 One of their own people will lead them;
their ruler will come from among them.
He will come near to me when I invite
him.
Who would dare to come to me
uninvited?" says the LORD.
22 "So you will be my people,
and I will be your God."

23 Look! It is a storm from the LORD!
He is angry and has gone out to punish
the people.
Punishment will come like a storm
crashing down on the evil people.
24 The LORD will stay angry
until he finishes punishing the people.
He will stay angry
until he finishes the punishment he
planned.
When that day comes,
you will understand this.

THE NEW ISRAEL

31 The LORD says, "At that time I will be
God of all Israel's family groups, and
they will be my people."
2 This is what the LORD says:
"The people who were not killed by the
enemy's sword
found help in the desert.
I came to give rest to Israel."
3 And from far away the LORD appeared to
his people and said,
"I love you people
with a love that will last forever.
That is why I have continued
showing you kindness.
4 People of Israel, I will build you up again,

and you will be rebuilt.
You will pick up your tambourines again
and dance with those who are joyful.
5 You will plant vineyards again
on the hills around Samaria.
The farmers will plant them
and enjoy their fruit.
6 There will be a time when watchmen in
the mountains of Ephraim shout this
message:
'Come, let's go up to Jerusalem to
worship the LORD our God!'"
7 This is what the LORD says:
"Be happy and sing for the people of
Jacob.
Shout for Israel, the greatest of the
nations.
Sing your praises and shout this:
'LORD, save your people,
those who are left alive from the nation
of Israel!'
8 Look, I will soon bring Israel from the
country in the north,
and I will gather them from the faraway
places on earth.
Some of the people are blind and crippled.
Some of the women are pregnant, and
some are ready to give birth.
A great many people will come back.
9 They will be crying as they come,
but they will pray as I bring them back.
I will lead those people by streams of
water
on an even road where they will not
stumble.
I am Israel's father,
and Israel is my firstborn son.

10 "Nations, listen to the message from the
LORD.
Tell this message in the faraway lands
by the sea:
'The one who scattered the people of
Israel will bring them back,
and he will watch over his people like a
shepherd.'
11 The LORD will pay for the people of
Jacob
and will buy them back from people
stronger than they were.
12 The people of Israel will come to the high
points of Jerusalem
and shout for joy.

Their faces will shine with happiness
about all the good things from the
LORD:
the grain, new wine, oil, young sheep,
and young cows.
They will be like a garden that has plenty
of water,
and they will not be troubled anymore.
13 Then young women of Israel will be
happy and dance,
the young men and old men also.
I will change their sadness into
happiness;

I will give them comfort and joy instead
of sadness.
14 The priests will have more than enough
sacrifices,
and my people will be filled with the
good things I give them!" says the
LORD.
15 This is what the LORD says:
"A voice was heard in Ramah
of painful crying and deep sadness:
Rachel crying for her children.
She refused to be comforted,
because her children are dead!"

DO YOU KNOW HIM?

the longest time

FULFILLMENT

JEREMIAH 31:3

The Hebrew concept of time seems quite strange to us. While "lasts forever" means "the indefinite future" in more than three hundred occurrences, it also can mean "a particular point in the distant past" (twenty occurrences). As if that were not confusing enough, the word is also translated as "since" and "until." No matter which *direction* the temporal idea points toward, one thing is common. It is a long period; even longer than most lifetimes can imagine.

This is the sense of the passage in Jeremiah. God's love lasts a long, long time. This word tells us that his love extends to the very limits of human history. And it also extends to the very limits of the future of humanity. It embraces all of what we know or will know about God's interaction with humanity. It is a love that "never fails."

But there is a theological sense that extends this word beyond even these limits. The Bible tells us that the motive behind all of God's creative actions, behind the very decision to make anything at all, is love. The range of human temporal measurement does not limit God's love. God is Love. God's love extends into the infinite past because love is a characteristic of who God is. And his love will go on and on forever into the future because Love is who God is. Love is the basis of existence. The next time your world seems constrained by temporal limits, remember that God's love covers it all.

reflect: Remind yourself that the love of God is boundless toward you today.
Go to **Lamentations 3:37.**

16But this is what the LORD says:
"Stop crying;
  don't let your eyes fill with tears.
You will be rewarded for your work!" says
  the LORD.
  "The people will return from their
    enemy's land.
17 So there is hope for you in the future,"
  says the LORD.
  "Your children will return to their own
    land.

18 "I have heard Israel moaning:
  'LORD, you punished me, and I have
    learned my lesson.
  I was like a calf that had never been
    trained.
  Take me back so that I may come back.
  You truly are the LORD my God.
19 LORD, after I wandered away from you,
  I changed my heart and life.
After I understood,
  I beat my breast with sorrow.
I was ashamed and disgraced,
  because I suffered for the foolish things
    I did when I was young.'

20 "You know that Israel is my dear son,
  The child I love.
Yes, I often speak against Israel,
  but I still remember him.
I love him very much,
  and I want to comfort him," says the
    LORD.

21 "People of Israel, fix the road signs.
  Put up signs to show you the way home.
Watch the road.
  Pay attention to the road on which you
    travel.
People of Israel, come home,
  come back to your towns.
22 You are an unfaithful daughter.
  How long will you wander before you
    come home?
The LORD has made something new
  happen in the land:
  A woman will go seeking a man."

23The LORD All-Powerful, the God of Israel, says: "I will again do good things for the
people of Judah. At that time the people in
the land of Judah and its towns will again use
these words: 'May the LORD bless you, home
of what is good, holy mountain.' 24People in
all the towns of Judah will live together in
peace. Farmers and those who move around
with their flocks will live together in peace.
25I will give rest and strength to those who
are weak and tired."

26After hearing that, I, Jeremiah, woke up
and looked around. My sleep had been very
pleasant.

27The LORD says, "The time is coming
when I will help the families of Israel and
Judah and their children and animals to
grow. 28In the past I watched over Israel and
Judah, to pull them up and tear them down,
to destroy them and bring them disaster. But
now I will watch over them to build them up
and make them strong," says the LORD.

29"At that time people will no longer say:
  'The parents have eaten sour grapes,
    and that caused the children to grind
      their teeth from the sour taste.'
30Instead, each person will die for his own
sin; the person who eats sour grapes will
grind his own teeth.

THE NEW AGREEMENT

31 "Look, the time is coming," says the LORD,
  "when I will make a new agreement
    with the people of Israel
    and the people of Judah.
32 It will not be like the agreement
    I made with their ancestors
  when I took them by the hand
    to bring them out of Egypt.
  I was a husband to them,
    but they broke that agreement," says the
      LORD.
33 "This is the agreement I will make
    with the people of Israel at that time,"
      says the LORD:
  "I will put my teachings in their minds
    and write them on their hearts.
  I will be their God,
    and they will be my people.
34 People will no longer have to teach their
      neighbors and relatives
    to know the LORD,
  because all people will know me,
    from the least to the most important,"
      says the LORD.
  "I will forgive them for the wicked things
      they did,
    and I will not remember their sins
      anymore."

THE LORD WILL NEVER LEAVE ISRAEL

35 The LORD makes the sun shine in the day
  and the moon and stars to shine at
    night.
He stirs up the sea so that its waves crash
    on the shore.
  The LORD All-Powerful is his name.
  This is what the LORD says:
36 "Only if these laws should ever fail,"
  says the LORD,
"will Israel's descendants ever stop
  being a nation before me."
37 This is what the LORD says:
"Only if people can measure the sky above

and learn the secrets of the earth below,
  will I reject all the descendants of Israel
  because of what they have done," says
    the LORD.

THE NEW JERUSALEM

38 The LORD says, "The time is coming
when Jerusalem will be rebuilt for me—everything from the Tower of Hananel to the Corner Gate. 39 The measuring line will stretch
from the Corner Gate straight to the hill of
Gareb. Then it will turn to the place named
Goah. 40 The whole valley where dead bodies
and ashes are thrown, and all the terraces out
to the Kidron Valley on the east as far as the

UNDERSTANDING AUTHORITY

extraordinary heart

FAMILY

By Larry Stockstill

JEREMIAH 31:33

Your physical body relies on a healthy heart to function properly, and you keep your physical heart healthy by proper diet, exercise, and avoiding harmful things. The condition of your emotional and spiritual heart is vital to healthy relationships, and there are things you must do to keep your spirit healthy and prevent bitterness. Examine your heart and preserve a free flow of the Holy Spirit in your life.

Power struggles have no place within a family. Neither does selfishness. When you are in relationship with people, your decisions and actions not only involve you, but they also affect everyone around you. You cannot be selfish without affecting others.

Wounds from rejection can control your heart and cause barriers to healthy relationships. If you have suffered from rejection, then you might unknowingly behave in a way that causes people to reject you in a destructive cycle. Let the Lord heal you so this pain will not control you.

Forgiveness is a choice, not an emotion. Make a decision to move past the heartaches and injustices of life, and keep free from bitterness. Forgive when someone hurts you. Jesus is able to change a stony heart to one of flesh. Keep him first in your life and experience extraordinary, healthy relationships full of life and love.

reflect: What fitness program do you use to preserve the health of your spiritual heart?

Go to **Matthew 12:34–37.**

corner of the Horse Gate—all that area will be holy to the LORD. The city of Jerusalem will never again be torn down or destroyed."

JEREMIAH BUYS A FIELD

32 This is the word the LORD spoke to Jeremiah in the tenth year Zedekiah was king of Judah, which was the eighteenth year of Nebuchadnezzar. ²At that time the army of the king of Babylon was surrounding Jerusalem. Jeremiah the prophet was under arrest in the courtyard of the guard, which was at the palace of the king of Judah.

³Zedekiah king of Judah had put Jeremiah in prison there. Zedekiah had asked, "Why have you prophesied the things you have?" (Jeremiah had said, "This is what the LORD says: 'I will soon hand the city of Jerusalem over to the king of Babylon, and he will capture it. ⁴Zedekiah king of Judah will not escape from the Babylonian army, but he will surely be handed over to the king of Babylon. And he will speak to the king of Babylon face to face and see him with his own eyes. ⁵The king will take Zedekiah to Babylon, where he will stay until I have punished him,' says the LORD. 'If you fight against the Babylonians, you will not succeed.'")

⁶While Jeremiah was in prison, he said, "The LORD spoke this word to me: ⁷Your cousin Hanamel, son of your uncle Shallum, will come to you soon. Hanamel will say to you, 'Jeremiah, you are my nearest relative, so buy my field near the town of Anathoth. It is your right and your duty to buy that field.'

⁸"Then it happened just as the LORD had said. My cousin Hanamel came to me in the courtyard of the guard and said to me, 'Buy for yourself my field near Anathoth in the land of Benjamin. It is your right and duty to buy it and own it.' So I knew this was a message from the LORD.

⁹"I bought the field at Anathoth from my cousin Hanamel, weighing out seven ounces of silver for him. ¹⁰I signed the record and sealed it and had some people witness it. I also weighed out the silver on the scales. ¹¹Then I took both copies of the record of ownership—the one that was sealed that had the demands and limits of ownership, and the one that was not sealed. ¹²And I gave them to Baruch son of Neriah, the son of Mahseiah. My cousin Hanamel, the other

witnesses who signed the record of ownership, and many Jews sitting in the courtyard of the guard saw me give the record of ownership to Baruch.

¹³"With all the people watching, I told Baruch, ¹⁴'This is what the LORD All-Powerful, the God of Israel, says: Take both copies of the record of ownership—the sealed copy and the copy that was not sealed—and put them in a clay jar so they will last a long time. ¹⁵This is what the LORD All-Powerful, the God of Israel, says: In the future my people will once again buy houses and fields for grain and vineyards in the land of Israel.'

¹⁶"After I gave the record of ownership to Baruch son of Neriah, I prayed to the LORD, ¹⁷Oh, Lord GOD, you made the skies and the earth with your very great power. There is nothing too hard for you to do. ¹⁸You show love and kindness to thousands of people, but you also bring punishment to children for their parents' sins. Great and powerful God, your name is the LORD All-Powerful. ¹⁹You plan and do great things. You see everything that people do, and you reward people for the way they live and for what they do. ²⁰You did miracles and wonderful things in the land of Egypt. You have continued doing them in Israel and among the other nations even until today. So you have become well known. ²¹You brought your people, the Israelites, out of Egypt using signs and miracles and your great power and strength. You brought great terror on everyone. ²²You gave them this land that you promised to their ancestors long ago, a fertile land. ²³They came into this land and took it for their own, but they did not obey you or follow your teachings. They did not do everything you commanded. So you made all these terrible things happen to them.

²⁴"Look! The enemy has surrounded the city and has built roads to the top of the walls to capture it. Because of war, hunger, and terrible diseases, the city will be handed over to the Babylonians who are attacking it. You said this would happen, and now you see it is happening. ²⁵But now, Lord GOD, you tell me, 'Buy the field with silver and call in witnesses.' You tell me this while the Babylonian army is ready to capture the city."

²⁶Then the LORD spoke this word to Jeremiah: ²⁷"I am the LORD, the God of every person on the earth. Nothing is impossible

for me. 28So this is what the LORD says: I will soon hand over the city of Jerusalem to the Babylonian army and to Nebuchadnezzar king of Babylon, who will capture it. 29The Babylonian army is already attacking the city of Jerusalem. They will soon enter it and start a fire to burn down the city and its houses. The people of Jerusalem offered sacrifices to Baal on the roofs[n] of those same houses and poured out drink offerings to other idols to make me angry. 30From their youth, the people of Israel and Judah have done only the things I said were wrong. They have made me angry by worshiping idols made with their own hands," says the LORD. 31"From the day Jerusalem was built until now, this city has made me angry, so angry that I must remove it from my sight. 32I will destroy it, because of all the evil the people of Israel and Judah have done. The people, their kings and officers, their priests and prophets, all the people of Judah, and the people of Jerusalem have made me angry. 33They turned their backs to me, not their faces. I tried to teach them again and again, but they wouldn't listen or learn. 34They put their hateful idols in the place where I have chosen to be worshiped, so they made it unclean. 35In the Valley of Ben Hinnom they built places to worship Baal so they could burn their sons and daughters as sacrifices to Molech. But I never commanded them to do such a hateful thing. It never entered my mind that they would do such a thing and cause Judah to sin.

36"You are saying, 'Because of war, hunger, and terrible diseases, the city will be handed over to the king of Babylon.' But the LORD, the God of Israel, says about Jerusalem: 37I forced the people of Israel and Judah to leave their land, because I was furious and very angry with them. But soon I will gather them from all the lands where I forced them to go, and I will bring them back to this place, where they may live in safety. 38The people of Israel and Judah will be my people, and I will be their God. 39I will make them truly want to be one people with one goal. They will truly want to worship me all their lives, for their own good and for the good of their children after them.

40"I will make an agreement with them that will last forever. I will never turn away from them; I will always do good to them. I will make them want to respect me so they will never turn away from me. 41I will enjoy doing good to them. And with my whole being I will surely plant them in this land and make them grow."

42This is what the LORD says: "I have brought this great disaster to the people of Israel and Judah. In the same way I will bring the good things that I promise to do for them. 43You are saying, 'This land is an empty desert, without people or animals. It has been handed over to the Babylonians.' But in the future, people will again buy fields in this land. 44They will use their money to buy fields. They will sign and seal their agreements and call in witnesses. They will again buy fields in the land of Benjamin, in the area around Jerusalem, in the towns of Judah and in the mountains, in the western hills, and in southern Judah. I will make everything as good for them as it once was," says the LORD.

THE PROMISE OF THE LORD

33 While Jeremiah was still locked up in the courtyard of the guards, the LORD spoke his word to him a second time: 2"These are the words of the LORD, who made the earth, shaped it, and gave it order, whose name is the LORD: 3'Judah, pray to me, and I will answer you. I will tell you important secrets you have never heard before.' 4This is what the LORD, the God of Israel, says about the houses in Jerusalem and the royal palaces of Judah that have been torn down to be used in defense of the attack by the Babylonian army: 5'Some people will come to fight against the Babylonians. They will fill these houses with the bodies of people I killed in my hot anger. I have turned away from this city because of all the evil its people have done.

6"But then I will bring health and healing to the people there. I will heal them and let them enjoy great peace and safety. 7I will bring Judah and Israel back from captivity and make them strong countries as in the past. 8They sinned against me, but I will wash away that sin. They did evil and turned

---

32:29 roofs In Bible times houses were built with flat roofs. The roof was used for drying things such as flax and fruit. And it was used as an extra room, as a place for worship, and as a cool place to sleep in the summer.

away from me, but I will forgive them. ⁹Then "Jerusalem" will be to me a name that brings joy! And people from all nations of the earth will praise it when they hear about the good things I am doing there. They will be surprised and shocked at all the good things and the peace I will bring to Jerusalem.'

¹⁰"You are saying, 'Our country is an empty desert, without people or animals.' But this is what the LORD says: It is now quiet in the streets of Jerusalem and in the towns of Judah, without people or animals, but it will be noisy there soon! ¹¹There will be sounds of joy and gladness and the happy sounds of brides and bridegrooms. There will be the sounds of people bringing to the Temple of the LORD their offerings of thanks to the LORD. They will say,

'Praise the LORD All-Powerful,
    because the LORD is good!
His love continues forever!'

They will say this because I will again do good things for Judah, as I did in the beginning," says the LORD.

¹²This is what the LORD All-Powerful says: "This place is empty now, without people or animals. But there will be shepherds in all the towns of Judah and pastures where they let their flocks rest. ¹³Shepherds will again count their sheep as the sheep walk in front of them. They will count them in the mountains and in the western hills, in southern Judah and the land of Benjamin, and around Jerusalem and the other towns of Judah!" says the LORD.

THE GOOD BRANCH

¹⁴The LORD says, "The time is coming when I will do the good thing I promised to the people of Israel and Judah.

¹⁵ In those days and at that time,
    I will make a good branch sprout from
        David's family.
    He will do what is fair and right in the
        land.
¹⁶ At that time Judah will be saved,
    and the people of Jerusalem will live in
        safety.
The branch will be named:
    The LORD Does What Is Right."

¹⁷This is what the LORD says: "Someone from David's family will always sit on the throne of the family of Israel. ¹⁸And there will always be priests from the family of Levi. They will always stand before me to offer burnt offerings and grain offerings and sacrifices to me."

¹⁹The LORD spoke his word to Jeremiah, saying: ²⁰"This is what the LORD says: I have an agreement with day and night that they will always come at the right times. If you could change that agreement, ²¹only then could you change my agreement with David and Levi. Only then would my servant David not have a descendant ruling as king on David's throne. And only then would the family of Levi not be priests serving me in the Temple. ²²But I will give many descendants to my servant David and to the family group of Levi who serve me in the Temple. They will be as many as the stars in the sky that no one can count. They will be as many as the grains of sand on the seashore that no one can measure."

²³The LORD spoke his word to Jeremiah, saying: ²⁴"Jeremiah, have you heard what the people are saying? They say: 'The LORD turned away from the two families of Israel and Judah that he chose.' Now they don't think of my people as a nation anymore!"

²⁵This is what the LORD says: "If I had not made my agreement with day and night, and if I had not made the laws for the sky and earth, ²⁶only then would I turn away from Jacob's descendants. And only then would I not let the descendants of David my servant rule over the descendants of Abraham, Isaac, and Jacob. But I will be kind to them and cause good things to happen to them again."

A WARNING TO ZEDEKIAH

34 The LORD spoke his word to Jeremiah when Nebuchadnezzar king of Babylon was fighting against Jerusalem and all the towns around it. Nebuchadnezzar had with him all his army and the armies of all the kingdoms and peoples he ruled. ²This is what the LORD, the God of Israel, said: "Jeremiah, go to Zedekiah king of Judah and tell him: 'This is what the LORD says: I will soon hand the city of Jerusalem over to the king of Babylon, and he will burn it down! ³You will not escape from the king of Babylon; you will surely be captured and handed over to him. You will see the king of Babylon with your own eyes, and he will talk to you face to face. And you will go to Babylon. ⁴But, Zedekiah king of Judah, listen to the promise of the LORD. This is what the LORD says about you: You will not be killed with a sword. ⁵You will die in a peaceful way. As people made funeral fires to honor your ancestors, the kings who ruled before you, so people will make a funeral fire to honor you. They will cry for you and sadly say, "Ah, master!" I myself make this promise to you, says the LORD.'"

⁶So Jeremiah the prophet gave this message to Zedekiah in Jerusalem. ⁷This was while the army of the king of Babylon was fighting against Jerusalem and the cities of Judah that had not yet been taken—Lachish and Azekah. These were the only strong, walled cities left in the land of Judah.

SLAVES ARE MISTREATED

⁸The LORD spoke his word to Jeremiah. This was after King Zedekiah had made an agreement with all the people in Jerusalem to free all the Hebrew slaves. ⁹Everyone was supposed to free his Hebrew slaves, both male and female. No one was to keep a fellow Jew as a slave. ¹⁰All the officers and all the people accepted this agreement; they agreed to free their male and female slaves and no longer keep them as slaves. So all the slaves were set free. ¹¹But after that, the people who had slaves changed their minds. So they took back the people they had set free and made them slaves again.

¹²Then the LORD spoke his word to Jeremiah: ¹³"This is what the LORD, the God of Israel, says: I brought your ancestors out of Egypt where they were slaves and made an agreement with them. ¹⁴I said to your ancestors: 'At the end of every seven years, each one of you must set his Hebrew slaves free. If a fellow Hebrew has sold himself to you, you must let him go free after he has served you for six years.' But your ancestors did not listen or pay attention to me. ¹⁵A short time ago you changed your hearts and did what I say is right. Each of you gave freedom to his fellow Hebrews who were slaves. And you even made an agreement before me in the place where I have chosen to be worshiped. ¹⁶But now you have changed your minds. You have shown you do not honor me. Each of you has taken back the male and female slaves you had set free, and you have forced them to become your slaves again.

¹⁷"So this is what the LORD says: You have not obeyed me. You have not given freedom to your fellow Hebrews, neither relatives nor friends. But now I will give freedom, says the LORD, to war, to terrible diseases, and to hunger. I will make you hated by all the kingdoms of the earth. ¹⁸I will hand over the men who broke my agreement, who have not kept the promises they made before me. They cut a calf into two pieces before me and walked between the pieces.ⁿ ¹⁹These people made the agreement before me by walking between the pieces of the calf: the leaders of Judah and Jerusalem, the officers of the court, the priests, and all the people of the land. ²⁰So I will hand them over to their enemies and to everyone who wants to kill them. Their bodies will become food for the birds of the air and for the wild animals of the earth. ²¹I will hand Zedekiah king of Judah and his officers over to their enemies, and to everyone who wants to kill them, and to the army of the king of Babylon, even though they have left Jerusalem. ²²I will give the order, says the LORD, to bring the Babylonian army back to Jerusalem. It will fight against Jerusalem, capture it, set it on fire, and burn it down. I will destroy the towns in Judah so that they become ruins where no one lives!"

THE RECABITE FAMILY OBEYS GOD

35 When Jehoiakim son of Josiah was king of Judah, the LORD spoke his word to Jeremiah, saying: ²"Go to the family of Recab. Invite them to come to one of the side rooms of the Temple of the LORD, and offer them wine to drink."

³So I went to get Jaazaniah son of Jeremiah,ⁿ the son of Habazziniah. And I gathered all of Jaazaniah's brothers and sons and the whole family of the Recabites together. ⁴Then I brought them into the Temple of the LORD. We went into the room of the sons of Hanan son of Igdaliah, who was a man of God. The room was next to the one where the officers stay and above the room of Maaseiah son of Shallum, the doorkeeper

---

34:18 They . . . pieces. This showed that the men were willing to be killed, like this animal, if they did not keep their agreement. **35:3 Jeremiah** Not the prophet Jeremiah, but a different man with the same name.

in the Temple. ⁵Then I put some bowls full of wine and some cups before the men of the Recabite family. And I said to them, "Drink some wine."

⁶But the Recabite men answered, "We never drink wine. Our ancestor Jonadab son of Recab gave us this command: 'You and your descendants must never drink wine. ⁷Also you must never build houses, plant seeds, or plant vineyards, or do any of those things. You must live only in tents. Then you will live a long time in the land where you are wanderers.' ⁸So we Recabites have obeyed everything Jonadab our ancestor commanded us. Neither we nor our wives, sons, or daughters ever drink wine. ⁹We never build houses in which to live, or own fields or vineyards, or plant crops. ¹⁰We have lived in tents and have obeyed everything our ancestor Jonadab commanded us. ¹¹But when Nebuchadnezzar king of Babylon attacked Judah, we said to each other, 'Come, we must enter Jerusalem so we can escape the Babylonian army and the Aramean army.' So we have stayed in Jerusalem."

¹²Then the LORD spoke his word to Jeremiah: ¹³"This is what the LORD All-Powerful, the God of Israel, says: Jeremiah, go and tell the men of Judah and the people of Jerusalem: 'You should learn a lesson and obey my message,' says the LORD. ¹⁴Jonadab son of Recab ordered his descendants not to drink wine, and that command has been obeyed. Until today they have obeyed their ancestor's command; they do not drink wine. But I, the LORD, have given you messages again and again, but you did not obey me. ¹⁵I sent all my servants the prophets to you again and again, saying, "Each of you must stop doing evil. You must change and be good. Do not follow other gods to serve them. If you obey me, you will live in the land I have given to you and your ancestors." But you have not listened to me or paid attention to my message. ¹⁶The descendants of Jonadab son of Recab obeyed the commands their ancestor gave them, but the people of Judah have not obeyed me.'

¹⁷"So the LORD God All-Powerful, the God of Israel, says: 'I will soon bring every disaster I said would come to Judah and to everyone living in Jerusalem. I spoke to those people, but they refused to listen. I called out to them, but they did not answer me.'"

¹⁸Then Jeremiah said to the Recabites, "This is what the LORD All-Powerful, the God of Israel, says: 'You have obeyed the commands of your ancestor Jonadab and have followed all of his teachings; you have done everything he commanded.' ¹⁹So this is what the LORD All-Powerful, the God of Israel, says: 'There will always be a descendant of Jonadab son of Recab to serve me.'"

JEHOIAKIM BURNS JEREMIAH'S SCROLL

36 The LORD spoke this word to Jeremiah during the fourth year that Jehoiakim son of Josiah was king of Judah: ²"Get a scroll. Write on it all the words I have spoken to you about Israel and Judah and all the nations. Write everything from when I first spoke to you, when Josiah was king, until now. ³Maybe the family of Judah will hear what disasters I am planning to bring on them and will stop doing wicked things. Then I would forgive them for the sins and the evil things they have done."

⁴So Jeremiah called for Baruch son of Neriah. Jeremiah spoke the messages the LORD had given him, and Baruch wrote those messages on the scroll. ⁵Then Jeremiah commanded Baruch, "I cannot go to the Temple of the LORD. I must stay here. ⁶So I want you to go to the Temple of the LORD on a day when the people are fasting. Read from the scroll to all the people of Judah who come into Jerusalem from their towns. Read the messages from the LORD, which are the words you wrote on the scroll as I spoke them to you. ⁷Perhaps they will ask the LORD to help them. Perhaps each one will stop doing wicked things, because the LORD has announced that he is very angry with them." ⁸So Baruch son of Neriah did everything Jeremiah the prophet told him to do. In the LORD's Temple he read aloud the scroll that had the LORD's messages written on it.

⁹In the ninth month of the fifth year that Jehoiakim son of Josiah was king, a fast was announced. All the people of Jerusalem and everyone who had come into Jerusalem from the towns of Judah were supposed to give up eating to honor the LORD. ¹⁰At that time Baruch read to all the people there the scroll containing Jeremiah's words. He read the scroll in the Temple of the LORD in the room of Gemariah son of Shaphan, a royal

secretary. That room was in the upper court-yard at the entrance of the New Gate of the Temple.

¹¹Micaiah son of Gemariah, the son of Shaphan, heard all the messages from the LORD that were on the scroll. ¹²Micaiah went down to the royal secretary's room in the king's palace where all of the officers were sitting: Elishama the royal secretary; Delaiah son of Shemaiah; Elnathan son of Acbor; Gemariah son of Shaphan; Zedekiah son of Hananiah; and all the other officers. ¹³Micaiah told those officers everything he had heard Baruch read to the people from the scroll.

¹⁴Then the officers sent a man named Jehudi son of Nethaniah to Baruch. (Nethaniah was the son of Shelemiah, who was the son of Cushi.) Jehudi said to Baruch, "Bring the scroll that you read to the people and come with me."

So Baruch son of Neriah took the scroll and went with Jehudi to the officers. ¹⁵Then the officers said to Baruch, "Please sit down and read the scroll to us."

So Baruch read the scroll to them. ¹⁶When the officers heard all the words, they became afraid and looked at each other. They said to Baruch, "We must certainly tell the king about these words." ¹⁷Then the officers asked Baruch, "Tell us, please, where did you get all these words you wrote on the scroll? Did you write down what Jeremiah said to you?"

¹⁸"Yes," Baruch answered. "Jeremiah spoke them all to me, and I wrote them down with ink on this scroll."

¹⁹Then the officers said to Baruch, "You and Jeremiah must go and hide, and don't tell anyone where you are."

²⁰The officers put the scroll in the room of Elishama the royal secretary. Then they went to the king in the courtyard and told him all about the scroll. ²¹So King Jehoiakim sent Jehudi to get the scroll. Jehudi brought the scroll from the room of Elishama the royal secretary and read it to the king and to all the officers who stood around the king. ²²It was the ninth month of the year, so King Jehoiakim was sitting in the winter apartment. There was a fire burning in a small firepot in front of him. ²³After Jehudi had read three or four columns, the king cut those columns off of the scroll with a penknife and threw them into the firepot. Finally, the whole scroll

was burned in the fire. ²⁴King Jehoiakim and his servants heard everything that was said, but they were not frightened! They did not tear their clothes to show their sorrow. ²⁵Elnathan, Delaiah, and Gemariah even tried to talk King Jehoiakim out of burning the scroll, but he would not listen to them. ²⁶Instead, the king ordered Jerahmeel son of the king, Seraiah son of Azriel, and Shelemiah son of Abdeel to arrest Baruch the secretary and Jeremiah the prophet. But the LORD had hidden them.

²⁷So King Jehoiakim burned the scroll where Baruch had written all the words Jeremiah had spoken to him. Then the LORD spoke his word to Jeremiah: ²⁸"Get another scroll. Write all the words on it that were on the first scroll that Jehoiakim king of Judah burned up. ²⁹Also say this to Jehoiakim king of Judah: 'This is what the LORD says: You burned up that scroll and said, "Why, Jeremiah, did you write on it 'the king of Babylon will surely come and destroy this land and the people and animals in it'?" ³⁰So this is what the LORD says about Jehoiakim king of Judah: Jehoiakim's descendants will not sit on David's throne. When Jehoiakim dies, his body will be thrown out on the ground. It will be left out in the heat of the day and in the cold frost of the night. ³¹I will punish Jehoiakim and his children and his servants, because they have done evil things. I will bring disasters upon them and upon all the people in Jerusalem and Judah—everything I promised but which they refused to hear.'"

³²So Jeremiah took another scroll and gave it to Baruch son of Neriah, his secretary. As Jeremiah spoke, Baruch wrote on the scroll the same words that were on the scroll Jehoiakim king of Judah had burned in the fire. And many similar words were added to the second scroll.

JEREMIAH IN PRISON

37 Nebuchadnezzar king of Babylon had appointed Zedekiah son of Josiah to be king of Judah. Zedekiah took the place of Jehoiachin son of Jehoiakim. ²But Zedekiah, his servants, and the people of Judah did not listen to the words the LORD had spoken through Jeremiah the prophet.

³Now King Zedekiah sent Jehucal son of Shelemiah and the priest Zephaniah son of

Maaseiah with a message to Jeremiah the prophet. This was the message: "Jeremiah, please pray to the LORD our God for us."

4At that time Jeremiah had not yet been put into prison. So he was free to go anywhere he wanted. 5The army of the king of Egypt had marched from Egypt toward Judah. Now the Babylonian army had surrounded the city of Jerusalem. When they heard about the Egyptian army marching toward them, the Babylonian army left Jerusalem.

6The LORD spoke his word to Jeremiah the prophet: 7"This is what the LORD, the God of Israel, says: Jehucal and Zephaniah, I know Zedekiah king of Judah sent you to seek my help. Tell this to King Zedekiah: 'The army of the king of Egypt came here to help you, but they will go back to Egypt. 8After that, the Babylonian army will return and attack Jerusalem and capture it and burn it down.'

9"This is what the LORD says: People of Jerusalem, do not fool yourselves. Don't say, 'The Babylonian army will surely leave us alone.' They will not! 10Even if you defeated all of the Babylonian army that is attacking you and there were only a few injured men left in their tents, they would come from their tents and burn down Jerusalem!"

11So the Babylonian army left Jerusalem to fight the army of the king of Egypt. 12Now Jeremiah tried to travel from Jerusalem to the land of Benjamin to get his share of the property that belonged to his family. 13When Jeremiah got to the Benjamin Gate of Jerusalem, the captain in charge of the guards arrested him. The captain's name was Irijah son of Shelemiah son of Hananiah. Irijah said, "You are leaving us to join the Babylonians!"

14But Jeremiah said to Irijah, "That's not true! I am not leaving to join the Babylonians." Irijah refused to listen to Jeremiah, so he arrested Jeremiah and took him to the officers of Jerusalem. 15Those rulers were very angry with Jeremiah and beat him. Then they put him in jail in the house of Jonathan the royal secretary, which had been made into a prison. 16So those people put Jeremiah into a cell in a dungeon, and Jeremiah was there for a long time.

17Then King Zedekiah sent for Jeremiah and had him brought to the palace. Zedekiah asked him in private, "Is there any message from the LORD?"

Jeremiah answered, "Yes, there is. Zedekiah, you will be handed over to the king of Babylon." 18Then Jeremiah said to King Zedekiah, "What crime have I done against you or your officers or the people of Jerusalem? Why have you thrown me into prison? 19Where are your prophets that prophesied this message to you: 'The king of Babylon will not attack you or this land of Judah'? 20But now, my master, king of Judah, please listen to me, and please do what I ask of you. Do not send me back to the house of Jonathan the royal secretary, or I will die there!"

21So King Zedekiah gave orders for Jeremiah to be put under guard in the courtyard of the guard and to be given bread each day from the street of the bakers until there was no more bread in the city. So he stayed under guard in the courtyard of the guard.

JEREMIAH IS THROWN INTO A WELL

38 Shephatiah son of Mattan, Gedaliah son of Pashhur, Jehucal son of Shelemiah, and Pashhur son of Malkijah heard what Jeremiah was telling all the people. He said: 2"This is what the LORD says: 'Everyone who stays in Jerusalem will die from war, or hunger, or terrible diseases. But everyone who surrenders to the Babylonian army will live; they will escape with their lives and live.' 3And this is what the LORD says: 'This city of Jerusalem will surely be handed over to the army of the king of Babylon. He will capture this city!'"

4Then the officers said to the king, "Jeremiah must be put to death! He is discouraging the soldiers who are still in the city, and all the people, by what he is saying to them. He does not want good to happen to us; he wants to ruin us."

5King Zedekiah said to them, "Jeremiah is in your control. I cannot do anything to stop you."

6So the officers took Jeremiah and put him into the well of Malkijah, the king's son, which was in the courtyard of the guards. The officers used ropes to lower Jeremiah into the well, which did not have any water in it, only mud. And Jeremiah sank down into the mud.

7But Ebed-Melech, a Cushite and a servant in the palace, heard that the officers had put Jeremiah into the well. As King Zedekiah was sitting at the Benjamin Gate, [8]Ebed-Melech left the palace and went to the king. Ebed-Melech said to him, [9]"My master and king, these rulers have acted in an evil way. They have treated Jeremiah the prophet badly. They have thrown him into a well and left him there to die! When there is no more bread in the city, he will starve to death."

[10]Then King Zedekiah commanded Ebed-Melech the Cushite, "Take thirty men from the palace and lift Jeremiah the prophet out of the well before he dies."

[11]So Ebed-Melech took the men with him and went to a room under the storeroom in the palace. He took some old rags and worn-out clothes from that room. Then he let those rags down with some ropes to Jeremiah in the well. [12]Ebed-Melech the Cushite said to Jeremiah, "Put these old rags and worn-out clothes under your arms to be pads for the ropes." So Jeremiah did as Ebed-Melech said. [13]The men pulled Jeremiah up with the ropes and lifted him out of the well. And Jeremiah stayed under guard in the courtyard of the guard.

ZEDEKIAH QUESTIONS JEREMIAH

[14]Then King Zedekiah sent someone to get Jeremiah the prophet and bring him to the third entrance to the Temple of the LORD. The king said to Jeremiah, "I am going to ask you something. Do not hide anything from me, but tell me everything honestly."

[15]Jeremiah said to Zedekiah, "If I give you an answer, you will surely kill me. And even if I give you advice, you will not listen to me."

[16]But King Zedekiah made a secret promise to Jeremiah, "As surely as the LORD lives who has given us breath and life, I will not kill you. And I promise not to hand you over to the officers who want to kill you."

[17]Then Jeremiah said to Zedekiah, "This is what the LORD God All-Powerful, the God of Israel, says: 'If you surrender to the officers of the king of Babylon, your life will be saved. Jerusalem will not be burned down, and you and your family will live. [18]But if you refuse to surrender to the officers of the king of Babylon, Jerusalem will be handed over to the Babylonian army, and they will burn it

down. And you yourself will not escape from them.'"

[19]Then King Zedekiah said to Jeremiah, "I'm afraid of some Jews who have already gone over to the side of the Babylonian army. If the Babylonians hand me over to them, they will treat me badly."

[20]But Jeremiah answered, "The Babylonians will not hand you over to the Jews. Obey the LORD by doing what I tell you. Then things will go well for you, and your life will be saved. [21]But if you refuse to surrender to the Babylonians, the LORD has shown me what will happen. [22]All the women left in the palace of the king of Judah will be brought out and taken to the important officers of the king of Babylon. Your women will make fun of you with this song:

'Your good friends misled you
    and were stronger than you.
While your feet were stuck in the mud,
    they left you.'

[23]"All your wives and children will be brought out and given to the Babylonian army. You yourself will not even escape from them. You will be taken prisoner by the king of Babylon, and Jerusalem will be burned down."

[24]Then Zedekiah said to Jeremiah, "Do not tell anyone that I have been talking to you, or you will die. [25]If the officers find out I talked to you, they will come to you and say, 'Tell us what you said to King Zedekiah and what he said to you. Don't keep any secrets from us. If you don't tell us everything, we will kill you.' [26]If they ask you, tell them, 'I was begging the king not to send me back to Jonathan's house to die.'"

[27]All the officers did come to question Jeremiah. So he told them everything the king had ordered him to say. Then the officers said no more to Jeremiah, because no one had heard what Jeremiah and the king had discussed.

[28]So Jeremiah stayed under guard in the courtyard of the guard until the day Jerusalem was captured.

THE FALL OF JERUSALEM

39
This is how Jerusalem was captured: Nebuchadnezzar king of Babylon marched against Jerusalem with his whole army and surrounded the city to attack it.

This was during the tenth month of the ninth year Zedekiah was king of Judah. ²This lasted until the ninth day of the fourth month in Zedekiah's eleventh year. Then the city wall was broken through. ³And all these officers of the king of Babylon came into Jerusalem and sat down at the Middle Gate: Nergal-Sharezer of the district of Samgar; Nebo-Sarsekim, a chief officer; Nergal-Sharezer, an important leader; and all the other important officers.

⁴When Zedekiah king of Judah and all his soldiers saw them, they ran away. They left Jerusalem at night and went out from the king's garden. They went through the gate that was between the two walls and then headed toward the Jordan Valley. ⁵But the Babylonian army chased them and caught up with Zedekiah in the plains of Jericho. They captured him and took him to Nebuchadnezzar king of Babylon, who was at the town of Riblah in the land of Hamath. There Nebuchadnezzar passed his sentence on Zedekiah. ⁶At Riblah the king of Babylon killed Zedekiah's sons and all the important officers of Judah as Zedekiah watched. ⁷Then he put out Zedekiah's eyes. He put bronze chains on Zedekiah and took him to Babylon.

⁸The Babylonians set fire to the palace and to the houses of the people, and they broke down the walls around Jerusalem. ⁹Nebuzaradan, commander of the king's special guards, took the people left in Jerusalem, those captives who had surrendered to him earlier, and the rest of the people of Jerusalem, and he took them all away to Babylon. ¹⁰But Nebuzaradan, commander of the guard, left some of the poorest people of Judah behind. They owned nothing, but that day he gave them vineyards and fields.

¹¹Nebuchadnezzar king of Babylon had given these orders about Jeremiah through Nebuzaradan, commander of the guard: ¹²"Find Jeremiah and take care of him. Do not hurt him, but do for him whatever he asks you." ¹³So Nebuchadnezzar sent these men for Jeremiah: Nebuzaradan, commander of the guards; Nebushazban, a chief officer; Nergal-Sharezer, an important leader; and all the other officers of the king of Babylon. ¹⁴They had Jeremiah taken out of the courtyard of the guard. Then they turned him over to Gedaliah son of Ahikam son of Shaphan, who had orders to take Jeremiah back home.

So they took him home, and he stayed among the people left in Judah.

¹⁵While Jeremiah was guarded in the courtyard, the LORD spoke his word to him: ¹⁶"Jeremiah, go and tell Ebed-Melech the Cushite this message: 'This is what the LORD All-Powerful, the God of Israel, says: Very soon I will make my words about Jerusalem come true through disaster, not through good times. You will see everything come true with your own eyes. ¹⁷But I will save you on that day, Ebed-Melech, says the LORD. You will not be handed over to the people you fear. ¹⁸I will surely save you, Ebed-Melech. You will not die from a sword, but you will escape and live. This will happen because you have trusted in me, says the LORD.'"

JEREMIAH IS SET FREE

40 The LORD spoke his word to Jeremiah after Nebuzaradan, commander of the guards, had set Jeremiah free at the city of Ramah. He had found Jeremiah in Ramah bound in chains with all the captives from Jerusalem and Judah who were being taken away to Babylon. ²When commander Nebuzaradan found Jeremiah, Nebuzaradan said to him, "The LORD your God announced this disaster would come to this place. ³And now the LORD has done everything he said he would do. This disaster happened because the people of Judah sinned against the LORD and did not obey him. ⁴But today I am freeing you from the chains on your wrists. If you want to, come with me to Babylon, and I will take good care of you. But if you don't want to come, then don't. Look, the whole country is open to you. Go wherever you wish." ⁵Before Jeremiah turned to leave, Nebuzaradan said, "Or go back to Gedaliah son of Ahikam, the son of Shaphan. The king of Babylon has chosen him to be governor over the towns of Judah. Go and live with Gedaliah among the people, or go anywhere you want."

Then Nebuzaradan gave Jeremiah some food and a present and let him go. ⁶So Jeremiah went to Gedaliah son of Ahikam at Mizpah and stayed with him there. He lived among the people who were left behind in Judah.

THE SHORT RULE OF GEDALIAH

⁷Some officers and their men from the army of Judah were still out in the open

country. They heard that the king of Babylon had put Gedaliah son of Ahikam in charge of the people who were left in the land: the men, women, and children who were the poorest. They were the ones who were not taken to Babylon as captives. 8So these soldiers came to Gedaliah at Mizpah: Ishmael son of Nethaniah, Johanan and Jonathan sons of Kareah, Seraiah son of Tanhumeth, the sons of Ephai the Netophathite, Jaazaniah son of the Maacathite, and their men.

9Gedaliah son of Ahikam, the son of Shaphan, made a promise to them, saying, "Do not be afraid to serve the Babylonians. Stay in the land and serve the king of Babylon. Then everything will go well for you. 10I myself will live in Mizpah and will speak for you before the Babylonians who come to us here. Harvest the wine, the summer fruit, and the oil, and put what you harvest in your storage jars. Live in the towns you control."

11The Jews in Moab, Ammon, Edom, and other countries also heard that the king of Babylon had left a few Jews alive in the land. And they heard the king of Babylon had chosen Gedaliah as governor over them. (Gedaliah was the son of Ahikam, the son of Shaphan.) 12When the people of Judah heard this news, they came back to Judah from all the countries where they had been scattered. They came to Gedaliah at Mizpah and gathered a large harvest of wine and summer fruit.

13Johanan son of Kareah and all the army officers of Judah still in the open country came to Gedaliah at Mizpah. 14They said to him, "Don't you know that Baalis king of the Ammonite people wants you dead? He has sent Ishmael son of Nethaniah to kill you." But Gedaliah son of Ahikam did not believe them.

15Then Johanan son of Kareah spoke to Gedaliah in private at Mizpah. He said, "Let me go and kill Ishmael son of Nethaniah. No one will know anything about it. We should not let Ishmael kill you. Then all the Jews gathered around you would be scattered to different countries again, and the few people of Judah who are left alive would be lost."

16But Gedaliah son of Ahikam said to Johanan son of Kareah, "Do not kill Ishmael! The things you are saying about Ishmael are not true."

41 In the seventh month Ishmael son of Nethaniah and ten of his men came to Gedaliah son of Ahikam at Mizpah. (Nethaniah was the son of Elishama.) Now Ishmael was a member of the king's family and had been one of the officers of the king of Judah. While they were eating a meal with Gedaliah at Mizpah, 2Ishmael and his ten men got up and killed Gedaliah son of Ahikam, the son of Shaphan, with a sword. (Gedaliah was the man the king of Babylon had chosen as governor over Judah.) 3Ishmael also killed all the Jews and the Babylonian soldiers who were there with Gedaliah at Mizpah.

4The day after Gedaliah was murdered, before anyone knew about it, 5eighty men came to Mizpah bringing grain offerings and incense to the Temple of the LORD. Those men from Shechem, Shiloh, and Samaria had shaved off their beards, torn their clothes, and cut themselves.[n] 6Ishmael son of Nethaniah went out from Mizpah to meet them, crying as he walked. When he met them, he said, "Come with me to meet Gedaliah son of Ahikam." 7So they went into Mizpah. Then Ishmael son of Nethaniah and his men killed seventy of them and threw the bodies into a deep well. 8But the ten men who were left alive said to Ishmael, "Don't kill us! We have wheat and barley and oil and honey that we have hidden in a field." So Ishmael let them live and did not kill them with the others. 9Now the well where he had thrown all the bodies had been made by King Asa as a part of his defenses against Baasha king of Israel. But Ishmael son of Nethaniah put dead bodies in it until it was full.

10Ishmael captured all the other people in Mizpah: the king's daughters and all the other people who were left there. They were the ones whom Nebuzaradan commander of the guard had chosen Gedaliah son of Ahikam to take care of. So Ishmael son of Nethaniah captured those people, and he started to cross over to the country of the Ammonites.

11Johanan son of Kareah and all his army officers with him heard about all the evil things Ishmael son of Nethaniah had done. 12So they took their men and went to fight

---

41:5 shaved . . . themselves The men did this to show they were sad about the Temple in Jerusalem being destroyed.

Ishmael son of Nethaniah and caught him near the big pool of water at Gibeon. ¹³When the captives Ishmael had taken saw Johanan and the army officers, they were glad. ¹⁴So all the people Ishmael had taken captive from Mizpah turned around and ran to Johanan son of Kareah. ¹⁵But Ishmael son of Nethaniah and eight of his men escaped from Johanan and ran away to the Ammonites.

¹⁶So Johanan son of Kareah and all his army officers saved the captives that Ishmael son of Nethaniah had taken from Mizpah after he murdered Gedaliah son of Ahikam. Among those left alive were soldiers, women, children, and palace officers. And Johanan brought them back from the town of Gibeon.

THE ESCAPE TO EGYPT

¹⁷⁻¹⁸Johanan and the other army officers were afraid of the Babylonians. Since the king of Babylon had chosen Gedaliah son of Ahikam to be governor of Judah but Ishmael son of Nethaniah had murdered him, Johanan was afraid that the Babylonians would be angry. So they decided to run away to Egypt. On the way they stayed at Geruth Kimham, near the town of Bethlehem.

42 While there, Johanan son of Kareah and Jezaniah son of Hoshaiah went to Jeremiah the prophet. All the army officers and all the people, from the least important to the greatest, went along, too. ²They said to him, "Jeremiah, please listen to what we ask. Pray to the LORD your God for all the people left alive from the family of Judah. At one time there were many of us, but you can see that there are few of us now. ³So pray that the LORD your God will tell us where we should go and what we should do."

⁴Then Jeremiah the prophet answered, "I understand what you want me to do. I will pray to the LORD your God as you have asked. I will tell you everything he says and not hide anything from you."

⁵Then the people said to Jeremiah, "May the LORD be a true and loyal witness against us if we don't do everything the LORD your God sends you to tell us. ⁶It does not matter if we like the message or not. We will obey the LORD our God, to whom we are sending you. We will obey what he says so good things will happen to us."

⁷Ten days later the LORD spoke his word to Jeremiah. ⁸Then Jeremiah called for Johanan son of Kareah, the army officers with him, and all the other people, from the least important to the greatest. ⁹Jeremiah said to them, "You sent me to ask the LORD for what you wanted. This is what the God of Israel says: ¹⁰'If you will stay in Judah, I will build you up and not tear you down. I will plant you and not pull you up, because I am sad about the disaster I brought on you. ¹¹Now you fear the king of Babylon, but don't be afraid of him. Don't be afraid of him,' says the LORD, 'because I am with you. I will save you and rescue you from his power. ¹²I will be kind to you, and he will also treat you with mercy and let you stay in your land.'

¹³"But if you say, 'We will not stay in Judah,' you will disobey the LORD your God. ¹⁴Or you might say, 'No, we will go and live in Egypt. There we will not see war, or hear the trumpets of war, or be hungry.' ¹⁵If you say that, listen to the message of the LORD, you who are left alive from Judah. This is what the LORD All-Powerful, the God of Israel, says: 'If you make up your mind to go and live in Egypt, these things will happen: ¹⁶You are afraid of war, but it will find you in the land of Egypt. And you are worried about hunger, but it will follow you into Egypt, and you will die there. ¹⁷Everyone who goes to live in Egypt will die in war or from hunger or terrible disease. No one who goes to Egypt will live; no one will escape the terrible things I will bring to them.'

¹⁸"This is what the LORD All-Powerful, the God of Israel, says: 'I showed my anger against the people of Jerusalem. In the same way I will show my anger against you when you go to Egypt. Other nations will speak evil of you. People will be shocked by what will happen to you. You will become a curse word, and people will insult you. And you will never see Judah again.'

¹⁹"You who are left alive in Judah, the LORD has told you, 'Don't go to Egypt.' Be sure you understand this; I warn you today ²⁰that you are making a mistake that will cause your deaths. You sent me to the LORD your God, saying, 'Pray to the LORD our God for us. Tell us everything the LORD our God says, and we will do it.' ²¹So today I have told you, but you have not obeyed the LORD your God in all that he sent me to tell you. ²²So now be sure

you understand this: You want to go to live in Egypt, but you will die there by war, hunger, or terrible diseases."

43 So Jeremiah finished telling the people the message from the LORD their God; he told them everything the LORD their God had sent him to tell them.

²Azariah son of Hoshaiah, Johanan son of Kareah, and some other men were too proud. They said to Jeremiah, "You are lying! The LORD our God did not send you to say, 'You must not go to Egypt to live there.' ³Baruch son of Neriah is causing you to be against us. He wants you to hand us over to the Babylonians so they can kill us or capture us and take us to Babylon."

⁴So Johanan, the army officers, and all the people disobeyed the LORD's command to stay in Judah. ⁵But Johanan son of Kareah and the army officers led away those who were left alive from Judah. They were the people who had run away from the Babylonians to other countries but then had come back to live in Judah. ⁶They led away the men, women, and children, and the king's daughters. Nebuzaradan commander of the guard had put Gedaliah son of Ahikam son of Shaphan in charge of those people. Johanan also took Jeremiah the prophet and Baruch son of Neriah. ⁷These people did not listen to the LORD. So they all went to Egypt to the city of Tahpanhes.

⁸In Tahpanhes the LORD spoke his word to Jeremiah: ⁹"Take some large stones. Bury them in the clay in the brick pavement in front of the king of Egypt's palace in Tahpanhes. Do this while the Jews are watching you. ¹⁰Then say to them, 'This is what the LORD All-Powerful, the God of Israel, says: I will soon send for my servant, Nebuchadnezzar king of Babylon. I will set his throne over these stones I have buried, and he will spread his covering for shade above them. ¹¹He will come here and attack Egypt. He will bring death to those who are supposed to die. He will make prisoners of those who are to be taken captive, and he will bring war to those who are to be killed with a sword. ¹²Nebuchadnezzar will set fire to the temples of the gods of Egypt and burn them. And he will take the idols away as captives. As a shepherd wraps himself in his clothes, so Nebuchadnezzar will wrap Egypt around him. Then he

will safely leave Egypt. ¹³He will destroy the stone pillars in the temple of the sun god in Egypt, and he will burn down the temples of the gods of Egypt.'"

DISASTER IN EGYPT

44 Jeremiah received a message from the LORD for all the Jews living in Egypt—in the cities of Migdol, Tahpanhes, Memphis, and in southern Egypt. This was the message: ²"The LORD All-Powerful, the God of Israel, says: You saw all the terrible things I brought on Jerusalem and the towns of Judah, which are ruins today with no one living in them. ³It is because the people who lived there did evil. They made me angry by burning incense and worshiping other gods that neither they nor you nor your ancestors ever knew. ⁴I sent all my servants, the prophets, to you again and again. By them I said to you, 'Don't do this terrible thing that I hate.' ⁵But they did not listen or pay attention. They did not stop doing evil things and burning incense to other gods. ⁶So I showed my great anger against them. I poured out my anger in the towns of Judah and the streets of Jerusalem so they are only ruins and piles of stones today.

⁷"Now the LORD All-Powerful, the God of Israel, says: Why are you doing such great harm to yourselves? You are cutting off the men and women, children and babies from the family of Judah, leaving yourselves without anyone from the family of Judah. ⁸Why do you want to make me angry by making idols? Why do you burn incense to the gods of Egypt, where you have come to live? You will destroy yourselves. Other nations will speak evil of you and make fun of you. ⁹Have you forgotten about the evil things your ancestors did? And have you forgotten the evil the kings and queens of Judah did? Have you forgotten about the evil you and your wives did? These things were done in the country of Judah and in the streets of Jerusalem. ¹⁰Even to this day the people of Judah are still too proud. They have not learned to respect me or to follow my teachings. They have not obeyed the laws I gave you and your ancestors.

¹¹"So this is what the LORD All-Powerful, the God of Israel, says: I am determined to bring disasters on you. I will destroy the

whole family of Judah. ¹²The few who were left alive from Judah were determined to go to Egypt and settle there, but they will all die in Egypt. They will be killed in war or die from hunger. From the least important to the greatest, they will be killed in war or die from hunger. Other nations will speak evil about them. People will be shocked by what has happened to them. They will become a curse word, and people will insult them. ¹³I will punish those people who have gone to live in Egypt, just as I punished Jerusalem, using swords, hunger, and terrible diseases. ¹⁴Of the people of Judah who were left alive and have gone to live in Egypt, none will escape my punishment. They want to return to Judah and live there, but none of them will live to return to Judah, except a few people who will escape."

¹⁵A large group of the people of Judah who lived in southern Egypt were meeting together. Among them were many women of Judah who were burning incense to other gods, and their husbands knew it. All these people said to Jeremiah, ¹⁶"We will not listen to the message from the LORD that you spoke to us. ¹⁷We promised to make sacrifices to the Queen Goddess, and we will certainly do everything we promised. We will burn incense and pour out drink offerings to worship her, just as we, our ancestors, kings, and officers did in the past. All of us did these things in the towns of Judah and in the streets of Jerusalem. At that time we had plenty of food and were successful, and nothing bad happened to us. ¹⁸But since we stopped making sacrifices to the Queen Goddess and stopped pouring out drink offerings to her, we have had great problems. Our people have also been killed in war and by hunger."

¹⁹The women said, "Our husbands knew what we were doing. We had their permission to burn incense to the Queen Goddess and to pour out drink offerings to her. Our husbands knew we were making cakes that looked like her and were pouring out drink offerings to her."

²⁰Then Jeremiah spoke to all the people—men and women—who answered him. ²¹He said to them, "The LORD remembered that you and your ancestors, kings and officers, and the people of the land burned incense in the towns of Judah and in the streets of Je-

rusalem. He remembered and thought about it. ²²Then he could not be patient with you any longer. He hated the terrible things you did. So he made your country an empty desert, where no one lives. Other people curse that country. And so it is today. ²³All this happened because you burned incense to other gods. You sinned against the LORD. You did not obey him or follow his teachings or the laws he gave you. You did not keep your part of the agreement with him. So this disaster has happened to you. It is there for you to see."

²⁴Then Jeremiah said to all those men and women, "People of Judah who are now in Egypt, hear the word of the LORD: ²⁵The LORD All-Powerful, the God of Israel, says: You and your wives did what you said you would do. You said, 'We will certainly keep the promises we made. We promised to make sacrifices to the Queen Goddess and to pour out drink offerings to her.' So, go ahead. Do the things you promised, and keep your promises. ²⁶But hear the word of the LORD. Listen, all you Jews living in Egypt. The LORD says, 'I have sworn by my great name: The people of Judah now living in Egypt will never again use my name to make promises. They will never again say in Egypt, "As surely as the Lord GOD lives..." ²⁷I am watching over them, not to take care of them, but to hurt them. The Jews who live in Egypt will die from swords or hunger until they are all destroyed. ²⁸A few will escape being killed by the sword and will come back to Judah from Egypt. Then, of the people of Judah who came to live in Egypt, those who are left alive will know if my word or their word came true. ²⁹I will give you a sign that I will punish you here in Egypt,' says the LORD. 'When you see it happen, you will know that my promises to hurt you will really happen.' ³⁰This is what the LORD says: 'Hophra king of Egypt has enemies who want to kill him. Soon I will hand him over to his enemies just as I handed Zedekiah king of Judah over to Nebuchadnezzar king of Babylon, who wanted to kill him.'"

A MESSAGE TO BARUCH

45 It was the fourth year that Jehoiakim son of Josiah was king of Judah. Jeremiah the prophet told these things to

Baruch son of Neriah, and Baruch wrote them on a scroll: ²"This is what the LORD, the God of Israel, says to you, Baruch: ³You have said, 'How terrible it is for me! The LORD has given me sorrow along with my pain. I am tired because of my suffering and cannot rest.'"

⁴The LORD said, "Say this to Baruch: 'This is what the LORD says: I will soon tear down what I have built, and I will pull up what I have planted everywhere in Judah. ⁵Baruch, you are looking for great things for yourself. Don't look for them, because I will bring disaster on all the people, says the LORD. You will have to go many places, but I will let you escape alive wherever you go.'"

MESSAGES TO THE NATIONS

46 The LORD spoke this word to Jeremiah the prophet about the nations:

²This message is to Egypt. It is about the army of Neco king of Egypt, which was defeated at the city of Carchemish on the Euphrates River by Nebuchadnezzar king of Babylon. This was in the fourth year that Jehoiakim son of Josiah was king of Judah. This is the LORD's message to Egypt:

³ "Prepare your shields, large and small,
    and march out for battle!
⁴ Harness the horses
    and get on them!
Go to your places for battle
    and put on your helmets!
Polish your spears.
    Put on your armor!
⁵ What do I see?
    That army is terrified,
and the soldiers are running away.
    Their warriors are defeated.
They run away quickly
    without looking back.
    There is terror on every side!" says the
    LORD.
⁶ "The fast runners cannot run away;
    the strong soldiers cannot escape.
They stumble and fall
    in the north, by the Euphrates River.
⁷ Who is this, rising up like the Nile River,
    like strong, fast rivers?
⁸ Egypt rises up like the Nile River,
    like strong, fast rivers.
Egypt says, 'I will rise up and cover the
    earth.

I will destroy cities and the people in
    them!'
⁹ Horsemen, charge into battle!
    Chariot drivers, drive hard!
March on, brave soldiers—
    soldiers from the countries of Cush and
    Put who carry shields,
    soldiers from Lydia who use bows.

¹⁰ "But that day belongs to the Lord GOD
    All-Powerful.
At that time he will give those people
    the punishment they deserve.
The sword will kill until it is finished,
    until it satisfies its thirst for their blood.
The Lord GOD All-Powerful will offer a
    sacrifice
in the land of the north, by the
    Euphrates River.

¹¹ "Go up to Gilead and get some balm,
    people of Egypt!
You have prepared many medicines,
    but they will not work;
    you will not be healed.
¹² The nations have heard of your shame,
    and your cries fill all the earth.
One warrior has run into another;
    both of them have fallen down
    together!"

¹³This is the message the LORD spoke to Jeremiah the prophet about Nebuchadnezzar king of Babylon's coming to attack Egypt:
¹⁴ "Announce this message in Egypt, and
    preach it in Migdol.
    Preach it also in the cities of Memphis
    and Tahpanhes:
'Get ready for war,
    because the battle is all around you.'
¹⁵ Egypt, why were your warriors killed?
    They could not stand because the LORD
    pushed them down.
¹⁶ They stumbled again and again
    and fell over each other.
They said, 'Get up. Let's go back
    to our own people and our homeland.
    We must get away from our enemy's
    sword!'
¹⁷ In their homelands those soldiers called
    out,
'The king of Egypt is only a lot of noise.
    He missed his chance for glory!'"

18 The King's name is the LORD
All-Powerful.
He says, "As surely as I live,
a powerful leader will come.
He will be like Mount Tabor among the
mountains,
like Mount Carmel by the sea.
19 People of Egypt, pack your things
to be taken away as captives,
because Memphis will be destroyed.
It will be a ruin, and no one will live
there.

20 "Egypt is like a beautiful young cow,
but a horsefly is coming
from the north to attack her.
21 The hired soldiers in Egypt's army
are like fat calves,
because even they all turn and run away
together;
they do not stand strong against the
attack.
Their time of destruction is coming;
they will soon be punished.
22 Egypt is like a hissing snake that is trying
to escape.
The enemy comes closer and closer.
They come against Egypt with axes
like men who cut down trees.
23 They will chop down Egypt's army
as if it were a great forest," says the
LORD.
"There are more enemy soldiers than
locusts;
there are too many to count.
24 The people of Egypt will be ashamed.
They will be handed over to the enemy
from the north."

25 The LORD All-Powerful, the God of Israel, says: "Very soon I will punish Amon, the
god of the city of Thebes. And I will punish
Egypt, her kings, her gods, and the people
who depend on the king. 26 I will hand those
people over to their enemies, who want to
kill them. I will give them to Nebuchadnezzar king of Babylon and his officers. But in
the future, Egypt will live in peace as it once
did," says the LORD.

A MESSAGE TO ISRAEL
27 "People of Jacob, my servants, don't be
afraid;
don't be frightened, Israel.

I will surely save you from those faraway
places
and your children from the lands where
they are captives.
The people of Jacob will have peace and
safety again,
and no one will make them afraid.
28 People of Jacob, my servants, do not be
afraid,
because I am with you," says the LORD.
"I will completely destroy the many
different nations
where I scattered you.
But I will not completely destroy you.
I will punish you fairly,
but I will not let you escape your
punishment."

A MESSAGE TO THE PHILISTINES

47 Before the king of Egypt attacked the
city of Gaza, the LORD spoke his word
to Jeremiah the prophet. This message is to
the Philistine people.
2 This is what the LORD says:
"See, the enemy is gathering in the north
like rising waters.
They will become like an overflowing
stream
and will cover the whole country like a
flood,
even the towns and the people living in
them.
Everyone living in that country
will cry for help;
the people will cry painfully.
3 They will hear the sound of the running
horses
and the noisy chariots
and the rumbling chariot wheels.
Parents will not help their children to
safety,
because they will be too weak to help.
4 The time has come
to destroy all the Philistines.
It is time to destroy all who are left alive
who could help the cities of Tyre and
Sidon.
The LORD will soon destroy the
Philistines,
those left alive from the island of
Crete.
5 The people from the city of Gaza will be
sad and shave their heads.

The people from the city of Ashkelon
  will be made silent.
Those left alive from the valley,
  how long will you cut yourselves?[n]

6 "You cry, 'Sword of the LORD,
  how long will you keep fighting?
Return to your holder.
  Stop and be still.'
7 But how can his sword rest
  when the LORD has given it a command?
He has ordered it
  to attack Ashkelon and the seacoast."

A MESSAGE TO MOAB

48 This message is to the country of Moab.

This is what the LORD All-Powerful, the God of Israel, says:

"How terrible it will be for the city of
  Nebo,
  because it will be ruined.
The town of Kiriathaim will be disgraced
  and captured;
  the strong city will be disgraced and
  shattered.
2 Moab will not be praised again.
  Men in the town of Heshbon plan
  Moab's defeat.
  They say, 'Come, let us put an end to
  that nation!'
Town of Madmen,[n] you will also be
  silenced.
  The sword will chase you.
3 Listen to the cries from the town of
  Horonaim,
  cries of much confusion and destruction.
4 Moab will be broken up.
  Her little children will cry for help.
5 Moab's people go up the path to the town
  of Luhith,
  crying loudly as they go.
On the road down to Horonaim,
  cries of pain and suffering can be heard.
6 Run! Run for your lives!
  Go like a bush being blown through the
  desert.
7 You trust in the things you do and in your
  wealth,
  so you also will be captured.
The god Chemosh will go into captivity
  and his priests and officers with him.
8 The destroyer will come against every
  town;

not one town will escape.
The valley will be ruined,
  and the high plain will be destroyed,
  as the LORD has said.
9 Give wings to Moab,
  because she will surely leave her land.
Moab's towns will become empty,
  with no one to live in them.
10 A curse will be on anyone who doesn't do
  what the LORD says,
  and a curse will be on anyone who
  holds back his sword from killing.

11 "The people of Moab have never known
  trouble.
  They are like wine left to settle;
they have never been poured from one jar
  to another.
  They have not been taken into captivity.
So they taste as they did before,
  and their smell has not changed.
12 A time is coming," says the LORD,
  "When I will send people to pour you
  from your jars.
They will empty Moab's jars
  and smash her jugs.
13 The people of Israel trusted that god in
  the town of Bethel,
  and they were ashamed when there was
  no help.
In the same way Moab will be ashamed
  of their god Chemosh.

14 "You cannot say, 'We are warriors!
  We are brave men in battle!'
15 The destroyer of Moab and her towns has
  arrived.
  Her best young men will be killed!" says
  the King,
  whose name is the LORD All-Powerful.
16 "The end of Moab is near,
  and she will soon be destroyed.
17 All you who live around Moab,
  all you who know her, cry for her.
Say, 'The ruler's power is broken;
  Moab's power and glory are gone.'

18 "You people living in the town of Dibon,
  come down from your place of honor
  and sit on the dry ground,

47:5 sad and . . . yourselves The people did these things to show their sadness. **48:2 Madmen** This name sounds like the Hebrew word for "be silenced."

843

because the destroyer of Moab has come
  against you.
  And he has destroyed your strong,
    walled cities.
19 You people living in the town of Aroer,
  stand next to the road and watch.
  See the man running away and the
    woman escaping.
  Ask them, 'What happened?'
20 Moab is filled with shame, because she is
  ruined.
  Cry, Moab, cry out!
  Announce at the Arnon River
    that Moab is destroyed.
21 People on the high plain have been
  punished.
  Judgment has come to these towns:
    Holon, Jahzah, and Mephaath;
22   Dibon, Nebo, and Beth Diblathaim;
23   Kiriathaim, Beth Gamul, and Beth
    Meon;
24   Kerioth and Bozrah.
  Judgment has come to all the towns of
    Moab, far and near.
25 Moab's strength has been cut off,
  and its arm broken!" says the LORD.

26 "The people of Moab thought they were
  greater than the LORD,
  so punish them until they act as if they
    are drunk.
  Moab will fall and roll around in its own
    vomit,
  and people will even make fun of it.
27 Moab, you made fun of Israel.
  Israel was caught in the middle of a
    gang of thieves.
  When you spoke about Israel,
    you shook your head and acted as if you
    were better than it.
28 People in Moab, leave your towns empty
  and go live among the rocks.
  Be like a dove that makes its nest
    at the entrance of a cave.
29 "We have heard that the people of Moab
  are proud,
  very proud.
  They are proud, very proud,
    and in their hearts they think they are
    important."
30 The LORD says,
  "I know Moab's great pride, but it is
    useless.

Moab's bragging accomplishes nothing.
31 So I cry sadly for Moab,
  for everyone in Moab.
  I moan for the people from the town of
    Kir Hareseth.
32 I cry with the people of the town of Jazer
  for you, the grapevines of the town of
    Sibmah.
  In the past your vines spread all the way
    to the sea,
  as far as the sea of Jazer.
  But the destroyer has taken over
    your fruit and grapes.
33 Joy and happiness are gone
  from the large, rich fields of Moab.
  I have stopped the flow of wine from the
    winepresses.
  No one walks on the grapes with shouts
    of joy.
  There are shouts,
    but not shouts of joy.

34 "Their crying can be heard from Moabite
  towns,
  from Heshbon to Elealeh and Jahaz.
  It can be heard from Zoar as far away as
    Horonaim and Eglath Shelishiyah.
  Even the waters of Nimrim are dried
    up.
35 I will stop Moab
  from making burnt offerings at the
    places of worship
  and from burning incense to their
    gods," says the LORD.

36 "My heart cries sadly for Moab like a flute
  playing a funeral song.
  It cries like a flute for the people from
    Kir Hareseth.
  The money they made has all been
    taken away.
37 Every head has been shaved
  and every beard cut off.
  Everyone's hands are cut,
    and everyone wears rough cloth around
    his waist.[n]
38 People are crying on every roof[n] in Moab
  and in every public square.

48:37 Every head . . . waist. The people did these
things to show their sadness for those who had died.
48:38 roof In Bible times houses were built with flat
roofs. The roof was used for drying things such as flax
and fruit. And it was used as an extra room, as a place for
worship, and as a cool place to sleep in the summer.

There is nothing but sadness,
  because I have broken Moab
  like a jar no one wants," says the LORD.
39 "Moab is shattered! The people are
    crying!
  Moab turns away in shame!
People all around her make fun of her.
  The things that happened fill them with
    great fear."

40This is what the LORD says:
"Look! Someone is coming, like an eagle
    diving down from the sky
  and spreading its wings over Moab.
41 The towns of Moab will be captured,
  and the strong, walled cities will be
    defeated.
At that time Moab's warriors will be
    frightened,
  like a woman who is having a baby.
42 The nation of Moab will be destroyed,
  because they thought they were greater
    than the LORD.
43 Fear, deep pits, and traps wait for you,
  people of Moab," says the LORD.
44 "People will run from fear,
  but they will fall into the pits.
Anyone who climbs out of the pits
  will be caught in the traps.
I will bring the year of punishment to
    Moab," says the LORD.

45 "People have run from the powerful
    enemy
  and have gone to Heshbon for safety.
But fire started in Heshbon;
  a blaze has spread from the hometown
    of Sihon king of Moab.
It burned up the leaders of Moab
  and destroyed those proud people.
46 How terrible it is for you, Moab!
  The people who worship Chemosh
    have been destroyed.
Your sons have been taken captive,
  and your daughters have been taken
    away.

47 "But in days to come,
  I will make good things happen again to
    Moab," says the LORD.

This ends the judgment on Moab.

A MESSAGE TO AMMON

49 This message is to the Ammonite
    people.
  This is what the LORD says:
"Do you think that Israel has no children?
  Do you think there is no one to take the
    land when the parents die?
If that were true, why did Molech take
    Gad's land
  and why did Molech's people settle in
    Gad's towns?"
2 The LORD says,
"The time will come when I will make
    Rabbah,
  the capital city of the Ammonites, hear
    the battle cry.
It will become a hill covered with ruins,
  and the towns around it will be burned.
Those people forced Israel out of that land,
  but now Israel will force them out!"
    says the LORD.
3 "People in the town of Heshbon, cry sadly
  because the town of Ai is destroyed!
Those who live in Rabbah, cry out!
Put on your rough cloth to show your
    sadness, and cry loudly.
Run here and there for safety inside the
    walls,
  because Molech will be taken captive
  and his priests and officers with him.
4 You brag about your valleys
  and about the fruit in your valleys.
You are like an unfaithful child
  who believes his treasures will save him.
  You think, 'Who would attack me?'
5 I will soon bring terror on you
  from everyone around you,"
    says the Lord GOD All-Powerful.
"You will all be forced to run away,
  and no one will be able to gather you.

6 "But the time will come
  when I will make good things happen
    to the Ammonites again,"
    says the LORD.

A MESSAGE TO EDOM

7This message is to Edom. This is what
the LORD All-Powerful says:
"Is there no more wisdom in the town of
    Teman?
  Can the wise men of Edom no longer
    give good advice?
  Have they lost their wisdom?

8 You people living in the town of Dedan,
    run away and hide in deep caves,
  because I will bring disaster on the people
    of Esau.
    It is time for me to punish them.
9 If workers came and picked the grapes
    from your vines,
    they would leave a few grapes behind.
  If robbers came at night,
    they would steal only enough for
      themselves.
10 But I will strip Edom bare.
    I will find all their hiding places,
    so they will not be able to hide from me.
  The children, relatives, and neighbors will
    die,
    and Edom will be no more.
11 Leave the orphans, and I will take care of
    them.
    Your widows also can trust in me."

12This is what the LORD says: "Some people did not deserve to be punished, but they
had to drink from the cup of suffering anyway. People of Edom, you deserve to be punished, so you will not escape punishment.
You must certainly drink from the cup of suffering." 13The LORD says, "I swear by my own
name that the city of Bozrah will become a
pile of ruins! People will be shocked by what
happened there. They will insult that city
and speak evil of it. And all the towns around
it will become ruins forever."

14 I have heard a message from the LORD.
    A messenger has been sent among the
      nations, saying,
  "Gather your armies to attack it!
    Get ready for battle!"

15 "Soon I will make you the smallest of
    nations,
    and you will be greatly hated by
      everyone.
16 Edom, you frightened other nations,
    but your pride has fooled you.
  You live in the hollow places of the cliff
    and control the high places of the hills.
  Even if you build your home as high as an
    eagle's nest,
    I will bring you down from there," says
      the LORD.
17 "Edom will be destroyed.
    People who pass by will be shocked to
      see the destroyed cities,

and they will be amazed at all her
  injuries.
18 Edom will be destroyed like the cities of
    Sodom and Gomorrah
    and the towns around them," says the
      LORD.
  "No one will live there!
    No one will stay in Edom.
19 "Like a lion coming up from the thick
    bushes near the Jordan River
    to attack a strong pen for sheep,
  I will suddenly chase Edom from its land.
    Who is the one I have chosen to do this?
  There is no one like me,
    no one who can take me to court.
  None of their leaders can stand up
    against me."
20 So listen to what the LORD has planned to
    do against Edom.
    Listen to what he has decided to do to
      the people in the town of Teman.
  He will surely drag away the young ones
    of Edom.
    Their hometowns will surely be
      shocked at what happens to them.
21 At the sound of Edom's fall, the earth will
    shake.
    Their cry will be heard all the way to
      the Red Sea.
22 The LORD is like an eagle swooping down
    and spreading its wings over the city of
      Bozrah.
  At that time Edom's soldiers will become
    very frightened,
    like a woman having a baby.

A MESSAGE TO DAMASCUS

23This message is to the city of Damascus:
  "The towns of Hamath and Arpad are put
    to shame,
    because they have heard bad news.
  They are discouraged.
    They are troubled like the tossing sea.
24 The city of Damascus has become weak.
    The people want to run away;
    they are ready to panic.
  The people feel pain and suffering,
    like a woman giving birth to a baby.
25 Damascus was a city of my joy.
    Why have the people not left that
      famous city yet?

26 Surely the young men will die in the city
  squares,
    and all her soldiers will be killed at that
    time," says the LORD All-Powerful.
27 "I will set fire to the walls of Damascus,
    and it will completely burn the strong
    cities of King Ben-Hadad."

A MESSAGE TO KEDAR AND HAZOR

28 This message is to the tribe of Kedar
and the kingdoms of Hazor, which Nebuchadnezzar king of Babylon defeated. This is
what the LORD says:

  "Go and attack the people of Kedar,
    and destroy the people of the East.
29 Their tents and flocks will be taken
  away.
    Their belongings will be carried off—
    their tents, all their goods, and their
    camels.
  Men will shout to them,
    'Terror on every side!'

30 "Run away quickly!
    People in Hazor, find a good place to
    hide!" says the LORD.
  "Nebuchadnezzar king of Babylon has
    made plans against you
    and wants to defeat you.

31 "Get up! Attack the nation that is
  comfortable,
    that is sure no one will defeat it," says
    the LORD.
  "It does not have gates or fences to
    protect it.
    Its people live alone.
32 The enemy will steal their camels
    and their large herds of cattle as war
    prizes.
  I will scatter the people who cut their hair
    short to every part of the earth,
    and I will bring disaster on them from
    everywhere," says the LORD.
33 "The city of Hazor will become a home
  for wild dogs;
    it will be an empty desert forever.
  No one will live there,
    and no one will stay in it."

A MESSAGE TO ELAM

34 Soon after Zedekiah became king of Judah, the LORD spoke this word to Jeremiah
the prophet. This message is to the nation of
Elam.

35 This is what the LORD All-Powerful
says:
  "I will soon break Elam's bow,
    its greatest strength.
36 I will bring the four winds against Elam
    from the four corners of the skies.
  I will scatter its people everywhere the
    four winds blow;
    its captives will go to every nation.
37 I will terrify Elam in front of their
    enemies,
    who want to destroy them.
  I will bring disaster to Elam
    and show them how angry I am!" says
    the LORD.
  "I will send a sword to chase Elam
    until I have killed them all.
38 I will set up my throne in Elam to show
    that I am king,
    and I will destroy its king and its
    officers!" says the LORD.

39 "But I will make good things happen to
    Elam again
    in the future," says the LORD.

A MESSAGE TO BABYLON

50 This is the message the LORD spoke
to Babylon and the Babylonian people through Jeremiah the prophet.
2 "Announce this to the nations.
    Lift up a banner and tell them.
    Speak the whole message and say:
  'Babylon will be captured.
    The god Bel will be put to shame,
    and the god Marduk will be afraid.
  Babylon's gods will be put to shame,
    and her idols will be afraid!'
3 A nation from the north will attack
    Babylon
    and make it like an empty desert.
  No one will live there;
    both people and animals will run away."

4 The LORD says, "At that time
    the people of Israel and Judah will
    come together.
  They will cry and look for the LORD
    their God.
5 Those people will ask how to go to
    Jerusalem
    and will start in that direction.
  They will come and join themselves to the
    LORD.

They will make an agreement with him
that will last forever,
an agreement that will never be
forgotten.

6 "My people have been like lost sheep.
Their leaders have led them in the
wrong way
and made them wander around in the
mountains and hills.
They forgot where their resting place
was.
7 Whoever saw my people hurt them.
And those enemies said, 'We did
nothing wrong.
Those people sinned against the LORD,
their true resting place,
the God their fathers trusted.'

8 "Run away from Babylon,
and leave the land of the
Babylonians.
Be like the goats that lead the flock.
9 I will soon bring against Babylon
many great nations from the north.
They will take their places for war against
it,
and it will be captured by people from
the north.
Their arrows are like trained soldiers
who do not return from war with empty
hands.
10 The enemy will take all the wealth from
the Babylonians.
Those enemy soldiers will get all they
want," says the LORD.

11 "Babylon, you are excited and happy,
because you took my land.
You dance around like a young cow in the
grain.
Your laughter is like the neighing of
male horses.
12 Your mother will be very ashamed;
the woman who gave birth to you will
be disgraced.
Soon Babylonia will be the least important
of all the nations.
She will be an empty, dry desert.
13 Because of the LORD's anger,
no one will live there.
She will be completely empty.
Everyone who passes by Babylon will be
shocked.

They will shake their heads when they
see all her injuries.

14 "Take your positions for war against
Babylon,
all you soldiers with bows.
Shoot your arrows at Babylon! Do not save
any of them,
because Babylon has sinned against the
LORD.
15 Soldiers around Babylon, shout the war
cry!
Babylon has surrendered, her towers
have fallen,
and her walls have been torn down.
The LORD is giving her people the
punishment they deserve.
You nations should give her what she
deserves;
do to her what she has done to others.
16 Don't let the people from Babylon plant
their crops
or gather the harvest.
The soldiers treated their captives cruelly.
Now, let everyone go back home.
Let everyone run to his own country.

17 "The people of Israel are like a flock of
sheep that are scattered
from being chased by lions.
The first lion to eat them up
was the king of Assyria.
The last lion to crush their bones
was Nebuchadnezzar king of Babylon."
18 So this is what the LORD All-Powerful,
the God of Israel, says:
"I will punish the king of Babylon and his
country
as I punished the king of Assyria.
19 But I will bring the people of Israel back
to their own pasture.
They will eat on Mount Carmel and in
Bashan.
They will eat and be full
on the hills of Ephraim and Gilead."
20 The LORD says,
"At that time people will try to find
Israel's guilt,
but there will be no guilt.
People will try to find Judah's sins,
but no sins will be found,
because I will leave a few people alive
from Israel and Judah,
and I will forgive their sins.

21 "Attack the land of Merathaim.
  Attack the people who live in Pekod.
Chase them, kill them, and completely
    destroy them.
  Do everything I commanded you!" says
    the LORD.
22 "The noise of battle can be heard all over
    the country;
  it is the noise of much destruction.
23 Babylon was the hammer of the whole
    earth,
  but how broken and shattered that
    hammer is now.
It is truly the most ruined
  of all the nations.
24 Babylon, I set a trap for you,
  and you were caught before you knew
    it.
You fought against the LORD,
  so you were found and taken prisoner.
25 The LORD has opened up his storeroom
  and brought out the weapons of his
    anger,
because the Lord GOD All-Powerful has
  work to do
  in the land of the Babylonians.
26 Come against Babylon from far away.
  Break open her storehouses of grain.
Pile up her dead bodies like heaps of
  grain.
Completely destroy Babylon
  and do not leave anyone alive.
27 Kill all the young men in Babylon;
  let them be killed like animals.
How terrible it will be for them, because
  the time has come for their defeat;
  it is time for them to be punished.
28 Listen to the people running to escape the
    country of Babylon!
  They are telling Jerusalem
how the LORD our God is punishing
  Babylon as it deserves
  for destroying his Temple.
29 "Call for the archers
  to come against Babylon.
Tell them to surround the city,
  and let no one escape.
Pay her back for what she has done;
  do to her what she has done to other
    nations.
Babylon acted with pride against the
  LORD,

the Holy One of Israel.
30 So her young men will be killed in her
    streets.
  All her soldiers will die on that day,"
    says the LORD.
31 "Babylon, you are too proud, and I am
    against you,"
  says the Lord GOD All-Powerful.
  "The time has come
    for you to be punished.
32 Proud Babylon will stumble and fall,
  and no one will help her get up.
I will start a fire in her towns,
  and it will burn up everything around
    her."
33 This is what the LORD All-Powerful
says:
  "The people of Israel
    and Judah are slaves.
The enemy took them as prisoners
  and won't let them go.
34 But God is strong and will buy them back.
  His name is the LORD All-Powerful.
He will surely defend them with power
  so he can give rest to their land.
  But he will not give rest to those living
    in Babylon."
35 The LORD says,
"Let a sword kill the people living in
    Babylon
  and her officers and wise men!
36 Let a sword kill her false prophets,
  and they will become fools.
Let a sword kill her warriors,
  and they will be full of terror.
37 Let a sword kill her horses and chariots
  and all the soldiers hired from other
    countries!
  Then they will be like frightened
    women.
Let a sword attack her treasures,
  so they will be taken away.
38 Let a sword attack her waters
  so they will be dried up.
She is a land of idols,
  and the people go crazy with fear over
    them.
39 "Desert animals and hyenas will live there,
  and owls will live there,
but no people will ever live there again.
  She will never be filled with people
    again.

40 God completely destroyed the cities of
　　Sodom and Gomorrah
　　and the towns around them," says the
　　　LORD.
　"In the same way no people will live in
　　Babylon,
　　and no human being will stay there.

41 "Look! An army is coming from the north.
　　A powerful nation and many kings
　　are coming together from all around the
　　　world.
42 Their armies have bows and spears.
　　The soldiers are cruel and have no
　　　mercy.
　As the soldiers come riding on their
　　horses,
　　the sound is loud like the roaring sea.
　They stand in their places, ready for battle.
　They are ready to attack you, city of
　　Babylon.
43 The king of Babylon heard about those
　　armies,
　　and he became helpless with fear.
　Distress has gripped him.
　　His pain is like that of a woman giving
　　　birth to a baby.

44 "Like a lion coming up from the thick
　　bushes near the Jordan River
　　to attack a strong pen for sheep,
　I will suddenly chase the people of
　　Babylon from their land.
　　Who is the one I have chosen to do this?
　There is no one like me,
　　no one who can take me to court.
　None of their leaders can stand up
　　against me."

45 So listen to what the LORD has planned to
　　do against Babylon.
　Listen to what he has decided to do to
　　the people in the city of Babylon.
　He will surely drag away the young ones
　　of Babylon.
　　Their hometowns will surely be
　　　shocked at what happens to them.
46 At the sound of Babylon's capture, the
　　earth will shake.
　People in all nations will hear Babylon's
　　cry of distress.

51 This is what the LORD says:
　　"I will soon cause a destroying
　　　wind to blow

against Babylon and the Babylonian
　people.
2 I will send foreign people to destroy
　　Babylon
　like a wind that blows chaff away.
　They will destroy the land.
　Armies will surround the city
　　when the day of disaster comes upon
　　　her.
3 Don't let the Babylonian soldiers prepare
　　their bows to shoot.
　　Don't even let them put on their armor.
　Don't feel sorry for the young men of
　　Babylon,
　　but completely destroy her army.
4 They will be killed in the land of the
　　Babylonians
　　and will die in her streets.
5 The Lord GOD All-Powerful
　　did not leave Israel and Judah,
　even though they were completely guilty
　　in the presence of the Holy One of
　　　Israel.

6 "Run away from Babylon
　　and save your lives!
　　Don't stay and be killed because of
　　　Babylon's sins.
　It is time for the LORD to punish Babylon;
　　he will give Babylon the punishment
　　　she deserves.
7 Babylon was like a gold cup in the LORD's
　　hand
　　that made the whole earth drunk.
　The nations drank Babylon's wine,
　　so they went crazy.
8 Babylon has suddenly fallen and been
　　broken.
　　Cry for her!
　Get balm for her pain,
　　and maybe she can be healed.

9 "Foreigners in Babylon say, 'We tried to
　　heal Babylon,
　　but she cannot be healed.
　So let us leave her and each go to his own
　　country.
　　Babylon's punishment is as high as the
　　　sky;
　　it reaches to the clouds.'

10 "The people of Judah say, 'The LORD has
　　shown us to be right.
　Come, let us tell in Jerusalem
　　what the LORD our God has done.'

11 "Sharpen the arrows!
   Pick up your shields!
The LORD has stirred up the kings of the
   Medes,
because he wants to destroy Babylon.
The LORD will punish them as they
   deserve
   for destroying his Temple.
12 Lift up a banner against the walls of
   Babylon!
   Bring more guards.
Put the watchmen in their places,
   and get ready for a secret attack!
The LORD will certainly do what he has
   planned
   and what he said he would do against
   the people of Babylon.
13 People of Babylon, you live near much
   water
   and are rich with many treasures,
but your end as a nation has come.
   It is time to stop you from robbing other
   nations.
14 The LORD All-Powerful has promised in
   his own name:
   'Babylon, I will surely fill you with so
   many enemy soldiers they will be like
   a swarm of locusts.
   They will stand over you and shout
   their victory.'

15 "The LORD made the earth by his power.
   He used his wisdom to build the world
   and his understanding to stretch out the
   skies.
16 When he thunders, the waters in the skies
   roar.
   He makes clouds rise in the sky all over
   the earth.
He sends lightning with the rain
   and brings out the wind from his
   storehouses.

17 "People are so stupid and know so little.
   Goldsmiths are made ashamed by their
   idols,
   because those statues are only false gods.
   They have no breath in them.
18 They are worth nothing; people make fun
   of them.
   When they are judged, they will be
   destroyed.
19 But God, who is Jacob's Portion, is not like
   the idols.

He made everything,
   and he chose Israel to be his special
   people.
   The LORD All-Powerful is his name.

20 "You are my war club,
   my battle weapon.
   I use you to smash nations.
   I use you to destroy kingdoms.
21 I use you to smash horses and riders.
   I use you to smash chariots and drivers.
22 I use you to smash men and women.
   I use you to smash old people and
   young people.
   I use you to smash young men and
   young women.
23 I use you to smash shepherds and flocks.
   I use you to smash farmers and oxen.
   I use you to smash governors and
   officers.

24 "But I will pay back Babylon and all the
Babylonians for all the evil things they did to
Jerusalem in your sight," says the LORD.
   25 The LORD says,
"Babylon, you are a destroying mountain,
   and I am against you.
   You have destroyed the whole land.
I will put my hand out against you.
   I will roll you off the cliffs,
   and I will make you a burned-out
   mountain.
26 People will not find any rocks in Babylon
   big enough for cornerstones.
   People will not take any rocks from
   Babylon to use for the foundation of
   a building,
   because your city will be just a pile of
   ruins forever," says the LORD.

27 "Lift up a banner in the land!
   Blow the trumpet among the nations!
Get the nations ready for battle against
   Babylon.
Call these kingdoms of Ararat, Minni,
   and Ashkenaz to fight against her.
Choose a commander to lead the army
   against Babylon.
   Send so many horses that they are like a
   swarm of locusts.
28 Get the nations ready for battle against
   Babylon—
   the kings of the Medes,
their governors and all their officers,
   and all the countries they rule.

29 The land shakes and moves in pain,
because the LORD will do what he has
planned to Babylon.
He will make Babylon an empty desert,
where no one will live.
30 Babylon's warriors have stopped fighting.
They stay in their protected cities.
Their strength is gone,
and they have become like frightened
women.
Babylon's houses are burning.
The bars of her gates are broken.
31 One messenger follows another;
messenger follows messenger.
They announce to the king of Babylon
that his whole city has been captured.
32 The river crossings have been captured,
and the swamplands are burning.
All of Babylon's soldiers are terribly
afraid."

33 This is what the LORD All-Powerful, the
God of Israel, says:
"The city of Babylon is like a threshing
floor,
where people crush the grain at harvest
time.
The time to harvest Babylon is coming
soon."

34 "Nebuchadnezzar king of Babylon has
defeated and destroyed us.
In the past he took our people away,
and we became like an empty jar.
He was like a giant snake that swallowed
us.
He filled his stomach with our best
things.
Then he spit us out.
35 Babylon did terrible things to hurt us.
Now let those things happen to
Babylon,"
say the people of Jerusalem.
"The people of Babylon killed our people.
Now let them be punished for what
they did," says Jerusalem.
36 So this is what the LORD says:
"I will soon defend you, Judah,
and make sure that Babylon is
punished.
I will dry up Babylon's sea
and make her springs become dry.
37 Babylon will become a pile of ruins,
a home for wild dogs.

People will be shocked by what happened
there.
No one will live there anymore.
38 Babylon's people roar like young lions;
they growl like baby lions.
39 While they are stirred up,
I will give a feast for them
and make them drunk.
They will shout and laugh.
And they will sleep forever and never
wake up!" says the LORD.
40 "I will take the people of Babylon to be
killed.
They will be like lambs,
like sheep and goats waiting to be
killed.

41 "How Babylon has been defeated!
The pride of the whole earth has been
taken captive.
People from other nations are shocked at
what happened to Babylon,
and the things they see make them
afraid.
42 The sea has risen over Babylon;
its roaring waves cover her.
43 Babylon's towns are ruined and empty.
It has become a dry, desert land,
a land where no one lives.
People do not even travel through
Babylon.
44 I will punish the god Bel in Babylon.
I will make him spit out what he has
swallowed.
Nations will no longer come to Babylon;
even the wall around the city will fall.

45 "Come out of Babylon, my people!
Run for your lives!
Run from the LORD's great anger.
46 Don't lose courage;
rumors will spread through the land,
but don't be afraid.
One rumor comes this year, and another
comes the next year.
There will be rumors of terrible fighting
in the country,
of rulers fighting against rulers.
47 The time will surely come
when I will punish the idols of
Babylon,
and the whole land will be disgraced.
There will be many dead people lying
all around.

48 Then heaven and earth and all that is in
them
will shout for joy about Babylon.
They will shout because the army comes
from the north
to destroy Babylon," says the LORD.

49 "Babylon must fall, because she killed
people from Israel.
She killed people from everywhere on
earth.

50 You who have escaped being killed with
swords,
leave Babylon! Don't wait!
Remember the LORD in the faraway
land
and think about Jerusalem."

51 "We people of Judah are disgraced,
because we have been insulted.
We have been shamed,
because strangers have gone into
the holy places of the LORD's Temple!"

52 So the LORD says, "The time is coming
soon
when I will punish the idols of Babylon.
Wounded people will cry with pain
all over that land.

53 Even if Babylon grows until she touches
the sky,
and even if she makes her highest cities
strong,
I will send people to destroy her," says
the LORD.

54 "Sounds of people crying are heard in
Babylon.
Sounds of people destroying things
are heard in the land of the Babylonians.

55 The LORD is destroying Babylon
and making the loud sounds of the city
become silent.
Enemies come roaring in like ocean waves.
The roar of their voices is heard all
around.

56 The army has come to destroy Babylon.
Her soldiers have been captured,
and their bows are broken,
because the LORD is a God who punishes
people for the evil they do.
He gives them the full punishment they
deserve.

57 I will make Babylon's rulers and wise men
drunk,

and her governors, officers, and
soldiers, too.
Then they will sleep forever and never
wake up," says the King,
whose name is the LORD All-Powerful.

58 This is what the LORD All-Powerful
says:
"Babylon's thick wall will be completely
pulled down
and her high gates burned.
The people will work hard, but it won't
help;
their work will only become fuel for the
flames!"

A MESSAGE TO BABYLON

59 This is the message that Jeremiah the
prophet gave to the officer Seraiah son of
Neriah, who was the son of Mahseiah. Seraiah went to Babylon with Zedekiah king of
Judah in the fourth year Zedekiah was king
of Judah. His duty was to arrange the king's
food and housing on the trip. 60 Jeremiah had
written on a scroll all the terrible things that
would happen to Babylon, all these words
about Babylon. 61 Jeremiah said to Seraiah,
"As soon as you come to Babylon, be sure to
read this message so all the people can hear
you. 62 Then say, 'LORD, you have said that
you will destroy this place so that no people
or animals will live in it. It will be an empty
ruin forever.' 63 After you finish reading this
scroll, tie a stone to it and throw it into the
Euphrates River. 64 Then say, 'In the same
way Babylon will sink and will not rise again
because of the terrible things I will make
happen here. Her people will fall.'"
The words of Jeremiah end here.

THE FALL OF JERUSALEM

52 Zedekiah was twenty-one years old
when he became king, and he was
king in Jerusalem for eleven years. His
mother's name was Hamutal daughter of
Jeremiah,[n] and she was from Libnah. 2 Zedekiah did what the LORD said was wrong, just
as Jehoiakim had done. 3 All this happened in
Jerusalem and Judah because the LORD was
angry with them. Finally, he threw them out
of his presence.
Zedekiah turned against the king of

52:1 **Jeremiah** This is not the prophet Jeremiah but a
different man with the same name.

Babylon. ⁴Then Nebuchadnezzar king of Babylon marched against Jerusalem with his whole army. They made a camp around the city and built devices all around the city walls to attack it. This happened on Zedekiah's ninth year, tenth month, and tenth day as king. ⁵And the city was under attack until Zedekiah's eleventh year as king.

⁶By the ninth day of the fourth month, the hunger was terrible in the city; there was no food for the people to eat. ⁷Then the city wall was broken through, and the whole army of Judah ran away at night. They left the city through the gate between the two walls by the king's garden. Even though the Babylonians were surrounding the city, Zedekiah and his men headed toward the Jordan Valley.

⁸But the Babylonian army chased King Zedekiah and caught him in the plains of Jericho. All of his army was scattered from him. ⁹So the Babylonians captured Zedekiah and took him to the king of Babylon at the town of Riblah in the land of Hamath. There he passed sentence on Zedekiah. ¹⁰At Riblah the king of Babylon killed Zedekiah's sons as he watched. The king also killed all the officers of Judah. ¹¹Then he put out Zedekiah's eyes, and put bronze chains on him, and took him to Babylon. And the king kept Zedekiah in prison there until the day he died.

¹²Nebuzaradan, commander of the king's special guards and servant of the king of Babylon, came to Jerusalem on the tenth day of the fifth month. This was in Nebuchadnezzar's nineteenth year as king of Babylon. ¹³Nebuzaradan set fire to the Temple of the LORD, the palace, and all the houses of Jerusalem; every important building was burned. ¹⁴The whole Babylonian army, led by the commander of the king's special guards, broke down all the walls around Jerusalem. ¹⁵Nebuzaradan, the commander of the king's special guards, took captive some of the poorest people, those who were left in Jerusalem, those who had surrendered to the king of Babylon, and the skilled craftsmen who were left in Jerusalem. ¹⁶But Nebuzaradan left behind some of the poorest people of the land to take care of the vineyards and fields.

¹⁷The Babylonians broke into pieces the bronze pillars, the bronze stands, and the large bronze bowl, called the Sea, which were in the Temple of the LORD. Then they carried all the bronze pieces to Babylon. ¹⁸They also took the pots, shovels, wick trimmers, bowls, dishes, and all the bronze objects used to serve in the Temple. ¹⁹The commander of the king's special guards took away bowls, pans for carrying hot coals, large bowls, pots, lampstands, pans, and bowls used for drink offerings. He took everything that was made of pure gold or silver.

²⁰There was so much bronze that it could not be weighed: two pillars, the large bronze bowl called the Sea with the twelve bronze bulls under it, and the movable stands, which King Solomon had made for the Temple of the LORD. ²¹Each of the pillars was about twenty-seven feet high, eighteen feet around, and hollow inside. The wall of each pillar was three inches thick. ²²The bronze capital on top of the one pillar was about seven and one-half feet high. It was decorated with a net design and bronze pomegranates all around it. The other pillar also had pomegranates and was like the first pillar. ²³There were ninety-six pomegranates on the sides of the pillars. There was a total of a hundred pomegranates above the net design.

²⁴The commander of the king's special guards took as prisoners Seraiah the chief priest, Zephaniah the priest next in rank, and the three doorkeepers. ²⁵He also took from the city the officer in charge of the soldiers, seven people who advised the king, the royal secretary who selected people for the army, and sixty other men from Judah who were in the city when it fell. ²⁶Nebuzaradan, the commander, took these people and brought them to the king of Babylon at the town of Riblah. ²⁷There at Riblah, in the land of Hamath, the king had them killed.

So the people of Judah were led away from their country as captives. ²⁸This is the number of the people Nebuchadnezzar took away as captives: in the seventh year, 3,023 Jews; ²⁹in Nebuchadnezzar's eighteenth year, 832 people from Jerusalem; ³⁰in Nebuchadnezzar's twenty-third year, Nebuzaradan, commander of the king's special guards, took 745 Jews as captives.

In all 4,600 people were taken captive.

JEHOIACHIN IS SET FREE

[31] Jehoiachin king of Judah was in prison in Babylon for thirty-seven years. The year Evil-Merodach became king of Babylon he let Jehoiachin king of Judah out of prison. He set Jehoiachin free on the twenty-fifth day of the twelfth month. [32] Evil-Merodach spoke kindly to Jehoiachin and gave him a seat of honor above the seats of the other kings who were with him in Babylon. [33] So Jehoiachin put away his prison clothes, and for the rest of his life, he ate at the king's table. [34] Every day the king of Babylon gave Jehoiachin an allowance. This lasted as long as he lived, until the day Jehoiachin died.

lamentations

SAD SONGS ABOUT JERUSALEM

JERUSALEM CRIES OVER HER LOSS

1 Jerusalem once was full of people,
  but now the city is empty.
Jerusalem once was a great city among
    the nations,
  but now she[n] is like a widow.
She was like a queen of all the other
    cities,
  but now she is a slave.

2 She cries loudly at night,
  and tears are on her cheeks.
There is no one to comfort her;
  all who loved her are gone.
All her friends have turned against her
  and are now her enemies.

3 Judah has gone into captivity
  where she suffers and works hard.
She lives among other nations,
  but she has found no rest.
Those who chased her caught her
  when she was in trouble.

4 The roads to Jerusalem are sad,
  because no one comes for the feasts.
No one passes through her gates.
  Her priests groan,
her young women are suffering,
  and Jerusalem suffers terribly.

5 Her foes are now her masters.
  Her enemies enjoy the wealth they have
    taken.
The LORD is punishing her
  for her many sins.
Her children have gone away
  as captives of the enemy.

6 The beauty of Jerusalem
  has gone away.
Her rulers are like deer
  that cannot find food.
They are weak
  and run from the hunters.

7 Jerusalem is suffering and homeless.
  She remembers all the good things
    from the past.

But her people were defeated by the
    enemy,
  and there was no one to help her.
When her enemies saw her,
  they laughed to see her ruined.

8 Jerusalem sinned terribly,
  so she has become unclean.
Those who honored her now hate her,
  because they have seen her nakedness.
She groans
  and turns away.

9 She made herself dirty by her sins
  and did not think about what would
      happen to her.
Her defeat was surprising,
  and no one could comfort her.
She says, "LORD, see how I suffer,
  because the enemy has won."

10 The enemy reached out and took
  all her precious things.
She even saw foreigners
  enter her Temple.
The LORD had commanded foreigners
  never to enter the meeting place of his
      people.

11 All of Jerusalem's people groan,
  looking for bread.
They are trading their precious things for
    food
  so they can stay alive.
The city says, "Look, LORD, and see.
  I am hated."

12 Jerusalem says, "You who pass by on the
    road don't seem to care.
  Come, look at me and see:
Is there any pain like mine?
  Is there any pain like that he has caused
    me?
The LORD has punished me
  on the day of his great anger.

1:1 she In this poem the city of Jerusalem is described
as a woman.

856

13 "He sent fire from above
    that went down into my bones.
He stretched out a net for my feet
    and turned me back.
He made me so sad and lonely
    that I am weak all day.

14 "He has noticed my sins;
    they are tied together by his hands;
they hang around my neck.
    He has turned my strength into
      weakness.
The Lord has handed me over
    to those who are stronger than I.

15 "The Lord has rejected
    all my mighty men inside my walls.
He brought an army against me
    to destroy my young men.
As if in a winepress, the Lord has crushed
    the capital city of Judah.

16 "I cry about these things;
    my eyes overflow with tears.
There is no one near to comfort me,
    no one who can give me strength
      again.
My children are left sad and lonely,
    because the enemy has won."

17 Jerusalem reaches out her hands,
    but there is no one to comfort her.
The Lord commanded the people of
    Jacob
    to be surrounded by their enemies.
Jerusalem is now unclean
    like those around her.

18 Jerusalem says, "The Lord is right,
    but I refused to obey him.
Listen, all you people,
    and look at my pain.
My young women and men
    have gone into captivity.

19 "I called out to my friends,
    but they turned against me.
My priests and my elders
    have died in the city
while looking for food
    to stay alive.

20 "Look at me, Lord. I am upset
    and greatly troubled.
My heart is troubled,
    because I have been so stubborn.

Out in the streets, the sword kills;
    inside the houses, death destroys.

21 "People have heard my groaning,
    and there is no one to comfort me.
All my enemies have heard of my trouble,
    and they are happy you have done this
      to me.
Now bring that day you have announced
    so that my enemies will be like me.

22 "Look at all their evil.
    Do to them what you have done to me
    because of all my sins.
I groan over and over again,
    and I am afraid."

THE LORD DESTROYED JERUSALEM

2 Look how the Lord in his anger
    has brought Jerusalem to shame.
He has thrown down the greatness of Israel
    from the sky to the earth;
he did not remember the Temple, his
      footstool,
    on the day of his anger.

2 The Lord swallowed up without mercy
    all the houses of the people of Jacob;
in his anger he pulled down
    the strong places of Judah.
He threw her kingdom and its rulers
    down to the ground in dishonor.

3 In his anger he has removed
    all the strength of Israel;
he took away his power from Israel
    when the enemy came.
He burned against the people of Jacob
    like a flaming fire
    that burns up everything around it.

4 Like an enemy, he prepared to shoot his
      bow,
    and his hand was against us.
Like an enemy, he killed
    all the good-looking people;
he poured out his anger like fire
    on the tents of Jerusalem.

5 The Lord was like an enemy;
    he swallowed up Israel.
He swallowed up all her palaces
    and destroyed all her strongholds.
He has caused more moaning and
      groaning
    for Judah.

6 He cut down his Temple like a garden;
  he destroyed the meeting place.
The LORD has made Jerusalem forget
  the set feasts and Sabbath days.
He has rejected the king and the priest
  in his great anger.

7 The Lord has rejected his altar
  and abandoned his Temple.
He has handed over to the enemy
  the walls of Jerusalem's palaces.
Their uproar in the LORD's Temple
  was like that of a feast day.

8 The LORD planned to destroy
  the wall around Jerusalem.
He measured the wall
  and did not stop himself from
    destroying it.
He made the walls and defenses sad;
  together they have fallen.

9 Jerusalem's gates have fallen to the
    ground;
  he destroyed and smashed the bars of
    the gates.
Her king and her princes are among the
    nations.
  The teaching of the LORD has stopped,
and the prophets do not have
  visions from the LORD.

10 The elders of Jerusalem
  sit on the ground in silence.
They throw dust on their heads
  and put on rough cloth to show their
    sadness.
The young women of Jerusalem
  bow their heads to the ground in
    sorrow.

11 My eyes have no more tears,
  and I am sick to my stomach.
I feel empty inside,
  because my people have been
    destroyed.
Children and babies are fainting
  in the streets of the city.

12 They ask their mothers,
  "Where is the grain and wine?"
They faint like wounded soldiers
  in the streets of the city
  and die in their mothers' arms.

13 What can I say about you, Jerusalem?

What can I compare you to?
What can I say you are like?
  How can I comfort you, Jerusalem?
Your ruin is as deep as the sea.
  No one can heal you.

14 Your prophets saw visions,
  but they were false and worth nothing.
They did not point out your sins
  to keep you from being captured.
They preached what was false
  and led you wrongly.

15 All who pass by on the road
  clap their hands at you;
they make fun of Jerusalem
  and shake their heads.
They ask, "Is this the city that people
    called
  the most beautiful city,
  the happiest place on earth?"

16 All your enemies open their mouths
  to speak against you.
They make fun and grind their teeth in
    anger.
  They say, "We have swallowed you up.
This is the day we were waiting for!
  We have finally seen it happen."

17 The LORD has done what he planned;
  he has kept his word
  that he commanded long ago.
He has destroyed without mercy,
  and he has let your enemies laugh at
    you.
He has strengthened your enemies.

18 The people cry out to the Lord.
  Wall of Jerusalem,
let your tears flow
  like a river day and night.
Do not stop
  or let your eyes rest.

19 Get up, cry out in the night,
  even as the night begins.
Pour out your heart like water
  in prayer to the Lord.
Lift up your hands in prayer to him
  for the life of your children
who are fainting with hunger
  on every street corner.

20 Jerusalem says: "Look, LORD, and see
  to whom you have done this.

Women eat their own babies,
the children they have cared for.
Priests and prophets are killed
in the Temple of the Lord.

21 "People young and old
lie outside on the ground.
My young women and young men
have been killed by the sword.
You killed them on the day of your anger;
you killed them without mercy.

22 "You invited terrors to come against me
on every side,
as if you were inviting them to a feast.
No one escaped or remained alive
on the day of the LORD's anger.
My enemy has killed
those I cared for and brought up."

THE MEANING OF SUFFERING

3 I am a man who has seen the suffering
that comes from the rod of the LORD's
anger.
2 He led me
into darkness, not light.
3 He turned his hand against me
again and again, all day long.

4 He wore out my flesh and skin
and broke my bones.
5 He surrounded me with sadness
and attacked me with grief.
6 He made me sit in the dark,
like those who have been dead a long
time.

7 He shut me in so I could not get out;
he put heavy chains on me.
8 I cry out and beg for help,
but he ignores my prayer.
9 He blocked my way with a stone wall
and led me in the wrong direction.

10 He is like a bear ready to attack me,
like a lion in hiding.
11 He led me the wrong way and let me stray
and left me without help.
12 He prepared to shoot his bow
and made me the target for his arrows.

13 He shot me in the kidneys
with the arrows from his bag.
14 I was a joke to all my people,
who make fun of me with songs all day
long.

15 The LORD filled me with misery;
he made me drunk with suffering.
16 He broke my teeth with gravel
and trampled me into the dirt.
17 I have no more peace.
I have forgotten what happiness is.
18 I said, "My strength is gone,
and I have no hope in the LORD."

19 LORD, remember my suffering and my
misery,
my sorrow and trouble.
20 Please remember me
and think about me.
21 But I have hope
when I think of this:

22 The LORD's love never ends;
his mercies never stop.
23 They are new every morning;
LORD, your loyalty is great.
24 I say to myself, "The LORD is mine,
so I hope in him."

25 The LORD is good to those who hope in
him,
to those who seek him.
26 It is good to wait quietly
for the LORD to save.
27 It is good for someone to work hard
while he is young.

28 He should sit alone and be quiet;
the LORD has given him hard work to
do.
29 He should bow down to the ground;
maybe there is still hope.
30 He should let anyone slap his cheek;
he should be filled with shame.

31 The Lord will not reject
his people forever.
32 Although he brings sorrow,
he also has mercy and great love.
33 He does not like to punish people
or make them sad.

34 He sees if any prisoner of the earth
is crushed under his feet;
35 he sees if someone is treated
unfairly
before the Most High God;
36 the Lord sees
if someone is cheated in his case in
court.

37 Nobody can speak and have it happen
   unless the Lord commands it.
38 Both bad and good things
   come by the command of the Most
   High God.
39 No one should complain
   when he is punished for his sins.

40 Let us examine and see what we have
   done
   and then return to the LORD.
41 Let us lift up our hands and pray from our
   hearts
   to God in heaven:
42 "We have sinned and turned against
   you,
   and you have not forgiven us.

43 "You wrapped yourself in anger and
   chased us;
   you killed us without mercy.
44 You wrapped yourself in a cloud,
   and no prayer could get through.
45 You made us like scum and trash
   among the other nations.

46 "All of our enemies
   open their mouths and speak against us.
47 We have been frightened and fearful,
   ruined and destroyed."
48 Streams of tears flow from my eyes,
   because my people are destroyed.

49 My tears flow continually,
   without stopping,
50 until the LORD looks down

DO YOU KNOW HIM?

FULFILLMENT

God's in control

LAMENTATIONS 3:37

The Book of Lamentations consists of five poems. They are laments about the destruction of Solomon's Temple built to the honor of God. These poems were read every year at a national day of mourning. They described suffering on a national scale.

This verse of scripture is a rhetorical question. That means it is a question that implies an expected answer. The answer that is expected is this: There is no one who makes anything happen unless God allows it to happen. The reason that this implication is important to the Jewish national day of mourning is that it reassures the people that the destruction of the Temple occurred only because God allowed it to occur. It was not accident, tragedy, fate, or the will of evil people.

Often we feel that bad things are out of control. Terrorism, catastrophes, genocide, and all kinds of individual and corporate disasters seem to challenge our faith in God's care. But all the while God is available to help the hurting. We can mourn, grieve, and lament. And God will hear us. Life is not out of control. We are not left helpless.

reflect: Give thanks to God that he has not left you helpless or hopeless today.
Go to **FULFILLMENT:** "Are You Programmed for Stress?" at **Philippians 2:5–11.**

and sees from heaven.
⁵¹ I am sad when I see
what has happened to all the women of
my city.

⁵² Those who are my enemies for no reason
hunted me like a bird.
⁵³ They tried to kill me in a pit;
they threw stones at me.
⁵⁴ Water came up over my head,
and I said, "I am going to die."
⁵⁵ I called out to you, LORD,
from the bottom of the pit.
⁵⁶ You heard me calling, "Do not close your
ears
and ignore my gasps and shouts."
⁵⁷ You came near when I called to you;
you said, "Don't be afraid."

⁵⁸ Lord, you have taken my case
and given me back my life.
⁵⁹ LORD, you have seen how I have been
wronged.
Now judge my case for me.
⁶⁰ You have seen how my enemies took
revenge on me
and made evil plans against me.

⁶¹ LORD, you have heard their insults
and all their evil plans against me.
⁶² The words and thoughts of my enemies
are against me all the time.
⁶³ Look! In everything they do
they make fun of me with songs.

⁶⁴ Pay them back, LORD,
for what they have done.
⁶⁵ Make them stubborn,
and put your curse on them.
⁶⁶ Chase them in anger, LORD,
and destroy them from under your
heavens.

THE ATTACK ON JERUSALEM

4 See how the gold has lost its shine,
how the pure gold has dulled!
The stones of the Temple are scattered
at every street corner.

² The precious people of Jerusalem
were more valuable than gold,
but now they are thought of as clay jars
made by the hands of a potter.

³ Even wild dogs give their milk
to feed their young,

but my people are cruel
like ostriches in the desert.

⁴ The babies are so thirsty
their tongues stick to the roofs of their
mouths.
Children beg for bread,
but no one gives them any.

⁵ Those who once ate fine foods
are now starving in the streets.
People who grew up wearing nice clothes
now pick through trash piles.

⁶ My people have been punished
more than Sodom was.
Sodom was destroyed suddenly,
and no hands reached out to help her.

⁷ Our princes were purer than snow,
and whiter than milk.
Their bodies were redder than rubies;
they looked like sapphires.

⁸ But now they are blacker than coal,
and no one recognizes them in the
streets.
Their skin hangs on their bones;
it is as dry as wood.

⁹ Those who were killed in the war were
better off
than those killed by hunger.
They starve in pain and die,
because there is no food from the field.

¹⁰ With their own hands kind women
cook their own children.
They became food
when my people were destroyed.

¹¹ The LORD turned loose all of his anger;
he poured out his strong anger.
He set fire to Jerusalem,
burning it down to the foundations.

¹² Kings of the earth and people of the world
could not believe
that enemies and foes
could enter the gates of Jerusalem.

¹³ It happened because her prophets sinned
and her priests did evil.
They killed in the city
those who did what was right.

¹⁴ They wandered in the streets
as if they were blind.

They were dirty with blood,
    so no one would touch their clothes.

¹⁵ "Go away! You are unclean," people
    shouted at them.
    "Get away! Get away! Don't touch us!"
So they ran away and wandered.
    Even the other nations said, "Don't stay
    here."

¹⁶ The LORD himself scattered them
    and did not look after them anymore.
No one respects the priests
    or honors the elders.

¹⁷ Also, our eyes grew tired,
    looking for help that never came.
We kept watch from our towers
    for a nation to save us.

GOD'S PURPOSE FOR YOUR LIFE

FUTURE

generational curses,
no excuses

LAMENTATIONS 5:7   By Larry Huch

If you have a recurring physical ailment, your doctor asks you for your family
medical history. Doctors need this information to help identify your present
problem. Likewise, the Great Physician, Jesus, asks, "Is there any family history of a
problem you seem plagued with and cannot get rid of?"

The Word teaches us that problems in our lives are sometimes caused by sins in our
family's past (see Lamentations 5:7 and Leviticus 26:39). His Holy Spirit helps us to
recognize these harmful characteristics or curses and teaches us how to destroy works
of the devil in our lives.

It does not matter whether you suffer as a result of something you have done or
something your ancestors have done, the Son of God, the Anointed One, has come to
set you free. Jesus Christ's sacrificial death and resurrected life give you the authority to
cast out the enemy forces attacking your family, home, or business. His blood paid for
your salvation and deliverance so you do not have to pay the penalty for generational
curses any longer. Jesus died on the cross to free you from every sin or curse (1 Peter
1:18–19).

Just remember, no matter what wrongs have been passed down to you, you are the
one responsible for your actions now. Recognize why you have been behaving in a
certain way, forgive without blaming others, and use your authority to sever that chain
of bondage. God's restoration through Jesus transforms you from the inside out. You
cannot change the past, but you can change your future. (From *Free at Last*)

---

reflect: What may be causing you to think and behave in an ungodly manner?
Go to **Matthew 19:26.**

18 Our enemies hunted us,
　so we could not even walk in the streets.
Our end is near. Our time is up.
　Our end has come.

19 Those who chased us
　were faster than eagles in the sky.
They ran us into the mountains
　and ambushed us in the desert.

20 The LORD's appointed king, who was our
　very breath,
　was caught in their traps.
We had said about him, "We will be
　protected by him
　among the nations."

21 Be happy and glad, people of Edom,
　you who live in the land of Uz.
The cup of God's anger will come to you;
　then you will get drunk and go naked.

22 Your punishment is complete, Jerusalem.
　He will not send you into captivity
　again.
But the LORD will punish the sins of
　Edom;
　he will uncover your evil.

A PRAYER TO THE LORD

5 Remember, LORD, what happened to us.
　Look and see our disgrace.
2 Our land has been turned over to
　strangers;
　our houses have been given to
　foreigners.
3 We are like orphans with no father;
　our mothers are like widows.
4 We have to buy the water we drink;
　we must pay for the firewood.
5 Those who chase after us want to catch us
　by the neck.

We are tired and find no rest.
6 We made an agreement with Egypt
　and with Assyria to get enough food.
7 Our ancestors sinned against you, but they
　are gone;
　now we suffer because of their sins.
8 Slaves have become our rulers,
　and no one can save us from them.
9 We risk our lives to get our food;
　we face death in the desert.
10 Our skin is hot like an oven;
　we burn with starvation.
11 The enemy abused the women of
　Jerusalem
　and the girls in the cities of Judah.
12 Princes were hung by the hands;
　they did not respect our elders.
13 The young men ground grain at the mill,
　and boys stumbled under loads of
　wood.
14 The elders no longer sit at the city gates;
　the young men no longer sing.
15 We have no more joy in our hearts;
　our dancing has turned to sadness.
16 The crown has fallen from our head.
　How terrible it is because we sinned.
17 Because of this we are afraid,
　and now our eyes are dim.
18 Mount Zion is empty,
　and wild dogs wander around it.

19 But you rule forever, LORD.
　You will be King from now on.
20 Why have you forgotten us for so long?
　Have you left us forever?
21 Bring us back to you, LORD, and we will
　return.
　Make our days as they were before,
22 or have you completely rejected us?
　Are you so angry with us?

ezekiel

GOD'S MESSAGE TO THE CAPTIVES

EZEKIEL'S VISION OF LIVING CREATURES

1 It was the thirtieth year, on the fifth day of the fourth month of our captivity. I was by the Kebar River among the people who had been carried away as captives. The sky opened, and I saw visions of God.

2 It was the fifth day of the month of the fifth year that King Jehoiachin had been a prisoner. 3 The LORD spoke his word to Ezekiel son of Buzi in the land of the Babylonians by the Kebar River. There he felt the power of the LORD.

4 When I looked, I saw a stormy wind coming from the north. There was a great cloud with a bright light around it and fire flashing out of it. Something that looked like glowing metal was in the center of the fire. 5 Inside the cloud was what looked like four living creatures, who were shaped like humans, 6 but each of them had four faces and four wings. 7 Their legs were straight. Their feet were like a calf's hoofs and sparkled like polished bronze. 8 The living creatures had human hands under their wings on their four sides. All four of them had faces and wings, 9 and their wings touched each other. The living creatures did not turn when they moved, but each went straight ahead.

10 Their faces looked like this: Each living creature had a human face and the face of a lion on the right side and the face of an ox on the left side. And each one also had the face of an eagle. 11 That was what their faces looked like. Their wings were spread out above. Each had two wings that touched one of the other living creatures and two wings that covered its body. 12 Each went straight ahead. Wherever the spirit would go, the living creatures would also go, without turning. 13 The living creatures looked like burning coals of fire or like torches. Fire went back and forth among the living creatures. It was bright, and lightning flashed from it. 14 The living creatures ran back and forth like bolts of lightning.

15 Now as I looked at the living creatures, I saw a wheel on the ground by each of the living creatures with its four faces. 16 The wheels and the way they were made were like this: They looked like sparkling chrysolite. All four of them looked the same, like one wheel crossways inside another wheel. 17 When they moved, they went in any one of the four directions, without turning as they went. 18 The rims of the wheels were high and frightening and were full of eyes all around.

19 When the living creatures moved, the wheels moved beside them. When the living creatures were lifted up from the ground, the wheels also were lifted up. 20 Wherever the spirit would go, the living creatures would go. And the wheels were lifted up beside them, because the spirit of the living creatures was in the wheels. 21 When the living creatures moved, the wheels moved. When the living creatures stopped, the wheels stopped. And when the living creatures were lifted from the ground, the wheels were lifted beside them, because the spirit of the living creatures was in the wheels.

22 Now, over the heads of the living creatures was something like a dome that sparkled like ice and was frightening. 23 And under the dome the wings of the living creatures were stretched out straight toward one another. Each living creature also had two wings covering its body. 24 I heard the sound of their wings, like the roaring sound of the sea, as they moved. It was like the voice of God Almighty, a roaring sound like a noisy army. When the living creatures stopped, they lowered their wings.

25 A voice came from above the dome over the heads of the living creatures. When the living creatures stopped, they lowered their wings. 26 Now above the dome there was something that looked like a throne. It looked like a sapphire gem. And on the throne was a shape like a human. 27 Then I noticed that from the waist up the shape looked like glowing metal with fire inside. From the waist down it looked like fire, and a bright light was

all around. ²⁸The surrounding glow looked like the rainbow in the clouds on a rainy day. It seemed to look like the glory of the LORD. So when I saw it, I bowed facedown on the ground and heard a voice speaking.

THE LORD SPEAKS TO EZEKIEL

2 He said to me, "Human, stand up on your feet so I may speak with you." ²While he spoke to me, the Spirit entered me and put me on my feet. Then I heard the LORD speaking to me.

³He said, "Human, I am sending you to the people of Israel. That nation has turned against me and broken away from me. They and their ancestors have sinned against me until this very day. ⁴I am sending you to people who are stubborn and who do not obey. You will say to them, 'This is what the Lord GOD says.' ⁵They may listen, or they may not, since they are a people who have turned against me. But they will know that a prophet has been among them. ⁶You, human, don't be afraid of the people or their words. Even though they may be like thorny branches and stickers all around you, and though you may feel like you live with poisonous insects, don't be afraid. Don't be afraid of their words or their looks, because they are a people who turn against me. ⁷But speak my words to them. They may listen, or they may not, because they turn against me. ⁸But you, human, listen to what I say to you. Don't turn against me as those people do. Open your mouth and eat what I am giving you."

⁹Then I looked and saw a hand stretched out to me, and a scroll was in it. ¹⁰He opened the scroll in front of me. Funeral songs, sad writings, and words about troubles were written on the front and back.

3 Then the LORD said to me, "Human, eat what you find; eat this scroll. Then go and speak to the people of Israel." ²So I opened my mouth, and he gave me the scroll to eat.

³He said to me, "Human, eat this scroll which I am giving you, and fill your stomach with it." Then I ate it, and it was as sweet as honey in my mouth.

⁴Then he said to me, "Human, go to the people of Israel, and speak my words to them. ⁵You are not being sent to people whose speech you can't understand, whose language is difficult. You are being sent to Is-

rael. ⁶You are not being sent to many nations whose speech you can't understand, whose language is difficult, whose words you cannot understand. If I had sent you to them, they would have listened to you. ⁷But the people of Israel will not be willing to listen to you, because they are not willing to listen to me. Yes, all the people of Israel are stubborn and will not obey. ⁸See, I now make you as stubborn and as hard as they are. ⁹I am making you as hard as a diamond, harder than stone. Don't be afraid of them or be frightened by them, though they are a people who turn against me."

¹⁰Also, he said to me, "Human, believe all the words I will speak to you, and listen carefully to them. ¹¹Then go to the captives, your own people, and say to them, 'The Lord GOD says this.' Tell them this whether they listen or not."

¹²Then the Spirit lifted me up, and I heard a loud rumbling sound behind me, saying, "Praise the glory of the LORD in heaven." ¹³I heard the wings of the living creatures touching each other and the sound of the wheels by them. It was a loud rumbling sound. ¹⁴So the Spirit lifted me up and took me away. I was unhappy and angry, and I felt the great power of the LORD. ¹⁵I came to the captives from Judah, who lived by the Kebar River at Tel Abib. I sat there seven days where these people lived, feeling shocked.

ISRAEL'S WARNING

¹⁶After seven days the LORD spoke his word to me again. He said, ¹⁷"Human, I now make you a watchman for Israel. Any time you hear a word from my mouth, warn them for me. ¹⁸When I say to the wicked, 'You will surely die,' you must warn them so they may live. If you don't speak out to warn the wicked to stop their evil ways, they will die in their sin. But I will hold you responsible for their death. ¹⁹If you warn the wicked and they do not turn from their wickedness or their evil ways, they will die because of their sin. But you will have saved your life.

²⁰"Again, those who do right may turn away from doing good and do evil. If I make something bad happen to them, they will die. Because you have not warned them, they will die because of their sin, and the good they did will not be remembered. But I will

hold you responsible for their deaths. ²¹But if you have warned those good people not to sin, and they do not sin, they will surely live, because they believed the warning. And you will have saved your life."

²²Then I felt the power of the LORD there. He said to me, "Get up and go out to the plain. There I will speak to you." ²³So I got up and went out to the plain. I saw the glory of the LORD standing there, like the glory I saw by the Kebar River, and I bowed facedown on the ground.

²⁴Then the Spirit entered me and made me stand on my feet. He spoke to me and said, "Go, shut yourself up in your house. ²⁵As for you, human, the people will tie you up with ropes so that you will not be able to go out among them. ²⁶Also, I will make your tongue stick to the roof of your mouth so you will be silent. You will not be able to argue with the people, even though they turn against me. ²⁷But when I speak to you, I will open your mouth, and you will say to them, 'The Lord GOD says this.' Those who will listen, let them listen. Those who refuse, let them refuse, because they are a people who turn against me.

THE MAP OF JERUSALEM

4 "Now, human, get yourself a brick, put it in front of you, and draw a map of Jerusalem on it. ²Then surround it with an army. Build battle works against the city and a dirt road to the top of the city walls. Set up camps around it, and put heavy logs in place to break down the walls. ³Then get yourself an iron plate and set it up like an iron wall between you and the city. Turn your face toward the city as if to attack it and then attack. This is a sign to Israel.

⁴"Then lie down on your left side, and take the guilt of Israel on yourself. Their guilt will be on you for the number of days you lie on your left side. ⁵I have given you the same number of days as the years of the people's sin. So you will have the guilt of Israel's sin on you for three hundred ninety days.

⁶"After you have finished these three hundred ninety days, lie down a second time, on your right side. You will then have the guilt of Judah on you. I will give it to you for forty days, a day for each year of their sin. ⁷Then you will look toward Jerusalem, which is being attacked. With your arm bare, you will prophesy against Jerusalem. ⁸I will put ropes on you so you cannot turn from one side to the other until you have finished the days of your attack on Jerusalem.

⁹"Take wheat, barley, beans, small peas, and millet seeds, and put them in one bowl, and make them into bread for yourself. You will eat it the three hundred ninety days you lie on your side. ¹⁰You will eat eight ounces of food every day at set times. ¹¹You will drink about two-thirds of a quart of water every day at set times. ¹²Eat your food as you would eat a barley cake, baking it over human dung where the people can see." ¹³Then the LORD said, "In the same way Israel will eat unclean food among the nations where I force them to go."

¹⁴But I said, "No, Lord GOD! I have never been made unclean. From the time I was young until now I've never eaten anything that died by itself or was torn by animals. Unclean meat has never entered my mouth."

¹⁵"Very well," he said. "Then I will give you cow's dung instead of human dung to use for your fire to bake your bread."

¹⁶He also said to me, "Human, I am going to cut off the supply of bread to Jerusalem. They will eat the bread that is measured out to them, and they will worry as they eat. They will drink water that is measured out to them, and they will be in shock as they drink it. ¹⁷This is because bread and water will be hard to find. The people will be shocked at the sight of each other, and they will become weak because of their sin.

EZEKIEL CUTS HIS HAIR

5 "Now, human, take a sharp sword, and use it like a barber's razor to shave your head and beard. Then take scales and weigh and divide the hair. ²Burn one-third with fire in the middle of the city when the days of the attack on Jerusalem are over. Then take one-third and cut it up with the knife all around the city. And scatter one-third to the wind. This is how I will chase them with a sword. ³Also take a few of these hairs and tie them in the folds of your clothes. ⁴Take a few more and throw them into the fire and burn them up. From there a fire will spread to all the people of Israel.

⁵"This is what the Lord GOD says: This

is Jerusalem. I have put her at the center of the nations with countries all around her. ⁶But she has refused to obey my laws and has been more evil than the nations. She has refused to obey my rules, even more than nations around her. The people of Jerusalem have rejected my laws and have not lived by my rules.

⁷"So this is what the Lord GOD says: You have caused more trouble than the nations around you. You have not followed my rules or obeyed my laws. You have not even obeyed the laws of the nations around you.

⁸"So this is what the Lord GOD says: I myself am against you, and I will punish you as the nations watch. ⁹I will do things among you that I have not done before and that I will never do anything like again, because you do the things I hate. ¹⁰So parents among you will eat their children, and children will eat their parents. I will punish you and will scatter to the winds all who are left alive. ¹¹So the Lord GOD says: You have made my Temple unclean with all your evil idols and the hateful things you do. Because of this, as surely as I live, I will cut you off. I will have no pity, and I will show no mercy. ¹²A third of you will die by disease or be destroyed by hunger inside your walls. A third will fall dead by the sword outside your walls. And a third I will scatter in every direction as I chase them with a sword. ¹³Then my anger will come to an end. I will use it up against them, and then I will be satisfied. Then they will know that I, the LORD, have spoken. After I have carried out my anger against them, they will know how strongly I felt.

¹⁴"I will make you a ruin and a shame among the nations around you, to be seen by all who pass by. ¹⁵Then the nations around you will shame you and make fun of you. You will be a warning and a terror to them. This will happen when I punish you in my great anger. I, the LORD, have spoken. ¹⁶I will send a time of hunger to destroy you, and then I will make your hunger get even worse, and I will cut off your supply of food. ¹⁷I will send a time of hunger and wild animals against you, and they will kill your children. Disease and death will sweep through your people, and I will bring the sword against you to kill you. I, the LORD, have spoken."

PROPHECIES AGAINST THE MOUNTAINS

6 Again the LORD spoke his word to me, saying: ²"Human, look toward the mountains of Israel, and prophesy against them. ³Say, 'Mountains of Israel, listen to the word of the Lord GOD. The Lord GOD says this to the mountains, the hills, the ravines, and the valleys: I will bring a sword against you, and I will destroy your places of idol worship. ⁴Your altars will be destroyed and your incense altars broken down. Your people will be killed in front of your idols. ⁵I will lay the dead bodies of the Israelites in front of their idols, and I will scatter your bones around your altars. ⁶In all the places you live, cities will become empty. The places of idol worship will be ruined; your altars will become lonely ruins. Your idols will be broken and brought to an end. Your incense altars will be cut down, and the things you made will be wiped out. ⁷Your people will be killed and fall among you. Then you will know that I am the LORD.

⁸"'But I will leave some people alive; some will not be killed by the nations when you are scattered among the foreign lands. ⁹Then those who have escaped will remember me, as they live among the nations where they have been taken as captives. They will remember how I was hurt because they were unfaithful to me and turned away from me and desired to worship their idols. They will hate themselves because of the evil things they did that I hate. ¹⁰Then they will know that I am the LORD. I did not bring this terrible thing on them for no reason.

¹¹"'This is what the Lord GOD says: Clap your hands, stamp your feet, and groan because of all the hateful, evil things the people of Israel have done. They will die by war, hunger, and disease. ¹²The person who is far away will die by disease. The one who is nearby will die in war. The person who is still alive and has escaped these will die from hunger. So I will carry out my anger on them. ¹³Their people will lie dead among their idols around the altars, on every high hill, on all the mountain tops, and under every green tree and leafy oak—all the places where they offered sweet-smelling incense to their idols. Then you will know that I am the LORD. ¹⁴I will use my power against them to make the land empty and wasted from the desert to

Diblah, wherever they live. Then they will know that I am the LORD.'"

EZEKIEL TELLS OF THE END

7 Again the LORD spoke his word to me, saying: ²"Human, the Lord GOD says this to the land of Israel: An end! The end has come on the four corners of the land. ³Now the end has come for you, and I will send my anger against you. I will judge you for the way you have lived, and I will make you pay for all your actions that I hate. ⁴I will have no pity on you; I will not hold back punishment from you. Instead, I will make you pay for the way you have lived and for your actions that I hate. Then you will know that I am the LORD.

⁵"This is what the Lord GOD says: Disaster on top of disaster is coming. ⁶The end has come! The end has come! It has stirred itself up against you! Look! It has come! ⁷Disaster has come for you who live in the land! The time has come; the day of confusion is near. There will be no happy shouting on the mountains. ⁸Soon I will pour out my anger against you; I will carry out my anger against you. I will judge you for the way you have lived and will make you pay for everything you have done that I hate. ⁹I will show no pity, and I will not hold back punishment. I will pay you back for the way you have lived and the things you have done that I hate. Then you will know that I am the LORD who punishes.

¹⁰"Look, the day is here. It has come. Disaster has come, violence has grown, and there is more pride than ever. ¹¹Violence has grown into a weapon for punishing wickedness. None of the people will be left—none of that crowd, none of their wealth, and nothing of value. ¹²The time has come; the day has arrived. Don't let the buyer be happy or the seller be sad, because my burning anger is against the whole crowd. ¹³Sellers will not return to the land they have sold as long as they live, because the vision against all that crowd will not be changed. Because of their sins, they will not save their lives. ¹⁴They have blown the trumpet, and everything is ready. But no one is going to the battle, because my anger is against all that crowd.

¹⁵"The sword is outside, and disease and hunger are inside. Whoever is in the field will die by the sword. Hunger and disease will destroy those in the city. ¹⁶Those who are left alive and who escape will be on the mountains, moaning like doves of the valleys about their own sin. ¹⁷All hands will hang weakly with fear, and all knees will become weak as water. ¹⁸They will put on rough cloth to show how sad they are. They will tremble all over with fear. Their faces will show their shame, and all their heads will be shaved. ¹⁹The people will throw their silver into the streets, and their gold will be like trash. Their silver and gold will not save them from the LORD's anger. It will not satisfy their hunger or fill their stomachs, because it caused them to fall into sin. ²⁰They were proud of their beautiful jewelry and used it to make their idols and their evil statues, which I hate. So I will turn their wealth into trash. ²¹I will give it to foreigners as loot from war and to the most evil people in the world as treasure, and they will dishonor it. ²²I will also turn away from the people of Israel, and they will dishonor my treasured place. Then robbers will enter and dishonor it.

²³"Make chains for captives, because the land is full of bloody crimes and the city is full of violence. ²⁴So I will bring the worst of the nations to take over the people's houses. I will also end the pride of the strong, and their holy places will be dishonored. ²⁵When the people are suffering greatly, they will look for peace, but there will be none. ²⁶Disaster will come on top of disaster, and rumor will be added to rumor. Then they will try to get a vision from a prophet; the teachings of God from the priest and the advice from the elders will be lost. ²⁷The king will cry greatly, the prince will give up hope, and the hands of the people who own land will shake with fear. I will punish them for the way they have lived. The way they have judged others is the way I will judge them. Then they will know that I am the LORD."

EZEKIEL'S VISION OF JERUSALEM

8 It was the sixth year, on the fifth day of the sixth month of our captivity. I was sitting in my house with the elders of Judah in front of me. There I felt the power of the Lord GOD. ²I looked and saw something that looked like a human. From the waist down it looked like fire, and from the waist

up it looked like bright glowing metal. ³It stretched out the shape of a hand and caught me by the hair on my head. The Spirit lifted me up between the earth and the sky. He took me in visions of God to Jerusalem, to the entrance to the north gate of the inner court-yard of the Temple. In the courtyard was the idol that caused God to be jealous. ⁴I saw the glory of the God of Israel there, as I had seen on the plain.

⁵Then he said to me, "Human, now look toward the north." So I looked up toward the north, and in the entrance north of the gate of the altar was the idol that caused God to be jealous.

⁶He said to me, "Human, do you see what they are doing? Do you see how many hate-ful things the people of Israel are doing here that drive me far away from my Temple? But you will see things more hateful than these."

⁷Then he brought me to the entry of the courtyard. When I looked, I saw a hole in the wall. ⁸He said to me, "Human, dig through the wall." So I dug through the wall and saw an entrance.

⁹Then he said to me, "Go in and see the hateful, evil things they are doing here." ¹⁰So I entered and looked, and I saw every kind of crawling thing and hateful beast and all the idols of the people of Israel, carved on the wall all around. ¹¹Standing in front of these carvings and idols were seventy of the elders of Israel and Jaazaniah son of Shaphan. Each man had his pan for burning incense in his hand, and a sweet-smelling cloud of incense was rising.

¹²Then he said to me, "Human, have you seen what the elders of Israel are doing in the dark? Have you seen each man in the room of his own idol? They say, 'The LORD doesn't see us. The LORD has left the land.'" ¹³He also said to me, "You will see even more hateful things that they are doing."

¹⁴Then he brought me to the entrance of the north gate of the Temple of the LORD, where I saw women sitting and crying for Tammuz." ¹⁵He said to me, "Do you see, hu-man? You will see things even more hateful than these."

¹⁶Then he brought me into the inner courtyard of the Temple. There I saw about twenty-five men at the entrance to the Tem-ple of the LORD, between the porch and the altar. With their backs turned to the Temple of the LORD, they faced east and were wor-shiping the sun in the east.

¹⁷He said to me, "Do you see, human? Is it unimportant that the people of Judah are do-ing the hateful things they have done here? They have filled the land with violence and made me continually angry. Look, they are insulting me every way they can. ¹⁸So I will act in anger. I will have no pity, nor will I show mercy. Even if they shout in my ears, I won't listen to them."

VISION OF THE ANGELS

9 Then he shouted with a loud voice in my ears, "You who are chosen to punish this city, come near with your weapon in your hand." ²Then six men came from the direc-tion of the upper gate, which faces north, each with his powerful weapon in his hand. Among them was a man dressed in linen with a writing case at his side. The men went in and stood by the bronze altar.

³Then the glory of the God of Israel went up from above the creatures with wings, where it had been, to the place in the Temple where the door opened. He called to the man dressed in linen who had the writing case at his side. ⁴He said to the man, "Go through Jerusalem and put a mark on the foreheads of the people who groan and cry about all the hateful things being done among them."

⁵As I listened, he said to the other men, "Go through the city behind the man dressed in linen and kill. Don't pity anyone, and don't show mercy. ⁶Kill and destroy old men, young men and women, little children, and older women, but don't touch any who have the mark on them. Start at my Temple." So they started with the elders who were in front of the Temple.

⁷Then he said to the men, "Make the Temple unclean, and fill the courtyards with those who have been killed. Go out!" So the men went out and killed the people in the city. ⁸While the men were killing the people, I was left alone. I bowed facedown on the ground and I cried out, "Oh, Lord GOD! Will you destroy everyone left alive

---

8:14 Tammuz Tammuz was a god in Babylon. Every year people thought this god died when the plants died. After they cried for him, they believed he came back to life, and the plants lived again.

in Israel when you turn loose your anger on Jerusalem?"

9Then he said to me, "The sin of the people of Israel and Judah is very great. The land is filled with people who murder, and the city is full of people who are not fair. The people say, 'The LORD has left the land, and the LORD does not see.' 10But I will have no pity, nor will I show mercy. I will bring their evil back on their heads."

11Then the man dressed in linen with the writing case at his side reported, "I have done just as you commanded me."

THE COALS OF FIRE

10 Then I looked and saw in the dome above the heads of the living creatures something like a sapphire gem which looked like a throne. 2The LORD said to the man dressed in linen, "Go in between the wheels under the living creatures, fill your hands with coals of fire from between the living creatures, and scatter the coals over the city."

As I watched, the man with linen clothes went in. 3Now the living creatures were standing on the south side of the Temple when the man went in. And a cloud filled the inner courtyard. 4Then the glory of the LORD went up from the living creatures and stood over the door of the Temple. The Temple was filled with the cloud, and the courtyard was full of the brightness from the glory of the LORD. 5The sound of the wings of the living creatures was heard all the way to the outer courtyard. It was like the voice of God Almighty when he speaks.

6When the LORD commanded the man dressed in linen, "Take fire from between the wheels, from between the living creatures," the man went in and stood by a wheel. 7One living creature put out his hand to the fire that was among them, took some of the fire, and put it in the hands of the man dressed in linen. Then the man took the fire and went out.

THE WHEELS AND THE CREATURES

8Something that looked like a human hand could be seen under the wings of the living creatures. 9I saw the four wheels by the living creatures, one wheel by each living creature. The wheels looked like shining chrysolite. 10All four wheels looked alike:

Each looked like a wheel crossways inside another wheel. 11When the wheels moved, they went in any of the directions that the four living creatures faced. The wheels did not turn about, and the living creatures did not turn their bodies as they went. 12All their bodies, their backs, their hands, their wings, and the wheels were full of eyes all over. Each of the four living creatures had a wheel. 13I heard the wheels being called "whirling wheels." 14Each living creature had four faces. The first face was the face of a creature with wings. The second face was a human face, the third was the face of a lion, and the fourth was the face of an eagle.

15Then the living creatures flew up. They were the same living creatures I had seen by the Kebar River. 16When the living creatures moved, the wheels moved beside them. When the living creatures lifted their wings to fly up from the ground, the wheels did not leave their place beside them. 17When the living creatures stopped, the wheels stopped. When the creatures went up, the wheels went up also, because the spirit of the living creatures was in the wheels.

18Then the glory of the LORD left the door of the Temple and stood over the living creatures. 19As I watched, the living creatures spread their wings and flew up from the ground, with the wheels beside them. They stood where the east gate of the Temple of the LORD opened, and the glory of the God of Israel was over them.

20These were the living creatures I had seen under the God of Israel by the Kebar River. I knew they were called cherubim. 21Each one had four faces and four wings, and under their wings were things that looked like human hands. 22Their faces looked the same as the ones I had seen by the Kebar River. They each went straight ahead.

PROPHECIES AGAINST EVIL LEADERS

11 The Spirit lifted me up and brought me to the front gate of the Temple of the LORD, which faces east. I saw twenty-five men where the gate opens, among them Jaazaniah son of Azzur and Pelatiah son of Benaiah, who were leaders of the people. 2Then the LORD said to me, "Human, these are the men who plan evil and give wicked advice in this city of Jerusalem. 3They say, 'It is almost time for us to build houses. This city is like a cooking pot, and we are like the best meat.' 4So prophesy against them, prophesy, human."

5Then the Spirit of the LORD entered me and told me to say: "This is what the LORD says: You have said these things, people of Israel, and I know what you are thinking. 6You have killed many people in this city, filling its streets with their bodies.

7"So this is what the Lord GOD says: Those people you have killed and left in the middle of the city are like the best meat, and this city is like the cooking pot. But I will force you out of the city. 8You have feared the sword, but I will bring a sword against you, says the Lord GOD. 9I will force you out of the city and hand you over to strangers and punish you. 10You will die by the sword. I will punish you at the border of Israel so you will know that I am the LORD. 11This city will not be your cooking pot, and you will not be the best meat in the middle of it. I will punish you at the border of Israel. 12Then you will know that I am the LORD. You did not live by my rules or obey my laws. Instead, you did the same things as the nations around you."

13As I prophesied, Pelatiah son of Benaiah died. Then I bowed facedown on the ground and shouted with a loud voice, "Oh no, Lord GOD! Will you completely destroy the Israelites who are left alive?"

PROMISE TO THOSE REMAINING

14The LORD spoke his word to me, saying, 15"Human, the people still in Jerusalem have spoken about your own relatives and all the people of Israel who are captives with you, saying, 'They are far from the LORD. This land has been given to us as our property.'

16"So say, 'This is what the Lord GOD says: I sent the people far away among the nations and scattered them among the countries. But for a little while I have become a Temple to them in the countries where they have gone.'

17"So say: 'This is what the Lord GOD says: I will gather you from the nations and bring you together from the countries where you have been scattered. Then I will give you back the land of Israel.'

18"When they come to this land, they will remove all the evil idols and all the hateful images. 19I will give them a desire to respect

me completely, and I will put inside them a new way of thinking. I will take out the stubborn heart of stone from their bodies, and I will give them an obedient heart of flesh. 20Then they will live by my rules and obey my laws and keep them. They will be my people, and I will be their God. 21But those who want to serve their evil statues and hateful idols, I will pay back for their evil ways, says the Lord GOD."

EZEKIEL'S VISION ENDS

22Then the living creatures lifted their wings with the wheels beside them, and the glory of the God of Israel was above them. 23The glory of the LORD went up from inside Jerusalem and stopped on the mountain on the east side of the city. 24The Spirit lifted me up and brought me to the captives who had been taken from Judah to Babylonia. This happened in a vision given by the Spirit of God, and then the vision I had seen ended. 25And I told the captives from Judah all the things the LORD had shown me.

EZEKIEL MOVES OUT

12 Again the LORD spoke his word to me, saying: 2"Human, you are living among a people who refuse to obey. They have eyes to see, but they do not see, and they have ears to hear, but they do not hear, because they are a people who refuse to obey.

3"So, human, pack your things as if you will be taken away captive, and walk away like a captive in the daytime with the people watching. Move from your place to another with the people watching. Maybe they will understand, even though they are a people who refuse to obey. 4During the day when the people are watching, bring out the things you would pack as captive. At evening, with the people watching, leave your place like those who are taken away as captives from their country. 5Dig a hole through the wall while they watch, and bring your things out through it. 6Lift them onto your shoulders with the people watching, and carry them out in the dark. Cover your face so you cannot see the ground, because I have made you a sign to the people of Israel."

7I did these things as I was commanded. In the daytime I brought what I had packed as if I were being taken away captive. Then in the evening I dug through the wall with my hands. I brought my things out in the dark and carried them on my shoulders as the people watched.

8Then in the morning the LORD spoke his word to me, saying: 9"Human, didn't Israel, who refuses to obey, ask you, 'What are you doing?'

10"Say to them, 'This is what the Lord GOD says: This message is about the king in Jerusalem and all the people of Israel who live there.' 11Say, 'I am a sign to you.'

"The same things I have done will be done to the people in Jerusalem. They will be taken away from their country as captives. 12The king among them will put his things on his shoulder in the dark and will leave. The people will dig a hole through the wall to bring him out. He will cover his face so he cannot see the ground. 13But I will spread my net over him, and he will be caught in my trap. Then I will bring him to Babylon in the land of the Babylonians. He will not see that land, but he will die there. 14All who are around the king—his helpers and all his army—I will scatter in every direction, and I will chase them with a sword.

15"They will know that I am the LORD when I scatter them among the nations and spread them among the countries. 16But I will save a few of them from the sword and from hunger and disease. Then they can tell about their hateful actions among the nations where they go. Then they will know that I am the LORD."

THE LESSON OF EZEKIEL'S SHAKING

17The LORD spoke his word to me, saying: 18"Human, tremble as you eat your food, and shake with fear as you drink your water. 19Then say to the people of the land: 'This is what the Lord GOD says about the people who live in Jerusalem in the land of Israel: They will eat their food with fear and drink their water in shock, because their land will be stripped bare because of the violence of the people who live in it. 20The cities where people live will become ruins, and the land will become empty. Then you will know that I am the LORD.'"

THE VISIONS WILL COME TRUE

21The LORD spoke his word to me, saying: 22"Human, what is this saying you have in the land of Israel: 'The days go by and every vision comes to nothing'? 23So say to them, 'This is what the Lord GOD says: I will make them stop saying this, and nobody in Israel will use this saying anymore.' But tell them, 'The time is near when every vision will come true. 24There will be no more false visions or pleasing prophecies inside the nation of Israel, 25but I, the LORD, will speak. What I say will be done, and it will not be delayed. You refuse to obey, but in your time I will say the word and do it, says the Lord GOD.'"

26The LORD spoke his word to me, saying: 27"Human, the people of Israel are saying, 'The vision that Ezekiel sees is for a time many years from now. He is prophesying about times far away.'

28"So say to them: 'The Lord GOD says this: None of my words will be delayed anymore. What I have said will be done, says the Lord GOD.'"

EZEKIEL SPEAKS AGAINST FALSE PROPHETS

13 The LORD spoke his word to me, saying: 2"Human, prophesy against the prophets of Israel. Say to those who make up their own prophecies: 'Listen to the word of the LORD. 3This is what the Lord GOD says: How terrible it will be for the foolish prophets who follow their own ideas and have not seen a vision from me! 4People of Israel, your prophets have been like wild dogs hunting to kill and eat among ruins. 5Israel is like a house in ruins, but you have not gone up into the broken places or repaired the wall. So how can Israel hold back the enemy in the battle on the LORD's day of judging? 6Your prophets see false visions and prophesy lies. They say, "This is the message of the LORD," when the LORD has not sent them. But they still hope their words will come true. 7You said, "This is the message of the LORD," but that is a false vision. Your prophecies are lies, because I have not spoken.

8"'So this is what the Lord GOD says: Because you prophets spoke things that are false and saw visions that do not come true, I am against you, says the Lord GOD. 9I will punish the prophets who see false visions and prophesy lies. They will have no place among my people. Their names will not be written on the list of the people of Israel, and they will not enter the land of Israel. Then you will know that I am the Lord GOD.

10"'It is because they lead my people the wrong way by saying, "Peace!" when there is no peace. When the people build a weak wall, the prophets cover it with whitewash to make it look strong. 11So tell those who cover a weak wall with whitewash that it will fall down. Rain will pour down, hailstones will fall, and a stormy wind will break the wall down. 12When the wall has fallen, people will ask you, "Where is the whitewash you used on the wall?"

13"'So this is what the Lord GOD says: I will break the wall with a stormy wind. In my anger rain will pour down, and hailstones will destroy the wall. 14I will tear down the wall on which you put whitewash. I will level it to the ground so that people will see the wall's foundation. And when the wall falls, you will be destroyed under it. Then you will know that I am the LORD. 15So I will carry out my anger on the wall and against those who covered it with whitewash. Then I will tell you, "The wall is gone, and those who covered it with whitewash are gone. 16The prophets of Israel who prophesy to Jerusalem and who see visions of peace for the city, when there is no peace, will be gone, says the Lord GOD."'

FALSE WOMEN PROPHETS

17"Now, human, look toward the women among your people who make up their own prophecies. Prophesy against them. 18Say, 'This is what the Lord GOD says: How terrible it will be for women who sew magic charms on their wrists and make veils of every length to trap people! You ruin the lives of my people but try to save your own lives. 19For handfuls of barley and pieces of bread, you have dishonored me among my people. By lying to my people, who listen to lies, you have killed people who should not die, and you have kept alive those who should not live.

20"'So this is what the Lord GOD says: I am against your magic charms, by which you trap people as if they were birds. I will tear those charms off your arms, and I will free those people you have trapped like birds. 21I will also tear off your veils and save my people from your hands. They will no longer be trapped by your power. Then you will know that I am the LORD. 22By your lies you have caused those who did right to be sad,

when I did not make them sad. And you have encouraged the wicked not to stop being wicked, which would have saved their lives. 23So you will not see false visions or prophesy anymore, and I will save my people from your power so you will know that I am the LORD.'"

STOP WORSHIPING IDOLS

14 Some of the elders of Israel came to me and sat down in front of me. 2Then the LORD spoke his word to me, saying: 3"Human, these people want to worship idols. They put up evil things that cause people to sin. Should I allow them to ask me for help? 4So speak to them and tell them, 'This is what the Lord GOD says: When any of the people of Israel want to worship idols and put up evil things that cause people to sin and then come to the prophet, I, the LORD, will answer them myself for worshiping idols. 5Then I will win back my people Israel, who have left me because of all their idols.'

6"So say to the people of Israel, 'This is what the Lord GOD says: Change your hearts and lives, and stop worshiping idols. Stop doing all the things I hate. 7Any of the Israelites or foreigners in Israel can separate themselves from me by wanting to worship idols or by putting up the things that cause people to sin. Then if they come to the prophet to ask me questions, I, the LORD, will answer them myself. 8I will reject them. I will make them a sign and an example, and I will separate them from my people. Then you will know that I am the LORD.

9"'But if the prophet is tricked into giving a prophecy, it is because I, the LORD, have tricked that prophet to speak. Then I will use my power against him and destroy him from among my people Israel. 10The prophet will be as guilty as the one who asks him for help; both will be responsible for their guilt. 11Then the nation of Israel will not leave me anymore or make themselves unclean anymore with all their sins. They will be my people, and I will be their God, says the Lord GOD.'"

JERUSALEM WILL NOT BE SPARED

12The LORD spoke his word to me, saying: 13"Human, if the people of a country sin against me by not being loyal, I will use my power against them. I will cut off their supply of food and send a time of hunger, destroying both people and animals. ¹⁴Even if three great men like Noah, Daniel, and Job were in that country, their goodness could save only themselves, says the Lord GOD.

¹⁵"Or I might send wild animals into that land, leaving the land empty and without children. Then no one would pass through it because of the animals. ¹⁶As surely as I live, says the Lord GOD, even if Noah, Daniel, and Job were in the land, they could not save their own sons or daughters. They could save only themselves, but that country would become empty.

¹⁷"Or I might bring a war against that country. I might say, 'Let a war be fought in that land,' in this way destroying its people and its animals. ¹⁸As surely as I live, says the Lord GOD, even if those three men were in the land, they could not save their sons or daughters. They could save only themselves.

¹⁹"Or I might cause a disease to spread in that country. I might pour out my anger against it, destroying and killing people and animals. ²⁰As surely as I live, says the Lord GOD, even if Noah, Daniel, and Job were in the land, they could not save their son or daughter. They could save only themselves because they did what was right.

²¹"This is what the Lord GOD says: My plans for Jerusalem are much worse! I will send my four terrible punishments against it—war, hunger, wild animals, and disease—to destroy its people and animals. ²²But some people will escape; some sons and daughters will be led out. They will come out to you, and you will see what happens to people who live as they did. Then you will be comforted after the disasters I have brought against Jerusalem, after all the things I have brought against it. ²³You will be comforted when you see what happens to them for living as they did, because you will know there was a good reason for what I did to Jerusalem, says the Lord GOD."

STORY OF THE VINE

15 The LORD spoke his word to me, saying: ²"Human, is the wood of the vine better than the wood of any tree in the forest? ³Can wood be taken from the vine to make anything? Can you use it to make a peg on which to hang something? ⁴If the vine is thrown into the fire for fuel, and the fire burns up both ends and starts to burn the middle, is it useful for anything? ⁵When the vine was whole, it couldn't be made into anything. When the fire has burned it completely, it certainly cannot be made into anything."

⁶So this is what the Lord GOD says: "Out of all the trees in the forest, I have given the wood of the vine as fuel for fire. In the same way I have given up the people who live in Jerusalem ⁷and will turn against them. Although they came through one fire, fire will still destroy them. When I turn against them, you will know that I am the LORD. ⁸So I will make the land empty, because the people have not been loyal, says the Lord GOD."

THE LORD'S KINDNESS TO JERUSALEM

16 The LORD spoke his word to me, saying: ²"Human, tell Jerusalem about her hateful actions. ³Say, 'This is what the Lord GOD says to Jerusalem: Your beginnings and your ancestors were in the land of the Canaanites. Your father was an Amorite, and your mother was a Hittite. ⁴On the day you were born, your cordⁿ was not cut. You were not washed with water to clean you. You were not rubbed with salt or wrapped in cloths. ⁵No one felt sorry enough for you to do any of these things for you. No, you were thrown out into the open field, because you were hated on the day you were born.

⁶"'When I passed by and saw you kicking about in your blood, I said to you, "Live!" ⁷I made you grow like a plant in the field. You grew up and became tall and became like a beautiful jewel. Your breasts formed, and your hair grew, but you were naked and without clothes.

⁸"'Later when I passed by you and looked at you, I saw that you were old enough for love. So I spread my robe over you and covered your nakedness. I also made a promise to you and entered into an agreement with you so that you became mine, says the Lord GOD.

⁹"'Then I bathed you with water, washed all the blood off of you, and put oil on you. ¹⁰I put beautiful clothes made with needlework on you and put sandals of fine leather on your feet. I wrapped you in fine linen and covered

---

16:4 cord The umbilical cord that gives the unborn baby food and air from its mother.

you with silk. ¹¹I put jewelry on you: brace-lets on your arms, a necklace around your neck, ¹²a ring in your nose, earrings in your ears, and a beautiful crown on your head. ¹³So you wore gold and silver. Your clothes were made of fine linen, silk, and beautiful needlework. You ate fine flour, honey, and olive oil. You were very beautiful and became a queen. ¹⁴Then you became famous among the nations, because you were so beautiful. Your beauty was perfect, because of the glory I gave you, says the Lord GOD.

JERUSALEM BECOMES A PROSTITUTE

¹⁵"'But you trusted in your beauty. You became a prostitute, because you were so famous. You had sexual relations with any-one who passed by. ¹⁶You took some of your clothes and made your places of worship colorful. There you carried on your prostitu-tion. These things should not happen; they should never occur. ¹⁷You also took your beautiful jewelry, made from my gold and sil-ver I had given you, and you made for your-selves male idols so you could be a prostitute with them. ¹⁸Then you took your clothes with beautiful needlework and covered the idols. You gave my oil and incense as an offer-ing to them. ¹⁹Also, you took the bread I gave you, the fine flour, oil, and honey I gave you to eat, and you offered them before the gods as a pleasing smell. This is what happened, says the Lord GOD.

²⁰"'But your sexual sins were not enough for you. You also took your sons and daugh-ters who were my children, and you sacri-ficed them to the idols as food. ²¹You killed my children and offered them up in fire to the idols. ²²While you did all your hateful acts and sexual sins, you did not remember when you were young, when you were naked and had no clothes and were left in your blood.

²³"'How terrible! How terrible it will be for you, says the Lord GOD. After you did all these evil things, ²⁴you built yourself a place to worship gods. You made for yourself a place of worship in every city square. ²⁵You built a place of worship at the beginning of every street. You made your beauty hateful, offering your body for sex to anyone who passed by, so your sexual sins became worse and worse. ²⁶You also had sexual relations with the Egyptians, who were your neigh-bors and partners in sexual sin. Your sexual sins became even worse, and they caused me to be angry. ²⁷So then, I used my power against you and took away some of your land. I let you be defeated by those who hate you, the Philistine women, who were ashamed of your evil ways. ²⁸Also, you had sexual rela-tions with the Assyrians, because you could not be satisfied. Even though you had sexual relations with them, you still were not sat-isfied. ²⁹You did many more sexual sins in Babylonia, the land of traders, but even this did not satisfy you.

³⁰"'Truly your will is weak, says the Lord GOD. You do all the things a stubborn prosti-tute does. ³¹You built your place to worship gods at the beginning of every street, and you made places of worship in every city square. But you were not like a prostitute when you refused to accept payment.

³²"'You are a wife who is guilty of adul-tery. You desire strangers instead of your husband. ³³Men pay prostitutes, but you pay all your lovers to come to you. And they come from all around for sexual relations. ³⁴So you are different from other prostitutes. No man asks you to be a prostitute, and you pay money instead of having money paid to you. Yes, you are different.

THE PROSTITUTE IS JUDGED

³⁵"'So, prostitute, hear the word of the LORD. ³⁶This is what the Lord GOD says: You showed your nakedness to other countries. You uncovered your body in your sexual sins with them as your lovers and with all your hateful idols. You killed your children and offered their blood to your idols. ³⁷So I will gather all your lovers with whom you found pleasure. Yes, I will gather all those you loved and those you hated. I will gather them against you from all around, and I will strip you naked in front of them so they can see your nakedness. ³⁸I will punish you as women guilty of adultery or as murderers are punished. I will put you to death because I am angry and jealous. ³⁹I will also hand you over to your lovers. They will tear down your places of worship and destroy other places where you worship gods. They will tear off your clothes and take away your jew-elry, leaving you naked and bare. ⁴⁰They will bring a crowd against you to throw stones

at you and to cut you into pieces with their swords. **41**They will burn down your houses and will punish you in front of many women. I will put an end to your sexual sins, and you will no longer pay your lovers. **42**Then I will rest from my anger against you, and I will stop being jealous. I will be quiet and not angry anymore.

43"Because you didn't remember when you were young, but have made me angry in all these ways, I will repay you for what you have done, says the Lord GOD. Didn't you add sexual sins to all your other acts which I hate?

44"Everyone who uses wise sayings will say this about you: "The daughter is like her mother." **45**You are like your mother, who hated her husband and children. You are also like your sisters, who hated their husbands and children. Your mother was a Hittite, and your father was an Amorite. **46**Your older sister is Samaria, who lived north of you with her daughters; your younger sister is Sodom, who lived south of you with her daughters. **47**You not only followed their ways and did the hateful things they did, but you were soon worse than they were in all your ways. **48**As surely as I live, says the Lord GOD, this is true. Your sister Sodom and her daughters never did what you and your daughters have done.

49"This was the sin of your sister Sodom: She and her daughters were proud and had plenty of food and lived in great comfort, but she did not help the poor and needy. **50**So Sodom and her daughters were proud and did things I hate in front of me. So I got rid of them when I saw what they did. **51**Also, Samaria did not do half the sins you do; you have done more hateful things than they did. So you make your sisters look good because of all the hateful things you have done. **52**You will suffer disgrace, because you have provided an excuse for your sisters. They are better than you are. Your sins were even more terrible than theirs. Feel ashamed and suffer disgrace, because you made your sisters look good.

53"But I will give back to Sodom and her daughters the good things they once had. I will give back to Samaria and her daughters the good things they once had. And with them I will also give back the good things

you once had **54**so you may suffer disgrace and feel ashamed for all the things you have done. You even gave comfort to your sisters in their sins. **55**Your sisters, Sodom with her daughters and Samaria with her daughters, will return to what they were before. You and your daughters will also return to what you were before. **56**You humiliated your sister Sodom when you were proud, **57**before your evil was uncovered. And now the Edomite women and their neighbors humiliate you. Even the Philistine women humiliate you. Those around you hate you. **58**This is your punishment for your terrible sins and for actions that I hate, says the LORD.

GOD KEEPS HIS PROMISES

59"This is what the Lord GOD says: I will do to you what you have done. You hated and broke the agreement you promised to keep. **60**But I will remember my agreement I made with you when you were young, and I will make an agreement that will continue forever with you. **61**Then you will remember what you have done and feel ashamed when you receive your sisters—both your older and your younger sisters. I will give them to you like daughters, but not because they share in my agreement with you. **62**I will set up my agreement with you, and you will know that I am the LORD. **63**You will remember what you did and feel ashamed. You will not open your mouth again because of your shame, when I forgive you for all the things you have done, says the Lord GOD.'"

THE EAGLE AND THE VINE

17 The LORD spoke his word to me, saying: **2**"Human, give a riddle and tell a story to the people of Israel. **3**Say, 'This is what the Lord GOD says: A giant eagle with big wings and long feathers of many different colors came to Lebanon and took hold of the top of a cedar tree. **4**He pulled off the top branch and brought it to a land of traders, where he planted it in a city of traders.

5"The eagle took some seed from the land and planted it in a good field near plenty of water. He planted it to grow like a willow tree. **6**It sprouted and became a low vine that spread over the ground. The branches turned toward the eagle, but the roots were under the eagle. So the seed became a vine, and its branches grew, sending out leaves.

7 "But there was another giant eagle with big wings and many feathers. The vine then bent its roots toward this eagle. It sent out its branches from the area where it was planted toward the eagle so he could water it. 8It had been planted in a good field by plenty of water so it could grow branches and give fruit. It could have become a fine vine.'

9 "Say to them, 'This is what the Lord GOD says: The vine will not continue to grow. The first eagle will pull up the vine's roots and strip off its fruit. Then the vine and all its new leaves will dry up and die. It will not take a strong arm or many people to pull the vine up by its roots. 10Even if it is planted again, it will not continue to grow. It will completely dry up and die when the east wind hits it in the area where it grew.'"

ZEDEKIAH AGAINST NEBUCHADNEZZAR

11Then the LORD spoke his word to me, saying: 12"Say now to the people who refuse to obey: 'Do you know what these things mean?' Say: 'The king of Babylon came to Jerusalem and took the king and important men of Jerusalem and brought them to Babylon. 13Then he took a member of the family of the king of Judah and made an agreement with him, forcing him to take an oath. The king also took away the leaders of Judah 14to make the kingdom weak so it would not be strong again. Then the kingdom of Judah could continue only by keeping its agreement with the king of Babylon. 15But the king of Judah turned against the king of Babylon by sending his messengers to Egypt and asking them for horses and many soldiers. Will the king of Judah succeed? Will the one who does such things escape? He cannot break the agreement and escape.

16 "As surely as I live, says the Lord GOD, he will die in Babylon, in the land of the king who made him king of Judah. The king of Judah hated his promise to the king of Babylon and broke his agreement with him. 17The king of Egypt with his mighty army and many people will not help the king of Judah in the war. The Babylonians will build devices to attack the cities and to kill many people. 18The king of Judah showed that he hated the promise by breaking the agreement. He promised to support Babylon, but he did all these things. So he will not escape.

19 "So this is what the Lord GOD says: As surely as I live, this is true: I will pay back the king of Judah for hating my promise and breaking my agreement. 20I will spread my net over him, and he will be caught in my trap. Then I will bring him to Babylon, where I will punish him for the unfaithful acts he did against me. 21All the best of his soldiers who escape will die by the sword, and those who live will be scattered to every wind. Then you will know that I, the LORD, have spoken.

22 "This is what the Lord GOD says: I myself will also take a young branch from the top of a cedar tree, and I will plant it. I will cut off a small twig from the top of the tree's young branches, and I will plant it on a very high mountain. 23I will plant it on the high mountain of Israel. Then it will grow branches and give fruit and become a great cedar tree. Birds of every kind will build nests in it and live in the shelter of the tree's branches. 24Then all the trees in the countryside will know that I am the LORD. I bring down the high tree and make the low tree tall. I dry up the green tree and make the dry tree grow. I am the LORD. I have spoken, and I will do it.'"

GOD IS FAIR

18

The LORD spoke his word to me, saying: 2"What do you mean by using this saying about the land of Israel:

'The parents have eaten sour grapes,
    and that caused the children to grind
        their teeth from the sour taste'?

3 "As surely as I live, says the Lord GOD, this is true: You will not use this saying in Israel anymore. 4Every living thing belongs to me. The life of the parent is mine, and the life of the child is mine. The person who sins is the one who will die.

5 "Suppose a person is good and does what is fair and right. 6He does not eat at the mountain places of worship. He does not look to the idols of Israel for help. He does not have sexual relations with his neighbor's wife or with a woman during her time of monthly bleeding. 7He does not mistreat anyone but returns what was given as a promise for a loan. He does not rob other people. He gives bread to the hungry and clothes to those who have none. 8He does not lend money to get too much interest or profit. He keeps his

hand from doing wrong. He judges fairly between one person and another. [9]He lives by my rules and obeys my laws faithfully. Whoever does these things is good and will surely live, says the Lord God.

[10]"But suppose this person has a wild son who murders people and who does any of these other things. [11](But the father himself has not done any of these things.) This son eats at the mountain places of worship. He has sexual relations with his neighbor's wife. [12]He mistreats the poor and needy. He steals and refuses to return what was promised for a loan. He looks to idols for help. He does things which I hate. [13]He lends money for too much interest and profit. Will this son live? No, he will not live! He has done all these hateful things, so he will surely be put to death. He will be responsible for his own death.

[14]"Now suppose this son has a son who has seen all his father's sins, but after seeing them does not do those things. [15]He does not eat at the mountain places of worship. He does not look to the idols of Israel for help. He does not have sexual relations with his neighbor's wife. [16]He does not mistreat anyone or keep something promised for a loan or steal. He gives bread to the hungry and clothes to those who have none. [17]He keeps his hand from doing wrong. He does not take too much interest or profit when he lends money. He obeys my laws and lives by my rules. He will not die for his father's sin; he will surely live. [18]But his father took other people's money unfairly and robbed his brother and did what was wrong among his people. So he will die for his own sin.

[19]"But you ask, 'Why is the son not punished for the father's sin?' The son has done what is fair and right. He obeys all my rules, so he will surely live. [20]The person who sins is the one who will die. A child will not be punished for a parent's sin, and a parent will not be punished for a child's sin. Those who do right will enjoy the results of their own goodness; evil people will suffer the results of their own evil.

[21]"But suppose the wicked stop doing all the sins they have done and obey all my rules and do what is fair and right. Then they will surely live; they will not die. [22]Their sins will be forgotten. Because they have done what is right, they will live. [23]I do not really want the wicked to die, says the Lord God. I want them to stop their bad ways and live.

[24]"But suppose good people stop doing good and do wrong and do the same hateful things the wicked do. Will they live? All their good acts will be forgotten, because they became unfaithful. They have sinned, so they will die because of their sins.

[25]"But you say, 'What the Lord does isn't fair.' Listen, people of Israel. I am fair. It is what you do that is not fair! [26]When good people stop doing good and do wrong, they will die because of it. They will die, because they did wrong. [27]When the wicked stop being wicked and do what is fair and right, they will save their lives. [28]Because they thought about it and stopped doing all the sins they had done, they will surely live; they will not die. [29]But the people of Israel still say, 'What the Lord does isn't fair.' People of Israel, I am fair. It is what you do that is not fair.

[30]"So I will judge you, people of Israel; I will judge each of you by what you do, says the Lord God. Change your hearts and stop all your sinning so sin will not bring your ruin. [31]Get rid of all the sins you have done, and get for yourselves a new heart and a new way of thinking. Why do you want to die, people of Israel? [32]I do not want anyone to die, says the Lord God, so change your hearts and lives so you may live.

A SAD SONG FOR ISRAEL

19 "Sing a funeral song for the leaders of Israel. [2]Say:

'Your mother was like a female lion.
She lay down among the young lions.
　She had many cubs.
[3] When she brought up one of her cubs,
　he became a strong lion.
He learned to tear the animals he hunted,
　and he ate people.
[4] The nations heard about him.
　He was trapped in their pit,
and they brought him with hooks
　to the land of Egypt.

[5] "'The mother lion waited and saw
　that there was no hope for her cub.
So she took another one of her cubs
　and made him a strong lion.
[6] This cub roamed among the lions.
　He was now a strong lion.

He learned to tear the animals he hunted,
and he ate people.
7 He tore down their strong places
and destroyed their cities.
The land and everything in it
were terrified by the sound of his roar.
8 Then the nations came against him
from areas all around,
and they spread their net over him.
He was trapped in their pit.
9 Then they put him into a cage with chains
and brought him to the king of Babylon.
They put him into prison
so his roar could not be heard again
on the mountains of Israel.

10 " 'Your mother was like a vine in your
vineyard,
planted beside the water.
The vine had many branches and gave
much fruit,
because there was plenty of water.
11 The vine had strong branches,
good enough for a king's scepter.
The vine became tall
among the thick branches.
And it was seen, because it was tall
with many branches.
12 But it was pulled up by its roots in anger
and thrown down to the ground.
The east wind dried it up.
Its fruit was torn off.
Its strong branches were broken off
and burned up.
13 Now the vine is planted in the desert,
in a dry and thirsty land.
14 Fire spread from the vine's main branch,
destroying its fruit.
There is not a strong branch left on it
that could become a scepter for a king.'
This is a funeral song; it is to be used as a funeral song."

ISRAEL HAS REFUSED GOD

20 It was the seventh year of our captivity, in the fifth month, on the tenth day of the month. Some of the elders of Israel came to ask about the LORD and sat down in front of me.

2 The LORD spoke his word to me, saying: 3 "Human, speak to the elders of Israel and say to them: 'This is what the Lord GOD says: Did you come to ask me questions? As surely as I live, I will not let you ask me questions.'

4 "Will you judge them? Will you judge them, human? Let them know the hateful things their ancestors did. 5 Say to them: 'This is what the Lord GOD says: When I chose Israel, I made a promise to the descendants of Jacob. I made myself known to them in Egypt, and I promised them, "I am the LORD your God." 6 At that time I promised them I would bring them out of Egypt into a land I had found for them, a fertile land, the best land in the world. 7 I said to them, "Each one of you must throw away the hateful idols you have seen and liked. Don't make yourselves unclean with the idols of Egypt. I am the LORD your God."

8 " 'But they turned against me and refused to listen to me. They did not throw away the hateful idols which they saw and liked; they did not give up the idols of Egypt. Then I decided to pour out my anger against them while they were still in Egypt. 9 But I acted for the sake of my name so it would not be dishonored in full view of the nations where the Israelites lived. I made myself known to the Israelites with a promise to bring them out of Egypt while the nations were watching. 10 So I took them out of Egypt and brought them into the desert. 11 I gave them my rules and told them about my laws, by which people will live if they obey them. 12 I also gave them my Sabbaths to be a sign between us so they would know that I am the LORD who made them holy.

13 " 'But in the desert Israel turned against me. They did not follow my rules, and they rejected my laws, by which people will live if they obey them. They dishonored my Sabbaths. Then I decided to pour out my anger against them and destroy them in the desert. 14 But I acted for the sake of my name so it would not be dishonored in full view of the nations who watched as I had brought the Israelites out of Egypt. 15 And in the desert I swore to the Israelites that I would not bring them into the land I had given them. It is a fertile land, the best land in the world. 16 This was because they rejected my laws and did not follow my rules. They dishonored my Sabbaths and wanted to worship their idols. 17 But I had pity on them. I did not destroy them or put an end to them in the desert. 18 I said to their children in the desert, "Don't live by the rules of your parents, or obey their

laws. Don't make yourselves unclean with their idols. ¹⁹I am the LORD your God. Live by my rules, obey my laws, and follow them. ²⁰Keep my Sabbaths holy, and they will be a sign between me and you. Then you will know that I am the LORD your God."

²¹"But the children turned against me. They did not live by my rules, nor were they careful to obey my laws, by which people will live if they obey them. They dishonored my Sabbaths. So I decided to pour out my anger against them in the desert. ²²But I held back my anger. I acted for the sake of my name so it would not be dishonored in full view of the nations who watched as I brought the Israelites out. ²³And in the desert I swore to the Israelites that I would scatter them among the nations and spread them among the countries, ²⁴because they had not obeyed my laws. They had rejected my rules and dishonored my Sabbaths and worshiped the idols of their parents. ²⁵I also allowed them to follow rules that were not good and laws by which they could not live. ²⁶I let the Israelites make themselves unclean by the gifts they brought to their gods when they sacrificed their first children in the fire. I wanted to terrify them so they would know that I am the LORD.'

²⁷"So, human, speak to the people of Israel. Say to them, 'This is what the Lord GOD says: Your ancestors spoke against me by being unfaithful to me in another way. ²⁸When I had brought them into the land I promised to give them, they saw every high hill and every leafy tree. There they offered their sacrifices to gods. They brought offerings that made me angry and burned their incense and poured out their drink offerings. ²⁹Then I said to them: What is this high place where you go to worship?'" (It is still called High Place today.)

³⁰"So say to the people of Israel: 'This is what the Lord GOD says: Are you going to make yourselves unclean as your ancestors did? Are you going to be unfaithful and desire their hateful idols? ³¹When you offer your children as gifts and sacrifice them in the fire, you are making yourselves unclean with all your idols even today. So, people of Israel, should I let you ask me questions? As surely as I live, says the Lord GOD, I will not accept questions from you.

³²"What you want will not come true. You say, "We want to be like the other nations, like the people in other lands. We want to worship idols made of wood and stone." ³³As surely as I live, says the Lord GOD, I will use my great power and strength and anger to rule over you. ³⁴I will bring you out from the foreign nations. With my great power and strength and anger I will gather you from the lands where you are scattered. ³⁵I will bring you among the nations as I brought your ancestors into the desert with Moses. There I will judge you face to face. ³⁶I will judge you the same way I judged your ancestors in the desert of the land of Egypt, says the Lord GOD. ³⁷I will count you like sheep and will bring you into line with my agreement. ³⁸I will get rid of those who refuse to obey me and who turn against me. I will bring them out of the land where they are now living, but they will never enter the land of Israel. Then you will know that I am the LORD.

³⁹"This is what the Lord GOD says: People of Israel, go serve your idols for now. But later you will listen to me; you will not continue to dishonor my holy name with your gifts and gods. ⁴⁰On my holy mountain, the high mountain of Israel, all Israel will serve me in the land, says the Lord GOD. There I will accept you. There I will expect your offerings, the first harvest of your offerings, and all your holy gifts. ⁴¹I will accept you like the pleasing smell of sacrifices when I bring you out from the foreign nations and gather you from the lands where you are scattered. Then through you I will show how holy I am so the nations will see. ⁴²When I bring you into the land of Israel, the land I promised your ancestors, you will know that I am the LORD. ⁴³There you will remember everything you did that made you unclean, and then you will hate yourselves for all the evil things you have done. ⁴⁴I will deal with you for the sake of my name, not because of your evil ways or unclean actions. Then you will know I am the LORD, people of Israel, says the Lord GOD.'"

BABYLON, THE LORD'S SWORD

⁴⁵Now the LORD spoke his word to me, saying: ⁴⁶"Human, look toward the south. Prophesy against the south and against the forest of the southern area. ⁴⁷Say to that forest: 'Hear the word of the LORD. This is what

the Lord GOD says: I am ready to start a fire in you that will destroy all your green trees and all your dry trees. The flames that burn will not be put out. Every face from south to north will feel their heat. ⁴⁸Then all the people will see that I, the LORD, have started the fire. It will not be put out.'"

⁴⁹Then I said, "Ah, Lord GOD! The people are saying about me, 'He is only telling stories.'"

21 Then the LORD spoke his word to me, saying: ²"Human, look toward Jerusalem and speak against the holy place. Prophesy against the land of Israel. ³Say to Israel: 'This is what the LORD says: I am against you. I will pull my sword out of its holder, and I will cut off from you both the wicked and those who do right. ⁴Because I am going to cut off the wicked and those who do right, my sword will come out from its holder and attack all people from south to north. ⁵Then all people will know that I, the LORD, have pulled my sword out from its holder. My sword will not go back in again.'

⁶"So, human, groan with breaking heart and great sadness. Groan in front of the people. ⁷When they ask you, 'Why are you groaning?' you will say, 'Because of what I have heard is going to happen. When it happens, every heart will melt with fear, and all hands will become weak. Everyone will be afraid; all knees will become weak as water. Look, it is coming, and it will happen, says the Lord GOD.'"

⁸The LORD spoke his word to me, saying: ⁹"Human, prophesy and say, 'This is what the Lord says:

A sword, a sword,
    made sharp and polished.
¹⁰ It is made sharp for the killing.
    It is polished to flash like lightning.

"'You are not happy about this horrible punishment by the sword. But my son Judah, you did not change when you were only beaten with a rod.
¹¹ The sword should be polished.
    It is meant to be held in the hand.
It is made sharp and polished,
    ready for the hand of a killer.
¹² Shout and yell, human,
    because the sword is meant for my
        people,
    for all the rulers of Israel.

They will be killed by the sword,
    along with my people.
    So beat your chest in sadness.
¹³"'The test will come. And Judah, who is hated by the armies of Babylon, will not last, says the Lord GOD.'

¹⁴ "So, human, prophesy
    and clap your hands.
Let the sword strike
    two or three times.
It is a sword meant for killing,
    a sword meant for much killing.
This sword surrounds the people to be
    killed.
¹⁵ Their hearts will melt with fear,
    and many people will die.
I have placed the killing sword
    at all their city gates.
Oh! The sword is made to flash like
    lightning.
    It is held, ready for killing.
¹⁶ Sword, cut on the right side;
    then cut on the left side.
    Cut anywhere your blade is turned.
¹⁷ I will also clap my hands
    and use up my anger.
    I, the LORD, have spoken."

JERUSALEM TO BE DESTROYED

¹⁸The LORD spoke his word to me, saying: ¹⁹"Human, mark two roads that the king of Babylon and his sword can follow. Both of these roads will start from the same country. And make signs where the road divides and one way goes toward the city. ²⁰Mark one sign to show the road he can take with his sword to Rabbah in the land of the Ammonites. Mark the other sign to show the road to Judah and Jerusalem, which is protected with strong walls. ²¹The king of Babylon has come to where the road divides, and he is using magic. He throws lots with arrows and asks questions of his family idols. He looks at the liver of a sacrificed animal to learn where he should go. ²²The lot in his right hand tells him to go to Jerusalem. It tells him to use logs to break down the city gates, to shout the battle cry and give the order to kill, and to build a dirt road to the top of the walls and devices to attack the walls. ²³The people of Jerusalem have made agreements with other nations to help them fight Babylon. So they will think this prediction is wrong, but it

is really proof of their sin, and they will be captured.

24"So this is what the Lord GOD says: 'You have shown how sinful you are by turning against the LORD. Your sins are seen in all the things you do. Because of this proof against you, you will be taken captive by the enemy.

25" 'You unclean and evil leader of Israel, you will be killed! The time of your final punishment has come. 26This is what the Lord GOD says: Take off the royal turban, and remove the crown. Things will change. Those who are important now will be made unimportant, and those who are unimportant now will be made important. 27A ruin! A ruin! I will make it a ruin! This place will not be rebuilt until the one comes who has a right to be king. Then I will give him that right.'

THE PUNISHMENT OF AMMON

28"And you, human, prophesy and say: 'This is what the Lord GOD says about the people of Ammon and their insults:

A sword, a sword
　　is pulled out of its holder.
It is polished to kill and destroy,
　　to flash like lightning!
29 Prophets see false visions about you
　　and prophesy lies about you.
The sword will be put on the necks
　　of these unclean and evil people.
Their day of judging has come;
　　the time of final punishment has come.
30 Put the sword back in its holder.
　　I will judge you
in the place where you were created,
　　in the land where you were born.
31 I will pour out my anger against you
　　and blast you with the fire of my anger.
I will hand you over to cruel men,
　　experts in destruction.
32 You will be like fuel for the fire;
　　you will die in the land.
You will not be remembered,
　　because I, the LORD, have spoken.'"

THE SINS OF JERUSALEM

22 The LORD spoke his word to me, saying: 2"And you, human, will you judge? Will you judge the city of murderers? Then tell her about all her hateful acts. 3You are to say: 'This is what the Lord GOD says: You are a city that kills those who come to live there. You make yourself unclean by making idols.

4You have become guilty of murder and have become unclean by your idols which you have made. So you have brought your time of punishment near; you have come to the end of your years. That is why I have made you a shame to the nations and why all lands laugh at you. 5Those near and those far away laugh at you with your bad name, you city full of confusion.

6" 'Jerusalem, see how each ruler of Israel in you has been trying to kill people. 7The people in you hate their fathers and mothers. They mistreat the foreigners in you and wrong the orphans and widows in you. 8You hate my holy things and dishonor my Sabbaths. 9The men in you tell lies to cause the death of others. The people in you eat food offered to idols at the mountain places of worship, and they take part in sexual sins. 10The men in you have sexual relations with their fathers' wives and with women who are unclean, during their time of monthly bleeding. 11One man in you does a hateful act with his neighbor's wife, while another has shamefully made his daughter-in-law unclean sexually. And another forces his half sister to have sexual relations with him. 12The people in you take money to kill others. You take unfair interest and profits and make profits by mistreating your neighbor. And you have forgotten me, says the Lord GOD.

13" 'So, Jerusalem, I will shake my fist at you for stealing money and for murdering people. 14Will you still be brave and strong when I punish you? I, the LORD, have spoken, and I will act. 15I will scatter you among the nations and spread you through the countries. That is how I will get rid of your uncleanness. 16But you, yourself, will be dishonored in the sight of the nations. Then you will know that I am the LORD.'"

ISRAEL IS WORTHLESS

17The LORD spoke his word to me, saying: 18"Human, the people of Israel have become useless like scum to me. They are like the copper, tin, iron, and lead left in the furnace when silver is purified. 19So this is what the Lord GOD says: 'Because you have become useless like scum, I am going to put you together inside Jerusalem. 20People put silver, copper, iron, lead, and tin together inside a furnace to melt them down in a blazing fire.

In the same way I will gather you in my hot anger and put you together in Jerusalem and melt you down. 21I will put you together and make you feel the heat of my anger. You will be melted down inside Jerusalem. 22As silver is melted in a furnace, you will be melted inside the city. Then you will know that I, the LORD, have poured out my anger on you.'"

SINS OF THE PEOPLE

23The LORD spoke his word to me, saying: 24"Human, say to the land, 'You are a land that has not had rain or showers when God is angry.' 25Like a roaring lion that tears the animal it has caught, Israel's rulers make evil plans. They have destroyed lives and have taken treasure and valuable things. They have caused many women to become widows. 26Israel's priests do cruel things to my teachings and do not honor my holy things. They make no difference between holy and unholy things, and they teach there is no difference between clean and unclean things. They do not remember my Sabbaths, so I am dishonored by them. 27Like wolves tearing a dead animal, Jerusalem's leaders have killed people for profit. 28And the prophets try to cover this up by false visions and by lying messages. They say, 'This is what the Lord GOD says' when the LORD has not spoken. 29The people cheat others and steal. They hurt people who are poor and needy. They cheat foreigners and do not treat them fairly.

30"I looked for someone to build up the walls and to stand before me where the walls are broken to defend these people so I would not have to destroy them. But I could not find anyone. 31So I let them see my anger. I destroyed them with an anger that was like fire because of all the things they have done, says the Lord GOD."

SAMARIA AND JERUSALEM

23 The LORD spoke his word to me, saying: 2"Human, a woman had two daughters. 3While they were young, they went to Egypt and became prostitutes. They let men touch and hold their breasts. 4The older girl was named Oholah, and her sister was named Oholibah. They became my wives and had sons and daughters. Oholah is Samaria, and Oholibah is Jerusalem."[n]

5"While still my wife, Samaria had sexual relations with other men. She had great sexual desire for her lovers, men from Assyria. The Assyrians were warriors and 6wore blue uniforms. They were all handsome young captains and lieutenants riding on horseback. 7Samaria became a prostitute for all the important men in Assyria and made herself unclean with all the idols of everyone she desired. 8She continued the prostitution she began in Egypt. When she was young, she had slept with men, and they touched her breasts and had sexual relations with her.

9"So I handed her over to her lovers, the Assyrians, that she wanted so badly. 10They stripped her naked and took away her sons and daughters. Then they killed her with a sword. Women everywhere began talking about how she had been punished.

11"Her sister Jerusalem saw what happened, but she became worse than her sister in her sexual desire and prostitution. 12She also desired the Assyrians, who were all soldiers in beautiful uniforms—handsome young captains and lieutenants riding horses. 13I saw that both girls were alike; both were prostitutes.

14"But Jerusalem went even further. She saw carvings of Babylonian men on a wall. They wore red 15and had belts around their waists and turbans on their heads. They all looked like chariot officers born in Babylonia. 16When she saw them, she wanted to have sexual relations with them and sent messengers to them in Babylonia. 17So these Babylonian men came and had sexual relations with her and made her unclean. After that, she became sick of them. 18But she continued her prostitution so openly that everyone knew about it. And I finally became sick of her, as I had her sister. 19But she remembered how she was a young prostitute in Egypt, so she took part in even more prostitution. 20She wanted men who behaved like animals in their sexual desire. 21In the same way you desired to do the sinful things you had done in Egypt. There men touched and held your young breasts.

23:4 Oholah . . . Jerusalem Throughout this chapter Samaria is used in place of Oholah, and Jerusalem is used in place of Oholibah.

GOD'S JUDGMENT ON JERUSALEM

22"So, Jerusalem, this is what the Lord GOD says: You are tired of your lovers. So now I will make them angry with you and have them attack you from all sides. 23Men from Babylon and all Babylonia and men from Pekod, Shoa, and Koa will attack you. All the Assyrians will attack you: handsome young captains and lieutenants, all of them important men and all riding horses. 24Those men will attack with great armies and with their weapons, chariots, and wagons. They will surround you with large and small shields and with helmets. And I will give them the right to punish you, and they will give you their own kind of punishment. 25Then you will see how strong my anger can be when they punish you in their anger. They will cut off your noses and ears. They will take away your sons and daughters, and those who are left will be burned. 26They will take off your clothes and steal your jewelry. 27I will put a stop to the sinful life you began when you were in Egypt so that you will not desire it or remember Egypt anymore.

28"This is what the Lord GOD says: You became tired of your lovers, but I am going to hand you over to those men you now hate. 29They will treat you with hate and take away everything you worked for, leaving you empty and naked. Everyone will know about the sinful things you did. Your sexual sins 30have brought this on you. You have had sexual relations with the nations and made yourselves unclean by worshiping their idols. 31You did the same things your sister did, so you will get the same punishment, like a bitter cup to drink.

32"This is what the Lord GOD says:
You will drink the same cup your sister
  did,
  and that cup is deep and wide.
Everyone will make fun of you,
  because the cup is full.
33 It will make you miserable and drunk.
  It is the cup of fear and ruin.
  It is the cup of your sister Samaria.
34 You will drink everything in it,
  and then you will smash it
  and tear at your breasts.
I have spoken, says the Lord GOD.

35"So this is what the Lord GOD says: You have forgotten me and turned your back on me. So you will be punished for your sexual sins."

JUDGMENT ON SAMARIA AND JERUSALEM

36The LORD said to me: "Human, will you judge Samaria and Jerusalem, showing them their hateful acts? 37They are guilty of adultery and murder. They have taken part in adultery with their idols. They even offered our children as sacrifices in the fire to be food for these idols. 38They have also done this to me: They made my Temple unclean at the same time they dishonored my Sabbaths. 39They sacrificed their children to their idols. Then they entered my Temple at that very time to dishonor it. That is what they did inside my Temple!

40"They even sent for men from far away, who came after a messenger was sent to them. The two sisters bathed themselves for them, painted their eyes, and put on jewelry. 41They sat on a fine bed with a table set before it, on which they put my incense and my oil.

42"There was the noise of a reckless crowd in the city. Common people gathered, and drunkards were brought from the desert. They put bracelets on the wrists of the two sisters and beautiful crowns on their heads. 43Then I said about the one who was worn out by her acts of adultery, 'Let them continue their sexual sins with her. She is nothing but a prostitute.' 44They kept going to her as they would go to a prostitute. So they continued to go to Samaria and Jerusalem, these shameful women. 45But men who do right will punish them as they punish women who take part in adultery and who murder people, because they are guilty of adultery and murder.

46"This is what the Lord GOD says: Bring together a mob against Samaria and Jerusalem, and hand them over to be frightened and robbed. 47Let the mob kill them by throwing stones at them, and let them cut them down with their swords. Let them kill their sons and daughters and burn their houses down.

48"So I will put an end to sexual sins in the land. Then all women will be warned, and they will not do the sexual sins you have done. 49You will be punished for your sexual sins and the sin of worshiping idols. Then you will know that I am the Lord GOD."

THE POT AND THE MEAT

24 The LORD spoke his word to me in the ninth year of our captivity, in the tenth month, on the tenth day of the month. He said: 2"Human, write down today's date, this very date. The king of Babylon has surrounded Jerusalem this very day. 3And tell a story to the people who refuse to obey me. Say to them: 'This is what the Lord GOD says:

Put on the pot; put it on
    and pour water in it.
4 Put in the pieces of meat,
    the best pieces—the legs and the
        shoulders.
Fill it with the best bones.
5   Take the best of the flock,
    and pile wood under the pot.
    Boil the pieces of meat
    until even the bones are cooked.
6"'This is what the Lord GOD says:
How terrible it will be for the city of
        murderers!
    How terrible it will be for the rusty pot
    whose rust will not come off!
Take the meat out of it, piece by piece.
    Don't choose any special piece.

7 "'The blood from her killings is still in the
        city.
    She poured the blood on the bare rock.
She did not pour it on the ground
    where dust would cover it.
8 To stir up my anger and revenge,
    I put the blood she spilled on the bare
        rock
    so it will not be covered.
9"'So this is what the Lord GOD says:
How terrible it will be for the city of
        murderers!
    I myself will pile the wood high for
        burning.
10 Pile up the wood
    and light the fire.
Finish cooking the meat.
    Mix in the spices,
    and let the bones burn.
11 Then set the empty pot on the coals
    so it may become hot and its copper
        sides glow.
The dirty scum stuck inside it may then
        melt
    and its rust burn away.
12 But efforts to clean the pot have failed.

Its heavy rust cannot be removed,
    even in the fire.
13"'By your sinful action you have become unclean. I wanted to cleanse you, but you are still unclean. You will never be cleansed from your sin until my anger against you is carried out.

14"'I, the LORD, have spoken. The time has come for me to act. I will not hold back punishment or feel pity or change my mind. I will judge you by your ways and actions, says the Lord GOD.'"

THE DEATH OF EZEKIEL'S WIFE

15Then the LORD spoke his word to me, saying: 16"Human, I am going to take your wife from you, the woman you look at with love. She will die suddenly, but you must not be sad or cry loudly for her or shed any tears. 17Groan silently; do not cry loudly for the dead. Tie on your turban, and put your sandals on your feet. Do not cover your face, and do not eat the food people eat when they are sad about a death."

18So I spoke to the people in the morning, and my wife died in the evening. The next morning I did as I had been commanded.

19Then the people asked me, "Tell us, what do the things you are doing mean for us?"

20Then I said to them, "The LORD spoke his word to me. He said, 21Say to the people of Israel, This is what the Lord GOD says: I am going to dishonor my Temple. You think it gives you strength. You are proud of it, and you look at it with love and tenderness. But your sons and daughters that you left behind in Jerusalem will fall dead by the sword. 22When that happens, you are to act as I have: you are not to cover your face, and you are not to eat the food people eat when they are sad about a death. 23Your turbans must stay on your heads, and your sandals on your feet. You must not cry loudly, but you must rot away in your sins and groan to each other. 24So Ezekiel is to be an example for you. You must do all the same things he did. When all this happens, you will know that I am the Lord GOD.'

25"And as for you, human, this is how it will be. I will take away the Temple that gives them strength and joy, that makes them proud. They look at it with love, and it makes them happy. And I will take away their sons and daughters also. 26At that time a person who escapes will come to you with information for you to hear. 27At that very time your mouth will be opened. You will speak and be silent no more. So you will be a sign for them, and they will know that I am the LORD."

PROPHECY AGAINST AMMON

25 The LORD spoke his word to me, saying: 2"Human, look toward the people of Ammon and prophesy against them. 3Say to them, 'Hear the word of the Lord GOD. This is what the Lord GOD says: You are glad when my Temple was dishonored, when the land of Israel was ruined, and when the people of Judah were taken away as captives. 4So I am going to give you to the people of the East to be theirs. They will set up their camps among you and make their homes among you. They will eat your fruit and drink your milk. 5I will make the city of Rabbah a pasture for camels and the land of Ammon a resting place for sheep. Then you will know that I am the LORD. 6This is what the Lord GOD says: You have clapped your hands and stamped your feet; you have laughed about all the insults you made against the land of Israel. 7So I will use my power against you. I will give you to the nations as if you were treasures taken in war. I will wipe you out of the lands so you will no longer be a nation, and I will destroy you. Then you will know that I am the LORD.'

PROPHECY AGAINST MOAB AND EDOM

8"This is what the Lord GOD says: 'Moab and Edom say, "The people of Judah are like all the other nations."' 9So I am going to take away the cities that protect Moab's borders, the best cities in that land: Beth Jeshimoth, Baal Meon, and Kiriathaim. 10Then I will give Moab, along with the Ammonites, to the people of the East as their possession. Then, along with the Ammonites, Moab will not be a nation anymore. 11So I will punish the people of Moab, and they will know that I am the LORD.'

PROPHECY AGAINST EDOM

12"This is what the Lord GOD says: 'Edom took revenge on the people of Judah, and the Edomites became guilty because of it. 13So this is what the Lord GOD says: I will use my

power against Edom, killing every human and animal in it. And I will destroy Edom all the way from Teman to Dedan as they die in battle. 14I will use my people Israel to take revenge on Edom. So the Israelites will do to Edom what my hot anger demands. Then the Edomites will know what my revenge feels like, says the Lord GOD.'

PROPHECY AGAINST PHILISTIA

15"This is what the Lord GOD says: 'The Philistines have taken revenge with hateful hearts. Because of their strong hatred, they have tried to destroy Judah. 16So this is what the Lord GOD says: I will use my power against the Philistines. I will kill the Kerethites, and I will destroy those people still alive on the coast of the Mediterranean Sea. 17I will punish them in my anger and do great acts of revenge to them. They will know that I am the LORD when I take revenge on them.'"

PROPHECY AGAINST TYRE

26 It was the eleventh year of our captivity, on the first day of the month. The LORD spoke his word to me, saying: 2"Human, the city of Tyre has spoken against Jerusalem: 'The city that traded with the nations is destroyed. Now we can be the trading center. Since the city of Jerusalem is ruined, we can make money.' 3So this is what the Lord GOD says: I am against you, Tyre. I will bring many nations against you, like the sea beating its waves on your island shores. 4They will destroy the walls of Tyre and pull down her towers. I will also scrape away her ruins and make her a bare rock. 5Tyre will be an island where fishermen dry their nets. I have spoken, says the Lord GOD. The nations will steal treasures from Tyre. 6Also, her villages on the shore across from the island will be destroyed by war. Then they will know that I am the LORD.

NEBUCHADNEZZAR TO ATTACK TYRE

7"This is what the Lord GOD says: I will bring a king from the north against Tyre. He is Nebuchadnezzar king of Babylon, the greatest king, with his horses, chariots, horsemen, and a great army. 8He will fight a battle and destroy your villages on the shore across from the island. He will set up devices to attack you. He will build a road of earth to the top of the walls. He will raise his shields against you. 9He will bring logs to pound through your city walls, and he will break down your towers with his iron bars. 10His horses will be so many that they will cover you with their dust. Your walls will shake at the noise of horsemen, wagons, and chariots. The king of Babylon will enter your city gates as men enter a city where the walls are broken through. 11The hoofs of his horses will run over your streets. He will kill your army with the sword, and your strong pillars will fall down to the ground. 12Also, his men will take away your riches and will steal the things you sell. They will break down your walls and destroy your nice houses. They will throw your stones, wood, and trash into the sea. 13So I will stop your songs; the music of your harps will not be heard anymore. 14I will make you a bare rock, and you will be a place for drying fishing nets. You will not be built again, because I, the LORD, have spoken, says the Lord GOD.

15"This is what the Lord GOD says to Tyre: The people who live along the seacoast will shake with fear when they hear about your defeat. Those of you who are injured and dying will groan. 16Then all the leaders of the seacoast will get down from their thrones, take off their beautiful needlework clothes, and show how afraid they are. They will sit on the ground and tremble all the time. When they see you, they will be shocked. 17They will begin singing a funeral song about you and will say to you:

'Tyre, you famous city, you have been
    destroyed!
You have lost your sea power!
You and your people
    had great power on the seas.
You made everyone around you
    afraid of you.
18 Now the people who live by the coast
    tremble,
    now that you have fallen.
The islands of the sea
    are afraid because you have been
        defeated.'

19"This is what the Lord GOD says: I will make you an empty city, like cities that have no people living in them. I will bring the deep ocean waters over you, and the Mediterranean Sea will cover you. 20At that time I will send you down to the place of the dead to join those who died long ago. I will make you live with the dead below the earth in places that are like old ruins. You will not come back from there or have any place in the world of the living again. 21Other people will be afraid of what happened to you, and it will be the end of you. People will look for you, but they will never find you again, says the Lord GOD."

A FUNERAL SONG FOR TYRE

27 The LORD spoke his word to me, saying: 2"Human, sing a funeral song for the city of Tyre. 3Speak to Tyre, which has ports for the Mediterranean Sea and is a place for trade for the people of many lands along the seacoast. 'This is what the Lord GOD says:

Tyre, you have said,
    "I am like a beautiful ship."
4 You were at home on the high seas.
    Your builders made your beauty perfect.
5 They made all your boards
    of fir trees from Mount Hermon.
They took a cedar tree from Lebanon
    to make a ship's mast for you.
6 They made your oars
    from oak trees from Bashan.
They made your deck
    from cypress trees from the coast of
        Cyprus
    and set ivory into it.
7 Your sail of linen with designs sewed on it
    came from Egypt
    and became like a flag for you.
Your cloth shades over the deck were blue
    and purple
    and came from the island of Cyprus.
8 Men from Sidon and Arvad used oars to
    row you.
Tyre, your skilled men were the sailors
    on your deck.
9 Workers of Byblos were with you,
    putting caulk[n] in your ship's seams.
All the ships of the sea and their sailors
    came alongside to trade with you.

10 "'Men of Persia, Lydia, and Put
    were warriors in your navy
and hung their shields and helmets on
    your sides.

27:9 **caulk** Something like tar put between the boards of a ship to make it waterproof.

They made you look beautiful.
11 Men of Arvad and Cilicia
   guarded your city walls all around.
   Men of Gammad
      were in your watchtowers
and hung their shields around your walls.
   They made your beauty perfect.

12 "People of Tarshish became traders for you because of your great wealth. They traded your goods for silver, iron, tin, and lead.

13 "People of Greece, Tubal, and Meshech became merchants for you. They traded your goods for slaves and items of bronze.

14 "People of Beth Togarmah traded your goods for work horses, war horses, and mules.

15 "People of Rhodes became merchants for you, selling your goods on many coastlands. They brought back ivory tusks and valuable black wood as your payment.

16 "People of Aram became traders for you, because you had so many good things to sell. They traded your goods for turquoise, purple cloth, cloth with designs sewed on, fine linen, coral, and rubies.

17 "People of Judah and Israel became merchants for you. They traded your goods for wheat from Minnith, and for honey, olive oil, and balm.

18-19 "People of Damascus became traders for you because you have many good things and great wealth. They traded your goods for wine from Helbon, wool from Zahar, and barrels of wine from Izal. They received wrought iron, cassia, and sugar cane in payment for your good things.

20 "People of Dedan became merchants for you, trading saddle blankets for riding.

21 "People of Arabia and all the rulers of Kedar became traders for you. They received lambs, male sheep, and goats in payment for you.

22 "The merchants of Sheba and Raamah became merchants for you. They traded your goods for all the best spices, valuable gems, and gold.

23 "People of Haran, Canneh, Eden, and the traders of Sheba, Asshur, and Kilmad became merchants for you. 24 They were paid with the best clothes, blue cloth, cloth with designs sewed on, carpets of many colors, and tightly wound ropes.

25 "'Trading ships
   carried the things you sold.
You were like a ship full of heavy cargo
   in the middle of the sea.
26 The men who rowed you
   brought you out into the high seas,
but the east wind broke you to pieces
   in the middle of the sea.
27 Your wealth, your trade, your goods,
   your seamen, your sailors, your
      workers,
   your traders, your warriors,
      and everyone else on board
   sank into the sea
      on the day your ship was wrecked.
28 The people on the shore shake with fear
   when your sailors cry out.
29 All the men who row
   leave their ships;
   the seamen and the sailors of other ships
      stand on the shore.
30 They cry loudly about you;
   they cry very much.
   They throw dust on their heads
      and roll in ashes to show they are sad.
31 They shave their heads for you,
   and they put on rough cloth to show
      they are upset.
   They cry and sob for you;
      they cry loudly.
32 And in their loud crying
   they sing a funeral song for you:
   "No one was ever destroyed like Tyre,
      surrounded by the sea."
33 When the goods you traded went out over
      the seas,
   you met the needs of many nations.
   With your great wealth and goods,
      you made kings of the earth rich.
34 But now you are broken by the sea
   and have sunk to the bottom.
   Your goods and all the people on board
      have gone down with you.
35 All those who live along the shore
   are shocked by what happened to you.
   Their kings are terribly afraid,
      and their faces show their fear.
36 The traders among the nations hiss at you.
   You have come to a terrible end,
      and you are gone forever.'"

PROPHECY AGAINST THE KING OF TYRE

28 The LORD spoke his word to me, saying: [2]"Human, say to the ruler of Tyre: 'This is what the Lord GOD says:

Because you are proud,
   you say, "I am a god.
I sit on the throne of a god
   in the middle of the seas."
You think you are as wise as a god,
   but you are a human, not a god.
[3] You think you are wiser than Daniel.
   You think you can find out all secrets.
[4] Through your wisdom and understanding
   you have made yourself rich.
You have gained gold and silver
   and have saved it in your storerooms.
[5] Through your great skill in trading,
   you have made your riches grow.
You are too proud
   because of your riches.

[6] "So this is what the Lord GOD says:
You think you are wise
   like a god,
[7] but I will bring foreign people against you,
   the cruelest nation.
They will pull out their swords
   and destroy all that your wisdom has
      built,
   and they will dishonor your greatness.
[8] They will kill you;
   you will die a terrible death
   like those who are killed at sea.
[9] While they are killing you,
   you will not be able to say anymore, "I
      am a god."
You will be only a human, not a god,
   when your murderers kill you.
[10] You will die like an unclean person;
   foreigners will kill you.
I have spoken, says the Lord GOD.'"

[11]The LORD spoke his word to me, saying:
[12]"Human, sing a funeral song for the king of
Tyre. Say to him: 'This is what the Lord GOD
says:

You were an example of what was perfect,
   full of wisdom and perfect in beauty.
[13] You had a wonderful life,
   as if you were in Eden, the garden of
      God.
Every valuable gem was on you:
   ruby, topaz, and emerald,
   yellow quartz, onyx, and jasper,
   sapphire, turquoise, and chrysolite.

Your jewelry was made of gold.
   It was prepared on the day you were
      created.
[14] I appointed a living creature to guard you.
   I put you on the holy mountain of God.
You walked among the gems that
   shined like fire.
[15] Your life was right and good
   from the day you were created,
   until evil was found in you.
[16] Because you traded with countries far
      away,
   you learned to be cruel, and you sinned.
So I threw you down in disgrace from the
      mountain of God.
And the living creature who guarded
      you
   forced you out from among the gems
      that shined like fire.
[17] You became too proud
   because of your beauty.
You ruined your wisdom
   because of your greatness.
I threw you down to the ground.
   Your example taught a lesson to other
      kings.
[18] You dishonored your places of worship
   through your many sins and dishonest
      trade.
So I set on fire the place where you lived,
   and the fire burned you up.
I turned you into ashes on the ground
   for all those watching to see.
[19] All the nations who knew you
   are shocked about you.
Your punishment was so terrible,
   and you are gone forever.'"

PROPHECY AGAINST SIDON

[20]The LORD spoke his word to me, saying:
[21]"Human, look toward the city of Sidon and
prophesy against her. [22]Say: 'This is what the
Lord GOD says:

I am against you, Sidon,
   and I will show my glory among you.
People will know that I am the LORD
   when I have punished Sidon;
   I will show my holiness by defeating
      her.
[23] I will send diseases to Sidon,
   and blood will flow in her streets.
Those who are wounded in Sidon will fall
      dead,

attacked from all sides.
Then they will know that I am the LORD.

GOD WILL HELP ISRAEL

24"'No more will neighboring nations be like thorny branches or sharp stickers to hurt Israel. Then they will know that I am the Lord GOD.

25"'This is what the Lord GOD says: I will gather the people of Israel from the nations where they are scattered. I will show my holiness when the nations see what I do for my people. Then they will live in their own land—the land I gave to my servant Jacob. 26They will live safely in the land and will build houses and plant vineyards. They will live in safety after I have punished all the nations around who hate them. Then they will know that I am the LORD their God.'"

PROPHECY AGAINST EGYPT

29 It was the tenth year of our captivity, in the tenth month, on the twelfth day of the month. The LORD spoke his word to me, saying: 2"Human, look toward the king of Egypt, and prophesy against him and all Egypt. 3Say: 'This is what the Lord GOD says:
I am against you, king of Egypt.
  You are like a great crocodile that lies in the Nile River.
You say, "The Nile is mine;
  I made it for myself."
4 But I will put hooks in your jaws,
  and I will make the fish of the Nile stick to your sides.
I will pull you up out of your rivers,
  with all the fish sticking to your sides.
5 I will leave you in the desert,
  you and all the fish from your rivers.
You will fall onto the ground;
  you will not be picked up or buried.
I have given you to the wild animals
  and to the birds of the sky for food.
6Then all the people who live in Egypt will know that I am the LORD.

"'Israel tried to lean on you for help, but you were like a crutch made out of a weak stalk of grass. 7When their hands grabbed you, you splintered and tore open their shoulders. When they leaned on you, you broke and made all their backs twist.

8"'So this is what the Lord GOD says: I will cause an enemy to attack you and kill your people and animals. 9Egypt will become

an empty desert. Then they will know that I am the LORD.

"'Because you said, "The Nile River is mine, and I have made it," 10I am against you and your rivers. I will destroy the land of Egypt and make it an empty desert from Migdol in the north to Aswan in the south, all the way to the border of Cush. 11No person or animal will walk through it, and no one will live in Egypt for forty years. 12I will make the land of Egypt the most deserted country of all. Her cities will be the most deserted of all ruined cities for forty years. I will scatter the Egyptians among the nations, spreading them among the countries.

13"'This is what the Lord GOD says: After forty years I will gather Egypt from the nations where they have been scattered. 14I will bring back the Egyptian captives and make them return to southern Egypt, to the land they came from. They will become a weak kingdom there. 15It will be the weakest kingdom, and it will never again rule other nations. I will make it so weak it will never again rule over the nations. 16The Israelites will never again depend on Egypt. Instead, Egypt's punishment will remind the Israelites of their sin in turning to Egypt for help. Then they will know that I am the Lord GOD.'"

EGYPT IS GIVEN TO BABYLON

17It was the twenty-seventh year of our captivity, in the first month, on the first day of the month. The LORD spoke his word to me, saying: 18"Human, Nebuchadnezzar king of Babylon made his army fight hard against Tyre. Every soldier's head was rubbed bare, and every shoulder was rubbed raw. But Nebuchadnezzar and his army gained nothing from fighting Tyre. 19So this is what the Lord GOD says: I will give the land of Egypt to Nebuchadnezzar king of Babylon. He will take away Egypt's people and its wealth and its treasures as pay for his army. 20I am giving Nebuchadnezzar the land of Egypt as a reward for working hard for me, says the Lord GOD.

21"At that time I will make Israel grow strong again, and I will let you, Ezekiel, speak to them. Then they will know that I am the LORD."

EGYPT WILL BE PUNISHED

30 The LORD spoke his word to me, saying: 2"Human, prophesy and say, 'This is what the Lord GOD says:

Cry and say,
"The terrible day is coming."
3 The day is near;
the LORD's day of judging is near.
It is a cloudy day
and a time when the nations will be judged.
4 An enemy will attack Egypt,
and Cush will tremble with fear.
When the killing begins in Egypt,
her wealth will be taken away,
and her foundations will be torn down.
5Cush, Put, Lydia, Arabia, Libya, and some of my people who had made an agreement with Egypt will fall dead in war.
6"'This is what the LORD says:
Those who fight on Egypt's side will fall.
The power she is proud of will be lost.
The people in Egypt will fall dead in war
from Migdol in the north to Aswan in the south,
says the Lord GOD.
7 They will be the most deserted lands.
Egypt's cities will be the worst of cities
that lie in ruins.
8 Then they will know that I am the LORD
when I set fire to Egypt
and when all those nations on her side
are crushed.
9"'At that time I will send messengers in ships to frighten Cush, which now feels safe. The people of Cush will tremble with fear when Egypt is punished. And that time is sure to come.
10"'This is what the Lord GOD says:
I will destroy great numbers of people in Egypt
through the power of Nebuchadnezzar king of Babylon.
11 Nebuchadnezzar and his army,
the cruelest army of any nation,
will be brought in to destroy the land.
They will pull out their swords against Egypt
and will fill the land with those they kill.
12 I will make the streams of the Nile River become dry land,

and then I will sell the land to evil people.
I will destroy the land and everything in it
through the power of foreigners.
I, the LORD, have spoken.

EGYPT'S IDOLS ARE DESTROYED

13"'This is what the Lord GOD says:
I will destroy the idols
and take away the statues of gods from
the city of Memphis.
There will no longer be a leader in Egypt,
and I will spread fear through the land
of Egypt.
14 I will make southern Egypt empty
and start a fire in Zoan
and punish Thebes.
15 And I will pour out my anger against Pelusium,
the strong place of Egypt.
I will destroy great numbers of people
in Thebes.
16 I will set fire to Egypt.
Pelusium will be in great pain.
The walls of Thebes will be broken open,
and Memphis will have troubles every day.
17 The young men of Heliopolis and Bubastis
will fall dead in war,
and the people will be taken away as captives.
18 In Tahpanhes the day will be dark
when I break Egypt's power.
Then she will no longer be proud of her power.
A cloud will cover Egypt,
and her villages will be captured and taken away.
19 So I will punish Egypt,
and they will know I am the LORD.'"

EGYPT BECOMES WEAK

20It was in the eleventh year of our captivity, in the first month, on the seventh day of the month. The LORD spoke his word to me, saying: 21"Human, I have broken the powerful arm of the king of Egypt. It has not been tied up, so it will not get well. It has not been wrapped with a bandage, so it will not be strong enough to hold a sword in war. 22So this is what the Lord GOD says: I am against the king of Egypt. I will break his arms, both the strong arm and the broken arm, and I will make the sword fall from his hand. ²³I will scatter the Egyptians among the nations, spreading them among the countries. ²⁴I will make the arms of the king of Babylon strong and put my sword in his hand. But I will break the arms of the king of Egypt. Then when he faces the king of Babylon, he will cry out in pain like a dying person. ²⁵So I will make the arms of the king of Babylon strong, but the arms of the king of Egypt will fall. Then people will know that I am the LORD when I put my sword into the hand of the king of Babylon and he uses it in war against Egypt. ²⁶Then I will scatter the Egyptians among the nations, spreading them among the countries. Then they will know that I am the LORD."

A CEDAR TREE

31 It was in the eleventh year of our captivity, in the third month, on the first day of the month. The LORD spoke his word to me, saying: ²"Human, say to the king of Egypt and his people:
'No one is like you in your greatness.
³ Assyria was once like a cedar tree in
        Lebanon
    with beautiful branches that shaded the
        forest.
    It was very tall;
        its top was among the clouds.
⁴ Much water made the tree grow;
        the deep springs made it tall.
    Rivers flowed
        around the bottom of the tree
    and sent their streams
        to all other trees in the countryside.
⁵ So the tree was taller
        than all the other trees in the
        countryside.
    Its limbs became long and big
        because of so much water.
⁶ All the birds of the sky
        made their nests in the tree's limbs.
    And all the wild animals
        gave birth under its branches.
    All great nations
        lived in the tree's shade.
⁷ So the tree was great and beautiful,
        with its long branches,
        because its roots reached down to much
        water.
⁸ The cedar trees in the garden of God
        were not as great as it was.

The pine trees
        did not have such great limbs.
    The plane trees
        did not have such branches.
    No tree in the garden of God
        was as beautiful as this tree.
⁹ I made it beautiful
        with many branches,
    and all the trees of Eden in the garden of
        God
        wanted to be like it.

¹⁰"So this is what the Lord GOD says: The tree grew tall. Its top reached the clouds, and it became proud of its height. ¹¹So I handed it over to a mighty ruler of the nations for him to punish it. Because it was evil, I got rid of it. ¹²The cruelest foreign nation cut it down and left it. The tree's branches fell on the mountains and in all the valleys, and its broken limbs were in all the ravines of the land. All the nations of the earth left the shade of that tree. ¹³The birds of the sky live on the fallen tree. The wild animals live among the tree's fallen branches. ¹⁴So the trees that grow by the water will not be proud to be tall; they will not put their tops among the clouds. None of the trees that are watered well will grow that tall, because they all are meant to die and go under the ground. They will be with people who have died and have gone down to the place of the dead.

¹⁵"This is what the Lord GOD says: On the day when the tree went down to the place of the dead, I made the deep springs cry loudly. I covered them and held back their rivers, and the great waters stopped flowing. I dressed Lebanon in black to show her sadness about the great tree, and all the trees in the countryside were sad about it. ¹⁶I made the nations shake with fear at the sound of the tree falling when I brought it down to the place of the dead. It went to join those who have gone down to the grave. Then all the trees of Eden and the best trees of Lebanon, all the well-watered trees, were comforted in the place of the dead below the earth. ¹⁷These trees had also gone down with the great tree to the place of the dead. They joined those who were killed in war and those among the nations who had lived under the great tree's shade.

¹⁸"So no tree in Eden is equal to you, Egypt, in greatness and honor, but you will

go down to join the trees of Eden in the place below the earth. You will lie among unclean people, with those who were killed in war.

"'This is about the king of Egypt and all his people, says the Lord GOD.'"

A FUNERAL SONG

32 It was in the twelfth year of our captivity, in the twelfth month, on the first day of the month. The LORD spoke his word to me, saying: ²"Human, sing a funeral song about the king of Egypt. Say to him:

'You are like a young lion among the
    nations.
You are like a crocodile in the seas.
You splash around in your streams
    and stir up the water with your feet,
    making the rivers muddy.
³"This is what the Lord GOD says:
I will spread my net over you,
    and I will use a large group of people
    to pull you up in my net.
⁴ Then I will throw you on the land
    dropping you onto the ground.
I will let the birds of the sky rest on you
    and all the animals of the earth eat you
    until they are full.
⁵ I will scatter your flesh on the mountains
    and fill the valleys with what is left of
    you.
⁶ I will drench the land with your flowing
    blood
    as far as the mountains,
    and the ravines will be full of your flesh.
⁷ When I make you disappear,
    I will cover the sky and make the stars
    dark.
I will cover the sun with a cloud,
    and the moon will not shine.
⁸ I will make all the shining lights in the sky
    become dark over you;
I will bring darkness over your land,
    says the Lord GOD.
⁹ I will cause many people to be afraid
    when I bring you as a captive into other
    nations,
    to lands you have not known.
¹⁰ I will cause many people to be shocked
    about you.
Their kings will tremble with fear
    because of you
when I swing my sword in front of
    them.

They will shake every moment
    on the day you fall;
    each king will be afraid for his own life.
¹¹"So this is what the Lord GOD says:
The sword of the king of Babylon
    will attack you.
¹² I will cause your people to fall
    by the swords of mighty soldiers,
    the most terrible in the world.
They will destroy the pride of Egypt
    and all its people.
¹³ I will also destroy all Egypt's cattle
    which live alongside much water.
The foot of a human will not stir the water,
    and the hoofs of cattle will not muddy it
    anymore.
¹⁴ So I will let the Egyptians' water become
    clear.
I will cause their rivers to run as
    smoothly as olive oil,
    says the Lord GOD.
¹⁵ When I make the land of Egypt empty
    and take everything that is in the land,
when I destroy all those who live in
    Egypt,
    then they will know that I am the
    LORD.'

¹⁶"This is the funeral song people will sing for Egypt. The women of the nations will sing it; they will sing a funeral song for Egypt and all its people, says the Lord GOD."

EGYPT TO BE DESTROYED

¹⁷It was in the twelfth year of our captivity, on the fifteenth day of the month. The LORD spoke his word to me, saying: ¹⁸"Human, cry for the people of Egypt. Bring down Egypt, together with the women of the powerful nations; bring them down to the place of the dead below the earth to join those who go to the place of the dead. ¹⁹Say to them: 'Are you more beautiful than others? Go lie down in death with those who are unclean.' ²⁰The Egyptians will fall among those killed in war. The sword is ready; the enemy will drag Egypt and all her people away. ²¹From the place of the dead the leaders of the mighty ones will speak about the king of Egypt and the nations which help him: 'The unclean, those killed in war, have come down here and lie dead.'

²²"Assyria and all its army lie dead there. The graves of their soldiers are all around.

All were killed in war, 23and their graves were put in the deepest parts of the place of the dead. Assyria's army lies around its grave. When they lived on earth, they frightened people, but now all of them have been killed in war.

24"The nation of Elam is there with all its army around its grave. All of them were killed in war. They had frightened people on earth and were unclean, so they went down to the lowest parts of the place of the dead. They must carry their shame with those who have gone down to the place of the dead. 25A bed has been made for Elam with all those killed in war. The graves of her soldiers are all around her. All Elam's people are unclean, killed in war. They frightened people when they lived on earth, but now they must carry their shame with those who have gone down to the place of the dead. Their graves are with the rest who were killed.

26"Meshech and Tubal are there with the graves of all their soldiers around them. All of them are unclean and have been killed in war. They also frightened people when they lived on earth. 27But they are not buried with the other soldiers who were killed in battle long ago, those who went with their weapons of war to the place of the dead. These soldiers had their swords laid under their heads and their shields on their bodies. These mighty soldiers used to frighten people when they lived on earth.

28"You, king of Egypt, will be broken and lie among those who are unclean, who were killed in war.

29"Edom is there also, with its kings and all its leaders. They were mighty, but now they lie in death with those killed in war, with those who are unclean, with those who have gone down to the place of the dead.

30"All the rulers of the north and all the Sidonians are there. Their strength frightened people, but they have gone down in shame with those who were killed. They are unclean, lying with those killed in war. They carry their shame with those who have gone down to the place of the dead.

31"The king of Egypt and his army will see these who have been killed in war. Then he will be comforted for all his soldiers killed in war, says the Lord GOD. 32I made people afraid of the king of Egypt while he lived on earth. But he and all his people will lie among those who are unclean, who were killed in war, says the Lord GOD."

EZEKIEL IS WATCHMAN FOR ISRAEL

33 The LORD spoke his word to me, saying: 2"Human, speak to your people and say to them: 'Suppose I bring a war against a land. The people of the land may choose one of their men and make him their watchman. 3When he sees the enemy coming to attack the land, he will blow the trumpet and warn the people. 4If they hear the sound of the trumpet but do nothing, the enemy will come and kill them. They will be responsible for their own deaths. 5They heard the sound of the trumpet but didn't do anything. So they are to blame for their own deaths. If they had done something, they would have saved their own lives. 6But if the watchman sees the enemy coming to attack and does not blow the trumpet, the people will not be warned. Then if the enemy comes and kills any of them, they have died because of their own sin. But I will punish the watchman for their deaths.'

7"You, human, are the one I have made a watchman for Israel. If you hear a word from my mouth, you must warn them for me. 8Suppose I say to the wicked: 'Wicked people, you will surely die,' but you don't speak to warn the wicked to stop doing evil. Then they will die because they were sinners, but I will punish you for their deaths. 9But if you warn the wicked to stop doing evil and they do not stop, they will die because they were sinners. But you have saved your life.

10"So you, human, say to Israel: 'You have said: Surely our law-breaking and sins are hurting us. They will kill us. What can we do so we will live?' 11Say to them: 'The Lord GOD says: As surely as I live, I do not want any who are wicked to die. I want them to stop doing evil and live. Stop! Stop your wicked ways! You don't want to die, do you, people of Israel?'

12"Human, say to your people: 'The goodness of those who do right will not save them when they sin. The evil of wicked people will not cause them to be punished if they stop doing it. If good people sin, they will not be able to live by the good they did earlier.' 13If I tell good people, 'You will surely live,' they might think they have done enough good and then do evil. Then none of the good things they did will be remembered. They will die because of the evil they have done. ¹⁴Or, if I say to the wicked people, 'You will surely die,' they may stop sinning and do what is right and honest. ¹⁵For example, they may return what somebody gave them as a promise to repay a loan, or pay back what they stole. If they live by the rules that give life and do not sin, then they will surely live, and they will not die. ¹⁶They will not be punished for any of their sins. They now do what is right and fair, so they will surely live.

¹⁷"Your people say: 'The way of the Lord is not fair.' But it is their own ways that are not fair. ¹⁸When the good people stop doing good and do evil, they will die for their evil. ¹⁹But when the wicked stop doing evil and do what is right and fair, they will live. ²⁰You still say: 'The way of the Lord is not fair.' Israel, I will judge all of you by your own ways."

THE FALL OF JERUSALEM EXPLAINED

²¹It was in the twelfth year of our captivity, on the fifth day of the tenth month. A person who had escaped from Jerusalem came to me and said, "Jerusalem has been captured." ²²Now I had felt the power of the LORD on me the evening before. He had made me able to talk again before this person came to me. I could speak; I was not without speech anymore.

²³Then the LORD spoke his word to me, saying: ²⁴"Human, people who live in the ruins in the land of Israel are saying: 'Abraham was only one person, yet he was given the land as his own. Surely the land has been given to us, who are many, as our very own.' ²⁵So say to them: 'This is what the Lord GOD says: You eat meat with the blood still in it, you ask your idols for help, and you murder people. Should you then have the land as your very own? ²⁶You depend on your sword and do terrible things which I hate. Each of you has sexual relations with his neighbor's wife. So should you have the land?'

²⁷"Say to them: 'This is what the Lord GOD says: As surely as I live, those who are among the city ruins in Israel will be killed in war. I will cause those who live in the country to be eaten by wild animals. People hiding in the strongholds and caves will die of dis-

ease. ²⁸I will make the land an empty desert. The people's pride in the land's power will end. The mountains of Israel will become empty so that no one will pass through them. ²⁹They will know that I am the LORD when I make the land an empty desert because of the things they have done that I hate.'

³⁰"But as for you, human, your people are talking about you by the walls and in the doorways of houses. They say to each other: 'Come now, and hear the message from the LORD.' ³¹So they come to you in crowds as if they were really ready to listen. They sit in front of you as if they were my people and hear your words, but they will not obey them. With their mouths they tell me they love me, but their hearts desire their selfish profits. ³²To your people you are nothing more than a singer who sings love songs and has a beautiful voice and plays a musical instrument well. They hear your words, but they will not obey them.

³³"When this comes true, and it surely will happen, then the people will know that a prophet has been among them."

THE LEADERS ARE LIKE SHEPHERDS

34 The LORD spoke his word to me, saying: ²"Human, prophesy against the leaders of Israel, who are like shepherds. Prophesy and say to them: 'This is what the Lord GOD says: How terrible it will be for the shepherds of Israel who feed only themselves! Why don't the shepherds feed the flock? ³You eat the milk curds, and you clothe yourselves with the wool. You kill the fat sheep, but you do not feed the flock. ⁴You have not made the weak strong. You have not healed the sick or put bandages on those that were hurt. You have not brought back those who strayed away or searched for the lost. But you have ruled the sheep with cruel force. ⁵The sheep were scattered, because there was no shepherd, and they became food for every wild animal. ⁶My flock wandered over all the mountains and on every high hill. They were scattered all over the face of the earth, and no one searched or looked for them.

⁷"So, you shepherds, hear the word of the LORD. This is what the Lord GOD says: ⁸As surely as I live, my flock has been caught and eaten by all the wild animals, because the flock has no shepherd. The shepherds did not

search for my flock. No, they fed themselves instead of my flock. ⁹So, you shepherds, hear the word of the LORD. ¹⁰This is what the Lord GOD says: I am against the shepherds. I will blame them for what has happened to my sheep and will not let them tend the flock anymore. Then the shepherds will stop feeding themselves, and I will take my flock from their mouths so they will no longer be their food.

¹¹"'This is what the Lord GOD says: I, myself, will search for my sheep and take care of them. ¹²As a shepherd takes care of his scattered flock when it is found, I will take care of my sheep. I will save them from all the places where they were scattered on a cloudy and dark day. ¹³I will bring them out from the nations and gather them from the countries. I will bring them to their own land and pasture them on the mountains of Israel, in the ravines, and in all the places where people live in the land. ¹⁴I will feed them in a good pasture, and they will eat grass on the high mountains of Israel. They will lie down on good ground where they eat grass, and they will eat in rich grassland on the mountains of Israel. ¹⁵I will feed my flock and lead them to rest, says the Lord GOD. ¹⁶I will search for the lost, bring back those that strayed away, put bandages on those that were hurt, and make the weak strong. But I will destroy those sheep that are fat and strong. I will tend the sheep with fairness.

¹⁷"'This is what the Lord GOD says: As for you, my flock, I will judge between one sheep and another, between the male sheep and the male goats. ¹⁸Is it not enough for you to eat grass in the good land? Must you crush the rest of the grass with your feet? Is it not enough for you to drink clear water? Must you make the rest of the water muddy with your feet? ¹⁹Must my flock eat what you crush, and must they drink what you make muddy with your feet?

²⁰"'So this is what the Lord GOD says to them: I, myself, will judge between the fat sheep and the thin sheep. ²¹You push with your side and with your shoulder, and you knock down all the weak sheep with your horns until you have forced them away. ²²So I will save my flock; they will not be hurt anymore. I will judge between one sheep and another. ²³Then I will put over them one

shepherd, my servant David. He will feed them and tend them and be their shepherd. ²⁴Then I, the LORD, will be their God, and my servant David will be a ruler among them. I, the LORD, have spoken.

²⁵"'I will make an agreement of peace with my sheep and will remove harmful animals from the land. Then the sheep will live safely in the desert and sleep in the woods. ²⁶I will bless them and let them live around my hill. I will cause the rains to come when it is time; there will be showers to bless them. ²⁷Also the trees in the countryside will give their fruit, and the land will give its harvest. And the sheep will be safe on their land. Then they will know that I am the LORD when I break the bars of their captivity and save them from the power of those who made them slaves. ²⁸They will not be led captive by the nations again. The wild animals will not eat them, but they will live safely, and no one will make them afraid. ²⁹I will give them a place famous for its good crops, so they will no longer suffer from hunger in the land. They will not suffer the insults of other nations anymore. ³⁰Then they will know that I, the LORD their God, am with them. The nation of Israel will know that they are my people, says the Lord GOD. ³¹You, my human sheep, are the sheep I care for, and I am your God, says the Lord GOD.'"

PROPHECY AGAINST EDOM

35 The LORD spoke his word to me, saying: ²"Human, look toward Edom and prophesy against it. ³Say to it: 'This is what the Lord GOD says: I am against you, Edom. I will stretch out my hand against you and make you an empty desert. ⁴I will destroy your cities, and you will become empty. Then you will know that I am the LORD.

⁵"'You have always been an enemy of Israel. You let them be defeated in war when they were in trouble at the time of their final punishment. ⁶So the Lord GOD says, as surely as I live, I will let you be murdered. Murder will chase you. Since you did not hate murdering people, murder will chase you. ⁷I will make Edom an empty ruin and destroy everyone who goes in or comes out of it. ⁸I will fill its mountains with those who are killed. Those killed in war will fall on your hills, in your valleys, and in all your ravines. ⁹I will

Always on His Mind

By Ken Ulmer

EZEKIEL 34:11–16

Hold on, child of God, you are destined for victory! God knows the struggles you face. He has great plans for you, and he thinks about you. The great God of the universe, the Father of lights and Creator of everything, knows your name, and you are on his mind. God is building your good future, even when you cannot see it. He is in charge of the big picture, the broad perspective, and he is bringing all the different elements of your life together. You can take his Word for it.

It is not over. His plans for you are not to hurt you, but to give you a good future (Jeremiah 29:11). He will give you the ability by the power of the Holy Spirit to have peace on the inside. Peace is not the absence of adversity, but the presence of his assistance. It is the power of God that resides in you that allows you to fulfill the great plans God has made for you.

There may be things lacking in your life. Some things may even look dead, but when God gets through fixing them, you'll be left with a masterpiece of your life. He breathes life into you by the power of his strength.

Your time is not aimless or without strategy. Maybe you did not get an itinerary, but God did not plan for you to be lost. Even if your life is adrift because of sin, discouragement, opposition, or trials, do not worry. God is reaching for you, ready to set you on a new course.

Your Christian life is like a rowboat. God steers and you row—always moving forward, but looking backward. He sees your journey's good end and navigates you toward it.

Begin to praise him on the way to your victory; don't wait until the end of the journey.

God is faithful in what he has done and what he will do.

Focus on what you are going *to*, not *through*, and remember how far you have come. Praise God for all he has done for you in the past, and thank him for the hope of all he is getting ready to do. God specializes in creating something out of nothing. Just as with weaving on a loom, all we see sometimes is the tangled back of the tapestry. Turn around to the other side and see God's masterpiece. God isn't finished with you yet, so look on the other side. He takes the downtimes and even the low times and weaves them into a good life. God's goal is to give you a good future.

After everything you have been through, you are still here. It is not over. God has good plans for you, plans of blessing and peace. So keep breathing. God has not forgotten about you. You are always on his mind!

TO LEARN MORE ON WHAT THE BIBLE HAS TO SAY ABOUT **FULFILLMENT,** READ THE SCRIPTURES AND DEVOTIONALS AT **GENESIS 32:28, EXODUS 14:2, EXODUS 14:13–14, EXODUS 15:2, PSALM 9:9, 1 KINGS 9:1–5,** AND **2 CHRONICLES 16:9.**

make you a ruin forever; no one will live in your cities. Then you will know that I am the LORD.

10" 'You said, "These two nations, Israel and Judah, and these two lands will be ours. We will take them for our own." But the LORD was there. 11So this is what the Lord GOD says: As surely as I live, I will treat you just as you treated them. You were angry and jealous because you hated them. So I will punish you and show the Israelites who I am. 12Then you will know that I, the LORD, have heard all your insults against the mountains of Israel. You said, "They have been ruined. They have been given to us to eat." 13You have not stopped your proud talk against me. I have heard you. 14This is what the Lord GOD says: All the earth will be happy when I make you an empty ruin. 15You were happy when the land of Israel was ruined, but I will do the same thing to you. Mount Seir and all Edom, you will become an empty ruin. Then you will know that I am the LORD.'

ISRAEL TO COME HOME

36 "Human, prophesy to the mountains of Israel and say: 'Mountains of Israel, hear the word of the LORD. 2This is what the Lord GOD says: The enemy has said about you, "Now the old places to worship gods have become ours."' 3So prophesy and say: 'This is what the Lord GOD says: They have made you an empty ruin and have crushed you from all around. So you became a possession of the other nations. People have talked and whispered against you. 4So, mountains of Israel, hear the word of the Lord GOD. The Lord GOD speaks to the mountains, hills, ravines, and valleys, to the empty ruins and abandoned cities that have been robbed and laughed at by the other nations. 5This is what the Lord GOD says: I speak in hot anger against the other nations. I speak against the people of Edom, who took my land for themselves with joy and with hate in their hearts. They forced out the people and took their pastureland.' 6So prophesy about the land of Israel and say to the mountains, hills, ravines, and valleys: 'This is what the Lord GOD says: I speak in my jealous anger, because you have suffered the insults of the nations. 7So this is what the Lord GOD says: I promise that the nations around you will also have to suffer insults.

8" 'But you, mountains of Israel, will grow branches and fruit for my people, who will soon come home. 9I am concerned about you; I am on your side. You will be plowed, and seed will be planted in you. 10I will increase the number of people who live on you, all the people of Israel. The cities will have people living in them, and the ruins will be rebuilt. 11I will increase the number of people and animals living on you. They will grow and have many young. You will have people living on you as you did before, and I will make you better off than at the beginning. Then you will know that I am the LORD. 12I will cause my people Israel to walk on you and own you, and you will belong to them. You will never again take their children away from them.

13" 'This is what the Lord GOD says: People say about you, "You eat people and take children from your nation." 14But you will not eat people anymore or take away the children, says the Lord GOD. 15I will not make you listen to insults from the nations anymore; you will not suffer shame from them anymore. You will not cause your nation to fall anymore, says the Lord GOD.'"

THE LORD ACTS FOR HIMSELF

16The LORD spoke his word to me again, saying: 17"Human, when the nation of Israel was living in their own land, they made it unclean by their ways and the things they did. Their ways were like a woman's uncleanness in her time of monthly bleeding. 18So I poured out my anger against them, because they murdered in the land and because they made the land unclean with their idols. 19I scattered them among the nations, and they were spread through the countries. I punished them for how they lived and what they did. 20They dishonored my holy name in the nations where they went. The nations said about them, 'These are the people of the LORD, but they had to leave the land which he gave them.' 21But I had concern for my holy name, which the nation of Israel had dishonored among the nations where they went.

22"So say to the people of Israel, 'This is what the Lord GOD says: Israel, I am going to act, but not for your sake. I will do something to help my holy name, which you have dishonored among the nations where you went. 23I will prove the holiness of my great name, which has been dishonored among the nations. You have dishonored it among these nations, but the nations will know that I am the LORD when I prove myself holy before their eyes, says the Lord GOD.

24"I will take you from the nations and gather you out of all the lands and bring you back into your own land. 25Then I will sprinkle clean water on you, and you will be clean. I will cleanse you from all your uncleanness and your idols. 26Also, I will teach you to respect me completely, and I will put a new way of thinking inside you. I will take out the stubborn hearts of stone from your bodies, and I will give you obedient hearts of flesh. 27I will put my Spirit inside you and help you live by my rules and carefully obey my laws. 28You will live in the land I gave to your ancestors, and you will be my people, and I will be your God. 29So I will save you from all

---

GOD'S PURPOSE FOR YOUR LIFE

a new heart

FUTURE

By Claudio Freidzon

EZEKIEL 36:25-27

A sponge and a rock are placed into a fish tank filled with water to illustrate the different influence of the water on rock and sponge. When the rock is removed, it is wet on the outside, but when cracked open it remains dry and hard on the inside. The sponge, however, absorbs the water all the way through. It is completely wet and brings water with it to soak whatever it touches.

We may have hearts of rock and stone—we may be under the influence of God at church and even feel the living waters touch and bless us. But deep inside, we remain dry and brittle. God wants to change our hearts. No matter what circumstance has hardened our heart, God will replace it with a compassionate heart and a heart that forgives.

We must guard against things that wound and harden our hearts. Unforgiveness and sin can enter our spirits and steal our joy, love, strength, or authority. A bitter, hardened heart has no room for the Holy Spirit. A prepared heart welcomes his presence.

The Lord wants us to have a strong heart according to his heart. The attacks of the Enemy cannot prevail against a heart that really loves Jesus. A humble heart that is surrendered to God is full of joy, worship, and passion for the will of the Lord. Christians can say to the Lord, "I have really been hurt, but heal me." The Lord will renew your song, your excitement in him, and your strength.

reflect: Are you growing thirstier for the things of God?
Go to **Deuteronomy 11:19**.

your uncleanness. I will command the grain to come and grow; I will not allow a time of hunger to hurt you. 30I will increase the harvest of the field so you will never again suffer shame among the nations because of hunger. 31Then you will remember your evil ways and actions that were not good, and you will hate yourselves because of your sins and your terrible acts that I hate. 32I want you to know that I am not going to do this for your sake, says the Lord GOD. Be ashamed and embarrassed about your ways, Israel.

33"This is what the Lord GOD says: This is what will happen on the day I cleanse you from all your sins: I will cause the cities to have people living in them again, and the destroyed places will be rebuilt. 34The empty land will be plowed so it will no longer be a ruin for everyone who passes by to see. 35They will say, "This land was ruined, but now it has become like the garden of Eden. The cities were destroyed, empty, and ruined, but now they are protected and have people living in them." 36Then those nations still around you will know that I, the LORD, have rebuilt what was destroyed and have planted what was empty. I, the LORD, have spoken, and I will do it.'

37"This is what the Lord GOD says: I will let myself be asked by the people of Israel to do this for them again: I will make their people grow in number like a flock. 38They will be as many as the flocks brought to Jerusalem during her holy feasts. Her ruined cities will be filled with flocks of people. Then they will know that I am the LORD."

THE VISION OF DRY BONES

37 I felt the power of the LORD on me, and he brought me out by the Spirit of the LORD and put me down in the middle of a valley. It was full of bones. 2He led me around among the bones, and I saw that there were many bones in the valley and that they were very dry. 3Then he asked me, "Human, can these bones live?"

I answered, "Lord GOD, only you know."

4He said to me, "Prophesy to these bones and say to them, 'Dry bones, hear the word of the LORD. 5This is what the Lord GOD says to the bones: I will cause breath to enter you so you will come to life. 6I will put muscles on you and flesh on you and cover you with skin. Then I will put breath in you so you will come to life. Then you will know that I am the LORD.'"

7So I prophesied as I was commanded. While I prophesied, there was a noise and a rattling. The bones came together, bone to bone. 8I looked and saw muscles come on the bones, and flesh grew, and skin covered the bones. But there was no breath in them.

9Then he said to me, "Prophesy to the wind.n Prophesy, human, and say to the wind, 'This is what the Lord GOD says: Wind, come from the four winds, and breathe on these people who were killed so they can come back to life.'" 10So I prophesied as the LORD commanded me. And the breath came into them, and they came to life and stood on their feet, a very large army.

11Then he said to me, "Human, these bones are like all the people of Israel. They say, 'Our bones are dried up, and our hope has gone. We are destroyed.' 12So, prophesy and say to them, 'This is what the Lord GOD says: My people, I will open your graves and cause you to come up out of your graves. Then I will bring you into the land of Israel. 13My people, you will know that I am the LORD when I open your graves and cause you to come up from them. 14And I will put my Spirit inside you, and you will come to life. Then I will put you in your own land. And you will know that I, the LORD, have spoken and done it, says the LORD.'"

JUDAH AND ISRAEL BACK TOGETHER

15The LORD spoke his word to me, saying, 16"Human, take a stick and write on it, 'For Judah and all the Israelites with him.' Then take another stick and write on it, 'The stick of Ephraim, for Joseph and all the Israelites with him.' 17Then join them together into one stick so they will be one in your hand.

18"When your people say to you, 'Explain to us what you mean by this,' 19say to them, 'This is what the Lord GOD says: I will take the stick for Joseph and the tribes of Israel with him, which is in the hand of Ephraim, and I will put it with the stick of Judah. I will make them into one stick, and they will be one in my hand.' 20Hold the sticks on which

---

37:9 wind This Hebrew word could also mean "breath" or "spirit."

you wrote these names in your hand so the people can see them. ²¹Say to the people, 'This is what the Lord GOD says: I am going to take the people of Israel from among the nations where they have gone. I will gather them from all around and bring them into their own land. ²²I will make them one nation in the land, on the mountains of Israel. One king will rule all of them. They will never again be two nations; they will not be divided into two kingdoms anymore. ²³They will not continue to make themselves unclean by their idols, their statues of gods which I hate, or by their sins. I will save them from all the ways they sin and turn against me, and I will make them clean. Then they will be my people, and I will be their God.

²⁴"'My servant David will be their king, and they will all have one shepherd. They will live by my rules and obey my laws. ²⁵They will live on the land I gave to my servant Jacob, the land in which your ancestors lived. They will all live on the land forever: they, their children, and their grandchildren. David my servant will be their king forever. ²⁶I will make an agreement of peace with them, an agreement that continues forever. I will put them in their land and make them grow in number. Then I will put my Temple among them forever. ²⁷The place where I live will be with them. I will be their God, and they will be my people. ²⁸When my Temple is among them forever, the nations will know that I, the LORD, make Israel holy.'"

PROPHECY AGAINST GOG

38 The LORD spoke his word to me, saying, ²"Human, look toward Gog of the land of Magog, the chief ruler of the nations of Meshech and Tubal. Prophesy against him ³and say, 'The Lord GOD says this: I am against you, Gog, chief ruler of Meshech and Tubal. ⁴I will turn you around and put hooks in your jaws. And I will bring you out with all your army, horses, and horsemen, all of whom will be dressed in beautiful uniforms. They will be a large army with large and small shields and all having swords. ⁵Persia, Cush, and Put will be with them, all of them having shields and helmets. ⁶There will also be Gomer with all its troops and the nation of Togarmah from the far north with all its troops—many nations with you.

⁷"'Be prepared. Be prepared, you and all the armies that have come together to make you their commander. ⁸After a long time you will be called for service. After those years you will come into a land that has been rebuilt from war. The people in the land will have been gathered from many nations to the mountains of Israel, which were empty for a long time. These people were brought out from the nations, and they will all be living in safety. ⁹You will come like a storm. You, all your troops, and the many nations with you will be like a cloud covering the land.

¹⁰"'This is what the Lord GOD says: At that time ideas will come into your mind, and you will think up an evil plan. ¹¹You will say, "I will march against a land of towns without walls. I will attack those who are at rest and live in safety. All of them live without city walls or gate bars or gates. ¹²I will capture treasures and take loot. I will turn my power against the rebuilt ruins that now have people living in them. I will attack these people who have been gathered from the nations, who have become rich with farm animals and property, who live at the center of the world." ¹³Sheba, Dedan, and the traders of Tarshish, with all its villages, will say to you, "Did you come to capture treasure? Did you bring your troops together to take loot? Did you bring them to carry away silver and gold and to take away farm animals and property?"'

¹⁴"So prophesy, human, and say to Gog, 'This is what the Lord GOD says: Now that my people Israel are living in safety, you will know about it. ¹⁵You will come with many people from your place in the far north. You will have a large group with you, a mighty army, all riding on horses. ¹⁶You will attack my people Israel like a cloud that covers the land. This will happen in the days to come when I bring you against my land. Gog, then the nations will know me when they see me prove how holy I am in what I do through you.

¹⁷"'This is what the Lord GOD says: You are the one about whom I spoke in past days. I spoke through my servants, the prophets of Israel, who prophesied for many years that I would bring you against them. ¹⁸This is what will happen: On the day Gog attacks the land of Israel, I will become very angry, says the Lord GOD. ¹⁹With jealousy and great anger

I tell you that at that time there will surely be a great earthquake in Israel. **20**The fish of the sea, the birds of the sky, the wild animals, everything that crawls on the ground, and all the people on the earth will shake with fear before me. Also the mountains will be thrown down, the cliffs will fall, and every wall will fall to the ground. **21**Then I will call for a war against Gog on all my mountains, says the Lord GOD. Everyone's sword will attack the soldier next to him. **22**I will punish Gog with disease and death. I will send a heavy rain with hailstones and burning sulfur on Gog, his army, and the many nations with him. **23**Then I will show how great I am. I will show my holiness, and I will make myself known to the many nations that watch. Then they will know that I am the LORD.'

THE DEATH OF GOG AND HIS ARMY

39 "Human, prophesy against Gog and say, 'This is what the Lord GOD says: I am against you, Gog, chief ruler of Meshech and Tubal. **2**I will turn you around and lead you. I will bring you from the far north and send you to attack the mountains of Israel. **3**I will knock your bow out of your left hand and throw down your arrows from your right hand. **4**You, all your troops, and the nations with you will fall dead on the mountains of Israel. I will let you be food for every bird that eats meat and for every wild animal. **5**You will lie fallen on the ground, because I have spoken, says the Lord GOD. **6**I will send fire on Magog and those who live in safety on the coastlands. Then they will know that I am the LORD.

7"'I will make myself known among my people Israel, and I will not let myself be dishonored anymore. Then the nations will know that I am the LORD, the Holy One in Israel. **8**It is coming! It will happen, says the Lord GOD. The time I talked about is coming.

9"'Then those who live in the cities of Israel will come out and make fires with the enemy's weapons. They will burn them, both large and small shields, bows and arrows, war clubs, and spears. They will use the weapons to burn in their fires for seven years. **10**They will not need to take wood from the field or chop firewood from the forests, because they will make fires with the weapons. In this way

they will take the treasures of those who took their treasures; they will take the loot of those who took their loot, says the Lord GOD.

11"'At that time I will give Gog a burial place in Israel, in the Valley of the Travelers, east of the Dead Sea. It will block the road for travelers. Gog and all his army will be buried there, so people will call it The Valley of Gog's Army.

12"The people of Israel will be burying them for seven months to make the land clean again. **13**All the people in the land will bury them, and they will be honored on the day of my victory, says the Lord GOD.

14"'The people of Israel will choose men to work through the land to make it clean. Along with others, they will bury Gog's soldiers still lying dead on the ground. After the seven months are finished, they will still search. **15**As they go through the land, anyone who sees a human bone is to put a marker by it. The sign will stay there until the gravediggers bury the bone in The Valley of Gog's Army. **16**A city will be there named Hamonah. So they will make the land clean again.'

17"Human, this is what the Lord GOD says: Speak to every kind of bird and wild animal: 'Come together, come! Come together from all around to my sacrifice, a great sacrifice which I will prepare for you on the mountains of Israel. Eat flesh and drink blood! **18**You are to eat the flesh of the mighty and drink the blood of the rulers of the earth as if they were fat animals from Bashan: male sheep, lambs, goats, and bulls. **19**You are to eat and drink from my sacrifice which I have prepared for you, eating fat until you are full and drinking blood until you are drunk. **20**At my table you are to eat until you are full of horses and riders, mighty men and all kinds of soldiers,' says the Lord GOD.

21"I will show my glory among the nations. All the nations will see my power when I punish them. **22**From that time onward the people of Israel will know that I am the LORD their God. **23**The nations will know Israel was taken away captive because they turned against me. So I turned away from them and handed them over to their enemies until all of them died in war. **24**Because of their uncleanness and their sins, I punished them and turned away from them.

25"So this is what the Lord GOD says: Now

I will bring the people of Jacob back from captivity, and I will have mercy on the whole nation of Israel. I will not let them dishonor me. 26The people will forget their shame and how they rejected me when they live again in safety on their own land with no one to make them afraid. 27I will bring the people back from other lands and gather them from the lands of their enemies. So I will use my people to show many nations that I am holy. 28Then my people will know that I am the LORD their God, because I sent them into captivity among the nations, but then I brought them back to their own land, leaving no one behind. 29I will not turn away from them anymore, because I will put my Spirit into the people of Israel, says the Lord GOD."

THE NEW TEMPLE

40 It was the twenty-fifth year of our captivity, at the beginning of the year, on the tenth day of the month. It was in the fourteenth year after Jerusalem was captured. On that same day I felt the power of the LORD, and he brought me to Jerusalem. 2In the visions of God he brought me to the land of Israel and put me down on a very high mountain. On the south of the mountain there were some buildings that looked like a city. 3He took me closer to the buildings, and I saw a man who looked as if he were made of bronze, standing in the gateway. He had a cord made of linen and a stick in his hand, both for measuring. 4The man said to me, "Human, look with your eyes and hear with your ears. Pay attention to all that I will show you, because that's why you have been brought here. Tell the people of Israel all that you see."

THE EAST GATEWAY

5I saw a wall that surrounded the Temple area. The measuring stick in the man's hand was ten and one-half feet long. So the man measured the wall, which was ten and one-half feet thick and ten and one-half feet high. 6Then the man went to the east gateway. He went up its steps and measured the opening of the gateway. It was ten and one-half feet deep. 7The rooms for the guards were ten and one-half feet long and ten and one-half feet wide. The walls that came out between the guards' rooms were about nine

feet thick. The opening of the gateway next to the porch that faced the Temple was ten and one-half feet deep.

8Then the man measured the porch of the gateway. 9It was about fourteen feet deep, and its side walls were three and one-half feet thick. The porch of the gateway faced the Temple.

10On each side of the east gateway were three rooms, which measured the same on each side. The walls between each room were the same thickness. 11The man measured the width of the entrance to the gateway, which was seventeen and one-half feet wide. The width of the gate was about twenty-three feet. 12And there was a low wall about twenty-one inches high in front of each room. The rooms were ten and one-half feet on each side. 13The man measured the gateway from the roof of one room to the roof of the opposite room. It was about forty-four feet from one door to the opposite door. 14The man also measured the porch, which was about thirty-five feet wide. The courtyard was around the porch. 15From the front of the outer side of the gateway to the front of the porch of the inner side of the gateway was eighty-seven and one-half feet. 16The rooms and porch had small windows on both sides. The windows were narrower on the side facing the gateway. Carvings of palm trees were on each side wall of the rooms.

THE OUTER COURTYARD

17Then the man brought me into the outer courtyard where I saw rooms and a pavement of stones all around the court. Thirty rooms were along the edge of the paved walkway. 18The pavement ran alongside the gates and was as deep as the gates were wide. This was the lower pavement. 19Then the man measured from the outer wall to the inner wall. The outer court between these two walls was one hundred seventy-five feet on the east and on the north.

THE NORTH GATEWAY

20The man measured the length and width of the north gateway leading to the outer courtyard. 21Its three rooms on each side, its inner walls, and its porch measured the same as the first gateway. It was eighty-seven and one-half feet long and forty-four feet wide. 22Its windows, porch, and carvings of palm trees measured the same as the east gateway. Seven steps went up to the gateway, and the gateway's porch was at the inner end. 23The inner courtyard had a gateway across from the northern gateway like the one on the east. The man measured it and found it was one hundred seventy-five feet from inner gateway to outer gateway.

THE SOUTH GATEWAY

24Then the man led me south where I saw a gateway facing south. He measured its inner walls and its porch, and they measured the same as the other gateways. 25The gateway and its porch had windows all around like the other gateways. It was eighty-seven and one-half feet long and forty-four feet wide. 26Seven steps went up to this gateway. Its porch was at the inner end, and it had carvings of palm trees on its inner walls. 27The inner courtyard had a gateway on its south side. The man measured from gate to gate on the south side, which was one hundred seventy-five feet.

THE INNER COURTYARD

28Then the man brought me through the south gateway into the inner courtyard. The inner south gateway measured the same as the gateways in the outer wall. 29The inner south gateway's rooms, inner walls, and porch measured the same as the gateways in the outer wall. There were windows all around the gateway and its porch. The gateway was eighty-seven and one-half feet long and forty-four feet wide. 30Each porch of each inner gateway was about forty-four feet long and about nine feet wide. 31The inner south gateway's porch faced the outer courtyard. Carvings of palm trees were on its side walls, and its stairway had eight steps.

32The man brought me into the inner courtyard on the east side. He measured the inner east gateway, and it was the same as the other gateways. 33The inner east gateway's rooms, inside walls, and porch measured the same as the other gateways. Windows were all around the gateway and its porch. The inner east gateway was eighty-seven and one-half feet long and forty-four feet wide. 34Its porch faced the outer courtyard. Carvings of palm trees were on its inner walls on each side, and its stairway had eight steps.

35Then the man brought me to the inner north gateway. He measured it, and it was the same as the other gateways. 36Its rooms, inner walls, and porch measured the same as the other gateways. There were windows all around the gateway, which was eighty-seven and one-half feet long and forty-four feet wide. 37Its porch faced the outer courtyard. Carvings of palm trees were on its inner walls on each side, and its stairway had eight steps.

ROOMS FOR PREPARING SACRIFICES

38There was a room with a door that opened onto the porch of the inner north gateway. In this room the priests washed animals for the burnt offerings. 39There were two tables on each side of the porch, on which animals for burnt offerings, sin offerings, and penalty offerings were killed. 40Outside, by each side wall of the porch, at the entrance to the north gateway, were two more tables. 41So there were four tables inside the gateway, and four tables outside. In all there were eight tables on which the priests killed animals for sacrifices. 42There were four tables made of cut stone for the burnt offering. These tables were about three feet long, three feet wide, and about two feet high. On these tables the priests put their tools which they used to kill animals for burnt offerings and the other sacrifices. 43Double shelves three inches wide were put up on all the walls. The flesh for the offering was put on the tables.

THE PRIESTS' ROOMS

44There were two rooms in the inner courtyard. One was beside the north gateway and faced south. The other room was beside the south gateway and faced north. 45The man said to me, "The room which faces south is for the priests who serve in the Temple area, 46while the room that faces north is for the priests who serve at the altar. This second group of priests are descendants of Zadok, the only descendants of Levi who can come near the LORD to serve him."

47The man measured the inner courtyard. It was a square—one hundred seventy-five feet long and one hundred seventy-five feet wide. The altar was in front of the Temple.

THE TEMPLE PORCH

⁴⁸The man brought me to the porch of the Temple and measured each side wall of the porch. Each was about nine feet thick. The doorway was twenty-four and one-half feet wide. The side walls of the doorway were each about five feet wide. ⁴⁹The porch was thirty-five feet long and twenty-one feet wide, with ten steps leading up to it. Pillars were by the side walls, one on each side of the entrance.

THE HOLY PLACE OF THE TEMPLE

41 The man brought me to the Holy Place and measured its side walls, which were each ten and one-half feet thick. ²The entrance was seventeen and one-half feet wide. The walls alongside the entrance were each about nine feet wide. The man measured the Holy Place, which was seventy feet long and thirty-five feet wide.

³Then the man went inside and measured the side walls of the next doorway. Each was three and one-half feet thick. The doorway was ten and one-half feet wide, and the walls next to it were each more than twelve feet thick. ⁴Then the man measured the room at the end of the Holy Place. It was thirty-five feet long and thirty-five feet wide. The man said to me, "This is the Most Holy Place."

⁵Then the man measured the wall of the Temple, which was ten and one-half feet thick. There were side rooms seven feet wide all around the Temple. ⁶The side rooms were on three different stories, each above the other, with thirty rooms on each story. All around the Temple walls there were ledges for the side rooms. The upper rooms rested on the ledges but were not attached to the Temple walls. ⁷The side rooms around the Temple were wider on each higher story, so rooms were wider on the top story. A stairway went up from the lowest story to the highest through the middle story.

⁸I also saw that the Temple had a raised base all around. Its edge was the foundation for the side rooms, and it was ten and one-half feet thick. ⁹The outer wall of the side rooms was about nine feet thick. There was an open area between the side rooms of the Temple ¹⁰and some other rooms. It was thirty-five feet wide and went all around the Temple. ¹¹The side rooms had doors which led to the open area around the outside of the Temple. One door faced north, and the other faced south. The open area was about nine feet wide all around.

¹²The building facing the private area at the west side was one hundred twenty-two and one-half feet wide. The wall around the building was about nine feet thick and one hundred fifty-seven and one-half feet long.

¹³Then the man measured the Temple. It was one hundred seventy-five feet long. The private area, including the building and its walls, was in all one hundred seventy-five feet long. ¹⁴Also the front of the Temple and the private area on its east side were one hundred seventy-five feet wide.

¹⁵The man measured the length of the building facing the private area on the west side, and it was one hundred seventy-five feet from one wall to the other.

The Holy Place, the Most Holy Place, and the outer porch ¹⁶had wood panels on the walls. By the doorway, the Temple had wood panels on the walls. The wood covered all the walls from the floor up to the windows, ¹⁷up to the part of the wall above the entrance.

All the walls inside the Most Holy Place and the Holy Place, and on the outside, in the porch, ¹⁸had carvings of creatures with wings and palm trees. A palm tree was between each carved creature, and every creature had two faces. ¹⁹One was a human face looking toward the palm tree on one side. The other was a lion's face looking toward the palm tree on the other side. They were carved all around the Temple walls. ²⁰From the floor to above the entrance, palm trees and creatures with wings were carved. The walls of the Holy Place ²¹had square doorposts. In front of the Most Holy Place was something that looked like ²²an altar of wood. It was more than five feet high and three feet wide. Its corners, base, and sides were wood. The man said to me, "This is the table that is in the presence of the LORD." ²³Both the Holy Place and the Most Holy Place had double doors. ²⁴Each of the doors had two pieces that would swing open. ²⁵Carved on the doors of the Holy Place were palm trees and creatures with wings, like those carved on the walls. And there was a wood roof over the front Temple porch. ²⁶There were windows and palm trees on both side walls of the porch.

The side rooms of the Temple were also covered by a roof over the stairway.

THE PRIESTS' ROOMS

42 Then the man led me north out into the outer courtyard and to the rooms across from the private area and the building. ²These rooms on the north side were one hundred seventy-five feet long and eighty-seven and one-half feet wide. ³There was thirty-five feet of the inner courtyard between them and the Temple. On the other side, they faced the stone pavement of the outer courtyard. The rooms were built in three stories like steps and had balconies. ⁴There was a path on the north side of the rooms, which was seventeen and one-half feet wide and one hundred seventy-five feet long. Doors led into the rooms from this path. ⁵The top rooms were narrower, because the balconies took more space from them. The rooms on the first and second stories of the building were wider. ⁶The rooms were on three stories. They did not have pillars like the pillars of the courtyards. So the top rooms were farther back than those on the first and second stories. ⁷There was a wall outside parallel to the rooms and to the outer courtyard. It ran in front of the rooms for eighty-seven and one-half feet. ⁸The row of rooms along the outer courtyard was eighty-seven and one-half feet long, and the rooms that faced the Temple were about one hundred seventy-five feet long. ⁹The lower rooms had an entrance on the east side so a person could enter them from the outer courtyard, ¹⁰at the start of the wall beside the courtyard.

There were rooms on the south side, which were across from the private area and the building. ¹¹These rooms had a path in front of them. They were like the rooms on the north with the same length and width and the same doors. ¹²The doors of the south rooms were like the doors of the north rooms. There was an entrance at the open end of a path beside the wall, so a person could enter at the east end.

¹³The man said to me, "The north and south rooms across from the private area are holy rooms. There the priests who go near the LORD will eat the most holy offerings. There they will put the most holy offerings: the grain offerings, sin offerings, and the penalty offerings, because the place is holy. ¹⁴The priests who enter the Holy Place must leave their serving clothes there before they go into the outer courtyard, because these clothes are holy. After they put on other clothes, they may go to the part of the Temple area which is for the people."

OUTSIDE THE TEMPLE AREA

¹⁵When the man finished measuring inside the Temple area, he brought me out through the east gateway. He measured the area all around. ¹⁶The man measured the east side with the measuring stick; it was eight hundred seventy-five feet by the measuring stick. ¹⁷He measured the north side; it was eight hundred seventy-five feet by the measuring stick. ¹⁸He measured the south side; it was eight hundred seventy-five feet by the measuring stick. ¹⁹He went around to the west side; it measured eight hundred seventy-five feet by the measuring stick. ²⁰So he measured the Temple area on all four sides. The Temple area had a wall all around it that was eight hundred seventy-five feet long and eight hundred seventy-five feet wide. It separated what was holy from that which was not holy.

THE LORD AMONG HIS PEOPLE

43 Then the man led me to the outer east gateway, ²and I saw the glory of the God of Israel coming from the east. It sounded like the roar of rushing water, and its brightness made the earth shine. ³The vision I saw was like the vision I had seen when the LORD came to destroy the city and also like the vision I had seen by the Kebar River. I bowed facedown on the ground. ⁴The glory of the LORD came into the Temple area through the east gateway.

⁵Then the Spirit picked me up and brought me into the inner courtyard. There I saw the LORD's glory filling the Temple. ⁶As the man stood at my side, I heard someone speaking to me from inside the Temple. ⁷The voice from the Temple said to me, "Human, this is my throne and the place where my feet rest. I will live here among the Israelites forever. The people of Israel will not make my holy name unclean again. Neither the people nor their kings will make it unclean with their sexual sins or with the dead bodies of their kings. ⁸The kings made my name unclean by

putting their doorway next to my doorway, and their doorpost next to my doorpost so only a wall separated me from them. When they did their acts that I hate, they made my holy name unclean, and so I destroyed them in my anger. 9Now let them stop their sexual sins and take the dead bodies of their kings far away from me. Then I will live among them forever.

10"Human, tell the people of Israel about the Temple so they will be ashamed of their sins. Let them think about the plan of the Temple. 11If they are ashamed of all they have done, let them know the design of the Temple and how it is built. Show them its exits and entrances, all its designs, and also all its rules and teachings. Write the rules as they watch so they will obey all the teachings and rules about the Temple. 12This is the teaching about the Temple: All the area around the top of the mountain is most holy. This is the teaching about the Temple.

THE ALTAR

13"These are the measurements of the altar, using the measuring stick. The altar's gutter is twenty-one inches high and twenty-one inches wide, and its rim is about nine inches around its edge. And the altar is this tall: 14From the ground up to the lower ledge, it measures three and one-half feet. It is twenty-one inches wide. It measures seven feet from the smaller ledge to the larger ledge and is twenty-one inches wide. 15The place where the sacrifice is burned on the altar is seven feet high, with its four corners shaped like horns and reaching up above it. 16It is square, twenty-one feet long and twenty-one feet wide. 17The upper ledge is also square, twenty-four and one-half feet long and twenty-four and one-half feet wide. The rim around the altar is ten and one-half inches wide, and its gutter is twenty-one inches wide all around. Its steps are on the east side."

18Then the man said to me, "Human, this is what the Lord GOD says: These are the rules for the altar. When it is built, use these rules to offer burnt offerings and to sprinkle blood on it. 19You must give a young bull as a sin offering to the priests, the Levites who are from the family of Zadok and who come near me to serve me, says the Lord GOD.

20Take some of the bull's blood and put it on the four corners of the altar, on the four corners of the ledge, and all around the rim. This is how you will make the altar pure and ready for God's service. 21Then take the bull for the sin offering and burn it in the proper place in the Temple area, outside the Temple building.

22"On the second day offer a male goat that has nothing wrong with it for a sin offering. The priests will make the altar pure and ready for God's service as they did with the young bull. 23When you finish making the altar pure and ready, offer a young bull and a male sheep from the flock, which have nothing wrong with them. 24You must offer them in the presence of the LORD, and the priests are to throw salt on them and offer them as a burnt offering to the LORD.

25"You must prepare a goat every day for seven days as a sin offering. Also, the priests must prepare a young bull and male sheep from the flock, which have nothing wrong with them. 26For seven days the priests are to make the altar pure and ready for God's service. Then they will give the altar to God. 27After these seven days, on the eighth day, the priests must offer your burnt offerings and your fellowship offerings on the altar. Then I will accept you, says the Lord GOD."

THE OUTER EAST GATE

44 Then the man brought me back to the outer east gateway of the Temple area, but the gate was shut. 2The LORD said to me, "This gate will stay shut; it will not be opened. No one may enter through it, because the LORD God of Israel has entered through it. So it must stay shut. 3Only the ruler himself may sit in the gateway to eat a meal in the presence of the LORD. He must enter through the porch of the gateway and go out the same way."

4Then the man brought me through the outer north gate to the front of the Temple. As I looked, I saw the glory of the LORD filling the Temple of the LORD, and I bowed facedown on the ground.

5The LORD said to me, "Human, pay attention. Use your eyes to see, and your ears to hear. See and hear everything I tell you about all the rules and teachings of the Temple of the LORD. Pay attention to the entrance to the Temple and to all the exits from the Temple area. 6Then speak to those who refuse to obey. Say to the people of Israel, 'This is what the Lord GOD says: Stop doing all your acts that I hate, Israel! 7You brought foreigners into my Holy Place who were not circumcised in the flesh and had not given themselves to serving me. You dishonored my Temple when you offered me food, fat, and blood. You broke my agreement by all the things you did that I hate. 8You did not take care of my holy things yourselves but put foreigners in charge of my Temple. 9This is what the Lord GOD says: Foreigners who are not circumcised in flesh and who do not give themselves to serving me may not enter my Temple. Not even a foreigner living among the people of Israel may enter.

10"'But the Levites who stopped obeying me when Israel left me and who followed their idols must be punished for their sin. 11These Levites are to be servants in my Holy Place. They may guard the gates of the Temple and serve in the Temple area. They may kill the animals for the burnt offering and the sacrifices for the people. They may stand before the people to serve them. 12But these Levites helped the people worship their idols and caused the people of Israel to fall, so I make this promise: They will be punished for their sin, says the Lord GOD. 13They will not come near me to serve as priests, nor will they come near any of my holy things or the most holy offerings. But they will be made ashamed of the things they did that I hate. 14I will put them in charge of taking care of the Temple area, all the work that must be done in it.

15"'But the priests who are Levites and descendants of Zadok took care of my Holy Place when Israel left me, so they may come near to serve me. They may stand in my presence to offer me the fat and blood of the animals they sacrifice, says the Lord GOD. 16They are the only ones who may enter my Holy Place. Only they may come near my table to serve me and take care of the things I gave them to do.

17"'When they enter the gates of the inner courtyard, they must wear linen robes. They must not wear wool to serve at the gates of the inner courtyard or in the Temple. 18They will wear linen turbans on their heads and

linen underclothes. They will not wear anything that makes them perspire. 19When they go out into the outer courtyard to the people, they must take off their serving clothes before they go. They must leave these clothes in the holy rooms and put on other clothes. Then they will not let their holy clothes hurt the people.

20"'They must not shave their heads or let their hair grow long but must keep the hair of their heads trimmed. 21None of the priests may drink wine when they enter the inner courtyard. 22The priests must not marry widows or divorced women. They may marry only virgins from the people of Israel or widows of priests. 23They must teach my people the difference between what is holy and what is not holy. They must help my people know what is unclean and what is clean.

24"'In court they will act as judges. When they judge, they will follow my teachings. They must obey my laws and my rules at all my special feasts and keep my Sabbaths holy.

25"'They must not go near a dead person, making themselves unclean. But they are allowed to make themselves unclean if the dead person is their father, mother, son, daughter, brother, or a sister who has not married. 26After a priest has been made clean again, he must wait seven days. 27Then he may go into the inner courtyard to serve in the Temple, but he must offer a sin offering for himself, says the Lord GOD.

28"'These are the rules about the priests and their property: They will have me instead of property. You will not give them any land to own in Israel; I am what they will own. 29They will eat the grain offerings, sin offerings, and penalty offerings. Everything Israel gives to me will be theirs. 30The best fruits of all the first harvests and all the special gifts offered to me will belong to the priests. You will also give to the priests the first part of your grain that you grind and so bring a blessing on your family. 31The priests must not eat any bird or animal that died a natural death or one that has been torn by wild animals.

THE LAND IS DIVIDED

45 "'When you divide the land for the Israelite tribes by throwing lots, you must give a part of the land to belong to the

LORD. It will be about seven miles long and about six miles wide; all of this land will be holy. ²From this land, an area eight hundred seventy-five feet square will be for the Temple. There will be an open space around the Temple that is eighty-seven and one-half feet wide. ³In the holy area you will measure a part about seven miles long and three miles wide, and in it will be the Most Holy Place. ⁴This holy part of the land will be for the priests who serve in the Temple, who come near to the LORD to serve him. It will be a place for the priests' houses and for the Temple. ⁵Another area about seven miles long and more than three miles wide will be for the Levites, who serve in the Temple area. It will belong to them so they will have cities in which to live.

⁶"You must give the city an area that is about one and one-half miles wide and about seven miles long, along the side of the holy area. It will belong to all the people of Israel.

⁷"The ruler will have land on both sides of the holy area and the city. On the west of the holy area, his land will reach to the Mediterranean Sea. On the east of the holy area, his land will reach to the eastern border. It will be as long as the land given to each tribe. ⁸Only this land will be the ruler's property in Israel. So my rulers will not be cruel to my people anymore, but they will let each tribe in the nation of Israel have its share of the land.

⁹"This is what the Lord GOD says: You have gone far enough, you rulers of Israel! Stop being cruel and hurting people, and do what is right and fair. Stop forcing my people out of their homes, says the Lord GOD. ¹⁰You must have honest scales, an honest dry measurement and an honest liquid measurement. ¹¹The dry measure and the liquid measure will be the same: The liquid measure will always be a tenth of a homer,ⁿ and the ephah will always be a tenth of a homer. The measurement they follow will be the homer. ¹²The shekelⁿ will be worth twenty gerahs, and a mina will be worth sixty shekels.

OFFERINGS AND HOLY DAYS

¹³"This is the gift you should offer: a sixth of an ephah from every homer of wheat, and a sixth of an ephah from every homer of barley. ¹⁴The amount of oil you are to offer is

a tenth of a bath from each cor. (Ten baths make a homer and also make a cor.) ¹⁵You should give one sheep from each flock of two hundred from the watering places of Israel. All these are to be offered for the grain offerings, burnt offerings, and fellowship offerings to remove sins so you will belong to God, says the Lord GOD. ¹⁶All people in the land will give this special offering to the ruler of Israel. ¹⁷It will be the ruler's responsibility to supply the burnt offerings, grain offerings, and drink offerings. These offerings will be given at the feasts, at the New Moons, on the Sabbaths, and at all the other feasts of Israel. The ruler will supply the sin offerings, grain offerings, and fellowship offerings to pay for the sins of Israel.

¹⁸"This is what the Lord GOD says: On the first day of the first month take a young bull that has nothing wrong with it. Use it to make the Temple pure and ready for God's service. ¹⁹The priest will take some of the blood from this sin offering and put it on the doorposts of the Temple, on the four corners of the ledge of the altar, and on the posts of the gate to the inner courtyard. ²⁰You will do the same thing on the seventh day of the month for anyone who has sinned by accident or without knowing it. This is how you make the Temple pure and ready for God's service.

PASSOVER FEAST OFFERINGS

²¹"On the fourteenth day of the first month you will celebrate the Feast of Passover. It will be a feast of seven days when you eat bread made without yeast. ²²On that day the ruler must offer a bull for himself and for all the people of the land as a sin offering. ²³During the seven days of the feast he must offer seven bulls and seven male sheep that have nothing wrong with them. They will be burnt offerings to the LORD, which the ruler will offer every day of the seven days of the feast. He must also offer a male goat every day as a sin offering. ²⁴The ruler must give as a grain offering one-half

---

45:11 homer The Hebrew word means "donkey-load." It measured about five dry bushels or one hundred seventy-five liquid quarts. So an ephah was about one-half bushel, and a bath was about eighteen quarts.
45:12 shekel In Ezekiel's time a shekel weighed about two-fifths of an ounce.

bushel for each bull and one-half bushel for each sheep. He must give a gallon of olive oil for each half bushel.

25 "Beginning on the fifteenth day of the seventh month, when you celebrate the Feast of Shelters, the ruler will supply the same things for seven days: the sin offerings, burnt offerings, grain offerings, and the olive oil.

RULES FOR WORSHIP

46 "'This is what the Lord God says: The east gate of the inner courtyard will stay shut on the six working days, but it will be opened on the Sabbath day and on the day of the New Moon. 2The ruler will enter from outside through the porch of the gateway and stand by the gatepost, while the priests offer the ruler's burnt offering and fellowship offering. The ruler will worship at the entrance of the gateway, and then he will go out. But the gate will not be shut until evening. 3The people of the land will worship at the entrance of that gateway in the presence of the LORD on the Sabbaths and New Moons. 4This is the burnt offering the ruler will offer to the LORD on the Sabbath day: six male lambs that have nothing wrong with them and a male sheep that has nothing wrong with it. 5He must give a half-bushel grain offering with the male sheep, but he may give as much grain offering with the lambs as he pleases. He must also give a gallon of olive oil for each half bushel of grain. 6On the day of the New Moon he must offer a young bull that has nothing wrong with it. He must also offer six lambs and a male sheep that have nothing wrong with them. 7The ruler must give a half-bushel grain offering with the bull and one-half bushel with the male sheep. With the lambs, he may give as much grain as he pleases. But he must give a gallon of olive oil for each half bushel of grain. 8When the ruler enters, he must go in through the porch of the gateway, and he must go out the same way.

9 "When the people of the land come into the LORD's presence at the special feasts, those who enter through the north gate to worship must go out through the south gate. Those who enter through the south gate must go out through the north gate. They must not return the same way they entered; everyone must go out the opposite way. 10The ruler will

go in with the people when they go in and go out with them when they go out.

11 "At the feasts and regular times of worship one-half bushel of grain must be offered with a young bull, and one-half bushel of grain must be offered with a male sheep. But with an offering of lambs, the ruler may give as much grain as he pleases. He should give a gallon of olive oil for each half bushel of grain. 12The ruler may give an offering as a special gift to the LORD; it may be a burnt offering or fellowship offering. When he gives it to the LORD, the inner east gate is to be opened for him. He must offer his burnt offering or his fellowship offering as he does on the Sabbath day. Then he will go out, and the gate will be shut after he has left.

13 "Every day you will give a year-old lamb that has nothing wrong with it for a burnt offering to the LORD. Do it every morning. 14Also, you must offer a grain offering with the lamb every morning. For this you will give three and one-third quarts of grain and one and one-third quarts of olive oil, to make the fine flour moist, as a grain offering to the LORD. This is a rule that must be kept from now on. 15So you must always give the lamb, together with the grain offering and the olive oil, every morning as a burnt offering.

RULES FOR THE RULER

16 "This is what the Lord God says: If the ruler gives a gift from his land to any of his sons, that land will belong to the son and then to the son's children. It is their property passed down from their family. 17But if the ruler gives a gift from his land to any of his servants, that land will belong to the servant only until the year of freedom. Then the land will go back to the ruler. Only the ruler's sons may keep a gift of land from the ruler. 18The ruler must not take any of the people's land, forcing them out of their land. He must give his sons some of his own land so my people will not be scattered out of their own land.'"

THE SPECIAL KITCHENS

19The man led me through the entrance at the side of the gateway to the priests' holy rooms that face north. There I saw a place at the west end. 20The man said to me, "This is where the priests will boil the meat of the penalty offering and sin offering and bake the grain offering. Then they will not need to bring these holy offerings into the outer courtyard, because that would hurt the people."

²¹Then the man brought me out into the outer courtyard and led me to its four corners. In each corner of the courtyard was a smaller courtyard. ²²Small courtyards were in the four corners of the courtyard. Each small courtyard was the same size, seventy feet long and fifty-two and one-half feet wide. ²³A stone wall was around each of the four small courtyards, and places for cooking were built in each of the stone walls. ²⁴The man said to me, "These are the kitchens where those who work in the Temple will boil the sacrifices offered by the people."

THE RIVER FROM THE TEMPLE

47 The man led me back to the door of the Temple, and I saw water coming out from under the doorway and flowing east. (The Temple faced east.) The water flowed down from the south side wall of the Temple and then south of the altar. ²The man brought me out through the outer north gate and led me around outside to the outer east gate. I found the water coming out on the south side of the gate.

³The man went toward the east with a line in his hand and measured about one-third of a mile. Then he led me through water that came up to my ankles. ⁴The man measured about one-third of a mile again and led me through water that came up to my knees. Then he measured about one-third of a mile again and led me through water up to my waist. ⁵The man measured about one-third of a mile again, but it was now a river that I could not cross. The water had risen too high; it was deep enough for swimming; it was a river that no one could cross. ⁶The man asked me, "Human, do you see this?"

Then the man led me back to the bank of the river. ⁷As I went back, I saw many trees on both sides of the river. ⁸The man said to me, "This water will flow toward the eastern areas and go down into the Jordan Valley. When it enters the Dead Sea, it will become fresh. ⁹Everywhere the river goes, there will be many fish. Wherever this water goes the Dead Sea will become fresh, and so where the river goes there will be many living things. ¹⁰Fishermen will stand by the

Dead Sea. From En Gedi all the way to En Eglaim there will be places to spread fishing nets. There will be many kinds of fish in the Dead Sea, as many as in the Mediterranean Sea. ¹¹But its swamps and marshes will not become fresh; they will be left for salt. ¹²All kinds of fruit trees will grow on both banks of the river, and their leaves will not dry and die. The trees will have fruit every month, because the water for them comes from the Temple. The fruit from the trees will be used for food, and their leaves for medicine."

BORDERS OF THE LAND

¹³This is what the Lord GOD says: "These are the borders of the land to be divided among the twelve tribes of Israel. Joseph will have two parts of land. ¹⁴You will divide the land equally. I promised to give it to your ancestors, so this land will belong to you as family property.

¹⁵"This will be the border line of the land: "On the north side it will start at the Mediterranean Sea. It will go through Hethlon, toward Lebo Hamath and on to the towns of Zedad, ¹⁶Berothah, and Sibraim on the border between Damascus and Hamath. Then it will go on to the town of Hazer Hatticon on the border of the country of Hauran. ¹⁷So the border line will go from the Mediterranean Sea east to the town of Hazar Enan, where the land belonging to Damascus and Hamath lies on the north side. This will be the north side of the land.

¹⁸"On the east side the border runs south from a point between Hauran and Damascus. It will go along the Jordan between Gilead and the land of Israel and will continue to the town of Tamar on the Dead Sea. This will be the east side of the land.

¹⁹"On the south side the border line will go west from Tamar all the way to the waters of Meribah Kadesh. Then it will run along the brook of Egypt to the Mediterranean Sea. This will be the south side of the land.

²⁰"On the west side the Mediterranean Sea will be the border line up to a place across from Lebo Hamath. This will be the west side of your land.

²¹"You will divide this land among the tribes of Israel. ²²You will divide it as family property for yourselves and for the foreigners who live and have children among you.

You are to treat these foreigners the same as people born in Israel; they are to share the land with the tribes of Israel. 23In whatever tribe the foreigner lives, you will give him some land," says the Lord GOD.

DIVIDING THE LAND

48 "These are the areas of the tribes named here: Dan will have one share at the northern border. It will go from the sea through Hethlon to Lebo Hamath, all the way to Hazar Enan, where Damascus lies to the north. It will stop there next to Hamath. This will be Dan's northern border from the east side to the Mediterranean Sea on the west side.

2"South of Dan's border, Asher will have one share. It will go from the east side to the west side.

3"South of Asher's border, Naphtali will have one share. It will go from the east side to the west side.

4"South of Naphtali's border, Manasseh will have one share. It will go from the east side to the west side.

5"South of Manasseh's border, Ephraim will have one share. It will go from the east side to the west side.

6"South of Ephraim's border, Reuben will have one share. It will go from the east side to the west side.

7"South of Reuben's border, Judah will have one share. It will go from the east side to the west side.

8"South of Judah's border will be the holy area which you are to give. It will be about seven miles wide and as long and wide as one of the tribes' shares. It will run from the east side to the west side. The Temple will be in the middle of this area.

9"The share which you will give the LORD will be about seven miles long and three miles wide. 10The holy area will be divided among these people. The priests will have land about seven miles long on the north and south sides, and three miles wide on the west and east sides. The Temple of the LORD will be in the middle of it. 11This land is for the priests who are given the holy duty of serving the LORD. They are the descendants of Zadok who did my work and did not leave me when Israel and the Levites left me. 12They will have as their share a very holy part of the holy portion of the land. It will be next to the land of the Levites.

13"Alongside the land for the priests, the Levites will have a share about seven miles long and three miles wide; its full length will be about seven miles and its full width about three miles. 14The Levites are not to sell or trade any of this land. They are not to let anyone else own any of this best part of the land, because it belongs to the LORD.

CITY PROPERTY

15"The rest of the area will be about one and one-half miles wide and seven miles long. It will not be holy but will belong to the city and be used for homes and pastures. The city will be in the middle of it. 16These are the city's measurements: the north side will be about one mile, the south side about one mile, the east side about one mile, and the west side about one mile. 17The city's land for pastures will be about four hundred thirty-seven feet on the north, four hundred thirty-seven feet on the south, four hundred thirty-seven feet on the east, and four hundred thirty-seven feet on the west. 18Along the long side of the holy area there will be left three miles on the east and three miles on the west. It will be used to grow food for the city workers. 19The city workers from all the tribes of Israel will farm this land. 20This whole area will be square, seven miles by seven miles. You shall give to the LORD the holy share along with the city property.

21"Land that is left over on both sides of the holy area and city property will belong to the ruler. That land will extend east of the holy area to the eastern border and west of it to the Mediterranean Sea. Both of these areas run the length of the lands of the tribes, and they belong to the ruler. The holy area with the Holy Place of the Temple will be in the middle. 22The Levites' land and the city property will be in the middle of the lands belonging to the ruler. Those lands will be between Judah's border and Benjamin's border.

THE OTHER TRIBES' LAND

23"Here is what the rest of the tribes will receive: Benjamin will have one share. It will go from the east side to the Mediterranean Sea on the west side.

²⁴"South of Benjamin's land, Simeon will have one share. It will go from the east side to the west side.

²⁵"South of Simeon's land, Issachar will have one share. It will go from the east side to the west side.

²⁶"South of Issachar's land, Zebulun will have one share. It will go from the east side to the west side.

²⁷"South of Zebulun's land, Gad will have one share. It will go from the east side to the west side.

²⁸"The southern border of Gad's land will go east from Tamar on the Dead Sea to the waters of Meribah Kadesh. Then it will run along the brook of Egypt to the Mediterranean Sea.

²⁹"This is the land you will divide among the tribes of Israel to be their shares," says the Lord God.

THE GATES OF THE CITY

³⁰"These will be the outside borders of the city: The north side will measure more than one mile. ³¹There will be three gates facing north: Reuben's Gate, Judah's Gate, and Levi's Gate, named for the tribes of Israel.

³²"The east side will measure more than one mile. There will be three gates facing east: Joseph's Gate, Benjamin's Gate, and Dan's Gate.

³³"The south side will measure more than one mile. There will be three gates facing south: Simeon's Gate, Issachar's Gate, and Zebulun's Gate.

³⁴"The west side will measure more than one mile. There will be three gates facing west: Gad's Gate, Asher's Gate, and Naphtali's Gate.

³⁵"The city will measure about six miles around. From then on the name of the city will be The Lord Is There."

daniel

THE LIFE AND VISIONS OF DANIEL

DANIEL TAKEN TO BABYLON

1 During the third year that Jehoiakim was king of Judah, Nebuchadnezzar king of Babylon came to Jerusalem and surrounded it with his army. ²The Lord allowed Nebuchadnezzar to capture Jehoiakim king of Judah. Nebuchadnezzar also took some of the things from the Temple of God, which he

---

TURNING REVELATIONS INTO REVOLUTIONS

FITNESS

natural order

DANIEL 1:8–16

To understand more about how God ordained you to eat, think of the lesson of the commercially processed blueberry bagel. If you look at the ingredient list, blueberries are not even listed!

Rather, there are a number of chemical dyes combined with high fructose corn syrup to create what are called "blueberry flavored chips." Additionally, a number of other chemicals are added to preserve freshness.

So here's the lesson of the blueberry bagel, which will hopefully change the way you think about food and understand how God ordained for you to eat.

Natural order simply suggests: "Don't eat the unnatural blueberry bagels." Anything unnatural called a "coloring, chemical, preservative, or artificial ingredient" will cause a chemical reaction in your body. If it's "unnatural," then it can't be part of the natural order to swallow it.

With reference to spoilage, if something can naturally go bad, then it should be frozen or eaten before it spoils. To use chemicals to "retard spoilage" so that it stays edible is not natural. If it can sit on your shelf indefinitely so that even the bugs won't eat it, then neither should you.

The lesson to be learned from the blueberry bagel is that if God didn't make it, it likely isn't safe to eat.

reflect: Use wisdom when it comes to selecting what types of foods to digest.
Go to **Amos 6:1–6.**

carried to Babylonia and put in the temple of his gods.

3Then King Nebuchadnezzar ordered Ashpenaz, his chief officer, to bring some of the men of Judah into his palace. He wanted them to be from important families, including the family of the king of Judah. 4King Nebuchadnezzar wanted only young Israelite men who had nothing wrong with them. They were to be handsome and well educated, capable of learning and understanding, and able to serve in his palace. Ashpenaz was to teach them the language and writings of the Babylonians. 5The king gave the young men a certain amount of food and wine every day, just like the food he ate. The young men were to be trained for three years, and then they would become servants of the king of Babylon. 6Among those young men were Daniel, Hananiah, Mishael, and Azariah from the people of Judah.

7Ashpenaz, the chief officer, gave them Babylonian names. Daniel's new name was Belteshazzar, Hananiah's was Shadrach, Mishael's was Meshach, and Azariah's was Abednego.

8Daniel decided not to eat the king's food or drink his wine because that would make him unclean. So he asked Ashpenaz for permission not to make himself unclean in this way.

9God made Ashpenaz, the chief officer, want to be kind and merciful to Daniel, 10but Ashpenaz said to Daniel, "I am afraid of my master, the king. He ordered me to give you this food and drink. If you begin to look worse than other young men your age, the king will see this. Then he will cut off my head because of you."

11Ashpenaz had ordered a guard to watch Daniel, Hananiah, Mishael, and Azariah. 12Daniel said to the guard, "Please give us this test for ten days: Don't give us anything but vegetables to eat and water to drink. 13After ten days compare how we look with how the other young men look who eat the king's food. See for yourself and then decide how you want to treat us, your servants."

14So the guard agreed to test them for ten days. 15After ten days they looked healthier and better fed than all the young men who ate the king's food. 16So the guard took away the king's special food and wine, feeding them vegetables instead.

17God gave these four young men wisdom and the ability to learn many things that people had written and studied. Daniel could also understand visions and dreams.

18At the end of the time set for them by the king, Ashpenaz brought all the young men to King Nebuchadnezzar. 19The king talked to them and found that none of the young men were as good as Daniel, Hananiah, Mishael, and Azariah. So those four young men became the king's servants. 20Every time the king asked them about something important, they showed much wisdom and understanding. They were ten times better than all the fortune-tellers and magicians in his kingdom! 21So Daniel continued to be the king's servant until the first year Cyrus was king.

NEBUCHADNEZZAR'S DREAM

2 During Nebuchadnezzar's second year as king, he had dreams that bothered him and kept him awake at night. 2So the king called for his fortune-tellers, magicians, wizards, and wise men, because he wanted them to tell him what he had dreamed. They came in and stood in front of the king.

3Then the king said to them, "I had a dream that bothers me, and I want to know what it means."

4The wise men answered the king in the Aramaic language, "O king, live forever! Please tell us, your servants, your dream. Then we will tell you what it means."

5King Nebuchadnezzar said to them, "I meant what I said. You must tell me the dream and what it means. If you don't, I will have you torn apart, and I will turn your houses into piles of stones. 6But if you tell me my dream and its meaning, I will reward you with gifts and great honor. So tell me the dream and what it means."

7Again the wise men said to the king, "Tell us, your servants, the dream, and we will tell you what it means."

8King Nebuchadnezzar answered, "I know you are trying to get more time, because you know that I meant what I said. 9If you don't tell me my dream, you will be punished. You have all agreed to tell me lies and wicked things, hoping things will change.

Losing Weight

By Dr. Jim Garlow

DANIEL 1:8

I recently lost eighty pounds. Believe me, I am not proud of the fact that I was so overweight. And I realize that I am not an expert on weight loss. In fact, one of my friends said to me, "Now that you're losing all this weight, are you going to become 'preachy' to all of us?" I said, "Absolutely not. I've got years of failure and only a short time of success. I don't have enough credibility on this topic to become preachy." But I did come to realize some things from my weight-loss experience that have application to the spiritual arena of my life.

For starters, I wondered why I finally, after years of failure, successfully lost a lot of weight. After thinking it over, I realized that the number one answer was actually very simple—desperation. One day I said to myself, "I am not going to live like this the rest of my life." Are you desperate to grow spiritually? Psalmists wrote, "I thirst for you [that is, for God]." That's good desperation.

Second, I had to acknowledge my need for help. Many years ago I had lost some weight. I thought I could do it again. But I couldn't. I needed other people to help me. So I joined a weight-loss group. I had to humble myself and admit I couldn't do it on my own. What's that have to do with our spiritual life? A lot! We need the body of Christ. We need each other.

What's the third thing I learned? At our first weight-loss class the leader stood before us and said, "You don't have to have willpower to succeed. If you had willpower you wouldn't be in our class in the first place. But you do have to have skill power." *What's skill power?* I thought. Skill power, she explained, is doing what we tell you to do. And I resolved that moment, I'm going do exactly what they tell me to do, and I lost eighty pounds in the next twenty-two weeks.

What is the application spiritually? Well, it's all too obvious, isn't it? God says, "Obey me, and then these blessings will come to you. If you will obey me, then here's what will happen."

The fourth lesson I learned from this weight-loss experience was the value of weekly meetings. We were required to come once a week. Is the application evident again? Sure it is. Once every seven days I went to my weight-loss group. And God says, "If you want to grow spiritually, then once every seven days, be at the house of worship."

Finally, I realized the tremendous power of a vision. For me, the vision was a suit—a suit that I had purchased in London, England in 1976 as a graduate student. It was a beautiful black, European cut suit with wide pinstripes. I had not worn it for almost three decades. But I kept it in my closet. I can now wear that suit once again!

Do you have a vision—for your spiritual life? Can you get a glimpse of the dream that God has for you, what God originally envisioned for you? Let that dream grip you, and it will take you very far. These lessons I learned in my weight-loss period have direct spiritual applications for us all.

TO LEARN MORE ON WHAT THE BIBLE HAS TO SAY ABOUT **FITNESS**, READ THE SCRIPTURES AND DEVOTIONALS AT **ACTS 11:8–9, 2 TIMOTHY 4:7, ROMANS 12:1, 1 CORINTHIANS 3:16, 1 TIMOTHY 4:8,** AND **1 CORINTHIANS 6:20.**

Now, tell me the dream so that I will know you can tell me what it really means!"

¹⁰The wise men answered the king, saying, "No one on earth can do what the king asks! No great and powerful king has ever asked the fortune-tellers, magicians, or wise men to do this; ¹¹the king is asking something that is too hard. Only the gods could tell the king this, but the gods do not live among people."

¹²When the king heard their answer, he became very angry. He ordered that all the wise men of Babylon be killed. ¹³So King Nebuchadnezzar's order to kill the wise men was announced, and men were sent to look for Daniel and his friends to kill them.

¹⁴Arioch, the commander of the king's guards, was going to kill the wise men of Babylon. But Daniel spoke to him with wisdom and skill, ¹⁵saying, "Why did the king order such a terrible punishment?" Then Arioch explained everything to Daniel. ¹⁶So Daniel went to King Nebuchadnezzar and asked for an appointment so that he could tell the king what his dream meant.

¹⁷Then Daniel went to his house and explained the whole story to his friends Hananiah, Mishael, and Azariah. ¹⁸Daniel asked his friends to pray that the God of heaven would show them mercy and help them understand this secret so he and his friends would not be killed with the other wise men of Babylon.

¹⁹During the night God explained the secret to Daniel in a vision. Then Daniel praised the God of heaven. ²⁰Daniel said:

"Praise God forever and ever,
    because he has wisdom and power.
²¹ He changes the times and seasons of the
        year.
    He takes away the power of kings
    and gives their power to new kings.
    He gives wisdom to those who are
        wise
    and knowledge to those who
        understand.
²² He makes known secrets that are deep
        and hidden;
    he knows what is hidden in darkness,
    and light is all around him.
²³ I thank you and praise you, God of my
        ancestors,
    because you have given me wisdom and
        power.

You told me what we asked of you;
    you told us about the king's dream."

THE MEANING OF THE DREAM

²⁴Then Daniel went to Arioch, the man King Nebuchadnezzar had chosen to kill the wise men of Babylon. Daniel said to him, "Don't put the wise men of Babylon to death. Take me to the king, and I will tell him what his dream means."

²⁵Very quickly Arioch took Daniel to the king and said, "I have found a man among the captives from Judah who can tell the king what his dream means."

²⁶The king asked Daniel, who was also called Belteshazzar, "Are you able to tell me what I dreamed and what it means?"

²⁷Daniel answered, "No wise man, magician, or fortune-teller can explain to the king the secret he has asked about. ²⁸But there is a God in heaven who explains secret things, and he has shown King Nebuchadnezzar what will happen at a later time. This is your dream, the vision you saw while lying on your bed: ²⁹O king, as you were lying there, you thought about things to come. God, who can tell people about secret things, showed you what is going to happen. ³⁰God also told this secret to me, not because I have greater wisdom than any other living person, but so that you may know what it means. In that way you will understand what went through your mind.

³¹"O king, in your dream you saw a huge, shiny, and frightening statue in front of you. ³²The head of the statue was made of pure gold. Its chest and arms were made of silver. Its stomach and the upper part of its legs were made of bronze. ³³The lower part of the legs were made of iron, while its feet were made partly of iron and partly of baked clay. ³⁴While you were looking at the statue, you saw a rock cut free, but no human being touched the rock. It hit the statue on its feet of iron and clay and smashed them. ³⁵Then the iron, clay, bronze, silver, and gold broke to pieces at the same time. They became like chaff on a threshing floor in the summertime; the wind blew them away, and there was nothing left. Then the rock that hit the statue became a very large mountain that filled the whole earth.

³⁶"That was your dream. Now we will

tell the king what it means. ³⁷O king, you are the greatest king. God of heaven has given you a kingdom, power, strength, and glory. ³⁸Wherever people, wild animals, and birds live, God made you ruler over them. King Nebuchadnezzar, you are the head of gold on that statue.

³⁹"Another kingdom will come after you, but it will not be as great as yours. Next a third kingdom, the bronze part, will rule over the earth. ⁴⁰Then there will be a fourth kingdom, strong as iron. In the same way that iron crushes and smashes things to pieces, the fourth kingdom will smash and crush all the other kingdoms.

⁴¹"You saw that the statue's feet and toes were partly baked clay and partly iron. That means the fourth kingdom will be a divided kingdom. It will have some of the strength of iron in it, just as you saw iron was mixed with clay. ⁴²The toes of the statue were partly iron and partly clay. So the fourth kingdom will be partly strong like iron and partly breakable like clay. ⁴³You saw the iron mixed with clay, but iron and clay do not hold together. In the same way the people of the fourth kingdom will be a mixture, but they will not be united as one people.

⁴⁴"During the time of those kings, the God of heaven will set up another kingdom that will never be destroyed or given to another group of people. This kingdom will crush all the other kingdoms and bring them to an end, but it will continue forever.

⁴⁵"King Nebuchadnezzar, you saw a rock cut from a mountain, but no human being touched it. The rock broke the iron, bronze, clay, silver, and gold to pieces. In this way the great God showed you what will happen. The dream is true, and you can trust this explanation."

⁴⁶Then King Nebuchadnezzar fell facedown on the ground in front of Daniel. The king honored him and commanded that an offering and incense be presented to him. ⁴⁷Then the king said to Daniel, "Truly I know your God is the greatest of all gods, the Lord of all the kings. He tells people about things they cannot know. I know this is true, because you were able to tell these secret things to me."

⁴⁸Then the king gave Daniel many gifts plus an important position in his kingdom.

Nebuchadnezzar made him ruler over the whole area of Babylon and put him in charge of all the wise men of Babylon. ⁴⁹Daniel asked the king to make Shadrach, Meshach, and Abednego leaders over the area of Babylon, so the king did as Daniel asked. Daniel himself became one of the people who stayed at the royal court.

THE GOLD IDOL AND BLAZING FURNACE

3 King Nebuchadnezzar made a gold statue ninety feet high and nine feet wide and set it up on the plain of Dura in the area of Babylon. ²Then he called for the leaders: the governors, assistant governors, captains of the soldiers, people who advised the king, keepers of the treasury, judges, rulers, and all other officers in his kingdom. He wanted them to come to the special service for the statue he had set up. ³So they all came for the special service and stood in front of the statue that King Nebuchadnezzar had set up. ⁴Then the man who made announcements for the king said in a loud voice, "People, nations, and those of every language, this is what you are commanded to do: ⁵When you hear the sound of the horns, flutes, lyres, zithers,ⁿ harps, pipes, and all the other musical instruments, you must bow down and worship the gold statue that King Nebuchadnezzar has set up. ⁶Anyone who doesn't bow down and worship will immediately be thrown into a blazing furnace."

⁷Now people, nations, and those who spoke every language were there. When they heard the sound of the horns, flutes, lyres, zithers, pipes, and all the other musical instruments, they bowed down and worshiped the gold statue King Nebuchadnezzar had set up.

⁸Then some Babylonians came up to the king and began speaking against the men of Judah. ⁹They said to King Nebuchadnezzar, "O king, live forever! ¹⁰O king, you gave a command that everyone who heard the horns, lyres, zithers, harps, pipes, and all the other musical instruments would have to bow down and worship the gold statue. ¹¹Anyone who wouldn't do this was to be thrown into a blazing furnace. ¹²O king, there are some men

---

3:5 zithers Musical instruments with thirty to forty strings.

of Judah whom you made officers in the area of Babylon that did not pay attention to your order. Their names are Shadrach, Meshach, and Abednego. They do not serve your gods and do not worship the gold statue you have set up."

¹³Nebuchadnezzar became very angry and called for Shadrach, Meshach, and Abednego. When they were brought to the king, ¹⁴Nebuchadnezzar said, "Shadrach, Meshach, and Abednego, is it true that you do not serve my gods nor worship the gold statue I have set up? ¹⁵In a moment you will again hear the sound of the horns, flutes, lyres, zithers, harps, pipes, and all the other musical instruments. If you bow down and worship the statue I made, that will be good. But if you do not worship it, you will immediately be thrown into the blazing furnace. What god will be able to save you from my power then?"

¹⁶Shadrach, Meshach, and Abednego

SERVANT EVANGELISM

character is
the issue

FAITH

By Paul Louis Cole

DANIEL 3:16–30

The *New York Times* recently had this headline: "Character to Be Major Issue in Trial." Interestingly, the writer prefaced his article with this sentence: "The trial of yet another former executive begins today, and the outcome may well turn more on what jurors think about his character than on the facts."

Character is always the issue in family life, marriage, profession, and success. What is beginning to dawn on our secular culture is that character is, indeed, important. Character is that quality of faithfulness seen in what a man will do when all alone. When he knows the human consequences are legally permissible, though unethical, he has a choice. That choice is the difference between those who rise to greatness and those who just live life.

The character of a person is measured in faithfulness to virtue. Faithfulness is measured by obedience. Obedience is just doing the next little thing God asks you to do. Do what is right. That seems simple, yet we often follow the deception of our hearts, the pull of the world, the lure of the flesh.

Those who would follow godly examples, those who add courage to their faith, will change the world. You can be one of them. We must pursue the passion of knowing God and go after the elements that build real character. Strive for true intimacy with God and share the burdens of others. It really is all about character . . . and the jury is watching.

reflect: Are you the same person in and out of the public arena?
Go to **Obadiah 15.**

answered the king, saying, "Nebuchadnezzar, we do not need to defend ourselves to you. ¹⁷If you throw us into the blazing furnace, the God we serve is able to save us from the furnace. He will save us from your power, O king. ¹⁸But even if God does not save us, we want you, O king, to know this: We will not serve your gods or worship the gold statue you have set up."

¹⁹Then Nebuchadnezzar was furious with Shadrach, Meshach, and Abednego, and he changed his mind. He ordered the furnace to be heated seven times hotter than usual. ²⁰Then he commanded some of the strongest soldiers in his army to tie up Shadrach, Meshach, and Abednego and throw them into the blazing furnace.

²¹So Shadrach, Meshach, and Abednego were tied up and thrown into the blazing furnace while still wearing their robes, trousers, turbans, and other clothes. ²²The king's command was very strict, and the furnace was made so hot that the flames killed the strong soldiers who threw Shadrach, Meshach, and Abednego into the furnace. ²³Firmly tied, Shadrach, Meshach, and Abednego fell into the blazing furnace.

²⁴Then King Nebuchadnezzar was so surprised that he jumped to his feet. He asked the men who advised him, "Didn't we tie up only three men and throw them into the fire?"

They answered, "Yes, O king."

²⁵The king said, "Look! I see four men walking around in the fire. They are not tied up, and they are not burned. The fourth man looks like a son of the gods."

²⁶Then Nebuchadnezzar went to the opening of the blazing furnace and shouted, "Shadrach, Meshach, and Abednego, come out! Servants of the Most High God, come here!"

So Shadrach, Meshach, and Abednego came out of the fire. ²⁷When they came out, the governors, assistant governors, captains of the soldiers, and royal advisers crowded around them and saw that the fire had not harmed their bodies. Their hair was not burned, their robes were not burned, and they didn't even smell like smoke!

²⁸Then Nebuchadnezzar said, "Praise the God of Shadrach, Meshach, and Abednego. Their God has sent his angel and saved his servants from the fire! These three men trusted their God and refused to obey my command. They were willing to die rather than serve or worship any god other than their own. ²⁹So I now give this command: Anyone from any nation or language who says anything against the God of Shadrach, Meshach, and Abednego will be torn apart and have his house turned into a pile of stones. No other god can save his people like this." ³⁰Then the king promoted Shadrach, Meshach, and Abednego in the area of Babylon.

NEBUCHADNEZZAR'S DREAM OF A TREE

4 King Nebuchadnezzar sent this letter to the people, nations, and those who speak every language in all the world:

I wish you peace and great wealth!

²The Most High God has done miracles and wonderful things for me that I am happy to tell you about.
³ His wonderful acts are great,
  and his miracles are mighty.
 His kingdom goes on forever,
  and his rule continues from now on.
⁴I, Nebuchadnezzar, was happy and successful at my palace, ⁵but I had a dream that made me afraid. As I was lying on my bed, I saw pictures and visions in my mind that alarmed me. ⁶So I ordered all the wise men of Babylon to come to me and tell me what my dream meant. ⁷The fortune-tellers, magicians, and wise men came, and I told them about the dream. But they could not tell me what it meant.

⁸Finally, Daniel came to me. (I called him Belteshazzar to honor my god, because the spirit of the holy gods is in him.) I told my dream to him. ⁹I said, "Belteshazzar, you are the most important of all the fortune-tellers. I know that the spirit of the holy gods is in you, so there is no secret that is too hard for you to understand. This was what I dreamed; tell me what it means. ¹⁰These are the visions I saw while I was lying in my bed: I looked, and there in front of me was a tree standing in the middle of the earth. And it was very tall. ¹¹The tree grew large and strong. The top of the tree touched the sky and could be seen

from anywhere on earth. [12]The leaves of the tree were beautiful. It had plenty of good fruit on it, enough food for everyone. The wild animals found shelter under the tree, and the birds lived in its branches. Every animal ate from it.

[13]"As I was looking at those things in the vision while lying on my bed, I saw an observer, a holy angel coming down from heaven. [14]He spoke very loudly and said, 'Cut down the tree and cut off its branches. Strip off its leaves and scatter its fruit. Let the animals under the tree run away, and let the birds in its branches fly away. [15]But leave the stump and its roots in the ground with a band of iron and bronze around it; let it stay in the field with the grass around it.

" 'Let the man become wet with dew, and let him live among the animals and plants of the earth. [16]Let him not think like a human any longer, but let him have the mind of an animal for seven years.

[17]" 'The observers gave this command; the holy ones declared the sentence. This is so all people may know that the Most High God rules over every kingdom on earth. God gives those kingdoms to anyone he wants, and he chooses people to rule them who are not proud.'

[18]"That is what I, King Nebuchadnezzar, dreamed. Now Belteshazzar,[n] tell me what the dream means. None of the wise men in my kingdom can explain it to me, but you can, because the spirit of the holy gods is in you."

DANIEL EXPLAINS THE DREAM

[19]Then Daniel, who was called Belteshazzar, was very quiet for a while, because his understanding of the dream frightened him. So the king said, "Belteshazzar, do not let the dream or its meaning make you afraid."

Then Belteshazzar answered, "My master, I wish the dream were about your enemies, and I wish its meaning were for those who are against you! [20]You saw a tree in your dream that grew large and strong. Its top touched the sky, and it could be seen from all over the earth. [21]Its leaves were beautiful, and it had plenty of fruit for everyone to eat.

It was a home for the wild animals, and its branches were nesting places for the birds. [22]O king, you are that tree! You have become great and powerful, like the tall tree that touched the sky. Your power reaches to the far parts of the earth.

[23]"O king, you saw an observer, a holy angel, coming down from heaven who said, 'Cut down the tree and destroy it. But leave the stump and its roots in the ground with a band of iron and bronze around it; leave it in the field with the grass. Let him become wet with dew and live like a wild animal for seven years.'

[24]"This is the meaning of the dream, O king. The Most High God has commanded these things to happen to my master the king: [25]You will be forced away from people to live among the wild animals. People will feed you grass like an ox, and dew from the sky will make you wet. Seven years will pass, and then you will learn this lesson: The Most High God is ruler over every kingdom on earth, and he gives those kingdoms to anyone he chooses.

[26]"Since the stump of the tree and its roots were left in the ground, your kingdom will be given back to you when you learn that one in heaven rules your kingdom. [27]So, O king, please accept my advice. Stop sinning and do what is right. Stop doing wicked things and be kind to the poor. Then you might continue to be successful."

THE KING'S DREAM COMES TRUE

[28]All these things happened to King Nebuchadnezzar. [29]Twelve months later as he was walking on the roof[n] of his palace in Babylon, [30]he said, "I have built this great Babylon as my royal home. I built it by my power to show my glory and my majesty."

[31]The words were still in his mouth when a voice from heaven said, "King Nebuchadnezzar, these things will

---

4:18 Belteshazzar Another name for Daniel.   **4:29 roof** In Bible times houses were built with flat roofs. The roof was used for drying things such as flax and fruit. And it was used as an extra room, as a place for worship, and as a cool place to sleep in the summer.

happen to you: Your royal power has been taken away from you. ³²You will be forced away from people. You will live with the wild animals and will be fed grass like an ox. Seven years will pass before you learn this lesson: The Most High God rules over every kingdom on earth and gives those kingdoms to anyone he chooses."

³³Immediately the words came true. Nebuchadnezzar was forced to go away from people, and he began eating grass like an ox. He became wet from dew. His hair grew long like the feathers of an eagle, and his nails grew like the claws of a bird.

³⁴At the end of that time, I, Nebuchadnezzar, looked up toward heaven, and I could think normally again! Then I gave praise to the Most High God; I gave honor and glory to him who lives forever.

God's rule is forever,
   and his kingdom continues for all
     time.
³⁵People on earth
   are not truly important.
God does what he wants
   with the powers of heaven
   and the people on earth.
No one can stop his powerful hand
   or question what he does.

FINANCES

THE LAWS OF INCREASE

acknowledging
authority

DANIEL 4:30–37

What was the sin of Nebuchadnezzar? It certainly wasn't wealth or power or influence. It wasn't unjust decisions or illegitimate wars or economic oppression. God judged the king for one thing: his failure to understand and acknowledge authority. His sin was much more serious than being proud of his accomplishments. His sin was thinking that he was responsible for his success. In other words, Nebuchadnezzar thought that he was the one in control.

Notice God's judgment of Nebuchadnezzar. God declares that the king's royal *authority* was to be taken from him. The king failed to see that all he had was the result of authority given to him by God. It was never about control. It was about the proper exercise of *authority*. God never gives us control. He grants us authority.

God always has the control, but at times he allows us to act as channels of his control by granting us authority over some of his realm. The real power behind our authority is God. What we have is a gift from him. God entrusts us with authority in order that we may serve and honor him with it. Ask yourself what God expects you to do with the authority he has given you today.

reflect: Think about the important difference between authority and control.
Go to **FINANCES:** "Handling Money God's Way" at **Deuteronomy 15:6.**

36At that time I could think normally again, and God gave back my great honor and power and returned the glory to my kingdom. The people who advised me and the royal family came to me for help again. I became king again and was even greater and more powerful than before. 37Now I, Nebuchadnezzar, give praise and honor and glory to the King of heaven. Everything he does is right and fair, and he is able to make proud people humble.

THE WRITING ON THE WALL

5 King Belshazzar gave a big banquet for a thousand royal guests and drank wine with them. 2As Belshazzar was drinking his wine, he gave orders to bring the gold and silver cups that his ancestor Nebuchadnezzar had taken from the Temple in Jerusalem. This was so the king, his royal guests, his wives, and his slave women could drink from those cups. 3So they brought the gold cups that had been taken from the Temple of God in Jerusalem. And the king and his royal guests, his wives, and his slave women drank from them. 4As they were drinking, they praised their gods, which were made from gold, silver, bronze, iron, wood, and stone.

5Suddenly the fingers of a person's hand appeared and began writing on the plaster of the wall, near the lampstand in the royal palace. The king watched the hand as it wrote.

6King Belshazzar was very frightened. His face turned white, his knees knocked together, and he could not stand up because his legs were too weak. 7The king called for the magicians, wise men, and wizards of Babylon and said to them, "Anyone who can read this writing and explain it will receive purple clothes fit for a king and a gold chain around his neck. And I will make that person the third highest ruler in the kingdom."

8Then all the king's wise men came in, but they could not read the writing or tell the king what it meant. 9King Belshazzar became even more afraid, and his face became even whiter. His royal guests were confused.

10Then the king's mother, who had heard the voices of the king and his royal guests, came into the banquet room. She said, "O king, live forever! Don't be afraid or let your face be white with fear! 11There is a man in your kingdom who has the spirit of the holy gods. In the days of your father, this man showed understanding, knowledge, and wisdom like the gods. Your father, King Nebuchadnezzar, put this man in charge of all the wise men, fortune-tellers, magicians, and wizards. 12The man I am talking about is named Daniel, whom the king named Belteshazzar. He was very wise and had knowledge and understanding. He could explain dreams and secrets and could answer very hard problems. Call for Daniel. He will tell you what the writing on the wall means."

13So they brought Daniel to the king, and the king asked, "Is your name Daniel? Are you one of the captives my father the king brought from Judah? 14I have heard that the spirit of the gods is in you, and that you are very wise and have knowledge and extraordinary understanding. 15The wise men and magicians were brought to me to read this writing and to explain what it means, but they could not explain it. 16I have heard that you are able to explain what things mean and can find the answers to hard problems. Read this writing on the wall and explain it to me. If you can, I will give you purple clothes fit for a king and a gold chain to wear around your neck. And you will become the third highest ruler in the kingdom."

17Then Daniel answered the king, "You may keep your gifts for yourself, or you may give those rewards to someone else. But I will read the writing on the wall for you and will explain to you what it means.

18"O king, the Most High God made your father Nebuchadnezzar a great, important, and powerful king. 19Because God made him important, all the people, nations, and those who spoke every language were very frightened of Nebuchadnezzar. If he wanted someone to die, he killed that person. If he wanted someone to live, he let that person live. Those he wanted to promote, he promoted. Those he wanted to be less important, he made less important.

20"But Nebuchadnezzar became too proud and stubborn, so he was taken off his royal throne. His glory was taken away. 21He was forced away from people, and his mind became like the mind of an animal. He lived with the wild donkeys and was fed grass like an ox and became wet with dew. These things happened to him until he learned his lesson: The Most High God rules over every kingdom on earth, and he sets anyone he chooses over those kingdoms.

22"Belshazzar, you already knew these things, because you are a descendant of Nebuchadnezzar. Still you have not been sorry for what you have done. 23Instead, you have set yourself against the Lord of heaven. You ordered the drinking cups from the Temple of the Lord to be brought to you. Then you and your royal guests, your wives, and your slave women drank wine from them. You praised the gods of silver, gold, bronze, iron, wood, and stone that are not really gods; they cannot see or hear or understand anything. You did not honor God, who has power over your life and everything you do. 24So God sent the hand that wrote on the wall.

25"These are the words that were written on the wall: 'Mene, mene, tekel, and parsin.'

26"This is what the words mean: Mene: God has counted the days until your kingdom will end. 27Tekel: You have been weighed on the scales and found not good enough. 28Parsin: Your kingdom is being divided and will be given to the Medes and the Persians."

29Then Belshazzar gave an order for Daniel to be dressed in purple clothes and to have a gold chain put around his neck. And it was announced that Daniel was the third highest ruler in the kingdom. 30That very same night Belshazzar, king of the Babylonian people, was killed. 31So Darius the Mede became the new king when he was sixty-two years old.

DANIEL AND THE LIONS

6 Darius thought it would be a good idea to choose one hundred twenty governors who would rule his kingdom. 2He chose three men as supervisors over those governors, and Daniel was one of the supervisors. The supervisors were to ensure that the governors did not try to cheat the king. 3Daniel showed that he could do the work better than the other supervisors and governors, so the king planned to put Daniel in charge of the whole kingdom. 4Because of this, the other supervisors and governors tried to find reasons to accuse Daniel about his work in the government. But they could not find anything wrong with him or any reason to accuse him, because he was trustworthy and not lazy or

dishonest. 5Finally these men said, "We will never find any reason to accuse Daniel unless it is about the law of his God."

6So the supervisors and governors went as a group to the king and said: "King Darius, live forever! 7The supervisors, assistant governors, governors, the people who advise you, and the captains of the soldiers have all agreed that you should make a new law for everyone to obey: For the next thirty days no one should pray to any god or human except to you, O king. Anyone who doesn't obey will be thrown into the lions' den. 8Now, O king, make the law and sign your name to it so that it cannot be changed, because then it will be a law of the Medes and Persians and cannot be canceled." 9So King Darius signed the law.

10Even though Daniel knew that the new law had been written, he went to pray in an upstairs room in his house, which had windows that opened toward Jerusalem. Three times each day Daniel would kneel down to pray and thank God, just as he always had done.

11Then those men went as a group and found Daniel praying and asking God for help. 12So they went to the king and talked to him about the law he had made. They said, "Didn't you sign a law that says no one may pray to any god or human except you, O king? Doesn't it say that anyone who disobeys during the next thirty days will be thrown into the lions' den?"

The king answered, "Yes, that is the law, and the laws of the Medes and Persians cannot be canceled."

13Then they said to the king, "Daniel, one of the captives from Judah, is not paying attention to you, O king, or to the law you signed. Daniel still prays to his God three times every day." 14The king became very upset when he heard this. He wanted to save Daniel, and he worked hard until sunset trying to think of a way to save him.

15Then those men went as a group to the king. They said, "Remember, O king, the law of the Medes and Persians says that no law or command given by the king can be changed."

16So King Darius gave the order, and Daniel was brought in and thrown into the lions' den. The king said to Daniel, "May the God you serve all the time save you!" 17A big stone was brought and placed over the opening of the lions' den. Then the king used his signet ring and the rings of his royal officers to put special seals on the rock. This ensured that no one would move the rock and bring Daniel out. ¹⁸Then King Darius went back to his palace. He did not eat that night, he did not have any entertainment brought to him, and he could not sleep.

¹⁹The next morning King Darius got up at dawn and hurried to the lions' den. ²⁰As he came near the den, he was worried. He called out to Daniel, "Daniel, servant of the living God! Has your God that you always worship been able to save you from the lions?"

²¹Daniel answered, "O king, live forever! ²²My God sent his angel to close the lions' mouths. They have not hurt me, because my God knows I am innocent. I never did anything wrong to you, O king."

²³King Darius was very happy and told his servants to lift Daniel out of the lions' den. So they lifted him out and did not find any injury on him, because Daniel had trusted in his God.

²⁴Then the king commanded that the men who had accused Daniel be brought to the lions' den. They, their wives, and their children were thrown into the den. The lions grabbed them before they hit the floor of the den and crushed their bones.

²⁵Then King Darius wrote a letter to all people and all nations, to those who spoke every language in the world:

I wish you great peace and wealth.

²⁶I am making a new law for people in every part of my kingdom. All of you must fear and respect the God of Daniel.

Daniel's God is the living God;
    he lives forever.
His kingdom will never be destroyed,
    and his rule will never end.
²⁷ God rescues and saves people
    and does mighty miracles
    in heaven and on earth.
He is the one who saved Daniel
    from the power of the lions.

²⁸So Daniel was successful during the time Darius was king and when Cyrus the Persian was king.

DANIEL'S DREAM ABOUT FOUR ANIMALS

7 In Belshazzar's first year as king of Babylon, Daniel had a dream. He saw visions as he was lying on his bed, and he wrote down what he had dreamed.

²Daniel said: "I saw my vision at night. In the vision the wind was blowing from all four directions, which made the sea very rough. ³I saw four huge animals come up from the sea, and each animal was different from the others.

⁴"The first animal looked like a lion, but had wings like an eagle. I watched this animal until its wings were torn off. It was lifted from the ground so that it stood up on two feet like a human, and it was given the mind of a human.

⁵"Then I saw a second animal before me that looked like a bear. It was raised up on one of its sides and had three ribs in its mouth between its teeth. It was told, 'Get up and eat all the meat you want!'

⁶"After that, I looked, and there before me was another animal. This animal looked like a leopard with four wings on its back that looked like a bird's wings. This animal had four heads and was given power to rule.

⁷"After that, in my vision at night I saw in front of me a fourth animal that was cruel, terrible, and very strong. It had large iron teeth. It crushed and ate what it killed, and then it walked on whatever was left. This fourth animal was different from any animal I had seen before, and it had ten horns.

⁸"While I was thinking about the horns, another horn grew up among them. It was a little horn with eyes like a human's eyes. It also had a mouth, and the mouth was bragging. The little horn pulled out three of the other horns.

⁹"As I looked,
thrones were put in their places,
    and God, the Eternal One, sat on his
        throne.
His clothes were white like snow,
    and the hair on his head was white like
        wool.
His throne was made from fire,
    and the wheels of his throne were
        blazing with fire.
¹⁰ A river of fire was flowing
    from in front of him.

Many thousands of angels were serving
him,
and millions of angels stood before him.
Court was ready to begin,
and the books were opened.

11"I kept on looking because the little horn was bragging. I kept watching until finally the fourth animal was killed. Its body was destroyed, and it was thrown into the burning fire. **12**(The power and rule of the other animals had been taken from them, but they were permitted to live for a certain period of time.)

13"In my vision at night I saw in front of me someone who looked like a human being coming on the clouds in the sky. He came near God, who has been alive forever, and he was led to God. **14**He was given authority, glory, and the strength of a king. People of every tribe, nation, and language will serve him. His rule will last forever, and his kingdom will never be destroyed.

THE MEANING OF THE DREAM

15"I, Daniel, was worried. The visions that went through my mind frightened me. **16**I came near one of those standing there and asked what all this meant.

"So he told me and explained to me what these things meant: **17**'The four great animals are four kingdoms that will come from the earth. **18**But the holy people who belong to the Most High God will receive the power to rule and will have the power to rule forever, from now on.'

19"Then I wanted to know what the fourth animal meant, because it was different from all the others. It was very terrible and had iron teeth and bronze claws. It was the animal that crushed and ate what it killed and then walked on whatever was left. **20**I also wanted to know about the ten horns on its head and about the little horn that grew there. It had pulled out three of the other ten horns and looked greater than the others. It had eyes and a mouth that kept bragging. **21**As I watched, the little horn began making war against God's holy people and was defeating them **22**until God, who has been alive forever, came. He judged in favor of the holy people who belong to the Most High God; then the time came for them to receive the power to rule.

23"And he explained this to me: 'The fourth animal is a fourth kingdom that will come on the earth. It will be different from all the other kingdoms and will destroy people all over the world. It will walk on and crush the whole earth. **24**The ten horns are ten kings who will come from this fourth kingdom. After those ten kings are gone, another king will come. He will be different from the kings who ruled before him, and he will defeat three of the other kings. **25**This king will speak against the Most High God, and he will hurt and kill God's holy people. He will try to change times and laws that have already been set. The holy people that belong to God will be in that king's power for three and one-half years.

26"'But the court will decide what should happen. The power of the king will be taken away, and his kingdom will be completely destroyed. **27**Then the holy people who belong to the Most High God will have the power to rule. They will rule over all the kingdoms under heaven with power and greatness, and their power to rule will last forever. People from all the other kingdoms will respect and serve them.'

28"That was the end of the dream. I, Daniel, was very afraid. My face became white from fear, but I kept everything to myself."

DANIEL'S VISION

8 During the third year of King Belshazzar's rule, I, Daniel, saw another vision, which was like the first one. **2**In this vision I saw myself in the capital city of Susa, in the area of Elam. I was standing by the Ulai Canal **3**when I looked up and saw a male sheep standing beside the canal. It had two long horns, but one horn was longer and newer than the other. **4**I watched the sheep charge to the west, the north, and the south. No animal could stand before him, and none could save another animal from his power. He did whatever he wanted and became very powerful.

5While I was watching this, I saw a male goat come from the west. This goat had one large horn between his eyes that was easy to see. He crossed over the whole earth so fast that his feet hardly touched the ground.

6In his anger the goat charged the sheep with the two horns that I had seen standing by the canal. ⁷I watched the angry goat attack the sheep and break the sheep's two horns. The sheep was not strong enough to stop it. The goat knocked the sheep to the ground and then walked all over him. No one was able to save the sheep from the goat, ⁸so the male goat became very great. But when he was strong, his big horn broke off and four horns grew in place of the one big horn. Those four horns pointed in four different directions and were easy to see.

⁹Then a little horn grew from one of those four horns, and it became very big. It grew to the south, the east, and toward the beautiful land of Judah. ¹⁰That little horn grew until it reached to the sky. It even threw some of the army of heaven to the ground and walked on them! ¹¹That little horn set itself up as equal to God, the Commander of heaven's armies. It stopped the daily sacrifices that were offered to him, and the Temple, the place where people worshiped him, was pulled down. ¹²Because there was a turning away from God, the people stopped the daily sacrifices. Truth was thrown down to the ground, and the horn was successful in everything it did.

¹³Then I heard a holy angel speaking. Another holy angel asked the first one, "How long will the things in this vision last—the daily sacrifices, the turning away from God that brings destruction, the Temple being pulled down, and the army of heaven being walked on?"

¹⁴The angel said to me, "This will happen for twenty-three hundred evenings and mornings. Then the holy place will be repaired."

¹⁵I, Daniel, saw this vision and tried to understand what it meant. In it I saw someone who looked like a man standing near me. ¹⁶And I heard a man's voice calling from the Ulai Canal: "Gabriel, explain the vision to this man."

¹⁷Gabriel came to where I was standing. When he came close to me, I was very afraid and bowed facedown on the ground. But Gabriel said to me, "Human being, understand that this vision is about the time of the end."

¹⁸While Gabriel was speaking, I fell into a deep sleep with my face on the ground. Then he touched me and lifted me to my feet. ¹⁹He said, "Now, I will explain to you what will happen in the time of God's anger. Your vision was about the set time of the end.

²⁰"You saw a male sheep with two horns, which are the kings of Media and Persia. ²¹The male goat is the king of Greece, and the big horn between its eyes is the first king. ²²The four horns that grew in the place of the broken horn are four kingdoms. Those four kingdoms will come from the nation of the first king, but they will not be as strong as the first king.

²³"When the end comes near for those kingdoms, a bold and cruel king who tells lies will come. This will happen when many people have turned against God. ²⁴This king will be very powerful, but his power will not come from himself. He will cause terrible destruction and will be successful in everything he does. He will destroy powerful people and even God's holy people. ²⁵This king will succeed by using lies and force. He will think that he is very important. He will destroy many people without warning; he will try to fight even the Prince of princes! But that cruel king will be destroyed, and not by human power.

²⁶"The vision that has been shown to you about these evenings and mornings is true. But seal up the vision, because those things won't happen for a long time."

²⁷I, Daniel, became very weak and was sick for several days after that vision. Then I got up and went back to work for the king, but I was very upset about the vision. I didn't understand what it meant.

DANIEL'S PRAYER

9 These things happened during the first year Darius son of Xerxes was king over Babylon. He was a descendant of the Medes. ²During Darius' first year as king, I, Daniel, was reading the Scriptures. I saw that the LORD told Jeremiah that Jerusalem would be empty ruins for seventy years.

³Then I turned to the Lord God and prayed and asked him for help. To show my sadness, I fasted, put on rough cloth, and sat in ashes. ⁴I prayed to the LORD my God and told him about all of our sins. I said, "Lord, you are a great God who causes fear and wonder. You keep your agreement of love with all who love you and obey your commands.

5"But we have sinned and done wrong. We have been wicked and turned against you, your commands, and your laws. 6We did not listen to your servants, the prophets, who spoke for you to our kings, our leaders, our ancestors, and all the people of the land.

7"Lord, you are good and right, but we are full of shame today—the people of Judah and Jerusalem, all the people of Israel, those near and far whom you scattered among many nations because they were not loyal to you. 8LORD, we are all ashamed. Our kings and leaders and our fathers are ashamed, because we have sinned against you.

9"But, Lord our God, you show us mercy and forgive us even though we have turned against you. 10We have not obeyed the LORD our God or the teachings he gave us through his servants, the prophets. 11All the people of Israel have disobeyed your teachings and have turned away, refusing to obey you. So you brought on us the curses and promises of punishment written in the Teachings of Moses, the servant of God, because we sinned against you.

12"You said these things would happen to us and our leaders, and you made them happen; you brought on us a great disaster. Nothing has ever been done on earth like what was done to Jerusalem. 13All this disaster came to us just as it is written in the Teachings of Moses. But we have not pleaded with the LORD our God. We have not stopped sinning. We have not paid attention to your truth. 14The LORD was ready to bring the disaster on us, and he did it because the LORD our God is right in everything he does. But we still did not obey him.

15"Lord our God, you used your power and brought us out of Egypt. Because of that, your name is known even today. But we have sinned and have done wrong. 16Lord, you do what is right, but please do not be angry with Jerusalem, your city on your holy hill. Because of our sins and the evil things done by our ancestors, people all around insult and make fun of Jerusalem and your people.

17"Now, our God, hear the prayers of your servant. Listen to my prayer for help, and for your sake do good things for your holy place that is in ruins. 18My God, pay attention and hear me. Open your eyes and see all the terrible things that have happened to us. See how our lives have been ruined and what has happened to the city that is called by your name. We do not ask these things because we are good; instead, we ask because of your mercy. 19Lord, listen! Lord, forgive! Lord, hear us and do something! For your sake, don't wait, because your city and your people are called by your name."

GABRIEL'S EXPLANATION

20While I was saying these things in my prayer to the LORD, my God, confessing my sins and the sins of the people of Israel and praying for God's holy hill, 21Gabriel came to me. (I had seen him in my last vision.) He came flying quickly to me about the time of the evening sacrifice, while I was still praying. 22He taught me and said to me, "Daniel, I have come to give you wisdom and to help you understand. 23When you first started praying, an answer was given, and I came to tell you, because God loves you very much. So think about the message and understand the vision.

24"God has ordered four hundred ninety years for your people and your holy city for these reasons: to stop people from turning against God; to put an end to sin; to take away evil; to bring in goodness that continues forever; to bring about the vision and prophecy; and to appoint a most holy place.

25"Learn and understand these things. A command will come to rebuild Jerusalem. The time from this command until the appointed leader comes will be forty-nine years and four hundred thirty-four years. Jerusalem will be rebuilt with streets and a trench filled with water around it, but it will be built in times of trouble. 26After the four hundred thirty-four years the appointed leader will be killed; he will have nothing. The people of the leader who is to come will destroy the city and the holy place. The end of the city will come like a flood, and war will continue until the end. God has ordered that place to be completely destroyed. 27That leader will make firm an agreement with many people for seven years. He will stop the offerings and sacrifices after three and one-half years. A destroyer will do blasphemous things until the ordered end comes to the destroyed city."

DANIEL'S VISION OF A MAN

10 During Cyrus' third year as king of Persia, Daniel, whose name was Belteshazzar, received a vision about a great war. It was a true message that Daniel understood.

²At that time I, Daniel, had been very sad for three weeks. ³I did not eat any fancy food or meat, or drink any wine, or use any perfumed oil for three weeks.

⁴On the twenty-fourth day of the first month, I was standing beside the great Tigris River. ⁵While standing there, I looked up and saw a man dressed in linen clothes with a belt of fine gold wrapped around his waist. ⁶His body was like shiny yellow quartz. His face was bright like lightning, and his eyes were like fire. His arms and legs were shiny like polished bronze, and his voice sounded like the roar of a crowd.

⁷I, Daniel, was the only person who saw the vision. The men with me did not see it, because they were so frightened that they ran away and hid. ⁸So I was left alone, watching this great vision. I lost my strength, my face turned white like a dead person, and I was helpless. ⁹Then I heard the man in the vision speaking. As I listened, I fell into a deep sleep with my face on the ground.

¹⁰Then a hand touched me and set me on my hands and knees. I was so afraid that I was shaking. ¹¹The man in the vision said to me, "Daniel, God loves you very much. Think carefully about the words I will speak to you, and stand up, because I have been sent to you." When he said this, I stood up, but I was still shaking.

¹²Then the man said to me, "Daniel, do not be afraid. Some time ago you decided to get understanding and to humble yourself before your God. Since that time God has listened to you, and I have come because of your prayers. ¹³But the prince of Persia has been fighting against me for twenty-one days. Then Michael, one of the most important angels, came to help me, because I had been left there with the king of Persia. ¹⁴Now I have come to explain to you what will happen to your people, because the vision is about a time in the future."

¹⁵While he was speaking to me, I bowed facedown and could not speak. ¹⁶Then one who looked like a man touched my lips, so I opened my mouth and started to speak. I said to the one standing in front of me, "Master, I am upset and afraid because of what I saw in the vision. I feel helpless. ¹⁷Master, how can I, your servant, talk with you? My strength is gone, and it is hard for me to breathe."

¹⁸The one who looked like a man touched me again and gave me strength. ¹⁹He said, "Daniel, don't be afraid. God loves you very much. Peace be with you. Be strong now; be courageous."

When he spoke to me, I became stronger and said, "Master, speak, since you have given me strength."

²⁰Then he said, "Daniel, do you know why I have come to you? Soon I must go back to fight against the prince of Persia. When I go, the prince of Greece will come, ²¹but I must first tell you what is written in the Book of Truth. No one stands with me against these enemies except Michael, the angel ruling over your people.

11 In the first year that Darius the Mede was king, I stood up to support Michael in his fight against the prince of Persia.

KINGDOMS OF THE SOUTH AND NORTH

²"Now then, Daniel, I tell you the truth: Three more kings will rule in Persia, and then a fourth king will come. He will be much richer than all the kings of Persia before him and will use his riches to get power. He will stir up everyone against the kingdom of Greece. ³Then a mighty king will come, who will rule with great power and will do anything he wants. ⁴After that king has come, his kingdom will be broken up and divided out toward the four parts of the world. His kingdom will not go to his descendants, and it will not have the power that he had, because his kingdom will be pulled up and given to other people.

⁵"The king of the South will become strong, but one of his commanders will become even stronger. He will begin to rule his own kingdom with great power. ⁶Then after a few years, a new friendship will develop. The daughter of the king of the South will marry the king of the North in order to bring peace. But she will not keep her power, and his family will not last. She, her husband, her child, and those who brought her to that country will be killed.

⁷"But a person from her family will

become king of the South and will attack the armies of the king of the North. He will go into that king's strong, walled city and will fight and win. ⁸He will take their gods, their metal idols, and their valuable things made of silver and gold back to Egypt. Then he will not bother the king of the North for a few years. ⁹Next, the king of the North will attack the king of the South, but he will be beaten back to his own country.

¹⁰"The sons of the king of the North will prepare for war. They will get a large army together that will move through the land very quickly, like a powerful flood. Later, that army will come back and fight all the way to the strong, walled city of the king of the South. ¹¹Then the king of the South will become very angry and will march out to fight against the king of the North. The king of the North will have a large army, but he will lose the battle, ¹²and the soldiers will be carried away. The king of the South will then be very proud and will kill thousands of soldiers from the northern army, but he will not continue to be successful. ¹³The king of the North will gather another army, larger than the first one. After several years he will attack with a large army and many weapons.

¹⁴"In those times many people will be against the king of the South. Some of your own people who love to fight will turn against the king of the South, thinking it is time for God's promises to come true. But they will fail. ¹⁵Then the king of the North will come. He will build ramps to the tops of the city walls and will capture a strong, walled city. The southern army will not have the power to fight back; even their best soldiers will not be strong enough to stop the northern army. ¹⁶So the king of the North will do whatever he wants; no one will be able to stand against him. He will gain power and control in the beautiful land of Israel and will have the power to destroy it. ¹⁷The king of the North will decide to use all his power to fight against the king of the South, but he will make a peace agreement with the king of the South. The king of the North will give one of his daughters as a wife to the king of the South so that he can defeat him. But those plans will not succeed or help him. ¹⁸Then the king of the North will turn his attention to cities along the coast of the Mediterranean

Sea and will capture them. But a commander will put an end to the pride of the king of the North, turning his pride back on him. ¹⁹After that happens the king of the North will go back to the strong, walled cities of his own country, but he will lose his power. That will be the end of him.

²⁰"The next king of the North will send out a tax collector so he will have plenty of money. In a few years that ruler will be killed, although he will not die in anger or in a battle.

²¹"That ruler will be followed by a very cruel and hated man, who will not have the honor of being from a king's family. He will attack the kingdom when the people feel safe, and he will take power by lying to the people. ²²He will sweep away in defeat large and powerful armies and even a prince who made an agreement. ²³Many nations will make agreements with that cruel and hated ruler, but he will lie to them. He will gain much power, but only a few people will support him. ²⁴The richest areas will feel safe, but that cruel and hated ruler will attack them. He will succeed where his ancestors did not. He will rob the countries he defeats and will give those things to his followers. He will plan to defeat and destroy strong cities, but he will be successful for only a short time.

²⁵"That very cruel and hated ruler will have a large army that he will use to stir up his strength and courage. He will attack the king of the South. The king of the South will gather a large and very powerful army and prepare for war. But the people who are against him will make secret plans, and the king of the South will be defeated. ²⁶People who were supposed to be his good friends will try to destroy him. His army will be swept away in defeat; many of his soldiers will be killed in battle. ²⁷Those two kings will want to hurt each other. They will sit at the same table and lie to each other, but it will not do either one any good, because God has set a time for their end to come. ²⁸The king of the North will go back to his own country with much wealth. Then he will decide to go against the holy agreement. He will take action and then return to his own country.

²⁹"At the right time the king of the North will attack the king of the South again, but

this time he will not be successful as he was before. 30Ships from the west will come and fight against the king of the North, so he will be afraid. Then he will return and show his anger against the holy agreement. He will be good to those who have stopped obeying the holy agreement.

31"The king of the North will send his army to make the Temple in Jerusalem unclean. They will stop the people from offering the daily sacrifice, and then they will set up a blasphemous object that brings destruction. 32The king of the North will tell lies and cause those who have not obeyed God to be ruined. But those who know God and obey him will be strong and fight back.

33"Those who are wise will help the others understand what is happening. But they will be killed with swords, or burned, or taken captive, or robbed of their homes and possessions. These things will continue for many days. 34When the wise ones are suffering, they will get a little help, but many who join the wise ones will not help them in their time of need. 35Some of the wise ones will be killed. But the hard times must come so they can be made stronger and purer and without faults until the time of the end comes. Then, at the right time, the end will come.

THE KING WHO PRAISES HIMSELF

36"The king of the North will do whatever he wants. He will brag about himself and praise himself and think he is even better than a god. He will say things against the God of gods that no one has ever heard. And he will be successful until all the bad things have happened. Then what God has planned to happen will happen. 37The king of the North will not care about the gods his ancestors worshiped or the god that women worship. He won't care about any god. Instead, he will make himself more important than any god. 38The king of the North will worship power and strength, which his ancestors did not worship. He will honor the god of power with gold and silver, expensive jewels and gifts. 39That king will attack strong, walled cities with the help of a foreign god. He will give much honor to the people who join him, making them rulers in charge of many other people. And he will make them pay him for the land they rule.

40"At the time of the end, the king of the South will fight a battle against the king of the North. The king of the North will attack with chariots, soldiers on horses, and many large ships. He will invade many countries and sweep through their lands like a flood. 41The king of the North will attack the beautiful land of Judah. He will defeat many countries, but Edom, Moab, and the leaders of Ammon will be saved from him. 42The king of the North will show his power in many countries; Egypt will not escape. 43The king will get treasures of gold and silver and all the riches of Egypt. The Libyan and Nubian people will obey him. 44But the king of the North will hear news from the east and the north that will make him afraid and angry. He will go to destroy completely many nations. 45He will set up his royal tents between the sea and the beautiful mountain where the holy Temple is built. But, finally, his end will come, and no one will help him.

THE TIME OF THE END

12 "At that time Michael, the great prince who protects your people, will stand up. There will be a time of much trouble, the worst time since nations have been on earth, but your people will be saved. Everyone whose name is written in God's book will be saved. 2Many people who have already died will live again. Some of them will wake up to have life forever, but some will wake up to find shame and disgrace forever. 3The wise people will shine like the brightness of the sky. Those who teach others to live right will shine like stars forever and ever.

4"But you, Daniel, close up the book and seal it. These things will happen at the time of the end. Many people will go here and there to find true knowledge."

5Then I, Daniel, looked, and saw two other men. One was standing on my side of the river, and the other was standing on the far side. 6The man who was dressed in linen was standing over the water in the river. One of the two men spoke to him and asked, "How long will it be before these amazing things come true?"

7The man dressed in linen, who stood over the water, raised his hands toward heaven. And I heard him swear by the name of God who lives forever, "It will be for three and one-half years. The power of the holy people will finally be broken, and then all these things will come true."

[8]I heard the answer, but I did not really understand, so I asked, "Master, what will happen after all these things come true?"

[9]He answered, "Go your way, Daniel. The message is closed up and sealed until the time of the end. [10]Many people will be made clean, pure, and spotless, but the wicked will continue to be wicked. Those wicked people will not understand these things, but the wise will understand them.

[11]"The daily sacrifice will be stopped. Then, after 1,290 days from that time, a blasphemous object that brings destruction will be set up. [12]Those who wait for the end of the 1,335 days will be happy.

[13]"As for you, Daniel, go your way until the end. You will get your rest, and at the end you will rise to receive your reward."

1 The LORD spoke his word to Hosea son of Beeri during the time that Uzziah, Jotham, Ahaz, and Hezekiah were kings of Judah and Jeroboam son of Jehoash was king of Israel.

HOSEA'S WIFE AND CHILDREN

2When the LORD began speaking through Hosea, the LORD said to him, "Go, and marry an unfaithful woman and have unfaithful children, because the people in this country have been completely unfaithful to the LORD." 3So Hosea married Gomer daughter of Diblaim, and she became pregnant and gave birth to Hosea's son.

4The LORD said to Hosea, "Name him Jezreel, because soon I will punish the family of Jehu for the people they killed at Jezreel. In the future I will put an end to the kingdom of Israel 5and break the power of Israel's army in the Valley of Jezreel."

6Gomer became pregnant again and gave birth to a daughter. The LORD said to Hosea, "Name her Lo-Ruhamah,[n] because I will not pity Israel anymore, nor will I forgive them. 7But I will show pity to the people of Judah. I will save them, but not by using bows or swords, horses or horsemen, or weapons of war. I, the LORD their God, will save them."

8After Gomer had stopped nursing Lo-Ruhamah, she became pregnant again and gave birth to another son. 9The LORD said, "Name him Lo-Ammi,[n] because you are not my people, and I am not your God.

GOD'S PROMISE TO ISRAEL

10"But the number of the Israelites will become like the grains of sand of the sea, which no one can measure or count. They were called, 'You are not my people,' but later they will be called 'children of the living God.' 11The people of Judah and Israel will join together again and will choose one leader for themselves. They will come up from the land, because the day of Jezreel[n] will be truly great.

2 "You are to call your brothers, 'my people,' and your sisters, 'you have been shown pity.'

GOD SPEAKS ABOUT ISRAEL

2 "Plead with your mother.[n]
  Accuse her, because she is no longer my wife,
    and I am no longer her husband.
  Tell her to stop acting like a prostitute,
    to stop behaving like an unfaithful wife.
3 If she refuses, I will strip her naked
    and leave her bare like the day she was born.
  I will make her dry like a desert,
    like a land without water,
    and I will kill her with thirst.
4 I will not take pity on her children,
    because they are the children of a prostitute.
5 Their mother has acted like a prostitute;
    the one who became pregnant with them has acted disgracefully.
  She said, 'I will chase after my lovers,[n]
    who give me my food and water,
  wool and flax, wine and olive oil.'
6 So I will block her road with thornbushes;
    I will build a wall around her
    so she cannot find her way.
7 She will run after her lovers,
    but she won't catch them.
  She will look for them,
    but she won't find them.
  Then she will say, 'I will go back to my first husband,[n]
    because life was better then for me than it is now.'
8 But she does not know that I was the one
    who gave her grain, new wine, and oil.

1:6 **Lo-Ruhamah** This name in Hebrew means "not pitied." 1:9 **Lo-Ammi** This name in Hebrew means "not my people." 1:11 **Jezreel** This name in Hebrew means "God plants." 2:2 **mother** Refers to the nation of Israel here. 2:5 **lovers** Refers to the nations surrounding Israel, who led Israel to worship false gods. 2:7 **husband** Refers to God here.

I gave her much silver and gold,
    but she used it for Baal.

9 "So I will come back and take away my
    grain at harvest time
and my new wine when it is ready.
I will take back my wool and linen
    that covered her nakedness.
10 So I will show her nakedness to her
    lovers,
and no one will save her from me.
11 I will put an end to all her celebrations:
    her yearly festivals, her New Moon
    festivals, and her Sabbaths.
I will stop all of her special feasts.
12 I will destroy her vines and fig trees,
    which she said were her pay from her
    lovers.
I will turn them into a forest,
    and wild animals will eat them.
13 I will punish her for all the times
    she burned incense to the Baals.
She put on her rings and jewelry
    and went chasing after her lovers,
but she forgot me!"
    says the LORD.

14 "So I am going to attract her;
    I will lead her into the desert
    and speak tenderly to her.
15 There I will give her back her vineyards,
    and I will make the Valley of Trouble a
    door of hope.
There she will respond as when she was
    young,
    as when she came out of Egypt."

16 The LORD says, "In the future she will call
    me 'my husband';
no longer will she call me 'my baal.'[n]
17 I will never let her say the names of Baal
    again;
people won't use their names anymore.
18 At that time I will make an agreement for
    them
with the wild animals, the birds, and
    the crawling things.
I will smash from the land
    the bow and the sword and the
    weapons of war,
so my people will live in safety.
19 And I will make you my promised bride
    forever.
I will be good and fair;

I will show you my love and mercy.
20 I will be true to you as my promised
    bride,
and you will know the LORD.

21 "At that time I will speak to you," says the
    LORD.
"I will speak to the skies,
    and they will give rain to the earth.
22 The earth will produce grain, new wine,
    and oil;
much will grow because my people are
    called Jezreel.[n]
23 I will plant my people in the land,
    and I will show pity to the one I had
    called 'not shown pity.'
I will say, 'You are my people'
    to those I had called 'not my people.'
And they will say to me, 'You are our
    God.'"

HOSEA BUYS A WIFE

3 The LORD said to me again, "Go, show your love to a woman loved by someone else, who has been unfaithful to you. In the same way the LORD loves the people of Israel, even though they worship other gods and love to eat the raisin cakes."[n]

2 So I bought her for six ounces of silver and ten bushels of barley. 3 Then I told her, "You must wait for me for many days. You must not be a prostitute, and you must not have sexual relations with any other man. I will act the same way toward you."

4 In the same way Israel will live many days without a king or leader, without sacrifices or holy stone pillars, and without the holy vest or an idol. 5 After this, the people of Israel will return to the LORD their God and follow him and the king from David's family. In the last days they will turn in fear to the LORD, and he will bless them.

THE LORD'S WORD AGAINST ISRAEL

4 People of Israel, listen to the LORD's
    message.
The LORD has this
    against you who live in the land:
"The people are not true, not loyal to God,

2:16 **baal** Another Hebrew word for husband, but it was the same word as the false god Baal. 2:22 **Jezreel** This name in Hebrew means "God plants." 3:1 **raisin cakes** This food was eaten in the feasts that honored false gods.

nor do those who live in the land even
    know him.
2 Cursing, lying, killing, stealing and
    adultery are everywhere.
  One murder follows another.
3 Because of this the land dries up,
    and all its people are dying.
  Even the wild animals and the birds of
    the air
  and the fish of the sea are dying.

GOD'S CASE AGAINST THE PRIESTS

4 "No one should accuse
    or blame another person.
  Don't blame the people, you priests,
    when they quarrel with you.
5 You will be ruined in the day,
    and your prophets will be ruined with
    you in the night.
  I will also destroy your mother.[n]
6 My people will be destroyed,
    because they have no knowledge.
  You have refused to learn,
    so I will refuse to let you be priests to
    me.
  You have forgotten the teachings of your
    God,
    so I will forget your children.
7 The more priests there are,
    the more they sin against me.
  I will take away their honor
    and give them shame.
8 Since the priests live off the sin offerings
    of the people,
  they want the people to sin more and
    more.
9 The priests are as wrong as the people,
    and I will punish them both for what
    they have done.
  I will repay them for the wrong they
    have done.
10 "They will eat
    but not have enough;
  they will have sexual relations with the
    prostitutes,
  but they will not have children,
  because they have left the LORD
    to give themselves to [n]prostitution,
to old and new wine,
  which take away their ability to
    understand.

GOD'S CASE AGAINST THE PEOPLE

12 "My people ask wooden idols for advice;
  they ask those sticks of wood to advise
    them!
  Like prostitutes, they have chased after
    other gods
  and have left their own God.
13 They make sacrifices on the tops of the
    mountains.
  They burn offerings on the hills,
  under oaks, poplars, and other trees,
    because their shade is nice.
  So your daughters become prostitutes,
    and your daughters-in-law are guilty of
    adultery.

14 "But I will not punish your daughters
    for becoming prostitutes,
  nor your daughters-in-law
    for their sins of adultery.
  I will not punish them,
    because the men have sexual relations
    with prostitutes
  and offer sacrifices with the temple
    prostitutes.
    A foolish people will be ruined.

15 "Israel, you act like a prostitute,
    but do not be guilty toward the LORD.
  Don't go to Gilgal
    or go up to Beth Aven.[n]
  Don't make promises,
    saying, 'As surely as the LORD lives . . .'
16 The people of Israel are stubborn
    like a stubborn young cow.
  Now the LORD will feed them
    like lambs in the open country.
17 The Israelites have chosen to worship
    idols,
  so leave them alone.
18 When they finish their drinking,
    they completely give themselves to
    being prostitutes;
  they love these disgraceful ways.
19 They will be swept away as if by a
    whirlwind,
  and their sacrifices will bring them only
    shame.

4:5 mother Refers to the nation of Israel here.
4:15 Gilgal . . . Beth Aven Cities in Israel where people
worshiped false gods.

GOD'S WORD AGAINST THE LEADERS

5 "Listen, you priests.
Pay attention, people of Israel.
Listen, royal family,
because you will all be judged.
You have been like a trap at Mizpah
and like a net spread out at Mount
Tabor.
2 You have done many evil things,
so I will punish you all.
3 I know all about the people of Israel;
what they have done is not hidden from
me.
Now that Israel acts like a prostitute,
it has made itself unclean.

4 "They will not give up their deeds
and return to their God.
They are determined to be unfaithful to
me;
they do not know the LORD.
5 Israel's pride testifies against them.
The people of Israel will stumble
because of their sin,
and the people of Judah will stumble
with them.
6 They will come to worship the LORD,
bringing their flocks and herds,
but they will not be able to find him,
because he has left them.
7 They have not been true to the LORD;
they are children who do not belong to
him.
So their false worship
will destroy them and their land.

8 "Blow the horn in Gibeah
and the trumpet in Ramah.
Give the warning at Beth Aven,
and be first into battle, people of
Benjamin.
9 Israel will be ruined
on the day of punishment.
To the tribes of Israel
I tell the truth.
10 The leaders of Judah are like those
who steal other people's land.
I will pour my punishment over them
like a flood of water.
11 Israel is crushed by the punishment,
because it decided to follow idols.
12 I am like a moth to Israel,
like a rot to the people of Judah.

13 "When Israel saw its illness
and Judah saw its wounds,
Israel went to Assyria for help
and sent to the great king of Assyria.
But he cannot heal you
or cure your wounds.
14 I will be like a lion to Israel,
like a young lion to Judah.
I will attack them
and tear them to pieces.
I will drag them off,
and no one will be able to save them.
15 Then I will go back to my place
until they suffer for their guilt and turn
back to me.
In their trouble they will look for me."

THE PEOPLE ARE NOT FAITHFUL

6 "Come, let's go back to the LORD.
He has hurt us, but he will heal us.
He has wounded us, but he will
bandage our wounds.
2 In two days he will put new life in us;
on the third day he will raise us up
so that we may live in his presence 3and
know him.
Let's try to learn about the LORD;
he will come to us as surely as the dawn
comes.
He will come to us like rain,
like the spring rain that waters the
ground."

4 The LORD says, "Israel, what should I do
with you?
Judah, what should I do with you?
Your faithfulness is like a morning mist,
like the dew that goes away early in the
day.
5 I have warned you by my prophets
that I will kill you and destroy you.
My justice comes out like bright
light.
6 I want faithful love
more than I want animal sacrifices.
I want people to know me
more than I want burnt offerings.
7 But they have broken the agreement as
Adam did;
they have been unfaithful to me.
8 Gilead is a city of people who do evil;
their footprints are bloody.
9 The priests are like robbers waiting to
attack people;

they murder people on the road to
  Shechem[n]
  and do wicked things.
[10] I have seen horrible things in Israel.
  Look at Israel's prostitution;
  Israel has become unclean.

[11] "Judah, I have set a harvest time for you
  when I will make the lives of my people
  good again.

7 When I heal Israel,
  Israel's sin will go away,
  and so will Samaria's evil.

"They cheat a lot!
  Thieves break into houses,
  and robbers are in the streets.
[2] It never enters their minds
  that I remember all their evil deeds.
  The bad things they do are all around
  them;
  they are right in front of me.

ISRAEL'S EVIL KINGS

[3] "They make the king happy with their
  wickedness;
  their rulers are glad with their lies.
[4] But all of them are traitors.
  They are like an oven heated by a
  baker.
  While he mixes the dough,
  he does not need to stir up the fire.
[5] The kings get so drunk they get sick every
  day.
  The rulers become crazy with wine;
  they make agreements with those who
  do not know the true God.
[6] They burn like an oven;
  their hearts burn inside them.
  All night long their anger is low,
  but when morning comes, it becomes a
  roaring fire.
[7] All these people are as hot as an oven;
  they burn up their rulers.
  All their kings fall,
  and no one calls on me.

ISRAEL AND THE OTHER NATIONS

[8] "Israel mixes with other nations;
  he is like a pancake cooked only on one
  side.
[9] Foreign nations have eaten up his
  strength,
  but he doesn't know it.
  Israel is weak and feeble, like an old man,

but he doesn't know it.
[10] Israel's pride will cause their defeat;
  they will not turn back to the LORD
  their God
  or look to him for help in all this.
[11] Israel has become like a pigeon—
  easy to fool and stupid.
  First they call to Egypt for help.
  Then they run to Assyria.
[12] When they go, I will catch them in a net,
  I will bring them down like birds from
  the sky;
  I will punish them countless times for
  their evil.
[13] How terrible for them because they left
  me!
  They will be destroyed, because they
  turned against me.
  I want to save them,
  but they have spoken lies against me.
[14] They do not call to me from their hearts.
  They just lie on their beds and cry.
  They come together to ask for grain and
  new wine,
  but they really turn away from me.
[15] Though I trained them and gave them
  strength,
  they have made evil plans against me.
[16] They did not turn to the Most High God.
  They are like a loose bow that can't
  shoot.
  Because their leaders brag about their
  strength,
  they will be killed with swords,
  and the people in Egypt
  will laugh at them.

ISRAEL HAS TRUSTED WRONG THINGS

8 "Put the trumpet to your lips and give
  the warning!
  The enemy swoops down on the LORD's
  people like an eagle.
  The Israelites have broken my agreement
  and have turned against my teachings.
[2] They cry out to me,
  'Our God, we in Israel know you!'
[3] But Israel has rejected what is good,
  so the enemy will chase them.
[4] They chose their own kings
  without asking my permission.

6:9 Shechem A city of safety where people could go for
protection.

They chose their own leaders,
people I did not know.
They made their silver and gold into idols,
and for all this they will be destroyed.
5 I hate the calf-shaped idol of Israel!
I am very angry with the people.
How long will they remain unclean?
6 The idol is something a craftsman made;
it is not God.
Israel's calf-shaped idol
will surely be smashed to pieces.

7 "Israel's foolish plans are like planting the
wind,
but they will harvest a storm.
Like a stalk with no head of grain,
it produces nothing.
Even if it produced something,
other nations would eat it.
8 Israel is eaten up;
the people are mixed among the other
nations
and have become useless to me.
9 Israel is like a wild donkey all by itself.
They have run to Assyria;
They have hired other nations to
protect them.
10 Although Israel is mixed among the
nations,
I will gather them together.
They will become weaker and weaker
as they suffer under the great king of
Assyria.

11 "Although Israel built more altars to
remove sin,
they have become altars for sinning.
12 I have written many teachings for them,
but they think the teachings are strange
and foreign.
13 The Israelites offer sacrifices to me as
gifts
and eat the meat,
but the Lord is not pleased with them.
He remembers the evil they have done,
and he will punish them for their sins.
They will be slaves again as they were
in Egypt.
14 Israel has forgotten their Maker and has
built palaces;
Judah has built many strong, walled
cities.
But I will send fire on their cities
and destroy their strong buildings."

ISRAEL'S PUNISHMENT

9 Israel, do not rejoice;
don't shout for joy as the other
nations do.
You have been like a prostitute against
your God.
You love the pay of prostitutes on every
threshing floor.
2 But the threshing floor and the winepress
will not feed the people,
and there won't be enough new wine.
3 The people will not stay in the Lord's land.
Israel will return to being captives as
they were in Egypt,
and in Assyria they will eat food that
they are not allowed to eat.
4 The Israelites will not give offerings of
wine to the Lord;
they will not give him sacrifices.
Their sacrifices will be like food that is
eaten at a funeral;
it is unclean, and everyone who eats it
becomes unclean.
Their food will only satisfy their hunger;
they cannot sacrifice it in the Temple.
5 What will you do then on the day of feasts
and on the day of the Lord's festival?
6 Even if the people are not destroyed,
Egypt will capture them;
Memphis[n] will bury them.
Weeds will grow over their silver
treasures,
and thorns will drive them out of their
tents.
7 The time of punishment has come,
the time to pay for sins.
Let Israel know this:
You think the prophet is a fool,
and you say the spiritual person is crazy.
You have sinned very much,
and your hatred is great.
8 Is Israel a watchman?
Are God's people prophets?
Everywhere Israel goes, traps are set for
him.
He is an enemy in God's house.
9 The people of Israel have gone deep into
sin
as the people of Gibeah[n] did.

9:6 Memphis A city in Egypt famous for its tombs.
9:9 Gibeah The sins of the people of Gibeah caused a
civil war. See Judges 19–21.

The Lord will remember the evil things
  they have done,
  and he will punish their sins.

10 "When I found Israel,
  it was like finding grapes in the desert.
Your ancestors were like
  finding the first figs on the fig tree.
But when they came to Baal Peor,
  they began worshiping an idol,
  and they became as hateful as the thing
  they worshiped.

11 Israel's glory will fly away like a bird;
  there will be no more pregnancy,
  no more births, no more getting
  pregnant.

12 But even if the Israelites bring up
  children,
  I will take them all away.
How terrible it will be for them
  when I go away from them!

13 I have seen Israel, like Tyre,
  given a pleasant place.
But the people of Israel will soon bring
  out
  their children to be killed."

14 LORD, give them what they should have.
  What will you give them?
  Make their women unable to have
  children;
  give them dried-up breasts that cannot
  feed their babies.

15 "The Israelites were very wicked in
  Gilgal,
  so I have hated them there.
Because of the sinful things they have
  done,
  I will force them to leave my land.
I will no longer love them;
  their leaders have turned against me.

16 Israel is beaten down;
  its root is dying, and it has no fruit.
If they have more children,
  I will kill the children they love."

17 God will reject them,
  because they have not obeyed him;
  they will wander among the nations.

ISRAEL WILL PAY FOR SIN

10 Israel is like a large vine
  that produced plenty of fruit.
As the people became richer,
  they built more altars for idols.

As their land became better,
  they put up better stone pillars to honor
  gods.

2 Their heart was false,
  and now they must pay for their guilt.
The LORD will break down their altars;
  he will destroy their holy stone pillars.

3 Then they will say, "We have no king,
  because we didn't honor the LORD.
As for the king,
  he couldn't do anything for us."

4 They make many false promises
  and agreements which they don't keep.
So people sue each other in court;
  they are like poisonous weeds growing
  in a plowed field.

5 The people from Israel are worried about
  the calf-shaped idol at Beth Aven.
The people will cry about it,
  and the priests will cry about it.
They used to shout for joy about its
  glory,

6 but it will be carried off to Assyria
  as a gift to the great king.
Israel will be disgraced,
  and the people will be ashamed for not
  obeying.

7 Israel will be destroyed;
  its king will be like a chip of wood
  floating on the water.

8 The places of false worship will be
  destroyed,
  the places where Israel sins.
Thorns and weeds will grow up
  and cover their altars.
Then they will say to the mountains,
  "Cover us!"
  and to the hills, "Fall on us!"

9 "Israel, you have sinned since the time of
  Gibeah,[n]
  and the people there have continued
  sinning.
But war will surely overwhelm them in
  Gibeah,
  because of the evil they have done
  there.

10 When I am ready,
  I will come to punish them.
Nations will come together against them,

10:9 **Gibeah** The sins of the people of Gibeah caused a
civil war. See Judges 19–21.

and they will be punished for their
double sins.

[11] Israel is like a well-trained young cow
that likes to thresh grain.
I will put a yoke on her neck
and make her work hard in the field.
Israel will plow,
and Judah will break up the ground.

[12] I said, 'Plant goodness,
harvest the fruit of loyalty,
plow the new ground of knowledge.
Look for the LORD until he comes
and pours goodness on you like water.'

[13] But you have plowed evil
and harvested trouble;
you have eaten the fruit of your lies.
Because you have trusted in your own
power
and your many soldiers,

[14] your people will hear the noise of battle,
and all your strong, walled cities will be
destroyed.
It will be like the time King Shalman
destroyed Beth Arbel in battle,
when mothers and their children were
bashed to death.

[15] The same will happen to you, people of
Bethel,
because you did so much evil.
When the sun comes up,
the king of Israel will die.

GOD'S LOVE FOR ISRAEL

11 "When Israel was a child, I loved him,
and I called my son out of Egypt.

[2] But when I called the people of Israel,
they went away from me.
They offered sacrifices to the Baals
and burned incense to the idols.

[3] It was I who taught Israel to walk,
and I took them by the arms,
but they did not understand
that I had healed them.

[4] I led them with cords of human kindness,
with ropes of love.
I lifted the yoke from their neck
and bent down and fed them.

[5] "The Israelites will become captives
again, as they were in Egypt,
and Assyria will become their king,
because they refuse to turn back to God.

[6] War will sweep through their cities
and will destroy them

and kill them because of their wicked
plans.

[7] My people have made up their minds
to turn away from me.
The prophets call them to turn to me,
but none of them honors me at all.

[8] "Israel, how can I give you up?
How can I give you away, Israel?
I don't want to make you like Admah
or treat you like Zeboiim.[n]
My heart beats for you,
and my love for you stirs up my pity.

[9] I won't punish you in my anger,
and I won't destroy Israel again.
I am God and not a human;
I am the Holy One, and I am among
you.
I will not come against you in anger.

[10] They will go after the LORD,
and he will roar like a lion.
When he roars,
his children will hurry to him from the
west.

[11] They will come swiftly
like birds from Egypt
and like doves from Assyria.
I will settle them again in their homes,"
says the LORD.

THE LORD IS AGAINST ISRAEL

[12] Israel has surrounded me with lies;
the people have made evil plans.
And Judah turns against God,
the faithful Holy One.

12 What Israel does is as useless as
chasing the wind;
he chases the east wind all day.
They tell more and more lies
and do more and more violence.
They make agreements with Assyria,
and they send a gift of olive oil to
Egypt.

[2] The LORD also has some things against
Judah.
He will punish Israel for what they
have done;
he will give them what they deserve.

[3] Their ancestor Jacob held on to his
brother's heel
while the two of them were being born.

11:8 Admah . . . Zeboiim Two other cities destroyed
when God destroyed Sodom and Gomorrah.

When he grew to be a man,
he wrestled with God.
4 When Jacob wrestled with the angel and
won,
he cried and asked for his blessing.
Later, God met with him at Bethel
and spoke with him there.
5 It was the LORD God All-Powerful;
the LORD is his great name.
6 You must return to your God;
love him, do what is just,
and always trust in him as your God.

7 The merchants use dishonest scales;
they like to cheat people.
8 Israel said, "I am rich! I am someone with
power!"
All their money will do them no good
because of the sins they have done.

9 "But I am the LORD your God,
who brought you out of Egypt.
I will make you live in tents again
as you used to do on worship days.
10 I spoke to the prophets
and gave them many visions;
through them, I taught my lessons to
you."

11 The people of Gilead are evil,
worth nothing.
Though people sacrifice bulls at Gilgal,
their altars will become like piles of
stone
in a plowed field.
12 Your ancestor Jacob fled to Northwest
Mesopotamia
where he worked to get a wife;
he tended sheep to pay for her.
13 Later the LORD used a prophet
to bring Jacob's descendants out of
Egypt;
he used a prophet
to take care of the Israelites.
14 But the Israelites made the Lord angry
when they killed other people,
and they deserve to die for their crimes.
The Lord will make them pay
for the disgraceful things they have
done.

THE FINAL WORD AGAINST ISRAEL

13 People used to fear the tribe of
Ephraim;
they were important people in Israel.

But they sinned by worshiping Baal,
so they must die.
2 But they still keep on sinning more and
more.
They make idols of their silver,
idols that are cleverly made,
the work of a craftsman.
Yet the people of Israel say to each other,
"Kiss those calf idols and sacrifice to
them."
3 So those people will be like the morning
mist;
they will disappear like the morning
dew.
They will be like chaff blown from the
threshing floor,
like smoke going out a window.

4 "I, the LORD, have been your God
since you were in the land of Egypt.
You should have known no other God
except me.
I am the only one who saves.
5 I cared for them in the desert
where it was hot and dry.
6 I gave them food, and they became full
and satisfied.
But then they became too proud and
forgot me.
7 That is why I will be like a lion to them,
like a leopard waiting by the road.
8 I will attack like a bear robbed of her cubs,
ripping their bodies open.
I will devour them like a lion
and tear them apart like a wild animal.

9 "Israel, I will destroy you.
Who will be your helper then?
10 What good is your king?
Can he save you in any of your towns?
What good are your leaders?
You said, 'Give us a king and leaders.'
11 So I gave you a king, but only in anger,
and I took him away in my great anger.
12 The sins of Israel are on record,
stored away, waiting for punishment.
13 The pain of birth will come for him,
but he is like a foolish baby
who won't come out of its mother's
womb.
14 Will I save them from the place of the
dead?
Will I rescue them from death?
Where is your sickness, death?

941

Where is your pain, place of death?
I will show them no mercy.

15 Israel is doing well among the nations,
but the LORD will send a wind from the
east,
coming from the desert,
that will dry up his springs and wells of
water.
He will destroy from their treasure houses
everything of value.

16 The nation of Israel will be ruined,
because it fought against God.
The people of Israel will die in war;
their children will be torn to pieces,
and their pregnant women will be
ripped open."

ISRAEL RETURNS TO GOD

14 Israel, return to the LORD your God,
because your sins have made you
fall.

2 Come back to the LORD
and say these words to him:
"Take away all our sin
and kindly receive us,
and we will keep the promises we made
to you.

3 Assyria cannot save us,
nor will we trust in our horses.
We will not say again, 'Our gods,'
to the things our hands have made.
You show mercy to orphans."

4 The LORD says,
"I will forgive them for leaving me
and will love them freely,
because I am not angry with them
anymore.

5 I will be like the dew to Israel,
and they will blossom like a lily.
Like the cedar trees in Lebanon,
their roots will be firm.

6 They will be like spreading branches,
like the beautiful olive trees
and the sweet-smelling cedars in
Lebanon.

7 The people of Israel will again live under
my protection.
They will grow like the grain,
they will bloom like a vine,
and they will be as famous as the wine
of Lebanon.

8 Israel, have nothing to do with idols.
I, the LORD, am the one who answers
your prayers and watches over you.
I am like a green pine tree;
your blessings come from me."

9 A wise person will know these things,
and an understanding person will take
them to heart.
The LORD's ways are right.
Good people live by following them,
but those who turn against God die
because of them.

LOCUSTS DESTROY THE CROPS

1 The LORD spoke his word to Joel son of Pethuel:

2 Elders, listen to this message.
> Listen to me, all you who live in the
> land.
> Nothing like this has ever happened
> during your lifetime
> or during your ancestors' lifetimes.

3 Tell your children about these things,
> let your children tell their children,
> and let your grandchildren tell their
> children.

4 What the cutting locusts have left,
> the swarming locusts have eaten;
> what the swarming locusts have left,
> the hopping locusts have eaten,
> and what the hopping locusts have left,
> the destroying locusts[n] have eaten.

5 Drunks, wake up and cry!
> All you people who drink wine, cry!
> Cry because your wine
> has been taken away from your mouths.

6 A powerful nation has come into my land
> with too many soldiers to count.
> It has teeth like a lion,
> jaws like a female lion.

7 It has made my grapevine a waste
> and made my fig tree a stump.
> It has stripped all the bark off my trees
> and left the branches white.

8 Cry as a young woman cries
> when the man she was going to marry
> has died.

9 There will be no more grain or drink
> offerings
> to offer in the Temple of the LORD.
> Because of this, the priests,
> the servants of the LORD, are sad.

10 The fields are ruined;
> the ground is dried up.
> The grain is destroyed,
> the new wine is dried up,
> and the olive oil runs out.

11 Be sad, farmers.
> Cry loudly, you who grow grapes.

> Cry for the wheat and the barley.
> Cry because the harvest of the field is
> lost.

12 The vines have become dry,
> and the fig trees are dried up.
> The pomegranate trees, the date palm
> trees, the apple trees—
> all the trees in the field have died.
> And the happiness of the people has died,
> too.

13 Priests, put on your rough cloth and cry to
> show your sadness.
> Servants of the altar, cry out loud.
> Servants of my God,
> keep your rough cloth on all night to
> show your sadness.
> Cry because there will be no more grain
> or drink offerings
> to offer in the Temple of your God.

14 Call for a day when everyone fasts!
> Tell everyone to stop work!
> Bring the elders
> and everyone who lives in the land
> to the Temple of the LORD your God,
> and cry out to the LORD.

15 What a terrible day it will be!
> The LORD's day of judging is near,
> when punishment will come
> like a destroying attack from the
> Almighty.

16 Our food is taken away
> while we watch.
> Joy and happiness are gone
> from the Temple of our God.

17 Though we planted fig seeds,
> they lie dry and dead in the dirt.
> The barns are empty and falling down.
> The storerooms for grain have been
> broken down,
> because the grain has dried up.

18 The animals are groaning!

1:4 cutting . . . locusts These are different names for an insect like a large grasshopper. The locust can quickly destroy trees, plants, and crops, and in this destruction, Joel sees a warning. God will cause this type of destruction when he punishes his people.

The herds of cattle wander around
confused,
because they have no grass to eat;
even the flocks of sheep suffer.
¹⁹ Lᴏʀᴅ, I am calling to you for help,
because fire has burned up the open
pastures,
and flames have burned all the trees in
the field.
²⁰ Wild animals also need your help.
The streams of water have dried up,
and fire has burned up the open
pastures.

THE COMING DAY OF JUDGMENT

2 Blow the trumpet in Jerusalem;
shout a warning on my holy mountain.
Let all the people who live in the land
shake with fear,
because the Lᴏʀᴅ's day of judging is
coming;
it is near.
² It will be a dark, gloomy day,
cloudy and black.
Like the light at sunrise,
a great and powerful army will spread
over the mountains.
There has never been anything like it
before,
and there will never be anything like it
again.
³ In front of them a fire destroys;
in back of them a flame burns.
The land in front of them is like the
garden of Eden;
the land behind them is like an empty
desert.
Nothing will escape from them.
⁴ They look like horses,
and they run like war horses.
⁵ It is like the noise of chariots
rumbling over the tops of the
mountains,
like the noise of a roaring fire
burning dry stalks.
They are like a powerful army lined up for
battle.
⁶ When they see them, nations shake with
fear,
and everyone's face becomes pale.
⁷ They charge like soldiers;
they climb over the wall like warriors.

They all march straight ahead
and do not move off their path.
⁸ They do not run into each other,
because each walks in line.
They break through all efforts to stop
them
and keep coming.
⁹ They run into the city.
They run at the wall
and climb into the houses,
entering through windows like thieves.
¹⁰ Before them, earth and sky shake.
The sun and the moon become dark,
and the stars stop shining.
¹¹ The Lᴏʀᴅ shouts out orders
to his army.
His army is very large!
Those who obey him are very strong!
The Lᴏʀᴅ's day of judging
is an overwhelming and terrible day.
No one can stand up against it!

CHANGE YOUR HEARTS

¹² The Lᴏʀᴅ says, "Even now, come back to
me with all your heart.
Fast, cry, and be sad."

¹³ Tearing your clothes is not enough to
show you are sad;
let your heart be broken.
Come back to the Lᴏʀᴅ your God,
because he is kind and shows mercy.
He doesn't become angry quickly,
and he has great love.
He can change his mind about doing
harm.
¹⁴ Who knows? Maybe he will turn back to
you
and leave behind a blessing for you.
Grain and drink offerings belong to the
Lᴏʀᴅ your God.

¹⁵ Blow the trumpet in Jerusalem;
call for a day when everyone fasts.
Tell everyone to stop work.
¹⁶ Bring the people together
and make the meeting holy for the
Lᴏʀᴅ.
Bring together the elders,
as well as the children,
and even babies that still feed at their
mothers' breasts.
The bridegroom should come from his
room,

the bride from her bedroom.

17 The priests, the LORD's servants, should cry

between the altar and the entrance to the Temple.

They should say, "LORD, have mercy on your people.

Don't let them be put to shame;
don't let other nations make fun of them.

Don't let people in other nations ask,
'Where is their God?'"

THE LORD RESTORES THE LAND

18 Then the LORD became concerned about his land
and felt sorry for his people.

19 He said to them:

"I will send you grain, new wine, and olive oil,
so that you will have plenty.

No more will I shame you
among the nations.

20 I will force the army from the north to leave your land
and go into a dry, empty land.

Their soldiers in front will be forced into the Dead Sea,
and those in the rear into the Mediterranean Sea.

Their bodies will rot and stink.
The LORD has surely done a wonderful thing!"

21 Land, don't be afraid;
be happy and full of joy,
because the LORD has done a wonderful thing.

22 Wild animals, don't be afraid,
because the open pastures have grown grass.

The trees have given fruit;
the fig trees and the grapevines have grown much fruit.

23 So be happy, people of Jerusalem;
be joyful in the LORD your God.

Because he does what is right,
he has brought you rain;
he has sent the fall rain
and the spring rain for you, as before.

24 And the threshing floors will be full of grain;
the barrels will overflow with new wine and olive oil.

THE LORD SPEAKS

25 "Though I sent my great army against you—
those swarming locusts and hopping locusts,
the destroying locusts and the cutting locusts[n] that ate your crops—

I will pay you back
for those years of trouble.

26 Then you will have plenty to eat
and be full.

You will praise the name of the LORD your God,
who has done miracles for you.

My people will never again be shamed.

27 Then you will know that I am among the people of Israel,
that I am the LORD your God,
and there is no other God.

My people will never be shamed again.

28 "After this,
I will pour out my Spirit on all kinds of people.

Your sons and daughters will prophesy,
your old men will dream dreams,
and your young men will see visions.

29 At that time I will pour out my Spirit
also on male slaves and female slaves.

30 I will show miracles
in the sky and on the earth:
blood, fire, and thick smoke.

31 The sun will become dark,
the moon red as blood,
before the overwhelming and terrible day of the LORD comes.

32 Then anyone who calls on the LORD
will be saved,
because on Mount Zion and in Jerusalem
there will be people who will be saved,
just as the LORD has said.

Those left alive after the day of punishment
are the people whom the LORD called.

PUNISHMENT FOR JUDAH'S ENEMIES

3 "In those days and at that time,
when I will make things better for Judah and Jerusalem,

2:25 swarming . . . locusts These are different names for an insect like a large grasshopper. The locust can quickly destroy trees, plants, and crops, and in this destruction, Joel sees a warning. God will cause this type of destruction when he punishes his people.

² I will gather all the nations together
    and bring them down into the Valley
      Where the Lord Judges.
    There I will judge them,
  because those nations scattered my own
      people Israel
  and forced them to live in other nations.
  They divided up my land
³ and threw lots for my people.
  They traded boys for prostitutes,
    and they sold girls to buy wine to drink.
⁴"Tyre and Sidon and all of you regions of Philistia! What did you have against me? Were you punishing me for something I did, or were you doing something to hurt me? I will very quickly do to you what you have done to me. ⁵You took my silver and gold, and you put my precious treasures in your temples. ⁶You sold the people of Judah and Jerusalem to the Greeks so that you could send them far from their land.

⁷"You sent my people to that faraway place, but I will get them and bring them back, and I will do to you what you have done to them. ⁸I will sell your sons and daughters to the people of Judah, and they will sell them to the Sabean people far away." The Lord said this.

GOD JUDGES THE NATIONS
⁹ Announce this among the nations:
    Prepare for war!
  Wake up the soldiers!
    Let all the men of war come near and
      attack.
¹⁰ Make swords from your plows,
    and make spears from your hooks for
      trimming trees.
  Let even the weak person say,
  "I am a soldier."
¹¹ All of you nations, hurry,
    and come together in that place.
  Lord, send your soldiers
    to gather the nations.

¹² "Wake up, nations,
    and come to attack in the Valley Where
      the Lord Judges.
  There I will sit to judge
    all the nations on every side.
¹³ Swing the cutting tool,
    because the harvest is ripe.
  Come, walk on them as you would walk
    on grapes to get their juice,

  because the winepress is full
    and the barrels are spilling over,
  because these people are so evil!"

¹⁴ There are huge numbers of people
    in the Valley of Decision,ⁿ
  because the Lord's day of judging is
    near
  in the Valley of Decision.
¹⁵ The sun and the moon will become dark,
    and the stars will stop shining.
¹⁶ The Lord will roar like a lion from
    Jerusalem;
  his loud voice will thunder from that
    city,
  and the sky and the earth will shake.
  But the Lord will be a safe place for his
    people,
  a strong place of safety for the people
    of Israel.

¹⁷ "Then you will know that I, the Lord
    your God,
  live on my holy Mount Zion.
  Jerusalem will be a holy place,
    and strangers will never even go
      through it again.

A NEW LIFE PROMISED FOR JUDAH
¹⁸ "On that day wine will drip from the
    mountains,
  milk will flow from the hills,
  and water will run through all the
    ravines of Judah.
  A fountain will flow from the Temple of
    the Lord
  and give water to the valley of acacia
    trees.
¹⁹ But Egypt will become empty,
    and Edom an empty desert,
  because they were cruel to the people of
    Judah.
  They killed innocent people in that
    land.
²⁰ But there will always be people living in
    Judah,
  and people will live in Jerusalem from
    now on.
²¹ Egypt and Edom killed my people,
    so I will definitely punish them."

The Lord lives in Jerusalem!

3:14 Valley of Decision This is like the name "Valley Where the Lord Judges" in 3:2 and 3:12.

1 These are the words of Amos, one of the shepherds from the town of Tekoa. He saw this vision about Israel two years before the earthquake. It was at the time Uzziah was king of Judah and Jeroboam son of Jehoash was king of Israel.

[2]Amos said,

"The LORD will roar from Jerusalem;
  he will send his voice from Jerusalem.
The pastures of the shepherds will
    become dry,
  and even the top of Mount Carmel will
    dry up."

ISRAEL'S NEIGHBORS ARE PUNISHED

THE PEOPLE OF ARAM

[3]This is what the LORD says:
"For the many crimes of Damascus,
  I will punish them.
They drove over the people of Gilead
  with threshing boards that had iron
    teeth.
[4] So I will send fire upon the house of
    Hazael
  that will destroy the strong towers of
    Ben-Hadad.
[5] I will break down the bar of the gate to
    Damascus
  and destroy the king who is in the
    Valley of Aven,
as well as the leader of Beth Eden.
  The people of Aram will be taken
    captive to the country of Kir," says the
LORD.

THE PEOPLE OF PHILISTIA

[6]This is what the LORD says:
"For the many crimes of Gaza,
  I will punish them.
They sold all the people of one area
  as slaves to Edom.
[7] So I will send a fire on the walls of Gaza
  that will destroy the city's strong
    buildings.
[8] I will destroy the king of the city of
    Ashdod,

as well as the leader of Ashkelon.
Then I will turn against the people of the
    city of Ekron,
  and the last of the Philistines will die,"
  says the Lord GOD.

THE PEOPLE OF PHOENICIA

[9]This is what the LORD says:
"For the many crimes of Tyre,
  I will punish them.
They sold all the people of one area
  as slaves to Edom,
  and they forgot the agreement among
    relatives they had made with Israel.
[10] So I will send fire on the walls of Tyre
  that will destroy the city's strong
    buildings."

THE PEOPLE OF EDOM

[11]This is what the LORD says:
"For the many crimes of Edom,
  I will punish them.
They hunted down their relatives, the
    Israelites, with the sword,
  showing them no mercy.
They were angry all the time
  and kept on being very angry.
[12] So I will send fire on the city of Teman
  that will even destroy the strong
    buildings of Bozrah."[n]

THE PEOPLE OF AMMON

[13]This is what the LORD says:
"For the many crimes of Ammon,
  I will punish them.
They ripped open the pregnant women in
    Gilead
  so they could take over that land
  and make their own country larger.
[14] So I will send fire on the city wall of
    Rabbah
  that will destroy its strong buildings.
It will come during a day of battle,

1:12 Teman . . . Bozrah Since Teman was in northern Edom and Bozrah was in southern Edom, this means the whole country will be destroyed.

during a stormy day with strong winds.
¹⁵ Then their king and leaders will be taken
captive;
they will all be taken away together,"
says the LORD.

THE PEOPLE OF MOAB

2 This is what the LORD says:
"For the many crimes of Moab,
I will punish them.
They burned the bones of the king of
Edom into lime.
² So I will send fire on Moab
that will destroy the strong buildings of
the city of Kerioth.
The people of Moab will die in a great
noise,
in the middle of the sounds of war and
trumpets.
³ So I will bring an end to the king of Moab,
and I will kill all its leaders with him,"
says the LORD.

THE PEOPLE OF JUDAH

⁴This is what the LORD says:
"For the many crimes of Judah,
I will punish them.
They rejected the teachings of the LORD
and did not keep his commands;
they followed the same gods
as their ancestors had followed.
⁵ So I will send fire on Judah,
and it will destroy the strong buildings
of Jerusalem."

ISRAEL IS PUNISHED

⁶This is what the LORD says:
"For the many crimes of Israel,
I will punish them.
For silver, they sell people who have done
nothing wrong;
they sell the poor to buy a pair of
sandals.
⁷ They walk on poor people as if they were
dirt,
and they refuse to be fair to those who
are suffering.
Fathers and sons have sexual relations
with the same woman,
and so they ruin my holy name.
⁸ As they worship at their altars,
they lie down on clothes taken from the
poor.
They fine people,

and with that money they buy wine to
drink in the house of their god.

⁹ "But it was I who destroyed the Amorites
before them,
who were tall like cedar trees and as
strong as oaks—
I destroyed them completely.
¹⁰ It was I who brought you from the land of
Egypt
and led you for forty years through the
desert
so I could give you the land of the
Amorites.
¹¹ I made some of your children to be
prophets
and some of your young people to be
Nazirites.
People of Israel, isn't this true?" says the
LORD.
¹² "But you made the Nazirites drink wine
and told the prophets not to prophesy.
¹³ Now I will make you get stuck,
as a wagon loaded with grain gets stuck.
¹⁴ No one will escape, not even the fastest
runner.
Strong people will not be strong
enough;
warriors will not be able to save
themselves.
¹⁵ Soldiers with bows and arrows will not
stand and fight,
and even fast runners will not get away;
soldiers on horses will not escape alive.
¹⁶ At that time even the bravest warriors
will run away without their armor," says
the LORD.

WARNING TO ISRAEL

3 Listen to this word that the LORD has spoken against you, people of Israel, against
the whole family he brought out of Egypt.
² "I have chosen only you
out of all the families of the earth,
so I will punish you
for all your sins."

³ Two people will not walk together
unless they have agreed to do so.
⁴ A lion in the forest does not roar
unless it has caught an animal;
it does not growl in its den
when it has caught nothing.
⁵ A bird will not fall into a trap

The **Extra Mile**
Marriage

By Drs. Les and Leslie Parrott

FAMILY

AMOS 3:3

"It is easier in these United States to walk away from a marriage than from a commitment to purchase a used car," said an attorney at a conference we attended. "Most contracts cannot be unilaterally terminated. A marriage commitment, however, can be broken by practically anyone at any time, and without cause."

He is right. A friend of ours went to traffic court where he heard two divorce decrees from the judge before his turn came to be heard. He dropped by our office later to tell us about his experience. He said, "I told my wife when I got home that we could have had a divorce any number of times if those reasons I heard in court were good enough for a legal separation."

The "till death do us part" of marriage, however, is not an ideal. It is a reality that is insured by an unswerving commitment—a willful agreement to keep love alive. "Two people will not walk together unless they have agreed to do so," said the prophet Amos (Amos 3:3). Commitment is the cerebral part of love. It is the part that comes more from our mind than from our heart.

But that kind of commitment doesn't come naturally. As a matter of fact, it was exactly what Jesus was talking about when he shocked the crowds with this statement: "If someone forces you to go with him one mile, go with him two miles" (Matthew 5:41). This simple principle holds enough power to revolutionize your marriage.

Every husband and every wife knows how to walk the first mile. After all, our relationships couldn't exist without it. The first mile is what we know we have to do. So, what's the second mile?

At the time Jesus made this statement, the Roman army had a pesky practice of forcing men and boys who were nearby to carry their soldiers' packs. Being more civilized than other armies, the Romans limited the task to one mile. And every boy under Roman rule knew exactly how far that was. In fact, as a marker, most boys drove a stake into the ground precisely one mile from their house. This way, when a soldier required the task, the boy would walk exactly a mile down the road to the stake, set the pack on the other side and be done with it. That was all he was required, and nobody expected more.

Jesus used this illustration to point out that we sometimes do the same thing in our relationships. We measure out exactly how much is expected and do just that, nothing more. Jesus, however, said there is a better way—to do more than the minimum.

Why do so many marriage commitments fall flat these days? Because they are commitments to do only the "bare minimum." Imagine what would happen if you *and* your spouse made a commitment to walk the extra mile—*together*. At the very minimum, it would deprive the divorce courts of another set of victims. Most likely, it would turn responsibility into opportunity. So why not start today?

TO LEARN MORE ON WHAT THE BIBLE HAS TO SAY ABOUT **FAMILY,** READ THE SCRIPTURES AND DEVOTIONALS AT **NUMBERS 26:58, RUTH 1:16, 2 SAMUEL 12:7–15, 1 CHRONICLES 29:11–12, JOB 12:12,** AND **PSALM 37:24.**

where there is no bait;
the trap will not spring shut
if there is nothing to catch.
6 When a trumpet blows a warning in a city,
the people tremble.
When trouble comes to a city,
the Lord has caused it.
7 Before the Lord God does anything,
he tells his plans to his servants the
prophets.
8 The lion has roared!
Who wouldn't be afraid?
The Lord God has spoken.
Who will not prophesy?

9 Announce this to the strong buildings of
Ashdod
and to the strong buildings of Egypt:
"Come to the mountains of Samaria,
where you will see great confusion
and people hurting others."
10 "The people don't know how to do what
is right," says the Lord.
"Their strong buildings are filled with
treasures they took by force from
others."
11So this is what the Lord God says:
"An enemy will take over the land
and pull down your strongholds;
he will take the treasures out of your
strong buildings."
12This is what the Lord says:
"A shepherd might save from a lion's
mouth
only two leg bones or a scrap of an ear
of his sheep.
In the same way only a few Israelites in
Samaria will be saved—
people who now sit on their beds
and on their couches."
13"Listen and be witnesses against the
family of Jacob," says the Lord God, the God
All-Powerful.
14 "When I punish Israel for their sins,
I will also destroy the altars at Bethel.
The corners of the altar will be cut off,
and they will fall to the ground.
15 I will tear down the winter house,
together with the summer house.
The houses decorated with ivory will be
destroyed,
and the great houses will come to an
end," says the Lord.

ISRAEL WILL NOT RETURN

4 Listen to this message, you cows of
Bashan[n] on the Mountain of Samaria.
You take things from the poor
and crush people who are in need.
Then you command your husbands,
"Bring us something to drink!"
2 The Lord God has promised this:
"Just as surely as I am a holy God,
the time will come
when you will be taken away by hooks,
and what is left of you with fishhooks.
3 You will go straight out of the city
through holes in the walls,
and you will be thrown on the garbage
dump," says the Lord.

4 "Come to the city of Bethel and sin;
come to Gilgal and sin even more.
Offer your sacrifices every morning,
and bring one-tenth of your crops every
three days.
5 Offer bread made with yeast as a sacrifice
to show your thanks,
and brag about the special offerings you
bring,
because this is what you love to do,
Israelites," says the Lord God.

6 "I did not give you any food in your cities,
and there was not enough to eat in any
of your towns,
but you did not come back to me," says
the Lord.
7 "I held back the rain from you
three months before harvest time.
Then I let it rain on one city
but not on another.
Rain fell on one field,
but another field got none and dried up.
8 People weak from thirst went from town
to town for water,
but they could not get enough to drink.
Still you did not come back to me," says
the Lord.
9 "I made your crops die from disease and
mildew.
When your gardens and your vineyards
got larger,
locusts ate your fig and olive trees.

4:1 Bashan Amos compares the rich, lazy women of
Samaria to well-fed cows from Bashan, a place known for
its rich animal pastures.

But still you did not come back to me,"
  says the LORD.
10 "I sent disasters against you,
  as I did to Egypt.
I killed your young men with swords,
  and your horses were taken from you.
I made you smell the stink from all the
  dead bodies,
  but still you did not come back to me,"
  says the LORD.
11 "I destroyed some of you
  as I destroyed Sodom and Gomorrah.
You were like a burning stick pulled from
  a fire,
  but still you did not come back to me,"
  says the LORD.

12 "So this is what I will do to you, Israel;
  because I will do this to you,
  get ready to meet your God, Israel."

13 He is the one who makes the mountains
  and creates the wind
  and makes his thoughts known to
  people.
He changes the dawn into darkness
  and walks over the mountains of the
  earth.
His name is the LORD God All-Powerful.

ISRAEL NEEDS TO REPENT

5 Listen to this funeral song that I sing
  about you, people of Israel.
2 "The young girl Israel has fallen,
  and she will not rise up again.
She was left alone in her own land,
  and there is no one to help her up."
3 This is what the Lord GOD says:
"If a thousand soldiers leave a city,
  only a hundred will return;
if a hundred soldiers leave a city,
  only ten will return."

4 This is what the LORD says to the nation
of Israel:
"Come to me and live.
5   But do not look in Bethel
or go to Gilgal,
  and do not go down to Beersheba.
The people of Gilgal will be taken away as
  captives,
  and Bethel will become nothing."
6 Come to the LORD and live,
  or he will move like fire against the
  descendants of Joseph.

The fire will burn Bethel,
  and there will be no one to put it out.
7 You turn justice upside down,
  and you throw on the ground what is
  right.

8 God is the one who made the star groups
  Pleiades and Orion;
he changes darkness into the morning
  light,
  and the day into dark night.
He calls for the waters of the sea
  to pour out on the earth.
The LORD is his name.
9 He destroys the protected city;
  he ruins the strong, walled city.

10 You hate those who speak in court against
  evil,
  and you can't stand those who tell the
  truth.
11 You walk on poor people,
  forcing them to give you grain.
You have built fancy houses of cut stone,
  but you will not live in them.
You have planted beautiful vineyards,
  but you will not drink the wine from
  them.
12 I know your many crimes,
  your terrible sins.
You hurt people who do right,
  you take money to do wrong,
  and you keep the poor from getting
  justice in court.
13 In such times the wise person will keep
  quiet,
  because it is a bad time.

14 Try to do good, not evil,
  so that you will live,
  and the LORD God All-Powerful will be
  with you
  just as you say he is.
15 Hate evil and love good;
  be fair in the courts.
Maybe the LORD God All-Powerful will
  be kind
  to the people of Joseph who are left
  alive.

16 This is what the Lord, the LORD God
All-Powerful, says:
"People will be crying in all the streets;
  they will be saying, 'Oh, no!' in the
  public places.

They will call the farmers to come and weep
and will pay people to cry out loud for them.
¹⁷ People will be crying in all the vineyards,
because I will pass among you to punish you," says the LORD.

THE LORD'S DAY OF JUDGING

¹⁸ How terrible it will be for you who want the LORD's day of judging to come.
Why do you want that day to come?
It will bring darkness for you, not light.
¹⁹ It will be like someone who runs from a lion
and meets a bear,
or like someone who goes into his house and puts his hand on the wall,
and then is bitten by a snake.
²⁰ So the LORD's day of judging will bring darkness, not light;
it will be very dark, not light at all.

²¹ The LORD says, "I hate and reject your feasts;
I cannot stand your religious meetings.
²² If you offer me burnt offerings and grain offerings,
I won't accept them.
You bring your best fellowship offerings of fattened cattle,
but I will ignore them.
²³ Take the noise of your songs away from me!
I won't listen to the music of your harps.
²⁴ But let justice flow like a river,
and let goodness flow like a never-ending stream.

²⁵ "People of Israel, you did not bring me sacrifices and offerings
while you traveled in the desert for forty years.
²⁶ You have carried with you
your king, the god Sakkuth,
and Kaiwan your idol,
and the star gods you have made.
²⁷ So I will send you away as captives beyond Damascus,"
says the LORD, whose name is the God All-Powerful.

ISRAEL WILL BE DESTROYED

6 How terrible it will be for those who have an easy life in Jerusalem,
for those who feel safe living on Mount Samaria.
You think you are the important people of the best nation in the world;
the Israelites come to you for help.
² Go look at the city of Calneh,
and from there go to the great city Hamath;
then go down to Gath of the Philistines.
You are no better than these kingdoms.
Your land is no larger than theirs.
³ You put off the day of punishment,
but you bring near the day when you can do evil to others.
⁴ You lie on beds decorated with ivory
and stretch out on your couches.
You eat tender lambs
and fattened calves.
⁵ You make up songs on your harps,
and, like David, you compose songs on musical instruments.
⁶ You drink wine by the bowlful
and use the best perfumed lotions.
But you are not sad over the ruin of Israel,
⁷ so you will be some of the first ones taken as slaves.
Your feasting and lying around will come to an end.

⁸The Lord GOD made this promise; the LORD God All-Powerful says:
"I hate the pride of the Israelites,
and I hate their strong buildings,
so I will let the enemy take the city
and everything in it."

⁹At that time there might be only ten people left alive in just one house, but they will also die. ¹⁰When the relatives come to get the bodies to take them outside, one of them will call to the other and ask, "Are there any other dead bodies with you?"

That person will answer, "No."

Then the one who asked will say, "Hush! We must not say the name of the LORD."

¹¹ The LORD has given the command;
the large house will be broken into pieces,
and the small house into bits.

12 Horses do not run on rocks,
    and people do not plow rocks with
        oxen.
But you have changed fairness into
        poison;
    you have changed what is right into a
        bitter taste.
13 You are happy that the town of Lo Debar
        was captured,
    and you say, "We have taken Karnaim[n]
        by our own strength."
14 The LORD God All-Powerful says,
    "Israel, I will bring a nation against
        you
    that will make your people suffer from
        Lebo Hamath in the north
    to the valley south of the Dead Sea."

THE VISION OF LOCUSTS

7 This is what the Lord GOD showed me:
He was forming a swarm of locusts, after
the king had taken his share of the first crop
and the second crop had just begun growing. 2When the locusts ate all the crops in the
country, I said, "Lord GOD, forgive us. How
could Israel live through this? It is too small
already!"

3So the LORD changed his mind about
this. "It will not happen," said the LORD.

THE VISION OF FIRE

4This is what the Lord GOD showed me:
The Lord GOD was calling for fire to come

6:13 Lo Debar ... Karnaim These were two not especially
significant cities that the Israelites had captured in war.

TURNING REVELATIONS INTO REVOLUTIONS

couch potatoes

FITNESS

AMOS 6:1-6

B efore the miracle of modern media, spoken words had to communicate visual
images. The prophet Amos chose some very picturesque words to create this
scene. He wanted to impress upon the people of the kingdom that their pursuit of
pleasure and luxury was going to be their downfall. Their reckless abandonment of
God's way would lead to punishment and destruction.

So he chose a word that means "excessive, unrestrained, or beyond bounds." Amos
says that these people were out of control in satisfying their desires. They were what
we would call "couch potatoes," drinking, eating, and lounging, instead of doing what
God designed them to do. The only god in their lives was their flesh. Consequently, the
people were judged for their hedonistic lifestyle and finally destroyed as a result of it.

God designed us for conquests, but too often we are willing to settle for counterfeits.
God's standard is to be our signpost—not that of our selfish society. The kingdom of
God wasn't designed for "sprawlers." So don't be surprised if God starts speaking to
you about getting rid of the sprawl in your life.

reflect: Think of how you could become more active in the kingdom of God.
Go to **Matthew 6:21.**

down like rain. It burned up the deep water and was going to burn up the land. ⁵Then I cried out, "Lord GOD, stop! How could Israel live through this? It is too small already."

⁶So the LORD changed his mind about this too. "It will not happen," said the Lord GOD.

THE VISION OF THE PLUMB LINE

⁷This is what he showed me: The Lord stood by a straight wall, with a plumb line in his hand. ⁸The LORD said to me, "Amos, what do you see?"

I said, "A plumb line."

Then the Lord said, "See, I will put a plumb line among my people Israel to show how crooked they are. I will not look the other way any longer.

⁹ "The places where Isaac's descendants
worship will be destroyed,
Israel's holy places will be turned into
ruins,
and I will attack King Jeroboam's
family with the sword."

AMAZIAH SPEAKS AGAINST AMOS

¹⁰Amaziah, a priest at Bethel, sent this message to Jeroboam king of Israel: "Amos is making evil plans against you with the people of Israel. He has been speaking so much that this land can't hold all his words. ¹¹This is what Amos has said:

'Jeroboam will die by the sword,
and the people of Israel will be taken as
captives
out of their own country.'"

¹²Then Amaziah said to Amos, "Seer, go back right now to Judah. Do your prophesying and earn your living there, ¹³but don't prophesy anymore here at Bethel. This is the king's holy place, and it is the nation's temple."

¹⁴Then Amos answered Amaziah, "I do not make my living as a prophet, nor am I a member of a group of prophets. I make my living as a shepherd, and I take care of sycamore trees. ¹⁵But the LORD took me away from tending the flock and said to me, 'Go, prophesy to my people Israel.' ¹⁶So listen to the LORD's word. You tell me,

'Don't prophesy against Israel,
and stop prophesying against the
descendants of Isaac.'

¹⁷"Because you have said this, the LORD says:

'Your wife will become a prostitute in the
city,
and your sons and daughters will be
killed with swords.
Other people will measure your land and
divide it among themselves,
and you will die in a foreign country.
The people of Israel will definitely be
taken
from their own land as captives.'"

THE VISION OF RIPE FRUIT

8 This is what the Lord GOD showed me: a basket of summer fruit. ²He said to me, "Amos, what do you see?"

I said, "A basket of summer fruit."

Then the LORD said to me, "An end[n] has come for my people Israel, because I will not overlook their sins anymore.

³"On that day the palace songs will become funeral songs," says the Lord GOD. "There will be dead bodies thrown everywhere! Silence!"

⁴ Listen to me, you who walk on helpless
people,
you who are trying to destroy the poor
people of this country, saying,
⁵ "When will the New Moon festival be
over
so we can sell grain?
When will the Sabbath be over
so we can bring out wheat to sell?
We can charge them more
and give them less,
and we can change the scales to cheat
the people.
⁶ We will buy poor people for silver,
and needy people for the price of a pair
of sandals.
We will even sell the wheat that was
swept up from the floor."
⁷The LORD has sworn by his name, the Pride of Jacob, "I will never forget everything that these people did.
⁸ The whole land will shake because of it,
and everyone who lives in the land will
cry for those who died.
The whole land will rise like the Nile;
it will be shaken, and then it will fall
like the Nile River in Egypt."

8:2 end The Hebrew word for "end" sounds like the Hebrew word for "summer fruit."

⁹The Lord GOD says:
"At that time I will cause the sun to go
  down at noon
  and make the earth dark on a bright day.
¹⁰ I will change your festivals into days of
    crying for the dead,
  and all your songs will become songs of
    sadness.
  I will make all of you wear rough cloth to
    show your sadness;
  I will make you shave your heads as
    well.
  I will make it like a time of crying for the
    death of an only son,
  and its end like the end of an awful day."

¹¹ The Lord GOD says: "The days are coming
    when I will cause a time of hunger in
    the land.
  The people will not be hungry for bread
    or thirsty for water,
  but they will be hungry for words from
    the LORD.
¹² They will wander from the
    Mediterranean Sea to the Dead Sea,
  from the north to the east.
  They will search for the word of the
    LORD,
  but they won't find it.
¹³ At that time the beautiful young women
    and the young men
  will become weak from thirst.
¹⁴ They make promises by the idol in
    Samaria
  and say, 'As surely as the god of Dan
    lives . . .'
  and, 'As surely as the god of Beersheba[n]
    lives, we promise . . .'
  So they will fall
  and never get up again."

ISRAEL WILL BE DESTROYED

9 I saw the Lord standing by the altar, and
he said:
"Smash the top of the pillars
  so that even the bottom of the doors
    will shake.
  Make the pillars fall on the people's heads;
    anyone left alive I will kill with a sword.
  Not one person will get away;
    no one will escape.
² If they dig down as deep as the place of
    the dead,
  I will pull them up from there.

If they climb up into heaven,
  I will bring them down from there.
³ If they hide at the top of Mount Carmel,
  I will find them and take them away.
  If they try to hide from me at the bottom
    of the sea,
  I will command a snake to bite them.
⁴ If they are captured and taken away by
    their enemies,
  I will command the sword to kill them.
  I will keep watch over them,
    but I will keep watch to give them
    trouble, not to do them good."

⁵ The Lord GOD All-Powerful touches the
    land,
  and the land shakes.
  Then everyone who lives in the land
    cries for the dead.
  The whole land rises like the Nile River
    and falls like the river of Egypt.
⁶ The LORD builds his upper rooms above
    the skies;
  he sets their foundations on the earth.
  He calls for the waters of the sea
    and pours them out on the land.
  The LORD is his name.
⁷The LORD says,
"Israel, you are no different to me than
    the people of Cush.
  I brought Israel out of the land of Egypt,
    and the Philistines from Crete,
    and the Arameans from Kir.
⁸ I, the Lord GOD, am watching the sinful
    kingdom Israel.
  I will destroy it
    from off the earth,
  but I will not completely destroy
    Jacob's descendants," says the LORD.
⁹ "I am giving the command
    to scatter the nation of Israel among all
    nations.
  It will be like someone shaking grain
    through a strainer,
  but not even a tiny stone falls through.
¹⁰ All the sinners among my people
  will die by the sword—
  those who say,
  'Nothing bad will happen to us.'

8:14 Dan . . . Beersheba Dan was the city farthest north
in Israel, and Beersheba was the city farthest south.

THE LORD PROMISES TO RESTORE ISRAEL

11 "The kingdom of David is like a fallen
tent,
  but in that day I will set it up again
  and mend its broken places.
I will rebuild its ruins
  as it was before.
12 Then Israel will take over what is left of
Edom
  and the other nations that belong to
  me,"
says the LORD,
  who will make it happen.

13 The LORD says, "The time is coming when
there will be all kinds of food.
People will still be harvesting crops
  when it's time to plow again.

People will still be taking the juice from
grapes
  when it's time to plant again.
Wine will drip from the mountains
  and pour from the hills.
14 I will bring my people Israel back from
captivity;
  they will build the ruined cities again,
  and they will live in them.
They will plant vineyards and drink the
  wine from them;
  they will plant gardens and eat their
  fruit.
15 I will plant my people on their land,
  and they will not be pulled out again
  from the land which I have given them,"
  says the LORD your God.

obadiah

GOD WILL PUNISH EDOM

THE LORD WILL PUNISH THE EDOMITES

1 This is the vision of Obadiah.

This is what the Lord GOD says about Edom:[n]

We have heard a message from the LORD.
A messenger has been sent among the nations, saying,
"Attack! Let's go attack Edom!"

THE LORD SPEAKS TO THE EDOMITES

2 "Soon I will make you the smallest of nations.
You will be greatly hated by everyone.
3 Your pride has fooled you,
you who live in the hollow places of the cliff.
Your home is up high,
you who say to yourself,
'No one can bring me down to the ground.'
4 Even if you fly high like the eagle
and make your nest among the stars,
I will bring you down from there," says the LORD.
5 "You will really be ruined!
If thieves came to you,
if robbers came by night,
they would steal only enough for themselves.
If workers came and picked the grapes from your vines,
they would leave a few behind.
6 But you, Edom, will really lose everything!
People will find all your hidden treasures!
7 All the people who are your friends
will force you out of the land.
The people who are at peace with you
will trick you and defeat you.
Those who eat your bread with you now
are planning a trap for you,
and you will not notice it."

8 The LORD says, "On that day
I will surely destroy the wise people from Edom,

and those with understanding from the mountains of Edom.
9 Then, city of Teman, your best warriors will be afraid,
and everyone from the mountains of Edom will be killed.
10 You did violence to your relatives, the Israelites,
so you will be covered with shame
and destroyed forever.
11 You stood aside without helping
while strangers carried Israel's treasures away.
When foreigners entered Israel's city gate
and threw lots to decide what part of Jerusalem they would take,
you were like one of them.

COMMANDS THAT EDOM BROKE

12 "Edom, do not laugh at your brother Israel in his time of trouble
or be happy about the people of Judah when they are destroyed.
Do not brag when cruel things are done to them.
13 Do not enter the city gate of my people in their time of trouble
or laugh at their problems in their time of trouble.
Do not take their treasures in their time of trouble.
14 Do not stand at the crossroads
to destroy those who are trying to escape.
Do not capture those who escape alive
and turn them over to their enemy in their time of trouble.

THE NATIONS WILL BE JUDGED

15 "The LORD's day of judging is coming soon
to all the nations.

---

1 Edom The Edomites were the people who came from Esau, Jacob's twin brother. They were enemies of the Israelites.

The same evil things you did to other
people
will happen to you;
they will come back upon your own
head.
16 Because you drank in my Temple,
all the nations will drink on and on.
They will drink and drink
until they disappear.
17 But on Mount Zion some will escape the
judgment,
and it will be a holy place.
The people of Jacob will take back their
land

from those who took it from them.
18 The people of Jacob will be like a fire
and the people of Joseph[n] like a
flame.
But the people of Esau[n] will be like dry
stalks.
The people of Jacob will set them on
fire and burn them up.
There will be no one left of the people of
Esau."

---

18 **people of Jacob . . . Joseph** The people who came
from Jacob and Joseph, or the Israelites. 18 **people
of Esau** The people who came from Esau, or the
Edomites.

FAITH

SERVANT EVANGELISM

the "**upside-down** golden rule"

OBADIAH 15

Obadiah's writing is the shortest book in the Old Testament, but it carries one of
the most important messages. God is the judge of all humankind and no nation
escapes his judgment.

We often think that "nations" is restricted to those political entities that color our world
map. But Obadiah's warning was about a group of people that God saw as a nation, not
necessarily a political entity. God viewed those who were of a particular culture and
background as a "nation."

God sees all Christians as a nation, one body of one culture with one purpose. And the
behavior of those calling themselves Christians sometimes leaves a lot to be desired.
Were it not for the mercy of God, Obadiah's upside-down Golden Rule ("The same evil
things you did to other people will happen to you") would become a terrible judgment
on the body of Christ.

The reason we need salvation is not because we need to be better people. We need
salvation because we are dead in our sins. We will never be good enough on our own!
The good news is that God has judged us through the death, burial, and resurrection of
Jesus, and we are free to follow the original Golden Rule through the love of Christ.

reflect: Give thanks for the grace and mercy of God toward you today.
Go to **Habakkuk 2:4.**

This will happen because the Lord has said it.

19 Then God's people will regain southern Judah from Edom;
   they will take back the mountains of Edom.
They will take back the western hills from the Philistines.
They will regain the lands of Ephraim and Samaria,
   and Benjamin will take over Gilead.
20 People from Israel who once were forced to leave their homes
will take the land of the Canaanites, all the way to Zarephath.
People from Judah who once were forced to leave Jerusalem and live in Sepharad
will take back the cities of southern Judah.
21 Powerful warriors will go up on Mount Zion,
   where they will rule the people living on Edom's mountains.
And the kingdom will belong to the Lord.

jonah

A PROPHET RUNS FROM GOD

GOD CALLS AND JONAH RUNS

1 The Lord spoke his word to Jonah son of Amittai: ²"Get up, go to the great city of Nineveh, and preach against it, because I see the evil things they do."

³But Jonah got up to run away from the Lord by going to Tarshish. He went to the city of Joppa, where he found a ship that was going to the city of Tarshish. Jonah paid for the trip and went aboard, planning to go to Tarshish to run away from the Lord.

⁴But the Lord sent a great wind on the sea, which made the sea so stormy that the ship was in danger of breaking apart. ⁵The sailors were afraid, and each man cried to his own god. They began throwing the cargo from the ship into the sea to make the ship lighter.

But Jonah had gone down far inside the ship to lie down, and he fell fast asleep. ⁶The captain of the ship came and said, "Why are you sleeping? Get up and pray to your god! Maybe your god will pay attention to us, and we won't die!"

⁷Then the men said to each other, "Let's throw lots to see who caused these troubles to happen to us."

When they threw lots, the lot showed that the trouble had happened because of Jonah. ⁸Then they said to him, "Tell us, who caused our trouble? What is your job? Where do you come from? What is your country? Who are your people?"

⁹Then Jonah said to them, "I am a Hebrew. I fear the Lord, the God of heaven, who made the sea and the land."

¹⁰The men were very afraid, and they asked Jonah, "What terrible thing did you do?" (They knew he was running away from the Lord because he had told them.)

¹¹Since the wind and the waves of the sea were becoming much stronger, they said to him, "What should we do to you to make the sea calm down for us?"

¹²Jonah said to them, "Pick me up, and throw me into the sea, and then it will calm down. I know it is my fault that this great storm has come on you."

¹³Instead, the men tried to row the ship back to the land, but they could not, because the sea was becoming more stormy.

JONAH'S PUNISHMENT

¹⁴So the men cried to the Lord, "Lord, please don't let us die because of this man's life; please don't think we are guilty of killing an innocent person. Lord, you have caused all this to happen; you wanted it this way." ¹⁵So they picked up Jonah and threw him into the sea, and the sea became calm. ¹⁶Then they began to fear the Lord very much; they offered a sacrifice to the Lord and made promises to him.

¹⁷The Lord caused a big fish to swallow Jonah, and Jonah was inside the fish three days and three nights.

2 While Jonah was inside the fish, he prayed to the Lord his God and said,

² "When I was in danger,
  I called to the Lord,
  and he answered me.
I was about to die,
  so I cried to you,
  and you heard my voice.
³ You threw me into the sea,
  down, down into the deep sea.
The water was all around me,
  and your powerful waves flowed over
    me.
⁴ I said, 'I was driven out of your presence,
  but I hope to see your Holy Temple
    again.'
⁵ The waters of the sea closed around my
    throat.
The deep sea was all around me;
  seaweed was wrapped around my head.
⁶ When I went down to where the
    mountains of the sea start to rise,
  I thought I was locked in this prison
    forever,
but you saved me from the pit of death,
  Lord my God.

7 "When my life had almost gone,
   I remembered the LORD.
I prayed to you,
   and you heard my prayers in your Holy
     Temple.

8 "People who worship useless idols
   give up their loyalty to you.
9 But I will praise and thank you
   while I give sacrifices to you,
   and I will keep my promises to you.

FOR YOUR OWN GOOD

show mercy

FULFILLMENT

JONAH 4:2

Today we do not speak much about the mercy of God, but it is one of the key attributes of our loving heavenly Father. In this day when movies and television shows call for characters to show no mercy, the understanding of this vital attribute is often not comprehended. The church talks and sings of the love of God, but we often forget that his love is demonstrated through mercy. The Bible says that while we were still sinners Christ died for us. Now that is real mercy!

When was the last time you were merciful to someone? When your child broke the window, did you show mercy or wrath? When your spouse forgot your anniversary, were you merciful or resentful? It is very important to express this attribute we share with God, especially in the negative society that surrounds us.

The Bible is full of stories of God's mercy in action. For example, when David became king, he could have destroyed all who were his enemies, which was the custom for that time. But, instead, he sought out the family of Saul and blessed Mephibosheth, the lame son of Jonathan, offering him a place at his own table and restoring all the possessions of Saul to him. In the Psalms, David wrote of the mercy of God over and over again.

Peter was also shown the Lord's mercy even after he denied Jesus three times. Peter was in close personal contact with Jesus for three years, yet when the time to stand for Jesus came, Peter denied him. Peter's heart was heavily grieved, and he felt that all he deserved was judgment; but the Lord himself in his great mercy appeared to Peter after his resurrection and asked him to take care of his sheep. The mercy of God is so great that Jesus asked him three times to match the three times Peter had denied him. Afterward, Peter was a changed man as a result of the mercy of God.

reflect: Extend the mercy of God to someone today.
Go to **Psalm 150:6.**

Salvation comes from the LORD!"

¹⁰Then the LORD spoke to the fish, and the fish threw up Jonah onto the dry land.

GOD CALLS AND JONAH OBEYS

3 The LORD spoke his word to Jonah again and said, ²"Get up, go to the great city Nineveh, and preach to it what I tell you to say."

³So Jonah obeyed the LORD and got up and went to Nineveh. It was a very large city; just to walk across it took a person three days. ⁴After Jonah had entered the city and walked for one day, he preached to the people, saying, "After forty days, Nineveh will be destroyed!"

⁵The people of Nineveh believed God. They announced that they would fast for a while, and they put on rough cloth to show their sadness. All the people in the city did this, from the most important to the least important.

⁶When the king of Nineveh heard this news, he got up from his throne, took off his robe, and covered himself with rough cloth and sat in ashes to show how upset he was. ⁷He sent this announcement through Nineveh:

By command of the king and his important men: No person or animal, herd or flock, will be allowed to taste anything. Do not let them eat food or drink water. ⁸But every person and animal should be covered with rough cloth, and people should cry loudly to God. Everyone must turn away from evil living and stop doing harm all the time. ⁹Who knows? Maybe God will change his mind. Maybe he will stop being angry, and then we will not die.

¹⁰When God saw what the people did, that they stopped doing evil, he changed his mind and did not do what he had warned. He did not punish them.

GOD'S MERCY MAKES JONAH ANGRY

4 But this made Jonah very unhappy, and he became angry. ²He prayed to the LORD, "When I was still in my own country this is what I said would happen, and that is why I quickly ran away to Tarshish. I knew that you are a God who is kind and shows mercy. You don't become angry quickly, and you have great love. I knew you would choose not to cause harm. ³So now I ask you, LORD, please kill me. It is better for me to die than to live."

⁴Then the LORD said, "Do you think it is right for you to be angry?"

⁵Jonah went out and sat down east of the city. There he made a shelter for himself and sat in the shade, waiting to see what would happen to the city. ⁶The LORD made a plant grow quickly up over Jonah, which gave him shade and helped him to be more comfortable. Jonah was very pleased to have the plant. ⁷But the next day when the sun rose, God sent a worm to attack the plant so that it died.

⁸As the sun rose higher in the sky, God sent a very hot east wind to blow, and the sun became so hot on Jonah's head that he became very weak and wished he were dead. He said, "It is better for me to die than to live."

⁹But God said to Jonah, "Do you think it is right for you to be angry about the plant?"

Jonah answered, "It is right for me to be angry! I am so angry I could die!"

¹⁰And the LORD said, "You are so concerned for that plant even though you did nothing to make it grow. It appeared one day, and the next day it died. ¹¹Then shouldn't I show concern for the great city Nineveh, which has more than one hundred twenty thousand people who do not know right from wrong, and many animals, too?"

micah

ASSYRIA WILL PUNISH ISRAEL AND JUDAH

SAMARIA AND ISRAEL TO BE PUNISHED

1 During the time that Jotham, Ahaz, and Hezekiah were kings of Judah, the word of the LORD came to Micah, who was from Moresheth. He saw these visions about Samaria and Jerusalem.

2 Hear this, all you nations;
    listen, earth and all you who live on it.
The Lord GOD will be a witness against
    you,
    the Lord from his Holy Temple.
3 See, the LORD is coming out of his place;
    he is coming down to walk on the tops
        of the mountains.
4 The mountains will melt under him,
    and the valleys will crack open,
like wax near a fire,
    like water running down a hillside.
5 All this is because of Jacob's sin,
    because of the sins of the nation of
        Israel.
    What is the place of Jacob's sin?
    Isn't it Samaria?
    What is Judah's place of idol worship?
    Isn't it Jerusalem?

THE LORD SPEAKS

6 "So I will make Samaria a pile of ruins in
        the open country,
    a place for planting vineyards.
I will pour her stones down into the
        valley
    and strip her down to her foundations.
7 All her idols will be broken into pieces;
    all the gifts to her idols will be burned
        with fire.
    I will destroy all her idols,
and because Samaria earned her money
        by being unfaithful to me,
    this money will be carried off by others
        who are not faithful to me."

MICAH'S GREAT SADNESS

8 I will moan and cry because of this evil,
    going around barefoot and naked.
I will cry loudly like the wild dogs
    and make sad sounds like the owls do,

9 because Samaria's wound cannot be
        healed.
    It will spread to Judah;
it will reach the city gate of my people,
    all the way to Jerusalem.
10 Don't tell it in Gath.[n]
    Don't cry in Acco.[n]
Roll in the dust
    at Beth Ophrah.[n]
11 Pass on your way, naked and ashamed,
    you who live in Shaphir.[n]
Those who live in Zaanan[n]
    won't come out.
The people in Beth Ezel[n] will cry,
    but they will not give you any support.
12 Those who live in Maroth[n]
    will be anxious for good news to come,
because trouble will come from the LORD,
    all the way to the gate of Jerusalem.
13 You people living in Lachish,[n]
    harness the fastest horse to the chariot.
Jerusalem's sins started in you;
    yes, Israel's sins were found in you.
14 So you must give farewell gifts
    to Moresheth[n] in Gath.
The houses in Aczib[n] will be false help
    to the kings of Israel.
15 I will bring against you people who will
        take your land,
    you who live in Mareshah.[n]
The glory of Israel
    will go in to Adullam.

1:10 Gath This name sounds like the Hebrew word for "tell." **1:10 Acco** This name sounds like the Hebrew word for "cry." **1:10 Beth Ophrah** This name means "house of dust." **1:11 Shaphir** This name means "beautiful." **1:11 Zaanan** This name sounds like the Hebrew word for "come out." **1:11 Beth Ezel** This name means "house by the side of another," suggesting help or support. **1:12 Maroth** This name sounds like the Hebrew word for "sad" or "miserable." **1:13 Lachish** This name sounds like the Hebrew word for "horses." **1:14 Moresheth** This may be a play on the word "engaged," referring to a farewell gift to a bride. **1:14 Aczib** This name means "lie" or "trick." **1:15 Mareshah** This name sounds like the Hebrew word for a person who captures other cities and lands.

16 Cut off your hair to show you are sad
     for the children you love.
   Make yourself bald like the eagle,
     because your children will be taken
       away to a foreign land.

THE EVIL PLANS OF PEOPLE

2 How terrible it will be for people who
     plan wickedness,
   who lie on their beds and make evil
     plans.
   When the morning light comes, they do
     what they planned,
     because they have the power to do so.
2 They want fields, so they take them;
     they want houses, so they take them
       away.
   They cheat people to get their houses;
     they rob them even of their property.
   3That is why the LORD says:
   "Look, I am planning trouble against such
       people,
     and you won't be able to save
       yourselves.
   You will no longer walk proudly,
     because it will be a terrible time.
4 At that time people will make fun of you
     and sing this sad song about you:
   'We are completely ruined;
     the LORD has taken away my people's
       land.
   Yes, he has taken it away from me
     and divided our fields among our
       enemies!'"
5 So you will have no one from the LORD's
       people
     to throw lots to divide the land.

MICAH IS ASKED NOT TO PROPHESY

6 The prophets say, "Don't prophesy to us!
     Don't prophesy about these things!
     Nothing to make us feel bad will
       happen!"
7 But I must say this, people of Jacob:
     The LORD is becoming angry about
       what you have done.
   My words are welcome
     to the person who does what is right.
8 But you are fighting against my people
     like an enemy.
     You take the coats from people who
       pass by;
   you rob them of their safety;
     you plan war.

9 You've forced the women of my people
     from their nice houses;
   you've taken my glory
     from their children forever.
10 Get up and leave.
   This is not your place of rest anymore.
   You have made this place unclean,
     and it is doomed to destruction.
11 But you people want a false prophet
     who will tell you nothing but lies.
   You want one who promises to prophesy
       good things for you
     if you give him wine and beer.
   He's just the prophet for you.

THE LORD PROMISES TO RESCUE HIS PEOPLE

12 "Yes, people of Jacob, I will bring all of
       you together;
     I will bring together all those left alive
       in Israel.
   I will put them together like sheep in a
       pen,
     like a flock in its pasture;
     the place will be filled with many
       people.
13 Someone will open the way and lead the
       people out.
     The people will break through the gate
       and leave the city where they were
         held captive.
   Their king will go out in front of them,
     and the LORD will lead them."

THE LEADERS OF ISRAEL ARE GUILTY OF EVIL

3 Then I said,
   "Listen, leaders of the people of Jacob;
     listen, you rulers of the nation of Israel.
   You should know how to decide cases
       fairly,
2 but you hate good and love evil.
   You skin my people alive
     and tear the flesh off their bones.
3 You eat my people's flesh
     and skin them and break their bones;
   you chop them up like meat for the pot,
     like meat in a cooking pan.
4 They will cry to the LORD,
     but he won't answer them.
   At that time he will hide his face from
       them,
     because what they have done is evil."
5The LORD says this about the prophets who teach his people the wrong way of
living:

"If these prophets are given food to eat,
they shout, 'Peace!'
But if someone doesn't give them what
they ask for,
they call for a holy war against that
person.
⁶ So it will become like night for them,
without visions.
It will become dark for them, without
any way to tell the future.
The sun is about to set for the prophets;
their day will become dark.
⁷ The seers will be ashamed;
the people who see the future will be
embarrassed.
Yes, all of them will cover their mouths,
because there will be no answer from
God."

MICAH IS AN HONEST PROPHET OF GOD

⁸ But I am filled with power,
with the Spirit of the LORD,
and with justice and strength,
to tell the people of Jacob how they have
turned against God,
and the people of Israel how they have
sinned.
⁹ Leaders of Jacob and rulers of Israel,
listen to me,
you who hate fairness
and twist what is right.
¹⁰ You build Jerusalem by murdering
people;
you build it with evil.
¹¹ Its judges take money
to decide who wins in court.
Its priests only teach for pay,
and its prophets only look into the
future when they get paid.
But they lean on the LORD and say,
"The LORD is here with us,
so nothing bad will happen to us."
¹² Because of you,
Jerusalem will be plowed like a field.
The city will become a pile of rocks,
and the hill on which the Temple stands
will be covered with bushes.

THE MOUNTAIN OF THE LORD

4 In the last days
the mountain on which the LORD's
Temple stands
will become the most important of all
mountains.

It will be raised above the hills,
and people from other nations will
come streaming to it.
² Many nations will come and say,
"Come, let us go up to the mountain of
the LORD,
to the Temple of the God of Jacob,
so that he can teach us his ways,
and we can obey his teachings."
His teachings will go out from Jerusalem,
the word of the LORD from that city.
³ The Lord will judge many nations;
he will make decisions about strong
nations that are far away.
They will hammer their swords into plow
blades
and their spears into hooks for
trimming trees.
Nations will no longer raise swords
against other nations;
they will not train for war anymore.
⁴ Everyone will sit under his own vine and
fig tree,
and no one will make him afraid,
because the LORD All-Powerful has
said it.
⁵ All other nations may follow their own gods,
but we will follow the LORD our God
forever and ever.
⁶ The LORD says, "At that time,
I will gather the crippled;
I will bring together those who were
sent away,
those whom I caused to have trouble.
⁷ I will keep alive those who were crippled,
and I will make a strong nation of those
who were sent away.
The LORD will be their king in Mount
Zion from now on and forever.
⁸ And you, watchtower of the flocks,ⁿ hill of
Jerusalem,
to you will come the kingdom as in the
past.
Jerusalem, the right to rule will come
again to you."

WHY THE ISRAELITES MUST GO TO BABYLON

⁹ Now, why do you cry so loudly?
Is your king gone?

4:8 watchtower . . . flocks This probably means a part
of Jerusalem. The leaders would be like shepherds in a
tower watching their sheep.

Have you lost your helper,
  so that you are in pain, like a woman
    trying to give birth?
¹⁰ People of Jerusalem, strain and be in pain.
  Be like a woman trying to give birth,
    because now you must leave the city
      and live in the field.
  You will go to Babylon,
    but you will be saved from that place.
  The LORD will go there
    and buy you back from your enemies.

¹¹ But now many nations
  have come to fight against you,
    saying, "Let's destroy Jerusalem.
      We will look at her and be glad we have
        defeated her."
¹² But they don't know
  what the LORD is thinking;
    they don't understand his plan.
      He has gathered them like bundles of
        grain to the threshing floor.
¹³ "Get up and beat them, people of
    Jerusalem.
  I will make you strong as if you had
    horns of iron
  and hoofs of bronze.
    You will beat many nations into small
      pieces
  and give their wealth to the LORD,
    their treasure to the Lord of all the
      earth."

5 So, strong city, gather your soldiers
    together,
  because we are surrounded and
    attacked.
  They will hit the leader of Israel
    in the face with a club.

THE RULER TO BE BORN IN BETHLEHEM
² "But you, Bethlehem Ephrathah,
  though you are too small to be among
    the army groups from Judah,
  from you will come one who will rule
    Israel for me.
  He comes from very old times,
    from days long ago."

³ The LORD will give up his people
  until the one who is having a baby gives
    birth;
  then the rest of his relatives will return
    to the people of Israel.

⁴ At that time the ruler of Israel will stand
  and take care of his people
  with the LORD's strength
    and with the power of the name of the
      LORD his God.
  The Israelites will live in safety,
    because his greatness will reach all over
      the earth.
⁵ He will bring peace.

RESCUE AND PUNISHMENT
Assyria will surely come into our country
  and walk over our large buildings.
  We will set up seven shepherds,
    eight leaders of the people.
⁶ They will destroy the Assyrians with their
    swords;
  they will conquer the land of Assyria
    with their swords drawn.
  They will rescue us from the Assyrians
    when they come into our land,
  when they walk over our borders.

⁷ Then the people of Jacob who are left
    alive
  will be to other people
  like dew from the LORD
    or rain on the grass—
  it does not wait for human beings;
    it does not pause for any person.
⁸ Those of Jacob's people who are left alive
  will be scattered among many nations
    and peoples.
  They will be like a lion among the animals
    of the forest,
  like a young lion in a flock of sheep:
  As it goes, it jumps on them
    and tears them to pieces,
    and no one can save them.
⁹ So you will raise your fist in victory over
    your enemies,
  and all your enemies will be destroyed.

¹⁰ The LORD says, "At that time,
  I will take your horses from you
  and destroy your chariots.
¹¹ I will destroy the cities in your country
  and tear down all your defenses.
¹² I will take away the magic charms you use
  so you will have no more
    fortune-tellers.
¹³ I will destroy your statues of gods
  and the stone pillars you worship
  so that you will no longer worship

what your hands have made.

¹⁴ I will tear down Asherah idols from you
and destroy your cities.

¹⁵ In my anger and rage,
I will pay back the nations that have not
listened."

THE LORD'S CASE

6 Now hear what the LORD says:
"Get up; plead your case in front of the
mountains;
let the hills hear your story.

² Mountains, listen to the LORD's legal case.
Foundations of the earth, listen.
The LORD has a legal case against his
people,
and he will accuse Israel."

³ He says, "My people, what did I do to you?
How did I make you tired of me?
Tell me.

⁴ I brought you from the land of Egypt
and freed you from slavery;
I sent Moses, Aaron, and Miriam to you.

⁵ My people, remember
the evil plans of Balak king of Moab
and what Balaam son of Beor told
Balak.
Remember what happened from Acacia
to Gilgal
so that you will know the LORD does
what is right!"

⁶ You say, "What can I bring with me
when I come before the LORD,
when I bow before God on high?
Should I come before him with burnt
offerings,
with year-old calves?

⁷ Will the LORD be pleased with a thousand
male sheep?
Will he be pleased with ten thousand
rivers of oil?
Should I give my first child for the evil I
have done?
Should I give my very own child for my
sin?"

⁸ The LORD has told you, human, what is
good;
he has told you what he wants from
you:
to do what is right to other people,
love being kind to others,
and live humbly, obeying your God.

⁹ The voice of the LORD calls to the city,
and the wise person honors him.
So pay attention to the rod of punishment;
pay attention to the One who threatens
to punish.

¹⁰ Are there still in the wicked house
wicked treasures
and the cursed false measure?

¹¹ Can I forgive people who cheat others
with wrong weights and scales?

¹² The rich people of the city
do cruel things.
Its people tell lies;
they do not tell the truth.

¹³ As for me, I will make you sick.
I will attack you, ruining you because of
your sins.

¹⁴ You will eat, but you won't become full;
you will still be hungry and empty.
You will store up, but save nothing,
and what you store up, the sword will
destroy.

¹⁵ You will plant,
but you won't harvest.
You will step on your olives,
but you won't get any oil from them.
You will crush the grapes,
but you will not drink the new wine.

¹⁶ This is because you obey the laws of King
Omri
and do all the things that Ahab's family
does;
you follow their advice.
So I will let you be destroyed.
The people in your city will be laughed
at,
and other nations will make fun of you.

THE EVIL THAT PEOPLE DO

7 Poor me! I am like a hungry man,
and all the summer fruit has been
picked—
there are no grapes left to eat,
none of the early figs I love.

² All of the faithful people are gone;
there is not one good person left in this
country.
Everyone is waiting to kill someone;
everyone is trying to trap someone else.

³ With both hands they are doing evil.
Rulers ask for money,
and judges' decisions are bought for a
price.

Rich people tell what they want,
and they get it.
4 Even the best of them is like a thornbush;
the most honest of them is worse than a
prickly plant.
The day that your watchmen[n] warned you
about has come.
Now they will be confused.
5 Don't believe your neighbor

or trust a friend.
Don't say anything,
even to your wife.
6 A son will not honor his father,
a daughter will turn against her mother,

7:4 watchmen Another name for prophets. The prophets were like guards who stood on a city's wall and watched for trouble coming from far away.

ARE YOU PROGRAMMED FOR STRESS?

FULFILLMENT

forgiving

MICAH 7:18–19

Micah tells us that God "throws away" our sins. When they are forgiven, they are pushed away—so far away that it is as if they have been lost in the depths of the ocean. They will never come back to incriminate us. God leaves them for dead.

Of course, we love to play the resurrecting god. So we have the habit of bringing our sins back to life. If you really think about it, sin is the only thing we can really claim is ours alone. God gave us everything else as a gift. But we created our sins without his help. So these are the only things that we could bring back to life. They are the only things we have mastery over. Imagine how ridiculous we are—raising our sins from the dead actually kills us!

God's forgiveness is an incredible thing. God casts away my sins when I come to him in true repentance and remorse. God forgets all about them. God does not need to remember how I hurt him with my sins. He does not bear a grudge toward me. He is not interested in punishing me. He wants me to embrace him as Father, so he throws away everything about my rebellion against him. As far as he is concerned, my sins are gone for good.

Oh, if only I could forgive like that. If only I could throw away those insults and infractions and aggravations that others have done to me so that as far as I was concerned, they would be gone for good. That's what God did for me. God's action gave me a standard for my actions—to forgive means "to cast it away" for good. If you are harboring some old hurts, cast them away. Be like your Father. He did it for you.

reflect: Quit resurrecting your sins and reminding God about them.
Go to **Matthew 3:13–17.**

and a daughter-in-law will be against her
   mother-in-law;
  a person's enemies will be members of
   his own family.

THE LORD'S KINDNESS

7 Israel says, "I will look to the LORD for
   help.
  I will wait for God to save me;
   my God will hear me.
8 Enemy, don't laugh at me.
  I have fallen, but I will get up again.
I sit in the shadow of trouble now,
  but the LORD will be a light for me.
9 I sinned against the LORD,
  so he was angry with me,
but he will defend my case in court.
  He will bring about what is right for me.
Then he will bring me out into the light,
  and I will see him set things right.
10 Then my enemies will see this,
  and they will be ashamed,
those who said to me,
  'Where is the LORD your God?'
I will look down on them.
  They will get walked on, like mud in the
   street."

ISRAEL WILL RETURN

11 The time will come when your walls will
   be built again,
  when your country will grow.
12 At that time your people will come back
   to you
  from Assyria and the cities of Egypt,
  and from Egypt to the Euphrates River,
  and from sea to sea and mountain to
   mountain.
13 The earth will be ruined for the people
   who live in it
  because of their deeds.

A PRAYER TO GOD

14 So shepherd your people with your
   stick;
  tend the flock of people who belong to
   you.
That flock now lives alone in the forest
  in the middle of a garden land.
Let them feed in Bashan and Gilead
  as in days long ago.

15 "As in the days when I brought you out of
   Egypt,
  I will show them miracles."

16 When the nations see those miracles,
  they will no longer brag about their
   power.
They will put their hands over their
   mouths,
  refusing to listen.
17 They will crawl in the dust like a snake,
  like insects crawling on the ground.
They will come trembling from their
   holes to the LORD our God
  and will turn in fear before you.
18 There is no God like you.
  You forgive those who are guilty of
   sin;
you don't look at the sins of your people
  who are left alive.
You will not stay angry forever,
  because you enjoy being kind.
19 You will have mercy on us again;
  you will conquer our sins.
You will throw away all our sins
  into the deepest part of the sea.
20 You will be true to the people of Jacob,
  and you will be kind to the people of
   Abraham
as you promised to our ancestors long
  ago.

nahum

GOD WILL PUNISH ASSYRIA

1 This is the message for the city of Nineveh.[n] This is the book of the vision of Nahum, who was from the town of Elkosh.

THE LORD IS ANGRY WITH NINEVEH

2 The LORD is a jealous God who punishes;
the LORD punishes and is filled with anger.
The LORD punishes those who are against him,
and he stays angry with his enemies.
3 The LORD does not become angry quickly,
and his power is great.
The LORD will not let the guilty go unpunished.
Where the LORD goes, there are whirlwinds and storms,
and the clouds are the dust beneath his feet.
4 He speaks to the sea and makes it dry;
he dries up all the rivers.
The areas of Bashan and Carmel dry up,
and the flowers of Lebanon dry up.
5 The mountains shake in front of him,
and the hills melt.
The earth trembles when he comes;
the world and all who live in it shake with fear.
6 No one can stay alive when he is angry;
no one can survive his strong anger.
His anger is poured out like fire;
the rocks are smashed by him.

7 The LORD is good,
giving protection in times of trouble.
He knows who trusts in him.
8 But like a rushing flood,
he will completely destroy Nineveh;
he will chase his enemies until he kills them.

9 The LORD will completely destroy anyone making plans against him.
Trouble will not come a second time.
10 Those people will be like tangled thorns
or like people drunk from their wine;
they will be burned up quickly like dry weeds.

11 Someone has come from Nineveh
who makes evil plans against the LORD
and gives wicked advice.
12 This is what the LORD says:
"Although Assyria is strong and has many people,
it will be defeated and brought to an end.
Although I have made you suffer, Judah,
I will make you suffer no more.
13 Now I will free you from their control
and tear away your chains."

14 The LORD has given you this command, Nineveh:
"You will not have descendants to carry on your name.
I will destroy the idols and metal images
that are in the temple of your gods.
I will make a grave for you,
because you are wicked."

15 Look, there on the hills,
someone is bringing good news!
He is announcing peace!
Celebrate your feasts, people of Judah,
and give your promised sacrifices to God.
The wicked will not come to attack you again;
they have been completely destroyed.

NINEVEH WILL BE DEFEATED

2 The destroyer[n] is coming to attack you, Nineveh.
Guard the defenses.
Watch the road.
Get ready.
Gather all your strength!
2 Destroyers have destroyed God's people
and ruined their vines,
but the LORD will bring back Jacob's greatness
like Israel's greatness.

1:1 Nineveh The capital city of the country of Assyria. Nahum uses Nineveh to stand for all of Assyria.
2:1 destroyer The Babylonians, the Scythians, and the Medes destroyed Nineveh.

3 The shields of his soldiers are red;
   the army is dressed in red.
The metal on the chariots flashes like fire
   when they are ready to attack;
   their horses are excited.
4 The chariots race through the streets
   and rush back and forth through the
      city squares.
They look like torches;
   they run like lightning.

5 He[n] calls his officers,
   but they stumble on the way.
They hurry to the city wall,
   and the shield is put into place.
6 The river gates are thrown open,
   and the palace is destroyed.
7 It has been announced that the people of
      Nineveh
   will be captured and carried away.
The slave girls moan like doves
   and beat their breasts, because they are
      sad.
8 Nineveh is like a pool,
   and now its water is draining away.
"Stop! Stop!" the people yell,
   but no one turns back.
9 Take the silver!
   Take the gold!
There is no end to the treasure—
   piles of wealth of every kind.
10 Nineveh is robbed, ruined, and destroyed.
   The people lose their courage, and their
      knees knock.
   Stomachs ache, and everyone's face
      grows pale.

11 Where is the lions'[n] den
   and the place where they feed their
      young?
Where did the lion, lioness, and cubs go
   without being afraid?
12 The lion killed enough for his cubs,
   enough for his mate.
He filled his cave with the animals he
      caught;
   he filled his den with meat he had
      killed.

13 "I am against you, Nineveh,"
   says the Lord All-Powerful.
"I will burn up your chariots in smoke,
   and the sword will kill your young
      lions.

I will stop you from hunting down
      others on the earth,
and your messengers' voices
   will no longer be heard."

IT WILL BE TERRIBLE FOR NINEVEH

3 How terrible it will be for the city that
   has killed so many.
It is full of lies
   and goods stolen from other countries.
It is always killing somebody.
2 Hear the sound of whips
   and the noise of the wheels.
Hear horses galloping
   and chariots bouncing along!
3 Horses are charging,
   swords are shining,
   spears are gleaming!
Many are dead;
   their bodies are piled up—
too many to count.
   People stumble over the dead bodies.
4 The city was like a prostitute;
   she was charming and a lover of magic.
She made nations slaves with her
      prostitution
   and her witchcraft.

5 "I am against you, Nineveh," says the
   Lord All-Powerful.
"I will pull your dress up over your face
and show the nations your nakedness
   and the kingdoms your shame.
6 I will throw filthy garbage on you
   and make a fool of you.
I will make people stare at you.
7 Everyone who sees you will run away and
      say,
   'Nineveh is in ruins. Who will cry for
      her?'
Nineveh, where will I find anyone to
      comfort you?"

8 You are no better than Thebes,[n]
   who sits by the Nile River
   with water all around her.
The river was her defense;
   the waters were like a wall around her.
9 Cush and Egypt gave her endless strength;
   Put and Libya supported her.

2:5 **He** This probably means the king of Assyria.
2:11 **lions'** The symbol of Assyria was the lion.
3:8 **Thebes** A great city in Egypt.

10 But Thebes was captured
    and went into captivity.
Her small children were beaten to death
    at every street corner.
Lots were thrown for her important men,
    and all of her leaders were put in
    chains.

11 Nineveh, you will be drunk, too.
    You will hide;
    you will look for a place safe from the
    enemy.
12 All your defenses are like fig trees with
    ripe fruit.
    When the tree is shaken, the figs fall
    into the mouth of the eater.
13 Look at your soldiers.
    They are all women!
The gates of your land
    are wide open for your enemies;
    fire has burned the bars of your gates.

14 Get enough water before the long war
    begins.
    Make your defenses strong!
Get mud,
    mix clay,
    make bricks!

15 There the fire will burn you up.
    The sword will kill you;
    like grasshoppers eating crops, the
    battle will completely destroy you.
Grow in number like hopping locusts;
    grow in number like swarming locusts!
16 Your traders are more than the stars in the
    sky,
    but like locusts, they strip the land and
    then fly away.
17 Your guards are like locusts.
    Your officers are like swarms of locusts
    that hang on the walls on a cold day.
When the sun comes up, they fly away,
    and no one knows where they have
    gone.
18 King of Assyria, your rulers are asleep;
    your important men lie down to rest.
Your people have been scattered on the
    mountains,
    and there is no one to bring them
    back.
19 Nothing can heal your wound;
    your injury will not heal.
Everyone who hears about you applauds,
    because everyone has felt your endless
    cruelty.

habakkuk

LEARNING HOW TO TRUST GOD

1 This is the message Habakkuk the prophet received.

HABAKKUK COMPLAINS

2 Lord, how long must I ask for help
and you ignore me?
I cry out to you about violence,
but you do not save us!
3 Why do you make me see wrong things
and make me look at trouble?
People are destroying things and hurting
others in front of me;
they are arguing and fighting.
4 So the teachings are weak,
and justice never comes.
Evil people gain while good people lose;
the judges no longer make fair
decisions.

THE LORD ANSWERS

5 "Look at the nations!
Watch them and be amazed and
shocked.
I will do something in your lifetime
that you won't believe even when you
are told about it.
6 I will use the Babylonians,
those cruel and wild people
who march across the earth
and take lands that don't belong to
them.
7 They scare and frighten people.
They do what they want to do
and are good only to themselves.
8 Their horses are faster than leopards
and quicker than wolves at sunset.
Their horse soldiers attack quickly;
they come from places far away.
They attack quickly, like an eagle
swooping down for food.
9 They all come to fight.
Nothing can stop them.
Their prisoners are as many as the
grains of sand.
10 They laugh at kings
and make fun of rulers.
They laugh at all the strong, walled cities

and build dirt piles to the top of the
walls to capture them.
11 Then they leave like the wind and move
on.
They are guilty of worshiping their own
strength."

HABAKKUK COMPLAINS AGAIN

12 Lord, you live forever,
my God, my holy God.
We will not die.
Lord, you have chosen the Babylonians to
punish people;
our Rock, you picked them to punish.
13 Your eyes are too good to look at evil;
you cannot stand to see those who do
wrong.
So how can you put up with those evil
people?
How can you be quiet when the wicked
swallow up people who are better
than they are?
14 You treat people like fish in the sea,
like sea animals without a leader.
15 The enemy brings them in with hooks.
He catches them in his net
and drags them in his fishnet.
So he rejoices and sings for joy.
16 The enemy offers sacrifices to his net
and burns incense to worship it,
because it lets him live like the rich
and enjoy the best food.
17 Will he keep on taking riches with his
net?
Will he go on destroying people
without showing mercy?

2 I will stand like a guard to watch
and place myself at the tower.
I will wait to see what he will say to me;
I will wait to learn how God will answer
my complaint.

THE LORD ANSWERS

2 The Lord answered me:
"Write down the vision;
write it clearly on clay tablets

so whoever reads it can run to tell
others.
³ It is not yet time for the message to come
true,
but that time is coming soon;
the message will come true.
It may seem like a long time,
but be patient and wait for it,
because it will surely come;
it will not be delayed.
⁴ The evil nation is very proud of itself;
it is not living as it should.
But those who are right with God will
live by faith.

⁵ "Just as wine can trick a person,
those who are too proud will not last,

because their desire is like a grave's desire
for death,
and like death they always want more.
They gather other nations for
themselves
and collect for themselves all the
countries.
⁶ But all the nations the Babylonians have
hurt will laugh at them.
They will make fun of the Babylonians
and say, 'How terrible it will be for the
one that steals many things.
How long will that nation get rich by
forcing others to pay them?'

⁷ "One day the people from whom you have
taken money will turn against you.

SERVANT EVANGELISM

FAITH

living by faith

HABAKKUK 2:4

If I read, "Those who are right with God will live by faith," I might think that faith is
something that I have to do in order to live. I have to perform "faith" as my way of
living. So I might conclude that I have to pray the right things, believe the right things,
say the right things—I have to do all those "religious" things that will make me "right
with God."

But some scholars think that the verse should be read, "The one who is right with God
by his faith shall live." The difference is hard to grasp, but it is important. We don't
become justified because we "perform" acts of faith. That would shift the justification
onto me and onto what I do. No, God gives us the status of "not guilty" in spite of our
sinful actions, precisely when we are guilty.

Faith is agreeing with God that we deserved punishment. We didn't earn anything, even
if that "earning" came by doing faithful things. We gratefully receive his gift of acquittal.
That is faith. And that is why we are justified. We didn't do anything. He did it. And,
now, because of his decision to change our status from "guilty" to "not guilty," we can
go about living. We are alive! And it's all because of him.

reflect: Praise God for his indescribable love for you and the rest of his creation.
Go to **FAITH:** "God's Ultimate Sacrifice" at **Acts 17:25.**

They will realize what is happening and
make you shake with fear.
Then they will take everything you
have.

8 Because you have stolen from many
nations,
those who are left will take much from
you.
This is because you have killed many
people,
destroying countries and cities and
everyone in them.

9 "How terrible it will be for the nation that
becomes rich by doing wrong,
thinking they will live in a safe place
and escape harm.
10 Because you have made plans to destroy
many people,
you have made your own houses
ashamed of you.
Because of it, you will lose your lives.
11 The stones of the walls will cry out
against you,
and the boards that support the roof
will agree that you are wrong.

12 "How terrible it will be for the nation that
kills people to build a city,
that wrongs others to start a town.
13 The LORD All-Powerful will send fire
to destroy what those people have
built;
all the nations' work will be for nothing.
14 Then, just as water covers the sea,
people everywhere will know the
LORD's glory.

15 "How terrible for the nation that makes
its neighbors drink,
pouring from the jug of wine until they
are drunk
so that it can look at their naked bodies.
16 You Babylonians will be filled with
disgrace, not respect.
It's your turn to drink and fall to the
ground like a drunk person.
The cup of anger from the LORD's right
hand is coming around to you.
You will receive disgrace, not respect.
17 You hurt many people in Lebanon,
but now you will be hurt.
You killed many animals there,
and now you must be afraid

because of what you did
to that land, those cities, and the people
who lived in them.

THE MESSAGE ABOUT IDOLS

18 "An idol does no good, because a human
made it;
it is only a statue that teaches lies.
The one who made it expects his own
work to help him,
but he makes idols that can't even
speak!
19 How terrible it will be for the one who
says to a wooden statue, 'Come to
life!'
How terrible it will be for the one who
says to a silent stone, 'Get up!'
It cannot tell you what to do.
It is only a statue covered with gold and
silver;
there is no life in it.
20 The LORD is in his Holy Temple;
all the earth should be silent in his
presence."

HABAKKUK'S PRAYER

3 This is the prayer of Habakkuk the
prophet, on shigionoth.
2 LORD, I have heard the news about you;
I am amazed at what you have done.
LORD, do great things once again in our
time;
make those things happen again in our
own days.
Even when you are angry,
remember to be kind.

3 God is coming from Teman;
the Holy One comes from Mount
Paran. [n]   *Selah*
His glory covers the skies,
and his praise fills the earth.
4 He is like a bright light.
Rays of light shine from his hand,
and there he hides his power.
5 Sickness goes before him,
and disease follows behind him.
6 He stands and shakes the earth.
He looks, and the nations shake with
fear.

3:3 Teman...Paran God is seen as again coming from
the direction of Mount Sinai. He came from Sinai when
he rescued his people from Egypt.

The mountains, which stood for ages,
  break into pieces;
the old hills fall down.
God has always done this.

7 I saw that the tents of Cushan were in
    trouble
  and that the tents of Midian trembled.
8 LORD, were you angry at the rivers,
  or were you angry at the streams?
Were you angry with the sea
  when you rode your horses and chariots
    of victory?[n]
9 You uncovered your bow
  and commanded many arrows to be
    brought to you.   Selah
You split the earth with rivers.
10 The mountains saw you and shook with
    fear.
  The rushing water flowed.
    The sea made a loud noise,
    and its waves rose high.
11 The sun and moon stood still in the sky;
  they stopped when they saw the flash of
    your flying arrows
  and the gleam of your shining spear.
12 In anger you marched on the earth;
  in anger you punished the nations.
13 You came out to save your people,
  to save your chosen one.
You crushed the leader of the wicked
    ones
  and took everything he had, from head
    to toe.   Selah
14 With the enemy's own spear you stabbed
    the leader of his army.

His soldiers rushed out like a storm to
    scatter us.
They were happy
  as they were robbing the poor people in
    secret.
15 But you marched through the sea with
    your horses,
  stirring the great waters.

16 I hear these things, and my body
    trembles;
  my lips tremble when I hear the sound.
My bones feel weak,
  and my legs shake.

But I will wait patiently for the day of
    disaster
  that will come to the people who attack
    us.
17 Fig trees may not grow figs,
  and there may be no grapes on the
    vines.
There may be no olives growing
  and no food growing in the fields.
There may be no sheep in the pens
  and no cattle in the barns.
18 But I will still be glad in the LORD;
  I will rejoice in God my Savior.
19 The Lord GOD is my strength.
  He makes me like a deer that does not
    stumble
  so I can walk on the steep mountains.
  For the director of music. On my stringed
instruments.

3:8 sea . . . victory This is probably talking about the
Israelites crossing the Red Sea.

zephaniah

GOD WILL JUDGE THE WORLD

1 This is the word of the LORD that came through Zephaniah while Josiah son of Amon was king of Judah. Zephaniah was the son of Cushi, who was the son of Gedaliah. Gedaliah was the son of Amariah, who was the son of Hezekiah.

THE LORD'S JUDGMENT

2 "I will sweep away everything
   from the earth," says the LORD.
3 "I will sweep away the people and
      animals;
   I will destroy the birds in the air
   and the fish of the sea.
   I will ruin the evil people,
   and I will remove human beings from
      the earth," says the LORD.

THE FUTURE OF JUDAH

4 "I will punish Judah
   and all the people living in Jerusalem.
   I will remove from this place
   all signs of Baal, the false priests, and
      the other priests.
5 I will destroy those who worship
   the stars from the roofs,[n]
   and those who worship and make
      promises
   by both the LORD and the god Molech,
6 and those who turned away from the
      LORD,
   and those who quit following the LORD
   and praying to him for direction.
7 Be silent before the Lord GOD,
   because the LORD's day for judging
      people is coming soon.
   The LORD has prepared a sacrifice;
   he has made holy his invited guests.
8 On the day of the LORD's sacrifice,
   I, the LORD, will punish the princes and
      the king's sons
   and all those who wear foreign clothes.
9 On that day I will punish those who
      worship Dagon,
   those who hurt others and tell lies in
      the temples of their gods.

10 "On that day," says the LORD,
   "a cry will be heard at the Fish Gate.
   A wail will come from the new area of
      the city,
   and a loud crash will echo from the
      hills.
11 Cry, you people living in the market area,
   because all the merchants will be dead;
   all the silver traders will be gone.
12 At that time I, the LORD, will search
      Jerusalem with lamps.
   I will punish those who are satisfied
      with themselves,
   who think, 'The LORD won't help us or
      punish us.'
13 Their wealth will be stolen
   and their houses destroyed.
   They may build houses,
   but they will not live in them.
   They may plant vineyards,
   but they will not drink any wine from
      them.

THE LORD'S DAY OF JUDGING

14 "The LORD's day of judging is coming
      soon;
   it is near and coming fast.
   The cry will be very sad on the day of the
      LORD;
   even soldiers will cry.
15 That day will be a day of anger,
   a day of terror and trouble,
   a day of destruction and ruin,
   a day of darkness and gloom,
   a day of clouds and blackness,
16 a day of alarms and battle cries.
   'Attack the strong, walled cities!
   Attack the corner towers!'
17 I will make life hard on the people;
   they will walk around like the blind,
   because they have sinned against the
      LORD.

1:5 roofs In Bible times houses were built with flat roofs. The roof was used for drying things such as flax and fruit. And it was used as an extra room, as a place for worship, and as a cool place to sleep in the summer.

Their blood will be poured out like dust,
and their insides will be dumped like
trash.

18 On the day that God will show his anger,
neither their silver nor gold will save
them.
The LORD's anger will be like a fire
that will burn up the whole world;
suddenly he will bring an end, yes, an end
to everyone on earth."

THE LORD ASKS PEOPLE TO CHANGE

2 Gather together, gather,
you unwanted people.
2 Do it before it's too late,
before you are blown away like chaff,
before the LORD's terrible anger reaches
you,
before the day of the LORD's anger
comes to you.
3 Come to the LORD, all you who are not
proud,
who obey his laws.
Do what is right. Learn to be humble.
Maybe you will escape
on the day the LORD shows his anger.

PHILISTIA WILL BE PUNISHED

4 No one will be left in the city of Gaza,
and the city of Ashkelon will be
destroyed.
Ashdod will be empty by noon,
and the people of Ekron will be chased
away.
5 How terrible it will be for you who live by
the Mediterranean Sea,
you Philistines!
The word of the LORD is against you,
Canaan, land of the Philistines.

"I will destroy you
so that no one will be left."
6 The land by the Mediterranean Sea, in
which you live,
will become pastures, fields for
shepherds, and pens for sheep.
7 It will belong to the descendants of Judah
who are left alive.
There they will let their sheep eat grass.
At night they will sleep
in the houses of Ashkelon.
The LORD their God will pay attention to
them
and will make their life good again.

MOAB AND AMMON WILL BE PUNISHED

8 "I have heard the insults of the country of
Moab
and the threats of the people of
Ammon.
They have insulted my people
and have taken their land."
9 So the LORD All-Powerful, the God of
Israel, says,
"As surely as I live,
Moab will be destroyed like Sodom,
and Ammon will be destroyed like
Gomorrah[n]—
a heap of weeds, a pit of salt,
and a ruin forever.
Those of my people who are left alive will
take whatever they want from them;
those who are left from my nation will
take their land."

10 This is what Moab and Ammon get for
being proud,
because they insulted and made fun of
the people of the LORD All-Powerful.
11 The LORD will frighten them,
because he will destroy all the gods of
the earth.
Then everyone in faraway places
will worship him wherever they are.

CUSH AND ASSYRIA WILL BE DESTROYED

12 "You Cushites also
will be killed by my sword."
13 Then the LORD will turn against the
north
and destroy Assyria.
He will make Nineveh
a ruin as dry as a desert.
14 Flocks and herds will lie down there,
and all wild animals.
The owls and crows will sit
on the stone pillars.
The owl will hoot through the windows,
trash will be in the doorways,
and the wooden boards of the buildings
will be gone.
15 This is the happy and safe city
that thinks there is no one else as strong
as it is.
But what a ruin it will be,
a place where wild animals live.

2:9 Sodom . . . Gomorrah Two cities God destroyed
because the people were so evil.

All those who pass by will make fun
and shake their fists.

JERUSALEM WILL BE PUNISHED

3 How terrible for the wicked, stubborn
city of Jerusalem,
which hurts its own people.
2 It obeys no voice;
it can't be taught to do right.
It doesn't trust the LORD;
it doesn't worship its God.
3 Its officers are like roaring lions.
Its rulers are like hungry wolves that
attack in the evening,
and in the morning nothing is left of
those they attacked.
4 Its prophets are proud;
they are people who cannot be
trusted.
Its priests don't respect holy things;
they break God's teachings.
5 But the LORD is good, and he is there in
that city.
He does no wrong.
Every morning he governs the people
fairly;
every day he can be trusted.
But evil people are not ashamed of what
they do.

6 "I have destroyed nations;
their towers were ruined.
I made their streets empty
so no one goes there anymore.
Their cities are ruined;
no one lives there at all.
7 I said, 'Surely now Jerusalem will respect
me
and will accept my teaching.'
Then the place where they lived would
not be destroyed,
and I would not have to punish them.
But they were still eager
to do evil in everything they did.
8 Just wait," says the LORD.
"Someday I will stand up as a witness.
I have decided that I will gather nations
and assemble kingdoms.
I will pour out my anger on them,
all my strong anger.
My anger will be like fire
that will burn up the whole world.

A NEW DAY FOR GOD'S PEOPLE

9 "Then I will give the people of all nations
pure speech
so that all of them will speak the name
of the LORD
and worship me together.
10 People will come from where the Nile
River begins;
my scattered people will come with
gifts for me.
11 Then Jerusalem will not be ashamed
of the wrongs done against me,
because I will remove from this city
those who like to brag;
there will never be any more proud people
on my holy mountain in Jerusalem.
12 But I will leave in the city
the humble and those who are not
proud,
and they will trust in the LORD.
13 Those who are left alive in Israel won't do
wrong or tell lies;
they won't trick people with their words.
They will eat and lie down
with no one to make them afraid."

A HAPPY SONG

14 Sing, Jerusalem.
Israel, shout for joy!
Jerusalem, be happy
and rejoice with all your heart.
15 The LORD has stopped punishing you;
he has sent your enemies away.
The King of Israel, the LORD, is with you;
you will never again be afraid of being
harmed.
16 On that day Jerusalem will be told,
"Don't be afraid, city of Jerusalem.
Don't give up.
17 The LORD your God is with you;
the mighty One will save you.
He will rejoice over you.
You will rest in his love;
he will sing and be joyful about you."
18 "I will take away the sadness planned for
you,
which would have made you very
ashamed.
19 At that time I will punish
all those who harmed you.
I will save my people who cannot walk
and gather my people who have been
thrown out.

I will give them praise and honor
in every place where they were shamed.
20 At that time I will gather you;
at that time I will bring you back home.
I will give you honor and praise

from people everywhere
when I make things go well again for
you,
as you will see with your own eyes,"
says the LORD.

FUTURE

BUILDING MOMENTUM THROUGH TEAMWORK

the importance
of affirmation

ZEPHANIAH 3:17

By Bill McCartney

In order to keep good team members who are committed to your vision, you must be able to relate to them well. Indeed, the word "relate" forms an acrostic that you can easily remember:

R – Respect. Offer respect to your team members. Everyone deserves respect; they should not have to "earn" it.

E – Encourage. Be an encourager. Look out for those who are lagging behind the rest of the group and coax them along. Carry them if you must. The benefit of the goal is the same for the whole group, no matter how each individual gets to it.

L – Listen. Every great leader is a great listener. To listen well, you must "listen to understand, not to respond." Listen to your team members; don't just wait for the opportunity to throw in your two cents' worth unless you are asked for your opinion. The greatest value you can give to someone is to show that person he is worth listening to.

A – Affirm. Believe in your team members. Tell them that you believe in them. Take the time to check on them. They need to know that their leader is concerned for their welfare.

T – Time. Time is a valuable commodity. Giving your time to your team members increases their worth.

E – Expect. Your team members may already be giving you most of what they've got. If you raise the expectations you have for them, they will give you more. Good leaders can relate to people effectively. Relate well to your team members, and they will respond well to you.

reflect: Do you relate well to the people you are leading?
Go to **Ephesians 5:17.**

---

haggai

THE TEMPLE IS REBUILT

IT IS TIME TO BUILD THE TEMPLE

1 The prophet Haggai spoke the word of the LORD to Zerubbabel son of Shealtiel, the governor of Judah, and to Joshua son of Jehozadak, the high priest. This message came in the second year that Darius was king, on the first day of the sixth month:

2"This is what the LORD All-Powerful says: 'The people say the right time has not come to rebuild the Temple of the LORD.'"

3Then Haggai the prophet spoke the word of the LORD: 4"Is it right for you to be living in fancy houses while the Temple is still in ruins?"

5This is what the LORD All-Powerful says: "Think about what you have done. 6You have planted much, but you harvest little. You eat, but you do not become full. You drink, but you are still thirsty. You put on clothes, but you are not warm enough. You earn money, but then you lose it all as if you had put it into a purse full of holes."

7This is what the LORD All-Powerful says: "Think about what you have done. 8Go up to the mountains, bring back wood, and build the Temple. Then I will be pleased with it and be honored," says the LORD. 9"You look for much, but you find little. When you bring it home, I destroy it. Why?" asks the LORD All-Powerful. "Because you all work hard for your own houses while my house is still in ruins! 10Because of what you have done, the sky holds back its rain and the ground holds back its crops. 11I have called for a time without rain on the land, and on the mountains, and on the grain, the new wine, the olive oil, the plants which the earth produces, the people, the farm animals, and all the work of your hands."

12Zerubbabel son of Shealtiel and Joshua son of Jehozadak, the high priest, and all the rest of the people who were left alive obeyed the LORD their God and the message from Haggai the prophet, because the LORD their God had sent him. And the people feared the LORD.

13Haggai, the LORD's messenger, gave the LORD's message to the people, saying, "The LORD says, 'I am with you.'" 14The LORD stirred up Zerubbabel son of Shealtiel, the governor of Judah, and Joshua son of Jehozadak, the high priest, and all the rest of the people who were left alive. So they came and worked on the Temple of their God, the LORD All-Powerful. 15They began on the twenty-fourth day of the sixth month in the second year Darius was king.

THE BEAUTY OF THE TEMPLE

2 On the twenty-first day of the seventh month, the LORD spoke his word through Haggai the prophet, saying, 2"Speak to Zerubbabel son of Shealtiel, governor of Judah, and to Joshua son of Jehozadak, the high priest, and to the rest of the people who are left alive. Say, 3'Do any of you remember how great the Temple was before it was destroyed? What does it look like now? Doesn't it seem like nothing to you?' 4But the LORD says, 'Zerubbabel, be brave. Also, Joshua son of Jehozadak, the high priest, be brave. And all you people who live in the land, be brave,' says the LORD. 'Work, because I am with you,' says the LORD All-Powerful. 5'I made a promise to you when you came out of Egypt, and my Spirit is still with you. So don't be afraid.'

6"This is what the LORD All-Powerful says: 'In a short time I will once again shake the heavens and the earth, the sea and the dry land. 7I will shake all the nations, and they will bring their wealth. Then I will fill this Temple with glory,' says the LORD All-Powerful. 8'The silver is mine, and the gold is mine,' says the LORD All-Powerful. 9'The new Temple will be greater than the one before,' says the LORD All-Powerful. 'And in this place I will give peace,' says the LORD All-Powerful."

10On the twenty-fourth day of the ninth month in the second year Darius was king, the LORD spoke his word to Haggai the prophet, saying, ¹¹"This is what the Lord All-Powerful says: 'Ask the priests for a teaching. ¹²Suppose a person carries in the fold of his clothes some meat made holy for the Lord. If that fold touches bread, cooked food, wine, olive oil, or some other food, will that be made holy?'"

The priests answered, "No."

¹³Then Haggai said, "A person who touches a dead body will become unclean. If he touches any of these foods, will it become unclean, too?"

The priests answered, "Yes, it would become unclean."

FINANCES

HANDLING MONEY GOD'S WAY

the "right to use" clause

HAGGAI 2:8

I n the U.S., the word "real" in real estate comes from the word "royal," meaning it really belongs to the government. If you don't believe that, don't pay your property taxes and see who ends up owning your land. Haggai's imagery makes it clear. We don't own the property. We only have a "right to use" clause. We are tenants in this world.

Therefore, we are subject to the rules of the lease agreement. We are here to demonstrate our faithfulness in the redistribution of God's property. For some period of time, he grants us the right to gather, consume, replenish, and restore his goods. Sometimes he gives us temporary custody over vast amounts, sometimes over only a little. But the purpose is the same: He wants us to learn how to treat his creation the same way he does.

Consider the gold and silver in your life. If this imagery represents your financial assets, are you managing what has been placed into your custody the way the Owner would? Are you using his property to further his objectives and purposes? Or have you been distracted by the accounting statements and decided that this property really belongs to you? That kind of thinking usually results in statements like this: "It's my money. I can do what I want with it."

The truth is a little different. It's not your money. It is God's. Amazingly, once we begin to treat his possessions properly, we discover that he is not stingy at all. He loves for his children to exercise proper stewardship over his creation. More often than not, when we demonstrate we can handle the responsibility, he gives us even more to take care of.

reflect: Realize that God is providing you with possessions for a purpose.
Go to **Malachi 3:3.**

[14]Then Haggai answered, "The LORD says, 'This is also true for the people of this nation. They are unclean, and everything they do with their hands is unclean to me. Whatever they offer at the altar is also unclean.

[15]"'Think about this from now on! Think about how it was before you started laying stones on top of stones to build the Temple of the LORD. [16]A person used to come to a pile of grain expecting to find twenty basketfuls, but there were only ten. And a person used to come to the wine vat to take out fifty jarfuls, but only twenty were there. [17]I destroyed your work with diseases, mildew, and hail, but you still did not come back to me,' says the LORD. [18]'It is the twenty-fourth day of the ninth month, the day in which the people finished working on the foundation of the Temple of the LORD. From now on, think about these things: [19]Do you have seeds for crops still in the barn? Your vines, fig trees, pomegranates, and olive trees have not given fruit yet. But from now on I will bless you!'"

THE LORD MAKES A PROMISE TO ZERUBBABEL

[20]Then the LORD spoke his word a second time to Haggai on the twenty-fourth day of the month. He said, [21]"Tell Zerubbabel, the governor of Judah, 'I am going to shake the heavens and the earth. [22]I will destroy the foreign kingdoms and take away the power of the kingdoms of the nations. I will destroy the chariots and their riders. The horses will fall with their riders, as people kill each other with swords.' [23]The LORD All-Powerful says, 'On that day I will take you, Zerubbabel son of Shealtiel, my servant,' says the LORD, 'and I will make you important like my signet ring, because I have chosen you!' says the LORD All-Powerful."

zechariah

ENCOURAGING THE PEOPLE

THE LORD CALLS HIS PEOPLE BACK

1 In the eighth month of the second year Darius was king, the LORD spoke his word to the prophet Zechariah son of Berekiah, who was the son of Iddo. The LORD said, 2"The LORD was very angry with your ancestors. 3So tell the people: This is what the LORD All-Powerful says: 'Return to me, and I will return to you,' says the LORD All-Powerful. 4Don't be like your ancestors. In the past the prophets said to them: This is what the LORD All-Powerful says: 'Stop your evil ways and evil actions.' But they wouldn't listen or pay attention to me, says the LORD. 5Your ancestors are dead, and those prophets didn't live forever. 6I commanded my words and laws to my servants the prophets, and they preached to your ancestors, who returned to me. They said, 'The LORD All-Powerful did as he said he would. He punished us for the way we lived and for what we did.'"

THE VISION OF THE HORSES

7It was on the twenty-fourth day of the eleventh month, which is the month of Shebat, in Darius's second year as king. The LORD spoke his word to the prophet Zechariah son of Berekiah, who was the son of Iddo.

8During the night I had a vision. I saw a man riding a red horse. He was standing among some myrtle trees in a ravine, with red, brown, and white horses behind him. 9I asked, "What are these, sir?"

The angel who was talking with me answered, "I'll show you what they are."

10Then the man standing among the myrtle trees explained, "They are the ones the LORD sent through all the earth."

11Then they spoke to the LORD's angel, who was standing among the myrtle trees. They said, "We have gone through all the earth, and everything is calm and quiet."

12Then the LORD's angel asked, "LORD All-Powerful, how long will it be before you show mercy to Jerusalem and the cities of Judah? You have been angry with them for seventy years now." 13So the LORD answered the angel who was talking with me, and his words were comforting and good.

14Then the angel who was talking to me said to me, "Announce this: This is what the LORD All-Powerful says: 'I have a strong love for Jerusalem. 15And I am very angry with the nations that feel so safe. I was only a little angry at them, but they made things worse.'

16"So this is what the LORD says: 'I will return to Jerusalem with mercy. My Temple will be rebuilt,' says the LORD All-Powerful, 'and the measuring line will be used to rebuild Jerusalem.'

17"Also announce: This is what the LORD All-Powerful says: 'My towns will be rich again. The LORD will comfort Jerusalem again, and I will again choose Jerusalem.'"

THE VISION OF THE HORNS

18Then I looked up and saw four animal horns. 19I asked the angel who was talking with me, "What are these?"

He said, "These are the horns that scattered the people of Judah, Israel, and Jerusalem."

20Then the LORD showed me four craftsmen. 21I asked, "What are they coming to do?"

He answered, "They have come to scare and throw down the horns. These horns scattered the people of Judah so that no one could even lift up his head. These horns stand for the nations that attacked the people of Judah and scattered them."

THE VISION OF THE MEASURING LINE

2 Then I looked up and saw a man holding a line for measuring things. 2I asked him, "Where are you going?"

He said to me, "I am going to measure Jerusalem, to see how wide and how long it is."

3Then the angel who was talking with me left, and another angel came out to meet him. 4The second angel said to him, "Run and tell that young man, 'Jerusalem will become a city without walls, because there will be so many people and cattle in it. 5I will be a wall of fire around it,' says the LORD. 'And I will be the glory within it.'

6"Oh no! Oh no! Run away from Babylon, because I have scattered you like the four winds of heaven," says the LORD.

7"Oh no, Jerusalem! Escape, you who live right in Babylon." 8This is what the LORD All-Powerful says: "After he has honored me and sent me against the nations who took your possessions—because whoever touches you hurts what is precious to me—9I will shake my hand against them so that their slaves will rob them."

Then you will know that the LORD All-Powerful sent me.

10"Shout and be glad, Jerusalem. I am coming, and I will live among you," says the LORD. 11"At that time people from many nations will join with the LORD and will become my people. Then I will live among you, and you will know that the LORD All-Powerful has sent me to you. 12The LORD will take Judah as his own part of the holy land, and Jerusalem will be his chosen city again. 13Be silent, everyone, in the presence of the LORD. He is coming out of the holy place where he lives."

THE VISION OF THE HIGH PRIEST

3 Then he showed me Joshua, the high priest, standing in front of the LORD's angel. And Satan was standing by Joshua's right side to accuse him. 2The LORD said to Satan, "The LORD says no to you, Satan! The LORD who has chosen Jerusalem says no to you! This man was like a burning stick pulled from the fire."

3Joshua was wearing dirty clothes and was standing in front of the angel. 4The angel said to those standing in front of him, "Take off those dirty clothes."

Then the angel said to Joshua, "Look, I have taken away your sin from you, and I am giving you beautiful, fine clothes."

5Then I said, "Put a clean turban on his head." So they put a clean turban on his head and dressed him while the LORD's angel stood there.

6Then the LORD's angel said to Joshua, 7"This is what the LORD All-Powerful says: 'If you do as I tell you and serve me, you will be

in charge of my Temple and my courtyards. And I will let you be with these angels who are standing here.

8"'Listen, Joshua, the high priest, and your friends who are sitting in front of you. They are symbols of what will happen. I am going to bring my servant called the Branch. 9Look, I put this stone in front of Joshua, a stone with seven sides. I will carve a message on it,' says the LORD All-Powerful. 'And in one day I will take away the sin of this land.'

10"The LORD All-Powerful says, 'In that day, each of you will invite your neighbor to sit under your own grapevine and under your own fig tree.'"

THE VISION OF THE LAMPSTAND

4 Then the angel who was talking with me returned and woke me up as if I had been asleep. 2He asked me, "What do you see?"

I said, "I see a solid gold lampstand with a bowl at the top. And there are seven lamps and also seven places for wicks. 3There are two olive trees by it, one on the right of the bowl and the other on the left."

4I asked the angel who talked with me, "Sir, what are these?"

5The angel said, "Don't you know what they are?"

"No, sir," I said.

6Then he told me, "This is the word of the LORD to Zerubbabel: 'You will not succeed by your own strength or by your own power, but by my Spirit,' says the LORD All-Powerful.

7"Who are you, big mountain? In front of Zerubbabel you will become flat land, and he will bring out the topmost stone, shouting, 'It's beautiful! It's beautiful!'"

8Then the LORD spoke his word to me again, saying, 9"Zerubbabel has laid the foundation of this Temple, and he will complete it. Then you will know that the LORD All-Powerful has sent me to you.

10"The people should not think that small beginnings are unimportant. They will be happy when they see Zerubbabel with tools, building the Temple.

"(These are the seven eyes of the LORD, which look back and forth across the earth.)"

11Then I asked the angel, "What are the two olive trees on the right and left of the lampstand?"

¹²I also asked him, "What are the two olive branches beside the two gold pipes, from which the olive oil flows to the lamps?"

¹³He answered, "Don't you know what they are?"

"No, sir," I said.

¹⁴So he said, "They are symbols of the two who have been appointed to serve the Lord of all the earth."

THE VISION OF THE FLYING SCROLL

5 I looked up again and saw a flying scroll. ²The angel asked me, "What do you see?"

I answered, "I see a flying scroll, thirty feet long and fifteen feet wide."

³And he said to me, "This is the curse that will go all over the land. One side says every thief will be taken away. The other side says everyone who makes false promises will be taken away. ⁴The LORD All-Powerful says, 'I will send it to the houses of thieves and to those who use my name to make false promises. The scroll will stay in that person's house and destroy it with its wood and stones.'"

THE VISION OF THE WOMAN

⁵Then the angel who was talking with me came forward and said to me, "Look up and see what is going out."

⁶"What is it?" I asked.

He answered, "It is a measuring basket going out." He also said, "It is a symbol of the people's sins in all the land."

⁷Then the lid made of lead was raised, and there was a woman sitting inside the basket. ⁸The angel said, "The woman stands for wickedness." Then he pushed her back into the basket and put the lid back down.

⁹Then I looked up and saw two women going out with the wind in their wings. Their wings were like those of a stork, and they lifted up the basket between earth and the sky.

¹⁰I asked the angel who was talking with me, "Where are they taking the basket?"

¹¹"They are going to Babylonia to build a temple for it," he answered. "When the temple is ready, they will set the basket there in its place."

THE VISION OF THE FOUR CHARIOTS

6 I looked up again and saw four chariots going out between two mountains, mountains of bronze. ²Red horses pulled the first chariot. Black horses pulled the second chariot. ³White horses pulled the third chariot, and strong, spotted horses pulled the fourth chariot. ⁴I asked the angel who was talking with me, "What are these, sir?"

⁵He said, "These are the four spirits of heaven. They have just come from the presence of the Lord of the whole world. ⁶The chariot pulled by the black horses will go to the land of the north. The white horses will go to the land of the west, and the spotted horses will go to the land of the south."

⁷When the powerful horses went out, they were eager to go through all the earth. So he said, "Go through all the earth," and they did.

⁸Then he called to me, "Look, the horses that went north have caused my spirit to rest in the land of the north."

A CROWN FOR JOSHUA

⁹The LORD spoke his word to me, saying, ¹⁰"Take silver and gold from Heldai, Tobijah, and Jedaiah, who were captives in Babylon. Go that same day to the house of Josiah son of Zephaniah, who came from Babylon. ¹¹Make the silver and gold into a crown, and put it on the head of Joshua son of Jehozadak, the high priest. ¹²Tell him this is what the LORD All-Powerful says: 'A man whose name is the Branch will branch out from where he is, and he will build the Temple of the LORD. ¹³One man[n] will build the Temple of the LORD, and the other[n] will receive honor. One man will sit on his throne and rule, and the other will be a priest on his throne. And these two men will work together in peace.' ¹⁴The crown will be kept in the Temple of the LORD to remind Heldai, Tobijah, Jedaiah, and Josiah son of Zephaniah. ¹⁵People living far away will come and build the Temple of the LORD. Then you will know the LORD All-Powerful has sent me to you. This will happen if you completely obey the LORD your God."

THE PEOPLE SHOULD SHOW MERCY

7 In the fourth year Darius was king, on the fourth day of the ninth month, which is called Kislev, the LORD spoke his word to Zechariah. ²The city of Bethel sent Sharezer, Regem-Melech, and their men to ask the

---

6:13 One man This probably refers to Zerubbabel.
6:13 other This probably refers to Joshua.

LORD a question. ³They went to the prophets and priests who were at the Temple of the LORD All-Powerful. The men said, "For years in the fifth month of each year we have shown our sadness and fasted. Should we continue to do this?"

⁴The LORD All-Powerful spoke his word to me, saying, ⁵"Tell the priests and the people in the land: 'For seventy years you fasted and cried in the fifth and seventh months, but that was not really for me. ⁶And when you ate and drank, it was really for yourselves. ⁷The LORD used the earlier prophets to say the same thing, when Jerusalem and the surrounding towns were at peace and wealthy, and people lived in the southern area and the western hills.'"

⁸And the LORD spoke his word to Zechariah again, saying, ⁹"This is what the LORD All-Powerful says: 'Do what is right and true. Be kind and merciful to each other. ¹⁰Don't hurt widows and orphans, foreigners or the poor; don't even think of doing evil to somebody else.'

¹¹"But they refused to pay attention; they were stubborn and did not want to listen anymore. ¹²They made their hearts as hard as rock and would not listen to the teachings of the LORD All-Powerful. And they would not hear the words he sent by his Spirit through the earlier prophets. So the LORD All-Powerful became very angry.

¹³"When I called to them, they would not listen. So when they called to me, I would not listen,' says the LORD All-Powerful. ¹⁴'I scattered them like a hurricane to other countries they did not know. This good land was left so ruined behind them that no one could live there. They had made the desired land a ruin.'"

THE LORD WILL BLESS JERUSALEM

8 The LORD All-Powerful spoke his word, saying, ²This is what the LORD All-Powerful says: "I have a very strong love for Jerusalem. My strong love for her is like a fire burning in me."

³This is what the LORD says: "I will return to Jerusalem and live in it. Then it will be called the City of Truth, and the mountain of the LORD All-Powerful will be called the Holy Mountain."

⁴This is what the LORD All-Powerful says:

"Old men and old women will again sit along Jerusalem's streets, each carrying a cane because of age. ⁵And the streets will be filled with boys and girls playing."

⁶This is what the LORD All-Powerful says: "Those who are left alive then may think it is too difficult to happen, but it is not too difficult for me," says the LORD All-Powerful. ⁷This is what the LORD All-Powerful says: "I will save my people from countries in the east and west. ⁸I will bring them back, and they will live in Jerusalem. They will be my people, and I will be their good and loyal God."

⁹This is what the LORD All-Powerful says: "Work hard, you who are hearing these words today. The prophets spoke these words when the foundation was laid for the house of the LORD All-Powerful, for the building of the Temple. ¹⁰Before that time there was no money to hire people or animals. People could not safely come and go because of the enemies; I had turned everyone against his neighbor. ¹¹But I will not do to these people who are left what I did in the past," says the LORD All-Powerful.

¹²"They will plant their seeds in peace, their grapevines will have fruit, the ground will give good crops, and the sky will send rain. I will give all this to the people who are left alive. ¹³Judah and Israel, your names have been used as curses in other nations. But I will save you, and you will become a blessing. So don't be afraid; work hard."

¹⁴This is what the LORD All-Powerful says: "When your ancestors made me angry, I planned to punish you. I did not change my mind," says the LORD All-Powerful. ¹⁵"But now I will do something different. I am planning to do good to Jerusalem and Judah. So don't be afraid. ¹⁶These are the things you should do: Tell each other the truth. In the courts judge with truth and complete fairness. ¹⁷Do not make plans to hurt your neighbors, and don't love false promises. I hate all these things," says the LORD.

¹⁸The LORD All-Powerful spoke his word to me again. ¹⁹This is what the LORD All-Powerful says: "The special days when you fast in the fourth, fifth, seventh, and tenth months will become good, joyful, happy feasts in Judah. But you must love truth and peace."

²⁰This is what the LORD All-Powerful says: "Many people from many cities will still come to Jerusalem. ²¹People from one city will go and say to those from another city, 'We are going to pray to the LORD and to ask the LORD All-Powerful for help. Come and go with us.' ²²Many people and powerful nations will come to worship the LORD All-Powerful in Jerusalem and to pray to the LORD for help."

²³This is what the LORD All-Powerful says: "At that time, ten men from different countries will come and take hold of a Judean by his coat. They will say to him, 'Let us go with you, because we have heard that God is with you.'"

PUNISHMENT ON ISRAEL'S ENEMIES

9 This message is the word of the LORD.

The message is against the land of Hadrach
and the city of Damascus.
The tribes of Israel and all people
belong to the LORD.
² The message is also against the city of Hamath, on the border,
and against Tyre and Sidon, with their skill.
³ Tyre has built a strong wall for herself.
She has piled up silver like dust
and gold like the mud in the streets.
⁴ But the Lord will take away all she has
and destroy her power on the sea.
That city will be destroyed by fire.
⁵ The city of Ashkelon will see it and be afraid.
The people of Gaza will shake with fear,
and the people of Ekron will lose hope.
No king will be left in Gaza,
and no one will live in Ashkelon anymore.
⁶ Foreigners will live in Ashdod,
and I will destroy the pride of the Philistines.
⁷ I will stop them from drinking blood
and from eating forbidden food.
Those left alive will belong to God.
They will be leaders in Judah,
and Ekron will become like the Jebusites.
⁸ I will protect my Temple
from armies who would come or go.

No one will hurt my people again,
because now I am watching them.

THE KING IS COMING

⁹ Rejoice greatly, people of Jerusalem!
Shout for joy, people of Jerusalem!
Your king is coming to you.
He does what is right, and he saves.
He is gentle and riding on a donkey,
on the colt of a donkey.
¹⁰ I will take away the chariots from Ephraim
and the horses from Jerusalem.
The bows used in war will be broken.
The king will talk to the nations about peace.
His kingdom will go from sea to sea,
and from the Euphrates River to the ends of the earth.

¹¹ As for you, because of the blood of the agreement with you
I will set your prisoners free from the waterless pit.
¹² You prisoners who have hope,
return to your place of safety.
Today I am telling you
that I will give you back twice as much as before.
¹³ I will use Judah like a bow
and Ephraim like the arrows.
Jerusalem, I will use your men
to fight the men of Greece.
I will use you like a warrior's sword.

¹⁴ Then the LORD will appear above them,
and his arrows will shoot like lightning.
The Lord GOD will blow the trumpet,
and he will march in the storms of the south.
¹⁵ The LORD All-Powerful will protect them;
they will destroy the enemy with slingshots.
They will drink and shout like drunks.
They will be filled like a bowl
used for sprinkling blood at the corners of the altar.
¹⁶ On that day the LORD their God will save them
as if his people were sheep.
They will shine in his land
like jewels in a crown.
¹⁷ They will be so pretty and beautiful.

The young men will grow strong on the
grain
and the young women on new wine.

THE LORD'S PROMISES

10 Ask the LORD for rain during the
springtime rains.
The LORD is the one who makes the
clouds.
He sends the showers
and gives everyone green fields.
2 Idols tell lies;
fortune-tellers see false visions
and tell about false dreams.
The comfort they give is worth nothing.
So the people are like lost sheep.
They are abused, because there is no
shepherd.

3 The LORD says, "I am angry at my
shepherds,
and I will punish the leaders.
I, the LORD All-Powerful, care
for my flock, the people of Judah.
I will make them like my proud war
horses.
4 From Judah will come the cornerstone,
and the tent peg,
the battle bow,
and every ruler.
5 Together they will be like soldiers
marching to battle through muddy
streets.
The LORD is with them,
so they will fight and defeat the
horsemen.

6 "I will strengthen the people of Judah
and save the people of Joseph.
I will bring them back,
because I care about them.
It will be as though
I had never left them,
because I am the LORD their God,
and I will answer them.
7 The people of Ephraim will be strong like
soldiers;
they will be glad as when they have
drunk wine.
Their children will see it and rejoice;
they will be happy in the LORD.
8 I will call my people
and gather them together.
I will save them,

and they will grow in number as they
grew in number before.
9 I have scattered them among the
nations,
but in those faraway places, they will
remember me.
They and their children will live and
return.
10 I will bring them back from the land of
Egypt
and gather them from Assyria.
I will bring them to Gilead and Lebanon
until there isn't enough room for them
all.
11 They will come through the sea of
trouble.
The waves of the sea will be calm,
and the Nile River will dry up.
I will defeat Assyria's pride
and destroy Egypt's power over other
countries.
12 I will make my people strong,
and they will live as I say," says the
LORD.

11 Lebanon, open your gates
so fire may burn your cedar trees.[n]
2 Cry, pine trees, because the cedar has
fallen,
because the tall trees are ruined.
Cry, oaks in Bashan,
because the mighty forest has been cut
down.
3 Listen to the shepherds crying
because their rich pastures are
destroyed.
Listen to the lions roaring
because the lovely land of the Jordan
River is ruined.

THE TWO SHEPHERDS

4 This is what the LORD my God says:
"Feed the flock that are about to be killed.
5 Their buyers kill them and are not punished.
Those who sell them say, 'Praise the LORD, I
am rich.' Even the shepherds don't feel sorry
for their sheep. 6 I don't feel sorry anymore
for the people of this country," says the LORD.
"I will let everyone be under the power of his
neighbor and king. They will bring trouble to

11:1 trees In this poem, trees, bushes, and animals stand
for leaders of countries around Judah.

the country, and I will not save anyone from them."

⁷So I fed the flock about to be killed, particularly the weakest ones. Then I took two sticks; I called one Pleasant and the other Union, and I fed the flock. ⁸In one month I got rid of three shepherds. The flock did not pay attention to me, and I got impatient with them. ⁹I said, "I will no longer take care of you like a shepherd. Let those that are dying die, and let those that are to be destroyed be destroyed. Let those that are left eat each other."

¹⁰Then I broke the stick named Pleasant to break the agreement God made with all the nations. ¹¹That day it was broken. The weak ones in the flock who were watching me knew this message was from the LORD.

¹²Then I said, "If you want to pay me, pay me. If not, then don't." So they paid me thirty pieces of silver.

¹³The LORD said to me, "Throw the money to the potter." That is how little they thought I was worth.ⁿ So I took the thirty pieces of silver and threw them to the potter in the Temple of the LORD.

¹⁴Then I broke the second stick, named Union, to break the brotherhood between Judah and Israel.

¹⁵Then the LORD said to me, "Get the things used by a foolish shepherd again, ¹⁶because I am going to get a new shepherd for the country. He will not care for the dying sheep, or look for the young ones, or heal the injured ones, or feed the healthy. But he will eat the best sheep and tear off their hoofs.
¹⁷ "How terrible it will be for the useless shepherd
  who abandoned the flock.
A sword will strike his arm and his right eye.
His arm will lose all its strength,
  and his right eye will go blind."

JERUSALEM WILL BE SAVED

12 This message is the word of the LORD to Israel. This is what the LORD says, who stretched out the skies, and laid the foundations of the earth, and put the human spirit within: ²"I will make Jerusalem like a cup of poison to the nations around her. They will come and attack Jerusalem and Judah. ³One day all the nations on earth will come together to attack Jerusalem, but I will make it like a heavy rock; anyone who tries to move it will get hurt. ⁴At that time I will confuse every horse and cause its rider to go crazy," says the LORD. "I will watch over Judah, but I will blind all the horses of the enemies. ⁵Then the leaders of Judah will say to themselves, 'The people of Jerusalem are strong, because the LORD All-Powerful is their God.'

⁶"At that time I will make the leaders of Judah like a fire burning a stack of wood or like a fire burning straw. They will destroy all the people around them left and right. But the people of Jerusalem will remain safe.

⁷"The LORD will save the homes of Judah first so that the honor given to David's family and to the people of Jerusalem won't be greater than the honor given to Judah. ⁸At that time the LORD will protect the people in Jerusalem. Then even the weakest of them will be strong like David. And the family of David will be like God, like an angel of the LORD in front of them. ⁹At that time I will go to destroy all the nations that attack Jerusalem.

CRYING FOR THE ONE THEY STABBED

¹⁰"I will pour out on David's family and the people in Jerusalem a spirit of kindness and mercy. They will look at me, the one they have stabbed, and they will cry like someone crying over the death of an only child. They will be as sad as someone who has lost a firstborn son. ¹¹At that time there will be much crying in Jerusalem, like the crying for Hadad Rimmon in the plain of Megiddo. ¹²The land will cry, each family by itself: the family of David by itself and their wives by themselves, the family of Nathan by itself and their wives by themselves, ¹³the family of Levi by itself and their wives by themselves, the family of Shimei by itself and their wives by themselves, ¹⁴and all the rest of the families by themselves and their wives by themselves.

13 "At that time a fountain will be open for David's descendants and for the people of Jerusalem to cleanse them of their sin and uncleanness."

²The LORD All-Powerful says, "At that

11:13 **worth** This was a small amount. It was about the price paid for a slave.

time I will get rid of the names of the idols from the land; no one will remember them anymore. I will also remove the prophets and unclean spirits from the land. ³If a person continues to prophesy, his own father and mother, the ones who gave birth to him, will tell him, 'You have told lies using the Lord's name, so you must die.' When he prophesies, his own father and mother who gave birth to him will stab him.

⁴"At that time the prophets will be ashamed of their visions and prophecies. They won't wear the prophet's clothes made of hair to trick people. ⁵Each of them will say, 'I am not a prophet. I am a farmer and have been a farmer since I was young.' ⁶But someone will ask, 'What are the deep cuts on your body?' And each will answer, 'I was hurt at my friend's house.'

THE SHEPHERD IS KILLED

⁷ "Sword, hit the shepherd.
  Attack the man who is my friend,"
  says the Lord All-Powerful.
"Kill the shepherd,
  and the sheep will scatter,
  and I will punish the little ones."
⁸ The Lord says, "Two-thirds of the people
    through all the land will die. They will
      be gone,
  and one-third will be left.
⁹ The third that is left I will test with fire,
  purifying them like silver,
  testing them like gold.
Then they will call on me,
  and I will answer them.
I will say, 'You are my people,'
  and they will say, 'The Lord is our
    God.'"

THE DAY OF PUNISHMENT

14 The Lord's day of judging is coming when the wealth you have taken will be divided among you.

²I will bring all the nations together to fight Jerusalem. They will capture the city and rob the houses and attack the women. Half the people will be taken away as captives, but the rest of the people won't be taken from the city.

³Then the Lord will go to war against those nations; he will fight as in a day of battle. ⁴On that day he will stand on the Mount of Olives, east of Jerusalem. The Mount of Olives will split in two, forming a deep valley that runs east and west. Half the mountain will move toward the north, and half will move toward the south. ⁵You will run through this mountain valley to the other side, just as you ran from the earthquake when Uzziah was king of Judah. Then the Lord my God will come and all the holy ones with him.

⁶On that day there will be no light, cold, or frost. ⁷There will be no other day like it, and the Lord knows when it will come. There will be no day or night; even at evening it will still be light.

⁸At that time fresh water will flow from Jerusalem. Half of it will flow east to the Dead Sea, and half will flow west to the Mediterranean Sea. It will flow summer and winter.

⁹Then the Lord will be king over the whole world. At that time there will be only one Lord, and his name will be the only name.

¹⁰All the land south of Jerusalem from Geba to Rimmon will be turned into a plain. Jerusalem will be raised up, but it will stay in the same place. The city will reach from the Benjamin Gate and to the First Gate to the Corner Gate, and from the Tower of Hananel to the king's winepresses. ¹¹People will live there, and it will never be destroyed again. Jerusalem will be safe.

¹²But the Lord will bring a terrible disease on the nations that fought against Jerusalem. Their flesh will rot away while they are still standing up. Their eyes will rot in their sockets, and their tongues will rot in their mouths. ¹³At that time the Lord will cause panic. Everybody will grab his neighbor, and they will attack each other. ¹⁴The people of Judah will fight in Jerusalem. And the wealth of the nations around them will be collected—much gold, silver, and clothes. ¹⁵A similar disease will strike the horses, mules, camels, donkeys, and all the animals in the camps.

¹⁶All of those left alive of the people who came to fight Jerusalem will come back to Jerusalem year after year to worship the King, the Lord All-Powerful, and to celebrate the Feast of Shelters. ¹⁷Anyone from the nations who does not go to Jerusalem to worship the King, the Lord All-Powerful, will not have

rain fall on his land. **18**If the Egyptians do not go to Jerusalem, they will not have rain. Then the LORD will send them the same terrible disease he sent the other nations that did not celebrate the Feast of Shelters. **19**This will be the punishment for Egypt and any nation which does not go to celebrate the Feast of Shelters.

20At that time the horses' bells will have written on them: HOLY TO THE LORD. The cooking pots in the Temple of the Lord will be like the holy altar bowls. **21**Every pot in Jerusalem and Judah will be holy to the LORD All-Powerful, and everyone who offers sacrifices will be able to take food from them and cook in them. At that time there will not be any buyers or sellers in the Temple of the LORD All-Powerful.

1 This message is the word of the LORD given to Israel through Malachi.

GOD LOVES ISRAEL

²The LORD said, "I have loved you."

But you ask, "How have you loved us?"

The LORD said, "Esau and Jacob were brothers. I loved Jacob, ³but I hated Esau. I destroyed his mountain country and left his land to the wild dogs of the desert."

⁴The people of Edom might say, "We were destroyed, but we will go back and rebuild the ruins."

But the LORD All-Powerful says, "If they rebuild them, I will destroy them. People will say, 'Edom is a wicked country. The LORD is always angry with the Edomites.' ⁵You will see these things with your own eyes. And you will say, 'The LORD is great, even outside the borders of Israel!'"

THE PRIESTS DON'T RESPECT GOD

⁶The LORD All-Powerful says, "A son honors his father, and a servant honors his master." I am a father, so why don't you honor me? I am a master, so why don't you respect me? You priests do not respect me.

"But you ask, 'How have we shown you disrespect?'

⁷"You have shown it by bringing unclean food to my altar.

"But you ask, 'What makes it unclean?'

"It is unclean because you don't respect the altar of the LORD. ⁸When you bring blind animals as sacrifices, that is wrong. When you bring crippled and sick animals, that is wrong. Try giving them to your governor. Would he be pleased with you? He wouldn't accept you," says the LORD All-Powerful.

⁹"Now ask God to be kind to you, but he won't accept you with such offerings," says the LORD All-Powerful.

¹⁰"I wish one of you would close the Temple doors so that you would not light useless fires on my altar! I am not pleased with you and will not accept your gifts," says the LORD All-Powerful. ¹¹"From the east to the west I will be honored among the nations. Everywhere they will bring incense and clean offerings to me, because I will be honored among the nations," says the LORD All-Powerful.

¹²"But you don't honor me. You say about the Lord's altar, 'It is unclean, and the food has no worth.' ¹³You say, 'We are tired of doing this,' and you sniff at it in disgust," says the LORD All-Powerful.

"And you bring hurt, crippled, and sick animals as gifts. You bring them as gifts, but I won't accept them from you," says the LORD. ¹⁴"The person who cheats will be cursed. He has a male animal in his flock and promises to offer it, but then he offers to the Lord an animal that has something wrong with it. I am a great king," says the LORD All-Powerful, "and I am feared by all the nations.

RULES FOR PRIESTS

2 "Priests, this command is for you. ²Listen to me. Pay attention to what I say. Honor my name," says the LORD All-Powerful. "If you don't, I will send a curse on you and on your blessings. I have already cursed them, because you don't pay attention to what I say.

³"I will punish your descendants. I will smear your faces with the animal insides left from your feasts, and you will be thrown away with it. ⁴Then you will know that I am giving you this command so my agreement with Levi will continue," says the LORD All-Powerful. ⁵"My agreement for priests was with the tribe of Levi. I promised them life and peace so they would honor me. And they did honor me and fear me. ⁶They taught the true teachings and spoke no lies. With peace and honesty they did what I said they should do, and they kept many people from sinning.

⁷"A priest should teach what he knows, and people should learn the teachings from him, because he is the messenger of the LORD All-Powerful. ⁸But you priests have stopped obeying me. With your teachings you have

caused many people to do wrong. You have broken the agreement with the tribe of Levi!" says the LORD All-Powerful. 9"You have not been careful to do what I say, but instead you take sides in court cases. So I have caused you to be hated and disgraced in front of everybody."

JUDAH WAS NOT LOYAL TO GOD

10We all have the same father; the same God made us. So why do people break their promises to each other and show no respect for the agreement our ancestors made with God? 11The people of Judah have broken their promises. They have done something God hates in Israel and Jerusalem: The people of Judah did not respect the Temple that the LORD loves, and the men of Judah married women who worship foreign gods. 12Whoever does this might bring offerings to the LORD All-Powerful, but the LORD will still cut that person off from the community of Israel.

GUILT AND GRACE

priority
in marriage

FAMILY

MALACHI 2:15

By Jimmy Evans

When God created the institution of marriage, he had a plan. Immediately following the creation of Adam and Eve, God ordained laws for marriage to operate within. Just like the natural laws that guide and guard creation, these laws provide the foundation and protection for marriage. With these laws, marriage is safe and beautiful; without them, marriage is dangerous and painful.

In the law of priority, a man and a woman leave their parents and cleave to each other. To leave in this context means to loosen or to relinquish. God designed marriage to operate as the number one priority in life, except for God. Marriage cannot function properly in any other position. There is such a thing as legitimate jealousy, which is a protective warning device. Listen to it or there will be damaging results. Priority in marriage must be established in real terms, not just in words.

Four ways we prove our priority for our marriage partner are: sacrifice, time, energy, and attitude. These indicators show interest and a willingness to meet the spouse's needs above all else; they are positive and affirming.

Priorities must be constantly protected from good things that are not in their proper place. Right priorities are God, marriage, children, church, extended family and friends, work, hobbies, and other interests. When we protect these rightly ordered priorities, God will bless our marriage.

reflect: Have you made your spouse the number one priority in your life?
Go to **Exodus 34:6-7.**

By Gary D. Chapman

I met Glenn on an airplane traveling from Dallas to Greensboro. When he found out I was a marriage counselor, he began to tell me about his parents' divorce. It was obvious he was deeply disturbed by the breakup of his parents' marriage. Near the end of the conversation, he asked me a question I have never forgotten. "Is it possible in today's world to have a lifelong loving marriage?" It was obvious to me that Glenn wanted that kind of marriage.

A recent survey indicated that among never-married singles between the ages of twenty and thirty, 87 percent said, "I want to have one marriage that will last a lifetime." They have seen their parents divorce, and they don't want to experience it themselves. The problem is they haven't the foggiest idea of how to have a lifelong marriage. I believe the answer to Glenn's question is found in understanding the biblical concept of marriage. Consider the words of Paul in Romans 12:2: "Do not be shaped by this world; instead be changed within by a new way of thinking."

If there is an arena in which the church is in danger of being molded by the world, it is in the area of marriage. Just as Israel often became estranged from God, we often struggle in our marriages. The reason is the same: We move away from God's instructions and try to do it our way. We are often influenced by the world around us.

Ours is a contract society. We make lease contracts, sales contracts, and service contracts. Legally, marriage is a contract. That's why we must get a license. That's why certain laws regulate marriage. So, in other words, we often treat our relationships like contracts. But for the Christian, marriage is more than a contract. It is a covenant. Here are just a few of the differences:

1. *Contracts* are made for a limited period of time, but *covenants* view commitment as permanent.
2. *Contracts* deal with specific actions, but *covenants* are built on steadfast love.
3. *Contracts* are conditional, but *covenants* contain unconditional promises.
4. *Contracts* are motivated by the desire to get something we want, but *covenants* are initiated for the benefit of the other person.
5. And, perhaps most importantly, *covenants* require confrontation and forgiveness, whereas *contracts* require neither.

It's easy to see how the contract mentality has influenced our view of marriage. I wish someone had told me about covenant marriage when I was young. Had I understood the biblical view of marriage, I'm sure our adjustments in the early years would have been easier. Perhaps that is why I am so committed to sharing the message of covenant marriage with the next generation.

I believe that thousands of Christians have a very faulty view of marriage, influenced far more by culture than by scripture. That is why I challenge you to continue to explore the biblical view of marriage until it becomes a part of who you are—and then share it with others. Will you make a fresh commitment to a biblical marriage? Walk through these five characteristics. Confess your failures, and recommit yourself to a covenant marriage. (From *Covenant Marriage*)

TO LEARN MORE ON WHAT THE BIBLE HAS TO SAY ABOUT **FAMILY,** READ THE SCRIPTURES AND DEVOTIONALS AT **DEUTERONOMY 11:18–25, PSALM 19:7–11, MARK 3:25, 2 JOHN 2, JOHN 2:1–4, JOHN 4:14,** AND **REVELATION 19:11.**

¹³This is another thing you do. You cover the LORD's altar with your tears. You cry and moan, because he does not accept your offerings and is not pleased with what you bring. ¹⁴You ask, "Why?" It is because the LORD sees how you treated the wife you married when you were young. You broke your promise to her, even though she was your partner and you had an agreement with her. ¹⁵God made husbands and wives to become one body and one spirit for his purpose—so they would have children who are true to God.

So be careful, and do not break your promise to the wife you married when you were young. ¹⁶The LORD God of Israel says, "I hate divorce. And I hate people who do cruel things as easily as they put on clothes," says the LORD All-Powerful.

So be careful. And do not break your trust.

THE SPECIAL DAY OF JUDGING

¹⁷You have tired the LORD with your words.

HANDLING MONEY GOD'S WAY

FINANCES

making it pure

MALACHI 3:3

The Bible uses the imagery of a refiner's fire in order to show us how important it is to remove the impurities in our lives. God expects pure product. What isn't pure needs to be burned away. But I wonder if we have considered the possibility that financial wealth (silver and gold) can easily be part of the fire, not the result. We hear story after story of people whose wealth led them to one problem after another. We know that scores of wealthy people live under constant threat. We hear the rumors of how unhappy the lives of the rich and famous really are.

It certainly seems that great wealth is more like fire than it is like peaceful repose. Jesus even said that great wealth is a severe stumbling block to finding the kingdom of heaven. With all of this evidence, do you ever wonder why we are still so consumed with accumulating money? Do you really think money will make you happy?

The way to remove the power of money over our lives is to pull it down from the pedestal it occupies in this world. How do we do that? Simple. We give it away. Nothing reduces the power of money more than giving it to someone else. Maybe that's the real purpose of money—to turn it into just one more vehicle of God's grace. What would happen to your attitude about living if you gave away all the money you made above the amount required for your needs? When God says that he loves a cheerful giver, does that thrill you, or do you feel a twinge of panic?

reflect: Has money become a stumbling block to you?
Go to **1 Timothy 3:1-4.**

You ask, "How have we tired him?"

You did it by saying, "The LORD thinks anyone who does evil is good, and he is pleased with them." Or you asked, "Where is the God who is fair?"

3 The LORD All-Powerful says, "I will send my messenger, who will prepare the way for me. Suddenly, the Lord you are looking for will come to his Temple; the messenger of the agreement, whom you want, will come." ²No one can live through that time; no one can survive when he comes. He will be like a purifying fire and like laundry soap. ³Like someone who heats and purifies silver, he will purify the Levites and make them pure like gold and silver. Then they will bring offerings to the LORD in the right way. ⁴And the LORD will accept the offerings from Judah and Jerusalem, as it was in the past. ⁵The LORD All-Powerful says, "Then I will come to you and judge you. I will be quick to testify against those who take part in evil magic,

---

HANDLING MONEY GOD'S WAY

what is necessary for family partnership?

FINANCES

By Elmer Towns

MALACHI 3:8–12

Faith in God's provision is the "glue" that keeps Christian families together. The family partnership is built upon these important points:

1. *God is the owner of everything we have, and we are merely managers.* In the parable found in Matthew 25:15–18, the owner gave three servants different amounts of gold (Matthew 25:15–18). Similarly, God gives each family different resources to manage according to his principles.

2. *God has a right to check up on everyone.* The family that manages wisely usually gets more. The family that squanders resources usually loses them.

3. *We must trust God's rules and live by them.* God is too wise to lead us astray and too loving to hurt us. If we follow his rules, but suffer losses, we should not be anxious. If we prosper, we should give God the glory and not become proud. Faith is applying God's principles and leaving the results to him.

4. *Every spending decision is a spiritual decision.* The Holy Spirit should control every decision, whether buying a house or something small.

5. *God uses money as a tool to teach us how to follow him.* Our stewardship is a reflection of our walk with God. Our heavenly father promises to meet our needs if we manage our resources according to his principles (Malachi 3:11).

---

reflect: Will you trust God to provide for you and your family today?
Go to **Matthew 5:5.**

adultery, and lying under oath, those who cheat workers of their pay and who cheat widows and orphans, those who are unfair to foreigners, and those who do not respect me.

STEALING FROM GOD

6"I the LORD do not change. So you descendants of Jacob have not been destroyed. 7Since the time of your ancestors, you have disobeyed my rules and have not kept them. Return to me, and I will return to you," says the LORD All-Powerful.

"But you ask, 'How can we return?'

8"Should a person rob God? But you are robbing me.

"You ask, 'How have we robbed you?'

"You have robbed me in your offerings and the tenth of your crops. 9So a curse is on you, because the whole nation has robbed me. 10Bring to the storehouse a full tenth of what you earn so there will be food in my house. Test me in this," says the LORD All-Powerful. "I will open the windows of heaven for you and pour out all the blessings you need. 11I will stop the insects so they won't eat your crops. The grapes won't fall from your vines before they are ready to pick," says the LORD All-Powerful. 12"All the nations will call you blessed, because you will have a pleasant country," says the LORD All-Powerful.

THE LORD'S PROMISE OF MERCY

13The LORD says, "You have said terrible things about me.

"But you ask, 'What have we said about you?'

14"You have said, 'It is useless to serve God. It did no good to obey his laws and to show the LORD All-Powerful that we were sorry for what we did. 15So we say that proud people are happy. Evil people succeed. They challenge God and get away with it.'"

16Then those who honored the LORD spoke with each other, and the LORD listened and heard them. The names of those who honored the LORD and respected him were written in his presence in a book to be remembered.

17The LORD All-Powerful says, "They belong to me; on that day they will be my very own. As a parent shows mercy to his child who serves him, I will show mercy to my people. 18You will again see the difference between good and evil people, between those who serve God and those who don't.

THE DAY OF THE LORD'S JUDGING

4 "There is a day coming that will burn like a hot furnace, and all the proud and evil people will be like straw. On that day they will be completely burned up so that not a root or branch will be left," says the LORD All-Powerful. 2"But for you who honor me, goodness will shine on you like the sun, with healing in its rays. You will jump around, like well-fed calves. 3Then you will crush the wicked like ashes under your feet on the day I will do this," says the LORD All-Powerful.

4"Remember the teaching of Moses my servant, those laws and rules I gave to him on Mount Sinai for all the Israelites.

5"But I will send you Elijah the prophet before that great and terrifying day of the LORD's judging. 6Elijah will help parents love their children and children love their parents. Otherwise, I will come and put a curse on the land."

the **new testament**

matthew

THE FAMILY HISTORY OF JESUS

1 This is the family history of Jesus Christ. He came from the family of David, and David came from the family of Abraham.

2 Abraham was the father[n] of Isaac.

Isaac was the father of Jacob.

Jacob was the father of Judah and his brothers.

3 Judah was the father of Perez and Zerah. (Their mother was Tamar.)

Perez was the father of Hezron.

Hezron was the father of Ram.

4 Ram was the father of Amminadab.

Amminadab was the father of Nahshon.

Nahshon was the father of Salmon.

5 Salmon was the father of Boaz. (Boaz's mother was Rahab.)

Boaz was the father of Obed. (Obed's mother was Ruth.)

Obed was the father of Jesse.

6 Jesse was the father of King David.

David was the father of Solomon. (Solomon's mother had been Uriah's wife.)

7 Solomon was the father of Rehoboam.

Rehoboam was the father of Abijah.

Abijah was the father of Asa.[n]

8 Asa was the father of Jehoshaphat.

Jehoshaphat was the father of Jehoram.

Jehoram was the ancestor of Uzziah.

9 Uzziah was the father of Jotham.

Jotham was the father of Ahaz.

Ahaz was the father of Hezekiah.

10 Hezekiah was the father of Manasseh.

Manasseh was the father of Amon.

Amon was the father of Josiah.

11 Josiah was the grandfather of Jehoiachin[n] and his brothers. (This was at the time that the people were taken to Babylon.)

12 After they were taken to Babylon:

Jehoiachin was the father of Shealtiel.

Shealtiel was the grandfather of Zerubbabel.

13 Zerubbabel was the father of Abiud.

Abiud was the father of Eliakim.

Eliakim was the father of Azor.

14 Azor was the father of Zadok.

Zadok was the father of Akim.

Akim was the father of Eliud.

15 Eliud was the father of Eleazar.

Eleazar was the father of Matthan.

Matthan was the father of Jacob.

16 Jacob was the father of Joseph.

Joseph was the husband of Mary, and Mary was the mother of Jesus.

Jesus is called the Christ.

17 So there were fourteen generations from Abraham to David. And there were fourteen generations from David until the people were taken to Babylon. And there were fourteen generations from the time when the people were taken to Babylon until Christ was born.

THE BIRTH OF JESUS CHRIST

18 This is how the birth of Jesus Christ came about. His mother Mary was engaged[n] to marry Joseph, but before they married, she learned she was pregnant by the power of the Holy Spirit. 19 Because Mary's husband, Joseph, was a good man, he did not want to disgrace her in public, so he planned to divorce her secretly.

20 While Joseph thought about these things, an angel of the Lord came to him in a dream. The angel said, "Joseph, descendant of David, don't be afraid to take Mary as your wife, because the baby in her is from the Holy Spirit. 21 She will give birth to a son, and you will name him Jesus,[n] because he will save his people from their sins."

22 All this happened to bring about what

1:2 father "Father" in Jewish lists of ancestors can sometimes mean grandfather or more distant relative. **1:7 Asa** Some Greek copies read "Asaph," another name for Asa (see 1 Chronicles 3:10). **1:11 Jehoiachin** The Greek reads "Jeconiah," another name for Jehoiachin (see 2 Kings 24:6 and 1 Chronicles 3:16). **1:18 engaged** For the Jewish people an engagement was a lasting agreement, which could only be broken by a divorce. If a bride-to-be was unfaithful, it was considered adultery, and she could be put to death. **1:21 Jesus** The name "Jesus" means "salvation."

the Lord had said through the prophet: 23"The virgin will be pregnant. She will have a son, and they will name him Immanuel,"[n] which means "God is with us."

24When Joseph woke up, he did what the Lord's angel had told him to do. Joseph took Mary as his wife, 25but he did not have sexual relations with her until she gave birth to the son. And Joseph named him Jesus.

WISE MEN COME TO VISIT JESUS

2 Jesus was born in the town of Bethlehem in Judea during the time when Herod was king. When Jesus was born, some wise men from the east came to Jerusalem. 2They asked, "Where is the baby who was born to be the king of the Jews? We saw his star in the east and have come to worship him."

3When King Herod heard this, he was troubled, as were all the people in Jerusalem. 4Herod called a meeting of all the leading priests and teachers of the law and asked them where the Christ would be born. 5They answered, "In the town of Bethlehem in Judea. The prophet wrote about this in the Scriptures:

6 'But you, Bethlehem, in the land of Judah,
    are not just an insignificant village in
        Judah.
  A ruler will come from you
    who will be like a shepherd for my
        people Israel.'"   *Micah 5:2*

7Then Herod had a secret meeting with the wise men and learned from them the exact time they first saw the star. 8He sent the wise men to Bethlehem, saying, "Look carefully for the child. When you find him, come tell me so I can worship him too."

9After the wise men heard the king, they left. The star that they had seen in the east went before them until it stopped above the place where the child was. 10When the wise men saw the star, they were filled with joy. 11They came to the house where the child was and saw him with his mother, Mary, and they bowed down and worshiped him. They opened their gifts and gave him treasures of gold, frankincense, and myrrh. 12But God warned the wise men in a dream not to go back to Herod, so they returned to their own country by a different way.

JESUS' PARENTS TAKE HIM TO EGYPT

13After they left, an angel of the Lord came to Joseph in a dream and said, "Get up!

Take the child and his mother and escape to Egypt, because Herod is starting to look for the child so he can kill him. Stay in Egypt until I tell you to return."

14So Joseph got up and left for Egypt during the night with the child and his mother. 15And Joseph stayed in Egypt until Herod died. This happened to bring about what the Lord had said through the prophet: "I called my son out of Egypt."[n]

HEROD KILLS THE BABY BOYS

16When Herod saw that the wise men had tricked him, he was furious. So he gave an order to kill all the baby boys in Bethlehem and in the surrounding area who were two years old or younger. This was in keeping with the time he learned from the wise men. 17So what God had said through the prophet Jeremiah came true:

18 "A voice was heard in Ramah
    of painful crying and deep sadness:
  Rachel crying for her children.
    She refused to be comforted,
    because her children are dead."
                        Jeremiah 31:15

JOSEPH AND MARY RETURN

19After Herod died, an angel of the Lord spoke to Joseph in a dream while he was in Egypt. 20The angel said, "Get up! Take the child and his mother and go to the land of Israel, because the people who were trying to kill the child are now dead."

21So Joseph took the child and his mother and went to Israel. 22But he heard that Archelaus was now king in Judea since his father Herod had died. So Joseph was afraid to go there. After being warned in a dream, he went to the area of Galilee, 23to a town called Nazareth, and lived there. And so what God had said through the prophets came true: "He will be called a Nazarene."[n]

THE WORK OF JOHN THE BAPTIST

3 About that time John the Baptist began preaching in the desert area of Judea. 2John said, "Change your hearts and lives

---

1:23 **"The virgin . . . Immanuel"** Quotation from Isaiah 7:14. 2:15 **"I called . . . Egypt."** Quotation from Hosea 11:1. 2:23 **Nazarene** A person from the town of Nazareth. Matthew may be referring to Isaiah 11:1, where the Hebrew word translated "branch" sounds like "Nazarene."

because the kingdom of heaven is near." ³John the Baptist is the one Isaiah the prophet was talking about when he said:

"This is a voice of one
who calls out in the desert:
'Prepare the way for the Lord.
Make the road straight for him.'"

Isaiah 40:3

⁴John's clothes were made from camel's hair, and he wore a leather belt around his waist. For food, he ate locusts and wild honey. ⁵Many people came from Jerusalem and Judea and all the area around the Jordan River to hear John. ⁶They confessed their sins, and he baptized them in the Jordan River.

⁷Many of the Pharisees and Sadducees came to the place where John was baptizing people. When John saw them, he said,

"You are snakes! Who warned you to run away from God's coming punishment? ⁸Do the things that show you really have changed your hearts and lives. ⁹And don't think you can say to yourselves, 'Abraham is our father.' I tell you that God could make children for Abraham from these rocks. ¹⁰The ax is now ready to cut down the trees, and every tree that does not produce good fruit will be cut down and thrown into the fire.ⁿ

¹¹"I baptize you with water to show that your hearts and lives have changed. But there is one coming after me who is greater than I am, whose sandals I am not good enough to carry. He will baptize you with the Holy Spirit and fire. ¹²He will come ready to clean

---

3:10 The ax . . . fire. This means that God is ready to punish his people who do not obey him.

---

let the rest go

FULFILLMENT

MATTHEW 3:13–17

John saw Jesus coming to him to be baptized. John protested, "No, Lord. You should be baptizing me." But Jesus said, "John, it's okay. *Let it go.* Release yourself to my desire. I know what is needed. Just do what I ask."

Jesus knew that life begins with letting it be. He came to John in humility and asked John just to do what he wanted to be done. "Don't worry, John. I know what is necessary. I am in control here. Just follow me," he declared.

How often have we been confronted by this simple request? "Just do what I ask," says Jesus. And we hesitate. "No, Lord. It doesn't seem right to me. You must be mistaken." But, of course, he isn't. He knows exactly what he is asking. So he reminds us, "Just let it be."

Jesus comes to you and to me. He asks only one thing: "Just do what I ask. Let the rest go." Will you be able to do what John did? Standing before him was the Son of God. John understood it, and he let it go. John took Jesus at his word and fulfilled Jesus' desire. That is all we need to do. Let the rest go.

reflect: Decide to let Jesus have his will and way in your life today.
Go to **Matthew 7:29.**

the grain, separating the good grain from the chaff. He will put the good part of the grain into his barn, but he will burn the chaff with a fire that cannot be put out.'"[n]

JESUS IS BAPTIZED BY JOHN

[13]At that time Jesus came from Galilee to the Jordan River and wanted John to baptize him. [14]But John tried to stop him, saying, "Why do you come to me to be baptized? I need to be baptized by you!"

[15]Jesus answered, "Let it be this way for now. We should do all things that are God's will." So John agreed to baptize Jesus.

[16]As soon as Jesus was baptized, he came up out of the water. Then heaven opened, and he saw God's Spirit coming down on him like a dove. [17]And a voice from heaven said, "This is my Son, whom I love, and I am very pleased with him."

THE TEMPTATION OF JESUS

4 Then the Spirit led Jesus into the desert to be tempted by the devil. [2]Jesus fasted for forty days and nights. After this, he was very hungry. [3]The devil came to Jesus to tempt him, saying, "If you are the Son of God, tell these rocks to become bread."

[4]Jesus answered, "It is written in the Scriptures, 'A person lives not on bread alone, but by everything God says.'"[n]

[5]Then the devil led Jesus to the holy city of Jerusalem and put him on a high place of the Temple. [6]The devil said, "If you are the Son of God, jump down, because it is written in the Scriptures:

'He has put his angels in charge of you.
    They will catch you in their hands
so that you will not hit your foot on a
    rock.'" *Psalm 91:11–12*

[7]Jesus answered him, "It also says in the Scriptures, 'Do not test the Lord your God.'"[n]

[8]Then the devil led Jesus to the top of a very high mountain and showed him all the kingdoms of the world and all their splendor. [9]The devil said, "If you will bow down and worship me, I will give you all these things."

[10]Jesus said to the devil, "Go away from me, Satan! It is written in the Scriptures, 'You must worship the Lord your God and serve only him.'"[n]

[11]So the devil left Jesus, and angels came and took care of him.

JESUS BEGINS WORK IN GALILEE

[12]When Jesus heard that John had been put in prison, he went back to Galilee. [13]He left Nazareth and went to live in Capernaum, a town near Lake Galilee, in the area near Zebulun and Naphtali. [14]Jesus did this to bring about what the prophet Isaiah had said:

[15] "Land of Zebulun and land of Naphtali
    along the sea,
  beyond the Jordan River.
    This is Galilee where the non-Jewish
        people live.
[16] These people who live in darkness
        will see a great light.
  They live in a place covered with the
        shadows of death,
    but a light will shine on them."
                        Isaiah 9:1–2

JESUS CHOOSES SOME FOLLOWERS

[17]From that time Jesus began to preach, saying, "Change your hearts and lives, because the kingdom of heaven is near."

[18]As Jesus was walking by Lake Galilee, he saw two brothers, Simon (called Peter) and his brother Andrew. They were throwing a net into the lake because they were fishermen. [19]Jesus said, "Come follow me, and I will make you fish for people." [20]So Simon and Andrew immediately left their nets and followed him.

[21]As Jesus continued walking by Lake Galilee, he saw two other brothers, James and John, the sons of Zebedee. They were in a boat with their father Zebedee, mending their nets. Jesus told them to come with him. [22]Immediately they left the boat and their father, and they followed Jesus.

JESUS TEACHES AND HEALS PEOPLE

[23]Jesus went everywhere in Galilee, teaching in the synagogues, preaching the Good News about the kingdom of heaven, and healing all the people's diseases and sicknesses. [24]The news about Jesus spread all over Syria, and people brought all the sick to him. They were suffering from different

---

3:12 He will . . . out. This means that Jesus will come to separate good people from bad people, saving the good and punishing the bad.   **4:4 'A person . . . says.'** Quotation from Deuteronomy 8:3.   **4:7 'Do . . . God.'** Quotation from Deuteronomy 6:16.   **4:10 'You . . . him.'** Quotation from Deuteronomy 6:13.

kinds of diseases. Some were in great pain, some had demons, some were epileptics,[n] and some were paralyzed. Jesus healed all of them. 25Many people from Galilee, the Ten Towns,[n] Jerusalem, Judea, and the land across the Jordan River followed him.

JESUS TEACHES THE PEOPLE

5 When Jesus saw the crowds, he went up on a hill and sat down. His followers came to him, 2and he began to teach them, saying:

3 "They are blessed who realize their spiritual poverty,
for the kingdom of heaven belongs to them.
4 They are blessed who grieve,
for God will comfort them.

5 They are blessed who are humble,
for the whole earth will be theirs.
6 They are blessed who hunger and thirst after justice,
for they will be satisfied.
7 They are blessed who show mercy to others,
for God will show mercy to them.
8 They are blessed whose thoughts are pure,
for they will see God.
9 They are blessed who work for peace,
for they will be called God's children.

4:24 epileptics People with a disease that causes them sometimes to lose control of their bodies and maybe faint, shake strongly, or not be able to move. **4:25 Ten Towns** In Greek, called "Decapolis." It was an area east of Lake Galilee that once had ten main towns.

HANDLING MONEY GOD'S WAY

response **options**

FINANCES

MATTHEW 5:5

This beatitude is about a change in perspective when life forces affliction upon us. How we respond to that is our choice and responsibility. The Old Testament context of this word means that we will see life in a way different from stoic resignation to abuse. We will see that the world is God's and that he causes us to prevail. We will see that submission is the hallmark of victory because it places our will in his. Finally, we will see that our response to trials and tribulations must come from his direction, not ours.

The humble are not people who lie down without a fight. These are not spiritual wimps. These are men and women who acknowledge the Lord God as their protector, who submit to his will for their lives while battles rage in heavenly places. They are the true soldiers of the kingdom, willing to give up their lives for their king.

Do we really live with the attitude that affliction is a way for us to grow in God's grace, or do we complain to God about how "unfair" life has become? Do we see our trials as opportunities for God to shape us into men and women who reflect his image, or are we kicking and screaming our way into his presence?

reflect: How has adversity helped shape your character?
Go to **Song of Songs 8:6–7.**

10 They are blessed who are persecuted for
   doing good,
   for the kingdom of heaven belongs to
   them.
11"People will insult you and hurt you.
They will lie and say all kinds of evil things
about you because you follow me. But when
they do, you will be blessed. 12Rejoice and be
glad, because you have a great reward waiting
for you in heaven. People did the same evil
things to the prophets who lived before you.

YOU ARE LIKE SALT AND LIGHT

13"You are the salt of the earth. But if the
salt loses its salty taste, it cannot be made
salty again. It is good for nothing, except to
be thrown out and walked on.

14"You are the light that gives light to the
world. A city that is built on a hill cannot be
hidden. 15And people don't hide a light under
a bowl. They put it on a lampstand so the
light shines for all the people in the house.
16In the same way, you should be a light for
other people. Live so that they will see the
good things you do and will praise your Father in heaven.

THE IMPORTANCE OF THE LAW

17"Don't think that I have come to destroy the law of Moses or the teaching of the

---

GOD'S ULTIMATE SACRIFICE

FAITH

connected
to the **source**

MATTHEW 5:14–16   By Elmer Towns

A missionary told about a native who stole a light switch, wire, and lightbulb. He
ran to the jungle and showed it to his tribe. Attaching the switch to his grass hut
and hanging the lightbulb from the ceiling, he flipped the switch. Nothing happened.
This native didn't realize that he needed a power source.

Some ridicule Christianity because they previously read the Bible or prayed without
results. They say, "I knew it wouldn't work." In that statement, they deny the faith
needed to get light. They protest, "I tried it once and it did not work," or "I had a friend
who tried it and didn't get it, so I know it won't work for me."

Light does not come from the switch alone. You have to accept the existence of
electricity and the necessity of having wires and a bulb. When all the conditions are
met, and the switch is turned on, there will be light. Faith is much like this. There are
conditions to faith, just as there are conditions to getting light in the room. Faith must
be attached to God, just as the light must be attached to electricity.

There may be a source of power, wires, a light fixture, and a switch. However, to have
light, someone must turn on the switch. Faith links the riches of God to our spiritual
poverty. The spiritual lines are humming with power, but we will remain impoverished if
we do not act in faith.

---

reflect: Have you activated the switch of faith in your life and ministry?
Go to **Matthew 16:25.**

prophets. I have not come to destroy them but to bring about what they said. ¹⁸I tell you the truth, nothing will disappear from the law until heaven and earth are gone. Not even the smallest letter or the smallest part of a letter will be lost until everything has happened. ¹⁹Whoever refuses to obey any command and teaches other people not to obey that command will be the least important in the kingdom of heaven. But whoever obeys the commands and teaches other people to obey them will be great in the kingdom of heaven. ²⁰I tell you that if you are no more obedient than the teachers of the law and the Pharisees, you will never enter the kingdom of heaven.

JESUS TEACHES ABOUT ANGER

²¹"You have heard that it was said to our people long ago, 'You must not murder anyone.'ⁿ Anyone who murders another will be judged.' ²²But I tell you, if you are angry with a brother or sister,ⁿ you will be judged. If you say bad things to a brother or sister, you will be judged by the council. And if you call someone a fool, you will be in danger of the fire of hell.

²³"So when you offer your gift to God at the altar, and you remember that your brother or sister has something against you, ²⁴leave your gift there at the altar. Go and make peace with that person, and then come and offer your gift.

²⁵"If your enemy is taking you to court, become friends quickly, before you go to court. Otherwise, your enemy might turn you over to the judge, and the judge might give you to a guard to put you in jail. ²⁶I tell you the truth, you will not leave there until you have paid everything you owe.

JESUS TEACHES ABOUT SEXUAL SIN

²⁷"You have heard that it was said, 'You must not be guilty of adultery.'ⁿ ²⁸But I tell you that if anyone looks at a woman and wants to sin sexually with her, in his mind he has already done that sin with the woman. ²⁹If your right eye causes you to sin, take it out and throw it away. It is better to lose one part of your body than to have your whole body thrown into hell. ³⁰If your right hand causes you to sin, cut it off and throw it away. It is better to lose one part of your body than for your whole body to go into hell.

JESUS TEACHES ABOUT DIVORCE

³¹"It was also said, 'Anyone who divorces his wife must give her a written divorce paper.'ⁿ ³²But I tell you that anyone who divorces his wife forces her to be guilty of adultery. The only reason for a man to divorce his wife is if she has sexual relations with another man. And anyone who marries that divorced woman is guilty of adultery.

MAKE PROMISES CAREFULLY

³³"You have heard that it was said to our people long ago, 'Don't break your promises, but keep the promises you make to the Lord.'ⁿ ³⁴But I tell you, never swear an oath. Don't swear an oath using the name of heaven, because heaven is God's throne. ³⁵Don't swear an oath using the name of the earth, because the earth belongs to God. Don't swear an oath using the name of Jerusalem, because that is the city of the great King. ³⁶Don't even swear by your own head, because you cannot make one hair on your head become white or black. ³⁷Say only yes if you mean yes, and no if you mean no. If you say more than yes or no, it is from the Evil One.

DON'T FIGHT BACK

³⁸"You have heard that it was said, 'An eye for an eye, and a tooth for a tooth.'ⁿ ³⁹But I tell you, don't stand up against an evil person. If someone slaps you on the right cheek, turn to him the other cheek also. ⁴⁰If someone wants to sue you in court and take your shirt, let him have your coat also. ⁴¹If someone forces you to go with him one mile, go with him two miles. ⁴²If a person asks you for something, give it to him. Don't refuse to give to someone who wants to borrow from you.

LOVE ALL PEOPLE

⁴³"You have heard that it was said, 'Love your neighborⁿ and hate your enemies.' ⁴⁴But I say to you, love your enemies. Pray for those

---

5:21 'You . . . anyone.' Quotation from Exodus 20:13; Deuteronomy 5:17. **5:22 sister** Some Greek copies continue, "without a reason." **5:27 'You . . . adultery.'** Quotation from Exodus 20:14; Deuteronomy 5:18. **5:31 'Anyone . . . divorce paper.'** Quotation from Deuteronomy 24:1. **5:33 'Don't . . . Lord.'** This refers to Leviticus 19:12; Numbers 30:2; Deuteronomy 23:21. **5:38 'An eye . . . tooth.'** Quotation from Exodus 21:24; Leviticus 24:20; Deuteronomy 19:21. **5:43 'Love your neighbor'** Quotation from Leviticus 19:18.

who hurt you.[n] 45If you do this, you will be true children of your Father in heaven. He causes the sun to rise on good people and on evil people, and he sends rain to those who do right and to those who do wrong. 46If you love only the people who love you, you will get no reward. Even the tax collectors do that. 47And if you are nice only to your friends, you are no better than other people. Even those who don't know God are nice to their friends. 48So you must be perfect, just as your Father in heaven is perfect.

JESUS TEACHES ABOUT GIVING

6 "Be careful! When you do good things, don't do them in front of people to be seen by them. If you do that, you will have no reward from your Father in heaven.

2"When you give to the poor, don't be like the hypocrites. They blow trumpets in the synagogues and on the streets so that people will see them and honor them. I tell you the truth, those hypocrites already have their full reward. 3So when you give to the poor, don't let anyone know what you are doing. 4Your giving should be done in secret. Your Father can see what is done in secret, and he will reward you.

JESUS TEACHES ABOUT PRAYER

5"When you pray, don't be like the hypocrites. They love to stand in the synagogues and on the street corners and pray so people will see them. I tell you the truth, they already have their full reward. 6When you pray, you should go into your room and close the door and pray to your Father who cannot be seen. Your Father can see what is done in secret, and he will reward you.

7"And when you pray, don't be like those people who don't know God. They continue saying things that mean nothing, thinking that God will hear them because of their many words. 8Don't be like them, because your Father knows the things you need before you ask him. 9So when you pray, you should pray like this:

'Our Father in heaven,
may your name always be kept holy.
10 May your kingdom come
and what you want be done,
here on earth as it is in heaven.
11 Give us the food we need for each day.
12 Forgive us for our sins,

just as we have forgiven those who sinned against us.
13 And do not cause us to be tempted,
but save us from the Evil One.' [The kingdom, the power, and the glory are yours forever. Amen.][n]

14Yes, if you forgive others for their sins, your Father in heaven will also forgive you for your sins. 15But if you don't forgive others, your Father in heaven will not forgive your sins.

JESUS TEACHES ABOUT WORSHIP

16"When you fast,[n] don't put on a sad face like the hypocrites. They make their faces look sad to show people they are fasting. I tell you the truth, those hypocrites already have their full reward. 17So when you fast, comb your hair and wash your face. 18Then people will not know that you are fasting, but your Father, whom you cannot see, will see you. Your Father sees what is done in secret, and he will reward you.

GOD IS MORE IMPORTANT THAN MONEY

19"Don't store treasures for yourselves here on earth where moths and rust will destroy them and thieves can break in and steal them. 20But store your treasures in heaven where they cannot be destroyed by moths or rust and where thieves cannot break in and steal them. 21Your heart will be where your treasure is.

22"The eye is a light for the body. If your eyes are good, your whole body will be full of light. 23But if your eyes are evil, your whole body will be full of darkness. And if the only light you have is really darkness, then you have the worst darkness.

24"No one can serve two masters. The person will hate one master and love the other, or will follow one master and refuse to follow the other. You cannot serve both God and worldly riches.

DON'T WORRY

25"So I tell you, don't worry about the food or drink you need to live, or about the clothes you need for your body. Life is more

---

5:44 **you** Some Greek copies continue, "Bless those who curse you, do good to those who hate you." Compare Luke 6:28. **6:13 The . . . Amen.** Some Greek copies do not contain the bracketed text. **6:16 fast** The people would give up eating for a special time of prayer and worship to God. It was also done to show sadness and disappointment.

than food, and the body is more than clothes. ²⁶Look at the birds in the air. They don't plant or harvest or store food in barns, but your heavenly Father feeds them. And you know that you are worth much more than the birds. ²⁷You cannot add any time to your life by worrying about it.

²⁸"And why do you worry about clothes? Look at how the lilies in the field grow. They don't work or make clothes for themselves. ²⁹But I tell you that even Solomon with his riches was not dressed as beautifully as one of these flowers. ³⁰God clothes the grass in the field, which is alive today

---

TURNING REVELATIONS INTO REVOLUTIONS

a **change** of **heart**

FITNESS

MATTHEW 6:21

Deep inside, people recognize the gap between how they are acting and how God *planned* for them to be acting. We know the plan that God has for our behaviors, but our actions just refuse to follow along. We believe in God's plan, but we do something else. Why don't we do what we believe? It is because we value something else.

We *say* what we believe, but we *do* what we value. Our values determine our behaviors, and how we behave regularly forms our habits. Therefore, someone might *say,* "Exercise is important" or "People shouldn't eat fast food," but, if they don't value their bodies more than they value watching television or satiating cravings, they'll rarely exercise and they'll give in to the smell of fried grease in a moment's notice.

Similarly, you may know you should spend more time with your family, but if you don't value those relationships more than you value work, money, and hobbies, then you will become yet another person lying in the hospital one day *not* saying, "I should have spent more time at the office, golf course, and watching television."

Our heads may know what to do, but our hearts are stricken with the dead weight of misdirected values. Therefore, you'll never have a change of habits until you have a change of heart. The heart is the wellspring of your values. Your head may keep saying you're going to change, but without a change in what you value, you'll only be writing another verbal check you can't cash.

If you begin to value God, your family, and your future more then you do fast food, sleeping in, and televised reruns, you surely will begin to exercise regularly, cut down on your calorie allotment, and prioritize date times with your spouse and children. It's not what you say that's important, but what you do. Your lifestyle is simply an expression of your heart and the values and the habits it produces.

reflect: Become a person who walks the walk, and not simply one who talks the talk.
Go to **FITNESS:** "The Longevity Factor" at **Deuteronomy 8:11-19.**

Fear of the Future

By James Merritt

By now you are probably all too familiar with the Homeland Security Advisory System. But what you may not be aware of is the fact that every day of your life you use the same system to chart your own anxiety level. And the relative ease and speed at which we can go from Anxiety Level Green (Low) to Anxiety Level Red (Severe) is astounding.

Some people call it tension. Others call it stress or anxiety. Jesus called it worry. I call it the fear of the future, and we are all susceptible. For example, did you know that in every presidential election, the number one concern for voters is the economy? It's sad, but true. People vote according to their pocketbooks. We worry about our financial, vocational, material, and professional futures.

However, let me clarify the difference between concern and worry. There is nothing wrong with concern. For example, lack of concern for the safety of your children playing in a street during business traffic is foolish. In other words, there is a difference between being carefree and being careless.

There are daily concerns that we all should have. Legitimate concerns are wise. But illegitimate worries are foolish. How can you tell the difference? Concerns focus on the present. Worries focus on the future. That's why Jesus took worry head-on: "So don't worry about tomorrow, because tomorrow will have its own worries. Each day has enough trouble of its own."

Someone has defined worry as "the interest we pay in advance today for the trouble that may never come tomorrow." In reality, worry is the act of a spiritual orphan or an atheist. Worry professes that either God cannot or will not take care of me, or that there isn't even a God up there who cares.

As someone who naturally worries about everything, I've developed three practical steps to help overcome this illegitimate "fear of the future." Try these for yourself:

1 **Remember how God has performed in the past.** You're alive now, aren't you? Despite troubles, problems, and speed bumps, you've survived. God has taken care of you. As recorded in Deuteronomy 1:29-33, Moses learned this lesson well and taught it to the people of Israel. Need more proof? Read the words of God in Isaiah 46:3-4.

2 **Realize what God has promised in the present.** Look at verses such as Psalm 32:8 or Deuteronomy 31:8. God's promise for you is that he will be with you and take care of you. God will *not* break his promise. He is faithful. If he takes care of the birds, don't you think he will take care of you?

3 **Rely on what God has planned for the future.** If you are a child of God, I can guarantee you that everything that happens to you in your future—regardless of how tough it may seem at the moment—will work out for your good. That's the money-back guarantee of Romans 8:28.

As you work through these three simple steps, you will find your anxiety levels decreasing every day. Remember, worry is an optional misery. So put worry aside and learn to trust God with yesterday, today, and tomorrow.

TO LEARN MORE ON WHAT THE BIBLE HAS TO SAY ABOUT **FULFILLMENT**, READ THE SCRIPTURES AND DEVOTIONALS AT **JOB 22:26, PSALM 4:4-5, PSALM 7:11-17, PSALM 23:5, PSALM 30:5, PSALM 46:1,** AND **PSALM 51:10.**

but tomorrow is thrown into the fire. So you can be even more sure that God will clothe you. Don't have so little faith! ³¹Don't worry and say, 'What will we eat?' or 'What will we drink?' or 'What will we wear?' ³²The people who don't know God keep trying to get these things, and your Father in heaven knows you need them. ³³Seek first God's kingdom and what God wants. Then all your other needs will be met as well. ³⁴So don't worry about tomorrow, because tomorrow will have its own worries. Each day has enough trouble of its own.

BE CAREFUL ABOUT JUDGING OTHERS

7 "Don't judge others, or you will be judged. ²You will be judged in the same way that you judge others, and the amount you give to others will be given to you.

³"Why do you notice the little piece of dust in your friend's eye, but you don't notice the big piece of wood in your own eye? ⁴How can you say to your friend, 'Let me take that little piece of dust out of your eye'? Look at yourself! You still have that big piece of wood in your own eye. ⁵You hypocrite! First, take the wood out of your own eye. Then you will see clearly to take the dust out of your friend's eye.

THE LONGEVITY FACTOR

are stimulants
good for **you?**

FITNESS

MATTHEW 6:33

Dr. B. J. Palmer, whose family founded the chiropractic profession, said, "Get the big idea, and all else follows." Of course, the Bible always seems to have said every great thing first. Dr. Palmer's statement is very similar to this verse, *"Seek first God's kingdom and . . . all your other needs will be met as well."* The idea here is that if you can understand the big picture, you'll understand how life operates, and everything else will fall into place.

All good things come from lining yourself up with God's intentions for your life . . . and bad things come when you're out of alignment. The "big idea" when it comes to your health is that there is a natural, God-given balance that all men and women should "seek first" to establish. Anything that helps to restore this balance is good, and anything opposed can bring only bad.

Knowing that a drug, caffeine, artificial ingredients, or sugar will all create imbalance, the "big idea" tells us that these things run contrary to God's intent for your body and are out of alignment. So, while there may be elements in stimulants that provide benefit, these are outweighed by the fact that there are also several other elements that provide damage. When you really start to seek God's authority with how you care for your body, you start by honoring it, not poisoning it, and making sure that your lifestyle is aligned with his design.

reflect: Order your diet around godly principles and reap the rewards.
Go to **Luke 6:12.**

⁶"Don't give holy things to dogs, and don't throw your pearls before pigs. Pigs will only trample on them, and dogs will turn to attack you.

ASK GOD FOR WHAT YOU NEED

⁷"Ask, and God will give to you. Search, and you will find. Knock, and the door will open for you. ⁸Yes, everyone who asks will receive. Everyone who searches will find. And everyone who knocks will have the door opened.

⁹"If your children ask for bread, which of you would give them a stone? ¹⁰Or if your children ask for a fish, would you give them a snake? ¹¹Even though you are bad, you know how to give good gifts to your children. How

---

FINANCES

UNDERSTANDING FREEDOM

the **high value** of healthy **ambition**

MATTHEW 7:12   By Bob Russell

The Book of Proverbs says a lot about the correlation between hard work and achievement. Solomon had little patience for the lazy; he had high praise for the ambitious.

"Lazy people sleep a lot, and idle people will go hungry" (Proverbs 19:15).

"If you love to sleep, you will be poor. If you stay awake, you will have plenty of food" (Proverbs 20:13).

These verses warn against laziness. In today's economy, most of us work for someone else; we are not farmers. All too often, however, we don't give our best effort at work; we take that next paycheck for granted. We need a good dose of healthy ambition. What is it? Simply put, it's the Golden Rule. You already have healthy ambition if you:

1. Go to work every day.
2. Show up on time.
3. Always give your best effort.
4. Help others.
5. Make your supervisor look good.
6. Get along with people.
7. Give attention to your family after work.
8. Let your record speak for itself.
9. Live a life of integrity.
10. Work as though the Lord were your supervisor.

"In all the work you are doing, work the best you can. Work as if you were doing it for the Lord, not for people" (Colossians 3:23). That's a gentle reminder that can have life-changing consequences. Ann Landers once said, "The harder you work, the luckier you will get." Solomon would probably put it another way: The harder you work, the more God will bless.

reflect: What are some ways you could improve your work ethic?
Go to **Matthew 25:14–30.**

much more your heavenly Father will give good things to those who ask him!

THE MOST IMPORTANT RULE

12"Do to others what you want them to do to you. This is the meaning of the law of Moses and the teaching of the prophets.

THE WAY TO HEAVEN IS HARD

13"Enter through the narrow gate. The gate is wide and the road is wide that leads to hell, and many people enter through that gate. 14But the gate is small and the road is narrow that leads to true life. Only a few people find that road.

PEOPLE KNOW YOU BY YOUR ACTIONS

15"Be careful of false prophets. They come to you looking gentle like sheep, but they are really dangerous like wolves. 16You will know these people by what they do. Grapes don't come from thornbushes, and figs don't come from thorny weeds. 17In the same way, every good tree produces good fruit, but a bad tree produces bad fruit. 18A good tree cannot produce bad fruit, and a bad tree cannot produce

BRAVE JOY

you **have** a **choice**

FAITH

By John Ed Mathison

MATTHEW 7:13–14

You're driving down the freeway and you have two lanes from which to choose: the first lane, the "fast lane," is wide and well traveled; the second lane is narrow and not crowded at all. The first lane leads to destruction; the other lane, the "faith lane," leads to eternal life. You must choose one or the other.

What do you have if you choose the "faith" lane? You have *confidence*: confidence in the blood of Jesus and the forgiveness of your sins; confidence in a new and living way that Christ has for you. You cannot make this way yourself (despite what countless "self-help" books will tell you). There is confidence in Jesus as a new high priest. Thanks to his death on the cross, no mediator is needed to approach him. You can come before him, confident that he will hear you.

You have *certainty*. There is a certainty that comes when you accept Jesus as your savior. You have assurance of your salvation.

You have *commitment*. God's commitment to you is unconditional. God is faithful. In return, he wants you to commit to him.

You have *community*. It's your church. Within this community of believers, you encourage one another. You stimulate each other to do good works. A church is a group of individuals joined like links in a chain fence. A single link can do little; but a community of links can do many things.

reflect: Do you need to get out of the "fast" lane and into the "faith" lane?
Go to **Romans 6:23**.

good fruit. ¹⁹Every tree that does not produce good fruit is cut down and thrown into the fire. ²⁰In the same way, you will know these false prophets by what they do.

²¹"Not all those who say 'You are our Lord' will enter the kingdom of heaven. The only people who will enter the kingdom of heaven are those who do what my Father in heaven wants. ²²On the last day many people will say to me, 'Lord, Lord, we spoke for you, and through you we forced out demons and did many miracles.' ²³Then I will tell them clearly, 'Get away from me, you who do evil. I never knew you.'

TWO KINDS OF PEOPLE

²⁴"Everyone who hears my words and obeys them is like a wise man who built his house on rock. ²⁵It rained hard, the floods came, and the winds blew and hit that house. But it did not fall, because it was built on rock. ²⁶Everyone who hears my words and does not obey them is like a foolish man who built his house on sand. ²⁷It rained hard, the floods came, and the winds blew and hit that house, and it fell with a big crash."

²⁸When Jesus finished saying these things, the people were amazed at his teaching,

---

ARE YOU PROGRAMMED FOR STRESS?

FULFILLMENT

positive stress

MATTHEW 7:29   By Edwin Louis Cole

Change is a normal and necessary part of life, and stress is a consequence of change. Every generation has faced stress; it is nothing new. America's forefathers lived through stressful situations fighting for freedom and opening new frontiers. Stress is normal to life. But God always starts on the positive, and he will always end on the positive. You can spend time in prayer and lose yourself in your identity with Jesus Christ to overcome stress.

Jesus had no personal stress in himself, even though he bore the sins of the world. Regardless of the turmoil, he was secure in his established purpose, identity, and authority. Jesus did not need to manipulate, threaten, or give ultimatums. He spoke and taught "like a person who had authority" (Matthew 7:29). His confidence and ability to exercise his authority came, in part, from knowing who he was and being in perfect agreement with God's plan and will for his life.

The right amount of tension in a guitar or piano string is necessary for fine-tuning. Pressure makes the difference between a lump of coal and a diamond. The more pressure something is able to withstand, the more valuable it becomes. People are the same.

It is the nature of God to change things in your life for the good. Remember, while change brings pressure, you can be secure in your relationship with God the Father. You can resolve to withstand the fires of pressure, to overcome stress, and to grow stronger.

reflect: How have you become stronger by overcoming a stressful situation?
Go to **Matthew 25:44–45.**

[29] because he did not teach like their teachers of the law. He taught like a person who had authority.

JESUS HEALS A SICK MAN

8 When Jesus came down from the hill, great crowds followed him. [2] Then a man with a skin disease came to Jesus. The man bowed down before him and said, "Lord, you can heal me if you will."

[3] Jesus reached out his hand and touched the man and said, "I will. Be healed!" And immediately the man was healed from his disease. [4] Then Jesus said to him, "Don't tell anyone about this. But go and show yourself to the priest[n] and offer the gift Moses commanded[n] for people who are made well. This will show the people what I have done."

JESUS HEALS A SOLDIER'S SERVANT

[5] When Jesus entered the city of Capernaum, an army officer came to him, begging for help. [6] The officer said, "Lord, my servant is at home in bed. He can't move his body and is in much pain."

[7] Jesus said to the officer, "I will go and heal him."

[8] The officer answered, "Lord, I am not worthy for you to come into my house. You only need to command it, and my servant will be healed. [9] I, too, am a man under the authority of others, and I have soldiers under my command. I tell one soldier, 'Go,' and he goes. I tell another soldier, 'Come,' and he comes. I say to my servant, 'Do this,' and my servant does it."

[10] When Jesus heard this, he was amazed. He said to those who were following him, "I tell you the truth, this is the greatest faith I have found, even in Israel. [11] Many people will come from the east and from the west and will sit and eat with Abraham, Isaac, and Jacob in the kingdom of heaven. [12] But those people who should be in the kingdom will be thrown outside into the darkness, where people will cry and grind their teeth with pain."

[13] Then Jesus said to the officer, "Go home. Your servant will be healed just as you believed he would." And his servant was healed that same hour.

JESUS HEALS MANY PEOPLE

[14] When Jesus went to Peter's house, he saw that Peter's mother-in-law was sick in bed with a fever. [15] Jesus touched her hand, and the fever left her. Then she stood up and began to serve Jesus.

[16] That evening people brought to Jesus many who had demons. Jesus spoke and the demons left them, and he healed all the sick. [17] He did these things to bring about what Isaiah the prophet had said:

"He took our suffering on him
   and carried our diseases."   *Isaiah 53:4*

PEOPLE WANT TO FOLLOW JESUS

[18] When Jesus saw the crowd around him, he told his followers to go to the other side of the lake. [19] Then a teacher of the law came to Jesus and said, "Teacher, I will follow you any place you go."

[20] Jesus said to him, "The foxes have holes to live in, and the birds have nests, but the Son of Man has no place to rest his head."

[21] Another man, one of Jesus' followers, said to him, "Lord, first let me go and bury my father."

[22] But Jesus told him, "Follow me, and let the people who are dead bury their own dead."

JESUS CALMS A STORM

[23] Jesus got into a boat, and his followers went with him. [24] A great storm arose on the lake so that waves covered the boat, but Jesus was sleeping. [25] His followers went to him and woke him, saying, "Lord, save us! We will drown!"

[26] Jesus answered, "Why are you afraid? You don't have enough faith." Then Jesus got up and gave a command to the wind and the waves, and it became completely calm.

[27] The men were amazed and said, "What kind of man is this? Even the wind and the waves obey him!"

JESUS HEALS TWO MEN WITH DEMONS

[28] When Jesus arrived at the other side of the lake in the area of the Gadarene[n] people, two men who had demons in them met him. These men lived in the burial caves and were

---

8:4 show . . . priest The Law of Moses said a priest must say when a Jewish person with a skin disease was well. **8:4 Moses commanded** Read about this in Leviticus 14:1–32. **8:28 Gadarene** From Gadara, an area southeast of Lake Galilee. The exact location is uncertain and some Greek copies read "Gergesene"; others read "Gerasene."

so dangerous that people could not use the road by those caves. [29]They shouted, "What do you want with us, Son of God? Did you come here to torture us before the right time?"

[30]Near that place there was a large herd of pigs feeding. [31]The demons begged Jesus, "If you make us leave these men, please send us into that herd of pigs."

[32]Jesus said to them, "Go!" So the demons left the men and went into the pigs. Then the whole herd rushed down the hill into the lake and were drowned. [33]The herdsmen ran away and went into town, where they told about all of this and what had happened to the men who had demons. [34]Then the whole town went out to see Jesus. When they saw him, they begged him to leave their area.

JESUS HEALS A PARALYZED MAN

9 Jesus got into a boat and went back across the lake to his own town. [2]Some people brought to Jesus a man who was paralyzed and lying on a mat. When Jesus saw the faith of these people, he said to the paralyzed man, "Be encouraged, young man. Your sins are forgiven."

[3]Some of the teachers of the law said to themselves, "This man speaks as if he were God. That is blasphemy!"[n]

[4]Knowing their thoughts, Jesus said, "Why are you thinking evil thoughts? [5]Which is easier: to say, 'Your sins are forgiven,' or to tell him, 'Stand up and walk'? [6]But I will prove to you that the Son of Man has authority on earth to forgive sins." Then Jesus said to the paralyzed man, "Stand up, take your mat, and go home." [7]And the man stood up and went home. [8]When the people saw this, they were amazed and praised God for giving power like this to human beings.

JESUS CHOOSES MATTHEW

[9]When Jesus was leaving, he saw a man named Matthew sitting in the tax collector's booth. Jesus said to him, "Follow me," and he stood up and followed Jesus.

[10]As Jesus was having dinner at Matthew's house, many tax collectors and "sinners" came and ate with Jesus and his followers. [11]When the Pharisees saw this, they asked Jesus' followers, "Why does your teacher eat with tax collectors and sinners?"

[12]When Jesus heard them, he said, "It is not the healthy people who need a doctor, but the sick. [13]Go and learn what this means: 'I want kindness more than I want animal sacrifices.'[n] I did not come to invite good people but to invite sinners."

JESUS' FOLLOWERS ARE CRITICIZED

[14]Then the followers of John[n] came to Jesus and said, "Why do we and the Pharisees often fast[n] for a certain time, but your followers don't?"

[15]Jesus answered, "The friends of the bridegroom are not sad while he is with them. But the time will come when the bridegroom will be taken from them, and then they will fast.

[16]"No one sews a patch of unshrunk cloth over a hole in an old coat. If he does, the patch will shrink and pull away from the coat, making the hole worse. [17]Also, people never pour new wine into old leather bags. Otherwise, the bags will break, the wine will spill, and the wine bags will be ruined. But people always pour new wine into new wine bags. Then both will continue to be good."

JESUS GIVES LIFE TO A DEAD GIRL AND HEALS A SICK WOMAN

[18]While Jesus was saying these things, a leader of the synagogue came to him. He bowed down before Jesus and said, "My daughter has just died. But if you come and lay your hand on her, she will live again." [19]So Jesus and his followers stood up and went with the leader.

[20]Then a woman who had been bleeding for twelve years came behind Jesus and touched the edge of his coat. [21]She was thinking, "If I can just touch his clothes, I will be healed."

[22]Jesus turned and saw the woman and said, "Be encouraged, dear woman. You are made well because you believed." And the woman was healed from that moment on.

[23]Jesus continued along with the leader and went into his house. There he saw the funeral musicians and many people crying. [24]Jesus said, "Go away. The girl is not dead,

---

9:3 blasphemy Saying things against God or not showing respect for God. **9:13 'I want ... sacrifices.'** Quotation from Hosea 6:6. **9:14 John** John the Baptist, who preached to people about Christ's coming (Matthew 3, Luke 3). **9:14 fast** The people would give up eating for a special time of prayer and worship to God. It was also done to show sadness and disappointment.

only asleep." But the people laughed at him. [25]After the crowd had been thrown out of the house, Jesus went into the girl's room and took hold of her hand, and she stood up. [26]The news about this spread all around the area.

JESUS HEALS MORE PEOPLE

[27]When Jesus was leaving there, two blind men followed him. They cried out, "Have mercy on us, Son of David!"

[28]After Jesus went inside, the blind men went with him. He asked the men, "Do you believe that I can make you see again?"

They answered, "Yes, Lord."

[29]Then Jesus touched their eyes and said, "Because you believe I can make you see again, it will happen." [30]Then the men were able to see. But Jesus warned them strongly, saying, "Don't tell anyone about this." [31]But the blind men left and spread the news about Jesus all around that area.

[32]When the two men were leaving, some people brought another man to Jesus. This man could not talk because he had a demon in him. [33]After Jesus forced the demon to leave the man, he was able to speak. The crowd was amazed and said, "We have never seen anything like this in Israel."

[34]But the Pharisees said, "The prince of demons is the one that gives him power to force demons out."

[35]Jesus traveled through all the towns and villages, teaching in their synagogues, preaching the Good News about the kingdom, and healing all kinds of diseases and sicknesses. [36]When he saw the crowds, he felt sorry for them because they were hurting and helpless, like sheep without a shepherd. [37]Jesus said to his followers, "There are many people to harvest but only a few workers to help harvest them. [38]Pray to the Lord, who owns the harvest, that he will send more workers to gather his harvest."[n]

JESUS SENDS OUT HIS APOSTLES

10 Jesus called his twelve followers together and gave them authority to drive out evil spirits and to heal every kind of disease and sickness. [2]These are the names of the twelve apostles: Simon (also called Peter) and his brother Andrew; James son of Zebedee, and his brother John; [3]Philip and Bartholomew; Thomas and Matthew, the tax collector; James son of Alphaeus, and Thaddaeus; [4]Simon the Zealot and Judas Iscariot, who turned against Jesus.

[5]Jesus sent out these twelve men with the following order: "Don't go to the non-Jewish people or to any town where the Samaritans live. [6]But go to the people of Israel, who are like lost sheep. [7]When you go, preach this: 'The kingdom of heaven is near.' [8]Heal the sick, raise the dead to life again, heal those who have skin diseases, and force demons out of people. I give you these powers freely, so help other people freely. [9]Don't carry any money with you—gold or silver or copper. [10]Don't carry a bag or extra clothes or sandals or a walking stick. Workers should be given what they need.

[11]"When you enter a city or town, find some worthy person there and stay in that home until you leave. [12]When you enter that home, say, 'Peace be with you.' [13]If the people there welcome you, let your peace stay there. But if they don't welcome you, take back the peace you wished for them. [14]And if a home or town refuses to welcome you or listen to you, leave that place and shake its dust off your feet.[n] [15]I tell you the truth, on the Judgment Day it will be better for the towns of Sodom and Gomorrah[n] than for the people of that town.

JESUS WARNS HIS APOSTLES

[16]"Listen, I am sending you out like sheep among wolves. So be as clever as snakes and as innocent as doves. [17]Be careful of people, because they will arrest you and take you to court and whip you in their synagogues. [18]Because of me you will be taken to stand before governors and kings, and you will tell them and the non-Jewish people about me. [19]When you are arrested, don't worry about what to say or how to say it. At that time you will be given the things to say. [20]It will not really be you speaking but the Spirit of your Father speaking through you.

[21]"Brothers will give their own brothers to be killed, and fathers will give their own

---

9:37–38 "There are . . . harvest." As a farmer sends workers to harvest the grain, Jesus sends his followers to bring people to God. **10:14 shake . . . feet** A warning. It showed that they had rejected these people. **10:15 Sodom and Gomorrah** Two cities that God destroyed because the people were so evil.

children to be killed. Children will fight against their own parents and have them put to death. ²²All people will hate you because you follow me, but those people who keep their faith until the end will be saved. ²³When you are treated badly in one city, run to another city. I tell you the truth, you will not finish going through all the cities of Israel before the Son of Man comes.

²⁴"A student is not better than his teacher, and a servant is not better than his master. ²⁵A student should be satisfied to become like his teacher; a servant should be satisfied to become like his master. If the head of the family is called Beelzebul, then the other members of the family will be called worse names!

FEAR GOD, NOT PEOPLE

²⁶"So don't be afraid of those people, because everything that is hidden will be shown. Everything that is secret will be made known. ²⁷I tell you these things in the dark, but I want you to tell them in the light. What you hear whispered in your ear you should shout from the housetops. ²⁸Don't be afraid of people, who can kill the body but cannot kill the soul. The only one you should fear is the one who can destroy the soul and the body in hell. ²⁹Two sparrows cost only a penny, but not even one of them can die without your Father's knowing it. ³⁰God even knows how many hairs are on your head. ³¹So don't be afraid. You are worth much more than many sparrows.

TELL PEOPLE ABOUT YOUR FAITH

³²"All those who stand before others and say they believe in me, I will say before my Father in heaven that they belong to me. ³³But all who stand before others and say they do not believe in me, I will say before my Father in heaven that they do not belong to me.

³⁴"Don't think that I came to bring peace to the earth. I did not come to bring peace, but a sword. ³⁵I have come so that

'a son will be against his father,
　a daughter will be against her mother,
　a daughter-in-law will be against her
　　mother-in-law.
³⁶　A person's enemies will be members of
　　his own family.'
　　　　　　　　　　　　　　Micah 7:6

³⁷"Those who love their father or mother more than they love me are not worthy to be my followers. Those who love their son

or daughter more than they love me are not worthy to be my followers. ³⁸Whoever is not willing to carry the cross and follow me is not worthy of me. ³⁹Those who try to hold on to their lives will give up true life. Those who give up their lives for me will hold on to true life. ⁴⁰Whoever accepts you also accepts me, and whoever accepts me also accepts the One who sent me. ⁴¹Whoever meets a prophet and accepts him will receive the reward of a prophet. And whoever accepts a good person because that person is good will receive the reward of a good person. ⁴²Those who give one of these little ones a cup of cold water because they are my followers will truly get their reward."

JESUS AND JOHN THE BAPTIST

11 After Jesus finished telling these things to his twelve followers, he left there and went to the towns in Galilee to teach and preach.

²John the Baptist was in prison, but he heard about what the Christ was doing. So John sent some of his followers to Jesus. ³They asked him, "Are you the One who is to come, or should we wait for someone else?"

⁴Jesus answered them, "Go tell John what you hear and see: ⁵The blind can see, the crippled can walk, and people with skin diseases are healed. The deaf can hear, the dead are raised to life, and the Good News is preached to the poor. ⁶Those who do not stumble in their faith because of me are blessed."

⁷As John's followers were leaving, Jesus began talking to the people about John. Jesus said, "What did you go out into the desert to see? A reed[n] blown by the wind? ⁸What did you go out to see? A man dressed in fine clothes? No, those who wear fine clothes live in kings' palaces. ⁹So why did you go out? To see a prophet? Yes, and I tell you, John is more than a prophet. ¹⁰This was written about him:

'I will send my messenger ahead of you,
　who will prepare the way for you.'
　　　　　　　　　　　　　　Malachi 3:1

¹¹I tell you the truth, John the Baptist is greater than any other person ever born, but even the least important person in the king-

---

11:7 reed It means that John was not ordinary or weak like grass blown by the wind.

dom of heaven is greater than John. [12]Since the time John the Baptist came until now, the kingdom of heaven has been going forward in strength, and people have been trying to take it by force. [13]All the prophets and the law of Moses told about what would happen until the time John came. [14]And if you will believe what they said, you will believe that John is Elijah, whom they said would come. [15]Let those with ears use them and listen!

[16]"What can I say about the people of this time? What are they like? They are like children sitting in the marketplace, who call out to each other,

[17] 'We played music for you, but you did not dance;

we sang a sad song, but you did not cry.'
[18]John came and did not eat or drink like other people. So people say, 'He has a demon.' [19]The Son of Man came, eating and drinking, and people say, 'Look at him! He eats too much and drinks too much wine, and he is a friend of tax collectors and sinners.' But wisdom is proved to be right by what she does."

JESUS WARNS UNBELIEVERS

[20]Then Jesus criticized the cities where he did most of his miracles, because the people did not change their lives and stop sinning. [21]He said, "How terrible for you, Korazin! How terrible for you, Bethsaida! If the same miracles I did in you had happened in Tyre and Sidon,[n] those people would have changed their lives a long time ago. They would have worn rough cloth and put ashes on themselves to show they had changed. [22]But I tell you, on the Judgment Day it will be better for Tyre and Sidon than for you. [23]And you, Capernaum,[n] will you be lifted up to heaven? No, you will be thrown down to the depths. If the miracles I did in you had happened in Sodom,[n] its people would have stopped sinning, and it would still be a city today. [24]But I tell you, on the Judgment Day it will be better for Sodom than for you."

JESUS OFFERS REST TO PEOPLE

[25]At that time Jesus said, "I praise you, Father, Lord of heaven and earth, because you have hidden these things from the people who are wise and smart. But you have shown them to those who are like little children. [26]Yes, Father, this is what you really wanted.

[27]"My Father has given me all things. No one knows the Son, except the Father. And no one knows the Father, except the Son and those whom the Son chooses to tell.

[28]"Come to me, all of you who are tired and have heavy loads, and I will give you rest. [29]Accept my teachings and learn from me, because I am gentle and humble in spirit, and you will find rest for your lives. [30]The burden that I ask you to accept is easy; the load I give you to carry is light."

JESUS IS LORD OF THE SABBATH

12 At that time Jesus was walking through some fields of grain on a Sabbath day. His followers were hungry, so they began to pick the grain and eat it. [2]When the Pharisees saw this, they said to Jesus, "Look! Your followers are doing what is unlawful to do on the Sabbath day."

[3]Jesus answered, "Have you not read what David did when he and the people with him were hungry? [4]He went into God's house, and he and those with him ate the holy bread, which was lawful only for priests to eat. [5]And have you not read in the law of Moses that on every Sabbath day the priests in the Temple break this law about the Sabbath day? But the priests are not wrong for doing that. [6]I tell you that there is something here that is greater than the Temple. [7]The Scripture says, 'I want kindness more than I want animal sacrifices.'[n] You don't really know what those words mean. If you understood them, you would not judge those who have done nothing wrong.

[8]"So the Son of Man is Lord of the Sabbath day."

JESUS HEALS A MAN'S HAND

[9]Jesus left there and went into their synagogue, [10]where there was a man with a crippled hand. They were looking for a reason to accuse Jesus, so they asked him, "Is it right to heal on the Sabbath day?"[n]

[11]Jesus answered, "If any of you has a sheep, and it falls into a ditch on the Sabbath

---

11:21 Tyre and Sidon Towns where wicked people lived. **11:21, 23 Korazin . . . Bethsaida . . . Capernaum** Towns by Lake Galilee where Jesus preached to the people. **11:23 Sodom** A city that God destroyed because the people were so evil. **12:7 'I . . . sacrifices.'** Quotation from Hosea 6:6. **12:10 Is it right . . . day?** It was against Jewish Law to work on the Sabbath day.

day, you will help it out of the ditch. [12]Surely a human being is more important than a sheep. So it is lawful to do good things on the Sabbath day."

[13]Then Jesus said to the man with the crippled hand, "Hold out your hand." The man held out his hand, and it became well again, like the other hand. [14]But the Pharisees left and made plans to kill Jesus.

JESUS IS GOD'S CHOSEN SERVANT

[15]Jesus knew what the Pharisees were doing, so he left that place. Many people followed him, and he healed all who were sick. [16]But Jesus warned the people not to tell who he was. [17]He did these things to bring about what Isaiah the prophet had said:

[18] "Here is my servant whom I have chosen.

I love him, and I am pleased with him.
I will put my Spirit upon him,
and he will tell of my justice to all people.

[19] He will not argue or cry out;
no one will hear his voice in the streets.

[20] He will not break a crushed blade of grass
or put out even a weak flame
until he makes justice win the victory.

[21] In him will the non-Jewish people find hope."   *Isaiah 42:1–4*

JESUS' POWER IS FROM GOD

[22]Then some people brought to Jesus a man who was blind and could not talk, because he had a demon. Jesus healed the man so that he could talk and see. [23]All the people were amazed and said, "Perhaps this man is the Son of David!"

[24]When the Pharisees heard this, they said, "Jesus uses the power of Beelzebul, the ruler of demons, to force demons out of people."

[25]Jesus knew what the Pharisees were thinking, so he said to them, "Every kingdom that is divided against itself will be destroyed. And any city or family that is divided against itself will not continue. [26]And if Satan forces out himself, then Satan is divided against himself, and his kingdom will not continue. [27]You say that I use the power of Beelzebul to force out demons. If that is true, then what power do your people use to force out demons? So they will be your judges. [28]But if I use the power of God's Spirit to force out demons, then the kingdom of God has come to you.

[29]"If anyone wants to enter a strong person's house and steal his things, he must first tie up the strong person. Then he can steal the things from the house.

[30]"Whoever is not with me is against me. Whoever does not work with me is working against me. [31]So I tell you, people can be forgiven for every sin and everything they say against God. But whoever speaks against the Holy Spirit will not be forgiven. [32]Anyone who speaks against the Son of Man can be forgiven, but anyone who speaks against the Holy Spirit will not be forgiven, now or in the future.

PEOPLE KNOW YOU BY YOUR WORDS

[33]"If you want good fruit, you must make the tree good. If your tree is not good, it will have bad fruit. A tree is known by the kind of fruit it produces. [34]You snakes! You are evil people, so how can you say anything good? The mouth speaks the things that are in the heart. [35]Good people have good things in their hearts, and so they say good things. But evil people have evil in their hearts, so they say evil things. [36]And I tell you that on the Judgment Day people will be responsible for every careless thing they have said. [37]The words you have said will be used to judge you. Some of your words will prove you right, but some of your words will prove you guilty."

THE PEOPLE ASK FOR A MIRACLE

[38]Then some of the Pharisees and teachers of the law answered Jesus, saying, "Teacher, we want to see you work a miracle as a sign."

[39]Jesus answered, "Evil and sinful people are the ones who want to see a miracle for a sign. But no sign will be given to them, except the sign of the prophet Jonah. [40]Jonah was in the stomach of the big fish for three days and three nights. In the same way, the Son of Man will be in the grave three days and three nights. [41]On the Judgment Day the people from Nineveh[n] will stand up with you people who live now, and they will show that you are guilty. When Jonah preached

---

12:41 Nineveh The city where Jonah preached to warn the people. Read Jonah 3.

to them, they were sorry and changed their lives. And I tell you that someone greater than Jonah is here. 42On the Judgment Day, the Queen of the South[n] will stand up with you people who live today. She will show that you are guilty, because she came from far away to listen to Solomon's wise teaching. And I tell you that someone greater than Solomon is here.

PEOPLE TODAY ARE FULL OF EVIL

43"When an evil spirit comes out of a person, it travels through dry places, looking for a place to rest, but it doesn't find it. 44So the spirit says, 'I will go back to the house I left.' When the spirit comes back, it finds the house still empty, swept clean, and made neat. 45Then the evil spirit goes out and brings seven other spirits even more evil than it is, and they go in and live there. So the person has even more trouble than before. It is the same way with the evil people who live today."

12:42 Queen of the South The Queen of Sheba. She traveled a thousand miles to learn God's wisdom from Solomon. Read 1 Kings 10:1–13.

UNDERSTANDING AUTHORITY

extraordinary
communications

FAMILY

By Larry Stockstill

MATTHEW 12:34–37

Words are a serious matter. They are powerful for both good and evil. When you use words to bless and encourage your spouse or children, you release a power in their lives that is greater than you realize. Spoken words have power in the spiritual world.

You have free choice to build or destroy every relationship in your life. Whereas God is the giver of speech and language, you are the one who chooses the particular words you say. Your words arise from your heart and are a reflection of your inner beliefs and attitudes. If your words are hurtful, you may have to deal with the issues of your heart to change the way you speak.

Everyone likes to speak, yet James 1:19 tells us it is important to listen. To build a healthy relationship, take the time to pay attention to what the other person is really saying. Be sure of what you hear before you speak, and choose the right words for each situation. Then, let your own words be few and well thought out, and people will pay attention to what you have to say. If you talk nonstop, other people will begin to tune you out and will no longer value what you are saying.

If you can control your words, you will lessen the chance of saying something you do not mean or of saying it in a way that offends someone. You can speak life or you can speak death. Ask the Holy Spirit to help you choose life.

reflect: Do you listen first to discover what others have to say?
Go to **Revelation 21:7.**

JESUS' TRUE FAMILY

⁴⁶While Jesus was talking to the people, his mother and brothers stood outside, trying to find a way to talk to him. ⁴⁷Someone told Jesus, "Your mother and brothers are standing outside, and they want to talk to you."[n]

⁴⁸He answered, "Who is my mother? Who are my brothers?" ⁴⁹Then he pointed to his followers and said, "Here are my mother and my brothers. ⁵⁰My true brother and sister and mother are those who do what my Father in heaven wants."

A STORY ABOUT PLANTING SEED

13 That same day Jesus went out of the house and sat by the lake. ²Large crowds gathered around him, so he got into a boat and sat down, while the people stood on the shore. ³Then Jesus used stories to teach them many things. He said: "A farmer went out to plant his seed. ⁴While he was planting, some seed fell by the road, and the birds came and ate it all up. ⁵Some seed fell on rocky ground, where there wasn't much dirt. That seed grew very fast, because the ground was not deep. ⁶But when the sun rose, the plants dried up, because they did not have deep roots. ⁷Some other seed fell among thorny weeds, which grew and choked the good plants. ⁸Some other seed fell on good ground where it grew and produced a crop. Some plants made a hundred times more, some made sixty times more, and some made thirty times more. ⁹Let those with ears use them and listen."

WHY JESUS USED STORIES TO TEACH

¹⁰The followers came to Jesus and asked, "Why do you use stories to teach the people?"

¹¹Jesus answered, "You have been chosen to know the secrets about the kingdom of heaven, but others cannot know these secrets. ¹²Those who have understanding will be given more, and they will have all they need. But those who do not have understanding, even what they have will be taken away from them. ¹³This is why I use stories to teach the people: They see, but they don't really see. They hear, but they don't really hear or understand. ¹⁴So they show that the things Isaiah said about them are true:

'You will listen and listen, but you will not understand.

You will look and look, but you will not learn.

¹⁵ For the minds of these people have become stubborn.

They do not hear with their ears, and they have closed their eyes.

Otherwise they might really understand what they see with their eyes and hear with their ears.

They might really understand in their minds and come back to me and be healed.'

Isaiah 6:9–10

¹⁶But you are blessed, because you see with your eyes and hear with your ears. ¹⁷I tell you the truth, many prophets and good people wanted to see the things that you now see, but they did not see them. And they wanted to hear the things that you now hear, but they did not hear them.

JESUS EXPLAINS THE SEED STORY

¹⁸"So listen to the meaning of that story about the farmer. ¹⁹What is the seed that fell by the road? That seed is like the person who hears the message about the kingdom but does not understand it. The Evil One comes and takes away what was planted in that person's heart. ²⁰And what is the seed that fell on rocky ground? That seed is like the person who hears the teaching and quickly accepts it with joy. ²¹But he does not let the teaching go deep into his life, so he keeps it only a short time. When trouble or persecution comes because of the teaching he accepted, he quickly gives up. ²²And what is the seed that fell among the thorny weeds? That seed is like the person who hears the teaching but lets worries about this life and the temptation of wealth stop that teaching from growing. So the teaching does not produce fruit[n] in that person's life. ²³But what is the seed that fell on the good ground? That seed is like the person who hears the teaching and understands it. That person grows and produces fruit, sometimes a hundred times more, sometimes sixty times more, and sometimes thirty times more."

12:47 Someone . . . you." Some Greek copies do not have verse 47. **13:22 produce fruit** To produce fruit means to have in your life the good things God wants.

A STORY ABOUT WHEAT AND WEEDS

²⁴Then Jesus told them another story: "The kingdom of heaven is like a man who planted good seed in his field. ²⁵That night, when everyone was asleep, his enemy came and planted weeds among the wheat and then left. ²⁶Later, the wheat sprouted and the heads of grain grew, but the weeds also grew. ²⁷Then the man's servants came to him and said, 'You planted good seed in your field. Where did the weeds come from?' ²⁸The man answered, 'An enemy planted weeds.' The servants asked, 'Do you want us to pull up the weeds?' ²⁹The man answered, 'No, because when you pull up the weeds, you might also pull up the wheat. ³⁰Let the weeds and the wheat grow together until the harvest time. At harvest time I will tell the workers, "First gather the weeds and tie them together to be burned. Then gather the wheat and bring it to my barn." ' "

STORIES OF MUSTARD SEED AND YEAST

³¹Then Jesus told another story: "The kingdom of heaven is like a mustard seed that a man planted in his field. ³²That seed is the smallest of all seeds, but when it grows, it is one of the largest garden plants. It becomes big enough for the wild birds to come and build nests in its branches."

³³Then Jesus told another story: "The kingdom of heaven is like yeast that a woman took and hid in a large tub of flour until it made all the dough rise."

³⁴Jesus used stories to tell all these things to the people; he always used stories to teach them. ³⁵This is as the prophet said:

"I will speak using stories;
    I will tell things that have been secret
        since the world was made." *Psalm 78:2*

JESUS EXPLAINS ABOUT THE WEEDS

³⁶Then Jesus left the crowd and went into the house. His followers came to him and said, "Explain to us the meaning of the story about the weeds in the field."

³⁷Jesus answered, "The man who planted the good seed in the field is the Son of Man. ³⁸The field is the world, and the good seed are all of God's children who belong to the kingdom. The weeds are those people who belong to the Evil One. ³⁹And the enemy who planted the bad seed is the devil. The harvest time is the end of the age, and the workers who gather are God's angels.

⁴⁰"Just as the weeds are pulled up and burned in the fire, so it will be at the end of the age. ⁴¹The Son of Man will send out his angels, and they will gather out of his kingdom all who cause sin and all who do evil. ⁴²The angels will throw them into the blazing furnace, where the people will cry and grind their teeth with pain. ⁴³Then the good people will shine like the sun in the kingdom of their Father. Let those with ears use them and listen.

STORIES OF A TREASURE AND A PEARL

⁴⁴"The kingdom of heaven is like a treasure hidden in a field. One day a man found the treasure, and then he hid it in the field again. He was so happy that he went and sold everything he owned to buy that field.

⁴⁵"Also, the kingdom of heaven is like a man looking for fine pearls. ⁴⁶When he found a very valuable pearl, he went and sold everything he had and bought it.

A STORY OF A FISHING NET

⁴⁷"Also, the kingdom of heaven is like a net that was put into the lake and caught many different kinds of fish. ⁴⁸When it was full, the fishermen pulled the net to the shore. They sat down and put all the good fish in baskets and threw away the bad fish. ⁴⁹It will be this way at the end of the age. The angels will come and separate the evil people from the good people. ⁵⁰The angels will throw the evil people into the blazing furnace, where people will cry and grind their teeth with pain."

⁵¹Jesus asked his followers, "Do you understand all these things?"

They answered, "Yes, we understand."

⁵²Then Jesus said to them, "So every teacher of the law who has been taught about the kingdom of heaven is like the owner of a house. He brings out both new things and old things he has saved."

JESUS GOES TO HIS HOMETOWN

⁵³When Jesus finished teaching with these stories, he left there. ⁵⁴He went to his hometown and taught the people in the synagogue, and they were amazed. They said, "Where did this man get this wisdom and this power to do miracles? ⁵⁵He is just the son of a carpenter. His mother is Mary, and his brothers are James, Joseph, Simon, and Judas. ⁵⁶And all his sisters are here with us. Where

then does this man get all these things?" [57]So the people were upset with Jesus.

But Jesus said to them, "A prophet is honored everywhere except in his hometown and in his own home."

[58]So he did not do many miracles there because they had no faith.

HOW JOHN THE BAPTIST WAS KILLED

14 At that time Herod, the ruler of Galilee, heard the reports about Jesus. [2]So he said to his servants, "Jesus is John the Baptist, who has risen from the dead. That is why he can work these miracles."

[3]Sometime before this, Herod had arrested John, tied him up, and put him into prison. Herod did this because of Herodias, who had been the wife of Philip, Herod's brother. [4]John had been telling Herod, "It is not lawful for you to be married to Herodias." [5]Herod wanted to kill John, but he was afraid of the people, because they believed John was a prophet.

[6]On Herod's birthday, the daughter of Herodias danced for Herod and his guests, and she pleased him. [7]So he promised with an oath to give her anything she wanted. [8]Herodias told her daughter what to ask for, so she said to Herod, "Give me the head of John the Baptist here on a platter." [9]Although King Herod was very sad, he had made a promise, and his dinner guests had heard him. So Herod ordered that what she asked for be done. [10]He sent soldiers to the prison to cut off John's head. [11]And they brought it on a platter and gave it to the girl, and she took it to her mother. [12]John's followers came and got his body and buried it. Then they went and told Jesus.

MORE THAN FIVE THOUSAND FED

[13]When Jesus heard what had happened to John, he left in a boat and went to a lonely place by himself. But the crowds heard about it and followed him on foot from the towns. [14]When he arrived, he saw a great crowd waiting. He felt sorry for them and healed those who were sick.

[15]When it was evening, his followers came to him and said, "No one lives in this place, and it is already late. Send the people away so they can go to the towns and buy food for themselves."

[16]But Jesus answered, "They don't need to go away. You give them something to eat."

[17]They said to him, "But we have only five loaves of bread and two fish."

[18]Jesus said, "Bring the bread and the fish to me." [19]Then he told the people to sit down on the grass. He took the five loaves and the two fish and, looking to heaven, he thanked God for the food. Jesus divided the bread and gave it to his followers, who gave it to the people. [20]All the people ate and were satisfied. Then the followers filled twelve baskets with the leftover pieces of food. [21]There were about five thousand men there who ate, not counting women and children.

JESUS WALKS ON THE WATER

[22]Immediately Jesus told his followers to get into the boat and go ahead of him across the lake. He stayed there to send the people home. [23]After he had sent them away, he went by himself up into the hills to pray. It was late, and Jesus was there alone. [24]By this time, the boat was already far away from land. It was being hit by waves, because the wind was blowing against it.

[25]Between three and six o'clock in the morning, Jesus came to them, walking on the water. [26]When his followers saw him walking on the water, they were afraid. They said, "It's a ghost!" and cried out in fear.

[27]But Jesus quickly spoke to them, "Have courage! It is I. Do not be afraid."

[28]Peter said, "Lord, if it is really you, then command me to come to you on the water."

[29]Jesus said, "Come."

And Peter left the boat and walked on the water to Jesus. [30]But when Peter saw the wind and the waves, he became afraid and began to sink. He shouted, "Lord, save me!"

[31]Immediately Jesus reached out his hand and caught Peter. Jesus said, "Your faith is small. Why did you doubt?"

[32]After they got into the boat, the wind became calm. [33]Then those who were in the boat worshiped Jesus and said, "Truly you are the Son of God!"

[34]When they had crossed the lake, they came to shore at Gennesaret. [35]When the people there recognized Jesus, they told people all around there that Jesus had come, and they brought all their sick to him. [36]They begged Jesus to let them touch just the edge of his coat, and all who touched it were healed.

OBEY GOD'S LAW

15 Then some Pharisees and teachers of the law came to Jesus from Jerusalem. They asked him, [2]"Why don't your followers obey the unwritten laws which have been handed down to us? They don't wash their hands before they eat."

[3]Jesus answered, "And why do you refuse to obey God's command so that you can follow your own teachings? [4]God said, 'Honor your father and your mother,'[n] and 'Anyone who says cruel things to his father or mother must be put to death.'[n] [5]But you say a person can tell his father or mother, 'I have something I could use to help you, but I have given it to God already.' [6]You teach that person not to honor his father or his mother. You rejected what God said for the sake of your own rules. [7]You are hypocrites! Isaiah was right when he said about you:

[8] 'These people show honor to me with words,
but their hearts are far from me.
[9] Their worship of me is worthless.
The things they teach are nothing but human rules.'"   *Isaiah 29:13*

[10]After Jesus called the crowd to him, he said, "Listen and understand what I am saying. [11]It is not what people put into their mouths that makes them unclean. It is what comes out of their mouths that makes them unclean."

[12]Then his followers came to him and asked, "Do you know that the Pharisees are angry because of what you said?"

[13]Jesus answered, "Every plant that my Father in heaven has not planted himself will be pulled up by the roots. [14]Stay away from the Pharisees; they are blind leaders.[n] And if a blind person leads a blind person, both will fall into a ditch."

[15]Peter said, "Explain the example to us."

[16]Jesus said, "Do you still not understand? [17]Surely you know that all the food that enters the mouth goes into the stomach and then goes out of the body. [18]But what people say with their mouths comes from the way they think; these are the things that make people unclean. [19]Out of the mind come evil thoughts, murder, adultery, sexual sins, stealing, lying, and speaking evil of others. [20]These things make people unclean; eating with unwashed hands does not make them unclean."

JESUS HELPS A NON-JEWISH WOMAN

[21]Jesus left that place and went to the area of Tyre and Sidon. [22]A Canaanite woman from that area came to Jesus and cried out, "Lord, Son of David, have mercy on me! My daughter has a demon, and she is suffering very much."

[23]But Jesus did not answer the woman. So his followers came to Jesus and begged him, "Tell the woman to go away. She is following us and shouting."

[24]Jesus answered, "God sent me only to the lost sheep, the people of Israel."

[25]Then the woman came to Jesus again and bowed before him and said, "Lord, help me!"

[26]Jesus answered, "It is not right to take the children's bread and give it to the dogs."

[27]The woman said, "Yes, Lord, but even the dogs eat the crumbs that fall from their masters' table."

[28]Then Jesus answered, "Woman, you have great faith! I will do what you asked." And at that moment the woman's daughter was healed.

JESUS HEALS MANY PEOPLE

[29]After leaving there, Jesus went along the shore of Lake Galilee. He went up on a hill and sat there.

[30]Great crowds came to Jesus, bringing with them the lame, the blind, the crippled, those who could not speak, and many others. They put them at Jesus' feet, and he healed them. [31]The crowd was amazed when they saw that people who could not speak before were now able to speak. The crippled were made strong. The lame could walk, and the blind could see. And they praised the God of Israel for this.

MORE THAN FOUR THOUSAND FED

[32]Jesus called his followers to him and said, "I feel sorry for these people, because they have already been with me three days, and they have nothing to eat. I don't want to send them away hungry. They might faint while going home."

[33]His followers asked him, "How can we

15:4 'Honor . . . mother.' Quotation from Exodus 20:12; Deuteronomy 5:16. **15:4 'Anyone . . . death.'** Quotation from Exodus 21:17. **15:14 leaders** Some Greek copies continue, "of blind people."

get enough bread to feed all these people? We are far away from any town."

34 Jesus asked, "How many loaves of bread do you have?"

They answered, "Seven, and a few small fish."

35 Jesus told the people to sit on the ground. 36 He took the seven loaves of bread and the fish and gave thanks to God. Then he divided the food and gave it to his followers, and they gave it to the people. 37 All the people ate and were satisfied. Then his followers filled seven baskets with the leftover pieces of food. 38 There were about four thousand men there who ate, besides women and children. 39 After sending the people home, Jesus got into the boat and went to the area of Magadan.

THE LEADERS ASK FOR A MIRACLE

16 The Pharisees and Sadducees came to Jesus, wanting to trick him. So they asked him to show them a miracle from God.

2 Jesus answered,[n] "At sunset you say we will have good weather, because the sky is red. 3 And in the morning you say that it will be a rainy day, because the sky is dark and red. You see these signs in the sky and know what they mean. In the same way, you see the things that I am doing now, but you don't know their meaning. 4 Evil and sinful people ask for a miracle as a sign, but they will not be given any sign, except the sign of Jonah."[n] Then Jesus left them and went away.

GUARD AGAINST WRONG TEACHINGS

5 Jesus' followers went across the lake, but they had forgotten to bring bread. 6 Jesus said to them, "Be careful! Beware of the yeast of the Pharisees and the Sadducees."

7 His followers discussed the meaning of this, saying, "He said this because we forgot to bring bread."

8 Knowing what they were talking about, Jesus asked them, "Why are you talking about not having bread? Your faith is small. 9 Do you still not understand? Remember the five loaves of bread that fed the five thousand? And remember that you filled many baskets with the leftovers? 10 Or the seven loaves of bread that fed the four thousand and the many baskets you filled then also? 11 I was not talking to you about bread. Why don't you understand that? I am telling you to beware of the yeast of the Pharisees and the Sadducees." 12 Then the followers understood that Jesus was not telling them to beware of the yeast used in bread but to beware of the teaching of the Pharisees and the Sadducees.

PETER SAYS JESUS IS THE CHRIST

13 When Jesus came to the area of Caesarea Philippi, he asked his followers, "Who do people say the Son of Man is?"

14 They answered, "Some say you are John the Baptist. Others say you are Elijah, and still others say you are Jeremiah or one of the prophets."

15 Then Jesus asked them, "And who do you say I am?"

16 Simon Peter answered, "You are the Christ, the Son of the living God."

17 Jesus answered, "You are blessed, Simon son of Jonah, because no person taught you that. My Father in heaven showed you who I am. 18 So I tell you, you are Peter.[n] On this rock I will build my church, and the power of death will not be able to defeat it. 19 I will give you the keys of the kingdom of heaven; the things you don't allow on earth will be the things that God does not allow, and the things you allow on earth will be the things that God allows." 20 Then Jesus warned his followers not to tell anyone he was the Christ.

JESUS SAYS THAT HE MUST DIE

21 From that time on Jesus began telling his followers that he must go to Jerusalem, where the Jewish elders, the leading priests, and the teachers of the law would make him suffer many things. He told them he must be killed and then be raised from the dead on the third day.

22 Peter took Jesus aside and told him not to talk like that. He said, "God save you from those things, Lord! Those things will never happen to you!"

23 Then Jesus said to Peter, "Go away from me, Satan![n] You are not helping me! You don't

---

16:2–3 answered Some Greek copies do not have the rest of verse 2 and verse 3. **16:4 sign of Jonah** Jonah's three days in the fish are like Jesus' three days in the tomb. The story about Jonah is in the Book of Jonah. **16:18 Peter** The Greek name "Peter," like the Aramaic name "Cephas," means "rock." **16:23 Satan** Name for the devil, meaning "the enemy." Jesus means that Peter was talking like Satan.

care about the things of God, but only about the things people think are important."

²⁴Then Jesus said to his followers, "If people want to follow me, they must give up the things they want. They must be willing even to give up their lives to follow me. ²⁵Those who want to save their lives will give up true life, and those who give up their lives for me will have true life. ²⁶It is worthless to have the whole world if they lose their souls. They could never pay enough to buy back their souls. ²⁷The Son of Man will come again with his Father's glory and with his angels. At that time, he will reward them for what they have done. ²⁸I tell you the truth, some people standing here will see the Son of Man coming with his kingdom before they die."

JESUS TALKS WITH MOSES AND ELIJAH

17 Six days later, Jesus took Peter, James, and John, the brother of James, up on a high mountain by themselves. ²While they watched, Jesus' appearance was changed; his face became bright like the sun, and his clothes became white as light. ³Then Moses and Elijah[n] appeared to them, talking with Jesus.

⁴Peter said to Jesus, "Lord, it is good that we are here. If you want, I will put up three tents here—one for you, one for Moses, and one for Elijah."

⁵While Peter was talking, a bright cloud covered them. A voice came from the cloud

---

17:3 Moses and Elijah Two of the most important Jewish leaders in the past. God had given Moses the Law, and Elijah was an important prophet.

GOD'S ULTIMATE SACRIFICE

losing your life

FAITH

MATTHEW 16:25

This verse talks about a complete change from one form of being to another. It describes the new creation and redeemed men and women in their renewed bodies. In this verse, Jesus promises that surrendering our lives as an act of obedience to him will result in our finding new life, life that we cannot have if we continue to search for our own answers.

No person in recovery could deny this principle of life. All of us thought we could find the fantasy life we desired, but the more we chased the dream, the more our lives became a nightmare. What we sought so hard slipped faster and faster through our fingers until there was nothing left but the emptiness. When we finally realized that there was no escape from ourselves, many of us sought to lose our lives. Jesus knows that helpless feeling of utter despair.

One of life's sacred paradoxes is that if I want to live, I must be willing to die to any attempt at self-control, self-recovery, and self-deceit. Recovery is first dying to my old way so that I can find God's way. My old life must be destroyed in order for my new life to be born. Perhaps the concept of being "born again" is not so strange after all.

reflect: Yield your life to Christ today, and experience the renewal that results.
Go to **Matthew 17:20.**

and said, "This is my Son, whom I love, and I am very pleased with him. Listen to him!"

⁶When his followers heard the voice, they were so frightened they fell to the ground. ⁷But Jesus went to them and touched them and said, "Stand up. Don't be afraid." ⁸When they looked up, they saw Jesus was now alone.

⁹As they were coming down the mountain, Jesus commanded them not to tell anyone about what they had seen until the Son of Man had risen from the dead.

¹⁰Then his followers asked him, "Why do the teachers of the law say that Elijah must come first?"

¹¹Jesus answered, "They are right to say that Elijah is coming and that he will make everything the way it should be. ¹²But I tell you that Elijah has already come, and they did not recognize him. They did to him whatever they wanted to do. It will be the same with the Son of Man; those same people will make the Son of Man suffer." ¹³Then the followers understood that Jesus was talking about John the Baptist.

JESUS HEALS A SICK BOY

¹⁴When Jesus and his followers came back to the crowd, a man came to Jesus and bowed before him. ¹⁵The man said, "Lord, have mercy on my son. He has epilepsy[n] and is suffering very much, because he often falls into the fire or into the water. ¹⁶I brought him to your followers, but they could not cure him."

¹⁷Jesus answered, "You people have no faith, and your lives are all wrong. How long must I put up with you? How long must I continue to be patient with you? Bring the boy here." ¹⁸Jesus commanded the demon inside the boy. Then the demon came out, and the boy was healed from that time on.

¹⁹The followers came to Jesus when he was alone and asked, "Why couldn't we force the demon out?"

²⁰Jesus answered, "Because your faith is too small. I tell you the truth, if your faith is as big as a mustard seed, you can say to this mountain, 'Move from here to there,' and it will move. All things will be possible for you. [²¹That kind of spirit comes out only if you use prayer and fasting.]"[n]

JESUS TALKS ABOUT HIS DEATH

²²While Jesus' followers were gathering in Galilee, he said to them, "The Son of Man will be handed over to people, ²³and they will kill him. But on the third day he will be raised from the dead." And the followers were filled with sadness.

JESUS TALKS ABOUT PAYING TAXES

²⁴When Jesus and his followers came to Capernaum, the men who collected the Temple tax came to Peter. They asked, "Does your teacher pay the Temple tax?"

²⁵Peter answered, "Yes, Jesus pays the tax."

Peter went into the house, but before he could speak, Jesus said to him, "What do you think? The kings of the earth collect different kinds of taxes. But who pays the taxes—the king's children or others?"

²⁶Peter answered, "Other people pay the taxes."

Jesus said to Peter, "Then the children of the king don't have to pay taxes. ²⁷But we don't want to upset these tax collectors. So go to the lake and fish. After you catch the first fish, open its mouth and you will find a coin. Take that coin and give it to the tax collectors for you and me."

WHO IS THE GREATEST?

18 At that time the followers came to Jesus and asked, "Who is greatest in the kingdom of heaven?"

²Jesus called a little child to him and stood the child before his followers. ³Then he said, "I tell you the truth, you must change and become like little children. Otherwise, you will never enter the kingdom of heaven. ⁴The greatest person in the kingdom of heaven is the one who makes himself humble like this child.

⁵"Whoever accepts a child in my name accepts me. ⁶If one of these little children believes in me, and someone causes that child to sin, it would be better for that person to have a large stone tied around the neck and be drowned in the sea. ⁷How terrible for the people of the world because of the things that cause them to sin. Such things will happen, but how terrible for the one who causes

---

17:15 epilepsy A disease that causes a person sometimes to lose control of his body and maybe faint, shake strongly, or not be able to move. **17:21 That . . . fasting.** Some Greek copies do not contain the bracketed text.

them to happen! [8]If your hand or your foot causes you to sin, cut it off and throw it away. It is better for you to lose part of your body and live forever than to have two hands and two feet and be thrown into the fire that burns forever. [9]If your eye causes you to sin, take it out and throw it away. It is better for you to have only one eye and live forever than to have two eyes and be thrown into the fire of hell.

A LOST SHEEP

[10]"Be careful. Don't think these little children are worth nothing. I tell you that they have angels in heaven who are always with my Father in heaven. [[11]The Son of Man came to save lost people.][n]

[12]"If a man has a hundred sheep but one of the sheep gets lost, he will leave the other ninety-nine on the hill and go to look for the lost sheep. [13]I tell you the truth, if he finds it he is happier about that one sheep than about the ninety-nine that were never lost. [14]In the same way, your Father in heaven does not want any of these little children to be lost.

18:11 The ... people. Some Greek copies do not contain the bracketed text.

GOD'S ULTIMATE SACRIFICE

moving **mountains**

FAITH

By Elmer Towns

MATTHEW 17:20

God has given many qualities to Christians, as demonstrated in his giving the fruit of the Spirit and the gifts of the Spirit. These qualities are given to help us relate to ourselves, to other Christians, or to our service for God, but faith is a quality with a different dimension. Faith is the one thing that moves God. Faith pleases God, and faith, correctly exercised, moves the mountains that face us. The Bible seems to teach that we need greater faith to accomplish greater works (John 14:12).

Dr. Howard Hendricks of Dallas Theological Seminary once preached a sermon that balanced this perspective. He told the audience, "Don't seek greater faith," explaining that if we do, we have then focused on man and not on God. Dr. Hendricks pointed us to the source of faith. "We don't need greater faith—we need a greater understanding of God in our lives."

Faith is a gift from God, a "knowing" in our spirit. How do we get this "knowing"? Usually, it results from reading God's Word. Then we can pray in faith for anything in his revealed will, unless it violates another person's free will. Sometimes God's will is not clearly stated in Scripture. In these situations, we take small steps according to the will of God that we know. Then we take bigger steps, according to the faith we have. Eventually, we find that we have overcome the mountain, all because we acted on the faith that we were given.

reflect: Do you need a greater understanding of God in your life?
Go to **Mark 1:35.**

WHEN A PERSON SINS AGAINST YOU

15"If your fellow believer sins against you,[n] go and tell him in private what he did wrong. If he listens to you, you have helped that person to be your brother or sister again. 16But if he refuses to listen, go to him again and take one or two other people with you. 'Every case may be proved by two or three witnesses.'[n] 17If he refuses to listen to them, tell the church. If he refuses to listen to the church, then treat him like a person who does not believe in God or like a tax collector.

18"I tell you the truth, the things you don't allow on earth will be the things God does not allow. And the things you allow on earth will be the things that God allows.

19"Also, I tell you that if two of you on earth agree about something and pray for it, it will be done for you by my Father in heaven. 20This is true because if two or three people come together in my name, I am there with them."

AN UNFORGIVING SERVANT

21Then Peter came to Jesus and asked, "Lord, when my fellow believer sins against me, how many times must I forgive him? Should I forgive him as many as seven times?"

22Jesus answered, "I tell you, you must forgive him more than seven times. You must forgive him even if he wrongs you seventy times seven.

23"The kingdom of heaven is like a king who decided to collect the money his servants owed him. 24When the king began to collect his money, a servant who owed him several million dollars was brought to him. 25But the servant did not have enough money to pay his master, the king. So the master ordered that everything the servant owned should be sold, even the servant's wife and children. Then the money would be used to pay the king what the servant owed.

26"But the servant fell on his knees and begged, 'Be patient with me, and I will pay you everything I owe.' 27The master felt sorry for his servant and told him he did not have to pay it back. Then he let the servant go free.

28"Later, that same servant found another servant who owed him a few dollars. The servant grabbed him around the neck and said, 'Pay me the money you owe me!'

29"The other servant fell on his knees and begged him, 'Be patient with me, and I will pay you everything I owe.'

30"But the first servant refused to be patient. He threw the other servant into prison until he could pay everything he owed. 31When the other servants saw what had happened, they were very sorry. So they went and told their master all that had happened.

32"Then the master called his servant in and said, 'You evil servant! Because you begged me to forget what you owed, I told you that you did not have to pay anything. 33You should have showed mercy to that other servant, just as I showed mercy to you.' 34The master was very angry and put the servant in prison to be punished until he could pay everything he owed.

35"This king did what my heavenly Father will do to you if you do not forgive your brother or sister from your heart."

JESUS TEACHES ABOUT DIVORCE

19 After Jesus said all these things, he left Galilee and went into the area of Judea on the other side of the Jordan River. 2Large crowds followed him, and he healed them there.

3Some Pharisees came to Jesus and tried to trick him. They asked, "Is it right for a man to divorce his wife for any reason he chooses?"

4Jesus answered, "Surely you have read in the Scriptures: When God made the world, 'he made them male and female.'[n] 5And God said, 'So a man will leave his father and mother and be united with his wife, and the two will become one body.'[n] 6So there are not two, but one. God has joined the two together, so no one should separate them."

7The Pharisees asked, "Why then did Moses give a command for a man to divorce his wife by giving her divorce papers?"

8Jesus answered, "Moses allowed you to divorce your wives because you refused to accept God's teaching, but divorce was not allowed in the beginning. 9I tell you that

---

18:15 against you Some Greek copies do not have "against you." **18:16 'Every . . . witnesses.'** Quotation from Deuteronomy 19:15. **19:4 'he made . . . female'** Quotation from Genesis 1:27 or 5:2. **19:5 'So . . . body.'** Quotation from Genesis 2:24.

anyone who divorces his wife and marries another woman is guilty of adultery.[n] The only reason for a man to divorce his wife is if his wife has sexual relations with another man."

[10]The followers said to him, "If that is the only reason a man can divorce his wife, it is better not to marry."

[11]Jesus answered, "Not everyone can accept this teaching, but God has made some able to accept it. [12]There are different reasons why some men cannot marry. Some men were

19:9 adultery Some Greek copies continue, "And anyone who marries a divorced woman is guilty of adultery." Compare Matthew 5:32.

---

what is **covenant marriage?**

FAMILY

By Gary Chapman

MATTHEW 19:4–6

The number of divorces among Christians, including missionaries and ministers, calls for a return to the biblical mandate of covenant marriage. God chose the marriage metaphor as a picture of his agreement with Israel. "The God who made you is like your husband. His name is the LORD All-Powerful" (Isaiah 54:5). In order to understand covenant marriage, Christians must understand these five characteristics of God's covenants, or agreements:

1. Covenants were initiated for the benefit of the other person. God initiated the covenants with his people for their benefit, not his own.

2. Covenants involved unconditional promises. In Exodus 19, God did not withdraw his promises when the Israelites left him. He remained faithful and ready to fulfill his promises if the Israelites returned.

3. God's covenants were built on steadfast love. In the Old Agreement, this love was expressed as *hesed*, or compassion. In the New Agreement, it is expressed as *agape*. This type of love is not a feeling, but a commitment to the other person's well-being.

4. Covenants were permanent. Only death could end the covenant.

5. Covenants required confrontation and renewal. Just as God did not ignore the failures of his people, covenant marriage requires that spouses lovingly confront and forgive each other.

Covenant marriage requires confrontation, confession, repentance, and forgiveness. Walk through these five characteristics with your spouse, confessing your failures to each other and recommitting yourselves to a covenant marriage.

reflect: Will you make a fresh commitment to biblical marriage?

Go to **FAMILY**: "Covenant Marriage" at **Malachi 2:14–16**.

The **Ultimate Investment**

By Bob Russell

Imagine that you've taken a quantum leap back in time and landed in Richmond, Virginia, circa 1861. You find a great-great-great-grandfather and introduce yourself as a "distant" relative. After a prolonged discussion, he informs you (with some obvious pride) that he is worth more than two million dollars. Since he's talking about your future inheritance, you really sit up and take notice. But your heart sinks when you learn that his entire life-savings is in Confederate bills hidden away in a household safe.

What would you say to your ancient ancestor? Undoubtedly, you would do your best to persuade him to exchange the Confederate bills for a more permanent commodity. You'd tell him, "Buy gold or invest in real estate but, whatever you do, get rid of those ridiculous Confederate bills as fast as you can. They are soon going to be worthless!"

Jesus Christ told a rich young man, "If you want to be perfect, then go and sell your possessions and give the money to the poor. If you do this, you will have treasure in heaven. Then come and follow me" (Matthew 19:21). Jesus saw people's lives from the eternal perspective. He knew the world and its pleasures would soon pass away.

That's why he continually warned against hoarding anything on this earth. Anything we store here will soon be eaten by moths, corroded by rust, or stolen by thieves. Since he wanted the best for us, he kept saying, "Give it away!

Help those in need and you will be investing in heaven." When you make an investment in heaven, your wealth will last. The Bible assures us it will never perish, spoil, or fade. It is kept in heaven for you.

What you invest in heaven will multiply in value. Jesus taught that everyone who left family or fields for his sake "will get much more than they left" (Matthew 19:29). If that's true, it's dumber to accumulate possessions on earth than it was for our forefathers to hoard Confederate money. Most importantly, when you invest in heaven it will tug at your heart. Jesus said, "Your heart will be where your treasure is" (Matthew 6:21). Investing in the things of God will get your mind off earthly things and onto heavenly things. It helps you to seek first the kingdom of God.

The rich young man just couldn't do what Jesus requested. He was too ingrained in the world's value system. He had too many years of instruction in materialism just to give it away. It was so counter to his instincts that "he left sorrowfully, because he was rich" (Matthew 19:22).

If he had only been willing to see things from an eternal perspective, he could have easily made the ultimate investment. And he would have discovered the joy in knowing that not only had his generosity helped someone else, but he had been, in fact, laying up a permanent treasure in heaven.

TO LEARN MORE ON WHAT THE BIBLE HAS TO SAY ABOUT **FINANCES,** READ THE SCRIPTURES AND DEVOTIONALS AT **JOB 42:2, ECCLESIASTES 9:7–9, PSALM 69:33, PSALM 106:3, PSALM 144:13–15,** AND **MARK 10:21.**

born without the ability to become fathers. Others were made that way later in life by other people. And some men have given up marriage because of the kingdom of heaven. But the person who can marry should accept this teaching about marriage."[n]

JESUS WELCOMES CHILDREN

[13]Then the people brought their little children to Jesus so he could put his hands on them[n] and pray for them. His followers told them to stop, [14]but Jesus said, "Let the little children come to me. Don't stop them, because the kingdom of heaven belongs to people who are like these children." [15]After Jesus put his hands on the children, he left there.

A RICH YOUNG MAN'S QUESTION

[16]A man came to Jesus and asked, "Teacher, what good thing must I do to have life forever?"

[17]Jesus answered, "Why do you ask me about what is good? Only God is good. But if you want to have life forever, obey the commands."

[18]The man asked, "Which commands?"

Jesus answered, "'You must not murder anyone; you must not be guilty of adultery; you must not steal; you must not tell lies about your neighbor; [19]honor your father and mother;[n] and love your neighbor as you love yourself.'"[n]

[20]The young man said, "I have obeyed all these things. What else do I need to do?"

[21]Jesus answered, "If you want to be perfect, then go and sell your possessions and give the money to the poor. If you do this, you will have treasure in heaven. Then come and follow me."

[22]But when the young man heard this, he left sorrowfully, because he was rich.

[23]Then Jesus said to his followers, "I tell you the truth, it will be hard for a rich person to enter the kingdom of heaven. [24]Yes, I tell you that it is easier for a camel to go through the eye of a needle than for a rich person to enter the kingdom of God."

[25]When Jesus' followers heard this, they were very surprised and asked, "Then who can be saved?"

[26]Jesus looked at them and said, "For people this is impossible, but for God all things are possible."

[27]Peter said to Jesus, "Look, we have left everything and followed you. So what will we have?"

[28]Jesus said to them, "I tell you the truth, when the age to come has arrived, the Son of Man will sit on his great throne. All of you who followed me will also sit on twelve thrones, judging the twelve tribes of Israel. [29]And all those who have left houses, brothers, sisters, father, mother,[n] children, or farms to follow me will get much more than they left, and they will have life forever. [30]Many who are first now will be last in the future. And many who are last now will be first in the future.

A STORY ABOUT WORKERS

20 "The kingdom of heaven is like a person who owned some land. One morning, he went out very early to hire some people to work in his vineyard. [2]The man agreed to pay the workers one coin[n] for working that day. Then he sent them into the vineyard to work. [3]About nine o'clock the man went to the marketplace and saw some other people standing there, doing nothing. [4]So he said to them, 'If you go and work in my vineyard, I will pay you what your work is worth.' [5]So they went to work in the vineyard. The man went out again about twelve o'clock and three o'clock and did the same thing. [6]About five o'clock the man went to the marketplace again and saw others standing there. He asked them, 'Why did you stand here all day doing nothing?' [7]They answered, 'No one gave us a job.' The man said to them, 'Then you can go and work in my vineyard.'

[8]"At the end of the day, the owner of the vineyard said to the boss of all the workers, 'Call the workers and pay them. Start with the last people I hired and end with those I hired first.'

[9]"When the workers who were hired at five o'clock came to get their pay, each

---

19:12 But . . . marriage. This may also mean, "The person who can accept this teaching about not marrying should accept it." **19:13 put his hands on them** Showing that Jesus gave special blessings to these children. **19:19 'You . . . mother.'** Quotation from Exodus 20:12–16; Deuteronomy 5:16–20. **19:19 'love . . . yourself'** Quotation from Leviticus 19:18. **19:29 mother** Some Greek copies continue, "or wife." **20:2 coin** A Roman denarius. One coin was the average pay for one day's work.

received one coin. ¹⁰When the workers who were hired first came to get their pay, they thought they would be paid more than the others. But each one of them also received one coin. ¹¹When they got their coin, they complained to the man who owned the land. ¹²They said, 'Those people were hired last and worked only one hour. But you paid them the same as you paid us who worked hard all day in the hot sun.' ¹³But the man who owned the vineyard said to one of those workers, 'Friend, I am being fair to you. You agreed to work for one coin. ¹⁴So take your pay and go. I want to give the man who was hired last the same pay that I gave you. ¹⁵I can do what I want with my own money. Are you jealous because I am good to those people?'

¹⁶"So those who are last now will someday be first, and those who are first now will someday be last."

JESUS TALKS ABOUT HIS OWN DEATH

¹⁷While Jesus was going to Jerusalem, he took his twelve followers aside privately and

---

GOD'S PURPOSE FOR YOUR LIFE

FUTURE

take **heart**

MATTHEW 19:26

By Bob Russell

Many people are discouraged these days. Political and economic realities cause anxiety. Wayward children, failing health, imperfect marriages, and other personal struggles make it difficult to be of good cheer. Even so, Jesus assures us in the Book of John that he has overcome the world. Moreover, Jesus personally prayed for you and me! (John 17:20).

Jesus told his followers to anticipate trouble, but promised that God can change any situation in order to fulfill his plan. Though you think your situation is hopeless, Jesus offers assurance. "For people this is impossible, but with God all things are possible" (Matthew 19:26).

The Bible has many examples of God turning negative situations into positive ones. Joseph's brothers sold him as a slave, but God caused Joseph to become prime minister of Egypt. Daniel was thrown to the lions, but God shut the mouths of the lions, causing Darius to make a law respecting Daniel's God. The enemies of Jesus crucified him, but God used the cross to reconcile the world to himself. Saul persecuted Christians, but God saved him, gave him a new name (Paul), and sent him forth as a missionary.

We must remember that God's plan cannot be thwarted. We must say, as the apostle Paul did, "We have troubles all around us, but we are not defeated. We do not know what to do, but we do not give up the hope of living. We are persecuted, but God does not leave us. We are hurt sometimes, but we are not destroyed" (2 Corinthians 4:8–9).

reflect: Are you willing to focus more on the solution than the situation?
Go to **Matthew 22:21.**

said to them, [18]"Look, we are going to Jerusalem. The Son of Man will be turned over to the leading priests and the teachers of the law, and they will say that he must die. [19]They will give the Son of Man to the non-Jewish people to laugh at him and beat him with whips and crucify him. But on the third day, he will be raised to life again."

A MOTHER ASKS JESUS A FAVOR

[20]Then the wife of Zebedee came to Jesus with her sons. She bowed before him and asked him to do something for her.

[21]Jesus asked, "What do you want?"

She said, "Promise that one of my sons will sit at your right side and the other will sit at your left side in your kingdom."

[22]But Jesus said, "You don't understand what you are asking. Can you drink the cup that I am about to drink?"[n]

The sons answered, "Yes, we can."

[23]Jesus said to them, "You will drink from my cup. But I cannot choose who will sit at my right or my left; those places belong to those for whom my Father has prepared them."

[24]When the other ten followers heard this, they were angry with the two brothers.

[25]Jesus called all the followers together and said, "You know that the rulers of the non-Jewish people love to show their power over the people. And their important leaders love to use all their authority. [26]But it should not be that way among you. Whoever wants to become great among you must serve the rest of you like a servant. [27]Whoever wants to become first among you must serve the rest of you like a slave. [28]In the same way, the Son of Man did not come to be served. He came to serve others and to give his life as a ransom for many people."

JESUS HEALS TWO BLIND MEN

[29]When Jesus and his followers were leaving Jericho, a great many people followed him. [30]Two blind men sitting by the road heard that Jesus was going by, so they shouted, "Lord, Son of David, have mercy on us!"

[31]The people warned the blind men to be quiet, but they shouted even more, "Lord, Son of David, have mercy on us!"

[32]Jesus stopped and said to the blind men, "What do you want me to do for you?"

[33]They answered, "Lord, we want to see."

[34]Jesus felt sorry for the blind men and touched their eyes, and at once they could see. Then they followed Jesus.

JESUS ENTERS JERUSALEM AS A KING

21 As Jesus and his followers were coming closer to Jerusalem, they stopped at Bethphage at the hill called the Mount of Olives. From there Jesus sent two of his followers [2]and said to them, "Go to the town you can see there. When you enter it, you will quickly find a donkey tied there with its colt. Untie them and bring them to me. [3]If anyone asks you why you are taking the donkeys, say that the Master needs them, and he will send them at once."

[4]This was to bring about what the prophet had said:

[5] "Tell the people of Jerusalem,
'Your king is coming to you.
He is gentle and riding on a donkey,
    on the colt of a donkey.'"
                    Isaiah 62:11; Zechariah 9:9

[6]The followers went and did what Jesus told them to do. [7]They brought the donkey and the colt to Jesus and laid their coats on them, and Jesus sat on them. [8]Many people spread their coats on the road. Others cut branches from the trees and spread them on the road. [9]The people were walking ahead of Jesus and behind him, shouting,

"Praise[n] to the Son of David!
God bless the One who comes in the name
    of the Lord!   *Psalm 118:26*
Praise to God in heaven!"

[10]When Jesus entered Jerusalem, all the city was filled with excitement. The people asked, "Who is this man?"

[11]The crowd said, "This man is Jesus, the prophet from the town of Nazareth in Galilee."

JESUS GOES TO THE TEMPLE

[12]Jesus went into the Temple and threw out all the people who were buying and selling there. He turned over the tables of those who were exchanging different kinds of money, and he upset the benches of those

---

20:22 **drink . . . drink** Jesus used the idea of drinking from a cup to ask if they could accept the same terrible things that would happen to him. 21:9 **Praise** Literally, "Hosanna," a Hebrew word used at first in praying to God for help. At this time it was probably a shout of joy used in praising God or his Messiah.

who were selling doves. ¹³Jesus said to all the people there, "It is written in the Scriptures, 'My Temple will be called a house for prayer.'[n] But you are changing it into a 'hideout for robbers.' "[n]

¹⁴The blind and crippled people came to Jesus in the Temple, and he healed them. ¹⁵The leading priests and the teachers of the law saw that Jesus was doing wonderful things and that the children were praising him in the Temple, saying, "Praise[n] to the Son of David." All these things made the priests and the teachers of the law very angry.

¹⁶They asked Jesus, "Do you hear the things these children are saying?"

Jesus answered, "Yes. Haven't you read in the Scriptures, 'You have taught children and babies to sing praises'?"[n]

¹⁷Then Jesus left and went out of the city to Bethany, where he spent the night.

THE POWER OF FAITH

¹⁸Early the next morning, as Jesus was going back to the city, he became hungry. ¹⁹Seeing a fig tree beside the road, Jesus went to it, but there were no figs on the tree, only leaves. So Jesus said to the tree, "You will never again have fruit." The tree immediately dried up.

²⁰When his followers saw this, they were amazed. They asked, "How did the fig tree dry up so quickly?"

²¹Jesus answered, "I tell you the truth, if you have faith and do not doubt, you will be able to do what I did to this tree and even more. You will be able to say to this mountain, 'Go, fall into the sea.' And if you have faith, it will happen. ²²If you believe, you will get anything you ask for in prayer."

LEADERS DOUBT JESUS' AUTHORITY

²³Jesus went to the Temple, and while he was teaching there, the leading priests and the elders of the people came to him. They said, "What authority do you have to do these things? Who gave you this authority?"

²⁴Jesus answered, "I also will ask you a question. If you answer me, then I will tell you what authority I have to do these things. ²⁵Tell me: When John baptized people, did that come from God or just from other people?"

They argued about Jesus' question, saying, "If we answer, 'John's baptism was from God,' Jesus will say, 'Then why didn't you believe him?' ²⁶But if we say, 'It was from people,' we

are afraid of what the crowd will do because they all believe that John was a prophet."

²⁷So they answered Jesus, "We don't know."

Jesus said to them, "Then I won't tell you what authority I have to do these things.

A STORY ABOUT TWO SONS

²⁸"Tell me what you think about this: A man had two sons. He went to the first son and said, 'Son, go and work today in my vineyard.' ²⁹The son answered, 'I will not go.' But later the son changed his mind and went. ³⁰Then the father went to the other son and said, 'Son, go and work today in my vineyard.' The son answered, 'Yes, sir, I will go and work,' but he did not go. ³¹Which of the two sons obeyed his father?"

The priests and leaders answered, "The first son."

Jesus said to them, "I tell you the truth, the tax collectors and the prostitutes will enter the kingdom of God before you do. ³²John came to show you the right way to live. You did not believe him, but the tax collectors and prostitutes believed him. Even after seeing this, you still refused to change your ways and believe him.

A STORY ABOUT GOD'S SON

³³"Listen to this story: There was a man who owned a vineyard. He put a wall around it and dug a hole for a winepress and built a tower. Then he leased the land to some farmers and left for a trip. ³⁴When it was time for the grapes to be picked, he sent his servants to the farmers to get his share of the grapes. ³⁵But the farmers grabbed the servants, beat one, killed another, and then killed a third servant with stones. ³⁶So the man sent some other servants to the farmers, even more than he sent the first time. But the farmers did the same thing to the servants that they had done before. ³⁷So the man decided to send his son to the farmers. He said, 'They will respect my son.' ³⁸But when the farmers saw the son, they said to each other, 'This son will inherit

---

21:13 'My Temple . . . prayer.' Quotation from Isaiah 56:7. **21:13** 'hideout for robbers' Quotation from Jeremiah 7:11. **21:15 Praise** Literally, "Hosanna," a Hebrew word used at first in praying to God for help. At this time it was probably a shout of joy used in praising God or his Messiah. **21:16** 'You . . . praises.' Quotation from the Septuagint (Greek) version of Psalm 8:2.

the vineyard. If we kill him, it will be ours!' ³⁹Then the farmers grabbed the son, threw him out of the vineyard, and killed him. ⁴⁰So what will the owner of the vineyard do to these farmers when he comes?"

⁴¹The priests and leaders said, "He will surely kill those evil men. Then he will lease the vineyard to some other farmers who will give him his share of the crop at harvest time."

⁴²Jesus said to them, "Surely you have read this in the Scriptures:

'The stone that the builders rejected
    became the cornerstone.

The Lord did this,
    and it is wonderful to us.'

Psalm 118:22–23

⁴³"So I tell you that the kingdom of God will be taken away from you and given to people who do the things God wants in his kingdom. ⁴⁴The person who falls on this stone will be broken, and on whomever that stone falls, that person will be crushed.'"ⁿ

⁴⁵When the leading priests and the

21:44 The . . . crushed. Some Greek copies do not have verse 44.

JESUS, WHO WAS, AND IS, AND IS TO COME

the **challenge** of **prayer**

〜〜 FAITH

By Gini Smith

MATTHEW 21:22

We can be thankful that God doesn't answer all of our prayers. In his mercy, he only answers those in alignment to his will. You can't manipulate God. You can't beg or cry out until you get your way. If your prayers aren't being answered, ask for forgiveness of anything that is blocking your communication, and align your will with God's heart.

God is a good Father; he cares about his children and loves to hear from you, his child. God can make sense of your ramblings. He just likes to listen to your voice and to hear you talk about everything, even if you are childish sometimes. It is all about your heart. Your words don't have to be perfect.

Prayer is not a selective responsibility for a privileged few; it is our means of communication with the living God. Not praying is like being married to someone and not talking to him or her. Communication is necessary to develop a successful relationship with anyone, but particularly with God.

If the Enemy says you're not worthy to speak to God, simply agree with him. No one is worthy to speak to God, but by the blood of Jesus our unworthiness doesn't count—his worthiness does! It is not your words; it is your heart. Grace is given so we can obey and live the life God has planned. It is not necessary to be good enough for grace; he gives grace so we can be good.

reflect: When was the last time you prayed out loud in a group situation?
Go to **1 Peter 3:8–12**.

Pharisees heard these stories, they knew Jesus was talking about them. [46]They wanted to arrest him, but they were afraid of the people, because the people believed that Jesus was a prophet.

A STORY ABOUT A WEDDING FEAST

22 Jesus again used stories to teach them. He said, [2]"The kingdom of heaven is like a king who prepared a wedding feast for his son. [3]The king invited some people to the feast. When the feast was ready, the king sent his servants to tell the people, but they refused to come.

[4]"Then the king sent other servants, saying, 'Tell those who have been invited that my feast is ready. I have killed my best bulls and calves for the dinner, and everything is ready. Come to the wedding feast.'

[5]"But the people refused to listen to the servants and left to do other things. One went to work in his field, and another went to his business. [6]Some of the other people grabbed the servants, beat them, and killed them. [7]The king was furious and sent his army to kill the murderers and burn their city.

[8]"After that, the king said to his servants, 'The wedding feast is ready. I invited those people, but they were not worthy to come. [9]So go to the street corners and invite everyone you find to come to my feast.' [10]So the servants went into the streets and gathered all the people they could find, both good and bad. And the wedding hall was filled with guests.

[11]"When the king came in to see the guests, he saw a man who was not dressed for a wedding. [12]The king said, 'Friend, how were you allowed to come in here? You are not dressed for a wedding.' But the man said nothing. [13]So the king told some servants, 'Tie this man's hands and feet. Throw him out into the darkness, where people will cry and grind their teeth with pain.'

[14]"Yes, many are invited, but only a few are chosen."

IS IT RIGHT TO PAY TAXES OR NOT?

[15]Then the Pharisees left that place and made plans to trap Jesus in saying something wrong. [16]They sent some of their own followers and some people from the group called Herodians.[n] They said, "Teacher, we know that you are an honest man and that you teach the truth about God's way. You are not afraid of what other people think about you, because you pay no attention to who they are. [17]So tell us what you think. Is it right to pay taxes to Caesar or not?"

[18]But knowing that these leaders were trying to trick him, Jesus said, "You hypocrites! Why are you trying to trap me? [19]Show me a coin used for paying the tax." So the men showed him a coin.[n] [20]Then Jesus asked, "Whose image and name are on the coin?"

[21]The men answered, "Caesar's."

Then Jesus said to them, "Give to Caesar the things that are Caesar's, and give to God the things that are God's."

[22]When the men heard what Jesus said, they were amazed and left him and went away.

SOME SADDUCEES TRY TO TRICK JESUS

[23]That same day some Sadducees came to Jesus and asked him a question. (Sadducees believed that people would not rise from the dead.) [24]They said, "Teacher, Moses said if a married man dies without having children, his brother must marry the widow and have children for him. [25]Once there were seven brothers among us. The first one married and died. Since he had no children, his brother married the widow. [26]Then the second brother also died. The same thing happened to the third brother and all the other brothers. [27]Finally, the woman died. [28]Since all seven men had married her, when people rise from the dead, whose wife will she be?"

[29]Jesus answered, "You don't understand, because you don't know what the Scriptures say, and you don't know about the power of God. [30]When people rise from the dead, they will not marry, nor will they be given to someone to marry. They will be like the angels in heaven. [31]Surely you have read what God said to you about rising from the dead. [32]God said, 'I am the God of Abraham, the God of Isaac, and the God of Jacob.'[n] God is the God of the living, not the dead."

[33]When the people heard this, they were amazed at Jesus' teaching.

22:16 Herodians A political group that followed Herod and his family. **22:19 coin** A Roman denarius. One coin was the average pay for one day's work. **22:32 'I am . . . Jacob.'** Quotation from Exodus 3:6.

THE MOST IMPORTANT COMMAND

³⁴When the Pharisees learned that the Sadducees could not argue with Jesus' answers to them, the Pharisees met together. ³⁵One Pharisee, who was an expert on the law of Moses, asked Jesus this question to test him: ³⁶"Teacher, which command in the law is the most important?"

³⁷Jesus answered, "'Love the Lord your God with all your heart, all your soul, and all your mind.'*ⁿ* ³⁸This is the first and most important command. ³⁹And the second command is like the first: 'Love your neighbor as you love yourself.'*ⁿ* ⁴⁰All the law and the writings of the prophets depend on these two commands."

JESUS QUESTIONS THE PHARISEES

⁴¹While the Pharisees were together, Jesus asked them, ⁴²"What do you think about the Christ? Whose son is he?"

They answered, "The Christ is the Son of David."

22:37 'Love . . . mind.' Quotation from Deuteronomy 6:5. **22:39 'Love . . . yourself.'** Quotation from Leviticus 19:18.

GOD'S PURPOSE FOR YOUR LIFE

civic **responsibility**

FUTURE

By Joel Hunter

MATTHEW 22:21

The Scriptures teach that followers of Christ are to be good citizens, as well as good worshipers. There has always been some debate as to whether we should pay any attention to worldly matters like participation in civic duties. We "render to Caesar" not only our taxes, but also a voice and a vote that is a part of our witness for Christ (Acts 1:8).

If we care about the future, we must help shape it. If we are to love our neighbors as ourselves (Matthew 22:39), we must help shape policies to address the general societal concerns God has always had on his heart: poverty (Deuteronomy 15:11), injustice (Psalm 82:3–4), pollution (Genesis 2:15), and more.

While we should not confuse political power with kingdom power (John 18:36), we must always recognize that part of our responsibility is to make this earth more like heaven (Matthew 6:10). Every place and every person ought to be better off because we follow Jesus. In caring for everyone, not just ourselves or our group, we are reflecting the heart of the God who loved the world and sacrificed for all (John 3:16).

It's important not to forget one more aspect of shaping the future as Christian citizens: all of our participation must be done with humility and love. Power is to be exercised within the context of service (Mark 10:42–45), and our views must always be put forth with an attitude of respect for those who differ from us (1 Peter 2:17).

reflect: What are some ways you can fulfill your civic responsibility?

Go to **FUTURE:** "Who Are You?" at **John 14:27.**

43Then Jesus said to them, "Then why did David call him 'Lord'? David, speaking by the power of the Holy Spirit, said,

44 'The Lord said to my Lord,

"Sit by me at my right side,
until I put your enemies under your
control." '   *Psalm 110:1*

45David calls the Christ 'Lord,' so how can the Christ be his son?"

46None of the Pharisees could answer Jesus' question, and after that day no one was brave enough to ask him any more questions.

JESUS ACCUSES SOME LEADERS

23 Then Jesus said to the crowds and to his followers, 2"The teachers of the law and the Pharisees have the authority to tell you what the law of Moses says. 3So you should obey and follow whatever they tell you, but their lives are not good examples for you to follow. They tell you to do things, but they themselves don't do them. 4They make strict rules and try to force people to obey them, but they are unwilling to help those who struggle under the weight of their rules.

5"They do good things so that other people will see them. They enlarge the little boxes[n] holding Scriptures that they wear, and they make their special prayer clothes very long. 6Those Pharisees and teachers of the law love to have the most important seats at feasts and in the synagogues. 7They love people to greet them with respect in the marketplaces, and they love to have people call them 'Teacher.'

8"But you must not be called 'Teacher,' because you have only one Teacher, and you are all brothers and sisters together. 9And don't call any person on earth 'Father,' because you have one Father, who is in heaven. 10And you should not be called 'Master,' because you have only one Master, the Christ. 11Whoever is your servant is the greatest among you. 12Whoever makes himself great will be made humble. Whoever makes himself humble will be made great.

13"How terrible for you, teachers of the law and Pharisees! You are hypocrites! You close the door for people to enter the kingdom of heaven. You yourselves don't enter, and you stop others who are trying to enter. [14How terrible for you, teachers of the

law and Pharisees. You are hypocrites. You take away widows' houses, and you say long prayers so that people will notice you. So you will have a worse punishment.][n]

15"How terrible for you, teachers of the law and Pharisees! You are hypocrites! You travel across land and sea to find one person who will change to your ways. When you find that person, you make him more fit for hell than you are.

16"How terrible for you! You guide the people, but you are blind. You say, 'If people swear by the Temple when they make a promise, that means nothing. But if they swear by the gold that is in the Temple, they must keep that promise.' 17You are blind fools! Which is greater: the gold or the Temple that makes that gold holy? 18And you say, 'If people swear by the altar when they make a promise, that means nothing. But if they swear by the gift on the altar, they must keep that promise.' 19You are blind! Which is greater: the gift or the altar that makes the gift holy? 20The person who swears by the altar is really using the altar and also everything on the altar. 21And the person who swears by the Temple is really using the Temple and also everything in the Temple. 22The person who swears by heaven is also using God's throne and the One who sits on that throne.

23"How terrible for you, teachers of the law and Pharisees! You are hypocrites! You give to God one-tenth of everything you earn—even your mint, dill, and cumin.[n] But you don't obey the really important teachings of the law—justice, mercy, and being loyal. These are the things you should do, as well as those other things. 24You guide the people, but you are blind! You are like a person who picks a fly out of a drink and then swallows a camel![n]

25"How terrible for you, teachers of the law and Pharisees! You are hypocrites! You wash the outside of your cups and dishes, but

---

23:5 boxes Small leather boxes containing four important Scriptures. Some Jews tied these to their foreheads and left arms, probably to show they were very religious. **23:14 How . . . punishment.** Some Greek copies do not contain the bracketed text. **23:23 mint, dill, and cumin** Small plants grown in gardens and used for spices. Only very religious people would be careful enough to give a tenth of these plants. **23:24 You . . . camel!** Meaning, "You worry about the smallest mistakes but commit the biggest sin."

inside they are full of things you got by cheating others and by pleasing only yourselves. [26]Pharisees, you are blind! First make the inside of the cup clean, and then the outside of the cup can be truly clean.

[27]"How terrible for you, teachers of the law and Pharisees! You are hypocrites! You are like tombs that are painted white. Outside, those tombs look fine, but inside, they are full of the bones of dead people and all kinds of unclean things. [28]It is the same with you. People look at you and think you are good, but on the inside you are full of hypocrisy and evil.

[29]"How terrible for you, teachers of the law and Pharisees! You are hypocrites! You build tombs for the prophets, and you show honor to the graves of those who lived good lives. [30]You say, 'If we had lived during the time of our ancestors, we would not have helped them kill the prophets.' [31]But you give proof that you are descendants of those who murdered the prophets. [32]And you will complete the sin that your ancestors started.

[33]"You are snakes! A family of poisonous snakes! How are you going to escape God's judgment? [34]So I tell you this: I am sending to you prophets and wise men and teachers. Some of them you will kill and crucify. Some of them you will beat in your synagogues and chase from town to town. [35]So you will be guilty for the death of all the good people who have been killed on earth—from the murder of that good man Abel to the murder of Zechariah[n] son of Berakiah, whom you murdered between the Temple and the altar. [36]I tell you the truth, all of these things will happen to you people who are living now.

JESUS FEELS SORRY FOR JERUSALEM

[37]"Jerusalem, Jerusalem! You kill the prophets and stone to death those who are sent to you. Many times I wanted to gather your people as a hen gathers her chicks under her wings, but you did not let me. [38]Now your house will be left completely empty. [39]I tell you, you will not see me again until that time when you will say, 'God bless the One who comes in the name of the Lord.'"[n]

THE TEMPLE WILL BE DESTROYED

24 As Jesus left the Temple and was walking away, his followers came up to show him the Temple's buildings. [2]Jesus asked, "Do you see all these buildings? I tell you the truth, not one stone will be left on another. Every stone will be thrown down to the ground."

[3]Later, as Jesus was sitting on the Mount of Olives, his followers came to be alone with him. They said, "Tell us, when will these things happen? And what will be the sign that it is time for you to come again and for this age to end?"

[4]Jesus answered, "Be careful that no one fools you. [5]Many will come in my name, saying, 'I am the Christ,' and they will fool many people. [6]You will hear about wars and stories of wars that are coming, but don't be afraid. These things must happen before the end comes. [7]Nations will fight against other nations; kingdoms will fight against other kingdoms. There will be times when there is no food for people to eat, and there will be earthquakes in different places. [8]These things are like the first pains when something new is about to be born.

[9]"Then people will arrest you, hand you over to be hurt, and kill you. They will hate you because you believe in me. [10]At that time, many will lose their faith, and they will turn against each other and hate each other. [11]Many false prophets will come and cause many people to believe lies. [12]There will be more and more evil in the world, so most people will stop showing their love for each other. [13]But those people who keep their faith until the end will be saved. [14]The Good News about God's kingdom will be preached in all the world, to every nation. Then the end will come.

[15]"Daniel the prophet spoke about 'a blasphemous object that brings destruction.'[n] You will see this standing in the holy place." (You who read this should understand what it means.) [16]"At that time, the people in Judea should run away to the mountains. [17]If people are on the roofs[n] of their houses,

---

23:35 Abel . . . Zechariah In the order of the books of the Hebrew Old Testament, the first and last men to be murdered. **23:39 'God . . . Lord.'** Quotation from Psalm 118:26. **24:15 'a blasphemous object that brings destruction'** Mentioned in Daniel 9:27; 12:11 (see also Daniel 11:31). **24:17 roofs** In Bible times houses were built with flat roofs. The roof was used for drying things such as flax and fruit. And it was used as an extra room, as a place for worship, and as a cool place to sleep in the summer.

they must not go down to get anything out of their houses. ¹⁸If people are in the fields, they must not go back to get their coats. ¹⁹At that time, how terrible it will be for women who are pregnant or have nursing babies! ²⁰Pray that it will not be winter or a Sabbath day when these things happen and you have to run away, ²¹because at that time there will be much trouble. There will be more trouble than there has ever been since the beginning of the world until now, and nothing as bad will ever happen again. ²²God has decided to make that terrible time short. Otherwise, no one would go on living. But God will make that time short to help the people he has chosen. ²³At that time, someone might say to you, 'Look, there is the Christ!' Or another person might say, 'There he is!' But don't believe them. ²⁴False Christs and false prophets will come and perform great wonders and miracles. They will try to fool even the people God has chosen, if that is possible. ²⁵Now I have warned you about this before it happens.

²⁶"If people tell you, 'The Christ is in the

FAMILY

LOVE IS MORE THAN GIVING

extraordinary
emotions

MATTHEW 23:37

By Larry Stockstill

Emotions are a very important part of who you are and are good and necessary in relationships. God created you to have emotions because he has them, too. Jesus was a man of intense emotion, and he was not afraid to express it (Matthew 23:37).

People's emotions reflect the health and depth of a relationship. When you are aware of another's emotions and respond accordingly, your relationship begins to grow and deepen. The Holy Spirit can help you learn to be sensitive and choose reactions that please, support, or affirm the other person.

There are times when emotions are soft and vulnerable. There are times when they are angry and full of pain. Relationships do not exist in a sterile vacuum where they remain dull, expressionless, and monotonous. Healthy emotions embrace the fullness of life to enhance, please, and empower; unhealthy emotions languish, squelch joy, and destroy. Where there is no crying, laughing, sadness, or dancing, relationships die. Where you find shared joy and sorrow, you find fully functional people sharing life together in extraordinary relationships.

It is like a door. You can open the door into someone's life and share both the joy and sorrow. You can also refuse to open the door and remain outside where you will always be a stranger. If you are committed to developing extraordinary relationships, fling that door open wide, run through it and be a full partaker of life with the people God has given you.

reflect: What emotional season are you living in today?
Go to **Song of Songs 7:10.**

desert,' don't go there. If they say, 'The Christ is in the inner room,' don't believe it. ²⁷When the Son of Man comes, he will be seen by everyone, like lightning flashing from the east to the west. ²⁸Wherever the dead body is, there the vultures will gather.

²⁹"Soon after the trouble of those days,

'the sun will grow dark,
and the moon will not give its light.
The stars will fall from the sky.
And the powers of the heavens will be
   shaken.' *Isaiah 13:10; 34:4*

³⁰"At that time, the sign of the Son of Man will appear in the sky. Then all the peoples of the world will cry. They will see the Son of Man coming on clouds in the sky with great power and glory. ³¹He will use a loud trumpet to send his angels all around the earth, and they will gather his chosen people from every part of the world.

³²"Learn a lesson from the fig tree: When its branches become green and soft and new leaves appear, you know summer is near. ³³In the same way, when you see all these things happening, you will know that the time is near, ready to come. ³⁴I tell you the truth, all these things will happen while the people of this time are still living. ³⁵Earth and sky will be destroyed, but the words I have said will never be destroyed.

WHEN WILL JESUS COME AGAIN?

³⁶"No one knows when that day or time will be, not the angels in heaven, not even the Son.ⁿ Only the Father knows. ³⁷When the Son of Man comes, it will be like what happened during Noah's time. ³⁸In those days before the flood, people were eating and drinking, marrying and giving their children to be married, until the day Noah entered the boat. ³⁹They knew nothing about what was happening until the flood came and destroyed them. It will be the same when the Son of Man comes. ⁴⁰Two men will be in the field. One will be taken, and the other will be left. ⁴¹Two women will be grinding grain with a mill.ⁿ One will be taken, and the other will be left.

⁴²"So always be ready, because you don't know the day your Lord will come. ⁴³Remember this: If the owner of the house knew what time of night a thief was coming, the owner would watch and not let the thief break in.

⁴⁴So you also must be ready, because the Son of Man will come at a time you don't expect him.

⁴⁵"Who is the wise and loyal servant that the master trusts to give the other servants their food at the right time? ⁴⁶When the master comes and finds the servant doing his work, the servant will be blessed. ⁴⁷I tell you the truth, the master will choose that servant to take care of everything he owns. ⁴⁸But suppose that evil servant thinks to himself, 'My master will not come back soon,' ⁴⁹and he begins to beat the other servants and eat and get drunk with others like him? ⁵⁰The master will come when that servant is not ready and is not expecting him. ⁵¹Then the master will cut him in pieces and send him away to be with the hypocrites, where people will cry and grind their teeth with pain.

A STORY ABOUT TEN BRIDESMAIDS

25 "At that time the kingdom of heaven will be like ten bridesmaids who took their lamps and went to wait for the bridegroom. ²Five of them were foolish and five were wise. ³The five foolish bridesmaids took their lamps, but they did not take more oil for the lamps to burn. ⁴The wise bridesmaids took their lamps and more oil in jars. ⁵Because the bridegroom was late, they became sleepy and went to sleep.

⁶"At midnight someone cried out, 'The bridegroom is coming! Come and meet him!' ⁷Then all the bridesmaids woke up and got their lamps ready. ⁸But the foolish ones said to the wise, 'Give us some of your oil, because our lamps are going out.' ⁹The wise bridesmaids answered, 'No, the oil we have might not be enough for all of us. Go to the people who sell oil and buy some for yourselves.'

¹⁰"So while the five foolish bridesmaids went to buy oil, the bridegroom came. The bridesmaids who were ready went in with the bridegroom to the wedding feast. Then the door was closed and locked.

¹¹"Later the others came back and said, 'Sir, sir, open the door to let us in.' ¹²But the bridegroom answered, 'I tell you the truth, I don't want to know you.'

24:36 not even the Son Some Greek copies do not have this phrase. **24:41 mill** Two large, round, flat rocks used for grinding grain to make flour.

¹³"So always be ready, because you don't know the day or the hour the Son of Man will come.

A STORY ABOUT THREE SERVANTS

¹⁴"The kingdom of heaven is like a man who was going to another place for a visit. Before he left, he called for his servants and told them to take care of his things while he was gone. ¹⁵He gave one servant five bags of gold, another servant two bags of gold, and a third servant one bag of gold, to each one as much as he could handle. Then he left. ¹⁶The servant who got five bags went quickly to invest the money and earned five more bags. ¹⁷In the same way, the servant who had two

UNDERSTANDING FREEDOM

FINANCES

good stewardship

MATTHEW 25:14-30

By Elmer Towns

Take a few moments to determine if you are a good steward of what God has given you by using the following seven principles as a self-test to determine your answer. Good stewards live in a way that says:

- God is the owner of everything we have. Christians should recognize that God is the owner of everything in their life—home, car, even spouse and children.

- God gives us things and expects us to manage them for him. No matter what resources or how much money a family has, they must submit to God's principles and manage their resources for God's glory.

- God has a right to check up on everyone. Because God is the owner of everything we have, he has the right to monitor how we use the resources he leaves in our care.

- We must trust God's rules and live by them. Faith is applying God's principles to our lives and leaving the results to him.

- Every spending decision is a spiritual decision. This means the Holy Spirit should control every decision, large or small.

- God uses possessions to prepare us for the future kingdom. How a person handles present opportunities determines future rewards; this includes money. How we handle it now determines our reward in heaven later.

- God uses money as a tool to teach us how to follow him. God uses our pocketbooks to get our attention!

reflect: Are you a good steward?
Go to **Mark 4:26-29.**

bags invested them and earned two more. [18]But the servant who got one bag went out and dug a hole in the ground and hid the master's money.

[19]"After a long time the master came home and asked the servants what they did with his money. [20]The servant who was given five bags of gold brought five more bags to the master and said, 'Master, you trusted me to care for five bags of gold, so I used your five bags to earn five more.' [21]The master answered, 'You did well. You are a good and loyal servant. Because you were loyal with small things, I will let you care for much greater things. Come and share my joy with me.'

[22]"Then the servant who had been given two bags of gold came to the master and said, 'Master, you gave me two bags of gold to care for, so I used your two bags to earn two more.' [23]The master answered, 'You did well. You are a good and loyal servant. Because you were loyal with small things, I will let you care for much greater things. Come and share my joy with me.'

[24]"Then the servant who had been given one bag of gold came to the master and said, 'Master, I knew that you were a hard man. You harvest things you did not plant. You gather crops where you did not sow any seed. [25]So I was afraid and went and hid your money in the ground. Here is your bag of gold.' [26]The master answered, 'You are a wicked and lazy servant! You say you knew that I harvest things I did not plant and that I gather crops where I did not sow any seed. [27]So you should have put my gold in the bank. Then, when I came home, I would have received my gold back with interest.'

[28]"So the master told his other servants, 'Take the bag of gold from that servant and give it to the servant who has ten bags of gold. [29]Those who have much will get more, and they will have much more than they need. But those who do not have much will have everything taken away from them.' [30]Then the master said, 'Throw that useless servant outside, into the darkness where people will cry and grind their teeth with pain.'

THE KING WILL JUDGE ALL PEOPLE

[31]"The Son of Man will come again in his great glory, with all his angels. He will be King and sit on his great throne. [32]All the nations of the world will be gathered before him, and he will separate them into two groups as a shepherd separates the sheep from the goats. [33]The Son of Man will put the sheep on his right and the goats on his left.

[34]"Then the King will say to the people on his right, 'Come, my Father has given you his blessing. Receive the kingdom God has prepared for you since the world was made. [35]I was hungry, and you gave me food. I was thirsty, and you gave me something to drink. I was alone and away from home, and you invited me into your house. [36]I was without clothes, and you gave me something to wear. I was sick, and you cared for me. I was in prison, and you visited me.'

[37]"Then the good people will answer, 'Lord, when did we see you hungry and give you food, or thirsty and give you something to drink? [38]When did we see you alone and away from home and invite you into our house? When did we see you without clothes and give you something to wear? [39]When did we see you sick or in prison and care for you?'

[40]"Then the King will answer, 'I tell you the truth, anything you did for even the least of my people here, you also did for me.'

[41]"Then the King will say to those on his left, 'Go away from me. You will be punished. Go into the fire that burns forever that was prepared for the devil and his angels. [42]I was hungry, and you gave me nothing to eat. I was thirsty, and you gave me nothing to drink. [43]I was alone and away from home, and you did not invite me into your house. I was without clothes, and you gave me nothing to wear. I was sick and in prison, and you did not care for me.'

[44]"Then those people will answer, 'Lord, when did we see you hungry or thirsty or alone and away from home or without clothes or sick or in prison? When did we see these things and not help you?'

[45]"Then the King will answer, 'I tell you the truth, anything you refused to do for even the least of my people here, you refused to do for me.'

[46]"These people will go off to be punished forever, but the good people will go to live forever."

THE PLAN TO KILL JESUS

26 After Jesus finished saying all these things, he told his followers, ²"You know that the day after tomorrow is the day of the Passover Feast. On that day the Son of Man will be given to his enemies to be crucified."

³Then the leading priests and the elders had a meeting at the palace of the high priest, named Caiaphas. ⁴At the meeting, they planned to set a trap to arrest Jesus and kill him. ⁵But they said, "We must not do it during the feast, because the people might cause a riot."

PERFUME FOR JESUS' BURIAL

⁶Jesus was in Bethany at the house of Simon, who had a skin disease. ⁷While Jesus was there, a woman approached him with an alabaster jar filled with expensive perfume. She poured this perfume on Jesus' head while he was eating.

⁸His followers were upset when they saw the woman do this. They asked, "Why waste that perfume? ⁹It could have been sold for a great deal of money and the money given to the poor."

¹⁰Knowing what had happened, Jesus said, "Why are you troubling this woman? She did an excellent thing for me. ¹¹You will always have the poor with you, but you will not always have me. ¹²This woman poured perfume on my body to prepare me for burial. ¹³I tell you the truth, wherever the Good News is preached in all the world, what this

ARE YOU PROGRAMMED FOR STRESS?

FULFILLMENT

helping
those in **need**

MATTHEW 25:44-45

If you see someone who is in need and you are capable of helping that person, you should do so. When you do such acts, you should do them as to the Lord; and if you ignore them, you are rejecting the needs of the Lord. Think about how many times you have seen people in need and you passed them by because you were too busy.

Is there anyone beneath you who isn't smart enough, important enough, attractive enough for your time or attention? Are there people you know who can barely pay their bills and can afford no luxury while you live in abundance? Are there annoying people or people you don't like who need the grace of God?

In this passage, Jesus is looking for us to be his hands and feet. We are called to be Jesus with skin on. We are called to care for the fatherless, the widow, and those that can't, or don't know how to, help themselves. Such people are those whom Jesus came to rescue.

Only what is done for Christ will last. And what is done in the name of Jesus is done for the "least" of those you know. Grace and mercy are gifts we don't deserve but have been given. Who will you give these gifts to in return?

reflect: Consider how you can bless someone in need today.
Go to **Mark 9:23.**

woman has done will be told, and people will remember her."

JUDAS BECOMES AN ENEMY OF JESUS

[14]Then one of the twelve apostles, Judas Iscariot, went to talk to the leading priests. [15]He said, "What will you pay me for giving Jesus to you?" And they gave him thirty silver coins. [16]After that, Judas watched for the best time to turn Jesus in.

JESUS EATS THE PASSOVER MEAL

[17]On the first day of the Feast of Unleavened Bread, the followers came to Jesus. They said, "Where do you want us to prepare for you to eat the Passover meal?"

[18]Jesus answered, "Go into the city to a certain man and tell him, 'The Teacher says: "The chosen time is near. I will have the Passover with my followers at your house." ' "

[19]The followers did what Jesus told them to do, and they prepared the Passover meal.

[20]In the evening Jesus was sitting at the table with his twelve followers. [21]As they were eating, Jesus said, "I tell you the truth, one of you will turn against me."

[22]This made the followers very sad. Each one began to say to Jesus, "Surely, Lord, I am not the one who will turn against you, am I?"

[23]Jesus answered, "The man who has dipped his hand with me into the bowl is the one who will turn against me. [24]The Son of Man will die, just as the Scriptures say. But how terrible it will be for the person who hands the Son of Man over to be killed. It would be better for him if he had never been born."

[25]Then Judas, who would give Jesus to his enemies, said to Jesus, "Teacher, surely I am not the one, am I?"

Jesus answered, "Yes, it is you."

THE LORD'S SUPPER

[26]While they were eating, Jesus took some bread and thanked God for it and broke it. Then he gave it to his followers and said, "Take this bread and eat it; this is my body."

[27]Then Jesus took a cup and thanked God for it and gave it to the followers. He said, "Every one of you drink this. [28]This is my blood which is the new[n] agreement that God makes with his people. This blood is poured out for many to forgive their sins. [29]I tell you this: I will not drink of this fruit of the vine[n]

again until that day when I drink it new with you in my Father's kingdom."

[30]After singing a hymn, they went out to the Mount of Olives.

JESUS' FOLLOWERS WILL LEAVE HIM

[31]Jesus told his followers, "Tonight you will all stumble in your faith on account of me, because it is written in the Scriptures:

'I will kill the shepherd,
  and the sheep will scatter.'

Zechariah 13:7

[32]But after I rise from the dead, I will go ahead of you into Galilee."

[33]Peter said, "Everyone else may stumble in their faith because of you, but I will not."

[34]Jesus said, "I tell you the truth, tonight before the rooster crows you will say three times that you don't know me."

[35]But Peter said, "I will never say that I don't know you! I will even die with you!" And all the other followers said the same thing.

JESUS PRAYS ALONE

[36]Then Jesus went with his followers to a place called Gethsemane. He said to them, "Sit here while I go over there and pray." [37]He took Peter and the two sons of Zebedee with him, and he began to be very sad and troubled. [38]He said to them, "My heart is full of sorrow, to the point of death. Stay here and watch with me."

[39]After walking a little farther away from them, Jesus fell to the ground and prayed, "My Father, if it is possible, do not give me this cup[n] of suffering. But do what you want, not what I want." [40]Then Jesus went back to his followers and found them asleep. He said to Peter, "You men could not stay awake with me for one hour? [41]Stay awake and pray for strength against temptation. The spirit wants to do what is right, but the body is weak."

[42]Then Jesus went away a second time and prayed, "My Father, if it is not possible for this painful thing to be taken from me, and if I must do it, I pray that what you want will be done."

26:28 new Some Greek copies do not have this word. Compare Luke 22:20. **26:29 fruit of the vine** Product of the grapevine; this may also be translated "wine." **26:39 cup** Jesus is talking about the terrible things that will happen to him. Accepting these things will be very hard, like drinking a cup of something bitter.

⁴³Then he went back to his followers, and again he found them asleep, because their eyes were heavy. ⁴⁴So Jesus left them and went away and prayed a third time, saying the same thing.

⁴⁵Then Jesus went back to his followers and said, "Are you still sleeping and resting? The time has come for the Son of Man to be handed over to sinful people. ⁴⁶Get up, we must go. Look, here comes the man who has turned against me."

JESUS IS ARRESTED

⁴⁷While Jesus was still speaking, Judas, one of the twelve apostles, came up. With him were many people carrying swords and clubs who had been sent from the leading priests and the Jewish elders of the people. ⁴⁸Judas had planned to give them a signal, saying, "The man I kiss is Jesus. Arrest him." ⁴⁹At once Judas went to Jesus and said, "Greetings, Teacher!" and kissed him.

⁵⁰Jesus answered, "Friend, do what you came to do."

Then the people came and grabbed Jesus and arrested him. ⁵¹When that happened, one of Jesus' followers reached for his sword and pulled it out. He struck the servant of the high priest and cut off his ear.

⁵²Jesus said to the man, "Put your sword back in its place. All who use swords will be killed with swords. ⁵³Surely you know I could ask my Father, and he would give me more than twelve armies of angels. ⁵⁴But it must happen this way to bring about what the Scriptures say."

⁵⁵Then Jesus said to the crowd, "You came to get me with swords and clubs as if I were a criminal. Every day I sat in the Temple teaching, and you did not arrest me there. ⁵⁶But all these things have happened so that it will come about as the prophets wrote." Then all of Jesus' followers left him and ran away.

JESUS BEFORE THE LEADERS

⁵⁷Those people who arrested Jesus led him to the house of Caiaphas, the high priest, where the teachers of the law and the elders were gathered. ⁵⁸Peter followed far behind to the courtyard of the high priest's house, and he sat down with the guards to see what would happen to Jesus.

⁵⁹The leading priests and the whole Jewish council tried to find something false against Jesus so they could kill him. ⁶⁰Many people came and told lies about him, but the council could find no real reason to kill him. Then two people came and said, ⁶¹"This man said, 'I can destroy the Temple of God and build it again in three days.'"

⁶²Then the high priest stood up and said to Jesus, "Aren't you going to answer? Don't you have something to say about their charges against you?" ⁶³But Jesus said nothing.

Again the high priest said to Jesus, "I command you by the power of the living God: Tell us if you are the Christ, the Son of God."

⁶⁴Jesus answered, "Those are your words. But I tell you, in the future you will see the Son of Man sitting at the right hand of God, the Powerful One, and coming on clouds in the sky."

⁶⁵When the high priest heard this, he tore his clothes and said, "This man has said things that are against God! We don't need any more witnesses; you all heard him say these things against God. ⁶⁶What do you think?"

The people answered, "He should die."

⁶⁷Then the people there spat in Jesus' face and beat him with their fists. Others slapped him. ⁶⁸They said, "Prove to us that you are a prophet, you Christ! Tell us who hit you!"

PETER SAYS HE DOESN'T KNOW JESUS

⁶⁹At that time, as Peter was sitting in the courtyard, a servant girl came to him and said, "You also were with Jesus of Galilee."

⁷⁰But Peter said to all the people there that he was never with Jesus. He said, "I don't know what you are talking about."

⁷¹When he left the courtyard and was at the gate, another girl saw him. She said to the people there, "This man was with Jesus of Nazareth."

⁷²Again, Peter said he was never with him, saying, "I swear I don't know this man Jesus!"

⁷³A short time later, some people standing there went to Peter and said, "Surely you are one of those who followed Jesus. The way you talk shows it."

⁷⁴Then Peter began to place a curse on himself and swear, "I don't know the man." At once, a rooster crowed. ⁷⁵And Peter remembered what Jesus had told him: "Before the rooster crows, you will say three times that you don't know me." Then Peter went outside and cried painfully.

JESUS IS TAKEN TO PILATE

27 Early the next morning, all the leading priests and elders of the people decided that Jesus should die. [2]They tied him, led him away, and turned him over to Pilate, the governor.

JUDAS KILLS HIMSELF

[3]Judas, the one who had given Jesus to his enemies, saw that they had decided to kill Jesus. Then he was very sorry for what he had done. So he took the thirty silver coins back to the priests and the leaders, [4]saying, "I sinned; I handed over to you an innocent man."

The leaders answered, "What is that to us? That's your problem, not ours."

[5]So Judas threw the money into the Temple. Then he went off and hanged himself.

[6]The leading priests picked up the silver coins in the Temple and said, "Our law does not allow us to keep this money with the Temple money, because it has paid for a man's death." [7]So they decided to use the coins to buy Potter's Field as a place to bury strangers who died in Jerusalem. [8]That is why that field is still called the Field of Blood. [9]So what Jeremiah the prophet had said came true: "They took thirty silver coins. That is how little the Israelites thought he was worth. [10]They used those thirty silver coins to buy the potter's field, as the Lord commanded me."[n]

PILATE QUESTIONS JESUS

[11]Jesus stood before Pilate the governor, and Pilate asked him, "Are you the king of the Jews?"

Jesus answered, "Those are your words."

[12]When the leading priests and the elders accused Jesus, he said nothing.

[13]So Pilate said to Jesus, "Don't you hear them accusing you of all these things?"

[14]But Jesus said nothing in answer to Pilate, and Pilate was very surprised at this.

PILATE TRIES TO FREE JESUS

[15]Every year at the time of Passover the governor would free one prisoner whom the people chose. [16]At that time there was a man in prison, named Barabbas,[n] who was known to be very bad. [17]When the people gathered at Pilate's house, Pilate said, "Whom do you want me to set free: Barabbas[n] or Jesus who is called the Christ?" [18]Pilate knew that they turned Jesus in to him because they were jealous.

[19]While Pilate was sitting there on the judge's seat, his wife sent this message to him: "Don't do anything to that man, because he is innocent. Today I had a dream about him, and it troubled me very much."

[20]But the leading priests and elders convinced the crowd to ask for Barabbas to be freed and for Jesus to be killed.

[21]Pilate said, "I have Barabbas and Jesus. Which do you want me to set free for you?"

The people answered, "Barabbas."

[22]Pilate asked, "So what should I do with Jesus, the one called the Christ?"

They all answered, "Crucify him!"

[23]Pilate asked, "Why? What wrong has he done?"

But they shouted louder, "Crucify him!"

[24]When Pilate saw that he could do nothing about this and that a riot was starting, he took some water and washed his hands[n] in front of the crowd. Then he said, "I am not guilty of this man's death. You are the ones who are causing it!"

[25]All the people answered, "We and our children will be responsible for his death."

[26]Then he set Barabbas free. But Jesus was beaten with whips and handed over to the soldiers to be crucified.

[27]The governor's soldiers took Jesus into the governor's palace, and they all gathered around him. [28]They took off his clothes and put a red robe on him. [29]Using thorny branches, they made a crown, put it on his head, and put a stick in his right hand. Then the soldiers bowed before Jesus and made fun of him, saying, "Hail, King of the Jews!" [30]They spat on Jesus. Then they took his stick and began to beat him on the head. [31]After they finished, the soldiers took off the robe and put his own clothes on him again. Then they led him away to be crucified.

JESUS IS CRUCIFIED

[32]As the soldiers were going out of the city with Jesus, they forced a man from Cyrene, named Simon, to carry the cross for Jesus.

27:9–10 **"They . . . commanded me."** See Zechariah 11:12–13 and Jeremiah 32:6–9. **27:16–17 Barabbas** Some Greek copies read "Jesus Barabbas." **27:24 washed his hands** He did this as a sign to show that he wanted no part in what the people did.

[33]They all came to the place called Golgotha, which means the Place of the Skull. [34]The soldiers gave Jesus wine mixed with gall[n] to drink. He tasted the wine but refused to drink it. [35]When the soldiers had crucified him, they threw lots to decide who would get his clothes.[n] [36]The soldiers sat there and continued watching him. [37]They put a sign above Jesus' head with a charge against him. It said: THIS IS JESUS, THE KING OF THE JEWS. [38]Two robbers were crucified beside Jesus, one on the right and the other on the left. [39]People walked by and insulted Jesus and shook their heads, [40]saying, "You said you could destroy the Temple and build it again in three days. So save yourself! Come down from that cross if you are really the Son of God!"

[41]The leading priests, the teachers of the law, and the Jewish elders were also making fun of Jesus. [42]They said, "He saved others, but he can't save himself! He says he is the king of Israel! If he is the king, let him come down now from the cross. Then we will believe in him. [43]He trusts in God, so let God save him now, if God really wants him. He himself said, 'I am the Son of God.'" [44]And in the same way, the robbers who were being crucified beside Jesus also insulted him.

JESUS DIES

[45]At noon the whole country became dark, and the darkness lasted for three hours. [46]About three o'clock Jesus cried out in a loud voice, "Eli, Eli, lama sabachthani?" This means, "My God, my God, why have you abandoned me?"

[47]Some of the people standing there who heard this said, "He is calling Elijah."

[48]Quickly one of them ran and got a sponge and filled it with vinegar and tied it to a stick and gave it to Jesus to drink. [49]But the others said, "Don't bother him. We want to see if Elijah will come to save him."

[50]But Jesus cried out again in a loud voice and died.

[51]Then the curtain in the Temple[n] was torn into two pieces, from the top to the bottom. Also, the earth shook and rocks broke apart. [52]The graves opened, and many of God's people who had died were raised from the dead. [53]They came out of the graves after Jesus was raised from the dead and went into the holy city, where they appeared to many people.

[54]When the army officer and the soldiers guarding Jesus saw this earthquake and everything else that happened, they were very frightened and said, "He really was the Son of God!"

[55]Many women who had followed Jesus from Galilee to help him were standing at a distance from the cross, watching. [56]Mary Magdalene, and Mary the mother of James and Joseph, and the mother of James and John were there.

JESUS IS BURIED

[57]That evening a rich man named Joseph, a follower of Jesus from the town of Arimathea, came to Jerusalem. [58]Joseph went to Pilate and asked to have Jesus' body. So Pilate gave orders for the soldiers to give it to Joseph. [59]Then Joseph took the body and wrapped it in a clean linen cloth. [60]He put Jesus' body in a new tomb that he had cut out of a wall of rock, and he rolled a very large stone to block the entrance of the tomb. Then Joseph went away. [61]Mary Magdalene and the other woman named Mary were sitting near the tomb.

THE TOMB OF JESUS IS GUARDED

[62]The next day, the day after Preparation Day, the leading priests and the Pharisees went to Pilate. [63]They said, "Sir, we remember that while that liar was still alive he said, 'After three days I will rise from the dead.' [64]So give the order for the tomb to be guarded closely till the third day. Otherwise, his followers might come and steal the body and tell people that he has risen from the dead. That lie would be even worse than the first one."

[65]Pilate said, "Take some soldiers and go guard the tomb the best way you know." [66]So they all went to the tomb and made it safe from thieves by sealing the stone in the entrance and putting soldiers there to guard it.

27:34 gall Probably a drink of wine mixed with drugs to help a person feel less pain. **27:35 clothes** Some Greek copies continue, "So what God said through the prophet came true, 'They divided my clothes among them, and they threw lots for my clothing.' " See Psalm 22:18. **27:51 curtain in the Temple** A curtain divided the Most Holy Place from the other part of the Temple. That was the special building in Jerusalem where God commanded the Jewish people to worship him.

JESUS RISES FROM THE DEAD

28 The day after the Sabbath day was the first day of the week. At dawn on the first day, Mary Magdalene and another woman named Mary went to look at the tomb.

²At that time there was a strong earthquake. An angel of the Lord came down from heaven, went to the tomb, and rolled the stone away from the entrance. Then he sat on the stone. ³He was shining as bright as lightning, and his clothes were white as snow. ⁴The soldiers guarding the tomb shook with fear because of the angel, and they became like dead men.

⁵The angel said to the women, "Don't be afraid. I know that you are looking for Jesus, who has been crucified. ⁶He is not here. He has risen from the dead as he said he would. Come and see the place where his body was. ⁷And go quickly and tell his followers, 'Jesus has risen from the dead. He is going into Galilee ahead of you, and you will see him there.'" Then the angel said, "Now I have told you."

⁸The women left the tomb quickly. They were afraid, but they were also very happy.

HOPE IN THE HOLY SPIRIT

develop a **life mission**

FUTURE

By Dr. Ronnie Floyd

MATTHEW 28:16-20

What in the world are you doing on this planet? Why do you exist?

Tough questions, but questions we all need to ponder. And next to beginning your day with God, understanding and articulating your life mission is the most critical thing you can do to insure that you are making a difference in this life. As I think about the possible answers to these questions in my own life, I am immediately reminded of Jesus:

"Didn't you know that I must be in my Father's house?" (Luke 2:49). Even at the age of twelve, Jesus had already begun to understand why he was here. He had sight of his mission. And in Matthew 20:28, Jesus made it crystal clear that he was not on the earth to prove his importance or to have others wait on him. He was here to serve, to pay the ransom for our souls.

"The Son of Man came to find lost people and save them" (Luke 19:10). Jesus came to pursue and to rescue those who are ruined . . . those who are being destroyed by sin...those who are lost to God. That is the nature of humanity without Christ—ruined, destroyed, lost. But hope is not lost, because Jesus pursues us! He came to save us. His life mission was very clear.

What can you learn from this clarity of purpose and vision? Simple: Be intentional about discovering and pursuing your life mission.

reflect: Are you purposing to become more like Jesus?
Go to **1 Thessalonians 4:15–18.**

They ran to tell Jesus' followers what had happened. ⁹Suddenly, Jesus met them and said, "Greetings." The women came up to him, took hold of his feet, and worshiped him. ¹⁰Then Jesus said to them, "Don't be afraid. Go and tell my followers to go on to Galilee, and they will see me there."

THE SOLDIERS REPORT TO THE LEADERS

¹¹While the women went to tell Jesus' followers, some of the soldiers who had been guarding the tomb went into the city to tell the leading priests everything that had happened. ¹²Then the priests met with the elders and made a plan. They paid the soldiers a large amount of money ¹³and said to them, "Tell the people that Jesus' followers came during the night and stole the body while you were asleep. ¹⁴If the governor hears about this, we will satisfy him and save you from trouble." ¹⁵So the soldiers kept the money and did as they were told. And that story is still spread among the people even today.

JESUS TALKS TO HIS FOLLOWERS

¹⁶The eleven followers went to Galilee to the mountain where Jesus had told them to go. ¹⁷On the mountain they saw Jesus and worshiped him, but some of them did not believe it was really Jesus. ¹⁸Then Jesus came to them and said, "All power in heaven and on earth is given to me. ¹⁹So go and make followers of all people in the world. Baptize them in the name of the Father and the Son and the Holy Spirit. ²⁰Teach them to obey everything that I have taught you, and I will be with you always, even until the end of this age."

JOHN PREPARES FOR JESUS

1 This is the beginning of the Good News about Jesus Christ, the Son of God,[n] ²as the prophet Isaiah wrote:

"I will send my messenger ahead of you,
who will prepare your way."

Malachi 3:1

³"This is a voice of one
who calls out in the desert:
'Prepare the way for the Lord.
Make the road straight for him.'"

Isaiah 40:3

⁴John was baptizing people in the desert and preaching a baptism of changed hearts and lives for the forgiveness of sins. ⁵All the people from Judea and Jerusalem were going out to him. They confessed their sins and were baptized by him in the Jordan River. ⁶John wore clothes made from camel's hair, had a leather belt around his waist, and ate locusts and wild honey. ⁷This is what John preached to the people: "There is one coming after me who is greater than I; I am not good enough even to kneel down and untie his sandals. ⁸I baptize you with water, but he will baptize you with the Holy Spirit."

JESUS IS BAPTIZED

⁹At that time Jesus came from the town of Nazareth in Galilee and was baptized by John in the Jordan River. ¹⁰Immediately, as Jesus was coming up out of the water, he saw heaven open. The Holy Spirit came down on him like a dove, ¹¹and a voice came from heaven: "You are my Son, whom I love, and I am very pleased with you."

¹²Then the Spirit sent Jesus into the desert. ¹³He was in the desert forty days and was tempted by Satan. He was with the wild animals, and the angels came and took care of him.

JESUS CHOOSES SOME FOLLOWERS

¹⁴After John was put in prison, Jesus went into Galilee, preaching the Good News from God. ¹⁵He said, "The right time has come. The kingdom of God is near. Change your hearts and lives and believe the Good News!"

¹⁶When Jesus was walking by Lake Galilee, he saw Simon[n] and his brother Andrew throwing a net into the lake because they were fishermen. ¹⁷Jesus said to them, "Come follow me, and I will make you fish for people." ¹⁸So Simon and Andrew immediately left their nets and followed him.

¹⁹Going a little farther, Jesus saw two more brothers, James and John, the sons of Zebedee. They were in a boat, mending their nets. ²⁰Jesus immediately called them, and they left their father in the boat with the hired workers and followed Jesus.

JESUS FORCES OUT AN EVIL SPIRIT

²¹Jesus and his followers went to Capernaum. On the Sabbath day he went to the synagogue and began to teach. ²²The people were amazed at his teaching, because he taught like a person who had authority, not like their teachers of the law. ²³Just then, a man was there in the synagogue who had an evil spirit in him. He shouted, ²⁴"Jesus of Nazareth! What do you want with us? Did you come to destroy us? I know who you are—God's Holy One!"

²⁵Jesus commanded the evil spirit, "Be quiet! Come out of the man!" ²⁶The evil spirit shook the man violently, gave a loud cry, and then came out of him.

²⁷The people were so amazed they asked each other, "What is happening here? This man is teaching something new, and with authority. He even gives commands to evil spirits, and they obey him." ²⁸And the news about Jesus spread quickly everywhere in the area of Galilee.

JESUS HEALS MANY PEOPLE

²⁹As soon as Jesus and his followers left the synagogue, they went with James and John to the home of Simon[n] and Andrew. ³⁰Simon's mother-in-law was sick in bed with a fever, and the people told Jesus about her. ³¹So Jesus went to her bed, took her hand,

---

1:1 **the Son of God** Some Greek copies do not have this phrase. 1:16, 29 **Simon** Simon's other name was Peter.

and helped her up. The fever left her, and she began serving them.

³²That evening, after the sun went down, the people brought to Jesus all who were sick and had demons in them. ³³The whole town gathered at the door. ³⁴Jesus healed many who had different kinds of sicknesses, and he forced many demons to leave people. But he would not allow the demons to speak, because they knew who he was.

³⁵Early the next morning, while it was still dark, Jesus woke and left the house. He went to a lonely place, where he prayed. ³⁶Simon and his friends went to look for Jesus. ³⁷When they found him, they said, "Everyone is looking for you!"

³⁸Jesus answered, "We should go to other towns around here so I can preach there too. That is the reason I came." ³⁹So he went everywhere in Galilee, preaching in the synagogues and forcing out demons.

JESUS HEALS A SICK MAN

⁴⁰A man with a skin disease came to Jesus. He fell to his knees and begged Jesus, "You can heal me if you will."

GOD'S ULTIMATE SACRIFICE

FAITH

your **wake-up** call

MARK 1:35

Have you ever asked yourself, *What made Jesus wake up each morning?* It certainly wasn't an alarm clock. Time after time, Jesus was up before anyone else, praying to his Father. What do you think made him wake up so early? My guess is that the Father woke him.

Jesus practiced full dependence. He learned obedience to his earthly father and his heavenly Father. I am sure that Joseph had a hand in waking Jesus for many years. But I am just as confident that the Father continued to wake him and call him to prayer. The Greek word gives us the proper picture. It means "to stand again." The Father whispered to Jesus, "It's time to stand again."

This verse introduces us to the daily orientation of a Christian. When we stand again, we take up the cross for one more day. We renew our submission to God's authority and we align ourselves to his purposes for the new day. Have you noticed this silent alarm clock in your life? Do you often just wake up while it is still dark, before the clock sounds or the smell of coffee fills the air?

Consider it God's whisper. He is reminding you that before anything else, the day begins with him. While it is still dark and the rest of the world sleeps, you have been called to seek his face in prayer. God is waking you in order that you can stand again with him.

reflect: Wake up with Jesus, and face the day knowing he is in your corner.
Go to **Joshua 22:5.**

[41]Jesus felt sorry for the man, so he reached out his hand and touched him and said, "I will. Be healed!" [42]Immediately the disease left the man, and he was healed.

[43]Jesus told the man to go away at once, but he warned him strongly, [44]"Don't tell anyone about this. But go and show yourself to the priest. And offer the gift Moses commanded for people who are made well.[n] This will show the people what I have done." [45]The man left there, but he began to tell everyone that Jesus had healed him, and so he spread the news about Jesus. As a result, Jesus could not enter a town if people saw him. He stayed in places where nobody lived, but people came to him from everywhere.

JESUS HEALS A PARALYZED MAN

2 A few days later, when Jesus came back to Capernaum, the news spread that he was at home. [2]Many people gathered together so that there was no room in the house, not even outside the door. And Jesus was teaching them God's message. [3]Four people came, carrying a paralyzed man. [4]Since they could not get to Jesus because of the crowd, they dug a hole in the roof right above where he was speaking. When they got through, they lowered the mat with the paralyzed man on it. [5]When Jesus saw the faith of these people, he said to the paralyzed man, "Young man, your sins are forgiven."

[6]Some of the teachers of the law were sitting there, thinking to themselves, [7]"Why does this man say things like that? He is speaking as if he were God. Only God can forgive sins."

[8]Jesus knew immediately what these teachers of the law were thinking. So he said to them, "Why are you thinking these things? [9]Which is easier: to tell this paralyzed man, 'Your sins are forgiven,' or to tell him, 'Stand up. Take your mat and walk'? [10]But I will prove to you that the Son of Man has authority on earth to forgive sins." So Jesus said to the paralyzed man, [11]"I tell you, stand up, take your mat, and go home." [12]Immediately the paralyzed man stood up, took his mat, and walked out while everyone was watching him.

The people were amazed and praised God. They said, "We have never seen anything like this!"

[13]Jesus went to the lake again. The whole crowd followed him there, and he taught them. [14]While he was walking along, he saw a man named Levi son of Alphaeus, sitting in the tax collector's booth. Jesus said to him, "Follow me," and he stood up and followed Jesus.

[15]Later, as Jesus was having dinner at Levi's house, many tax collectors and "sinners" were eating there with Jesus and his followers. Many people like this followed Jesus. [16]When the teachers of the law who were Pharisees saw Jesus eating with the tax collectors and "sinners," they asked his followers, "Why does he eat with tax collectors and sinners?"

[17]Jesus heard this and said to them, "It is not the healthy people who need a doctor, but the sick. I did not come to invite good people but to invite sinners."

JESUS' FOLLOWERS ARE CRITICIZED

[18]Now the followers of John[n] and the Pharisees often fasted[n] for a certain time. Some people came to Jesus and said, "Why do John's followers and the followers of the Pharisees often fast, but your followers don't?"

[19]Jesus answered, "The friends of the bridegroom do not fast while the bridegroom is still with them. As long as the bridegroom is with them, they cannot fast. [20]But the time will come when the bridegroom will be taken from them, and then they will fast.

[21]"No one sews a patch of unshrunk cloth over a hole in an old coat. Otherwise, the patch will shrink and pull away—the new patch will pull away from the old coat. Then the hole will be worse. [22]Also, no one ever pours new wine into old leather bags. Otherwise, the new wine will break the bags, and the wine will be ruined along with the bags. But new wine should be put into new leather bags."

JESUS IS LORD OF THE SABBATH

[23]One Sabbath day, as Jesus was walking through some fields of grain, his followers

---

1:44 Moses . . . well Read about this in Leviticus 14:1–32. **2:18 John** John the Baptist, who preached to the Jewish people about Christ's coming (Mark 1:4–8). **2:18 fasted** The people would give up eating for a special time of prayer and worship to God. It was also done to show sadness and disappointment.

For Your **Own Good**

This is one of those chapters that give Pharisees a bad name. Mark tells four quick stories about the teachers of the Jewish law who tried to trap Jesus with some legalistic doctrine, and each time Jesus simply and quickly pointed them toward a higher spiritual plane. If you think about it, each time the Pharisees spoke, they were trying to limit the work of God. In their world, there would be no healing, no regard for the weak and poor, no celebration, and no freedom. Thankfully, Jesus had a better plan for all of us to follow.

But look especially at the way this chapter ends, with Jesus saying, "The Sabbath day was made to help people; [people] were not made to be ruled by the Sabbath day" (Mark 2:27). In one sentence, he rearranges our whole understanding of the purpose of the law. God's instructions are meant for our good. They are meant to make our lives better—more stable, more successful, more satisfying.

From "You must not have any other gods except me" to "You must not want anything that belongs to your neighbor," God's law serves us by ordering our lives around his good principles. We don't serve his commandments; his commandments serve us. He planned it that way. Too often in Christian circles, however, Jesus' words here are taken to mean that the Sabbath is unimportant. Too often, instead of using this verse to refine our understanding of the Sabbath, we use it to neglect the Sabbath.

Doing so is a huge mistake. The Sabbath was made for us, so we need to understand its place in our lives. We don't need to be scared of it, and we don't need to idolize it. But we do need to keep it, just as we do the rest of the Ten Commandments. God wants us to rest, to be rejuvenated and restored, and to renew our focus on him.

Remember, in the center of the Garden of Eden were two trees: the tree of the knowledge of good and evil and the tree of life. With most issues in life, we are constantly choosing to live by one of the two trees. With an issue like the Sabbath, the tree of the knowledge of good and evil will lead us to silly, inconsequential details about what we can and cannot do on our days of rest: Can I wash my car? Walk my dog? Help my kids with their homework? If we approach the Sabbath in this way, we're headed for trouble, just like the Pharisees.

But if we live by the tree of life, and if we choose innocence, we can see that something like the Sabbath can be a wonderful benefit to us, our families, and God's purposes for our lives. The Sabbath was made for us, so let's figure out how to keep it.

TO LEARN MORE ON WHAT THE BIBLE HAS TO SAY ABOUT **FULFILLMENT,** READ THE SCRIPTURES AND DEVOTIONALS AT **PSALM 56:11, PSALM 61:1–4, PSALM 100, JONAH 4:2, PSALM 150:6, PROVERBS 2:1–5,** AND **ECCLESIASTES 2:24–26.**

began to pick some grain to eat. 24The Pharisees said to Jesus, "Why are your followers doing what is not lawful on the Sabbath day?"

25Jesus answered, "Have you never read what David did when he and those with him were hungry and needed food? 26During the time of Abiathar the high priest, David went into God's house and ate the holy bread, which is lawful only for priests to eat. And David also gave some of the bread to those who were with him."

27Then Jesus said to the Pharisees, "The Sabbath day was made to help people; they were not made to be ruled by the Sabbath day. 28So then, the Son of Man is Lord even of the Sabbath day."

JESUS HEALS A MAN'S HAND

3 Another time when Jesus went into a synagogue, a man with a crippled hand was there. 2Some people watched Jesus closely to see if he would heal the man on the Sabbath day so they could accuse him.

3Jesus said to the man with the crippled hand, "Stand up here in the middle of everyone."

4Then Jesus asked the people, "Which is lawful on the Sabbath day: to do good or to do evil, to save a life or to kill?" But they said nothing to answer him.

5Jesus was angry as he looked at the people, and he felt very sad because they were stubborn. Then he said to the man, "Hold out your hand." The man held out his hand and it was healed. 6Then the Pharisees left and began making plans with the Herodians[n] about a way to kill Jesus.

MANY PEOPLE FOLLOW JESUS

7Jesus left with his followers for the lake, and a large crowd from Galilee followed him. 8Also many people came from Judea, from Jerusalem, from Idumea, from the lands across the Jordan River, and from the area of Tyre and Sidon. When they heard what Jesus was doing, many people came to him. 9When Jesus saw the crowds, he told his followers to get a boat ready for him to keep people from crowding against him. 10He had healed many people, so all the sick were pushing toward him to touch him. 11When evil spirits saw Jesus, they fell down before him and shouted, "You are the Son of God!"

12But Jesus strongly warned them not to tell who he was.

JESUS CHOOSES HIS TWELVE APOSTLES

13Then Jesus went up on a mountain and called to him those he wanted, and they came to him. 14Jesus chose twelve and called them apostles.[n] He wanted them to be with him, and he wanted to send them out to preach 15and to have the authority to force demons out of people. 16These are the twelve men he chose: Simon (Jesus named him Peter), 17James and John, the sons of Zebedee (Jesus named them Boanerges, which means "Sons of Thunder"), 18Andrew, Philip, Bartholomew, Matthew, Thomas, James the son of Alphaeus, Thaddaeus, Simon the Zealot, 19and Judas Iscariot, who later turned against Jesus.

SOME PEOPLE SAY JESUS HAS A DEVIL

20Then Jesus went home, but again a crowd gathered. There were so many people that Jesus and his followers could not eat. 21When his family heard this, they went to get him because they thought he was out of his mind. 22But the teachers of the law from Jerusalem were saying, "Beelzebul is living inside him! He uses power from the ruler of demons to force demons out of people."

23So Jesus called the people together and taught them with stories. He said, "Satan will not force himself out of people. 24A kingdom that is divided cannot continue, 25and a family that is divided cannot continue. 26And if Satan is against himself and fights against his own people, he cannot continue; that is the end of Satan. 27No one can enter a strong person's house and steal his things unless he first ties up the strong person. Then he can steal things from the house. 28I tell you the truth, all sins that people do and all the things people say against God can be forgiven. 29But anyone who speaks against the Holy Spirit will never be forgiven; he is guilty of a sin that continues forever."

30Jesus said this because the teachers of the law said that he had an evil spirit inside him.

3:6 **Herodians** A political group that followed Herod and his family. 3:14 **and called them apostles** Some Greek copies do not have this phrase.

JESUS' TRUE FAMILY

³¹Then Jesus' mother and brothers arrived. Standing outside, they sent someone in to tell him to come out. ³²Many people were sitting around Jesus, and they said to him, "Your mother and brothers[n] are waiting for you outside."

³³Jesus asked, "Who are my mother and my brothers?" ³⁴Then he looked at those sitting around him and said, "Here are my mother and my brothers! ³⁵My true brother and sister and mother are those who do what God wants."

A STORY ABOUT PLANTING SEED

4 Again Jesus began teaching by the lake. A great crowd gathered around him, so he sat down in a boat near the shore. All the people stayed on the shore close to the water. ²Jesus taught them many things, using stories. He said, ³"Listen! A farmer went out to plant his seed. ⁴While he was planting, some seed fell by the road, and the birds

3:32 brothers Some Greek copies continue, "and sisters."

COVENANT MARRIAGE

FAMILY

rearing **great children** as you build a **great marriage**

MARK 3:25

By Jimmy Evans

C hildren are a blessing from God and one of the greatest joys in marriage. However, they also bring challenges and changes to a marriage. Two principles promote the well-being of your marriage and your children. The key issue that determines how successful we will be as parents is whether or not our marriage and children are growing and developing properly.

You are not succeeding if your children or your marriage is being ignored or suffering for the sake of the other. It is very common in marriage to ignore either the marriage or the children. Time reveals the truth about whether we have failed or succeeded. If we respect and obey these two principles, we will succeed. If we don't, both our marriage and our children will suffer.

The first principle is that marriage must be understood and practiced as a higher priority than children. However, nothing besides our relationship with God or our spouse is more important than our children. God's law of priority is inviolable. When it is violated, marriage suffers. God has established the priority of marriage, and we must respect it. Our proper relationship with God and our spouse is what makes us a good parent. Rearing children is a temporary task. Marriage is for a lifetime.

The second principle is unity. Children instinctively know how to divide their parents and how to exploit any division. We must never allow a division to compromise our marriage or our ability to parent.

reflect: Do you have proper priorities in your marriage?
Go to **2 John 2.**

Mentoring **World Changers** for **Christ**

By Peter Lowe

MARK 4:13–20

When Jesus mentored his followers, he used parables (stories) to teach them principles. The first one was about success and failure—the parable of the farmer and the four soils. The last seed fell on good soil and produced lasting success. That's what we want to see when we mentor people. We want what we sow into the hearts of others to take root, spring up, and produce a crop that will feed other people in the world.

As mentors, we are like the farmer and our seed is the Word of God. We may be the ones who sow God's Word, but only God can prepare the soil of the hearts to receive it and produce a crop. Only God can prepare hearts so that what we say is not quickly scattered and stolen by the devil, snuffed out by trouble or persecution because it did not take root, or choked out by the cares of this world.

Mentoring world changers begins with a work first being done in us. This was even true of Billy Graham. Back in 1949, he had a great crusade in Los Angeles. Right before that crusade, he struggled with the reality of the Word of God being a seed. He went out into the moonlight and prayed. He confessed his sin in trying to win people to God in his own power and agreed with God that the Bible is God's Word—that it has power to change people. The sermons in that crusade were more powerful than any he had preached before. They were the same sermons, but the difference was in Billy Graham's reliance on God's Word to accomplish God's purpose. That crusade helped establish Billy Graham as one of the greatest evangelists in the history of Christianity.

If we are to see abundant and lasting fruit in our own ministries, we, like Billy Graham, must come to that place where we rely on God rather than on our own strength. We, too, must be in agreement with the fact that it is God's Word, not us, that has the power to bring about lasting change in people and ultimately bring about change in the world.

We first are used by God to bring about change in them by sowing God's Word into their hearts. When God's Word begins to take root, the change has begun in them. Then, when other people notice that change, the tender plants are beginning to peek out from the ground of their hearts. When those plants bear fruit, they nourish other people and bring about change in the world. The goal of mentoring world changers, then, is for the fruit produced in the hearts of those we mentor to consistently nourish change in the world.

To mentor world changers, we must know the Word of God, use it, rely on it, and mentor others to do the same. In times of stress, we all tend to go back to what has been easiest for us, and many times that means returning to self-reliance. When we find ourselves returning to relying upon our own strength, we must quickly get out of our comfort zone and return to wholly relying on God. We must ensure that we are watering and fertilizing the hearts of those we mentor with the Word of God.

TO LEARN MORE ON WHAT THE BIBLE HAS TO SAY ABOUT **FUTURE**, READ THE SCRIPTURES AND DEVOTIONALS AT **PSALM 94:12, PSALM 133:1–3, JOSHUA 23:6, PROVERBS 3:5–6, PROVERBS 16:18–19,** AND **2 THESSALONIANS 3:5.**

came and ate it up. ⁵Some seed fell on rocky ground where there wasn't much dirt. That seed grew very fast, because the ground was not deep. ⁶But when the sun rose, the plants dried up because they did not have deep roots. ⁷Some other seed fell among thorny weeds, which grew and choked the good plants. So those plants did not produce a crop. ⁸Some other seed fell on good ground and began to grow. It got taller and produced a crop. Some plants made thirty times more, some made sixty times more, and some made a hundred times more."

⁹Then Jesus said, "Let those with ears use them and listen!"

JESUS TELLS WHY HE USED STORIES

¹⁰Later, when Jesus was alone, the twelve apostles and others around him asked him about the stories.

¹¹Jesus said, "You can know the secret about the kingdom of God. But to other people I tell everything by using stories ¹²so that:

'They will look and look, but they will not learn.
They will listen and listen, but they will not understand.
If they did learn and understand, they would come back to me and be forgiven.'"   *Isaiah 6:9–10*

JESUS EXPLAINS THE SEED STORY

¹³Then Jesus said to his followers, "Don't you understand this story? If you don't, how will you understand any story? ¹⁴The farmer is like a person who plants God's message in people. ¹⁵Sometimes the teaching falls on the road. This is like the people who hear the teaching of God, but Satan quickly comes and takes away the teaching that was planted in them. ¹⁶Others are like the seed planted on rocky ground. They hear the teaching and quickly accept it with joy. ¹⁷But since they don't allow the teaching to go deep into their lives, they keep it only a short time. When trouble or persecution comes because of the teaching they accepted, they quickly give up. ¹⁸Others are like the seed planted among the thorny weeds. They hear the teaching, ¹⁹but the worries of this life, the temptation of wealth, and many other evil desires keep the teaching from growing and producing fruit[n] in their lives. ²⁰Others are like the seed

planted in the good ground. They hear the teaching and accept it. Then they grow and produce fruit—sometimes thirty times more, sometimes sixty times more, and sometimes a hundred times more."

USE WHAT YOU HAVE

²¹Then Jesus said to them, "Do you hide a lamp under a bowl or under a bed? No! You put the lamp on a lampstand. ²²Everything that is hidden will be made clear and every secret thing will be made known. ²³Let those with ears use them and listen!

²⁴"Think carefully about what you hear. The way you give to others is the way God will give to you, but God will give you even more. ²⁵Those who have understanding will be given more. But those who do not have understanding, even what they have will be taken away from them."

JESUS USES A STORY ABOUT SEED

²⁶Then Jesus said, "The kingdom of God is like someone who plants seed in the ground. ²⁷Night and day, whether the person is asleep or awake, the seed still grows, but the person does not know how it grows. ²⁸By itself the earth produces grain. First the plant grows, then the head, and then all the grain in the head. ²⁹When the grain is ready, the farmer cuts it, because this is the harvest time."

A STORY ABOUT MUSTARD SEED

³⁰Then Jesus said, "How can I show you what the kingdom of God is like? What story can I use to explain it? ³¹The kingdom of God is like a mustard seed, the smallest seed you plant in the ground. ³²But when planted, this seed grows and becomes the largest of all garden plants. It produces large branches, and the wild birds can make nests in its shade."

³³Jesus used many stories like these to teach the crowd God's message—as much as they could understand. ³⁴He always used stories to teach them. But when he and his followers were alone, Jesus explained everything to them.

JESUS CALMS A STORM

³⁵That evening, Jesus said to his followers, "Let's go across the lake." ³⁶Leaving the crowd behind, they took him in the boat just

---

4:19 producing fruit To produce fruit means to have in your life the good things God wants.

as he was. There were also other boats with them. [37]A very strong wind came up on the lake. The waves came over the sides and into the boat so that it was already full of water. [38]Jesus was at the back of the boat, sleeping with his head on a cushion. His followers woke him and said, "Teacher, don't you care that we are drowning!"

[39]Jesus stood up and commanded the wind and said to the waves, "Quiet! Be still!" Then the wind stopped, and it became completely calm.

[40]Jesus said to his followers, "Why are you afraid? Do you still have no faith?"

[41]The followers were very afraid and asked each other, "Who is this? Even the wind and the waves obey him!"

A MAN WITH DEMONS INSIDE HIM

5 Jesus and his followers went to the other side of the lake to the area of the Gerasene[n] people. [2]When Jesus got out of the boat, instantly a man with an evil spirit came to him from the burial caves. [3]This man lived in the caves, and no one could tie him up, not even with a chain. [4]Many times people had used chains to tie the man's hands and feet, but he always broke them off. No one was strong enough to control him. [5]Day and night he would wander around the burial caves and on the hills, screaming and cutting himself

---

5:1 Gerasene From Gerasa, an area southeast of Lake Galilee. The exact location is uncertain and some Greek copies read "Gergesene"; others read "Gadarene."

UNDERSTANDING FREEDOM

waiting for **increase**

FINANCES

By Larry Stockstill

MARK 4:26-29

It seems like every day of our lives we are forced to wait for something, and waiting is something nobody likes to do. However, in the process of sowing and reaping, you have to understand the ingredient of "waiting." Without it you will not see increase in your finances, character, or souls won to Christ.

There is a natural progression to growth, and it can't be altered. Sowing your seed is the easy part. Looking down the road to see the harvest that will come is the fun part. But in between is the period of time called "waiting." God works in your life while you are waiting, testing you to see if he can trust you with a bountiful harvest.

God wants to make sure the motives of your heart are right—that you are obedient and willing to be a good steward. Think about this: If you received millions of dollars to give to world missions, would you? Could you really give it away? Or would you squander it on material things?

God will test your faithfulness, looking for signs of disobedience. Keep your promises to him, and set your face like flint to serve him. He will test your patience, but he will also help you if you ask. God will bless you; he promised!

reflect: What area of your life needs an increase?
Go to **Mark 5:1–20.**

with stones. ⁶While Jesus was still far away, the man saw him, ran to him, and fell down before him.

⁷The man shouted in a loud voice, "What do you want with me, Jesus, Son of the Most High God? I command you in God's name not to torture me!" ⁸He said this because Jesus was saying to him, "You evil spirit, come out of the man."

⁹Then Jesus asked him, "What is your name?"

He answered, "My name is Legion,ⁿ because we are many spirits." ¹⁰He begged Jesus again and again not to send them out of that area.

¹¹A large herd of pigs was feeding on a hill near there. ¹²The demons begged Jesus, "Send us into the pigs; let us go into them." ¹³So Jesus allowed them to do this. The evil spirits left the man and went into the pigs. Then the herd of pigs—about two thousand of them—rushed down the hill into the lake and were drowned.

5:9 Legion Means very many. A legion was about five thousand men in the Roman army.

UNDERSTANDING FREEDOM

FINANCES

stand **firm**

MARK 5:1–20   By Wendell Smith

Faith is holding steady in the face of contradiction, and faith is vision before provision. Don't say to God: "If you bless me I'll give more to you," because that is not true. If you don't give it now, you won't give it then. You have to sow for the vision in order to reap the provision.

Money is not what really supports your ministry. Faith does. It doesn't matter if you need eight million dollars or eight dollars; if God has really called you to do something, if it is truly his will and you are faithful in what you do have, he will provide the resources. If it is his plan, then it will have his backing. He supports what he inspires.

In the story of the man of Gerasene in Mark 5, Jesus and his followers got in the boat, weathered the storm, crossed to the other side, met one demon-possessed man, cast out the demons, destroyed a herd of pigs, aggravated the locals, and then returned to the starting place.

After a while, if you go back and forth from side to side a few different times you might begin to think, *OK, Lord, now make up your mind, what side do you want me on?* The issue is sometimes that you just do what he tells you to do. We do the ridiculous; he does the miraculous. Stand firm. He'll pay for the cruise if he wants you to go to the other side.

reflect: Can you see the hand of God in whatever situation you are facing?
Go to **Luke 18:17.**

[14]The herdsmen ran away and went to the town and to the countryside, telling everyone about this. So people went out to see what had happened. [15]They came to Jesus and saw the man who used to have the many evil spirits, sitting, clothed, and in his right mind. And they were frightened. [16]The people who saw this told the others what had happened to the man who had the demons living in him, and they told about the pigs. [17]Then the people began to beg Jesus to leave their area.

[18]As Jesus was getting back into the boat, the man who was freed from the demons begged to go with him.

[19]But Jesus would not let him. He said, "Go home to your family and tell them how much the Lord has done for you and how he has had mercy on you." [20]So the man left and began to tell the people in the Ten Towns[n] about what Jesus had done for him. And everyone was amazed.

JESUS GIVES LIFE TO A DEAD GIRL AND HEALS A SICK WOMAN

[21]When Jesus went in the boat back to the other side of the lake, a large crowd gathered around him there. [22]A leader of the synagogue, named Jairus, came there, saw Jesus, and fell at his feet. [23]He begged Jesus, saying again and again, "My daughter is dying. Please come and put your hands on her so she will be healed and will live." [24]So Jesus went with him.

A large crowd followed Jesus and pushed very close around him. [25]Among them was a woman who had been bleeding for twelve years. [26]She had suffered very much from many doctors and had spent all the money she had, but instead of improving, she was getting worse. [27]When the woman heard about Jesus, she came up behind him in the crowd and touched his coat. [28]She thought, "If I can just touch his clothes, I will be healed." [29]Instantly her bleeding stopped, and she felt in her body that she was healed from her disease.

[30]At once Jesus felt power go out from him. So he turned around in the crowd and asked, "Who touched my clothes?"

[31]His followers said, "Look at how many people are pushing against you! And you ask, 'Who touched me?'"

[32]But Jesus continued looking around to see who had touched him. [33]The woman, knowing that she was healed, came and fell at Jesus' feet. Shaking with fear, she told him the whole truth. [34]Jesus said to her, "Dear woman, you are made well because you believed. Go in peace; be healed of your disease."

[35]While Jesus was still speaking, some people came from the house of the synagogue leader. They said, "Your daughter is dead. There is no need to bother the teacher anymore."

[36]But Jesus paid no attention to what they said. He told the synagogue leader, "Don't be afraid; just believe."

[37]Jesus let only Peter, James, and John the brother of James go with him. [38]When they came to the house of the synagogue leader, Jesus found many people there making lots of noise and crying loudly. [39]Jesus entered the house and said to them, "Why are you crying and making so much noise? The child is not dead, only asleep." [40]But they laughed at him. So, after throwing them out of the house, Jesus took the child's father and mother and his three followers into the room where the child was. [41]Taking hold of the girl's hand, he said to her, "Talitha, koum!" (This means, "Young girl, I tell you to stand up!") [42]At once the girl stood right up and began walking. (She was twelve years old.) Everyone was completely amazed. [43]Jesus gave them strict orders not to tell people about this. Then he told them to give the girl something to eat.

JESUS GOES TO HIS HOMETOWN

6 Jesus left there and went to his hometown, and his followers went with him. [2]On the Sabbath day he taught in the synagogue. Many people heard him and were amazed, saying, "Where did this man get these teachings? What is this wisdom that has been given to him? And where did he get the power to do miracles? [3]He is just the carpenter, the son of Mary and the brother of James, Joseph, Judas, and Simon. And his sisters are here with us." So the people were upset with Jesus.

[4]Jesus said to them, "A prophet is honored everywhere except in his hometown and

---

5:20 Ten Towns In Greek, called "Decapolis." It was an area east of Lake Galilee that once had ten main towns.

with his own people and in his own home." [5]So Jesus was not able to work any miracles there except to heal a few sick people by putting his hands on them. [6]He was amazed at how many people had no faith.

Then Jesus went to other villages in that area and taught. [7]He called his twelve followers together and got ready to send them out two by two and gave them authority over evil spirits. [8]This is what Jesus commanded them: "Take nothing for your trip except a walking stick. Take no bread, no bag, and no money in your pockets. [9]Wear sandals, but take only the clothes you are wearing. [10]When you enter a house, stay there until you leave that town. [11]If the people in a certain place refuse to welcome you or listen to you, leave that place. Shake its dust off your feet[n] as a warning to them."[n]

[12]So the followers went out and preached that people should change their hearts and lives. [13]They forced many demons out and put olive oil on many sick people and healed them.

HOW JOHN THE BAPTIST WAS KILLED

[14]King Herod heard about Jesus, because he was now well known. Some people said,[n] "He is John the Baptist, who has risen from the dead. That is why he can work these miracles."

[15]Others said, "He is Elijah."[n]

Other people said, "Jesus is a prophet, like the prophets who lived long ago."

[16]When Herod heard this, he said, "I killed John by cutting off his head. Now he has risen from the dead!"

[17]Herod himself had ordered his soldiers to arrest John and put him in prison in order to please his wife, Herodias. She had been the wife of Philip, Herod's brother, but then Herod had married her. [18]John had been telling Herod, "It is not lawful for you to be married to your brother's wife." [19]So Herodias hated John and wanted to kill him. But she couldn't, [20]because Herod was afraid of John and protected him. He knew John was a good and holy man. Also, though John's preaching always bothered him, he enjoyed listening to John.

[21]Then the perfect time came for Herodias to cause John's death. On Herod's birthday, he gave a dinner party for the most important government leaders, the commanders of his army, and the most important people in Galilee. [22]When the daughter of Herodias[n] came in and danced, she pleased Herod and the people eating with him.

So King Herod said to the girl, "Ask me for anything you want, and I will give it to you." [23]He promised her, "Anything you ask for I will give to you—up to half of my kingdom."

[24]The girl went to her mother and asked, "What should I ask for?"

Her mother answered, "Ask for the head of John the Baptist."

[25]At once the girl went back to the king and said to him, "I want the head of John the Baptist right now on a platter."

[26]Although the king was very sad, he had made a promise, and his dinner guests had heard it. So he did not want to refuse what she asked. [27]Immediately the king sent a soldier to bring John's head. The soldier went and cut off John's head in the prison [28]and brought it back on a platter. He gave it to the girl, and the girl gave it to her mother. [29]When John's followers heard this, they came and got John's body and put it in a tomb.

MORE THAN FIVE THOUSAND FED

[30]The apostles gathered around Jesus and told him about all the things they had done and taught. [31]Crowds of people were coming and going so that Jesus and his followers did not even have time to eat. He said to them, "Come away by yourselves, and we will go to a lonely place to get some rest."

[32]So they went in a boat by themselves to a lonely place. [33]But many people saw them leave and recognized them. So from all the towns they ran to the place where Jesus was going, and they got there before him. [34]When he arrived, he saw a great crowd waiting. He felt sorry for them, because they were like sheep without a shepherd. So he began to teach them many things.

6:11 Shake…feet A warning. It showed that they were rejecting these people. **6:11 them** Some Greek copies continue, "I tell you the truth, on the Judgment Day it will be better for the towns of Sodom and Gomorrah than for the people of that town." See Matthew 10:15. **6:14 Some people said** Some Greek copies read "He said." **6:15 Elijah** A great prophet who spoke for God and who lived hundreds of years before Christ. See 1 Kings 17. **6:22 When…Herodias** Some Greek copies read "When his daughter Herodias."

35When it was late in the day, his followers came to him and said, "No one lives in this place, and it is already very late. 36Send the people away so they can go to the countryside and towns around here to buy themselves something to eat."

37But Jesus answered, "You give them something to eat."

They said to him, "We would all have to work a month to earn enough money to buy that much bread!"

38Jesus asked them, "How many loaves of bread do you have? Go and see."

When they found out, they said, "Five loaves and two fish."

39Then Jesus told his followers to have the people sit in groups on the green grass. 40So they sat in groups of fifty or a hundred. 41Jesus took the five loaves and two fish and, looking up to heaven, he thanked God for the food. He divided the bread and gave it to his followers for them to give to the people. Then he divided the two fish among them all. 42All the people ate and were satisfied. 43The followers filled twelve baskets with the leftover pieces of bread and fish. 44There were five thousand men who ate.

JESUS WALKS ON THE WATER

45Immediately Jesus told his followers to get into the boat and go ahead of him to Bethsaida across the lake. He stayed there to send the people home. 46After sending them away, he went into the hills to pray.

47That night, the boat was in the middle of the lake, and Jesus was alone on the land. 48He saw his followers struggling hard to row the boat, because the wind was blowing against them. Between three and six o'clock in the morning, Jesus came to them, walking on the water, and he wanted to walk past the boat. 49But when they saw him walking on the water, they thought he was a ghost and cried out. 50They all saw him and were afraid. But quickly Jesus spoke to them and said, "Have courage! It is I. Do not be afraid." 51Then he got into the boat with them, and the wind became calm. The followers were greatly amazed. 52They did not understand about the miracle of the five loaves, because their minds were closed.

53When they had crossed the lake, they came to shore at Gennesaret and tied the boat there. 54When they got out of the boat, people immediately recognized Jesus. 55They ran everywhere in that area and began to bring sick people on mats wherever they heard he was. 56And everywhere he went—into towns, cities, or countryside—the people brought the sick to the marketplaces. They begged him to let them touch just the edge of his coat, and all who touched it were healed.

OBEY GOD'S LAW

7 When some Pharisees and some teachers of the law came from Jerusalem, they gathered around Jesus. 2They saw that some of Jesus' followers ate food with hands that were not clean, that is, they hadn't washed them. 3(The Pharisees and all the Jews never eat before washing their hands in the way required by their unwritten laws. 4And when they buy something in the market, they never eat it until they wash themselves in a special way. They also follow many other unwritten laws, such as the washing of cups, pitchers, and pots."[n])

5The Pharisees and the teachers of the law said to Jesus, "Why don't your followers obey the unwritten laws which have been handed down to us? Why do your followers eat their food with hands that are not clean?"

6Jesus answered, "Isaiah was right when he spoke about you hypocrites. He wrote,

'These people show honor to me with words,
    but their hearts are far from me.
7 Their worship of me is worthless.
    The things they teach are nothing but
      human rules.'   *Isaiah 29:13*

8You have stopped following the commands of God, and you follow only human teachings."[n]

9Then Jesus said to them, "You cleverly ignore the commands of God so you can follow your own teachings. 10Moses said, 'Honor your father and your mother,'[n] and 'Anyone who says cruel things to his father or mother must be put to death.'[n] 11But you say a person can tell his father or mother,

---

7:4 pots Some Greek copies continue, "and dining couches." **7:8 teachings** Some Greek copies continue, "You wash pitchers and jugs and do many other such things." **7:10 'Honor . . . mother.'** Quotation from Exodus 20:12; Deuteronomy 5:16. **7:10 'Anyone . . . death.'** Quotation from Exodus 21:17.

'I have something I could use to help you, but it is Corban—a gift to God.' ¹²You no longer let that person use that money for his father or his mother. ¹³By your own rules, which you teach people, you are rejecting what God said. And you do many things like that."

¹⁴After Jesus called the crowd to him again, he said, "Every person should listen to me and understand what I am saying. ¹⁵There is nothing people put into their bodies that makes them unclean. People are made unclean by the things that come out of them. [¹⁶Let those with ears use them and listen.]"ⁿ

¹⁷When Jesus left the people and went into the house, his followers asked him about this story. ¹⁸Jesus said, "Do you still not understand? Surely you know that nothing that enters someone from the outside can make that person unclean. ¹⁹It does not go into the mind, but into the stomach. Then it goes out of the body." (When Jesus said this, he meant that no longer was any food unclean for people to eat.)

²⁰And Jesus said, "The things that come out of people are the things that make them unclean. ²¹All these evil things begin inside people, in the mind: evil thoughts, sexual sins, stealing, murder, adultery, ²²greed, evil actions, lying, doing sinful things, jealousy, speaking evil of others, pride, and foolish living. ²³All these evil things come from inside and make people unclean."

JESUS HELPS A NON-JEWISH WOMAN

²⁴Jesus left that place and went to the area around Tyre.ⁿ When he went into a house, he did not want anyone to know he was there, but he could not stay hidden. ²⁵A woman whose daughter had an evil spirit in her heard that he was there. So she quickly came to Jesus and fell at his feet. ²⁶She was Greek, born in Phoenicia, in Syria. She begged Jesus to force the demon out of her daughter.

²⁷Jesus told the woman, "It is not right to take the children's bread and give it to the dogs. First let the children eat all they want."

²⁸But she answered, "Yes, Lord, but even the dogs under the table can eat the children's crumbs."

²⁹Then Jesus said, "Because of your answer, you may go. The demon has left your daughter."

³⁰The woman went home and found her daughter lying in bed; the demon was gone.

JESUS HEALS A DEAF MAN

³¹Then Jesus left the area around Tyre and went through Sidon to Lake Galilee, to the area of the Ten Towns.ⁿ ³²While he was there, some people brought a man to him who was deaf and could not talk plainly. The people begged Jesus to put his hand on the man to heal him.

³³Jesus led the man away from the crowd, by himself. He put his fingers in the man's ears and then spit and touched the man's tongue. ³⁴Looking up to heaven, he sighed and said to the man, "Ephphatha!" (This means, "Be opened.") ³⁵Instantly the man was able to hear and to use his tongue so that he spoke clearly.

³⁶Jesus commanded the people not to tell anyone about what happened. But the more he commanded them, the more they told about it. ³⁷They were completely amazed and said, "Jesus does everything well. He makes the deaf hear! And those who can't talk he makes able to speak."

MORE THAN FOUR THOUSAND PEOPLE FED

8 Another time there was a great crowd with Jesus that had nothing to eat. So Jesus called his followers and said, ²"I feel sorry for these people, because they have already been with me for three days, and they have nothing to eat. ³If I send them home hungry, they will faint on the way. Some of them live a long way from here."

⁴Jesus' followers answered, "How can we get enough bread to feed all these people? We are far away from any town."

⁵Jesus asked, "How many loaves of bread do you have?"

They answered, "Seven."

⁶Jesus told the people to sit on the ground. Then he took the seven loaves, gave thanks to God, and divided the bread. He gave the pieces to his followers to give to the people, and they did so. ⁷The followers also had a few small fish. After Jesus gave thanks for the fish, he told his followers to give them to the people also. ⁸All the people ate and were satisfied. Then his followers filled seven baskets with the leftover pieces of food. ⁹There were

---

7:16 **Let . . . listen.** Some Greek copies do not contain the bracketed text. 7:24 **Tyre** Some Greek copies continue, "and Sidon." 7:31 **Ten Towns** In Greek, called "Decapolis." It was an area east of Lake Galilee that once had ten main towns.

about four thousand people who ate. After they had eaten, Jesus sent them home. 10Then right away he got into a boat with his followers and went to the area of Dalmanutha.

THE LEADERS ASK FOR A MIRACLE

11The Pharisees came to Jesus and began to ask him questions. Hoping to trap him, they asked Jesus for a miracle from God. 12Jesus sighed deeply and said, "Why do you people ask for a miracle as a sign? I tell you the truth, no sign will be given to you." 13Then Jesus left the Pharisees and went in the boat to the other side of the lake.

GUARD AGAINST WRONG TEACHINGS

14His followers had only one loaf of bread with them in the boat; they had forgotten to bring more. 15Jesus warned them, "Be careful! Beware of the yeast of the Pharisees and the yeast of Herod."

16His followers discussed the meaning of this, saying, "He said this because we have no bread."

17Knowing what they were talking about, Jesus asked them, "Why are you talking about not having bread? Do you still not see or understand? Are your minds closed? 18You have eyes, but you don't really see. You have ears, but you don't really listen. Remember when 19I divided five loaves of bread for the five thousand? How many baskets did you fill with leftover pieces of food?"

They answered, "Twelve."

20"And when I divided seven loaves of bread for the four thousand, how many baskets did you fill with leftover pieces of food?"

They answered, "Seven."

21Then Jesus said to them, "Don't you understand yet?"

JESUS HEALS A BLIND MAN

22Jesus and his followers came to Bethsaida. There some people brought a blind man to Jesus and begged him to touch the man. 23So Jesus took the blind man's hand and led him out of the village. Then he spit on the man's eyes and put his hands on the man and asked, "Can you see now?"

24The man looked up and said, "Yes, I see people, but they look like trees walking around."

25Again Jesus put his hands on the man's eyes. Then the man opened his eyes wide and

they were healed, and he was able to see everything clearly. 26Jesus told him to go home, saying, "Don't go into the town."[n]

PETER SAYS JESUS IS THE CHRIST

27Jesus and his followers went to the towns around Caesarea Philippi. While they were traveling, Jesus asked them, "Who do people say I am?"

28They answered, "Some say you are John the Baptist. Others say you are Elijah,[n] and others say you are one of the prophets."

29Then Jesus asked, "But who do you say I am?"

Peter answered, "You are the Christ."

30Jesus warned his followers not to tell anyone who he was.

31Then Jesus began to teach them that the Son of Man must suffer many things and that he would be rejected by the Jewish elders, the leading priests, and the teachers of the law. He told them that the Son of Man must be killed and then rise from the dead after three days. 32Jesus told them plainly what would happen. Then Peter took Jesus aside and began to tell him not to talk like that. 33But Jesus turned and looked at his followers. Then he told Peter not to talk that way. He said, "Go away from me, Satan![n] You don't care about the things of God, but only about things people think are important."

34Then Jesus called the crowd to him, along with his followers. He said, "If people want to follow me, they must give up the things they want. They must be willing even to give up their lives to follow me. 35Those who want to save their lives will give up true life. But those who give up their lives for me and for the Good News will have true life. 36It is worthless to have the whole world if they lose their souls. 37They could never pay enough to buy back their souls. 38The people who live now are living in a sinful and evil time. If people are ashamed of me and my teaching, the Son of Man will be ashamed of them when he comes with his Father's glory and with the holy angels."

8:26 **town** Some Greek copies continue, "Don't even go and tell anyone in the town." 8:28 **Elijah** A man who spoke for God and who lived hundreds of years before Christ. See 1 Kings 17. 8:33 **Satan** Name for the devil meaning "the enemy." Jesus means that Peter was talking like Satan.

9
Then Jesus said to the people, "I tell you the truth, some people standing here will see the kingdom of God come with power before they die."

JESUS TALKS WITH MOSES AND ELIJAH

²Six days later, Jesus took Peter, James, and John up on a high mountain by themselves. While they watched, Jesus' appearance was changed. ³His clothes became shining white, whiter than any person could make them. ⁴Then Elijah and Moses[n] appeared to them, talking with Jesus.

⁵Peter said to Jesus, "Teacher, it is good that we are here. Let us make three tents—one for you, one for Moses, and one for Elijah." ⁶Peter did not know what to say, because he and the others were so frightened.

⁷Then a cloud came and covered them, and a voice came from the cloud, saying, "This is my Son, whom I love. Listen to him!"

⁸Suddenly Peter, James, and John looked around, but they saw only Jesus there alone with them.

⁹As they were coming down the mountain, Jesus commanded them not to tell anyone about what they had seen until the Son of Man had risen from the dead.

¹⁰So the followers obeyed Jesus, but they discussed what he meant about rising from the dead.

¹¹Then they asked Jesus, "Why do the teachers of the law say that Elijah must come first?"

¹²Jesus answered, "They are right to say that Elijah must come first and make everything the way it should be. But why does the Scripture say that the Son of Man will suffer much and that people will treat him as if he were nothing? ¹³I tell you that Elijah has already come. And people did to him whatever they wanted to do, just as the Scriptures said it would happen."

JESUS HEALS A SICK BOY

¹⁴When Jesus, Peter, James, and John came back to the other followers, they saw a great crowd around them and the teachers of the law arguing with them. ¹⁵But as soon as the crowd saw Jesus, the people were surprised and ran to welcome him.

¹⁶Jesus asked, "What are you arguing about?"

¹⁷A man answered, "Teacher, I brought my son to you. He has an evil spirit in him that stops him from talking. ¹⁸When the spirit attacks him, it throws him on the ground. Then my son foams at the mouth, grinds his teeth, and becomes very stiff. I asked your followers to force the evil spirit out, but they couldn't."

¹⁹Jesus answered, "You people have no faith. How long must I stay with you? How long must I put up with you? Bring the boy to me."

²⁰So the followers brought him to Jesus. As soon as the evil spirit saw Jesus, it made the boy lose control of himself, and he fell down and rolled on the ground, foaming at the mouth.

²¹Jesus asked the boy's father, "How long has this been happening?"

The father answered, "Since he was very young. ²²The spirit often throws him into a fire or into water to kill him. If you can do anything for him, please have pity on us and help us."

²³Jesus said to the father, "You said, 'If you can!' All things are possible for the one who believes."

²⁴Immediately the father cried out, "I do believe! Help me to believe more!"

²⁵When Jesus saw that a crowd was quickly gathering, he ordered the evil spirit, saying, "You spirit that makes people unable to hear or speak, I command you to come out of this boy and never enter him again!"

²⁶The evil spirit screamed and caused the boy to fall on the ground again. Then the spirit came out. The boy looked as if he were dead, and many people said, "He is dead!" ²⁷But Jesus took hold of the boy's hand and helped him to stand up.

²⁸When Jesus went into the house, his followers began asking him privately, "Why couldn't we force that evil spirit out?"

²⁹Jesus answered, "That kind of spirit can only be forced out by prayer."[n]

JESUS TALKS ABOUT HIS DEATH

³⁰Then Jesus and his followers left that place and went through Galilee. He didn't want anyone to know where he was, ³¹because he was teaching his followers. He

---

9:4 Elijah and Moses Two of the most important Jewish leaders in the past. God had given Moses the Law, and Elijah was an important prophet. **9:29 prayer** Some Greek copies continue, "and fasting."

said to them, "The Son of Man will be handed over to people, and they will kill him. After three days, he will rise from the dead." ³²But the followers did not understand what Jesus meant, and they were afraid to ask him.

WHO IS THE GREATEST?

³³Jesus and his followers went to Capernaum. When they went into a house there, he asked them, "What were you arguing about on the road?" ³⁴But the followers did not answer, because their argument on the road was about which one of them was the greatest.

³⁵Jesus sat down and called the twelve apostles to him. He said, "Whoever wants to be the most important must be last of all and servant of all."

³⁶Then Jesus took a small child and had him stand among them. Taking the child in his arms, he said, ³⁷"Whoever accepts a child like this in my name accepts me. And whoever accepts me accepts the One who sent me."

ANYONE NOT AGAINST US IS FOR US

³⁸Then John said, "Teacher, we saw someone using your name to force demons out of a person. We told him to stop, because he does not belong to our group."

³⁹But Jesus said, "Don't stop him, because anyone who uses my name to do powerful

---

ARE YOU PROGRAMMED FOR STRESS?

become a **goal setter**

FULFILLMENT

By Dr. Ronnie Floyd

MARK 9:23

Have you ever thought about the fact that a goal is a statement of your faith?

If you have the faith to set goals for your life—goals that are based on something God has put deep within you—then even though human reason and your abilities make them seem impossible, God will be there to make them possible.

Too often we think that setting goals means we lack faith or that we aren't being led by the Spirit. But, think about this: God planned everything. He is the most orderly Being in the universe. Being led by the Spirit does not mean chaos. That's opposite of New Testament teaching. A Spirit-led person knows the direction of his or her life generally and follows God's leading in every step. God puts a vision in your heart as part of that process. Yes, there will be setbacks—that's part of the process, not an indication that you've missed God. We all failed many times learning to walk, to read, to play, to learn, to love.

That's what goal setting is all about—listening for what God will say to me. But, when we fail to listen for his voice and do not set goals, we are in essence placing our faith in ourselves and in what we can do. Goals, on the other hand, are statements of faith in God and in his purpose and plan for our lives.

reflect: Are your goals a statement of faith about what God has placed in you?
Go to **Mark 11:23–25.**

things will not easily say evil things about me. ⁴⁰Whoever is not against us is with us. ⁴¹I tell you the truth, whoever gives you a drink of water because you belong to the Christ will truly get his reward.

⁴²"If one of these little children believes in me, and someone causes that child to sin, it would be better for that person to have a large stone tied around his neck and be drowned in the sea. ⁴³If your hand causes you to sin, cut it off. It is better for you to lose part of your body and live forever than to have two hands and go to hell, where the fire never goes out. [⁴⁴In hell the worm does not die; the fire is never put out.]ⁿ ⁴⁵If your foot causes you to sin, cut it off. It is better for you to lose part of your body and to live forever than to have two feet and be thrown into hell. [⁴⁶In hell the worm does not die;

9:44 In . . . out. Some Greek copies do not contain the bracketed text.

FAMILY

SHOWING APPROVAL FOR YOUR HUSBAND

overcoming barriers to **sexual fulfillment**

MARK 10:6–8   By Jimmy Evans

Sex is what keeps marriage from becoming a business relationship. If you're not enjoying your physical relationship, you're missing what God has for you. Sex is a beautiful thing that God wants us to enjoy.

In order to enjoy sex, we have to remove the barriers to fulfillment. Sex is not only about our physical natures. It's also about our spiritual, mental, emotional, and volitional (will) dimensions. There's no such thing as ignoring certain dimensions of your marriage and then having great sex. Great sex is the fruit of a tree well tended. Listed here for your reference are the five barriers to sexual fulfillment:

1. *Lack of spiritual intimacy.* Pray together. Invite your spouse into your own "Most Holy Place."

2. *Past sin.* Your sin affects everyone and divides you from others. God wants us to confess our sin so he can forgive us.

3. *Unforgiveness.* You must forgive everyone, especially family members. Walk in love every day, or you won't be able to express healthy sexuality.

4. *Bad company.* Bad company corrupts good morals. Your close friendships should be at church. Good marriages and sexual maturity run in groups.

5. *Violation of the marriage covenant.* In marriage, you surrender the rights to your own body. You have a sacred duty to fulfill your spouse's needs.

reflect: Are you committed to overcoming the barriers to sexual fulfillment?
Go to **Hebrews 13:4.**

the fire is never put out.][n] [47]If your eye causes you to sin, take it out. It is better for you to enter the kingdom of God with only one eye than to have two eyes and be thrown into hell. [48]In hell the worm does not die; the fire is never put out. [49]Every person will be salted with fire.

[50]"Salt is good, but if the salt loses its salty taste, you cannot make it salty again. So, be full of salt, and have peace with each other."

JESUS TEACHES ABOUT DIVORCE

10 Then Jesus left that place and went into the area of Judea and across the Jordan River. Again, crowds came to him, and he taught them as he usually did.

[2]Some Pharisees came to Jesus and tried to trick him. They asked, "Is it right for a man to divorce his wife?"

[3]Jesus answered, "What did Moses command you to do?"

[4]They said, "Moses allowed a man to write out divorce papers and send her away."[n]

[5]Jesus said, "Moses wrote that command for you because you were stubborn. [6]But when God made the world, 'he made them male and female.'[n] [7]'So a man will leave his father and mother and be united with his wife,[n] [8]and the two will become one body.'[n] So there are not two, but one. [9]God has joined the two together, so no one should separate them."

[10]Later, in the house, his followers asked Jesus again about the question of divorce. [11]He answered, "Anyone who divorces his wife and marries another woman is guilty of adultery against her. [12]And the woman who divorces her husband and marries another man is also guilty of adultery."

JESUS ACCEPTS CHILDREN

[13]Some people brought their little children to Jesus so he could touch them, but his followers told them to stop. [14]When Jesus saw this, he was upset and said to them, "Let the little children come to me. Don't stop them, because the kingdom of God belongs to people who are like these children. [15]I tell you the truth, you must accept the kingdom of God as if you were a little child, or you will never enter it." [16]Then Jesus took the children in his arms, put his hands on them, and blessed them.

A RICH YOUNG MAN'S QUESTION

[17]As Jesus started to leave, a man ran to him and fell on his knees before Jesus. The man asked, "Good teacher, what must I do to have life forever?"

[18]Jesus answered, "Why do you call me good? Only God is good. [19]You know the commands: 'You must not murder anyone. You must not be guilty of adultery. You must not steal. You must not tell lies about your neighbor. You must not cheat. Honor your father and mother.'"[n]

[20]The man said, "Teacher, I have obeyed all these things since I was a boy."

[21]Jesus, looking at the man, loved him and said, "There is one more thing you need to do. Go and sell everything you have, and give the money to the poor, and you will have treasure in heaven. Then come and follow me."

[22]He was very sad to hear Jesus say this, and he left sorrowfully, because he was rich.

[23]Then Jesus looked at his followers and said, "How hard it will be for the rich to enter the kingdom of God!"

[24]The followers were amazed at what Jesus said. But he said again, "My children, it is very hard[n] to enter the kingdom of God! [25]It is easier for a camel to go through the eye of a needle than for a rich person to enter the kingdom of God."

[26]The followers were even more surprised and said to each other, "Then who can be saved?"

[27]Jesus looked at them and said, "For people this is impossible, but for God all things are possible."

[28]Peter said to Jesus, "Look, we have left everything and followed you."

[29]Jesus said, "I tell you the truth, all those who have left houses, brothers, sisters, mother, father, children, or farms for me and for the Good News [30]will get more than they left. Here in this world they will have a hundred times more homes, brothers, sisters,

---

9:46 In . . . out. Some Greek copies do not contain the bracketed text. **10:4 "Moses . . . away."** Quotation from Deuteronomy 24:1. **10:6 'he made . . . female'** Quotation from Genesis 1:27. **10:7 and . . . wife** Some Greek copies do not have this phrase. **10:7–8 'So . . . body.'** Quotation from Genesis 2:24. **10:19 'You . . . mother.'** Quotation from Exodus 20:12–16; Deuteronomy 5:16–20. **10:24 hard** Some Greek copies continue, "for those who trust in riches."

mothers, children, and fields. And with those things, they will also suffer for their belief. But in this age they will have life forever. ³¹Many who are first now will be last in the future. And many who are last now will be first in the future."

JESUS TALKS ABOUT HIS DEATH

³²As Jesus and the people with him were on the road to Jerusalem, he was leading the way. His followers were amazed, but others in the crowd who followed were afraid. Again Jesus took the twelve apostles aside and began to tell them what was about to happen in Jerusalem. ³³He said, "Look, we are going to Jerusalem. The Son of Man will be turned over to the leading priests and the teachers of the law. They will say that he must die, and they will turn him over to the non-Jewish people, ³⁴who will laugh at him and spit on him. They will beat him with whips and

THE ULTIMATE INVESTMENT

FINANCES

fulfilling treasures

MARK 10:21

The world places considerable emphasis on wealth. Some people spend their lives trying to accumulate vast fortunes. The sight is not always pretty. When Saddam Hussein was captured, he had $750,000 in cash with him in hopes of buying his freedom. For most people, that represents considerable wealth. But as this proverb suggests, it was wealth that produced nothing but trouble.

God is also interested in wealth. The only difference is that his view of wealth is not limited to economics. The Bible uses a word that means "treasure" or "storehouse." But this treasure is one that cannot be lost, stolen, or corrupted. Jesus used the same concept when he taught us about the true motivation of our hearts. What kind of treasure can never be taken away? The treasure of faith, hope, and love in our hearts and lives.

Jesus said something else about the relationship between wealth and genuine treasure. He commented that great financial wealth can be a significant hindrance to experiencing God's treasures, if one doesn't guard against it. God's treasures are found in a life of humility, a life that has left self-sufficiency behind.

But great wealth easily seduces us into self-reliance. Wealth can be a substitute for dependence on God. It is a trap for pride. Relatively few can handle wealth and remain servants of God. Have you been absorbed with the treasure syndrome? Examine your heart to see where your treasure lies and determine whether you need to make some adjustments.

reflect: Ask God to help you maintain the proper perspective toward wealth.
Go to **FINANCES:** "The Laws of Increase" at **Leviticus 26:1–13.**

crucify him. But on the third day, he will rise to life again."

TWO FOLLOWERS ASK JESUS A FAVOR

[35]Then James and John, sons of Zebedee, came to Jesus and said, "Teacher, we want to ask you to do something for us."

[36]Jesus asked, "What do you want me to do for you?"

[37]They answered, "Let one of us sit at your right side and one of us sit at your left side in your glory in your kingdom."

[38]Jesus said, "You don't understand what you are asking. Can you drink the cup that I must drink? And can you be baptized with the same kind of baptism that I must go through?"[n]

[39]They answered, "Yes, we can."

Jesus said to them, "You will drink the same cup that I will drink, and you will be baptized with the same baptism that I must go through. [40]But I cannot choose who will sit at my right or my left; those places belong to those for whom they have been prepared."

[41]When the other ten followers heard this, they began to be angry with James and John.

[42]Jesus called them together and said, "The other nations have rulers. You know that those rulers love to show their power over the people, and their important leaders love to use all their authority. [43]But it should not be that way among you. Whoever wants to become great among you must serve the rest of you like a servant. [44]Whoever wants to become the first among you must serve all of you like a slave. [45]In the same way, the Son of Man did not come to be served. He came to serve others and to give his life as a ransom for many people."

JESUS HEALS A BLIND MAN

[46]Then they came to the town of Jericho. As Jesus was leaving there with his followers and a great many people, a blind beggar named Bartimaeus son of Timaeus was sitting by the road. [47]When he heard that Jesus from Nazareth was walking by, he began to shout, "Jesus, Son of David, have mercy on me!"

[48]Many people warned the blind man to be quiet, but he shouted even more, "Son of David, have mercy on me!"

[49]Jesus stopped and said, "Tell the man to come here."

So they called the blind man, saying, "Cheer up! Get to your feet. Jesus is calling you." [50]The blind man jumped up, left his coat there, and went to Jesus.

[51]Jesus asked him, "What do you want me to do for you?"

The blind man answered, "Teacher, I want to see."

[52]Jesus said, "Go, you are healed because you believed." At once the man could see, and he followed Jesus on the road.

JESUS ENTERS JERUSALEM AS A KING

11 As Jesus and his followers were coming closer to Jerusalem, they came to the towns of Bethphage and Bethany near the Mount of Olives. From there Jesus sent two of his followers [2]and said to them, "Go to the town you can see there. When you enter it, you will quickly find a colt tied, which no one has ever ridden. Untie it and bring it here to me. [3]If anyone asks you why you are doing this, tell him its Master needs the colt, and he will send it at once."

[4]The followers went into the town, found a colt tied in the street near the door of a house, and untied it. [5]Some people were standing there and asked, "What are you doing? Why are you untying that colt?" [6]The followers answered the way Jesus told them to answer, and the people let them take the colt.

[7]They brought the colt to Jesus and put their coats on it, and Jesus sat on it. [8]Many people spread their coats on the road. Others cut branches in the fields and spread them on the road. [9]The people were walking ahead of Jesus and behind him, shouting,

"Praise God!
God bless the One who comes in the name
    of the Lord!   *Psalm 118:26*
[10] God bless the kingdom of our father David!
    That kingdom is coming!
Praise[n] to God in heaven!"

[11]Jesus entered Jerusalem and went into the Temple. After he had looked at everything, since it was already late, he went out to Bethany with the twelve apostles.

10:38 Can you . . . through? Jesus was asking if they could suffer the same terrible things that would happen to him. **11:10 Praise** Literally, "Hosanna," a Hebrew word used at first in praying to God for help, but at this time it was probably a shout of joy used in praising God or his Messiah.

Have **Faith** in **God**

By Reinhard Bonnke

MARK 11:22–24

Personal relationships, either with people or God, cannot exist without faith. Friends honor one another with mutual trust. God invites us to trust him as a friend. Naturally, as Hebrews 11:6 says, "Without faith no one can please God."

Scripture gives us assurance of God's competency with his 7,847 (counted) express promises. Most are fulfilled; some are being fulfilled daily, millions of times over. Whatever we know about a person's past, we have to trust God for their future. The Bible's central verse enshrines its central message: "It is better to trust the LORD than to trust people" (Psalm 118:8).

Faith is a natural gift of God, like seeing and hearing. Every moment, in everything we touch and do, we believe. We trust that food and transportation are good and safe. We don't think twice about leaving our money in the bank or trusting ourselves in the hands of doctors. If we don't trust somebody, it is by choice; and it is by choice if we don't trust God. It suggests a hostile attitude.

Sometimes people explain that they have no faith, and that's the way they are by nature, made that way. Unfortunately, that is not an explanation. It is an admission. Christ said, "Only believe," meaning we *can* believe. It is an act, a decision, and not to believe is also a decision. It may seem unconscious, but Christ sent the Holy Spirit into the world to expose unbelief as a reflection upon the integrity of God. The Bible

describes our nature as fallen, faulty. We need divine grace to rectify our sensitivity and disposition.

Faith is not a mental exercise for believing the impossible, believing what we know is not true. It is not believing "something" at all. Faith is trust in God. It is personal. In the Gospels, Jesus never talked about believing something would happen, a miracle perhaps, but only about believing him.

Our destiny rests on faith. We are saved by faith. "Those who believe in the Son have eternal life" (John 3:36). We simply cannot expect God ever to welcome us if we have no trust in him. Heaven would not be big enough for a man so cynical about God.

In Scripture, faith in God particularly relates to salvation, a major biblical theme. But it is more than a conversion experience. Salvation is God taking responsibility for us in all we do, for all our lives, and for eternity. It is his saving care at work. The New Testament, written in Greek, speaks of faith as both our single act, and as our continuous stance.

The Gospel of John, a special faith book, always speaks of "believing" and of receiving life while believing. By faith we receive what otherwise we cannot conceive, to know God and Jesus Christ as Savior and Lord. The God we are to put our trust in is worthy as the God who loved us and gave his Son to bear our sins on the cross.

TO LEARN MORE ON WHAT THE BIBLE HAS TO SAY ABOUT **FAITH,** READ THE SCRIPTURES AND DEVOTIONALS AT **PSALM 103:8, JEREMIAH 12:3, JEREMIAH 23:24, PROVERBS 3:21, ISAIAH 44:21,** AND **MARK 15:34.**

[12]The next day as Jesus was leaving Bethany, he became hungry. [13]Seeing a fig tree in leaf from far away, he went to see if it had any figs on it. But he found no figs, only leaves, because it was not the right season for figs. [14]So Jesus said to the tree, "May no one ever eat fruit from you again." And Jesus' followers heard him say this.

JESUS GOES TO THE TEMPLE

[15]When Jesus returned to Jerusalem, he went into the Temple and began to throw out those who were buying and selling there. He turned over the tables of those who were exchanging different kinds of money, and he upset the benches of those who were selling doves. [16]Jesus refused to allow anyone to carry goods through the Temple courts. [17]Then he taught the people, saying, "It is written in the Scriptures, 'My Temple will be called a house for prayer for people from all nations.'[n] But you are changing God's house into a 'hideout for robbers.'"[n]

[18]The leading priests and the teachers of the law heard all this and began trying to find a way to kill Jesus. They were afraid of him, because all the people were amazed at his teaching. [19]That evening, Jesus and his followers[n] left the city.

THE POWER OF FAITH

[20]The next morning as Jesus was passing by with his followers, they saw the fig tree dry and dead, even to the roots. [21]Peter remembered the tree and said to Jesus, "Teacher, look! The fig tree you cursed is dry and dead!"

[22]Jesus answered, "Have faith in God. [23]I tell you the truth, you can say to this mountain, 'Go, fall into the sea.' And if you have no doubts in your mind and believe that what you say will happen, God will do it for you. [24]So I tell you to believe that you have received the things you ask for in prayer, and God will give them to you. [25]When you are praying, if you are angry with someone, forgive him so that your Father in heaven will also forgive your sins. [[26]But if you don't forgive other people, then your Father in heaven will not forgive your sins.]"[n]

LEADERS DOUBT JESUS' AUTHORITY

[27]Jesus and his followers went again to Jerusalem. As Jesus was walking in the Temple, the leading priests, the teachers of the law, and the elders came to him. [28]They said to him, "What authority do you have to do these things? Who gave you this authority?"

[29]Jesus answered, "I will ask you one question. If you answer me, I will tell you what authority I have to do these things. [30]Tell me: When John baptized people, was that authority from God or just from other people?"

[31]They argued about Jesus' question, saying, "If we answer, 'John's baptism was from God,' Jesus will say, 'Then why didn't you believe him?' [32]But if we say, 'It was from other people,' the crowd will be against us." (These leaders were afraid of the people, because all the people believed that John was a prophet.)

[33]So they answered Jesus, "We don't know."

Jesus said to them, "Then I won't tell you what authority I have to do these things."

A STORY ABOUT GOD'S SON

12 Jesus began to use stories to teach the people. He said, "A man planted a vineyard. He put a wall around it and dug a hole for a winepress and built a tower. Then he leased the land to some farmers and left for a trip. [2]When it was time for the grapes to be picked, he sent a servant to the farmers to get his share of the grapes. [3]But the farmers grabbed the servant and beat him and sent him away empty-handed. [4]Then the man sent another servant. They hit him on the head and showed no respect for him. [5]So the man sent another servant, whom they killed. The man sent many other servants; the farmers beat some of them and killed others.

[6]"The man had one person left to send, his son whom he loved. He sent him last of all, saying, 'They will respect my son.'

[7]"But the farmers said to each other, 'This son will inherit the vineyard. If we kill him, it will be ours.' [8]So they took the son, killed him, and threw him out of the vineyard.

[9]"So what will the owner of the vineyard do? He will come and kill those farmers and will give the vineyard to other farmers.

11:17 'My Temple . . . nations.' Quotation from Isaiah 56:7. **11:17 'hideout for robbers'** Quotation from Jeremiah 7:11. **11:19 his followers** Some Greek copies mention only Jesus here. **11:26 But . . . sins.** Some Greek copies do not contain the bracketed text.

¹⁰Surely you have read this Scripture:
'The stone that the builders rejected
became the cornerstone.
¹¹ The Lord did this,
and it is wonderful to us.'"
Psalm 118:22–23

¹²The Jewish leaders knew that the story was about them. So they wanted to find a way to arrest Jesus, but they were afraid of the people. So the leaders left him and went away.

IS IT RIGHT TO PAY TAXES OR NOT?

¹³Later, the Jewish leaders sent some Pharisees and Herodians[n] to Jesus to trap him in saying something wrong. ¹⁴They came to him and said, "Teacher, we know that you are an honest man. You are not afraid of what other people think about you, because you pay no attention to who they are. And you teach the truth about God's way. Tell us: Is it right to pay taxes to Caesar or not? ¹⁵Should we pay them, or not?"

But knowing what these men were really trying to do, Jesus said to them, "Why are you trying to trap me? Bring me a coin to look at." ¹⁶They gave Jesus a coin, and he asked, "Whose image and name are on the coin?"

They answered, "Caesar's."

¹⁷Then Jesus said to them, "Give to Caesar

12:13 Herodians A political group that followed Herod and his family.

FULFILLMENT

ARE YOU PROGRAMMED FOR STRESS?

two **principles** of **faith**

MARK 11:23-25

By Billy Joe Daugherty

One of the first principles you need to apply in order to put your faith into action is found in Mark 11:23. Jesus said, "I tell you the truth, you can say to this mountain, 'Go fall in the sea.' And if you have no doubts in your mind and believe that what you say will happen, God will do it for you." Speak to your mountain, whether it is sickness, lack, difficulties in your marriage or family, or any other area. And believe that it will do as it is told. It is not you, but your faith it will obey.

Then put the second principle into play—faith works through love. "The important thing is faith—the kind of faith that works through love" (Galatians 5:6). For your faith to work, your heart must be free of all unforgiveness. Just as a car needs gasoline to run, the fuel that causes your faith to work is love. Mark 11:25 says, "When you are praying, if you are angry with someone, forgive him so that your Father in heaven will also forgive your sins."

If you are going to live by faith (and the Bible says the just will live by faith), do not speak the circumstances or words of unbelief, regardless of the mountain of challenge you are facing. Believe and speak the promises of God's Word, and trust that God will hasten to perform his word that you think in your heart and speak from your lips.

reflect: Why do you think it is so important to watch how you talk about a situation?
Go to **FULFILLMENT:** "Five Ingredients of Peace by God" at **Hebrews 6:19.**

the things that are Caesar's, and give to God the things that are God's." The men were amazed at what Jesus said.

SOME SADDUCEES TRY TO TRICK JESUS

18Then some Sadducees came to Jesus and asked him a question. (Sadducees believed that people would not rise from the dead.) 19They said, "Teacher, Moses wrote that if a man's brother dies, leaving a wife but no children, then that man must marry the widow and have children for his brother. 20Once there were seven brothers. The first brother married and died, leaving no children. 21So the second brother married the widow, but he also died and had no children. The same thing happened with the third brother. 22All seven brothers married her and died, and none of the brothers had any children. Finally the woman died too. 23Since all seven brothers had married her, when people rise from the dead, whose wife will she be?"

24Jesus answered, "Why don't you understand? Don't you know what the Scriptures say, and don't you know about the power of God? 25When people rise from the dead, they will not marry, nor will they be given to someone to marry. They will be like the angels in heaven. 26Surely you have read what God said about people rising from the dead. In the book in which Moses wrote about the burning bush,[n] it says that God told Moses, 'I am the God of Abraham, the God of Isaac, and the God of Jacob.'[n] 27God is the God of the living, not the dead. You Sadducees are wrong!"

THE MOST IMPORTANT COMMAND

28One of the teachers of the law came and heard Jesus arguing with the Sadducees. Seeing that Jesus gave good answers to their questions, he asked Jesus, "Which of the commands is most important?"

29Jesus answered, "The most important command is this: 'Listen, people of Israel! The Lord our God is the only Lord. 30Love the Lord your God with all your heart, all your soul, all your mind, and all your strength.'[n] 31The second command is this: 'Love your neighbor as you love yourself.'[n] There are no commands more important than these."

32The man answered, "That was a good answer, Teacher. You were right when you said God is the only Lord and there is no other God besides him. 33One must love God with all his heart, all his mind, and all his strength. And one must love his neighbor as he loves himself. These commands are more important than all the animals and sacrifices we offer to God."

34When Jesus saw that the man answered him wisely, Jesus said to him, "You are close to the kingdom of God." And after that, no one was brave enough to ask Jesus any more questions.

35As Jesus was teaching in the Temple, he asked, "Why do the teachers of the law say that the Christ is the son of David? 36David himself, speaking by the Holy Spirit, said:

'The Lord said to my Lord,
"Sit by me at my right side,
until I put your enemies under your
control." '   *Psalm 110:1*

37David himself calls the Christ 'Lord,' so how can the Christ be his son?" The large crowd listened to Jesus with pleasure.

38Jesus continued teaching and said, "Beware of the teachers of the law. They like to walk around wearing fancy clothes, and they love for people to greet them with respect in the marketplaces. 39They love to have the most important seats in the synagogues and at feasts. 40But they cheat widows and steal their houses and then try to make themselves look good by saying long prayers. They will receive a greater punishment."

TRUE GIVING

41Jesus sat near the Temple money box and watched the people put in their money. Many rich people gave large sums of money. 42Then a poor widow came and put in two small copper coins, which were only worth a few cents.

43Calling his followers to him, Jesus said, "I tell you the truth, this poor widow gave more than all those rich people. 44They gave only what they did not need. This woman is very poor, but she gave all she had; she gave all she had to live on."

12:26 burning bush Read Exodus 3:1–12 in the Old Testament. **12:26 'I am . . . Jacob.'** Quotation from Exodus 3:6. **12:29–30 'Listen . . . strength.'** Quotation from Deuteronomy 6:4–5. **12:31 'Love . . . yourself.'** Quotation from Leviticus 19:18.

THE TEMPLE WILL BE DESTROYED

13 As Jesus was leaving the Temple, one of his followers said to him, "Look, Teacher! How beautiful the buildings are! How big the stones are!"

2 Jesus said, "Do you see all these great buildings? Not one stone will be left on another. Every stone will be thrown down to the ground."

3 Later, as Jesus was sitting on the Mount of Olives, opposite the Temple, he was alone with Peter, James, John, and Andrew. They asked Jesus, 4 "Tell us, when will these things happen? And what will be the sign that they are going to happen?"

5 Jesus began to answer them, "Be careful that no one fools you. 6 Many people will come in my name, saying, 'I am the One,' and they will fool many people. 7 When you hear about wars and stories of wars that are coming, don't be afraid. These things must happen before the end comes. 8 Nations will fight against other nations, and kingdoms against other kingdoms. There will be earthquakes in different places, and there will be times when there is no food for people to eat. These things are like the first pains when something new is about to be born.

9 "You must be careful. People will arrest you and take you to court and beat you in their synagogues. You will be forced to stand before kings and governors, to tell them about me. This will happen to you because you follow me. 10 But before these things happen, the Good News must be told to all people. 11 When you are arrested and judged, don't worry ahead of time about what you should say. Say whatever is given you to say at that time, because it will not really be you speaking; it will be the Holy Spirit.

12 "Brothers will give their own brothers to be killed, and fathers will give their own children to be killed. Children will fight against their own parents and cause them to be put to death. 13 All people will hate you because you follow me, but those people who keep their faith until the end will be saved.

14 "You will see 'a blasphemous object that brings destruction'[n] standing where it should not be." (You who read this should understand what it means.) "At that time, the people in Judea should run away to the mountains. 15 If people are on the roofs[n] of their houses, they must not go down or go inside to get anything out of their houses. 16 If people are in the fields, they must not go back to get their coats. 17 At that time, how terrible it will be for women who are pregnant or have nursing babies! 18 Pray that these things will not happen in winter, 19 because those days will be full of trouble. There will be more trouble than there has ever been since the beginning, when God made the world, until now, and nothing as bad will ever happen again. 20 God has decided to make that terrible time short. Otherwise, no one would go on living. But God will make that time short to help the people he has chosen. 21 At that time, someone might say to you, 'Look, there is the Christ!' Or another person might say, 'There he is!' But don't believe them. 22 False Christs and false prophets will come and perform great wonders and miracles. They will try to fool even the people God has chosen, if that is possible. 23 So be careful. I have warned you about all this before it happens.

24 "During the days after this trouble comes,

'the sun will grow dark,
    and the moon will not give its light.
25 The stars will fall from the sky.
    And the powers of the heavens will be
        shaken.'   *Isaiah 13:10; 34:4*

26 "Then people will see the Son of Man coming in clouds with great power and glory. 27 Then he will send his angels all around the earth to gather his chosen people from every part of the earth and from every part of heaven.

28 "Learn a lesson from the fig tree: When its branches become green and soft and new leaves appear, you know summer is near. 29 In the same way, when you see these things happening, you will know that the time is near, ready to come. 30 I tell you the truth, all these things will happen while the people of this time are still living. 31 Earth and sky will be destroyed, but the words I have said will never be destroyed.

32 "No one knows when that day or time

13:14 'a blasphemous object that brings destruction' Mentioned in Daniel 9:27; 12:11 (cf. Daniel 11:31).
13:15 roofs In Bible times houses were built with flat roofs. The roof was used for drying things such as flax and fruit. And it was used as an extra room, as a place for worship, and as a cool place to sleep in the summer.

will be, not the angels in heaven, not even the Son. Only the Father knows. [33]Be careful! Always be ready,[n] because you don't know when that time will be. [34]It is like a man who goes on a trip. He leaves his house and lets his servants take care of it, giving each one a special job to do. The man tells the servant guarding the door always to be watchful. [35]So always be ready, because you don't know when the owner of the house will come back. It might be in the evening, or at midnight, or in the morning while it is still dark, or when the sun rises. [36]Always be ready. Otherwise he might come back suddenly and find you sleeping. [37]I tell you this, and I say this to everyone: 'Be ready!'"

THE PLAN TO KILL JESUS

14 It was now only two days before the Passover and the Feast of Unleavened Bread. The leading priests and teachers of the law were trying to find a trick to arrest Jesus and kill him. [2]But they said, "We must not do it during the feast, because the people might cause a riot."

A WOMAN WITH PERFUME FOR JESUS

[3]Jesus was in Bethany at the house of Simon, who had a skin disease. While Jesus was eating there, a woman approached him with an alabaster jar filled with very expensive perfume, made of pure nard. She opened the jar and poured the perfume on Jesus' head.

[4]Some who were there became upset and said to each other, "Why waste that perfume? [5]It was worth a full year's work. It could have been sold and the money given to the poor." And they got very angry with the woman.

[6]Jesus said, "Leave her alone. Why are you troubling her? She did an excellent thing for me. [7]You will always have the poor with you, and you can help them anytime you want. But you will not always have me. [8]This woman did the only thing she could do for me; she poured perfume on my body to prepare me for burial. [9]I tell you the truth, wherever the Good News is preached in all the world, what this woman has done will be told, and people will remember her."

JUDAS BECOMES AN ENEMY OF JESUS

[10]One of the twelve apostles, Judas Iscariot, went to talk to the leading priests to offer to hand Jesus over to them. [11]These priests were pleased about this and promised to pay Judas money. So he watched for the best time to turn Jesus in.

JESUS EATS THE PASSOVER MEAL

[12]It was now the first day of the Feast of Unleavened Bread when the Passover lamb was sacrificed. Jesus' followers said to him, "Where do you want us to go and prepare for you to eat the Passover meal?"

[13]Jesus sent two of his followers and said to them, "Go into the city and a man carrying a jar of water will meet you. Follow him. [14]When he goes into a house, tell the owner of the house, 'The Teacher says: "Where is my guest room in which I can eat the Passover meal with my followers?"' [15]The owner will show you a large room upstairs that is furnished and ready. Prepare the food for us there."

[16]So the followers left and went into the city. Everything happened as Jesus had said, so they prepared the Passover meal.

[17]In the evening, Jesus went to that house with the twelve. [18]While they were all eating, Jesus said, "I tell you the truth, one of you will turn against me—one of you eating with me now."

[19]The followers were very sad to hear this. Each one began to say to Jesus, "I am not the one, am I?"

[20]Jesus answered, "It is one of the twelve—the one who dips his bread into the bowl with me. [21]The Son of Man will die, just as the Scriptures say. But how terrible it will be for the person who hands the Son of Man over to be killed. It would be better for him if he had never been born."

THE LORD'S SUPPER

[22]While they were eating, Jesus took some bread and thanked God for it and broke it. Then he gave it to his followers and said, "Take it; this is my body."

[23]Then Jesus took a cup and thanked God for it and gave it to the followers, and they all drank from the cup.

[24]Then Jesus said, "This is my blood which is the new[n] agreement that God makes

---

13:33 **ready** Some Greek copies continue, "and pray."
14:24 **new** Some Greek copies do not have this word. Compare Luke 22:20.

with his people. This blood is poured out for many. ²⁵I tell you the truth, I will not drink of this fruit of the vine[n] again until that day when I drink it new in the kingdom of God."

²⁶After singing a hymn, they went out to the Mount of Olives.

JESUS' FOLLOWERS WILL LEAVE HIM

²⁷Then Jesus told the followers, "You will all stumble in your faith, because it is written in the Scriptures:

'I will kill the shepherd,
and the sheep will scatter.'
Zechariah 13:7

²⁸But after I rise from the dead, I will go ahead of you into Galilee."

²⁹Peter said, "Everyone else may stumble in their faith, but I will not."

14:25 fruit of the vine Product of the grapevine; this may also be translated "wine."

THE LIFE YOU WERE BORN TO LIVE

FITNESS

sweet **quality**

MARK 14:3–9

It's well known that the best place in the world from which to purchase the highest quality, most diverse technology is Japan. However, what is not as well known is the fact that at the end of the world wars Japan was the home of electronics with relatively poor quality and limited ability, whereas America was considered the best and brightest at the time.

Ironically, an American, Dr. Edward Demming, was the one who turned Japan around. He came in and rebuilt, reengineered, and redesigned everything Japan was thinking and doing. He resurrected Japan using one single concept: uncompromising quality in all areas of product and procedure.

In our times, quality often is the last thing on people's mind. Here are some examples:

1. Insurance: People buy the cheapest possible policy, all the while expecting cheap insurance to provide quality coverage.

2. Food: People compromise quality for speed by consuming fast food as a regular part of their dietary program.

The result of a "faster and/or cheaper is better" mentality is that you spend 25 percent more in the long run because you have to buy it twice. What is worse is that you live a 25 percent shorter life with 50 percent less quality. God wants you to be a good steward with your money, but God wants quality. Quality and not price alone should be the priority, particularly when it comes to your health.

reflect: Think about changes you could make to improve your quality of life.
Go to **Psalm 139:14.**

[30]Jesus answered, "I tell you the truth, tonight before the rooster crows twice you will say three times you don't know me."

[31]But Peter insisted, "I will never say that I don't know you! I will even die with you!" And all the other followers said the same thing.

JESUS PRAYS ALONE

[32]Jesus and his followers went to a place called Gethsemane. He said to them, "Sit here while I pray." [33]Jesus took Peter, James, and John with him, and he began to be very sad and troubled. [34]He said to them, "My heart is full of sorrow, to the point of death. Stay here and watch."

[35]After walking a little farther away from them, Jesus fell to the ground and prayed that, if possible, he would not have this time of suffering. [36]He prayed, "Abba,[n] Father! You can do all things. Take away this cup[n] of suffering. But do what you want, not what I want."

[37]Then Jesus went back to his followers and found them asleep. He said to Peter, "Simon, are you sleeping? Couldn't you stay awake with me for one hour? [38]Stay awake and pray for strength against temptation. The spirit wants to do what is right, but the body is weak."

[39]Again Jesus went away and prayed the same thing. [40]Then he went back to his followers, and again he found them asleep, because their eyes were very heavy. And they did not know what to say to him.

[41]After Jesus prayed a third time, he went back to his followers and said to them, "Are you still sleeping and resting? That's enough. The time has come for the Son of Man to be handed over to sinful people. [42]Get up, we must go. Look, here comes the man who has turned against me."

JESUS IS ARRESTED

[43]At once, while Jesus was still speaking, Judas, one of the twelve apostles, came up. With him were many people carrying swords and clubs who had been sent from the leading priests, the teachers of the law, and the Jewish elders.

[44]Judas had planned a signal for them, saying, "The man I kiss is Jesus. Arrest him and guard him while you lead him away." [45]So Judas went straight to Jesus and said, "Teacher!" and kissed him. [46]Then the peo-ple grabbed Jesus and arrested him. [47]One of his followers standing nearby pulled out his sword and struck the servant of the high priest and cut off his ear.

[48]Then Jesus said, "You came to get me with swords and clubs as if I were a criminal. [49]Every day I was with you teaching in the Temple, and you did not arrest me there. But all these things have happened to make the Scriptures come true." [50]Then all of Jesus' followers left him and ran away.

[51]A young man, wearing only a linen cloth, was following Jesus, and the people also grabbed him. [52]But the cloth he was wearing came off, and he ran away naked.

JESUS BEFORE THE LEADERS

[53]The people who arrested Jesus led him to the house of the high priest, where all the leading priests, the elders, and the teachers of the law were gathered. [54]Peter followed far behind and entered the courtyard of the high priest's house. There he sat with the guards, warming himself by the fire.

[55]The leading priests and the whole Jewish council tried to find something that Jesus had done wrong so they could kill him. But the council could find no proof of anything. [56]Many people came and told false things about him, but all said different things—none of them agreed.

[57]Then some people stood up and lied about Jesus, saying, [58]"We heard this man say, 'I will destroy this Temple that people made. And three days later, I will build another Temple not made by people.'" [59]But even the things these people said did not agree.

[60]Then the high priest stood before them and asked Jesus, "Aren't you going to answer? Don't you have something to say about their charges against you?" [61]But Jesus said nothing; he did not answer.

The high priest asked Jesus another question: "Are you the Christ, the Son of the blessed God?"

[62]Jesus answered, "I am. And in the future you will see the Son of Man sitting at the right hand of God, the Powerful One, and coming on clouds in the sky."

14:36 Abba Name that a Jewish child called his father.
14:36 cup Jesus is talking about the terrible things that will happen to him. Accepting these things will be very hard, like drinking a cup of something bitter.

63When the high priest heard this, he tore his clothes and said, "We don't need any more witnesses! 64You all heard him say these things against God. What do you think?"

They all said that Jesus was guilty and should die. 65Some of the people there began to spit at Jesus. They blindfolded him and beat him with their fists and said, "Prove you are a prophet!" Then the guards led Jesus away and beat him.

PETER SAYS HE DOESN'T KNOW JESUS

66While Peter was in the courtyard, a servant girl of the high priest came there. 67She saw Peter warming himself at the fire and looked closely at him.

Then she said, "You also were with Jesus, that man from Nazareth."

68But Peter said that he was never with Jesus. He said, "I don't know or understand what you are talking about." Then Peter left and went toward the entrance of the courtyard. And the rooster crowed.[n]

69The servant girl saw Peter there, and again she said to the people who were standing nearby, "This man is one of those who followed Jesus." 70Again Peter said that it was not true.

A short time later, some people were standing near Peter saying, "Surely you are one of those who followed Jesus, because you are from Galilee, too."

71Then Peter began to place a curse on himself and swear, "I don't know this man you're talking about!"

72At once, the rooster crowed the second time. Then Peter remembered what Jesus had told him: "Before the rooster crows twice, you will say three times that you don't know me." Then Peter lost control of himself and began to cry.

PILATE QUESTIONS JESUS

15 Very early in the morning, the leading priests, the elders, the teachers of the law, and all the Jewish council decided what to do with Jesus. They tied him, led him away, and turned him over to Pilate, the governor.

2Pilate asked Jesus, "Are you the king of the Jews?"

Jesus answered, "Those are your words."

3The leading priests accused Jesus of many things. 4So Pilate asked Jesus another question, "You can see that they are accusing you of many things. Aren't you going to answer?"

5But Jesus still said nothing, so Pilate was very surprised.

PILATE TRIES TO FREE JESUS

6Every year at the time of the Passover the governor would free one prisoner whom the people chose. 7At that time, there was a man named Barabbas in prison who was a rebel and had committed murder during a riot. 8The crowd came to Pilate and began to ask him to free a prisoner as he always did.

9So Pilate asked them, "Do you want me to free the king of the Jews?" 10Pilate knew that the leading priests had turned Jesus in to him because they were jealous. 11But the leading priests had persuaded the people to ask Pilate to free Barabbas, not Jesus.

12Then Pilate asked the crowd again, "So what should I do with this man you call the king of the Jews?"

13They shouted, "Crucify him!"

14Pilate asked, "Why? What wrong has he done?"

But they shouted even louder, "Crucify him!"

15Pilate wanted to please the crowd, so he freed Barabbas for them. After having Jesus beaten with whips, he handed Jesus over to the soldiers to be crucified.

16The soldiers took Jesus into the governor's palace (called the Praetorium) and called all the other soldiers together. 17They put a purple robe on Jesus and used thorny branches to make a crown for his head. 18They began to call out to him, "Hail, King of the Jews!" 19The soldiers beat Jesus on the head many times with a stick. They spit on him and made fun of him by bowing on their knees and worshiping him. 20After they finished, the soldiers took off the purple robe and put his own clothes on him again. Then they led him out of the palace to be crucified.

JESUS IS CRUCIFIED

21A man named Simon from Cyrene, the father of Alexander and Rufus, was coming from the fields to the city. The soldiers forced

---

14:68 And the rooster crowed. Some Greek copies do not have this phrase.

Simon to carry the cross for Jesus. ²²They led Jesus to the place called Golgotha, which means the Place of the Skull. ²³The soldiers tried to give Jesus wine mixed with myrrh to drink, but he refused. ²⁴The soldiers crucified Jesus and divided his clothes among themselves, throwing lots to decide what each soldier would get.

²⁵It was nine o'clock in the morning when they crucified Jesus. ²⁶There was a sign with this charge against Jesus written on it: THE KING OF THE JEWS. ²⁷They also put two robbers on crosses beside Jesus, one on the right, and the other on the left. [²⁸And the Scripture came true that says, "They put him with criminals."]ⁿ ²⁹People walked by and insulted Jesus and shook their heads, saying, "You said you could destroy the Temple and build it again in three days. ³⁰So save yourself! Come down from that cross!"

³¹The leading priests and the teachers of the law were also making fun of Jesus. They said to each other, "He saved other people, but he can't save himself. ³²If he is really the Christ, the king of Israel, let him come down now from the cross. When we see this, we will believe in him." The robbers who were being crucified beside Jesus also insulted him.

JESUS DIES

³³At noon the whole country became dark, and the darkness lasted for three hours. ³⁴At three o'clock Jesus cried in a loud voice, "Eloi, Eloi, lama sabachthani." This means, "My God, my God, why have you abandoned me?" ³⁵When some of the people standing

---

15:28 And . . . criminals. Some Greek copies do not contain the bracketed text, which quotes from Isaiah 53:12.

---

abandoned by God

FAITH

MARK 15:34

"My God, my God, why have you *abandoned* me?" But we know why Jesus cried out from the cross, don't we? God abandoned Jesus in that moment because of your sins and mine. The suffering servant is the dying Messiah. He dies because of our rejection of God's love. Our sins carried him to the cross. Our sins drove the nails into his hands and feet. And our sins brought about the greatest tragedy—and the greatest triumph—the world has ever known.

Jesus suffered because of our rejection of him. He accepted every one of those blows because we refused to bow. He paid the debt for us. We forsook the Savior while he patiently waited for each of us to say, "Forgive me, I did not know what I was doing."

On the cross, the Messiah looked our rejection right in the face and said, "I'll bear the burden of your soul." He was forsaken so we could be forgiven. That was victory, for me and for you. Isaiah said it well: "He was hated and rejected by people. . . . He had much pain and suffering." Yes, that is our Savior and our Lord.

reflect: Spend some time reflecting on how much God loves you today.
Go to **FAITH:** "Servant Evangelism" at **John 13:3-17.**

there heard this, they said, "Listen! He is calling Elijah."

³⁶Someone there ran and got a sponge, filled it with vinegar, tied it to a stick, and gave it to Jesus to drink. He said, "We want to see if Elijah will come to take him down from the cross."

³⁷Then Jesus cried in a loud voice and died.

³⁸The curtain in the Temple*ⁿ* was torn into two pieces, from the top to the bottom. ³⁹When the army officer who was standing in front of the cross saw what happened when Jesus died,*ⁿ* he said, "This man really was the Son of God!"

⁴⁰Some women were standing at a distance from the cross, watching; among them were Mary Magdalene, Salome, and Mary the mother of James and Joseph. (James was her youngest son.) ⁴¹These women had followed Jesus in Galilee and helped him. Many other women were also there who had come with Jesus to Jerusalem.

JESUS IS BURIED

⁴²This was Preparation Day. (That means the day before the Sabbath day.) That evening, ⁴³Joseph from Arimathea was brave enough to go to Pilate and ask for Jesus' body. Joseph, an important member of the Jewish council, was one of the people who was waiting for the kingdom of God to come. ⁴⁴Pilate was amazed that Jesus would have already died, so he called the army officer who had guarded Jesus and asked him if Jesus had already died. ⁴⁵The officer told Pilate that he was dead, so Pilate told Joseph he could have the body. ⁴⁶Joseph bought some linen cloth, took the body down from the cross, and wrapped it in the linen. He put the body in a tomb that was cut out of a wall of rock. Then he rolled a very large stone to block the entrance of the tomb. ⁴⁷And Mary Magdalene and Mary the mother of Joseph saw the place where Jesus was laid.

JESUS RISES FROM THE DEAD

16 The day after the Sabbath day, Mary Magdalene, Mary the mother of James, and Salome bought some sweet-smelling spices to put on Jesus' body. ²Very early on that day, the first day of the week, soon after sunrise, the women were on their way to the tomb. ³They said to each other, "Who will roll away for us the stone that covers the entrance of the tomb?"

⁴Then the women looked and saw that the stone had already been rolled away, even though it was very large. ⁵The women entered the tomb and saw a young man wearing a white robe and sitting on the right side, and they were afraid.

⁶But the man said, "Don't be afraid. You are looking for Jesus from Nazareth, who has been crucified. He has risen from the dead; he is not here. Look, here is the place they laid him. ⁷Now go and tell his followers and Peter, 'Jesus is going into Galilee ahead of you, and you will see him there as he told you before.'"

⁸The women were confused and shaking with fear, so they left the tomb and ran away. They did not tell anyone about what happened, because they were afraid.

Verses 9–20 are not included in some of the earliest surviving Greek copies of Mark.

SOME FOLLOWERS SEE JESUS

[⁹After Jesus rose from the dead early on the first day of the week, he showed himself first to Mary Magdalene. One time in the past, he had forced seven demons out of her. ¹⁰After Mary saw Jesus, she went and told his followers, who were very sad and were crying. ¹¹But Mary told them that Jesus was alive. She said that she had seen him, but the followers did not believe her.

¹²Later, Jesus showed himself to two of his followers while they were walking in the country, but he did not look the same as before. ¹³These followers went back to the others and told them what had happened, but again, the followers did not believe them.

JESUS TALKS TO THE APOSTLES

¹⁴Later Jesus showed himself to the eleven apostles while they were eating, and he criticized them because they had no faith. They were stubborn and refused to believe those who had seen him after he had risen from the dead.

15:38 curtain in the Temple A curtain divided the Most Holy Place from the other part of the Temple. That was the special building in Jerusalem where God commanded the Jewish people to worship him. **15:39 when Jesus died** Some Greek copies read "when Jesus cried out and died."

[15]Jesus said to his followers, "Go everywhere in the world, and tell the Good News to everyone. [16]Anyone who believes and is baptized will be saved, but anyone who does not believe will be punished. [17]And those who believe will be able to do these things as proof: They will use my name to force out demons. They will speak in new languages.[n] [18]They will pick up snakes and drink poison without being hurt. They will touch the sick, and the sick will be healed."

[19]After the Lord Jesus said these things to his followers, he was carried up into heaven, and he sat at the right side of God. [20]The followers went everywhere in the world and told the Good News to people, and the Lord helped them. The Lord proved that the Good News they told was true by giving them power to work miracles.]

16:17 languages This can also be translated "tongues."

luke

LUKE TELLS ABOUT JESUS
THE SAVIOR FOR ALL PEOPLE

LUKE WRITES ABOUT JESUS' LIFE

1 Many have tried to report on the things that happened among us. ²They have written the same things that we learned from others—the people who saw those things from the beginning and served God by telling people his message. ³Since I myself have studied everything carefully from the beginning, most excellent[n] Theophilus, it seemed good for me to write it out for you. I arranged it in order, ⁴to help you know that what you have been taught is true.

ZECHARIAH AND ELIZABETH

⁵During the time Herod ruled Judea, there was a priest named Zechariah who belonged to Abijah's group.[n] Zechariah's wife, Elizabeth, came from the family of Aaron. ⁶Zechariah and Elizabeth truly did what God said was good. They did everything the Lord commanded and were without fault in keeping his law. ⁷But they had no children, because Elizabeth could not have a baby, and both of them were very old.

⁸One day Zechariah was serving as a priest before God, because his group was on duty. ⁹According to the custom of the priests, he was chosen by lot to go into the Temple of the Lord and burn incense. ¹⁰There were a great many people outside praying at the time the incense was offered. ¹¹Then an angel of the Lord appeared to Zechariah, standing on the right side of the incense table. ¹²When he saw the angel, Zechariah was startled and frightened. ¹³But the angel said to him, "Zechariah, don't be afraid. God has heard your prayer. Your wife, Elizabeth, will give birth to a son, and you will name him John. ¹⁴He will bring you joy and gladness, and many people will be happy because of his birth. ¹⁵John will be a great man for the Lord. He will never drink wine or beer, and even from birth, he will be filled with the Holy Spirit. ¹⁶He will help many people of Israel return to the Lord their God. ¹⁷He will go before the Lord in spirit and power like Elijah. He will make peace between parents and their children and will bring those who are not obeying God back to the right way of thinking, to make a people ready for the coming of the Lord."

¹⁸Zechariah said to the angel, "How can I know that what you say is true? I am an old man, and my wife is old, too."

¹⁹The angel answered him, "I am Gabriel. I stand before God, who sent me to talk to you and to tell you this good news. ²⁰Now, listen! You will not be able to speak until the day these things happen, because you did not believe what I told you. But they will really happen."

²¹Outside, the people were still waiting for Zechariah and were surprised that he was staying so long in the Temple. ²²When Zechariah came outside, he could not speak to them, and they knew he had seen a vision in the Temple. He could only make signs to them and remained unable to speak. ²³When his time of service at the Temple was finished, he went home.

²⁴Later, Zechariah's wife, Elizabeth, became pregnant and did not go out of her house for five months. Elizabeth said, ²⁵"Look what the Lord has done for me! My people were ashamed[n] of me, but now the Lord has taken away that shame."

AN ANGEL APPEARS TO MARY

²⁶During Elizabeth's sixth month of pregnancy, God sent the angel Gabriel to Nazareth, a town in Galilee, ²⁷to a virgin. She was engaged to marry a man named Joseph from the family of David. Her name was Mary. ²⁸The angel came to her and said, "Greetings! The Lord has blessed you and is with you."

1:3 excellent This word was used to show respect to an important person like a king or ruler. **1:5 Abijah's group** The Jewish priests were divided into twenty-four groups. See 1 Chronicles 24. **1:25 ashamed** The Jewish people thought it was a disgrace for women not to have children.

²⁹But Mary was very startled by what the angel said and wondered what this greeting might mean.

³⁰The angel said to her, "Don't be afraid, Mary; God has shown you his grace. ³¹Listen! You will become pregnant and give birth to a son, and you will name him Jesus. ³²He will be great and will be called the Son of the Most High. The Lord God will give him the throne of King David, his ancestor. ³³He will rule over the people of Jacob forever, and his kingdom will never end."

³⁴Mary said to the angel, "How will this happen since I am a virgin?"

³⁵The angel said to Mary, "The Holy Spirit will come upon you, and the power of the Most High will cover you. For this reason the baby will be holy and will be called the Son of God. ³⁶Now Elizabeth, your relative, is also pregnant with a son though she is very old. Everyone thought she could not have a baby, but she has been pregnant for six months. ³⁷God can do anything!"

³⁸Mary said, "I am the servant of the Lord. Let this happen to me as you say!" Then the angel went away.

MARY VISITS ELIZABETH

³⁹Mary got up and went quickly to a town in the hills of Judea. ⁴⁰She came to Zechariah's house and greeted Elizabeth. ⁴¹When Elizabeth heard Mary's greeting, the unborn baby inside her jumped, and Elizabeth was filled with the Holy Spirit. ⁴²She cried out in a loud voice, "God has blessed you more than any other woman, and he has blessed the baby to which you will give birth. ⁴³Why has this good thing happened to me, that the mother of my Lord comes to me? ⁴⁴When I heard your voice, the baby inside me jumped with joy. ⁴⁵You are blessed because you believed that what the Lord said to you would really happen."

MARY PRAISES GOD

⁴⁶Then Mary said,

"My soul praises the Lord;
⁴⁷   my heart rejoices in God my Savior,
⁴⁸ because he has shown his concern for his
      humble servant girl.
From now on, all people will say that I am
      blessed,
⁴⁹   because the Powerful One has done
      great things for me.
   His name is holy.

⁵⁰ God will show his mercy forever and ever
      to those who worship and serve him.
⁵¹ He has done mighty deeds by his power.
   He has scattered the people who are
      proud
   and think great things about themselves.
⁵² He has brought down rulers from their
      thrones
   and raised up the humble.
⁵³ He has filled the hungry with good things
   and sent the rich away with nothing.
⁵⁴ He has helped his servant, the people of
      Israel,
   remembering to show them mercy
⁵⁵ as he promised to our ancestors,
   to Abraham and to his children forever."

⁵⁶Mary stayed with Elizabeth for about three months and then returned home.

THE BIRTH OF JOHN

⁵⁷When it was time for Elizabeth to give birth, she had a boy. ⁵⁸Her neighbors and relatives heard how good the Lord was to her, and they rejoiced with her.

⁵⁹When the baby was eight days old, they came to circumcise him. They wanted to name him Zechariah because this was his father's name, ⁶⁰but his mother said, "No! He will be named John."

⁶¹The people said to Elizabeth, "But no one in your family has this name." ⁶²Then they made signs to his father to find out what he would like to name him.

⁶³Zechariah asked for a writing tablet and wrote, "His name is John," and everyone was surprised. ⁶⁴Immediately Zechariah could talk again, and he began praising God. ⁶⁵All their neighbors became alarmed, and in all the mountains of Judea people continued talking about all these things. ⁶⁶The people who heard about them wondered, saying, "What will this child be?" because the Lord was with him.

ZECHARIAH PRAISES GOD

⁶⁷Then Zechariah, John's father, was filled with the Holy Spirit and prophesied:
⁶⁸ "Let us praise the Lord, the God of Israel,
   because he has come to help his people
   and has given them freedom.
⁶⁹ He has given us a powerful Savior
   from the family of God's servant David.
⁷⁰ He said that he would do this
   through his holy prophets who lived
      long ago:

71 He promised he would save us from our enemies
and from the power of all those who hate us.
72 He said he would give mercy to our ancestors
and that he would remember his holy promise.
73 God promised Abraham, our father,
74 that he would save us from the power of our enemies
so we could serve him without fear,
75 being holy and good before God as long as we live.
76 "Now you, child, will be called a prophet of the Most High God.
You will go before the Lord to prepare his way.
77 You will make his people know that they will be saved
by having their sins forgiven.
78 With the loving mercy of our God,
a new day from heaven will dawn upon us.
79 It will shine on those who live in darkness, in the shadow of death.
It will guide us into the path of peace."

80 And so the child grew up and became strong in spirit. John lived in the desert until the time when he came out to preach to Israel.

THE BIRTH OF JESUS

2 At that time, Augustus Caesar sent an order that all people in the countries under Roman rule must list their names in a register. 2This was the first registration;[n] it was taken while Quirinius was governor of Syria. 3And all went to their own towns to be registered.

4So Joseph left Nazareth, a town in Galilee, and went to the town of Bethlehem in Judea, known as the town of David. Joseph went there because he was from the family of David. 5Joseph registered with Mary, to whom he was engaged[n] and who was now pregnant. 6While they were in Bethlehem, the time came for Mary to have the baby, 7and she gave birth to her first son. Because there were no rooms left in the inn, she wrapped the baby with pieces of cloth and laid him in a feeding trough.

SHEPHERDS HEAR ABOUT JESUS

8That night, some shepherds were in the fields nearby watching their sheep. 9Then an angel of the Lord stood before them. The glory of the Lord was shining around them, and they became very frightened. 10The angel said to them, "Do not be afraid. I am bringing you good news that will be a great joy to all the people. 11Today your Savior was born in the town of David. He is Christ, the Lord. 12This is how you will know him: You will find a baby wrapped in pieces of cloth and lying in a feeding box."

13Then a very large group of angels from heaven joined the first angel, praising God and saying:

14 "Give glory to God in heaven,
and on earth let there be peace among the people who please God."[n]

15When the angels left them and went back to heaven, the shepherds said to each other, "Let's go to Bethlehem. Let's see this thing that has happened which the Lord has told us about."

16So the shepherds went quickly and found Mary and Joseph and the baby, who was lying in a feeding trough. 17When they had seen him, they told what the angels had said about this child. 18Everyone was amazed at what the shepherds said to them. 19But Mary treasured these things and continued to think about them. 20Then the shepherds went back to their sheep, praising God and thanking him for everything they had seen and heard. It had been just as the angel had told them.

21When the baby was eight days old, he was circumcised and was named Jesus, the name given by the angel before the baby began to grow inside Mary.

JESUS IS PRESENTED IN THE TEMPLE

22When the time came for Mary and Joseph to do what the law of Moses taught about being made pure,[n] they took Jesus to Jerusalem to present him to the Lord. 23(It

---

2:2 registration Census. A counting of all the people and the things they own. 2:5 engaged For the Jewish people, an engagement was a lasting agreement. It could only be broken by divorce. 2:14 and . . . God Some Greek copies read "and on earth let there be peace and goodwill among people." 2:22 pure The Law of Moses said that forty days after a Jewish woman gave birth to a son, she must be cleansed by a ceremony at the Temple. Read Leviticus 12:2–8.

is written in the law of the Lord: "Every firstborn male shall be given to the Lord.")[n] [24]Mary and Joseph also went to offer a sacrifice, as the law of the Lord says: "You must sacrifice two doves or two young pigeons."[n]

SIMEON SEES JESUS

[25]In Jerusalem lived a man named Simeon who was a good man and godly. He was waiting for the time when God would take away Israel's sorrow, and the Holy Spirit was in him. [26]Simeon had been told by the Holy Spirit that he would not die before he saw the Christ promised by the Lord. [27]The Spirit led Simeon to the Temple. When Mary and Joseph brought the baby Jesus to the Temple to do what the law said they must do, [28]Simeon took the baby in his arms and thanked God:

[29] "Now, Lord, you can let me, your servant,
   die in peace as you said.
[30] With my own eyes I have seen your
   salvation,
[31]   which you prepared before all people.
[32] It is a light for the non-Jewish people to
   see
   and an honor for your people, the
      Israelites."

[33]Jesus' father and mother were amazed at what Simeon had said about him. [34]Then Simeon blessed them and said to Mary, "God has chosen this child to cause the fall and rise of many in Israel. He will be a sign from God that many people will not accept [35]so that the thoughts of many will be made known. And the things that will happen will make your heart sad, too."

ANNA SEES JESUS

[36]There was a prophetess, Anna, from the family of Phanuel in the tribe of Asher. Anna was very old. She had once been married for seven years. [37]Then her husband died, and she was a widow for eighty-four years. Anna never left the Temple but worshiped God, going without food and praying day and night. [38]Standing there at that time, she thanked God and spoke about Jesus to all who were waiting for God to free Jerusalem.

JOSEPH AND MARY RETURN HOME

[39]When Joseph and Mary had done everything the law of the Lord commanded, they went home to Nazareth, their own town in Galilee. [40]The little child grew and became strong. He was filled with wisdom, and God's goodness was upon him.

JESUS AS A BOY

[41]Every year Jesus' parents went to Jerusalem for the Passover Feast. [42]When he was twelve years old, they went to the feast as they always did. [43]After the feast days were over, they started home. The boy Jesus stayed behind in Jerusalem, but his parents did not know it. [44]Thinking that Jesus was with them in the group, they traveled for a whole day. Then they began to look for him among their family and friends. [45]When they did not find him, they went back to Jerusalem to look for him there. [46]After three days they found Jesus sitting in the Temple with the teachers, listening to them and asking them questions. [47]All who heard him were amazed at his understanding and answers. [48]When Jesus' parents saw him, they were astonished. His mother said to him, "Son, why did you do this to us? Your father and I were very worried about you and have been looking for you."

[49]Jesus said to them, "Why were you looking for me? Didn't you know that I must be in my Father's house?" [50]But they did not understand the meaning of what he said.

[51]Jesus went with them to Nazareth and was obedient to them. But his mother kept in her mind all that had happened. [52]Jesus became wiser and grew physically. People liked him, and he pleased God.

THE PREACHING OF JOHN

3 It was the fifteenth year of the rule of Tiberius Caesar. These men were under Caesar: Pontius Pilate, the ruler of Judea; Herod, the ruler of Galilee; Philip, Herod's brother, the ruler of Iturea and Traconitis; and Lysanias, the ruler of Abilene. [2]Annas and Caiaphas were the high priests. At this time, the word of God came to John son of Zechariah in the desert. [3]He went all over the area around the Jordan River preaching a baptism of changed hearts and lives for the forgiveness of sins. [4]As it is written in the book of Isaiah the prophet:

"This is a voice of one
   who calls out in the desert:
'Prepare the way for the Lord.
   Make the road straight for him.

2:23 **"Every . . . Lord."** Quotation from Exodus 13:2.
2:24 **"You . . . pigeons."** Quotation from Leviticus 12:8.

5 Every valley should be filled in,
    and every mountain and hill should be
    made flat.
Roads with turns should be made straight,
    and rough roads should be made
    smooth.
6 And all people will know about the
    salvation of God!'"   Isaiah 40:3–5

7 To the crowds of people who came to be baptized by John, he said, "You are all snakes! Who warned you to run away from God's coming punishment? 8 Do the things that show you really have changed your hearts and lives. Don't begin to say to yourselves, 'Abraham is our father.' I tell you that God could make children for Abraham from these rocks. 9 The ax is now ready to cut down the trees, and every tree that does not produce good fruit will be cut down and thrown into the fire.'"[n]

10 The people asked John, "Then what should we do?"

11 John answered, "If you have two shirts, share with the person who does not have one. If you have food, share that also."

12 Even tax collectors came to John to be baptized. They said to him, "Teacher, what should we do?"

13 John said to them, "Don't take more taxes from people than you have been ordered to take."

14 The soldiers asked John, "What about us? What should we do?"

John said to them, "Don't force people to give you money, and don't lie about them. Be satisfied with the pay you get."

15 Since the people were hoping for the Christ to come, they wondered if John might be the one.

16 John answered everyone, "I baptize you with water, but there is one coming who is greater than I am. I am not good enough to untie his sandals. He will baptize you with the Holy Spirit and fire. 17 He will come ready to clean the grain, separating the good grain from the chaff. He will put the good part of the grain into his barn, but he will burn the chaff with a fire that cannot be put out.'"[n]

18 And John continued to preach the Good News, saying many other things to encourage the people.

19 But John spoke against Herod, the governor, because of his sin with Herodias, the wife of Herod's brother, and because of the many other evil things Herod did. 20 So Herod did something even worse: He put John in prison.

JESUS IS BAPTIZED BY JOHN

21 When all the people were being baptized by John, Jesus also was baptized. While Jesus was praying, heaven opened 22 and the Holy Spirit came down on him in the form of a dove. Then a voice came from heaven, saying, "You are my Son, whom I love, and I am very pleased with you."

THE FAMILY HISTORY OF JESUS

23 When Jesus began his ministry, he was about thirty years old. People thought that Jesus was Joseph's son.
Joseph was the son[n] of Heli.
24 Heli was the son of Matthat.
Matthat was the son of Levi.
Levi was the son of Melki.
Melki was the son of Jannai.
Jannai was the son of Joseph.
25 Joseph was the son of Mattathias.
Mattathias was the son of Amos.
Amos was the son of Nahum.
Nahum was the son of Esli.
Esli was the son of Naggai.
26 Naggai was the son of Maath.
Maath was the son of Mattathias.
Mattathias was the son of Semein.
Semein was the son of Josech.
Josech was the son of Joda.
27 Joda was the son of Joanan.
Joanan was the son of Rhesa.
Rhesa was the son of Zerubbabel.
Zerubbabel was the grandson of Shealtiel.
Shealtiel was the son of Neri.
28 Neri was the son of Melki.
Melki was the son of Addi.
Addi was the son of Cosam.
Cosam was the son of Elmadam.
Elmadam was the son of Er.
29 Er was the son of Joshua.
Joshua was the son of Eliezer.
Eliezer was the son of Jorim.
Jorim was the son of Matthat.

3:9 The ax . . . fire. This means that God is ready to punish his people who do not obey him. 3:17 He will . . . out. This means that Jesus will come to separate good people from bad people, saving the good and punishing the bad. 3:23 son "Son" in Jewish lists of ancestors can sometimes mean grandson or more distant relative.

Matthat was the son of Levi.
30 Levi was the son of Simeon.
Simeon was the son of Judah.
Judah was the son of Joseph.
Joseph was the son of Jonam.
Jonam was the son of Eliakim.
31 Eliakim was the son of Melea.
Melea was the son of Menna.
Menna was the son of Mattatha.
Mattatha was the son of Nathan.
Nathan was the son of David.
32 David was the son of Jesse.
Jesse was the son of Obed.
Obed was the son of Boaz.
Boaz was the son of Salmon.[n]
Salmon was the son of Nahshon.
33 Nahshon was the son of Amminadab.
Amminadab was the son of Admin.
Admin was the son of Arni.
Arni was the son of Hezron.
Hezron was the son of Perez.
Perez was the son of Judah.
34 Judah was the son of Jacob.
Jacob was the son of Isaac.
Isaac was the son of Abraham.
Abraham was the son of Terah.
Terah was the son of Nahor.
35 Nahor was the son of Serug.
Serug was the son of Reu.
Reu was the son of Peleg.
Peleg was the son of Eber.
Eber was the son of Shelah.
36 Shelah was the son of Cainan.
Cainan was the son of Arphaxad.
Arphaxad was the son of Shem.
Shem was the son of Noah.
Noah was the son of Lamech.
37 Lamech was the son of Methuselah.
Methuselah was the son of Enoch.
Enoch was the son of Jared.
Jared was the son of Mahalalel.
Mahalalel was the son of Kenan.
38 Kenan was the son of Enosh.
Enosh was the son of Seth.
Seth was the son of Adam.
Adam was the son of God.

JESUS IS TEMPTED BY THE DEVIL

4 Jesus, filled with the Holy Spirit, returned from the Jordan River. The Spirit led Jesus into the desert 2 where the devil tempted Jesus for forty days. Jesus ate nothing during that time, and when those days were ended, he was very hungry.

3 The devil said to Jesus, "If you are the Son of God, tell this rock to become bread."

4 Jesus answered, "It is written in the Scriptures: 'A person does not live on bread alone.'"[n]

5 Then the devil took Jesus and showed him all the kingdoms of the world in an instant. 6 The devil said to Jesus, "I will give you all these kingdoms and all their power and glory. It has all been given to me, and I can give it to anyone I wish. 7 If you worship me, then it will all be yours."

8 Jesus answered, "It is written in the Scriptures: 'You must worship the Lord your God and serve only him.'"[n]

9 Then the devil led Jesus to Jerusalem and put him on a high place of the Temple. He said to Jesus, "If you are the Son of God, jump down. 10 It is written in the Scriptures:

'He has put his angels in charge of you
    to watch over you.'   *Psalm 91:11*

11 It is also written:

'They will catch you in their hands
    so that you will not hit your foot on a
    rock.'"   *Psalm 91:12*

12 Jesus answered, "But it also says in the Scriptures: 'Do not test the Lord your God.'"[n]

13 After the devil had tempted Jesus in every way, he left him to wait until a better time.

JESUS TEACHES THE PEOPLE

14 Jesus returned to Galilee in the power of the Holy Spirit, and stories about him spread all through the area. 15 He began to teach in their synagogues, and everyone praised him.

16 Jesus traveled to Nazareth, where he had grown up. On the Sabbath day he went to the synagogue, as he always did, and stood up to read. 17 The book of Isaiah the prophet was given to him. He opened the book and found the place where this is written:

18 "The Lord has put his Spirit in me,
    because he appointed me to tell the
    Good News to the poor.
He has sent me to tell the captives they
    are free
and to tell the blind that they can see
    again.   *Isaiah 61:1*

3:32 **Salmon** Some Greek copies read "Sala." 4:4 **'A person . . . alone.'** Quotation from Deuteronomy 8:3. 4:8 **'You . . . him.'** Quotation from Deuteronomy 6:13. 4:12 **'Do . . . God.'** Quotation from Deuteronomy 6:16.

God sent me to free those who have been
   treated unfairly   *Isaiah 58:6*
19   and to announce the time when the
   Lord will show his kindness."

                                        Isaiah 61:2

20 Jesus closed the book, gave it back to
the assistant, and sat down. Everyone in the
synagogue was watching Jesus closely. 21 He
began to say to them, "While you heard these
words just now, they were coming true!"

22 All the people spoke well of Jesus and
were amazed at the words of grace he spoke.
They asked, "Isn't this Joseph's son?"

23 Jesus said to them, "I know that you will
tell me the old saying: 'Doctor, heal yourself.'
You want to say, 'We heard about the things
you did in Capernaum. Do those things here
in your own town!'" 24 Then Jesus said, "I tell
you the truth, a prophet is not accepted in his
hometown. 25 But I tell you the truth, there
were many widows in Israel during the time
of Elijah. It did not rain in Israel for three
and one-half years, and there was no food
anywhere in the whole country. 26 But Elijah
was sent to none of those widows, only to a
widow in Zarephath, a town in Sidon. 27 And
there were many with skin diseases living in
Israel during the time of the prophet Elisha.
But none of them were healed, only Naaman,
who was from the country of Syria."

28 When all the people in the synagogue
heard these things, they became very angry.
29 They got up, forced Jesus out of town, and
took him to the edge of the cliff on which the
town was built. They planned to throw him
off the edge, 30 but Jesus walked through the
crowd and went on his way.

JESUS FORCES OUT AN EVIL SPIRIT

31 Jesus went to Capernaum, a city in Galilee, and on the Sabbath day, he taught the
people. 32 They were amazed at his teaching, because he spoke with authority. 33 In
the synagogue a man who had within him
an evil spirit shouted in a loud voice, 34 "Jesus of Nazareth! What do you want with us?
Did you come to destroy us? I know who you
are—God's Holy One!"

35 Jesus commanded the evil spirit, "Be
quiet! Come out of the man!" The evil spirit
threw the man down to the ground before
all the people and then left the man without
hurting him.

36 The people were amazed and said to
each other, "What does this mean? With authority and power he commands evil spirits,
and they come out." 37 And so the news about
Jesus spread to every place in the whole
area.

JESUS HEALS MANY PEOPLE

38 Jesus left the synagogue and went to
the home of Simon.[n] Simon's mother-in-law
was sick with a high fever, and they asked
Jesus to help her. 39 He came to her side and
commanded the fever to leave. It left her, and
immediately she got up and began serving
them.

40 When the sun went down, the people
brought those who were sick to Jesus. Putting his hands on each sick person, he healed
every one of them. 41 Demons came out of
many people, shouting, "You are the Son of
God." But Jesus commanded the demons and
would not allow them to speak, because they
knew Jesus was the Christ.

42 At daybreak, Jesus went to a lonely
place, but the people looked for him. When
they found him, they tried to keep him from
leaving. 43 But Jesus said to them, "I must
preach about God's kingdom to other towns,
too. This is why I was sent."

44 Then he kept on preaching in the synagogues of Judea.[n]

JESUS' FIRST FOLLOWERS

5 One day while Jesus was standing beside Lake Galilee, many people were
pressing all around him to hear the word of
God. 2 Jesus saw two boats at the shore of the
lake. The fishermen had left them and were
washing their nets. 3 Jesus got into one of the
boats, the one that belonged to Simon,[n] and
asked him to push off a little from the land.
Then Jesus sat down and continued to teach
the people from the boat.

4 When Jesus had finished speaking, he
said to Simon, "Take the boat into deep water, and put your nets in the water to catch
some fish."

5 Simon answered, "Master, we worked
hard all night trying to catch fish, and we
caught nothing. But you say to put the nets in

4:38 Simon Simon's other name was Peter. **4:44 Judea**
Some Greek copies read "Galilee." **5:3 Simon** Simon's
other name was Peter.

the water, so I will." ⁶When the fishermen did as Jesus told them, they caught so many fish that the nets began to break. ⁷They called to their partners in the other boat to come and help them. They came and filled both boats so full that they were almost sinking.

⁸When Simon Peter saw what had happened, he bowed down before Jesus and said, "Go away from me, Lord. I am a sinful man!" ⁹He and the other fishermen were amazed at the many fish they caught, as were ¹⁰James and John, the sons of Zebedee, Simon's partners.

Jesus said to Simon, "Don't be afraid. From now on you will fish for people." ¹¹When the men brought their boats to the shore, they left everything and followed Jesus.

JESUS HEALS A SICK MAN

¹²When Jesus was in one of the towns, there was a man covered with a skin disease. When he saw Jesus, he bowed before him and begged him, "Lord, you can heal me if you will."

¹³Jesus reached out his hand and touched the man and said, "I will. Be healed!" Immediately the disease disappeared. ¹⁴Then Jesus said, "Don't tell anyone about this, but go and show yourself to the priest[n] and offer a gift for your healing, as Moses commanded.[n] This will show the people what I have done."

5:14 show . . . priest The Law of Moses said a priest must say when a Jewish person with a skin disease was well.   **5:14 Moses commanded** Read about this in Leviticus 14:1–32.

SOWING AND REAPING

the **obedience** that leads to **abundance**

FINANCES

By Larry Stockstill   LUKE 5:1-11

People crowded around Jesus on the seashore. Down the beach, two men washed their nets, their boats alongside. They were not particularly interested in Jesus; they were just pursuing their livelihood. Can you imagine Jesus walking down the beach, coming up to Peter, and asking to use his boat? Think about it. That's a pretty big request because Peter, earned his living with that boat. It provided his income. The men were tired, and it is a lot of work to set sail. Peter had many reasons to say no. Instead, he offered Jesus his most important resource. That was the greatest decision of his life!

That boat represented Peter's need. He had fished all night and caught nothing. Jesus asked for the one valuable resource Peter still had left: his boat. In essence, Peter took his need and his energy and invested it into the kingdom of God.

When you freely give an offering of time or resources to God and plant a seed from your need, the Lord responds delightedly. He longs to jump in the boat with you, take you out to the deepest waters, and fill you to overflowing with his abundance. What a blessing to know that God is on your side. I don't know about you, but I could use a boat-sinking harvest in my finances, my family, my ministry, and in every area of my life!

reflect: What are you willing to invest for eternal rewards?
Go to **Genesis 8:22.**

¹⁵But the news about Jesus spread even more. Many people came to hear Jesus and to be healed of their sicknesses, ¹⁶but Jesus often slipped away to be alone so he could pray.

JESUS HEALS A PARALYZED MAN

¹⁷One day as Jesus was teaching the people, the Pharisees and teachers of the law from every town in Galilee and Judea and from Jerusalem were there. The Lord was giving Jesus the power to heal people. ¹⁸Just then, some men were carrying on a mat a man who was paralyzed. They tried to bring him in and put him down before Jesus. ¹⁹But because there were so many people there, they could not find a way in. So they went up on the roof and lowered the man on his mat through the ceiling into the middle of the crowd right before Jesus. ²⁰Seeing their faith, Jesus said, "Friend, your sins are forgiven."

²¹The Jewish teachers of the law and the Pharisees thought to themselves, "Who is this man who is speaking as if he were God? Only God can forgive sins."

²²But Jesus knew what they were thinking and said, "Why are you thinking these things? ²³Which is easier: to say, 'Your sins are forgiven,' or to say, 'Stand up and walk'? ²⁴But I will prove to you that the Son of Man has authority on earth to forgive sins." So Jesus said to the paralyzed man, "I tell you, stand up, take your mat, and go home."

²⁵At once the man stood up before them, picked up his mat, and went home, praising God. ²⁶All the people were fully amazed and began to praise God. They were filled with much respect and said, "Today we have seen amazing things!"

LEVI FOLLOWS JESUS

²⁷After this, Jesus went out and saw a tax collector named Levi sitting in the tax collector's booth. Jesus said to him, "Follow me!" ²⁸So Levi got up, left everything, and followed him.

²⁹Then Levi gave a big dinner for Jesus at his house. Many tax collectors and other people were eating there, too. ³⁰But the Pharisees and the men who taught the law for the Pharisees began to complain to Jesus' followers, "Why do you eat and drink with tax collectors and sinners?"

³¹Jesus answered them, "It is not the healthy people who need a doctor, but the sick. ³²I have not come to invite good people but sinners to change their hearts and lives."

JESUS ANSWERS A QUESTION

³³They said to Jesus, "John's followers often fast[n] for a certain time and pray, just as the Pharisees do. But your followers eat and drink all the time."

³⁴Jesus said to them, "You cannot make the friends of the bridegroom fast while he is still with them. ³⁵But the time will come when the bridegroom will be taken away from them, and then they will fast."

³⁶Jesus told them this story: "No one takes cloth off a new coat to cover a hole in an old coat. Otherwise, he ruins the new coat, and the cloth from the new coat will not be the same as the old cloth. ³⁷Also, no one ever pours new wine into old leather bags. Otherwise, the new wine will break the bags, the wine will spill out, and the leather bags will be ruined. ³⁸New wine must be put into new leather bags. ³⁹No one after drinking old wine wants new wine, because he says, 'The old wine is better.'"

JESUS IS LORD OVER THE SABBATH

6 One Sabbath day Jesus was walking through some fields of grain. His followers picked the heads of grain, rubbed them in their hands, and ate them. ²Some Pharisees said, "Why do you do what is not lawful on the Sabbath day?"

³Jesus answered, "Have you not read what David did when he and those with him were hungry? ⁴He went into God's house and took and ate the holy bread, which is lawful only for priests to eat. And he gave some to the people who were with him." ⁵Then Jesus said to the Pharisees, "The Son of Man is Lord of the Sabbath day."

JESUS HEALS A MAN'S HAND

⁶On another Sabbath day Jesus went into the synagogue and was teaching, and a man with a crippled right hand was there. ⁷The teachers of the law and the Pharisees were watching closely to see if Jesus would heal on the Sabbath day so they could accuse him. ⁸But he knew what they were thinking, and

---

5:33 fast The people would give up eating for a special time of prayer and worship to God. It was also done to show sadness and disappointment.

he said to the man with the crippled hand, "Stand up here in the middle of everyone." The man got up and stood there. ⁹Then Jesus said to them, "I ask you, which is lawful on the Sabbath day: to do good or to do evil, to save a life or to destroy it?" ¹⁰Jesus looked around at all of them and said to the man, "Hold out your hand." The man held out his hand, and it was healed.

¹¹But the Pharisees and the teachers of the law were very angry and discussed with each other what they could do to Jesus.

JESUS CHOOSES HIS APOSTLES

¹²At that time Jesus went off to a mountain to pray, and he spent the night praying to God. ¹³The next morning, Jesus called his followers to him and chose twelve of them, whom he named apostles: ¹⁴Simon (Jesus named him Peter), his brother Andrew, James, John, Philip, Bartholomew, ¹⁵Matthew, Thomas, James son of Alphaeus, Simon (called the Zealot), ¹⁶Judas son of James, and Judas Iscariot, who later turned Jesus over to his enemies.

JESUS TEACHES AND HEALS

¹⁷Jesus and the apostles came down from the mountain, and he stood on level ground. A large group of his followers was there, as well as many people from all around Judea, Jerusalem, and the seacoast cities of Tyre and

---

THE LONGEVITY FACTOR

the **seeds** of **health**

FITNESS

LUKE 6:12

During the time that Jesus spent on earth with his followers, he walked with the people, talked with them, and ate with them on a daily basis. Healing flowed from his hands, and deliverance came from the words that he spoke. He continually gave of himself, as he taught his followers to do. Yet Jesus also encouraged his followers to take time to rest and pray.

Jesus himself took time to be alone with his Father; even though Jesus was God, he still was a man on this earth and had to have the rest and rejuvenation that spending time alone gave him. Jesus knew the human body could not continue to give out without taking time to be replenished by seeking time alone with the Father. He understood this so well that he often walked away from people who desperately needed him all because he knew that, without rest, he could not complete his mission.

You need to take time for yourself to allow your body to recuperate and build up a reserve to be able to handle the things that daily life brings you. Life's worries, daily living, and even pleasures, will take a toll on you, hindering you from becoming a mature Christian and walking in the fullness of the Lord. The Scriptures instruct us to rest in the Lord, and he will help us learn to rest. Perhaps the best way for us to succeed and grow in health is not more work, but rather rest.

reflect: Learn to lighten up and rest in the Lord.
Go to **Luke 19:1–6.**

Sidon. ¹⁸They all came to hear Jesus teach and to be healed of their sicknesses, and he healed those who were troubled by evil spirits. ¹⁹All the people were trying to touch Jesus, because power was coming from him and healing them all.

²⁰Jesus looked at his followers and said,

"You people who are poor are blessed,
because the kingdom of God belongs
to you.
²¹ You people who are now hungry are
blessed,
because you will be satisfied.
You people who are now crying are
blessed,
because you will laugh with joy.

²²"People will hate you, shut you out, insult you, and say you are evil because you follow the Son of Man. But when they do, you will be blessed. ²³Be full of joy at that time, because you have a great reward in heaven. Their ancestors did the same things to the prophets.

²⁴ "But how terrible it will be for you who
are rich,
because you have had your easy life.
²⁵ How terrible it will be for you who are full
now,
because you will be hungry.
How terrible it will be for you who are
laughing now,
because you will be sad and cry.

²⁶"How terrible when everyone says only good things about you, because their ancestors said the same things about the false prophets.

LOVE YOUR ENEMIES

²⁷"But I say to you who are listening, love your enemies. Do good to those who hate you, ²⁸bless those who curse you, pray for those who are cruel to you. ²⁹If anyone slaps you on one cheek, offer him the other cheek, too. If someone takes your coat, do not stop him from taking your shirt. ³⁰Give to everyone who asks you, and when someone takes something that is yours, don't ask for it back. ³¹Do to others what you would want them to do to you. ³²If you love only the people who love you, what praise should you get? Even sinners love the people who love them. ³³If you do good only to those who do good to you, what praise should you get? Even sin-

ners do that! ³⁴If you lend things to people, always hoping to get something back, what praise should you get? Even sinners lend to other sinners so that they can get back the same amount! ³⁵But love your enemies, do good to them, and lend to them without hoping to get anything back. Then you will have a great reward, and you will be children of the Most High God, because he is kind even to people who are ungrateful and full of sin. ³⁶Show mercy, just as your Father shows mercy.

LOOK AT YOURSELVES

³⁷"Don't judge others, and you will not be judged. Don't accuse others of being guilty, and you will not be accused of being guilty. Forgive, and you will be forgiven. ³⁸Give, and you will receive. You will be given much. Pressed down, shaken together, and running over, it will spill into your lap. The way you give to others is the way God will give to you."

³⁹Jesus told them this story: "Can a blind person lead another blind person? No! Both of them will fall into a ditch. ⁴⁰A student is not better than the teacher, but the student who has been fully trained will be like the teacher. ⁴¹"Why do you notice the little piece of dust in your friend's eye, but you don't notice the big piece of wood in your own eye? ⁴²How can you say to your friend, 'Friend, let me take that little piece of dust out of your eye' when you cannot see that big piece of wood in your own eye! You hypocrite! First, take the wood out of your own eye. Then you will see clearly to take the dust out of your friend's eye.

TWO KINDS OF FRUIT

⁴³"A good tree does not produce bad fruit, nor does a bad tree produce good fruit. ⁴⁴Each tree is known by its own fruit. People don't gather figs from thornbushes, and they don't get grapes from bushes. ⁴⁵Good people bring good things out of the good they stored in their hearts. But evil people bring evil things out of the evil they stored in their hearts. People speak the things that are in their hearts.

TWO KINDS OF PEOPLE

⁴⁶"Why do you call me, 'Lord, Lord,' but do not do what I say? ⁴⁷I will show you what everyone is like who comes to me and hears

my words and obeys. [48]That person is like a man building a house who dug deep and laid the foundation on rock. When the floods came, the water tried to wash the house away, but it could not shake it, because the house was built well. [49]But the one who hears my words and does not obey is like a man who built his house on the ground without a foundation. When the floods came, the house quickly fell and was completely destroyed."

JESUS HEALS A SOLDIER'S SERVANT

7 When Jesus finished saying all these things to the people, he went to Capernaum. [2]There was an army officer who had a servant who was very important to him. The servant was so sick he was nearly dead. [3]When the officer heard about Jesus, he sent some Jewish elders to him to ask Jesus to come and heal his servant. [4]The men went to Jesus and begged him, saying, "This officer is worthy of your help. [5]He loves our people, and he built us a synagogue."

[6]So Jesus went with the men. He was getting near the officer's house when the officer sent friends to say, "Lord, don't trouble yourself, because I am not worthy to have you come into my house. [7]That is why I did not come to you myself. But you only need to command it, and my servant will be healed. [8]I, too, am a man under the authority of others, and I have soldiers under my command. I tell one soldier, 'Go,' and he goes. I tell another soldier, 'Come,' and he comes. I say to my servant, 'Do this,' and my servant does it."

[9]When Jesus heard this, he was amazed. Turning to the crowd that was following him, he said, "I tell you, this is the greatest faith I have found anywhere, even in Israel."

[10]Those who had been sent to Jesus went back to the house where they found the servant in good health.

JESUS BRINGS A MAN BACK TO LIFE

[11]Soon afterwards Jesus went to a town called Nain, and his followers and a large crowd traveled with him. [12]When he came near the town gate, he saw a funeral. A mother, who was a widow, had lost her only son. A large crowd from the town was with the mother while her son was being carried out. [13]When the Lord saw her, he felt very sorry for her and said, "Don't cry." [14]He went up and touched the coffin, and the people who were carrying it stopped. Jesus said, "Young man, I tell you, get up!" [15]And the son sat up and began to talk. Then Jesus gave him back to his mother.

[16]All the people were amazed and began praising God, saying, "A great prophet has come to us! God has come to help his people."

[17]This news about Jesus spread through all Judea and into all the places around there.

JOHN ASKS A QUESTION

[18]John's followers told him about all these things. He called for two of his followers [19]and sent them to the Lord to ask, "Are you the One who is to come, or should we wait for someone else?"

[20]When the men came to Jesus, they said, "John the Baptist sent us to you with this question: 'Are you the One who is to come, or should we wait for someone else?'"

[21]At that time, Jesus healed many people of their sicknesses, diseases, and evil spirits, and he gave sight to many blind people. [22]Then Jesus answered John's followers, "Go tell John what you saw and heard here. The blind can see, the crippled can walk, and people with skin diseases are healed. The deaf can hear, the dead are raised to life, and the Good News is preached to the poor. [23]Those who do not stumble in their faith because of me are blessed!"

[24]When John's followers left, Jesus began talking to the people about John: "What did you go out into the desert to see? A reed[n] blown by the wind? [25]What did you go out to see? A man dressed in fine clothes? No, people who have fine clothes and much wealth live in kings' palaces. [26]But what did you go out to see? A prophet? Yes, and I tell you, John is more than a prophet. [27]This was written about him:

'I will send my messenger ahead of you,
who will prepare the way for you.'

Malachi 3:1

[28]I tell you, John is greater than any other person ever born, but even the least important person in the kingdom of God is greater than John."

7:24 reed It means that John was not ordinary or weak like grass blown by the wind.

29(When the people, including the tax collectors, heard this, they all agreed that God's teaching was good, because they had been baptized by John. 30But the Pharisees and experts on the law refused to accept God's plan for themselves; they did not let John baptize them.)

31Then Jesus said, "What shall I say about the people of this time? What are they like? 32They are like children sitting in the marketplace, calling to one another and saying,

'We played music for you, but you did not dance;

we sang a sad song, but you did not cry.'

33John the Baptist came and did not eat bread or drink wine, and you say, 'He has a demon in him.' 34The Son of Man came eating and drinking, and you say, 'Look at him! He eats too much and drinks too much wine, and he is a friend of tax collectors and sinners!' 35But wisdom is proved to be right by what it does."

A WOMAN WASHES JESUS' FEET

36One of the Pharisees asked Jesus to eat with him, so Jesus went into the Pharisee's house and sat at the table. 37A sinful woman in the town learned that Jesus was eating at the Pharisee's house. So she brought an alabaster jar of perfume 38and stood behind Jesus at his feet, crying. She began to wash his feet with her tears, and she dried them with her hair, kissing them many times and rubbing them with the perfume. 39When the Pharisee who asked Jesus to come to his house saw this, he thought to himself, "If Jesus were a prophet, he would know that the woman touching him is a sinner!"

40Jesus said to the Pharisee, "Simon, I have something to say to you."

Simon said, "Teacher, tell me."

41Jesus said, "Two people owed money to the same banker. One owed five hundred coins[n] and the other owed fifty. 42They had no money to pay what they owed, but the banker told both of them they did not have to pay him. Which person will love the banker more?"

43Simon, the Pharisee, answered, "I think it would be the one who owed him the most money."

Jesus said to Simon, "You are right." 44Then Jesus turned toward the woman and said to Simon, "Do you see this woman? When I came into your house, you gave me no water for my feet, but she washed my feet with her tears and dried them with her hair. 45You gave me no kiss of greeting, but she has been kissing my feet since I came in. 46You did not put oil on my head, but she poured perfume on my feet. 47I tell you that her many sins are forgiven, so she showed great love. But the person who is forgiven only a little will love only a little."

48Then Jesus said to her, "Your sins are forgiven."

49The people sitting at the table began to say among themselves, "Who is this who even forgives sins?"

50Jesus said to the woman, "Because you believed, you are saved from your sins. Go in peace."

THE GROUP WITH JESUS

8 After this, while Jesus was traveling through some cities and small towns, he preached and told the Good News about God's kingdom. The twelve apostles were with him, 2and also some women who had been healed of sicknesses and evil spirits: Mary, called Magdalene, from whom seven demons had gone out; 3Joanna, the wife of Cuza (the manager of Herod's house); Susanna; and many others. These women used their own money to help Jesus and his apostles.

A STORY ABOUT PLANTING SEED

4When a great crowd was gathered, and people were coming to Jesus from every town, he told them this story:

5"A farmer went out to plant his seed. While he was planting, some seed fell by the road. People walked on the seed, and the birds ate it up. 6Some seed fell on rock, and when it began to grow, it died because it had no water. 7Some seed fell among thorny weeds, but the weeds grew up with it and choked the good plants. 8And some seed fell on good ground and grew and made a hundred times more."

As Jesus finished the story, he called out, "Let those with ears use them and listen!"

9Jesus' followers asked him what this story meant.

7:41 **coins** Roman denarii. One coin was the average pay for one day's work.

¹⁰Jesus said, "You have been chosen to know the secrets about the kingdom of God. But I use stories to speak to other people so that:

'They will look, but they may not see.
They will listen, but they may not understand.'   *Isaiah 6:9*

¹¹"This is what the story means: The seed is God's message. ¹²The seed that fell beside the road is like the people who hear God's teaching, but the devil comes and takes it away from them so they cannot believe it and be saved. ¹³The seed that fell on rock is like those who hear God's teaching and accept it gladly, but they don't allow the teaching to go deep into their lives. They believe for a while, but when trouble comes, they give up. ¹⁴The seed that fell among the thorny weeds is like those who hear God's teaching, but they let the worries, riches, and pleasures of this life keep them from growing and producing good fruit. ¹⁵And the seed that fell on the good ground is like those who hear God's teaching with good, honest hearts and obey it and patiently produce good fruit.

USE WHAT YOU HAVE

¹⁶"No one after lighting a lamp covers it with a bowl or hides it under a bed. Instead, the person puts it on a lampstand so those who come in will see the light. ¹⁷Everything that is hidden will become clear, and every secret thing will be made known. ¹⁸So be careful how you listen. Those who have understanding will be given more. But those who do not have understanding, even what they think they have will be taken away from them."

JESUS' TRUE FAMILY

¹⁹Jesus' mother and brothers came to see him, but there was such a crowd they could not get to him. ²⁰Someone said to Jesus, "Your mother and your brothers are standing outside, wanting to see you."

²¹Jesus answered them, "My mother and my brothers are those who listen to God's teaching and obey it!"

JESUS CALMS A STORM

²²One day Jesus and his followers got into a boat, and he said to them, "Let's go across the lake." And so they started across. ²³While they were sailing, Jesus fell asleep. A very strong wind blew up on the lake, causing the boat to fill with water, and they were in danger.

²⁴The followers went to Jesus and woke him, saying, "Master! Master! We will drown!"

Jesus got up and gave a command to the wind and the waves. They stopped, and it became calm. ²⁵Jesus said to his followers, "Where is your faith?"

The followers were afraid and amazed and said to each other, "Who is this that commands even the wind and the water, and they obey him?"

A MAN WITH DEMONS INSIDE HIM

²⁶Jesus and his followers sailed across the lake from Galilee to the area of the Gerasene[n] people. ²⁷When Jesus got out on the land, a man from the town who had demons inside him came to Jesus. For a long time he had worn no clothes and had lived in the burial caves, not in a house. ²⁸When he saw Jesus, he cried out and fell down before him. He said with a loud voice, "What do you want with me, Jesus, Son of the Most High God? I beg you, don't torture me!" ²⁹He said this because Jesus was commanding the evil spirit to come out of the man. Many times it had taken hold of him. Though he had been kept under guard and chained hand and foot, he had broken his chains and had been forced by the demon out into a lonely place.

³⁰Jesus asked him, "What is your name?"

He answered, "Legion,"[n] because many demons were in him. ³¹The demons begged Jesus not to send them into eternal darkness.[n] ³²A large herd of pigs was feeding on a hill, and the demons begged Jesus to allow them to go into the pigs. So Jesus allowed them to do this. ³³When the demons came out of the man, they went into the pigs, and the herd ran down the hill into the lake and was drowned.

³⁴When the herdsmen saw what had happened, they ran away and told about this in the town and the countryside. ³⁵And people

---

8:26 Gerasene From Gerasa, an area southeast of Lake Galilee. The exact location is uncertain and some Greek copies read "Gadarene"; others read "Gergesene." **8:30 Legion** Means very many. A legion was about five thousand men in the Roman army. **8:31 eternal darkness** Literally, "the abyss," something like a pit or a hole that has no end.

went to see what had happened. When they came to Jesus, they found the man sitting at Jesus' feet, clothed and in his right mind, because the demons were gone. But the people were frightened. 36The people who saw this happen told the others how Jesus had made the man well. 37All the people of the Gerasene country asked Jesus to leave, because they were all very afraid. So Jesus got into the boat and went back to Galilee.

38The man whom Jesus had healed begged to go with him, but Jesus sent him away, saying, 39"Go back home and tell people how much God has done for you." So the man went all over town telling how much Jesus had done for him.

JESUS GIVES LIFE TO A DEAD GIRL AND HEALS A SICK WOMAN

40When Jesus got back to Galilee, a crowd welcomed him, because everyone was waiting for him. 41A man named Jairus, a leader of the synagogue, came to Jesus and fell at his feet, begging him to come to his house. 42Jairus' only daughter, about twelve years old, was dying.

While Jesus was on his way to Jairus' house, the people were crowding all around him. 43A woman was in the crowd who had been bleeding for twelve years,[n] but no one was able to heal her. 44She came up behind Jesus and touched the edge of his coat, and instantly her bleeding stopped. 45Then Jesus said, "Who touched me?"

When all the people said they had not touched him, Peter said, "Master, the people are all around you and are pushing against you."

46But Jesus said, "Someone did touch me, because I felt power go out from me." 47When the woman saw she could not hide, she came forward, shaking, and fell down before Jesus. While all the people listened, she told why she had touched him and how she had been instantly healed. 48Jesus said to her, "Dear woman, you are made well because you believed. Go in peace."

49While Jesus was still speaking, someone came from the house of the synagogue leader and said to him, "Your daughter is dead. Don't bother the teacher anymore."

50When Jesus heard this, he said to Jairus, "Don't be afraid. Just believe, and your daughter will be well."

51When Jesus went to the house, he let only Peter, John, James, and the girl's father and mother go inside with him. 52All the people were crying and feeling sad because the girl was dead, but Jesus said, "Stop crying. She is not dead, only asleep."

53The people laughed at Jesus because they knew the girl was dead. 54But Jesus took hold of her hand and called to her, "My child, stand up!" 55Her spirit came back into her, and she stood up at once. Then Jesus ordered that she be given something to eat. 56The girl's parents were amazed, but Jesus told them not to tell anyone what had happened.

JESUS SENDS OUT THE APOSTLES

9 Jesus called the twelve apostles together and gave them power and authority over all demons and the ability to heal sicknesses. 2He sent the apostles out to tell about God's kingdom and to heal the sick. 3He said to them, "Take nothing for your trip, neither a walking stick, bag, bread, money, or extra clothes. 4When you enter a house, stay there until it is time to leave. 5If people do not welcome you, shake the dust off of your feet[n] as you leave the town, as a warning to them."

6So the apostles went out and traveled through all the towns, preaching the Good News and healing people everywhere.

HEROD IS CONFUSED ABOUT JESUS

7Herod, the governor, heard about all the things that were happening and was confused, because some people said, "John the Baptist has risen from the dead." 8Others said, "Elijah has come to us." And still others said, "One of the prophets who lived long ago has risen from the dead." 9Herod said, "I cut off John's head, so who is this man I hear such things about?" And Herod kept trying to see Jesus.

MORE THAN FIVE THOUSAND FED

10When the apostles returned, they told Jesus everything they had done. Then Jesus took them with him to a town called Bethsaida where they could be alone together. 11But the people learned where Jesus went and followed him. He welcomed them and

---

8:43 years Some Greek copies continue, "and she had spent all the money she had on doctors." **9:5 shake ... feet** A warning. It showed that they had rejected these people.

talked with them about God's kingdom and healed those who needed to be healed.

[12]Late in the afternoon, the twelve apostles came to Jesus and said, "Send the people away. They need to go to the towns and countryside around here and find places to sleep and something to eat, because no one lives in this place."

[13]But Jesus said to them, "You give them something to eat."

They said, "We have only five loaves of bread and two fish, unless we go buy food for all these people." [14](There were about five thousand men there.)

Jesus said to his followers, "Tell the people to sit in groups of about fifty people."

[15]So the followers did this, and all the people sat down. [16]Then Jesus took the five loaves of bread and two fish, and looking up to heaven, he thanked God for the food. Then he divided the food and gave it to the followers to give to the people. [17]They all ate and were satisfied, and what was left over was gathered up, filling twelve baskets.

JESUS IS THE CHRIST

[18]One time when Jesus was praying alone, his followers were with him, and he asked them, "Who do the people say I am?"

[19]They answered, "Some say you are John the Baptist. Others say you are Elijah.[n] And others say you are one of the prophets from long ago who has come back to life."

[20]Then Jesus asked, "But who do you say I am?"

Peter answered, "You are the Christ from God."

[21]Jesus warned them not to tell anyone, saying, [22]"The Son of Man must suffer many things. He will be rejected by the Jewish elders, the leading priests, and the teachers of the law. He will be killed and after three days will be raised from the dead."

[23]Jesus said to all of them, "If people want to follow me, they must give up the things they want. They must be willing to give up their lives daily to follow me. [24]Those who want to save their lives will give up true life. But those who give up their lives for me will have true life. [25]It is worthless to have the whole world if they themselves are destroyed or lost. [26]If people are ashamed of me and my teaching, then the Son of Man will be ashamed of them when he comes in his glory and with the glory of the Father and the holy angels. [27]I tell you the truth, some people standing here will see the kingdom of God before they die."

JESUS TALKS WITH MOSES AND ELIJAH

[28]About eight days after Jesus said these things, he took Peter, John, and James and went up on a mountain to pray. [29]While Jesus was praying, the appearance of his face changed, and his clothes became shining white. [30]Then two men, Moses and Elijah,[n] were talking with Jesus. [31]They appeared in heavenly glory, talking about his departure which he would soon bring about in Jerusalem. [32]Peter and the others were very sleepy, but when they awoke fully, they saw the glory of Jesus and the two men standing with him. [33]When Moses and Elijah were about to leave, Peter said to Jesus, "Master, it is good that we are here. Let us make three tents—one for you, one for Moses, and one for Elijah." (Peter did not know what he was talking about.)

[34]While he was saying these things, a cloud came and covered them, and they became afraid as the cloud covered them. [35]A voice came from the cloud, saying, "This is my Son, whom I have chosen. Listen to him!"

[36]When the voice finished speaking, only Jesus was there. Peter, John, and James said nothing and told no one at that time what they had seen.

JESUS HEALS A SICK BOY

[37]The next day, when they came down from the mountain, a large crowd met Jesus. [38]A man in the crowd shouted to him, "Teacher, please come and look at my son, because he is my only child. [39]An evil spirit seizes my son, and suddenly he screams. It causes him to lose control of himself and foam at the mouth. The evil spirit keeps on hurting him and almost never leaves him. [40]I begged your followers to force the evil spirit out, but they could not do it."

9:19 Elijah A man who spoke for God and who lived hundreds of years before Christ. See 1 Kings 17. **9:30 Moses and Elijah** Two of the most important Jewish leaders in the past. God had given Moses the Law, and Elijah was an important prophet.

Do You **Know Him?**

By H. B. London

Several years ago at the National Religious Broadcasters meeting, Dr. Richard Halverson, chaplain of the U.S. Senate, told this most insightful story.

It seems his small son was playing in the backyard with his friends when the conversation turned to one of those "my dad can whip your dad" routines. Halverson overheard one boy say, "My dad knows the mayor of our city!" Another said, "That's nothing — my dad knows the governor of our state!" Then Halverson heard his son say, "That's nothing — my dad knows God!"

Dr. Halverson reported that he slipped away from his place of eavesdropping with hot tears streaming down his cheeks. When he reached his study, he fell on his knees and earnestly prayed, "Oh, God, I pray that my boy will always be able to say, 'My dad knows God.'"

How important it is for us to be a spiritual example for our children, the same example Jesus was for his followers and for us: "He took Peter, John, and James and went up on a mountain to pray. While Jesus was praying, the appearance of his face changed, and his clothes became shining white" (Luke 9:28–29).

Jesus did nothing without the Father. He spent hours in prayer, garnering strength, courage, and wisdom to do the Father's will. And he modeled this for his followers on many occasions. Clearly, he showed us how to know God—and the proper way to lead!

Unfortunately, for many leaders, we spend more time being swept away by an ambition that has often been referred to as the "walk on the water" syndrome. So often, the people we lead expect the miraculous, and we do not want to disappoint them. Instead of trying to "know God," we spend all our time trying to "play God." That's unhealthy, at best. I know, because I nearly destroyed my health trying to "walk on water." But you are not a super-being and neither am I. Ask yourself the following questions:

- What and who do you live for?
- What and who would you die for?
- What are your first thought when you awake and your last thought before you sleep?
- What are your dreams?
- What is your treasure in life?

The answers to these questions will show you whether or not you are focusing on the wrong goals. Do you like them? If not, then change them! You may not be able to walk on water, but you serve a super God whose powerful Holy Spirit dwells within you. Why not focus on knowing him intimately by following Jesus' example? Establish your own "mountain of prayer," a special time and place to get to know the Father. Then, let him be praised and glorified through you as you do your best to obey and please him each day.

TO LEARN MORE ON WHAT THE BIBLE HAS TO SAY ABOUT **FULFILLMENT,** READ THE SCRIPTURES AND DEVOTIONALS AT **ISAIAH 41:10, ISAIAH 43:1, ISAIAH 52:7, LEVITICUS 16:20–22, JEREMIAH 3:22, JEREMIAH 31:3,** AND **LAMENTATIONS 3:37.**

41Jesus answered, "You people have no faith, and your lives are all wrong. How long must I stay with you and put up with you? Bring your son here."

42While the boy was coming, the demon threw him on the ground and made him lose control of himself. But Jesus gave a strong command to the evil spirit and healed the boy and gave him back to his father. 43All the people were amazed at the great power of God.

JESUS TALKS ABOUT HIS DEATH

While everyone was wondering about all that Jesus did, he said to his followers, 44"Don't forget what I tell you now: The Son of Man will be handed over to people." 45But the followers did not understand what this meant; the meaning was hidden from them so they could not understand. But they were afraid to ask Jesus about it.

WHO IS THE GREATEST?

46Jesus' followers began to have an argument about which one of them was the greatest. 47Jesus knew what they were thinking, so he took a little child and stood the child beside him. 48Then Jesus said, "Whoever accepts this little child in my name accepts me. And whoever accepts me accepts the One who sent me, because whoever is least among you all is really the greatest."

ANYONE NOT AGAINST US IS FOR US

49John answered, "Master, we saw someone using your name to force demons out of people. We told him to stop, because he does not belong to our group."

50But Jesus said to him, "Don't stop him, because whoever is not against you is for you."

A TOWN REJECTS JESUS

51When the time was coming near for Jesus to depart, he was determined to go to Jerusalem. 52He sent some messengers ahead of him, who went into a town in Samaria to make everything ready for him. 53But the people there would not welcome him, because he was set on going to Jerusalem. 54When James and John, followers of Jesus, saw this, they said, "Lord, do you want us to call fire down from heaven and destroy those people?"n

55But Jesus turned and scolded them. [And Jesus said, "You don't know what kind of spirit you belong to. 56The Son of Man did not come to destroy the souls of people but

to save them."]n Then they went to another town.

FOLLOWING JESUS

57As they were going along the road, someone said to Jesus, "I will follow you any place you go."

58Jesus said to them, "The foxes have holes to live in, and the birds have nests, but the Son of Man has no place to rest his head."

59Jesus said to another man, "Follow me!"

But he said, "Lord, first let me go and bury my father."

60But Jesus said to him, "Let the people who are dead bury their own dead. You must go and tell about the kingdom of God."

61Another man said, "I will follow you, Lord, but first let me go and say good-bye to my family."

62Jesus said, "Anyone who begins to plow a field but keeps looking back is of no use in the kingdom of God."

JESUS SENDS OUT THE SEVENTY-TWO

10 After this, the Lord chose seventy-twon others and sent them out in pairs ahead of him into every town and place where he planned to go. 2He said to them, "There are a great many people to harvest, but there are only a few workers. So pray to God, who owns the harvest, that he will send more workers to help gather his harvest. 3Go now, but listen! I am sending you out like sheep among wolves. 4Don't carry a purse, a bag, or sandals, and don't waste time talking with people on the road. 5Before you go into a house, say, 'Peace be with this house.' 6If peace-loving people live there, your blessing of peace will stay with them, but if not, then your blessing will come back to you. 7Stay in the same house, eating and drinking what the people there give you. A worker should be given his pay. Don't move from house to house. 8If you go into a town and the people welcome you, eat what they give you. 9Heal the sick who live there, and tell them, 'The kingdom of God is near you.' 10But if you go into a town, and the people don't welcome you, then go into the streets and say, 11"Even

---

9:54 people Some Greek copies continue "as Elijah did." **9:55–56 And . . . them."** Some Greek copies do not contain the bracketed text. **10:1 seventy-two** Some Greek copies read "seventy."

the dirt from your town that sticks to our feet we wipe off against you."[n] But remember that the kingdom of God is near.' [12]I tell you, on the Judgment Day it will be better for the people of Sodom[n] than for the people of that town.

JESUS WARNS UNBELIEVERS

[13]"How terrible for you, Korazin! How terrible for you, Bethsaida! If the miracles I did in you had happened in Tyre and Sidon,[n] those people would have changed their lives long ago. They would have worn rough cloth and put ashes on themselves to show they had changed. [14]But on the Judgment Day it will be better for Tyre and Sidon than for you. [15]And you, Capernaum,[n] will you be lifted up to heaven? No! You will be thrown down to the depths!

[16]"Whoever listens to you listens to me, and whoever refuses to accept you refuses to accept me. And whoever refuses to accept me refuses to accept the One who sent me."

SATAN FALLS

[17]When the seventy-two[n] came back, they were very happy and said, "Lord, even the demons obeyed us when we used your name!"

[18]Jesus said, "I saw Satan fall like lightning from heaven. [19]Listen, I have given you power to walk on snakes and scorpions, power that is greater than the enemy has. So nothing will hurt you. [20]But you should not be happy because the spirits obey you but because your names are written in heaven."

JESUS PRAYS TO THE FATHER

[21]Then Jesus rejoiced in the Holy Spirit and said, "I praise you, Father, Lord of heaven and earth, because you have hidden these things from the people who are wise and smart. But you have shown them to those who are like little children. Yes, Father, this is what you really wanted.

[22]"My Father has given me all things. No one knows who the Son is, except the Father. And no one knows who the Father is, except the Son and those whom the Son chooses to tell."

[23]Then Jesus turned to his followers and said privately, "You are blessed to see what you now see. [24]I tell you, many prophets and kings wanted to see what you now see, but they did not, and they wanted to hear what you now hear, but they did not."

THE GOOD SAMARITAN

[25]Then an expert on the law stood up to test Jesus, saying, "Teacher, what must I do to get life forever?"

[26]Jesus said, "What is written in the law? What do you read there?"

[27]The man answered, "Love the Lord your God with all your heart, all your soul, all your strength, and all your mind."[n] Also, "Love your neighbor as you love yourself."[n]

[28]Jesus said to him, "Your answer is right. Do this and you will live."

[29]But the man, wanting to show the importance of his question, said to Jesus, "And who is my neighbor?"

[30]Jesus answered, "As a man was going down from Jerusalem to Jericho, some robbers attacked him. They tore off his clothes, beat him, and left him lying there, almost dead. [31]It happened that a priest was going down that road. When he saw the man, he walked by on the other side. [32]Next, a Levite[n] came there, and after he went over and looked at the man, he walked by on the other side of the road. [33]Then a Samaritan[n] traveling down the road came to where the hurt man was. When he saw the man, he felt very sorry for him. [34]The Samaritan went to him, poured olive oil and wine[n] on his wounds, and bandaged them. Then he put the hurt man on his own donkey and took him to an inn where he cared for him. [35]The next day, the Samaritan brought out two coins,[n] gave them to the innkeeper, and said, 'Take care of this man. If you spend more money on him, I will pay it back to you when I come again.'"

10:11 dirt . . . you A warning. It showed that they had rejected these people. **10:12 Sodom** City that God destroyed because the people were so evil. **10:13 Tyre and Sidon** Towns where wicked people lived. **10:13, 15 Korazin, Bethsaida, Capernaum** Towns by Lake Galilee where Jesus preached to the people. **10:17 seventy-two** Some Greek copies read "seventy." **10:27 "Love . . . mind."** Quotation from Deuteronomy 6:5. **10:27 "Love . . . yourself."** Quotation from Leviticus 19:18. **10:32 Levite** Levites were members of the tribe of Levi who helped the Jewish priests with their work in the Temple. Read 1 Chronicles 23:24–32. **10:33 Samaritan** Samaritans were people from Samaria. These people were part Jewish, but the Jews did not accept them as true Jews. Samaritans and Jews disliked each other. **10:34 olive oil and wine** Oil and wine were used like medicine to soften and clean wounds. **10:35 coins** Roman denarii. One coin was the average pay for one day's work.

36Then Jesus said, "Which one of these three men do you think was a neighbor to the man who was attacked by the robbers?"

37The expert on the law answered, "The one who showed him mercy."

Jesus said to him, "Then go and do what he did."

MARY AND MARTHA

38While Jesus and his followers were traveling, Jesus went into a town. A woman named Martha let Jesus stay at her house. 39Martha had a sister named Mary, who was sitting at Jesus' feet and listening to him teach. 40But Martha was busy with all the work to be done. She went in and said, "Lord, don't you care that my sister has left me alone to do all the work? Tell her to help me."

41But the Lord answered her, "Martha, Martha, you are worried and upset about many things. 42Only one thing is important. Mary has chosen the better thing, and it will never be taken away from her."

JESUS TEACHES ABOUT PRAYER

11 One time Jesus was praying in a certain place. When he finished, one of his followers said to him, "Lord, teach us to pray as John taught his followers."

2Jesus said to them, "When you pray, say:
'Father, may your name always be kept holy.
  May your kingdom come.
3 Give us the food we need for each day.
4 Forgive us for our sins,
    because we forgive everyone who has
        done wrong to us.
  And do not cause us to be tempted.'"n

11:2–4 'Father...tempted.' Some Greek copies include phrases from Matthew's version of this prayer (Matthew 6:9–13).

FIVE INGREDIENTS OF PEACE BY GOD

too **busy**

FULFILLMENT

By Claudio Freidzon

LUKE 10:38–42

Martha certainly had a lot to do to prepare for Jesus' visit. Not only was he coming, but since everyone traveled in large groups in those days, he was bringing company. He was probably bringing his followers and their families and other friends, easily fifteen to twenty people. Martha anxiously strapped on her apron, grabbed Mary, and got very busy.

But Jesus was in the house, just in the other room, and Mary wanted to be with him. She took off her apron and ran from the busy kitchen. She sought a precious, intimate communion and fellowship with Jesus himself, not his dirty dishes. After all, he was there *in person*.

There are moments when the Lord wants to touch you and gaze at your face, but you are too busy. Learn from Mary. She went to where Jesus was and hung on his every word. The Lord wants you to enjoy a new relationship with him so that he can fill your heart even more.

reflect: Are you willing to spend time communing with Jesus?
Go to **Luke 17:12–19**.

CONTINUE TO ASK

⁵Then Jesus said to them, "Suppose one of you went to your friend's house at midnight and said to him, 'Friend, loan me three loaves of bread. ⁶A friend of mine has come into town to visit me, but I have nothing for him to eat.' ⁷Your friend inside the house answers, 'Don't bother me! The door is already locked, and my children and I are in bed. I cannot get up and give you anything.' ⁸I tell you, if friendship is not enough to make him get up to give you the bread, your boldness will make him get up and give you whatever you need. ⁹So I tell you, ask, and God will give to you. Search, and you will find. Knock, and the door will open for you. ¹⁰Yes, everyone who asks will receive. The one who searches will find. And everyone who knocks will have the door opened. ¹¹If your children ask for[n] a fish, which of you would give them a snake instead? ¹²Or, if your children ask for an egg, would you give them a scorpion? ¹³Even though you are bad, you know how to give good things to your children. How much more your heavenly Father will give the Holy Spirit to those who ask him!"

JESUS' POWER IS FROM GOD

¹⁴One time Jesus was sending out a demon who could not talk. When the demon came out, the man who had been unable to speak, then spoke. The people were amazed. ¹⁵But some of them said, "Jesus uses the power of Beelzebul, the ruler of demons, to force demons out of people."

¹⁶Other people, wanting to test Jesus, asked him to give them a sign from heaven. ¹⁷But knowing their thoughts, he said to them, "Every kingdom that is divided against itself will be destroyed. And a family that is divided against itself will not continue. ¹⁸So if Satan is divided against himself, his kingdom will not continue. You say that I use the power of Beelzebul to force out demons. ¹⁹But if I use the power of Beelzebul to force out demons, what power do your people use to force demons out? So they will be your judges. ²⁰But if I use the power of God to force out demons, then the kingdom of God has come to you.

²¹"When a strong person with many weapons guards his own house, his possessions are safe. ²²But when someone stronger comes and defeats him, the stronger one will take away the weapons the first man trusted and will give away the possessions.

²³"Anyone who is not with me is against me, and anyone who does not work with me is working against me.

THE EMPTY PERSON

²⁴"When an evil spirit comes out of a person, it travels through dry places, looking for a place to rest. But when it finds no place, it says, 'I will go back to the house I left.' ²⁵And when it comes back, it finds that house swept clean and made neat. ²⁶Then the evil spirit goes out and brings seven other spirits more evil than it is, and they go in and live there. So the person has even more trouble than before."

PEOPLE WHO ARE TRULY BLESSED

²⁷As Jesus was saying these things, a woman in the crowd called out to Jesus, "Blessed is the mother who gave birth to you and nursed you."

²⁸But Jesus said, "No, blessed are those who hear the teaching of God and obey it."

THE PEOPLE WANT A MIRACLE

²⁹As the crowd grew larger, Jesus said, "The people who live today are evil. They want to see a miracle for a sign, but no sign will be given them, except the sign of Jonah.[n] ³⁰As Jonah was a sign for those people who lived in Nineveh, the Son of Man will be a sign for the people of this time. ³¹On the Judgment Day the Queen of the South[n] will stand up with the people who live now. She will show they are guilty, because she came from far away to listen to Solomon's wise teaching. And I tell you that someone greater than Solomon is here. ³²On the Judgment Day the people of Nineveh will stand up with the people who live now, and they will show that you are guilty. When Jonah preached to them, they were sorry and changed their lives. And I tell you that someone greater than Jonah is here.

11:11 for Some Greek copies include the phrase "for bread, which of you would give them a stone, or if they ask for . . ." **11:29 sign of Jonah** Jonah's three days in the fish are like Jesus' three days in the tomb. See Matthew 12:40. **11:31 Queen of the South** The Queen of Sheba. She traveled a thousand miles to learn God's wisdom from Solomon. Read 1 Kings 10:1–3.

BE A LIGHT FOR THE WORLD

33"No one lights a lamp and puts it in a secret place or under a bowl, but on a lampstand so the people who come in can see. 34Your eye is a light for the body. When your eyes are good, your whole body will be full of light. But when your eyes are evil, your whole body will be full of darkness. 35So be careful not to let the light in you become darkness. 36If your whole body is full of light, and none of it is dark, then you will shine bright, as when a lamp shines on you."

JESUS ACCUSES THE PHARISEES

37After Jesus had finished speaking, a Pharisee asked Jesus to eat with him. So Jesus went in and sat at the table. 38But the Pharisee was surprised when he saw that Jesus did not wash his hands[n] before the meal. 39The Lord said to him, "You Pharisees clean the outside of the cup and the dish, but inside you are full of greed and evil. 40You foolish people! The same one who made what is outside also made what is inside. 41So give what is in your dishes to the poor, and then you will be fully clean. 42How terrible for you Pharisees! You give God one-tenth of even your mint, your rue, and every other plant in your garden. But you fail to be fair to others and to love God. These are the things you should do while continuing to do those other things. 43How terrible for you Pharisees, because you love to have the most important seats in the synagogues, and you love to be greeted with respect in the marketplaces. 44How terrible for you, because you are like hidden graves, which people walk on without knowing."

JESUS TALKS TO EXPERTS ON THE LAW

45One of the experts on the law said to Jesus, "Teacher, when you say these things, you are insulting us, too."

46Jesus answered, "How terrible for you, you experts on the law! You make strict rules that are very hard for people to obey, but you yourselves don't even try to follow those rules. 47How terrible for you, because you build tombs for the prophets whom your ancestors killed! 48And now you show that you approve of what your ancestors did. They killed the prophets, and you build tombs for them! 49This is why in his wisdom God said, 'I will send prophets and apostles to them.

They will kill some, and they will treat others cruelly.' 50So you who live now will be punished for the deaths of all the prophets who were killed since the beginning of the world— 51from the killing of Abel to the killing of Zechariah,[n] who died between the altar and the Temple. Yes, I tell you that you who are alive now will be punished for them all.

52"How terrible for you, you experts on the law. You have taken away the key to learning about God. You yourselves would not learn, and you stopped others from learning, too."

53When Jesus left, the teachers of the law and the Pharisees began to give him trouble, asking him questions about many things, 54trying to catch him saying something wrong.

DON'T BE LIKE THE PHARISEES

12 So many thousands of people had gathered that they were stepping on each other. Jesus spoke first to his followers, saying, "Beware of the yeast of the Pharisees, because they are hypocrites. 2Everything that is hidden will be shown, and everything that is secret will be made known. 3What you have said in the dark will be heard in the light, and what you have whispered in an inner room will be shouted from the housetops.

4"I tell you, my friends, don't be afraid of people who can kill the body but after that can do nothing more to hurt you. 5I will show you the one to fear. Fear the one who has the power to kill you and also to throw you into hell. Yes, this is the one you should fear.

6"Five sparrows are sold for only two pennies, and God does not forget any of them. 7But God even knows how many hairs you have on your head. Don't be afraid. You are worth much more than many sparrows.

DON'T BE ASHAMED OF JESUS

8"I tell you, all those who stand before others and say they believe in me, I, the Son of Man, will say before the angels of God that they belong to me. 9But all who stand before others and say they do not believe in me, I will say before the angels of God that they do not belong to me.

11:38 **wash his hands** This was a Jewish religious custom that the Pharisees thought was very important.
11:51 **Abel...Zechariah** In the Hebrew Old Testament, the first and last men to be murdered.

¹⁰"Anyone who speaks against the Son of Man can be forgiven, but anyone who speaks against the Holy Spirit will not be forgiven.

¹¹"When you are brought into the synagogues before the leaders and other powerful people, don't worry about how to defend yourself or what to say. ¹²At that time the Holy Spirit will teach you what you must say."

JESUS WARNS AGAINST SELFISHNESS

¹³Someone in the crowd said to Jesus, "Teacher, tell my brother to divide with me the property our father left us."

¹⁴But Jesus said to him, "Who said I should judge or decide between you?" ¹⁵Then Jesus said to them, "Be careful and guard against all kinds of greed. Life is not measured by how much one owns."

¹⁶Then Jesus told this story: "There was a rich man who had some land, which grew a good crop. ¹⁷He thought to himself, 'What will I do? I have no place to keep all my crops.' ¹⁸Then he said, 'This is what I will do: I will tear down my barns and build bigger ones, and there I will store all my grain and other goods. ¹⁹Then I can say to myself, "I have

---

UNDERSTANDING FREEDOM

FINANCES

a **nice** portfolio

LUKE 12:13-34

By Joseph Stowell

When we read Luke 12:13-21, this question jumps out at us: "Who's really in charge of your money—your portfolio?" Then these words of Jesus in verses 22-34 further challenge us: Why are you so distracted from kingdom work by earth-side realities? Why are you so worried about stuff? Your Father knows your needs. Go after him, and he'll take care of you! For true followers of Christ, God measures our lives by the faithful pursuit of the kingdom.

You see, a kingdom has a king. It's not a democracy. You don't vote Jesus out one day. It's a monarchy. It's a benevolent dictatorship, if you please. In a kingdom, one person is totally in charge.

When it comes to money, the kingdom of God has backward-sounding rules: Give it away, and it will be given to you. The kingdom has an economy, a supply-side economy. You give it away, and God supplies it from behind; you give it away, and God pours it back in. The kingdom not only has a king, rules, and an economy, but it also has terms and term limits. What are the terms of the kingdom? Eternity. Being a kingdom person means asking what you will be doing for eternity. That's why Christ closed this section of Luke 12 by saying, "Get for yourselves purses that will not wear out, the treasure in heaven that never runs out, where thieves can't steal and moths can't destroy. Your heart will be where your treasure is" (verse 34).

reflect: Who manages your investment portfolio?

Go to **FINANCES:** "Sowing and Reaping" at **Galatians 6:9.**

---

enough good things stored to last for many years. Rest, eat, drink, and enjoy life!'"

²⁰"But God said to him, 'Foolish man! Tonight your life will be taken from you. So who will get those things you have prepared for yourself?'

²¹"This is how it will be for those who store up things for themselves and are not rich toward God."

DON'T WORRY

²²Jesus said to his followers, "So I tell you, don't worry about the food you need to live, or about the clothes you need for your body. ²³Life is more than food, and the body is more than clothes. ²⁴Look at the birds. They don't plant or harvest, they don't have storerooms or barns, but God feeds them. And you are worth much more than birds. ²⁵You cannot add any time to your life by worrying about it. ²⁶If you cannot do even the little things, then why worry about the big things? ²⁷Consider how the lilies grow; they don't work or make clothes for themselves. But I tell you that even Solomon with his riches was not dressed as beautifully as one of these flowers. ²⁸God clothes the grass in the field, which is alive today but tomorrow is thrown into the fire. So how much more will God clothe you? Don't have so little faith! ²⁹Don't always think about what you will eat or what you will drink, and don't keep worrying. ³⁰All the people in the world are trying to get these things, and your Father knows you need them. ³¹But seek God's kingdom, and all your other needs will be met as well.

DON'T TRUST IN MONEY

³²"Don't fear, little flock, because your Father wants to give you the kingdom. ³³Sell your possessions and give to the poor. Get for yourselves purses that will not wear out, the treasure in heaven that never runs out, where thieves can't steal and moths can't destroy. ³⁴Your heart will be where your treasure is.

ALWAYS BE READY

³⁵"Be dressed, ready for service, and have your lamps shining. ³⁶Be like servants who are waiting for their master to come home from a wedding party. When he comes and knocks, the servants immediately open the door for him. ³⁷They will be blessed when their master comes home, because he sees

that they were watching for him. I tell you the truth, the master will dress himself to serve and tell the servants to sit at the table, and he will serve them. ³⁸Those servants will be blessed when he comes in and finds them still waiting, even if it is midnight or later.

³⁹"Remember this: If the owner of the house knew what time a thief was coming, he would not allow the thief to enter his house. ⁴⁰So you also must be ready, because the Son of Man will come at a time when you don't expect him!"

WHO IS THE TRUSTED SERVANT?

⁴¹Peter said, "Lord, did you tell this story to us or to all people?"

⁴²The Lord said, "Who is the wise and trusted servant that the master trusts to give the other servants their food at the right time? ⁴³When the master comes and finds the servant doing his work, the servant will be blessed. ⁴⁴I tell you the truth, the master will choose that servant to take care of everything he owns. ⁴⁵But suppose the servant thinks to himself, 'My master will not come back soon,' and he begins to beat the other servants, men and women, and to eat and drink and get drunk. ⁴⁶The master will come when that servant is not ready and is not expecting him. Then the master will cut him in pieces and send him away to be with the others who don't obey.

⁴⁷"The servant who knows what his master wants but is not ready, or who does not do what the master wants, will be beaten with many blows! ⁴⁸But the servant who does not know what his master wants and does things that should be punished will be beaten with few blows. From everyone who has been given much, much will be demanded. And from the one trusted with much, much more will be expected.

JESUS CAUSES DIVISION

⁴⁹"I came to set fire to the world, and I wish it were already burning! ⁵⁰I have a baptismⁿ to suffer through, and I feel very troubled until it is over. ⁵¹Do you think I came to give peace to the earth? No, I tell you, I came to divide it. ⁵²From now on, a family with five people will be divided, three against

---

12:50 I…baptism Jesus was talking about the suffering he would soon go through.

two, and two against three. ⁵³They will be divided: father against son and son against father, mother against daughter and daughter against mother, mother-in-law against daughter-in-law and daughter-in-law against mother-in-law."

UNDERSTANDING THE TIMES

⁵⁴Then Jesus said to the people, "When you see clouds coming up in the west, you say, 'It's going to rain,' and it happens. ⁵⁵When you feel the wind begin to blow from the south, you say, 'It will be a hot day,' and it happens. ⁵⁶Hypocrites! You know how to understand the appearance of the earth and sky. Why don't you understand what is happening now?

SETTLE YOUR PROBLEMS

⁵⁷"Why can't you decide for yourselves what is right? ⁵⁸If your enemy is taking you to court, try hard to settle it on the way. If you don't, your enemy might take you to the judge, and the judge might turn you over to the officer, and the officer might throw you into jail. ⁵⁹I tell you, you will not get out of there until you have paid everything you owe."

CHANGE YOUR HEARTS

13 At that time some people were there who told Jesus that Pilate[n] had killed some people from Galilee while they were

13:1 **Pilate** Pontius Pilate was the Roman governor of Judea from A.D. 26 to A.D. 36.

SOWING AND REAPING

FINANCES

defining **success**

LUKE 12:42–48

By Joseph Stowell

Picture yourself totally alone in a room. In that room is a table with everything you have on it . . . everything. Nothing stays under the table and nothing in the closet. It's all there. You hear a knock on the door, go to the door, you open it up, and guess who's standing there? It's Jesus. He wants to come in. Obviously, we are going to let him in, right? So you let Jesus in, shut the door behind him, and he looks at everything on your table.

Do you feel a little threatened by that? Well, you ought to. If you see Jesus as merely a comfortable, cuddly, encouraging companion for life and have never seen Jesus as a threat, then you have never met the authentic Jesus of Scripture. As soon as he walks into that room where you and he and all of your things are, he demands to be in control. That is what is threatening about him.

You say, "I'll just hire him as a consultant; that's what I'll do. I'm going to make Jesus the consultant of all my success." But he doesn't hire out as a consultant. He walks in as the chairman of the board. He walks in as the commander-in-chief. He wants to rearrange what's on your table, so that you can be pleasing in his sight and give a good account to him.

reflect: What have you done with what you have been given?
Go to **Luke 16:9–13.**

worshiping. He mixed their blood with the blood of the animals they were sacrificing to God. ²Jesus answered, "Do you think this happened to them because they were more sinful than all others from Galilee? ³No, I tell you. But unless you change your hearts and lives, you will be destroyed as they were! ⁴What about those eighteen people who died when the tower of Siloam fell on them? Do you think they were more sinful than all the others who live in Jerusalem? ⁵No, I tell you. But unless you change your hearts and lives, you will all be destroyed too!"

THE USELESS TREE

⁶Jesus told this story: "A man had a fig tree planted in his vineyard. He came looking for some fruit on the tree, but he found none. ⁷So the man said to his gardener, 'I have been looking for fruit on this tree for three years, but I never find any. Cut it down. Why should it waste the ground?' ⁸But the servant answered, 'Master, let the tree have one more year to produce fruit. Let me dig up the dirt around it and put on some fertilizer. ⁹If the tree produces fruit next year, good. But if not, you can cut it down.'"

JESUS HEALS ON THE SABBATH

¹⁰Jesus was teaching in one of the synagogues on the Sabbath day. ¹¹A woman was there who, for eighteen years, had an evil spirit in her that made her crippled. Her back was always bent; she could not stand up straight. ¹²When Jesus saw her, he called her over and said, "Woman, you are free from your sickness." ¹³Jesus put his hands on her, and immediately she was able to stand up straight and began praising God.

¹⁴The synagogue leader was angry because Jesus healed on the Sabbath day. He said to the people, "There are six days when one has to work. So come to be healed on one of those days, and not on the Sabbath day."

¹⁵The Lord answered, "You hypocrites! Doesn't each of you untie your work animals and lead them to drink water every day— even on the Sabbath day? ¹⁶This woman that I healed, a daughter of Abraham, has been held by Satan for eighteen years. Surely it is not wrong for her to be freed from her sickness on a Sabbath day!" ¹⁷When Jesus said this, all of those who were criticizing him were ashamed, but the entire crowd re-joiced at all the wonderful things Jesus was doing.

STORIES OF MUSTARD SEED AND YEAST

¹⁸Then Jesus said, "What is God's kingdom like? What can I compare it with? ¹⁹It is like a mustard seed that a man plants in his garden. The seed grows and becomes a tree, and the wild birds build nests in its branches."

²⁰Jesus said again, "What can I compare God's kingdom with? ²¹It is like yeast that a woman took and hid in a large tub of flour until it made all the dough rise."

THE NARROW DOOR

²²Jesus was teaching in every town and village as he traveled toward Jerusalem. ²³Someone said to Jesus, "Lord, will only a few people be saved?"

Jesus said, ²⁴"Try hard to enter through the narrow door, because many people will try to enter there, but they will not be able. ²⁵When the owner of the house gets up and closes the door, you can stand outside and knock on the door and say, 'Sir, open the door for us.' But he will answer, 'I don't know you or where you come from.' ²⁶Then you will say, 'We ate and drank with you, and you taught in the streets of our town.' ²⁷But he will say to you, 'I don't know you or where you come from. Go away from me, all you who do evil!' ²⁸You will cry and grind your teeth with pain when you see Abraham, Isaac, Jacob, and all the prophets in God's kingdom, but you yourselves thrown outside. ²⁹People will come from the east, west, north, and south and will sit down at the table in the kingdom of God. ³⁰There are those who are last now who will be first in the future. And there are those who are first now who will be last in the future."

JESUS WILL DIE IN JERUSALEM

³¹At that time some Pharisees came to Jesus and said, "Go away from here! Herod wants to kill you!"

³²Jesus said to them, "Go tell that fox Herod, 'Today and tomorrow I am forcing demons out and healing people. Then, on the third day, I will reach my goal.' ³³Yet I must be on my way today and tomorrow and the next day. Surely it cannot be right for a prophet to be killed anywhere except in Jerusalem.

[34]"Jerusalem, Jerusalem! You kill the prophets and stone to death those who are sent to you. Many times I wanted to gather your people as a hen gathers her chicks under her wings, but you would not let me. [35]Now your house is left completely empty. I tell you, you will not see me until that time when you will say, 'God bless the One who comes in the name of the Lord.'"[n]

HEALING ON THE SABBATH

14 On a Sabbath day, when Jesus went to eat at the home of a leading Pharisee, the people were watching Jesus very closely. [2]And in front of him was a man with dropsy.[n] [3]Jesus said to the Pharisees and experts on the law, "Is it right or wrong to heal on the Sabbath day?" [4]But they would not answer his question. So Jesus took the man, healed him, and sent him away. [5]Jesus said to the Pharisees and teachers of the law, "If your child[n] or ox falls into a well on the Sabbath day, will you not pull him out quickly?" [6]And they could not answer him.

DON'T MAKE YOURSELF IMPORTANT

[7]When Jesus noticed that some of the guests were choosing the best places to sit, he told this story: [8]"When someone invites you to a wedding feast, don't take the most important seat, because someone more important than you may have been invited. [9]The host, who invited both of you, will come to you and say, 'Give this person your seat.' Then you will be embarrassed and will have to move to the last place. [10]So when you are invited, go sit in a seat that is not important. When the host comes to you, he may say, 'Friend, move up here to a more important place.' Then all the other guests will respect you. [11]All who make themselves great will be made humble, but those who make themselves humble will be made great."

YOU WILL BE REWARDED

[12]Then Jesus said to the man who had invited him, "When you give a lunch or a dinner, don't invite only your friends, your family, your other relatives, and your rich neighbors. At another time they will invite you to eat with them, and you will be repaid. [13]Instead, when you give a feast, invite the poor, the crippled, the lame, and the blind. [14]Then you will be blessed, because they have nothing and cannot pay you back. But you will be repaid when the good people rise from the dead."

A STORY ABOUT A BIG BANQUET

[15]One of those at the table with Jesus heard these things and said to him, "Blessed are the people who will share in the meal in God's kingdom."

[16]Jesus said to him, "A man gave a big banquet and invited many people. [17]When it was time to eat, the man sent his servant to tell the guests, 'Come. Everything is ready.'

[18]"But all the guests made excuses. The first one said, 'I have just bought a field, and I must go look at it. Please excuse me.' [19]Another said, 'I have just bought five pairs of oxen; I must go and try them. Please excuse me.' [20]A third person said, 'I just got married; I can't come.' [21]So the servant returned and told his master what had happened. Then the master became angry and said, 'Go at once into the streets and alleys of the town, and bring in the poor, the crippled, the blind, and the lame.' [22]Later the servant said to him, 'Master, I did what you commanded, but we still have room.' [23]The master said to the servant, 'Go out to the roads and country lanes, and urge the people there to come so my house will be full. [24]I tell you, none of those whom I invited first will eat with me.'"

THE COST OF BEING JESUS' FOLLOWER

[25]Large crowds were traveling with Jesus, and he turned and said to them, [26]"If anyone comes to me but loves his father, mother, wife, children, brothers, or sisters—or even life—more than me, he cannot be my follower. [27]Whoever is not willing to carry his cross and follow me cannot be my follower. [28]If you want to build a tower, you first sit down and decide how much it will cost, to see if you have enough money to finish the job. [29]If you don't, you might lay the foundation, but you would not be able to finish. Then all who would see it would make fun of you, [30]saying, 'This person began to build but was not able to finish.'

[31]"If a king is going to fight another king, first he will sit down and plan. He will decide

---

13:35 'God . . . Lord.' Quotation from Psalm 118:26. **14:2 dropsy** A sickness that causes the body to swell larger and larger. **14:5 child** Some Greek copies read "donkey."

if he and his ten thousand soldiers can defeat the other king who has twenty thousand soldiers. [32]If he can't, then while the other king is still far away, he will send some people to speak to him and ask for peace. [33]In the same way, you must give up everything you have to be my follower.

DON'T LOSE YOUR INFLUENCE

[34]"Salt is good, but if it loses its salty taste, you cannot make it salty again. [35]It is no good for the soil or for manure; it is thrown away.

"Let those with ears use them and listen."

A LOST SHEEP, A LOST COIN

15 The tax collectors and sinners all came to listen to Jesus. [2]But the Pharisees and the teachers of the law began to complain: "Look, this man welcomes sinners and even eats with them."

[3]Then Jesus told them this story: [4]"Suppose one of you has a hundred sheep but loses one of them. Then he will leave the other ninety-nine sheep in the open field and go out and look for the lost sheep until he finds it. [5]And when he finds it, he happily puts it on his shoulders [6]and goes home. He calls to his friends and neighbors and says, 'Be happy with me because I found my lost sheep.' [7]In the same way, I tell you there is more joy in heaven over one sinner who changes his heart and life, than over ninety-nine good people who don't need to change.

[8]"Suppose a woman has ten silver coins,[n] but loses one. She will light a lamp, sweep the house, and look carefully for the coin until she finds it. [9]And when she finds it, she will call her friends and neighbors and say, 'Be happy with me because I have found the coin that I lost.' [10]In the same way, there is joy in the presence of the angels of God when one sinner changes his heart and life."

THE SON WHO LEFT HOME

[11]Then Jesus said, "A man had two sons. [12]The younger son said to his father, 'Give me my share of the property.' So the father divided the property between his two sons. [13]Then the younger son gathered up all that was his and traveled far away to another country. There he wasted his money in foolish living. [14]After he had spent everything, a time came when there was no food anywhere in the country, and the son was poor and hun-

gry. [15]So he got a job with one of the citizens there who sent the son into the fields to feed pigs. [16]The son was so hungry that he wanted to eat the pods the pigs were eating, but no one gave him anything. [17]When he realized what he was doing, he thought, 'All of my father's servants have plenty of food. But I am here, almost dying with hunger. [18]I will leave and return to my father and say to him, "Father, I have sinned against God and against you. [19]I am no longer worthy to be called your son, but let me be like one of your servants."' [20]So the son left and went to his father.

"While the son was still a long way off, his father saw him and felt sorry for his son. So the father ran to him and hugged and kissed him. [21]The son said, 'Father, I have sinned against God and against you. I am no longer worthy to be called your son.'[n] [22]But the father said to his servants, 'Hurry! Bring the best clothes and put them on him. Also, put a ring on his finger and sandals on his feet. [23]And get our fat calf and kill it so we can have a feast and celebrate. [24]My son was dead, but now he is alive again! He was lost, but now he is found!' So they began to celebrate.

[25]"The older son was in the field, and as he came closer to the house, he heard the sound of music and dancing. [26]So he called to one of the servants and asked what all this meant. [27]The servant said, 'Your brother has come back, and your father killed the fat calf, because your brother came home safely.' [28]The older son was angry and would not go in to the feast. So his father went out and begged him to come in. [29]But the older son said to his father, 'I have served you like a slave for many years and have always obeyed your commands. But you never gave me even a young goat to have at a feast with my friends. [30]But your other son, who wasted all your money on prostitutes, comes home, and you kill the fat calf for him!' [31]The father said to him, 'Son, you are always with me, and all that I have is yours. [32]We had to celebrate and be happy because your brother was dead, but now he is alive. He was lost, but now he is found.'"

15:8 silver coins Roman denarii. One coin was the average pay for one day's work. **15:21 son** Some Greek copies continue, "but let me be like one of your servants" (see verse 19).

TRUE WEALTH

16 Jesus also said to his followers, "Once there was a rich man who had a manager to take care of his business. This manager was accused of cheating him. ²So he called the manager in and said to him, 'What is this I hear about you? Give me a report of what you have done with my money, because you can't be my manager any longer.' ³The manager thought to himself, 'What will I do since my master is taking my job away from me? I am not strong enough to dig ditches, and I am ashamed to beg. ⁴I know what I'll do so that when I lose my job people will welcome me into their homes.'

⁵"So the manager called in everyone who owed the master any money. He asked the first one, 'How much do you owe?' ⁶He answered, 'Eight hundred gallons of olive oil.' The manager said to him, 'Take your bill, sit down quickly, and write four hundred gallons.' ⁷Then the manager asked another one, 'How much do you owe?' He answered, 'One thousand bushels of wheat.' Then the manager said to him, 'Take your bill and write eight hundred bushels.' ⁸So, the master praised the dishonest manager for being clever. Yes, worldly people are more clever with their own kind than spiritual people are.

⁹"I tell you, make friends for yourselves using worldly riches so that when those riches are gone, you will be welcomed in those homes that continue forever. ¹⁰Whoever can be trusted with a little can also be trusted with a lot, and whoever is dishonest with a little is dishonest with a lot. ¹¹If you cannot be trusted with worldly riches, then who will trust you with true riches? ¹²And if you cannot be trusted with things that belong to someone else, who will give you things of your own?

¹³"No servant can serve two masters. The servant will hate one master and love the other, or will follow one master and refuse to follow the other. You cannot serve both God and worldly riches."

GOD'S LAW CANNOT BE CHANGED

¹⁴The Pharisees, who loved money, were listening to all these things and made fun of Jesus. ¹⁵He said to them, "You make yourselves look good in front of people, but God knows what is really in your hearts. What is important to people is hateful in God's sight.

¹⁶"The law of Moses and the writings of the prophets were preached until John[n] came. Since then the Good News about the kingdom of God is being told, and everyone tries to enter it by force. ¹⁷It would be easier for heaven and earth to pass away than for the smallest part of a letter in the law to be changed.

DIVORCE AND REMARRIAGE

¹⁸"If a man divorces his wife and marries another woman, he is guilty of adultery, and the man who marries a divorced woman is also guilty of adultery."

THE RICH MAN AND LAZARUS

¹⁹Jesus said, "There was a rich man who always dressed in the finest clothes and lived in luxury every day. ²⁰And a very poor man named Lazarus, whose body was covered with sores, was laid at the rich man's gate. ²¹He wanted to eat only the small pieces of food that fell from the rich man's table. And the dogs would come and lick his sores. ²²Later, Lazarus died, and the angels carried him to the arms of Abraham. The rich man died, too, and was buried. ²³In the place of the dead, he was in much pain. The rich man saw Abraham far away with Lazarus at his side. ²⁴He called, 'Father Abraham, have mercy on me! Send Lazarus to dip his finger in water and cool my tongue, because I am suffering in this fire!' ²⁵But Abraham said, 'Child, remember when you were alive you had the good things in life, but bad things happened to Lazarus. Now he is comforted here, and you are suffering. ²⁶Besides, there is a big pit between you and us, so no one can cross over to you, and no one can leave there and come here.' ²⁷The rich man said, 'Father, then please send Lazarus to my father's house. ²⁸I have five brothers, and Lazarus could warn them so that they will not come to this place of pain.' ²⁹But Abraham said, 'They have the law of Moses and the writings of the prophets; let them learn from them.' ³⁰The rich man said, 'No, father Abraham! If someone goes to them from the dead, they would believe and change their hearts and lives.' ³¹But Abraham said to him, 'If they will not listen to Moses and the prophets, they will not listen to someone who comes back from the dead.'"

16:16 John John the Baptist, who preached to people about Christ's coming (Matthew 3, Luke 3).

SIN AND FORGIVENESS

17 Jesus said to his followers, "Things that cause people to sin will happen, but how terrible for the person who causes them to happen! ²It would be better for you to be thrown into the sea with a large stone around your neck than to cause one of these little ones to sin. ³So be careful!

"If another follower sins, warn him, and if he is sorry and stops sinning, forgive him. ⁴If he sins against you seven times in one day and says that he is sorry each time, forgive him."

HOW BIG IS YOUR FAITH?

⁵The apostles said to the Lord, "Give us more faith!"

⁶The Lord said, "If your faith were the size of a mustard seed, you could say to this mulberry tree, 'Dig yourself up and plant yourself in the sea,' and it would obey you.

BE GOOD SERVANTS

⁷"Suppose one of you has a servant who has been plowing the ground or caring for the sheep. When the servant comes in from working in the field, would you say, 'Come in and sit

SOWING AND REAPING

extraordinary
finances

FINANCES

By Larry Stockstill

LUKE 16:9–13

Absolutely everything belongs to God and we possess nothing. We are simply caretakers of whatever God entrusts to us. The world cannot understand this philosophy. However, if you have been born anew into God's family, you recognize it is a divine guide to the use of worldly resources.

God has the right to do whatever he wants with your possessions. The wonderful part of this is that he also bears the responsibility of providing for you. When you accept that the Lord is your shepherd and you are accountable to live within his standards, rest assured that you also will have everything you need. God will help you live in the faith that he will provide if you will acknowledge that all of your possessions and financial dealings belong to him in the first place.

A truly wise person focuses on the value of people over material goods. When possessions are your highest priority in life, your interactions with people suffer. One or the other is going to take priority. Money without healthy relationships is meaningless. People to love and to give you love are what bring you richness and fulfillment in life. Your personal relationship with God and others fills the void in your human heart.

God designed money to be a tool to bless your family and neighbors, not a weapon. Hold it lightly and never let it gain an unhealthy importance in your life. Your real wealth is not money or material things. Your earthly happiness results from your faith and your healthy, rewarding relationships.

reflect: Are you esteeming material things instead of other people?
Go to **Luke 5:1–11.**

down to eat'? ⁸No, you would say to him, 'Prepare something for me to eat. Then get yourself ready and serve me. After I finish eating and drinking, you can eat.' ⁹The servant does not get any special thanks for doing what his master commanded. ¹⁰It is the same with you. When you have done everything you are told to do, you should say, 'We are unworthy servants; we have only done the work we should do.'"

BE THANKFUL

¹¹While Jesus was on his way to Jerusalem, he was going through the area between Samaria and Galilee. ¹²As he came into a small town, ten men who had a skin disease met him there. They did not come close to Jesus ¹³but called to him, "Jesus! Master! Have mercy on us!"

¹⁴When Jesus saw the men, he said, "Go and show yourselves to the priests."

FULFILLMENT

FIVE INGREDIENTS OF PEACE BY GOD

honoring God for his mercy

LUKE 17:12-19

As you grow and mature as a believer, you realize that thankfulness is a foundational part of your Christian life. Giving thanks to God is an attentive reply that comes from looking beyond your blessings to the source of your blessings. As a Christian, you have been forgiven of your sins, saved from death, and healed of your diseases. That is a great reason to be thankful.

In the days of Jesus, lepers were social outcasts. Leprosy was a disease that was highly contagious, and, due to their condition, lepers were set apart from the ones they loved. During those days, they kept to themselves in camps and did not mingle with society.

When the ten lepers in this passage heard about Jesus, they found him and asked for mercy. Jesus told them what to do and as they obeyed they were healed. Imagine the joy and jubilation that must have filled them when they saw that they were healed!

Only one of the lepers stopped and ran back to Jesus to give him thanks. This man was a Samaritan and was normally shunned by the Jews, but Jesus had compassion and healed him. However, the other nine failed to thank Jesus for what he had done for them. Ten lepers were enjoying their newfound health. Ten were joyfully sharing the good news with their family and friends. But only one looked to the giver of that blessing and stopped to thank the one who had given him back his life.

You, too, have been healed and set free by the Lord. You are free to enjoy life and the blessings that he has given you. Do you, like the nine lepers, rush off to glory in your blessings without stopping to give thanks to your precious Lord? Don't forget the source of all the blessings you enjoy. Take the time and thank God daily for all he has done.

reflect: Give God glory for the blessings in your life.

Go to **John 8:36.**

As the ten men were going, they were healed. [15]When one of them saw that he was healed, he went back to Jesus, praising God in a loud voice. [16]Then he bowed down at Jesus' feet and thanked him. (And this man was a Samaritan.) [17]Jesus said, "Weren't ten men healed? Where are the other nine? [18]Is this Samaritan the only one who came back to thank God?" [19]Then Jesus said to him, "Stand up and go on your way. You were healed because you believed."

GOD'S KINGDOM IS WITHIN YOU

[20]Some of the Pharisees asked Jesus, "When will the kingdom of God come?"

Jesus answered, "God's kingdom is coming, but not in a way that you will be able to see with your eyes. [21]People will not say, 'Look, here it is!' or, 'There it is!' because God's kingdom is within[n] you."

[22]Then Jesus said to his followers, "The time will come when you will want very much to see one of the days of the Son of Man. But you will not see it. [23]People will say to you, 'Look, there he is!' or, 'Look, here he is!' Stay where you are; don't go away and search.

WHEN JESUS COMES AGAIN

[24]"When the Son of Man comes again, he will shine like lightning, which flashes across the sky and lights it up from one side to the other. [25]But first he must suffer many things and be rejected by the people of this time. [26]When the Son of Man comes again, it will be as it was when Noah lived. [27]People were eating, drinking, marrying, and giving their children to be married until the day Noah entered the boat. Then the flood came and killed them all. [28]It will be the same as during the time of Lot. People were eating, drinking, buying, selling, planting, and building. [29]But the day Lot left Sodom,[n] fire and sulfur rained down from the sky and killed them all. [30]This is how it will be when the Son of Man comes again.

[31]"On that day, a person who is on the roof and whose belongings are in the house should not go inside to get them. A person who is in the field should not go back home. [32]Remember Lot's wife.[n] [33]Those who try to keep their lives will lose them. But those who give up their lives will save them. [34]I tell you, on that night two people will be sleeping in one bed; one will be taken and the other will be left. [35]There will be two women grinding grain together; one will be taken, and the other will be left. [[36]Two people will be in the field. One will be taken, and the other will be left.][n]

[37]The followers asked Jesus, "Where will this be, Lord?"

Jesus answered, "Where there is a dead body, there the vultures will gather."

GOD WILL ANSWER HIS PEOPLE

18 Then Jesus used this story to teach his followers that they should always pray and never lose hope. [2]"In a certain town there was a judge who did not respect God or care about people. [3]In that same town there was a widow who kept coming to this judge, saying, 'Give me my rights against my enemy.' [4]For a while the judge refused to help her. But afterwards, he thought to himself, 'Even though I don't respect God or care about people, [5]I will see that she gets her rights. Otherwise she will continue to bother me until I am worn out.'"

[6]The Lord said, "Listen to what the unfair judge said. [7]God will always give what is right to his people who cry to him night and day, and he will not be slow to answer them. [8]I tell you, God will help his people quickly. But when the Son of Man comes again, will he find those on earth who believe in him?"

BEING RIGHT WITH GOD

[9]Jesus told this story to some people who thought they were very good and looked down on everyone else: [10]"A Pharisee and a tax collector both went to the Temple to pray. [11]The Pharisee stood alone and prayed, 'God, I thank you that I am not like other people who steal, cheat, or take part in adultery, or even like this tax collector. [12]I fast[n] twice a week, and I give one-tenth of everything I get!'

17:14 show ... priests The Law of Moses said a priest must say when a person with a skin disease became well. **17:21 within** Or "among." **17:29 Sodom** City that God destroyed because the people were so evil. **17:32 Lot's wife** A story about what happened to Lot's wife is found in Genesis 19:15–17, 26. **17:36 Two ... left.** Some Greek copies do not contain the bracketed text. **18:12 fast** The people would give up eating for a special time of prayer and worship to God. It was also done to show sadness and disappointment.

¹³"The tax collector, standing at a distance, would not even look up to heaven. But he beat on his chest because he was so sad. He said, 'God, have mercy on me, a sinner.' ¹⁴I tell you, when this man went home, he was right with God, but the Pharisee was not. All who make themselves great will be made humble, but all who make themselves humble will be made great."

WHO WILL ENTER GOD'S KINGDOM?

¹⁵Some people brought even their babies to Jesus so he could touch them. When the followers saw this, they told them to stop. ¹⁶But Jesus called for the children, saying, "Let the little children come to me. Don't stop them, because the kingdom of God belongs to people who are like these children. ¹⁷I tell you the truth, you must accept the kingdom of God as if you were a child, or you will never enter it."

A RICH MAN'S QUESTION

¹⁸A certain leader asked Jesus, "Good Teacher, what must I do to have life forever?" ¹⁹Jesus said to him, "Why do you call me

---

UNDERSTANDING FREEDOM

FINANCES

receive your increase

LUKE 18:17

By Larry Stockstill

For some of us, receiving is a hard thing. We value our independence and do not want to take anything from anybody. We want to take care of ourselves. To a degree, that is good. We should not lie around and want whatever we can get from whoever will give it to us. That is lazy and selfish. However, there is a time and a place for receiving.

Sometimes we think that if God blesses us, there will not be enough for someone else who "really needs it." God is limitless in his resources. Giving to you does not diminish him in any way.

God says to believe that you *have* received what you are praying for. He is waiting for you to realize that you *already have* received, instead of *hoping to* receive. The Word speaks of a positive, already accomplished action, not something in the future. There is a very important difference between the two.

Like a loving father, God wants you to have what you need and sometimes what you want. God cannot bless you if you are full of greed, envy, or pride. If you remain humble and childlike in your relationship with the Lord, he can't wait to bless you. When you line up with his will, you can pray in confidence that he will answer. If your heart is pure, full of right motives, and passionate for the things of God, God will bless you with an abundant increase. It is just a matter of time.

reflect: Are you prepared to receive the blessings of God?

Go to **Luke 12:13–34.**

good? Only God is good. 20You know the commands: 'You must not be guilty of adultery. You must not murder anyone. You must not steal. You must not tell lies about your neighbor. Honor your father and mother.'"[n]

21But the leader said, "I have obeyed all these commands since I was a boy."

22When Jesus heard this, he said to him, "There is still one more thing you need to do. Sell everything you have and give it to the poor, and you will have treasure in heaven. Then come and follow me." 23But when the man heard this, he became very sad, because he was very rich.

24Jesus looked at him and said, "It is very hard for rich people to enter the kingdom of God. 25It is easier for a camel to go through the eye of a needle than for a rich person to enter the kingdom of God."

WHO CAN BE SAVED?

26When the people heard this, they asked, "Then who can be saved?"

27Jesus answered, "The things impossible for people are possible for God."

28Peter said, "Look, we have left everything and followed you."

29Jesus said, "I tell you the truth, all those who have left houses, wives, brothers, parents, or children for the kingdom of God 30will get much more in this life. And in the age that is coming, they will have life forever."

JESUS WILL RISE FROM THE DEAD

31Then Jesus took the twelve apostles aside and said to them, "We are going to Jerusalem. Everything the prophets wrote about the Son of Man will happen. 32He will be turned over to those who are evil. They will laugh at him, insult him, spit on him, 33beat him with whips, and kill him. But on the third day, he will rise to life again." 34The apostles did not understand this; the meaning was hidden from them, and they did not realize what was said.

JESUS HEALS A BLIND MAN

35As Jesus came near the city of Jericho, a blind man was sitting beside the road, begging. 36When he heard the people coming down the road, he asked, "What is happening?"

37They told him, "Jesus, from Nazareth, is going by."

38The blind man cried out, "Jesus, Son of David, have mercy on me!"

39The people leading the group warned the blind man to be quiet. But the blind man shouted even more, "Son of David, have mercy on me!"

40Jesus stopped and ordered the blind man to be brought to him. When he came near, Jesus asked him, 41"What do you want me to do for you?"

He said, "Lord, I want to see."

42Jesus said to him, "Then see. You are healed because you believed."

43At once the man was able to see, and he followed Jesus, thanking God. All the people who saw this praised God.

ZACCHAEUS MEETS JESUS

19 Jesus was going through the city of Jericho. 2A man was there named Zacchaeus, who was a very important tax collector, and he was wealthy. 3He wanted to see who Jesus was, but he was not able because he was too short to see above the crowd. 4He ran ahead to a place where Jesus would come, and he climbed a sycamore tree so he could see him. 5When Jesus came to that place, he looked up and said to him, "Zacchaeus, hurry and come down! I must stay at your house today."

6Zacchaeus came down quickly and welcomed him gladly. 7All the people saw this and began to complain, "Jesus is staying with a sinner!"

8But Zacchaeus stood and said to the Lord, "I will give half of my possessions to the poor. And if I have cheated anyone, I will pay back four times more."

9Jesus said to him, "Salvation has come to this house today, because this man also belongs to the family of Abraham. 10The Son of Man came to find lost people and save them."

A STORY ABOUT THREE SERVANTS

11As the people were listening to this, Jesus told them a story because he was near Jerusalem and they thought God's kingdom would appear immediately. 12He said: "A very important man went to a country far away to be made a king and then to return home. 13So

---

18:20 'You . . . mother.' Quotation from Exodus 20:12–16; Deuteronomy 5:16–20.

he called ten of his servants and gave a coin[n] to each servant. He said, 'Do business with this money until I get back.' [14]But the people in the kingdom hated the man. So they sent a group to follow him and say, 'We don't want this man to be our king.'

[15]"But the man became king. When he returned home, he said, 'Call those servants who have my money so I can know how much they earned with it.'

[16]"The first servant came and said, 'Sir, I earned ten coins with the one you gave me.'

[17]The king said to the servant, 'Excellent! You are a good servant. Since I can trust you with small things, I will let you rule over ten of my cities.'

[18]"The second servant said, 'Sir, I earned five coins with your one.' [19]The king said to this servant, 'You can rule over five cities.'

[20]"Then another servant came in and said to the king, 'Sir, here is your coin which

---

19:13 coin A Greek "mina." One mina was enough money to pay a person for working three months.

THE LONGEVITY FACTOR

-•\/\•-

FITNESS

hurry and worry

LUKE 19:1-6

Hurry up! Get going! Move along! One of the ubiquitous elements of our lives is **hurry.** We are so busy with life that we don't have time to live. We are so pressed with schedules and tasks and deadlines that we don't have time to work. We are inundated with the demand for instant everything.

This describes Zacchaeus perfectly. He ran to get ahead of the crowd. He scrambled up the tree. Jesus saw him and told him to hasten down. So he went as fast as he could. He rushed to his home to prepare for Jesus' arrival. He was the man in a hurry. But when Jesus arrived, life for Zacchaeus changed.

If you think about the lifestyle of Jesus, you will discover that he didn't hurry. He was radically relaxed about life. He didn't seem to worry or hurry about anything. Why do you suppose that the man on the world's greatest mission never rushed?

The answer is so obvious that it shocks us. Jesus was and is the totally dependent man. He is the very opposite of our rush to take care of everything. Jesus is never in a hurry because he is completely committed to God's care. And God doesn't seem to consider "hurry" a priority either. Do you suppose that God has a bigger perspective on things?

How would your life be different today if you really believed that God's care for you meant you didn't have to hurry? You'd probably stop and make some time to take care of yourself and others around you. So stop speeding through life and start enjoying it.

reflect: Think of several ways you can slow down the pace of life today.
Go to **John 5:6.**

I wrapped in a piece of cloth and hid. ²¹I was afraid of you, because you are a hard man. You even take money that you didn't earn and gather food that you didn't plant.' ²²Then the king said to the servant, 'I will condemn you by your own words, you evil servant. You knew that I am a hard man, taking money that I didn't earn and gathering food that I didn't plant. ²³Why then didn't you put my money in the bank? Then when I came back, my money would have earned some interest.'

²⁴"The king said to the men who were standing by, 'Take the coin away from this servant and give it to the servant who earned ten coins.' ²⁵They said, 'But sir, that servant already has ten coins.' ²⁶The king said, 'Those who have will be given more, but those who do not have anything will have everything taken away from them. ²⁷Now where are my enemies who didn't want me to be king? Bring them here and kill them before me.'"

JESUS ENTERS JERUSALEM AS A KING

²⁸After Jesus said this, he went on toward Jerusalem. ²⁹As Jesus came near Bethphage

---

TOTAL CHRISTIAN FITNESS

mission-centered life

FITNESS

LUKE 19:10

History books are filled with stories of people who faced life-threatening illness or injury, yet lived into their eighties and nineties too bound to their mission to leave the planet. There's something about a purpose that keeps you not just alive, but also kicking lively.

On the other hand, there is an eerie and common occurrence among people who retire: a tremendous percentage of these people die within the very next year. Perhaps they've left not only their careers but also their missions.

It's hard to imagine someone on a mission chronically unhappy and in need of mood-altering medication. The phrase "on a mission" conjures up an image of someone fired up, energetic, and ready to take on the world. It certainly doesn't paint a picture of someone depressed, fatigued, and hunched over on a barstool or in a medical waiting room.

Mission is defined as "the sending or self-imposed charge to *perform* a specific duty or service [purpose, object, or aim]." A military mission is a sworn duty. There are no intentions or aims, only results—or you die trying. It's a high calling and high commitment.

It's not just purpose; it's sworn and lasting purpose. There's focus, there's excitement, and there's a never-stop, never-quit attitude that causes you to learn, adapt, and persevere no matter the circumstance. Your mission is a command you keep in your heart no matter what comes.

reflect: Define your mission, and live it daily through the grace of God.
Go to **Colossians 2:19.**

and Bethany, towns near the hill called the Mount of Olives, he sent out two of his followers. ³⁰He said, "Go to the town you can see there. When you enter it, you will find a colt tied there, which no one has ever ridden. Untie it and bring it here to me. ³¹If anyone asks you why you are untying it, say that the Master needs it."

³²The two followers went into town and found the colt just as Jesus had told them. ³³As they were untying it, its owners came out and asked the followers, "Why are you untying our colt?"

³⁴The followers answered, "The Master needs it." ³⁵So they brought it to Jesus, threw their coats on the colt's back, and put Jesus on it. ³⁶As Jesus rode toward Jerusalem, others spread their coats on the road before him.

³⁷As he was coming close to Jerusalem, on the way down the Mount of Olives, the whole crowd of followers began joyfully shouting praise to God for all the miracles they had seen. ³⁸They said,

"God bless the king who comes in the
　　name of the Lord!　　　*Psalm 118:26*
There is peace in heaven and glory to God!"

³⁹Some of the Pharisees in the crowd said to Jesus, "Teacher, tell your followers not to say these things."

⁴⁰But Jesus answered, "I tell you, if my followers didn't say these things, then the stones would cry out."

JESUS CRIES FOR JERUSALEM

⁴¹As Jesus came near Jerusalem, he saw the city and cried for it, ⁴²saying, "I wish you knew today what would bring you peace. But now it is hidden from you. ⁴³The time is coming when your enemies will build a wall around you and will hold you in on all sides. ⁴⁴They will destroy you and all your people, and not one stone will be left on another. All this will happen because you did not recognize the time when God came to save you."

JESUS GOES TO THE TEMPLE

⁴⁵Jesus went into the Temple and began to throw out the people who were selling things there. ⁴⁶He said, "It is written in the Scriptures, 'My Temple will be a house for prayer.'ⁿ But you have changed it into a 'hideout for robbers'!"ⁿ

⁴⁷Jesus taught in the Temple every day. The leading priests, the experts on the law, and some of the leaders of the people wanted to kill Jesus. ⁴⁸But they did not know how they could do it, because all the people were listening closely to him.

JEWISH LEADERS QUESTION JESUS

20 One day Jesus was in the Temple, teaching the people and telling them the Good News. The leading priests, teachers of the law, and elders came up to talk with him, ²saying, "Tell us what authority you have to do these things? Who gave you this authority?"

³Jesus answered, "I will also ask you a question. Tell me: ⁴When John baptized people, was that authority from God or just from other people?"

⁵They argued about this, saying, "If we answer, 'John's baptism was from God,' Jesus will say, 'Then why did you not believe him?' ⁶But if we say, 'It was from other people,' all the people will stone us to death, because they believe John was a prophet." ⁷So they answered that they didn't know where it came from.

⁸Jesus said to them, "Then I won't tell you what authority I have to do these things."

A STORY ABOUT GOD'S SON

⁹Then Jesus told the people this story: "A man planted a vineyard and leased it to some farmers. Then he went away for a long time. ¹⁰When it was time for the grapes to be picked, he sent a servant to the farmers to get some of the grapes. But they beat the servant and sent him away empty-handed. ¹¹Then he sent another servant. They beat this servant also, and showed no respect for him, and sent him away empty-handed. ¹²So the man sent a third servant. The farmers wounded him and threw him out. ¹³The owner of the vineyard said, 'What will I do now? I will send my son whom I love. Maybe they will respect him.' ¹⁴But when the farmers saw the son, they said to each other, 'This son will inherit the vineyard. If we kill him, it will be ours.' ¹⁵So the farmers threw the son out of the vineyard and killed him.

19:46 'My Temple . . . prayer.' Quotation from Isaiah 56:7. **19:46 'hideout for robbers'** Quotation from Jeremiah 7:11.

"What will the owner of this vineyard do to them? 16He will come and kill those farmers and will give the vineyard to other farmers."

When the people heard this story, they said, "Let this never happen!"

17But Jesus looked at them and said, "Then what does this verse mean:

'The stone that the builders rejected
    became the cornerstone'? *Psalm 118:22*
18Everyone who falls on that stone will be broken, and the person on whom it falls, that person will be crushed!"

19The teachers of the law and the leading priests wanted to arrest Jesus at once, because they knew the story was about them. But they were afraid of what the people would do.

IS IT RIGHT TO PAY TAXES OR NOT?

20So they watched Jesus and sent some spies who acted as if they were sincere. They wanted to trap Jesus in saying something wrong so they could hand him over to the authority and power of the governor. 21So the spies asked Jesus, "Teacher, we know that what you say and teach is true. You pay no attention to who people are, and you always teach the truth about God's way. 22Tell us, is it right for us to pay taxes to Caesar or not?"

23But Jesus, knowing they were trying to trick him, said, 24"Show me a coin. Whose image and name are on it?"

They said, "Caesar's."

25Jesus said to them, "Then give to Caesar the things that are Caesar's, and give to God the things that are God's."

26So they were not able to trap Jesus in anything he said in the presence of the people. And being amazed at his answer, they became silent.

SOME SADDUCEES TRY TO TRICK JESUS

27Some Sadducees, who believed people would not rise from the dead, came to Jesus. 28They asked, "Teacher, Moses wrote that if a man's brother dies and leaves a wife but no children, then that man must marry the widow and have children for his brother. 29Once there were seven brothers. The first brother married and died, but had no children. 30Then the second brother married the widow, and he died. 31And the third brother married the widow, and he died. The same

thing happened with all seven brothers; they died and had no children. 32Finally, the woman died also. 33Since all seven brothers had married her, whose wife will she be when people rise from the dead?"

34Jesus said to them, "On earth, people marry and are given to someone to marry. 35But those who will be worthy to be raised from the dead and live again will not marry, nor will they be given to someone to marry. 36In that life they are like angels and cannot die. They are children of God, because they have been raised from the dead. 37Even Moses clearly showed that the dead are raised to life. When he wrote about the burning bush,[n] he said that the Lord is 'the God of Abraham, the God of Isaac, and the God of Jacob.'[n] 38God is the God of the living, not the dead, because all people are alive to him."

39Some of the teachers of the law said, "Teacher, your answer was good." 40No one was brave enough to ask him another question.

IS THE CHRIST THE SON OF DAVID?

41Then Jesus said, "Why do people say that the Christ is the Son of David? 42In the book of Psalms, David himself says:

'The Lord said to my Lord,
    "Sit by me at my right side,
43   until I put your enemies under your
        control." '[n]   *Psalm 110:1*
44David calls the Christ 'Lord,' so how can the Christ be his son?"

JESUS ACCUSES SOME LEADERS

45While all the people were listening, Jesus said to his followers, 46"Beware of the teachers of the law. They like to walk around wearing fancy clothes, and they love for people to greet them with respect in the marketplaces. They love to have the most important seats in the synagogues and at feasts. 47But they cheat widows and steal their houses and then try to make themselves look good by saying long prayers. They will receive a greater punishment."

20:37 burning bush Read Exodus 3:1–12 in the Old Testament. **20:37 'the God of . . . Jacob'** These words are taken from Exodus 3:6. **20:43 until . . . control** Literally, "until I make your enemies a footstool for your feet."

TRUE GIVING

21 As Jesus looked up, he saw some rich people putting their gifts into the Temple money box.[n] 2Then he saw a poor widow putting two small copper coins into the box. 3He said, "I tell you the truth, this poor widow gave more than all those rich people. 4They gave only what they did not need. This woman is very poor, but she gave all she had to live on."

THE TEMPLE WILL BE DESTROYED

5Some people were talking about the Temple and how it was decorated with beautiful stones and gifts offered to God.

But Jesus said, 6"As for these things you are looking at, the time will come when not one stone will be left on another. Every stone will be thrown down."

7They asked Jesus, "Teacher, when will these things happen? What will be the sign that they are about to take place?"

8Jesus said, "Be careful so you are not fooled. Many people will come in my name, saying, 'I am the One' and, 'The time has come!' But don't follow them. 9When you hear about wars and riots, don't be afraid, because these things must happen first, but the end will come later."

10Then he said to them, "Nations will fight against other nations, and kingdoms against other kingdoms. 11In various places there will be great earthquakes, sicknesses, and a lack of food. Fearful events and great signs will come from heaven.

12"But before all these things happen, people will arrest you and treat you cruelly. They will judge you in their synagogues and put you in jail and force you to stand before kings and governors, because you follow me. 13But this will give you an opportunity to tell about me. 14Make up your minds not to worry ahead of time about what you will say. 15I will give you the wisdom to say things that none of your enemies will be able to stand against or prove wrong. 16Even your parents, brothers, relatives, and friends will turn against you, and they will kill some of you. 17All people will hate you because you follow me. 18But none of these things can really harm you. 19By continuing to have faith you will save your lives.

JERUSALEM WILL BE DESTROYED

20"When you see armies all around Jerusalem, you will know it will soon be destroyed. 21At that time, the people in Judea should run away to the mountains. The people in Jerusalem must get out, and those who are near the city should not go in. 22These are the days of punishment to bring about all that is written in the Scriptures. 23How terrible it will be for women who are pregnant or have nursing babies! Great trouble will come upon this land, and God will be angry with these people. 24They will be killed by the sword and taken as prisoners to all nations. Jerusalem will be crushed by non-Jewish people until their time is over.

DON'T FEAR

25"There will be signs in the sun, moon, and stars. On earth, nations will be afraid and confused because of the roar and fury of the sea. 26People will be so afraid they will faint, wondering what is happening to the world, because the powers of the heavens will be shaken. 27Then people will see the Son of Man coming in a cloud with power and great glory. 28When these things begin to happen, look up and hold your heads high, because the time when God will free you is near!"

JESUS' WORDS WILL LIVE FOREVER

29Then Jesus told this story: "Look at the fig tree and all the other trees. 30When their leaves appear, you know that summer is near. 31In the same way, when you see these things happening, you will know that God's kingdom is near.

32"I tell you the truth, all these things will happen while the people of this time are still living. 33Earth and sky will be destroyed, but the words I have spoken will never be destroyed.

BE READY ALL THE TIME

34"Be careful not to spend your time feasting, drinking, or worrying about worldly things. If you do, that day might come on you suddenly, 35like a trap on all people on earth. 36So be ready all the time. Pray that you will be strong enough to escape all these things that will happen and that you will be able to stand before the Son of Man."

21:1 money box A special box in the Jewish place of worship where people put their gifts to God.

37During the day, Jesus taught the people in the Temple, and at night he went out of the city and stayed on the Mount of Olives. 38Every morning all the people got up early to go to the Temple to listen to him.

JUDAS BECOMES AN ENEMY OF JESUS

22 It was almost time for the Feast of Unleavened Bread, called the Passover Feast. 2The leading priests and teachers of the law were trying to find a way to kill Jesus, because they were afraid of the people.

3Satan entered Judas Iscariot, one of Jesus' twelve apostles. 4Judas went to the leading priests and some of the soldiers who guarded the Temple and talked to them about a way to hand Jesus over to them. 5They were pleased and agreed to give Judas money. 6He agreed and watched for the best time to hand Jesus over to them when he was away from the crowd.

JESUS EATS THE PASSOVER MEAL

7The Day of Unleavened Bread came when the Passover lambs had to be sacrificed. 8Jesus said to Peter and John, "Go and prepare the Passover meal for us to eat."

9They asked, "Where do you want us to prepare it?" 10Jesus said to them, "After you go into the city, a man carrying a jar of water will meet you. Follow him into the house that he enters, 11and tell the owner of the house, 'The Teacher says: "Where is the guest room in which I may eat the Passover meal with my followers?" ' 12Then he will show you a large, furnished room upstairs. Prepare the Passover meal there."

13So Peter and John left and found everything as Jesus had said. And they prepared the Passover meal.

THE LORD'S SUPPER

14When the time came, Jesus and the apostles were sitting at the table. 15He said to them, "I wanted very much to eat this Passover meal with you before I suffer. 16I will not eat another Passover meal until it is given its true meaning in the kingdom of God."

17Then Jesus took a cup, gave thanks, and said, "Take this cup and share it among yourselves. 18I will not drink again from the fruit of the vine[n] until God's kingdom comes."

19Then Jesus took some bread, gave thanks, broke it, and gave it to the apostles,

saying, "This is my body,[n] which I am giving for you. Do this to remember me." 20In the same way, after supper, Jesus took the cup and said, "This cup is the new agreement that God makes with his people. This new agreement begins with my blood which is poured out for you."

WHO WILL TURN AGAINST JESUS?

21"But one of you will turn against me, and his hand is with mine on the table. 22What God has planned for the Son of Man will happen, but how terrible it will be for that one who turns against the Son of Man."

23Then the apostles asked each other which one of them would do that.

BE LIKE A SERVANT

24The apostles also began to argue about which one of them was the most important. 25But Jesus said to them, "The kings of the non-Jewish people rule over them, and those who have authority over others like to be called 'friends of the people.' 26But you must not be like that. Instead, the greatest among you should be like the youngest, and the leader should be like the servant. 27Who is more important: the one sitting at the table or the one serving? You think the one at the table is more important, but I am like a servant among you.

28"You have stayed with me through my struggles. 29Just as my Father has given me a kingdom, I also give you a kingdom 30so you may eat and drink at my table in my kingdom. And you will sit on thrones, judging the twelve tribes of Israel.

DON'T LOSE YOUR FAITH!

31"Simon, Simon, Satan has asked to test all of you as a farmer sifts his wheat. 32I have prayed that you will not lose your faith! Help your brothers be stronger when you come back to me."

33But Peter said to Jesus, "Lord, I am ready to go with you to prison and even to die with you!"

34But Jesus said, "Peter, before the rooster crows this day, you will say three times that you don't know me."

22:18 fruit of the vine Product of the grapevine; this may also be translated "wine." **22:19b–20 body** Some Greek copies do not have the rest of verse 19 or verse 20.

BE READY FOR TROUBLE

[35] Then Jesus said to the apostles, "When I sent you out without a purse, a bag, or sandals, did you need anything?"

They said, "No."

[36] He said to them, "But now if you have a purse or a bag, carry that with you. If you don't have a sword, sell your coat and buy one. [37] The Scripture says, 'He was treated like a criminal,'[n] and I tell you this scripture must have its full meaning. It was written about me, and it is happening now."

[38] His followers said, "Look, Lord, here are two swords."

He said to them, "That is enough."

JESUS PRAYS ALONE

[39] Jesus left the city and went to the Mount of Olives, as he often did, and his followers went with him. [40] When he reached the place, he said to them, "Pray for strength against temptation."

[41] Then Jesus went about a stone's throw

22:37 '**He . . . criminal.**' Quotation from Isaiah 53:12.

FUTURE

WHO ARE YOU?

Jesus won back our **willpower**

LUKE 22:42-44   By Larry Huch

You can have the willpower to change your life because Jesus shed his blood as part of God's plan for your restoration. You can say yes to the will of God in your life and no to the Enemy of your life.

The first Adam surrendered to Satan in the Garden of Eden. Adam chose his will over the will of God and sacrificed man's willpower in every area. With Adam's disobedience, the Enemy gained control over humanity's ability to say yes to all of God's goodness and no to the bad the enemy wants us to do. The second Adam, Jesus, restored your willpower in the Garden of Gethsemane by agreeing to fulfill God's plan.

Jesus sweat drops of his perfect blood in the Garden of Gethsemane. Doctors have confirmed that at times of intense agony or torment, blood vessels can break beneath the skin so that blood literally seeps out of the pores like sweat. That night there was an extreme struggle going on inside Jesus—the will of the Father versus the will of man.

The same conflict faced Adam and often faces us today: whether to follow our desires or the desires of God. Jesus knew what was going to happen to him. His spirit and his flesh battled, but he won when he submitted to the will of the Father. We do not need to try to change our lives in our own strength. The power of Jesus' blood returned our willpower and now strengthens us to walk in liberty. (From *Free at Last*)

reflect: What type of behavior do you want to see changed in your life?
Go to **1 Corinthians 15:10.**

away from them. He kneeled down and prayed, [42]"Father, if you are willing, take away this cup[n] of suffering. But do what you want, not what I want." [43]Then an angel from heaven appeared to him to strengthen him. [44]Being full of pain, Jesus prayed even harder. His sweat was like drops of blood falling to the ground. [45]When he finished praying, he went to his followers and found them asleep because of their sadness. [46]Jesus said to them, "Why are you sleeping? Get up and pray for strength against temptation."

JESUS IS ARRESTED

[47]While Jesus was speaking, a crowd came up, and Judas, one of the twelve apostles, was leading them. He came close to Jesus so he could kiss him.

[48]But Jesus said to him, "Judas, are you using the kiss to give the Son of Man to his enemies?"

[49]When those who were standing around him saw what was happening, they said, "Lord, should we strike them with our swords?" [50]And one of them struck the servant of the high priest and cut off his right ear.

[51]Jesus said, "Stop! No more of this." Then he touched the servant's ear and healed him.

[52]Those who came to arrest Jesus were the leading priests, the soldiers who guarded the Temple, and the elders. Jesus said to them, "You came out here with swords and clubs as though I were a criminal. [53]I was with you every day in the Temple, and you didn't arrest me there. But this is your time—the time when darkness rules."

PETER SAYS HE DOESN'T KNOW JESUS

[54]They arrested Jesus, and led him away, and brought him into the house of the high priest. Peter followed far behind them. [55]After the soldiers started a fire in the middle of the courtyard and sat together, Peter sat with them. [56]A servant girl saw Peter sitting there in the firelight, and looking closely at him, she said, "This man was also with him."

[57]But Peter said this was not true; he said, "Woman, I don't know him."

[58]A short time later, another person saw Peter and said, "You are also one of them."

But Peter said, "Man, I am not!"

[59]About an hour later, another man insisted, "Certainly this man was with him, because he is from Galilee, too."

[60]But Peter said, "Man, I don't know what you are talking about!"

At once, while Peter was still speaking, a rooster crowed. [61]Then the Lord turned and looked straight at Peter. And Peter remembered what the Lord had said: "Before the rooster crows this day, you will say three times that you don't know me." [62]Then Peter went outside and cried painfully.

THE PEOPLE MAKE FUN OF JESUS

[63]The men who were guarding Jesus began making fun of him and beating him. [64]They blindfolded him and said, "Prove that you are a prophet, and tell us who hit you." [65]They said many cruel things to Jesus.

JESUS BEFORE THE LEADERS

[66]When day came, the council of the elders of the people, both the leading priests and the teachers of the law, came together and led Jesus to their highest court. [67]They said, "If you are the Christ, tell us."

Jesus said to them, "If I tell you, you will not believe me. [68]And if I ask you, you will not answer. [69]But from now on, the Son of Man will sit at the right hand of the powerful God."

[70]They all said, "Then are you the Son of God?"

Jesus said to them, "You say that I am."

[71]They said, "Why do we need witnesses now? We ourselves heard him say this."

PILATE QUESTIONS JESUS

23 Then the whole group stood up and led Jesus to Pilate.[n] [2]They began to accuse Jesus, saying, "We caught this man telling things that mislead our people. He says that we should not pay taxes to Caesar, and he calls himself the Christ, a king."

[3]Pilate asked Jesus, "Are you the king of the Jews?"

Jesus answered, "Those are your words."

[4]Pilate said to the leading priests and the people, "I find nothing against this man."

[5]They were insisting, saying, "But Jesus makes trouble with the people, teaching all around Judea. He began in Galilee, and now he is here."

22:42 cup Jesus is talking about the painful things that will happen to him. Accepting these things will be hard, like drinking a cup of something bitter. **23:1 Pilate** Pontius Pilate was the Roman governor of Judea from A.D. 26 to A.D. 36.

PILATE SENDS JESUS TO HEROD

⁶Pilate heard this and asked if Jesus was from Galilee. ⁷Since Jesus was under Herod's authority, Pilate sent Jesus to Herod, who was in Jerusalem at that time. ⁸When Herod saw Jesus, he was very glad, because he had heard about Jesus and had wanted to meet him for a long time. He was hoping to see Jesus work a miracle. ⁹Herod asked Jesus many questions, but Jesus said nothing. ¹⁰The leading priests and teachers of the law were standing there, strongly accusing Jesus. ¹¹After Herod and his soldiers had made fun of Jesus, they dressed him in a kingly robe and sent him back to Pilate. ¹²In the past, Pilate and Herod had always been enemies, but on that day they became friends.

JESUS MUST DIE

¹³Pilate called the people together with the leading priests and the rulers. ¹⁴He said to them, "You brought this man to me, saying he makes trouble among the people. But I have questioned him before you all, and I have not found him guilty of what you say. ¹⁵Also, Herod found nothing wrong with him; he sent him back to us. Look, he has done nothing for which he should die. ¹⁶So, after I punish him, I will let him go free." [¹⁷Every year at the Passover Feast, Pilate had to release one prisoner to the people.]ⁿ

¹⁸But the people shouted together, "Take this man away! Let Barabbas go free!" ¹⁹(Barabbas was a man who was in prison for his part in a riot in the city and for murder.)

²⁰Pilate wanted to let Jesus go free and told this to the crowd. ²¹But they shouted again, "Crucify him! Crucify him!"

²²A third time Pilate said to them, "Why? What wrong has he done? I can find no reason to kill him. So I will have him punished and set him free."

²³But they continued to shout, demanding that Jesus be crucified. Their yelling became so loud that ²⁴Pilate decided to give them what they wanted. ²⁵He set free the man who was in jail for rioting and murder, and he handed Jesus over to them to do with him as they wished.

JESUS IS CRUCIFIED

²⁶As they led Jesus away, Simon, a man from Cyrene, was coming in from the fields. They forced him to carry Jesus' cross and to walk behind him.

²⁷A large crowd of people was following Jesus, including some women who were sad and crying for him. ²⁸But Jesus turned and said to them, "Women of Jerusalem, don't cry for me. Cry for yourselves and for your children. ²⁹The time is coming when people will say, 'Blessed are the women who cannot have children and who have no babies to nurse.' ³⁰Then people will say to the mountains, 'Fall on us!' And they will say to the hills, 'Cover us!' ³¹If they act like this now when life is good, what will happen when bad times come?"ⁿ

³²There were also two criminals led out with Jesus to be put to death. ³³When they came to a place called the Skull, the soldiers crucified Jesus and the criminals—one on his right and the other on his left. ³⁴Jesus said, "Father, forgive them, because they don't know what they are doing."ⁿ

The soldiers threw lots to decide who would get his clothes. ³⁵The people stood there watching. And the leaders made fun of Jesus, saying, "He saved others. Let him save himself if he is God's Chosen One, the Christ."

³⁶The soldiers also made fun of him, coming to Jesus and offering him some vinegar. ³⁷They said, "If you are the king of the Jews, save yourself!" ³⁸At the top of the cross these words were written: THIS IS THE KING OF THE JEWS.

³⁹One of the criminals on a cross began to shout insults at Jesus: "Aren't you the Christ? Then save yourself and us."

⁴⁰But the other criminal stopped him and said, "You should fear God! You are getting the same punishment he is. ⁴¹We are punished justly, getting what we deserve for what we did. But this man has done nothing wrong." ⁴²Then he said, "Jesus, remember me when you come into your kingdom."

⁴³Jesus said to him, "I tell you the truth, today you will be with me in paradise."ⁿ

JESUS DIES

⁴⁴It was about noon, and the whole land became dark until three o'clock in the

---

23:17 Every . . . people. Some Greek copies do not contain the bracketed text. **23:31 If . . . come?** Literally, "If they do these things in the green tree, what will happen in the dry?" **23:34 Jesus . . . doing."** Some Greek copies do not have this first part of verse 34. **23:43 paradise** Another word for heaven.

afternoon, [45]because the sun did not shine. The curtain in the Temple[n] was torn in two. [46]Jesus cried out in a loud voice, "Father, I give you my life." After Jesus said this, he died.

[47]When the army officer there saw what happened, he praised God, saying, "Surely this was a good man!"

[48]When all the people who had gathered there to watch saw what happened, they returned home, beating their chests because they were so sad. [49]But those who were close friends of Jesus, including the women who had followed him from Galilee, stood at a distance and watched.

JOSEPH TAKES JESUS' BODY

[50]There was a good and religious man named Joseph who was a member of the council. [51]But he had not agreed to the other leaders' plans and actions against Jesus. He was from the town of Arimathea and was waiting for the kingdom of God to come. [52]Joseph went to Pilate to ask for the body of Jesus. [53]He took the body down from the cross, wrapped it in cloth, and put it in a tomb that was cut out of a wall of rock. This tomb had never been used before. [54]This was late on Preparation Day, and when the sun went down, the Sabbath day would begin.

[55]The women who had come from Galilee with Jesus followed Joseph and saw the tomb and how Jesus' body was laid. [56]Then the women left to prepare spices and perfumes.

On the Sabbath day they rested, as the law of Moses commanded.

JESUS RISES FROM THE DEAD

24 Very early on the first day of the week, at dawn, the women came to the tomb, bringing the spices they had prepared. [2]They found the stone rolled away from the entrance of the tomb, [3]but when they went in, they did not find the body of the Lord Jesus. [4]While they were wondering about this, two men in shining clothes suddenly stood beside them. [5]The women were very afraid and bowed their heads to the ground. The men said to them, "Why are you looking for a living person in this place for the dead? [6]He is not here; he has risen from the dead. Do you remember what he told you in Galilee? [7]He said the Son of Man must be handed over to sinful people, be crucified, and rise from

the dead on the third day." [8]Then the women remembered what Jesus had said.

[9]The women left the tomb and told all these things to the eleven apostles and the other followers. [10]It was Mary Magdalene, Joanna, Mary the mother of James, and some other women who told the apostles everything that had happened at the tomb. [11]But they did not believe the women, because it sounded like nonsense. [12]But Peter got up and ran to the tomb. Bending down and looking in, he saw only the cloth that Jesus' body had been wrapped in. Peter went away to his home, wondering about what had happened.

JESUS ON THE ROAD TO EMMAUS

[13]That same day two of Jesus' followers were going to a town named Emmaus, about seven miles from Jerusalem. [14]They were talking about everything that had happened. [15]While they were talking and discussing, Jesus himself came near and began walking with them, [16]but they were kept from recognizing him. [17]Then he said, "What are these things you are talking about while you walk?"

The two followers stopped, looking very sad. [18]The one named Cleopas answered, "Are you the only visitor in Jerusalem who does not know what just happened there?"

[19]Jesus said to them, "What are you talking about?"

They said, "About Jesus of Nazareth. He was a prophet who said and did many powerful things before God and all the people. [20]Our leaders and the leading priests handed him over to be sentenced to death, and they crucified him. [21]But we were hoping that he would free Israel. Besides this, it is now the third day since this happened. [22]And today some women among us amazed us. Early this morning they went to the tomb, [23]but they did not find his body there. They came and told us that they had seen a vision of angels who said that Jesus was alive! [24]So some of our group went to the tomb, too. They found it just as the women said, but they did not see Jesus."

[25]Then Jesus said to them, "You are foolish and slow to believe everything the

---

23:45 curtain in the Temple A curtain divided the Most Holy Place from the other part of the Temple, the special building in Jerusalem where God commanded the Jewish people to worship him.

prophets said. 26They said that the Christ must suffer these things before he enters his glory." 27Then starting with what Moses and all the prophets had said about him, Jesus began to explain everything that had been written about himself in the Scriptures.

28They came near the town of Emmaus, and Jesus acted as if he were going farther. 29But they begged him, "Stay with us, because it is late; it is almost night." So he went in to stay with them.

30When Jesus was at the table with them, he took some bread, gave thanks, divided it, and gave it to them. 31And then, they were allowed to recognize Jesus. But when they saw who he was, he disappeared. 32They said to each other, "It felt like a fire burning in us when Jesus talked to us on the road and explained the Scriptures to us."

33So the two followers got up at once and went back to Jerusalem. There they found the eleven apostles and others gathered. 34They were saying, "The Lord really has risen from the dead! He showed himself to Simon."

35Then the two followers told what had happened on the road and how they recognized Jesus when he divided the bread.

JESUS APPEARS TO HIS FOLLOWERS

36While the two followers were telling this, Jesus himself stood right in the middle of them and said, "Peace be with you."

37They were fearful and terrified and thought they were seeing a ghost. 38But Jesus said, "Why are you troubled? Why do you doubt what you see? 39Look at my hands and my feet. It is I myself! Touch me and see, because a ghost does not have a living body as you see I have."

40After Jesus said this, he showed them his hands and feet. 41While they still could not believe it because they were amazed and happy, Jesus said to them, "Do you have any food here?" 42They gave him a piece of broiled fish. 43While the followers watched, Jesus took the fish and ate it.

44He said to them, "Remember when I was with you before? I said that everything written about me must happen—everything in the law of Moses, the books of the prophets, and the Psalms."

45Then Jesus opened their minds so they could understand the Scriptures. 46He said to them, "It is written that the Christ would suffer and rise from the dead on the third day 47and that a change of hearts and lives and forgiveness of sins would be preached in his name to all nations, starting at Jerusalem. 48You are witnesses of these things. 49I will send you what my Father has promised, but you must stay in Jerusalem until you have received that power from heaven."

JESUS GOES BACK TO HEAVEN

50Jesus led his followers as far as Bethany, and he raised his hands and blessed them. 51While he was blessing them, he was separated from them and carried into heaven. 52They worshiped him and returned to Jerusalem very happy. 53They stayed in the Temple all the time, praising God.

CHRIST COMES TO THE WORLD

1 In the beginning there was the Word.[n] The Word was with God, and the Word was God. [2]He was with God in the beginning. [3]All things were made by him, and nothing was made without him. [4]In him there was life, and that life was the light of all people. [5]The Light shines in the darkness, and the darkness has not overpowered[n] it.

[6]There was a man named John[n] who was sent by God. [7]He came to tell people the truth about the Light so that through him all people could hear about the Light and believe. [8]John was not the Light, but he came to tell people the truth about the Light. [9]The true Light that gives light to all was coming into the world!

[10]The Word was in the world, and the world was made by him, but the world did not know him. [11]He came to the world that was his own, but his own people did not accept him. [12]But to all who did accept him and believe in him he gave the right to become children of God. [13]They did not become his children in any human way—by any human parents or human desire. They were born of God.

[14]The Word became a human and lived among us. We saw his glory—the glory that belongs to the only Son of the Father—and he was full of grace and truth. [15]John tells the truth about him and cries out, saying, "This is the One I told you about: 'The One who comes after me is greater than I am, because he was living before me.'"

[16]Because he was full of grace and truth, from him we all received one gift after another. [17]The law was given through Moses, but grace and truth came through Jesus Christ. [18]No one has ever seen God. But God the only Son is very close to the Father,[n] and he has shown us what God is like.

JOHN TELLS PEOPLE ABOUT JESUS

[19]Here is the truth John[n] told when the leaders in Jerusalem sent priests and Levites to ask him, "Who are you?"

[20]John spoke freely and did not refuse to answer. He said, "I am not the Christ."

[21]So they asked him, "Then who are you? Are you Elijah?"[n]

He answered, "No, I am not."

"Are you the Prophet?"[n] they asked.

He answered, "No."

[22]Then they said, "Who are you? Give us an answer to tell those who sent us. What do you say about yourself?"

[23]John told them in the words of the prophet Isaiah:

"I am the voice of one
    calling out in the desert:
'Make the road straight for the Lord.'"

Isaiah 40:3

[24]Some Pharisees who had been sent asked John: [25]"If you are not the Christ or Elijah or the Prophet, why do you baptize people?"

[26]John answered, "I baptize with water, but there is one here with you that you don't know about. [27]He is the One who comes after me. I am not good enough to untie the strings of his sandals."

[28]This all happened at Bethany on the other side of the Jordan River, where John was baptizing people.

[29]The next day John saw Jesus coming toward him. John said, "Look, the Lamb of God,[n] who takes away the sin of the world!

1:1 Word The Greek word is "logos," meaning any kind of communication; it could be translated "message." Here, it means Christ, because Christ was the way God told people about himself. **1:5 overpowered** This can also be translated, "understood." **1:6 John** John the Baptist, who preached to people about Christ's coming (Matthew 3, Luke 3). **1:18 But . . . Father** This could be translated, "But the only God is very close to the Father." Also, some Greek copies read "But the only Son is very close to the Father." **1:19 John** John the Baptist, who preached to people about Christ's coming (Matthew 3, Luke 3). **1:21 Elijah** A prophet who spoke for God. He lived hundreds of years before Christ and was expected to return before Christ (Malachi 4:5–6). **1:21 Prophet** They probably meant the prophet that God told Moses he would send (Deuteronomy 18:15–19). **1:29 Lamb of God** Name for Jesus. Jesus is like the lambs that were offered for a sacrifice to God.

A **Partnership** with **God**

FAITH

By Elmer Towns

JOHN 1:12

Many church members claim to have a relationship with God, but not all are born-again Christians. Just because a person claims to be a Christian or a member of the church does not mean he or she is in partnership with God. One plus one does not necessarily equal two. Here's how to be sure.

God is in partnership with those related to him through the new birth. The Bible teaches that we can be related to God by receiving Jesus Christ. "But to all who did accept him and believe in him he gave the right to become children of God" (John 1:12). We become related to him by believing in Jesus Christ.

God is a partner to those doing the right things. There are many who have come to a saving knowledge of Jesus Christ. But that does not mean they have joined hands with God to serve him daily. Paul could say to the believers in Corinth, "We are God's workers, working together" (1 Corinthians 3:9). Paul and the church at Corinth had formed a partnership to serve God. In a real sense, our availability to serve God is greater than our ability to serve God.

God is a partner with those who love others. To be in a partnership with God, we must not be guilty of narcissism, which is love of self. Instead, we find true love as we give ourselves to other people. Jesus said, "The greatest love a person can show is to die for his friends" (John 15:13). Later, John,

writing on the same theme, said, "This is how we know what real love is: Jesus gave his life for us. So we should give our lives for our brothers and sisters" (1 John 3:16).

God is a partner with those who do his work. When we join forces with God to carry out his work, all of those who join us become partners together with God. "We are God's workers, working together; you are like God's farm, God's house" (1 Corinthians 3:9).

God is in partnership with those who give him glory. Jesus taught us to pray, "Our Father in heaven, may your name always be kept holy" (Matthew 6:9). When we pray the first petition of the Lord's Prayer we give glory to the Father. All who join in glorifying the Father are in partnership. The family members who pray together are taking steps toward a spiritual partnership that will bond them to one another and to God.

God enters partnership with any who meet his conditions. Jesus told followers to "follow me." On another occasion he told his listeners that people who want to follow him "must be willing to give up their lives daily" (Luke 9:23). In many different ways, the challenge is given for people to follow Jesus Christ by partnering with him. In the same way, that challenge is given to young families today. Those families that respond positively should sign an agreement with God.

TO LEARN MORE ON WHAT THE BIBLE HAS TO SAY ABOUT **FAITH,** READ THE SCRIPTURES AND DEVOTIONALS AT **ROMANS 5:6, ROMANS 10:9, 2 CORINTHIANS 4:13, 2 CORINTHIANS 12:9, EPHESIANS 1:22,** AND **EPHESIANS 2:8-9.**

[30]This is the One I was talking about when I said, 'A man will come after me, but he is greater than I am, because he was living before me.' [31]Even I did not know who he was, although I came baptizing with water so that the people of Israel would know who he is."

[32-33]Then John said, "I saw the Spirit come down from heaven in the form of a dove and rest on him. Until then I did not know who the Christ was. But the God who sent me to baptize with water told me, 'You will see the Spirit come down and rest on a man; he is the One who will baptize with the Holy Spirit.' [34]I have seen this happen, and I tell you the truth: This man is the Son of God."[n]

THE FIRST FOLLOWERS OF JESUS

[35]The next day John[n] was there again with two of his followers. [36]When he saw Jesus walking by, he said, "Look, the Lamb of God!"[n]

[37]The two followers heard John say this, so they followed Jesus. [38]When Jesus turned and saw them following him, he asked, "What are you looking for?"

They said, "Rabbi, where are you staying?" ("Rabbi" means "Teacher.")

[39]He answered, "Come and see." So the two men went with Jesus and saw where he was staying and stayed there with him that day. It was about four o'clock in the afternoon.

[40]One of the two men who followed Jesus after they heard John speak about him was Andrew, Simon Peter's brother. [41]The first thing Andrew did was to find his brother Simon and say to him, "We have found the Messiah." ("Messiah" means "Christ.")

[42]Then Andrew took Simon to Jesus. Jesus looked at him and said, "You are Simon son of John. You will be called Cephas." ("Cephas" means "Peter."[n])

[43]The next day Jesus decided to go to Galilee. He found Philip and said to him, "Follow me."

[44]Philip was from the town of Bethsaida, where Andrew and Peter lived. [45]Philip found Nathanael and told him, "We have found the man that Moses wrote about in the law, and the prophets also wrote about him. He is Jesus, the son of Joseph, from Nazareth."

[46]But Nathanael said to Philip, "Can anything good come from Nazareth?"

Philip answered, "Come and see."

[47]As Jesus saw Nathanael coming toward him, he said, "Here is truly an Israelite. There is nothing false in him."

[48]Nathanael asked, "How do you know me?"

Jesus answered, "I saw you when you were under the fig tree, before Philip told you about me."

[49]Then Nathanael said to Jesus, "Teacher, you are the Son of God; you are the King of Israel."

[50]Jesus said to Nathanael, "Do you believe simply because I told you I saw you under the fig tree? You will see greater things than that." [51]And Jesus said to them, "I tell you the truth, you will all see heaven open and 'angels of God going up and coming down'[n] on the Son of Man."

THE WEDDING AT CANA

2 Two days later there was a wedding in the town of Cana in Galilee. Jesus' mother was there, [2]and Jesus and his followers were also invited to the wedding. [3]When all the wine was gone, Jesus' mother said to him, "They have no more wine."

[4]Jesus answered, "Dear woman, why come to me? My time has not yet come."

[5]His mother said to the servants, "Do whatever he tells you to do."

[6]In that place there were six stone water jars that the Jews used in their washing ceremony.[n] Each jar held about twenty or thirty gallons.

[7]Jesus said to the servants, "Fill the jars with water." So they filled the jars to the top.

[8]Then he said to them, "Now take some out and give it to the master of the feast."

So they took the water to the master. [9]When he tasted it, the water had become wine. He did not know where the wine came from, but the servants who had brought the water knew. The master of the wedding

---

1:34 the Son of God Some Greek copies read "God's Chosen One." **1:35 John** John the Baptist, who preached to people about Christ's coming (Matthew 3, Luke 3). **1:36 Lamb of God** Name for Jesus. Jesus is like the lambs that were offered for a sacrifice to God. **1:42 Peter** The Greek name "Peter," like the Aramaic name "Cephas," means "rock." **1:51 'angels . . . down'** These words are from Genesis 28:12. **2:6 washing ceremony** The Jewish people washed themselves in special ways before eating, before worshiping in the Temple, and at other special times.

called the bridegroom ¹⁰and said to him, "People always serve the best wine first. Later, after the guests have been drinking awhile, they serve the cheaper wine. But you have saved the best wine till now."

¹¹So in Cana of Galilee Jesus did his first miracle. There he showed his glory, and his followers believed in him.

JESUS IN THE TEMPLE

¹²After this, Jesus went to the town of Capernaum with his mother, brothers, and followers. They stayed there for just a few days. ¹³When it was almost time for the Jewish Passover Feast, Jesus went to Jerusalem. ¹⁴In the Temple he found people selling cattle, sheep, and doves. He saw others sitting at tables, exchanging different kinds of money. ¹⁵Jesus made a whip out of cords and forced all of them, both the sheep and cattle, to leave the Temple. He turned over the tables and scattered the money of those who were exchanging it. ¹⁶Then he said to those who were selling pigeons, "Take these things

---

COVENANT MARRIAGE

changing
relationships

FAMILY

JOHN 2:1-4

Jesus is not being harsh here. He uses this same word for "woman" in moments of great tenderness; for example, when he transfers responsibility for care of his mother to John as he is dying on the cross. It is not a cold and sterile rejection. But the question following this address indicates that there has been a change in Jesus' relationship with his mother.

He is deliberately stepping away from those family associations. He is beginning a new chapter in his life. His old relationships are being altered. The course of his life is to be directed by the Father. Even though there is tenderness in his address to Mary, nothing will distract him from doing the will of his Father.

Most of our relationships to other people require accommodations. God knows all about that fact, and he gives us plenty of useful information about how we are to conduct those relationships. Husbands, love your wives. Wives, obey your husbands. Children, honor your parents. Lots of accommodations.

But there is one relationship that must never be compromised, even if intimate family members are in the mix. The admonition to "love the Lord your God with all your heart, all your soul, all your mind, and all your strength" (Mark 12:30) does not give room for diverting attention to someone else. God is to come first, always. Old relationships must change if we are to separate ourselves to God's purposes. Tenderness must meet commitment.

reflect: Consider in what areas you need to give God greater place in your life.

Go to **John 4:14.**

out of here! Don't make my Father's house a place for buying and selling!"

[17]When this happened, the followers remembered what was written in the Scriptures: "My strong love for your Temple completely controls me."[n]

[18]Some of his people said to Jesus, "Show us a miracle to prove you have the right to do these things."

[19]Jesus answered them, "Destroy this temple, and I will build it again in three days."

[20]They answered, "It took forty-six years to build this Temple! Do you really believe you can build it again in three days?"

[21](But the temple Jesus meant was his own body. [22]After Jesus was raised from the dead, his followers remembered that Jesus had said this. Then they believed the Scripture and the words Jesus had said.)

[23]When Jesus was in Jerusalem for the Passover Feast, many people believed in him because they saw the miracles he did. [24]But Jesus did not believe in them because he knew them all. [25]He did not need anyone to tell him about people, because he knew what was in people's minds.

NICODEMUS COMES TO JESUS

3There was a man named Nicodemus who was one of the Pharisees and an important Jewish leader. [2]One night Nicodemus came to Jesus and said, "Teacher, we know you are a teacher sent from God, because no one can do the miracles you do unless God is with him."

[3]Jesus answered, "I tell you the truth, unless you are born again, you cannot be in God's kingdom."

[4]Nicodemus said, "But if a person is already old, how can he be born again? He cannot enter his mother's womb again. So how can a person be born a second time?"

[5]But Jesus answered, "I tell you the truth, unless you are born from water and the Spirit, you cannot enter God's kingdom. [6]Human life comes from human parents, but spiritual life comes from the Spirit. [7]Don't be surprised when I tell you, 'You must all be born again.' [8]The wind blows where it wants to and you hear the sound of it, but you don't know where the wind comes from or where it is going. It is the same with every person who is born from the Spirit."

[9]Nicodemus asked, "How can this happen?"

[10]Jesus said, "You are an important teacher in Israel, and you don't understand these things? [11]I tell you the truth, we talk about what we know, and we tell about what we have seen, but you don't accept what we tell you. [12]I have told you about things here on earth, and you do not believe me. So you will not believe me if I tell you about things of heaven. [13]The only one who has ever gone up to heaven is the One who came down from heaven—the Son of Man.[n]

[14]"Just as Moses lifted up the snake in the desert,[n] the Son of Man must also be lifted up. [15]So that everyone who believes can have eternal life in him.

[16]"God loved the world so much that he gave his one and only Son so that whoever believes in him may not be lost, but have eternal life. [17]God did not send his Son into the world to judge the world guilty, but to save the world through him. [18]People who believe in God's Son are not judged guilty. Those who do not believe have already been judged guilty, because they have not believed in God's one and only Son. [19]They are judged by this fact: The Light has come into the world, but they did not want light. They wanted darkness, because they were doing evil things. [20]All who do evil hate the light and will not come to the light, because it will show all the evil things they do. [21]But those who follow the true way come to the light, and it shows that the things they do were done through God."

JESUS AND JOHN THE BAPTIST

[22]After this, Jesus and his followers went into the area of Judea, where he stayed with his followers and baptized people. [23]John was also baptizing in Aenon, near Salim, because there was plenty of water there. People were going there to be baptized. [24](This was before John was put into prison.)

[25]Some of John's followers had an argument with a Jew about religious washing.[n] [26]So they came to John and said, "Teacher,

2:17 **"My...me."** Quotation from Psalm 69:9. **3:13 the Son of Man** Some Greek copies continue, "who is in heaven." **3:14 Moses...desert** When the Israelites were dying from snakebites, God told Moses to put a bronze snake on a pole. The people who looked at the snake were healed (Numbers 21:4–9). **3:25 religious washing** The Jewish people washed themselves in special ways before eating, before worshiping in the Temple, and at other special times.

remember the man who was with you on the other side of the Jordan River, the one you spoke about so much? He is baptizing, and everyone is going to him."

[27] John answered, "A man can get only what God gives him. [28] You yourselves heard me say, 'I am not the Christ, but I am the one sent to prepare the way for him.' [29] The bride

GOD'S ULTIMATE SACRIFICE

FAITH

leap of faith

JOHN 3:31–36   By Elmer Towns

A father wanted to teach his son about faith. He placed him on the table, backed up a few feet, and told the little fellow to jump.

The son shook his head. "I'm afraid."

"Jump and I'll catch you," the father said. "Trust me."

The child was ready to jump but looked down and cried, "I'm afraid!"

"Didn't I tell you I would catch you?" the father said. "Would Papa trick you?"

The boy shook his head. He was having a hard time believing his father, so the father encouraged him, "Look me in the eye and jump. I will catch you."

The little fellow got ready a third time but froze again. "I'm afraid."

The promise of the father was not enough. The boy was hesitant to do what he had never done, so the father asked, "Have I ever hurt you?"

"No."

"Will you obey me?"

"Yes."

"Jump!" The father held out his arms.

The boy finally leaped into his father's arms. The father and son both laughed and hugged. This small child had learned the lesson of faith. Immediately, he said, "Let me jump again."

His father put him on the table, and he jumped into his father's arms many more times. The father stepped further back, and the boy still jumped. He had learned to trust his father.

Those who have learned to trust in God have put their seal upon the truthfulness of God. Unbelief says, "I can't," while faith says, "I will."

reflect: Are you willing to take the leap of faith into the will of God?
Go to **FAITH:** "Brave Joy" at **Genesis 32:22–32.**

belongs only to the bridegroom. But the friend who helps the bridegroom stands by and listens to him. He is thrilled that he gets to hear the bridegroom's voice. In the same way, I am really happy. 30He must become greater, and I must become less important.

THE ONE WHO COMES FROM HEAVEN

31"The One who comes from above is greater than all. The one who is from the earth belongs to the earth and talks about things on the earth. But the One who comes from heaven is greater than all. 32He tells what he has seen and heard, but no one accepts what he says. 33Whoever accepts what he says has proven that God is true. 34The One whom God sent speaks the words of God, because God gives him the Spirit fully. 35The Father loves the Son and has given him power over everything. 36Those who believe in the Son have eternal life, but those who do not obey the Son will never have life. God's anger stays on them."

JESUS AND A SAMARITAN WOMAN

4 The Pharisees heard that Jesus was making and baptizing more followers than John, 2although Jesus himself did not baptize people, but his followers did. 3Jesus knew that the Pharisees had heard about him, so he left Judea and went back to Galilee. 4But on the way he had to go through the country of Samaria.

5In Samaria Jesus came to the town called Sychar, which is near the field Jacob gave to his son Joseph. 6Jacob's well was there. Jesus was tired from his long trip, so he sat down beside the well. It was about twelve o'clock noon. 7When a Samaritan woman came to the well to get some water, Jesus said to her, "Please give me a drink." 8(This happened while Jesus' followers were in town buying some food.)

9The woman said, "I am surprised that you ask me for a drink, since you are a Jewish man and I am a Samaritan woman." (Jewish people are not friends with Samaritans.n)

10Jesus said, "If you only knew the free gift of God and who it is that is asking you for water, you would have asked him, and he would have given you living water."

11The woman said, "Sir, where will you get this living water? The well is very deep, and you have nothing to get water with. 12Are you greater than Jacob, our father, who gave us this well and drank from it himself along with his sons and flocks?"

13Jesus answered, "Everyone who drinks this water will be thirsty again, 14but whoever drinks the water I give will never be thirsty. The water I give will become a spring of water gushing up inside that person, giving eternal life."

15The woman said to him, "Sir, give me this water so I will never be thirsty again and will not have to come back here to get more water."

16Jesus told her, "Go get your husband and come back here."

17The woman answered, "I have no husband."

Jesus said to her, "You are right to say you have no husband. 18Really you have had five husbands, and the man you live with now is not your husband. You told the truth."

19The woman said, "Sir, I can see that you are a prophet. 20Our ancestors worshiped on this mountain, but you say that Jerusalem is the place where people must worship."

21Jesus said, "Believe me, woman. The time is coming when neither in Jerusalem nor on this mountain will you actually worship the Father. 22You Samaritans worship something you don't understand. We understand what we worship, because salvation comes from the Jews. 23The time is coming when the true worshipers will worship the Father in spirit and truth, and that time is here already. You see, the Father too is actively seeking such people to worship him. 24God is spirit, and those who worship him must worship in spirit and truth."

25The woman said, "I know that the Messiah is coming." (Messiah is the One called Christ.) "When the Messiah comes, he will explain everything to us."

26Then Jesus said, "I am he—I, the one talking to you."

27Just then his followers came back from town and were surprised to see him talking with a woman. But none of them asked, "What do you want?" or "Why are you talking with her?"

4:9 Jewish people . . . Samaritans. This can also be translated "Jewish people don't use things that Samaritans have used."

²⁸Then the woman left her water jar and went back to town. She said to the people, ²⁹"Come and see a man who told me everything I ever did. Do you think he might be the Christ?" ³⁰So the people left the town and went to see Jesus.

³¹Meanwhile, his followers were begging him, "Teacher, eat something."

³²But Jesus answered, "I have food to eat that you know nothing about."

³³So the followers asked themselves, "Did somebody already bring him food?"

³⁴Jesus said, "My food is to do what the One who sent me wants me to do and to finish his work. ³⁵You have a saying, 'Four more months till harvest.' But I tell you, open your eyes and look at the fields ready for harvest now. ³⁶Already, the one who harvests is being paid and is gathering crops for eternal life. So the one who plants and the one who harvests celebrate at the same time. ³⁷Here the saying is true, 'One person plants, and another harvests.' ³⁸I sent you to harvest a crop that you did not work on. Others did

BRAVE JOY

FAITH

JOHN 4:10

listening to God

The story of the woman at the well is so familiar that we often overlook this critical verse. When Jesus begins to talk to this woman about the real meaning of life, he points out that her biggest problem is ignorance. She just doesn't know about God's gift. If she did, her life would be completely different. This woman hears what he says but she doesn't get it at all. She thinks she needs more information. But the word Jesus uses tells us that what she needs she will never find by gathering facts. She needs a different kind of "knowing." So do we.

The Greek language has several verbs for "know." The one we are most familiar with is *ginosko*. *Ginosko* describes the kind of knowledge that we collect from experience. It is knowledge that we accumulate from trial and error. It is experiential knowing. That's what this woman wants. She asks for information.

But Jesus uses the verb *eido*. *Eido* implies intuitive, full knowledge. The word is used to describe Jesus' knowledge of the Father. Jesus is not suggesting that this woman needs more information. What she needs is to be fully aware.

"If you [fully understood] the gift of God . . . ." We come to God with our needs. We think we need more information. We search for answers. We construct theological solutions. We write rules for living. Jesus makes a startling announcement here. Life is not discovered. It is revealed. God reveals the truth as a gift to you. God is the active agent. You are the recipient. The only real question is this: are you listening?

reflect: Seek to know the will of God for your life by asking him to reveal it to you.
Go to **John 13:34–35.**

the work, and you get to finish up their work."[n]

[39]Many of the Samaritans in that town believed in Jesus because of what the woman said: "He told me everything I ever did." [40]When the Samaritans came to Jesus, they begged him to stay with them, so he stayed there two more days. [41]And many more believed because of the things he said.

[42]They said to the woman, "First we believed in Jesus because of what you said, but now we believe because we heard him our-

selves. We know that this man really is the Savior of the world."

JESUS HEALS AN OFFICER'S SON

[43]Two days later, Jesus left and went to Galilee. [44](Jesus had said before that a prophet is not respected in his own country.) [45]When Jesus arrived in Galilee, the people there welcomed him. They had seen all the

---

4:38 I . . . their work. As a farmer sends workers to harvest grain, Jesus sends his followers out to bring people to God.

---

the **woman** at the **well**

FAMILY

By Jimmy Evans

JOHN 4:14

The story of the Samaritan woman at the well is often preached, but rarely within its true context. This story reveals Jesus as a marriage counselor to a woman who had had five husbands and was living with a man out of wedlock. Everything Jesus said was designed to fix the core problem that was causing her failures in relationships. Jesus' ministry to the woman was healing her of the wounds in her life that were keeping her from entering into healthy relationships.

Even though few of us can relate to the situation the woman was in, all of us identify with being hurt in relationships, with marriage being the greatest challenge of all. Everything Jesus said to the woman relates to every relationship. What he said reveals God's design for relationships and exposes the most important issue that determines success or failure in marriage.

There are three important truths revealed through this story. First, is the compassion of Jesus to those who have failed in marriage. Second, marriage was created by God and is only successful when it honors his plan and includes his presence. Third, the most important issue is a personal relationship with Jesus Christ.

We all have four basic needs. They are acceptance, identity, security, and purpose. If we don't trust Jesus to meet those needs, we will transfer the expectation of getting those needs met to our parents, spouses, or others. However, no one but Jesus can truly meet those needs.

reflect: Who are you trusting to meet your needs?
Go to **Revelation 19:11.**

things he did at the Passover Feast in Jerusalem, because they had been there, too.

⁴⁶Jesus went again to visit Cana in Galilee where he had changed the water into wine. One of the king's important officers lived in the city of Capernaum, and his son was sick. ⁴⁷When he heard that Jesus had come from Judea to Galilee, he went to Jesus and begged him to come to Capernaum and heal his son, because his son was almost dead. ⁴⁸Jesus said to him, "You people must see signs and miracles before you will believe in me."

⁴⁹The officer said, "Sir, come before my child dies."

⁵⁰Jesus answered, "Go. Your son will live."

The man believed what Jesus told him and went home. ⁵¹On the way the man's servants came and met him and told him, "Your son is alive."

⁵²The man asked, "What time did my son begin to get well?"

They answered, "Yesterday at one o'clock the fever left him."

⁵³The father knew that one o'clock was the exact time that Jesus had said, "Your son will live." So the man and all the people who lived in his house believed in Jesus.

⁵⁴That was the second miracle Jesus did after coming from Judea to Galilee.

JESUS HEALS A MAN AT A POOL

5 Later Jesus went to Jerusalem for a special feast. ²In Jerusalem there is a pool with five covered porches, which is called Bethesda[n] in the Hebrew language.[n] This pool is near the Sheep Gate. ³Many sick people were lying on the porches beside the pool. Some were blind, some were crippled, and some were paralyzed [, and they waited for the water to move. ⁴Sometimes an angel of the Lord came down to the pool and stirred up the water. After the angel did this, the first person to go into the pool was healed from any sickness he had].[n] ⁵A man was lying there who had been sick for thirty-eight years. ⁶When Jesus saw the man and knew that he had been sick for such a long time, Jesus asked him, "Do you want to be well?"

⁷The sick man answered, "Sir, there is no one to help me get into the pool when the water starts moving. While I am coming to the water, someone else always gets in before me."

⁸Then Jesus said, "Stand up. Pick up your mat and walk." ⁹And immediately the man was well; he picked up his mat and began to walk.

The day this happened was a Sabbath day. ¹⁰So the Jews said to the man who had been healed, "Today is the Sabbath. It is against our law for you to carry your mat on the Sabbath day."

¹¹But he answered, "The man who made me well told me, 'Pick up your mat and walk.'"

¹²Then they asked him, "Who is the man who told you to pick up your mat and walk?"

¹³But the man who had been healed did not know who it was, because there were many people in that place, and Jesus had left.

¹⁴Later, Jesus found the man at the Temple and said to him, "See, you are well now. Stop sinning so that something worse does not happen to you."

¹⁵Then the man left and told his people that Jesus was the one who had made him well.

¹⁶Because Jesus was doing this on the Sabbath day, some evil people began to persecute him. ¹⁷But Jesus said to them, "My Father never stops working, and so I keep working, too."

¹⁸This made them try still harder to kill him. They said, "First Jesus was breaking the law about the Sabbath day. Now he says that God is his own Father, making himself equal with God!"

JESUS HAS GOD'S AUTHORITY

¹⁹But Jesus said, "I tell you the truth, the Son can do nothing alone. The Son does only what he sees the Father doing, because the Son does whatever the Father does. ²⁰The Father loves the Son and shows the Son all the things he himself does. But the Father will show the Son even greater things than this so that you can all be amazed. ²¹Just as the Father raises the dead and gives them life, so also the Son gives life to those he wants to. ²²In fact, the Father judges no one, but he has given the Son power to do all the judging ²³so that all people

---

5:2 Bethesda Some Greek copies read "Bethzatha" or "Bethsaida," different names for the pool of Bethesda. **5:2 Hebrew language** Or Aramaic, the languages of many people in this region in the first century. **5:3–4 and . . . had** Some Greek copies do not contain all or most of the bracketed text.

will honor the Son as much as they honor the Father. Anyone who does not honor the Son does not honor the Father who sent him.

²⁴"I tell you the truth, whoever hears what I say and believes in the One who sent me has eternal life. That person will not be judged guilty but has already left death and entered life. ²⁵I tell you the truth, the time is coming and is already here when the dead will hear the voice of the Son of God, and those who hear will have life. ²⁶Life comes from the Father himself, and he has allowed the Son to have life in himself as well. ²⁷And the Father has given the Son the approval to judge, because he is the Son of Man. ²⁸Don't be surprised at this: A time is coming when all who are dead and in their graves will hear his voice. ²⁹Then they will come out of their graves. Those who did good will rise and have life forever, but those who did evil will rise to be judged guilty.

JESUS IS GOD'S SON

³⁰"I can do nothing alone. I judge only the way I am told, so my judgment is fair. I don't

---

THE LONGEVITY FACTOR

do you **want** to be **well?**

FITNESS

JOHN 5:6

There is more to Jesus' question than a qualification of willingness. The Greek makes it clear that Jesus did not ask simply if the man wanted to be healed. The question really was, "Are you willing to be generated whole?" The word translated "be generated" means "to begin to be" or "to come into existence." It is the Greek word *genesthai*. We identify it from its transliteration: *genesis*. Are you completely willing to begin to be? Are you totally committed to a new existence, a genesis, a new beginning starting right now?

The Greek word that we translate "well" is *hugies*. It means "healthy, sound, and whole." The New Testament places significant emphasis on health and well-being. The very fact that Jesus brought wholeness to many as a sign of God's grace and power underlines Jesus' role as the liberator of a new life that embraces the whole man, body and soul.

Jesus asked this man about his motives, his passion, and his commitment to restoration. But Jesus may well have intended more than the obvious recovery of this man's health, for the question reached far below the surface. Jesus asked him if he was ready to be reborn into a whole person, the person God intended him to be.

Just how ready are we to do whatever is required to be generated whole? This man was ready. The encounter with Jesus changed everything about his life. The most absurd question was exactly the one that needed to be asked. Are we willing to be made whole?

reflect: Yield your entire being to God so that you can become entirely whole.
Go to **Acts 2:24.**

try to please myself, but I try to please the One who sent me.

31"If only I tell people about myself, what I say is not true. 32But there is another who tells about me, and I know that the things he says about me are true.

33"You have sent people to John, and he has told you the truth. 34It is not that I need what humans say; I tell you this so you can be saved. 35John was like a burning and shining lamp, and you were happy to enjoy his light for a while.

36"But I have a proof about myself that is greater than that of John. The things I do, which are the things my Father gave me to do, prove that the Father sent me. 37And the Father himself who sent me has given proof about me. You have never heard his voice or seen what he looks like. 38His teaching does not live in you, because you don't believe in the One the Father sent. 39You carefully study the Scriptures because you think they give you eternal life. They do in fact tell about me, 40but you refuse to come to me to have that life.

41"I don't need praise from people. 42But I know you—I know that you don't have God's love in you. 43I have come from my Father and speak for him, but you don't accept me. But when another person comes, speaking only for himself, you will accept him. 44You try to get praise from each other, but you do not try to get the praise that comes from the only God. So how can you believe? 45Don't think that I will stand before the Father and say you are wrong. The one who says you are wrong is Moses, the one you hoped would save you. 46If you really believed Moses, you would believe me, because Moses wrote about me. 47But if you don't believe what Moses wrote, how can you believe what I say?"

MORE THAN FIVE THOUSAND FED

6 After this, Jesus went across Lake Galilee (or, Lake Tiberias). 2Many people followed him because they saw the miracles he did to heal the sick. 3Jesus went up on a hill and sat down there with his followers. 4It was almost the time for the Jewish Passover Feast.

5When Jesus looked up and saw a large crowd coming toward him, he said to Philip, "Where can we buy enough bread for all these people to eat?" 6(Jesus asked Philip this question to test him, because Jesus already knew what he planned to do.)

7Philip answered, "Someone would have to work almost a year to buy enough bread for each person to have only a little piece."

8Another one of his followers, Andrew, Simon Peter's brother, said, 9"Here is a boy with five loaves of barley bread and two little fish, but that is not enough for so many people."

10Jesus said, "Tell the people to sit down." There was plenty of grass there, and about five thousand men sat down there. 11Then Jesus took the loaves of bread, thanked God for them, and gave them to the people who were sitting there. He did the same with the fish, giving as much as the people wanted.

12When they had all had enough to eat, Jesus said to his followers, "Gather the leftover pieces of fish and bread so that nothing is wasted." 13So they gathered up the pieces and filled twelve baskets with the pieces left from the five barley loaves.

14When the people saw this miracle that Jesus did, they said, "He must truly be the Prophet[n] who is coming into the world."

15Jesus knew that the people planned to come and take him by force and make him their king, so he left and went into the hills alone.

JESUS WALKS ON THE WATER

16That evening Jesus' followers went down to Lake Galilee. 17It was dark now, and Jesus had not yet come to them. The followers got into a boat and started across the lake to Capernaum. 18By now a strong wind was blowing, and the waves on the lake were getting bigger. 19When they had rowed the boat about three or four miles, they saw Jesus walking on the water, coming toward the boat. The followers were afraid, 20but Jesus said to them, "It is I. Do not be afraid." 21Then they were glad to take him into the boat. At once the boat came to land at the place where they wanted to go.

THE PEOPLE SEEK JESUS

22The next day the people who had stayed on the other side of the lake knew that Jesus

---

6:14 **Prophet** They probably meant the prophet that God told Moses he would send (Deuteronomy 18:15–19).

had not gone in the boat with his followers but that they had left without him. And they knew that only one boat had been there. 23But then some boats came from Tiberias and landed near the place where the people had eaten the bread after the Lord had given thanks. 24When the people saw that Jesus and his followers were not there now, they got into boats and went to Capernaum to find Jesus.

JESUS, THE BREAD OF LIFE

25When the people found Jesus on the other side of the lake, they asked him, "Teacher, when did you come here?"

26Jesus answered, "I tell you the truth, you aren't looking for me because you saw me do miracles. You are looking for me because you ate the bread and were satisfied. 27Don't work for the food that spoils. Work for the food that stays good always and gives eternal life. The Son of Man will give you this food, because on him God the Father has put his power."

28The people asked Jesus, "What are the things God wants us to do?"

29Jesus answered, "The work God wants you to do is this: Believe the One he sent."

30So the people asked, "What miracle will you do? If we see a miracle, we will believe you. What will you do? 31Our ancestors ate the manna in the desert. This is written in the Scriptures: 'He gave them bread from heaven to eat.'n"

32Jesus said, "I tell you the truth, it was not Moses who gave you bread from heaven; it is my Father who is giving you the true bread from heaven. 33God's bread is the One who comes down from heaven and gives life to the world."

34The people said, "Sir, give us this bread always."

35Then Jesus said, "I am the bread that gives life. Whoever comes to me will never be hungry, and whoever believes in me will never be thirsty. 36But as I told you before, you have seen me and still don't believe. 37The Father gives me the people who are mine. Every one of them will come to me, and I will always accept them. 38I came down from heaven to do what God wants me to do, not what I want to do. 39Here is what the One who sent me wants me to do: I must not lose even one whom God gave me, but I must raise them all on the last day. 40Those who see the Son and believe in him have eternal life, and I will raise them on the last day. This is what my Father wants."

41Some people began to complain about Jesus because he said, "I am the bread that comes down from heaven." 42They said, "This is Jesus, the son of Joseph. We know his father and mother. How can he say, 'I came down from heaven'?"

43But Jesus answered, "Stop complaining to each other. 44The Father is the One who sent me. No one can come to me unless the Father draws him to me, and I will raise that person up on the last day. 45It is written in the prophets, 'They will all be taught by God.'n Everyone who listens to the Father and learns from him comes to me. 46No one has seen the Father except the One who is from God; only he has seen the Father. 47I tell you the truth, whoever believes has eternal life. 48I am the bread that gives life. 49Your ancestors ate the manna in the desert, but still they died. 50Here is the bread that comes down from heaven. Anyone who eats this bread will never die. 51I am the living bread that came down from heaven. Anyone who eats this bread will live forever. This bread is my flesh, which I will give up so that the world may have life."

52Then the evil people began to argue among themselves, saying, "How can this man give us his flesh to eat?"

53Jesus said, "I tell you the truth, you must eat the flesh of the Son of Man and drink his blood. Otherwise, you won't have real life in you. 54Those who eat my flesh and drink my blood have eternal life, and I will raise them up on the last day. 55My flesh is true food, and my blood is true drink. 56Those who eat my flesh and drink my blood live in me, and I live in them. 57The living Father sent me, and I live because of the Father. So whoever eats me will live because of me. 58I am not like the bread your ancestors ate. They ate that bread and still died. I am the bread that came down from heaven, and whoever eats this bread will live forever." 59Jesus said all these things while he was teaching in the synagogue in Capernaum.

6:31 'He gave . . . eat.' Quotation from Psalm 78:24.
6:45 'They . . . God.' Quotation from Isaiah 54:13.

THE WORDS OF ETERNAL LIFE

60When the followers of Jesus heard this, many of them said, "This teaching is hard. Who can accept it?"

61Knowing that his followers were complaining about this, Jesus said, "Does this teaching bother you? 62Then will it also bother you to see the Son of Man going back to the place where he came from? 63It is the Spirit that gives life. The flesh doesn't give life. The words I told you are spirit, and they give life. 64But some of you don't believe." (Jesus knew from the beginning who did not believe and who would turn against him.) 65Jesus said, "That is the reason I said, 'If the Father does not bring a person to me, that one cannot come.'"

66After Jesus said this, many of his followers left him and stopped following him.

67Jesus asked the twelve followers, "Do you want to leave, too?"

68Simon Peter answered him, "Lord, who would we go to? You have the words that give eternal life. 69We believe and know that you are the Holy One from God."

70Then Jesus answered, "I chose all twelve of you, but one of you is a devil." 71Jesus was talking about Judas, the son of Simon Iscariot. Judas was one of the twelve, but later he was going to turn against Jesus.

JESUS' BROTHERS DON'T BELIEVE

7 After this, Jesus traveled around Galilee. He did not want to travel in Judea, because some evil people there wanted to kill him. 2It was time for the Feast of Shelters. 3So Jesus' brothers said to him, "You should leave here and go to Judea so your followers there can see the miracles you do. 4Anyone who wants to be well known does not hide what he does. If you are doing these things, show yourself to the world." 5(Even Jesus' brothers did not believe in him.)

6Jesus said to his brothers, "The right time for me has not yet come, but any time is right for you. 7The world cannot hate you, but it hates me, because I tell it the evil things it does. 8So you go to the feast. I will not go yet[n] to this feast, because the right time for me has not yet come." 9After saying this, Jesus stayed in Galilee.

10But after Jesus' brothers had gone to the feast, Jesus went also. But he did not let people see him. 11At the feast some people were looking for him and saying, "Where is that man?"

12Within the large crowd there, many people were whispering to each other about Jesus. Some said, "He is a good man."

Others said, "No, he fools the people." 13But no one was brave enough to talk about Jesus openly, because they were afraid of the elders.

JESUS TEACHES AT THE FEAST

14When the feast was about half over, Jesus went to the Temple and began to teach. 15The people were amazed and said, "This man has never studied in school. How did he learn so much?"

16Jesus answered, "The things I teach are not my own, but they come from him who sent me. 17If people choose to do what God wants, they will know that my teaching comes from God and not from me. 18Those who teach their own ideas are trying to get honor for themselves. But those who try to bring honor to the one who sent them speak the truth, and there is nothing false in them. 19Moses gave you the law,[n] but none of you obeys that law. Why are you trying to kill me?"

20The people answered, "A demon has come into you. We are not trying to kill you."

21Jesus said to them, "I did one miracle, and you are all amazed. 22Moses gave you the law about circumcision. (But really Moses did not give you circumcision; it came from our ancestors.) And yet you circumcise a baby boy on a Sabbath day. 23If a baby boy can be circumcised on a Sabbath day to obey the law of Moses, why are you angry at me for healing a person's whole body on the Sabbath day? 24Stop judging by the way things look, but judge by what is really right."

IS JESUS THE CHRIST?

25Then some of the people who lived in Jerusalem said, "This is the man they are trying to kill. 26But he is teaching where everyone can see and hear him, and no one is trying to stop him. Maybe the leaders have decided he really is the Christ. 27But we

---

7:8 yet Some Greek copies do not have this word.
7:19 law Moses gave God's people the Law that God gave him on Mount Sinai (Exodus 34:29–32).

know where this man is from. Yet when the real Christ comes, no one will know where he comes from."

28Jesus, teaching in the Temple, cried out, "Yes, you know me, and you know where I am from. But I have not come by my own authority. I was sent by the One who is true, whom you don't know. 29But I know him, because I am from him, and he sent me."

30When Jesus said this, they tried to seize him. But no one was able to touch him, because it was not yet the right time. 31But many of the people believed in Jesus. They said, "When the Christ comes, will he do more miracles than this man has done?"

THE LEADERS TRY TO ARREST JESUS

32The Pharisees heard the crowd whispering these things about Jesus. So the leading priests and the Pharisees sent some Temple guards to arrest him. 33Jesus said, "I will be with you a little while longer. Then I will go back to the One who sent me. 34You will look for me, but you will not find me. And you cannot come where I am."

35Some people said to each other, "Where will this man go so we cannot find him? Will he go to the Greek cities where our people live and teach the Greek people there? 36What did he mean when he said, 'You will look for me, but you will not find me,' and 'You cannot come where I am'?"

JESUS TALKS ABOUT THE SPIRIT

37On the last and most important day of the feast Jesus stood up and said in a loud voice, "Let anyone who is thirsty come to me and drink. 38If anyone believes in me, rivers of living water will flow out from that person's heart, as the Scripture says." 39Jesus was talking about the Holy Spirit. The Spirit had not yet been given, because Jesus had not yet been raised to glory. But later, those who believed in Jesus would receive the Spirit.

THE PEOPLE ARGUE ABOUT JESUS

40When the people heard Jesus' words, some of them said, "This man really is the Prophet."[n]

41Others said, "He is the Christ."

Still others said, "The Christ will not come from Galilee. 42The Scripture says that the Christ will come from David's family and from Bethlehem, the town where David lived." 43So the people did not agree with each other about Jesus. 44Some of them wanted to arrest him, but no one was able to touch him.

SOME LEADERS WON'T BELIEVE

45The Temple guards went back to the leading priests and the Pharisees, who asked, "Why didn't you bring Jesus?"

46The guards answered, "The words he says are greater than the words of any other person who has ever spoken!"

47The Pharisees answered, "So Jesus has fooled you also! 48Have any of the leaders or the Pharisees believed in him? No! 49But these people, who know nothing about the law, are under God's curse."

50Nicodemus, who had gone to see Jesus before, was in that group.[n] He said, 51"Our law does not judge a person without hearing him and knowing what he has done."

52They answered, "Are you from Galilee, too? Study the Scriptures, and you will learn that no prophet comes from Galilee."

Some of the earliest surviving Greek copies do not contain 7:53—8:11.

[53And everyone left and went home.

THE WOMAN CAUGHT IN ADULTERY

8 Jesus went to the Mount of Olives. 2But early in the morning he went back to the Temple, and all the people came to him, and he sat and taught them. 3The teachers of the law and the Pharisees brought a woman who had been caught in adultery. They forced her to stand before the people. 4They said to Jesus, "Teacher, this woman was caught having sexual relations with a man who is not her husband. 5The law of Moses commands that we stone to death every woman who does this. What do you say we should do?" 6They were asking this to trick Jesus so that they could have some charge against him.

But Jesus bent over and started writing on the ground with his finger. 7When they continued to ask Jesus their question, he raised up and said, "Anyone here who has

---

7:40 Prophet They probably meant the prophet God told Moses he would send (Deuteronomy 18:15–19).
7:50 Nicodemus...group. The story about Nicodemus going and talking to Jesus is in John 3:1–21.

never sinned can throw the first stone at her." [8]Then Jesus bent over again and wrote on the ground.

[9]Those who heard Jesus began to leave one by one, first the older men and then the others. Jesus was left there alone with the woman standing before him. [10]Jesus raised up again and asked her, "Woman, where are they? Has no one judged you guilty?"

[11]She answered, "No one, sir."

Then Jesus said, "I also don't judge you guilty. You may go now, but don't sin anymore."]

JESUS IS THE LIGHT OF THE WORLD

[12]Later, Jesus talked to the people again, saying, "I am the light of the world. The person who follows me will never live in darkness but will have the light that gives life."

[13]The Pharisees said to Jesus, "When you talk about yourself, you are the only one to say these things are true. We cannot accept what you say."

[14]Jesus answered, "Yes, I am saying these things about myself, but they are true. I know where I came from and where I am going. But you don't know where I came from or where I am going. [15]You judge by human standards. I am not judging anyone. [16]But when I do judge, I judge truthfully, because I am not alone. The Father who sent me is with me. [17]Your own law says that when two witnesses say the same thing, you must accept what they say. [18]I am one of the witnesses who speaks about myself, and the Father who sent me is the other witness."

[19]They asked, "Where is your father?"

Jesus answered, "You don't know me or my Father. If you knew me, you would know my Father, too." [20]Jesus said these things while he was teaching in the Temple, near where the money is kept. But no one arrested him, because the right time for him had not yet come.

THE PEOPLE MISUNDERSTAND JESUS

[21]Again, Jesus said to the people, "I will leave you, and you will look for me, but you will die in your sins. You cannot come where I am going."

[22]So the Jews asked, "Will he kill himself? Is that why he said, 'You cannot come where I am going'?"

[23]Jesus said, "You people are from here below, but I am from above. You belong to this world, but I don't belong to this world. [24]So I told you that you would die in your sins. Yes, you will die in your sins if you don't believe that I am he."

[25]They asked, "Then who are you?"

Jesus answered, "I am what I have told you from the beginning. [26]I have many things to say and decide about you. But I tell people only the things I have heard from the One who sent me, and he speaks the truth."

[27]The people did not understand that he was talking to them about the Father. [28]So Jesus said to them, "When you lift up the Son of Man, you will know that I am he. You will know that these things I do are not by my own authority but that I say only what the Father has taught me. [29]The One who sent me is with me. I always do what is pleasing to him, so he has not left me alone." [30]While Jesus was saying these things, many people believed in him.

FREEDOM FROM SIN

[31]So Jesus said to the Jews who believed in him, "If you continue to obey my teaching, you are truly my followers. [32]Then you will know the truth, and the truth will make you free."

[33]They answered, "We are Abraham's children, and we have never been anyone's slaves. So why do you say we will be free?"

[34]Jesus answered, "I tell you the truth, everyone who lives in sin is a slave to sin. [35]A slave does not stay with a family forever, but a son belongs to the family forever. [36]So if the Son makes you free, you will be truly free. [37]I know you are Abraham's children, but you want to kill me because you don't accept my teaching. [38]I am telling you what my Father has shown me, but you do what your father has told you."

[39]They answered, "Our father is Abraham."

Jesus said, "If you were really Abraham's children, you would do[n] the things Abraham did. [40]I am a man who has told you the truth which I heard from God, but you are trying to kill me. Abraham did nothing like that.

8:39 If...do Some Greek copies read "If you are really Abraham's children, you will do."

[41]So you are doing the things your own father did."

But they said, "We are not like children who never knew who their father was. God is our Father; he is the only Father we have."

[42]Jesus said to them, "If God were really your Father, you would love me, because I came from God and now I am here. I did not come by my own authority; God sent me. [43]You don't understand what I say, because you cannot accept my teaching. [44]You belong to your father the devil, and you want to do what he wants. He was a murderer from the beginning and was against the truth, because there is no truth in him. When he tells a lie, he shows what he is really like, because he is a liar and the father of lies. [45]But because I speak the truth, you don't believe me. [46]Can any of you prove that I am guilty of sin? If I am telling the truth, why don't you believe me? [47]The person who belongs to God accepts what God says. But you don't accept what God says, because you don't belong to God."

JESUS IS GREATER THAN ABRAHAM

[48]They answered, "We say you are a Samaritan and have a demon in you. Are we not right?"

FIVE INGREDIENTS OF PEACE BY GOD

free, indeed

FULFILLMENT

JOHN 8:36

Freedom is an important concept in modern times. Many believe it to be a God-given right worth fighting for. Jesus believed that freedom was important, too. But his view was a little different from ours. We might think we are free because we believe we are independent, but God's reality says otherwise.

Until we are "set free" by the Son, we are in the grip of an evil master whose only purpose is to destroy us. Our pursuit of political or economic freedom as an end in itself is folly—we are chasing goals that are tied to a defective world, a world that is already in slavery. Death is the power it holds over all of us. Even if we win, we lose.

Jesus is telling us that if he sets us free, we will no longer be under the power of death. The ultimate form of captivity will be broken. No one is finally, really free until the power of death over life has been broken for that person. No matter what a person's status in this world, death has him or her in its clutches.

You are never free until you are no longer a subject of death's realm. When death knocks, all of your efforts to gain control over your world will come to nothing unless you have already been released from those chains. Only one person can really set us free. And when he does, we will be really free no matter what chains the world has put around us. His freedom is freedom from fear.

reflect: Thank God that he has freed you from the fear and snare of death.
Go to **John 10:14–15.**

[49]Jesus answered, "I have no demon in me. I give honor to my Father, but you dishonor me. [50]I am not trying to get honor for myself. There is One who wants this honor for me, and he is the judge. [51]I tell you the truth, whoever obeys my teaching will never die."

[52]They said to Jesus, "Now we know that you have a demon in you! Even Abraham and the prophets died. But you say, 'Whoever obeys my teaching will never die.' [53]Do you think you are greater than our father Abraham, who died? And the prophets died, too. Who do you think you are?"

[54]Jesus answered, "If I give honor to myself, that honor is worth nothing. The One who gives me honor is my Father, and you say he is your God. [55]You don't really know him, but I know him. If I said I did not know him, I would be a liar like you. But I do know him, and I obey what he says. [56]Your father Abraham was very happy that he would see my day. He saw that day and was glad."

[57]They said to him, "You have never seen Abraham! You are not even fifty years old."

[58]Jesus answered, "I tell you the truth, before Abraham was even born, I am!" [59]When Jesus said this, the people picked up stones to throw at him. But Jesus hid himself, and then he left the Temple.

JESUS HEALS A MAN BORN BLIND

9 As Jesus was walking along, he saw a man who had been born blind. [2]His followers asked him, "Teacher, whose sin caused this man to be born blind—his own sin or his parents' sin?"

[3]Jesus answered, "It is not this man's sin or his parents' sin that made him blind. This man was born blind so that God's power could be shown in him. [4]While it is daytime, we must continue doing the work of the One who sent me. Night is coming, when no one can work. [5]While I am in the world, I am the light of the world."

[6]After Jesus said this, he spit on the ground and made some mud with it and put the mud on the man's eyes. [7]Then he told the man, "Go and wash in the Pool of Siloam." (Siloam means Sent.) So the man went, washed, and came back seeing.

[8]The neighbors and some people who had earlier seen this man begging said, "Isn't this the same man who used to sit and beg?"

[9]Some said, "He is the one," but others said, "No, he only looks like him."

The man himself said, "I am the man."

[10]They asked, "How did you get your sight?"

[11]He answered, "The man named Jesus made some mud and put it on my eyes. Then he told me to go to Siloam and wash. So I went and washed, and then I could see."

[12]They asked him, "Where is this man?"

"I don't know," he answered.

PHARISEES QUESTION THE HEALING

[13]Then the people took to the Pharisees the man who had been blind. [14]The day Jesus had made mud and healed his eyes was a Sabbath day. [15]So now the Pharisees asked the man, "How did you get your sight?"

He answered, "He put mud on my eyes, I washed, and now I see."

[16]So some of the Pharisees were saying, "This man does not keep the Sabbath day, so he is not from God."

But others said, "A man who is a sinner can't do miracles like these." So they could not agree with each other.

[17]They asked the man again, "What do you say about him since it was your eyes he opened?"

The man answered, "He is a prophet."

[18]These leaders did not believe that he had been blind and could now see again. So they sent for the man's parents [19]and asked them, "Is this your son who you say was born blind? Then how does he now see?"

[20]His parents answered, "We know that this is our son and that he was born blind. [21]But we don't know how he can now see. We don't know who opened his eyes. Ask him. He is old enough to speak for himself." [22]His parents said this because they were afraid of the elders, who had already decided that anyone who said Jesus was the Christ would be avoided. [23]That is why his parents said, "He is old enough. Ask him."

[24]So for the second time, they called the man who had been blind. They said, "You should give God the glory by telling the truth. We know that this man is a sinner."

[25]He answered, "I don't know if he is a sinner. One thing I do know: I was blind, and now I see."

²⁶They asked, "What did he do to you? How did he make you see again?"

²⁷He answered, "I already told you, and you didn't listen. Why do you want to hear it again? Do you want to become his followers, too?"

²⁸Then they insulted him and said, "You are his follower, but we are followers of Moses. ²⁹We know that God spoke to Moses, but we don't even know where this man comes from."

³⁰The man answered, "This is a very strange thing. You don't know where he comes from, and yet he opened my eyes. ³¹We all know that God does not listen to sinners, but he listens to anyone who worships and obeys him. ³²Nobody has ever heard of anyone giving sight to a man born blind. ³³If this man were not from God, he could do nothing."

³⁴They answered, "You were born full of sin! Are you trying to teach us?" And they threw him out.

SPIRITUAL BLINDNESS

³⁵When Jesus heard that they had thrown him out, Jesus found him and said, "Do you believe in the Son of Man?"

³⁶He asked, "Who is the Son of Man, sir, so that I can believe in him?"

³⁷Jesus said to him, "You have seen him. The Son of Man is the one talking with you."

³⁸He said, "Lord, I believe!" Then the man worshiped Jesus.

³⁹Jesus said, "I came into this world so that the world could be judged. I came so that the blind[n] would see and so that those who see will become blind."

⁴⁰Some of the Pharisees who were nearby heard Jesus say this and asked, "Are you saying we are blind, too?"

⁴¹Jesus said, "If you were blind, you would not be guilty of sin. But since you keep saying you see, your guilt remains."

THE SHEPHERD AND HIS SHEEP

10 Jesus said, "I tell you the truth, the person who does not enter the sheepfold by the door, but climbs in some other way, is a thief and a robber. ²The one who enters by the door is the shepherd of the sheep. ³The one who guards the door opens it for him. And the sheep listen to the voice of the shepherd. He calls his own sheep by name and leads them out. ⁴When he brings all his sheep out, he goes ahead of them, and they follow him because they know his voice. ⁵But they will never follow a stranger. They will run away from him because they don't know his voice." ⁶Jesus told the people this story, but they did not understand what it meant.

JESUS IS THE GOOD SHEPHERD

⁷So Jesus said again, "I tell you the truth, I am the door for the sheep. ⁸All the people who came before me were thieves and robbers. The sheep did not listen to them. ⁹I am the door, and the person who enters through me will be saved and will be able to come in and go out and find pasture. ¹⁰A thief comes to steal and kill and destroy, but I came to give life—life in all its fullness.

¹¹"I am the good shepherd. The good shepherd gives his life for the sheep. ¹²The worker who is paid to keep the sheep is different from the shepherd who owns them. When the worker sees a wolf coming, he runs away and leaves the sheep alone. Then the wolf attacks the sheep and scatters them. ¹³The man runs away because he is only a paid worker and does not really care about the sheep.

¹⁴"I am the good shepherd. I know my sheep, and my sheep know me, ¹⁵just as the Father knows me, and I know the Father. I give my life for the sheep. ¹⁶I have other sheep that are not in this flock, and I must bring them also. They will listen to my voice, and there will be one flock and one shepherd. ¹⁷The Father loves me because I give my life so that I can take it back again. ¹⁸No one takes it away from me; I give my own life freely. I have the right to give my life, and I have the right to take it back. This is what my Father commanded me to do."

¹⁹Again the leaders did not agree with each other because of these words of Jesus. ²⁰Many of them said, "A demon has come into him and made him crazy. Why listen to him?"

²¹But others said, "A man who is crazy with a demon does not say things like this. Can a demon open the eyes of the blind?"

9:39 blind Jesus is talking about people who are spiritually blind, not physically blind.

JESUS IS REJECTED

²²The time came for the Feast of Dedication at Jerusalem. It was winter, ²³and Jesus was walking in the Temple in Solomon's Porch. ²⁴Some people gathered around him and said, "How long will you make us wonder about you? If you are the Christ, tell us plainly."

²⁵Jesus answered, "I told you already, but you did not believe. The miracles I do in my Father's name show who I am. ²⁶But you don't believe, because you are not my sheep. ²⁷My sheep listen to my voice; I know them, and they follow me. ²⁸I give them eternal life, and they will never die, and no one can steal them out of my hand. ²⁹My Father gave my sheep to me. He is greater than all, and no person can steal my sheep out of my Father's hand. ³⁰The Father and I are one."

³¹Again some of the people picked up stones to kill Jesus. ³²But he said to them, "I have done many good works from the Father. Which of these good works are you killing me for?"

³³They answered, "We are not killing you because of any good work you did, but because you speak against God. You are only a human, but you say you are the same as God!"

³⁴Jesus answered, "It is written in your

FIVE INGREDIENTS OF PEACE BY GOD

the
shepherd's tenet

FULFILLMENT

JOHN 10:14-15

A shepherd guides his sheep toward the places he knows will bring them good food, comfort, security, and safety. His only role in life is to keep and protect the flock and look after its well-being at all times. If sheep stray, he finds them and brings them back to the fold. If they are hurt, he sees that they get treated. If they are in danger, he fights off the predator or removes the sheep from harm's way.

The sheep trust the shepherd to do all these things. Like a baby sleeping safely in his crib or a child riding comfortably in the backseat of a car, the sheep have total faith that their needs are always going to be met. They are not concerned about the place they are in life, as they trust they are exactly where they should be. They willingly follow the shepherd and innocently believe they are headed in the right direction. They have confidence they will get to their destination precisely on time.

You can startle sheep, but the shepherd always returns peace to the flock. They have no reason to fear any harm, for they know the shepherd is always right there with them. Even if there is great danger, they know their enemies stand no chance against the shepherd's staff. Allow God—the Good Shepherd—to provide loving protection for you. Follow him like a sheep of his own flock. You will be blessed with safety, peace, and joy in your life.

reflect: What do you need protection from right now?

Go to **John 14:27.**

law that God said, 'I said, you are gods.'[n] [35]This Scripture called those people gods who received God's message, and Scripture is always true. [36]So why do you say that I speak against God because I said, 'I am God's Son'? I am the one God chose and sent into the world. [37]If I don't do what my Father does, then don't believe me. [38]But if I do what my Father does, even though you don't believe in me, believe what I do. Then you will know and understand that the Father is in me and I am in the Father."

[39]They tried to take Jesus again, but he escaped from them.

[40]Then he went back across the Jordan River to the place where John had first baptized. Jesus stayed there, [41]and many people came to him and said, "John never did a miracle, but everything John said about this man is true." [42]And in that place many believed in Jesus.

THE DEATH OF LAZARUS

11 A man named Lazarus was sick. He lived in the town of Bethany, where Mary and her sister Martha lived. [2]Mary was the woman who later put perfume on the Lord and wiped his feet with her hair. Mary's brother Lazarus was the man who was now sick. [3]So Mary and Martha sent someone to tell Jesus, "Lord, the one you love is sick."

[4]When Jesus heard this, he said, "This sickness will not end in death. It is for the glory of God, to bring glory to the Son of God." [5]Jesus loved Martha and her sister and Lazarus. [6]But when he heard that Lazarus was sick, he stayed where he was for two more days. [7]Then Jesus said to his followers, "Let's go back to Judea."

[8]The followers said, "But Teacher, some people there tried to stone you to death only a short time ago. Now you want to go back there?"

[9]Jesus answered, "Are there not twelve hours in the day? If anyone walks in the daylight, he will not stumble, because he can see by this world's light. [10]But if anyone walks at night, he stumbles because there is no light to help him see."

[11]After Jesus said this, he added, "Our friend Lazarus has fallen asleep, but I am going there to wake him."

[12]The followers said, "But, Lord, if he is only asleep, he will be all right."

[13]Jesus meant that Lazarus was dead, but his followers thought he meant Lazarus was really sleeping. [14]So then Jesus said plainly, "Lazarus is dead. [15]And I am glad for your sakes I was not there so that you may believe. But let's go to him now."

[16]Then Thomas (the one called Didymus) said to the other followers, "Let us also go so that we can die with him."

JESUS IN BETHANY

[17]When Jesus arrived, he learned that Lazarus had already been dead and in the tomb for four days. [18]Bethany was about two miles from Jerusalem. [19]Many of the Jews had come there to comfort Martha and Mary about their brother.

[20]When Martha heard that Jesus was coming, she went out to meet him, but Mary stayed home. [21]Martha said to Jesus, "Lord, if you had been here, my brother would not have died. [22]But I know that even now God will give you anything you ask."

[23]Jesus said, "Your brother will rise and live again."

[24]Martha answered, "I know that he will rise and live again in the resurrection[n] on the last day."

[25]Jesus said to her, "I am the resurrection and the life. Those who believe in me will have life even if they die. [26]And everyone who lives and believes in me will never die. Martha, do you believe this?"

[27]Martha answered, "Yes, Lord. I believe that you are the Christ, the Son of God, the One coming to the world."

JESUS CRIES

[28]After Martha said this, she went back and talked to her sister Mary alone. Martha said, "The Teacher is here and he is asking for you." [29]When Mary heard this, she got up quickly and went to Jesus. [30]Jesus had not yet come into the town but was still at the place where Martha had met him. [31]The Jews were with Mary in the house, comforting her. When they saw her stand and leave quickly, they followed her, thinking she was going to the tomb to cry there.

[32]But Mary went to the place where Jesus

10:34 'I . . . gods.' Quotation from Psalm 82:6. **11:24 resurrection** Being raised from the dead to live again.

was. When she saw him, she fell at his feet and said, "Lord, if you had been here, my brother would not have died."

33When Jesus saw Mary crying and the Jews who came with her also crying, he was upset and was deeply troubled. 34He asked, "Where did you bury him?"

"Come and see, Lord," they said.

35Jesus cried.

36So the Jews said, "See how much he loved him."

37But some of them said, "If Jesus opened the eyes of the blind man, why couldn't he keep Lazarus from dying?"

JESUS RAISES LAZARUS

38Again feeling very upset, Jesus came to the tomb. It was a cave with a large stone covering the entrance. 39Jesus said, "Move the stone away."

Martha, the sister of the dead man, said, "But, Lord, it has been four days since he died. There will be a bad smell."

40Then Jesus said to her, "Didn't I tell you that if you believed you would see the glory of God?"

41So they moved the stone away from the entrance. Then Jesus looked up and said, "Father, I thank you that you heard me. 42I know that you always hear me, but I said these things because of the people here around me. I want them to believe that you sent me."

43After Jesus said this, he cried out in a loud voice, "Lazarus, come out!" 44The dead man came out, his hands and feet wrapped with pieces of cloth, and a cloth around his face. Jesus said to them, "Take the cloth off of him and let him go."

THE PLAN TO KILL JESUS

45Many of the people, who had come to visit Mary and saw what Jesus did, believed in him. 46But some of them went to the Pharisees and told them what Jesus had done. 47Then the leading priests and Pharisees called a meeting of the council. They asked, "What should we do? This man is doing many miracles. 48If we let him continue doing these things, everyone will believe in him. Then the Romans will come and take away our Temple and our nation."

49One of the men there was Caiaphas, the high priest that year. He said, "You people know nothing! 50You don't realize that it is better for one man to die for the people than for the whole nation to be destroyed."

51Caiaphas did not think of this himself. As high priest that year, he was really prophesying that Jesus would die for their nation 52and for God's scattered children to bring them all together and make them one.

53That day they started planning to kill Jesus. 54So Jesus no longer traveled openly among the people. He left there and went to a place near the desert, to a town called Ephraim and stayed there with his followers.

55It was almost time for the Passover Feast. Many from the country went up to Jerusalem before the Passover to do the special things to make themselves pure. 56The people looked for Jesus and stood in the Temple asking each other, "Is he coming to the Feast? What do you think?" 57But the leading priests and the Pharisees had given orders that if anyone knew where Jesus was, he must tell them. Then they could arrest him.

JESUS WITH FRIENDS IN BETHANY

12 Six days before the Passover Feast, Jesus went to Bethany, where Lazarus lived. (Lazarus is the man Jesus raised from the dead.) 2There they had a dinner for Jesus. Martha served the food, and Lazarus was one of the people eating with Jesus. 3Mary brought in a pint of very expensive perfume made from pure nard. She poured the perfume on Jesus' feet, and then she wiped his feet with her hair. And the sweet smell from the perfume filled the whole house.

4Judas Iscariot, one of Jesus' followers who would later turn against him, was there. Judas said, 5"This perfume was worth an entire year's wages. Why wasn't it sold and the money given to the poor?" 6But Judas did not really care about the poor; he said this because he was a thief. He was the one who kept the money box, and he often stole from it.

7Jesus answered, "Leave her alone. It was right for her to save this perfume for today, the day for me to be prepared for burial. 8You will always have the poor with you, but you will not always have me."

THE PLOT AGAINST LAZARUS

9A large crowd of people heard that Jesus was in Bethany. So they went there to see not only Jesus but Lazarus, whom Jesus raised from the dead. [10]So the leading priests made plans to kill Lazarus, too. [11]Because of Lazarus many of the Jews were leaving them and believing in Jesus.

JESUS ENTERS JERUSALEM

[12]The next day a great crowd who had come to Jerusalem for the Passover Feast heard that Jesus was coming there. [13]So they took branches of palm trees and went out to meet Jesus, shouting,

"Praise[n] God!
God bless the One who comes in the name of the Lord!
God bless the King of Israel!"
Psalm 118:25–26

[14]Jesus found a colt and sat on it. This was as the Scripture says,

[15] "Don't be afraid, people of Jerusalem!
Your king is coming,
sitting on the colt of a donkey."
Zechariah 9:9

[16]The followers of Jesus did not understand this at first. But after Jesus was raised to glory, they remembered that this had been written about him and that they had done these things to him.

PEOPLE TELL ABOUT JESUS

[17]There had been many people with Jesus when he raised Lazarus from the dead and told him to come out of the tomb. Now they were telling others about what Jesus did. [18]Many people went out to meet Jesus, because they had heard about this miracle. [19]So the Pharisees said to each other, "You can see that nothing is going right for us. Look! The whole world is following him."

JESUS TALKS ABOUT HIS DEATH

[20]There were some Greek people, too, who came to Jerusalem to worship at the Passover Feast. [21]They went to Philip, who was from Bethsaida in Galilee, and said, "Sir, we would like to see Jesus." [22]Philip told Andrew, and then Andrew and Philip told Jesus.

[23]Jesus said to them, "The time has come for the Son of Man to receive his glory. [24]I tell you the truth, a grain of wheat must fall to the ground and die to make many seeds. But if it never dies, it remains only a single seed. [25]Those who love their lives will lose them, but those who hate their lives in this world

will keep true life forever. [26]Whoever serves me must follow me. Then my servant will be with me everywhere I am. My Father will honor anyone who serves me.

[27]"Now I am very troubled. Should I say, 'Father, save me from this time'? No, I came to this time so I could suffer. [28]Father, bring glory to your name!"

Then a voice came from heaven, "I have brought glory to it, and I will do it again."

[29]The crowd standing there, who heard the voice, said it was thunder.

But others said, "An angel has spoken to him."

[30]Jesus said, "That voice was for your sake, not mine. [31]Now is the time for the world to be judged; now the ruler of this world will be thrown down. [32]If I am lifted up from the earth, I will draw all people toward me." [33]Jesus said this to show how he would die.

[34]The crowd said, "We have heard from the law that the Christ will live forever. So why do you say, 'The Son of Man must be lifted up'? Who is this 'Son of Man'?"

[35]Then Jesus said, "The light will be with you for a little longer, so walk while you have the light. Then the darkness will not catch you. If you walk in the darkness, you will not know where you are going. [36]Believe in the light while you still have it so that you will become children of light." When Jesus had said this, he left and hid himself from them.

SOME PEOPLE WON'T BELIEVE IN JESUS

[37]Though Jesus had done many miracles in front of the people, they still did not believe in him. [38]This was to bring about what Isaiah the prophet had said:

"Lord, who believed what we told them?
Who saw the Lord's power in this?"
Isaiah 53:1

[39]This is why the people could not believe: Isaiah also had said,

[40] "He has blinded their eyes,
and he has closed their minds.
Otherwise they would see with their eyes
and understand in their minds
and come back to me and be healed."
Isaiah 6:10

12:13 Praise Literally, "Hosanna," a Hebrew word used at first in praying to God for help, but at this time it was probably a shout of joy used in praising God or his Messiah.

[41]Isaiah said this because he saw Jesus' glory and spoke about him.

[42]But many believed in Jesus, even many of the leaders. But because of the Pharisees, they did not say they believed in him for fear they would be put out of the synagogue. [43]They loved praise from people more than praise from God.

[44]Then Jesus cried out, "Whoever believes in me is really believing in the One who sent me. [45]Whoever sees me sees the One who sent me. [46]I have come as light into the world so that whoever believes in me would not stay in darkness.

[47]"Anyone who hears my words and does not obey them, I do not judge, because I did not come to judge the world, but to save the world. [48]There is a judge for those who refuse to believe in me and do not accept my words. The word I have taught will be their judge on the last day. [49]The things I taught were not from myself. The Father who sent me told me what to say and what to teach. [50]And I know that eternal life comes from what the Father commands. So whatever I say is what the Father told me to say."

JESUS WASHES HIS FOLLOWERS' FEET

13 It was almost time for the Passover Feast. Jesus knew that it was time for him to leave this world and go back to the Father. He had always loved those who were his own in the world, and he loved them all the way to the end.

[2]Jesus and his followers were at the evening meal. The devil had already persuaded Judas Iscariot, the son of Simon, to turn against Jesus. [3]Jesus knew that the Father had given him power over everything and that he had come from God and was going back to God. [4]So during the meal Jesus stood up and took off his outer clothing. Taking a towel, he wrapped it around his waist. [5]Then he poured water into a bowl and began to wash the followers' feet, drying them with the towel that was wrapped around him.

[6]Jesus came to Simon Peter, who said to him, "Lord, are you going to wash my feet?"

[7]Jesus answered, "You don't understand now what I am doing, but you will understand later."

[8]Peter said, "No, you will never wash my feet."

Jesus answered, "If I don't wash your feet, you are not one of my people."

[9]Simon Peter answered, "Lord, then wash not only my feet, but wash my hands and my head, too!"

[10]Jesus said, "After a person has had a bath, his whole body is clean. He needs only to wash his feet. And you men are clean, but not all of you." [11]Jesus knew who would turn against him, and that is why he said, "Not all of you are clean."

[12]When he had finished washing their feet, he put on his clothes and sat down again. He asked, "Do you understand what I have just done for you? [13]You call me 'Teacher' and 'Lord,' and you are right, because that is what I am. [14]If I, your Lord and Teacher, have washed your feet, you also should wash each other's feet. [15]I did this as an example so that you should do as I have done for you. [16]I tell you the truth, a servant is not greater than his master. A messenger is not greater than the one who sent him. [17]If you know these things, you will be blessed if you do them.

[18]"I am not talking about all of you. I know those I have chosen. But this is to bring about what the Scripture said: 'The man who ate at my table has turned against me.'[n] [19]I am telling you this now before it happens so that when it happens, you will believe that I am he. [20]I tell you the truth, whoever accepts anyone I send also accepts me. And whoever accepts me also accepts the One who sent me."

JESUS TALKS ABOUT HIS DEATH

[21]After Jesus said this, he was very troubled. He said openly, "I tell you the truth, one of you will turn against me."

[22]The followers all looked at each other, because they did not know whom Jesus was talking about. [23]One of the followers sitting[n] next to Jesus was the follower Jesus loved. [24]Simon Peter motioned to him to ask Jesus whom he was talking about.

[25]That follower leaned closer to Jesus and asked, "Lord, who is it?"

[26]Jesus answered, "I will dip this bread into the dish. The man I give it to is the man

---

13:18 '**The man . . . me.**' Quotation from Psalm 41:9.
13:23 **sitting** Literally, "lying." The people of that time ate lying down and leaning on one arm.

Servant Evangelism

By Steve Sjogren

JOHN 13:3–17

Cincinnati is a cold city, and I'm not just talking about the weather. It was a really difficult place to plant a church because the people are so very skeptical of anything new. For example, when I told people that I was starting a new church that would be fun to go to, where the worship would sound like James Taylor, and messages would be practical, the response was fairly consistent: "Sounds like a cult to me. . . . " Honestly.

I talked to two thousand people during two years using traditional church planting methods, and at our first meeting we had thirty-seven people show up. That's about a 99 percent rejection rate. That'll send anyone to the analyst's couch.

Then one day—it was ten degrees below zero—I was performing my duties as a school bus driver and complaining to God: *God, there's got to be a more lucrative way to be miserable.* It was in that frozen moment that I felt God inspiring me to build a different kind of church: a "go-and-do," not a "come-and-see," church. What we were doing was simply not interesting to people. I was ready to try anything.

My first idea was to do things that were FREE for people and that would help them. Jesus washed feet, so I decided to wash people's mode of transportation: their cars. When I mentioned the idea to our "congregation," about one-third of our group got so upset that they left the church! Our "blessed reduction" left us with twenty-four.

Nevertheless, we plowed ahead. We managed to wash about twenty cars. But the experience had some unexpected consequences that have guided us ever since. I realized that the best thing that happens when you do servant evangelism is that it actually impacts you a lot more than it impacts those you are serving.

Those twenty-four servants were so inspired by the experience that they began coming up with their own ideas. We now have a Web site dedicated to sharing some of our best ideas from the years: www.servantevangelism.com.

Our second big idea was to go after poor, needy, forgotten, and marginalized people, giving them food. The results were amazing. Between the free service projects and helping the needy through some very creative means, we couldn't keep people away! We even told people *not* to come to our church because we were still so small and goofy.

None of us knew what were doing. We passed out "connection cards" with the names and addresses of other churches written on them! But it didn't seem to matter; they came anyway.

Throughout the years, we've built a culture around servant evangelism and we've come to believe some very simple truths about serving. First, small things done with great love will change the world. I realize that I can't really do big things. But if I do small things, in the right direction, repeatedly, they become big things in Christ!

Second, we must demonstrate God's love by offering to do some humble act of service with no strings attached. These simple truths have changed our church and our lives. If implemented, I believe they can do the same for you.

TO LEARN MORE ON WHAT THE BIBLE HAS TO SAY ABOUT **FAITH,** READ THE SCRIPTURES AND DEVOTIONALS AT **ISAIAH 56:7, ISAIAH 61:8, JEREMIAH 17:9, DANIEL 3:16–30, OBADIAH 15,** AND **HABAKKUK 2:4.**

who will turn against me." So Jesus took a piece of bread, dipped it, and gave it to Judas Iscariot, the son of Simon. [27]As soon as Judas took the bread, Satan entered him. Jesus said to him, "The thing that you will do—do it quickly." [28]No one at the table understood why Jesus said this to Judas. [29]Since he was the one who kept the money box, some of the followers thought Jesus was telling him to buy what was needed for the feast or to give something to the poor.

[30]Judas took the bread Jesus gave him and immediately went out. It was night.

[31]When Judas was gone, Jesus said, "Now the Son of Man receives his glory, and God receives glory through him. [32]If God receives glory through him,[n] then God will give glory to the Son through himself. And God will give him glory quickly."

[33]Jesus said, "My children, I will be with you only a little longer. You will look for me, and what I told the Jews, I tell you now: Where I am going you cannot come.

[34]"I give you a new command: Love each other. You must love each other as I have loved you. [35]All people will know that you are my followers if you love each other."

PETER WILL SAY HE DOESN'T KNOW JESUS

[36]Simon Peter asked Jesus, "Lord, where are you going?"

Jesus answered, "Where I am going you cannot follow now, but you will follow later."

[37]Peter asked, "Lord, why can't I follow you now? I am ready to die for you!"

[38]Jesus answered, "Are you ready to die for me? I tell you the truth, before the rooster

---

13:32 If . . . him Some Greek copies do not have this phrase.

FAITH

BRAVE JOY

what would
Jesus do?

JOHN 13:34–35

What would Jesus do? That's a great question. Most likely, if he passed you on the street or in the mall or he was sitting next to you on the bus, he would probably look you in the eye and ask you about your life, or something like that. He is all about expressing love and valuing relationships.

When people travel around the world, the first thing most observe is the differences in the attitudes of the people they meet. While certain countries are said to be friendlier, or to the contrary, less polite than others, what you will really find is that mostly people return about the same level of love as they are given.

Give and it shall be given to you. If you live large, you will reap large rewards in return. This is one of the consequences of being a servant of all. There are vast areas of untapped reserves in the soul of every person. It takes the mind of Christ to look deeply within and see where God wants to confirm, exhort, encourage, or challenge. When you do this, you will be practicing what Jesus would do.

reflect: Ask God to show you how to minister to others as Jesus would.
Go to **John 14:16–17.**

crows, you will say three times that you don't know me."

JESUS COMFORTS HIS FOLLOWERS

14 Jesus said, "Don't let your hearts be troubled. Trust in God, and trust in me. ²There are many rooms in my Father's house; I would not tell you this if it were not true. I am going there to prepare a place for you. ³After I go and prepare a place for you, I will come back and take you to be with me so that you may be where I am. ⁴You know the way to the place where I am going."[n]

⁵Thomas said to Jesus, "Lord, we don't know where you are going. So how can we know the way?"

⁶Jesus answered, "I am the way, and the truth, and the life. The only way to the Father is through me. ⁷If you really knew me, you would know my Father, too. But now you do know him, and you have seen him."

⁸Philip said to him, "Lord, show us the Father. That is all we need."

⁹Jesus answered, "I have been with you a long time now. Do you still not know me,

---

14:4 You...going. Some Greek copies read "You know where I am going and the way to the place I am going."

BRAVE JOY

I **believe** in the **Holy Spirit**

FAITH

By Jack Hayford   JOHN 14:16-17

I **believe the Holy Spirit is an individual whom I can understand.** He is one person with the Father and the Son. The trinity is almighty, all-knowing, and always present. Because I believe this, I worship and welcome him in all aspects and affairs of my life. The Holy Spirit instructs and teaches me. His constant presence glorifies the Lord Jesus in me and bears witness to the Lord Jesus through me.

I believe the love of the Holy Spirit identifies me with the body of Christ, and his presence pours God's love into my heart. His work produces new life and guides my obedience to the Father's Word. Because I believe this, I cherish the Holy Spirit's presence in my heart. I respect and respond to him as he teaches me to turn from sin and develops his fruit in my character.

I believe the power of the Holy Spirit anointed Jesus' ministry and that Jesus himself baptizes me so I can receive him. By this empowering, I am able to do the works that Christ did and expect to do even greater things through the gifts of the Holy Spirit.

My desire and prayer is that Christ my Lord will overflow my life with his Holy Spirit and I will see the fullness of Jesus' love and power demonstrated in my life. I bow in humble submission to his authority as I grow in tender sensitivity to his love and surrender myself to his power.

---

reflect: Where in your life do you need the help of the Holy Spirit?
Go to **John 15:7.**

Who Are You?

By John Hagee

JOHN 14:27

Y ou cannot change that which you will not confront. Confront yourself and discover who you are. It is an identity that is more authentic than describing what you do. Who are you? What is your divine purpose? If you do not like what you find, there is a better way available to you.

Focus on what God wants, and you will no longer need to be all things to all people. You can be anything you set yourself to be, but not everything. God made every man and woman an original; there is not another person like you. To regain the love, joy, and excitement of the Holy Spirit you had when you first came to believe, revisit the message from God, the Bible. It is fresh fire from heaven for you.

The Bible is the most powerful weapon God allows man to handle. This Book is the living, breathing Word of God. It is the two-edged sword that separates light from darkness and heaven from hell. It is your combat manual for warfare, breaking the fetters of sin, taking gloom from the grave, and guaranteeing your victory over the world, flesh, and the devil.

The Scriptures hold the blueprint for a perfect society. God's Word is meat for the mature and milk for babes. It is a stream in the desert and greater than any other book. In fact, we judge other books by this Book—the living, breathing

Word of God. The Holy Bible is superior to any other book, just as the sun is greater than a single candle and the ocean is greater than a dripping faucet.

You are who the Bible says you are, and you can do what it says you can do. You have the authority to lay hands on the sick and see them recover, and you can cast out demons with a word. You are a child of the King and an heir with Jesus, and you have the royal blood of heaven flowing in your veins.

At the cross, Jesus crushed the head of the serpent. Satan is defeated, humiliated, and conquered. He cannot intimidate you with fear, control you with deceit, manipulate you with death, threaten you with sickness, or steal your financial inheritance because you are covered by the blood of Jesus Christ.

Because of Jesus' victory on the cross, you have everlasting life and peace. His peace is not found in a prescription or a platitude designed to make you feel good. True peace is found in acknowledging your salvation in Jesus Christ and in submission to him as Lord of your life. You are a child of the living God. When you get your life right with Christ, you will overflow with the peace that is beyond understanding.

TO LEARN MORE ON WHAT THE BIBLE HAS TO SAY ABOUT **FUTURE,** READ THE SCRIPTURES AND DEVOTIONALS AT **LUKE 22:42–44, 1 CORINTHIANS 15:10, ACTS 9:1–22, ROMANS 1:3–4, ROMANS 3:21–26,** AND **JOB 13:15.**

Philip? Whoever has seen me has seen the Father. So why do you say, 'Show us the Father'? [10]Don't you believe that I am in the Father and the Father is in me? The words I say to you don't come from me, but the Father lives in me and does his own work. [11]Believe me when I say that I am in the Father and the Father is in me. Or believe because of the miracles I have done. [12]I tell you the truth, whoever believes in me will do the same things that I do. Those who believe will do even greater things than these, because I am going to the Father. [13]And if you ask for anything in my name, I will do it for you so that the Father's glory will be shown through the Son. [14]If you ask me for anything in my name, I will do it.

THE PROMISE OF THE HOLY SPIRIT

[15]"If you love me, you will obey my commands. [16]I will ask the Father, and he will give you another Helper[n] to be with you forever— [17]the Spirit of truth. The world cannot accept him, because it does not see him or know him. But you know him, because he lives with you and he will be in you.

[18]"I will not leave you all alone like orphans; I will come back to you. [19]In a little while the world will not see me anymore, but you will see me. Because I live, you will live, too. [20]On that day you will know that I am in my Father, and that you are in me and I am in you. [21]Those who know my commands and obey them are the ones who love me, and my Father will love those who love me. I will love them and will show myself to them."

[22]Then Judas (not Judas Iscariot) said, "But, Lord, why do you plan to show yourself to us and not to the rest of the world?"

[23]Jesus answered, "If people love me, they will obey my teaching. My Father will love them, and we will come to them and make our home with them. [24]Those who do not love me do not obey my teaching. This teaching that you hear is not really mine; it is from my Father, who sent me.

[25]"I have told you all these things while I am with you. [26]But the Helper will teach you everything and will cause you to remember all that I told you. This Helper is the Holy Spirit whom the Father will send in my name.

[27]"I leave you peace; my peace I give you. I do not give it to you as the world does. So don't let your hearts be troubled or afraid. [28]You heard me say to you, 'I am going, but I am coming back to you.' If you loved me, you should be happy that I am going back to the Father, because he is greater than I am. [29]I have told you this now, before it happens, so that when it happens, you will believe. [30]I will not talk with you much longer, because the ruler of this world is coming. He has no power over me, [31]but the world must know that I love the Father, so I do exactly what the Father told me to do.

"Come now, let us go."

JESUS IS LIKE A VINE

15 "I am the true vine; my Father is the gardener. [2]He cuts off every branch of mine that does not produce fruit. And he trims and cleans every branch that produces fruit so that it will produce even more fruit. [3]You are already clean because of the words I have spoken to you. [4]Remain in me, and I will remain in you. A branch cannot produce fruit alone but must remain in the vine. In the same way, you cannot produce fruit alone but must remain in me.

[5]"I am the vine, and you are the branches. If any remain in me and I remain in them, they produce much fruit. But without me they can do nothing. [6]If any do not remain in me, they are like a branch that is thrown away and then dies. People pick up dead branches, throw them into the fire, and burn them. [7]If you remain in me and follow my teachings, you can ask anything you want, and it will be given to you. [8]You should produce much fruit and show that you are my followers, which brings glory to my Father. [9]I loved you as the Father loved me. Now remain in my love. [10]I have obeyed my Father's commands, and I remain in his love. In the same way, if you obey my commands, you will remain in my love. [11]I have told you these things so that you can have the same joy I have and so that your joy will be the fullest possible joy.

[12]"This is my command: Love each other as I have loved you. [13]The greatest love a person can show is to die for his friends. [14]You are my friends if you do what I command you. [15]I no longer call you servants, because a servant

---

14:16 Helper "Counselor" or "Comforter." Jesus is talking about the Holy Spirit.

does not know what his master is doing. But I call you friends, because I have made known to you everything I heard from my Father. 16You did not choose me; I chose you. And I gave you this work: to go and produce fruit, fruit that will last. Then the Father will give you anything you ask for in my name. 17This is my command: Love each other.

JESUS WARNS HIS FOLLOWERS

18"If the world hates you, remember that it hated me first. 19If you belonged to the world, it would love you as it loves its own. But I have chosen you out of the world, so you don't belong to it. That is why the world hates you. 20Remember what I told you: A servant is not greater than his master. If people did wrong to me, they will do wrong to you, too. And if they obeyed my teaching, they will obey yours, too. 21They will do all this to you on account of me, because they do not know the One who sent me. 22If I had not come and spoken to them, they would not be guilty of sin, but now they have no excuse for their sin. 23Whoever hates me also hates my Father. 24I did works among them

---

FIVE INGREDIENTS OF PEACE BY GOD

FULFILLMENT

peace, not **bliss**

JOHN 14:27

The Greek word for "peace" is *eirene*. In classic Greek, it meant "the absence of war." By implication, it came to mean "health, well-being, and prosperity." But the Greek meaning is a description of external or internal conditions. When the word was used in the New Testament, the Hebrew influence changed this context. The word took on the sense of relationships, not of conditions.

In the New Testament, the word is not primarily associated with resolution of political conflict, good health, personal well-being, or even prosperity. It is associated with words like love, grace, glory, honor, righteousness, and mercy. Its opposites are also words about relationships: anxiety, anguish, fear, confusion, division, distress.

Jesus is not telling his followers that he is leaving them in a state of blessed euphoria. He is not granting them a condition of happiness or bliss. He says that he is leaving them *his* peace. He is leaving them a special relationship made possible only because he is finishing his mission.

Notice that Jesus "gives" this peace and "leaves" this peace with us. It is not an announcement that we have accomplished something. It is a gift left behind for us to enjoy. Jesus is giving his followers a going-away present. That present is unbroken fellowship with God. It is a present that we can experience right now and that will last forever. It places a safety net over our lives that nothing can take away.

reflect: Celebrate the gift of peace that God has given you through Christ.
Go to **John 15:15.**

that no one else has ever done. If I had not done these works, they would not be guilty of sin. But now they have seen what I have done, and yet they have hated both me and my Father. 25But this happened so that what is written in their law would be true: 'They hated me for no reason.'[n]

26"I will send you the Helper[n] from the Father; he is the Spirit of truth who comes from the Father. When he comes, he will tell about me, 27and you also must tell people about me, because you have been with me from the beginning.

16 "I have told you these things to keep you from giving up. 2People will put you out of their synagogues. Yes, the time is coming when those who kill you will think they are offering service to God. 3They will do this because they have not known the Father and they have not known me. 4I have told you these things now so that when the time comes you will remember that I warned you.

15:25 'They . . . reason.' These words could be from Psalm 35:19 or Psalm 69:4. **15:26 Helper** "Counselor" or "Comforter." Jesus is talking about the Holy Spirit.

BRAVE JOY

fellowship with God

FAITH

JOHN 15:7

In John's Gospel, the same harmony and fellowship that Jesus experienced with the Father is offered to Jesus' followers. This unity of wills is the basis for the promise offered in the verse. St. Augustine said, "Love God and do as you please." The key is to love God, for if we truly love God, what we are pleased to do is his will, not ours.

There is a simple, powerful truth to accepting Jesus into your life—forgiveness of sins. The next step, however, in the Christian maturation process is becoming aware of the dead weight of our sinful nature. The addressing of sins and mistakes one at a time is frustrating and ineffective. Issues and problems in our thoughts and behavior come from the deep place where our heart lies. Change your heart and change your character.

In this verse, Jesus simply says that the deep spiritual fellowship that is available to us will not only change our life, but our desires about life. It will enable us to ask for those things that God wants and we want. Formerly, our hearts held us captive to fantasy fulfillment, fantasy that could never or should never be fulfilled, and it always left us wanting more.

Here Christ promises true reality fulfillment; but, unlike our fantasies, these desires will come to be. Surrendering to God releases our desires from the tyranny of sin and allows God to give us all the real desires of our heart—desires for love, freedom, and wholeness.

reflect: Remember that the best of living is available to each of us as believers.
Go to **Matthew 7:13-14.**

THE WORK OF THE HOLY SPIRIT

"I did not tell you these things at the beginning, because I was with you then. ⁵Now I am going back to the One who sent me. But none of you asks me, 'Where are you going?' ⁶Your hearts are filled with sadness because I have told you these things. ⁷But I tell you the truth, it is better for you that I go away. When I go away, I will send the Helper[n] to you. If I do not go away, the Helper will not come. ⁸When the Helper comes, he will prove to the people of the world the truth about sin, about being right with God, and about judgment. ⁹He will prove to them that sin is not believing in me. ¹⁰He will prove to them that being right with God comes from my going to the Father and not being seen anymore. ¹¹And the Helper will prove to them that judgment happened when the ruler of this world was judged.

¹²"I have many more things to say to you, but they are too much for you now. ¹³But when the Spirit of truth comes, he will lead you into all truth. He will not speak his own words, but he will speak only what he hears, and he will tell you what is to come. ¹⁴The Spirit of truth will bring glory to me, because he will take what I have to say and tell it to you. ¹⁵All that the Father has is mine. That is why I said that the Spirit will take what I have to say and tell it to you.

SADNESS WILL BECOME HAPPINESS

¹⁶"After a little while you will not see me,

16:7 Helper "Counselor" or "Comforter." Jesus is talking about the Holy Spirit.

FIVE INGREDIENTS OF PEACE BY GOD

FULFILLMENT

what a **friend**

JOHN 15:15   By Joseph Stowell

Some time ago, I was flying from Europe back to the United States when I found myself sitting next to a little girl who never stopped talking from the moment she sat down next to me. I got the history of her family. She told me her little Rottweiler pup, Duke, was down in the hold of the plane. We took off, and she began, "Look at this, look at that . . . ." I'm thinking, *Eight hours!*

So we played games and chatted until she suddenly got quiet. I thought maybe she was going to doze off. She pulled her blanket up a little bit. I reached for a magazine, and as I did, I got a little elbow in my side. I looked down at her as she threw out her little hand and said, "Want to be friends?" My heart melted. "Sure, Stephanie, let's be friends," I said, and I was reminded of Jesus.

In the midst of life, often when we really think we want to be left alone, Jesus throws out his nail-scarred hand and invites us to be his friend. And the great surprise is that once we accept, we finally begin to understand the old song that simply says, "What a Friend We Have in Jesus . . . "

reflect: Will you spend time today with your friend Jesus?
Go to **FULFILLMENT:** "Peace by God" at **1 Peter 4:19.**

and then after a little while you will see me again."

[17]Some of the followers said to each other, "What does Jesus mean when he says, 'After a little while you will not see me, and then after a little while you will see me again'? And what does he mean when he says, 'Because I am going to the Father'?" [18]They also asked, "What does he mean by 'a little while'? We don't understand what he is saying."

[19]Jesus saw that the followers wanted to ask him about this, so he said to them, "Are you asking each other what I meant when I said, 'After a little while you will not see me, and then after a little while you will see me again'? [20]I tell you the truth, you will cry and be sad, but the world will be happy. You will be sad, but your sadness will become joy. [21]When a woman gives birth to a baby, she has pain, because her time has come. But when her baby is born, she forgets the pain, because she is so happy that a child has been born into the world. [22]It is the same with you. Now you are sad, but I will see you again and you will be happy, and no one will take away your joy. [23]In that day you will not ask me for anything. I tell you the truth, my Father will give you anything you ask for in my name. [24]Until now you have not asked for anything in my name. Ask and you will receive, so that your joy will be the fullest possible joy.

VICTORY OVER THE WORLD

[25]"I have told you these things indirectly in stories. But the time will come when I will not use stories like that to tell you things; I will speak to you in plain words about the Father. [26]In that day you will ask the Father for things in my name. I mean, I will not need to ask the Father for you. [27]The Father himself loves you. He loves you because you loved me and believed that I came from God. [28]I came from the Father into the world. Now I am leaving the world and going back to the Father."

[29]Then the followers of Jesus said, "You are speaking clearly to us now and are not using stories that are hard to understand. [30]We can see now that you know all things. You can answer a person's question even before it is asked. This makes us believe you came from God."

[31]Jesus answered, "So now you believe? [32]Listen to me; a time is coming when you will be scattered, each to your own home. That time is now here. You will leave me alone, but I am never really alone, because the Father is with me.

[33]"I told you these things so that you can have peace in me. In this world you will have trouble, but be brave! I have defeated the world."

JESUS PRAYS FOR HIS FOLLOWERS

17 After Jesus said these things, he looked toward heaven and prayed, "Father, the time has come. Give glory to your Son so that the Son can give glory to you. [2]You gave the Son power over all people so that the Son could give eternal life to all those you gave him. [3]And this is eternal life: that people know you, the only true God, and that they know Jesus Christ, the One you sent. [4]Having finished the work you gave me to do, I brought you glory on earth. [5]And now, Father, give me glory with you; give me the glory I had with you before the world was made.

[6]"I showed what you are like to those you gave me from the world. They belonged to you, and you gave them to me, and they have obeyed your teaching. [7]Now they know that everything you gave me comes from you. [8]I gave them the teachings you gave me, and they accepted them. They knew that I truly came from you, and they believed that you sent me. [9]I am praying for them. I am not praying for people in the world but for those you gave me, because they are yours. [10]All I have is yours, and all you have is mine. And my glory is shown through them. [11]I am coming to you; I will not stay in the world any longer. But they are still in the world. Holy Father, keep them safe by the power of your name, the name you gave me, so that they will be one, just as you and I are one. [12]While I was with them, I kept them safe by the power of your name, the name you gave me. I protected them, and only one of them, the one worthy of destruction, was lost so that the Scripture would come true.

[13]"I am coming to you now. But I pray these things while I am still in the world so that these followers can have all of my joy in them. [14]I have given them your teaching. And the world has hated them, because they don't belong to the world, just as I don't belong to the world. [15]I am not asking you to

take them out of the world but to keep them safe from the Evil One. 16They don't belong to the world, just as I don't belong to the world. 17Make them ready for your service through your truth; your teaching is truth. 18I have sent them into the world, just as you sent me into the world. 19For their sake, I am making myself ready to serve so that they can be ready for their service of the truth.

20"I pray for these followers, but I am also praying for all those who will believe in me because of their teaching. 21Father, I pray that they can be one. As you are in me and I am in you, I pray that they can also be one in us. Then the world will believe that you sent me. 22I have given these people the glory that you gave me so that they can be one, just as you and I are one. 23I will be in them and you will be in me so that they will be completely one. Then the world will know that you sent me and that you loved them just as much as you loved me.

24"Father, I want these people that you gave me to be with me where I am. I want them to see my glory, which you gave me because you loved me before the world was made. 25Father, you are the One who is good. The world does not know you, but I know you, and these people know you sent me. 26I showed them what you are like, and I will show them again. Then they will have the same love that you have for me, and I will live in them."

JESUS IS ARRESTED

18 When Jesus finished praying, he went with his followers across the Kidron Valley. On the other side there was a garden, and Jesus and his followers went into it.

2Judas knew where this place was, because Jesus met there often with his followers. Judas was the one who turned against Jesus. 3So Judas came there with a group of soldiers and some guards from the leading priests and the Pharisees. They were carrying torches, lanterns, and weapons.

4Knowing everything that would happen to him, Jesus went out and asked, "Who is it you are looking for?"

5They answered, "Jesus from Nazareth."

"I am he," Jesus said. (Judas, the one who turned against Jesus, was standing there with them.) 6When Jesus said, "I am he," they moved back and fell to the ground.

7Jesus asked them again, "Who is it you are looking for?"

They said, "Jesus of Nazareth."

8"I told you that I am he," Jesus said. "So if you are looking for me, let the others go." 9This happened so that the words Jesus said before would come true: "I have not lost any of the ones you gave me."

10Simon Peter, who had a sword, pulled it out and struck the servant of the high priest, cutting off his right ear. (The servant's name was Malchus.) 11Jesus said to Peter, "Put your sword back. Shouldn't I drink the cup[n] the Father gave me?"

JESUS IS BROUGHT BEFORE ANNAS

12Then the soldiers with their commander and the guards arrested Jesus. They tied him 13and led him first to Annas, the father-in-law of Caiaphas, the high priest that year. 14Caiaphas was the one who told the Jews that it would be better if one man died for all the people.

PETER SAYS HE DOESN'T KNOW JESUS

15Simon Peter and another one of Jesus' followers went along after Jesus. This follower knew the high priest, so he went with Jesus into the high priest's courtyard. 16But Peter waited outside near the door. The follower who knew the high priest came back outside, spoke to the girl at the door, and brought Peter inside. 17The girl at the door said to Peter, "Aren't you also one of that man's followers?"

Peter answered, "No, I am not!"

18It was cold, so the servants and guards had built a fire and were standing around it, warming themselves. Peter also was standing with them, warming himself.

THE HIGH PRIEST QUESTIONS JESUS

19The high priest asked Jesus questions about his followers and his teaching. 20Jesus answered, "I have spoken openly to everyone. I have always taught in synagogues and in the Temple, where all the Jews come together. I never said anything in secret. 21So why do you question me? Ask the people who heard my teaching. They know what I said."

18:11 cup Jesus is talking about the painful things that will happen to him. Accepting these things will be very hard, like drinking a cup of something bitter.

22When Jesus said this, one of the guards standing there hit him. The guard said, "Is that the way you answer the high priest?"

23Jesus answered him, "If I said something wrong, then show what it was. But if what I said is true, why do you hit me?"

24Then Annas sent Jesus, who was still tied, to Caiaphas the high priest.

PETER SAYS AGAIN HE DOESN'T KNOW JESUS

25As Simon Peter was standing and warming himself, they said to him, "Aren't you one of that man's followers?"

Peter said it was not true; he said, "No, I am not."

26One of the servants of the high priest was there. This servant was a relative of the man whose ear Peter had cut off. The servant said, "Didn't I see you with him in the garden?"

27Again Peter said it wasn't true. At once a rooster crowed.

JESUS IS BROUGHT BEFORE PILATE

28Early in the morning they led Jesus from Caiaphas's house to the Roman governor's palace. They would not go inside the palace, because they did not want to make themselves unclean;[n] they wanted to eat the Passover meal. 29So Pilate went outside to them and asked, "What charges do you bring against this man?"

30They answered, "If he were not a criminal, we wouldn't have brought him to you."

31Pilate said to them, "Take him yourselves and judge him by your own law."

"But we are not allowed to put anyone to death," the Jews answered. 32(This happened so that what Jesus said about how he would die would come true.)

33Then Pilate went back inside the palace and called Jesus to him and asked, "Are you the king of the Jews?"

34Jesus said, "Is that your own question, or did others tell you about me?"

35Pilate answered, "I am not one of you. It was your own people and their leading priests who handed you over to me. What have you done wrong?"

36Jesus answered, "My kingdom does not belong to this world. If it belonged to this world, my servants would have fought to keep me from being given over to the Jewish leaders. But my kingdom is from another place."

37Pilate said, "So you are a king!"

Jesus answered, "You are the one saying I am a king. This is why I was born and came into the world: to tell people the truth. And everyone who belongs to the truth listens to me."

38Pilate said, "What is truth?" After he said this, he went out to the crowd again and said to them, "I find nothing against this man. 39But it is your custom that I free one prisoner to you at Passover time. Do you want me to free the 'king of the Jews'?"

40They shouted back, "No, not him! Let Barabbas go free!" (Barabbas was a robber.)

19 Then Pilate ordered that Jesus be taken away and whipped. 2The soldiers made a crown from some thorny branches and put it on Jesus' head and put a purple robe around him. 3Then they came to him many times and said, "Hail, King of the Jews!" and hit him in the face.

4Again Pilate came out and said to them, "Look, I am bringing Jesus out to you. I want you to know that I find nothing against him." 5So Jesus came out, wearing the crown of thorns and the purple robe. Pilate said to them, "Here is the man!"

6When the leading priests and the guards saw Jesus, they shouted, "Crucify him! Crucify him!"

But Pilate answered, "Crucify him yourselves, because I find nothing against him."

7The leaders answered, "We have a law that says he should die, because he said he is the Son of God."

8When Pilate heard this, he was even more afraid. 9He went back inside the palace and asked Jesus, "Where do you come from?" But Jesus did not answer him. 10Pilate said, "You refuse to speak to me? Don't you know I have power to set you free and power to have you crucified?"

11Jesus answered, "The only power you have over me is the power given to you by God. The man who turned me in to you is guilty of a greater sin."

12After this, Pilate tried to let Jesus go. But some in the crowd cried out, "Anyone who makes himself king is against Caesar. If you let this man go, you are no friend of Caesar."

18:28 unclean Going into the Roman palace would make them unfit to eat the Passover Feast, according to their Law.

[13]When Pilate heard what they were saying, he brought Jesus out and sat down on the judge's seat at the place called The Stone Pavement. (In the Hebrew language[n] the name is Gabbatha.) [14]It was about noon on Preparation Day of Passover week. Pilate said to the crowd, "Here is your king!"

[15]They shouted, "Take him away! Take him away! Crucify him!"

Pilate asked them, "Do you want me to crucify your king?"

The leading priests answered, "The only king we have is Caesar."

[16]So Pilate handed Jesus over to them to be crucified.

JESUS IS CRUCIFIED

The soldiers took charge of Jesus. [17]Carrying his own cross, Jesus went out to a place called The Place of the Skull, which in the Hebrew language[n] is called Golgotha. [18]There they crucified Jesus. They also crucified two other men, one on each side, with Jesus in the middle. [19]Pilate wrote a sign and put it on the cross. It read: JESUS OF NAZARETH, THE KING OF THE JEWS. [20]The sign was written in Hebrew, in Latin, and in Greek. Many of the people read the sign, because the place where Jesus was crucified was near the city. [21]The leading priests said to Pilate, "Don't write, 'The King of the Jews.' But write, 'This man said, "I am the King of the Jews."'"

[22]Pilate answered, "What I have written, I have written."

[23]After the soldiers crucified Jesus, they took his clothes and divided them into four parts, with each soldier getting one part. They also took his long shirt, which was all one piece of cloth, woven from top to bottom. [24]So the soldiers said to each other, "We should not tear this into parts. Let's throw lots to see who will get it." This happened so that this Scripture would come true:

"They divided my clothes among them,
    and they threw lots for my clothing."
                                    Psalm 22:18

So the soldiers did this.

[25]Standing near his cross were Jesus' mother, his mother's sister, Mary the wife of Clopas, and Mary Magdalene. [26]When Jesus saw his mother and the follower he loved standing nearby, he said to his mother, "Dear woman, here is your son." [27]Then he said to the follower, "Here is your mother." From that time on, the follower took her to live in his home.

JESUS DIES

[28]After this, Jesus knew that everything had been done. So that the Scripture would come true, he said, "I am thirsty."[n] [29]There was a jar full of vinegar there, so the soldiers soaked a sponge in it, put the sponge on a branch of a hyssop plant, and lifted it to Jesus' mouth. [30]When Jesus tasted the vinegar, he said, "It is finished." Then he bowed his head and died.

[31]This day was Preparation Day, and the next day was a special Sabbath day. Since the religious leaders did not want the bodies to stay on the cross on the Sabbath day, they asked Pilate to order that the legs of the men be broken[n] and the bodies be taken away. [32]So the soldiers came and broke the legs of the first man on the cross beside Jesus. Then they broke the legs of the man on the other cross beside Jesus. [33]But when the soldiers came to Jesus and saw that he was already dead, they did not break his legs. [34]But one of the soldiers stuck his spear into Jesus' side, and at once blood and water came out. [35](The one who saw this happen is the one who told us this, and whatever he says is true. And he knows that he tells the truth, and he tells it so that you might believe.) [36]These things happened to make the Scripture come true: "Not one of his bones will be broken."[n] [37]And another Scripture says, "They will look at the one they stabbed."[n]

JESUS IS BURIED

[38]Later, Joseph from Arimathea asked Pilate if he could take the body of Jesus. (Joseph was a secret follower of Jesus, because he was afraid of some of the leaders.) Pilate gave his permission, so Joseph came and took Jesus' body away. [39]Nicodemus, who earlier had come to Jesus at night, went with Joseph. He

---

19:13, 17 Hebrew language Or Aramaic, the languages of many people in this region in the first century. **19:28 "I am thirsty."** Read Psalms 22:15; 69:21. **19:31 broken** The breaking of their bones would make them die sooner. **19:36 "Not one . . . broken."** Quotation from Psalm 34:20. The idea is from Exodus 12:46; Numbers 9:12. **19:37 "They . . . stabbed."** Quotation from Zechariah 12:10.

brought about seventy-five pounds of myrrh and aloes. [40]These two men took Jesus' body and wrapped it with the spices in pieces of linen cloth, which is how they bury the dead. [41]In the place where Jesus was crucified, there was a garden. In the garden was a new tomb that had never been used before. [42]The men laid Jesus in that tomb because it was nearby, and they were preparing to start their Sabbath day.

JESUS' TOMB IS EMPTY

20 Early on the first day of the week, Mary Magdalene went to the tomb while it was still dark. When she saw that the large stone had been moved away from the tomb, [2]she ran to Simon Peter and the follower whom Jesus loved. Mary said, "They have taken the Lord out of the tomb, and we don't know where they have put him."

[3]So Peter and the other follower started for the tomb. [4]They were both running, but the other follower ran faster than Peter and reached the tomb first. [5]He bent down and looked in and saw the strips of linen cloth lying there, but he did not go in. [6]Then following him, Simon Peter arrived and went into the tomb and saw the strips of linen lying there. [7]He also saw the cloth that had been around Jesus' head, which was folded up and laid in a different place from the strips of linen. [8]Then the other follower, who had reached the tomb first, also went in. He saw and believed. [9](They did not yet understand from the Scriptures that Jesus must rise from the dead.)

JESUS APPEARS TO MARY MAGDALENE

[10]Then the followers went back home. [11]But Mary stood outside the tomb, crying. As she was crying, she bent down and looked inside the tomb. [12]She saw two angels dressed in white, sitting where Jesus' body had been, one at the head and one at the feet.

[13]They asked her, "Woman, why are you crying?"

She answered, "They have taken away my Lord, and I don't know where they have put him." [14]When Mary said this, she turned around and saw Jesus standing there, but she did not know it was Jesus.

[15]Jesus asked her, "Woman, why are you crying? Whom are you looking for?"

Thinking he was the gardener, she said to him, "Did you take him away, sir? Tell me where you put him, and I will get him."

[16]Jesus said to her, "Mary."

Mary turned toward Jesus and said in the Hebrew language,[n] "Rabboni." (This means "Teacher.")

[17]Jesus said to her, "Don't hold on to me, because I have not yet gone up to the Father. But go to my brothers and tell them, 'I am going back to my Father and your Father, to my God and your God.'"

[18]Mary Magdalene went and said to the followers, "I saw the Lord!" And she told them what Jesus had said to her.

JESUS APPEARS TO HIS FOLLOWERS

[19]When it was evening on the first day of the week, Jesus' followers were together. The doors were locked, because they were afraid of the elders. Then Jesus came and stood right in the middle of them and said, "Peace be with you." [20]After he said this, he showed them his hands and his side. His followers were thrilled when they saw the Lord.

[21]Then Jesus said again, "Peace be with you. As the Father sent me, I now send you." [22]After he said this, he breathed on them and said, "Receive the Holy Spirit. [23]If you forgive anyone his sins, they are forgiven. If you don't forgive them, they are not forgiven."

JESUS APPEARS TO THOMAS

[24]Thomas (called Didymus), who was one of the twelve, was not with them when Jesus came. [25]The other followers kept telling Thomas, "We saw the Lord."

But Thomas said, "I will not believe it until I see the nail marks in his hands and put my finger where the nails were and put my hand into his side."

[26]A week later the followers were in the house again, and Thomas was with them. The doors were locked, but Jesus came in and stood right in the middle of them. He said, "Peace be with you." [27]Then he said to Thomas, "Put your finger here, and look at my hands. Put your hand here in my side. Stop being an unbeliever and believe."

[28]Thomas said to him, "My Lord and my God!"

20:16 Hebrew language Or Aramaic, the languages of many people in this region in the first century.

²⁹Then Jesus told him, "You believe because you see me. Those who believe without seeing me will be truly blessed."

WHY JOHN WROTE THIS BOOK

³⁰Jesus did many other miracles in the presence of his followers that are not written in this book. ³¹But these are written so that you may believe that Jesus is the Christ, the Son of God. Then, by believing, you may have life through his name.

JESUS APPEARS TO SEVEN FOLLOWERS

21 Later, Jesus showed himself to his followers again—this time at Lake Galilee.ⁿ This is how he showed himself: ²Some of the followers were together: Simon Peter, Thomas (called Didymus), Nathanael from Cana in Galilee, the two sons of Zebedee, and two other followers. ³Simon Peter said, "I am going out to fish."

The others said, "We will go with you." So they went out and got into the boat. They fished that night but caught nothing.

⁴Early the next morning Jesus stood on the shore, but the followers did not know it was Jesus. ⁵Then he said to them, "Friends, did you catch any fish?"

They answered, "No."

21:1 Lake Galilee Literally, "Sea of Tiberias."

PEACE BY GOD

FULFILLMENT

he **knows**
your **name**

JOHN 20:16

Mary Magdalene became a follower of Jesus, and she loved him dearly. Jesus saved her from being stoned and delivered her so she could be free. Jesus accepted her even though she had a troubled past. When Jesus gave her a second chance at life, she changed and wanted what he had to offer. No one else treated her as kindly as Jesus had done.

All her life she had been misused and abused by those people who were around her until the day that Jesus came into her life. Can you imagine the helplessness she felt when she had to watch Jesus die on the cross? There was nothing she could do for him. Here the one who had been so kind to her had to suffer and die a horrific death, and she would never again hear him call her name. She was devastated. The day she went to the tomb to put incense and fragrances on his body and found that he was not there must have caused her agonizing desperation. Then he called her name.

He knows your name. No matter what we have done in our past, he accepts us where we are and reaches his hand out to us to lift us up out of the pit that we have made for ourselves. Without that acceptance, we would be hopeless, living in a world of darkness and pain. What would have happened if Christ had not reached out to us? Where would we be? Are you as accepting of others as Christ is of you?

reflect: Think about the fact that Jesus knows you by name.
Go to **John 20:22-23.**

⁶He said, "Throw your net on the right side of the boat, and you will find some." So they did, and they caught so many fish they could not pull the net back into the boat.

⁷The follower whom Jesus loved said to Peter, "It is the Lord!" When Peter heard him say this, he wrapped his coat around himself. (Peter had taken his clothes off.) Then he jumped into the water. ⁸The other followers went to shore in the boat, dragging the net full of fish. They were not very far from shore, only about a hundred yards. ⁹When the followers stepped out of the boat and onto the shore, they saw a fire of hot coals. There were fish on the fire, and there was bread.

¹⁰Then Jesus said, "Bring some of the fish you just caught."

¹¹Simon Peter went into the boat and pulled the net to the shore. It was full of big fish, one hundred fifty-three in all, but even though there were so many, the net did not tear. ¹²Jesus said to them, "Come and eat." None of the followers dared ask him, "Who

PEACE BY GOD

the **principle** of **release**

FULFILLMENT

By Edwin Louis Cole

JOHN 20:22-23

It is extremely simple, profound, and true. The sins you forgive are released, and the sins you do not forgive are retained in your life. Releasing sin frees you from a host of negative attitudes that have their roots in unforgiveness. The worst part is that while you harbor pain from the offenses of someone, intending to use the hurts as weapons, the object of your hate is unaffected.

Your mind, body, and soul are the ones poisoned from feeding on hostility and hardheartedness. The one you hold sin against goes about daily life oblivious to distress, while you reap bitterness and hatred that stunt your spiritual growth. You remain connected to the offense and to the person in an unhealthy bondage.

You must accept responsibility for your life, no matter who has done what to you and regardless of who was right or wrong. Your refusal to accept that responsibility or attempt to relieve yourself of it by blaming someone else will block your maturity.

Maturity does not come with age; it comes with the acceptance of responsibility. The principle of release is vital. It keeps you free from other people's sins all your life. It helps you mature and move from one stage of development to the next.

You can do what Jesus said to do. By faith, receive God's Holy Spirit and power in your life and forgive others so you can release their sins and not retain them for your own harm!

reflect: Whom do you need to forgive in order to free yourself from bitterness today?
Go to **Romans 6:12-14.**

Inspire Your Team to Realize the Dream

By Bill McCartney

JOHN 21:6

A good leader has the ability to see what a vision of perfection is supposed to look like, and he or she will not compromise on the requirements of that vision. As a leader, you must not only have this vision, but you also must bring people onto your team who can share this vision with you. They may not see your vision at first, but your enthusiasm for it will eventually enable them to see it, too. Before your team can share your vision, there are three things you must do:

1 **See it clearly**. Until you envision it, it will be impossible for you to get there. Stay focused on your vision. Be aware of the risks, but take them on as a challenge. Your vision will give way to a passion that, in turn, will be contagious to your team.

2 **Show it creatively**. Your team members will be affected by your enthusiasm, but they most likely will be ready to commit to your vision if you can show them the "big picture" that is, the reward waiting for them at the end.

3 **Say it constantly**. Repetition works like a charm! The key to explaining your vision to others is to speak of it tirelessly. Don't quit presenting it. See the vision. Then, find the people who can see it in you.

Great leaders are what they are because they bring out their team's potential for greatness. When the leader is effective, the individuals on the team work together as one. An effective leader needs four key ingredients to bring out the best in his team:

First, you need **character.** Can you be trusted? Is your word your bond? Are you sincere?

Second, you need **competence**. You may be of unimpeachable character, but can you do your job? Are you good at what you do? Character is good, but it's not effective unless it is paired with competence. The same is true the other way around.

Third, you need **chemistry**. Do you believe in the character and the competence of your team's folks? Do you tell them that you believe in them? Do you give them your respect? Do you encourage them? The words "I believe in you" can go a long way toward raising the worth of your team members in their own eyes and in yours.

Fourth, you need **commitment**. Are you committed to your vision? It's similar to the difference between renting a home and buying one. Do your team members see the "pride of ownership" that you have with them? Do they know you will "stick with it"? If you, as an effective leader, can believe in your team members and inspire them to work together, then you will realize your dream.

TO LEARN MORE ON WHAT THE BIBLE HAS TO SAY ABOUT **FUTURE**, READ THE SCRIPTURES AND DEVOTIONALS AT **ISAIAH 40:11, ISAIAH 42:10–16, ISAIAH 57:15, ISAIAH 30:21, 1 KINGS 18:41–46,** AND **JEREMIAH 29:14.**

are you?" because they knew it was the Lord. [13]Jesus came and took the bread and gave it to them, along with the fish.

[14]This was now the third time Jesus showed himself to his followers after he was raised from the dead.

JESUS TALKS TO PETER

[15]When they finished eating, Jesus said to Simon Peter, "Simon son of John, do you love me more than these?"

He answered, "Yes, Lord, you know that I love you."

Jesus said, "Feed my lambs."

[16]Again Jesus said, "Simon son of John, do you love me?"

He answered, "Yes, Lord, you know that I love you."

Jesus said, "Take care of my sheep."

[17]A third time he said, "Simon son of John, do you love me?"

Peter was hurt because Jesus asked him the third time, "Do you love me?" Peter said, "Lord, you know everything; you know that I love you!"

He said to him, "Feed my sheep. [18]I tell you the truth, when you were younger, you tied your own belt and went where you wanted. But when you are old, you will put out your hands and someone else will tie you and take you where you don't want to go." [19](Jesus said this to show how Peter would die to give glory to God.) Then Jesus said to Peter, "Follow me!"

[20]Peter turned and saw that the follower Jesus loved was walking behind them. (This was the follower who had leaned against Jesus at the supper and had said, "Lord, who will turn against you?") [21]When Peter saw him behind them, he asked Jesus, "Lord, what about him?"

[22]Jesus answered, "If I want him to live until I come back, that is not your business. You follow me."

[23]So a story spread among the followers that this one would not die. But Jesus did not say he would not die. He only said, "If I want him to live until I come back, that is not your business."

[24]That follower is the one who is telling these things and who has now written them down. We know that what he says is true.

[25]There are many other things Jesus did. If every one of them were written down, I suppose the whole world would not be big enough for all the books that would be written.

acts

THE GOOD NEWS OF JESUS SPREADS

LUKE WRITES ANOTHER BOOK

1 To Theophilus.
The first book I wrote was about everything Jesus began to do and teach ²until the day he was taken up into heaven. Before this, with the help of the Holy Spirit, Jesus told the apostles he had chosen what they should do. ³After his death, he showed himself to them and proved in many ways that he was alive. The apostles saw Jesus during the forty days after he was raised from the dead, and he spoke to them about the kingdom of God. ⁴Once when he was eating with them, he told them not to leave Jerusalem. He said, "Wait here to receive the promise from the Father which I told you about. ⁵John baptized people with water, but in a few days you will be baptized with the Holy Spirit."

JESUS IS TAKEN UP INTO HEAVEN

⁶When the apostles were all together, they asked Jesus, "Lord, are you now going to give the kingdom back to Israel?"

⁷Jesus said to them, "The Father is the only One who has the authority to decide dates and times. These things are not for you to know. ⁸But when the Holy Spirit comes to you, you will receive power. You will be my witnesses—in Jerusalem, in all of Judea, in Samaria, and in every part of the world."

⁹After he said this, as they were watching, he was lifted up, and a cloud hid him from their sight. ¹⁰As he was going, they were looking into the sky. Suddenly, two men wearing white clothes stood beside them. ¹¹They said, "Men of Galilee, why are you standing here looking into the sky? Jesus, whom you saw taken up from you into heaven, will come back in the same way you saw him go."

A NEW APOSTLE IS CHOSEN

¹²Then they went back to Jerusalem from the Mount of Olives. (This mountain is about half a mile from Jerusalem.) ¹³When they entered the city, they went to the upstairs room where they were staying. Peter, John, James, Andrew, Philip, Thomas, Bartholomew, Mat-

thew, James son of Alphaeus, Simon (known as the Zealot), and Judas son of James were there. ¹⁴They all continued praying together with some women, including Mary the mother of Jesus, and Jesus' brothers.

¹⁵During this time there was a meeting of the believers (about one hundred twenty of them). Peter stood up and said, ¹⁶⁻¹⁷"Brothers and sisters, in the Scriptures the Holy Spirit said through David something that must happen involving Judas. He was one of our own group and served together with us. He led those who arrested Jesus." ¹⁸(Judas bought a field with the money he got for his evil act. But he fell to his death, his body burst open, and all his intestines poured out. ¹⁹Everyone in Jerusalem learned about this so they named this place Akeldama. In their language Akeldama means "Field of Blood.")

²⁰"In the Book of Psalms," Peter said, "this is written:

'May his place be empty;
   leave no one to live in it.'   *Psalm 69:25*
And it is also written:
'Let another man replace him as leader.'
                        Psalm 109:8

²¹⁻²²So now a man must become a witness with us of Jesus' being raised from the dead. He must be one of the men who were part of our group during all the time the Lord Jesus was among us—from the time John was baptizing people until the day Jesus was taken up from us to heaven."

²³They put the names of two men before the group. One was Joseph Barsabbas, who was also called Justus. The other was Matthias. ²⁴⁻²⁵The apostles prayed, "Lord, you know the thoughts of everyone. Show us which one of these two you have chosen to do this work. Show us who should be an apostle in place of Judas, who turned away and went where he belongs." ²⁶Then they used lots to choose between them, and the lots showed that Matthias was the one. So he became an apostle with the other eleven.

THE COMING OF THE HOLY SPIRIT

2 When the day of Pentecost came, they were all together in one place. ²Suddenly a noise like a strong, blowing wind came from heaven and filled the whole house where they were sitting. ³They saw something like flames of fire that were separated and stood over each person there. ⁴They were all filled with the Holy Spirit, and they began to speak different languages[n] by the power the Holy Spirit was giving them.

⁵There were some religious Jews staying in Jerusalem who were from every country in the world. ⁶When they heard this noise, a crowd came together. They were all surprised, because each one heard them speaking in his own language. ⁷They were completely amazed at this. They said, "Look! Aren't all these people that we hear speaking from Galilee? ⁸Then how is it possible that we each hear them in our own languages? We are from different places: ⁹Parthia, Media, Elam, Mesopotamia, Judea, Cappadocia, Pontus, Asia, ¹⁰Phrygia, Pamphylia, Egypt, the areas of Libya near Cyrene, Rome ¹¹(both Jews and those who had become Jews), Crete, and Arabia. But we hear them telling in our own languages about the great things God has done!" ¹²They were all amazed and confused, asking each other, "What does this mean?"

¹³But others were making fun of them, saying, "They have had too much wine."

2:4 **languages** This can also be translated "tongues."

THE ONE PERCENT SOLUTION

good medicine

FITNESS

ACTS 1:14

More then ever in history, people are operating from a place of fear, panic, and anxiety. This comes from a sense that we're lost and alone, and that is why the most profitable medications being sold today are for depression. We weren't created to be alone.

Alone and prosperous, we hoard our money and attempt to build security, fill personal needs, and build gates to block ourselves further from the rest of the world. Alone and in crisis, we take on illness, crisis, and despair all by ourselves, further suffering as a result.

We were created for relationships and to focus on the power of God instead of our own. Together, by giving and interacting with others, we can go from addition to multiplication in our own health, as well as utilize our success for the very reason God blessed us with it in the first place—to serve him and the people in need.

As a result, we find peace and power rather than panic and powerlessness. We find hope, worthiness, and value, and we discover all kinds of people around us willing to contribute to our recovery. We're in crisis, but we're not alone. We're experiencing trauma, but we are loved, cared for, and protected. That's good medicine.

reflect: Trust God to be everything you need regardless of the circumstances.
Go to **2 Corinthians 13:5**.

PETER SPEAKS TO THE PEOPLE

¹⁴But Peter stood up with the eleven apostles, and in a loud voice he spoke to the crowd: "My fellow Jews, and all of you who are in Jerusalem, listen to me. Pay attention to what I have to say. ¹⁵These people are not drunk, as you think; it is only nine o'clock in the morning! ¹⁶But Joel the prophet wrote about what is happening here today:

¹⁷ 'God says: In the last days
    I will pour out my Spirit on all kinds of
      people.
  Your sons and daughters will prophesy.
    Your young men will see visions,
    and your old men will dream dreams.
¹⁸ At that time I will pour out my Spirit
    also on my male slaves and female
      slaves,
    and they will prophesy.
¹⁹ I will show miracles
    in the sky and on the earth:
    blood, fire, and thick smoke.
²⁰ The sun will become dark,
    the moon red as blood,
    before the overwhelming and glorious
      day of the Lord will come.
²¹ Then anyone who calls on the Lord will
      be saved.'   *Joel 2:28–32*

²²"People of Israel, listen to these words: Jesus from Nazareth was a very special man. God clearly showed this to you by the miracles, wonders, and signs he did through Jesus. You all know this, because it happened right here among you. ²³Jesus was given to you, and with the help of those who don't know the law, you put him to death by nailing him to a cross. But this was God's plan which he had made long ago; he knew all this would happen. ²⁴God raised Jesus from the dead and set him free from the pain of death, because death could not hold him. ²⁵For David said this about him:

'I keep the Lord before me always.
  Because he is close by my side,
  I will not be hurt.
²⁶ So I am glad, and I rejoice.
  Even my body has hope,
²⁷ because you will not leave me in the grave.
  You will not let your Holy One rot.
²⁸ You will teach me how to live a holy life.
  Being with you will fill me with joy.'
      Psalm 16:8–11

²⁹"Brothers and sisters, I can tell you truly that David, our ancestor, died and was buried. His grave is still here with us today. ³⁰He was a prophet and knew God had promised him that he would make a person from David's family a king just as he was.[n] ³¹Knowing this before it happened, David talked about the Christ rising from the dead. He said:

'He was not left in the grave.
  His body did not rot.'

³²So Jesus is the One whom God raised from the dead. And we are all witnesses to this. ³³Jesus was lifted up to heaven and is now at God's right side. The Father has given the Holy Spirit to Jesus as he promised. So Jesus has poured out that Spirit, and this is what you now see and hear. ³⁴David was not the one who was lifted up to heaven, but he said:

'The Lord said to my Lord,
  "Sit by me at my right side,
³⁵   until I put your enemies under your
      control." '[n]   *Psalm 110:1*

³⁶"So, all the people of Israel should know this truly: God has made Jesus—the man you nailed to the cross—both Lord and Christ."

³⁷When the people heard this, they felt guilty and asked Peter and the other apostles, "What shall we do?"

³⁸Peter said to them, "Change your hearts and lives and be baptized, each one of you, in the name of Jesus Christ for the forgiveness of your sins. And you will receive the gift of the Holy Spirit. ³⁹This promise is for you, for your children, and for all who are far away. It is for everyone the Lord our God calls to himself."

⁴⁰Peter warned them with many other words. He begged them, "Save yourselves from the evil of today's people!" ⁴¹Then those people who accepted what Peter said were baptized. About three thousand people were added to the number of believers that day. ⁴²They spent their time learning the apostles' teaching, sharing, breaking bread,[n] and praying together.

THE BELIEVERS SHARE

⁴³The apostles were doing many miracles and signs, and everyone felt great respect for God. ⁴⁴All the believers were together and

---

2:30 God . . . was See 2 Samuel 7:13; Psalm 132:11. **2:35 until . . . control** Literally, "until I make your enemies a footstool for your feet." **2:42 breaking bread** This may mean a meal as in verse 46, or the Lord's Supper, the special meal Jesus told his followers to eat to remember him (Luke 22:14–20).

shared everything. ⁴⁵They would sell their land and the things they owned and then divide the money and give it to anyone who needed it. ⁴⁶The believers met together in the Temple every day. They ate together in their homes, happy to share their food with joyful hearts. ⁴⁷They praised God and were liked by all the people. Every day the Lord added those who were being saved to the group of believers.

PETER HEALS A CRIPPLED MAN

3 One day Peter and John went to the Temple at three o'clock, the time set each day for the afternoon prayer service. ²There, at the Temple gate called Beautiful Gate, was a man who had been crippled all his life. Every day he was carried to this gate to beg for money from the people going into the Temple. ³The

man saw Peter and John going into the Temple and asked them for money. ⁴Peter and John looked straight at him and said, "Look at us!" ⁵The man looked at them, thinking they were going to give him some money. ⁶But Peter said, "I don't have any silver or gold, but I do have something else I can give you. By the power of Jesus Christ from Nazareth, stand up and walk!" ⁷Then Peter took the man's right hand and lifted him up. Immediately the man's feet and ankles became strong. ⁸He jumped up, stood on his feet, and began to walk. He went into the Temple with them, walking and jumping and praising God. ⁹⁻¹⁰All the people recognized him as the crippled man who always sat by the Beautiful Gate begging for money. Now they saw this same man walking and praising God, and they were amazed. They wondered how this could happen.

THE LONGEVITY FACTOR

pain and agony

FITNESS

ACTS 2:24

The word "pain" in this verse is used to describe the pain of childbirth. It is also used to describe the sorrows of war and the trauma of famine and other disasters. Here we are reminded that all humanity lives under the destructive and merciless power of death. It is a power that seeks only one thing: agony. The letter to the Hebrews tells us that we were held prisoners by death all of our lives.

But God did something about all this. This verse tells us that God put an end to this agony. The Greek word used here means "broke loose the bonds." Notice that the verse does not tell us that God put an end to death. What God did is put an end to the *agony* of death. It is no longer a sorrow, an agony, a torment, or a disaster. It still happens to each of us, but we no longer fear it.

We don't know when death will strike. We do know that if we're not good stewards of our bodies, it may happen sooner and more painfully than expected. Our relationship with Jesus Christ qualifies us for heaven, but we don't want an unhealthy lifestyle to hasten our journey there!

reflect: Thank God for putting an end to the agony of death through Jesus Christ.
Go to **Acts 10:14–15.**

PETER SPEAKS TO THE PEOPLE

[11]While the man was holding on to Peter and John, all the people were amazed and ran to them at Solomon's Porch. [12]When Peter saw this, he said to them, "People of Israel, why are you surprised? You are looking at us as if it were our own power or goodness that made this man walk. [13]The God of Abraham, Isaac, and Jacob, the God of our ancestors, gave glory to Jesus, his servant. But you handed him over to be killed. Pilate decided to let him go free, but you told Pilate you did not want Jesus. [14]You did not want the One who is holy and good but asked Pilate to give you a murderer[n] instead. [15]And so you killed the One who gives life, but God raised him from the dead. We are witnesses to this. [16]It was faith in Jesus that made this crippled man well. You can see this man, and you know him. He was made completely well because of trust in Jesus, and you all saw it happen!

[17]"Brothers and sisters, I know you did those things to Jesus because neither you nor your leaders understood what you were doing. [18]God said through the prophets that his Christ would suffer and die. And now God has made these things come true in this way. [19]So you must change your hearts and lives! Come back to God, and he will forgive your sins. Then the Lord will send the time of rest. [20]And he will send Jesus, the One he chose to be the Christ. [21]But Jesus must stay in heaven until the time comes when all things will be made right again. God told about this time long ago when he spoke through his holy prophets. [22]Moses said, 'The Lord your God will give you a prophet like me, who is one of your own people. You must listen to everything he tells you. [23]Anyone who does not listen to that prophet will die, cut off from God's people.'[n] [24]Samuel, and all the other prophets who spoke for God after Samuel, told about this time now. [25]You are descendants of the prophets. You have received the agreement God made with your ancestors. He said to your father Abraham, 'Through your descendants all the nations on the earth will be blessed.'[n] [26]God has raised up his servant Jesus and sent him to you first to bless you by turning each of you away from doing evil."

PETER AND JOHN AT THE COUNCIL

4 While Peter and John were speaking to the people, priests, the captain of the soldiers that guarded the Temple, and Sadducees came up to them. [2]They were upset because the two apostles were teaching the people and were preaching that people will rise from the dead through the power of Jesus. [3]The older leaders grabbed Peter and John and put them in jail. Since it was already night, they kept them in jail until the next day. [4]But many of those who had heard Peter and John preach believed the things they said. There were now about five thousand in the group of believers.

[5]The next day the rulers, the elders, and the teachers of the law met in Jerusalem. [6]Annas the high priest, Caiaphas, John, and Alexander were there, as well as everyone from the high priest's family. [7]They made Peter and John stand before them and then asked them, "By what power or authority did you do this?"

[8]Then Peter, filled with the Holy Spirit, said to them, "Rulers of the people and you elders, [9]are you questioning us about a good thing that was done to a crippled man? Are you asking us who made him well? [10]We want all of you and all the people to know that this man was made well by the power of Jesus Christ from Nazareth. You crucified him, but God raised him from the dead. This man was crippled, but he is now well and able to stand here before you because of the power of Jesus. [11]Jesus is

'the stone[n] that you builders rejected,
which has become the cornerstone.'

Psalm 118:22

[12]Jesus is the only One who can save people. No one else in the world is able to save us."

[13]The leaders saw that Peter and John were not afraid to speak, and they understood that these men had no special training or education. So they were amazed. Then they realized that Peter and John had been with Jesus. [14]Because they saw the healed man standing there beside the two apostles,

---

3:14 murderer Barabbas, the man the crowd asked Pilate to set free instead of Jesus (Luke 23:18). **3:22–23 'The Lord . . . people.'** Quotation from Deuteronomy 18:15, 19. **3:25 'Through . . . blessed.'** Quotation from Genesis 22:18; 26:4. **4:11 stone** A symbol meaning Jesus.

they could say nothing against them. 15After the leaders ordered them to leave the meeting, they began to talk to each other. 16They said, "What shall we do with these men? Everyone in Jerusalem knows they have done a great miracle, and we cannot say it is not true. 17But to keep it from spreading among the people, we must warn them not to talk to people anymore using that name."

18So they called Peter and John in again and told them not to speak or to teach at all in the name of Jesus. 19But Peter and John answered them, "You decide what God would want. Should we obey you or God? 20We cannot keep quiet. We must speak about what we have seen and heard." 21The leaders warned the apostles again and let them go free. They could not find a way to punish them, because all the people were praising God for what had been done. 22The man who received the miracle of healing was more than forty years old.

THE BELIEVERS PRAY

23After Peter and John left the meeting of leaders, they went to their own group and told them everything the leading priests and the elders had said to them. 24When the believers heard this, they prayed to God together, "Lord, you are the One who made the sky, the earth, the sea, and everything in them. 25By the Holy Spirit, through our father David your servant, you said:

'Why are the nations so angry?
  Why are the people making useless plans?
26 The kings of the earth prepare to fight,
  and their leaders make plans together
    against the Lord
      and his Christ.'   *Psalm 2:1–2*

27These things really happened when Herod, Pontius Pilate, and some Jews and non-Jews all came together against Jesus here in Jerusalem. Jesus is your holy servant, the One you made to be the Christ. 28These people made your plan happen because of your power and your will. 29And now, Lord, listen to their threats. Lord, help us, your servants, to speak your word without fear. 30Show us your power to heal. Give proofs and make miracles happen by the power of Jesus, your holy servant."

31After they had prayed, the place where they were meeting was shaken. They were all filled with the Holy Spirit, and they spoke God's word without fear.

THE BELIEVERS SHARE

32The group of believers were united in their hearts and spirit. All those in the group acted as though their private property belonged to everyone in the group. In fact, they shared everything. 33With great power the apostles were telling people that the Lord Jesus was truly raised from the dead. And God blessed all the believers very much. 34There were no needy people among them. From time to time those who owned fields or houses sold them, brought the money, 35and gave it to the apostles. Then the money was given to anyone who needed it.

36One of the believers was named Joseph, a Levite born in Cyprus. The apostles called him Barnabas (which means "one who encourages"). 37Joseph owned a field, sold it, brought the money, and gave it to the apostles.

ANANIAS AND SAPPHIRA DIE

5 But a man named Ananias and his wife Sapphira sold some land. 2He kept back part of the money for himself; his wife knew about this and agreed to it. But he brought the rest of the money and gave it to the apostles. 3Peter said, "Ananias, why did you let Satan rule your thoughts to lie to the Holy Spirit and to keep for yourself part of the money you received for the land? 4Before you sold the land, it belonged to you. And even after you sold it, you could have used the money any way you wanted. Why did you think of doing this? You lied to God, not to us!" 5-6When Ananias heard this, he fell down and died. Some young men came in, wrapped up his body, carried it out, and buried it. And everyone who heard about this was filled with fear.

7About three hours later his wife came in, but she did not know what had happened. 8Peter said to her, "Tell me, was the money you got for your field this much?"

Sapphira answered, "Yes, that was the price."

9Peter said to her, "Why did you and your husband agree to test the Spirit of the Lord? Look! The men who buried your husband are at the door, and they will carry you out." 10At that moment Sapphira fell down by his feet and died. When the young men came in and saw that she was dead, they carried her out and buried her beside her husband. [11]The whole church and all the others who heard about these things were filled with fear.

THE APOSTLES HEAL MANY

[12]The apostles did many signs and miracles among the people. And they would all meet together on Solomon's Porch. [13]None of the others dared to join them, but all the people respected them. [14]More and more men and women believed in the Lord and were added to the group of believers. [15]The people placed their sick on beds and mats in the streets, hoping that when Peter passed by at least his shadow might fall on them. [16]Crowds came from all the towns around Jerusalem, bringing their sick and those who were bothered by evil spirits, and all of them were healed.

LEADERS TRY TO STOP THE APOSTLES

[17]The high priest and all his friends (a group called the Sadducees) became very jealous. [18]They took the apostles and put them in jail. [19]But during the night, an angel of the Lord opened the doors of the jail and led the apostles outside. The angel said, [20]"Go stand in the Temple and tell the people everything about this new life." [21]When the apostles heard this, they obeyed and went into the Temple early in the morning and continued teaching.

When the high priest and his friends arrived, they called a meeting of the leaders and all the important elders. They sent some men to the jail to bring the apostles to them. [22]But, upon arriving, the officers could not find the apostles. So they went back and reported to the leaders. [23]They said, "The jail was closed and locked, and the guards were standing at the doors. But when we opened the doors, the jail was empty!" [24]Hearing this, the captain of the Temple guards and the leading priests were confused and wondered what was happening.

[25]Then someone came and told them, "Listen! The men you put in jail are standing in the Temple teaching the people." [26]Then the captain and his men went out and brought the apostles back. But the soldiers did not use force, because they were afraid the people would stone them to death.

[27]The soldiers brought the apostles to the meeting and made them stand before the leaders. The high priest questioned them, [28]saying, "We gave you strict orders not to continue teaching in that name. But look, you have filled Jerusalem with your teaching and are trying to make us responsible for this man's death."

[29]Peter and the other apostles answered, "We must obey God, not human authority! [30]You killed Jesus by hanging him on a cross. But God, the God of our ancestors, raised Jesus up from the dead! [31]Jesus is the One whom God raised to be on his right side, as Leader and Savior. Through him, all people could change their hearts and lives and have their sins forgiven. [32]We saw all these things happen. The Holy Spirit, whom God has given to all who obey him, also proves these things are true."

[33]When the leaders heard this, they became angry and wanted to kill them. [34]But a Pharisee named Gamaliel stood up in the meeting. He was a teacher of the law, and all the people respected him. He ordered the apostles to leave the meeting for a little while. [35]Then he said, "People of Israel, be careful what you are planning to do to these men. [36]Remember when Theudas appeared? He said he was a great man, and about four hundred men joined him. But he was killed, and all his followers were scattered; they were able to do nothing. [37]Later, a man named Judas came from Galilee at the time of the registration.[n] He also led a group of followers and was killed, and all his followers were scattered. [38]And so now I tell you: Stay away from these men, and leave them alone. If their plan comes from human authority, it will fail. [39]But if it is from God, you will not be able to stop them. You might even be fighting against God himself!"

The leaders agreed with what Gamaliel said. [40]They called the apostles in, beat them, and told them not to speak in the name of Jesus again. Then they let them go free. [41]The apostles left the meeting full of joy because they were given the honor of suffering disgrace for Jesus. [42]Every day in the Temple and in people's homes they continued teaching the people and telling the Good News—that Jesus is the Christ.

5:37 registration Census. A counting of all the people and the things they own.

SEVEN LEADERS ARE CHOSEN

6 The number of followers was growing. But during this same time, the Greek-speaking followers had an argument with the other followers. The Greek-speaking widows were not getting their share of the food that was given out every day. [2]The twelve apostles called the whole group of followers together and said, "It is not right for us to stop our work of teaching God's word in order to serve tables. [3]So, brothers and sisters, choose seven of your own men who are good, full of the Spirit and full of wisdom. We will put them in charge of this work. [4]Then we can continue to pray and to teach the word of God."

[5]The whole group liked the idea, so they chose these seven men: Stephen (a man with great faith and full of the Holy Spirit), Philip,[n] Procorus, Nicanor, Timon, Parmenas, and Nicolas (a man from Antioch who had become a follower of the Jewish religion). [6]Then they put these men before the apostles, who prayed and laid their hands[n] on them.

[7]The word of God was continuing to spread. The group of followers in Jerusalem increased, and a great number of the Jewish priests believed and obeyed.

STEPHEN IS ACCUSED

[8]Stephen was richly blessed by God who gave him the power to do great miracles and signs among the people. [9]But some people were against him. They belonged to the synagogue of Free Men[n] (as it was called), which included people from Cyrene, Alexandria, Cilicia, and Asia. They all came and argued with Stephen.

[10]But the Spirit was helping him to speak with wisdom, and his words were so strong that they could not argue with him. [11]So they secretly urged some men to say, "We heard Stephen speak against Moses and against God."

[12]This upset the people, the elders, and the teachers of the law. They came and grabbed Stephen and brought him to a meeting of the leaders. [13]They brought in some people to tell lies about Stephen, saying, "This man is always speaking against this holy place and the law of Moses. [14]We heard him say that Jesus from Nazareth will destroy this place and that Jesus will change the customs Mo-

ses gave us." [15]All the people in the meeting were watching Stephen closely and saw that his face looked like the face of an angel.

STEPHEN'S SPEECH

7 The high priest said to Stephen, "Are these things true?"

[2]Stephen answered, "Brothers and fathers, listen to me. Our glorious God appeared to Abraham, our ancestor, in Mesopotamia before he lived in Haran. [3]God said to Abraham, 'Leave your country and your relatives, and go to the land I will show you.'[n] [4]So Abraham left the country of Chaldea and went to live in Haran. After Abraham's father died, God sent him to this place where you now live. [5]God did not give Abraham any of this land, not even a foot of it. But God promised that he would give this land to him and his descendants, even before Abraham had a child. [6]This is what God said to him: 'Your descendants will be strangers in a land they don't own. The people there will make them slaves and will mistreat them for four hundred years. [7]But I will punish the nation where they are slaves. Then your descendants will leave that land and will worship me in this place.'[n] [8]God made an agreement with Abraham, the sign of which was circumcision. And so when Abraham had his son Isaac, Abraham circumcised him when he was eight days old. Isaac also circumcised his son Jacob, and Jacob did the same for his sons, the twelve ancestors[n] of our people.

[9]"Jacob's sons became jealous of Joseph and sold him to be a slave in Egypt. But God was with him [10]and saved him from all his troubles. The king of Egypt liked Joseph and respected him because of the wisdom God gave him. The king made him governor of Egypt and put him in charge of all the people in his palace.

[11]"Then all the land of Egypt and Canaan became so dry that nothing would grow, and

---

6:5 Philip Not the apostle named Philip. **6:6 laid their hands** The laying on of hands had many purposes, including the giving of a blessing, power, or authority. **6:9 Free Men** Jewish people who had been slaves or whose fathers had been slaves, but were now free. **7:3 'Leave . . . you.'** Quotation from Genesis 12:1. **7:6-7 'Your descendants . . . place.'** Quotation from Genesis 15:13-14 and Exodus 3:12. **7:8 twelve ancestors** Important ancestors of the people of Israel; the leaders of the twelve tribes of Israel.

Building **Momentum** Through **Teamwork**

By Tom Mullins

To be effective in the 21st century, ministry leaders must know how to lead ministry teams. The first step in leading a team is building it. The building blocks are the people who make up the team. For the team to be strong, the blocks must be positioned in the right places. Leaders who recognize the God-given strengths of their team members and then build their teams in a way that matches those strengths with corresponding positions on the team will inspire the individuals and knit the team unit together in a way that makes it inherently strong.

Good Christian leaders will go beyond seeing the potential of their members. They will communicate what they see in a way that celebrates the strengths in each member. This will inspire people to use their own strengths and encourage team members to value and draw upon one another's strengths.

As team members are inspired to get into their personal and corporate strength zones in this way, they will be naturally motivated to get on board with the game plan. Being part of the fulfillment of that plan will not be drudgery for team members because their strengths are being utilized in a way that matches God's purposes for their lives. Because they have been properly fitted into the unit, they will tend to celebrate the successes of other team members rather than feel threatened by them.

To sustain momentum and keep morale high, however, the team leader must also map out and clearly communicate the team's game plan. This map includes where the team is going, why, and how. It also includes who will be doing what and when. The details of the game plan should be constantly evaluated and refined. Involving team members in the refining of the details of the game plan that are in their areas of responsibility or expertise will deepen their commitment to the execution of the plan and contribute to its success.

Successes of individuals and of the team should be recognized and celebrated often. This does not mean waiting to celebrate until the game plan has been fully played out. Instead, it means celebrating small successes all along the way. In some cases, it can be as informal as a pat on the back in front of coworkers; in other cases, it can be as formal as a press release announcing the names of those who contributed to the accomplishment of a particular goal.

Enthusiastically filling team members with the confidence needed to take on the challenges and maintain a can-do attitude will keep them motivated to stay focused on fulfilling their part of the game plan as they thrive individually and as a team. If leaders are consistently using their strengths to optimally fulfill God's plan for their own lives, they will consistently motivate the people on their teams to do the same.

TO LEARN MORE ON WHAT THE BIBLE HAS TO SAY ABOUT **FUTURE**, READ THE SCRIPTURES AND DEVOTIONALS AT **2 CORINTHIANS 3:18, ZEPHANIAH 3:17, EPHESIANS 5:17, 1 JOHN 5:1-5, 2 CORINTHIANS 5:17,** AND **GALATIANS 4:1-7.**

---

the people suffered very much. Jacob's sons, our ancestors, could not find anything to eat. [12]But when Jacob heard there was grain in Egypt, he sent his sons there. This was their first trip to Egypt. [13]When they went there a second time, Joseph told his brothers who he was, and the king learned about Joseph's family. [14]Then Joseph sent messengers to invite Jacob, his father, to come to Egypt along with all his relatives (seventy-five persons altogether). [15]So Jacob went down to Egypt, where he and his sons died. [16]Later their bodies were moved to Shechem and put in a grave there. (It was the same grave Abraham had bought for a sum of money from the sons of Hamor in Shechem.)

[17]"The promise God made to Abraham was soon to come true, and the number of people in Egypt grew large. [18]Then a new king, who did not know who Joseph was, began to rule Egypt. [19]This king tricked our people and was cruel to our ancestors, forcing them to leave their babies outside to die. [20]At this time Moses was born, and he was very beautiful. For three months Moses was cared for in his father's house. [21]When they put Moses outside, the king's daughter adopted him and raised him as if he were her own son. [22]The Egyptians taught Moses everything they knew, and he was a powerful man in what he said and did.

[23]"When Moses was about forty years old, he thought it would be good to visit his own people, the people of Israel. [24]Moses saw an Egyptian mistreating one of his people, so he defended the Israelite and punished the Egyptian by killing him. [25]Moses thought his own people would understand that God was using him to save them, but they did not. [26]The next day when Moses saw two men of Israel fighting, he tried to make peace between them. He said, 'Men, you are brothers. Why are you hurting each other?' [27]The man who was hurting the other pushed Moses away and said, 'Who made you our ruler and judge? [28]Are you going to kill me as you killed the Egyptian yesterday?'[n] [29]When Moses heard him say this, he left Egypt and went to live in the land of Midian where he was a stranger. While Moses lived in Midian, he had two sons.

[30]"Forty years later an angel appeared to Moses in the flames of a burning bush as he was in the desert near Mount Sinai. [31]When Moses saw this, he was amazed and went near to look closer. Moses heard the Lord's voice say, [32]'I am the God of your ancestors, the God of Abraham, Isaac, and Jacob.'[n] Moses began to shake with fear and was afraid to look. [33]The Lord said to him, 'Take off your sandals, because you are standing on holy ground. [34]I have seen the troubles my people have suffered in Egypt. I have heard their cries and have come down to save them. And now, Moses, I am sending you back to Egypt.'[n]

[35]"This Moses was the same man the two men of Israel rejected, saying, 'Who made you a ruler and judge?'[n] Moses is the same man God sent to be a ruler and savior, with the help of the angel that Moses saw in the burning bush. [36]So Moses led the people out of Egypt. He worked miracles and signs in Egypt, at the Red Sea, and then in the desert for forty years. [37]This is the same Moses that said to the people of Israel, 'God will give you a prophet like me, who is one of your own people.'[n] [38]This is the Moses who was with the gathering of the Israelites in the desert. He was with the angel that spoke to him at Mount Sinai, and he was with our ancestors. He received commands from God that give life, and he gave those commands to us.

[39]"But our ancestors did not want to obey Moses. They rejected him and wanted to go back to Egypt. [40]They said to Aaron, 'Make us gods who will lead us. Moses led us out of Egypt, but we don't know what has happened to him.'[n] [41]So the people made an idol that looked like a calf. Then they brought sacrifices to it and were proud of what they had made with their own hands. [42]But God turned against them and did not try to stop them from worshiping the sun, moon, and stars. This is what is written in the book of the prophets: God says,

'People of Israel, you did not bring me
    sacrifices and offerings
while you traveled in the desert for
    forty years.

7:27–28 'Who . . . yesterday?' Quotation from Exodus 2:14. 7:32 'I am . . . Jacob.' Quotation from Exodus 3:6. 7:33–34 'Take . . . Egypt.' Quotation from Exodus 3:5–10. 7:35 'Who . . . judge?' Quotation from Exodus 2:14. 7:37 'God . . . people.' Quotation from Deuteronomy 18:15. 7:40 'Make . . . him.' Quotation from Exodus 32:1.

43 You have carried with you
  the tent to worship Molech
  and the idols of the star god Rephan
    that you made to worship.
So I will send you away beyond Babylon.'

Amos 5:25–27

44"The Holy Tent where God spoke to our ancestors was with them in the desert. God told Moses how to make this Tent, and he made it like the plan God showed him. 45Later, Joshua led our ancestors to capture the lands of the other nations. Our people went in, and God forced the other people out. When our people went into this new land, they took with them this same Tent they had received from their ancestors. They kept it until the time of David, 46who pleased God and asked God to let him build a house for him, the God of Jacob.[n] 47But Solomon was the one who built the Temple.

48"But the Most High does not live in houses that people build with their hands. As the prophet says:

49 'Heaven is my throne,
  and the earth is my footstool.
So do you think you can build a house for
  me? says the Lord.
  Do I need a place to rest?
50 Remember, my hand made all these
    things!'"   *Isaiah 66:1–2*

51Stephen continued speaking: "You stubborn people! You have not given your hearts to God, nor will you listen to him! You are always against what the Holy Spirit is trying to tell you, just as your ancestors were. 52Your ancestors tried to hurt every prophet who ever lived. Those prophets said long ago that the One who is good would come, but your ancestors killed them. And now you have turned against and killed the One who is good. 53You received the law of Moses, which God gave you through his angels, but you haven't obeyed it."

STEPHEN IS KILLED

54When the leaders heard this, they became furious. They were so mad they were grinding their teeth at Stephen. 55But Stephen was full of the Holy Spirit. He looked up to heaven and saw the glory of God and Jesus standing at God's right side. 56He said, "Look! I see heaven open and the Son of Man standing at God's right side."

57Then they shouted loudly and covered their ears and all ran at Stephen. 58They took him out of the city and began to throw stones at him to kill him. And those who told lies against Stephen left their coats with a young man named Saul. 59While they were throwing stones, Stephen prayed, "Lord Jesus, receive my spirit." 60He fell on his knees and cried in a loud voice, "Lord, do not hold this sin against them." After Stephen said this, he died.

8 Saul agreed that the killing of Stephen was good.

TROUBLES FOR THE BELIEVERS

On that day the church of Jerusalem began to be persecuted, and all the believers, except the apostles, were scattered throughout Judea and Samaria.

2And some religious people buried Stephen and cried loudly for him. 3Saul was also trying to destroy the church, going from house to house, dragging out men and women and putting them in jail. 4And wherever they were scattered, they told people the Good News.

PHILIP PREACHES IN SAMARIA

5Philip went to the city of Samaria and preached about the Christ. 6When the people there heard Philip and saw the miracles he was doing, they all listened carefully to what he said. 7Many of these people had evil spirits in them, but Philip made the evil spirits leave. The spirits made a loud noise when they came out. Philip also healed many weak and crippled people there. 8So the people in that city were very happy.

9But there was a man named Simon in that city. Before Philip came there, Simon had practiced magic and amazed all the people of Samaria. He bragged and called himself a great man. 10All the people—the least important and the most important—paid attention to Simon, saying, "This man has the power of God, called 'the Great Power'!" 11Simon had amazed them with his magic so long that the people became his followers. 12But when Philip told them the Good News about the kingdom of God and the power of Jesus Christ, men and women believed Philip and were baptized. 13Simon himself believed, and

---

7:46 Jacob Some Greek copies read "the house of Jacob." This means the people of Israel.

after he was baptized, he stayed very close to Philip. When he saw the miracles and the powerful things Philip did, Simon was amazed.

¹⁴When the apostles who were still in Jerusalem heard that the people of Samaria had accepted the word of God, they sent Peter and John to them. ¹⁵When Peter and John arrived, they prayed that the Samaritan believers might receive the Holy Spirit. ¹⁶These people had been baptized in the name of the Lord Jesus, but the Holy Spirit had not yet come upon any of them. ¹⁷Then, when the two apostles began laying their hands on the people, they received the Holy Spirit.

¹⁸Simon saw that the Spirit was given to people when the apostles laid their hands on them. So he offered the apostles money, ¹⁹saying, "Give me also this power so that anyone on whom I lay my hands will receive the Holy Spirit."

²⁰Peter said to him, "You and your money should both be destroyed, because you thought you could buy God's gift with money. ²¹You cannot share with us in this work since your heart is not right before God. ²²Change your heart! Turn away from this evil thing you have done, and pray to the Lord. Maybe he will forgive you for thinking this. ²³I see that you are full of bitter jealousy and ruled by sin."

²⁴Simon answered, "Both of you pray for me to the Lord so the things you have said will not happen to me."

²⁵After Peter and John told the people what they had seen Jesus do and after they had spoken the message of the Lord, they went back to Jerusalem. On the way, they went through many Samaritan towns and preached the Good News to the people.

PHILIP TEACHES AN ETHIOPIAN

²⁶An angel of the Lord said to Philip, "Get ready and go south to the road that leads down to Gaza from Jerusalem—the desert road." ²⁷So Philip got ready and went. On the road he saw a man from Ethiopia, a eunuch. He was an important officer in the service of Candace, the queen of the Ethiopians; he was responsible for taking care of all her money. He had gone to Jerusalem to worship. ²⁸Now, as he was on his way home, he was sitting in his chariot reading from the Book of Isaiah,

the prophet. ²⁹The Spirit said to Philip, "Go to that chariot and stay near it."

³⁰So when Philip ran toward the chariot, he heard the man reading from Isaiah the prophet. Philip asked, "Do you understand what you are reading?"

³¹He answered, "How can I understand unless someone explains it to me?" Then he invited Philip to climb in and sit with him. ³²The portion of Scripture he was reading was this:

"He was like a sheep being led to be killed.
He was quiet, as a lamb is quiet while its wool is being cut;
he never opened his mouth.
³³   He was shamed and was treated unfairly.
He died without children to continue his family.
His life on earth has ended."

Isaiah 53:7–8

³⁴The officer said to Philip, "Please tell me, who is the prophet talking about—himself or someone else?" ³⁵Philip began to speak, and starting with this same Scripture, he told the man the Good News about Jesus.

³⁶While they were traveling down the road, they came to some water. The officer said, "Look, here is water. What is stopping me from being baptized?" [³⁷Philip answered, "If you believe with all your heart, you can." The officer said, "I believe that Jesus Christ is the Son of God."]ⁿ ³⁸Then the officer commanded the chariot to stop. Both Philip and the officer went down into the water, and Philip baptized him. ³⁹When they came up out of the water, the Spirit of the Lord took Philip away; the officer never saw him again. And the officer continued on his way home, full of joy. ⁴⁰But Philip appeared in a city called Azotus and preached the Good News in all the towns on the way from Azotus to Caesarea.

SAUL IS CONVERTED

9 In Jerusalem Saul was still threatening the followers of the Lord by saying he would kill them. So he went to the high priest ²and asked him to write letters to the synagogues in the city of Damascus. Then if Saul

---

8:37 **Philip . . . God."** Some Greek copies do not contain the bracketed text.

found any followers of Christ's Way, men or women, he would arrest them and bring them back to Jerusalem.

³So Saul headed toward Damascus. As he came near the city, a bright light from heaven suddenly flashed around him. ⁴Saul fell to the ground and heard a voice saying to him, "Saul, Saul! Why are you persecuting me?"

⁵Saul said, "Who are you, Lord?"

The voice answered, "I am Jesus, whom you are persecuting. ⁶Get up now and go into the city. Someone there will tell you what you must do."

⁷The people traveling with Saul stood there but said nothing. They heard the voice, but they saw no one. ⁸Saul got up from the ground and opened his eyes, but he could not see. So those with Saul took his hand and led him into Damascus. ⁹For three days Saul could not see and did not eat or drink.

¹⁰There was a follower of Jesus in Damascus named Ananias. The Lord spoke to Ananias in a vision, "Ananias!"

Ananias answered, "Here I am, Lord."

¹¹The Lord said to him, "Get up and go to Straight Street. Find the house of Judas,ⁿ and ask for a man named Saul from the city of Tarsus. He is there now, praying. ¹²Saul has seen a vision in which a man named Ananias

---

9:11 Judas This is not either of the apostles named Judas.

FUTURE

WHO ARE YOU?

change comes from the core

ACTS 9:1-22

Many people say they go through what they call a "life-changing experience" when they are almost killed in an accident or barely survive a heart attack. They say they are different as a result. For a while, they may be more positive or start living a healthier lifestyle, but eventually they go back to their old attitudes and bad habits. The same thing often occurs after someone reads a motivational book, hears an inspiring sermon, or listens to an uplifting song.

However, change does not necessarily come as a result of such revelations, as they are epiphanies based on experiences. On the other hand, a true change of heart makes you different at the very core of your being. You truly look at life and other people in a more accepting, loving, patient, and compassionate way. With a real change of heart, your perception of everything improves.

Real change requires time: time to learn, practice, and examine life in an effort to improve ourselves. This is called acquiring wisdom, and it is particularly helpful in the area of finances. To grow in financial wisdom, we must revolutionize our belief system according to biblical principles. Remember, the most powerful part of the Bible is not what we learn from it, but what we live from it.

---

reflect: Meditate on scriptural principles to change your financial belief system.
Go to **Romans 1:3–4**.

---

comes to him and lays his hands on him. Then he is able to see again."

¹³But Ananias answered, "Lord, many people have told me about this man and the terrible things he did to your holy people in Jerusalem. ¹⁴Now he has come here to Damascus, and the leading priests have given him the power to arrest everyone who worships you."

¹⁵But the Lord said to Ananias, "Go! I have chosen Saul for an important work. He must tell about me to those who are not Jews, to kings, and to the people of Israel. ¹⁶I will show him how much he must suffer for my name."

¹⁷So Ananias went to the house of Judas. He laid his hands on Saul and said, "Brother Saul, the Lord Jesus sent me. He is the one you saw on the road on your way here. He sent me so that you can see again and be filled with the Holy Spirit." ¹⁸Immediately, something that looked like fish scales fell from Saul's eyes, and he was able to see again! Then Saul got up and was baptized. ¹⁹After he ate some food, his strength returned.

SAUL PREACHES IN DAMASCUS

Saul stayed with the followers of Jesus in Damascus for a few days. ²⁰Soon he began to preach about Jesus in the synagogues, saying, "Jesus is the Son of God."

²¹All the people who heard him were amazed. They said, "This is the man who was in Jerusalem trying to destroy those who trust in this name! He came here to arrest the followers of Jesus and take them back to the leading priests."

²²But Saul grew more powerful. His proofs that Jesus is the Christ were so strong that his own people in Damascus could not argue with him.

²³After many days, they made plans to kill Saul. ²⁴They were watching the city gates day and night, but Saul learned about their plan. ²⁵One night some followers of Saul helped him leave the city by lowering him in a basket through an opening in the city wall.

SAUL PREACHES IN JERUSALEM

²⁶When Saul went to Jerusalem, he tried to join the group of followers, but they were all afraid of him. They did not believe he was really a follower. ²⁷But Barnabas accepted Saul and took him to the apostles. Barnabas

explained to them that Saul had seen the Lord on the road and the Lord had spoken to Saul. Then he told them how boldly Saul had preached in the name of Jesus in Damascus.

²⁸And so Saul stayed with the followers, going everywhere in Jerusalem, preaching boldly in the name of the Lord. ²⁹He would often talk and argue with the Jewish people who spoke Greek, but they were trying to kill him. ³⁰When the followers learned about this, they took Saul to Caesarea and from there sent him to Tarsus.

³¹The church everywhere in Judea, Galilee, and Samaria had a time of peace and became stronger. Respecting the Lord by the way they lived, and being encouraged by the Holy Spirit, the group of believers continued to grow.

PETER HEALS AENEAS

³²As Peter was traveling through all the area, he visited God's people who lived in Lydda. ³³There he met a man named Aeneas, who was paralyzed and had not been able to leave his bed for the past eight years. ³⁴Peter said to him, "Aeneas, Jesus Christ heals you. Stand up and make your bed." Aeneas stood up immediately. ³⁵All the people living in Lydda and on the Plain of Sharon saw him and turned to the Lord.

PETER HEALS TABITHA

³⁶In the city of Joppa there was a follower named Tabitha (whose Greek name was Dorcas). She was always doing good deeds and kind acts. ³⁷While Peter was in Lydda, Tabitha became sick and died. Her body was washed and put in a room upstairs. ³⁸Since Lydda is near Joppa and the followers in Joppa heard that Peter was in Lydda, they sent two messengers to Peter. They begged him, "Hurry, please come to us!" ³⁹So Peter got ready and went with them. When he arrived, they took him to the upstairs room where all the widows stood around Peter, crying. They showed him the shirts and coats Tabitha had made when she was still alive. ⁴⁰Peter sent everyone out of the room and kneeled and prayed. Then he turned to the body and said, "Tabitha, stand up." She opened her eyes, and when she saw Peter, she sat up. ⁴¹He gave her his hand and helped her up. Then he called the saints and the widows into the room and showed them that Tabitha was alive. ⁴²People

everywhere in Joppa learned about this, and many believed in the Lord. ⁴³Peter stayed in Joppa for many days with a man named Simon who was a tanner.

PETER TEACHES CORNELIUS

10 At Caesarea there was a man named Cornelius, an officer in the Italian group of the Roman army. ²Cornelius was a religious man. He and all the other people who lived in his house worshiped the true God. He gave much of his money to the poor and prayed to God often. ³One afternoon about three o'clock, Cornelius clearly saw a vision. An angel of God came to him and said, "Cornelius!"

⁴Cornelius stared at the angel. He became afraid and said, "What do you want, Lord?"

The angel said, "God has heard your prayers. He has seen that you give to the poor, and he remembers you. ⁵Send some men now to Joppa to bring back a man named Simon who is also called Peter. ⁶He is staying with a man, also named Simon, who is a tanner and has a house beside the sea." ⁷When the angel who spoke to Cornelius left, Cornelius called two of his servants and a soldier, a religious man who worked for him. ⁸Cornelius explained everything to them and sent them to Joppa.

⁹About noon the next day as they came near Joppa, Peter was going up to the roof[n] to pray. ¹⁰He was hungry and wanted to eat, but while the food was being prepared, he had a vision. ¹¹He saw heaven opened and something coming down that looked like a big sheet being lowered to earth by its four corners. ¹²In it were all kinds of animals, reptiles, and birds. ¹³Then a voice said to Peter, "Get up, Peter; kill and eat."

¹⁴But Peter said, "No, Lord! I have never eaten food that is unholy or unclean."

¹⁵But the voice said to him again, "God has made these things clean, so don't call them 'unholy'!" ¹⁶This happened three times, and at once the sheet was taken back to heaven.

¹⁷While Peter was wondering what this vision meant, the men Cornelius sent had found Simon's house and were standing at the gate. ¹⁸They asked, "Is Simon Peter staying here?"

¹⁹While Peter was still thinking about the vision, the Spirit said to him, "Listen, three men are looking for you. ²⁰Get up and go downstairs. Go with them without doubting, because I have sent them to you."

²¹So Peter went down to the men and said, "I am the one you are looking for. Why did you come here?"

²²They said, "A holy angel spoke to Cornelius, an army officer and a good man; he worships God. All the people respect him. The angel told Cornelius to ask you to come to his house so that he can hear what you have to say." ²³So Peter asked the men to come in and spend the night.

The next day Peter got ready and went with them, and some of the followers from Joppa joined him. ²⁴On the following day they came to Caesarea. Cornelius was waiting for them and had called together his relatives and close friends. ²⁵When Peter entered, Cornelius met him, fell at his feet, and worshiped him. ²⁶But Peter helped him up, saying, "Stand up. I too am only a human." ²⁷As he talked with Cornelius, Peter went inside where he saw many people gathered. ²⁸He said, "You people understand that it is against our law for Jewish people to associate with or visit anyone who is not Jewish. But God has shown me that I should not call any person 'unholy' or 'unclean.' ²⁹That is why I did not argue when I was asked to come here. Now, please tell me why you sent for me."

³⁰Cornelius said, "Four days ago, I was praying in my house at this same time—three o'clock in the afternoon. Suddenly, there was a man standing before me wearing shining clothes. ³¹He said, 'Cornelius, God has heard your prayer and has seen that you give to the poor and remembers you. ³²So send some men to Joppa and ask Simon Peter to come. Peter is staying in the house of a man, also named Simon, who is a tanner and has a house beside the sea.' ³³So I sent for you immediately, and it was very good of you to come. Now we are all here before God to hear everything the Lord has commanded you to tell us."

³⁴Peter began to speak: "I really understand now that to God every person is the same. ³⁵In every country God accepts anyone

---

10:9 roof In Bible times houses were built with flat roofs. The roof was used for drying things such as flax and fruit. And it was used as an extra room, as a place for worship, and as a cool place to sleep in the summer.

who worships him and does what is right. [36]You know the message that God has sent to the people of Israel is the Good News that peace has come through Jesus Christ. Jesus is the Lord of all people! [37]You know what has happened all over Judea, beginning in Galilee after John[n] preached to the people about baptism. [38]You know about Jesus from Nazareth, that God gave him the Holy Spirit and power. You know how Jesus went everywhere doing good and healing those who

10:37 John John the Baptist, who preached to people about Christ's coming (Luke 3).

THE LONGEVITY FACTOR

the **un**-diet

FITNESS

ACTS 10:14–15

Diets never work. Eating God's way is the opposite of dieting. In fact, it's the Un-diet.

Myth #1: Dieting equals deprivation.

Truth: Healthy eating is not about eating only bland and tasteless foods, restricting portions, or cutting calories.

Myth #2: Eat like an elephant; look like an elephant.

Truth: If you are eating the foods God intended you to eat and/or eating the way he intended you to eat them, you will *never* look like an elephant.

Myth #3: If you crave, you cave. Once you cheat or go off your diet, it's over.

Truth: Taking short vacations from proper eating is part of life. Eating a food you crave is actually part of the plan.

Myth #4: You can trick the body into better health.

Truth: God's body cannot be tricked; it must be treated with respect. Diets that restrict foods or use only one kind of food category, such as a protein-only diet, may trick the body into change in the short-term. However, they *never* work in the long-term. Eliminating an entire food group cannot be healthy because God would not have placed those foods on the face of the earth in the first place if they were not to be eaten at all.

Always use a balance of God's foods, including fruits, vegetables, whole grains, and fresh meats to create real, lasting health.

reflect: Eat something good for your health today, and you'll reap the results later.
Go to **FITNESS:** "Losing Weight" at **Daniel 1:8.**

were ruled by the devil, because God was with him. [39]We saw what Jesus did in Judea and in Jerusalem, but the Jews in Jerusalem killed him by hanging him on a cross. [40]Yet, on the third day, God raised Jesus to life and caused him to be seen, [41]not by all the people, but only by the witnesses God had already chosen. And we are those witnesses who ate and drank with him after he was raised from the dead. [42]He told us to preach to the people and to tell them that he is the one whom God chose to be the judge of the living and the dead. [43]All the prophets say it is true that all who believe in Jesus will be forgiven of their sins through Jesus' name."

[44]While Peter was still saying this, the Holy Spirit came down on all those who were listening. [45]The Jewish believers who came with Peter were amazed that the gift of the Holy Spirit had been given even to the nations. [46]These believers heard them speaking in different languages[n] and praising God. Then Peter said, [47]"Can anyone keep these people from being baptized with water? They have received the Holy Spirit just as we did!" [48]So Peter ordered that they be baptized in the name of Jesus Christ. Then they asked Peter to stay with them for a few days.

PETER RETURNS TO JERUSALEM

11 The apostles and the believers in Judea heard that some who were not Jewish had accepted God's teaching too. [2]But when Peter came to Jerusalem, some people argued with him. [3]They said, "You went into the homes of people who are not circumcised and ate with them!"

[4]So Peter explained the whole story to them. [5]He said, "I was in the city of Joppa, and while I was praying, I had a vision. I saw something that looked like a big sheet being lowered from heaven by its four corners. It came very close to me. [6]I looked inside it and saw animals, wild beasts, reptiles, and birds. [7]I heard a voice say to me, 'Get up, Peter. Kill and eat.' [8]But I said, 'No, Lord! I have never eaten anything that is unholy or unclean.' [9]But the voice from heaven spoke again, 'God has made these things clean, so don't call them unholy.' [10]This happened three times. Then the whole thing was taken back to heaven. [11]Right then three men who were sent to me from Caesarea came to the house where I was staying. [12]The Spirit told me to go with them without doubting. These six believers here also went with me, and we entered the house of Cornelius. [13]He told us about the angel he saw standing in his house. The angel said to him, 'Send some men to Joppa and invite Simon Peter to come. [14]By the words he will say to you, you and all your family will be saved.' [15]When I began my speech, the Holy Spirit came on them just as he came on us at the beginning. [16]Then I remembered the words of the Lord. He said, 'John baptized with water, but you will be baptized with the Holy Spirit.' [17]Since God gave them the same gift he gave us who believed in the Lord Jesus Christ, how could I stop the work of God?"

[18]When the believers heard this, they stopped arguing. They praised God and said, "So God is allowing even other nations to turn to him and live."

THE GOOD NEWS COMES TO ANTIOCH

[19]Many of the believers were scattered when they were persecuted after Stephen was killed. Some of them went as far as Phoenicia, Cyprus, and Antioch telling the message to others, but only to Jews. [20]Some of these believers were people from Cyprus and Cyrene. When they came to Antioch, they spoke also to Greeks,[n] telling them the Good News about the Lord Jesus. [21]The Lord was helping the believers, and a large group of people believed and turned to the Lord.

[22]The church in Jerusalem heard about all of this, so they sent Barnabas to Antioch. [23-24]Barnabas was a good man, full of the Holy Spirit and full of faith. When he reached Antioch and saw how God had blessed the people, he was glad. He encouraged all the believers in Antioch always to obey the Lord with all their hearts, and many people became followers of the Lord.

[25]Then Barnabas went to the city of Tarsus to look for Saul, [26]and when he found Saul, he brought him to Antioch. For a whole year Saul and Barnabas met with the church and taught many people there. In Antioch the followers were called Christians for the first time.

10:46 languages This can also be translated "tongues."
11:20 Greeks Some Greek copies read "Hellenists," non-Greeks who spoke Greek.

²⁷About that time some prophets came from Jerusalem to Antioch. ²⁸One of them, named Agabus, stood up and spoke with the help of the Holy Spirit. He said, "A very hard time is coming to the whole world. There will be no food to eat." (This happened when Claudius ruled.) ²⁹The followers all decided to help the believers who lived in Judea, as much as each one could. ³⁰They gathered the money and gave it to Barnabas and Saul, who brought it to the elders in Judea.

HEROD AGRIPPA HURTS THE CHURCH

12 During that same time King Herod began to mistreat some who belonged to the church. ²He ordered James, the brother of John, to be killed by the sword. ³Herod saw that some of the people liked this, so he decided to arrest Peter, too. (This happened during the time of the Feast of Unleavened Bread.)

⁴After Herod arrested Peter, he put him in jail and handed him over to be guarded by sixteen soldiers. Herod planned to bring Peter before the people for trial after the Passover Feast. ⁵So Peter was kept in jail, but the church prayed earnestly to God for him.

PETER LEAVES THE JAIL

⁶The night before Herod was to bring him to trial, Peter was sleeping between two soldiers, bound with two chains. Other soldiers were guarding the door of the jail. ⁷Suddenly, an angel of the Lord stood there, and a light shined in the cell. The angel struck Peter on the side and woke him up. "Hurry! Get up!" the angel said. And the chains fell off Peter's hands. ⁸Then the angel told him, "Get dressed and put on your sandals." And Peter did. Then the angel said, "Put on your coat and follow me." ⁹So Peter followed him out, but he did not know if what the angel was doing was real; he thought he might be seeing a vision. ¹⁰They went past the first and second guards and came to the iron gate that separated them from the city. The gate opened by itself for them, and they went through it. When they had walked down one street, the angel suddenly left him.

¹¹Then Peter realized what had happened. He thought, "Now I know that the Lord really sent his angel to me. He rescued me from Herod and from all the things the people thought would happen."

¹²When he considered this, he went to

LOSING WEIGHT

it's all **good,**
but is it all **right?**

FITNESS

ACTS 11:8-9

I n his infinite wisdom concerning all of life, health, and longevity, God mentions that "the pig . . . is unclean for you" (Leviticus 11:7) and that "you must hate any animal in the water that does not have fins and scales [such as crabs, clams, mussels, and lobsters]" (Leviticus 11:12).

While under the New Agreement, we know that eating meat from the aforementioned animals doesn't keep you out of heaven or make you a bad person, avoiding such animals and the toxic chemicals that typically go along with these foods is still a good idea, no, a "God idea."

reflect: Consider changing your diet if you consume foods of a questionable nature.
Go to **2 Timothy 4:7.**

the home of Mary, the mother of John Mark. Many people were gathered there, praying. [13]Peter knocked on the outside door, and a servant girl named Rhoda came to answer it. [14]When she recognized Peter's voice, she was so happy she forgot to open the door. Instead, she ran inside and told the group, "Peter is at the door!"

[15]They said to her, "You are crazy!" But she kept on saying it was true, so they said, "It must be Peter's angel."

[16]Peter continued to knock, and when they opened the door, they saw him and were amazed. [17]Peter made a sign with his hand to tell them to be quiet. He explained how the Lord led him out of the jail, and he said, "Tell James and the other believers what happened." Then he left to go to another place.

[18]The next day the soldiers were very upset and wondered what had happened to Peter. [19]Herod looked everywhere for him but could not find him. So he questioned the guards and ordered that they be killed.

THE DEATH OF HEROD AGRIPPA

Later Herod moved from Judea and went to the city of Caesarea, where he stayed. [20]Herod was very angry with the people of Tyre and Sidon, but the people of those cities all came in a group to him. After convincing Blastus, the king's personal servant, to be on their side, they asked Herod for peace, because their country got its food from his country.

[21]On a chosen day Herod put on his royal robes, sat on his throne, and made a speech to the people. [22]They shouted, "This is the voice of a god, not a human!" [23]Because Herod did not give the glory to God, an angel of the Lord immediately caused him to become sick, and he was eaten by worms and died.

[24]God's message continued to spread and reach people.

[25]After Barnabas and Saul finished their task in Jerusalem, they returned to Antioch, taking John Mark with them.

BARNABAS AND SAUL ARE CHOSEN

13 In the church at Antioch there were these prophets and teachers: Barnabas, Simeon (also called Niger), Lucius (from the city of Cyrene), Manaen (who had grown up with Herod, the ruler), and Saul. [2]They were all worshiping the Lord and fasting[n] for a

certain time. During this time the Holy Spirit said to them, "Set apart for me Barnabas and Saul to do a special work for which I have chosen them."

[3]So after they fasted and prayed, they laid their hands on[n] Barnabas and Saul and sent them out.

BARNABAS AND SAUL IN CYPRUS

[4]Barnabas and Saul, sent out by the Holy Spirit, went to the city of Seleucia. From there they sailed to the island of Cyprus. [5]When they came to Salamis, they preached the Good News of God in the synagogues. John Mark was with them to help.

[6]They went across the whole island to Paphos where they met a magician named Bar-Jesus. He was a false prophet [7]who always stayed close to Sergius Paulus, the governor and a smart man. He asked Barnabas and Saul to come to him, because he wanted to hear the message of God. [8]But Elymas, the magician, was against them. (Elymas is the name for Bar-Jesus in the Greek language.) He tried to stop the governor from believing in Jesus. [9]But Saul, who was also called Paul, was filled with the Holy Spirit. He looked straight at Elymas [10]and said, "You son of the devil! You are an enemy of everything that is right! You are full of evil tricks and lies, always trying to change the Lord's truths into lies. [11]Now the Lord will touch you, and you will be blind. For a time you will not be able to see anything—not even the light from the sun."

Then everything became dark for Elymas, and he walked around, trying to find someone to lead him by the hand. [12]When the governor saw this, he believed because he was amazed at the teaching about the Lord.

PAUL AND BARNABAS LEAVE CYPRUS

[13]Paul and those with him sailed from Paphos and came to Perga, in Pamphylia. There John Mark left them to return to Jerusalem. [14]They continued their trip from Perga and went to Antioch, a city in Pisidia. On the Sabbath day they went into the synagogue

---

13:2 fasting The people would give up eating for a special time of prayer and worship to God. It was also done sometimes to show sadness and disappointment.
13:3 laid their hands on The laying on of hands had many purposes, including the giving of a blessing, power, or authority.

and sat down. [15]After the law of Moses and the writings of the prophets were read, the leaders of the synagogue sent a message to Paul and Barnabas: "Brothers, if you have any message that will encourage the people, please speak."

[16]Paul stood up, raised his hand, and said, "You Israelites and you who worship God, please listen! [17]The God of the Israelites chose our ancestors. He made the people great during the time they lived in Egypt, and he brought them out of that country with great power. [18]And he was patient with them[n] for forty years in the desert. [19]God destroyed seven nations in the land of Canaan and gave the land to his people. [20]All this happened in about four hundred fifty years.

"After this, God gave them judges until the time of Samuel the prophet. [21]Then the people asked for a king, so God gave them Saul son of Kish. Saul was from the tribe of Benjamin and was king for forty years. [22]After God took him away, God made David their king. God said about him: 'I have found in David son of Jesse the kind of man I want. He will do all I want him to do.' [23]So God has brought Jesus, one of David's descendants, to Israel to be its Savior, as he promised. [24]Before Jesus came, John[n] preached to all the people of Israel about a baptism of changed hearts and lives. [25]When he was finishing his work, he said, 'Who do you think I am? I am not the Christ. He is coming later, and I am not worthy to untie his sandals.'

[26]"Brothers, sons of the family of Abraham, and others who worship God, listen! The news about this salvation has been sent to us. [27]Those who live in Jerusalem and their leaders did not realize that Jesus was the Savior. They did not understand the words that the prophets wrote, which are read every Sabbath day. But they made them come true when they said Jesus was guilty. [28]They could not find any real reason for Jesus to be put to death, but they asked Pilate to have him killed. [29]When they had done to him all that the Scriptures had said, they took him down from the cross and laid him in a tomb. [30]But God raised him up from the dead! [31]After this, for many days, those who had gone with Jesus from Galilee to Jerusalem saw him. They are now his witnesses to the people. [32]We tell you the Good News

about the promise God made to our ancestors. [33]God has made this promise come true for us, his children, by raising Jesus from the dead. We read about this also in Psalm 2:

'You are my Son.
Today I have become your Father.'

Psalm 2:7

[34]God raised Jesus from the dead, and he will never go back to the grave and become dust. So God said:

'I will give you the holy and sure blessings
that I promised to David.'   *Isaiah 55:3*

[35]But in another place God says:

'You will not let your Holy One rot.'

Psalm 16:10

[36]David did God's will during his lifetime. Then he died and was buried beside his ancestors, and his body did rot in the grave. [37]But the One God raised from the dead did not rot in the grave. [38-39]Brothers, understand what we are telling you: You can have forgiveness of your sins through Jesus. The law of Moses could not free you from your sins. But through Jesus everyone who believes is free from all sins. [40]Be careful! Don't let what the prophets said happen to you:

[41]'Listen, you people who doubt!
You can wonder, and then die.
I will do something in your lifetime
that you won't believe even when you
are told about it!'"   *Habakkuk 1:5*

[42]While Paul and Barnabas were leaving the synagogue, the people asked them to tell them more about these things on the next Sabbath. [43]When the meeting was over, many people with those who had changed to worship God followed Paul and Barnabas from that place. Paul and Barnabas were persuading them to continue trusting in God's grace.

[44]On the next Sabbath day, almost everyone in the city came to hear the word of the Lord. [45]Seeing the crowd, the Jewish people became very jealous and said insulting things and argued against what Paul said. [46]But Paul and Barnabas spoke very boldly, saying, "We must speak the message of God to you first. But you refuse to listen. You are judging yourselves not worthy of having eternal life! So we will now go to the people of other

---

13:18 And . . . them Some Greek copies read "And he cared for them." **13:24 John** John the Baptist, who preached to people about Christ's coming (Luke 3).

Early, First, or Nothing

By Dr. Ronnie Floyd

FAITH

ACTS 13:22

I must know that I am making a difference. The very thought that my life is not really making a difference to those around me would be more than I could bear. And the truth is, I *have* seen the Lord do amazing and exciting things in me, around me, and through me. But it isn't for reasons that you might think.

When I look at the one thing in my life that has made the greatest impression, that has had the greatest influence, that above all others has helped assure me that I am truly making a difference, it is being able to begin each of my days with God.

One of my favorite heroes of the faith is David, the only man about whom God said, "I have found in David son of Jesse the kind of man I want. He will do all I want him to do" (Acts 13:22).

This word about David ought to arrest us. I can't think of a better commendation in the world. I want to be the kind of man whom God wants, the kind of man who resonates with the very heart of God. And the Book of Psalms tells us David's secret to becoming that kind of person: Begin your day with God.

Of course, David isn't the only one who knew this secret. In the Bible we also see the testimony of the world's most important figure, Jesus. "Early the next morning, while it was still dark, Jesus woke and left the house. He went to a lonely place, where he prayed" (Mark 1:35).

It's amazing that any of us think we can begin our day without leaning on the Father. If Jesus needed to do it, what makes us think we can do any less? This is what I call the "first or nothing"

principle. You start your day with God—regardless of when you get up—or you will get little or nothing from your life.

But why the importance of *starting* our day with God? Why not simply ensure that we make time for God within each day? There are at least four good reasons:

1 Priority—If Jesus is the center of our lives, the *priority* of our lives, then we need to act like it. Is Jesus first, or is the morning paper or a cup of coffee?

2 Power—You will be faced with challenges all day. How much *power* will you need in dealing with those things?

3 Perspective—By beginning your day with God you are able to judge more clearly the day's events and circumstances from God's *perspective* instead of your own.

4 Purity—Most of us have been stained by the patterns of this world, but exposure to God's presence cleans and reinforces our commitment to *purity*.

It all comes back to whether or not we want God to expand his influence in and through us. God's favor comes upon the lives of those who are willing to spend time with him, to give the firstfruits of their day to him and him alone. What we give God only grows with time.

TO LEARN MORE ON WHAT THE BIBLE HAS TO SAY ABOUT **FAITH,** READ THE SCRIPTURES AND DEVOTIONALS AT **3 JOHN 2, PSALM 17:3, PSALM 28:6–7, PSALM 27:1, PSALM 41:4,** AND **PSALM 50:12.**

nations. [47]This is what the Lord told us to do, saying:

'I have made you a light for the nations;
you will show people all over the world
the way to be saved.'" *Isaiah 49:6*

[48]When those who were not Jewish heard Paul say this, they were happy and gave honor to the message of the Lord. And the people who were chosen to have life forever believed the message.

[49]So the message of the Lord was spreading through the whole country. [50]But the Jewish people stirred up some of the important religious women and the leaders of the city. They started trouble against Paul and Barnabas and forced them out of their area. [51]So Paul and Barnabas shook the dust off their feet[n] and went to Iconium. [52]But the followers were filled with joy and the Holy Spirit.

PAUL AND BARNABAS IN ICONIUM

14 In Iconium, Paul and Barnabas went as usual to the synagogue. They spoke so well that a great many Jews and Greeks believed. [2]But some people who did not believe excited the others and turned them against the believers. [3]Paul and Barnabas stayed in Iconium a long time and spoke bravely for the Lord. He showed that their message about his grace was true by giving them the power to work miracles and signs. [4]But the city was divided. Some of the people agreed with the Jews, and others believed the apostles.

[5]Some who were not Jews, some Jews, and some of their rulers wanted to mistreat Paul and Barnabas and to stone them to death. [6]When Paul and Barnabas learned about this, they ran away to Lystra and Derbe, cities in Lycaonia, and to the areas around those cities. [7]They announced the Good News there, too.

PAUL IN LYSTRA AND DERBE

[8]In Lystra there sat a man who had been born crippled; he had never walked. [9]As this man was listening to Paul speak, Paul looked straight at him and saw that he believed God could heal him. [10]So he cried out, "Stand up on your feet!" The man jumped up and began walking around. [11]When the crowds saw what Paul did, they shouted in the Lycaonian language, "The gods have become like humans and have come down to us!" [12]Then the people began to call Barnabas "Zeus"[n] and Paul "Hermes,"[n] because he was the main speaker.

[13]The priest in the temple of Zeus, which was near the city, brought some bulls and flowers to the city gates. He and the people wanted to offer a sacrifice to Paul and Barnabas. [14]But when the apostles, Barnabas and Paul, heard about it, they tore their clothes. They ran in among the people, shouting, [15]"Friends, why are you doing these things? We are only human beings like you. We are bringing you the Good News and are telling you to turn away from these worthless things and turn to the living God. He is the One who made the sky, the earth, the sea, and everything in them. [16]In the past, God let all the nations do what they wanted. [17]Yet he proved he is real by showing kindness, by giving you rain from heaven and crops at the right times, by giving you food and filling your hearts with joy." [18]Even with these words, they were barely able to keep the crowd from offering sacrifices to them.

[19]Then some evil people came from Antioch and Iconium and persuaded the people to turn against Paul. So they threw stones at him and dragged him out of town, thinking they had killed him. [20]But the followers gathered around him, and he got up and went back into the town. The next day he and Barnabas left and went to the city of Derbe.

THE RETURN TO ANTIOCH IN SYRIA

[21]Paul and Barnabas told the Good News in Derbe, and many became followers. Paul and Barnabas returned to Lystra, Iconium, and Antioch, [22]making the followers of Jesus stronger and helping them stay in the faith. They said, "We must suffer many things to enter God's kingdom." [23]They chose elders for each church, by praying and fasting[n] for a certain time. These elders had trusted the Lord, so Paul and Barnabas put them in the Lord's care.

[24]Then they went through Pisidia and came to Pamphylia. [25]When they had preached the message in Perga, they went down to

---

13:51 shook . . . feet A warning. It showed that they had rejected these people. **14:12 "Zeus"** The Greeks believed in many false gods, of whom Zeus was most important. **14:12 "Hermes"** The Greeks believed he was a messenger for the other gods. **14:23 fasting** The people would give up eating for a special time of prayer and worship to God. It was also done sometimes to show sadness and disappointment.

Attalia. 26And from there they sailed away to Antioch where the believers had put them into God's care and had sent them out to do this work. Now they had finished.

27When they arrived in Antioch, Paul and Barnabas gathered the church together. They told the church all about what God had done with them and how God had made it possible for those who were not Jewish to believe. 28And they stayed there a long time with the followers.

THE MEETING AT JERUSALEM

15 Then some people came to Antioch from Judea and began teaching the non-Jewish believers: "You cannot be saved if you are not circumcised as Moses taught us." 2Paul and Barnabas were against this teaching and argued with them about it. So the church decided to send Paul, Barnabas, and some others to Jerusalem where they could talk more about this with the apostles and elders.

3The church helped them leave on the trip, and they went through the countries of Phoenicia and Samaria, telling all about how the other nations had turned to God. This made all the believers very happy. 4When they arrived in Jerusalem, they were welcomed by the apostles, the elders, and the church. Paul, Barnabas, and the others told about everything God had done with them. 5But some of the believers who belonged to the Pharisee group came forward and said, "The non-Jewish believers must be circumcised. They must be told to obey the law of Moses."

6The apostles and the elders gathered to consider this problem. 7After a long debate, Peter stood up and said to them, "Brothers, you know that in the early days God chose me from among you to preach the Good News to the nations. They heard the Good News from me, and they believed. 8God, who knows the thoughts of everyone, accepted them. He showed this to us by giving them the Holy Spirit, just as he did to us. 9To God, those people are not different from us. When they believed, he made their hearts pure. 10So now why are you testing God by putting a heavy load around the necks of the non-Jewish believers? It is a load that neither we nor our ancestors were able to carry. 11But we be-

lieve that we and they too will be saved by the grace of the Lord Jesus."

12Then the whole group became quiet. They listened to Paul and Barnabas tell about all the miracles and signs that God did through them among the people. 13After they finished speaking, James said, "Brothers, listen to me. 14Simon has told us how God showed his love for those people. For the first time he is accepting from among them a people to be his own. 15The words of the prophets agree with this too:

16 'After these things I will return.

> The kingdom of David is like a fallen tent.

But I will rebuild its ruins,
> and I will set it up.

17 Then those people who are left alive may
> ask the Lord for help,

and the other nations that belong to me,
says the Lord,
> who will make it happen.

18 And these things have been known for a
> long time.'   *Amos 9:11–12*

19"So I think we should not bother the other people who are turning to God. 20Instead, we should write a letter to them telling them these things: Stay away from food that has been offered to idols (which makes it unclean), any kind of sexual sin, eating animals that have been strangled, and blood. 21They should do these things, because for a long time in every city the law of Moses has been taught. And it is still read in the synagogue every Sabbath day."

LETTER TO NON-JEWISH BELIEVERS

22The apostles, the elders, and the whole church decided to send some of their men with Paul and Barnabas to Antioch. They chose Judas Barsabbas and Silas, who were respected by the believers. 23They sent the following letter with them:

From the apostles and elders, your brothers.

To all the non-Jewish believers in Antioch, Syria, and Cilicia:

Greetings!

24We have heard that some of our group have come to you and said things that trouble and upset you. But we did not tell them to do this. 25We have all agreed to choose some messengers and send them to you with our dear friends Barnabas and Paul— [26]people who have given their lives to serve our Lord Jesus Christ. [27]So we are sending Judas and Silas, who will tell you the same things. [28]It has pleased the Holy Spirit that you should not have a heavy load to carry, and we agree. You need to do only these things: [29]Stay away from any food that has been offered to idols, eating any animals that have been strangled, and blood, and any kind of sexual sin. If you stay away from these things, you will do well.

Good-bye.

[30]So they left Jerusalem and went to Antioch where they gathered the church and gave them the letter. [31]When they read it, they were very happy because of the encouraging message. [32]Judas and Silas, who were also prophets, said many things to encourage the believers and make them stronger. [33]After some time Judas and Silas were sent off in peace by the believers, and they went back to those who had sent them [, [34]but Silas decided to remain there].[n]

[35]But Paul and Barnabas stayed in Antioch and, along with many others, preached the Good News and taught the people the message of the Lord.

PAUL AND BARNABAS SEPARATE

[36]After some time, Paul said to Barnabas, "We should go back to all those towns where we preached the message of the Lord. Let's visit the believers and see how they are doing."

[37]Barnabas wanted to take John Mark with them, [38]but he had left them at Pamphylia; he did not continue with them in the work. So Paul did not think it was a good idea to take him. [39]Paul and Barnabas had such a serious argument about this that they separated and went different ways. Barnabas took Mark and sailed to Cyprus, [40]but Paul chose Silas and left. The believers in Antioch put Paul into the Lord's care, [41]and he went through Syria and Cilicia, giving strength to the churches.

TIMOTHY GOES WITH PAUL

16 Paul came to Derbe and Lystra, where a follower named Timothy lived. Timothy's mother was Jewish and a believer, but his father was a Greek.

[2]The believers in Lystra and Iconium respected Timothy and said good things about him. [3]Paul wanted Timothy to travel with him, but all the people living in that area knew that Timothy's father was Greek. So Paul circumcised Timothy to please his mother's people. [4]Paul and those with him traveled from town to town and gave the decisions made by the apostles and elders in Jerusalem for the people to obey. [5]So the churches became stronger in the faith and grew larger every day.

PAUL IS CALLED OUT OF ASIA

[6]Paul and those with him went through the areas of Phrygia and Galatia since the Holy Spirit did not let them preach the Good News in Asia. [7]When they came near the country of Mysia, they tried to go into Bithynia, but the Spirit of Jesus did not let them. [8]So they passed by Mysia and went to Troas. [9]That night Paul saw in a vision a man from Macedonia. The man stood and begged, "Come over to Macedonia and help us." [10]After Paul had seen the vision, we immediately prepared to leave for Macedonia, understanding that God had called us to tell the Good News to those people.

LYDIA BECOMES A CHRISTIAN

[11]We left Troas and sailed straight to the island of Samothrace. The next day we sailed to Neapolis.[n] [12]Then we went by land to Philippi, a Roman colony[n] and the leading city in that part of Macedonia. We stayed there for several days.

[13]On the Sabbath day we went outside the city gate to the river where we thought we would find a special place for prayer. Some women had gathered there, so we sat down and talked with them. [14]One of the listeners was a woman named Lydia from the city of Thyatira whose job was selling purple cloth. She worshiped God, and he opened her mind to pay attention to what Paul was saying. [15]She and all the people in her house were baptized. Then she invited us to her home, saying, "If you think I am truly a believer in

---

15:34 but . . . there Some Greek copies do not contain the bracketed text. **16:11 Neapolis** City in Macedonia. It was the first city Paul visited on the continent of Europe. **16:12 Roman colony** A town begun by Romans with Roman laws, customs, and privileges.

the Lord, then come stay in my house." And she persuaded us to stay with her.

PAUL AND SILAS IN JAIL

16Once, while we were going to the place for prayer, a servant girl met us. She had a special spirit[n] in her, and she earned a lot of money for her owners by telling fortunes. 17This girl followed Paul and us, shouting, "These men are servants of the Most High God. They are telling you how you can be saved."

18She kept this up for many days. This bothered Paul, so he turned and said to the spirit, "By the power of Jesus Christ, I command you to come out of her!" Immediately, the spirit came out.

19When the owners of the servant girl saw this, they knew that now they could not use her to make money. So they grabbed Paul and Silas and dragged them before the city rulers in the marketplace. 20They brought Paul and Silas to the Roman rulers and said, "These men are Jews and are making trouble in our city. 21They are teaching things that are not right for us as Romans to do."

22The crowd joined the attack against them. The Roman officers tore the clothes of Paul and Silas and had them beaten with rods. 23Then Paul and Silas were thrown into jail, and the jailer was ordered to guard them carefully. 24When he heard this order, he put them far inside the jail and pinned their feet down between large blocks of wood.

25About midnight Paul and Silas were praying and singing songs to God as the other prisoners listened. 26Suddenly, there was a strong earthquake that shook the foundation of the jail. Then all the doors of the jail broke open, and all the prisoners were freed from their chains. 27The jailer woke up and saw that the jail doors were open. Thinking that the prisoners had already escaped, he got his sword and was about to kill himself.[n] 28But Paul shouted, "Don't hurt yourself! We are all here."

29The jailer told someone to bring a light. Then he ran inside and, shaking with fear, fell down before Paul and Silas. 30He brought them outside and said, "Men, what must I do to be saved?"

31They said to him, "Believe in the Lord Jesus and you will be saved—you and all the people in your house." 32So Paul and Silas told the message of the Lord to the jailer and all the people in his house. 33At that hour of the night the jailer took Paul and Silas and washed their wounds. Then he and all his people were baptized immediately. 34After this the jailer took Paul and Silas home and gave them food. He and his family were very happy because they now believed in God.

35The next morning, the Roman officers sent the police to tell the jailer, "Let these men go free."

36The jailer said to Paul, "The officers have sent an order to let you go free. You can leave now. Go in peace."

37But Paul said to the police, "They beat us in public without a trial, even though we are Roman citizens.[n] And they threw us in jail. Now they want to make us go away quietly. No! Let them come themselves and bring us out."

38The police told the Roman officers what Paul said. When the officers heard that Paul and Silas were Roman citizens, they were afraid. 39So they came and told Paul and Silas they were sorry and took them out of jail and asked them to leave the city. 40So when they came out of the jail, they went to Lydia's house where they saw some of the believers and encouraged them. Then they left.

PAUL AND SILAS IN THESSALONICA

17 Paul and Silas traveled through Amphipolis and Apollonia and came to Thessalonica where there was a synagogue. 2Paul went into the synagogue as he always did, and on each Sabbath day for three weeks, he talked with his fellow Jews about the Scriptures. 3He explained and proved that the Christ must die and then rise from the dead. He said, "This Jesus I am telling you about is the Christ." 4Some of them were convinced and joined Paul and Silas, along with many of the Greeks who worshiped God and many of the important women.

5But some others became jealous. So they got some evil men from the marketplace,

---

16:16 spirit This was a spirit from the devil, which caused her to say she had special knowledge. **16:27 kill himself** He thought the leaders would kill him for letting the prisoners escape. **16:37 Roman citizens** Roman law said that Roman citizens must not be beaten before they had a trial.

Lessons from the Battlefield

By Steve Hill

ACTS 16:22–30

Christianity isn't always smooth, easy sailing. The moment you become a Christian, you sign up to fight in the greatest and longest war in the history of humanity. It's the battle of the ages between good and evil. And the conflict often seems dark and stormy. But I've got good news for you. Satan is a defeated foe, and you have authority over him through Jesus Christ!

The question is, how do you make that victory a reality in your life? Let me share some lessons I've learned from the battlefield and from the Bible. First, lift your vision to see the big picture and quiet your spirit before the Lord. Remember, the situation you're now going through is just one conflict, not the whole war. We will win in the end. He brought you through yesterday's battles, and he'll bring you through today's, as well.

Divert your attention from your problem and onto the Lord through praise and worship. Acknowledge that he is your healer, deliverer, and strength. Paul and Silas did this when they were chained in prison. During their midnight hour, they prayed and sang praises to God, and heaven responded by sending an earthquake to deliver them! It's important that you don't take your present situation out of context. This is just a season, and it will pass.

Psalm 91:1 promises, "Those who go to God Most High for safety will be protected by the Almighty." One of the most powerful weapons the Lord has given you is his Word. Ephesians 6:17 refers to the Word of God as "the sword of the Spirit." This sword enables you to defeat your enemy. Use it to protect your heart. Keep it sharp. Use it daily.

Jesus Christ is your Commander-in-Chief. That means you must obey him. When you disobey his commands, you set yourself up for guaranteed defeat. Satan's strategy is to reroute you, then ruin you. But as you obey the Lord and stay true to his plan for your life, you will stay on course.

Second Corinthians 2:14 says, "But thanks be to God who always leads us as captives in Christ's victory parade. . . . " Are you in a battle right now? God will always lead you! Is the enemy pressing upon you? The Lord already has won the victory for your salvation!

Come before the Lord with a childlike heart and say, "Jesus, I shut everything out and draw close to you. You are my refuge. You are my peace. You are the lover of my soul."

As you draw near to him in that secret place, you will hear the soothing, steady beat of his heart. And there, in that quiet place, he will meet with you.

TO LEARN MORE ON WHAT THE BIBLE HAS TO SAY ABOUT **FUTURE**, READ THE SCRIPTURES AND DEVOTIONALS AT **1 PETER 1:12, EPHESIANS 5:15–16, GALATIANS 2:20, 1 JOHN 2:13–14, 2 TIMOTHY 1:3,** AND **HEBREWS 10:23–25.**

formed a mob, and started a riot. They ran to Jason's house, looking for Paul and Silas, wanting to bring them out to the people. ⁶But when they did not find them, they dragged Jason and some other believers to the leaders of the city. The people were yelling, "These people have made trouble everywhere in the world, and now they have come here too! ⁷Jason is keeping them in his house. All of them do things against the laws of Caesar, saying there is another king, called Jesus."

⁸When the people and the leaders of the city heard these things, they became very upset. ⁹They made Jason and the others put up a sum of money. Then they let the believers go free.

PAUL AND SILAS GO TO BEREA

¹⁰That same night the believers sent Paul and Silas to Berea where they went to the synagogue. ¹¹These people were more willing to listen than the people in Thessalonica. The Bereans were eager to hear what Paul and Silas said and studied the Scriptures every day to find out if these things were true. ¹²So, many of them believed, as well as many important Greek women and men. ¹³But the people in Thessalonica learned that Paul was preaching the word of God in Berea, too. So they came there, upsetting the people and making trouble. ¹⁴The believers quickly sent Paul away to the coast, but Silas and Timothy stayed in Berea. ¹⁵The people leading Paul went with him to Athens. Then they carried a message from Paul back to Silas and Timothy for them to come to him as soon as they could.

PAUL PREACHES IN ATHENS

¹⁶While Paul was waiting for Silas and Timothy in Athens, he was troubled because he saw that the city was full of idols. ¹⁷In the synagogue, he talked with the Jews and the Greeks who worshiped God. He also talked every day with people in the marketplace. ¹⁸Some of the Epicurean and Stoic philosophers[n] argued with him, saying, "This man doesn't know what he is talking about. What is he trying to say?" Others said, "He seems to be telling us about some other gods," because Paul was telling them about Jesus and his rising from the dead. ¹⁹They got Paul and took him to a meeting of the Areopagus,[n] where they said, "Please explain to us this new idea you have been teaching. ²⁰The things you are saying are new to us, and we want to know what this teaching means." ²¹(All the people of Athens and those from other countries who lived there always used their time to talk about the newest ideas.)

²²Then Paul stood before the meeting of the Areopagus and said, "People of Athens, I can see you are very religious in all things. ²³As I was going through your city, I saw the objects you worship. I found an altar that had these words written on it: TO A GOD WHO IS NOT KNOWN. You worship a god that you don't know, and this is the God I am telling you about! ²⁴The God who made the whole world and everything in it is the Lord of the land and the sky. He does not live in temples built by human hands. ²⁵This God is the One who gives life, breath, and everything else to people. He does not need any help from them; he has everything he needs. ²⁶God began by making one person, and from him came all the different people who live everywhere in the world. God decided exactly when and where they must live. ²⁷God wanted them to look for him and perhaps search all around for him and find him, though he is not far from any of us: ²⁸'By his power we live and move and exist.' Some of your own poets have said: 'For we are his children.' ²⁹Since we are God's children, you must not think that God is like something that people imagine or make from gold, silver, or rock. ³⁰In the past, people did not understand God, and he ignored this. But now, God tells all people in the world to change their hearts and lives. ³¹God has set a day that he will judge all the world with fairness, by the man he chose long ago. And God has proved this to everyone by raising that man from the dead!"

³²When the people heard about Jesus being raised from the dead, some of them laughed. But others said, "We will hear more about this from you later." ³³So Paul went away from them. ³⁴But some of the people believed Paul and joined him. Among those

---

17:18 Epicurean and Stoic philosophers Philosophers were those who searched for truth. Epicureans believed that pleasure, especially pleasures of the mind, were the goal of life. Stoics believed that life should be without feelings of joy or grief. **17:19 Areopagus** A council or group of important leaders in Athens. They were like judges.

God's **Ultimate** Sacrifice

FAITH

By James Davis

ACTS 17:25

God measures things completely differently from the way people do. His agenda is all about you coming over to his side and his plan. Become faithful to what God has planned for your life, and he will use you for his glory. You cannot conquer sin or difficulties in your own strength. If there is going to be victory, then God will have to give you the victory.

Faith in a great God is different from a great faith in God. If you put faith in yourself, you get what you can do. Put faith in a business or organization and you will get what the business or organization can do. However, when you put your faith in God, be prepared to get what God can do. And God can do anything. Centuries ago, in the Book of Genesis, when a man sinned, he brought an offering as covering for his sin. The man sacrificed a lamb: one lamb per man.

In the Book of Exodus, we learn that one lamb covered one family. As the Israelites were getting ready to leave Egypt, there was the first Passover. Each family feasted on lamb and put some of the blood of the lamb on the doorpost. How did they get out of Egyptian bondage? They went out under the blood. How do you get out of bondage? By coming under the blood of Jesus Christ in your heart.

The Bible tells us the Israelites eventually made it to Canaan, and they had a Passover again; this time it was one lamb for an entire nation. It had taken forty years for the Israelites to get right with the Lord and to conquer the giants in Canaan.

Another thousand years went by and the Israelites celebrated Passover every year—one lamb for one nation. Then John the Baptist preached not one lamb per man, one lamb per family, or one lamb per nation. John the Baptist declared, "Look, the Lamb of God, who takes away the sin of the world!" (John 1:29). God's careful planning brought release from sin to the entire human race, one lamb at a time until the arrival of the perfect Lamb of God—one lamb for all of humanity.

Every time a sin, nation, or person lines up against God, he brings them down. God is looking for people who put their faith in him. Give the great God all your problems and all that is against you. Your great and all-powerful God can cause the angels of heaven to fight for you if needed. It does not matter what you own, how powerful your weapons or who you command, God controls the universe. Nothing ever catches God by surprise. He knows the end while his plans are still beginning. And his plans for you are incredible!

TO LEARN MORE ON WHAT THE BIBLE HAS TO SAY ABOUT **FAITH,** READ THE SCRIPTURES AND DEVOTIONALS AT **MATTHEW 5:14–16, MATTHEW 16:25, MATTHEW 17:20, MARK 1:35, JOSHUA 22:5,** AND **JOHN 3:31–36.**

who believed was Dionysius, a member of the Areopagus, a woman named Damaris, and some others.

PAUL IN CORINTH

18 Later Paul left Athens and went to Corinth. [2]Here he met a Jew named Aquila who had been born in the country of Pontus. But Aquila and his wife, Priscilla, had recently moved to Corinth from Italy, because Claudius[n] commanded that all Jews must leave Rome. Paul went to visit Aquila and Priscilla. [3]Because they were tentmakers, just as he was, he stayed with them and worked with them. [4]Every Sabbath day he talked with the Jews and Greeks in the synagogue, trying to persuade them to believe in Jesus.

[5]Silas and Timothy came from Macedonia and joined Paul in Corinth. After this, Paul spent all his time telling people the Good News, showing them that Jesus is the Christ. [6]But they would not accept Paul's teaching and said some evil things. So he shook off the dust from his clothes[n] and said to them, "If you are not saved, it will be your own fault! I have done all I can do! After this, I will go to other nations." [7]Paul left the synagogue and moved into the home of Titius Justus, next to the synagogue. This man worshiped God. [8]Crispus was the leader of that synagogue, and he and all the people living in his house believed in the Lord. Many others in Corinth also listened to Paul and believed and were baptized.

[9]During the night, the Lord told Paul in a vision: "Don't be afraid. Continue talking to people and don't be quiet. [10]I am with you, and no one will hurt you because many of my people are in this city." [11]Paul stayed there for a year and a half, teaching God's word to the people.

PAUL IS BROUGHT BEFORE GALLIO

[12]When Gallio was the governor of the country of Southern Greece, some people came together against Paul and took him to the court. [13]They said, "This man is teaching people to worship God in a way that is against our law."

[14]Paul was about to say something, but Gallio spoke, saying, "I would listen to you if you were complaining about a crime or some wrong. [15]But the things you are saying are only questions about words and names—arguments about your own law. So you must solve this problem yourselves. I don't want to be a judge of these things." [16]And Gallio made them leave the court.

[17]Then they all grabbed Sosthenes, the leader of the synagogue, and beat him there before the court. But this did not bother Gallio.

PAUL RETURNS TO ANTIOCH

[18]Paul stayed with the believers for many more days. Then he left and sailed for Syria, with Priscilla and Aquila. At Cenchrea Paul cut off his hair,[n] because he had made a promise to God. [19]Then they went to Ephesus, where Paul left Priscilla and Aquila. While Paul was there, he went into the synagogue and talked with the people. [20]When they asked him to stay with them longer, he refused. [21]But as he left, he said, "I will come back to you again if God wants me to." And so he sailed away from Ephesus.

[22]When Paul landed at Caesarea, he went and gave greetings to the church in Jerusalem. After that, Paul went to Antioch. [23]He stayed there for a while and then left and went through the regions of Galatia and Phrygia. He traveled from town to town in these regions, giving strength to all the followers.

APOLLOS IN EPHESUS AND CORINTH

[24]A Jew named Apollos came to Ephesus. He was born in the city of Alexandria and was a good speaker who knew the Scriptures well. [25]He had been taught about the way of the Lord and was always very excited when he spoke and taught the truth about Jesus. But the only baptism Apollos knew about was the baptism that John[n] taught. [26]Apollos began to speak very boldly in the synagogue, and when Priscilla and Aquila heard him, they took him to their home and helped him better understand the way of God. [27]Now Apollos wanted to go to the country of Southern Greece. So the believers helped him and wrote a letter to the followers there, asking

---

18:2 Claudius The emperor (ruler) of Rome, A.D. 41–54. **18:6 shook . . . clothes** This was a warning to show that Paul was finished talking to the people in that city. **18:18 cut . . . hair** Jews did this to show that the time of a special promise to God was finished. **18:25 John** John the Baptist, who preached to people about Christ's coming (Luke 3).

them to accept him. These followers had believed in Jesus because of God's grace, and when Apollos arrived, he helped them very much. [28]He argued very strongly with the Jews before all the people, clearly proving with the Scriptures that Jesus is the Christ.

PAUL IN EPHESUS

19 While Apollos was in Corinth, Paul was visiting some places on the way to Ephesus. There he found some followers [2]and asked them, "Did you receive the Holy Spirit when you believed?"

They said, "We have never even heard of a Holy Spirit."

[3]So he asked, "What kind of baptism did you have?"

They said, "It was the baptism that John taught."

[4]Paul said, "John's baptism was a baptism of changed hearts and lives. He told people to believe in the one who would come after him, and that one is Jesus."

[5]When they heard this, they were baptized in the name of the Lord Jesus. [6]Then Paul laid his hands on them,[n] and the Holy Spirit came upon them. They began speaking different languages[n] and prophesying. [7]There were about twelve people in this group.

[8]Paul went into the synagogue and spoke out boldly for three months. He talked with the people and persuaded them to accept the things he said about the kingdom of God. [9]But some of them became stubborn. They refused to believe and said evil things about the Way of Jesus before all the people. So Paul left them, and taking the followers with him, he went to the school of a man named Tyrannus. There Paul talked with people every day [10]for two years. Because of his work, every Jew and Greek in Asia heard the word of the Lord.

THE SONS OF SCEVA

[11]God used Paul to do some very special miracles. [12]Some people took handkerchiefs and clothes that Paul had used and put them on the sick. When they did this, the sick were healed and evil spirits left them.

[13]But some people also were traveling around and making evil spirits go out of people. They tried to use the name of the Lord Jesus to force the evil spirits out. They would say, "By the same Jesus that Paul talks about,

I order you to come out!" [14]Seven sons of Sceva, a leading priest, were doing this.

[15]But one time an evil spirit said to them, "I know Jesus, and I know about Paul, but who are you?"

[16]Then the man who had the evil spirit jumped on them. Because he was so much stronger than all of them, they ran away from the house naked and hurt. [17]All the people in Ephesus—Jews and Greeks—learned about this and were filled with fear and gave great honor to the Lord Jesus. [18]Many of the believers began to confess openly and tell all the evil things they had done. [19]Some of them who had used magic brought their magic books and burned them before everyone. Those books were worth about fifty thousand silver coins.[n]

[20]So in a powerful way the word of the Lord kept spreading and growing.

[21]After these things, Paul decided to go to Jerusalem, planning to go through the countries of Macedonia and Southern Greece and then on to Jerusalem. He said, "After I have been to Jerusalem, I must also visit Rome." [22]Paul sent Timothy and Erastus, two of his helpers, ahead to Macedonia, but he himself stayed in Asia for a while.

TROUBLE IN EPHESUS

[23]And during that time, there was some serious trouble in Ephesus about the Way of Jesus. [24]A man named Demetrius, who worked with silver, made little silver models that looked like the temple of the goddess Artemis.[n] Those who did this work made much money. [25]Demetrius had a meeting with them and some others who did the same kind of work. He told them, "Men, you know that we make a lot of money from our business. [26]But look at what this man Paul is doing. He has convinced and turned away many people in Ephesus and in almost all of Asia! He says the gods made by human hands are not real. [27]There is a danger that our business will lose its good name, but there is also another

---

19:6 laid his hands on them The laying on of hands had many purposes, including the giving of a blessing, power, or authority. **19:6 languages** This can also be translated "tongues." **19:19 fifty thousand silver coins** Probably drachmas. One coin was enough to pay a worker for one day's labor. **19:24 Artemis** A Greek goddess that the people of Asia Minor worshiped.

danger: People will begin to think that the temple of the great goddess Artemis is not important. Her greatness will be destroyed, and Artemis is the goddess that everyone in Asia and the whole world worships."

28When the others heard this, they became very angry and shouted, "Artemis, the goddess of Ephesus, is great!" 29The whole city became confused. The people grabbed Gaius and Aristarchus, who were from Macedonia and were traveling with Paul, and ran to the theater. 30Paul wanted to go in and talk to the crowd, but the followers did not let him. 31Also, some leaders of Asia who were friends of Paul sent him a message, begging him not to go into the theater. 32Some people were shouting one thing, and some were shouting another. The meeting was completely confused; most of them did not know why they had come together. 33They put a man named Alexander in front of the people, and some of them told him what to do. Alexander waved his hand so he could explain things to the people. 34But when they saw that Alexander was a Jew, they all shouted the same thing for two hours: "Great is Artemis of Ephesus!"

35Then the city clerk made the crowd be quiet. He said, "People of Ephesus, everyone knows that Ephesus is the city that keeps the temple of the great goddess Artemis and her holy stone[n] that fell from heaven. 36Since no one can say this is not true, you should be quiet. Stop and think before you do anything. 37You brought these men here, but they have not said anything evil against our goddess or stolen anything from her temple. 38If Demetrius and those who work with him have a charge against anyone they should go to the courts and judges where they can argue with each other. 39If there is something else you want to talk about, it can be decided at the regular town meeting of the people. 40I say this because some people might see this trouble today and say that we are rioting. We could not explain this, because there is no real reason for this meeting." 41After the city clerk said these things, he told the people to go home.

PAUL IN MACEDONIA AND GREECE

20 When the trouble stopped, Paul sent for the followers to come to him. After he encouraged them and then told them goodbye, he left and went to the country of Macedonia. 2He said many things to strengthen the followers in the different places on his way through Macedonia. Then he went to Greece, 3where he stayed for three months. He was ready to sail for Syria, but some evil people were planning something against him. So Paul decided to go back through Macedonia to Syria. 4The men who went with him were Sopater son of Pyrrhus, from the city of Berea; Aristarchus and Secundus, from the city of Thessalonica; Gaius, from Derbe; Timothy; and Tychicus and Trophimus, two men from Asia. 5These men went on ahead and waited for us at Troas. 6We sailed from Philippi after the Feast of Unleavened Bread. Five days later we met them in Troas, where we stayed for seven days.

PAUL'S LAST VISIT TO TROAS

7On the first day of the week,[n] we all met together to break bread,[n] and Paul spoke to the group. Because he was planning to leave the next day, he kept on talking until midnight. 8We were all together in a room upstairs, and there were many lamps in the room. 9A young man named Eutychus was sitting in the window. As Paul continued talking, Eutychus was falling into a deep sleep. Finally, he went sound asleep and fell to the ground from the third floor. When they picked him up, he was dead. 10Paul went down to Eutychus, knelt down, and put his arms around him. He said, "Don't worry. He is alive now." 11Then Paul went upstairs again, broke bread, and ate. He spoke to them a long time, until it was early morning, and then he left. 12They took the young man home alive and were greatly comforted.

THE TRIP FROM TROAS TO MILETUS

13We went on ahead of Paul and sailed for the city of Assos, where he wanted to join us on the ship. Paul planned it this way because he wanted to go to Assos by land. 14When he met us there, we took him aboard and went to Mitylene. 15We sailed from Mitylene and the

---

19:35 holy stone Probably a meteorite or stone that the people thought looked like Artemis.   **20:7 first day of the week** Sunday, which for Jews began at sunset on our Saturday. But if in this part of Asia a different system of time was used, then the meeting was on our Sunday night.   **20:7 break bread** Probably the Lord's Supper, the special meal that Jesus told his followers to eat to remember him (Luke 22:14–20).

next day came to a place near Kios. The following day we sailed to Samos, and the next day we reached Miletus. [16]Paul had already decided not to stop at Ephesus, because he did not want to stay too long in Asia. He was hurrying to be in Jerusalem on the day of Pentecost, if that were possible.

THE ELDERS FROM EPHESUS

[17]Now from Miletus Paul sent to Ephesus and called for the elders of the church. [18]When they came to him, he said, "You know about my life from the first day I came to Asia. You know the way I lived all the time I was with you. [19]The evil people made plans against me, which troubled me very much. But you know I always served the Lord unselfishly, and I often cried. [20]You know I preached to you and did not hold back anything that would help you. You know that I taught you in public and in your homes. [21]I warned both Jews and Greeks to change their lives and turn to God and believe in our Lord Jesus. [22]But now I must obey the Holy Spirit and go to Jerusalem. I don't know what will happen to me there. [23]I know only that in every city the Holy Spirit tells me that troubles and even jail wait for me. [24]I don't care about my own life. The most important thing is that I complete my mission, the work that the Lord Jesus gave me—to tell people the Good News about God's grace.

[25]"And now, I know that none of you among whom I was preaching the kingdom of God will ever see me again. [26]So today I tell you that if any of you should be lost, I am not responsible, [27]because I have told you everything God wants you to know. [28]Be careful for yourselves and for all the people the Holy Spirit has given to you to oversee. You must be like shepherds to the church of God,[n] which he bought with the death of his own son. [29]I know that after I leave, some people will come like wild wolves and try to destroy the flock. [30]Also, some from your own group will rise up and twist the truth and will lead away followers after them. [31]So be careful! Always remember that for three years, day and night, I never stopped warning each of you, and I often cried over you.

[32]"Now I am putting you in the care of God and the message about his grace. It is able to give you strength, and it will give you

the blessings God has for all his holy people. [33]When I was with you, I never wanted anyone's money or fine clothes. [34]You know I always worked to take care of my own needs and the needs of those who were with me. [35]I showed you in all things that you should work as I did and help the weak. I taught you to remember the words Jesus said: 'It is more blessed to give than to receive.'"

[36]When Paul had said this, he knelt down with all of them and prayed. [37-38]And they all cried because Paul had said they would never see him again. They put their arms around him and kissed him. Then they went with him to the ship.

PAUL GOES TO JERUSALEM

21 After we all said good-bye to them, we sailed straight to the island of Cos. The next day we reached Rhodes, and from there we went to Patara. [2]There we found a ship going to Phoenicia, so we went aboard and sailed away. [3]We sailed near the island of Cyprus, seeing it to the north, but we sailed on to Syria. We stopped at Tyre because the ship needed to unload its cargo there. [4]We found some followers in Tyre and stayed with them for seven days. Through the Holy Spirit they warned Paul not to go to Jerusalem. [5]When we finished our visit, we left and continued our trip. All the followers, even the women and children, came outside the city with us. After we all knelt on the beach and prayed, [6]we said good-bye and got on the ship, and the followers went back home.

[7]We continued our trip from Tyre and arrived at Ptolemais, where we greeted the believers and stayed with them for a day. [8]The next day we left Ptolemais and went to the city of Caesarea. There we went into the home of Philip the preacher, one of the seven helpers,[n] and stayed with him. [9]He had four unmarried daughters who had the gift of prophesying. [10]After we had been there for some time, a prophet named Agabus arrived from Judea. [11]He came to us and borrowed Paul's belt and used it to tie his own hands and feet. He said, "The Holy Spirit says, 'This is how evil people in Jerusalem will tie up

---

20:28 **of God** Some Greek copies read "of the Lord."
21:8 **helpers** The seven men chosen for a special work described in Acts 6:1–6. Sometimes they are called "deacons."

the man who wears this belt. Then they will give him to the older leaders.'"

[12]When we all heard this, we and the people there begged Paul not to go to Jerusalem. [13]But he said, "Why are you crying and making me so sad? I am not only ready to be tied up in Jerusalem, I am ready to die for the Lord Jesus!"

[14]We could not persuade him to stay away from Jerusalem. So we stopped begging him and said, "We pray that what the Lord wants will be done."

[15]After this, we got ready and started on our way to Jerusalem. [16]Some of the followers from Caesarea went with us and took us to the home of Mnason, where we would stay. He was from Cyprus and was one of the first followers.

PAUL VISITS JAMES

[17]In Jerusalem the believers were glad to see us. [18]The next day Paul went with us to visit James, and all the elders were there. [19]Paul greeted them and told them everything God had done among the other nations through him. [20]When they heard this, they praised God. Then they said to Paul, "Brother, you can see that many thousands of our people have become believers. And they think it is very important to obey the law of Moses. [21]They have heard about your teaching, that you tell our people who live among the nations to leave the law of Moses. They have heard that you tell them not to circumcise their children and not to obey customs. [22]What should we do? They will learn that you have come. [23]So we will tell you what to do: Four of our men have made a promise to God. [24]Take these men with you and share in their cleansing ceremony.[n] Pay their expenses so they can shave their heads.[n] Then it will prove to everyone that what they have heard about you is not true and that you follow the law of Moses in your own life. [25]We have already sent a letter to the non-Jewish believers. The letter said: 'Do not eat food that has been offered to idols, or blood, or animals that have been strangled. Do not take part in sexual sin.'"

[26]The next day Paul took the four men and shared in the cleansing ceremony with them. Then he went to the Temple and announced the time when the days of the cleansing ceremony would be finished. On the last day an offering would be given for each of the men.

[27]When the seven days were almost over, some of his people from Asia saw Paul at the Temple. They caused all the people to be upset and grabbed Paul. [28]They shouted, "People of Israel, help us! This is the man who goes everywhere teaching against the law of Moses, against our people, and against this Temple. Now he has brought some Greeks into the Temple and has made this holy place unclean!" [29](They said this because they had seen Trophimus, a man from Ephesus, with Paul in Jerusalem. They thought that Paul had brought him into the Temple.)

[30]All the people in Jerusalem became upset. Together they ran, took Paul, and dragged him out of the Temple. The Temple doors were closed immediately. [31]While they were trying to kill Paul, the commander of the Roman army in Jerusalem learned that there was trouble in the whole city. [32]Immediately he took some officers and soldiers and ran to the place where the crowd was gathered. When the people saw them, they stopped beating Paul. [33]The commander went to Paul and arrested him. He told his soldiers to tie Paul with two chains. Then he asked who he was and what he had done wrong. [34]Some in the crowd were yelling one thing, and some were yelling another. Because of all this confusion and shouting, the commander could not learn what had happened. So he ordered the soldiers to take Paul to the army building. [35]When Paul came to the steps, the soldiers had to carry him because the people were ready to hurt him. [36]The whole mob was following them, shouting, "Kill him!"

[37]As the soldiers were about to take Paul into the army building, he spoke to the commander, "May I say something to you?"

The commander said, "Do you speak Greek? [38]I thought you were the Egyptian who started some trouble against the government not long ago and led four thousand killers out to the desert."

[39]Paul said, "No, I am a Jew from Tarsus

21:24 cleansing ceremony The special things Jews did to end the Nazirite promise. **21:24 shave their heads** Jews did this to show that their promise was finished.

in the country of Cilicia. I am a citizen of that important city. Please, let me speak to the people."

⁴⁰The commander gave permission, so Paul stood on the steps and waved his hand to quiet the people. When there was silence, he spoke to them in the Hebrew language.

PAUL SPEAKS TO THE PEOPLE

22 Paul said, "Brothers and fathers, listen to my defense to you." ²When they heard him speaking the Hebrew language,[n] they became very quiet. Paul said, ³"I am a Jew, born in Tarsus in the country of Cilicia, but I grew up in this city. I was a student of Gamaliel,[n] who carefully taught me everything about the law of our ancestors. I was very serious about serving God, just as are all of you here today. ⁴I persecuted the people who followed the Way of Jesus, and some of them were even killed. I arrested men and women and put them in jail. ⁵The high priest and the whole council of elders can tell you this is true. They gave me letters to the brothers in Damascus. So I was going there to arrest these people and bring them back to Jerusalem to be punished.

⁶"About noon when I came near Damascus, a bright light from heaven suddenly flashed all around me. ⁷I fell to the ground and heard a voice saying, 'Saul, Saul, why are you persecuting me?' ⁸I asked, 'Who are you, Lord?' The voice said, 'I am Jesus from Nazareth whom you are persecuting.' ⁹Those who were with me did not understand the voice, but they saw the light. ¹⁰I said, 'What shall I do, Lord?' The Lord answered, 'Get up and go to Damascus. There you will be told about all the things I have planned for you to do.' ¹¹I could not see, because the bright light had made me blind. So my companions led me into Damascus.

¹²"There a man named Ananias came to me. He was a religious man; he obeyed the law of Moses, and all the Jews who lived there respected him. ¹³He stood by me and said, 'Brother Saul, see again!' Immediately I was able to see him. ¹⁴He said, 'The God of our ancestors chose you long ago to know his plan, to see the Righteous One, and to hear words from him. ¹⁵You will be his witness to all people, telling them about what you have seen and heard. ¹⁶Now, why wait any longer? Get up, be baptized, and wash your sins away, trusting in him to save you.'

¹⁷"Later, when I returned to Jerusalem, I was praying in the Temple, and I saw a vision. ¹⁸I saw the Lord saying to me, 'Hurry! Leave Jerusalem now! The people here will not accept the truth about me.' ¹⁹But I said, 'Lord, they know that in every synagogue I put the believers in jail and beat them. ²⁰They also know I was there when Stephen, your witness, was killed. I stood there agreeing and holding the coats of those who were killing him!' ²¹But the Lord said to me, 'Leave now. I will send you far away to the other nations.'"

²²The crowd listened to Paul until he said this. Then they began shouting, "Get rid of him! He doesn't deserve to live!" ²³They shouted, threw off their coats,[n] and threw dust into the air.[n]

²⁴Then the commander ordered the soldiers to take Paul into the army building and beat him. He wanted to make Paul tell why the people were shouting against him like this. ²⁵But as the soldiers were tying him up, preparing to beat him, Paul said to an officer nearby, "Do you have the right to beat a Roman citizen[n] who has not been proven guilty?"

²⁶When the officer heard this, he went to the commander and reported it. The officer said, "Do you know what you are doing? This man is a Roman citizen."

²⁷The commander came to Paul and said, "Tell me, are you really a Roman citizen?"

He answered, "Yes."

²⁸The commander said, "I paid a lot of money to become a Roman citizen."

But Paul said, "I was born a citizen."

²⁹The men who were preparing to question Paul moved away from him immediately. The commander was frightened because he had already tied Paul, and Paul was a Roman citizen.

22:2 **Hebrew language** Or Aramaic, the languages of many people in this region in the first century. 22:3 **Gamaliel** A very important teacher of the Pharisees, a Jewish religious group (Acts 5:34). 22:23 **threw off their coats** This showed that the people were very angry with Paul. 22:23 **threw dust into the air** This showed even greater anger. 22:25 **Roman citizen** Roman law said that Roman citizens must not be beaten before they had a trial.

PAUL SPEAKS TO LEADERS

30The next day the commander decided to learn why the Jews were accusing Paul. So he ordered the leading priests and the council to meet. The commander took Paul's chains off. Then he brought Paul out and stood him before their meeting.

23 Paul looked at the council and said, "Brothers, I have lived my life without guilt feelings before God up to this day." 2Ananias,[n] the high priest, heard this and told the men who were standing near Paul to hit him on the mouth. 3Paul said to Ananias, "God will hit you, too! You are like a wall that has been painted white. You sit there and judge me, using the law of Moses, but you are telling them to hit me, and that is against the law."

4The men standing near Paul said to him, "You cannot insult God's high priest like that!"

5Paul said, "Brothers, I did not know this man was the high priest. It is written in the Scriptures, 'You must not curse a leader of your people.'"[n]

6Some of the men in the meeting were Sadducees, and others were Pharisees. Knowing this, Paul shouted to them, "My brothers, I am a Pharisee, and my father was a Pharisee. I am on trial here because I believe that people will rise from the dead."

7When Paul said this, there was an argument between the Pharisees and the Sadducees, and the group was divided. 8(The Sadducees do not believe in angels or spirits or that people will rise from the dead. But the Pharisees believe in them all.) 9So there was a great uproar. Some of the teachers of the law, who were Pharisees, stood up and argued, "We find nothing wrong with this man. Maybe an angel or a spirit did speak to him."

10The argument was beginning to turn into such a fight that the commander was afraid some evil people would tear Paul to pieces. So he told the soldiers to go down and take Paul away and put him in the army building.

11The next night the Lord came and stood by Paul. He said, "Be brave! You have told people in Jerusalem about me. You must do the same in Rome."

12In the morning some evil people made a plan to kill Paul, and they took an oath not to eat or drink anything until they had killed

him. 13There were more than forty men who made this plan. 14They went to the leading priests and the elders and said, "We have taken an oath not to eat or drink until we have killed Paul. 15So this is what we want you to do: Send a message to the commander to bring Paul out to us as though you want to ask him more questions. We will be waiting to kill him while he is on the way here."

16But Paul's nephew heard about this plan and went to the army building and told Paul. 17Then Paul called one of the officers and said, "Take this young man to the commander. He has a message for him."

18So the officer brought Paul's nephew to the commander and said, "The prisoner, Paul, asked me to bring this young man to you. He wants to tell you something."

19The commander took the young man's hand and led him to a place where they could be alone. He asked, "What do you want to tell me?"

20The young man said, "The Jews have decided to ask you to bring Paul down to their council meeting tomorrow. They want you to think they are going to ask him more questions. 21But don't believe them! More than forty men are hiding and waiting to kill Paul. They have all taken an oath not to eat or drink until they have killed him. Now they are waiting for you to agree."

22The commander sent the young man away, ordering him, "Don't tell anyone that you have told me about their plan."

PAUL IS SENT TO CAESAREA

23Then the commander called two officers and said, "I need some men to go to Caesarea. Get two hundred soldiers, seventy horsemen, and two hundred men with spears ready to leave at nine o'clock tonight. 24Get some horses for Paul to ride so he can be taken to Governor Felix safely." 25And he wrote a letter that said:

26From Claudius Lysias.
To the Most Excellent Governor Felix: Greetings.
27Some of the Jews had taken this man and planned to kill him. But I learned that

---

23:2 **Ananias** This is not the same man named Ananias in Acts 22:12. **23:5 'You . . . people.'** Quotation from Exodus 22:28.

he is a Roman citizen, so I went with my soldiers and saved him. 28I wanted to know why they were accusing him, so I brought him before their council meeting. 29I learned that these people said Paul did some things that were wrong by their own laws, but no charge was worthy of jail or death. 30When I was told that some of them were planning to kill Paul, I sent him to you at once. I also told them to tell you what they have against him.

31So the soldiers did what they were told and took Paul and brought him to the city of Antipatris that night. 32The next day the horsemen went with Paul to Caesarea, but the other soldiers went back to the army building in Jerusalem. 33When the horsemen came to Caesarea and gave the letter to the governor, they turned Paul over to him. 34The governor read the letter and asked Paul, "What area are you from?" When he learned that Paul was from Cilicia, 35he said, "I will hear your case when those who are against you come here, too." Then the governor gave orders for Paul to be kept under guard in Herod's palace.

PAUL IS ACCUSED

24 Five days later Ananias, the high priest, went to the city of Caesarea with some of the elders and a lawyer named Tertullus. They had come to make charges against Paul before the governor. 2Paul was called into the meeting, and Tertullus began to accuse him, saying, "Most Excellent Felix! Our people enjoy much peace because of you, and many wrong things in our country are being made right through your wise help. 3We accept these things always and in every place, and we are thankful for them. 4But not wanting to take any more of your time, I beg you to be kind and listen to our few words. 5We have found this man to be a troublemaker, stirring up his people everywhere in the world. He is a leader of the Nazarene group. 6Also, he was trying to make the Temple unclean, but we stopped him. [And we wanted to judge him by our own law. 7 But the officer Lysias came and used much force to take him from us. 8And Lysias commanded those who wanted to accuse Paul to come to you.]n By asking him questions yourself, you can decide if all these things are true." 9The

others agreed and said that all of this was true.

10When the governor made a sign for Paul to speak, Paul said, "Governor Felix, I know you have been a judge over this nation for a long time. So I am happy to defend myself before you. 11You can learn for yourself that I went to worship in Jerusalem only twelve days ago. 12Those who are accusing me did not find me arguing with anyone in the Temple or stirring up the people in the synagogues or in the city. 13They cannot prove the things they are saying against me now. 14But I will tell you this: I worship the God of our ancestors as a follower of the Way of Jesus. The others say that the Way of Jesus is not the right way. But I believe everything that is taught in the law of Moses and that is written in the books of the Prophets. 15I have the same hope in God that they have—the hope that all people, good and bad, will surely be raised from the dead. 16This is why I always try to do what I believe is right before God and people.

17"After being away from Jerusalem for several years, I went back to bring money to my people and to offer sacrifices. 18I was doing this when they found me in the Temple. I had finished the cleansing ceremony and had not made any trouble; no people were gathering around me. 19But there were some people from Asia who should be here, standing before you. If I have really done anything wrong, they are the ones who should accuse me. 20Or ask these people here if they found any wrong in me when I stood before the council in Jerusalem. 21But I did shout one thing when I stood before them: 'You are judging me today because I believe that people will rise from the dead!'"

22Felix already understood much about the Way of Jesus. He stopped the trial and said, "When commander Lysias comes here, I will decide your case." 23Felix told the officer to keep Paul guarded but to give him some freedom and to let his friends bring what he needed.

PAUL SPEAKS TO FELIX AND HIS WIFE

24After some days Felix came with his wife, Drusilla, who was Jewish, and asked

---

24:6–8 And . . . you. Some Greek copies do not contain the bracketed text.

for Paul to be brought to him. He listened to Paul talk about believing in Christ Jesus. 25But Felix became afraid when Paul spoke about living right, self-control, and the time when God will judge the world. He said, "Go away now. When I have more time, I will call for you." 26At the same time Felix hoped that Paul would give him some money, so he often sent for Paul and talked with him.

27But after two years, Felix was replaced by Porcius Festus as governor. But Felix had left Paul in prison to please the Jews.

PAUL ASKS TO SEE CAESAR

25 Three days after Festus became governor, he went from Caesarea to Jerusalem. 2There the leading priests and the important leaders made charges against Paul before Festus. 3They asked Festus to do them a favor. They wanted him to send Paul back to Jerusalem, because they had a plan to kill him on the way. 4But Festus answered that Paul would be kept in Caesarea and that he himself was returning there soon. 5He said, "Some of your leaders should go with me. They can accuse the man there in Caesarea, if he has really done something wrong."

6Festus stayed in Jerusalem another eight or ten days and then went back to Caesarea. The next day he told the soldiers to bring Paul before him. Festus was seated on the judge's seat 7when Paul came into the room. The people who had come from Jerusalem stood around him, making serious charges against him, which they could not prove. 8This is what Paul said to defend himself: "I have done nothing wrong against the law, against the Temple, or against Caesar."

9But Festus wanted to please the people. So he asked Paul, "Do you want to go to Jerusalem for me to judge you there on these charges?"

10Paul said, "I am standing at Caesar's judgment seat now, where I should be judged. I have done nothing wrong to them; you know this is true. 11If I have done something wrong and the law says I must die, I do not ask to be saved from death. But if these charges are not true, then no one can give me to them. I want Caesar to hear my case!"

12Festus talked about this with his advisers. Then he said, "You have asked to see Caesar, so you will go to Caesar!"

PAUL BEFORE KING AGRIPPA

13A few days later King Agrippa and Bernice came to Caesarea to visit Festus. 14They stayed there for some time, and Festus told the king about Paul's case. Festus said, "There is a man that Felix left in prison. 15When I went to Jerusalem, the leading priests and the elders there made charges against him, asking me to sentence him to death. 16But I answered, 'When a man is accused of a crime, Romans do not hand him over until he has been allowed to face his accusers and defend himself against their charges.' 17So when these people came here to Caesarea for the trial, I did not waste time. The next day I sat on the judge's seat and commanded that the man be brought in. 18They stood up and accused him, but not of any serious crime as I thought they would. 19The things they said were about their own religion and about a man named Jesus who died. But Paul said that he is still alive. 20Not knowing how to find out about these questions, I asked Paul, 'Do you want to go to Jerusalem and be judged there?' 21But he asked to be kept in Caesarea. He wants a decision from the emperor.[n] So I ordered that he be held until I could send him to Caesar."

22Agrippa said to Festus, "I would also like to hear this man myself."

Festus said, "Tomorrow you will hear him."

23The next day Agrippa and Bernice appeared with great show, acting like very important people. They went into the judgment room with the army leaders and the important men of Caesarea. Then Festus ordered the soldiers to bring Paul in. 24Festus said, "King Agrippa and all who are gathered here with us, you see this man. All the people, here and in Jerusalem, have complained to me about him, shouting that he should not live any longer. 25When I judged him, I found no reason to order his death. But since he asked to be judged by Caesar, I decided to send him. 26But I have nothing definite to write the emperor about him. So I have brought him before all of you—especially you, King Agrippa. I hope you can question him and give me something to write. 27I think it is

---

25:21 emperor The ruler of the Roman Empire, which was almost all the known world.

foolish to send a prisoner to Caesar without telling what charges are against him."

PAUL DEFENDS HIMSELF

26 Agrippa said to Paul, "You may now speak to defend yourself."

Then Paul raised his hand and began to speak. [2]He said, "King Agrippa, I am very blessed to stand before you and will answer all the charges the evil people make against me. [3]You know so much about all the customs and the things they argue about, so please listen to me patiently.

[4]"All my people know about my whole life, how I lived from the beginning in my own country and later in Jerusalem. [5]They have known me for a long time. If they want to, they can tell you that I was a good Pharisee. And the Pharisees obey the laws of my tradition more carefully than any other group. [6]Now I am on trial because I hope for the promise that God made to our ancestors. [7]This is the promise that the twelve tribes of our people hope to receive as they serve God day and night. My king, they have accused me because I hope for this same promise! [8]Why do any of you people think it is impossible for God to raise people from the dead?

[9]"I, too, thought I ought to do many things against Jesus from Nazareth. [10]And that is what I did in Jerusalem. The leading priests gave me the power to put many of God's people in jail, and when they were being killed, I agreed it was a good thing. [11]In every synagogue, I often punished them and tried to make them speak against Jesus. I was so angry against them I even went to other cities to find them and punish them.

[12]"One time the leading priests gave me permission and the power to go to Damascus. [13]On the way there, at noon, I saw a light from heaven. It was brighter than the sun and flashed all around me and those who were traveling with me. [14]We all fell to the ground. Then I heard a voice speaking to me in the Hebrew language,[n] saying, 'Saul, Saul, why are you persecuting me? You are only hurting yourself by fighting me.' [15]I said, 'Who are you, Lord?' The Lord said, 'I am Jesus, the one you are persecuting. [16]Stand up! I have chosen you to be my servant and my witness—you will tell people the things that you have seen and the things that I will show

you. This is why I have come to you today. [17]I will keep you safe from your own people and also from the others. I am sending you to them [18]to open their eyes so that they may turn away from darkness to the light, away from the power of Satan and to God. Then their sins can be forgiven, and they can have a place with those people who have been made holy by believing in me.'

[19]"King Agrippa, after I had this vision from heaven, I obeyed it. [20]I began telling people that they should change their hearts and lives and turn to God and do things to show they really had changed. I told this first to those in Damascus, then in Jerusalem, and in every part of Judea, and also to the other people. [21]This is why the Jews took me and were trying to kill me in the Temple. [22]But God has helped me, and so I stand here today, telling all people, small and great, what I have seen. But I am saying only what Moses and the prophets said would happen— [23]that the Christ would die, and as the first to rise from the dead, he would bring light to all people."

PAUL TRIES TO PERSUADE AGRIPPA

[24]While Paul was saying these things to defend himself, Festus said loudly, "Paul, you are out of your mind! Too much study has driven you crazy!"

[25]Paul said, "Most excellent Festus, I am not crazy. My words are true and sensible. [26]King Agrippa knows about these things, and I can speak freely to him. I know he has heard about all of these things, because they did not happen off in a corner. [27]King Agrippa, do you believe what the prophets wrote? I know you believe."

[28]King Agrippa said to Paul, "Do you think you can persuade me to become a Christian in such a short time?"

[29]Paul said, "Whether it is a short or a long time, I pray to God that not only you but every person listening to me today would be saved and be like me—except for these chains I have."

[30]Then King Agrippa, Governor Festus, Bernice, and all the people sitting with them stood up [31]and left the room. Talking to each

---

26:14 Hebrew language Or Aramaic, the languages of many people in this region in the first century.

other, they said, "There is no reason why this man should die or be put in jail." [32]And Agrippa said to Festus, "We could let this man go free, but he has asked Caesar to hear his case."

PAUL SAILS FOR ROME

27 It was decided that we would sail for Italy. An officer named Julius, who served in the emperor's[n] army, guarded Paul and some other prisoners. [2]We got on a ship that was from the city of Adramyttium and was about to sail to different ports in Asia. Aristarchus, a man from the city of Thessalonica in Macedonia, went with us. [3]The next day we came to Sidon. Julius was very good to Paul and gave him freedom to go visit his friends, who took care of his needs. [4]We left Sidon and sailed close to the island of Cyprus, because the wind was blowing against us. [5]We went across the sea by Cilicia and Pamphylia and landed at the city of Myra, in Lycia. [6]There the officer found a ship from Alexandria that was going to Italy, so he put us on it.

[7]We sailed slowly for many days. We had a hard time reaching Cnidus because the wind was blowing against us, and we could not go any farther. So we sailed by the south side of the island of Crete near Salmone. [8]Sailing past it was hard. Then we came to a place called Fair Havens, near the city of Lasea.

[9]We had lost much time, and it was now dangerous to sail, because it was already after the Day of Cleansing.[n] So Paul warned them, [10]"Men, I can see there will be a lot of trouble on this trip. The ship, the cargo, and even our lives may be lost." [11]But the captain and the owner of the ship did not agree with Paul, and the officer believed what the captain and owner of the ship said. [12]Since that harbor was not a good place for the ship to stay for the winter, most of the men decided that the ship should leave. They hoped we could go to Phoenix and stay there for the winter. Phoenix, a city on the island of Crete, had a harbor which faced southwest and northwest.

THE STORM

[13]When a good wind began to blow from the south, the men on the ship thought, "This is the wind we wanted, and now we have it." So they pulled up the anchor, and we sailed very close to the island of Crete. [14]But then a very strong wind named the "northeaster" came from the island. [15]The ship was caught in it and could not sail against it. So we stopped trying and let the wind carry us. [16]When we went below a small island named Cauda, we were barely able to bring in the lifeboat. [17]After the men took the lifeboat in, they tied ropes around the ship to hold it together. The men were afraid that the ship would hit the sandbanks of Syrtis,[n] so they lowered the sail and let the wind carry the ship. [18]The next day the storm was blowing us so hard that the men threw out some of the cargo. [19]A day later with their own hands they threw out the ship's equipment. [20]When we could not see the sun or the stars for many days, and the storm was very bad, we lost all hope of being saved.

[21]After the men had gone without food for a long time, Paul stood up before them and said, "Men, you should have listened to me. You should not have sailed from Crete. Then you would not have all this trouble and loss. [22]But now I tell you to cheer up because none of you will die. Only the ship will be lost. [23]Last night an angel came to me from the God I belong to and worship. [24]The angel said, 'Paul, do not be afraid. You must stand before Caesar. And God has promised you that he will save the lives of everyone sailing with you.' [25]So men, have courage. I trust in God that everything will happen as his angel told me. [26]But we will crash on an island."

[27]On the fourteenth night we were still being carried around in the Adriatic Sea.[n] About midnight the sailors thought we were close to land, [28]so they lowered a rope with a weight on the end of it into the water. They found that the water was one hundred twenty feet deep. They went a little farther and lowered the rope again. It was ninety feet deep. [29]The sailors were afraid that we would hit the rocks, so they threw four anchors into the water and prayed for daylight to come. [30]Some of the sailors wanted to leave the ship, and they lowered the lifeboat, pretending they were throwing more anchors

---

27:1 **emperor** The ruler of the Roman Empire, which was almost all the known world. 27:9 **Day of Cleansing** An important Jewish holy day in the fall of the year. This was the time of year that bad storms arose on the sea. 27:17 **Syrtis** Shallow area in the sea near the Libyan coast. 27:27 **Adriatic Sea** The sea between Greece and Italy, including the central Mediterranean.

from the front of the ship. [31]But Paul told the officer and the other soldiers, "If these men do not stay in the ship, your lives cannot be saved." [32]So the soldiers cut the ropes and let the lifeboat fall into the water.

[33]Just before dawn Paul began persuading all the people to eat something. He said, "For the past fourteen days you have been waiting and watching and not eating. [34]Now I beg you to eat something. You need it to stay alive. None of you will lose even one hair off your heads." [35]After he said this, Paul took some bread and thanked God for it before all of them. He broke off a piece and began eating. [36]They all felt better and started eating, too. [37]There were two hundred seventy-six people on the ship. [38]When they had eaten all they wanted, they began making the ship lighter by throwing the grain into the sea.

THE SHIP IS DESTROYED

[39]When daylight came, the sailors saw land. They did not know what land it was, but they saw a bay with a beach and wanted to sail the ship to the beach if they could. [40]So they cut the ropes to the anchors and left the anchors in the sea. At the same time, they untied the ropes that were holding the rudders. Then they raised the front sail into the wind and sailed toward the beach. [41]But the ship hit a sandbank. The front of the ship stuck there and could not move, but the back of the ship began to break up from the big waves.

[42]The soldiers decided to kill the prisoners so none of them could swim away and escape. [43]But Julius, the officer, wanted to let Paul live and did not allow the soldiers to kill the prisoners. Instead he ordered everyone who could swim to jump into the water first and swim to land. [44]The rest were to follow using wooden boards or pieces of the ship. And this is how all the people made it safely to land.

PAUL ON THE ISLAND OF MALTA

28 When we were safe on land, we learned that the island was called Malta. [2]The people who lived there were very good to us. Because it was raining and very cold, they made a fire and welcomed all of us. [3]Paul gathered a pile of sticks and was putting them on the fire when a poisonous snake came out because of the heat and bit him on the hand. [4]The people living on the island saw the snake hanging from Paul's hand and said to each other, "This man must be a murderer! He did not die in the sea, but Justice[n] does not want him to live." [5]But Paul shook the snake off into the fire and was not hurt. [6]The people thought that Paul would swell up or fall down dead. They waited and watched him for a long time, but nothing bad happened to him. So they changed their minds and said, "He is a god!"

[7]There were some fields around there owned by Publius, an important man on the island. He welcomed us into his home and was very good to us for three days. [8]Publius' father was sick with a fever and dysentery.[n] Paul went to him, prayed, and put his hands on the man and healed him. [9]After this, all the other sick people on the island came to Paul, and he healed them, too. [10-11]The people on the island gave us many honors. When we were ready to leave, three months later, they gave us the things we needed.

PAUL GOES TO ROME

We got on a ship from Alexandria that had stayed on the island during the winter. On the front of the ship was the sign of the twin gods.[n] [12]We stopped at Syracuse for three days. [13]From there we sailed to Rhegium. The next day a wind began to blow from the south, and a day later we came to Puteoli. [14]We found some believers there who asked us to stay with them for a week. Finally, we came to Rome. [15]The believers in Rome heard that we were there and came out as far as the Market of Appius[n] and the Three Inns[n] to meet us. When Paul saw them, he was encouraged and thanked God.

PAUL IN ROME

[16]When we arrived at Rome, Paul was allowed to live alone, with the soldier who guarded him.

[17]Three days later Paul sent for the leaders there. When they came together, he said, "Brothers, I have done nothing against our people or the customs of our ancestors. But

---

28:4 Justice The people thought there was a god named Justice who would punish bad people. **28:8 dysentery** A sickness like diarrhea. **28:10–11 twin gods** Statues of Castor and Pollux, gods in old Greek tales. **28:15 Market of Appius** A town about twenty-seven miles from Rome. **28:15 Three Inns** A town about thirty miles from Rome.

I was arrested in Jerusalem and given to the Romans. ¹⁸After they asked me many questions, they could find no reason why I should be killed. They wanted to let me go free, ¹⁹but the evil people there argued against that. So I had to ask to come to Rome to have my trial before Caesar. But I have no charge to bring against my own people. ²⁰That is why I wanted to see you and talk with you. I am bound with this chain because I believe in the hope of Israel."

²¹They answered Paul, "We have received no letters from Judea about you. None of our Jewish brothers who have come from there brought news or told us anything bad about you. ²²But we want to hear your ideas, because we know that people everywhere are speaking against this religious group."

²³Paul and the people chose a day for a meeting and on that day many more of the Jews met with Paul at the place he was staying. He spoke to them all day long. Using the law of Moses and the prophets' writings, he explained the kingdom of God, and he tried

FAMILY

LOVE IS MORE THAN GIVING

Jesus won back our **dominion**

ACTS 28:8-9

By Larry Huch

God placed all authority in the hands of human beings (Genesis 1:26-28), but they disobeyed God. As a result, human authority was lost and Satan became the god of the world until about two thousand years ago, when Jesus was crucified and crushed Satan. The blood shed from the crucifixion of Jesus paid for the return of humanity's authority.

Many people still try to run and hide from the devil, but they cannot run fast enough. Some just hold their ground and keep quiet, but the devil will not ignore them. As a child of God, you need not be timid, on the defensive, or stuck in neutral. Overcome the enemy who wants to destroy you. Take the offensive to thwart Satan's tactics. Jesus' blood gives you the authority to defeat the devil.

Lay hands on your family, business, and home and pray the blood of Jesus over them to break curses off them. Speak the Word over your children. The blood of Jesus breaks the chains of sin and bondage the moment you take authority over the enemy and releases the Holy Spirit to bring God's promises to pass in your life. Why? It is not simply a ritual, but a right, because authority has been returned. Whatever evil you encounter, you have the authority in Jesus' name to render it harmless.

The Word of God says you have been bought by the blood of Jesus. Authority is yours. Dominion is yours. Take your hands and lay them on all that is yours and claim the promises of God with authority, by the blood, and in the name of Jesus Christ. (From *Free at Last*)

reflect: What are some things you can do to exercise your authority today?
Go to **Matthew 23:37.**

to persuade them to believe these things about Jesus. [24]Some believed what Paul said, but others did not. [25]So they argued and began leaving after Paul said one more thing to them: "The Holy Spirit spoke the truth to your ancestors through Isaiah the prophet, saying,

[26] 'Go to this people and say:
You will listen and listen, but you will not understand.
You will look and look, but you will not learn,
[27] because these people have become stubborn.
They don't hear with their ears,
and they have closed their eyes.
Otherwise, they might really understand what they see with their eyes

and hear with their ears.
They might really understand in their minds
and come back to me and be healed.'
Isaiah 6:9–10

[28]"I want you to know that God has also sent his salvation to all nations, and they will listen!" [[29]After Paul said this, the Jews left. They were arguing very much with each other.][n]

[30]Paul stayed two full years in his own rented house and welcomed all people who came to visit him. [31]He boldly preached about the kingdom of God and taught about the Lord Jesus Christ, and no one stopped him.

28:29 After . . . other. Some Greek copies do not contain the bracketed text.

1 From Paul, a servant of Christ Jesus. God called me to be an apostle and chose me to tell the Good News.

²God promised this Good News long ago through his prophets, as it is written in the Holy Scriptures. ³⁻⁴The Good News is about God's Son, Jesus Christ our Lord. As a man, he was born from the family of David. But through the Spirit of holiness he was declared to be God's Son with great power by rising from the dead. ⁵Through Christ, God gave me the special work of an apostle, which was to lead people of all nations to believe and obey. I do this work for him. ⁶And you who are in Rome are also called to belong to Jesus Christ.

⁷To all of you in Rome whom God loves and has called to be his holy people:

Grace and peace to you from God our Father and the Lord Jesus Christ.

A PRAYER OF THANKS

⁸First I want to say that I thank my God through Jesus Christ for all of you, because people everywhere in the world are talking about your faith. ⁹God, whom I serve with my whole heart by telling the Good News about his Son, knows that I always mention you ¹⁰every time I pray. I pray that I will be allowed to come to you, and this will happen if God wants it. ¹¹I want very much to see you, to give you some spiritual gift to make you strong. ¹²I mean that I want us to help each other with the faith we have. Your faith will help me, and my faith will help you. ¹³Brothers and sisters, I want you to know that I planned many times to come to you, but this has not been possible. I wanted to come so that I could help you grow spiritually as I have helped the other non-Jewish people.

¹⁴I have a duty to all people—Greeks and those who are not Greeks, the wise and the foolish. ¹⁵That is why I want so much to preach the Good News to you in Rome.

¹⁶I am not ashamed of the Good News, because it is the power God uses to save everyone who believes—to save the Jews first, and then to save non-Jews. ¹⁷The Good News shows how God makes people right with himself—that it begins and ends with faith. As the Scripture says, "But those who are right with God will live by faith."[n]

ALL PEOPLE HAVE DONE WRONG

¹⁸God's anger is shown from heaven against all the evil and wrong things people do. By their own evil lives they hide the truth. ¹⁹God shows his anger because some knowledge of him has been made clear to them. Yes, God has shown himself to them. ²⁰There are things about him that people cannot see—his eternal power and all the things that make him God. But since the beginning of the world those things have been easy to understand by what God has made. So people have no excuse for the bad things they do. ²¹They knew God, but they did not give glory to God or thank him. Their thinking became useless. Their foolish minds were filled with darkness. ²²They said they were wise, but they became fools. ²³They traded the glory of God who lives forever for the worship of idols made to look like earthly people, birds, animals, and snakes.

²⁴Because they did these things, God left them and let them go their sinful way, wanting only to do evil. As a result, they became full of sexual sin, using their bodies wrongly with each other. ²⁵They traded the truth of God for a lie. They worshiped and served what had been created instead of the God who created those things, who should be praised forever. Amen.

²⁶Because people did those things, God left them and let them do the shameful things they wanted to do. Women stopped having natural sex and started having sex with other women. ²⁷In the same way, men stopped having natural sex and began wanting each

---

1:17 "But those . . . faith." Quotation from Habakkuk 2:4.

other. Men did shameful things with other men, and in their bodies they received the punishment for those wrongs.

²⁸People did not think it was important to have a true knowledge of God. So God left them and allowed them to have their own worthless thinking and to do things they should not do. ²⁹They are filled with every kind of sin, evil, selfishness, and hatred. They are full of jealousy, murder, fighting, lying, and thinking the worst about each other. They gossip ³⁰and say evil things about each other. They hate God. They are rude and conceited and brag about themselves. They invent ways of doing evil. They do not obey their parents. ³¹They are foolish, they do not keep their promises, and they show no kindness or mercy to others. ³²They know God's law says that those who live like this should die. But they themselves not only continue to do these evil things, they applaud others who do them.

YOU PEOPLE ALSO ARE SINFUL

2 If you think you can judge others, you are wrong. When you judge them, you are really judging yourself guilty, because you do the same things they do. ²God judges those who do wrong things, and we know that his judging is right. ³You judge those who do wrong, but you do wrong yourselves.

WHO ARE YOU?

I **believe** in the **resurrection**

FUTURE

By Jack Hayford   ROMANS 1:3–4

I believe in the resurrection of Jesus Christ, the Son of God; that he physically and actually died and rose from the dead. I believe that his resurrection conquered death and hell, and all who believe this in their heart are saved. Because I believe this, I confess with my mouth the Lord Jesus and worship the Son of God, risen from the grave and ascended upon high in triumph above all the powers of darkness.

I believe in the resurrection of all humanity and on the last day, I will stand before the throne of God and give an account for my deeds done on earth. Because of Jesus' death and resurrection, I look forward to that day with joy and without fear of death. I know I will receive everlasting delight instead of everlasting shame. I believe that at Christ's return, I will be changed into the image of his glorious and perfect resurrected body, and I will receive a perfect and undying body that will never decay so that I can be with and serve the living God forever (Psalm 16:8–11).

Because I believe this, I walk in faith and clear-headedness, knowing that my motives as well as my deeds, and my thoughts as well as my words, represent the eternal values that I either serve or shirk and according to which I will be judged before the loving and righteous Father. With such expectations, I praise my resurrected Savior who gives me a never-ending hope and fills me with power to live daily in his victory.

reflect: What does it mean to you for Jesus to be your best friend?
Go to **Romans 3:21–26.**

Understanding
Authority

ROMANS 1:28-32

Parents everywhere rejoice! In his letter to the Romans—right in the middle of a long list of bad people and evil deeds—the apostle Paul includes that "they do not obey their parents." Along with murderers, haters of God, and people who gossip and slander, we have people who won't do what mom and dad tell them to do. In the apostle's mind, disobedient children were right up there with the worst of the worst. They were counted among those who "did not think it was important to have a true knowledge of God" (Romans 1:28-32).

Respecting our elders is a huge deal to God and says something about God's larger plan for the way authority should work in our lives.

God has set up several levels of authority to protect, guide, correct, and instruct us throughout our lives. National and local governments, places of work, schools, and churches all play some authoritative role in our lives, and the sooner we learn to respect these authorities and respond correctly to them, the sooner we will live steady, peaceful lives. We all know people who never figure out how to respond properly to a speeding ticket or to a word of correction from their boss. They never learn what authority is for, and because of that, their lives are always off the mark.

But learning to respect authority doesn't come natural. It must be purposely instilled into us, and that work begins at home. Family life is the best training ground for learning to respond to the people God places over us. Through our parents, we learn how to take instruction, how to follow orders, and how to deal with punishment. We also learn how to be generous with the faults of our leaders—kids become very familiar with their parents' strengths and weaknesses.

But this isn't just kids' stuff. God wants all of us to respect our parents—to listen to them, speak well of them, honor their names, and never do anything to bring them shame or grief.

Need more evidence that this issue matters to God? Check out the Ten Commandments. "Honor your father and your mother" is right in there. From very, very early in human history, God began speaking to us about the importance of respecting our parents. It's one of the top ten things we're supposed to do. It's as important as being faithful to our spouses, worshiping the one true God, telling the truth, and, yes, not taking someone else's life. It's a big, big deal.

So, in this letter to the Romans, the apostle Paul is no doubt taking a cue directly from the Jewish law he knew so well. He's warning all of us to understand our relationship to authority and saying that, if we don't, we're keeping some pretty questionable company.

TO LEARN MORE ON WHAT THE BIBLE HAS TO SAY ABOUT **FAMILY,** READ THE SCRIPTURES AND DEVOTIONALS AT **PROVERBS 27:17, ECCLESIASTES 4:12, JEREMIAH 3:19, JEREMIAH 31:33, MATTHEW 12:34-37, REVELATION 21:7,** AND **MATTHEW 19:4-6.**

Do you think you will be able to escape the judgment of God? [4]He has been very kind and patient, waiting for you to change, but you think nothing of his kindness. Perhaps you do not understand that God is kind to you so you will change your hearts and lives. [5]But you are stubborn and refuse to change, so you are making your own punishment even greater on the day he shows his anger. On that day everyone will see God's right judgments. [6]God will reward or punish every person for what that person has done. [7]Some people, by always continuing to do good, live for God's glory, for honor, and for life that has no end. God will give them life forever. [8]But other people are selfish. They refuse to follow truth and, instead, follow evil. God will give them his punishment and anger. [9]He will give trouble and suffering to everyone who does evil—to the Jews first and also to those who are not Jews. [10]But he will give glory, honor, and peace to everyone who does good—to the Jews first and also to those who are not Jews. [11]For God judges all people in the same way.

[12]People who do not have the law and who are sinners will be lost, although they do not have the law. And, in the same way, those who have the law and are sinners will be judged by the law. [13]Hearing the law does not make people right with God. It is those who obey the law who will be right with him. [14](Those who are not Jews do not have the law, but when they freely do what the law commands, they are the law for themselves. This is true even though they do not have the law. [15]They show that in their hearts they know what is right and wrong, just as the law commands. And they show this by their consciences. Sometimes their thoughts tell them they did wrong, and sometimes their thoughts tell them they did right.) [16]All these things will happen on the day when God, through Christ Jesus, will judge people's secret thoughts. The Good News that I preach says this.

THE JEWS AND THE LAW

[17]What about you? You call yourself a Jew. You trust in the law of Moses and brag that you are close to God. [18]You know what he wants you to do and what is important, because you have learned the law. [19]You think you are a guide for the blind and a light for those who are in darkness. [20]You think you can show foolish people what is right and teach those who know nothing. You have the law; so you think you know everything and have all truth. [21]You teach others, so why don't you teach yourself? You tell others not to steal, but you steal. [22]You say that others must not take part in adultery, but you are guilty of that sin. You hate idols, but you steal from temples. [23]You brag about having God's law, but you bring shame to God by breaking his law, [24]just as the Scriptures say: "Those who are not Jews speak against God's name because of you."[n]

[25]If you follow the law, your circumcision has meaning. But if you break the law, it is as if you were never circumcised. [26]People who are not Jews are not circumcised, but if they do what the law says, it is as if they were circumcised. [27]You Jews have the written law and circumcision, but you break the law. So those who are not circumcised in their bodies, but still obey the law, will show that you are guilty. [28]They can do this because a person is not a true Jew if he is only a Jew in his physical body; true circumcision is not only on the outside of the body. [29]A person is a Jew only if he is a Jew inside; true circumcision is done in the heart by the Spirit, not by the written law. Such a person gets praise from God rather than from people.

3 So, do Jews have anything that other people do not have? Is there anything special about being circumcised? [2]Yes, of course, there is in every way. The most important thing is this: God trusted the Jews with his teachings. [3]If some Jews were not faithful to him, will that stop God from doing what he promised? [4]No! God will continue to be true even when every person is false. As the Scriptures say:

"So you will be shown to be right when
    you speak,
    and you will win your case." *Psalm 51:4*

[5]When we do wrong, that shows more clearly that God is right. So can we say that God is wrong to punish us? (I am talking as people might talk.) [6]No! If God could not punish us, he could not judge the world.

2:24 **"Those . . . you."** Quotation from Isaiah 52:5; Ezekiel 36:20.

[7]A person might say, "When I lie, it really gives him glory, because my lie shows God's truth. So why am I judged a sinner?" [8]It would be the same to say, "We should do evil so that good will come." Some people find fault with us and say we teach this, but they are wrong and deserve the punishment they will receive.

ALL PEOPLE ARE GUILTY

[9]So are we Jews better than others? No! We have already said that Jews and those who are not Jews are all guilty of sin. [10]As the Scriptures say:

"There is no one who always does what
is right,
not even one.
[11] There is no one who understands.
There is no one who looks to God for
help.
[12] All have turned away.
Together, everyone has become useless.
There is no one who does anything good;
there is not even one."   *Psalm 14:1–3*
[13] "Their throats are like open graves;
they use their tongues for telling lies."
Psalm 5:9
"Their words are like snake poison."
Psalm 140:3
[14]   "Their mouths are full of cursing and
hate."   *Psalm 10:7*
[15] "They are always ready to kill people.
[16]   Everywhere they go they cause ruin
and misery.
[17] They don't know how to live in peace."
Isaiah 59:7–8
[18]   "They have no fear of God." *Psalm 36:1*

[19]We know that the law's commands are for those who have the law. This stops all excuses and brings the whole world under God's judgment, [20]because no one can be made right with God by following the law. The law only shows us our sin.

HOW GOD MAKES PEOPLE RIGHT

[21]But God has a way to make people right with him without the law, and he has now shown us that way which the law and the prophets told us about. [22]God makes people right with himself through their faith in Jesus Christ. This is true for all who believe in Christ, because all people are the same: [23]Everyone has sinned and fallen short of God's glorious standard, [24]and all need to be made right with God by his grace, which is a free gift. They need to be made free from sin through Jesus Christ. [25]God sent him to die in our place to take away our sins. We receive forgiveness through faith in the blood of Jesus' death. This showed that God always does what is right and fair, as in the past when he was patient and did not punish people for their sins. [26]And God gave Jesus to show today that he does what is right. God did this so he could judge rightly and so he could make right any person who has faith in Jesus.

[27]So do we have a reason to brag about ourselves? No! And why not? It is the way of faith that stops all bragging, not the way of trying to obey the law. [28]A person is made right with God through faith, not through obeying the law. [29]Is God only the God of the Jews? Is he not also the God of those who are not Jews? [30]Of course he is, because there is only one God. He will make Jews right with him by their faith, and he will also make those who are not Jews right with him through their faith. [31]So do we destroy the law by following the way of faith? No! Faith causes us to be what the law truly wants.

THE EXAMPLE OF ABRAHAM

4 So what can we say that Abraham,[n] the father of our people, learned about faith? [2]If Abraham was made right by the things he did, he had a reason to brag. But this is not God's view, [3]because the Scripture says, "Abraham believed God, and God accepted Abraham's faith, and that faith made him right with God."[n]

[4]When people work, their pay is not given as a gift, but as something earned. [5]But people cannot do any work that will make them right with God. So they must trust in him, who makes even evil people right in his sight. Then God accepts their faith, and that makes them right with him. [6]David said the same thing. He said that people are truly blessed when God, without paying attention to their deeds, makes people right with himself.
[7] "Blessed are they
whose sins are forgiven,
whose wrongs are pardoned.

4:1 Abraham Most respected ancestor of the Jews. Every Jew hoped to see Abraham. **4:3 "Abraham . . . God."** Quotation from Genesis 15:6.

8 Blessed is the person
    whom the Lord does not consider
    guilty." *Psalm 32:1–2*
9Is this blessing only for those who are circumcised or also for those who are not circumcised? We have already said that God accepted Abraham's faith and that faith made him right with God. 10So how did this happen? Did God accept Abraham before or after he was circumcised? It was before his circumcision. 11Abraham was circumcised to show that he was right with God through faith before he was circumcised. So Abraham is the father of all those who believe but are not circumcised; he is the father of all believers who are accepted as being right with God.

12And Abraham is also the father of those who have been circumcised and who live following the faith that our father Abraham had before he was circumcised.

GOD KEEPS HIS PROMISE

13Abraham[n] and his descendants received the promise that they would get the whole world. He did not receive that promise through the law, but through being right with God by his faith. 14If people could receive what God promised by following the law, then faith is worthless. And God's promise to Abraham is worthless, 15because the law can

---

4:13 Abraham Most respected ancestor of the Jews. Every Jew hoped to see Abraham.

WHO ARE YOU?

I **believe** in Jesus Christ

FUTURE

By Jack Hayford

ROMANS 3:21–26

I believe Jesus Christ is the Son of God; the gift of the Father for the salvation of this world; and the Word of God who was with the Father in the beginning. Because I believe this, I worship him as Alpha and Omega—the beginning and the end—the one who is and was and is coming. I receive and acknowledge him as the savior of all people, and that includes me. I honor him as Lord and praise his name.

I believe Jesus Christ became a man and his mother Mary was a virgin. I believe he took the full weight and consequence of all my sins when he was crucified, and his blood justifies me before God. I am forgiven and cleansed in heart and conscience. I acknowledge that Jesus Christ paid for my sins, and I accept the freedom from all guilt or condemnation. Because of Jesus, the Father sees me as if I have never sinned.

I believe Jesus Christ is the living Lord and risen from the dead. He is victorious over hell's every power. He ascended to the Father's right hand, where he rules in might and ceaselessly intercedes for his people. Because I believe this, I walk free of fear and as one delivered from darkness. I am secure in his power, authority, and constant watch over me. With Jesus as my king and my friend, I can live in peace because he is completing the good work he started in me and continues until the day of his return.

reflect: What can you do to strengthen your confidence in the finished work of God?
Go to **Job 13:15.**

only bring God's anger. But if there is no law, there is nothing to disobey.

[16]So people receive God's promise by having faith. This happens so the promise can be a free gift. Then all of Abraham's children can have that promise. It is not only for those who live under the law of Moses but for anyone who lives with faith like that of Abraham, who is the father of us all. [17]As it is written in the Scriptures: "I am making you a father of many nations."[n] This is true before God, the God Abraham believed, the God who gives life to the dead and who creates something out of nothing.

[18]There was no hope that Abraham would have children. But Abraham believed God and continued hoping, and so he became the father of many nations. As God told him, "Your descendants also will be too many to count."[n] [19]Abraham was almost a hundred years old, much past the age for having children, and Sarah could not have children. Abraham thought about all this, but his faith in God did not become weak. [20]He never doubted that God would keep his promise, and he never stopped believing. He grew stronger in his faith and gave praise to God. [21]Abraham felt sure that God was able to do what he had promised. [22]So, "God accepted Abraham's faith, and that faith made him right with God."[n] [23]Those words ("God accepted Abraham's faith") were written not only for Abraham [24]but also for us. God will accept us also because we believe in the One who raised Jesus our Lord from the dead. [25]Jesus was given to die for our sins, and he was raised from the dead to make us right with God.

RIGHT WITH GOD

5 Since we have been made right with God by our faith, we have[n] peace with God. This happened through our Lord Jesus Christ, [2]who through our faith[n] has brought us into that blessing of God's grace that we now enjoy. And we are happy because of the hope we have of sharing God's glory. [3]We also have joy with our troubles, because we know that these troubles produce patience. [4]And patience produces character, and character produces hope. [5]And this hope will never disappoint us, because God has poured out his love to fill our hearts. He gave us his love through the Holy Spirit, whom God has given to us.

[6]When we were unable to help ourselves, at the right time, Christ died for us, although we were living against God. [7]Very few people will die to save the life of someone else. Although perhaps for a good person someone might possibly die. [8]But God shows his great love for us in this way: Christ died for us while we were still sinners.

[9]So through Christ we will surely be saved from God's anger, because we have been made right with God by the blood of Christ's death. [10]While we were God's enemies, he made us his friends through the death of his Son. Surely, now that we are his friends, he will save us through his Son's life. [11]And not only that, but now we are also very happy in God through our Lord Jesus Christ. Through him we are now God's friends again.

ADAM AND CHRIST COMPARED

[12]Sin came into the world because of what one man did, and with sin came death. This is why everyone must die—because everyone sinned. [13]Sin was in the world before the law of Moses, but sin is not counted against us as breaking a command when there is no law. [14]But from the time of Adam to the time of Moses, everyone had to die, even those who had not sinned by breaking a command, as Adam had.

Adam was like the One who was coming in the future. [15]But God's free gift is not like Adam's sin. Many people died because of the sin of that one man. But the grace from God was much greater; many people received God's gift of life by the grace of the one man, Jesus Christ. [16]After Adam sinned once, he was judged guilty. But the gift of God is different. God's free gift came after many sins, and it makes people right with God. [17]One man sinned, and so death ruled all people because of that one man. But now those people who accept God's full grace and the great gift of being made right with him will surely have true life and rule through the one man, Jesus Christ.

4:17 "I . . . nations." Quotation from Genesis 17:5.
4:18 "Your . . . count." Quotation from Genesis 15:5.
4:22 "God . . . God." Quotation from Genesis 15:6.
5:1 **we have** Some Greek copies read "let us have."
5:2 **through our faith** Some Greek copies do not have this phrase.

¹⁸So as one sin of Adam brought the punishment of death to all people, one good act that Christ did makes all people right with God. And that brings true life for all. ¹⁹One man disobeyed God, and many became sinners. In the same way, one man obeyed God, and many will be made right. ²⁰The law came to make sin worse. But when sin grew worse, God's grace increased. ²¹Sin once used death to rule us, but God gave people more of his grace so that grace could rule by making people right with him. And this brings life forever through Jesus Christ our Lord.

DEAD TO SIN BUT ALIVE IN CHRIST

6 So do you think we should continue sinning so that God will give us even more grace? ²No! We died to our old sinful lives, so how can we continue living with sin? ³Did you forget that all of us became part of Christ when we were baptized? We shared his death in our baptism. ⁴When we were baptized, we were buried with Christ and shared his death. So, just as Christ was raised from the dead by the wonderful power of the Father, we also can live a new life.

⁵Christ died, and we have been joined with him by dying too. So we will also be joined with him by rising from the dead as he did. ⁶We know that our old life died with Christ on the cross so that our sinful selves would have no power over us and we would not be slaves to sin. ⁷Anyone who has died is made free from sin's control.

⁸If we died with Christ, we know we will also live with him. ⁹Christ was raised from the dead, and we know that he cannot die again. Death has no power over him now.

A PARTNERSHIP WITH GOD

we are **unable**

FAITH

ROMANS 5:6

In the New Testament, the word "unable" is most often translated by our English word "weak." There are four different senses of weakness in the New Testament. This word describes physical weakness of the whole person. It describes sickness. It describes an inner poverty or incapacity. Finally, it is used of economic poverty.

In this verse, Paul is speaking of our spiritual incapacity to do anything about our condition of separation from God and from our true selves. The amazing proclamation of the Bible is that God rescued us precisely because we had absolutely no ability to save ourselves. Anyone who has honestly faced the reality of an addiction knows exactly this feeling of complete powerlessness.

Admitting that we are weak beyond hope in ourselves is the first step of recovery. It is important to recognize that many of us have experienced all four meanings of this word. Our lifestyles left us physically destroyed, spiritually bankrupt, sick, and poor. Yet Christ died to redeem us from each of those conditions. Helplessness was our pathway to grace. How can we ever thank him enough? He has given us back our lives!

reflect: Thank God for rescuing you from yourself and your wayward lifestyle.
Go to **Romans 10:9.**

¹⁰Yes, when Christ died, he died to defeat the power of sin one time—enough for all time. He now has a new life, and his new life is with God. ¹¹In the same way, you should see yourselves as being dead to the power of sin and alive with God through Christ Jesus.

¹²So, do not let sin control your life here on earth so that you do what your sinful self wants to do. ¹³Do not offer the parts of your body to serve sin, as things to be used in doing evil. Instead, offer yourselves to God as people who have died and now live. Offer the parts of your body to God to be used in doing good. ¹⁴Sin will not be your master, because you are not under law but under God's grace.

BE SLAVES OF RIGHTEOUSNESS

¹⁵So what should we do? Should we sin because we are under grace and not under law? No! ¹⁶Surely you know that when you give yourselves like slaves to obey someone, then you are really slaves of that person. The person you obey is your master. You can follow sin, which brings spiritual death, or

---

PEACE BY GOD

FULFILLMENT

no **truce**

ROMANS 6:12–14   By Edwin Louis Cole

A **truce is no substitute for victory.** Jesus did not declare a truce when Satan offered him a compromise on the Mount of Temptation (Matthew 4:1-11). Instead, he gave his life to win victory over the Enemy and to claim his birthright as the Prince of Peace.

Jesus is a gentle man but not a soft man. A gentle man is strong and never declares a truce when it is difficult to declare victory. God wants you to fight in the power of his Son, Jesus, until you have triumph over your sin. Then you can live in peace. God calls you to be a peacemaker, not a truce maker.

Prayer is your invisible weapon. People who pray spend time talking to God as a friend. You become more than a conqueror because you know God is with you, and you do not fear anyone or anything that is against you. God wants you to settle for nothing less than an intimate relationship with him. He made this possible through Jesus, whose victory over sin and death restores you to God.

Jesus also teaches that God requires ruthlessness. Be ruthless with your sins and shortcomings. When you are tempted to do what is not right, have the determination and self-discipline to distance yourself from it. Whatever is causing you to commit sin, sever it from your life. You can have victory if you do not settle for less. Declare victory, not compromise. Never settle for truce in place of peace.

---

reflect: Where have you compromised truth for convenience lately?
Go to **Romans 8:28.**

you can obey God, which makes you right with him. ¹⁷In the past you were slaves to sin—sin controlled you. But thank God, you fully obeyed the things that you were taught. ¹⁸You were made free from sin, and now you are slaves to goodness. ¹⁹I use this example because this is hard for you to understand. In the past you offered the parts of your body to be slaves to sin and evil; you lived only for evil. In the same way now you must give yourselves to be slaves of goodness. Then you will live only for God.

²⁰In the past you were slaves to sin, and goodness did not control you. ²¹You did evil things, and now you are ashamed of them. Those things only bring death. ²²But now you are free from sin and have become slaves of God. This brings you a life that is only for God, and this gives you life forever. ²³The payment for sin is death. But God gives us the free gift of life forever in Christ Jesus our Lord.

AN EXAMPLE FROM MARRIAGE

7 Brothers and sisters, all of you understand the law of Moses. So surely you know that the law rules over people only while they are alive. ²For example, a woman must stay married to her husband as long as he is alive. But if her husband dies, she is free from the law of marriage. ³But if she marries another man while her husband is still alive, the law says she is guilty of adultery. But if her husband dies, she is free from the law of marriage. Then if she marries another man, she is not guilty of adultery.

⁴In the same way, my brothers and sisters, your old selves died, and you became free from the law through the body of Christ. This happened so that you might belong to someone else—the One who was raised from the dead—and so that we might be used in service to God. ⁵In the past, we were ruled by our sinful selves. The law made us want to do sinful things that controlled our bodies, so

BRAVE JOY

receiving the **gift**

FAITH

By Elmer Towns

ROMANS 6:23

The faith that leads to salvation has often been compared to receiving a gift. Consider this analogy: A convict had been confined to a prison cell for many years, but one day the jailer brought him a pardon. The convict could not go free until he received the pardon. Even though the pardon was immediately valid when signed by the governor, it did not become effective until the convict accepted it and walked out of the prison.

Saving faith is like this. It is simply receiving God's pardon for sin, a pardon accomplished by Christ's death on the cross. Forgiveness, like all spiritual reality, is of no effect unless accepted by the person who needs it. It is important to understand that God initiated this pardon; it is ready and waiting for you. He has already offered it by sending his Son to pay the penalty for your sin. Receive God's gift of forgiveness today and find freedom and a fresh start.

reflect: Have you accepted the gracious gift of God's forgiveness and freedom?
Go to **FAITH:** "A Partnership with God" at **John 1:12.**

the things we did were bringing us death. [6]In the past, the law held us like prisoners, but our old selves died, and we were made free from the law. So now we serve God in a new way with the Spirit, and not in the old way with written rules.

OUR FIGHT AGAINST SIN

[7]You might think I am saying that sin and the law are the same thing. That is not true. But the law was the only way I could learn what sin meant. I would never have known what it means to want to take something belonging to someone else if the law had not said, "You must not want to take your neighbor's things."[n] [8]And sin found a way to use that command and cause me to want all kinds of things I should not want. But without the law, sin has no power. [9]I was alive before I knew the law. But when the law's command came to me, then sin began to live, [10]and I died. The command was meant to bring life, but for me it brought death. [11]Sin found a way to fool me by using the command to make me die.

[12]So the law is holy, and the command is holy and right and good. [13]Does this mean that something that is good brought death to me? No! Sin used something that is good to bring death to me. This happened so that I could see what sin is really like; the command was used to show that sin is very evil.

THE WAR WITHIN US

[14]We know that the law is spiritual, but I am not spiritual since sin rules me as if I were its slave. [15]I do not understand the things I do. I do not do what I want to do, and I do the things I hate. [16]And if I do not want to do the hated things I do, that means I agree that the law is good. [17]But I am not really the one who is doing these hated things; it is sin living in me that does them. [18]Yes, I know that nothing good lives in me—I mean nothing good lives in the part of me that is earthly and sinful. I want to do the things that are good, but I do not do them. [19]I do not do the good things I want to do, but I do the bad things I do not want to do. [20]So if I do things I do not want to do, then I am not the one doing them. It is sin living in me that does those things.

[21]So I have learned this rule: When I want to do good, evil is there with me. [22]In my mind, I am happy with God's law. [23]But I see another law working in my body, which

makes war against the law that my mind accepts. That other law working in my body is the law of sin, and it makes me its prisoner. [24]What a miserable man I am! Who will save me from this body that brings me death? [25]I thank God for saving me through Jesus Christ our Lord!

So in my mind I am a slave to God's law, but in my sinful self I am a slave to the law of sin.

BE RULED BY THE SPIRIT

8 So now, those who are in Christ Jesus are not judged guilty.[n] [2]Through Christ Jesus the law of the Spirit that brings life made you[n] free from the law that brings sin and death. [3]The law was without power, because the law was made weak by our sinful selves. But God did what the law could not do. He sent his own Son to earth with the same human life that others use for sin. By sending his Son to be an offering for sin, God used a human life to destroy sin. [4]He did this so that we could be the kind of people the law correctly wants us to be. Now we do not live following our sinful selves, but we live following the Spirit.

[5]Those who live following their sinful selves think only about things that their sinful selves want. But those who live following the Spirit are thinking about the things the Spirit wants them to do. [6]If people's thinking is controlled by the sinful self, there is death. But if their thinking is controlled by the Spirit, there is life and peace. [7]When people's thinking is controlled by the sinful self, they are against God, because they refuse to obey God's law and really are not even able to obey God's law. [8]Those people who are ruled by their sinful selves cannot please God.

[9]But you are not ruled by your sinful selves. You are ruled by the Spirit, if that Spirit of God really lives in you. But the person who does not have the Spirit of Christ does not belong to Christ. [10]Your body will always be dead because of sin. But if Christ is in you, then the Spirit gives you life, because Christ made you right with God. [11]God raised Jesus from the dead, and if God's Spirit is living in

---

7:7 "You . . . things." Quotation from Exodus 20:17. **8:1 guilty** Some Greek copies continue, "those who do not live in the power of their sinful selves, but in the power of the Spirit." **8:2 you** Some Greek copies read "me."

Hope in the Holy Spirit

By Claudio Freidzon

As Christian believers, we turn darkness upside down. We prayerfully seek the Holy Spirit because he has the power and is the one who renews us. The Holy Spirit is not just a force we meet on Sunday; he is as real as any other person in our lives. His friendship is a relationship that truly is always with us and deepens as we walk and talk with him.

The invisible, eternal things of God have power to change what is visible in your life. Do not lose hope because of what your physical eyes perceive; things will not stay like that forever. The Spirit of God will manifest, and he has promised you favor, mercy, kindness, and power.

Pray and seek God's plans. Ask him to give you relief from confusion and sadness. In spite of what the devil tells you, or the barriers and hardships you face, you can say, "The Holy Spirit will lead me from victory to victory. He will give me the support to finish projects and the creativity to solve problems. He will show and tell me how to do things."

God protects our lives. The power from the Holy Spirit cancels all voices of death and destruction and gives us promises of good. Any evil spirits of depression, fear, or discouragement must flee from us. As believers, we stand firm and hold onto God's authority and the blessings of the Holy Spirit.

The fire of the Holy Spirit burns out all ungodly thoughts within us. This fire will dominate and drown all other fires. Panic attacks disappear, chronic depression is broken, and thoughts of death and suicide must depart. Because our good health and well-being is his concern, the Lord says "no more" to the Enemy!

As friends of the Holy Spirit, we speak words of life over each other, families, spouses, and children concerning health and finances. Whatever the situations, we declare resurrection life and pray for each other to break bondages and the chains of hell. We worship the Lord with praise songs and joy in order to strengthen our declarations in the name of Jesus Christ.

Under the authority of God, the Holy Spirit enables us to conquer all things through the work of Jesus Christ and cancel all curses, and we receive and enjoy abundant life. Bind yourself to hope and let the Holy Spirit unchain you. Do not fear defeat or anguish, and no longer call yourself poor, depressed, or sorrowful. You are a person of hope with the power of the Holy Spirit on your side!

TO LEARN MORE ON WHAT THE BIBLE HAS TO SAY ABOUT **FUTURE,** READ THE SCRIPTURES AND DEVOTIONALS AT **HEBREWS 13:20–21, JAMES 1:14, JAMES 3:10, MATTHEW 28:16–20, 1 THESSALONIANS 4:15–18,** AND **REVELATION 21:3–5.**

you, he will also give life to your bodies that die. God is the One who raised Christ from the dead, and he will give life through[n] his Spirit that lives in you.

[12]So, my brothers and sisters, we must not be ruled by our sinful selves or live the way our sinful selves want. [13]If you use your lives to do the wrong things your sinful selves want, you will die spiritually. But if you use the Spirit's help to stop doing the wrong things you do with your body, you will have true life.

[14]The true children of God are those who let God's Spirit lead them. [15]The Spirit we received does not make us slaves again to fear; it makes us children of God. With that Spirit we cry out, "Father."[n] [16]And the Spirit himself joins with our spirits to say we are God's children. [17]If we are God's children, we will receive blessings from God together with Christ. But we must suffer as Christ suffered so that we will have glory as Christ has glory.

OUR FUTURE GLORY

[18]The sufferings we have now are nothing compared to the great glory that will be shown to us. [19]Everything God made is waiting with excitement for God to show his children's glory completely. [20]Everything God made was changed to become useless, not by its own wish but because God wanted it and because all along there was this hope: [21]that everything God made would be set free from ruin to have the freedom and glory that belong to God's children.

[22]We know that everything God made has been waiting until now in pain, like a woman ready to give birth. [23]Not only the world, but we also have been waiting with pain inside us. We have the Spirit as the first part of God's promise. So we are waiting for God to finish making us his own children, which means our bodies will be made free. [24]We were saved, and we have this hope. If we see what we are waiting for, that is not really hope. People do not hope for something they already have. [25]But we are hoping for something we do not have yet, and we are waiting for it patiently.

[26]Also, the Spirit helps us with our weakness. We do not know how to pray as we should. But the Spirit himself speaks to God for us, even begs God for us with deep feel-

ings that words cannot explain. [27]God can see what is in people's hearts. And he knows what is in the mind of the Spirit, because the Spirit speaks to God for his people in the way God wants.

[28]We know that in everything God works for the good of those who love him.[n] They are the people he called, because that was his plan. [29]God knew them before he made the world, and he chose them to be like his Son so that Jesus would be the firstborn[n] of many brothers and sisters. [30]God planned for them to be like his Son; and those he planned to be like his Son, he also called; and those he called, he also made right with him; and those he made right, he also glorified.

GOD'S LOVE IN CHRIST JESUS

[31]So what should we say about this? If God is for us, no one can defeat us. [32]He did not spare his own Son but gave him for us all. So with Jesus, God will surely give us all things. [33]Who can accuse the people God has chosen? No one, because God is the One who makes them right. [34]Who can say God's people are guilty? No one, because Christ Jesus died, but he was also raised from the dead, and now he is on God's right side, appealing to God for us. [35]Can anything separate us from the love Christ has for us? Can troubles or problems or sufferings or hunger or nakedness or danger or violent death? [36]As it is written in the Scriptures:

"For you we are in danger of death all the time.
People think we are worth no more than sheep to be killed." *Psalm 44:22*

[37]But in all these things we are completely victorious through God who showed his love for us. [38]Yes, I am sure that neither death, nor life, nor angels, nor ruling spirits, nothing now, nothing in the future, no powers, [39]nothing above us, nothing below us, nor anything else in the whole world will ever be able to separate us from the love of God that is in Christ Jesus our Lord.

8:11 through Some Greek copies read "because of." **8:15 "Father"** Literally, "Abba, Father." Jewish children called their fathers "Abba." **8:28 We . . . him.** Some Greek copies read "We know that everything works together for good for those who love God." **8:29 firstborn** Here this probably means that Christ was the first in God's family to share God's glory.

GOD AND THE JEWISH PEOPLE

9 I am in Christ, and I am telling you the truth; I do not lie. My conscience is ruled by the Holy Spirit, and it tells me I am not lying. ²I have great sorrow and always feel much sadness. ³I wish I could help my Jewish brothers and sisters, my people. I would even wish that I were cursed and cut off from Christ if that would help them. ⁴They are the people of Israel, God's chosen children. They have seen the glory of God, and they have the agreements that God made between himself and his people. God gave them the law of Moses and the right way of worship and his promises. ⁵They are the descendants of our great ancestors, and they are the earthly family into which Christ was born, who is God over all. Praise him forever!ⁿ Amen.

9:5 born . . . forever! This can also mean "born. May God, who rules over all things, be praised forever!"

PEACE BY GOD

four types of **stress**

FULFILLMENT

By Dr. Sheri Lerner

ROMANS 8:28

There are four types of stress:

1. Positive Stress (Eustress): this is a stressful situation that you tend to feel good about and adapt to in a healthy manner. Eustress can be associated with things like getting married or landing a dream job.

2. Negative Stress (Distress): distress may be associated with work overload, financial difficulties, a sick child, or a broken relationship. Your body doesn't adapt to negative stress in a healthy manner. Instead, it prolongs it and may manifest itself in feelings of failure, anger, or fear.

3. Physical Stress: a result of exercise or manual labor done too rigorously. Over time, this type of physical activity can be abusive to your joints, muscles, and tendons. You may also experience physical stress by *not* doing any physical activity.

4. Toxic (Chemical) Stress: comes from things like smoking, drugs, environmental pollution, toxins in household and personal hygiene products, and chemical-laden foods.

When it comes to stress, relax—you're in the Father's hands. He knew there would be repercussions to your body if you allowed stress to get out of hand. That's why he gave you the gift of prayer. When you are so stressed that even burned toast upsets you, you should stop everything you are doing and pray. The Holy Spirit will help you by expressing what you cannot, due to your inability to see the situation clearly, and he will give you the peace you need in order to deal with your stressful situations.

---

reflect: Why don't you deliver the stresses of the day over to God?

Go to **Isaiah 45:7.**

⁶It is not that God failed to keep his promise to them. But only some of the people of Israel are truly God's people,[n] ⁷and only some of Abraham's[n] descendants are true children of Abraham. But God said to Abraham: "The descendants I promised you will be from Isaac."[n] ⁸This means that not all of Abraham's descendants are God's true children. Abraham's true children are those who become God's children because of the promise God made to Abraham. ⁹God's promise to Abraham was this: "At the right time I will return, and Sarah will have a son."[n] ¹⁰And that is not all. Rebekah's sons had the same father, our father Isaac. ¹¹⁻¹²But before the two boys were born, God told Rebekah, "The older will serve the younger."[n] This was before the boys had done anything good or bad. God said this so that the one chosen would be chosen because of God's own plan. He was chosen because he was the one God wanted to call, not because of anything he did. ¹³As the Scripture says, "I loved Jacob, but I hated Esau."[n]

¹⁴So what should we say about this? Is God unfair? In no way. ¹⁵God said to Moses, "I will show kindness to anyone to whom I want to show kindness, and I will show mercy to anyone to whom I want to show mercy."[n] ¹⁶So God will choose the one to whom he decides to show mercy; his choice does not depend on what people want or try to do. ¹⁷The Scripture says to the king of Egypt: "I made you king for this reason: to show my power in you so that my name will be talked about in all the earth."[n] ¹⁸So God shows mercy where he wants to show mercy, and he makes stubborn the people he wants to make stubborn.

¹⁹So one of you will ask me: "Then why does God blame us for our sins? Who can fight his will?" ²⁰You are only human, and human beings have no right to question God. An object should not ask the person who made it, "Why did you make me like this?" ²¹The potter can make anything he wants to make. He can use the same clay to make one thing for special use and another thing for daily use.

²²It is the same way with God. He wanted to show his anger and to let people see his power. But he patiently stayed with those people he was angry with—people who were made ready to be destroyed. ²³He waited with patience so that he could make known his rich glory to the people who receive his mercy. He has prepared these people to have his glory, ²⁴and we are those people whom God called. He called us not from the Jews only but also from those who are not Jews. ²⁵As the Scripture says in Hosea:

"I will say, 'You are my people'
   to those I had called 'not my people.'
And I will show my love
   to those people I did not love."
                        Hosea 2:1, 23

²⁶ "They were called,
   'You are not my people,'
but later they will be called
   'children of the living God.'" *Hosea 1:10*

²⁷And Isaiah cries out about Israel:
"The people of Israel are many,
   like the grains of sand by the sea.
But only a few of them will be saved,
²⁸   because the Lord will quickly and
      completely punish the people on the
      earth." *Isaiah 10:22–23*

²⁹It is as Isaiah said:
"The Lord All-Powerful
   allowed a few of our descendants to
      live.
Otherwise we would have been
   completely destroyed
like the cities of Sodom and
   Gomorrah."[n] *Isaiah 1:9*

³⁰So what does all this mean? Those who are not Jews were not trying to make themselves right with God, but they were made right with God because of their faith. ³¹The people of Israel tried to follow a law to make themselves right with God. But they did not succeed, ³²because they tried to make themselves right by the things they did instead of trusting in God to make them right. They stumbled over the stone that causes people to stumble. ³³As it is written in the Scripture:

9:6 God's people Literally, "Israel," the people God chose to bring his blessings to the world. **9:7 Abraham** Most respected ancestor of the Jews. Every Jew hoped to see Abraham. **9:7 "The descendants . . . Isaac."** Quotation from Genesis 21:12. **9:9 "At . . . son."** Quotation from Genesis 18:10, 14. **9:11–12 "The older . . . younger."** Quotation from Genesis 25:23. **9:13 "I . . . Esau."** Quotation from Malachi 1:2–3. **9:15 "I . . . mercy."** Quotation from Exodus 33:19. **9:17 "I . . . earth."** Quotation from Exodus 9:16. **9:29 Sodom and Gomorrah** Two cities that God destroyed because the people were so evil.

"I will put in Jerusalem a stone that
  causes people to stumble,
  a rock that makes them fall.
Anyone who trusts in him will never be
  disappointed."   *Isaiah 8:14; 28:16*

10 Brothers and sisters, the thing I want most is for all the Jews to be saved. That is my prayer to God. ²I can say this about them: They really try to follow God, but they do not know the right way. ³Because they did not know the way that God makes people right with him, they tried to make themselves right in their own way. So they did not accept God's way of making people right. ⁴Christ ended the law so that everyone who believes in him may be right with God.

⁵Moses writes about being made right by following the law. He says, "A person who obeys these things will live because of them."ⁿ ⁶But this is what the Scripture says about being made right through faith: "Don't say to yourself, 'Who will go up into heaven?'" (That means, "Who will go up to heaven and bring Christ down to earth?") ⁷"And do not say, 'Who will go down into the world below?'" (That means, "Who will go down and bring Christ up from the dead?") ⁸This is what the Scripture says: "The word is near you; it is in your mouth and in your heart."ⁿ That is the teaching of faith that we are telling. ⁹If you declare with your mouth, "Jesus is Lord," and if you believe in your heart that God raised Jesus from the dead, you will be saved. ¹⁰We believe with our

---

10:5 "A person . . . them." Quotation from Leviticus 18:5. **10:6–8 But . . . heart."** Quotations from Deuteronomy 9:4; 30:12–14; Psalm 107:26.

A PARTNERSHIP WITH GOD

confession

FAITH

ROMANS 10:9

When did we begin to imagine that confession only meant speaking? It's true that the Greek word *homologeo* literally means "to say the same thing." It implies speaking in agreement with someone or something. But "confession" in the first century meant a great deal more than verbal assent.

Calling someone "lord" was the equivalent of naming that person as divine. The Greek translation of the Old Testament uses the word "Lord" as the name of God more than six thousand times. In Paul's world, the Roman emperor was routinely called "lord" as a designation of his divinity. To call someone "lord" was to *confess* that all of your life was in his service and under his authority. Confession was about naming your god.

When the Christians were persecuted in the early church, confession became the determination of their fate. If they would not *confess* the emperor, they were often tortured and put to death. Those simple words, "Jesus is Lord," became the words of life or death. The New Testament meaning of the word has not changed. It still implies total service and total authority, and it influences how we will live and how we will die.

reflect: Make Jesus the Lord of your entire life: spirit, soul, and body.
Go to **2 Corinthians 4:13.**

hearts, and so we are made right with God. And we declare with our mouths that we believe, and so we are saved. [11]As the Scripture says, "Anyone who trusts in him will never be disappointed."[n] [12]That Scripture says "anyone" because there is no difference between those who are Jews and those who are not. The same Lord is the Lord of all and gives many blessings to all who trust in him, [13]as the Scripture says, "Anyone who calls on the Lord will be saved."[n]

[14]But before people can ask the Lord for help, they must believe in him; and before they can believe in him, they must hear about him; and for them to hear about the Lord, someone must tell them; [15]and before someone can go and tell them, that person must be sent. It is written, "How beautiful is the person who comes to bring good news."[n] [16]But not all the Jews accepted the good news. Isaiah said, "Lord, who believed what we told them?"[n] [17]So faith comes from hearing the Good News, and people hear the Good News when someone tells them about Christ.

[18]But I ask: Didn't people hear the Good News? Yes, they heard—as the Scripture says:

"Their message went out through all the
    world;
  their words go everywhere on earth."
                              Psalm 19:4

[19]Again I ask: Didn't the people of Israel understand? Yes, they did understand. First, Moses says:

"I will use those who are not a nation to
    make you jealous.
I will use a nation that does not
    understand to make you angry."
                        Deuteronomy 32:21

[20]Then Isaiah is bold enough to say:

"I was found by those who were not
    asking me for help.
I made myself known to people who
    were not looking for me."   *Isaiah 65:1*

[21]But about Israel God says,

"All day long I stood ready to accept
  people who disobey and are stubborn."
                              Isaiah 65:2

GOD SHOWS MERCY TO ALL PEOPLE

11 So I ask: Did God throw out his people? No! I myself am an Israelite from the family of Abraham, from the tribe of Benjamin. [2]God chose the Israelites to be his

people before they were born, and he has not thrown his people out. Surely you know what the Scripture says about Elijah, how he prayed to God against the people of Israel. [3]"Lord," he said, "they have killed your prophets, and they have destroyed your altars. I am the only prophet left, and now they are trying to kill me, too."[n] [4]But what answer did God give Elijah? He said, "But I have left seven thousand people in Israel who have never bowed down before Baal."[n] [5]It is the same now. There are a few people that God has chosen by his grace. [6]And if he chose them by grace, it is not for the things they have done. If they could be made God's people by what they did, God's gift of grace would not really be a gift.

[7]So this is what has happened: Although the Israelites tried to be right with God, they did not succeed, but the ones God chose did become right with him. The others were made stubborn and refused to listen to God. [8]As it is written in the Scriptures:

"God gave the people a dull mind so they
    could not understand."   *Isaiah 29:10*
"He closed their eyes so they could not
    see
  and their ears so they could not hear.
This continues until today."
                        Deuteronomy 29:4

[9]And David says:

"Let their own feasts trap them and cause
    their ruin;
  let their feasts cause them to stumble
    and be paid back.
[10] Let their eyes be closed so they cannot see
  and their backs be forever weak from
    troubles."   *Psalm 69:22–23*

[11]So I ask: When the Jews fell, did that fall destroy them? No! But their failure brought salvation to those who are not Jews, in order to make the Jews jealous. [12]The Jews' failure brought rich blessings for the world, and the Jews' loss brought rich blessings for the non-Jewish people. So surely the world will receive much richer blessings when enough Jews become the kind of people God wants.

10:11 **"Anyone . . . disappointed."** Quotation from Isaiah 28:16. 10:13 **"Anyone . . . saved."** Quotation from Joel 2:32. 10:15 **"How . . . news."** Quotation from Isaiah 52:7. 10:16 **"Lord, . . . them?"** Quotation from Isaiah 53:1. 11:3 **"they . . . too"** Quotation from 1 Kings 19:10, 14. 11:4 **"But . . . Baal."** Quotation from 1 Kings 19:18.

¹³Now I am speaking to you who are not Jews. I am an apostle to those who are not Jews, and since I have that work, I will make the most of it. ¹⁴I hope I can make my own people jealous and, in that way, help some of them to be saved. ¹⁵When God turned away from the Jews, he became friends with other people in the world. So when God accepts the Jews, surely that will bring them life after death.

¹⁶If the first piece of bread is offered to God, then the whole loaf is made holy. If the roots of a tree are holy, then the tree's branches are holy too.

¹⁷It is as if some of the branches from an olive tree have been broken off. You non-Jewish people are like the branch of a wild olive tree that has been joined to that first tree. You now share the strength and life of the first tree, the Jews. ¹⁸So do not brag about those branches that were broken off. If you brag, remember that you do not support the root, but the root supports you. ¹⁹You will say, "Branches were broken off so that I could be joined to their tree." ²⁰That is true. But those branches were broken off because they did not believe, and you continue to be part of the tree only because you believe. Do not be proud, but be afraid. ²¹If God did not let the natural branches of that tree stay, then he will not let you stay if you don't believe.

²²So you see that God is kind and also very strict. He punishes those who stop following him. But God is kind to you, if you continue following in his kindness. If you do not, you will be cut off from the tree. ²³And if the Jews will believe in God again, he will accept them back. God is able to put them back where they were. ²⁴It is not natural for a wild branch to be part of a good tree. And you who are not Jews are like a branch cut from a wild olive tree and joined to a good olive tree. But since those Jews are like a branch that grew from the good tree, surely they can be joined to their own tree again.

²⁵I want you to understand this secret, brothers and sisters, so you will understand that you do not know everything: Part of Israel has been made stubborn, but that will change when many who are not Jews have come to God. ²⁶And that is how all Israel will be saved. It is written in the Scriptures:

"The Savior will come from Jerusalem;
  he will take away all evil from the
    family of Jacob.ⁿ
²⁷ And I will make this agreement with
    those people
  when I take away their sins."
Isaiah 59:20–21; 27:9

²⁸The Jews refuse to accept the Good News, so they are God's enemies. This has happened to help you who are not Jews. But the Jews are still God's chosen people, and he loves them very much because of the promises he made to their ancestors. ²⁹God never changes his mind about the people he calls and the things he gives them. ³⁰At one time you refused to obey God. But now you have received mercy, because those people refused to obey. ³¹And now the Jews refuse to obey, because God showed mercy to you. But this happened so that they also canⁿ receive mercy from him. ³²God has given all people over to their stubborn ways so that he can show mercy to all.

PRAISE TO GOD

³³Yes, God's riches are very great, and his wisdom and knowledge have no end! No one can explain the things God decides or understand his ways. ³⁴As the Scripture says,

"Who has known the mind of the Lord,
  or who has been able to give him
    advice?"   *Isaiah 40:13*
³⁵ "No one has ever given God anything
  that he must pay back."   *Job 41:11*
³⁶Yes, God made all things, and everything continues through him and for him. To him be the glory forever! Amen.

GIVE YOUR LIVES TO GOD

12 So brothers and sisters, since God has shown us great mercy, I beg you to offer your lives as a living sacrifice to him. Your offering must be only for God and pleasing to him, which is the spiritual way for you to worship. ²Do not be shaped by this world; instead be changed within by a new way of thinking. Then you will be able to decide what God wants for you; you will know what is good and pleasing to him and what is perfect. ³Because God has given me a special gift,

---

11:26 **Jacob** Father of the twelve family groups of Israel, the people God chose to be his people. 11:31 **can** Some Greek copies read "can now."

I have something to say to everyone among you. Do not think you are better than you are. You must decide what you really are by the amount of faith God has given you. ⁴Each one of us has a body with many parts, and these parts all have different uses. ⁵In the same way, we are many, but in Christ we are all one body. Each one is a part of that body, and each part belongs to all the other parts. ⁶We all have different gifts, each of which came because of the grace God gave us. The person who has the gift of prophecy should use that gift in agreement with the faith. ⁷Anyone who has the gift of serving should serve. Anyone who has the gift of teaching should teach. ⁸Whoever has the gift of encouraging others should encourage. Whoever has the gift of giving to others should give freely. Anyone who has the gift of being a leader should try hard when he leads. Whoever has the gift of showing mercy to others should do so with joy.

⁹Your love must be real. Hate what is evil, and hold on to what is good. ¹⁰Love each other like brothers and sisters. Give each

LOSING WEIGHT

a **worthy** body

ROMANS 12:1

In the Greek language, the word for "body" is *soma* (translated "lives" in the New Century Version). It is where we get the English word "psychosomatic"—a combination of two Greek words meaning "soul over body," an illness of the body that is really in the mind. There is a bit of Greek history behind this word. In Greek philosophy, the body and the mind were separate realities. This separation was the result of the Greek belief that the body represented all of the lower and despicable things of life. It was subject to illness and injury. It was full of cravings and desires. It had to be fed, clothed, and cared for incessantly.

The mind, on the other hand, could contemplate lofty ideals, achieve great thoughts, and transport a person out of the world of toil and trouble. The body was considered nothing more than an annoying shell in which the soul was trapped. Denying the body was an important part of Greek religion. By denying oneself, one could free one's mind of the earthly realm.

Christianity completely rejects this dualism between body and mind. So, when Paul tells Christians to present their lives (bodies) as a living sacrifice to God, he said something that no Greek would ever even have considered. How could God be interested in the useless, worthless shell that surrounds the soul? Paul suggests God is so interested in our physical being that he wants us to bring it to him as our gift. Yet God wants far more from us than our mind and our soul. He wants all of us!

reflect: Glorify God with the gift of your life—spirit, soul, and body—today.
Go to **1 Corinthians 3:16.**

Understanding
Freedom

By Leon Fontaine

ROMANS 12:2

I don't believe that the world or the church truly understands *freedom*. Most people think it's the absence of work or the ability to disregard laws, but that's ridiculous! Either of those behaviors takes freedom away from people. We won't understand or enjoy freedom until we understand God's perspective and take a look at why he created man. Here are seven things that will help us understand true freedom.

1 **We were created for freedom.** Not one person on earth was designed to be dominated by another. On another note, Adam, created perfectly and designed with freedom, was also created to work.

2 **Giving Adam the freedom (power of choice) is what activated his will.** Without the freedom to make his own choices, Adam's will would have been irrelevant. Our choices have consequences. And, as became evident in the Garden of Eden, handling real freedom takes maturity and wisdom.

3 **Walking in freedom means shouldering its responsibilities.** Adam was given the responsibilities to guard, work, and enjoy the garden. He simply had to stay away from one tree. Even in freedom, his irresponsibility led to his downfall.

4 **Deliverance and freedom are not the same.** Skip forward to the birth of Israel as a nation. The Israelites were in bondage to Egypt, and God used Moses to deliver them out of slavery. However, Israel never came to understand or experience the freedom that God offered. Still today, there are Christians who have been delivered from the power of darkness, yet aren't free because they're still controlled by many bondages.

5 **Real freedom starts in the spirit, moves to the soul, and only then can be enjoyed physically.** After finding spiritual freedom through a relationship with God, you can begin "working out" your freedom in your soul (mind). As you do that, you'll finally begin to enjoy the physical benefits of true freedom.

6 **True freedom must be personally managed.** Many times the only difference between a person who is living a significant life and impacting people and somebody barely getting by is simply the fact that significant people manage themselves with excellence. Therefore, they're free to pursue their gifts and abilities.

7 **Freedom develops through three phases of responsibility.** The Israelites' journey to the Promised Land began in *Egypt*, where, as slaves, they had no responsibility except to obey or die. Next came the *Red Sea*, the site of Israelites' deliverance and the beginning of miracles that secured their survival. In this phase, God provided just what they needed, right on time. Finally, Israel entered *Canaan*, a land flowing with milk and honey. But here the Israelites had to learn to manage themselves to possess the blessing that was available! In the Promised Land, God wants you to take responsibility and learn to manage yourself!

We're going to be held accountable for the incredible freedom we have. We can impact a nation! We can even impact the world, as we Christians wake up and walk through these steps of freedom. Remember these seven key aspects of freedom, and you'll never again settle for or be forced to live with less than God's very best for your life.

TO LEARN MORE ON WHAT THE BIBLE HAS TO SAY ABOUT **FINANCES**, READ THE SCRIPTURES AND DEVOTIONALS AT **MATTHEW 7:12, MATTHEW 25:14-30, MARK 4:26-29, MARK 5:1-20, LUKE 18:17,** AND **LUKE 12:13-34.**

other more honor than you want for yourselves. [11]Do not be lazy but work hard, serving the Lord with all your heart. [12]Be joyful because you have hope. Be patient when trouble comes, and pray at all times. [13]Share with God's people who need help. Bring strangers in need into your homes.

[14]Wish good for those who harm you; wish them well and do not curse them. [15]Be happy with those who are happy, and be sad with those who are sad. [16]Live in peace with each other. Do not be proud, but make friends with those who seem unimportant. Do not think how smart you are.

[17]If someone does wrong to you, do not pay him back by doing wrong to him. Try to do what everyone thinks is right. [18]Do your best to live in peace with everyone. [19]My friends, do not try to punish others when they wrong you, but wait for God to punish them with his anger. It is written: "I will punish those who do wrong; I will repay them,"[n] says the Lord. [20]But you should do this:

"If your enemy is hungry, feed him;
        if he is thirsty, give him a drink.
Doing this will be like pouring burning
        coals on his head." *Proverbs 25:21–22*

[21]Do not let evil defeat you, but defeat evil by doing good.

CHRISTIANS SHOULD OBEY THE LAW

13 All of you must yield to the government rulers. No one rules unless God has given him the power to rule, and no one rules now without that power from God. [2]So those who are against the government are really against what God has commanded. And they will bring punishment on themselves. [3]Those who do right do not have to fear the rulers; only those who do wrong fear them. Do you want to be unafraid of the rulers? Then do what is right, and they will praise you. [4]The ruler is God's servant to help you. But if you do wrong, then be afraid. He has the power to punish; he is God's servant to punish those who do wrong. [5]So you must yield to the government, not only because you might be punished, but because you know it is right.

[6]This is also why you pay taxes. Rulers are working for God and give their time to their work. [7]Pay everyone, then, what you owe. If you owe any kind of tax, pay it. Show respect and honor to them all.

LOVING OTHERS

[8]Do not owe people anything, except always owe love to each other, because the person who loves others has obeyed all the law. [9]The law says, "You must not be guilty of adultery. You must not murder anyone. You must not steal. You must not want to take your neighbor's things."[n] All these commands and all others are really only one rule: "Love your neighbor as you love yourself."[n] [10]Love never hurts a neighbor, so loving is obeying all the law.

[11]Do this because we live in an important time. It is now time for you to wake up from your sleep, because our salvation is nearer now than when we first believed. [12]The "night"[n] is almost finished, and the "day"[n] is almost here. So we should stop doing things that belong to darkness and take up the weapons used for fighting in the light. [13]Let us live in a right way, like people who belong to the day. We should not have wild parties or get drunk. There should be no sexual sins of any kind, no fighting or jealousy. [14]But clothe yourselves with the Lord Jesus Christ and forget about satisfying your sinful self.

DO NOT CRITICIZE OTHER PEOPLE

14 Accept into your group someone who is weak in faith, and do not argue about opinions. [2]One person believes it is right to eat all kinds of food.[n] But another, who is weak, believes it is right to eat only vegetables. [3]The one who knows that it is right to eat any kind of food must not reject the one who eats only vegetables. And the person who eats only vegetables must not think that the one who eats all foods is wrong, because God has accepted that person. [4]You cannot judge another person's servant. The master decides if the servant is doing well or not. And the Lord's servant will do well because the Lord helps him do well.

[5]Some think that one day is more important than another, and others think that every

---

12:19 "I . . . them." Quotation from Deuteronomy 32:35. **13:9 "You . . . things."** Quotation from Exodus 20:13–15, 17. **13:9 "Love . . . yourself."** Quotation from Leviticus 19:18. **13:12 "night"** This is used as a symbol of the sinful world we live in. This world will soon end. **13:12 "day"** This is used as a symbol of the good time that is coming, when we will be with God. **14:2 all . . . food** The Jewish law said there were some foods Jews should not eat. When Jews became Christians, some of them did not understand they could now eat all foods.

day is the same. Let all be sure in their own mind. [6]Those who think one day is more important than other days are doing that for the Lord. And those who eat all kinds of food are doing that for the Lord, and they give thanks to God. Others who refuse to eat some foods do that for the Lord, and they give thanks to God. [7]We do not live or die for ourselves. [8]If we live, we are living for the Lord, and if we die, we are dying for the Lord. So living or dying, we belong to the Lord.

[9]The reason Christ died and rose from the dead to live again was so he would be Lord over both the dead and the living. [10]So why do you judge your brothers or sisters in Christ? And why do you think you are better than they are? We will all stand before God to be judged, [11]because it is written in the Scriptures:

"'As surely as I live,' says the Lord,
'Everyone will bow before me;
everyone will say that I am God.'"

Isaiah 45:23

[12]So each of us will have to answer to God.

DO NOT CAUSE OTHERS TO SIN

[13]For that reason we should stop judging each other. We must make up our minds not to do anything that will make another Christian sin. [14]I am in the Lord Jesus, and I know that there is no food that is wrong to eat. But if a person believes something is wrong, that thing is wrong for him. [15]If you hurt your brother's or sister's faith because of something you eat, you are not really following the way of love. Do not destroy someone's faith by eating food he thinks is wrong, because Christ died for him. [16]Do not allow what you think is good to become what others say is evil. [17]In the kingdom of God, eating and drinking are not important. The important things are living right with God, peace, and joy in the Holy Spirit. [18]Anyone who serves Christ by living this way is pleasing God and will be accepted by other people.

[19]So let us try to do what makes peace and helps one another. [20]Do not let the eating of food destroy the work of God. All foods are all right to eat, but it is wrong to eat food that causes someone else to sin. [21]It is better not to eat meat or drink wine or do anything that will cause your brother or sister to sin.

[22]Your beliefs about these things should be kept secret between you and God. People are happy if they can do what they think is right without feeling guilty. [23]But those who eat something without being sure it is right are wrong because they did not believe it was right. Anything that is done without believing it is right is a sin.

15 We who are strong in faith should help the weak with their weaknesses, and not please only ourselves. [2]Let each of us please our neighbors for their good, to help them be stronger in faith. [3]Even Christ did not live to please himself. It was as the Scriptures said: "When people insult you, it hurts me."[n] [4]Everything that was written in the past was written to teach us. The Scriptures give us patience and encouragement so that we can have hope. [5]May the patience and encouragement that come from God allow you to live in harmony with each other the way Christ Jesus wants. [6]Then you will all be joined together, and you will give glory to God the Father of our Lord Jesus Christ. [7]Christ accepted you, so you should accept each other, which will bring glory to God. [8]I tell you that Christ became a servant of the Jews to show that God's promises to the Jewish ancestors are true. [9]And he also did this so that those who are not Jews could give glory to God for the mercy he gives to them. It is written in the Scriptures:

"So I will praise you among the non-Jewish people.
I will sing praises to your name."

Psalm 18:49

[10]The Scripture also says,

"Be happy, you who are not Jews,
together with his people."

Deuteronomy 32:43

[11]Again the Scripture says,

"All you who are not Jews, praise the Lord.
All you people, sing praises to him."

Psalm 117:1

[12]And Isaiah says,

"A new king will come from the family of Jesse.[n]
He will come to rule over the non-Jewish people,
and they will have hope because of him."

Isaiah 11:10

15:3 "When . . . me." Quotation from Psalm 69:9.
15:12 Jesse Jesse was the father of David, king of Israel. Jesus was from their family.

[13]I pray that the God who gives hope will fill you with much joy and peace while you trust in him. Then your hope will overflow by the power of the Holy Spirit.

PAUL TALKS ABOUT HIS WORK

[14]My brothers and sisters, I am sure that you are full of goodness. I know that you have all the knowledge you need and that you are able to teach each other. [15]But I have written to you very openly about some things I wanted you to remember. I did this because God gave me this special gift: [16]to be a minister of Christ Jesus to those who are not Jews. I served God by teaching his Good News, so that the non-Jewish people could be an offering that God would accept—an offering made holy by the Holy Spirit.

[17]So I am proud of what I have done for God in Christ Jesus. [18]I will not talk about anything except what Christ has done through me in leading those who are not Jews to obey God. They have obeyed God because of what I have said and done, [19]because of the power of miracles and the great things they saw, and because of the power of the Holy Spirit. I preached the Good News from Jerusalem all the way around to Illyricum, and so I have finished that part of my work. [20]I always want to preach the Good News in places where people have never heard of Christ, because I do not want to build on the work someone else has already started. [21]But it is written in the Scriptures:

"Those who were not told about him will
     see,
  and those who have not heard about
     him will understand."   *Isaiah 52:15*

PAUL'S PLAN TO VISIT ROME

[22]This is the reason I was stopped many times from coming to you. [23]Now I have finished my work here. Since for many years I have wanted to come to you, [24]I hope to visit you on my way to Spain. After I enjoy being with you for a while, I hope you can help me on my trip. [25]Now I am going to Jerusalem to help God's people. [26]The believers in Macedonia and Southern Greece were happy to give their money to help the poor among God's people at Jerusalem. [27]They were happy to do this, and really they owe it to them. These who are not Jews have shared in the Jews' spiritual blessings, so they should use their material possessions to help the Jews. [28]After I am sure the poor in Jerusalem get the money that has been given for them, I will leave for Spain and stop and visit you. [29]I know that when I come to you I will bring Christ's full blessing.

[30]Brothers and sisters, I beg you to help me in my work by praying to God for me. Do this because of our Lord Jesus and the love that the Holy Spirit gives us. [31]Pray that I will be saved from the nonbelievers in Judea and that this help I bring to Jerusalem will please God's people there. [32]Then, if God wants me to, I will come to you with joy, and together you and I will have a time of rest. [33]The God who gives peace be with you all. Amen.

GREETINGS TO THE CHRISTIANS

16 I recommend to you our sister Phoebe, who is a helper[n] in the church in Cenchrea. [2]I ask you to accept her in the Lord in the way God's people should. Help her with anything she needs, because she has helped me and many other people also.

[3]Give my greetings to Priscilla and Aquila, who work together with me in Christ Jesus [4]and who risked their own lives to save my life. I am thankful to them, and all the non-Jewish churches are thankful as well. [5]Also, greet for me the church that meets at their house.

Greetings to my dear friend Epenetus, who was the first person in Asia to follow Christ. [6]Greetings to Mary, who worked very hard for you. [7]Greetings to Andronicus and Junia, my relatives, who were in prison with me. They are very important apostles. They were believers in Christ before I was. [8]Greetings to Ampliatus, my dear friend in the Lord. [9]Greetings to Urbanus, a worker together with me for Christ. And greetings to my dear friend Stachys. [10]Greetings to Apelles, who was tested and proved that he truly loves Christ. Greetings to all those who are in the family of Aristobulus. [11]Greetings to Herodion, my fellow citizen. Greetings to all those in the family of Narcissus who belong to the Lord. [12]Greetings to Tryphena and Tryphosa, women who work very hard for the Lord. Greetings to my

---

16:1 helper Literally, "deaconess." This might mean the same as one of the special women helpers in 1 Timothy 3:11.

dear friend Persis, who also has worked very hard for the Lord. [13]Greetings to Rufus, who is a special person in the Lord, and to his mother, who has been like a mother to me also. [14]Greetings to Asyncritus, Phlegon, Hermes, Patrobas, Hermas, and all the brothers and sisters who are with them. [15]Greetings to Philologus and Julia, Nereus and his sister, and Olympas, and to all God's people with them. [16]Greet each other with a holy kiss. All of Christ's churches send greetings to you.

[17]Brothers and sisters, I ask you to look out for those who cause people to be against each other and who upset other people's faith. They are against the true teaching you learned, so stay away from them. [18]Such people are not serving our Lord Christ but are only doing what pleases themselves. They use fancy talk and fine words to fool the minds of those who do not know about evil. [19]All the believers have heard that you obey, so I am very happy because of you. But I want you to be wise in what is good and innocent in what is evil.

[20]The God who brings peace will soon defeat Satan and give you power over him.

The grace of our Lord Jesus be with you.

[21]Timothy, a worker together with me, sends greetings, as well as Lucius, Jason, and Sosipater, my relatives.

[22]I am Tertius, and I am writing this letter from Paul. I send greetings to you in the Lord.

[23]Gaius is letting me and the whole church here use his home. He also sends greetings to you, as do Erastus, the city treasurer, and our brother Quartus. [[24]The grace of our Lord Jesus Christ be with all of you. Amen.][n]

[25]Glory to God who can make you strong in faith by the Good News that I tell people and by the message about Jesus Christ. The message about Christ is the secret that was hidden for long ages past but is now made known. [26]It has been made clear through the writings of the prophets. And by the command of the eternal God it is made known to all nations that they might believe and obey.

[27]To the only wise God be glory forever through Jesus Christ! Amen.

16:24 The . . . Amen. Some Greek copies do not contain the bracketed text.

1 corinthians

HELP FOR A CHURCH WITH PROBLEMS

1 From Paul. God called me to be an apostle of Christ Jesus because that is what God wanted. Also from Sosthenes, our brother in Christ.

²To the church of God in Corinth, to you who have been made holy in Christ Jesus. You were called to be God's holy people with all people everywhere who pray in the name of the Lord Jesus Christ—their Lord and ours:

³Grace and peace to you from God our Father and the Lord Jesus Christ.

PAUL GIVES THANKS TO GOD

⁴I always thank my God for you because of the grace God has given you in Christ Jesus. ⁵I thank God because in Christ you have been made rich in every way, in all your speaking and in all your knowledge. ⁶Just as our witness about Christ has been guaranteed to you, ⁷so you have every gift from God while you wait for our Lord Jesus Christ to come again. ⁸Jesus will keep you strong until the end so that there will be no wrong in you on the day our Lord Jesus Christ comes again. ⁹God, who has called you into fellowship with his Son, Jesus Christ our Lord, is faithful.

PROBLEMS IN THE CHURCH

¹⁰I beg you, brothers and sisters, by the name of our Lord Jesus Christ that all of you agree with each other and not be split into groups. I beg that you be completely joined together by having the same kind of thinking and the same purpose. ¹¹My brothers and sisters, some people from Chloe's family have told me quite plainly that there are quarrels among you. ¹²This is what I mean: One of you says, "I follow Paul"; another says, "I follow Apollos"; another says, "I follow Peter"; and another says, "I follow Christ." ¹³Christ has been divided up into different groups! Did Paul die on the cross for you? No! Were you baptized in the name of Paul? No! ¹⁴I thank God I did not baptize any of you except Crispus and Gaius ¹⁵so that now no one can say you were baptized in my name. ¹⁶(I also baptized the family of Stephanas, but I do not remember that I baptized anyone else.) ¹⁷Christ did not send me to baptize people but to preach the Good News. And he sent me to preach the Good News without using words of human wisdom so that the cross[n] of Christ would not lose its power.

CHRIST IS GOD'S POWER AND WISDOM

¹⁸The teaching about the cross is foolishness to those who are being lost, but to us who are being saved it is the power of God. ¹⁹It is written in the Scriptures:

"I will cause the wise to lose their wisdom;
    I will make the wise unable to
        understand."   *Isaiah 29:14*

²⁰Where is the wise person? Where is the educated person? Where is the skilled talker of this world? God has made the wisdom of the world foolish. ²¹In the wisdom of God the world did not know God through its own wisdom. So God chose to use the message that sounds foolish to save those who believe. ²²The Jews ask for miracles, and the Greeks want wisdom. ²³But we preach a crucified Christ. This causes the Jews to stumble and is foolishness to non-Jews. ²⁴But Christ is the power of God and the wisdom of God to those people God has called—Jews and Greeks. ²⁵Even the foolishness of God is wiser than human wisdom, and the weakness of God is stronger than human strength.

²⁶Brothers and sisters, look at what you were when God called you. Not many of you were wise in the way the world judges wisdom. Not many of you had great influence. Not many of you came from important families. ²⁷But God chose the foolish things of the world to shame the wise, and he chose the weak things of the world to shame the strong. ²⁸He chose what the world thinks is unimportant and what the world looks down

---

1:17 cross Paul uses the cross as a picture of the Good News, the story of Christ's death and rising from the dead for people's sins. The cross, or Christ's death, was God's way to save people.

on and thinks is nothing in order to destroy what the world thinks is important. ²⁹God did this so that no one can brag in his presence. ³⁰Because of God you are in Christ Jesus, who has become for us wisdom from God. In Christ we are put right with God, and have been made holy, and have been set free from sin. ³¹So, as the Scripture says, "If people want to brag, they should brag only about the Lord."ⁿ

THE MESSAGE OF CHRIST'S DEATH

2 Dear brothers and sisters, when I came to you, I did not come preaching God's secretⁿ with fancy words or a show of human wisdom. ²I decided that while I was with you I would forget about everything except Jesus Christ and his death on the cross. ³So when I came to you, I was weak and fearful and trembling. ⁴My teaching and preaching were not with words of human wisdom that persuade people but with proof of the power that the Spirit gives. ⁵This was so that your faith would be in God's power and not in human wisdom.

GOD'S WISDOM

⁶However, I speak a wisdom to those who are mature. But this wisdom is not from this world or from the rulers of this world, who are losing their power. ⁷I speak God's secret wisdom, which he has kept hidden. Before the world began, God planned this wisdom for our glory. ⁸None of the rulers of this world understood it. If they had, they would not have crucified the Lord of glory. ⁹But as it is written in the Scriptures:

"No one has ever seen this,
    and no one has ever heard about it.
No one has ever imagined
    what God has prepared for those who
        love him."   *Isaiah 64:4*

¹⁰But God has shown us these things through the Spirit.

The Spirit searches out all things, even the deep secrets of God. ¹¹Who knows the thoughts that another person has? Only a person's spirit that lives within him knows his thoughts. It is the same with God. No one knows the thoughts of God except the Spirit of God. ¹²Now we did not receive the spirit of the world, but we received the Spirit that is from God so that we can know all that God has given us. ¹³And we speak about these

things, not with words taught us by human wisdom but with words taught us by the Spirit. And so we explain spiritual truths to spiritual people. ¹⁴A person who does not have the Spirit does not accept the truths that come from the Spirit of God. That person thinks they are foolish and cannot understand them, because they can only be judged to be true by the Spirit. ¹⁵The spiritual person is able to judge all things, but no one can judge him. The Scripture says:

¹⁶ "Who has known the mind of the Lord?
    Who has been able to teach him?"
                              Isaiah 40:13

But we have the mind of Christ.

FOLLOWING PEOPLE IS WRONG

3 Brothers and sisters, in the past I could not talk to you as I talk to spiritual people. I had to talk to you as I would to people without the Spirit—babies in Christ. ²The teaching I gave you was like milk, not solid food, because you were not able to take solid food. And even now you are not ready. ³You are still not spiritual, because there is jealousy and quarreling among you, and this shows that you are not spiritual. You are acting like people of the world. ⁴One of you says, "I belong to Paul," and another says, "I belong to Apollos." When you say things like this, you are acting like people of the world.

⁵Is Apollos important? No! Is Paul important? No! We are only servants of God who helped you believe. Each one of us did the work God gave us to do. ⁶I planted the seed, and Apollos watered it. But God is the One who made it grow. ⁷So the one who plants is not important, and the one who waters is not important. Only God, who makes things grow, is important. ⁸The one who plants and the one who waters have the same purpose, and each will be rewarded for his own work. ⁹We are God's workers, working together; you are like God's farm, God's house.

¹⁰Using the gift God gave me, I laid the foundation of that house like an expert builder. Others are building on that foundation, but all people should be careful how they build on it. ¹¹The foundation that has

---

1:31 **"If . . . Lord."** Quotation from Jeremiah 9:24.
2:1 **God's secret** Some Greek copies read "God's message."

already been laid is Jesus Christ, and no one can lay down any other foundation. ¹²But if people build on that foundation, using gold, silver, jewels, wood, grass, or straw, ¹³their work will be clearly seen, because the Day of Judgment[n] will make it visible. That Day will appear with fire, and the fire will test everyone's work to show what sort of work it was. ¹⁴If the building that has been put on the foundation still stands, the builder will get a reward. ¹⁵But if the building is burned up, the builder will suffer loss. The builder will be saved, but it will be as one who escaped from a fire.

¹⁶Don't you know that you are God's temple and that God's Spirit lives in you? ¹⁷If anyone destroys God's temple, God will destroy that person, because God's temple is holy and you are that temple.

¹⁸Do not fool yourselves. If you think you are wise in this world, you should become a fool so that you can become truly wise, ¹⁹because the wisdom of this world is foolishness with God. It is written in the Scriptures, "He catches those who are wise in their own clever traps."[n] ²⁰It is also written in the Scriptures, "The Lord knows what wise people think. He knows their thoughts are just a puff of wind."[n] ²¹So you should not brag about human leaders. All things belong to you: ²²Paul, Apollos, and Peter; the world, life, death, the present, and the future—all these belong to

---

3:13 Day of Judgment The day Christ will come to judge all people and take his people home to live with him. **3:19 "He . . . traps."** Quotation from Job 5:13. **3:20 "The Lord . . . wind."** Quotation from Psalm 94:11.

LOSING WEIGHT

FITNESS

God's house

1 CORINTHIANS 3:16

Many of us wake up in the morning and make a checklist for the day. The one item that is missing from many of our lists is something to improve our health. Why is it that we do not include something daily for the good of our very lives? Is it because we forget? Could it be we do not care? Maybe we have never been taught. Or it may be that we have never identified a big enough reason to do it. Perhaps all of these reasons contribute to our lack of effort to live healthy.

As this scripture points out, our bodies actually house God. With this understanding, it becomes much easier to take care of our bodies. Imagine if God were to knock on the front door of your house. If you were like most people, you would run around the house picking up, so the house would be presentable.

We would do this because we would never want God to think that we did not keep a clean house. What if the house we lived in were God's house and we were staying in it temporarily? We would never think of messing up God's house. Yet the truth is that our body is God's house and we need to take care of it.

reflect: Do at least one activity today that enhances your overall health.
Go to **1 Timothy 4:8.**

you. ²³And you belong to Christ, and Christ belongs to God.

APOSTLES ARE SERVANTS OF CHRIST

4 People should think of us as servants of Christ, the ones God has trusted with his secrets. ²Now in this way those who are trusted with something valuable must show they are worthy of that trust. ³As for myself, I do not care if I am judged by you or by any human court. I do not even judge myself. ⁴I know of no wrong I have done, but this does not make me right before the Lord. The Lord is the One who judges me. ⁵So do not judge before the right time; wait until the Lord comes. He will bring to light things that are now hidden in darkness, and will make known the secret purposes of people's hearts. Then God will praise each one of them.

⁶Brothers and sisters, I have used Apollos and myself as examples so you could learn through us the meaning of the saying, "Follow only what is written in the Scriptures." Then you will not be more proud of one person than another. ⁷Who says you are better than others? What do you have that was not given to you? And if it was given to you, why do you brag as if you did not receive it as a gift?

⁸You think you already have everything you need. You think you are rich. You think you have become kings without us. I wish you really were kings so we could be kings together with you. ⁹But it seems to me that God has put us apostles in last place, like those sentenced to die. We are like a show for the whole world to see—angels and people. ¹⁰We are fools for Christ's sake, but you are very wise in Christ. We are weak, but you are strong. You receive honor, but we are shamed. ¹¹Even to this very hour we do not have enough to eat or drink or to wear. We are often beaten, and we have no homes in which to live. ¹²We work hard with our own hands for our food. When people curse us, we bless them. When they hurt us, we put up with it. ¹³When they tell evil lies about us, we speak nice words about them. Even today, we are treated as though we were the garbage of the world—the filth of the earth.

¹⁴I am not trying to make you feel ashamed. I am writing this to give you a warning as my own dear children. ¹⁵For though you may have ten thousand teachers in Christ, you do not have many fathers. Through the Good News I became your father in Christ Jesus, ¹⁶so I beg you, please follow my example. ¹⁷That is why I am sending to you Timothy, my son in the Lord. I love Timothy, and he is faithful. He will help you remember my way of life in Christ Jesus, just as I teach it in all the churches everywhere.

¹⁸Some of you have become proud, thinking that I will not come to you again. ¹⁹But I will come to you very soon if the Lord wishes. Then I will know what the proud ones do, not what they say, ²⁰because the kingdom of God is present not in talk but in power. ²¹Which do you want: that I come to you with punishment or with love and gentleness?

WICKEDNESS IN THE CHURCH

5 It is actually being said that there is sexual sin among you. And it is a kind that does not happen even among people who do not know God. A man there has his father's wife. ²And you are proud! You should have been filled with sadness so that the man who did this should be put out of your group. ³I am not there with you in person, but I am with you in spirit. And I have already judged the man who did that sin as if I were really there. ⁴When you meet together in the name of our Lord Jesus, and I meet with you in spirit with the power of our Lord Jesus, ⁵then hand this man over to Satan. So his sinful selfⁿ will be destroyed, and his spirit will be saved on the day of the Lord.

⁶Your bragging is not good. You know the saying, "Just a little yeast makes the whole batch of dough rise." ⁷Take out all the old yeast so that you will be a new batch of dough without yeast, which you really are. For Christ, our Passover lamb, has been sacrificed. ⁸So let us celebrate this feast, but not with the bread that has the old yeast—the yeast of sin and wickedness. Let us celebrate this feast with the bread that has no yeast—the bread of goodness and truth.

⁹I wrote you in my earlier letter not to associate with those who sin sexually. ¹⁰But I did not mean you should not associate with those of this world who sin sexually, or with

---

5:5 sinful self Literally, "flesh." This could also mean his body.

the greedy, or robbers, or those who worship idols. To get away from them you would have to leave this world. [11]I am writing to tell you that you must not associate with those who call themselves believers in Christ but who sin sexually, or are greedy, or worship idols, or abuse others with words, or get drunk, or cheat people. Do not even eat with people like that.

[12-13]It is not my business to judge those who are not part of the church. God will judge them. But you must judge the people who are part of the church. The Scripture says, "You must get rid of the evil person among you."[n]

JUDGING PROBLEMS AMONG CHRISTIANS

6When you have something against another Christian, how can you bring yourself to go before judges who are not right with God? Why do you not let God's people decide who is right? [2]Surely you know that God's people will judge the world. So if you are to judge the world, are you not able to judge small cases as well? [3]You know that in the future we will judge angels, so surely we can judge the ordinary things of this life. [4]If you have ordinary cases that must be judged, are you going to appoint people as judges who mean nothing to the church? [5]I say this to shame you. Surely there is someone among you wise enough to judge a complaint between believers. [6]But now one believer goes to court against another believer—and you do this in front of unbelievers!

[7]The fact that you have lawsuits against each other shows that you are already defeated. Why not let yourselves be wronged? Why not let yourselves be cheated? [8]But you yourselves do wrong and cheat, and you do this to other believers!

[9-10]Surely you know that the people who do wrong will not inherit God's kingdom. Do not be fooled. Those who sin sexually, worship idols, take part in adultery, those who are male prostitutes, or men who have sexual relations with other men, those who steal, are greedy, get drunk, lie about others, or rob—these people will not inherit God's kingdom. [11]In the past, some of you were like that, but you were washed clean. You were made holy, and you were made right with God in the name of the Lord Jesus Christ and in the Spirit of our God.

USE YOUR BODIES FOR GOD'S GLORY

[12]"I am allowed to do all things," but not all things are good for me to do. "I am allowed to do all things," but I will not let anything make me its slave. [13]"Food is for the stomach, and the stomach for food," but God will destroy them both. The body is not for sexual sin but for the Lord, and the Lord is for the body. [14]By his power God has raised the Lord from the dead and will also raise us from the dead. [15]Surely you know that your bodies are parts of Christ himself. So I must never take the parts of Christ and join them to a prostitute! [16]It is written in the Scriptures, "The two will become one body."[n] So you should know that anyone who joins with a prostitute becomes one body with the prostitute. [17]But the one who joins with the Lord is one spirit with the Lord.

[18]So run away from sexual sin. Every other sin people do is outside their bodies, but those who sin sexually sin against their own bodies. [19]You should know that your body is a temple for the Holy Spirit who is in you. You have received the Holy Spirit from God. So you do not belong to yourselves, [20]because you were bought by God for a price. So honor God with your bodies.

ABOUT MARRIAGE

7Now I will discuss the things you wrote me about. It is good for a man not to have sexual relations with a woman. [2]But because sexual sin is a danger, each man should have his own wife, and each woman should have her own husband. [3]The husband should give his wife all that he owes her as his wife. And the wife should give her husband all that she owes him as her husband. [4]The wife does not have full rights over her own body; her husband shares them. And the husband does not have full rights over his own body; his wife shares them. [5]Do not refuse to give your bodies to each other, unless you both agree to stay away from sexual relations for a time so you can give your time to prayer. Then come together again so Satan cannot tempt you because of a lack of self-control. [6]I say this to give you permission to stay away from sexual

---

5:12–13 "You . . . you." Quotation from Deuteronomy 17:7; 19:19; 22:21, 24; 24:7. **6:16 "The two . . . body."** Quotation from Genesis 2:24.

relations for a time. It is not a command to do so. **7**I wish that everyone were like me, but each person has his own gift from God. One has one gift, another has another gift.

8Now for those who are not married and for the widows I say this: It is good for them to stay unmarried as I am. **9**But if they cannot control themselves, they should marry. It is better to marry than to burn with sexual desire.

10Now I give this command for the married people. (The command is not from me; it is from the Lord.) A wife should not leave her husband. **11**But if she does leave, she must not marry again, or she should make up with her husband. Also the husband should not divorce his wife.

12For all the others I say this (I am saying this, not the Lord): If a Christian man has a wife who is not a believer, and she is happy to live with him, he must not divorce her. **13**And if a Christian woman has a husband who is not a believer, and he is happy to live with her, she must not divorce him. **14**The husband who is not a believer is made holy through his believing wife. And the wife who is not a believer is made holy through her believing husband. If this were not true, your children would not be clean, but now your children are holy.

15But if those who are not believers decide to leave, let them leave. When this happens, the Christian man or woman is free. But God called us[n] to live in peace. **16**Wife, you don't know; maybe you will save your husband. And husband, you don't know; maybe you will save your wife.

7:15 us Some Greek copies read "you."

---

inspiration over motivation

FITNESS

1 CORINTHIANS 6:20

The Bible tells us to "honor God with your bodies." When we understand that the body is by God and is his temple, it's a lot easier to become not only motivated to take care of it short-term, but inspired to take care of it long-term.

God's love for us is not altered by what we look like or our fitness levels. Yet our good health and optimum longevity are certainly important and pleasing to God. It's easy for Christians to neglect their bodies when they think that the spirit is what is of primary importance.

But the results of bad health apply to families of believers and nonbelievers alike. A forty-year-old dying of cancer or a four-year-old with leukemia is horrifying, no matter what your beliefs are. If we care for our children's health, how much more so must our Father in heaven care for our health? You, your body by God, and your health, mean everything to God. Make God happy. In addition to having faith in him, honor him by honoring your body by God.

reflect: Honor God with your body by taking good care of it today.
Go to **FITNESS:** "The One Percent Solution" at **2 Peter 1:5.**

LIVE AS GOD CALLED YOU

¹⁷But in any case each one of you should continue to live the way God has given you to live—the way you were when God called you. This is a rule I make in all the churches. ¹⁸If a man was already circumcised when he was called, he should not undo his circumcision. If a man was without circumcision when he was called, he should not be circumcised. ¹⁹It is not important if a man is circumcised or not. The important thing is obeying God's commands. ²⁰Each one of you should stay the way you were when God called you. ²¹If you were a slave when God called you, do not let that bother you. But if you can be free, then make good use of your freedom. ²²Those who were slaves when the Lord called them are free persons who belong to the Lord. In the same way, those who were free when they were called are now Christ's slaves. ²³You all were bought at a great price, so do not become slaves of people. ²⁴Brothers and sisters, each of you should stay as you were when you were called, and stay there with God.

QUESTIONS ABOUT GETTING MARRIED

²⁵Now I write about people who are not married. I have no command from the Lord about this; I give my opinion. But I can be trusted, because the Lord has shown me mercy. ²⁶The present time is a time of trouble,

---

FAMILY

LOVE IS MORE THAN GIVING

understanding and meeting your spouse's needs

1 CORINTHIANS 7:4   By Jimmy Evans

There are certain needs in your life that no human being can meet: identity, security, acceptance, and purpose. Only Jesus Christ can meet these needs. However, you have needs that your spouse has to meet. These are legitimate needs that both of you need to meet for each other. This is part of God's design for marriage, as it establishes a bond of intimacy that cannot be penetrated by anyone or anything else. Meeting each other's needs creates and maintains the attraction, intimacy, and satisfaction of the relationship and minimizes the risk of outside attraction and affairs.

Major problems can be encountered in trying to meet each other's needs. Foremost is the failure to understand inherent differences between the sexes. Men and women are different by God's design. Accept and understand the differences between you and your spouse. One of a man's primary needs is sex. One of a woman's primary needs is affection. When we try to translate their need into our language, it results in rejection. We both say what we need, but we don't believe each other.

If you're selfish, you resent being told what your spouse's needs are. You are insensitive and uncaring about the needs of your spouse. The four major needs of a man are honor, sex, kindred fellowship, and domestic support. The four major needs of a woman are security, affection, honest communication, and leadership.

reflect: Are you meeting the needs of your spouse daily?

Go to **Colossians 3:18.**

so I think it is good for you to stay the way you are. ²⁷If you have a wife, do not try to become free from her. If you are not married, do not try to find a wife. ²⁸But if you decide to marry, you have not sinned. And if a girl who has never married decides to marry, she has not sinned. But those who marry will have trouble in this life, and I want you to be free from trouble.

²⁹Brothers and sisters, this is what I mean: We do not have much time left. So starting now, those who have wives should live as if they had no wives. ³⁰Those who are crying should live as if they were not crying. Those who are happy should live as if they were not happy. Those who buy things should live as if they own nothing. ³¹Those who use the things of the world should live as if they were not using them, because this world in its present form will soon be gone.

³²I want you to be free from worry. A man who is not married is busy with the Lord's work, trying to please the Lord. ³³But a man who is married is busy with things of the world, trying to please his wife. ³⁴He must think about two things—pleasing his wife and pleasing the Lord. A woman who is not married or a girl who has never married is busy with the Lord's work. She wants to be holy in body and spirit. But a married woman is busy with things of the world, as to how she can please her husband. ³⁵I am saying this to help you, not to limit you. But I want you to live in the right way, to give yourselves fully to the Lord without concern for other things.

³⁶If a man thinks he is not doing the right thing with the girl he is engaged to, if she is almost past the best age to marry and he feels he should marry her, he should do what he wants. They should get married. It is no sin. ³⁷But if a man is sure in his mind that there is no need for marriage, and has his own desires under control, and has decided not to marry the one to whom he is engaged, he is doing the right thing. ³⁸So the man who marries his girl does right, but the man who does not marry will do better.

³⁹A woman must stay with her husband as long as he lives. But if her husband dies, she is free to marry any man she wants, but she must marry another believer. ⁴⁰The woman is happier if she does not marry again. This is my opinion, but I believe I also have God's Spirit.

ABOUT FOOD OFFERED TO IDOLS

8 Now I will write about meat that is sacrificed to idols. We know that "we all have knowledge." Knowledge puffs you up with pride, but love builds up. ²If you think you know something, you do not yet know anything as you should. ³But if any person loves God, that person is known by God.

⁴So this is what I say about eating meat sacrificed to idols: We know that an idol is really nothing in the world, and we know there is only one God. ⁵Even though there are things called gods, in heaven or on earth (and there are many "gods" and "lords"), ⁶for us there is only one God—our Father. All things came from him, and we live for him. And there is only one Lord—Jesus Christ. All things were made through him, and we also were made through him.

⁷But not all people know this. Some people are still so used to idols that when they eat meat, they still think of it as being sacrificed to an idol. Because their conscience is weak, when they eat it, they feel guilty. ⁸But food will not bring us closer to God. Refusing to eat does not make us less pleasing to God, and eating does not make us better in God's sight.

⁹But be careful that your freedom does not cause those who are weak in faith to fall into sin. ¹⁰Suppose one of you who has knowledge eats in an idol's temple.ⁿ Someone who is weak in faith might see you eating there and be encourag to eat meat sacrificed to idols while thin   it is wrong to do so. ¹¹This weak believ   whom Christ died is ruined because of   "knowledge." ¹²When you sin against   brothers and sisters in Christ like this and cause them to do what they feel is wrong, you are also sinning against Christ. ¹³So if the food I eat causes them to fall into sin, I will never eat meat again so that I will not cause any of them to sin.

PAUL IS LIKE THE OTHER APOSTLES

9 I am a free man. I am an apostle. I have seen Jesus our Lord. You people are all an example of my work in the Lord. ²If others do not accept me as an apostle, surely you do, because you are proof that I am an apostle in the Lord.

8:10 idol's temple Building where a god is worshiped.

³This is the answer I give people who want to judge me: ⁴Do we not have the right to eat and drink? ⁵Do we not have the right to bring a believing wife with us when we travel as do the other apostles and the Lord's brothers and Peter? ⁶Are Barnabas and I the only ones who must work to earn our living? ⁷No soldier ever serves in the army and pays his own salary. No one ever plants a vineyard without eating some of the grapes. No person takes care of a flock without drinking some of the milk.

⁸I do not say this by human authority; God's law also says the same thing. ⁹It is written in the law of Moses: "When an ox is working in the grain, do not cover its mouth to keep it from eating."ⁿ When God said this, was he thinking only about oxen? No. ¹⁰He was really talking about us. Yes, that Scripture was written for us, because it goes on to say: "The one who plows and the one who works in the grain should hope to get some of the grain for their work." ¹¹Since we planted spiritual seed among you, is it too much if we should harvest material things? ¹²If others have the right to get something from you, surely we have this right, too. But we do not use it. No, we put up with everything ourselves so that we will not keep anyone from believing the Good News of Christ. ¹³Surely you know that those who work at the Temple get their food from the Temple, and those who serve at the altar get part of what is offered at the altar. ¹⁴In the same way, the Lord has commanded that those who tell the Good News should get their living from this work.

¹⁵But I have not used any of these rights. And I am not writing this now to get anything from you. I would rather die than to have my reason for bragging taken away. ¹⁶Telling the Good News does not give me any reason for bragging. Telling the Good News is my duty—something I must do. And how terrible it will be for me if I do not tell the Good News. ¹⁷If I preach because it is my own choice, I have a reward. But if I preach and it is not my choice to do so, I am only doing the duty that was given to me. ¹⁸So what reward do I get? This is my reward: that when I tell the Good News I can offer it freely. I do not use my full rights in my work of preaching the Good News.

¹⁹I am free and belong to no one. But I make myself a slave to all people to win as many as I can. ²⁰To the Jews I became like a Jew to win the Jews. I myself am not ruled by the law. But to those who are ruled by the law I became like a person who is ruled by the law. I did this to win those who are ruled by the law. ²¹To those who are without the law I became like a person who is without the law. I did this to win those people who are without the law. (But really, I am not without God's law—I am ruled by Christ's law.) ²²To those who are weak, I became weak so I could win the weak. I have become all things to all people so I could save some of them in any way possible. ²³I do all this because of the Good News and so I can share in its blessings.

²⁴You know that in a race all the runners run, but only one gets the prize. So run to win! ²⁵All those who compete in the games use self-control so they can win a crown. That crown is an earthly thing that lasts only a short time, but our crown will never be destroyed. ²⁶So I do not run without a goal. I fight like a boxer who is hitting something—not just the air. ²⁷I treat my body hard and make it my slave so that I myself will not be disqualified after I have preached to others.

WARNINGS FROM ISRAEL'S PAST

10 Brothers and sisters, I want you to know what happened to our ancestors who followed Moses. They were all under the cloud and all went through the sea. ²They were all baptized as followers of Moses in the cloud and in the sea. ³They all ate the same spiritual food, ⁴and all drank the same spiritual drink. They drank from that spiritual rock that followed them, and that rock was Christ. ⁵But God was not pleased with most of them, so they died in the desert.

⁶And these things happened as examples for us, to stop us from wanting evil things as those people did. ⁷Do not worship idols, as some of them did. Just as it is written in the Scriptures: "They sat down to eat and drink, and then they got up and sinned sexually."ⁿ ⁸We must not take part in sexual sins, as some of them did. In one day twenty-three thousand of them died because of their sins.

9:9 "When an ox . . . eating." Quotation from Deuteronomy 25:4. 10:7 "They . . . sexually." Quotation from Exodus 32:6.

⁹We must not test Christ as some of them did; they were killed by snakes. ¹⁰Do not complain as some of them did; they were killed by the angel that destroys.

¹¹The things that happened to those people are examples. They were written down to teach us, because we live in a time when all these things of the past have reached their goal. ¹²If you think you are strong, you should be careful not to fall. ¹³The only temptation that has come to you is that which everyone has. But you can trust God, who will not permit you to be tempted more than you can stand. But when you are tempted, he will also give you a way to escape so that you will be able to stand it.

¹⁴So, my dear friends, run away from the worship of idols. ¹⁵I am speaking to you as to reasonable people; judge for yourselves what I say. ¹⁶We give thanks for the cup of

---

THE ONE PERCENT SOLUTION

losing weight

FITNESS

By Jim Garlow

1 CORINTHIANS 9:24-27

Our weight-loss experiences can have applications to the spiritual arena of our lives.

Why do some people, after years of failure, successfully lose a lot of weight? The first reason is simple—desperation. When they finally decide they are tired of being overweight, they do something. Are you desperate to grow spiritually? The psalmist wrote, "I thirst for the living God" (Psalm 42:2). That's good desperation.

The second reason is acknowledgement of a need for help. People have to humble themselves and admit they can't do it alone. What's that have to do with our spiritual lives? A lot! We need Christ.

The third reason is application of certain skills. Amazingly, if we do what we're supposed to do, the pounds drop off. What's the spiritual application? God says, "If you obey me, these blessings will come to you."

The fourth reason is the help that comes from meeting with others. If people go to a weight-loss group, others help and encourage them. The spiritual application: God says, "If you want to grow spiritually, then once every seven days be at the house of worship."

Finally, there is tremendous power in a vision. People who want to lose weight have a vision of themselves all decked out in the latest fashions and in a smaller size. Do you have a vision for your spiritual life? Can you get a glimpse of the dream that God has for you? Let that dream grip you, and it will take you where you want to go.

reflect: Are you desperate to become all that God has designed you to be?
Go to **Titus 2:12**.

blessing,[1] which is a sharing in the blood of Christ. And the bread that we break is a sharing in the body of Christ. [17]Because there is one loaf of bread, we who are many are one body, because we all share that one loaf.

[18]Think about the Israelites: Do not those who eat the sacrifices share in the altar? [19]I do not mean that the food sacrificed to an idol is important. I do not mean that an idol is anything at all. [20]But I say that what is sacrificed to idols is offered to demons, not to God. And I do not want you to share anything with de-

mons. [21]You cannot drink the cup of the Lord and the cup of demons also. You cannot share in the Lord's table and the table of demons. [22]Are we trying to make the Lord jealous? We are not stronger than he is, are we?

HOW TO USE CHRISTIAN FREEDOM

[23]"We are allowed to do all things," but not all things are good for us to do. "We are

---

10:16 cup of blessing The cup of the fruit of the vine that Christians thank God for and drink at the Lord's Supper.

SOWING AND REAPING

the **promise** of **protection**

1 CORINTHIAN   3

One of the ways that God is faithful is in protecting us from temptations that we just can't handle. God is the God of true fidelity. He is completely dependable, acting with confident assurance that his promises will be fulfilled. His promises are worthy, steadfast, truthful, sincere, and irrevocable. The call for us to have faith is of the same character as God's faithfulness toward us. While we can often only wish that we were unalterably reliable, our vacillation in believing simply strengthens how unwavering God is toward us. God never falters in his love for us.

This verse is especially important for those of us who are leaving behind a past of bad decisions. It tells us immediately that we are not alone—that our problems are common to humanity and that God recognizes their ubiquity. But more than this, God promises to protect us even in our temptations to succumb to sin. He is faithful never to allow a temptation to become so overpowering that it entices us beyond our limits.

He will always be there, ready to help, prepared to do battle for us, available to support us through the struggle. This does not promise that the temptation will vanish but that we will have victory within it, that we will endure it and learn surrender in the process. We can count on him to see us through.

No area of modern life is more subject to temptation than finances. But even here, God promises to protect us. We can rejoice that he has not given us more than we can handle. Life is not about accumulation of wealth, but about submission to divine will.

reflect: Trust God to deliver you from every temptation that you face in life.
Go to **2 Corinthians 5:18.**

allowed to do all things," but not all things help others grow stronger. 24Do not look out only for yourselves. Look out for the good of others also.

25Eat any meat that is sold in the meat market. Do not ask questions about it. 26You may eat it, "because the earth belongs to the Lord, and everything in it."[n]

27Those who are not believers may invite you to eat with them. If you want to go, eat anything that is put before you. Do not ask questions about it. 28But if anyone says to you, "That food was offered to idols," do not eat it. Do not eat it because of that person who told you and because eating it might be thought to be wrong. 29I don't mean you think it is wrong, but the other person might. But why, you ask, should my freedom be judged by someone else's conscience? 30If I eat the meal with thankfulness, why am I criticized because of something for which I thank God?

31The answer is, if you eat or drink, or if you do anything, do it all for the glory of God. 32Never do anything that might hurt others— Jews, Greeks, or God's church— 33just as I, also, try to please everybody in every way. I am not trying to do what is good for me but what is good for most people so they can be saved.

11 Follow my example, as I follow the example of Christ.

BEING UNDER AUTHORITY

2I praise you because you remember me in everything, and you follow closely the teachings just as I gave them to you. 3But I want you to understand this: The head of every man is Christ, the head of a woman is the man,[n] and the head of Christ is God. 4Every man who prays or prophesies with his head covered brings shame to his head. 5But every woman who prays or prophesies with her head uncovered brings shame to her head. She is the same as a woman who has her head shaved. 6If a woman does not cover her head, she should have her hair cut off. But since it is shameful for a woman to cut off her hair or to shave her head, she should cover her head. 7But a man should not cover his head, because he is the likeness and glory of God. But woman is man's glory. 8Man did not come from woman, but woman

came from man. 9And man was not made for woman, but woman was made for man. 10So that is why a woman should have a symbol of authority on her head, because of the angels.

11But in the Lord women are not independent of men, and men are not independent of women. 12This is true because woman came from man, but also man is born from woman. But everything comes from God. 13Decide this for yourselves: Is it right for a woman to pray to God with her head uncovered? 14Even nature itself teaches you that wearing long hair is shameful for a man. 15But long hair is a woman's glory. Long hair is given to her as a covering. 16Some people may still want to argue about this, but I would add that neither we nor the churches of God have any other practice.

THE LORD'S SUPPER

17In the things I tell you now I do not praise you, because when you come together you do more harm than good. 18First, I hear that when you meet together as a church you are divided, and I believe some of this. 19(It is necessary to have differences among you so that it may be clear which of you really have God's approval.) 20When you come together, you are not really eating the Lord's Supper.[n] 21This is because when you eat, each person eats without waiting for the others. Some people do not get enough to eat, while others have too much to drink. 22You can eat and drink in your own homes! You seem to think God's church is not important, and you embarrass those who are poor. What should I tell you? Should I praise you? I do not praise you for doing this.

23The teaching I gave you is the same teaching I received from the Lord: On the night when the Lord Jesus was handed over to be killed, he took bread 24and gave thanks for it. Then he broke the bread and said, "This is my body; it is[n] for you. Do this to remember me." 25In the same way, after they ate, Jesus took the cup. He said, "This cup is the new agreement that is sealed with the blood of my death. When you drink this, do it

---

10:26 "because . . . it" Quotation from Psalms 24:1; 50:12; 89:11. **11:3 the man** This could also mean "her husband." **11:20 Lord's Supper** The meal Jesus told his followers to eat to remember him (Luke 22:14–20). **11:24 it is** Some Greek copies read "it is broken."

to remember me." ²⁶Every time you eat this bread and drink this cup you are telling others about the Lord's death until he comes.

²⁷So a person who eats the bread or drinks the cup of the Lord in a way that is not worthy of it will be guilty of sinning against the body and the blood of the Lord. ²⁸Look into your own hearts before you eat the bread and drink the cup, ²⁹because all who eat the bread and drink the cup without recognizing the body eat and drink judgment against themselves. ³⁰That is why many in your group are

sick and weak, and some of you have died. ³¹But if we judged ourselves in the right way, God would not judge us. ³²But when the Lord judges us, he disciplines us so that we will not be destroyed along with the world.

³³So my brothers and sisters, when you come together to eat, wait for each other. ³⁴Anyone who is too hungry should eat at home so that in meeting together you will not bring God's judgment on yourselves. I will tell you what to do about the other things when I come.

GUILT AND GRACE

FAMILY

becoming a **helper**

1 CORINTHIANS 11:7–9

In Genesis 2:18, God says, "I will make a helper who is right for [the man]." There were many choices for the correct word to use in this verse about God's decision to make a woman. The Bible could have used "woman," "wife," "female," or something else. But God chose the Hebrew word for helper, *ezer*. This is quite an unusual choice.

First, *ezer* is masculine gender. Like most Romance languages, nouns are either masculine or feminine, even if they are about tables and chairs. Here, the noun is masculine, but it is about "woman."

Second, this same noun is used to describe God's relationship to Israel. God is the *helper* of his chosen people. Finally, other uses of this word in the Bible give the sense of "save from danger," "deliver from death," and "succor." The context shows that this word carries the idea of help from one who has superior strength.

God is so clever. Here, at the creation of "woman," he taught us that she is the one who will be our strength, who will deliver and save us. Moreover, by using the masculine noun, God tells us that she is completely equal. Finally, God reminds us that she plays the same role with men as he does with Israel. All of this is buried in one small word.

How did we ever come to think women were not equal, were not important, or were not to be respected? God never endorsed any of those lies. God created the perfect match for a man. And she is called "woman."

reflect: Thank God for the gift of women and for the strength they provide as helpers.
Go to **Song of Songs 5:1.**

GIFTS FROM THE HOLY SPIRIT

12 Now, brothers and sisters, I want you to understand about spiritual gifts. ²You know the way you lived before you were believers. You let yourselves be influenced and led away to worship idols—things that could not speak. ³So I want you to understand that no one who is speaking with the help of God's Spirit says, "Jesus be cursed." And no one can say, "Jesus is Lord," without the help of the Holy Spirit.

⁴There are different kinds of gifts, but they are all from the same Spirit. ⁵There are different ways to serve but the same Lord to serve. ⁶And there are different ways that God works through people but the same God. God works in all of us in everything we do. ⁷Something from the Spirit can be seen in each person, for the common good. ⁸The Spirit gives one person the ability to speak with wisdom, and the same Spirit gives another the ability to speak with knowledge. ⁹The same Spirit gives faith to one person. And, to another, that one Spirit gives gifts of healing. ¹⁰The Spirit gives to another person the power to do miracles, to another the ability to prophesy. And he gives to another the ability to know the difference between good and evil spirits. The Spirit gives one person the ability to speak in different kinds of languages[n] and to another the ability to interpret those languages. ¹¹One Spirit, the same Spirit, does all these things, and the Spirit decides what to give each person.

THE BODY OF CHRIST WORKS TOGETHER

¹²A person's body is one thing, but it has many parts. Though there are many parts to a body, all those parts make only one body. Christ is like that also. ¹³Some of us are Jews, and some are Greeks. Some of us are slaves, and some are free. But we were all baptized into one body through one Spirit. And we were all made to share in the one Spirit.

¹⁴The human body has many parts. ¹⁵The foot might say, "Because I am not a hand, I am not part of the body." But saying this would not stop the foot from being a part of the body. ¹⁶The ear might say, "Because I am not an eye, I am not part of the body." But saying this would not stop the ear from being a part of the body. ¹⁷If the whole body were an eye, it would not be able to hear. If the whole body were an ear, it would not be able to smell. ¹⁸⁻¹⁹If each part of the body were the same part, there would be no body. But truly God put all the parts, each one of them, in the body as he wanted them. ²⁰So then there are many parts, but only one body.

²¹The eye cannot say to the hand, "I don't need you!" And the head cannot say to the foot, "I don't need you!" ²²No! Those parts of the body that seem to be the weaker are really necessary. ²³And the parts of the body we think are less deserving are the parts to which we give the most honor. We give special respect to the parts we want to hide. ²⁴The more respectable parts of our body need no special care. But God put the body together and gave more honor to the parts that need it ²⁵so our body would not be divided. God wanted the different parts to care the same for each other. ²⁶If one part of the body suffers, all the other parts suffer with it. Or if one part of our body is honored, all the other parts share its honor.

²⁷Together you are the body of Christ, and each one of you is a part of that body. ²⁸In the church God has given a place first to apostles, second to prophets, and third to teachers. Then God has given a place to those who do miracles, those who have gifts of healing, those who can help others, those who are able to govern, and those who can speak in different languages.[n] ²⁹Not all are apostles. Not all are prophets. Not all are teachers. Not all do miracles. ³⁰Not all have gifts of healing. Not all speak in different languages. Not all interpret those languages. ³¹But you should truly want to have the greater gifts.

LOVE IS THE GREATEST GIFT

And now I will show you the best way of all.

13 I may speak in different languages[n] of people or even angels. But if I do not have love, I am only a noisy bell or a crashing cymbal. ²I may have the gift of prophecy. I may understand all the secret things of God and have all knowledge, and I may have faith so great I can move mountains. But even with all these things, if I do not have love, then I

12:10; 12:28; 13:1 **languages** This can also be translated "tongues."

am nothing. ³I may give away everything I have, and I may even give my body as an offering to be burned.ⁿ But I gain nothing if I do not have love.

⁴Love is patient and kind. Love is not jealous, it does not brag, and it is not proud. ⁵Love is not rude, is not selfish, and does not get upset with others. Love does not count up wrongs that have been done. ⁶Love takes no pleasure in evil but rejoices over the truth. ⁷Love patiently accepts all things. It always trusts, always hopes, and always endures.

⁸Love never ends. There are gifts of prophecy, but they will be ended. There are gifts of speaking in different languages, but those gifts will stop. There is the gift of knowledge, but it will come to an end. ⁹The reason is that our knowledge and our ability to prophesy are not perfect. ¹⁰But when perfection comes, the things that are not perfect will end. ¹¹When I was a child, I talked like a child, I thought like a child, I reasoned like a child. When I became a man, I stopped those childish ways. ¹²It is the same with us. Now we see a dim reflection, as if we were looking into a mirror, but then we shall see clearly. Now I know only a part, but then I will know fully, as God has known me. ¹³So these three things continue forever: faith, hope, and love. And the greatest of these is love.

DESIRE SPIRITUAL GIFTS

14 You should seek after love, and you should truly want to have the spiritual gifts, especially the gift of prophecy. ²I will explain why. Those who have the gift of speaking in different languagesⁿ are not speaking to people; they are speaking to God. No one understands them; they are speaking secret things through the Spirit. ³But those who prophesy are speaking to people to give them strength, encouragement, and comfort. ⁴The ones who speak in different languages are helping only themselves, but those who prophesy are helping the whole church. ⁵I wish all of you had the gift of speaking in different kinds of languages, but more, I wish you would prophesy. Those who prophesy are greater than those who can only speak in different languages—unless someone is there who can explain what is said so that the whole church can be helped.

⁶Brothers and sisters, will it help you if I come to you speaking in different languages? No! It will help you only if I bring you a new truth or some new knowledge, or prophecy, or teaching. ⁷It is the same as with lifeless things that make sounds—like a flute or a harp. If they do not make clear musical notes, you will not know what is being played. ⁸And in a war, if the trumpet does not give a clear sound, who will prepare for battle? ⁹It is the same with you. Unless you speak clearly with your tongue, no one can understand what you are saying. You will be talking into the air! ¹⁰It may be true that there are all kinds of sounds in the world, and none is without meaning. ¹¹But unless I understand the meaning of what someone says to me, we will be like foreigners to each other. ¹²It is the same with you. Since you want spiritual gifts very much, seek most of all to have the gifts that help the church grow stronger.

¹³The one who has the gift of speaking in a different language should pray for the gift to interpret what is spoken. ¹⁴If I pray in a different language, my spirit is praying, but my mind does nothing. ¹⁵So what should I do? I will pray with my spirit, but I will also pray with my mind. I will sing with my spirit, but I will also sing with my mind. ¹⁶If you praise God with your spirit, those persons there without understanding cannot say amenⁿ to your prayer of thanks, because they do not know what you are saying. ¹⁷You may be thanking God in a good way, but the other person is not helped.

¹⁸I thank God that I speak in different kinds of languages more than all of you. ¹⁹But in the church meetings I would rather speak five words I understand in order to teach others than thousands of words in a different language.

²⁰Brothers and sisters, do not think like children. In evil things be like babies, but in your thinking you should be like adults. ²¹It is written in the Scriptures:

"With people who use strange words and
   foreign languages

13:3 give...burned Other Greek copies read "hand over my body in order that I may brag." **14:2 languages** This can also be translated "tongues." **14:16 amen** To say amen means to agree with the things that were said.

I will speak to these people.
But even then they will not listen to me,"
Isaiah 28:11–12
says the Lord.

22So the gift of speaking in different kinds of languages is a sign for those who do not believe, not for those who do believe. And prophecy is for people who believe, not for those who do not believe. 23Suppose the whole church meets together and everyone speaks in different languages. If some people come in who do not understand or do not believe, they will say you are crazy. 24But suppose everyone is prophesying and some people come in who do not believe or do not understand. If everyone is prophesying, their sin will be shown to them, and they will be judged by all that they hear. 25The secret things in their hearts will be made known. So they will bow down and worship God saying, "Truly, God is with you."

MEETINGS SHOULD HELP THE CHURCH

26So, brothers and sisters, what should you do? When you meet together, one person has a song, and another has a teaching. Another has a new truth from God. Another speaks in a different language,[n] and another person interprets that language. The purpose of all these things should be to help the church grow strong. 27When you meet together, if anyone speaks in a different language, it should be only two, or not more than three, who speak. They should speak one after the other, and someone should interpret. 28But if there is no interpreter, then those who speak in a different language should be quiet in the church meeting. They should speak only to themselves and to God.

29Only two or three prophets should speak, and the others should judge what they say. 30If a message from God comes to another person who is sitting, the first speaker should stop. 31You can all prophesy one after the other. In this way all the people can be taught and encouraged. 32The spirits of prophets are under the control of the prophets themselves. 33God is not a God of confusion but a God of peace.

As is true in all the churches of God's people, 34women should keep quiet in the church meetings. They are not allowed to speak, but they must yield to this rule as the law says. 35If they want to learn something, they should ask their own husbands at home. It is shameful for a woman to speak in the church meeting. 36Did God's teaching come from you? Or are you the only ones to whom it has come?

37Those who think they are prophets or spiritual persons should understand that what I am writing to you is the Lord's command. 38Those who ignore this will be ignored by God.[n]

39So my brothers and sisters, you should truly want to prophesy. But do not stop people from using the gift of speaking in different kinds of languages. 40But let everything be done in a right and orderly way.

THE GOOD NEWS ABOUT CHRIST

15 Now, brothers and sisters, I want you to remember the Good News I brought to you. You received this Good News and continue strong in it. 2And you are being saved by it if you continue believing what I told you. If you do not, then you believed for nothing.

3I passed on to you what I received, of which this was most important: that Christ died for our sins, as the Scriptures say; 4that he was buried and was raised to life on the third day as the Scriptures say; 5and that he was seen by Peter and then by the twelve apostles. 6After that, Jesus was seen by more than five hundred of the believers at the same time. Most of them are still living today, but some have died. 7Then he was seen by James and later by all the apostles. 8Last of all he was seen by me—as by a person not born at the normal time. 9All the other apostles are greater than I am. I am not even good enough to be called an apostle, because I persecuted the church of God. 10But God's grace has made me what I am, and his grace to me was not wasted. I worked harder than all the other apostles. (But it was not I really; it was God's grace that was with me.) 11So if I preached to you or the other apostles preached to you, we all preach the same thing, and this is what you believed.

WE WILL BE RAISED FROM THE DEAD

12Now since we preached that Christ was raised from the dead, why do some of you say

---

14:26 language This can also be translated "tongue."
14:38 Those . . . God. Some Greek copies read "Those who are ignorant of this will stay ignorant."

that people will not be raised from the dead? [13]If no one is ever raised from the dead, then Christ has not been raised. [14]And if Christ has not been raised, then our preaching is worth nothing, and your faith is worth nothing. [15]And also, we are guilty of lying about God, because we testified of him that he raised Christ from the dead. But if people are not raised from the dead, then God never raised Christ. [16]If the dead are not raised, Christ has not been raised either. [17]And if Christ has not been raised, then your faith has nothing to it;

you are still guilty of your sins. [18]And those in Christ who have already died are lost. [19]If our hope in Christ is for this life only, we should be pitied more than anyone else in the world.

[20]But Christ has truly been raised from the dead—the first one and proof that those who sleep in death will also be raised. [21]Death has come because of what one man did, but the rising from death also comes because of one man. [22]In Adam all of us die. In the same way, in Christ all of us will be made

WHO ARE YOU?

who's stopping you?

FUTURE

1 CORINTHIANS 15:10

Whether it is your health, your wealth, your relationships, or your emotions, there is only one thing on this planet that can stop you . . . you! At some point in history, someone sicker than you recovered, someone poorer than you became rich, someone lonelier than you discovered a relationship, and someone more miserable than you found happiness.

People who feel they have been dealt an insurmountable, unfixable, permanently *lousy* hand, simply believe that they are stuck with the problem and can't make a change or a comeback, no matter how hard they try.

The problem is that people think that issues and illnesses come from outside of them. Then they assume that cures must also come from outside of them. Faulty thinking like this is a disastrous epidemic.

If you believe that positive outcomes and great health are just going to come to you, then you have a slightly less than 10 percent chance of being happy and healthy. However, if you believe that you create health and happiness, you have slightly more than 90 percent chance of finding out it's true.

Take responsibility and authority for your life. Don't give it to anyone else; don't take it from anyone else. God can do anything for you if you'll simply trust him. The power of God inside of you is greater than any outside force arrayed against you.

reflect: Thank God that he is greater than any problem you'll ever face.
Go to **Acts 9:1–22.**

alive again. [23]But everyone will be raised to life in the right order. Christ was first to be raised. When Christ comes again, those who belong to him will be raised to life, [24]and then the end will come. At that time Christ will destroy all rulers, authorities, and powers, and he will hand over the kingdom to God the Father. [25]Christ must rule until he puts all enemies under his control. [26]The last enemy to be destroyed will be death. [27]The Scripture says that God put all things under his control.[n] When it says "all things" are under him, it is clear this does not include God himself. God is the One who put everything under his control. [28]After everything has been put under the Son, then he will put himself under God, who had put all things under him. Then God will be the complete ruler over everything.

[29]If the dead are never raised, what will people do who are being baptized for the dead? If the dead are not raised at all, why are people being baptized for them?

[30]And what about us? Why do we put ourselves in danger every hour? [31]I die every day. That is true, brothers and sisters, just as it is true that I brag about you in Christ Jesus our Lord. [32]If I fought wild animals in Ephesus only with human hopes, I have gained nothing. If the dead are not raised, "Let us eat and drink, because tomorrow we will die."[n]

[33]Do not be fooled: "Bad friends will ruin good habits." [34]Come back to your right way of thinking and stop sinning. Some of you do not know God—I say this to shame you.

WHAT KIND OF BODY WILL WE HAVE?

[35]But someone may ask, "How are the dead raised? What kind of body will they have?" [36]Foolish person! When you sow a seed, it must die in the ground before it can live and grow. [37]And when you sow it, it does not have the same "body" it will have later. What you sow is only a bare seed, maybe wheat or something else. [38]But God gives it a body that he has planned for it, and God gives each kind of seed its own body. [39]All things made of flesh are not the same: People have one kind of flesh, animals have another, birds have another, and fish have another. [40]Also there are heavenly bodies and earthly bodies. But the beauty of the heavenly bodies is one kind, and the beauty of the earthly bodies is another. [41]The sun has one kind of beauty, the moon has another beauty, and the stars have another. And each star is different in its beauty.

[42]It is the same with the dead who are raised to life. The body that is "planted" will ruin and decay, but it is raised to a life that cannot be destroyed. [43]When the body is "planted," it is without honor, but it is raised in glory. When the body is "planted," it is weak, but when it is raised, it is powerful. [44]The body that is "planted" is a physical body. When it is raised, it is a spiritual body.

There is a physical body, and there is also a spiritual body. [45]It is written in the Scriptures: "The first man, Adam, became a living person."[n] But the last Adam became a spirit that gives life. [46]The spiritual did not come first, but the physical and then the spiritual. [47]The first man came from the dust of the earth. The second man came from heaven. [48]People who belong to the earth are like the first man of earth. But those people who belong to heaven are like the man of heaven. [49]Just as we were made like the man of earth, so we will[n] also be made like the man of heaven.

[50]I tell you this, brothers and sisters: Flesh and blood cannot have a part in the kingdom of God. Something that will ruin cannot have a part in something that never ruins. [51]But look! I tell you this secret: We will not all sleep in death, but we will all be changed. [52]It will take only a second—as quickly as an eye blinks—when the last trumpet sounds. The trumpet will sound, and those who have died will be raised to live forever, and we will all be changed. [53]This body that can be destroyed must clothe itself with something that can never be destroyed. And this body that dies must clothe itself with something that can never die. [54]So this body that can be destroyed will clothe itself with that which can never be destroyed, and this body that dies will clothe itself with that which can never die. When this happens, this Scripture will be made true:

15:27 God put...control. From Psalm 8:6. **15:32 "Let us...die."** Quotation from Isaiah 22:13; 56:12. **15:45 "The first...person."** Quotation from Genesis 2:7. **15:49 so we will** Some Greek copies read "so let us."

"Death is destroyed forever in victory."
Isaiah 25:8

⁵⁵ "Death, where is your victory?

Death, where is your pain?" *Hosea 13:14*

⁵⁶Death's power to hurt is sin, and the power of sin is the law. ⁵⁷But we thank God! He gives us the victory through our Lord Jesus Christ.

⁵⁸So my dear brothers and sisters, stand strong. Do not let anything move you. Always give yourselves fully to the work of the Lord, because you know that your work in the Lord is never wasted.

THE GIFT FOR OTHER BELIEVERS

16 Now I will write about the collection of money for God's people. Do the same thing I told the Galatian churches to do: ²On the first day of every week, each one of you should put aside money as you have been blessed. Save it up so you will not have to collect money after I come. ³When I arrive, I will send whomever you approve to take your gift to Jerusalem. I will send them with letters of introduction, ⁴and if it seems good for me to go also, they will go along with me.

A FAMILY CHANGED

FAMILY

conscience of
champions

1 CORINTHIANS 15:34

By Edwin Louis Cole

Your conscience is programmed like a computer—Garbage In, Garbage Out. That is why God gave us his Word. It washes our minds and programs our consciences to operate in righteousness. The restraint of the Holy Spirit keeps us pure before God in thought, word, and deed.

Everything God made, he made perfect, including the act of sex. God's intention for sex is to enable a man and a woman, in the union of marriage, to give themselves unreservedly to each other for mutual benefit and blessing. God's prohibition of sex outside marriage protects sex from the very errors we see because of immorality today, including venereal disease, emotional distress, abortion, divorce, rape, molestation, pornography, and homosexuality. Sin blights and distorts what God creates.

Sexual sins like pornography, homosexuality, and promiscuity are idolatrous. Indulging in perverted fantasies or activities produces a stronghold in your mind and a snare to your life. Sin always promises to please and serve, but, in reality, it always enslaves and dominates. Immorality pollutes. It contaminates and infects your mind and spirit and endangers your body.

Live a life of freedom and fulfillment in the light of God's truth. Program your conscience to righteousness by the Word of God so that you can appreciate and take advantage of God's wonderful gifts.

---

reflect: How might you attune your conscience to righteousness today?

Go to **Proverbs 12:14.**

The **Road** to **Success**

By Dr. Ben Lerner

1 CORINTHIANS 15:58

As first a personal trainer, then a nutritionist, a chiropractor, and business coach, I've always lived in an alternative universe. What I know through training and experience that people need almost always runs counter to what they want or think they need. Additionally, the values I want to instill in them almost always run counter to the values that they're fighting so hard to maintain. In all of these careers, I've had three choices:

1. To abandon my values for others.

2. To compromise my values.

3. To maintain my values.

Ironically, when I do 1 and 2, I usually end up with a whole lot of what I'm trying to avoid. In an effort to make people happy, give them what they "think" they want, and just do or be what they ask, everyone ends up miserable.

As a chiropractor, I often hear people say that they want to be free from pain in a hurry.

However, there is typically an underlying issue that needs to be corrected and maintained in order to substantiate and sustain good health.

As a business coach, my major goal is to help leaders be "service minded." Their attitude may be, however, that they hired me to help them make more, not serve more. If I choose their values, they may make more, but it will be as, or even more, dysfunctional a situation as before, and their team will be even unhappier. If they choose mine, they make a whole lot more, everyone is more fulfilled, and, while it's not always easier, it's more gratifying.

Anyone who compromises his values in thinking that he'll avoid confrontation or gain a shortcut to success, typically ends up with a whole lot of what he has been trying to avoid: more pain, more time, and more controversy. Even if it works in the short run, in the long run quick fixes and flexible integrity always bring disaster. Remember, whatever you compromise to keep, you lose in the process.

TO LEARN MORE ON WHAT THE BIBLE HAS TO SAY ABOUT **FUTURE,** READ THE SCRIPTURES AND DEVOTIONALS AT **PSALM 16:11, PSALM 23:1, PSALM 32:8, PSALM 58:1–3,** AND **DEUTERONOMY 1:8.**

PAUL'S PLANS

⁵I plan to go through Macedonia, so I will come to you after I go through there. ⁶Perhaps I will stay with you for a time or even all winter. Then you can help me on my trip, wherever I go. ⁷I do not want to see you now just in passing. I hope to stay a longer time with you if the Lord allows it. ⁸But I will stay at Ephesus until Pentecost, ⁹because a good opportunity for a great and growing work has been given to me now. And there are many people working against me.

¹⁰If Timothy comes to you, see to it that he has nothing to fear with you, because he is working for the Lord just as I am. ¹¹So none of you should treat Timothy as unimportant, but help him on his trip in peace so that he can come back to me. I am expecting him to come with the brothers.

¹²Now about our brother Apollos: I strongly encouraged him to visit you with the other brothers. He did not at all want to come now; he will come when he has the opportunity.

PAUL ENDS HIS LETTER

¹³Be alert. Continue strong in the faith. Have courage, and be strong. ¹⁴Do everything in love.

¹⁵You know that the family of Stephanas were the first believers in Southern Greece and that they have given themselves to the service of God's people. I ask you, brothers and sisters, ¹⁶to follow the leading of people like these and anyone else who works and serves with them.

¹⁷I am happy that Stephanas, Fortunatus, and Achaicus have come. You are not here, but they have filled your place. ¹⁸They have refreshed my spirit and yours. You should recognize the value of people like these.

¹⁹The churches in Asia send greetings to you. Aquila and Priscilla greet you in the Lord, as does the church that meets in their house. ²⁰All the brothers and sisters here send greetings. Give each other a holy kiss when you meet.

²¹I, Paul, am writing this greeting with my own hand.

²²If anyone does not love the Lord, let him be separated from God—lost forever!

Come, O Lord!

²³The grace of the Lord Jesus be with you.

²⁴My love be with all of you in Christ Jesus.ⁿ

16:24 My ... Jesus. Some Greek copies add "Amen."

2 corinthians

PAUL ANSWERS THOSE WHO ACCUSE HIM

1 From Paul, an apostle of Christ Jesus. I am an apostle because that is what God wanted. Also from Timothy our brother in Christ.

To the church of God in Corinth, and to all of God's people everywhere in Southern Greece:

²Grace and peace to you from God our Father and the Lord Jesus Christ.

PAUL GIVES THANKS TO GOD

³Praise be to the God and Father of our Lord Jesus Christ. God is the Father who is full of mercy and all comfort. ⁴He comforts us every time we have trouble, so when others have trouble, we can comfort them with the same comfort God gives us. ⁵We share in the many sufferings of Christ. In the same way, much comfort comes to us through Christ. ⁶If we have troubles, it is for your comfort and salvation, and if we have comfort, you also have comfort. This helps you to accept patiently the same sufferings we have. ⁷Our hope for you is strong, knowing that you share in our sufferings and also in the comfort we receive.

⁸Brothers and sisters, we want you to know about the trouble we suffered in Asia. We had great burdens there that were beyond our own strength. We even gave up hope of living. ⁹Truly, in our own hearts we believed we would die. But this happened so we would not trust in ourselves but in God, who raises people from the dead. ¹⁰God saved us from these great dangers of death, and he will continue to save us. We have put our hope in him, and he will save us again. ¹¹And you can help us with your prayers. Then many people will give thanks for us—that God blessed us because of their many prayers.

THE CHANGE IN PAUL'S PLANS

¹²This is what we are proud of, and I can say it with a clear conscience: In everything we have done in the world, and especially with you, we have had an honestⁿ and sincere heart from God. We did this by God's grace,

not by the kind of wisdom the world has. ¹³⁻¹⁴We write to you only what you can read and understand. And I hope that as you have understood some things about us, you may come to know everything about us. Then you can be proud of us, as we will be proud of you on the day our Lord Jesus Christ comes again.

¹⁵I was so sure of all this that I made plans to visit you first so you could be blessed twice. ¹⁶I planned to visit you on my way to Macedonia and again on my way back. I wanted to get help from you for my trip to Judea. ¹⁷Do you think that I made these plans without really meaning it? Or maybe you think I make plans as the world does, so that I say yes, yes and at the same time no, no.

¹⁸But since you can believe God, you can believe that what we tell you is never both yes and no. ¹⁹The Son of God, Jesus Christ, that Silas and Timothy and I preached to you, was not yes and no. In Christ it has always been yes. ²⁰The yes to all of God's promises is in Christ, and through Christ we say yes to the glory of God. ²¹Remember, God is the One who makes you and us strong in Christ. God made us his chosen people. ²²He put his mark on us to show that we are his, and he put his Spirit in our hearts to be a guarantee for all he has promised.

²³I tell you this, and I ask God to be my witness that this is true: The reason I did not come back to Corinth was to keep you from being punished or hurt. ²⁴We are not trying to control your faith. You are strong in faith. But we are workers with you for your own joy.

2 So I decided that my next visit to you would not be another one to make you sad. ²If I make you sad, who will make me glad? Only you can make me glad—particularly the person whom I made sad. ³I wrote you a letter for this reason: that when I came to you I would not be made sad by the people

---

1:12 honest Some Greek copies read "holy."

who should make me happy. I felt sure of all of you, that you would share my joy. ⁴When I wrote to you before, I was very troubled and unhappy in my heart, and I wrote with many tears. I did not write to make you sad, but to let you know how much I love you.

FORGIVE THE SINNER

⁵Someone there among you has caused sadness, not to me, but to all of you. I mean he caused sadness to all in some way. (I do not want to make it sound worse than it really is.) ⁶The punishment that most of you gave him is enough for him. ⁷But now you should forgive him and comfort him to keep him from having too much sadness and giving up completely. ⁸So I beg you to show that you love him. ⁹I wrote you to test you and to see if you obey in everything. ¹⁰If you forgive someone, I also forgive him. And what I have forgiven—if I had anything to forgive—I forgave it for you, as if Christ were with me.

¹¹I did this so that Satan would not win anything from us, because we know very well what Satan's plans are.

PAUL'S CONCERN IN TROAS

¹²When I came to Troas to preach the Good News of Christ, the Lord gave me a good opportunity there. ¹³But I had no peace, because I did not find my brother Titus. So I said good-bye to them at Troas and went to Macedonia.

VICTORY THROUGH CHRIST

¹⁴But thanks be to God, who always leads us as captives in Christ's victory parade. God uses us to spread his knowledge everywhere like a sweet-smelling perfume. ¹⁵Our offering to God is this: We are the sweet smell of Christ among those who are being saved and among those who are being lost. ¹⁶To those who are lost, we are the smell of death that brings death, but to those who are being

---

UNWAVERING FAITH

FAITH

the **gift** of **encouragement**

2 CORINTHIANS 1:3-4

Once upon a time five frogs were traveling through the woods. Two of the frogs fell into a deep pit. The other frogs saw how deep the pit was and told the two frogs at the bottom that they would never get out. The two frogs ignored the words that were spoken and tried as hard as they could to get out of the pit. The others kept telling them that they were as good as dead.

One of the frogs listened to what the group was saying and finally gave up. He fell down and died. But the frog that was left kept jumping as hard as he could. Finally, the little frog jumped out. The group of frogs went over to him and asked, "Why didn't you listen to us and stop jumping?" The little frog told them that he was hard of hearing and he thought that they were cheering for him.

What kind of encouragement are you giving to those who look up to you? Do they need to be deaf to your words to get the right message? Or are you really cheering for them?

reflect: Give someone you love the gift of genuine encouragement today.

Go to **2 Samuel 22:4.**

saved, we are the smell of life that brings life. So who is able to do this work? ¹⁷We do not sell the word of God for a profit as many other people do. But in Christ we speak the truth before God, as messengers of God.

SERVANTS OF THE NEW AGREEMENT

3 Are we starting to brag about ourselves again? Do we need letters of introduction to you or from you, like some other people? ²You yourselves are our letter, written on our hearts, known and read by everyone. ³You show that you are a letter from Christ sent through us. This letter is not written with ink but with the Spirit of the living God. It is not written on stone tablets[n] but on human hearts.

⁴We can say this, because through Christ we feel certain before God. ⁵We are not saying that we can do this work ourselves. It is God who makes us able to do all that we do. ⁶He made us able to be servants of a new agreement from himself to his people. This new agreement is not a written law, but it is of the Spirit. The written law brings death, but the Spirit gives life.

⁷The law that brought death was written in words on stone. It came with God's glory, which made Moses' face so bright that the Israelites could not continue to look at it. But that glory later disappeared. ⁸So surely the new way that brings the Spirit has even more glory. ⁹If the law that judged people guilty of sin had glory, surely the new way that makes people right with God has much greater glory. ¹⁰That old law had glory, but it really loses its glory when it is compared to the much greater glory of this new way. ¹¹If that law which disappeared came with glory, then this new way which continues forever has much greater glory.

¹²We have this hope, so we are very bold.

3:3 **stone tablets** Meaning the Law of Moses that was written on stone tablets (Exodus 24:12; 25:16).

God **doesn't** do **remodeling**

FUTURE

2 CORINTHIANS 3:18

Changing the way you think is not simply a matter of being a better person or trying a little harder. This is not remodeling. God doesn't take the old stuff and change a little of it. He starts over with brand-new materials and a brand-new plan. When we are instructed to renew our minds, we need to remember that the old patterns need to be scrapped so new ones can be put in place.

God never settles for substandard foundations. He builds new construction. That's why the process can be painful at times. The old has to be demolished, not just reconfigured. The old pattern is not up to code. It has to go.

Anytime you find yourself hanging onto some of that old structure, realize that God is building you into exactly what you are designed to be—a brand-new creation with no compromises. It isn't worth sacrificing a new mansion to salvage some old masonry.

reflect: Renew your mind by building your life upon the foundation of God.
Go to **Zephaniah 3:17**.

¹³We are not like Moses, who put a covering over his face so the Israelites would not see it. The glory was disappearing, and Moses did not want them to see it end. ¹⁴But their minds were closed, and even today that same covering hides the meaning when they read the old agreement. That covering is taken away only through Christ. ¹⁵Even today, when they read the law of Moses, there is a covering over their minds. ¹⁶But when a person changes and follows the Lord, that covering is taken away. ¹⁷The Lord is the Spirit, and where the Spirit of the Lord is, there is freedom. ¹⁸Our faces, then, are not covered. We all show the Lord's glory, and we are being changed to be like him. This change in us brings ever greater glory, which comes from the Lord, who is the Spirit.

PREACHING THE GOOD NEWS

4 God, with his mercy, gave us this work to do, so we don't give up. ²But we have turned away from secret and shameful ways.

We use no trickery, and we do not change the teaching of God. We teach the truth plainly, showing everyone who we are. Then they can know in their hearts what kind of people we are in God's sight. ³If the Good News that we preach is hidden, it is hidden only to those who are lost. ⁴The devil who rules this world has blinded the minds of those who do not believe. They cannot see the light of the Good News—the Good News about the glory of Christ, who is exactly like God. ⁵We do not preach about ourselves, but we preach that Jesus Christ is Lord and that we are your servants for Jesus. ⁶God once said, "Let the light shine out of the darkness!" This is the same God who made his light shine in our hearts by letting us know the glory of God that is in the face of Christ.

SPIRITUAL TREASURE IN CLAY JARS

⁷We have this treasure from God, but we are like clay jars that hold the treasure. This shows that the great power is from God, not

---

THE ONE PERCENT SOLUTION

FITNESS

Jesus with skin on

2 CORINTHIANS 4:7

I t's next to impossible to have long-term physical health without a strong spiritual component. And it's next to impossible to function well, mentally or spiritually, when the body is unhealthy, overstressed, and depleted of what it needs.

While the non-Christian world must understand point one, that all fails without God, the Christian world often needs to understand more of point two. We don't want to be so heavenly minded that we're no earthly good. To be sound, effective Christ followers, and to be a support and not a burden on our families, we must do all we can to keep our lives and our bodies in order.

Jesus is the treasure, but your life and your body are the jar in which others find him. How that clay is molded is up to you. What do your life and your lifestyle look like when you decide to become Jesus with skin on?

reflect: Meditate about what it means for you to be "Jesus with skin on."
Go to **Acts 1:14.**

from us. ⁸We have troubles all around us, but we are not defeated. We do not know what to do, but we do not give up the hope of living. ⁹We are persecuted, but God does not leave us. We are hurt sometimes, but we are not destroyed. ¹⁰We carry the death of Jesus in our own bodies so that the life of Jesus can also be seen in our bodies. ¹¹We are alive, but for Jesus we are always in danger of death so that the life of Jesus can be seen in our bodies that die. ¹²So death is working in us, but life is working in you.

¹³It is written in the Scriptures, "I believed, so I spoke."ⁿ Our faith is like this, too. We believe, and so we speak. ¹⁴God raised the Lord Jesus from the dead, and we know that God will also raise us with Jesus. God will bring us together with you, and we will stand before him. ¹⁵All these things are for you. And so the grace of God that is being given to more and more people will bring increasing thanks to God for his glory.

4:13 **"I ... spoke."** Quotation from Psalm 116:10.

A PARTNERSHIP WITH GOD

victory in Jesus

FAITH

By Billy Joe Daugherty   2 CORINTHIANS 4:13

Faith believes what God says in his Word, agrees with it, speaks it, and then acts upon it. Paul describes the spirit of faith in 2 Corinthians 4:13: "I believed, so I spoke." Your faith is like this, also. You believe and so you speak. You speak to your mountain whether it is sickness, financial need, difficulties in your marriage or family, or any other area. You tell it to move, leave, increase, or be repaired. And it does (Mark 11:22-24).

While ministering once I felt prompted to say, "There is someone with a cancer blockage inside of you and God is removing it." There was a woman listening who had been diagnosed with cancer and scheduled for surgery. That word of knowledge took root in her heart, and immediately she responded, "That's me! I claim it!" This woman later had the surgery and her doctor's report was that "a ball of cancer" literally fell out of her body.

Watch your words! You live by faith, so speak from your lips only the promises of God's Word. Free your heart of all unforgiveness so that your faith can operate. A car requires gasoline to run and the fuel that causes your faith to work is *love*. "The important thing is faith—the kind of faith that works through love" (Galatians 5:6). Regardless of the challenging mountains you face, believe and speak the promises of God's Word, and believe that God will quickly carry out his Word.

reflect: Is there a mountain in your life that needs to be moved?
Go to **2 Corinthians 12:9.**

LIVING BY FAITH

¹⁶So we do not give up. Our physical body is becoming older and weaker, but our spirit inside us is made new every day. ¹⁷We have small troubles for a while now, but they are helping us gain an eternal glory that is much greater than the troubles. ¹⁸We set our eyes not on what we see but on what we cannot see. What we see will last only a short time, but what we cannot see will last forever.

5 We know that our body—the tent we live in here on earth—will be destroyed. But when that happens, God will have a house for us. It will not be a house made by human hands; instead, it will be a home in heaven that will last forever. ²But now we groan in this tent. We want God to give us our heavenly home, ³because it will clothe us so we will not be naked. ⁴While we live in this body, we have burdens, and we groan. We do not want to be naked, but we want to be clothed with our heavenly home. Then this body that dies will be fully covered with life. ⁵This is what God made us for, and he has given us the Spirit to be a guarantee for this new life.

⁶So we always have courage. We know that while we live in this body, we are away from the Lord. ⁷We live by what we believe, not by what we can see. ⁸So I say that we have courage. We really want to be away from this body and be at home with the Lord. ⁹Our only goal is to please God whether we live here or there, ¹⁰because we must all stand before Christ to be judged. Each of us will receive what we should get—good or bad—for the things we did in the earthly body.

BECOMING FRIENDS WITH GOD

¹¹Since we know what it means to fear the Lord, we try to help people accept the truth about us. God knows what we really are, and I hope that in your hearts you know, too. ¹²We are not trying to prove ourselves to you again, but we are telling you about ourselves so you will be proud of us. Then you will have an answer for those who are proud about things that

---

BUILDING MOMENTUM THROUGH TEAMWORK

FUTURE

your **new** suit

2 CORINTHIANS 5:17

When we become new people in Christ, our old habits, our old desires, our old character, and our old attitude are changed. But it's more than being totally washed clean and brand-new. We are new creatures. That means we are a new species. We are unique. There is no one else exactly like us. We shed off the old nature like a snake sheds its skin.

Years ago in London, there was a homeless man dressed in tattered clothes. Someone pointed to him and said, "Communism will put a new suit on that man." A Christian standing nearby said, "Yes, but Christ will put a new man in that suit." That is what God will do in our lives if we will let him have control over us. God will change us from the inside out, not from the outside in. Take on your daily duties as a new person, letting God do what he wants with you. Rejoice because you have a new slate to start out with.

reflect: Meditate on what it means to be a new creature in Christ.
Go to **Galatians 4:1-7.**

can be seen rather than what is in the heart. [13]If we are out of our minds, it is for God. If we have our right minds, it is for you. [14]The love of Christ controls us, because we know that One died for all, so all have died. [15]Christ died for all so that those who live would not continue to live for themselves. He died for them and was raised from the dead so that they would live for him.

[16]From this time on we do not think of anyone as the world does. In the past we thought of Christ as the world thinks, but we no longer think of him in that way. [17]If anyone belongs to Christ, there is a new creation. The old things have gone; everything is made new! [18]All this is from God. Through Christ, God made peace between us and himself, and God gave us the work of telling everyone about the peace we can have with him. [19]God was in Christ, making peace between the world and himself. In Christ, God did not hold the world guilty of its sins. And he gave us this message of peace. [20]So we have been sent to speak for Christ. It is as if God is calling to you through

SOWING AND REAPING

debts **paid**

FINANCES

2 CORINTHIANS 5:18

Bankruptcy! Most of us have emotional reactions to that word. We think about the damage to our credit, the embarrassment, and the endless negotiating that will follow. Jesus once told the story of a debtor who was bankrupt. He could not ever repay his debt. But in Jesus' time, there were no bankruptcy laws. If you couldn't pay, you went to prison, and everything you had, including your wife and children, were sold to pay the debt. In Jesus' story, the debtor went to the king and pleaded for mercy. And, amazingly, the king set *aside* the entire debt. That is the Greek word for "reconcile," *katallasso.*

Likewise, this verse tells us that our debt has been completely taken care of by Jesus Christ. There are no strings attached. It is over and done with. It is more than getting rid of a debt. *Allasso* is a verb that means to transform something or to change from what is worse to what is better. It also is used for the idea of exchanging one thing for another.

When we file for bankruptcy, all we do is set aside the collection of the debts we owe. We still owe them, but we prevent the creditors from collecting. But that is not how God works. God transforms our terrible debtor condition into something much better— the state of being completely forgiven. How can he do this? He pays the debt for us. It is fully satisfied. He exchanges the life of his Son for our lives. Reconciliation is the act of actually paying the price for us. We owed debt we could not pay, so Jesus paid debt he did not owe, all for us!

reflect: Meditate on the goodness and faithfulness of God toward humanity.

Go to **FINANCES:** "Attaining Financial Freedom" at **1 Timothy 6:6–10.**

us. We speak for Christ when we beg you to be at peace with God. ²¹Christ had no sin, but God made him become sin so that in Christ we could become right with God.

6 We are workers together with God, so we beg you: Do not let the grace that you received from God be for nothing. ²God says,

"At the right time I heard your prayers.
On the day of salvation I helped you."

Isaiah 49:8

I tell you that the "right time" is now, and the "day of salvation" is now.

³We do not want anyone to find fault with our work, so nothing we do will be a problem for anyone. ⁴But in every way we show we are servants of God: in accepting many hard things, in troubles, in difficulties, and in great problems. ⁵We are beaten and thrown into prison. We meet those who become upset with us and start riots. We work hard, and sometimes we get no sleep or food. ⁶We show we are servants of God by our pure lives, our understanding, patience, and kindness, by the Holy Spirit, by true love, ⁷by speaking the truth, and by God's power. We use our right living to defend ourselves against everything. ⁸Some people honor us, but others blame us. Some people say evil things about us, but others say good things. Some people say we are liars, but we speak the truth. ⁹We are not known, but we are well known. We seem to be dying, but we continue to live. We are punished, but we are not killed. ¹⁰We have much sadness, but we are always rejoicing. We are poor, but we are making many people rich in faith. We have nothing, but really we have everything.

¹¹We have spoken freely to you in Corinth and have opened our hearts to you. ¹²Our feelings of love for you have not stopped, but you have stopped your feelings of love for us. ¹³I speak to you as if you were my children. Do to us as we have done—open your hearts to us.

WARNING ABOUT NON-CHRISTIANS

¹⁴You are not the same as those who do not believe. So do not join yourselves to them. Good and bad do not belong together. Light and darkness cannot share together. ¹⁵How can Christ and Belial, the devil, have any agreement? What can a believer have together with a nonbeliever? ¹⁶The temple of

God cannot have any agreement with idols, and we are the temple of the living God. As God said: "I will live with them and walk with them. And I will be their God, and they will be my people."ⁿ

¹⁷ "Leave those people,
and be separate, says the Lord.
Touch nothing that is unclean,
and I will accept you." *Isaiah 52:11;*
Ezekiel 20:34, 41

¹⁸ "I will be your father,
and you will be my sons and daughters,
says the Lord Almighty." *2 Samuel 7:14*

7 Dear friends, we have these promises from God, so we should make ourselves pure—free from anything that makes body or soul unclean. We should try to become holy in the way we live, because we respect God.

PAUL'S JOY

²Open your hearts to us. We have not done wrong to anyone, we have not ruined the faith of anyone, and we have not cheated anyone. ³I do not say this to blame you. I told you before that we love you so much we would live or die with you. ⁴I feel very sure of you and am very proud of you. You give me much comfort, and in all of our troubles I have great joy.

⁵When we came into Macedonia, we had no rest. We found trouble all around us. We had fighting on the outside and fear on the inside. ⁶But God, who comforts those who are troubled, comforted us when Titus came. ⁷We were comforted, not only by his coming but also by the comfort you gave him. Titus told us about your wish to see me and that you are very sorry for what you did. He also told me about your great care for me, and when I heard this, I was much happier.

⁸Even if my letter made you sad, I am not sorry I wrote it. At first I was sorry, because it made you sad, but you were sad only for a short time. ⁹Now I am happy, not because you were made sad, but because your sorrow made you change your lives. You became sad in the way God wanted you to, so you were not hurt by us in any way. ¹⁰The kind of sorrow God wants makes people change their hearts and lives. This leads to salvation, and

---

6:16 "I . . . people." Quotation from Leviticus 26:11–12; Jeremiah 32:38; Ezekiel 37:27.

Love Is More Than Giving

By Gary Edmonds

2 CORINTHIANS 6:13

My wife Tricia and I have four grown children. They are great kids, great spouses, and great parents. One day last year we were all talking about what it meant to *feel* loved—not merely to *know* that you are loved, but actually to *experience* that you are loved. What I heard from them surprised me.

We talked about the wonderful times that we had spent together: family vacations, skiing trips, dinners around the kitchen table, wrestling on the living room floor, hosting foreign visitors in our home. But the one thing that made a difference in helping them "feel" loved was when we let them love us on their terms and in their style.

Our youngest son talked about the time when he was about three years old. He had one of those perpetual runny noses from a childhood cold. But it was Mother's Day, and he wanted to do something special for his mom. Upstairs he went to get an already used sheet of computer paper. In typical three-year-old fashion, he grabbed his crayons and scribbled lines and circles on the page.

After the masterpiece was created, he went to the backyard to pick a bunch of dandelions. Into the house he marched. With dandelions in one hand, the "masterpiece" in the other, and snot running from his nose, he proudly declared, "Mom, I love you." Then he planted a big wet kiss on my wife's lips. My wife did the most loving act that I have ever seen. She accepted all the treasures and expression of love and returned the kiss, with the words, "Thank you so much for loving me."

Our little runny-nosed three-year-old beamed. Why? Because my wife received with humble gratitude his expression of love. It hit me at that moment that one of the most significant ways that we can show love to our children and spouse is to receive and accept with gratitude the gifts they offer to us. Rather than saying, "Oh, you shouldn't have done that," we say, "Thank you so much for showing love to me." Rather than pretending that we are mature and do not need to know love from others, we humbly and gratefully accept their expressions of affection.

In the church at Corinth, the apostle Paul met a group of Christians who pretended to be superspiritual by operating in a self-reliant and aloof manner. Paul challenged them to "do to us as we have done—open your hearts to us" (2 Corinthians 6:13). He told them to stop traveling the self-destructive path of independence and accept the love, affirmation, and gifts of others. Until we learn how to be loved, we will never love others well.

This is especially true in the family context. Here we are vulnerable. Here it is hard to hide and pretend. Yet, it is precisely in this dynamic that we learn to accept the good, yet still imperfect, gifts of others. It is in a family that we can learn to open our hearts and receive from each other.

TO LEARN MORE ON WHAT THE BIBLE HAS TO SAY ABOUT **FAMILY,** READ THE SCRIPTURES AND DEVOTIONALS AT **ACTS 28:8–9, MATTHEW 23:37, SONG OF SONGS 7:10, 1 CORINTHIANS 7:4, COLOSSIANS 3:18,** AND **EPHESIANS 5:31.**

you cannot be sorry for that. But the kind of sorrow the world has brings death. [11]See what this sorrow—the sorrow God wanted you to have—has done to you: It has made you very serious. It made you want to restore yourselves. It made you angry and afraid. It made you want to see me. It made you care. It made you want to do the right thing. In every way you have regained your innocence. [12]I wrote that letter, not because of the one who did the wrong or because of the person who was hurt. I wrote the letter so you could see, before God, the great care you have for us. [13]That is why we were comforted.

Not only were we very comforted, we were even happier to see that Titus was so happy. All of you made him feel much better. [14]I bragged to Titus about you, and you showed that I was right. Everything we said to you was true, and you have proved that what we bragged about to Titus is true. [15]And his love for you is stronger when he remembers that you were all ready to obey. You welcomed him with respect and fear. [16]I am very happy that I can trust you fully.

CHRISTIAN GIVING

8 And now, brothers and sisters, we want you to know about the grace God gave the churches in Macedonia. [2]They have been tested by great troubles, and they are very poor. But they gave much because of their great joy. [3]I can tell you that they gave as much as they were able and even more than they could afford. No one told them to do it. [4]But they begged and pleaded with us to let them share in this service for God's people. [5]And they gave in a way we did not expect: They first gave themselves to the Lord and to us. This is what God wants. [6]So we asked Titus to help you finish this special work of grace since he is the one who started it. [7]You are rich in everything—in faith, in speaking, in knowledge, in truly wanting to help, and in the love you learned from us.[n] In the same way, be strong also in the grace of giving.

[8]I am not commanding you to give. But I want to see if your love is true by comparing you with others that really want to help. [9]You know the grace of our Lord Jesus Christ. You know that Christ was rich, but for you he became poor so that by his becoming poor you might become rich.

[10]This is what I think you should do: Last year you were the first to want to give, and you were the first who gave. [11]So now finish the work you started. Then your "doing" will be equal to your "wanting to do." Give from what you have. [12]If you want to give, your gift will be accepted. It will be judged by what you have, not by what you do not have. [13]We do not want you to have troubles while other people are at ease, but we want everything to be equal. [14]At this time you have plenty. What you have can help others who are in need. Then later, when they have plenty, they can help you when you are in need, and all will be equal. [15]As it is written in the Scriptures, "The person who gathered more did not have too much, nor did the person who gathered less have too little."[n]

TITUS AND HIS COMPANIONS HELP

[16]I thank God because he gave Titus the same love for you that I have. [17]Titus accepted what we asked him to do. He wanted very much to go to you, and this was his own idea. [18]We are sending with him the brother who is praised by all the churches because of his service in preaching the Good News. [19]Also, this brother was chosen by the churches to go with us when we deliver this gift of money. We are doing this service to bring glory to the Lord and to show that we really want to help.

[20]We are being careful so that no one will criticize us for the way we are handling this large gift. [21]We are trying hard to do what the Lord accepts as right and also what people think is right.

[22]Also, we are sending with them our brother, who is always ready to help. He has proved this to us in many ways, and he wants to help even more now, because he has much faith in you. [23]Now about Titus—he is my partner who is working with me to help you. And about the other brothers—they are sent from the churches, and they bring glory to Christ. [24]So show these men the proof of your love and the reason we are proud of you. Then all the churches can see it.

8:7 in . . . us Some Greek copies read "in your love for us." **8:15 "The person . . . little."** Quotation from Exodus 16:18.

HELP FOR FELLOW CHRISTIANS

9 I really do not need to write you about this help for God's people. ²I know you want to help. I have been bragging about this to the people in Macedonia, telling them that you in Southern Greece have been ready to give since last year. And your desire to give has made most of them ready to give also. ³But I am sending the brothers to you so that our bragging about you in this will not be empty words. I want you to be ready, as I said you would be. ⁴If any of the people from Macedonia come with me and find that you are not ready, we will be ashamed that we were so sure of you. (And you will be ashamed, too!) ⁵So I thought I should ask these brothers to go to you before we do. They will finish getting in order the generous gift you promised so it will be ready when we come. And it will be a generous gift—not one that you did not want to give.

⁶Remember this: The person who plants a little will have a small harvest, but the person who plants a lot will have a big harvest. ⁷Each of you should give as you have decided in your heart to give. You should not be sad when you give, and you should not give because you feel forced to give. God loves the person who gives happily. ⁸And God can give you more blessings than you need. Then you will always have plenty of everything— enough to give to every good work. ⁹It is written in the Scriptures:

"He gives freely to the poor.
The things he does are right and will
continue forever."   *Psalm 112:9*

¹⁰God is the One who gives seed to the farmer and bread for food. He will give you all the

---

ATTAINING FINANCIAL FREEDOM

how do **you give?**

FINANCES

2 CORINTHIANS 8:5

Giving is not an obligation. If you give because you think you have to, then it is not a gift, but a payment. Paul commends these believers because of their attitude about giving. They had a deep desire to share what they had for the expansion of God's kingdom. God certainly counted them as cheerful givers.

Today we find many who believe that giving to God is like a magic financial formula. They seem to think of God as some investment broker. So they give out of a desire for personal gain. Or they give out of guilt. Either way, their gifts are nothing but payments. They do not come with a generous and gracious heart.

One of the basic principles of finance under the banner of God's authority is giving. But God is far more interested in the attitude and motive than in the amount. When you give to his work, no one will know why you wrote that check except you and him. But without an attitude check to go along with the bank check, it might just be a false statement. When you genuinely give from your heart, you give it cheerfully and with no strings attached.

reflect: Give to God with a generous and gracious heart of thankfulness.

Go to **2 Corinthians 9:7.**

seed you need and make it grow so there will be a great harvest from your goodness. ¹¹He will make you rich in every way so that you can always give freely. And your giving through us will cause many to give thanks to God. ¹²This service you do not only helps the needs of God's people, it also brings many more thanks to God. ¹³It is a proof of your faith. Many people will praise God because you obey the Good News of Christ—the gospel you say you believe—and because you freely share with them and with all others. ¹⁴And when they pray, they will wish they could be with you because of the great grace that God has given you. ¹⁵Thanks be to God for his gift that is too wonderful for words.

PAUL DEFENDS HIS MINISTRY

10 I, Paul, am begging you with the gentleness and the kindness of Christ. Some people say that I am easy on you when I am with you and bold when I am away. ²They think we live in a worldly way, and I plan to be very bold with them when I come. I beg you that when I come I will not need to use that same boldness with you. ³We do live in the world, but we do not fight in the same way the world fights. ⁴We fight with weapons that are different from those the world uses. Our weapons have power from God that can destroy the enemy's strong places. We destroy people's arguments ⁵and every proud thing that raises itself against the knowledge

FINANCES

ATTAINING FINANCIAL FREEDOM

cheerful giving

2 CORINTHIANS 9:7

Are you a cheerful giver? Or do you give out of a sense of obligation or guilt? When you hear about tithing, are you delighted or chagrined? When the request comes to give to a charity, are you anxious to come up with more ways to provide, or do you worry about how you will make ends meet?

God's Word makes it fairly clear that *attitude* is the key to giving. You can give, without giving it a thought. God doesn't want your money. He wants your heart. And if you have given him your heart, you realize that what you give of your money will never be enough to repay the debt you owe him. Cheerful giving comes from the realization that all that we have is his gift to us. How can we ever give enough to repay him for saving our lives?

If God is the Creator, he owns everything. If he is the Creator, he is quite capable of doing anything he wishes. Technically, he doesn't need us at all. He certainly doesn't *need* our money. But he has arranged the universe in such a way that we have the opportunity to express our love to him by giving back to him what he gave to us in the first place. How awesome is that? He even gets excited for us as we give it back to him. We become cheerful givers by simply changing our perspective from getting to giving.

reflect: Give happily, and giving will become a blessing instead of a burden.
Go to **Galatians 4:18.**

of God. We capture every thought and make it give up and obey Christ. 6We are ready to punish anyone there who does not obey, but first we want you to obey fully.

7You must look at the facts before you. If you feel sure that you belong to Christ, you must remember that we belong to Christ just as you do. 8It is true that we brag freely about the authority the Lord gave us. But this authority is to build you up, not to tear you down. So I will not be ashamed. 9I do not want you to think I am trying to scare you with my letters. 10Some people say, "Paul's letters are powerful and sound important, but when he is with us, he is weak. And his speaking is nothing." 11They should know this: We are not there with you now, so we say these things in letters. But when we are there with you, we will show the same authority that we show in our letters.

12We do not dare to compare ourselves with those who think they are very important. They use themselves to measure themselves, and they judge themselves by what they themselves are. This shows that they know nothing. 13But we will not brag about things outside the work that was given us to do. We will limit our bragging to the work that God gave us, and this includes our work with you. 14We are not bragging too much, as we would be if we had not already come to you. But we have come to you with the Good News of Christ. 15We limit our bragging to the work that is ours, not what others have done. We hope that as your faith continues to grow, you will help our work to grow much larger. 16We want to tell the Good News in the areas beyond your city. We do not want to brag about work that has already been done in another person's area. 17But, "If people want to brag, they should brag only about the Lord."n 18It is not those who say they are good who are accepted but those the Lord thinks are good.

PAUL AND THE FALSE APOSTLES

11 I wish you would be patient with me even when I am a little foolish, but you are already doing that. 2I am jealous over you with a jealousy that comes from God. I promised to give you to Christ, as your only husband. I want to give you as his pure bride. 3But I am afraid that your minds will be led away from your true and pure following of Christ just as Eve was tricked by the snake with his evil ways. 4You are very patient with anyone who comes to you and preaches a different Jesus from the one we preached. You are very willing to accept a spirit or gospel that is different from the Spirit and Good News you received from us.

5I do not think that those "great apostles" are any better than I am. 6I may not be a trained speaker, but I do have knowledge. We have shown this to you clearly in every way.

7I preached God's Good News to you without pay. I made myself unimportant to make you important. Do you think that was wrong? 8I accepted pay from other churches, taking their money so I could serve you. 9If I needed something when I was with you, I did not trouble any of you. The brothers who came from Macedonia gave me all that I needed. I did not allow myself to depend on you in any way, and I will never depend on you. 10No one in Southern Greece will stop me from bragging about that. I say this with the truth of Christ in me. 11And why do I not depend on you? Do you think it is because I do not love you? God knows that I love you.

12And I will continue doing what I am doing now, because I want to stop those people from having a reason to brag. They would like to say that the work they brag about is the same as ours. 13Such men are not true apostles but are workers who lie. They change themselves to look like apostles of Christ. 14This does not surprise us. Even Satan changes himself to look like an angel of light.n 15So it does not surprise us if Satan's servants also make themselves look like servants who work for what is right. But in the end they will be punished for what they do.

PAUL TELLS ABOUT HIS SUFFERINGS

16I tell you again: No one should think I am a fool. But if you think so, accept me as you would accept a fool. Then I can brag a little, too. 17When I brag because I feel sure of myself, I am not talking as the Lord would talk but as a fool. 18Many people are bragging about their lives in the world. So I will brag

---

10:17 "If . . . Lord." Quotation from Jeremiah 9:24.
11:14 angel of light Messenger from God. The devil fools people so that they think he is from God.

Beating the Burnout Blues

By Paul L. Walker

2 CORINTHIANS 11:21–33

O n a rainy morning in Georgia, an over-worked, hassled pastor got out of bed, made sure his wife had gone to work and his children had left for school, took the telephone off the hook, and then went back to bed. In his words, "I was burned out. Two months later I resigned from the ministry. Now, what do I do?"

By definition, burnout is perhaps best described as emotional fatigue. It is a kind of exhaustion marked by chronic negativism toward work, life, and other people. It is a persistent feeling of gloom that threatens our lifestyles and changes our moods. Our spirits are down, and we feel like giving up. This condition is sometimes referred to as the burnout blues.

This poses the question: How do we beat the burnout blues? To start with, it is important for us to strive to practice what we preach. This means we turn to the living Word of God to find the for-mula to live a life that beats the burnout problem.

In this regard, the apostle Paul is our model. Here was a man called of God who was literally stretched to the limit. In comparing himself to the parade of false prophets in the church of Corinth, he presented a resume with all the potentiality not only for burnout but a disastrous flameout (2 Corinthians 11:21–33).

As we read this account, we have to ask, "What was the formula that enabled him to hang tough in the face of such adversity? What can we learn from him that will help us beat the burnout blues?" In response, we pick up the story in the Roman jail when Paul was faced with a death sentence for preaching the Good News.

While there, he wrote to the church in Philippi and made a startling statement for a person fac-ing execution—"Be full of joy in the Lord always. I will say again, be full of joy" (Philippians 4:4). From the natural standpoint, such an affirmation makes no sense, but from a spiritual standpoint, the apostle Paul found a formula that gave him the inner resources he needed regardless of the circumstances or situation. Look at verses 6–8:

Do not worry about anything, but pray and ask God for everything you need, always giving thanks. And God's peace, which is so great we cannot understand it, will keep your hearts and minds in Christ Jesus. Brothers and sisters, think about the things that are good and worthy of praise. Think about the things that are true and honorable and right and pure and beautiful and respected.

As a clarion call to each one of us, we hear Paul say that *this* is the way to beat the burnout blues: pray in detail, practice the peace of God and pro-gram your thinking.

Yes, it sounds simple, but it will work! It simply means we have to trust the Holy Spirit to tran-scend whatever the causal factors may be in the burnout experience. It is a matter of growing in grace and living by faith. It is breaking through to a new interactive relationship of communication with God. It is taking God at his Word that we can cast our anxieties on him because he cares for us. With God as our source, we can beat the burnout blues!

TO LEARN MORE ON WHAT THE BIBLE HAS TO SAY ABOUT **FULFILLMENT,** READ THE SCRIPTURES AND DEVOTIONALS AT **1 THESSALONIANS 5:18, 2 TIMOTHY 2:16–17, HEBREWS 3:1, HEBREWS 4:12, 1 JOHN 3:1,** AND **JUDE 24.**

too. [19]You are wise, so you will gladly be patient with fools! [20]You are even patient with those who order you around, or use you, or trick you, or think they are better than you, or hit you in the face. [21]It is shameful to me to say this, but we were too "weak" to do those things to you!

But if anyone else is brave enough to brag, then I also will be brave and brag. (I am talking as a fool.) [22]Are they Hebrews?[n] So am I. Are they Israelites? So am I. Are they from Abraham's family? So am I. [23]Are they serving

Christ? I am serving him more. (I am crazy to talk like this.) I have worked much harder than they. I have been in prison more often. I have been hurt more in beatings. I have been near death many times. [24]Five times the Jews have given me their punishment of thirty-nine lashes with a whip. [25]Three different times I was beaten with rods. One time I was almost stoned to death. Three times I was in

11:22 Hebrews A name for the Jews that some Jews were very proud of.

A PARTNERSHIP WITH GOD

the **power** of **Christ**

FAITH

2 CORINTHIANS 12:9

There is wonderful imagery in the Greek for this verse's word "live" that we just don't see in English. The word is *episkenoo*. It literally means "to pitch a tent in." We don't know what kind of a tentmaker Paul was in the physical world, but in the spiritual world his failure as a tentmaker was the very reason that Jesus could set up a tent in his life.

If you look at this kind of imagery in the Gospels, you will find the same root word "lived" in John 1:14 ("The Word became a human and lived among us"). It is a direct image drawn from the Old Testament idea of the Meeting Tent. God lived in the midst of his people, in the tent he had set up, and now God lives in us, inside the tent he makes in the place where we were unable to cleanse ourselves. You also can say, "I am very happy to brag about my weaknesses. Then Christ's power can live in me."

Do you realize just how powerful this upside-down reality is? Jesus is at home where you feel out of place! When you are sitting in your comfort zone, where you have control of your castle, there's no room for the Meeting Tent of God. God dwells in the midst of *need!* And the reason God doesn't remove that need is because that's his home. Jesus resides in those places where you are least comfortable with your life— where you long to straighten things up and clean house. His glory shines through your inglorious inadequacies.

reflect: Invite God to inhabit every part of the house that is your heart.
Go to **Ephesians 1:22.**

ships that wrecked, and one of those times I spent a night and a day in the sea. 26I have gone on many travels and have been in danger from rivers, thieves, my own people, the Jews, and those who are not Jews. I have been in danger in cities, in places where no one lives, and on the sea. And I have been in danger with false Christians. 27I have done hard and tiring work, and many times I did not sleep. I have been hungry and thirsty, and many times I have been without food. I have been cold and without clothes. 28Besides all this, there is on me every day the load of my concern for all the churches. 29I feel weak every time someone is weak, and I feel upset every time someone is led into sin.

30If I must brag, I will brag about the things that show I am weak. 31God knows I am not lying. He is the God and Father of the Lord Jesus Christ, and he is to be praised forever. 32When I was in Damascus, the governor under King Aretas wanted to arrest me, so he put guards around the city. 33But my friends lowered me in a basket through a hole in the city wall. So I escaped from the governor.

A SPECIAL BLESSING IN PAUL'S LIFE

12 I must continue to brag. It will do no good, but I will talk now about visions and revelations[n] from the Lord. 2I know a man in Christ who was taken up to the third heaven fourteen years ago. I do not know whether the man was in his body or out of his body, but God knows. 3-4And I know that this man was taken up to paradise.[n] I don't know if he was in his body or away from his body, but God knows. He heard things he is not able to explain, things that no human is allowed to tell. 5I will brag about a man like that, but I will not brag about myself, except about my weaknesses. 6But if I wanted to brag about myself, I would not be a fool, because I would be telling the truth. But I will not brag about myself. I do not want people to think more of me than what they see me do or hear me say.

7So that I would not become too proud of the wonderful things that were shown to me, a painful physical problem[n] was given to me. This problem was a messenger from Satan, sent to beat me and keep me from being too proud. 8I begged the Lord three times to take this problem away from me. 9But he said to me, "My grace is enough for you. When you are weak, my power is made perfect in you." So I am very happy to brag about my weaknesses. Then Christ's power can live in me. 10For this reason I am happy when I have weaknesses, insults, hard times, sufferings, and all kinds of troubles for Christ. Because when I am weak, then I am truly strong.

PAUL'S LOVE FOR THE CHRISTIANS

11I have been talking like a fool, but you made me do it. You are the ones who should say good things about me. I am worth nothing, but those "great apostles" are not worth any more than I am! 12When I was with you, I patiently did the things that prove I am an apostle—signs, wonders, and miracles. 13So you received everything that the other churches have received. Only one thing was different: I was not a burden to you. Forgive me for this!

14I am now ready to visit you the third time, and I will not be a burden to you. I want nothing from you, except you. Children should not have to save up to give to their parents. Parents should save to give to their children. 15So I am happy to give everything I have for you, even myself. If I love you more, will you love me less?

16It is clear I was not a burden to you, but you think I was tricky and lied to catch you. 17Did I cheat you by using any of the messengers I sent to you? No, you know I did not. 18I asked Titus to go to you, and I sent our brother with him. Titus did not cheat you, did he? No, you know that Titus and I did the same thing and with the same spirit.

19Do you think we have been defending ourselves to you all this time? We have been speaking in Christ and before God. You are our dear friends, and everything we do is to make you stronger. 20I am afraid that when I come, you will not be what I want you to be, and I will not be what you want me to be. I am afraid that among you there may be arguing, jealousy, anger, selfish fighting, evil talk, gossip, pride, and confusion. 21I am afraid that when I come to you again, my God will

---

12:1 **revelations** Revelation is making known a truth that was hidden. 12:3–4 **paradise** Another word for heaven. 12:7 **painful physical problem** Literally, "thorn in the flesh."

make me ashamed before you. I may be saddened by many of those who have sinned because they have not changed their hearts or turned from their sexual sins and the shameful things they have done.

FINAL WARNINGS AND GREETINGS

13 I will come to you for the third time. "Every case must be proved by two or three witnesses."[n] ²When I was with you the second time, I gave a warning to those who had sinned. Now I am away from you, and I give a warning to all the others. When I come to you again, I will not be easy with them. ³You want proof that Christ is speaking through me. My proof is that he is not weak among you, but he is powerful. ⁴It is true that he was weak when he was killed on the cross, but he lives now by God's power. It is true that we are weak in Christ, but for you we will be alive in Christ by God's power.

⁵Look closely at yourselves. Test yourselves to see if you are living in the faith. You know that Jesus Christ is in you—unless you fail the test. ⁶But I hope you will see that we ourselves have not failed the test. ⁷We pray to God that you will not do anything wrong. It is not important to see that we have passed

13:1 **"Every . . . witnesses."** Quotation from Deuteronomy 19:15.

THE ONE PERCENT SOLUTION

spiritual biopsy

FITNESS

2 CORINTHIANS 13:5

Paul is exhorting us to do a little surgery here. He tells us to make a tiny cut into our outer façade and look under the skin. What do we find? Do we see a man dedicated to God's purposes, or do we find a man who wants God to help him with his own plans? Do we see a woman whose focus is on inner beauty, or do we find a woman who continually worries about her appearance? Do we find people who are willing to stand up for faith, or do we find people who adopt the "don't ask, don't tell" philosophy?

Without a look under the skin, there is no self-examination. We've got to perforate the surface before we can see the real story of dedication, commitment, and repentance. All of us know how easy it is to talk the talk. Paul tells us that life in Christ means more than spouting creeds or following crowds. Life in Christ is about love, joy, peace, patience, kindness, goodness, faithfulness, gentleness, and self-control. Without these fruit of the Spirit, we fail the test.

Are you willing to let the Word of God cut into you like a two-edged sword, exposing your heart of hearts? God is asking you to do a spiritual biopsy. Take a sample of your heart tissue and see if it is clean or cancerous. There is nothing worse than living with an untreated ailment when a cure is readily available.

reflect: Examine your spiritual condition today in light of the Word of God.
Go to **Galatians 6:10.**

the test, but it is important that you do what is right, even if it seems we have failed. ⁸We cannot do anything against the truth, but only for the truth. ⁹We are happy to be weak, if you are strong, and we pray that you will become complete. ¹⁰I am writing this while I am away from you so that when I come I will not have to be harsh in my use of authority. The Lord gave me this authority to build you up, not to tear you down.

¹¹Now, brothers and sisters, I say goodbye. Live in harmony. Do what I have asked you to do. Agree with each other, and live in peace. Then the God of love and peace will be with you.

¹²Greet each other with a holy kiss. ¹³All of God's holy people send greetings to you.

¹⁴The grace of the Lord Jesus Christ, the love of God, and the fellowship of the Holy Spirit be with you all.

CHRISTIANS ARE SAVED BY GRACE

1 From Paul, an apostle. I was not chosen to be an apostle by human beings, nor was I sent from human beings. I was made an apostle through Jesus Christ and God the Father who raised Jesus from the dead. [2]This letter is also from all those of God's family[n] who are with me.

To the churches in Galatia:[n]

[3]Grace and peace to you from God our Father and the Lord Jesus Christ. [4]Jesus gave himself for our sins to free us from this evil world we live in, as God the Father planned. [5]The glory belongs to God forever and ever. Amen.

THE ONLY GOOD NEWS

[6]God, by his grace through Christ, called you to become his people. So I am amazed that you are turning away so quickly and believing something different than the Good News. [7]Really, there is no other Good News. But some people are confusing you; they want to change the Good News of Christ. [8]We preached to you the Good News. So if we ourselves, or even an angel from heaven, should preach to you something different, we should be judged guilty! [9]I said this before, and now I say it again: You have already accepted the Good News. If anyone is preaching something different to you, let that person be judged guilty!

[10]Do you think I am trying to make people accept me? No, God is the One I am trying to please. Am I trying to please people? If I still wanted to please people, I would not be a servant of Christ.

PAUL'S AUTHORITY IS FROM GOD

[11]Brothers and sisters, I want you to know that the Good News I preached to you was not made up by human beings. [12]I did not get it from humans, nor did anyone teach it to me, but Jesus Christ showed it to me.

[13]You have heard about my past life in the Jewish religion. I attacked the church of God and tried to destroy it. [14]I was becoming a leader in the Jewish religion, doing bet-

ter than most other Jews of my age. I tried harder than anyone else to follow the teachings handed down by our ancestors.

[15]But God had special plans for me and set me apart for his work even before I was born. He called me through his grace [16]and showed his son to me so that I might tell the Good News about him to those who are not Jewish. When God called me, I did not get advice or help from any person. [17]I did not go to Jerusalem to see those who were apostles before I was. But, without waiting, I went away to Arabia and later went back to Damascus.

[18]After three years I went to Jerusalem to meet Peter and stayed with him for fifteen days. [19]I met no other apostles, except James, the brother of the Lord. [20]God knows that these things I write are not lies. [21]Later, I went to the areas of Syria and Cilicia.

[22]In Judea the churches in Christ had never met me. [23]They had only heard it said, "This man who was attacking us is now preaching the same faith that he once tried to destroy." [24]And these believers praised God because of me.

OTHER APOSTLES ACCEPTED PAUL

2 After fourteen years I went to Jerusalem again, this time with Barnabas. I also took Titus with me. [2]I went because God showed me I should go. I met with the believers there, and in private I told their leaders the Good News that I preach to the non-Jewish people. I did not want my past work and the work I am now doing to be wasted. [3]Titus was with me, but he was not forced to be circumcised, even though he was a Greek. [4]We talked about this problem because some false believers had come into our group secretly. They came in like spies to overturn the freedom we have in Christ Jesus. They wanted to make us slaves. [5]But we

---

1:2 those . . . family The Greek text says "brothers."
1:2 Galatia Probably the same country where Paul preached and began churches on his first missionary trip. Read the Book of Acts, chapters 13 and 14.

did not give in to those false believers for a minute. We wanted the truth of the Good News to continue for you.

⁶Those leaders who seemed to be important did not change the Good News that I preach. (It doesn't matter to me if they were "important" or not. To God everyone is the same.) ⁷But these leaders saw that I had been given the work of telling the Good News to those who are not Jewish, just as Peter had the work of telling the Jews. ⁸God gave Peter the power to work as an apostle for the Jewish people. But he also gave me the power to work as an apostle for those who are not Jews. ⁹James, Peter, and John, who seemed to be the leaders, understood that God had given me this special grace, so they accepted Barnabas and me. They agreed that they would go to the Jewish people and that we should go to those who are not Jewish. ¹⁰The only thing they asked us was to remember to help the poor—something I really wanted to do.

PAUL SHOWS THAT PETER WAS WRONG

¹¹When Peter came to Antioch, I challenged him to his face, because he was wrong.

LESSONS FROM THE BATTLEFIELD

FUTURE

the **passions** of **life**

GALATIANS 2:20

Some people were perplexed by the title of the popular film, *The Passion of the Christ.* The Greek word for passion is *pathematon,* and it means "sufferings." It is not the emotional experience that we have come to associate with the word "passion." The Greeks saw *passions* as those experiences that overtook life and overwhelmed their abilities to maintain life's balance, including the experiences of fear and pain. Paul points us toward an incredible fact of Christian living: We are called toward suffering as part of the plan of God's purpose to bring us into conformity with the image of his Son.

Too much of our lives is devoted to avoiding the "passions." We run from these intersections with crisis. Yet don't forget that God is good, and all of the time, not just part of it. Therefore, what appears bad—your enemies, your setbacks, and your failures—is only part of the process of God's good plan. What other people mean for bad, God can only have meant for good, because he is good and only does good.

Paul understood this well. If we are to be stripped of our self-sufficiency and wayward independence from God, we often need to embrace pain and fear as part of the roadway of discipleship and maturity. God doesn't always take us this way. There are exceptions to the rule. But for most of us, learning to rely entirely on him will mean some difficult and agonizing days. We are to trust God *through* the passions of this life, just as Jesus did.

reflect: Realize that the path to maturity often involves sharing the sufferings of Christ.
Go to **1 John 2:13-14.**

[12]Peter ate with the non-Jewish people until some Jewish people sent from James came to Antioch. When they arrived, Peter stopped eating with those who weren't Jewish, and he separated himself from them. He was afraid of the Jews. [13]So Peter was a hypocrite, as were the other Jewish believers who joined with him. Even Barnabas was influenced by what these Jewish believers did. [14]When I saw they were not following the truth of the Good News, I spoke to Peter in front of them all. I said, "Peter, you are a Jew, but you are not living like a Jew. You are living like those who are not Jewish. So why do you now try to force those who are not Jewish to live like Jews?"

[15]We were not born as non-Jewish "sinners," but as Jews. [16]Yet we know that a person is made right with God not by following the law, but by trusting in Jesus Christ. So we, too, have put our faith in Christ Jesus, that we might be made right with God because we trusted in Christ. It is not because we followed the law, because no one can be made right with God by following the law.

[17]We Jews came to Christ, trying to be made right with God, and it became clear that we are sinners, too. Does this mean that Christ encourages sin? No! [18]But I would really be wrong to begin teaching again those things that I gave up. [19]It was the law that put me to death, and I died to the law so that I can now live for God. [20]I was put to death on the cross with Christ, and I do not live anymore—it is Christ who lives in me. I still live in my body, but I live by faith in the Son of God who loved me and gave himself to save me. [21]By saying these things I am not going against God's grace. Just the opposite, if the law could make us right with God, then Christ's death would be useless.

BLESSING COMES THROUGH FAITH

3 You people in Galatia were told very clearly about the death of Jesus Christ on the cross. But you were foolish; you let someone trick you. [2]Tell me this one thing: How did you receive the Holy Spirit? Did you receive the Spirit by following the law? No, you received the Spirit because you heard the Good News and believed it. [3]You began your life in Christ by the Spirit. Now are you trying to make it complete by your own power?

That is foolish. [4]Were all your experiences wasted? I hope not! [5]Does God give you the Spirit and work miracles among you because you follow the law? No, he does these things because you heard the Good News and believed it.

[6]The Scriptures say the same thing about Abraham: "Abraham believed God, and God accepted Abraham's faith, and that faith made him right with God."[n] [7]So you should know that the true children of Abraham are those who have faith. [8]The Scriptures, telling what would happen in the future, said that God would make the non-Jewish people right through their faith. This Good News was told to Abraham beforehand, as the Scripture says: "All nations will be blessed through you."[n] [9]So all who believe as Abraham believed are blessed just as Abraham was. [10]But those who depend on following the law to make them right are under a curse, because the Scriptures say, "Anyone will be cursed who does not always obey what is written in the Book of the Law."[n] [11]Now it is clear that no one can be made right with God by the law, because the Scriptures say, "Those who are right with God will live by faith."[n] [12]The law is not based on faith. It says, "A person who obeys these things will live because of them."[n] [13]Christ took away the curse the law put on us. He changed places with us and put himself under that curse. It is written in the Scriptures, "Anyone whose body is displayed on a tree[n] is cursed." [14]Christ did this so that God's blessing promised to Abraham might come through Jesus Christ to those who are not Jews. Jesus died so that by our believing we could receive the Spirit that God promised.

THE LAW AND THE PROMISE

[15]Brothers and sisters, let us think in human terms: Even an agreement made between two persons is firm. After that agreement is accepted by both people, no one can stop it or add anything to it. [16]God made

---

3:6 "Abraham . . . God." Quotation from Genesis 15:6.
3:8 "All . . . you." Quotation from Genesis 12:3 and 18:18.
3:10 "Anyone . . . Law." Quotation from Deuteronomy 27:26. **3:11 "Those . . . faith."** Quotation from Habakkuk 2:4. **3:12 "A person . . . them."** Quotation from Leviticus 18:5. **3:13 displayed on a tree** Deuteronomy 21:22–23 says that when a person was killed for doing wrong, the body was hung on a tree to show shame. Paul means that the cross of Jesus was like that.

promises both to Abraham and to his descendant. God did not say, "and to your descendants." That would mean many people. But God said, "and to your descendant." That means only one person; that person is Christ. [17]This is what I mean: God had an agreement with Abraham and promised to keep it. The law, which came four hundred thirty years later, cannot change that agreement and so destroy God's promise to Abraham. [18]If the law could give us Abraham's blessing, then the promise would not be necessary. But that is not possible, because God freely gave his blessings to Abraham through the promise he had made.

[19]So what was the law for? It was given to show that the wrong things people do are against God's will. And it continued until the special descendant, who had been promised, came. The law was given through angels who used Moses for a mediator[n] to give the law to people. [20]But a mediator is not needed when there is only one side, and God is only one.

3:19 mediator A person who helps one person talk to or give something to another person.

BUILDING MOMENTUM THROUGH TEAMWORK

a **great life** requires **management**

GALATIANS 4:1-7

By Leon Fontaine

Would you give your toddler an open jar of peanut butter and let him play on your brand-new living room carpet? Absolutely not! At that age, kids are still learning to control themselves. They can't properly understand the purpose of the peanut butter. However, someday that will change, and they'll grow and learn how to manage lots of things.

When we came to know God and became part of his family, there were many things we needed to learn about management. God's Son died for us to provide for our adoption into his family. All his resources are rightfully available to us. He expects us to move beyond the survival stage and develop the ability to manage our own physical and spiritual affairs.

God's Word is our blueprint. The Bible shows us a way to manage everything—love, health, family, money—and grow into the amazing life that God has planned! Dynamic Christian conferences, books, and teaching CDs supply opportunities to increase our management skills. Our life is designed for blessing and abundance, but it absolutely needs management.

God, the ruler of the universe, calls us his children. He sent Jesus and his Spirit to help us, as his heirs, learn to manage with excellence. When we reach spiritual maturity, we can receive and manage our full inheritance, and his promised blessings will overflow our lives.

reflect: How can you grow your God-given abilities?

Go to **FUTURE:** "Lessons from the Battlefield" at **Acts 16:22–30.**

THE PURPOSE OF THE LAW OF MOSES

[21]Does this mean that the law is against God's promises? Never! That would be true only if the law could make us right with God. But God did not give a law that can bring life. [22]Instead, the Scriptures showed that the whole world is bound by sin. This was so the promise would be given through faith to people who believe in Jesus Christ.

[23]Before this faith came, we were all held prisoners by the law. We had no freedom until God showed us the way of faith that was coming. [24]In other words, the law was our guardian leading us to Christ so that we could be made right with God through faith. [25]Now the way of faith has come, and we no longer live under a guardian.

[26-27]You were all baptized into Christ, and so you were all clothed with Christ. This means that you are all children of God through faith in Christ Jesus. [28]In Christ, there is no difference between Jew and Greek, slave and free person, male and female. You are all the same in Christ Jesus. [29]You belong to Christ, so you are Abraham's descendants. You will inherit all of God's blessings because of the promise God made to Abraham.

4 I want to tell you this: While those who will inherit their fathers' property are still children, they are no different from slaves. It does not matter that the children own everything. [2]While they are children, they must obey those who are chosen to care for them. But when the children reach the age set by their fathers, they are free. [3]It is the same for us. We were once like children, slaves to the useless rules of this world. [4]But when the right time came, God sent his Son who was born of a woman and lived under the law. [5]God did this so he could buy freedom for those who were under the law and so we could become his children.

[6]Since you are God's children, God sent the Spirit of his Son into your hearts, and the Spirit cries out, "Father."[n] [7]So now you are not a slave; you are God's child, and God will give you the blessing he promised, because you are his child.

PAUL'S LOVE FOR THE CHRISTIANS

[8]In the past you did not know God. You were slaves to gods that were not real. [9]But now you know the true God. Really, it is God who knows you. So why do you turn back to those weak and useless rules you followed before? Do you want to be slaves to those things again? [10]You still follow teachings about special days, months, seasons, and years. [11]I am afraid for you, that my work for you has been wasted.

[12]Brothers and sisters, I became like you, so I beg you to become like me. You were very good to me before. [13]You remember that it was because of an illness that I came to you the first time, preaching the Good News. [14]Though my sickness was a trouble for you, you did not hate me or make me leave. But you welcomed me as an angel from God, as if I were Jesus Christ himself! [15]You were very happy then, but where is that joy now? I am ready to testify that you would have taken out your eyes and given them to me if that were possible. [16]Now am I your enemy because I tell you the truth?

[17]Those people[n] are working hard to persuade you, but this is not good for you. They want to persuade you to turn against us and follow only them. [18]It is good for people to show interest in you, but only if their purpose is good. This is always true, not just when I am with you. [19]My little children, again I feel the pain of childbirth for you until you truly become like Christ. [20]I wish I could be with you now and could change the way I am talking to you, because I do not know what to think about you.

THE EXAMPLE OF HAGAR AND SARAH

[21]Some of you still want to be under the law. Tell me, do you know what the law says? [22]The Scriptures say that Abraham had two sons. The mother of one son was a slave woman, and the mother of the other son was a free woman. [23]Abraham's son from the slave woman was born in the normal human way. But the son from the free woman was born because of the promise God made to Abraham.

[24]This story teaches something else: The two women are like the two agreements between God and his people. One agreement is the law that God made on Mount Sinai,[n] and the people who are under this agreement are

---

4:6 "Father" Literally, "Abba, Father." Jewish children called their fathers "Abba." **4:17 Those people** They are the false teachers who were bothering the believers in Galatia (Galatians 1:7). **4:24 Mount Sinai** Mountain in Arabia where God gave his Law to Moses (Exodus 19 and 20).

like slaves. The mother named Hagar is like that agreement. 25She is like Mount Sinai in Arabia and is a picture of the earthly city of Jerusalem. This city and its people are slaves to the law. 26But the heavenly Jerusalem, which is above, is like the free woman. She is our mother. 27It is written in the Scriptures:

"Be happy, Jerusalem.
    You are like a woman who never gave
        birth to children.
    Start singing and shout for joy.
    You never felt the pain of giving birth,
    but you will have more children
        than the woman who has a husband."
                                    Isaiah 54:1

28My brothers and sisters, you are God's children because of his promise, as Isaac was

then. 29The son who was born in the normal way treated the other son badly. It is the same today. 30But what does the Scripture say? "Throw out the slave woman and her son. The son of the slave woman should not inherit anything. The son of the free woman should receive it all.'" 31So, my brothers and sisters, we are not children of the slave woman, but of the free woman.

KEEP YOUR FREEDOM

5 We have freedom now, because Christ made us free. So stand strong. Do not change and go back into the slavery of the law. 2Listen, I Paul tell you that if you go back to the law by being circumcised, Christ does

---

4:30 **"Throw . . . all."** Quotation from Genesis 21:10.

ATTAINING FINANCIAL FREEDOM

FINANCES

prosperity on
purpose

GALATIANS 4:18

When you are in a managerial position it is very challenging to motivate your staff to work with zeal and do a job with excellence. There are many ways leaders try to motivate people. There is the hard way: through enforcing tough rules and regulations. Or there is the easy way: through bonuses and positive reinforcement. Both ways seem to meet with limitations over time or even backfire altogether.

The godly way to inspire is by helping people find their purpose. Rules won't do it. And money only does it if they can feel fulfilled in making it. We're all born to serve God's purposes. That is why people have an attraction to a group bigger than themselves with a purpose bigger then their own. Helping people realize why God put them on earth and helping them see how they can really make a difference in even the little things they do every day will fire them up and cause them to want to do a great job for you.

If you want to make a ton of money, get some people excited about your vision and the purpose you serve. We were all put here to be wildly successful at serving the purpose God has for us. Even more, we were meant to enjoy it, work hard at it, and sustain it. An employee on purpose is one who stays and one who pays.

---

reflect: Motivate others by getting them to pursue their purpose.

Go to **Galatians 5:1.**

you no good. ³Again, I warn every man: If you allow yourselves to be circumcised, you must follow all the law. ⁴If you try to be made right with God through the law, your life with Christ is over—you have left God's grace. ⁵But we have the true hope that comes from being made right with God, and by the Spirit we wait eagerly for this hope. ⁶When we are in Christ Jesus, it is not important if we are circumcised or not. The important thing is faith—the kind of faith that works through love.

⁷You were running a good race. Who stopped you from following the true way? ⁸This change did not come from the One who chose you. ⁹Be careful! "Just a little yeast makes the whole batch of dough rise." ¹⁰But

I trust in the Lord that you will not believe those different ideas. Whoever is confusing you with such ideas will be punished.

¹¹My brothers and sisters, I do not teach that a man must be circumcised. If I teach circumcision, why am I still being attacked? If I still taught circumcision, my preaching about the cross would not be a problem. ¹²I wish the people who are bothering you would castrate[n] themselves!

¹³My brothers and sisters, God called you to be free, but do not use your freedom

5:12 castrate To cut off part of the male sex organ. Paul uses this word because it is similar to "circumcision." Paul wanted to show that he is very upset with the false teachers.

ATTAINING FINANCIAL FREEDOM

standing strong

 FINANCES

GALATIANS 5:1

Paul was a theologically educated Jew. He knew that the idea of standing strong was used in the Greek translation of the Old Testament to describe the stability of God's agreement with his people. God's promises stand strong. Nothing can overthrow them. God actively involves himself in the process of accomplishing his promises in the agreement. God does not stand still. He is the God who acts. Paul exhorts Christians to take the same posture toward their own commitment. In this sense, standing strong is a description of power, not just of resolute confrontation.

Standing strong is applied to several important concepts in the Christian's life. First, the Bible says that God himself stands strong on his Word. Second, the church stands strong on its foundation in Jesus. Marriage is the opportunity to stand strong in personal commitment to another. Standing strong in faith brings joy and grace.

Christians must stand strong on the message of the Good News in Jesus Christ. Prayer helps us stand strong. All of this practice will help us stand against evil. Finally, the day will come when we will stand before God's judgment. In modern terms, we might say something like this: Take a stand for your beliefs. Stand up and be counted. But you don't stand alone. God is standing strong right beside you.

reflect: Are you standing strong on the promises of God?
Go to **Proverbs 11:28.**

Sowing and Reaping

FINANCES

By James Robison

GALATIANS 6:9

The concept of sowing and reaping is an important aspect of giving. In 2 Corinthians 9, the apostle Paul gives the framework for the law of the harvest. Unfortunately, this biblical principle has become so distorted in recent years that many people have missed out on the intended meaning. Clearly, Paul's focus is on giving, not receiving.

Have you ever met a farmer? He prepares the ground, plants the seed, tends to it, prays for sun and rain—and he will plant again. If his field gets hailed out, stormed out, stomped out, or washed out, he's still going to plant again. Why? He's a farmer, not a miner.

I can take you to Colorado and show you more abandoned mine shafts than you might imagine. Or we can go to the fertile foothills of Colorado and see where farmers invested in the land that will sell for hundreds of thousands of dollars because it's been well taken care of.

A miner seeks to extract resources for his own benefit, whereas a farmer continually invests in the ground, improving it and trusting God for the increase. If you become a farmer because someone said you can make a hundredfold return on your harvest, the first time you hit trouble, you won't farm again.

Another known fact about farming is that farmers don't yield the same amount of crops. One of the huge deceptions in some personal prosperity teaching is the notion that everybody is going to have a big house, big car, or big income. This concept promotes a "sameness" mentality, and it is simply not scriptural.

No two farmers get exactly the same amount of rain and exactly the same yield in their crop. In fact, godly farmers may not have as good a harvest as their ungodly neighbors. It happens!

Some people—even righteous individuals—will be tested. They may seem to have problems, challenges, and pressures that others don't battle. It may seem unfair, but remember, God is in control. Through life's challenges, the Lord often gives people an opportunity to share a powerful testimony that will minister to others.

Giving is the essence of life. Jesus wants us to understand this principle. If we release that which he has freely given us, I believe with all my heart he will increase it—for his purpose. It isn't so that we can build bigger barns, but so we can know what it means to live life abundantly.

Those who focus on earthly treasures and receiving a blessing may get a lot of stuff, but they will not experience fullness of life nor fullness of joy. In the end, they will rot with their stuff. Imagine how much the Father in heaven wants to bless children who can be trusted to release his resources to kingdom purposes.

Where is your heart? If you're just looking for a return, you're a miner. God wants us to be farmers for kingdom purpose. If you will be faithful, Scripture says "at the right time" you will reap a harvest. "We must not become tired of doing good. We will receive our harvest of eternal life at the right time if we do not give up" (Galatians 6:9).

TO LEARN MORE ON WHAT THE BIBLE HAS TO SAY ABOUT **FINANCES,** READ THE SCRIPTURES AND DEVOTIONALS AT **LUKE 12:42–48, LUKE 16:9–13, LUKE 5:1–11, GENESIS 8:22, 1 CORINTHIANS 10:13,** AND **2 CORINTHIANS 5:18.**

as an excuse to do what pleases your sinful self. Serve each other with love. ¹⁴The whole law is made complete in this one command: "Love your neighbor as you love yourself."ⁿ ¹⁵If you go on hurting each other and tearing each other apart, be careful, or you will completely destroy each other.

THE SPIRIT AND HUMAN NATURE

¹⁶So I tell you: Live by following the Spirit. Then you will not do what your sinful selves want. ¹⁷Our sinful selves want what is against the Spirit, and the Spirit wants what is against our sinful selves. The two are against each other, so you cannot do just what you please. ¹⁸But if the Spirit is leading you, you are not under the law.

¹⁹The wrong things the sinful self does are clear: being sexually unfaithful, not being

5:14 **"Love . . . yourself."** Quotation from Leviticus 19:18.

THE ONE PERCENT SOLUTION

God's **involvement**

FITNESS

GALATIANS 6:10

Stress is something we all face regularly. The only ones without it are running with the angels. Stress is incredibly dangerous to our bodies. Stress causes weight gain, aging, arthritis, high blood pressure, high cholesterol, and many other indicators of poor health. Stress becomes dangerous when we feel hopeless, overpowered, and overwhelmed, and we feel this way when we lose sight of the awesome power of our closest friend, God.

So even if we're fit, if we're not focused on God, we won't be entirely healthy. Living without God as the focal point for our lives is like walking on a tight rope in a blasting wind—without a net. It's scary, there's no support, no hope, and the possibility of a tragic ending is ever present in our minds. This type of stress, the kind in which we've lost sight of God's faithfulness, we've forgotten his support, and we've failed to remember his promises, can be deadly.

We all experience times in which we lose our awareness that God is there, helping us keep our balance, quieting the winds, and catching us if we fall. It is during those times of separation that life gets hard. Church is good for us because it reconnects us with this power, grants us peace of mind, and helps us not to underestimate the supernatural ability of God to preserve us for his purposes.

Going to church actually helps us to live longer. Secular research proves this point. Research studies done at major universities show that involving God in our lives is not just good for the soul, but it's also great for our health.

reflect: Worship God by spending time fellowshiping with other believers.
Go to **FITNESS:** "Total Christian Fitness" at **3 John 2.**

pure, taking part in sexual sins, ²⁰worshiping gods, doing witchcraft, hating, making trouble, being jealous, being angry, being selfish, making people angry with each other, causing divisions among people, ²¹feeling envy, being drunk, having wild and wasteful parties, and doing other things like these. I warn you now as I warned you before: Those who do these things will not inherit God's kingdom. ²²But the Spirit produces the fruit of love, joy, peace, patience, kindness, goodness, faithfulness, ²³gentleness, self-control. There is no law that says these things are wrong. ²⁴Those who belong to Christ Jesus have crucified their own sinful selves. They have given up their old selfish feelings and the evil things they wanted to do. ²⁵We get our new life from the Spirit, so we should follow the Spirit. ²⁶We must not be proud or make trouble with each other or be jealous of each other.

HELP EACH OTHER

6 Brothers and sisters, if someone in your group does something wrong, you who are spiritual should go to that person and gently help make him right again. But be careful, because you might be tempted to sin, too. ²By helping each other with your troubles, you truly obey the law of Christ. ³If anyone thinks he is important when he really is not, he is only fooling himself. ⁴Each person should judge his own actions and not compare himself with others. Then he can be proud for what he himself has done. ⁵Each person must be responsible for himself.

⁶Anyone who is learning the teaching of God should share all the good things he has with his teacher.

LIFE IS LIKE PLANTING A FIELD

⁷Do not be fooled: You cannot cheat God. People harvest only what they plant. ⁸If they plant to satisfy their sinful selves, their sinful selves will bring them ruin. But if they plant to please the Spirit, they will receive eternal life from the Spirit. ⁹We must not become tired of doing good. We will receive our harvest of eternal life at the right time if we do not give up. ¹⁰When we have the opportunity to help anyone, we should do it. But we should give special attention to those who are in the family of believers.

PAUL ENDS HIS LETTER

¹¹See what large letters I use to write this myself. ¹²Some people are trying to force you to be circumcised so the Jews will accept them. They are afraid they will be attacked if they follow only the cross of Christ.ⁿ ¹³Those who are circumcised do not obey the law themselves, but they want you to be circumcised so they can brag about what they forced you to do. ¹⁴I hope I will never brag about things like that. The cross of our Lord Jesus Christ is my only reason for bragging. Through the cross of Jesus my world was crucified, and I died to the world. ¹⁵It is not important if a man is circumcised or uncircumcised. The important thing is being the new people God has made. ¹⁶Peace and mercy to those who follow this rule—and to all of God's people.

¹⁷So do not give me any more trouble. I have scars on my body that showⁿ I belong to Christ Jesus.

¹⁸My brothers and sisters, the grace of our Lord Jesus Christ be with your spirit. Amen.

6:12 cross of Christ Paul uses the cross as a picture of the Good News, the story of Christ's death and rising from the dead to pay for our sins. The cross, or Christ's death, was God's way to save us. **6:17 that show** Many times Paul was beaten and whipped by people who were against him because he was teaching about Christ. The scars were from these beatings.

GOD UNITES HIS PEOPLE

1 From Paul, an apostle of Christ Jesus. I am an apostle because that is what God wanted.

To God's holy people living in Ephesus,[n] believers in Christ Jesus:

2Grace and peace to you from God our Father and the Lord Jesus Christ.

SPIRITUAL BLESSINGS IN CHRIST

3Praise be to the God and Father of our Lord Jesus Christ. In Christ, God has given us every spiritual blessing in the heavenly world. 4That is, in Christ, he chose us before the world was made so that we would be his holy people—people without blame before him. 5Because of his love, God had already decided to make us his own children through Jesus Christ. That was what he wanted and what pleased him, 6and it brings praise to God because of his wonderful grace. God gave that grace to us freely, in Christ, the One he loves. 7In Christ we are set free by the blood of his death, and so we have forgiveness of sins. How rich is God's grace, 8which he has given to us so fully and freely. God, with full wisdom and understanding, 9let us know his secret purpose. This was what God wanted, and he planned to do it through Christ. 10His goal was to carry out his plan, when the right time came, that all things in heaven and on earth would be joined together in Christ as the head.

11In Christ we were chosen to be God's people, because from the very beginning God had decided this in keeping with his plan. And he is the One who makes everything agree with what he decides and wants. 12We are the first people who hoped in Christ, and we were chosen so that we would bring praise to God's glory. 13So it is with you. When you heard the true teaching—the Good News about your salvation—you believed in Christ. And in Christ, God put his special mark of ownership on you by giving you the Holy Spirit that he had promised. 14That Holy Spirit is the guarantee that we will receive what God promised for his people until God

gives full freedom to those who are his—to bring praise to God's glory.

PAUL'S PRAYER

15That is why since I heard about your faith in the Lord Jesus and your love for all God's people, 16I have not stopped giving thanks to God for you. I always remember you in my prayers, 17asking the God of our Lord Jesus Christ, the glorious Father, to give you a spirit of wisdom and revelation so that you will know him better. 18I pray also that you will have greater understanding in your heart so you will know the hope to which he has called us and that you will know how rich and glorious are the blessings God has promised his holy people. 19And you will know that God's power is very great for us who believe. That power is the same as the great strength 20God used to raise Christ from the dead and put him at his right side in the heavenly world. 21God has put Christ over all rulers, authorities, powers, and kings, not only in this world but also in the next. 22God put everything under his power and made him the head over everything for the church, 23which is Christ's body. The church is filled with Christ, and Christ fills everything in every way.

WE NOW HAVE LIFE

2 In the past you were spiritually dead because of your sins and the things you did against God. 2Yes, in the past you lived the way the world lives, following the ruler of the evil powers that are above the earth. That same spirit is now working in those who refuse to obey God. 3In the past all of us lived like them, trying to please our sinful selves and doing all the things our bodies and minds wanted. We should have suffered God's anger because we were sinful by nature. We were the same as all other people.

4But God's mercy is great, and he loved

1:1 in Ephesus Some Greek copies do not have this phrase.

us very much. ⁵Though we were spiritually dead because of the things we did against God, he gave us new life with Christ. You have been saved by God's grace. ⁶And he raised us up with Christ and gave us a seat with him in the heavens. He did this for those in Christ Jesus ⁷so that for all future time he could show the very great riches of his grace by being kind to us in Christ Jesus. ⁸I mean that you have been saved by grace through believing. You did not save yourselves; it was a gift from God. ⁹It was not the result of your own efforts, so you cannot brag about it. ¹⁰God has made us what we are. In Christ Jesus, God made us to do good works, which God planned in advance for us to live our lives doing.

ONE IN CHRIST

¹¹You were not born Jewish. You are the people the Jews call "uncircumcised."ⁿ Those who call you "uncircumcised" call themselves "circumcised." (Their circumcision is only something they themselves do on their bodies.) ¹²Remember that in the past you were without Christ. You were not citizens of Israel, and you had no part in the agreementsⁿ with the promise that God made to his people. You had no hope, and you did not know God. ¹³But now in Christ Jesus, you who were far away from God are

---

2:11 "uncircumcised" People not having the mark of circumcision as the Jews had. **2:12 agreements** The agreements that God gave to his people in the Old Testament.

A PARTNERSHIP WITH GOD

FAITH

it's **mine!**

EPHESIANS 1:22

"It's mine!" "No, it's mine!" Have you ever listened to children argue about power and possession?** They intuitively know that it is a matter of forced subjection. It's one person's will against another's. This is the sense of the word *hypotasso* in the New Testament. You will find it in Romans 8:20, Philippians 3:21, 1 Peter 3:22, and 1 Corinthians 15:25, and here in Ephesians 1:22.

God is the absolute Ruler of all creation. He has put everything in subjection to his Son. Not just some of this and some of that. Everything. Including death. Not one thing that ever happens, exists, or comes to be is outside of the authority of Jesus. Jesus is in charge of it all.

We struggle greatly with the things of this world. We fight to survive. We complain. We get tossed back and forth by emotions. We wonder where that peace that passes understanding really is. We have not fully begun to embrace living until we realize we have a special friend who is the Man really in charge of the universe. When do you suppose we will grow up beyond the "I have to do it myself" and "It's mine and not yours" attitude and realize that it's all in his hands and it's all his?

---

reflect: Think of the areas of your life that you need to give the Lord control over.
Go to **Ephesians 2:8–9.**

---

brought near through the blood of Christ's death. ¹⁴Christ himself is our peace. He made both Jewish people and those who are not Jews one people. They were separated as if there were a wall between them, but Christ broke down that wall of hate by giving his own body. ¹⁵The Jewish law had many commands and rules, but Christ ended that law. His purpose was to make the two groups of people become one new people in him and in this way make peace. ¹⁶It was also Christ's purpose to end the hatred between the two groups, to make them into one body, and to bring them back to God. Christ did all this with his death on the cross. ¹⁷Christ came and preached peace to you who were far away from God, and to those who were near to God. ¹⁸Yes, it is through Christ we all have the right to come to the Father in one Spirit.

¹⁹Now you who are not Jewish are not foreigners or strangers any longer, but are citizens together with God's holy people. You belong to God's family. ²⁰You are like a building that was built on the foundation of the

A PARTNERSHIP WITH GOD

grace **all** the time

FAITH

EPHESIANS 2:8–9

"**G**race" is a very familiar word to readers of the New Testament. It comes from the Greek word *charis*, which is where we get the word "charity." It means giving out of love—whether it was earned, deserved, or not—without intent to get in return. This word comes from the same group as the words for rejoice, joy, give freely, bestow favor, bless, and gift. When we partake of the Lord's Supper, we celebrate the "Eucharist," a word that comes from the same root and means thanksgiving or gratitude. Jesus' grace meal is the bread and wine, the body and the blood.

Paul made great use of the word for grace. For him, grace was the joy of faith and the gift of the Spirit. Paul relates the word to freedom and hope, both now and in the future. If God had a Web site, its domain name might be grace.com. All of God's activities are derived from his character, and grace is central to who God is. That's why grace is so vitally important in the daily life of a follower of Christ.

Paul makes it clear that grace comes from outside. You can think of grace like gravity. It surrounds us and everything about us. It is the bonding agent that keeps us in alignment with God. It is the force that gives structure to all of our relationships. To be cut loose from grace is to be free-floating in space, disconnected, disoriented, and dismayed. There is no life with God without grace. It is either "grace all the time" or spinning out of control.

reflect: Today you can thank God for grace—and know that thanking him is just one more aspect of grace itself.

Go to **FAITH:** "Unwavering Faith" at **Hebrews 11:32–40.**

apostles and prophets. Christ Jesus himself is the most important stone[n] in that building, [21]and that whole building is joined together in Christ. He makes it grow and become a holy temple in the Lord. [22]And in Christ you, too, are being built together with the Jews into a place where God lives through the Spirit.

PAUL'S WORK IN TELLING THE GOOD NEWS

3 So I, Paul, am a prisoner of Christ Jesus for you who are not Jews. [2]Surely you have heard that God gave me this work to tell you about his grace. [3]He let me know his secret by showing it to me. I have already written a little about this. [4]If you read what I wrote then, you can see that I truly understand the secret about the Christ. [5]People who lived in other times were not told that secret. But now, through the Spirit, God has shown that secret to his holy apostles and prophets. [6]This is that secret: that through the Good News those who are not Jews will share with the Jews in God's blessing. They belong to the same body, and they share together in the promise that God made in Christ Jesus.

[7]By God's special gift of grace given to me through his power, I became a servant to tell that Good News. [8]I am the least important of all God's people, but God gave me this gift—to tell those who are not Jews the Good News about the riches of Christ, which are too great to understand fully. [9]And God gave me the work of telling all people about the plan for his secret, which has been hidden in him since the beginning of time. He is the One who created everything. [10]His purpose was that through the church all the rulers and powers in the heavenly world will now know God's wisdom, which has so many forms. [11]This agrees with the purpose God had since the beginning of time, and he carried out his plan through Christ Jesus our Lord. [12]In Christ we can come before God with freedom and without fear. We can do this through faith in Christ. [13]So I ask you not to become discouraged because of the sufferings I am having for you. My sufferings are for your glory.

THE LOVE OF CHRIST

[14]So I bow in prayer before the Father [15]from whom every family in heaven and on earth gets its true name. [16]I ask the Father in his great glory to give you the power to be strong inwardly through his Spirit. [17]I pray that Christ will live in your hearts by faith and that your life will be strong in love and be built on love. [18]And I pray that you and all God's holy people will have the power to understand the greatness of Christ's love—how wide and how long and how high and how deep that love is. [19]Christ's love is greater than anyone can ever know, but I pray that you will be able to know that love. Then you can be filled with the fullness of God.

[20]With God's power working in us, God can do much, much more than anything we can ask or imagine. [21]To him be glory in the church and in Christ Jesus for all time, forever and ever. Amen.

THE UNITY OF THE BODY

4 I am in prison because I belong to the Lord. Therefore I urge you who have been chosen by God to live up to the life to which God called you. [2]Always be humble, gentle, and patient, accepting each other in love. [3]You are joined together with peace through the Spirit, so make every effort to continue together in this way. [4]There is one body and one Spirit, and God called you to have one hope. [5]There is one Lord, one faith, and one baptism. [6]There is one God and Father of everything. He rules everything and is everywhere and is in everything.

[7]Christ gave each one of us the special gift of grace, showing how generous he is. [8]That is why it says in the Scriptures,

"When he went up to the heights,
　he led a parade of captives,
　and he gave gifts to people." *Psalm 68:18*

[9]When it says, "He went up," what does it mean? It means that he first came down to the earth. [10]So Jesus came down, and he is the same One who went up above all the heaven. Christ did that to fill everything with his presence. [11]And Christ gave gifts to people—he made some to be apostles, some to be prophets, some to go and tell the Good News, and some to have the work of caring for and teaching God's people. [12]Christ gave those gifts to prepare God's holy people for the work of serving, to make the body of

---

2:20 most important stone Literally, "cornerstone." The first and most important stone in a building.

Christ stronger. ¹³This work must continue until we are all joined together in the same faith and in the same knowledge of the Son of God. We must become like a mature person, growing until we become like Christ and have his perfection.

¹⁴Then we will no longer be babies. We will not be tossed about like a ship that the waves carry one way and then another. We will not be influenced by every new teaching we hear from people who are trying to fool us. They make plans and try any kind of trick to fool people into following the wrong path.

¹⁵No! Speaking the truth with love, we will grow up in every way into Christ, who is the head. ¹⁶The whole body depends on Christ, and all the parts of the body are joined and held together. Each part does its own work to make the whole body grow and be strong with love.

THE WAY YOU SHOULD LIVE

¹⁷In the Lord's name, I tell you this. Do not continue living like those who do not believe. Their thoughts are worth nothing. ¹⁸They do not understand, and they know nothing,

---

UNWAVERING FAITH

God is **big**

FAITH

By Wendell Smith

EPHESIANS 3:14–21

Have you noticed that the Bible doesn't talk about the devil nearly as much as it **talks about God?** God is a great, big God, but the devil is little-bitty. The devil is small enough to fit under your feet, but God fills the earth and even the heavens can't contain him. Keep the devil where he should be and God where he should be. Your Christian faith is in a Person, not a creed. The Bible is his Word, but we don't worship the Bible; we use the Bible to worship the Person of God.

In the Old Testament, all God had to do was touch a mountain and it smoked! He was always hidden in clouds and darkness with great lightning and thundering. This was done to protect the people because if his glory was revealed directly it would kill them. He had to cloak himself.

Jesus is the exact image of the Father and the reflection of God in the New Testament.

When you see Jesus, you see God the Father. When God became Jesus, he put on flesh. He is the same power, purity, and holiness cloaked with skin. When he shed his blood to pay for our sins, he provided his blood as a shield for us so we could see God's glory.

After Pentecost, by the power of the Holy Spirit, we have glimpses of heaven that grow brighter as we spend time in praise and prayer and the study of God's Word. It's all because of the marvelous love of a great, big God!

reflect: How powerful do you allow God to be in your life?
Go to **2 Corinthians 1:3–4.**

because they refuse to listen. So they cannot have the life that God gives. [19]They have lost all feeling of shame, and they use their lives for doing evil. They continually want to do all kinds of evil. [20]But what you learned in Christ was not like this. [21]I know that you heard about him, and you are in him, so you were taught the truth that is in Jesus. [22]You were taught to leave your old self—to stop living the evil way you lived before. That old self becomes worse, because people are fooled by the evil things they want to do. [23]But you were taught to be made new in your hearts, [24]to become a new person. That new person is made to be like God—made to be truly good and holy.

[25]So you must stop telling lies. Tell each other the truth, because we all belong to each other in the same body.[n] [26]When you are angry, do not sin, and be sure to stop being angry before the end of the day. [27]Do not give the devil a way to defeat you. [28]Those who are stealing must stop stealing and start working. They should earn an honest living for themselves. Then they will have something to share with those who are poor.

[29]When you talk, do not say harmful things, but say what people need—words that will help others become stronger. Then what you say will do good to those who listen to you. [30]And do not make the Holy Spirit sad. The Spirit is God's proof that you belong to him. God gave you the Spirit to show that God will make you free when the final day comes. [31]Do not be bitter or angry or mad. Never shout angrily or say things to hurt others. Never do anything evil. [32]Be kind and loving to each other, and forgive each other just as God forgave you in Christ.

LIVING IN THE LIGHT

5 You are God's children whom he loves, so try to be like him. [2]Live a life of love just as Christ loved us and gave himself for us as a sweet-smelling offering and sacrifice to God.

[3]But there must be no sexual sin among you, or any kind of evil or greed. Those things are not right for God's holy people. [4]Also, there must be no evil talk among you, and you must not speak foolishly or tell evil jokes. These things are not right for you. Instead, you should be giving thanks to God. [5]You can be sure of this: No one will have a place in the kingdom of Christ and of God who sins sexu-

ally, or does evil things, or is greedy. Anyone who is greedy is serving a false god.

[6]Do not let anyone fool you by telling you things that are not true, because these things will bring God's anger on those who do not obey him. [7]So have nothing to do with them. [8]In the past you were full of darkness, but now you are full of light in the Lord. So live like children who belong to the light. [9]Light brings every kind of goodness, right living, and truth. [10]Try to learn what pleases the Lord. [11]Have nothing to do with the things done in darkness, which are not worth anything. But show that they are wrong. [12]It is shameful even to talk about what those people do in secret. [13]But the light makes all things easy to see, [14]and everything that is made easy to see can become light. This is why it is said:

"Wake up, sleeper!
  Rise from death,
  and Christ will shine on you."

[15]So be very careful how you live. Do not live like those who are not wise, but live wisely. [16]Use every chance you have for doing good, because these are evil times. [17]So do not be foolish but learn what the Lord wants you to do. [18]Do not be drunk with wine, which will ruin you, but be filled with the Spirit. [19]Speak to each other with psalms, hymns, and spiritual songs, singing and making music in your hearts to the Lord. [20]Always give thanks to God the Father for everything, in the name of our Lord Jesus Christ.

WIVES AND HUSBANDS

[21]Yield to obey each other as you would to Christ.

[22]Wives, yield to your husbands, as you do to the Lord, [23]because the husband is the head of the wife, as Christ is the head of the church. And he is the Savior of the body, which is the church. [24]As the church yields to Christ, so you wives should yield to your husbands in everything.

[25]Husbands, love your wives as Christ loved the church and gave himself for it [26]to make it belong to God. Christ used the word to make the church clean by washing it with water. [27]He died so that he could give the church to himself like a bride in all her beauty. He died so that the church could be

---

4:25 Tell . . . body. Quotation from Zechariah 8:16.

pure and without fault, with no evil or sin or any other wrong thing in it. ²⁸In the same way, husbands should love their wives as they love their own bodies. The man who loves his wife loves himself. ²⁹No one ever hates his own body, but feeds and takes care of it. And that is what Christ does for the church, ³⁰because we are parts of his body. ³¹The Scripture says, "So a man will leave his father and mother and be united with his wife, and the two will become one body."ⁿ ³²That secret is very important—I am talking about Christ and the church. ³³But each one of you must love his wife as he loves himself, and a wife must respect her husband.

CHILDREN AND PARENTS

6 Children, obey your parents as the Lord wants, because this is the right thing to do. ²The command says, "Honor your father and mother."ⁿ This is the first command that

---

5:31 "So . . . body." Quotation from Genesis 2:24.
6:2 "Honor . . . mother." Quotation from Exodus 20:12; Deuteronomy 5:16.

LESSONS FROM THE BATTLEFIELD

now FUTURE

By Robert Barriger

EPHESIANS 5:15-16

A **sign posted above a tree in a nursery asks, "When is the best time to plant a tree?"** and below that the answer reads, "Ten years ago" . . . Further along, another sign reads, "When is the *next* best time to plant a tree?" The answer: "Today." In other words, a tree planted ten years ago bears fruit and provides shade and beauty today, and if you plant a tree today, it will be ready to bear fruit ten years from now.

Suppose a pastor asks his congregation for someone to play the piano and a young man comes forward and says, "I am your man." The pastor asks, "Great. Do you play piano?" And his answer is, "No, but I will learn." When is the best time to learn piano, if the need is for today? Ten years ago?

Look at the amazing changes in the church during the last ten years, and according to the promises in God's Word, the best is still to come. The Lord has prepared exciting and wonderful things for his children. The greatest church is yet to be planted, the best books are yet to be written, and the best worship songs are yet to be sung. We have to prepare today in order to be ready for the future.

Preparation is evidence that you believe something is coming. So when is the best time to fix your marriage? When is the best time to lose weight and exercise? When is the best time to start something good? Maybe it was ten years ago. When is the *next* best time? NOW!

---

reflect: When do you think is the best time to study the Bible?
Go to **Galatians 2:20.**

has a promise with it— [3]"Then everything will be well with you, and you will have a long life on the earth."[n]

[4]Fathers, do not make your children angry, but raise them with the training and teaching of the Lord.

SLAVES AND MASTERS

[5]Slaves, obey your masters here on earth with fear and respect and from a sincere heart, just as you obey Christ. [6]You must do this not only while they are watching you, to please them. With all your heart you must do what God wants as people who are obeying Christ. [7]Do your work with enthusiasm. Work as if you were serving the Lord, not as if you were serving only men and women. [8]Remember that the Lord will give a reward to everyone, slave or free, for doing good.

[9]Masters, in the same way, be good to your slaves. Do not threaten them. Remember that the One who is your Master and their Master is in heaven, and he treats everyone alike.

WEAR THE FULL ARMOR OF GOD

[10]Finally, be strong in the Lord and in his great power. [11]Put on the full armor of God so that you can fight against the devil's evil tricks. [12]Our fight is not against people on

---

6:3 "Then . . . earth." Quotation from Exodus 20:12; Deuteronomy 5:16.

FUTURE

BUILDING MOMENTUM THROUGH TEAMWORK

finding what God has called you to do

EPHESIANS 5:17

By Truett Cathy

Even though we have our own goals for our lives, we must be sensitive to the fact that the Lord may be leading us down a different path through unexpected **opportunities.** He has a plan for each of us. If you're not happy in what you're doing, you probably have not found his plan for your life.

Life is a great journey, and all of us are called in various ways. The Lord wants us to make use of our abilities and talents, since he has made them available to us. Whatever God has called you to do, it is a high calling, because all work is an opportunity to minister to others. Those who preach and teach the Word are to be commended, but biblical principles can be followed in any work.

God has called each of us to our own profession, and he wants us to be successful. He is honored by success, not by failure. Three things are needed to be successful. First, we have to want to do whatever it is we're doing. Second, we have to develop the skills and the "know-how" required for the job. Third, we have to get up and do it.

Ask yourself: Why am I here? What is my purpose? Our purpose must be to glorify God and to be a faithful steward of all that the Lord has entrusted to our care, so that we might have a positive influence on the people we come in contact with.

---

reflect: Do you know what your purpose is, and are you pursuing it?
Go to **1 John 5:1–5.**

earth but against the rulers and authorities and the powers of this world's darkness, against the spiritual powers of evil in the heavenly world. ¹³That is why you need to put on God's full armor. Then on the day of evil you will be able to stand strong. And when you have finished the whole fight, you will still be standing. ¹⁴So stand strong, with the belt of truth tied around your waist and the protection of right living on your chest. ¹⁵On your feet wear the Good News of peace to help you stand strong. ¹⁶And also use the shield of faith with which you can stop all the burning arrows of the Evil One. ¹⁷Accept God's salvation as your helmet, and take the sword of the Spirit, which is the word of God. ¹⁸Pray in the Spirit at all times with all kinds of prayers, asking for everything you need. To do this you must always be ready and never give up. Always pray for all God's people.

¹⁹Also pray for me that when I speak, God will give me words so that I can tell the secret of the Good News without fear. ²⁰I have been sent to preach this Good News, and I

LOVE IS MORE THAN GIVING

the **law** of **pursuit**

FAMILY

By Jimmy Evans

EPHESIANS 5:31

The law of pursuit in marriage says that a man shall cleave to (NCV: "be united with") his wife, with the word "cleave" meaning "to pursue with energy." This affirms the fact that marriage is work. When you work, it works. When you don't work, it doesn't.

A problem with the law of pursuit is that we pursue until we get what we want, but then we get lazy and take each other for granted. Furthermore, there are some misconceptions in our society about love and marriage. One misconception is that if we marry the right person, the emotions will happen naturally. But emotions can't fuel a relationship long-term; only commitment can do that.

Another misconception is that if our emotions change toward our spouse, we must have married the wrong person. This is satanic deception that brings divorce and heartache. Satan always wants us to believe that the grass is greener on the other side. The truth is that when it looks greener, it's time to water your own yard. Totally focus and commit to your relationship. Don't get in a vicious cycle of following your emotions. Marriage operates on the Manna Principle: You must work at it every day.

Another misconception is that when we experience no emotions for a while there is no way to get the love back. The truth is that you fell in love because you worked at it. God can restore your marriage. The formula is: Remember. Repent. Redo.

reflect: Are you working at your marriage every day?
Go to **FAMILY:** "Showing Approval for Your Husband" at **Hebrews 3:13.**

am doing that now, here in prison. Pray that when I preach the Good News I will speak without fear, as I should.

FINAL GREETINGS

²¹I am sending to you Tychicus, our brother whom we love and a faithful servant of the Lord's work. He will tell you everything that is happening with me. Then you will know how I am and what I am doing. ²²I am sending him to you for this reason—so that you will know how we are, and he can encourage you.

²³Peace and love with faith to you brothers and sisters from God the Father and the Lord Jesus Christ. ²⁴Grace to all of you who love our Lord Jesus Christ with love that never ends.

FINANCES

ATTAINING FINANCIAL FREEDOM

who's the **boss?**

EPHESIANS 6:5–8

Paul is talking to slaves here. He is telling them that accepting Christ is meant to change their attitude and actions. In so many words, he tells them that before Jesus became the Lord of their lives, they used to work only when someone was watching them. They worked just to make sure that the boss was pleased. But now things have changed. He admonishes them to do their work as though God employed them, for he is the one they really work for. They are to act like they work for God and not for men.

How many times have we only done what we needed to do? How many times have we kept up the pretense of work while the boss was watching? One cartoon shows the boss standing by a desk, with the employee saying, "Well, I would have been working if I knew you were coming." Paul tells us that God's purpose changes everything about us, including the way we work. When God puts us into circumstances that he engineers just for us, we are to work from a heart that is guided by him. Who cares if our human boss is watching? Our heavenly boss is watching all the time!

reflect: Work for the Lord, and you'll never worry about who else may be watching.
Go to **FINANCES:** "What Jesus Wants" at **Revelation 3:15–16.**

1 From Paul and Timothy, servants of Christ Jesus.

To all of God's holy people in Christ Jesus who live in Philippi, including your overseers and deacons:

2Grace and peace to you from God our Father and the Lord Jesus Christ.

PAUL'S PRAYER

3I thank my God every time I remember you, 4always praying with joy for all of you. 5I thank God for the help you gave me while I preached the Good News—help you gave from the first day you believed until now. 6God began doing a good work in you, and I am sure he will continue it until it is finished when Jesus Christ comes again.

7And I know that I am right to think like this about all of you, because I have you in my heart. All of you share in God's grace with me while I am in prison and while I am defending and proving the truth of the Good News. 8God knows that I want to see you very much, because I love all of you with the love of Christ Jesus.

9This is my prayer for you: that your love will grow more and more; that you will have knowledge and understanding with your love; 10that you will see the difference between good and bad and will choose the good; that you will be pure and without wrong for the coming of Christ; 11that you will be filled with the good things produced in your life by Christ to bring glory and praise to God.

PAUL'S TROUBLES HELP THE WORK

12I want you brothers and sisters to know that what has happened to me has helped to spread the Good News. 13All the palace guards and everyone else knows that I am in prison because I am a believer in Christ. 14Because I am in prison, most of the believers have become more bold in Christ and are not afraid to speak the word of God.

15It is true that some preach about Christ because they are jealous and ambitious, but others preach about Christ because they want to help. 16They preach because they have love, and they know that God gave me the work of defending the Good News. 17But the others preach about Christ for selfish and wrong reasons, wanting to make trouble for me in prison.

18But it doesn't matter. The important thing is that in every way, whether for right or wrong reasons, they are preaching about Christ. So I am happy, and I will continue to be happy. 19Because you are praying for me and the Spirit of Jesus Christ is helping me, I know this trouble will bring my freedom. 20I expect and hope that I will not fail Christ in anything but that I will have the courage now, as always, to show the greatness of Christ in my life here on earth, whether I live or die. 21To me the only important thing about living is Christ, and dying would be profit for me. 22If I continue living in my body, I will be able to work for the Lord. I do not know what to choose—living or dying. 23It is hard to choose between the two. I want to leave this life and be with Christ, which is much better, 24but you need me here in my body. 25Since I am sure of this, I know I will stay with you to help you grow and have joy in your faith. 26You will be very happy in Christ Jesus when I am with you again.

27Only one thing concerns me: Be sure that you live in a way that brings honor to the Good News of Christ. Then whether I come and visit you or am away from you, I will hear that you are standing strong with one purpose, that you work together as one for the faith of the Good News, 28and that you are not afraid of those who are against you. All of this is proof that your enemies will be destroyed but that you will be saved by God. 29God gave you the honor not only of believing in Christ but also of suffering for him, both of which bring glory to Christ. 30When I was with you, you saw the struggles I had, and you hear about the struggles I am having now. You yourselves are having the same kind of struggles.

Are You **Programmed** for **Stress?**

FULFILLMENT

By Dr. Ben Lerner

The way you look at the world you live in has, in many ways, been programmed. Think of it as "Perception Software." In most cases, it is your *point of view* of people, issues, and events, and not the people, issues, and events themselves, that determines how you react to them, define them, and create your version of the story.

Continuing the analogy, your Perception Software can be generalized to fit into three basic areas:

> *History Software.* Your experience with certain circumstances, people, events, conflicts, and education make up your History Software. These past experiences will often determine how you feel about every new experience.

> *Cultural Software.* Your family, occupation, peer group, geographic area, school, and religion (together or individually) make up your Cultural Software. For example, my family grew up in New York City. The tendency is for people in that culture not to express love openly, to be fast to judge, to be cynical, and to have high and unrealistic expectations of others. The world-famous "New York attitude" is really a result of cultural programming.

> *Self-Esteem Software.* How you see yourself and how you feel others see you makes up your Self-Esteem Software. How you envision yourself will definitely influence what future goals you feel you are capable of attaining.

Because of the power and saturated influence of Perception Software, stressful times and events in your life may lead you to feel overpowered and overwhelmed. When you perceive that you are a victim of circumstances, the resulting stress can be extremely dangerous. When you see your problems as being in control of your emotions, health, and success, the physical and mental damage of stress will run rampant.

In other words, it isn't stress until you *call* it stress; and you call 'em as you *see* 'em.

For your world to improve and your stress to be reduced, you must begin *seeing* life from a totally different perspective. To change your perspective, you must change your perception software . . . you must change the way you are programmed. And this is exactly the type of change that the apostle Paul seemed to have in mind.

> "Do not be shaped by this world; instead be **changed within by a new way of thinking.** Then you will be able to decide what God wants for you; you will know what is good and pleasing to him and what is perfect" (Romans 12:2, emphasis added).

Did you catch that? Be changed from *within* by a *new way of thinking.* Reprogram your brain! All your Perception Software issues *can* be fixed. While installing new software may be more difficult to do on a person than on a computer (maybe), the reality is that you *can* be reprogrammed. If the Bible says that we must be changed within and learn to think and act like Christ Jesus, you can be sure that it is not only possible, but that it is part of God's purpose and plan for your life!

TO LEARN MORE ON WHAT THE BIBLE HAS TO SAY ABOUT **FULFILLMENT,** READ THE SCRIPTURES AND DEVOTIONALS AT **MICAH 7:18–19, MATTHEW 3:13–17, MATTHEW 7:29, MATTHEW 25:44–45, MARK 9:23,** AND **MARK 11:23–25.**

2 Does your life in Christ give you strength? Does his love comfort you? Do we share together in the spirit? Do you have mercy and kindness? ²If so, make me very happy by having the same thoughts, sharing the same love, and having one mind and purpose. ³When you do things, do not let selfishness or pride be your guide. Instead, be humble and give more honor to others than to yourselves. ⁴Do not be interested only in your own life, but be interested in the lives of others.

BE UNSELFISH LIKE CHRIST

⁵In your lives you must think and act like Christ Jesus.

⁶ Christ himself was like God in everything.
But he did not think that being equal with God was something to be used for his own benefit.

⁷ But he gave up his place with God and made himself nothing.
He was born as a man
and became like a servant.

⁸ And when he was living as a man,
he humbled himself and was fully obedient to God,
even when that caused his death—death on a cross.

⁹ So God raised him to the highest place.
God made his name greater than every other name

¹⁰ so that every knee will bow to the name of Jesus—

WHAT JESUS WANTS

work is not about us

FINANCES

PHILIPPIANS 2:12

Our lives are dominated by a Greek outlook on work. One Greek poet coined the phrase "known by their works." We carry the same orientation today when we use the formula greeting, "What do you do?" We are simply suggesting that people are measured by their work. A better question is, "Who are you?" or "What do you stand for?"

For the Hebrews, "work" was a word that was ultimately about God, not about us. God always has been a God of activity. He always has been known by his work. Of course, this began with Creation. Even today, his handiwork is seen in every aspect of creation, in every moment and every detail. God is continuously involved in the making of this world—including judgment, redemption, direction, and restoration. Jesus confirmed this view of God when he said, "My Father never stops working" (John 5:17).

In the New Testament, the work of a believer is always ultimately an expression of the activity of God. This means that no matter what trade, occupation, skill, or activity you name in answer to the question, "What do you do?" the believer understands that his or her activity is first and foremost service to God. Since work is an extension of belief in the active, living God, there is no discrepancy between "faith" and "works." One is a reflection of the other.

reflect: Make your work an accurate reflection of your relationship with God.
Go to **Philippians 3:12-14.**

everyone in heaven, on earth, and under the earth.

¹¹ And everyone will confess that Jesus
  Christ is Lord
  and bring glory to God the Father.

BE THE PEOPLE GOD WANTS YOU TO BE

¹²My dear friends, you have always obeyed God when I was with you. It is even more important that you obey now while I am away from you. Keep on working to complete your salvation with fear and trembling, ¹³because God is working in you to help you want to do and be able to do what pleases him.

¹⁴Do everything without complaining or arguing. ¹⁵Then you will be innocent and without any wrong. You will be God's children without fault. But you are living with crooked and mean people all around you, among whom you shine like stars in the dark world. ¹⁶You offer the teaching that gives life. So when Christ comes again, I can be happy because my work was not wasted. I ran the race and won.

¹⁷Your faith makes you offer your lives as a sacrifice in serving God. If I have to offer my own blood with your sacrifice, I will be happy and full of joy with all of you. ¹⁸You also should be happy and full of joy with me.

TIMOTHY AND EPAPHRODITUS

¹⁹I hope in the Lord Jesus to send Timothy to you soon. I will be happy to learn how you are. ²⁰I have no one else like Timothy, who truly cares for you. ²¹Other people are interested only in their own lives, not in the work of Jesus Christ. ²²You know the kind of person Timothy is. You know he has served with me in telling the Good News, as a son serves his father. ²³I plan to send him to you quickly when I know what will happen to me. ²⁴I am sure that the Lord will help me to come to you soon.

²⁵Epaphroditus, my brother in Christ, works and serves with me in the army of Christ. When I needed help, you sent him to me. I think now that I must send him back to you, ²⁶because he wants very much to see all of you. He is worried because you heard that he was sick. ²⁷Yes, he was sick, and nearly died, but God had mercy on him and me too so that I would not have more sadness. ²⁸I want very much to send him to you so that when you see him you can be happy, and I can stop worrying about you. ²⁹Welcome him in the Lord with much joy. Give honor to people like him, ³⁰because he almost died for the work of Christ. He risked his life to give me the help you could not give in your service to me.

THE IMPORTANCE OF CHRIST

3 My brothers and sisters, be full of joy in the Lord. It is no trouble for me to write the same things to you again, and it will help you to be more ready. ²Watch out for those who do evil, who are like dogs, who demand to cut[n] the body. ³We are the ones who are truly circumcised. We worship God through his Spirit, and our pride is in Christ Jesus. We do not put trust in ourselves or anything we can do, ⁴although I might be able to put trust in myself. If anyone thinks he has a reason to trust in himself, he should know that I have greater reason for trusting in myself. ⁵I was circumcised eight days after my birth. I am from the people of Israel and the tribe of Benjamin. I am a Hebrew, and my parents were Hebrews. I had a strict view of the law, which is why I became a Pharisee. ⁶I was so enthusiastic I tried to hurt the church. No one could find fault with the way I obeyed the law of Moses. ⁷Those things were important to me, but now I think they are worth nothing because of Christ. ⁸Not only those things, but I think that all things are worth nothing compared with the greatness of knowing Christ Jesus my Lord. Because of him, I have lost all those things, and now I know they are worthless trash. This allows me to have Christ ⁹and to belong to him. Now I am right with God, not because I followed the law, but because I believed in Christ. God uses my faith to make me right with him. ¹⁰I want to know Christ and the power that raised him from the dead. I want to share in his sufferings and become like him in his death. ¹¹Then I have hope that I myself will be raised from the dead.

CONTINUING TOWARD OUR GOAL

¹²I do not mean that I am already as God wants me to be. I have not yet reached that goal, but I continue trying to reach it and to make it mine. Christ wants me to do that, which is the reason he made me his. ¹³Broth-

---

3:2 cut The word in Greek is like the word "circumcise," but it means "to cut completely off."

ers and sisters, I know that I have not yet reached that goal, but there is one thing I always do. Forgetting the past and straining toward what is ahead, ¹⁴I keep trying to reach the goal and get the prize for which God called me through Christ to the life above.

¹⁵All of us who are spiritually mature should think this way, too. And if there are things you do not agree with, God will make them clear to you. ¹⁶But we should continue following the truth we already have.

¹⁷Brothers and sisters, all of you should try to follow my example and to copy those who live the way we showed you. ¹⁸Many people live like enemies of the cross of Christ. I have often told you about them, and it makes me cry to tell you about them now.

¹⁹In the end, they will be destroyed. They do whatever their bodies want, they are proud of their shameful acts, and they think only about earthly things. ²⁰But our homeland is in heaven, and we are waiting for our Savior, the Lord Jesus Christ, to come from heaven. ²¹By his power to rule all things, he will change our humble bodies and make them like his own glorious body.

WHAT THE CHRISTIANS ARE TO DO

4 My dear brothers and sisters, I love you and want to see you. You bring me joy and make me proud of you, so stand strong in the Lord as I have told you.

²I ask Euodia and Syntyche to agree in the Lord. ³And I ask you, my faithful friend, to

WHAT JESUS WANTS

keep your **eye** on the **ball**

FINANCES

By Howard Dayton

PHILIPPIANS 3:12–14

Growing up playing Little League baseball was the love of one young boy's life. He played on a huge baseball diamond with a towering fence in the outfield. This youngster was not a very good hitter, but one time he succeeded in hitting it over the fence. Even today, a mental picture of that hit still plays in his mind.

A trip to that baseball field many years later brought back memories. There was a mental replay of that exhilarating hit. It was hard to believe how much that field had shrunk after thirty years. It was so small it was possible to step over that fence in the outfield!

Standing on the pitcher's mound, it immediately struck the now middle-aged ballplayer that much of life was like that. What may seem so large and momentous today, with a few years retrospect, will shrink in importance. This thought should help us gain a healthy fear. To be face-to-face with Christ, realizing this life is not everything there is, prompts a look back to see how we have invested our time, our creativity, and our resources.

Most of our investments, unfortunately, are in really *small things*. The challenge to all of us is to invest our lives in the *big things* when we are face-to-face with Christ. What is truly important today? Keep your eye on the ball, and don't get sidetracked by the little stuff.

reflect: Are you majoring on the minor issues of life?
Go to **Philippians 4:5**.

help these women. They served with me in telling the Good News, together with Clement and others who worked with me, whose names are written in the book of life.[n]

4Be full of joy in the Lord always. I will say again, be full of joy.

5Let everyone see that you are gentle and kind. The Lord is coming soon. 6Do not worry about anything, but pray and ask God for everything you need, always giving thanks. 7And God's peace, which is so great we cannot understand it, will keep your hearts and minds in Christ Jesus.

8Brothers and sisters, think about the things that are good and worthy of praise. Think about the things that are true and honorable and right and pure and beautiful and respected. 9Do what you learned and received from me, what I told you, and what you saw me do. And the God who gives peace will be with you.

PAUL THANKS THE CHRISTIANS

10I am very happy in the Lord that you have shown your care for me again. You continued to care about me, but there was no way for you to show it. 11I am not telling you this because I need anything. I have learned to be satisfied with the things I have and with everything that happens. 12I know how to

4:3 **book of life** God's book that has the names of all God's chosen people (Revelation 3:5; 21:27).

WHAT JESUS WANTS

FINANCES

intense moderation

PHILIPPIANS 4:5

Have you ever heard of "intense moderation"? I don't think so. But that's exactly the sense of this verse. Intense moderation is about being entirely fair, going out of the way to be truthful and equitable. It is not a matter of being calm in the middle or living a dutiful but bland life. Paul was anything but bland. This is a word that calls for real action. It means "make sure that your life stands for justice." And, by the way, let it make such a strong statement that everyone will know you by your behavior.

In our society, there are plenty of people clamoring for justice. There are lots of causes that ask for our support. But "moderation" means a lot more than waving banners and protesting. It also means "to be lenient, yielding, and unassertive." How can that be? How can I stand up for justice and at the same time be lenient and yielding?

The answer is found by asking, "Whose justice am I passionate about?" If my passion is aimed at achieving justice for myself or for my cause, it is motivated by human concerns. That kind of justice is only interested in demands. But if my passion for justice is to see God's will done on earth, then my efforts are in line with the Founder of the universe—and his justice embraces mercy. Power and patience go together when God is the Judge.

reflect: Stand up for the cause of Christ and motivate others to notice your stand.
Go to **Colossians 1:9.**

live when I am poor, and I know how to live when I have plenty. I have learned the secret of being happy at any time in everything that happens, when I have enough to eat and when I go hungry, when I have more than I need and when I do not have enough. 13I can do all things through Christ, because he gives me strength.

14But it was good that you helped me when I needed it. 15You Philippians remember when I first preached the Good News there. When I left Macedonia, you were the only church that gave me help. 16Several times you sent me things I needed when I was in Thessalonica. 17Really, it is not that I want to receive gifts from you, but I want you to have the good that comes from giving. 18And now I have everything, and more. I have all I need, because Epaphroditus brought your gift to me. It is like a sweet-smelling sacrifice offered to God, who accepts that sacrifice and is pleased with it. 19My God will use his wonderful riches in Christ Jesus to give you everything you need. 20Glory to our God and Father forever and ever! Amen.

21Greet each of God's people in Christ Jesus. Those who are with me send greetings to you. 22All of God's people greet you, particularly those from the palace of Caesar.

23The grace of the Lord Jesus Christ be with you all.

colossians

ONLY CHRIST CAN SAVE PEOPLE

1 From Paul, an apostle of Christ Jesus. I am an apostle because that is what God wanted. Also from Timothy, our brother.

²To the holy and faithful brothers and sisters in Christ that live in Colossae:

Grace and peace to you from God our Father.[n]

³In our prayers for you we always thank God, the Father of our Lord Jesus Christ, ⁴because we have heard about the faith you have in Christ Jesus and the love you have for all of God's people. ⁵You have this faith and love because of your hope, and what you hope for is kept safe for you in heaven. You learned about this hope when you heard the message about the truth, the Good News ⁶that was told to you. Everywhere in the world that Good News is bringing blessings and is growing. This has happened with you, too, since you heard the Good News and understood the truth about the grace of God. ⁷You learned about God's grace from Epaphras, whom we love. He works together with us and is a faithful servant of Christ for us.[n] ⁸He also told us about the love you have from the Holy Spirit.

⁹Because of this, since the day we heard about you, we have continued praying for you, asking God that you will know fully what he wants. We pray that you will also have great wisdom and understanding in spiritual things ¹⁰so that you will live the kind of life that honors and pleases the Lord in every way. You will produce fruit in every good work and grow in the knowledge of God. ¹¹God will strengthen you with his own great power so that you will not give up when troubles come, but you will be patient. ¹²And you will joyfully give thanks to the Father who has made you[n] able to have a share in all that he has prepared for his people in the kingdom of light. ¹³God has freed us from the power of darkness, and he brought us into the kingdom of his dear Son. ¹⁴The Son paid for our sins,[n] and in him we have forgiveness.

THE IMPORTANCE OF CHRIST

¹⁵No one can see God, but Jesus Christ is exactly like him. He ranks higher than everything that has been made. ¹⁶Through his power all things were made—things in heaven and on earth, things seen and unseen, all powers, authorities, lords, and rulers. All things were made through Christ and for Christ. ¹⁷He was there before anything was made, and all things continue because of him. ¹⁸He is the head of the body, which is the church. Everything comes from him. He is the first one who was raised from the dead. So in all things Jesus has first place. ¹⁹God was pleased for all of himself to live in Christ. ²⁰And through Christ, God has brought all things back to himself again—things on earth and things in heaven. God made peace through the blood of Christ's death on the cross.

²¹At one time you were separated from God. You were his enemies in your minds, and the evil things you did were against God. ²²But now God has made you his friends again. He did this through Christ's death in the body so that he might bring you into God's presence as people who are holy, with no wrong, and with nothing of which God can judge you guilty. ²³This will happen if you continue strong and sure in your faith. You must not be moved away from the hope brought to you by the Good News that you heard. That same Good News has been told to everyone in the world, and I, Paul, help in preaching that Good News.

PAUL'S WORK FOR THE CHURCH

²⁴I am happy in my sufferings for you. There are things that Christ must still suffer through his body, the church. I am accepting, in my body, my part of these things

---

1:2 Father Some Greek copies continue, "and the Lord Jesus Christ." **1:7 for us** Some Greek copies read "for you." **1:12 you** Some Greek copies read "us." **1:14 sins** Some Greek copies continue, "with his blood."

that must be suffered. ²⁵I became a servant of the church because God gave me a special work to do that helps you, and that work is to tell fully the message of God. ²⁶This message is the secret that was hidden from everyone since the beginning of time, but now it is made known to God's holy people. ²⁷God decided to let his people know this rich and glorious secret which he has for all people. This secret is Christ himself, who is in you. He is our only hope for glory. ²⁸So we continue to preach Christ to each person, using all wisdom to warn and to teach everyone, in order to bring each one into God's presence as a mature person in Christ. ²⁹To do this, I work and struggle, using Christ's great strength that works so powerfully in me.

2 I want you to know how hard I work for you, those in Laodicea, and others who have never seen me. ²I want them to be strengthened and joined together with love

so that they may be rich in their understanding. This leads to their knowing fully God's secret, that is, Christ himself. ³In him all the treasures of wisdom and knowledge are safely kept.

⁴I say this so that no one can fool you by arguments that seem good, but are false. ⁵Though I am absent from you in my body, my heart is with you, and I am happy to see your good lives and your strong faith in Christ.

CONTINUE TO LIVE IN CHRIST

⁶As you received Christ Jesus the Lord, so continue to live in him. ⁷Keep your roots deep in him and have your lives built on him. Be strong in the faith, just as you were taught, and always be thankful.

⁸Be sure that no one leads you away with false and empty teaching that is only human, which comes from the ruling spirits of this world, and not from Christ. ⁹All of God

WHAT JESUS WANTS

wisdom in work

FINANCES

COLOSSIANS 1:9

T he Greek word *sophia* means wisdom, skill, and expertise. It may refer to practical wisdom, or what we call "street smarts," in the world of commerce and work. The word can also refer to higher understanding, such as wisdom about spiritual matters. This sort of wisdom is a gift of God and influences one's lifestyle.

And God gives us exactly what we need to live successfully. In the Old Testament, God asked Solomon what one thing he wished to possess and Solomon answered "wisdom," which is the ability to know God's will in the circumstances of life. The good news is that the wisdom of God is available to us today also, simply for the asking.

In this passage, Paul prays that all believers will be filled with wisdom and spiritual understanding. Without it, we are directionless, like compasses without a true north. But with it, we can experience God's direction in every situation, no matter the circumstance.

reflect: Ask God for the wisdom you need to make good, godly decisions.
Go to **Colossians 4:2.**

lives fully in Christ (even when Christ was on earth), ¹⁰and you have a full and true life in Christ, who is ruler over all rulers and powers.

¹¹Also in Christ you had a different kind of circumcision, a circumcision not done by hands. It was through Christ's circumcision, that is, his death, that you were made free from the power of your sinful self. ¹²When you were baptized, you were buried with Christ, and you were raised up with him through your faith in God's power that was shown when he raised Christ from the dead. ¹³When you were spiritually dead because of your sins and because you were not free from the power of your sinful self, God made you alive with Christ, and he forgave all our sins. ¹⁴He canceled the debt, which listed all the rules we failed to follow. He took away that record with its rules and nailed it to the cross. ¹⁵God stripped the spiritual rulers and powers of their authority. With the cross, he won the victory and showed the world that they were powerless.

DON'T FOLLOW PEOPLE'S RULES

¹⁶So do not let anyone make rules for you about eating and drinking or about a religious feast, a New Moon Festival, or a Sabbath day. ¹⁷These things were like a shadow of what was to come. But what is true and

---

TOTAL CHRISTIAN FITNESS

FITNESS

connected to **God**

COLOSSIANS 2:19

Think about it. There was a time when there was no such thing as manufactured food preservatives. God never designed the human body to ingest such things. He did not make human beings and then say, "Let there now be processed food for them to eat." When we cease to live our life by design, we begin to disconnect from God.

Anytime we get out of alignment with God's plan, particularly when it comes to our physical health, there will be negative effects due to that disconnection. One particular area of disconnection that modern nutrition has created is in our use of fats.

Natural meats, fish, and dairy products contain healthy fats that assist our bodies in building tissue, supporting growth, and providing functionality. These healthy, God-intended fats are anti-inflammatory and pro-immunity, and, therefore, disease preventing. On the other hand, fats consumed from commercialized food products are inflammatory and anti-immunity, and, therefore, are disease promoting.

It is all connected. If God didn't design us to physically do it, sooner or later we'd become disconnected from his plan. Our bodies would no longer grow the way he designed them to grow and we'd suffer the consequences. The challenge is for us to choose God's way and reap the rewards.

---

reflect: Consider ways to wean yourself from unhealthy eating practices.
Go to **Hebrews 12:1–3.**

real has come and is found in Christ. ¹⁸Do not let anyone disqualify you by making you humiliate yourself and worship angels. Such people enter into visions, which fill them with foolish pride because of their human way of thinking. ¹⁹They do not hold tightly to Christ, the head. It is from him that all the parts of the body are cared for and held together. So it grows in the way God wants it to grow.

²⁰Since you died with Christ and were made free from the ruling spirits of the world, why do you act as if you still belong to this world by following rules like these: ²¹"Don't handle this," "Don't taste that," "Don't even touch that thing"? ²²These rules refer to earthly things that are gone as soon as they are used. They are only human commands and teachings. ²³They seem to be wise, but they are only part of a human religion. They make people pretend not to be proud and make them punish their bodies, but they do not really control the evil desires of the sinful self.

YOUR NEW LIFE IN CHRIST

3 Since you were raised from the dead with Christ, aim at what is in heaven, where Christ is sitting at the right hand of God. ²Think only about the things in heaven, not the things on earth. ³Your old sinful self has died, and your new life is kept with Christ in

---

SHOWING APPROVAL FOR YOUR HUSBAND

compassion

FAMILY

COLOSSIANS 3:12

How we long to feel compassion! And for good reason. Life is difficult. Maybe that isn't quite strong enough. Life is often difficult to the point of emotional and spiritual exhaustion. Those are the moments when we need the gentle touch of someone who has deep concern for us, someone who knows our pain and is ready to lift our burden.

The word "compassion" emphasizes the deep emotional response on behalf of someone else, a response that finds its ultimate origination in the heart of God. Compassion is central to the heart of God. It is the choice to act graciously on behalf of another without the expectation of compensation. It is doing what is best for someone else no matter what the cost to self. It is a selfless, urgent rush to help.

When God chose us, he set the example for the way we should act. And how does God act? He is moved by the plight of his children. He springs to action. He can't wait to rescue. His feelings for us burst forth in deliberate, direct intervention. God rushes to help.

Is that an accurate picture of you and me? Are we rushing to help? Have we made the heart of compassion a priority in our family? Compassion is action, not just feelings. It can be seen every time we put our agenda on the shelf in order to lift someone else.

---

reflect: Transfer the compassion that God has for you and help another person.
Go to **Mark 10:6–8.**

the **yielded** wife

COLOSSIANS 3:18

By Diana Hagee

God prepared the woman for a role of influence and honor. He intended the husband to have leadership accountability for his family. God expects the wife to submit to her husband. Yet, the act of yielding to your husband's headship is often difficult to accept as a necessary part of God's plan.

Wifely obedience is a position of strength and not inferiority or abuse. It requires an act of ultimate discipline to crucify one's will at the cross of Christ and to follow another's leadership with pure submission. Yielding to your husband shows God's power acting through you.

Submission to another's lead is not accomplished by yielding flesh to flesh. That is impossible! True submission is a condition of the heart and is only accomplished when we first yield to our Lord and Savior and his will for our lives. Genuine submission is personal and quiet. Sincere yielding is humble, and it is a private deed between you and Jesus.

When you yield to God, whether you agree with your husband's leadership or not, God gives you the grace to yield to his divinely appointed leadership. It is never a good thing to say you are submissive when you are not. It is far better to admit you struggle with surrendering your personal agenda to another's than to submit falsely . . . remember, God always knows the true motive of your heart.

When you and your husband come before the throne of God in agreement, the Lord sees one flesh, one entity, and it pleases him, for the Word says where there is unity, the Lord will command a blessing. Listen to the voice of God though your husband and agree with him in prayer. Your actions and strengths should complement him, not compete with him. God created you to be a helpmate to your husband. Learn to be comfortable in that distinctive role.

If you feel your godly husband is leading you in the wrong direction, allow God to deal with him in his own way and in his own time. Your responsibility as a godly wife is to maintain the proper line of submission under the ultimate authority of God.

Yield yourself to the Lord, and he will reward you with a life filled with mercy, love, and grace. If you find yielding too difficult, learn to be honest with him. He knows your heart, and he is faithful to empower you to accomplish that which he has ordained you to do.

reflect: Are you submitted to the will of God for your life?
Go to **Ephesians 5:31.**

God. [4]Christ is your[n] life, and when he comes again, you will share in his glory.

[5]So put all evil things out of your life: sexual sinning, doing evil, letting evil thoughts control you, wanting things that are evil, and greed. This is really serving a false god. [6]These things make God angry.[n] [7]In your past, evil life you also did these things.

[8]But now also put these things out of your life: anger, bad temper, doing or saying things to hurt others, and using evil words when you talk. [9]Do not lie to each other. You have left your old sinful life and the things you did before. [10]You have begun to live the new life, in which you are being made new and are becoming like the One who made you. This new life brings you the true knowledge of God. [11]In the new life there is no difference between Greeks and Jews, those who are circumcised and those who are not circumcised, or people who are foreigners, or Scythians.[n] There is no difference between slaves and free people. But Christ is in all believers, and Christ is all that is important.

[12]God has chosen you and made you his holy people. He loves you. So you should always clothe yourselves with mercy, kindness, humility, gentleness, and patience. [13]Bear with each other, and forgive each other. If someone does wrong to you, forgive that person because the Lord forgave you. [14]Even more than all this, clothe yourself in love. Love is what holds you all together in perfect unity. [15]Let the peace that Christ gives control your thinking, because you were all called together in one body[n] to have peace. Always be thankful. [16]Let the teaching of Christ live in you richly. Use all wisdom to teach and instruct each other by singing psalms, hymns, and spiritual songs with thankfulness in your hearts to God. [17]Everything you do or say should be done to obey Jesus your Lord. And in all you do, give thanks to God the Father through Jesus.

YOUR NEW LIFE WITH OTHER PEOPLE

[18]Wives, yield to the authority of your husbands, because this is the right thing to do in the Lord.

[19]Husbands, love your wives and be gentle with them.

[20]Children, obey your parents in all things, because this pleases the Lord.

[21]Fathers, do not nag your children. If you are too hard to please, they may want to stop trying.

[22]Slaves, obey your masters in all things. Do not obey just when they are watching you, to gain their favor, but serve them honestly, because you respect the Lord. [23]In all the work you are doing, work the best you can. Work as if you were doing it for the Lord, not for people. [24]Remember that you will receive your reward from the Lord, which he promised to his people. You are serving the Lord Christ. [25]But remember that anyone who does wrong will be punished for that wrong, and the Lord treats everyone the same.

4 Masters, give what is good and fair to your slaves. Remember that you have a Master in heaven.

WHAT THE CHRISTIANS ARE TO DO

[2]Continue praying, keeping alert, and always thanking God. [3]Also pray for us that God will give us an opportunity to tell people his message. Pray that we can preach the secret that God has made known about Christ. This is why I am in prison. [4]Pray that I can speak in a way that will make it clear, as I should.

[5]Be wise in the way you act with people who are not believers, making the most of every opportunity. [6]When you talk, you should always be kind and pleasant so you will be able to answer everyone in the way you should.

NEWS ABOUT THE PEOPLE WITH PAUL

[7]Tychicus is my dear brother in Christ and a faithful minister and servant with me in the Lord. He will tell you all the things that are happening to me. [8]This is why I am sending him: so you may know how we are[n] and he may encourage you. [9]I send him with Onesimus, a faithful and dear brother in Christ, and one of your group. They will tell you all that has happened here.

[10]Aristarchus, a prisoner with me, and Mark, the cousin of Barnabas, greet you. (I

3:4 your Some Greek copies read "our." **3:6 These . . . angry** Some Greek copies continue, "against the people who do not obey God." **3:11 Scythians** The Scythians were known as very wild and cruel people. **3:15 body** The spiritual body of Christ, meaning the church or his people. **4:8 so . . . are** Some Greek copies read "so he may know how you are."

have already told you what to do about Mark. If he comes, welcome him.) ¹¹Jesus, who is called Justus, also greets you. These are the only Jewish believers who work with me for the kingdom of God, and they have been a comfort to me.

¹²Epaphras, a servant of Jesus Christ, from your group, also greets you. He always prays for you that you will grow to be spiritually mature and have everything God wants for you. ¹³I know he has worked hard for you and the people in Laodicea and in Hierapolis.

¹⁴Demas and our dear friend Luke, the doctor, greet you.

¹⁵Greet the brothers and sisters in Laodicea. And greet Nympha and the church that meets in her house. ¹⁶After this letter is read to you, be sure it is also read to the church in Laodicea. And you read the letter that I wrote to Laodicea. ¹⁷Tell Archippus, "Be sure to finish the work the Lord gave you."

¹⁸I, Paul, greet you and write this with my own hand. Remember me in prison. Grace be with you.

WHAT JESUS WANTS

FINANCES

the **prayer** strategy

COLOSSIANS 4:2

There are certain birds that make their nest without having a perch. In order to get into the nest, the bird has to fly directly into the hole without halting; otherwise, he would miss the mark. Can you imagine how the entry must be? The bird must try to learn how to hit the mark. Surely the bird will make a few mistakes, but with time and practice the bird will be able to enter his nest with no difficulty.

There's a saying, "Show me a beggar with goals, and I'll soon show you a millionaire. Show me a millionaire without goals, and I'll soon show you a beggar." Having goals, specific aims in life, will make you like these birds—you'll hit the mark. Writing not only the goals, but also the specific strategies to reach the goals, will make your dreams a reality. But don't blur the edges. If your strategy has you getting up at five o'clock, don't hit the snooze button for extra sleep. If you're supposed to make five sales calls, don't settle for four.

Be specific in your prayers, as well. They should be a focused part of your strategy for success. If you want your business to earn a million dollars, pray for that daily and diligently. Have others put that in their prayer time. God is a God of specifics. When you pray, make the most correct and direct approach you can so that your prayers can more surely hit their target.

---

reflect: Pray with directness and diligence on a daily basis.

Go to **1 Timothy 6:17.**

1 thessalonians

1 From Paul, Silas, and Timothy.

To the church in Thessalonica, the church in God the Father and the Lord Jesus Christ:

Grace and peace to you.

THE FAITH OF THE THESSALONIANS

[2] We always thank God for all of you and mention you when we pray. [3] We continually recall before God our Father the things you have done because of your faith and the work you have done because of your love. And we thank him that you continue to be strong because of your hope in our Lord Jesus Christ.

[4] Brothers and sisters, God loves you, and we know he has chosen you, [5] because the Good News we brought to you came not only with words, but with power, with the Holy Spirit, and with sure knowledge that it is true. Also you know how we lived when we were with you in order to help you. [6] And you became like us and like the Lord. You suffered much, but still you accepted the teaching with the joy that comes from the Holy Spirit. [7] So you became an example to all the believers in Macedonia and Southern Greece. [8] And the Lord's teaching spread from you not only into Macedonia and Southern Greece, but now your faith in God has become known everywhere. So we do not need to say anything about it. [9] People everywhere are telling about the way you accepted us when we were there with you. They tell how you stopped worshiping idols and began serving the living and true God. [10] And you wait for God's Son, whom God raised from the dead, to come from heaven. He is Jesus, who saves us from God's angry judgment that is sure to come.

PAUL'S WORK IN THESSALONICA

2 Brothers and sisters, you know our visit to you was not a failure. [2] Before we came to you, we suffered in Philippi. People there insulted us, as you know, and many people were against us. But our God helped us to be brave and to tell you his Good News. [3] Our appeal does not come from lies or wrong reasons, nor were we trying to trick you. [4] But we

speak the Good News because God tested us and trusted us to do it. When we speak, we are not trying to please people, but God, who tests our hearts. [5] You know that we never tried to influence you by saying nice things about you. We were not trying to get your money; we had no selfishness to hide from you. God knows that this is true. [6] We were not looking for human praise, from you or anyone else, [7] even though as apostles of Christ we could have used our authority over you.

But we were very gentle with you,[n] like a mother caring for her little children. [8] Because we loved you, we were happy to share not only God's Good News with you, but even our own lives. You had become so dear to us! [9] Brothers and sisters, I know you remember our hard work and difficulties. We worked night and day so we would not burden any of you while we preached God's Good News to you.

[10] When we were with you, we lived in a holy and honest way, without fault. You know this is true, and so does God. [11] You know that we treated each of you as a father treats his own children. [12] We encouraged you, we urged you, and we insisted that you live good lives for God, who calls you to his glorious kingdom.

[13] Also, we always thank God because when you heard his message from us, you accepted it as the word of God, not the words of humans. And it really is God's message which works in you who believe. [14] Brothers and sisters, your experiences have been like those of God's churches in Christ that are in Judea.[n] You suffered from the people of your own country, as they suffered from the Jews [15] who killed both the Lord Jesus and the prophets and forced us to leave that country. They do not please God and are against all people. [16] They try to stop us from teaching those who are not Jews so they may be saved. By doing this, they are increasing their

---

2:7 But . . . you Some Greek copies read "But we were like infants among you." **2:14 Judea** The Jewish land where Jesus lived and taught and where the church first began.

sins to the limit. The anger of God has come to them at last.

PAUL WANTS TO VISIT THEM AGAIN

[17]Brothers and sisters, though we were separated from you for a short time, our thoughts were still with you. We wanted very much to see you and tried hard to do so. [18]We wanted to come to you. I, Paul, tried to come more than once, but Satan stopped us. [19]You are our hope, our joy, and the crown we will take pride in when our Lord Jesus Christ comes. [20]Truly you are our glory and our joy.

3 When we could not wait any longer, we decided it was best to stay in Athens alone [2]and send Timothy to you. Timothy, our brother, works with us for God and helps us tell people the Good News about Christ. We sent him to strengthen and encourage you in your faith [3]so none of you would be upset by these troubles. You yourselves know that we must face these troubles. [4]Even when we were with you, we told you we all would have to suffer, and you know it has happened. [5]Because of this, when I could wait no longer, I sent Timothy to you so I could learn about your faith. I was afraid the devil had tempted you, and perhaps our hard work would have been wasted.

[6]But Timothy now has come back to us from you and has brought us good news about your faith and love. He told us that you always remember us in a good way and that you want to see us just as much as we want to see you. [7]So, brothers and sisters, while we have much trouble and suffering, we are encouraged about you because of your faith. [8]Our life is really full if you stand strong in the Lord. [9]We have so much joy before our God because of you. We cannot thank him enough for all the joy we feel. [10]Night and day we continue praying with all our heart that we can see you again and give you all the things you need to make your faith strong.

[11]Now may our God and Father himself and our Lord Jesus prepare the way for us to come to you. [12]May the Lord make your love grow more and multiply for each other and for all people so that you will love others as we love you. [13]May your hearts be made strong so that you will be holy and without fault before our God and Father when our Lord Jesus comes with all his holy ones.

A LIFE THAT PLEASES GOD

4 Brothers and sisters, we taught you how to live in a way that will please God, and you are living that way. Now we ask and encourage you in the Lord Jesus to live that way even more. [2]You know what we told you to do by the authority of the Lord Jesus. [3]God wants you to be holy and to stay away from sexual sins. [4]He wants each of you to learn to control your own body[n] in a way that is holy and honorable. [5]Don't use your body for sexual sin like the people who do not know God. [6]Also, do not wrong or cheat another Christian in this way. The Lord will punish people who do those things as we have already told you and warned you. [7]God called us to be holy and does not want us to live in sin. [8]So the person who refuses to obey this teaching is disobeying God, not simply a human teaching. And God is the One who gives us his Holy Spirit.

[9]We do not need to write you about having love for your Christian family, because God has already taught you to love each other. [10]And truly you do love the Christians in all of Macedonia. Brothers and sisters, now we encourage you to love them even more.

[11]Do all you can to live a peaceful life. Take care of your own business, and do your own work as we have already told you. [12]If you do, then people who are not believers will respect you, and you will not have to depend on others for what you need.

THE LORD'S COMING

[13]Brothers and sisters, we want you to know about those Christians who have died so you will not be sad, as others who have no hope. [14]We believe that Jesus died and that he rose again. So, because of him, God will raise with Jesus those who have died. [15]What we tell you now is the Lord's own message. We who are living when the Lord comes again will not go before those who have already died. [16]The Lord himself will come down from heaven with a loud command, with the voice of the archangel,[n] and with the trumpet call of God. And those who have died believing in Christ will rise first. [17]After that, we who are still alive will be gathered up with

---

4:4 learn . . . body This might also mean "learn to live with your own wife." **4:16 archangel** The leader among God's angels or messengers.

them in the clouds to meet the Lord in the air. And we will be with the Lord forever. ¹⁸So encourage each other with these words.

BE READY FOR THE LORD'S COMING

5 Now, brothers and sisters, we do not need to write you about times and dates. ²You know very well that the day the Lord comes again will be a surprise, like a thief that comes in the night. ³While people are saying, "We have peace and we are safe," they will be destroyed quickly. It is like pains that come quickly to a woman having a baby. Those people will not escape. ⁴But you, brothers and sisters, are not living in darkness, and so that day will not surprise you like a thief. ⁵You are all people who belong to the light and to the day. We do not belong to the night or to dark-

ness. ⁶So we should not be like other people who are sleeping, but we should be alert and have self-control. ⁷Those who sleep, sleep at night. Those who get drunk, get drunk at night. ⁸But we belong to the day, so we should control ourselves. We should wear faith and love to protect us, and the hope of salvation should be our helmet. ⁹God did not choose us to suffer his anger but to have salvation through our Lord Jesus Christ. ¹⁰Jesus died for us so that we can live together with him, whether we are alive or dead when he comes. ¹¹So encourage each other and give each other strength, just as you are doing now.

FINAL INSTRUCTIONS AND GREETINGS

¹²Now, brothers and sisters, we ask you to appreciate those who work hard among you,

---

HOPE IN THE HOLY SPIRIT

I **believe** in the **second coming** of **Jesus Christ**

FUTURE

By Jack Hayford

1 THESSALONIANS 4:15–18

I believe in the second coming of Jesus Christ. I believe he literally and physically ascended from the Mount of Olives and that he will come again the same way. His physical return is possible at any moment, and I wait with eager expectation until the trumpet sounds and he descends from heaven with a shout. Because I believe this, I reject any human proposal that predicts a day or date of his return.

I believe he is coming for his church like a bridegroom seeking a pure and devoted bride. I believe in his promise never to abandon us and to keep us on a path of growth and holiness so we will be ready for him when he returns. Because I believe this, I live each day as a wise servant awaiting his return. I walk with him in fellowship and my heart talks to him daily in prayer (Luke 12:35–38).

I believe he will establish his perfect kingdom upon the whole earth and that our decisions today determine our reign with him. Because I believe this, I serve him faithfully in his kingdom activities, doing his business reaching the lost and teaching his life and love by every means. With such hope as this, I live in assurance that he has prepared a place for me and is coming again to bring me home (Philippians 3:20).

reflect: What are you doing to prepare for the second coming of Jesus?
Go to **Revelation 21:3–5.**

who lead you in the Lord and teach you. ¹³Respect them with a very special love because of the work they do.

Live in peace with each other. ¹⁴We ask you, brothers and sisters, to warn those who do not work. Encourage the people who are afraid. Help those who are weak. Be patient with everyone. ¹⁵Be sure that no one pays back wrong for wrong, but always try to do what is good for each other and for all people.

¹⁶Always be joyful. ¹⁷Pray continually, ¹⁸and give thanks whatever happens. That is what God wants for you in Christ Jesus.

¹⁹Do not hold back the work of the Holy Spirit. ²⁰Do not treat prophecy as if it were unimportant. ²¹But test everything. Keep what is good, ²²and stay away from everything that is evil.

²³Now may God himself, the God of peace, make you pure, belonging only to him. May your whole self—spirit, soul, and body—be kept safe and without fault when our Lord Jesus Christ comes. ²⁴You can trust the One who calls you to do that for you.

²⁵Brothers and sisters, pray for us. ²⁶Give each other a holy kiss when you meet. ²⁷I tell you by the authority of the Lord to read this letter to all the believers.

²⁸The grace of our Lord Jesus Christ be with you.

BEATING THE BURNOUT BLUES

FULFILLMENT

don't forget to say "thank you"

1 THESSALONIANS 5:18

As we appreciate God as the source from whom all blessings flow, we give him glory. The expressions of thanks are evidences that we appreciate what God has done for us. Through his writings, Paul put a special emphasis on being thankful. For example, in the Book of Ephesians, Paul wrote about being filled with the Spirit and giving thanks always and in everything.

Superabundance of thanksgiving is the apostle's constant plea. In the Book of Philippians, he expresses that by prayer and petition with thanksgiving, we are to ask God for everything we need. Notice that our thanks should go before, or at least accompany, our requests to God. We can always thank him again for answering our requests when they are answered.

Giving thanks to God is a necessary act for a number of reasons. It reminds us of his goodness, it acknowledges him as the giver of gifts, and it helps to remind us of our dependency upon him. Giving thanks to God is a sign that we realize without him we are nothing. Salvation is the most important reason why we should thank God, for without the shed blood of Jesus Christ, we would not be able to enjoy eternal life with the Father. The greater this realization comes to us, the more sincere our heartfelt thanks to our Father will be.

reflect: Learn to give thanks to God for big and small blessings.

Go to **2 Timothy 2:16–17**.

2 thessalonians

THE PROBLEMS OF NEW CHRISTIANS

1 From Paul, Silas, and Timothy.

To the church in Thessalonica in God our Father and the Lord Jesus Christ:

²Grace and peace to you from God the Father and the Lord Jesus Christ.

PAUL TALKS ABOUT GOD'S JUDGMENT

³We must always thank God for you, brothers and sisters. This is only right, because your faith is growing more and more, and the love that every one of you has for each other is increasing. ⁴So we brag about you to the other churches of God. We tell them about the way you continue to be strong and have faith even though you are being treated badly and are suffering many troubles.

⁵This is proof that God is right in his judgment. He wants you to be counted worthy of his kingdom for which you are suffering. ⁶God will do what is right. He will give trouble to those who trouble you. ⁷And he will give rest to you who are troubled and to us also when the Lord Jesus appears with burning fire from heaven with his powerful angels. ⁸Then he will punish those who do not know God and who do not obey the Good News about our Lord Jesus Christ. ⁹Those people will be punished with a destruction that continues forever. They will be kept away from the Lord and from his great power. ¹⁰This will happen on the day when the Lord Jesus comes to receive glory because of his holy people. And all the people who have believed will be amazed at Jesus. You will be in that group, because you believed what we told you.

¹¹That is why we always pray for you, asking our God to help you live the kind of life he called you to live. We pray that with his power God will help you do the good things you want and perform the works that come from your faith. ¹²We pray all this so that the name of our Lord Jesus Christ will have glory in you, and you will have glory in him. That glory comes from the grace of our God and the Lord Jesus Christ.

EVIL THINGS WILL HAPPEN

2 Brothers and sisters, we have something to say about the coming of our Lord Jesus Christ and the time when we will meet together with him. ²Do not become easily upset in your thinking or afraid if you hear that the day of the Lord has already come. Someone may have said this in a prophecy or in a message or in a letter as if it came from us. ³Do not let anyone fool you in any way. That day of the Lord will not come until the turning away[n] from God happens and the Man of Evil,[n] who is on his way to hell, appears. ⁴He will be against and put himself above any so-called god or anything that people worship. And that Man of Evil will even go into God's Temple and sit there and say that he is God.

⁵I told you when I was with you that all this would happen. Do you not remember? ⁶And now you know what is stopping that Man of Evil so he will appear at the right time. ⁷The secret power of evil is already working in the world, but there is one who is stopping that power. And he will continue to stop it until he is taken out of the way. ⁸Then that Man of Evil will appear, and the Lord Jesus will kill him with the breath that comes from his mouth and will destroy him with the glory of his coming. ⁹The Man of Evil will come by the power of Satan. He will have great power, and he will do many different false miracles, signs, and wonders. ¹⁰He will use every kind of evil to trick those who are lost. They will die, because they refused to love the truth. (If they loved the truth, they would be saved.) ¹¹For this reason God sends them something powerful that leads them away from the truth so they will believe a lie. ¹²So all those will be judged guilty who did not believe the truth, but enjoyed doing evil.

2:3 **turning away** Or "the rebellion." 2:3 **Man of Evil** Some Greek copies read "Man of Sin."

YOU ARE CHOSEN FOR SALVATION

¹³Brothers and sisters, whom the Lord loves, God chose you from the beginning⁷ to be saved. So we must always thank God for you. You are saved by the Spirit that makes you holy and by your faith in the truth. ¹⁴God used the Good News that we preached to call you to be saved so you can share in the glory of our Lord Jesus Christ. ¹⁵So, brothers and sisters, stand strong and continue to believe the teachings we gave you in our speaking and in our letter.

¹⁶⁻¹⁷May our Lord Jesus Christ himself and God our Father encourage you and strengthen you in every good thing you do and say. God loved us, and through his grace he gave us a good hope and encouragement that continues forever.

PRAY FOR US

3 And now, brothers and sisters, pray for us that the Lord's teaching will continue to spread quickly and that people will give honor to that teaching, just as happened with you. ²And pray that we will be protected from stubborn and evil people, because not all people believe.

³But the Lord is faithful and will give you strength and will protect you from the Evil One. ⁴The Lord makes us feel sure that you are doing and will continue to do the things we told you. ⁵May the Lord lead your hearts into God's love and Christ's patience.

2:13 God . . . beginning Some Greek copies read "God chose you as the firstfruits of the harvest."

FAITH

UNWAVERING FAITH

how **faith** works

2 THESSALONIANS 2:13–15

By Wendell Smith

Faith is not just for you personally. Faith is not just to get rid of your headache or to make sure all of your bills get paid. It is not a magic wand so that you can go through life without too many problems and be a happy person. Jesus doesn't grant faith to you just so you can shake off that heavy feeling.

Faith is part of God's grand purpose to save the world. God is trying to stir faith in us so that all men and women might be saved. He wants to move us into a level of faith that can embrace his plans, so that there can be an expansion in our vision. Faith can grasp the reality that multitudes of people can come into the kingdom of heaven. That is faith. Faith is always tied into God's great objectives.

Faith is also action. Once you have heard a word from God, and you really know what he wants you to do, you actually have to do it. Just like Peter did, you have to step out of the boat and onto the water, something nobody could ever do unless the act is based on a word from Jesus. When you hear his voice, by faith and in complete trust, you can stir yourself up and actually step out onto the water. If Jesus calls you, you can say, "Yes, Lord! Here I come!"

---

reflect: Whom might you share your faith with today?

Go to **1 Timothy 6:12.**

THE DUTY TO WORK

⁶Brothers and sisters, by the authority of our Lord Jesus Christ we command you to stay away from any believer who refuses to work and does not follow the teaching we gave you. ⁷You yourselves know that you should live as we live. We were not lazy when we were with you. ⁸And when we ate another person's food, we always paid for it. We worked very hard night and day so we would not be an expense to any of you. ⁹We had the right to ask you to help us, but we worked to take care of ourselves so we would be an example for you to follow. ¹⁰When we were with you, we gave you this rule: "Anyone who refuses to work should not eat."

¹¹We hear that some people in your group refuse to work. They do nothing but busy themselves in other people's lives. ¹²We command those people and beg them in the Lord Jesus Christ to work quietly and earn their own food. ¹³But you, brothers and sisters, never become tired of doing good.

¹⁴If some people do not obey what we tell you in this letter, then take note of them. Have nothing to do with them so they will feel ashamed. ¹⁵But do not treat them as enemies. Warn them as fellow believers.

MENTORING WORLD CHANGERS FOR CHRIST

where is your team going?

FUTURE

By Bill McCartney

2 THESSALONIANS 3:5

Are you the leader of a team? Ask yourself a few questions. Who are you? Where are you going? It's time to take inventory. No matter your level of success in the past, you have to be ready to take things to a different level. Maybe you think you are already successful. How do you measure success? You can only measure success by improvement. You have to get better every day.

Sometimes a team doesn't know where it wants to go. Even if the players do know where they want to go, they usually don't know how to get there. Leaders take others where they don't know how to get or maybe don't want to go.

Your team can't succeed if the members don't work together. Everyone on the team has to be able to look into the eyes of the other members. The eyes tell the story. The eyes approve, accept, embrace, and deny. We have to be able to look each other in the eyes and find acceptance. We need to be able to trust each other when our backs are turned, instead of putting each other down.

We need to support each other and champion each other. When our backs are turned, when we're back to back, that effort to champion each other needs to happen or we won't have anything. If one falls, the other must help him up. We have to work together and have each other's best interests at heart. Can your team do that? Can you?

reflect: Are you the type of leader others will follow faithfully?
Go to **FUTURE:** "Inspire Your Team to Realize the Dream" at **John 21:6.**

FINAL WORDS

¹⁶Now may the Lord of peace give you peace at all times and in every way. The Lord be with all of you.

¹⁷I, Paul, end this letter now in my own handwriting. All my letters have this to show they are from me. This is the way I write.

¹⁸The grace of our Lord Jesus Christ be with you all.

1 From Paul, an apostle of Christ Jesus, by the command of God our Savior and Christ Jesus our hope.

²To Timothy, a true child to me because you believe:

Grace, mercy, and peace from God the Father and Christ Jesus our Lord.

WARNING AGAINST FALSE TEACHING

³I asked you to stay longer in Ephesus when I went into Macedonia so you could command some people there to stop teaching false things. ⁴Tell them not to spend their time on stories that are not true and on long lists of names in family histories. These things only bring arguments; they do not help God's work, which is done in faith. ⁵The purpose of this command is for people to have love, a love that comes from a pure heart and a good conscience and a true faith. ⁶Some people have missed these things and turned to useless talk. ⁷They want to be teachers of the law, but they do not understand either what they are talking about or what they are sure about.

⁸But we know that the law is good if someone uses it lawfully. ⁹We also know that the law is not made for good people but for those who are against the law and for those who refuse to follow it. It is for people who are against God and are sinful, who are unholy and ungodly, who kill their fathers and mothers, who murder, ¹⁰who take part in sexual sins, who have sexual relations with people of the same sex, who sell slaves, who tell lies, who speak falsely, and who do anything against the true teaching of God. ¹¹That teaching is part of the Good News of the blessed God that he gave me to tell.

THANKS FOR GOD'S MERCY

¹²I thank Christ Jesus our Lord, who gave me strength, because he trusted me and gave me this work of serving him. ¹³In the past I spoke against Christ and persecuted him and did all kinds of things to hurt him. But God showed me mercy, because I did not know what I was doing. I did not believe. ¹⁴But the grace of our Lord was fully given to me, and with that grace came the faith and love that are in Christ Jesus.

¹⁵What I say is true, and you should fully accept it: Christ Jesus came into the world to save sinners, of whom I am the worst. ¹⁶But I was given mercy so that in me, the worst of all sinners, Christ Jesus could show that he has patience without limit. His patience with me made me an example for those who would believe in him and have life forever. ¹⁷To the King that rules forever, who will never die, who cannot be seen, the only God, be honor and glory forever and ever. Amen.

¹⁸Timothy, my child, I am giving you a command that agrees with the prophecies that were given about you in the past. I tell you this so you can follow them and fight the good fight. ¹⁹Continue to have faith and do what you know is right. Some people have rejected this, and their faith has been shipwrecked. ²⁰Hymenaeus and Alexander have done that, and I have given them to Satan so they will learn not to speak against God.

SOME RULES FOR MEN AND WOMEN

2 First, I tell you to pray for all people, asking God for what they need and being thankful to him. ²Pray for rulers and for all who have authority so that we can have quiet and peaceful lives full of worship and respect for God. ³This is good, and it pleases God our Savior, ⁴who wants all people to be saved and to know the truth. ⁵There is one God and one mediator so that human beings can reach God. That way is through Christ Jesus, who is himself human. ⁶He gave himself as a payment to free all people. He is proof that came at the right time. ⁷That is why I was chosen to tell the Good News and to be an apostle. (I am telling the truth; I am not lying.) I was chosen to teach those who are not Jews to believe and to know the truth.

⁸So, I want the men everywhere to pray, lifting up their hands in a holy manner, without anger and arguments.

9Also, women should wear proper clothes that show respect and self-control, not using braided hair or gold or pearls or expensive clothes. 10Instead, they should do good deeds, which is right for women who say they worship God.

11Let a woman learn by listening quietly and being ready to cooperate in everything. 12But I do not allow a woman to teach or to have authority over a man, but to listen quietly, 13because Adam was formed first and then Eve. 14And Adam was not tricked, but the woman was tricked and became a sinner. 15But she will be saved through having children if she continues in faith, love, and holiness, with self-control.

ELDERS IN THE CHURCH

3 What I say is true: Anyone wanting to become an overseer desires a good work. 2An overseer must not give people a reason to

---

FINANCES

HANDLING MONEY GOD'S WAY

how the **father leads** the family in **finances**

1 TIMOTHY 3:1-4

By Elmer Towns

Every man has the responsibility of leading his family in the management of finances. How does he do this?

First, he leads by yielding himself to God. In 2 Corinthians 8:5, the Christians "first gave themselves to the Lord." A man must yield himself before he can lead others or yield anything else.

Second, the father leads family members to yield themselves to God. Romans 12:1 commands, "Offer your lives as a living sacrifice to him." Scripture teaches that money alone is not enough. The father must teach his family that God is more interested in having our hearts than our money.

Third, the father focuses the family finances. He communicates the importance of giving to God's work and puts the envelope into the offering plate on Sunday morning. He teaches the children about tithing and helps the children prepare their offerings each week. The father exercises financial self-discipline. When family members see that he doesn't buy everything he wants, even though he controls the finances, they will follow his example.

Fourth, the father prays about finances. He prays for guidance, including the incurring of debt. He prays for the financial needs of the church, for the family as a whole, and for each individual family member. He leads the family to ask God to supply those financial needs.

Last, the father gives to others. He helps needy relatives and the needy in the community. This giving is beyond the church and may involve both Christian and secular charities.

reflect: Are you an example of godly leadership when it comes to finances?
Go to **Malachi 3:8–12.**

criticize him, and he must have only one wife. He must be self-controlled, wise, respected by others, ready to welcome guests, and able to teach. ³He must not drink too much wine or like to fight, but rather be gentle and peaceable, not loving money. ⁴He must be a good family leader, having children who cooperate with full respect. ⁵(If someone does not know how to lead the family, how can that person take care of God's church?) ⁶But an elder must not be a new believer, or he might be too proud of himself and be judged guilty just as the devil was. ⁷An elder must also have the respect of people who are not in the church so he will not be criticized by others and caught in the devil's trap.

DEACONS IN THE CHURCH

⁸In the same way, deacons must be respected by others, not saying things they do not mean. They must not drink too much wine or try to get rich by cheating others. ⁹With a clear conscience they must follow the secret of the faith that God made known to us. ¹⁰Test them first. Then let them serve as deacons if you find nothing wrong in them. ¹¹In the same way, womenⁿ must be respected by others. They must not speak evil of others. They must be self-controlled and trustworthy in everything. ¹²Deacons must have only one wife and be good leaders of their children and their own families. ¹³Those who serve well as deacons are making an honorable place for themselves, and they will be very bold in their faith in Christ Jesus.

THE SECRET OF OUR LIFE

¹⁴Although I hope I can come to you soon, I am writing these things to you now. ¹⁵Then, even if I am delayed, you will know how to live in the family of God. That family is the church of the living God, the support and foundation of the truth. ¹⁶Without doubt, the secret of our life of worship is great:

Heⁿ was shown to us in a human body,
    proved right in spirit,
and seen by angels.
    He was proclaimed to the nations,
believed in by the world,
    and taken up in glory.

A WARNING ABOUT FALSE TEACHERS

4 Now the Holy Spirit clearly says that in the later times some people will stop believing the faith. They will follow spirits that lie and teachings of demons. ²Such teachings come from the false words of liars whose consciences are destroyed as if by a hot iron. ³They forbid people to marry and tell them not to eat certain foods which God created to be eaten with thanks by people who believe and know the truth. ⁴Everything God made is good, and nothing should be refused if it is accepted with thanks, ⁵because it is made holy by what God has said and by prayer.

BE A GOOD SERVANT OF CHRIST

⁶By telling these things to the brothers and sisters, you will be a good servant of Christ Jesus. You will be made strong by the words of the faith and the good teaching which you have been following. ⁷But do not follow foolish stories that disagree with God's truth, but train yourself to serve God. ⁸Training your body helps you in some ways, but serving God helps you in every way by bringing you blessings in this life and in the future life, too. ⁹What I say is true, and you should fully accept it. ¹⁰This is why we work and struggle:ⁿ We hope in the living God who is the Savior of all people, especially of those who believe.

¹¹Command and teach these things. ¹²Do not let anyone treat you as if you are unimportant because you are young. Instead, be an example to the believers with your words, your actions, your love, your faith, and your pure life. ¹³Until I come, continue to read the Scriptures to the people, strengthen them, and teach them. ¹⁴Use the gift you have, which was given to you through prophecy when the group of elders laid their hands onⁿ you. ¹⁵Continue to do those things; give your life to doing them so your progress may be seen by everyone. ¹⁶Be careful in your life and in your teaching. If you continue to live and teach rightly, you will save both yourself and those who listen to you.

RULES FOR LIVING WITH OTHERS

5 Do not speak angrily to an older man, but plead with him as if he were your father. Treat younger men like brothers, ²older

---

3:11 women This might mean the wives of the deacons, or it might mean women who serve in the same way as deacons. **3:16 He** Some Greek copies read "God." **4:10 struggle** Some Greek copies read "suffer." **4:14 laid their hands on** The laying on of hands had many purposes, including the giving of a blessing, power, or authority.

women like mothers, and younger women like sisters. Always treat them in a pure way.

³Take care of widows who are truly widows. ⁴But if a widow has children or grandchildren, let them first learn to do their duty to their own family and to repay their parents or grandparents. That pleases God. ⁵The true widow, who is all alone, puts her hope in God and continues to pray night and day for God's help. ⁶But the widow who uses her life to please herself is really dead while she is alive. ⁷Tell the believers to do these things so that no one can criticize them. ⁸Whoever does not care for his own relatives, especially his own family members, has turned against

the faith and is worse than someone who does not believe in God.

⁹To be on the list of widows, a woman must be at least sixty years old. She must have been faithful to her husband. ¹⁰She must be known for her good works—works such as raising her children, welcoming strangers, washing the feet of God's people, helping those in trouble, and giving her life to do all kinds of good deeds.

¹¹But do not put younger widows on that list. After they give themselves to Christ, they are pulled away from him by their physical desires, and then they want to marry again. ¹²They will be judged for not doing what

---

FITNESS

LOSING WEIGHT

take a **first step** toward **total fitness**

1 TIMOTHY 4:8 — By Lynne Dugan

You can experience the truth of Paul's words to Timothy, "Training your body helps you in some ways, but serving God helps you in every way by bringing you blessings in this life and in the future life, too" (1 Timothy 4:8).

My own first step in "training my body" was all it took to get me started on the road to total fitness—spiritual, mental, physical, and social—after a step on the scale revealed I was thirty-five pounds overweight and a look in the mirror revealed that the reflection I was seeing just had to change.

I was on my way to total fitness after reading an article on jogging. Although shortness of breath quickly reduced my jog to a labored walk around the block, I refused to give up so easily and added one block to my regimen each week until the blocks I was jogging added up to miles. The pounds of fat and the weight of stress dropped off all along the way. I went from a size 14 to a size 4 and am still there today.

During the past twenty-five years, what began as a small amount of self-discipline to go for a jog expanded to include a daily exercise routine that honors God in the other areas of my life. The key for me was not to count as unimportant the day of "small beginnings" (Zechariah 4:10).

reflect: What can you do to start fitness training today?
Go to **1 Corinthians 6:20.**

they first promised to do. ¹³Besides that, they learn to waste their time, going from house to house. And they not only waste their time but also begin to gossip and busy themselves with other people's lives, saying things they should not say. ¹⁴So I want the younger widows to marry, have children, and manage their homes. Then no enemy will have any reason to criticize them. ¹⁵But some have already turned away to follow Satan.

¹⁶If any woman who is a believer has widows in her family, she should care for them herself. The church should not have to care for them. Then it will be able to take care of those who are truly widows.

¹⁷The elders who lead the church well should receive double honor, especially those who work hard by speaking and teaching, ¹⁸because the Scripture says: "When an ox is working in the grain, do not cover its mouth

---

UNWAVERING FAITH

the **day** things
changed

FAITH

1 TIMOTHY 6:12

---

*F*ight: agonizomai—contend in a contest, labor fervently, strive to obtain; to be purpose-driven.

Life is a battle. But what fight are you fighting? Paul reminds Timothy of a critical event in Timothy's life, the day that he embraced eternal life by agreeing with the good words in front of witnesses. This was the day of Timothy's conversion. It was public. It was a significant transition. And it had eternal results.

Every believer has a personal God-day. It is the day that you turned your design for living over to the Designer so that his pattern could be woven into your fabric. The church celebrates these days with public declarations such as baptism, confirmation, and membership. These are all important.

But the day does not become "your day" until God comes to reign in your life. The day is God's day for you when you agree with God. He is right about you and about what you need. He is right about your status in life without him. He is right about a lot of things that you thought you knew better. That day is the beginning of the real you: the "you" God designed you to be.

One day life changes. It's the day when you enlist in God's army. It's the day you stop fighting a war for material accumulation and begin fighting a war for spiritual aspiration. It's the day you're ready to fight a "good" fight—a more noble, praiseworthy, pure, honorable, precious, loving fight. To be *driven* toward the character of God and develop your *purpose* in the midst of the on-going battle is to resist the ways of the world.

reflect: Ask yourself whether God is winning the battle for your life today.
Go to **Titus 1:2**.

Attaining Financial Freedom

FINANCES

By Sunday Adelaja

1 TIMOTHY 6:6-10

The Bible says that money answers for everything in the material world. We will always need money, even though we are spiritual beings, because money is a major means of resolving problems and issues on the earth. There is no doubt that money answers for a lot of problems of the world; but, on the other hand, money is not always the answer to everything in life. Where money fails, God cannot fail. God does what money cannot do.

We should also know that God is the source of all wealth, including money. He brings us wealth and money so we can overcome obstacles and hindrances in order for us to be effective in serving him and bringing his will to pass on earth. Money is dangerous if its purpose is not known. The purpose of money is to facilitate the kingdom of God on earth. Money is only a tool that we use to please God. The kingdom of God is the ultimate purpose of human love on earth.

Financial freedom is not a mystery. Money comes to those who practice the laws of money. One of the greatest laws of money is sowing and reaping. Another major law of money is savings and investments. The money that comes to our hand should not only be expended, but it also should work for us and be multiplied.

Build a foundation of mental victory over money. You must be able to look at a million dollars as if it is just paper. If you are moved or driven by it, you will be captivated, and it will become your master. Become a person who is rich within so you can administer money. Then wealth will have no power to destroy.

The key to not being captivated by money is to be wealthy with spiritual principles before trying to be rich with material possessions. Real wealth is found in heart contentment. If your heart is rich with the golden rules of the kingdom, you will be able to rule over money. If you do not apply those principles, money will rule you!

Life and money become enjoyable only when we allow money to serve us instead of our serving money. We are made to be masters of money—it should never master us! Never give money too important of a position in your heart. It should be regarded as a tool to meeting your needs. The most important place in your heart should always belong to God and his principles.

It is important to be satisfied in life with godliness. Do not expect money to become your source of satisfaction. Money can only temporarily gratify, as it can never give lasting satisfaction. Money is only a tool for accomplishing the purposes and will of God on the earth. Never give it too great a place in your heart, realizing that money is a bad master, but a good servant.

TO LEARN MORE ON WHAT THE BIBLE HAS TO SAY ABOUT **FINANCES,** READ THE SCRIPTURES AND DEVOTIONALS AT **2 CORINTHIANS 8:5, 2 CORINTHIANS 9:7, GALATIANS 4:18, GALATIANS 5:1, PROVERBS 11:28,** AND **EPHESIANS 6:5–8.**

to keep it from eating,"[n] and "A worker should be given his pay."[n]

[19] Do not listen to someone who accuses an elder, without two or three witnesses. [20] Tell those who continue sinning that they are wrong. Do this in front of the whole church so that the others will have a warning.

[21] Before God and Christ Jesus and the chosen angels, I command you to do these things without showing favor of any kind to anyone.

[22] Think carefully before you lay your hands on[n] anyone, and don't share in the sins of others. Keep yourself pure.

[23] Stop drinking only water, but drink a little wine to help your stomach and your frequent sicknesses.

5:18 "When . . . eating." Quotation from Deuteronomy 25:4. **5:18 "A worker . . . pay."** Quotation from Luke 10:7. **5:22 lay your hands on** The laying on of hands had many purposes, including the giving of a blessing, power, or authority.

WHAT JESUS WANTS

no such thing as "**financial security**"

FINANCES

1 TIMOTHY 6:17

The New Testament insists that we not be conformed to the patterns of this world. But patterns of this world are not limited to obvious immoral behaviors. In this verse, Paul exposes another pattern—one that is perhaps more damaging than any violation of moral code. It is the pattern of self-security.

There really is no such thing as financial security. If you don't have money, you're insecure in that you don't know if your needs will be met. If you do have it, you're afraid you might lose it. Security placed in wealth is security that stands on a completely false foundation. No matter how much money you have, it provides no real protection in life. Sickness, calamity, natural disaster, accident, and death cannot be thwarted by wealth.

Trusting in wealth is a pattern of the world that destroys every particle of peace the life of God gives. Paul reminds us that riches are the least tangible of assets. They are a vapor of economic agreement, subject to every kind of market, social, and political pressure. Real treasure is what God values, not what humanity desires.

This pattern is very difficult to counteract. We all see its simple truth, yet we all tend to view our lives on the measurement scale of buying power. That leaves us in a constant state of fear, far from the peace of God. In order for us to overcome this pattern, we must believe what God says, not what we see. But isn't that what genuine faith requires?

reflect: Believe God to provide all of your needs, both temporal and eternal ones.

You have completed the **FINANCES** readings. Now go to **FITNESS:** "When Your Way Isn't God's Way" at **Job 10:8–9.**

²⁴The sins of some people are easy to see even before they are judged, but the sins of others are seen only later. ²⁵So also good deeds are easy to see, but even those that are not easily seen cannot stay hidden.

6 All who are slaves under a yoke should show full respect to their masters so no one will speak against God's name and our teaching. ²The slaves whose masters are believers should not show their masters any less respect because they are believers. They should serve their masters even better, because they are helping believers they love.

You must teach and preach these things.

FALSE TEACHING AND TRUE RICHES

³Anyone who has a different teaching does not agree with the true teaching of our Lord Jesus Christ and the teaching that shows the true way to serve God. ⁴This person is full of pride and understands nothing, but is sick with a love for arguing and fighting about words. This brings jealousy, fighting, speaking against others, evil mistrust, ⁵and constant quarrels from those who have evil minds and have lost the truth. They think that serving God is a way to get rich.

⁶Serving God does make us very rich, if we are satisfied with what we have. ⁷We brought nothing into the world, so we can take nothing out. ⁸But, if we have food and clothes, we will be satisfied with that. ⁹Those who want to become rich bring temptation to themselves and are caught in a trap. They want many foolish and harmful things that ruin and destroy people. ¹⁰The love of money causes all kinds of evil. Some people have left the faith, because they wanted to get more money, but they have caused themselves much sorrow.

SOME THINGS TO REMEMBER

¹¹But you, man of God, run away from all those things. Instead, live in the right way, serve God, have faith, love, patience, and gentleness. ¹²Fight the good fight of faith, grabbing hold of the life that continues forever. You were called to have that life when you confessed the good confession before many witnesses. ¹³In the sight of God, who gives life to everything, and of Christ Jesus, I give you a command. Christ Jesus made the good confession when he stood before Pontius Pilate. ¹⁴Do what you were commanded to do without wrong or blame until our Lord Jesus Christ comes again. ¹⁵God will make that happen at the right time. He is the blessed and only Ruler, the King of all kings and the Lord of all lords. ¹⁶He is the only One who never dies. He lives in light so bright no one can go near it. No one has ever seen God, or can see him. May honor and power belong to God forever. Amen.

¹⁷Command those who are rich with things of this world not to be proud. Tell them to hope in God, not in their uncertain riches. God richly gives us everything to enjoy. ¹⁸Tell the rich people to do good, to be rich in doing good deeds, to be generous and ready to share. ¹⁹By doing that, they will be saving a treasure for themselves as a strong foundation for the future. Then they will be able to have the life that is true life.

²⁰Timothy, guard what God has trusted to you. Stay away from foolish, useless talk and from the arguments of what is falsely called "knowledge." ²¹By saying they have that "knowledge," some have missed the true faith.

Grace be with you.

2 timothy

1 From Paul, an apostle of Christ Jesus by the will of God. God sent me to tell about the promise of life that is in Christ Jesus.

[2] To Timothy, a dear child to me:

Grace, mercy, and peace to you from God the Father and Christ Jesus our Lord.

ENCOURAGEMENT FOR TIMOTHY

[3] I thank God as I always mention you in my prayers, day and night. I serve him, doing what I know is right as my ancestors did. [4] Remembering that you cried for me, I want very much to see you so I can be filled with joy. [5] I remember your true faith. That faith first lived in your grandmother Lois and in your mother Eunice, and I know you now have that same faith. [6] This is why I remind you to keep using the gift God gave you when I laid my hands on[n] you. Now let it grow, as a small flame grows into a fire. [7] God did not give us a spirit that makes us afraid but a spirit of power and love and self-control.

[8] So do not be ashamed to tell people about our Lord Jesus, and do not be ashamed of me, in prison for the Lord. But suffer with me for the Good News. God, who gives us the strength to do that, [9] saved us and made us his holy people. That was not because of anything we did ourselves but because of God's purpose and grace. That grace was given to us through Christ Jesus before time began, [10] but it is now shown to us by the coming of our Savior Christ Jesus. He destroyed death, and through the Good News he showed us the way to have life that cannot be destroyed. [11] I was chosen to tell that Good News and to be an apostle and a teacher. [12] I am suffering now because I tell the Good News, but I am not ashamed, because I know Jesus, the One in whom I have believed. And I am sure he is able to protect what he has trusted me with until that day.[n] [13] Follow the pattern of true teachings that you heard from me in faith and love, which are in Christ Jesus. [14] Protect the truth that you were given; protect it with the help of the Holy Spirit who lives in us.

[15] You know that everyone in Asia has left me, even Phygelus and Hermogenes. [16] May the Lord show mercy to the family of Onesiphorus, who has often helped me and was not ashamed that I was in prison. [17] When he came to Rome, he looked eagerly for me until he found me. [18] May the Lord allow him to find mercy from the Lord on that day. You know how many ways he helped me in Ephesus.

A LOYAL SOLDIER OF CHRIST JESUS

2 You then, Timothy, my child, be strong in the grace we have in Christ Jesus. [2] You should teach people whom you can trust the things you and many others have heard me say. Then they will be able to teach others. [3] Share in the troubles we have like a good soldier of Christ Jesus. [4] A soldier wants to please the enlisting officer, so no one serving in the army wastes time with everyday matters. [5] Also an athlete who takes part in a contest must obey all the rules in order to win. [6] The farmer who works hard should be the first person to get some of the food that was grown. [7] Think about what I am saying, because the Lord will give you the ability to understand everything.

[8] Remember Jesus Christ, who was raised from the dead, who is from the family of David. This is the Good News I preach, [9] and I am suffering because of it to the point of being bound with chains like a criminal. But God's teaching is not in chains. [10] So I patiently accept all these troubles so that those whom God has chosen can have the salvation that is in Christ Jesus. With that salvation comes glory that never ends.

[11] This teaching is true:
If we died with him, we will also live with
    him.
[12] If we accept suffering, we will also rule
    with him.

1:6 laid my hands on The laying on of hands had many purposes, including the giving of a blessing, power, or authority. **1:12 day** The day Christ will come to judge all people and take his people to live with him.

If we say we don't know him, he will say
he doesn't know us.
13 If we are not faithful, he will still be
faithful,
because he must be true to who he is.

A WORKER PLEASING TO GOD

14Continue teaching these things, warning people in God's presence not to argue about words. It does not help anyone, and it ruins those who listen. 15Make every effort to give yourself to God as the kind of person he will approve. Be a worker who is not ashamed and who uses the true teaching in the right way. 16Stay away from foolish, useless talk, because that will lead people further away

from God. 17Their evil teaching will spread like a sickness inside the body. Hymenaeus and Philetus are like that. 18They have left the true teaching, saying that the rising from the dead has already taken place, and so they are destroying the faith of some people. 19But God's strong foundation continues to stand. These words are written on the seal: "The Lord knows those who belong to him,"[n] and "Everyone who wants to belong to the Lord must stop doing wrong."

20In a large house there are not only things made of gold and silver, but also things made

2:19 "The Lord . . . him." Quotation from Numbers 16:5.

LESSONS FROM THE BATTLEFIELD

FUTURE

playing for God

2 TIMOTHY 1:3

If you ever played high school football, you soon discovered that there was always a coach up in the stands recording every play. While the parents sat in the stands cheering on the team and hoping their boys would do well, little did they know that there was a camera judging every move their children were making.

As a player, you always have a subtle awareness that every move is being watched. While the video of the games sometimes misses a good play, it never seems to miss a mistake. After each game, the coaches review the tape to determine how each of the players executed his plays. Then the team gets together to look at the film with the coaches.

During the game, it is often hard to figure out who messed up. If it was you, you could lie about it, hide it, deny it, or point fingers. However, on Monday afternoons, the truth comes out. The coach will always say, "The eye in the sky doesn't lie."

You can fool some of the people all of the time, you can fool all of the people some of the time, and you can even fool yourself part of the time, but you can't fool God any time. If you play the game of life with that in mind, you will play a much better game.

reflect: Live your life continually aware of the presence of God, and you'll experience fewer regrets.
Go to **Hebrews 10:23–25.**

of wood and clay. Some things are used for special purposes, and others are made for ordinary jobs. ²¹All who make themselves clean from evil will be used for special purposes. They will be made holy, useful to the Master, ready to do any good work.

²²But run away from the evil desires of youth. Try hard to live right and to have faith, love, and peace, together with those who trust in the Lord from pure hearts. ²³Stay away from foolish and stupid arguments, because you know they grow into quarrels. ²⁴And a servant of the Lord must not quarrel but must be kind to everyone, a good teacher, and patient. ²⁵The Lord's servant must gently teach those who disagree. Then maybe God will let them change their minds so they can accept the truth. ²⁶And they may wake up

and escape from the trap of the devil, who catches them to do what he wants.

THE LAST DAYS

3 Remember this! In the last days there will be many troubles, ²because people will love themselves, love money, brag, and be proud. They will say evil things against others and will not obey their parents or be thankful or be the kind of people God wants. ³They will not love others, will refuse to forgive, will gossip, and will not control themselves. They will be cruel, will hate what is good, ⁴will turn against their friends, and will do foolish things without thinking. They will be conceited, will love pleasure instead of God, ⁵and will act as if they serve God but will not have his power. Stay away from those people. ⁶Some of them go into homes and get

---

BEATING THE BURNOUT BLUES

foolish, useless talk

FULFILLMENT

2 TIMOTHY 2:16-17

The Word of God tells us to avoid foolish, useless talk. What is foolish, useless talk? It is talk about things that are not of a constructive nature. It is talk that is defeatist or negative. It is acceptable in society continually to offer jokes at another person's expense. We see it on a daily basis on the television advertisements. The people who watch these shows have the idea this is an acceptable way to live. However, that is not what is told to us in the Scriptures. The apostle Paul tells us not to allow any word to come out of our mouths that is not beneficial to others.

One of the most feared diseases today is cancer. But foolish, useless talk is linguistic cancer and just as deadly. The Lord is adamant about the fact that talking like this is evil. In the Gospels, the Pharisees were debating the Scripture with Jesus. They attempted to trap him in a discussion about a woman with seven consecutive husbands. Jesus told them that they erred. Jesus saw that their talk was not motivated by a desire to know God but rather by a desire to boost ego. Endless debates may cause us to stray from our faith. It is our motivation that matters. If our talk causes dissension among our brothers and sisters in Christ, we need to cease from it.

reflect: Speak words that are full of life instead of death.
Go to **Hebrews 3:1.**

control of silly women who are full of sin and are led by many evil desires. 7These women are always learning new teachings, but they are never able to understand the truth fully. 8Just as Jannes and Jambres were against Moses, these people are against the truth. Their thinking has been ruined, and they have failed in trying to follow the faith. 9But they will not be successful in what they do, because as with Jannes and Jambres, everyone will see that they are foolish.

OBEY THE TEACHINGS

10But you have followed what I teach, the way I live, my goal, faith, patience, and love. You know I never give up. 11You know how I have been hurt and have suffered, as in Antioch, Iconium, and Lystra. I have suffered, but the Lord saved me from all those troubles. 12Everyone who wants to live as God desires, in Christ Jesus, will be persecuted. 13But people who are evil and cheat others will go from bad to worse. They will fool others, but they will also be fooling themselves.

14But you should continue following the teachings you learned. You know they are true, because you trust those who taught you. 15Since you were a child you have known the Holy Scriptures which are able to make you wise. And that wisdom leads to salvation through faith in Christ Jesus. 16All Scripture is inspired by God and is useful for teaching, for showing people what is wrong in their lives, for correcting faults, and for teaching how to live right. 17Using the Scriptures, the person who serves God will be capable, having all that is needed to do every good work.

4 I give you a command in the presence of God and Christ Jesus, the One who will judge the living and the dead, and by his coming and his kingdom: 2Preach the Good News. Be ready at all times, and tell people what they need to do. Tell them when they are wrong. Encourage them with great

---

FITNESS

LOSING WEIGHT

we're informed **beyond** our level of **discipline**

2 TIMOTHY 4:7

In the classic movie *Karate Kid*, when Mr. Miaggi asked Daniel-san if he was ready to start his karate training, the boy answered, "I guess so." Mr. Miaggi explained that it is fine if you walk on the right side of the road and fine if you walk on the left side of the road, but if you walk down the middle of the road, it is not fine.

We've got to learn what it takes to honor our commitments. It is important for us to understand what it means to develop maturely enough so that we have the discipline to finish what we started. We need to learn either not to begin a task or to complete what we set out to accomplish.

The importance of our bodies goes beyond our current level of awareness. That is to say, we unconsciously make decisions about what we do with our bodies every day. Our bodies are important to God, the people we serve, and the people who care about us.

reflect: Commit yourself to maintaining your health with the help of God.
Go to **Romans 12:1.**

patience and careful teaching, 3because the time will come when people will not listen to the true teaching but will find many more teachers who please them by saying the things they want to hear. 4They will stop listening to the truth and will begin to follow false stories. 5But you should control yourself at all times, accept troubles, do the work of telling the Good News, and complete all the duties of a servant of God.

6My life is being given as an offering to God, and the time has come for me to leave this life. 7I have fought the good fight, I have finished the race, I have kept the faith. 8Now, a crown is being held for me—a crown for being right with God. The Lord, the judge who judges rightly, will give the crown to me on that day[n]—not only to me but to all those who have waited with love for him to come again.

PERSONAL WORDS

9Do your best to come to me as soon as you can, 10because Demas, who loved this world, left me and went to Thessalonica. Crescens went to Galatia, and Titus went to Dalmatia. 11Luke is the only one still with me. Get Mark and bring him with you when you come, because he can help me in my work here. 12I sent Tychicus to Ephesus. 13When I was in Troas, I left my coat there with Carpus. So when you come, bring it to me, along with my books, particularly the ones written on parchment.[n]

14Alexander the metalworker did many harmful things against me. The Lord will punish him for what he did. 15You also should be careful that he does not hurt you, because he fought strongly against our teaching.

16The first time I defended myself, no one helped me; everyone left me. May they be forgiven. 17But the Lord stayed with me and gave me strength so I could fully tell the Good News to all those who are not Jews. So I was saved from the lion's mouth. 18The Lord will save me when anyone tries to hurt me, and he will bring me safely to his heavenly kingdom. Glory forever and ever be the Lord's. Amen.

FINAL GREETINGS

19Greet Priscilla and Aquila and the family of Onesiphorus. 20Erastus stayed in Corinth, and I left Trophimus sick in Miletus. 21Try as hard as you can to come to me before winter.

Eubulus sends greetings to you. Also Pudens, Linus, Claudia, and all the brothers and sisters in Christ greet you.

22The Lord be with your spirit. Grace be with you.

4:8 day The day Christ will come to judge all people and take his people to live with him. **4:13 parchment** A writing paper made from the skins of sheep.

titus

PAUL INSTRUCTS TITUS

1 From Paul, a servant of God and an apostle of Jesus Christ. I was sent to help the faith of God's chosen people and to help them know the truth that shows people how to serve God. ²That faith and that knowledge come from the hope for life forever, which God promised to us before time began. And God cannot lie. ³At the right time God let the world know about that life through preaching. He trusted me with that work, and I preached by the command of God our Savior.

⁴To Titus, my true child in the faith we share:

Grace and peace from God the Father and Christ Jesus our Savior.

TITUS' WORK IN CRETE

⁵I left you in Crete so you could finish doing the things that still needed to be done and so you could appoint elders in every town, as I directed you. ⁶An elder must not be guilty of doing wrong, must have only one wife, and must have believing children.

UNWAVERING FAITH

FAITH

the **whole** truth

TITUS 1:2

What would it be like to have a friend who could never lie? Even the best of our friends don't always tell the truth. They may have good reasons to shield us from reality, but in the end, all good reasons for lying still cover up what we need to know in order to live completely. The power of a lie is always in the secret it holds. But God *cannot* lie. Lying is not even a possibility for him. The word here literally says that God can never be false. What God says is always 100 percent true.

Imagine how life would change if we really believed this. God tells us not to worry about our needs. Do we trust him accordingly? God says that we have truly been forgiven. Do we let go of the guilt and shame? God says that those who live without his grace are doomed. Do we feel the obligation to tell others? God says that we will give an account of every act of our lives. Are we careful about what we do and say? God says that there is no way for favor with him except through his Son. Do we choose to accept that remedy? God says that self-sacrifice is the mark of a Christian. Are we so abandoned to him that we do not hold on to our own plans and desires?

reflect: Rejoice in the fact that you can trust God with every detail of your life.

Go to **FAITH:** "Jesus, Who Was, and Is, and Is to Come" at **Revelation 1:8.**

They must not be known as children who are wild and do not cooperate. ⁷As God's managers, overseers must not be guilty of doing wrong, being selfish, or becoming angry quickly. They must not drink too much wine, like to fight, or try to get rich by cheating others. ⁸Overseers must be ready to welcome guests, love what is good, be wise, live right, and be holy and self-controlled. ⁹By holding on to the trustworthy word just as we teach it, overseers can help people by using true teaching, and they can show those who are against the true teaching that they are wrong.

¹⁰There are many people who refuse to cooperate, who talk about worthless things and lead others into the wrong way—mainly those who insist on circumcision to be saved. ¹¹These people must be stopped, because they are upsetting whole families by teaching things they should not teach, which they do to get rich by cheating people. ¹²Even one of their own prophets said, "Cretans are always liars, evil animals, and lazy people who do nothing but

---

THE ONE PERCENT SOLUTION

sluggish **body**, sluggish **mind**

FITNESS

By Doug Stringer

TITUS 2:12

We all want to think clearly and possess enough energy to engage fully with **people** and accomplish what we need to accomplish. The key to these things is making sure your body is in good condition. The benefits to taking care of your physical health are many, including stress management, better blood circulation, and improved relaxation and sleep. Proper diet and activity help control weight loss or gain and bolster your psychological well-being, enthusiasm, and optimism.

There is no overnight way to gain good condition. However, everyone can develop a fitness discipline to improve overall personal health and fitness. You will feel better while you firm, tone, and condition your physical body, and you will develop disciplines for your spiritual body, as well.

Even if you've learned to enjoy things that are harmful to your body and spirit, there is hope. The Holy Spirit will help you discipline your body, attitudes, and thinking patterns. Your first priority is your spirit being, and your exercises in discipline must include spiritual fitness.

Physical training, like spiritual growth, becomes a way of life if practiced on a regular basis. Like good eating habits, physical and spiritual routines are a lifetime commitment. When your life is in order and you keep your body and spirit in balance, you will experience total health as a child of God created in his image.

reflect: What is the next step you can take to improve your overall fitness?
Go to **2 Corinthians 4:7**.

eat." ¹³The words that prophet said are true. So firmly tell those people they are wrong so they may become strong in the faith, ¹⁴not accepting Jewish false stories and the commands of people who reject the truth. ¹⁵To those who are pure, all things are pure, but to those who are full of sin and do not believe, nothing is pure. Both their minds and their consciences have been ruined. ¹⁶They say they know God, but their actions show they do not accept him. They are hateful people, they refuse to obey, and they are useless for doing anything good.

FOLLOWING THE TRUE TEACHING

2 But you must tell everyone what to do to follow the true teaching. ²Teach older men to be self-controlled, serious, wise, strong in faith, in love, and in patience.

³In the same way, teach older women to be holy in their behavior, not speaking against others or enslaved to too much wine, but teaching what is good. ⁴Then they can teach the young women to love their husbands, to love their children, ⁵to be wise and pure, to be good workers at home, to be kind, and to yield to their husbands. Then no one will be able to criticize the teaching God gave us.

⁶In the same way, encourage young men to be wise. ⁷In every way be an example of doing good deeds. When you teach, do it with honesty and seriousness. ⁸Speak the truth so that you cannot be criticized. Then those who are against you will be ashamed because there is nothing bad to say about us.

⁹Slaves should yield to their own masters at all times, trying to please them and not

---

JESUS, WHO WAS, AND IS, AND IS TO COME

FAITH

right path thinking

TITUS 3:3

Have you noticed something important in Paul's list? The first three words are all about mental processes, not about behavior. The third word means "to be led astray." It comes from a word that means "to wander out of the right way." This is the first word in the list that is *passive*. It is something done to you, not something you do. Who makes you wander out of the right way? Who leads you astray?

Jesus gives us the answer in his instruction on prayer in Matthew 6:13: "And do not cause us to be tempted, but save us from the Evil One." Jesus' prayer asks God to give us guidance that will not let us wander and to deliver us from the one who wants us to wander. On another occasion Jesus made it very clear when he called Satan the father of lies and the great deceiver.

Satan knows well that the battle is about your mind. When Paul told us that we would become new creatures through the renewal of the *mind*, he acknowledged the scene of the battle. Don't bother with counting merit badges for outward action. Ask the tough questions: How is my attitude? What is my mind-set? How am I thinking?

reflect: Think godly thoughts today instead of thoughts that will lead you astray.
Go to **Hebrews 11:1–2.**

arguing with them. ¹⁰They should not steal from them but should show their masters they can be fully trusted so that in everything they do they will make the teaching of God our Savior attractive.

¹¹That is the way we should live, because God's grace that can save everyone has come. ¹²It teaches us not to live against God nor to do the evil things the world wants to do. Instead, that grace teaches us to live in the present age in a wise and right way and in a way that shows we serve God. ¹³We should live like that while we wait for our great hope and the coming of the glory of our great God and Savior Jesus Christ. ¹⁴He gave himself for us so he might pay the price to free us from all evil and to make us pure people who belong only to him—people who are always wanting to do good deeds.

¹⁵Say these things and encourage the people and tell them what is wrong in their lives, with all authority. Do not let anyone treat you as if you were unimportant.

THE RIGHT WAY TO LIVE

3 Remind the believers to yield to the authority of rulers and government leaders, to obey them, to be ready to do good, ²to speak no evil about anyone, to live in peace, and to be gentle and polite to all people.

³In the past we also were foolish. We did not obey, we were wrong, and we were slaves to many things our bodies wanted and enjoyed. We spent our lives doing evil and being jealous. People hated us, and we hated each other. ⁴But when the kindness and love of God our Savior was shown, ⁵he saved us because of his mercy. It was not because of good deeds we did to be right with him. He saved us through the washing that made us new people through the Holy Spirit. ⁶God poured out richly upon us that Holy Spirit through Jesus Christ our Savior. ⁷Being made right with God by his grace, we could have the hope of receiving the life that never ends.

⁸This teaching is true, and I want you to be sure the people understand these things. Then those who believe in God will be careful to use their lives for doing good. These things are good and will help everyone.

⁹But stay away from those who have foolish arguments and talk about useless family histories and argue and quarrel about the law. Those things are worth nothing and will not help anyone. ¹⁰After a first and second warning, avoid someone who causes arguments. ¹¹You can know that such people are evil and sinful; their own sins prove them wrong.

SOME THINGS TO REMEMBER

¹²When I send Artemas or Tychicus to you, make every effort to come to me at Nicopolis, because I have decided to stay there this winter. ¹³Do all you can to help Zenas the lawyer and Apollos on their journey so that they have everything they need. ¹⁴Our people must learn to use their lives for doing good deeds to provide what is necessary so that their lives will not be useless.

¹⁵All who are with me greet you. Greet those who love us in the faith.

Grace be with you all.

philemon

A SLAVE BECOMES A CHRISTIAN

¹From Paul, a prisoner of Christ Jesus, and from Timothy, our brother.

To Philemon, our dear friend and worker with us; ²to Apphia, our sister; to Archippus, a worker with us; and to the church that meets in your home:

³Grace and peace to you from God our Father and the Lord Jesus Christ.

PHILEMON'S LOVE AND FAITH

⁴I always thank my God when I mention you in my prayers, ⁵because I hear about the love you have for all God's holy people and the faith you have in the Lord Jesus. ⁶I pray that the faith you share may make you understand every blessing we have in Christ. ⁷I have great joy and comfort, my brother, because the love you have shown to God's people has refreshed them.

ACCEPT ONESIMUS AS A BROTHER

⁸So, in Christ, I could be bold and order you to do what is right. ⁹But because I love you, I am pleading with you instead. I, Paul, an old man now and also a prisoner for Christ Jesus, ¹⁰am pleading with you for my child Onesimus, who became my child while I was in prison. ¹¹In the past he was useless to you, but now he has become useful for both you and me.

¹²I am sending him back to you, and with him I am sending my own heart. ¹³I wanted to keep him with me so that in your place he might help me while I am in prison for the Good News. ¹⁴But I did not want to do anything without asking you first so that any good you do for me will be because you want to do it, not because I forced you. ¹⁵Maybe Onesimus was separated from you for a short time so you could have him back forever— ¹⁶no longer as a slave, but better than a slave, as a loved brother. I love him very much, but you will love him even more, both as a person and as a believer in the Lord.

¹⁷So if you consider me your partner, welcome Onesimus as you would welcome me. ¹⁸If he has done anything wrong to you or if he owes you anything, charge that to me. ¹⁹I, Paul, am writing this with my own hand. I will pay it back, and I will say nothing about what you owe me for your own life. ²⁰So, my brother, I ask that you do this for me in the Lord: Refresh my heart in Christ. ²¹I write this letter, knowing that you will do what I ask you and even more.

²²One more thing—prepare a room for me in which to stay, because I hope God will answer your prayers and I will be able to come to you.

FINAL GREETINGS

²³Epaphras, a prisoner with me for Christ Jesus, sends greetings to you. ²⁴And also Mark, Aristarchus, Demas, and Luke, workers together with me, send greetings.

²⁵The grace of our Lord Jesus Christ be with your spirit.

ANGER MANAGEMENT

healing your spirit

FITNESS

By Phil Pringle

PHILEMON 17–21

The physical and spiritual healing processes are often similar. When your flesh is cut, the wound has to be cleansed so it will not become infected. Whether the wound is deep or superficial, it is closed somehow, either by stitching it together or by drawing it together with a bandage.

You close and heal cuts in your spirit by forgiving and forgetting. It can be an extremely difficult thing to let go of unkind words, unfair treatment, or actions that have wounded your spirit. These offenses seem to surface time and again in your memory and cause the pain to be relived over and over. If you desire to be free from this hurt, it is very important that you forgive whoever caused the wound and forget his or her words and actions.

Forgiveness is the key to healing. Jesus tells us that if we expect forgiveness from God, then we must be forgiving toward those who have wronged us (Matthew 6:12). To forgive is to stand in the presence of God in prayer and say, "I forgive so and so. I bless that person in the name of Jesus." This is not some superstitious ritual, but the ripping up of any IOUs. It is being able to state there is not a soul on earth whom you hold any grudge against, and no one owes you an apology.

After you close the wounds with forgiveness, surround yourself with positive and spiritually healthy people. And actively worship God. This acts as an antiseptic to prevent infection. You will be restored when you apply the medications that bring healing.

reflect: What offense do you need to forgive and forget today?
Go to **FITNESS:** "The Life You Were Born to Live" at **Jeremiah 29:11.**

hebrews

A BETTER LIFE THROUGH CHRIST

GOD SPOKE THROUGH HIS SON

1 In the past God spoke to our ancestors through the prophets many times and in many different ways. [2]But now in these last days God has spoken to us through his Son. God has chosen his Son to own all things, and through him he made the world. [3]The Son reflects the glory of God and shows exactly what God is like. He holds everything together with his powerful word. When the Son made people clean from their sins, he sat down at the right side of God, the Great One in heaven. [4]The Son became much greater than the angels, and God gave him a name that is much greater than theirs.

[5]This is because God never said to any of the angels,

"You are my Son.
Today I have become your Father."
Psalm 2:7

Nor did God say of any angel,

"I will be his Father,
and he will be my Son."   *2 Samuel 7:14*

[6]And when God brings his firstborn Son into the world, he says,

"Let all God's angels worship him."[n]
Psalm 97:7

[7]This is what God said about the angels:

"God makes his angels become like winds.
He makes his servants become like
flames of fire."   *Psalm 104:4*

[8]But God said this about his Son:

"God, your throne will last forever and ever.
You will rule your kingdom with fairness.
[9] You love right and hate evil,
so God has chosen you from among
your friends;
he has set you apart with much joy."
Psalm 45:6–7

[10]God also says,

"Lord, in the beginning you made the earth,
and your hands made the skies.
[11] They will be destroyed, but you will remain.
They will all wear out like clothes.
[12] You will fold them like a coat.
And, like clothes, you will change them.

But you never change,
and your life will never end."
Psalm 102:25–27

[13]And God never said this to an angel:

"Sit by me at my right side
until I put your enemies under your
control."[n]   *Psalm 110:1*

[14]All the angels are spirits who serve God and are sent to help those who will receive salvation.

OUR SALVATION IS GREAT

2 So we must be more careful to follow what we were taught. Then we will not stray away from the truth. [2]The teaching God spoke through angels was shown to be true, and anyone who did not follow it or obey it received the punishment that was earned. [3]So surely we also will be punished if we ignore this great salvation. The Lord himself first told about this salvation, and those who heard him testified it was true. [4]God also testified to the truth of the message by using wonders, great signs, many kinds of miracles, and by giving people gifts through the Holy Spirit, just as he wanted.

CHRIST BECAME LIKE HUMANS

[5]God did not choose angels to be the rulers of the new world that was coming, which is what we have been talking about. [6]It is written in the Scriptures,

"Why are people even important to you?
Why do you take care of human beings?
[7] You made them a little lower than the
angels
and crowned them with glory and
honor.[n]
[8] You put all things under their control."
Psalm 8:4–6

1:6 "Let . . . him." These words are found in Deuteronomy 32:43 in the Septuagint, the Greek version of the Old Testament, and in a Hebrew copy among the Dead Sea Scrolls. **1:13 until . . . control** Literally, "until I make your enemies a footstool for your feet." **2:7 You . . . honor.** Some Greek copies continue, "You put them in charge of everything you made." See Psalm 8:6.

When God put everything under their control, there was nothing left that they did not rule. Still, we do not yet see them ruling over everything. ⁹But we see Jesus, who for a short time was made lower than the angels. And now he is wearing a crown of glory and honor because he suffered and died. And by God's grace, he died for everyone.

¹⁰God is the One who made all things, and all things are for his glory. He wanted to have many children share his glory, so he made the One who leads people to salvation perfect through suffering.

¹¹Jesus, who makes people holy, and those who are made holy are from the same family. So he is not ashamed to call them his brothers and sisters. ¹²He says,

"Then, I will tell my brothers and sisters
   about you;
I will praise you in the public meeting."
                              Psalm 22:22

¹³He also says,

"I will trust in God."   *Isaiah 8:17*

And he also says,

"I am here, and with me are the children
   God has given me."   *Isaiah 8:18*

¹⁴Since these children are people with physical bodies, Jesus himself became like them. He did this so that, by dying, he could destroy the one who has the power of death—the devil— ¹⁵and free those who were like slaves all their lives because of their fear of death. ¹⁶Clearly, it is not angels that Jesus helps, but the people who are from Abraham.ⁿ ¹⁷For this reason Jesus had to be made like his brothers and sisters in every way so he could be their merciful and faithful high priest in service to God. Then Jesus could die in their place to take away their sins. ¹⁸And now he can help those who are tempted, because he himself suffered and was tempted.

JESUS IS GREATER THAN MOSES

3 So all of you holy brothers and sisters, who were called by God, think about Jesus, who was sent to us and is the high priest of our faith. ²Jesus was faithful to God as Moses was in God's family. ³Jesus has more honor than Moses, just as the builder of a house has more honor than the house itself. ⁴Every house is built by someone, but the builder of everything is God himself. ⁵Moses was faithful in God's family as a servant, and

he told what God would say in the future. ⁶But Christ is faithful as a Son over God's house. And we are God's house if we confidently maintain our hope.

WE MUST CONTINUE TO FOLLOW GOD

⁷So it is as the Holy Spirit says:

"Today listen to what he says.
⁸ Do not be stubborn as in the past
   when you turned against God,
when you tested God in the desert.
⁹ There your ancestors tried me and
      tested me
and saw the things I did for forty years.
¹⁰ I was angry with them.
   I said, 'They are not loyal to me
   and have not understood my ways.'
¹¹ I was angry and made a promise,
   'They will never enter my rest.'"ⁿ
                              Psalm 95:7–11

¹²So brothers and sisters, be careful that none of you has an evil, unbelieving heart that will turn you away from the living God. ¹³But encourage each other every day while it is "today."ⁿ Help each other so none of you will become hardened because sin has tricked you. ¹⁴We all share in Christ if we keep till the end the sure faith we had in the beginning. ¹⁵This is what the Scripture says:

"Today listen to what he says.
   Do not be stubborn as in the past
   when you turned against God."
                              Psalm 95:7–8

¹⁶Who heard God's voice and was against him? It was all those people Moses led out of Egypt. ¹⁷And with whom was God angry for forty years? He was angry with those who sinned, who died in the desert. ¹⁸And to whom was God talking when he promised that they would never enter his rest? He was talking to those who did not obey him. ¹⁹So we see they were not allowed to enter and have God's rest, because they did not believe.

4 Now, since God has left us the promise that we may enter his rest, let us be very careful so none of you will fail to enter. ²The Good News was preached to us just as it was to them. But the teaching they heard did not

---

2:16 Abraham Most respected ancestor of the Jews. Every Jew hoped to see Abraham. **3:11 rest** A place of rest God promised to give his people. **3:13 "today"** This word is taken from verse 7. It means that it is important to do these things now.

help them, because they heard it but did not accept it with faith.[n] ³We who have believed are able to enter and have God's rest. As God has said,

> "I was angry and made a promise,
> 'They will never enter my rest.'"
>
> *Psalm 95:11*

But God's work was finished from the time he made the world. ⁴In the Scriptures he talked about the seventh day of the week: "And on the seventh day God rested from all his works."[n] ⁵And again in the Scripture God said, "They will never enter my rest."

⁶It is still true that some people will enter God's rest, but those who first heard the way to be saved did not enter, because they did not obey. ⁷So God planned another day, called "today." He spoke about that day through David a long time later in the same Scripture used before:

> "Today listen to what he says.
> Do not be stubborn." *Psalm 95:7–8*

4:2 **because . . . faith** Some Greek copies read "because they did not share the faith of those who heard it."
4:4 **"And . . . works."** Quotation from Genesis 2:2.

FULFILLMENT

BEATING THE BURNOUT BLUES

passport to
fulfillment

HEBREWS 3:1

What does it mean to have a passport? Most of us think of passports in association with travel. But a passport is not a ticket. It is a statement of national identity. A passport is an official document that indicates you are a citizen of a certain country.

Every Christian has a passport issued by God. You stand before the world as one who belongs to God's realm and rule. You no longer carry the documentation of the old way of life. You have been transferred to a new kingdom, a kingdom that supplants all others. You are a citizen of heaven.

As Christians, we can be easily confused about where we really belong. When you decide to agree with God's assessment of your life, the world doesn't suddenly change color or turn upside down. Things still "feel" pretty normal. But slowly you begin to realize that what you thought was "normal" is now very foreign to your spirit. After a while, you discover that you don't belong.

Your passport allows you to travel here on earth, but you realize you aren't at home. Home is where your spirit can resonate without disturbance with the one who has called you. God's passport allows you to be an influence wherever he guides you. But don't forget what the passport means. You are just traveling through. Your real home is with him in heaven.

---

reflect: Consider what it means for you to be a citizen of a heavenly kingdom.
Go to **Hebrews 4:12.**

Showing **Approval** for Your **Husband**

FAMILY

By Dr. Gary Smalley

HEBREWS 3:13

Men hunger for appreciation from others. They will gladly receive recognition from employers, employees, friends, or anyone else willing to give it. When a man knows his wife approves of him, he enjoys her companionship. He will find himself spontaneously complimenting her in response to the approval she gives.

One way to show approval is the "direct" approach—expressing esteem for your husband verbally or through letters, love notes, and cards. I'm looking at two cards my wife sent me last month. In the past, I would have opened them and thought, *Isn't that nice?* before tossing them into the nearest trash can.

But the more cards and letters I receive from Norma, the more anxious I am to reciprocate her "written praise." When she sends cards that cite specific qualities she appreciates in me, I feel inspired to think about her praiseworthy qualities and reciprocate with a card.

Of course, men think differently from women and not all men like the same form of appreciation. Be careful to avoid forms your husband might find overly sentimental. You can discern what will encourage your husband and what will embarrass him by trying several ways until a few really hit home.

The "indirect" approach is another way to show approval for your husband. Norma's mother had this approach down pat years ago. Through good grooming and a timely greeting, she showed "indirect" approval for her husband. Every day she prepared for his homecoming by bathing and putting on fresh clothing. Norma says she can't remember a single time when her mother greeted her father with problems or complaints. Instead, she let him relax and made him feel important by the extra time and effort she spent to make one part of his day happy.

I could list a thousand indirect ways to show approval for your husband. Norma knows plenty of them: She welcomes my suggestions about her wardrobe; she introduces me to new friends with a tone of voice that reflects admiration for me; and she constantly tells our children how much she appreciates me.

You can make it a point to praise your husband to his male friends and their wives. Just think what good gossip you'll spread when you say positive things about your spouse. Quite a switch from the usual complaints! Consider making a long list of the indirect ways you can show approval for your husband. Pick two or three of the best ones, and be sure to apply them during the next week.

TO LEARN MORE ON WHAT THE BIBLE HAS TO SAY ABOUT **FAMILY,** READ THE SCRIPTURES AND DEVOTIONALS AT **COLOSSIANS 3:12, MARK 10:6–8, HEBREWS 13:4, 1 PETER 3:1–2,** AND **1 JOHN 4:7–12.**

[8]We know that Joshua[n] did not lead the people into that rest, because God spoke later about another day. [9]This shows that the rest[n] for God's people is still coming. [10]Anyone who enters God's rest will rest from his work as God did. [11]Let us try as hard as we can to enter God's rest so that no one will fail by following the example of those who refused to obey.

[12]God's word is alive and working and is sharper than a double-edged sword. It cuts all the way into us, where the soul and the spirit are joined, to the center of our joints and bones. And it judges the thoughts and feelings in our hearts. [13]Nothing in all the world can be hidden from God. Everything is clear and lies open before him, and to him we must explain the way we have lived.

JESUS IS OUR HIGH PRIEST

[14]Since we have a great high priest, Jesus the Son of God, who has gone into heaven, let us hold on to the faith we have. [15]For our high priest is able to understand our weaknesses. He was tempted in every way that we are, but he did not sin. [16]Let us, then, feel very sure that we can come before God's throne where there is grace. There we can

---

4:8 Joshua After Moses died, Joshua became leader of the Jewish people and led them into the land that God promised to give them.   **4:9 rest** Literally, "sabbath rest," meaning a sharing in the rest that God began after he created the world.

BEATING THE BURNOUT BLUES

FULFILLMENT

the **Word** of **God**

HEBREWS 4:12

By Diana Hagee

It is of constant amazement to me that the sacred Scriptures desire to say so much more to us than what we first casually read in passing. When we take the time to study God's Word, he reveals much more to the believer in order to broaden our knowledge of his infinite power and as a way of increasing the love we have for him.

The Word of God is the protoplasm of life—dynamic and in constant motion. The Word of God will transform itself and become whatever we need, whenever we need it. The Word of God will always restore our souls, whatever our conditions.

When we lack anything, the Word of God is our abundance. When we are weak, the Word of God is our strength. When we are hungry, the Word of God is our nourishment. His Word is milk for babes and meat for mature believers. When we are lost, the Word of God is our compass.

When we are discouraged, the Word of God is our joy. When we lack insight, the Word of God is our wisdom. When we are lonely, the Word of God is our companion. When we need protection, the Word of God is our shelter. The Word of God is whatever we need, whenever we need it.

reflect: Will you seek to study the Word of God today?
Go to **1 John 3:1.**

receive mercy and grace to help us when we need it.

5 Every high priest is chosen from among other people. He is given the work of going before God for them to offer gifts and sacrifices for sins. [2]Since he himself is weak, he is able to be gentle with those who do not understand and who are doing wrong things. [3]Because he is weak, the high priest must offer sacrifices for his own sins and also for the sins of the people.

[4]To be a high priest is an honor, but no one chooses himself for this work. He must be called by God as Aaron[n] was. [5]So also Christ did not choose himself to have the honor of being a high priest, but God chose him. God said to him,

"You are my Son.
   Today I have become your Father."
                                    Psalm 2:7

[6]And in another Scripture God says,

"You are a priest forever,
   a priest like Melchizedek."[n] *Psalm 110:4*

[7]While Jesus lived on earth, he prayed to God and asked God for help. He prayed with loud cries and tears to the One who could save him from death, and his prayer was heard because he trusted God. [8]Even though Jesus was the Son of God, he learned obedience by what he suffered. [9]And because his obedience was perfect, he was able to give eternal salvation to all who obey him. [10]In this way God made Jesus a high priest, a priest like Melchizedek.

WARNING AGAINST FALLING AWAY

[11]We have much to say about this, but it is hard to explain because you are so slow to understand. [12]By now you should be teachers, but you need someone to teach you again the first lessons of God's message. You still need the teaching that is like milk. You are not ready for solid food. [13]Anyone who lives on milk is still a baby and knows nothing about right teaching. [14]But solid food is for those who are grown up. They are mature enough to know the difference between good and evil.

6 So let us go on to grown-up teaching. Let us not go back over the beginning lessons we learned about Christ. We should not again start teaching about faith in God and about turning away from those acts that lead to death. [2]We should not return to the teaching about baptisms,[n] about laying on of hands,[n] about the raising of the dead and eternal judgment. [3]And we will go on to grown-up teaching if God allows.

[4]Some people cannot be brought back again to a changed life. They were once in God's light, and enjoyed heaven's gift, and shared in the Holy Spirit. [5]They found out how good God's word is, and they received the powers of his new world. [6]But they fell away from Christ. It is impossible to bring them back to a changed life again, because they are nailing the Son of God to a cross again and are shaming him in front of others.

[7]Some people are like land that gets plenty of rain. The land produces a good crop for those who work it, and it receives God's blessings. [8]Other people are like land that grows thorns and weeds and is worthless. It is about to be cursed by God and will be destroyed by fire.

[9]Dear friends, we are saying this to you, but we really expect better things from you that will lead to your salvation. [10]God is fair; he will not forget the work you did and the love you showed for him by helping his people. And he will remember that you are still helping them. [11]We want each of you to go on with the same hard work all your lives so you will surely get what you hope for. [12]We do not want you to become lazy. Be like those who through faith and patience will receive what God has promised.

[13]God made a promise to Abraham. And as there is no one greater than God, he used himself when he swore to Abraham, [14]saying, "I will surely bless you and give you many descendants."[n] [15]Abraham waited patiently for this to happen, and he received what God promised.

[16]People always use the name of someone greater than themselves when they

---

5:4 Aaron Moses' brother and the first Jewish high priest.   **5:6 Melchizedek** A priest and king who lived in the time of Abraham. (Read Genesis 14:17–24.)   **6:2 baptisms** The word here may refer to Christian baptism, or it may refer to the Jewish ceremonial washings.   **6:2 laying on of hands** The laying on of hands had many purposes, including the giving of a blessing, power, or authority.   **6:14 "I . . . descendants."** Quotation from Genesis 22:17.

swear. The oath proves that what they say is true, and this ends all arguing. [17]God wanted to prove that his promise was true to those who would get what he promised. And he wanted them to understand clearly that his purposes never change, so he made an oath. [18]These two things cannot change: God cannot lie when he makes a promise, and he cannot lie when he makes an oath. These things encourage us who came to God for safety. They give us strength to hold on to the hope we have been given. [19]We have this hope as an anchor for the soul, sure

and strong. It enters behind the curtain in the Most Holy Place in heaven, [20]where Jesus has gone ahead of us and for us. He has become the high priest forever, a priest like Melchizedek.[n]

THE PRIEST MELCHIZEDEK

7 Melchizedek[n] was the king of Salem and a priest for God Most High. He met Abraham when Abraham was coming back after defeating the kings. When

---

6:20; 7:1 Melchizedek A priest and king who lived in the time of Abraham. (Read Genesis 14:17–24.)

TOTAL CHRISTIAN FITNESS

FITNESS

magic bullets

HEBREWS 5:9

We are in a society that craves the magic bullet. What is the magic bullet? It is the instant fix for whatever ails you. Rather then promoting an effort to get to the complex, underlying cause of symptoms, we now have a pill for every ill, a lotion for every motion, and a potion for every emotion.

Do you want flat, rippled abdominal muscles? There is a quick fix for that, too. Strap a machine on your stomach and it will contract your abs for you! And there are quick fixes for dieting, also. Don't eat healthier—pop a pill, have surgery, or follow some new fad diet. Unfortunately, the bottom line is that there are no shortcuts to anywhere worth going. Magic bullets are rarely magical, and, like all bullets, they are rather deadly projectiles.

A pastor once asked in church the question of all questions: "Why wasn't Jesus ever sick?" The group gave answers like, "He is the Son of God. He is Jesus. He walked in the Spirit." No one gave the answer the pastor was looking for. With much anxiety the group waited. Finally, the pastor responded, "Jesus walked in obedience."

Obedience is the only way. Follow Jesus' health program. Obedience may seem like the long way instead of the shortcut to the things we desire, but it's the only route that actually takes you where you want to go without taking on the shrapnel of magic bullets.

reflect: Bypass shortcuts and follow Jesus' directions for living holy and healthy.
Go to **James 5:16.**

Five Ingredients of Peace by God

By Dr. Sheri Lerner

HEBREWS 6:19

There are five basic ingredients of peace by God. Once you understand them, you can fully appreciate the tremendous gift God has given you. Let's examine these gifts within the gift of peace that work together to produce peace.

Ingredient 1
Acceptance

Peace with God comes from approaching him on his terms, meeting and knowing him on a personal basis, recognizing him as your God, and trusting him on a moment-by-moment basis for everything you need. As a Christian, you're accepted. Regardless of your past, your bank account, your weight, your car, or your achievements, you're loved unconditionally by God. He loves you not for what you do, but for who you are. While few, if any, people can love you like that, God can. He loves you at the core.

Ingredient 2
Faith

The letters in the word faith stand for the true definition of the word: *Forsaking All, I Trust Him*. Sometimes all you can do is just that: *hang on and trust God*. He does know the end from the beginning, after all, and even the faith to believe in God is a gift from him. God has made certain promises to his children; and he is not only able to deliver on those promises, but *wants* to do so.

Ingredient 3
Love

The way God loves us is on a totally different plane from human love. His love is eternal, but it is also a *tough*

love, pointing out things in our lives we need to attend to for our own good and protecting us from injury and harmful situations by taking us down paths that we don't understand. Know that you are loved: deeply, enduringly, and with great joy on his part.

Ingredient 4
Hope

Hope is the thing that keeps you from giving up when all the odds are stacked against you. It's very much like faith, but there are slight differences. Faith carries with it the idea of assurance; hope is more of an expectation or anticipation. Faith confirms that we were *right* in hoping. God doesn't hope, because he *knows*. He has given us every coping tool we need for life's twists and turns, both good and not-so-good. That should give you both hope and peace.

Ingredient 5
Security

We can know we are secure because God has promised, "I will never leave you; I will never abandon you" (Hebrews 13:5). Security means we don't have a thing to worry about if we have given God control of our lives. Security is having our needs met time after time after time. Security is knowing that we are abundantly blessed, giving us enough to share with others. Security is great!

TO LEARN MORE ON WHAT THE BIBLE HAS TO SAY ABOUT **FULFILLMENT,** READ THE SCRIPTURES AND DEVOTIONALS AT **LUKE 10:38–42, LUKE 17:12–19, JOHN 8:36, JOHN 10:14–15, JOHN 14:27,** AND **JOHN 15:15.**

they met, Melchizedek blessed Abraham, [2]and Abraham gave him a tenth of everything he had brought back from the battle. First, Melchizedek's name means "king of goodness," and he is king of Salem, which means "king of peace." [3]No one knows who Melchizedek's father or mother was,[n] where he came from, when he was born, or when he died. Melchizedek is like the Son of God; he continues being a priest forever.

[4]You can see how great Melchizedek was. Abraham, the great father, gave him a tenth of everything that he won in battle. [5]Now the law says that those in the tribe of Levi who become priests must collect a tenth from the people—their own people—even though the priests and the people are from the family of Abraham. [6]Melchizedek was not from the tribe of Levi, but he collected a tenth from Abraham. And he blessed Abraham, the man who had God's promises. [7]Now everyone knows that the more important person blesses the less important person. [8]Priests receive a tenth, even though they are only men who live and then die. But Melchizedek, who received a tenth from Abraham, continues living, as the Scripture says. [9]We might even say that Levi, who receives a tenth, also paid it when Abraham paid Melchizedek a tenth. [10]Levi was not yet born, but he was in the body of his ancestor when Melchizedek met Abraham.

[11]The people were given the law[n] concerning the system of priests from the tribe of Levi, but they could not be made perfect through that system. So there was a need for another priest to come, a priest like Melchizedek, not Aaron. [12]And when a different kind of priest comes, the law must be changed, too. [13]We are saying these things about Christ, who belonged to a different tribe. No one from that tribe ever served as a priest at the altar. [14]It is clear that our Lord came from the tribe of Judah, and Moses said nothing about priests belonging to that tribe.

JESUS IS LIKE MELCHIZEDEK

[15]And this becomes even more clear when we see that another priest comes who is like Melchizedek.[n] [16]He was not made a priest by human rules and laws but through the power of his life, which continues forever. [17]It is said about him,

"You are a priest forever,
    a priest like Melchizedek." *Psalm 110:4*
[18]The old rule is now set aside, because it was weak and useless. [19]The law of Moses could not make anything perfect. But now a better hope has been given to us, and with this hope we can come near to God. [20]It is important that God did this with an oath. Others became priests without an oath, [21]but Christ became a priest with God's oath. God said:

"The Lord has made a promise
    and will not change his mind.
'You are a priest forever.'"   *Psalm 110:4*
[22]This means that Jesus is the guarantee of a better agreement[n] from God to his people.

[23]When one of the other priests died, he could not continue being a priest. So there were many priests. [24]But because Jesus lives forever, he will never stop serving as priest. [25]So he is able always to save those who come to God through him because he always lives, asking God to help them.

[26]Jesus is the kind of high priest we need. He is holy, sinless, pure, not influenced by sinners, and he is raised above the heavens. [27]He is not like the other priests who had to offer sacrifices every day, first for their own sins, and then for the sins of the people. Christ offered his sacrifice only once and for all time when he offered himself. [28]The law chooses high priests who are people with weaknesses, but the word of God's oath came later than the law. It made God's Son to be the high priest, and that Son has been made perfect forever.

JESUS IS OUR HIGH PRIEST

8 Here is the point of what we are saying: We have a high priest who sits on the right side of God's throne in heaven. [2]Our high priest serves in the Most Holy Place, the true place of worship that was made by God, not by humans.

[3]Every high priest has the work of offering gifts and sacrifices to God. So our high

---

7:3 No . . . was Literally, "Melchizedek was without father, without mother, without genealogy." **7:11 The . . . law** This refers to the people of Israel who were given the Law of Moses. **7:15 Melchizedek** A priest and king who lived in the time of Abraham. (Read Genesis 14:17–24.) **7:22 agreement** God gives a contract or agreement to his people. For the Jews, this agreement was the Law of Moses. But now God has given a better agreement to his people through Christ.

priest must also offer something to God. ⁴If our high priest were now living on earth, he would not be a priest, because there are already priests here who follow the law by offering gifts to God. ⁵The work they do as priests is only a copy and a shadow of what is in heaven. This is why God warned Moses when he was ready to build the Holy Tent: "Be very careful to make everything by the plan I showed you on the mountain."ⁿ ⁶But the priestly work that has been given to Jesus is much greater than the work that was given to the other priests. In the same way, the new agreement that Jesus brought from God to his people is much greater than the old one. And the new agreement is based on promises of better things.

⁷If there had been nothing wrong with the first agreement,ⁿ there would have been no need for a second agreement. ⁸But God found something wrong with his people. He says:ⁿ

"Look, the time is coming, says the Lord,
when I will make a new agreement
with the people of Israel
and the people of Judah.
⁹ It will not be like the agreement
I made with their ancestors
when I took them by the hand
to bring them out of Egypt.
But they broke that agreement,
and I turned away from them, says the
Lord.
¹⁰ This is the agreement I will make
with the people of Israel at that time,
says the Lord.
I will put my teachings in their minds
and write them on their hearts.
I will be their God,
and they will be my people.
¹¹ People will no longer have to teach their
neighbors and relatives
to know the Lord,
because all people will know me,
from the least to the most important.
¹² I will forgive them for the wicked things
they did,
and I will not remember their sins
anymore."   *Jeremiah 31:31–34*

¹³God called this a new agreement, so he has made the first agreement old. And anything that is old and worn out is ready to disappear.

THE OLD AGREEMENT

9 The first agreementⁿ had rules for worship and a place on earth for worship. ²The Holy Tent was set up for this. The first area in the Tent was called the Holy Place. In it were the lamp and the table with the bread that was made holy for God. ³Behind the second curtain was a room called the Most Holy Place. ⁴In it was a golden altar for burning incense and the Ark covered with gold that held the old agreement. Inside this Ark was a golden jar of manna, Aaron's rod that once grew leaves, and the stone tablets of the old agreement. ⁵Above the Ark were the creatures that showed God's glory, whose wings reached over the lid. But we cannot tell everything about these things now.

⁶When everything in the Tent was made ready in this way, the priests went into the first room every day to worship. ⁷But only the high priest could go into the second room, and he did that only once a year. He could never enter the inner room without taking blood with him, which he offered to God for himself and for sins the people did without knowing they did them. ⁸The Holy Spirit uses this to show that the way into the Most Holy Place was not open while the system of the old Holy Tent was still being used. ⁹This is an example for the present time. It shows that the gifts and sacrifices offered cannot make the conscience of the worshiper perfect. ¹⁰These gifts and sacrifices were only about food and drink and special washings. They were rules for the body, to be followed until the time of God's new way.

THE NEW AGREEMENT

¹¹But when Christ came as the high priest of the good things we now have,ⁿ he entered the greater and more perfect tent. It is not made by humans and does not belong to this world. ¹²Christ entered the Most Holy Place only once—and for all time. He did not take with him the blood of goats and calves. His

---

8:5 **"Be . . . mountain."** Quotation from Exodus 25:40. 8:7; 9:1 **first agreement** The contract God gave the Jewish people when he gave them the Law of Moses. 8:8 **But . . . says** Some Greek copies read "But God found something wrong and says to his people." 9:11 **good . . . have** Some Greek copies read "good things that are to come."

sacrifice was his own blood, and by it he set us free from sin forever. [13]The blood of goats and bulls and the ashes of a cow are sprinkled on the people who are unclean, and this makes their bodies clean again. [14]How much more is done by the blood of Christ. He offered himself through the eternal Spirit[n] as a perfect sacrifice to God. His blood will make our consciences pure from useless acts so we may serve the living God.

[15]For this reason Christ brings a new agreement from God to his people. Those who are called by God can now receive the blessings he has promised, blessings that will last forever. They can have those things because Christ died so that the people who lived under the first agreement could be set free from sin.

[16]When there is a will,[n] it must be proven that the one who wrote that will is dead. [17]A will means nothing while the person is alive; it can be used only after the person dies. [18]This is why even the first agreement could not begin without blood to show death. [19]First, Moses told all the people every command in the law. Next he took the blood of calves and mixed it with water. Then he used red wool and a branch of the hyssop plant to sprinkle it on the book of the law and on all the people. [20]He said, "This is the blood that begins the Agreement that God commanded you to obey."[n] [21]In the same way, Moses sprinkled the blood on the Holy Tent and over all the things used in worship. [22]The law says that almost everything must be made clean by blood, and sins cannot be forgiven without blood to show death.

CHRIST'S DEATH TAKES AWAY SINS

[23]So the copies of the real things in heaven had to be made clean by animal sacrifices. But the real things in heaven need much better sacrifices. [24]Christ did not go into the Most Holy Place made by humans, which is only a copy of the real one. He went into heaven itself and is there now before God to help us. [25]The high priest enters the Most Holy Place once every year with blood that is not his own. But Christ did not offer himself many times. [26]Then he would have had to suffer many times since the world was made. But Christ came only once and for all time at just the right time to take away

all sin by sacrificing himself. [27]Just as everyone must die once and then be judged, [28]so Christ was offered as a sacrifice one time to take away the sins of many people. And he will come a second time, not to offer himself for sin, but to bring salvation to those who are waiting for him.

10 The law is only an unclear picture of the good things coming in the future; it is not the real thing. The people under the law offer the same sacrifices every year, but these sacrifices can never make perfect those who come near to worship God. [2]If the law could make them perfect, the sacrifices would have already stopped. The worshipers would be made clean, and they would no longer have a sense of sin. [3]But these sacrifices remind them of their sins every year, [4]because it is impossible for the blood of bulls and goats to take away sins.

[5]So when Christ came into the world, he said:

"You do not want sacrifices and offerings,
　but you have prepared a body for me.
[6] You do not ask for burnt offerings
　and offerings to take away sins.
[7] Then I said, 'Look, I have come.
　It is written about me in the book.
　God, I have come to do what you
　　want.'"　　　　*Psalm 40:6–8*
[8]In this Scripture he first said, "You do not want sacrifices and offerings. You do not ask for burnt offerings and offerings to take away sins." (These are all sacrifices that the law commands.) [9]Then he said, "Look, I have come to do what you want." God ends the first system of sacrifices so he can set up the new system. [10]And because of this, we are made holy through the sacrifice Christ made in his body once and for all time.

[11]Every day the priests stand and do their religious service, often offering the same sacrifices. Those sacrifices can never take away sins. [12]But after Christ offered one sacrifice for sins, forever, he sat down at the right side of God. [13]And now Christ waits there for his

---

9:14 **Spirit** This refers to the Holy Spirit, to Christ's own spirit, or to the spiritual and eternal nature of his sacrifice. 9:16 **will** A legal document that shows how a person's money and property are to be distributed at the time of death. This is the same word in Greek as "agreement" in verse 15. 9:20 **"This . . . obey."** Quotation from Exodus 24:8.

enemies to be put under his power. ¹⁴With one sacrifice he made perfect forever those who are being made holy.

¹⁵The Holy Spirit also tells us about this. First he says:

¹⁶ "This is the agreement[n] I will make
    with them at that time, says the Lord.
I will put my teachings in their hearts
    and write them on their minds."

Jeremiah 31:33

¹⁷Then he says:

"Their sins and the evil things they do—

I will not remember anymore."

Jeremiah 31:34

¹⁸Now when these have been forgiven, there is no more need for a sacrifice for sins.

CONTINUE TO TRUST GOD

¹⁹So, brothers and sisters, we are completely free to enter the Most Holy Place

10:16 agreement God gives a contract or agreement to his people. For the Jews, this agreement was the Law of Moses. But now God has given a better agreement to his people through Christ.

LESSONS FROM THE BATTLEFIELD

building your own culture

FUTURE

HEBREWS 10:23–25

When the culture you are living in stops working for you, then you need to form your own culture. When the fast-paced, goal-oriented, achievement-based, possession-centered lifestyle so common to most modern people is no longer sufficient to inspire or sustain you, then the only option left to you is to change your culture. In your own culture with your friends and family, you can develop a better way of life than the rest of the world.

Think about what matters most to you, and then take steps to form your own culture around that. What is it that you really want? And how do you get it while still maintaining the things that are really most important in your life? Answering these questions as part of your new culture is a giant leap toward reducing stress, increasing peace, and living and dying happy.

This process is the essential idea behind the church. The church is a place where a new culture is built around the values God endorses. The culture of the church does not reflect the tired and worn-out answers that the world offers. It marches to the beat of a different drum. It is countercultural.

If you think that you can modify your own culture and find a more satisfying life, but you neglect to put yourself in the mix with those who are reorienting their lives around God's values, you're being foolish. Culture is the interlaced fabric of many relationships. God knew that we needed to be established together, not as independent individuals.

reflect: Choose God's culture of church, which runs counter to the world's culture.
Go to **FUTURE:** "Hope in the Holy Spirit" at **Romans 8:11.**

without fear because of the blood of Jesus' death. [20]We can enter through a new and living way that Jesus opened for us. It leads through the curtain—Christ's body. [21]And since we have a great priest over God's house, [22]let us come near to God with a sincere heart and a sure faith, because we have been made free from a guilty conscience, and our bodies have been washed with pure water. [23]Let us hold firmly to the hope that we have confessed, because we can trust God to do what he promised.

[24]Let us think about each other and help each other to show love and do good deeds. [25]You should not stay away from the church meetings, as some are doing, but you should meet together and encourage each other. Do this even more as you see the day[n] coming.

[26]If we decide to go on sinning after we have learned the truth, there is no longer any sacrifice for sins. [27]There is nothing but fear in waiting for the judgment and the terrible fire that will destroy all those who live against God. [28]Anyone who refused to obey the law of Moses was found guilty from the proof given by two or three witnesses. He was put to death without mercy. [29]So what do you think should be done to those who do not respect the Son of God, who look at the blood of the agreement that made them holy as no different from others' blood, who insult the Spirit of God's grace? Surely they should have a much worse punishment. [30]We know that God said, "I will punish those who do wrong; I will repay them."[n] And he also said, "The Lord will judge his people."[n] [31]It is a terrible thing to fall into the hands of the living God.

[32]Remember those days in the past when you first learned the truth. You had a hard struggle with many sufferings, but you continued strong. [33]Sometimes you were hurt and attacked before crowds of people, and sometimes you shared with those who were being treated that way. [34]You helped the prisoners. You even had joy when all that you owned was taken from you, because you knew you had something better and more lasting.

[35]So do not lose the courage you had in the past, which has a great reward. [36]You must hold on, so you can do what God wants and receive what he has promised. [37]For in a very short time,

"The One who is coming will come
 and will not be delayed.
[38]Those who are right with me
 will live by faith.
But if they turn back with fear,
 I will not be pleased with them."

Habakkuk 2:3–4

[39]But we are not those who turn back and are lost. We are people who have faith and are saved.

WHAT IS FAITH?

11Faith means being sure of the things we hope for and knowing that something is real even if we do not see it. [2]Faith is the reason we remember great people who lived in the past.

[3]It is by faith we understand that the whole world was made by God's command so what we see was made by something that cannot be seen.

[4]It was by faith that Abel offered God a better sacrifice than Cain did. God said he was pleased with the gifts Abel offered and called Abel a good man because of his faith. Abel died, but through his faith he is still speaking.

[5]It was by faith that Enoch was taken to heaven so he would not die. He could not be found, because God had taken him away. Before he was taken, the Scripture says that he was a man who truly pleased God. [6]Without faith no one can please God. Anyone who comes to God must believe that he is real and that he rewards those who truly want to find him.

[7]It was by faith that Noah heard God's warnings about things he could not yet see. He obeyed God and built a large boat to save his family. By his faith, Noah showed that the world was wrong, and he became one of those who are made right with God through faith.

[8]It was by faith Abraham obeyed God's call to go to another place God promised to give him. He left his own country, not knowing where he was to go. [9]It was by faith that he lived like a foreigner in the country God promised to give him. He lived in tents with

---

10:25 day The day Christ will come to judge all people and take his people to live with him. **10:30 "I . . . them."** Quotation from Deuteronomy 32:35. **10:30 "The Lord . . . people."** Quotation from Deuteronomy 32:36; Psalm 135:14.

Isaac and Jacob, who had received that same promise from God. [10]Abraham was waiting for the city[n] that has real foundations—the city planned and built by God.

[11]He was too old to have children, and Sarah could not have children. It was by faith that Abraham was made able to become a father, because he trusted God to do what he had promised.[n] [12]This man was so old he was almost dead, but from him came as many descendants as there are stars in the sky. Like the sand on the seashore, they could not be counted.

[13]All these great people died in faith. They did not get the things that God promised his people, but they saw them coming far in the future and were glad. They said they were like visitors and strangers on earth. [14]When people say such things, they show they are looking for a country that will be their own. [15]If they had been thinking about the country

---

11:10 city The spiritual "city" where God's people live with him. Also called "the heavenly Jerusalem." (See Hebrews 12:22.) **11:11 It . . . promised.** Some Greek copies refer to Sarah's faith, rather than Abraham's.

JESUS, WHO WAS, AND IS, AND IS TO COME

faith **is**

FAITH

By Wendell Smith   HEBREWS 11:1-2

Everything we do in our Christian life is done by faith. We are baptized by faith, and we receive the Holy Spirit by faith. Our attendance at church is done by faith that God will speak to us, that we will receive a word to help build our faith. Tithes and offerings are given by faith; we believe that by giving money away, all our needs will be met.

As Christians, we partake of the Lord's Supper by faith, believing that the elements have more meaning than just crackers and juice. We believe in the broken body and shed blood of our Lord and Savior Jesus Christ. We read the Bible by faith, trusting it is the divinely inspired word of the living God. We bow our knees by faith, praying and seeking God's plans for ourselves and others. We believe in the power of the Good News and its impact on the human heart.

By faith, we sing songs and lift holy hands, believing we are transformed into God's image through praise. We lay hands on the sick in faith, pray by faith and expect them to recover, believing the stripes that were inflicted on the back of Jesus heal our bodies.

It is our faith that has engaged the unseen realities and embraced them as real, true, and valid. This is the lifestyle that we have chosen as believers and followers of Jesus Christ. We are witnesses in our everyday life that those who are right with God will live by faith.

---

reflect: Are you waiting in faith for a prodigal child to return home?
Go to **James 1:2-8.**

Unwavering Faith

By John Ed Mathison

The number one New Year's resolution for many Americans is "to lose weight and start exercising." There's nothing wrong with keeping your physical body fit, but God has an "exercise program" for your spiritual body, too.

First, you must discipline yourself for the purpose of godliness; that is, to become more like God. Paul instructed Timothy that "serving God helps you in every way by bringing you blessings in this life and in the future life, too" (1 Timothy 4:8).

To become more like God, you must have nourishment for your soul. You must maintain a balanced diet. Don't look to the world as an authority on this kind of nutrition! You will receive good nourishment through your daily study of Scripture. You can then apply it to your everyday life in outreach opportunities.

You must avoid worldliness. Remember, it's not all about you; it's all about God. Focus on God. Take care of those around you, and God will take care of you. The byproduct of being consistently fueled by God rather than by the world will be a dependence on God that nourishes an unwavering faith that is only possible through uninterrupted and undistracted intimacy with Jesus Christ.

This unwavering faith doesn't know **when**. "God, when will you do this thing for me?" Jesus' followers wanted to know when he would return and set up his kingdom (Acts 1:6–8). Jesus instructed them that only God had that answer. In the meantime, his followers were to do his work and be ready, awake, and alert as though his

return would be at any moment. Faith doesn't tell us when . . . but faith is prepared for anything.

This unwavering faith doesn't know **where**. God doesn't expect us to know where to go when he calls, but he does expect us to obey him. One of the biggest deterrents to the joy of discovering God's purpose for our lives is our reluctance to leave our "comfort zone" for fear of failure. Faith is the perfect antidote for this fear. You were not made to stay in one place; trust God to lead you where you should go.

This unwavering faith doesn't know **why**. Faith just trusts God. Having faith is not a guarantee that things won't go wrong. However, God does promise that he will be with you to see you through when bad things happen.

This unwavering faith **does** *know* **who** . . . *Jesus Christ*. Faith is knowing Jesus Christ in an intimate way. If you have this personal relationship with Christ, you can face the uncertainties of the "when, where, and why." With faith in Jesus, you can face anything.

You will become more genuine as a person. Your spiritual gifts will be better developed. You will become an influence to ensure salvation for those who know you.

You are redeemed by the living Word of God—not by earthly possessions, power, and pleasure that are temporary and cannot be compared to the benefits today and eternal rewards tomorrow of a life of faith that has been wholly dependent upon and intimate with Jesus Christ.

TO LEARN MORE ON WHAT THE BIBLE HAS TO SAY ABOUT **FAITH,** READ THE SCRIPTURES AND DEVOTIONALS AT **EPHESIANS 3:14–21, 2 CORINTHIANS 1:3-4, 2 SAMUEL 22:4, 2 THESSALONIANS 2:13–15, 1 TIMOTHY 6:12,** AND **TITUS 1:2.**

they had left, they could have gone back. [16]But they were waiting for a better country—a heavenly country. So God is not ashamed to be called their God, because he has prepared a city for them.

[17]It was by faith that Abraham, when God tested him, offered his son Isaac as a sacrifice. God made the promises to Abraham, but Abraham was ready to offer his own son as a sacrifice. [18]God had said, "The descendants I promised you will be from Isaac."[n] [19]Abraham believed that God could raise the dead, and really, it was as if Abraham got Isaac back from death.

[20]It was by faith that Isaac blessed the future of Jacob and Esau. [21]It was by faith that Jacob, as he was dying, blessed each one of Joseph's sons. Then he worshiped as he leaned on the top of his walking stick.

[22]It was by faith that Joseph, while he was dying, spoke about the Israelites leaving Egypt and gave instructions about what to do with his body.

[23]It was by faith that Moses' parents hid him for three months after he was born. They saw that Moses was a beautiful baby, and they were not afraid to disobey the king's order.

[24]It was by faith that Moses, when he grew up, refused to be called the son of the king of Egypt's daughter. [25]He chose to suffer with God's people instead of enjoying sin for a short time. [26]He thought it was better to suffer for the Christ than to have all the treasures of Egypt, because he was looking for God's reward. [27]It was by faith that Moses left Egypt and was not afraid of the king's anger. Moses continued strong as if he could see the God that no one can see. [28]It was by faith that Moses prepared the Passover and spread the blood on the doors so the one who brings death would not kill the firstborn sons of Israel.

[29]It was by faith that the people crossed the Red Sea as if it were dry land. But when the Egyptians tried it, they were drowned.

[30]It was by faith that the walls of Jericho fell after the people had marched around them for seven days.

[31]It was by faith that Rahab, the prostitute, welcomed the spies and was not killed with those who refused to obey God.

[32]Do I need to give more examples? I do not have time to tell you about Gideon, Barak, Samson, Jephthah, David, Samuel, and the prophets. [33]Through their faith they defeated kingdoms. They did what was right, received God's promises, and shut the mouths of lions. [34]They stopped great fires and were saved from being killed with swords. They were weak, and yet were made strong. They were powerful in battle and defeated other armies. [35]Women received their dead relatives raised back to life. Others were tortured and refused to accept their freedom so they could be raised from the dead to a better life. [36]Some were laughed at and beaten. Others were put in chains and thrown into prison. [37]They were stoned to death, they were cut in half,[n] and they were killed with swords. Some wore the skins of sheep and goats. They were poor, abused, and treated badly. [38]The world was not good enough for them! They wandered in deserts and mountains, living in caves and holes in the earth.

[39]All these people are known for their faith, but none of them received what God had promised. [40]God planned to give us something better so that they would be made perfect, but only together with us.

FOLLOW JESUS' EXAMPLE

12 We are surrounded by a great cloud of people whose lives tell us what faith means. So let us run the race that is before us and never give up. We should remove from our lives anything that would get in the way and the sin that so easily holds us back. [2]Let us look only to Jesus, the One who began our faith and who makes it perfect. He suffered death on the cross. But he accepted the shame as if it were nothing because of the joy that God put before him. And now he is sitting at the right side of God's throne. [3]Think about Jesus' example. He held on while wicked people were doing evil things to him. So do not get tired and stop trying.

GOD IS LIKE A FATHER

[4]You are struggling against sin, but your struggles have not yet caused you to be killed. [5]You have forgotten the encouraging words that call you his children:

11:18 "The descendants . . . Isaac." Quotation from Genesis 21:12. **11:37 they were cut in half** Some Greek copies also include, "they were tested."

"My child, don't think the Lord's
    discipline is worth nothing,
    and don't stop trying when he corrects
        you.
6 The Lord disciplines those he loves,
    and he punishes everyone he accepts as
        his child."   *Proverbs 3:11–12*

7So hold on through your sufferings, because they are like a father's discipline. God is treating you as children. All children are disciplined by their fathers. 8If you are never disciplined (and every child must be disciplined), you are not true children. 9We have all had fathers here on earth who disciplined us, and we respected them. So it is even more important that we accept disci-

pline from the Father of our spirits so we will have life. 10Our fathers on earth disciplined us for a short time in the way they thought was best. But God disciplines us to help us, so we can become holy as he is. 11We do not enjoy being disciplined. It is painful at the time, but later, after we have learned from it, we have peace, because we start living in the right way.

BE CAREFUL HOW YOU LIVE

12You have become weak, so make yourselves strong again. 13Keep on the right path, so the weak will not stumble but rather be strengthened.

14Try to live in peace with all people, and try to live free from sin. Anyone whose life is

---

TOTAL CHRISTIAN FITNESS

FITNESS

running

HEBREWS 12:1–3   By Bob Roberts

O ne of the greatest "spiritual" disciplines is running. Yes, you read it right running! Holiness is not merely attitudes, but acts and lifestyle. Holiness is tied to discipline, be it watching your weight, managing your money, or anything else. So, as you pursue the discipline of running, simply work your way up to the amount that is right for you.

The discipline required to run daily will affect other areas of your life. It will become easier to manage your money and your time. God wants us to be disciplined. No one will change the world unless he or she is disciplined and focused. There's enough time to change the world, be a good family person, and enjoy life, but there is no time to waste.

When you run, you can think more clearly about life than at any other time. Start your day with prayer and the Word for an hour, perhaps journaling about challenges, events, and people. Then, when you run, think about it all. When you run, chemicals called endorphins are released in your brain, and it has a positive impact on your thinking. Problem-solving ability will be enhanced. To pray, think, run, and understand how God would have us interact with the people around us—this is a lifestyle that pleases the Lord.

reflect: Is running an activity that you might start as a daily discipline?
Go to **Hebrews 5:9.**

not holy will never see the Lord. [15]Be careful that no one fails to receive God's grace and begins to cause trouble among you. A person like that can ruin many of you. [16]Be careful that no one takes part in sexual sin or is like Esau and never thinks about God. As the oldest son, Esau would have received everything from his father, but he sold all that for a single meal. [17]You remember that after Esau did this, he wanted to get his father's blessing, but his father refused. Esau could find no way to change what he had done, even though he wanted the blessing so much that he cried.

[18]You have not come to a mountain that can be touched and that is burning with fire. You have not come to darkness, sadness, and storms. [19]You have not come to the noise of a trumpet or to the sound of a voice like the one the people of Israel heard and begged not to hear another word. [20]They did not want to hear the command: "If anything, even an animal, touches the mountain, it must be put to death with stones."[n] [21]What they saw was so terrible that Moses said, "I am shaking with fear."[n]

[22]But you have come to Mount Zion,[n] to the city of the living God, the heavenly Jerusalem. You have come to thousands of angels gathered together with joy. [23]You have

12:20 **"If . . . stones."** Quotation from Exodus 19:12–13.
12:21 **"I . . . fear."** Quotation from Deuteronomy 9:19.
12:22 **Mount Zion** Another name for Jerusalem, here meaning the spiritual city of God's people.

SHOWING APPROVAL FOR YOUR HUSBAND

the **marriage** bed

 **FAMILY**

HEBREWS 13:4

In the Greek text, the idea behind this verse is about impurity. The moral concept of "stain" always means *pollution* by sin. So, here, the word carries the idea that the marriage is to be pure and unstained by sin. Actually, the word is even more specific because it is associated with the sexual relationship in marriage. The author of Hebrews continues this thought by saying that God will judge those who defile this sacred union.

This is about as clear as it gets. Sex in marriage is absolutely exclusive. Christians have always known this. But the implication is far greater than a prohibition against adultery.

If we think of it in terms of the picture of staining, we can see that even the slightest color added to clear glass would alter its transparency.

There is a reason that Paul pleads with us to renew our minds. "Undefiled" is a description of God's holiness. Marriage has always been used as a religious symbol of God's covenant relationship to his people. Just as God tolerates no pollution of that relationship, neither should we tolerate anything that stains our sexuality in marriage. It is designed to be a permanent "one-flesh" arrangement.

reflect: Commit yourself anew to the sanctity of your marriage vows today.
Go to **1 Peter 3:1–2.**

come to the meeting of God's firstborn[n] children whose names are written in heaven. You have come to God, the judge of all people, and to the spirits of good people who have been made perfect. [24]You have come to Jesus, the One who brought the new agreement from God to his people, and you have come to the sprinkled blood[n] that has a better message than the blood of Abel.[n]

[25]So be careful and do not refuse to listen when God speaks. Others refused to listen to him when he warned them on earth, and they did not escape. So it will be worse for us if we refuse to listen to God who warns us from heaven. [26]When he spoke before, his voice shook the earth, but now he has promised,

"Once again I will shake not only the earth but also the heavens."[n] [27]The words "once again" clearly show us that everything that was made—things that can be shaken—will be destroyed. Only the things that cannot be shaken will remain.

[28]So let us be thankful, because we have a kingdom that cannot be shaken. We should worship God in a way that pleases him with

---

12:23 firstborn The first son born in a Jewish family was given the most important place in the family and received special blessings. All of God's children are like that. **12:24 sprinkled blood** The blood of Jesus' death. **12:24 Abel** The son of Adam and Eve, who was killed by his brother Cain (Genesis 4:8). **12:26 "Once . . . heavens."** Quotation from Haggai 2:6, 21.

FUTURE

HOPE IN THE HOLY SPIRIT

fully equipped
for the **job**

HEBREWS 13:20–21

The author of Hebrews concludes his letter with a prayer. It is a prayer that God will completely outfit those who read his letter to do God's will. Don't we often struggle with the question, What is God's will for me? Here we see a prayer and a promise. God is training and equipping his followers with everything they need to do what he wants them to do. This is God's role and his responsibility.

He wants us to become artisans for performing his will. Even more importantly, we are told that God is equipping us with every *good* thing needed to accomplish our task. God makes craftsmen of his children. There are no apprentices when he is done. He produces only ace students, completely ready to take on his tasks.

A famous billionaire was once asked, "What do you look for in the people you work with?" He immediately said, "Follow-through. If we're supposed to have a lunch meeting and you have to reschedule, I don't hire you . . . or you're fired."

Today we can have confidence that God is making us into completely fit and sufficient stewards. We won't lack anything to accomplish his purpose for us. So go ahead and follow through. You have every good thing going for you.

---

reflect: Rest in the knowledge that God has equipped you for greatness.
Go to **James 1:14.**

respect and fear, ²⁹because our God is like a fire that burns things up.

13 Keep on loving each other as brothers and sisters. ²Remember to welcome strangers, because some who have done this have welcomed angels without knowing it. ³Remember those who are in prison as if you were in prison with them. Remember those who are suffering as if you were suffering with them.

⁴Marriage should be honored by everyone, and husband and wife should keep their marriage pure. God will judge as guilty those who take part in sexual sins. ⁵Keep your lives free from the love of money, and be satisfied with what you have. God has said,

"I will never leave you;
I will never abandon you."

Deuteronomy 31:6

⁶So we can be sure when we say,

"I will not be afraid, because the Lord is
my helper.
People can't do anything to me."

Psalm 118:6

⁷Remember your leaders who taught God's message to you. Remember how they lived and died, and copy their faith. ⁸Jesus Christ is the same yesterday, today, and forever.

⁹Do not let all kinds of strange teachings lead you into the wrong way. Your hearts should be strengthened by God's grace, not by obeying rules about foods, which do not help those who obey them.

¹⁰We have a sacrifice, but the priests who serve in the Holy Tent cannot eat from it. ¹¹The high priest carries the blood of animals into the Most Holy Place where he offers this blood for sins. But the bodies of the animals are burned outside the camp. ¹²So Jesus also suffered outside the city to make his people holy with his own blood. ¹³So let us go to Jesus outside the camp, holding on as he did when we are abused.

¹⁴Here on earth we do not have a city that lasts forever, but we are looking for the city that we will have in the future. ¹⁵So through Jesus let us always offer to God our sacrifice of praise, coming from lips that speak his name. ¹⁶Do not forget to do good to others, and share with them, because such sacrifices please God.

¹⁷Obey your leaders and act under their authority. They are watching over you, because they are responsible for your souls. Obey them so that they will do this work with joy, not sadness. It will not help you to make their work hard.

¹⁸Pray for us. We are sure that we have a clear conscience, because we always want to do the right thing. ¹⁹I especially beg you to pray so that God will send me back to you soon.

²⁰⁻²¹I pray that the God of peace will give you every good thing you need so you can do what he wants. God raised from the dead our Lord Jesus, the Great Shepherd of the sheep, because of the blood of his death. His blood began the eternal agreement that God made with his people. I pray that God will do in us what pleases him, through Jesus Christ, and to him be glory forever and ever. Amen.

²²My brothers and sisters, I beg you to listen patiently to this message I have written to encourage you, because it is not very long. ²³I want you to know that our brother Timothy has been let out of prison. If he arrives soon, we will both come to see you.

²⁴Greet all your leaders and all of God's people. Those from Italy send greetings to you.

²⁵Grace be with you all.

james

HOW TO LIVE AS A CHRISTIAN

1 From James, a servant of God and of the Lord Jesus Christ.

To all of God's people who are scattered everywhere in the world:

Greetings.

FAITH AND WISDOM

²My brothers and sisters, when you have many kinds of troubles, you should be full of joy, ³because you know that these troubles test your faith, and this will give you patience. ⁴Let your patience show itself perfectly in

---

JESUS, WHO WAS, AND IS, AND IS TO COME

FAITH

one **enemy** of **faith**

JAMES 1:2–8

By Wendell Smith

Of all the great struggles of faith, the biggest problem occurs when faith doesn't work. That's pretty simple, right? All of a sudden there is a reversal of fortunes—your finances are lacking, or your body is sick. Sometimes your circumstances just don't line up, and heaviness and oppression lie heavy on your heart. It is tempting to be depressed and feel insufficient when it seems your prayers are not answered.

The majority of the greatest things to be learned about faith are not learned from large victories. You frequently learn more from the most humiliating defeats. It is often in those dark times that you learn what true faith is.

You don't need faith when times are going great, your finances are flowing, your body is healthy, and circumstances are lining up. It is easy to feel joyous and independent if everything is going your way. You don't need a lot of faith when life is going well—but you need faith in impossible situations. In bad times and during tests and trials, your faith will see you through into God's light and victory.

If there were no enemies, there would be no need for faith. It is in the valleys and the shadows that you become familiar with God's presence. When you see his hand in yours and trust him, all of a sudden your table is beautiful and the feast tastes better and you begin thinking, *My God, you are with me everywhere all the time.*

reflect: Are you in a position to trust God in your faith adventure today?
Go to **Matthew 21:22.**

what you do. Then you will be perfect and complete and will have everything you need. ⁵But if any of you needs wisdom, you should ask God for it. He is generous to everyone and will give you wisdom without criticizing you. ⁶But when you ask God, you must believe and not doubt. Anyone who doubts is like a wave in the sea, blown up and down by the wind. ⁷⁻⁸Such doubters are thinking two different things at the same time, and they cannot decide about anything they do. They should not think they will receive anything from the Lord.

TRUE RICHES

⁹Believers who are poor should take pride that God has made them spiritually rich. ¹⁰Those who are rich should take pride that

God has shown them that they are spiritually poor. The rich will die like a wild flower in the grass. ¹¹The sun rises with burning heat and dries up the plants. The flower falls off, and its beauty is gone. In the same way the rich will die while they are still taking care of business.

TEMPTATION IS NOT FROM GOD

¹²When people are tempted and still continue strong, they should be happy. After they have proved their faith, God will reward them with life forever. God promised this to all those who love him. ¹³When people are tempted, they should not say, "God is tempting me." Evil cannot tempt God, and God himself does not tempt anyone. ¹⁴But people are tempted when their own evil desire leads them away

HOPE IN THE HOLY SPIRIT

don't take the bait

FUTURE

JAMES 1:14

James is telling us as it is. Those inner impulses and desires that are designed to drag us off the right road are not wonderful, exciting, enjoyable hopes and dreams. They are bait. They're part of a trap! It's very hard to see things for what they really are. It's like a magic act. What you see isn't what you get. Magic works only when it makes you believe that you see something that isn't really there. That is what our inner impulses and desires do to us.

So how do we avoid these traps? How do we turn away from the bait? There are two clear methods.

The first method for avoiding traps is to look somewhere else. Actually, the Bible tells us that the way to stay on the right road is to use God's word as our light. "Your word is like a lamp for my feet" (Psalm 119:105) is a useful simile. Lost in the dark, there is nothing better than a good old lantern. It provides lots of nice, bright light for us to make it back to camp in the dark. Next time you spot a trap, turn on the light.

Second, any fisherman knows that the fish don't bite when they're not hungry. So lesson number two is to fill up your life with God and his love. Bait isn't so tempting when your heart is already full.

reflect: Resist temptation by focusing your attention on the goodness of God.
Go to **James 3:10.**

and traps them. [15]This desire leads to sin, and then the sin grows and brings death.

[16]My dear brothers and sisters, do not be fooled about this. [17]Every good action and every perfect gift is from God. These good gifts come down from the Creator of the sun, moon, and stars, who does not change like their shifting shadows. [18]God decided to give us life through the word of truth so we might be the most important of all the things he made.

LISTENING AND OBEYING

[19]My dear brothers and sisters, always be willing to listen and slow to speak. Do not become angry easily, [20]because anger will not help you live the right kind of life God wants. [21]So put out of your life every evil thing and every kind of wrong. Then in gentleness accept God's teaching that is planted in your hearts, which can save you.

[22]Do what God's teaching says; when you only listen and do nothing, you are fooling yourselves. [23]Those who hear God's teaching and do nothing are like people who look at themselves in a mirror. [24]They see their faces and then go away and quickly forget what they looked like. [25]But the truly happy people are those who carefully study God's perfect law that makes people free, and they continue to study it. They do not forget what they heard, but they obey what God's teaching says. Those who do this will be made happy.

THE TRUE WAY TO WORSHIP GOD

[26]People who think they are religious but say things they should not say are just fooling themselves. Their "religion" is worth nothing. [27]Religion that God accepts as pure and without fault is this: caring for orphans or widows who need help, and keeping yourself free from the world's evil influence.

LOVE ALL PEOPLE

2 My dear brothers and sisters, as believers in our glorious Lord Jesus Christ, never think some people are more important than others. [2]Suppose someone comes into your church meeting wearing nice clothes and a gold ring. At the same time a poor person comes in wearing old, dirty clothes. [3]You show special attention to the one wearing nice clothes and say, "Please, sit here in this good seat." But you say to the poor person, "Stand over there," or, "Sit on the floor by my feet." [4]What are you doing? You are making some people more important than others, and with evil thoughts you are deciding that one person is better.

[5]Listen, my dear brothers and sisters! God chose the poor in the world to be rich with faith and to receive the kingdom God promised to those who love him. [6]But you show no respect to the poor. The rich are always trying to control your lives. They are the ones who take you to court. [7]And they are the ones who speak against Jesus, who owns you.

[8]This royal law is found in the Scriptures: "Love your neighbor as you love yourself."[n] If you obey this law, you are doing right. [9]But if you treat one person as being more important than another, you are sinning. You are guilty of breaking God's law. [10]A person who follows all of God's law but fails to obey even one command is guilty of breaking all the commands in that law. [11]The same God who said, "You must not be guilty of adultery,"[n] also said, "You must not murder anyone."[n] So if you do not take part in adultery but you murder someone, you are guilty of breaking all of God's law. [12]In everything you say and do, remember that you will be judged by the law that makes people free. [13]So you must show mercy to others, or God will not show mercy to you when he judges you. But the person who shows mercy can stand without fear at the judgment.

FAITH AND GOOD WORKS

[14]My brothers and sisters, if people say they have faith, but do nothing, their faith is worth nothing. Can faith like that save them? [15]A brother or sister in Christ might need clothes or food. [16]If you say to that person, "God be with you! I hope you stay warm and get plenty to eat," but you do not give what that person needs, your words are worth nothing. [17]In the same way, faith by itself— that does nothing—is dead.

[18]Someone might say, "You have faith, but I have deeds." Show me your faith without doing anything, and I will show you my faith by what I do. [19]You believe there is one God. Good! But the demons believe that, too, and they tremble with fear.

2:8 "Love . . . yourself." Quotation from Leviticus 19:18. **2:11 "You . . . adultery."** Quotation from Exodus 20:14 and Deuteronomy 5:18. **2:11 "You . . . anyone."** Quotation from Exodus 20:13 and Deuteronomy 5:17.

[20]You foolish person! Must you be shown that faith that does nothing is worth nothing? [21]Abraham, our ancestor, was made right with God by what he did when he offered his son Isaac on the altar. [22]So you see that Abraham's faith and the things he did worked together. His faith was made perfect by what he did. [23]This shows the full meaning of the Scripture that says: "Abraham believed God, and God accepted Abraham's faith, and that faith made him right with God."[n] And Abraham was called God's friend.[n] [24]So you see that people are made right with God by what they do, not by faith only.

[25]Another example is Rahab, a prostitute, who was made right with God by something she did. She welcomed the spies into her home and helped them escape by a different road. [26]Just as a person's body that does not have a spirit is dead, so faith that does nothing is dead!

CONTROLLING THE THINGS WE SAY

3 My brothers and sisters, not many of you should become teachers, because you know that we who teach will be judged more strictly. [2]We all make many mistakes. If people never said anything wrong, they would be perfect and able to control their entire selves, too. [3]When we put bits into the mouths of horses to make them obey us, we can control their whole bodies. [4]Also a ship is very big, and it is pushed by strong winds. But a very small rudder controls that big ship, making it go wherever the pilot wants. [5]It is the same with the tongue. It is a small part of the body, but it brags about great things.

A big forest fire can be started with only a little flame. [6]And the tongue is like a fire. It is a whole world of evil among the parts of our bodies. The tongue spreads its evil through the whole body. The tongue is set on fire by hell, and it starts a fire that influences all of life. [7]People can tame every kind of wild animal, bird, reptile, and fish, and they have tamed them, [8]but no one can tame the tongue. It is wild and evil and full of deadly poison. [9]We use our tongues to praise our Lord and Father, but then we curse people, whom God made like himself. [10]Praises and curses come from the same mouth! My brothers and sisters, this should not happen. [11]Do good and bad water flow from the same spring? [12]My brothers and sisters, can a fig tree make olives, or can a grapevine make figs? No! And a well full of salty water cannot give good water.

TRUE WISDOM

[13]Are there those among you who are truly wise and understanding? Then they should show it by living right and doing good things with a gentleness that comes from wisdom. [14]But if you are selfish and have bitter jealousy in your hearts, do not brag. Your bragging is a lie that hides the truth. [15]That kind of "wisdom" does not come from God but from the world. It is not spiritual; it is from the devil. [16]Where jealousy and selfishness are, there will be confusion and every kind of evil. [17]But the wisdom that comes from God is first of all pure, then peaceful, gentle, and easy to please. This wisdom is always ready to help those who are troubled and to do good for others. It is always fair and honest. [18]People who work for peace in a peaceful way plant a good crop of right-living.

GIVE YOURSELVES TO GOD

4 Do you know where your fights and arguments come from? They come from the selfish desires that war within you. [2]You want things, but you do not have them. So you are ready to kill and are jealous of other people, but you still cannot get what you want. So you argue and fight. You do not get what you want, because you do not ask God. [3]Or when you ask, you do not receive because the reason you ask is wrong. You want things so you can use them for your own pleasures.

[4]So, you are not loyal to God! You should know that loving the world is the same as hating God. Anyone who wants to be a friend of the world becomes God's enemy. [5]Do you think the Scripture means nothing that says, "The Spirit that God made to live in us wants us for himself alone"?[n] [6]But God gives us even more grace, as the Scripture says,

> "God is against the proud,
> but he gives grace to the humble."
>
> *Proverbs 3:34*

[7]So give yourselves completely to God. Stand against the devil, and the devil will run

---

2:23 "Abraham . . . God." Quotation from Genesis 15:6. **2:23 God's friend** These words about Abraham are found in 2 Chronicles 20:7 and Isaiah 41:8. **4:5 "The Spirit . . . alone."** These words may be from Exodus 20:5.

from you. ⁸Come near to God, and God will come near to you. You sinners, clean sin out of your lives. You who are trying to follow God and the world at the same time, make your thinking pure. ⁹Be sad, cry, and weep! Change your laughter into crying and your joy into sadness. ¹⁰Humble yourself in the Lord's presence, and he will honor you.

YOU ARE NOT THE JUDGE

¹¹Brothers and sisters, do not tell evil lies about each other. If you speak against your fellow believers or judge them, you are judg-ing and speaking against the law they follow. And when you are judging the law, you are no longer a follower of the law. You have become a judge. ¹²God is the only Lawmaker and Judge. He is the only One who can save and destroy. So it is not right for you to judge your neighbor.

LET GOD PLAN YOUR LIFE

¹³Some of you say, "Today or tomorrow we will go to some city. We will stay there a year, do business, and make money." ¹⁴But you do not know what will happen tomor-

---

HOPE IN THE HOLY SPIRIT

FUTURE

gossip

JAMES 3:10

By Diana Hagee

God intended your words to express love where there is rejection, to comfort where there is pain, to bestow blessings where there are only curses and, ultimately, to be a witness of him to the world around you. The words of a Christian have a powerful effect on others.

Your conversation should always benefit God's kingdom and God's people. When your words do not lift up the name of God, they are irreverent and blasphemous. If your conversation harms the reputation of the person you are talking about, it is slander and gossip. Gossip is defined as idle words involving rumors about others.

Check your motive in answering a question or speaking your opinion. If your words do not bring comfort or edification, then keep from saying them. If a person is eager to share something negative with you about someone else, eventually that person will say something negative about you, as well. You are not immune from the sin of gossip. If someone wants to draw you into gossip, end the conversation swiftly, for to listen in silence is to take part in gossip by default.

Be mindful not to hide behind self-righteousness. Even if you repeat the truth, it is still gossip if the words spoken are not meant for good toward the person you are speaking with or for the one you are speaking about. God, our Father, always knows our motive, and one day he will reward or judge us by those motives.

reflect: When was the last time you spoke words of blessing to someone?
Go to **Matthew 28:16–20.**

row! Your life is like a mist. You can see it for a short time, but then it goes away. 15So you should say, "If the Lord wants, we will live and do this or that." 16But now you are proud and you brag. All of this bragging is wrong. 17Anyone who knows the right thing to do, but does not do it, is sinning.

A WARNING TO THE RICH

5 You rich people, listen! Cry and be very sad because of the troubles that are coming to you. 2Your riches have rotted, and your clothes have been eaten by moths. 3Your gold and silver have rusted, and that rust will be a proof that you were wrong. It will eat your bodies like fire. You saved your treasure for the last days. 4The pay you did not give the workers who mowed your fields cries out against you, and the cries of the workers have been heard by the Lord All-Powerful. 5Your life on earth was full of rich living and pleasing yourselves with everything you wanted. You made yourselves fat, like an animal ready to be killed. 6You have judged guilty and then murdered innocent people, who were not against you.

TOTAL CHRISTIAN FITNESS

I believe in God's will to heal

FITNESS

By Jack Hayford

JAMES 5:16

I believe it is God's will to heal and deliver the sick and tormented and that he has revealed his healing purpose in his Son, Jesus Christ. I believe it is God's nature to heal by every possible means and that his mercy and loving-kindness provide grace for the relief of human need, pain, misery, and sin.

Because I believe this, I praise the Creator who made all things. Sickness and pain are a result of humanity's fallen condition and not God's will or desire for humanity. I praise him for providing natural recovery processes: climate and diet, hospitals, doctors, and medicine, and for the divine healing gifts of the Holy Spirit in the name of Jesus.

I believe in the power of Jesus Christ's name to heal the sick and afflicted and to break any satanic bondage. I believe Jesus' power is as freely available today as it was during his own earthly ministry. Because of his death on the cross, I expect and receive healing and deliverance just as I receive forgiveness and blessing.

I believe in the power of God's Word and Spirit to supply health. I reject any teaching that produces guilt when Jesus does not seem to perform physical healing or personal deliverance from sickness or any other torment. I am convinced that where victory is not clearly evident, the divine grace of Almighty God is providing a victory of another sort.

This is my faith. I practice the ministry of prayer, faith, and healing so that Jesus Christ is glorified.

reflect: What area of your life needs divine healing today?
Go to **1 Peter 1:3.**

BE PATIENT

7Brothers and sisters, be patient until the Lord comes again. A farmer patiently waits for his valuable crop to grow from the earth and for it to receive the autumn and spring rains. 8You, too, must be patient. Do not give up hope, because the Lord is coming soon. 9Brothers and sisters, do not complain against each other or you will be judged guilty. And the Judge is ready to come! 10Brothers and sisters, follow the example of the prophets who spoke for the Lord. They suffered many hard things, but they were patient. 11We say they are happy because they did not give up. You have heard about Job's patience, and you know the Lord's purpose for him in the end. You know the Lord is full of mercy and is kind.

BE CAREFUL WHAT YOU SAY

12My brothers and sisters, above all, do not use an oath when you make a promise. Don't use the name of heaven, earth, or anything else to prove what you say. When you mean yes, say only yes, and when you mean no, say only no so you will not be judged guilty.

THE POWER OF PRAYER

13Anyone who is having troubles should pray. Anyone who is happy should sing praises. 14Anyone who is sick should call the church's elders. They should pray for and pour oil on the person[n] in the name of the Lord. 15And the prayer that is said with faith will make the sick person well; the Lord will heal that person. And if the person has sinned, the sins will be forgiven. 16Confess your sins to each other and pray for each other so God can heal you. When a believing person prays, great things happen. 17Elijah was a human being just like us. He prayed that it would not rain, and it did not rain on the land for three and a half years! 18Then Elijah prayed again, and the rain came down from the sky, and the land produced crops again.

SAVING A SOUL

19My brothers and sisters, if one of you wanders away from the truth, and someone helps that person come back, 20remember this: Anyone who brings a sinner back from the wrong way will save that sinner's soul from death and will cause many sins to be forgiven.

5:14 pour oil on the person Oil was used in the name of the Lord as a sign that the person was now set apart for God's special attention and care.

1 From Peter, an apostle of Jesus Christ.

To God's chosen people who are away from their homes and are scattered all around Pontus, Galatia, Cappadocia, Asia, and Bithynia. ²God planned long ago to choose you by making you his holy people, which is the Spirit's work. God wanted you to obey him and to be made clean by the blood of the death of Jesus Christ.

Grace and peace be yours more and more.

WE HAVE A LIVING HOPE

³Praise be to the God and Father of our Lord Jesus Christ. In God's great mercy he has caused us to be born again into a living

TOTAL CHRISTIAN FITNESS

regeneration by adoption

FITNESS

1 PETER 1:3

The literal word in this verse is "again generated." This is the technical term for "born again." It is a Greek word that Peter used. It is not the term that Jesus used in John 3, where Jesus told Nicodemus, "You all must be born again." But it is clear from the reply of Nicodemus that he meant "born a second time." In the Greek mystery religions, regeneration was associated with the idea that the divine spark in humanity was recirculated from one life to the next. Divinity, dispersed across the animated souls of people, was collected at death and returned in the birth of another. Many of the current ideas of past lives and reincarnation are really very old forms of Greek mystery cults.

But here the meaning is legal rather than mystical. When a convert comes into the faith, that individual's moral status before God is renewed. As now part of the true religion, he or she becomes a new person in God's eyes. Peter avoids the mystical meaning of this term by pointing to the resurrection as the means of regeneration.

Being "born again" is God's act, not ours. It does not occur because we follow some initiation rite or make vows or work ourselves into a fervent condition. God empowers regeneration because he is merciful and for no other reason.

If God has regenerated us on the inside, then we have the power and the ability to make the changes necessary to honor him on the outside. We don't need a motivational tape to get moving; we simply need to realize that God has gotten the process started for us.

reflect: Apply the power of God to your life, and watch how it naturally changes.

You have completed the **FITNESS** readings. Now go to **FULFILLMENT:** "Always on His Mind" at **Ezekiel 34:11–16.**

hope, because Jesus Christ rose from the dead. [4]Now we hope for the blessings God has for his children. These blessings, which cannot be destroyed or be spoiled or lose their beauty, are kept in heaven for you. [5]God's power protects you through your faith until salvation is shown to you at the end of time. [6]This makes you very happy, even though now for a short time different kinds of troubles may make you sad. [7]These troubles come to prove that your faith is pure. This purity of faith is worth more than gold, which can be proved to be pure by fire but will ruin. But the purity of your faith will bring you praise and glory and honor when Jesus Christ is shown to you. [8]You have not seen Christ, but still you love him. You cannot see him now, but you believe in him. So you are filled with a joy that cannot be explained, a joy full of glory. [9]And you are receiving the goal of your faith—the salvation of your souls.

[10]The prophets searched carefully and tried to learn about this salvation. They prophesied about the grace that was coming to you. [11]The Spirit of Christ was in the prophets, telling in advance about the sufferings of Christ and about the glory that would follow those sufferings. The prophets tried to learn about what the Spirit was showing them, when those things would happen, and what the world would be like at that time. [12]It was shown them that their service was not for themselves but for you, when they told about the truths you have now heard. Those who preached the Good News to you told you those things with the help of the Holy Spirit who was sent from heaven—things into which angels desire to look.

A CALL TO HOLY LIVING

[13]So prepare your minds for service and have self-control. All your hope should be for the gift of grace that will be yours when Jesus Christ is shown to you. [14]Now that you are obedient children of God do not live as you did in the past. You did not understand, so you did the evil things you wanted. [15]But be holy in all you do, just as God, the One who called you, is holy. [16]It is written in the Scriptures: "You must be holy, because I am holy."[n]

[17]You pray to God and call him Father, and he judges each person's work equally. So while you are here on earth, you should live with respect for God. [18]You know that in the past you were living in a worthless way, a way passed down from the people who lived before you. But you were saved from that useless life. You were bought, not with something that ruins like gold or silver, [19]but with the precious blood of Christ, who was like a pure and perfect lamb. [20]Christ was chosen before the world was made, but he was shown to the world in these last times for your sake. [21]Through Christ you believe in God, who raised Christ from the dead and gave him glory. So your faith and your hope are in God.

[22]Now that your obedience to the truth has purified your souls, you can have true love for your Christian brothers and sisters. So love each other deeply with all your heart. [n] [23]You have been born again, and this new life did not come from something that dies, but from something that cannot die. You were born again through God's living message that continues forever. [24]The Scripture says,

"All people are like the grass,
and all their glory is like the flowers of
the field.
The grass dies and the flowers fall,
[25] but the word of the Lord will live
forever."   *Isaiah 40:6–8*

And this is the word that was preached to you.

JESUS IS THE LIVING STONE

2 So then, rid yourselves of all evil, all lying, hypocrisy, jealousy, and evil speech. [2]As newborn babies want milk, you should want the pure and simple teaching. By it you can mature in your salvation, [3]because you have already examined and seen how good the Lord is.

[4]Come to the Lord Jesus, the "stone"[n] that lives. The people of the world did not want this stone, but he was the stone God chose, and he was precious. [5]You also are like living stones, so let yourselves be used to build a spiritual temple—to be holy priests who offer spiritual sacrifices to God. He will accept those sacrifices through Jesus Christ.

1:16 "You must be . . . holy." Quotation from Leviticus 11:45; 19:2; 20:7. **1:22 with all your heart** Some Greek copies read "with a pure heart." **2:4 "stone"** The most important stone in God's spiritual temple or house (his people).

⁶The Scripture says:
"I will put a stone in the ground in
Jerusalem.
Everything will be built on this
important and precious rock.
Anyone who trusts in him
will never be disappointed."
Isaiah 28:16
⁷This stone is worth much to you who believe. But to the people who do not believe,
"the stone that the builders rejected
has become the cornerstone."
Psalm 118:22
⁸Also, he is
"a stone that causes people to stumble,
a rock that makes them fall." *Isaiah 8:14*
They stumble because they do not obey what

God says, which is what God planned to
happen to them.

⁹But you are a chosen people, royal
priests, a holy nation, a people for God's own
possession. You were chosen to tell about
the wonderful acts of God, who called you
out of darkness into his wonderful light. ¹⁰At
one time you were not a people, but now you
are God's people. In the past you had never
received mercy, but now you have received
God's mercy.

LIVE FOR GOD

¹¹Dear friends, you are like foreigners and
strangers in this world. I beg you to avoid
the evil things your bodies want to do that
fight against your soul. ¹²People who do not

LESSONS FROM THE BATTLEFIELD

heaven is a
place to learn

FUTURE

By Bob Russell

1 PETER 1:12

The Bible does not provide much detail about heaven, but there is enough
information to stimulate interest. One thing that is going to be exciting there is
the opportunity for learning. Some people believe that when Christians get to heaven
they will immediately know everything.

That is not true. If we were to know everything, we would be as great as God. In the
context of Ephesians 2:7, "show" means to reveal in an ongoing, progressive way.
Clearly, all believers will be in a continual state of learning when they are in heaven.

The angels live in heaven, but even they did not know everything about the plan of
redemption until it actually unfolded. First Peter 1:12 reveals that angels desired to look
into those things. If the angels are still learning, there will certainly be things in heaven
for humans to learn. No one will know it all instantly.

Heaven is going to be an exciting place of deepening relationships, fulfilling activities,
healthy laughter, inspirational worship, incredible beauty, and productive work.
However, one of the primary reasons to set affections on things above is that in the
coming ages, God will teach everyone the incomparable riches of his grace!

reflect: What are some things you want to learn when you get to heaven?
Go to **Ephesians 5:15–16.**

believe are living all around you and might say that you are doing wrong. Live such good lives that they will see the good things you do and will give glory to God on the day when Christ comes again.

YIELD TO EVERY HUMAN AUTHORITY

13For the Lord's sake, yield to the people who have authority in this world: the king, who is the highest authority, 14and the leaders who are sent by him to punish those who do wrong and to praise those who do right. 15It is God's desire that by doing good you should stop foolish people from saying stupid things about you. 16Live as free people, but do not use your freedom as an excuse to do evil. Live as servants of God. 17Show respect for all people: Love the brothers and sisters of God's family, respect God, honor the king.

FOLLOW CHRIST'S EXAMPLE

18Slaves, yield to the authority of your masters with all respect, not only those who are good and kind, but also those who are dishonest. 19A person might have to suffer even when it is unfair, but if he thinks of God and can stand the pain, God is pleased. 20If you are beaten for doing wrong, there is no reason to praise you for being patient in your punishment. But if you suffer for doing good, and you are patient, then God is pleased. 21This is what you were called to do, because Christ suffered for you and gave you an example to follow. So you should do as he did.
22 "He had never sinned,
    and he had never lied."   *Isaiah 53:9*
23People insulted Christ, but he did not insult them in return. Christ suffered, but he did not threaten. He let God, the One who judges rightly, take care of him. 24Christ carried our sins in his body on the cross so we would stop living for sin and start living for what is right. And you are healed because of his wounds. 25You were like sheep that wandered away, but now you have come back to the Shepherd and Overseer of your souls.

WIVES AND HUSBANDS

3 In the same way, you wives should yield to your husbands. Then, if some husbands do not obey God's teaching, they will be persuaded to believe without anyone's saying a word to them. They will be persuaded by the way their wives live. 2Your husbands will

see the pure lives you live with your respect for God. 3It is not fancy hair, gold jewelry, or fine clothes that should make you beautiful. 4No, your beauty should come from within you—the beauty of a gentle and quiet spirit that will never be destroyed and is very precious to God. 5In this same way the holy women who lived long ago and followed God made themselves beautiful, yielding to their own husbands. 6Sarah obeyed Abraham, her husband, and called him her master. And you women are true children of Sarah if you always do what is right and are not afraid.

7In the same way, you husbands should live with your wives in an understanding way, since they are weaker than you. But show them respect, because God gives them the same blessing he gives you—the grace that gives true life. Do this so that nothing will stop your prayers.

SUFFERING FOR DOING RIGHT

8Finally, all of you should be in agreement, understanding each other, loving each other as family, being kind and humble. 9Do not do wrong to repay a wrong, and do not insult to repay an insult. But repay with a blessing, because you yourselves were called to do this so that you might receive a blessing. 10The Scripture says,

"A person must do these things
    to enjoy life and have many happy days.
He must not say evil things,
    and he must not tell lies.
11 He must stop doing evil and do good.
    He must look for peace and work for it.
12 The Lord sees the good people
    and listens to their prayers.
But the Lord is against
    those who do evil."   *Psalm 34:12–16*
13If you are trying hard to do good, no one can really hurt you. 14But even if you suffer for doing right, you are blessed.
"Don't be afraid of what they fear;
    do not dread those things."
                                 Isaiah 8:12–13
15But respect Christ as the holy Lord in your hearts. Always be ready to answer everyone who asks you to explain about the hope you have, 16but answer in a gentle way and with respect. Keep a clear conscience so that those who speak evil of your good life in Christ will be made ashamed. 17It is better to suffer for

doing good than for doing wrong if that is what God wants. ¹⁸Christ himself suffered for sins once. He was not guilty, but he suffered for those who are guilty to bring you to God. His body was killed, but he was made alive in the spirit. ¹⁹And in the spirit he went and preached to the spirits in prison ²⁰who refused to obey God long ago in the time of Noah. God was waiting patiently for them while Noah was building the boat. Only a few people—eight in all—were saved by water. ²¹And that water is like baptism that now saves you—not the washing of dirt from the body, but the promise made to God from a good conscience. And this is because Jesus Christ was raised from the dead. ²²Now Jesus has gone into heaven and is at God's right side ruling over angels, authorities, and powers.

CHANGE YOUR LIVES

4 Since Christ suffered while he was in his body, strengthen yourselves with the same way of thinking Christ had. The person who has suffered in the body is finished with sin. ²Strengthen yourselves so that you will

---

SHOWING APPROVAL FOR YOUR HUSBAND

submission **still** works

FAMILY

By Bob Russell

1 PETER 3:1–2

The world scoffs at passages that instruct wives to submit to their husbands. In this era of women's liberation, the idea that a wife should respect her husband's leadership seems so antiquated that even many Christians apologize for it or try to explain it away.

Some Christian teachers are quick to point out that the Bible says we are all to be submissive to one another, and that the wife is not a doormat, nor the husband a dictator. They are correct. However, one major factor needs to be considered before discarding this passage: submission still works! It is truly amazing what happens when we take God at his Word.

Some husbands may be so hardhearted that they will never change. But the chances of a transformation are greatly enhanced if the wife follows the counsel of God's Word. A wife's humble, patient, submissive spirit is still very effective. That is better than the bickering and alienation that often result when spouses demand their rights. "Loving God means obeying his commands. And God's commands are not too hard for us" (1 John 5:3).

Wives, if your husband is not a believer, don't pout, complain, rebel, whine, criticize, or leave little passages of Scripture on his pillow. You probably will not influence him by any power play. Instead, follow the advice in 1 Peter 3. Submit to your husband. Let the beauty of your gentle and quiet spirit shine. In this way, God is glorified. Try it. It works!

---

reflect: What areas of your life need to be submitted to the authority of God?
Go to **1 John 4:7–12.**

live here on earth doing what God wants, not the evil things people want. ³In the past you wasted too much time doing what nonbelievers enjoy. You were guilty of sexual sins, evil desires, drunkenness, wild and drunken parties, and hateful idol worship. ⁴Nonbelievers think it is strange that you do not do the many wild and wasteful things they do, so they insult you. ⁵But they will have to explain this to God, who is ready to judge the living and the dead. ⁶For this reason the Good News was preached to those who are now dead. Even though they were judged like all people, the Good News was preached to them so they could live in the spirit as God lives.

USE GOD'S GIFTS WISELY

⁷The time is near when all things will end. So think clearly and control yourselves so you will be able to pray. ⁸Most importantly, love each other deeply, because love will cause people to forgive each other for many sins. ⁹Open your homes to each other, without complaining. ¹⁰Each of you has received a gift to use to serve others. Be good servants of God's various gifts of grace. ¹¹Anyone who speaks should speak words

---

JESUS, WHO WAS, AND IS, AND IS TO COME

FAITH

brotherly love

1 PETER 3:8–12

This is a word you are not likely to forget, once you know what it is. The word is *philadelphio*. We have a city in Pennsylvania by that name. It literally means "brotherly love." This word combines the word *adelphia* (brothers) and *philo* (love). Peter tells us that brotherly (or family) love is a mark of our faithfulness to Christ. He knows this from personal experience.

There are few joys more satisfying than the embrace of friends, people you know you can count on, people who have been woven into the fabric of your life. Sharing our lives with others who are on the same path toward heaven is a great comfort and a wonderful reward. As far as the Bible is concerned, my real family is made up of those who are traveling to the same destination in Christ. That's the only family resemblance that matters.

We were created for relationship. Being a Christian is a commitment to community. God planned it that way. We are a family of the forgiven. Once we truly understand what that means, we recognize that the greatest evil is anything that works to tear us apart. All of the distinctions that the world wants to use to separate one group from another really don't come into play for us. My display of brotherly love is for all the brothers and sisters in my family, and I don't care where they came from or how they got there. I'm just glad that I'm included.

reflect: Consider how you can actively grow in community with others today.
You have completed the **FAITH** readings. Now go to **FAMILY:** "Guilt and Grace" at **Proverbs 3:13–18.**

Peace by God

By Dr. Ben Lerner

1 PETER 4:19

Stress is not just something the advertising wizards on Madison Avenue cooked up to sell more aspirin. It's the "real deal," and it is incredibly damaging to your body. Stress is something you must drastically minimize in order not just to stay sane, but also to stay healthy.

However, to change your stress levels really requires a moment of awakening. It takes a time when you look around you and finally realize that you are not a victim of your crises, you are at the root of them. Of course, the challenge is that we humans often need to face complete and total destruction before we are willing to consider this revelational kick in the head.

Peter seemed to exhibit this same problem in Matthew 14. It was one of those nights when everything seemed to be going wrong. Jesus had rushed Peter and the other followers out of the area (see Matthew 14:22), and now they were trapped in the middle of the lake with a major storm threatening to drown them all. Then, as if out of thin air, Jesus came walking across the water. Talk about stress . . . the disciples were scared half to death, convinced that they were seeing a ghost!

> But Jesus quickly spoke to them, "Have courage! It is I. Do not be afraid."
> Peter said, "Lord, if it is really you, then command me to come to you on the water."
> Jesus said, "Come." And Peter left the boat and walked on the water to Jesus. (Matthew 14:27–29)

So far, so good. Sure, Peter was stressed out, but he could see Jesus through the storm. He took a step of faith and accomplished something no other mere mortal has ever accomplished. Then came the relapse.

> But when Peter saw the wind and the waves, he became afraid and began to sink. He shouted, "Lord, save me!" (Matthew 14:30)

Peter looked around and saw himself as a victim of the wind and waves—the same wind and waves that he was currently overcoming! Peter "saw" the circumstances and got stressed out all over again, even after demonstrating that the wind and waves had no power over his faith. Peter's stress-filled *reaction* to the elements could have killed him had it not been for the hand of Christ.

You see, stress is created when forces *outside* a person overwhelm the mind and the senses and cause a reaction *inside* a person. That stress reaction can have a tremendously negative impact on your health. You don't have to be sinking in a stormy lake to have stress put you in harm's way.

Eventually, Peter had his "moment of awakening" and was able to say with confidence that "those who suffer as God wants should trust their souls to the faithful Creator as they continue to do what is right" (1 Peter 4:19). And if Peter can exercise enough peace to walk on water in the middle of a raging storm, surely you and I can allow God's peace to rule and reign in the midst of our own daily struggles.

TO LEARN MORE ON WHAT THE BIBLE HAS TO SAY ABOUT **FULFILLMENT,** READ THE SCRIPTURES AND DEVOTIONALS AT **JOHN 20:16, JOHN 20:22–23, ROMANS 6:12-14, ROMANS 8:28, ISAIAH 45:7,** AND **ISAIAH 26:3.**

from God. Anyone who serves should serve with the strength God gives so that in everything God will be praised through Jesus Christ. Power and glory belong to him forever and ever. Amen.

SUFFERING AS A CHRISTIAN

12My friends, do not be surprised at the terrible trouble which now comes to test you. Do not think that something strange is happening to you. 13But be happy that you are sharing in Christ's sufferings so that you will be happy and full of joy when Christ comes again in glory. 14When people insult you because you follow Christ, you are blessed, because the glorious Spirit, the Spirit of God, is with you. 15Do not suffer for murder, theft, or any other crime, nor because you trouble other people. 16But if you suffer because you are a Christian, do not be ashamed. Praise God because you wear that name. 17It is time for judgment to begin with God's family. And if that judging begins with us, what will happen to those people who do not obey the Good News of God?

18 "If it is very hard for a good person to be
>saved,
>the wicked person and the sinner will
>surely be lost!"[n]

19So those who suffer as God wants should trust their souls to the faithful Creator as they continue to do what is right.

THE FLOCK OF GOD

5 Now I have something to say to the elders in your group. I also am an elder. I have seen Christ's sufferings, and I will share in the glory that will be shown to us. I beg you to 2shepherd God's flock, for whom you are responsible. Watch over them because you want to, not because you are forced. That is how God wants it. Do it because you are happy to serve, not because you want money. 3Do not be like a ruler over people you are re-

sponsible for, but be good examples to them. 4Then when Christ, the Chief Shepherd, comes, you will get a glorious crown that will never lose its beauty.

5In the same way, younger people should be willing to be under older people. And all of you should be very humble with each other.

"God is against the proud,
>but he gives grace to the humble."

Proverbs 3:34

6Be humble under God's powerful hand so he will lift you up when the right time comes. 7Give all your worries to him, because he cares about you.

8Control yourselves and be careful! The devil, your enemy, goes around like a roaring lion looking for someone to eat. 9Refuse to give in to him, by standing strong in your faith. You know that your Christian family all over the world is having the same kinds of suffering.

10And after you suffer for a short time, God, who gives all grace, will make everything right. He will make you strong and support you and keep you from falling. He called you to share in his glory in Christ, a glory that will continue forever. 11All power is his forever and ever. Amen.

FINAL GREETINGS

12I wrote this short letter with the help of Silas, who I know is a faithful brother in Christ. I wrote to encourage you and to tell you that this is the true grace of God. Stand strong in that grace.

13The church in Babylon, who was chosen like you, sends you greetings. Mark, my son in Christ, also greets you. 14Give each other a kiss of Christian love when you meet.

Peace to all of you who are in Christ.

4:18 "If . . . lost!" Quotation from Proverbs 11:31 in the Septuagint, the Greek version of the Old Testament.

2 peter

CORRECTING FALSE TEACHINGS

1 From Simon Peter, a servant and apostle of Jesus Christ.

To you who have received a faith as valuable as ours, because our God and Savior Jesus Christ does what is right.

²Grace and peace be given to you more and more, because you truly know God and Jesus our Lord.

GOD HAS GIVEN US BLESSINGS

³Jesus has the power of God, by which he has given us everything we need to live and to serve God. We have these things because we know him. Jesus called us by his glory and goodness. ⁴Through these he gave us the very great and precious promises. With these gifts you can share in God's nature, and the world will not ruin you with its evil desires.

⁵Because you have these blessings, do your best to add these things to your lives: to your faith, add goodness; and to your goodness, add knowledge; ⁶and to your knowledge, add self-control; and to your self-control, add patience; and to your patience, add service for God; ⁷and to your service for God, add kindness for your brothers and sisters in Christ; and to this kindness, add love. ⁸If all these things are in you and are growing, they will help you to be useful and productive in your knowledge of our Lord Jesus Christ. ⁹But anyone who does not have these things cannot see clearly. He is blind and has forgotten that he was made clean from his past sins.

¹⁰My brothers and sisters, try hard to be certain that you really are called and chosen by God. If you do all these things, you will never fall. ¹¹And you will be given a very great welcome into the eternal kingdom of our Lord and Savior Jesus Christ.

¹²You know these things, and you are very strong in the truth, but I will always help you remember them. ¹³I think it is right for me to help you remember as long as I am in this body. ¹⁴I know I must soon leave this body, as our Lord Jesus Christ has shown me. ¹⁵I will try my best so that you may be able to remember these things even after I am gone.

WE SAW CHRIST'S GLORY

¹⁶When we told you about the powerful coming of our Lord Jesus Christ, we were not telling just clever stories that someone invented. But we saw the greatness of Jesus with our own eyes. ¹⁷Jesus heard the voice of God, the Greatest Glory, when he received honor and glory from God the Father. The voice said, "This is my Son, whom I love, and I am very pleased with him." ¹⁸We heard that voice from heaven while we were with Jesus on the holy mountain.

¹⁹This makes us more sure about the message the prophets gave. It is good for you to follow closely what they said as you would follow a light shining in a dark place, until the day begins and the morning star rises in your hearts. ²⁰Most of all, you must understand this: No prophecy in the Scriptures ever comes from the prophet's own interpretation. ²¹No prophecy ever came from what a person wanted to say, but people led by the Holy Spirit spoke words from God.

FALSE TEACHERS

2 There used to be false prophets among God's people, just as you will have some false teachers in your group. They will secretly teach things that are wrong—teachings that will cause people to be lost. They will even refuse to accept the Master, Jesus, who bought their freedom. So they will bring quick ruin on themselves. ²Many will follow their evil ways and say evil things about the way of truth. ³Those false teachers only want your money, so they will use you by telling you lies. Their judgment spoken against them long ago is still coming, and their ruin is certain.

⁴When angels sinned, God did not let them go free without punishment. He sent them to hell and put them in caves[n] of darkness where they are being held for judgment. ⁵And God punished the world long ago when he brought a flood to the world that was full of people who were against him. But God

---

2:4 caves Some Greek copies read "chains."

The **One Percent** Solution

FITNESS

By Dr. Ben Lerner

2 PETER 1:5

In the short span of a single week, I review dozens of diets or case histories. Due to the constantly growing number of things that taste good, I come across countless new addictions on an almost daily basis.

Nearly all of us face addiction issues when it comes to food. Foods with caffeine, sugar, and things with caffeine and sugar in them are your more popular addictions. We find them in foods like coffee, cookies, sodas, candy, ice cream, and bread.

Sadly, when you look at our national health and social problems—obesity, heart disease, cancer, divorce, crime, depression—you see the side effects of our addictions at the root of many of them. Recognizing this is all well and good, but how do you actually *change* addictions? The very word "addiction" means that you are completely devoted to the issue. It's hard to get away from something you are completely devoted to.

I have several suggestions, but my key one is finding *something* or *someone* you are devoted to, more than you are devoted to chocolate or cookies.

My father was never "just eating." He was either on a diet or off of a diet. He really struggled with his weight, and it hurt me to watch him do so. His struggle is one of the many reasons I ended up getting into the healthcare field. When I was 12 years old, my father came up to me and said, "If I have to keep dieting in order to live longer, I do not want to live longer."

I thought at the time that he made a valid point. He hated dieting. This was especially true because, to my father, eating properly *did* mean deprivation. There were no healthy substitutes at the time. There were only carrot sticks and celery or junk food as far as my dad knew.

My thought for overcoming addictions is this: As a result of my dad's lifestyle, he died at 52. He left behind a young wife and three kids. My youngest brother found my dad on the lawn where he had died of his heart attack. I had a great dad who loved his family—but I wish my dad had thought about us when he decided he would stop trying.

I know how hard it is to get rid of the negative things we are so devoted to. A great first step is to step outside of yourself and think of how it affects everyone around you—now and in the future. Then become devoted/addicted to learning and improving from there.

Remember, the journey to health doesn't happen all at once, it's comprised of small successes, compounded day in and day out across the years. That's why we advocate the "1 Percent Solution": just concentrate on getting 1 percent better for God in this area today. Then tomorrow, strive to get 1 percent better still. It may not sound like much, but at the end of 40 days you can be 40 percent better for God—and that's pretty impressive. Breaking the power of food addictions isn't about perfection; it's about progress—1 percent at a time.

TO LEARN MORE ON WHAT THE BIBLE HAS TO SAY ABOUT **FITNESS,** READ THE SCRIPTURES AND DEVOTIONALS AT **1 CORINTHIANS 9:24–27, TITUS 2:12, 2 CORINTHIANS 4:7, ACTS 1:14, 2 CORINTHIANS 13:5,** AND **GALATIANS 6:10.**

saved Noah, who preached about being right with God, and seven other people with him. 6And God also destroyed the evil cities of Sodom and Gomorrah[n] by burning them until they were ashes. He made those cities an example of what will happen to those who are against God. 7But he saved Lot from those cities. Lot, a good man, was troubled because of the filthy lives of evil people. 8(Lot was a good man, but because he lived with evil people every day, his good heart was hurt by the evil things he saw and heard.) 9So the Lord knows how to save those who serve him when troubles come. He will hold evil people and punish them, while waiting for the Judgment Day. 10That punishment is especially for those who live by doing the evil things their sinful selves want and who hate authority.

These false teachers are bold and do anything they want. They are not afraid to speak against the angels. 11But even the angels, who are much stronger and more powerful than false teachers, do not accuse them with insults before[n] the Lord. 12But these people speak against things they do not understand. They are like animals that act without thinking, animals born to be caught and killed. And, like animals, these false teachers will be destroyed. 13They have caused many people to suffer, so they themselves will suffer. That is their pay for what they have done. They take pleasure in openly doing evil, so they are like dirty spots and stains among you. They delight in deceiving you while eating meals with you. 14Every time they look at a woman they want her, and their desire for sin is never satisfied. They lead weak people into the trap of sin, and they have taught their hearts to be greedy. God will punish them! 15These false teachers left the right road and lost their way, following the way Balaam went. Balaam was the son of Beor, who loved being paid for doing wrong. 16But a donkey, which cannot talk, told Balaam he was sinning. It spoke with a man's voice and stopped the prophet's crazy thinking.

17Those false teachers are like springs without water and clouds blown by a storm. A place in the blackest darkness has been kept for them. 18They brag with words that mean nothing. By their evil desires they lead people into the trap of sin—people who are just beginning to escape from others who live in error. 19They promise them freedom, but they themselves are not free. They are slaves of things that will be destroyed. For people are slaves of anything that controls them. 20They were made free from the evil in the world by knowing our Lord and Savior Jesus Christ. But if they return to evil things and those things control them, then it is worse for them than it was before. 21Yes, it would be better for them to have never known the right way than to know it and to turn away from the holy teaching that was given to them. 22What they did is like this true saying: "A dog goes back to what it has thrown up,"[n] and, "After a pig is washed, it goes back and rolls in the mud."

JESUS WILL COME AGAIN

3 My friends, this is the second letter I have written you to help your honest minds remember. 2I want you to think about the words the holy prophets spoke in the past, and remember the command our Lord and Savior gave us through your apostles. 3It is most important for you to understand what will happen in the last days. People will laugh at you. They will live doing the evil things they want to do. 4They will say, "Jesus promised to come again. Where is he? Our fathers have died, but the world continues the way it has been since it was made." 5But they do not want to remember what happened long ago. By the word of God heaven was made, and the earth was made from water and with water. 6Then the world was flooded and destroyed with water. 7And that same word of God is keeping heaven and earth that we now have in order to be destroyed by fire. They are being kept for the Judgment Day and the destruction of all who are against God.

8But do not forget this one thing, dear friends: To the Lord one day is as a thousand years, and a thousand years is as one day. 9The Lord is not slow in doing what he promised—the way some people understand slowness. But God is being patient with you. He does not want anyone to be lost, but he wants all people to change their hearts and lives.

2:6 Sodom and Gomorrah Two cities God destroyed because the people were so evil. **2:11 before** Some Greek copies read "from." **2:22 "A dog . . . up."** Quotation from Proverbs 26:11.

[10]But the day of the Lord will come like a thief. The skies will disappear with a loud noise. Everything in them will be destroyed by fire, and the earth and everything in it will be exposed.[n] [11]In that way everything will be destroyed. So what kind of people should you be? You should live holy lives and serve God, [12]as you wait for and look forward to the coming of the day of God. When that day comes, the skies will be destroyed with fire, and everything in them will melt with heat. [13]But God made a promise to us, and we are waiting for a new heaven and a new earth where goodness lives.

[14]Dear friends, since you are waiting for this to happen, do your best to be without sin and without fault. Try to be at peace with God. [15]Remember that we are saved because our Lord is patient. Our dear brother Paul told you the same thing when he wrote to you with the wisdom that God gave him. [16]He writes about this in all his letters. Some things in Paul's letters are hard to understand, and people who are ignorant and weak in faith explain these things falsely. They also falsely explain the other Scriptures, but they are destroying themselves by doing this.

[17]Dear friends, since you already know about this, be careful. Do not let those evil people lead you away by the wrong they do. Be careful so you will not fall from your strong faith. [18]But grow in the grace and knowledge of our Lord and Savior Jesus Christ. Glory be to him now and forever! Amen.

3:10 and . . . exposed Some Greek copies read "and everything in it will be burned up."

1 We write you now about what has always existed, which we have heard, we have seen with our own eyes, we have looked at, and we have touched with our hands. We write to you about the Word[n] that gives life. [2]He who gives life was shown to us. We saw him and can give proof about it. And now we announce to you that he has life that continues forever. He was with God the Father and was shown to us. [3]We announce to you what we have seen and heard, because we want you also to have fellowship with us. Our fellowship is with God the Father and with his Son, Jesus Christ. [4]We write this to you so we may be full of joy.[n]

GOD FORGIVES OUR SINS

[5]Here is the message we have heard from Christ and now announce to you: God is light,[n] and in him there is no darkness at all. [6]So if we say we have fellowship with God, but we continue living in darkness, we are liars and do not follow the truth. [7]But if we live in the light, as God is in the light, we can share fellowship with each other. Then the blood of Jesus, God's Son, cleanses us from every sin.

[8]If we say we have no sin, we are fooling ourselves, and the truth is not in us. [9]But if we confess our sins, he will forgive our sins, because we can trust God to do what is right. He will cleanse us from all the wrongs we have done. [10]If we say we have not sinned, we make God a liar, and we do not accept God's teaching.

JESUS IS OUR HELPER

2 My dear children, I write this letter to you so you will not sin. But if anyone does sin, we have a helper in the presence of the Father—Jesus Christ, the One who does what is right. [2]He died in our place to take away our sins, and not only our sins but the sins of all people.

[3]We can be sure that we know God if we obey his commands. [4]Anyone who says, "I know God," but does not obey God's commands is a liar, and the truth is not in that person. [5]But if someone obeys God's teaching, then in that person God's love has truly reached its goal. This is how we can be sure we are living in God: [6]Whoever says that he lives in God must live as Jesus lived.

THE COMMAND TO LOVE OTHERS

[7]My dear friends, I am not writing a new command to you but an old command you have had from the beginning. It is the teaching you have already heard. [8]But also I am writing a new command to you, and you can see its truth in Jesus and in you, because the darkness is passing away, and the true light is already shining.

[9]Anyone who says, "I am in the light,"[n] but hates a brother or sister, is still in the darkness. [10]Whoever loves a brother or sister lives in the light and will not cause anyone to stumble in his faith. [11]But whoever hates a brother or sister is in darkness, lives in darkness, and does not know where to go, because the darkness has made that person blind.

[12] I write to you, dear children,
because your sins are forgiven through Christ.
[13] I write to you, fathers,
because you know the One who existed from the beginning.
I write to you, young people,
because you have defeated the Evil One.
[14] I write to you, children,
because you know the Father.
I write to you, fathers,
because you know the One who existed from the beginning.
I write to you, young people,
because you are strong;
the teaching of God lives in you,
and you have defeated the Evil One.
[15]Do not love the world or the things in

1:1 Word The Greek word is "logos," meaning any kind of communication. Here, it means Christ, who was the way God told people about himself. **1:4 so...joy** Some Greek copies read "so you may be full of joy." **1:5; 2:9 light** Here, it is used as a symbol of God's goodness or truth.

the world. If you love the world, the love of the Father is not in you. ¹⁶These are the ways of the world: wanting to please our sinful selves, wanting the sinful things we see, and being too proud of what we have. None of these come from the Father, but all of them come from the world. ¹⁷The world and everything that people want in it are passing away, but the person who does what God wants lives forever.

REJECT THE ENEMIES OF CHRIST

¹⁸My dear children, these are the last days. You have heard that the enemy of Christ is coming, and now many enemies of Christ are already here. This is how we know that these are the last days. ¹⁹These enemies of Christ

---

LESSONS FROM THE BATTLEFIELD

FUTURE

young but able

1 JOHN 2:13-14

You are never too young to serve the Lord. The Bible tells us that even though Timothy was a young man, he earnestly wanted to serve the Lord. Most young people feel that they are incompetent to be in a position of leadership. Timothy was just as insecure; he felt that his age was a major factor, and he doubted he could do the job that the Lord had called him to do.

Paul encouraged Timothy to continue in his zeal and to trust in what God was doing with him. Again Timothy was urged to live above what the critics could say about him. He was instructed to be strong in grace and to take his share of hardships and suffering as a good soldier. He was told to live a life that others could follow and that he should be a model for the others in the church. Paul was very personal in his instruction of Timothy concerning the qualifications of church office. He also offered instruction about his responsibility and duties as a minister of the Good News.

As you seek to follow the Lord, are you looking at yourself as a person who is too young to serve the Lord in the capacity that he would want you to serve? Do you feel that the way of the world is easier? Remember that as a young person you have qualifications that supersede your age.

If you feel that you have missed the mark or maybe your education level is not high enough, those are all excuses that can hinder your walk with God. Don't let this intimidate you from following God's will for you. What you feel is an inferior area could be the very means God uses to demonstrate his strength through you. Whether you are young or not as educated as you feel you should be, allow God to mold you and shape you into what he wants you to be, and just do it.

reflect: Meditate on whom God had made you in Christ.

Go to **2 Timothy 1:3.**

were in our fellowship, but they left us. They never really belonged to us; if they had been a part of us, they would have stayed with us. But they left, and this shows that none of them really belonged to us.

20You have the gift[n] that the Holy One gave you, so you all know the truth.[n] 21I do not write to you because you do not know the truth but because you do know the truth. And you know that no lie comes from the truth.

22Who is the liar? It is the person who does not accept Jesus as the Christ. This is the enemy of Christ: the person who does not accept the Father and his Son. 23Whoever does not accept the Son does not have the Father. But whoever confesses the Son has the Father, too.

24Be sure you continue to follow the teaching you heard from the beginning. If you continue to follow what you heard from the beginning, you will stay in the Son and in the Father. 25And this is what the Son promised to us—life forever.

26I am writing this letter about those people who are trying to lead you the wrong way. 27Christ gave you a special gift that is still in you, so you do not need any other teacher. His gift teaches you about everything, and it is true, not false. So continue to live in Christ, as his gift taught you.

28Yes, my dear children, live in him so that when Christ comes back, we can be without fear and not be ashamed in his presence. 29Since you know that Christ is righteous, you know that all who do right are God's children.

WE ARE GOD'S CHILDREN

3 The Father has loved us so much that we are called children of God. And we really are his children. The reason the people in the world do not know us is that they have not known him. 2Dear friends, now we are children of God, and we have not yet been shown what we will be in the future. But we know that when Christ comes again, we will be like him, because we will see him as he really is. 3Christ is pure, and all who have this hope in Christ keep themselves pure like Christ.

4The person who sins breaks God's law. Yes, sin is living against God's law. 5You know that Christ came to take away sins and that there is no sin in Christ. 6So anyone who lives

in Christ does not go on sinning. Anyone who goes on sinning has never really understood Christ and has never known him.

7Dear children, do not let anyone lead you the wrong way. Christ is righteous. So to be like Christ a person must do what is right. 8The devil has been sinning since the beginning, so anyone who continues to sin belongs to the devil. The Son of God came for this purpose: to destroy the devil's work.

9Those who are God's children do not continue sinning, because the new life from God remains in them. They are not able to go on sinning, because they have become children of God. 10So we can see who God's children are and who the devil's children are: Those who do not do what is right are not God's children, and those who do not love their brothers and sisters are not God's children.

WE MUST LOVE EACH OTHER

11This is the teaching you have heard from the beginning: We must love each other. 12Do not be like Cain who belonged to the Evil One and killed his brother. And why did he kill him? Because the things Cain did were evil, and the things his brother did were good.

13Brothers and sisters, do not be surprised when the people of the world hate you. 14We know we have left death and have come into life because we love each other. Whoever does not love is still dead. 15Everyone who hates a brother or sister is a murderer,[n] and you know that no murderers have eternal life in them. 16This is how we know what real love is: Jesus gave his life for us. So we should give our lives for our brothers and sisters. 17Suppose someone has enough to live and sees a brother or sister in need, but does not help. Then God's love is not living in that person. 18My children, we should love people not only with words and talk, but by our actions and true caring.

19-20This is the way we know that we belong to the way of truth. When our hearts make us feel guilty, we can still have peace

---

2:20 gift This might mean the Holy Spirit, or it might mean teaching or truth as in verse 24. **2:20 you . . . truth** Some Greek copies read "so you know all things." **3:15 Everyone . . . murderer** If one person hates a brother or sister, then in the heart that person has killed that brother or sister. Jesus taught about this sin to his followers (Matthew 5:21–26).

before God. God is greater than our hearts, and he knows everything. 21My dear friends, if our hearts do not make us feel guilty, we can come without fear into God's presence. 22And God gives us what we ask for because we obey God's commands and do what pleases him. 23This is what God commands: that we believe in his Son, Jesus Christ, and that we love each other, just as he commanded. 24The people who obey God's commands live in God, and God lives in them. We know that God lives in us because of the Spirit God gave us.

WARNING AGAINST FALSE TEACHERS

4 My dear friends, many false prophets have gone out into the world. So do not believe every spirit, but test the spirits to see if they are from God. 2This is how you can know God's Spirit: Every spirit who confesses that Jesus Christ came to earth as a human is from God. 3And every spirit who refuses to say this about Jesus is not from God. It is the spirit of the enemy of Christ, which you have heard is coming, and now he is already in the world.

4My dear children, you belong to God and have defeated them; because God's Spirit, who is in you, is greater than the devil, who is in the world. 5And they belong to the world, so what they say is from the world, and the world listens to them. 6But we belong to God, and those who know God listen to us. But those who are not from God do not listen to us. That is how we know the Spirit that is true and the spirit that is false.

BEATING THE BURNOUT BLUES

FULFILLMENT

rewrite your life

1 JOHN 3:1

We are the children of God, not because we did anything to deserve being his children but simply because we were favored with his love gift to us. In this verse, John expresses how unimaginably wonderful it is to know that God the Father loved us so much he chose to bless us with the gift of his Son, a gift so perfect that we became his adopted children by accepting his gift.

This proclamation of God's love toward us tells us something very important about who we are. It tells us that we matter to God. In fact, God places so high a value on us that he gave us the best gift he could—the gift that would bring us back to him. When we are trapped in destructive lives, we are often faced with the despair of worthlessness. But God says that we are worthy of his love. Think how great a love that is!

The only book that can create a completely new you is the one God wrote. The Bible is the only Book that lets God rewrite your life. And that's what we need. We are only able to remodel the mess we've made. God is able to do reconstruction. We don't need self-help. It was the "self" that was causing the problems. We need God to give us a new "self." The old one just couldn't do the job. We become new people through Christ.

reflect: Consider what it means to become a new creation being through Christ.

Go to **Jude 24.**

LOVE COMES FROM GOD

⁷Dear friends, we should love each other, because love comes from God. Everyone who loves has become God's child and knows God. ⁸Whoever does not love does not know God, because God is love. ⁹This is how God showed his love to us: He sent his one and only Son into the world so that we could have life through him. ¹⁰This is what real love is: It is not our love for God; it is God's love for us. He sent his Son to die in our place to take away our sins.

¹¹Dear friends, if God loved us that much we also should love each other. ¹²No one has ever seen God, but if we love each other, God lives in us, and his love is made perfect in us.

¹³We know that we live in God and he lives in us, because he gave us his Spirit. ¹⁴We have seen and can testify that the Father sent his Son to be the Savior of the world. ¹⁵Whoever confesses that Jesus is the Son of God has God living inside, and that person lives in God. ¹⁶And so we know the love that God has for us, and we trust that love.

God is love. Those who live in love live in God, and God lives in them. ¹⁷This is how love is made perfect in us: that we can be without

---

SHOWING APPROVAL FOR YOUR HUSBAND

building **lasting** love

FAMILY

By Jimmy Evans   1 JOHN 4:7–12

When we see people in love, we say, "Aren't they lucky?" Actually, love has nothing to do with luck. If you don't know what *love* is, you will be open to deception. Hosea 4:6 says the people perish for lack of knowledge. A lack of knowledge can destroy your marriage.

Amos 3:3 says two cannot walk together unless they are in agreement. You and your spouse have to come to agreement on the definition of *love* so you can rescue the destiny of your relationship.

The English language is deficient in words that adequately express what we mean by *love*. However, the Greek language has several words for it. The first, *eros*, refers to sexual attraction. Another word refers to family love. Still another word is *philia*, which is the love between friends. None of these is the word for God's love. The word for God's love is *agape*, as in John 3:16.

God commands us to have this kind of love for him and for each other. This is Christian love, but it is also used in the Bible to talk about the love between a husband and wife. *Agape* is a permanent, self-sacrificing commitment to act in the best interest of the other person, regardless of negative emotions or difficult circumstances. *Agape* love is the greatest type of love, and it is the only love that can help a marriage last.

---

reflect: Have you made an absolute commitment to your spouse until death?

You have completed the **FAMILY** readings. Now go to **FINANCES**: "The Favor of God" at **Genesis 16:1–13**.

fear on the day God judges us, because in this world we are like him. ¹⁸Where God's love is, there is no fear, because God's perfect love drives out fear. It is punishment that makes a person fear, so love is not made perfect in the person who fears.

¹⁹We love because God first loved us. ²⁰If people say, "I love God," but hate their brothers or sisters, they are liars. Those who do not love their brothers and sisters, whom they have seen, cannot love God, whom they have never seen. ²¹And God gave us this command: Those who love God must also love their brothers and sisters.

FAITH IN THE SON OF GOD

5 Everyone who believes that Jesus is the Christ is God's child, and whoever loves the Father also loves the Father's children. ²This is how we know we love God's children: when we love God and obey his commands. ³Loving God means obeying his commands. And God's commands are not too hard for us, ⁴because everyone who is a child of God

---

BUILDING MOMENTUM THROUGH TEAMWORK

FUTURE

guaranteed to win

1 JOHN 5:1-5   By John Ed Mathison

Here's the good news: you're already a winner if you have committed your life to Jesus Christ. However, your work has just begun! Here's how to live your life in a winning way for him:

Control yourself. Like an invading army seeking a weakness in a city's protective wall, Satan knows how to attack you at the point where you have the least self-control. Your temper, your tongue, your appetites, your attitudes, your emotions, and your thoughts must be guarded carefully against temptation.

Contend for an eternal prize. You are redeemed, not by perishable things, but by the living Word of God. The Olympic athletes in Paul's time competed for a wreath of ivy that did not last long. The earthly rewards of possessions, power, and pleasure are temporary. Investing in eternal rewards will guarantee a victory (1 Peter 1:4).

Compete with purpose in every step. Do not run about aimlessly (1 Corinthians 9:26). God created you for a purpose. Ask him to reveal this purpose to you.

Commit to discipline and training. "Anyone who loves learning accepts correction, but a person who hates being corrected is stupid" (Proverbs 12:1). Discipline is hard, and there's no instant gratification. It's a gradual process. God wants us to be trained in his way. He wants to take the things that connect us to him and train us to use these things wisely.

If you have a relationship with Jesus Christ, you are guaranteed to win for eternity!

---

reflect: Are you prepared to do what is necessary to experience victory?
Go to **2 Corinthians 5:17.**

conquers the world. And this is the victory that conquers the world—our faith. [5]So the one who conquers the world is the person who believes that Jesus is the Son of God.

[6]Jesus Christ is the One who came by water[n] and blood.[n] He did not come by water only, but by water and blood. And the Spirit says that this is true, because the Spirit is the truth. [7]So there are three witnesses:[n] [8]the Spirit, the water, and the blood; and these three witnesses agree. [9]We believe people when they say something is true. But what God says is more important, and he has told us the truth about his own Son. [10]Anyone who believes in the Son of God has the truth that God told us. Anyone who does not believe makes God a liar, because that person does not believe what God told us about his Son. [11]This is what God told us: God has given us eternal life, and this life is in his Son. [12]Whoever has the Son has life, but whoever does not have the Son of God does not have life.

WE HAVE ETERNAL LIFE NOW

[13]I write this letter to you who believe in the Son of God so you will know you have eternal life. [14]And this is the boldness we have in God's presence: that if we ask God for anything that agrees with what he wants, he hears us. [15]If we know he hears us every time we ask him, we know we have what we ask from him.

[16]If anyone sees a brother or sister sinning (sin that does not lead to eternal death), that person should pray, and God will give the sinner life. I am talking about people whose sin does not lead to eternal death. There is sin that leads to death. I do not mean that a person should pray about that sin. [17]Doing wrong is always sin, but there is sin that does not lead to eternal death.

[18]We know that those who are God's children do not continue to sin. The Son of God keeps them safe, and the Evil One cannot touch them. [19]We know that we belong to God, but the Evil One controls the whole world. [20]We also know that the Son of God has come and has given us understanding so that we can know the True One. And our lives are in the True One and in his Son, Jesus Christ. He is the true God and the eternal life.

[21]So, dear children, keep yourselves away from false gods.

5:6 water This probably means the water of Jesus' baptism. **5:6 blood** This probably means the blood of Jesus' death. **5:7–8 So . . . witnesses** A few very late Greek copies and the Latin Vulgate continue, "in heaven: the Father, the Word, and the Holy Spirit, and these three witnesses agree. [8]And there are three witnesses on earth:"

2 john

DO NOT HELP FALSE TEACHERS

[1]From the Elder.[n]
To the chosen lady[n] and her children:
I love all of you in the truth,[n] and all those who know the truth love you. [2]We love you because of the truth that lives in us and will be with us forever.

[3]Grace, mercy, and peace from God the Father and his Son, Jesus Christ, will be with us in truth and love.

[4]I was very happy to learn that some of your children are following the way of truth,

---

1 Elder "Elder" means an older person. It can also mean a special leader in the church (as in Titus 1:5). **1 lady** This might mean a woman, or in this letter it might mean a church. If it is a church, then "her children" would be the people of the church. **1 truth** The truth or "Good News" about Jesus Christ that joins all believers together.

FAMILY

COVENANT MARRIAGE

setting **new** boundaries

2 JOHN 2   By Drs. Les and Leslie Parrott

A man made his living by raising ducks, but he had a problem. He only had one pond, but he had several different kinds of ducks, and they would peck at each other. Wanting to keep the ducks separate, he ran fences through the water. When he was finished, he had fences going in every direction. He thought all the ducks would feel safe in their own section.

Sometimes couples do the same thing. Spouses erect fences and build walls around parts of themselves to keep from getting hurt. In some marriages, the fences run in every direction. If that sounds like you, it is time to consider doing something about those fences.

The man who raised the ducks later discovered that they were not doing well. Some seemed feeble because they did not have enough room to swim. The man did not know what to do. It would have been difficult to rip out all the fences. Then he came up with a solution: raise the level of the water. What a difference! The water eventually submerged the fences, and the ducks had plenty of room to swim, yet keep their distance.

Spouses have the same option. You might be tempted to tear down your partner's fence, but nobody likes someone else messing with his boundaries. On the other hand, you can raise the level of love in your marriage until the fences cannot be seen. When love is deep, the divisions become less important.

---

reflect: Do you have fences in your marriage that need to be flooded by love?
Go to **John 2:1–4.**

as the Father commanded us. [5]And now, dear lady, this is not a new command but is the same command we have had from the beginning. I ask you that we all love each other. [6]And love means living the way God commanded us to live. As you have heard from the beginning, his command is this: Live a life of love.

[7]Many false teachers are in the world now who do not confess that Jesus Christ came to earth as a human. Anyone who does not confess this is a false teacher and an enemy of Christ. [8]Be careful yourselves that you do not lose everything you[n] have worked for, but that you receive your full reward.

[9]Anyone who goes beyond Christ's teaching and does not continue to follow only his teaching does not have God. But whoever continues to follow the teaching of Christ has both the Father and the Son. [10]If someone comes to you and does not bring this teaching, do not welcome or accept that person into your house. [11]If you welcome such a person, you share in the evil work.

[12]I have many things to write to you, but I do not want to use paper and ink. Instead, I hope to come to you and talk face to face so we can be full of joy. [13]The children of your chosen sister[n] greet you.

---

8 you Some Greek copies read "we." **13 sister** Sister of the "lady" in verse 1. This might be another woman or another church.

3 john

HELP CHRISTIANS WHO TEACH TRUTH

¹From the Elder.ⁿ

To my dear friend Gaius, whom I love in the truth:ⁿ

²My dear friend, I know your soul is doing fine, and I pray that you are doing well in every way and that your health is good. ³I was very happy when some brothers and sisters came and told me about the truth in your life and how you are following the way of truth. ⁴Nothing gives me greater joy than to hear that my children are following the way of truth.

⁵My dear friend, it is good that you help the brothers and sisters, even those you do not know. ⁶They told the church about your love. Please help them to continue their trip in a way worthy of God. ⁷They started out in service to Christ, and they have been accepting nothing from nonbelievers. ⁸So we should help such people;

---

1 Elder "Elder" means an older person. It can also mean a special leader in the church (as in Titus 1:5).
1 truth The truth or "Good News" about Jesus Christ that joins all believers together.

EARLY, FIRST, OR NOTHING

FAITH

inside changes

3 JOHN 2

People have been searching for the answers to life and all of its mysteries for years. We often look to books and movies on the outside to make us happy on the inside. In fact, society as a whole concentrates on outward needs. Many people look for happiness by receiving a rose, watching a child playing, or observing a beautiful sunset with their loved one. There are countless outward activities that influence us on some level.

Some people look at outward activities and contend that it is all of the beautiful things in life that make them happy. But none of that truly has the power to make us happy. The truth is that we need to discover who we are in God to be happy. The real power of God to grant happiness is in making us happy with whom we are. We need to realize that God doesn't love us based on our achievements, but on the basis of whom he made us to be, flaws and all.

All of the wonderful things God has given us to enjoy are amazing and are there for our good pleasure. However, we can't become very happy by appreciating "stuff" only. First, we must more fully accept the person he has created each one of us to be. And that is an "inside" job.

---

reflect: Think about how special you are to God and his grand design.
Go to **Psalm 17:3.**

Total Christian Fitness

By Tommy Barnett

Isn't it ironic that most people spend the first half of their life neglecting health in order to accumulate wealth and the second half spending their wealth to try and buy back some health? God paid a great price for your soul, but he's also concerned about more than just your soul. And he has shown his concern by commanding you to glorify him in your body.

Some people actually think that it is sinful to be concerned about the body. Nothing could be further from the truth. If we don't include body, we've missed the wholeness of the Good News, because our bodies are the servants of our spirit and soul. Of course, our bodies are also very unforgiving if we mistreat them. Too often we try to break God's natural laws concerning the body and then get mad at doctors and the government who can't put Humpty Dumpty back together. So I want to give you four principles of fitness to help you take care of your bodies.

First, fitness is a matter of Discipline. You cannot call yourself a disciple unless you are disciplined. The two are linked. That includes discipline in at least three areas: *Diet* (1 Corinthians 10:31), *Exercise* (1 Timothy 4:8), and *Rest* (Psalm 127:2). Successful people discipline themselves and prioritize their schedules in order to get the proper amount of diet, exercise, and rest their bodies need.

Second, fitness is a matter of Disposition. There are two kinds of emotions: positive and negative. And, believe it or not, you have the power to choose your emotions—just like you choose your friends! The Bible commands us to think in certain ways. To rejoice is a choice. But if your disposition is sour, it will cause you a whole host of health problems.

Third, fitness is a matter of Decision. The Bible speaks clearly about those who know to do good but don't do it. Now, once you make the decision, it really is fun to be healthy! The hardest part of exercise is getting started. But once you get started, you'll get hooked. You'll feel better and look better.

And last, but most importantly, fitness is a matter of Devotion. When you put God first, he helps you by giving you what you need in order to take care of the rest. In other words, loving God will make you more fit than the average person. You see, with my *spirit*, I know the world above me. With my *soul*, I know the world around me. With my *body*, I relate to the world beneath me. Therefore,

- When my spirit is right, I'm holy.
- When my soul is right, I'm happy.
- When my body is right, I'm healthy.

So you are perfectly tuned—aligned with God's will for your life—when you are holy, happy, and healthy. And that's what it means to embrace total Christian fitness.

TO LEARN MORE ON WHAT THE BIBLE HAS TO SAY ABOUT **FITNESS,** READ THE SCRIPTURES AND DEVOTIONALS AT **LUKE 19:10, COLOSSIANS 2:19, HEBREWS 12:1–3, HEBREWS 5:9, JAMES 5:16,** AND **1 PETER 1:3.**

when we do, we share in their work for the truth.

⁹I wrote something to the church, but Diotrephes, who loves to be their leader, will not listen to us. ¹⁰So if I come, I will talk about what Diotrephes is doing, about how he lies and says evil things about us. But more than that, he refuses to accept the other brothers and sisters; he even stops those who do want to accept them and puts them out of the church.

¹¹My dear friend, do not follow what is bad; follow what is good. The one who does good belongs to God. But the one who does evil has never known God.

¹²Everyone says good things about Demetrius, and the truth agrees with what they say. We also speak well of him, and you know what we say is true.

¹³I have many things I want to write you, but I do not want to use pen and ink. ¹⁴I hope to see you soon and talk face to face. ¹⁵Peace to you. The friends here greet you. Please greet each friend there by name.

¹From Jude, a servant of Jesus Christ and a brother of James.

To all who have been called by God. God the Father loves you, and you have been kept safe in Jesus Christ:

²Mercy, peace, and love be yours richly.

GOD WILL PUNISH SINNERS

³Dear friends, I wanted very much to write you about the salvation we all share. But I felt the need to write you about something else: I want to encourage you to fight hard for the faith that was given the holy people of God once and for all time. ⁴Some people have secretly entered your group. Long ago the prophets wrote about these people who will be judged guilty. They are against God and have changed the grace of our God into a reason for sexual sin. They also refuse to accept Jesus Christ, our only Master and Lord.

⁵I want to remind you of some things you already know: Remember that the Lord[n] saved his people by bringing them out of the land of Egypt. But later he destroyed all those who did not believe. ⁶And remember the angels who did not keep their place of power but left their proper home. The Lord has kept these angels in darkness, bound with everlasting chains, to be judged on the great day. ⁷Also remember the cities of Sodom and Gomorrah[n] and the other towns around them. In the same way they were full of sexual sin and people who desired sexual relations that God does not allow. They suffer the punishment of eternal fire, as an example for all to see.

⁸It is the same with these people who have entered your group. They are guided by dreams and make themselves filthy with sin. They reject God's authority and speak against the angels. ⁹Not even the archangel[n] Michael, when he argued with the devil about who would have the body of Moses, dared to judge the devil guilty. Instead, he said, "The Lord punish you." ¹⁰But these people speak against things they do not understand. And what they do know, by feeling, as dumb animals know things, are the very things that destroy them. ¹¹It will be terrible for them. They have followed the way of Cain, and for money they have given themselves to doing the wrong that Balaam did. They have fought against God as Korah did, and like Korah, they surely will be destroyed. ¹²They are like dirty spots in your special Christian meals you share. They eat with you and have no fear, caring only for themselves. They are clouds without rain, which the wind blows around. They are autumn trees without fruit that are pulled out of the ground. So they are twice dead. ¹³They are like wild waves of the sea, tossing up their own shameful actions like foam. They are like stars that wander in the sky. A place in the blackest darkness has been kept for them forever.

¹⁴Enoch, the seventh descendant from Adam, said about these people: "Look, the Lord is coming with many thousands of his holy angels to ¹⁵judge every person. He is coming to punish all who are against God for all the evil they have done against him. And he will punish the sinners who are against God for all the evil they have said against him."

¹⁶These people complain and blame others, doing the evil things they want to do. They brag about themselves, and they flatter others to get what they want.

A WARNING AND THINGS TO DO

¹⁷Dear friends, remember what the apostles of our Lord Jesus Christ said before. ¹⁸They said to you, "In the last times there will be people who laugh about God, following their own evil desires which are against God." ¹⁹These are the people who divide you, people whose thoughts are only of this world, who do not have the Spirit.

²⁰But dear friends, use your most holy faith to build yourselves up, praying in the

---

5 the Lord Some Greek copies read "Jesus." **7 Sodom and Gomorrah** Two cities God destroyed because they were so evil. **9 archangel** The leader among God's angels or messengers.

Holy Spirit. **21**Keep yourselves in God's love as you wait for the Lord Jesus Christ with his mercy to give you life forever.

22Show mercy to some people who have doubts. **23**Take others out of the fire, and save them. Show mercy mixed with fear to others, hating even their clothes which are dirty from sin.

PRAISE GOD

24God is strong and can help you not to fall. He can bring you before his glory without any wrong in you and can give you great joy. **25**He is the only God, the One who saves us. To him be glory, greatness, power, and authority through Jesus Christ our Lord for all time past, now, and forever. Amen.

BEATING THE BURNOUT BLUES

FULFILLMENT

no stumbling

JUDE 24

G od is the motivating power behind walking without stumbling. When we were blind, we constantly crashed into life, stumbling and falling with injuries. But God has made us able to walk with sight. We don't stumble because we now can see where we are going.

The Greek text actually says "to keep you *without* stumbling." It is not that God always directs us in ways that give us a nice, smooth path. It is rather that wherever we walk, we do not stumble because he keeps watch over us. It is his guarding power that sets our footing firmly, even if the path we tread is full of pitfalls and obstacles. The path of a Christian is a new way, a way we would never have considered. It is often very treacherous, but the dangers are overcome because God guards our steps.

God's ways require diligence and attention. We can't gaze off while we're moving or else we'll be likely to stumble. But God promises that his ways will be infinitely more satisfying and joyful. With him guiding us, life will become a breathtaking adventure full of twists and turns, and we won't stumble if we'll simply follow his footsteps.

reflect: Walk with God today and watch how adventuresome life becomes.

You have completed the **FULFILLMENT** readings. Now go to **FUTURE:** "The Product of Present Obedience" at **1 Kings 19:1–18.**

revelation

JOHN TELLS ABOUT THIS BOOK

1 This is the revelation[n] of Jesus Christ, which God gave to him, to show his servants what must soon happen. And Jesus sent his angel to show it to his servant John, [2] who has told everything he has seen. It is the word of God; it is the message from Jesus Christ. [3] Blessed is the one who reads the words of God's message, and blessed are the people who hear this message and do what is written in it. The time is near when all of this will happen.

JESUS' MESSAGE TO THE CHURCHES

[4] From John.

To the seven churches in Asia:

Grace and peace to you from the One who is and was and is coming, and from the seven spirits before his throne, [5] and from Jesus Christ. Jesus is the faithful witness, the first among those raised from the dead. He is the ruler of the kings of the earth.

He is the One who loves us, who made us free from our sins with the blood of his death. [6] He made us to be a kingdom of priests who serve God his Father. To Jesus Christ be glory and power forever and ever! Amen.

[7] Look, Jesus is coming with the clouds, and everyone will see him, even those who stabbed him. And all peoples of the earth will cry loudly because of him. Yes, this will happen! Amen.

[8] The Lord God says, "I am the Alpha and the Omega.[n] I am the One who is and was and is coming. I am the Almighty."

[9] I, John, am your brother. All of us share with Christ in suffering, in the kingdom, and in patience to continue. I was on the island of Patmos,[n] because I had preached the word of God and the message about Jesus. [10] On the Lord's day I was in the Spirit, and I heard a loud voice behind me that sounded like a trumpet. [11] The voice said, "Write what you see in a book and send it to the seven churches: to Ephesus, Smyrna, Pergamum, Thyatira, Sardis, Philadelphia, and Laodicea."

[12] I turned to see who was talking to me. When I turned, I saw seven golden lampstands [13] and someone among the lampstands who was "like a Son of Man."[n] He was dressed in a long robe and had a gold band around his chest. [14] His head and hair were white like wool, as white as snow, and his eyes were like flames of fire. [15] His feet were like bronze that glows hot in a furnace, and his voice was like the noise of flooding water. [16] He held seven stars in his right hand, and a sharp double-edged sword came out of his mouth. He looked like the sun shining at its brightest time.

[17] When I saw him, I fell down at his feet like a dead man. He put his right hand on me and said, "Do not be afraid. I am the First and the Last. [18] I am the One who lives; I was dead, but look, I am alive forever and ever! And I hold the keys to death and to the place of the dead. [19] So write the things you see, what is now and what will happen later. [20] Here is the secret of the seven stars that you saw in my right hand and the seven golden lampstands: The seven lampstands are the seven churches, and the seven stars are the angels of the seven churches.

TO THE CHURCH IN EPHESUS

2 "Write this to the angel of the church in Ephesus:

"The One who holds the seven stars in his right hand and walks among the seven golden lampstands says this: [2] I know what you do, how you work hard and never give up. I know you do not put up with the false teachings of evil people. You have tested those who say they are apostles but really are not, and you found they are liars. [3] You have patience and have suffered troubles for my name and have not given up.

[4] "But I have this against you: You have left the love you had in the beginning. [5] So

---

1:1 revelation Making known truth that has been hidden. **1:8 Alpha and the Omega** The first and last letters of the Greek alphabet. This means "the beginning and the end." **1:9 Patmos** A small island in the Aegean Sea, near the coast of Asia Minor (modern Turkey). **1:13 "like . . . Man"** "Son of Man" is a name Jesus called himself.

Jesus, Who **Was**, and **Is**, and **Is to Come**

FAITH

By Jack Hayford

REVELATION 1:8

I believe Jesus Christ is the Son of God; the gift of the Father for the salvation of this world; and the Word of God who was with the Father in the beginning. Because I believe this, I worship him and I receive and acknowledge him as the savior of all people and that includes me. I honor him as Lord and praise his name.

I believe Jesus became a man and his mother Mary was a virgin. I believe he took the full weight and consequence of all my sins when he was crucified and his blood justifies me before God. I am forgiven and cleansed in heart and conscience. I acknowledge Jesus paid for my sins and I accept the freedom from all guilt or condemnation. Because of Jesus, the Father sees me as if I never sinned.

I believe in the resurrection of Jesus Christ, the Son of God; that he physically and actually died and rose from the dead. I believe in the second coming of Jesus Christ. I believe he literally and physically ascended from the Mount of Olives and that he will come again the same way. His physical return is possible at any moment and I wait with eager expectation until the trumpet sounds and he descends from heaven. Because I believe this, I reject any human proposal that predicts a day or date of his return.

I believe he is coming for his church like a bridegroom seeking a pure and devoted bride. I believe in his promise never to abandon us and to keep us on a path of growth and holiness so we will be ready for him when he returns. I believe he will establish his perfect kingdom upon the whole earth and that our decisions today determine our reign with him.

I believe in the resurrection of all humanity and on the last day, I will stand before the Throne of God and give an account for my deeds done on earth. I look forward to that day with joy and without fear because of Jesus' work on the cross. I know I will receive everlasting delight instead of everlasting shame.

I believe that at Christ's return, I will be changed into the image of his glorious and perfect resurrected body and I will receive a perfect and undying body that will never decay so that I can be with and serve the living God forever. With Jesus as my king and my friend, I can live in peace because he is completing the good work he started in me and continues until the day of his return.

TO LEARN MORE ON WHAT THE BIBLE HAS TO SAY ABOUT **FAITH,** READ THE SCRIPTURES AND DEVOTIONALS AT **TITUS 3:3, HEBREWS 11:1-2, JAMES 1:2-8, MATTHEW 21:22,** AND **1 PETER 3:8-12.**

remember where you were before you fell. Change your hearts and do what you did at first. If you do not change, I will come to you and will take away your lampstand from its place. 6But there is something you do that is right: You hate what the Nicolaitans[n] do, as much as I.

7"Every person who has ears should listen to what the Spirit says to the churches. To those who win the victory I will give the right to eat the fruit from the tree of life, which is in the garden of God.

TO THE CHURCH IN SMYRNA

8"Write this to the angel of the church in Smyrna:

"The One who is the First and the Last, who died and came to life again, says this: 9I know your troubles and that you are poor, but really you are rich! I know the bad things some people say about you. They say they are Jews, but they are not true Jews. They are a synagogue that belongs to Satan. 10Do not be afraid of what you are about to suffer. I tell you, the devil will put some of you in prison to test you, and you will suffer for ten days. But be faithful, even if you have to die, and I will give you the crown of life.

11"Everyone who has ears should listen to what the Spirit says to the churches. Those who win the victory will not be hurt by the second death.

TO THE CHURCH IN PERGAMUM

12"Write this to the angel of the church in Pergamum:

"The One who has the sharp, double-edged sword says this: 13I know where you live. It is where Satan has his throne. But you are true to me. You did not refuse to tell about your faith in me even during the time of Antipas, my faithful witness who was killed in your city, where Satan lives.

14"But I have a few things against you: You have some there who follow the teaching of Balaam. He taught Balak how to cause the people of Israel to sin by eating food offered to idols and by taking part in sexual sins. 15You also have some who follow the teaching of the Nicolaitans.[n] 16So change your hearts and lives. If you do not, I will come to you quickly and fight against them with the sword that comes out of my mouth.

17"Everyone who has ears should listen to what the Spirit says to the churches.

"I will give some of the hidden manna to everyone who wins the victory. I will also give to each one who wins the victory a white stone with a new name written on it. No one knows this new name except the one who receives it.

TO THE CHURCH IN THYATIRA

18"Write this to the angel of the church in Thyatira:

"The Son of God, who has eyes that blaze like fire and feet like shining bronze, says this: 19I know what you do. I know about your love, your faith, your service, and your patience. I know that you are doing more now than you did at first.

20"But I have this against you: You let that woman Jezebel spread false teachings. She says she is a prophetess, but by her teaching she leads my people to take part in sexual sins and to eat food that is offered to idols. 21I have given her time to change her heart and turn away from her sin, but she does not want to change. 22So I will throw her on a bed of suffering. And all those who take part in adultery with her will suffer greatly if they do not turn away from the wrongs she does. 23I will also kill her followers. Then all the churches will know I am the One who searches hearts and minds, and I will repay each of you for what you have done.

24"But others of you in Thyatira have not followed her teaching and have not learned what some call Satan's deep secrets. I say to you that I will not put any other load on you. 25Only continue in your loyalty until I come.

26"I will give power over the nations to everyone who wins the victory and continues to be obedient to me until the end.

27 'You will rule over them with an iron rod,
    as when pottery is broken into pieces.'
                                    Psalm 2:9

28This is the same power I received from my Father. I will also give him the morning star. 29Everyone who has ears should listen to what the Spirit says to the churches.

TO THE CHURCH IN SARDIS

3 "Write this to the angel of the church in Sardis:

"The One who has the seven spirits and the seven stars says this: I know what you do.

2:6, 15 Nicolaitans This is the name of a religious group that followed false beliefs and ideas.

People say that you are alive, but really you are dead. ²Wake up! Strengthen what you have left before it dies completely. I have found that what you are doing is less than what my God wants. ³So do not forget what you have received and heard. Obey it, and change your hearts and lives. So you must wake up, or I will come like a thief, and you will not know when I will come to you. ⁴But you have a few there in Sardis who have kept their clothes unstained, so they will walk with me and will wear white clothes, because they are worthy. ⁵Those who win the victory will be dressed in white clothes like them. And I will not erase their names from the book of life, but I will say they belong to me before my Father and before his angels. ⁶Everyone who has ears should listen to what the Spirit says to the churches.

TO THE CHURCH IN PHILADELPHIA

⁷"Write this to the angel of the church in Philadelphia:

"This is what the One who is holy and true, who holds the key of David, says. When he opens a door, no one can close it. And when he closes it, no one can open it. ⁸I know what you do. I have put an open door before you, which no one can close. I know you have little strength, but you have obeyed my teaching and were not afraid to speak my name. ⁹Those in the synagogue that belongs to Satan say they are Jews, but they are not true Jews; they are liars. I will make them come before you and bow at your feet, and they will know that I have loved you. ¹⁰You have obeyed my teaching about not giving up your faith. So I will keep you from the time of trouble that will come to the whole world to test those who live on earth.

¹¹"I am coming soon. Continue strong in your faith so no one will take away your crown. ¹²I will make those who win the victory pillars in the temple of my God, and they will never have to leave it. I will write on them the name of my God and the name of the city of my God, the new Jerusalem,ⁿ that comes down out of heaven from my God. I will also write on them my new name. ¹³Everyone who has ears should listen to what the Spirit says to the churches.

TO THE CHURCH IN LAODICEA

¹⁴"Write this to the angel of the church in Laodicea:

"The Amen,ⁿ the faithful and true witness, the ruler of all God has made, says this: ¹⁵I know what you do, that you are not hot or cold. I wish that you were hot or cold! ¹⁶But because you are lukewarm—neither hot, nor cold—I am ready to spit you out of my mouth. ¹⁷You say, 'I am rich, and I have become wealthy and do not need anything.' But you do not know that you are really miserable, pitiful, poor, blind, and naked. ¹⁸I advise you to buy from me gold made pure in fire so you can be truly rich. Buy from me white clothes so you can be clothed and so you can cover your shameful nakedness. Buy from me medicine to put on your eyes so you can truly see.

¹⁹"I correct and punish those whom I love. So be eager to do right, and change your hearts and lives. ²⁰Here I am! I stand at the door and knock. If you hear my voice and open the door, I will come in and eat with you, and you will eat with me.

²¹"Those who win the victory will sit with me on my throne in the same way that I won the victory and sat down with my Father on his throne. ²²Everyone who has ears should listen to what the Spirit says to the churches."

JOHN SEES HEAVEN

4 After the vision of these things I looked, and there before me was an open door in heaven. And the same voice that spoke to me before, that sounded like a trumpet, said, "Come up here, and I will show you what must happen after this." ²Immediately I was in the Spirit, and before me was a throne in heaven, and someone was sitting on it. ³The One who sat on the throne looked like precious stones, like jasper and carnelian. All around the throne was a rainbow the color of an emerald. ⁴Around the throne there were twenty-four other thrones with twenty-four elders sitting on them. They were dressed in white and had golden crowns on their heads. ⁵Lightning flashes and noises and thunder came from the throne. Before the throne seven lamps were burning, which are the seven spirits of God. ⁶Also before the throne

---

3:12 Jerusalem This name is used to mean the spiritual city God built for his people. See Revelation 21–22.
3:14 Amen Used here as a name for Jesus; it means to agree fully that something is true.

What Jesus **Wants**

FINANCES

By Joseph Stowell

REVELATION 3:15–16

I have a friend who happens to be a very wealthy man who's been blessed of God and is generous with the kingdom. One day we were out for coffee, just horsing around, when he got serious, and I'll never forget what he said: "I wonder sometimes if anybody likes me for who I am, or I just wonder if everybody wants to hang out with me because of my money."

Do you ever feel that way? More importantly, have you ever felt that way about Jesus?

All he wants is my money. I wonder if he'd like me if I didn't have any money. Now listen, you didn't bring your money to the cross, did you? No. We all come the same way: humble, poor, wretched, repentant sinners. Lay aside those thoughts, and we'll talk about what Jesus really wants when he walks into your life.

The Book of Revelation contains letters to the seven churches of Asia. Most of these letters have commendations *and* reproofs, but only one of those letters has *only* reproof: The letter to Laodicea. They had a huge problem. The other churches had problems, sure. Yet when the Lord talked to the church of Laodicea, he was upset with them more than with any other church:

"I know what you do, that you are not hot or cold. I wish that you were hot or cold! But because you are lukewarm—neither hot, nor cold—I am ready to spit you out of my mouth" (Revelation

3:15–16). What he essentially said is, "You make me sick. When I think about you, I feel like vomiting." What on earth did the church of Laodicea do? Jesus said, "You say, 'I am rich, and I have become wealthy and do not need anything,'" not even God.

One of the great dangers of wonderful, phenomenal financial success is the sin of self-sufficiency. We tend to forget that every good thing we have comes from God (James 1:17). Believe me, you wouldn't have a dime to your name or a thread of clothes on your back if it weren't for the grace of God in your life providing everything you need in abundance. It's all from him. But we get so caught up in the gifts that we forget the giver.

That's the danger that offends Jesus: We have forgotten that we are nothing without him. We act as though we don't need or want him. We've lost him under the piles of stuff. We need to put Jesus back in the center.

Toward the end of this letter to the Laodiceans Jesus said, "Here I am! I stand at the door and knock." Where was Jesus? Their self-sufficiency had shut him out. But do you know what's most interesting in this text? He didn't want their money. He wanted them. He wants a relationship with you. If he is first in your life and you are in relationship with him, all the other stuff of life will take care of itself.

TO LEARN MORE ON WHAT THE BIBLE HAS TO SAY ABOUT **FINANCES,** READ THE SCRIPTURES AND DEVOTIONALS AT **PHILIPPIANS 2:12, PHILIPPIANS 3:12–14, PHILIPPIANS 4:5, COLOSSIANS 1:9, COLOSSIANS 4:2,** AND **1 TIMOTHY 6:17.**

there was something that looked like a sea of glass, clear like crystal.

In the center and around the throne were four living creatures with eyes all over them, in front and in back. [7]The first living creature was like a lion. The second was like a calf. The third had a face like a man. The fourth was like a flying eagle. [8]Each of these four living creatures had six wings and was covered all over with eyes, inside and out. Day and night they never stop saying:

"Holy, holy, holy is the Lord God
　　Almighty.
He was, he is, and he is coming."

[9]These living creatures give glory, honor, and thanks to the One who sits on the throne, who lives forever and ever. [10]Then the twenty-four elders bow down before the One who sits on the throne, and they worship him who lives forever and ever. They put their crowns down before the throne and say:

[11] "You are worthy, our Lord and God,
　　to receive glory and honor and power,
　because you made all things.
　　Everything existed and was made,
　　because you wanted it."

5 Then I saw a scroll in the right hand of the One sitting on the throne. The scroll had writing on both sides and was kept closed with seven seals. [2]And I saw a powerful angel calling in a loud voice, "Who is worthy to break the seals and open the scroll?" [3]But there was no one in heaven or on earth or under the earth who could open the scroll or look inside it. [4]I cried bitterly because there was no one who was worthy to open the scroll or look inside. [5]But one of the elders said to me, "Do not cry! The Lion[n] from the tribe of Judah, David's descendant, has won the victory so that he is able to open the scroll and its seven seals."

[6]Then I saw a Lamb standing in the center of the throne and in the middle of the four living creatures and the elders. The Lamb looked as if he had been killed. He had seven horns and seven eyes, which are the seven spirits of God that were sent into all the world. [7]The Lamb came and took the scroll from the right hand of the One sitting on the throne. [8]When he took the scroll, the four living creatures and the twenty-four elders bowed down before the Lamb. Each one of them had a harp and golden bowls full of

incense, which are the prayers of God's holy people. [9]And they all sang a new song to the Lamb:

"You are worthy to take the scroll
　　and to open its seals,
because you were killed,
　　and with the blood of your death you
　　　bought people for God
　　from every tribe, language, people, and
　　　nation.
[10] You made them to be a kingdom of priests
　　　for our God,
　　and they will rule on the earth."

[11]Then I looked, and I heard the voices of many angels around the throne, and the four living creatures, and the elders. There were thousands and thousands of angels, [12]saying in a loud voice:

"The Lamb who was killed is worthy
to receive power, wealth, wisdom, and
　　strength,
honor, glory, and praise!"

[13]Then I heard all creatures in heaven and on earth and under the earth and in the sea saying:

"To the One who sits on the throne
　　and to the Lamb
be praise and honor and glory and power
　　forever and ever."

[14]The four living creatures said, "Amen," and the elders bowed down and worshiped.

6 Then I watched while the Lamb opened the first of the seven seals. I heard one of the four living creatures say with a voice like thunder, "Come!" [2]I looked, and there before me was a white horse. The rider on the horse held a bow, and he was given a crown, and he rode out, determined to win the victory.

[3]When the Lamb opened the second seal, I heard the second living creature say, "Come!" [4]Then another horse came out, a red one. Its rider was given power to take away peace from the earth and to make people kill each other, and he was given a big sword.

[5]When the Lamb opened the third seal, I heard the third living creature say, "Come!" I looked, and there before me was a black horse, and its rider held a pair of scales in his hand. [6]Then I heard something that sounded like a voice coming from the middle of the four living creatures. The voice said, "A quart

---

5:5 **Lion** Here refers to Christ.

of wheat for a day's pay, and three quarts of barley for a day's pay, and do not damage the olive oil and wine!"

[7]When the Lamb opened the fourth seal, I heard the voice of the fourth living creature say, "Come!" [8]I looked, and there before me was a pale horse. Its rider was named death, and Hades[n] was following close behind him. They were given power over a fourth of the earth to kill people by war, by starvation, by disease, and by the wild animals of the earth.

[9]When the Lamb opened the fifth seal, I saw under the altar the souls of those who had been killed because they were faithful to the word of God and to the message they had received. [10]These souls shouted in a loud voice, "Holy and true Lord, how long until you judge the people of the earth and punish them for killing us?" [11]Then each one of them was given a white robe and was told to wait a short time longer. There were still some of their fellow servants and brothers and sisters in the service of Christ who must be killed as they were. They had to wait until all of this was finished.

[12]Then I watched while the Lamb opened the sixth seal, and there was a great earthquake. The sun became black like rough black cloth, and the whole moon became red like blood. [13]And the stars in the sky fell to the earth like figs falling from a fig tree when the wind blows. [14]The sky disappeared as a scroll when it is rolled up, and every mountain and island was moved from its place.

[15]Then the kings of the earth, the rulers, the generals, the rich people, the powerful people, the slaves, and the free people hid themselves in caves and in the rocks on the mountains. [16]They called to the mountains and the rocks, "Fall on us. Hide us from the face of the One who sits on the throne and from the anger of the Lamb! [17]The great day for their anger has come, and who can stand against it?"

THE 144,000 PEOPLE OF ISRAEL

7 After the vision of these things I saw four angels standing at the four corners of the earth. The angels were holding the four winds of the earth to keep them from blowing on the land or on the sea or on any tree. [2]Then I saw another angel coming up from the east who had the seal of the living God.

And he called out in a loud voice to the four angels to whom God had given power to harm the earth and the sea. [3]He said to them, "Do not harm the land or the sea or the trees until we mark with a sign the foreheads of the people who serve our God." [4]Then I heard how many people were marked with the sign. There were one hundred forty-four thousand from every tribe of the people of Israel.

[5] From the tribe of Judah twelve thousand were marked with the sign,
from the tribe of Reuben twelve thousand,
from the tribe of Gad twelve thousand,
[6] from the tribe of Asher twelve thousand,
from the tribe of Naphtali twelve thousand,
from the tribe of Manasseh twelve thousand,
[7] from the tribe of Simeon twelve thousand,
from the tribe of Levi twelve thousand,
from the tribe of Issachar twelve thousand,
[8] from the tribe of Zebulun twelve thousand,
from the tribe of Joseph twelve thousand,
and from the tribe of Benjamin twelve thousand were marked with the sign.

THE GREAT CROWD WORSHIPS GOD

[9]After the vision of these things I looked, and there was a great number of people, so many that no one could count them. They were from every nation, tribe, people, and language of the earth. They were all standing before the throne and before the Lamb, wearing white robes and holding palm branches in their hands. [10]They were shouting in a loud voice, "Salvation belongs to our God, who sits on the throne, and to the Lamb." [11]All the angels were standing around the throne and the elders and the four living creatures. They all bowed down on their faces before the throne and worshiped God, [12]saying, "Amen! Praise, glory, wisdom, thanks, honor, power, and strength belong to our God forever and ever. Amen!"

6:8 Hades The unseen world of the dead.

[13]Then one of the elders asked me, "Who are these people dressed in white robes? Where did they come from?"

[14]I answered, "You know, sir."

And the elder said to me, "These are the people who have come out of the great distress. They have washed their robes[n] and made them white in the blood of the Lamb. [15]Because of this, they are before the throne of God. They worship him day and night in his temple. And the One who sits on the throne will be present with them. [16]Those people will never be hungry again, and they will never be thirsty again. The sun will not hurt them, and no heat will burn them, [17]because the Lamb at the center of the throne will be their shepherd. He will lead them to springs of water that give life. And God will wipe away every tear from their eyes."

THE SEVENTH SEAL

8 When the Lamb opened the seventh seal, there was silence in heaven for about half an hour. [2]And I saw the seven angels who stand before God and to whom were given seven trumpets.

[3]Another angel came and stood at the altar, holding a golden pan for incense. He was given much incense to offer with the prayers of all God's holy people. The angel put this offering on the golden altar before the throne. [4]The smoke from the incense went up from the angel's hand to God with the prayers of God's people. [5]Then the angel filled the incense pan with fire from the altar and threw it on the earth, and there were flashes of lightning, thunder and loud noises, and an earthquake.

THE SEVEN ANGELS AND TRUMPETS

[6]Then the seven angels who had the seven trumpets prepared to blow them.

[7]The first angel blew his trumpet, and hail and fire mixed with blood were poured down on the earth. And a third of the earth, and all the green grass, and a third of the trees were burned up.

[8]Then the second angel blew his trumpet, and something that looked like a big mountain, burning with fire, was thrown into the sea. And a third of the sea became blood, [9]a third of the living things in the sea died, and a third of the ships were destroyed.

[10]Then the third angel blew his trumpet, and a large star, burning like a torch, fell from the sky. It fell on a third of the rivers and on the springs of water. [11]The name of the star is Wormwood.[n] And a third of all the water became bitter, and many people died from drinking the water that was bitter.

[12]Then the fourth angel blew his trumpet, and a third of the sun, and a third of the moon, and a third of the stars were struck. So a third of them became dark, and a third of the day was without light, and also the night.

[13]While I watched, I heard an eagle that was flying high in the air cry out in a loud voice, "Trouble! Trouble! Trouble for those who live on the earth because of the remaining sounds of the trumpets that the other three angels are about to blow!"

9 Then the fifth angel blew his trumpet, and I saw a star fall from the sky to the earth. The star was given the key to the deep hole that leads to the bottomless pit. [2]Then it opened up the hole that leads to the bottomless pit, and smoke came up from the hole like smoke from a big furnace. Then the sun and sky became dark because of the smoke from the hole. [3]Then locusts came down to the earth out of the smoke, and they were given the power to sting like scorpions.[n] [4]They were told not to harm the grass on the earth or any plant or tree. They could harm only the people who did not have the sign of God on their foreheads. [5]These locusts were not given the power to kill anyone, but to cause pain to the people for five months. And the pain they felt was like the pain a scorpion gives when it stings someone. [6]During those days people will look for a way to die, but they will not find it. They will want to die, but death will run away from them.

[7]The locusts looked like horses prepared for battle. On their heads they wore what looked like crowns of gold, and their faces looked like human faces. [8]Their hair was like women's hair, and their teeth were like lions' teeth. [9]Their chests looked like iron breastplates, and the sound of their wings was like the noise of many horses and chariots hurrying into battle. [10]The locusts had tails with stingers like scorpions, and in their tails was

---

7:14 washed their robes This means they believed in Jesus so that their sins could be forgiven by Christ's blood. **8:11 Wormwood** Name of a very bitter plant; used here to give the idea of bitter sorrow. **9:3 scorpions** A scorpion is an insect that stings with a bad poison.

their power to hurt people for five months. [11]The locusts had a king who was the angel of the bottomless pit. His name in the Hebrew language is Abaddon and in the Greek language is Apollyon.[n]

[12]The first trouble is past; there are still two other troubles that will come.

[13]Then the sixth angel blew his trumpet, and I heard a voice coming from the horns on the golden altar that is before God. [14]The voice said to the sixth angel who had the trumpet, "Free the four angels who are tied at the great river Euphrates." [15]And they let loose the four angels who had been kept ready for this hour and day and month and year so they could kill a third of all people on the earth. [16]I heard how many troops on horses were in their army—two hundred million.

[17]The horses and their riders I saw in the vision looked like this: They had breastplates that were fiery red, dark blue, and yellow like sulfur. The heads of the horses looked like heads of lions, with fire, smoke, and sulfur coming out of their mouths. [18]A third of all the people on earth were killed by these three terrible disasters coming out of the horses' mouths: the fire, the smoke, and the sulfur. [19]The horses' power was in their mouths and in their tails; their tails were like snakes with heads, and with them they hurt people.

[20]The other people who were not killed by these terrible disasters still did not change their hearts and turn away from what they had made with their own hands. They did not stop worshiping demons and idols made of gold, silver, bronze, stone, and wood—things that cannot see or hear or walk. [21]These people did not change their hearts and turn away from murder or evil magic, from their sexual sins or stealing.

THE ANGEL AND THE SMALL SCROLL

10 Then I saw another powerful angel coming down from heaven dressed in a cloud with a rainbow over his head. His face was like the sun, and his legs were like pillars of fire. [2]The angel was holding a small scroll open in his hand. He put his right foot on the sea and his left foot on the land. [3]Then he shouted loudly like the roaring of a lion. And when he shouted, the voices of seven thunders spoke. [4]When the seven thunders spoke, I started to write. But I heard a voice from

heaven say, "Keep hidden what the seven thunders said, and do not write them down."

[5]Then the angel I saw standing on the sea and on the land raised his right hand to heaven, [6]and he made a promise by the power of the One who lives forever and ever. He is the One who made the skies and all that is in them, the earth and all that is in it, and the sea and all that is in it. The angel promised, "There will be no more waiting! [7]In the days when the seventh angel is ready to blow his trumpet, God's secret will be finished. This secret is the Good News God told to his servants, the prophets."

[8]Then I heard the same voice from heaven again, saying to me: "Go and take the open scroll that is in the hand of the angel that is standing on the sea and on the land."

[9]So I went to the angel and told him to give me the small scroll. And he said to me, "Take the scroll and eat it. It will be sour in your stomach, but in your mouth it will be sweet as honey." [10]So I took the small scroll from the angel's hand and ate it. In my mouth it tasted sweet as honey, but after I ate it, it was sour in my stomach. [11]Then I was told, "You must prophesy again about many peoples, nations, languages, and kings."

THE TWO WITNESSES

11 I was given a measuring stick like a rod, and I was told, "Go and measure the temple of God and the altar, and count the people worshiping there. [2]But do not measure the yard outside the temple. Leave it alone, because it has been given to those who are not God's people. And they will trample on the holy city for forty-two months. [3]And I will give power to my two witnesses to prophesy for one thousand two hundred sixty days, and they will be dressed in rough cloth to show their sadness."

[4]These two witnesses are the two olive trees and the two lampstands that stand before the Lord of the earth. [5]And if anyone tries to hurt them, fire comes from their mouths and kills their enemies. And if anyone tries to hurt them in whatever way, in that same way that person will die. [6]These witnesses have the power to stop the sky from raining during the time they are prophesying. And

---

9:11 Abaddon, Apollyon Both names mean "Destroyer."

they have power to make the waters become blood, and they have power to send every kind of trouble to the earth as many times as they want.

7When the two witnesses have finished telling their message, the beast that comes up from the bottomless pit will fight a war against them. He will defeat them and kill them. 8The bodies of the two witnesses will lie in the street of the great city where the Lord was killed. This city is named Sodom[n] and Egypt, which has a spiritual meaning. 9Those from every race of people, tribe, language, and nation will look at the bodies of the two witnesses for three and one-half days, and they will refuse to bury them. 10People who live on the earth will rejoice and be happy because these two are dead. They will send each other gifts, because these two prophets brought much suffering to those who live on the earth.

11But after three and one-half days, God put the breath of life into the two prophets again. They stood on their feet, and everyone who saw them became very afraid. 12Then the two prophets heard a loud voice from heaven saying, "Come up here!" And they went up into heaven in a cloud as their enemies watched.

13In the same hour there was a great earthquake, and a tenth of the city was destroyed. Seven thousand people were killed in the earthquake, and those who did not die were very afraid and gave glory to the God of heaven.

14The second trouble is finished. Pay attention: The third trouble is coming soon.

THE SEVENTH TRUMPET

15Then the seventh angel blew his trumpet. And there were loud voices in heaven, saying:

"The power to rule the world now
 belongs to our Lord and his Christ,
 and he will rule forever and ever."

16Then the twenty-four elders, who sit on their thrones before God, bowed down on their faces and worshiped God. 17They said:

"We give thanks to you, Lord God
 Almighty,
 who is and who was,
because you have used your great power
 and have begun to rule!

18The people of the world were angry,
 but your anger has come.
The time has come to judge the dead,
 and to reward your servants the
 prophets
and your holy people,
 all who respect you, great and small.
The time has come to destroy those who
 destroy the earth!"

19Then God's temple in heaven was opened. The Ark that holds the agreement God gave to his people could be seen in his temple. Then there were flashes of lightning, noises, thunder, an earthquake, and a great hailstorm.

THE WOMAN AND THE DRAGON

12 And then a great wonder appeared in heaven: A woman was clothed with the sun, and the moon was under her feet, and a crown of twelve stars was on her head. 2She was pregnant and cried out with pain, because she was about to give birth. 3Then another wonder appeared in heaven: There was a giant red dragon with seven heads and seven crowns on each head. He also had ten horns. 4His tail swept a third of the stars out of the sky and threw them down to the earth. He stood in front of the woman who was ready to give birth so he could eat her baby as soon as it was born. 5Then the woman gave birth to a son who will rule all the nations with an iron rod. And her child was taken up to God and to his throne. 6The woman ran away into the desert to a place God prepared for her where she would be taken care of for one thousand two hundred sixty days.

7Then there was a war in heaven. Michael[n] and his angels fought against the dragon, and the dragon and his angels fought back. 8But the dragon was not strong enough, and he and his angels lost their place in heaven. 9The giant dragon was thrown down out of heaven. (He is that old snake called the devil or Satan, who tricks the whole world.) The dragon with his angels was thrown down to the earth.

10Then I heard a loud voice in heaven saying:

11:8 Sodom City that God destroyed because the people were so evil. **12:7 Michael** The archangel—leader among God's angels or messengers (Jude 9).

"The salvation and the power and the
kingdom of our God
and the authority of his Christ have
now come.
The accuser of our brothers and sisters,
who accused them day and night before
our God,
has been thrown down.
[11] And our brothers and sisters defeated him
by the blood of the Lamb's death
and by the message they preached.
They did not love their lives so much
that they were afraid of death.
[12] So rejoice, you heavens
and all who live there!
But it will be terrible for the earth and the
sea,
because the devil has come down to
you!
He is filled with anger,
because he knows he does not have
much time."

[13]When the dragon saw he had been
thrown down to the earth, he hunted for
the woman who had given birth to the son.
[14]But the woman was given the two wings of
a great eagle so she could fly to the place prepared for her in the desert. There she would
be taken care of for three and one-half years,
away from the snake. [15]Then the snake poured
water out of its mouth like a river toward the
woman so the flood would carry her away.
[16]But the earth helped the woman by opening its mouth and swallowing the river that
came from the mouth of the dragon. [17]Then
the dragon was very angry at the woman, and
he went off to make war against all her other
children—those who obey God's commands
and who have the message Jesus taught.
[18]And the dragon[n] stood on the seashore.

THE TWO BEASTS

13 Then I saw a beast coming up out of
the sea. It had ten horns and seven
heads, and there was a crown on each horn.
A name against God was written on each
head. [2]This beast looked like a leopard, with
feet like a bear's feet and a mouth like a lion's
mouth. And the dragon gave the beast all of
his power and his throne and great authority. [3]One of the heads of the beast looked as if
it had been killed by a wound, but this death
wound was healed. Then the whole world

was amazed and followed the beast. [4]People
worshiped the dragon because he had given
his power to the beast. And they also worshiped the beast, asking, "Who is like the
beast? Who can make war against it?"

[5]The beast was allowed to say proud words
and words against God, and it was allowed to
use its power for forty-two months. [6]It used
its mouth to speak against God, against God's
name, against the place where God lives,
and against all those who live in heaven. [7]It
was given power to make war against God's
holy people and to defeat them. It was given
power over every tribe, people, language,
and nation. [8]And all who live on earth will
worship the beast—all the people since the
beginning of the world whose names are not
written in the Lamb's book of life. The Lamb
is the One who was killed.

[9]Anyone who has ears should listen:
[10] If you are to be a prisoner,
then you will be a prisoner.
If you are to be killed with the sword,
then you will be killed with the sword.
This means that God's holy people must have
patience and faith.

[11]Then I saw another beast coming up out
of the earth. It had two horns like a lamb, but
it spoke like a dragon. [12]This beast stands before the first beast and uses the same power
the first beast has. By this power it makes everyone living on earth worship the first beast,
who had the death wound that was healed.
[13]And the second beast does great miracles
so that it even makes fire come down from
heaven to earth while people are watching. [14]It fools those who live on earth by the
miracles it has been given the power to do.
It does these miracles to serve the first beast.
The second beast orders people to make an
idol to honor the first beast, the one that was
wounded by the deadly sword but sprang
to life again. [15]The second beast was given
power to give life to the idol of the first one
so that the idol could speak. And the second
beast was given power to command all who
will not worship the image of the beast to be
killed. [16]The second beast also forced all people, small and great, rich and poor, free and
slave, to have a mark on their right hand or
on their forehead. [17]No one could buy or sell

12:18 the dragon Some Greek copies read "I."

without this mark, which is the name of the beast or the number of its name. [18]This takes wisdom. Let the one who has understanding find the meaning of the number, which is the number of a person. Its number is 666.[n]

THE SONG OF THE SAVED

14 Then I looked, and there before me was the Lamb standing on Mount Zion.[n] With him were one hundred forty-four thousand people who had his name and his Father's name written on their foreheads. [2]And I heard a sound from heaven like the noise of flooding water and like the sound of loud thunder. The sound I heard was like people playing harps. [3]And they sang a new song before the throne and before the four living creatures and the elders. No one could learn the new song except the one hundred forty-four thousand who had been bought from the earth. [4]These are the ones who did not do sinful things with women, because they kept themselves pure. They follow the Lamb every place he goes. These one hundred forty-four thousand were bought from among the people of the earth as people to be offered to God and the Lamb. [5]They were not guilty of telling lies; they are without fault.

THE THREE ANGELS

[6]Then I saw another angel flying high in the air. He had the eternal Good News to preach to those who live on earth—to every nation, tribe, language, and people. [7]He preached in a loud voice, "Fear God and give him praise, because the time has come for God to judge all people. So worship God who made the heavens, and the earth, and the sea, and the springs of water."

[8]Then the second angel followed the first angel and said, "Ruined, ruined is the great city of Babylon! She made all the nations drink the wine of the anger of her adultery."

[9]Then a third angel followed the first two angels, saying in a loud voice: "If anyone worships the beast and his idol and gets the beast's mark on the forehead or on the hand, [10]that one also will drink the wine of God's anger, which is prepared with all its strength in the cup of his anger. And that person will be put in pain with burning sulfur before the holy angels and the Lamb. [11]And the smoke from their burning pain will rise forever and ever. There will be no rest, day or night, for

those who worship the beast and his idol or who get the mark of his name." [12]This means God's holy people must be patient. They must obey God's commands and keep their faith in Jesus.

[13]Then I heard a voice from heaven saying, "Write this: Blessed are the dead who die from now on in the Lord."

The Spirit says, "Yes, they will rest from their hard work, and the reward of all they have done stays with them."

THE EARTH IS HARVESTED

[14]Then I looked, and there before me was a white cloud, and sitting on the white cloud was One who looked like a Son of Man.[n] He had a gold crown on his head and a sharp sickle[n] in his hand. [15]Then another angel came out of the temple and called out in a loud voice to the One who was sitting on the cloud, "Take your sickle and harvest from the earth, because the time to harvest has come, and the fruit of the earth is ripe." [16]So the One who was sitting on the cloud swung his sickle over the earth, and the earth was harvested.

[17]Then another angel came out of the temple in heaven, and he also had a sharp sickle. [18]And then another angel, who has power over the fire, came from the altar. This angel called to the angel with the sharp sickle, saying, "Take your sharp sickle and gather the bunches of grapes from the earth's vine, because its grapes are ripe." [19]Then the angel swung his sickle over the earth. He gathered the earth's grapes and threw them into the great winepress of God's anger. [20]They were trampled in the winepress outside the city, and blood flowed out of the winepress as high as horses' bridles for a distance of about one hundred eighty miles.

THE LAST TROUBLES

15 Then I saw another wonder in heaven that was great and amazing. There were seven angels bringing seven disasters. These are the last disasters, because after them, God's anger is finished.

13:18 **666** Some Greek copies read "616." 14:1 **Mount Zion** Another name for Jerusalem; here meaning the spiritual city of God's people. 14:14 **Son of Man** "Son of Man" is a name Jesus called himself. 14:14 **sickle** A farming tool with a curved blade. It was used to harvest grain.

[2]I saw what looked like a sea of glass mixed with fire. All of those who had won the victory over the beast and his idol and over the number of his name were standing by the sea of glass. They had harps that God had given them. [3]They sang the song of Moses, the servant of God, and the song of the Lamb:

"You do great and wonderful things,
                    Psalm 111:2
Lord God Almighty.   *Amos 3:13*
Everything the Lord does is right and
   true,   *Psalm 145:17*
King of the nations."[n]
[4] Everyone will respect you, Lord,
                   Jeremiah 10:7
and will honor you.
Only you are holy.
All the nations will come
   and worship you,   *Psalm 86:9–10*
because the right things you have done
   are now made known."
               Deuteronomy 32:4

[5]After this I saw that the temple (the Tent of the Agreement) in heaven was opened. [6]And the seven angels bringing the seven disasters came out of the temple. They were dressed in clean, shining linen and wore golden bands tied around their chests. [7]Then one of the four living creatures gave to the seven angels seven golden bowls filled with the anger of God, who lives forever and ever. [8]The temple was filled with smoke from the glory and the power of God, and no one could enter the temple until the seven disasters of the seven angels were finished.

THE BOWLS OF GOD'S ANGER

16 Then I heard a loud voice from the temple saying to the seven angels, "Go and pour out the seven bowls of God's anger on the earth."

[2]The first angel left and poured out his bowl on the land. Then ugly and painful sores came upon all those who had the mark of the beast and who worshiped his idol.

[3]The second angel poured out his bowl on the sea, and it became blood like that of a dead man, and every living thing in the sea died.

[4]The third angel poured out his bowl on the rivers and the springs of water, and they became blood. [5]Then I heard the angel of the waters saying:

"Holy One, you are the One who is and
   who was.
You are right to decide to punish these
   evil people.
[6] They have poured out the blood of your
   holy people and your prophets.
So now you have given them blood to
   drink as they deserve."

[7]And I heard a voice coming from the altar saying:

"Yes, Lord God Almighty,
   the way you punish evil people is right
   and fair."

[8]The fourth angel poured out his bowl on the sun, and he was given power to burn the people with fire. [9]They were burned by the great heat, and they cursed the name of God, who had control over these disasters. But the people refused to change their hearts and lives and give glory to God.

[10]The fifth angel poured out his bowl on the throne of the beast, and darkness covered its kingdom. People gnawed their tongues because of the pain. [11]They also cursed the God of heaven because of their pain and the sores they had, but they refused to change their hearts and turn away from the evil things they did.

[12]The sixth angel poured out his bowl on the great river Euphrates so that the water in the river was dried up to prepare the way for the kings from the east to come. [13]Then I saw three evil spirits that looked like frogs coming out of the mouth of the dragon, out of the mouth of the beast, and out of the mouth of the false prophet. [14]These evil spirits are the spirits of demons, which have power to do miracles. They go out to the kings of the whole world to gather them together for the battle on the great day of God Almighty.

[15]"Listen! I will come as a thief comes! Blessed are those who stay awake and keep their clothes on so that they will not walk around naked and have people see their shame."

[16]Then the evil spirits gathered the kings together to the place that is called Armageddon in the Hebrew language.

[17]The seventh angel poured out his bowl into the air. Then a loud voice came out of

---

15:3 King . . . nations Some Greek copies read "King of the ages."

the temple from the throne, saying, "It is finished!" ¹⁸Then there were flashes of lightning, noises, thunder, and a big earthquake—the worst earthquake that has ever happened since people have been on earth. ¹⁹The great city split into three parts, and the cities of the nations were destroyed. And God remembered the sins of Babylon the Great, so he gave that city the cup filled with the wine of his terrible anger. ²⁰Then every island ran away, and mountains disappeared. ²¹Giant hailstones, each weighing about a hundred pounds, fell from the sky upon people. People cursed God for the disaster of the hail, because this disaster was so terrible.

THE WOMAN ON THE ANIMAL

17 Then one of the seven angels who had the seven bowls came and spoke to me. He said, "Come, and I will show you the punishment that will be given to the great prostitute, the one sitting over many waters. ²The kings of the earth sinned sexually with her, and the people of the earth became drunk from the wine of her sexual sin."

³Then the angel carried me away by the Spirit to the desert. There I saw a woman sitting on a red beast. It was covered with names against God written on it, and it had seven heads and ten horns. ⁴The woman was dressed in purple and red and was shining with the gold, precious jewels, and pearls she was wearing. She had a golden cup in her hand, a cup filled with evil things and the uncleanness of her sexual sin. ⁵On her forehead a title was written that was secret. This is what was written:

THE GREAT BABYLON
MOTHER OF PROSTITUTES
AND OF THE EVIL THINGS OF THE EARTH

⁶Then I saw that the woman was drunk with the blood of God's holy people and with the blood of those who were killed because of their faith in Jesus.

When I saw the woman, I was very amazed. ⁷Then the angel said to me, "Why are you amazed? I will tell you the secret of this woman and the beast she rides—the one with seven heads and ten horns. ⁸The beast you saw was once alive but is not alive now. But soon it will come up out of the bottomless pit and go away to be destroyed. There are people who live on earth whose names have not been written in the book of life since the beginning of the world. They will be amazed when they see the beast, because he was once alive, is not alive now, but will come again.

⁹"You need a wise mind to understand this. The seven heads on the beast are seven mountains where the woman sits. ¹⁰And they are seven kings. Five of the kings have already been destroyed, one of the kings lives now, and another has not yet come. When he comes, he must stay a short time. ¹¹The beast that was once alive, but is not alive now, is also an eighth king. He belongs to the first seven kings, and he will go away to be destroyed.

¹²"The ten horns you saw are ten kings who have not yet begun to rule, but they will receive power to rule with the beast for one hour. ¹³All ten of these kings have the same purpose, and they will give their power and authority to the beast. ¹⁴They will make war against the Lamb, but the Lamb will defeat them, because he is Lord of lords and King of kings. He will defeat them with his called, chosen, and faithful followers."

¹⁵Then the angel said to me, "The waters that you saw, where the prostitute sits, are peoples, races, nations, and languages. ¹⁶The ten horns and the beast you saw will hate the prostitute. They will take everything she has and leave her naked. They will eat her body and burn her with fire. ¹⁷God made the ten horns want to carry out his purpose by agreeing to give the beast their power to rule, until what God has said comes about. ¹⁸The woman you saw is the great city that rules over the kings of the earth."

BABYLON IS DESTROYED

18 After the vision of these things, I saw another angel coming down from heaven. This angel had great power, and his glory made the earth bright. ²He shouted in a powerful voice:

"Ruined, ruined is the great city of
  Babylon!
 She has become a home for demons
 and a prison for every evil spirit,
  and a prison for every unclean bird and
   unclean beast.
³ She has been ruined, because all the
  peoples of the earth

have drunk the wine of the desire of her
sexual sin.
She has been ruined also because the
kings of the earth
have sinned sexually with her,
and the merchants of the earth
have grown rich from the great wealth
of her luxury."

⁴Then I heard another voice from heaven
saying:

"Come out of that city, my people,
so that you will not share in her sins,
so that you will not receive the disasters
that will come to her.
⁵ Her sins have piled up as high as the sky,
and God has not forgotten the wrongs
she has done.
⁶ Give that city the same as she gave to
others.
Pay her back twice as much as she did.
Prepare wine for her that is twice as
strong
as the wine she prepared for others.
⁷ She gave herself much glory and rich
living.
Give her that much suffering and
sadness.
She says to herself, 'I am a queen sitting
on my throne.
I am not a widow; I will never be sad.'
⁸ So these disasters will come to her in one
day:
death, and crying, and great hunger,
and she will be destroyed by fire,
because the Lord God who judges her is
powerful."

⁹The kings of the earth who sinned sexually with her and shared her wealth will see
the smoke from her burning. Then they will
cry and be sad because of her death. ¹⁰They
will be afraid of her suffering and stand far
away and say:

"Terrible! How terrible for you, great city,
powerful city of Babylon,
because your punishment has come in
one hour!"

¹¹And the merchants of the earth will cry
and be sad about her, because now there is no
one to buy their cargoes— ¹²cargoes of gold,
silver, jewels, pearls, fine linen, purple cloth,
silk, red cloth; all kinds of citron wood and all
kinds of things made from ivory, expensive
wood, bronze, iron, and marble; ¹³cinnamon,

spice, incense, myrrh, frankincense, wine, olive oil, fine flour, wheat, cattle, sheep, horses,
carriages, slaves, and human lives.

¹⁴The merchants will say,

"Babylon, the good things you wanted are
gone from you.
All your rich and fancy things have
disappeared.
You will never have them again."

¹⁵The merchants who became rich from selling to her will be afraid of her suffering and
will stand far away. They will cry and be sad
¹⁶and say:

"Terrible! How terrible for the great city!
She was dressed in fine linen, purple
and red cloth,
and she was shining with gold, precious
jewels, and pearls!
¹⁷ All these riches have been destroyed in
one hour!"

Every sea captain, every passenger, the
sailors, and all those who earn their living
from the sea stood far away from Babylon.
¹⁸As they saw the smoke from her burning,
they cried out loudly, "There was never a city
like this great city!" ¹⁹And they threw dust on
their heads and cried out, weeping and being
sad. They said:

"Terrible! How terrible for the great city!
All the people who had ships on the sea
became rich because of her wealth!
But she has been destroyed in one hour!
²⁰ Be happy because of this, heaven!
Be happy, God's holy people and
apostles and prophets!
God has punished her because of what
she did to you."

²¹Then a powerful angel picked up a large
stone, like one used for grinding grain, and
threw it into the sea. He said:

"In the same way, the great city of
Babylon will be thrown down,
and it will never be found again.
²² The music of people playing harps
and other instruments, flutes, and
trumpets,
will never be heard in you again.
No workman doing any job
will ever be found in you again.
The sound of grinding grain
will never be heard in you again.
²³ The light of a lamp
will never shine in you again,

and the voices of a bridegroom and bride
will never be heard in you again.
Your merchants were the world's great
people,
and all the nations were tricked by your
magic.
24 You are guilty of the death of the prophets
and God's holy people
and all who have been killed on earth."

PEOPLE IN HEAVEN PRAISE GOD

19 After this vision and announcement I
heard what sounded like a great many
people in heaven saying:
"Hallelujah!"
Salvation, glory, and power belong to our
God,
2 because his judgments are true and
right.
He has punished the prostitute
who made the earth evil with her
sexual sin.
He has paid her back for the death of his
servants."
3Again they said:
"Hallelujah!
She is burning, and her smoke will rise
forever and ever."
4Then the twenty-four elders and the four
living creatures bowed down and worshiped
God, who sits on the throne. They said:
"Amen, Hallelujah!"
5Then a voice came from the throne,
saying:
"Praise our God, all you who serve him
and all you who honor him, both small
and great!"
6Then I heard what sounded like a great
many people, like the noise of flooding water, and like the noise of loud thunder. The
people were saying:
"Hallelujah!
Our Lord God, the Almighty, rules.
7 Let us rejoice and be happy
and give God glory,
because the wedding of the Lamb has
come,
and the Lamb's bride has made herself
ready.
8 Fine linen, bright and clean, was given to
her to wear."
(The fine linen means the good things done
by God's holy people.)

9And the angel said to me, "Write this:
Blessed are those who have been invited to
the wedding meal of the Lamb!" And the angel said, "These are the true words of God."
10Then I bowed down at the angel's feet to
worship him, but he said to me, "Do not worship me! I am a servant like you and your brothers and sisters who have the message of Jesus.
Worship God, because the message about Jesus is the spirit that gives all prophecy."

THE RIDER ON THE WHITE HORSE

11Then I saw heaven opened, and there
before me was a white horse. The rider on
the horse is called Faithful and True, and he
is right when he judges and makes war. 12His
eyes are like burning fire, and on his head
are many crowns. He has a name written on
him, which no one but himself knows. 13He
is dressed in a robe dipped in blood, and his
name is the Word of God. 14The armies of
heaven, dressed in fine linen, white and clean,
were following him on white horses. 15Out of
the rider's mouth comes a sharp sword that
he will use to defeat the nations, and he will
rule them with a rod of iron. He will crush
out the wine in the winepress of the terrible
anger of God the Almighty. 16On his robe and
on his upper leg was written this name: KING
OF KINGS AND LORD OF LORDS.
17Then I saw an angel standing in the sun,
and he called with a loud voice to all the birds
flying in the sky: "Come and gather together
for the great feast of God 18so that you can eat
the bodies of kings, generals, mighty people,
horses and their riders, and the bodies of all
people—free, slave, small, and great."
19Then I saw the beast and the kings of
the earth. Their armies were gathered together to make war against the rider on the
horse and his army. 20But the beast was captured and with him the false prophet who did
the miracles for the beast. The false prophet
had used these miracles to trick those who
had the mark of the beast and worshiped his
idol. The false prophet and the beast were
thrown alive into the lake of fire that burns
with sulfur. 21And their armies were killed
with the sword that came out of the mouth
of the rider on the horse, and all the birds ate
the bodies until they were full.

19:1 Hallelujah This means "praise God!"

THE THOUSAND YEARS

20 I saw an angel coming down from heaven. He had the key to the bottomless pit and a large chain in his hand. ²The angel grabbed the dragon, that old snake who is the devil and Satan, and tied him up for a thousand years. ³Then he threw him into the bottomless pit, closed it, and locked it over him. The angel did this so he could not trick the people of the earth anymore until the thousand years were ended. After a thousand years he must be set free for a short time.

⁴Then I saw some thrones and people sitting on them who had been given the power to judge. And I saw the souls of those who had been killed because they were faithful to the message of Jesus and the message from God. They had not worshiped the beast or his idol, and they had not received the mark of the beast on their foreheads or on their hands. They came back to life and ruled with Christ for a thousand years. ⁵(The oth-

ers that were dead did not live again until the thousand years were ended.) This is the first raising of the dead. ⁶Blessed and holy are those who share in this first raising of the dead. The second death has no power over them. They will be priests for God and for Christ and will rule with him for a thousand years.

⁷When the thousand years are over, Satan will be set free from his prison. ⁸Then he will go out to trick the nations in all the earth—Gog and Magog—to gather them for battle. There are so many people they will be like sand on the seashore. ⁹And Satan's army marched across the earth and gathered around the camp of God's people and the city God loves. But fire came down from heaven and burned them up. ¹⁰And Satan, who tricked them, was thrown into the lake of burning sulfur with the beast and the false prophet. There they will be punished day and night forever and ever.

COVENANT MARRIAGE

caring enough to commit

FAMILY

By Drs. Les and Leslie Parrott

REVELATION 19:11

The reason that so many marriages fail is that promises are made without trusting the promises of God. We need to "hold firmly to the hope that we have confessed, because we can trust God to do what he promised" (Hebrews 10:23). The commitment of spouses to their marriage is sustained by God's model of faithfulness. When a man and woman come into agreement with one another, God promises faithfulness to them. (See 1 Corinthians 1:9.)

The centrality of commitment in God's character cannot be overemphasized. It is woven into every part of the Bible—from Genesis, where God initiates his promise of faithfulness, through Revelation, where John's vision depicts a white horse with a rider called Faithful and True (Revelation 19:11). Are you struggling in your own marriage? Seek God's grace. He will be faithful to you.

reflect: What are some ways you can grow in commitment to your spouse?
Go to **FAMILY:** "Love Is More Than Giving" at **2 Corinthians 6:13.**

PEOPLE OF THE WORLD ARE JUDGED

[11]Then I saw a great white throne and the One who was sitting on it. Earth and sky ran away from him and disappeared. [12]And I saw the dead, great and small, standing before the throne. Then books were opened, and the book of life was opened. The dead were judged by what they had done, which was written in the books. [13]The sea gave up the dead who were in it, and Death and Hades[n] gave up the dead who were in them. Each person was judged by what he had done. [14]And Death and Hades were thrown into the lake of fire. The lake of fire is the second death. [15]And anyone whose name was not found written in the book of life was thrown into the lake of fire.

THE NEW JERUSALEM

21 Then I saw a new heaven and a new earth. The first heaven and the first earth had disappeared, and there was no sea anymore. [2]And I saw the holy city, the new Jerusalem,[n] coming down out of heaven from God. It was prepared like a bride dressed for her husband. [3]And I heard a loud voice from the throne, saying, "Now God's presence is with people, and he will live with them, and

20:13 Hades The place of the dead.　**21:2 new Jerusalem** The spiritual city where God's people live with him.

FUTURE

HOPE IN THE HOLY SPIRIT

things that **won't** be in **heaven**

REVELATION 21:3-5　　　　　　　　　　　　　By Bob Russell

In this passage of Scripture, John describes heaven:

"And I heard a loud voice from the throne, saying, 'Now God's presence is with people, and he will live with them, and they will be his people. God himself will be with them and will be their God. He will wipe away every tear from their eyes, and there will be no more death, sadness, crying, or pain, because all the old ways are gone.' The One who was sitting on the throne said, 'Look! I am making everything new!'"

John helps us picture heaven by telling us what will not be there: death, mourning, crying, pain.

> No dust, no rust, no rats, no rot; no raucous rock, no potent pot.
> No growing old with weakened sight; no dentures slipping when you bite.
> No bombs, no guns, no courts, no jails; where all succeed and no one fails.
> No strikes, no layoffs, full employment; and everyone with job enjoyment.
> All tell the truth, state only facts; no wars, no debts, no income tax.
> According to this dream of mine; in heaven no one stands in line.
> And there are only smiling faces; and lots and lots of parking places!

reflect: What do you most look forward to about heaven?

You have completed the **FUTURE** readings. Now go to **FAITH:** "The Extraordinary in the Mundane" at **Joshua 2:1-21.**

they will be his people. God himself will be with them and will be their God.[n] 4He will wipe away every tear from their eyes, and there will be no more death, sadness, crying, or pain, because all the old ways are gone."

5The One who was sitting on the throne said, "Look! I am making everything new!" Then he said, "Write this, because these words are true and can be trusted."

6The One on the throne said to me, "It is finished. I am the Alpha and the Omega,[n] the Beginning and the End. I will give free water from the spring of the water of life to anyone who is thirsty. 7Those who win the victory will receive this, and I will be their God, and they will be my children. 8But cowards, those who refuse to believe, who do evil

things, who kill, who sin sexually, who do evil magic, who worship idols, and who tell lies—all these will have a place in the lake of burning sulfur. This is the second death."

9Then one of the seven angels who had the seven bowls full of the seven last troubles came to me, saying, "Come with me, and I will show you the bride, the wife of the Lamb." 10And the angel carried me away by the Spirit to a very large and high mountain. He showed me the holy city, Jerusalem, coming down out of heaven from God. 11It was shining with the glory of God and was bright like a very

---

21:3 and . . . God Some Greek copies do not have this phrase. **21:6 Alpha and the Omega** The first and last letters of the Greek alphabet. This means "the beginning and the end."

UNDERSTANDING AUTHORITY

children **at last**

FAMILY

REVELATION 21:7

The purpose of life is to become a child. We have it all backward. We think that life is about growing up and becoming adults. But this is not so. Our goal must be to become children again—children of God. In this verse, John sees the final days of judgment. Those who have followed Jesus are ushered into the New Jerusalem where God is the ever-present King.

And God announces the most wondrous proclamation that could ever be heard by the ears of the faithful: "I will be your God, and you will be my children." After thousands of generations, the promise made to Abraham will be finally fulfilled. We will live with the Father in his house, brothers and sisters of his Son, as one immense family. Someday we will all be children again.

If this doesn't give you delight over the children God has graciously put under your care, nothing ever will. If this doesn't make you want to honor their childhood, nurture their dependence, praise their carefree play, and celebrate their innocence, you have not understood the meaning of this verse. Thank God for children. They are the signposts to heaven. God is going in their direction. And a child shall lead them.

reflect: Celebrate the gift of the children in your life and imitate their humility.
Go to **Matthew 19:4–6.**

expensive jewel, like a jasper, clear as crystal. [12]The city had a great high wall with twelve gates with twelve angels at the gates, and on each gate was written the name of one of the twelve tribes of Israel. [13]There were three gates on the east, three on the north, three on the south, and three on the west. [14]The walls of the city were built on twelve foundation stones, and on the stones were written the names of the twelve apostles of the Lamb.

[15]The angel who talked with me had a measuring rod made of gold to measure the city, its gates, and its wall. [16]The city was built in a square, and its length was equal to its width. The angel measured the city with the rod. The city was 1,500 miles long, 1,500 miles wide, and 1,500 miles high. [17]The angel also measured the wall. It was 216 feet high, by human measurements, which the angel was using. [18]The wall was made of jasper, and the city was made of pure gold, as pure as glass. [19]The foundation stones of the city walls were decorated with every kind of jewel. The first foundation was jasper, the second was sapphire, the third was chalcedony, the fourth was emerald, [20]the fifth was onyx, the sixth was carnelian, the seventh was chrysolite, the eighth was beryl, the ninth was topaz, the tenth was chrysoprase, the eleventh was jacinth, and the twelfth was amethyst. [21]The twelve gates were twelve pearls, each gate having been made from a single pearl. And the street of the city was made of pure gold as clear as glass.

[22]I did not see a temple in the city, because the Lord God Almighty and the Lamb are the city's temple. [23]The city does not need the sun or the moon to shine on it, because the glory of God is its light, and the Lamb is the city's lamp. [24]By its light the people of the world will walk, and the kings of the earth will bring their glory into it. [25]The city's gates will never be shut on any day, because there is no night there. [26]The glory and the honor of the nations will be brought into it. [27]Nothing unclean and no one who does shameful things or tells lies will ever go into it. Only those whose names are written in the Lamb's book of life will enter the city.

22 Then the angel showed me the river of the water of life. It was shining like crystal and was flowing from the throne of God and of the Lamb [2]down the middle of the street of the city. The tree of life was on each side of the river. It produces fruit twelve times a year, once each month. The leaves of the tree are for the healing of all the nations. [3]Nothing that God judges guilty will be in that city. The throne of God and of the Lamb will be there, and God's servants will worship him. [4]They will see his face, and his name will be written on their foreheads. [5]There will never be night again. They will not need the light of a lamp or the light of the sun, because the Lord God will give them light. And they will rule as kings forever and ever.

[6]The angel said to me, "These words can be trusted and are true." The Lord, the God of the spirits of the prophets, sent his angel to show his servants the things that must happen soon.

[7]"Listen! I am coming soon! Blessed is the one who obeys the words of prophecy in this book."

[8]I, John, am the one who heard and saw these things. When I heard and saw them, I bowed down to worship at the feet of the angel who showed these things to me. [9]But the angel said to me, "Do not worship me! I am a servant like you, your brothers the prophets, and all those who obey the words in this book. Worship God!"

[10]Then the angel told me, "Do not keep secret the words of prophecy in this book, because the time is near for all this to happen. [11]Let whoever is doing evil continue to do evil. Let whoever is unclean continue to be unclean. Let whoever is doing right continue to do right. Let whoever is holy continue to be holy."

[12]"Listen! I am coming soon! I will bring my reward with me, and I will repay each one of you for what you have done. [13]I am the Alpha and the Omega,[n] the First and the Last, the Beginning and the End.

[14]"Blessed are those who wash their robes[n] so that they will receive the right to eat the fruit from the tree of life and may go through the gates into the city. [15]Outside the

---

22:13 Alpha and the Omega The first and last letters of the Greek alphabet. This means "the beginning and the end." **22:14 wash their robes** This means they believed and obeyed Jesus so that their sins could be forgiven by Christ's blood. The "washing" may refer to baptism (Acts 22:16).

city are the evil people, those who do evil magic, who sin sexually, who murder, who worship idols, and who love lies and tell lies.

¹⁶"I, Jesus, have sent my angel to tell you these things for the churches. I am the descendant from the family of David, and I am the bright morning star."

¹⁷The Spirit and the bride say, "Come!" Let the one who hears this say, "Come!" Let whoever is thirsty come; whoever wishes may have the water of life as a free gift.

¹⁸I warn everyone who hears the words of the prophecy of this book: If anyone adds anything to these words, God will add to that person the disasters written about in this book. ¹⁹And if anyone takes away from the words of this book of prophecy, God will take away that one's share of the tree of life and of the holy city, which are written about in this book.

²⁰Jesus, the One who says these things are true, says, "Yes, I am coming soon."

Amen. Come, Lord Jesus!

²¹The grace of the Lord Jesus be with all. Amen.

resources

FOR MAXIMIZED LIVING

vitalistic and mechanistic thinking vs. maximized living, hope, and healing

BY DR. BEN LERNER

> Don't depend on your own wisdom.
>   Respect the LORD and refuse to do wrong.
> Then your body will be healthy,
>   and your bones will be strong. (PROVERBS 3:7–8)

We face two challenges in our search for personal health and wellness:

1. Common misconceptions about modern medicine
2. New age philosophy

Our bodies are made in an amazing and wonderful way. We're literally designed by God to be healthy. So what we need is maximized living and not simply treatment of symptoms.

Healing doesn't come from a pill, a shot, a vitamin, or a specialist of any kind. It can only come from God. Maximized living doesn't treat the symptom or the illness; maximized living doesn't cure the illness. This can only come from God's power. God doesn't need any help to get us well or keep us well. What he needs is no interference on our part. Maximized living is a healthy lifestyle that removes interference from the equation.

Throughout God's Word, we see people healed and overcoming their circumstances through faith and the adoption of a godly lifestyle. The Bible reveals to us that we as human beings are far more than merely a collection of raw materials. We have a supernatural quality given to us by our Creator. Scripture also shows that what we sow into our bodies determines the results we reap in life.

Unfortunately, modern medicine fails to look at the spiritual makeup of humankind; and, as a result, today's miracle drug becomes tomorrow's class action lawsuit. This mechanistic philosophy views your body as merely a frail biochemical machine controlled by genes and predestined either to fail or succeed, be happy or sad, be ill or well. While this type of health care can be of great benefit in the case of emergencies and other extreme circumstances, because it is not considerate of natural, God-given function, there are always dangerous "side effects."

Meanwhile, new age philosophy is essentially a modern manifestation of Satan's old lie: "you will be like God." It puts man in the center of the universe. And it would be laughable if it weren't so dangerous: we didn't create ourselves, and we cannot heal ourselves. We miss the "maximized" in maximized living without a vital relationship with the one true living God.

New age dogma does recognize the spiritual truth that life cannot be explained solely by mechanistic thinking, and it acknowledges the important role of natural living in creating wellness. Unfortunately, God is not at the center of this thinking. Rather, his sovereignty is replaced by terms like "vitalism," "metaphysics," or "universalism." In addition to the clear moral and spiritual dilemma beliefs like this have foisted on us, new age also places the focus of healing outside of the authority of God.

Conversely, maximized living recognizes that we are God's creation—we are amazingly and wonderfully made. We are much more than a machine—but we are also stewards of our bodies. As stewards, it is our duty to take the best possible care of our bodies so they can perform exactly the way God designed them to perform.

Because we are God's children (if we've trusted Jesus as our Savior), we have exceedingly great and precious promises. He heals us when we're sick. He brings us peace when we're anxious. He blesses us with every spiritual blessing in Christ because he is the best Father of all. So, working along with our good stewardship, he can break the power of "genetic tendencies" . . . and scientific evidence shows us that. Cancer, heart disease, diabetes, spinal degeneration, and even depression can all be changed by God and overcome through maximized living.

Unlike mechanistic thinking, the Word of God shows us that we are not weak or preprogrammed, but vital and powerful beyond what we can ever fully fathom. There is something supernatural about us and our bodies that goes far beyond genetics, chemistry, biology, and physics. And, unlike new age philosophers, we Christians also know this power comes through God.

Our genetics are a tendency, not a death sentence; and, in fact, science shows us that only 2 percent of any conditions have to do with a single gene disorder. Therefore, we know that 98 percent of the time we have something to say about our future by how we believe and live our lives.

Sadly, living a healthy, natural lifestyle has often been misconstrued as "new age" or "alternative living." However, it is the Bible that touts honoring the body, godly living, and natural healing. Gyms, health food stores, and natural health care providers should all be Christian stores, businesses, and clinics—not new age or alternative living practices.

More and more studies are showing that when you line up your lifestyle and the environment within your body next to God's natural intentions, well-being is the result. When there is harmony inside, health is expressed outside. On the other hand, when disharmony exists, it will show up as pain, depression, disease, and generally a failure to thrive.

Throughout history, it has been the tendency of people to turn toward the outside as a means of treating the condition, using bloodletting, drugs, surgery, herbs, vitamins, idols, needles, and crystals. However, these things don't bring back order or establish health. While some may treat symptoms, patch dysfunction, or supplement an inadequate diet, only God heals.

Additionally, any time you put the focus of health and healing in someone or something that comes from outside the body and away from God's power working inside the body, you will fail to achieve the desired results and "side effects" will arise.

Healing in the Bible means "restoring" or "making whole." It's God's life power alone that's keeping you alive and that will keep you or make you whole. For example, if paramedics arrive at the scene of an accident and find two victims, one who is dead and one who is barely surviving, and then begin surgically sealing all of the wounds and administering first aid, which one has the only chance of making it? Obviously, barring resurrection, the survivor is the only one with a chance because he still has the divine spark of life given him by the Creator.

Through maximized living, we understand that there is more to life than physical law, and we distinguish between manmade treatments from the outside and God-given intelligence from the inside. From a Christian perspective, the modifications that are encouraged to bring healing are ones that allow the healing process to take place naturally by respecting the normal way God created the body to function.

When adjustments are made to the body, or when nutrition and lifestyle changes are utilized, it is not for the purpose of treating symptoms, but for restoring balance and establishing health and wholeness. By working to get well and stay well, there is hope. When we prevail, we glorify the restoring power of God to make us healthy and whole.

Here are some essentials to know about establishing health through maximized living:

- **Commit to a relationship with Jesus Christ.** Health outside a relationship with Christ is not really wholeness. This intentional, prayerful connection helps you prioritize your time, establish healthy relationships, and experience a key area of wellness—peace. Only Jesus has the power to heal!
- **Cooperate with the design of your body.** Healthy posture, structural integrity of the spine and nervous system, the right quality and quantity of nutrients, stress management, and cardiovascular and muscle function obtained through regular physical activity all lead to personal wellness.

- **Cultivate a nontoxic internal environment for your cells.** Key toxins that interfere with normal function of the body include medications, refined foods, sugar, additives, colorings, preservatives, alcohol, and smoke.

Practicing these principles will produce the inherent consequence of a natural lifestyle that respects your body and falls into alignment with the ultimate intent God has for your life. Remember, health and happiness are your alternatives; they are available realities through Jesus Christ, and the results of the maximized living tools found in this Bible.

peace management:

YOUR LIFE IS ON FIRE!

BY DR. BEN LERNER

MOTIVATE

Are you rightly related to the people in your life?

W. Oscar Thompson, Jr., wrote a book called *Concentric Circles of Concern*. In the book, Dr. Thompson explained how we must be rightly related to those in our sphere of influence. We must first meet the needs of close family members, then meet the needs of our friends, and then, if time permits, focus on all others, moving outward in concentric circles. At the center of the circle, however, was self. The self must be rightly related to God before we can move outward to build and repair personal relationships, which is necessary if we are to have peace.

EDUCATE

2 Samuel 18:33—19:14

The head coach of a professional baseball team lost his 18-year-old son to suicide. At the funeral, the bereaved father addressed the parents: "God can provide joy in the midst of a sad occasion. The challenge is to find that joy. I urge you not to take your relations for granted. Parents, hug your kids every chance you get. Tell them you love them each chance you get. You don't know when it's going to be the last time."

The parent-child relationship is one of the closest and most important relationships of our lives. Though children can disappoint us despite our best efforts, failing to develop a right relationship with our children will always lead to problems. Second Samuel tells us, in chapters 15—18, that King David's son Absalom conspired to take over his father's kingdom. What kind of father-son relationship did they have?

Despite the fact that David was called "the kind of man God wanted" (Acts 13:22), he had many faults. We can speculate that David did not devote the time he should have

to the important job of forming a relationship with this son. Nevertheless, David loved his son. When he heard that Absalom had been killed, he cried, "My son Absalom, my son Absalom! I wish I had died and not you. Absalom, my son, my son!" (2 Samuel 18:33). Surely, David must have spent many hours wondering "what if" he had done things differently.

When Absalom died, David was so caught up in his grief that he did not remember to acknowledge the loyal subjects who had fought Absalom so that David might keep his kingdom. When the people saw David's grief, they crept into their houses quietly instead of celebrating their great victory over the rebels. Because of this, Joab reprimanded David.

He said, "Today you have shamed all your men. They saved your life and the lives of your sons, daughters, wives, and slave women. You have shamed them because you love those who hate you, and you hate those who love you. Today you have made it clear that your commanders and men mean nothing to you. What if Absalom had lived and all of us were dead? I can see you would be pleased. Now go out and encourage your servants" (2 Samuel 19:5–7). It was too late for David to mend the relationship with his son, but it was not too late to work on the relationship with his friends and supporters. So David went out and sat in the gate, and everyone came to see him.

Beyond his family and friends, David had to repair the relationship with everyone else, including his former enemies. He was able to win back the support of Absalom's former followers, although that was not the end of his problems. David, like all of us, had to be constantly on guard, putting out many relationship fires. To do so required time and effort; but, as it still is today, a satisfying life depends on good relationships.

ILLUSTRATE

Wake Up and Smell the Smoke

To change your stress levels requires a moment of awakening. It takes a moment when you look around and finally realize that you are not a victim of your crises, you are the root of them. It seems to be human nature to come near to complete destruction before we finally stop looking at everyone and everything around us for the answer to our problems and start looking at the person in the mirror.

If you are like most people, you need lightning to strike twice, make the walls come tumbling down, set your whole world on fire, and fill your entire life with smoke before you ever wake up and say to God, "Are you talking to *me*?"

The most common crises seem to be in the area of relationships. Maybe you think the cause of your problems is all the crazy, needy, incompetent people around you. Take another look. You might be surprised to realize that *you* are the one making them crazy, needy, and incompetent. It takes pain after pain, broken heart after broken heart, and circumstance after circumstance before we finally wake up to the fact that the reason we have so much stress from relationships is that we do not know how to relate.

You can begin living in a whole new world when you wake up and realize the smoke that is surrounding you is coming from fires that you helped to ignite. God can help you pull the matches out of your hand and save you from the slow and painful death of smoke inhalation.

As you wake up and smell the smoke rising off the blazing infernos of past relationships and clouding every room of your life, you may realize that you were not the victim of bad relationships; you were the arsonist.

ACTIVATE

Think of some broken relationships in your life. List the names of these people in each circle. Then pray about how to mend those relationships.

[Draw four concentric circles, with a small circle in the middle. The middle circle should be labeled *self*, the next one *family*, then *friends*, and finally *acquaintances*.]

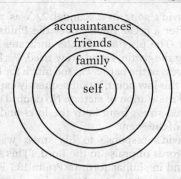

Begin to take responsibility for your problems and the ripple effect occurs. As you change, the concentric circles around you change—starting with the people in the nearest circle to you—the ones that are most important. When you change who you are in the world, the world you are in changes.

I WILL CALL TO THE LORD

MOTIVATE

David wrote this song of praise to God who saved him:

> I will call to the LORD, who is worthy of praise,
>   and I will be saved from my enemies....
> The LORD lives!
>   May my Rock be praised!
>   Praise God, the Rock, who saves me!

The whole song (2 Samuel 22:2–51) is an effective reminder that we must call upon God when we need help and praise him before and after he helps us.

EDUCATE

2 Samuel 22

The great King David knew a lot about stress. He had problems in his family life, as well as enemies who wanted to kill him. In addition, he suffered stress from his own failings and sins. Despite his many troubles, David's life and his psalms are a testimony to his constant dependence on God to relieve his worries and conquer his fears. Time after time, David turned to praising God as the way to find peace in trying circumstances.

David's song in 2 Samuel 22 was written after a great victory over the Philistine giants. The previous chapter indicates that during the battle, David grew tired. Perhaps the stress of the battle was too much for him. From this low point, he subsequently experienced the elation of victory. No doubt David suffered stress from both the lows and the highs of the event.

David's response to his stress was to sing words of praise to the Lord. (This song is found in similar form in Psalm 18.) First, David praised the greatness of God, recognizing that the Lord had saved him from his enemies (verses 2–4). Then David described the seriousness of his situation and said that in his distress, he had called upon the Lord, who had heard him (verses 5–7). He said that after the Lord heard him, everything changed (verses 8–20).

David recognized that one reason he gained the Lord's favor was that he had been living a clean life. He had kept the Lord's commandments (verses 21–25). David surely had learned by this late stage of his life that sin does not pay and that it is wise to be obedient to God's Word. This is an important factor in experiencing a peaceful life.

Equally important was David's recognition that God would notice David's treatment of others (verses 26–28). David knew that God valued mercy, loyalty, purity, and humility (verses 26–28). Then David spoke of the many ways God had enabled him to triumph in various situations. God enabled David to do almost anything, while protecting him. Finally, the end of the song reverts to pure praise: "The Lord lives! May my Rock be praised! Praise God, the Rock, who saves me!" (verse 47). David knew he served a living God who was interested and involved in the lives of those who loved and served him. This knowledge brought David peace.

ILLUSTRATE

Stress Is a Self-Inflicted Wound

All of us face many of the same outside factors that cause stress. Work, relationships, school, personal and family health problems, money issues, and even positive events like weddings and parties can all be stress-producing circumstances. However, none of these things are necessarily *bad*.

Both happy events and tragedies cause a stress response in the body. Some stress is unavoidable. The only way to have zero stress is not to get up in the morning! On the other hand, stress becomes negative only when your response to it is negative. The condition we call stress is entirely self-induced. It is how each individual responds to stress, and not the stress itself, that causes a negative reaction in the body. Stress is not a person, a condition, or an event. Stress is a reaction to a person, a condition, or an event. Just how negative this reaction is will determine the amount of emotional turmoil.

Effectively, any injury induced by stress is a self-inflicted wound. Whether something is stressful or not is determined by the interpretation of the individual. The level of stress and change in the emotional sector is determined by each person's reaction to outside forces—not by the outside forces themselves.

The only reaction that can really bring lasting peace is to call on God. Scripture says, "You, Lord, give true peace to those who depend on you, because they trust you" (Isaiah 26:3).

Healing Self-inflicted Wounds

You may have faced many unbearable tragedies in your life and may be dealing with them even today. Some tragedies have left indelible footprints and scars upon your life. Nevertheless, you are still the one who chooses whether to cower and let life's challenges defeat you or to stand happy, grateful, and triumphant.

Any time you are looking at life and thinking about yourself and your problems, you become stressed and miserable, but when you choose to focus on relieving the troubles of others, you can find yourself energetic and motivated. Always do your best not to look at yourself so much; instead, care for the people around you.

While you will have moments of fear, self-pity, and regret, you must not forget that the stress is not the issue. Call on God. Praise him and recognize his power and love for you. God and others are counting on you to move forward and to function at your best. Get your attention back on those who need you, and the stress will begin to fade.

ACTIVATE

Write your own song of praise to God. Praise him for who he is and for what he's done for you in the past. In the song, review the right things you have done in your life and how God has rewarded you. Write about your commitment to deal rightly with all the people around you. Then write more words of praise to the rock of *your* salvation.

PEACE MAKES YOUR BODY HAPPY

MOTIVATE

It only takes a few minutes of searching on the Internet to find articles about how deadly stress is to our physical health. Stress can be a contributing factor in heart problems, arthritis, digestive problems, and nerve disorders.

EDUCATE

Psalms 31:9–24; 32:1–4; 55:4–7; 102:3–7; 109:22–25; 139:13–16

In the days of King David, people struggled with worry, anger, and guilt. They also suffered the physical effects of these stressors just as we do today. David and other psalmists were aware of the health-damaging effects of being overcome by negative emotions and wrote of these in some of their psalms.

Often, David wrote about the guilt he felt because of his sin. Before he confessed his sin to God, he "felt weak" and his "strength was gone as in the summer heat" (Psalm 32:3–4). On other occasions, David recognized that his sickness was a direct result of his sin. He said, "My body is sick from your punishment. Even my bones are not healthy because of my sin. . . . My sores stink and become infected . . . I am bent over and bowed down . . . I am burning with fever and my whole body is sore . . . My heart pounds, and my strength is gone" (Psalm 38:1–10).

When worried, fearful, and troubled because of his enemies, David said, "My whole being is tired from grief. . . . My troubles are using up my strength, and my bones are getting weaker. . . . I am like a piece of a broken pot" (Psalm 31:9–12). In a time of great discouragement, another psalmist wrote: "My bones are burned up with fire. My heart is like grass that has been cut and dried. I forget to eat. Because of my grief, my skin hangs on my bones" (Psalm 102:3–5). When praying for protection from an enemy, David's health was so affected by his distress that he said, "I am dying like an evening shadow; I am shaken off like a locust. My knees are weak from fasting, and I have grown thin" (Psalm 109:22–24).

David knew that God had given him a wonderful body. He appreciated the fact that God knew about every part of him. His wonderful testimony to the handiwork of God in Psalm 139:13–15 says, "You made my whole being; you formed me in my mother's body. I praise you because you made me in an amazing and wonderful way. What you have done is wonderful. I know this very well. You saw my bones being formed as I took shape in my mother's body. When I was put together there, you saw my body as it was formed."

Surely, David knew that his worries, fears, and guilt were taking a toll on his health, and he struggled to find peace by turning to God. He says to all of us: "Give your worries to the LORD, and he will take care of you" (Psalm 55:22).

ILLUSTRATE

Stress Changes the Chemistry of Your Body

One of the most destructive effects negative stress has within the body is the alteration of normal internal chemistry. The chemicals within the body, such as insulin, estrogen, testosterone, adrenaline, dopamine, and cholesterol regulate everything from heart rate, breathing, and digestion to thinking, moving, and even going to the bathroom.

Under normal circumstances, the cells and chemicals within the body have unique formulas, solutions, and molecular structures. A normal balance is present when things inside the body are operating properly.

However, when the effect of a negative stress response is introduced upon the body's many operating systems, those cells and chemicals get out of balance and actually transform.

The Structural Effects of Stress

Internal factors that are associated with stress can create many outward effects on the body. Wrinkles, skin discoloration, changes in hair and nails, along with many other signs of aging, can all be associated with the internal tension created by stress.

The appearance of a stressed-out person is quite distinct: hunched shoulders, bad posture, tightened muscles, and a tense expression on the face. Constant poor spinal posture and muscle strain will speed the degenerative process and lead to pain, stiffness, joint deterioration, and even serious neurological problems.

Stress Affects the Nervous System

When under a negative stress reaction, the nervous system sends the body into an emergency mode called "fight or flight." When the body is put into a state of emergency, it prepares to defend itself or run from an attack. All the energy necessary to prepare for rage or sudden movement is released. To maximize the release of energy, this mechanism also responds by shutting or slowing down the systems designed for storing and reserving energy.

All the changes in chemical levels, organ function, and muscle tension during a fight-or-flight response are there to support movement or action. If these changes occur while someone is neither fighting nor fleeing, but working on a computer to meet a deadline, getting angry with their spouse, being aggravated in traffic, or acting upset with an irate customer, it can be extremely dangerous.

The adrenal glands respond to stress by placing more adrenaline into the bloodstream. When excess adrenaline is put into the system without using it in physical activity, there is injury to the heart and associated blood vessels. The damage increases every time this occurs, until it eventually becomes fatal. The damage caused by stress is cumulative. Each time you experience anger, resentment, worry, and fear, you create more and more destruction to the body.

Stress Depletes Nutrient Storage

The strain placed on the body during times of stress will drain essential nutrients. Nutrient depletion has a significant effect on the immune system. Common outward side effects of stress, such as flu symptoms, cold sores, skin problems, pain, and illness, are all evidence of how stress can suppress the immune system. A weakened immune system can cause cancer and autoimmune diseases.

With all the negative effects the body endures when in a state of anxiety, immune system defense is needed more than ever. Yet, in fact, just the opposite is taking place. When stressed, the immune system is weakened, putting the entire body in an extremely vulnerable state.

ACTIVATE

Do you currently have a health problem? Do some research and see if stress could be a factor in your illness.

YOU ARE AN "UPGRADE" IN PROGRESS

MOTIVATE

The wide world of computers has its own language and touches many areas of our lives. While computers are truly amazing, even the most sophisticated system is only as good as its programming. The common saying is: "Garbage in, garbage out." This is true for our individual thoughts, as well.

EDUCATE

Acts 9:1–30

Saul (later called the apostle Paul) had been raised and trained to hate anything that was contrary to his strict religious education as a Pharisee. He was obsessed with hunting out Christian believers and saw to their arrests. He considered himself a good man and believed his right to defend his faith justified his intense prejudice and hatred of the early Christians.

(verses 3–8) However, God had other plans for him. If you had been one of the soldiers or servants traveling with Saul on the way to Damascus, what would you have thought about the mighty and relentless Saul lying on the ground, apparently talking to someone they could not see? Would you have been scared? Would you have dared laugh?

(verse 8) At that time, Saul was an influential member of the privileged class. He had power and education, and important people took orders from him. How do you think he felt when he became blind and helplessly dependent on others to lead him by the hand?

(verses 9 and 17) Why did God choose such a dramatic way to get Saul's attention and then give him three days to think about their conversation? Do you think Saul would have listened to Ananias under other circumstances?

(verses 21 and 26) After his change of heart, Saul encountered difficulties persuading the followers that he had, indeed, given up his prejudices and become a believer. What would have convinced you he was serious?

ILLUSTRATE

All our perceptions are *limited* to what we have encountered in life. When you develop a viewpoint based on *limited* knowledge, it is called a "prejudice." *Prejudice* is defined as "an opinion formed without adequate reason or substantial information—usually negative."

We are all programmed by our life experiences to live and think a certain way, much like a computer is programmed by various software applications. Understanding your programming or your Perception Software should help you begin to understand others', as well. We all come from different places. We all have different programming based on our individual backgrounds.

This is important to remember when you see someone handling issues or behaving in a manner you do not agree with. Quite likely, if you had their Perception Programming, you would respond and behave in the same manner. You would *see* the world as they *see* it.

All our words and actions are *limited* by our different Perception Software. We are all drastically influenced by the way each of us is programmed to see the world. By under-

standing this, hopefully you can delete your prejudices and improve your reactions to other people and events.

Deleting prejudiced programming means making an effort to understand where other people are coming from and gaining more knowledge about other individuals, professions, groups, organizations, and circumstances before forming an opinion or making a judgment about them. There is a more heavenly perception: "Even God waits until the end before judging."

In all areas of your life, some of your greatest limitations to success are the walls your perceptions build around you. If you examine your life carefully, as you should each day, quite frequently you should come to the conclusion that certain areas are not working out as they should and that some of the things you do don't make sense.

When I look at kids wearing pants around their knees, poking holes all over their bodies, depressed over a lack of popularity, taking drugs, dropping out of school, or doing all sorts of tragic things with their lives, I realize that they are just programmed by the wrong *software*. Something about their history, their culture around them, and/or their self-esteem has *programmed* them to think that some terrible things, awful goals, and the need to be accepted by teenagers or to be in love at sixteen actually "make sense."

As adults, we are often not much different. We live in a world where our health, our finances, our emotional state, our families, and our planet's peace are in constant turmoil. Yet very few people ever change their course. Many have become programmed to take pills rather than change their health, to accept limited financial resources and depression rather than change their views and occupation, to get married and divorced too easily, and to blame others for our wars rather than looking in the mirror at our own internal wars first.

In order to see a change in your life, you must change the way you are programmed. You must begin to identify the components of your Perception Software that must be deleted and what new modules or elements must be downloaded in order for you to go to the next level.

All your Perception Software issues *can* be fixed. Whereas deleting and downloading new software may be more difficult to do on a person than on a computer, due to all of our hard drive (head) problems, the reality is that you *can* be reprogrammed.

Reprogramming requires looking at the world from a totally different place and angle than you have ever looked at it before. It requires that you continually reexamine your thoughts, emotions, and reactions, to determine where they are coming from. Once you have identified the source of your programming and you become convinced that your reactions are, in fact, programmed, you can begin to work on deleting the faulty programming and downloading more positive, peaceful files.

ACTIVATE

Begin to create more peace by downloading new software from heaven. A good place to start is studying the Book of Proverbs, especially Proverbs 1:33 and Proverbs 2:2, 9–11. New and godly wisdom is important and readily available for the asking (James 1:5). In your process, never forget Luke 18:27: "The things impossible for people are possible for God."

HOW JOB HANDLED STRESS

MOTIVATE

In late August 2005, Hurricane Katrina moved ashore in New Orleans, and about a month later, Hurricane Rita made landfall in the same region. The devastation from these two storms and their aftermath produced a great deal of stress among both victims and those viewing the events on television and the Internet or hearing firsthand accounts.

What were your reactions? What did you think should have been done for the people who needed to be rescued?

EDUCATE

The Book of Job

In the Book of Job, we see devastation attack an unsuspecting man. We can study eight dif-

ferent reactions to stress through the views and opinions of Satan, Job, Job's wife, Eliphaz, Bildad, Zophar, Elihu, and God.

In Job 1:8 and again in Job 2:3, God is bragging on Job as being an excellent and blameless man. How does Satan see Job's friendship with God? (Job 1:9–11; 2:4–5). How does he want to prove his point?

Job's reaction to the death of his sons is typical of his culture. Do you think you could worship God in the midst of such tragedy as Job does in 1:20–21? Was this more to relieve his own pain or to glorify God? Do you think he found comfort in this previously established relationship with God?

(2:9–10) Job's wife is the first to contradict his point of view. In her grief and pain, she strikes out at God and her husband. Do you think her reaction is based on her anger or on God's righteousness? Would cursing God actually relieve Job's or her suffering or reverse the circumstances?

(chapters 4—25) The advice and opinions of his friends upset Job rather than comfort him. Their points of view may have been politically correct and even sensible from some standpoints—their logic contained grains of truth—but it was still an earthly, human perspective. What are some of the truths sprinkled through their advice that would apply to Job's life? How do they suggest Job end his suffering?

By Job 26—31, Job is still passionately sure of his innocence. He knows his past; he knows his relationship with God. Even if he was, indeed, guilty, Job knew God and knew that God would not punish him in this manner after Job asked for forgiveness. If you were his lawyer in Job 31:35, how would you argue his case?

(32:3) Elihu is a young man with an opinion. Who do you think he is angriest with: Job for being self-righteous, or the others for placing blame? What does this show about his judgment?

(chapters 38—41) Finally, God displays his truth and power. How does he reveal himself to Job and his friends? As you read these chapters, think about how you would react if this were your best friend speaking or, perhaps, if it was someone you had never heard of before.

(chapter 42) At the end of this book, how

is God's goodness revealed? Is Job's integrity confirmed? How do you think his relationship with God and his outlook are adjusted?

ILLUSTRATE

In many ways, your emotions have been *programmed* into you, just like a computer. The way you look at the world you live in reflects this programming.

Learning to deprogram or reprogram yourself from feeling the effects and triggers of stress will save you from much of the serious physical damage stress can cause and drastically improve your life. Clearing your internal hard drive will leave you plenty of room to download newer and better files and feel the peace you are lacking in your life.

You have Perception Software that has been downloaded into you throughout your life, and it determines how you see the world. Perception is an innate aspect of human nature. In most cases, it is your *point of view* of people, issues, and events and not the people, issues, and events themselves that will determine how you react to them and create your version of the story.

Your Perception Software has programmed your point of view, which ultimately determines your emotional responses. Most everyone looks at life's circumstances differently. Like the characters in Job's situation, different people look at the same incident and, due to their different perceptions, report completely different versions of the situation. What happened, who's at fault, and almost every other detail, will vary from person to person.

It is your *perceptions* that often decide whether something is positive or negative to you. Some people see a challenge or conflict as an overwhelming problem; some see the same scenario as being small; and some do not see it as a problem at all.

This viewpoint programming determines how swiftly and confidently you act and on what scale you measure the issues that affect your life. It influences your expectations of people, how you manage controversy, how you judge and treat others, and how you handle relationships in the different areas of your life.

In many ways, your programming determines your success in life. If you put someone with a poverty mind-set in a wealthy area, he or she will find a way to live in poverty. On the contrary, if you put someone with a wealthy mind-set in an impoverished area, that person will soon own half the real estate and be renting it out to the people with the poverty mind-sets. This program can, however, be uninstalled and upgraded.

ACTIVATE

Job handled his stress by turning to God. He had already established a close relationship with God's principles and requirements. His first reaction was to worship God, acknowledging his goodness and sovereignty. After coming face-to-face with God, Job acknowledged his own limitations and helplessness compared to the Creator.

Reprogram the way you look at others, the way you react, by learning more about who God really is. Practice making your first reaction one of "Praise God" rather than "Why me?"

"YOU CALL 'EM AS YOU SEE 'EM!"

MOTIVATE

It is the final inning of the final game in the World Series, and the score is tied. The bases are loaded, there are two outs, and the final batter now has three balls and two strikes. The next pitch will most likely decide the game and the Series. The final pitch is thrown, the batter does not swing, and the catcher is holding onto the ball. You can hear a pin drop in the sold-out stadium as everyone waits for the umpire to make the call. When he doesn't say anything, a fan finally screams, "Well, what is it?" The umpire says, "It ain't nothing until I call it."

EDUCATE

Mark 8:14–21; 6:3; 9:34–35

Mark 8:14–21

Jesus' followers seemed to have trouble remembering his supernatural abilities. They had lived their lives without personal displays of God's power. They had been "programmed" to expect limitations. Jesus tried to reprogram them to expect and accept another level of relationship with him and also the supernatural intervention of God when needed. What else could they expect once they accepted this idea? Why would this be important when these followers reached the Crucifixion?

Mark 6:3

Why do you suppose it was so difficult for the townspeople to accept that one of them was the Messiah? Did they worry he would embarrass their village? Do you think some people may have worried that Jesus knew too much about them and would confront them? And if he was the Son of God, what did that make them?

What would be your reaction if, without any publicity or preparation, one of the shop owners in your neighborhood stood up in church one day and made Jesus' proclamation? Would you be jealous? Skeptical? Proud? What would you accept as proof?

Mark 9:34–35

In the midst of the awe and wonder of daily fellowship with the Son of God, Jesus' friends were competing with each other for ranking. What do you think Jesus intended for them? Do you think he hoped their goals related to spreading his works or adding a title to their name?

ILLUSTRATE

Things are not always negative or positive, or black or white. How you see things depends on what kind of glasses you are wearing. Your internal programming or Perception Software defines your eyewear prescription. The way you look at the world you live in has, in many ways, been programmed like computer software. This programming can, however, be uninstalled and upgraded if necessary.

Your experience with circumstances, people, events, conflicts, and education make up your History Software. These experiences affect how you feel about every new experience.

If you have a history of dealing with complex or uncertain events like a flat tire or a stock market crash, then you know what to do and you have some idea how it turns out. As a result, your history programming allows you to handle the situation more easily and with less stress.

Your family, occupation, peer group, geographic area, school, and religion are all components of your Cultural Software.

Different cultures put tremendous importance on certain ideas and have very specific ways, rules, and, in some cases, strict laws, regarding how people should behave, how they should work, and how they should treat others.

If the culture you grew up in believes that good people wear only black hats, dress in green clothes, eat blue food, and are accountants, you will be programmed to think that anyone who wears a red hat, dresses in yellow clothes, eats pink food, or is a fireman is bad.

The intensity of your desire to obtain your wants and needs makes up your Goal Software.

The level of your desire to obtain wealth, meet needs, be on time, find perfection, and your intensity in pursuing ethical or religious standards determines the effects of your Goal Software on your perceptions.

If someone is meticulous about every detail or obsessive about order, their Goal Software has programmed them for severe inner turmoil from something as simple as a typo on a page, a disorderly desk, or a messy kitchen. On the other hand, others who are not programmed this way will feel little or no stress in the same situations.

How you see yourself and how you feel others see you make up your Self-Esteem Software.

How you envision yourself influences what you feel your capabilities are. Your Self-Esteem Software determines your choices for college, occupation, and marriage partner.

The key to experiencing good relationships in your life is not based on the performance of others. Your Self-Esteem Software programs your own confidence and feelings of worthiness, and that is the greatest factor in determining how well you relate to others.

Stressful times and events in your life can only injure you if you feel overpowered by them. When the glasses you are looking through see you as a *victim* of stress, that is the only time stress is necessarily bad. When you see your problems as being in control of your emotions, health, and success, that is the only time when the physical and mental damage of stress applies.

For your world to improve and your stress to be reduced, you must begin seeing life through a totally different pair of glasses from those you are used to wearing, or at least start changing the prescription for your lenses. To change your prescription, you must change your Perception Software.

It isn't stress until you call it stress; and you call 'em as you see 'em.

ACTIVATE

Romans 12:2, Ephesians 4:23–24, and Titus 3:5 all tell us that not only is it possible to "reprogram" your life, but that as believers we should expect to renew our hearts and minds. Commit yourself to change with God's help. Ask the Holy Spirit to lead you and to help you understand the teachings of Scripture. There is a wealth of help available through your church pastor and other leaders, as well as through books and study programs. Just as you load necessary software into your computer to do the things you want, you can program your mind and body to maintain the lifestyle God has blessed you with. Take care of your spiritual life. You can beat stress.

ten peace principles

BY DR. BEN LERNER

I. Thou Shalt Be Appearance-less
(See 1 Samuel 16:7.)

Our infatuation with how we look never leads down a smooth and peaceful path. Relying on our appearance to decide how to feel makes us only a zit or a bad-hair-day away from misery. Beauty is totally unreliable. You cannot count on it from one day or one decade to the next. Yet people spend endless hours and countless dollars on improving how they look.

It is not a bad thing always to try to look your best. But when you allow your appearance to determine who you are, how you feel about yourself, your health, or your success, you limit yourself and build on a very fragile, shaky foundation. Too much concern about appearance sets you up for a life full of stress, illness, and many falls from grace.

My elementary school took a class picture at the end of every year. In these pictures, the tallest kids were in the back row and the shortest were in the front. I started out in kindergarten toward the tall row, but by the second grade, I had made my way all the way down to the very front. In fact, eventually, I was not only in the front row, I was front and center, where only the shortest of the short reside.

In addition to being vertically challenged, I had a large, curly red afro, freckles from forehead to toe, and my parents apparently enjoyed plaid. As years went by, things slowly improved. I eventually discovered regular haircuts, sunscreen, and solid colors.

Unfortunately, visually, I was still very different from my classmates. Clothing and better hairstyles could not change the fact that I was a short guy with red hair. For years, I often wished I were somebody else. I wanted to be taller, have better hair, a cooler personality, and parents with better taste. Then I had a son.

My little boy, Skylar, has good hair, and I hate plaid. He is beautiful, charming, and well dressed. The reality is that, regardless of what he looks or acts like, I love him just the same. I have come to realize that a father's love surpasses all appearances. Of far greater importance than what he looks like is who he is himself. When it comes to my son, I look right through what other people see. I see what they do not see, and I love what he looks like no matter what.

Today, I no longer feel peculiar; I feel special. I know that when my Father God looks at me, he loves what he has created. He loves what he sees, even when I have a zit or bad hair. Knowing that, I don't wish I were someone else anymore. I am now much more appearance-less. (Although I still wouldn't mind being just a little bit taller.) I do all I can to look my best, but I try not to allow my appearance to determine who I am or what I feel like.

II. Thou Shalt Be Want-less
(See Psalm 23:1.)

To create peace, learn to become both ambitious and content. Set goals, but be happy with what you already possess and be want-less. You were born wanting. The dilemma begins when you go from *needing* food and a dry diaper to *wanting* a nicer car, bigger home, different job, better body, larger bank account, tropical vacation, and the latest electronic gadget.

As you desire more and more, what you desire begins to drive your thoughts, control your actions, and determine the direction you and your emotions take. When you measure your success by how much you have of what you want or how close you are to getting it, you have become a slave to your wants. Ultimately, your wants or desires become your shepherd.

Constantly seeking more will often cause you to look past what is truly important. If you believe you must reach your goals to be worthy or satisfied with life, you will rarely, if ever, find peace. The miserable achiever is practically a proverb.

People often think they need financial freedom; they believe money will bring them peace. The problem is, there is no such thing as financial freedom. If you do not have money, you worry about where you are going to get it. If you have it, you worry about it being taken away. The tragedy of getting what you want is that cars get old, gadgets get broken, and vacations end. Acquisitions rarely bring lasting joy and usually bring with them even more concerns about, and focus on, money.

It does not matter how noble or worthy something you want may be, your wanting it brings stress and frustration. Only after you decide to let all your wants go and you realize that all you really need is God's will, can you sit back, do what he puts in front of you, relax, and patiently wait for it to come about.

If you have no need to desire anything, then nothing can be taken from you. Everything *you* want can be taken from you, but nothing can be taken if *God* wants you to have it. You begin to determine your own direction when you are no longer a slave to the wants in your life. Make God, and not some craving, your shepherd, and trust that you have everything you actually need. While you may not get the fleeting things you want, you get everything God desires for you.

If you want better health, focus on the activities connected with achieving better health, not on illness. If you want more loving, committed relationships, focus on being more loving and being more committed, not on loneliness and strife. If you want more success in your work, focus on perfecting your skills and improving your work habits, not on failure.

The mission of life is to serve God, care for others, and build and rebuild your self. Desire what God wants to give you, and he will give you everything you need—and more than you ever wanted.

III. Thou Shalt Be Acceptance-less (See Ephesians 3:16.)

Opinions are like noses. Everyone's got one and they smell, so choose the opinions you value very carefully. Being a crowd-pleaser and choosing jobs, classes, attitudes, and lifestyles that are favored by others and not desired by you sets you up for failure.

Just because something is popular doesn't make it right, and just because something is not popular doesn't make it wrong. Defining yourself or the people around you based on popular opinion is wrong. It may sometimes make you popular, but it will rarely allow you to like yourself. The desire for acceptance has caused kids to steal candy; teenagers to take drugs, smoke, drink, and engage in premarital sex; and adults to end up in a place that has left them impoverished and in despair.

Acceptance by others is biased, fleeting, and often holds no real reason or value. If you seek acceptance by others, you will often be without peace. Jesus knew this, and so would not seek acceptance from those around him, only from God. God's outlook is perfect.

In order to become completely free from the need for acceptance, you must discover who you really are and what you should be like. Once you understand what are good and proper goals for your life and your behavior, you can stop following the crowd and begin following your heart.

There is truly only one "right" way to act. Act like God. You are not God, but you can try to copy him. In your life, try to behave as if you are a mirror held up in front of God. Then attempt to let everything you say and do be a reflection of his qualities. God is humble, gentle, patient, loving, faithful, good, kind, true, noble, right, pure, lovely, admirable, excellent, praiseworthy, and peaceful.

When someone judges or criticizes you, if his or her suggestion represents a quality of God, prayerfully heed it. If it does not, ignore it. Choosing to mirror God rather than mirror the crowd is called integrity. Living with integrity and standing by godly principles, no matter what, gives you a much more secure foundation than fluctuating with every fleeting fad of others. You may not always be popular or successful in the short run, but integrity always wins out in the long run and gains a lasting trust and respect of others.

When you build the peace and confidence necessary not to be controlled by the need to have the approval of others, you can rightfully enjoy honest appreciation. You can lovingly express sincere gratitude and encouragement to others around you. Do not withhold praise from your wife, husband, children, coworkers, barber, or grocery store clerk. In fact, over-praise whenever possible. And be acceptance-less yourself. Do not follow the blind; lead them.

IV. Thou Shalt Be Result-less
(See Genesis 41:38.)

The story of Joseph is a story of being result-less. God shows us through Joseph that you should not worry about the results of a single game, but focus instead on how the entire season turns out. Defeat is often opportunity in disguise. God has a purpose for everything. All things, even losses, can be used for his good. The history books are jam-packed with people who used immense defeats to create incredible victories. While losses may at first appear to be failures, often they become God's road signs, leading us in the direction we need to go so that he wins *big*.

You can look at trials in your life and wonder why God does not let you off the hook. You can look at people and be angry at them for the turmoil they cause. Yet it may be God's will that you are handed these losses. The things that come against you and cause defeats may be the actual instruments God is using to put you in a place where you can do his work—and be successful. It is often within defeat and frustration that God can turn your heart and your focus in the proper direction.

In professional baseball, if a player gets one hit out of every three times he bats, he's an all-star. If he fails twice as often as he succeeds, he is considered one of the best baseball players in the world. Even more, if he were to fail as often as he succeeds, get one hit out of every two at bats, they would name the stadium, the airport, and half the roads in the city after him!

If a doctor, lawyer, coach, salesman, teacher, or athlete is happy only when he succeeds, or when other people are appreciative of him, he will live a roller-coaster life of highs, lows, and frequent breakdowns. Peace is spoiled by focusing just on the results of your efforts. The reality in the game of life is that you are going to strike out once in a while. You are going to lose some games, possibly more than you will win. If your peace of mind and happiness are strictly tied to

winning, life is going to be a long and painful season.

To enjoy every part of life, you have to detach yourself from results and pay more attention to the joy of playing the game and less attention to how it turns out. Become result-less. A result-less life is a lot more fun and a lot less stressful.

How you play the game often determines how you answer God's call. When the score is taken at the end of your life, let it be said that you won some and lost some. But don't let it be said that you never even came off the bench. Sometimes, all that matters in life is forgetting the consequences and going for it. Remember, only God never loses.

V. Thou Shalt Be Pride-less
(See Proverbs 3:34.)

It is amazing how much pride can fit inside a three-year-old. Each night before I'd put my young son Skylar to bed, I would ask him questions and expect "God" as the answer. One evening, I asked one of my typical questions, "Who made the moon?" He answered mischievously, "Skylar did it."

Then I said, "Come on, who made the moon?" Again he answered, "Skylar did it."

Next I said, "Then who made the sun?" To which he answered, "Skylar did it."

Finally, I said, "Come on, Skylar, who made the sun, the moon, and everything on the earth?" To which he answered once again, "Skylar did it."

The next evening, when I came home from my clinic and walked into the living room, I kicked over a "sippy" cup that was left on the floor and sent its juicy contents flying all over the rug and wall. I immediately turned to Skylar and said, "Who left that cup on the floor?" To which he promptly answered, "God did it!"

I've always been inspired by the fact that all the really cool, well-known athletes who came from the bottom and won championships and medals were people who always gave the glory to God. I also have always been inspired by the fact that all the really bad, well-known evil dictators who once were on top, and fell, always glorified themselves.

God is moving millions of people in billions of directions and knows the outcome of every move made. Humans have a "God complex." We tend to think we are so brilliant, so judicious, and so capable, we can run the show for ourselves. However, we truly do not have even a glimmer of understanding of God's grand plan for this world.

God is big. There is no leader more farsighted, no boss more empowering, no book more motivating, no friend less judging, no family member more supporting, and no one who understands you more or knows your needs as well as God.

We, on the other hand, are quite small. We are extremely shortsighted in our thinking regarding our own lives and the lives of others. We are almost totally unaware of how our thoughts, actions, and interactions impact the world and our future. If we depend on only what we see and understand, it is impossible not to make error after error and confront failure after failure.

Many of life's circumstances are so totally overwhelming that we cannot even begin to comprehend how to change them. Unless you and I can release all leadership responsibilities to God, we stop his plan from achieving its ultimate success in our lives and in the lives of others. We create stress instead of peace. We need to be pride-less and realize that what we see as the right way of thinking or acting may be totally wrong. Try to look at things from God's perspective. God is not limited by time and space. God uses no excuses. Turning things over to God is called peace.

VI. Thou Shalt Be Time-less
(See Matthew 6:34.)

Life is a game. Some people play the doctor game, the sales game, the athlete game, the student game, or the no job or ambition game. It doesn't matter who you are or what you do, it is still a game.

Some games appear more important than other games. Surgeons have people's hearts in their hands, clergy have people's souls on their minds, and chiropractors watch people's backs. A president's and a parent's work determine the future, and a high school dropout and drug dealer may have no future. But it is still a game.

You can do better or worse in the game than others. You can get in great shape or out of shape, achieve or lose many things, create new ideas or never think at all. You can become a pauper or a king. You can beat others in many different ways or lose to others for many different reasons. But it is still a game.

Your life is definitely a game because in the end, as in any game, you go back in the box. No matter what type of game you played, how well you think you played it, what you won, who you lost to, or who you appeared to be, in the end, you go back in the box. Sooner or later, time is going to run out.

Usually the goal of any game is to win. Nevertheless, the reality of the game of life is that you never really win what you think you are playing for. You can win money, fame, houses, cars, hotels, but in the end, they become someone else's and you go back in the box. Knowing that, it really does not make sense to take yourself, or your time here, too seriously. That is, except for preparing for the reality of heaven.

You should always play to win. Just remember the real point of a game is not really annihilating your opponent, but having as much fun as possible for as long as possible. If you are not having fun, then you are not playing the game right—or you are not playing the right game. Don't waste time worrying about winning. The game moves pretty fast, so enjoy every moment of it that you can. When the game of life is over, there are no overtimes or extra innings.

Make sure to play the game by the rules, that is, by God's rules. Others deserve to enjoy the game and have a chance to win, too. Since the game here doesn't last long, you will want to remember what will happen when it's all over and you go back in the box.

Do not get too stressed if it's a long time between wins, or if you occasionally miss a turn. Just play the game you are best at, the very best you can. Take every turn you can get, and always play your game full out for God. And let the good times roll!

VII. Thou Shalt Be Hate-less
(See 1 Corinthians 13:13.)

Love has been at the core of almost every poem, book, song, psalm, and movie since the beginning of time. Many authors, doctors, and researchers have dedicated their lives throughout history searching for its source and its meaning. The apostle Paul describes love perfectly in 1 Corinthians 13, otherwise known as the "love chapter."

Love is an extremely difficult commitment. Love is constantly under fire. Your enemies, the people around you, and especially your family and friends will constantly challenge your ability to love them.

Most people would say that they are "loving." The problem is that their love has limits. God's love, the love he has commanded us to aspire to, is limitless and without condition. While you can upset him and separate yourself from him, he is slow to anger and quick to forgive. His love endures forever.

I was reminded of the limits and challenges involved with human love one evening when a family I provided care for invited me over to dinner. When I arrived, both of the adults were working hard in the kitchen and told me to have a seat in the living room. While I was waiting, their young daughter came running in to see me. She gave me a big hug and then said that her mother told her to ask me if I liked broccoli.

I said, "Broccoli? I love broccoli!"

The little girl responded, "I love broccoli, too!"

For the next half hour while dinner was cooking, she ran around the house yelling and singing, "Broccoli, broccoli, I love broccoli."

When the meal was ready, I could barely wait to serve this girl some broccoli. Immediately after sitting down, I picked up the broccoli bowl and asked her how much she wanted. Her shocking reply was, "I don't want any."

Totally bewildered, I said, "You don't want any? I thought you loved broccoli?"

To which she exclaimed, "I do love broccoli. But not enough to eat it!"

Most of us love other people right up until we have to endure their issues and shortcomings. Then love ends and judgment and un-forgiveness begins. We love broccoli, but not enough to eat it.

"Love each other" is a tall order. People have their limits; no one on this planet is faultless. Only Jesus is perfect. Accepting others' limitations develops patience, tolerance, and compassion for everyone. As we learn and practice loving people despite their sometimes unlovable tastes, colors, or textures, we begin to love as God loves. He made broccoli and everything and everyone else on the planet—and he loves it all.

God's love is perfect. Even if we are not perfect, God wants us to get better at loving each other. The better we get at loving others with his love, the better we also get at loving him. As we learn how to get closer to people, we learn how to get closer to God.

VIII. Thou Shalt Be Fear-less
(See Joshua 1:9.)

God knew you would enter into a world filled with challenges, change, and chaos. He never promised it would be easy, but he did promise he would be with you every step of the way. God did design the human mind to be resilient and resistant to any forces that occur outside of it. In order to know you can overcome any obstacle, you must understand that the problems ahead of you are never as great as the power behind you. Life comes with difficulties built into it. However, you can face life heroically, knowing God is behind you.

Stress is not the enemy. No matter what the cause or reason, stress is only dangerous when you wrongly feel powerless against it. Stress cannot hurt you once you realize that all of the challenges and changes that occur in life cannot only be survived, but overcome, as well. The truth is, only small-minded people are tamed by adversity, whereas great minds rise above it.

God does not allow a problem for which he has no solution. There is not a single crisis or circumstance in existence that someone has not triumphed over or gone around, and there is no disease that the body has not cured.

Living life for God gives you freedom and fearlessness. When you turn your life and everything in it over to God, you grant him the opportunity and authority to bless it and confirm that you trust in his way and his time to take care of it.

When things are not going as smoothly in my work, with my family, or with my life in general, I have learned to say, "It's God's office," or "God, this is your family, life, and so on." Then I have released it. If it's his, I can trust him to handle both the process and the results. All I have to do is show up and *fearlessly* do my job.

When you maintain ownership over things in your life, you take control away from God. When he has no control, you do not allow his perfect will and plan to unfold in your life. You stop the flow of blessings.

Call your wife or husband, "God's wife/husband." Call your money, "God's money." Call your children, "God's children." Call your work, "God's work." Call your body, "God's body." Call your life, "God's life."

When you trust everything to God, in his time, the supernatural, right things will happen. When everything becomes God's responsibility and you have him behind you, there is no enemy you cannot defeat and no task you cannot accomplish.

IX. Thou Shalt Be Faithful
(See 2 Timothy 1:7.)

The superhero Superman is not courageous. He just has no fear. He is the man of steel and knows he cannot be hurt. So why should he be afraid or be courageous?

Courage doesn't mean you are not afraid. It means you are afraid—and you do what you need to do anyway. Courage means that while you know you are weak, you know you can be hurt, and you know you don't have much game, you charge straight ahead anyway. You do this because you have faith that God is strong and will bring you to victory.

Let's take a look at three members of the animal world: the rhino, the wild boar, and the llama. Their reactions to danger can help us understand three types of faith: No Faith, Weak Faith, and Strong Faith.

THE RHINO:

The rhino has massive girth, blazing speed, thick protective hide, and extremely dangerous weaponry. If it is attacked or threatened, it charges.

THE BOAR:

The boar is only about four feet long and three feet high; however, its lower teeth grow into strong, sharp tusks that, while mostly designed for digging, can present a significant element of danger to humans or other animals. If the boar is attacked or threatened, it also charges.

THE LLAMA:

The llama has a relatively unsubstantial stature and possesses no battle skills, weaponry, or defense systems of any kind. The llama has no real power or ability. Despite all of its limitations, when an enemy threatens, just like the boar and the rhino, the llama charges.

Because of its incredible power, the rhino has complete faith in itself. This is *no faith*. The rhino currently faces extinction.

Regardless of its small size, the boar charges because it has faith in its own weapons and determination. This is *weak faith*. The boar population has become limited in certain parts of the world.

The llama has absolutely no power, strength, or strategy, and, thus, could not possibly have any faith in its own ability to fight. Even though the llama has absolutely no game, it charges enemies that it could not possibly defeat, totally relying on this tactic to win. The llama has *strong faith*. Predators see the confidence of the llama charges and they retreat! As a result of its faith, the llama is in abundance today.

It's not faith if you know you can do it on your own! It is not courage if you have no fear of failure. Don't be a rhino or a boar—be a llama. With llamalike faith, you can charge head-on into your life and watch your enemies retreat. When you are faithful and trust God for your weapons, protection, and plans, you are the true, courageous superhero.

X. Thou Shalt Be Hopeful
(See Hebrews 6:19.)

Fearful times can become fascinating if you see them as puzzles to be solved and a chance to test your faith. Seeing the world as fearful, depressing, and full of opposition and failure doesn't solve anything and can actually hinder the realization of amazing discoveries.

Sometimes things just do not work out. Having a "Positive Mental Attitude" (PMA) usually means you are figuring everything will eventually go your way. Regrettably, sometimes it won't. PMA is "Peace by Man," not "Peace by Messiah."

Hope is more than just being positive or having a PMA. Being hopeful means that no matter what happens, you trust God has a plan that always works out for the ultimate good. You may have no idea what God is doing with your life, or if he is even a part of your life at all, but he knows and he is right there. It will be the best plan for you—and for everyone around you. Therefore, you have hope in all situations and circumstances.

In order to live in this world, you have to face monstrous injustice and fierce opposition. On the other hand, God loves you. He loves you even more than you do, and he deeply desires that your life should work out. Thus, you have hope, in spite of tests and frustrations.

When a child is taking illegal drugs, failing in school, or headed in the wrong direction, the father of that child loves that child's body, life, and future more than the child does. It is exactly the same with your Father in heaven. When he sees you in trouble or falling short of your potential, he wants much more for you than even you do.

The Bible says, "The LORD your God is with you; the mighty One will save you. He will rejoice over you. You will rest in his love; he will sing and be joyful about you" (Zephaniah 3:17). He not only loves you; he rejoices in you and is joyful about you. He even sings about you. It is very unlikely that you love yourself so much that you are willing to sing about yourself. But God does love you that much.

No matter how steep or treacherous a mountain gets, you can keep moving up it with your eyes focused on God. You can move up the mountain with your family, your health, your relationships, your finances, and your dreams. When you get stressed because you are running late, worried that you may run out of money, or something is going wrong with your family, job, or your life, be hopeful. God wants you to get to the top even more than you do.

It is through your eyes, your mouth, and your hands that God often gets things done in this world. So continue to hope and trust in God's help to do anything. And you can accomplish all that he asks.

time managment

STARTING A REVOLUTION
BY DR. BEN LERNER

MOTIVATE

Are you managing your time or is your time managing you?

Look at the phrases below and on a scale of 1–10, circle which is more like you:

Being Late, Rushing, Missing Appointments	1	2	3	4	5	6	7	8	9	10	Planning and Organization
Doctor Visits, Pharmacy Visits	1	2	3	4	5	6	7	8	9	10	Healthy Lifestyle
Auto Mechanic, Repairs	1	2	3	4	5	6	7	8	9	10	Maintenance of Cars and Equipment
Marital Counseling, Divorce, Fights	1	2	3	4	5	6	7	8	9	10	Relationship Building
Children Failing School, Conflicts	1	2	3	4	5	6	7	8	9	10	Relationship Building, Coaching with Successful Parents
Employment Dissatisfaction	1	2	3	4	5	6	7	8	9	10	Exploring New Opportunities, Skill Sharpening, New Skill Development, Coaching
Overweight, Pain and Illness, Fatigue	1	2	3	4	5	6	7	8	9	10	Healthy Lifestyle, Spiritual Growth, Coaching
Low Self-Esteem, Irritable, Depressed	1	2	3	4	5	6	7	8	9	10	Reprogrammed Perception of Self, Coaching

Now total up your score: _____
* 0–27: Time has you by the throat.
* 28–54: You may be down, but you are not out yet.
* 55–72: You are on your way to using time wisely.
* 73+: You've nearly mastered time.

EDUCATE

Ephesians 5:15–17

So be very careful how you live. Do not live like those who are not wise, but live wisely. (Ephesians 5:15)

What does it mean to live "wisely"?

Paul could have used any number of Greek words in encouraging his readers to be careful about their lifestyles, focusing on living wisely. He could have used *phren*, which means "to be careful to live thoughtfully or discreetly" (implying a cautious character), or he could have used *sunetos*, which means "to be careful to live intelligently, mentally sharp."

Instead, Paul used a simple Greek word, *sophos*, which implies practical skill, that is, common sense.

From a biblical perspective, what are some characteristics of living with "common sense"?

Use every chance you have for doing good, because these are evil times. (Ephesians 5:16)

Once again, a peek into the Greek language helps clarify Paul's intent.

There are actually two primary words in the Greek language that can be translated as "time." *Chronos* is literal clock time: seconds, minutes, hours, weeks, and so on. By definition *chronos* is linear and bidirectional. *Chronos* can be measured with some precision forwards or backwards, like a ruler. *Chronos* then serves as a model or container in which God can implement his purposes.

Kairos infers that which is convenient, appropriate, and decisive. It is that defining moment in which an action takes place that has long-term consequences. It is the "window of opportunity" in which we have the ability to do something significant with the circumstances that have presented themselves. Whereas *chronos* ticks on and on unaffected by our actions, *kairos* is literally defined by our actions.

In Ephesians 5:16, Paul used the word *kairos* and encouraged his readers to "use every chance you have for doing good." The Greek says literally to continually participate in the act of redeeming/buying up/ransoming/rescuing those *kairos* opportunities for your own benefit.

So from God's perspective, it is not the passage of clock time (*chronos*) that is important but the completion of purposeful events (*kairos*) that matters most. Why? Because the days are evil.

So do not be foolish but learn what the Lord wants you to do. (Ephesians 5:17)

In this final verse concerning the specifics of time management, Paul once again contrasted foolishness, only this time it is contrasted against a second idea: Learning to do what the Lord wants you to do.

How is it that a lack of focus on God's will for your life could be considered foolish?

How can an understanding of God's will, coupled with an understanding of God's emphasis on windows of opportunity (*kairos*) affect the way you conduct your day-to-day affairs?

ILLUSTRATE

To Have Time for My Four Full-Time Jobs, I Must Find Time by God

Managing your time is perhaps the most significant aspect of managing your life. If you had 48 hours a day to get things done instead of 24, your stress would already be reduced, you'd eat less fast food, and you'd probably even exercise more. Although it may not appear that way right now, this is possible. The time is there; all you have to do is make twice as much use out of your time.

For example, I take care of patients, I write, I am a speaker/consultant, and I am also focused on maintaining a thriving family and athletic life. I really have four full-time jobs. To do all of the things that I do full-time, I need to get 160 hours out of a 40-hour workweek. While I am able to take good care of my patients, have a quality family life, successful business ventures, and stay in top, competitive shape, most people I work with feel that they do not have the time to do even one thing with excellence.

The truth is that all people have the time; they just don't know how to manage the time effectively. Why is this? Because typically you are not managing your time; it is managing you. Think about it. Much of your time is centered on handling all of the issues and "emergencies" you face with your relationships, your health, your work, and your stressful outlook on life. In a life like that, you end up so focused on just getting *through* your day that you forget about getting *from* your day. The result of that kind of focus is more issues and "emergencies" that use up even more time.

The Time by God system will show you how to get in and stay in great health, be a successful student, focus on career, and be an incredible spouse and parent, without feeling like you are using more time than you are right now.

To get four times more done in a week than you ever thought possible, you must begin using time the way God intended. You must begin using Time by God (*kairos*) and stop spending Time by man (*chronos*).

When your time is managing you, that is Time by man. Time by man leaves precious little time for what is really important in life. By contrast, Time by God is managing your time so that you can do what is necessary to create health, peace, success, better relationships, or anything else that is good for your future.

In summary, you do not stumble onto health and happiness; you schedule it.

Time management turns resolutions into revolutions. Resolutions are quickly broken. But when you learn to manage your time so that you get your life back under control, you are starting a revolution! It takes real planning to have a personal revolution and experience a real-life transformation. Time management creates consistency and real long-term change.

ACTIVATE

Start today by thinking about the things in life that are the most important to both you and God. Next, take a look at your weekly calendar (*chronos*) and begin looking for ways you can carve out "windows of opportunity" to focus on those most important things (*kairos*).

DEFINE THE DIFFERENT ROLES IN YOUR LIFE
MOTIVATE

You're a busy person—chances are, very busy. Take a moment now and list your roles and responsibilities:

1. _____ 2. _____ 3. _____

4. _____ 5. _____ 6. _____

7. _____ 8. _____ 9. _____

Are you busier than you are successful?

The simplest advice you can give to someone in need is to ask them to consider this question: "How can I best use my time to meet this need?" If they are looking for the right relationship, then where can they go to spend the most time around the type of people for whom they are looking? If they're having financial problems, how can they spend the most time doing what makes them the most money? It's simple advice, *but effective.*

The irony of today is that we live in a world of plentiful information on dieting, nutrition, fitness, and emotional management, yet we're more overweight, have more nutrition-related illness, and are more tired and depressed then ever before.

Did you ever wonder why, with all of the millions of books, tapes, and programs on physical and mental health being sold on television, the Internet, in bookstores, and in malls, that we're failing more than at any other time in recorded history to be healthy—physically and mentally?

The answer is that our personal culture just doesn't support wellness. People are extraordinarily busy, but what are they busy doing? Clearly, it's not exercising, spending time with their family, praying, or really focusing on sharpening the necessary skills for success. When I see a poor, overweight, unhealthy, unhappy person talking on the cell phone, I want to say, "Hey, who you talking to? Unless it's the president, your pastor, or your personal trainer—hang up!"

In these Bible studies, I want to show you the secrets I've found to help you become more successful—and less busy.

EDUCATE

Luke 10—Mary and Martha, Part 1

While Jesus and his followers were traveling, Jesus went into a town. A woman named Martha let Jesus stay at her house. (Luke 10:38)

By the time this event took place, Jesus had been traveling all over the region performing many miracles. No doubt, word traveled quickly about this mysterious individual. He was a celebrity in every sense of the word. As Jesus arrived in town, presumably in Bethany (see John 11), Martha must have been one of the first to meet him. As was the polite custom of the day, she invited Jesus and his followers to her home, and when he accepted the invitation, you can only imagine her response.

Have you ever had important guests over for dinner or even to lodge? What was the atmosphere like as you prepared for your guests' arrival? Buzzing? Exciting? Busy? Tense?

Martha had a sister named Mary, who was sitting at Jesus' feet and listening to him teach. But Martha was busy with all the work to be done. She went in and said, "Lord, don't you care that my sister has left me alone to do all the work? Tell her to help me." (Luke 10:39–40)

Traditionally, Martha gets a bad rap for her behavior in this situation, but stop and think. How many times have you been working insanely in the kitchen, making last-minute preparations, while your spouse, children, or siblings were in the living room, hanging out with the guests? How did this make you feel?

On the flip side, maybe you are always the one sitting in the living room while others scurry around, working frantically. How do you feel? Do you ever dread the looks you might get or the cold shoulder after the guests have gone? Do you ever feel guilty for not helping more?

But the Lord answered her, "Martha, Martha, you are worried and upset about many things. Only one thing is important. Mary has chosen the better thing, and it will never be taken away from her." (Luke 10:41–42)

Notice that Jesus did not directly condemn or chastise either Mary or Martha. Why do you think that is so? The Greek here is very interesting. Literally, it would read something like this: *There is only one business/duty/affair, and Mary has chosen the more pleasant part.* In other words, both the work and the worship, the list and the listening, *are important parts of one whole.* Mary just happened to choose the more pleasant parts—the worship and the listening.

What does this say to you about prioritizing your "hats" when it seems that they are all equally important? In other words, how could Mary and Martha both have shared the pleasant and unpleasant parts of this event?

ILLUSTRATE

All of us have multiple important areas and roles that we play: spouse, parent, employee, facilitator, and civic leader are just some of the lives we may lead. As the founder of Body by God, I have multiple areas of my life that I consider to be firmly planted in time by God. It is critical to me that each of these areas be done well. In order to do this, I have to look at myself as almost having split personalities. I literally have seven roles or "lives":

1. Spiritual Life
2. Family Life
3. Personal Health-and-Fitness Life
4. Patient-Care Life

5. Author Life
6. Lecturer Life
7. Consultant Life

All of these lives help others and serve God, so each is worthy of being done with excellence. Each of them revolves around the 6 F's of Maximized Living—Faith, Family, Fitness, Finance, Future, and Fulfillment. All of my lives together, and the F's therein, make up my mission. Not everything I do is "pleasant" or relaxing, but it is all important and necessary. So, in order to maintain a positive attitude and experience, each of these lives needs to be protected.

This is why planning is so important. It is in the planning process that we can take a proactive stance in choosing the things we focus on. With the speed of information and the number of opportunities that present themselves to us on a daily basis, we need to have an awareness of what impact an impromptu choice (such as inviting an important guest to dinner) will have.

Each month we need to examine how we are doing in the lives that we live. Are we fulfilling the expectations that we have set in each area of life? What areas can we improve? For instance, can you become a better listener in your family life? Do you need to spend more time in the Word and in prayer in your spiritual life? Have you spent enough time in your physical life to keep your body at its peak potential?

There is always enough time to get the important things done. The problem is never truly that there is not enough time; the problem is that there is not enough time *management*. All of us are busy, but those who are busy and successful have learned how to compartmentalize their time so they can get *multiple* things done better than many people can get *one* thing done.

ACTIVATE

Make a list of your different roles or "lives" by filling out the "Identifying Your Lives" chart. Now look at your calendar for the rest of this week. How will certain events impact each of these "hats," and how can you prioritize your schedule so that you are able to get the *lists* checked off that serve them?

To Identify Your "Lives" Think about Your:
Roles
Responsibilities
Relationships

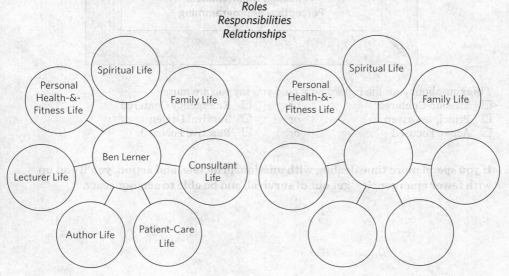

PAINT SOLID YELLOW LINES AROUND YOUR LIVES

MOTIVATE

How many times each day are you interrupted from important tasks in order to attend to "urgent" tasks?

THE "TIME ZONES"
HOW TO GET 160 HOURS FROM A 40-HOUR WORKWEEK

ZONE 1
TIME BY MAN

- Emergency Centered (Time, Relationships, Personal)
- Survival Driven • Reactive Focused

DISTRACTIONS: Technology and Hobbies, News and World Events, Treatment for Illness, Emotional Challenges, Fringe Business

ZONE 2
TIME BY GOD

- Mission Centered • Principle Driven
- Cause-Active Focused

MISSION-ARY WORK: Healthy Lifestyle, Spiritual Growth, Relationship Building, Social and Community Involvement, Skill Sharpening and New Skill Development, Opportunity, Planning & Organizing, Coaching, Maintenance, Perception Reprogramming

---

Thinking about your life right now, would you say you are more:

☐ Mission Centered   or   ☐ Emergency Centered
☐ Principle Driven   or   ☐ Survival Driven
☐ Active Focused   or   ☐ Reactive Focused

If you spend more time dealing with mission, principle, and action, you'll end up with fewer emergencies, get out of survival, and be able to act, not react.

EDUCATE

John 11—Mary and Martha, Part 2

In Luke 10, where Jesus first met Mary and Martha, we learn about the importance of defining our lives so that we can experience the worship without neglecting the work. In John 11, Jesus' next encounter with Mary and Martha, we learn the next step in this process.

A man named Lazarus was sick. He lived in the town of Bethany, where Mary and her sister Martha lived. Mary was the woman who later put perfume on the Lord and wiped his feet with her hair. Mary's brother was Lazarus, the man who was now sick. So Mary and Martha sent someone to tell Jesus, "Lord, the one you love is sick." (John 11:1–3)

Why do you suppose Mary and Martha felt that it was important to say, "the one you love is sick," rather than simply saying Lazarus's name (common name issues aside)?

Have you ever tried to contact someone important only to meet with a closed door or a full schedule? In the times where you were able to "get through," what gave you the extra push? Was it a special relationship or a unique circumstance? Could it be that Mary and Martha were using the same tactic?

Skip to verse 5 for now.

Jesus loved Martha and her sister and Lazarus. But when he heard that Lazarus was sick, he stayed where he was for two more days. (John 11:5–6)

Again the Greek here is telling. John used the word *meno*, meaning that Jesus continued whatever it was he was doing for two more days. Consider what John could have said, but didn't: *epimeno*, meaning that Jesus forced himself to stay, perservering, as it were; *hupomeno*, meaning that Jesus stayed *instead of* leaving; or *prosmeno*, meaning that he stayed *longer* than he wanted.

Now look back at verse 4. Why do you think John used the word *meno* to describe Jesus' actions?

Then Jesus said to his followers, "Let's go back to Judea. . . . Lazarus is dead. And I am glad for your sakes I was not there so that you may believe."

[Jesus] cried out in a loud voice, "Lazarus, come out!" The dead man came out, his hands and feet wrapped with pieces of cloth, and a cloth around his face. Jesus said to them, "Take the cloth off of him and let him go." (John 11:7–15, 43–44)

Do you find it difficult or easy to manage the "tyranny of the urgent" as it crops up in your life?

Do you find it difficult to identify the difference between things that are truly urgent (and require "flexibility" in your schedule) and things that simply seem urgent on the surface?

ILLUSTRATE

The nature of this particular event in John 11 (control over life and death) is something with which we cannot identify. But that's what makes it such a great illustration. For you and me, this would have been catastrophic, but for someone with the power to raise the dead at will, Jesus demonstrated a principle of time management that is applicable for us all. Whatever Jesus' business was, it was equally important to the situation with Lazarus. Because Jesus had the ability to manage both, he did just that—without allowing the "urgency" of Lazarus's sickness to dictate his time and make him miserable or stressed out (as if that were possible).

As the founder of Body by God, I lead many lives: spiritual life, family life, personal health-and-fitness life, patient-care life, author life, lecturer life, and consultant life.

It would be easy to look at my many lives and say that I must be overworked and miserable. Not that I never am. Who isn't overworked and miserable at some point in their lives? But it is not very often. Through proper compartmentalization and delegation, my life is actually fun and fairly easy to manage.

The important thing to do is to draw lines around each life. When you are driving, if there is a dotted line, you can pass or cross over into the other lane. However, if there is a solid yellow line, you cannot legally pass and you cannot legally cross over. Others cannot legally pass or cross over, either. I paint solid yellow lines around each of my lives and the work they contain. That way, other lives cannot pass or cross over and I cannot pass or cross over into them.

For example, on Monday morning, I have my Spiritual Life, my Author Life, and my Patient-Care Life. In order for me to accomplish all three of these important lives successfully, I must create focused time for each one.

From 5:00 to 6:00 A.M. is my Spiritual Life. At that time, I am nothing else. I draw a solid yellow line next to that life so that I am not a doctor, author, or speaker: I am a student of the Bible and a prayer warrior . . . nothing else. No other life is allowed in at that time. I do not take calls, the kids aren't up yet (hopefully), and I do not look at e-mail. My day (and week) continues along this path according to a specific schedule, strategically placed so that all that needs to be accomplished is done well.

Obviously, it doesn't always work out so perfectly. Sometimes a child wakes up during times designated for reading, or an extremely urgent issue pops up that cannot be handled by the people to whom I have delegated authority. At those times, I have to practice flexibility. I do not want to get massively stressed when something or someone tries to pass me in the "no passing lane."

If lives "cross over" into one another, as they occasionally will, I try to remember the saying "That's life." I work to get past the issues and try to get everyone and everything back in their lanes as quickly as possible before there is an accident!

Jesus painted yellow lines around his time in the city and around his time with Lazarus. He knew he was capable of managing both if he was strategic and purposeful. And by his actions, Jesus set another example for you and me to follow in managing our time.

ACTIVATE

Review the lives that you lead, the goals you have set for each of those lives, and paint solid yellow lines around those areas—by which I mean, commit to not let anything detour or disrupt you from devoting the necessary time to succeed in these areas. It will help you develop the discipline of doing this each week. The most important aspect of weekly planning is that you set up a regular time for this type of planning and that you do it at the same time each week. Your goal with weekly planning should be to spend 15 to 20 minutes each week in this process. In fact, if you are just beginning to do this, schedule weekly planning at the same time for the next four weeks to develop the habit.

The schedule below shows I how I budget my time.

Generalized Personal Time Chart—Dr. Ben Lerner

MORNING/AFTERNOON				
Time: 5-6 AM	Time: 6-6:45 AM	Time: 6:45-11 AM	Time: 11 AM-1 PM	Time: 1-1:45 PM
Life: Spiritual	Life: Author	Life: Doctor	Life: Consultant	Life: Health

AFTERNOON/EVENING				
Time: 2-6 PM	Time: 6-9 PM	Time: 9-10 PM	Time: 10 PM	Time:
Life: Doctor	Life: Family	Life: Lecturer	Life: Sleep	Life:

(SYL)   (SYL)   (SYL)   (SYL)

SOLID YELLOW LINE (SYL)

Now use the blank chart below to schedule your day.

Generalized Personal Time Chart

MORNING/AFTERNOON				
Time:	Time:	Time:	Time:	Time:
Life:	Life:	Life:	Life:	Life:

AFTERNOON/EVENING				
Time:	Time:	Time:	Time:	Time:
Life:	Life:	Life:	Life:	Life:

(SYL)   (SYL)   (SYL)   (SYL)

SOLID YELLOW LINE (SYL)

SCHEDULE AWAY THE STRESS

MOTIVATE

Who, exactly, *are* the Joneses . . . and why are we killing ourselves to keep up with them?
List the three things in life that tend to cause you the most stress.
1.
2.
3.
Now list the three things in life that tend to bring you the most peace.
1.
2.
3.
Finally, estimate how much time you invest per week in each of these six items. Compare the numbers.

EDUCATE

Matthew 6:19–34

"Don't store treasures for yourselves here on earth where moths and rust will destroy them and thieves can break in and steal them. But store your treasures in heaven where they cannot be destroyed by moths or rust and where thieves cannot break in and steal them. Your heart will be where your treasure is." (Matthew 6:19–21)

This is certainly one of the most recognizable passages in the New Testament (yet, interestingly enough, only Matthew recorded it). Why do you suppose our hearts always tend to navigate toward "treasure"? For example, have you ever met anyone who doesn't seem to be interested in money?

First Timothy 6:10 says that *"the love of money causes all kinds of evil. Some people have left the faith, because they wanted to get more money, but they have caused themselves much sorrow."* What does that tell you about Jesus' advice in Matthew 6:21?

Do you think most people are interested in money for money's sake, or could there be another reason for its mysterious appeal?

The Bible tells us clearly that it is a limited record (John 21:25). Imagine how many books it would take to record all the conversations and activities concerning Jesus! I can imagine that after verse 21 of Matthew 6, there was plenty of discussion. It's possible that some in the crowd were arguing for the value of pursuing both God and money—within balance and reason.

After all, money is simply a tool that can be used for lots of good and necessary things. That might explain why Jesus said, *"No one can serve two masters. The person will hate one master and love the other, or will follow one master and refuse to follow the other. You cannot serve both God and worldly riches"* (Matthew 6:24).

Be honest. Doesn't that strike you as ridiculous . . . *almost* foolish? How could anyone survive if she chose to take this advice seriously? How would you explain this "upside-down" thinking to a nonbeliever?

Jesus attempts to explain his thinking in verses 25–34:

"So I tell you, don't worry about the food or drink you need to live, or about the clothes you need for your body. . . . You cannot add any time to your life by worrying about it. . . . The people who don't know God keep trying to get these things, and your Father in heaven knows you need them. Seek first God's kingdom and what God wants. Then all your other needs will be met as well. So don't worry about tomorrow, because tomorrow will have its own worries. Each day has enough trouble of its own."

Can't you just picture a little rat, running frantically around a maze, trying to gather up every morsel possible before time runs out—all the while missing the best pieces that are hidden just overhead? Could it be that we are missing the best things in life by wasting all our time in pursuit of the things that matter least?

What would happen to your stress levels if you changed the way you invested your time and began to trust God with the rest?

ILLUSTRATE

If You Think You're Always Running Out of Time, You Are Right

Time management *is* stress management.

Think about it: The goal of technology is to make work, travel, food preparation, and communication more time-efficient. This is done in an effort to give us more time. That doesn't seem to work out so well. Now, everyone feels as if they have *less time*. And that means *more stress!*

You most likely wake up by an alarm, get paid by the hour, and eat by the clock. Everyone is always in a hurry. The dilemma is, this feeling that you have less time or are running out of time possibly creates more stress than any other one thing. The stress created by hurry is so intense, it can literally be deadly. See if any of the following scenarios connect with you:

Your mornings typically start out with instant oatmeal, microwaved waffles, and automatic coffee that brewed while you slept. Then you race off to work and get caught in rush-hour traffic. Because you can't wait to get to work to start making calls, you use a cell phone. To save time, you use automatic speed dial.

When you are at work, you one-minute manage, make instant copies, use memos instead of meetings, use high-speed Internet access, and you instant message, e-mail, or voice-mail people instead of waiting to actually talk to them. You take five-minute breaks, go out to lunch at restaurants that promise a ten-minute meal, or order twenty-minute pizza delivery.

When you drive, you are constantly on the lookout for police, get money from the automatic teller, and get pay-at-the-pump gas so you don't have to waste time going inside and actually interacting with someone.

You try to avoid shopping for dinner if you can by stopping at a convenience store or picking up some fast food. At night, you watch news clips and instant replays of the life and the games you didn't have enough time to watch.

When you do have to go shopping, you try to get just enough food to go into the express lane. If this fails, you attempt to locate the smallest line. While in line, you watch people who got in a different line at the same time as you and pray that you beat them out of the store. Silently, you wish the elderly lady in front of you would use cash instead of a check card and for the bagger to hurry. If the lady fumbles around with her wallet or the bagger likes to talk, you begin to get stressed as you watch the people who got in the other lines at the same time as you begin moving ahead faster. If they beat you out of the store, you are actually a little depressed.

When you come to a stoplight, you swerve into the lane with the smallest number of cars. If there is a tie, you get behind what looks to be the latest model or fastest car. If you can see the drivers, you get behind the youngest, most daring-looking one. Should someone hesitate at the green light, they get the wrath of your horn.

Everyone is so busy. The problem is, if the beginning of your day is like someone just turned over an hourglass and you are trying to finish before the sand runs out, life is going to be stressful. That's why (as I've said before), that managing your time is perhaps the most significant aspect of managing your life. The key, then, to stress management is to organize and strategize your time so it is focused on activities that relate to *"God's kingdom and doing what God wants."*

ACTIVATE

Spend some time thinking about the things that the Bible mentions as priorities, such as daily time with God, ministry to others, and so on. Now take the time to schedule each of these things into your daily and weekly routines . . . in Solid Yellow Lines.

DISCIPLINE IS FREEDOM

MOTIVATE

Which of the following words best defines "discipline" in your eyes: training, order, obedience, rules, control, or punishment?

Now think of the most *disciplined* person you know. Does that person's life typify the definition of discipline you chose from the list above? If not, how would you describe the discipline that so identifies this person?

EDUCATE

1 Corinthians 9:24–27

Corinth was the sin city of its time—infamous as a city of commercialized pleasure. Corinth knew how to show sailors a good time and how to cater to the desires of tourists and traveling salesmen; and as a result, it was known as the most wicked city in Greece—if not the empire. In fact, in the ancient world, the phrase, to *live as a Corinthian,* was used to refer to a lifestyle that was at once luxurious and wicked. What happened in Corinth stayed in Corinth.

Corinth was dominated by an impregnable mountain fortress—the Acrocorinth—which was never taken by force until the invention of gunpowder. On the slopes of this fortress was the infamous temple to Aphrodite, the goddess of erotic love. This "temple" housed approximately 1,000 sacred prostitutes who were known as temple slaves. To commit fornication with these prostitutes was considered to be an act of religious devotion. These prostitutes were so well known that it was common for Grecians to refer to any prostitute as simply a "Corinthian girl."

Interestingly enough, the city known for its excesses was also known for the Isthmian Games, second only in popularity to the Olympics in Athens, but equally as competitive. It's within this cultural landscape that Paul had to communicate the Good News.

You know that in a race all the runners run, but only one gets the prize. So run to win! (1 Corinthians 9:24)

The Corinthians obviously understood the importance of winning. So why do you think Paul felt the need to remind them?

Can you think of a time in your own life when you allowed certain circumstances or attitudes to prevent you from giving a 100 percent effort?

All those who compete in the games use self-control so they can win a crown. That crown is an earthly thing that lasts only a short time, but our crown will never be destroyed. (1 Corinthians 9:25)

Paul used the Greek word *agonizomai* to communicate the idea of competition. It literally means to fight/labor fervently. You might recognize the English word "agonize" here. Paul, of course, used the games as a metaphor for life. So here's the question: What battle are you agonizing over in your own life?

You *will* agonize at some point. It's part of the game. And it is precisely at that point where self-control becomes the determinate factor. Paul said that world-class athletes—such as those who compete in the Olympics—use self-control to overcome the agony of competition. When you are too tired to go another step, self-control pulls you through.

Can you think of an example from your own life in which exercising self-discipline under extreme pressure caused you to move forward or ahead in a critical matter?

So I do not run without a goal. I fight like a boxer who is hitting something—not just the air. I treat my body hard and make it my slave so that I myself will not be disqualified after I have preached to others. (1 Corinthians 9:26–27)

Think of a big goal that you have in your life. List three ways a lack of self-discipline could cause you to be disqualified from attaining that prize.

1.
2.
3.

ILLUSTRATE

People think I am very disciplined. In one instance, a person introducing me onstage to speak at a seminar stated as part of the introduction, "Dr. Ben is the most disciplined guy I know." However, the truth is, I am not as disciplined as you'd think. Just ask my wife. I am terrible about putting my shoes back in the closet, rinsing out my oatmeal bowl, and filling the car with gas.

However, I do have a desire to be obedient. I want to attain the crown Paul talked about in his letter to the Corinthians. I desire to do what pleases God and supports his work here on earth and beyond. That desire is inspired by a love for God. And as a result, the Holy Spirit helps me to be disciplined in the areas of my life that matter most.

Regular people normally fail at the things they have made commitments to, such as diet, exercise, and marriage, because they have committed to these things for themselves. These types of commitments require discipline.

On the other hand, Bible heroes did not fail at their commitments because they were committing for the Lord. They loved God so much that they were inspired to be obedient. As Proverbs 16:3 says, "Depend on the Lord in whatever you do, and your plans will succeed." As a result, the Lord Himself supplied them with the self-discipline necessary to be obedient and complete the task.

When it comes to levels of stress, body weight, relationships, finances, or fitness levels, you did not just end up with them; you created them. If you are having problems in any or all of these areas, you may have identified the problem as a lack of discipline. The important thing to remember is that most of the really cool Bible heroes got off to some pretty slow starts.

Some of them had pretty bad middles, as well. This is great news because if you are like me, you have gotten off to some bad starts and had some rough middles, too. Fortunately, the most important part of a race is not the beginning or the middle . . . it is the finish. And God wants to help you achieve the self-discipline necessary to get there!

Just think of yourself as a construction zone. You are a "work in progress." While your body and your life may look as if they have just been hit by a wrecking ball, remember that for a beautiful new building to be erected, sometimes the old, worn-out structure that was standing there has to be destroyed. For the beautiful, new butterfly to be born and soar to another level, the ugly, old caterpillar has to die. That takes discipline. But it's worth it. Discipline allows us to be free to live the life that we want.

Those who exercise discipline in managing their time have the freedom to be healthy, enjoy a peaceful relationship with God, and experience joy in their relationships.

ACTIVATE

Maintain solid-yellow cautionary lines protecting your health life, spiritual life, and relationship life.

Health Life: Schedule two or three aerobic exercise sessions each week, at least one resistance exercise day each week, and time each week for nutrition planning, shopping, preparing, and cooking.

Spiritual Life: Schedule time for reading Scripture and the Ten Peace Principles.

Relationship Life: A special time set aside each week for each family member, friend, and/or special someone with an additional daily focused time with the family (focus means no television, Internet, cell phone, and so on).

Take this opportunity to again fill in the following solid yellow line chart with all of these vital lives protected.

Generalized Personal Time Chart

MORNING/AFTERNOON				
Time:	Time:	Time:	Time:	Time:
Life:	Life:	Life:	Life:	Life:

AFTERNOON/EVENING				
Time:	Time:	Time:	Time:	Time:
Life:	Life:	Life:	Life:	Life:

(SYL)   (SYL)   (SYL)   (SYL)

SOLID YELLOW LINE (SYL)

THE POWER OF COMMITMENT

MOTIVATE

Have you ever felt like giving up?

List three things in life that you've "given up" on that have permanently changed your course.

1447

1.

2.

3.

Now list three things in life that you did not give up on. How have those three things changed your course?

1.

2.

3.

Is "giving up" always a bad thing?

EDUCATE

"We must not become tired of doing good. We will receive our harvest of eternal life at the right time if we do not give up." (Galatians 6:9)

Despite what you may hear from the world, there are absolutes: God is sovereign; The Bible is God's Word; Jesus is the only way to salvation; and many more. But determination is not an absolute.

Surprising? Paul makes it easy for us:

Don't give up when it comes to doing good . . .

Being determined to finish that last piece of pie or to spend every penny in your account are not good things.

Being determined to read every last word of *War and Peace* may not be a worthwhile pursuit.

Being determined to achieve executive status in your company may not even be advisable.

But being determined to do that which is "good" (something only the Bible can define with absolute clarity) is essential and critical for both now and the hereafter.

So why is it that those "good" things are so often the hardest to endure? Paul again has the answer but you have to think backwards:

"We will receive . . . if we do not give up."

At first glance, this doesn't really help. But the word Paul uses (*ekluo*) literally means "to fall apart or break down."

So, if you mix up the order of Galatians 6:9, it starts to makes sense:

Don't fall apart mentally, and you won't wind up quitting before you reach the prize.

Need an example? Bookmark this page and go read 1 Kings 18–19.

First Kings 18 is set during the reign of King Ahab and Queen Jezebel. What did Jezebel do that could have made most people want to give up on being a servant of the Lord?

Obadiah, who was in charge of the king's palace, was understandably reluctant to tell Ahab that he had seen Elijah. But Elijah reassured him, and the meeting finally took place between Ahab and the prophet Elijah. That's when Elijah set up the challenge against the 450 prophets of Baal.

Would you have been willing to meet with Ahab? Do you think that was courageous on the part of Elijah? What about the challenge itself? . . . What do you think it was like, standing around with 450 demon-possessed men calling on a false god, cutting themselves, screaming, chanting, and who knows what else? Is that the kind of event you would look forward to attending?

Now, look at verse 27, which shows the absolute confidence and determination in the heart of Elijah:

At noon Elijah began to make fun of them. "Pray louder!" he said. "If Baal really is a god, maybe he is thinking, or busy, or traveling! Maybe he is sleeping so you will have to wake him!" The prophets prayed louder, cutting themselves with swords and spears until their blood flowed, which was the way they worshiped.

Of course, you know the rest of the story. God came through (as always), showing up for

Elijah and making believers out of the Israelites who had been led astray by the prophets of Baal. Then Elijah personally killed all 450 false prophets.

Have you ever known anyone who acted with such unbelievable strength of character, faith, and commitment to righteousness? Can you imagine yourself behaving so boldly?

Now here's the real kicker. After all that faith and power, 1 Kings 19:1–3 says, "King Ahab told Jezebel every thing Elijah had done and how Elijah had killed all the prophets with a sword. So Jezebel sent a messenger to Elijah, saying, 'May the gods punish me terribly if by this time tomorrow I don't kill you just as you killed those prophets.' When Elijah heard this, he was afraid and ran for his life, taking his servant with him."

Somewhere between mowing down the false prophets and his sprint to Jezreel, Elijah began to fall apart mentally. Maybe it was just fatigue, but the result was a complete breakdown of his faith and valor. The Bible says that he spent the entire day wandering in the desert wanting to die because he had "had enough."

Elijah gave up on trying to do good. Thankfully, though, God did not give up on Elijah, and Elijah eventually claimed a great prize in eternity!

ILLUSTRATE

One thing that Elijah's story should teach us is that there is no failure, only times when focus dims. We all have times at work, with our relationships, and with our yard and housework when we are not enthusiastic, focused, or doing the things that make these areas successful. However, we do not quit our job, quit on our families, or quit taking care of business—it just dims once in a while.

The same goes for your yellow lines. Expect to get lost, expect low times, and expect what look like endings or failures. But by being inspired to live for God and the people you love and serve, you eventually get back to some degree of commitment to your yellow lines and eventually you get back all the way.

Remember, there are at least six areas of your life in which it will take a firm commitment from you in order to draw those solid yellow lines and see the kind of success that God has in store:

1. Faith (relationship and trust in God)
2. Family (quantity and quality time)
3. Fitness (nutrition, exercise, stress management, and structural wellbeing)
4. Finance (stewardship with your money and optimum accumulation)
5. Future (mission and purpose)
6. Fulfillment (time management, peace of mind, and fun in life)

Commit to not cross, blur (make shaky), or blot out the yellow lines. The integrity of those lines equals the integrity of your life and your future. Commitment has genius, power, and magic in it.

Be inspired for life. Elijah's level of commitment was critical for the success of those who came after him, such as Elisha. In the same way, God—and all of us—are counting on you to be committed in these most critical areas of your life.

ACTIVATE

Remember the rule of the road: do not blur or cross your solid yellow lines. Pull out your calendar and schedule your commitment to spiritual times, health times, and relationship times. Go ahead and put these things on your schedule for at least 40 days. Five to six weeks is the time the Bible often utilizes and science proves is needed to create new habits, and as a result, transformation in your life. Determine that you will not quit until you have turned your determination into a habit.

30 days with Jesus

READING PLAN

1. John 1:1–51
2. Luke 2:1–52
3. Mark 1:1–11
4. Luke 4:1–44
5. John 3:1–36
6. Luke 5:1–39
7. John 4:1–54
8. Luke 6:1–49
9. Luke 7:1–50
10. Luke 8:1–56

11. Mark 8:1–38
12. Luke 10:1–42
13. Matthew 5:1–48
14. Matthew 6:1–34
15. Matthew 7:1–29
16. Luke 14:1–35
17. Luke 15:1–32
18. Luke 16:1–31
19. John 8:1–59
20. Luke 17:1–37

21. Luke 18:1–43
22. John 9:1–41
23. Luke 19:1–48
24. Luke 20:1–47
25. John 10:1–42
26. John 11:1–57
27. Mark 13:1–37
28. Luke 22:1–71
29. Matthew 27:1–66
30. Luke 24:1–53

60 days with Paul

READING PLAN

1. Romans 1:16–32
2. Romans 2:1–16
3. Romans 3:21–31
4. Romans 4:1–25
5. Romans 5:12–21
6. Romans 6:1–23
7. Romans 7:1–25
8. Romans 8:18–39
9. Romans 10:1–21
10. Romans 12:1–21
11. Romans 13:1–14
12. Romans 14:1—15:6
13. 1 Corinthians 1:10–31
14. 1 Corinthians 2:1–16
15. 1 Corinthians 3:1–23
16. 1 Corinthians 7:1–24
17. 1 Corinthians 7:25–40
18. 1 Corinthians 9:19—10:13
19. 1 Corinthians 12:1–31
20. 1 Corinthians 13:1–13

21. 1 Corinthians 15:1–28
22. 2 Corinthians 1:3–14
23. 2 Corinthians 1:15—2:11
24. 2 Corinthians 4:1–18
25. 2 Corinthians 5:1—6:2
26. 2 Corinthians 6:14—7:1
27. 2 Corinthians 8:1–15
28. Galatians 2:11–21
29. Galatians 3:19—4:7
30. Galatians 5:1–26
31. Galatians 6:1–10
32. Ephesians 1:3–14
33. Ephesians 1:15—2:10
34. Ephesians 5:1–20
35. Ephesians 5:21—6:9
36. Ephesians 6:10–20
37. Philippians 1:3–26
38. Philippians 1:27—2:18
39. Philippians 3:1–16
40. Philippians 3:17—4:9

41. Philippians 4:10–23
42. Colossians 1:15–23
43. Colossians 2:6–23
44. Colossians 3:1–17
45. Colossians 3:18—4:6
46. 1 Thessalonians 1:1–10
47. 1 Thessalonians 4:1–18
48. 1 Thessalonians 5:1–28
49. 2 Thessalonians 2:1–17
50. 2 Thessalonians 3:1–15
51. 1 Timothy 2:1–15
52. 1 Timothy 3:1–16
53. 1 Timothy 4:1–16
54. 1 Timothy 5:1–22
55. 1 Timothy 6:3–21
56. 2 Timothy 1:3–18
57. 2 Timothy 2:1—3:9
58. 2 Timothy 4:1–8
59. Titus 1:1–16
60. Titus 2:1—3:11

90-day overview

1. Genesis 1:1—2:3
2. Genesis 3:1-24
3. Genesis 6:9—7:24
4. Genesis 8:1—9:17
5. Genesis 17:1-22
6. Genesis 22:1-19
7. Genesis 25:19-34
8. Genesis 27:1—28:9
9. Genesis 37:1-36
10. Genesis 41:1-57
11. Genesis 45:1-28
12. Exodus 1:8—2:15
13. Exodus 3:1—4:17
14. Exodus 5:1—6:13
15. Exodus 12:1-42
16. Exodus 13:17—14:31
17. Exodus 20:1-21
18. Numbers 13:1-33
19. Joshua 2:1-24
20. Joshua 6:1-27
21. Judges 16:4-31
22. 1 Samuel 1:1-28
23. 1 Samuel 3:1-21
24. 1 Samuel 10:1-27
25. 1 Samuel 16:1-13
26. 1 Samuel 17:1-58
27. 1 Samuel 24:1-22
28. 2 Samuel 11:1—12:25
29. 1 Kings 3:1-28
30. 1 Kings 17:8-24

31. 1 Kings 18:1-46
32. 2 Kings 2:1-18
33. 2 Kings 4:8-37
34. 2 Chronicles 35:20—36:23
35. Esther 2:1-23
36. Esther 6:1—8:8
37. Job 1:1—2:13; 42:1-17
38. Psalm 23:1-6
39. Psalm 51:1-19
40. Psalm 100:1-5
41. Psalm 121:1-8
42. Psalm 145:1-21
43. Proverbs 4:1-27
44. Ecclesiastes 11:9—12:14
45. Isaiah 53:1-12
46. Daniel 1:1-21
47. Daniel 3:1-30
48. Daniel 6:1-28
49. Jonah 1:1—4:11
50. Matthew 1:18—2:23
51. Matthew 5:1-16; 6:1—7:12
52. Matthew 14:13-36
53. Matthew 21:1-17
54. Matthew 26:47-75
55. Matthew 27:15-66
56. Matthew 28:1-20
57. Mark 1:1-20
58. Mark 4:1-20
59. Luke 1:26-56; 2:1-20
60. Luke 10:25-42; 14:25-35

61. Luke 15:1-32
62. Luke 22:1-23
63. Luke 24:13-53
64. John 1:1-18
65. John 3:1-21
66. John 4:1-42
67. John 8:1-11
68. John 11:1-44
69. John 14:1-31
70. Acts 1:1-11
71. Acts 2:1-47
72. Acts 8:26-40
73. Acts 9:1-31
74. Acts 11:1-18
75. Acts 16:11-40
76. Romans 3:1-31
77. Romans 8:1-39
78. Romans 12:1-21
79. 1 Corinthians 13:1-13
80. 1 Corinthians 15:1-58
81. Ephesians 2:1-22; 6:10-20
82. Philippians 3:1—4:9
83. Colossians 3:1—4:1
84. 1 Thessalonians 4:1-18
85. Hebrews 11:1-40
86. James 1:1-27
87. James 3:1-18
88. 1 Peter 1:3-25
89. 1 John 1:1—2:17
90. Revelation 21:1—22:21

365 days

THROUGH THE WHOLE BIBLE

DATE	REFERENCE	DATE	REFERENCE	DATE	REFERENCE
Jan. 1	Genesis 1:1—3:24	Feb. 18	Judges 1:1—3:6	Apr. 7	2 Chronicles 36:1-23
Jan. 2	Genesis 4:1—5:32	Feb. 19	Judges 3:7—8:35	Apr. 8	Ezra 1:1—2:70
Jan. 3	Genesis 6:1—8:22	Feb. 20	Judges 9:1—12:15	Apr. 9	Ezra 3:1—6:22
Jan. 4	Genesis 9:1—11:32	Feb. 21	Judges 13:1—16:31	Apr. 10	Ezra 7:1—8:36
Jan. 5	Genesis 12:1—14:24	Feb. 22	Judges 17:1—21:25	Apr. 11	Ezra 9:1—10:44
Jan. 6	Genesis 15:1—17:27	Feb. 23	Ruth 1:1—4:22	Apr. 12	Nehemiah 1:1—2:10
Jan. 7	Genesis 18:1—20:18	Feb. 24	1 Samuel 1:1—3:21	Apr. 13	Nehemiah 2:11—3:32
Jan. 8	Genesis 21:1—23:20	Feb. 25	1 Samuel 4:1—7:17	Apr. 14	Nehemiah 4:1—7:73
Jan. 9	Genesis 24:1—28:9	Feb. 26	1 Samuel 8:1—12:25	Apr. 15	Nehemiah 8:1—10:39
Jan. 10	Genesis 28:10—30:43	Feb. 27	1 Samuel 13:1—15:35	Apr. 16	Nehemiah 11:1—13:31
Jan. 11	Genesis 31:1—36:43	Feb. 28	1 Samuel 16:1—17:58	Apr. 17	Esther 1:1—2:23
Jan. 12	Genesis 37:1—41:57	Mar. 1	1 Samuel 18:1—20:42	Apr. 18	Esther 3:1—4:17
Jan. 13	Genesis 42:1—45:28	Mar. 2	1 Samuel 21:1—26:25	Apr. 19	Esther 5:1—10:3
Jan. 14	Genesis 46:1—50:26	Mar. 3	1 Samuel 27:1—31:13	Apr. 20	Job 1:1—2:13
Jan. 15	Exodus 1:1—4:31	Mar. 4	2 Samuel 1:1—4:12	Apr. 21	Job 3:1—14:22
Jan. 16	Exodus 5:1—7:13	Mar. 5	2 Samuel 5:1—7:29	Apr. 22	Job 15:1—21:34
Jan. 17	Exodus 7:14—12:30	Mar. 6	2 Samuel 8:1—10:19	Apr. 23	Job 22:1—31:40
Jan. 18	Exodus 12:31—18:27	Mar. 7	2 Samuel 11:1—12:31	Apr. 24	Job 32:1—37:24
Jan. 19	Exodus 19:1—24:18	Mar. 8	2 Samuel 13:1—14:33	Apr. 25	Job 38:1—41:34
Jan. 20	Exodus 25:1—31:18	Mar. 9	2 Samuel 15:1—20:26	Apr. 26	Job 42:1-17
Jan. 21	Exodus 32:1—34:35	Mar. 10	2 Samuel 21:1—24:25	Apr. 27	Psalms 1:1—4:8
Jan. 22	Exodus 35:1—40:38	Mar. 11	1 Kings 1:1—4:34	Apr. 28	Psalms 5:1—8:9
Jan. 23	Leviticus 1:1—7:38	Mar. 12	1 Kings 5:1—8:66	Apr. 29	Psalms 9:1—12:8
Jan. 24	Leviticus 8:1—10:20	Mar. 13	1 Kings 9:1—11:43	Apr. 30	Psalms 13:1—16:11
Jan. 25	Leviticus 11:1—17:16	Mar. 14	1 Kings 12:1—16:34	May 1	Psalms 17:1—20:9
Jan. 26	Leviticus 18:1—22:33	Mar. 15	1 Kings 17:1—19:21	May 2	Psalms 21:1—24:10
Jan. 27	Leviticus 23:1—25:55	Mar. 16	1 Kings 20:1—22:53	May 3	Psalms 25:1—28:9
Jan. 28	Leviticus 26:1—27:34	Mar. 17	2 Kings 1:1—8:15	May 4	Psalms 29:1—32:11
Jan. 29	Numbers 1:1—4:49	Mar. 18	2 Kings 8:16—10:36	May 5	Psalms 33:1—36:12
Jan. 30	Numbers 5:1—10:10	Mar. 19	2 Kings 11:1—13:25	May 6	Psalms 37:1—41:13
Jan. 31	Numbers 10:11—14:45	Mar. 20	2 Kings 14:1—17:41	May 7	Psalms 42:1—45:17
Feb. 1	Numbers 15:1—21:35	Mar. 21	2 Kings 18:1—21:26	May 8	Psalms 46:1—49:20
Feb. 2	Numbers 22:1—25:18	Mar. 22	2 Kings 22:1—25:30	May 9	Psalms 50:1—53:6
Feb. 3	Numbers 26:1—31:54	Mar. 23	1 Chronicles 1:1—9:44	May 10	Psalms 54:1—56:13
Feb. 4	Numbers 32:1—34:29	Mar. 24	1 Chronicles 10:1—12:40	May 11	Psalms 57:1—59:17
Feb. 5	Numbers 35:1—36:13	Mar. 25	1 Chronicles 13:1—17:27	May 12	Psalms 60:1—62:12
Feb. 6	Deuteronomy 1:1—5:33	Mar. 26	1 Chronicles 18:1—21:30	May 13	Psalms 63:1—65:13
Feb. 7	Deuteronomy 6:1—11:32	Mar. 27	1 Chronicles 22:1—27:34	May 14	Psalms 66:1—68:35
Feb. 8	Deuteronomy 12:1—16:17	Mar. 28	1 Chronicles 28:1—29:30	May 15	Psalms 69:1—72:20
Feb. 9	Deuteronomy 16:18—20:20	Mar. 29	2 Chronicles 1:1—5:1	May 16	Psalms 73:1—75:10
Feb. 10	Deuteronomy 21:1—26:19	Mar. 30	2 Chronicles 5:2—9:31	May 17	Psalms 76:1—78:72
Feb. 11	Deuteronomy 27:1—30:20	Mar. 31	2 Chronicles 10:1—14:1	May 18	Psalms 79:1—81:16
Feb. 12	Deuteronomy 31:1—34:12	Apr. 1	2 Chronicles 14:2—16:14	May 19	Psalms 82:1—84:12
Feb. 13	Joshua 1:1—5:12	Apr. 2	2 Chronicles 17:1—21:3	May 20	Psalms 85:1—89:52
Feb. 14	Joshua 5:13—8:35	Apr. 3	2 Chronicles 21:4—24:27	May 21	Psalms 90:1—92:15
Feb. 15	Joshua 9:1—12:24	Apr. 4	2 Chronicles 25:1—28:27	May 22	Psalms 93:1—95:11
Feb. 16	Joshua 13:1—19:51	Apr. 5	2 Chronicles 29:1—32:33	May 23	Psalms 96:1—98:9
Feb. 17	Joshua 20:1—24:33	Apr. 6	2 Chronicles 33:1—35:27	May 24	Psalms 99:1—101:8

DATE . . . . .REFERENCE	DATE . . . . .REFERENCE	DATE . . . . .REFERENCE
May 25 . . . . . . Psalms 102:1—104:35	**July 19** . . . . Isaiah 28:1—31:9	**Sept. 12** . . . . . . Matthew 8:1—10:42
May 26 . . . . . . Psalms 105:1—106:48	**July 20** . . . . Isaiah 32:1—35:10	**Sept. 13** . . . . . . Matthew 11:1—13:52
May 27 . . . . . . Psalms 107:1—109:31	**July 21** . . . . Isaiah 36:1—39:8	**Sept. 14** . . . . . Matthew 13:53—15:39
May 28 . . . . . . Psalms 110:1—112:10	**July 22** . . . . Isaiah 40:1—48:22	**Sept. 15** . . . . . . Matthew 16:1—18:35
May 29 . . . . . . Psalms 113:1—115:18	**July 23** . . . . Isaiah 49:1—52:12	**Sept. 16** . . . . . . Matthew 19:1—20:34
May 30 . . . . . . Psalms 116:1—118:29	**July 24** . . . . . . Isaiah 52:13—55:13	**Sept. 17** . . . . . . Matthew 21:1—23:39
May 31 . . . . Psalm 119:1-176	**July 25** . . . . Isaiah 56:1—59:21	**Sept. 18** . . . . . . Matthew 24:1—25:46
June 1 . . . . Psalms 120:1—124:8	**July 26** . . . . Isaiah 60:1—66:24	**Sept. 19** . . . . . . Matthew 26:1—28:20
June 2 . . . . Psalms 125:1—129:8	**July 27** . . . . Jeremiah 1:1—6:30	**Sept. 20** . . . . Mark 1:1—3:35
June 3 . . . . Psalms 130:1—134:3	**July 28** . . . . . . Jeremiah 7:1—10:25	**Sept. 21** . . . . Mark 4:1—7:23
June 4 . . . . Psalms 135:1—137:9	**July 29** . . . . . . Jeremiah 11:1—15:21	**Sept. 22** . . . . Mark 7:24—9:1
June 5 . . . . . . Psalms 138:1—140:13	**July 30** . . . . . . Jeremiah 16:1—20:18	**Sept. 23** . . . . Mark 9:2—10:52
June 6 . . . . . . Psalms 141:1—144:15	**July 31** . . . . . . Jeremiah 21:1—24:10	**Sept. 24** . . . . Mark 11:1—12:44
June 7 . . . . . . Psalms 145:1—150:6	**Aug. 1** . . . . . . Jeremiah 25:1—29:32	**Sept. 25** . . . . .Mark 13:1-37
June 8 . . . . Proverbs 1:1-33	**Aug. 2** . . . . . . Jeremiah 30:1—33:26	**Sept. 26** . . . . . . .Mark 14:1—16:20
June 9 . . . . Proverbs 2:1-22	**Aug. 3** . . . . . . Jeremiah 34:1—38:28	**Sept. 27** . . . . Luke 1:1—4:13
June 10 . . . . Proverbs 3:1-35	**Aug. 4** . . . . . . .Jeremiah 39:1—45:5	**Sept. 28** . . . . . . Luke 4:14—6:49
June 11 . . . . Proverbs 4:1-27	**Aug. 5** . . . . . . Jeremiah 46:1—52:34	**Sept. 29** . . . . Luke 7:1—9:50
June 12 . . . . Proverbs 5:1-23	**Aug. 6** . . . . . Lamentations 1:1—5:22	**Sept. 30** . . . . . . Luke 9:51—10:42
June 13 . . . . Proverbs 6:1-35	**Aug. 7** . . . . Ezekiel 1:1—3:27	**Oct. 1** . . . . Luke 11:1-54
June 14 . . . . Proverbs 7:1-27	**Aug. 8** . . . . Ezekiel 4:1—11:25	**Oct. 2** . . . . Luke 12:1-59
June 15 . . . . Proverbs 8:1-36	**Aug. 9** . . . . . . Ezekiel 12:1—17:24	**Oct. 3** . . . . . . Luke 13:1—14:35
June 16 . . . . Proverbs 9:1-18	**Aug. 10** . . . . . . Ezekiel 18:1—24:27	**Oct. 4** . . . . . . .Luke 15:1—16:31
June 17 . . . . Proverbs 10:1-32	**Aug. 11** . . . . . . Ezekiel 25:1—32:32	**Oct. 5** . . . . . . .Luke 17:1—19:27
June 18 . . . . Proverbs 11:1-31	**Aug. 12** . . . . . . Ezekiel 33:1—39:29	**Oct. 6** . . . . . Luke 19:28—21:38
June 19 . . . . Proverbs 12:1-28	**Aug. 13** . . . . . . Ezekiel 40:1—48:35	**Oct. 7** . . . . Luke 22:1-71
June 20 . . . . Proverbs 13:1-25	**Aug. 14** . . . . . . .Daniel 1:1—3:30	**Oct. 8** . . . . . . .Luke 23:1-56
June 21 . . . . Proverbs 14:1-35	**Aug. 15** . . . . . . Daniel 4:1—6:28	**Oct. 9** . . . . . . .Luke 24:1-53
June 22 . . . . Proverbs 15:1-33	**Aug. 16** . . . . . . Daniel 7:1—12:13	**Oct. 10** . . . . John 1:1—2:12
June 23 . . . . Proverbs 16:1-33	**Aug. 17** . . . . . . .Hosea 1:1—3:5	**Oct. 11** . . . . . . .John 2:13—3:36
June 24 . . . . Proverbs 17:1-28	**Aug. 18** . . . . . . .Hosea 4:1—5:15	**Oct. 12** . . . . John 4:1-45
June 25 . . . . Proverbs 18:1-24	**Aug. 19** . . . . . . Hosea 6:1—10:15	**Oct. 13** . . . . . . John 4:46—6:71
June 26 . . . . Proverbs 19:1-29	**Aug. 20** . . . . . . Hosea 11:1—14:9	**Oct. 14** . . . . . . John 7:1—10:42
June 27 . . . . . . .Proverbs 20:1-30	**Aug. 21** . . . . Joel 1:1—2:27	**Oct. 15** . . . . . . John 11:1—12:50
June 28 . . . . . . .Proverbs 21:1-31	**Aug. 22** . . . . . . Joel 2:28—3:21	**Oct. 16** . . . . . . John 13:1—14:31
June 29 . . . . Proverbs 22:1-29	**Aug. 23** . . . . Amos 1:1—2:16	**Oct. 17** . . . . . . John 15:1—17:26
June 30 . . . . Proverbs 23:1-35	**Aug. 24** . . . . Amos 3:1—6:14	**Oct. 18** . . . . . . John 18:1—19:42
July 1 . . . . Proverbs 24:1-34	**Aug. 25** . . . . Amos 7:1—9:15	**Oct. 19** . . . . . . John 20:1—21:25
July 2 . . . . Proverbs 25:1-28	**Aug. 26** . . . . Obadiah 1-21	**Oct. 20** . . . . Acts 1:1—4:37
July 3 . . . . Proverbs 26:1-28	**Aug. 27** . . . . Jonah 1:1—2:10	**Oct. 21** . . . . . . .Acts 5:1—7:60
July 4 . . . . Proverbs 27:1-27	**Aug. 28** . . . . Jonah 3:1—4:11	**Oct. 22** . . . . . . Acts 8:1—12:24
July 5 . . . . Proverbs 28:1-28	**Aug. 29** . . . . Micah 1:1—2:13	**Oct. 23** . . . . . Acts 12:25—15:35
July 6 . . . . Proverbs 29:1-27	**Aug. 30** . . . . Micah 3:1—5:15	**Oct. 24** . . . . . Acts 15:36—18:23
July 7 . . . . Proverbs 30:1-33	**Aug. 31** . . . . Micah 6:1—7:20	**Oct. 25** . . . . . .Acts 18:24—21:16
July 8 . . . . .Proverbs 31:1-31	**Sept. 1** . . . . Nahum 1:1—3:19	**Oct. 26** . . . . . .Acts 21:17—28:31
July 9 . . . . . . Ecclesiastes 1:1—2:26	**Sept. 2** . . . . . . .Habakkuk 1:1—3:19	**Oct. 27** . . . . . . Romans 1:1—3:20
July 10 . . . . . .Ecclesiastes 3:1—5:20	**Sept. 3** . . . . . . Zephaniah 1:1—3:20	**Oct. 28** . . . . . Romans 3:21—5:21
July 11 . . . . . . Ecclesiastes 6:1—8:17	**Sept. 4** . . . . Haggai 1:1—2:23	**Oct. 29** . . . . . . Romans 6:1—8:39
July 12 . . . . . Ecclesiastes 9:1—12:14	**Sept. 5** . . . . . . Zechariah 1:1—8:23	**Oct. 30** . . . . . Romans 9:1—11:36
July 13 . . . . . Song of Songs 1:1—8:14	**Sept. 6** . . . . . . .Zechariah 9:1—14:21	**Oct. 31** . . . . . Romans 12:1—16:27
July 14 . . . . Isaiah 1:1—6:13	**Sept. 7** . . . . Malachi 1:1—4:6	**Nov. 1** . . . . . . .1 Corinthians 1:1—4:21
July 15 . . . . Isaiah 7:1—12:6	**Sept. 8** . . . . . . .Matthew 1:1—4:25	**Nov. 2** . . . . . . 1 Corinthians 5:1—6:20
July 16 . . . . . . .Isaiah 13:1—18:7	**Sept. 9** . . . . . . Matthew 5:1-48	**Nov. 3** . . . . . . .1 Corinthians 7:1-40
July 17 . . . . . . .Isaiah 19:1—23:18	**Sept. 10** . . . . . . Matthew 6:1-34	**Nov. 4** . . . . 1 Corinthians 8:1—11:1
July 18 . . . . Isaiah 24:1—27:13	**Sept. 11** . . . . . . .Matthew 7:1-29	**Nov. 5** . . . . . 1 Corinthians 11:2—14:40

DATE . . . . .REFERENCE	DATE . . . . .REFERENCE	DATE . . . . .REFERENCE
Nov. 6 . . . . . 1 Corinthians 15:1—16:24	**Nov. 25** . . . . . 2 Thessalonians 3:1-18	**Dec. 14** . . . . 1 Peter 2:11—4:19
Nov. 7 . . . . 2 Corinthians 1:1—2:11	**Nov. 26** . . . . 1 Timothy 1:1-20	**Dec. 15** . . . . 1 Peter 5:1-14
Nov. 8 . . . . . 2 Corinthians 2:12—7:16	**Nov. 27** . . . . . .1 Timothy 2:1—3:16	**Dec. 16** . . . . 2 Peter 1:1-21
Nov. 9 . . . . . . 2 Corinthians 8:1—9:15	**Nov. 28** . . . . 1 Timothy 4:1—6:21	**Dec. 17** . . . . 2 Peter 2:1-22
Nov. 10 . . . . 2 Corinthians 10:1—13:14	**Nov. 29** . . . . 2 Timothy 1:1—2:26	**Dec. 18** . . . . 2 Peter 3:1-18
Nov. 11 . . . . Galatians 1:1—2:21	**Nov. 30** . . . . 2 Timothy 3:1—4:22	**Dec. 19** . . . . 1 John 1:1—2:27
Nov. 12 . . . . .Galatians 3:1—4:31	**Dec. 1** . . . . Titus 1:1-16	**Dec. 20** . . . . . . .1 John 2:28—4:21
Nov. 13 . . . . .Galatians 5:1—6:18	**Dec. 2** . . . . Titus 2:1-15	**Dec. 21** . . . . 1 John 5:1-21
Nov. 14 . . . . .Ephesians 1:1—3:21	**Dec. 3** . . . . Titus 3:1-15	**Dec. 22** . . . . . . 2 John 1—3 John 15
Nov. 15 . . . . Ephesians 4:1—6:24	**Dec. 4** . . . . .Philemon 1-25	**Dec. 23** . . . . Jude 1-25
Nov. 16 . . . . .Philippians 1:1-30	**Dec. 5** . . . . Hebrews 1:1—2:18	**Dec. 24** . . . . . . Revelation 1:1—3:22
Nov. 17 . . . . Philippians 2:1-30	**Dec. 6** . . . . Hebrews 3:1—4:13	**Dec. 25** . . . . . . Revelation 4:1—5:14
Nov. 18 . . . . .Philippians 3:1—4:1	**Dec. 7** . . . . Hebrews 4:14—7:28	**Dec. 26** . . . . . . .Revelation 6:1—8:5
Nov. 19 . . . . Philippians 4:2-23	**Dec. 8** . . . . Hebrews 8:1—10:18	**Dec. 27** . . . . . .Revelation 8:6—11:19
Nov. 20 . . . . . . Colossians 1:1—2:23	**Dec. 9** . . . . . .Hebrews 10:19—13:25	**Dec. 28** . . . . . .Revelation 12:1—14:20
Nov. 21 . . . . .Colossians 3:1—4:18	**Dec. 10** . . . . James 1:1-27	**Dec. 29** . . . . . . Revelation 15:1—16:21
Nov. 22 . . . . 1 Thessalonians 1:1—3:13	**Dec. 11** . . . . James 2:1—3:12	**Dec. 30** . . . . . .Revelation 17:1—20:15
Nov. 23 . . . 1 Thessalonians 4:1—5:28	**Dec. 12** . . . . James 3:13—5:20	**Dec. 31** . . . . . . .Revelation 21:1—22:21
Nov. 24 . . . .2 Thessalonians 1:1—2:17	**Dec. 13** . . . . .1 Peter 1:1—2:10	